February 8–12, 2012
Seattle, WA, USA

Association for Computing Machinery

Advancing Computing as a Science & Profession

WSDM 2012 SEATTLE

Proceedings of the 5th ACM International Conference on

Web Search and Data Mining

Sponsored by:

ACM SIGIR, ACM SIGKDD, ACM SIGMOD, & ACM SIGWEB

Supported by:

Microsoft Research, eBay, Yahoo! Labs, Google, Surf Canyon, Yandex, & Bing

I0882254

Association for
Computing Machinery

Advancing Computing as a Science & Profession

The Association for Computing Machinery
2 Penn Plaza, Suite 701
New York, New York 10121-0701

Copyright © 2012 by the Association for Computing Machinery, Inc. (ACM). Permission to make digital or hard copies of portions of this work for personal or classroom use is granted without fee provided that copies are not made or distributed for profit or commercial advantage and that copies bear this notice and the full citation on the first page. Copyright for components of this work owned by others than ACM must be honored. Abstracting with credit is permitted. To copy otherwise, to republish, to post on servers or to redistribute to lists, requires prior specific permission and/or a fee. Request permission to republish from: permissions@acm.org or Fax +1 (212) 869-0481.

For other copying of articles that carry a code at the bottom of the first or last page, copying is permitted provided that the per-copy fee indicated in the code is paid through www.copyright.com.

Notice to Past Authors of ACM-Published Articles
ACM intends to create a complete electronic archive of all articles and/or other material previously published by ACM. If you have written a work that has been previously published by ACM in any journal or conference proceedings prior to 1978, or any SIG Newsletter at any time, and you do NOT want this work to appear in the ACM Digital Library, please inform permissions@acm.org, stating the title of the work, the author(s), and where and when published.

ISBN: 978-1-4503-0747-5 (Digital)

ISBN: 978-1-4503-1367-4 (Print)

Additional copies may be ordered prepaid from:

ACM Order Department
PO Box 30777
New York, NY 10087-0777, USA

Phone: 1-800-342-6626 (USA and Canada)
+1-212-626-0500 (Global)
Fax: +1-212-944-1318
E-mail: acmhelp@acm.org
Hours of Operation: 8:30 am – 4:30 pm ET

ACM Order Number: 618123

Printed in the USA

Foreword from the General Chairs

On behalf of the Organizing Committee, we would like to extend a warm welcome to the Fifth ACM International Conference on Web Search and Data Mining (WSDM 2012), in Seattle, Washington, USA, held February 8–12, 2012.

WSDM is the premier annual international ACM conference for presenting the very best research innovations and other significant work covering areas in search and data mining on the Web and the Social Web, with an emphasis on practical but principled novel models of search, retrieval and data mining, algorithm design and analysis, economics implications, and in-depth experimental analysis of accuracy and performance. The goal of WSDM 2012 is to provide a forum for researchers, practitioners, and professionals to identify challenging issues in these areas, to share the latest ideas and results, to shape research directions, and to inspire future breakthroughs.

Eytan Adar
General Co-Chair
University of Michigan
Ann Arbor, MI, USA

Following the successes of Stanford, California, USA (WSDM 2008), Barcelona, Spain (WSDM 2009), New York, New York, USA (WSDM 2010), and Hong Kong (WSDM 2011), Seattle, WA, USA was chosen as the location for WSDM 2012. Nestled in a beautiful natural setting, Seattle is the major economic, cultural, and educational center in the Pacific Northwest. Seattle and its suburbs house many technology companies, including sponsors Microsoft, Bing, Google, and Yahoo. There are also a number of local universities in the area, including the University of Washington, Seattle University, and Seattle Pacific University. Many members of these communities are actively involved in the organization of WSDM 2012 and are attending the conference.

Jaime Teevan
General Co-Chair
Microsoft Research
Redmond, WA, USA

WSDM 2012 features a top-quality and excellent technical program. In keeping with previous instances of WSDM, the main conference is three days, single track, and consists primarily of paper presentations with two keynote lectures. Some of the highlights of the program include:

- Focused single-track sessions
- Variable length plenary paper presentations
- Interactive poster-based discussion for all papers
- Two excellent keynote speakers
- Outstanding workshops and tutorials
- The inaugural WSDM Doctoral Consortium

A shared experience for all attendees is a valuable part of what makes WSDM what it is. Last year, in order to retain the single track format while maintaining a reasonable acceptance rate, only a subset of accepted papers were presented in full length plenary presentations. Instead, many papers were presented in interactive paper presentations focused around posters. These sessions provided a good opportunity for paper presenters to discuss their research in a more collaborative manner than typical. Building on the experiences from last year, WSDM 2012 features variable length paper presentations and interactive discussion for all papers during an evening poster session. 30 papers will be presented in traditional, full length plenary sessions, and 45 will be presented via shorter spotlight presentations with extended time immediately following for interactive discussion.

New to the program this year is the WSDM 2012 Doctoral Consortium. Intended to increase student involvement at the conference, the one-day pre-conference event provides doctoral students with a unique opportunity to have substantive interaction with other researchers regarding their proposed dissertation research.

The 2012 ACM Conference on Computer Supported Cooperative Work (CSCW) is also being held in the Seattle area coincidental with WSDM. CSCW is a premier venue for presenting research in the design and use of technologies that affect groups, organizations, and communities. The co-location of these conferences provides an excellent opportunity for two relatively disjoint communities with strongly overlapping interests to forge new bridges and connections. With the organizers of CSCW, we have coordinated a co-occurring workshop program, holding the WSDM workshops after the main conference instead of before. We have also made it possible for people attending CSCW to cross-register for the last day of the WSDM main program, and have included the research presentations most related to the social web in the program that day. Saturday evening Microsoft Research will host a Social-Search Social cocktail event for attendees of CSCW and WSDM.

It is the strong WSDM program that makes the conference a success. We would like to thank all the members of the Organizing Committee for their dedication and hard work in ensuring an excellent technical program. In particular, we would like to thank our Program Co-Chairs, Eugene Agichtein and Yoelle Maarek, the 25 Senior PC members, the 175 PC members, and other reviewers for their great efforts in providing WSDM 2012 with an excellent technical program. We also thank the authors of submitted papers for their contributions, and the delegates for their participation.

Our most sincere thanks goes to the following Organizing Committee members for their dedication and support in making WSDM 2012 a great success: Treasurer, Krysta Svore; Local Chairs, Misha Bilenko and Jeff Huang; Workshop Chair, Diane Kelly; Tutorial Chair Paul Bennett; Doctoral Consortium Chairs, Brian Davison and Susan Dumais; Proceedings Chair, Alice Oh; Registration Chair, Smriti Bhagat; and Best Paper Chair, Andrew Tomkins. We are deeply grateful to our two distinguished speakers, Hal Varian and Hilary Mason for their insightful keynote talks that highlight state of the art research work in web search and mining.

We would also like to thank the sponsors of WSDM 2012: Microsoft Research, eBay, Google, Yahoo! Labs, Surf Canyon, SIGIR, SIGKDD, SIGMOD, SIGWEB, and ACM. Our special thanks go to Microsoft Research for sponsoring the Best Paper and Best Student Paper Awards. In addition, Bing is providing travel support for a number of students in attendance this year, and Microsoft Research is hosting a Women's Lunch on the first day of the main program. All of these organizations' generous sponsorship and support contribute immensely to the success of the conference.

Once again, we welcome you to WSDM 2012, and wish you a stimulating, productive, and fruitful experience in Seattle!

Eytan Adar and Jaime Teevan, General Chairs

http://www.cond.org

http://research.microsoft.com/~teevan

Welcome from the Program Chairs

We are delighted to welcome you to the Fifth ACM International Conference on Web Search and Data Mining (WSDM 2012) held on February 8–12, 2012 in Seattle, Washington. As in the previous years, WSDM has attracted an impressive number of submissions tackling the most recent technical challenges in Web search and data mining, with an ever-growing interest in their social aspects. Now in its fifth year, the conference has reached maturity and has become a leading forum for reporting the latest research developments in the field. We are happy to present here the proceedings of the conference.

Eugene Agichtein
Program co-chair
Emory University
USA

We received a total of 362 submissions from 38 countries and regions, out of which 75 were accepted for full paper publication in the proceedings, thus reaching an acceptance rate of 20.7% (compared to 22.3% last year). The accepted papers are from 17 countries, spanning four continents – making this a truly international forum. Oral presentation slots were allocated to all papers. Yet, in order to maintain the single track model that most attendees prefer, we introduced this year a "spotlight" type of oral presentation. Out of the 75 accepted papers, 45 were assigned such a "spotlight" slot, while 30 were assigned a plenary slot. The type of slot was chosen by the Senior PC members and Program chairs, mostly based on whether the topic and the content of the paper were best suited for a large group presentation or for a more focused and interactive "spotlight" style of presentation.

Yoelle Maarek
Program co-chair
Yahoo! Research
ISRAEL

We would like to acknowledge the tremendous work of the 175 members of the international Program Committee (representing 20 countries), and in particular the effort of the 25 Senior PC members. They should be credited for the high quality of the program this year. We would also like to thank the general chairs, Eytan Adar and Jaime Teevan who were wonderful partners in getting this program together, always looking for creative solutions to improve the quality of the conference. Finally, we are in debt to the authors and attendees, who are the ones who make this conference possible and have allowed WSDM to become a wonderful forum to advance Web research and the premier ACM conference in the field.

We hope that you will find this program interesting and thought-provoking. Our goal was not only to give you the opportunity to share ideas with other researchers and practitioners from around the world, but also to foster new research and innovation in this fascinating Web era.

Eugene Agichtein and Yoelle Maarek, Program Chairs

http://www.mathcs.emory.edu/~eugene/
http://yoelle.com

Table of Contents

Session 3: Web Search I

Session 4: Web Information Extraction and Data Mining

Session 5: Spotlight on Search and Advertising

Session 6: Web Search II

Session 7: Web Advertising and Finance

Session 8: Social I

Session 9: Spotlight on Social

Session 10: Social II

Keynote Address 2

Doctoral Consortium

Tutorials

Workshops

WSDM 2012 Organization

General Chairs:	Eytan Adar (University of Michigan, USA) Jaime Teevan (Microsoft Research, USA)
Program Chairs:	Eugene Agichtein (Emory University, USA) Yoelle Maarek (Yahoo! Research, Israel)
Tutorial Chair:	Paul Bennett (Microsoft Research, USA)
Proceedings/Presentations Chair:	Alice Oh (KAIST, Korea)
Doctoral Consortium Chairs:	Brian Davison (Lehigh University, USA) Susan Dumais (University of Washington, USA)
Local Chairs:	Misha Bilenko (Microsoft Research, USA) Jeff Huang (University of Washington, USA)
Registration Chair:	Smriti Bhagat (Technicolor, USA)
Treasurer:	Krysta Svore (Microsoft Research, USA)
Workshop Chair:	Diane Kelly (University of North Carolina at Chapel Hill, USA)
Steering Committee:	Rakesh Agrawal (Microsoft, USA) Ricardo Baeza-Yates (Yahoo! & University of Chile, Spain) Ziv Bar-Yossef (Technion & Google, Israel) Soumen Chakrabarti (IIT Bombay, India) Monika Henzinger (EPFL & Google, Switzerland) Jon Kleinberg (Cornell University, USA) Marc Najork (Microsoft, USA)

Senior Program Committee:

Lada Adamic (University of Michigan, USA)
Ziv Bar-Yossef (Technion and Google, Israel)
András Benczúr (Hungarian Academy of Sciences, Hungary)
Paolo Boldi (University of Milano, Italy)
Ed Chang (Google Beijing, China)
Charles Clarke (University of Waterloo, Canada)
Nick Craswell (Microsoft, USA)
Fernando Diaz (Yahoo! Labs, USA)
Evgeniy Gabrilovich (Yahoo!, USA)
Vanja Josifovski (Yahoo! Research, USA)
Irwin King (Chinese University of Hong Kong and AT&T Labs Research, Hong Kong/USA)
Mounia Lalmas (Yahoo! Research Barcelona, Spain)
Ronny Lempel (Yahoo!, Israel)
Jure Lescovec (Stanford, USA)
Hang Li (Microsoft Research Asia, China)
Ee-Peng Lim (Singapore Management University, Singapore)
Kevin McCurley (Google, USA)
Marc Najork (Microsoft Research, USA)
Wolfgang Nejdl (Leibniz Universität Hannover, Germany)
Filip Radlinski (Microsoft, Canada)
Chua Tat-Seng (National University of Singapore, Singapore)
Andrew Tomkins (Google, USA)
Gerhard Weikum (Max-Planck-Institut fur Informatik, Germany)
Ryen White (Microsoft Research, USA)
ChengXiang Zhai (University of Illinois at Urbana-Champaign, USA)

Program Committee:

Nir Ailon (Technion, Israel)
Virgilio Almeida (UFMG, Brazil)
Aris Anagnostopoulos (Sapienza University of Rome, Italy)
Jaime Arguello (Carnegie Mellon University, USA)
Lars Backstrom (Facebook, USA)
Ricardo Baeza-Yates (Yahoo! Research, Spain)
Krisztian Balog (Norwegian University of Science & Technology, Norway)
Judit Bar-Ilan (Bar-Ilan University, Israel)
Roberto Bayardo (Google, USA)
Behshad Behzadi (Google Inc., Switzerland)
Nicholas Belkin (Rutgers University, USA)
Klaus Berberich (Max-Planck Institute for Informatics, Germany)
Mikhail Bilenko (Microsoft Research, USA)
Edward Bortnikov (Yahoo!, Israel)
Pavel Braslavski (Yandex, Russian Federation)
Michael Cafarella (University of Michigan, USA)
B. Barla Cambazoglu (Yahoo! Research, Spain)
David Carmel (IBM Research Lab in Haifa, Israel)
Carlos Castillo (Yahoo! Research, Spain)
Yi Chang (Yahoo, USA)
Kevin Chang (UIUC, USA)
Longbin Chen (Microsoft Bing, USA)
Ed H. Chi (Google, USA)
Yejin Choi (Stony Brook University, USA)
David Crandall (Cornell University, USA)
Fabio Crestani (University of Lugano, Switzerland)
Bruce Croft (University of Massachusetts Amherst, USA)
Hang Cui (Google, USA)
Atish Das Sarma (Georgia Institute of Technology, USA)
Anish Das Sarma (Stanford University, USA)
Anirban Dasgupta (Yahoo! Research, USA)
Brian Davison (Lehigh University, USA)
Munmun De Choudhury (Microsoft Research, USA)
Hongbo Deng (UIUC, USA)
Debora Donato (Yahoo! Research Barcelona, USA)
Doug Downey (Northwestern University, USA)
Gideon Dror (The Academic College of Tel-Aviv-Yaffo, Israel)
Georges Dupret (Yahoo! Labs, USA)
Alex Fabrikant (Google, USA)
Wei Fan (IBM Watson, USA)
Hui Fang (University of Delaware, USA)
Dennis Fetterly (Microsoft Research, USA)
Marcus Fontoura (Google Research, USA)
Patrick Gallinari (LIP6 - University of Paris 6, France)
Aristides Gionis (Yahoo! Research Barcelona, Spain)

Program Committee:

Natalie Glance (Google, USA)
Sharad Goel (Yahoo! Research, USA)
Sreenivas Gollapudi (Microsoft Research, USA)
Gregory Grefenstette, (Exalead, France)
Antonio Gulli (Microsoft, Italy)
Krishna Gummadi (MPI-SWS, Germany)
Fan Guo (Carnegie Mellon University, USA)
Maxim Gurevich (Yahoo! Research, USA)
Zoltan Gyongyi (Google Research, USA)
Marti Hearst (University of California, Berkeley, USA)
Monika Henzinger (University of Vienna, Austria)
Jake Hofman (Yahoo! Research, USA)
Vagelis Hristidis (FIU, USA)
Xuanjing Huang (Fudan University, China)
Jimmy Huang (York University, Canada)
Matthew Hurst (Microsoft, USA)
Jeremy Hylton (Google, USA)
Nicole Immorlica (Northwestern University, USA)
Joemon Jose (University of Glasgow, United Kingdom)
Flavio Junqueira (Yahoo! Research, Spain)
Jaap Kamps (University of Amsterdam, Netherlands)
Evangelos Kanoulas (University of Sheffield, United Kingdom)
Gabriella Kazai (Microsoft Research, United Kingdom)
Diane Kelly (University of North Carolina, USA)
Krishnaram Kenthapadi (Microsoft Research, USA)
Emre Kiciman (Microsoft Research, USA)
Arnd Christian König (Microsoft Research, USA)
Marijn Koolen (University of Amsterdam, Netherlands)
Yehuda Koren (Yahoo! Research, Israel)
Nick Koudas (U Toronto, Canada)
Georgia Koutrika (IBM Almaden Research Center, USA)
Ravi Kumar (Yahoo! Research, USA)
Oren Kurland (Technion, Israel Institute of Technology, Israel)
Kevin Lang (Yahoo! Research, USA)
Silvio Lattanzi (Google, USA)
Hady W. Lauw (Microsoft Research, Singapore)
Lihong Li (Yahoo! Research, USA)
Ping Li (Cornell University, USA)
Edo Liberty (Yahoo Labs, Israel)
Tie-Yan Liu (Microsoft Research Asia, China)
Bing Liu (University of Illinois at Chicago, USA)
Wei-Ying Ma (Microsoft Research Asia, China)
Michael Mahoney (Stanford University, USA)

Program Committee:

Mark Manasse (Microsoft Research, USA)
Amelie Marian (Rutgers University, USA)
Winter Mason (Yahoo! Research, USA)
Qiaozhu Mei (University of Michigan, USA)
Massimo Melucci (University of Padua, Italy)
Donald Metzler (University of Southern California, USA)
Nina Mishra (Microsoft, USA)
Alistair Moffat (University of Melbourne, Australia)
Vanessa Murdock (Yahoo! Research Barcelona, Spain)
Uri Nadav (Yahoo! Research, USA)
Michael Nelson (Old Dominion University, USA)
Alexandros Ntoulas (Zynga, USA)
Jeffrey Junfeng Pan (Google Inc., USA)
Sandeep Pandey (Yahoo! Research, USA)
Bo Pang (Yahoo! Research, USA)
Srinivasan Parthasarathy (Ohio State University, USA)
Dmitry Pechyony (Akamai Technologies, USA)
Jan Pedersen (Microsoft, USA)
Jian Pei (Simon Fraser University, Canada)
Dan Pelleg (Yahoo! Research, USA)
Kunal Punera (Yahoo! Research, USA)
Balazs Racz (Google Switzerland GmbH, Switzerland)
Hema Raghavan (Yahoo! Research, USA)
Ashwin Ram (Georgia Institute of Technology, USA)
Berthier Ribeiro-Neto (Google Engineering Belo Horizonte & CS Department, UFMG, Belo Horizonte, Brazil)
Matthew Richardson (Microsoft Research, USA)
Marco Rosa (Università degli Studi di Milano, Italy)
Tetsuya Sakai (Microsoft Research Asia, China)
Mark Sanderson (RMIT University, Australia)
Tamas Sarlos (Yahoo! Research, USA)
Uri Schonfeld (UCLA, USA)
Dou Shen (Microsoft, USA)
Milad Shokouhi (Microsoft Research, United Kingdom)
Edleno Silva De Moura (UFMG, Brazil)
Fabrizio Silvestri (ISTI - CNR, Italy)
D Sivakumar (Yahoo!, USA)
Sergej Sizov (University of Koblenz-Landau, Germany)
Alan Smeaton (Dublin City University, Ireland)
Alex Smola (Yahoo, USA)
Ian Soboroff (NIST, USA)
Aya Soffer (IBM, Israel)
Oren Somekh (Yahoo! Labs, Israel)
Marc Spaniol (Max-Planck-Institut für Informatik, Germany)
Steffen Staab (University of Koblenz-Landau, Germany)

Program Committee: Fabian M. Suchanek (INRIA Saclay, France)
Aixin Sun (Nanyang Technological University, Singapore)
Martin Theobald, Max-Planck-Institut Informatik, Germany)
Hanghang Tong, Carnegie Mellon University, USA)
Panayiotis Tsaparas (Microsoft Search Labs, USA)
Sergei Vassilvitskii (Yahoo! Research, USA)
Sebastiano Vigna (Universita' degli Studi di Milano, Italy)
Kuansan Wang (Microsoft Research, USA)
Ingmar Weber (Yahoo! Research Barcelona, Spain)
Danny Wyatt (Google, USA)
Josiane Xavier Parreira (National University of Ireland, Galway, Ireland)
Jun Xu (Microsoft Research Asia, China)
Emine Yilmaz (Microsoft Research Cambridge, United Kingdom)
Elad Yom-Tov (Yahoo Research, USA)
Cong Yu (Google Research, USA)
Philip Yu (UI Chicago, USA)
Yisong Yue (Carnegie Mellon University, USA)
Dell Zhang, Birkbeck (University of London, United Kingdom)
Zhaohui Zheng (Yahoo!, USA)
Feida Zhu (Singapore Management University, Singapore)

WSDM 2012 Sponsors & Supporters

WSDM 2012 is grateful for the support of our sponsors

ACM Sponsors	SIGIR Special Interest Group on Information Retrieval	KDD.org
	ACM SIGMOD	sigweb
Platinum Sponsors	Microsoft Research	ebay
Gold Sponsors	YAHOO! LABS	Google
Bronze Sponsors	SURFCANYON	Yandex
Student Travel Grants Sponsored by	bing	

Support for best paper awards provided by
Microsoft Research and
additional student funding by Google

Nowcasting the Macroeconomy with Search Engine Data

Hal R. Varian
Google, Inc.
hal@google.com

ABSTRACT

It is now possible to acquire real time information on economic variables of interest from various commercial sources. I illustrate how one can use Google Trends data to measure the state of the macroeconomy in various sectors, and discuss some of the ramifications for research and policy.

Categories and Subject Descriptors

J.4 [Social and Behavioral Science]: *Economics*

General Terms:

Economics, Measurement

Keywords:

Forecasting

Copyright is held by the author/owner(s).
WSDM'12, February 8–12, 2012, Seattle, Washington, USA.
ACM 978-1-4503-0747-5/12/02.

Spatially-aware Indexing for Image Object Retrieval

Roelof van Zwol
Yahoo! Research
Santa Clara, CA, USA
roelof@yahoo-inc.com

Lluis Garcia Pueyo
Yahoo! Research
Santa Clara, CA, USA
lluis@yahoo-inc.com

ABSTRACT

The success of image object retrieval systems relies on the visual bag-of-words paradigm, which allows image retrieval systems to adopt a retrieval strategy analogous to text retrieval. In this paper we propose two spatially-aware retrieval strategies for image object retrieval that replaces the vector space model. The advantage of the proposed spatially-aware indexing and retrieval strategies are three-fold: (1) It allows for the deployment of small visual vocabularies, (2) the number of images evaluated at retrieval time is significantly reduced, and (3) it eliminates the need for a post-retrieval phase, which is normally used to test the spatial composition of the visual words in the retrieved images.

The first spatially-aware retrieval strategy explores the direct neighbourhood of two local features for common visual words to determine the similarity of the region surrounding the local features. The second strategy embeds the spatial composition of its neighbourhood directly in the index using edge signatures. Both strategies rely on the coherence of the neighbourhood of points in different images containing similar objects. The comparison of the spatially-aware retrieval strategies against the vector space baseline shows a significant improvement in terms of early precision, and at the same time significantly reduce the number of candidates to be considered at retrieval time.

Categories and Subject Descriptors

H.3.3 [**Information Storage and Retrieval**]: Information Search and Retrieval; I.5.4 [**Pattern Recognition**]: General

General Terms

Algorithms, Experimentation

Keywords

image retrieval, spatially-aware indexing, quantization error

Permission to make digital or hard copies of all or part of this work for personal or classroom use is granted without fee provided that copies are not made or distributed for profit or commercial advantage and that copies bear this notice and the full citation on the first page. To copy otherwise, to republish, to post on servers or to redistribute to lists, requires prior specific permission and/or a fee.
WSDM'12, February 8–12, 2012, Seattle, Washingtion, USA.
Copyright 2012 ACM 978-1-4503-0747-5/12/02 ...$10.00.

1. INTRODUCTION

In this paper we study the problem of object-based image retrieval in large image collections. Web-based image search engines and social media sharing sites allow users to search for images using a keyword combination. Recently, a small selection of search engines also allow the user to request similar images using one of the initially retrieved images. With our research we want to push this one step further, where a user can select an object or region in the image, and search for similar objects.

Figure 1: Sample image .

Consider for example a user who is searching for pictures of the Golden Gate Bridge. One of the images returned by the search engine is the image depicted at the top of Figure 1, where a boat is passing under the bridge. The image is definitely relevant to the query "Golden Gate Bridge", and the view point of the bridge is exactly right. Unfortunately the user was looking for an image without the boat in it. Allowing the user to select a region in the image that is of particular interest allows for a visual refinement of the original information request.

To support this type of queries, state-of-the-art in image object retrieval has progressed significantly since 2003, when the visual bag-of-words paradigm of image object retrieval was first introduced by Sivic et al. [19]. In essence, local features are extracted from the images and translated into a so called visual word, using quantization techniques such as k-means clustering [21] or locality-sensitive hashing [9]. An image is then represented as a visual bag-of-words. Similarly, the query is also represented as a visual bag-of-words, consisting of the local features that lay within the selected query region. From here on forward, existing retrieval strategies for text retrieval can be used to retrieve images containing the query object. To make this work in practice, a post-retrieval filtering step is often needed to remove false positives from the ranking.

Expanding on this initial framework, a large body of research has focussed on (1) improving the local feature descriptors [4, 14], which are also known as interest points, (2) enhancing the quantization techniques to produce a more reliable visual vocabulary [2, 16], and (3) introducing more refined post retrieval filtering methods [7].

The contributions of the research presented in this paper are twofold. First, we propose an alternative retrieval strategy that can replace the vector space model for the initial retrieval of relevant images. This strategy is specifically designed to address the in-ability of the vector space model to effectively separate the relevant images from the non-relevant images, by introducing a spatially aware matching strategy. Second, we propose to create a spatially aware index, by indexing the edges between two interest points, rather than the individual interest points. The approach preserves the rotation and invariance, and is to a certain degree also scale invariant.

The vector space model treats an image as a bag-of-words, and allows for the retrieval of images containing similar point patches. When the vocabulary size is small, many instances need to be processed at query time. Simply increasing the k-means quantization space will make the quantizations more specific, and it has been shown to improve the retrieval performance. However, increasing the quantization space will also increase the quantization error when two local features, which are highly similar in the Euclidean space, are separated into different visual words.

To address this problem, we propose the neighbourhood similarity matching strategy which allows small visual vocabularies to be used effectively. It is based on the principle that if two interest points have the same quantization id, and are describing the same object, then they are likely to share neighbours with similar quantization ids. Similarly, if they accidentally have the same quantization ids but belong to different objects, it is unlikely that their neighbours will have the same quantization id. The number of matching neighbours can then be directly used to score the point similarity of a query interest point, and the best matching interest point in a candidate image.

Inspired by the neighbourhood similarity matching strategy we then introduce the concept of edge indexing, where each point in an image and its N nearest neighbours form *directed* edges. This will linearly expand the size of the index, and quadratically increase the size of the quantization space, without increasing the quantization error. With some small adjustments of the neighbourhood similarity matching strategy, we can then effectively reduce the number of neighbouring points that need to be tested at query time. The bottom part of Figure 1 shows an example of the edges corresponding to the query region selected by the user.

In the remainder of this paper, we will first discuss the related work in Section 2, followed by a detailed description of the visual bag-of-words approach for image object retrieval in Section 3. Section 4 will present the neighbourhood similarity matching strategy, and our approach for edge indexing. The two spatially aware retrieval strategies are then evaluated in a retrieval performance experiment in Section 5. Finally, we'll present the conclusions in Section 6.

2. RELATED WORK

One long-standing goal of computer vision is certainly object recognition. A significant amount of research has been dedicated to image object retrieval in general and to different related sub-domains such as logo-recognition. Nevertheless the task remains challenging, both in terms of the reported retrieval performance, and in the scalability aspects of the system.

Visual Bag-of-Word Approach.

A turning point in scalable image object retrieval, which also provides the basis for our approach is the introduction of the visual bag-of-words approach [19, 20]. At the core of the visual bag-of-words approach is the quantization of local features, such as SIFT [14] and SURF [4] descriptors for efficient indexing instead of matching the raw descriptors directly. The descriptors are quantized to discrete visual words that form a vocabulary, which usually is derived through k-means clustering. Similar images can then be retrieved using retrieval strategies that have initially been developed for text retrieval, such as the vector-space model [3]. However due to the bag-of-words representation of an image, the visual composition of the local features is lost. Therefore one or more expensive post-retrieval filters are often used to reconstruct the spatial arrangement of the query features over the candidate images retrieved. In particular the spatial consistency filter as proposed by Sivic and Zisserman [20] is of interest in relation to our approach. The principle behind spatial consistency states that two matching interest points, describing the same object, share neighbouring interest points with the same quantization class. We adopt this principle, but rather than using it in a post-retrieval step, we embed the neighbourhood scoring function as part of the neighbourhood similarity matching strategy, which then replaces the vector-space model. As a consequence the retrieval strategy becomes spatially aware, and significantly reduces the amount of irrelevant images retrieved without deploying a post-filtering step.

More recent methods extend the basic model by grouping visual words. For instance, Yuan et al. [22] define *visual phrases* as frequent co-occurring visual word groups, extracted via *frequent itemset mining*. However, the authors do not use visual phrases for indexing; they rather only use them for top-down refinement of the visual codebook.

With the research presented in this paper, we question the effectiveness of the vector-space model, and propose an alternative retrieval strategy, that largely eliminates the need for a post retrieval step. Using the neighbourhood similarity matching strategy, we can directly provide a ranking of similar images that uses the geometric arrangement of the neighbouring quantization ids.

Interest Point Grouping.

There has been a lot of work recently in grouping *interest points* [5, 6, 10, 12, 18, 15]. However, all these methods work directly on the *descriptor space* after combining interest points.

Therefore they are impractical in a large scale retrieval scenario, where quantization using a *visual codebook* seems unavoidable.

Indexing Geometry.

The need for embedding geometry in the index has appeared recently, with datasets scaling up to millions. The bag-of-words model fails, due to the high number of features extracted from the image, and the limited expressiveness of the visual vocabulary. Perdoch et al. [16] discretize local feature shape (ellipses) to save memory. On the other hand, Avrithis et al. [2] incorporate global geometry in the index by means of feature map hashing.

Inspired by the neighbourhood similarity matching strategy, we propose the construction of an edge index, where the quantization of neighbouring point-pairs is encoded in edge signatures. Rather than using the global geometry of an image, we propose to explore the immediate neighbourhood of the local features. This also makes our approach more suitable for image object retrieval.

Poullot et al. [17] group spatially neighbouring local features and index triangles. Instead of a trained visual codebook they use bucketing and extract a compact binary signature to represent local feature appearance. This representation is highly discriminative, but poses invariance limitations and is very sensitive to outliers. This is not an issue when dealing with near-duplicate detection, but in our problem the limitations would be prohibitive.

Similar in spirit is the work of Lan et al. [11]. In their work they propose to model spatial relationships between matching primitives using a local bi-gram representation consisting of transition probabilities between neighbouring primitives. Similar objects are retrieved by finding trees of matching primitives in an image that obey the model learned for a specific object class. Liu et al. [13] propose a ranking strategy which adopts a progressive exploration, similar to the concept of boosting, of the spatial neighbourhood when there are matching interest points. Although computing and weighting spatial relationships at retrieval time is too expensive, the solution of Lui et al. is very well suited for object classification problems. Our approach does not require object classes to be learned a-priori, making it more fitted for Web-scale search applications.

Zheng and Gao [23] propose to construct visual phrases for object image retrieval based on the adjacency and size of the interest points. The adjacent pairs then form a phrase which is indexed and retrieved using the vector space model. As a consequence the size of the index will increase significantly, as is the case with our approach. However, as we will explain in detail in Section 5.1, the vector space model does not allow them to filter for coincidental matches at query time.

3. IMAGE OBJECT RETRIEVAL

The basis for our approach is derived from the bag-of-words paradigm [19]. At the core of the visual bag-of-words approach is the quantization of local features for efficient indexing instead of matching the raw descriptors directly. The descriptors are quantized to discrete visual words that form a vocabulary, often derived through k-means clustering. An image is then represented by the quantized interest points, and similar images can be retrieved using well known retrieval models, such as the vector space model.

3.1 Feature Extraction

Advances in computer vision research have produced a number of highly accurate and efficient local image- and video descriptors. A good comparison of the available interest point detectors and descriptors is provided by Gil et al. [8]. Based on their review, and an internal small scale experiment we selected the SURF descriptor for our research. The SURF descriptor is initially proposed by Bay et al [4], and provides a scale- and rotation invariant detector and descriptor that performs competitively to other interest point detectors. Among other fields, the SURF descriptor contains the x, y coordinates of the point of interest detected in the image, the scale space of the interest point, the sign of the Laplacian, and a 64 dimensional descriptor, which is based on the sums of the Haar wavelet components. The sign of the Laplacian can be used to distinguish bright blobs on dark backgrounds from the reverse situation. If one uses the sign of the Laplacian in the quantization as is discussed below, inversion invariance is lost, but precision can be enhanced significantly.

3.2 K-Means Quantization

Various strategies have been proposed to quantize the interest point descriptors, including locality sensitive hashing, and different types of k-means clustering. For our research we rely on a basic k-means clustering implementation, where the training of the models is seeded with a random selection of 1 million 64-dimensional SURF descriptors. We trained a large number of models of various sizes ($K = \{2.000..50.000\}$), each using up to 200 iterations to minimize the mean square error of the clustering.

Each SURF descriptor is then quantized using one of the k-means models, and is assigned an initial quantization id (> 0). Following the suggestion of Bay et al. [4] we then multiple the quantization id with the sign of the Laplacian. If two SURF descriptors would have the same quantization id, but a different sign of the Laplacian, it would not make sense to compare them. This effectively doubles the quantization space ($K' = \{4.000..100.000\}$), and directly divides the average number of interest points that need to be tested at retrieval time in half. We believe that we are the first to apply this principle in practice.

Figure 2 shows the distribution of number of interest points per quantization class in descending order. A small fraction of the quantization classes have a large number of instances. These classes are ignored at retrieval time, as they can be considered the equivalent of stop words in text retrieval [19]. As depicted in the figure, a threshold of 12.500 is used to discard high-frequent classes when using the 50.000 k-means model.

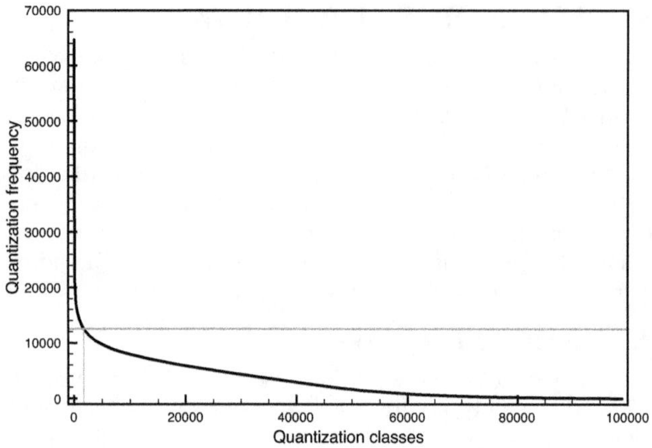

Figure 2: Distribution of point quantizations.

3.3 Ranking Candidate Images

After the quantization of the interest points, a visual vocabulary is created where each image is represented by a bag of visual words. Following the bag-of-words approach that underlies many text retrieval systems, similar images can be retrieved using for instance the vector-space model. In our case, we use a user-defined bounding box over the image as the query object. The query then consists of all interest points that lay within the bounding box. Typically a query consists of 40 - 800 visual words, which is many times more complex than the average textual query entered by a user. A *tfidf* vector is constructed for the query and candidate images. Next, the candidate images are ranked using the cosine similarity of the query and the image [3].

Typically image object retrieval systems deploy a post retrieval filter to reduce the number of false positive matches. The literature on this topic is extensive. By far the most popular approach for post retrieval filtering is based on RANdom SAmple Consensus (RANSAC) [7]. Although RANSAC can easily by deployed for our purposes to reduce the number of irrelevant images in the ranking, we have decided **not** to use RANSAC, or any other post-retrieval filter for the systems described. In this paper we are explicitly focussing on the efficient indexing and initial retrieval of images. Adding any post-retrieval filtering to our system, would mean that we're adding an additional variable to our performance evaluation.

4. SPATIALLY AWARE INDEXING

In this section we present how to take advantage of the geometric arrangement of neighbouring points in an image when matching a query interest point with one or more candidate points. The resulting neighbourhood similarity matching strategy replaces the vector space model. Next, we'll discuss how exploration of the neighbourhood of an interest point can be used to create a spatially-aware index, which will allow us to significantly reduce the amount of data to be processed during the retrieval process.

4.1 Neighbourhood Similarity Matching

Our neighbourhood similarity matching is based on the assumption that two matching interest points, describing the same object share neighbouring interest points with the same quantization class. This principle was first introduced by Sivic and Zisserman [20]. The essential difference however is that we propose to use this principle directly in the ranking function which completely replaces the vector-space model, and it also eliminates the need to apply a very expensive post-retrieval spatial consistency test. The illustration of Figure 3 shows two images, a query image and a candidate image. The dashed box indicates the query bounding box. Within the bounding box one of the query interest point is selected (green dot). The candidate image contains two interest points with the same quantization id as the query interest point. For both the query and candidate interest points we then consider the N nearest neighbours (in the figure, N=5). If none of the neighbouring quantization ids match between two interest points, we decide that they are not similar, despite their matching quantization ids. If in a candidate image, more than one interest point corresponds with the query interest point, we only keep the candidate interest point with the maximum number of corresponding neighbours. In Figure 3 the matching neighbours are indicated by the same colours. The neighbourhood similarity score assigned is the maximum number of corresponding neighbours. In the example, the maximum score for the two matching candidate points is 4, and that would be the similarity score for this query - candidate point pair.

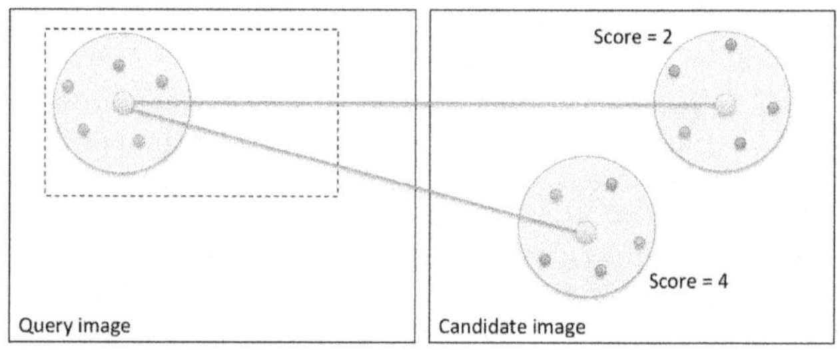

Figure 3: Matching based on neighbourhood similarity.

Algorithm 1 gives a formal description of the matching strategy, where threshold *nnth* is used as the minimum number of near neighbours a query point and candidate point must have in common for the pair to be considered as valid in terms of the matching score. Algorithm 2 presents the function to test the neighbourhood similarity of two interest points. Cost for the complete algorithm is $O(n^3)$.

Optimization. The neighbourhood similarity matching has two intrinsic variables, the number of nearest neighbours used for matching, and a threshold determining when a pair of interest points is considered similar. Furthermore, the performance of the matching strategy depends on the size of the visual vocabulary. Large visual vocabulary sizes are normally preferred for image object retrieval as they drastically reduce the quantization noise, i.e. the number of false positive matches, and the number of instances that need to be tested at retrieval time. However the quantization error is likely to increase, when increasing the vocabulary size. The quantization error causes two SURF descriptors that are very similar in Euclidean space to receive different quantization ids, when the two points lays in between two centroids of the k-means model. This can then negatively affect the neighbourhood similarity matching strategy. In

Algorithm 1 Neighbourhood similarity

```
scores ← ∅
qPoints ← getQueryPoints()
for all qPoint in qPoints do
  qPointScores ← ∅
  cPoints ← getCandidatePoints(qPoint.class)
  for all cPoint in cPoints do
    score = neighbourScore(qPoint, cPoint)
    if score > nnth then
      maxS = max(qPointScores[cPoint.image], score)
      qPointScores[cpoint.image] = maxS
    end if
  end for
  for all image in qPointScores do
    scores[image] += qPointScores[image]
  end for
end for
```

Algorithm 2 function neighbourScore(qPoint,cPoint)

```
q ← sort(qPoint.neighbours)
c ← sort(cPoint.neighbours)
score = 0
while notEmpty(q) and notEmpty(c) do
  if q.top().class == c.top().class then
    q.pop()
    c.pop()
    score = score + 1
  else if q.top().class > c.top().class then
    q.pop()
  else if q.top().class < c.top().class then
    c.pop()
  end if
end while
return score
```

addition, we believe that increasing the size of the visual vocabulary through deployment of larger K-Means models[1] will cause a loss in the viewpoint variation of the images returned.

To determine the optimal configuration, in a visual similarity search scenario, we ran a parameter sweep with varying the number of neighbours ($nn = \{5, 10, 15, 20\}$), the nearest neighbour threshold ($nnth = \{1, 2\}$), and the size of the vocabulary ($K = \{3000, 5000, 7500, 10000, 12500, 20000\}$). Figure 4 shows the mean average precision (MAP) for different vocabulary sizes when using $nn = 10$, which was the best performing combination. From the figure, we can conclude that the impact of the quantization error using $nn = 10$ is minimized when choosing a vocabulary size of $K = 10000$. On our test collection, we found an optimal performance using $K = 10000$, $nn = 10$ and $nnth = 1$.

4.2 Edge Indexing

As an alternative to storing neighbours in every single point for the index, we propose to embed spatial information in the quantization itself by storing edges. Given a point in an image, the *base* point, there are N outgoing edges that connect to the N nearest neighbours, which are referred to as *offset* points. With this approach, every *base* point results

[1]E.g. in literature vocabularies of up to 1M words have been reported

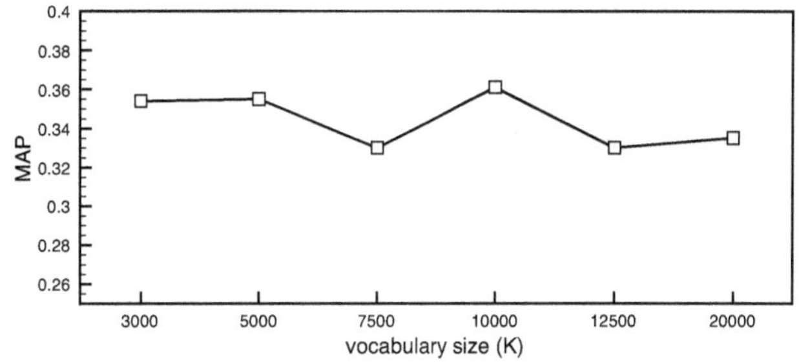

Figure 4: Mean average precision for nearest neighbour matching with varying vocabulary size.

in N entries in the index, and the quantization class for every entry is a combination of *base* and *offset* quantizations, also called the *edgesignature*.

The rationale to use this method is exactly the same as for the neighbourhood similarity matching: similar edges are likely to be found in similar objects and a matching *base* point is likely to contain one or more *offset* points as nearest neighbours. In this scenario, using two quantizations to create a signature introduces a higher degree of specificity that results in less candidates per index entry. This also results in the deletion of noise, as only coherent pairs will be considered when matching. The reduction of candidates to be processed at query time is critical in image object retrieval given the large amount of descriptors extracted from a single image.

The number of possible signatures using a vocabulary of size K is K^2 when no other information is used. In our case, the sign of the Laplacian in the descriptor for *base* and *offset* points is also used, which causes the number of possible quantization entries to grow to $(2 * K)^2$.

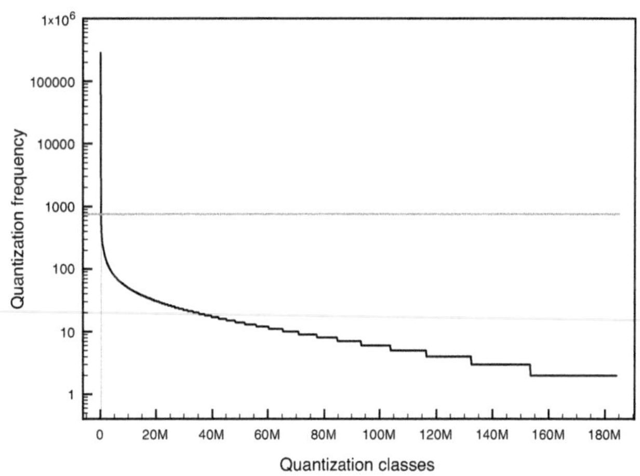

Figure 5: Distribution of edge quantizations.

Figure 5 shows the distribution of number of edges per quantization entry. As can be observed, the number of elements per entry quickly decreases and the number of non-empty classes does not span the entire space of quantization entries. This point will be discussed in more detail in Section 5.1.

Given a *base* point and one of its *offset* points, the edge signature is created using the binary representation of the single quantizations and concatenating them in a single number. Besides, the sign of the Laplacian of the descriptor is added at the end of the representation, creating different signatures for same *base* and *offset* classes with a different Laplacian sign. Figure 6 contains examples of edge signatures for three different *base* - *offset* point pairs.

Matching Edges.

Algorithm 3 gives a formal description of how edge matching between the query image and documents in the collection is calculated. At query time, N signatures are created for every query point and its N nearest neighbours. Query signatures are grouped by <*base*,*x*,*y*>. The maximum number of matching *offset* points per group and candidate image is the *score* credited for that query point and the corresponding candidate image. The algorithm cost is $O(n^3)$, same as for the neighbourhood similarity matching, but the number of candidates returned by *getCandidatePoints*(...) is significantly smaller due to its quantization specificity.

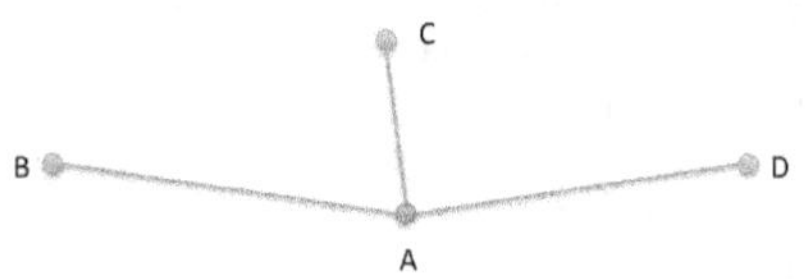

Base	Offset	Base Binary	Offset Binary	Base Sign	Offset Sign	Quantization
A = -123	B = -3454	0111 1011	1101 0111 1110	0	0	1101 0111 1110 0000 0111 1011 0 0 = 56590828
A = -123	C = 3454	0111 1011	1101 0111 1110	0	1	1101 0111 1110 0000 0111 1011 1 0 = 56590830
A = -123	D = 2057	0111 1011	1000 0000 1001	0	1	1000 0000 1001 0000 0111 1011 1 0 = 33702382

Figure 6: Creating edge signatures.

5. EVALUATION

In this section we first examine the effect of edge-based indexing by the hand of a quantization and index characterisation. Thereafter, we'll present the retrieval performance experiment that was conducted to analyse the impact in terms of precision/recall.

5.1 Quantization and Index Characteristics

To get a better understanding of the three different retrieval strategies, we present a short characterisation of the visual vocabulary and number of instances per quantization class in the index. We have selected 4 different system configurations for the comparison:

- **50k-tfidf**: Our baseline system, using a 50K k-means classification model, with the vector space matching strategy.
- **10k-nn10**: The optimal configuration of the nearest neighbour matching strategy, using a k-means model with $K = 10000$, $nn = 10$, and $nnth = 1$.
- **3k-edge10**: The edge-based configuration with the smallest vocabulary size, and the number of edges per point equals to 10 ($edge = 10$).
- **10k-edge10**: The edge-based equivalent of the optimal nearest neighbour matching strategy, using a k-means model with $K = 10000$, and the number of edges per points equals to 10 ($edge = 10$).

Algorithm 3 Edge based similarity

```
scores ← ∅
bases ← ∅
qEdges ← getQueryEdges()
for all qEdge in qEdges do
  base = getBase(qEdge.signature)
  bases[< base, qEdge.x, qEdge.y >].add(qEdge)
end for
for all < base, x, y > in bases do
  eqEdges ← bases[< base, x, y >]
  tScores ← ∅
  for all eqEdge in eqEdges do
    cEdges ← getCandidateEdges(eqEdge.signature)
    for all cEdge in cEdges do
      cbase = getBase(cEdge.signature)
      key = < cbase, cEdge.x, cEdge.y >
      tScores[cEdge.image][key] += 1
    end for
  end for
  {Post-condition: tScores contains the number of matching neighbours for each candidate base point (< base, x, y >)}
  for all image in tScores do
    score[image] += max(tScores[image])
  end for
end for
```

Table 1 presents the theoretical (Q_T) and actual (Q_A) vocabulary size of the four different system configurations. In addition, the total number of quantization entries (Q_{total}) in the index, the average number of instances per quantization class (Q_{avg}) and their corresponding standard deviations (Q_{stdev}) are reported in the table.

System	Q_T	Q_A	Q_{total}	Q_{avg}	Q_{stdev}
50k-tfidf	100K	99K	309M	3117	3650
10k-nn10	20K	20K	309M	30874	27509
3k-edge10	36M	31M	3.090M	98	620
10k-edge10	400M	183M	3.090M	16	139

Table 1: Characterisation of the retrieval systems.

For the 10k-tfidf and the 10-nn10 systems the theoretical quantization space, e.g. size of the visual vocabulary, equals $2 * K$, with K the number of clusters in the k-means model and when using the sign of the Laplacian of the SURF descriptor to double the original quantization space. For the edge-based configurations the theoretical quantization space is much larger: $(2 * k)^2$. As shown in the table using $309M$ interest points, almost the entire quantization space is used, in case of the 50k-tfidf and 10k-nn10 runs, while only 85% and 46% of the quantization space is used for the 3k-edge10 and 10k-edge10 runs respectively. In the latter case the index contains a total of 3.090M edge quantizations. Though the size of the index is expanded with a factor of 10 in case of the edge-based configuration, the average number of instances per quantization class (Q_{avg} are reduced with a factor of 32 and 195, respectively for the 3k-edge10 and 10k-edge10 systems, when compared against the 50k-tfidf baseline.

Effectively, this means that *at retrieval time* we're reducing the number of candidate interest points tested with a factor of 19.5 when processing a query. If our theory holds in practice we have successfully eliminated all false-positive hits when comparing the edge-based strategy to the nearest neighbour similarity matching strategy. The retrieval performance experiment will allow us to validate this.

5.2 Retrieval Performance Experiment

In this section we describe the retrieval performance experiment that we have performed to compare the neighbourhood similarity matching strategy and the edge indexing against the baseline approach with the vector-space model.

5.2.1 Experimental Setup

Task.

The task at hand is to retrieve images that contain a specific object or image region of interest, which is defined by a user bounding box over a query image.

Collection.

We base the evaluation of our systems on the EC1M - Flickr image collection that was composed by Avrithis et al. [1]. This data-set consists of 909,940 geo-tagged images spread over 22 European cities, which have been crawled from Flickr using geographic queries covering a window of each city center. Note that we do not use the geo-tagging information, nor other image meta-data for the research presented here. We crawled the medium sized (500px) images from Flickr, and extracted the SURF descriptor using the default settings.

Topics.

As we are interested in image object retrieval rather than image similarity, we could not re-use the topics and assessments that are provided with the EC1M collection. We therefore created a new set of 25 topics, consisting of an image, and a bounding box over the image that specifically identifies the object of interest. Figure 7 provides a visual impression of the 25 topics, and their bounding boxes[2]. Following the order in the figure, the topic titles are: Vatican stairs, London Eye, Ampersand, Van Gogh, Belvedere Palace, Guinness, Tour Eiffel, Big Ben, Florence's Duomo, Budweiser, Mona Lisa, Battistero San Giovanni, Scott Monument, Tower Bridge, Underground sign, Colloseum, TDK/Sanyo, Acropolis, Arc de Triomphe, Palazzo Bovolo's stairs, Basilique Saint Etienne, British museum, Atomic Clock, Mosaic glass Notre Dame, Clock.

Systems.

Central in this evaluation are three system configurations that have been introduced in Section 5.1: **50k-tfidf** (baseline), **10k-nn10**, and **10k-edge10**. The objective is to compare the performance of the neighbourhood similarity matching approach against the baseline system that uses a larger initial quantization space in combination with the vector space model for ranking the images. In addition we test the performance of the edge-based retrieval strategy, which should give similar performance to the neighbourhood similarity matching strategy, but at lower cost. Note that we can easily *achieve the exact same performance* between the 10k-nn10, and 10k-edge10 systems, by indexing only those edges in the 10k-edge10 system, which are composed of the valid visual words of the 10k-nn10 system. The difference in performance between the two systems is only caused by the removal of visual stop words as depicted in Figures 2 and 5.

Metrics.

We have adopted a blind pooling method, as commonly used for the evaluation of retrieval systems. The top 50 results per topic were collected for each of the system configurations tested. The assessors were then asked to provide a binary relevance judgement for each image retrieved. In total 24.5K relevance judgements are collected for the 25 topics. For the evaluation of the systems, we'll report the mean-average precision (MAP) and the *precision at document cut-off (P@N)*. The latter metric provides more detailed information on the ability of a system to rank relevant images at the top of the ranking[3].

5.2.2 Retrieval Performance Evaluation

We'll analyse the results in three phases. First we will provide a short summary of the retrieval performance of the different systems focussing on MAP, P@5, and P@25. Followed by a more in depth analysis of the precision at different points in the ranking, and finally we'll inspect the retrieval performance on each of the 25 topics.

Results Summary.

Table 2 presents the overall results of the retrieval performance experiment. Though the results do not vary that much, it is interesting to see that the edge-based run has the highest number of relevant results retrieved and the highest mean average precision. Most notably are the differences in the performance at the early positions in the ranking. Using a paired T-test with significance level $p < 0.05$ we observe that the P@5 of the 10k-nn10 and 10k-edge10 runs is significantly better than for the baseline run, using 50k-tfidf. As expected, we did not find any significant differences between the neighbourhood similarity matching, and the edge-based retrieval strategy.

Table 2: Overview of retrieval performance.

System	50k-tfidf	10k-nn10	10k-edge10
Retrieved	1250	1247	1246
Relevant	1724	1724	1724
Relevant Retrieved	587	572	**597**
MAP	0.3682	0.3561	**0.3703**
P@5	0.78	**0.89**	0.86
P@25	0.59	**0.62**	0.61

To give a visual impression of the retrieval performance the top 10 results for three of the topics are shown in Figure 8. These results have been obtained with the 10k-nn10 system configuration. It underlines that the performance is good on different type of objects, e.q. landmarks, paintings, and to discriminate structures that do not contain a lot of visual variation. In Section 5.2.2 we will present a more detailed analysis of the performance on the different topics.

[2]To enhance the reproducibility of the research presented in this paper, the topics and relevance judgements are publicly available for download at `http://to-be-provided/`.

Figure 7: Image topics.

Figure 8: Top 10 image results for the topics: Tower bridge (top), Mona Lisa (middle), and British museum (bottom) using the 10k-nn10 system.

Precision at Document Cut Off.

Figure 9 presents the precision at different positions in the ranking. It allows for a detailed analysis of the 'early precision'. From this perspective, the 10k-nn10 is performing best with a near-optimal precision (0.96) at the first position in the ranking, which then gradually degrades to a precision of 0.88 after having seen the first 5 results in the ranking.

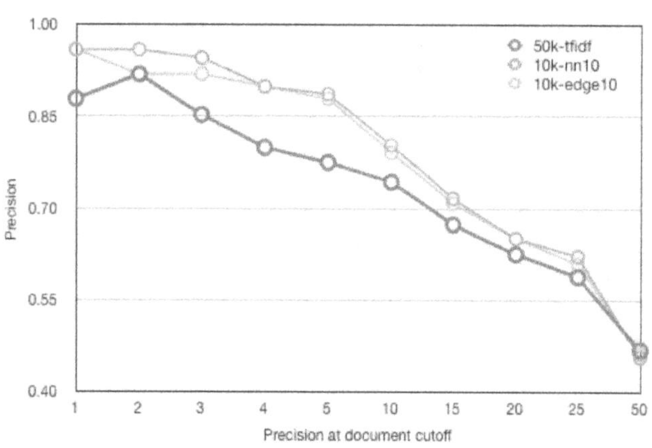

Figure 9: Precision @ document cut off.

The performance of the 10k-edge10 run closely follows the 10k-nn10 run, with a small dip at P@2. This confirms our expectations regarding the comparison of the performance of the edge-based retrieval strategy versus the neighbourhood similarity matching. The small differences observed can be explained by the different thresholds used, when fetching candidate points or edges from the index. At the early positions in the ranking, the difference with the 50k-tfidf run is largest, which indicates that the 10k-nn10 and 10k-edge10 runs are better at ranking the relevant results at the top of the ranking. This is most likely the effect of the spatial-awareness of those two approaches.

Precision per Topic.

We will conclude our analysis of the results with an inspection of the P@25 for each of the topics at Figure 10. We choose this metric as it approximates the number of elements returned in a single page by the most image search engines. As can be observed, there are very few cases where the baseline 50k-tfidf outperforms the spatially-aware approaches and, when it does, the difference is not huge. On the other hand, the inverse case can be observed specially for two topics, $BritishMuseum$ and $TDKSanyo$, where spatial awareness is critical due to the pattern repetition in the first topic and the lack of descriptiveness in the second.

For those topics with low precision, considered as difficult queries for all systems, spatial aware systems generally outperforms the baseline, which gives and indication of spatial coherence used for 10k-nn10 and spatial coherence and noise deletion for 10k-edge10.

10k-edge10 system has comparable scores for all topics with the other systems, even when its precision scores are lower. This indicates that less candidates are processed per signature.

Spatially aware systems outperform the baseline overall for the P@25 metric, as can be observed in the last column of Figure 10.

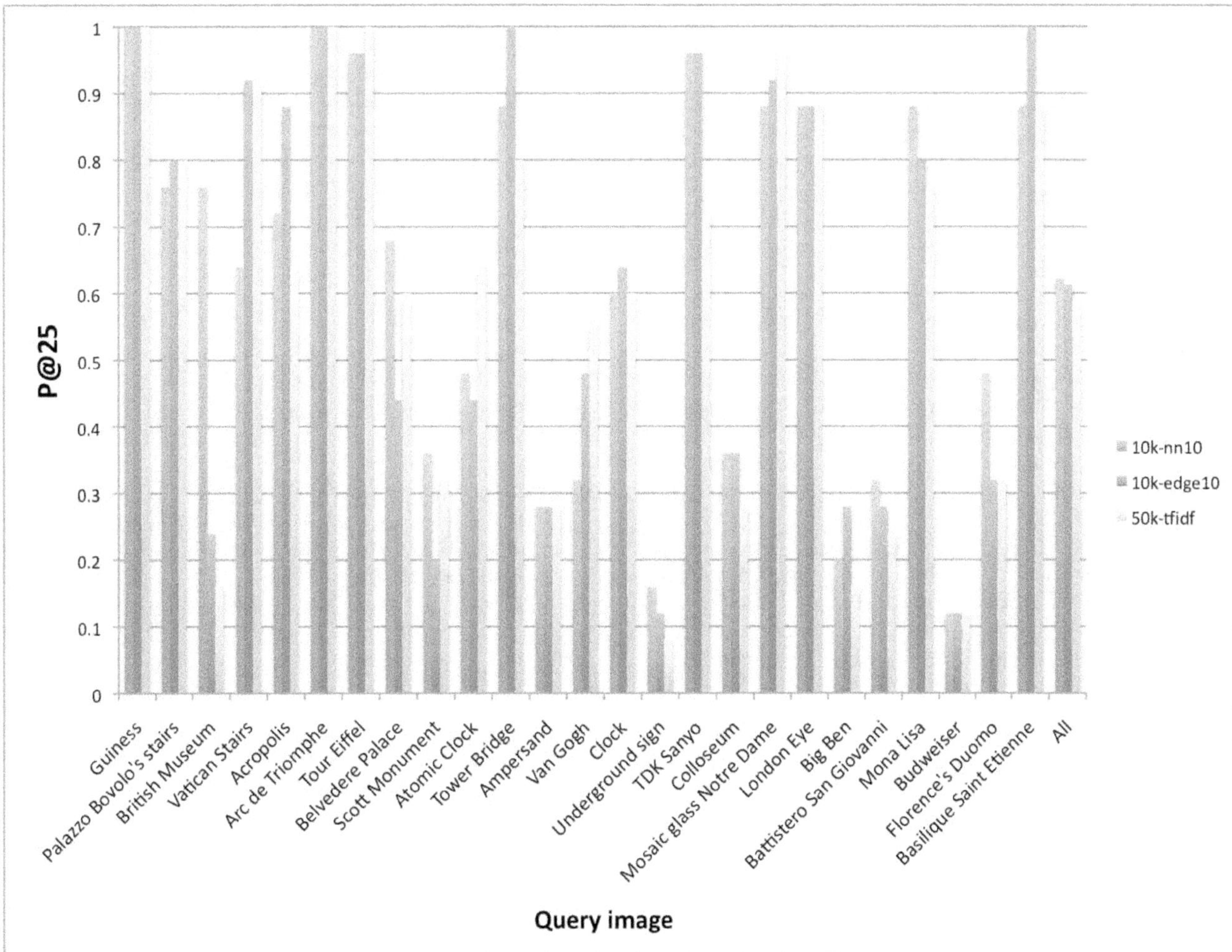

Figure 10: P@25 per topic.

6. CONCLUSIONS

Since the initial introduction of the visual bag-of-words approach for image object retrieval, a large number of enhancements have have been proposed to improve the retrieval performance. These advances include improved and reliable feature detection, more sophisticated quantization techniques, and the use of post-retrieval filters to eliminate irrelevant results from the ranking.

In this paper we have looked at the actual retrieval phase and we propose to replace the traditional vector space model with a novel neighbourhood similarity matching strategy. Key to the neighbourhood similarity matching is the use of the quantization ids of the points surrounding both the query interest point and a candidate interest point. When the two points share neighbours with the same quantization id, they are credited. The neighbourhood exploration is particularly important when for a given query point there is more than one candidate interest point per image. In that case the neighbourhood similarity algorithm will select the candidate point with the best matching neighbourhood, while for the vector space model there is no such discriminating power.

The outcome of the retrieval performance experiment clearly demonstrates that the neighbourhood similarity matching strategy outperforms the vector space model in terms of precision at the top of the ranking P@{1..10}. Moreover, we have demonstrated that we can achieve this using a relatively small vocabulary size, compared to the trend that can be observed in literature concerning the size of the visual vocabularies used there.

Our second major contribution is the introduction of a spatially aware index, where instead of indexing interest points, we store edge signatures. The edge indexing technique, and corresponding retrieval strategy mimics the neighbourhood similarity matching strategy. By embedding the geometric arrangement of the neighbouring quantization ids into the index, we can reduce the average number of candidate edges that need to be processed at query time with a factor of 19.5, in comparison to the vector space approach (10k-edge10 vs 50k-tfidf). When inspecting the retrieval performance of the edge-indexing strategy we find a statistically in-significant difference with the neighbourhood similarity matching strategy, as was predicted.

In summary we have proposed a spatially-aware indexing technique and corresponding retrieval strategy for image (object) retrieval that can effectively replace the vector space model in terms of retrieval performance, and at the same time significantly reduce the number of computations that need to be performed at query time, without using a post-retrieval method.

Future Work. As indicated before, there are many aspects that influence the retrieval performance. Therefore we will continue our research and reconsider other steps that potentially have a big impact on the retrieval performance without jeopardizing the scalability of the system. To that end, we will conduct additional experimentation with alternative feature descriptors, i.e. color sift, explore alternative quantization techniques, using locality sensitive hashing, and deploy lightweight post-retrieval filtering methods.

7. REFERENCES

[1] Y. Avrithis, Y. Kalantidis, G. Tolias, and E. Spyrou. Retrieving landmark and non-landmark images from community photo collections. In *in Proceedings of ACM Multimedia (Full paper) (MM 2010)*, Firenze, Italy, October 2010.

[2] Y. Avrithis, G. Tolias, and Y. Kalantidis. Feature map hashing: Sub-linear indexing of appearance and global geometry. In *ACM Multimedia*, 2010.

[3] R. Baeza-Yates and B. Ribeiro-Neto. *Modern Information Retrieval.* Addison-Wesley Longman Publishing Co., Inc., Boston, MA, USA, 1999.

[4] H. Bay, A. Ess, T. Tuytelaars, and L. V. Gool. Speeded-up robust features (surf). *Computer Vision and Image Understanding*, 110(3):346 – 359, 2008.

[5] M. Brown and D. Lowe. Invariant features from interest point groups. In *BMVC*, 2002.

[6] V. Ferrari, T. Tuytelaars, and L. Van Gool. Simultaneous object recognition and segmentation by image exploration. *ECCV*, 2004.

[7] M. A. Fischler and R. C. Bolles. Random sample consensus: a paradigm for model fitting with applications to image analysis and automated cartography. *Commun. ACM*, 24:381–395, June 1981.

[8] A. Gil, O. Mozos, M. Ballesta, and O. Reinoso. A comparative evaluation of interest point detectors and local descriptors for visual slam. *Machine Vision and Applications*, 21:905–920, 2010.

[9] A. Gionis, P. Indyk, and R. Motwani. Similarity search in high dimensions via hashing. In *Proceedings of the 25th International Conference on Very Large Data Bases*, VLDB '99, pages 518–529, San Francisco, CA, USA, 1999. Morgan Kaufmann Publishers Inc.

[10] K. Grauman and T. Darrell. Unsupervised learning of categories from sets of partially matching image features. 2006.

[11] X. Lan, L. Zitnick, and R. Szeliski. Local bi-gram model for object recognition. Technical Report MSR-TR-2007-54, Microsoft Research, November 2007.

[12] S. Lazebnik, C. Schmid, and J. Ponce. Semi-local affine parts for object recognition. In *BMVC*, 2004.

[13] D. Liu, G. Hua, P. Viola, and T. Chen. Integrated feature selection and higher-order spatial feature extraction for object categorization. *Computer Vision and Pattern Recognition, IEEE Computer Society Conference on*, 0:1–8, 2008.

[14] D. Lowe. Distinctive image features from scale-invariant keypoints. *IJCV*, 60(2):91–110, 2004.

[15] E. Ng and N. Kingsbury. Matching of interest point groups with pairwise spatial constraints. In *Proceedings of the 17th International Conference on Image Processing (ICIP)*, ICIP'10, Hong Kong, 2010. IEEE.

[16] M. Perd'och, O. Chum, and J. Matas. Efficient representation of local geometry for large scale object retrieval. In *CVPR*, 2009.

[17] S. Poullot, M. Crucianu, and S. Satoh. Indexing local configurations of features for scalable content-based video copy detection. In *ACM workshop on Large-scale Multimedia Retrieval and Mining*, 2009.

[18] Y. Shen and H. Foroosh. View-invariant action recognition using fundamental ratios. In *CVPR*, 2008.

[19] J. Sivic and A. Zisserman. Video Google: A text retrieval approach to object matching in videos. In *ICCV*, 2003.

[20] J. Sivic and A. Zisserman. Efficient visual search of videos cast as text retrieval. *IEEE Transactions on Pattern Analysis and Machine Intelligence*, 31:591–606, 2009.

[21] P.-N. Tan, M. Steinbach, and V. Kumar. *Introduction to Data Mining.* Addison-Wesley, 2006.

[22] J. Yuan, Y. Wu, and M. Yang. Discovery of collocation patterns: from visual words to visual phrases. In *CVPR*, 2007.

[23] Q.-F. Zheng and W. Gao. Constructing visual phrases for effective and efficient object-based image retrieval. *ACM Trans. Multimedia Comput. Commun. Appl.*, 5:7:1–7:19, October 2008.

Auralist: Introducing Serendipity into Music Recommendation

Yuan Cao Zhang[§] Diarmuid Ó Séaghdha[§] Daniele Quercia[§] Tamas Jambor[‡]
[§]Computer Laboratory, University of Cambridge, UK
[‡]Department of Computer Science, University College London, UK
ycz20@cantab.net, do242@cam.ac.uk, dq209@cl.cam.ac.uk, t.jambor@cs.ucl.ac.uk

ABSTRACT

Recommendation systems exist to help users discover content in a large body of items. An ideal recommendation system should mimic the actions of a trusted friend or expert, producing a personalised collection of recommendations that balance between the desired goals of accuracy, diversity, novelty and serendipity. We introduce the *Auralist* recommendation framework, a system that – in contrast to previous work – attempts to balance and improve all four factors simultaneously. Using a collection of novel algorithms inspired by principles of 'serendipitous discovery', we demonstrate a method of successfully injecting serendipity, novelty and diversity into recommendations whilst limiting the impact on accuracy. We evaluate *Auralist* quantitatively over a broad set of metrics and, with a user study on music recommendation, show that *Auralist*'s emphasis on serendipity indeed improves user satisfaction.

Categories and Subject Descriptors

H.3.3 [**Information Storage and Retrieval**]: Information Retrieval and Search; H.2.8 [**Database applications**]: Data mining; I.2.6 [**Artificial Intelligence**]: Learning—*Knowledge Acquisition*

General Terms

Algorithms, Experimentation, Human Factors

Keywords

Collaborative filtering, diversification, serendipity, novelty, accuracy, recommender systems, metrics

1. INTRODUCTION

In an era of increasing choice, recommender systems have emerged as an important tool to help consumers manage the dizzying array of options presented by digitised markets and communities. Recommender systems generate prioritised list of unseen items by trying to predict a user's preferences based upon their profile. Such systems can now be seen in numerous applications (recommending, e.g., music, books), and have been shown to aid online sales [21].

Until recently, the vast majority of previous research has focused on improving the accuracy of recommendation: better modelling user preference so as to produce individually more enjoyable items. A growing trend, however, is to consider factors other than accuracy that contribute towards the quality of recommendation [15]. Notions of diversity, novelty and serendipity have been recently explored [8] as objectives that often conflict with the drive for accuracy.

The dangers of an overt focus on accuracy are twofold. Firstly, in failing to consider human desires for variety, discovery and change, accuracy-focused recommenders may forfeit an overall improved user experience, producing boring and ineffective recommendations. Secondly, in considering that recommendations have the power to shape user consumption patterns, there is an aesthetic concern that too much personalisation and pandering to a user's existing tastes harms a user's personal growth and experience. The extreme concept of a *"filter bubble"* describes the idea that users could be trapped in a self-reinforcing cycle of opinion, never being pushed to discover alternative genres or viewpoints [17].

It is important, then, that systems are designed with such alternative qualities in mind. We introduce a series of novel and well-grounded approaches that together compose the *Auralist* recommender, a system that explicitly balances the conflicting goals of accuracy, diversity, novelty and serendipity. Whereas prior research has often focused on these factors individually (as we shall see in our discussion of related work in Section 2), we use a range of metrics to measure all three non-accuracy factors simultaneously. Our methods are introduced as part of a hybrid framework that can combine a variety of algorithms to achieve the desired mix of qualities.

We address the issue of non-accuracy factors by focusing on techniques that simultaneously inject novelty, diversity, and serendipity into the recommendation process. In this way, we hope to actively counteract the constricting effects of personalisation. More specifically, we make three main contributions:

Auralist Framework. Auralist uses hybrid rank-interpolation to combine the output of three constituent algorithms in four different combinations: 1) *Basic Auralist* employs solely a new item-based col-

Permission to make digital or hard copies of all or part of this work for personal or classroom use is granted without fee provided that copies are not made or distributed for profit or commercial advantage and that copies bear this notice and the full citation on the first page. To copy otherwise, to republish, to post on servers or to redistribute to lists, requires prior specific permission and/or a fee.
WSDM'12, February 8–12, 2012, Seattle, Washington, USA.
Copyright 2012 ACM 978-1-4503-0747-5/12/02 ...$10.00.

laborative filtering algorithm called *Artist-based LDA* based on *Latent Dirichlet Allocation* [3] (Section 4.1); 2) *Community-Aware Auralist* combines *Artist-based LDA* with a new algorithm called *Listener Diversity* that promotes artists with "diverse" listenerships (Section 4.2.1); 3) *Bubble-Aware Auralist* combines *Artist-based LDA* with the new *Declustering* algorithm that identifies and counteracts a user's "music bubble" (Section 4.2.2); and 4) *Full Auralist* is the combination of all three algorithms (*Artist-based LDA*, *Listener Diversity*, and *Declustering*) together.

Quantitative evaluation of Auralist. We evaluate the different versions of Auralist using a comprehensive set of metrics that simultaneously assess accuracy, diversity, novelty and serendipity in user recommendation results (Section 5). We find that *Basic Auralist* produces recommendations that are as accurate as those produced by the state-of-the art *Implicit SVD* algorithm [10], and that both *Community-Aware Auralist* and *Bubble-Aware Auralist* greatly improve all three qualities of diversity, novelty and serendipity with differing trade-offs in accuracy.

Qualitative evaluation of Auralist. We conduct a user study to assess the objective qualities of enjoyment, real-world novelty, serendipity and overall user satisfaction (Section 6). We find that *Full Auralist*, although having lower accuracy and individual item enjoyment, is significantly more serendipitous and proves more satisfying overall than *Basic Auralist*.

Before concluding, we discuss the practical implications of our findings that go beyond music recommendation (Section 7).

2. RELATED WORK

Our research builds upon previous work attempting to quantify and measure the additional factors influencing end-user recommendation quality. We also draw inspiration from the implementation of algorithms designed to retain or enhance such qualities.

The techniques we propose belong to a family of model-based techniques for collaborative filtering [22]. Item-based [20] approaches in particular have found use in a number of commercial applications, being pioneered for Amazon.com product recommendations [13]. The possible use of *LDA* for recommendation was touched upon by Blei [3] in his initial formulation of the model, but it was later research by Hoffman [9] that established the use of Latent semantic models (in the form of the PLSI topic model) as tools for collaborative filtering.

Early concepts of novelty and serendipity were described by Herlocker [8] in his seminal survey of recommendation evaluation techniques, with other authors contributing quantitative measures and definitions [29, 27, 24, 16]. More recently, Vargas and Castells [25] attempt to formally unify diversity and novelty in a single evaluation framework. Our framework takes the straightforward approach of selecting a single metric to measure each evaluation independently.

The idea of balancing multiple objectives in recommendation has a strong basis in previous research. Adomavicius and Kwon [1] introduce a re-ranking method of diversity-improvement by applying a number of simple re-ranking algorithms to the output of accuracy-focused collaborative filtering algorithms. The diversity-accuracy tradeoff is controlled by restricting the re-ranking to the *top-N* most accurate items, thus restricting the maximum movement of an item. They show substantial improvements in the number of distinct items recommended in the *top-N* lists of users.

Jambor and Wang [11] frame conflicting objectives as a series of optimisation constraints, for use in a matrix factorisation algorithm. In one such experiment, the authors introduce constraints related to novelty and diversity, which are able to alter the distribution of popular items within a *top-N* list with little impact on accuracy. Ziegler *et al.* [29] use a topic diversification algorithm to rank items according to dissimilarity to preceding items in the recommendation set, integrating this information into recommendations through a rank-interpolation method; an approach that we reproduce, but across a wider set of objectives. A similar strategy appears in Zhou and Kuscik [27], where two graph-spreading algorithms that specialise in terms of accuracy and novelty performance respectively are hybridised in order to produce a recommender with the properties of both. Their results suggest that interpolation is indeed a viable method of producing balanced recommendations.

It is unclear, however, if multiple properties in addition to accuracy can be promoted at once. We present next a detailed description of the three properties of diversity, novelty and serendipity (Section 3) and a selection of algorithms that attempt to incorporate those properties in the recommendation process (Section 4).

3. WHY ACCURACY IS NOT ENOUGH

Before defining the three properties, we introduce two widely-used measures of accuracy and explain when they fall short of what is needed to measure the effectiveness of recommender systems.

Traditionally, recommendation quality is measured using one of a number of accuracy metrics, which assess how well the predictive output of a system matches a proportion of known, withheld items for each user. Examples of accuracy metrics include average *Top-N Recall* and the average *Rank* score proposed by Hu *et al.* [10]. Recall-based metrics measure the proportion of a user's test-set that appear within a *Top-N* recommendation list – a *Top-20* list that successfully includes 5 out of 10 test-set items will score a single-user recall of 0.5. These metrics we describe using a set of common symbols in Table 1.

$$\overline{Top\text{-}20\ Recall} = \frac{1}{|S|}\sum_{u\in S}\frac{|R_{u,20}\cap W_u|}{|W_u|} \qquad (1)$$

The average *Rank* score measures the average percentage rank of withheld items in a user's history, weighted by (positive) preference (for boolean preferences, the average *Rank* is simply the average rank of all history items). Unlike $\overline{Top\text{-}20\ Recall}$, $\overline{Rank}$ assesses how accurate a system is at modelling a user's entire history, not just the most easily recommended items. It also takes into account the full recommendation ranking, which complements recall-based assessments of only the top (observable) items:

$$\overline{Rank} = \frac{1}{|S|}\sum_{u\in S}\frac{\sum_{j\in N} P_{j,u}\,rank_{j,u}}{\sum_{j\in N} P_{j,u}} \qquad (2)$$

S	Set of all users
P	Preference matrix, where $P_{i,u}$ is the preference given by user u for item i (with our boolean preference system, $P_{i,u} = 1$ if the item is preferred by the user, and 0 otherwise)
R	*Top-N* function, where $R_{u,n}$ gives the top n recommended items for user u
N	Set of all items
W_u	Withheld item history of user u (set not used for training)
H_u	Non-withheld item history of user u
pop_i	Fraction of (all) preferences directed at item i
T	Set of *LDA* topics (the number of topics is 200).
L	*LDA* item-topic matrix, where $L_{i,t}$ represents the composition proportion assigned to topic t for item i
C_i	Number of artist i's unique listeners

Table 1: Symbols.

$$rank_{j,u} = \frac{\text{Index of item } j \text{ in ordered list for } u}{|N|}$$

Other metrics, such as *RMSE* (which measures the standard error of predicted preferences) have also seen widespread use. The above metrics, however, are better suited to handle the boolean nature of our dataset, which is described further in Section 5.1. The use of accuracy as a performance metric is well-grounded; previous user studies, such as the one conducted by Swearingen and Sinha [23] indicate that recommendation accuracy is a primary factor behind user satisfaction with recommendation systems. This has led to a focus on improving accuracy in recommendation algorithms; state-of-the-art systems score very highly indeed [10]. However, this is not to say that accuracy alone guarantees satisfactory recommendations.

There is a growing argument that factors other than accuracy also influence recommendation quality [15, 8, 29, 5, 19]. Recommendation techniques that focus purely on accuracy may neglect such alternative qualities and produce recommendations that appear superficially "good" but are in fact inferior in terms of actual user satisfaction. An extreme example of this may be a recommendation set consisting of entirely Beatles songs - the recommendations themselves may be accurate, but users will rapidly become bored with a collection of such similar and generic items.

To fix this problem, the three criteria of diversity, novelty and serendipity have been introduced by researchers. These assess the major factors influencing recommendation satisfaction alongside accuracy. Unlike previous work which has often considered only one or two such factors, we measure our improvements against a comprehensive assessment of each. To better characterise likely usage scenarios, all our metrics are applied to the *Top-20* recommendation list for each user, representing the fact that in a realistic application users are unlikely to be exposed to anything below the very top of the rankings.

Diversity represents the variety present in a list of recommendations. A diverse list can be seen to counteract user satiety with (homogeneous) recommendations. The aforementioned all-Beatles recommendation list, for example, is much less diverse than a list containing a wider assortment of artists. Previous research has shown that users will actively choose less-preferred items in an effort to improve the variety of consumption [19, 29]. We measure diversity through the *Intra-List Similarity* metric introduced by Ziegler *et al.* [28, 29], using (binary) cosine similarity (*CosSim*) to judge the similarity between items. *Intra-List Similarity* essentially sums the pairwise similarity of all items in a set (simplified in our case due to a symmetric similarity measure). Intuitively, the greater the proportion of preferring users two items have in common, the greater the similarity value *CosSim* will register. A recommendation list with groups of very similar items will score a high intra-list similarity compared to a list that has more dispersed and diverse recommendations.

$$\overline{Intra\text{-}List\ Similarity} = \frac{1}{|S|}\sum_{u\in S}\ \sum_{i,j\in R_{u,20}, j<i} CosSim(i,j) \quad (3)$$

$$CosSim(i,j) = \frac{\#\text{ users who like both } i \text{ and } j}{\sqrt{\#\text{ prefs in } i} \times \sqrt{\#\text{ prefs in } j}} \quad (4)$$

Novelty can be seen as the ability of a recommender to introduce users to items that they have not previously experienced before in real life (such experiences may be outside the system itself; e.g., music listened to whilst not on a computer). A recommendation that is accurate but not novel will include items that the user enjoys, but already knows of. A limited proportion of such recommendations has been shown [23, 18] to have a positive, trust-building impact on user satisfaction, but it can also be seen that to be useful a recommender needs to suggest previously unknown items. We measure novelty with a metric previously introduced by Zhuo and Kuscik [27]:

$$\overline{Novelty} = \frac{1}{|S|}\sum_{u\in S}\ \sum_{i\in R_{u,20}} \frac{\log_2 pop_i}{20} \quad (5)$$

This novelty metric quantifies the average information content of recommendation events – higher values mean that more globally "unexplored" items are being recommended. Under the assumption that the likelihood a user has experienced an item is proportional to its global popularity, this serves an approximation of true novelty. We measure actual novelty on an individual basis in our user study (Section 6).

Serendipity represents the "unusualness" or "surprise" of recommendations. Unlike novelty, serendipity encompasses the semantic content of items, and can be imagined as the distance between recommended items and their expected contents. A recommendation of *John Lennon* to listeners of *The Beatles* may well be accurate and novel, but hardly constitutes an original or surprising recommendation. A serendipitous system will challenge users to expand their tastes and hopefully provide more interesting recommendations, qualities that can help improve recommendation satisfaction [23]. We assess serendipity through a new *Unserendipity* metric, which uses *CosSim* to measure the average similarity between items in a user's history H_u and new recommendations. Lower values indicate that recommendations deviate from a user's traditional behaviour, and hence are more surprising:

$$\overline{Unserendipity} = \sum_{u \in S} \frac{1}{|S||H_u|} \sum_{h \in H_u} \sum_{i \in R_{u,20}} \frac{CosSim(i,h)}{20} \quad (6)$$

This metric bears some similarities to the distance-based novelty family of metrics seen in Vargas *et al.* [25].

4. THE AURALIST FRAMEWORK

At heart, the *Auralist* framework is an experiment in combining distinctive recommendation algorithms to improve overall (serendipitous) performance. Here, we introduce three techniques for generating recommendation rankings (*Artist-based LDA*, *Listener Diversity* and *Declustering*) that are paired to create different flavours of *Auralist*. *Basic Auralist* (Section 4.1) incorporates the so-called *Artist-based LDA* technique and is intended as a standalone recommender system. *Community-Aware* (Section 4.2.1) and *Bubble-Aware* (Section 4.2.2) *Auralist* versions interpolate *Artist-based LDA* with *Listener Diversity* and *Declustering* rankings respectively. These versions combine small elements of a serendipity-focused algorithm to reorder the basic algorithm's recommendations. A final *Full Auralist* recommender combines all three sub-algorithms.

4.1 Basic Auralist

Basic Auralist is an item-based recommender system that employs *Latent Dirichlet Allocation* as a technique for computing item features. We call this approach *Artist-based LDA* and present it next.

LDA has been used traditionally in topic-modeling, being a fully generative model for document production [3]. Under this framework, words within a large document set can be clustered into topics based upon co-occurrence, each topic being a probabilistic distribution over word tokens. A "topic composition vector" can then be determined for each document, indicating the estimated level of influence each "topic" would have if the document were to be generated using the *LDA* model. Both topic clustering and document composition can be computed stochastically using the *Gibbs Sampling* algorithm (described in Griffiths and Steyvers [7]) in an unsupervised manner over a training dataset.

Our approach applies *Gibbs Sampling* to the unary preferences of our *Last.fm* dataset (described in Section 5.1) using the MALLET toolkit [14]. We note two straightforward means of framing user-artist preferences in a manner suitable for *LDA*. In a *User-based LDA* model, users are treated as *LDA* documents and preferred artists as words. This produces a series of artist topics corresponding roughly to artist genre, but does not tell us anything about the artists themselves. Conversely, the inverse *Artist-based LDA* model treats artists as documents and preferring users as words, producing a fixed-length topic composition vector for each item. Topics in the artist-based model can be imagined to represent *user-communities*, clustering together users with similar preferences. Topic vectors thus represent the distribution of the listener base of an artist, and can be used to characterise them. We then define a *LDA* similarity metric as the (real-valued) cosine similarity between **artist** topic vectors:

$$LDASim(i,j) = \frac{\sum_{t \in T} L_{i,t} \times L_{j,t}}{\sqrt{\sum_{t \in T} (L_{i,t})^2} \sqrt{\sum_{t \in T} (L_{j,t})^2}} \quad (7)$$

This similarity metric is then used directly for item-based recommendation by defining $Basic(u,i)$, which is the score that user u associates to item i:

$$Basic(u,i) = \sum_{h \in H_u} LDASim(i,h) \quad (8)$$

All artists can be sorted (in descending order) by the sum-total of their similarity with items in a user's existing history [13]. This produces a $rank_{Basic,u,i}$ for each item i, with the most similar items awarded the smallest percentage ranks.

By generalising user "topics", we aim to both smooth the data and generate less obvious and more serendipitous recommendations compared to more naïve techniques, as connections can now be made through similar, but not directly related users. We note also that *Basic Auralist* built on *Artist-based LDA* inherits two main benefits common to *model-based* recommenders: faster online performance (if item-item similarities are not precomputed) and a compact semantic representation of the data (in this case, in terms of listener composition). This semantic representation is exploited in the following subsection to further influence recommendation.

4.2 Two hybrid versions of Auralist

To increase the novelty, diversity, and serendipity of *Basic Auralist*'s recommendations, we combine *Artist-based LDA* recommendation with two new algorithms. The first is called *Listener Diversity* and aims to prioritise for recommendation artists with particularly diverse listener communities, encouraging users to explore beyond a given niche. The combination of *Artist-based LDA* and *Listener Diversity* is called *Community-Aware Auralist* (Section 4.2.1).

The second algorithm is called *Declustering* and aims to determine a user's "musical bubbles" (clusters of artists that the user listens to) and then recommend artists outside established cluster groups (hence *Declustering*). The combination of *Artist-based LDA* and *Declustering* is called *Bubble-Aware Auralist* (Section 4.2.2).

We combine the different *Auralist* algorithms by merging their individual rank outputs. One way of doing so is to produce a hybrid score for each item (artist) [29]. Intuitively, the hybrid ranking score of an item i can be taken as a linear interpolation of the percentage [0,1) rank the item has in the output of each of the contributing algorithms. A set of interpolation coefficients λ_a over a set of algorithms A controls the influence of each individual algorithm. In the case of the generalised *Full Auralist* recommender, we have three λ coefficients governing an algorithm set A that includes *Artist-based LDA*, *Listener Diversity* and *Declustering*.

$$Hybrid(u,i) = \sum_{a \in A} \lambda_a (rank_{a,u,i})$$

The final recommendation output consists of the item list sorted by the hybrid rank score. The "hybridisation" of recommendation allows an accuracy-focused *Basic Auralist* to be combined with small proportions of diversity or serendipity promoting algorithms, in order to improve the overall balance of qualities.

4.2.1 Community-Aware Auralist

Community-Aware Auralist introduces the *Listener Diversity* metric for artists, which is used to produce a ranked list of the most diverse artists. This list is blended with *Basic Auralist* to promote more diverse artists in recommendation.

We recall that for the *Artist LDA* model, topics are formed over "user communities", groups of users that share common item preferences. An artist in the *LDA* recommender is represented by a vector of topic proportions indicating how listeners of that artist are distributed amongst these "user communities".

Such a representation offers us a unique perspective on the demographics of listeners, not visible when observing the raw vector of preferences. Certain artists, whilst popular in their own right, might have a listener base concentrated in only a few user communities, whereas the listeners of another artist might be more widely distributed.

Given that a *LDA* topic vector is a probability distribution summing to 1, we use the entropy of such a distribution to measure its skewedness. A distribution focused on only a few outcomes will score a less negative entropy; a more evenly and widely distributed event will produce a greater negative entropy. We thus introduce the *Listener Diversity* of an artist i as the entropy over its topic distribution:

$$Listener\ Diversity(i) = -\sum_{t \in T} L_{i,t} \log_2(L_{i,t})$$

What does Listener Diversity represent in terms of recommendation quality? Intuitively, we can imagine it as being a measure of nicheness - how polarising a given performer is. A Ukrainian bagpipe metal band[1] is unlikely to spark broad appeal compared to, say, *The Beatles*. However, that is not to say that the former should not be recommended, if the user belongs to the limited demographic following that style of music. In the context of serendipitous recommendations, however, we seek to expand a user's music taste beyond that of his comfort zone. A strategy for this would be to highlight more diverse artists that include a user's established music communities, but also introduce elements of ones the user may be unfamiliar with. This balance can be achieved by interpolating the output of a *Listener Diversity*-sorted list with that of a conventional accuracy-focused algorithm; the former boosting the rank of more diverse artists whilst the latter ensures that ranking artists are still enjoyable:

$$Community(u,i) = (1-\lambda) rank_{Basic,u,i} + \lambda rank_{Diversity,i}$$

Analysis of *Listener Diversity*'s relationship with other factors shows that *Listener Diversity* tends to bias towards globally popular artists. This should be unsurprising, as such artists will garner more exposure and attract a naturally wider fan base. We compensate for this by discounting an artist's original *Listener Diversity* with a popularity-diversity regression function, highlighting artists that are diverse for their popularity level (popularity being the number C_i of the artist's unique listeners). The resulting adjusted *Listener Diversity* is:

$$Listener\ Diversity'(i) = Listener\ Diversity(i) - Offset_{pop}(i) \tag{9}$$

In our dataset (which will be described in Section 5.1), following a linear regression, we find the following coefficients for $Offset_{pop}(i)$:

$$Offset_{pop}(i) = 0.462 \log(C_i) - 1.326. \tag{10}$$

4.2.2 Bubble-Aware Auralist

As a counterpart to *Listener Diversity*, we introduce a graph-based algorithm termed *Declustering*. *Declustering* produces a ranked list of the least "clustered" or "boring" items for a user and is interpolated with *Basic Auralist* to form *Bubble-Aware Auralist*:

$$Bubble(u,i) = (1-\lambda) rank_{Basic,u,i} + \lambda rank_{Declustering,u,i}$$

We compute *Declustering* scores over what we call the "Artist Graph". Formally, this is a graph $G = (N, E)$ where each node $i \in N$ is an artist and edges $(i, j, weight) \in E$ are drawn between artists that have non-zero similarity, according to a similarity metric $weight = sim(i,j)$ computed with the previously defined *LDASim* (Equation 7). Intuitively, framing recommendations in this format allows us to apply network-based analysis techniques to (prospective) items. Such a model has been used previously by Celma *et al.* [5, 4] to investigate the long-tail properties of music recommendation in terms of network links. We further introduce the idea of a user's "*local preference graph*", which can also be seen as a user's "music bubble". This is the subgraph $G_u = (H_u, E_u)$ of the artist G consisting only of the nodes $i \in H_u$ that are found in the preference history of the user.

The *Declustering* algorithm attempts to identify nodes that lie on the edge of clusters in a user's graph, avoiding heavy concentrations of previous activity ("boring" recommendations) whilst still maintaining overall similarity. In this way we hope to help users expand their music taste, literally pushing the boundaries of the region their behaviour occupies in the feature-space. This recommendation strategy is motivated by concepts of social network theory such as clustering and brokerage [6].

In analysing the Artist Graph, we find that the *Last.fm* dataset has a power-law distribution of node degrees, suggesting it may have "small-world" properties [26]. This implies a graph structure similar to that of a social network, with nodes being clustered around a series of high-degree "hubs". Therefore, we employ a metric commonly used in social-network analysis to measure how clustered nodes in a network are. The clustering coefficient of a node i is defined as:

$$Clustering(i) = \frac{2 \times |\{(j,k) \in E_u | j, k \in \text{neighbours}(i)\}|}{|\text{neighbours}(i)| \times (|\text{neighbours}(i)| - 1)} \tag{11}$$

where *neighbours(i)* is the set of nodes that are neighbours of item i in the local preference graph. The clustering coefficient of a node measures the proportion of possible interconnections that exist amongst neighbours of a node. A node with a high clustering coefficient is surrounded by tightly interconnected nodes (i.e., in the centre of a near-clique) whereas a node with a lower clustering coefficient might have neighbours split between multiple clusters or lie on the edge of an existing cluster.

[1] www.holyblood.com.ua

```
foreach item pair j, k in H_u do
    total+= LDASim(j, k);
    count+=1;
end
avgSim = total/count;
foreach item i in candidate set for user u do
    foreach item pair j, k in neighbours(i) do
        if LDASim(j, k) > avgSim then
            edgeTotal+=1;
        end
        edgeCount+=1;
    end
    cluster(i) = edgeTotal/edgeCount;
    recommendations.add(cluster(i), i);
end
recommendations.sortBy(cluster, ascending);
```

Algorithm 1: Pseudo-code for *Declustering.*

The *Declustering* algorithm (Algorithm 1) considers in turn all the prospective recommendations for a user. For each item, it temporarily adds the item to the graph and computes the clustering coefficient of that node with respect to the existing elements of the user's local preference graph. The output of the algorithm is an ordered list of the most "cluster-avoiding" artists in the candidate set, which (as with *Listener Diversity*) can be interpolated with a conventional recommender to apply counter-clustering pressure to recommendation items. As the clustering coefficient operates over unweighted edges, we threshold edges in the local preference graph according to whether a similarity weight indicates unusual significance. An *LDASim* weight that exceeds the average for a particular user is considered significant for the purposes of computing the clustering coefficient. This has the effect of removing the majority of (weak) edges in the graph. We can also adjust the threshold in terms of standard deviations from the average; this affects the sensitivity of cluster detection and should be experimentally determined. *Declustering*'s emphasis on low clustering scores reflects the desire to dissuade the recommendation of artists that are too deeply embedded in a genre cluster with respect to a particular user. Such artists are likely accurate but not serendipitous, being too similar to a great many of user's existing artists.

In the next section, we prove the effectiveness of our techniques by apply to them the evaluation metrics introduced in Section 3.

5. EVALUATION

The goals of our evaluation are to assess: 1) to which extent the *Auralist* framework produces diverse, novel, and serendipitous recommendations; 2) at which cost for accuracy *Auralist* produces such recommendations; and 3) the best combination of algorithms that produces an overall more satisfying recommender. To meet these goals, we employ the suite of metrics described in Section 3 to quantitatively measure the performance of both a set of baseline recommenders as well as various interpolations of our serendipity-enhancing techniques.

5.1 Dataset

Our experiments are conducted over a 360k *Last.fm* user[2] dataset [12], collected by Òscar Celma in 2008 [3]. This contains the `user.getTopArtists()` output for each user from the *Last.fm* API, which is a list of previously listened-to artists and play-counts derived from both *Last.fm*'s online radio services and media player plugins.

In contrast to other publicly available datasets, the *Last.fm* dataset consists of implicit observations of user preference through prior behaviour. This means that there is no explicit ratings scale associated with preferences and that preferences themselves can be considered noisy - track metadata may be incorrect, songs may be left on loop/shuffle and user history lengths will vary. We clean the dataset to remove non-artist items, misspelled artist names and extremely unpopular artists, leaving us with 48,988 possible recommendation items. We take our implicit preferences to be **unary** (1 or nothing), which lends itself well to the processing techniques we introduced in Section 4.

5.2 Basic Auralist Recommendation

We evaluate the effectiveness of *Artist-LDA* recommendation method against the state-of-the art *Implicit SVD* method introduced by Hu, Koren and Valinsky [10]. We adapt this model to incorporate the implicit artist play-count as a confidence weight in the matrix factorisation cost function. Metrics are computed over random subsamples of 35k users; larger samples only marginally improve performance. 20% of each user's preferences were randomly withheld as a training sample. One feature of *LDA* that we leverage is the fact that Gibbs Sampling runs relatively quickly even on large user samples, compared to other model-based techniques. We thus bootstrap the *LDA* topic training step with the full 360k user dataset, which completes 1000 iterations in under an hour on an Intel Core^{TM}i5 2.8GHz processor.

Our experimental results are reported in Table 2 and show that *Basic Auralist* produces the most overall accurate rankings for user histories ($\overline{Rank}$ = 0.0194) whilst *Implicit SVD* produces the highest $\overline{\textit{Top-20 Recall}}$ scores (0.174). Both algorithms score comparatively in diversity ($\overline{\textit{Intra-List Similarity}}$), whereas *Implicit SVD* has improved serendipity and *Basic Auralist* has slightly improved novelty.

The combination of accuracy scores seem to indicate that *Implicit SVD* does a better job of including items in the *Top-20* list. However, it may be argued that for the use-case of *serendipitous* recommendation, a high recall is not necessary; recall indicates that similar, already known items are being placed in the *Top-20* list, displacing the recommendation of novel items. By contrast, *Basic Auralist* broadly characterises what a user has previously liked ($\overline{Rank}$) without being overtly sycophantic. Interestingly, of the items *Implicit SVD* does recommend, the registered $\overline{\textit{Unserendipity}}$ is somewhat lower, implying that the generalisation of matrix factorisation does result in some less obvious recommendations as well. We exceed this serendipity value with later versions of *Auralist.*

[2] `http://www.last.fm`

[3] `http://www.dtic.upf.edu/~ocelma/MusicRecommendationDataset/`

	$\overline{Rank}$	$\overline{Top\text{-}20\ Recall}$	$\overline{Intra\text{-}List\ Similarity}$	$\overline{Novelty}$	$\overline{Unserendipity}$
Basic Auralist	**0.019** ±0.0004	0.157 ±0.004	**14.4** ±0.2	**11.8** ±0.06	0.060 ±0.0004
Implicit SVD	0.039 ± 0.0008	**0.174** ±0.002	14.7 ±0.1	10.9 ±0.03	**0.046** ±0.0002
Community-aware(λ=0.05)	0.023 ±0.02	0.030 ±0.0009	3.4 ±0.06	17.2 ±0.1	0.047 ±0.0003
Bubble-aware(λ=0.2)	0.021 ±0.0002	0.029 ±0.0006	3.4 ±0.05	14.2 ±0.1	0.035 ±0.0002
Full Auralist	0.025	0.008	1.54	17.3	0.039

Table 2: Performance results for *Basic Auralist*, the state-of-the-art *Implicit SVD*, and *Full Auralist*.

5.3 Hybrid versions of Auralist

Figures 1 and 2 show the performance results for *Community-Aware* and *Bubble-Aware Auralist*. Table 2 also includes their performance at points of interest along the λ curve (note at λ=0, both algorithms reduce to *Basic Auralist*).

Given that both hybrid versions of Auralist attempt to bias towards serendipitous recommendations at the expense of more "easily accurate" items, it should be unsurprising that both exhibit an accuracy-serendipity trade-off. More interestingly, both methods increase novelty and diversity, and do so at different rates.

As the *Listener Diversity* interpolation increases, *Community-Aware Auralist*'s rapid improvements in non-accuracy scores (Figures 2(a), 2(b), 2(c)) are tracked by decays in recall (Figure 1(b)) and to a lesser extent $\overline{Rank}$ (Figure 1(a)), tailing off at higher proportions. *Community-Aware Auralist* hence represents a direct trade-off between accuracy and non-accuracy performance, with the most activity occurring in the $0 < \lambda < 0.05$ range of Figures 1 and 2. Compared with the other graphs, *Community-Aware Auralist* maintains a consistently sizable lead over *Bubble-Aware Auralist* in terms of novelty (Figure 2(b)), likely due to the popularity correction $Offset_{pop}$ we introduced in Section 4.2.1 (Equation 10).

As with *Community-Aware Auralist*, the *Bubble-Aware Auralist*'s performance curves for serendipity, novelty and diversity track that of $\overline{Top\text{-}20\ Recall}$. Unlike *Community-Aware Auralist*, however, *Bubble-Aware Auralist*'s $\overline{Rank}$ decays at a much slower rate, and the performance curves possess sigmoid-like qualities, experiencing the greatest rate of change after about $\lambda = 0.1$ and diminishing returns afterwards. We propose that this is the point when the *Declustering* algorithm is able to successfully overcome the bias towards recommendations embedded within preference clusters and is able to successfully recommend cluster-bordering items. The nature of the $\overline{Rank}$ curve indicates that the bulk of this benefit can be achieved without an overwhelming effect on overall accuracy, suggesting that *Bubble-Aware Auralist* may be able to supply "almost free" serendipity, diversity and novelty.

Bubble-Aware Auralist manages to surpass *Community-Aware Auralist* in terms of serendipity relatively quickly ($\lambda \sim 0.15$), continuing to improve even after *Community-Aware Auralist*'s performance begins to plateau. This suggests that the serendipity improvement is not merely incidental (i.e., from declining accuracy), and is actively being promoted by *Declustering*.

To sum up, these findings indicate that *Community-Aware Auralist* is best used at smaller interpolations (0–0.05) as a roughly even trade between accuracy and non-accuracy qualities and as a broad stroke in changing the (accuracy/non-accuracy) focus of a recommender. They also suggest that using *Bubble-Aware Auralist* during the peak rate of change before significant $\overline{Rank}$ penalties (Figure 1(a)) accrue can improve non-accuracy qualities at very little cost. At $\lambda = 0.2$, a mere 0.7% increase in average history rank is accompanied by a 77% decrease in $\overline{Intra\text{-}List\ Similarity}$, 20% increase in novelty and a 42% decrease in measured unserendipity. Overall, both methods prove to be able to successfully improve diversity, novelty and serendipity.

6. USER STUDY

Alongside our quantitative measurements, we further conduct a user study to validate the effectiveness of *Auralist* (and indeed, serendipity-orientated recommendation in general) in real-life situations. We measure the perceived serendipity, enjoyment, novelty and overall qualitative satisfaction associated with a refined version of the hybrid recommender.

The *Full Auralist* recommender combines *Artist-LDA*, *Listener Diversity*, and *Declustering* in proportions of $\lambda_{1,2} = (0.03, 0.20)$ respectively (motivated by the results of the previous section) and demonstrates overall superior non-accuracy performance compared to our previous methods (Table 2):

$$\begin{aligned} Full_{u,i} =& (1 - \lambda_1 - \lambda_2) rank_{Basic,u,i} \\ & + \lambda_1 rank_{Diversity,u,i} + \lambda_2 rank_{Declustering,u,i} \end{aligned}$$

6.1 Experimental Method

The user study involved 21 participants, the majority of which are current university students. This included a mix of under/post graduates and men/women between the ages of 18-27, of varying nationalities. Each participant was asked to name six pre-2008 artists that represented his/her music tastes, which were used as "seed" histories for recommendation. Volunteers suggested a very wide range of artists, across many musical genres. Users were then presented with two (unlabelled) *Top-20* recommendation lists, generated by *Basic Auralist* and *Full Auralist* respectively. The lists were presented in a randomly determined order for each participant.

Users were instructed to listen to at least two 30-second song samples from each unknown artist and to fill in an accompanying survey[4]. Survey questions assess individually for each recommendation how enjoyable (Dislike the song... Will definitely listen again), serendipitous (Exactly what I listen to normally... Something I would never have listened to otherwise) and novel an artist is. The former two are assessed using 5-point Likert scales, whereas novelty is multiple choice.

6.2 User Ratings

For each user, we compute the average enjoyment and serendipity ratings given to the artists in each list. The results are summarised in Table 3 and show that there is a substantial difference in scores given to *Basic Auralist* and

[4]`http://tinyurl.com/ycz20`

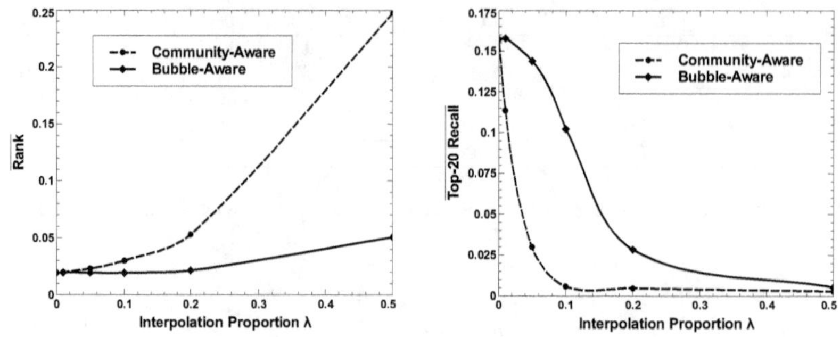

(a) $\overline{Rank}$ accuracy (b) $\overline{Top\text{-}20\ Recall}$ accuracy

Figure 1: Accuracy performance of *Community-Aware Auralist* and *Bubble-Aware Auralist* as the contribution λ of the corresponding serendipity-enhancing technique increases.

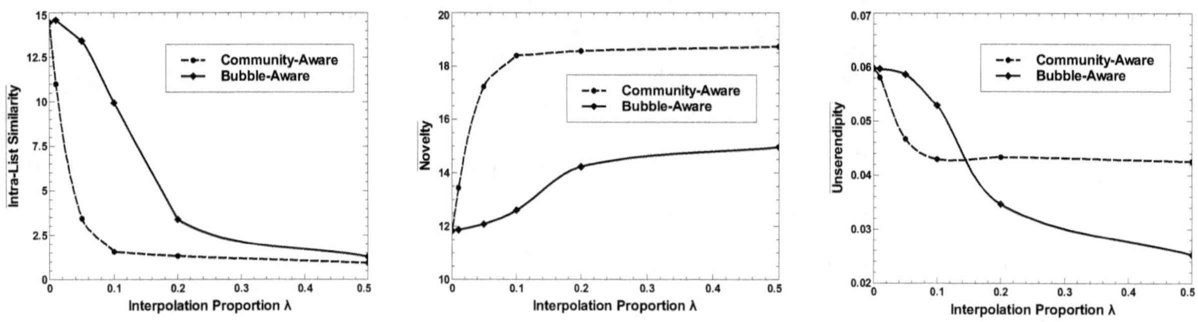

(a) Diversity (b) Novelty (c) Serendipity

Figure 2: Diversity, novelty, and serendipity performance of *Community-Aware Auralist* and *Bubble-Aware Auralist* as the contribution λ of the corresponding serendipity-enhancing technique increases.

	Basic Auralist	Full Auralist
Serendipity Rating	2.08 (±0.77)	2.96 (±0.69)
Enjoyment Rating	4.21 (±0.54)	3.82 (±0.53)
# Useful Recommendations	2.90 (±2.61)	5.86 (±3.05)
# Serendipitous Recomm.s	1.81 (±1.86)	4.14 (±2.90)
# Familiar Recomm.s	12.62 (±4.14)	7.43 (±5.07)

Table 3: Summary of the results from our user study. Values in brackets are standard deviations.

Full Auralist. Compared to the basic accuracy-focused system, *Full Auralist* manages to score much higher in terms of *Serendipity* (+0.88), but sacrifices a proportion of average *Enjoyment* (−0.39) in doing so. A plot of the difference between these two variables can be seen in Figure 3(a).

Whilst the variance of reported results may appear high, we recall that the study was conducted as a repeated measures experiment. Therefore, we test the significance of a findings using a one-tailed pairwise *t-test.* Our tests show that *Full Auralist* does indeed exhibit greater serendipity ($p = 0.00002$) and reduced accuracy ($p = 0.004$) compared to *Basic Auralist.*

In addition to raw serendipity/enjoyment scores, we also measure the average number of *Useful*, *Serendipitous* and *Familiar* recommendations issued to each user by the recommenders. We classify as *Useful* any recommendation that is not "Already Known" to the user, and is rated a 4 or 5 in enjoyment ("Already Known" recommendations with 4/5 in enjoyment are instead classified as *Familiar* recommendations). *Serendipitous* recommendations are those *Useful* recommendations that satisfy the additional requirement of being rated a 4 or 5 in serendipity. Useful items represent successful recommendations made to the user, whilst Serendipitous items detail how many managed to both satisfy the user and expand his/her tastes at the same time. Familiar items represent the "trust-building" items described in Swearingen [23] that do not increase utility but improve user satisfaction with the system.

Full Auralist is shown to improve significantly on the basic version in terms of the number of Useful and Serendipitous recommendations, with *t-test* confidence values of $p < 0.001$. Indeed, *Full Auralist* produces on average double the number of Useful and Serendipitous recommendations compared to *Basic Auralist*, with the proportion of Serendipitous artists within the set of Useful artist being higher as well (71% compared to 62%). Despite this, *Full Auralist* still manages to produce a substantial number of Familiar recommendations (7.43). The overall novelty of *Full Auralist*'s recommendations is vastly superior - Figure 3(b) shows that the system reduces the number of "Already Known" artists in recommendation lists by an absolute percentage of over 25%.

6.3 User Satisfaction

Quantitative analysis of survey results have shown that, whilst featuring a reduction in perceived *Enjoyment*, *Full*

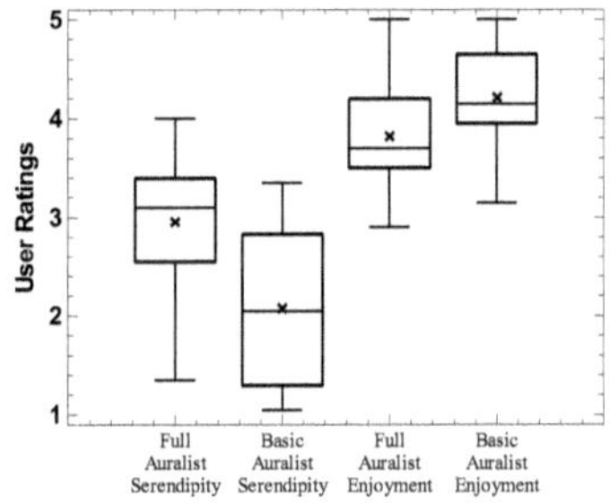

(a) *Serendipity* and *Enjoyment* ratings

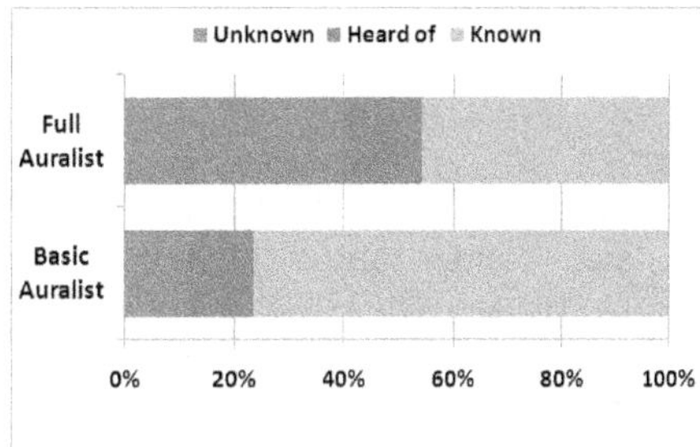

(b) Fraction of novel recommendations

Figure 3: Results for user satisfaction. (a) *Serendipity* and *Enjoyment* user ratings for *Basic Auralist* and *Full Auralist* on a 1-5 Likert scale. (b) Fraction of recommended artists that are *"Previously Known"*, *"Heard of, but not listened to"* and *"Completely Unknown"* for *Basic Auralist* and *Full Auralist*.

Auralist significantly improves upon perceived *Serendipity* and *Novelty*, as well as the overall number of *Useful* recommendations. We show below a selection of comments participants made with regards to which recommendation algorithm they thought was more satisfying:

> *"[Full Auralist] was more satisfying because it introduced me to new artists. [Basic] was filled entirely with new artists which, while very good, were things that I listened to all the time on a regular basis. [Full Auralist] had artists that were of the same quality of those I listen to but which I'd never heard of."*

> *"I found [the Full Auralist list] more surprising than [Basic]. Most artists I had not heard of (which is what I prefer). Listening to them gave me at least five new artists I could look into and use in the future."*

> *"While I enjoyed the songs on the [Full Auralist] list less, I liked that there was more new music on it than the first list. So I'm going to say that I preferred the [Full Auralist] list."*

> *"[The Basic list was better], more familiar music & more my taste, although [Full Auralist] introduced me to a few good bands."*

> *"[The Full Auralist list] was way too jazzy, and had very few artists I connected with immediately. While [the Basic list] had a vast majority of artists I knew well and have opinions of, the few unknowns were really very congenial."*

In analysing these and other comments, we see two broad consensuses amongst the opinions of participants. A majority(12) of users prefer *Full Auralist*, appreciating the novelty and serendipity of the recommendations made. A substantial minority(7), however, prefer the baseline system due to its comparatively better modelling of their own tastes. Two gave neutral preferences. Whether a user falls into the first or second camp may well depend on three main factors - the user's prior convictions, emotional state, and social context, as recent work has suggested [2].

The dichotomy in preference seems to suggest that an adaptive recommendation system, where users can individually tune the level of "wildness" in recommendations, may find success. This could be offered as a series of recommendation lists, or perhaps be controlled by a sliding scale. In both cases, the hybrid model of recommendation would be particularly effective, as different levels of serendipity can be implemented simply by adjusting the interpolation parameters.

7. DISCUSSION

Our user study shows that *Full Auralist* produces significantly more serendipitous recommendations at the cost of some accuracy. We also show that, despite the reduced accuracy, a large number of participants expressed greater satisfaction with *Full Auralist*'s recommendations. These conclusions are consistent with previous user studies [29, 23, 19]. In particular, we support Ziegler [29] and Ratner [19]'s findings that users are willing to sacrifice some amount of accuracy for improved novelty/diversity/serendipity performance, and that such systems are more satisfying overall. Qualitative comments seem to indicate that serendipity is usually, but not consistently, a positive contributor to this.

The nature of this experiment also demonstrates that Auralist functions well as a practical recommender, even with the "cold-start problem" of limited initial history. It is likely that much of the results variance comes from users' choice of initial artists, with some users suggesting a wider range of genres. Additional history data, perhaps pulled from a *Last.fm* profile, would allow us to better model a user's preferences and thus generate both more accurate and more serendipitous items.

Perhaps our most interesting discovery is that novelty, diversity and serendipity can be improved simultaneously, without any apparent trade-off between the three qualities. One may argue that this is because all three benefit from a departure from pure accuracy – all three qualities, though different, represent facets of a notion of "discovery" that diametrically oppose the notion of "familiarity" that accuracy represents. This does not mean individual qualities cannot be emphasised, however - hybridising a popularity-sorted ranking list will primarily improve novelty, whereas a topic diversification method (such as Ziegler's [29]) will mostly improve diversity.

Our algorithms represents a direct attempt at countering

what appears to be an increasing trend by websites and social media to filter what people see - recommending only "safe" items by clustering like-minded users [17]. This behaviour is concerning because it prevents established ideas and norms from being challenged, fostering partisanship and impeding mutual understanding. We hope that even as algorithms are becoming more accurate, additional consideration is given to ensuring this accuracy is also used to introduce users to new content. Despite being designed for music recommendation, *Auralist* has the potential to be adapted for a great many other fields; practically, the *Declustering* algorithm could be readily applied to many existing item-based recommendation algorithms (with domain-dependent similarity metrics). By mapping out a user's preference space and deliberately trying to expand it, one could effectively promote personalised exploration balanced with satisfaction.

8. CONCLUSION

We introduced *Auralist* as a novel recommendation framework that generates diverse, novel and serendipitous recommendations, at a slight cost to accuracy. To aid quantitative analysis, we described a series of metrics designed to assess both accuracy and the three additional qualities of diversity, novelty and serendipity.

We further presented two novel serendipity-enhancing techniques that can be combined with existing ranking methods through "hybridisation". Both *Community-Aware Auralist* and the *Bubble-Aware Auralist* prove to effectively boost novelty, diversity and serendipity scores, with the latter offering a better trade-off with regards to accuracy.

Through a user study on the *Full Auralist* recommender employing all three techniques, we conclusively show that our methods are able to produce more serendipitous recommendations. In addition, despite a noted decrease in the average enjoyment of artists, we show that our serendipity-enhancing techniques improve overall user satisfaction.

We believe our findings are valuable for any kind of consumer-facing recommendation system, where a user's previous history may increasingly constrain their recommendations. Our techniques offer a simple and well-grounded way to diffuse the effects of the so-called "filter bubble".

Although we investigate only two serendipity-enhancing methods here, additional techniques can easily be introduced to achieve other performance goals. Of particular interest then would be a framework that allows explicit user feedback to shape the algorithm interpolation for individual users, allowing the system to adapt to the adventurousness and mood of different personalities. This could be integrated into a system that maintains serendipity over time, perhaps by cycling through genres or recommendation flavours. Allowing users to direct their own musical growth (through interactive questions or target genres) may also be a way of increasing user satisfaction and promoting musical diversity. Finally, we suggest that a consistent and validated set of performance metrics would greatly aid future work in recommender balance.

Acknowledgments. This work was in part funded by RCUK through the Horizon Digital Economy Research grant (EP/G065802/1). We also thank Òscar Celma for making the dataset publicly available, Stephen Clark for his support, and Toby Moncaster and Jon Crowcroft for their comments. We finally thank the anonymous reviewers.

9. REFERENCES

[1] G. Adomavicius and Y. O. Kwon. Towards more diverse recommendations: Item re-ranking methods for recommender systems. In *Workshop on Information Technologies and Systems*, 2009.

[2] J. An, D. Quercia, and J. Crowcroft. This paper won't change your mind, but...: Why individuals seek diverse opinions (or why they don't). In *Technical Report of the University of Cambridge*, 2012.

[3] D. M. Blei, A. Y. Ng, and M. I. Jordan. Latent dirichlet allocation. *Joural of Machine Learning Research*, 2003.

[4] O. Celma and P. Cano. From hits to niches?: or how popular artists can bias music recommendation and discovery. In *ACM NETFLIX*, 2008.

[5] O. Celma and P. Herrera. A new approach to evaluating novel recommendations. In *ACM RecSys*, 2008.

[6] D. A. Easley and J. M. Kleinberg. *Networks, Crowds, and Markets - Reasoning About a Highly Connected World.* Cambridge University Press, 2010.

[7] T. L. Griffiths and M. Steyvers. Finding scientific topics. *PNAS*, 2004.

[8] J. L. Herlocker, J. A. Konstan, L. G. Terveen, and J. T. Riedl. Evaluating collaborative filtering recommender systems. *ACM Transactions of Information Systems*, 2004.

[9] T. Hofmann. Latent semantic models for collaborative filtering. *ACM Transactions of Information Systems*, 2004.

[10] Y. Hu, Y. Koren, and C. Volinsky. Collaborative filtering for implicit feedback datasets. In *Proceedings of the 2008 Eighth IEEE International Conference on Data Mining*, 2008.

[11] T. Jambor and J. Wang. Optimizing multiple objectives in collaborative filtering. In *ACM RecSys*, 2010.

[12] M. Levy and K. Bosteels. Music recommendation and the long tail. In *WOMRAD*, 2010.

[13] G. Linden, B. Smith, and J. York. Amazon.com recommendations: Item-to-item collaborative filtering. *IEEE Internet Computing*, 2003.

[14] A. K. McCallum. Mallet: A machine learning for language toolkit. `http://mallet.cs.umass.edu`, 2002.

[15] S. M. McNee, J. Riedl, and J. A. Konstan. Being accurate is not enough: how accuracy metrics have hurt recommender systems. In *ACM CHI EA*, 2006.

[16] T. Murakami, K. Mori, and R. Orihara. Metrics for evaluating the serendipity of recommendation lists. In *JSAI*, 2007.

[17] E. Pariser. *The Filter Bubble: What the Internet Is Hiding from You.* Penguin Group USA, 2011.

[18] P. Pu and L. Chen. A user-centric evaluation framework of recommender systems. In *UCERSTI Workshop*, ACM RecSys, 2010.

[19] R. K. Ratner, B. E. Kahn, and D. Kahneman. Choosing less-preferred experiences for the sake of variety. *The Journal of Consumer Research*, 1999.

[20] B. Sarwar, G. Karypis, J. Konstan, and J. Reidl. Item-based collaborative filtering recommendation algorithms. In *ACM WWW*, 2001.

[21] J. B. Schafer, J. Konstan, and J. Riedi. Recommender systems in e-commerce. In *ACM EC*, 1999.

[22] X. Su and T. M. Khoshgoftaar. A survey of collaborative filtering techniques. *Advances in Artificial Intelligence*, 2009.

[23] K. Swearingen and R. Sinha. Beyond Algorithms: An HCI Perspective on Recommender Systems. *SIGIR*, 2001.

[24] K. O. Takayuki Akiyama and M. Tanizaki. Proposal and evaluation of serendipitous recommendation method using general unexpectedness. In *PRSAT*, 2010.

[25] S. Vargas and P. Castells. Rank and relevance in novelty and diversity metrics for recommender systems. ACM RecSys, 2011.

[26] D. J. Watts and S. H. Strogatz. Collective dynamics of 'small-world' networks. *Nature*, 1998.

[27] T. Zhuo, Z. Kuscik, J.-G. Liu, M. Medo, J. R. Wakeling, and Y.-C. Zhang. Solving the apparent diversity-accuracy dilemma of recommender systems. *PNAS*, 2010.

[28] C.-N. Ziegler, G. Lausen, and S.-T. Lars. Taxonomy-driven computation of product recommendations. In *ACM CIKM*, 2004.

[29] C.-N. Ziegler, S. M. McNee, J. A. Konstan, and G. Lausen. Improving recommendation lists through topic diversification. In *ACM WWW*, 2005.

Efficient Misbehaving User Detection in Online Video Chat Services

Hanqiang Cheng[1], Yu-Li Liang[2], Xinyu Xing[3], Xue Liu[1],Richard Han[2], Qin Lv[2], Shivakant Mishra[2]
[1]School of Computer Science, McGill University
[2]Department of Computer Science, University of Colorado at Boulder
[3]School of Computer Science, Georgia Institute of Technology
hanqiang.cheng@mail.mcgill.ca, yu-li.liang@colorado.edu, xxing8@gatech.edu
xueliu@cs.mcgill.ca, {rick.han, qin.lv, Shivakaht.Mishra}@colorado.edu

ABSTRACT

Online video chat services, such as Chatroulette, Omegle, and vChatter are becoming increasingly popular and have attracted millions of users. One critical problem encountered in such applications is the presence of misbehaving users ("flashers") and obscene content. Automatically filtering out obscene content from these systems in an *efficient* manner poses a difficult challenge. This paper presents a novel Fine-Grained Cascaded (FGC) classification solution that significantly speeds up the compute-intensive process of classifying misbehaving users by dividing image feature extraction into multiple stages and filtering out easily classified images in earlier stages, thus saving unnecessary computation costs of feature extraction in later stages. Our work is further enhanced by integrating new webcam-related contextual information (illumination and color) into the classification process, and a 2-stage soft margin SVM algorithm for combining multiple features. Evaluation results using real-world data set obtained from Chatroulette show that the proposed *FGC* based classification solution significantly outperforms state-of-the-art techniques.

Categories and Subject Descriptors

K.4.1 [**Computers and Society**]: Abuse and crime involving computers

General Terms

Algorithms, Performance, Design, Experimentation

1. INTRODUCTION

Online video chatting has grown rapidly in popularity in recent years. The number of websites that provide an environment for users to chat online by video has expanded substantially since 2010, with websites such as Chatroulette [2], Myyearbook [22], Omegle [24], TinyChat [28], etc. experiencing aggressive membership growth. In an online video chat service, strangers from around the world are randomly paired together for webcam-based conversations. Visitors who are looking for entertainment go to the website and randomly begin a conversation (via video, audio, and text) with another visitor. Such websites are typically offered for free, and are easy to use, which enhances their popularity and implies a great market for advertisement. Online video chatting's appeal is based on providing a real-time video environment for a rich interactive experience via face-to-face conversations, gestures, and manners that extend beyond what mere text or audio chat can offer.

However, the presence of misbehaving users ("flashers" who display obscene content) is a serious problem in these video chat services. Figure 1 shows some snapshot image samples that we have observed in one of the video chat websites (Chatroulette). We could see that misbehaving users display obscene content, such as genitalia or exhibit inappropriate behavior, while normal users do not. To make the problem even worse, a significant fraction of video chat participants are underage minors, whose exposure to such obscene content may cause legal problems. An instance is iChatr, an iphone application similar to Chatroulette that randomly pairs iphone users for video chat. iChatr was excluded from Apple's application store due to the transmission of obscene content.

In this paper, our goal is to investigate mechanisms that can *efficiently* detect obscene content in online video chat systems with high accuracy. We have experimented with a variety of approaches based on prior work to address the problem of misbehaving user detection, and found them to be insufficient. Prior work is ill-suited to the demanding real-world classification scenario posed by video chat streams. For example, the statistical skin-color model approach for pornography detection [12] does not work well with online video chat data, due to diverse illumination conditions. SafeVchat [33] is the first software that achieves reasonable performance for detecting obscene content in online video chat systems and is deployed in the world-largest online video chat website - Chatroulette. However, the software requires a large amount of computation resources and involves high computation latency, which makes some online video chat websites such as Omegle refuse its deployment. As a result, there is a strong motivation for us to improve its efficiency. In addition to these two approaches above, we further investigate the technique which uses Scale-Invariant Feature Transform (SIFT [20]) along with Bag-of-Visual-Words (BoVW [3, 6]) framework because SIFT is broadly used for pornographic content detection [5, 19] and achieve acceptable detection accuracy. Unfortunately, SIFT based solution is still not the answer for misbehaving user detec-

Permission to make digital or hard copies of all or part of this work for personal or classroom use is granted without fee provided that copies are not made or distributed for profit or commercial advantage and that copies bear this notice and the full citation on the first page. To copy otherwise, or republish, to post on servers or to redistribute to lists, requires prior specific permission and/or a fee.
WSDM'12 February 8-12, 2012, Seattle, Washington, USA.
Copyright 2012 ACM 978-1-4503-0747-5/12/02...$10.00.

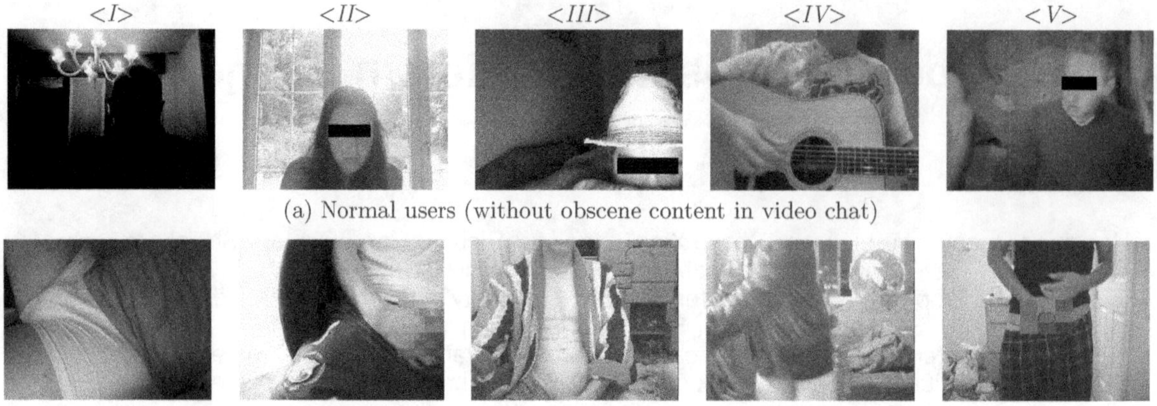

(a) Normal users (without obscene content in video chat)

(b) Misbehaving users (with obscene content in video chat)

Figure 1: Snapshot image samples from online video chat systems.

tion in online video chat systems. The detailed analysis and investigation of these techniques are presented in Section 2.

To detect misbehaving users in online video chat systems, this paper proposes a solution which (1) introduces a novel Fine-Grained Cascaded (FGC) classification which systematically generates the optimal combination of partial image features for classification and thus significantly improve classification efficiency without sacrificing classification precision/recall; and (2) achieves better classification performance in terms of precision and recall.

This paper makes the following contributions:

- We propose a novel *Fine-Grained Cascaded* (FGC) classification approach to significantly improve classification efficiency without sacrificing classification precision and recall. The FGC classification approach systematically evaluates the classification capacities of different features and automatically generates the optimal feature extraction order to allow for earlier classification with partial features.

- We identify two new contextual features which are significant for discriminating misbehaving users from normal ones and incorporate these new features into an enhanced combination algorithm for misbehaving user classification.

- We present key observations from over a half-year study of users on the Chatroulette system, the world's largest online video chat system. These long-term key observations inspire the design of our FGC classification approach.

The rest of this paper is organized as follows. Section 2 discusses related work. Section 3 introduces the properties of online video chat systems, real-world experimental data, and the classification workflow of our proposed solution. Section 4 describes how our solution achieves high classification precision and recall by integrating two novel contextual features using a 2-stage soft margin SVM algorithm. Section 5 presents our innovative "Fine-Grained Cascaded (FGC)" classification approach for improved efficiency. Section 6 evaluates the precision, recall, and latency of our solution. Finally, Section 7 concludes the paper.

2. RELATED WORK

Over the past decade, a number of techniques have been introduced for detecting objectionable content, especially in the context of pornographic images. Recent work leverages different types of information such as text, image, and URL [9, 18]. In online video chat systems, only a small number of users use text for chatting, so detecting misbehaving users via text analysis is not effective. Furthermore, the large scale of video chat systems makes real-time video analysis infeasible. Any practical solution including ours for detecting misbehaving users needs to focus on individual snapshot images of each chatter. Therefore, we focus on image-based objectionable content filtering techniques, and summarize the ones that are most relevant to our proposed solution and their limitations under video chat scenarios.

For pornographic image detection, skin color based detection is the most widely used technique and achieves acceptable performance in this scenario [12, 7, 34, 16]. The basic idea of skin color based detection is to identify skin exposure regions in images based on a statistical color model that is trained from manually labeled data. Area size and shape of detected pixels are sometimes considered to further improve the skin color detection results. However, approaches based on statistical skin-color models, such as PicBlock [1], have been shown to be insufficient for identifying obscene content in video chat systems, due to the diverse quality and content of snapshot images captured from online video chat systems [33], A recent survey [13] concludes that skin detection methods may only be used as a preprocessor for obscene content detection, and other content types such as text [10] and motion analysis [11] may be incorporated to improve accuracy.

SafeVchat [33], an obscene content detection system we have recently developed for online video chat systems, is the first solution that addresses this difficult problem. It has been successfully deployed in the Chatroulette online video chat system. Unfortunately, this solution is highly compute-intensive, requiring over a hundred servers running continuously 24 × 7 to filter out misbehaving users. Moreover, the system's ability to classify misbehaving users is still weak. As a result, the software must be backed up by a second round of expensive human screeners. Together, these limitations make the SafeVchat solution too expensive at present for most online video chat services. For example, Omegle is not able to implement our solution because it is too heavyweight and costly for them. Thus, there is a strong need to improve upon the state of the art.

We further investigate Scale Invariant Feature Transform (SIFT) descriptors [20] along with the Bag-of-Visual-Words (BoVW) framework [3, 6], which was shown to work well in two recently-proposed pornography detectors [5, 19]. However, the classification performance of these two detectors is fairly poor when using them in the context of online video chat systems. There are several reasons behind the poor performance. First, though SIFT descriptors are keypoint descriptors that are good at describing salient regions, the salient regions of our snapshot images are not obvious in the context of online video chat systems. Second, SIFT descriptors are sparse and not uniformly distributed, which causes only few keypoints are extracted. Finally, the problem we face here is more difficult than the pornography classification problem due to the smaller inter-class distance between different categories. For example, the "difference", or visual distance, between pornography categories (e.g. fully-clothed and nude body trunk) is large. However, for our problem, the difference between misbehaving and normal users is not that clear. Figure 1 shows some snapshot image samples in our data set with obscene parts being blurred. As we can observe, the characteristics of misbehaving users are quite similar to those of normal users. For example, both misbehaving and normal users could be dressed, show their faces, and expose large skin area (normal users show their hands and upper chest while misbehaving users show their genitalia).

3. OVERVIEW

In this section, we start with an overview of online video chat systems and our real-world experimental data sets. We then present our key observations and the proposed Fine-Grained Cascaded (FGC) classification workflow.

3.1 Online Video Chat Systems and Experimental Data Sets

To support online video chat among a large number of users, all online video chat systems are designed to use a peer-to-peer architecture. As a result, it is infeasible to obtain continuous video chat streams between any two peers for analysis at a central server. To detect misbehaving users, online video chat systems utilize an HTTP polling method to obtain periodic snapshot images from users' video chat streams. For example, in Chatroulette, users' snapshots are captured every 30 seconds and forwarded to a central server. Such periodic snapshot images are thus what we can use for classifying misbehaving users.

To support our study, Andrey Ternovskiy, the founder of Chatroulette, has kindly provided us with these otherwise unobtainable internal data traces containing 20,000 users' snapshot images (with the resolution of 320×240 pixels) as well as Chatroulette computation resources. We conducted our experiments on the Chatroulette platform using these real-world data traces, in which 15% of users are misbehaving and the rest are normal. We have divided these data traces evenly into five sets – three sets for training, one for evaluation, and one for testing. To reduce variability, multiple rounds of cross-validation over the 20,000 users' data traces are performed in our experiments.

3.2 Key Observations

In conjunction with Chatroulette's human moderation team, we conducted a half-year study of the world's largest online video chat system – Chatroulette. Through this long-term study, we have made a number of key observations, which

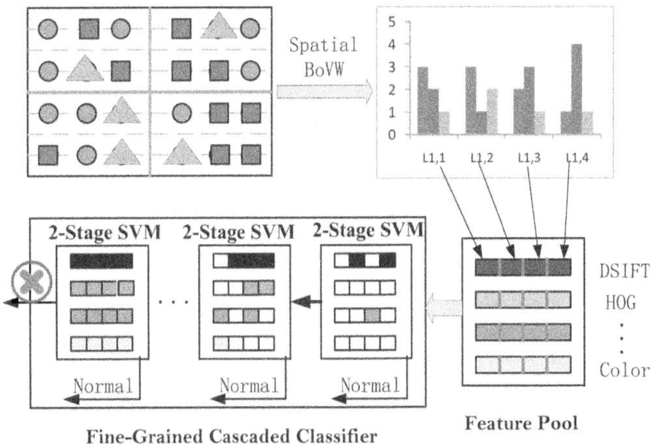

Figure 2: Fine-Grained Cascaded (FGC) classification workflow for efficient misbehavior detection.

significantly inspired our solution for classifying misbehaving users in online video chat systems. We summarize our key observations as follows.

(1) The fundamental observation from online video chat systems is that misbehaving users expose themselves in front of webcams while normal users are fully-clothed. In addition, the Chatroulette moderation team observed that normal users on their system usually maintain a stable posture while misbehaving users do not.

(2) Misbehaving users usually attempt to point their webcams downwards, while normal users typically point their webcams upwards. The reason is that webcams usually have a very narrow field of vision and users cannot present their full body in their video. This motivates us to identify the orientation of users' webcams and classify a user to be normal (misbehaving) if his/her webcam points upward (downward). The webcam orientation usually correlates strongly with the illumination context of a snapshot image. For normal users, a bright illumination area usually appears either on the top (from the ceiling light) or the side area (from open windows) of the snapshot image when users point their webcams upwards (e.g., <I> in Figure 1(a)). These bright illumination areas can be used to infer that the webcam is oriented upwards and thus the users are normal. In contrast, we observed that some misbehaving users typically stay in a dark environment but present themselves in a centered bright area (e.g., <I> in Figure 1(b)).

(3) Misbehaving users generally do not expose themselves in an outdoor environment. The color characteristics of an outdoor scene is significantly different from that of an indoor scene. As shown in <II> of Figure 1(a), an outdoor scene usually includes green trees – green area in the top of a snapshot image.

(4) Another surprising observation illustrates that users in a room with dark red lighting (e.g., in a bar) are unlikely to be misbehaving users (<V> in Figure 1(a)). This is because misbehaving users usually expose themselves in their bedrooms, and bedrooms typically have white or yellow lighting instead of dark red lighting.

3.3 Classification Workflow

Figure 2 illustrates the workflow of our Fine-Grained Cascaded (FGC) classification solution for efficient detection of misbehaving users. It consists of four key steps.

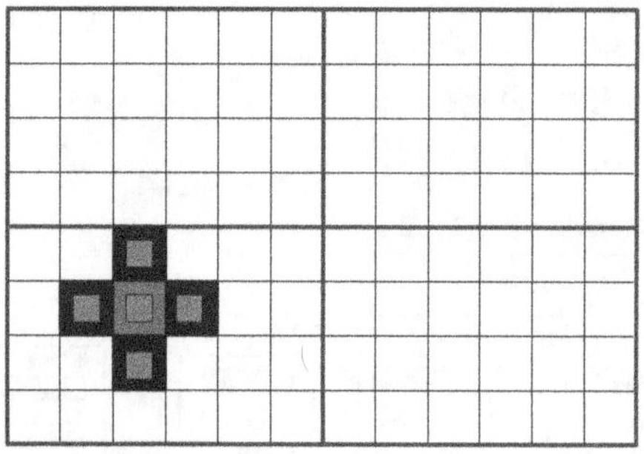

Figure 3: Illumination feature extraction. The dense grid is also used for the calculation of other descriptors.

Step 1 (*Upper Left*): Each user's snapshot image is first partitioned into several spatial regions ($2 \times 2 = 4$ regions in the example). We then use the Bag-of-Visual-Words framework [3, 6] to extract visual words (e.g., $\circ$, $\triangle$, and $\square$) in each region for each feature descriptor. We also propose two new contextual descriptors (illumination and color) for better classification accuracy (Section 4).

Step 2 (*Upper Right*): For each region, we generate one histogram based on the frequencies of different visual words.

Step 3 (*Lower Right*): Each histogram is a "*regional feature*" for a specific descriptor. If we use four descriptors to describe a snapshot image with four regions, then the snapshot image has $4 \times 4 = 16$ *regional features* (histograms).

Step 4 (*Lower Left*): The proposed Fine-Grained Cascaded (FGC) classifier is utilized to distinguish misbehaving users from normal ones. FGC selects multiple sets of appropriate *regional features*, combines features in each set using a 2-stage soft margin SVM algorithm (Section 4), and computes the optimal ordering of classification stages (each stage uses one set of combined features) in order to achieve high quality and high efficiency for classification (Section 5).

4. BOOSTING CLASSIFICATION PERFORMANCE

We first focus on how to boost classification performance, i.e., classify misbehaving users with high precision and high recall. We propose two new contextual feature descriptors based on illumination and color, and a 2-stage soft margin SVM algorithm to combine these features. The efficiency and effectiveness of the feature descriptors as well as our combination algorithm are validated in Section 6.

4.1 Feature Descriptors

A significant number of feature descriptors used in computer vision and image processing have been introduced for the purpose of object detection. Based on our observations in Section 3.2, we select the following three feature descriptors for classifying misbehaving users.

1. Dense SIFT (DSIFT). Dense SIFT [29] is one of the most effective descriptors used for a wide variety of object/scene classification applications. Compared with traditional SIFT [20], it is more efficient and can achieve higher classification performance.

2. Histogram of oriented gradient (HOG). Based on our observations described in Section 3.2, normal chatters habitually maintain a stable posture (i.e., sitting in front of a webcam). We choose HOG since it has been used successfully for capturing stable posture or shape [4].

3. Local Binary Patterns (LBP). The fundamental difference between misbehaving and normal users is that normal users are generally fully-clothed, while misbehaving ones are not. The texture between large skin exposure and clothes is discriminative. Therefore LBP is chosen to capture texture information.

In addition to these three feature descriptors, we introduce two new contextual descriptors that can obviously boost the classification performance. These two feature descriptors represent illumination context and color context.

4.1.1 *Illumination Contextual Descriptor*

Our observations in Section 3.2 illustrate that the orientation of users' webcams can be used to discriminate normal users from misbehaving ones, and the webcam orientation usually correlates strongly with the illumination context of a snapshot image. Therefore, we propose a new illumination contextual descriptor that can be used for discriminating normal users from misbehaving ones.

To reduce noise in a snapshot image caused by low-quality webcams, we first smooth the snapshot image by averaging its value with the neighboring pixels (i.e., on a 3×3 patch). After smoothing, we compute illumination contextual descriptors on a dense grid of uniformly spaced cells. Each illumination contextual descriptor is defined as the brightest light intensity value on a smaller patch (shown as blue patches in Figure 3) in a grid cell. Mathematically, the illumination descriptor on patch K (Figure 3: blue patch in the red cell) $I(K)$ is computed as follows:

$$I(K) = \alpha \cdot I_0(K) + (1 - \alpha) \cdot \frac{I_{neighbor}(K)}{4} \quad (1)$$

$$I_0(K) = \max(\max(v_R(K)), \max(v_G(K)), \max(v_B(K))) \quad (2)$$

$$I_{neighbor}(K) = \sum_{i \in \{Up, Down, Left, Right\}} I_0(i) \quad (3)$$

where α is a scaling factor for further noise reduction, and $v_R(K)$, $v_G(K)$, $v_B(K)$ denote the R,G,B values on patch K, respectively. $I_{neighbor}(K)$ represents the sum of the four neighbor descriptors' I_0 (Figure 3: blue patches in black cells). Figure 4(a) and Figure 4(b) show the average illumination contextual descriptors of normal users' snapshots and that of misbehaving users' snapshots, respectively [1]. It is obvious that our illumination contextual descriptors clearly capture the illumination difference between normal users and misbehaving users, which is also consistent with our observation in Section 3.2.

4.1.2 *Color Contextual Descriptor*

Since the observations in Section 3.2 also indicate that the color presented in a snapshot image can be harnessed to identify normal and misbehaving users, we propose a color contextual descriptor. Similar to the illumination contextual descriptor, we sample color descriptors on a dense grid of uniformly spaced cells. Since illumination intensity can significantly affect the color appearance, we only utilize Hue

[1]The illumination values have been scaled to illustrate the contrast of the illumination contextual descriptors.

(a) Normal users

(b) Misbehaving users

Figure 4: Comparison of average illumination contextual descriptors of normal and misbehaving users.

and Saturation in the HSV color space. Each color descriptor therefore is represented as a two-element vector (hue and saturation). The color contextual descriptors are further quantized (mapped) to the most similar major colors, which are generated using k-means clustering algorithm.

4.1.3 *Usage of Feature Descriptors*

Bag-of-Visual-Words framework is used to represent each type of descriptors [3, 6]. Since the spatial information is useful for boosting classification performance, a 3-level Spatial Pyramid Matching [15] is used to process the feature descriptors above[2].

A 3-level Spatial Pyramid is composed of level-0, level-1, and level-2. In each level, a given image is evenly partitioned into several blocks. The number of blocks for each level is: level-0: ($1 \times 1 = 1$ block), level-1: ($2 \times 2 = 4$ blocks), and level-2: ($4 \times 4 = 16$ blocks). In Figure 2, the upper left diagram shows an image with level-1 partition ($2 \times 2 = 4$ blocks). For each block, one histogram of visual word frequency is created. For example, the upper right diagram in Figure 2 describes four histograms for DSIFT descriptor. For a 3-level spatial pyramid, there are totally 21 histograms from all 3 levels (i.e., 1(level-0)+4(level-1)+16(level-2)= 21). Therefore, for an image which is partitioned using a 3-level spatial pyramid, each type of feature descriptor can be projected to 21 histograms.

4.2 Feature Combination

Given the five different types of features described above, our goal is to combine multiple features and achieve better performance for the classification of misbehaving users. This is accomplished through a 2-stage soft margin SVM classifier, which is inspired by a recently proposed multiple feature combination algorithm, Linear Programming Boosting algorithm (LPBoost) [8] .

LPBoost was originally designed for very high dimensional heterogeneous visual feature combination and has demonstrated better performance than multiple kernel learning (MKL) [8]. Since *norm-1* constrained variables tend to have a sparse optimal solution [27], LPBoost searches for a sparse optimal set of combination coefficients, which improves the interpretability of features for a classification problem. However, when applying LPBoost to combine both weak and much stronger features (e.g., DSIFT is much stronger in misbehaving users detection than other four features), the combination coefficients of the strong feature(s) can carry much larger weights than that of the weak feature(s), thus limiting the contributions of the weak features in terms of boosting

[2][15] indicates the L-level spatial pyramid can achieve good classification performance when $L = 3$.

the classification performance. To address this problem, we extend LPBoost to *norm-2* and reformulate LPBoost with ℓ_2-norm constraint on combination coefficients [3], which is inspired by l_p-norm multiple kernel learning [14]. In this paper, we refer to the original LPBoost and the 2-stage soft margin SVM as LPBoost-ℓ_1 and 2-Stage SVM, respectively.

Similar to LPBoost-ℓ_1, our 2-stage SVM also contains two separate steps. In the first step, classifier f_m for each type of feature is trained in a labeled sample set $D = \{(x_{i,m}, y_i)\}_{i=1,2,...,N}$ (where $x_{i,m}$ is the mth type of feature for snapshot i and y_i is the corresponding label – misbehaving or normal user). Subsequently we optimize over combination coefficients $\beta = \{\beta_1, \beta_2, ..., \beta_F\}$ as follows:

$$\min_{\beta,\xi} \sum_{m=1}^{F} \beta_m^2 + \frac{1}{\nu N} \sum_{i=1}^{N} \xi_i \tag{4}$$

$$sb.t.\ \ y_i(\sum_{i=1}^{F} \beta_m f_m(x_i) + b) + \xi_i \geq 1, \quad i = 1, 2, ..., N \tag{5}$$

$$\|\beta\|_2^2 \leq 1, \quad \beta_m \geq 0, \qquad \xi_i \geq 0, \tag{6}$$

with $\xi = \{\xi_1, \xi_2, ..., \xi_N\}$ being slack variables. Here, ν denotes the parameter that controls the tradeoff between the margin of the boosting classifier and misclassification penalty, and $f_m(x_i)$ represents the output of the mth individual classifier for the ith training sample. Different from LPBoost-ℓ_1 which employs regularizers of the form $\|\beta\|_1$ to promote sparse combination, our 2-stage SVM uses smooth convex regularizers of the form $\|\beta\|_2$, allowing for non-sparse solutions.

5. REDUCING CLASSIFICATION LATENCY

We now focus on the problem of reducing the classification latency, which is particularly important given the large scale of online video chat services. To answer this question, we revisit and analyze the classification technique that we proposed in Section 4. Based on our analysis, we propose a Fine-Grained Cascaded (FGC) classification scheme to reduce the computation latency that our misbehaving user classification technique involves.

5.1 Classification Analysis

In general, there are three steps for classifying images using the Bag-of-Visual-Words framework: 1) descriptor extraction, 2) descriptor projection, and 3) feature classification. In the first step, certain types of descriptors (e.g., DSIFT, HOG, etc.) are computed from an image. In the second step, the Bag-of-Visual-Words framework projects the extracted descriptors to corresponding visual words which are further used to generate corresponding features. Based on the features, the final step uses a classification algorithm to classify images into different classes, in our case, misbehaving or normal users.

A number of research efforts have been made to accelerate the procedure above. Vedaldi and Zisserman introduce an explicit feature map approximating non-linear kernels (e.g., intersection kernel and chi kernel) by a linear kernel [32], which reduces the feature classification latency for those widely used kernel based classification algorithms (such as SVM and LPBoost). Furthermore, the feature map generally does not have negative impacts on classification performance in terms of precision and recall. Another pioneering

[3]*norm-2* is a quadratic optimization problem, which is easy to solve.

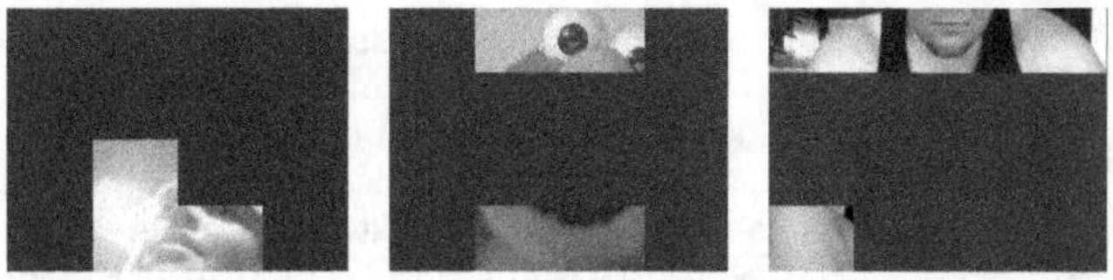

(a) (b) (c)

Figure 5: Using partial blocks of snapshots to discriminate normal users from misbehaving ones.

work uses a vocabulary tree to reduce the computation latency for descriptor projection [25]. Uijlings et al. designed fast SIFT descriptors, which significantly reduces the computation latency of widely used SIFT descriptors [29]. All these approaches are incorporated in our solution introduced in Section 4, and this new implementation reduces the computation latency by three times over previous approaches such as SafeVchat.

A closer analysis reveals that there is a substantial opportunity to further reduce the latency in the descriptor extraction step. In comparison with descriptor projection and feature classification, we observe that descriptor extraction is usually the most compute-intensive step and involves the highest computation latency. For example, gray DSIFT descriptor extraction takes 0.06 seconds (see Table 1), while the corresponding descriptor projection and classification latency are 0.01 and 0.004 seconds, respectively. Computation latency of classification in general is one magnitude smaller than that of feature extraction. Therefore, the main goal of our work is to reduce the computation latency in the process of descriptor extraction. While Uijlings et al. introduced two approaches to reduce the computation latency for SIFT descriptor extraction [29], these two approaches cannot be used for other types of descriptors (e.g., HOG). Furthermore, these approaches can sacrifice classification precision and recall.

5.2 Fine-Grained Cascaded Classification

Recall our classification approach where the classification process uses 4×21 *regional features* that are generated from 4 descriptors (DSIFT, HOG, color and illumination) in 21 regions defined in a 3-level spatial pyramid (see Section 4.1.3). Note our experiment in Section 6 indicates LBP descriptor is not necessary for our classification. Inspired by the *"image guessing game"* where a player guesses the content of images that are partially blocked, we optimize our classification approach and thus reduce computation latency. Figure 5, for example, shows some snapshot samples where only partial blocks are revealed. Reviewing these partially revealed blocks, one can easily label Figure 5(a) and 5(b) as "normal" with high confidence but may not be able to determine whether obscene content is presented in Figure 5(c). Therefore, more blocks on the third snapshot are revealed in the next-round of image guessing. The guessing game continues until all the images are labeled or all the images are completely revealed. Imagine extending this game in the procedure of misbehaving user classification. Since there are partial snapshot images classified by our classification approach in each round of "guessing", descriptor computation for these snapshot images is not intensive because descriptors are only extracted from the revealed blocks of these images. Given a snapshot image, the computation for a specific descriptor gradually increases with the rounds of the "guessing" game, because more blocks on the snapshot image are revealed if the image cannot be classified in the previous rounds of "guessing". According to the characteristics of the guessing game, we name our misbehaving user classification as Fine-Grained Cascaded (FGC) classification.

Our FGC classification has to satisfy two criteria – (1) minimizing the computation latency for descriptor extraction; and (2) maintaining high classification performance in terms of precision and recall. To minimize computation latency, we have to determine which blocks of a snapshot image should be revealed first (i.e., determining which *regional features* should be selected first for misbehaving user classification). This is because different regional features may involve different computation latency (e.g., Table 1 shows that feature extraction for gray DSIFT is faster than HOG) and have different classification capacities. To maintain the same classification precision and recall as the classification approach introduced in Section 4, we have to ensure that the snapshot images that are classified as "normal" in each round of "guessing" have higher classification precision. This is because low recall causes misbehaving users to be mistakenly classified as normal, and adversely affects the overall classification precision and recall for misbehaving user classification. In other words, we want those obscene snapshot images, which are rarer than normal snapshots, to be classified at the last rounds of the "guessing".

Accordingly, we propose a latency-driven method that can automatically select the appropriate regional feature set (i.e., blocks of snapshot images that need to be revealed) at each round of "guessing". It is difficult to globally optimize the regional feature sets for each round of "guessing". Therefore, our latency-driven method selects locally optimal regional features at each round of "guessing". In other words, we first choose the regional feature set for the first round and then choose the regional feature set for the second round, and so on. The criterion for regional feature selection at each round of "guessing" considers the following three factors: (1) the computation latency of the selected regional features; (2) the proportion of the snapshot images that can be classified by using the selected regional features; and (3) the proportion of the snapshot images that are mistakenly classified as "normal".

For an online video chat system like Chatroulette, it usually sets up a *maximum tolerable average latency* for classifying a snapshot image. Here we refer to this latency as T_1. When optimizing our classification approach, the average classification latency for a snapshot image should be less than T_1. To satisfy this and minimize the computation latency of descriptor extraction, we select regional features by maximizing the *maximal tolerable latency* at the next round of "guessing". This is illustrated by the following example. Suppose that an online video chat system needs to classify 100 snapshots and the *maximal tolerable latency of the online video chat system* is 50 milliseconds per snapshot. If the descriptor extraction takes 20 milliseconds per snapshot at the first round of "guessing" and classifies 40 snapshots as "normal", then the maximal tolerable latency at the second round of "guessing" is $\frac{(50-20)\times 100}{100-40}$ [4]. We further explain our computation for this example as follows. The online video chat system allocates a total of 50×100 milliseconds for the classification process. In the first round, the process of descriptor extraction needs to go through all the snapshot images, which takes 20×100 milliseconds, and so 30×100 milliseconds are remaining for the next rounds of "guessing".

[4]To simplify our computation, we ignore the latency for descriptor projection and feature classification.

Since 40 snapshot images have been classified in the first round, there are 30×100 milliseconds which can be spent on classifying the remaining 60 snapshot images. Therefore, the average tolerable latency (i.e., the maximal tolerable latency at the second round) left for classifying each snapshot image is $\frac{(50-20)\times 100}{100-40}$ milliseconds.

Let s be the sth round of "guessing". We formulate the maximal tolerable latency for the $(s+1)^{th}$ round of "guessing" as follows.

$$T_{s+1} = (T_s - f(sel_s) - c_s) \cdot \frac{p_s}{r_s \cdot p_{(s-1)}} \tag{7}$$

where $f(sel_s)$ is the computation latency of descriptor extraction for selected feature set sel_s at the sth round of "guessing". c_s denotes the computation latency that descriptor projection and feature classification involve at the sth round of "guessing". p_s and r_s represent the precision and recall for classifying obscene snapshot images at the sth round of "guessing", respectively. In Equation 7, $\frac{p_s}{r_s \cdot p_{(s-1)}}$ is equal to $\frac{N_{(s-1)}}{N_s}$. Here, $N_{(s-1)}$ and N_s are the number of snapshot images that are classified at the $(s-1)^{th}$ and s^{th} round of "guessing", respectively. Note that N_0 is the total number of snapshot images that an online video chat system obtains, and p_0 is the proportion of the obscene snapshot images.

Since it is possible to mistakenly classify obscene snapshot images as "normal" in each round of "guessing", we add a penalty factor $w_s(r_s)$ at the sth round of "guessing". The penalty factor is a function of r_s – $w_s(r_s) = \alpha^{100\times(1-r_s)}$ where α is a constant and $\alpha < 1$. By combining penalty factor $w_s(r_s)$ with maximal tolerable latency T_s at the sth round of "guessing", we formulate the objective function of regional feature selection as follows.

$$\max_{sel} \quad w_s(r_s) \cdot T_{s+1}, \tag{8}$$

$$sb.t. \quad sel_s \subseteq X - \bigcup_{m=1}^{s-1} sel_m \tag{9}$$

$$p_s, r_s := boost(\bigcup_{m=1}^{s-1} sel_m, sel_s) \tag{10}$$

$$T_{s+1} = (T_s - f(sel_s) - c_s) \cdot \frac{p_s}{r_s \cdot p_{s-1}} \tag{11}$$

where X is the power set that contains all candidate regional feature sets. sel_m represents the selected regional feature set at the mth round of "guessing", and $\bigcup_{m=1}^{s-1} sel_m = sel_1 \cup sel_2 \cup \cdots \cup sel_{s-1}$. Equation 10 indicates that precision p_s and recall r_s at the sth round are obtained using a boosting algorithm to combine all the regional features that we used from the first to the $(s-1)^{th}$ round of "guessing" as well as the regional features that we use at the sth round.

To obtain a global optimal for this optimization problem, the straightforward approach is to exhaustively search for optimal regional feature set in power set X. However, exhaustive search is not applicable for the problem where the number of candidate regional feature sets is large. To address the searching problem, sequential forward search [26] is adopted. The pseudo-code is described in Algorithm 1. Sequential forward search is a greedy algorithm, which starts from a null feature set and adds locally optimal feature(s) into the feature set one by one until the expected precision and recall are satisfied. The expected precision and recall are defined based on the maximum number of "guessing" rounds

Inputs;
er: expected recall at the sth round;
ep: expected precision at the sth round;
p_{s-1}: precision at the $(s-1)^{th}$ round;
T_s: maximal tolerable latency at the sth round;
$avail_s$: feature sets that can be selected at the sth round;
Outputs;
$avail_{s+1}$: feature sets that can be selected at the $(s+1)^{th}$ round;
sel_s: selected feature sets at the sth round;
Initialization;
$p = 0, r = 0$;
$sel_s = \emptyset$;
$avail_{s+1} = avail_s$;
while $p < ep \,\&\, r < er \,\&\, avail_{s+1} \neq \emptyset$ **do**
  for $i = 1 : length(avail_{s+1})$ **do**
    $p, r := boost(\bigcup_{m=1}^{s} sel_m, avail_s(i))$;
    $t = (T_s - f(avail_s(i)) - c_s) \cdot \frac{p}{r \cdot p_{s-1}}$;
    $score(i) = w_s(r)t$;
  end
  $feat := regional\ feature\ with\ maximal\ score$;
  $avail_{s+1} = avail_{s+1} - feat$;
  $sel_s = sel_s \cup feat$;
  $p, r := boost(\bigcup_{m=1}^{s} sel_m, sel)$;
end
return $avail_{s+1}$, sel_s;

Algorithm 1: Selecting feature set at the sth round.

as well as the precision and recall that the non-cascaded solution introduced in Section 4 can achieve. Let P and R be the precision and recall of the non-cascaded solution, respectively. The maximum number of guessing rounds is N. Then, the expected precision ep_s and recall er_s at the sth round are

$$ep_s = P_0 + \frac{s}{N}(P - P_0) \tag{12}$$

$$er_s = R^{1/N} \tag{13}$$

where P_0 is the proportion of obscene snapshot images. The value for the maximum number of guessing rounds can be empirically chosen by selecting the value which achieves the least classification latency.

6. EVALUATION

In this section, using real-world data sets (Section 3) , we evaluate the proposed Fine-Grained Cascaded (FGC) classification solution for misbehaving user detection in online video chat services. Specifically, we validate the effectiveness and efficiency of the new contextual feature descriptors (illumination and color) we have proposed, the 2-stage soft margin SVM algorithm, and our innovative FGC classification scheme.

We have implemented all the descriptors that we introduced in Section 4. The dense SIFT descriptor is implemented in three different color spaces (Gray, HSV and RGB) based on the real time dense SIFT descriptor of the VLFeat library [30]. The HOG descriptor is implemented based on the PHOG descriptor of Vgg MKL [31], and the LBP descriptor is based on the uniform rotation invariant $LBP_{8,1}$ [23]. The parameters used in these descriptors are all empirically tuned to obtain an optimal tradeoff between classification quality and classification efficiency.

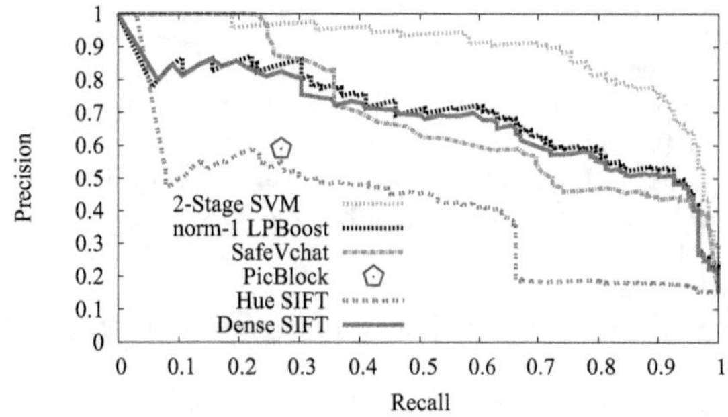

Figure 6: Classification performance comparison.

6.1 Classification Precision and Recall

To evaluate the feature descriptors and the improved combination algorithm, we conduct several experiments and compare our combination algorithm with the state-of-the-art pornographic content detection techniques. Table 1 shows the latency of feature extraction using our implementation. In addition, the Pearson correlations between features and the label of snapshot images (i.e., misbehaving or normal users) are also calculated. As shown in the table, the Pearson correlations are either moderate or medium.

We can observe that the features we use for the classification of misbehaving users are meaningful and the correlations between the features and the snapshot labels (i.e., flasher or not) are not a chance occurrence. Before combining these features, a multicollinearity diagnosis however is necessary, because strong correlations among these features may impose multicollinearity threats. Our Pearson correlation calculation among all the features identifies a few highly-correlated features. Specifically, gray DSIFT has high Pearson correlation values with rgb and hsv DSIFT ($corr = 0.854$ and $corr = 0.746$), and the Pearson correlation value between rgb and hsv DSIFT is also fairly high ($corr = 0.851$). To avoid the multicollinearity threat, the most straightforward approach is to drop any two of DSIFT features. As shown in Table 1, gray DSIFT has higher Pearson correlation than DSIFT feature in rgb and hsv color spaces, which indicates better classification precision and recall. Further, the feature extraction latency for hsv and rgb DSIFT is three times the extraction latency of gray DSIFT. Therefore, we drop rgb and hsv DSIFT features and do not consider them in our combination algorithm.

Combining the features (i.e., gray DSIFT, illumination context, color context, HOG and LBP) using 2-stage SVM, as shown in Figure 6, significantly outperforms the state-of-the-art skin color based detection technique (PicBlock [1] [5]), because the skin colors in snapshot images captured from online video chat systems are diverse and thus the statistical skin-color model used in PicBlock cannot provide effective discriminative characteristics for misbehaving user classification.

In addition to the skin color based detection techniques, we also compare our solution with the state-of-the-art Hue SIFT based pornographic content detection technique [19]. Figure 6 shows that the Hue SIFT based technique provides poor classification performance in terms of precision and recall. The reason behind this poor classification performance is that the SIFT descriptor is a sparse feature representation which may cause the loss of some discriminative characteristics. To address this issue, the most straightforward solution is to simply replace the SIFT descriptor with the Dense SIFT descriptor. We repeated the experiment that we conducted for the SIFT descriptor using the Dense SIFT descriptor. We observe that the classification performance in terms of precision and recall is significantly improved and approximately the same as SafeVchat (see Figure 6). However, the classification performance of this straightforward improvement is still lower than our combined solution – combining five features including gray DSIFT, illumination, color, HOG and LBP using 2-stage SVM, because snapshot images have smaller inter-class distance between normal and misbehaving users.

We also compare the performance between the actively deployed SafeVchat [21] and our new solution introduced in Section 4. Figure 6 shows a significant performance improvement in terms of precision and recall. Since SafeVchat uses facial features to discriminate normal users from misbehaving ones, normal users might be mistakenly classified as misbehaving ones when facial features are not presented in the normal users' snapshots. This results in the lower classification performance of SafeVchat. On the other hand, the new solution which combines five features using 2-stage SVM uses other discriminative features to classify misbehaving users. Though the individual features among the five features do not show strong classification capacity (see Table 1), the combination of the features achieves higher classification performance in terms of precision and recall.

To demonstrate that the 2-stage SVM can achieve significant performance improvement, we use the traditional LPBoost algorithm to combine the same features that 2-stage SVM combines. As shown in Figure 6, the classification precision and recall for 2-stage SVM are significantly improved in comparison with the traditional LPBoost algorithm (norm-1 LPBoost). As shown in Table 1, the classification capacity of the features that the combination algorithms use are fairly diverse. For example, Gray DSIFT has strong classification capacity ($corr = 0.552$) while the classification capacity for HOG is weak ($corr = 0.202$). The classification results for traditional LPBoost can be easily biased by the feature with strong classification capacity (i.e., gray DSIFT), while our two stage SVM can balance well the weights of the features and thus achieves higher precision and recall.

Finally, we evaluate the contribution of each feature for classification performance improvement when using 2-stage SVM. Figure 7 shows the incremental classification performance improvement by adding features one by one in the following order – gray DSIFT, illumination, color context,

Descriptor	Latency (sec.)	Correlation
Gray DSIFT	.06	.552**
RGB DSIFT	.18	.460**
HSV DSIFT	.18	.354**
HOG	.22	.202**
LBP	.08	.251**
Color Context	.02	.284**
Illumination Context	.01	.271**
** Correlation is significant at the 0.01 level (2-tailed).		

Table 1: Latency of feature extraction and Pearson Correlation.

[5] PicBlock is a commercial software and we are not able to obtain the whole precision-recall curve.

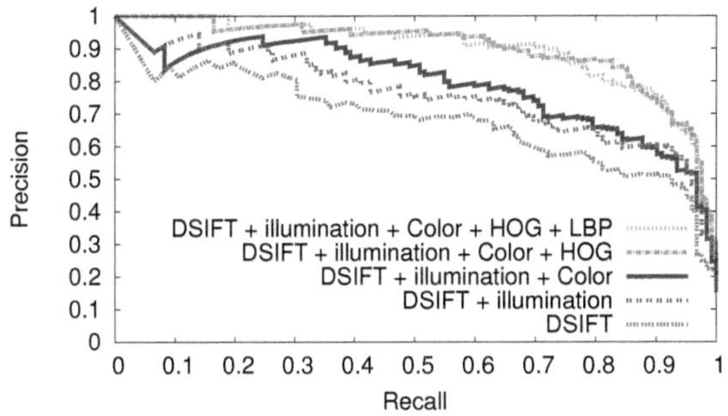

Figure 7: Classification performance variation of 2-stage SVM algorithm using different feature sets.

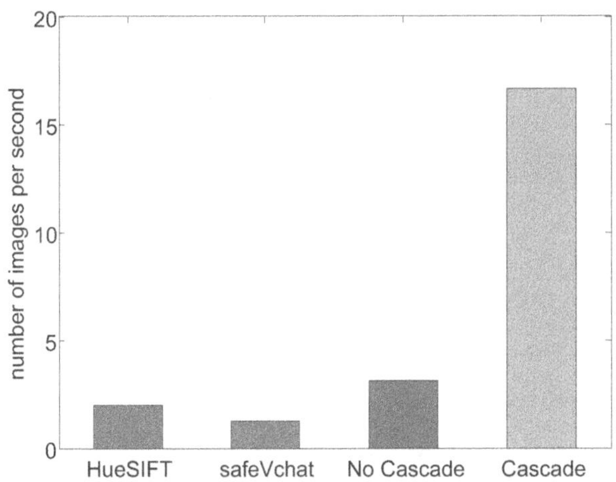

Figure 8: Comparison of classification efficiency. ("Cascade" = classifier with FGC scheme)

HOG, and LBP. As shown in the figure, sequentially adding the features - illumination, color context, and HOG - on gray DSIFT feature significantly boosts the classification performance in terms of precision and recall. However, the classification performance improvement, as shown in Figure 7, is not significant when combining the LBP feature with the other four features. To balance the need for accuracy on one hand and the need for efficiency on the other hand, we therefore do not consider the LBP feature in the classification of misbehaving users.

6.2 Classification Latency

To evaluate the classification latency of our FGC scheme, the *Maximal tolerable latency of the online video chat system* T_1 is set based on the requirements of Chatroulette.

Figure 8 compares of classification efficiency of different schemes, i.e., number of snapshot images that can be classified per second. We observe that FGC classification (cascaded classification) enables one Chatroulette computation infrastructure to classify approximately 17 snapshot images per second. Compared with the SafeVchat deployment [33] and the state-of-the-art pornographic content detection technique (Hue SIFT) [19], FGC classification achieves 92% and 89% reduction in computation latency, respectively. The reason behind this significant improvement in terms of classification efficiency is quite straightforward – both SafeVchat and Hue SIFT involve compute-intensive feature extraction procedures.

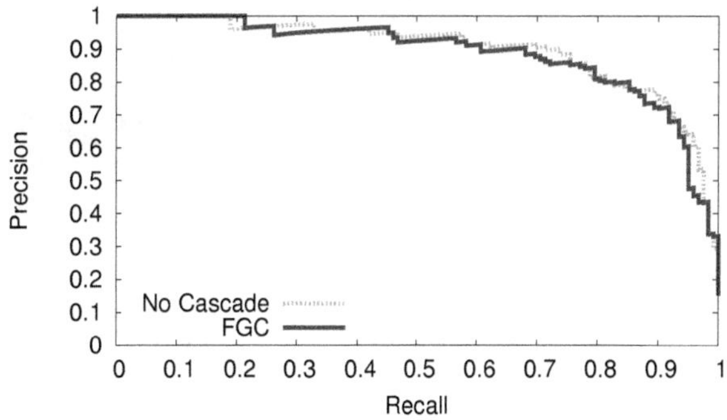

Figure 9: Classification precision and recall (FGC classification vs. No-cascaded classification.

We also observe that our FGC classification achieves significant efficiency improvement in comparison with the non-cascaded classification (82% reduction in computation latency). To understand the reason behind this efficiency improvement, we show the selected regional feature set, partial classified snapshots and partial non-classified snapshots in the first round (see Figure 10). The selected regional feature set by FGC classification in the first round contains the DSIFT feature in six regional blocks (i.e., the areas without blue screen in Figure 10). The first interesting observation here is that, among all the trained DSIFT features, some features capture the ceiling-like line structure and are more abundant in the snapshots from normal users (shown as green "□" in Figure 10(a)). Since ceiling information can infer the upward orientation of webcams and thus identify the snapshots as "normal", the snapshots shown in Figure 10(a) can be classified as "normal" and thus reduce computation latency for these snapshots. While non-cascaded classification can also obtain the same classification results based on the ceiling information, it needs to process the whole snapshot image (all blocks) rather than partial (revealed) blocks in the snapshot image. Likewise, some DSIFT features capture the texture of hairy skin (shown as red "+" in Figure 10(b)). Since the snapshots with hairy skin are more likely to contain obscene content, those snapshot images are passed to the subsequent rounds of "guessing". For those snapshot images that cannot be classified by using a few revealed blocks, the computation latency involved in FGC classification remains the same as that in non-cascaded classification. Therefore, the overall efficiency improvement is contributed by those snapshot images that can be classified using only a few of blocks of the images.

Finally, we compare classification precision and recall for our FGC classification with non-cascaded classification (See Figure 9). We can see that the precision and recall in FGC classification are similar to those in non-cascaded classification. Our feature descriptors are designed based on discriminative characteristics and the presence of the discriminative characteristics at certain regions of an snapshot image dominates the classification result. As a result, using certain regions of snapshot images to classify obscene and normal snapshot images can obtain approximately the same classification performance in terms of precision and recall.

7. CONCLUSION

This paper presents a novel solution to identify misbehaving users efficiently and accurately in online video chat sys-

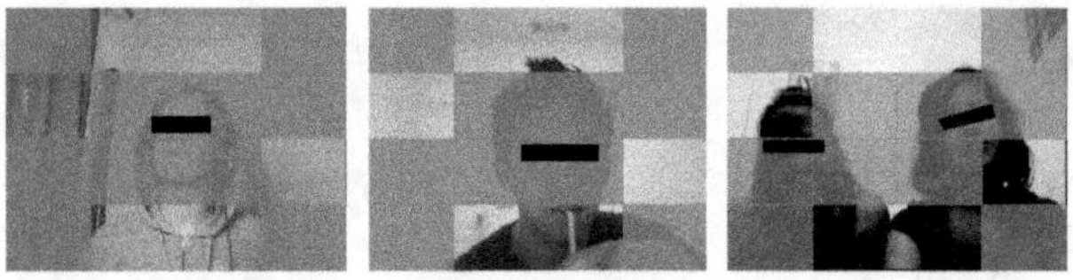

(a) Normal users

(b) Misbehaving users

Figure 10: FGC classification results at the first round of the "guessing".

tems. Two new contextual features, illumination and color contextual features are introduced. Combining these two new features along with a few existing features using a 2-stage SVM algorithm, the proposed solution can discriminate misbehaving users from normal ones with high classification performance in terms of precision and recall. To achieve higher classification efficiency, the paper further proposes a new fine-grained cascaded (FGC) classification approach, which orders the compute-intensive feature extraction process into multiple rounds and allows normal users to be classified in fewer rounds. Experimental results using real-world data demonstrate that our solution can significantly improve the classification precision and recall as well as reduce classification latency.

Acknowledgment

We thank Andrey Ternovskiy (Founder of Chatroulette.com) and Kirill Gura (CTO of Chatroulette.com) for providing us with these otherwise unobtainable internal data traces and computation resources. This work is supported in part by the unrestricted gift funds from Chatroulette.

8. REFERENCES

[1] Picblock web site. http://www.cinchworks.com/.

[2] Chatroulette web site. http://www.chatroulette.com/.

[3] G. Csurka, C. Dance, L. Fan, J. Willamowski, and C. Bray. Visual categorization with bags of keypoints. In *Workshop on statistical learning in computer vision, ECCV*, volume 1, page 22, 2004.

[4] N. Dalal and B. Triggs. Histograms of oriented gradients for human detection. In *CVPR*, volume 1, pages 886 -893 vol. 1, june 2005.

[5] T. Deselaers, L. Pimenidis, and H. Ney. Bag-of-visual-words models for adult image classification and filtering. In *ICPR 2008.*, pages 1 -4, dec. 2008.

[6] L. Fei-Fei and P. Perona. A bayesian hierarchical model for learning natural scene categories. In *CVPR*, volume 2, pages 524 – 531 vol. 2, june 2005.

[7] M. Fleck, D. Forsyth, and C. Bregler. Finding naked people. In *ECCV' 96*, pages 593–602. Springer Berlin / Heidelberg, 1996.

[8] P. Gehler and S. Nowozin. On feature combination for multiclass object classification. In *ICCV*, pages 221–228. IEEE, 2009.

[9] M. Hammami, Y. Chahir, and L. Chen. Webguard: A web filtering engine combining textual, structural, and visual content-based analysis. *IEEE Trans. on Knowl. and Data Eng.*, 18:272–284, February 2006.

[10] W. Hu, O. Wu, Z. Chen, Z. Fu, and S. Maybank. Recognition of pornographic web pages by classifying texts and images. *IEEE Transactions on Pattern Analysis and Machine Intelligence*, pages 1019–1034, 2007.

[11] C. Jansohn, A. Ulges, and T. M. Breuel. Detecting Pornographic Video Content by Combining Image Features with Motion Information. In *Proceeding of the seventeen ACM international conference on Multimedia*, 2009.

[12] M. J. Jones and J. M. Rehg. Statistical color models with application to skin detection. In *International Journal of Computer Vision*, pages 274–280, 1999.

[13] P. Kakumanu, S. Makrogiannis, and N. Bourbakis. A survey of skin-color modeling and detection methods. *Pattern Recognition*, 40(3):1106–1122, 2007.

[14] M. Kloft, U. Brefeld, S. Sonnenburg, P. Laskov, K. R. Müller, and A. Zien. Efficient and accurate lp-norm multiple kernel learning. *NIPS*, 22(22):997–1005, 2009.

[15] S. Lazebnik, C. Schmid, and J. Ponce. Beyond bags of features: Spatial pyramid matching for recognizing natural scene categories. In *CVPR*, volume 2, pages 2169 – 2178, 2006.

[16] J.-S. Lee, Y.-M. Kuo, P.-C. Chung, and E.-L. Chen. Naked image detection based on adaptive and extensible skin color model. *Pattern Recognition*, 40(8):2261 – 2270, 2007.

[17] P. Lee, S. Hui, and A. Fong. An intelligent categorization engine for bilingual web content filtering. *IEEE Transactions on Multimedia*, 7(6):1183 – 1190, dec. 2005.

[18] A. Lopes, S. de Avila, A. Peixoto, R. Oliveira, and A. Araújo. A bag-of-features approach based on hue-sift descriptor for nude detection. In *Proceedings of the 17th European Signal Processing Conference, Glasgow, Scotland*, 2009.

[19] D. Lowe. Object recognition from local scale-invariant features. In *ICCV*, volume 2, pages 1150 -1157 vol.2, 1999.

[20] Flasher detection algorithm aims to clean up video chat. January 19, 2011. http://www.technologyreview.com/blog/arxiv/26281/.

[21] Myyearbook live web site. http://live.myyearbook.com/.

[22] T. Ojala, M. PietikÃd'inen, and D. Harwood. A comparative study of texture measures with classification based on featured distributions. *Pattern Recognition*, pages 51–59, 1996.

[23] Omegle web site. http://www.omegle.com/.

[24] J. Philbin, O. Chum, M. Isard, J. Sivic, and A. Zisserman. Object retrieval with large vocabularies and fast spatial matching. In *ICCV*, pages 1–8, 2007.

[25] P. Pudil, J. Novovicová, and J. Kittler. Floating search methods in feature selection. *Pattern recognition letters*, 15(11):1119–1125, 1994.

[26] G. Ratsch. Robust boosting via convex optimization: Theory and applications. PhD thesis, University of Potsdam, Potsdam, Germany, 2001.

[27] Tinychat web site. http://tinychat.com/.

[28] J. Uijlings, A. Smeulders, and R. Scha. Real-time bag of words, approximately. In *Proceeding of the ACM International Conference on Image and Video Retrieval*, page 6. ACM, 2009.

[29] A. Vedaldi and B. Fulkerson. VLFeat: An open and portable library of computer vision algorithms. `http://www.vlfeat.org/`, 2011.

[30] A. Vedaldi, V. Gulshan, M. Varma, and A. Zisserman. Multiple kernels for object detection. In *ICCV*, 2009.

[31] A. Vedaldi and A. Zisserman. Efficient additive kernels via explicit feature maps. In *CVPR*, pages 3539–3546. IEEE, 2010.

[32] X. Xing, Y.-l. Liang, H. Cheng, J. Dang, R. Han, X. Liu, Q. Lv, and S. Mishra. Safevchat: Detecting obscene content and misbehaving users in online video chat services. In *WWW*, 2011.

[33] J. Ze Wang, J. Li, G. Wiederhold, and O. Firschein. System for screening objectionable images. *Computer Communications*, 21(15):1355–1360, 1998.

Beyond Co-occurrence: Discovering and Visualizing Tag Relationships from Geo-spatial and Temporal Similarities

Haipeng Zhang, Mohammed Korayem, Erkang You, David J. Crandall
School of Informatics & Computing
Indiana University
Bloomington, IN
{zhanhaip,mkorayem,erkyou,djcran}@indiana.edu

ABSTRACT

Studying relationships between keyword tags on social sharing websites has become a popular topic of research, both to improve tag suggestion systems and to discover connections between the concepts that the tags represent. Existing approaches have largely relied on tag co-occurrences. In this paper, we show how to find connections between tags by comparing their distributions over time and space, discovering tags with similar geographic and temporal patterns of use. Geo-spatial, temporal and geo-temporal distributions of tags are extracted and represented as vectors which can then be compared and clustered. Using a dataset of tens of millions of geo-tagged Flickr photos, we show that we can cluster Flickr photo tags based on their geographic and temporal patterns, and we evaluate the results both qualitatively and quantitatively using a panel of human judges. We also develop visualizations of temporal and geographic tag distributions, and show that they help humans recognize semantic relationships between tags. This approach to finding and visualizing similar tags is potentially useful for exploring any data having geographic and temporal annotations.

Categories and Subject Descriptors

H.2.8 [**Database applications**]: Data mining

General Terms

Measurement, Theory.

Keywords

tag semantics and visualization, Flickr, geo-spatial and temporal clustering

1. INTRODUCTION

Online photo sharing is booming: as of late 2010, Flickr hosted over 5 billion photos and users were uploading more than 3,000 new images every minute [29]. In addition to simply hosting images, these sites include social features that allow users to annotate photos in a variety of ways, including adding descriptive keywords (called *tags*), titles, captions, quality scores, and free-form comments. In the particular case of tags, empirical studies of Flickr have shown that users add tags for a variety of reasons, including to indicate geographic locations, descriptions of actions and events, identities of objects, people, and groups, and so on [30]. Thus tags provide a rich (albeit noisy, incomplete and inconsistent) source of information about the semantic content of photos. Tags have been used in the data mining community to study the properties of online photo collections, including identifying temporal bursts of photographic activity corresponding to important events [26], finding geo-spatial peaks of activity corresponding to important landmarks [22], selecting iconic images to represent particular places [6], and even predicting product adoption rates by monitoring the popularity of product photos [14].

A major theme of this existing work has been to study *tag co-occurrences*, finding tags that frequently occur with one another on the same photograph as a means of identifying semantically-related tags. Co-occurrence has been particularly helpful for suggesting new tags based on the existing tags of a photo [11, 18, 30]. Other work has applied clustering algorithms to find semantically-related concepts by looking for groups of tags that frequently co-occur [3, 28]. While these approaches often yield reasonable results, they make the assumption that tags are related only if they co-occur often on the same photographs. But some related tags may seldom co-occur: the Statue of Liberty and Central Park are clearly related – both are major New York City landmarks – but the tags *statueofliberty* and *centralpark* do not have many co-occurrences because it is nearly impossible to take a photo that includes both. Moreover, co-occurrences give little information about the nature of the relationship – i.e. *why* two tags are related.

In this paper, we explore other more specific types of connections between tags – and, by extension, between the concepts that the tags represent – by comparing the spatial and temporal distributions of tags instead of their co-occurrences. The intuition here is that related concepts have similar geo-temporal distributions because they occur at about the same times and places, even if they rarely co-occur on photos. Our work takes advantage of the rich metadata available on photo-sharing sites like Flickr, including the timestamps recorded by modern digital cameras, and the geo-tags specifying the latitude and longitude of where a photo was taken. Geo-spatial and temporal properties of tags have been studied in existing work (e.g. [14, 22, 26]), but we are not aware of work that has used these properties to quantify connections between tags. We also present methods for visualizing the relationships between tags by comparing their geo-temporal distributions. These techniques complement other methods like tag clouds [16] and temporal tag evolution [8] to help people find and visualize the relationships between tags.

Permission to make digital or hard copies of all or part of this work for personal or classroom use is granted without fee provided that copies are not made or distributed for profit or commercial advantage and that copies bear this notice and the full citation on the first page. To copy otherwise, to republish, to post on servers or to redistribute to lists, requires prior specific permission and/or a fee.
WSDM'12, February 8–12, 2012, Seattle, Washington, USA.
Copyright 2012 ACM 978-1-4503-0747-5/12/02 ...$10.00.

In the remainder of this paper, we describe an approach that finds relationships between tags from geo-spatial and temporal similarities, and we apply this approach on a large dataset of tens of millions of photos downloaded from Flickr. After surveying related work in Section 2, we show how to define feature vectors to compactly represent geo-temporal distributions and cluster tags based on these features (Section 3). We then present qualitative visualizations of the resulting clusters as well as a more quantitative evaluation using a panel of human judges in Section 4.

2. RELATED WORK

Tags on social sharing systems have been studied extensively. Here we review the work most relevant to studying tag semantics and relationships in photo collections.

Clustering tags based on co-occurrences. Much work has been based on photo tag co-occurrences, mostly in the context of tag suggestion systems. Garg and Weber [11] use tag co-occurrences to suggest additional tags for a new image. Sigurbjörnsson and Van Zwol [30] take a similar approach but also conduct a study of tagging behavior on Flickr. Liu *et al* [18] rank tags by performing Pagerank-like random walks on tag graphs where the edge weights are frequency of co-occurrence. Other work has clustered tags using co-occurrence features in order to find groups of semantically-related tags. Shepitsen *et al* [28] use TF-IDF to build trees of del.icio.us and Last.Fm tags, and then partition them into homogeneous clusters. Begelman *et al* [3] partition tag graphs using spectral clustering. These papers inspired our idea of clustering tags, but our work differs in that we use features other than co-occurrence, instead looking for tags with second-order connections like similarities in spatial and/or temporal distributions.

Temporal and geo-spatial properties of tags. Timestamps and geo-tags of photos have been used to study temporal and geo-spatial distributions of individual tags, often in order to identify peaks in the temporal distribution (corresponding to events) and/or in the geo-spatial distribution (corresponding to cities and popular landmarks). Rattenbury *et al* [26] use burst detection techniques to find tags with significant peaks in time and space, while Moxley *et al* [22] build on this work by using entropy analysis on a quadtree data structure to improve performance. Chen and Roy [4] model tag occurrences as points in a 3D geo-temporal space, use wavelet transform-based techniques to find tags with bursts in both temporal and spatial distributions, and then cluster these tags using DBSCAN. Ahern *et al* [1] cluster photos to find dense areas based on geo-tags and find representative tags for the areas using TF-IDF, while Moxley *et al* [21] use a similar approach to rank local tags. Crandall *et al* [6] and Kennedy *et al* [17] find both distinctive tags and images for clusters of photos found based on geo-tags. While these papers analyze geo-spatial and temporal attributes of photos, they are primarily focused on finding and studying "event" tags corresponding to peaks in the geo-temporal tag usage distributions, whereas we are interested in comparing and grouping larger and more general sets of tags.

Visualizing tag clusters. The usual method to visualize tags is to draw tag clouds [16], while Dubinko *et al* [8] visualize interesting Flickr tags that evolve over time through animations. In this paper we propose visualizations of the temporal semantics of tag clusters by plotting time series representing their usage along time, and the geo-spatial semantics of tag clusters in a 3-D space over a map to represent their usage across space. We also show that the visualizations can help humans understand subtle semantic relationships.

Spatial clustering and co-location pattern mining. Our work is reminiscent of spatial clustering [24, 27] which groups together similar spatial data points based on their locations, but differs from our problem in that it clusters spatial data points while we cluster spatial distributions. Our goal is more related to co-location pattern mining [9, 10, 13, 35], in which the goal is to identify features that are often located near one another. Clustering is not used by Xiao *et al* [35], while Huang and Zhang [13] and Estivill-Castro *et al* [9, 10] take different clustering approaches. We are not aware of work that applies these techniques to vast datasets of user-generated social media content as we do here.

Studies of query logs, tweets and news articles. Temporal and geo-spatial patterns have been studied to discover concept relationships in other domains, including tweets, news articles, and queries in search engine logs. Radinsky *et al* [25] extend Explicit Semantic Analysis to represent concepts as time series of word occurrences in the New York Times archive. Vlachos *et al* [33] use frequency-space analysis of search query time series to identify bursts and semantically-similar queries. Chien and Immorlica [5] use similar techniques but perform an experimental evaluation, and find that for 70% of the queries, at least three of the top ten keywords identified by temporal similarity are semantically related. The geo-spatial distributions of search engine queries were studied by Backstrom *et al* [2], who estimate geographic centers and dispersions of queries. Vadrevu *et al* [32] use the co-occurrence of a query term with place names in a region to determine whether the query is related to this region. Perhaps most similar to ours is very recent work in the domains of search engine queries and Twitter hashtags. Mohebbi *et al* [20] developed a tool which takes a search engine query and finds other queries with similar temporal or spatial distributions. They quantize the weekly time series data and state-by-state usage data of individual queries into vectors to represent temporal and spatial distributions, and then apply K-means clustering and an approximate nearest neighbor alogorithm to look up similar vectors efficiently. Meanwhile, Yang and Leskovec [36] cluster Twitter hashtags and short phrases in news documents to identify their temporal patterns and the dynamics of human attention they receive. Neither of these latter two papers evaluates the semantic quality of the resulting clusters and connections, whereas we use panels of human judges to evaluate our results.

Finally, our work is related in spirit to that of Wu *et al* [34], who compute the "Flickr distance" between a pair of tags by computing the visual similarity of photos having those tags, and then cluster tags based on this score. Our work is similar in that it defines connections between tags using a property other than co-occurrence, but is complementary in that we define similarity metrics based on metadata like timestamps and geo-tags instead of the visual content of images. This both allows us to discover connections that may not be apparent from visual features, and also allows our techniques to scale to much larger datasets (having tens of millions of photographs) because processing metadata is much more efficient than visual analysis.

3. DISCOVERING TAG RELATIONSHIPS

We assume that we have a dataset of online objects (e.g. photos), each of which has a user id of the person generating the object (e.g. the photographer), a timestamp specifying when the object was created, a geo-tag specifying latitude-longitude coordinates for the object, and a set of zero or more text tags. To define this formally, it is useful to think of tagging *events* – individual acts of a user tagging a photo with a text tag. The information associated with a particular event includes the tag that was applied, the photo to which the tag was applied, the user who uploaded the tagged photo, the geographic location of the tagged photo, and the timestamp indicating when the photo was taken. Letting $\mathcal{T}$ be the set of all possible text tags, then the set of tagging actions $\mathcal{A} = \{a_1, a_2, ..., a_q\}$ can be defined as a set of tuples of the form $a_i = (u_i, t_i, \tau_i, g_i)$, where u_i is a user, $t_i \in \mathcal{T}$ is a tag, τ_i is a timestamp, and $g_i \in \mathcal{R} \times \mathcal{R}$ is a geo-tag (latitude-longitude coordinate).

Given a collection of tagged objects, our goal is to cluster the tags based on their geo-spatial and temporal properties. To do this, we first extract a geo or temporal signature for each tag and represent it with a corresponding feature vector, and then we cluster the feature vectors using an unsupervised algorithm like k-means [19]. In addition to finding the geo-spatial and temporal distributions of each tag, we also compute a feature vector based on the cross-product of these two attributes, which allows us to represent a tag's joint geo-temporal distribution – i.e. the "motion" of how a tag's spatial distribution changes over time. The following three subsections explain the geo, temporal, and motion feature vectors in turn.

3.1 Geo-spatial feature vectors

Since different types of tags have different geographical distributions, our first feature aims to characterize the geographical distribution of a tag. Because the distribution of photographs over the world is highly non-uniform, with most of the photographic activity concentrated in cities, many areas of the world have very few photos. It is thus useful to aggregate photos together into coarse geo-spatial buckets instead of clustering using raw geo-tags. (Quantization of geo-tags also reduces the impact of noise in the geo-tags.) To do this, we divide the world into n bins, each with s degrees of latitude by s degrees of longitude. We assign each of the bins a unique index number in the range $[1, n]$, and define a quantization function $q_G(g)$ that maps a latitude-longitude coordinate g into the index number of the corresponding geo bin. In the results presented in this paper, we use $s = 1$ degree, which corresponds to grid cells of roughly 100 km $\times$ 100 km at the middle latitudes. Note that the bins do not have the same surface area because degrees of longitude became closer together near the poles; this tends not to be a problem in practice because the vast majority of photos are taken near the middle latitudes. An equal-area partitioning of the globe [12] would address this issue and is a direction for future work.

To compute a geo feature vector for tag t, we first count the number of unique users who have used that tag in each geo bin g,

$$U_G(g, t) = || \{u_i | (u_i, t_i, \tau_i, g_i) \in \mathcal{A}, t_i = t, g = q_G(g_i)\} ||.$$

We count the number of *users* who applied a tag within a geographic area instead of the number of photos in order to prevent high-activity users from biasing the distribution [1]. (This can be thought of as giving each user a single "vote" for whether or not a tag applies to a given geographic area.) Then we normalize the vector to get the geo feature $v^G(t)$ of tag t,

$$v_i^G(t) = \frac{U_G(i, t)}{\sqrt{\sum_{j=1}^{n} U_G^2(j, t)}}.$$

Normalization is necessary since tags sharing similar geo distributions might have different overall frequencies of occurrence. While other work has found that L1 normalization works better in high dimensional spaces [7, 23], we found that L2 normalization works better in our context. (For example, for the clustering results presented in Section 4, we found that L2 norm generates clusters that have more uniform and moderate sizes. When clustering 2000 tags into 50 clusters, L1 norm produces 17 singletons (clusters that contain only one tag) while L2 norm produces no singletons. L1 norm cluster sizes also have much greater variation: their standard deviation is 127.8 while the standard deviation of L2 norm is 54.1.)

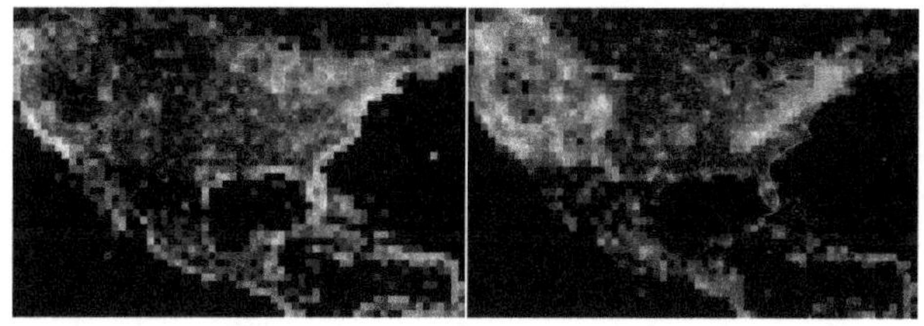

Figure 1: Geographic distributions for tag "beach" (left) and "mountains" (right).

As an example, Figures 1 visualizes the normalized matrices for tags "beach" and "mountains" over North America, in which greater intensity indicates that more users applied the tag to photos in a given geo-bin. Notice that the Appalachian and Rocky Mountain ranges are immediately apparent in the "mountains" map, while the "beach" map highlights the coastline of North America.

3.2 Temporal feature vectors

Tags also have different temporal distributions, because some tags (and semantic concepts) are much more popular at certain times than others — for example, we might expect "beach" to be used more often during the summer than in the winter, while "restaurant" might occur more often during the meal times of the day. As with the geographic feature vectors described above, with temporal features it is also useful to aggregate photos together into coarse temporal bins. Let $q_T(\tau)$ be a quantization function that maps a timestamp τ into one of m temporal bins, returning a bin index in the range $[1, m]$. This quantization function could be designed to operate at different levels of granularity, for example mapping timestamps to hours of the day, days of the week, months of the year, etc. For any tag t, we then build an m-dimensional vector, again counting the number of unique users who have used the tag in each temporal period p,

$$U_T(p, t) = || \{u_i | (u_i, t_i, \tau_i, g_i) \in \mathcal{A}, t_i = t, p = q_T(\tau_i)\} ||,$$

and then normalize to produce an m-dimensional temporal feature vector $v^T(t)$,

$$v_i^T(t) = \frac{U_T(i, t)}{\sqrt{\sum_{j=1}^{m} U_T^2(j, t)}}.$$

In this paper we primarily use a quantization function that maps timestamps into one of 26 two-week periods of the year: January 1-14, January 15-28, etc. We disregard the specific year and as a result, all the data is merged together into a single year – for example, photos taken on January 1, 2008 and January 1, 2009 will be mapped to the same cell. In addition to the 26-dimensional 2-week vectors, we also create 7-dimensional day-of-week vectors and 24-dimensional hour-of-day vectors.

Flickr users are significantly more active at certain times of the year than others, as illustrated in Figure 2: note that nearly twice as many users take photos during the first two weeks of July (period 14) than in early February (period 3). To correct for this effect, in practice we normalize the temporal counts for tag t and period p, $U_T(p, t)$, by the total number of photos taken in North America during p, before applying L2 normalization to produce v^T. Figure 3 shows the process of obtaining temporal feature vectors.

3.3 Geo-temporal (motion) features

Finally, we also want to produce a signature for a tag based on

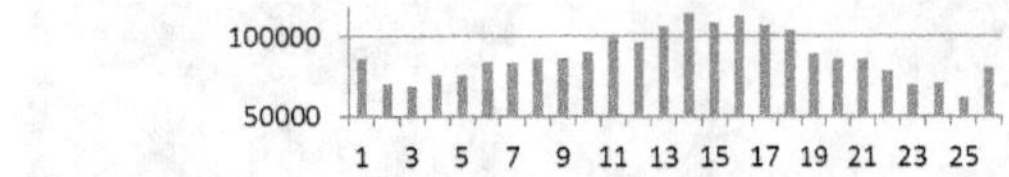

Figure 2: Number of unique Flickr users active in North America, for each 2-week period of the year.

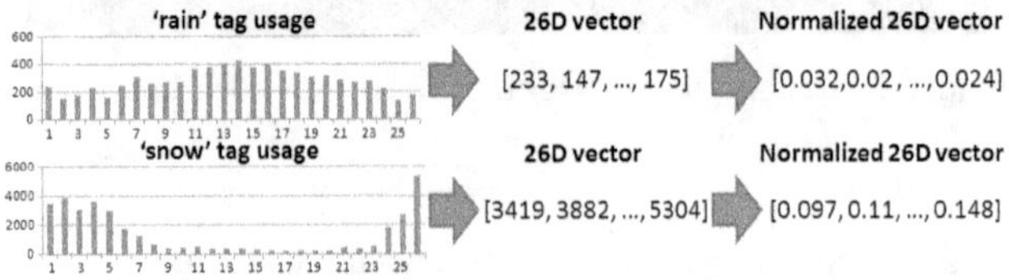

Figure 3: Computing temporal feature vectors.

its joint geo-temporal distribution – that is, how the geo-spatial distribution of the tag varies over the course of a year (or equivalently, how the temporal distribution varies with spatial location). We call these geo-temporal signatures our "motion" features. Given geo and temporal quantization functions q_G and q_T (described above) that map geo-tags into one of n bins and timestamps into one of m bins, a motion feature vector has one bin per entry in the cross product of these two sets of indices, or mn dimensions total. More precisely, we define a motion quantization function that maps a geo-tag g_i and timestamp τ_i to a bin index in $[1, mn]$,

$$q_M(g_i, \tau_i) = m \times (q_G(g_i) - 1) + q_T(\tau_i),$$

then count the number of unique users who used a given tag t in each geo-temporal bin,

$$U_M(m,t) = || \{u_i | (u_i, t_i, \tau_i, g_i) \in \mathcal{A}, t_i = t, m = q_M(g_i, \tau_i)\} ||,$$

and take the L2 norm (as above) to define a final motion feature vector, v^M. For the experiments in this paper, this vector has $mn = 124,800$ dimensions. As with the geo feature vectors, we remove empty dimensions (geo-temporal cells having no photos) as an optimization.

3.4 Co-occurrence features

For comparison purposes, we also define similarity metrics using using two more traditional techniques. First, the pairwise co-occurrence between two tags t_1 and t_2, co_occur(t_1, t_2), is computed by simply counting the number of photos that are tagged with both t_1 and t_2. A disadvantage of this simple co-occurrence measure is that it favors pairs of tags that occur very often, since very frequent tags will co-occur more often than infrequent tags even if they are unrelated. Thus we include a second baseline feature, mutual information, which overcomes this problem by normalizing the co-occurrence measures by the overall frequency of the tags [3],

$$\text{mutual\_info}(t_1, t_2) = \log\left(\frac{\text{co\_occur}(t_1, t_2)}{\text{occur}(t_1) \times \text{occur}(t_2)}\right)$$

where occur(t) is the total number of photos having tag t. This score can be thought of as a measure of the independence of the two tags: it is minimized if the two tags are completely independent (never co-occur), and is maximized if the tags are strongly correlated (always co-occur).

4. EXPERIMENTS AND VISUALIZATIONS

To test our techniques for characterizing tags based on geo and temporal signatures, we used a dataset of geo-tagged, time-stamped photos downloaded from Flickr through the site's public API interface, using a crawling technique similar to that described in [6]. We collected the following information for each photo: the geo-tag (latitude and longitude) of where the photo was taken, the timestamp of when it was taken, and the set of textual tags (if any) associated with the photo. From this collection of nearly 80 million photos, we selected only the photos in North America (which we defined to be a rectangular region spanning from 10 degrees north, -130 degrees west to 70 degrees north, -50 degrees west).

We then computed the top 2000 most frequent text tags (ranked by the number of unique users applying the tag) in North America. (We chose this relatively small number of tags so that our geo-temporal distributions would have substantial mass (each of these tags has been used by at least 1,100 unique Flickr users), and to make human evaluation tractable. Note that the majority (66.7%) of photos on Flickr are tagged with at least one of these 2,000 tags since Flickr tag frequency follows a long tailed distribution [30].) For each of these tags, we extracted the geo feature vectors, temporal feature vectors and motion vectors described in Section 3. In preparation for geo feature vector extraction, we filtered the data by removing photos with geotag precision less than about city-scale (according to the precision reported by Flickr), resulting in a dataset with about 44 million photos. For the temporal feature vectors, we removed photos with inaccurate or suspicious timestamps (including photos supposedly taken in the future or distant past), resulting in about 41 million photos; for the motion feature vectors, both of these filters were applied, yielding about 39 million photos.

4.1 Tag relationships

We can use the similarity metrics defined in Section 3 to find pairs of similar tags. Given a tag t', we can find a list of related tags using each of the distances defined above, including geo-spatial, temporal, and geo-temporal. To do this, we compute the feature vectors $v^G(t)$, $v^T(t)$, and $v^M(t)$ for each tag t, and then compute the pairwise Euclidean distances between these vectors and those of t'. The tags are ranked according to their distances to t' in ascending order, and the k tags with lowest distance are found. For the co-occurrence and mutual information features, we compute the similarity for each tag t using the co_occur(t, t') and mutual_info(t, t') functions, and then rank the tags in increasing order of similarity.

As an example, Table 1 lists the tags that are most similar to the tag "cherryblossoms" under the various measures of similarity. The first column shows the 20 most similar tags according to the geo-spatial similarity metric. Most of these tags are strongly related to Washington, DC (which is of course famous for its annual cherry blossom festival in April), including "president," "whitehouse," "smithsonian," and "lincolnmemorial," among others. The second column shows tags having high temporal similarity, including "easter," "spring," "april," and "magnolia". The list of tags under motion similarity appear to be a mixture of geographically similar tags and temporally similar tags. In contrast, the co-occurrence list has arguably much lower quality: "canon," "water," and "usa" are popular tags that also co-occur with many other tags, and are not particularly relevant to "cherryblossoms." Mutual information gives more meaningful results compared to raw co-occurrence, but some tags such as "lions" and "drops" cannot be interpreted easily and do not have clear geo-spatial or temporal relationships to cherry blossoms. Moreover, the mutual information list missed tags like "whitehouse," "april", and "kite" which were picked up by the temporal and geo-spatial analyses. These tags do not frequently co-occur with "cherryblossoms" on the same photos, but do share similar geo and/or temporal patterns.

4.2 Clustering tags

The analysis in the last section can be used to compute the sim-

Table 1: **Top 20 most similar tags to "cherryblossoms" using different similarity metrics. The columns rank the tags according to (from left): geo-spatial, temporal, motion (geo-temporal), co-occurrence, and mutual information.**

	Geo-spatial		Temporal		Motion		Co-occurrence		Mutual information	
1.	president	0.321	cherry	0.451	cherry	0.291	washingtondc	4568	blossoms	-10.577
2.	whitehouse	0.321	blossoms	0.505	blossoms	0.417	dc	3443	cherry	-11.004
3.	monument	0.323	blossom	0.612	blossom	0.546	spring	2319	washingtonmonument	-11.355
4.	smithsonian	0.324	easter	0.636	jefferson	0.673	washington	2089	buds	-12.289
5.	memorial	0.324	spring	0.638	kite	0.868	flowers	1969	washingtondc	-12.456
6.	georgetown	0.325	april	0.654	washingtonmonument	0.908	blossoms	1367	dc	-12.580
7.	washingtonmonument	0.327	magnolia	0.735	monument	0.990	pink	1007	hearts	-12.622
8.	dc	0.327	buds	0.758	magnolia	0.998	trees	979	jefferson	-12.657
9.	lincolnmemorial	0.328	washingtonmonument	0.813	spring	1.026	canon	754	blossom	-12.659
10.	wwii	0.331	tulip	0.822	bloom	1.042	cherry	753	spring	-12.760
11.	washingtondc	0.332	jefferson	0.837	memorial	1.057	tree	703	lions	-12.785
12.	jefferson	0.367	egg	0.858	lincolnmemorial	1.085	usa	610	pink	-12.845
13.	arlington	0.370	tulips	0.862	washingtondc	1.086	flower	560	bloom	-12.884
14.	lincoln	0.372	bloom	0.868	dc	1.091	washingtonmonument	552	petals	-12.955
15.	mall	0.392	break	0.869	whitehouse	1.092	water	498	poppy	-13.051
16.	capitol	0.401	poppy	0.870	mall	1.096	2007	415	flowers	-13.263
17.	soldier	0.407	eggs	0.883	festival	1.103	unitedstates	412	drops	-13.283
18.	war	0.421	bud	0.895	tulip	1.106	festival	379	branches	-13.327
19.	cherry	0.429	kite	0.922	government	1.121	nature	377	japan	-13.381
20.	capital	0.448	olympics	0.924	capital	1.122	brooklyn	347	shell	-13.385

ilarity between any arbitrary pair of tags, but it is difficult to visualize or quantify the performance of these results directly because there are so many possible pairs. In past work, tag similarity results have been summarized by grouping tags into a small number of similar clusters, typically using co-occurrence information (e.g. [5]). We follow a similar strategy and cluster Flickr tags according to each of our three types of distance metrics (temporal, geo-spatial, geo-temporal) as well as traditional co-occurrence and mutual information measures.

For each feature vector type, we clustered the 2000 tags using k-means [19]. Squared Euclidean distance was used to measure distances between vectors. Since k-means clustering is sensitive to the initial choice of centroids, we ran k-means five times with different random initial cluster centers and chose the best result (in this case, choosing the clustering with the minimum total vector-to-centroid distance). Of course, this clustering algorithm requires an *a priori* choice of the number of clusters (k). For the purposes of this paper, where our primary focus is on presenting techniques for comparing tags based on their geo and temporal distributions and not on presenting an end-to-end system for tag analysis, we simply set k to a value (50) that gave reasonable results in our subjective judgment. Various techniques exist for selecting k automatically based on properties of a dataset (see e.g. [31]) and these techniques could easily be applied to our work.

As we show in the next few sections, the overall "shape" of the geo-spatial and temporal distributions varies dramatically from tag to tag and cluster to cluster: some clusters contain tags that are diffuse across space and time (like "canon", "geotagged", "blackandwhite", etc.), while other distributions are very "peaky" ("newyorkcity", "washingtondc", etc.), and others are somewhere in between ("usa", "newengland", etc.). It is thus useful to compute a statistical measure of the peakiness of a distribution, in order to compactly characterize its overall "shape". We measure the peakiness of a vector v by computing its second moment,

$$\text{second\_moment}(v) = v \cdot v = \sum_{i=1}^{n} v_i^2,$$

and measure the peakiness of a cluster of tags C as the average second moment of the vectors that it contains,

$$\frac{\sum_{v \in C} \text{second\_moment}(v)}{|C|}.$$

Peaky distributions will have higher second moment values, while distributions close to uniform will have low second moment. (Note that the second moment of a discrete probability distribution is the likelihood of sampling twice from the distribution and drawing the same value both times.) The second moment gives a statistic by which to rank clusters, as clusters with high average peakiness usually have bursts in temporal distributions or geo-spatial distributions which indicate particularly interesting clusters.

We present sample results and visualizations for several sample tag clusters in the following sections. Due to space limitations we do not show all the tag clusters generated from the three different perspectives, but these and other detailed results are available at `http://vision.soic.indiana.edu/tagclusters`.

4.2.1 *Geo-spatial clusters*

Figure 4 shows visualizations of several tag clusters produced by analyzing geo-spatial distributions. The visualizations were created by taking a cluster centroid and converting it back to a two-dimensional matrix: i.e. for each geo bin, we find the corresponding latitude-longitude coordinates for the bin center and plot them together with their values in a 3D space over a schematic map of North America. The result is a topographical visual effect with the heights of the peaks as well as the intensity of red color indicating the usage of the tags in the cluster at corresponding locations underneath. The figure shows three sample clusters. Figure 4(a) consists of tags from the New York City area. Some not very obvious tags are: "soho" which is a shopping area in New York City, "bull" which is the Wall Street Bull and "ground" which relates to Ground Zero referring to World Trade Center site. This cluster is ranked 10th out of 50 clusters by second moment. Figure 4(b) visualizes the cluster in which most tags are related to zoos and animals and others are related to airports. As a result, the visualization peaks at major US cities with famous zoos and airports. It is ranked 37th. Figure 4(c) displays the cluster of tags that occur predominantly in national parks. This cluster is ranked 27th.

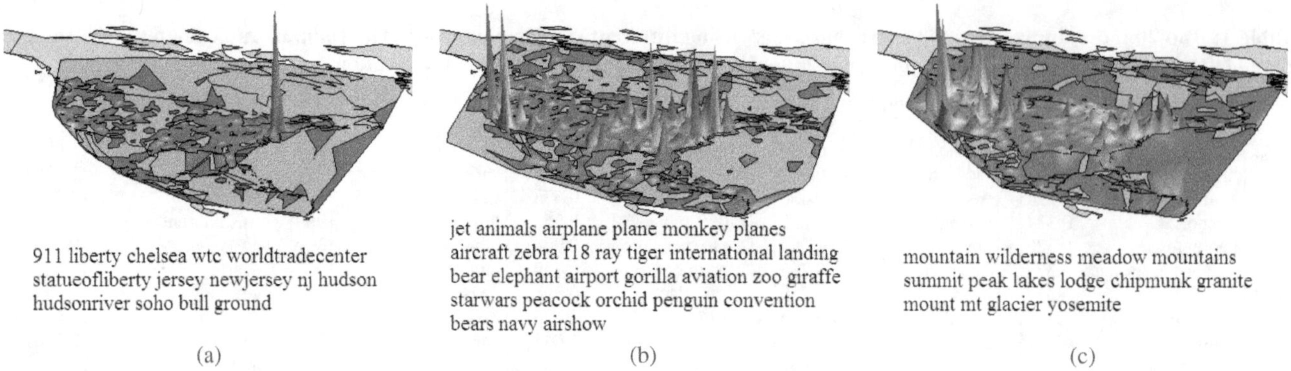

Figure 4: Visualizations of sample clusters produced by analyzing similarity of geo-spatial distributions. The clusters seem to correspond to (a) tags related to New York City, (b) tags related to cities with popular zoos and airports, and (c) tags related to national parks and outdoor areas. Best viewed in color.

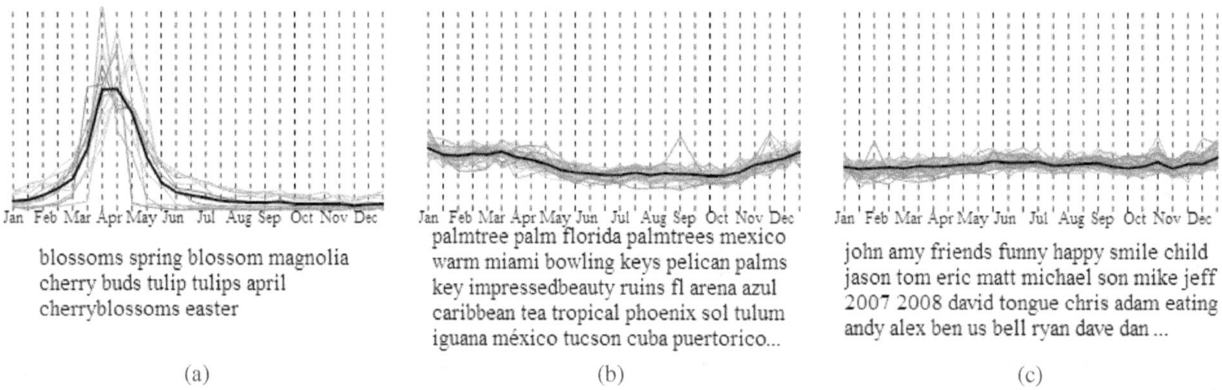

Figure 5: Visualizations of three clusters produced by analyzing similarity of temporal distributions: (a) tags related to spring, (b) tags related to winter, (c) tags related to gatherings of friends.

Images that record the visualizations of all the 50 geo clusters are available at the above website. The top ranked clusters by second moment are more concentrated geographically. From these top clusters, we see state clusters, city clusters, zoo clusters, park clusters, northern city clusters, coastal area clusters and so on. For lower ranked clusters, the tags are more geographically distributed, such as a cluster of rural regions and a cluster of urban regions.

4.2.2 *Temporal clusters*

Figure 5 shows visualizations of three of the clusters produced by the temporal similarity metric. For each temporal cluster, we plot the cluster centroid as well as the distributions of the individual tags within the cluster, with each point representing the usage in the corresponding two-week period. Figure 5(a) displays the cluster with a strong peak during spring. The thick black curve corresponds to the cluster centroid while the other curves correspond to the signals for individual tags. This cluster is ranked 11th out of 50 clusters by second moment. Figure 5(b) visualizes a cluster with a shallow peak during the winter season. Most tags are related to winter vacations in warm locales. This cluster is ranked 34th. The cluster in Figure 5(c) (ranked 48th by second moment) seems to correspond to family gatherings, with slight temporal peaks around Thanksgiving and Christmas. There are also some year tags (e.g. "2008", "2009", etc.) which appear frequently around New Year's Day. Visualizations of all 50 temporal clusters are available at the website above. We see that top ranked clusters of tags have sharp bursts in smaller time windows and lower ranked clusters have more general seasonal patterns.

We also clustered the data according to temporal features at other time scales, including 7-dimensional day-of-week vectors and 24-dimensional hours-of-day vectors. Due to space constraints we do not present detailed results, but instead mention a few interesting findings. For day-of-week vectors, we are able to see weekday clusters such as "work office desk students commute" and weekend clusters such as "live sushi gallery concert macys highschool moma". For hours-of-day clusters, we see clusters peak at different time of the day, such as a morning cluster, "early sunrise dawn morning," and a nighttime cluster, "lightning concert longexposure campfire nighttime nightphotography exposure live".

4.2.3 *Geo-temporal clusters*

Tags within a motion cluster typically share either geo and temporal similarities, or both. Cluster "vegas lasvegas las bellagio strip paris casino nevada fountains flamingo" captures Las Vegas and its hotels and casinos which has a counterpart in geo clusters. It is ranked 5th out of 50. Cluster "christmas holiday xmas holidays christmastree christmaslights december decorations ornament decoration cookies gift santa fireplace" captures Christmas which has a counterpart in temporal clusters and is ranked 31st. We observe that top ranked clusters are more likely to have obvious geographic connections while the clusters having temporal patterns are ranked

Top 10 temporal clusters

	Tags in cluster	# tags	2nd moment
1	**4th fourthofjuly 4thofjuly independenceday july4th**	7	0.578
2	**january newyearseve**	2	0.5
3	**turkey thanksgiving november**	3	0.355
4	**august**	1	0.2785
5	iris may dandelion graduation memorialday	5	0.269
6	**costume costumes halloween**	3	0.223
7	**christmastree christmaslights christmas ornament holidays**	9	0.215
8	pride june	2	0.206
9	**fallcolors pumpkins autumn fall foliage**	7	0.190
10	irish march	2	0.144

Top 10 geo-spatial clusters

	Tags in cluster	# tags	2nd moment
1	*toronto niagara niagarafalls cntower falls*	9	0.415
2	*golden cablecar francisco sanfrancisco sf*	27	0.402
3	*los angeles santamonica la losangeles*	8	0.397
4	*broadway brooklyn empire cab empirestatebuilding*	34	0.394
5	*strip paris vegas las lasvegas*	10	0.379
6	*seattle needle pugetsound spaceneedle wa*	8	0.374
7	*chicago bean searstower illinois il*	7	0.366
8	*ma massachusetts boston cambridge newengland*	6	0.332
9	prairie pennsylvania pa philadelphia philly	58	0.287
10	*911 liberty chelsea wtc worldtradecenter*	14	0.276

Top 10 motion (geo-temporal) clusters

	Tags in cluster	# tags	2nd moment
1	*losangeles angeles santamonica los la*	7	0.021
2	*taxi broadway empirestatebuilding brooklyn empire*	38	0.01693
3	*tx texas austin houston dallas*	5	0.01691
4	*chicago searstower bean illinois il*	7	0.01679
5	*vegas lasvegas las bellagio strip*	10	0.01671
6	*alberta calgary banff*	3	0.01606
7	*francisco sanfrancisco goldengatebridge goldengate berkeley*	30	0.0158
8	*pa philadelphia philly pennsylvania*	4	0.0157
9	*statueofliberty liberty newjersey jersey nj*	13	0.0148
10	ski skiing snowboarding tahoe fdsflickrtoys	73	0.0138

10 randomly-chosen co-occurrence clusters

	Tags in cluster	# tags
1	*sea ocean beach boat island*	41
2	*coast waves sun shore pier*	41
3	*washington statue museum sculpture washingtondc*	41
4	people model female face hair	43
5	*vacation travel trip desert arizona*	41
6	*water canada winter sky nature*	41
7	*trees mountains mountain hiking hike*	41
8	party wedding friends love dance	40
9	light city night bed sleep	39
10	geotagged us building architecture canon	41

10 randomly-chosen mutual information clusters

	Tags in cluster	# tags
1	rails rail railway train railroad	36
2	**independenceday july4th fourthofjuly 4th weird**	39
3	*marriage rings groom love couple*	38
4	plane jet aviation aircraft planes	38
5	furry sleepy pet kitten fur	38
6	jeans jacket socks shoes feet	39
7	furniture toilet sink seat couch	34
8	*tide waves surf ocean wave*	41
9	*rockies rockymountains peak glacier summit*	38
10	*sail port harbor docks sailing*	37

Figure 6: Comparison of clusters produced by different similarity metrics: temporal (top left), geo-spatial (top right), and geo-temporal (center). Clusters judged to be temporally significant by human judges are printed in blue boldface, while clusters judged to be geographically related are printed in *red boldface italics*. Clusters are sorted in decreasing order of second moment. For comparison, also shown are clusters produced by co-occurrence (bottom left) and mutual information (bottom right). For each cluster, up to 5 top ranked tags are displayed. Relevancy was judged by users without visualizations being shown.

in the middle. All the motion clusters can also be found at the website above.

4.3 Evaluation

We evaluated the idea of finding similar tags using geo-spatial and temporal features by comparing the clustering results from our proposed methods with those of the co-occurrence based techniques. Because it is difficult to define the quality of a tag cluster objectively, we involved humans in our experiments to judge the geo-spatial and temporal relevance of the clusters we found. We then used the human judgment as ground truth to compute the precisions and recalls when the task is to retrieve semantically meaningful clusters in time and/or space by thresholding the average second moment values. The goal of this evaluation was to test whether our techniques produce coherent tag clusters that correspond to intuitive geo-spatial and temporal concepts, and how these clusters compare to traditional techniques that use co-occurrence. We also showed our visualizations of geo-spatial and temporal tag distributions to a subset of the human judges, to try to measure how well these visualizations could help people appreciate subtle semantic connections between tags.

4.3.1 Clustering based on tag co-occurrences

As a baseline we used the method based on tag co-occurrence described in [3] to cluster the top 2000 tags into 50 clusters for a fair comparison. In particular, we constructed an undirected graph of tags, weighted the edges between tags by metrics of their co-occurrences and removed weak edges by thresholding the weights. We then applied a graph partitioning program, KMETIS [15], to partition the graph into clusters. We tried two different methods to weight the edges, one by raw co-occurrence counts and the other by mutual information (defined in Section 3). As a result, we generated two sets of 50 clusters: co-occurrence clusters and mutual information clusters. For each cluster, we ranked its tags by the numbers of edges inside the cluster: tags with more edges are considered to be more representative.

4.3.2 Ground truth from human judgment

To conduct the human judgment study at a large scale, we used

Amazon's Mechanical Turk service, asking users to judge the geo coherence and temporal coherence of clusters produced by the various similarity metrics that we propose. To improve the quality of the human judgment, we required users to be in the United States (so that they would be familiar with North American geography and cultural events) and have a good (>=95%) historical approval rate. For each cluster discovered by our methods, we selected its ten top ranked tags to present to the user.

For each geo, motion, co-occurrence and mutual information cluster, we asked the users to judge its geo relevance among the following three options: "more than 50% of its tag representatives represents a specific geographic area such as NYC", "more than 50% of its tag representatives represents an abstract geographic concept such as ocean," or "not geo relevant." Similarly, for each cluster we also asked the users to judge its temporal relevance according to the scale: "more than 50% of its tag representatives represents a specific temporal event such as Thanksgiving", "more than 50% of its tag representatives represents a broad temporal indication such as spring", "not temporally relevant". For both the geo and temporal relevance questions, if at least 80% of the users choose the first or second option for a cluster, we consider it to be geo or temporally relevant respectively. We put the clusters in 16 batches of 25 clusters per assignment and each batch was assigned to up to 20 Mechanical Turk users. On average, each cluster was judged by 19.9 users. Users were shown only the top ten tags associated with each cluster. We conducted two independent sets of experiments, one in which the 20 users were not shown the visualization graphs described above, and another in which a separate group of 20 users were shown the visualizations, to quantify how useful the visualizations might be in practice.

4.3.3 Evaluation results

The evaluation found that geo-spatial and motion clustering were more effective in finding geo relevant clusters than the other techniques: 29 (58%) of the geo clusters were found to be geo relevant by the human judges who were not shown the visualizations, compared to 30 (60%) of motion clusters, 11 (22%) of the co-occurrence clusters, and 11 (22%) of the mutual information clusters. A case study of some geo-temporal clusters judged not to be geo or temporally relevant showed the visualizations gave hints to people and helped understand the not-so-obvious semantics behind the clusters. For the geo clusters, among the top 31 clusters ranked by average second moment, 28 were judged to be geo relevant. We examined the 3 clusters that were judged to be "not geo relevant," and even these appeared to have interesting geographical semantics that were likely not obvious to the human judges. Visualizations for these 3 clusters are shown in Figure 7. The cluster in Figure 7(a) has an obvious peak in San Diego. The terms "polarbear" and "border" may not be immediately associated with San Diego, but in fact they refer to the San Diego Zoo's famous polar bears while the tag "border" refers to the Mexican border which is just a few miles away. In Figure 7(b), most tags are state or city names. They are in one cluster as their geographical distributions are very concentrated resulting in very peaky geo vectors which are not far from each other as measured by Euclidean distances. In Figure 7(c), there is a peak in Northern California and the tags are related to wine. Northern California is famous for its wine industry (Wine Country). Some other lower ranked clusters judged to be "not geo relevant" also show some geographical signal, such as the cluster displayed in Figure 4(b), which highlights zoos and airports.

Temporal clustering also found more temporally-relevant clusters than other techniques: 13 (26%) of the clusters produced by the temporal similarity metric were found to be temporally relevant, versus 5 (10%) of motion clusters and only 1 (2%) of the co-occurrence clusters and 6 (12%) of the mutual information clusters. We examined the temporal clusters judged not to be temporally relevant and found that some did have temporal patterns that were hard to observe when only the text tags were presented to users. We present three such clusters in Figure 8. The cluster in Figure 8(a) has bursts around important dates for the Presidential election. The cluster in Figure 8(b) has an autumn pattern and includes mostly insects and plants that are active or increasing in autumn. Finally, the cluster in Figure 8(c) has a January and February pattern, with tags related to the Chinese New Year and the Super Bowl. Some other such examples can be found in Figure 5(b) and (c) which were also judged to be "not temporally relevant."

In all of these cases, the visualizations of geo and temporal clusters were helpful for us to discover the hidden semantics behind the tag clusters. To try to measure the effectiveness of these visualizations, we conducted two separate evaluations on Mechanical Turk, one in which the visualizations were shown and another in which they were suppressed. The results suggested that the visualizations were helpful; the results only differed in that some of the clusters that were judged to be "not geo relevant" or "not temporally relevant" by the group who did not see visualizations were judged to be "geo relevant" or "temporally relevant" by the group that did. For geo clusters, 2 more high-ranked clusters (ranked 11 and 31 by second moment) mentioned above and visualized in Figure 7(a) and (c) were judged to be "geo relevant," which gave in total 62% of the 50 clusters judged to be "geo relevant." For temporal clusters, 6 more clusters (ranked in top 21) were judged to be "temporally relevant," which gave in total 38% of the clusters judged to be "temporally relevant" and 18 out the 22 top ranked clustered were "temporally relevant." Clusters displayed in Figures 8(a) and (b) and Figure 5(b) and (c) are examples of the 6 clusters. Though the cluster in Figure 8(c) was still judged to be "not temporally relevant," 65% of the users who saw the visualizations judged it to be "temporally relevant" versus the 40% who did not. On average, for each geo cluster, 66.7% of the users who saw visualizations judged it to be "geo relevant," compared with 64.4%; for each temporal cluster, 56.9% of the users who saw visualizations judged it to be "temporally relevant", comparing with 49.7%.

Motion clustering found both geographically and temporally relevant clusters. However, no motion clusters were judged to be both geo *and* temporally relevant. Mutual information clustering and co-occurrence clustering found the same number of geo relevant clusters, but mutual information clustering found 5 more temporally relevant clusters. Using this measurement, mutual information clustering performed better in finding temporally relevant clusters than co-occurrence clustering.

A subset of the evaluation results are shown in more detail in Figure 6. The figure shows the top 10 clusters produced by the geo-spatial, temporal, motion, co-occurrence, and mutual information analyses, and indicates which of these clusters were found to be geo or temporally significant by the panel of human judges which did not see the visualizations.

4.3.4 Geo and temporally relevant cluster retrieval

We observed that the average second moment of the geo-spatial, temporal, and motion clusters appears to be a good indicator of whether a cluster will be judged to be geo or temporally relevant. We quantified this relevance by studying a retrieval problem, in which the task is to find relevant clusters using different average second moment thresholds. Clusters are considered to be retrieved if their average second moment is equal to or above a certain threshold. We can then summarize the results in terms of standard pre-

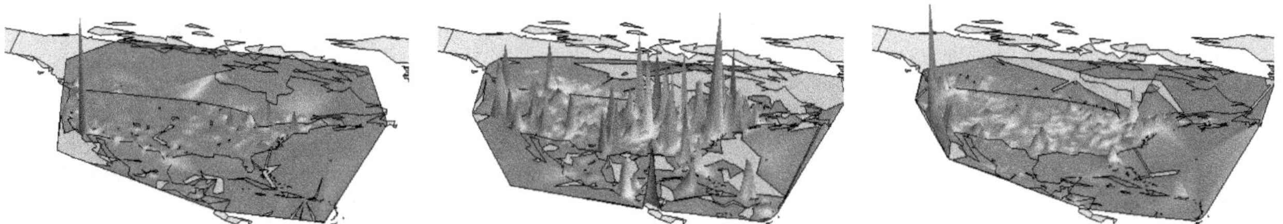

diego sandiego polarbear border (a)

prairie pennsylvania pa philadelphia philly rainforest dam cottage wisconsin maryland missouri michigan volcano madison ... (b)

wine grapes vines barrel cows winery vineyard cattle ranch (c)

Figure 7: Sample geo clusters judged to be not geo relevant with high average second moment by users who were not shown the visualizations. The clusters correspond to (a) tags related to San Diego, (b) tags related to cities and states, and (c) tags related to Northern California Wine Country. Best viewed in color.

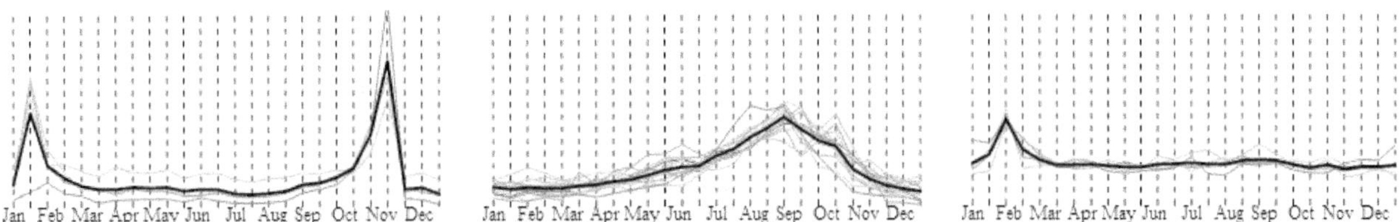

obama barackobama president election (a)

spider fair spiderweb web rides grapes monarch grasshopper peppers tomatoes corn airshow sunflower (b)

chinatown chinese super dragon bowl (c)

Figure 8: Sample temporal clusters judged to be not temporal relevant by users who were not shown the visualizations. The clusters correspond to (a) tags related to the Presidential election, (b) tags related to autumn, (c) tags related to Jan and Feb.

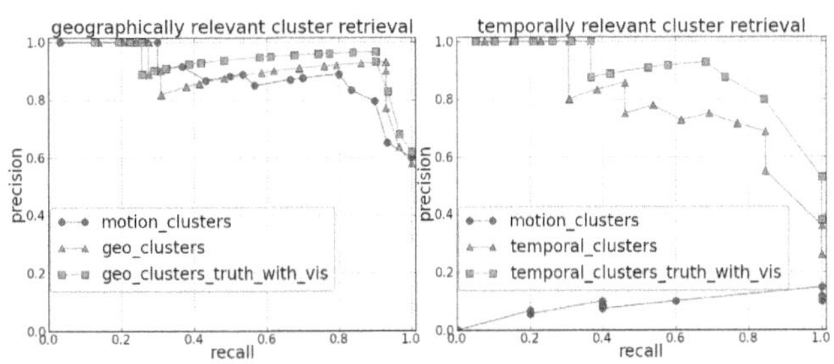

Figure 9: Precision-recall curves for retrieving geographically (left) and temporally (right) relevant clusters.

cision and recall statistics. The precision and recall for geographically relevant cluster retrieval is computed as:

$$\text{precision} = \frac{|R \cap G|}{|R|} \qquad \text{recall} = \frac{|R \cap G|}{|G|}$$

where R is the set of retrieved clusters and G is the set of clusters judged to be geographically relevant. The precision and recall for temporally relevant cluster retrieval are computed in a similar way.

Figure 9(left) shows the precision-recall curves for retrieving geo relevant clusters, in which the average second moment threshold decreases from left to right on each curve. For example, for geo clusters in geo relevant cluster retrieval, when the average second moment threshold is 0.04, both the precision and recall are 93.1%. Motion clusters performed slightly worse at high recalls.

Figure 9(right) shows the precision-recall curves for retrieving temporally relevant clusters. The precisions and recalls for temporal clusters are worse than geo relevant cluster retrieval. When the average second moment threshold is 0.07, the precision is 71.4% and recall is 76.9%. Motion clusters performed much worse, because (as we discussed above) for motion clusters the average second moment does not have strong correlation with temporal relevance. In the ground truth, only 5 clusters were judged to be temporally relevant and their average second moment ranks ranged from 13 to 33. As future work, it would be interesting to study alternative statistics other than second moment that may perform better for motion clusters.

We found that the retrieval statistics were best when ground truth was defined by the group of users who were shown our visualizations; when the recall is 90.3%, the precision reaches 96.6% for the geo-spatial clusters, and reached 68.4% recall and 92.9% precision for the temporal features. This result suggests that the visualizations helped users see subtle geospatial or temporal connections between tags in a cluster.

5. CONCLUSION

In this paper, we proposed techniques to measure the semantic similarity of tags by comparing geo-spatial, temporal, and geo-temporal patterns of use. We used these techniques on a large dataset from Flickr to cluster tags using geo-temporal distributions and proposed novel methods to visualize the resulting clusters. An evaluation and case study showed the overall high quality of the semantics mined by our approach, and that the second moment served as a simple filtering measurement that achieved promising performance in selecting geographically- and temporally-relevant clusters. A case study suggests that our visualizations of tag semantics can help people understand subtle geo-temporal relationships between tags.

There are many possible improvements and future directions for this research. Currently, we are using only North American data and clustering the top 2000 most used tags into 50 clusters. It would be interesting to apply our approach within a more flexible framework, deciding the number of tags and the number of clusters in an automatic way. It would also be interesting to build a tag recommendation system that integrates our techniques, using multiple kinds of tag similarity metrics to improve results and give corresponding visualizations to the user. Finally, our approach could be applied to other collections of objects with geographical and temporal attributes, such as data from Wikipedia or Twitter.

6. ACKNOWLEDGEMENTS

We thank Prof. Andrew Hanson for discussions and advice on visualization, and the anonymous reviewers for their helpful comments. This work was supported in part by a grant from the Lilly Endowment Inc. and by the Data to Insight Center at Indiana University.

7. REFERENCES

[1] S. Ahern, M. Naaman, R. Nair, and J. Yang. World explorer: Visualizing aggregate data from unstructured text in geo-referenced collections. In *JCDL*, 2007.

[2] L. Backstrom, J. Kleinberg, R. Kumar, and J. Novak. Spatial variation in search engine queries. In *WWW*, 2008.

[3] G. Begelman, P. Keller, and F. Smadja. Automated tag clustering: Improving search and exploration in the tag space. In *Collaborative Web Tagging Workshop*, 2006.

[4] L. Chen and A. Roy. Event detection from flickr data through wavelet-based spatial analysis. In *CIKM*, 2009.

[5] S. Chien and N. Immorlica. Semantic similarity between search engine queries using temporal correlation. In *WWW*, 2005.

[6] D. Crandall, L. Backstrom, D. Huttenlocher, and J. Kleinberg. Mapping the world's photos. In *WWW*, 2009.

[7] C. Ding, D. Zhou, X. He, and H. Zha. R1-PCA: Rotational invariant L1-norm Principal Component Analysis for robust subspace factorization. In *ICML*, 2006.

[8] M. Dubinko, R. Kumar, J. Magnani, J. Novak, P. Raghavan, and A. Tomkins. Visualizing tags over time. *ACM Transactions on the Web*, 1(2), 2007.

[9] V. Estivill-Castro and I. Lee. Data mining techniques for autonomous exploration of large volumes of geo-referenced crime data. In *Intl. Conf. on Geocomputation*, 2001.

[10] V. Estivill-Castrol and A. Murray. Discovering associations in spatial data – an efficient medoid based approach. In *PAKDD*, 1998.

[11] N. Garg and I. Weber. Personalized tag suggestion for Flickr. In *WWW*, 2008.

[12] K. M. Górski, E. Hivon, A. J. Banday, B. D. Wandelt, F. K. Hansen, M. Reinecke, and M. Bartelmann. Healpix: A framework for high-resolution discretization and fast analysis of data distributed on the sphere. *The Astrophysical Journal*, 622(2), 2005.

[13] Y. Huang and P. Zhang. On the relationships between clustering and spatial co-location pattern mining. In *ICTAI*, 2006.

[14] X. Jin, A. C. Gallagher, L. Cao, J. Luo, and J. Han. The wisdom of social multimedia: using Flickr for prediction and forecast. In *ACM MM*, 2010.

[15] G. Karypis and V. Kumar. Parallel multilevel k-way partitioning scheme for irregular graphs. In *Proc. Supercomputing*, 1996.

[16] O. Kaser and D. Lemire. Tag-cloud drawing: Algorithms for cloud visualization. In *WWW Workshop on Tagging and Metadata for Social Information Organization*, 2007.

[17] L. Kennedy, M. Naaman, S. Ahern, R. Nair, and T. Rattenbury. How flickr helps us make sense of the world: context and content in community-contributed media collections. In *ACM MM*, 2007.

[18] D. Liu, X.-S. Hua, L. Yang, M. Wang, and H.-J. Zhang. Tag ranking. In *WWW*, 2009.

[19] J. MacQueen. Some methods for classification and analysis of multivariate observations. In *Berkeley Symposium on Mathematical Statistics and Probability*, 1967.

[20] M. Mohebbi, D. Vanderkam, J. Kodysh, R. Schonberger, H. Choi, and S. Kumar. Google correlate whitepaper. http://www.google.com/trends/correlate/whitepaper.pdf, 2011.

[21] E. Moxley, J. Kleban, and B. S. Manjunath. Spirittagger: a geo-aware tag suggestion tool mined from flickr. In *MIR*, 2008.

[22] E. Moxley, J. Kleban, J. Xu, and B. S. Manjunath. Not all tags are created equal: Learning Flickr tag semantics for global annotation. In *ICME*, 2009.

[23] A. Ng. Feature selection, L1 vs. L2 regularization, and rotational invariance. In *ICML*, 2004.

[24] R. Ng and J. Han. Efficient and effective clustering methods for spatial data mining. In *VLDB*, 1994.

[25] K. Radinsky, E. Agichtein, E. Gabrilovich, and S. Markovitch. A word at a time: computing word relatedness using temporal semantic analysis. In *WWW*, 2011.

[26] T. Rattenbury, N. Good, and M. Naaman. Towards automatic extraction of event and place semantics from Flickr tags. In *SIGIR*, 2007.

[27] J. Sander, M. Ester, and H. P. Kriegel. Density-based clustering in spatial databases: A new algorithm and its applications. *Data Mining and Knowledge Discovery*, 1998.

[28] A. Shepitsen, J. Gemmell, B. Mobasher, and R. D. Burke. Personalized recommendation in social tagging systems using hierarchical clustering. In *Proc. ACM Conf. on Recommender Systems*, 2008.

[29] Z. Sheppard. Flickr blog: 5,000,000,000. http://blog.flickr.net/en/2010/09/19/5000000000/, 2010.

[30] B. Sigurbjörnsson and R. V. Zwol. Flickr tag recommendation based on collective knowledge. In *WWW*, 2008.

[31] C. A. Sugar and G. M. James. Finding the number of clusters in a data set: An information theoretic approach. *Journal of the American Statistical Association*, 98, 2003.

[32] S. Vadrevu, Y. Zhang, B. Tseng, G. Sun, and X. Li. Identifying regional sensitive queries in web search. In *WWW*, 2008.

[33] M. Vlachos, C. Meek, Z. Vagena, and D. Gunopulos. Identifying similarities, periodicities and bursts for online search queries. In *SIGMOD*, 2004.

[34] L. Wu, X. Hua, N. Yu, W.-Y. Ma, and S. Li. Flickr distance. In *ACM MM*, 2008.

[35] X. Xiao, X. Xie, Q. Luo, and W.-Y. Ma. Density based co-location pattern discovery. In *Intl. Conf. on Advances in Geographic Information Systems*, 2008.

[36] J. Yang and J. Leskovec. Patterns of temporal variation in online media. In *WSDM*, 2011.

Object Matching in Tweets with Spatial Models

Nilesh Dalvi Ravi Kumar Bo Pang
Yahoo! Research
701 First Avenue
Sunnyvale, CA 94089.
{ndalvi,ravikumar,bopang}@yahoo-inc.com

ABSTRACT

Despite their 140-character limitation, tweets embody a lot of valuable information, especially temporal and spatial. In this paper we study the geographic aspects of tweets, for a given object domain. We propose a user-level model for spatial encoding in tweets that goes beyond the explicit geocoding or place name mentions; this model can be used to match objects to tweets. We illustrate our model and methodology using restaurants as the objects, and show a significant improvement in performance over using standard language models. En route, we obtain a method to geolocate users who tweet about geolocated objects; this may be of independent interest.

Categories and Subject Descriptors. H.3.m [**Information Storage and Retrieval**]: Miscellaneous

General Terms. Algorithms, Experimentation, Measurements

Keywords. Tweets, Spatial model, Language model, Object matching

1. INTRODUCTION

Tweets are steadily being treated as information sources and there is a growing body of research work to understand and use them in web applications. Tweets provide information that, in a sense, is complementary to what other web sources provide. For example, a user may review a restaurant only once, but may tweet about the same restaurant multiple times. A particular Twitter application that is becoming popular is topic- and object-recognition: identify which object the tweet is about. The broad success of `tweetbeat.com` during the 2010 World Cup Soccer, where the *aboutness* of tweets had to be determined, is a testament to the importance of this application. Motivated by applications such as these, in this paper we study the object matching problem in tweets.

Most of the research so far has been to study individual tweets from an information retrieval and content analysis points of view, to use the set of tweets from a user for recommendation purposes, and to get insights into the social processes behind tweeting. The 140-character limitation on tweets makes many of these tasks already challenging: there is hardly any room to provide complete information about anything, even if the author of the tweet so desired. Given that many of the tweets are content-free,[1] there is a real limitation on how far tweets by themselves can be used for interesting applications such as object matching.

Fortunately, there are two redeeming aspects to tweets: their volume and the context in which they are generated. By context, we mean the metadata about the author of the tweet and the spatial/temporal information associated with each tweet. A judicious filtering of the content-free tweets combined with a careful use of its context opens up new possibilities for using the information tweets contain.

Geographic information is a vital component of the context of a tweet. More than one-third of all Twitter users have a valid geographical location and more than half of them have a geographical location that is at a city level; of course, these are based on self-reporting and hence could be erroneous. (More on these numbers in Section 3.2.) And, 3–4% of all tweets have a latitude-longitude (lat-lon) associated with them. This fraction will grow with the proliferation of GPS-enabled devices and social applications such as Foursquare or Gowalla.[2] Furthermore, even when such information is not explicitly declared, it can be possible to infer it from the location of places a user typically tweets about. All of these raise the possibility of using geographic information in an intrinsic manner in order to improve the usability of tweets as information.

In this paper we consider a genre of applications, where the goal is to match a tweet to an object, if possible, where the object is from a list of objects in a given domain. We assume that the geographic location of the entities is known. For this object matching task, we develop a user model that utilizes geographic information in an intrinsic way: the probability of a user tweeting about the object depends on the distance between the user's location and the object's location. We illustrate our model and method by using restaurants as the object domain. There have been a few recent attempts to incorporate geography into topic modeling and

Permission to make digital or hard copies of all or part of this work for personal or classroom use is granted without fee provided that copies are not made or distributed for profit or commercial advantage and that copies bear this notice and the full citation on the first page. To copy otherwise, to republish, to post on servers or to redistribute to lists, requires prior specific permission and/or a fee.
WSDM'12, February 8–12, 2012, Seattle, Washington, USA.
Copyright 2012 ACM 978-1-4503-0747-5/12/02 ...$10.00.

[1] A Pear Analytics study from 2009 (`http://www.pearanalytics.com/blog/wp-content/uploads/2010/05/Twitter-Study-August-2009.pdf`) argues that over 40% of the tweets are small talk.

[2] According to `http://www.pewinternet.org/~/media/Files/Reports/2010/PIP-Location-based-services.pdf`, on each day, 1% of the online population uses these services.

related tasks but none of these is particularly suitable for our application (more on this in Section 2).

Main contributions. We formulate a simple user model for generating a tweet about an object. In our model, there are three quantities: each user is associated with an interest in the set of objects (say, restaurants) that captures the propensity of the user to tweet about an object from the set, each object has an associated popularity, and each user and each object have their own geographic locations (locations of objects are given as input to the model, whereas locations of users need to be inferred). Now, the probability that the user tweets about an object is a product of the user's interest in the object, the popularity of the object, and a decreasing function of the distance between the user and object locations.

With this model, we show an estimation procedure based on the EM algorithm. Unfortunately, the estimation can be computationally challenging. We then show that under reasonable simplifying assumptions on the distribution of users and objects, a computationally efficient method can be used to learn the parameters of the model. As a byproduct, we also obtain a principled method to geolocate tweets: infer the location of a user based on the tweets about geolocated objects.

Our experiments on a large-scale collection of tweets that show our geography-enabled model is able to achieve significant performance gains over geography-less models. We also show that our method to infer geolocation of the users performs well in practice: in our restaurant-related dataset, for users with three or more tweets, the median error between the user's self-reported location and the location inferred by our method is around 10 miles.

Organization. In Section 2, we discuss the related work on topic models that incorporate geography, matching objects in short user-generated content, and geolocating user-generated content. In Section 3, we argue why our problem is hard and why traditional methods will not be applicable. In Section 4, we present the basic model that consists of a distance component based on the user model described above and a language model component that models textual information. In Section 5, we develop a method to estimate the parameters of the model in a principled manner; here, we make certain simplifying assumptions that make the estimation procedure computationally tractable so that it can be applied to a large domain such as tweets. In Section 6, we describe the data source and its properties. In Section 7, we examine properties of our distance model and in Section 8, we study the performance of the full model on the matching task, focusing on the performance improvements enabled by the combination of the distance model with the language model. Concluding remarks are presented in Section 9.

2. RELATED WORK

The line of work closest to ours is that of topic models that incorporate geography. O'Connor et al. study the geographic linguistic variation in tweets [8, 11]. They propose a geographic topic model that incorporates regional vocabulary variations in the way the tweet text is generated. They use the geotagged tweets in their study and their model can be used to classify a tweet into a geographic region. Extending topic modeling to incorporate geographic information has been recently addressed in general information retrieval and NLP contexts. Mei et al. [10] postulate a model in which the distribution of topics is conditioned on geographical location; however they assume that the set of locations is given. Sizov [14] combines text and geographic information, where each topic generates latitude and longitude from two topic-specific Gaussian distributions. He shows that this improves tasks such as tag recommendation and clustering. Yin et al. [17] also study a similar problem but the geographic topic regions are discovered in a more systematic manner. Our work differs from these in the following ways: their granularities are much coarser than what we can afford, they do not incorporate the location of a user, and their goal is not to do object matching.

The question of matching objects to short text such as reviews and blogs was recently addressed in [6, 5], where simple translation models were proposed for the matching; such models served as motivation behind our language model. These papers, however, do not attempt to model the geographic aspects of the data, which is unique to our setting.

The geographic information that is present in tweets and in other user-generated content has lent itself to many interesting data mining studies. Backstrom et al. [1] studied the role of geography in search engine queries. Crandall et al. [4] studied similar questions for geotagged images. They used text tags of images and geospatial data to find out the location of photos; see also the work of Rattenbury et al. [12] on Flickr tags. Backstrom et al. [2] proposed a method to infer the geographic location of users based on the stated locations of their social connections; their method is based on postulating a friendship creation model that resembles the geographic component of our model. Recently, Wing and Baldridge [15] proposed a text-based supervised method for geolocating tweets; their method obtains a median error of 479km.[3] All these papers focus only on locating an object in the space using several clues about them. We, on the other hand, make this location detection as part of our model, with the end goal of matching entities to tweets. Finin et al. [9] tried to use crowd-sourcing in order to extract named entities in tweets; they do not use any geographic information. Tweets are being studied from a sociological point of view: there is a growing literature on this and we refer the readers to [3, 16, 13] and the references therein.

3. A CLOSER LOOK AT THE PROBLEM

In this section, we discuss motivations of our modeling choices.

3.1 Is text enough?

We can cast our problem as matching unstructured text such as tweets with structured entities in a database listing (e.g., restaurants with attributes like name, address, and cuisine). This can be seen as a cross of two problems: entity matching in databases, which matches pairs of structured entities, and document retrieval in IR, which matches unstructured queries with unstructured documents. Previous work [5, 6] has looked into matching unstructured text reviews with structured entities. The main idea behind these

[3]As we will see in Section 7, our geolocation method has a median error of below 10 miles; however, these results are not comparable since [15] use all tweets of the user whereas we focus only on restaurant-related tweets.

Figure 1: A sample restaurant tweet.

approaches is to treat the text as a bag of words, which is generated from the mixture of two distributions: an entity-independent review language model and an entity-specific model. In the simpler case [5], the entity-specific model is a distribution over words in the attributes of the entity. The matching problem is to find the entity that maximizes the probability of a given text being generated from it. These previous models focused on the textual information in reviews and did not incorporate contextual information such as metadata about reviewers.

A fundamental challenge in applying these techniques to tweets is the lack of information redundancy since tweets are so short. Figure 1 shows an example of a tweet about a restaurant named `Ronnarong`. Based on text matching alone, this tweet could potentially match three businesses is our database: `Yum Thai`, `Thai Tapas`, and `Ronnarong`. In full-length reviews, term frequency can help reveal the correct entity. E.g. a full-length review of `Ronnarong` might mention the name (or other attributes) several times. But in a short tweet, this does not hold. Using a bag of words model, it is difficult to distinguish between the three matches, each appearing exactly once in the tweet.

One way to combat this is to go for a deeper analysis of the text and take advantage of more structured representations such as a dependency parse of the text. However, given the informal nature of the medium, a full-blown parser is unlikely to fare well. Identifying noun phrases using a light-weight part-of-speech tagging would be insufficient, as we need to distinguish noun phrases that are menu items or location names from noun phrases that are restaurant names.

We develop two techniques to address the challenge posed by short tweets. First, we consider a generative language model *based on bigrams*. Note that the bigram mixture model we consider here is not just allowing each component model to include bigrams; in a way, we also model transitions between different components (see Section 4.2.2 for more details). As an example, our bigram mixture model can be implicitly distinguishing between different types of noun phrases. E.g., we can learn that `at` is a common word preceding a restaurant name, `in` commonly succeeds a restaurant name, `yum` commonly precedes a menu item but not a restaurant, etc. Thus, the more fine-grained modeling of the textual information partially compensates for the lack of repetition in tweets.

The second, and the main technique of this paper, involves *incorporating locations of the users* in the matching. Using our language model, we might be able to correctly identify `Ronnarong` as the restaurant name. However, we still need to figure out which specific entity in the database it refers to—there can be several restaurants with the same name (but in different cities) in our database. Given the short nature of the tweets, the full address of the business, even at the city level, is often missing from the text.[4] As such, knowledge of user locations can immensely help us in disambiguating between the matching restaurants.

As an example, suppose we know the location of the user in the tweet above to be `Somerville, MA`. Then, we can match the tweet to `Ronnarong` in `Somerville` with higher confidence than `Ronnarong` in other locations. This can also help us further lower the confidence over `Yum Thai` and `Thai Tapas`, if those restaurants are not near Somerville.

3.2 Can users be geolocated?

In the previous section, we argued that knowledge over user locations can be very helpful for the matching task. Is it trivial to identify obtain this information at a useful granularity? One obvious source seems to be the profile information, which is part of the meta-information accompanying each tweet. However, not all users report their locations in their profiles. Based on an analysis of one month of tweet feed (June, 2010), out of the 22 million unique users who tweeted in this period, 44% of the users did not specify location in their profile. This accounted for 19.4% of the total tweet traffic.

Among the users who do have non-empty location field, not all of the specified location values correspond to valid geographical locations, e.g., `Next to you`. We applied the Yahoo! Geolocation API, and obtained the country and city information from the profile locations when the API was able to recognize one.[5] We found that overall, 33% of the profiles contain recognizable country names, and only 20% (accounting 25% of the tweet traffic) contain city names. There are also twitter clients that let users with a geo-enabled device to set an exact latitude and longitude as their location, but they amount to less than 2% of users. If we were to depend on the self-reported locations in user profiles, clearly we miss out on 80% of the users (75% of the tweets), not to mention tweets where the self-reported locations do not reflect the actual place the user resides in.

In this work we take a different approach. Instead of relying on self-reported locations, we try to infer the location of a user based on the geo-locations of entities the user tweets about. This presents a technical challenge: we need the user location to compute accurate matches, and we need correct matches to infer the location. Our approach is to use a probabilistic model that combines the language model with the distance model, and jointly infer the location of the users and the matches between tweets and entities. We experimentally demonstrate that our model is very effective in inferring user locations, and for many of the users we can identify the location to within 10 miles. Thus, our technique for location inference helps even for users with valid reported locations. E.g., we might identify that a user with a reported location in `New York` is in fact in `Lower Manhattan`. In the next section, we describe our joint model.

4. MODEL

Let U be a set of users, where each user $u \in U$ has a location $\ell(u)$. Let E be a set of entities, where each entity $e \in E$ has a set of attributes including its location $\ell(e)$ Finally, let T be a set of tweets, where each tweet $t \in T$

[4]The tweet in Figure 1 mentions a landmark `Union Sq.`, but it does not help as it is not part of the address we have in our database.

[5]Since this API does not work with foreign text, we removed those profile location that contained non-ASCII characters.

consists of a piece of text, and is associated with a user $u \in U$, and needs to be matched to an entity $e \in E$.

We assume there is an underlying distribution $\mathbf{P}$ over the set $T \times U \times E$. Our goal is to model $\mathbf{P}$. This will enable us to compute $\mathbf{P}(e \mid t, u)$ for a triple (t, u, e) drawn from this distribution, so that we can predict the best e^* for an observed tweet–user pair (t, u).

There are two components of the probabilistic model.

(i) The *distance model* captures the relationship between U and E. It is given by $\mathbf{P}(e, u)$, which captures the propensity of a user u tweeting about an entity e.

(ii) The *language model* captures the relationship between E and T. It is given by $\mathbf{P}(t \mid e, u)$, which captures the distribution of words in a tweet t corresponding to a user u and an entity e.

The complete model that captures the probability distribution over $T \times U \times E$ can be expressed as

$$\mathbf{P}(e, t, u) = \mathbf{P}(t \mid e, u)\mathbf{P}(e, u). \quad (1)$$

We now discuss the distance model (Section 4.1) and the language model (Section 4.2) in more detail.

4.1 Distance model

In this section we present our model for $\mathbf{P}(e, u)$, which captures the propensity of a user tweeting about an entity. We expect the geographical distance between a user u and an entity e to play an important role in this model, and use $d(e, u)$ to denote the distance between $\ell(u)$ and $\ell(e)$.

We assume that each user u is associated with an *interest* $\alpha(u)$ with respect to the entity set E, e.g., if E is the set of restaurants, then $\alpha(u)$ will capture the interest of the user u in tweeting about restaurants. Similarly, we assume that each entity e has a *popularity* $\beta(e)$. Finally, the probability of observing a pair (e, u) is directly proportional to the interest of the user and the popularity of the entity and monotonically decreases with the distance between them. Assuming a polynomial decay, we have

$$\mathbf{P}(e, u) \propto \alpha(u)\beta(e)(d_0 + d(e, u))^{-k}, \quad (2)$$

where d_0 and k are parameters that govern how fast the probability drops with distance.

We can normalize the above equation by summing over all pairs of entities and users. Let

$$g(e, u) = \alpha(u)\beta(e)(d_0 + d(e, u))^{-k}, \quad (3)$$

we have

$$\mathbf{P}(e, u) = \frac{g(e, u)}{\sum_{(e', u') \in E \times U} g(e', u')}. \quad (4)$$

Note that we use a distance function that exhibits a polynomial decay with respect to the distance between the user and the entity. Alternatively, we could have used, say, an exponentially decaying function. Here, we give the theoretical rationale for our distance function; Section 7 provides more empirical evidence for our choice.

In theory, exponentially decaying function does not lead to intuitive properties that we expect. For instance, suppose we have a model where the probability of a user u visiting an entity e is proportional to $e^{-kd(e,u)}$. Consider the case when we have a user u and two entities e_1 and e_2 that are d_1 and d_2 away from u. Suppose they are all located on the same line, with $d_2 = d_1 + y$. If y is a constant $\frac{\log 2}{k}$, we have $\frac{P(e_1,u)}{P(e_2,u)} = e^{-k(d_1-d_2)} = e^{ky} = 2$. That is, the user is twice as likely to visit e_1 than e_2, irrespective of d_1. This behavior is counter-intuitive: when a user is really far away from both entities ($d_1 >> y$), we expect them to visit the two entities with almost equal probability. This property makes an exponential model (or, for that matter, any superpolynomial model) undesirable.

4.2 Language models

In this work we do not attempt to model the differences in the language usage of different users. That is, we assume that the language model is independent of the user. Formally, given the entity, the probability of observing a given text is independent of the user:

$$\mathbf{P}(t \mid e, u) = \mathbf{P}(t \mid e). \quad (5)$$

This is a reasonable assumption — otherwise we will run into data sparsity issues since most of the users will not have sufficiently many tweets to learn user-specific language models. Under this assumption, Equation (1) is reduced to

$$\mathbf{P}(e, t, u) = \mathbf{P}(t \mid e, u)\mathbf{P}(e, u) = \mathbf{P}(t \mid e)\mathbf{P}(e, u). \quad (6)$$

Given an entity e and a tweet t, $\mathbf{P}(t \mid e)$ denotes the probability of observing the words in the textual content of the tweet, given that the tweet is about entity e. For example, if E is the set of restaurants and e is a specific restaurant, then the tweet is likely to include words from the attributes such as *name*, *address*, and *cuisine* of e, as well as generic words such as `dinner` and `delicious` that are associated with restaurants.

Several unigram-based language models have been considered in the past for entity-matching, including simple term-frequency based models [5] as well as more advanced translation models [6]. We consider a model that is an extension of the language model proposed by Dalvi et al. [5], which we refer to as the *unigram mixture model*. We briefly describe the model here.

4.2.1 Unigram mixture model

Given a set of known entities from a specific category, e.g., a set of restaurants, the unigram mixture model represents the probability distribution of documents (in our case, tweets) that are about these entities. Here, both the document and the entities are modeled as a bag of words. Given a document t about an entity e, each word in t is drawn randomly from a mixture of two language models: a generic unigram language model $\mathbf{P}_{\text{lm}}$ for the domain which is independent of e (e.g., words related to restaurants) and an entity-specific language model $\mathbf{P}_e$ which is a distribution over words in e (e.g., the name and address of e). Given a mixture coefficient $\theta \in (0, 1)$, it assigns

$$\mathbf{P}(t \mid e) = \prod_{w \in t} (\theta \cdot \mathbf{P}_e(w) + (1 - \theta) \cdot \mathbf{P}_{\text{lm}}(w)).$$

$\mathbf{P}_{\text{lm}}$ can be learnt by counting the word frequencies of documents in the collection, while $\mathbf{P}_e$ can simply be taken as the uniform distribution over the set of words in e.[6]

Modeling documents and entities as bags of words (unigrams) leads to the loss of sequential information. In the

[6]If we have different attributes in e, we can give different weights to words in different attributes in $\mathbf{P}_e$, e.g., words in names can have more weight than the words in addresses.

case of full-length documents, the redundancy in the document compensates for this information loss in representation. However, in our setting, since the tweets are very short and most of the times entity names are mentioned just once, we need to make use of the context of name mentions to improve accuracy. Thus, we consider an extension which we will refer to as the *bigram mixture model.*

4.2.2 Bigram mixture model

Bigram language models (more generally, n-gram language models) are well-studied, but combining them into a generative mixture model for entities is tricky. Standard bigram language models represents the probability of a sequence of words $w_1, \ldots, w_n$ as

$$\mathbf{P}(w_1, \ldots, w_n) = \prod_i \mathbf{P}(w_i \mid w_{i-1}).$$

Let $f(w_i \mid w_{i-1})$ be the frequentist estimation, which is the number of occurrences of the sequence (w_{i-1}, w_i) divided by the number of occurrences of w_{i-1} in the data. Usually this is smoothed with a unigram term due to data sparsity,

$$\mathbf{P}(w_i \mid w_{i-1}) = \delta \cdot f(w_i \mid w_{i-1}) + (1 - \delta) \cdot f(w_i). \quad (7)$$

Let $\mathbf{P}_{\text{lm}}$ and $\mathbf{P}_e$ be the bigram language models for the generic language and entity e. We need to adapt the standard bigram language models to account for the fact that w_i and w_{i-1} can be drawn from either $\mathbf{P}_{\text{lm}}$ or $\mathbf{P}_e$. For each w_i, there are four possibilities: it is a continuation of a bigram from $\mathbf{P}_{\text{lm}}$, it is a continuation of a bigram from $\mathbf{P}_e$, it is the start of a new bigram from $\mathbf{P}_{\text{lm}}$ while the previous word was from the entity e, or it is the start of a new bigram from $\mathbf{P}_e$ while the previous word was from the generic language.

To take this into account in defining the bigram mixture model, we introduce a new token called ENTITY, which stands for the entity words. In $\mathbf{P}_{\text{lm}}$, in addition to the usual bigram sequences (w, w'), we also have bigrams of the form (w, ENTITY) and (ENTITY, w). Thus, in our model, in addition to better modeling the sequential information in language usage, we model to an extent the context for an entity mention. For instance, for restaurants, we expect a high probability for bigrams such as (`at`, ENTITY), (`in`, ENTITY), and (ENTITY, `has`).

Let $q_e(w)$ denote the posterior of w being drawn from $\mathbf{P}_e$. We have

$$\mathbf{P}(t \mid e) = \prod_i \left(q_e(w_{i-1}) \cdot A + (1 - q_e(w_{i-1})) \cdot B\right),$$

where

$$\begin{aligned} A &= \theta \cdot \mathbf{P}_e(w_i \mid w_{i-1}) + (1-\theta) \cdot \mathbf{P}_{\text{lm}}(w_i \mid \text{ENTITY}), \\ B &= \theta \cdot \mathbf{P}_{\text{lm}}(\text{ENTITY} \mid w_{i-1}) + (1-\theta) \cdot \mathbf{P}_{\text{lm}}(w_i \mid w_{i-1}), \\ q_e(w_i) &= q_e(w_{i-1}) \cdot \theta \cdot \mathbf{P}_e(w_i \mid w_{i-1}) \\ &\quad + (1 - q_e(w_{i-1})) \cdot \theta \cdot \mathbf{P}_{\text{lm}}(\text{ENTITY} \mid w_{i-1}). \end{aligned}$$

4.3 The estimation and inference problems

Let Δ denote the parameters of the distance model that include the set $\{\alpha(u) \mid u \in U\}$, the set $\{\beta(e) \mid e \in E\}$, d_0, and k (from Equation (2)). Let Λ denote the parameters of the language model that include $\mathbf{P}_{\text{lm}}$, $\mathbf{P}_e$, and θ. Note that Δ and Λ completely specify the probability model.

We assume that we know the location $\ell(e)$ of each entity $e \in E$, which can be obtained by geomapping its physical address. However, the locations $\ell(\cdot)$ of users are unknown; let L denote the mapping of all users to locations. Let T be a set of tweets consisting of (t, u) pairs (note that we do not have any (entity) labels for the tweets). We consider the following estimation problem.

PROBLEM 1. *(Estimation) Given T, determine parameters Δ, Λ, and the locations of users L that maximizes the likelihood of observing T.*

Once we learn the model, we want to use it to match tweets with entities. Given a tweet t and a user u, we want to find the most likely restaurant (if at all) the tweet is about. This leads to the following inferencing problem.

PROBLEM 2. *(Inference) Given a tweet t and a user u, compute*

$$\arg\max_{e \in E} \mathbf{P}(e \mid t, u), \quad (8)$$

i.e., the most likely entity given t and u.

5. MODEL ESTIMATION

Given a set T of tweet–user pairs, we want to estimate parameters Δ, Λ, and the locations L of all users that maximize the likelihood of observing T, i.e., find

$$\arg\max_{\Delta, \Lambda, L} \prod_{(t,u) \in T} \mathbf{P}(t, u).$$

We have $\mathbf{P}(t, u) = \sum_{e \in E} \mathbf{P}(e, t, u)$, where $\mathbf{P}(e, t, u)$ is given by Equation (6). Thus, we want

$$\arg\max_{\Delta, \Lambda, L} \prod_{(t,u) \in T} \sum_e \mathbf{P}(t \mid e) \mathbf{P}(e, u). \quad (9)$$

The main difficulty in solving Equation (9) lies in the normalization term in Equation (4). Since the term depends on the specific location of each user and each entity in relation to each other, it is hard to compute it exactly. We therefore introduce a set of simplifying assumptions that lead to reasonable interpretations of the model in order to make the problem tractable.

5.1 Making the estimation tractable

We make the following smoothness assumptions to make the model tractable while remaining interesting and useful.

1. We assume that the density of entities in any small neighborhood is proportional to the density of users in that neighborhood.
2. Given any region, the α values of the users come from a distribution Γ_u, which is independent of the region.
3. Given any region, the β values of the entities come from a distribution Γ_e, which is independent of the region.

The first assumption is intuitive, as densely populated regions have more businesses. The second assumption states that each region has a similar mix of users in terms of their interests in tweeting about restaurants. Likewise, the third assumption states that each user has access to a similar mix of popular and unpopular entities. These are intuitively true for any given region. Now, we describe how these assumptions lead to a natural interpretation for the α and β parameters, and how they can be estimated efficiently.

Recall the definition of $g(e,u)$ given in Equation (3). For a user u, define

$$F(u) = \sum_e \beta(e)(d_0 + d(e,u))^{-k}.$$

Similarly, for an entity e, define

$$G(e) = \sum_u \alpha(u)(d_0 + d(e,u))^{-k}.$$

Also, while the entities and users are discrete points in space, we approximate their distributions Γ_u and Γ_e by assuming them as continuous functions. Let γ_u and γ_e be the means of the distributions Γ_u and Γ_e respectively. For simplicity, the rest of this section assumes that the densities of the entities and the users are constant, and given by τ_e and τ_u respectively. The analysis can be extended to the case when the ratio of the user density to the restaurant density is a global constant.

First, we show that under our assumptions, $F(u)$ is a constant independent of u.

LEMMA 3.

$$F(u) = \frac{2\pi\tau_e\gamma_e}{(k-1)(k-2)d_0^{k-2}}.$$

PROOF. Since we assume a continuous distribution of entities in the plane, to compute $F(u)$, we integrate it over the plane. Consider a small disc centered at $\ell(u)$ of radius x and infinitesimal width dx. The area of the disc is $2\pi x dx$. Total number of entities in the disc equals $\tau_e \cdot 2\pi x dx$. The average value of $\beta(e)$ in this region is γ_e. Thus, we have

$$F(u) = \int_0^\infty \gamma_e (d_0 + x)^{-k} \cdot \tau_e \cdot 2\pi x dx$$

Solving the above integral gives us the expression in the lemma. □

Likewise, we show that under our assumptions, $G(e)$ is a constant independent of e.

LEMMA 4.

$$G(e) = \frac{2\pi\tau_u\gamma_u}{(k-1)(k-2)d_0^{k-2}}.$$

PROOF. Similar to the above. □

The main conclusion of the above two lemmas is that the terms $F(u)$ and $G(e)$ can be assumed to be constant over the set of users and set of entities respectively. This allows us to interpret $\alpha(u)$ and $\beta(e)$ naturally. For example,

$$\mathbf{P}(e) = \sum_u \alpha(u)\beta(e)(d_0 + d(e,u))^{-k} = \beta(e)G(e) \propto \beta(e),$$

since $G(e)$ is independent of e by Lemma 4. Also, the parameters α and β are scale invariant model parameters, i.e., if we scale each α by some constant and, independently, each β by another constant, we get back the same model. Thus, we can take $\beta(e)$ to be exactly equal to $\mathbf{P}(e)$, i.e., the probability that a random tweet is about the entity e. Similarly, $\alpha(u)$ can be taken as simply the probability that a random tweet is from the user u.

5.2 Learning the parameters

In this section we describe how to solve Equation (9). We can write the objective function as

$$\prod_{(t,u)\in T} \sum_e \mathbf{P}(t \mid e)\mathbf{P}(e,u) = \prod_u \mathbf{P}(u) \prod_{(t,u)\in T} \sum_e \mathbf{P}(t \mid e)\mathbf{P}(e \mid u).$$

Note that $\mathbf{P}(u) = \alpha(u)$ as we approximated in the previous section. Similarly, $\mathbf{P}(e \mid u) = \beta(u)(d_0 + d(u,e))^{-k}/G(e)$, which does not depend on the α parameters. Thus, we can independently optimize the first product and the rest of the expression, since they do not share parameters. Since $\alpha(u) = \mathbf{P}(u)$, we can estimate it as the fraction of all tweets that are by the user u, which can be directly computed from the set T of tweets. For the rest of the section we focus on the following optimization:

$$\arg\max_{\Delta,\Lambda,L} \prod_{(t,u)\in T} \sum_e \mathbf{P}(t \mid e)\mathbf{P}(e \mid u).$$

Since the optimization function is in a product of sum form which is difficult to optimize directly, we apply the expectation-maximization (EM) method to simplify its form. We define a *hidden* random variable $\pi(t,u,e)$ for each triplet:

$$\pi(t,u,e) = \begin{cases} 1 & \text{if } (t,u) \text{ is about } e, \\ 0 & \text{otherwise.} \end{cases}$$

Then, we can write our objective function as

$$\arg\max_{\Delta,\Lambda,L} \prod_{(t,u)\in T} \prod_e (\mathbf{P}(t \mid e)\mathbf{P}(e \mid u))^{\pi(t,u,e)}.$$

Now we can apply EM iteratively.

E step. In the E step, we assume some initial value of the parameters, say Δ_0, Λ_0, L_0 and find the expected value of the hidden variables. We have,

$$\mathbf{E}(\pi(t,u,e)) = \mathbf{P}(e \mid t,u) = \frac{\mathbf{P}(e,t,u)}{\sum_{e'} \mathbf{P}(e',t,u)}.$$

Using the current values of the parameters, we can compute the above expression. In theory, this can be done by iterating over each entity for each tweet (t,u). This, however, will be infeasible in practice. Instead, for each tweet, we maintain a set of candidate entities that have a non-trivial overlap with the text of the tweet, and assume the probability of match to be 0 for all other entities.

M step. In the M step, we use the values $f(t,u,e) = \mathbf{E}(\pi(t,u,e))$ and find the parameters Δ, Λ, L that maximize the following function:

$$\prod_{(t,u),e} (\mathbf{P}(t \mid e)\mathbf{P}(e \mid u))^{f(t,u,e)}$$

$$= \left(\prod_{(t,u),e} \mathbf{P}(t \mid e)^{f(t,u,e)}\right)\left(\prod_{(t,u),e} \mathbf{P}(e \mid u)^{f(t,u,e)}\right) \quad (10)$$

We see that the first product only involves the language parameters Λ, while the second product only involves Δ and L, the parameters of the distance model. Thus, we can separately optimize the language model and the distance model.

Learning the distance model. We learn d_0 and k by directly fitting the observed data, as described in Section 7. For user locations, we take all possible locations of the tweets (i.e., locations of all possible candidate entity matches for the tweet) from the user and compute the second product in Equation (10) from each of the locations to find the optimal location of the user.

Learning the language model. We can learn the bigram language model by a simple frequency counting. We keep a count of all the bigrams. Consider a (t, e) pair, along with the value $f(t, u, e)$ as computed in the **E** step. First, we look for the name of entity e in the tweet, and replace it by a single token called ENTITY. If there is no exact match, we look at the maximal common substring of tokens between the tweet and the entity, and treat that as the reference to the entity name. After the replacement, for each bigram in the tweet, we add an amount of $f(t, u, e)$ to the global count of that bigram. We process all the (t, e) pairs, and finally, normalize all the bigram counts to sum up to 1. The resulting distribution is the language model $\mathbf{P}_{\text{lm}}$ that maximizes the first product term in the **M** step.

6. DATA

In this section we first describe the data, which consists of tens of billions of tweets recorded over a year. The set of entities we consider are the restaurants in the continental United States.

We use the Twitter data, which consists of all the tweets with the associated metadata such as the name of the user, location of the user (if available), time, etc. We considered the data from December 2009 to January 2011. We consider the set of restaurants in the US, where each restaurant is associated with metadata such as the name, address, phone number, cuisine, etc. This data is obtained from Yahoo! Local (`local.yahoo.com`) and consists of about 750K restaurants.

To illustrate the efficacy of our methods, we focus on tweets that pertain to restaurants. Given the large volume of tweets, only a small portion of them will be about restaurants. Ideally we would like to focus only on tweets that have a non-negligible chance of being about restaurants. Developing a highly accurate classifier for this purpose is not easy. Previous work has exploited the hashtags in tweets to generate labels for certain classification tasks [7]; for example, tweets with the hashtag `#hcr` can largely be assumed to be related to the health-care reform. Most of these hashtags have evolved by convention and usage. Unfortunately, we are not aware of a set of good hashtags that can help in our restaurant classification task. In fact, the top hashtags for the restaurant-related tweets (as determined by the filtering method described below) are `#Yelp`, `#coupon`, `#food`, `#restaurant`, `#coupon`, and they cover less than 15% of the tweets. Since the main focus in this paper is to investigate the effectiveness of our model, we consider developing such classifiers as an orthogonal (but interesting) effort to solve the final task, and opted for a simple keyword-based filtering scheme as described below.

We obtained the textual content of about 300K Yelp restaurant reviews used in [5], and picked the top occurring words in the reviews (discarding the stopwords) as our keyword list. The keywords are: {`cafe`, `restaurant`, `club`, `bar`, `lounge`, `dinner`, `lunch`, `food`, `pizza`, `grill`, `coffee`, `sushi`, `tavern`, `kitchen`, `breakfast`, `diner`, `yelp`, `taco`, `burger`, `drinks`, `drink`, `brunch`, `bbq`, `bakery`, `yummy`, `burrito`, `cheese`, `tasty`, `delicious`, `crowded`, `eat`, `eating`}. Tweets that do not contain any of these keywords were filtered out from our collection. As we will discuss in Section 8, even this seemingly strict filtering scheme results in many tweets that are not about restaurants.

We collected all tweets with a non-trivial match to a restaurant name from our set of restaurants (i.e., matching words more uncommon than `food`, which is the name of three restaurants in our set of restaurants). This yielded a dataset of over 200 million tweets, authored by close to 14 million users.

7. EXPERIMENTS: DISTANCE MODEL

In this section we examine the distance model with which we infer the geographic locations of users. We perform two experiments. The first examines how well our polynomial distance model fits the data. The second examines how accurate the inferred user locations are.

We first look at how our distance model fits the observed data in terms of the distribution of user–entity distance. More specifically, suppose we have an oracle tweet–location mapping (e.g., using tweets that are geotagged), does the polynomial decay function in the distance model accurately explains the observed data? We consider the subsets of tweets that are geotagged; around 3% of all tweets fall into this category. For each unique user who authored one of these tweets, we compute the user location by optimizing the EM objective function given by our distance model. We then compute the distance of each tweet to the inferred location of its author. Figure 2 shows the resulting distribution. We also plot the distribution as predicted by the model, i.e., $(d_0 + x)^{-k} \cdot x$: the probability that a user tweets about a restaurant at a distance x is proportional to $(d_0 + x)^{-k}$, and the number of entities at distance x is proportional to x, assuming a uniform distribution of entities. We compute the parameters d_0 and k that best fit the data. Figure 2 plots both the observed and the theoretical distributions, and we see that predicted distribution fits the observed distribution closely; here, $d_0 = 6$ and $k = 3$.

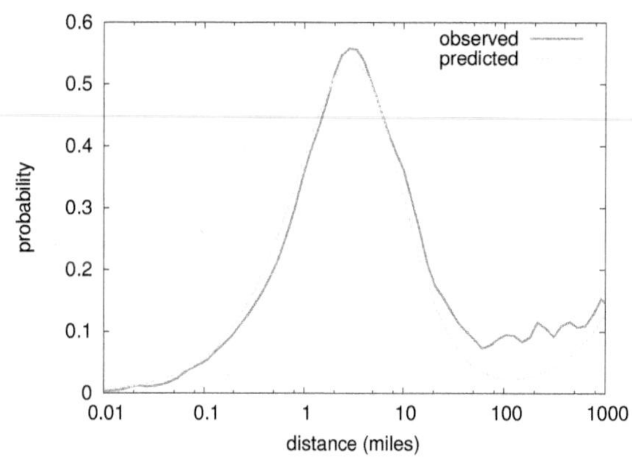

Figure 2: Observed probability distribution vs. distance model.

In the second experiment, we measure the performance of our distance model in inferring the actual user locations.

To this end, we focus on users who have issued at least one restaurant-related tweet (of a restaurant in our collection) and have self-reported their geolocations by explicitly specifying a latitude-longitude pair. Since each qualifying tweet carries a user location in the metadata, we obtain a distribution over locations for each such user; let $\ell(u, \cdot)$ denote this distribution. This serves as the ground-truth. We then apply the distance model to infer the location of each user in this collection, withholding the ground-truth location from the model. We measure the error of the inferred location $\ell'(u)$ against the ground-truth in two ways. In the *min* measure, the error is the minimum distance between $\ell'(u)$ and p, where p is in the support of $\ell(u, \cdot)$, i.e., $\ell(u, p) > 0$. In the *mode* measure, it is the distance between $\ell'(u)$ and p where p is the mode of the distribution $\ell'(u, \cdot)$.

Figure 3 shows the performance curves as a cumulative fraction: the x-axis is the distance in miles and the y-axis is the fraction of users whose error is within the distance. We study the error for users with at least 3 and at least 10

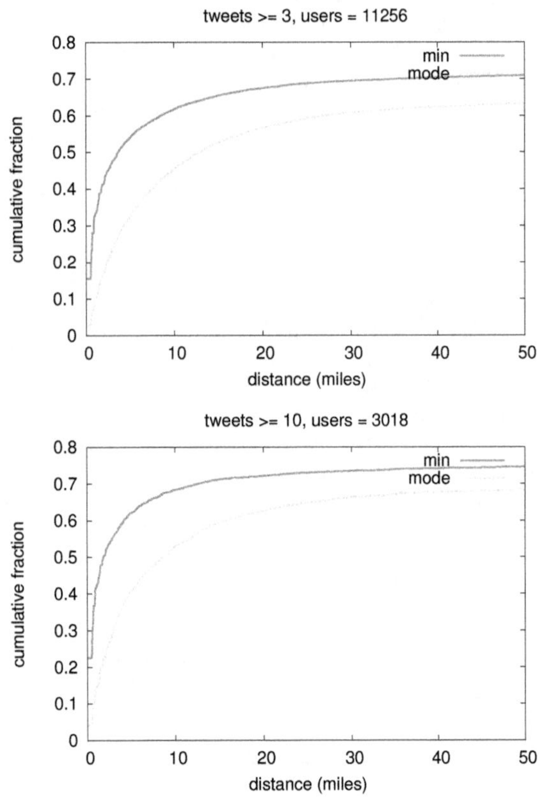

Figure 3: User locations: self-reported vs inferred.

restaurant tweets. For users with at least 3 tweets, about 50% of the users have an error of at most 10 miles under the stricter mode measure. The fraction jumps to 70% if we consider the min measure for users with at least 10 restaurant tweets. Note that our model can still be quite accurate when the user moves about. Figure 4 shows the restaurants tweets for a peripatetic user with a self-reported location in Atlanta. Even though the restaurant tweets are emanating from disparate locations, the inferred user location is within a mile of the self-reported location.

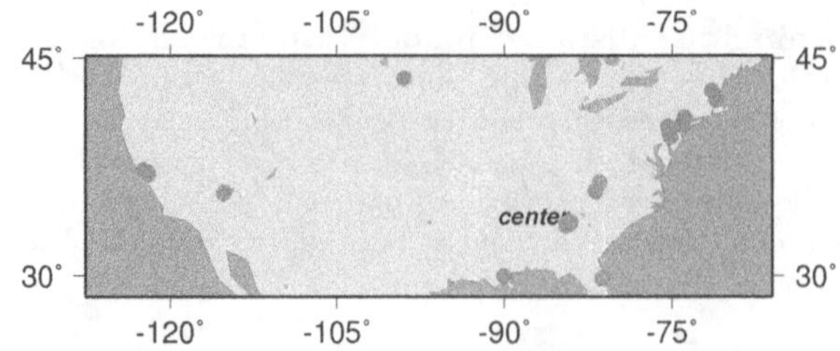

Figure 4: Location of the restaurant tweets for a user from Atlanta, GA.

These experiments illustrate that our distance model not only accurately captures the true distance distribution of tweet-user pairs but also is useful in obtaining the actual location of the user fairly accurately.

8. EXPERIMENTS: MATCHING

8.1 Experimental setup

In this section we evaluate the performance of the model for the matching task. Note that our model outputs the entity e that maximizes the probability of generating a given tweet. However, for some tweets, we want to return a "no match", if the most likely entity results in a low probability. To this end, we add a dummy entity in our collection, NONRESTAURANT, which has no distance model but has a language model consisting of the entity-independent language $\mathbf{P}_{\mathrm{lm}}$. In addition, we assign a prior probability c to this object. The higher the value of c, the more likely a random tweet is non-restaurant. If during matching, the most likely entity is found to be NONRESTAURANT, we say that the tweet has "no match". As default, we set $\theta = 0.2, c = 0.999$.

Test data. If we randomly sample from the tweet collection that has been filtered by the keyword list as described in Section 6, then most are either non-restaurant or do not contain a match to any of the candidate restaurants in our restaurant set. On the other hand, if we take only the tweet–match pairs with the highest confidence, then we do not get to evaluate our performance on the low-confidence end. In order to obtain a reasonable amount of positive data points with limited human labeling effort, we need to select across the board. To this end, we took the raw score produced by the model in [5], ranked the tweet–match pairs according to this raw matching score[7], and selected the same amount of examples to label from each of the following buckets: top 2%, 2–5%, 5–30%, and the rest. We filtered out users with more than 10K tweets as these users are less likely to be real users. 490 tweets sampled this way were labeled in the following procedure. Each tweet, along with all candidate restaurants, is presented to annotators, who either label the tweet as not about any of the candidates (e.g., not a restaurant tweet), or choose one of the candidates as the correct match. The location information of the user, if available, is also presented. In order to give more contextual information

[7]Note that the original model was developed to select the best matching restaurant for documents that are known to be restaurant reviews, thus the raw score is not optimal for this purpose. Nonetheless, it is a good surrogate to obtain a reasonable sample from the dataset.

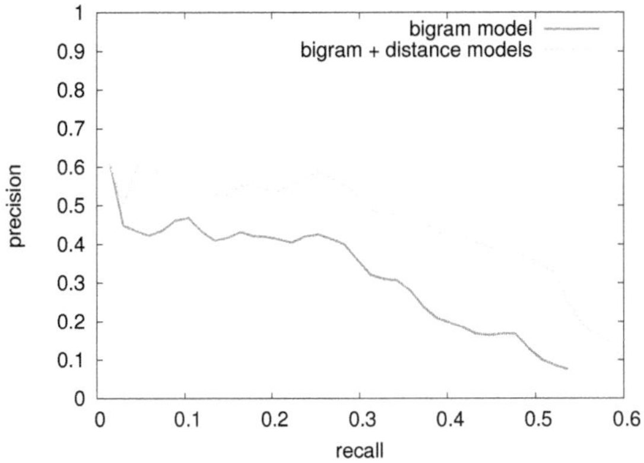

Figure 5: Performance: $\theta = 0.2, c = 0.999$.

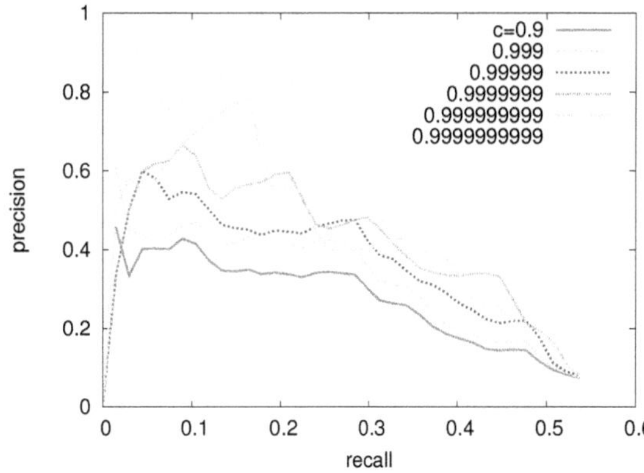

Figure 7: Effect of different values of c for $\theta = 0.2$.

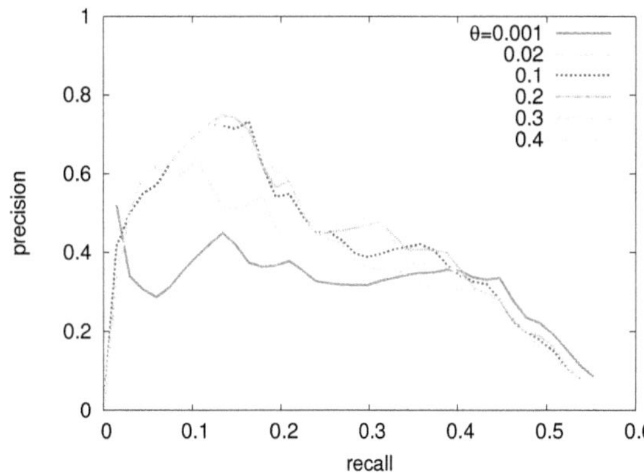

Figure 8: Effect of different values of θ for $c =$ 0.99999999.

about the user, we also provide other tweets written by the user in the past.

We compare different methods by comparing the precision–recall curves. We compute the precision–recall curve in the following manner. For each tweet t, we take the candidate restaurant r with the highest matching probability p and form a $\langle t, r, p\rangle$ tuple. For a given threshold τ, we output r for t if $p > \tau$ and for all tweets with $p \leq \tau$, output "no match". If r is the match chosen for t by annotators, we consider this to be a correct match. Note that this slightly differs from a standard precision–recall curve in that the recall may not reach 1 as we lower τ: if a tweet has an incorrect candidate ranked ahead of the correct one, it will never be correctly "retrieved", no matter how low τ is.

8.2 Results

First, we compare the performance of the language model with and without the distance model. As we can see in Figure 5, with our default parameter setting ($\theta = 0.2, c = 0.999$), we observe clear improvements in the precision–recall curve by utilizing the distance model. This trend is consistent for other c values as well (Figures 6(a) and 6(b)).

In addition, we investigate the effect of using different parameters. This set of comparison is done without using the distance model. First, we fix $\theta = 0.2$ and experiment with different values of c. As shown in Figure 7, we achieve better performance with large values of c. If we hope to maintain at least 50% in recall, then the optimal value for c ranges between $1 - 10^{-7}$ and $1 - 10^{-9}$. As we increase c to $1 - 10^{-10}$, we observe a clear degradation in performance on the higher recall range. Indeed, for c ranging from $1 - 10^{-6}$ to $1 - 10^{-10}$, we observe higher c values performing better at the lower end of recall and lower c values performing better at the higher end of recall. This is a reasonable behavior since higher c values are in effect favoring tweets with extremely high confidence in the matching, and user locations are in turn computed with more accurate matches.

We then compare different values of θ for $c = 1 - 10^{-9}$. Figure 8 shows that for a wide range of θ values (0.2–0.4), the performance is quite stable.

Finally, We observe that the performance degrade if we switch to the unigram model. Using the default parameter setting, we see that the bigram model outperforms the unigram model when used on its own (Figure 9(a)) as well as when used in conjunction with the distance model (Figure 9(b)). While the distance model improves both the unigram and the bigram models, the gap between them is larger in Figure 9(b). This trend is more pronounced for a higher value of c; we omit these plots due to space constraints.

9. CONCLUSIONS

In this paper we formulated a user model for generating a tweet about an object. Our model depends on three intuitive quantities: the propensity of a user to tweet about an object, the object's inherent popularity, and the distance between the user and object's geographic location. We obtained an efficient estimation algorithm that can infer the model parameters. We then used this algorithm to match objects to tweets, focusing on the restaurant domain. Our experiments indicate that the model and methodology we developed work well in practice. As a byproduct of our modeling, we also obtained a principled method to infer the location of a user using the restaurant tweets; this inference method may be of independent interest.

This object matching primitive is essential for applications that associate an object with tweets. These applications promise to be useful to the web community at large. Future work includes fine-tuning the model to take into account multiple locations for a user (home vs office, travel, etc) and including a user-specific popularity for a restaurant (preference for a cuisine, decor, etc).

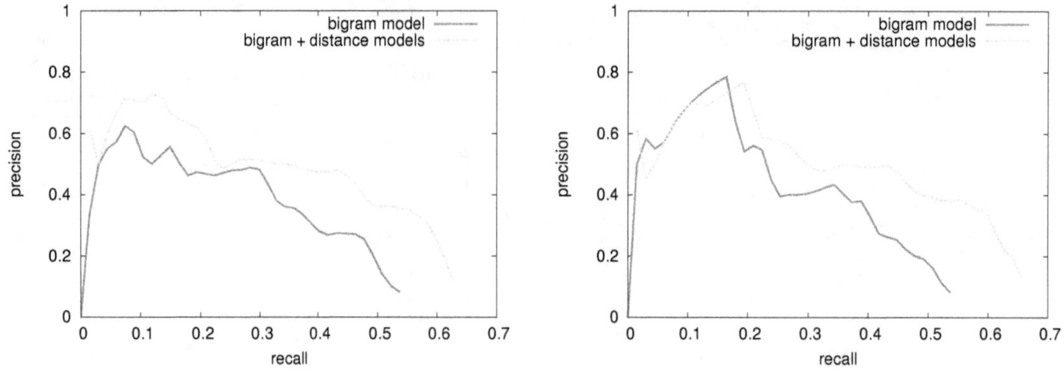

(a) $\theta = 0.2, c = 0.999999$ (b) $\theta = 0.2, c = 0.999999999$

Figure 6: Effect of distance models.

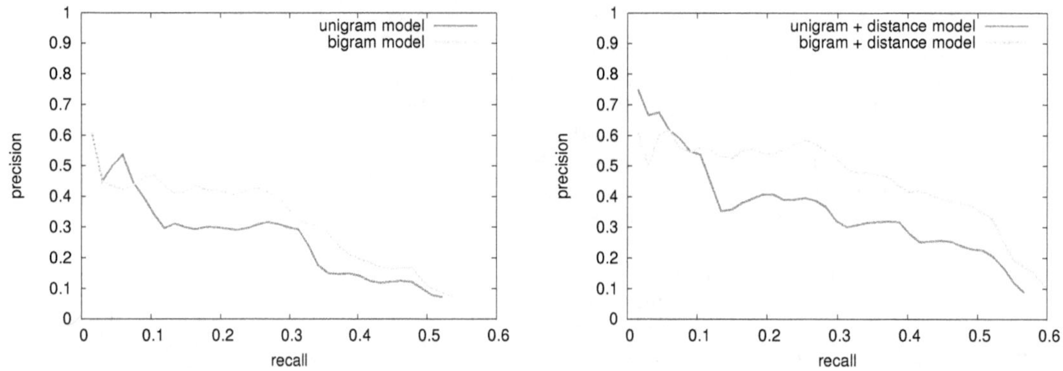

(a) (b)

Figure 9: Unigram vs. Bigram model, $\theta = 0.2, c = 0.999$.

10. REFERENCES

[1] L. Backstrom, J. M. Kleinberg, R. Kumar, and J. Novak. Spatial variation in search engine queries. In *WWW*, pages 357–366, 2008.

[2] L. Backstrom, E. Sun, and C. Marlow. Find me if you can: Improving geographical prediction with social and spatial proximity. In *WWW*, pages 61–70, 2010.

[3] E. Bakshy, J. M. Hofman, W. A. Mason, and D. J. Watts. Everyone's an influencer: Quantifying influence on Twitter. In *WSDM*, pages 65–74, 2011.

[4] D. J. Crandall, L. Backstrom, D. P. Huttenlocher, and J. M. Kleinberg. Mapping the world's photos. In *WWW*, pages 761–770, 2009.

[5] N. N. Dalvi, R. Kumar, B. Pang, and A. Tomkins. Matching reviews to objects using a language model. In *EMNLP*, pages 609–618, 2009.

[6] N. N. Dalvi, R. Kumar, B. Pang, and A. Tomkins. A translation model for matching reviews to objects. In *CIKM*, pages 167–176, 2009.

[7] D. Davidov, O. Tsur, and A. Rappoport. Enhanced sentiment learning using Twitter hashtags and smileys. In *COLING*, pages 241–249, 2010.

[8] J. Eisenstein, B. O'Connor, N. A. Smith, and E. P. Xing. A latent variable model for geographic lexical variation. In *EMNLP*, pages 1277–1287, 2010.

[9] T. Finin, W. Murnane, A. Karandikar, N. Keller, J. Martineau, and M. Dredze. Annotating named entites in twitter data with crowdsourcing. In *Workshop on Creating Speech and Language Data with Mechanical Turk at NAACL-HLT*, 2010.

[10] Q. Mei, C. Liu, H. Su, and C. Zhai. A probabilistic approach to spatiotemporal theme pattern mining on weblogs. In *WWW*, pages 533–542, 2006.

[11] B. O'Connor, J. Eisenstein, E. P. Xing, and N. A. Smith. Discovering demographic language variation. In *Workshop on Machine Learning for Social Computing at NIPS*, 2010.

[12] T. Rattenbury, N. Good, and M. Naaman. Towards automatic extraction of event and place semantics from flickr tags. In *SIGIR*, pages 103–110, 2007.

[13] D. Romero, B. Meeder, and J. Kleinberg. Differences in the mechanics of information diffusion across topics: Idioms, political hashtags, and complex contagion on Twitter. In *WWW*, pages 695–704, 2011.

[14] S. Sizov. Geofolk: Latent spatial semantics with Web 2.0 social media. In *WSDM*, pages 281–290, 2010.

[15] B. Wing and J. Baldridge. Simple supervised document geolocation with geodesic grids. In *ACL*, pages 955–964, 2011.

[16] S. Wu, J. M. Hofman, W. Mason, and D. J. Watts. Says what to whom on Twitter. In *WWW*, pages 705–714, 2011.

[17] Z. Yin, L. Cao, J. Han, C. Zhai, and T. Huang. Geographic topic discovery and comparison. In *WWW*, pages 247–256, 2011.

Beyond 100 Million Entities: Large-scale Blocking-based Resolution for Heterogeneous Data

George Papadakis[$,♯], Ekaterini Ioannou[◇],
Claudia Niederée[♯], Themis Palpanas[‡], and Wolfgang Nejdl[♯]

[$] National Technical University of Athens, Greece gpapadis@mail.ntua.gr
[◇] Technical University of Crete, Greece ioannou@softnet.tuc.gr
[♯] L3S Research Center, Germany {surname}@L3S.de
[‡] University of Trento, Italy themis@disi.unitn.eu

ABSTRACT

A prerequisite for leveraging the vast amount of data available on the Web is Entity Resolution, i.e., the process of identifying and linking data that describe the same real-world objects. To make this inherently quadratic process applicable to large data sets, blocking is typically employed: entities (records) are grouped into clusters - the *blocks* - of matching candidates and only entities of the same block are compared. However, novel blocking techniques are required for dealing with the noisy, heterogeneous, semi-structured, user-generated data in the Web, as traditional blocking techniques are inapplicable due to their reliance on schema information. The introduction of redundancy, improves the robustness of blocking methods but comes at the price of additional computational cost.

In this paper, we present methods for enhancing the efficiency of redundancy-bearing blocking methods, such as our attribute-agnostic blocking approach. We introduce novel blocking schemes that build blocks based on a variety of evidences, including entity identifiers and relationships between entities; they significantly reduce the required number of comparisons, while maintaining blocking effectiveness at very high levels. We also introduce two theoretical measures that provide a reliable estimation of the performance of a blocking method, without requiring the analytical processing of its blocks. Based on these measures, we develop two techniques for improving the performance of blocking: combining individual, complementary blocking schemes, and purging blocks until given criteria are satisfied. We test our methods through an extensive experimental evaluation, using a voluminous data set with 182 million heterogeneous entities. The outcomes of our study show the applicability and the high performance of our approach.

Categories and Subject Descriptors

H.3.3 [**Information Search and Retrieval**]: Information filtering

General Terms

Algorithms, Experimentation, Performance

Keywords

Data Cleaning, Entity Resolution, Attribute-Agnostic Blocking

Permission to make digital or hard copies of all or part of this work for personal or classroom use is granted without fee provided that copies are not made or distributed for profit or commercial advantage and that copies bear this notice and the full citation on the first page. To copy otherwise, to republish, to post on servers or to redistribute to lists, requires prior specific permission and/or a fee.
WSDM'12, February 8–12, 2012, Seattle, Washingtion, USA.
Copyright 2012 ACM 978-1-4503-0747-5/12/02 ...$10.00.

1. INTRODUCTION

The Linked Data principles[1] are of central importance for the effective re-use of the (semi-)structured, heterogeneous data that are increasingly becoming available in the Web. They enable exposing, sharing, and connecting these data, thus making it possible to leverage the investment in creating and collecting them [2]. However, the currently available Web data are not as "linked" as this paradigm envisions; content providers tend to use their own entity (resource) identifiers and schemata rather than re-using existing ones. As a result, the Web of Data ends up consisting of heterogeneous, overlapping islands of knowledge that pose significant challenges in the effort to combine entity information from different sources [9].

To remedy this problem, *Entity Resolution* (ER) is typically used; it is the process of automatically identifying sets of entities that correspond to the same real-world object. In principle, ER is a task of quadratic complexity, as it requires comparing each entity with all others. To scale it to large data collections, approximate ER methods drastically reduce the required number of comparisons, sacrificing some of their effectiveness (i.e., number of detected duplicates) in order to enhance their efficiency. Among these methods, *data blocking* is the most prevalent one: it clusters data into blocks, such that potential duplicates are placed in the same block with a high probability. Thus, instead of operating on the entire collection, it suffices to handle the data inside each block separately [6].

However, generating and processing blocks for large heterogeneous data sets imposes serious, new challenges; their inherent characteristics - i.e., loose schema binding, noise, missing or inconsistent values, as well as unprecedented levels of heterogeneity - break the fundamental assumptions of existing blocking techniques and turn them inapplicable [19]. To deal with these settings, blocking methods typically rely on *redundancy* (i.e., the common practice of placing each entity in multiple blocks); a representative example is the *attribute-agnostic blocking* approach [19], which achieves higher performance by splitting its functionality in two layers: (i) the *effectiveness layer*, which minimizes the likelihood of missed matches with the help of redundancy, and (ii) the *efficiency layer*, which employs a series of techniques to scale up the ER process by saving a large portion of the unnecessary comparisons (i.e., repeated ones or comparisons between non-matching entities) [20, 21]. Through these layers, we are able to handle large volumes of noisy and heterogeneous data, without relying on any assumptions about their schemata.

In more detail, we introduce blocking mechanisms for heterogeneous data that keep redundancy under control, without diminishing the blocking effectiveness of our attribute blocking approach.

[1] http://en.wikipedia.org/wiki/Linked_data#Principles

We actually aim at enhancing the blocking efficiency at no impact on the number of duplicates that share at least one block. In particular, we present novel, schema-independent blocking schemes that operate at a higher level of granularity, distinguishing three sources of evidence in entity profiles: (a) strings used for entity identification (typically URIs), (b) entity identifiers used for linking entities with each other (relationships), and (c) literal values used in entity descriptions. The use of these evidences in blocking significantly reduces the resulting number of required comparisons, thus offering substantially higher efficiency. However, they are less robust in isolation, since they make more assumptions on the entity profiles than attribute-agnostic blocking. Therefore, we experiment with *composite blocking schemes*, which combine the functionality of two or more - preferably complementary - individual blocking techniques in order to ensure increased robustness.

We also introduce two theoretical measures for a priori estimating the performance of a blocking method, without requiring any analytical processing of its blocks. We verify the high correlation of these metrics with the blocking effectiveness and efficiency, and demonstrate how they can be employed in the context of *block purging* [19], i.e., the process of discarding oversized blocks in order to save superfluous comparisons at a limited and controllable cost in effectiveness.

The main contributions of this paper are as follows:

1. We introduce two theoretical metrics that quantitatively capture the trade-off between blocking effectiveness and efficiency. Their values provide a reliable estimation of the performance of a blocking method, without requiring any analytical block examination. Therefore, they are suitable for a-priori estimating the best performing among a set of blocking methods.
2. We present a set of atomic blocking schemes that are crafted for large-scale ER within heterogeneous collections of data. They rely on different aspects of entity descriptions and, thus, can be combined into composite schemes of higher robustness and enhanced performance.
3. We introduce an intelligent technique for block purging that enhances the efficiency of a blocking method at a negligible and controllable cost in its effectiveness. It relies on our theoretical metrics in order to discard the excessively large blocks and save the superfluous comparisons they entail.
4. We apply our techniques on a real-world data set that comprises 182 million entities, which are described by 1.15 billion statements - the largest entity collection ever employed in the context of Entity Resolution. The overall evaluation demonstrates the utility of the proposed theoretical metrics and verifies the higher efficiency of our blocking techniques in comparison with attribute-agnostic blocking.

The rest of the paper is organized as follows: Section 2 discusses the related work, while Section 3 defines the problem. In Section 4 we propose three new blocking methods, we explain the benefits of merging them into composite ones, and we present a new algorithm for block purging. Section 5 reports the results of our experimental evaluation, while Section 6 provides conclusions and discusses future work.

2. RELATED WORK

Being a traditional problem of Computer Science, a variety of methods for ER have already been proposed in the literature. They employ a rich diversity of techniques that - among others - include string similarity metrics [4], similarity methods that rely on transformations [23], as well as relationships among entities [5]. A comprehensive overview of the most important works in this domain can be found in [6].

The most important ER blocking methods are summarized in [3]. They typically associate each record with a *Blocking Key Value* (BKV), which summarizes the values of selected attributes, and operate exclusively on it [6]. For instance, the Sorted Neighborhood approach [10] orders records according to their BKV and then slides a window of fixed size over them, comparing the records it contains. The StringMap method [14] maps the BKV of each record to a multi-dimensional, Euclidean space and employs suitable data structures to efficiently identify pairs of similar records. The q-grams blocking technique [7] builds overlapping clusters of records that share at least one q-gram (i.e., sub-string of length q) of their BKV. Canopy clustering [16] employs a cheap string similarity metric for building high-dimensional overlapping blocks, whereas the Suffix Arrays approach [24] considers the suffixes of the BKV instead. Whang et al. [25] explores another aspect of these blocking approaches, arguing that more duplicates can be detected and more pair-wise comparisons can be saved through the iterative distribution of identified matches to subsequently (re-)processed blocks. The same principle lies at the core of HARRA [13], a suite of LSH-based, iterative blocking algorithms that scale well in the context of homogeneous information spaces. [22] presents a principled framework for parallelizing any sound ER method at a minimum message passing cost. Note, though, that all these methods are not suitable for handling the heterogeneous entity collections of the Web of Data, due to their core assumption that entities are described by the same schema(ta), and that the quality of the individual attributes is known a priori.

In addition, the vast majority of the above methods depends on fine-tuning several application- and data-specific parameters in order to achieve their optimal performance [24]. To automate the parameter setting procedure, existing methods typically model it as a machine learning problem. For instance, [17] defines it as learning disjunctive sets of conjunctions that consist of an attribute (used for blocking) and a method (used for comparing the corresponding values). Similarly, [1] considers disjunctions of *blocking predicates* (i.e., conjunctions of attributes and methods) along with predicates combined in disjunctive normal form (DNF). These approaches, however, are only applicable to data sets involving a restricted number of distinct attributes. Otherwise, they have to consider an excessively high number of attribute combinations. They do not scale, therefore, in the context of heterogeneous information spaces.

In sharp contrast to existing approaches, attribute-agnostic blocking requires no fine-tuning, while assuming no background knowledge of the data at hand [19]. Instead, it completely disregards the schemata of the heterogeneous information spaces and solely considers the values of their entity profiles. It ensures high robustness and blocking effectiveness (i.e., the vast majority of the matching entities have at least one block in common), by creating one block for each token that appears in at least two entity profiles. Although this approach scales well to middle-sized entity collections (with few million entities), its fine granularity conveys extremely high levels of redundancy when applied to large entity collections, like the BTC09.

In this work, we argue that Heterogeneous Information Spaces allow for blocking schemes of higher granularity that involve substantially lower levels of redundancy. They are, thus, more efficient, while maintaining high levels of blocking effectiveness. In addition, they can be arbitrarily combined, forming more robust and more effective blocking methods, which are more efficient than the original attribute-agnostic blocking. To the best of our knowledge, there is no prior work on blocking techniques that can handle hundreds of millions of entities described by arbitrary schemata.

3. PROBLEM DEFINITION

To describe the problem succinctly, we follow the unifying data model that was introduced in [19]. Entity profiles are basically composed of a globally unique identifier (e.g. URIs) coupled with a set of attributes names and the values that accompany them. We assume the existence of an infinite set of attribute names $\mathcal{AN}$, along with an infinite set of possible values $\mathcal{V}$ and an infinite set of identifiers $\mathcal{ID}$.

DEFINITION 1. *An **entity profile** $\mathbf{p_{id}}$ is a tuple $\langle id, A_{p_{id}} \rangle$, where $id \in \mathcal{ID}$ is a globally unique identifier of the profile, and $A_{p_{id}}$ is a set of attributes a_i. Each **attribute** $a_i \in A_{p_{id}}$ is a tuple $\langle n_i, v_i \rangle$, consisting of an **attribute name** $n_i \in \mathcal{AN}$ and an **attribute value** $v_i \in (\mathcal{V} \cup \mathcal{ID})$.*

The simplicity of this model enables it to accommodate entities in more complex formats, such as RDF and XML, and to represent data both in Web [26] and dataspace applications [8, 11]. For example, multiple values can be assigned to the same attribute name, while the attribute name can be a mere empty string, thus allowing for *tag-style attributes* (i.e., no associated attribute name). In addition, attribute values can contain entity identifiers, enabling the representation of relationships between entities.

DEFINITION 2. *An **entity collection** $\mathcal{E}$ is a tuple $\langle AN_\mathcal{E}, V_\mathcal{E}, ID_\mathcal{E}, P_\mathcal{E} \rangle$, where $AN_\mathcal{E} \subseteq \mathcal{AN}$ is the set of attribute names appearing in it, $V_\mathcal{E} \subseteq (\mathcal{V} \cup \mathcal{ID})$ is the set of values used in it, $ID_\mathcal{E} \subseteq \mathcal{ID}$ is the set of global identifiers contained in it, and $P_\mathcal{E} \subseteq ID_\mathcal{E} \times \wp(AN_\mathcal{E} \times V_\mathcal{E})$ is the set of entity profiles that it comprises.*

3.1 Resolution through Blocking Techniques

We expect that data aggregated from diverse sources contain duplicate entity profiles, which describe the same real-world objects. Two such profiles p_i and p_j are said to *match*, a situation that is denoted as $\mathbf{p_i \equiv p_j}$. The general problem of entity resolution can, thus, be defined as follows:

PROBLEM STATEMENT 1 (ENTITY RESOLUTION). *Given an entity collection $\mathcal{E}$ that contains duplicates, detect all matches as effectively (i.e., with high recall) and efficiently (i.e., with few entity comparisons) as possible.*

In this work, we focus on two particular cases of Entity Resolution: (i) the *Dirty-Clean ER*, where the goal is to identify the matching entities among a duplicate-free (i.e., clean) entity collection and another collection containing duplicates (i.e., dirty), and (ii) the *Dirty-Dirty ER*, which deals with the resolution of two dirty collections. Both cases are equivalent to detecting the duplicates within a single dirty entity collection that is derived from the union of the individual input data sets (i.e., *Dirty ER*). Therefore, in the following, we assume that the input to our blocking methods comprises a single set of - possibly matching - entities.

ER apparently constitutes a quadratic problem, whose naive solution (i.e., comparing each entity with all others) does not scale to large entity collections. To reduce the number of comparisons, we follow the paradigm of data blocking: our goal is to define methods that group the given set of profiles into blocks according to a blocking scheme. For our purposes, we model a blocking scheme as a combination of two functions:

DEFINITION 3. *A **blocking scheme** $\mathbf{bs_{t,c}}$ for an entity collection $\mathcal{E}$ is defined by a transformation function $f_t : \mathcal{E} \mapsto T$ and a set of constraint functions $f_c^i : T \times T \mapsto \{true, false\}$, where T stands for the space of all possible blocking representations for entity profiles. The **transformation function** $\mathbf{f_t}$ derives the appropriate representation for blocking from the complete entity profile (or parts of it). The **constraint function** $\mathbf{f_c^i}$ is a transitive and symmetric function, encapsulating the condition that has to be satisfied by two entities, if they are to be placed in the same block b_i.*

To elucidate this definition, consider a homogeneous data collection of demographic data; a possible blocking scheme could comprise a transformation function that represents each person through her/his zip code, and a set of constraint functions that define blocks on the equality of the zip code (each constraint function corresponds to a single zip code, and, thus, to a single block). However, for heterogeneous data sets, other, less attribute dependent transformation functions are required.

Applying a blocking scheme $bs_{t,c}$ to an entity collection $\mathcal{E}$ yields a set of blocks $\mathbf{B_{t,c}^\mathcal{E}}$, whose instances are defined as follows:

DEFINITION 4. *A **block** $b_i \in B_{t,c}^\mathcal{E}$ is a maximal subset of the given entity collection $\mathcal{E}$ - having a minimum cardinality of 2 - that is defined by the blocking scheme $bs_{t,c}$, i.e., by the transformation function f_t and the constraint functions f_c^i: $b_i \subseteq \mathcal{E} \wedge \forall p_1, p_2 \in \mathcal{E} : f_c^i(f_t(p_1), f_t(p_2)) = true \Rightarrow p_1, p_2 \in b_i$.*

The challenge in developing an efficacious blocking method - including a blocking scheme and a method for block processing - is to successfully balance the trade-off between the following two competing quality targets [1, 17, 19, 24]:

Pair Completeness: Duplicates should share at least one common block, otherwise they cannot be detected. A blocking method should, therefore, minimize the matching entities that have no block in common. This requirement is expressed through the metric of *Pair Completeness* (**PC**), which is formally defined as $PC = dm/rm$, where dm denotes the detected matches (i.e., the number of matches that share at least one block), and rm represents the number of real matches. It takes values in the interval $[0, 1]$, with higher values indicating higher *effectiveness* of the blocking method. Note that PC is comparable to the Recall metric of Information Retrieval (i.e., Blocking Recall), but is different from the Recall of the entire ER process, though having a direct impact on it.

Reduction Ratio: Each block should contain as few irrelevant entities as possible, in order to reduce the number of unnecessary pair-wise comparisons. This requirement is typically measured with respect to a baseline blocking method through the metric of *Reduction Ratio* (**RR**); this measure is defined as $RR = 1 - mc/bc$, where mc stands for the method's number of comparisons and bc for the number of baseline comparisons. RR takes values in the interval $[0, 1]$ (for $mc \leq bc$), with higher values denoting higher *efficiency* of the blocking scheme.

In this context, the formal definition of the problem we are tackling in this work is the following:

PROBLEM STATEMENT 2 (BLOCKING FOR ENTITY RESOLUTION). *Given an entity collection $\mathcal{E}$ that contains duplicates and a baseline blocking method, cluster its entities into blocks, such that Pair Completeness and Reduction Ratio are maximized.*

Maximizing RR means that the process of Entity Resolution can be efficiently applied to large data sets, while maximizing PC satisfies the application requirements (i.e., an acceptable level of effectiveness for heterogeneous data sets).

3.2 Metric Space for Blocking Techniques

To meet the goal of high PC in the context of noisy or heterogeneous information spaces, blocking methods typically rely on *redundancy*: entities are associated with multiple, overlapping blocks, thus minimizing the likelihood of missed matches [3, 19, 24, 25]. In this way, effectiveness is significantly enhanced, though at the cost of the second target: redundancy has a substantial impact on efficiency, due to the increased number of comparisons between

entities. There is, therefore, a clear trac
gets: higher blocking redundancy incre
vice versa.

To concretely express this general
measures that a priori assess the perf
ods. The first one - called *Blocking Ca.*
proportional relationship between redi
blocks associated with each entity, on a

Definition 5. *Given an entity colle*
*ing scheme $bs_{t,c}$, the **Blocking Cardin.***
set of blocks $\mathcal{B}^{\mathcal{E}}_{t,c}$ is defined as the avera
an entity profile $p_{id} \in \mathcal{E}$ is placed in:

$$BC^{\mathcal{E}}_{t,c} = \frac{\sum_{p_{id}\in\mathcal{E}} |b_i \in \mathcal{B}^{\mathcal{E}}_{t,c} : p_{id} \in b_i|}{|\mathcal{E}|} = \frac{\sum_{b_i\in\mathcal{B}^{\mathcal{E}}_{t,c}} |b_i|}{|\mathcal{E}|},$$

where $|\mathcal{E}|$ denotes the size of the given entity collection $\mathcal{E}$, and $|b_i|$ the size of block b_i.

BC takes values in the interval $[0, |\mathcal{E}| - 1]$, with higher values denoting higher levels of redundancy. A value of 1 denotes a technique that is close to a *partitioning blocking method* (i.e., one that partitions the given entity collection into non-overlapping blocks). Values lower than 1 indicate blocking methods that fail to place each entity in at least one block; this is possible, for instance, with blocking techniques that exclusively rely on a single attribute and ignore entity profiles that do not possess it. The maximum value of BC is set to $|\mathcal{E}| - 1$, since there is no point in associating every entity with all others more than once.

Another crucial factor for the performance of a blocking method is the distribution of block sizes: a large set of individually small blocks is substantially more efficient than a set of few, but extremely large blocks, even if these sets share the same BC value. To quantify this notion, we introduce the metric of *Comparisons Cardinality* (**CC**):

Definition 6. *Given an entity collection $\mathcal{E}$ along with a blocking scheme $bs_{t,c}$, the **Comparisons Cardinality** ($\mathbf{CC}^{\mathcal{E}}_{\mathbf{t,c}}$) of the resulting set of blocks $\mathcal{B}^{\mathcal{E}}_{t,c}$ is defined as the ratio between the sum of block sizes and the total number of comparisons entailed in $\mathcal{B}^{\mathcal{E}}_{t,c}$:*

$$CC^{\mathcal{E}}_{t,c} = \frac{\sum_{b_i\in\mathcal{B}^{\mathcal{E}}_{t,c}} |b_i|}{\sum_{b_i\in\mathcal{B}^{\mathcal{E}}_{t,c}} |b_i| \cdot (|b_i| - 1)/2},$$

where $|b_i|$ denotes the size of block b_i.

In essence, CC denotes the number of *block assignments* (i.e., associations between a block and an entity) that account for a single comparison. It takes values in the interval $[0, 2]$, with higher values corresponding to block size distributions that are dominated by small blocks, and, thus, are more efficient. In fact, its maximum value $CC_{max} = 2$ corresponds to the ideal case of a blocking method that associates each entity of the input collection $\mathcal{E}$ with a single block that contains just another entity: $CC = \frac{|\mathcal{E}|}{|\mathcal{E}|/2} = 2$. In contrast, for a blocking method that places all given entity profiles in a single block, we have $CC_{max} = \frac{|\mathcal{E}|}{|\mathcal{E}|\cdot(|\mathcal{E}|-1)/2} = \frac{2}{|\mathcal{E}|-1} \ll CC_{max}$. On the whole, the closer the CC is to CC_{max}, the more efficient the corresponding blocking method is.

Note that both the BC and the CC depend on the input entity collection as well as the blocking method at hand: the same blocking scheme can yield different levels of redundancy and different block size distributions, when applied to different entity collections.

The combination of these two metrics - BC and CC - captures in a comprehensive way the trade-off between effectiveness and efficiency, that is inherent in any blocking method. This trade-off can be actually visualized by mapping a blocking method onto a

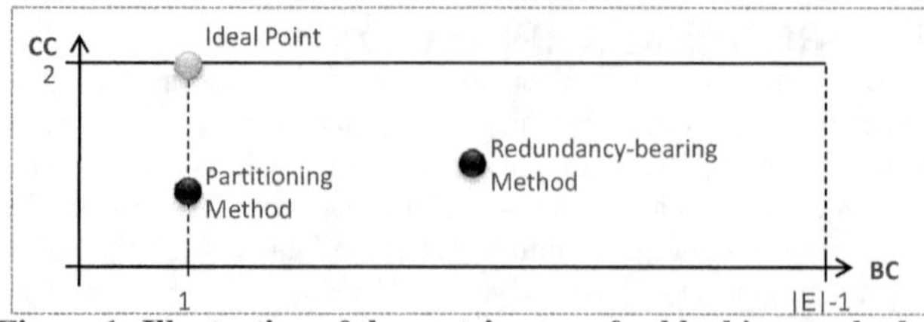

Figure 1: Illustration of the metric space for blocking methods.

Cartesian space, with its X-axis corresponding to BC values, and its Y-axis corresponding to CC values. We call it the **BC-CC space** (see Figure 1). A partitioning method has a BC value of 1, while its CC value depends on the distribution of block sizes; thus, it is mapped to some point on the $x = 1$ line. The *ideal point* (i.e., point (1,2)) corresponds to the ideal case of a partitioning method that completely disregards non-matching entities and builds a block of minimum size for each pair of duplicates. A typical redundancy-bearing blocking method is mapped to a point lying somewhere between the lines $x = 1$ and $x = |\mathcal{E}| - 1$.

In the following, we demonstrate that the conjunction of the BC and CC metrics is appropriate not only for describing blocking methods, but also for providing a reliable estimation of their actual performance. There is indeed a high correlation between the BC value of a blocking method and its effectiveness (i.e., Pair Completeness). The same holds true for CC and its relation to the efficiency of a method. The metric space of BC-CC can be used, therefore, for comparing a priori a set of blocking methods: the closer a blocking method is to the ideal point (1,2), the better its performance. The main advantage of this methodology is its negligible cost: both metrics are computed in linear time, $O(|\mathcal{B}^{\mathcal{E}}_{t,c}|)$, simply by passing over the given set of blocks in order to record their size[2]. Below we also explain how the BC-CC mapping of a blocking method can be used as a guide for further enhancements in its performance, such as in block purging.

4. BLOCKING TECHNIQUES

Our approach to blocking for large-scale heterogeneous data sets is inspired by three observations: (i) The data sets we are considering entail loose schema binding and unprecedented levels of heterogeneity. The latter pertains to the schemata describing the same entity types as well as to different profiles describing the same entity. Google Base[3], for instance, encompasses 100,000 distinct schemata that correspond to 10,000 entity types [15]. Consequently, these conditions strongly oppose to a crucial role of attributes in blocking and duplicate detection. (ii) Many identifiers in the Web of Data, (i.e., URIs) contain semantics, thus constituting a strong basis on which entities can be matched. This was experimentally verified in [18], where a large-scale analysis of matching entities according to the semantics of their identifiers had a precision well over 90% and a recall exceeding 70%. (iii) Relationships between entities provide important evidences for matching them and can be exploited in numerous ways. For example, after detecting a pair of duplicates, positive and negative evidences can be propagated across related entities in order to increase the precision and recall of ER [5].

Based on the above observations, we developed a set of blocking schemes that are robust enough to tolerate high schema heterogeneity, as well as inconsistencies and noise (i.e., missing or incorrect values in the entity profiles). Observation (i) inspired us

[2]This is the reason why CC considers the entire amount of comparisons, including the redundant ones: its value is derived from the plain inspection of the blocks at hand, without looking into the entities they contain.

[3]http://www.google.com/base

	Prefix	Infix	Suffix
(a)	http://dblp.l3s.de/d2r/resource/publications/books/sp/wooldridgeV99	/ThalmannN99	
	http://bibsonomy.org/uri/bibtexkey/books/sp/wooldridgeV99	/ThalmannN99	/dblp

	Prefix	Infix	Suffix
(b)	http://liris.cnrs.fr	/olivier.aubert	/foaf.rdf#me
	http://bat710.univ-lyon1.fr	/˜oaubert	/foaf.rdf#me

Figure 2: Examples of URI pairs in the PI(S) form that refer to the same real-world entity.

to develop techniques that completely ignore the schema information and exclusively rely on the values of entity profiles [19]; all blocking schemes that are presented in the following adhere to this principle. Observation (ii) advocates the creation of blocks on the basis of evidence drawn from the semantics of entity identifiers (Blocking Scheme A.1). In view of observation (iii), we additionally consider blocking schemes that rely on the relationships between entities, exploiting the semantics contained in the identifiers of affiliated resources (Blocking Scheme A.2).

4.1 Preliminaries: Entity Identifier Analysis

Even though the *W3C* explicitly discourages users from incorporating semantics into URIs [12], the latter often contain substrings that provide clues about the corresponding entity. These substrings usually stem from well-established, often hierarchical, human labeling schemes (e.g., names, titles, or addresses), or explicit standardization efforts (e.g., industry-wide product codes or digital object identifiers - DOI). Hence, they constitute a natural source of evidence appropriate for matching duplicate entities. Indeed, [18] verified experimentally that approximately 66% of the 182 million URIs of the BTC09 data set[4] follow a common pattern: the *Prefix-Infix(-Suffix) scheme* - PI(S) for short. Each component of this form plays a special role: the *Prefix* part contains information about the source (i.e., domain) of the URI, the *Infix* part is a sort of local identifier, and the optional *Suffix* part contains either details about the format (e.g., `.rdf` and `.n3`), or a named anchor.

Our approach builds upon this pattern in order to extract matching evidences from entity identifiers. We actually expect the Infixes of URIs, which are more *source-independent* than the Prefixes and the Suffixes, to contain the most discriminative information for our purpose within a URI [18]. As an example, consider the duplicate pairs shown in Figure 2. Pair (a) shows that despite the high heterogeneity in the Prefixes of the URIs, the Infix remains the same. Moreover, the Suffix (e.g., `dblp`) is optional and can be ignored when matching URIs. Pair (b) illustrates the limitations of the approach: non-identical Infixes such as (`olivier.aubert` and `˜oaubert`) can only be matched with the help of appropriate similarity methods. In the following, we explain how this situation can be resolved through blocking methods that combine evidence from different aspects of entity profiles.

4.2 Atomic Blocking Schemes

Given an entity profile p_{id}, our blocking schemes disregard all schema information (i.e., attribute names), and rely exclusively on the remaining description items that are illustrated in Figure 3: the identifier *id* of the profile (its Infix, in particular), the URIs contained in p_{id} as values for denoting entity relationships, and the *literal values*[5] that are used to represent textual values of attributes. Blocking methods that rely solely on one category of the aforementioned information are **atomic blocking schemes**, in contrast to **composite blocking schemes**, which consider evidence from two or more of the above information sources.

To apply our blocking schemes to a collection of RDF data, we generate the entity profiles from its statements in line with Definition 1: all triples with a particular subject s, form the basis for an entity profile p_s that has s as its identifier, while the respective predicates and objects correspond to the set A_{p_s} of the name-value pairs of p_s.

In the following, we formally define our blocking schemes A.1 to A.3. For this purpose, we use two functions: $Infix(id)$[6], which extracts the Infix from the given entity identifier *id*, and *tokenize*(v), which tokenizes a string value v on all special characters (i.e., characters that are neither letters nor digits).

A.1. Infix Blocking. This blocking scheme conveys a *transformation function* that extracts the Infix from the *id* of each entity profile: $f_t(p_{id}) = Infix(id)$. Its *constraint functions* define blocks on the equivalence of Infixes: every block is associated with an Infix and contains all entities that share it. More formally, $f_c^i(p_{id_1}, p_{id_2}) = ((i = Infix(id_1)) \wedge (i = Infix(id_2)))$, where i is an Infix.

Apparently, this blocking scheme places each entity in just one block, thus resulting in non-overlapping blocks, i.e., $BC \leq 1$. For example, the entity of Figure 3, is placed solely in the block that corresponds to the Infix "Barack_Obama", together with all other entities sharing the same Infix. Values lower than 1 denote that the given entity collection contains profiles, whose URIs lack an Infix. The absence of redundancy together with the discriminative information of Infixes ensure blocks of small size and high CC values (i.e., high Reduction Ratio). However, its blocking effectiveness as well as its robustness is expected to be limited, as a side-effect of its low BC value. For instance, it does not apply to entities with a blank node[7] or a random URI as their *id*; the reason is that, in these cases, the corresponding identifier has merely a local scope, thus not providing a meaningful Infix for entity matching.

A.2. Infix Profile Blocking. The *Infix Profile* of an entity profile p_{id} - denoted by $IP_{p_{id}}$ - is the set of the Infixes of all URIs contained in p_{id} as attribute values, with the exception of its own identifier (i.e., *id*): $IP_{p_{id}} = \{Infix(id_i) : \exists n_i :< n_i, id_i >\in A_{p_{id}} \wedge id_i \neq id\}$.

Based on this concept, we can define a blocking scheme with a *transformation function* that represents each entity profile p_{id} by its $IP_{p_{id}}$ (i.e., $f_t(p_{id}) = IP_{p_{id}}$), and a set of *constraint functions* that form blocks on Infix equality: $f_c^i(p_{id_1}, p_{id_2}) = ((i \in IP_{p_{id_1}}) \wedge (i \in IP_{p_{id_2}}))$, where i is an Infix.

The cardinality of an $IP_{p_{id}}$ can be larger than one, since an entity is typically associated with multiple entities. Hence, every entity with a non-empty Infix Profile can be placed in multiple blocks, which are now overlapping (i.e., $BC \geq 1$ if all entities have a non-empty Infix Profile). For example, the entity of Figure 3, is contained in three blocks: those corresponding to the Infixes "Michelle_Obama", "Hawaii", and "Joe_Biden". This redundancy leads to larger blocks - on average - and inevitably to a lower CC value than Infix Blocking. RR is, therefore, lower to the benefit of higher PC and robustness. This blocking scheme has actually the potential to cover duplicates, where pure Infix Blocking is inappli-

[4] http://vmlion25.deri.ie.

[5] In RDF statements, these are objects that are neither URIs nor blank nodes.

[6] See [18] for an efficient approach to splitting a collection of URIs into the PI(S) form in order to extract the Infix from the individual URIs.

[7] Blank nodes constitute anonymous nodes in an RDF graph that are typically used whenever there is no information available about the corresponding resource. Consequently, their identifiers do not carry any semantics.

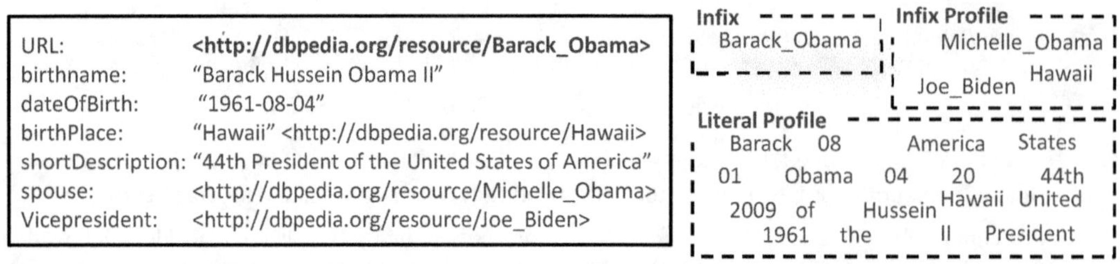

Figure 3: Illustration of the description items of an entity profile that are used by our blocking schemes.

cable: even though blank nodes and numerical URIs have no Infix, their Infix Profile can be non-empty. The same applies to matching entities with non-identical Infixes: their Infix Profile is likely to share at least one Infix of a related entity. Regarding its mapping to the BC-CC space, this schema is placed to the right of A.1 on the X-axis and lower than it on the Y-axis (assuming that both schemes are applied to the same entity collection).

However, the coverage of this strategy is also limited: entities with numerical/arbitrary URIs tend to be related to other numerical/arbitrary URIs of the same domain, thus lacking an Infix Profile, unless they are used in multiple domains. Moreover, it cannot cover the cases of entity profiles that lack an Infix Profile (e.g., profiles that solely contain literal values).

A.3. Literal Profile Blocking. The Literal Profile of an entity profile p_{id} - denoted by $LP_{p_{id}}$ - comprises the set of all tokens of the literal values contained in it: $LP_{p_{id}} = \{t_i : \exists n_i, v_i :< n_i, v_i >\in A_{p_{id}} \wedge t_i \in tokenize(v_i) \wedge v_i \notin \mathcal{ID}\}$.

This textual information can be employed in the context of a blocking method that has the following *transformation function*: $f_t(p_{id}) = LP_{p_{id}}$. Blocks are based on the equality of tokens, with each block corresponding to a single token and each entity associated with multiple blocks. For instance, in Figure 3 we can see that the depicted entity will be placed in 18 blocks, one for each token in its Literal Profile. More formally, the *constraint functions* are defined as follows: $f_c^{t_i}(p_{id_1}, p_{id_2}) = ((t_i \in LP_{p_{id_1}}) \wedge (t_i \in LP_{p_{id_2}}))$, where t_i is a token.

Note that this blocking scheme is similar to that presented in [19] with the difference that it does not tokenize the URIs contained in entity profiles as values. It is expected, therefore, to be inapplicable to cases where a profile has no literal values. Still, PC is potentially higher than that of A.1 and A.2, as the only prerequisite for an eligible entity profile is to contain at least one literal value that is shared with other entities. However, its efficiency (i.e., RR) is expected to be lower, due to the higher degree of redundancy: each block corresponds to a single token, with the number of entities sharing a token being typically higher than those sharing an Infix (Infixes normally consist of several tokens concatenated together, and are less common than individual tokens). This results in blocks that are larger, on average, thus reducing the value of CC. Its mapping to the BC-CC space is placed to the right of A.1 on the X-axis and lower than it on the Y-axis (assuming that both schemes are applied to the same entity collection).

4.3 Enhancing Effectiveness: Composite Blocking Schemes

In isolation, the individual atomic blocking schemes are of limited robustness, with their effectiveness depending upon the characteristics of the entity collections at hand. To remedy this situation, we propose the combination of atomic blocking schemes into composite ones. Given that the individual blocking schemes rely on different aspects of entity profiles, they are *complementary*. Thus, the composite blocking schemes derived from their union are expected to exhibit significantly higher robustness, leading to significantly higher PC. This is at the cost of efficiency, however, since the new scheme entails more blocks that are larger in size, due to the common constraint functions (i.e., those stemming from different atomic blocking schemes, but corresponding to the same token or Infix).

In Figure 4, we illustrate the effect of merging atomic blocking schemes into composite ones on the BC-CC space: combining $Method_1$ with $Method_2$ leads to $Method_3$ that has increased BC value (i.e., higher redundancy) and lower CC value (i.e., restricted efficiency), due to the larger - on average - blocks.

In the following paragraphs, we present all four possible combinations of the above atomic schemes and explain the rationale behind them. Note that all of them produce overlapping blocks.

B.1. Complete Infix Blocking. This blocking scheme is derived from the combination of the schemes A.1 and A.2. Thus, the *transformation function* extracts from an entity profile the union of its Infix and its Infix Profile: $f_t(p_{id}) = Infix(id) \cup IP_{p_{id}}$. Blocks are again built on the equivalence of Infixes, with each block corresponding to a single Infix and each entity potentially placed in multiple blocks: $f_c^i(p_{id_1}, p_{id_2}) = ((i = Infix(id_1) \vee i \in IP_{p_{id_1}}) \wedge (i = Infix(id_2) \vee i \in IP_{p_{id_2}})$, where i is an Infix.

Compared to Infix Blocking, it covers profiles with a synthetic identifier (i.e., a blank node or a random URI) and is able to match entities with non-identical Infixes. Compared to Infix Profile Blocking, it applies to entities with empty Infix Profiles which, nevertheless, have an Infix. The only case that this scheme is not applicable is for entities that lack any meaningful URI in their profile; these are entities that have arbitrary, synthetic URIs as ids and are solely associated with identifiers of the same kind as well as with literal values. Most importantly, though, this combination takes advantage of Infixes that originally did not result in blocks, due to their scarcity in the individual blocking schemes (i.e., they appeared in just one profile). As verified in Section 5, this results in significantly higher robustness that brings about higher PC, as well.

B.2. Infix-Literal Profile Blocking. This scheme results from the combination of A.1 with A.3: its *transformation function* represents each entity by the union of its Infix and its Literal Profile: $f_t(p_{id}) = Infix(id) \cup LP_{p_{id}}$, while its *constraint functions* build blocks on the equality of Infixes or tokens: $f_c^i(p_{id_1}, p_{id_2}) = ((i = Infix(id_1) \vee i \in LP_{p_{id_1}}) \wedge (i = Infix(id_2) \vee i \in LP_{p_{id_2}}))$, where i is an Infix and/or a token.

It is worth noting that the merge of these two atomic schemes is more than just the union of the blocks of the individual schemes: some Infixes merely consist of a single token, leading to some constraint functions that are common among both schemes (e.g., the Infix "Hawaii" of the entity in Figure 3 appears as a token of a literal value, as well). Thus, this composite scheme involves blocks common among the atomic ones; these blocks have a larger size than before, entailing more comparisons and resulting in lower efficiency and lower CC values. However, robustness and effectiveness are substantially enhanced: the only profiles that are not covered by this composite scheme are those having a blank node or a random URI as id, while containing no literal values in their set of attribute values. Apparently, this case is highly unlikely.

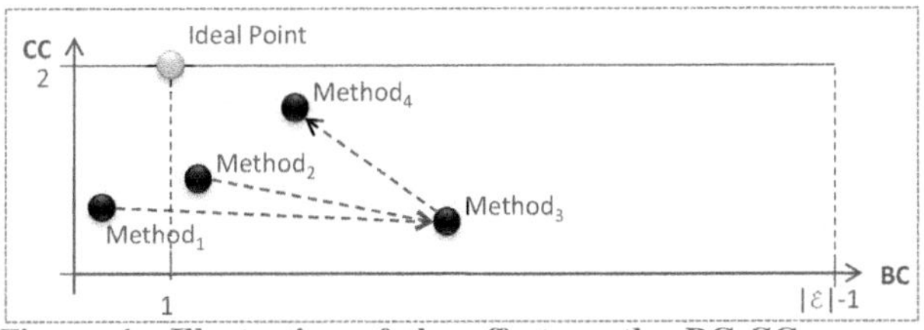

Figure 4: Illustration of the effect on the BC-CC space of two optimization techniques: (i) merging individual blocking schemes ($Method_1$ and $Method_2$) into composite ones ($Method_3$), and (ii) purging the oversized blocks of a blocking technique ($Method_3$) to produce a more efficient one ($Method_4$).

B.3. Infix Profile-Literal Profile Blocking. This scheme is derived from the combination of the schemes A.2 and A.3. Similar to B.2, the *transformation function* extracts from an entity profile the union of its Infix and its Literal profile (i.e., $f_t(p_{id}) = IP_{p_{id}} \cup LP_{p_{id}}$), while the *constraint functions* define blocks on the equality of Infixes or tokens: $f_c^i(p_{id_1}, p_{id_2}) = ((i \in IP_{p_{id_1}} \lor i \in LP_{p_{id_1}}) \land (i \in IP_{p_{id_2}} \lor i \in LP_{p_{id_2}}))$, where i is an Infix and/or a token.

For the reasons explained in B.2, it exhibits higher redundancy (i.e., higher BC value) than the individual blocking schemes it comprises, thus involving higher robustness coupled with higher effectiveness. The main difference between B.2 and B.3 lies in the cases that B.3 does not cover: this scheme does not apply to profiles whose set of attribute values contains solely blank nodes and random URIs.

B.4. Total Description Blocking. This blocking scheme is formed by the combination of all atomic ones. Thus, it represents entities by the Infixes of all URIs contained in their profiles and the tokens of all their literal values: $f_t(p_{id}) = Infix(id) \cup IP_{p_{id}} \cup LP_{p_{id}}$. Blocks are then defined on the equality of tokens or Infixes: $f_c^i(p_{id_1}, p_{id_2}) = ((i = Infix(id_1) \lor i \in IP_{p_{id_1}} \lor i \in LP_{p_{id_1}}) \land (i = Infix(id_2) \lor i \in IP_{p_{id_2}} \lor i \in LP_{p_{id_2}}))$, where i is an Infix and/or a token.

The interplay of all atomic blocking methods leads to the highest robustness among all schemes presented in this paper: this combination fails only in the highly unlikely cases where an entity profile has a non-meaningful identifier as its id and exclusively contains identifiers of this kind in its set of attribute values. This results not only in the highest effectiveness among all methods, but also in the highest BC value: it entails the highest number of blocks, which are also expected to be larger - on average - than the blocks of the other schemes. They entail, therefore, a considerably higher number of comparisons that leads to lower efficiency and lower CC values.

4.4 Enhancing Efficiency: Block Purging

BC and CC are useful not only for assessing the performance of blocking techniques, but also for improving it. In fact, they can be employed in the context of *block purging*, a method introduced in [19] as a way of increasing the efficiency of redundancy-bearing blocking methods. In essence, it is based on the observation that very large blocks entail a high cost (in terms of comparisons), although they have a negligible contribution to Pair Completeness (i.e. it is very unlikely that they contain duplicates that have no other block in common). Based on this observation, Block Purging specifies an upper limit on the size of the blocks that are processed, and discards all blocks that exceed it.

The effect of this approach on the BC-CC space is illustrated in Figure 4 by $Method_3$ and $Method_4$. With the removal of any block, the overall number of block assignments is reduced together with Blocking Cardinality (as its denominator remains stable); thus, the BC-CC mapping of a blocking method moves to the left on the X-axis. On the other hand, CC increases, as the removal of large blocks leads to a more even distribution of block assignments across the remaining collection of blocks. In the general case, therefore, block purging moves the original method ($Method_3$) to the direction of $Method_4$ (i.e., closer to the ideal point (1,2)).

Algorithm 1: Tuning for Block Purging.

```
Input:  B a set of blocks
Output: optimalBlockSize the optimal, maximum block size for block purging
1  B' ← orderBySize(B);
2  blockAssignments ← 0;
3  comparisons ← 0;
4  lastBlockSize ← 2;
5  index ← 0;
6  statistics[] ← {};
7  foreach b_i ∈ B' do
8      if lastBlockSize < b_i.size() then
9          statistics[index].size = lastBlockSize;
10         statistics[index].cc = blockAssignments / comparisons;
11         index++;
12         lastBlockSize ← b_i.size();
13     blockAssignments ← blockAssignments + b_i.size();
14     comparisons ← comparisons + b_i.size()·(b_i.size()−1) / 2;
15 statistics[index].size = lastBlockSize;
16 statistics[index].cc = blockAssignments / comparisons;
17 optimalBlockSize ← lastBlockSize;
18 for i ← statistics.size()-1 to 1 do
19     if statistics[i].cc ≈ statistics[i − 1].cc then
20         optimalBlockSize ← statistics[i].size;
21         break;
22 return optimalBlockSize;
```

The key for successfully applying this technique is the selection of the upper limit on block sizes. A simple method for this task was introduced in [19], but it is crafted for the Clean-Clean case of ER and is not applicable to the Dirty ER we are considering. To replace it, we introduce a novel method for selecting the optimal threshold on the maximum block size that relies on the CC metric. It is based on the following observation: starting with the exclusion of the largest block and going down towards the smaller ones, the value of Comparisons Cardinality slowly increases. This is because the removal of large blocks (i.e., blocks with $|b_i| \gg 2$) decreases its denominator (i.e., number of comparisons - $\sum_{b_i \in B} |b_i| \cdot (|b_i| - 1)/2$) faster than its numerator (i.e., number of block assignments - $\sum_{b_i \in B} |b_i|$). Block purging should stop, therefore, as soon as there is no more increase in the value of CC to be expected; discarding additional blocks would just reduce BC and, consequently, PC, while having a negligible effect - if any - on RR. For this reason, we use the following termination criterion: block purging stops as soon as two consecutive block sizes have the same value for CC.

The outline of our approach to Block Purging is presented in Algorithm 22. Line 1 orders the given collection of blocks B in ascending order of block sizes, and, thus, makes it possible to calculate the Comparisons Cardinality value for each block size with a single pass (Lines 2-19). Lines 15-16 ensure that the last block is also taken into account in the computation of the statistics. Starting from the largest block size, the CC values of consecutive sizes are then compared in Lines 17-22. The procedure is terminated as soon as the CC value remains stable. Apparently, the complexity of our algorithm is dominated by the initial sorting and is equivalent to $O(|B| \log |B|)$, where $|B|$ stands for the size of the given collection of blocks B.

5. EVALUATION

5.1 Setup

Baseline. Previous studies have shown that — in the context of heterogeneous information spaces — existing blocking methods, which rely on schema information, exhibit high efficiency (i.e., very few entities per block), but they suffer from remarkably poor recall (i.e., PC): they place less than half the matching entities into (at least) one common block [19]. In this paper, we do not repeat the comparison experiments to such blocking methods. Instead we use as baseline for our experiments the original attribute-agnostic blocking method of [19], which outperforms previous techniques. It is denoted by **Total Tokenizer** and essentially works as follows: given an entity profile, this blocking scheme tokenizes all the values it contains on their special values and defines blocks on the equality of tokens. The only values that are excluded from this procedure are the URIs that correspond to blank nodes. As stated above, the goal is to prove that the blocking schemes presented in this paper provide a better balance between PC and RR: they maintain blocking effectiveness at equally high levels, while requiring a significantly lower amount of pair-wise entity comparisons.

Performance Metrics. To assess our blocking techniques, we employ the two metrics that have been established in the blocking literature and were introduced in Section 3.1: Pair Completeness and Reduction Ratio. The former estimates the ratio between the true matches that share at least one block and the true matches in the entire data set; the latter measures the reduction in the number of pair-wise comparisons the examined blocking method achieves with respect to the baseline one. Note that we follow the literature [1, 17, 19, 24], and focus on the performance of the blocking methods, thus ignoring the precision of entity matching techniques. The latter is actually out of the scope of this paper, as the proposed schemes can be integrated with any entity comparison method.

Technical Metrics. The second group of metrics we consider elucidates important technical characteristics of blocking methods, providing the grounds for their measured performance. The considered measures are the following: **(i)** *Method Coverage* denotes the portion of the given entities that qualify for the respective blocking method, **(ii)** *Blocks Coverage* expresses the percentage of entities that are placed in at least one block. In conjunction with Method Coverage, it estimates those entities that qualify for the blocking scheme, but share no description item(s) with any other entity[8], **(iii)** *Disk Space* occupied on the hard drive, **(iv)** *Average Block Size* denotes the average entities per block, **(v)** *Number of Blocks* generated by the technique.

The first two measures are indicative of the robustness of a blocking scheme, with higher values corresponding to more robust methods. The remaining ones are related to the efficiency aspects of a method (including storage efficiency), with higher values corresponding to lower efficiency; for example, the larger the blocks of a blocking method are on average, the more comparisons they entail and the lower its efficiency is.

Large-scale Data Set. We evaluated our approaches on the real-world data set of BTC09, the largest one ever used in the context of Entity Resolution. It comprises more than 182 million distinct entities that are described by 1.15 billion RDF statements. They have been crawled from several thousand sources of the Semantic Web, each having its unique characteristics for the format and the quality of the contained information. As a result, BTC09 constitutes a sizeable and representative heterogeneous information space, which is suitable for deriving safe conclusions about the generality of our blocking techniques.

As ground-truth we employed two collections of matching entities: the first one - denoted by **SameAs** - was derived from the explicit `owl:sameAs` statements and encompasses 5.99 million matches of the form $p_i \equiv p_j$ that, in total, involve 8.67 million distinct entities. The second ground-truth set - symbolized as **IFP** - was inferred from the implicit equivalence relationships of the InverseFunctionalProperties[9] and contains $11,553$ matches among $17,990$ distinct entities.

The reason for considering two sources of ground-truth is the bias that is perhaps lurking in the explicit equivalence relationships: it is possible that some of them consist of machine-generated same-as statements, which typically follow specific URI patterns (i.e., they change solely the Prefix and the Suffix of a URI, leaving the Infix intact). This is the case, for instance, with the transformation of Wikipedia URIs to DBPedia ones. To have a better understanding of the general performance and the robustness of our algorithm, we need, therefore, an additional data set that involves a higher variety of equivalence relationships, derived from a rich diversity of sources. The ground-truth set of implicit equivalence relationships (i.e., IFP) serves this need perfectly.

5.2 Blocking Schemes Performance

Technical Metrics. The technical metrics of our thorough experimental comparisons are presented in the left side of Table 1. Regarding Method Coverage, we can see that the atomic blocking schemes individually cover less than 2/3 of all entities, while their combinations have substantially higher coverage - well over 90% in most of the cases. Nevertheless, the coverage of Infix and Infix Profile blocking alone is larger than one would expect. To explain this phenomenon, we investigated the extent to which blank nodes are used as ids, not only for uniquely identifying entities, but also for expressing the associations between entities. We found out that, among all data sources of BTC09, less than a third of their entities (32.61%) have a blank node as an id, and a mere 4.99% of their statements have a blank node as their object. Consequently, blank nodes are completely outweighed by real URIs, and have a restricted impact on the applicability of our method.

The values of Blocks Coverage follow the same pattern as those of Method Coverage: they are slightly lower than 66% for atomic blocking schemes, but significantly higher for the composite ones. It is worth noting that - in almost all the cases - the value of Blocks Coverage is around 2% lower than that of Method Coverage. This means that our blocking schemes place almost all entities that contain the required description item(s) in at least one block. The only exception to this is Infix Blocking: there is a discrepancy of 36% between its Blocks and its Method Coverage. This is caused not only by the arbitrary entity identifiers (i.e., random or numerical URIs), but also by the scarcity of Infixes (i.e., a considerable part of Infixes appears in just one entity identifier, thus not forming a block).

It is interesting to examine why this does not apply to Infix Profile Blocking, as well. A possible reason is the connectivity of the resources contained in BTC09; in fact, it was reported in [18] that 12.55% of the resources appear only as subjects, 30.49% appear solely as objects, while the rest (56.96%) appear both as subjects and objects. This evidence suggests that there are strong connections between the nodes of the RDF graph and, consequently, many relations between the entities of different domains. Therefore, sources with synthetic URIs are connected to other domains that do not necessarily follow the same methodology for generating identifiers. Thus, they pose no serious threat to the robustness of Infix Profile blocking and the blocking schemes built on it.

The results on the efficiency characteristics are quite intuitive:

[8]Note that each block has to contain at least 2 entities.

[9]InverseFunctionalProperties (IFPs) provide a reliable means of discovering *implicit* equivalence relationships in the Semantic Web: *any two resources that share the same value for an IFP are, actually, identical.*

Blocking Scheme	Method Coverage	Blocks Coverage	Disk Space (GB)	Blocks ($\times 10^6$)	Av. Block Size	RR	PC_{IFP} (%)	PC_{SameAs} (%)	BC	CC ($\times 10^{-7}$)
	Technical Metrics					Performance Metrics				
Infix	67.20%	31.32%	13	15.34	3.83	99.98	59.31	49.60	0.32	94.20
Infix Profile	66.17%	64.84%	26	23.59	17.80	95.86	84.19	43.78	2.30	3.92
Literal Profile	55.63%	54.95%	59	17.83	111.39	89.68	94.49	24.51	10.90	7.43
Complete Infix	98.91%	97.25%	33	68.87	8.13	95.77	85.16	87.14	3.07	5.10
Infix-Literal Pr.	91.88%	74.18%	65	27.90	74.07	87.46	96.43	65.67	11.34	6.36
Infix Pr.-Literal Pr.	69.29%	68.13%	75	38.44	62.14	85.30	96.64	52.09	13.11	6.61
Total Description	99.66%	98.90%	83	81.08	31.05	84.96	97.98	91.13	13.82	6.13
Total Tokenizer	100.00%	100.00%	114	31.16	112.45	-	99.32	92.26	19.23	1.35

Table 1: General statistics and performance of the proposed blocking schemes in comparison with the baseline method.

composite blocking schemes have more blocks, which are larger in size (on average) and occupy more disk space. Their efficiency is, therefore, lower than that of the atomic schemes. The baseline method is the least efficient, as it requires more than 25% additional disk space and has the largest average block size. This is a side-effect of its low-granularity, which results in rather frequent blocking units (e.g., most of the URIs contain the token "http"). This also explains why the average size of its blocks is only comparable to that of Literal Profile: they both rely on the same blocking units. However, the latter involves a lower number of tokens and can be combined with the other atomic blocking schemes to produce blocks of smaller - on average - size, thus increasing its efficiency.

Performance Metrics. The actual performance of our blocking schemes is presented on the right side of Table 1. We notice that RR takes values over 85% in all cases (there is no RR value for Total Tokenizer, since it is the baseline against which RR is computed). This means, the Total Tokenizer performs an order of magnitude more comparisons than those required by the other methods. In absolute values, the former involves 2.59×10^{16} comparisons, while the comparisons for our methods range from 6.24×10^{12} (Infix Blocking) to 3.90×10^{15} (Total Description); that is, the required pair-wise comparisons per entity drop from 10^7 to a value between 10^4 and 10^6 (we further reduce these numbers to a significant extent in Section 5.4). The very low efficiency of Total Tokenizer is depicted in its CC value as well: it is the lowest by far, while Infix Blocking has the highest one - almost an order of magnitude higher.

Regarding effectiveness, we can see that - independently of the ground-truth set - PC is quite low for the atomic blocking schemes, but substantially higher for the composite ones. This pattern actually constitutes a strong evidence in favor of merging complementary blocking schemes: their PC is always considerably larger than the maximum value of the individual schemes comprising them. For this reason, the highest PC is achieved by the method that combines all three atomic schemes (i.e., *Total Description*), being lower than Total Tokenizer by just 1%, for both benchmark sets. Note also that there is a clear association between the values of PC and BC, with high BC values conveying high PC ones. This interesting association is analytically discussed in the following section.

Overall, we note that the atomic blocking schemes exhibit the highest levels of efficiency, but suffer from deficient robustness and effectiveness. The composite blocking methods improve on both of these weaknesses, without a significant sacrifice of their efficiency. In fact, the method that encompasses all atomic schemes exhibits similar levels of robustness and effectiveness with Total Tokenizer, while saving almost 85% of all comparisons. Thus, it achieves our goal by having two crucial differences from the baseline: first, it considers the Infix of URIs that appear as attribute values, instead of extracting all tokens from them, and second, it exploits the URIs that are used as entity identifiers, extracting their Infixes, as well.

5.3 BC-CC mapping vs Real Performance

In this section, we experimentally verify that the combination of BC and CC metrics provides a highly accurate estimation of a blocking method's real performance. The values of BC actually exhibit a high correlation with those of PC, while the same applies for CC and RR. Our analysis relies on the *Pearson correlation coefficient* ($\rho_{X,Y}$), a well established measure for estimating the linear dependency between two variables X and Y. It takes values in the interval $[-1, 1]$, and the higher its absolute value is, the stronger the correlation of the given variables is. A value of $|\rho_{X,Y}| = 1$ indicates a completely linear relationship of the form $X = \alpha \cdot Y + \beta$, where $\alpha, \beta \in \mathcal{R}$ and $0 < \alpha$ if $\rho_{X,Y} = 1$, while $\alpha < 0$ if $\rho_{X,Y} = -1$.

Our analysis consists of two parts: first, we measure the correlation between the above metrics with respect to different blocking schemes. We also investigate to which extent the BC and CC metrics can identify the best performing among a set of blocking methods; to this end, we examine the relation between a blocking method's distance from the ideal point of the BC-CC space (i.e., (1,2)) and its deviation from the optimal real performance (i.e., PC=100% and RR=100%). Second, we analyze the same correlations in the context of block purging, i.e., with respect to the same blocking scheme, for various thresholds on the maximum size of the blocks. Our goal is to demonstrate the usefulness of BC and CC for determining the optimal cutting point for this process.

For the first case, Pearson's ρ can be derived directly from the values in the right part of Table 1. We have: $\rho_{PC_{IFP},BC} = 0.84$, $\rho_{PC_{SameAs},BC} = 0.37$, and $\rho_{RR,CC} = 0.63$. We can see that BC accurately predicts the value of PC with respect to IFP, but this applies to a minor extent for the SameAs ground-truth set. In both cases, however, there is a positive correlation between these two metrics, with an average value of $\rho_{P\bar{C},BC} = 0.61$. This is sufficiently high for a good and valuable estimation, given that BC can be easily derived from a simple inspection of the blocks at hand. The same applies to the correlation between CC and RR. We can, thus, deduce that BC and CC can discern the best technique among a set of blocking methods with a relatively high accuracy.

This conclusion is also advocated by the positive correlation between a blocking method's deviation from its optimal performance and its distance from the ideal point of the BC-CC space. To quantify this correlation, we consider the **PC-RR space**: a two-dimensional space defined by PC on the X-axis and RR on the Y-axis. Apparently, the optimal point in this space is (100,100), which corresponds to the perfect blocking efficiency and effectiveness. Based on the numbers of Table 1, the correlation between the distances from the ideal points of the PC-RR and the BC-CC space was found to be $\rho_{IFP} = 0.49$ and $\rho_{SameAs} = 0.45$ with respect to the IFP and the Same-As ground-truth sets, respectively. There is, therefore, an indisputably positive correlation between these distances, which is high enough (0.47 on average) for discerning between the low and the high performing blocking schemes.

To evaluate the functionality of the BC-CC mapping in the context of block purging, we systematically applied various upper limits on the block size of all blocking schemes and estimated the resulting PC and BC values (we ignored the efficiency metrics CC

	$\rho_{PC_{IFP},BC}$	$\rho_{PC_{SameAs},BC}$
Infix	0.99	0.76
Infix Profile	0.97	0.82
Literal Profile	0.67	0.89
Complete Infix	0.97	0.73
Infix-Literal Pr.	0.71	0.67
Infix Pr.-Literal Pr.	0.75	0.66
Total Description	0.77	0.56
Total Tokenizer	0.68	0.93

Table 2: Pearson Correlation between PC and BC.

and RR, since RR is at nearly 100% for all block sizes due to the high reduction). To ensure a large variety of block sizes, we determined the maximum block size according to the following formula: $|b_{i_{max}}| = 10^{\log|\mathcal{E}|/d_i}$, where $|b_{i_{max}}|$ is the maximum block size, $|\mathcal{E}|$ is the size of the input entity collection, and d_i is an integer that takes all values in the interval $[1, 10]$. The outcomes of our analysis are presented in Table 2. The average correlation of BC and PC is $\rho_{\bar{PC}_{IFP},BC} = 0.83$ and $\rho_{\bar{PC}_{SameAs},BC} = 0.73$, with respect to the IFP and to the SameAs ground-truth sets, respectively. On the average case (across both ground-truth sets), it is equal to $\rho_{\bar{PC},BC} = 0.78$. These high values lead to the safe conclusion that the BC metric accurately determines whether a cutting point for block purging has a significantly negative impact on Pair Completeness. In this case, a higher value for the block size threshold is required.

5.4 Block Purging Performance

To check the performance of Algorithm 22, we applied it to all the aforementioned blocking schemes, and the outcomes are presented in Table 3. Note that, instead of RR values, we present the absolute number of pair-wise comparisons, because RR had the maximum value (i.e., 100%) for all blocking schemes. The required number of comparisons actually dropped by four orders of magnitude in all cases (e.g., from 10^{12} to 10^8 for Infix blocking). At the core of this substantial improvement lies the restriction imposed by block purging on the maximum block sizes: from several millions entities they were reduced to several thousands of entities.

Most importantly, though, we can see that block purging achieves a better balance between Pair Completeness and Reduction Ratio: although the latter is greatly enhanced, there is a negligible decrease in the former; the values of PC are lower than in Table 1 by just 1% or 2%, in most of the cases. The only exceptions to this rule are the Infix Profile and the Complete Infix with respect to the IFP, and the Total Tokenizer with respect to the SameAs golden standard. This is a strong indication of limited robustness for the corresponding methods, as their initially high effectiveness extensively depends on their oversized blocks. In complete contrast, Total Description is the only one that retains its PC (i.e., around 90%) for both ground-truth sets, thus constituting the most robust of the proposed blocking schemes. Note also that our experimental results verify the behavior of block purging on the BC-CC space, as demonstrated in Figure 4: the BC values move to the left of the X-axis, while the CC values move higher on the Y-axis.

6. CONCLUSIONS

We introduced novel blocking schemes tailored for heterogeneous data. Individually, they achieve high efficiency, but suffer from low robustness. To enhance it, we combine them into composite, more effective blocking methods and discard the largest of their blocks, thus boosting their efficiency as well. The trade-off between Pair Completeness and Reduction Ratio led to the idea of introducing two blocking scheme assessment metrics (BC and CC), which are easily derived from the external characteristics of a set of blocks. Their values are highly correlated with the actual performance of a blocking method and provide a quite accurate, a priori estimation for it. Our techniques were thoroughly tested on the largest, real-world data collection ever used for this task, and the

	Comp. ($\times 10^{11}$)	PC_{IFP} (%)	PC_{SameAs} (%)	BC	CC ($\times 10^{-4}$)
Infix	0.004	58.85	49.54	0.28	1144.70
Infix Profile	1.62	76.53	41.36	1.42	15.97
Literal Profile	9.37	94.34	18.29	2.90	5.63
Complete Infix	1.69	72.64	86.60	2.14	23.21
Infix-Literal Pr.	8.79	94.48	63.75	3.07	6.38
Infix Pr.-Literal Pr.	12.00	93.57	50.03	4.29	6.52
Total Description	11.64	95.37	89.35	4.96	7.77
Total Tokenizer	15.49	96.79	60.52	4.31	5.07

Table 3: Performance of our Block Purging algorithm for all blocking schemes.

outcomes verified the usefulness of our metrics The main conclusion is that combining Total Description with Block Purging yields a blocking method that excels in all aspects of performance (i.e., robustness, efficiency and effectiveness). In the future, we intend to investigate ways of parallelizing the required pair-wise comparisons, based on the MapReduce paradigm.

Acknowledgments. This work is partly funded by the European Commission under the FP7 EU Project GLOCAL (Contract No. 248984).

References

[1] M. Bilenko, B. Kamath, and R. J. Mooney. Adaptive blocking: Learning to scale up record linkage. In *ICDM*, 2006.

[2] C. Bizer, T. Heath, and T. Berners-Lee. Linked data - the story so far. *Int. J. Semantic Web Inf. Syst.*, 5(3), 2009.

[3] P. Christen. A survey of indexing techniques for scalable record linkage and deduplication. *IEEE Transactions on Knowledge and Data Engineering*, 2011.

[4] W. W. Cohen, P. D. Ravikumar, and S. E. Fienberg. A comparison of string distance metrics for name-matching tasks. In *IIWeb*, 2003.

[5] X. Dong, A. Halevy, and J. Madhavan. Reference reconciliation in complex information spaces. In *SIGMOD*, 2005.

[6] A. K. Elmagarmid, P. G. Ipeirotis, and V. S. Verykios. Duplicate record detection: A survey. *TKDE*, 19(1), 2007.

[7] L. Gravano, P. Ipeirotis, H. Jagadish, N. Koudas, S. Muthukrishnan, and D. Srivastava. Approximate string joins in a database (almost) for free. In *VLDB*, 2001.

[8] A. Y. Halevy, M. J. Franklin, and D. Maier. Principles of dataspace systems. In *PODS*, 2006.

[9] O. Hassanzadeh, A. Kementsietsidis, L. Lim, R. J. Miller, and M. Wang. A framework for semantic link discovery over relational data. In *CIKM*, 2009.

[10] M. A. Hernández and S. J. Stolfo. The merge/purge problem for large databases. In *SIGMOD Conference*, 1995.

[11] E. Ioannou, W. Nejdl, C. Niederée, and Y. Velegrakis. On-the-fly entity-aware query processing in the presence of linkage. *PVLDB*, 3(1), 2010.

[12] I. Jacobs and N. Walsh. Architecture of the world wide web, volume one. *W3C Recommendation*, December 2004.

[13] H. Kim and D. Lee. HARRA: fast iterative hashed record linkage for large-scale data collections. In *EDBT*, 2010.

[14] C. Li, L. Jin, and S. Mehrotra. Supporting efficient record linkage for large data sets using mapping techniques. *WWW Journal*, 9(4), 2006.

[15] J. Madhavan, S. Cohen, X. Dong, A. Halevy, S. Jeffery, D. Ko, and C. Yu. Web-scale data integration: You can afford to pay as you go. In *CIDR*, 2007.

[16] A. McCallum, K. Nigam, and L. H. Ungar. Efficient clustering of high-dimensional data sets with application to reference matching. In *KDD*, 2000.

[17] M. Michelson and C. A. Knoblock. Learning blocking schemes for record linkage. In *AAAI*, 2006.

[18] G. Papadakis, G. Demartini, P. Kärger, and P. Fankhauser. The missing links: Discovering hidden same-as links among a billion of triples. In *iiWAS*, 2010.

[19] G. Papadakis, E. Ioannou, C. Niederée, and P. Fankhauser. Efficient entity resolution for large heterogeneous information spaces. In *WSDM*, 2011.

[20] G. Papadakis, E. Ioannou, C. Niederée, T. Palpanas, and W. Nejdl. Eliminating the redundancy in blocking-based entity resolution methods. In *JCDL*, pages 85–94, 2011.

[21] G. Papadakis, E. Ioannou, C. Niederée, T. Palpanas, and W. Nejdl. To compare or not to compare: making entity resolution more efficient. In *SWIM Workshop, co-located with SIGMOD*, 2011.

[22] V. Rastogi, N. N. Dalvi, and M. N. Garofalakis. Large-scale collective entity matching. *PVLDB*, 4(4), 2011.

[23] S. Tejada, C. A. Knoblock, and S. Minton. Learning domain-independent string transformation weights for high accuracy object identification. In *KDD*, 2002.

[24] T. Vries, H. Ke, S. Chawla, and P. Christen. Robust record linkage blocking using suffix arrays. In *CIKM*, 2009.

[25] S. E. Whang, D. Menestrina, G. Koutrika, M. Theobald, and H. Garcia-Molina. Entity resolution with iterative blocking. In *SIGMOD Conference*, 2009.

[26] M. Zhong, M. Liu, and Q. Chen. Modeling heterogeneous data in dataspace. In *IRI*, 2008.

Mining Contrastive Opinions on Political Texts using Cross-Perspective Topic Model

Yi Fang†, Luo Si†, Naveen Somasundaram†, Zhengtao Yu‡
† Department of Computer Science, Purdue University, West Lafayette, IN 47907, USA
‡ Kunming University of Science and Technology, Kunming, China
†{fangy, lsi, nsomasun}@cs.purdue.edu; ‡ztyu@bit.edu.cn

ABSTRACT

This paper presents a novel opinion mining research problem, which is called Contrastive Opinion Modeling (COM). Given any query topic and a set of text collections from multiple perspectives, the task of COM is to present the opinions of the individual perspectives on the topic, and furthermore to quantify their difference. This general problem subsumes many interesting applications, including opinion summarization and forecasting, government intelligence and cross-cultural studies. We propose a novel unsupervised topic model for contrastive opinion modeling. It simulates the generative process of how opinion words occur in the documents of different collections. The ad hoc opinion search process can be efficiently accomplished based on the learned parameters in the model. The difference of perspectives can be quantified in a principled way by the Jensen-Shannon divergence among the individual topic-opinion distributions. An extensive set of experiments have been conducted to evaluate the proposed model on two datasets in the political domain: 1) statement records of U.S. senators; 2) world news reports from three representative media in U.S., China and India, respectively. The experimental results with both qualitative and quantitative analysis have shown the effectiveness of the proposed model.

Categories and Subject Descriptors

H.3.3 [**Information Storage and Retrieval**]: Information Search and Retrieval—*Retrieval models*; G.3 [**Probability and Statistics**]: Probabilistic algorithms; I.2.7 [**Artificial Intelligence**]: Natural Language Processing—*Text analysis*

General Terms

Algorithms, Experimentation

Keywords

contrastive opinions, opinion mining, topic modeling, opinion retrieval

Permission to make digital or hard copies of all or part of this work for personal or classroom use is granted without fee provided that copies are not made or distributed for profit or commercial advantage and that copies bear this notice and the full citation on the first page. To copy otherwise, to republish, to post on servers or to redistribute to lists, requires prior specific permission and/or a fee.
WSDM'12, February 8–12, 2012, Seattle, Washington, USA.
Copyright 2012 ACM 978-1-4503-0747-5/12/02 ...$10.00.

1. INTRODUCTION

Opinion mining is concerned with extracting and analyzing judgments on various aspects of given items from a set of text documents. It is an important task in information retrieval and data mining as it aims at finding subjective information, which may be more relevant to users than factual information in many applications. While there has been much research in opinion mining, most of them focus on analyzing opinions at the word-level, sentence-level or document-level. This paper studies a novel opinion mining problem which examines opinions at the collection-level with each text collection coming from a different perspective. We refer to the task as Contrastive Opinion Modeling (COM): given any query topic and a set of text collections from multiple perspectives, the task is to demonstrate the difference among the perspectives' opinions on the topic. Specifically, COM discovers the common topics across all the perspectives. For each discovered topic or any ad hoc query topic, the task involves: 1) presenting the opinions from each perspective; 2) quantifying their difference. COM models opinions against a whole collection/perspective which potentially consists of a large number of documents. Therefore, it can answer a wide range of opinion analysis requests about the perspective.

There exists much work on opinion retrieval such as the subtask in TREC Blog track [23]. In the TREC task, a set of opinionated documents are returned and users often have to go through the documents to look for the opinions expressed by the perspective of interest. In COM, opinions (in the form of opinion words) are directly returned in response to the user query. For example, it can address a user request like "what are the respective opinions of U.S., China and India (e.g., from news agencies) on *Dalai Lama* and how much difference among them?". To answer this request, the opinion words are returned like "nonviolent" for U.S., "rebellious" for China and "Holy" for India, and a diversity score is also presented so that users can clearly know the degree of discordance among the perspectives. Thus, COM can provide more direct opinion search than the existing work.

Furthermore, a lot of current opinion mining work focuses on mining review data and solving classification problems. As we go beyond product reviews, only knowing sentiment orientations such as positive, negative and neutral is not enough in many cases. This is especially true in the domain of politics where the wording is often sensitive. For example, with respect to healthcare reform in U.S., a Republican might often say "we want responsible healthcare reform based on private insurance"[1], while a Democrat might of-

[1]http://www.gop.gov/solutions/healthcare

ten say "we want universal healthcare reform with a public government-run health insurance agency"[2]. Both statements can be viewed as positive on healthcare reform in general, but the opinion words "responsible" and "private" vs "universal" and "public" reflect their huge difference on the issue. Therefore, in COM, the opinions of interest are represented by opinion words which are directly returned to users.

To tackle the task of contrastive opinion modeling, we propose a novel topic model, called Cross-Perspective Topic (CPT) model. The model simulates the generative process of how opinion words appear in the documents. It not only discovers topics but also models the corresponding opinions across multiple perspectives. In CPT, the generative process of opinion words are separated from the generative process of topic words. As a result, besides the word distribution of each topic, we can obtain the opinion distribution for each topic as well. These distributions manifest the associations between topics and opinions, and enable us to accomplish a variety of opining mining tasks including COM. Our contributions in this paper can be summarized as follows:

1. We define and study a novel opinion mining task: contrastive opinion modeling, which aims to directly find the opinions of multiple perspectives with respect to a given topic and quantify their difference on the topic.

2. We propose a fully unsupervised topic model requiring no labeled data for COM. The proposed model is estimated by the Gibbs Sampling algorithm. The opinions on any ad hoc query can be efficiently determined based on the learned parameters.

3. Based on the proposed model, we define a diversity metric of multiple perspectives on a given topic by the Jensen-Shannon divergence among the individual topic-opinion distributions.

4. We conduct an extensive set of experiments with both qualitative and quantitative evaluations on two datasets in the political domain: 1) statement records of U.S. senators; 2) world news reports from three representative media in U.S., China and India, respectively.

2. RELATED WORK

Opinion mining and sentiment analysis have been extensively studied in the recent years. For a general survey, please refer to [24]. The early work focused on identifying the polarity of opinions at the word level [9], at the sentence level [13] and at the document level [25]. These methods do not consider the dependence of opinions on topics.

In [11], topicality and polarity are first combined together to form the notion of opinion retrieval, i.e., to find opinionated documents about a given topic. One early ranking formula is introduced in [6] as the cross entropy of topics and sentiments under a generative model. In 2006, the Text REtrieval Conference (TREC) introduced a Blog Track with a major task of opinion retrieval [23]. An opinion retrieval system is required to locate blog documents expressing opinions. The opinion retrieval task has been approached as a two-stage task: first, retrieving topically relevant documents, and then reranking the documents by the opinion scores. One popular method to identify opinionated content is by matching the documents with a sentiment word dictionary and calculating term frequency [38]. There are also some interesting work on modeling the topic and sentiment of documents in a unified way [37]. The task of opinion retrieval here is essentially a document retrieval process, without opinions directly returned in response to a search request. Similar to the TREC effort, NTCIR launched the Opinion Analysis Task [29] in 2007 with multilingual testbeds in Chinese, Japanese, and English. One subtask involves detection of opinionated sentences and opinion fragments within opinionated sentences, which is closer to our task while we directly target on opinion words.

Another body of related research is around feature based opinion mining which identifies opinions about the features or attributes of a product instead of giving an overall evaluation. The early representative work is the association rule mining based method [10], and template extraction based method [28]. However, these product opinion features are highly dependent on the training data sets, and thus the methods are not flexible to deal with ad hoc queries and topics. The same problem is shared with [35]. Our work finds the underlying topics (equivalent to features) automatically through topic models and can be applied to ad hoc queries.

Latent Dirichlet Allocation (LDA) [2] is one of the earliest topic models and many variants of LDA have been proposed. Among them, the Correspondence Latent Dirichlet Allocation (corrLDA) model [1] resembles our model in spirit. However, corrLDA models the joint distribution of images (with Gaussian distribution) and their annotations (with multinomial distribution), while our model targets on the generative process of opinions (with multinomial distributions over both opinions and topic words). Furthermore, our model differentiates the perspectives of documents. Several topic models have been proposed for opinion mining. Topic-Sentiment Model [22] calculates sentiment coverage of documents by jointly modeling the mixture of topics and sentiment predictions. Similarly, the Joint Sentiment Topic model [16] is proposed and can directly predict the sentiment orientation at the document level. Considering the hierarchy structure between objects and their associated aspects, the Multi-Grain Latent Dirichlet Allocation model [32] was proposed to find ratable aspects from global topics. They later proposed Multi-Aspect Sentiment model [31] which summarizes sentiment texts by aggregating on each ratable aspects. Recently, the Aspect and Sentiment Unification Model [12] is proposed to model sentiments toward different aspects of an entity. The major difference of all the above work from ours is that the existing work does not retrieve opinion words on ad hoc queries. In addition, they do not model contrastive opinions and are not able to quantify the difference between perspectives.

On the other hand, current opinion mining work mostly focuses on mining product review data [5], because of the wide availability of review data and their relatively obvious sentiment orientations such as good, bad and so on. In this paper, we move beyond the review data and target on the political domain where merely identifying the opinion polarity is not sufficient. In the recent years, political data are increasingly available to the public from a wide range of sources such as political blogs, news media, user comments,

[2]http://en.wikipedia.org/wiki/Public_health_insurance_option

and the Open Government Data Initiative[3]. The emerging political data open new opportunities as well as unique challenges for opinion mining and sentiment analysis, which results in an increased interest in the area. For example, in [30] and [4], they study the language and ideology issues on congressional speeches by investigating the contributions of words on ideology. In [34], topic models are proposed to model the discussions in online political blogs and predicts responses to the blog posts. In [3], the opinion scoring models are constructed to extract statements which best express opinionists' standpoints on certain topics. In [18, 19], statistical models are proposed to identify the political perspective of a document or a collection. All the above works do not either generalize to ad hoc query topics nor model contrastive opinions.

There are several studies conducted on comparing texts or opinions. In [20], a system is presented for analyzing and comparing consumer opinions of competing products. In [15], a weakly-supervised bootstrapping method is proposed to identify comparative questions and entities. A probabilistic model for comparing text collections was previously introduced in [36] for a problem called comparative text mining. Given news articles from different sources (about the same event), the model can extract what is common to all the sources and what is unique to one specific source. The model is extended in [26] to detect cultural differences from people's experiences in various countries. In [14] and [27], they tackle the problem of contrastive summarization, which jointly generates summaries for two entities in order to highlight their differences. However, the above works do not quantify the differences, which makes the differences not measurable or comparable among multiple requests. Moreover, they cannot deal with ad hoc queries.

3. CROSS-PERSPECTIVE TOPIC MODEL

Latent Dirichlet Allocation (LDA) [2] is one of the most popular topic models based upon the assumption that documents are mixture of topics, where a topic is a probability distribution over words. LDA is a powerful tool for topic modeling, but it is not well fitted for opinion modeling. A topic in LDA not only contains the words that describe the topic, but also the words that express the opinions about the topic. In other words, LDA does not differentiate opinion words from topic words, which makes both opinions and topics obscure for opinion mining. The problem is even exacerbated when opinions come from multiple different perspectives. In this case, a standard LDA will have severe limitations because it does not directly model the opinions and thus different opinions could be mixed together in the same topics.

In this section, we introduce the Cross-Perspective Topic (CPT) model for contrastive opinion modeling. This model directly depicts how opinions are generated in the documents of different perspectives. In CPT, the opinion generation process is separated from the topic term generation process. We assume that topics are expressed through noun words in the documents, and opinions are conveyed through adjective, verb and adverb words. Section 4.2 gives a detailed description of how to extract the opinion words and topic words from the documents.

The imaginary generative process of the opinions in a document is: a person first chooses a topic based on the document, and then she selects a topic word based on the topic. After choosing all the topic words in the document, she selects a topic to express the opinions. The choice of the topic for a opinion word is based on the actual frequency of the topic occurring in the document. Under this topic, she then selects a opinion word based on her perspective. In this model, it is assumed that topics are shared among all the documents, regardless the perspective of the document. Therefore, the topic words are drawn from the shared topic-word distribution. On the other hand, the opinions from different perspective could be different. Thus, the opinion words are drawn from the topic-opinion distribution conditioned on the perspective. Specifically, the topic word w is modeled by a shared LDA across perspectives. The opinion word o is drawn conditioned on the topic x which is uniformly sampled from the topics learned from the topic words in document d. For simplicity of presentation, we only consider two perspectives, but the model can be straightforwardly generalized to more perspectives. The index of the perspective is denoted by the superscript of the variable instance (e.g., w^1 is a topic word in perspective/collection C^1). The generative process in CPT can be described as follows.

1. Draw a perspective-independent multinomial topic word distribution ϕ from Dirichlet(β) for each topic z
2. Draw a perspective-specific multinomial opinion word distribution ϕ_o^i from Dirichlet(β_o^i) for each topic z^i for the perspective C^i
3. For each document d, choose a topic mixture θ from Dirichlet(α)
4. For each topic word w in d
   (a) Draw a topic z from Multinomial(θ)
   (b) Draw a word w from Multinomial(ϕ) conditional on z
5. For each opinion word o in $d \in C^i$,
   (a) draw a topic x^i from Uniform($z_{w_1}, z_{w_2}, \ldots\ldots, z_{w_{N_{t,d}}}$)
   (b) draw a opinion word o^i from Multinomial(ϕ_o^i) conditional on x^i

The graphical model corresponding to this process is shown in Figure 1 with the notations summarized in Table 1. The dashed line from θ to z_2 means that a document can only

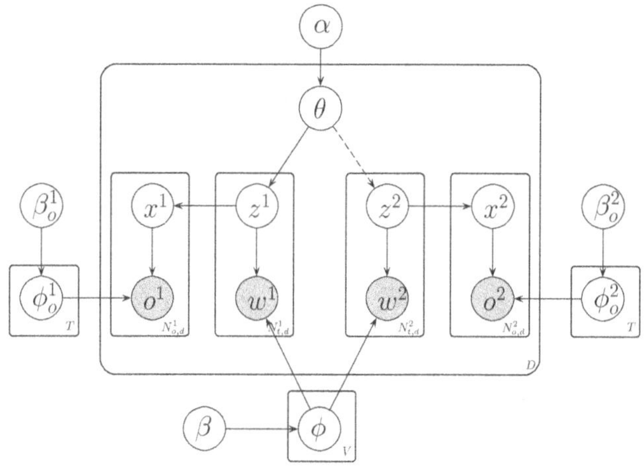

Figure 1: The plate notation of the Cross-Perspective Topic model. The shaded nodes are observed variables.

[3]http://www.data.gov and http://data.gov.uk

come from a single perspective/collection (either C^1 or C^2 in this figure).

3.1 Parameter Estimation

The CPT model has four parameters to estimate: i.e., the document-topic distribution θ, the topic-word distribution ϕ, and the topic-opinion distributions ϕ^1 and ϕ^2. Several methods have been developed for estimating the parameters in LDA, such as Gibbs sampling [8] and variational EM [2]. We employ Gibbs sampling in this paper, because it is comparable in speed to other estimation methods and it approximates a global maximum (whereas EM algorithms may only converge to a local maximum).

Gibbs sampling is a type of Markov chain Monte Carlo algorithm. In a Gibbs sampler, one iteratively samples new assignments of hidden variables by drawing from the distributions conditioned on the previous state of the model. In the Gibbs Sampling procedure of CPT, additional Markov chains are introduced for simulating the opinion generation. We derive the Gibbs sampling equations for our model as follows. The major notations used in the following equations are explained in Table 1.

- Sampling equation of the topic variable z for each topic word w_i:

$$p(z_i = k|w_i = v, \boldsymbol{z}_{-i}, \boldsymbol{w}_{-i}, \alpha, \beta)$$
$$\propto \frac{n_{kd,-i} + \alpha}{\sum_{k=1}^{K} n_{kd,-i} + K\alpha} \times \frac{n_{vk} + \beta}{\sum_{v=1}^{V} n_{vk} + V\beta}$$

- Sampling equation of the opinion topic variable x^1 in the perspective C^1 (the similar equation can be derived for C^2):

$$p(x_i^1 = s|o_i = r, \boldsymbol{x}_{-i}^1, \boldsymbol{o}_{-i}, \beta, \beta_o)$$
$$\propto \frac{n_{rs,-i} + \beta_o^1}{\sum_{r=1}^{T} n_{rs,-i} + T\beta_o^1} \times \frac{n_{sd}}{N_{t,d}}$$

After a set of sampling processes based on the posterior distributions calculated with the above equations, we can estimate the four parameters for any single sample using the following equations:

$$\theta_{kd} = \frac{n_{kd,-i} + \alpha}{\sum_{k=1}^{K} n_{kd,-i} + K\alpha}, \qquad \phi_{vk} = \frac{n_{vk} + \beta}{\sum_{v=1}^{V} n_{vk} + V\beta}$$
$$\phi_{o,rs}^1 = \frac{n_{o,rs} + \beta_o^1}{\sum_{r=1}^{T} n_{o,rs} + T\beta_o^1}, \qquad \phi_{o,rs}^2 = \frac{n_{o,rs} + \beta_o^2}{\sum_{r=1}^{T} n_{o,rs} + T\beta_o^2}$$

3.2 Inference for Contrastive Opinion Modeling

The CPT model estimates soft associations between latent topics and observed opinions across different perspectives. These associations are the basis for a number of operations relevant to opinion mining. In this subsection, we present methods to tackle the contrastive opinion modeling problem by utilizing the estimated parameters in the model.

As shown in Introduction, the ad hoc opinion search task in COM is to present the most relevant opinion words to users with respect to a given query topic (and a particular

Table 1: Notations in the Cross-Perspective Topic model

d, v, r, k, s	Instance of a variable: d for document, v for topic word, r for opinion, k for topic of topic word, s for topic of opinion word
D, K	Number of documents and topics
V, T	Size of topic word vocabulary and opinion word vocabulary
$\boldsymbol{w}_{-i}$, $\boldsymbol{z}_{-i}$, $\boldsymbol{o}_{-i}$	The vector values of $\boldsymbol{w}$, $\boldsymbol{z}_i$ and $\boldsymbol{o}_i$ on all the other dimensions except i
$N_{t,d}$	Number of topic words in document d
$N_{o,d}$	Number of opinion words in document d
$n_{kd,-i}$	Number of times topic k has occurred in document d, except the current instance
$n_{vk,-i}$	Number of times word v is assigned to topic k, without counting the current instance
$n_{rs,-i}$	Number of times opinion r is assigned to topic s, without counting the current instance
n_{sd}	Number of times topic s occurs in document d
θ	$D \times K$ matrix for document-topic distribution
ϕ	$K \times V$ matrix for topic-word distribution
ϕ_o^1, ϕ_o^2	$K \times T$ matrices for topic-opinion distribution

perspective C^i). Based on the estimated CPT model, this can be done by calculating a predictive likelihood $p(o = r|q, C^i)$ that the opinion word r could be generated by the query q as follows:

$$\begin{aligned} p(o = r|q, C^i) &= \sum_{k=1}^{K} p(o = r|z = k)p(z = k|q) \\ &= \sum_{k=1}^{K} p(o = r|z = k)\frac{p(q|z = k)p(z = k)}{p(q)} \\ &\propto \sum_{k=1}^{K} \phi_{o,rk}^i \phi_{qk} n_k \end{aligned} \quad (1)$$

In the above derivation, the Bayes' rule is used, $p(q)$ is constant for the same query, and the unconditional topic probability $p(z = k) \propto n_k$, where n_k is the perspective-wide total number of words associated with topic k. $\phi_{o,rk}^i$ and ϕ_{qk} are topic-opinion distribution and topic-word distribution, respectively, which are the parameters estimated in the CPT training process. The opinion words are then ranked according to the descending order of $p(o = r|q, C^i)$ in response to query q. Intuitively, Eqn. (1) is a weighted inner product between two vectors that penalizes weak topics. Moreover, it is worth noticing that $\phi_{o,rk}^i$, ϕ_{qk} and n_k are all computed offline, which makes the opinion search process very efficient.

As discussed in Section 1, another important aspect of contrastive opinion modeling is to quantify the difference between different perspectives' stance on the topic. In fact, $p(o = r|q, C^1)$ provides the basis for accomplishing the task, because $p(o = r|q, C^1)$ is essentially the probability that perspective C^1 uses the word r to express her opinions on the issue q. The perspectives with similar opinions will have similar $p(o|q)$ and the perspectives with contrary opinions will have very different $p(o|q)$. Therefore, we can compare the distributions of different perspectives, i.e., $p(o|q, C^1)$ vs $p(o|q, C^2)$, to find out their difference.

A natural and well studied "distance" between distributions is the Kullback-Leibler (KL) divergence. However, the KL-divergence suffers from two drawbacks: 1) it is not symmetric in its arguments and 2) it does not naturally generalize to measuring the divergence among more than two distributions. We instead employ the related Jensen-Shannon divergence [17]. Formally, we define a diversity metric between multiple perspectives on a topic by the Jensen-Shannon divergence. Given a set of query-opinion distributions $\{p(o^1|q), ..., p(o^m|q)\}$ from m perspectives, let $\bar{p}$ be the average (centroid) of these distributions. The Jensen-Shannon divergence JS among these distributions is then defined as the average of the KL-divergences of each distribution to this average distribution as follows:

$$JS(C^1, ..., C^m) = \frac{1}{m}\sum_{j=1}^{m} KL\Big(p(o^j|q)||\bar{p}\Big)$$

where

$$KL\Big(p(o^j|q)||\bar{p}\Big) = \sum_{o=1}^{T} p(o^j|q)\log\frac{p(o^j|q)}{\bar{p}}$$

$$\bar{p} = \frac{1}{m}\sum_{j=1}^{m} p(o^j|q)$$

4. EXPERIMENTAL SETUP

4.1 Data Collections

We create two datasets for the evaluation of the proposed model. The first dataset contains the statement records of U.S. senators crawled from the Project Vote Smart[4] website. These statement records present the political stances of senators. The second dataset includes the international headline news published in New York Times[5], Xinhua News[6] and The Hindu[7] during the period of January 2009 - December 2010. The three news agencies are the influential media in US, China, and India, respectively, and usually express representative opinions for these three countries. These world news are all in English and are reported around the same period. The topics covered are thus expected to be largely overlapped. Both datasets were automatically tokenized and sentence split. Table 2 gives detailed statistics of the collections. Before applying the topic models we removed punctuation and also removed stop words using the standard list of stop words[8] [9].

The CPT model has four Dirichlet hyper parameters α, β, β^1 and β^2. Previous research found that these hype parameters only affect the convergence of Gibbs sampling but not much the output results [8]. We fix them to $\alpha = 50/K$ and $\beta = \beta^1 = \beta^2 = 0.02$ according to [8] for all the experiments.

4.2 Opinion Word Extraction

We treat all the nouns in the documents as the topic words. For the opinion words, we use the adjectives, verbs and adverbs that only appear in the opinion sentences, because these words are more likely to convey the opinions. To judge whether a sentence expresses an opinion or not, we choose the opinion clues as basic criteria. Opinion clues are used in [7] to extract opinion sentences from blog pages and are also used in [3] to extract statements which best express opinionists' standpoints on certain topics. Following these work, we use the rule-based method to define opinion clues. More details can be found in [7, 3]. In addition, we also augment the opinion clues by adding their synonyms through WordNet[10] and those opinion words included in MPQA Opinion Corpus[11] [33]. To classify tokens into nouns, adjectives, verbs and adverbs, we use the Part-of-Speech tagging function provided by the MontyLingua Python library[12].

4.3 Research Questions

An extensive set of experiments are designed to address the following questions of the proposed research:

- Can the CPT model effectively discover the shared topics across multiple perspectives and accurately capture the opinions expressed by different perspectives on the topics? (Section 5.2)
- Can CPT have improved predictive performance over other methods for opinion modeling? (Section 5.1.1)
- Can CPT effectively present opinion words for ad hoc queries? (Section 5.1.2)
- Can the diversity metric derived from the learned model parameters characterize the difference of multiple perspectives? (Section 5.2.1)

5. EXPERIMENTS

In this section we present both quantitative and qualitative experiments on the two testbeds. For the quantitative evaluation, we show that CPT performs substantially better than the baseline methods. For the qualitative analysis we show that the opinions inferred by CPT do accurately correspond to their perspectives on the topics.

5.1 Quantitative Evaluation

5.1.1 Opinion Perplexity

In this experiment, we use perplexity as the criterion for model evaluation. Perplexity is a quantitative measure for comparing language models and is often used to compare the predictive performance of topic models [8]. The value of perplexity reflects the ability of a model to generalize to unseen data. A lower perplexity score indicates better generalization performance. In our case, perplexity reflects the ability of a model to predict opinion words for new unseen documents. The perplexity is algebraically equivalent to the inverse of the geometric mean of per-word (per-opinion word in our case) likelihood. Formally, the perplexity for a set of test documents D_{test} is calculated as follows:

$$perplexity(D_{test}) = \exp - \frac{\sum_{d=1}^{|D_{test}|}\log\left(p(\mathbf{o}_d)\right)}{\sum_{d=1}^{|D_{test}|} N_{o,d}} \quad (2)$$

[4]http://www.votesmart.org
[5]http://www.nytimes.com/pages/world
[6]http://www.xinhuanet.com/english2010/world
[7]http://www.thehindu.com/news/international
[8]http://ir.dcs.gla.ac.uk/resources/linguistic_utils/stop_words
[9]We removed the stop words after extracting the opinion sentences in Section 4.2 because some stop words are indicative opinion clues such as "should" and "must"

[10]http://wordnet.princeton.edu
[11]http://www.cs.pitt.edu/mpqa/databaserelease
[12]http://web.media.mit.edu/hugo/montylingua/index.html

Table 2: Statistics of the Senate and News testbeds

	Senate			News			
	Republican	Democrat	Total	NYT	Xinhua	Hindu	Total
Number of documents	4,097	9,876	13,973	8,225	4,177	3,731	16,133
Number of sentences	137,688	285,804	423,492	219,766	48,111	57,513	325,390
Number of words	3,358,239	7,340,255	10,698,494	5,753,693	1,715,817	599,222	7,868,732
Number of topic words	697,003	1,546,911	2,243,914	1,185,518	396,464	125,804	1,707,786
Number of opinion words	768,367	347,709	1,116,076	573,560	200,546	158,176	932,282

Table 3: 20 ad hoc queries for each testbed

Senate	News
immigration, Iraq war, abortion, healthcare, education, veteran, agriculture, censorship, drugs, taxes, stem cell, minimum wage, trade, financial market, climate change, guns, death penalty, judges, prayer, affirmative action	Dalai Lama, Kashmir, Wikileaks, nuclear weapon, iphone, climate change, terrorism, Haiti earthquake, Iran, WTO, Xiaobo Liu, Islam, corruption, Google, energy, communist, education, censorship, population control, globalization

where

$$p(\boldsymbol{o}_d) = \prod_{i=1}^{N_{o,d}} \sum_{k=1}^{K} p(o_i|z_i = k)p(z_i = k|d) \quad (3)$$

In the above equation $\boldsymbol{o}_d$ is the set of opinion words appearing in the test document d. The probability $p(o_i|z_i = k)$ is learned from the training process, and $p(z_i = k|d)$ is inferred from a Gibbs Sampling process on the test data based on the parameters learned from training data. We randomly select 20% of the documents as a held-out test data and train the model on the remaining 80%.

In topic models, we need to select the number of topics. A range of 50 to 300 topics is typically used in the literature. 50 topics are often used for relatively small collections and 300 for large collections. We test the perplexity of the trained model on the test data for different topic numbers K. Figure 2 shows the perplexities in five different settings of K for the Senate dataset. We can see that in general the perplexity scores for all the settings decrease over the iterations. The algorithm tends to converge after about 100 iterations. Along the iterations, larger topic number usually leads to smaller perplexity value, indicating a better prediction performance. This is due to the fact that the increased topic number reduces the uncertainty in training. The effect of increase in topic number on perplexity value gets smaller when the topic number gets larger. When the topic number set to 160, the perplexity value increases. Therefore, we set the topic number $K = 120$ which leads to a near-minimum perplexity. The topic number selection process for the News dataset is similar and the results are also shown in Figure 2.

In this subsection, we compare CPT with LDA and corrLDA on the metric of perplexity. In the experiments, we adapt corrLDA to opinion modeling by changing the Gaussian distribution over image features to multinomial distribution over topic words. The Gibbs sampling procedure can be similarly derived. As discussed in Section 3, in LDA, topic words and opinion words are mixed together and generated from a single distribution. Therefore, it is not an appropriate comparison with CPT if we use $p(o)$ in LDA to calculate the perplexity (because $\sum_o p(o) < 1$). Instead, we train a LDA model only on the opinion words, which make it use the same opinion word vocabulary with CPT.

Figure 3 plots the perplexity results for each model over different topic numbers. The iteration numbers for both models are set to 120. From the plots, we can see that CPT achieves the minimum perplexity on both testbeds among the three models. When the number of topics is small, CPT and corrLDA yield similar performance. When K gets large, the gap between CPT and corrLDA is generally widened. These results may be explained by the fact that corrLDA does not differentiate the perspectives of documents while CPT does. In consequence, when finer granularity of topics is present, CPT can yield better predicative performance than corrLDA because opinions for a more focused topic are generally more homogeneous. Furthermore, CPT and corrLDA seem less affected by the topic number. In fact, CPT and corrLDA shows consistent performance in a wide range of topic numbers from 100 to 200. In addition, on both datasets, LDA achieves its minimum with a smaller topic number than CPT and corrLDA. This may be explained by the fact the topics in LDA derived from the opinion words while the topics in CPT and corrLDA come from the topic words. There are more topic words than opinion words (as shown in Table 2), which probably results in more heterogeneous topics in CPT and corrLDA.

5.1.2 Ad hoc Queries

In this subsection, we conduct quantitative experiments to evaluate the retrieval performance of CPT on ad hoc query topics. Table 3 shows the 20 ad hoc queries for each testbed. These queries are chosen based on several knowledge sources[13] and they are perceived to have varied degree of different stances among the perspectives. When selecting these queries, we did not know what topics would be learned from the model. For each query, the model returns a ranked list of opinion words for each perspective. The results are judged by two people who are familiar with the query topics. A binary judgment (i.e. "relevant" or "not relevant") is made for each opinion word against the query topic. The evaluation metrics are Precision at 5 (P@5), Precision at 10 (P@10) Precision at 20 (P@20), Mean Reciprocal Rank (MRR), and normalized Discounted Cumulative Gain at 20 (nDCG@20).

In Table 4, we compare the models with and without ap-

[13]http://www.americanpolitics.com/030499dictionary.html http://www.diffen.com/difference/Democrat_vs_Republican http://www.cfr.org/india/india-china-united-states-delicate-balance/p9962

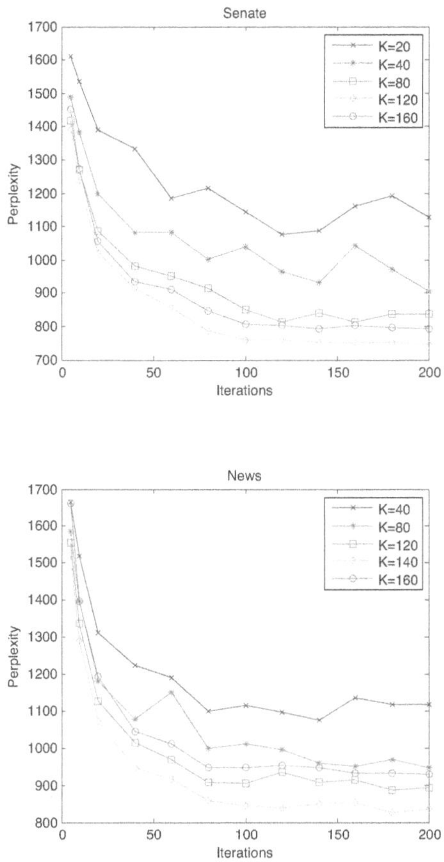

Figure 2: The perplexity results of the Cross-Perspective Topic model on the two testbeds for six different topic numbers K over the iterations. Top: Senate dataset. Bottom: News dataset.

plying the opinion word extraction procedure presented in Section 4.2. "FULL" represents the opinion words come from the whole document. "OS" represents the opinion words only come from the extracted opinion sentences. By comparing "OS" with "FULL", we can see quite a big positive impact from our opinion word extraction method.

To compare CPT with other methods, we use LDA and corrLDA as two baselines. Specifically, we train LDA and corrLDA models on the whole collection of each perspective and then calculate $p(w|q)$ in a similar way as shown in Eqn. (1). Because the words in LDA contain both topic and opinion words, we only focus on the opinion words and rank them according to $p(w|q)$. In addition, we design another two retrieval based baselines for comparison as follows. For each query topic, we retrieve 50 documents from each perspective by BM25 [21]. We then extract the opinion words using the procedure in Section 4.2. For the first baseline ("freq"), we rank the opinion words by frequency in each perspective. For the second baseline ("mutual"), we rank the opinion words by mutual information with respect to each perspective. Mutual information measures how much information (in the information-theoretic sense) an opinion word contains about the perspective [21]. Table 5 presents the comparison of the five methods.

From the table, we can see that CPT achieves the best

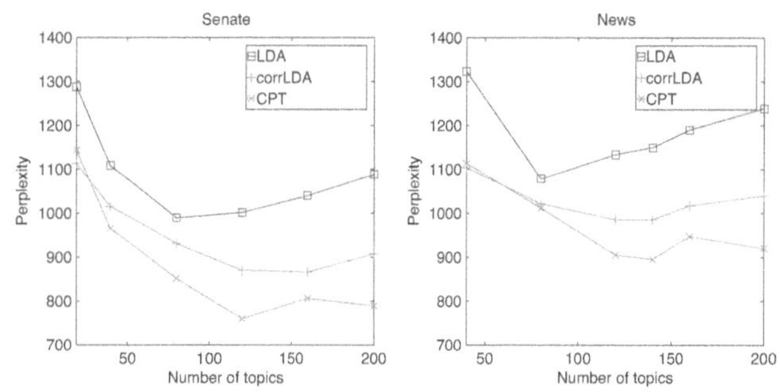

Figure 3: The perplexity results of LDA, corrLDA and CPT on the two testbeds. Left: Senate dataset with topic number K=20, 40, 80, 120, 160 and 200. Right: News dataset with topic number K=40, 80, 120, 140, 160 and 200

Table 4: Evaluation results of CPT with and without extracting opinion sentences. Best results on each testbed are highlighted. The †symbol indicates statistical significance (by two-tailed Student's t-test) of "FULL" against "OS" at 0.95 confidence interval.

	P@5	P@10	P@20	MRR	nDCG
Senate					
FULL	0.835	0.786	0.688	0.911	0.773
OS	**0.896†**	**0.824**	**0.727**	**0.952†**	**0.822†**
News					
FULL	0.764	0.745	0.639	0.875	0.714
OS	**0.822†**	**0.782**	**0.674**	**0.901**	**0.768†**

results on both testbeds in all the evaluation metrics. By comparing CPT with the baselines, we can see that CPT has substantial improvement especially on P@5, MRR and nDCG@20, which indicates CPT is effective to return the relevant results to the top of the list. corrLDA generates the second best results after CPT, while there exists noticeable gaps between these two methods. For the retrieval based method, "mutual" generally yields better results than "freq", and "freq" yields similar performance than LDA on both testbeds. Another observation is that the performance on the News dataset is worse than on the Senate dataset. This can be explained by the fact that Republican and Democratic senators usually have shared issues to discuss which enables the models to learn more representative topics and more logically connected opinions. In contrast, the news coverage of the three news agencies could be more diverse. This observation is also consistent with the perplexity results in Figure 3.

5.2 Qualitative Analysis

In this subsection, we show the discovered topics and the corresponding opinions by the Cross-Perspective Topic model. The model is trained on the whole collections with the parameters chosen based on the experimental results in Section 5.1.1. Table 6 contains a sample of topics and the corresponding opinions on the Senate dataset. The top 5 words from the shared topic-word distribution $p(w|z)$ and the top 5 words from the topic-opinion distribution $p(o|z)$ are shown for each perspective. The coupling between $p(w|z)$ and $p(o|z)$ can illustrate each perspective's opinions o on the topic z represented by the word w. By looking at the ta-

Table 6: A sample of topics and the corresponding opinions from Republican and Democratic parties. Shown are the top 5 words from the shared topic-word distribution $p(w|z)$ and the top 5 words from the topic-opinion distribution $p(o|z)$ for each party.

		Republican		Democrat	
TOPIC 9					
Word	**Prob.**	**Opinion**	**Prob.**	**Opinion**	**Prob.**
immigration	0.1165	illegal	0.0370	comprehensive	0.0330
border	0.0761	alien	0.0362	legal	0.0275
reform	0.0415	secure	0.0317	fair	0.0251
security	0.0285	comprehensive	0.0290	undocumented	0.0204
visa	0.0277	enforce	0.0286	temporary	0.0202
TOPIC 26					
insurance	0.1255	small	0.0344	uninsured	0.0393
health	0.1227	private	0.0198	federal	0.0281
coverage	0.0732	eligible	0.0181	affordable	0.0205
care	0.0394	responsible	0.0177	expand	0.0187
medicaid	0.0358	individual	0.0175	public	0.0185
TOPIC 39					
Word	**Prob.**	**Opinion**	**Prob.**	**Opinion**	**Prob.**
trade	0.1449	global	0.0195	domestic	0.0198
agreement	0.0604	developing	0.0190	unfair	0.0187
china	0.0331	unfair	0.0163	lost	0.0171
manufacturing	0.0255	manipulate	0.0161	fair	0.0169
world	0.0179	competitive	0.0160	environmental	0.0146
TOPIC 75					
Word	**Prob.**	**Opinion**	**Prob.**	**Opinion**	**Prob.**
iraq	0.1692	military	0.0296	military	0.0177
war	0.0614	supplemental	0.0156	failed	0.0164
security	0.0189	win	0.0151	end	0.0157
afghanistan	0.0171	critical	0.0147	change	0.0147
saddam	0.0170	secure	0.0147	withdraw	0.0145

Table 5: Comparison of CPT with other methods for each testbed. Best results on each testbed are highlighted. The †symbol indicates statistical significance (by two-tailed Student's t-test) of "CPT" against "freq" at 0.95 confidence interval.

	P@5	P@10	P@20	MRR	nDCG
Senate					
freq	0.818	0.769	0.672	0.875	0.771
mutual	0.832	0.788	0.685	0.896	0.778
LDA	0.812	0.764	0.672	0.882	0.759
corrLDA	0.859†	0.798	0.701	0.922†	0.802
CPT	**0.896†**	**0.824†**	**0.727**	**0.952†**	**0.822†**
News					
freq	0.758	0.740	0.638	0.853	0.711
mutual	0.767	0.748	0.645	0.879	0.721
LDA	0.751	0.738	0.642	0.857	0.717
corrLDA	0.792	0.766	0.659	0.886†	0.730
CPT	**0.822†**	**0.782**	**0.674**	**0.901†**	**0.768†**

ble we can see some clear differences between Republicans and Democrats. For example, in Topic 9 which is about immigration, Republican senators often used the words "illegal aliens" while Democratic senators probably prefer to use "undocumented" workers/immigrants. In fact, the choice of words can reflect their stance on the issue[14]. In addition, Republicans seem to emphasize more on the "secure" aspect of the immigration reform while Democrats more on the "legal" and "fair" aspect. In Topic 26 which is about health insurance, "private" and "individual" vs "public" and "federal" probably indicates the two parties' difference on the role of government in this issue. Topic 39 is about the trade with China and both parties seem to think it is "unfair" while the other opinion words are different. In Topic 75 about Iraq war, "win" vs "failed" and "supplemental" vs "withdraw" also illustrate their different attitudes towards the war.

Table 7 presents a sample of topics and the corresponding opinions from the News dataset. From the table, it is interesting to see the media bias on the issues. For example, topic 40 is about 2010 Nobel Peace Prize laureate Liu Xiaobo (actually the 7th top word is "xiaobo" which is not shown in the table). In this topic, we can clearly see the huge discrepancy between New York Times (The Hindu) and Xinhua on this issue. The difference is also manifested in Topic 54 which is about Iran uranium enrichment. New York Times probably reports more on potential "military" operations while Xinhua emphasizes on "peaceful", "diplomatic" and "negotiate" aspects. Hindu seems to have a middle ground perspective between NYT and Xinhua. In Topic 68 which is about Kashmir in Pakistan, all the top 5 opinion words from the three news agencies are different, which may indicate their different views on this issue. In Topic 81 which is about China, although "economic" is the top word in all the three perspectives, the other opinion words clearly show their differences especially between Xinhua and the other two media. For example, the American and India media often use the word "rising" while the Chinese media uses "developing". This can be explained by the fact that "China's peaceful rise" was replaced in Chinese government parlance from 2004 by "China's peaceful development", to emphasize that China poses no threat to the established order[15].

[14] The term "illegal aliens" is considered offensive to some Latinos: https://www.spj.org/quill_issue.asp?ref=1745

[15] http://en.wikipedia.org/wiki/China's_peaceful_rise

Table 7: A sample of topics and the corresponding opinions from the three media: New York Times in US, Xinhua News in China and The Hindu in India. Shown are the top 5 words from the shared topic-word distribution $p(w|z)$ and the top 5 words from the topic-opinion distribution $p(o|z)$ for each news agency.

		New York Times		Xinhua News		The Hindu	
TOPIC 40							
WORD	PROB.	OPINION	PROB.	OPINION	PROB.	OPINION	PROB.
peace	0.0573	dissident	0.0116	convicted	0.0163	jailed	0.0168
prize	0.0533	awarded	0.0101	arrogant	0.0114	dissident	0.0077
nobel	0.0425	democratic	0.0078	political	0.0092	criticised	0.0062
liu	0.0391	imprisoned	0.0068	interfere	0.0092	unaware	0.0062
committee	0.0281	pro-democracy	0.0049	internal	0.0085	imprisoned	0.0046
TOPIC 54							
WORD	PROB.	OPINION	PROB.	OPINION	PROB.	OPINION	PROB.
iran	0.2209	military	0.0765	peaceful	0.1065	diplomatic	0.0713
program	0.0391	impose	0.0623	diplomatic	0.0128	international	0.0496
tehran	0.0334	stop	0.0442	negotiate	0.0121	military	0.0367
uranium	0.0305	diplomatic	0.0307	civilian	0.0113	constructive	0.0299
ahmadinejad	0.0195	financial	0.0225	unilateral	0.0109	regional	0.0186
TOPIC 68							
WORD	PROB.	OPINION	PROB.	OPINION	PROB.	OPINION	PROB.
kashmir	0.0404	ethnic	0.0147	indian-controlled	0.0205	democratic	0.0275
pakistan	0.0388	killed	0.0147	moderate	0.0198	civil	0.0215
constitution	0.0222	disputed	0.0145	end	0.0162	insurgent	0.0201
violence	0.0193	peaceful	0.0145	infiltrate	0.0156	separate	0.0195
valley	0.0157	tibetan	0.0142	bilateral	0.0151	military	0.0184
TOPIC 81							
WORD	PROB.	OPINION	PROB.	OPINION	PROB.	OPINION	PROB.
china	0.2414	economic	0.1133	economic	0.1175	economic	0.1147
chinese	0.1063	state-run	0.0165	western	0.0520	communist	0.0193
beijing	0.0672	rising	0.0159	peaceful	0.0180	growing	0.0186
government	0.0213	manipulate	0.0156	positive	0.0171	rising	0.0180
currency	0.0109	controlled	0.0154	developing	0.0160	territorial	0.0179

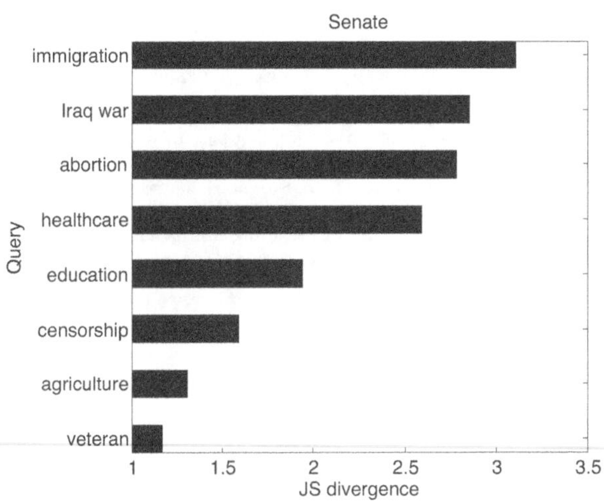

Figure 4: Quantitative differences between Republican senators and Democratic senators on 8 ad hoc queries

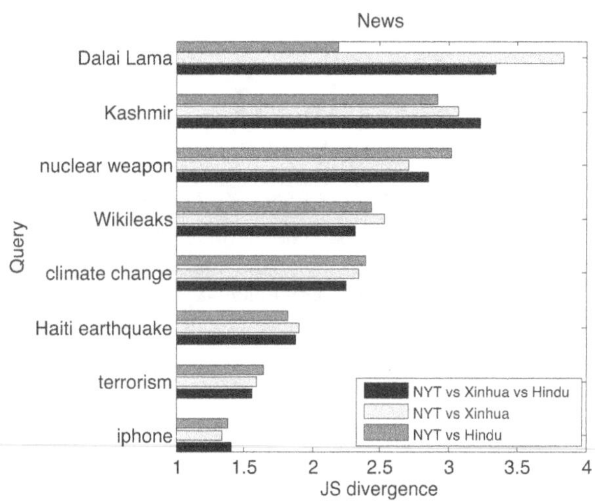

Figure 5: Quantitative differences among New York Times, Xinhua News and The Hindu on 8 ad hoc queries

5.2.1 *Diversity Metric*

In this subsection, we use the diversity metric based on the Jensen-Shannon divergence (defined in Section 3.2) to quantify the dissimilarities between different perspectives with respect to various query topics. Due to space constraints, we only present 8 queries for each testbed. These queries are ad hoc as well, although some of them may correspond to the conceptual topics learned from the model. Figure 4 shows the results for the Senate dataset. From Figure 4, we can see that the Republic and Democratic parties have quite different stances on the queries "immigration", "Iraq war", "abortion" and "healthcare". On the other hand, two parties have quite similar stances on "censorship", "agriculture" and "veteran". With respect to the query "education", the two parties have mild differences. These findings are consistent with what are commonly perceived about the two parties. Figure 5 shows the results for the News dataset. Besides showing the Jensen-Shannon divergence among the three news agencies (i.e., NYT vs Xinhua vs Hindu), we also show the JS divergence between NYT and Xinhua, and the divergence between NYT and Hindu. Overall, we can see that the three agencies have very different opinions on the queries "Dalai Lama", "Kashmir", and "nuclear weapon". They have quite similar opinions on "iphone", "terrorism" and "Haiti earthquake", and have mild difference on "Wikileaks" and "climate change". By looking at the pair comparison, we can see that some big JS divergences are caused by pairwise difference. For example, NYT and Hindu actually have similar opinions on "Dalai Lama", while the JS divergence of the three agencies on the topic is the largest. On the other hand, on the query topic "nuclear weapon", NYT and Xihuna have more similar opinions. From Figure 5, we can see that generally NYT and Hindu share more similar stances on the issues while NYT and Xinhua hold more different opinions. From Figure 4 and Figure 5, we can easily identify the controversial and consensual issues among different perspectives. They could be a visualization tool to help reduce users' cognitive efforts.

6. CONCLUSIONS AND FUTURE WORK

In this paper, we study a novel opining mining problem referred to as contrastive opining modeling. The work reported in this paper is just an initial step towards a promising new direction. There are many interesting future research directions. It is worth exploring the applicability of the CPT model to large-scale Web documents such as blogs and reviews. It is also interesting to see the proposed model to serve as a data mining tool for comparative research in social science such as cross-culture, cross-religion, and cross-country studies.

7. ACKNOWLEDGMENTS

The authors would like to thank John Haller for making relevance judgements. This research is supported by the following NSF research grants: IIS-0746830, CNS-1012208 and IIS-1017837. This work is partially supported by the Center for Science of Information (CSoI), an NSF Science and Technology Center, under grant agreement CCF-0939370, and the National Natural Science Foundation of China (61175068).

8. REFERENCES

[1] D. Blei and M. Jordan. Modeling annotated data. In *SIGIR*, pages 127–134. ACM, 2003.

[2] D. Blei, A. Ng, and M. Jordan. Latent dirichlet allocation. *The Journal of Machine Learning Research*, 3:993–1022, 2003.

[3] B. Chen, L. Zhu, D. Kifer, and D. Lee. What is an opinion about? exploring political standpoints using opinion scoring model. In *AAAI*, pages 1007–1012.

[4] D. Diermeier, J. Godbout, B. Yu, and S. Kaufmann. Language and ideology in Congress. In *Annual Meeting of the Midwest Political Science Association*, 2007.

[5] X. Ding, B. Liu, and P. Yu. A holistic lexicon-based approach to opinion mining. In *WSDM*, pages 231–240, 2008.

[6] K. Eguchi and V. Lavrenko. Sentiment retrieval using generative models. In *EMNLP*, pages 345–354, 2006.

[7] O. Furuse, N. Hiroshima, S. Yamada, and R. Kataoka. Opinion sentence search engine on open-domain blog. In *IJCAI*, pages 2760–2765, 2007.

[8] T. Griffiths and M. Steyvers. Finding scientific topics. *PNAS*, 101:5228, 2004.

[9] V. Hatzivassiloglou and K. McKeown. Predicting the semantic orientation of adjectives. In *EACL*, pages 174–181, 1997.

[10] M. Hu and B. Liu. Mining opinion features in customer reviews. In *AAAI*, pages 755–760, 2004.

[11] M. Hurst and K. Nigam. Retrieving topical sentiments from online document collections. In *Document Recognition and Retrieval XI*, pages 27–34, 2004.

[12] Y. Jo and A. Oh. Aspect and sentiment unification model for online review analysis. In *WSDM*, pages 815–824, 2011.

[13] S. Kim and E. Hovy. Determining the sentiment of opinions. In *COLING*, pages 1367–1374, 2004.

[14] K. Lerman and R. McDonald. Contrastive summarization: an experiment with consumer reviews. In *NAACL/HLT*, pages 113–116, 2009.

[15] S. Li, C. Lin, Y. Song, and Z. Li. Comparable entity mining from comparative questions. In *ACL*, pages 650–658. Association for Computational Linguistics, 2010.

[16] C. Lin and Y. He. Joint sentiment/topic model for sentiment analysis. In *CIKM*, pages 375–384. ACM, 2009.

[17] J. Lin. Divergence measures based on the Shannon entropy. *IEEE Transactions on Information Theory*, 37(1):145–151, 2002.

[18] W. Lin and A. Hauptmann. Are these documents written from different perspectives?: a test of different perspectives based on statistical distribution divergence. In *ACL*, pages 1057–1064, 2006.

[19] W. Lin, T. Wilson, J. Wiebe, and A. Hauptmann. Which side are you on?: identifying perspectives at the document and sentence levels. In *CoNLL*, pages 109–116. Association for Computational Linguistics, 2006.

[20] B. Liu, M. Hu, and J. Cheng. Opinion observer: Analyzing and comparing opinions on the web. In *WWW*, pages 342–351, 2005.

[21] C. Manning, P. Raghavan, and H. Schutze. *Introduction to information retrieval*. Cambridge University Press, UK, 2008.

[22] Q. Mei, X. Ling, M. Wondra, H. Su, and C. Zhai. Topic sentiment mixture: modeling facets and opinions in weblogs. In *WWW*, pages 171–180, 2007.

[23] I. Ounis, M. Rijke, C. Macdonald, G. Mishne, and I. Soboroff. Overview of the TREC-2006 Blog Track. In *TREC*, pages 15–27, 2006.

[24] B. Pang and L. Lee. Opinion mining and sentiment analysis. *Foundations and Trends in Information Retrieval*, 2(1-2):1–135, 2008.

[25] B. Pang, L. Lee, and S. Vaithyanathan. Thumbs up?: sentiment classification using machine learning techniques. In *EMNLP*, pages 79–86, 2002.

[26] M. Paul and R. Girju. Cross-cultural analysis of blogs and forums with mixed-collection topic models. In *EMNLP*, pages 1408–1417, 2009.

[27] M. Paul, C. Zhai, and R. Girju. Summarizing contrastive viewpoints in opinionated text. In *EMNLP*, pages 66–76, 2010.

[28] A. Popescu and O. Etzioni. Extracting product features and opinions from reviews. In *HLT/EMNLP*, pages 339–346, 2005.

[29] Y. Seki, D. Evans, L. Ku, H. Chen, N. Kando, and C. Lin. Overview of opinion analysis pilot task at NTCIR-6. In *NTCIR-6*, pages 265–278, 2007.

[30] M. Thomas, B. Pang, and L. Lee. Get out the vote: Determining support or opposition from Congressional floor-debate transcripts. In *EMNLP*, pages 327–335, 2006.

[31] I. Titov and R. McDonald. A joint model of text and aspect ratings for sentiment summarization. In *ACL*, page 308, 2008.

[32] I. Titov and R. McDonald. Modeling online reviews with multi-grain topic models. In *WWW*, pages 111–120, 2008.

[33] T. Wilson, P. Hoffmann, S. Somasundaran, J. Kessler, J. Wiebe, Y. Choi, C. Cardie, E. Riloff, and S. Patwardhan. OpinionFinder: A system for subjectivity analysis. In *HLT/EMNLP*, pages 34–35, 2005.

[34] T. Yano, W. Cohen, and N. Smith. Predicting response to political blog posts with topic models. In *NAACL/HLT*, pages 477–485, 2009.

[35] J. Yi, T. Nasukawa, R. Bunescu, and W. Niblack. Sentiment analyzer: Extracting sentiments about a given topic using natural language processing techniques. In *ICDM*, pages 427–434. IEEE, 2003.

[36] C. Zhai, A. Velivelli, and B. Yu. A cross-collection mixture model for comparative text mining. In *SIGKDD*, pages 743–748, 2004.

[37] M. Zhang and X. Ye. A generation model to unify topic relevance and lexicon-based sentiment for opinion retrieval. In *SIGIR*, pages 411–418. ACM, 2008.

[38] W. Zhang, C. Yu, and W. Meng. Opinion retrieval from blogs. In *CIKM*, pages 831–840. ACM, 2007.

Coupled Temporal Scoping of Relational Facts

Partha Pratim Talukdar
Carnegie Mellon University
5000 Forbes Avenue
Pittsburgh, PA
ppt@cs.cmu.edu

Derry Wijaya
Carnegie Mellon University
5000 Forbes Avenue
Pittsburgh, PA
dwijaya@cs.cmu.edu

Tom Mitchell
Carnegie Mellon University
5000 Forbes Avenue
Pittsburgh, PA
tom.mitchell@cs.cmu.edu

ABSTRACT

Recent research has made significant advances in automatically constructing knowledge bases by extracting relational facts (e.g., Bill Clinton-presidentOf-US) from large text corpora. Temporally scoping such relational facts in the knowledge base (i.e., determining that Bill Clinton-presidentOf-US is true only during the period 1993 - 2001) is an important, but relatively unexplored problem. In this paper, we propose a joint inference framework for this task, which leverages fact-specific temporal constraints, and weak supervision in the form of a few labeled examples. Our proposed framework, CoTS (Coupled Temporal Scoping), exploits temporal containment, alignment, succession, and mutual exclusion constraints among facts from within and across relations. Our contribution is multi-fold. Firstly, while most previous research has focused on micro-reading approaches for temporal scoping, we pose it in a macro-reading fashion, as a change detection in a time series of facts' features computed from a large number of documents. Secondly, to the best of our knowledge, there is no other work that has used joint inference for temporal scoping. We show that joint inference is effective compared to doing temporal scoping of individual facts independently. We conduct our experiments on large scale open-domain publicly available time-stamped datasets, such as English Gigaword Corpus and Google Books Ngrams, demonstrating CoTS's effectiveness.

Categories and Subject Descriptors

H.4 [**Information Systems Applications**]: Miscellaneous; I.2.6 [**Artificial Intelligence**]: Learning

General Terms

Algorithms,Experimentation

Keywords

Temporal Scoping,Joint Inference,Knowledge Base

Permission to make digital or hard copies of all or part of this work for personal or classroom use is granted without fee provided that copies are not made or distributed for profit or commercial advantage and that copies bear this notice and the full citation on the first page. To copy otherwise, to republish, to post on servers or to redistribute to lists, requires prior specific permission and/or a fee.
WSDM'12, February 8–12, 2012, Seattle, Washington, USA.
Copyright 2012 ACM 978-1-4503-0747-5/12/02 ...$10.00.

1. INTRODUCTION

There has been much research on extracting relational facts from both structured and unstructured text. Systems such as YAGO [21], KnowItAll [10], TextRunner [4], and NELL [7] gather entities and factual relations between entities from Web sources. However, much of the effort has been focused on gathering facts without their temporal scope. Facts are treated as time-invariant when in reality they dynamically change with time. New facts arise while others cease to be valid or change over time. Knowledge grows in various dimensions, and completely new entity types, relation types or knowledge structures may arise with time [28]. For example, the fact that Bill Clinton is a US President is only valid from the year 1993 to 2001. Such temporally scoped facts are useful for many reasons. Temporal information can be used as a dimension along which facts can be organized, ranked, or explored. Time can be helpful for relevancy ranking purposes. Presenting facts in a timeline can greatly benefit user experience in their exploration of knowledge evolution [2]. In a search or question answering system, time-sensitive queries such as business-intelligence queries (e.g., when did certain companies acquire other companies?) or medical queries (e.g., when did a certain vaccine become available?) will also benefit from temporally scoped facts. Temporal scoping of facts can also benefit other natural language applications, such as document summarization where the temporal information of facts mentioned in sentences can be used to generate better sentence ordering.

Despite the importance of time in any information space, gathering and distilling temporal knowledge from Web sources remains a major research challenge [28]. To the best of our knowledge, Timely YAGO [27] and PRAVDA [26], two recently proposed techniques, are the only systems which try to harvest temporal facts. Timely YAGO tries to automatically scope facts using regular expressions in Wikipedia infoboxes, and hence is not applicable to widely available free text. PRAVDA, a promising recent approach, uses a combination of textual patterns and graph-based re-ranking techniques to harvest facts and their temporal points at the same time. However, it is not immediately clear how this approach could be used to temporally scope facts in an existing knowledge base. Other works on temporal information extraction have tackled partial aspects of the problem such as temporal relations identification between events [6, 14, 5, 16, 8, 29, 13]. However, these other works are not sufficient to temporally scope facts as they are all focused on micro-reading of time at a single document or sentence level, i.e., temporal expressions and relations are normalized and identified based

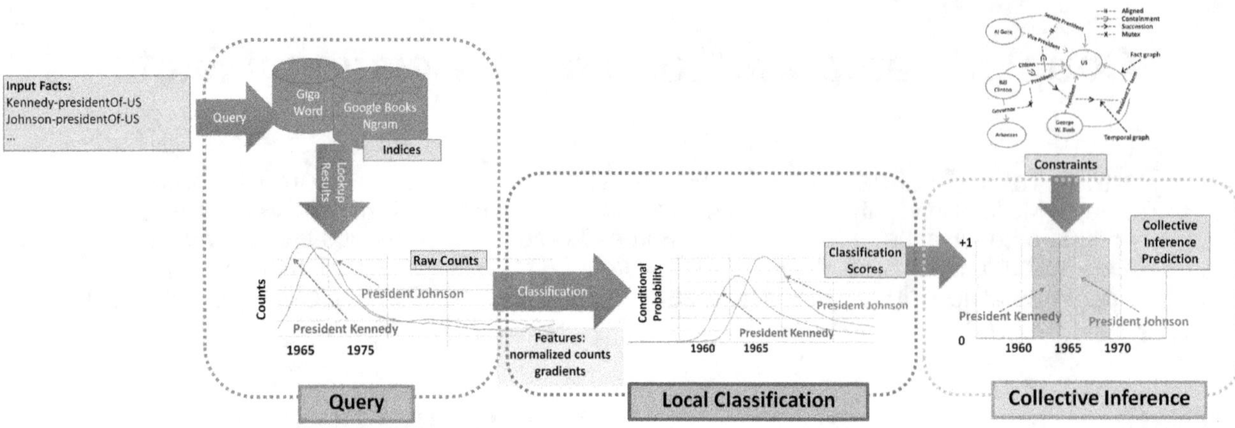

Figure 1: Architecture of the CoTS system (see Section 2 for an overview). Details of the Local Classification and Collective Inference modules are presented in Section 3.1 and Section 3.2, respectively.

only on features derived from the document. However, web is unique in that it typically offers ample redundancy, and hence it only seems natural to aggregate many observed cues for a temporal fact in a statistical manner [28]. This is what we attempt to do in our work, a macro-reading of temporal information from large-scale sources such as Google Books Ngram [15] and newswire text in Gigaword [12] using their document creation times (DCTs) to temporally scope facts.

Our contribution to this important but largely unexplored problem of temporal scoping is to propose a novel system, CoTS (Coupled Temporal Scoping), with multi-fold benefits.

- Firstly, in the spirit of macro-reading, CoTS uses a statistical approach to the problem, by using simple counts of facts in documents over time as cues to their temporal validity. Without going into document content, CoTS represents a fact by a time series of its counts over time. We believe time series is a natural way of representing a fact as it models directly the dynamic nature of the fact, its rise and fall over time. Evidence of change in time series is used as cues to classify whether the fact is active or not at any given time.

- Secondly, CoTS is novel in that we introduce collective[1] temporal inference over multiple temporally correlated facts to aggregate many observed cues for improved time scoping. Independent activation scores of facts are input to a collective inference framework, and Integer Linear Programming (ILP) is used to infer the temporal scope of facts while respecting various temporal dependencies among those facts, such containment, alignment, succession, and mutual exclusion.

- Thirdly, CoTS is weakly supervised: we need only a few labeled examples to train a local classifier (one for each relation), the only supervised component in CoTS. Moreover, CoTS provides a flexible framework where prior knowledge about the temporal dependencies among facts can be easily specified.

- Lastly, through experiments on interesting open-domain datasets such as the Google Books Ngram Corpus and the Gigaword Newswire Corpus, we demonstrate CoTS' effectiveness in improved temporal scoping, highlighting benefits of scoping multiple temporally related facts jointly, rather than scoping each such fact in isolation.

2. CoTS OVERVIEW

2.1 Challenges & Motivation

The problem of macro-reading the temporal scope of a fact from its counts in documents is a difficult one as these counts can be noisy, lagging in time, or sparse. A fact may still be found in documents (i.e., its count is not zero) even after it ceases to be valid. For example, some documents discuss the presidency of Kennedy even after his death. The document creation time may also lag behind a fact's activation time. For example, books about President Clinton may only be published some months after his inauguration (since books often take longer time to print and publish than news). Some facts are not mentioned enough in documents, leading to the sparsity of their counts. For example, unlike the President relation, the US Secretary of State relation may not be mentioned as frequently in documents.

These challenges of the problem motivate our approach. Firstly, to deal with the issue of time lag, especially in books data, we use also the change in the counts over time to capture the activation of a fact. A positive gradient in the time series of a fact's counts indicates that the fact is increasingly being talked about in documents, which may signal its activation time. Using positive gradients as additional information can capture change points based on the moment they start to be increasingly mentioned in data.

Secondly, to deal with the noise and sparsity of counts, we conduct collective inference to temporally scope several facts jointly. The advantage of doing collective inference is multifold. By utilizing temporal constraints between correlated facts, collective inference can bind the temporal scope of noisy facts by ensuring temporal consistency between facts, or inform the time scope of a sparse fact from the time scope of other, temporally correlated facts.

For example, in a functional relation (e.g., US presiden-

[1]In this paper, we shall use the terms collective inference, coupled inference, and joint inference interchangeably.

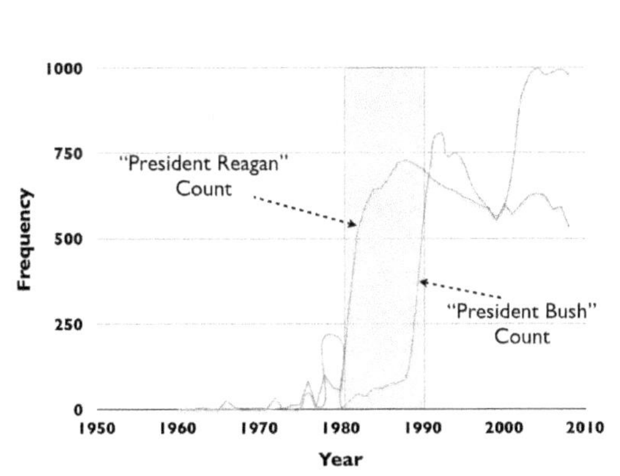

Figure 2: Temporal profiles of two facts demonstrating potential benefit of collective inference: considering 'President Bush' during inference can help determine the end of Reagan's presidency (shaded region).

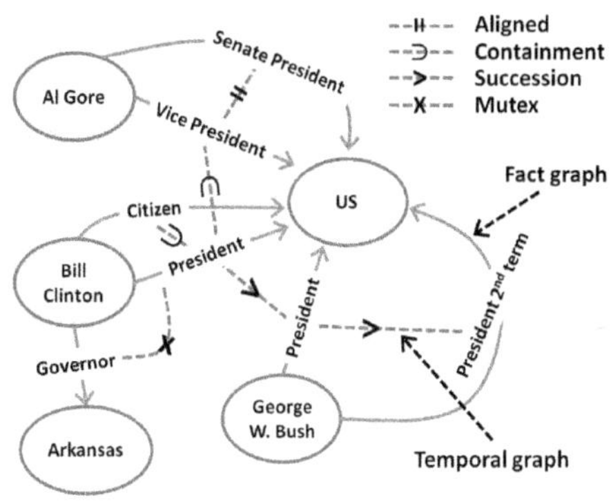

Figure 3: Temporal graph (dotted red edges) imposed over a factual graph (blue solid edges). Edges in the temporal graph correspond to constraints in CoTS, the proposed system.

tial relation), knowing the time scope of one instance of the relation can bind the time scope of another instance of the same relation since no two instances of a functional relation can be true at the same time (i.e., no two persons can be US president at the same time). This constraint is great to bind noisy, frequently mentioned facts. For example, although documents may still refer to Kennedy as 'President Kennedy' even after his death, knowing that Johnson's presidency began in 1963 and that his presidency succeeded Kennedy's can help bind the time scope of Kennedy's presidency. For example, in Figure 2, we can see how knowing the start of Bush's presidency can bind the end of Reagan's presidency, even though 'President Reagan' continues to be mentioned in documents even after his presidency.

Conversely, for facts that are sparse (e.g., those belonging to the US vice president relation), knowing the time scope of a correlated fact can help infer the time scope of the sparse fact. For example, the time scope of Clinton's presidency can be used to infer the time scope of Gore's vice presidency knowing that Gore served under Clinton's presidency.

Allowing users to specify temporal constraints between facts is also a natural way of adding prior knowledge to the task of temporal scoping. In Figure 3, we illustrate various temporal constraints that can be specified for US administration relations. Solid lines indicate factual relations (entity-relation-entity triplets) while dashed lines indicate temporal constraints between these facts. As we can see from Figure 3, temporal alignment between VicePresident and SenatePresident relations indicates that Al Gore must be vice president of the US at the same time that he is the president of US senate. Temporal mutual exclusion between President and Governor relations indicates that Bill Clinton cannot be both President of the US and Governor of Arkansas at the same time. Temporal containment between Citizen and President relations indicates that Bill Clinton must be a President of the US within the period that he is a citizen of the US. Temporal succession between facts indicates that the time scope of Bush-presidentOf-US follows the time scope of Clinton-presidentOf-US.

2.2 System Architecture

Figure 1 summarizes the high level architecture of our work to temporally scope facts, which involves the following pipeline of operations:

1. **Query**: To macro-read the temporal scope of a fact, we first construct a query to represent the fact. For example, the fact: 'Kennedy-presidentOf-US' is represented by the query 'President Kennedy'. Then we do a lookup of the query on the indices we have built for Google Books Ngram and Gigaword datasets. We gather raw counts of the results: i.e., the number of n-grams containing the query (for Google Books) and the number of times a query is found in the news documents (for GigaWord). Each fact is thus represented by a time series of its query counts, normalized over its total query counts.

2. **Local Classification**: Normalized counts and gradients of each fact are then input to a Maximum Entropy classifier which computes the conditional probability that the fact s from relation r is active at a given time t, i.e., $p_r(+1|s,t)$. As discussed previously, gradient information is included as a feature in this classification to capture the informative signal of increasing counts which may indicate the start of the fact's activation. Using only normalized counts and where they peak to classify start time may not be sufficient, as the peak may not always coincide with the start time due to possible time difference (lag) between the actual start time and the document creation time.

3. **Collective Inference**: Individual classification scores of the facts, $p_r(+1|s,t)$ and $p_r(-1|s,t)$, are then input to a collective inference engine (in our case, an Integer Linear Program (ILP)) together with the temporal constraints we have described and illustrated in Figure 3. ILP then predicts which facts are active at which times, based on the input classification scores and the specified temporal constraints. The outputs are then the facts and the times for which they are active.

3. SYSTEM DESCRIPTION

In this section, we present detailed descriptions of the three main modules in the CoTS system.

Notations

- Let $\{S^1, \ldots, S^m\}$ be sets of facts, one set for each of the m relations. We would like to temporally scope each fact $s \in S^r$, $\forall 1 \leq r \leq m$. In this paper, we shall use the relation index, r, also to refer to the relation name itself.

- Let B and E be the beginning and end of the timespan over which the temporal scoping is currently performed. We shall assume that any time instant $t \in \{B, \ldots, E\}$ is discretized at an appropriate granularity, which for the experiments in this paper is at the year level.

- $p_r(+1|s,t)$ is the local classification score specific to relation r, which measures whether the fact $s \in S^r$ is true at time t. Please refer to Section 3.1 for a discussion on estimating such scores.

- $x_{r,s,t} \in \{0,1\}$ is a binary integer variable, where $x_{r,s,t} = 1$ indicates that fact $s \in S^r$ is true at time $t \in \{B \ldots E\}$, and false otherwise.

- $z^b_{r,s,t} \in \{0,1\}$ is a binary integer variable, where $z^b_{r,s,t} = 1$ indicates that fact s started to be true at time t.

- Similarly, $z^e_{r,s,t} \in \{0,1\}$ is a binary integer variable, where $z^e_{r,s,t} = 1$ indicates that fact s ceased to be true at time t.

3.1 Local Classification Scores

In this section, we describe how we estimate the initial score, $p_r(+1|s,t) \in [0,1]$, which measures the probability of fact $s \in S^r$ being true at time t. We obtain these initial scores by training a Maximum Entropy (MaxEnt) classifier, separately for each relation r. For each relation r, we assume that we are given a set of training instances $T_r = \{(\phi_r(s,t,y), y)\}$, where $\phi_r(s,t,y) \in R^d$ is the d-dimensional representation of fact $s \in S^r$ at time t, and $y \in \{-1,+1\}$ is its label, with $y = 1$ suggesting that the fact is true at time t, and -1 otherwise.

For each relation r, these labeled instances are then used to estimate parameters $\mathbf{w}_r$ of corresponding MaxEnt classifier. The classifier can then be applied to classify an unlabeled instance u at time t using Equation 1.

$$p_r(+1|u,t) = \frac{\exp(\mathbf{w}_r^T \cdot \phi_r(u,t,+1))}{\sum_y \exp(\mathbf{w}_r^T \cdot \phi_r(u,t,y))} \quad (1)$$

This score gives an estimate of how likely it is that fact u from relation r is true at time t. We note that $p_r(+1|u,t)$ is a probability distribution and hence it is bounded in $[0,1]$. We use both positive and negative real numbers as the values for our features. The actual features that we use for the experiments in this paper are described below.

Features:

Using the Query module described in Section 2.2, we obtain a timeline L_u for each fact u, where $L_u(t)$ returns the (normalized) count of fact u at time t. We use $L_u(t)$ as the **count feature**. We also compute the gradient over L_u at t, and use the gradient value as the **gradient feature**. This feature helps in adapting the classifier to adapt to time-lag issues as described in Section 2.1. We use only these two features in the local classifier. Since the local classifier estimates its parameters from a very small number of labeled instances, we wanted to make sure the the local classifier doesn't overfit severely which is possible in the presence of large numbers of features.

3.2 Collective Inference

In our system, time scoping each fact in isolation corresponds to making the final scoping decisions based purely on the scores $p_r(+1|u,t)$ as described in previous section. While such scores provide useful discriminating information, they are often noisy, leading to incorrect time scoping decisions. Lack of discriminating features, paucity of labeled training data, and inherent hardness of the classification task itself could be one of several reasons leading to these noisy predictions. While obtaining large amounts of labeled data may not be practical, incremental improvements may be possible by employing more sophisticated features. We take a different approach and as motivated in previous sections, we introduce here a way to use these prediction scores, and at the same time exploit available domain-specific constraints. To this effect, in this section, we present the Integer Linear Program (ILP)-based collective inference module of our system. First, we present the constraints that can be specified in our system, and then present the objective which is ultimately optimized subject to the constraints.

3.2.1 Constraints

Constraints in the CoTS system can be categorized into the following two classes:

1. **Intra Relation Constraints**: These constraints regulate the temporal scoping of one or more facts from a single relation. For example, Functional constraints (described below) belong to this category, which can enforce the requirement that at most one fact from the relation can be true at any given time. For example, there is only one US President at any given time. Please note that such requirements can be enforced only if multiple facts from the same relation are considered jointly during temporal scoping, which is strictly not possible in case of temporal scoping of each fact in isolation.

2. **Cross Relation Constraints**: Constraints in this category couple temporal scoping of facts from multiple relations. For example, we may want to enforce the requirement that Al Gore's Vice Presidency aligned exactly with Bill Clinton's Presidency. Aligned constraints (described below) operating over the Vice President and President relations can be used to enforce such requirement.

Please note that all our constraints are specified at the fact level, even though they may affect one or more facts from the same or multiple relations. Below, we present examples of different constraints exploited by the CoTS system for the experiments in this paper.

- Consistency: The following constraints make sure that the begin ($z^b_{r,s,t}$) and end ($z^e_{r,s,t}$) variables are consistent with the $x_{r,s,t}$ variables.
  - BeginConsistency1: For a fact to start at a given time, the fact should also be true at that time.

$$z^b_{r,s,t} \leq x_{r,s,t},\ \forall s \in S^r,\ t \in \{B, \ldots, E\}$$

- BeginConsistency2: For a fact to begin at time t, the fact should not be true at time $t-1$ and become true at t. We use the boundary condition $x_{r,s,(B-1)} = 0$.

$$z^b_{r,s,t} \geq x_{r,s,t} - x_{r,s,(t-1)},\ \forall s, t \in \{B \ldots E\}$$

- EndConsistency1: For a fact to end at a given time, the fact should also be true until that time.

$$z^e_{r,s,t} \leq x_{r,s,t},\ \forall s \in S^r, \text{and } t$$

- EndConsistency2: For a fact to end at time t, the fact should be true at time t and not true at $t+1$. We use the boundary condition $x_{r,s,(E+1)} = 0$.

$$z^e_{r,s,t} \geq x_{r,s,t} - x_{r,s,(t+1)},\ \forall t \in \{B \ldots E\}$$

- Functional: For a given relation r, these constraints enforce the requirement that no two facts from r be true at the same time.

$$\textstyle\sum_s x_{r,s,t} \leq 1,\ \ \forall t \in B \ldots E$$

As an example, Functional constraints can be used to enforce the fact that there can be at most one Vice President in USA at any given time. Functional constraints are Intra Relation in nature.

- SingleSpan: These constraints make sure that any fact from a relation r is true continuously for a single span of time, without any interruption in between. For example, US presidencies tend to be a single continuous span of time. SingleSpan, another member of the Intra Relation constraint class, is actually a set of constraints, which we describe below. Below, we shall assume that the fact belongs to relations r.

  - SingleBegin: For each fact, there is at most one beginning. This is "at most" and not "equal" as the fact may not be activated during the time interval $B \ldots E$.

$$\textstyle\sum_t z^b_{r,s,t} \leq 1,\ \forall s \in S^r$$

  - SingleEnd: For each facts, there is at most one end.

$$\textstyle\sum_t z^e_{r,s,t} \leq 1,\ \forall s \in S^r$$

  - EndAfterBegin: End of the fact should happen after its beginning.

$$\textstyle\sum_t t * z^e_{r,s,t} - \sum_t t * z^b_{r,s,t} \geq 0,\ \forall s \in S^r$$

- Point: This constraint is useful when the fact is true only at one instant of time, i.e., the temporal span has unit length. For example, even though Steven Spielberg has multiple Academy Award for Best Director, length of temporal scope of each win is of unit length, at the year granularity.

$$\textstyle\sum_t x_{r,u,t} \leq 1,\ \forall u \in S^r$$

Please note that this is different from the Functional constraint as the sum here is over all $t \in \{B \ldots E\}$, as opposed to all facts s in case of Functional. Point constraints are Intra Class.

- Aligned: This constraint is useful whenever two facts (from same or different relations) have exactly same temporal span. For example, George H.W. Bush was the Vice President throughout Ronald Reagan's presidency. In other words, if facts $u \in S^a$ and $v \in S^c$ are temporally aligned, then $x_{a,u,t} = x_{c,v,t},\ \forall t$. We enforce this through two inequality constraints.

$$x_{a,u,t} \leq x_{c,v,t}, \text{ and } x_{c,v,t} \leq x_{a,u,t},\ \forall t \in \{B \ldots E\}$$

- Containment: Suppose, we want to express the fact that Al Gore's Vice Presidency was contained within Bill Clinton's Presidency, even though we don't exactly know the time span of either fact. The Containment temporal constraint can be used to achieve this. If the timespan of fact $u \in S^a$ is contained within the time span of fact $v \in S^c$, then we the Containment constraint is of the form:

$$x_{a,u,t} \leq x_{c,v,t},\ \forall t \in \{B \ldots E\}$$

We can verify that this constraint will be violated only when $x_{a,u,t} = 1$ and $x_{c,v,t} = 0$, the only undesirable case. Containment can be both Intra Relation as well as Cross Relation.

- Succession: This constraint is useful when we want to express the requirement that one fact ($v \in S^c$) from relation c happened after another fact ($u \in S^a$) from relation a, e.g., Ronald Reagan became president after Henry Kissinger was the Secretary of State.

$$\textstyle\sum_t t * z^e_{a,u,t} - \sum_t t * z^b_{c,v,t} \leq 0$$

Please note that the above constraint is effective only in conjunction with SingleSpan constraint.

- Mutex: Suppose, we want to enforce the requirement that George H. W. Bush can't be US President and Vice President at the same time. This can be achieved through the Mutex constraint. This constraint ensures that two facts, $u \in S^a$ and $v \in S^c$, are not true at the same time.

$$x_{a,u,t} + x_{c,v,t} \leq 1,\ \forall t \in \{B \ldots E\}$$

Mutex can be both Intra ($a = c$) as well as Cross Relational ($a \neq c$).

Please note that choice of constraints finally used in any given inference is dependent on the type of relation(s) involved. Moreover, the temporal constraints presented above are not meant to be exhaustive, as depending on the domain and type of relation(s), new constrains may have to introduced. We hope that CoTS' linear constraint specification is flexible enough to support a majority of such extensions.

3.2.2 *Objective*

Subject to the constraints mentioned above, CoTS optimizes the following objective,

$$\max_{\{x_{r,s,t}\}} \sum_{r,s,t} p_r(+1|s,t) * x_{r,s,t} + \lambda * p_r(-1|s,t) * (1 - x_{r,s,t})$$

where $\lambda \in [0, 1]$ is the tradeoff weight which controls the relative importance of the two terms in the objective. The first term in the objective encourages the optimization to respect the classification scores $p_r(+1|s,t)$; while the second term encourages the inference to abstain from over-predicting in case the local MAXENT classifier is not confident enough. This become more apparent after the following analysis.

$$\begin{aligned} & p_r(+1|s,t) * x_{r,s,t} + \lambda * p_r(-1|s,t) * (1 - x_{r,s,t}) \\ = \; & p_r(+1|s,t) * x_{r,s,t} + \lambda * (1 - p_r(+1|s,t) * (1 - x_{r,s,t}) \\ = \; & ((1+\lambda) * p_r(+1|s,t) - \lambda) * x_{r,s,t} + \lambda * (1 - p_r(+1|s,t)) \\ = \; & ((1+\lambda) * p_r(+1|s,t) - \lambda) * x_{r,s,t} + \text{Constant} \end{aligned}$$

The optimization can ignore the second constant term as it is not dependent on $x_{r,s,t}$. Since the objective is one of maximization sense, there is incentive to set $x_{r,s,t} = 1$ (subject to constraint satisfaction) iff

$$\begin{aligned} (1+\lambda) * p_r(+1|s,t) - \lambda &> 0 \\ p_r(+1|s,t) &> \frac{\lambda}{1+\lambda} \end{aligned}$$

With $\lambda = 1$, we observe that $x_{r,s,t} = 1$ is a candidate for prediction if $p_r(+1|s,t) > 0.5$, i.e., $p_r(+1|s,t) > p_r(-1|s,t)$. By varying λ, we can control how much confidence collective inference rests on the local classification scores. It is interesting to note that all these fall out naturally from the formulation of the objective. This built-in mechanism against over-prediction is a desirable property of CoTS, which is lacking in the other systems we compare against, and as we shall see in Section 4, it results in better temporal scoping.

4. EXPERIMENTS

In this section, we investigate the following:

- Does adding gradient-based features in the local classifier lead to improved temporal scoping? (Section 4.2)
- Does coupled temporal scoping (i.e., joint inference involving multiple instances from same as well different relations) help improve performance? (Section 4.3)
- What are the effects of different types of constraints on CoTS's performance? (Section 4.4)
- Is CoTS's Collective inference module fast enough? (Section 4.5)

4.1 Experimental Setup

4.1.1 *Relations and Facts*

Relation names and the number of facts from these relations which were used in the experiments in this section are presented in Table 1. Please note that CoTS assumes that these facts have already been extracted, and it instead focuses only on temporally scoping them. Facts from the US Administration domain (i.e., facts from the relations US President, US Vice President, and US Secretary of State) were temporally scoped together, while facts from the Academy Awards domain (i.e., Best Director and Best Movie) were scoped jointly. True temporal scope of each fact was determined manually, which in turn was used for training and evaluation purposes. Facts from the US Administration domain spanned the period 1961 - 2008, while facts from the Academy Awards domain spanned the period 1995 - 2008.

Relation Name	Number of Facts
US President	9
US Vice President	12
US Secretary of State	27
Best Director	14
Best Movie	14

Table 1: Relations and the number of facts from these relations used in the experiments in Section 4.

4.1.2 *Query Module*

Queries: As described in Section 2, in order to get the temporal profile of a fact (see Figure 2), we first construct a query to represent the fact. In the following description, we shall use the notation {q} to denote a query, whose keywords and operators are stored in q as per Lucene's query syntax [11]. For the three US Administration office relations in Table 1, we use the query template: Office LastName. So, the fact Bill Clinton-presidentOf-US is represented by the query {"president clinton"}. Similarly, {"vice president gore"}, and {"secretary albright"}. For the Academy Awards Best Movie relation, we used the query template {"academy award" AND movieName}, which resulted in queries of the form {"academy award" AND "a beautiful mind"}. The goal behind using this query is to retrieve documents containing both phrases: "academy award" and "a beautiful mind". Similarly, for the Academy Award Best Directory relation, the query template {"academy award" AND directorLastName} was used, which resulted in queries of the form {"academy award" AND "spielberg"}.

Time-Stamped Corpus: Once a query is generated from a fact as described above, we construct a temporal profile of the fact from the document creation times (DCTs) of documents retrieved by its query. In order to retrieve such documents for a given query, we use Lucene [11] to index time-stamped documents and look the query up against that index. We use the following two sources of time-stamped documents:

- **Google Books Ngram**[2] [15] is a corpus of about 5 million digitized books. The resulting corpus contains over 500 billion words in several languages. The data is released in the form of n-gram (n = 1 to 5) and three different counts of each of these n-grams are available per year: (1) the number of times the n-gram is found in books published in the year; (2) the number of pages that contain the n-gram in books published in the year; and (3) the number of books published in the year that contain the n-gram. An interesting feature of this data set is its extended time coverage spanning from 1500s to 2008.
- **Gigaword**[3] [12] contains English newswire text data acquired from four international newswire services, spanning the period from 1994 to 2008. Unlike Google Books Ngrams, Gigaword contains full time-stamped newswire documents and not just ngrams extracted from them. However, compared to the Google Books Ngrams dataset, it is much smaller in size and has smaller time coverage.

[2]http://books.google.com/ngrams/datasets
[3]LDC Gigaword: http://bit.ly/vZFoJ6

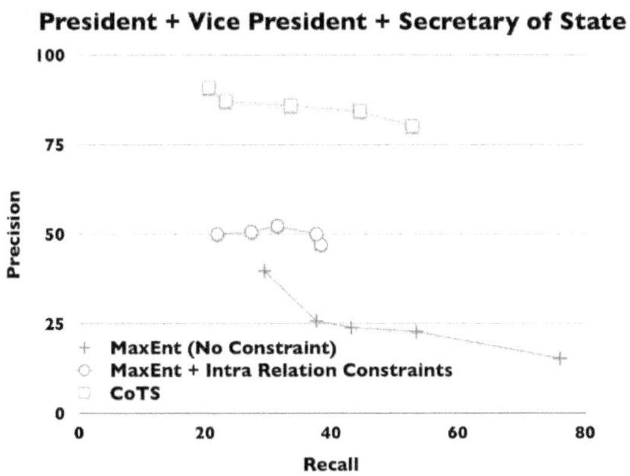

Figure 4: Precision-Recall plot for temporal scoping of US President, Vice President and Secretary of State relations. CoTS is the system proposed in this paper. (see Section 4.3)

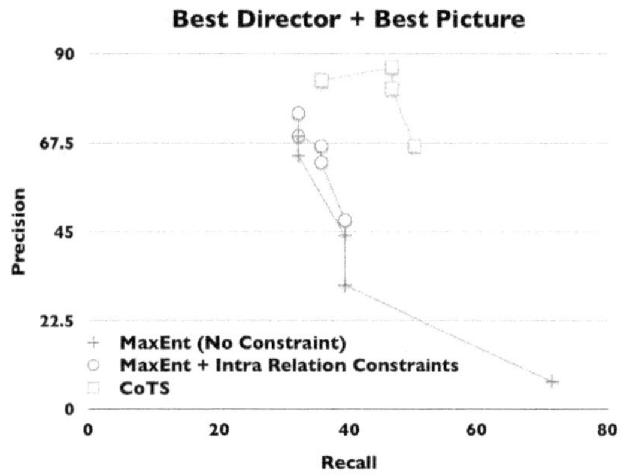

Figure 5: Precision-Recall plot for temporal scoping of Academy Award Best Director and Best Picture relations. CoTS is the system proposed in this paper. (see Section 4.3)

In case of Google Books Ngram dataset, each (unique) ngram is considered a document. Per year data from these two datasets are (separately) indexed using Lucene as mentioned above. For Google Books Ngrams dataset, we index only the English 5-grams published during the period 1960 - 2008. We consider 5-grams as they can accommodate longer queries. We use the Google Books Ngram dataset for the three US Administration relations in Table 1, as temporal scope of facts from these three relations span 1961 - 2008, which is beyond the temporal coverage of Gigaword (1994 - 2008). We use the Gigaword corpus for the two Academy Awards relations in Table 1, as the combined temporal span of facts from these two relations (as considered in this section) are aligned with that of Gigaword.

4.1.3 *Training Local Classifier*

Once the temporal profiles of facts are generated as described above, we next train a relation-specific local classifier by deriving features from these temporal profiles (Section 3.1). For each relation experimented with in this paper (Table 1), we use a single temporally scoped fact from this relation to generate all training data needed to train the corresponding relation-specific local classifier (MaxEnt, see Section 3.1). For example, for the US President relation, we derive training data from the temporally scoped fact: President Kennedy (1961 - 1963). In this case, all instances in the span [1961,1963] correspond to positive instances ($y = +1$), while everything outside this range correspond to negative instances ($y = +1$). Please note that all the classifiers in these experiments are trained from such limited amount of training data, demonstrating the real-world applicability of CoTS, the proposed method.

4.1.4 *Metrics*

As mentioned in Section 4.1.1, true temporal scopes of all facts in Table 1 were determined by a human annotator. Prediction from CoTS (or any of the baselines) that a fact is true at a given time is matched against this gold-standard to determine prediction correctness. Based on this, Precision (P), Recall (R), and F1 ($\frac{2*P*R}{(P+R)}$) are computed, which are used as the final evaluation metrics. Also, all evaluations are performed at the year level, as that is the finest granularity common to the two time-stamped datasets (Section 4.1.2).

In order to generate different Precision-Recall plots, we vary the λ parameter over the local classifier's scores, as described in Section 3.2.2.

4.2 Effect of Gradient Feature

Relations	F1 (No Gradient)	F1 (With Gradient)
President, V. President, Sec. of State	42.8	**63.63**
Best Director, Best Picture	4.26	**60.47**

Table 2: Effect of using gradient information during temporal scoping of different relations from two domains.

In this section, we evaluate the effect of gradient-based features in the local classifier (Section 3.1) can have on collective inference. We use the full CoTS with and without gradient features in the local classifier, and apply it on relations from two domains. F1 results are presented in Table 2. We observe that gradient features can significantly improve temporal scoping performance. This validates our motivation behind using gradient-based features in the local classifier, as it can help get rid of the publication lag issues in the books data and for certain domains in the newswire.

Based on these results, in all subsequent experiments, we include gradient-based features in CoTS's local classifier.

4.3 Effect of Coupling Constraints

In this section, we evaluate the effect of Cross Relational coupling constraints on temporal scoping. We compare the performance of CoTS against other systems exploiting either no constraint (MaxEnt, the local classifier in Section 3.1), or a subset of constraints (Intra Relation, Section 3.2.1) but without any cross relation coupling constraints. Examples of a few manually-specified coupling constraints used by CoTS for these experiments are presented in Table 3.

President, Vice President, Secretary of State		
Fact	Temporal Constraint	Fact
President Clinton	Containment	Vice President Gore
President Reagan	Containment	Vice President Bush
President Reagan	Succession	Secretary Kissinger
Best Director, Best Picture		
Director Cameron	Aligned	Titanic
Director Howard	Aligned	A Beautiful Mind

Table 3: Examples of coupling constraints used by CoTS for the experiments in Section 4.3. For brevity, we represent the facts by the queries used to compute their counts from the timestamped datasets (Section 4.1.2).

The Precision-Recall plots for these comparisons over facts from the two sets of relations in Table 1 are reported in Figure 4 and Figure 5, respectively. From these plots, we observe that CoTS, which exploits cross relational coupling constraints, significantly outperforms other baselines which either don't use any constraint (MaxEnt), or use only a subset of constraints exploited by CoTS.

4.4 Constraint Ablation Study

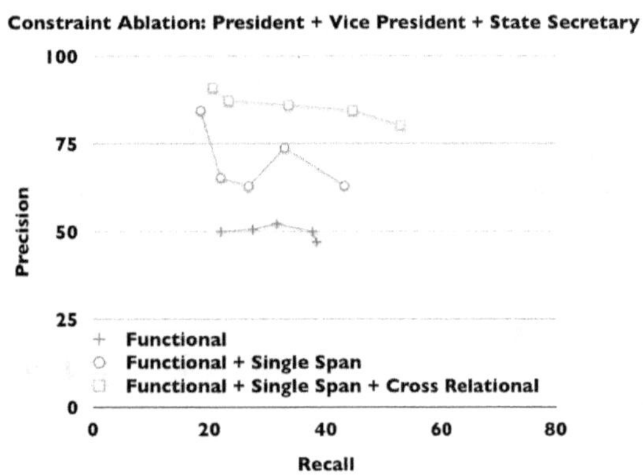

Figure 6: Constraint ablation results for temporal scoping over US President, Vice President and Secretary of State relations.

In this section, we report results from constraint ablation studies involving CoTS. The goal is to study the effect of different constraint types on CoTS's performance. Results from two different sets of relations are reported in Figure 6 and Figure 7. For the politics domain (President, Vice President, Sec. of State), we use the SingleSpan constraint as facts in that domain tend to be true for a contiguous single span (e.g., presidency usually lasts multiple consecutive years, and one is president for a single span). This is in contrast to the temporal spans of the two relations in the movies domain whose spans are usually a unit length, and where one could win the same award multiple times in one's lifetime, and hence the choice of the Point constraint.

From the results in Figure 6 and Figure 7, we observe that CoTS's performance improves as more prior knowledge is injected through additional coupling constraints. This

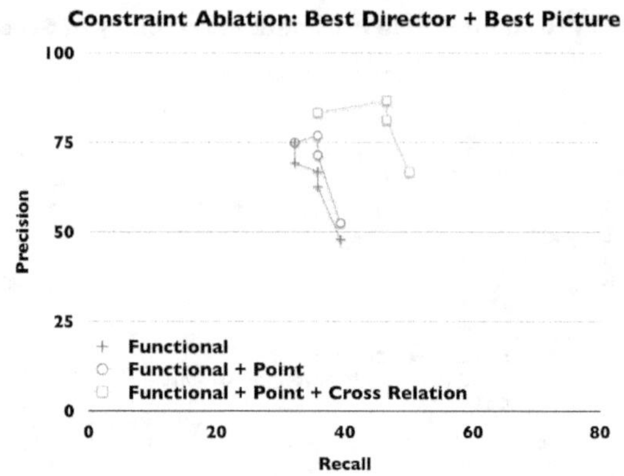

Figure 7: Constraint ablation results for temporal scoping over Academy Award winner Best Director and Best Picture relations.

justifies our design choice of using coupled (joint) inference for more accurate temporal scoping.

4.5 Running time of ILP

For all the problems in our experiments, CoTS's collective inference took on average 0.25 sec, with inference over the largest problem involving 2334 variables and 3804 constraints taking only 2.6 sec. This demonstrates the practicality of CoTS's inference scheme.

5. RELATED WORK

Even though time is an important dimension in any information space, and knowledge of temporal scopes of facts can be useful for better information retrieval systems, and user experience [2], temporal scoping of knowledge base facts is an area that is still largely unexplored. Only recently, a few research papers have started to address this problem [13, 27, 26]. Otherwise, most previous work on temporal information extraction has been focused largely on temporal representations [17], temporal relation identification [6, 14, 5, 16], and ensuring temporal consistency between extracted temporal relations [8, 29, 13]. We shall review some of the more recently proposed (and more relevant) approaches first, and then compare CoTS against the other previous work on temporal relation identification.

Timely YAGO [27] is similar in spirit to CoTS in that its objective is also temporal grounding of facts. As in CoTS, a fact in Timely YAGO refers to an instance of a binary relation between entities (entity-relation-entity triplet). Facts and their temporal information in Timely YAGO are extracted from semi-structured text in the infoboxes and category information in Wikipedia using regular expression matching. In contrast, CoTS is applicable more widely and is not limited to Wikipedia texts alone. Moreover, instead of using any regular expression based extractors, CoTS aggregates document-level metadata (viz., document creation time) based evidences to temporally scope multiple temporally related facts at the same time.

A method to temporally scope facts and reason over such scoped facts is presented in [25]. Given a target fact, the method in [25] attempts to gather count-based evidence for the begin, active and end time of this fact. These possibly inconsistent evidences are then aggregated using a set of heuristics to determine the final interval over which the target fact is likely to be true. Instead of temporally scoping each fact in isolation as in [25], CoTS performs joint inference to temporally scope multiple facts at the same time while exploiting temporal dependencies among those facts, resulting in more accurate temporal scoping as demonstrated through the experiments in this paper.

The Temporal Information Extraction (TIE) system [13] attempts to output a maximal set of events and their temporal relations as directly implied in a given sentence. TIE uses joint transitivity inference to bind the start and end times for each event. As in TIE, and instead of Allen-style intervals [1], CoTS uses a real-valued point-based temporal representation. While TIE is a micro-reading system which processes a single (or a set of) sentences at once, CoTS works at the macro-reading level, aggregating evidences from a large number of documents to temporally scope a set of facts.

PRAVDA is a recently proposed method to harvest temporal facts from free text [26]. PRAVDA uses textual patterns to generate candidate temporal facts, which are then re-ranked using a graph-based label propagation algorithm adapted from a recently proposed graph transduction algorithm [22]. PRAVDA is probably the prior work which is closest in spirit to CoTS. However, unlike PRAVDA, CoTS exploits temporal dependencies among facts to scope them jointly, a strategy that we have found to be quite effective as demonstrated in Section 4.

We note that Timely Yago [27], TIE [13], and PRAVDA [26] are complementary to CoTS, as extractions from these three systems can be used as additional evidence (features) in CoTS's local classifier, with potential for more accurate temporal scoping.

Learning and inference in CoTS is similar in spirit to the CCM framework [9, 20]. However, unlike existing CCM models, CoTS uses additional variables to define more expressive constraints, and applies them to the novel problem of temporally scoping relation facts, which is beyond the scope of current CCM-based models. Similar to CoTS, the SCAD system [3] also uses ILP to improve on the predictions from a weakly-supervised local classifier. However, the two systems address very different problems with completely different motivations.

Previous works on temporal relation identification have been largely spurred by the release of TimeML [17], a notable markup language for events and temporal expressions in natural language, the availability of tools such as TARSQI [24] to automatically annotate events and times in TimeML, and the release of TimeBank [18], a TimeML annotated corpora for training and testing. The TimeBank corpus consists of 186 news articles that are annotated for events, time expressions and temporal relations between events and times. Most previous work on temporal relation identification is based on the TimeBank corpus [6, 14, 8]. These approaches build temporal relation classifier over the corpus relations and making either local pairwise decisions of temporal relations between events [6, 14], or jointly informed decision to impose transitivity constraints (A before B and B before C implies A before C) between locally discovered temporal relations [8]. Aside from transitivity constraint, temporal expression normalization (e.g., "last year" is before "last month") are also used to discover implicit time-time relation in the document to enrich temporal network between events and times in TimeBank.

Other works on temporal relation identification [5, 16, 29] have been conducted for the tasks of TempEval Challenge [23]. TempEval challenge uses training and test sets encoded in a subset of TimeML, and is divided into three subtasks: to identify temporal relations 1) between a specific event and a time expression in the same sentence, 2) between a specific event and the Document Creation Time (DCT), and 3) between the provided main events in two adjacent sentences. The event is specified per sentence by the main verb in the sentence. Some approaches use relation classification on each subtask independently by using either a pure machine learning approach [5], or a combination of rule based and machine learning [16]. Another approach attempts to solve the three subtasks jointly [29] by learning a single probabilistic model for all three tasks, incorporating formulas of temporal transitivity that should hold across tasks.

Please note that there are fundamental differences between these temporal relation identification approaches and CoTS. Firstly, an event in these approaches is usually a tensed verb, which is different from the notion of relational facts in CoTS. Moreover, unlike these previous approaches, CoTS attempts to temporally ground facts on the timeline, and not just infer temporal dependencies among events (and time). However, these approaches could be complementary to CoTS in the sense that the temporal relations inferred by these approaches could potentially be used as additional constraints in CoTS's collective inference engine.

6. CONCLUSION

Despite the benefits of temporally scoped facts in knowledge bases, temporal scoping of facts is a research area that has been largely unexplored, with the exception of a few recent proposals [27, 26]. In this paper we propose CoTS (Coupled Temporal Scoping), a novel way of temporally scoping facts by exploiting a variety of signals: counts of mentions of the fact in large open domain data sources such as Google Books Ngram corpus and Gigaword Corpus; and by exploiting temporal relationships between the fact and other facts from the same or different relations.

CoTS poses the task of temporal scoping as a change detection in the temporal profile of the fact. To aggregate redundant observed cues (e.g., gradients and counts from the temporal profile) for a fact, CoTS uses Integer Linear Program (ILP) to jointly infer the time scopes of multiple temporally related facts while respecting any temporal constraints among them. CoTS is a weakly supervised system in that it only needs a few labeled examples per relation to make decision on the temporal scope of facts.

There are several avenues for improving CoTS, and overcoming fact count sparseness is one of them. Some queries such as those related to the 'defenseSecretaryOf' relation return very few results in both Google Books and Gigaword datasets. Although temporal scope of sparse facts can be inferred from the temporal scope of other related facts via coupling, sparsity of counts may still hamper temporal scoping of facts that have little or no other correlated facts. To overcome this problem, we are planning to (1) derive counts from a larger number of time-stamped sources; and (2) use semi-supervised learning algorithms to gather fact counts even from non time-stamped documents.

Furthermore, in the current CoTS system, temporal constraints among facts are specified manually based on users' prior knowledge. In the future, we would like to automatically acquire such relation and fact specific constraints, for example, by learning temporal relationships among facts in a semi-supervised fashion, such as in NELL [7].

Acknowledgments

This research has been supported in part by DARPA (under contract number FA8750-09-C-0179), Google, and Fulbright. Any opinions, findings, conclusions and recommendations expressed in this paper are the authors' and do not necessarily reflect those of the sponsors. We are thankful to Lei Li (CMU) for useful discussions, and to the four anonymous reviewers for their constructive comments.

7. REFERENCES

[1] J.F. Allen. Maintaining knowledge about temporal intervals. *Communications of the ACM*, 26(11), 1983.

[2] O. Alonso, M. Gertz, and R. Baeza-Yates. On the value of temporal information in information retrieval. In *ACM SIGIR Forum*, volume 41. ACM, 2007.

[3] A. Bakalov, A. Fuxman, P.P. Talukdar, and S. Chakrabarti. Scad: Collective discovery of attribute values. In *Proceedings of WWW*, 2011.

[4] M. Banko, M.J. Cafarella, S. Soderland, M. Broadhead, and O. Etzioni. Open information extraction from the web. *Proceedings of IJCAI*, 2007.

[5] S. Bethard and J.H. Martin. Cu-tmp: Temporal relation classification using syntactic and semantic features. In *In SemEval-2007*, 2007.

[6] B. Boguraev and R.K. Ando. Timeml-compliant text analysis for temporal reasoning. In *Proceedings of IJCAI*, 2005.

[7] A. Carlson, J. Betteridge, B. Kisiel, B. Settles, E.R. Hruschka Jr, and T.M. Mitchell. Toward an architecture for never-ending language learning. In *Proceedings of AAAI*, 2010.

[8] N. Chambers and D. Jurafsky. Jointly combining implicit constraints improves temporal ordering. In *Proceedings of EMNLP*, 2008.

[9] M.W. Chang, L. Ratinov, N. Rizzolo, and D. Roth. Learning and inference with constraints. In *Proceedings of the 23rd National Conference on Artificial intelligence*, 2008.

[10] O. Etzioni, M. Cafarella, D. Downey, S. Kok, A.M. Popescu, T. Shaked, S. Soderland, D.S. Weld, and A. Yates. Web-scale information extraction in knowitall:(preliminary results). In *Proceedings of WWW*, 2004.

[11] O. Gospodnetic, E. Hatcher, et al. *Lucene in action.* Manning, 2005.

[12] D. Graff, J. Kong, K. Chen, and K. Maeda. English gigaword. *Linguistic Data Consortium, Philadelphia*, 2003.

[13] X. Ling and D.S. Weld. Temporal information extraction. In *Proceedings of AAAI*, 2010.

[14] I. Mani, M. Verhagen, B. Wellner, C.M. Lee, and J. Pustejovsky. Machine learning of temporal relations. In *Proceedings of the ACL*, 2006.

[15] J.B. Michel, Y.K. Shen, A.P. Aiden, A. Veres, M.K. Gray, J.P. Pickett, D. Hoiberg, D. Clancy, P. Norvig, J. Orwant, et al. Quantitative analysis of culture using millions of digitized books. *Science*, 331(6014), 2011.

[16] G. Puscasu. Wvali: Temporal relation identification by syntactico-semantic analysis. In *Proceedings of the 4th International Workshop on SemEval*, 2007.

[17] J. Pustejovsky, J. Castano, R. Ingria, R. Saurí, R. Gaizauskas, A. Setzer, G. Katz, and D. Radev. Timeml: Robust specification of event and temporal expressions in text. In *Fifth International Workshop on Computational Semantics*, 2003.

[18] J. Pustejovsky, P. Hanks, R. Sauri, A. See, R. Gaizauskas, A. Setzer, D. Radev, B. Sundheim, D. Day, L. Ferro, et al. The timebank corpus. In *Corpus Linguistics*, 2003.

[19] M. Richardson and P. Domingos. Markov logic networks. *Machine Learning*, 62(1), 2006.

[20] D. Roth and W. Yih. A linear programming formulation for global inference in natural language tasks.

[21] F.M. Suchanek, G. Kasneci, and G. Weikum. Yago: a core of semantic knowledge. In *Proceedings of WWW*, 2007.

[22] P. Talukdar and K. Crammer. New regularized algorithms for transductive learning. In *Proceedings of ECML*, 2009.

[23] M. Verhagen, R. Gaizauskas, F. Schilder, M. Hepple, G. Katz, and J. Pustejovsky. Semeval-2007 task 15: Tempeval temporal relation identification. In *Proceedings of the 4th International Workshop on Semantic Evaluations*, 2007.

[24] M. Verhagen, I. Mani, R. Sauri, R. Knippen, S.B. Jang, J. Littman, A. Rumshisky, J. Phillips, and J. Pustejovsky. Automating temporal annotation with tarsqi. In *Proceedings of the ACL Session on Interactive poster and demonstration sessions*, 2005.

[25] Y. Wang, M. Yahya, and M. Theobald. Time-aware reasoning in uncertain knowledge bases. In *MUD Workshop*, 2010.

[26] Y. Wang, B. Yang, L. Qu, M. Spaniol, and G. Weikum. Harvesting facts from textual web sources by constrained label propagation. In *Proceedings of CIKM*, 2011.

[27] Y. Wang, M. Zhu, L. Qu, M. Spaniol, and G. Weikum. Timely yago: harvesting, querying, and visualizing temporal knowledge from wikipedia. In *Proceedings of the 13th International Conference on Extending Database Technology*, 2010.

[28] G. Weikum, S. Bedathur, and R. Schenkel. Temporal knowledge for timely intelligence. *Enabling Real-Time Business Intelligence*, 2011.

[29] K. Yoshikawa, S. Riedel, M. Asahara, and Y. Matsumoto. Jointly identifying temporal relations with markov logic. In *Proceedings of ACL*, 2009.

Overcoming Browser Cookie Churn with Clustering

Anirban Dasgupta Maxim Gurevich Liang Zhang Belle Tseng Achint O. Thomas
Yahoo! Research
701 First Avenue
Sunnyvale, CA 94089
{anirban,maximg,liangzha,belle,aothomas}@yahoo-inc.com

ABSTRACT

Many large Internet websites are accessed by users anonymously, without requiring registration or logging-in. However, to provide personalized service these sites build anonymous, yet persistent, user models based on repeated user visits. Cookies, issued when a web browser first visits a site, are typically employed to anonymously associate a website visit with a distinct user (web browser). However, users may reset cookies, making such association short-lived and noisy. In this paper we propose a solution to the cookie churn problem: a novel algorithm for grouping similar cookies into clusters that are more persistent than individual cookies. Such clustering could potentially allow more robust estimation of the number of unique visitors of the site over a certain long time period, and also better user modeling which is key to plenty of web applications such as advertising and recommender systems.

We present a novel method to cluster browser cookies into groups that are likely to belong to the same browser based on a statistical model of browser visitation patterns. We address each step of the clustering as a binary classification problem estimating the probability that two different subsets of cookies belong to the same browser. We observe that our clustering problem is a generalized interval graph coloring problem, and propose a greedy heuristic algorithm for solving it. The scalability of this method allows us to cluster hundreds of millions of browser cookies and provides significant improvements over baselines such as constrained K-means.

Categories and Subject Descriptors

I.5.3 [**Pattern Recognition**]: Clustering—*Algorithms, similarity measures*; D.1.3 [**Programming Techniques**]: Concurrent Programming—*Distributed programming*

General Terms

Algorithms, Experimentation

1. INTRODUCTION

The World Wide Web (WWW) has been growing extremely fast in recent years and large websites such as Yahoo!, Google and MSN attract hundreds of millions of unique visitors every month. These user visits are logged anonymously by the websites, with an aim to measure user engagement and to improve user experience. When a web browser visits a website for the first time, the website creates and assigns the browser a unique identifier (cookie), which is sent to the website on consecutive visits until it expires or is deleted by user through the browser interface or otherwise.

Cookies help websites to better estimate various user engagement metrics e.g. the number of unique visitors, the average engagement time of an user, and the number of repeat visitors to the site. These metrics are important both for assessing website popularity and for measuring the effectiveness of display advertisements, which is a large source of revenue for Internet companies. Maintaining anonymous user profiles associated with each cookie allows a website to improve user experience, e.g. to personalize the stories displayed on a web-page based on the user's past history [2], even to the users that have not explicitly registered or otherwise identified themselves to the website.

However, cookies do not last forever: some browsers are set up to clear cookies when the browser is closed; cookies can be deleted by user request; cookies expire after some predefined period. A study released by `comScore` in 2007 [1] indicates that around 31 percent of U.S. Internet users clear their first-party cookies within a month. The conclusion drawn in the study is that cookie-based unique visitor counting systems, which are widely implemented by many websites, usually overestimate the number of unique visitors by large factors. We refer to problem of frequent cookie deletion as "cookie churn" in this paper. Figure 1 shows that a significant fraction of Yahoo! Toolbar users clears cookies at least once a day, and even more do so weekly and monthly. It aligns well with the findings in [1].

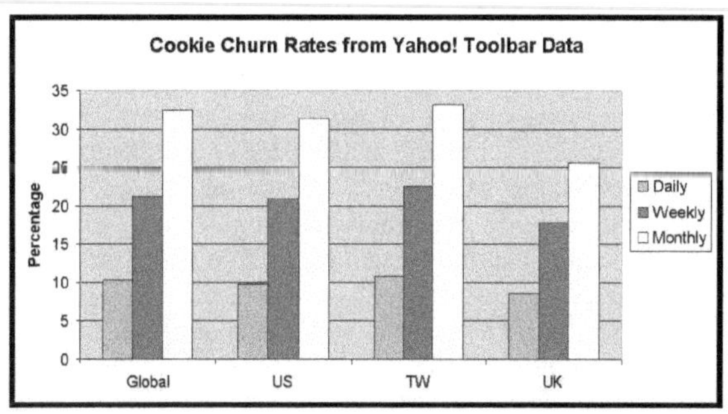

Figure 1: Fraction of Yahoo! Toolbar users that clear cookies.

In addition to causing overestimation of the number of unique visitors, the cookie churn problem also impacts the effectiveness of user-targeting models and applications. In user behavioral model-

Permission to make digital or hard copies of all or part of this work for personal or classroom use is granted without fee provided that copies are not made or distributed for profit or commercial advantage and that copies bear this notice and the full citation on the first page. To copy otherwise, to republish, to post on servers or to redistribute to lists, requires prior specific permission and/or a fee.
WSDM'12, February 8–12, 2012, Seattle, Washington, USA.
Copyright 2012 ACM 978-1-4503-0747-5/12/02 ...$10.00.

ing, recently-created cookies have little history to learn from (a.k.a. the "cold-start" problem, see [17, 30, 2, 36]), which negatively affects model performance. In online advertising, advertisers are interested to know the joint distribution of how many users have been exposed to ads from a campaign (*reach*), and how many times individual users have been exposed to the campaign (*frequency*). Under cookie churn, estimating these metrics is hard. In fact, neither of the above two problems – *user-modeling* or *reach-frequency* curve estimation – can be solved by only estimating a scaling parameter (e.g. average number of cookies used by a user); we do need some approximate grouping of the cookies in order to solve either.

Although the cookie churn problem is important for many applications, there is little research done on this problem, other than by companies e.g. `comScore` and `Nielsen`, who are engaged in estimating user metrics. A popular approach used by these companies is to recruit panelists to estimate cookie-visitor ratios, and then inferring the number of unique visitors to a site based on the number of unique cookies and these ratios. A similar work by [15] tries to find the cookie-visitor or IP-visitor ratios and uses these to normalize the number of cookies. As we mentioned, such ratio-based methods are applicable only to coarse grained user counting and not to the user behavioral modeling or the reach and frequency problems. Another interesting related work is a public web tool built by the Electronic Frontier Foundation [13] that defines the concept of "browser fingerprints" using a number of browser features such as user agent, http accept headers, browser plugins, screen resolution, and third party cookies. The authors claim that among a sample of around 470K browsers they have collected, 83.6% of them have unique fingerprints. Thus, such fingerprint could serve as a potential identifier of a browser. However, their estimation of uniqueness is built on a miscalculation of entropy that assumes the browser features to be independent of each other – in general this is not true. Also, for large sites with hundreds of millions of visitors every month, the collision rate is expected to be high. Lastly, the fingerprint are based on browser properties that are not accessible to most websites unless explicitly authorized by the users and the instrumentation to collect them exists, and thus cannot be used in practice. We aim to construct similar browser fingerprints, but based on features that are much more benign and less discriminative. One of the contributions of this work is to show that even using a seemingly benign set of features enables us to identify browsers with high accuracy.

Our approach. Our broad approach in solving the cookie churn problem in the settings of user-modeling and reach-frequency estimation from ad campaign is to create **clusters of cookies** based on a behavioral profile – each cluster ideally will represent all and only the cookies associated with a single browser.

To solve the cookie clustering problem, one important observation is that the lifetimes of cookies (the lifetime is defined as time elapsed between cookie creation and the last pageview) in a cluster can not overlap, i.e., a browser has to clear the previous cookie to generate a new one. This induces a set of hard *cannot-link* constraints among cookies. Additional cannot-link constraints are derived from the fact that the operating system (OS) or the browser-types of cookies in a cluster have to be the same.

Challenges. There are several major challenges we face when tackling this problem in a clustering framework. First, the solution has to scale well to be able to process hundreds of millions of cookies created every month at major websites. Most clustering algorithms do not scale to this level. Secondly, since each cluster represents a browser, the number of clusters is unknown – in fact, one of the outputs of our method is an estimate of the number of underlying browsers. This is a major issue for most clustering algorithms – often solved using model-selection approaches, or simply by trying out different values for the number of clusters. Moreover, in our setting the number of clusters is of the same order of magnitude as the number of cookies, an atypical setting for many clustering algorithms like K-means or spectral clustering. Third, in large websites that have millions of simultaneous visitors, the number of cannot-link constraints (due to lifetime and OS and browser types) is *quadratic* in the number of cookies, stressing scalability even more. The hard cannot-link constraints are known to be difficult to satisfy if the number of clusters is pre-specified [10]. Fourth, due to the short lifetime of the majority of cookies, the amount of useful information in their profiles is low, making it hard to extract meaningful cookie profiles and to design accurate similarity measure among these profiles. All of the above challenges make off-the-shelf clustering algorithms ineffective, necessitating a specialized solution.

Our solution. We propose a novel and scalable method which overcomes all the above challenges and is able to cluster hundreds of millions of browser cookies, essentially predicting "typical" browser identifiers spanning multiple cookie sessions. We observe that while in general clustering with cannot-link constraints is a hard problem, the non-overlap constraints induce an interval graph [16], where each cookie is an interval defined by its lifetime. Interval graphs have an elegant structure admitting an optimal greedy graph coloring algorithm that essentially partitions the graph into the provably minimal number of groups of cookies where the lifetimes of all cookies in a group do not overlap. However, the coloring algorithm does not use cookie profile information, which as we show reduces clustering accuracy. To embed cookie profile similarity into clustering, we need to solve an augmented coloring problem using binary classification model that predicts the likelihood of a cookie to belong to one of the several candidate clusters. Hence we propose a greedy heuristic algorithm that is inspired by the interval graph coloring algorithm. We define a set of cookie profile features such as cookie lifetime, number of page views, OS type, distribution of IP addresses, categories of visited webpages, etc. We propose two profile similarity measures, one based on L_2 distance between profile vectors, and the other by further embedding Bayes factors into the similarity measure. Both measure are learned through logistic regression [27] using some training data.

We evaluated our algorithm on a dataset extracted from one months of web logs of Yahoo! websites (clean of the majority of bot traffic), containing 200M cookies. For training the similarity measure as well as evaluating our clustering algorithm, we use the Yahoo! Toolbar web logs where we use Toolbar ID is used as the ground truth browser identifier. Although the Toolbar data likely carries some bias and does not accurately represent user population, the bias problem is orthogonal to the techniques we develop in this work, and can be dealt with independently using existing bias removal approaches, e.g., [3].

Our contributions. In summary, our major contributions in this work are: (a) We formalize the problem of dealing with cookie churn by creating clusters of cookies using a constrained clustering framework. (b) We define a simple browser model for cookie lifetimes and also uses real-world data to validate our assumption. This model is also used to derive theoretical intuitions behind our clustering algorithm. (c) We define a set of cookie profile features and propose an efficient and scalable clustering algorithm based on interval graph coloring and cookie profile similarities; we also show how to learn the parameters of such similarity measures from the training data. (d) We evaluate our algorithms on the real-world Yahoo! data and show that it outperforms various baseline methods.

User privacy. Today's Internet users are aware of their privacy when online, which explains the findings by comScore and us that many users clear cookies often. We reiterate that cookie profiles that we use are completely anonymized and cannot be tracked to individual users. In particular, they are not linked to the richer user profiles of registered users. Furthermore, given the increasing importance of personalization as a business strategy, research in exposing the tradeoff between privacy and value-addition is inevitable and important. By showing the feasibility of browser identification using a weak set of features, we also see our work as a step towards exposing this tradeoff, demonstrating the need for improved anonymization techniques if privacy is desired.

2. COOKIE CLUSTERING

In this section we describe our clustering algorithm. We start from describing the basic interval graph coloring algorithm [16]. By using a simplified cookie generation model, we show that for the problem of estimating the number of unique browsers in the data, this algorithm is an effective one if we have observed the data for a sufficiently long time. However, the coloring algorithm alone does not consider cookie profile similarities, and may group cookies with very different profiles. Obviously, this reduces clustering accuracy as we later demonstrate in our experimental evaluation.

We thus augment the coloring technique with a profile similarity measure (discussed in Section 3), such that we group cookies in the same cluster only if they satisfy the cannot-link constraints *and* their profile similarity are above some threshold. Finally, we show a componentization algorithm that splits the input sets of cookies into several smaller subsets on which the clustering algorithm can be run in parallel.

There are two types of cannot-link constraints we need to incorporate in the clustering – the constraints due to OS and browser-type mismatch, and those due to overlap in the cookie lifetimes. We incorporate the OS and browser-type mismatch simply by partitioning the set of cookies such that cookies with different OS-browser values fall in different partitions. This is achieved by our componentization algorithm in Section 2.3. In this section, we show how to incorporate the lifetime overlap constraints and the cookie profile similarity measure in our clustering algorithm. In order to handle overlap constraints efficiently, we resort to the coloring problem in interval graphs.

2.1 Interval Graphs

A graph $G(V, E)$ over a set of vertices V and a set of edges E is an interval graph if each vertex corresponds to a connected interval on the real line, i.e. each $v_i \in V$ can be associated with $[s_i, t_i] \in \Re^1$ such that $(v_i, v_j) \in E$ iff $[s_i, t_i] \cap [s_j, t_j] \neq \emptyset$. We naturally represent each cookie by the interval corresponding to the lifetime of the cookie. The lifetime constraints are then obeyed if the clustering of the cookies corresponds to a coloring of this interval graph. Since interval graphs are perfect graphs, finding a coloring with the minimal number of colors can be done optimally in time $O(|V|\log(|V|) + |E|)$, by a clever greedy algorithm given in Algorithm 1. In Section 2.2 we show how we obtain our clustering heuristic by modifying this coloring algorithm.

Before presenting our modification of the coloring algorithm, we present some theoretical results that justify the importance of the lifetime constraints for partitioning cookies into browsers. Using the interval representation of the cookies, the minimum number of colors that is required to color the cookies is a lower bound to the underlying number of browsers. This is because, assigning an unique color to all the cookies from one browser creates a consistent coloring of the graph. On the other hand, this lower bound might be weak, as the cookies generated by two browsers might not overlap in time – either because both are infrequent visitors, or because their lifetimes are too short.

Algorithm 1 IntervalColor

Input: Set of intervals S
Output: A partition of S that is a valid minimal coloring of S
Let $\Phi = \{C_1, \ldots, C_k\}$ be the coloring up until the current step. Initialize $\Phi = \emptyset$.
Sort the intervals in S by their starting point
for all $c \in S$ in the ascending order of starting point **do**
  if there exists a color $C \in \Phi$ such that c does not overlap with any $c' \in C$, **then**
    Assign c to the color C, i.e., $C \leftarrow C \cup \{c\}$
  else
    Assign a new color to c, i.e., add $\{c\}$ to Φ.
return Φ.

We next formalize the above intuition. We first formulate a simple browser model and check its validity by using the real-world data. We then use this model to derive theoretical results to build connections between the minimal number of colors and the underlying number of browsers. Note that the underlying number of browsers is only one of our major interests: clustering cookies into browsers would give more benefits on problems such as personalized ad serving and calculating reach-frequency in ad campaigns.

Browser Model. For a single browser, each visit to the website that created the cookie is an observed event. Each browser is associated with two parameters λ and p. We make a simple assumption that the inter-visit times of the browser follow an exponential distribution with the parameter λ. Thus, the number of visits made in any time interval t follows a Poisson distribution with parameter λt. Each visit of a browser is assumed to be associated with a cookie. If a cookie does not exist, it is created by the website automatically at the time of this event. In addition, each browser has a parameter $p \in [0, 1]$ that controls the probability of clearing cookies. Each visit is independently categorized to be of type *clearing* with probability p and *non-clearing* with probability $1-p$. If a visit is non-clearing, the browser does not clear the cookie at the time of this visit. On the other hand, for each clearing visit, the existing cookie is cleared by the browser immediately after the observed visit. In particular, if a cookie did not exist prior to the visit, it is first created and then cleared, resulting in cookie lifetime of zero. We note that although the real cookie clearing time is usually not coupled with browser visiting time, in this paper we assume they are coupled since there is no way to observe the real cookie clearing time. What we do observe instead is a browser uses one cookie to visit Yahoo! and later uses another cookie to visit again, hence in our real-world data cookie clearing is already coupled with visits.

Denote the set of cookies generated by a browser by $[1, \ldots, n]$. For every cookie i, let f_i be the first event associated with this cookie, and let ℓ_i be the last event associated with the cookie, i.e., the first *clearing* event following f_i (if f_i is clearing then $\ell_i = f_i$). Let the lifetime interval of cookie i be $[f_i, \ell_i]$, and let the lifetime of i be $d_i = \ell_i - f_i$. We now derive the distribution of d_i.

LEMMA 1. *Suppose a browser has the visit-distribution $Exp(\lambda)$ and the cookie-clearing probability p for each visit. Suppose the first visit time and last visit time of the ith cookie from this browser are denoted by f_i and ℓ_i respectively, and WLOG let $f_i = 0$. Then,*

- *The fraction of cookies that have lifetime $d_i = 0$ is p^2.*
- *For the cookies with positive lifetime, the lifetime d_i is distributed as $Exp(\lambda p)$.*

- *The intervals $f_{i+k} - \ell_i$, where cookie $i+k$ is the first cookie following i that has positive lifetime (i.e., skipping all cookies $i+1, \ldots, i+k-1$ that have zero lifetimes), are distributed as $Exp((1-p)\lambda)$.*

PROOF. First, the number of cookies that are cleared immediately and thus have zero lifetime can be computed as the fraction of clearing events minus the fraction of clearing events preceded by a non-clearing event (as the latter clearing events clear a cookie with non-zero lifetime). This value is $p - p(1-p) = p^2$, which shows the first claim.

Now, the partitioning of the set of visits into clearing and non-clearing can be seen as the splitting of the Poisson visitation process into two random parts – i.i.d. with probability p. Thus, each of the two clearing and non-clearing events can thus be seen as an independent Poisson process – with rates λp and $\lambda(1-p)$, and thus have interarrival times exponentially distributed also. Thus, for the cookie i, the next clearing event after f_i arrives at time exponentially distributed as λp – this by definition is the event ℓ_i. Hence $d_i \sim Exp(\lambda p)$. Similar argument shows the distribution of $f_{i+1} - \ell_i$. □

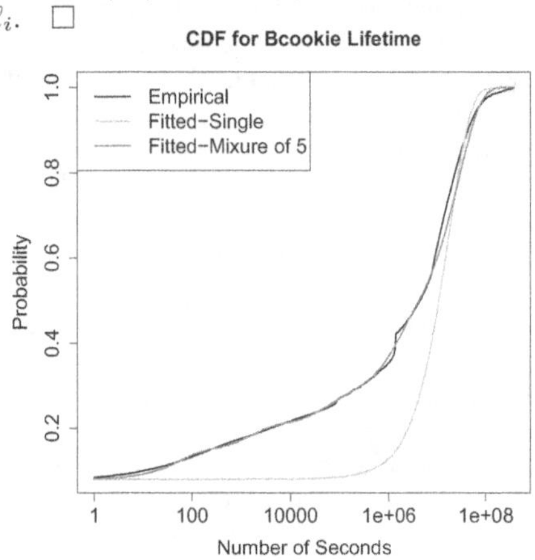

Figure 2: The empirical cdf of the observed cookie lifetime d_i based on a sample of cookies visiting Yahoo! (black curve). The green curve is the optimal fitted cdf by using a single λp. The red curve is the optimal fitted cdf by using a mixture of 5 λp's.

To validate the above model, we extracted a random sample of cookies that visited Yahoo! on Mar 1, 2011, and track the visits of these cookies for the next 3 months. We note that around 8% of the observed cookies have zero lifetime. In Figure 2 we show the empirical cumulative distribution function (cdf) of the observed cookie lifetime d_i in the sample (black curve). Recall from the lemma that the positive cookie lifetime has a distribution $Exp(\lambda p)$. We then fitted an exponential distribution by considering the point-mass at zero, and finding λp that minimizes the K-L divergence to the empirical density, and plot the fitted cdf (green curve) in Figure 2. Obviously, the fitted curve does not match the true distribution. However, we can obtain a very close fit using a mixture of five exponential distributions (red curve). The means of the five distributions, i.e. $1/(\lambda p)$, are 50 seconds (6% of the cookies), 25 minutes (7% of the cookies), 14 hours (7% of the cookies), 15 days (18% of the cookies), and 337 days (62% of the cookies). This is very intuitive since we know different people have different cookie clearing browser settings and preferences, hence trying to find global values of λ and p do not bring success.

Next, we show that under such a random data generation model, the interval coloring algorithm gives a good estimate of the number of underlying browsers. We assume that each browser b is characterized by parameters (p_b, λ_b), and that the observed cookies are generated by a set of k browsers, each acting independently according to its parameters. We also assume that we observe the data for a sufficiently long time. Under these assumptions, the following theorem says that the number of colors required to color the observed interval graph is a good estimate of the number of browsers.

THEOREM 1. *Let $\epsilon > 0, \delta < 1$ be two constants. Suppose there are k browsers, with parameters (p_b, λ_b) for browser b, and that for each b, $p_b < 2\epsilon$. Then, in the steady state, if the cookies are observed for a time period $T = \Theta(1/\delta)$, then with probability $1-\delta$, the resulting interval graph needs at least $(1-\epsilon)k$ and at most k colors for a proper coloring.*

We relegate the proof of this theorem to the Appendix.

2.2 Clustering by Intervals and Similarities

Clearly, using interval graph coloring alone is suboptimal in our setting as it ignores cookie profile similarity and is likely to assign unrelated cookies to the same cluster merely by virtue of non-overlapping. In this section we combine the interval graph coloring approach with the cookie profile similarity measure.

Let S be the set of observed cookies. Let $I(c)$ be the $[f_c, \ell_c]$ interval corresponding to the lifetime of a cookie c, and for $C \subseteq S$ let $I(C)$ be the minimal interval containing $I(c)$ of all $c \in C$. The objective of the algorithm we propose is to cluster the set of cookies S into a set of clusters Φ such that each cookie from S belongs to one cluster $C \in \Phi$, and the lifetimes of all pairs of cookies in C are non-overlapping. Additionally, we want to maximize similarity measure of cookies in each cluster:

$$\max \sum_{C\in\Phi} \sum_{i=2}^{|C|} \mathtt{sim}(C[1,\ldots,(i-1)], C[i,i]), \tag{1}$$

where $\mathtt{sim}$ is the profile similarity measure we describe in Section 3, and $C[a,b]$ denotes the subset of cookies in C starting from a-th cookie and up to b-th cookie when ordered by their timestamps (the order is unique since lifetimes of cookies in C do not overlap).

The clustering algorithm assumes access to an oracle function $\mathtt{sim}(C,c) \in (-\infty, \infty)$ that given a set of cookies C and a single cookie c, returns a real valued similarity score which reflects the likelihood of C and c belonging to the same browser. We experiment with several implementation of function $\mathtt{sim}$ to evaluate different strategies for cookie clustering. One implementation $\mathtt{sim}_I$, based on the time gaps between lifetimes, gives higher score to the clusters with endpoints closer to cookie's first page view time. Let $\ell(C) = \max_{c\in C} \ell_c$, and let the gap between C and c be

$$\mathtt{timegap}(C,c) = f_c - \ell(C). \tag{2}$$

Then,

$$\mathtt{sim}_I(C,c) = \begin{cases} 1/\mathtt{timegap}(C,c) & \mathtt{timegap}(C,c) > 0 \\ -\infty & \text{otherwise.} \end{cases}$$

We discuss all other implementations of $\mathtt{sim}$ using cookie profile features in Section 3.

The greedy one-pass clustering algorithm (Algorithm 2) maintains the set of clusters created so far (denoted as Φ), and processes cookies in the ascending order based on their creation time. For each new cookie c, the algorithm collects the set A of non-overlapping clusters in Φ, picks the cluster with the highest similarity to the cookie, and then appends the cookie to this cluster if the similarity score is above a predefined threshold θ. If A is empty or all the similarity scores are below θ, we create a new cluster with this cookie. Intuitively, the higher is the threshold the more "reluctant" is the algorithm to assign a cookie to an existing cluster versus creating a new cluster. In our experiments we pick multiple thresholds to allow the trade-off between precision and recall.

Clearly, Algorithm 2 satisfies the lifetime non-overlap constraints. As for maximizing objective (1), although the algorithm does not guarantee to reach the optimal solution, each iteration of the algorithm either increases the function in (1) or does not change it. The advantage of such a one-pass greedy algorithm is obvious in the setting where the input size is large so that any additional passes or reassignments of cookies to different clusters is expensive.

Algorithm 2 ClusterBrowsers

```
Input: Set of cookies S, threshold θ
Output: Subsets of cookies, each likely to belong to the same
    browser
Φ be the set of clusters formed up until now
Sort all the cookies in S by their creation time
for all c ∈ S in the ascending order of creation time do
    A ← {C ∈ Φ, I(c) ∩ I(C) = ∅}
    C* ← arg max_{C∈A} sim(C, {c})
    if A ≠ ∅ AND sim(C*, {c}) ≥ θ then
        Remove C* from Φ and add C* ∪ c
    else
        Add a new cluster {c} to Φ.
return Φ
```

Reducing the number of candidates. The naive implementation of Algorithm 2 does not scale to the input size we consider (hundreds of millions of cookies) due to the need to evaluate the measure sim for each candidate cluster in A, which has the same order as the input size. We thus limit the number of candidate clusters by considering only the ones where the last cookie has at least one profile features equal to that of cookie c (e.g. IP, OS, browser type). Note that this directly exploits the properties of the implementations of sim in Section 3. Thus by ignoring clusters having no common features with c the probability of missing the cluster C with the highest $\mathtt{sim}(C, c)$ is low. We consider such pruning of the candidate clusters as a pre-screening step, thus using it in conjunction with sim we get a more efficient algorithm.

2.3 Partitioning for Parallel Clustering

Although the one-pass Algorithm 2 is quite efficient as it considers each cookie only once, it is inherently serial. Since the number of cookies visiting a large website is tremendous, such a serial algorithm does not scale at all. We thus propose the following heuristic algorithm which can be run in parallel and also ensures that the OS and browser constraints are satisfied.

The parallel clustering algorithm shown in Algorithm 3 consists of two phases – in the first phase we partition the set of cookies into chunks of manageable sizes while trying to keep cookies of the same browser in the same partition. The second phase invokes an instance of the clustering Algorithm 2 for each partition, where each instance gets an independent set of cookies and thus can be run in parallel, e.g., on top of the Map-Reduce framework.

For the first phase the algorithm creates a bipartite graph of cookies on one side and (IP, OS, browser-type) tuples on the other, and connects undirected edges between a cookie c and a (IP, OS, browser-type) tuple if either f_c or ℓ_c was observed with this (IP, OS, browser-type). Connected components of cookies can thus be built to serve as input to run Algorithm 2 in parallel.

vfill

Algorithm 3 ClusterBrowsersParallel

```
Input: Set of cookies S
Output: Subsets of cookies, each likely to belong to the same
    browser
Create a bipartite graph with the cookies S on one side and (IP,
    OS, browser-type) tuples on the other side
Add an edge between cookie c and a (IP, OS, browser-type)
    tuple if either f_c or ℓ_c was observed with this (IP, OS, browser-
    type).
Let G_1, ... G_k be the connected components in the graph
For each i, in parallel, B_i ← ClusterBrowsers(G_i)
return the union of all B_i's
```

3. COOKIE PROFILE SIMILARITY

In this section we discuss the form of $\mathtt{sim}(C, C')$, the cookie profile similarity measure for two sets of cookies such that $C \cup C'$ satisfies the cannot-link constraints. For ease of exposition, we describe our features while implicitly assuming that C' is a non-empty set of cookies. When we train and apply the model, C' always contains one cookie.

Each cookie c is associated with a profile composed of several features. For a set of cookies C, let $\boldsymbol{x}$ denote a feature set such that x_{ij} is the ith feature of the jth cookie in C. Examples of features are the number of page views, lifetime length, etc. Note that x_{ij} can also be multi-dimensional, e.g. the IP usage pattern of a cookie is represented by a sparse vector containing 1 at the positions corresponding to the IPs that the cookie was observed at. If there are n cookies in C, denote the values of the ith feature in cookies in C by $\boldsymbol{x}_i = \{x_{i1}, \ldots, x_{in}\}$.

Given the feature sets $\boldsymbol{x}$ and $\boldsymbol{x}'$ for C and C', one common way to define set-similarity measure is using the distance between centroids of $\boldsymbol{x}$ and $\boldsymbol{x}'$; the distance can be Euclidean distance (L_2 norm) or the Manhattan distance (L_1 norm). Another measure, the Mahalanobis distance [26], defines the distance between two centroids $\hat{\boldsymbol{x}}$ and $\hat{\boldsymbol{x}'}$ as $\sqrt{(\hat{\boldsymbol{x}} - \hat{\boldsymbol{x}'})^T M (\hat{\boldsymbol{x}} - \hat{\boldsymbol{x}'})}$, where the positive-semi-definite matrix M can be learned from labeled data (e.g. [35] for k-nearest neighbor classification). However, learning the full matrix M is not generally considered in constrained clustering scenarios. We thus learn a simpler form of the Mahalanobis distance, where M is diagonal.

We define our similarity function as follows:

$$\mathtt{sim}(C, C') = s(\boldsymbol{x}, \boldsymbol{x}') = \sum_i \beta_i s_i(\boldsymbol{x}_i, \boldsymbol{x}'_i). \quad (3)$$

Hence, if for each feature type i, $-s_i(\boldsymbol{x}_i, \boldsymbol{x}'_i)$ is the Euclidean distance between the centroids and $\beta_i = 1$, we obtain the simple Euclidean distance and a (diagonal) Mahalanobis distance for general β_i.

For simple numerical features such as the average number of page views, using Euclidean distance for $s_i(\boldsymbol{x}_i, \boldsymbol{x}'_i)$ may be good enough. However, for features like webpage category visiting pattern and IP address usage pattern, we need to incorporate the following information in the measure: (a) a webpage category which is frequently visited (such as Yahoo! Frontpage) should be weighted lower than another category that is seldom visited, i.e. if two cookies both visit the Yahoo! Frontpage, that may be less significant, than if they both visit the Yahoo! Groups → Table Tennis; (b) The frequency information matters: a cookie with only 1 page view on the Yahoo! Groups → Table Tennis may not mean much, but 1000 page views on that webpage category means this person really enjoys this category and it becomes a meaningful behavioral feature. Therefore, simply using Euclidean distance for these kind of features may not work well since it is not trivial to incorporate the above information into the measure. TF-IDF [31] satisfies requirement (a) but it does not consider (b). Hence we propose to construct some of cookie behavior feature similarities using *Bayes factors* [21] from model selection in statistics literature.

3.1 Bayes Factors

We first briefly introduce Bayes factors [21] which is a popular approach in model selection and hypothesis testing. Given the two sets of cookie profiles $\boldsymbol{x}$ and $\boldsymbol{x}'$, consider the ith feature types $\boldsymbol{x}_i$ and $\boldsymbol{x}'_i$. Our goal is to use $\boldsymbol{x}_i$ and $\boldsymbol{x}'_i$ to test the hypothesis of whether the two sets of cookies belong to the same browser. Naturally, the null hypothesis H_0 becomes that these two sets of cookies are from the same browser, and the alternative hypothesis H_1 becomes that they are from two different browsers. The Bayes factor for feature type i is defined as

$$BF_i = \frac{p(\boldsymbol{x}_i \cup \boldsymbol{x}'_i|H_0)}{p(\boldsymbol{x}_i|H_1)p(\boldsymbol{x}'_i|H_1)} \quad (4)$$
$$= \frac{\int p(\boldsymbol{x}_i \cup \boldsymbol{x}'_i|\gamma_i, H_0)p(\gamma_i)d\gamma_i}{\int p(\boldsymbol{x}_i|\gamma_i, H_1)p(\gamma_i)d\gamma_i \int p(\boldsymbol{x}'_i|\gamma_i, H_1)p(\gamma_i)d\gamma_i},$$

where $p(\boldsymbol{x}_i|\gamma_i, H_1)$ and $p(\boldsymbol{x}'_i|\gamma_i, H_1)$ are two independent probability models for feature $\boldsymbol{x}_i$ and $\boldsymbol{x}'_i$ given the parameter set γ_i since they are from two different browsers (hypothesis H_1). $p(\boldsymbol{x}_i \cup \boldsymbol{x}'_i|\gamma_i, H_0)$ is the probability model for the single browser by merging the features $\boldsymbol{x}_i$ and $\boldsymbol{x}'_i$ (hypothesis H_0), and $p(\gamma_i)$ is the prior distribution of γ_i. The Bayes factors give a natural way of incorporating both prior knowledge and the observed data into hypothesis testing. In this paper we use the $\log(BF)$ as the similarity measure for several feature types.

3.2 Feature Construction

In this paper we consider the following cookie profile features along with definition of similarity measures:

Lifetime gap: For two sets of cookies C and C', assuming all cookies in C' are created after the last timestamp of cookies in C (i.e., C and C' do not overlap), the lifetime gap is defined as $\texttt{timegap}(C, C')$, as in Equation (2). The intuition behind this feature is that if a browser is visiting the web site and clears its cookies, there is a high chance that this browser will generate another page view after short time with a new cookie.

Lifetime length: The lifetime length is defined as the last page view timestamp of a cookie minus its creation time. We use simple Euclidean distance between centroids.

Number of page views: We use logarithm of the number of page views of a cookie and apply Euclidean distance between centroids.

Operating system type (OS): Since the OS is a cannot-link constraint, i.e. cookies with different operation system can not have the same browser, for Euclidean distance we do not need to use this feature. However, using Bayes factors we incorporate the prior knowledge of the popularity of the OS into the similarity measure, i.e. the OS $o|\boldsymbol{p}_o \sim Multinomial(\boldsymbol{p}_o)$, where $\boldsymbol{p}_o$ is the apriori known probability vector reflecting popularity of the OS. The logarithm of the Bayes factor for OS type o_j is hence $-\log p_{o,j}$, i.e. if o_j is popular such that $p_{o,j}$ is large, $-\log p_{o,j}$ is relatively small; on the other hand if $p_{o,j}$ is very small for some non-popular OS, $-\log p_{o,j}$ becomes large.

Web browser type: For Euclidean distance we do not need this feature since browser type is a cannot-link constraint. However, using Bayes factors we can similarly incorporate prior knowledge of the popularity of the browser type into the similarity measure.

IP addresses usage pattern: We denote the IP address usage pattern for a set of n cookies as $\boldsymbol{f} = \{\boldsymbol{f}_1, ..., \boldsymbol{f}_n\}$. Assume there are p IP addresses. For cookie j, $\boldsymbol{f}_j$ is a length-p vector where each element indicates the number of page views allocated for this IP address. For Euclidean distance, we naturally define the centroid as $(\sum_{j=1}^{n} \boldsymbol{f}_j)/(\sum_{j=1}^{n}\sum_{k=1}^{p} f_{jk})$, and the distance between two sets of cookies is the Euclidean distance between their centroids. For similarity measure construction via Bayes factors, let the number of page views for cookie j be $v_j = \sum_{k=1}^{p} f_{jk}$, we assume $\boldsymbol{f}_j|v_j, \boldsymbol{p}_f \sim Multinomial(v_j, \boldsymbol{p}_f)$, and the unknown mean probability vector $\boldsymbol{p}_f$ has a prior $\boldsymbol{p}_f \sim Dirichlet(\boldsymbol{\alpha}_f s_f)$. The parameter $\boldsymbol{\alpha}_f$ is a vector of the prior mean probabilities of IP address usage which is obtained from the data, and $\sum_k \alpha_{f,k} = 1$. s_f is the prior sample size and we set $s_f = 1$. Note that for this model the interactions among the IP addresses are ignored, e.g. in reality IP addresses from the same IP subnet are more likely to show up together. However, since IP addresses are hashed due to privacy concerns, IP subnets can not be recovered.

Webpage category visiting pattern: The similarity measure for this feature is similar to the IP address feature shown above. Note that the Multinomial-Dirichlet probability model also ignores the interactions among the categories, e.g. users who visit Yahoo! Frontpage may also visit Yahoo! Search. The prior sample size (like s_f in the IP addresses usage pattern) is also set to be 1 in our experiments.

3.3 Learning Weights

The raw training data we use consists of cookies with their behavior pattern features in a certain time period (a week in this paper). For a small subset of cookies (around 1%) we know their true browser IDs (the Yahoo! Toolbar IDs). To train the similarity measure $\texttt{sim}(C, C')$ we need to create a sample of pairs of subsets (C, C') distributed similarly to the distribution of pairs for which $\texttt{sim}(C, C')$ is called by the clustering algorithm. One way is to sample pairs for with non-overlapping lifetimes and that share the same OS and browser type. Such a sampling is difficult to do efficiently without introducing some bias. In practice, we bias the sampling towards the desired distribution by simply running the clustering algorithm (Section 2) on the training data using the following similarity function: $\texttt{sim}(C, c) = \infty$ if all cookies in $C \cup c$ have the same Toolbar ID and $-\infty$ otherwise. We then output the sets of candidates (A in Algorithm 2) that the clustering algorithm faces, and sample pairs (C, c) to obtain the training data.

Since the training data constructed has binary responses, binary classification models such as logistic regression [27] and support vector machines [19] can naturally be used to learn the β_i's in Equation (3) by treating each $s_i(\boldsymbol{x}_i, \boldsymbol{x}'_i)$ as a feature. In this paper we use the logistic regression model. Specifically, let y be the binary response which tells whether the two sets of cookies belong to the same browser,

$$P[y = 1] = 1/(1 + exp(-\sum_i \beta_i s_i(\boldsymbol{x}_i, \boldsymbol{x}'_i))). \quad (5)$$

4. RELATED WORK

In this section we discuss the related clustering algorithms in the literature and explain the reason why these algorithms can not be directly applied to this problem. The two typical clustering algorithms K-means [25] and EM algorithm [9] require the knowledge of number of clusters K which is not available in our problem. The density-based clustering algorithms such as DBSCAN [14] and

OPTICS [5] do not require the input K but the maximum neighborhood distance (radius) and the minimum number of points to form a cluster. Large-scale text clustering algorithms such as [8] usually form "shingles" (hashed feature sets of web documents) and construct pair-wise document similarity if the two documents share some common shingles. However, none of the above approach directly handles cannot-link constraints in the clustering.

Due to the important role that the constraints play in this problem, the existing constraint-based clustering algorithms are more related to this work. The constrained K-means by [34] modifies K-means to allow hard constraints. However, it still requires the knowledge of K, and most importantly, for each iteration and each point, it takes complexity $O(K)$ in the worst case to find the nearest candidate cluster and to check for the violation of the constraints for all candidates. Therefore, for n points (cookies) and K clusters, the complexity of the algorithm can be $O(nK)$ for each iteration. Davidson et. al. [10] prove the cannot-link feasibility problem is NP-complete and connect this to the graph coloring problem. [12] modifies the clustering objective function so it includes a penalty term for satisfying specified constraints, but still it needs the input K. Correlation clustering [7] is another technique for incorporating both negative and positive constraints. There are algorithms with theoretically proven guarantees for correlation clustering – for general constraint graphs with weights, this would require solving a linear program [11], and is thus infeasible in our setting. There are also proposed constrained spectral clustering algorithms [23, 24]. However, these algorithms require manipulations on the pairwise $n \times n$ similarity matrix such as eigenvalue decomposition so it is not feasible when you have hundreds of millions of cookies to cluster. In this paper, we compare our clustering method with constrained K-means by [34] and show improvements, assuming K is known. More details are provided in Section 5.

5. EXPERIMENTS

In this section we first describe the dataset we used for evaluating our algorithms, then evaluate several profile similarity measures and finally evaluate the cookie clustering algorithm comparing with constrained K-means.

5.1 Data Sets

We generated our datasets from two months of web logs of Yahoo! websites during April-May 2011. After removing cookies with bot-like behavior, we created a subsample of 200 million cookies for our experiments. This dataset contains information such as the cookie id, timestamps of the first and the last pageviews, hashed IP address, webpage categories visited, OS type, etc. For most of the cookies in this data set, we do not know which cookies actually belong to the same browser. However, for a small subset of cookies (around 1%) that belong to Yahoo! Toolbar users, we consider cookies having the same Toolbar ID to be the ground-truth clusters. In this work we ignore any bias inherent to the Toolbar users and we consider correcting the bias as future work (one solution is to use [3]). We trained parameters of the profile similarity measures using a subset of the data for April, and evaluated the clustering algorithms using the entire month of May.

5.2 Learning Profile Similarity Parameters

We train feature weights β_i's using logistic regression as specified in Equation (5). We used a sample of 1.7 million pairs of sets of cookies from which 75% were used for learnig the weights, and 25% for evaluating the accuracy of similarity measures (for details of the sampling process see Section 3.3). We compare 3 similarity measures: Pure Euclidean distance (**Euclidean**), the special case of Mahalanobis with M diagonal and the diagonal entries from β_i's (**Mahalanobis**), and the Bayes factors similarity measure (**Bayes**). The ROC curves of these three similarity measures are shown in Figure 3. Clearly, the **Bayes** measure that uses Bayes factors for some feature types such as IP usage pattern or webpage category visiting pattern significantly improves over the other two traditional distance measures. Going forward, we use only the **Mahalanobis** and the **Bayes** similarity functions for clustering.

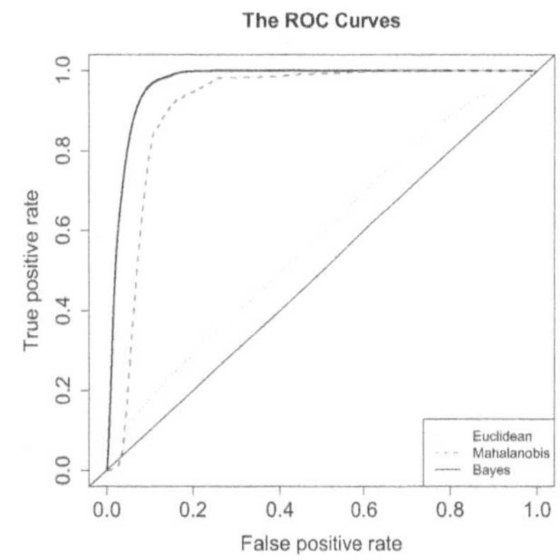

Figure 3: The ROC curves of the three similarity measure.

5.3 Clustering Evaluation Metrics

There are many types of clustering evaluation metrics. Representative metrics include purity and inverse purity [37], Van Rijsbergen's F measure [33, 22], pairwise items counting metrics [18, 28], entropy-based metrics [32], BCubed precision and recall metrics [6]. The authors of [4] defined a set of formal constraints that an evaluation metric should satisfy and showed that among all these different measures, BCubed precision and recall is the only type of existing metrics that satisfy all the defined constraints. Therefore, we use the BCubed precision and recall to evaluate the accuracy of different clustering algorithms. Specifically, for cookie c denote $L(c)$ and $O(c)$ as the true browser id and the created cluster id. Define the clustering correctness function $f(c, c')$ for a pair of cookies c and c' as: If $L(c) = L(c')$ and $O(c) = O(c')$ then $f(c, c') = 1$, otherwise $f(c, c') = 0$. The BCubed precision and recall can be thus defined as follows:

$$\texttt{Precision} = \texttt{Avg}_c[\texttt{Avg}_{c', O(c)=O(c')}[f(c, c')]],$$

$$\texttt{Recall} = \texttt{Avg}_c[\texttt{Avg}_{c', L(c)=L(c')}[f(c, c')]].$$

Since in our dataset only a small subset of cookies have true browser labels, each cluster can contain both cookies with labels and without labels. If cookie c has a label and c' does not, although we do not know $L(c')$ we do know that $L(c) \neq L(c')$; otherwise c' would have the same label as c. Therefore, we modify the BCubed precision and recall as

$$\texttt{Precision} = \texttt{Avg}_{c, L(c) exists}[\texttt{Avg}_{c', O(c)=O(c')}[f(c, c')]],$$

$$\texttt{Recall} = \texttt{Avg}_{c, L(c) exists}[\texttt{Avg}_{c', L(c)=L(c')}[f(c, c')]].$$

5.4 Clustering Evaluation Results

We next compare the accuracy of the clustering algorithms in predicting the true clusters according to the above metric. We consider the following algorithms with roughly increasing complexity:

`Ip-os`: Every cookie is assigned to only one (IP,OS) tuple from which it has made the maximum number of visits – these (IP,OS) tuples form the clusters. Note that this algorithm ignores the cookie lifetime as well as browser type cannot-link constraints.
`Naive`: A modification of the coloring algorithm where each cookie is assigned to a random cluster that satisfies all cannot-link constraints and also shares (IP, OS) with the last cookies in the cluster.
`Time`: The coloring algorithm as in **Naive** but with the similarity function $\mathtt{sim}_I$, i.e., cookie is assigned to the candidate cluster with which it has the shortest `timegap`.
`Mahalanobis` and **Bayes**: The coloring algorithm as in **Naive** that satisfies cannot-link constraints, but with cookie profile similarity function. A cookie is connected to the candidate cluster the lowest Mahalanobis distance, or with the highest Bayes similarity measure respectively.

In order to show the trade-off between precision and recall, we run each of the clustering algorithms, except for `Ip-os`, with a tunable parameter. For `Time`, `Mahanalobis` and `Bayes` we choose several different thresholds θ for `sim` in Algorithm 2. For `Naive`, for every cookie we first obtain a list of candidate clusters that share (IP,OS) and do not violate constraints, and then toss a coin with the probability equal to the tuning parameter to decide whether to connect to a random candidate (head), or to form a new cluster (tail).

The BCubed precision-recall curves are shown in Figure 4, where at the left-most point for all the four algorithms we never connect cookies so all formed clusters have only 1 cookie, and for the right-most points, we always connect to the cluster with highest `sim` (for `Time`, `Mahanalobis` and `Bayes`) or to a random cluster (for `Naive`) whenever cannot-link constraints are satisfied. `Ip-os` generates a single point, and is not shown in the plot, since the 0.74 precision at 0.69 recall is much lower than the corresponding performance obtained by other algorithms.

The relative high accuracy of `Naive` shows that simply obeying the hard cannot-link constraints (browser type and lifetime non-overlap) results in quite high clustering accuracy. `Time` further improves upon `Naive` – one possible explanation is that browsers clear cookies while still conducting the browsing activity. Lastly, the `Mahanalobis` and the `Bayes` algorithm perform best, with the `Bayes` being marginally yet consistently better – showing that incorporating the features provides a significant boost to the browser identification, and that incorporating Bayes factors into similarity measure is effective.

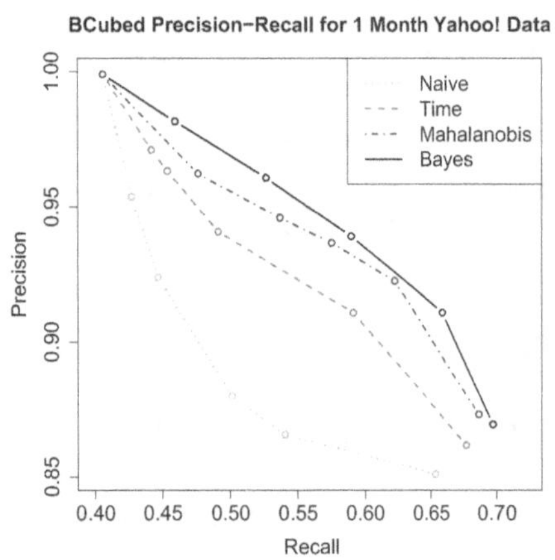

Figure 4: The BCubed precision-recall curves of cookie clustering algorithms. For `Ip-os` we obtain precision 0.74 and recall 0.69.

True Cluster Size	Percentage	Naive Precision	Naive Recall	Bayes Precision	Bayes Recall
1	23.0%	0.885	1.0	0.919	1.0
2-4	13.8%	0.812	0.735	0.886	0.766
5-9	7.4%	0.800	0.587	0.886	0.619
10-29	14.6%	0.814	0.479	0.900	0.501
30-99	19.9%	0.850	0.401	0.920	0.395
>99	12.3%	0.882	0.320	0.930	0.294
Overall	100%	0.851	0.654	0.911	0.659

Table 1: The BCubed precision, recall for `Naive` (right-most point of the green curve in Figure 4) and `Bayes` (second right-most point of the black curve in Figure 4) for different cookie segments based on true cluster size.

To further understand the performance of these algorithms we split the cookies that have Toolbar IDs (i.e., the ground truth clusters) into multiple segments based on the true cluster size. In Table 1 we show the precision and recall as a function of true cluster size for `Naive` (the right-most point in Figure 4) and `Bayes` (the second right-most point in Figure 4) since they share very similar overall recall (~ 0.65). Interestingly, for both `Naive` and `Bayes` the recall degrades as the true cluster size increases, but the precision remains at the same level. This phenomenon can be explained as follows: (a) The cannot-link constraints have a strong effect in preventing the algorithms from mistakenly connecting cookies to wrong clusters, even for the `Naive` approach. (b) To make our algorithms scale, we used a "divide-and-conquer" approach (see Algorithm 3). Using IP, OS, and browser types to partition cookies has a dramatic effect on scalability but leads to some recall loss, especially for browsers with large number of cookies. (c) The clustering problem naturally becomes more difficult as the true cluster size increases, and that contributes to the decreasing recall with the cluster size.

5.5 Comparison with Constrained K-means

We compare our proposed algorithm `Bayes` with another baseline algorithm: the constrained K-means from [34]. Since in our problem K is not known apriori, this algorithm could not be used in practice for cookie clustering. However, for the sake of comparison, we used the K computed from the output of the `Bayes` algorithm. Note that we actually need to provide the K for each connected component generated from Algorithm 3 as input to K-means. Since there can be millions of connected components, using constrained K-means by tuning K is infeasible.

Due to its iterative nature and frequent cookie reassignments, constrained K-means does not readily scale to the full size of our dataset. We thus ran constrained K-means for 20 iterations on around 1% of the data and compare it with our `Bayes` algorithm for various thresholds θ. We report the precision-recall numbers in Figure 5. It is obvious that even though we provided the K for each connected component and allowed the algorithm to reassess cookies between clusters for 20 iterations, the clustering is still less accurate than our one-pass `Bayes` algorithm.

6. CONCLUSION

In this paper, we formalized a large-scale clustering approach to deal with the problem of cookie churn. Our main contributions were in developing a set of features and defining similarity measures based on Bayes factors, formalizing the constraints in terms of interval graphs, and giving a novel clustering heuristic that is a generalization of the coloring algorithm on interval graphs.

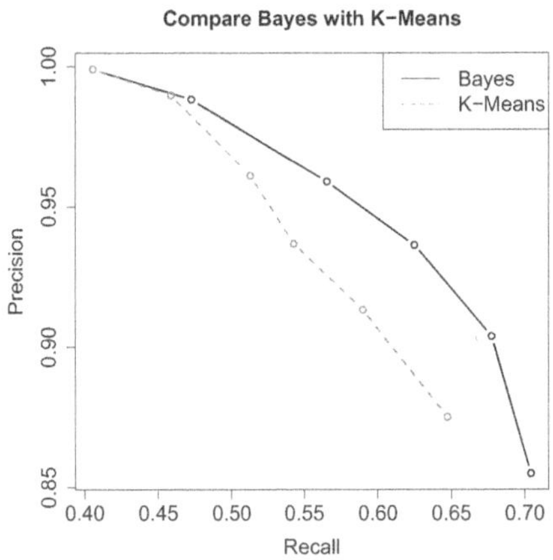

Figure 5: The BCubed precision-recall curves of cookie clustering algorithms `Bayes` and constrained K-means for around 1% of the data.

There are interesting open questions on improving accuracy and efficiency of cookie clustering, and on theoretical analysis and modeling of cookie observation and generation process.

7. APPENDIX

We use the following well-known fact ([29], Chapter 8) in our proof.

FACT 1. *If $X_1, \ldots, X_k$ are exponentially distributed random variables, $X_i \sim \lambda_i \exp(-\lambda_i t)$, then $\min_i\{X_i\}$ follows an exponential distribution, with parameter $\sum_i \lambda_i$. Also,* $\Pr[X_j = \min_i\{X_i\}] = \frac{\lambda_j}{\sum_i \lambda_i}$.

Proof of Theorem 1.

For simplicity of exposition, we first show the proof for the case when all browsers have the same set of parameters (p, λ) and then describe how to generalize for k different parameter tuples.

Let G be the observed interval graph of cookies generated by k browsers during time interval T. We show a lower bound on the number of colors $\chi(G)$ required to color G. Obviously $\chi(G) \leq k$. Define the *depth* at time t, $D(t)$, to be the number of browsers that have a cookie whose lifetime intersects t – we call such browsers (resp. cookies) "active" at time t. Cookie with zero lifetime intersection no t – thus a browser turns "active" from "inactive" only when it produces a cookie with positive lifetime.

Note that $\max_{t\in T} D(t)$ is a lower bound on the number of colors – since these many intervals intersect each other, at least these many colors must be used. $D(t)$ is a random variable that evolves as follows: at time $t+1$, any subset of the currently active browsers can clear their current cookie, and any subset of the currently inactive browsers can start a new non-zero-length cookie by having a non-clearing event. We first prove that the random variable $D(t)$ evolves as a continuous time Markov chain with the time spent at each state being distributed as a exponential distribution.

It is easy to see that $D(t)$ evolves as a Markov chain, since the next value of $D(t)$ depends only on the current state and not on past history. It is also easy to see that the state space is $\{0, \ldots, k\}$. Suppose we are at state i at time t (i.e. $D(t) = i$), where $i \notin \{0, k\}$ – there are i active browsers and $k-i$ inactive browsers. Let $t + X$ denote the time when the first one of these active browsers becomes inactive and $t+Y$ be the first time when the first of these inactive browsers becomes active. Then, by the memorylessness of the exponential distribution, X is distributed as the minimum of i exponentially distributed r.v.s with parameter $p\lambda$, and hence is distributed as $\lambda \exp(-p\lambda i)$. Similarly, $Y \sim \lambda \exp(-(1-p)(k-i)\lambda)$. From state i we can only move into state $i-1$ or $i+1$. Whether we move into state $i-1$ or $i+1$ from state i depends on which of X and Y is smaller. Again $\min(X, Y)$ is distributed as an exponential r.v. with p.d.f $\theta_i \exp(-\theta_i t)$ where $\theta_i = p\lambda i + (1-p)(k-i)\lambda$. For any $i, j \in \{0, k\}$, let p_{ij} denote the probability of moving from state i to state j. At the boundary, we have $p_{01} = 1$ and $p_{k,k-1} = 1$. For $i \in [0, k-1]$, $p_{i,i+1} = \Pr[Y < X] = \frac{(1-p)\lambda(k-i)}{\theta_i}$ and for $i \in [1, k]$, $p_{i,i-1} = \frac{p\lambda i}{\theta_i}$.

Let $\{\pi_0, \ldots, \pi_k\}$ denote the stationary distribution of the Markov chain. Using the property of the stationary distribution, we have that for $i \in [1, k-1]$, $\pi_i\theta_i = \pi_{i-1}\theta_{i-1}p_{i-1,i} + \pi_{i+1}\theta_{i+1}p_{i+1,i}$.

For the boundary states, $\pi_0\theta_0 = \pi_1\theta_1 p_{10} = \pi_i\lambda$, and hence $\pi_1 = \frac{k(1-p)\lambda}{p\lambda} = \frac{k(1-p)}{p}$. The following solution to the above equation can be verified using simple algebra: $\pi_{i+1} = \frac{(k-i)(1-p)\lambda}{(i+1)p\lambda}\pi_i = \binom{k}{i+1}(\frac{1-p}{p})^{i+1}\pi_0$. By using the fact that $\sum_{i\leq k}\binom{k}{i}(\frac{1-p}{p})^i = (1+(1-p)/p)^k = 1/p^k$, we get that $\pi_0 = p^k$. Thus, $\pi_{i+1} = p^k\binom{k}{i+1}(\frac{1-p}{p})^{i+1}$. Now, at steady state, π_i also denotes the expected fraction of time that the chain will be in state i. Thus, for $i \in [(1-\epsilon)k, k]$, we have that

$$\sum_{i\in[(1-\epsilon)k,k]} \pi_i = p^k \sum_{i\in[(1-\epsilon)k,k]} \binom{k}{i}((1-p)/p)^i.$$

We use the following result from [20]. Suppose $\alpha < 1$ and k' is such that $k' > \alpha k - \sqrt{k\alpha(1-\alpha)}$. Then,

$$\sum_{j\leq k'} \binom{k}{j}\alpha^j(1-\alpha)^{k-j} = \Theta(1).$$

In our case, define $\alpha = p$. Then

$$\sum_{i\in[(1-\epsilon)k,k]} \pi_i = p^k \sum_{i\in[(1-\epsilon)k,k]} \binom{k}{i}((1-p)/p)^i$$

$$= \sum_{i\in[(1-\epsilon)k,k]} \binom{k}{i}(1-p)^i p^{k-i}$$

$$= \sum_{i\in[(1-\epsilon)k,k]} \binom{k}{k-i}(1-p)^i p^{k-i} = \sum_{j\in[0,\epsilon k]} \binom{k}{j}(1-p)^{k-j}p^j,$$

where in the last step we just substituted $j = k - i$. Thus, if $\epsilon k > pk - \sqrt{kp(1-p)}$, we have $\sum_{i>\epsilon k} \pi_i = \Theta(1)$. For this, we need $\epsilon > p - \sqrt{p(1-p)/k} > p/2$ for $k > 4(1-p)$. To complete the proof, note that if $\sum_{i>\epsilon k} \pi_i = \Theta(1)$, then at the steady state, a constant fraction of time is spent in the states $[(1-\epsilon)k, k]$. Applying Markov's inequality to the indicator variable for the states $[(1-\epsilon)k, k]$ in a time period T, the expectation is $\Theta(T)$, and hence if $T = \Theta(1/\delta)$, with probability $1-\delta$, we will hit the states $[(1-\epsilon)k, k]$. We will then need at least $(1-\epsilon)k$ colors to color the corresponding interval graph.

In the general case, when each browser does not necessarily have the same parameter sets, we need to consider a different Markov chain. The states of the chain will be A, the set of "active" browsers – instead of the number of active browsers. We then have to define transitions p_{AB} for each set B such that either $|B \setminus A| = 1$, or $|A \setminus B| = 1$. We will have $\pi_A = \pi_\emptyset \Pi_{b\in A}\frac{1-p_b}{p_b}$ where $\pi_\emptyset$ is the stationary probability of the set $\emptyset$, and p_b is the clearing probability for browser b. We can then go through the same calculation to show the claim.

References

[1] http://www.comscore.com/Press_Events/Press_Releases/2007/04/comScore_Cookie_Deletion_Report.

[2] D. Agarwal and B. Chen. Regression-based latent factor models. In *Proceedings of the 15th ACM SIGKDD international conference on Knowledge discovery and data mining*, pages 19–28. ACM, 2009.

[3] D. Agarwal, L. Li, and A. Smola. Linear-time estimators for propensity scores. *Proceedings of the Fourteenth International Conference on Artificial Intelligence and Statistics*, 15:93–100, 2011.

[4] E. Amigó, J. Gonzalo, J. Artiles, and F. Verdejo. A comparison of extrinsic clustering evaluation metrics based on formal constraints. *Information Retrieval*, 12(4):461–486, 2009.

[5] M. Ankerst, M. Breunig, H. Kriegel, and J. Sander. OPTICS: ordering points to identify the clustering structure. In *Proceedings of the 1999 ACM SIGMOD international conference on Management of data*, pages 49–60. ACM, 1999.

[6] A. Bagga and B. Baldwin. Entity-based cross-document coreferencing using the vector space model. In *Proceedings of the 17th international conference on Computational linguistics-Volume 1*, pages 79–85. Association for Computational Linguistics, 1998.

[7] N. Bansal, A. Blum, and S. Chawla. Correlation clustering. *Machine Learning*, 56(1):89–113, 2004.

[8] A. Broder, S. Glassman, M. Manasse, and G. Zweig. Syntactic clustering of the web. *Computer Networks and ISDN Systems*, 29(8-13):1157–1166, 1997.

[9] G. Celeux and G. Govaert. *A classification EM algorithm for clustering and two stochastic versions*. Institut National de Recherche en Informatique et en Automatique, 1991.

[10] I. Davidson and S. Ravi. Clustering With Constraints: Feasibility Issues and the K-Means Algorithm. In *Proceedings of the Fifth SIAM International Conference on Data Mining*, page 138. Society for Industrial Mathematics, 2005.

[11] E. Demaine, D. Emanuel, A. Fiat, and N. Immorlica. Correlation clustering in general weighted graphs. *Theoretical Computer Science*, 361(2-3):172–187, 2006.

[12] A. Demiriz, K. Bennett, and M. Embrechts. Semi-supervised clustering using genetic algorithms. *Artificial neural networks in engineering (ANNIE-99)*, pages 809–814, 1999.

[13] P. Eckersley. How unique is your web browser? *http://panopticlick.eff.org/browser-uniqueness.pdf*.

[14] M. Ester, H. Kriegel, J. Sander, and X. Xu. A density-based algorithm for discovering clusters in large spatial databases with noise. In *Proc. KDD*, volume 96, pages 226–231, 1996.

[15] M. Fomitchev. Method and system for estimating unique visitors for internet sites. *United States Patent Application 20100228850*.

[16] M. Golumbic. *Algorithmic graph theory and perfect graphs*. North-Holland, 2004.

[17] N. Good, J. Schafer, J. Konstan, A. Borchers, B. Sarwar, J. Herlocker, and J. Riedl. Combining collaborative filtering with personal agents for better recommendations. In *Proceedings of the National Conference on Artificial Intelligence*, pages 439–446. JOHN WILEY & SONS LTD, 1999.

[18] M. Halkidi, Y. Batistakis, and M. Vazirgiannis. On clustering validation techniques. *Journal of Intelligent Information Systems*, 17(2):107–145, 2001.

[19] M. Hearst, S. Dumais, E. Osman, J. Platt, and B. Scholkopf. Support vector machines. *Intelligent Systems and their Applications, IEEE*, 13(4):18–28, 2002.

[20] E. Jeábek. Dual weak pigeonhole principle, Boolean complexity, and derandomization. *Annals of Pure and Applied Logic*, 129(1-3):1–37, 2004.

[21] R. Kass and A. Raftery. Bayes factors. *Journal of the American Statistical Association*, 90(430):773–795, 1995.

[22] B. Larsen and C. Aone. Fast and effective text mining using linear-time document clustering. In *Proceedings of the fifth ACM SIGKDD international conference on Knowledge discovery and data mining*, pages 16–22. ACM, 1999.

[23] Z. Li and J. Liu. Constrained clustering by spectral kernel learning. In *Computer Vision, 2009 IEEE 12th International Conference on*, pages 421–427. IEEE, 2010.

[24] Z. Lu and M. Carreira-Perpinán. Constrained spectral clustering through affinity propagation. In *Computer Vision and Pattern Recognition, 2008. CVPR 2008. IEEE Conference on*, pages 1–8. IEEE, 2008.

[25] J. MacQueen et al. Some methods for classification and analysis of multivariate observations. In *Proceedings of the fifth Berkeley symposium on mathematical statistics and probability*, volume 1, page 14. California, USA, 1967.

[26] P. Mahalanobis. On the generalized distance in statistics. In *Proceedings of the National Institute of Science, Calcutta*, volume 12, page 49, 1936.

[27] P. McCullagh and J. Nelder. *Generalized linear models*. Chapman & Hall, CRC, 1999.

[28] M. Meila. Comparing clusterings by the variation of information. In *Learning theory and Kernel machines: 16th Annual Conference on Learning Theory and 7th Kernel Workshop, COLT/Kernel 2003, Washington, DC, USA, August 24-27, 2003: proceedings*, page 173. Springer Verlag, 2003.

[29] M. Mitzenmacher and E. Upfal. *Probability and computing: Randomized algorithms and probabilistic analysis*. Cambridge Univ Pr, 2005.

[30] S. Park, D. Pennock, O. Madani, N. Good, and D. DeCoste. Naïve filterbots for robust cold-start recommendations. In *Proceedings of the 12th ACM SIGKDD international conference on Knowledge discovery and data mining*, pages 699–705. ACM, 2006.

[31] G. Salton and M. McGill. Introduction to modern information retrieval. *New York*, 1983.

[32] M. Steinbach, G. Karypis, and V. Kumar. A comparison of document clustering techniques. In *KDD workshop on text mining*, volume 34, page 35. Citeseer, 2000.

[33] C. Van Rijsbergen. Foundation of evaluation. *Journal of Documentation*, 30(4):365–373, 1993.

[34] K. Wagstaff, C. Cardie, S. Rogers, and S. Schrödl. Constrained k-means clustering with background knowledge. In *Proceedings of the Eighteenth International Conference on Machine Learning*, pages 577–584. Citeseer, 2001.

[35] K. Weinberger and L. Saul. Distance metric learning for large margin nearest neighbor classification. *The Journal of Machine Learning Research*, 10:207–244, 2009.

[36] L. Zhang, D. Agarwal, and B. Chen. Generalizing matrix factorization through flexible regression priors. In *Proceedings of the fifth ACM conference on Recommender systems*, pages 13–20. ACM, 2011.

[37] Y. Zhao and G. Karypis. *Criterion functions for document clustering*. Citeseer, 2005.

mTrust: Discerning Multi-Faceted Trust in a Connected World

Jiliang Tang
Computer Science & Engineering
Arizona State University
Tempe, AZ 85281
{Jiliang.Tang}@asu.edu

Huiji Gao
Computer Science & Engineering
Arizona State University
Tempe, AZ 85281
{Huiji.Gao}@asu.edu

Huan Liu
Computer Science & Engineering
Arizona State University
Tempe, AZ 85281
{Huan.Liu}@asu.edu

ABSTRACT

Traditionally, research about trust assumes a single type of trust between users. However, trust, as a social concept, inherently has many facets indicating multiple and heterogeneous trust relationships between users. Due to the presence of a large trust network for an online user, it is necessary to discern multi-faceted trust as there are naturally experts of different types. Our study in product review sites reveals that people place trust differently to different people. Since the widely used adjacency matrix cannot capture multi-faceted trust relationships between users, we propose a novel approach by incorporating these relationships into traditional rating prediction algorithms to reliably estimate their strengths. Our work results in interesting findings such as heterogeneous pairs of reciprocal links. Experimental results on real-world data from Epinions and Ciao show that our work of discerning multi-faceted trust can be applied to improve the performance of tasks such as rating prediction, facet-sensitive ranking, and status theory.

Categories and Subject Descriptors

H.3.3 [**Information Search and Retrieval**]: Information Filetering; H.5.3 [**Group and Organization Interfaces**]: Web-based interaction

General Terms

Algorithms, Experimentation, Human Factors

Keywords

Multi-faceted Trust, Multi-dimension Tie Strength, Trust Network, Heterogeneous Trust

1. INTRODUCTION

In recent years, the notion of trust has attracted more and more attention from the computer science community [6, 18]. Trust plays a central role in exchanging relationships involving unknown risk [4], which provides information about with whom we should share information and from whom we should accept information [5]. The role of trust is especially critical in some online communities such as e-commerce sites and product review sites, which has been described as the "wild wild west" of the 21st century [19].

Users in product review sites such as Epinions[1] can share their reviews about products. Also they can establish their trust networks from which they may seek advice to make decisions. Assuming that users are likely to have similar preferences with their trust networks, trust networks are widely exploited in collaborative filtering [8, 1], intelligent recommender systems [17, 5], review quality prediction [15] and viral marketing [22] to improve the accuracy.

Most of these works assume single and homogeneous trust relationships between users. However, trust, as a social concept, has many facets [5], indicating multiple and heterogeneous trust relationships between users. People's multi-faceted interests and experts of different types suggest that people may place trust differently to different people. Siegler et al. pointed out that there is a strong and significant correlation between trust and similarity [25]. The more similar two people are, the greater the trust between them exists. In the context of product review sites, trust relationships between users can be indicated by their rating similarities [1].

Figure 1(a) demonstrates single trust relationships between a real user from Epinions[2], represented by user 1, and her 20 representative friends. Figures 1(b) and 1(c) show their multi-faceted trust relationships in the categories of "Home & Garden" and "Restaurants", respectively[3]. The width of arcs in these figures indicates their trust strengths. The top 3 trustworthy people in Figures 1(a), 1(b) and 1(c) are users $\{7, 8, 18\}$, $\{19, 8, 6\}$ and $\{7, 9, 11\}$, respectively. They are very different from one another, which reveals the existence of multi-faceted and heterogeneous trust relationships. For instance, user 7 is the most trustworthy person when assuming a single trust relationship. However, he is not even in the top 3 people in "Home & Garden", in which user 19 is most trustable. We closely examine user 19 from Epinions and find that she is the lead reviewer in "Home & Garden". Thus the user should seek advice from user 19 in "Home & Garden" instead of user 7. Moreover, users

Permission to make digital or hard copies of all or part of this work for personal or classroom use is granted without fee provided that copies are not made or distributed for profit or commercial advantage and that copies bear this notice and the full citation on the first page. To copy otherwise, to republish, to post on servers or to redistribute to lists, requires prior specific permission and/or a fee.
WSDM'12, February 8–12, 2012, Seattle, Washington, USA.
Copyright 2012 ACM 978-1-4503-0747-5/12/02 ...$10.00.

[1]http://www.epinions.com
[2]http://www.epinions.com/user-nancy35c
[3]Figure 1 is drawn by Pajek (http://pajek.imfm.si)

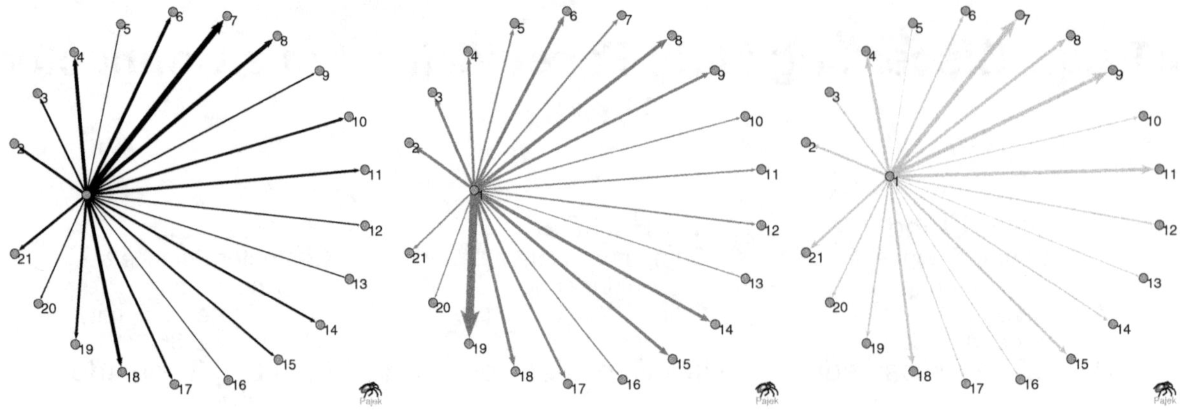

(a) Single Trust (b) Trust in Home & Garden (c) Trust in Restaurants

Figure 1: Single Trust and Multi-Faceted Trust Relationships of One User in Epinions

might trust some people more than others. For example, Figure 1(b) and 1(c) show that their trust strengths vary.

The example from Epinions suggests that single trust can't capture the real relationships between users. To obtain multi-faceted trust relationships between users, there are two challenges: 1) *how to represent multiple and heterogeneous trust relationships between users*? and 2) *how to estimate their strengths*? In this paper, we discern multi-faceted trust relationships in product review sites to improve data-mining related performance. Since an adjacency matrix cannot capture multi-faceted trust relationships, a fine-grained representation is proposed. By incorporating these relationships into rating prediction, their strengths are estimated. Experiments show that our work can improve the performance in various tasks such as rating prediction, facet-sensitive ranking, and status theory. Main contributions of this work include:

- Demonstrating that people with trust relationships have more similar multi-faceted interests than those without and show the existence of multi-faceted trust relationships in product review sites.
- Proposing a fine-gained representation to capture the multi-faceted trust relationships between users. By incorporating these relationships into rating prediction, their strengths are estimated.
- Presenting interesting findings from this multi-faceted trust study. For example, more than 17% of transitive trust relationships are heterogeneous, and more than 23% pairs of reciprocal links are heterogeneous.
- Showing various applications of mTrust such as rating prediction, facet-sensitive ranking and status theory and the experiments using real-world datasets.

The rest of paper is organized as follows. Section 2 describes the datasets used in our work, discusses multi-faceted interests and demonstrates multi-faceted trust relationships between users. Section 3 introduces a fine-grained representation for multi-faceted trust relationships and describes our method to estimate their strengths. Section 4 discusses applications of mTrust. Section 5 presents experimental results and findings. Section 6 briefly reviews related work. Finally, Section 7 concludes this study with future work.

Table 1: Statistics of the Datasets

	Epinions	Ciao
# of Users	22166	12375
# of Products	296277	106797
# of Catagories	27	28
# of Rating	922267	484086
# of Links	355813	237350
Ave Rating	4.05	4.21
Trust Network Density	0.0014	0.0031
Clustering Coefficient	0.1518	0.1969

2. DATASETS AND DATA ANALYSIS

For the purpose of this study, we crawled two datasets from two popular product review sites Epinions and Ciao[4] in the month of May, 2011. On both sites, people not only write critical reviews for various products but also read and rate the reviews written by others. Furthermore, people can add members to their trust networks or "Circle of Trust", if they find their reviews consistently interesting and helpful.

We started with a set of most active users and then did breadth-first search until no new users could be found. For each user, we collected information about profiles, trust networks, and product rating entries. For each product rating entry, we collected date, product name, *categories* of a product and its ratings. Users with fewer than 5 reviews are pruned. Some statistics of the datasets are shown in Table 1: Epinions has a much larger trust network while Ciao has more close-knit trust relationships, indicated by its higher clustering coefficient and network density.

Both sites employ a 5-star rating system. We investigate their rating distributions and find that more than **70%** ratings are 4 or 5. Many studies also reported this positive ratings phenomenon in online consumer ratings [1, 7].

[4]http://www.ciao.co.uk

19.8% and **21.3%** of users wrote **80%** reviews in Epinions and Ciao respectively.

2.1 Reciprocity in Trust Relationships

High reciprocity is reported in many relationships such as following relationships in Twitter [23]. We study the reciprocity of trust relationships by showing the correlation between the number of trustors and trustees for each user in Figure 2. The first observation is that most people have few trustors and trustees, while a few users have an extremely high number of trustees or trustors. We also compute the trustors and trustees for each user and the distributions are shown in Figure 3. These distributions suggest a power law distribution that is typical in social networks.

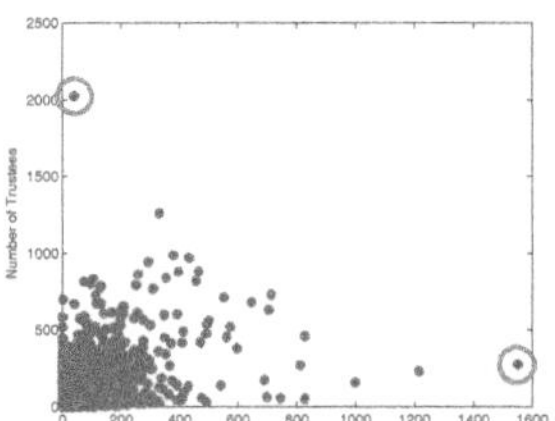

(a) Epinions

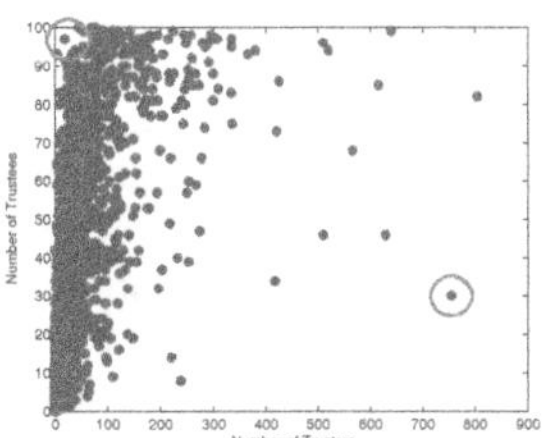

(b) Ciao

Figure 2: Number of Trustors vs Number of Trustees

Having many trustors does not necessarily mean having many trustees, and vice versa. Some representative users are indicated by red circles in Figure 2. Our closer examination reveals that the reciprocity is **19.28%** in Epinions and **23.77%** in Ciao.

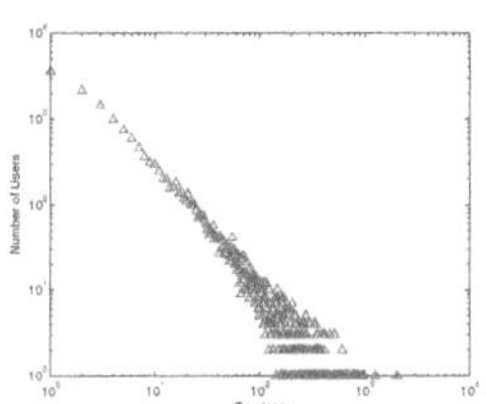

(a) Trustees(Epinions)

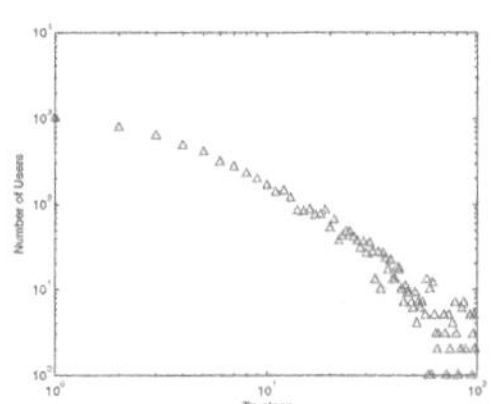

(b) Trustees(Ciao)

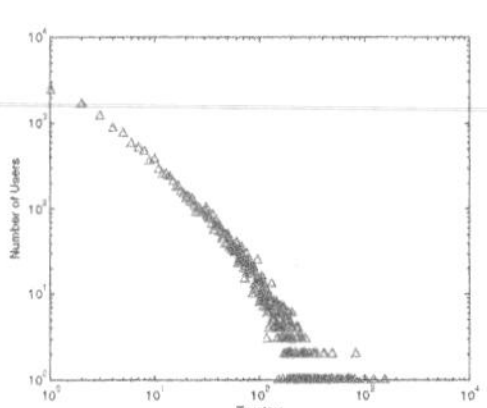

(c) Trustors(Epinions)

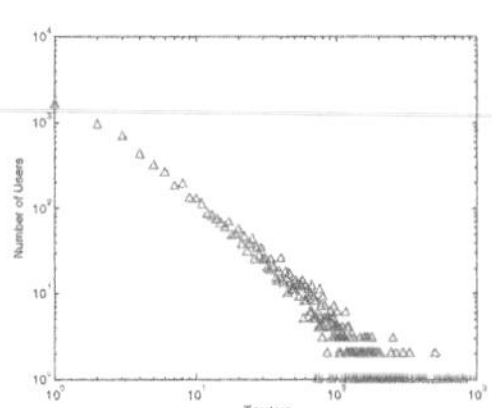

(d) Trustors(Ciao)

Figure 3: Trustors and Trustees Distributions in Epinions and Ciao

We also investigate the correlation between reciprocity and the number of trustors. The results are shown in Figure 4. We find that *people who have fewer trustors are more likely to trust their trustees*. It shows that people with many trustees are more likely to have bias or propensity to trust others [20]. Thus the ratios of reciprocal links for these people are low.

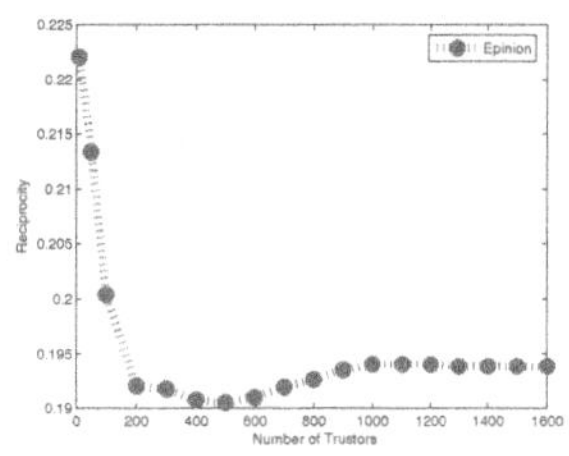

(a) Epinions

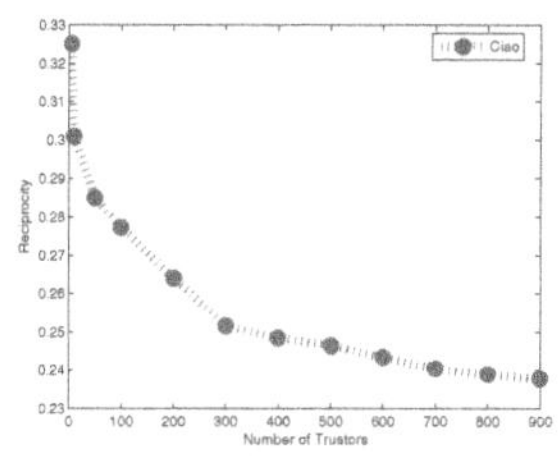

(b) Ciao

Figure 4: Reciprocity vs Number of Trustors

2.2 Multi-Faceted Interests

When people place multi-faceted trust to others, they are supposed to have similar multi-faceted interests with their trustees. In this section, we investigate the connection between multi-faceted interests and trust relationships. More specifically, we want to answer this question: *Do people with trust relationships have more similar multi-faceted interests than those without?*. To answer this question, we need to define facet in product review sites and how to measure the multi-faceted interests similarity between a pair of users.

Facet in product review sites is defined as a set of products which are similar to each other. In product review sites, the notion of category is used to organize products, and products in the same category have similar characteristics. Products are manually assigned to different categories by reviewers. Based on these facts, in our work, categories are regarded as facets. On average, people are interested in 6.3 and 5.8 facets in Epinions and Ciao, respectively.

Let $fd_i(k)$ be the probability that user i is interested in facet k, which is formally defined in Eq. (1)

$$fd_i(k) = \frac{n_i(k)}{n_i} \tag{1}$$

where n_i is the total number of products rated by user i and $n_i(k)$ is the number of products from facet k rated by user i. With the facet distribution for each user, *multi-faceted interests similarity(f_{dist}) between user i and user j can be measured based on the Jensen-Shannon Divergence between two facet distributions fd_i and fd_j.*

$$\begin{aligned} f_{dist} &= \sqrt{2 * D_{JS}(i,j)} \\ &= \sqrt{D_{KL}(fd_i \| m) + D_{KL}(fd_j \| m)} \end{aligned} \tag{2}$$

where m is the average of the two distributions, i.e., $m = \frac{1}{2}(fd_i + fd_j)$. D_{KL} is the Kullback-Leibler Divergence. For example $D_{KL}(fd_i \| m) = \sum_k fd_i(k) \log \frac{fd_i(k)}{m(k)}$

For each user i, we calculate two f_{dist}, i.e., $\mathbf{s}_t(i)$ and $\mathbf{s}_r(i)$. $\mathbf{s}_t(i)$ is the average f_{dist} between user i and his/her trust network, while $\mathbf{s}_r(i)$ is the average f_{dist} between user i and randomly chosen users, who are not in the trust network of user i. The number of these randomly chosen users is the same as the size of user i 's trust network.

For a visual comparison, in Figure 5 we plot the Kernel-smoothing density estimations based on the vectors $\mathbf{s}_t$ and

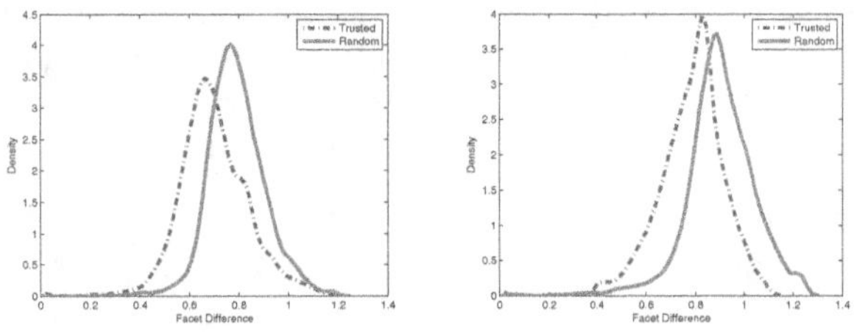

(a) Epinions (b) Ciao

Figure 5: Density Estimates of Users' *f-dist*

Table 2: Statistics of Chosen Categories

Order	Name	Products	Ratings	Ave Score
Epinions				
1	Electronics	9594	23571	3.96
2	Home & Garden	16029	28759	4.12
3	Computer Hardware	7584	17532	4.02
4	Hotels & Travel	11723	33410	4.15
5	Restaurants	14368	32477	3.91
6	Kids & Family	20926	50783	4.11
Ciao				
1	Entertainment	5059	14349	4.13
2	House & Garden	5805	15398	4.37
3	Household Apps	5334	14478	4.34
4	Electronics	4802	12426	4.41
5	Family	6227	18923	4.08
6	Games	6237	18491	4.31

$\mathbf{s}_r$. For both datasets, $\mathbf{s}_t$ have smaller concentrated values, i.e., smaller f_{dist}, compared with $\mathbf{s}_r$.

We also conduct a two sample t-test on the vectors $\mathbf{s}_t$ and $\mathbf{s}_r$. The null hypothesis is H_0: $\mathbf{s}_t = \mathbf{s}_r$, and the alternative hypothesis is H_1: $\mathbf{s}_t < \mathbf{s}_r$. For both datasets, the null hypothesis is rejected at significant level $\alpha = 0.01$ with p-value of 3.2e-7 and 1.3e-6 in Epinions and Ciao, respectively.

The evidence from both Figure 5 and t-test suggests a positive answer to the question: *with high probability, users with trust relationships have smaller f_{dist} than those without.* Based on this finding, we further study multi-faceted relationships in the next section.

2.3 Multi-Faceted Trust Relationships

In order to trust, people need some information usually based on the target person's current and previous experiences [2]. People with similar experiences are more likely to trust each other. In this section, we study rating similarity between users for each facet(*facet similarity*). Due to the strong correlation between user similarity and trust, multi-faceted trust relationships between users can be indicated by facet similarities.

We choose six representative facets (categories) from Epinions and Ciao to study multi-faceted trust relationships. The statistical information for these chosen facets is shown in Table 2. On average, each product receives more than two ratings. The average ratings for different facets are different and users have different preferences for different facets.

For each user, we calculate the average and the variance of similarities with her/his trust network(trust facet similarity) and randomly chosen users(random facet similarity) for each facet. Facet rating similarities between users are calculated by *cosine* similarity. Let $\mathbf{S}_t(i,k)$ and $\mathbf{S}_r(i,k)$ denote the average of trust facet similarities and random facet similarities of user i in facet k, respectively. $\mathbf{V}_t(i,k)$ and $\mathbf{V}_r(i,k)$ are their variances.

Let $\bar{\mathbf{s}}_t(k)$ denote the average of trust facet similarities of all users in facet k, which is formally defined as:

$$\bar{\mathbf{s}}_t(k) = \frac{\sum_{i=1}^{n} \mathbf{S}_t(i,k)}{n} \tag{3}$$

where n is the number of users. Let $\bar{\mathbf{s}}_r$ be the averages of random facet similarities, $\bar{\mathbf{v}}_t$ and $\bar{\mathbf{v}}_r$ be the averages of their variances, respectively. $\bar{\mathbf{s}}_r$, $\bar{\mathbf{v}}_t$ and $\bar{\mathbf{v}}_r$ can be obtained similarly as $\bar{\mathbf{s}}_t$. Table 3 shows the results in the Epinions dataset and we can get similar results in Ciao.

$\bar{\mathbf{s}}_t$ is always larger than $\bar{\mathbf{s}}_r$. This supports that *for each facet, users with trust relationships have more similar product ratings than those without.* $\bar{\mathbf{v}}_t$ is always larger than $\bar{\mathbf{v}}_r$, indicating that *users trust their friends differently and they have greater trust in some friends than in others.* The variance of facet similarity directly supports that the strengths of trust relationships vary between users.

Most of the time, the facet similarities are smaller than the overall similarity, while the facet variances are always larger than the overall variance. In other words, *for each facet, people only strongly trust a part of their trust networks*, or the existence of multi-faceted trust between users.

We also want to investigate whether distributions of facet similarities are significantly different. Thus for each pair of facets (i,j), we conduct a two-sample Kolmogorov-Smirnov(KS) test on their facet similarity vectors, i.e. $\{\mathbf{S}_t(:,i), \mathbf{S}_t(:,j)\}$. The p-value is shown in Table 4. The star next to the p-value means that there is strong evidence($p < 0.01$) that two samples come from different distributions.

The table shows that p-values for all pairs of facets are close to zero. This implies that the distributions for different facets are significantly different, indicating multi-faceted trust relationships in product review sites.

Evidence from Table 3 and KS-test suggests the existence of multi-faceted relationships between users in product review sites. In the next section, we present our method, mTrust, to model multi-faceted relationships, including a fine-grained representation and the estimation of their strengths.

3. MODELING mTrust RELATIONSHIPS

Before building the mathematical model, we would like to establish the notations that are used. Following the standard notations, scalars are denoted by low-case letters $(a, b, \ldots)$, vectors are written as low-case bold letters $(\mathbf{a}, \mathbf{b}, \ldots)$, matri-

Table 3: Average of Means and Variances of Facet Similarities in Epinions

Facets	Trust Network		Random	
	$\bar{\mathbf{s}}_t$	$\bar{\mathbf{v}}_t$	$\bar{\mathbf{s}}_r$	$\bar{\mathbf{v}}_r$
1	0.0128	0.0024	0.0056	0.0011
2	0.0067	0.0016	0.0025	0.0007
3	0.0051	0.0017	0.0016	0.0007
4	0.0053	0.0018	0.0018	0.0007
5	0.0150	0.0024	0.0064	0.0012
6	0.0171	0.0024	0.0077	0.0011
overall	0.0159	0.0017	0.0056	0.0005

Table 4: Statistics of Facet Similarity For Pairs of Facets

	Epinions(p-value)				
	2	3	4	5	6
1	5.51e-46*	1.77e-111*	5.14e-76*	2.35e-08*	2.15e-26*
2	-	7.67e-37*	3.65e-16*	2.21e-77*	5.56e-135*
3	-	-	7.91e-06*	4.39e-122*	2.36e-227*
4	-	-	-	3.90e-97*	1.83e-178*
5	-	-	-	-	7.88e-22*

	Ciao(p-value)				
	2	3	4	5	6
1	6.00e-24*	6.46e-97*	3.50e-69*	4.63e-7*	4.15e-20*
2	-	1.12e-33*	8.23e-16*	4.72e-26*	1.50e-80*
3	-	-	9.56e-05*	1.42e-92*	3.55e-184*
4	-	-	-	1.49e-69*	1.42e-154*
5	-	-	-	-	1.03e-19*

ces correspond to bold-face captitals($\mathbf{A}, \mathbf{B}, \ldots$), and tensors are written as calligraphic letters ($\mathcal{A}, \mathcal{B}, \ldots$). Also we represent the elements in a given above structure using a convention similar to *Matlab*. For example, $\mathbf{A}(i,j)$ is the entry at the ith row and j^{th} column of the matrix $\mathbf{A}$, $\mathbf{A}(i,:)$ is the ith row of $\mathbf{A}$ and $\mathbf{A}(:,j)$ is the jth column of $\mathbf{A}$ etc.

Let $\mathbf{u} = \{u_1, u_2, \ldots, u_n\}$ be the user set vector where n is the number of users. $\mathbf{e} = \{e_1, e_2, \ldots, e_m\}$ and $\mathbf{f} = \{f_1, f_2, \ldots, f_K\}$ denote the set of products and facets, respectively, where m is the number of products and K is the number of facets. We use $\mathbf{A} \in \mathbb{R}^{n \times n}$ to denote the adjacency matrix for the trust network, in which $\mathbf{A}(i,j) = 1$ if u_j trusts u_i and $\mathbf{A}(i,j) = 0$ otherwise. $\mathbf{R} \in \mathbb{R}^{n \times m}$ denotes the rating matrix and $\mathbf{R}(i,j)$ is the rating for the product e_j from u_i. $\mathbf{PF} \in \mathbb{R}^{m \times K}$ is the product-facet matrix. $\mathbf{PF}(i,k) = 1$ if e_i belongs to f_k and $\mathbf{PF}(i,k) = 0$, otherwise.

3.1 Tensor Representation for Multi-Faceted Trust Relationships

A trust network is often represented by an adjacency matrix with binary values. Multi-faceted trust between users is a **quadruple** {*user, user, facet, strength*}, which is out of the scope of what an adjacency matrix can capture. Thus we extend the *matrix* representation to a *tensor* representation by adding an extra dimension *facets*, as demonstrated in Figure 6.

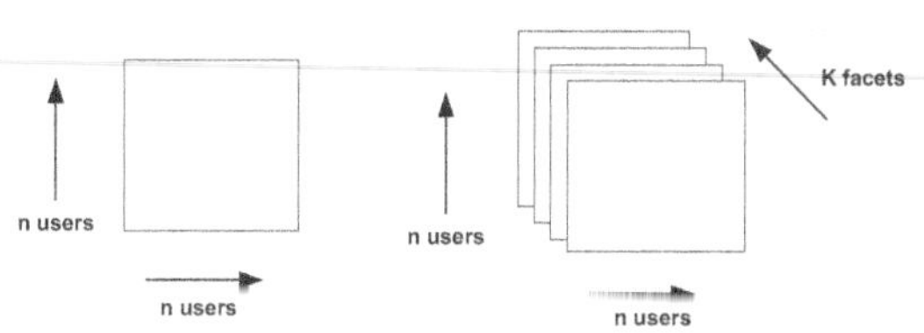

Figure 6: Matrix Representation(Left) vs Tensor Representation(Right)

We first briefly introduce some background on tensors. A *tensor*, also known as multidimensional matrix [3], is a higher order generalization of a vector (first order tensor) and a matrix (second order tensor). An Nth-order tensor $\mathcal{A}$ is denoted as $\mathcal{A} \in \mathbb{R}^{I_1 \times I_2 \times \ldots \times I_N}$. A generalization of the product of two matrices is the product of a tensor and a matrix. The mode-n product of a tensor $\mathcal{A} \in \mathbb{R}^{I_1 \times I_2 \times \ldots \times I_N}$ and a matrix $\mathbf{Q} \in \mathbb{R}^{J_n \times I_n}$ is a tensor, denoted as

$$\mathcal{A} \times_n \mathbf{Q} \in \mathbb{R}^{I_1 \times \ldots \times I_{n-1} \times J_n \times I_{n+1} \ldots I_N} \tag{4}$$

whose entries are given by

$$(\mathcal{A} \times_n \mathbf{Q})(i_1, \ldots, i_{n-1}, j_n, i_{n+1}, \ldots, i_N) = \sum_{i_n} \mathcal{A}(i_1, \ldots, i_{n-1}, i_n, i_{n+1}, \ldots, i_N)\mathbf{Q}(j_n, i_n) \tag{5}$$

The proposed representation, as shown in Figure 6 (**Right**), is a *third order* tensor. Let $\mathcal{A} \in \mathbb{R}^{n \times n \times K}$ represent multi-faceted trust relationships among n users in K facets. Each element $\mathcal{A}(i,j,k)$ indicates the strength that u_j trusts u_i in facet f_k. In the next section, we introduce a method to estimate the strengths of multi-faceted trust relationships, i.e., entities in $\mathcal{A}$.

3.2 Estimation of Strengths of Multi-faceted Trust Relationships

Due to the strong correlation between rating similarity and trust, it is desirable to understand strengths of a user's multi-faceted trust relations in the context of product rating prediction. The (u,i) pairs for which $\mathbf{R}(u,i)$ is known are stored in the set $\mathcal{O} = \{(u,i)|\mathbf{R}(u,i) \text{ } is \text{ } known\}$ and unknown pairs are stored in $\mathcal{U} = \{(u,i)|\mathbf{R}(u,i) \text{ } is \text{ } unknown\}$. We denote the predicted value of $\mathbf{R}(u,i)$ as $\hat{\mathbf{R}}(u,i)$.

One baseline method for rating prediction is based on users' preferences and products' characteristics [11]. Some users have propensity to give higher ratings than others and some products are more likely to receive higher ratings than others. Thus, the optimization formulation to estimate unknown rating $\hat{\mathbf{R}}(u,i)$ is shown below, accounting for both user and product effects:

$$\min_{\mathbf{b},\mathbf{c}} \sum_{(u,i)\in\mathcal{O}} (\mathbf{R}(u,i) - \hat{\mathbf{R}}(u,i))^2 + \lambda(\sum_u \mathbf{b}^2(u) + \sum_i \mathbf{c}^2(i)) \tag{6}$$

where $\hat{\mathbf{R}}(u,i) = \mu + \mathbf{b}(u) + \mathbf{c}(i)$. $\mathbf{b}(u)$ and $\mathbf{c}(i)$ indicate the bias of user u and product i respectively. μ is the average rating over all products and λ controls the regularized part to avoid overfitting.

Another baseline method based on trust networks is the nearest-neighbor algorithm. Let $N(u,i)$ be the set of users who are trusted by user u and have rated product i. Then the unknown rating from u to i can be calculated by:

$$\mathbf{R}(u,i) = \frac{\sum_{v\in N(u,i)} \mathbf{W}(v,u)\mathbf{R}(v,i)}{\sum_{v\in N(u,i)} \mathbf{W}(v,u)} \tag{7}$$

where $\mathbf{W}(v,u)$ is the strength of single trust from u to v.

We want to incorporate the notion of multiple facets into these two baseline methods. The first baseline method assumes that one user has the same bias to all products. However, from the data analysis section, we know that users might have different bias toward different facets. Also the average ratings for different facets are different. Thus $\hat{\mathbf{R}}(u,i)$ can be improved by considering facet differences:

$$\hat{\mathbf{R}}(u,i) = \mathbf{c}(i) + \frac{\sum_k \mathbf{PF}(i,k)(\mu(k) + \mathbf{B}(u,k))}{\sum_k \mathbf{PF}(i,k)} \tag{8}$$

where $\mu(k)$ is average rating for f_k and $\mathbf{B}(u,k)$ is the bias from u toward f_k.

The second baseline method assumes single trust relationships between users. Our tensor representation, i.e., multi-faceted trust relationships, can be easily incorporated into this method as follows:

$$\hat{\mathbf{R}}(u,i) = \frac{\sum_{k=1}^{K}\sum_{v\in N(u,i)}\mathbf{PF}(i,k)\mathcal{A}(v,u,k)\mathbf{R}(v,i)}{\sum_{k=1}^{K}\sum_{v\in N(u,i)}\mathbf{PF}(i,k)\mathcal{A}(v,u,k)} \quad (9)$$

The first model doesn't consider the trust network, while the latter one doesn't consider the bias from products and users. We believe that both factors are useful for rating prediction, thus the rating prediction algorithm to estimate strengths of multi-faceted trust are shown below:

$$\begin{aligned}\hat{\mathbf{R}}(u,i) = \alpha\Big(\frac{\sum_k \mathbf{PF}(i,k)(\mu(k)+\mathbf{B}(u,k))}{\sum_k \mathbf{PF}(i,k)} + \mathbf{c}(i)\Big) + \quad (10)\\ (1-\alpha)\frac{\sum_{k=1}^{K}\sum_{v\in N(u,i)}\mathbf{PF}(i,k)\mathcal{A}(v,u,k)\mathbf{R}(v,i)}{\sum_{k=1}^{K}\sum_{v\in N(u,i)}\mathbf{PF}(i,k)\mathcal{A}(v,u,k)}\end{aligned}$$

In this formulation, the rating u giving to i from f_k, $\hat{\mathbf{R}}(u,i)$, is determined by two factors. First, the rating is determined by the bias of u toward f_k and the characteristics of i. This factor is modeled as the first part of our formulation. Secondly, as mentioned above, users in product review sites always seek advice from their trust networks to make decisions. Thus $\hat{\mathbf{R}}(u,i)$ should be influenced by the trust network of u. $\mathcal{A}(v,u,k)$ indicates the strength of trust from u to v in f_k. If u strongly trusts v in f_k, $\hat{\mathbf{R}}(u,i)$ should be similar to $\mathbf{R}(v,i)$. The second part of our formulation is used to model this factor, which captures the influence from multi-faceted trust relationships between users. The parameter α controls the contributions of these two parts. Note that multi-faceted trust relationships can be incorporated into other more complex rating prediction methods, which we leave as our future work.

We define $\mathbf{E}(u,i)$, p and q as following:

$$\begin{aligned}\mathbf{E}(u,i) &\stackrel{\text{def}}{=} \mathbf{R}(u,i) - \hat{\mathbf{R}}(u,i)\\ p &\stackrel{\text{def}}{=} \textstyle\sum_{k=1}^{K}\sum_{v\in N(u,i)}\mathbf{PF}(i,k)\mathcal{A}(v,u,k)\\ q &\stackrel{\text{def}}{=} \textstyle\sum_{k=1}^{K}\sum_{v\in N(u,i)}\mathbf{PF}(i,k)\mathcal{A}(v,u,k)\mathbf{R}(v,i)\end{aligned}$$

To estimate the parameters $\{\mathbf{B},\mathbf{c},\mathcal{A}\}$, we solve the following optimization problem:

$$\begin{aligned}&\min_{\mathbf{B},\mathbf{c},\mathcal{A}} \textstyle\sum_{(u,i)\in\mathcal{O}} \mathbf{E}^2(u,i) + \lambda(\sum_{u,k}\mathbf{B}^2(u,k) + \sum_i \mathbf{c}^2(i))\\ &\quad s.t.\ \ \mathcal{A}(v,u,k)\in[0,1]\end{aligned} \quad (11)$$

We use projected gradient method to solve Eq. (11). Then the following rules are used to update $\{\mathbf{B}(u,k), \mathbf{c}(i), \mathcal{A}(v,u,k)\}$:

$$\begin{aligned}\mathbf{B}(u,k) &\leftarrow \mathbf{B}(u,k) - \beta_{\mathbf{B}}\nabla_{\mathbf{B}(u,k)} \quad (12)\\ \mathbf{c}(i) &\leftarrow \mathbf{c}(i) - \beta_{\mathbf{c}}\nabla_{\mathbf{c}(i)}\\ \mathcal{A}(v,u,k) &\leftarrow \begin{cases} 0 & \mathcal{A}(v,u,k) - \beta_{\mathcal{A}}\nabla_{\mathcal{A}(v,u,k)} < 0\\ 1 & \mathcal{A}(v,u,k) - \beta_{\mathcal{A}}\nabla_{\mathcal{A}(v,u,k)} > 1\\ \mathcal{A}(v,u,k) - \beta_{\mathcal{A}}\nabla_{\mathcal{A}(v,u,k)} & else\end{cases}\end{aligned}$$

where $\beta_{\mathbf{B}}$, $\beta_{\mathbf{c}}$ and $\beta_{\mathcal{A}}$ are the learning step sizes, which are chosen to satisfy *Goldstein Conditions*. $\nabla_{\mathbf{B}(u,k)}$, $\nabla_{\mathbf{c}(i)}$ and $\nabla_{\mathcal{A}(v,u,k)}$ are shown as follows:

$$\begin{aligned}\nabla_{\mathbf{B}(u,k)} &= -\alpha\mathbf{E}(u,i) + \lambda\frac{\mathbf{B}(u,k)}{\sum_k \mathbf{PF}(i,k)} \quad (13)\\ \nabla_{\mathbf{c}(i)} &= -\alpha\mathbf{E}(u,i) + \lambda\mathbf{c}(i)\\ \nabla_{\mathcal{A}(v,u,k)} &= (\alpha-1)\mathbf{E}(u,i)\frac{\mathbf{PF}(i,k)\mathbf{R}(v,i)p - q\mathbf{PF}(i,k)}{p^2}\end{aligned}$$

4. APPLYING mTrust

In this section, we apply mTrust to improve some data mining tasks on product review sites: rating prediction, facet-sensitive ranking, and strengthening status theory.

4.1 Rating Prediction

Users in product review sites are likely to refer to product reviews provided by their trust networks. Thus trust have been widely used to improve the performance of rating prediction [16]. Most of these approaches assume single trust relationships. However, our work indicates the existence of multi-faceted trust relationships between users, which can be used to further improve the performance of prediction.

In section 3.2, we have already shown how to model multi-faceted trust relationships to improve nearest-neighbor algorithm. Actually our multi-faceted trust relationships can also be incorporated into other complex rating prediction methods, such as latent factor model [11] as follows:

$$\hat{\mathbf{R}}(u,i) = \alpha\mathbf{p}_u^\top\mathbf{q}_i + (1-\alpha)\frac{\sum_{k=1}^{K}\sum_v \mathbf{PF}(i,k)\mathcal{A}(u,v,k)\mathbf{R}(v,i)}{\sum_{k=1}^{K}\sum_v \mathbf{PF}(i,k)\mathcal{A}(u,v,k)} \quad (14)$$

where $\mathbf{p}_u$ is a user-factors vector associated with user u and $\mathbf{q}_i$ is a product-factors vector with product i. α is also used to control the contributions of two factors in Eq. (14).

4.2 Facet-Sensitive Ranking

Ranking nodes in a network is an important problem, and *HITS* [10] and *PageRank* [21] are two very popular ranking techniques. Most traditional ranking techniques give higher ranks to nodes with better connectivity. However, from the analysis above, people trust others because they have more similar multi-faceted interests, which suggests that ranking algorithms in product review sites should consider both trust networks and people's interests. Multi-faceted trust relationships, which are estimated by taking into account both the link structure and people's multi-faceted interests, can be used for facet-sensitive ranking to improve the performance of ranking.

Let $\mathbf{FR}\in\mathbb{R}^{n\times K}$, each element of which, $\mathbf{FR}(i,k)$, denotes the ranking of u_i in f_k. The kth column of $\mathbf{FR}$, $\mathbf{FR}(:,k)$, represents the rankings of users in f_k. Based on the estimated $\mathcal{A}$, $\mathbf{FR}(:,k)$ can be calculated as following:

$$\mathbf{FR}(:,k) = d\times\mathcal{A}(:,:,k)\times\mathbf{FR}(:,k) + (1-d)\times\frac{\mathbf{e}}{n} \quad (15)$$

where $\mathbf{e}\in\mathbb{R}^n = \{1,1,\dots,1\}$ and the parameter d is used to control the probability that a user would "jump" to some users instead of following the trust relationships.

The overall rankings, $\mathbf{fr}\in\mathbb{R}^n$, can be obtained from the aggregation of the rankings in different facets.

$$\mathbf{fr} = \mathbf{FR}\times\mathbf{r} \quad (16)$$

where $\mathbf{r} \in \mathbb{R}^K$ is a weight vector and $\mathbf{r}(k)$ represents the weight assigned to f_k and associated $\mathbf{FR}(:, k)$.

With the rankings of users in each facet, it is easier for advertisers to differentiate effective users for their products propagation with different facets.

4.3 Strengthening Status Theory

One important social-psychological theory is status theory [13]. In this theory, u_i trusting u_k means that u_i regards u_k as having higher status than herself. However, this theory holds weakly on the subset of links in these networks that are reciprocated(consisting of directed links in both directions between two users) [13]. For example, if u_i trusts u_k and u_k also trusts u_i, as shown in the top subgraph of Figure 7, then it will be difficult for status theory to determine whose status is higher.

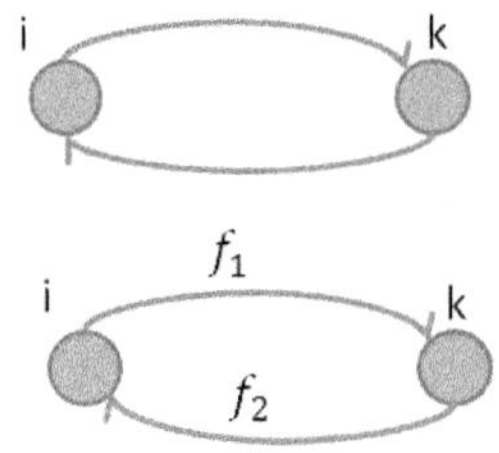

Figure 7: Reciprocity and Status Theory

In the data analysis section, we study reciprocity in trust networks in Epinions and Ciao. The reciprocity is **19.28%** in Epinions and **23.77%** in Ciao. Thus status theory might not hold strongly in both datasets. However, our work indicates that a pair of reciprocal links might be heterogeneous. As shown in the bottom subgraph of Figure 7, u_i trusts u_k in facet f_1 and u_k trusts u_i in facet f_2. According to status theory, u_i has a higher status in f_2 and u_k has a higher status in f_1. In this case, status theory holds for this pair of reciprocal links. Thus our work can be applied to strengthening status theory in networks with reciprocal links.

5. EXPERIMENTS AND FINDINGS

In this section, we describe in detail the findings and different experiments resulting from applying mTrust to the Epinions and Ciao datasets. Two parameters of mTrust, i.e., λ and α, are determined through cross validation.

5.1 Findings about mTrust

For this experiment, all ratings are used as training data to estimate $\mathcal{A}$, which indicates multi-faceted trust relationships between users. We observe the following about $\mathcal{A}$:

- In the studied six facets for both datasets, less than 1% of users trust their friends in all six facets. However, more than 70% of users trust their friends more than one facet. On average, people trust only 35.4% of their trust networks for a specific facet.

- We examine transitive and co-citation trust relationships in both datasets. 22.3% and 17.1% of transitive trust relationships are heterogeneous for Epinions and Ciao, respectively, while 13.1% and 11.7% of co-citation relationships are heterogeneous. Examples of heterogeneous transitive and co-citation trust relationships are shown in Figure 8. For example, a transitive trust relationship, $i \to j \to k$, is heterogeneous. u_i trusts u_j in f_1, however, u_j trusts u_k in f_2; a co-citation trust, $i_1 \to j_2$ and $i_2 \to j_2$, is heterogeneous.

- We study pairs of reciprocal links in the original networks and we find that 23.5% and 24.1% pairs of these links are heterogeneous in the Epinions and Ciao, respectively. As shown in the bottom subgraph of Figure 7, the link $i \to j$ and link $j \to i$ are different types.

- The original network is a big component for both datasets. However, we examine the trust relationships in each facet and there exist many components, most of which are singletons. For example, for the first facet in Epinions, 96.7% of these components are singletons and the biggest component contains 75.5% users.

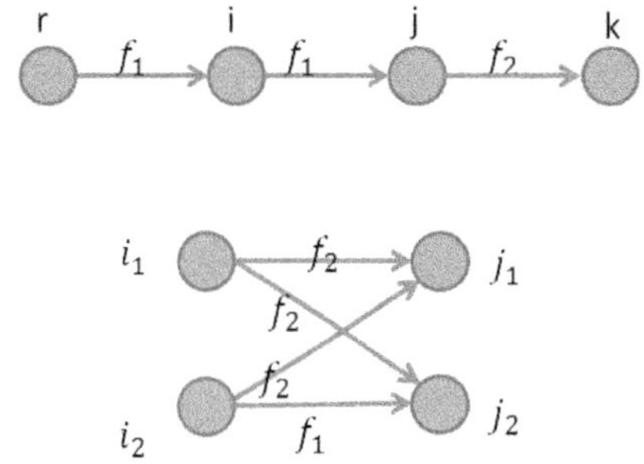

Figure 8: Heterogeneous Transitive and Co-citation Trust Relationships

5.2 Rating Prediction

The ratings in both datasets are sorted in *chronological order* and we choose the top 70% of the datasets as training data and the rest as testing data. Then the model parameters are estimated from *past* data and to predict *future* data. The estimated parameters, i.e., $\{\mathbf{B}, \mathbf{c}, \mathcal{A}\}$, can be used to predict unknown ratings. mTrust can be incoporated into other rating prediction methods thus our objective is not to compare rating prediction methods. Instead, we want to verify that considering multi-faceted trust relationships between users allows us to improve the performance of prediction. We use a common metric, Root Mean Squared Error(RMSE), to evaluate prediction accuracy.

$$RMSE(\mathcal{U}) = \sqrt{\frac{\sum_{(u,r)\in\mathcal{U}} (\mathbf{R}(u,i) - \hat{\mathbf{R}}(u,i))^2}{|\mathcal{U}|}} \quad (17)$$

where $|\mathcal{U}|$ is the size of testing data $\mathcal{U}$

Through cross validation, we set $\lambda = 0.05$. The parameter α controls the contributions of two factors of our formulation. We test different values of α to investigate the importance of these two factors in our study datasets. Results are shown in Figure 9. The methods mentioned in the figure are defined as follows:

- *Mean*: the rating of a product is predicted by the mean of known ratings of the product.

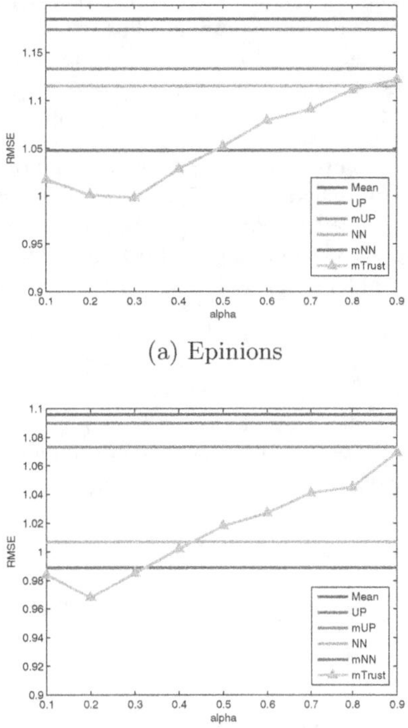

(a) Epinions

(b) Ciao

Figure 9: Performance of Rating Prediction in Epinions and Ciao

- *UP*: the rating of a product is predicted by Eq. (6) and this model assumes that one user has the same bias to all products.
- *mUP*: the model is a variant of *UP*, which incorporates the facet differences such as average facet ratings differences and users' facet bias differences.
- *NN*: it refers to the nearest neighbor algorithm, as shown in Eq. (7). *NN* assumes single trust relationships between users.
- *mNN*: the rating of a product is predicted by Eq. (9), which considers multi-faceted trust relationships between users.
- *mTrust*: the rating of a product is predicted by the combination of *mUP* and *mNN*, as shown in Eq (11).

The first observation is that *Mean* and *UP* are very close in performance on both datasets. Most of the time, the majority of users actual ratings are close to the average. As reported in the data analysis section, more than 70% users give a score of 4 or 5. When facet differences are incorporated into *UP*, the performance of *mUP* is apparently improved. This directly supports the existence of facet differences, i.e. average facet rating differences and facet bias differences.

The performance of *NN* is better than that of *mUP* especially on the Ciao dataset. People on product review sites often refer to the reviews from their trust networks. Thus their product ratings can be easily influenced by their trust networks. Ciao has more close-knit trust relationships and people are influenced more by their trust networks. We check the estimated single trust matrix $\mathbf{W}$ and find that the strengths of single trust relationships vary between users, i.e., people trust some people more than others.

The difference between *NN* and *mNN* is that *mNN* assumes multi-faceted trust relationships between users. Comparing the performance of *mNN* with *NN* on both datasets, we can see that *mNN* is always better. The experiments show that mTrust helps capture fine-grained relationships between users for better performance.

For both datasets, *mTrust* obtains the best performance. The algorithm achieves the peak performance with $\alpha = 0.3$ for Epinions dataset and $\alpha = 0.2$ for Ciao dataset. A small α means that a higher weight would be put on *mNN*. This suggests (1) the importance of trust networks in rating prediction, and (2) that an appropriate combination of these two factors is crucial to achieve better performance.

5.3 Facet-Sensitive Ranking

Facet-sensitive ranking, i.e., ranking users using multi-faceted trust relationships, is one important application of mTrust. For instance, advertisers can easily differentiate effective users for product propagation from different facets. Rankings of users in different facets can also be used for the recommendation of helpful reviews that may be buried in a large number of spam reviews [15].

Rankings in facet f_k, $\mathbf{FR}(:,k)$, are calculated by Eq. (15) and the overall rankings, $\mathbf{fr}$, are obtained by Eq. (16). The weight vector $\mathbf{r}$ is set as the probabilities of different facets' presence, calculated according to the number of rated products from corresponding facets. The multi-faceted trust relationships, $\mathcal{A}$, are estimated by all ratings and the damping factor d is set to 0.85. Due to the limitation of space, we only show the results in Epinions since we get similar results in Ciao. Table 5 lists top-5 users for the studied six facets in Epinions.

We observe that *the top ranking people are different for different facets.* In other words, people have different rankings in different facets. The ranking results of Epinions for each facet seem reasonable. For example, "Howard_Creech" is the lead reviewers in "Electronics". His reviews mainly focus on products in "Electronics" and most of his reviews are rated as very helpful. "dlstewart" is the leader in "Home & Garden". "popsrocks" is the leader in "Hotels & Travel" and among the top reviewers in "Restaurants". "Bryan_Carey" is the top 10 people in Epinions. He wrote 3,493 reviews about products from various facets such as "Restaurants" and "Hotels & Travel". The remaining of the top 5 users are also among the top advisors or top reviewers in their respective facets.

Although "jo.com" is the top 1 user in Epinions, she is not even among the top 5 users in some facets such as "Electronics" and "Computer Hardware". Facet-sensitive ranking for product review effectively take into account both link structure and people's multi-faceted interests.

It is beyond the scope of this paper to probe further causes of high rankings. However, we observe some commonalities among these top users:

- They usually registered at the sites very early. For example, "Howard_Creech" was a member of Epinions since Aug 16,1999 and "yusakugo" registered Epinions on Apr 14, 2000.

Table 5: Top 5 Users in Each Facet in Epinions

Electronics	Home & Garden	Computer Hardware	Hotels & Travel	Restaurants	Kids & Family	overall
Howard_Creech	dlstewart	yusakugo	popsrocks	Bryan_Carey	Freak369	Bryan_Carey
dkozin	Bryan_Carey	Gr8ful	mrkstvns	popsrocks	marytara	Freak369
yusakugo	mountainhigh	lawman67	AliventiAsylum	jo.com	melissasrn	popsrocks
nick1326	Freak369	ptiemann	Bryan_Carey	Bruguru	three_ster	yusakugo
paulphoto	michiman1	paulphoto	jo.com	AliventiAsylum	pippadaisy	marytara

- They contributed many reviews such as "Freak369" wrote 5,921 reviews and "popsrocks" wrote 2,651 reviews. More than 90% of their reviews are considered as very helpful. For example, 93% of reviews written by "dkozin" are rated very helpful by other users.
- They have many trustors. For example, "ptiemann" has 2,809 trustors and "Bryan_Carey" has 1,570 trustors.

5.4 Strengthening Status Theory in Networks with Reciprocal Links

Status theory is one of important social theories about social networks. It is reported in [13] that the theory of status holds weakly on these networks that are reciprocated. Here we show how mTrust can strengthen status theory in trust networks with reciprocal links.

In status theory, if u_i trusts u_j, it means that u_i regards u_j as having higher status than herself. In the context of product review sites, the facet-sensitive rankings for users can be considered as their statuses in each facet. if u_i trusts u_j in f_k then u_j should have a higher ranking than u_i in f_k, i.e., $\mathbf{FR}(j,k) > \mathbf{FR}(i,k)$.

For this experiment, multi-faced trust relationships, $\mathcal{A}$, are estimated by all ratings. Given the trust relationships in f_k, $\mathcal{A}(:,:,k)$, let $\mathcal{S}$ be the set of all occurrences of form $i \rightarrow j$ in $\mathcal{A}(:,:,k)$. We compute the ratio of trust relationships(RAT), on which status theory doesn't hold as Eq. (18):

$$RAT = \frac{\sum_{(i,j)\in\mathcal{S}} \varphi(\mathbf{FR}(j,k) - \mathbf{FR}(i,k))}{|\mathcal{S}|} \quad (18)$$

where $|\mathcal{S}|$ is the number of trust relationships. $\varphi(x)$ is a function defined as:

$$\varphi(x) = \begin{cases} 0, & if\ x > 0 \\ 1, & if\ x \leq 0 \end{cases} \quad (19)$$

The RAT and Reciprocity(RCT) for trust relationships in each facet and original networks in Epinions and Ciao datasets are reported in Table 6. The reciprocity in trust relationships for each facet is significantly reduced compared to the original trust networks for both datasets. The RAT for each facet is much less than that of the original network. As mentioned above, 23.5% and 24.1% pairs of reciprocal links are heterogeneous in Epinions and Ciao, respectively. With the help of mTrust, status theory becomes stronger in the trust networks with reciprocated links.

Table 6: Status Theory is Strengthened by mTrust

Epinions	overall	1	2	3	4	5	6
RAT	0.332	0.228	0.221	0.231	0.207	0.208	0.216
RCT(%)	19.28	14.27	14.23	14.27	14.15	14.16	14.18
Ciao	overall	1	2	3	4	5	6
RAT	0.359	0.259	0.263	0.271	0.265	0.265	0.259
RCT(%)	23.77	17.34	17.55	18.37	17.85	17.83	17.49

6. RELATED WORK

In recent years, the notion of trust has attracted more and more attention from computer science communities. [25, 5] investigated the connection between user similarity (such as ratings of movies) and trust. They found a strong and significant correlation between trust and similarity. The more similar two people are, the greater the trust between them is. Guha et al. developed a formal framework of trust propagation schemes [6]. It first separates trust and distrust matrix and then performs operations on them to obtain the transitive trust between two nodes. In [20], the authors propose a method to model and compute the bias or the truthfulness of a user in trust networks. The bias of users are their propensity to trust/distrust other users. They claimed that their model conforms well to other graph ranking algorithms and social theories such as the balance theory. In [14], the authors propose a classification approach to predict if a user trusts another user using features derived from his/her interactions with the latter as well as from the interactions with other uses. In addition, Leskovec et al. study how trust and distrust relations among users in social networks can be predicted using various topological features of a social network [12].

Trust network is an important characteristic of product review sites, where users rely on their trust networks to seek advice and make decisions. In [16], several methods for incorporating trust networks are proposed to improve the performance of collaborative filtering. Matsuo and Yamamoto study and modeled the bidirectional effects between trust relations and product rating [18]. Lu et al. propose a generic framework for incorporating social context information to improve review quality prediction [15]. However, these works assume binary trust relationships between users.

Another direction of related research is the prediction of tie strength. Tie strength prediction differs from trust relationship prediction. The former focuses on modeling the strength of existed links rather than link existence. Based on interaction data, a supervised method is proposed in [9] to distinguish strong ties from weak ties by predicting binary relationship strength between users. Xiang et al. develop a latent variable model to estimate relationship strength from interaction activities and user similarities [24]. In this model, relationship strength is modeled as the hidden effect of user similarities and it also impacts the nature and frequency of online interactions. Au et al. investigated strength of social influence in trust networks [1]. It shows that the strength of trust relation correlates with the similarity among the users. A modified matrix factorization technique is used to estimate strengths of trust relations.

This work assumes single and homogeneous trust relationships between users. However, we show that trust inherently has multiple facets and people may place trust differently to different people.

7. CONCLUSION

In this paper, we study multi-faceted trust between users in the domain of product review sites. A fine-grained approach, mTrust, is proposed to capture multi-faceted trust relationships. We apply mTrust to tasks such as rating prediction, facet-sensitive ranking, and strengthening status theory. Experiments on two real-world datasets show that mTrust effectively capture multi-faceted trust and can be applied to improve the performance of rating prediction, facet-sensitive ranking, and status theory.

There are new research directions to be investigated. First, mTrust does not consider temporal information related to trust networks and product ratings. When a longer time span is studied (e.g., a year), it would be wise to include temporal effects on trust between users. Second, the notion of multi-faceted trust may be applicable for other domains, e.g., following relationships in Twitter. Finally, sophisticated models can be explored to estimate the strengths of multi-faceted trust to advance research and development on trust propagation and trust relationships prediction.

Acknowledgments

The work is, in part, supported by ARO (#025071) and NSF (#0812551).

8. REFERENCES

[1] C. Au Yeung and T. Iwata. Strength of social influence in trust networks in product review sites. In *WSDM*, pages 495–504. ACM, 2011.

[2] K. Blomqvist. The many faces of trust. *Scandinavian journal of management*, 13(3):271–286, 1997.

[3] L. De Lathauwer, B. De Moor, and J. Vandewalle. A multilinear singular value decomposition. *SIAM Journal on Matrix Analysis and Applications*, 21(4):1253–1278, 2000.

[4] D. Gefen, E. Karahanna, and D. Straub. Trust and tam in online shopping: An integrated model. *Mis Quarterly*, pages 51–90, 2003.

[5] J. Golbeck. Trust and nuanced profile similarity in online social networks. *ACM Transactions on the Web*, 3(4):1–33, 2009.

[6] R. Guha, R. Kumar, P. Raghavan, and A. Tomkins. Propagation of trust and distrust. In *WWW*, pages 403–412. ACM, 2004.

[7] N. Hu, P. Pavlou, and J. Zhang. Can online reviews reveal a product's true quality?: empirical findings and analytical modeling of online word-of-mouth communication. In *Proceedings of the 7th ACM conference on Electronic commerce*, pages 324–330. ACM, 2006.

[8] M. Jamali and M. Ester. Trustwalker: a random walk model for combining trust-based and item-based recommendation. In *KDD*, pages 397–406. ACM, 2009.

[9] I. Kahanda and J. Neville. Using transactional information to predict link strength in online social networks. In *Proceedings of the Third International Conference on Weblogs and Social Media*, 2009.

[10] J. Kleinberg. Authoritative sources in a hyperlinked environment. *Journal of the ACM*, 46(5):604–632, 1999.

[11] Y. Koren. Factorization meets the neighborhood: a multifaceted collaborative filtering model. In *KDD*, pages 426–434. ACM, 2008.

[12] J. Leskovec, D. Huttenlocher, and J. Kleinberg. Predicting positive and negative links in online social networks. In *WWW*, 2010.

[13] J. Leskovec, D. Huttenlocher, and J. Kleinberg. Signed networks in social media. In *Proceedings of the 28th international conference on Human factors in computing systems*, pages 1361–1370. ACM, 2010.

[14] H. Liu, E. Lim, H. Lauw, M. Le, A. Sun, J. Srivastava, and Y. Kim. Predicting trusts among users of online communities: an epinions case study. In *Proceedings of the 9th ACM Conference on Electronic Commerce*, pages 310–319. ACM, 2008.

[15] Y. Lu, P. Tsaparas, A. Ntoulas, and L. Polanyi. Exploiting social context for review quality prediction. In *WWW*, pages 691–700. ACM, 2010.

[16] H. Ma, H. Yang, M. Lyu, and I. King. Sorec: social recommendation using probabilistic matrix factorization. In *Proceeding of the 17th ACM conference on Information and knowledge management*, pages 931–940. ACM, 2008.

[17] P. Massa and P. Avesani. Trust-aware recommender systems. In *Proceedings of the 2007 ACM conference on Recommender systems*, pages 17–24. ACM, 2007.

[18] Y. Matsuo and H. Yamamoto. Community gravity: measuring bidirectional effects by trust and rating on online social networks. In *WWW*, pages 751–760. ACM, 2009.

[19] D. McKnight, V. Choudhury, and C. Kacmar. Developing and validating trust measures for e-commerce: An integrative typology. *Information systems research*, 13(3):334–359, 2003.

[20] A. Mishra and A. Bhattacharya. Finding the bias and prestige of nodes in networks based on trust scores. In *WWW*, pages 567–576. ACM, 2011.

[21] L. Page, S. Brin, R. Motwani, and T. Winograd. The pagerank citation ranking: Bringing order to the web. 1999.

[22] M. Richardson and P. Domingos. Mining knowledge-sharing sites for viral marketing. In *Proceedings of the eighth ACM SIGKDD international conference on Knowledge discovery and data mining*, pages 61–70. ACM, 2002.

[23] J. Weng, E. Lim, J. Jiang, and Q. He. Twitterrank: finding topic-sensitive influential twitterers. In *Proceedings of the third ACM international conference on Web search and data mining*, pages 261–270. ACM, 2010.

[24] R. Xiang, J. Neville, and M. Rogati. Modeling relationship strength in online social networks. In *WWW*, 2010.

[25] C. Ziegler and J. Golbeck. Investigating interactions of trust and interest similarity. *Decision Support Systems*, 43(2):460–475, 2007.

Of Hammers and Nails: An Empirical Comparison of Three Paradigms for Processing Large Graphs

Marc Najork
Microsoft Research
Mountain View, CA, USA
najork@microsoft.com

Dennis Fetterly
Microsoft Research
Mountain View, CA, USA
fetterly@microsoft.com

Alan Halverson
Microsoft Corporation
Madison, WI, USA
alanhal@microsoft.com

Krishnaram Kenthapadi
Microsoft Research
Mountain View, CA, USA
krisken@microsoft.com

Sreenivas Gollapudi
Microsoft Research
Mountain View, CA, USA
sreenig@microsoft.com

ABSTRACT

Many phenomena and artifacts such as road networks, social networks and the web can be modeled as large graphs and analyzed using graph algorithms. However, given the size of the underlying graphs, efficient implementation of basic operations such as connected component analysis, approximate shortest paths, and link-based ranking (*e.g.*PageRank) becomes challenging.

This paper presents an empirical study of computations on such large graphs in three well-studied platform models, *viz.*, a relational model, a data-parallel model, and a special-purpose in-memory model. We choose a prototypical member of each platform model and analyze the computational efficiencies and requirements for five basic graph operations used in the analysis of real-world graphs *viz.*, PageRank, SALSA, Strongly Connected Components (SCC), Weakly Connected Components (WCC), and Approximate Shortest Paths (ASP). Further, we characterize each platform in terms of these computations using model-specific implementations of these algorithms on a large web graph. Our experiments show that there is no single platform that performs best across different classes of operations on large graphs. While relational databases are powerful and flexible tools that support a wide variety of computations, there are computations that benefit from using special-purpose storage systems and others that can exploit data-parallel platforms.

Categories and Subject Descriptors

G.2.2 [**Discrete mathematics**]: Graph Theory—*Graph algorithms, path and circuit problems*; H.2.4 [**Database management**]: Systems—*Distributed databases*

General Terms

Algorithms, Experimentation, Performance

Keywords

Very large graphs, graph algorithms, databases, data-parallel computing, graph servers

Permission to make digital or hard copies of all or part of this work for personal or classroom use is granted without fee provided that copies are not made or distributed for profit or commercial advantage and that copies bear this notice and the full citation on the first page. To copy otherwise, to republish, to post on servers or to redistribute to lists, requires prior specific permission and/or a fee.
WSDM'12, February 8–12, 2012, Seattle, Washington, USA.
Copyright 2012 ACM 978-1-4503-0747-5/12/02 ...$10.00.

1. INTRODUCTION

Large scale networks are increasingly finding their place beyond traditional networks such as the Internet and telecommunication networks. Social and professional networks such as Facebook and LinkedIn have seen explosive growth in recent years. The social graph of Facebook, for example, contains more than 750 million active users[1] and an average friend count of 130. The widespread use of GPS applications and devices is built upon the graph of roads, intersections, and topographical data. The underlying graph in all these networks allows a wide range of analyses to measure different properties of these networks such as communities, size of the largest component, and distances between nodes. For example, the affinity between people in a social network can be modeled as a connectivity problem between nodes in the underlying graph where edges denote shared interests between any two people in the network. Computation of the popularity of a web page and of the similarity between two web pages are widely studied problems.

The analysis of large graphs presents challenging algorithmic problems. Fundamental applications like component analysis using breadth-first search (BFS) or depth-first search (DFS), PageRank computation, and shortest path computation become prohibitively expensive in the absence of suitable representation of the underlying graph. For example, the classic algorithm of Dijkstra [11] would take days to run on a web graph containing tens of billions of nodes and trillions of edges. Even in a distributed setting, the sequentially dependent nature of Dijkstra's algorithm would require huge amounts of communication. For the analysis of large graphs, research has focused on the relational model, the streaming model, and other special-purpose and often application-specific models.

Given the explosive growth of both the number and size of graph datasets as well as the increased complexity of analyzing large graphs, choosing a scalable platform for graph data storage and analysis is of paramount importance. Data parallel computation models such as MapReduce [14] provide a natural candidate platform. However, the complexity of implementing diverse and rich graph applications as MapReduce jobs produces the need for a higher level language to express the implementations in. Several languages for data-parallel systems exist (e.g. Sawzall [30], Pig [27], and DryadLINQ [39]) with a common goal of providing a declarative programming surface that allows the programmer to ask for "what" data they want rather than "how" to get it. Many of these languages are inspired by SQL, the standard language surface of relational database management systems (RDBMS). Thirty years of

[1] `http://www.facebook.com/press/info.php?statistics`

RDBMS research experience suggest that it should be considered as a candidate platform as well. Still, sometimes the "how" of data retrieval and processing is important. For example, an in-memory graph store will be extremely efficient in retrieving the neighborhood of a random node and therefore a very effective model for component analysis in a graph. We therefore have a "hammers and nails" problem – that is, the hammers are the data storage and processing platforms and the nails are the graph applications to evaluate over the data. Given the collection of hammers and nails, how should we best match them for efficiency, cost, and performance?

In this study, we undertake an extensive empirical study of three representative systems of the above models and their effectiveness in solving some prototypical graph algorithms using a large web graph. The contributions of our study are two-fold. First, given the size of the graph, we tailored the graph algorithms to work on large-scale data under the three settings. Second, we provide a first-of-a-kind study to show the effectiveness of each model to solve different classes of graph algorithms. We describe the implementations of five basic graph algorithms, *viz.*, PageRank [28], SALSA [20, 25], SCC [36, 4], WCC [11], and ASP [13], on a prototypical member of each model and further compare these implementations in terms of performance, scalability, and ease of implementation.

2. RELATED WORK

Recently, a lot of research has been directed toward studying large-scale graph algorithms necessitated by applications in large networks such as road networks, wireless networks, the Internet, and social networks [21, 10, 32, 8, 12]. The implementations in these studies have mostly relied on application specific storage and access models for the underlying graphs. Studies have also focused on developing graph algorithms in the streaming model [16, 17].

On problems involving large data sets, studies using relational databases have focused on issues related to scale-up and scale-out. Traditional ways to scale a database included upgrading to faster CPUs, adding more RAM and disks. However, these approaches often run into technical and economic limitations. In the limit, twice the money does not buy twice the performance. Recently, there has been a plethora of work on "scaling out" as exemplified by systems such as Netezza, column-based storage systems [33, 2, 26, 9], and managing data in cloud databases [1].

In the class of data-parallel systems, MapReduce [14] is the first system to use clusters of commodity hardware for distributed computing on large data sets. The *map* step in a MapReduce system typically involves mapping different parts of the problem to different nodes in the system. Each subproblem is processed at the worker node. The *reduce* step involves the master node aggregating the answers from all the worker nodes and processing it to generate the final output. The order of computation and the dataflow between nodes is represented using a directed graph known as the *dataflow graph.* The scalability and simplicity of this paradigm led the open-source community to develop Hadoop [6]. In fact, there are hybrid architectures that combine a MapReduce framework with a RDBMS, such as HadoopDB [3], Hive [37], and Aster Data. One of the drawbacks of MapReduce and Hadoop is that the dataflow graph has a fixed topology. Dryad [18] was developed to overcome this drawback. The dataflow graph in Dryad is computed dynamically based on the data at run-time. There are related platforms that are built on top of either MapReduce, Hadoop, or Dryad. Sawzall [30] was developed as an interpreted procedural language to work on MapReduce; Pig [27] was developed for analyzing large data sets on Hadoop; and DryadLINQ [39] is a programming language developed for writing applications on Dryad.

In the space of special-purpose graph stores, the Connectivity Server [5] is a link-server built to access the linkage information for all web pages indexed by the AltaVista search engine. Suel and Yuan [35] built a similar server to store a compressed web graph consisting of several hundred million nodes and a billion links. A number of systems exploit different compression schemes to scale traditional in-memory stores to large graphs [31, 7]. The system that is representative of this class in our study is the Scalable Hyperlink Store [24]. It differs from the earlier in-memory stores in that it is distributed, following the client-server model.

Pavlo et al. [29] performed a similar study as ours in which they provide benchmarks for Hadoop, Vertica, and an unnamed RDBMS on an identical cluster of 100 commodity nodes. Their workload consisted of different flavors of `grep`, database queries with joins and simple aggregations on clickstream data. They showed that the RDBMS in general outperformed Hadoop. While we agree that databases are incredibly useful pieces of infrastructure that can support an extremely wide set of applications, there are applications when more specialized tools are more appropriate. One example is time-constraints – applications that have extremely low latency requirements but do not require the guarantees that come with databases, such as transactional semantics. Another example is economic constraints – when a service will be run on a million computers, the potential savings in capital expenditure justify the cost of implementing a bespoke solution. More recently, a pair of articles by Stonebraker et al. [34] and Dean and Ghemawat [15] appeared in CACM to continue the discussion by arguing both for and against the use of an RDBMS for general data processing, respectively. Stonebraker et al. argue that MapReduce provides an excellent extract-transform-load (ETL) tool for pre-processing data to load into an RDBMS, but question the repeated parsing of lines that the Hadoop implementation does. Dean and Ghemawat counter by pointing to their Protocol Buffer serialization for data as a way to avoid repeated line parsing, and provide guidelines for MapReduce system usage to avoid some of the overheads pointed out in [29]. In our study, we will focus on the special case of large graph storage and query processing in our three chosen platforms.

Another paradigm for graph computations that supports iterative processing of messages between vertices is proposed in [22]. In each iteration each vertex processes messages received in the previous iteration and sends out messages that can potentially change the graph topology. Finally, we note that there are many other graph databases based on the paradigms that we study in this paper. The reader is referred to the Wikipedia article on graph databases [38] and the references within. While comparing these products would be an interesting study in itself, we note that the focus of this work has been to study and compare three paradigms of computation on graph databases instead of the products themselves.

3. EXPERIMENTAL SETUP

This section describes the data sets we used as the input to our experiments, we hardware we ran them on, and the software platforms (SQL Server PDW, DryadLINQ, and SHS) on top of which we implemented the five graph algorithms.

3.1 The data sets

We perform our experiments on the ClueWeb09 datasets[2]. The larger "Category A" dataset was derived from 1 billion web pages crawled during January and February 2009. It is comprised of two files, one containing all unique URLs (325 GB uncompressed, 116 GB compressed) and the other containing all the outlinks (71 GB uncompressed, 29 GB compressed). The corresponding graph con-

[2] `http://boston.lti.cs.cmu.edu/Data/clueweb09/`

sists of 4.77 billion unique URLs and 7.94 billion edges. The maximum out-degree is 2,079 and the maximum in-degree is 6,445,063. The smaller "Category B" dataset contains the first 50 million English pages in Category A. It is comprised of two files, one containing all unique URLs (30 GB uncompressed, 9.7 GB compressed) and the other containing all the outlinks (3.8 GB uncompressed, 1.6 GB compressed). The corresponding graph consists of 428 million unique URLs and 454 million edges. The maximum out-degree is 1,055 and the maximum in-degree is 310,483.

For the evaluation of the SALSA algorithm, we use 171 queries sampled from the Bing query log. For each query, we extracted up to 5,000 top URLs (based on BM25F, a text-based ranking feature) from the ClueWeb09 Category A or B pages, thereby obtaining a total of 831,591 and 826,364 associated URLs, respectively.

3.2 The hardware

We performed all our experiments on a cluster of 17 Dell PowerEdge 2950 servers, all running Windows Server 2008 R2. Each server had two Intel Xeon E5430 processors clocked at 2.66 GHz, 16 GB of DDR2 RAM, and six 146 GB, 15K RPM SAS drives. The computers were each connected to a Force10 S50-01-GE-48T-AC 48-port full-crossbar Gigabit Ethernet switch via Gigabit Ethernet. For the set of experiments where we used a single server, we ran the client/control program on the same machine; otherwise we used 16 machines to run the platform and one machine to run the client.

3.3 The platforms

We next describe the three platforms we use, representing the three paradigms for processing large graphs. We also discuss how the web graph is preprocessed, loaded and distributed into each of the three systems, since the performance of the graph algorithms depends heavily on the way the data is configured on the systems.

SQL Server PDW

Microsoft SQL Server 2008 R2 Parallel Data Warehouse [23] (SQL Server PDW) is a multi-user client/server RDBMS developed and commercialized by Microsoft Corporation. It provides standard RDBMS functionality – transactions, concurrency control, recovery, and a SQL language surface plus extensions (T-SQL). The relational data model is at the heart of data processing for SQL Server PDW. Set-oriented operations are preferred to row-by-row processing due to overheads associated with query parsing, algebraization, optimization, and execution that are incurred for each SQL statement passed to the system. SQL Server PDW uses a Control Node to accept a user query, produces a parallel execution plan, and executes the plan on a set of Compute Nodes. The Control Node is also responsible for presenting a "single system image" to users of the system, allowing expression of T-SQL queries as if all data is stored in a single database instance. SQL Server PDW is an appliance product that provides a choice of hardware configurations to users. The experiments we performed for this paper utilized the hardware described in Section 3.2, and therefore cannot be considered indicative of real-world SQL Server PDW performance.

The chosen relational schema for the ClueWeb09 data contains two relations: the `nodes` relation with attributes `id` of type bigint and `url` of type VARCHAR(900)[3]; and the `edges` relation with attributes `src` and `dest`, both of type bigint. By contrast, the original ClueWeb09 edges file contains an adjacency list per source node. We partitioned the edges and nodes files into 8 pieces to facilitate a parallel bulk insert operation into SQL Server PDW.

[3]In SQL Server PDW, index keys are limited to 900 bytes, and providing efficient URL-to-ID lookups requires an index on URL.

DryadLINQ

DryadLINQ [39][4] is a system for large scale distributed data-parallel computing using a high-level programming language. Compared to programming environments such as SQL, MapReduce, and Dryad, DryadLINQ supports general-purpose imperative and declarative operations on datasets within a traditional high-level programming language and thereby provides a higher layer of abstraction. A DryadLINQ program is a sequential program composed of LINQ expressions and can be written and debugged using standard .NET development tools. LINQ expressions are similar to SQL statements, however they are commonly used in conjunction with lambda expressions (specified with => operators) where each expression will be applied to every element of the stream. DryadLINQ adds several methods to enable data-parallel computations, including `PartitionTable.Get` and `ToPartitionedTable` which will respectively read from and write to a data stream spread across multiple machines. Distribution of data is done using the `HashPartition` and `RangePartition` methods. The `Apply` method both consumes and produces a stream of elements, which is useful for algorithms that employ a sliding window. The DryadLINQ system automatically and transparently translates the data-parallel portions of the program into a distributed execution plan which is passed to the Dryad execution framework. By design, DryadLINQ is inherently specialized for streaming computations. In general, DryadLINQ is suitable for computations that can be expressed using LINQ constructs. However, executing a DryadLINQ program incurs at least a few seconds of overhead. Hence DryadLINQ is not appropriate for all applications, e.g. applications requiring low-latency distributed database lookups.

The processed ClueWeb09 data is partitioned into the cluster machines based on a hash value of the page identifier such that all pages and their associated link identifiers are present in the same machine. After the data is loaded into the cluster, whenever a new job is started, we incur a small overhead as the binaries need to be copied to all the machines.

Scalable Hyperlink Store

The Scalable Hyperlink Store (SHS) [24] is a distributed in-memory database for storing large portions of the web graph. It partitions the nodes (URLs) and the edges (hyperlinks) of the web graph over a set of servers, maintains all the data in main memory to allow extremely fast random access, and uses data compression techniques that leverage properties of the web graph (namely, the prevalence of relative links) to achieve fairly good compression. SHS was designed to enable research on structural properties of the web graph as well as new link-based ranking algorithms. It is not well suited for graph applications that require attaching arbitrary metadata to nodes and edges (such as anchor texts and weights) as doing so would result in decreased compression ratios. To achieve good compression, SHS maintains a bijection between textual URLs and numerical UIDs, and edges are represented in terms of UIDs. Initially the SHS Builder distributes the web graph data across a set of available SHS servers, by partitioning the URLs and their associated links according to the URLs' host components. This preserves link locality, that is, all URLs on a host and all links between pages on the same host are kept in the same SHS server. The clerk can determine the SHS server responsible for a URL by performing a local computation (hash function). Similarly the SHS server ID is encoded in UIDs, so that a client can determine the SHS server owning a UID locally. Client applications communicate with SHS via the `ShsClerk` class whose key methods are as follows:

[4]Available at `http://connect.microsoft.com/Dryad`

```
public class ShsClerk {
  public ShsClerk(string shsName) {...}
  public IEnumerable<long> Uids {...}
  public bool IsLastUid(long uid) {...}
  public long[] BatchedUrlToUid(string[] urls) {...}
  public string[] BatchedUidToUrl(long[] uids) {...}
  public long[][] BatchedGetLinks(bool fwd, long[] uids) {...}
  public long[][] BatchedSampleLinks(bool fwd, long[] uids,
      int numSamples, bool consistent) {...}
  public UidState<T> AllocateUidState<T>() {...}
  ...
}
public class UidState<T> {
  public void Dispose() {...}
  public T Get(long uid) {...}
  public void Set(long uid, T val) {...}
  public T[] GetMany(long[] uids) {...}
  public void SetMany(long[] uids, T[] vals) {...}
  public IEnumerable<UidVal<T>> GetAll() {...}
  public void SetAll(Func<long,T> f) {...}
}
public struct UidVal<T> {
  public readonly long uid;
  public readonly T val;
  public UidVal(long uid, T val) {...}
}
public struct UidBatch {
  public UidBatch(int sz) {...}
  public void Add(long uid) {...}
  public static implicit operator long[] (UidBatch x) {...}
  public bool Full { get {...} }
  public void Reset() {...}
}
public class UidMap {
  public UidMap(long[][] items) {...}
  public int this[long item] {...}
  public static implicit operator long[] (UidMap x) {...}
  ...
}
```

The `ShsClerk` constructor creates a new clerk object connected to the given SHS service. UIDs can be enumerated using the C# enumerator `Uids`, and `IsLastUid(u)` returns whether `u` is the final UID in that enumeration. `BatchedUrlToUid` and `BatchedUidToUrl` map URLs to UIDs and vice versa. The method `BatchedGetLinks` returns out-links/in-links associated with UIDs depending on the value of `fwd`. The method `BatchedSampleLinks` can be used to return either a uniformly random sample or a consistent sample of such links. The `Batched` methods allow clients to send many UIDs or URLs at once, thereby allowing them to amortize the RPC overhead, which is crucial for performance.

The version of SHS described in [24] provided a read-only store of the vertices and edges of the web graph. Since then, we have augmented the system to also provide a per-vertex read-write storage service. Calling `AllocateUidState<T>()` allocates a value of type `T` for each vertex in the graph, distributed over the SHS servers in the same way as the vertices themselves, and returns a `UidState` handle to this distributed mapping. The `UidState` provides a `Dispose` method for freeing up the server-side state, and methods for reading and updating the values. `Get` and `Set` read and update the value associated with a single UID, `GetMany` and `SetMany` read and update the values associated with a batch of UIDs, `GetAll` returns an enumeration of all UID/value pairs, and `SetAll` sets all values functionally dependent on their UIDs.

Among the auxiliary classes contained in the SHS package, two should be mentioned here: The `UidBatch` class makes it easy to aggregate UIDs into a bounded-size batch, for use with methods such as `BatchedGetLinks`. The `UidMap` class maps a multi-set of UIDs as returned by `BatchedGetLinks` to a set of UIDs realized as a `long` array that can be passed to `UidState.GetMany` and `UidState.SetMany`, and provides a way for obtaining the index of a given UID in that array.

We preprocess the ClueWeb09 dataset using DryadLINQ to produce a file containing the URLs of all pages and their links, which is then ingested by the SHS Builder to produce an SHS store.

4. ALGORITHM IMPLEMENTATION AND EVALUATION

We evaluated the five graph algorithms on the datasets described in Section 3.1 on each of the three systems. For each algorithm, we provide a short description of the graph algorithm and its implementation on each system. Before we delve into the details of our implementation of each algorithm, we describe the evaluation criteria, both quantitative and qualitative, for comparing the systems.

- Performance: We measure performance in terms of the running time for each implementation of each algorithm.
- Scalability: We characterize how the performance of each implementation changes as the size of the cluster and/or the size of the graph increases.
- Ease of implementation: We consider how elegant, concise and natural each implementation is.

We report performance in terms of running time in seconds. Table 1 shows the running time of the implementations of the five algorithms on each of the three platforms, processing the ClueWeb09 Category B graph using a single server. Table 2 shows running times of the same programs processing the same graph using sixteen servers. As the tables show, SHS experiences a substantial slowdown for every algorithm. The reasons for this are two-fold: first, SHS runs in client-server paradigm where the data resides in the servers and the computation happens in the client. Therefore, increasing the number of servers only scales up the available storage, but not the available computing resources, since the algorithms run on the client machine; On the other hand, both DryadLINQ and SQL Server PDW admit data-parallel computation and therefore scale up gracefully on both the data and computation as more servers are added to the system. We note that DryadLINQ is optimized for streaming access of data and this model is especially useful for computations like ASP and WCC where one needs to access all the nodes in the graph. However, this advantage is not present in the case of SALSA and to a lesser extent SCC where the access to nodes is mostly random. We would also like to point out that in the case of the single server, SHS also benefits from having the client and server running on the same machine.

Another key measure of effectiveness of an algorithm is its scalability. In our case, the key question to ask is *how does each of the platforms perform when the size of the graph increases*? Table 3 shows similar running times of the same programs processing the ClueWeb09 Category A graph using sixteen servers. We note that this graph has an order-of-magnitude more nodes than the ClueWeb09 Category B graph. While both DryadLINQ and SQL Server PDW scale gracefully on the larger data set, SHS suffers from the bottleneck introduced by having the computation performed in the client even as it scales well in terms of using more servers to handle the larger data. We discuss the scalability of each platform in more detail as we describe the implementation of each algorithm in the following sections.

Performance aside, we are also interested in how elegant and concise each implementation is. A quantitative measure of conciseness is the number of lines of code, which we report in Table 4. For the first algorithm (PageRank), we discuss the code in detail to give a flavor of implementations in each of the systems.

Algorithm	SQL Server PDW	DryadLINQ	SHS
PageRank	122,305	83,472	63,771
SALSA	5,873	4,843	37
SCC	1,147	3,243	94,346/816
WCC	63,972	74,359	1,801
ASP	138,911	175,839	77,214

Table 1: Running time in seconds for each algorithm implementation in each system, processing the Category B graph on one server.

Algorithm	SQL Server PDW	DryadLINQ	SHS
PageRank	8,970	4,513	90,942
SALSA	2,034	439	163
SCC	475	446	214,858/1,073
WCC	4,207	3,844	1,976
ASP	30,379	17,089	246,944

Table 2: Running time in seconds for each algorithm implementation in each system, processing the Category B graph on sixteen servers.

Algorithm	SQL Server PDW	DryadLINQ	SHS
PageRank	156,982	68,791	836,445
SALSA	2,199	2,211	124
SCC	7,306	6,294	-/15,903
WCC	214,479	160,168	26,210
ASP	671,142	749,016	2,381,278

Table 3: Running time in seconds for each algorithm implementation in each system, processing the Category A graph on sixteen servers.

Algorithm	SQL Server PDW	DryadLINQ	SHS
PageRank	34	23	38
SALSA	116	165	77
SCC	-/247	-/118	66/174
WCC	86	40	181
ASP	78	144	108

Table 4: Number of lines of code for each algorithm implementation in each system.

4.1 PageRank

PageRank [28] (Algorithm 1) computes a query-independent score of web pages based on endorsement (in the form of links) of each web page by other web pages. It is well-suited for data-parallel architectures, since links and one score vector can be easily streamed.

SQL Server PDW

The T-SQL implementation uses three temporary tables, for current (*score_cur*) and previous (*score_prev*) scores and the count of outlinks (*link_counts*) for each node. Pre-computing the outlink counts provides a straightforward way to normalize the score being passed from a source node to its destination outlinks. The *link_counts* table is sparse, meaning that only nodes with non-zero out-degree are present. In each iteration, the scores in *score_prev* are passed on to outlinks, and new rank is provided via the random jump probability as the two queries concatenated by the `UNION ALL` statement. The results are grouped by the node-id and summed to populate the *score_cur* table. At the end of each iteration, the *score_prev* table is dropped and the *score_cur* table is renamed to *score_prev*.

DryadLINQ

The DryadLINQ implementation creates a distributed stream of $\langle$*page-id*, *link-ids*$\rangle$ for each node in the graph and a distributed stream of $\langle id, score\rangle$ pairs such that each score is $1/n$ and a pair with a given *id* resides on the same machine as the link entry with the matching *page-id*. Each PageRank iteration is performed in parallel using a `join` of these two streams on *page-id* and *id*. All tuples with the same key u are aggregated in the machine responsible for u and then the join on u is locally computed on this machine. Denoting the adjacency list of u by $links[u]$, the output of the join is a new stream of $\langle v, score[u]/|links[u]|\rangle$ pairs for each node v in $links[u]$. Then all pairs in the new stream about the same node v are aggregated using a `group by` operation (so that the probability contributions from every in-link to v are grouped together) and the score for v is updated. At the end of each iteration, the scores are written to disks across the cluster. Note that the PageRank implementation makes full use of data-parallel computation in DryadLINQ.

SHS

The SHS implementation performs batched invocations to the server to amortize network latency. During each iteration, we enumerate the UIDs in a fixed order using the C# enumerator `Uids` and create batches of UIDs using a `UidBatch` object. Whenever the batch becomes full or the last UID is reached, we obtain the forward links for all UIDs in the batch using the method `BatchedGetLinks`. We then retrieve the scores corresponding to these links from the servers, update them appropriately, and send them back to the servers. After going through all the UIDs, the scores are retrieved from the servers and written to a file on the client's disk, which is then read in the next iteration in a streaming fashion. Writing to the disk avoids having to maintain two sets of scores in main memory.

Performance Evaluation

For PageRank computation, we observed that on a single server, SHS outperforms both DryadLINQ and SQL Server PDW. However, when either the number of machines or the data is increased, the other two platforms take advantage of the increase in storage and compute power and perform significantly better than SHS. The fact that PageRank is highly parallelizable is the main reason behind the improvement.

As can be seen from the code snippets for PageRank and from Table 4, all the algorithms could be implemented using a few lines of code on all the platforms. We notice that for each system, the algorithms that are most natural to that paradigm take the fewest lines of code to implement. In the case of SQL Server PDW, each row of the edges table is complete that is, the source and destination node IDs are both represented. This creates both opportunity and limitations for the programmer. For example, finding edges whose source node ID is greater than the destination node ID can be expressed as `SELECT src, dest FROM edges WHERE src > dest`. However, we need to keep the context explicit in the query, as the output schema is fixed. The programmer cannot query for a list of destination IDs for a given source ID when the list is of variable length depending upon the source ID. In the above example, it would be space-efficient to write `SELECT src, listOfDest FROM edges WHERE src > dest`. Some relational systems have been extended with arrays and/or nested relations to provide support for such operations, but code using these extensions is not portable.

4.2 SALSA

The Stochastic Approach to Link-Sensitivity Analysis (SALSA) [20] is a query-dependent link-based ranking algorithm inspired by HITS [19] and PageRank [28]. SALSA computes an authority score for each node in a query-specific neighborhood graph, by performing a random walk on the neighborhood graph (Algorithm 2). In the computation of this neighborhood graph, $C_t(X)$ refers to a consistent unbiased sample of t elements from set X, as described in [25]. We used consistent sampling parameters, $a = b = 5$. The random walk on the neighborhood graph commences on a node with in-degree greater than 0. Each step in the walk consists of following an edge in the backward direction and then following an edge in the forward direction. The stationary probability distribution of the random walk is returned as the authority score vector s. We next describe the implementations in the three systems.

Algorithm 1 PAGERANK(G)

Input: A directed graph $G = (V, E)$ with n nodes, random jump probability d, number of iterations z.
Output: A vector s of stationary probabilities for the nodes in G.

for each $u \in V$ **do**
  $s[u] := 1/n$, $s'[u] := 0$
for $k = 1$ to z **do**
  for each $u \in V$ **do**
    $links[u] := \{v \mid (u, v) \in E\}$
    for each $v \in links[u]$ **do**
      $s'[v] := s'[v] + \frac{s[u]}{|links[u]|}$
  for each $u \in V$ **do**
    $s[u] := d/n + (1-d)s'[u]$
    $s'[u] := 0$

```
public class ShsPageRank {
  private static string Name(int i) { return "scores-" + i; }
  public static void Main(string[] args) {
    Shs.ShsClerk shs = new Shs.ShsClerk(args[0]);
    double d = double.Parse(args[1]);
    long n = shs.NumUrls();
    var ob = new OutBuf(Name(0));
    for (long i = 0; i < n; i++) ob.WriteDouble(1.0 / n);
    ob.Close();
    var scores = shs.AllocateUidState<double>();
    var uidBatch = new Shs.UidBatch(50000);
    for (int k = 0; k < 100; k++) {
      scores.SetAll(x => d / n);
      var ib = new InBuf(Name(k));
      foreach (long u in shs.Uids) {
        uidBatch.Add(u);
        if (uidBatch.Full || shs.IsLastUid(u)) {
          var linkBatch = shs.BatchedGetLinks(true, uidBatch);
          var linkMap = new Shs.UidMap(linkBatch);
          var scoreArr = scores.GetMany(linkMap);
          foreach (var links in linkBatch) {
            double f = (1.0 - d) * ib.ReadDouble() / links.Length;
            foreach (long link in links) {
              scoreArr[linkMap[link]] += f;
            }
          }
          scores.SetMany(linkMap, scoreArr);
          uidBatch.Reset();
        }
      }
      ib.Close();
      ob = new OutBuf(Name(k+1));
      foreach (var us in scores.GetAll()) ob.WriteDouble(us.val);
      ob.Close();
      System.IO.File.Delete(Name(k));
    }
  }
}
```

SHS implementation of PageRank

```
CREATE TABLE link_counts WITH (DISTRIBUTION=HASH(id)) AS
      SELECT src AS id, COUNT(dest) AS cnt
      FROM edges GROUP BY src;
Declare @CNODES bigint = (SELECT COUNT_BIG(*) FROM nodes);
CREATE TABLE score_prev WITH (DISTRIBUTION=HASH(id)) AS
      SELECT n.id, 1.0 / @CNODES AS score FROM nodes n;
Declare @ITER int = 0, @d float = 0.15;
While @ITER < 100
BEGIN
      CREATE TABLE score_cur WITH (DISTRIBUTION=HASH(id)) AS
      SELECT s.curid AS id, SUM(s.newscore) AS score FROM
      (SELECT * FROM (
      SELECT e.dest AS curid,
            SUM((1.0-@d)*(sp.score/lc.cnt)) AS newscore
      FROM score_prev sp, edges e, link_counts lc
      WHERE sp.id = lc.id AND sp.id = e.src
      GROUP BY e.dest
      WITH (DISTRIBUTED_AGG)) A
      UNION ALL
      SELECT sp.id AS curid, (@d / @CNODES) AS newscore
      FROM score_prev sp
      WHERE sp.id <> @CNODES) s GROUP BY s.curid;

      INSERT INTO score_cur
      SELECT CAST(@CNODES AS bigint) AS id,
      SUM(CASE WHEN lc.cnt IS NULL
          THEN sp.score ELSE 0 END) * (1.0 - @d)
      FROM score_prev sp
          LEFT OUTER JOIN link_counts lc on sp.id = lc.id;

      DROP TABLE score_prev;
      RENAME OBJECT score_cur TO score_prev;
      SET @ITER += 1;
END
DROP TABLE link_counts; DROP TABLE score_prev;
```

SQL Server PDW implementation of PageRank

```
using LD = LinqToDryad.Pair<long, double>;
using GR = LinqToDryad.Pair<long, long[]>;

public class DryadLINQPageRank {
  public static IEnumerable<LD> InitScores(long n) {
    for (long i = 0; i < n; i++) yield return new LD(i, 1.0 / n);
  }
  static void Main(string[] args) {
    var pages = PartitionedTable.Get<GR>("tidyfs://cw-graph");
    long n = pages.LongCount();
    double d = double.Parse(args[0]);
    IQueryable<LD> scores = pages.Apply(x => InitScores(n))
         .HashPartition(x => x.Key, pages.PartitionCount)
         .ToPartitionedTable("tidyfs://scores-0");
    for (int i = 1; i <= 100; i++) {
      var scores1 = from p in pages
                    join s in scores on p.Key equals s.Key
                    from v in p.Value
                    select new LD(v, s.Value / p.Value.Length);
      scores = from s in scores1
               group s.Value by s.Key into g
               select new LD(g.Key, d / n + (1.0 - d) * g.Sum());
      scores.ToPartitionedTable("tidyfs://scores-" + i);
    }
  }
}
```

DryadLINQ implementation of PageRank

SQL Server PDW

The SALSA implementation for SQL Server PDW is a set-oriented implementation of the algorithm. For all input queries, we compute the graph based on the input URLs and random sampling of the edges, keeping track of which query-id the graph belongs to. We perform a random walk back and forth on the graphs 100 times and return the top input urls for each query according to the calculated score. Due to the interpreted nature of a T-SQL batch script in SQL

Algorithm 2 SALSA(G)

Input: A directed web graph $G = (V, E)$, a result set $R \subseteq V$ of URLs that satisfy a query q, consistent sampling parameters a, b.
Output: A vector s of SALSA authority scores for each URL in a query-specific neighborhood graph.

$V_R := \bigcup_{r \in R}\{r\} \cup C_a(\{u|(u,r) \in E\}) \cup C_b(\{v|(r,v) \in E\})$
$E_R := \{(u,v) \in E | u \in V_R \wedge v \in V_R\}$
$V_R^A := \{u \in V_R | in(u) > 0\}$
for each $u \in V_R$ **do**
  $s[u] := \frac{1}{|V_R^A|}$ if $u \in V_R^A$; 0 otherwise
repeat
  for each $u \in V_R^A$ **do**
    $s'[u] := \sum_{(v,u) \in E_R} \sum_{(u,w) \in E_R} \frac{s[w]}{out(v) \cdot in(w)}$
  for each $u \in V_R^A$ **do**
    $s[u] := s'[u]$
until s converges

Server PDW, each short random walk query is re-compiled and optimized. This adds some overhead to the total query execution time, but the overhead is amortized across all input queries.

The program performs consistent sampling by joining the edges table to a table containing a pre-computed mapping of node ids to random numbers, which are obtained in ascending order using a `ROW_NUMBER() OVER()` analytic function, and only the rows with a row number less than 5 are included in the graph.

DryadLINQ

The DryadLINQ implementation computes both the neighborhood graph and the SALSA authority scores in a distributed data-parallel fashion. First, a distributed stream of ⟨*page-id*, *link-ids*⟩ corresponding to graph G is created and then streams of forward and backward edges are generated from this stream. Similarly a distributed stream R_s of ⟨*query-id*,*page-id*⟩ pairs is generated by joining the ⟨*query-id*, *URL*⟩ dataset with the given URL/id mapping. The stream R_s is joined with streams of forward and backward edges and then sampled to generate the SALSA neighborhood set V_R associated with each query (as a stream). This neighborhood set stream is then joined with the forward graph stream to obtain the neighborhood graph stream for each query (a stream of ⟨*query-id*,*page-id*, *link-id*⟩ tuples). Using a series of distributed joins, we aggregate the relevant information for each query (query-id, result set R, neighborhood set V_R, and edge set E_R) at one cluster node and compute the SALSA authority scores locally on that node. Finally, we map the scores to the URLs by joining the stream of computed SALSA scores with the URL/id mapping. The implementation benefits tremendously from DryadLINQ's ability to perform distributed joins over data streams.

SHS

The SHS implementation computes the neighborhood graph by communicating with the SHS store and then performs the random walk locally. The neighborhood graph corresponding to the given set of result URLs is computed as follows. The set of result URLs is first converted to UIDs (using one invocation of `BatchedUrlToUid`). Then `BatchedSampleLinks` is called twice to obtain a random sample of forward and backward links for each URL in the result set. As the method `BatchedSampleLinks` performs sampling at the server end, the network overhead is kept to a minimum. Finally the set of URLs pointed to by the vertices in the neighborhood graph is obtained (using one invocation of `BatchedGetLinks`) for use in the remaining local computations. Thus batching over many UIDs (or URLs) helps to significantly reduce the RPC overhead.

Algorithm 3 SCC(G)

Input: A directed graph $G = (V, E)$.
Output: A list of SCCs where each SCC is represented as a set of nodes belonging to the SCC.

for each $u \in V$ **do**
  $fwdVisited[u] := false, fwdParent[u] := Nil$
$time := 0$
for each $u \in V$ **do**
  if $fwdVisited[u] = false$ **then**
    DFS-VISIT($u, E, fwdVisited, fwdParent, f$)
$E^T := \{(v,u)|(u,v) \in E\}$
for each $u \in V$ **do**
  $bwdVisited[u] := false, bwdParent[u] := Nil$
for each $u \in V$ in decreasing order of $f[u]$ **do**
  if $bwdVisited[u] = false$ **then**
    DFS-VISIT($u, E^T, bwdVisited, bwdParent, b$)
Output the vertices of each tree in the backward depth-first forest as a separate strongly connected component.

Algorithm 3 DFS-VISIT($u, E, visited, parent, f$)

$time := time + 1$
$links[u] := \{v|(u,v) \in E\}$
for each $v \in links[u]$ **do**
  if $visited[v] = false$ **then**
    $parent[v] := u$
    DFS-VISIT($v, E, visited, parent, f$)
$visited[u] := true, f[u] := time$

Performance Evaluation

We observe that SALSA is inherently based on random access to the node information. As noted earlier, SHS is very suitable for such applications. In fact, as both tables show SHS does indeed perform as much as 160 times better than both DryadLINQ and SQL Server PDW. SHS does not benefit from the increase in the number of servers from one to sixteen, while the other two platforms exploit the additional storage and compute power to their benefit. The performance difference between SQL Server PDW and DryadLINQ can be attributed to DryadLINQ performing the power iteration on a single machine instead of distributed over the cluster, whereas SQL Server PDW has to persist the result after each iteration to distributed storage.

4.3 Strongly Connected Components

We next consider the problem of decomposing a directed graph into its strongly connected components [36, 4]. This problem is important since many problems on large directed graphs require such a decomposition. Typically an original problem can be divided into subproblems, one for each strongly connected component.

The standard linear-time algorithm for computing strongly connected components in a directed graph (Algorithm 3) uses two depth-first searches, one on the graph and one on the transpose graph. However, depth-first search is highly sequential and hence this algorithm is not suitable for execution on very large graphs. We instead implement a "hybrid" version which copies a pruned version of the graph locally and runs Algorithm 3 locally. The graph is pruned as follows: All nodes with no outlinks (sinks) or no inlinks (sources) are guaranteed to be singleton SCCs and hence we rule out these nodes and their incident edges. As most of the nodes in a large web graph tend to be sinks, we get a substantial reduction in the graph size so that the new graph fits into memory and DFS computations can be performed locally. However this approach does not scale with the size of the graph. We briefly describe the SCC implementations in the three systems. We also implement the original version of Algorithm 3 on SHS.

SQL Server PDW

We describe the SQL Server PDW implementation of SCC using the hybrid version. First, SQL Server PDW is used to filter the nodes and edges to remove nodes that cannot possibly end up in an SCC larger than size 1. By definition, nodes in a multi-node SCC must have at least one outlink and at least one inlink other than a reflexive edge. The filtered node list comes from intersecting the src and dest sets in the edges table. To aid in the computation, a mapping function is constructed to a new, dense ID space. The edges are then filtered and mapped into the new ID space. Given the reduced size of the nodes and edges table, both are read out of SQL Server PDW into main memory where Algorithm 3 is performed. The edges are read into adjacency arrays twice, first ordered by src (forward direction), then by dest (backward direction).

DryadLINQ

We next describe the DryadLINQ implementation of the hybrid version of Algorithm 3. First we create a distributed stream of ⟨*page-id*, *link-ids*⟩ for each node in the graph and obtain the number of nodes using a `count` operation. We then create a stream of ⟨*source-id*, *destination-id*⟩ for edges in the graph, from which we generate streams of non-sink nodes (nodes with non-zero out-degree) and non-source nodes (nodes with non-zero in-degree) using `select` and `distinct` operations. Intersecting these two streams provides a stream of nodes in the pruned graph, which we then map to a new, dense ID space. Then we stream through the distributed stream of edges, loading the forward graph corresponding to the above nodes into main memory of the client machine, and locally perform forward DFS. Then we similarly load the backward graph into main memory and perform backward DFS locally. Finally the SCCs (including the singleton SCCs) are written to disk.

SHS

The SHS implementation of the original version of Algorithm 3 involves a clever implementation of depth-first search to handle the large graph size. As either out-links or in-links can be retrieved for each node, we do not have to compute the transpose graph G^T explicitly. In order to maintain the nodes in the order of their finishing times in the first DFS, we implement a custom stack that is optimized for disk access. Due to the sequential nature of depth-first search, we do not parallelize (batch) accesses and hence incur a significant network overhead.

We also implemented the hybrid version of Algorithm 3. We perform `BatchedGetDegree` requests to the store to obtain forward and backward degrees for all nodes, thereby determining nodes guaranteed to be singleton SCCs. We map the remaining nodes to a new, dense ID space. Then we load the forward graph into user space (main memory of the client machine) using a series of `BatchedGetLinks` requests, and perform forward DFS locally. Then we load the backward graph into user space (reusing memory) and perform backward DFS locally. While this approach improves the performance by about two orders of magnitude due to the reduced network overhead, it is inherently non-scalable.

Performance Evaluation

The performance of the non-hybrid SHS implementation of SCC is largely constrained by the exploration of one node at a time in DFS, which requires one roundtrip to the server per node in the DFS.

For the hybrid version, SHS performs best for the one server Category B experiment, but falls behind SQL Server PDW and DryadLINQ in both of the sixteen node experiments. The SCC implementation for all three platforms under study is identical, with the exception of the first phase. At the beginning, each implementation must prune out nodes that will be in singleton SCCs and remap the remaining node ids into a dense id space that starts with zero. The edges containing references to these nodes are then rewritten to use the mapped node ids as well. This allows a very compact in-memory representation – for example, even if the original node ids required an eight byte integer representation, the mapped ids can utilize a four byte integer. In the case of SQL Server PDW and DryadLINQ, this mapping effort can be done completely inside the cluster and only the mapped and pruned edges need be pulled out to the client SCC memory. By contrast, the SHS implementation must pull the forward and backward link counts for every node and build the id mapping in the client. It further must pull all of the links for any node found to have nonzero in and out degree, and is not able to prune the edges for those nodes on the server side.

Algorithm 4 WCC(G)

Input: A directed graph $G = (V,E)$ on n nodes, where $V = \{1,\dots,n\}$ and $E \subseteq V \times V$.
Output: A mapping *rep* where all nodes in the same WCC map to the same representative element.

for each $u \in V$ **do**
  $rep[u] := u$
repeat
  $progress := false$
  for each $u \in V$ **do**
    $links[u] := \{v | (u,v) \in E\}$
    $minid := rep[u]$
    for each $v \in links[u]$ **do**
      if $rep[v] \neq minid$ **then**
        $minid := \min(minid, rep[v])$
        $progress := true$
    $rep[u] := minid$
    for each $v \in links[u]$ **do**
      $rep[v] := minid$
until $\neg progress$

4.4 Weakly Connected Components

A related problem is to compute the weakly connected components in a directed graph. Determining the connected components and their sizes is crucial to understanding the network structure of massive graphs. Moreover other graph computations such as minimum spanning tree or approximate shortest path are defined only over individual components.

Weakly connected components can be computed by performing depth-first search or breadth-first search on the underlying undirected graph. Our algorithm uses the latter since all nodes in the BFS frontier can be explored in parallel. Algorithm 4 has resemblance to the algorithm for computing WCC using disjoint-set operations [11]. Initially each node is in its own connected component (with component value equal to itself). We then iterate until no component mapping gets updated. In each iteration, for each node u, we check whether any of its neighbors is mapped to a different component and if so, update the node and its neighbors to map to the smallest component value amongst them.

SQL Server PDW

The SQL Server PDW implementation of WCC starts by precomputing the "flattened graph" – that is, the union of the directed edge set with the set of edges reversed. To speed computation, all nodes not present in the flattened graph are removed from further processing since they are guaranteed to be in singleton WCCs. The propagation of the *minid* in each loop is done as a join of the current *id*-to-*minid* table with the flattened graph, UNIONed with the *id*-to-*minid* table. We perform a GROUP BY *id* with a MIN() function applied to the *minids* from that union-ed set. The loop continues until the *minid* for all *ids* does not change across an iteration.

DryadLINQ

The DryadLINQ implementation of WCC generates a distributed stream E of graph edges from the input graph and maintains a distributed stream C of $\langle node, componentID \rangle$ pairs. C is initialized with the identity mapping so that each node is in its own component. Then the components are merged by growing balls around the nodes and checking whether nodes in intersecting balls are assigned to the same component. This "growing" step is implemented as follows. Let C' denote the stream obtained by joining C with E ($C' = \{(y,id) | (x,id) \in C \wedge (x,y) \in E\}$). We compute the union $C' \cup C$ and then generate the stream with the new component mapping, $C_{new} = \{(x, minid) | minid = min(id : (x,id) \in C \cup C')\}$ using a `group by` operation. When all the components have been assigned correctly, C_{new} will be identical to C. If C_{new} is different from C, we update C to C_{new} and iterate. As the component ID for any node can only decrease, it is sufficient to check whether the sum of component IDs over all nodes has changed.

SHS

The SHS implementation of WCC is based on disjoint-set operations [11]. The union-find forest is represented as a distributed `UidState` array, which can be updated in constant time, and performance is further improved through batching.

Performance Evaluation

We observe that SHS dramatically outperforms SQL Server PDW and DryadLINQ, due to its ability to express the union-find algorithm. As described earlier, DryadLINQ is limited by the overhead associated with evaluating the loop termination. To amortize this overhead, the DryadLINQ program performs partial loop unrolling, checking the termination condition every five iterations. The SQL Server PDW implementation does the loop termination check on every iteration, and therefore suffers from an overhead that the DryadLINQ implementation does not.

4.5 Approximate Shortest Path

We next consider the problem of finding shortest paths between pairs of nodes in a large graph, which is a fundamental operation with many applications. However, for web-scale graphs, computation of exact shortest paths is challenging since these graphs do not fit in main memory on a single machine. Even in a distributed setting, the computation would require huge amounts of communication. Furthermore, in a real-time application, we would like to compute shortest paths with limited memory and processing resources. Hence we are interested in computing approximate shortest paths between nodes.

We use the algorithm proposed in [13]. The essential idea behind that algorithm is the following: In an offline computation, sample a small number of sets of nodes in the graph (sets of seed nodes). Then, for each node in the graph, find the closest seed in each of these seed sets. The sketch for a node is composed of the closest seeds, and the distance to these closest seeds. The offline steps are described in Algorithm 5. Then, in an online step, the sketches can be used to estimate the distance between any pair of nodes (as described in [13]). As the most important component of computation of the approximate shortest paths is computation of the offline

Algorithm 5 OFFLINE-SKETCH(G)

Input: An undirected graph $G = (V, E)$.
Output: Vectors of nearest seeds $seed[u]$ and their distances $dist[u]$ for each node u.

```
C := {u ∈ V | degree(u) ≥ 2}
I := {0, 1, ..., ⌊log|C|⌋}
for each i ∈ I do
    S_i := Random sample of 2^i elements of C
for each u ∈ V and each i ∈ I do
    seed[u][i] := u
    dist[u][i] := 0 if u ∈ S_i; ∞ otherwise
repeat
    progress := false
    for each (u, v) ∈ E and each i ∈ I do
        if dist[u][i] < dist[v][i] then
            seed[v][i] := seed[u][i]
            dist[v][i] := dist[u][i] + 1
            progress := true
until ¬progress
```

sketch for all nodes u, we perform our evaluations on this step, treating the graph as undirected.

SQL Server PDW

We have implemented ASP in T-SQL in an iterative manner. For each chosen seed set size, the next BFS search is computed in a single query for all seeds. When a given node is encountered along multiple paths originating from different seeds, the seed with the minimum ID value is chosen as the seed. Beyond this conversion, the algorithm is implemented in a straightforward manner.

DryadLINQ

The DryadLINQ implementation uses the input stream of graph edges to compute a stream of (undirected) degrees of nodes using a `group by` operation, and then obtains a stream of candidate nodes C by removing nodes with degree < 2. It then determines the count of C to to set $r = \lfloor \log |C| \rfloor$ and also to set the initial value of the number of nodes reachable from all the sampled sets. Next it samples sets of sizes, $1, 2, 2^2, 2^3, \ldots, 2^r$ by generating a stream of $\langle node, initial\text{-}sketch \rangle$ pairs, where for each node u, the corresponding *initial-sketch* represents membership of u in the r sampled sets. DryadLINQ's flexibility allows us to use a single series of joins to process all of the seed sets, thereby performing the BFSs for the $\log n$ seed sets in parallel. For each sampled set S, in parallel, we grow a ball around S and thereby compute distances of all other nodes to S. At the end of each iteration, we check whether the number of nodes reachable from all the sampled sets increases (using a distributed sum operation) and if not, terminate the loop.

SHS

First we compute the candidate set C by probing degrees of all nodes and ruling out nodes with degree < 2 and represent C using a bit vector. This step is batched to reduce network overhead. Then we sample sets of different sizes $(1, 2, 2^2, 2^3, \ldots)$ uniformly at random from the candidate set of vertices. For each sampled set S, we compute distances of all other nodes to S by growing a ball around S, until no new nodes are added to the ball (that is, when distances to all nodes from S have been computed). This step is also performed in batches.

Performance Evaluation

In this case, the trade-off in using SHS is in memory vs. roundtrips. The bulk of the relatively large cost of computing the approximate shortest paths for SHS can be attributed to computing the BFS one dimension at a time. This constraint arises because the entire sketch for all the nodes cannot be stored in memory on a single machine. Such a constraint does not exist in the case of DryadLINQ where the sketch is stored on disk and read and written in a streaming fashion, and all the dimensions can therefore be handled concurrently. This explains the relative speedup of DryadLINQ compared to SHS. The SQL Server PDW implementation processes one seed set at a time and therefore pays a sequential processing penalty that the DryadLINQ implementation avoids.

5. DISCUSSION AND CONCLUSION

This study compared the efficiency of three paradigms of computation on very large graphs used in real-world applications. We explained, using five basic graph algorithms, the effectiveness of each paradigm. The graph algorithms were chosen in a way to favor different data and computation models. For example, the efficiency of SALSA hinges on the random access to node data while ASP does not have such a restriction. In fact, ASP allows a natural streaming data model and data-parallel computation on this model. We conclude that SHS is a good platform choice when random access to the data is involved and relatively little computation is required (e.g. SALSA); DryadLINQ is a good choice for data-parallel computations on streaming data (e.g. PageRank); and is appropriate for scenarios where indices can be leveraged or transactions are required. DryadLINQ provides richer data types (e.g. arrays) and a more expressive language (C#) to programmers than SQL Server PDW does with T-SQL; but this flexibility comes at a price: programmers *can* optimize DryadLINQ programs by choosing the number of stream partitions or annotating user-defined operators with hints that trigger partial aggregation, but on the flip-side they *have to* perform these optimizations to extract the best performance from the system. SQL Server PDW, on the other hand, is much more of black box: programmers write their queries in a completely declarative fashion, and the system generates what it believes is the best query plan.

6. REFERENCES

[1] D. Abadi. Data management in the cloud: Limitations and opportunities. *IEEE Data Engineering Bulletin*, 32(1):3–12, 2009.

[2] D. J. Abadi, P. A. Boncz, and S. Harizopoulos. Column oriented database systems. In *VLDB*, 2009.

[3] A. Abouzeid, K. Bajda-Pawlikowski, D. Abadi, A. Silberschatz, and A. Rasin. HadoopDB: An architectural hybrid of MapReduce and DBMS technologies for analytical workloads. In *VLDB*, 2009.

[4] A. Aho, J. Hopcroft, and J. Ullman. *Data Structures and Algorithms*. Addison-Wesley, 1983.

[5] K. Bharat, A. Broder, M. Henzinger, P. Kumar, and S. Venkatasubramanian. The connectivity server: Fast access to linkage information on the web. In *WWW*, 1998.

[6] A. Bialecki, M. Cafarella, D. Cutting, and O. O-Malley. Hadoop: A framework for running applications on large clusters built of commodity hardware, 2005. `http://lucene.apache.org/hadoop/`.

[7] P. Boldi and S. Vigna. The webgraph framework I: Compression techniques. In *WWW*, 2004.

[8] A. Broder, R. Kumar, F. Maghoul, P. Raghavan, S. Rajagopalan, R. Stata, A. Tomkins, and J. Wiener. Graph structure in the web. In *WWW*, 2000.

[9] M. Castellanos, U. Dayal, and T. Sellis. Beyond conventional data warehousing–massively parallel data processing with greenplum database. In *BIRTE*, 2008.

[10] B. V. Cherkassky, L. Georgiadis, A. V. Goldberg, R. E. Tarjan, and R. F. F. Werneck. Shortest path feasibility algorithms: An experimental evaluation. In *ALENEX*, pages 118–132, 2008.

[11] T. Cormen, C. Leiserson, R. Rivest, and C. Stein. *Introduction to algorithms*. The MIT press, 2001.

[12] N. Craswell and M. Szummer. Random walks on the click graph. In *SIGIR*, pages 239–246, 2007.

[13] A. Das Sarma, S. Gollapudi, M. Najork, and R. Panigrahy. A sketch-based distance oracle for web-scale graphs. In *WSDM*, 2010.

[14] J. Dean and S. Ghemawat. Mapreduce: Simplified data processing on large clusters. In *OSDI*, 2004.

[15] J. Dean and S. Ghemawat. MapReduce: A flexible data processing tool. *Commun. ACM*, 53(1):72–77, 2010.

[16] J. Feigenbaum, S. Kannan, A. McGregor, S. Suri, and J. Zhang. On graph problems in a semi-streaming model. *Theor. Comput. Sci.*, 348(2-3):207–216, 2005.

[17] J. Feigenbaum, S. Kannan, A. McGregor, S. Suri, and J. Zhang. Graph distances in the data-stream model. *SIAM J. Comput.*, 38(5):1709–1727, 2008.

[18] M. Isard, M. Budiu, Y. Yu, A. Birrell, and D. Fetterly. Dryad: Distributed data-parallel programs from sequential building blocks. In *EuroSys*, 2007.

[19] J. Kleinberg. Authoritative sources in a hyperlinked environment. In *SODA*, 1998.

[20] R. Lempel and S. Moran. The stochastic approach for link-structure analysis (SALSA) and the TKC effect. *Computer Networks*, 33(1-6):387–401, 2000.

[21] M. W. Mahoney, L.-H. Lim, and G. E. Carlsson. Algorithmic and statistical challenges in modern large-scale data analysis are the focus of MMDS 2008. *CoRR*, abs/0812.3702, 2008.

[22] G. Malewicz, M. H. Austern, A. J. C. Bik, J. C. Dehnert, I. Horn, N. Leiser, and G. Czajkowski. Pregel: A System for Large-Scale Graph Processing. In *SIGMOD*, 2010.

[23] Microsoft SQL Server 2008 R2 Parallel Data Warehouse. `http://www.microsoft.com/sqlserver/en/us/solutions-technologies/data-warehousing/pdw.aspx`.

[24] M. Najork. The scalable hyperlink store. In *HT*, 2009.

[25] M. Najork, S. Gollapudi, and R. Panigrahy. Less is more: Sampling the neighborhood graph makes SALSA better and faster. In *WSDM*, 2009.

[26] S. Navathe, S. Ceri, G. Wiederhold, and J. Dou. Vertical partitioning algorithms for database design. *ACM Trans. Database Syst.*, 9(4):680–710, 1984.

[27] C. Olston, B. Reed, U. Srivastava, R. Kumar, and A. Tomkins. Pig Latin: A not-so-foreign language for data processing. In *SIGMOD*, 2008.

[28] L. Page, S. Brin, R. Motwani, and T. Winograd. The PageRank citation ranking: Bringing order to the web. Technical report, Stanford InfoLab, 1999.

[29] A. Pavlo, E. Paulson, A. Rasin, D. J. Abadi, D. J. DeWitt, S. Madden, and M. Stonebraker. A comparative study of approaches to cluster-based large scale data analysis. In *SIGMOD*, 2009.

[30] R. Pike, S. Dorward, R. Griesemer, and S. Quinlan. Interpreting the data: Parallel analysis with Sawzall. *Scientific Programming*, 13(4):277–298, 2005.

[31] K. Randall, R. Stata, J. Wiener, and R. Wickremesinghe. The link database: Fast access to graphs of the web. In *DCC*, 2002.

[32] S. D. Servetto and G. Barrenechea. Constrained random walks on random graphs: Routing algorithms for large scale wireless sensor networks. In *WSNA*, 2002.

[33] M. Stonebraker, D. J. Abadi, A. Batkin, X. Chen, M. Cherniack, M. Ferreira, E. Lau, A. Lin, S. Madden, E. O'Neil, P. O'Neil, A. Rasin, N. Tran, and S. Zdonik. C-Store: A column-oriented DBMS. In *VLDB*, 2005.

[34] M. Stonebraker, D. J. Abadi, D. J. DeWitt, S. Madden, E. Paulson, A. Pavlo, and A. Rasin. MapReduce and parallel DBMSs: Friends or foes? *Commun. ACM*, 53(1):64–71, 2010.

[35] T. Suel and J. Yuan. Compressing the graph structure of the web. In *DCC*, 2001.

[36] R. Tarjan. Depth-first search and linear graph algorithms. *SIAM Journal on Computing*, 1(2):146–160, 1972.

[37] A. Thusoo, J. S. Sarma, N. Jain, Z. Shao, P. Chakka, S. Anthony, H. Liu, P. Wyckoff, and R. Murthy. Hive: A warehousing solution over a Map-Reduce framework. In *VLDB*, 2009.

[38] Wikipedia. Graph database. `http://en.wikipedia.org/wiki/Graph_database`.

[39] Y. Yu, M. Isard, D. Fetterly, M. Budiu, U. Erlingsson, P. K. Gunda, and J. Currey. DryadLINQ: A system for general-purpose distributed data-parallel computing using a high-level language. In *OSDI*, 2008.

Pairwise Cross-Domain Factor Model for Heterogeneous Transfer Ranking

Bo Long
Yahoo! Labs
bolong@yahoo-inc.com

Yi Chang
Yahoo! Labs
yichang@yahoo-inc.com

Anlei Dong
Yahoo! Labs
anlei@yahoo-inc.com

Jianzhang He
Yahoo! Labs
jhe@yahoo-inc.com

ABSTRACT

Learning to rank arises in many information retrieval applications, ranging from Web search engine, online advertising to recommendation systems. Traditional ranking mainly focuses on one type of data source, and effective modeling relies on a sufficiently large number of labeled examples, which require expensive and time-consuming labeling process. However, in many real-world applications, ranking over multiple related heterogeneous domains becomes a common situation, where in some domains we may have a relatively large amount of training data while in some other domains we can only collect very little. Theretofore, how to leverage labeled information from related heterogeneous domain to improve ranking in a target domain has become a problem of great interests. In this paper, we propose a novel probabilistic model, pairwise cross-domain factor model, to address this problem. The proposed model learns latent factors(features) for multi-domain data in partially-overlapped heterogeneous feature spaces. It is capable of learning homogeneous feature correlation, heterogeneous feature correlation, and pairwise preference correlation for cross-domain knowledge transfer. We also derive two PCDF variations to address two important special cases. Under the PCDF model, we derive a stochastic gradient based algorithm, which facilitates distributed optimization and is flexible to adopt different loss functions and regularization functions to accommodate different data distributions . The extensive experiments on real world data sets demonstrate the effectiveness of the proposed model and algorithm.

Categories and Subject Descriptors

H.4 [**Information Systems Applications**]: Miscellaneous; I.5.1 [**Pattern Recognition**]: Models-statistical

General Terms

algorithms

Permission to make digital or hard copies of all or part of this work for personal or classroom use is granted without fee provided that copies are not made or distributed for profit or commercial advantage and that copies bear this notice and the full citation on the first page. To copy otherwise, to republish, to post on servers or to redistribute to lists, requires prior specific permission and/or a fee.
WSDM'12, February 8–12, 2012, Seattle, Washington, USA.
Copyright 2012 ACM 978-1-4503-0747-5/12/02 ...$10.00.

Keywords

Ranking, Homogeneous transfer ranking, Heterogeneous transfer ranking, Source Domain, Target Domain, Pairwise cross-domain factor model, Stochastic gradient descent.

1. INTRODUCTION

Ranking is the core component of many important information retrieval problems, such as web search, recommendation, computational advertising. Learning to rank represents an important class of supervised machine learning tasks with the goal of automatically constructing ranking functions from training data. As many other supervised machine learning problems, the quality of a ranking function is highly correlated with the amount of labeled data used to train the function. Due to the complexity of many ranking problems, a large amount of labeled training examples are usually required to learn a high quality ranking function. However, in general, it is very expensive and time-consuming to acquire labeled data.

On the other hand, in many real-world applications, ranking over multiple related domains becomes a common situation, where in some domains we may have a relatively large amount of training data while in some other domains we can only collect very little. In those situations, making use of labeled data from related domain to is a desirable direction to address the data scarcity in the target domain.

Besides ranking applications, this learning scenario is also popular for other applications and in general it has been studied as transfer learning in the literature. Existing transfer learning approaches mainly focus on knowledge transfer in the same feature space, i.e., the data from different domains are assumed in a common feature space (we refer to this scenario as *homogeneous transfer learning*). However, in practice, we often face the problem where the labeled data are scarce in their own feature space, whereas there may be a large amount of labeled heterogeneous data in another feature space. In fact, this problem arises frequently in today's information retrieval systems, such as search engines and recommendation systems. For example, a search engine system often conducts ranking learning tasks in various domains with different languages (e.g., English text search, Spanish text search, etc.), or different verticals/topics (e.g., news search, product search, etc.); here, data from an English language domain may be helpful for a Spanish language domain; however their data usually exist in different feature spaces which are language dependent. Similarly, different vertical search data could benefit each other with knowledge transfer; but they lie in different feature spaces. In such situations, it would be desirable to transfer the knowledge from heterogeneous domains to a target domain where we have relatively little training data available (we refer to this scenario as *heterogeneous transfer learning*). Note that unlike multiple view learning [7], there is no data instance correspondence between two domains in heterogeneous transfer learning.

For the homogeneous transfer learning, since the data are in a common feature space, the main challenge is to overcome the data distribution difference to learn domain correlation for knowledge transfer. On the other hand, for the heterogeneous transfer learning, the domain difference is beyond distribution difference, since distributions from heterogeneous spaces are not even comparable. Therefore, in general heterogeneous transfer learning is more challenging.

When it comes to ranking, the problem becomes *heterogeneous transfer ranking*, which is even more challenging due to the following facts. First, unlike in classification or regression, in ranking the labels (relevance scores) for different domains may not be comparable. For example, a domain can have five grade relevance scores; another domain can have binary relevance scores. In fact, since the relevance scores may be query-dependent, the absolute values are not important and the preference order between instances are more important. Therefore, heterogeneous transfer ranking needs to catch correlations between preference orders from different domains, instead the traditional label correlations in classification and regression. Second, in general, a ranking application needs thousands of (or millions of) training examples. It is important to develop the method that can scale well to large data sets.

In this paper, we propose a general probabilistic model, *Pairwise Cross-Domain Factor* (PCDF) model, for heterogeneous transfer ranking. PCDF model is a feature-based transfer ranking model that learns common latent factors (features) to transfer knowledge cross multiple heterogeneous ranking domains. PCDF assumes that (1) homogeneous features, heterogeneous features, and hidden relevance scores are generated conditioning on latent factors and (2) preference orders are generated conditioning on hidden relevance scores. Through direct and indirect parameter sharing for the generative processes in different domains, the latent factors catch different types of domain correlations to extract the common knowledge for different domains. Our contributions can be summarized as follows.

- We introduce the concepts of *two-component latent factor* and *hidden relevance score* as key concepts to model the the feature heterogeneity and preference pair in heterogeneous transfer ranking;
- We propose a novel heterogeneous transfer learning model, PCDF model, which is capable of learning homogeneous feature correlation, heterogeneous feature correlation, and preference order correlation. PCDF is applicable to various cross-domina ranking applications with different data distribution assumptions.
- We also derive two variations of the PCDF model to address two important special cases, which provide a new homogeneous transfer ranking model and a general transfer learning model beyond ranking applications.
- Under PCDF model, we derive an efficient stochastic gradient descent algorithm that is ready for distributed computation and is flexible to adopt different loss functions and regularization functions to accommodate different data distributions.

2. RELATED WORK

Transfer ranking is an overlapping field of , transfer learning, and learning to rank.

2.1 Transfer Learning

Transfer learning approaches can be mainly categorized into three classes.

A popular class of transfer learning methods is instance-based [4, 15, 31, 5, 25, 17, 35], which assumes that certain parts of the data in the source domain can be reused for the target domain by re-weighting. [26] proposed a heuristic method to remove "misleading" training instances from source domain so as to include "good" instances from labeled source-domain instances and unlabeled target-domain instances. [15] introduced a boosting algorithm, TrAdaBoost, which assumes that the source and target domain data use exactly the same set of features and labels, but the distributions of the data in the two domains are different. TrAdaBoost attempts to iteratively re-weight the source domain data and target domain data to reduce the effect of the "bad" source data while encourage the "good" source data to contribute more for the target domains. [4] proposed a framework to simultaneously re-weight the source domain data and train models on the re-weighted data with a kernel logistic regression classifier.

Another category of approaches can be viewed as model-based approaches [34, 28, 18, 8], which assumes that the source tasks and the target tasks share some parameters or priors of their models. An efficient algorithm MT-IVM [28], which is based on Gaussian Process (GP), was proposed to handle multi-domain learning case. MT-IVM tries to learn parameters of GP over multiple tasks by assigning the same GP prior to the tasks. Similarly, Hierarchical Bayes (HB) is used with GP for multi-task learning [34]. [18] borrowed the idea of [34] and used SVMs for multi-domain learning. The parameters of SVMs for each domain is assumed to be separable into two terms: a common term across tasks and a task specific term. [32] proposed a consensus regularization framework for transfer learning from multiple source domains to a target domain.

The third category of transfer learning approaches are feature based. [6, 33, 14, 1, 2, 3, 30], where a feature representation is learned for the target domain and used to transfer knowledge across domains. A structural correspondence learning (SCL) algorithm [6] is proposed to use unlabeled data from the target domain to extract features so as to reduce the difference between source and target domains. A simple kernel mapping function is introduced in [16], which maps the data from both domains to a high-dimensional feature space. [33] proposed to apply sparse coding, an unsupervised feature construction method, to learning higher level features across domain. On the other hand, heterogeneous transfer learning starts to attract attention very recently. We notice that [39] extends PLSA to a specific application, using social Web data to help image clustering; [37] proposes a manifold alignment based approach for heterogeneous domain adaptation; [24] formulates heterogeneous transfer learning as multi-task and multi-view learning and proposes a graph-based solution; [23] focus on single task learning with multiple outlooks, which is also related to heterogeneous transfer learning.

2.2 Learning to Rank

In recent years, the ranking problem is frequently formulated as a supervised machine learning problem [27, 9, 19, 38, 13, 41, 22]. These learning-to-rank approaches are capable of combining different kinds of features to train ranking functions. The problem of ranking can be formulated as that of learning a ranking function from pair-wise preference data. The idea is to minimize the number of contradicting pairs in training data. For example, RankSVM [27] uses support vector machines to learn a ranking function from preference data. RankNet [9] applies neural network and gradient descent to obtain a ranking function. RankBoost [19] applies the idea of boosting to construct an efficient ranking function from a set of weak ranking functions. The studies reported in [41] proposes a framework called GBRank using gradient descent in function spaces, which is able to learn relative ranking information in the context of web search. [10] proposes a new probabilistic method for listwise ranking. Specifically it introduces two probability models, respectively referred to as permutation probability and top k probability, to define a listwise loss function for learning.

A few studies have been applied the idea of transfer learning for learning to rank problem. Zha et al.[40] uses multi-task learning technique to incorporate query difference, where each query is regarded as a task. However, the objective of this work is to learn a single ranking function instead of multiple functions for multiple tasks. TransRank[11] considers cross-domain information to attack transfer learning problem for ranking, which utilizes the labeled data from a source domain to enhance the learning of ranking function in the target domain with augmented features. However, this approach does not make use of unlabeled data. Gao et al.[21] explore several model adaptation methods for Web search ranking. They trained two ranking functions separately, then interpolated the two functions for the final result, and their experiments show that the simple model interpolation method achieves the best results. Similarly, heterogeneous transfer ranking is rarely touched in the literature. We notice that [36] proposes a regularized framework to addresses ranking cross heterogeneous domains. It simultaneously minimize two loss functions corresponding to two related domains by mapping each domain onto a shared latent space.

Among those transfer learning approaches, in general instance-based and model-based approaches depend on the assumption of homogeneous feature more strongly than feature-based approaches. Another advantage of feature-based approaches is its flexibility of adopting different base ranking learners in real applications, i.e., after the common latent features learnt from different domains, it is flexible to use any ranking learner on the new training data with common latent features to train ranking functions. Those motivate us to focus on deriving a feature-based model in this study.

3. PCDF MODEL

3.1 Problem Formulation

For ease of exposition and to avoid notational clutter, we use the terms, *target domain* and *source domain*, to distinguish two given domains in a transfer learning task, though the discussions in this study are applicable to the situation that two domains are exchangeable and mutually helpful and can also be easily extended to multiple domains.

We begin with notations. We consider that the target domain data exist in a $d_t + d_c$ dimension space and the source domain data exist in a $d_s + d_c$ dimension space, where d_c is the number of dimensions for their overlapped feature space (denoted as $\mathcal{S}^c$); d_t and d_s are the number of dimensions for their dedicated feature spaces (denoted as $\mathcal{S}^t$ and $\mathcal{S}^d$), respectively. For traditional homogeneous transfer learning , all data are in the same feature space, i.e., $d_t = 0$ and $d_s = 0$. For totally heterogeneous transfer learning, the feature spaces for the different domains has no overlapping, i.e., $d_c = 0$. In this study, we consider the most general case, partially overlapped heterogeneous feature spaces, which arises frequently in real applications.

We let n_t and n_s denote the numbers of instances in the target domain and the source domain, respectively. We let $X^{(t)} = [X^{(td)}X^{(tc)}]$ denote the target domain data, where $X^{(td)} \in \mathbb{R}^{n_t \times d_t}$ denote the target domain data in its dedicated feature space, and $X^{(tc)} \in \mathbb{R}^{n_t \times d_c}$ denote target domain data in the common feature space. Similarly, $X^{(s)} = [X^{(sd)}X^{(sc)}]$ denotes the source domain data, where $X^{(sd)} \in \mathbb{R}^{n_s \times d_s}$ denote the source domain data in its dedicated feature space, and $X^{(sc)} \in \mathbb{R}^{n_s \times d_c}$ denote the source domain data in the overlapped feature space. To denote the ith data instance in the target domain or source domain, we use $X^{(t)}_{i.}$ or $X^{(s)}_{i.}$.

Furthermore, we let $R^{(t)}_{ij}$ denote the preference value between ith instance and jth instance in the target domain such that

$$R^{(t)}_{ij} \begin{cases} > 0 & \text{if } i\text{th instance is preferred over } j\text{th instance,} \\ = 0 & \text{if } i\text{th and } j\text{th instance are equally preferred,} \\ < 0 & \text{if } j\text{th instance is preferred over } i\text{th instance.} \end{cases} \quad (1)$$

where $1 \leq i, j \leq n_t$ (however it is not necessary that there is $R^{(t)}_{ij}$ for any pair of i and j in the data). In general $R^{(t)}_{ij} \in \mathbb{R}$. In the special case that only the preference order matters, $R^{(t)}_{ij} \in \{-1, 0, +1\}$. Note that even the data are given with relevance labels or lists of ordered instances, they can be easily converted to the pairwise preferences. Similarly, we let $R^{(s)}_{ij}$ denote the preference value between ith instance and jth instance in the source domain.

In heterogeneous transfer ranking, given target domain data, $X^{(td)}$, $X^{(tc)}$, and $R^{(t)}$, and source domain data, $X^{(sd)}$, $X^{(sc)}$, and $R^{(s)}$, they are three types of domain difference to impede us from directly applying target domain data to the target domain: different feature distributions in the shared feature space; different dedicated feature spaces; different distributions for pairwise preference values.

On the other hand, we need to catch three types of domain correlations for knowledge transfer. The first one is homogeneous feature correlation hidden in the overlapped feature space, i.e., correlation between $X^{(tc)}$ and $X^{(sc)}$, which is the focus of traditional homogeneous transfer learning. The second one is heterogeneous feature correlation hidden in the dedicated feature spaces, i.e., correlation between $X^{(td)}$ and $X^{(sd)}$. The third one is preference correlation, i.e., the correlation between $R^{(t)}$ and $R^{(s)}$.

3.2 Model Formulation

In this study, we consider a generative model, in which features and pairwise preferences are generated conditioning on the latent variables.

3.2.1 Feature Generating

Fist we assume that the two domains' features are generated conditioning on the common latent factors with maximum domain correlations and minimum domain differences. In heterogenous transfer ranking, there are two type of feature correlations between the two domains and intuitively it is difficult to catch them in one type of latent factor. Base on this observation, we propose of the concept, two-component latent factor. The two-component latent factors for the two domains are given as follows,

$$Z^{(t)} = [Z^{(td)} Z^{(tc)}] \tag{2}$$

and

$$Z^{(s)} = [Z^{(sd)} Z^{(sc)}], \tag{3}$$

where $Z^{(t)} \in \mathbb{R}^{n_t \times (k_d+k_c)}$, $Z^{(td)} \in \mathbb{R}^{n_d \times k_c}$, $Z^{(tc)} \in \mathbb{R}^{n_t \times k_c}$, $Z^{(s)} \in \mathbb{R}^{n_s \times (k_c+k_d)}$, $Z^{(sd)} \in \mathbb{R}^{n_s \times k_d}$, $Z^{(sc)} \in \mathbb{R}^{n_s \times k_c}$, k_c is the dimension of latent factors for the common features, and k_d is the dimensions of latent factors for the dedicated features. In the target domain latent factor $Z^{(t)}$, the component $Z^{(td)}$ is to catch heterogeneous feature correlation and the component $Z^{(tc)}$ is to catch homogeneous feature correlation.

Then, the common features in the overlapped feature space are generated according to the following probabilities,

$$X^{(tc)} \sim p(X^{(tc)}|f(Z^{(tc)}; P^{(c)})) \tag{4}$$

$$X^{(sc)} \sim p(X^{(sc)}|f(Z^{(sc)}; P^{(c)})), \tag{5}$$

where $f(\cdot)$ is a link function and $P^{(c)}$ is the function parameter. Through the shared parameter $P^{(c)}$, the latent factors $Z^{(tc)}$ and $Z^{(sc)}$ catch common knowledge from the two domains' common features.

However, for the dedicated features $X^{(td)}$ and $X^{(sd)}$, since they are in the different feature spaces, in general direct knowledge transfer by sharing the link function parameter is not feasible. For example, if $X^{(td)}$ and $X^{(sd)}$ have different dimensions and we use the popular linear link function such that $f(Z; P) = ZP$, then it is not feasible for a shared parameter matrix $P^{(c)}$ to make the latent factor $Z^{(td)}$ and $Z^{(sd)}$ have the same dimension k_d. In other words, the parameter sharing is a too strong assumption for the heterogeneous features. On the other hand, it is more reasonable to learn the heterogeneous feature correlation indirectly through the interaction between different types of latent factors and interaction between latent factors and pairwise preferences (we discuss more details later). Therefore, we assume that the dedicated features are generated with their own link function parameters as follows,

$$X^{(td)} \sim p(X^{(td)}|g(Z^{(td)}; P^{(td)})) \tag{6}$$

$$X^{(sd)} \sim p(X^{(sd)}|g(Z^{(sd)}; P^{(sd)})). \tag{7}$$

where $g(\cdot)$ is a link function and $P^{(td)}$ and $P^{(sd)}$ are the function parameters.

Furthermore, we assume prior distributions for $P^{(c)}$, $P^{(td)}$, and $P^{(sd)}$ to reduce over fitting,

$$P^{(c)} \sim p(P^{(c)}; \lambda_c), \tag{8}$$

$$P^{(td)} \sim p(P^{(td)}; \lambda_{td}), \tag{9}$$

$$P^{(sd)} \sim p(P^{(sd)}; \lambda_{sd}), \tag{10}$$

3.2.2 Pairwise Preferences Generating

To generate another observed variable, the pairwise preference score R_{ij}, we propose the concept of latent relevance score. We assume that each instance i has a latent relevance score y_i such that comparing a pair of y_i and y_j will give the pairwise preference between instance i and j.

In other words, we assume that Rij is generated conditioning on y_i and y_j for the both domains,

$$R_{ij}^{(t)} \sim p(R_{ij}^{(t)}|r(y_i^{(t)}, y_j^{(t)})). \tag{11}$$

$$R_{ij}^{(s)} \sim p(R_{ij}^{(s)}|r(y_i^{(s)}, y_j^{(s)})). \tag{12}$$

where r is a link function. An intuitive choice for r is the difference function, i.e., $r(a, b) = a - b$. For example, we can assume that the distribution of $\mathbb{R}_{ij}$ is the normal distribution with the difference of y_i and y_j as the mean such that

$$R_{ij}|y_i, y_j \sim \mathbf{N}(y_i - y_j, \sigma^2). \tag{13}$$

We further assume that the latent relevance score is generated conditioning on the latent factor.

$$y^{(t)} \sim p(y^{(t)}|h(Z^{(t)}; w)) \tag{14}$$

$$y^{(s)} \sim p(y^{(s)}|h(Z^{(s)}; w)), \tag{15}$$

where h(;) is a link function, $w \in \mathbb{R}^k$ is the function parameter, and $Z^{(t)}$ and $Z^{(s)}$ are defined as in (2) and (3). Therefore, through the latent relevance scores and the shared parameter w , the latent factor is able to catch the pairwise preference correlation in addition to homogeneous feature correlation and heterogeneous feature correlation.

Similarly, we assume prior distributions for $P^{(w)}$ to reduce over fitting,

$$w \sim p(w; \lambda_w), \tag{16}$$

3.2.3 PCDF and Its Variations

Figure 1 summarizes the PCDF mode as a Bayesian network. From Figure 1, we can observe that the two domains share two parameters $P^{(c)}$ and w, which are bridges of knowledge transfer. Through the information propagation among the Bayesian network, the two-component latent factors catch the three types of domain correlations, i.e., the common knowledge cross the two domains.

As a general model for heterogenous transfer ranking, PCDF can be easily modified to accommodate special cases.

First, it can be easily applied to homogeneous transfer ranking, i.e., two domains in a shared feature space. Figure 2 shows the PCDF model for homogenous data. From Figure 2, we observe that without the heterogeneous features and

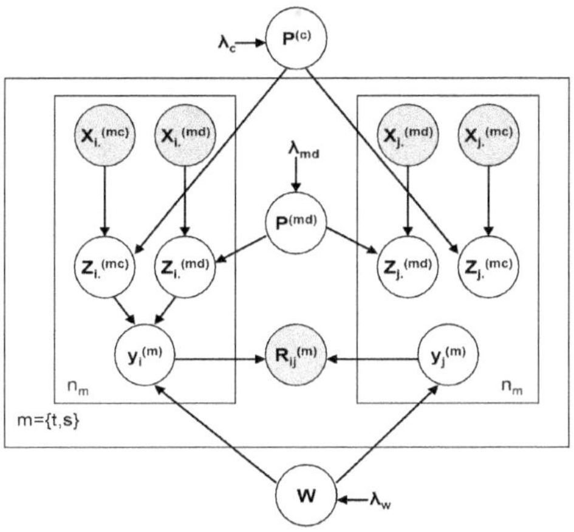

Figure 1: PCDF Bayesian network

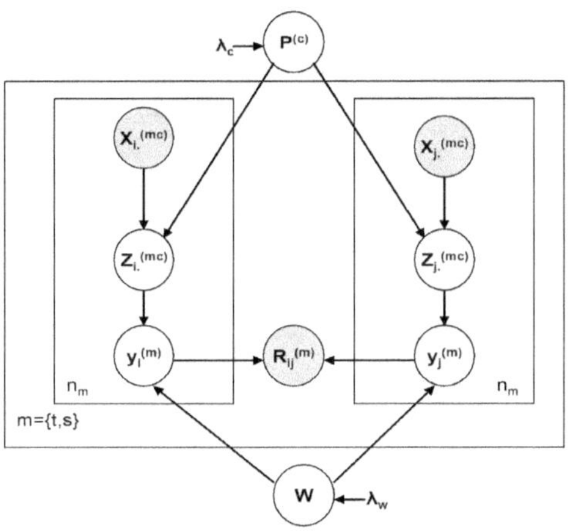

Figure 2: PCDF model for Homogeneous Data

heterogeneous latent factors, PCDF model is reduced to a new homogeneous transfer ranking model.

Second, with a little modification, the PCDF model can also be applied to the situation that data with absolute relevance scores. In such situation, $y^{(t)}$ and $y^{(s)}$ become observed variables and pairwise preferences are omitted. Hence, PCDF model is reduced to point-wise cross-domain factor model, which is shown in Figure 3. More interestingly, pointwise cross-domain factor model is beyond ranking applications, i.e., it can be directly applied to general regression and classification applications.

4. ALGORITHM DERIVATION

In this section, we derive the algorithm to learn the parameters for the PCDF model.

4.1 Objective Specification

The likelihood function of the PCDF model is given in Eq.(17), in which D denotes observed data; Ω denotes all parameters; Φ^m denotes the set of observed pairwise preferences of instances i and j for domain m.

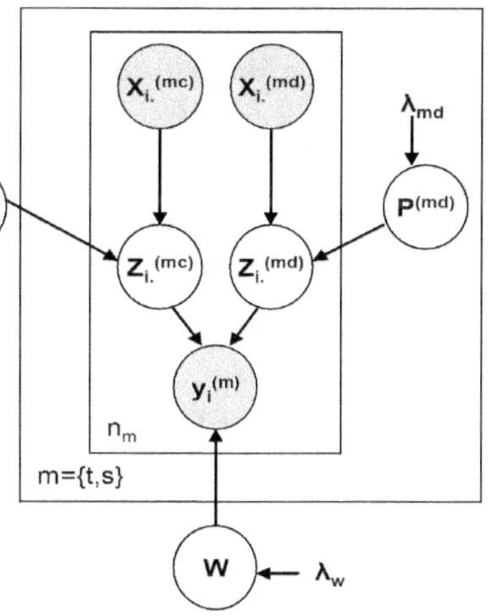

Figure 3: Pointwise Cross-domain Factor Model

$$\begin{aligned} p(D;\Omega) = \sum_{m=t,s} (\sum_{(i,j)\in\Phi^m} & (p(X_{i.}^{(mc)}|f(Z_{i.}^{(mc)};P^{(c)})) \\ & p(X_{i.}^{(md)}|g(Z_{i.}^{(md)};P^{(md)}))p(y_i^{(m)}|h(Z_{i.}^{(m)};w)) \\ & p(X_{j.}^{(mc)}|f(Z_{j.}^{(mc)};P^{(c)}))p(X_{j.}^{(md)}|g(Z_{j.}^{(md)};P^{(md)})) \\ & p(y_j^{(m)}|h(Z_{j.}^{(m)};w)))p(R_{ij}^{(m)}|r(y_i^{(m)},y_j^{(m)})) \\ & p(P^{(md)};\lambda_{md}))p(P^{(c)};\lambda_c)p(w;\lambda_w), \end{aligned} \tag{17}$$

Eq. (17) is a general objective function. In this study, to instantiate Eq. (17), we adopt popular linear function for the link functions f,g, and h; we use intuitive difference function for r. Furthermore, It has been observed in the literature [12] that maximizing likelihood under a certain distribution corresponds to minimizing distance under the corresponding distortion measure. For example, the normal distribution, Bernoulli distribution, multinormial distribution and exponential distribution correspond to Euclidean distance, logistic loss, KL-divergence and Itakura-Satio distance, respectively. Therefore, the problem of minimizing the the negative log posterior of PCDF boils down to the following objective:

$$\begin{aligned} \min_{\Omega} \sum_{m=t,s} (\sum_{(i,j)\in\Phi^m} & (\alpha_{mc} l(X_{i.}^{(mc)}, Z_{i.}^{(mc)}P^{(c)})+ \\ & \alpha_{md} l(X_{i.}^{(md)}, Z_{i.}^{(md)}P^{(md)}) + \beta_m l(y_i^{(m)}, Z_{i.}^{(m)}w)+ \\ & \alpha_{mc} l(X_{j}^{(mc)}, Z_{j}^{(mc)}P^{(c)})+ \\ & \alpha_{md} l(X_{j.}^{(md)}, Z_{j.}^{(md)}P^{(md)}) + \beta_m l(y_j^{(m)}, Z_{j.}^{(m)}w)+ \\ & \gamma_m l(R_{ij}^{(m)}, y_i^{(m)} - y_j^{(m)})) + \lambda_{md}\omega(P^{(md)})+ \\ & \lambda_c\omega(P^{(c)}) + \lambda_w\omega(w), \end{aligned} \tag{18}$$

where α, β, γ, and λ are trade-off parameters; $l(.,.)$ are the loss functions (for convenience, we use l for all terms; in general, it could be different for different terms) corresponding to conditional distributions in Eq. (17); $\omega(.)$ is the regularization loss function corresponding to the prior distribution in Eq. (17).

The motivations for a computational framework instead

of direct probabilistic inference are mainly two-fold: First, the two formulations are somewhat equivalent, i.e., the conditional distributions can be encoded precisely through the choice of loss functions; likewise, the prior distributions over parameters could also be readily translated into the regularization penalties. Secondly, computational models allow more scalable algorithms, e.g. via stochastic gradient descent, whereas probabilistic reasoning often requires Monte Carlo sampling or quite nontrivial variational approximations.

4.2 Optimization and Implementation

In general, minimizing (18) is a nonconvex problem regardless of the choice of the loss functions and regularizers. While there are convex reformulations for some settings, they tend to be computationally inefficient for large scale problems - the convex formulations require the manipulation of a full matrix which is impractical for anything beyond thousands of instances.

We established algorithms for distributed optimization based on the Hadoop MapReduce framework. The basic idea is to decompose the objective in (18) by optimizing with respect to each pairwise preference $R_{ij}^{(m)}$ and to combine the results for the parameters in the Reduce phase.

We briefly describe a stochastic gradient descent algorithm to solve the optimization of (18). The algorithm is computationally efficient and decouples different pairwise preferences. For a detailed discussion please see [42]. The algorithm loops over all the observations and updates the parameters by moving in the direction defined by negative gradient. Specifically, for each observation $R_{ij}^{(m)}$, the algorithm performs the following sequence of updating. First, the hidden variables related to instance i are updated as follows:

$$y_i^{(m)} = y_i^{(m)} - \delta(\beta_m l'(y_i^{(m)}, Z_{i.}^{(m)} w) + \gamma_m l'(R_{ij}^{(m)}, y_i^{(m)} - y_j^{(m)})); \tag{19}$$

$$Z_{i.}^{(md)} = Z_{i.}^{(md)} - \delta(\alpha_{md} l'(X_{i.}^{(md)}, Z_{i.}^{(md)} P^{(md)}) \odot P^{(md)} \mathbf{1} + \beta_m l'(y_i^{(m)}, Z_{i.}^{(md)} w^{(d)}) \odot w^{(d)}), \tag{20}$$

$$Z_{i.}^{(mc)} = Z_{i.}^{(mc)} - \delta(\alpha_{mc} l'(X_{i.}^{(mc)}, Z_{i.}^{(mc)} P^{(c)}) \odot P^{(c)} \mathbf{1} + \beta_m l'(y_i^{(m)}, Z_{i.}^{(mc)} w^{(c)}) \odot w^{(c)}), \tag{21}$$

where δ is the learning rate, $\odot$ denotes elementwise multiplication, $\mathbf{1}$ denotes vector of 1's, and for convenience we write w into $\left[\begin{smallmatrix} w^{(d)} \\ w^{(c)} \end{smallmatrix} \right]$.

Second, the latent variables related to instance j are updated as follows:

$$y_j^{(m)} = y_j^{(m)} - \delta(\beta_m l'(y_j^{(m)}, Z_{j.}^{(m)} w) - \gamma_m l'(R_{ij}^{(m)}, y_i^{(m)} - y_j^{(m)})); \tag{22}$$

$$Z_{j.}^{(md)} = Z_{j.}^{(md)} - \delta(\alpha_{md} l'(X_{j.}^{(md)}, Z_{j.}^{(md)} P^{(md)}) \odot P^{(md)} \mathbf{1} + \beta_m l'(y_j^{(m)}, Z_{j.}^{(md)} w^{(d)}) \odot w^{(d)}), \tag{23}$$

$$Z_{j.}^{(mc)} = Z_{j.}^{(mc)} - \delta(\alpha_{mc} l'(X_{j.}^{(mc)}, Z_{j.}^{(mc)} P^{(c)}) \odot P^{(c)} \mathbf{1} + \beta_m l'(y_j^{(m)}, Z_{j.}^{(mc)} w^{(c)}) \odot w^{(c)}), \tag{24}$$

Algorithm 1 General PCDF Algorithm

Input:$\{X^{(t)}, R^{(t)}, X^{(s)}, R^{(s)}\}$ and an integer b (number of instances for batch updating parameters).
Output:$\{P^{(td)}, P^{(sd)}, P^{(c)}, w\}$.
Method:

```
Initialize {Z^(t), Z^(s), y^(t), y^(s), P^(td), P^(sd), P^(c), w}
repeat
  for m=t,d do
    Randomly shuffle R^(m)
    Let count = 0
    for Each observed R_ij^(m) do
      Let count = count + 1
      Perform updating rules (19)-(21).
      Perform updating rules (22)-(24)
      if count%b == 0 then
        Perform updating rules (25)-(27)
      end if
    end for
  end for
until convergence
```

Third, the parameters are updated as follows:

$$P^{(md)} = P^{(md)} - \delta(\alpha_{md} l'(X^{(md)}, Z^{(md)} P^{(md)}) Z^{(md)} + \lambda_{md} \omega'(P^{(md)})), \tag{25}$$

$$P^{(c)} = P^{(c)} - \delta(\sum_{m=t,s} (\alpha_{mc} l'(X^{(mc)}, Z^{(mc)} P^{(c)}) Z^{(mc)}) + \lambda_c \omega'(P^{(c)})), \tag{26}$$

$$w = w - \delta(\sum_{m=t,s} (\beta_m l'(y^{(m)}, Z^{(m)} w) Z^{(m)}) + \lambda_w \omega'(w)). \tag{27}$$

In summary, the algorithm loops over all the $R_{ij}^{(m)}$'s to perform updating rules (19)-(27) until it converges. In practice, the algorithm may not need to update parameters for each $R_{ij}^{(m)}$, since the changes of parameters may not be significant for one observation. Instead it could be more efficient to perform updating rules (25)-(27) after performing updating rules (19)-(24) on a batch of observations. General PCDF algorithm is summarized in Algorithm 1. Note that following the similar procedure, it is easy to derive the algorithms for the variations of the PCDF model in Figure 2 and Figure 3, PCDF for homogenous data and point-wise (regression-based) cross-domain factor model.

The proposed stochastic gradient descent based algorithm has two desirable properties. First, it is ready for distributed optimization based on the Hadoop MapReduce framework, since it decouples different pairwise preference observations. Second, it is flexible to adopt different loss functions and regularization function for different types of data with different distributions.

5. EXPERIMENTAL EVALUATION

As a general heterogeneous ranking algorithm, PCDF can be applied to different ranking applications with different data distributions. In this section, we apply PCDF to Web search data to demonstrate the properties and effectiveness of PCDF.

Although PCDF model is flexible to adopt different loss and regularization functions, in this study we evaluate PCDF with the most popular loss function, L2 loss, corresponding to normal distribution, i.e., we use L2 loss for all l in minimization (18). For the regularization functions, we evaluate both L2 loss (normal distribution prior) and L1 loss (laplace distribution prior). We denote those two algorithms as *PCDF-n-he* and *PCDF-l-he* ("n" is for normal distribution prior; "l" is for laplace distribution prior; "he" is for heterogeneous ranking).

To our best knowledge, there is no existing transfer learning algorithms directly applicable to partially overlapped heterogeneous feature spaces (However, we thank an anonymous reviewer for pointing out very recent works, like [37] and [24], which may be modified to this learning situation). In this study, we use two state-of-the-art homogeneous transfer learning algorithm, Sparse Coding (called *SC-ho*)[33, 29] and multi-task feature learning (called *MTFL-ho*)[2] as comparisons. Furthermore, an intuitive way for heterogeneous transfer learning is to treat one domain's dedicated features in another domain as missing values and apply existing homogeneous transfer learning to the data with missing values; hence we modify the sparse coding algorithm (it is difficult to modify MFLF for this) to handle missing values (called *SC-he*) to evaluate this idea. Finally, the baseline is using the original target domain training data only (called *TD*) for ranking learning.

We also evaluate algorithms for two PCDF variations in Figure 2 and Figure 3 to gain deep understanding of PCDF itself. Similarly we use L2 loss for all the loss functions; L2 and L1 loss for the regularizer functions. For PCDF for homogeneous data in Figure 2, they are denoted as *PCDF-n-ho* and *PCDF-l-ho*, respectively; for regression based cross-domain factor model in Figure 3, they are denoted as *RCDF-n-he* and *RCDF-l-he*.

In summary, we compare ten algorithms: TD, SC-ho, SC-he, MTFL-ho, PCDF-n-ho, PCDF-l-ho, RCDF-n-he, RCDF-n-he, PCDF-n-he, and PCDF-l-he.

5.1 Data

We use Web search data from a commercial search engine system, which conducts ranking learning tasks in various domains with different languages or different verticals. The source domain (denoted as S0) is general Web search for an English speaking country, which has relatively large amount of labeled data. The first target domain (denoted as T1) is general Web search for a Spanish speaking country; the second target domain (denoted as T2) is news article search for the same country as S0; the third target domain (denoted as T3) is answer search (providing text search for knowledge-sharing community) for another non-English speaking country.

In the data, each query-document example is represented by a feature vector. Those query-document examples in domain S and T1 are originally labeled using a five-grade labeling scheme and those in domain T1 and T2 are originally labeled using a four-grade labeling scheme. We then transform them into pairwise preference data.

The features generally fall into the following three categories. Query features comprise features dependent on the query only and have constant values across all the documents, for example, the number of terms in the query, whether or not the query is a person name, etc. Document features comprise features dependent on the document only and have constant values across all the queries, for example, the number of inbound links pointing to the document, the amount of anchor-texts in bytes for the document, and the language identity of the document, etc. Query-document features comprise features dependent on the relation of the query with respect to the document d, for example, the number of times each term in the query appears in the document d, the number of times each term in the query appears in the anchor-texts of the document, etc.

The four domains have an overlapped feature space consisting of text match features, which describes various aspects of text match between a query and a document, such as title match and body match. Each domain has its own dedicated feature space. For example, all domains have their own dedicated features related to term segmentation in a query which is language dependent; T2 has its dedicated features related to news articles's freshness. Table 1 summarizes the data information for four domains. In our experiments, 20% of data for each target domain are used as training data (i.e., labeled data are very scarce in target domains); 80% of them are used as test data to make evaluation robust; all the source domain data are used as training data to help the target domains.

5.2 Experimental Setting

To evaluate those transfer learning algorithms, first, the new latent features and parameters are learnt by the algorithms; then source domain and target domain training data with the new latent features then are used by a base ranking learner to train a ranking model; third, the ranking model are tested on the test data of the target domain, which are also projected into the new feature space.

For the base ranking learner, we use Gradient Boosting Decision Tree (GBDT)[20]. For performance measure of the ranking models, we adopt widely used Discounted Cumulative Gain (DCG). Specifically, we sue DCG-k, since users of a search engine are only interested in the top k results of a query rather than a sorted order of the entire document collection. In this study, we select k as 5 and 1. For every experimental setting, 10 runs are repeated and the average DCG of 10 runs is reported for each experiment setting.

The gradient of L1 regularization function is the discontinuous sign function. We approximate it by a steep soft sign function $l(x) = \frac{1-\exp(-\theta x)}{1+\exp(-\theta x)}$, where θ is a positive number controlling the ramp of $l(x)$ (we use $\theta = 100$).

For the dimension of the latent factor, in our preliminary experiments we observe that the performance is not sensitive to it as long as it is not too small. In this study, we simply set $k_c = 20$ and $k_d = 20$. Other parameters, such as the learning rate, are selected by cross-validation.

5.3 Results and Discussions

The relative weight of source domain data w.r.t the target domain data controls how much the source domain affect the target domain. It is very important, since it is directly affect the efficiency of the knowledge transfer. For example, the low weight will impede the knowledge transfer no matter how close the two domains are.

We evaluate the effects of relative weights of the source

Data set	Number of examples	Number of Preference Pairs	Overlapped Features	Dedicated Features
S0	50,121	325,684	67	121
T1	5,112	26,534	67	81
T2	5,087	25,332	67	93
T3	5,124	26,898	67	76

Table 1: Data summary for one source domain and three target domains.

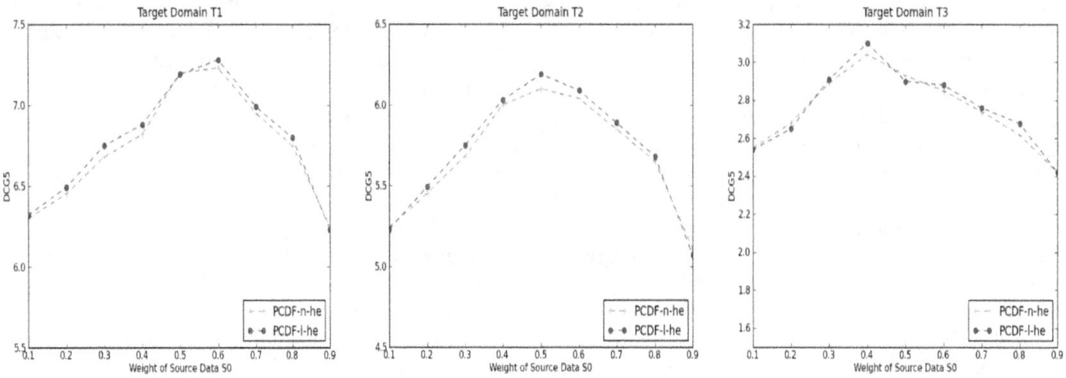

Figure 4: The effects of relative weights of source domain data on DCG5 performance.

domain data for PCDF-n-he and PCDF-l-he algorithms to illustrate this important aspect. Figure 4 shows The effects of relative weights of source domain data on DCG5 performance for all three target domains. From Figure 4, we observe that approximately the algorithms perform best at weight 0.6 for target domain T1, weight 0.5 for target domain T2, and weight 0.4 for target domain T3. The results implies that the T1 is the closest to the source domain, T2 is the second closest one, and T3 is the third closest one. This is consistent with our domain knowledge about the four domains. Note that it is flexible for PCDF algorithms to adopt the optimal relative weights that can be decided by cross-validation.

The DCG5 and DCG1 comparisons of the ten algorithms are shown in Figure 5 and Figure 6. From Figure 5 and Figure 6, we observe the following interesting facts:

- TD performs worst in all settings. This is due to insufficient training data for the target domains. This confirms the basic motivation of transfer ranking - to improve poor ranking performance in domains with insufficient training data.
- Overall PCDF-l-he performs best and PCDF-n-he performs second. This shows that PCDF can effectively catch domain correlations in both overlapped and heterogeneous feature spaces to improve learning in the target domain.
- PCDF-n-he and PCDF-l-he performs better than RCDF-n-he and RCDF-l-he. The possible reason is that PCDF catch correlations from preference orders, which matters more for ranking applications than absolute scores.
- PCDF-n-he and PCDF-l-he performs better than PCDF-n-ho and PCDF-l-ho, since PCDF-n-ho and PCDF-l-ho can use only features in the overlapped space and misses the knowledge transfer in the heterogenous feature spaces.
- PCDF-n-ho and PCDF-l-ho performs better than SC-ho and MTFL-ho. This shows that PCDF helps not only common knowledge learning cross heterogeneous feature spaces, but also in the same feature space, i.e., PCDF also provide an effective homogeneous transfer ranking model.
- MTFL algorithm performs better than SC algorithms. The possible reason for this is that as a supervised learning algorithm, MTFL learns the more informative latent features by making use of label information.
- SC-he does not perform better than SC-ho, even SC-he uses both overlapped features and heterogeneous features. This implies that simply treating one domain's dedicated features in another domain as missing values cannot effectively catch the the heterogeneous feature correlation.
- Overall, the L1 regularization algorithms performs better than L2 regularization algorithms. This shows that the choice of the regularization functions could have significant effects on the performance and hence, it is desirable for an algorithm to be flexible to adopt different regularization functions.

6. CONCLUSIONS

In this paper, we propose a novel probabilistic model, PCDF, for heterogeneous transfer ranking. The proposed model learns latent factors for multi-domain data in partially-overlapped heterogeneous feature spaces. It is capable of learning homogeneous feature correlation, heterogeneous feature correlation, and pairwise preference correlation for cross-domain knowledge transfer. We also derive two PCDF variations to address two important special cases. Under the PCDF model, we derive a stochastic gradient based algorithm, which facilitates distributed optimization and is flex-

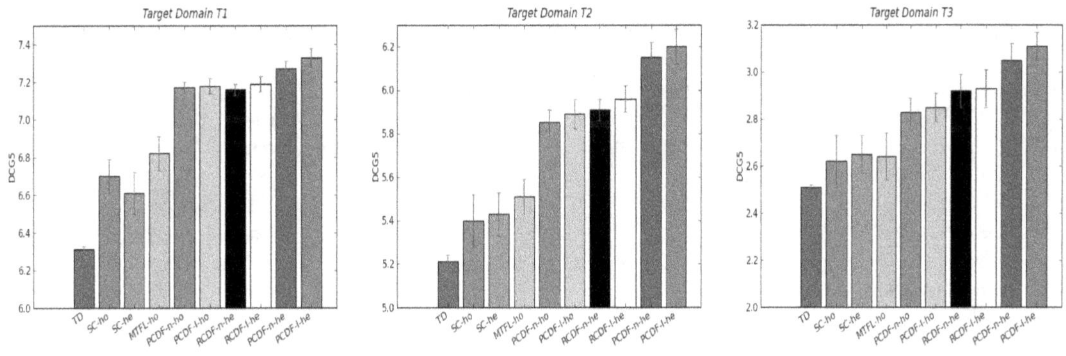

Figure 5: DCG5 comparisons of ten algorithms on the three target domains.

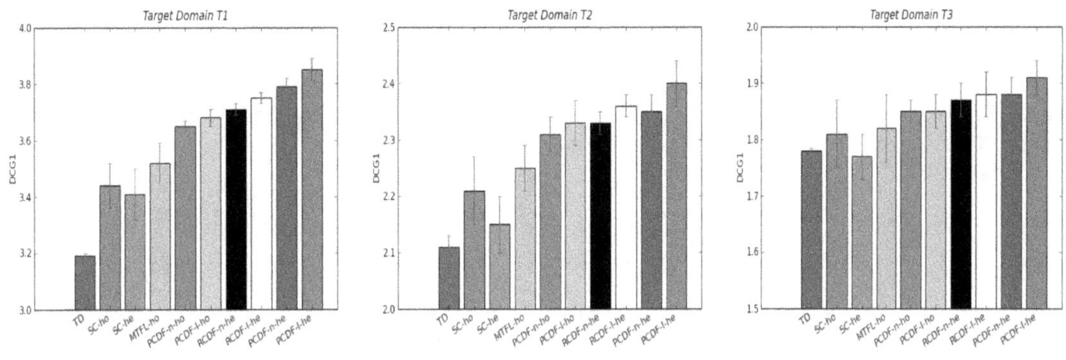

Figure 6: DCG1 comparisons of ten algorithms on the three target domains.

ible to adopt different loss functions and regularization functions to accommodate different data distributions . The extensive experiments on real Web search data sets demonstrate the effectiveness PCDF model and algorithms.

7. REFERENCES

[1] R. Ando and T. Zhang. A high-performance semi-supervised learning method for text chunking. In *Proceedings of the 43rd Annual Meeting on Association for Computational Linguistics*, pages 1–9. Association for Computational Linguistics Morristown, NJ, USA, 2005.

[2] A. Argyriou, T. Evgeniou, and M. Pontil. Multi-task feature learning. In *Advances in Neural Information Processing Systems: Proceedings of the 2006 Conference*, page 41. MIT Press, 2007.

[3] A. Argyriou, C. Micchelli, M. Pontil, and Y. Ying. A spectral regularization framework for multi-task structure learning. *Advances in Neural Information Processing Systems*, 20, 2008.

[4] S. Bickel, M. Brückner, and T. Scheffer. Discriminative learning for differing training and test distributions. In *Proceedings of the 24th international conference on Machine learning*, pages 81–88. ACM New York, NY, USA, 2007.

[5] J. Blitzer, K. Crammer, A. Kulesza, F. Pereira, and J. Wortman. Learning bounds for domain adaptation. *Advances in Neural Information Processing Systems*, 20, 2008.

[6] J. Blitzer, R. McDonald, and F. Pereira. Domain adaptation with structural correspondence learning. In *Proceedings of the Empirical Methods in Natural Language Processing (EMNLP)*, 2006.

[7] A. Blum and T. Mitchell. Combining labeled and unlabeled data with co-training. In *Proceedings of the eleventh annual conference on Computational learning theory*, COLT' 98, pages 92–100, 1998.

[8] E. Bonilla, K. Chai, and C. Williams. Multi-task gaussian process prediction. *Advances in Neural Information Processing Systems*, 20:153–160.

[9] C. Burges, T. Shaked, E. Renshaw, A. Lazier, M. Deeds, N. Hamilton, and G. Hullender. Learning to rank using gradient descent. In *Proceedings of the 22nd International Conference on Machine learning*, 2005.

[10] Z. Cao, T. Qin, T.-Y. Liu, M.-F. Tsai, and H. Li. Learning to rank: from pairwise approach to listwise approach. In *ICML '07*, pages 129–136, New York, NY, USA, 2007. ACM.

[11] D. Chen, J. Yan, G. Wang, Y. Xiong, W. Fan, and Z. Chen. TransRank: A Novel Algorithm for Transfer of Rank Learning. In *IEEE ICDM Workshops*, 2008.

[12] M. Collins, S. Dasgupta, and R. Reina. A generalizaionof principal component analysis to the exponential family. In *NIPS'01*, 2001.

[13] C. Cortes, M. Mohri, and A. Rastogi. Magnitude-preserving ranking algorithms. In *Proceedings of the 24th ICML*, 2007.

[14] W. Dai, G. Xue, Q. Yang, and Y. Yu. Co-clustering based classification for out-of-domain documents. In *Proceedings of the 13th ACM SIGKDD international conference on Knowledge discovery and data mining*, pages 210–219. ACM New York, NY, USA, 2007.

[15] W. Dai, Q. Yang, G. Xue, and Y. Yu. Boosting for transfer learning. In *Proceedings of the 24th international conference on Machine learning*, pages 193–200. ACM New York, NY, USA, 2007.

[16] H. Daume. Frustratingly easy domain adaptation. In *Annual meeting-association for computational linguistics*, volume 45, page 256, 2007.

[17] H. Daume III and D. Marcu. Domain adaptation for statistical classifiers. *Journal of Artificial Intelligence Research*, 26:101–126, 2006.

[18] T. Evgeniou and M. Pontil. Regularized multi-task learning. In *Proceedings of the tenth ACM SIGKDD international conference on Knowledge discovery and data mining*, pages 109–117. ACM New York, NY, USA, 2004.

[19] Y. Freund, R. Iyer, R. Schapire, and Y. Singer. An efficient boosting algorithm for combining preferences. In *Proceedings of the Fifteenth International Conference on Machine Learning*, 1998.

[20] J. Friedman. Greedy function approximation: a gradient boosting machine. *Annals of Statistics*, pages 1189–1232, 2001.

[21] J. Gao, Q. Wu, C. Burges, K. Svore, Y. Su, N. Khan, S. Shah, and H. Zhou. Model adaptation via model interpolation and boosting for web search ranking. In *Proceedings of conference on Empirical Methods in Natural Language Processing*, 2009.

[22] J. Guiver and E. Snelson. Learning to rank with SoftRank and Gaussian processes. In *Proceedings of the 31st annual international ACM SIGIR conference on Research and development in information retrieval*, 2008.

[23] M. Harel and S. Mannor. Learning from multiple outlooks. In L. Getoor and T. Scheffer, editors, *Proceedings of the 28th International Conference on Machine Learning (ICML-11)*, ICML '11, pages 401–408, New York, NY, USA, June 2011. ACM.

[24] J. He and R. Lawrence. A graph-based framework for multi-task multi-view learning. In L. Getoor and T. Scheffer, editors, *Proceedings of the 28th International Conference on Machine Learning (ICML-11)*, ICML '11, pages 25–32, New York, NY, USA, June 2011. ACM.

[25] J. Huang, A. Smola, A. Gretton, K. Borgwardt, and B. Scholkopf. Correcting sample selection bias by unlabeled data. *Advances in neural information processing systems*, 19:601, 2007.

[26] J. Jiang and C. Zhai. Instance weighting for domain adaptation in NLP. In *Annual meeting-assosciation for computational linguistics*, volume 45, page 264, 2007.

[27] T. Joachims. Optimizing search engines using clickthrough data. In *Proceedings of ACM SIGKDD*, 2002.

[28] N. Lawrence and J. Platt. Learning to learn with the informative vector machine. In *Proceedings of the twenty-first international conference on Machine learning*. ACM New York, NY, USA, 2004.

[29] H. Lee, A. Battle, R. Raina, and A. Y. Ng. Efficient sparse coding algorithms. In *In NIPS*, pages 801–808. NIPS, 2007.

[30] S. Lee, V. Chatalbashev, D. Vickrey, and D. Koller. Learning a meta-level prior for feature relevance from multiple related tasks. In *Proceedings of the 24th international conference on Machine learning*, pages 489–496. ACM New York, NY, USA, 2007.

[31] X. Liao, Y. Xue, and L. Carin. Logistic regression with an auxiliary data source. In *MACHINE LEARNING-INTERNATIONAL WORKSHOP THEN CONFERENCE-*, volume 22, page 505, 2005.

[32] P. Luo, F. Zhuang, H. Xiong, Y. Xiong, and Q. He. Transfer learning from multiple source domains via consensus regularization. In *CIKM '08: Proceeding of the 17th ACM conference on Information and knowledge management*, pages 103–112, New York, NY, USA, 2008. ACM.

[33] R. Raina, A. Battle, H. Lee, B. Packer, and A. Ng. Self-taught learning: Transfer learning from unlabeled data. In *Proceedings of the 24th international conference on Machine learning*, pages 759–766. ACM New York, NY, USA, 2007.

[34] A. Schwaighofer, V. Tresp, and K. Yu. Learning Gaussian process kernels via hierarchical Bayes. *Advances in Neural Information Processing Systems*, 17:1209–1216, 2005.

[35] M. Sugiyama, S. Nakajima, H. Kashima, P. von Bunau, and M. Kawanabe. Direct importance estimation with model selection and its application to covariate shift adaptation. *Advances in Neural Information Processing Systems*, 20, 2008.

[36] B. Wang, J. Tang, W. Fan, S. Chen, Z. Yang, and Y. Liu. Heterogeneous cross domain ranking in latent space. In *Proceeding of the 18th ACM conference on Information and knowledge management*, CIKM '09, pages 987–996, 2009.

[37] C. Wang and S. Mahadevan. Heterogeneous domain adaptation using manifold alignment. In *IJCAI*, pages 1541–1546, 2011.

[38] J. Xu and H. Li. Adarank: a boosting algorithm for information retrieval. In *Proceedings of the 30th ACM SIGIR*, 2007.

[39] Q. Yang, Y. Chen, G.-R. Xue, W. Dai, and Y. Yu. Heterogeneous transfer learning for image clustering via the social web. ACL '09, pages 1–9, 2009.

[40] H. Zha, Z. Zheng, H. Fu, and G. Sun. Incorporating query difference for learning retrieval functions in world wide web search. In *Proceedings of the 15th ACM CIKM conference*, 2006.

[41] Z. Zheng, K. Chen, G. Sun, and H. Zha. A regression framework for learning ranking functions using relative relevance judgments. In *SIGIR '07: Proceedings of the 30th annual international ACM SIGIR conference on Research and development in information retrieval*, pages 287–294, New York, NY, USA, 2007. ACM.

[42] M. Zinkevich, M. Weimer, A. Smola, and L. Li. Parallelized stochastic gradient descent. In J. Lafferty, C. K. I. Williams, J. Shawe-Taylor, R. Zemel, and A. Culotta, editors, *Advances in Neural Information Processing Systems 23*, pages 2595–2603, 2010.

Scalable Inference in Latent Variable Models

Amr Ahmed, Mohamed Aly, Joseph Gonzalez,* Shravan Narayanamurthy, Alexander Smola
Yahoo! Research, Santa Clara, CA, USA
{amahmed, aly, jegonzal, shravanm, smola}@yahoo-inc.com

ABSTRACT

Latent variable techniques are pivotal in tasks ranging from predicting user click patterns and targeting ads to organizing the news and managing user generated content. Latent variable techniques like topic modeling, clustering, and subspace estimation provide substantial insight into the latent structure of complex data with little or no external guidance making them ideal for reasoning about large-scale, rapidly evolving datasets. Unfortunately, due to the data dependencies and global state introduced by latent variables and the iterative nature of latent variable inference, latent-variable techniques are often prohibitively expensive to apply to large-scale, streaming datasets.

In this paper we present a scalable parallel framework for efficient inference in latent variable models over streaming web-scale data. Our framework addresses three key challenges: 1) *synchronizing the global state* which includes global latent variables (e.g., cluster centers and dictionaries); 2) *efficiently storing and retrieving the large local state* which includes the data-points and their corresponding latent variables (e.g., cluster membership); and 3) *sequentially incorporating streaming data* (e.g., the news). We address these challenges by introducing: 1) a novel delta-based aggregation system with a bandwidth-efficient communication protocol; 2) schedule-aware out-of-core storage; and 3) approximate forward sampling to rapidly incorporate new data. We demonstrate state-of-the-art performance of our framework by easily tackling datasets two orders of magnitude larger than those addressed by the current state-of-the-art. Furthermore, we provide an optimized and easily customizable open-source implementation of the framework [1].

Categories and Subject Descriptors

G.3 [**Probability And Statistics**]: Statistical Computing

General Terms

Algorithms, Experimentation, Performance

Keywords

Inference, Graphical Models, Large-scale Systems, Latent Models.

1. INTRODUCTION

In many cases, we are interested in reasoning about the underlying latent causes that give rise to the data we observe. For instance, when dealing with users we may want to elicit the underlying intents and interests that govern their activity and friendship patterns. Alternatively, we might want to discover the underlying topics of discussions on various pages across the web. More generally we may want to assign meaning to linked and interacting objects such as webpages, named entities, users, and their behavior.

Latent variable models have become an indispensable tool for reasoning about the latent causes that give rise to data in tasks ranging from text modeling [18, 3, 6] to bioinformatics [8, 21]. The popularity of latent variable models stems from their ability to easily encode rich structured priors and then infer latent properties of the data without requiring access to costly labels or editorial feedback.

Latent variable models are constructed by introducing unobserved (latent) variables which help explain the observed data and then coupling these latent variables (often by introducing additional latent variables) to capture the underlying problem structure. For example, in the mixture of Gaussians model there are two sets of latent variables. The first denotes the cluster membership of each data point while the second describes the shape and position of the Gaussian clusters and introduces dependencies between the data-points.

Latent variable inference is the process of estimating the most likely assignment (or posterior distribution) of all the latent variables. In the context of the mixture of Gaussians model, latent variable inference is the process of estimating the latent membership of each data-point as well as the center and shape of each cluster. Inference in latent variable models is typically computationally expensive, often requiring the solution to hard combinatorial search problems. As a consequence approximate inference algorithms are typically employed. Unfortunately, even approximate inference algorithms can be costly, requiring iterative transformations of the latent variable assignments (i.e., transforming large amounts of program state).

In most web-scale settings, data is not collected once and then processed offline; instead, data arrives continuously and

*Visiting on internship from CMU, Department of Machine Learning, Pittsburgh PA; jegonzal@cs.cmu.edu
[1] Available at https://github.com/shravanmn/Yahoo_LDA

Permission to make digital or hard copies of all or part of this work for personal or classroom use is granted without fee provided that copies are not made or distributed for profit or commercial advantage and that copies bear this notice and the full citation on the first page. To copy otherwise, to republish, to post on servers or to redistribute to lists, requires prior specific permission and/or a fee.
WSDM'12, February 8–12, 2012, Seattle, Washington, USA.
Copyright 2012 ACM 978-1-4503-0747-5/12/02 ...$10.00.

must be processed online and in real-time. The online setting presents unique challenges for latent variable models. As new data arrives new latent variables are introduced extending the model and requiring both the ability to quickly infer the values (or distributions) of the newly introduced latent variables as well as their effect on the existing model.

As a result of the computational cost of inference, the need to store and manage a massive amount of model state, and the added complexity of online data-processing, latent variable models are often abandoned in web-scale settings. However, [18] demonstrated that by exploiting massive scale parallelism through careful system engineering and the appropriate statistical approximations it is possible to apply latent variable techniques to web-scale problems.

In this paper we generalize the work of [18] by identifying the three principal challenges (Section 2) that must be addressed when applying any latent variable technique to web-scale problems. We then provide a general framework (Section 3) for addressing these challenges in a wide range of latent-variable models. Our general framework substantially extends [18] by introducing:

- A schedule aware disk-based cache for local (per-data) latent variables.
- A significantly improved general communications structure for asynchronously updating global variables.
- An efficient online algorithm for latent variable inference in streaming data.
- A new mechanism for fault-tolerance and fast recovery for large distributed global state.

We apply our framework (Section 4) to web-scale latent variable problems that are several order of magnitude larger than the largest problems previously tackled by [18]. To the best of our knowledge these are the largest to date reported estimation results for latent variable models.

Additionally, we provide an open-source implementation of our framework at `https://github.com/shravanmn/Yahoo_LDA`. Our code base is easily customizable, allowing researchers and engineers to easily encode new graphicals model and apply them on web-scale data sets.

2. LATENT VARIABLE MODELS

Graphical models provide a convenient language for describing latent variable models and so we will introduce some basic graphical model terminology. Graphical models encode probability distributions over large sets of random variables as a graph in which vertices correspond to random variables, both observed and unobserved, and edges encode dependencies. For simplicity we focus on *directed* graphical models (i.e., Bayesian networks), however the techniques we present can be easily applied to undirected models.

We can represent the mixture of Gaussians latent variable model as the directed graphical model:

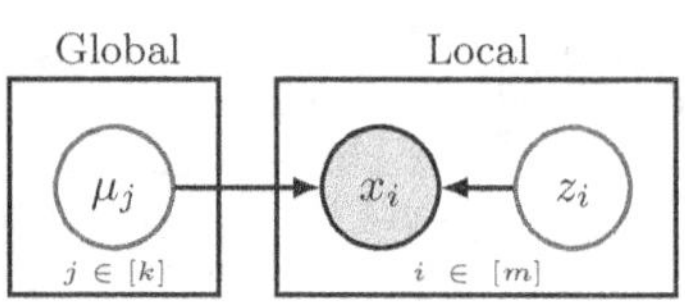

for m data points x_i. For each data point we introduce an unobserved latent variable z_i. In addition we introduce latent variables μ_j corresponding to the k cluster centers. We denote observed variables with shaded circles and unobserved (latent) variables with clear circles.

The boxes, referred to as *plates*, describe repeated (sets of) variables. For example, while there is only one circle μ_i the plate indicates that there are in fact k variables $\{\mu_1, \ldots, \mu_k\}$ all of which are connected to each of the $\{x_1, \ldots, x_m\}$. Note that each z_i is connected only to the corresponding x_i.

We have labeled the plates **Global** and **Local** to denote two general classes of latent variables. The global latent variables are those latent variables that are not directly associated with the data. The number of global latent variables is fixed or slowly increasing with the size of the dataset. Alternatively, the local latent variables are directly associated with each new record and grow directly with the dataset. There are often billions of local latent variables in web-scale problems.

The joint probability distribution for the mixture of Gaussian latent variable model is then given by:

$$\mathbf{P}(\{x_i\}_{i=1}^m, \{z_i\}_{i=1}^m, \{\mu_j\}_{j=1}^k) = \left(\prod_{j=1}^k \mathbf{P}(\mu_j)\right) \prod_{i=1}^m \mathbf{P}(z_i)\mathbf{P}(x_i \mid z_i, \{\mu_j\}_{j=1}^k)$$

where $\mathbf{P}(\mu_j)$ is the prior for each cluster center, $\mathbf{P}(z_i)$ is the latent cluster membership prior for each data-point, and $\mathbf{P}(x_i \mid z_i, \{\mu_j\}_{j=1}^k)$ is the probability of each data point given its cluster membership and the cluster centers.

Inference in the mixture of Gaussian model estimates the posterior conditional $\mathbf{P}(\{z_i\}_{i=1}^m, \{\mu_j\}_{j=1}^k \mid \{x_i\}_{i=1}^m)$ (or in many cases just the maximizing assignments). One of the most widely used interference technique is Gibbs sampling introduced by[9]. The Gibbs sampler iterates over the sets of latent variables, drawing one variable, or a small tractable subset of variables, at a time while keeping the remainder fixed. In the case of a Gaussian mixture model we would alternate between sampling:

$$\{\mu_j\}_{j=1}^k \sim \mathbf{P}(\{\mu_j\}_{j=1}^k \mid \{z_i\}_{i=1}^m, \{x_i\}_{i=1}^m) \quad (1)$$

$$\{z_i\}_{i=1}^m \sim \mathbf{P}(\{z_i\}_{i=1}^m \mid \{\mu_j\}_{j=1}^k \{x_i\}_{i=1}^m) \quad (2)$$

This process is *iterated a significant number of times* (depending on the complexity of the statistical model) until a sample that is approximately independent of the initial conditions can be drawn. Due to its popularity, performance, and general applicability we will focus on Gibbs sampling in this paper. However, many other approximate inference algorithm share similar computational patterns and would likely also benefit from the techniques discussed here.

In many cases the convergence of the Gibbs sampler can be greatly accelerated by analytically eliminating (collapsing) a subset of the latent variables. For example, if the normal inverse Wishart prior is placed on the Gaussian clusters, then we can analytically eliminate $\{\mu_j\}_{j=1}^k$ to construct the conditional $\mathbf{P}(z_i \mid z_{-i}, \{x_i\}_{i=1}^m)$ which couples each latent variable z_i with all the remaining latent variables z_{-i}. It is important to note that in most cases each variable z_i only depends on the remaining variable through sufficient statistics (e.g., the mean and variances). In this paper we will focus on the so called collapsed Gibbs sampler.

We now describe the three key challenges: 1) synchronizing the global state (e.g., $\{\mu_j\}_{j=1}^k$ or the sufficient statistics in the collapsed model); 2) efficiently storing and retrieving the large local state (e.g., $\{z_i\}_{i=1}^m$), and 3) sequentially incorporating streaming data (e.g., increasing (x_{m+1}, z_{m+1})).

2.1 Managing A Massive Local State

As discussed earlier the local state consists of the actual data and any latent variables directly associated with each data record (e.g., the data-points x_i and cluster memberships z_i). In web-scale applications the local state can be very large. For example, if we apply the popular LDA latent variable model to a web-scale text corpus with billions of documents we can end up facing in the orders of 10^{11} to 10^{12} local variables z_i (one for each unique word on each web-page) and corresponding textual data x_i. It is clearly infeasible to retain this amount of data in memory even on a very large cluster.

To make matters worse we will need to *repeatedly* read and *modify* the local latent variables z_i as we run our collapsed Gibbs sampler. At the same time our system must be robust to node failure which could lead to a partial loss of the local state z_i.

2.2 Synchronizing Global State

While the local state can be naturally partitioned over a large collection of distributed machines, the global state (e.g., the latent cluster center $\{\mu_j\}_{j=1}^k$ or the sufficient statistics in the collapsed modle) both depends on the assignments to the local variables. For example, in the mixture of Gaussians model, in order to estimate the value of each μ_j we need to know the location of all the datapoints x_i for which $z_i = j$ (i.e., the points assigned to cluster j). More generally, we will need to be able to estimate sufficient statistics over the entire cluster even as the values of the latent variables are changing and potentially new data is being introduced.

Even worse, as the Gibbs sampler redraws each local latent variable it will need access to the latest global variables (or the latests global sufficient statistics in the case of the collapsed Gibbs sampler). After each local variable is updated the global sufficient statistics and all other nodes on the cluster will need to be notified of the resulting change in the global statistics.

An effective solution to address these problem is to make local copies of the global variable and to keep these copies synchronized. Such a strategy is pursued e.g. by [18, 13, 17] using both synchronous and asynchronous communication patterns for reconciling local copies.

Matters are rather more complex whenever the global state is large. In this case aggressive synchronization may not be easily possible. In some cases, the global state may even be too large to be locally cached on a single machine. We will discuss both issues in the next section and show how a 'star of stars' communication architecture, paired with consistent hashing [12], and effective message ordering can be used to ensure good synchronization.

A final problem arises from the fact that modern microprocessors have many cores but the memory footprint of the models makes it impossible to store copies for each core separately. This requires that several cores access a shared state simultaneously. While read access is not a problem, simultaneous write access can lead to race conditions and correspondingly to unpredictable (and possibly wrong) state of the estimator. One means of dealing with this situation is to allow for diverging states and to decouple sampling from the application of the changes, both locally within a computer and between computers.

2.3 Online Data with Temporal Structure

A third problem arises when there is a significant sequential order inherent in the data which couples a lengthy chain of random variables. This problem is exacerbated whenever we wish to operate the system in a realtime setting where data is received continuously and needs to be annotated.

Example 1 (Latent Markov Chain) *Assume that a latent state (e.g. the distribution of words over topics, the interests of a user) exists that allows us to annotate a user's actions efficiently. Moreover assume that this latent change is allowed to change (smoothly) over time. Such a model can be represented as follows:*

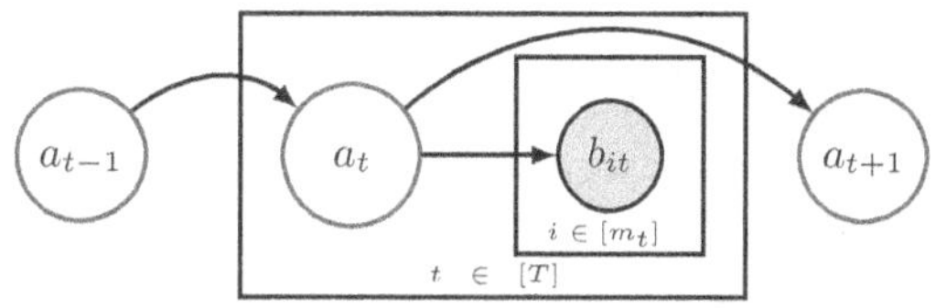

Here we observe b whereas a is latent and can only be inferred indirectly by inverting the 'emissions' model.

Techniques for dealing with such problems can be found in the use Sequential Monte Carlo estimation and in the approximation of using only a single particle whenever the state space is too large to perform proper particle filtering.

3. GENERAL FRAMEWORK

In the following we discuss a set of general techniques for obtaining efficient parallel algorithms for inference in web-scale latent variable models. These techniques address the core challenges presented in the previous section. Most of the discussion will be devoted to the synchronization of global variables and the associated systems aspects.

3.1 Global variables on a single machine

We begin by discussing the role of approximation in exposing parallelsim in collapsed Gibbs sampling. Recall that the uncollapsed Gibbs sampler typically alternates between sampling global (Eq. (1)) and local (Eq. (2)) latent variables. Because all the local variables are typically conditionally independent given the global variables (and vice versa), we can construct the following parallelization:

Fix all $\{z_i\}_{i=1}^m$
for all $j \in [k]$ **parallel do**
    Sample $\mu_j \sim \mathbf{P}(\mu_j \mid \{z_i\}_{i=1}^m, \{x_i\}_{i=1}^m)$
end for
Fix $\{\mu_j\}_{j=1}^k$.
for all $i \in [m]$ **parallel do**
    Sample $z_i \sim \mathbf{P}(z_i \mid \{\mu_j\}_{j=1}^k \{x_i\}_{i=1}^m)$.
end for

While this approach is both statistically sound and exposes considerable parallelism, especially when m and k are large, it does not leverage the greatly accelerated mixing [11] of the collapsed Gibbs sampler. The problem is that in this case the random variables $\{z_i\}_{i=1}^m$ are no longer independent and we obtain the following *sequential* sampling algorithm:

```
for all i ∈ [m] do
    Sample z_i ~ P(z_i | z_{-i}, {x_i}_{i=1}^m)
end forv
```

The above algorithm unfortunately is not amenable to multicore parallelization since only one variable may be changed at a time. However, if we are willing to admit a slight approximation we may parallelize this step in analogy to [15, 18, 5], simply by executing it for different z_i on several cores simultaneously:

```
Allocate a task pool T of m tasks
while T not empty do
    if core available then
        Remove i from T and draw:
            z_i ~ P(z_i | z_{-i}, {x_i}_{i=1}^m)
        Update sufficient statistics for {z_i}_{i=1}^m.
    end if
end while
```

Clearly the above is an approximation since z_i is drawn using partially stale sufficient statistics. However, whenever we have millions of z_i, the error in using a slightly stale distribution is negligible: the number of cores is small relative to the number of random variables. The only locking that occurs in this context is that writes to the sufficient statistics (as executed by an update thread) must not occur simultaneously as reads (as executed by the sampling threads). This, however, is much more benign since all but one thread only require read locks.

3.2 Global variables between machines

In principle, the same design decisions that guided the single core parallelism are also applicable to systems of many machines. However, what is a cheap in-memory operation for a multicore system becomes an excessively expensive operation when carried out across the network. Instead, we borrow an idea from dual decomposition methods [4] — we make local copies of the global variables and constrain the local copies to be consistent. The graph below explains the basic idea:

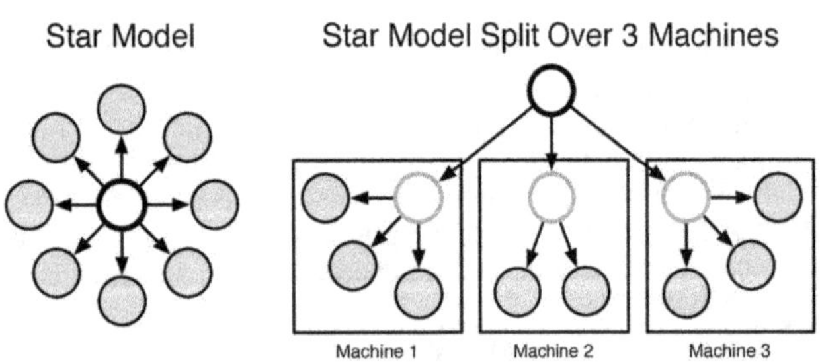

On the left we have a dependency structure with a shared global variable. On the right we inserted local copies (the clear vertices inside each box) per machine (the box) which are then synchronized with the original global variable. Note that this approach applies hierarchically whenever we face additional communications boundaries, e.g. when keeping sets of machines on different switches (or racks) synchronized.

We can actually express this transformed model in the context of a modified version of the original graphical model:

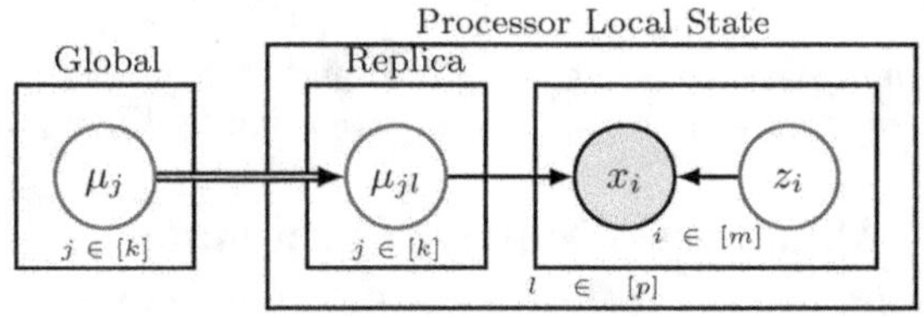

Here μ_{jl} denotes the *local* copy of the global variable μ_j. Note that our approach is quite different from [17] despite the similar structure. The key difference is that [17] assume that there exists a hierarchical generative process which led to divergent copies of the same random variable between different machines. In other words, they assume that the partitioning between machines is meaningful. Quite contrary to that, we simply assume that the variables may go out of sync due to insufficiently frequent communication between the machines. In other words, after complete synchronization we expect *equality* rather than just similarity between the global variable and its per-machine copies. This is made explicit by the double arrow connecting μ_j and μ_{jl}. To make the above concept practical we need to specify a) detailed update equations, b) a effective means of distributing global variables across many machines and c) a schedule to avoid communications overhead.

3.3 Asynchronous Delta Aggregation

The message passing system described by [18] suffers from high latency as a result of one sided communication through *memcached* (a distributed key-value store). In particular rather than using server-side transactional consistency, each node follows a remote lock-request-update-send-unlock protocol for each transaction. This introduces considerable latency since each of the lock, request, send, and unlock operations requires round-trip communication between the updating node and the hosting node. Furthermore, since many distributed key-value stores lack server-side processing, these problems cannot be addressed within the framework of [18] making it especially unsuitable for efficient synchronization of global state.

In addition the protocol described by [18] updates the global value on the client machine and then pushes the new global value back to the hosting machine. This leads to the need to potentially push more data than was changed in the update. Ideally, we would like to push only revisions to the global value (i.e., changes in components of the mean vector rather than the entire mean vector). With appropriate server-side processing we would like to be able to aggregate client side revisions before modifying the server-state.

We now present a substantially improved protocol which is over an order of magnitude faster in our experiments. Our new protocol applies whenever the global data μ_j is an element of an algebraic ring. Specifically we require that μ_j is closed under 'addition' and that an 'inverse' element exists. These conditions are satisfied for common operations like addition/subtraction in $\mathbb{R}$ $(+, \mathbb{R})$ or for multiplication/division in $\mathbb{R}^+$ $(\cdot, \mathbb{R}^+)$ allowing us to easily express the standard multiplicative or additive updates to s global sufficient statistic or latent variable estimates.

The algorithm below summarizes how the algebraic ring can be used to collect a change (δ) from a client, incorporate the change into the master version on the server node, and then update the clients to the change in the master value. We denote by μ_j the master value of the global variable. Moreover, μ_{jl} denotes the *local* copy of μ_j on machine l.

For the moment simply assume that there exists some easily identifiable server containing μ_j. Then the $(+, \mathbb{R})$ ring yields:

Initialization
for all $j \in [k], l \in [p]$ **do**
  $\mu_{jl}^{\text{old}} \leftarrow \mu_{jl} \leftarrow \mu_j$
  $s_{jl} \leftarrow$ FALSE (sent bit)
end for

ClientSend(l)
for all j **do**
  Acquire lock for s_{jl}
  if $s_{jl} =$ FALSE **then**
    Acquire lock for μ_{jl}
    Compute local change $\delta \leftarrow \mu_{jl} - \mu_{jl}^{\text{old}}$
    Release lock for μ_{jl}
    Server(j, l, δ)
    $s_{jl} \leftarrow$ TRUE (we sent a message)
    $\mu_{jl}^{\text{old}} \leftarrow \mu_{jl}^{\text{old}} + \delta$ (locally commit changes)
  end if
  Release lock for s_{jl}
end for

ClientReceive(j, l, μ^{new})
Acquire lock for s_{jl}
$s_{jl} \leftarrow$ FALSE (we received data)
Set write lock for b_{jl}
$\mu_{jl} \leftarrow \mu_{jl} + \mu^{\text{new}} - \mu_{jl}^{\text{old}}$ (get global changes)
$\mu_{jl}^{\text{old}} \leftarrow \mu^{\text{new}}$ (we are up to date)
Release write lock for μ_{jl} and s_{jl}

Server(j, l, δ) (buffered input)
$\mu_j \leftarrow \mu_j + \delta$
ClientReceive(j, l, μ_j)

Initially, the local copies and global state are set to the same values. Each client l cycles through its set of local copies and determines how much has changed locally since the previous communication round. It then transmits this information to a server and stores a backup of the local estimate. A sent bit s_{jl} ensures that no more than one message is 'in flight' from client to server. Note that the call to the server is *non blocking*, that is, we need not wait for the server to process the message. This fact is vital in designing synchronization algorithms which are bandwidth limited rather than latency limited (for comparison, [18] requires 4 TCP/IP roundtrips per variable).

The server incorporates the changes into its global state. This can be done efficiently since it only receives δ containing the change in state. Finally, it triggers a return message to the client. To see why the updates make sense assume for a moment that nothing changed after the client sent its changes: in this case we have $\mu_{jl}^{\text{old}} = \mu_{jl}$. Moreover, μ_j will contain all changes that locally occurred on μ_{jl} *and* all changes from other copies. Hence the update $\mu_{jl}^{\text{old}} \leftarrow \mu^{\text{new}}$ is valid. The update of μ_{jl} ensures that any local changes that might have occurred in the meantime are recorded and will be transmitted at the next step.

This approach dramatically reduces latency since the post to the server is non-blocking and the client is able to proceed processing using the freshly updated local copy. When the server completes the transaction it captures any additional changes made by other machines and then asynchronously notifies the other nodes in the cluster again with a non-blocking call. Because transactions are additive, they can be merged at bottlenecks in the network (e.g., switches) to reduce the necessary bandwidth between racks. Finally, for very large μ_j for which only small parts are changing, we need only send 'diffs' further reducing the bandwidth requirements.

3.4 Distribution and Scheduling

Now that we established *how* local copies of a global variable are kept synchronized we need to establish how to distribute the global copies over several servers: given p clients and k global variables the above algorithms creates $O(kp)$ traffic. If we select p servers (conveniently the same machines as the clients) we arrive at $O(k)$ traffic per server, provided that we are able to distribute the global variables uniformly over all servers. The latter is achieved by consistent hashing [12], i.e. by selecting server

$$s(j) = \underset{s \in \{1,\ldots,p\}}{\text{argmin}} \ \text{hash(s, j)}. \quad (3)$$

The advantage of (3) is that it does not require any additional storage to record the mapping of variables to servers. In expectation each server stores $\frac{k}{p}$ global variables. Since the assignment is randomized we can apply Chernoff bounds to show that with probability at least $1 - \gamma$ no machine receives more than $k/p + \sqrt{k}\,(\log p - \log \gamma)$. This follows from bounding the number of variables per server and by taking the union bound over p servers.

This strategy works well for up to $p = 100$ machines. At this point a secondary inefficiency becomes significant: Since each client is communicating with each server, it means that the amount of data exchanged between any pair of machines is $O(k/p)$. This means that the data *rate* between two machines *decreases* with $O(p^{-1})$ and that moreover the number of open network connections per machine increases with $O(p)$. Neither is good if we want to keep the communications overhead at a minimum (e.g. minimum packet size, collision avoidance, and sockets all contribute to a decreased efficiency as the rate decreases). In fact, for 1000 machines this overhead is quite substantial, hence the naive consistent hashing protocol requires an extension.

The key insight for improvement is that the synchronization occurs repeatedly and that we know for each machine which messages require sending beforehand. We therefore arrange the transmission of the messages in the synchronization algorithm of Section 3.3 such that we only communicate with one machine at a time. Consequently each client needs to keep only one connection to a server open at a time and we can transmit all data to be sent to this particular server jointly.

Unfortunately, this approach also has a subtle flaw: while we reduced the number of connections from p^2 to p, we obtain a rather nonuniform distribution in terms of the number of connections that each server has. For instance, if each client opens connections in a (different) random order, it follows that the open connections at any time are given by p draws with replacement from a set of p alternatives. Hence the probability of not receiving any data at all is given by $(1 - p^{-1})^p \approx e^{-1}$ per server. This is clearly inefficient — the problem is that we opened connections to *too few* servers. The solution is to communicate with $r \ll p$ servers simultaneously while selecting them in a random order.

RandomOrder(l, p)
for $i = 1$ **to** p **do**

```
    f[i] = crypt(i, range = p, key = l)
end for
return f
```

The above algorithm achieves precisely that by means of cryptography [14], e.g. via Feistel ciphers. The communication schedule for synchronization then works as follows:

```
ClientSend(l, p)
Generate s(j) for all j (compute machine keys)
Sort j into sets S_m with s(j) = m if j ∈ S_m.
f = RandomOrder(l, p)
for i = 1 to p step r do
    Variable pool S = ∪_{v=i}^{i+r-1} S_{f[v]}
    for all w ∈ S do
        Perform communication with server as before.
    end for
end for
```

The main modification to the plain communication algorithm is that we now synchronize the global variables in a specific prescribed order which ensures that at any given time we only open r random connections per machine. This ensures that we have fewer idle servers.

Lemma 1 *The efficiency (as measured by the expected proportion of bandwidth used) of communicating with r machines at a time is bounded in the limit of large p by:*

$$1 - e^{-r} \sum_{i=0}^{r} \left[1 - \frac{i}{r}\right] \frac{r^i}{i!} \leq \text{Eff} \leq 1 - e^{-r}$$

PROOF. The data flow is represented by a bipartite graph between p clients and p servers, where each client has r random connections to the set of servers. Randomness is assured by the random permutation over the order in which a given client connects to the servers, hence at any fixed instant in time the connectivity structure of each vertex is drawn iid from a uniform distribution over all servers. For any given server v the probability of not receiving any incoming edge is $\left(1 - \frac{1}{p}\right)^{pr} \rightarrow e^{-r}$. If each of the connected vertices receives data at full rate, this amounts to an efficiency of $1 - e^{-r}$. The maximally efficient communication order can be obtained by solving the optimal flow problem.

Now consider the model where the efficiency of the server is bounded by $\min(1, i/r)$. That is, the flow is linear in the number of incoming connections but never larger than the maximum flow. Using a Poisson approximation for the probability of receiving i incoming connections we see that $\mathbf{P}(i) = e^{-r} r^i / i!$ with expected number of incoming connections r. We can then compute the expected efficiency:

$$\begin{aligned}
\text{Eff} &\geq \sum_{i=0}^{\infty} \min\left(1, \frac{i}{r}\right) \mathbf{P}(i) = \sum_{i=0}^{\infty} \min\left(1, \frac{i}{r}\right) e^{-r} \frac{r^i}{i!} \\
&= e^{-r} \sum_{i=0}^{r} \frac{i}{r} \frac{r^i}{i!} + e^{-r} \sum_{i=r+1}^{\infty} \frac{r^i}{i!} \\
&= e^{-r} \sum_{i=0}^{r} \frac{i}{r} \frac{r^i}{i!} + 1 - e^{-r} \sum_{i=0}^{r} \frac{r^i}{i!} \\
&= 1 - e^{-r} \sum_{i=0}^{r} \left(1 - \frac{i}{r}\right) \frac{r^i}{i!} \qquad (4)
\end{aligned}$$

□

Plugging some numbers into the bounds obtained above shows that a small number of connections suffices to yield satisfactory efficiency:

r	1	2	3	4	5
lower bound	0.63	0.73	0.78	0.80	0.82
upper bound	0.63	0.86	0.95	0.98	0.99

3.5 Fault tolerance

An important issue in large distributed systems is fault tolerance. For instance, a job executed on 1000 machines lasting one day assumes that the mean time between failures should significantly exceed 3 years to make such experiments feasible without fault tolerance.

[18] were only able to provide a rather weak guarantee due to the fact that in case of a machine failure the entire global state needed to be regenerated from scratch. This is very costly. Instead, we take advantage of the fact that, unlike when using *memcached*, we are able to perform operations directly on the data store of the server. One fact that complicates matters is that whenever the global synchronization is executed it requires one full pass through the entire set of variables before all local copies are in sync. This can be costly since synchronization may take several minutes, thus making writing a checkpoint an exceedingly slow matter.

Instead we use the following strategy: at any given time when we want to compute a checkpoint we *halt* all communication and sampling and wait until the incoming message queues have been processed (this is easily satisfied by reaching a barrier). At this point each client and server simply write their state to the cloud file system (HadoopFS in our case). This means that we are able to checkpoint the distributed synchronized state. Recovery is simply possible by loading the state from file system.

3.6 Local variables and out of core storage

Quite often, evidence is associated with local latent variables. For instance, in topic models we may want to obtain a topic estimate for each word. This leads to a state space which typically exceeds the amount of RAM available. An option to deal with this issue is to store part of the latent state out of core and to stream evidence and latent variables from disk whenever they are required. This approach is effective since the typical schedule for the Gibbs sampler iterates over the variables in a fixed order. Consider the following variant of the model of Section 2.1.

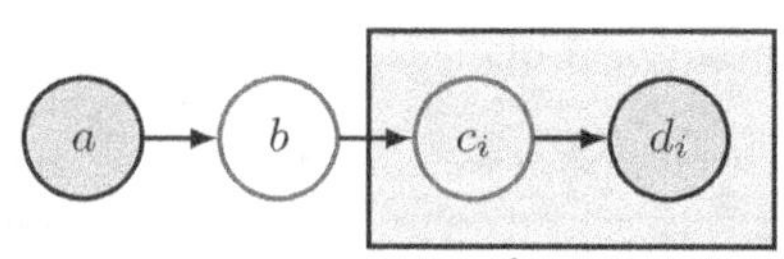

Here it suffices to traverse the local data sequentially.

```
for all i do
    buffered read c_i, d_i from storage
    sample c_i | d_i, b
    buffered write c_i
end for
```

Note that we only write the variable part of the state back to disc (the constant part is only read to avoid having to store the entire set of evidence nodes in memory). This strategy is very effective for document collections but less so, e.g. for highly interdependent entities such as social networks.

3.7 Sequential estimation

Often data comes with an additional sequential order as described in Section 2.3. Inference in this setting is possible, e.g. by the use of Sequential Monte Carlo estimation [7]. Given a model of the form

$$\mathbf{P}(a, b) = \mathbf{P}(a_0) \prod_t \mathbf{P}(a_t \mid a_{t-1})\mathbf{P}(b_t \mid a_t) \quad (5)$$

it is our goal to draw from $\mathbf{P}(a \mid b) \propto \mathbf{P}(a, b)$. In the following denote by $a^t := (a_0, \ldots, a_t)$ and $b^t := (b_1, \ldots, b_t)$ the sets of variables up to time t respectively. Assume that we draw from some proposal distribution

$$a_t \sim \pi_t(a_t \mid a^{t-1}, b^t). \quad (6)$$

In this case we need to re-weight the draw by

$$\beta := \frac{\mathbf{P}(a \mid b)}{\prod_t \pi_t(a_t \mid a^{t-1}, b^t)} = \frac{\mathbf{P}(a_0)}{\pi_0(a_0)} \prod_t \frac{\mathbf{P}(b_t \mid a_t)\mathbf{P}(a_t \mid a_{t-1})}{\pi(a_t \mid a^{t-1}, b^{-t})}$$

One may show [7] that the minimum variance draw is achieved by using as proposal distribution π_t the posterior $\mathbf{P}(a_t \mid a^{t-1}, b^t)$. Moreover, we set $\pi_0(a_0) = \mathbf{P}(a_0)$. By Bayes rule we have

$$\mathbf{P}(a_t \mid a^{t-1}, b^t) = \frac{\mathbf{P}(b_t \mid a_t)\mathbf{P}(a_t \mid a_{t-1})}{\mathbf{P}(b_t \mid a^{t-1} b^{t-1})} \quad (7)$$

Plugging this expansion back into β yields

$$\beta = \prod_t \mathbf{P}(b_t \mid a^{t-1} b^{t-1}). \quad (8)$$

In other words, we re-weight particles according to how well they explain future data while adjusting the parameter estimate at each step once we observe the evidence. [1] use this model to estimate topics and clusters on streaming news.

This procedure is carried out for a number of 'particles' which provide a discrete approximation of the posterior distribution over the latent variables. The computational cost scales linearly in the number of particles. However, we face two challenges: firstly every time some particles get too heavy we are forced to re-sample. This requires an update of the data structures. The latter is highly nontrivial since the state is distributed over many computers. Second, computing $\mathbf{P}(b_t \mid a^{t-1}, b^{t-1})$ is costly. Third, due to concentration of mass effects the behavior of the particles is quite similar ([1] show that even a small number of particles performs well).

Consequently we resort to a more drastic approximation: we only choose a single particle which avoids the need to track and recompute β. Such an approximation is justified for a number of reasons: firstly, we are primarily interested in the present estimate of a nonstationary distribution. For a contractive mapping the contribution of past errors decreases, hence the error arising from using a single particle diminishes. Finally, the single-particle approach is used in situations where the state of a particle is significant (e.g. all user actions of a given day). In this case concentration of measure effects allow us to show, e.g. via martingales, that all particles would perform extremely similarly, simply since the aggregate state is sufficiently large. Consequently, the single particle approach renders the problem amenable to practical implementation. This yields the following algorithm.

1: **for** $t = 1$ **to** T **do**
2: Sample $a_t \sim \mathbf{P}(a_t \mid a^{t-1}, b^t)$
3: **end for**

It proceeds in stages, using past latent and observed variables to sample the current set of parameters. We should stress here that the primitive Sample $a_t \sim \mathbf{P}(a_t \mid a^{t-1}, b^t)$ means perform a few Gibbs iterations over the Markov chain constructed over (a_t) where a_t is usually a set of hidden variables as we will show in Section 4.Running a Gibbs sweep over a_t using the state of the sampled values form earlier time steps (a^{t-1}) has been reported to work well in the literature [19, 20, 2, 1] especially if a_t depends on (a^{t-1}) via aggregates – which is true in many web applications. In other words, we design our sequential estimation primitives to perform well under the characteristics of our target applications.

4. APPLICATIONS

We now show based on a number of use-cases that the approximations above are effective at obtaining scalable estimates. More specifically, we give details on the improved variable replication strategy described in the previous section. Subsequently we show how the three primitives for dealing with local state, global state, and sequential order can be used in the context of dynamic user profiling.

4.1 Message Passing

To demonstrate the efficacy of the message passing scheme of Section 3.2 we briefly compare the algorithm described in [18] to the algorithm of Section 3.2. That is, we compare the performance of Yahoo's LDA implementation using both synchronization schemes.

We used 20 million news articles from Yahoo's news article collection, 100 computers, and 1000 topics. We performed 1000 iterations of collapsed Gibbs sampling for the documents and synchronization was carried by one of the following schedules:

Memcached: We use the schedule of [18]. That is, sufficient statistics are stored in *memcached*, a distributed (key,value) storage. Since *memcached* does not provide locking or versioning we emulate this as follows:

1: Set lock on *memcached* (fails if lock exists)
2: Get data from *memcached*
3: Update local values (no TCP/IP needed here)
4: Send data to *memcached*
5: Release lock record

As is evident this requires 4 TCP/IP roundtrips to update a single record. This means that the algorithm is considerably latency bound. We mitigate this effect by performing parallel synchronization with several threads simultaneously.

Ice: We implemented our own distributed (key,value) storage as part of the LDA codebase. To ensure that client and server remain synchronized we limit the number of tokens in flight at any given time, i.e. we limit the number of outstanding sent requests s_{jl} = TRUE that a client can have, e.g. $\sum_j s_{jl} \leq 100$. This is desirable since we want to ensure that messages are recent rather than being queued up for a long time. For communication we use the *ice* inter process communication library of zeroc.com.

Below we show how the time to complete a single synchronization pass change as we increases the number of machines while fixing the dataset characteristic. As we can see, the new architecture presented in this paper is actually able to leverage the increased number of machines more efficiently.

Protocol	*old*[18]			*new* (this paper)		
Machines	100	200	400	100	200	400
Sync time (sec)	155.61	131.47	149.14	33.2	28.22	24.12

The improved synchronization rate has additional desirable benefits — it significantly accelerates convergence of the sampler, as can be seen in Figure 1. More to the point, the sampler converges up to 5 times faster, due to an improved synchronization strategy: the negative log-likelihood using *ice* at 100 iterations is higher than what *memcached* reaches after 500 iterations. In other words, not only is the new scheme faster *per iteration*, it also converges faster, hence we may terminate the sampler earlier. Moreover, as evident from the Figure, as we increase the number of machines, the difference in performance gap between the old and new architecture increases significantly which suggests that the new architecture is more suitable for large-scale web application using large number of machines.

4.2 Message Scheduling

Next we tested the efficiency of the communication scheduling algorithm described in Section 3.4. For this purpose we used 150 machines and a dataset of 20 million documents with a vocabulary size of 3.5 million words. In particular, we compared the average time required for a synchronization pass when using no schedule and when using aggregate schedules for various aggregation factors p.

Schedule	none	$p = 2$	$p = 5$	$p = 10$
Sync time	231s	227s	**209s**	233s

As can be seen, using 5 machines at a time yields a 10% speedup in synchronization. This is desirable in its own right, however it also ensures somewhat faster convergence due to faster mixing. The reason that $p = 2$ and $p = 10$ show essentially no effect can be explained by a lack of enough connections (for $p = 2$) and overhead due to thread management and TCP/IP packet inefficiencies. We believe that the throughput can be improved further by adjusting the operating parameters of *ice* to force serialization of several messages into a single wire packet.

4.3 Temporal user profiling

The second application described in this paper is that of temporal user profiling. Here the goal is to obtain an estimate of the interest distribution of a user where the latter keeps on changing over time. The associated graphical model is given in Figure 2. Essentially each user i has an interest distribution θ_{it} which is a function of time t and which changes slowly. At any given moment the user draws a particular interest z_{itj} from this interest distribution and then he draws an action w_{itj} from the associated activity distribution ϕ_{tk}. Likewise the interest prior Ω_t depends on prior activity through the count variables m_t. The model is considerably more complicated than a conventional topic model due to the fact that now user interest, activity distribution and general topic distribution all become time-dependent random variables. Figure 2 provides a simplified version. For details of the full model see [2].

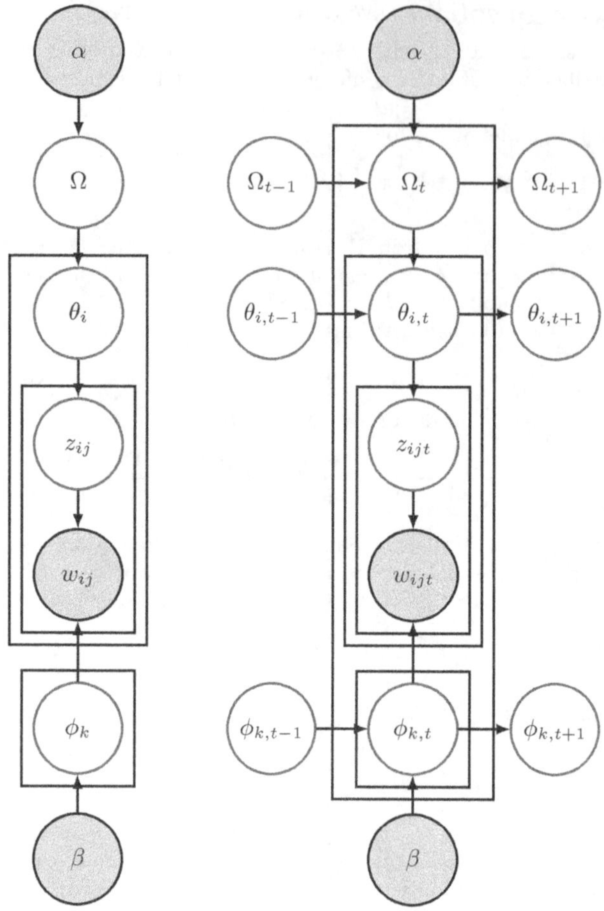

Figure 2: Left: Latent Dirichlet Allocation. Right: a simplified variant of Temporal LDA [2]. The key difference between both models is that in Temporal LDA, the prior over topics, the actual topic distribution and the activity distribution per topic depend on the past assignments which are summarized as m_t, n_t and β_t.

Scalability

The key motivation for discussing the model is that it demonstrates the interaction between all previously described approximations. In particular, we use the distributed LDA sampler described above as the main building block to perform inference on a daily basis. The state of the sampler comprises the topic-word counts matrix, and the document-topic counts matrix. The former is shared across users and is maintained in a distributed hash table as described in Section 3.2. The latter is document-specific and can be maintained locally in each client. We distribute the users at time t across N computers. Each client executes a foreground thread to resample a user for a given day and a background thread synchronizing its local copy of the topic-word counts matrix with the global copy.

Figure 3 confirms one of the most basic requirements of scalable inference — the amount of time required to process data scales *linearly* with the amount of data when keeping the computational resources fixed. Furthermore it also shows that while our algorithm does not scale perfectly, we lose only a small amount of performance when increasing

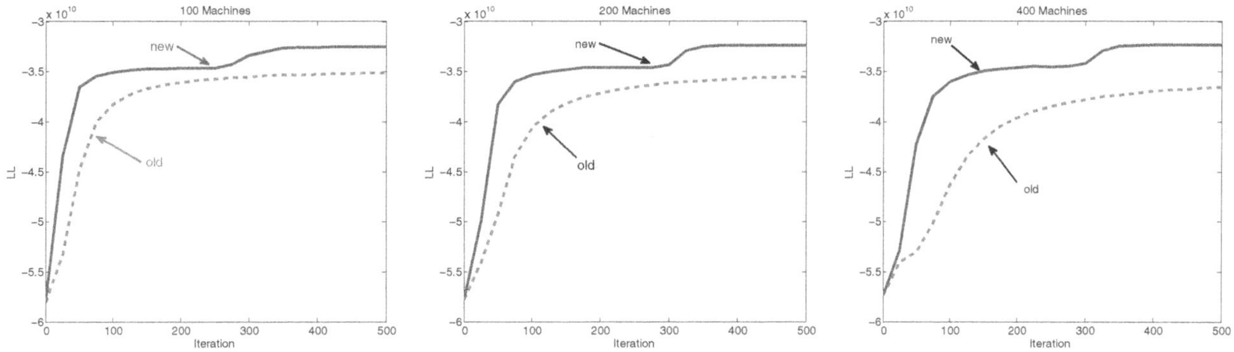

Figure 1: Log-likelihood of topic assignments during the sampling iterations. We compare the *old* architecture [18] and the *new* architecture described in this paper using LDA on 20 million news articles and1000 topics. We report results over 100, 200 and 400 machines. Note that the improved sampler converges approximately 5 times faster than the old *memcached* based variant. Moreover note that this gap increases as the number of machines increases, which suggests that the new architecture is more scalable than the old one

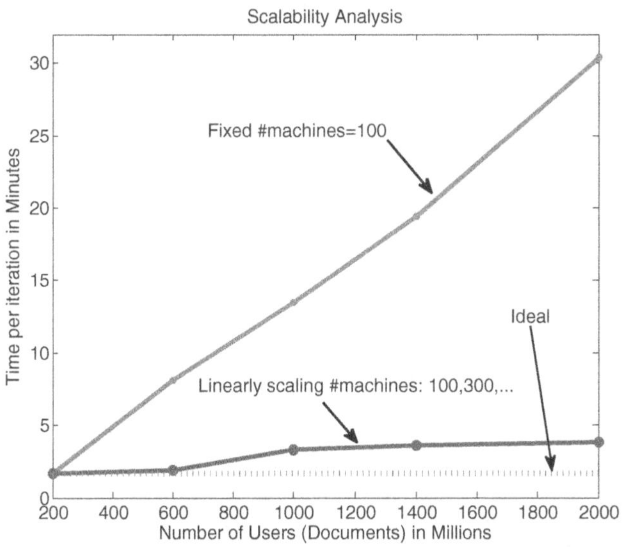

Figure 3: Time per iteration vs. millions of user days. When fixing the number of machines we observe a linear dependence between iteration time and the amount of data. The blue line depicts the time per iteration when keeping the data to machine ratio constant. That is, we use $\{100, 300, 500, 700, 1000\}$ machines such that each machine receives 2 million user days.

the data tenfold. We believe that some of the associated inefficiencies are due to the fact that the experiments were carried out on a production cluster where it would have been more difficult to allocate 1000 machines in close proximity on Hadoop. Hence the communications overhead arising from inter-rack communication would have had a significant impact on the runtime. Overall, the results show that we are able to process the equivalent of 2 billion documents (i.e. user days) on 1000 machines in a satisfactory time.

Resampling global parameters

As shown in Section 3.7, after each day (for each value of t), the random variables Ω_t should be sampled. However, Ω_t requires a *reduction* step across clients since it depends on the joint counts from all users across all clients. This is a classical Reduce operation. Using the distributed (key, value) storage it is implemented as follows: First each client writes its contribution for m_t based on its assinged users to the master, then the clients reach a *barrier* where they wait for each other to proceed to the next stage of the cycle. We implemented a sense-reversing barrier algorithm which arranges the nodes in a tree and thus has a latency that scales logarithmically with N [16]. After this barrier, all counts are in global storage and as such one client sums these counts to obtain m_t, use it to sample Ω_t, and finally writes it back. All other clients wait, then they read the new value of Ω_t and this finalizes a single cycle.

Performance

While desirable in terms of speed, we also need to resolve whether the aforementioned modifications affect the quality of the estimates. For this purpose we compared the results from [2] (old) to the current sampler (new) when applied to the problem of temporal user profiling. In other words, we did not change the model significantly but rather only changed the sampler to allow for faster synchronization.

For evaluation purposes we compute the ROC score when using simple bag of words features (BOW) as baseline, features from temporal LDA (TLDA), and a combination of both features (BOW+TLDA).

Feature set	BOW	TLDA		TLDA+BOW	
Variant		old [2]	new	old [2]	new
ROC score	57.03	58.70	60.2	60.38	**63.8**

The data we used for this experiment were 435GB of behavioral data spanning 44 days with 33.5 million users. It clearly shows that improving speed *also* improves performance in our case, thus giving us the best of both worlds.

Fault Tolerance

Finally, we need to address the issue of fault tolerance and recovery from failure. We described an improved mechanism of writing backup copies per server locally. As can be seen, this leads to a dramatic improvement in terms of recovery time by at least one order of magnitude. Since the time is primarily dominated by the vocabulary size and the number of topics we compared the times for a number of parameter combinations.

words	topics	machines	old [2]	new
1.5M	100	100	25.1 min	3 min
3M	100	100	64.2 min	3.5 min
5M	200	300	80.2 min	6.5 min

This improvement in terms of fault recovery (and correspondingly reduced time for taking snapshots of the current state) allows us to perform backups much more eagerly, thus allowing for a more stable production system.

5. DISCUSSION

In this paper we presented a number of powerful strategies for performing approximate inference on web-scale data collections. While quite effective in isolation, their joint use opens the door to the use of very sophisticated latent variable models in actual production settings in industry. To the best of our knowledge, the results presented here are on significantly much larger problems than the previously largest experiments of [18, 2].

To ensure widespread dissemination of these ideas we released an open-source implementation of our framework at `https://github.com/shravanmn/Yahoo_LDA`, together with the full documentation of the framework architecture, its different components, the steps to run it, and the mechanism of exapnding it with new graphical models. We believe this framework has the great potential of allowing, both researchers and practitioners, of easily tackling web-scale inference problems with little coding effort.

Note that the approximations are quite orthogonal to the approach of [10, 13] which focus heavily on graph partitioning for general graphs which are small enough to be retained in main memory and on efficient message passing schedules. Future work will be to combine these techniques with our approximations. We have reason to believe that this will yield an enterprise ready graphical model inference toolkit which is capable of analyzing data from hundreds of millions of users in social networks and billions of webpages.

Acknowledgments

We thank Yucheng Low and Tamas Sarlos for fruitful discussions. This work was supported by the ARC.

6. REFERENCES

[1] A. Ahmed, Q. Ho, C. H. Teo, J. Eisenstein, A. J. Smola and E. P. Xing. Online Inference for The Infinite Topic-cluster model: Storylines from Streaming Text. In *Artificial Intelligence and Statistics AISTATS*, 2011.

[2] A. Ahmed, Y. Low, M. Aly, V. Josifovski, and A. Smola. Scalable inference of dynamic user interests for behavioural targeting. In *Knowledge Discovery and Data Mining*, 2011. submitted.

[3] A. Asuncion, P. Smyth, and M. Welling. Asynchronous distributed learning of topic models. In D. Koller, D. Schuurmans, Y. Bengio, and L. Bottou, editors, *NIPS*, pages 81–88. MIT Press, 2008.

[4] S. Boyd and L. Vandenberghe. *Convex Optimization.* Cambridge University Press, Cambridge, 2004.

[5] J. K. Bradley, A. Kyrola, D. Bickson, and C. Guestrin. Parallel coordinate descent for l1-regularized loss minimization. In *International Conference on Machine Learning ICML*, Bellevue, WA, 2011.

[6] W. Chen, D. Zhang, and E. Chang. Combinational collaborative filtering for personalized community recommendation. In Y. Li, B. Liu, and S. Sarawagi, editors, *Proceedings of the 14th ACM SIGKDD International Conference on Knowledge Discovery and Data Mining*, pages 115–123. ACM, 2008.

[7] A. Doucet, N. de Freitas, and N. Gordon. *Sequential Monte Carlo Methods in Practice.* Springer-Verlag, 2001.

[8] R. Durbin, S. Eddy, A. Krogh, and G. Mitchison. *Biological Sequence Analysis: Probabilistic models of proteins and nucleic acids.* Cambridge University Press, 1998.

[9] S. Geman and D. Geman. Stochastic relaxation, Gibbs distributions, and the Bayesian restoration of images. *IEEE Transactions on Pattern Analysis and Machine Intelligence*, PAMI-6:721–741, 1984.

[10] J. Gonzalez, Y. Low, A. Gretton, and C. Guestrin. Parallel Gibbs Sampling: From Colored Fields to Thin Junction Trees. In *Artificial Intelligence and Statistics AISTATS*, 2011.

[11] T. Griffiths and M. Steyvers. Finding scientific topics. *Proceedings of the National Academy of Sciences*, 101:5228–5235, 2004.

[12] D. Karger, E. Lehman, T. Leighton, M. Levine, D. Lewin, and R. Panigrahy. Consistent hashing and random trees: Distributed caching protocols for relieving hot spots on the world wide web. In *Symposium on the Theory of Computing STOC*, pages 654–663, New York, May 1997. Association for Computing Machinery.

[13] Y. Low, J. Gonzalez, A. Kyrola, D. Bickson, C. Guestrin, and J. M. Hellerstein. GraphLab: A new parallel framework for machine learning. In *Conference on Uncertainty in Artificial Intelligence*, 2010.

[14] M. Luby and C. Rackoff. How to construct pseudorandom permutations from pseudorandom functions. *SIAM Journal on Computing*, 17(2):373–386, 1988.

[15] W. Macready, A. Siapas, and S. Kauffman. Criticality and parallelization in combinatorial optimization. *Science*, 271:56–59, 1996.

[16] J. Mellor-Crummey and M. Scott. Algorithms for scalable synchronization on shared-memory multiprocessors. *ACM Transactions on Computer Systems*, 9(1):21–65, Feb. 1991.

[17] D. Newman, A. Asuncion, P. Smyth, and M. Welling. Distributed algorithms for topic models. *Journal of Machine Learning Research*, 10:1801–1828, 2009.

[18] A. Smola and S. Narayanamurthy. An architecture for parallel topic models. In *Very Large Databases (VLDB)*, 2010.

[19] T. Iwata, T. Yamada, Y. Sakurai, and N. UedaOnline multiscale dynamic topic models. In *KDD*, 2010.

[20] N. Bartlett, D. Pfau, and F. Wood . Forgetting counts : Constant Memory inference for a dependent hierarchical Pitman-Yor Process In *ICML*, 2010.

[21] E. Xing, M. Jordan, and R. Sharan. Bayesian haplotype inference via the dirichlet process. *Journal of Computational Biology*, 14(3):267–284, 2007.

Learning Recommender Systems with Adaptive Regularization

Steffen Rendle
Social Network Analysis
University of Konstanz
78457 Konstanz, Germany
steffen.rendle@uni-konstanz.de

ABSTRACT

Many factorization models like matrix or tensor factorization have been proposed for the important application of recommender systems. The success of such factorization models depends largely on the choice of good values for the regularization parameters. Without a careful selection they result in poor prediction quality as they either underfit or overfit the data. Regularization values are typically determined by an expensive search that requires learning the model parameters several times: once for each tuple of candidate values for the regularization parameters. In this paper, we present a new method that adapts the regularization automatically while training the model parameters. To achieve this, we optimize simultaneously for two criteria: (1) as usual the model parameters for the regularized objective and (2) the regularization of future parameter updates for the best predictive quality on a validation set. We develop this for the generic model class of Factorization Machines which subsumes a wide variety of factorization models. We show empirically, that the advantages of our adaptive regularization method compared to expensive hyperparameter search do not come to the price of worse predictive quality. In total with our method, learning regularization parameters is as easy as learning model parameters and thus there is no need for any time-consuming search of regularization values because they are found on-the-fly. This makes our method highly attractive for practical use.

Categories and Subject Descriptors

I.2.6 [**Artificial Intelligence**]: Learning—*Parameter Learning*

General Terms

Algorithms, Experimentation, Measurement, Performance

Keywords

Regularization, Matrix Factorization, Tensor Factorization

Permission to make digital or hard copies of all or part of this work for personal or classroom use is granted without fee provided that copies are not made or distributed for profit or commercial advantage and that copies bear this notice and the full citation on the first page. To copy otherwise, to republish, to post on servers or to redistribute to lists, requires prior specific permission and/or a fee.
WSDM'12, February 8–12, 2012, Seattle, Washington, USA.
Copyright 2012 ACM 978-1-4503-0747-5/12/02 ...$10.00.

1. INTRODUCTION

Recommender systems are an important tool with many applications e.g. online-shopping, video rental, personalized web sites, etc. Recently factorization models became very popular due to their success in several challenges including the Netflix prize[1]. Most of the research in this field focuses on new and improved models, among them are matrix factorization [16, 12, 18], probabilistic latent semantic analysis (PLSA) [6], SVD++ [7], SoRec [11], time-variant matrix factorization [8] for collaborative filtering or Tucker decomposition [20, 10, 14] and pairwise interaction tensor factorization (PITF) [15] for tag recommendation. However, the success of all the mentioned factorization models depends largely on the right choice of their regularization values. The reason is that factorization models deal with a very large number of model parameters – e.g. many millions of model parameters for the winning approaches of the Netflix prize. This makes all factorization models very prone to overfitting, i.e. a low prediction error on the training data, but a high error on future test cases. L2-regularization is commonly applied where regularization parameters serve as a complexity control that can prevent overfitting. But if the regularization is chosen too large, the model will not learn (fit the training data) and if it is chosen too small the model will overfit. In both cases, the prediction quality will be poor and thus the choice of the regularization values is crucial. For factorization models, the common way to determine these regularization values is a time-consuming search over a set of candidates (often grid search [1]). For each candidate value, the model parameters are trained – a process that might take hours on large scale problems for each of the candidate values for the regularization. After learning several models, the regularization value with the best predictive quality on a withheld validation set is taken. This process is very time consuming because many models have to be learned.

Even though factorization models are very sensitive to the regularization values and the search for these values is very expensive, there is little research to overcome this issue. For the practical application of factorization models it is crucial to have a fast approach to determine regularization values. Even more because of the sensitivity it is desired that regularization values are chosen automatically such that wrong values cannot be set accidentally by inexperienced users. Finally, an automatic approach should work with several loss functions, be easy to implement and integrate into the prevalent existing algorithms.

In this work, we propose a new method that meets these

[1] `http://www.netflixprize.com/`

requirements. (1) It integrates the search for regularization values directly into the learning algorithm for model parameters. That means the model parameters have to be learned only once and during this process the regularization values are automatically found on-the-fly. This is done by adapting the regularization values such that in the next update step of model parameters the error on a validation set is minimized. (2) The runtime complexity of our proposed algorithm for adaptive regularization is the same as the one of standard stochastic gradient descent (SGD) which is the standard method for optimizing factorization models. This makes the algorithm applicable to large scale problems like recommender systems with millions of data records. (3) Compared to the common approach of expensive search over a set of candidate regularization values, our approach has also the advantage that it searches not just a predefined subspace of candidates, but the search space is unrestricted. Furthermore, models with many regularization parameters can be solved efficiently (e.g. one regularization parameter per factor dimension) which is not feasible with traditional grid search where the search space is exponential in the number of regularization parameters. (4) The proposed algorithm works with several losses and is easy to integrate into existing SGD algorithms. This makes our approach highly attractive for practical use of factorization models.

We analyze our proposed approach empirically on the Netflix and Movielens datasets and show that the prediction quality of adaptive regularization is comparable to models where the regularization values have been searched using expensive grid search.

2. RELATED WORK

2.1 Validation Set Based Approaches

Usually regularization values are determined by a search for optimal values using a withheld validation set. There are different approaches how the search is performed. The most common one is to search a space of candidate values for regularization and to learn a separate model for each candidate. Using the withheld validation set, the model for each regularization value can be evaluated and the best one is chosen. For factorization models, grid search [1] is usually performed where a predefined grid of candidates is set up and on each candidate a model is trained and evaluated (see fig. 1). Even though such an uninformed search is very expensive in terms of runtime, it is the dominating method for factorization models (e.g. [7, 15, 13]).

For other models, there are more sophisticated methods where an informed search is performed. Examples are Chapelle et al. [2] for SVMs and Larsen et al. [9] for neural networks. Both guide the search for regularization parameters by gradient methods: Chapelle et al. optimize the kernel parameters and Larsen et al. the weight decay. Although both work with different models, similar to us they alternate between optimizing regularization/ weight decay and model parameters. But unlike our approach both do not intertwine the adaptive regularization with the learning of model parameters. Instead they iterate between a complete training of model parameters and a complete training of regularization hyperparameters. Even though such an informed search reduces the number of models that have to be learned, still several models have to be fitted. And unlike grid search, learning these several models cannot be parallelized trivially. In contrast to this, our approach integrates both steps and requires only to learn a single model. Besides a more concise learning of model and regularization parameters, our intertwined approach benefits from its ongoing adaptation of both sets of parameters because the regularization can be adapted to the current state of the learning: At first, when the model parameters are far from convergence, regularization will be (almost) zero, increasing to its final level when the model parameters (start to) converge.

Also for support vector machines (SVMs), Hastie et al. [5] have proposed regularization paths that can be used for speeding up the search for the optimal regularization value. Regularization paths allow to find all possible solutions as a function of the regularization value and can be computed in the same complexity as fitting a single model. Like our approach, the runtime for finding the regularization values is roughly doubled compared to standard learning with predefined regularization values. Besides the different model of SVMs and factorization models, we deal with a large number of regularization parameters (see fig. 6).

In total, to the best of our knowledge our approach is the first one that allows to adapt regularization parameters efficiently for the prevalent model and learning method in recommender systems: i.e. factorization models with stochastic gradient descent learning.

2.2 Hierarchical Bayesian Approaches

Another direction to find regularization parameters are Bayesian approaches [3] that do not work with a validation set but use a hierarchical model with hyperpriors on the prior distribution (i.e. regularization). This allows to group parameters like we do and due to hyperpriors partial pooling is achieved which decreases overfitting. Salakhutdinov and Mnih [17] proposed a hierarchical Bayesian model for matrix factorization and Xiong et al. [21] for a three mode PARAFAC model but both are only applicable for least squares loss. Furthermore Bayesian approaches are typically optimized with Markov Chain Monte Carlo (MCMC) whereas most factorization models are optimized with SGD (e.g. [12, 11, 7, 8, 15]) due to its simplicity and low computational complexity. Our method allows to be integrated with little effort into such existing (S)GD methods for factorization models and work for different losses.

To summarize, our method integrates the search for regularization values directly into the learning algorithm of the model parameters, it allows to learn many regularization values and can be applied for several losses and finally is very easy to implement. We show this for Factorization Machines which generalize a wide variety of factorization models.

3. PROBLEM SETTING

Before introducing our method we shortly recapitulate some of the most successful factorization models for recommender systems and discuss how they are regularized and learned.

3.1 Factorization Models

Matrix Factorization (MF) [19] can be applied to settings with two variables over categorical domains, e.g. users U and items I in a recommender system. The matrix factorization model finds a latent description (a vector of k factors) for each entity, e.g. $\mathbf{v}_u \in \mathbb{R}^k$ for a user $u \in U$. The model

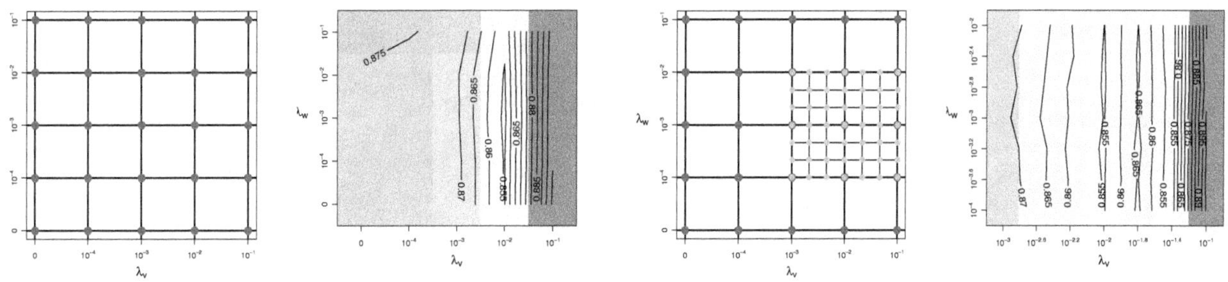

(a) Initial Grid (b) RMSE Heatmap (c) Refined Grid (d) RMSE Heatmap

Figure 1: Typical grid search for finding regularization values (here $\lambda \in \mathbb{R}^2$): (a) Grid of candidates $\Lambda = \{(0,0),(0,10^{-1}),(10^{-1},0),\ldots\}$. (b) For each candidate $\lambda \in \Lambda$, the model parameters are trained on S_T and their quality is measured on a withheld validation set S_V. (c) Finer grid in the neighborhood of the best value (here $\lambda = (0.01, 0.001)$). (d) For each of the new candidates model parameters are trained and tested.

equation corresponds to the dot product of two entities (e.g. a user u and an item i):

$$\hat{y}(u,i) := \langle \mathbf{v}_u, \mathbf{v}_i \rangle, \quad \mathbf{V} \in \mathbb{R}^{(U \cup I) \times k} \tag{1}$$

In this model, the latent factors $\mathbf{V}$ are the model parameters that have to be learned. Often bias terms are added to the matrix factorization model [12]: A global bias w_0 that usually holds the mean over the target. And secondly, bias terms for each entity are added, e.g. w_i for the item i. The matrix factorization model with such additional biases reads:

$$\hat{y}(u,i) := w_0 + w_i + w_u + \langle \mathbf{v}_u, \mathbf{v}_i \rangle. \tag{2}$$

Here $w_0 \in \mathbb{R}$ and $\mathbf{w} \in \mathbb{R}^{U \cup I}$ are additional model parameters.

For problems such as tag recommendation or context-awareness where more than two variables are involved, e.g. $C_1, \ldots, C_j$, tensor factorization models can be applied. Examples are Tucker Decomposition (TD) [20] or Parallel Factor Analysis (PARAFAC) [4]. For tag recommender systems, a model using pairwise interactions (PITF) [15] has been proposed and shown to outperform TD and PARAFAC on this task. The PITF model for j variables and biases can be written as:

$$\hat{y}(c_1,\ldots,c_j) := w_0 + \sum_{l=1}^{j} w_{c_l} + \sum_{l_1=1}^{j} \sum_{l_2>l_1}^{j} \langle \mathbf{v}_{c_{l_1}}, \mathbf{v}_{c_{l_2}} \rangle \tag{3}$$

where the model parameters are $w_0 \in \mathbb{R}$, $\mathbf{w} \in \mathbb{R}^{C_1 \cup \ldots C_j}$ and $\mathbf{V} \in \mathbb{R}^{(C_1 \cup \ldots C_j) \times k}$.

There are lots of specialized models that extend general factorization models for special cases. E.g. SVD++ [7] for movie recommendation that adds implicit feedback indicators to MF:

$$\hat{y}(u,i) := w_0 + w_i + w_u + \langle \mathbf{v}_u, \mathbf{v}_i \rangle + \frac{1}{\sqrt{N(u)}} \sum_{l \in N(u)} \langle \mathbf{v}_i, \mathbf{v}_l \rangle$$

where $N(u)$ is the set of all other items a user u has ever selected (e.g. rented or viewed). Or a k-nearest-neighbor (KNN) model [7] where neighborhood weights are treated as model parameters:

$$\hat{y}(u,i) := w_0 + w_i + w_u + \frac{1}{\sqrt{R(u)}} \sum_{l \in R(u)} w_{i,l,1}(y_{u,l} - b_{u,l}) + \frac{1}{\sqrt{N(u)}} \sum_{l \in N(u)} w_{i,l,2} \tag{4}$$

Here $R(u)$ is the set of items where the ratings are known.

The models described so far can be generalized to Factorization Machines (FM) [13] which work with real-valued input vectors $\mathbf{x} \in \mathbb{R}^p$. It has been shown [13] that FMs can mimic several factorization models among them are (biased) MF, SVD++, KNN and PITF, just by feature engineering, i.e. definition of the input vectors $\mathbf{x}$ using binary indicator variables (e.g. one variable for each user, each item, etc.). A FM models all nested d-way interactions between any combination of d variables with the target[2]. A 2-way FM is defined as:

$$\hat{y}(\mathbf{x}) := w_0 + \sum_{l=1}^{p} w_l \, x_l + \sum_{l_1=1}^{p} \sum_{l_2>l_1}^{p} \langle \mathbf{v}_{l_1}, \mathbf{v}_{l_2} \rangle \, x_{l_1} \, x_{l_2} \tag{5}$$

with model parameters $w_0 \in \mathbb{R}$, $\mathbf{w} \in \mathbb{R}^p$ and $\mathbf{V} \in \mathbb{R}^{p \times k}$. The model equation of FMs can be computed efficiently because eq. (5) is equivalent to:

$$\hat{y}(\mathbf{x}) = w_0 + \sum_{l=1}^{p} w_l \, x_l + \frac{1}{2} \sum_{f=1}^{k} \left(\left(\sum_{l=1}^{p} v_{l,f} \, x_l \right)^2 - \sum_{l=1}^{p} v_{l,f}^2 \, x_l^2 \right)$$

Due to the expressiveness of FMs, we develop our adaptive regularization approach for this model class. This leads to self-adaptive approaches of all subsumed models.

3.2 Optimization

Before a model can be applied, the values of the model parameters Θ (e.g. $\Theta = (w_0, \mathbf{w}, \mathbf{V})$ for FMs) have to be learned from a set of observed data S. Let S be a set of observed cases $(\mathbf{x}, y) \in \mathbb{R}^{p+1}$, where for classification $y \in \{-1, 1\}$.

3.2.1 Optimization Tasks

Optimality of model parameters is usually defined with a loss function l where the task is to minimize the sum of

[2]In this work, we will deal only with $d = 2$.

losses over the data S:

$$\textsc{Opt}(S) := \operatorname*{argmin}_{\Theta} \sum_{(\mathbf{x},y)\in S} l(\hat{y}(\mathbf{x}|\Theta), y). \tag{6}$$

Note that we add the model parameters Θ to the model equation and write $\hat{y}(\mathbf{x}|\Theta)$ when we want to stress that $\hat{y}$ depends on a certain choice of Θ. Depending on the task, the loss function can be chosen. E.g. for regression, least squares loss:

$$l^{\text{LS}}(y_1, y_2) := (y_1 - y_2)^2, \tag{7}$$

or for binary classification:

$$l^{\text{C}}(y_1, y_2) := -\ln \sigma(y_1\, y_2) \tag{8}$$

where $\sigma(x) = \frac{1}{1+e^{-x}}$ is the sigmoid/ logistic function.

3.2.2 *Regularization*

All the presented factorization models usually have a huge number of model parameters Θ – especially if k is chosen large enough. This makes them prone to overfitting. To overcome this, typically L2 regularization is applied which can be motivated by maximum-margin [19], Tikhonov regularization or MAP estimator with Gaussian priors [18]:

$$\textsc{OptReg}(S,\lambda) := \operatorname*{argmin}_{\Theta} \left(\sum_{(\mathbf{x},y)\in S} l(\hat{y}(\mathbf{x}|\Theta), y) + \sum_{\theta\in\Theta} \lambda_\theta \theta^2 \right). \tag{9}$$

Here $\lambda_\theta \in \mathbb{R}_+$ is the regularization parameter for the model parameter θ. The major issue of such regularization approaches is that their success depends largely on the choice of the value of the regularization parameter λ. If λ is chosen too large, the model cannot fit the training data and thus does not learn. If λ is chosen too small, the model overfits the training data which means the training error will be small but the error on future test cases will be large. As mentioned before, overfitting is easy to achieve with models of high expressiveness, i.e. lots of model parameters, like in factorization models. That means regularization succeeds only if λ is chosen correctly.

Multiple Priors.

In fact this problem even gets more difficult, as one does not deal with only one regularization parameter $\lambda \in \mathbb{R}_+$ that is shared by all model parameters, but instead model parameters are grouped and each group has an independent regularization parameter λ. So if there are c groups, λ is a c-dimensional vector: $\lambda \in \mathbb{R}_+^c$. A simple example for FMs would be that the global bias w_0 has its own regularization parameter λ_0, all bias parameters $w_1, \ldots, w_p$ share one regularization parameter λ_w and each level f of the k dimensions of the factors $\mathbf{V}$ share one parameter, e.g. λ_f for $v_{1,f}, \ldots, v_{p,f}$. In total this leads to $c = k+2$ regularization parameters. Such a grouping is typically chosen in advance because it stems from the structure of the factorization model. In the following, we will allow several regularization parameters and we denote with λ_θ the regularization parameter that belongs to the model parameter θ.

3.2.3 *Learning Algorithm*

For optimizing complex models with respect to $\textsc{OptReg}$, usually iterative algorithms are applied. Especially popular for factorization models are gradient descent (GD) methods because they are simple and are easily applicable to a wide variety of loss functions. This method has been shown to solve large problems e.g. the Netflix prize [12, 7, 8] efficiently. The idea of GD is that given a parameter setting Θ^t, the model parameters can be improved to Θ^{t+1} by performing a step in the opposite direction of the gradient of the loss function. To speed up learning, stochastic GD (SGD) is used where a case $(\mathbf{x}, y)$ is randomly drawn from the observed data S and the update is performed only with respect to this case:

$$\theta^{t+1} = \theta^t - \alpha \left(\frac{\partial}{\partial \theta^t} l(\hat{y}(\mathbf{x}|\Theta^t), y) + 2\,\lambda\,\theta^t \right) \tag{10}$$

where α is the learning rate or step size. GD works with any differentiable loss, e.g. for least squares, the gradient is

$$\frac{\partial}{\partial \theta} \left(\hat{y}(\mathbf{x}|\Theta) - y\right)^2 = 2\,\left(\hat{y}(\mathbf{x}|\Theta) - y\right)\, \frac{\partial}{\partial \theta}\hat{y}(\mathbf{x}|\Theta) \tag{11}$$

or for classification

$$\frac{\partial}{\partial \theta} - \ln \sigma\left(\hat{y}(\mathbf{x}|\Theta)\, y\right) = \left(\sigma\left(\hat{y}(\mathbf{x}|\Theta)\, y\right) - 1\right)\, y\, \frac{\partial}{\partial \theta}\hat{y}(\mathbf{x}|\Theta). \tag{12}$$

Finally, the gradients of the model equation for factorization machines are [13]:

$$\frac{\partial}{\partial \theta}\hat{y}(\mathbf{x}) = \begin{cases} 1, & \text{if } \theta \text{ is } w_0 \\ x_i, & \text{if } \theta \text{ is } w_i \\ x_i \left(\sum_{j=1} x_j\, v_{j,f} - x_i\, v_{i,f}\right), & \text{if } \theta \text{ is } v_{i,f} \end{cases} \tag{13}$$

Given these formulas, a SGD algorithm for factorization machines [13] can be sketched (see figure 2). Note that this algorithm also can learn all subsumed model classes (see section 3.1) like matrix factorization or PITF.

```
procedure SolveOptReg(S, λ)
    w_0 ← 0
    w ← (0, ..., 0)
    V ~ N(0, σ)
    repeat
        for (x, y) ∈ S do
            ∂_0 ← ∂/∂w_0 l(ŷ(x|Θ), y)
            w_0 ← w_0 − α (2 λ_0 w_0 + ∂_0)
            for i ∈ {1, ..., p} ∧ x_i ≠ 0 do
                ∂_i ← ∂/∂w_i l(ŷ(x|Θ), y)
                w_i ← w_i − α (2 λ_w w_i + ∂_i)
                for f ∈ {1, ..., k} do
                    ∂_{i,f} ← ∂/∂v_{i,f} l(ŷ(x|Θ), y)
                    v_{i,f} ← v_{i,f} − α (2 λ_f v_{i,f} + ∂_{i,f})
                end for
            end for
        end for
    until stopping criterion is met
    return Θ := (w_0, w, V)
end procedure
```

Figure 2: Learning model parameters Θ of a FM by stochastic gradient descent for OptReg (eq. 9) given a regularization vector $\lambda \in \mathbb{R}_+^c$.

4. ADAPTIVE REGULARIZATION

In the following, we show how the search for optimal regularization values can be integrated directly into SOLVEOPTREG (fig. 2). We start with the definition of the optimization task for regularization values and develop a fast and simple learning algorithm.

4.1 Optimization Task for Regularization

Typically, optimal regularization values $\lambda^* \in \mathbb{R}_+^c$ for factorization models are determined using a holdout method. Therefore the available data S is split into two disjoint data sets: $S = S_T \cup S_V$. On S_T, the model parameters are optimized for the regularized loss objective (OPTREG, eq. 9) given a regularization constant λ. Using the validation set S_V, the quality of the learned model parameters can be estimated. As the training S_T and validation S_V sets are disjoint, the quality on S_V gives a reliable estimate of the future success of the parameter setting – as long as the size of the validation set is sufficiently large and the future data is generated by the same process as the validation data S_V. Working with disjoint training and validation sets is one of the core principles in machine learning. In our case, the task is to find the regularization values λ^* that lead to the lowest error on the validation set

$$\lambda^* := \operatorname*{argmin}_{\lambda \in \mathbb{R}_+^c} \sum_{(\mathbf{x},y)\in S_V} l\left(\hat{y}(\mathbf{x}|\text{OPTREG}(S_T,\lambda)), y\right). \quad (14)$$

This is a nested optimization task where the outermost objective is to determine the best regularization values λ^* that minimize the loss on the validation set S_V. This loss on the validation set depends not directly on λ. Instead it depends on the model equation $\hat{y}$ which itself depends only on the model parameters. However, the model parameters are the solution of $\Theta^*|\lambda = \text{OPTREG}(S_T, \lambda)$, i.e. the regularized optimization criterion on the training data S_T, thus these optimal model parameters depend on λ. So in total, we are looking for a λ^* such that the corresponding optimal model parameters $\Theta^*|\lambda^*$ with respect to the regularized loss on S_T lead to a minimal error on the validation set S_V.

Alternating Optimization.

A straightforward idea is to use an alternating optimization, i.e. starting with an initial guess of (Θ, λ) and alternate between improving Θ while λ is fixed and improving λ while Θ is fixed. This process is repeated up to convergence. For the first task, i.e. optimizing Θ for a given λ, we already have a solution (alg. SolveOptReg). But the second task (eq. 14) is not trivial. If Θ is kept constant here, i.e. $\text{OPTREG}(S_T, \lambda)$ is replaced by the current model parameters Θ^t, then the optimization task (eq. 14) reads

$$\lambda^*|\Theta^t := \operatorname*{argmin}_{\lambda \in \mathbb{R}_+^c} \sum_{(\mathbf{x},y)\in S_V} l\left(\hat{y}(\mathbf{x}|\Theta^t)), y\right). \quad (15)$$

In this task the right hand side is independent of λ. This means the gradient vanishes

$$\frac{\partial}{\partial \lambda} L(S_V, \Theta^t) = \frac{\partial}{\partial \lambda} \sum_{(\mathbf{x},y)\in S_V} l(\hat{y}(\mathbf{x}|\Theta^t), y) = 0 \quad (16)$$

and thus every value $\lambda \in \mathbb{R}$ would be optimal w.r.t. equation (15) which is obviously not the right approach to solve the original task (eq. 14).

4.2 Optimizing Future Model Parameters

Alternating optimization using eqs. (9) and (14) seems to be impossible as the gradient of any λ vanishes when Θ is kept constant. The problem is that λ does not appear explicitly in the optimization formula (eq. 15). However if we remember the role of lambda in eq. (14), it can be seen that λ steers the search for the model parameters Θ on S_T which are then used in S_V. This can also be seen in the SGD update rule for the model parameters (eq. 10) where λ appears. That means with a simple trick, we can reformulate the model equation such that it depends explicitly on λ: It is known that after the next update on θ, the value of θ will be the one of eq. (10). This future value θ^{t+1} depends on λ. So the future model equation after updating the model parameters Θ can be written as:

$$\hat{y}(\mathbf{x}|\Theta^{t+1}) = w_0^{t+1} + \sum_{l=1}^{p} w_l^{t+1} x_l + \sum_{l_1=1}^{p} \sum_{l_2>l_1}^{p} \langle \mathbf{v}_{l_1}^{t+1}, \mathbf{v}_{l_2}^{t+1} \rangle x_{l_1} x_{l_2} \quad (17)$$

That means instead of expressing the model equation with the current parameters Θ^t, it can be formulated to depend on the parameters after the next update Θ^{t+1}. Replacing each θ^{t+1} in eq. (17) with the right hand side of eq. (10), results in a model equation which depends on λ:

$$\begin{aligned}\hat{y}(\mathbf{x}|\Theta^{t+1}) &= w_0^t - \alpha\left(\frac{\partial l(\hat{y}(\mathbf{x}|\Theta^t), y)}{\partial w_0^t} + 2\,\lambda_0\, w_0^t\right)\\ &+ \sum_{l=1}^{p} x_l \left(w_l^t - \alpha\left(\frac{\partial l(\hat{y}(\mathbf{x}|\Theta^t), y)}{\partial w_l^t} + 2\,\lambda_w\, w_l^t\right)\right)\\ &+ \sum_{l_1=1}^{p}\sum_{l_2>l_1}^{p}\sum_{f=1}^{k}\left[x_{l_1}\left(v_{l_1,f}^t - \alpha\left(\frac{\partial l(\hat{y}(\mathbf{x}|\Theta^t), y)}{\partial v_{l_1,f}^t} + 2\,\lambda_f\, v_{l_1,f}^t\right)\right)\right.\\ &\left.\quad x_{l_2}\left(v_{l_2,f}^t - \alpha\left(\frac{\partial l(\hat{y}(\mathbf{x}|\Theta^t), y)}{\partial v_{l_2,f}^t} + 2\,\lambda_f\, v_{l_2,f}^t\right)\right)\right] \end{aligned} \quad (18)$$

This future model equation $\hat{y}(\mathbf{x}|\Theta^{t+1})$ can be used in eq. (14), which results in the following task:

$$\lambda^*|\Theta^t := \operatorname*{argmin}_{\lambda \in \mathbb{R}_+^c} \sum_{(\mathbf{x},y)\in S_V} l\left(\hat{y}(\mathbf{x}|\Theta^{t+1}), y\right). \quad (19)$$

This optimization task answers the question: *What is the best value of λ such that the next update on Θ generates the smallest error on the validation set?* Now alternating between eqs. (9) and (19) is possible.

In general, this idea can be used for any iterative optimization algorithm where the update on the model parameter explicitly depends on the regularization value. In the following, we show how this can be done efficiently for SGD.

Gradients.

As the model parameters are usually optimized with SGD, we propose to use SGD as well for optimizing λ w.r.t. the task of eq. (19). The SGD-update for λ given a case $(\mathbf{x}, y) \in S_V$ is

$$\lambda^{t+1} = \lambda^t - \alpha \frac{\partial}{\partial \lambda} l\left(\hat{y}(\mathbf{x}|\Theta^{t+1}), y\right) \quad (20)$$

where the gradients of the loss function are the same as in

eqs. (11) and (12), e.g. for least squares it reads

$$\frac{\partial}{\partial \lambda}(\hat{y}(\mathbf{x}|\Theta^{t+1}) - y)^2 = 2\,(\hat{y}(\mathbf{x}|\Theta^{t+1}) - y)\frac{\partial}{\partial \lambda}\hat{y}(\mathbf{x}|\Theta^{t+1}),$$

and for logistic classification loss:

$$\frac{\partial}{\partial \lambda} - \ln \sigma\left(\hat{y}(\mathbf{x}|\Theta^{t+1})\,y\right)$$

$$= \left(\sigma\left(\hat{y}(\mathbf{x}|\Theta^{t+1})\,y\right) - 1\right)\,y\,\frac{\partial}{\partial \lambda}\hat{y}(\mathbf{x}|\Theta^{t+1}).$$

Finally, the gradients of the future model equation (eq. 17) w.r.t. λ have to be calculated. As the update equation of L2-regularized gradient descent is a linear function in λ and FMs are linear functions in each single model parameter, this is always easy to derive. We show this now for the example where there are $k+2$ regularization parameters: one parameter (λ_0) for w_0, one (λ_w) that is shared by $w_1, \ldots, w_p$ and for each of the factorization dimensionality $f = 1, \ldots, k$, there is one regularization parameter λ_f which is shared by $v_{1,f}, \ldots, v_{p,f}$. First, the gradient of λ_0 w.r.t. the future model equation (eq. 18) is

$$\frac{\partial}{\partial \lambda_0}\hat{y}(\mathbf{x}|\Theta^{t+1}) = -2\,\alpha\, w_0^t,$$

for λ_w the gradient reads

$$\frac{\partial}{\partial \lambda_w}\hat{y}(\mathbf{x}|\Theta^{t+1}) = -2\,\alpha \sum_{i=1}^{p} w_i^t x_i$$

and for each λ_f

$$\frac{\partial}{\partial \lambda_f}\hat{y}(\mathbf{x}|\Theta^{t+1}) = -2\alpha\left[\sum_{i=1} x_i v_{i,f}^{t+1} \sum_{j=1} x_j v_{j,f}^{t} - \sum_{j=1} x_j^2 v_{j,f}^{t+1} v_{j,f}^{t}\right]$$

Note that the derivative of factors depends both on current $v_{i,f}^t$ and future $v_{i,f}^{t+1}$ parameters (see eq. 10).

4.3 Alternating SGD Algorithm

These gradients allow to derive an alternating SGD algorithm for eq. (14). Instead of solving OPTREG (eq. 9) and the optimization for λ (eq. 19) one after another, they can be solved simultaneously by alternating single SGD-steps: i.e. drawing one case from S_T and perform an update step (eq. 10) on the model parameters Θ and then draw one case from S_V and perform an update on λ with eq. (20). This means while learning Θ, the regularization parameters are adapted.

Fast Computation.

Now only one issue in the optimization of λ remains. Each parameter θ^{t+1} in the future model eq. (18) depends on the gradient $\frac{\partial l(\hat{y}(\mathbf{x}|\Theta^t),y)}{\partial \theta^t}$ of the training case $(\mathbf{x}, y) \in S_T$ which will update θ next. Instead of computing this gradients for every θ^{t+1} on every λ-update, this value can be approximated by the last gradient of θ which we denote by ∂_θ. That means when a model parameter is updated in a θ-update step, its gradient is stored in ∂_θ and can be used later for the corresponding λ-updates where the approximated future model parameter $\tilde{\theta}^{t+1}$ is

$$\tilde{\theta}^{t+1} := \theta^t - \alpha\left(\partial_\theta + 2\,\lambda\,\theta^t\right) \approx \theta^{t+1} \qquad (21)$$

This approximation $\tilde{\theta}^{t+1}$ is used for the λ-steps, i.e. in eq. (18) and its derivatives (eq. 20). The size of the approximating error depends on the size of the change in the model parameters between updates. With a small step size α the approximation error is also small. Furthermore the approximation error decreases and finally vanishes in convergence of model parameters and regularization.

procedure SOLVEOPTADAPTIVEREG(S_T, S_V)
  $w_0 \leftarrow 0$
  $\mathbf{w} \leftarrow (0, \ldots, 0)$
  $\mathbf{V} \sim \mathcal{N}(0, \sigma)$
  $\lambda \leftarrow (0, \ldots, 0)$
  $\partial \leftarrow (0, \ldots, 0)$
  repeat
    for $(\mathbf{x}, y) \in S_T$ **do**
      $\partial_0 \leftarrow \frac{\partial}{\partial w_0} l(\hat{y}(\mathbf{x}|\Theta), y)$
      $w_0 \leftarrow w_0 - \alpha\,(2\,\lambda_0\,w_0 + \partial_0)$
      for $i \in \{1, \ldots, p\} \wedge x_i \neq 0$ **do**
        $\partial_i \leftarrow \frac{\partial}{\partial w_i} l(\hat{y}(\mathbf{x}|\Theta), y)$
        $w_i \leftarrow w_i - \alpha\,(2\,\lambda_w\,w_i + \partial_i)$
        for $f \in \{1, \ldots, k\}$ **do**
          $\partial_{i,f} \leftarrow \frac{\partial}{\partial v_{i,f}} l(\hat{y}(\mathbf{x}|\Theta), y)$
          $v_{i,f} \leftarrow v_{i,f} - \alpha\,(2\,\lambda_f\,v_{i,f} + \partial_{i,f})$
        end for
      end for
      $(\mathbf{x}', y') \sim S_V$ ▷ draw a case from valid. set
      $\lambda_0 \leftarrow \max\left(0, \lambda_0 - \alpha \frac{\partial}{\partial \lambda_0} l\left(\hat{y}(\mathbf{x}'|\tilde{\Theta}), y'\right)\right)$
      $\lambda_w \leftarrow \max\left(0, \lambda_w - \alpha \frac{\partial}{\partial \lambda_w} l\left(\hat{y}(\mathbf{x}'|\tilde{\Theta}), y'\right)\right)$
      for $f \in \{1, \ldots, k\}$ **do**
        $\lambda_f \leftarrow \max\left(0, \lambda_f - \alpha \frac{\partial}{\partial \lambda_f} l\left(\hat{y}(\mathbf{x}'|\tilde{\Theta}), y'\right)\right)$
      end for
    end for
  until stopping criterion is met
  return $\Theta := (w_0, \mathbf{w}, \mathbf{V})$
end procedure

Figure 3: Integrating the search for regularization parameters into the learning algorithm for model parameters. This way, adaptive regularization learns the regularization values automatically while learning the model parameters. See section 4.2 for the gradients.

Algorithm.

The final algorithm is very simple and requires only little extensions to the standard SGD algorithm.

1. Update model parameters as usual. Store for each model parameter the last gradient step, i.e. $\partial_\theta \leftarrow \frac{\partial l(\hat{y}(\mathbf{x}|\Theta^t),y)}{\partial \theta^t}$. As this value is anyway computed during the SGD on the model parameters, this has no extra overhead in runtime but doubles the number of parameters to store.

2. After each update on the model parameters, make an SGD-update on the regularization values (eq. 20) using the approximated future model parameter (eq. 21).

Figure 3 shows the extended SGD algorithm that adapts regularization during parameter learning. To shorten notation and because within the algorithm it does not make sense to keep track of time t, we replaced θ^t with θ and $\tilde{\theta}^{t+1}$ with $\tilde{\theta}$.

Table 1: Datasets statistics about the number of users, items and number of instances/ rows in the train, validation and test set.

Dataset	# users	# items	size train	size validation	size test
Movielens	6,040	3,900	792,164	8,002	200,042
Netflix	480,189	17,700	100,340,104	140,403	1,408,789

4.4 Properties of Adaptive Regularization

To summerize, adaptive regularization has the following properties:

1. The runtime complexity of adaptively regularized model parameter learning (fig. 3) is the same as the one of standard learning (fig. 2) where λ is fixed. The only computational overhead of adaptive regularization compared to the basic algorithm are the additional gradient steps on λ. In each update, computing the gradients for all regularization parameters has the same complexity as computing the gradients of the model parameters, i.e. $O(k\,m(\mathbf{x}))$[3]. As we propose to do a regularization update for each model update, the runtime is roughly doubled. Compared to this, learning hyperparameters with non-integrated approaches (e.g. grid-search, see fig. 1 or informed search) is much more time-consuming because it means learning one model for each of the candidates.

2. The proposed algorithm adapts the regularization values automatically that means there is no danger that an inexperienced user sets wrong values to these critical parameters.

3. Most optimization algorithms for factorization models are based on SGD. Our proposed approach is easy to integrate into such SGD algorithms and is applicable to many loss functions.

5. EVALUATION

In the evaluation, we investigate the predictive performance of our proposed adaptive regularization method (SGDA, fig. 3) compared to the standard approach of SGD (fig. 2) with expensive grid search. Moreover, we provide deeper insights into the process of learning optimal hyperparameters λ using SGDA.

5.1 Methodology

5.1.1 Experimental Reproducibility

For sake of experimental reproducibility we evaluate on two well-known datasets: Movielens 1M (ML1M) and Netflix (see table 1). We split Movielens into a train and test set using a random 80/20-split. Concerning Netflix we use the train (incl. *probe*) and quiz (the *leaderboard* set) split from the challenge as train and test data sets – this allows comparison to the results reported on the Netflix leaderboard. The experiments are conducted using the publicly available software LIBFM[4] that we extend with adaptive SGDA learning. We use the factorization machine of LIBFM to mimic biased matrix factorization (MF) (see eq. 2) and the KNN model with learned similarities (eq. 4) with implicit feedback (KNN++) and without (KNN) – we run it with a neighborhood size of 256 following the pruning protocol of Koren [7].

5.1.2 Protocol

For SGDA, we run SOLVEOPTADAPTIVEREG (fig. 3) to predict the test set. For ML1M we use a random subsample of 1% of the training data for validation S_V. For Netflix we use a 10% subsample of the Netflix *probe* set as validation set S_V because *probe* is representative for test[5]. As SGDA finds the regularization values automatically, there is no need to specify any regularization hyperparameter in advance. For determining the number of iterations, we use the predicted quality on the validation set S_V.

The setup for SGD is more complicated because regularization parameters have to be found. As the search for individual regularization parameters for each factor layer $f \in \{1, \ldots, k\}$ using grid search is not feasible, we restrict the search space and only search for λ_w and one shared λ_v for all factor layers. For Movielens, we apply a grid search like the one in fig. 1 using the 1% validation sample; the best values are $\lambda_w = 0$ and $\lambda_v = 0.01$ for the MF model. For the much larger and more time-consuming Netflix dataset, we rely on the hyperparameter search from [7]: for KNN we use $\lambda_w = 0.002$ and for MF $\lambda_w = \lambda_v = 0.04$ which was reported for the related SVD++ model. In favor of SGD, after regularization values have been searched, we retrain the models on the whole dataset (i.e. merging S_V and S_T) with the best λ found.

5.2 Results

5.2.1 Predictive Accuracy

Figure 4 compares the predictive accuracy of SGDA to SGD. It can be seen that on all variants, both methods perform comparable. Note that SGDA achieves this quality without any predefined regularization values which are crucial for SGD and very expensive to determine.

Despite SGDA variants make only use of 99% (ML1M) and 99.9% (Netflix) of the train data (1% and 0.1% of train become the validation datasets), they outperform their SGD counterparts slightly. The reason is that SGDA allows to use many regularization parameters without any additional cost: we use $k+1$ regularization parameters for SGDA (λ_w and λ_f, $f \in \{1, \ldots, k\}$). As described before, for SGD we use only two regularization parameters λ_w and λ_v due to the exponential complexity of grid search. The increased flexibility of SGDA in modeling the *importance*[6] of each latent dimension allows for more flexible regularization and thus better predictions with higher numbers of latent dimensions overcompensating the lack of 1% or 0.1% of the training

[3]Where $m(\mathbf{x})$ is the number of non-zero values in $\mathbf{x}$.

[4]`http://www.libfm.org/`

[5]The test set (qualify) of Netflix is a temporal split where rare users are oversampled which means a random subsample from train would not be a representative validation set.

[6]Higher regularization equals to lower importance and vice versa.

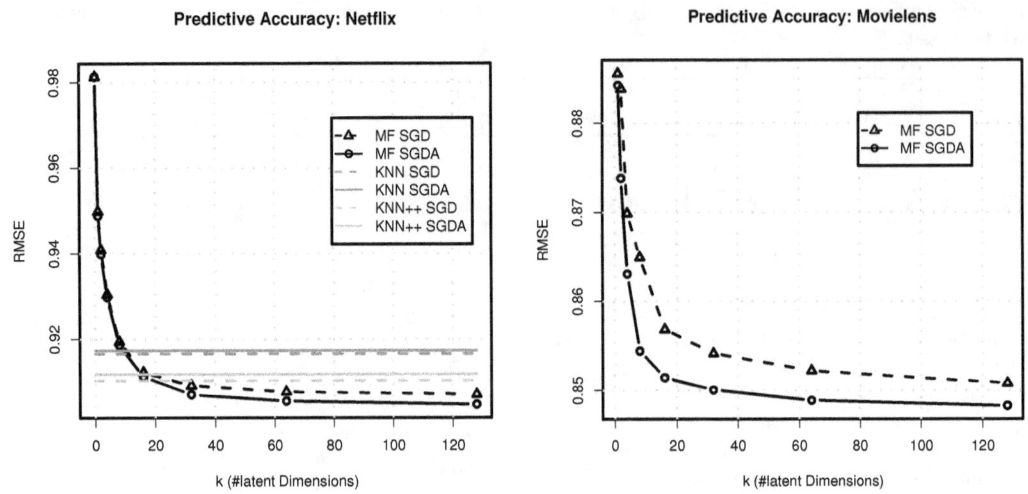

Figure 4: Predictive accuracy of Matrix Factorization and variants of learned KNN with 256 neighbors [7]. All methods are learned with SGD and SGDA. Despite SGDA does not perform any expensive hyperparameter search for regularization values, its predictive accuracy is as good as SGD which uses expensive grid search.

data. Moreover, instead of searching a grid of candidates like SGD, SGDA has an unrestricted search space for the regularization values which is another advantage of SGDA over grid-search based SGD.

Nearest neighbor models (KNN) [7] show another difference between SGD and SGDA. Since both methods have no factored features the number of regularization parameters is the same. Without the advantage of a more flexible regularization, SGDA suffers from the reduced amount of training data. Thus, SGDA performs slightly worse than SGD with optimal hyperparameters. A simple retraining of SGDA on the whole dataset S after λ has been found – like we have done for SGD – is expected to close the performance gap.

5.2.2 *Convergence*

When numerical optimization algorithms like gradient descent methods are applied the question of convergence arises automatically. Figure 5 shows for both evaluation datasets the relationship between train, validation and test error for SGDA based matrix factorization. Unlike the train error which is typically used for determining convergence, the validation error behaves identically to the test error. Shape and slope as a function of the number of iterations for validation and test are the same. Thus, the number of iterations necessary for SGDA can be determined automatically by monitoring the slope of the validation error.

5.2.3 *Evolution of* λ

Since one regularization parameter is learned per latent dimension, it is possible to assess single dimensions by the corresponding regularization parameter, i.e. more important latent dimensions have lower regularization values. These different regularization levels for each dimension are depicted in figure 6 which shows the distributions of regularization parameters per latent dimension sorted in ascending order of their mean value.

Since the different regularization values per dimension in this plot are the result of a learning process, they indicate that having more flexible regularization is better than one

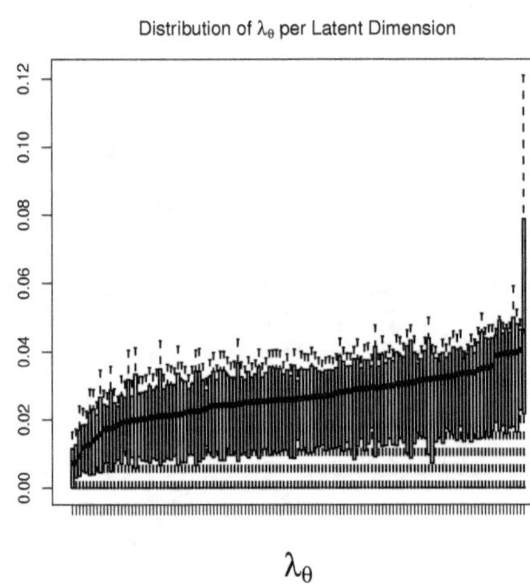

Figure 6: Series of boxplots showing distributions of all regularization values λ on Netflix for SGDA-MF with $k = 128$ features.

regularization value for all dimensions. In general, the more dimension enter a factorization model, the more regularization is necessary to avoid overfitting. However, instead of regularizing all dimensions equally like standard regularization search does, SGDA and its individually *optimized* regularization approach, do not assign the same regularization value to all dimensions but discriminate between more and less important dimensions.

5.2.4 *Size of Validation Set* S_V

Up to now, the size of the validation set was 1% and 0.1% of the training set for Movielens and Netflix respectively. Since the validation set guides the search for regularization values, we want to study the influence of different sizes (see fig. 7). First of all, the validation set should be representative for the test set. This way one can measure the quality of the current model parameters by predicting the validation

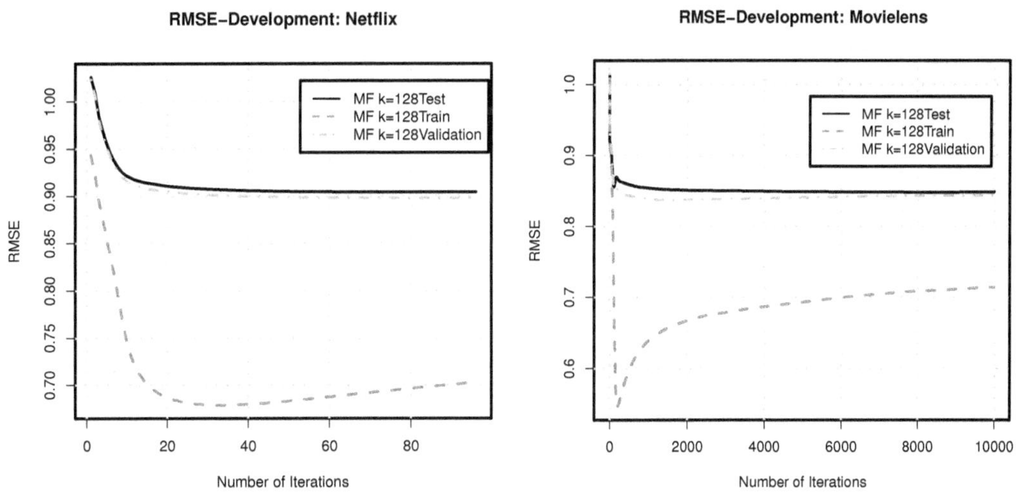

Figure 5: Development of RMSE relative to the number of full gradient descent iterations of SGDA. The quality on the validation set can be used for selecting the number of iterations.

set and see this as an approximation of the (unknown) test error. Furthermore, it has to be large enough that it cannot be overfit by the regularization values. As the regularization values are learned on the validation set, a large number of regularization values with a small validation set might lead to overfitting. Of course, the larger the validation set, the better the approximation is supposed to be. Figure 7 shows the Pearson correlation coefficient between the validation error measured after each full data iteration and the corresponding test error. While less than 100 validation instances do not suffice to accurately approximate the test error with the validation error, the approximation steadily improves by increasing the size of validation set $|S_V|$. Already 8000 cases (1% of train) have a correlation of 0.971 and 80,000 (10% of train) a correlation of 0.9996.

However, the improved approximation comes at the cost of higher test errors since the training data reduces. Figure 7 shows this trade-off for an MF model with $k = 32$ dimensions. Even though very small validation sets (e.g. 8 and 80 cases) allow to learn the model parameters from almost all data, they lead to low prediction quality because the validation set cannot find reliable regularization parameters. A validation set of 8000 cases which does not diminish the train data set too much, leads to the best test error as the approximation between validation error and test error is high 0.971 and the training set is still large (99%). Any further increase in the validation data set improves the approximation further, however, the final error increases as too much training data is used for the test error approximation and for learning the regularization values λ_θ but not for training the model parameters Θ.

Note that this trade-off between the size of the validation set and the prediction quality on test exists not just for SGDA but for any method that uses a validation set for hyperparameter tuning (also grid-search). The experiment shows that even though a trade-off exists, all reasonable choices (800 cases = 0.1% to 80,000 cases = 10%) lead to good results.

6. CONCLUSION AND FUTURE WORK

In this work, a new approach for finding regularization values for factorization models has been proposed. Our approach integrates the search for regularization values directly into the learning algorithm for model parameters. This avoids a time-consuming search for regularization values that is usually done by techniques like grid search and requires training the model parameters several times. Furthermore our adaptive regularization method can handle a large number of regularization parameters without any impact on the runtime complexity. We developed a learning algorithm with adaptive regularization for Factorization Machines that subsume a variety of factorization models including matrix factorization and specialized models. In our experiments, we have shown on the large Netflix dataset that our adaptive regularization method achieves similar predictive quality as the standard learning technique where the regularization parameters have been chosen carefully in advance by an expensive search.

Besides the regularization value, the learning rate is another hyperparameter of SGD algorithms. In basic factorization models like MF, there is typically only one parameter for the learning rate, however, more complex models like the integrated neighboorhood SVD++ model [7] use different learning rates. Studying adaption strategies for learning rates is an interesting direction for future research.

7. ACKNOWLEDGMENTS

I would like to thank Christoph Freudenthaler for many fruitful discussions and his valuable comments.

8. REFERENCES

[1] C.-C. Chang and C.-J. Lin. *LIBSVM: a library for support vector machines*, 2001. Software available at `http://www.csie.ntu.edu.tw/~cjlin/libsvm`.

[2] O. Chapelle, V. Vapnik, O. Bousquet, and S. Mukherjee. Choosing multiple parameters for support vector machines. *Machine Learning*, 46:131–159, 2002. 10.1023/A:1012450327387.

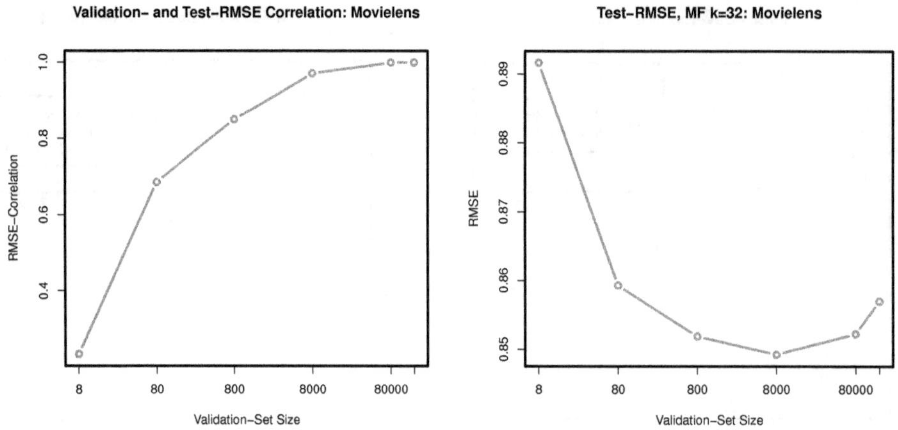

Figure 7: Influence of the size of the validation set. The left figure shows the correlation between the error on the validation set and the test set. The larger the validation data, the closer is its error to the test error. The right plot shows the test error depending on the validation size. As larger validation sets lead to smaller training sets, there is a trade-off between training and validation size.

[3] A. Gelman, J. B. Carlin, H. S. Stern, and D. B. Rubin. *Bayesian Data Analysis.* Chapman and Hall/CRC, 2nd edition, 2003.

[4] R. A. Harshman. Foundations of the parafac procedure: models and conditions for an 'exploratory' multimodal factor analysis. *UCLA Working Papers in Phonetics*, pages 1–84, 1970.

[5] T. Hastie, S. Rosset, R. Tibshirani, and J. Zhu. The entire regularization path for the support vector machine. *Journal of Machine Learning Research*, 5:1391–1415, December 2004.

[6] T. Hofmann. Latent semantic models for collaborative filtering. *ACM Trans. Inf. Syst.*, 22(1):89–115, 2004.

[7] Y. Koren. Factorization meets the neighborhood: a multifaceted collaborative filtering model. In *KDD '08: Proceeding of the 14th ACM SIGKDD international conference on Knowledge discovery and data mining*, pages 426–434, New York, NY, USA, 2008. ACM.

[8] Y. Koren. Collaborative filtering with temporal dynamics. In *KDD '09: Proceedings of the 15th ACM SIGKDD international conference on Knowledge discovery and data mining*, pages 447–456, New York, NY, USA, 2009. ACM.

[9] J. Larsen, C. Svarer, and L. N. Andersen. Adaptive regularization in neural network modeling. In *Neural Networks: Tricks of the Trade, Lecture Notes in Computer Science*, volume 1524, pages 113–132. Springer-Verlag, 1998.

[10] L. D. Lathauwer, B. D. Moor, and J. Vandewalle. A multilinear singular value decomposition. *SIAM J. Matrix Anal. Appl.*, 21(4):1253–1278, 2000.

[11] H. Ma, H. Yang, M. R. Lyu, and I. King. Sorec: social recommendation using probabilistic matrix factorization. In *Proceeding of the 17th ACM conference on Information and knowledge management*, CIKM '08, pages 931–940, New York, NY, USA, 2008. ACM.

[12] A. Paterek. Improving regularized singular value decomposition for collaborative filtering. In *Proc. KDD Cup Workshop at SIGKDD'07, 13th ACM Int. Conf. on Knowledge Discovery and Data Mining*, pages 39–42, 2007.

[13] S. Rendle. Factorization machines. In *Proceedings of the 10th IEEE International Conference on Data Mining*. IEEE Computer Society, 2010.

[14] S. Rendle, L. B. Marinho, A. Nanopoulos, and L. Schmidt-Thieme. Learning optimal ranking with tensor factorization for tag recommendation. In *KDD '09: Proceeding of the 15th ACM SIGKDD international conference on Knowledge discovery and data mining*, New York, NY, USA, 2009. ACM.

[15] S. Rendle and L. Schmidt-Thieme. Pairwise interaction tensor factorization for personalized tag recommendation. In *WSDM '10: Proceedings of the third ACM international conference on Web search and data mining*, pages 81–90, New York, NY, USA, 2010. ACM.

[16] J. D. M. Rennie and N. Srebro. Fast maximum margin matrix factorization for collaborative prediction. In *ICML '05: Proceedings of the 22nd international conference on Machine learning*, pages 713–719. ACM, 2005.

[17] R. Salakhutdinov and A. Mnih. Bayesian probabilistic matrix factorization using Markov chain Monte Carlo. In *Proceedings of the 25th International Conference on Machine Learning*, volume 25, 2008.

[18] R. Salakhutdinov and A. Mnih. Probabilistic matrix factorization. In *Advances in Neural Information Processing Systems*, volume 20, 2008.

[19] N. Srebro, J. D. M. Rennie, and T. S. Jaakola. Maximum-margin matrix factorization. In *Advances in Neural Information Processing Systems 17*, pages 1329–1336. MIT Press, 2005.

[20] L. Tucker. Some mathematical notes on three-mode factor analysis. *Psychometrika*, 31:279–311, 1966.

[21] L. Xiong, X. Chen, T.-K. Huang, J. Schneider, and J. G. Carbonell. Temporal collaborative filtering with bayesian probabilistic tensor factorization. 2010.

Collaborative Ranking

Suhrid Balakrishnan
AT&T Labs–Research
180 Park Ave.
Florham Park, NJ
suhrid@research.att.com

Sumit Chopra
AT&T Labs–Research
180 Park Ave.
Florham Park, NJ
schopra@research.att.com

ABSTRACT

Typical recommender systems use the root mean squared error (RMSE) between the predicted and actual ratings as the evaluation metric. We argue that RMSE is not an optimal choice for this task, especially when we will only recommend a few (top) items to any user. Instead, we propose using a ranking metric, namely normalized discounted cumulative gain (NDCG), as a better evaluation metric for this task. Borrowing ideas from the learning to rank community for web search, we propose novel models which approximately optimize NDCG for the recommendation task. Our models are essentially variations on matrix factorization models where we also additionally learn the features associated with the users and the items for the ranking task. Experimental results on a number of standard collaborative filtering data sets validate our claims. The results also show the accuracy and efficiency of our models and the benefits of learning features for ranking.

Categories and Subject Descriptors

H.2.8 [**Database Applications**]: Data Mining—*Collaborative Filtering and Ranking*; I.2.6 [**Learning**]: Connectionism and Neural Nets

General Terms

Algorithms

Keywords

Recommender Systems, Learning to Rank, Collaborative Ranking, NDCG, RMSE

1. INTRODUCTION AND MOTIVATION

The past decade has seen a large number of web-based recommendation systems deployed with great success in diverse domains. Their surge can be attributed to a variety of factors. Among them, a key factor is the rather limitless choice of items available to a user in a multitude of applications. A partial list of extremely popular web-based recommender services are: Netflix, for movies, Amazon.com for products, Pandora, Last.fm, and iTunes Genius for music, YouTube's Recommended For You, for online videos, Facebook's Other People You May Know, for social networking, What Should I Read Next, for books etc.

Before a typical recommender system can make personalized recommendations for a user, it needs to elicit that users preferences. This is done by soliciting numeric (and now ubiquitous) "star" ratings from the user for select items. For instance, Netflix makes this the first step for a user as soon as she creates an account on their website; they ask a new user to rate some minimum number of preselected movies/TV shows on a 5 point star scale ranging from 1 = *Hate it*, to 5 = *Love it*. After sufficiently many ratings have been collected, collaborative filtering (CF) [17] techniques are applied to the entire dataset (all users, all items). CF models form the core of most recommender systems. They work by extrapolating unobserved user-item preferences from preference information collected from the target user, and the preferences of all the other users. Finally, recommendations are made, and the user can be shown the items estimated to be the most preferred by her. This is usually done by using CF models to first estimate the preferences of all the items. Next, the items are sorted by these estimated preferences; and finally, a (small) subset of the top items are shown to the user as her recommendations.

Since many recommender systems operate in this paradigm of using explicit ratings as a surrogate for user preferences, a natural way to train and evaluate such systems has emerged. In this view, the recommendation task reduces to predicting the ratings for an unseen user-item pair. In order to evaluate the performance of such systems, the collected ratings data from all the users, is partitioned into a training portion (the training set) and a disjoint/non-overlapping testing portion (the test set). Models are learned on the training set and evaluated on the test set (held-out ratings not seen during training). Since the recommendation task is framed as predicting the ratings for unseen user-item pairs, evaluation consists of quantifying how well the recommender predicts the test user-item ratings. This is essentially a regression task, and the Mean Squared Error (MSE) between the model predictions and the actual test ratings is a natural choice for an evaluation metric. Models with lower test MSE have better predictions, on average, than models with higher MSE. Furthermore, once test MSE is the evaluation

Permission to make digital or hard copies of all or part of this work for personal or classroom use is granted without fee provided that copies are not made or distributed for prof t or commercial advantage and that copies bear this notice and the full citation on the f rst page. To copy otherwise, to republish, to post on servers or to redistribute to lists, requires prior specif c permission and/or a fee.
WSDM'12, February 8–12, 2012, Seattle, Washington, USA.
Copyright 2012 ACM 978-1-4503-0747-5/12/02 ...$10.00.

criterion, training MSE is also automatically the first choice for a loss function while training these models.

While this has been a completely valid and a successful approach to building recommender systems, we, along with a few other researchers [22, 6, 16, 21], believe that using MSE criteria to evaluate such systems is a suboptimal fit to the recommendation task. The reasons are two-fold. First, as mentioned earlier, the way most recommenders are used in practice is to generate a top-k list of the items to show each user. Therefore, only recommendations that the system estimates to be highly rated by her will ever be shown to a user. A user is never shown any item which the system believes she will not give a high rating to. Since MSE places equal emphasis on all the ratings, high and low, minimizing MSE results in training models that predict the low ratings as accurately as the high ones. Therefore it appears a lot of extra work is done unnecessarily, in trying to solve a harder problem than we need to. As an example, in the case of Netflix, since we know beforehand that we will only show (estimated) 4/5-star items to a user, requiring our system to be good at predicting a 1-star rating accurately seems wasteful of modeling capacity. The second main criticism of MSE as a training criterion is that most of the time, the actual predicted ratings values themselves are not even shown to the users directly (Netflix is a notable exception). If the only use for the numerical values of the predictions is generating a top-k list, precision in the predicted value of these ratings also doesn't seem to be necessary. Instead, getting the order of the items right seems critical. In particular, the correct order at the top of the list appears to be key.

For these reasons we argue that instead of using MSE, a ranking metric will be better suited to evaluating recommendation systems. In particular, in this paper we show that Normalized Discounted Cumulative Gain (NDCG) is a particularly good fit as a metric for evaluating such systems. NDCG (see Section 2.1 for mathematical details) was developed with ranking in information retrieval as the target application [12]. Given relevance values (typically on an ordinal scale) for a set of items (web-pages) returned as response to a search query, NDCG can be used to score any list of permutations of these items. NDCG was designed so that the list with the highest relevance items in the top ranked positions is the one which gets the maximum score. Since a recommender system will be used to show users only a few suggested items, our focus is also precisely on the items populating the top of the list. As long as low ranked items can be distinguished from the high ranked ones, estimating low scoring ratings is of little to no consequence to NDCG and hence to the ranking task. We call this ranking view to recommendation *Collaborative Ranking.*

Motivated by the work in the domain of learning-to-rank for web-search, we propose two classes of models for the collaborative ranking problem; point-wise models and pair-wise models. The idea behind both these models is to learn a parametric function which assigns a relevance score to every input, which is a user-item pair. The distinction between the two models lie in the way the parameters of the function are learned to optimize the ranking metric.

A key issue in using these models in the recommendation setting, as opposed to web-search ranking, is the lack of availability of explicit input features. To this end we propose a novel solution this problem, which involves learning these features while simultaneously learning the parameters of the ranking function during the optimization of the loss function. We validate our claims by running our models on a number of standard real-world collaborative filtering data sets. The results show the efficiency and accuracy of our models. We also show the benefits of learning the input features tuned to the ranking task at hand.

In Section 2 we briefly discuss the outline of the state of the learning-to-rank community and the types of models people use for web-search ranking. Section 3 discusses in detail the our proposed models for the collaborative ranking problem. We then discuss related work and evaluation in Section 4. Next, we turn to our experiments and results in Section 5. Finally, we end with our conclusions and discuss future work in Section 6.

2. LEARNING TO RANK

The web-search task concerns finding information on the Internet. In the standard setting, users provide a search engine with a set of search terms (the query), and the search engine returns a list of relevant hyperlinks (listings or impressions). The user may then follow hyperlinks that look relevant, or refine her search etc. Research effort has focused on many specific aspects of this task. One prominent area of recent research attention has been automated web-search result ranking. In particular, motivated by the observation that most users focus their attention on only a handful of impressions typically placed on the top of the first page of the search result, one desired characteristic is that this list of impressions returned by the search engine should be ranked according to their relevance to the search query. In the web-search literature this task, concerned with finding models that return listings by strongly taking into account their rank, is known as the "learning to rank" (LTR) problem.

Under most circumstances, in LTR, the ranking problem is treated as a supervised learning problem, where access to a labeled training data $\mathcal{D}$ is assumed. A canonical training data set $\mathcal{D}$ consists of a list of query-impression pairs (q_i, l_i) labeled with the corresponding relevance score y_i: $\mathcal{D} = \{(q_i, l_i, y_i) : i \in [1 \ldots n]\}$. The relevance labels, y_i are typically editorial judgments on some ordinal scale $\mathcal{Y}$ (e.g., $y = 1$, not relevant to $y = 5$, very relevant), and the query-impression pairs are represented by a fixed length feature vectors $\mathbf{x}_{ql} \in \mathbb{R}^d$. The exact features used by search engines are proprietary, but generally include quantities measuring the textual overlap between the query and the listing body text, anchor text, the URL and document title. They may also include quantities specific to the query, like length of the query, or quantities specific to the listing: it's pagerank, linkage characteristics etc. Learning involves estimating the parameters of a model which takes as input the features $\mathbf{x}_{ql}$ associated with the query-impression pair (q, l), and produces the correct relevance score y.

2.1 NDCG

Recall that our goal is to produce ranking mechanisms that position relevant impressions in the very top of a ranked list extremely well. As mentioned earlier, it is known that the top few impressions get much more attention (clicks as well as views) than impressions further down the page [19]. Further down the list attention drops off even more rapidly, and many users rarely go beyond the first page of results [19]. Reflecting these concerns, an evaluation metric that has become very popular in the LTR community is Normalized Discounted Cumulative Gain or NDCG [12].

One can calculate the NDCG scores for any permutation of a set of items whose relevance labels are known. NDCG has one user-defined parameter and two functions that make it desirable in the ranking setting. The parameter k is a cut-off parameter, and determines how many items in the ranked list to consider. The two functions are the *gain function* and the *discount function*. The gain function allows a user to set the significance of each relevance level. The discount function makes items lower down in the ranked list contribute less to the NDCG score. More specifically, let $\mathbf{y}$ be a vector of the relevance values for a sequence of items (e.g., the impressions associated with one query). Let π denote a permutation over the sequence of items in $\mathbf{y}$. π, for example, would be the order of the listings returned by a trained ranking algorithm. Then π_q is the index of the qth item in π and y_{π_q} is the actual relevance value of this item. The Discounted Cumulative Gain (DCG) for this permutation π is defined as:

$$\text{DCG@}k(\mathbf{y}, \pi) = \sum_{q=1}^{k} \frac{2^{y_{\pi_q}} - 1}{\log_2(2+q)}.$$

The gain function is a power of two in this definition (minus 1), and the discount function has a logarithmic decay as we move down the ranked list. Normalized Discounted Cumulative Gain (NDCG) can then be defined as:

$$\text{NDCG@}k(\mathbf{y}, \pi) = \frac{\text{DCG@}k(\mathbf{y}, \pi)}{\text{DCG@}k(\mathbf{y}, \pi^*)}, \tag{1}$$

where π^* is a permutation over the sequence of items which corresponds to any perfect ordering based on the relevance scores; an ordering where no item with a low relevance score appears earlier than any item with a higher relevance score in the ordering (in other words, with the items sorted by $\mathbf{y}$, and ties broken arbitrarily).

Ideally, one would like to learn the parameters of the ranking model so that it directly maximizes the NDCG of the predicted rankings. However the fact that the metric is discontinuous everywhere presents significant challenges while optimizing it. Furthermore, the inherent "sort" associated with it makes the design of smooth relaxations/approximations of this metric equally difficult. To this end several authors [5, 3, 15] have proposed a number of solutions for the LTR problem, which involve a surrogate loss function whose minimization will loosely approximate the maximization of the NDCG metric. We describe some of these LTR proposals at a high level next.

2.2 Learning to Rank Approaches

Models in the LTR paradigm can be grouped into three main categories: point-wise, pair-wise and the so called list-wise approaches. The differences are mainly with respect to the form of loss function and training data used.

Point-wise models estimate a parametric function $h(\mathbf{x}_{ql})$ that takes as input the features associated with each query-impression item and produce as output a relevance score. In order to train the parameters of this function, one can either use a regression loss when the predicted relevance scores are continuous ($h : \mathbb{R}^d \to \mathbb{R}$) [5], or a classification loss when the relevance scores are discrete ($h : \mathbb{R}^d \to \mathcal{Y}$) [15]. Typically, while training, the performance on a ranking metric, such as NDCG, is mimicked by the judicious choice of the target response. For instance in [5], the authors work with a exponentiation of the actual relevance values as the targets for regression. This rescales the relevance value y to a value closer to the numerator of the NDCG metric. Thus point-wise models are essentially regression/classification models for web-search query-impression, relevance data. Note that in point-wise models, the distinction between queries is typically expressed only through appropriate query-impression features, $\mathbf{x}_{ql}$. In other words, the query q and impression l only define appropriate features; these examples with their features $\mathbf{x}_{ql}$ and associated responses are subsequently modeled independently. Underlying the modeling is the assumption that the query-impression features $\mathbf{x}_{ql}$ are informative enough to distinguish their given relevance levels. For the models themselves, flexible and powerful (non-linear) regression/classification methods like gradient boosted regression trees are typically used. The advantage of such point-wise models is that learning models is relatively straightforward, and more importantly, these methods scale well to large size problems.

Pair-wise models also estimate a function, $g(\mathbf{x}_{ql})$ that scores each query-impression item[1] $g : \mathbb{R}^d \to \mathbb{R}$. However, the training loss for pair-wise models is based on pairs of impressions with the same query, $\{(q_i, \mathbf{x}_{q_i l_i}, y_i), (q_j, \mathbf{x}_{q_j l_j}, y_j)\}$ where $q_i = q_j$, but $l_i \neq l_j$. The pair-wise loss depends on the order of the relevance labels of the items in the pair. The loss is low when the predicted order is correct, or in other words, when the more relevant item in a pair is predicted to have a higher score than the less relevant item. In our example, with $y_j > y_i$ the loss would be low for $g(\mathbf{x}_{q_j l_j}) > g(\mathbf{x}_{q_i l_i})$. The loss would be high when there is a mistake in the order. For instance, in our previous example, when $y_j > y_i$, but $g(\mathbf{x}_{q_j l_j}) < g(\mathbf{x}_{q_i l_i})$. Examples of pairwise approaches are RankBoost [8], RankNet and LambdaRank [3]. The intuition for these models is that a function that can order well should also be able to rank the items well.

We also briefly give pointers to list-wise approaches, such as, AdaRank and PermuRank [23, 24] which are beyond the scope of our work (and may be an interesting avenue of future work). These methods have been devised to iteratively optimize specialized ranking performance measures like NDCG, mean-average precision etc.

We next proceed to outlining how these LTR approaches (point-wise and pair-wise) can be applied to the recommendation problem. A number of questions naturally crop up. How exactly do we set up the recommendation problem in an analogous fashion to ranking? What is the concept corresponding to a query in the collaborative filtering setting? What features can we use? What choice of parametric functions will perform well? How do we modify the point-wise and pair-wise loss to optimize performance on NDCG? We tackle these and other issues next.

3. COLLABORATIVE RANKING

Recall that the objective of a recommender system is to make effective recommendations given the ratings data R, on a set of m users $\mathcal{U}$, and n items $\mathcal{I}$. In our notation, we will use the index $j \in \mathcal{U}$ to index over the users and the index $i \in \mathcal{I}$ to index over the items. Thus, we can refer to

[1]There are analogous classification based pairwise models as well, but we will be concerned with regression models in this paper.

an individual rating for item i and user j by R_{ij}. Since in practice a typical user rates only a small set of items, the ratings data R is usually very sparse.

We first outline latent factor models [14], a standard class of collaborative filtering models that are very popular and effective. In a latent factor model, we learn d-dimensional vectors representing "factors" for each user and each item. Typically, d is much smaller than either m or n, and it models our belief that a small number of unobserved factors are sufficient to provide accurate ratings. We then make predictions for a rating $\hat{R}_{ij}$, by taking the dot product of the factors for item i and user j. Mathematically:

$$\hat{R}_{ij} = \mathbf{v}_i^{\mathrm{T}}\mathbf{u}_j,$$

where the factors for each item i and user j, are the d-dimensional vectors $\mathbf{v}_i$ and $\mathbf{u}_j$.[2] We will also refer to the collection of all the user factors with $\mathbf{U}$, and similarly the collection of all the item factors with $\mathbf{V}$.

When MSE is the evaluation and training criterion, this leads to parameter estimation using modifications of the following primary objective function:

$$\min_{\mathbf{u},\mathbf{v}} \sum_{\{i,j\}\in R} (R_{ij}-\mathbf{v}_i^{\mathrm{T}}\mathbf{u}_j)^2+\lambda\left(\sum_{i=1}^{n}||\mathbf{v}_i||^2+\sum_{j=1}^{m}||\mathbf{u}_j||^2\right). \quad (2)$$

The differences in various latent factor models are usually in the form of the regularization of the factors. In the formulation above, from Probabilistic Matrix Factorization (PMF, [20]) factor regularization is in the form of a squared ℓ_2 norm on the factors. We overload the notation of R to also denote indexing over the non-zero ratings in the sparse matrix ($\{i,j\} \in R$). Also, test MSE is given by $1/|R^*|\sum_{\{i,j\}\in R^*}(R^*_{ij} - \mathbf{v}_i^{\mathrm{T}}\mathbf{u}_j)^2$, again overloading the notation of the test ratings matrix R^*. In particular, $|R^*|$ denotes the number of test user-item pairs.

As argued earlier, we believe that the squared loss over the predicted and actual ratings is suboptimal for top-k recommendations. This is because MSE loss treats all wrongly predicted ratings equally. We instead propose to use mean NDCG@k (Equation 1) as the evaluation metric. We craft suitable ranking losses borrowing ideas from the LTR community in order to learn models which are more accurate for the ranking task. We call this paradigm collaborative ranking (as in [22]). Following LTR methods (see Section 2), we propose point-wise and pair-wise solutions to the problem.

3.1 Point-wise Models

The first set of methods we propose are similar to the regression based point-wise approaches used in the LTR community. The key insight is an idea proposed in [5] and also in [15]; perfect regression (or classification) will also result in perfect NDCG. Analyzing DCG, Cossock and Zhang were able to bound DCG errors by regression errors [5]. Similarly, Li et. al in [15] were able to bound DCG errors by classification errors. Practically, this implies that regression (or classification) is a feasible path towards optimizing for ranking. These results are favorable because both regression and classification are extremely well studied and scalable.

Recall that in the LTR setting, there are queries, impressions, and corresponding relevance labels, and that query-impression pairs give rise to the features in these models. For our recommender task however, we only have sparse ratings data R. Hence it is unclear how to directly apply the above regression (or classification) type approaches used in LTR to the collaborative ranking task. In particular, we need to clearly define the analogous concepts to a query, the query-impression features and the relevance values. Recall that LTR problem essentially involves ranking a set of impressions in response to a query. Analogously, one can view the problem of recommendations, as ranking a set of items for a particular user. Hence a user in the recommendation task correspond to a query in web-search. Next, while we wish to use mean test NDCG as an evaluation metric, unlike in LTR, we do not have explicit user-item features with which to train the models. Conveniently, this is exactly what we get as a result of training a latent factor model. Finally, with queries being equivalent to users, and features being defined, the relevance values for query-impressions, intuitively correspond to the user-item rating values that we have observed.

This leads to our first proposal. It is a two step procedure. The first step involves training a latent factor model using RMSE to obtain the user and item factors. In our experiments we used the PMF model described in Equation 2. After the model is trained, the factors for item i and user j are concatenated to form a feature vector associated with the item-user pair (i, j). These form "features" for each rating of the item-user pair. In the second step, using the features learned from the first step as input, we apply a regression based point-wise LTR algorithm to optimize for ranking. We call this simple two-stage method $\mathrm{CR}_{\triangleright\mathrm{MF}}$, where the $\triangleright$ symbol is used to denote that it is point-wise technique, and the MF stands for features estimated using matrix factorization.

We have found any class of regression function g that has sufficient capacity works well with $\mathrm{CR}_{\triangleright\mathrm{MF}}$. We experimented with various non-linear regressors with roughly equal success. In particular, we tried gradient boosted trees [9, 15], random forests [2, 18] and multi-layer neural networks [3].

In more detail, the procedure for training a $\mathrm{CR}_{\triangleright\mathrm{MF}}$ model based on a neural network for g is as follows:

1. Given ratings data R, we first train a d-dimensional factor model, such as PMF, which minimizes the objective function in Equation 2. This results in a set of item and user factors $\mathbf{V}$ and $\mathbf{U}$.

2. We then create a new training dataset $\mathcal{D}$ for rank-based training as follows: For every observed training rating R_{ij} from item i and user j, we create a single fixed length feature vector $\mathbf{x}_{ij} = [\mathbf{v}_i; \mathbf{u}_j]$ of length $2k$. The symbol ";" denotes column-wise concatenation. Further, for every target rating R_{ij} we also create a modified response y_{ij} given by $y_{ij} = 2^{R_{ij}} - 1$. This rescaling of the response to better reflect NDCG gain was suggested in [5] and was found to work well in [15]. Thus, we have a data set $\mathcal{D} = \{(\mathbf{x}_z, y_z)\}$ with $z = \{i, j\} \in R$, indexing all the training ratings.

3. Using this labeled data set $\mathcal{D}$ we then learn a suitable regression function g, with parameters $\boldsymbol{\theta}$, to map user-item features to the rescaled rating value. Thus g is a function such that $g : \mathbb{R}^{2k} \to \mathbb{R}$. Learning involves minimizing the squared error on the rescaled

[2] Note that an error term is also typically included to complete the model specification. Gaussian noise is typically the error form used.

responses:

$$\mathcal{L} = \sum_{(\mathbf{x}_z, y_z) \in \mathcal{D}} (y_z - g(\mathbf{x}_z))^2. \quad (3)$$

This minimization is accomplished using stochastic gradient descent. In particular, for every item-user pair (i, j), its feature vector $\mathbf{x}_{ij} = [\mathbf{v}_i; \mathbf{u}_j]$ is forward propagated through the function g to compute the output and the loss. The gradient of the loss with respect to the parameters of the function is computed using back-propagation, and the parameters $\boldsymbol{\theta}$ are updated. We use learning rate annealing and early stopping as a way to regularize the parameters. See Figure 1 for a schematic depiction of the model.

4. At test time, given a user-item pair to make a prediction for, we construct the corresponding user-item features, and obtain a score using the learnt function g.

5. Once our model has predicted the scores of all the item-user pairs, a ranked list of movies for any user can be trivially obtained by sorting the movies according to their scores for that user.

One issue with this model is its two step nature. In the first phase the features for $\text{CR}_{\triangleright\text{MF}}$ are learned using MSE minimization, and it is not clear that these are the optimal features to use for the ranking task. Ideally one would want to use features best suited for the final task at hand. Using neural networks as the ranking function provides us with an attractive opportunity of learning the parameters of the network while simultaneously learning the item-user feature representation tuned for the ranking task. This results in a unified model for this problem, which is entirely ranking based and estimated from the data. The feature learning aspect of this work is inspired by models for Natural Language Processing problems [1, 4].

We call this unified model $\text{CR}_{\triangleright\text{LF}}$ (LF for Learned Factors). At a high level, $\text{CR}_{\triangleright\text{LF}}$ is like a typical factor model, in that it has d-dimensional factors $\mathbf{U}$ and $\mathbf{V}$ for all training users and items. Additionally though, $\text{CR}_{\triangleright\text{LF}}$ has a set of parameters $\boldsymbol{\theta}$ that functionally determine how to compute predicted responses, which are scaled ratings. Both the factors and the model parameters $\boldsymbol{\theta}$, are learned simultaneously for the ranking task. We train this model using the following EM-like algorithm (see Figure 1):

1. We rescale the ratings as $y_{ij} = 2^{R_{ij}} - 1$.

2. The factors $\mathbf{U}$ and $\mathbf{V}$ are randomly initialized. One can potentially initialize the factors in other ways, such as, using the output of the matrix factorization procedure.

3. Next we fix the factors $\mathbf{U}$ and $\mathbf{V}$, and estimate the parameters $\boldsymbol{\theta}$ of the ranking function, which takes these features as input and produces a rescaled rating as output. This training is done by minimizing the squared error over the rescaled target response and the output of the regression function, using a stochastic gradient descent procedure (similar to what we described for $\text{CR}_{\triangleright\text{MF}}$).

4. After one epoch of parameter training in step 3, we fix the parameters $\boldsymbol{\theta}$ and train the features $\mathbf{U}$ and $\mathbf{V}$.

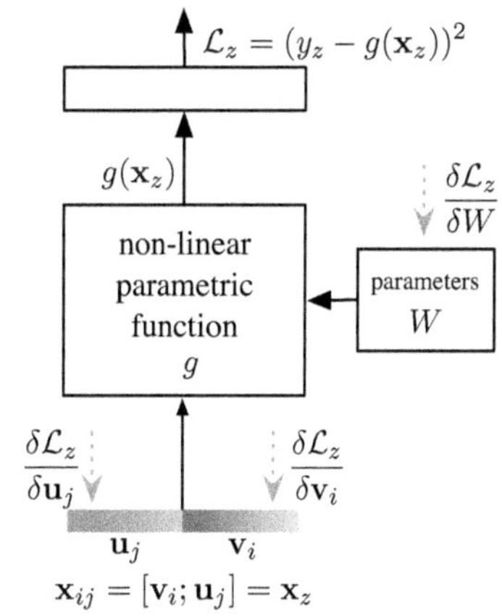

Figure 1: Schematic depiction of $\text{CR}_{\triangleright\text{MF}}$ and $\text{CR}_{\triangleright\text{LF}}$. User factors $\mathbf{u}_j$ and item factors $\mathbf{v}_i$ form the parameters $\mathbf{x}_z$, that are used by the model to compute a prediction $g(\mathbf{x}_z)$. Training for every sample involves back-propagating the gradients for the per-sample squared loss $\mathcal{L}_z = (y_z - g(\mathbf{x}_z))^2$, to update only the model parameters W (for $\text{CR}_{\triangleright\text{MF}}$), and additionally the item-user features $\mathbf{x}_z$ (for $\text{CR}_{\triangleright\text{LF}}$).

This step also uses stochastic gradient descent. However instead of computing the gradients respect to the parameters $\boldsymbol{\theta}$, we compute the gradient of the loss with respect to the feature vector $\mathbf{x}_{ij} = [\mathbf{v}_i; \mathbf{u}_j]$ using back-propagation and then update the feature vector.

5. We iterate steps 3 and 4 until validation error does not decrease and return the learned $\mathbf{U}$, $\mathbf{V}$ and $\boldsymbol{\theta}$.

Our experiments show this to be an accurate and efficient technique for collaborative ranking. We next turn to pair-wise approaches for collaborative ranking.

3.2 Pair-wise Models

Starting with [11], researchers have focused attention on pairwise training losses for the ranking problem. In the LTR community, SVMrank [13] by Joachims, RankNet and LambdaRank [3] by Burges et.al., have been particularly influential. Pair-wise techniques are attractive because eliciting explicit ratings (or relevance scores) suffers from a drawback known as *calibration* [10], which can be illustrated with two examples. First, users often have incompatible ratings on the same scale. For instance, on a ratings scale of 1 to 5, a rating of 4 for some user A might be comparable to a rating of 5 for another user B. Second, sometimes users start off by rating items in an overly generous (or harsh) manner and retrospectively come to regret those initial ratings after seeing some number of items. Instead of getting accurate predictions of relevance scores of individual items, pair-wise techniques bypass the issues associated with calibration by focusing directly on learning the rank order between a pair of items correctly.

As in the case of point-wise models, the ideas behind the pair-wise models introduced for the LTR problem can be directly applied for solving the collaborative ranking problem, so long as we can define appropriate user-item features. The procedure at the heart of a pair-wise approach is to learn a parametric function $g(\mathbf{x}) : \mathbb{R}^d \rightarrow \mathbb{R}$, parameterized by $\boldsymbol{\theta}$, which operates on single user-item feature vector $\mathbf{x}_{ij}$ and returns a score. However, the approach is pair-wise because the parameters $\boldsymbol{\theta}$ are trained using pairs of examples. This leads to a model that can make test predictions quickly, because it operates on a single user-item feature vector; pairs of examples are only used in training, they are not needed at test time.

Our first proposal is an analogous pair-wise extension to the two stage point-wise model $\mathrm{CR}_{\triangleright\mathrm{MF}}$. We denote this model with the symbol $\mathrm{CR}_{\bowtie\mathrm{MF}}$, where $\bowtie$ refers to pair-wise training. The detailed procedure is as follows:

1. Given the ratings data R, we first train a d-dimensional factor model to obtain item and user factors $\mathbf{V}$ and $\mathbf{U}$.

2. We then create a dataset $\mathcal{D}$, with the same features as the point-wise features, namely, for every item-user pair (i, j) we generate a feature vector $\mathbf{x}_{ij}$, obtained by concatenating the factors associated with item i and user j: $\mathbf{x}_{ij} = [\mathbf{v}_i; \mathbf{u}_j]$. The target response y_{ij} for this item-user pair is set to the original rating $y_{ij} = R_{ij}$ (no rescaling in this case). At the end of this step, we have a training data set $\mathcal{D} = \{(\mathbf{x}_z, y_z)\}$ with $z = \{i, j\} \in R$.

3. We then learn the parameters $\boldsymbol{\theta}$ of our scoring function $g(\mathbf{x})$, on pairs of examples from $\mathcal{D}$ by setting up an appropriate pair-wise probabilistic regression [3]. Let a pair of ratings from a particular user, on two different items be indexed by z_1 and z_2. Define $o_{z_1} = g(\mathbf{x}_{z_1})$ as the model output (the predicted rating score), and $o_{z_1 z_2} = g(\mathbf{x}_{z_1}) - g(\mathbf{x}_{z_2})$ as the difference between the predicted scores on a pair of items from the same user. Let $P_{z_1 > z_2}$ denote the probability under the model that item z_1 is ranked higher than item z_2 for this user. Following [3] we use a logistic function $\sigma(q) = \frac{1}{1+e^{-q}}$ to model this probability conditioned on the model outputs. Thus:

$$P_{z_1 > z_2} = \frac{e^{o_{z_1 z_2}}}{1 + e^{o_{z_1 z_2}}} = \frac{e^{g(\mathbf{x}_{z_1}) - g(\mathbf{x}_{z_2})}}{1 + e^{g(\mathbf{x}_{z_1}) - g(\mathbf{x}_{z_2})}}. \quad (4)$$

Learning the model involves estimating the parameters $\boldsymbol{\theta}$ of the score function g, such that the model produces a high probability $P_{z_1 > z_2}$ for a pair of samples for which $y_{z_1} > y_{z_2}$, and low probability when $y_{z_1} < y_{z_2}$. This is accomplished by minimizing the cross entropy loss. In particular, let $Y_{z_1 > z_2} = I(y_{z_1} - y_{z_2})$ be an indicator function which takes on the values in $\{0, 1\}$ depending on whether $y_{z_1} > y_{z_2}$ or not. Then the loss over a single pair of examples is given by:

$$\mathcal{L}_{z_1 z_2} = \log(1 + e^{o_{z_1 z_2}}) - Y_{z_1 > z_2} o_{z_1 z_2}. \quad (5)$$

We used a a multi-layer neural network for the scoring function g in our experiments, and we minimize the cross entropy loss using stochastic gradient descent. See Figure 2 for a schematic representation of the model and the training process.

4. Step 3 is repeated for all the pairs of examples for every user until the error on the validation set stops decreasing. The loss over the entire data set is given by

$$\mathcal{L} = \sum_{z_1, z_2 \in \mathcal{D}} (\log(1 + e^{o_{z_1 z_2}}) - Y_{z_1 > z_2} o_{z_1 z_2}). \quad (6)$$

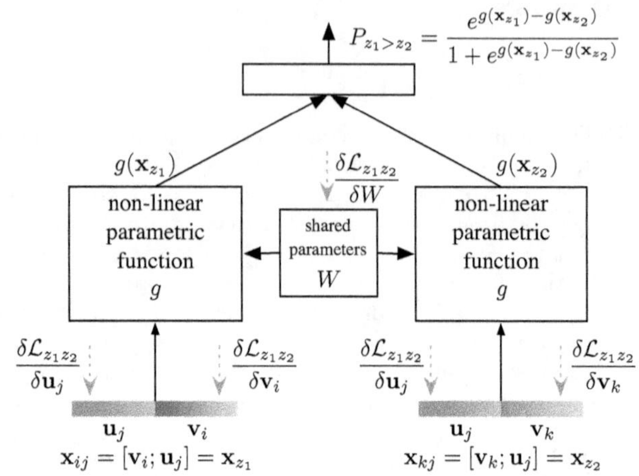

Figure 2: Figure illustrating the pair-wise models $\mathrm{CR}_{\bowtie\mathrm{MF}}$ and $\mathrm{CR}_{\bowtie\mathrm{LF}}$. In these models, pairs of ratings i and k, from the same user j define our input features $\mathbf{x}_{z_1}$ and $\mathbf{x}_{z_2}$. The identical function g estimates a score for both z_1 and z_2. The per-sample loss $\mathcal{L}_{z_1 z_2}$ (given by equation 5) is a function of the difference of these scores and the true ratings for i and k. Training for each pair of samples involve back-propagating the gradients of this loss only to the model parameters W (for $\mathrm{CR}_{\bowtie\mathrm{MF}}$), and additionally to the features $\mathbf{x}_{z_1}$ and $\mathbf{x}_{z_2}$ (for $\mathrm{CR}_{\bowtie\mathrm{LF}}$).

5. At test time, given a user-item pair to make a prediction for, we construct the corresponding user-item features, and obtain a prediction by the output of the function g with learned parameters θ. Ranking follows by sorting the predicted scores for each user.

Since we use neural networks for the function g, in a similar manner to the point-wise case, we have the ability to learn a unified model in the pair-wise setting too. We denote this proposal where we additionally learn the factors by $\mathrm{CR}_{\bowtie\mathrm{LF}}$, and the EM style algorithm to fit this model follows an analogous recipe: fix the factors $\mathbf{U}$, $\mathbf{V}$ and estimate $\boldsymbol{\theta}$; then fix $\boldsymbol{\theta}$ and estimate the factors $\mathbf{U}$, $\mathbf{V}$ (see Figure 2).

3.2.1 A Heuristic for Pair-wise Models

Careful readers would have observed that the complexity of the pair-wise procedures appears quite large; training on pairs of ratings is burdensome, especially when most collaborative filtering datasets have millions of observed ratings. We do point out that we only construct pairs from ratings by the same user, and so for our sparse ratings matrix, the number of such pairs far less than $O(|R|^2)$. However, considering even all ratings pairs from every user is quite challenging because many datasets contain many active/heavy users, who have thousands of ratings each.

Another issue associated with the pair-wise models, which was raised in the LambdaRank paper [3], bears resemblance to the issue with using MSE evaluation metric in the point-wise models. In particular, while training, giving equal emphasis to all the pairs per user might be suboptimal when NDCG is used as an evaluation metric[3]. This is because

[3]Note that LambdaRank was a web-search LTR proposal

NDCG cares more about higher rating values, both via the gain function, and the discount function (see Equation 1). In other words, trying to get g to learn an ordering between a pair of items rated '1' and '2' is not very useful. In LambdaRank, the authors address this shortcoming by modifying the gradient update steps while cycling through all (per user) pairs. In particular, they create all possible pairs for every user, but assign weights to each pair, so that the pairs involving higher ratings, such as ('5','4'), are assigned a higher weight than those involving lower ratings, such as ('2', '1'). During the gradient update of the parameters, this results in a larger gradient step (and thus a bigger change in g) for pairs involving higher ratings, and a smaller step for pairs involving lower ratings. In other words, pairs with higher ratings have more influence on g. They also show that empirically, this procedure leads to locally optimal NDCG [7].

We instead dispatch with both of these problems, namely, of large number of pairs and of dealing with non-informative pairs for NDCG, with one simple heuristic. For each user, instead of creating all pairs of items, we only create pairs which have at least one of the top ratings class the user has rated any item with. For instance, if a particular user has used values '5', '4', '3', '2', to rate various items, then for this user we only form pairs which consists of at least one item rated either a '5' or a '4'. The procedure is as follows:

1. For every user we collect all the items which she has rated and sort them according to their ratings. Let us denote this set of items by $\mathcal{S}_j$ for a user j.

2. We pick the highest rated item from $\mathcal{S}_j$, and pair it with all the items in the set which are rated less than the rating of the picked item.

3. We then remove this item from the set $\mathcal{S}_j$.

4. We repeat steps 2 and 3 until we have exhausted all the items corresponding to the top 2 rating classes for that user.

The intuition behind this is that the pairs containing the top two ratings classes for every user (say '4's and '5's), are what we need to be concerned with, when we are evaluating NDCG. As pointed out in [5] and [15], in order to have good test NDCG performance, the learned function necessarily need not have perfect regression (or classification) performance. For instance, adding the same constant to every rating score will not affect the NDCG performance. Indeed, what matters are just two things: A) The ability to accurately distinguish between the highly rated items, say, between an item rated '4' and an item rated '5'. B) The ability to accurately distinguish highly rated items from low rated items, say between an item rated a '4' and an item rated a '1'. Our heuristic captures both of these requirements. A. is addressed by making pairs of items with ratings of the form ('5','4'). B. is encoded by only makings pairs of items with at least one high rating, i.e., pairs of the form ('5','1') or ('4', '2'). Since being able to order a ('1', '2') pair is likely not useful at all to test NDCG, we don't create any such pairs with our heuristic.

and not about recommendations. We have taken the liberty of translating the ideas in question to our setting for clarity and continuity.

4. RELATED WORK AND EVALUATION

We now turn to related proposals in the literature. Indeed, not many other researchers have focused on matrix factorization from a ranking perspective. As we mentioned in the introduction, the de-facto standard is to perform matrix factorization using MSE/RMSE. But, before we discuss some of the related proposals, we point out here that evaluating recommenders on the ranking task is complicated by the fact that we have a fixed number of ratings to use both for training the models and evaluating them (as opposed to evaluating a deployed system on live users, for example). We address this issue next.

4.1 Evaluation

In particular, training and experimental evaluation with a single fixed ratings dataset suffers from a rather direct trade-off between having more ratings for training, and thus decreasing the bias in the model predictions, and having more ratings for testing, and decreasing the bias in the evaluation[4]. Our metric of choice, NDCG, is particularly vulnerable to this trade-off.

As an example, consider the standard training validation (probe) split for the Netflix dataset, where the validation dataset consists of about three ratings per user. In this case, after training on the training dataset, we wouldn't even be able to evaluate NDCG@10 on the validation dataset. As a more relevant example, using some fixed number of randomly sampled ratings for validation/testing, say 20 per user will result in high variance estimates of NDCG@10.

Since we are making the case for collaborative ranking, we prefer more accurate/lower variance evaluations, and thus our preferred train-test split has many more test ratings per user than training ratings. Indeed, this form of experimental setup (large test dataset, smaller training dataset) was also the one favored by CofiRank [22]. Cremonesi et al. [6], pursue a different form of evaluation. In what follows, we briefly outline these two proposals and highlight the similarities and differences compared to our methods.

4.2 Cremonesi et al.

In their recent paper, Cremonesi et al. point out the inadequacies of MSE/RMSE as an evaluation metric [6]. Like us, they argue that a top-k based recommendation scheme is a better and more natural fit with how the recommender will finally be used. In their paper, they show that methods trained to perform well on MSE/RMSE, do not behave particularly well on the top-k recommendation task. They further propose straightforward sparse SVD (as SVD requires a full rank matrix, the impute zero values for unseen ratings) as a competitive method for the top-k recommendation task. However, there are significant differences between their work and ours. The biggest difference is in how they evaluate their top-k recommenders. Cremonesi et al. do not consider NDCG; they evaluate using precision/recall on just a small number of high ratings and also a large number of items sampled at random. They settle on this scheme in order to train on a much larger set of ratings. While this is reasonable, we prefer our evaluation using NDCG which avoids random sampling and has very little bias. Another issue that Cremonesi et al. bring up is that popular items seem to heavily

[4]LTR approaches do not suffer from this issue as they simply evaluate on test/ independent queries

sway the performance of algorithms on their precision/recall evaluation metric. Again, we feel this is mainly due to the nature of their evaluation metric; in experiments we do not report, both sparse SVD and top-pop (a non-personalized recommender that simply returns the items sorted by the number of training occurrences) perform non-competitively compared to the methods we evaluate.

4.3 Cof Rank

A proposal much closer to our work is CofiRank [22]. The motivation and development of CofiRank is exactly the same as that of our models. They argue for NDCG being a better training/evaluation metric for recommendations, and the experimental protocol we follow is essentially the same as theirs (to allow for comparison). In CofiRank, the authors fit a maximum margin matrix factorization model (matrix factorization with a trace norm regularization on the factors) to minimize various losses including NDCG@k. There are a few very important differences between our proposals. Perhaps the biggest difference lies in our pair-wise and point-wise training loss which is different than CofiRank's proposal to directly minimize training NDCG@k. In the same way that evaluation is difficult in this setting, it is not clear that minimizing training NDCG@k will give a model that performs well on test NDCG@k, particularly when the train and test data are of different sizes. This may be why in the CofiRank paper, the authors report that Cofi with a regression (squared) loss (Cofi-reg) performs competitively/better that Cofi model trained using NDCG@k (Cofi-NDCG). In our experiments, we also consistently found Cofi-reg to be better than Cofi-NDCG. Other minor differences between CofiRank and us have to do with the form regularization used in the matrix factorization model. While Cofi uses MMMF, we use PMF [20], which has a slightly different form of regularization.

5. EXPERIMENTS

We now describe the experiments we performed to evaluate our methods. We evaluate our proposals on several well known collaborative filtering data sets. The data sets are primarily for movie (and TV shows on DVD) recommendation, and are comprised of a collection of ratings given by a set of users to a set of movies. In particular, we used the MovieLens data, and the EachMovie data. These data sets vary in their size and composition. Table 1 gives some basic statistics associated with each one.

Our experimental evaluation closely follows the experimental evaluations in the CofiRank paper. For every user, we randomly sample a fixed number N of ratings and place them in the training set. The remaining ratings by that user are placed in the test set. We experimented with $N = 10$, 20, and 50 training ratings per user. Since we evaluate NDCG@10, we require that users have rated at least 20, 30, and 60 items respectively. Users not meeting these requirements are dropped from both training and test data sets. In addition, we require that for an item to be considered, it should have been rated by at least 5 users in the data set (train+test). Items not meeting this criteria are also dropped. This filtering results in a slight decrease in the number of users and items in the data sets. The original number of users and items are reported in the first two columns of Table 1. For data sets corresponding to different values of N, the average number of users and items after filtering are reported in the last two columns of Table 1. For both the data sets, for different values of N, we generate 10 replicate data sets, each with a different random samples for the training and test set. We report the average NDCG@10 over these 10 replicates for each N. NDCG at other cutoffs gave us different numerical values but qualitative exactly the same results.

5.1 Results

In all our models the parametric scoring function g was a two layer fully connected neural network. The first layer (the hidden layer) was a standard perceptron layer consisting of a linear module followed by a tanh non-linearity applied component-wise to the output of the linear module. The second layer (the output layer) was a fully connected linear layer, which used the output of the hidden layer as input and produced a score. The number of units in the hidden layer were fixed for all the experiments and were set to 400. Since it is a scoring function, the output layer consisted of a single unit. Other hyper parameters associated with the model, such as the learning rates, and the number of training epochs for early stopping were chosen once per data set using a separate training/validation data set sampled with similar characteristics. We did not do further parameter optimization. The results shown are for models learned with these fixed parameters.

As the baseline model, we chose standard Probabilistic Matrix Factorization (PMF) which is fit by minimizing regularized MSE (Equation 2). We also compared our models against CofiRank [22]. We set the factor dimensionality, $d = 50$ in all our experiments. We trained and evaluated the point-wise models $CR_{\triangleright MF}$ and $CR_{\triangleright FL}$. We also trained and evaluated the pair-wise models $CR_{\bowtie MF}$ and $CR_{\bowtie FL}$. The features for $CR_{\triangleright MF}$ and $CR_{\bowtie MF}$ were obtained from the baseline PMF model.

Our results on the MovieLens, and EachMovie data sets are reported in Tables 2 and 3. Overall, the results show some intuitive patterns. All methods get better at making ranking recommendations with increasing number of available training ratings N per user. Furthermore, we see that the baseline results are quite reasonable. In other words, in line with our expectations, minimizing training MSE is not a terrible proxy to train on for providing ranking recommendations. Since training for min MSE is the de-facto standard, our results provide reassurance for using this approach. CofiRank did not do well in our evaluation. We trained all three versions of CofiRank discussed in [22], namely Cofi-NDCG, Cofi-ord (ordinal loss), and Cofi-reg. In our results, we report the performance of the best performing model of the three. We use the untuned hyper-parameter settings as described in [22]. In our experiments we found that in many cases, Cofi-reg was the best method.

However the models we propose in this paper are the clear winners. They provide superior ranking recommendation performance. We show substantial gains in NDCG even when we use the fixed factors obtained by minimizing the MSE, just by using a different yet straightforward predictive model such as $CR_{\triangleright MF}$. This validates our hypothesis that the MSE minimization is not optimal for making recommendations. Furthermore, tuning the factors according to the task at hand is critical and can lead to even more improvement. This is evident from the performance of our learned feature models, $CR_{\triangleright FL}$ and $CR_{\bowtie FL}$. Our experiments do not provide evidence for the superiority of pair-wise or point-wise models. As a practical suggestion, we thus recommend using point-wise models, over their pair-wise counterparts, due to their efficiency and scalability.

6. CONCLUSIONS AND FUTURE WORK

In this paper we argue for collaborative ranking as a better way to make recommendations. Inspired by recent work in the LTR community, we present novel models for the collaborative ranking problem, and their accompanying efficient algorithms. Our experiments show that our proposals are accurate and that learning features for the ranking task produces the best performing models. In future work, we would like to extend our models to richer models like list-wise LTR approaches. Other avenues for future work include analyzing and formalizing our pair-wise heuristic, and improving the scalability of the pair-wise algorithms. Lastly, we plan on extending these results to bigger data sets, such as Netflix, and to data sets from different domains, such as music recommendation, and book recommendations.

7. ACKNOWLEDGMENTS

We would like to acknowledge discussions with Bob Bell, always a source of great ideas and inspiration.

8. REFERENCES

[1] Y. Bengio, R. Ducharme, P. Vincent, and C. Janvin. A neural probabilistic language model. *Journal of Machine Learning Research*, 3:1137–1155, 2003.

[2] L. Breiman. Random forests. In *Machine Learning*, volume 45(1), 2001.

[3] C. Burges. From ranknet to lambdarank to lambdamart: An overview. In *Microsoft Research Technical Report MSR-TR-2010-82*, 2010.

[4] R. Collobert and J. Weston. A unified architecture for natural language processing: deep neural networks with multitask learning. In *ICML '08: Proceedings of the 25th international conference on Machine learning*, pages 160–167, New York, NY, USA, 2008. ACM.

[5] D. Cossock and T. Zhang. Statistical analysis of bayes optimal subset ranking. *IEEE Transactions on Information Theory*, 54(11):5140–5154, 2008.

[6] P. Cremonesi, Y. Koren, and R. Turrin. Performance of recommender algorithms on top-n recommendation tasks. In *Proceedings of the fourth ACM conference on Recommender systems*, RecSys '10, pages 39–46, New York, NY, USA, 2010. ACM.

[7] P. Donmez, K. M. Svore, and C. J. Burges. On the local optimality of lambdarank. In *Proceedings of the 32nd international ACM SIGIR conference on Research and development in information retrieval*, SIGIR '09, pages 460–467, New York, NY, USA, 2009. ACM.

[8] Y. Freund, R. Iyer, R. E. Schapire, and Y. Singer. An efficient boosting algorithm for combining preferences. *J. Mach. Learn. Res.*, 4:933–969, 2003.

[9] J. H. Friedman. Greedy function approximation: A gradient boosting machine. *Annals of Statistics*, 29:1189–1232, 2000.

[10] S. Hacker and L. von Ahn. Matchin: eliciting user preferences with an online game. In *CHI '09: Proceedings of the 27th international conference on Human factors in computing systems*, pages 1207 – 1216, New York, NY, USA, 2009. ACM.

[11] R. Herbrich, T. Graepel, and K. Obermayer. Large margin rank boundaries for ordinal regression. In P. J. Bartlett, B. Schölkopf, D. Schuurmans, and A. J. Smola, editors, *Advances in Large Margin Classifiers*, pages 115–132. MIT Press, 2000.

[12] K. Järvelin and J. Kekäläinen. Cumulated gain-based evaluation of ir techniques. *ACM Trans. Inf. Syst.*, 20:422–446, October 2002.

[13] T. Joachims. Optimizing search engines using clickthrough data. In *Proceedings of the eighth ACM SIGKDD international conference on Knowledge discovery and data mining*, KDD '02, pages 133–142, New York, NY, USA, 2002. ACM.

[14] Y. Koren, R. Bell, and C. Volinsky. Matrix Factorization Techniques for Recommender Systems. *Computer*, 42(8):30 – 37, 2009.

[15] P. Li, C. J. C. Burges, and Q. Wu. Mcrank: Learning to rank using multiple classification and gradient boosting, 2007.

[16] B. M. Marlin and R. S. Zemel. Collaborative prediction and ranking with non-random missing data. *Proceedings of the third ACM conference on Recommender systems (RecSys '09)*, 2009.

[17] P. Melville and V. Sindhwani. Recommender Systems. 2010.

[18] A. Mohan, Z. Chen, and K. Q. Weinberger. Web-search ranking with initialized gradient boosted regression trees. *Journal of Machine Learning Research, Workshop and Conference Proceedings*, 14:77–89, 2011.

[19] M. Richardson, E. Dominowska, and R. Ragno. Predicting clicks: estimating the click-through rate for new ads. In *Proceedings of the 16th international conference on World Wide Web*, WWW '07, pages 521–530, New York, NY, USA, 2007. ACM.

[20] R. Salakhutdinov and A. Mnih. Probabilistic matrix factorization. In *Neural Information Processing Systems (NIPS)*, 2007.

[21] H. Steck and R. S. Zemel. A generalized probabilistic framework and its variants for training top-k recommender systems. *Workshop on the Practical Use of Recommender Systems, Algorithms and Technologies (PRSAT 2010)in conjunction with RecSys 2010*, 2010.

[22] M. Weimer, A. Karatzoglou, Q. V. Le, and A. Smola. Cofi-rank: Maximum margin matrix factorization for collaborative ranking. In *Neural Information Processing Systems (NIPS)*, 2007.

[23] J. Xu and H. Li. Adarank: a boosting algorithm for information retrieval. In *Proceedings of the 30th annual international ACM SIGIR conference on Research and development in information retrieval*, SIGIR '07, pages 391–398, New York, NY, USA, 2007. ACM.

[24] J. Xu, T.-Y. Liu, M. Lu, H. Li, and W.-Y. Ma. Directly optimizing evaluation measures in learning to rank. In *Proceedings of the 31st annual international ACM SIGIR conference on Research and development in information retrieval*, SIGIR '08, pages 107–114, New York, NY, USA, 2008. ACM.

Table 1: **The table showing the statistics associated with the three data sets which we used in the experiments. The column "Avg. Users (10/20/50)" (and "Avg. Items (10/20/50)") reports the average number of users (and items) in the three data sets generated after randomly sampling 10, 20 and 50 ratings per user as part of the training data.**

Data set	No. of Users	No. of Items	No. of Ratings	Ratings Scale	Avg. Users (10/20/50)	Avg. Items (10/20/50)
MovieLens	943	1682	100000	1 – 5	941/743/496	1094/1205/1279
Eachmovie	61265	1623	2811718	0 – 1	36656/28170/14350	1526/1564/1592

Table 2: The table reports NDCG@10 by various models on the MovieLens data set using different training set sizes. The mean and the standard deviation over the 10 folds is reported.

Method	N = 10	N = 20	N = 50
Baseline	0.6916 ± 0.0051	0.7087 ± 0.0031	0.7317 ± 0.0053
CofiRank	0.6994 ± 0.0079	0.7125 ± 0.0031	0.7204 ± 0.0040
$CR_{\triangleright MF}$	0.7026 ± 0.0022	0.7103 ± 0.0021	0.7242 ± 0.0051
$CR_{\triangleright FL}$	**0.7220** ± 0.0043	**0.7202** ± 0.0031	**0.7316** ± 0.0070
$CR_{\bowtie MF}$	0.7023 ± 0.0040	0.7129 ± 0.0033	0.7312 ± 0.0053
$CR_{\bowtie FL}$	**0.7184** ± 0.0031	**0.7221** ± 0.0034	**0.7360** ± 0.0058

Table 3: The table reports NDCG@10 by various models on the EachMovie data set using different training set sizes. The mean and the standard deviation over the 10 folds is reported.

Method	N = 10	N = 20	N = 50
Baseline	0.6950 ± 0.0019	0.7028 ± 0.0006	0.7269 ± 0.0007
CofiRank	0.7109 ± 0.0050	0.7271 ± 0.0074	0.7346 ± 0.0077
$CR_{\triangleright MF}$	0.6959 ± 0.0021	0.7409 ± 0.0013	0.7469 ± 0.0013
$CR_{\triangleright FL}$	**0.7205** ± 0.0010	**0.7620** ± 0.0005	**0.7593** ± 0.0013
$CR_{\bowtie MF}$	0.7038 ± 0.0016	0.7359 ± 0.0007	0.7367 ± 0.0010
$CR_{\bowtie FL}$	**0.7200** ± 0.0012	**0.7442** ± 0.0004	**0.7503** ± 0.0006

From Chatter to Headlines: Harnessing the Real-Time Web for Personalized News Recommendation

Gianmarco De Francisci Morales
IMT & ISTI-CNR
Lucca & Pisa, Italy
gdfm@yahoo-inc.com

Aristides Gionis
Yahoo! Research
Barcelona, Spain
gionis@yahoo-inc.com

Claudio Lucchese
ISTI-CNR
Pisa, Italy
claudio.lucchese@isti.cnr.it

ABSTRACT

We propose a new methodology for recommending interesting news to users by exploiting the information in their twitter persona. We model relevance between users and news articles using a mix of signals drawn from the news stream and from twitter: the profile of the social neighborhood of the users, the content of their own tweet stream, and topic popularity in the news and in the whole twitter-land.

We validate our approach on a real-world dataset of approximately 40k articles coming from Yahoo! News and one month of crawled twitter data. We train our model using a learning-to-rank approach and support-vector machines. The train and test set are drawn from Yahoo! toolbar log data. We heuristically identify 3 214 users of twitter in the log and use their clicks on news articles to train our system.

Our methodology is able to predict with good accuracy the news articles clicked by the users and rank them higher than other news articles. The results show that the combination of various signals from real-time web and micro-blogging platforms can be a useful resource to understand user behavior.

Categories and Subject Descriptors

H.4.m [**Information Systems**]: Miscellaneous

General Terms

Algorithms, Experimentation

Keywords

recommendation systems, news recommendation, real-time web, micro-blogging applications, personalization

1. INTRODUCTION

Information overload is a term referring to the difficulty in taking decisions or understanding an issue when there is more information than one can handle. Information overload is not a new problem. The term itself precedes the Internet by several years [23]. However, digital and automated information processing has aggravated the problem to unprecedented levels, transforming it into one of the crucial issues in the modern information society.

In this work we focus on one of the most common daily activities: news reading. Every day the press produces thousands of news articles covering a wide spectrum of topics. For a user, finding relevant and interesting information in this ocean of news is a daunting task.

News portals like Yahoo! news and Google news often resort to recommender systems to help the user find relevant pieces of information. In recent years the most successful recommendation paradigm has been *collaborative filtering* [2]. Collaborative filtering requires the users to rate the items they like. The rating can be explicit (e.g., 'like', '+1', number of stars) or implicit (e.g., click on a link, download). In both cases, collaborative filtering leverages a closed feedback loop: user preferences are inferred by looking only at the user interaction with the system itself. This approach suffers from a data sparsity problem, namely it is hard to make recommendations for users for whom there is little available information or for brand new items, since little or no feedback is available for such "cold" items.

At the same time, at an increasingly rate, web users access news articles via micro-blogging services and the so-called real-time web. By subscribing to feeds of other users, such as friends, colleagues, domain experts and enthusiasts, as well as to organizations of interest, they obtain timely access to relevant and personalized information. Yet, information obtained by micro-blogging services is not complete as highly-relevant events could easily be missed by users if none of their contacts posts about these events.

We propose to recommend news articles to users by combining two sources of information, news streams and micro-blogs, and leveraging the best features of each. News streams have high *coverage* as they aggregate a very large volume of news articles obtained from many different news agencies. On the other hand, information obtained by micro-blogging services can be exploited to address the problems of *information filtering and personalization*, as users can be placed in the context of their social circles and personal interests.

Our approach has the following advantages. First, we are able to overcome the data-sparsity problem: if we do not have enough information for a user, there should be significantly more information from the social circle of the user, which is presumably relevant. Second, more than once it has been reported that news break out earlier on the real-time

Permission to make digital or hard copies of all or part of this work for personal or classroom use is granted without fee provided that copies are not made or distributed for profit or commercial advantage and that copies bear this notice and the full citation on the first page. To copy otherwise, to republish, to post on servers or to redistribute to lists, requires prior specific permission and/or a fee.
WSDM'12, February 8–12, 2012, Seattle, Washington, USA.
Copyright 2012 ACM 978-1-4503-0747-5/12/02 ...$10.00.

web than in traditional media, and we would like to harness this property to provide timely recommendations.

With more than 200 million users, twitter is currently the most popular real-time web service. Twitter is an emerging agora where users publish short text messages, also known as tweets, and organize themselves into social networks. Interestingly, in many cases, news have been published and commented on twitter before any other news agency, as in the case of Osama Bin-Laden's death in 2011,[1] or Tiger Wood's car crash in 2009.[2] Due to its popularity, traditional news providers, such as magazines, news agencies, have become twitter users: they exploit twitter and its social network to disseminate their contents.

Example. In Figure 1(a) we show the normalized number of tweets and news articles regarding "Osama Bin Laden" during the time period between May 1st and 4th, 2011. For the news, we also report the number of clicks in the same period. We notice that the number of relevant tweets ramps up earlier than news, meaning that the information spread through twitter even before any press release. Later on, while the number of tweets decreases quickly, and stabilizes around a relatively small number of tweets, the number of published news continues to be quite large. The number of clicks on news articles follows somewhat the number of published news, even though there is a significant delay until the time the users actually click and read an article on the topic. Figure 1(b) presents similar information for the "Joplin tornado." In this case, even though there is a great activity both on twitter and on news streams, users start reading the news only after one day. About 60% of the clicks on the news occur after 10 hours from its publication. □

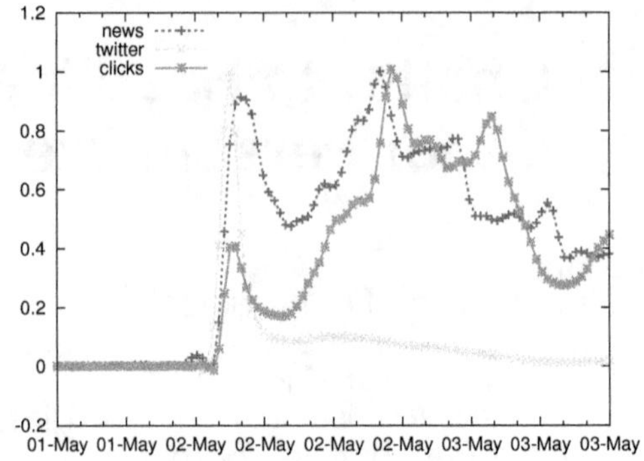

(a) *Osama Bin Laden*

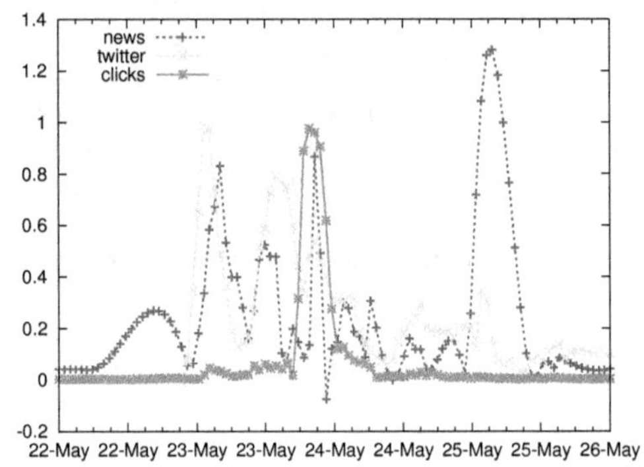

(b) *Joplin tornado*

Figure 1: Trends on twitter and news streams.

The goal of this work is to reduce the delay between the publication of a news and its access by a user. We aim at helping the users in finding relevant news as soon as they are published. Our envisioned application scenario is a feature operating on a news aggregator like Yahoo! news or Google news. Our objective is to develop a recommendation system that provides the users with fresh, relevant news by leveraging their tweet stream. Ideally, the users log in into the news portal and link their twitter account to their portal account in order to provide access to their tweet stream. The portal analyzes the tweet stream of the users and provides them personalized recommendations.

Solving this problem poses a number of research challenges. First, the volume of tweets and news is significantly large. It is necessary to design a scalable recommender system able to handle millions of users, tweets and news. Second, both tweets and news are unbounded streams of items arriving in real-time. The set of news from which to choose recommendations is highly dynamic. In fact, news are published continuously and, more importantly, they are related to events that cannot be predicted in advance. Also, by nature, news have a short life cycle, since they are replaced by updated news on the same topic, or because they become obsolete. Therefore, a recommender system should be able to find relevant news early, before they lose their value over time. Third, the nature of tweets, short and jargon-like, complicates the task of modeling the interests of users.

Finally, personalization should leverage user profiles to drive the user to less popular news. But it should not prevent from suggesting news of general interest, even when unrelated to the user profile, e.g., the Fukushima accident.

In summary, our contributions are the following.

- We propose a light-weight, adaptive, online recommendation system. In contrast, typical recommendation systems usually operate in offline mode.
- We present a new application of usage of tweets. Twitter has mainly been used to identify trending topics and analyzing information spread. Its application to recommendation has received little interest in the community. Our main recommendation system is called `T.Rex`, for *twitter-based news recommendation system.*
- Our system provides personalized recommendations by leveraging information from the tweet stream of users, as well as from the streams of their social circle. By incorporating social information we address the issue of data sparsity. When we do not have enough information for a user, for example for a new user or if a user rarely tweets, the available information in the social circle of the user provides a proxy to his interests.

The rest of the paper is organized as follows. In Section 2 we formalize the news recommendation problem, and introduce our proposed personalized news ranking function. In Section 3 we describe the learning process of the ranking function based on click data. In Section 4 we present the experimental setting used in the evaluation of our algorithms and our results. Finally, in Section 5 we discuss other work related to our paper, and Section 6 is a short conclusion.

[1] www.bbc.co.uk/news/technology-13257940

[2] techcrunch.com/2009/11/27/internet-twitter-tiger-woods

Table 1: Table of symbols.

Symbol	Definition
$\mathcal{N} = \{n_0, n_1, \ldots\}$	Stream of news
$\mathcal{T} = \{t_0, t_1, \ldots\}$	Stream of tweets
$\mathcal{U} = \{u_0, u_1, \ldots\}$	Set of users
$\mathcal{Z} = \{z_0, z_1, \ldots\}$	Set of entities
$\tau(n_i)$	Timestamp of the i-th news article n_i
$\tau(t_i)$	Timestamp of the i-th tweet t_i
$c(n_i)$	Timestamp of the click on n_i
S	Social network matrix
S^*	Social-influence network matrix
A	User × tweet authorship matrix
T	Tweet × entity relatedness matrix
N	Entity × news relatedness matrix
$M = T \cdot N$	Tweet × news relatedness matrix
$\Gamma = A \cdot M$	User × news content relatedness
$\Sigma = S^* \cdot A \cdot M$	User × news social relatedness
Z	Entity popularity
$\Pi = Z \cdot N$	News popularity
$R_\tau(u, n)$	Ranking score of news n for user u at time τ

2. MODEL

Our goal is to harness the information present in tweets posted by users and by their social circles in order to make relevant and timely recommendation of news articles. We proceed by introducing our notation and define formally the problem that we consider in this paper. For quick reference, our notation is also summarized in Table 1.

Definition 1 (News stream) *Let $\mathcal{N} = \{n_0, n_1, \ldots\}$ be an unbounded stream of news arriving from a set of news sources, where news article n_i is published at time $\tau(n_i)$.*

Definition 2 (Tweet stream) *Let $\mathcal{T} = \{t_0, t_1, \ldots\}$ be an unbounded stream of tweets arriving from the set of twitter users, where tweet t_i is published at time $\tau(t_i)$.*

It is worth noting that a tweet stream for a user is composed of tweets authored by the user and people in the social neighborhood of the user. This is an extension of the concept of "home timeline" as known in twitter.

Problem 1 (News recommendation problem) *Given a stream of news $\mathcal{N}$, a set of users $\mathcal{U} = \{u_0, u_1, \ldots\}$ and their stream of tweets $\mathcal{T}$, find the top-k most relevant news for user $u \in \mathcal{U}$ at time τ.*

We aim at exploiting the tweet and news streams to identify news of general interest, but also at exploiting a twitter-based user profile to provide personalized recommendations. That is, for any user $u \in \mathcal{U}$ at any given time τ, the problem requires to rank the stream of past news in $\mathcal{N}$ according to a user-dependent relevance criteria. We also aim at incorporating time recency into our model, so that our recommendations favor the most recently published news articles.

We now proceed to model the factors that affect the relevance of news for a given user. We first model the social-network aspect. In our case, the social component is induced by the twitter *following* relationship. We define S to be the social network adjacency matrix, were $S(i,j)$ is equal to 1 divided by the number of users followed by user u_i if u_i follows u_j, and 0 otherwise. We also adopt a functional ranking [5] that spreads the interests of a user among its neighbors recursively. By limiting the maximum hop distance d, we define the social influence in a network as follows.

Definition 3 (Social influence S^*) *Given a set of users $\mathcal{U} = \{u_0, u_1, \ldots\}$, organized in a social network where each user may express an interest to the content published by another user, we define the social influence model S^* as the $|\mathcal{U}| \times |\mathcal{U}|$ matrix where $S^*(i,j)$ measures the interest of user u_i to the content generated by user u_j and it is computed as*

$$S^* = \left(\sum_{i=1}^{i=d} \sigma^i S^i \right),$$

where S is the row-normalized adjacency matrix of the social network, d is the maximum hop-distance up to which users may influence their neighbors, and σ is a damping factor.

Next we model the profile of a user based on the content that the user has generated. We first define a binary authorship matrix A to capture the relationship between users and the tweets they produce.

Definition 4 (Tweet authorship A) *Let A be a $|\mathcal{U}| \times |\mathcal{T}|$ matrix where $A(i,j)$ is 1 if u_i is the author of t_j, and 0 otherwise.*

The matrix A can be extended to deal with different types of relationships between users and posts, e.g., weigh differently *re-tweets*, or *likes*. In this work, we limit the concept of authorship to the posts actually written by the user.

We observe that news and tweets often happen to deal with the same topic. Sometimes a given topic is pushed into twitter by a news source, and then it spread throughout the twitter social network. However sometimes a given topic is first discussed by twitter users, and it is later reflected in the news, which may or may not be published back on twitter. In both cases, it is important to discover which are the current trending entities in order to promptly recommend news of interest. We model the relationship between tweets and news by introducing an intermediate layer between the two streams. This layer is populated by what we call *entities*.

Definition 5 (Tweets-to-news model M) *Let $\mathcal{N}$ be a stream of news, $\mathcal{T}$ a stream of tweets, and $\mathcal{Z} = \{z_0, z_1, \ldots\}$ a set of entities. We model the relationship between tweets and news as a $|\mathcal{T}| \times |\mathcal{N}|$ matrix M, where $M(i,j)$ is the relatedness of tweet t_i to news n_j, and it is computed as*

$$M = T \cdot N,$$

where

T is a $|\mathcal{T}| \times |\mathcal{Z}|$ row-wise normalized matrix with $T(i,j)$ representing the relatedness of tweet t_i to entity z_j;

N is a $|\mathcal{Z}| \times |\mathcal{N}|$ column-wise normalized matrix with $N(i,j)$ representing the relatedness of entity z_i to news n_j.

The set of entities $\mathcal{Z}$ introduces a middle layer between the stream of news and the stream of tweets that allows us to generalize our analysis. First, this layer allows to overcome any vocabulary mismatch problem between the two streams, since the streams are mapped onto the entity space. Second, rather than monitoring the relevance of a specific news or a tweet, we propose to measure the relevance of an entity.

There are a number of techniques that can be used to extract entities from news and tweets. A naïve approach is to let each term in the dictionary play the role of an entity. In this case $T(t, z)$ can be estimated as the number of occurrences of the term z in the tweet t, or as a **tf·idf** score, and similarly for N. An alternative approach is to use probabilistic latent semantic indexing and map tweets and news onto a set of latent topics [13].

In this work we follow a third approach: we use an existing entity-extraction system. In particular we use the `Spectrum` system, which was proposed by Paranjpe [20]. Given any fragment of text, the `Spectrum` system identifies entities related to Wikipedia articles. Therefore, we assume that $\mathcal{Z}$ consists of the set of all titles of Wikipedia articles. This choice has some interesting advantages. First, once an entity is detected, it is easy to propose a meaningful *label* to the user. Second, it allows to include additional external knowledge into the ranking, such as geographic position, categorization, number of recent edits by Wikipedia users, and many others. Although we choose to use `Spectrum`, we note that our model is independent of the specific entity extraction technique employed.

Example. Consider the following tweet by user KimAKelly: "Miss Liberty is closed until further notice." The words "Miss Liberty" are mapped to the entity/Wikipedia page *Statue of Liberty*, which is an interesting topic, due to the just announced renovation. This allows to rank high news regarding the Statue of Liberty, e.g. "Statue of Liberty to Close for One Year after 125th Anniversary" by Fox news. Potentially, since the Wikipedia page is geo-referenced, it is possible to boost the ranking of the news for users living nearby, or being interested in the topic/entity *New York*. □

The three matrices S^*, A, M can be used to measure the relatedness of the news in $\mathcal{N}$ to the tweets posted by a user or her social neighborhood.

Definition 6 (Content-based relatedness Γ) *Given the tweet authorship matrix A and the tweets-to-news model M for a stream of news $\mathcal{N}$ and a stream of tweets $\mathcal{T}$ authored by users $\mathcal{U}$, the relatedness between $\mathcal{U}$ and $\mathcal{N}$ is defined as*

$$\Gamma = A \cdot M,$$

where Γ is a $|\mathcal{U}| \times |\mathcal{N}|$ matrix, where $\Gamma(u_i, n_j)$ is the relevance of news n_j for user u_i.

According to the definition of Γ, a news article n_j is relevant for user u_i, if the news discusses entities that have been discussed in the past by the user in her own tweets.

Definition 7 (Social-based relatedness Σ) *Given the tweet authorship matrix A, the tweets-to-news model M, and the social network S for a stream of news $\mathcal{N}$ and a stream of tweets $\mathcal{T}$ authored by users $\mathcal{U}$, the relatedness between $\mathcal{U}$ and $\mathcal{N}$ is defined as*

$$\Sigma = S^* \cdot A \cdot M,$$

where Σ is a $|\mathcal{U}| \times |\mathcal{N}|$ matrix, where $\Sigma(u_i, n_j)$ is the relevance of news n_j for user u_i.

In the case of social-based relatedness Σ, the relevance of a news is computed by taking into account the tweets authored by neighboring users.

The matrices Γ and Σ measure content-based similarity, with no reference to popularity or freshness of tweets, news articles, and entities. In order to provide timely recommendations and catch up with trending news, we introduce a popularity component, which combines the "hotness" of entities in the news stream and the tweet stream.

Definition 8 (Entity-based news popularity Π) *Given a stream of news $\mathcal{N}$, a set of entities $\mathcal{Z}$, and their relatedness matrix N, the popularity of $\mathcal{N}$ is defined as*

$$\Pi = Z \cdot N,$$

where Z is a row-wise vector of length $|\mathcal{Z}|$ and $Z(i)$ is a measure of the popularity of entity z_i. The resulting Π is a row-wise vector of length $|\mathcal{N}|$, where $\Pi(j)$ measures the popularity of the news article n_j.

The vector Z holds the popularity of each entity z_i. The counts of the popularity vector Z need to be updated as new entities of interest arise in the news stream $\mathcal{N}$ and the tweet stream $\mathcal{T}$. An important aspect in updating the popularity counts is to take into account recency: new entities of interest should dominate the popularity counts of older entities. In this paper, we choose to update the popularity counts using an exponential decay rule. We discuss the details in Section 2.1. However, note that the popularity update is independent of our recommendation model, and any other decaying function can be used.

Finally, we propose a ranking function for recommending news articles to users. The ranking function is linear combination of the scoring components described above.

Definition 9 (Recommendation ranking $R_\tau(u, n)$) *Given the components Σ_τ, Γ_τ and Π_τ, resulting form a stream of news $\mathcal{N}$ and a stream of tweets $\mathcal{T}$ authored by users $\mathcal{U}$ up to time τ, the recommendation score of a news article $n \in \mathcal{N}$ for a user $u \in \mathcal{U}$ at time τ is defined as*

$$R_\tau(u, n) = \alpha \cdot \Sigma_\tau(u, n) + \beta \cdot \Gamma_\tau(u, n) + \gamma \cdot \Pi_\tau(n),$$

where α, β, γ are coefficients that specify the relative weight of the components.

At any given time, the recommender system produces a set of news recommendation by ranking a set of candidate news, e.g., the most recent ones, according to the ranking function R. To motivate the proposed ranking function we note similarities with popular recommendation techniques. When $\beta = \gamma = 0$, the ranking function R resembles collaborative filtering, where user similarity is computed on the basis of their social circles. When $\alpha = \gamma = 0$, the function R implements a content-based recommender system, where a user is profiled by the bag-of-entities occurring in the tweets of the user. Finally, when $\alpha = \beta = 0$, the most popular items recommended, regardless of the user profile.

Note that Σ, Γ, Π and R are all time dependent. At any given time τ, the social network and the set of authored tweets vary, thus affecting Σ and Γ. More importantly, some entities may abruptly become popular, and therefore of interest to many user. This time dependency is modeled by Π. While the changes in Σ and Γ derive directly from the

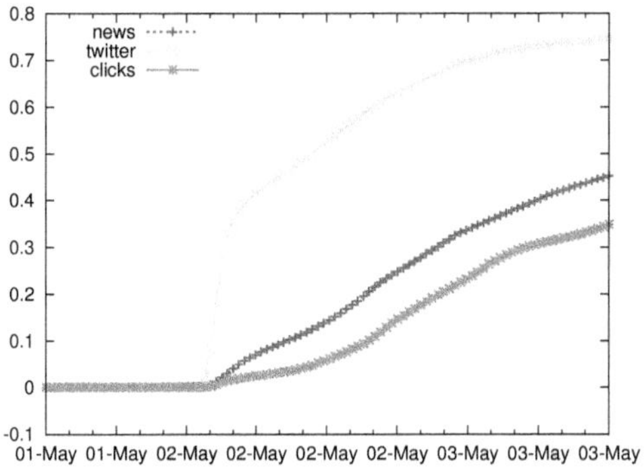

Figure 2: *Osama Bin Laden* trends on twitter and news streams.

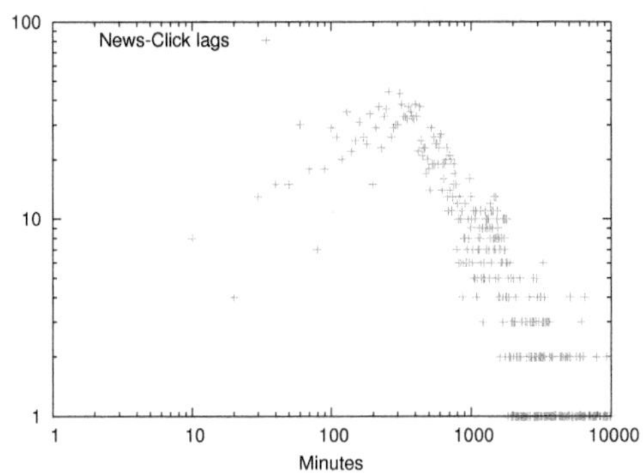

Figure 3: News clicks delay distribution.

tweet stream $\mathcal{T}$ and the social network S, the update of Π is crucial, and plays a fundamental role in the recommendation system that we describe in the next section.

2.1 Entity popularity

We complete the description of our model by discussing the update of the entity popularity counts. We motivate our approach by empirically observing how the user interest for particular entities decays over time.

In Figure 2 we show the cumulative distribution of occurrences and news clicks for the same entity in Figure 1(a) shown in the introduction. By using cumulative distribution, the fact the entity appears much earlier in twitter than in the news becomes more evident. If we consider the number of clicks on news as a surrogate of user interest, we notice that with a delay of about one day the entity receives a great deal of attention. This delay is probably due to the fact that the users have not been informed about the event yet. On the other hand, we observe that after two days the number of clicks drop, possibly the interest of users has been saturated or diverted to other events.

It turns out that the example above is not an exception, but it describes well the typical behavior of users with respect to clicking news articles. Figure 3 shows the distribution of the delay between the time that news articles are published the when they are clicked by users. The figure considers all the news articles and all the clicks in our dataset (see Section 4.1). We see that a very small number of news is clicked within the first hour from their publication. On the other hand, 76.7% of the clicks happen within 1 day (1,440 minutes) and 90.1% within 2 days (2,880 minutes).

From these empirical observations, we draw the following conclusions.

1. The increase in the number of tweets and news related to a given entity can be used to predict the increase of interest of the users.

2. News become stale after two days.

The first observation motivates us to inject a popularity component in our recommendation model. The second observation suggests updating popularity counts using a decaying function. We choose an exponentially-decaying function, which has the advantage of allowing to count efficiently frequent items in the data stream model, in order to monitor entity popularity in high-speed data streams [9].

Definition 10 (Popularity-update rule) *Given a stream of news $\mathcal{N}$ and a stream of tweets $\mathcal{T}$ at time τ, the popularity vector Z is computed at the end of every time window of fixed width ω as follows*

$$Z_\tau = \lambda Z_{\tau-1} + w_\mathcal{T} H_\mathcal{T} + w_\mathcal{N} H_\mathcal{N}.$$

The vectors $H_\mathcal{T}$ and $H_\mathcal{N}$ are estimates of the expected number of mentions of the entity occurring in tweets and news, respectively, during the latest time window. They are also called hotness *coefficients. The weights $w_\mathcal{T}$ and $w_\mathcal{N}$ measure the relative impact of news and tweets to the popularity count, and $\lambda < 1$ is an exponential forgetting factor.*

The popularity-update rule has the effect of promptly detecting entities becoming suddenly popular, and spreading this popularity in the subsequent time windows. According to our experimental evidence, we fix λ so that a signal is becomes negligible after two days. We set both coefficients $w_\mathcal{T}$ and $w_\mathcal{N}$ to 0.5 to give equal weight to tweets and news.

As shown by Asur et al. [4], the number of tweets for a trending topic grows linearly over time. Thus, we compute the expected number of mentions of the entity in tweets and news $H_\mathcal{T}$ and $H_\mathcal{N}$ by using the first order derivative of their cumulative counts, measured at the last time window $\tau - 1$.

3. LEARNING ALGORITHM

The next step is to estimate the parameters of the relevance model that we developed in the previous section. The parameters consist of the coefficients α, β, γ used to adjust the relative weight of the components of the ranking function R_τ. Another parameter is the damping factor used in the computation of social influence, but we empirically observed that it does not influence the results very much, so we used a default value of $\sigma = 0.85$. We consider only direct neighbors by setting the maximum hop distance $d = 1$.

Our approach is to learn the parameters of the model by using training data obtained from action logs. In particular, we use click-log data from Yahoo! toolbar as a source of user feedback. The Yahoo! toolbar anonymously collects clicks of several millions of users on the Web, including clicks on news. Our working hypothesis is that a high-quality news recommender ranks high the news that will be clicked by users. We actually formulate our recommendation task according to the learning-to-rank framework [16].

Consider a user $u \in \mathcal{U}$ and a news article $n \in \mathcal{N}$ with publication timestamp $\tau(n) \leq \tau$, where τ is the current time. We say that the news article n should be ranked in the i-th position of the recommendation list for user u, if it will be the i-th article to be clicked in the future by user u.

This formulation allows to define precedence constraints on the ranking function R_τ. Let $c(n)$ be the time at which the news n is clicked, and let $c(n) = +\infty$ if n is never clicked. At time τ, for two news n_i, n_j with $\tau(n_i) \leq \tau$ and $\tau(n_j) \leq \tau$, we obtain the following constraint:

$$\text{If } \tau \leq c(n_i) < c(n_j) \text{ then } R_\tau(u, n_i) > R_\tau(u, n_j). \quad (1)$$

The click stream from Yahoo! toolbar identifies a large number of constraints according to Equation (1) that the optimal ranking function must satisfy. As for the learning-to-rank problem [16], finding the optimal ranking function is an **NP**-hard problem. Additionally, considering that some of the constraints could be contradictory, a feasible solution may not exist. As usual, the learning problem is translated to a Ranking-SVM optimization problem.

Problem 2 (Recommendation Ranking Optimization)

$$\textit{Minimize: } V\left(\vec{\omega} \equiv \langle \alpha, \beta, \gamma \rangle, \vec{\xi}\right) = \frac{1}{2}\|\vec{\omega}\|^2 + C\sum \xi_{ij\tau}$$
$$\textit{Subject to: } R_\tau(u, n_i) > R_\tau(u, n_j) + 1 - \xi_{ij\tau}$$
$$\textit{for all } \tau, n_i \in \mathcal{N}, n_j \in \mathcal{N} \textit{ such that}$$
$$\tau(n_i) \leq \tau, \tau(n_j) \leq \tau, \tau \leq c(n_i) < c(n_j)$$
$$\xi_{ij\tau} \geq 0$$

As shown by Joachims [16], this optimization problem can be solved via classification SVM. In the following sections, we show how to generate the training set of the SVM classifier in order to keep a reasonably low amount of training instances, so as to speed-up convergence and support the scalability of the solution.

3.1 Constraint selection

The formulation of Problem 2 includes a potentially huge number of constraints. Every click occurring after time τ on a news n, generates a new constraints involving n and every other non-clicked news published before time τ. Such a large number of constraints also includes relationships on "stale" news articles, e.g., a non-clicked news article published weeks or months before τ. Since clicks are the informative signals driving the learning process, it is important to select pairs of clicked news articles that eliminate biases, such as the one caused by stale news articles. Clearly, the more constraints are taken into consideration during the learning process, the more robust is the final model. On the other hand, increasing the number of constraints affects the complexity of the minimization algorithm. We propose the following strategy in order to select only the most interesting constraints and thus simplify the optimization problem.

First, we evaluate the ranking function only at the time instants when a click happens. This selection does not actually change the set of constraints of Problem 2, but it helps in the generation of the constraints by focussing on specific time instants. If the user u clicks at the news article n_i at time $c(n_i)$, then the news article n_i must be the most relevant at that time. The following must hold.

$$R_{c(n_i)}(u, n_i) > R_{c(n_i)}(u, n_j) + 1 - \xi_{ijc(n_i)}$$
$$\text{for all } n_j \in \mathcal{N} \text{ such that } \tau(n_j) \leq c(n_i). \quad (2)$$

Whenever a click occurs at time $c(n_i)$, we add a set of constraint to the ranking function such that the clicked news article gets the largest score among any other news article published before time $c(\tau)$.

Second, we restrict the number of news articles to be compared with the clicked one. If a news article was published a long time before the click, then it can be easily filtered out, as it would not help the learning process. As we have shown in Section 2.1, users lose interest into news articles after a time interval $\hat{\tau}$ of two days. We can make use of this threshold into Equation (2) as follows:

$$R_{c(n_i)}(u, n_i) > R_{c(n_i)}(u, n_j) + 1 - \xi_{ijc(n_i)}$$
$$\text{for all } n_j \in \mathcal{N}\left[c(n_i) - \hat{\tau}, c(n_i)\right] \quad (3)$$

where $\mathcal{N}\left[c(n_i) - \hat{\tau}, c(n_i)\right]$ is the set of news published between time $c(n_i) - \hat{\tau}$ and $c(n_i)$.

Finally, we further restrict $\mathcal{N}\left[c(n_i) - \hat{\tau}, c(n_i)\right]$ by considering only those news articles that are relevant according to at least one of the three score components Σ_τ, Γ_τ, Π_τ. Let $\mathsf{Top}(k, \chi, \tau_a, \tau_b)$ be the set of k news articles with largest rank in the set $\mathcal{N}[\tau_a, \tau_b]$ according to the score component χ. We include into the optimization Problem 2 only the constraints:

$$R_{c(n_i)}(u, n_i) > R_{c(n_i)}(u, n_j) + 1 - \xi_{ijc(n_i)}$$
$$\text{for all } n_j \text{ s.t. } n_j \in \mathsf{Top}\left(k, \Sigma_{c(n_i)}, c(n_i) - \hat{\tau}, c(n_i)\right) \text{ or}$$
$$n_j \in \mathsf{Top}\left(k, \Gamma_{c(n_i)}, c(n_i) - \hat{\tau}, c(n_i)\right) \text{ or}$$
$$n_j \in \mathsf{Top}\left(k, \Pi_{c(n_i)}, c(n_i) - \hat{\tau}, c(n_i).\right) \quad (4)$$

By setting $k = 10$ we are able to reduce the number of constraints from more than 25 million to approximately 250 thousand, significantly reducing the training time.

3.2 Additional features

The system obtained by learning the model parameters using the SVM-Rank method is named `T.Rex`, and forms our main recommender. Additionally, we attempt to improve the accuracy of `T.Rex` by incorporating more features. To build this improved recommender we use exactly the same learning framework: we collect more features from the same training dataset and we learn their importance using the SVM-Rank algorithm. We choose three additional features: *age*, *hotness* and *click count*, which we describe below.

The *age* of a news article n is the time elapsed between the current time and the time n was published, that is, $\tau - \tau(n)$.

The *hotness* of a news article is a set of features extracted from the vectors $H_\mathcal{T}$ and $H_\mathcal{N}$, which keep the popularity counts for the entities in our model. For each news article n we compute the average and standard deviation of the vectors $H_\mathcal{T}$ and $H_\mathcal{N}$ over all entities extracted from article n. This process gives us four hotness features per news article.

Finally, the *click count* of a news article is simply the number of times that the article has been clicked by any users in the system up to time τ.

The system that we obtain by training our ranking function on these additional features is called `T.Rex+`.

4. EXPERIMENTS

4.1 Datasets

To build our recommendation system we need the following sources of information: twitter stream, news stream, the social network of users, and click-through data. We extract this information from three different data sources: twitter, Yahoo! news, and Yahoo! toolbar, respectively.

Twitter: We obtain tweets from twitter's public API by crawling users' timelines. We collect all tweets posted during May 2011 by our 3,214 target users (identified as described below). We also collect a random sample of tweets to track entity popularity across all twitter. We extract entities from tweets using the `Spectrum` method described by Paranjpe [20]. Overall we obtain about 1 million tweets in English, for which we are able to extract entities. Figure 4(a) shows the distribution of entities in the twitter dataset. The curve has a truncated power law shape.

Yahoo! news: We collect all news articles aggregated in the English site of Yahoo! news during May 2011. From the news articles we extract entities by using again the `Spectrum` algorithm. Overall we have about 28.5 million news articles, from which we keep only the articles that contain at least one entity contained in one of the tweets. In total we obtain about 40 thousand news articles. Figure 4(b) shows the distribution of entities in the Yahoo! news dataset. The shape of the distribution is similar to the one of twitter.

Yahoo! toolbar: We collect click information from the Yahoo! toolbar logs. The Yahoo! toolbar is a browser add-on that provides a set of browsing functionalities. The logs contain information about the browsing behavior of the users who have installed the toolbar, such as, user cookie id, url, referral url, event type, and so on. We collect all toolbar data occurring in May 2011. We use the first 80% in chronological order of the toolbar clicks to train our system.

Using a simple heuristic we identify a small set of users for whom we can link their toolbar cookie id, with their twitter user id. The heuristic is to identify which twitter account a user is visiting more often, discarding celebrity accounts and non-bijective mappings. The underlying assumption is that users visit more often their own accounts. In total we identify of set U_0 of 3,214 test users. The dataset used in this paper is the projection of all the data sources on the users of the set U_0, that is, for all the users in U_0 we collect all their tweets and all their clicks on Yahoo! news. Additionally, by employing snowball sampling on twitter we obtain the set of users U_1 who are followed by the set of users U_0. Then, by collecting all the tweets of the users in U_1, we form the social component for our set of users of interest U_0.

4.2 Test set

Evaluating a recommendation strategy is a complex task. The ideal evaluation method is to deploy a live system and gather click-through statistics. While such a deployment gives the best accuracy, it is also very expensive. An alternative evaluation method is via user studies. However, getting judgements from human experts does not scale well to a large number of recommendations. Furthermore, user studies cannot be automated, and they are impractical if more than one strategy or many parameters need to be tested.

For these reasons, we propose an automated method to evaluate our recommendation algorithm. The proposed evaluation method exploits the available click data collected by the Yahoo! toolbar, and it is similar in spirit with the learning process. Given a stream of news and a stream of tweets for the user, we identify an event that a user clicks at a news article n_*. Assume that such a click occurs at time $\tau = c(n_*)$. Suppose the user just logged in the system at time τ. Then the recommendation strategy should rank the news article n_* as high as possible.

To create a test instance, we collect all news articles that have been published within the time interval $[\tau - \tau^*, \tau]$, and select a subset as described by Equation (4): we pick the news with largest scores according to the components of content, social, popularity, and number of clicks until time τ. In total we generate a pool of $k = 1{,}000$ candidate news. All these news articles are ranked using our ranking function R_τ, and we then examine what is the ranking of the article n_* in the list.

The last 20%, in chronological order, of the Yahoo! toolbar data is used to test the `T.Rex` and `T.Rex`+ algorithms, as well as all the baselines.

4.3 Evaluation measures

Evaluating a ranking of items is a standard problem in information retrieval. In our setting we have only one correct answer per ranking — the news article n_* clicked by the user — and we care about the position of this item in the ranking, which we evaluate using the mean reciprocal rank (MRR) measure [24]:

$$\mathrm{MRR} = \frac{1}{|Q|}\sum_{i=1}^{Q}\frac{1}{r(n_*^i)},$$

where $r(n_*^i)$ is the rank of the news article n_*^i in the i-th event of the evaluation and Q is the set of all tests. The MRR measure is commonly used to evaluate question-answering (QA) systems, where only the first correct answer matters. MRR gives higher scores to correct results that are higher in the ranking and reduces the importance of correct predictions in the lower parts of the ranking.

We also compute the precision of our system at different levels. For our task we define the *precision-at-k* (P@k) as the fraction of rankings in which the clicked news is ranked in the top-k positions. We compute P@k for $k = 1$, 5, and 10.

There are cases in which the sparsity of the data prevents our system from providing recommendations. Therefore, we also evaluate the coverage of our recommendations. We define the coverage as the fraction of clicks for which we were able to provide some recommendation.

Finally, we note that when the user clicks on a news, the user is actually expressing interest in the entities mentioned in the news. We can argue that if a user clicks on a report on Fukushima from CNN, the user might equally be interested in a report on the same topic from BBC. In this case, we would like to predict the entities that the user is interested in, rather than the news articles themselves.

We use Jaccard overlap between the sets of entities mentioned in two news articles to measure the similarity between the articles themselves. We compute the similarity between each news article in the ranking and the clicked news. Then, we assign a relevance level to each news by binning the computed similarity into five levels. We use DCG [14] to measure the performance of the strategies on this multiple level

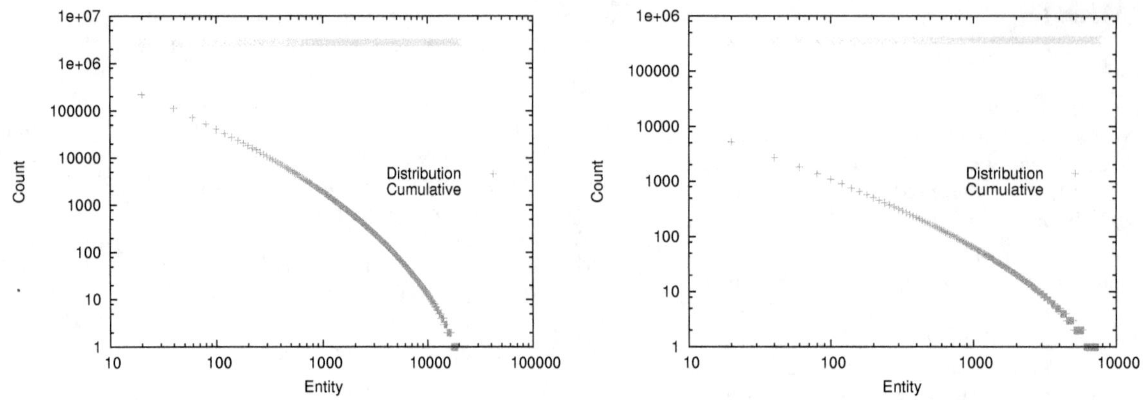

(a) Twitter.

(b) News.

Figure 4: Distribution of entities

Algorithm	MRR	P@1	P@5	P@10	Coverage
`Recency`	0.020	0.002	0.018	0.036	1.000
`ClickCount`	0.059	0.024	0.086	0.135	1.000
`Social`	0.017	0.002	0.018	0.036	0.606
`Content`	0.107	0.029	0.171	0.286	0.158
`Popularity`	0.008	0.003	0.005	0.012	1.000
`T.Rex`	0.107	0.073	0.130	0.168	1.000
`T.Rex`+	0.109	0.062	0.146	0.189	1.000

Table 2: MRR, precision and coverage.

relevance task:

$$\mathrm{DCG}[i] = \begin{cases} G[i] & \text{if } i = 1; \\ \mathrm{DCG}[i-1] + \frac{G[i]}{log_2 i} & \text{if } i > 1, \end{cases}$$

where $G[i]$ is the relevance of the document at position i in our ranking. We compute the DCG for the top 20 results averaged over all the rankings produced. If a strategy is not able to produce a ranking, we pad the ranking with non-relevant documents.

4.4 Baselines

We compare our system with other five ranking baselines:

`Recency`: it ranks news articles by time of publication (most recent first);

`ClickCount`: it ranks news articles by click count (highest count first);

`Social`: it ranks news articles by using our algorithm with $\beta = \gamma = 0$;

`Content`: it ranks news articles by using our algorithm with $\alpha = \gamma = 0$;

`Popularity`: it ranks news articles by using our algorithm with $\alpha = \beta = 0$.

4.5 Results

We report MRR, precision and coverage results in Table 2. We observe that the two variants of our model, `T.Rex` and `T.Rex`+, have overall the best results.

The `T.Rex`+ system has the highest MRR of all the alternatives. This result means that our model has a good overall performance across the dataset. `Content` has also a very high MRR. Unfortunately, the coverage level achieved by the `Content` strategy is very low. This issue is mainly caused by the sparsity of the user profiles. It is well know that most of twitter users belong to the "silent majority," and do not tweet very much.

The `Social` strategy is affected by the same problem, albeit to a much lesser extent. The reason for this difference is that `Social` draws from a large social neighborhood of user profiles, instead of just one. So it has more chances to provide a recommendation. The quality of the recommendation is however quite low, probably because the social-based profile only is not able to catch the specific user interests.

It is worth noting that in almost 20% of the cases, `T.Rex`+ was able to rank the clicked news in the top 10 results. Ranking by the `ClickCount` strategy is quite efficient despite being very simple. Interestingly, adding the `ClickCount` feature to our model does not improve the results significantly. In fact, the difference in P@10 between `T.Rex` and `T.Rex`+ is only about 2%. This suggests that the information contained in the click counts is already captured by our model, or cannot be effectively exploited by a linear combination. This issue deserves further investigation.

Figure 5 shows the DCG measure for the top 20 positions

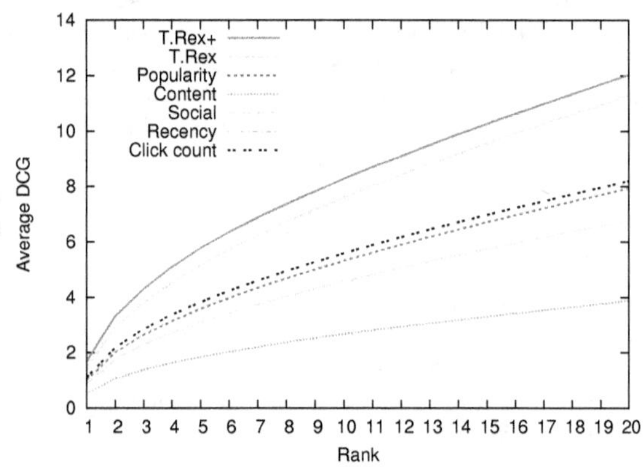

Figure 5: Average discounted cumulated gain on related entities on top 20 ranks.

in the rankings. From the figure we can see that `T.Rex` and `T.Rex`+ are able to suggest more related news than the other strategies. This result is expected, as our system is designed to exploit the concept of entities.

5. RELATED WORK

Recommender systems can be roughly divided in two large categories: content-based and collaborative filtering [12].

The large-scale system for generating personalized news recommendations proposed by Das et al. [10] falls in the second category. The authors exploit a linear combination of three different approaches: minhashing-based clustering of users, probabilistic latent semantic indexing of users and news, and news co-visitation count. All of the three approaches take advantage the user click-through data only, and therefore they are content agnostic. Even tough the system can update its recommendation immediately after a new click is observed, we have seen that click information arrives with a significant delay, and therefore it may fail in detecting emerging topics early.

Thus, for addressing emerging topics the idea of using twitter to provide *fresh* recommendations has recently become very appealing. A number of studies attempts to understand the twitter social network, the information-spreading process, and to discover emerging topics of interesest over such a network [6, 7, 15].

Chen et al. [8] propose a URL-recommender system from URLs posted in twitter. A user study shows that both the user content-based profile, and the user social neighborhood plays a role, but, the most important factor in the recommendation performance is given by the social ranking, i.e., the number of times a URL is mentioned among the neighborhood of a given user. The work presented by Esparza et al. [11] exploits data from a micro-blogging movie review service similar to twitter. The user profile is built on the basis of the user's posts. Similarly, a movie profile generated from the posts associated to the movie. The proposed prototype resembles a content-based recommender system, where users are matched against recommended items.

A small user study by Teevan et al. [22] reports that 49% of users search while looking for information related to news, or to topics gaining popularity, and in general to "to keep up with events." The analysis of a larger crawl of twitter by Kwak et al. [17] shows that about 85% of the twitter posts are about headlines or persistent news. The abundance of news-related content thus makes twitter the ideal source of information for the news recommendation task.

Akcora et al. [3] use twitter to detect abrupt opinion changes. Based on an *emotion-word corpus*, the proposed algorithm detects opinion changes, which can be related to publication of some interesting news. No actual automatic linking to news is produced. The system proposed by Phelan et al. [21] is a content-based approach that uses tweets to rank news using `tf·idf`. A given a set of tweets, either public or of a friend, is used to build a user profile, which is matched against the news coming from a set of user-defined RSS feeds. Mccreadie et al. [18] show that, even if useful, URL links present in blog posts may not be sufficient to identify interesting news due to their sparsity. Their approach exploits user posts as if they were votes for the news of a given day. The association between news and posts is achieved by exploiting a divergence from randomness model. They show that a Gaussian weighting scheme can profitably be used to predict the importance of a news on a given day, given the posts of a few previous days.

Our approach pursues the same direction, with the goal of exploiting twitter posts to predict news of interest. To this end, rather than analyzing the raw text of a tweet, we chose to extract the topics discussed in tweets. Indeed, twitter highlights in its web interfaces the so called *trending topics*, i.e., set of words occurring frequently in recent tweets. Asur et al. [4] crawled all the tweets containing the keywords identifying a twitter trending topic in the 20 minutes before the topic is detected by twitter. Authors found that the popularity of a topic can be described as a multiplicative growth process with noise. From this, it can be derived that the cumulative number of tweets related to a trending topic increases linearly with time. Another interesting study on a large crawl of twitter has been conducted by Kwak et al. [17], where a number of features and phenomena across the twitter social network have been analyzed. We highlight a few interesting findings. After the initial break-up, the cumulative number of tweets of a trending topic increases linearly, as suggested by Asur et al. [4], and independently of the number of users. Almost 80% of the trending topics have a single activity period, i.e., they occur in a single burst, and 93% of such activity periods last less than 10 days. Finally, once a tweet is published, half of its *re-tweets* occur within an hour and 75% within one day. Also, once re-tweeted, tweets quickly spread four hops away. These studies confirm the fast information spreading occurring on twitter.

In our work, we did not exploit the twitter *trending topics* for two reasons. First, because we need to discover interesting topics even before they are recognized as trending by twitter. Second, our system provides personalized recommendations based on users interests, while *trending topics* capture general interests and are not suitable for modeling a single user.

A basic approach for building topic-based user profiles from tweets is proposed by Michelson and Macskassy [19]. Each capitalized non-stopword is considered an entity. The entity is used as a query to Wikipedia and the categories of the retrieved page are used to update the list of topics of interest for the user who authored the tweet.

Abel et al. [1] propose a more sophisticated user model to support news recommendation for twitter users. They explore different ways of modeling use profiles by using hashtags, topics or entities and conclude that entity based modeling gives the best results. They employ a simple recommender algorithm that uses cosine similarity between user profiles and tweets. The authors recommend tweets containing news URLs and re-tweets are used as ground truth.

Similarly, we used the `Spectrum` system [20] to map every single tweet to a bag of entities, each corresponding to a Wikipedia page. In addition to the user-authored posts, we used her social network to further enrich the user profile. We apply the same entity-extraction process to the incoming stream of news, with the goal of overcoming the vocabulary mismatch problem by mapping both tweets and news in the same entity-based coordinate system.

Our proposed model borrows from the aforementioned works by exploiting a blend of content-based and social-based profile enrichment. But in addition to the state-of-the-art recommender systems, it is able to discover emerging trends on twitter by measuring their popularity and taking into account aging effects.

6. CONCLUSIONS AND FUTURE WORK

We presented a new method for making personalized recommendations of news articles, which leverages information found in real-time Web. We use data from twitter and Yahoo! news in order to build user profiles that model user interests, content found in the social neighborhood of users, and topic popularity. These signals are combined using a learning-to-rank approach with training data extracted from the Yahoo! toolbar logs. The resulting systems, `T.Rex` and its variant `T.Rex`+, are light-weight online recommenders that are able to predict with good accuracy the news articles clicked by the users and rank them higher.

A number of research questions deserve further investigation. First, we are interested to explore the effects of a different entity space, for instance, performing LSI-type of decompositions on the existing entity space, or using a higher level representation, for example, moving from wikipedia article titles to broad-level categories such as "US News," "movies," and "cooking." We also intend to test if the accuracy of the system can be improved by clustering the users and learning different parameters for each cluster. Note that such clusters do not need to be topical but behavioral. For example, one cluster may represent the users who have broad set of interests and gets influenced very little from their social neighborhood, and so on. Finally, we plan to investigate the effect of using other notions of social neighborhoods, such as geographic locations at a city, state, or country level.

Acknowledgements. Claudio Lucchese and Gianmarco De Francisci Morales were partially supported by the EU-FP7-250527 (Assets) and the POR-FESR 2007-2013 (VISITO Tuscany) projects. Aristides Gionis and Gianmarco De Francisci Morales were partially supported by the Torres Quevedo Program of the Spanish Ministry of Science and Innovation, co-funded by the European Social Fund, and by the Spanish Centre for the Development of Industrial Technology under the CENIT program, project CEN-20101037, "Social Media" (http://www.cenitsocialmedia.es/).

References

[1] F. Abel, Q. Gao, G. Houben, and K. Tao. Analyzing user modeling on twitter for personalized news recommendations. In *19th International Conference on User Modeling, Adaption and Personalization*, 2011.

[2] G. Adomavicius and A. Tuzhilin. Toward the Next Generation of Recommender Systems: A Survey of the State-of-the-Art and Possible Extensions. *IEEE Transactions on Knowledge and Data Engineering*, 17, 2005.

[3] C. Akcora, M. Bayir, M. Demirbas, and H. Ferhatosmanoglu. Identifying breakpoints in public opinion. In *1st Workshop on Social Media Analytics*, 2010.

[4] S. Asur, B. Huberman, G. Szabo, and C. Wang. Trends in social media: Persistence and decay. *Arxiv preprint arXiv:1102.1402*, 2011.

[5] R. Baeza-Yates, P. Boldi, and C. Castillo. Generalizing pagerank: Damping functions for link-based ranking algorithms. In *29th International Conference on Research and Development in Information Retrieval*, 2006.

[6] E. Bakshy, J. M. Hofman, W. A. Mason, and D. J. Watts. Everyone's an influencer: quantifying influence on twitter. In *4th International Conference on Web Search and Data Mining*, 2011.

[7] M. Cataldi, L. Di Caro, and C. Schifanella. Emerging topic detection on twitter based on temporal and social terms evaluation. In *10th International Workshop on Multimedia Data Mining*, 2010.

[8] J. Chen, R. Nairn, L. Nelson, M. Bernstein, and E. Chi. Short and tweet: experiments on recommending content from information streams. In *28th International Conference on Human Factors in Computing Systems*, 2010.

[9] G. Cormode, F. Korn, and S. Tirthapura. Exponentially decayed aggregates on data streams. In *24th International Conference on Data Engineering*, 2008.

[10] A. Das, M. Datar, A. Garg, and S. Rajaram. Google news personalization: scalable online collaborative filtering. In *16th International Conference on World Wide Web*, 2007.

[11] S. G. Esparza, M. O'Mahony, and B. Smyth. On the real-time web as a source of recommendation knowledge. *4th ACM Conference on Recommender Systems*, 2010.

[12] D. Goldberg, D. Nichols, B. M. Oki, and D. Terry. Using collaborative filtering to weave an information tapestry. *Communications of the ACM*, 35, 1992.

[13] T. Hofmann. Probabilistic latent semantic indexing. *22nd International Conference on Research and Development in Information Retrieval*, 1999.

[14] K. Järvelin and J. Kekäläinen. Cumulated gain-based evaluation of ir techniques. *ACM Transaction Information Systems*, 20, 2002.

[15] A. Java, X. Song, T. Finin, and B. Tseng. Why we twitter: understanding microblogging usage and communities. In *9th WebKDD and 1st SNA-KDD workshop on Web Mining and Social Network Analysis*, 2007.

[16] T. Joachims. Optimizing search engines using clickthrough data. In *8th International Conference on Knowledge Discovery and Data Mining*, 2002.

[17] H. Kwak, C. Lee, H. Park, and S. Moon. What is twitter, a social network or a news media? *19th International Conference on World Wide Web*, 2010.

[18] R. Mccreadie, C. Macdonald, and I. Ounis. News article ranking: leveraging the wisdom of bloggers. In *9th International Conference on Adaptivity, Personalization and Fusion of Heterogeneous Information*, 2010.

[19] M. Michelson and S. Macskassy. Discovering users' topics of interest on twitter: a first look. In *4th workshop on Analytics for noisy unstructured text data*, 2010.

[20] D. Paranjpe. Learning document aboutness from implicit user feedback and document structure. In *18th ACM Conference on Information and Knowledge Management*, 2009.

[21] O. Phelan, K. McCarthy, M. Bennett, and B. Smyth. Terms of a Feather : Content-Based News Recommendation and Discovery Using Twitter. *Advances in Information Retrieval*, 6611(07), 2011.

[22] J. Teevan, D. Ramage, and M. R. Morris. #twittersearch: a comparison of microblog search and web search. In *4th International Conference on Web Search and Data Mining*, 2011.

[23] A. Toffler. *Future shock*. Random House Publishing Group, 1984.

[24] E. M. Voorhees. The TREC-8 Question Answering Track Report. In *Text REtrieval Conference*, 1999.

ETF: Extended Tensor Factorization Model for Personalizing Prediction of Review Helpfulness

Samaneh Moghaddam
School of Computing Science
Simon Fraser University
Burnaby, BC, Canada
sam39@cs.sfu.ca

Mohsen Jamali
School of Computing Science
Simon Fraser University
Burnaby, BC, Canada
sja25@cs.sfu.ca

Martin Ester
School of Computing Science
Simon Fraser University
Burnaby, BC, Canada
ester@cs.sfu.ca

ABSTRACT

Online reviews are valuable sources of information for a variety of decision-making processes such as purchasing products. As the number of online reviews is growing rapidly, it becomes increasingly difficult for users to identify those that are helpful. This has motivated research into the problem of identifying high quality and helpful reviews automatically. The current methods assume that the helpfulness of a review is independent from the readers of that review. However, we argue that the quality of a review may not be the same for different users. For example, a professional and an amateur photographer may rate the helpfulness of a review very differently. In this paper, we introduce the problem of predicting a personalized review quality for recommendation of helpful reviews. To address this problem, we propose a series of increasingly sophisticated probabilistic graphical models, based on Matrix Factorization and Tensor Factorization. We evaluate the proposed models using a database of 1.5 million reviews and more than 13 million quality ratings obtained from Epinions.com. The experiments demonstrate that the proposed latent factor models outperform the state-of-the-art approaches using textual and social features. Finally, our experiments confirm that the helpfulness of a review is indeed not the same for all users and that there are some latent factors that affect a user's evaluation of the review quality.

Categories and Subject Descriptors

H.2.8.d [**Information Technology and System**]: Database Application—*Data Miming*; G.3 [**Mathematics of Computing**]: Probability and Statistics—*Statistical Computing, Multivariate Statistics*

General Terms

Algorithms, Design, Experimentation

Permission to make digital or hard copies of all or part of this work for personal or classroom use is granted without fee provided that copies are not made or distributed for profit or commercial advantage and that copies bear this notice and the full citation on the first page. To copy otherwise, to republish, to post on servers or to redistribute to lists, requires prior specific permission and/or a fee.
WSDM'12, February 8–12, 2012, Seattle, Washington, USA.
Copyright 2012 ACM 978-1-4503-0747-5/12/02 ...$10.00.

Keywords

Personalized Review Quality Prediction, Review Recommendation, Matrix Factorization, Tensor Factorization

1. INTRODUCTION

Other people's opinions have always played an important role in decision-making process [20, 21]. As online commerce activity continues to grow, the role of online reviews is expected to become increasingly important [17]. The number of online reviews has been increasing rapidly at websites such as Amazon[1], Epinions[2], Yelp[3], Ciao UK[4]. Due to the fact that most online reviews are written by non-professional authors, they tend to be of very different quality [22]. The growing importance of online reviews in the purchasing decision making process of users has also led to the creation of an ever growing number of spam reviews, which try to mislead online users [8]. Given the huge number of online reviews available and their greatly varying quality, it becomes more and more difficult to find high-quality, helpful reviews.

In an attempt to support their users in selecting helpful reviews, many reviewing websites allow users to rate the helpfulness of online reviews. Almost all of the reviewing websites collect users' opinions (as helpful or unhelpful votes, or quality ratings) about the provided reviews. While most of them only show the percentage of positive votes or the average quality rating to public users, some of them provide their log-in users with access to the individual ratings (quality rating of each user for each review), such as Epinions and Ciao UK. However, this feedback tends to be sparse, with many reviews (particularly newly written ones) failing to attract any feedback [23]. This sparsity is partly due to a rich-get-richer effect where the top reviews accumulate more and more feedback, while more recent reviews are rarely read and thus not rated [16]. While review ratings are far too sparse to allow users to find all helpful reviews, they can provide valuable input to learn a model for automatically predicting the quality of any review. This has inspired a new line of research on automatic review quality prediction.

Most previous works [10, 13, 2, 16, 30] attempt to predict the quality of reviews by extracting textual features (e.g. total number of tokens, ratio of nouns, adjectives, etc.) and learning a function of these features for predicting review quality. There are also some recent works [17, 28, 23, 15]

[1]http://www.amazon.com/
[2]http://www.epinions.com/
[3]http://www.yelp.com/
[4]http://www.ciao.co.uk/

utilizing social features (e.g. number of past reviews by reviewer, PageRank of the reviewer, etc.) in addition to the textual features to assess the quality of reviews.

To the best of our knowledge, all of the existing methods assume that the helpfulness of a review is the same for all users and determine the quality of a review in general (i.e. in a user unspecific way). However, this assumption may not be true in all cases. We argue that the quality of the same review may not be the same for different users. For example, a professional and an amateur photographer may rate the helpfulness of a review very differently. In Section 3 we will elaborate an example where different users evaluate the quality of a review differently because of their different evaluation criteria. We believe these differences in the users' criteria may result in different evaluations of a review.

In this paper, we introduce the new problem of personalized review quality prediction for recommendation of helpful reviews. To address this problem, we propose a series of increasingly sophisticated factorization models. These models are based on the assumption that the observed review ratings depend on latent features of the reviews, reviewers, raters, and products. These latent features have two crucial advantages compared to observed textual or social features:

- The latent user/rater features are user-specific and allow personalized recommendation.
- The use of latent features avoids the difficult choice of appropriate textual or social features. The difficulty of this choice is underlined by the fact that there is no consensus among the feature sets used in current review quality prediction methods.

We first present a model based on probabilistic Matrix Factorization (MF) (Section 4.1). The underlying assumption of this model is that both reviews and raters (review readers) can be modeled by a set of latent features. The MF model personalizes review quality prediction by decomposing the *rater* $\times$ *review* matrix and learning latent factors for each rater and each review. We also employ the concept of Tensor Factorization (TF) (Section 4.2). The TF based model assumes that the latent feature vector of each review is generated in a probabilistic way by aggregating the latent feature vector of its reviewer and the latent feature vector of the corresponding product (since each review is written by a reviewer about a product). That is, the *rater* $\times$ *review* two-dimensional matrix is converted into a three-dimensional tensor *rater* $\times$ *reviewer* $\times$ *product*. MF and TF have already been employed for item recommendation but not yet for review recommendation.

As our main contribution, we introduce two novel models for review recommendation. The *Extended Tensor Factorization (ETF)* model incorporates the overall rating of a product expressed in a review as another observed variable into the TF model. The ETF model assumes that the overall rating of a product given by the reviewer is generated in a probabilistic way by aggregating the product-specific and reviewer-specific latent feature vectors. We further improve the ETF model by capturing the biases associated with each factor that affect the rating values independent of any interaction between the factors. The *unBiased ETF (BETF)* model considers the rater's and review's biases in the estimation of review quality rating and also captures the reviewer's and product's biases in the learning of their feature vectors. We empirically verify that the BETF model improves ETF by capturing the factor's biases. We also verify that the ETF model improves MF, which does not take into account the product and reviewer factors, and also improves TF, which uses less observed data. In addition, our experiments demonstrate that latent factor models outperform the state-of-the-art non-personalized approaches using textual and social features. Thus, our experiments confirm that the helpfulness of a review is indeed not the same for all users, and there are some latent factors that affect a user's evaluation of review quality.

It should also be mentioned that factor models that have recently been used in the area of recommendation system [12, 9] for the purpose of item recommendation estimate the quality of an item based on the user preferences. On the other hand, our problem is to estimate the quality of a review (a reviewer's opinion about an item) based on the rater preferences. In other words, in item recommendation the feature vector of items is independent from the feature vector of users, while in our problem the feature vector of the review depends on the feature vector of the reviewer which makes the problem more complicated than item recommendation.

Automatic review quality prediction is useful in various contexts: 1) It enables reviewing websites to identify high quality reviews for users. 2) Predicting the quality of reviews can also resolve the rich-get-richer effect. 3) High quality reviews can be used in higher-level applications such as review summarization and opinion-based question answering. Note that throughout this paper, we use 'quality' and 'helpfulness' as synonyms. While review helpfulness is more specific than review quality, the term 'helpfulness' has been typically used for a binary scale (whether the review is helpful or not), but review quality can be on a larger scale (usually in the range from 1 to 5).

The remainder of the paper is organized as follows. The next section is devoted to related work. Section 3 introduces the problem definition and discusses a motivating example. Section 4 presents the basic factor models, MF and TF for the considered problem. In section 5 we extend the TF model by incorporating product rating as an additional input source (ETF) and capturing biases (BETF). In Section 6 we first describe the characteristics of our real-life dataset and then report the results of our experimental evaluation. Finally, Section 7 concludes the paper with a summary and discussion of future work.

2. RELATED WORK

The problem of automatically evaluating the quality of online reviews has recently attracted increasing attention. To the best of our knowledge, no previous study has addressed the problem of predicting a personalized quality rating for a review, but there are several lines of related work, predicting a general user-unspecific review quality, which we will review in this section. We also briefly discuss some recent work using factor models in the area of recommendation systems.

Most previous works have focused on automatically determining the quality (helpfulness) of reviews by using a set of observed features, i.e. textual and/or social features. Textual features include features that are based on text statistics, such as length of the review, the average length of a sentence, percentage of nouns or adjectives, etc. Social features, on the other hand, are related to the author of the review and are extracted from his social context, such as the number of past reviews by the author, in-degree and out-degree of the author in the social network, past average rating for the author, etc. Most of the current works have formulated the problem of evaluating review quality as a classification or regression problem using these observed features. In the following, we first review some recent classification-based and regression-based approaches and then describe the importance of our problem in other domains, i.e. recommendation systems, opinion retrieval, opinion question answering, etc.

The authors of [23, 16, 26, 28] propose classification-based approaches learning from annotated ground-truth. Tseng et al. in [28] and O'Mahony et al. in [23] use both textual and social features in the process of estimating review quality. Tseng et al. employ a multi-class support vector machine (SVM) model to categorize reviews in five classes. O'Mahony et al. claim to present a recommender system for reviews, but they actually present a non-personalized classifier. There are also some other works [16, 26] employing SVM to classify reviews as helpful or unhelpful. The model presented in [16] uses textual features while [26] uses a term-based representation of comments constructed using tf-idf.

Instead of classifying reviews as helpful or unhelpful, some recent works consider estimating a quality rating for each review using a regression model. The authors of [10, 29] apply support vector regression (SVR) and the authors of [2] apply linear regression (LR) on a variety of textual features to predict the quality of reviews. The method proposed in [30], which also uses textual features, compares the performance of SVR with simple LR. Experimental results show that SVR provides better estimation for quality of reviews than LR. The most recent work, [17], formulates this problem as a linear regression problem and mine combined textual and social context information to evaluate the quality of reviews. The results show that adding social context as additional features can improve predictions significantly over a text-only baseline. The authors also present an alternative use of the social context by defining a set of constraints for the text-based predictors, but none of them outperforms the combined predictor (using both textual and social features) when there is sufficient amount of training data.

There are also some analytical studies on the helpfulness of reviews. Liu et al. in [16] identify a "rich-get-richer" effect, where reviews accumulate quality ratings (helpfulness votes) more quickly depending on the number of votes they already have. This analysis strengthens the motivation for automatically determining the quality of reviews in order to avoid such biases. Mizil et al. [1] show that the helpfulness of a review depends not just on its content but also on users' social contexts. The authors of [5] also propose a simulation model to assess review quality by considering reviewer's behavior. These analyses clarify the relationship between the social context of the reviewer and the quality of the review.

The problem of assessing the quality of user-generated content is also critical in other domains. The works proposed in [4] and [19] consider the problem of product review search (opinion retrieval problem) and rank the retrieved reviews based on their quality. The authors of [27] consider the problem of finding good answers to a question using community question answering portals, e.g. Yahoo! Answers[5] (collaborative question answering problem). As part of their method, they determine the answer quality. The quality of an answer is determined by the answer content (textual features) as well as answerer expertise (social features). They apply the HITS model on the entire questioner and answerer database to determine the answerer expertise. In [14] another solution for the same problem has been proposed. They consider the sentences as authorities and question topic and opinion sentiments as hubs and apply the PageRank and HITS algorithm on the graph to find high quality answers for the given question. Jindal et al [8][7] also study the problem of opinion spam in the context of product reviews. They use textual and social features and employ a regression model to estimate the probability of each review being a spam.

Finally, regarding our approach which is based on factor models there are some related works in the area of recommendation systems. The matrix factorization (MF) model has been used in some recent work [25, 6, 12, 11] to factorize the user-item matrix. Tensor factorization (TF) [13] has also been used in the recommendation system area [9, 24] by adding a third dimension (e.g. context) to the user-item matrix. However, to the best of our knowledge there is no previous work employing factor models for evaluating the quality of online reviews.

[5]http://answers.yahoo.com/

3. PROBLEM DEFINITION

To the best of our knowledge, none of the existing methods estimates the helpfulness of a review for a specific user. All of the current works on review quality prediction assume that the helpfulness of a review is the same for all users. However, this assumption may not be true in all cases. Consider the following motivating example:

Motivating Example: Assume that a professional photographer, who has recently joined an online reviewing website, has written a review about his new digital camera. He covered the professional aspects of the camera such as manual focus quality. Three raters r_1, r_2, and r_3 read this review to make a purchase decision. Rater r_1 who is also a professional photographer assigns the review a high rating since it answers most of his questions about the advanced features of the product. Rater r_2 who is an amateur photographer and wants to know how easy to use the camera is and what general picture quality he gets for the price he pays, does not find the review very helpful. Finally, rater r_3 who tends to be skeptical of reviews by unknown reviewers, assigns the review a low rating because of the low popularity of its reviewer.

In the above example, helpfulness of the same review is evaluated differently because of raters' different evaluation criteria. We argue that in many cases the personalized review quality may be more accurate than its non-personalized counterpart and introduce the problem of user-specific review quality prediction.

Problem Statement: Given a set of N_p products from different categories $P = \{p_1, p_2, ..., p_{N_p}\}$, a set of N_r reviews $R = \{r_1, r_2, ..., r_{N_r}\}$ about these products, a set of N_v reviewers $V = \{v_1, v_2, ..., v_{N_v}\}$ who have written these reviews, and a set of N_u raters $U = \{u_1, u_2, ..., u_{N_u}\}$ who have read and rated some of the reviews, the task is to predict the quality rating (helpfulness) of a given review r_j for a given rater u_i.

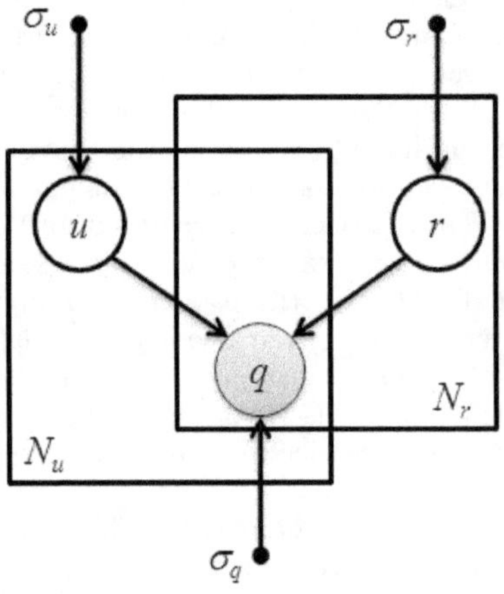

Figure 1: Matrix Factorization Model

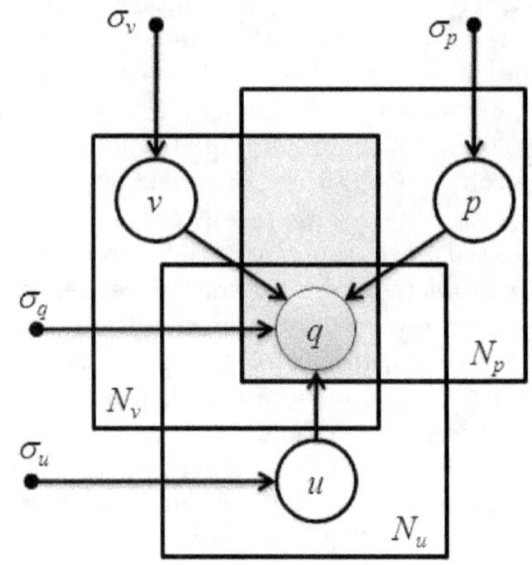

Figure 2: Tensor Factorization Model

4. BASIC FACTOR MODELS

In this section, we present two basic factor models for estimating review quality: A probabilistic matrix factorization (MF) model, and a tensor factorization (TF) model. Note that, while MF [25, 6, 12, 11] and TF [13, 9, 24] have already been used in the literature for item recommendation, these methods have not yet been explored for review recommendation.

In the following models, p, v, u, and r denote the latent variables for product, reviewer, rater, and review, respectively.

4.1 Matrix Factorization Model

In this section we employ MF to factorize the *rater* $\times$ *review* matrix for predicting review quality. The underlying assumption of this model is that both raters and reviews can be modeled by a set of latent features, which together determine the rating of a review in a probabilistic way.

Suppose we have a set of N_u raters and a set of N_r reviews. The quality ratings expressed by raters on reviews are given in a matrix $q = [q_{ij}]_{N_u \times N_r}$. In this matrix q_{ij} represents the quality rating of rater u_i for review r_j. q_{ij} can be any real number, but often ratings are integers in the range $[1, 5]$. In this paper, without loss of generality, we map the ratings to the interval $[0, 1]$ by normalizing the ratings. Let $u \in \mathbb{R}^{K \times N_u}$ and $r \in \mathbb{R}^{K \times N_r}$ be latent rater and review feature matrices, with column vector u_i representing K-dimensional rater-specific latent feature vectors of rater u_i and column vector r_j representing K-dimensional review-specific latent feature vectors of review r_j. The goal of MF is to learn these latent variables and exploit them for recommendation. Figure 1 shows the corresponding graphical model. Following the standard graphical model formalism, nodes represent random variables and edges indicate possible dependence. Shaded nodes are observed variables and unshaded nodes are latent variables. Finally, a box around a group of random variables is a 'plate' which denotes replication of these variables. The conditional probability of the observed ratings in our MF model is defined as:

$$P(q|u, r, \sigma_q^2) = \prod_i^{N_u} \prod_j^{N_r} [\mathcal{N}(q_{ij}|g(u_i^T r_j), \sigma_q^2)]^{I_{ij}^q} \quad (1)$$

where $\mathcal{N}(x|\mu, \sigma^2)$ is the probability density function of the Gaussian distribution with mean μ and variance σ^2, and I_{ij}^q is the indicator function that is equal to 1 if rater u_i rates review r_j (q_{ij} is observed) and equal to 0 otherwise. The function $g(x)$ is the logistic function $g(x) = 1/(1+exp(-x))$, which bounds the range of $u_i^T r_j$ within $[0, 1]$. We also place a zero-mean spherical Gaussian prior on rater and review feature vectors:

$$P(u|\sigma_u^2) = \prod_i^{N_u} \mathcal{N}(u_i|0, \sigma_u^2 \mathbf{I}), P(r|\sigma_r^2) = \prod_j^{N_r} \mathcal{N}(r_j|0, \sigma_r^2 \mathbf{I}) \quad (2)$$

Through a Bayesian inference, the log of the posterior distribution over rater and review features is obtained. Maximizing the log-posterior over the latent variables with hyperparameters kept fixed is equivalent to minimizing the following sum-of-squared-errors loss function with regularization terms:

$$E_{MF} = \frac{1}{2} \sum_i^{N_u} \sum_j^{N_r} I_{ij}^q (q_{ij} - g(u_i^T r_j))^2 + \frac{\lambda_u}{2} \sum_i^{N_u} \|u_i\|_{Fro}^2 + \frac{\lambda_r}{2} \sum_j^{N_r} \|r_j\|_{Fro}^2 \quad (3)$$

where $\lambda_u = \sigma_q^2/\sigma_u^2$, $\lambda_r = \sigma_q^2/\sigma_r^2$ and $\|.\|_{Fro}^2$ denotes the Frobenius norm. A local minimum of this objective function can be found by performing stochastic gradient descent.

4.2 Tensor Factorization Model

In this section, we employ TF to personalize review quality prediction. The underlying assumption of our model is that since each review is written by a reviewer about a product, the latent feature vector of a review can be generated in a probabilistic way by aggregating the latent feature vector of its reviewer and the latent feature vector of the corresponding product. That is, the *rater* $\times$ *review* two-dimensional matrix used as input in MF is converted into three-dimensional tensor *rater* $\times$ *reviewer* $\times$ *product*. Note that, in contrast to most of the TF-based recommendation system approaches which add a third dimension to the traditional user-item matrix, we propose to replace the *review* dimension in MF with *reviewer* × *product* in TF. Figure 2 shows the corresponding graphical model, where the shaded box represents reviews written by a reviewer about some product.

Suppose we have a set of N_u raters, a set of N_v reviewers, and a set of N_p products. The quality ratings expressed by raters on reviews written by reviewers about different products are given in a three-dimensional tensor $q = [q_{ijk}]_{N_u \times N_v \times N_p}$. In this tensor q_{ijk} represents the quality rating of rater u_i for the review written by reviewer v_j about product p_k. The three-dimensional tensor is factorized into three matrices and one central tensor. Let $u \in \mathbb{R}^{K \times N_u}$, $v \in \mathbb{R}^{K \times N_v}$, and $p \in \mathbb{R}^{K \times N_p}$ be latent rater, reviewer, and product feature matrices, with column vector u_i representing K-dimensional rater-specific latent feature vector of rater u_i, column vector v_j representing K-dimensional reviewer-specific latent feature vector of reviewer v_j, and column vector p_k representing K-dimensional product-specific latent feature vector of product p_k. Let also $s \in \mathbb{R}^{K \times K \times K}$ be the central tensor where K is the dimension of the model latent factors. The goal of tensor factorization is to learn these latent variables and exploit them for rating prediction. Given the feature matrices and the central tensor, the prediction can be made as follows:

$$h_{ijk} = \sum_{x=1}^{K} \sum_{y=1}^{K} \sum_{z=1}^{K} s_{xyz} u_{ix} v_{jy} p_{kz} \tag{4}$$

where h_{ijk} is the predicted value for q_{ijk}. To simplify Equation 4, we use the tensor-matrix product operator $\times_a$ to multiply a matrix on dimension a with a tensor [9], e.g. $t = s \times_u u_i$ is a $K \times K$ matrix where $t_{yz} = \sum_{x=1}^{K} s_{xyz} u_{ix}$. So, the prediction is made by multiplying the three feature matrices and the central tensor:

$$h_{ijk} = s \times_u u_i \times_v v_j \times_p p_k \tag{5}$$

Similar to MF, we minimize the sum-of-squared-errors between the observed rating q_{ijk} and the predicted rating $g(h_{ijk})$ [9]. We also add regularization terms to avoid overfitting. So, the objective function for the minimization problem is as follows:

$$\begin{aligned} E_{TF} = &\frac{1}{2} \sum_{i}^{N_u} \sum_{j}^{N_v} \sum_{k}^{N_p} I^q_{ijk} (q_{ijk} - g(h_{ijk}))^2 \\ &+ \frac{\lambda_u}{2} \sum_{i}^{N_u} \|u_i\|^2_{Fro} + \frac{\lambda_v}{2} \sum_{j}^{N_v} \|v_j\|^2_{Fro} \\ &+ \frac{\lambda_p}{2} \sum_{k}^{N_p} \|p_k\|^2_{Fro} + \frac{\lambda_s}{2} \sum_{ijk} \|s_{ijk}\|^2_{Fro} \end{aligned} \tag{6}$$

where I^q_{ijk} is the indicator function that is equal to 1 if q_{ijk} is observed (i.e. rater u_i rates the review written by reviewer v_j about product p_k) and equal to 0 otherwise. The function $g(x)$ is the logistic function defined in Section 4.1 which bound the range of h_{ijk} within $[0, 1]$. Again, to minimize the objective function, we perform stochastic gradient descent.

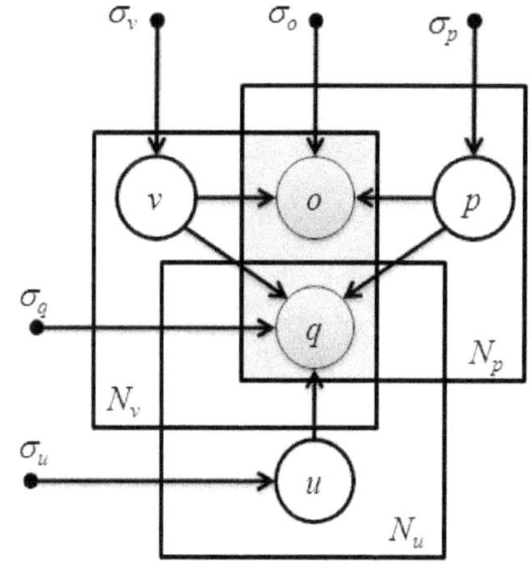

Figure 3: Extended Tensor Factorization Model

5. EXTENDED FACTOR MODELS

One benefit of the factor approaches is their flexibility in dealing with various data aspects and other application-specific requirements [12]. In this section, we introduce a novel model, Extended Tensor Factorization (ETF), which incorporates the overall rating of a product expressed in a review as another observed variable into the TF model. We further improve the ETF model by capturing the factor biases and propose the unBiased ETF (BETF).

5.1 Incorporating Product Rating

Typically, online reviews consist of a textual review and a numerical rating value indicating the overall evaluation of the reviewer for the reviewed product. We incorporate the overall rating of a product expressed in a review as another observed variable into our tensor factorization model and propose the Extended Tensor Factorization (ETF) model. The ETF model assumes that the overall rating of a product given by the reviewer is generated in a probabilistic way by aggregating the product and reviewer latent features. ETF uses this additional assumption to add a constraint on the TF model which promises to improve the accuracy of the learned model. Figure 3 shows the corresponding graphical model, where the shaded box represents reviews and the observed variable o denotes the overall product rating of that review.

Suppose we have a set of N_u raters, a set of N_v reviewers, and a set of N_p products. The quality ratings expressed by raters on reviews are given in a tensor $q = [q_{ijk}]_{N_u \times N_v \times N_p}$ where q_{ijk} represents the quality rating of rater u_i for the review written by reviewer v_j about product p_k. The overall ratings of products expressed by reviewers are given in a matrix $o = [o_{jk}]_{N_v \times N_p}$ where o_{jk} represents the overall rating assigned by reviewer v_j to product p_k. Similar to the TF model, the three-dimensional tensor q is factorized into three matrices u, v, and p and one central tensor s. The goal of the ETF model is to learn these latent variables and exploit them for rating prediction.

In analogy to MF and TF, our goal is to minimize the sum-of-squared-errors between the observed review rating q_{ijk} and the predicted rating $g(h_{ijk})$, and also between the observed product overall rating o_{jk} and the predicted rating $g(v_j^T p_k)$. Again, to avoid overfitting, we add regularization

Algorithm 1 Extended Tensor Factorization

Input: q, o, K
initialize $u \in \mathbb{R}^{K\times N_u}$, $v \in \mathbb{R}^{K\times N_v}$, $p \in \mathbb{R}^{K\times N_p}$, and $s \in \mathbb{R}^{K\times K\times K}$ with small random values
set $t = t_0$
repeat
  $\eta \leftarrow \frac{1}{\sqrt{t}}$ and $t \leftarrow t+1$
  for all (i,j,k) such that q_{ijk} is observed **do**
    $h_{ijk} = s \times_u u_i \times_v v_j \times_p p_k$
    $u_i \leftarrow u_i - \eta g'(h_{ijk})(g(h_{ijk}) - q_{ijk})(s \times_v v_j \times_p p_k)$
    $v_j \leftarrow v_j - \eta g'(h_{ijk})(g(h_{ijk}) - q_{ijk})(s \times_u u_i \times_p p_k)$
    $p_k \leftarrow p_k - \eta g'(h_{ijk})(g(h_{ijk}) - q_{ijk})(s \times_u u_i \times_v v_j)$
    $s \leftarrow s - \eta g'(h_{ijk})(g(h_{ijk}) - q_{ijk})(u_i \otimes v_j \otimes p_k)$
  end for
  for all (j,k) such that o_{jk} is observed **do**
    $v_j \leftarrow v_j - \eta g'(v_j^T p_k)(g(v_j^T p_k) - o_{jk})p_k$
    $p_k \leftarrow p_k - \eta g'(v_j^T p_k)(g(v_j^T p_k) - o_{jk})v_j$
  end for
  for each u_i in u **do**
    $u_i \leftarrow u_i - \eta\lambda_u u_i$
  for each v_j in v **do**
    $v_j \leftarrow v_j - \eta\lambda_v v_j$
  for each p_k in p **do**
    $p_k \leftarrow p_k - \eta\lambda_p p_k$
  $s \leftarrow s - \eta\lambda_s s$
until convergence
Output: u, v, p, s

terms to the error function. So, the objective function for the minimization problem is as follows:

$$E_{ETF} = \frac{1}{2}\sum_i^{N_u}\sum_j^{N_v}\sum_k^{N_p} I^q_{ijk}(q_{ijk} - g(h_{ijk}))^2 + \frac{1}{2}\sum_j^{N_v}\sum_k^{N_p} I^o_{jk}(o_{jk} - g(v_j^T p_k))^2 + \frac{\lambda_u}{2}\sum_i^{N_u}\|u_i\|^2_{Fro} + \frac{\lambda_v}{2}\sum_j^{N_v}\|v_j\|^2_{Fro} + \frac{\lambda_p}{2}\sum_k^{N_p}\|p_k\|^2_{Fro} + \frac{\lambda_s}{2}\sum_{ijk}\|s_{ijk}\|^2_{Fro} \quad (7)$$

To find a local minimum of the objective function, we perform stochastic gradient descent. In order to compute the updates for the stochastic gradient descent algorithm, we compute the derivative of the objective function with respect to the model parameters. The pseudo-code for the extended tensor factorization model is presented in Algorithm 1 where $\otimes$ is the matrix outer product and $g'(x)$ is the derivative of the logistic function defined in Section 4.1.

5.2 Capturing Biases

Koren et al. [11] showed that pure factor models capture well the interaction among factors. However, much of the observed variation in rating values is due to biases associated with the individual factors, independently of the interaction among factors [12]. While the ETF can model the interaction among reviewers, products, and raters accurately, it fails in capturing the biases associated with each

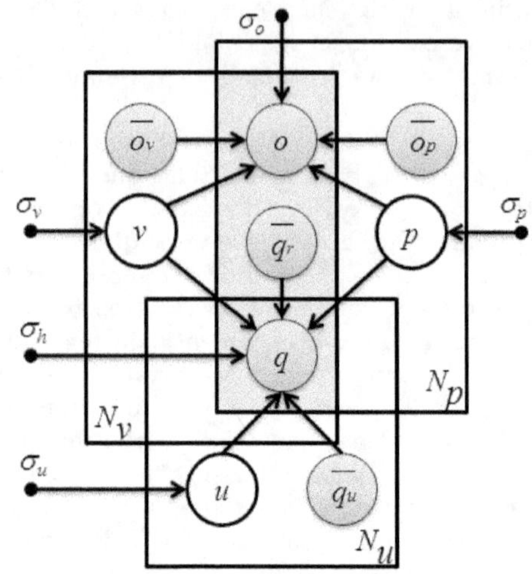

Figure 4: unBiased ETF Model

factor, such as tendencies of some raters/reviewers to give higher ratings than others, and for some products/reviews to receive higher ratings than others.

The ETF model proposed in the previous section explains the review quality rating and the product overall rating by interactions of the form $s \times_u u_i \times_v v_j \times_p p_k$ and $v_j^T p_k$, respectively. In this section we further improve the ETF model by capturing biases related to each factor. The *unBiased ETF model (BETF)* tries to identify the portion of the review quality rating, q_{ijk}, that individual rater or review biases can explain, as well as the portion of the product overall rating, o_{jk}, that individual reviewer or product biases can explain, and subjects only the true interaction portion of the data to factor modeling (Figure 4). A first-order approximation of the bias involved in review quality rating q_{ijk} is as follows:

$$b_{ijk} = \mu_q + \bar{q_{u_i}} + \bar{q_{r_{jk}}} \quad (8)$$

where μ_q is the average rating of all reviews over all raters, and $\bar{q_{u_i}}$ and $\bar{q_{r_{jk}}}$ indicate the average deviation (the bias) of rater u_i and review r_{jk} from μ_q, respectively. Review r_{jk} is the review that has been written by reviewer v_j about product p_k. In the same way, an approximation of the bias involved in product overall rating o_{jk} is as follows:

$$b_{jk} = \mu_o + \bar{o_{v_j}} + \bar{o_{p_k}} \quad (9)$$

where μ_o is the average rating of all products over all reviewers, and $\bar{o_{v_j}}$ and $\bar{o_{p_k}}$ indicate the average deviation (the bias) of reviewer v_j and product p_k from μ_o, respectively. We integrate these biases into the ETF factor model, and in the BETF model the rating is predicted as follows:

$$\hat{q_{ijk}} = \mu_q + \bar{q_{u_i}} + \bar{q_{r_{jk}}} + h_{ijk} \quad (10)$$

$$\hat{o_{jk}} = \mu_o + \bar{o_{v_j}} + \bar{o_{p_k}} + v_j^T p_k \quad (11)$$

where $\hat{q_{ijk}}$ and $\hat{o_{jk}}$ are the predicted review quality rating and product overall rating, respectively, and h_{ijk} is computed using Equation 5. Here, the observed review rating q_{ijk} is broken down into four components: global average μ_q, rater bias $\bar{q_{u_i}}$, review bias $\bar{q_{r_{jk}}}$, and rater-reviewer-product interaction h_{ijk}. Similarly, the observed product rating o_{jk} is broken down into global average μ_o, reviewer bias $\bar{o_{v_j}}$, product bias $\bar{o_{p_k}}$, and reviewer-product interaction $v_j^T p_k$. This allows each component to explain only the part of a rating relevant to it. The objective function for the minimization problem is updated as follows:

$$\begin{aligned} E_{BETF} &= \frac{1}{2}\sum_i^{N_u}\sum_j^{N_v}\sum_k^{N_p} I_{ijk}^q (q_{ijk} - g(\hat{q_{ijk}}))^2 \\ &+ \frac{1}{2}\sum_j^{N_v}\sum_k^{N_p} I_{jk}^o (o_{jk} - g(\hat{o_{jk}}))^2 \\ &+ \frac{\lambda_u}{2}\sum_i^{N_u}\|u_i\|_{Fro}^2 + \frac{\lambda_v}{2}\sum_j^{N_v}\|v_j\|_{Fro}^2 \\ &+ \frac{\lambda_p}{2}\sum_k^{N_p}\|p_k\|_{Fro}^2 + \frac{\lambda_s}{2}\sum_{ijk}\|s_{ijk}\|_{Fro}^2 \end{aligned} \quad (12)$$

where $\hat{q_{ijk}}$ and $\hat{o_{jk}}$ are computed using Equations 10 and 11. Again, to find a local minimum of the objective function, we perform stochastic gradient descent. The pseudo-code presented in Algorithm 1 can be used for the BETF model by replacing the h_{ijk} and $v_j^T p_k$ with $\hat{q_{ijk}}$ and $\hat{o_{jk}}$, respectively.

6. EXPERIMENTAL EVALUATION

In this section, we describe the real-life dataset we used for our experiments and present the results of our experimental evaluation and comparison with state-of-the-art methods.

6.1 Dataset

To evaluate the proposed models, we performed experiments on a dataset from the popular reviewing website Epinions.com. Epinions.com is a consumers opinion website where users can write reviews about products (such as digital cameras, laptops, books, movies, software, etc.) and assign them numeric ratings in the range from 1 to 5. It also allows users to express their feedback about the helpfulness of a review using numeric quality ratings. We used the version of the Epinions' dataset[6] published by the authors of [18]. This dataset was given directly by Epinions staff to the authors and, different from other publicly available Epinions datasets, contains ratings of reviews assigned by different users. This dataset does not have the text of the reviews, but it provides the review identifiers. We enhanced this dataset by downloading the review text from the Epinions website (using the available identifiers) and made the complete dataset publicly available for research purposes[7]. This dataset is very large and covers a very wide range of more than 200,000 products from different categories which can be considered as a collection of several review datasets.

Table 1 presents some statistics of our Epinions dataset. We can see that about 50% of the reviews have been rated by at least one rater. It is also shown that on average each rated review has been rated by 18 different raters which indicates the richness of this dataset.

[6]http://www.trustlet.org/wiki/Extended_Epinions_dataset
[7]http://www.sfu.ca/~sam39/Datasets/EpinionsReviews

Table 1: Statistics of the dataset

#Reviews	1,560,144
#Products	200,953
#Reviewers	326,983
#Raters	120,492
#Rated Reviews	755,760
#Ratings	13,668,320

Figure 5 shows some distributions of reviews, reviewers, raters, and products in this dataset. We first consider the following plots:

- Distribution of #reviews per reviewer (Fig. 5(a))
- Distribution of #reviews per product (Fig. 5(b))
- Distribution of #ratings per rater (Fig. 5(c))
- Distribution of #ratings per review (Fig. 5(d))

Not surprisingly, these distributions all follow a power law. We can see that a large number of reviewers write only a few reviews, and a few reviewers write a large number of reviews (Figure 5(a)). A similar property can be seen in the other three figures. The relationship between the number of reviews and the number of ratings (Figure 5(d)) is slightly lower than an ideal straight line for the first few points, which are mainly reviews with fewer than 5 ratings.

We also analyze the distribution of two of the most important properties of each review:

- Distribution of overall rating of products expressed in reviews (Fig. 5(e))
- Distribution of quality ratings of reviews (Fig. 5(f))

The overall rating of a product expressed in a review is assigned by its writer (reviewer) showing his overall satisfaction regarding the reviewed product. On the other hand, the quality rating of a review is assigned by the reader of that review (rater) showing the helpfulness of that review for him. Epinions uses a 5-point rating scale (ranging from 1 to 5) for both ratings. As we see in Figure 5(e), 46% of reviews in Epinions have an overall product rating of 5, which means that most of the reviews have high ratings and therefore most of the reviewers also have a high average rating assigned to products. Figure 5(f) shows a very similar distribution for the quality ratings. Again, 77% of quality ratings are 5 and therefore most of the raters have a high average rating assigned to reviews.

6.2 Experimental Setup

As pointed out already, all of the current works have formulated the problem of determining review quality as a classification or regression problem using a set of observed features, i.e. textual and/or social features. As discussed in Section 2, classification-based approaches mainly employ SVM for classifying reviews [28, 16, 26]. Our proposed models, on the other hand, predict real-value ratings which cannot be compared with the classification results. For a fair comparison, we use the regression version of SVM, Support Vector Regression (SVR), which is also used in some

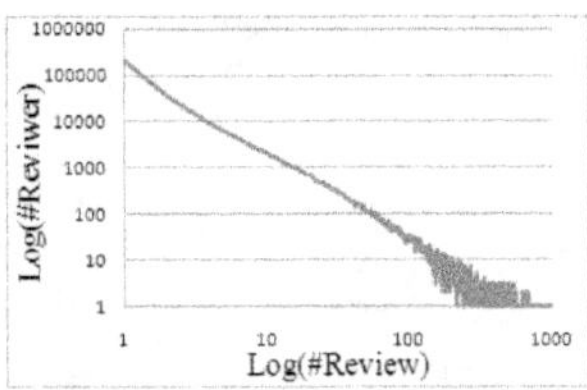

(a) Number of reviews per reviewer

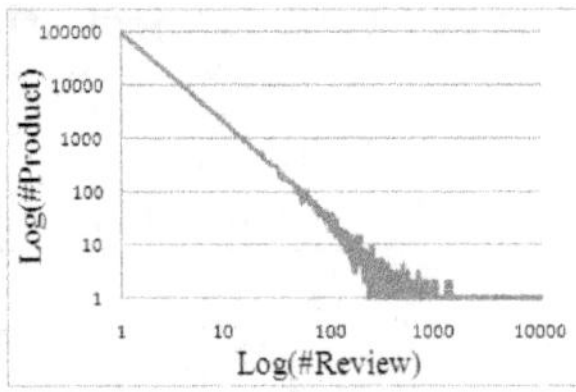

(b) Number of reviews per product

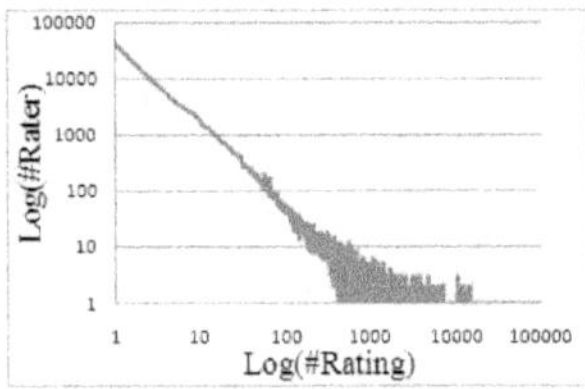

(c) Number of ratings per rater

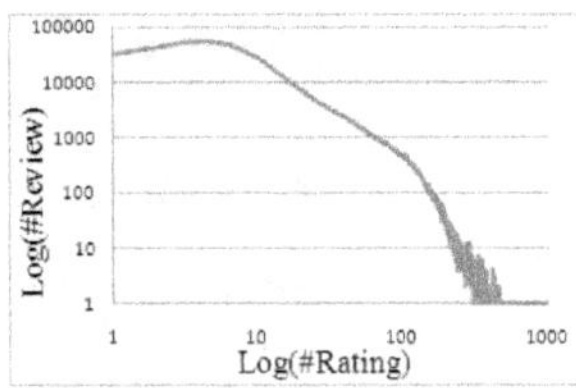

(d) Number of ratings per review

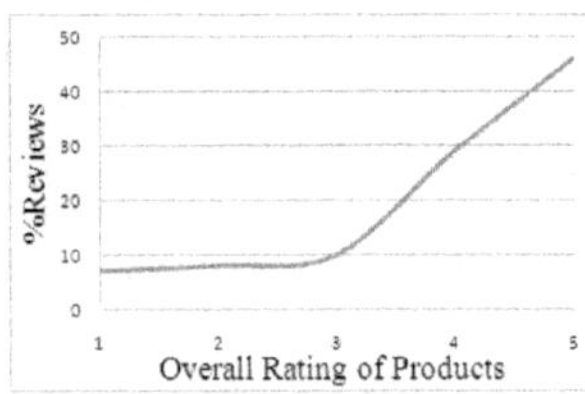

(e) Distribution of overall rating

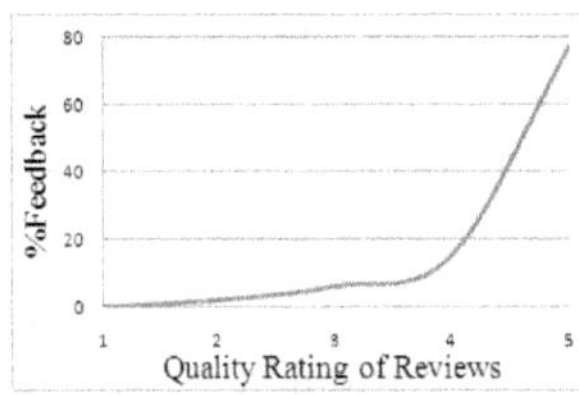

(f) Distribution of quality rating

Figure 5: Dataset Analysis

regression-based approaches [29, 10, 30]. Since other regression-based approaches mainly apply Linear Regression (LR) [17, 2, 30] to predict the quality rating of reviews, we use LR as another comparison partner.

As mentioned in Section 2, each work has defined a set of features to predict the quality of reviews. Most of them only use textual features [10, 13, 2, 16, 30] , while some of them combined both textual and social features [17, 28, 23]. Our proposed models do not use observed features, however our comparison partners need them to be learned. We use textual and social features defined in the most recent work [17] to implement our comparison partners. Textual features include total number of tokens and sentences, ratio of positive and negative sentiment words, ratio of verbs, adverbs, etc. Social features include number of past reviews by the reviewer, in-degree and out-degree of the reviewer, PageRank score of the reviewer, etc.

As further comparison partner, we choose the Collaborative Filtering (CF) method [3] which is widely used in the area of recommendation systems for the task of predicting the rating of an item. CF treats each review as an item and only uses their rating for the task of prediction, i.e. it uses neither observed textual/social features not latent factors. Finally, we use several baseline methods which use the average rating of reviews or raters for prediction. For the sake of clarity, we list all comparison partners as follows:

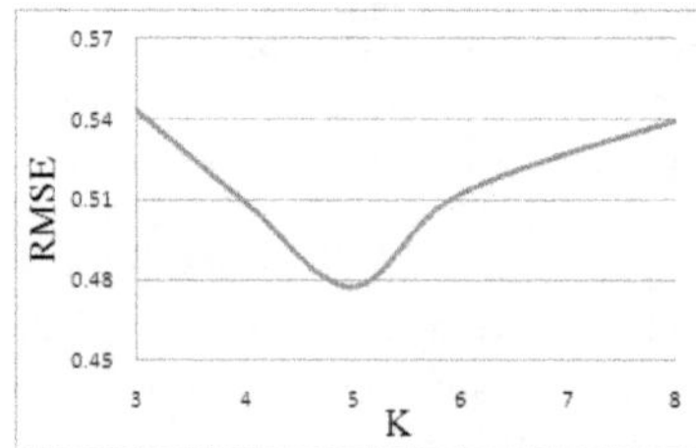

(a) RMSE of MF

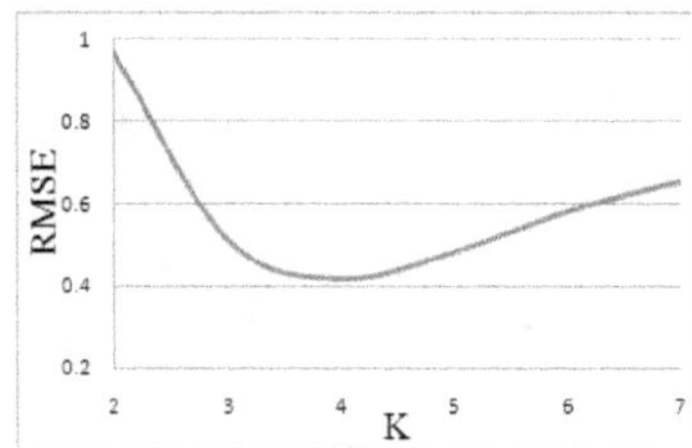

(b) RMSE of TF

Figure 6: Sensitivity analysis for RMSE of MF and TF models for different values of K

Avg-AllRev: A baseline method using the average quality ratings of all reviews as the predicted rating for all reviews and all raters.

Avg-AllRater: A baseline method using the average quality ratings of all raters as the predicted rating for all reviews and all raters.

Avg-Rev: A baseline method using the average quality ratings of a review as the predicted rating for all raters of that review.

Avg-Rater: A baseline method using the average ratings of a rater as the predicted rating for all reviews of that rater.

LR-Txt: Linear Regression on textual features.

LR-Soc: Linear Regression on social features.

LR-All: Linear Regression on textual and social features.

SVR-Txt: Support Vector Regression on textual features.

SVR-Soc: Support Vector Regression on social features.

SVR-All: Support Vector Regression on textual and social features.

CF: User-based Collaborative Filtering.

MF: Matrix factorization model described in Section 4.1.

TF: Tensor Factorization model described in Section 4.2.

ETF: Extended Tensor Factorization model described in Section 5.1.

BETF: unBiased ETF described in Section 5.2.

In our proposed models, the dimension of the latent factors, K, need to be specified as input. We perform sensitivity analysis to find the optimum value for K. Figure 6 shows the RMSE of MF and TF models for different values of K. MF performs best at $K = 5$ and TF reaches its minimum RMSE at $K = 4$. The BETF and ETF models, which are an extension of TF, also reach their minimum RMSE at $K = 4$. It should be noted that in our experiments we set all regularization parameters (λ's) to 0.1.

Table 2: RMSE of comparison partners for all raters and cold start raters

Method	All Raters	Cold Raters
Avg-AllRev	0.7487	1.0529
Avg-AllRater	0.7149	1.0619
Avg-Rater	0.7076	1.1943
Avg-Rev	0.6479	1.1415
LR-Txt	0.6339	1.0927
LR-Soc	0.5331	1.1054
LR-All	0.5230	1.1116
SVR-Txt	0.5665	1.1141
SVR-Soc	0.5176	1.0982
SVR-All	0.5018	1.0216
CF	0.4992	1.0874
MF	0.4774	0.8627
TF	0.4164	0.6749
ETF	0.3804	0.4591
BETF	0.3401	0.4128

6.3 Experimental Results

In this section, we report the results of our experimental evaluation for the comparison partners listed in Section 6.2. For evaluation, we performed 10-fold cross validation on the Epinions dataset. In each fold we used 90% of the data as the training set and the remaining 10% as the test set. The evaluation metric is Root Mean Squared Error (RMSE), the standard metric for evaluation of recommender systems, which is defined as:

$$RMSE = \sqrt{\frac{\sum_{D_{test}}(q-h)^2}{|D_{test}|}} \tag{13}$$

where q is the actual quality rating of a review for a specific user in the test set, h is the predicted value for q, and $|D_{test}|$ is the number of ratings in the test set.

As discussed in Section 6.1 and showed in Figure 5(c), most of the raters have rated only a small number of reviews. In the area of recommendation systems these users are called *Cold Start* users. As is common practice, we use the term 'cold start' for those raters who have rated less than 5 reviews. Predicting the quality rating of a review for cold start raters is more challenging than for normal raters, since the size of the training data is very small for these raters. In the Epinions dataset almost 60% of the raters are cold start, and hence accuracy of any quality prediction algorithm for these raters is very important. To this end, we separately evaluate the performance of the comparison partners for cold start raters. Table 2 and Figure 7 report the RMSE values for all comparison partners on the Epinions dataset for both all raters and cold start raters.

Analyzing the RMSE results for all raters, we observe that all of the comparison partners which model the relationship among reviews' features (textual and/or social) outperform the baseline methods which are only based on the reviews' rating. This improvement highlights the impact of review features in determining the quality of reviews. Our experiments also confirm the finding from the literature [17] that using the combination of textual and social features can improve the accuracy of prediction over the text-only

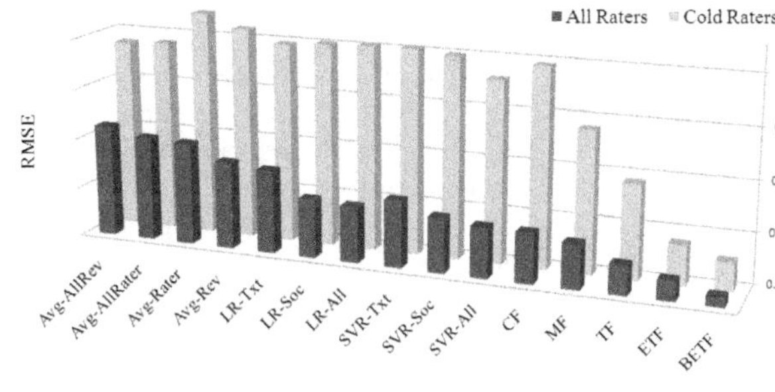

Figure 7: RMSE of comparison partners

and social-only methods. Moreover, the CF model performs better than both the LR and SVR methods. We believe the better performance of CF is due to its personalized prediction by identifying like-minded raters.

The MF model, which is learned based on rater and review latent factors, outperforms all of the existing non-personalized methods, showing the superior ability of latent factor models in personalized review quality prediction. As expected, the TF model outperforms the MF model, since TF decomposes the review latent factor into reviewer and product latent factors, providing a richer model of the effects underlying the observed data. The ETF model provides better prediction with lower RMSE than TF, because of using additional observed data (overall rating of products expressed in reviews). Finally, BETF provides the best personalized review quality prediction with the minimum RMSE. The improved performance of BETF over ETF can be explained by the ability of capturing biases by the BETF model.

We now analyze the performance for cold start raters separately. While all of the comparison partners clearly outperform the baseline methods for all raters, this is not the case for cold start raters. Compared to LR and SVR models, the baseline methods achieve pretty good performance, and even outperform them in some cases. This shows that methods using only observed features (either reviews' features as used in LR and SVR, or similar raters' ratings as used in CF) cannot accurately infer the preferences of cold start raters. On the other hand, the results for cold start raters in all our factor models (MF, TF, ETF, and BETF) are significantly better than those of the comparison partners. We believe this gain is due to the modeling and learning of the latent factors of review quality.

We summarize our experimental results as follows:

- All of the personalized methods outperform all of the non-personalized prediction methods.
- MF improves the RMSE of SVR-All, which has the highest accuracy among the state-of-the-art methods, by 5% on all raters and by 16% on cold start raters. TF outperforms MF on all raters and cold start raters by 13% and 22%, respectively.
- The proposed ETF model improves the RMSE of TF by 9% on all raters and by 32% on cold start raters. Finally, the gain of the BETF model over ETF is 11% on all raters and 10% on cold start raters.
- Compared to SVR-All, the best published method, the BETF model improves RMSE by 32% on all raters and by 60% on cold start raters.

7. SUMMARY AND FUTURE WORK

In this paper, we introduce the problem of personalized review quality prediction. To address this problem, we have proposed a series of probabilistic factorization models, MF, TF, ETF and BETF. Experiments on a real-life dataset from Epinions.com demonstrate that all of the proposed latent factor models outperform state-of-the-art comparison partners using observed features (LR, SVR, and CF). We also observed that TF performs better than MF by replacing the review latent factor with the reviewer and product latent factors, ETF performs better than TF by exploiting overall product ratings expressed in reviews in the learning process, and finally BETF outperforms ETF by capturing factor biases. Also, the gain achieved by factorization models over LR and SVR models for cold start raters is significantly higher than that of all raters. Finally, our experiments confirm that the helpfulness of a review is indeed not the same for all users and personalized predictions are more accurate.

This work suggests several interesting directions for future work. It is well-known that the information in social networks can improve the accuracy of product recommendation, and we plan to extend our approach by exploiting a social network among reviewers and raters. Moreover, since user preferences for reviews are changing as new reviews emerge, modeling the temporal dynamics for review recommendation can be another line of future work.

8. REFERENCES

[1] C. Danescu-Niculescu-Mizil, G. Kossinets, J. Kleinberg, and L. Lee. How opinions are received by online communities: a case study on amazon.com helpfulness votes. In *WWW '09*.

[2] A. Ghose and P. G. Ipeirotis. Estimating the helpfulness and economic impact of product reviews: Mining text and reviewer characteristics. *IEEE Transactions on Knowledge and Data Engineering*, 99, 2010.

[3] D. Goldberg, D. Nichols, B. M. Oki, and D. Terry. Using collaborative filtering to weave an information tapestry. *Commun. ACM*, 35, 1992.

[4] S. Huang, D. Shen, W. Feng, C. Baudin, and Y. Zhang. Improving product review search experiences on general search engines. In *ICEC '09*.

[5] S. Huang, D. Shen, W. Feng, Y. Zhang, and C. Baudin. Discovering clues for review quality from author's behaviors on e-commerce sites. In *ICEC '09*.

[6] M. Jamali and M. Ester. A matrix factorization technique with trust propagation for recommendation in social networks. In *ACM RecSys '10*.

[7] N. Jindal and B. Liu. Opinion spam and analysis. In *WSDM '08*.

[8] N. Jindal and B. Liu. Review spam detection. In *WWW '07*.

[9] A. Karatzoglou, X. Amatriain, L. Baltrunas, and N. Oliver. Multiverse recommendation: n-dimensional tensor factorization for context-aware collaborative filtering. In *ACM RecSys '10*.

[10] S.-M. Kim, P. Pantel, T. Chklovski, and M. Pennacchiotti. Automatically assessing review helpfulness. In *EMNLP '06*.

[11] Y. Koren. Collaborative filtering with temporal dynamics. In *KDD '09*.

[12] Y. Koren, R. Bell, and C. Volinsky. Matrix factorization techniques for recommender systems. *Computer Journal*, 42, 2009.

[13] L. D. Lathauwer, B. D. Moor, and J. Vandewalle. A multilinear singular value decomposition. *SIAM J. Matrix Anal. Appl.*, 21(4), 2000.

[14] F. Li, Y. Tang, M. Huang, and X. Zhu. Answering opinion questions with random walks on graphs. In *ACL-IJCNLP '09*.

[15] E.-P. Lim, V.-A. Nguyen, N. Jindal, B. Liu, and H. W. Lauw. Detecting product review spammers using rating behaviors. In *CIKM '10*.

[16] J. Liu, Y. Cao, C.-Y. Lin, Y. Huang, and M. Zhou. Low-quality product review detection in opinion summarization. In *EMNLP-CoNLL '07*.

[17] Y. Lu, P. Tsaparas, A. Ntoulas, and L. Polanyi. Exploiting social context for review quality prediction. In *WWW '10*.

[18] P. Massa and P. Avesani. Controversial users demand local trust metrics: an experimental study on epinions.com community. In *AAAI '05*.

[19] Q. Miao, Q. Li, and R. Dai. A unified framework for opinion retrieval. In *Proceedings of the 2008 IEEE/WIC/ACM International Conference on Web Intelligence and Intelligent Agent Technology - Volume 01*, 2008.

[20] S. Moghaddam and M. Ester. ILDA: interdependent lda model for learning latent aspects and their ratings from online product reviews. In *SIGIR '11*.

[21] S. Moghaddam and M. Ester. Opinion digger: an unsupervised opinion miner from unstructured product reviews. In *CIKM '10*.

[22] S. Moghaddam, M. Jamali, and M. Ester. Review recommendation: personalized prediction of the quality of online reviews. In *CIKM '11*.

[23] M. P. O'Mahony and B. Smyth. Learning to recommend helpful hotel reviews. In *ACM RecSys '09*.

[24] S. Rendle, L. Balby Marinho, A. Nanopoulos, and S.-T. Lars. Learning optimal ranking with tensor factorization for tag recommendation. In *KDD '09*.

[25] R. Salakhutdinov and A. Mnih. Probabilistic matrix factorization. In *NIPS '07*.

[26] S. Siersdorfer, S. Chelaru, W. Nejdl, and J. San Pedro. How useful are your comments?: analyzing and predicting youtube comments and comment ratings. In *WWW '10*.

[27] M. A. Suryanto, E. P. Lim, A. Sun, and R. H. L. Chiang. Quality-aware collaborative question answering: methods and evaluation. In *WSDM '09*.

[28] Y.-D. Tseng and C. C. Chen. Using an information quality framework to evaluate the quality of product reviews. In *AIRS '09*.

[29] X. Yu, Y. Liu, X. Huang, and A. An. A quality-aware model for sales prediction using reviews. In *WWW '10*.

[30] Z. Zhang and B. Varadarajan. Utility scoring of product reviews. In *CIKM '06*.

Multi-Relational Matrix Factorization using Bayesian Personalized Ranking for Social Network Data

Artus Krohn-Grimberghe, Lucas Drumond, Christoph Freudenthaler, and Lars Schmidt-Thieme
Information Systems and Machine Learning Lab, University of Hildesheim, Germany
{artus, ldrumond, freudenthaler, schmidt-thieme}@ismll.de

ABSTRACT

A key element of the social networks on the internet such as Facebook and Flickr is that they encourage users to create connections between themselves, other users and objects.

One important task that has been approached in the literature that deals with such data is to use social graphs to predict user behavior (e.g. joining a group of interest). More specifically, we study the cold-start problem, where users only participate in some relations, which we will call social relations, but not in the relation on which the predictions are made, which we will refer to as target relations.

We propose a formalization of the problem and a principled approach to it based on multi-relational factorization techniques. Furthermore, we derive a principled feature extraction scheme from the social data to extract predictors for a classifier on the target relation. Experiments conducted on real world datasets show that our approach outperforms current methods.

Categories and Subject Descriptors

H.3.3 [**Information Search and Retrieval**]: Information filtering; Search process

General Terms

Algorithms

Keywords

Recommender Systems, Cold-Start, Multi-Relational Learning, Social Network, Matrix Factorization, Item Prediction, Item Recommendation, Ranking, Joint Factorization

1. INTRODUCTION

Social media applications allow users to connect to each other and to interact with items of interest such as songs, videos, web pages, news, groups and the like. Users generally tend to connect to other users due to some commonalities they share, often reflected in similar interests. One of the most important applications in this domain is to provide each user with a list of items ranked according to the likelihood that they could be interesting to him or her. Moreover, in many real-life applications it may be the case that only social information about certain users is available while interaction data between the items and those users has not yet been observed. In this paper we address how to make use of social information on users for item prediction, especially when no collaborative information on the test users is available.

This task is exactly the one demanded of recommender systems, which are designed to predict whether and how much a user will like an item and, in some cases, whether she will buy, watch, use or evaluate it. Since users usually tend to connect with others due to common interests and preferences, the connections between them in social networks may contain useful information for predicting their preferences. In [3], it has been shown that such information may indeed help to improve the quality of rating prediction (i.e. estimating the rating that a user will give to an item), especially for cold start users. In this work we restrict ourselves to the related, but yet distinct task of item prediction, where we present users a ranked list of items that are likely to suit their interests. More specifically, we study the problem of recommending items to users where only social information is available, but no previous direct interactions with items has been recorded, i.e. the cold-start problem.

This problem has been approached by Tang and Liu [14][15], who extract user features from social networks and use them as predictors of a multi-label classifier that predicts whether each of the items is interesting to a given user.

One of the most prominent approaches for recommender systems is matrix factorization. Since social media data is usually presented as two or more matrices (the social and the target relation), in order to apply factorization approaches to social data, one has to resort to their multi-relational variants [12]. However, special care is necessary if, as in the cold-start scenario analyzed here, no information about the test users is given on the target relation.

Approaching this problem with multi-relational matrix factorization can be seen as a variant of [14], where both the feature extraction and the item prediction are performed by sparse factorization models. However, one crucial difference is that, whereas Tang and Liu perform the two steps sequentially, plain applications of multi-relational factorization methods simply simultaneously factorize all the matrices, which means that both feature extraction and item pre-

Permission to make digital or hard copies of all or part of this work for personal or classroom use is granted without fee provided that copies are not made or distributed for profit or commercial advantage and that copies bear this notice and the full citation on the first page. To copy otherwise, to republish, to post on servers or to redistribute to lists, requires prior specific permission and/or a fee.
WSDM'12, February 8–12, 2012, Seattle, Washington, USA.
Copyright 2012 ACM 978-1-4503-0747-5/12/02 ...$10.00.

diction are performed jointly. It is however unclear whether the sequential or the joint approach is more appropriate.

Since the task at hand is to rank items according to the preferences of a given user, it makes sense to optimize the models for a suitable criterion. The Bayesian personalized ranking (BPR) [9] has been shown to provide strong results in many item recommendation tasks [9][10]. We argue that it is a more suitable optimization criterion for the task analyzed and present an extension of it to the multi-relational case.

The main contributions of this work are:

1. We formalize the problem of recommendation in social networks as a multi-relational learning problem and present it in a multi-relational factorization framework;
2. We extend the Bayesian personalized ranking (BPR) framework to the multi-relational case and show how it can be adapted to optimize for different evaluation measures;
3. We provide empirical evidence that factorizing the relations jointly is at least as good as the sequential approach, yielding most of the times better results;
4. Our experiments show that our multi-relational BPR approach outperforms state-of-the-art approaches for recommendation in social networks and for cold-start recommendations in real world datasets.

2. RELATED WORK

The cold-start problem [11] has a long history in the area of recommender systems and several approaches both attribute-based and multi-relational have been proposed.

Tang and Liu [14, 15] offer two bi-relational approaches. Both methods can handle the cold-start problem when no information is present in the target relation for the entity receiving the predictions. In their setting, the first relation comprises two different entities, users and labels, whereas the second relation is an interaction between the users (friendship). They predict whether users should be connected to labels, and their methods treat this problem as a multi-label relational classification task, with the links between users and labels being the class labels. In both algorithms, the training data is derived from the friendship relation during a unique pre-processing step and fed into a SVM for learning. For modularity maximization (ModMax) [14], the training data are first k eigenvectors of the modularity matrix [8] of the friendship relation. For edge clustering [15], a sparse k-means clustering of the edges between the entities of the friendship relation is used as a training feature. The labels of the target relation are treated independently of each other; the ones with the highest scores are suggested to the user.

Gantner et al. [1] focus on cold-start item recommendations. Their work is different from the work of Tang and Liu insofar as they do not use auxiliary relational data but attributes instead. Furthermore, in their work the attributes belong to the items, but after a transposition of the user-item-relation this difference is removed. The method proposed by Gantner et al.—BPR-map—starts with a factorization of the sparse user-item matrix and subsequently learns a (linear) mapping on the user features from the factorization and the auxiliary user-attribute matrix. The attributes serve as predictors for the user features, making the model able to offer predictions for non-observed users; the user features predicted are in turn used to reconstruct the target relation.

Ma et al. [6, 5] exploit a friendship relation for rating prediction which is shown to be effective especially for users with few ratings. They do not evaluate full-on cold-start situations, though. SoRec [6] proposes a joint multi-relational factorization of both the user-item relation and the user-user relation. As a pre-processing step, they require a normalization of the user-user relation. STE (Social Trust Ensemble) [5] is a weighted combination of a factorization on the user-item relation and neighborhood score, derived from the sum of the dot products of the item and the friends.

Jamali and Ester [3] extend the work of Ma et al. on improving rating prediction by exploiting a social relation. Their method, SocialMF, employs an additional regularizer for a standard matrix factorization. The regularization term forces a user's features learnt during the factorization of the target relation to be similar to her friends' features. This is shown to improve rating prediction performance at least for users with few ratings. On the other hand, this method cannot work for users with no ratings for which only social information is available.

Singh and Gordon [12, 13] propose a framework for multi-relational factorization models. They subsume models on any number of relations as long as their loss function is a twice differentiable decomposable loss (including Bregman Divergences). In their work, they address both rating prediction and item recommendation.

Zhang et al [17] contribute an extension of the probabilistic matrix factorization to the multi-relational case. They propose sharing only the user features among different relations via a covariance matrix learnt from the data. Additionally, the authors review different link functions in order to transform the data within the relations, but their loss function is always the square loss. Interestingly, they propose breaking up the item dimension into several smaller dimensions (given additional information).

Yang et al. [16] model item prediction in a bi-relational social network as a problem that consists of multi-relational data and/or attribute data. They evaluate on a ranking measure but still use a logistic loss or square loss derivatives for learning. They also show that taking the non-negative structure of the data into account is rewarded with better prediction accuracy.

We will review the differences to our approach in section 3.2 after formulating the problem.

3. COLD-START ITEM RECOMMENDATION IN SOCIAL NETWORKS

3.1 Problem Formulation

This problem can be seen as a specific case of a more general relational learning setting. In the general case, there is a set of entity types $\mathcal{E} := \{E_1, E_2, ..., E_{|\mathcal{E}|}\}$. Each entity type is a set of entity instances $E_i := \{e_i^{(1)}, ..., e_i^{(|E_i|)}\}$. Entity types are related through a set of binary relations between them $\mathcal{R} = \{R_1, R_2, ..., R_{|\mathcal{R}|}\}$, where $R_m \subseteq E_i \times E_j$. For almost all applications, there is only one relation for which the model employed should make a prediction. Consequently, we call this relation the *target relation* and denote it by Y. The

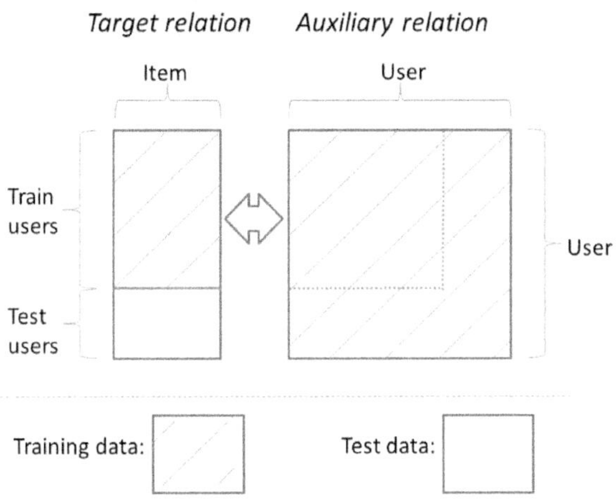

Figure 1: An overview of the multi-relational cold-start setting in social networks.

other relations are called *auxiliary relations* $\mathcal{A} := \mathcal{R} \setminus \{Y\}$ which contain information that is used to improve or enable the prediction of the target values. In the specific case considered in this work, there are two entities, $\mathcal{E} = \{U, I\}$, where U is the set of users and I is the set of items. The target relation represents information about interaction between users and items is represented as a set of pairs $Y \subseteq U \times I$. Finally, auxiliary information is available in the form a social relation $A \subseteq U \times U$, which represents the existence of a relationship between a pair of users, e.g. the users are friends. The items could be videos, for instance, blog posts, or communities that the users can join; the edges of A may represent friendship relationships among users; and the implicit feedback Y means that users have watched videos, read posts or joined communities, thus allowing one to assume that they are interested in them. Figure 1 depicts the general setting.

The task now is to derive a ranked list of items, sorted according to the likelihood that a given user will be interested in each of them. More formally, given a user u, the task is to derive a total order $>_u$ of all items I. In line with [9], this can be achieved by learning a scoring function $\hat{y} : U \times I \rightarrow \mathbb{R}$ capable of generating predictions for users U^{test} and sorting the items according to their scores.

In a full cold-start problem, the task gets increasingly intricate due to additional requirements on the training data: while auxiliary information in form of a social graph $G := (U, A)$ is still available for all users, the training data $Y \subseteq U^{train} \times I$ does not contain any information about the users U^{test}. Mitigating cold-start effects and the incorporation of information beyond the target relation are among the hardest problems in recommender systems nowadays. It should also be noted that besides a full cold-start, our approach also handles slow start situations when the first few user-item interactions become available as well as regular recommender scenarios.

3.2 State-of-the-Art Approaches

Table 1 lists three state-of-the-art approaches capable of cold-start item recommendations, namely *ModMax* [14], *edge clustering* [15], and *BPR-map* [1]. All of them follow a two step learning model. *ModMax* and *edge clustering* first extract user features from the social graph (the auxiliary relation) and then feed those features into a classifier that predicts whether each item will be interesting to a given user. Both approaches use a one-vs-rest linear SVM as a classifier, but they use different feature extraction approaches. *ModMax* works with the top-k eigenvectors of the modularity matrix of the social graph. *edge clustering* first clusters the edges in the *edge* $\times$ *user* representation of the auxiliary matrix, and then uses the resulting relation of users and their cluster membership as predictors. *BPR-map* differs from this in that it starts with learning from the target relation, first extracting latent user features and item features from the target relation using a factorization method. Subsequently, it learns a mapping between the user features as labels and the rows of the auxiliary matrix as predictors.

The predictions for the target relation are made by a (linear multi-label) SVM for *ModMax* and *edge clustering* and a (linear) BPR regression for *BPR-map* using the features learned from and the auxiliary relation.

The cited methods have in common that they learn their models from the target and auxiliary relations separately in a sequential way. In the next section, we propose to use an approach that is able to learn from both relations simultaneously and show how it can be generalized to the sequential case.

4. MULTI RELATIONAL LEARNING WITH BPR

Following the formalization in section 3, the recommendation task described here can be viewed as an instance of a multi-relational learning problem which consists of two entities, the users and the items, as well as of at least two relations, namely the auxiliary relation A (represented by the social graph) and the target relation Y, represented by the user-item interaction (figure 1).

Multi-relational matrix factorization models [12] provide a framework for jointly factorizing multiple relations. In this section we cast the problem of ranking in social networks as a multi-relational factorization problem and propose a model and learning algorithms for it that address the issues discussed here.

4.1 Ranking in Social Networks–A Multi-Relational Factorization Problem

Matrix factorization models [4] represent a matrix as the product of two lower-rank matrices. [1] The goal is, given a partially observed matrix $\mathbf{R}$, to find two matrices $\mathbf{E_1}$ and $\mathbf{E_2}$ such that

$$\underset{\mathbf{E_1},\mathbf{E_2}}{\operatorname{argmin}} L(\mathbf{R}, \mathbf{E_1}\mathbf{E_2}^T) + Reg(\mathbf{E_1}, \mathbf{E_2}) \qquad (1)$$

where L is a loss function that measures the reconstruction error of R given $\mathbf{E_1}$ and $\mathbf{E_2}$ and Reg a regularization term to prevent overfitting.

A matrix can be viewed as a relation between two entity types. When we follow equation (1), we may represent each entity type E_i by a matrix $\boldsymbol{E_i} \in \mathbb{R}^{|E_i| \times k}$ where the rows

[1] Matrices are denoted in bold face to avoid confusion with entity type and relation identifiers.

	ModMax	EdgeClustering	BPR-map
Target relation treatment	dense binary	dense binary	sparse unary
Model on target relation	N/A	N/A	matrix factorization
Aux. relation treatment	dense modularity matrix	dense graph	dense matrix
Model on aux. relation	PCA	k-means	N/A
Meta Model	eigenvectors as predictors to multi-class SVM with labels as classes	see ModMax	auxiliary matrix as predictor to a regression on latent user features

Table 1: Baseline methods for the cold-start item prediction task.

are latent feature vectors of the entity type instances and k is the number of latent features, chosen by model selection. The two entities participating in a relation R_i are denoted by E_{R_i1} and E_{R_i2}. Each relation R is represented by a matrix $\mathbf{R}^{|E_{R1}|\times|E_{R2}|}$ where each entry is given by

$$\mathbf{R}(e^{(i)}_{E_{R1}}, e^{(j)}_{E_{R2}}) := \begin{cases} 1 & \text{if } (e^{(i)}_{E_{R1}}, e^{(j)}_{E_{R2}}) \in R, \\ \text{unobserved} & \text{else} \end{cases}$$

Thus the factorization of relation R_i is given by $\mathbf{R_i} \approx \mathbf{E_{R_i1}} \mathbf{E_{R_i2}}^T$. To make notation simpler, we define the set of all model parameters $\Theta := \{\mathbf{E_1}, \ldots \mathbf{E}_{|\mathcal{E}|}\}$.

Singh and Gordon [12] generalized the problem in equation (1) in cases where there is more than one relation. The problem is now to find a set of matrices Θ that minimizes the sum of the losses on all relations:

$$\underset{\Theta}{\operatorname{argmin}} \sum_{R \in \mathcal{R}} \alpha_R L(\mathbf{R}, \mathbf{E_{R1}} \mathbf{E_{R2}}^T) + Reg(\Theta)$$

where α_R is an application specific weight for the loss of relation $\mathbf{R}$ and weights are normalized such that:

$$\sum_{R \in \mathcal{R}} \alpha_R = 1$$

In the specific case considered in this work, there are two entities, i.e $\mathcal{E} = \{U, I\}$ and two relations, $R = \{Y, A\}$. Consequently, the specific loss to the problem approached in this paper is the following:

$$\underset{(\mathbf{U},\mathbf{I})}{\operatorname{argmin}} \, \alpha_Y L(\mathbf{Y}, \mathbf{U}\mathbf{I}^T) + \alpha_A L(\mathbf{A}, \mathbf{U}\mathbf{U}^T) + Reg(\mathbf{U}, \mathbf{I}) \quad (2)$$

The advantage of formalizing the problem this way, in comparison to the multi-label classification view in [14, 15] is twofold. Firstly, it allows for a more straightforward way to incorporate new entities and relations into the model, as it would just require adding the loss for the new relation and the regularization terms for the new entities on the general loss. Secondly, the models in [14, 15] are able to generate predictions for one relation alone. With the formalization proposed here, recommendations can be made for all entities on all relations, without the need to retrain.

4.2 Multi-Relational Factorization with BPR

Since we are dealing with a ranking problem, it makes sense to use a loss function that is optimized for ranking. The Bayesian personalized ranking optimization criterion (BPR-Opt) [9] has been shown to be a suitable criterion for ranking in general and item prediction in particular. Another reason that makes BPR suitable for the task of ranking in social networks is that it is tailored to data where only positive feedback is available (unary data). In fact, for the task at hand the Y relation is a typical representative of positive feedback only recommender data. Thus, $(u, i) \in Y$ can be interpreted as a positive feedback given by the user u about item i. The opposite, however, $(u, j) \notin Y$, only tells us that the user has not yet interacted with item j. For most applications, it would be unjustified to treat all those j as being equally valued by the respective user, e.g., assign all items that he is unaware of and all those items explicitly ignored the same score (i.e. 0). The same holds true for the social relation: the fact that a connection between two users is not observed in the data does not necessarily imply that there is no connection in the real world.

BPR-Opt makes use of the assumption that, for a given user u, an item i where $(u, i) \in Y$ should be ranked higher than an item j where $(u, j) \notin Y$. For convenience, we define for each relation R, a set D_R as being the set of triples $D_R := \{(u, i, j) | (u, i) \in R \wedge (u, j) \notin R\}$. Throughout this section, we stick to the (u, i, j) notation, although these values do not necessarily denote users and items as in the example above; u nonetheless denotes an instance of the first entity involved in the relation, and i and j instances of the second entity.

If $\hat{r}(u, i)$ is the predicted score for the (u, i) pair on relation R and $\hat{x}^R_{u,i,j} = \hat{r}(u, i) - \hat{r}(u, j)$, BPR-Opt can be defined as in equation 3.

$$\text{BPR-Opt}(\mathbf{R}, \mathbf{E_{R1}} \mathbf{E_{R2}}^T) := \sum_{(u,i,j) \in D_R} \ln \sigma(\hat{x}^R_{u,i,j}) \quad (3)$$

where $\sigma(x) := \frac{1}{1+e^{-x}}$ is the sigmoid logistic function. It is worth noting that BPR-Opt should be maximized. Optimizing for BPR-Opt is a smoothed version of optimizing for the well-known ranking measure Area under the ROC Curve (AUC). For a proof and more details about BPR-Opt, please see [9].

Having chosen a loss function, an appropriate regularization term still needs to be chosen. In this case, we use L_2 regularization, since the L_2-regularization terms are differentiable, allowing us to apply gradient-based methods.

In the case of item recommendations for multi-relational cold-starts, there is more than one relation involved. Consequently, an extension of BPR-Opt for the multi-relational case is necessary. Following the framework of [12, 13], we propose the following extension for multi-relational ranking in social networks with Bayesian personalized ranking:

procedure LEARNMR-BPR($D, \mathcal{R}, \mathcal{E}$)
  initialize all $\mathbf{E} \in \Theta$
  repeat
    for $R \in \mathcal{R}$ **do**
      draw (u,i,j) from D_R
      $\Theta \leftarrow \Theta + \mu\left(\alpha_R \frac{e^{-\hat{x}^R_{uij}}}{1+e^{-\hat{x}^R_{uij}}} \cdot \frac{\partial}{\partial\Theta}\hat{x}^R_{uij} + \lambda_\Theta \cdot \Theta\right)$
    end for
  until convergence
  return Θ
end procedure

Figure 2: Multi-relational extension of the LearnBPR algorithm proposed in [9] with learning rate μ and regularization λ_Θ.

$$\text{MR-BPR}(\mathcal{R},\Theta) = \sum_{R\in\mathcal{R}} \alpha_R \,\text{BPR-Opt}(\mathbf{R}, \mathbf{E_{R1}}\mathbf{E_{R2}}^T) + \sum_{E\in\mathcal{E}} \lambda_E ||\mathbf{E}||^2 \qquad (4)$$

where λ_E is the regularization constant for entity E.

The optimization problem described in equation (4) can be solved using a stochastic gradient descent algorithm. In [9], just such an algorithm, called LearnBPR, is proposed for the unirelational case, i.e. when there is only one matrix to be factorized. Figure 2 provides an extension to LearnBPR that considers the multi-relational case. At each iteration, one sample is uniformly drawn from D_R for each relation R and the parameters are updated in the opposite direction of the loss function's gradient at the point sampled. The derivative of the loss function presented in equation (4) is:

$$\frac{\partial\,\text{MR-BPR}(\mathbf{R},u,i,j)}{\partial\Theta} = \alpha_R \frac{-e^{-\hat{x}^R_{uij}}}{1+e^{-\hat{x}^R_{uij}}} \cdot \frac{\partial}{\partial\Theta}\hat{x}^R_{uij} + \lambda_\Theta \cdot \Theta$$

The $\hat{x}^R_{uij}$ partial derivatives are:

$$\frac{\partial}{\partial\Theta}\hat{x}^R_{uij} = \begin{cases} (\mathbf{i}_f - \mathbf{i}_f) & \text{if } \theta = \mathbf{u}_f, \\ \mathbf{u}_f & \text{if } \theta = \mathbf{i}_f, \\ -\mathbf{u}_f & \text{if } \theta = \mathbf{j}_f, \\ 0 & \text{else} \end{cases}$$

where f denotes the f-th latent feature of the entity instance in question. The parameters are optimized using equation (4).

4.3 Pivotization

The problem of item recommendation can be viewed from two perspectives:

1. Given a user, which items could be interesting to her?
2. Given an item, which users could be interested in it?

The first perspective is the one taken into account for BPR optimization as presented before. This is reflected by the samples D_Y, which are composed of a user u and two items i and j, one a positive example, one a negative. In order to train a BPR model for the second perspective, $\mathbf{Y}$ can be transposed and samples drawn from $D_{Y^T} := \{(i,u,v)|i \in I \wedge u,v \in U \wedge (u,i) \in Y \wedge (v,i) \notin Y\}$. This is the perspective adopted in [14] and [15] by one of the evaluation criteria.

procedure LEARNMR-BPR-PIVOTIZATION($D, \mathcal{R}, \mathcal{E}$)
  initialize all $\mathbf{E} \in \Theta$
  repeat
    for $R \in \mathcal{R}$ **do**
      draw (u,i,j) from D_R
      $\Theta \leftarrow \Theta + \mu\left(\alpha_R \frac{e^{-\hat{x}^R_{uij}}}{1+e^{-\hat{x}^R_{uij}}} \cdot \frac{\partial}{\partial\Theta}\hat{x}^R_{uij} + \lambda_\Theta \cdot \Theta\right)$
      draw (i,u,v) from D_{R^T}
      $\Theta \leftarrow \Theta + \mu\left(\alpha_R \frac{e^{-\hat{x}^R_{iuv}}}{1+e^{-\hat{x}^R_{iuv}}} \cdot \frac{\partial}{\partial\Theta}\hat{x}^R_{iuv} + \lambda_\Theta \cdot \Theta\right)$
    end for
  until convergence
  return Θ
end procedure

Figure 3: Optimizing models for BPR with bootstrapping based stochastic gradient descent. With learning rate α and regularization λ_Θ.

The question is: which one of the perspectives is the most appropriate? Clearly, this depends on the measure employed to evaluate the algorithm. In a classical recommender scenario, where the ranking performance is evaluated per user and then averaged, it makes sense to resort to the first perspective. On the other hand, in an evaluation setup like the one in [14, 15] where the recommender performance is evaluated per item, learning under the second perspective should provide better results. We propose to take both views into account by sampling from D_R and D_{R^T} alternately, as described in Algorithm 3. We call this horizontal and vertical sampling *pivotization*.

4.4 Sequential Learning

The multi-relational extension of the LearnBPR algorithm, LearnMR-BPR (figure 2), goes in line with the guidelines in Singh and Gordon [12], where the parameters are learned simultaneously by sampling examples from all the relations. In order to investigate the benefits of this joint factorization approach, we propose to compare it with an analogous model that learns in a step-by-step fashion, such as *ModMax*, *edge clustering*, and *BPR-map*. In order to do this, we will first learn the user parameters on the auxiliary relation using the original LearnBPR algorithm, and then factorize the target relation with the traditional LearnBPR algorithm, making sure to only update the item parameters (keeping the user parameters constant at the values obtained during the factorization of the auxiliary relation).

Figure 4 details the sequential MR-BPR variant of our multi-relational learning approach.

5. EVALUATION

5.1 Datasets

We have three social network datasets: one from a larger blogging website (Blogcatalog), one from flickr.com (Flickr), and one crawled from youtube.com (YouTube); each dataset consists of two relations, with one relation between users and labels (target), and an additional social relation between users and other users (auxiliary). Table 2 shows detailed statistics.

Dataset	relation	dimensionality	# observations	avg. observations per user	avg. observations per label	sparsity
Blogcatalog	target	10312x39	14,476	1.4	371.2	96.40%
	auxiliary	10312^2	667,966	64.7 (med 21)	-	99.37%
Flickr	target	80513x195	107,741	1.3	552.5	99.31%
	auxiliary	80513^2	11,799,764	146.6 (med 46)	-	99.82%
YouTube	target	31,703x47	50,691	1.6	1,078.5	96.60%
	auxiliary	$1,138,499^2$	5,980,886	5.3 (med 1)	-	99,9995%

Table 2: Statistics of the BlogCatalog, Flickr, and YouTube datasets.

```
procedure LEARNBPR-SEQUENTIAL(D_Y, D_S, U, I)
    initialize U
    repeat
        draw (u, i, j) from D_S
        U ← U + μ(α_S · e^{-x̂^R_uij} / (1+e^{-x̂^R_uij}) · ∂/∂U x̂^R_uij + λ_U · U)
    until convergence
    initialize I
    repeat
        draw (u, i, j) from D_Y
        I ← I + μ(α_S · e^{-x̂^R_uij} / (1+e^{-x̂^R_uij}) · ∂/∂I x̂^R_uij + λ_I · I)
    until convergence
    return U, I
end procedure
```

Figure 4: Sequential MR-BPR learning algorith

The high sparsity of all relations is instantly noticeable, although there are some differences between the three datasets. In comparison with Blogcatalog, on Flickr the target relation is almost an order of magnitude sparser. Blogcatalog and YouTube show virtually the same sparsity level on the target relation, but YouTube is three orders of magnitude sparser on the network relation with a median of one user being connected to another.

5.2 Baseline Methods

For better evaluation of the proposed MR-BPR method, we will field the following well-known and strong baseline methods (already have been detailed in section 3.2):

- Modularity maximization (ModMax). ModMax [14] is essentially a PCA on the auxiliary matrix followed by a SVM-multilabel regression between the labels on the target relation and the top eigenvectors of the PCA as features. The interesting aspect of ModMax is that the auxiliary relation gets converted into a modularity matrix [8] before the eigenvectors are extracted. ModMax already outperforms wvRN, LBC, and other classical relational learning algorithms.

- Edge clustering. Edge clustering [15] does a k-means clustering of the edges of the auxiliary relation interpreted as a graph. The resulting sparse clusters are subsequently normalized in a row-wise manner and used as features for a multi-label SVM like with ModMax.

- BPR-map. BPR-map [1] also is a two-step process. In the first step, a factorization model is learnt on the observed (sparse) part of the target relation. As a regular factorization model, this does not yield any features for elements not observed in the training data. In the second step, a linear mapping between the user features from the factorization model and the corresponding entries in the auxiliary relation is learnt. The auxiliary relation serves as a predictor for this mapping and thus, given information in the auxiliary relation, the model is able to make predictions for users not observed in the initial factorization of the target relation.

5.3 Measures

For a consistent evaluation with the social analysis literature, two classical measures for multi-label classification are employed: Micro-F1 (cf. equation (7)) and Macro-F1 (cf. equation (6)).

To better capture the overall ranking performance of the algorithms, the area under the ROC curve, AUC (cf. equation (9)), is analyzed too.

$$F1(i) := \frac{2 * correct(i)}{true(i) + predicted(i)}, \tag{5}$$

$$MacroF1 := \frac{\sum_{i \in I} F1(i)}{|I|} \tag{6}$$

$$MicroF1 := \frac{2 * \sum_{i \in I} correct(i)}{\sum_{i \in I} true(i) + \sum_{i \in I} predicted(i)} \tag{7}$$

$$AUC(u) := \frac{1}{|I_u^+||I \setminus I_u^+|} \sum_{i \in I_u^+} \sum_{I \setminus I_u^+} \delta(\hat{x}_{uij} > 0), \tag{8}$$

$$AUC := \frac{\sum_{u \in U} AUC(u)}{|U|} \tag{9}$$

The functions *correct(i)* counts the "hits" of the prediction model for an item i where an element from the ground truth is among the elements predicted. The function *true(i)* emits the number of elements in the ground truth, and *predicted(i)* returns the number of elements in the respective recommendation list.

5.4 Experiment Protocol

For the experiment protocol, we follow [15] for better comparability.

We evaluated a cold-start scenario in which some users already have social information in the auxiliary relation but are not yet present in the target relation. The aim is to predict which labels the cold-start users interacted with on the target relation.

The experiments were set up as ten-fold cross-validated experiments at different train-test split ratios. For each train-test split ratio, the respective ratio of the available users in the target relation is used for training, together with all information from the social relation. The remaining percentage of users in the target relation was used as test data for evaluation. For each train-test split ratio, ten different splits were generated randomly and continued to provide equal conditions for all algorithms and to get more reliable performance estimates. Test data was never used during training.

As suggested in [15], we remove the dependency on the length of the top-N list for performance evaluation w.r.t. Micro-F1 and Macro-F1 by assuming that the number of true instances is known at prediction time.

On Blogcatalog we created nine different split percentages from 10% to 90% of the target relation being used for training. For Flickr and YouTube, we used 1% to 10%—a setting in which hardly any interaction information on the target relation remains available for training.

5.5 Results

The prediction performance on all three datasets is shown in figures 5–7. Consistent with [15] we did not run modularity maximization on the YouTube dataset due the to the vast runtime and memory requirements of the given method.

The overall picture is the same across all three datasets and all three evaluation criteria employed. In most cases, the BPR-map yields the lowest performance, although this method can sometimes tie with ModMax an/or edge clustering, in rare cases even outperform those methods. Edge clustering outperforms ModMax on Micro-F1 and Macro-F1, except on Blogcatalog, where they are tied (figures 5–6). For AUC, the performance is the complete opposite, with ModMax easily outpacing edge clustering (figure 7). Sequential MR-BPR is the runner-up method, while MR-BPR performs best.

From a datasets perspective, it is interesting to note that Flickr seems to be the toughest dataset with respect to Micro- and Macro-F1, but not so for AUC (where we even observe a reversal of the order of sequential MR-BPR and jointly learning MR-BPR). The top-performing methods on Flickr (AUC), MR-BPR and sequential MR-BPR, achieve very stable and highly correct ordering in pairs. By comparison, Blogcatalog and YouTube seem to be rather easy datasets, except for AUC. On Blogcatalog, edge clustering manages to tie with the proposed MR-BPR algorithms for the splits from 50% on for AUC.

The curves for the BPR-map and our MR-BPR are very similar across all datasets and evaluation measures. Nonetheless, the performance of both approaches is very different with MR-BPR easily outperforming BPR-map. Sequential MR-BPR manages to tie with the jointly learning MR-BPR on several occasions, such as on Flickr and YouTube AUC and on YouTube Micro-F1. Though, in general MR-BPR performs significantly better.

Finally, we note that for Macro-F1 the pivotization of MR-BPR (section 4.3) leads to significantly improved results for all three datasets compared to the version without pivotization. Results omitted for brevity.

Criterion	BPR-SVM	ModMax*	Edge Clustering*
MicroF1 @ 10%	0,2702	0,2756	0,2815
MicroF1 @ 90%	0,3838	0,3756	0,3592
MacroF1 @ 10%	0,1724	0,1735	0,1640
MacroF1 @ 90%	0,2697	0,2390	0,2477

Table 3: Using an SVM on top of features learnt through LearnBPR scheme vs. features learnt using modularity maximization and edge clustering. The results are on the Blogcatalog dataset. Methods with an (*) used optimized hyperparameters. Higher values are better.

5.6 Discussion

ModMax and edge clustering are strong state-of-the-art methods for the multi-relational cold-start item recommendation problem. Both are known to outperform classical relational learning algorithms in the present problem setting[15]. While BPR-map is also a strong method, it is not designed for a multi-relational setting, but rather for use with i.i.d. attributes as auxiliary information; this is reflected by the results it can achieve.

As the ModMax [14] algorithm proposes the conversion of the auxiliary relation into a dense modularity matrix [8], we wanted to investigate the strength of this pre-processing step. To do so, we replaced this feature extraction process with a plain factorization of the auxiliary relation. The user features learnt this way are treated as vectors, normalized by their norm and subsequently fed into the same multi-label SVM process as Tang and Liu (using the same hyper-parameters they report). From the results in table 3, it is clear that there is virtually no difference between the multi-label SVM on the expensive eigenvectors of the modularity matrix or the multi-label SVM on the user features from the factorization.

This is an interesting observation, as the sparse matrix decomposition [4] of the LearnBPR [9] methods is easy to implement, of low complexity and additionally very fast, yet principled. We may add that optimized hyper-parameters have not been searched - neither for the BPR factorization of the auxiliary relation nor for the SVM learning with the BPR features as parameters. Instead, we simply re-used the hyper-parameters from Tang and Liu for the SVM and from MR-BPR for the factorization.

An important factor in the performance we saw on the various datasets and evaluation methods, we believe, should be attributed to interpreting the underlying multi-relational data in a more appropriate way: BPR treats input data as sparse and unary. This benefits MR-BPR in two ways. Firstly, it treats the auxiliary relation as sparse and unary while BPR-map, ModMax, and edge clustering do not do so. Secondly, ModMax and edge clustering do not take this data property for the target relation into account, while MR-BPR and BPR-map do. We argue that edge clustering performs better than its cousin, ModMax, because it generates sparse features (from a dense interpretation of the matrix) for its final learning step. Further to this, we believe that the similarity in shape of the performance curves of BPR-map and MR-BPR may result from the conceptual similarity with respect to the interpretation of the target relation as positive-only feedback and the application of the BPR-Opt ranking criterion.

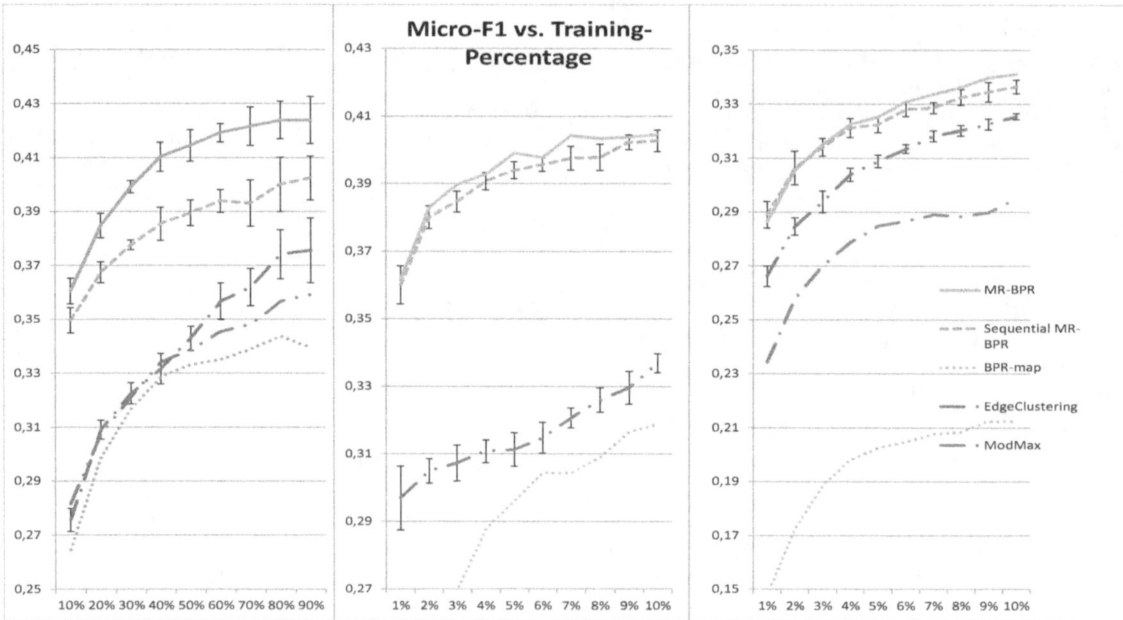

Figure 5: Micro-F1 results on a. Blogcatalog, b. YouTube, and c. Flickr vs. percentage of data used for training. The standard deviation is reported for some methods for better assessment of the statistical significance.

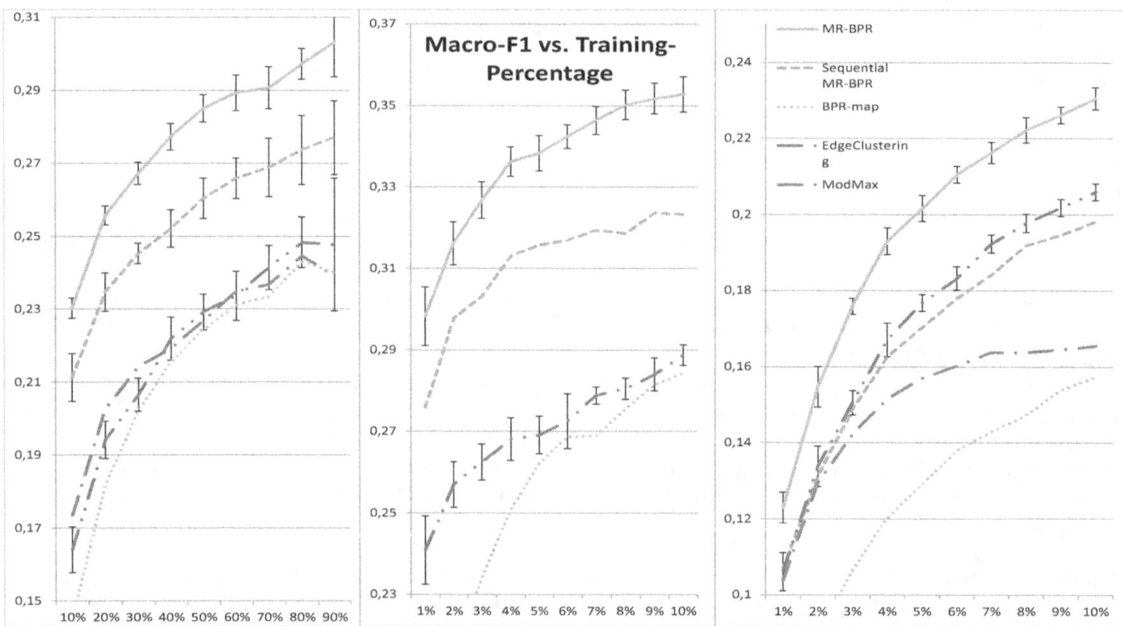

Figure 6: Macro-F1 results on a. Blogcatalog, b. YouTube, and c. Flickr vs. percentage of data used for training. The standard deviation is reported for some methods for better assessment of the statistical significance.

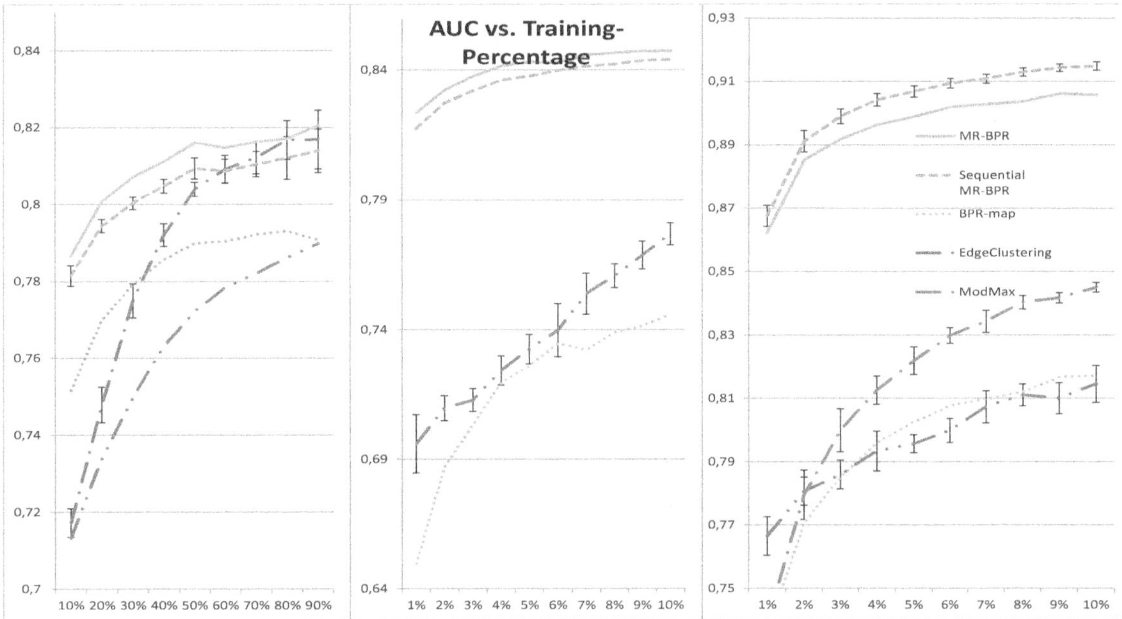

Figure 7: AUC results on a. Blogcatalog, b. YouTube, and c. Flickr vs. percentage of data used for training. The standard deviation is reported for some methods for better assessment of the statistical significance.

We should add that there may also have been more potential for edge clustering and ModMax (and BPR-SVM for that matter) if the parameters had been optimized for the F-measure evaluation scheme. Although it is hard to optimize directly for F-measure, Musicant et al. [7] have shown that for the SVM both, C_+ and C_- need to be searched for an approximate optimization. It is worth noting that the BPR learning framework does not directly optimize, but simply leaves enough room for general optimizations to arbitrary evaluation criteria. For that matter, all hyper-parameters for the BPR family algorithms have been searched such that optimized conditions for an evenly weighted combination of the evaluation criteria were created.

The joint learning of the full multi-relational factorization is what we consider a major improvement over previous methods. Not only is it in line with the findings from [12], but it is also highly scalable (i.e., virtually for free) and performs well. However, we do agree that it would be difficult for the competing SVM approaches to realize such joint learning without an expectation maximization approach. We would have expected the jointly learnt MR-BPR to outperform its sequentially learnt cousin on a more pronounced level. For this reason, more detailed research on this this trait will be a part of our work in future. Our conjecture is that a better factorization on the auxiliary matrix is meaningless when is not accompanied by an improved factorization on the target relation.

5.7 Reproducibility of the Experiments

For modularity maximization and edge clustering, the optimal hyper-parameters (the number of latent dimensions for the feature selection and the SVM cost parameter) for all datasets are taken from [15]. For BPR-map and MR-BPR, the optimal hyper-parameters have been estimated via grid search on the largest training split of each respective dataset. BPR-map has two sets of hyper-parameters, where the first set is used for the initial factorization of the target relation ($\mu = 0.01$, $\lambda_u = 0.01$, $\lambda_i = 0.01$, $\lambda_j = 0.00005$ and 300 iterations for all datasets and $k = 500$ for Blogcatalog, $k = 200$ for Flickr and YouTube) and the second set is used for the subsequent mapping of the latent feature to the auxiliary relation ($\lambda_u = 0.0025$, $\lambda_i = 0.0025$, $\lambda_j = 0.00025$, $\mu = 0.01$, 300 iterations, $\lambda_{mapping} = 0.01$, 15000 mapping iterations, $\mu_{mapping} = 0.1$ for all datasets and $k = 500$ for Blogcatalog and $k = 200$ for Flickr and YouTube). For MR-BPR the hyper-parameters are $k = 500$, $\mu = 0.02$, $\lambda_{user} = 0.0125$, $\lambda_{item} = 0.0005$, 300 iterations, $\alpha = 0.5$ for Blogcatalog; $k = 200$, $\mu = 0.05$, $\lambda_{user} = 0.005$, $\lambda_{item} = 0.0005$, $\alpha = 0.5$, 300 iterations for Flickr; and $k = 200$, $\mu = 0,1$, $\lambda = 0,0125$, $\lambda_{item} = 0,0125$, $\alpha = 0,5$ and 300 iterations for YouTube.

The code for MR-BPR is available at: `http://www.ismll.uni-hildesheim.de/software`.

The code for BPR-map is available in the MyMediaLite framework [2]. The code for ModMax and EdgeClustering is available from the homepage of the first author of [14].

The datasets are available from the homepage of the first author of [14].

6. CONCLUSION

In this work, we formalized the special link prediction task of item recommendation in social networks in a multi-relational framework. We then presented a multi-relational factorization approach to the problem. Since the task of item prediction is a ranking task, the Bayesian personalized ranking (BPR) framework was extended to the multi-relational case, so that the approach proposed here offers a model optimized for a ranking loss function.

Our experiments on real world datasets show that our approach outperforms state-of-the-art competitors in different evaluation measures without the need higher runtime.

One of the advantages of multi-relational matrix factorization techniques against state-of-the-art approaches like ModMax and edge clustering is that there is no need for any kind of preprocessing of the auxiliary relation, such as modularity matrix computation or clustering of edges. Instead of factorizing relations separately, our experiments suggest that learning them jointly yields at least comparable results. A thorough comparison between joint an sequential learning of the auxiliary and target relations is left for future work.

7. ACKNOWLEDGMENTS

The authors gratefully acknowledge the co-funding of their work by the Multi-relational Factorization Models project granted by the Deutsche Forschungsgesellschaft[2]. Lucas Drumond is sponsored by a scholarship from CNPq, a Brazilian government institution for scientific development. We also want to thank the reviewers for their comments and Lei Tang for providing the datasets, the implementations of his baseline methods and his friendly and swift replies to our questions and requests.

8. REFERENCES

[1] Z. Gantner, L. Drumond, C. Freudenthaler, S. Rendle, and L. Schmidt-Thieme. Learning attribute-to-feature mappings for cold-start recommendations. In *Proceedings of the 2010 IEEE International Conference on Data Mining*, ICDM '10, pages 176–185, Washington, DC, USA, 2010. IEEE Computer Society.

[2] Z. Gantner, S. Rendle, C. Freudenthaler, and L. Schmidt-Thieme. Mymedialite: A free recommender system library. In *Proceedings of the 5th ACM International Conference on Recommender Systems (RecSys 2011) (to appear)*, 2011.

[3] M. Jamali and M. Ester. A matrix factorization technique with trust propagation for recommendation in social networks. In *Proceedings of the fourth ACM conference on Recommender systems*, RecSys '10, pages 135–142, New York, NY, USA, 2010. ACM.

[4] Y. Koren, R. Bell, and C. Volinsky. Matrix factorization techniques for recommender systems. *Computer*, 42(8):30–37, 2009.

[5] H. Ma, I. King, and M. R. Lyu. Learning to recommend with social trust ensemble. In *Proceedings of the 32nd international ACM SIGIR conference on Research and development in information retrieval*, SIGIR '09, pages 203–210, New York, NY, USA, 2009. ACM.

[6] H. Ma, H. Yang, M. R. Lyu, and I. King. Sorec: social recommendation using probabilistic matrix factorization. In *Proceeding of the 17th ACM conference on Information and knowledge management*, CIKM '08, pages 931–940, New York, NY, USA, 2008. ACM.

[2]http://www.ismll.uni-hildesheim.de/projekte/dfg_multirel_en.html

[7] D. R. Musicant, V. Kumar, and A. Ozgur. Optimizing f-measure with support vector machines. In *Proceedings of the Sixteenth International Florida Artificial Intelligence Research Society Conference*, pages 356–360. Haller AAAI Press, 2003.

[8] M. E. J. Newman. Modularity and community structure in networks. *Proc. Natl. Acad. Sci. USA*, 103:8577–8582, 2006.

[9] S. Rendle, C. Freudenthaler, Z. Gantner, and L. Schmidt-Thieme. BPR: Bayesian personalized ranking from implicit feedback. In *Proceedings of the Twenty-Fifth Conference on Uncertainty in Artificial Intelligence*, UAI '09, pages 452–461, Arlington, Virginia, United States, 2009. AUAI Press.

[10] S. Rendle and L. Schmidt-Thieme. Pairwise interaction tensor factorization for personalized tag recommendation. In *Proceedings of the third ACM international conference on Web search and data mining*, WSDM '10, pages 81–90, New York, NY, USA, 2010. ACM.

[11] A. I. Schein, A. Popescul, L. H. Ungar, and D. M. Pennock. Methods and metrics for cold-start recommendations. In *Proceedings of the 25th annual international ACM SIGIR conference on Research and development in information retrieval*, SIGIR '02, pages 253–260, New York, NY, USA, 2002. ACM.

[12] A. P. Singh and G. J. Gordon. Relational learning via collective matrix factorization. In *Proceeding of the 14th ACM SIGKDD international conference on Knowledge discovery and data mining*, KDD '08, pages 650–658, New York, NY, USA, 2008. ACM.

[13] A. P. Singh and G. J. Gordon. A unified view of matrix factorization models. In *Proceedings of the European conference on Machine Learning and Knowledge Discovery in Databases - Part II*, ECML PKDD '08, pages 358–373, Berlin, Heidelberg, 2008. Springer-Verlag.

[14] L. Tang and H. Liu. Relational learning via latent social dimensions. In *Proceedings of the 15th ACM SIGKDD international conference on Knowledge discovery and data mining*, KDD '09, pages 817–826, New York, NY, USA, 2009. ACM.

[15] L. Tang and H. Liu. Scalable learning of collective behavior based on sparse social dimensions. In *Proceeding of the 18th ACM conference on Information and knowledge management*, CIKM '09, pages 1107–1116, New York, NY, USA, 2009. ACM.

[16] Yang, Long, Smola, Sadagopan, Zheng, and Zha. Like like alike – joint friendship and interest propagation in social networks. In *Proceedings of the WWW 2011*, 2011.

[17] Y. Zhang, B. Cao, and D.-Y. Yeung. Multi-domain collaborative filtering. In *Proceedings of the 26th Conference on Uncertainty in Artificial Intelligence (UAI)*, pages 725–732, Catalina Island, California, 2010.

Comment Spam Detection by Sequence Mining

Ravi Kant
Yahoo! Labs, Bangalore
rkant@yahoo-inc.com

Srinivasan H Sengamedu
Komli Labs, Bangalore
shs@yahoo-inc.com

Krishnan Kumar
Yahoo! Labs, Bangalore
krishsk@yahoo-inc.com

ABSTRACT

Comments are supported by several web sites to increase user participation. Users can usually comment on a variety of media types – photos, videos, news articles, blogs, etc. Comment spam is one of the biggest challenges facing this feature. The traditional approach to combat spam is to train classifiers using various machine learning techniques. Since the commonly used classifiers work on the entire comment text, it is easy to mislead them is by embedding spam content in good content.

In this paper, we make several contributions towards comment spam detection. (1) We propose a new framework for spam detection that is immune to embed attacks. We characterize spam by a set of frequently occurring sequential patterns. (2) We introduce a variant (called min-closed) of the frequent closed sequence mining problem that succinctly captures all the frequently occurring patterns. We prove as well as experimentally show that the set of min-closed sequences is an order of magnitude smaller than the set of closed sequences and yet has exactly the same coverage. (3) We describe MCPRISM, extension of the recently published PRISM algorithm that effectively mines min-closed sequences, using prime encoding. In the process, we solve the open problem of using the prime-encoding technique to speed up traditional closed sequence mining. (4) We finally need to whittle down the set of frequent subsequences to a small set without sacrificing coverage. This problem is NP-Hard but we show that the coverage function is submodular and hence the greedy heuristic gives a fast algorithm that is close to optimal. We then describe the experiments that were carried out on a large real world comment data and the publicly available Gazelle dataset. (1) We show that nearly 80% of spam on real world data can be effectively captured by the mined sequences at very low false positive rates. (2) The sequences mined are highly discriminative. (3) On Gazelle data, the proposed algorithmic enhancements are faster by at least by a factor and by an order of magnitude on the larger comment dataset.

Permission to make digital or hard copies of all or part of this work for personal or classroom use is granted without fee provided that copies are not made or distributed for profit or commercial advantage and that copies bear this notice and the full citation on the first page. To copy otherwise, to republish, to post on servers or to redistribute to lists, requires prior specific permission and/or a fee.
WSDM'12, February 8–12, 2012, Seattle, Washingtion, USA.
Copyright 2012 ACM 978-1-4503-0747-5/12/02 ...$10.00.

Categories and Subject Descriptors

H.2.8 [**Information Systems**]: Database Management

General Terms

Algorithms

Keywords

Comments Spam Detection, Frequent Subsequence Mining

1. INTRODUCTION

Comments provide a simple approach to increasing user engagement. Comments enable an informal and interactive way of sharing opinions. Commenters spontaneously voice their opinions, record their reactions, and share their knowledge. Readers get more information about the article/content from comments and can also post responses to comments. A very simple response to a comment is to rate it – give a "thumbs up" or "thumbs down" rating. More elaborate replies are also possible – leading to "comment threads". Hence comments provide a sense of community participation with a very low entry barrier.

Just like any other community feature, comments are susceptible to abuse – comment sections abound in hateful, out of topic, spam, etc. comments. The negative impact of spam are manifold.

- *Readers* are disincentivized to read comments because they have to sift through spam to get to good comments.
- *Commenters* are disincentivized to comment in a spammy ecosystem because of their comments are likely to be drowned in a sea of spam.
- *Publishers* or *Site owners* see poor user participation and eventually less quality traffic.

Hence detection and blocking of comment spam is essential for the success of comments.

Mail was the first application to be infested with spam. Spam caught up with other innovations like message boards, forums, comments, reviews, blogs, etc. Some of the common techniques that are broadly applicable for spam detection across different systems are [19, 2, 1]:

Velocity: If there are too many mails or comments from a single user or an IP address in a short time, then the source is likely to be an automated spam source.

Whitelists/blacklists: Known sources of good or spam

content are kept in black/white lists.
Keywords/Patterns: Comments containing URL patterns or specific keywords can be blocked.
Classifiers: We can train classifiers which classify spam and non-spam content using various machine learning techniques.
Reputation: Instead of black/white lists, we can associate a spam score with each source (user/IP address/site/etc.) and update the scores based on user action, connections, etc.

These methods are often used together in practice. In this paper, we focus on detection of comment spam using machine learned models. The following section captures the limitations of the current techniques.

1.1 Limitations of Existing Approaches

Spam being a very practical problem, there is extensive research work on this area. Section 2 reviews part of the relevant research in this area. Machine learning models typically learn to classify input content (email message, comment text, etc.) into spam or non-spam. Most of the classifiers we are aware of are *global* – they work on the entire comment text. It is very easy to mislead such classifiers by embedding spam in good content. For example, consider the following comment:

EXAMPLE 1. **[Spam Comment]** *Happy 2011 to everyone....My friend Vanessa, a 25 yrs lady, has announced her wedding with a millionaire young man Ronald who is the CEO of a MNC. It's amazing, she said she just posted her profile on a millionaire d'ating s'ite called ———-Celeb Mingle.CM——- - and received his chat invitations a few days later. Then, everything went so well that I can't believe it's true! Every love story will unfold on it's own...=====* **Happy to see she is progressing well. Also happy to see that most Americans reject the blame-the-conservatives crap that some (not all) liberals from all social strata were trying to promote for political gain.** □

Note that the comment contains good content (**in bold**) in addition to spam content. The spam content is hidden inside good content making it very hard to detect. Also, several variations of the comment text with changes in name, age, etc. are also posted. (Table 2 shows the sequence mined to capture this comment and other similar comments.) Traditionally, this problem has been approached in two different ways.
Hand-crafted features: The feature can be based on the presence or absence of patterns, e.g., url patterns.
Feature selection: Several classifiers like decision trees, boosting, etc. are capable of feature selection. So it is possible that features that correspond to spam are selected even if spam content is embedded in non-spam content.

Since spam is dynamic, hand-crafted features are difficult to maintain. Feature selection is usually implicit and may not pick higher-order features (like specific combinations of words) that characterize spam.

In addition to the above, the approaches based on machine learning have other disadvantages.
• Machine learning requires training data and, for complex problems, training data sizes can be very large.
• Most of the machine learned models are not interpretable. Hence updating them for specific failure cases can be very difficult.

1.2 Our Contributions

The work presented in this paper addresses the above issues. Before listing our contributions, we provide a formal description of the problem.

Problem Definition: Given a dataset $\mathcal{D}$ containing both spam and of non-spam comments, design a high-precision classifier that detects current and future spam comments. In this case, we are allowed to ask for label for "patterns" after we mine them. The comments again have time stamps. The specification of the time windows to use for mining is a problem that also has to be solved. □

The following is a summary of the main contributions of the paper.
1) We present a new framework for spam detection that uses local patterns (like `*happy 2011*friend*` for Example 1) instead of global classifiers for spam detection. Though using such patterns that have been manually identified is not new, what we present in this paper is a technique to mine such patterns very quickly, rather than depending on an expert to design them.
2) The sequence mining algorithms in the literature crash on Yahoo comment data. Even the best closed-sequence mining algorithm (BIDE [29]) is unable to handle a typical hour's data on Yahoo news. We explain their shortcomings and introduce an additional constraint – the notion of *min closed* sequences – and an algorithm for mining frequent sequences with this constraint, which effectively mines large volumes of Yahoo comments data. Our algorithm mines an entire day's comments in less than an hour on a desktop.
3) As a by product we solve an open problem mentioned in [10] – use the block encoding technique to speed up frequent closed sequence mining. Our algorithm is faster by a factor of 2-5 compared to state of art algorithms when evaluated on publicly available benchmarks and by an order of magnitude on comment datasets.
4) Frequent sequence mining algorithms often provide sequences which have overlapping coverage. Finding a small subset of patterns which maximize coverage is an NP Hard optimization problem. We show that the coverage function is submodular and hence there exists a fast approximation algorithm that comes close to optimal.
5) We show using real world data that comment spam is temporal in nature, and hence any techniques used should be highly adaptive – a condition which the techniques presented in this paper do satisfy.

Paper organization: This paper is organized as follows. Section 2 discussed related work in the areas of spam detection and frequent sequence mining. Section 3 defines Min-closed sequences and Section 4 outlines the algorithm for mining them. Section 6 discusses the selection of minimal number of non-redundant subsequences so that coverage is maximized. Section 7 contains the experimental results. Section 8 presents the conclusions and open issues. Appendix A presents background on frequent sequences mining and the standard concepts and notation in the literature and Appendix B contains proofs of the claims in the paper.

2. RELATED WORK

In this section we summarize the previous approaches to

spam, how our method differs from them, followed by related work on frequent sequence mining.

2.1 Spam detection

There are different types of spam: email [8], web [11], comment [31], review [15], blog spam [16], etc. In this paper, we focus primarily on comment spam. In addition to machine-learning based classifiers, several techniques like CAPTCHAs [28], reputation modeling and community moderation [30], etc. have been used to prevent/detect comment spam. CAPTCHAs can contribute a great deal towards spam prevention. Unfortunately, they are intrusive and impair the user experience. Reputation modeling techniques require sufficient data to build reliable reputation scores and hence leak initially. We consider these different approaches to be complementary and best deployed in conjunction. Our focus in this paper is on detecting comment spam through machine learned models.

Even in the machine learning framework, there are several approaches to spam detection: classification, language modeling, topic modeling, etc.

Language/topic modeling are generative techniques. In these approaches, language or topic models are learned for the two classes – spam and non-spam. A test document is labeled spam or non-spam depending on the probability of generation. [5], [17], [27], and [19] use language models for spam-detection in web sites or blogs. [4] uses topic models (more specifically, Latent Dirichlet Allocation) to learn spam and non-spam topics. They run topic model on spam and non-spam site to learn spam and non-spam topics. The proportion of these topics in a new site determines its class.

Classification techniques are discriminative. The naive-bayes classification has achieved a measure of success in spam detection [23, 24]. Some of the recent papers use co-classification (e.g., [6]) to classify spam content and spammers simultaneously.

Since spam is temporal, continual update of detection systems is important. [22] shows that it very easy create spam comments. Hence it is is very easy to change spam messages. [9] shows the importance of the age of training examples for spam classification. [7] proposes an ensemble of classifiers to detect classifier drift.

2.2 Frequent sequence mining

Frequent itemset and frequent sequence mining is a widely researched area. Some of the well-known algorithms in this area are: Apriori [25], GSP [26], PSP [18] etc. which work with the horizontal data format, SPADE [33], SPAM [3], PRISM [10] etc. which work use the vertical data format, and PrefixSpan [21] and related projection based methods.

We have enhanced cSPADE with a new constraint called min-closedness. These are described in detail in Sections 3 and 4.

3. MIN-CLOSED SEQUENCES

The notation and notions (like support, closed sequence, etc.) we use in this paper are standard in the sequence mining literature. See Appendix A, for details.

We start with the definition of Min Closed sequence.

DEFINITION 2. **[Min-l-Closed sequence]**: *Given a sequence database $\mathcal{D}$, a sequence s is defined to be min-l-closed iff all the following hold.*

1) $length(s) \geq l$
2) s is closed
3) There does not exist a closed subsequence $s' \preceq s$ with $length(s') \geq l$
In the rest of the paper we use the term min-closed when the parameter l is obvious from the context.

We now prove some theoretical properties of min-closedness that show that it is an ideal constraint for our application. Throughout we denote our sequence database by $\mathcal{D}$, support threshold by t, minimum length by l and the number of rows in the database by n. For our application $l \ll n$ and $t \ll n$.

Let $\mathcal{C}$ denote the set of frequent closed sequences of length $\geq l$ and let $\mathcal{C}_{min}$ denote the set of frequent min-closed sequences.

THEOREM 3.

$$Support(\mathcal{C}_{min}) = Support(\mathcal{C}).$$

Proof is in Appendix B.

The above theorem shows that by restricting ourselves to min-closed sequences rather than the set of closed sequences we do not lose any coverage.

THEOREM 4. $\frac{|\mathcal{C}|}{|\mathcal{C}_{min}|} \geq 1$. *The ratio can be exponentially large in the worst case (exponential in the number of rows in the database). Proof is in Appendix B.*

Even though the above theorem only gives a worst case exponential bound, is not very far removed from what is encountered in practice. During our experiments with Yahoo comments data we have observed that comments with common substrings occur quite often and cause all the standard min-closed miners to run out of memory as they generate several hundred GBs of frequent closed patterns from a few MB of real world comment data. This was the motivation for us to develop a new algorithm to mine Yahoo comment data. See Sections 7.2 and 7.4.2 for experimental results on this.

The theorems above show that the set of frequent min-closed sequences is a succinct collection with the same coverage as the set of all frequent sequences of length $\geq l$.

4. MINING MIN-CLOSED SEQUENCES

All known frequent sequence mining algorithms essentially traverse the subsequence partial order in either a depth-first or breadth-first manner and at each stage compute the support of the current node. If the support is less than the threshold, they prune the tree at this node. If not, they output the current node as a frequent sequence. In either case they proceed to the next node (in DFS/BFS order) if it exists. The aspect in which the existing methods differ from one another is the data structures they maintain for every node in order to do the support counting. BFS is not feasible on our data since the number of frequent sequences gets very large, hence we use DFS in our algorithm.

For mining closed sequences there are essentially two kinds of strategies in the literature.

1. The candidate-maintenance-and-test approach used, for example, in cloSPAN [32] (also used in pattern/itemset mining algorithms like CHARM [34], CLOSET [20] and TFP [13]). In this case, the algorithm maintains a

set of candidate closed sequences and prunes it using sub-pattern and super-pattern checking. If the number of candidates gets very large then this approach becomes infeasible.

2. On-the-fly closure checking used in BIDE [29]. In this case, additional processing is done on every node to determine if it is closed. This ensures that the memory usage is lower as compared to the previous approach. Also the backscan pruning method greatly reduces the number of nodes visited during the DFS traversal.

For mining min-closed sequences we use the second approach to prune our DFS. We need the following:

DEFINITION 5. **[Prefix-l-Closed]**: *A sequence s is defined to be prefix-l-closed iff all the following conditions are satisfied: 1) length$(s) \geq l$*
2) s is closed
3) There does not exist a prefix s' of s such that length$(s') \geq l$ and s' is closed
We drop the parameter l if it is obvious from the context.

Clearly s is min-l-closed $\implies$ s is prefix-l-closed.
Our algorithm modifies PRISM [10] in the following ways:

1. For on-the-fly closure checking, we use additional data structures. In the next section we show how an enhanced block-encoding can be used to do the bi-directional closure checking and backscan pruning described in [29].

2. We modify the pruning strategy for the DFS tree by taking advantage of the min-closed constraint. It is easy to check for a prefix-closed node on-the-fly – perform the bi-directional closure check for every node during the DFS and prune the traversal at the node iff it is closed and its length is $\geq l$.

3. We use a prefix sequence tree to store and update the set of prefix-closed sequences encountered in the previous step.

Let F_i be the set of all frequent sequences of length i.

1. We first build the sets F_1 and F_2 and their associated prime-block encodings. This can be done in 2 passes of the database.

2. We group the elements of F_2 by their first element. To be precise, we store F_2 as a hash map where the key is the first element shared by the group and the value is an array of all the elements of F_2 that have the key as their first element.

3. We start our modified DFS on the lexicographically ordered sequence tree. Our start node is the first node of F_1 in lexicographic order.

4. We now describe how our modified DFS processes every node. For the node $f \in F_i$ compute the join of f with every element of F_2 whose first element is equal to the last element of f. This gives us the prime-block encodings of all the children of f in our DFS tree. Use the block encodings to calculate support for each child and discard child sequences that are not frequent. If $i \geq l$ use the bi-directional closure check to determine if the current node is closed. If it is closed, update the prefix sequence tree that stores the prefix-closed sequences and prune the tree at this node. Continue the DFS.

Note: To handle max-gap constraint the only change that needs to be made is to construct F_2 to be the set of all sequences of length two which match $> t$ sequences such that in each match there are $<$ max-gap tokens between consecutive matches.

5. ON THE FLY CLOSURE CHECKING

A key step in the algorithm described in the previous section is closure checking which is an expensive operation. Using prime encodings, we can perform on the fly closure checking. The complete scheme is described in the Appendix C. We call the final algorithm MCPRISM.

6. MAXIMIZING COVERAGE

In case the number of min-closed sequences itself becomes large we need to prune our set to the desired size while minimizing the coverage loss. This motivates the following problem:

PROBLEM 6. *Given n sequences $S_1, \ldots, S_n$, a sequence database $\mathcal{C}$ and an integer k, output a set $\mathcal{S}$, of k strings $\{s_1, \ldots, s_k\}$, such that $\sigma_{\mathcal{C}}(\mathcal{S})$ is maximized.*

It is easy to see that the above problem includes SET COVER as a special case [14] and is thus NP-Hard.

However we can design a fast approximation algorithms for this problem which come close to optimal. We observe that

LEMMA 7. *The function $\sigma(S)$ is submodular. Proof is in Appendix B.*

So if we start with a set of candidate strings that includes the optimal set then we can (in $O(n \log n)$) compute a greedy set that is guaranteed to come within

$$(1 - (1 - \frac{1}{k})^k)$$

of the optimal set [14]. The typical value of k is 30-50, so we see that our solution is within 70% of the optimal.

7. EXPERIMENTAL RESULTS

We describe three sets of experiments:

1. **Coverage:** To evaluate the suitability of frequent subsequences as a spam detectors, we calculate the percentage of spam captured by them and editorial gain (:= average number of spam comments captured per subsequence). We show that subsequence mining as a standalone system detects approximately 80% of spam comments. The rest of the comments consist primarily of very small comments and abusive coments which can be caught by keyword-based detectors. We also find that the editorial gain is 27.96, the coverage increase is around 6% at very low false positive rate.

2. **Spam Trends:** We illustrate general properties of frequent sequences and the temporal trends observed. We show that spam patterns in comment data are highly

	TP	FP
MCPRISM	79.2%	0.2%
Baseline	73.3%	21.0%

Table 1: Coverage and False Positives

transient and subsequence mining is effective in capturing these short term trends. The insights from these experiments can be used to design a spam detection system based on the subsequence miner and tune its parameters.

3. **Min-Closed and Closed Mining:** We evaluate the impact of the proposed Min-Closed constraint on result size and the performance of the sequence mining algorithm itself. Additionally we evaluate the performance of MCPRISM and compare the run time with the best known closed sequence mining algorithm (BIDE).

Datasets: For the above experiments, we use two datasets. Comment Dataset: We use a subset of comments corresponding to 9 days consisting of about 2.3 million comments posted on `news.yahoo.com`. The comments corresponded to the period Feb - Mar 2011.

Gazelle: We use the Gazelle data set for our comparison the execution performance of our algorithm. It contains 59602 sequences, 497 distinct items and sequence lengths in the range $[1, 267]$. We use this dataset for scalability experiments because BIDE does not scale to the comments dataset. Gazelle was part of the KDD CUP 2000 challenge dataset and is commonly used to compare algorithms for closed sequence mining.

Baseline: We use an SVM-classifier trained on bag of words feature representation.

Subsequence miner settings: We have throughout used the following parameters for our subsequence miner: $min\_length = 5$, $min\_support = 5$, $max\_gap = 2$.

7.1 Coverage

We split the Comment Data into hourly chunks and mine the subsequences using MCPRISM. We create ground truth labels for all the comments in a few randomly chosen chunks.

We label a mined subsequence as spam if it matches with even one comment labeled spam. The comments matching even one subsequence labeled spam constutute the detected spam. We provide coverage and false positive estimates based on the detected spam.

Table 1 shows the spam coverage (TP) and false positive (FP) numbers for MCPRISM and the baseline SVM. The baseline has a very high false positive rate implying that the classifier learns from the non-spam cotent in the comments and incorrectly classifies several non-spam comments as spam. The baseline also has a lower TP rate.

Some of the detected subsequences are shown in Table 2. It can be seen that the sequences are long and hence have low false positive rate.

The average of the ratio of the length of the largest comment to that of the smallest comment is XXX. This shows that the detected commnets are non near-duplicates and hence are unlikely to be caught by such techniques.

Note that if we had used larger chunks instead of hourly chunks, the additional coverage would have been higher. See Section 7.3.2. We have done hourly data mining to reduce the editorial effort of generating ground truth.

7.1.1 Editorial Gains

As can be seen from the above description, each subsequence is editorially labeled just once and can be used to label several comments (in the same time slot or in other time slots) as spam. We define editorial gain as the ratio of the number of comments detected as spam by a set of subsequences to the total number of subsequences in the set. (Since each subsequence is shown just once to the editor, this also characterizes the amount of editorial effort required to label the set of subsequences.) We mined our Golden Set for frequent subsequences, manually labelled these subsequences as spam/non-spam and used these sequences on the entire corpus of 2.3 million comments. The editorial gain for this set was found to be 27.96.

7.2 Execution Performance

7.3 Spam Trends

In this section we describe two experiments. The first shows that frequent sequences are effective in discriminating spam from non-spam, the second shows that frequent patterns are highly transient.

7.3.1 Discriminative Power

It can be seen from Table 1 that MCPRISM has a very low false positive rate. In this section, we explore this aspect in more detail. We call a frequent subsequence **discriminative** if either (1)> 90% of its support is spam (in this case we will call it a "spam sequence", or (2) > 90% of its support is non-spam ("non-spam" sequence). Figure 1 shows the fraction of frequent sequences that were found to be discriminative for each day. Overall percentage of discriminative sequences was found to be 96.4%.

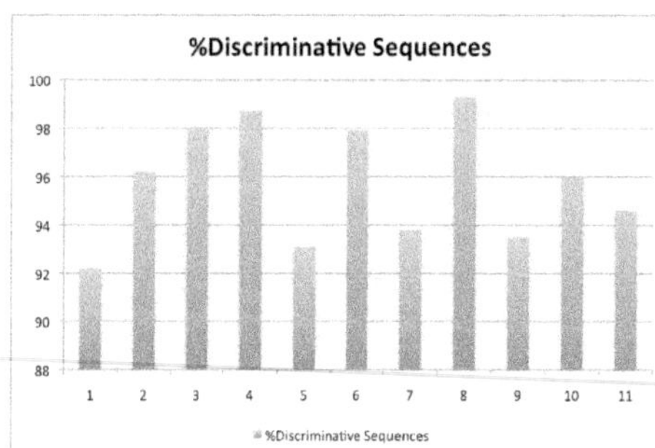

Figure 1: Percentage Discriminative Sequences

7.3.2 Temporal Localization

To elucidate the temporal patterns in spam comments, we conducted two sets of experiments. In the first experiment we mined the hourly trends and measured how long these trends last. The precise details are as follows.

1. Split all the hourly spam patterns into the following buckets depending on how many times the pattern appears in the data. E.g., if the pattern appears in only one hour place it in bucket 1, if it appears twice (say,

1. happy 2011 friend yrs lady announced wedding it' amazing posted received chat invitations days believe it' true love story unfold it' own

2. 3d toshiba laptop worth $1599 arrived paid $198 47 deal till neighbor told he' getting massive 42 inch 3dtv $192 74 delivered apartment tomorrow it' amazing feeling paying jacked prices public have-to started selling products staff i' killing look:

Table 2: Frequent subsequences which are spam. When matching, we use a wildcard ("*") between any two tokens in the sequence. The first sequence is derived from Example 1 and other similar comments.

in hour 30 and hour 32) then it is placed in bucket 2, and so on.

2. Plot a bar graph showing the percentage of spam patterns that fall in each bucket.

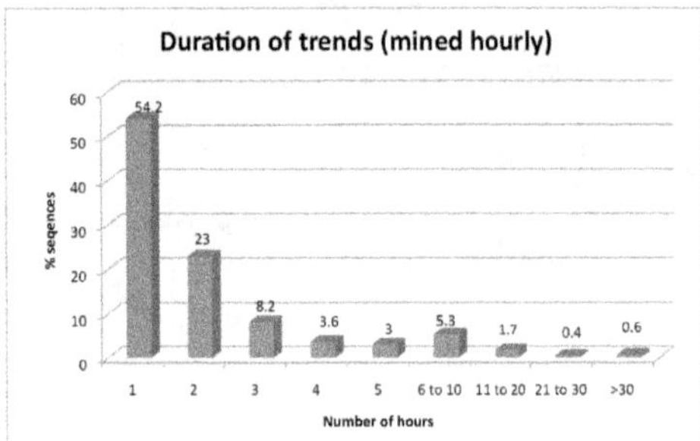

Figure 2: Duration of hourly trends

The graph is shown in Figure 2. As can be seen, over 85% of the mined sequences last for a maximum of three hours. This clearly implies specific spam types are short lived, and it is necessary for any algorithm to adapt very quickly to this rapidly changing behavior.

In the above experiment it is possible that some subsequences may be frequent globally but infrequent locally. In other words, they may lie below the support threshold every hour but may be spread out and over a period of several days they may outnumber the locally frequent patterns. If this is a common occurrence then this would violate our claim that frequently occurring patterns are localized. To test this possibility we conducted the following experiment:

1. Mine the cumulative data (from 5 consecutive days) all patterns that have coverage greater than the support threshold.

2. For each pattern compute the number of hours for which it has non zero coverage.

Figure 3 shows the graph that was obtained.

Again over 70% of the spam sequences last for three hours or less, and over 80% last for five hours or less. This implies that mining on a corpus of three to five hours will detect most spam sequences for a day.

7.4 Execution Performance of the Algorithm

In this section we evaluate our algorithm on two fronts on Gazelle dataset:

1. The running time of the algorithm with respect to the fastest closed sequence mining algorithm in the literature (BIDE).

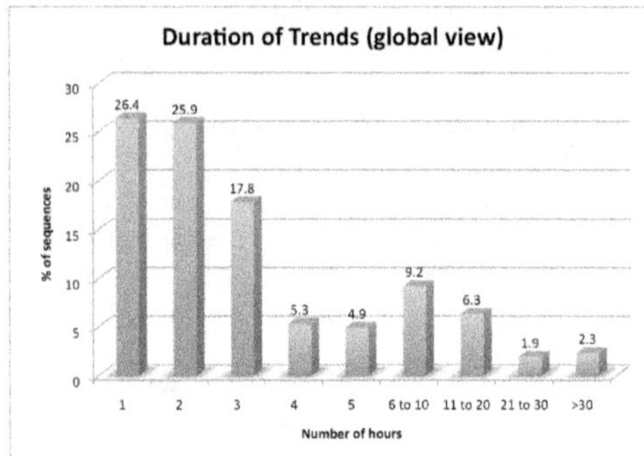

Figure 3: Duration of hourly trends

2. The efficacy of the min-closed criterion for pruning mining results.

7.4.1 Execution Time

One of our contributions is a new algorithm for mining frequent closed sequences. In this section we compare the running time of our algorithm with BIDE, the fastest algorithm for this problem in the literature.

We ran the two algorithms on a 3.4 GHz P6 system with 2GB RAM. Figure 4 shows the relative run times of the two algorithms. We observe that our algorithm is 2 to 2.5 times faster than BIDE on the Gazelle dataset.

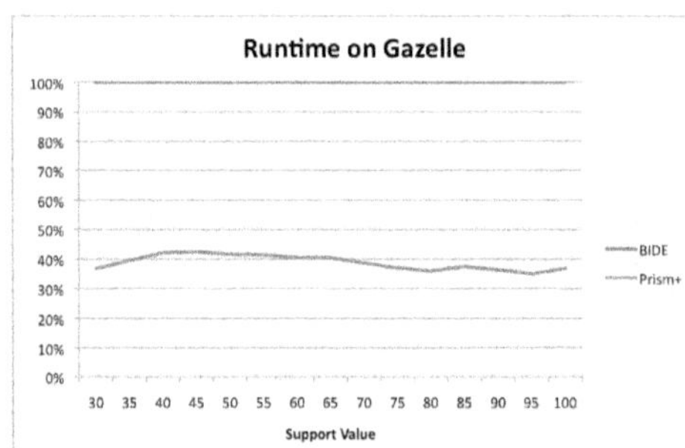

Figure 4: Relative Runtimes BIDE vs MCPRISM on Gazelle

7.4.2 Min Closed Pruning

In this section we evaluate the efficacy of the min closed pruning with respect to the following criteria:

1. **Result Size:** We show the relative sizes of the min closed and closed sets on the dataset Gazelle. In Figure 5 shows the relative sizes of the sets for a typical

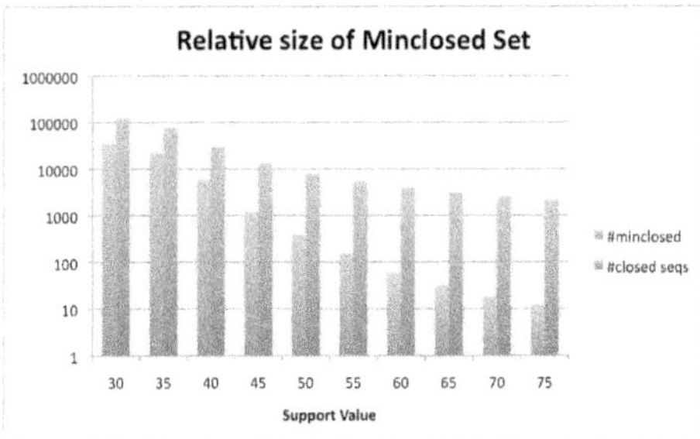

Figure 5: Relative size of closed and min-closed sets on Gazelle

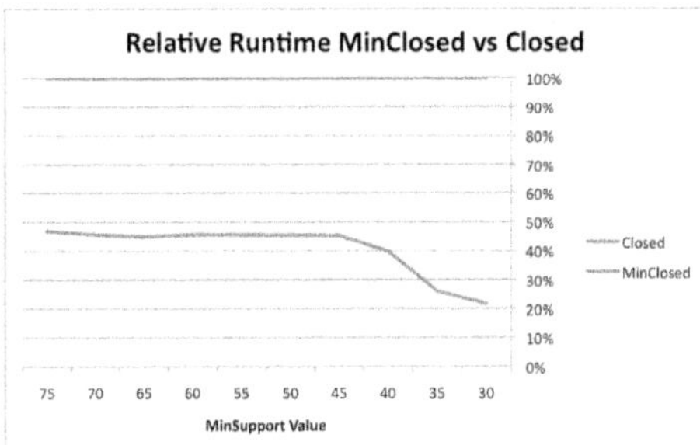

Figure 6: Relative Runtime of closed vs min-closed sets on Gazelle

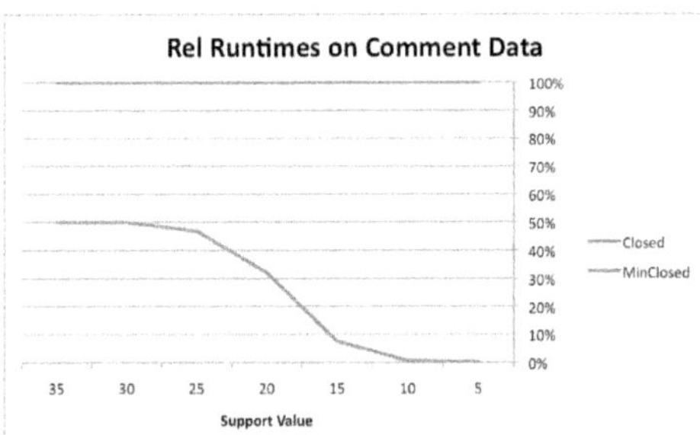

Figure 7: Relative Runtime of closed vs min-closed sets on our comments data

min len value (we used the value 5). It shows that the min closed set is an order of magnitude (or more) smaller than the corresponding closed set.

2. **Running Time:** Figure 6 show the relative running times of closed and minclosed sequence mining on the Gazelle dataset. We see that on this dataset the min closed pruning speeds the mining by a factor of 2 to 5. Figure 7 show the relative running times of closed and minclosed sequence mining on our comment dataset. We see that on this dataset the min closed pruning speeds the mining by a factor of over 1000 as the min support value gets smaller.

8. CONCLUSIONS

In this paper, we have proposed a spam detection framework based on frequent subsequence mining. The framework complements current techniques for spam detection including those based on machine learning. The existing sequence mining algorithms typically fail to operate under the settings needed for spam detection. We have proposed enhancements to both the problem setting wherein instead of using sequence pattern mining as is, we propose to mine min-closed sequences. Consequently, we have modified the PRISM algorithm to get a new algorithm called MCPRISM, which can mine frequent sequences from spam comments very efficiently. We have shown greedy selection of patterns gives good coverage of the spam data while minimizing the number of patterns. The technique reduces the editorial efforts by an order of magnitude. Hence this approach is especially applicable in the presence of trending patterns in spam. We have also demonstrated the scalability of MCPRISM on Gazelle dataset.

9. REFERENCES

[1] Six Apart Guide to Comment Spam. `http://www.sixapart.com/pronet/comment_spam`.

[2] Spam in blogs. `http://en.wikipedia.org/wiki/Spam_in_blogs`.

[3] J. Ayres, J. Flannick, J. Gehrke, and T. Yiu. Sequential pattern mining using a bitmap representation. In *SIGKDD*, 2002.

[4] I. Biro, J. Szabo, and A. A. Benczur. Latent dirichlet allocation in web spam filtering. In *AIRWeb*, 2008.

[5] T. Bogers and A. van den Bosch. Using language modeling for spam detection in social reference manager websites. In *DIR*, 2009.

[6] F. Chen, P.-N. Tan, and A. K. Jain. A co-classification framework for detecting web spam and spammers in social media web sites. In *CIKM*, 2009.

[7] D. Chinavle, P. Kolari, T. Oates, and T. Finin. Ensembles in adversarial classification for spam. In *CIKM*, 2009.

[8] G. V. Cormack. Email spam filtering: A systematic review. *Foundations and Trends in Information Retrieval*, 2007.

[9] G. V. Cormack and J.-M. M. da Cruz. On the relative age of spam and ham training samples for email filtering. In *SIGIR*, 2009.

[10] K. Gouda, M. Hassaan, and M. J. Zaki. Prism: A prime-encoding approach for frequent sequence mining. In *JCSS*, 2010.

[11] Z. Gyongyi and H. Garcia-Molina. Web spam taxonomy. In *WWW*, 2005.

[12] J. Han, J. Pei, B. Mortazavi-Asl, Q. Chen, U. Dayal, and M. Hsu. Freespan: Frequent pattern-projected sequential pattern mining. In *SIGKDD*, 2000.

[13] J. Han, J. Wang, Y. Lu, and P. Tzvetkov. Mining top-k frequent closed patterns without minimum support. In *ICDM*, 2002.

[14] D. Hochbaum. *Approximating covering and packing problems: Set Cover, vertex cover, independent set, and related problems.* 1997.

[15] N. Jindal and B. Liu. Review spam detection. In *WWW*, 2007.

[16] P. Kolari, T. Finin, and A. Joshi. SVMs for the Blogosphere: Blog Identification and Splog Detection. In *AAAI Spring Symposium on Computational Approaches to Analysing Weblogs*, 2006.

[17] J. Martinez-Romo and L. Araujo. Web spam identification through language model analysis. In *AIRWeb*, 2009.

[18] F. Masseglia, F. Cathala, and P. Poncelet. The psp approach for mining sequential patterns. In *PKDD*, London, UK, 1998. Springer-Verlag.

[19] G. Mishne, D. Carmel, and R. Lempel. Blocking blog spam with language model disagreement. In *AIRWeb*, 2005.

[20] J. Pei, J. Han, and R. Mao. Closet: An efficient algorithm for mining frequent closed itemsets. In *DKMD*, 2000.

[21] J. Pei, J. Han, B. Mortazavi-Asl, H. Pinto, Q.Chen, U. Dayal, and M.-C. Hsu. Prefixspan: Mining sequential

patterns efficiently by prefixprojected pattern growth. In *ICDE*, 2001.
[22] M. Ramilli and M. Prandini. Comment spam injection made easy. In *CCNC*, 2009.
[23] M. Sahami, S. Dumais, D. Heckerman, and E. Horvitz. A bayesian approach to filtering junk e-mail. In *AAAI Workshop on Learning for Text Categorization*, 1998.
[24] Y. Song, A. Kolcz, and C. L. Giles. Better naive bayes classification for high-precision spam detection. *Software: Practice and Experience*, 2009.
[25] R. Srikant and R. Agrawal. Mining sequential patterns. In *(ICDE)*, 1995.
[26] R. Srikant and R. Agrawal. Mining sequential patterns: Generalizations and Performance Improvements. In *EDBT*, 1996.
[27] E. Terra. Simple language models for spam detection. In *TREC*, 2005.
[28] L. von Ahn, M. Blum, N. Hopper, and J. Langford. CAPTCHA: Using Hard AI Problems for Security. In *Eurocrypt*, 2003.
[29] J. Wang and J. Han. Bide: Efficient mining of frequent closed sequences. In *ICDE*, 2004.
[30] P. J. Windley, K. Tew, and D. Daley. A framework for building reputation systems. In *WWW*, 2007.
[31] B. Wong, M. E. Locasto, and A. D. Keromytis. PalProtect: A collaborative security approach to comment spam. In *IEEE Information Assurance Workshop*, 2006.
[32] X. Yan, J. Han, and R. Afshar. Mining closed sequential patterns in large datasets. In *SDM*, 2003.
[33] M. Zaki. SPADE: An efficient algorithm for mining frequent sequences. In *Machine Learning Journal*, 2001.
[34] M. J. Zaki and C.-J. Hsiao. CHARM: An efficient algorithm for closed itemset mining. In *ICDM*, 2002.

APPENDIX

A. NOTATION AND DEFINITIONS

PROBLEM 8 (FREQUENT SEQUENCE MINING PROBLEM). *Given a sequence database (i.e., a database where each element is a sequence of normalized tokens), a frequency threshold t, and a length threshold l, output all the sequences of length $\geq l$, that occur as a subsequence in more than t sequences. Note that the subsequence need not be contiguous.*

The above is a fundamental data-mining problem and there are many well known algorithms that solve it: Apriori [25], GSP [26], FreeSpan [12], PrefixSpan [21], Spade [33], SPAM [3], PRISM [10].

DEFINITION 9. **[Sequence]**: *Let $I = \{i_1, \ldots, i_n\}$ be a set of* **items**. *A* **sequence** *is an ordered list of items and is denoted by $\langle s_1, \ldots, s_l\rangle$ where each s_j is an item. The* **length** *of the sequence is the number of items in the sequence.*

DEFINITION 10. *A* **sequence database** *is a set of tuples $\langle sid, s\rangle$ where sid is a unique* **sequence_id** *associated with the sequence s.*

EXAMPLE 11. *The following sequence database will function as our running example throughout the paper.* **Items**: *$I = \{A, B, C, D\}$*

Sequence_id	Sequence
1	$\langle A,B,C,A\rangle$
2	$\langle A,B,A\rangle$
3	$\langle B,A,C\rangle$
4	$\langle A,C,D,A\rangle$

DEFINITION 12. **[Subsequence relation]**: *A sequence $s = \langle s_1, \ldots, s_k\rangle$ is said to be a subsequence of the sequence $s' = \langle s'_1, \ldots, s'_l\rangle$ iff there exist indices $1 \leq i_1 < i_2 < \ldots < i_k \leq l$ such that $s_1 = s'_{i_1}, s_2 = s'_{i_2}, \ldots, s_k = s_{i_k}$. In this case we write $s \preceq s'$.*

For example, $\langle a,b,c,d\rangle \preceq \langle a,c,b,a,d,c,f,d\rangle$.
The subsequence relation induces a partial order over the set of all sequences. We refer to this as the **subsequence partial order**.

DEFINITION 13. **[Support]**: *$Support_{\mathcal{D}}(s)$ of a sequence, s with respect to a set $\mathcal{D} = \{d_1, \ldots, d_n\}$ of sequences defined to be:*

$$Support_{\mathcal{D}}(s) = \{d_i | d_i \in \mathcal{D} \text{ and } s \preceq d_i\}.$$

We generally omit the subscript $\mathcal{D}$ when the sequence database is obvious from the context.
If S is a set of sequences $\{s_1, \ldots, s_k\}$ then we extend the above definition to:

$$Support(S) = \{c_i | c_i \in \mathcal{D} \text{ and } s_j \preceq c_i \text{ for some } 1 \leq j \leq k\}.$$

We also define $\sigma(s) = \mid Support(s) \mid$ and $\sigma(S) = \mid Support(S) \mid$.

DEFINITION 14. **[Frequent Sequence]**: *Given a sequence database $\mathcal{D}$ and a support threshold t we call a sequence s frequent iff $Support_{\mathcal{D}}(s) \geq t$.*

DEFINITION 15. **[Closed sequence]**: *A sequence s is defined to be closed with respect to a set $\mathcal{D}$ if and only if there does not exist any sequence s' such that $s \preceq s'$ and $Support_{\mathcal{D}}(s) = Support_{\mathcal{D}}(s')$.*

In our running example we see that the set $\mathcal{C}$ of frequent closed sequences is $\{AA, ABA, AC, ACA, BA, BC, CA\}$.We have omitted commas and angular brackets for the sake of readability.

In our running example the set $\mathcal{C}_{min}$ of frequent min-closed sequences is $\{AA, ABA, AC, BA, BC, CA\}$. Note that the sequence ACA is not min-closed because it has a subsequence AC that is closed and of length 2.

Note that if we consider the restriction of the subsequence partial order to frequent closed sequences that are longer than l, then the set of min-closed sequences is the set of minimal elements in this partial order.

B. PROOFS

B.1 Proof of Theorem 1

$\mathcal{C}_{min} \subseteq \mathcal{C}$ so trivially we have

$$Support(\mathcal{C}_{min}) \subseteq Support(\mathcal{C}).$$

For every sequence $s \in \mathcal{C}$ there is a sequence $s' \in \mathcal{C}_{min}$ such that $s' \preceq s$ and it follows that $Support(s) \subseteq Support(s')$. Hence we can conclude:

$$\begin{aligned} Support(\mathcal{C}) &= \bigcup_{s \in \mathcal{C}} Support(s) \\ &\subseteq \bigcup_{s' \in \mathcal{C}_{min}} Support(s') \\ &\subseteq Support(\mathcal{C}_{min}) \end{aligned}$$

B.2 Proof of Theorem 2

The first statement is trivial. To see the second consider the following sequence database over the set of items $A = \{a_1, a_2, \ldots, a_n\}$.

$$\begin{aligned} s_1 &= \langle a_1, a_2, \ldots, a_{n-1} \rangle & (a_n \ missing) \\ s_2 &= \langle a_1, \ldots, a_{n-2}, a_n \rangle & (a_{n-1} \ missing) \\ &\vdots \\ s_n &= \langle a_2, \ldots, a_{n-1}, a_n \rangle & (a_1 \ missing) \end{aligned}$$

We assume that the elements of A are lexicographically ordered as $a_1 < a_2 < \cdots < a_n$. For any subset $S \subseteq A$ let $\tilde{S}$ denote the sequence that is obtained by lexicographically ordering the elements of S.

Now, clearly $Support(\tilde{S}) = n - |S|$. It follows that for every subset S such that $l \leq |S| \leq n - t$, $\tilde{S}$ is a frequent closed subsequence. Also, in this instance the set of frequent min-closed sequences $= \{\tilde{S} : S \subseteq A \text{ and } |S| = l\}$. Hence we have

$$\frac{|\mathcal{C}|}{|\mathcal{C}_{min}|} = \frac{\binom{n}{l} + \cdots \binom{n}{(n-t)}}{\binom{n}{1}}$$

Since $l \ll n$ and $t \ll n$,

$$\frac{|\mathcal{C}|}{|\mathcal{C}_{min}|} = \Omega(\frac{2^n}{n^l})$$

B.3 Proof of Lemma 6

Follows from the fact that for any two sets S, T, we have:

$$Support(S \cup T) = Support(S) \cup Support(T).$$

and

$$Support(S \cap T) = Support(S) \cap Support(T).$$

Hence we have:

$$\begin{aligned} \sigma(S \cup T) + \sigma(S \cap T) &= |\ Support(S) \cup Support(T)\ | + \\ & \quad |\ Support(S) \cap Support(T)\ | \\ &= |\ Support(S)\ | + |\ Support(T)\ | \\ &= \sigma(S) + \sigma(T). \end{aligned}$$

C. BLOCK ENCODING FOR CLOSED SEQUENCE MINING

We describe how the prime block encoding can be extended to efficiently mine closed sequences. We briefly review some basic concepts that will be referred to later. For a full description, see the original papers [33] and [10].

DEFINITION 16. *The temporal id list, also denoted by tid-list of a sequence s with respect to a sequence database S is the list of all pairs (i, j) where i is the sequence_id of a sequence s_i in S containing s, and j is an index such that the length j prefix of s_i contains s and the jth item in s_i is equal to the last item of s. Note that there can be more than one such j satisfying these conditions and in that case the list contains all such pairs (i, j)*

For our running example (Example 11), Table 3 shows the tid-lists.

PRISM [10] optimizes the task of computing the join of two tid-lists by encoding pairs as bitvectors, breaking the bit vectors up into fixed size blocks and precomputing the joins of these blocks. For example, if we choose block size 4,

sequence	tid-list
$\langle A \rangle$	(1, 1) (1, 4) (2, 1) (2, 3) (3, 2) (4, 1) (4, 4)
$\langle B \rangle$	(1, 2) (2, 2) (3, 1)
$\langle A, B \rangle$	(1, 2) (2, 2)

Table 3: Tid-lists

sequence_id	bit-encoded pos	prime encoded pos
1	1001	14
2	1010	10
3	0100	3
4	1001	14

Table 4: Position Encoding for $\langle A \rangle$

Table 4 show the bit encoded positions of the tid-list for $\langle A \rangle$ and Table 5 shows the corresponding sequence blocks. The prime block encoding is obtained by choosing the first four prime numbers (2, 3, 5, 7) to constitute our **base set** and multiplying the primes corresponding to the bit positions that are set to 1 in the bit encoded positions.

Table 6 shows the sequence and position blocks and their corresponding prime encodings. It is easy to see that the join of two tid-lists consists of the the following operations in the corresponding prime blocks: Define, $mask(i)$ = product of all the primes in our base set that are larger than the largest prime factor of i. The join of two blocks with prime encoding i, j is $gcd(mask(i), j)$. If we precompute these functions in a table with all possible values of i, j (for block size 4 this is a 16×16 table) we can replace the task of joining two tid-lists, which involves the linear traversal of the lists, by lookup operations. If the block size is k, then k comparisons are replaced by a single lookup. The additional memory required is $O(2^{2k})$. When $k = 8$ this is less than 200 KB.

Clearly this idea works with any efficiently computable integer function instead of the mask and gcd functions. In the rest of the section we show how on-the-fly closure checking can be optimized using the above idea.

We build on the concepts and results from [29]. See [29] for the complete details. We also need the following concepts and results from [29] which we reproduce for the sake of ease of exposition. Please see [29] for the complete details.

DEFINITION 17. **([29]: The i-th last-in-last appearance w.r.t. a sequence)** *Given a sequence $s = a_1a_2 \ldots a_p$ and a supersequence t, the i-th last-in-last appearance (denoted by LL_i) of s w.r.t. t is defined recursively as: (1) for $i = p$ LL_p is the last appearance of a_p in t. (2) For $1 \leq i < n$ LL_i is the last occurrence of a_i before LL_{i+1} .*

For example if the last-in-last appearances for different values of i for the strings s=abcbde, t=abaebcabcdeabdce are shown in Table 7

DEFINITION 18. **([29]: The i-th maximum period)**

bit-encoded sequence_id	prime encoded sequence_id
1111	210

Table 5: Sequence Encoding for $\langle A \rangle$

sequence	sequence blocks	position blocks
$\langle A \rangle$	210	14, 10, 3, 14
$\langle B \rangle$	30	3, 3, 2, 1
$\langle A, B \rangle$	6	3, 3, 1, 1

Table 6: Full Primal Blocks

i	LL_i (marked in bold)
6	a b a e b c a b c d e a b d c **e**
5	a b a e b c a b c d e a b **d** c e
4	a b a e b c a b c d e a **b** d c e
3	a b a e b c a b **c** d e a b d c e
2	a b a e b c a **b** c d e a b d c e
1	a b a e b c **a** b c d e a b d c e

Table 7: Last-in-Last Values for s=abcbde, t=abaebcabcdeabdce.

Given a sequence $s = a_1 a_2 \dots a_p$ and a supersequence t, the i-th maximum period of s w.r.t. t is defined as: (1) For $1 < i \leq n$ it is the portion of the sequence t lying in between the first instance of $a_1, \dots a_i$ in t (ie the shortest prefix of t containing it as a subsequence) and LL_i of s w.r.t. t.

Table 8 shows the i-th maximum periods for the strings in the above example

THEOREM 19. (**[29]**): *A sequence $s = a_1 a_2 \dots a_p$ is closed iff (1) There does not exist an element a such that $s' = a_1 a_2 \dots a_p a$ has the same support as s and (2) there does not exist an integer i and an element a such that for every supersequence t of s in the database, a appears in all the i-th maximum periods of s in t.*

DEFINITION 20. *Given a bit vector A we define $\rho(A) = \arg\max_i\{A[i] = 1\}$. We define the masking operator $(A)^{\triangleleft}$ as follows:*

$$(A)^{\triangleleft}[i] = \begin{cases} 0 & \text{if } i > \rho(A) \\ 1 & \text{otherwise} \end{cases}$$

Analogously we define $\lambda(A) = \arg\min_i\{A[i] = 1\}$ and the masking operator $(A)^{\triangleright}$:

$$(A)^{\triangleright}[i] = \begin{cases} 1 & \text{if } i > \lambda(A) \\ 0 & \text{otherwise} \end{cases}$$

LEMMA 21. *Given strings $s = a_1 a_2 \dots a_p \preceq t$, let A_i denote the bit vector representing the tid list of $a_1 a_2 \dots a_i$ for the string t. Define B_i, $1 \leq i < p$ recursively as follows:*

$$\begin{aligned} 1.B_p &= A_p \\ 2.B_i &= A_i \circ B_{i+1}^{\triangleleft} \quad 1 \leq i \leq p-1 \end{aligned}$$

where $\circ$ denotes the bitwise inner product operator.
Then $LL_i = \rho(B_i)$, for all $1 \leq i \leq p$

PROOF. We prove this by induction. Clearly for $i = p$, $LL_p = \rho(A_p) = \rho(B_p)$. Now, suppose $LL_i = \rho(B_i)$, from the definition 17, LL_{i-1} = the rightmost occurrence of a_{i-1} that lies to the left of LL_i. The masking vector $B_i^{\triangleleft}$ contains 1 on precisely all the valid positions for LL_{i-1}. The tid-list A_{i-1} contains all the valid endpoints of the subsequence matches of s in t and clearly that includes the last occurrence of a_{i-1} in t that lies to the left of LL_i. Thus we conclude that $LL_{i-1} = \rho(B_{i-1})$. □

The above lemma gives us a way of using the prime-block-encoding to compute all the LL_i values of a candidate substring for all the rows of the database. For this we need the following:

1. An additional table storing the $\triangleleft$ masks and the ρ values for all the possible prime blocks. PRISM uses a gcd table and a $\triangleright$ table storing the gcd values and the $\triangleright$ masks for all the possible prime blocks. This additional table adds a minimal space overhead – for block size 8 we just need to store 512 integer values.
2. Each subsequence stores a pointer to the prime blocks of all its prefixes. The space overhead for this is minimal as well.

The lemma shows that the LL_i computation can be done by simply performing gcd lookups using the $\triangleleft$ masks.
Analogously we observe the following:

LEMMA 22. *Given strings $s = a_1 a_2 \dots a_p \preceq t$, let A_i denote the bit vector representing the tid list of $a_1 a_2 \dots a_i$ for the string t. Define C_i, $1 \leq i < p$ recursively as follows:*

$$\begin{aligned} 1.C_1 &= A_1 \\ 2.C_{i+1} &= A_{i+1} \circ C_i^{\triangleright} \quad 1 < i \leq p-1 \end{aligned}$$

Then the first instance of a_i in t = $\lambda(C_i)$, for all $1 \leq i \leq p$.

PROOF. Very similar to the proof of Lemma 21. □

The above lemmas 21, 22 describe a mechanism of closure checking on the fly (without candidate maintenance).
This completes our description of the algorithm for mining min-closed sequences. As a by product we also observe that the above technique can also be used to enhance the PRISM algorithm to mine frequent closed sequences (by skipping the min-closed pruning step). In the experimental section we compare the performance of this algorithm with BIDE on the publicly available dataset Gazelle.

i	i-th max period (marked in bold)
6	a b a e b c a b c d e **a b d c** e
5	a b a e b c a b c d **e a b** d c e
4	a b a e b c a b **c d e a** b d c e
3	a b a e b c **a b** c d e a b d c e
2	a b **a e b c a** b c d e a b d c e
1	a **b a e b c** a b c d e a b d c e

Table 8: Max Period Values for s=abcbde, t=abaebcabcdeabdce.

Mining Slang and Urban Opinion Words and Phrases from cQA Services: An Optimization Approach

Hadi Amiri and Tat-Seng Chua
NUS Graduate School for Integrative Sciences and Engineering
Department of Computer Science, School of Computing
National University of Singapore
{hadi,chuats}@comp.nus.edu.sg

ABSTRACT
Current opinion lexicons contain most of the common opinion words, but they miss slang and so-called urban opinion words and phrases (e.g. *delish*, *cozy*, *yummy*, *nerdy*, and *yuck*). These subjectivity clues are frequently used in community questions and are useful for opinion question analysis. This paper introduces a principled approach to constructing an opinion lexicon for community-based question answering (cQA) services. We formulate the opinion lexicon induction as a semi-supervised learning task in the graph context. Our method makes use of existing opinion words to extract new opinion entities (slang and urban words/phrases) from community questions. It then models the opinion entities in a graph context to learn the polarity of the new opinion entities based on the graph connectivity information. In contrast to previous approaches, our method not only learns such polarities from the labeled data but also from the unlabeled data and is more feasible in the web context where the dictionary-based relations (such as *synonym*, *antonym*, or *hyponym*) between most words are not available for constructing a high quality graph. The experiments show that our approach is effective both in terms of the quality of the discovered new opinion entities as well as its ability in inferring their polarity. Furthermore, since the value of opinion lexicons lies in their usefulness in applications, we show the utility of the constructed lexicon in the sentiment classification task.

Categories and Subject Descriptors
I.2.7 [**Natural Language Processing**]: Text Analysis; H.3.3 [**Information Search and Retrieval**]: Text Mining

General Terms
Algorithms, Experimentation.

Keywords
Slang, Urban Word, Opinion Lexicon, Sentiment Orientation, Opinion Mining, Sentiment Analysis.

1. INTRODUCTION
Community-based Question Answering (cQA) services are web portals that allow users to post questions, respond to the previously asked questions, and rate/vote answers, etc. Well-known examples of such services are Yahoo! Answers[1], AnswerBag[2], and Baidu Zhidao[3]. The cQA questions usually contain a high amount of spelling errors and usage of slang. These issues make the analysis of such questions very difficult. Hence, the cQA data are triggering many innovative research scenarios in areas as diverse as user satisfaction [1], question recommendation [32], answer ranking and selection [23], and opinion summarization [27].

In this research we focus on the more fundamental issue of constructing an opinion lexicon from cQA questions. Opinion lexicons contain opinion words with their polarity labels, either positive or negative, and some scores that represent the strength of their polarity. Opinion lexicons are essential resources for almost all the tasks of sentiment analysis such as opinion mining [8], opinion retrieval [9], and opinion question answering [14]. In particular, in the cQA context, opinion lexicons can be used for discriminating opinion from factual questions [13], and answer summarization [27]. Given a question, a good cQA opinion lexicon can help determining the question as opinion or factual and deciding whether we should employ opinion-specific summarization methods in generating the answer or just rely on the traditional summarization techniques [2, 3].

There exist three approaches to opinion lexicon construction: manual, dictionary-based, and corpus-based approaches [19, 15]. The manual approach needs human annotators to tag the individual words as positive, negative or neutral. Dictionary-based approaches use a set of seeds (opinion words with already-known polarity) and search their synonyms and antonyms in dictionaries like WordNet[4] to find new opinion words [6, 10, 8, 24, 22, 21, 17]. An important shortcoming of the dictionary-based approaches is the limited vocabulary or coverage problem. In fact, the dictionary-based methods cannot find informal or so-called urban opinion words due to the fact that such words do not appear in the dictionaries. To address this problem, the corpus-based approaches are evolved that use synthetic or co-occurrence patterns in the text for constructing opinion lexicons [7, 11, 28, 29, 4]. The corpus-based approaches can help to find domain and context specific opinion words or phrases and their polarity orientations using a domain corpus. We review some of these works in the next section.

Permission to make digital or hard copies of all or part of this work for personal or classroom use is granted without fee provided that copies are not made or distributed for profit or commercial advantage and that copies bear this notice and the full citation on the first page. To copy otherwise, or republish, to post on servers or to redistribute to lists, requires prior specific permission and/or a fee.
WSDM'12, February 8–12, 2011, Seattle, Washington, USA.
Copyright 2012 ACM 978-1-4503-0747-5/12/02…$10.00.

[1] http://answers.yahoo.com/

[2] http://www.answerbag.com/

[3] http://zhidao.baidu.com/

[4] WordNet: http://wordnet.princeton.edu/

In this research we divide the cQA opinion lexicon construction task into two subtasks:

1. New Opinion Entity Detection: To the best of our knowledge, there is no principled approach to detect new *opinion entities* (words or phrases). Previous research either: (1) designed hand-crafted rules [7, 21, 11, 20], or (2) used dictionaries and WordNet relations [8, 26, 6, 22, 12] for this purpose. Each of the above two approaches has its own advantages and disadvantages. For instance both rule-based and dictionary-based approaches are precise, but rules are hard to design and dictionaries have limited vocabulary (coverage) problem. In this research, we propose a principled approach to detect new opinion entities in the cQA context. Our approach effectively combines the above-mentioned methods in a unified framework and is able to detect non-standard entities such as urban opinion words/phrases, slang and misspellings etc.

2. Polarity Inference: The association between seeds and new opinion entities provides a rich source of relationships. We model such relationships in a graph context to assign polarity to new opinion entities. Most of the previous methods only utilized labeled data (seeds) to predict such polarities [e.g. 28, 11], or used synonym, antonym, or hyponym relations available in dictionaries to construct a high quality graph [10, 24, 22, 17]. In contrast, we make use of both labeled and unlabeled data to predict the polarities, and construct the graph from the *polarity association* between the words. Our polarity inference method is more feasible in the Web context where the data contains many non-standard entities and the above dictionary-based relations are not available. We formulate the polarity inference task as a semi-supervised learning task in the graph context where the seeds and opinion entities are modeled as the graph nodes and the aim is to optimize the polarity of new opinion entities based on the graph connectivity information. Similar to [28, 4, 29] we use co-occurrence as the polarity association measure. This is because previous research shows that opinion words with opposite orientation tend not to co-occur in the same context, while opinion words with similar orientation tend to co-occur [4].

To summarize, the contributions of this paper are as follows:

- We propose a principled approach to mine new opinion words in the cQA context. Our approach can be used as a feature selection method for mining sentiment terminology.
- We present a novel adaptation of graph-based semi-supervised learning methods to learn the polarity of new opinion entities in the graph context.
- Our opinion lexicon contains non-standard entities such as urban opinion words/phrases, slang and misspellings etc that cannot be found in the current popular opinion lexicons.

The experiments show that our polarity inference method significantly improves the performance of the two baselines by 21.16% and 2.78% in F1 score. We also investigate the effect of unlabeled data in polarity inference and show that the above improvement comes from the optimization framework and learning from unlabeled data. In addition, the sentiment classification experiments show that our method is effective in detecting new opinion entities and constructing a high quality cQA opinion lexicon. Our best performing method significantly improves the performance of the baseline (seeds) by 5.89% in F1 score.

The rest of this paper is organized as follows. Section 2 surveys the related work. Section 3 gives an overview of our approach. Section 4 elaborates our method for mining new opinion entities and explains some linguistic considerations for this purpose. Section 5 describes our optimization framework for polarity inference. Section 6 reports the experimental settings and results on both polarity inference and sentiment classification tasks, and, finally, Section 7 concludes the paper and discusses future directions and plans.

2. RELATED WORK

As aforementioned, there are three approaches to opinion lexicon construction: manual, dictionary-based, and corpus-based approaches [19, 15].

As a dictionary-based approach for opinion lexicon construction, Hu and Liu [8] proposed to consider the synonyms and antonyms of seeds in WordNet as new opinion words. The synonyms and antonyms were accumulated in an opinion lexicon and the process was repeated until no new word could be added to the lexicon. Qiu et al. [21] used a similar method as [8], but their algorithm also exploits the relations between sentiment words and product features that the sentiment words modify. Kamps et al. [10] used WordNet to construct a graph of synonyms. They used the shortest paths from a given word to the seeds "*good*" and "*bad*" to determine the polarity of the word. They reported that in WordNet synonymy graph, the words "*good*" and "*bad*" themselves are quite close to each other and concluded that the shortest path in such a graph could be noisy. Rao and Ravichandran [22] used synonym and hyponym of seeds to construct the graph and utilized the label propagation technique proposed in [5] to propagate the polarity labels in the graph.

In contrast to dictionary-based approaches, corpus-based approaches use synthetic or co-occurrence patterns in the text. As a corpus-based approach, Hatzivassiloglou and McKeown [7] and Kanayama and Nasukawa [11] used seed opinion adjectives with conjunctions like "*and*", "*or*", "*but*", "*either-or*", and "*neither-nor*" to find more seeds. For example, "*and*" was used as an evidence of the same polarity ("*cheap and comfortable*"). So, if we know the polarity of one of the words in a conjunctive expression, we can deduce the polarity of the other word using the above clues. Kanayama and Nasukawa [11] further expanded the above heuristics to consider the proximity between the sentences in reviews based on the assumption that the same opinion orientation is usually expressed in a few consecutive sentences. The conjunction-based rules have been used in many research works as an aid to help developing opinion lexicons [26, 20].

Turney [28] and Turney and Littman [29] proposed to determine the polarity of a word/phrase by comparing whether it has a greater tendency to co-occur with positive opinion words (e.g. "*excellent*") or negative opinion words (e.g. "*poor*"). In particular, given a word w, they determined the polarity of w as the point-wise mutual information (PMI) between w and a fixed set of positive words minus the PMI between w and a fixed set of negative words. This approach is simple and feasible, but it does not guarantee that two highly co-related opinion words will be assigned the same polarity. In this paper, we utilize this approach as a feature selection method for mining opinion terminology and improve it by utilizing unlabeled data in an optimization framework.

Constructing opinion lexicons from the web content has been studied previously in [18] and [30]. Kaji and Kitsuregawa [18] focused on Japanese text and proposed a method to construct an opinion lexicon that only contains adjective phrases. They utilized seeds and HTML structural clues (such as *bulleted lists* and *tables*) to first extract opinion sentences from web pages. They then used a syntactic parser to extract opinion adjective phrases from the sentences. The polarity of a phrase was then determined using Turney's method [28]. In contrast, our research focus is on extracting any type of opinion entities from the cQA context where the only available information is the question threads.

Velikovich et al. [30] proposed a Graph Propagation (GP) technique to perform polarity inference in the graph context. They considered word n-grams as the nodes of a graph and weighted edges based on the cosine similarity between the context features of their nodes (extracted from Web n-grams for each node). They computed both positive and negative scores for each unlabeled node based on the maximum weighted paths between the node and all seeds. The polarity of the unlabeled node was then computed based on Turney's method, i.e. the difference between the two positive and negative scores. We show that our polarity inference approach better utilizes the unlabeled nodes by constructing a *smooth* polarity graph and outperforms the GP method in the polarity inference task.

3. OVERVIEW OF OUR APPROACH

This section presents an overview of our approach for constructing the cQA opinion lexicon. We construct the lexicon in two steps: (1) mining candidate opinion entities, and (2) inferring the polarity of the entities.

Step 1: We first extract a set of candidate opinion entities using seeds (the words with already-known polarity). Having two classes of positive and negative seeds, we extract entities (words or phrases) that frequently co-occur with one class (e.g. positive seeds) and rarely with its opposite class (e.g. negative seeds). We expect these entities to be rich in sentiment. We refer to such entities as *Significant Entities* (SEs) and consider them as candidate opinion entities. For instance "*cooool place*" and "*recommend*" are SE because they frequently co-occur with seeds like *fun, favorite etc* and rarely with *bad, terrible etc.* However, the entity "*to go*" (semi) equally co-occurs with both positive and negative seeds and cannot be a SE.

Step 2: In the next step, we construct a *polarity graph* from the seeds and the extracted SEs as depicted in Figure 1. In this Figure, the '+' and '-' nodes are labeled nodes (positive and negative seeds respectively), and the '?' nodes are SEs or unlabeled nodes. Each SE node is attached to a corresponding d-node (the black nodes) that contains an initial polarity prediction for the SE. The initial predictions are optional. We explain d-node prediction in Section 5.3. The solid edges in the graph reflect the *polarity association* between the nodes. The weight of such edges is computed as a function of the co-occurrence between their corresponding nodes. In our polarity graph, we restrict such edges to happen only between SEs and seeds, and any two seeds with the same polarity. This prevents the opposite seeds from directly propagating their labels through each other. Once the graph is constructed, the polarity inference problem can be best modeled as a semi-supervised learning task in the graph context where the labeled nodes are the seeds and the unlabeled nodes are SEs and the aim is to optimize the polarity of SEs based on the graph connectivity information. We treat the SEs with sufficiently high confidence as new opinion entities and add them to the cQA opinion lexicon.

The above two Steps construct the polarity graph without using any dictionary or dictionary-based relations between the nodes. As such, our method is more feasible in the Web context where

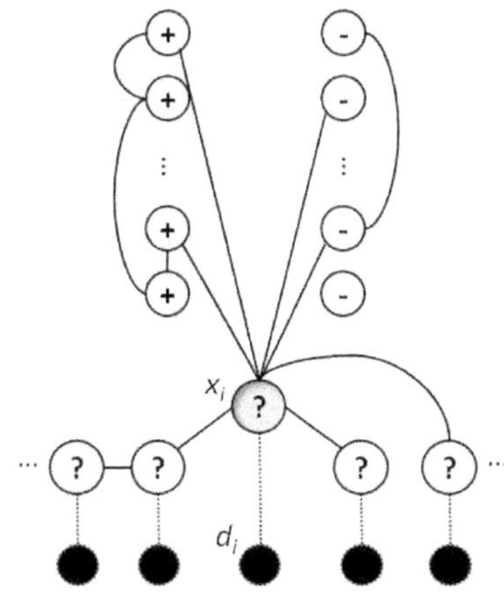

Figure 1. The connectivity information available in the polarity graph. '+' and '-' indicate positive and negative seeds respectively, '?' indicates SEs, and the black nodes are the initial polarity predictions for SEs.

such relations are generally not available among many non-standard entities.

4. MINING SIGNIFICANT ENTITIES

In this section, we aim to extract significant entities (SEs) and treat them as candidate opinion entities. We first explain some linguistic considerations and then describe our method for mining SEs.

4.1 Linguistic Considerations

We first utilize three sources of easy-to-collect information as seeds. These sources provide high quality seeds that have high confidence (precision) but low coverage (recall) in sentiment:

- **General Purpose Opinion Lexicons**: We consider those opinion words as seeds that are either labeled as strong in the General Inquirer [25] or subjectivity lexicon [33], or have positive or negative score of one in SentiWordNet [24]. For SentiWordNet, we only consider the first sense of the words.
- **Linguistic Rules**: As we mentioned before, previous research designed linguistic rules to detect more opinion words. For example, the affixes "*dis*" and "*mis*" were used as evidences for opposite polarities (*honest* ↔ *dishonest, fortune* ↔ *misfortune*). We use the above seeds and linguistic rules of [17] to find more high quality seeds.
- **WordNet Similarity**: We extract the synonym and antonym of each seed from WordNet and consider them as seeds too. The synonyms will be assigned the same polarity as their corresponding seeds, while the antonyms will receive the opposite polarity. We do not repeat this process because we want to ensure the high confidence (precision) of seeds.

The above sources provide an initial set of seeds. We only consider the seeds that occur more than once in our development corpus. These seeds will then be used to mine the significant entities.

In addition we found that *Negations* and *Disjunctive Clauses* are important factors to appropriately relate entities to seeds. For example, if a seed is negated, its context words tend to co-occur with the seed's antonym but not the seed itself. Sub-sentences of a disjunctive clause[5] also have opposite polarities. We explain below the way we handle negations and disjunctive clauses in detail:

Negations: Negation words/phrases such as *not*, *none*, *cannot*, *barely*, *lack of*, and *never* etc reverse the sentiment of the seed words. Parser toolkits are useful resources to detect negations and their dependencies in the text. We consider the *clause* that contains a negation word as the scope of the negation. However, because of the weak grammar and the presence of high amount of short-form texts in cQA data, we designed some manual rules to better tackle the negation. We also consider cases that the negation word is not negating the seeds such as "*not only ... but also ...*", "*last but not least ...*" etc. In total we compiled 36 negation words and rules.

Disjunctive Clauses: We consider disjunctions like *but*, *though*, *although*, *despite*, *in spite of*, *except for*, *except that* etc to relate the entities and seeds. Consider an opinion sentence with two clauses connected by the disjunction "*but*", such as "*CLAUSE1, but CLAUSE2*" where *CLAUSE1* contains the seed word *s*. These two clauses should have opposite sentiments because of the disjunction "*but*". Therefore, we can say that the entities of *CLAUSE2* co-occur with the antonym of *s* instead of *s*. For example given the sentence: "*I think it's stylish to hang artworks on walls, but nowadays it's kind of tacky to hang up posters*!" with the word "*stylish*" as its seed, the entities in the clause after "*but*" such as "*tacky*", "*it's kind of tacky*", *etc* should be related to the antonym of "*stylish*". We also designed a few manual rules to better detect and handle disjunctive clauses. We utilize Stanford toolkit to extract clauses and split questions and answers into sentences.

4.2 Significant Entity Extraction

As aforementioned, our assumption is that the entities that frequently co-occur with positive seeds and rarely (or never) with negative seeds are highly likely to be positive. Similarly, the entities that frequently co-occur with negative seeds and rarely (or never) with positive seeds are highly likely to be negative [28, 29, 30, 18].

We use Point-wise Mutual Information (PMI) as the measure of co-occurrence. PMI between two words *v* and *w* is defined as follows:

$$PMI(v,w) = log(\frac{P(v \,\&\, w)}{P(v)P(w)}) = log(\frac{Count(v \,\&\, w)M}{Count(v)Count(w)}) \quad (1)$$

where $P(v \,\&\, w)$ is the probability that the two words co-occur in the same context (e.g., a sentence or several consecutive sentences), and $P(v)$ and $P(w)$ are the probability of *v* and *w* occurring in the entire corpus respectively, and *M* is a constant (e.g. the number of terms in the corpus). PMI is a good measure to associate the words that frequently co-occur in the same context [29, 35].

We define an entity as any word *N-grams* (N = 1, 2, or 3) extracted from the cQA questions or their answers. Our aim is to use seeds to find SEs. For this purpose, for each seed s_i, we extract all the entities that occur in the context of s_i, compute their PMI with respect to s_i, and accumulate them in set N_{s_i} as the set of neighboring entities of s_i.

We consider the sentence that contains s_i and its previous sentence as the context of s_i. It is necessary to consider a set of consecutive sentences as the context of the seed words for the following 2 reasons: (1) many new opinion entities do not co-occur with any seed word at the sentence level, and (2) the same opinion orientation is usually expressed in a few consecutive sentences [11]. So we can expect the same orientation among the entities of consecutive sentences. However, we limit the above requirement as follows: (1) if the previous sentence contains a seed with opposite polarity with s_i, we do not consider that sentence in the context of s_i; and (2) if the current sentence contains two seeds with opposite polarities, we only consider the previous sentence as the context of the seed that appears first.

We create the entity pool *N* from the sets of neighboring entities as follows:

$$N = \cup_{\forall i} N_{s_i} \quad (2)$$

We then compute an *initial polarity score* for each entity $e_k \in N$. This score is computed as a function of entity's co-occurrence with positive and negative seeds as follows:

$$InitPScore_{e_k} = \sum_{s_i \in Pos} PMI(s_i, e_k) - \sum_{s_j \in Neg} PMI(s_j, e_k) \quad (3)$$

where *Pos* is the set of positive seeds and *Neg* is the set of negative seeds. In Equation (3), we only consider positive PMI values because it reflects positive co-relation between entities and seeds. The above Equation measures the tendency of the entities towards positive or negative classes of seeds. In the above Equation, $|InitPScore_{e_k}|$ will be high for entities that are highly associated with only one of the positive or negative classes. We first normalize the *InitPScore*s and then sort the entities in descending order of the *absolute* values of their *InitPScore*s. We then pick the *Top K* entities from this set and consider them as significant entities. These SEs are expected to be rich in sentiment.

5. POLARITY INFERENCE

The SEs and seeds provide a rich source of relationships. Such information can be readily encoded as a graph where the presence of an edge represents a relationship between the nodes (here polarity association) and the weight of the edge represents the strength of the relationship. This information can help to learn the polarity of candidate opinion entities when only a few seeds are present.

Formally, the polarity inference problem can be described as follows:

Assume that there exist *n* instances $\{x_1, \ldots, x_n\}$ in the dataset $\mathcal{X}$. Let the first *l* instances $\mathcal{X}^l = \{x_1, \ldots, x_l\}$ be the labeled data (seeds) and the remaining instance $\mathcal{X}^u = \{x_{l+1}, \ldots, x_n\}$ be the unlabeled data (the SEs). Let y_i indicates the label (polarity score) of x_i; with y_i=+1 for positive seeds and y_i=-1 for the negative seeds. The aim is to find a real-valued function $f: x \rightarrow \mathbb{R}$ that gives a continuous polarity score $f(x)$ to entity *x*. The value of function *f* on the labeled data x_i is the same as its initial label y_i, i.e. $f(x_i) = y_i$ for $i = 1, \ldots, l$. The problem is then to determine the polarity of the unlabeled nodes, i.e. $f(x_j), j = l+1, \ldots, n$.

[5] A disjunctive clause contains two sub-sentences connected by a disjunction (e.g. *but*).

This problem can best be modeled as a semi-supervised learning task in the graph context where the connectivity information of the graph can be utilized to estimate the polarity scores for the unlabeled data. We first construct the polarity graph from the SEs and seeds and then define the optimization criteria.

5.1 Polarity Graph Construction

Let G=(V, E) be an undirected edge-weighted graph defined on the dataset $\mathcal{X}$ with nodes V corresponding to the n entities of $\mathcal{X}$, and edges E that are weighted by an $n \times n$ symmetric weight matrix **W**. The weight of the edge $(v_i, v_j) \in E$, w_{ij}, indicates the polarity association between the nodes v_i and v_j and is obtained from PMI(v_i, v_j) as defined in Equation (1). Formally, we construct G as follows:

- Any $x_j \in \mathcal{X}^u$ is connected to all the $\mathcal{X}^u$ and $\mathcal{X}^l$ nodes that have positive PMI with x_j, and
- Any $x_i \in \mathcal{X}^l$ is connected to all the $\mathcal{X}^l$ nodes that have the same polarity and positive PMI with x_i .

If there is no edge between two nodes its corresponding weight is deemed to be 0. Note that the PMI function is a *symmetric function*, i.e. PMI (a, b) = PMI (b, a). The above configuration results in a large graph in which each unlabeled nodes (SE) is potentially connected to several labeled nodes and other unlabeled nodes through different edges/paths (see Figure 1).

Furthermore, we assume that, we have an initial polarity prediction (also called *dongle* node [34]) for each unlabeled node, i.e. $f(x_i) = \acute{y}_i$ for $i=l+1 \ldots n$. Each d-node is connected to its corresponding unlabeled node with the edge weight of 1 and acts as prior knowledge for the semi-supervised learning framework. $\acute{y}_i$ is set to zero when there is no initial prediction. We explain how to estimate the value of d-nodes in section 5.3.

5.2 Optimization Framework

The basic idea of the semi-supervised learning algorithms in the graph context is that the function $f(x)$ should be *smooth* with respect to the graph [5, 34, 31]. $f(x)$ is not smooth with respect to the graph if there is a heavy edge with weight w_{ij} between two nodes x_i and x_j, and the difference between $f(x_i)$ and $f(x_j)$ is large, i.e. $w_{ij}\,(f(x_i) - f(x_j))^2$ is large. Therefore, the aim of the optimization framework is to minimize the above value over all the edges in the polarity graph.

Assuming that the d-nodes in Figure 1 are connected to their corresponding unlabeled nodes with the weight of 1, our aim is to minimize the following *energy* function:

$$E(f) = \gamma \sum_{x_i \in \mathcal{X}^u} (f(x_i) - \acute{y}_i)^2 + (1-\gamma) \sum_{x_i \in \mathcal{X}^u} \left(\sum_{x_j \in Adj^l(x_i)} \alpha w_{ij} \left(f(x_i) - f(x_j)\right)^2 + \sum_{x_j \in Adj^u(x_i)} (1-\alpha) w_{ij} (f(x_i) - f(x_j))^2 \right) \tag{4}$$

where $Adj^l(x_i)$ and $Adj^u(x_i)$ are the sets of x_i's adjacent labeled and unlabeled nodes respectively, the parameter $\gamma \in [0,1]$ represents the influence of each source of learning (dongle node vs. adjacent nodes) on the polarity of x_i, and the coefficient $\alpha \in [0,1]$ controls the effect of labeled and unlabeled nodes on the polarity of the unlabeled node x_i. Equation (4) represents the requirements that for each unlabeled node $x_i \in \mathcal{X}^u$, we want $f(x_i)$ to be consistent with its d-node, and its neighbors. The greater values of α reduce the effect of the adjacent unlabeled nodes on the polarity of x_i, while smaller values of α increase such effects. Since the paths from unlabeled nodes could potentially be noisy, we set $\alpha \geq 0.5$ to produce better performance.

The optimization problem can be defined as follows:

$$\hat{f} = argmin_f\, E(f) \tag{5}$$

To find a closed-form solution to the above Equation, we define an $n \times n$ matrix $\boldsymbol{T}$ as follows:

$$T_{ij} = \begin{cases} 0, & i \in L, j \in L \\ \alpha(1-\gamma) w_{ij}, & i \in L, j \in U \\ \alpha(1-\gamma) w_{ij}, & i \in U, j \in L \\ 2(1-\alpha)(1-\gamma) w_{ij}, & i \in U, j \in U \end{cases} \tag{6}$$

where L= 1…l and U= l+1…n are the labeled and unlabeled node indices respectively. Let $\boldsymbol{D}$ be a diagonal matrix derived from $\boldsymbol{T}$ as follows:

$$D_{ii} = \sum_{j=l}^{n} T_{ij} \tag{7}$$

Let $\boldsymbol{\Omega} = \boldsymbol{D} - \boldsymbol{T}$ be the $n \times n$ *graph Laplacian* matrix [16], $\boldsymbol{f} = [f(x_1), \ldots, f(x_n)]^T$, and $\boldsymbol{y} = [y_1, \ldots, y_l, \acute{y}_{l+1}, \ldots, \acute{y}_n]^T$ where $f(x_i) = y_i$ for the labeled nodes (i=1…l), and $\acute{y}_j$ is the value of the dongle nodes for the unlabeled nodes (j=l+1…n). We can rewrite Equation (4) as follows where $\boldsymbol{I}$ is the $n \times n$ identity matrix (see Appendix A for the derivations):

$$E(f) = \gamma (\boldsymbol{f} - \boldsymbol{y})^T \boldsymbol{I}\, (\boldsymbol{f} - \boldsymbol{y}) + \boldsymbol{f}^T \boldsymbol{\Omega}\, \boldsymbol{f} \tag{8}$$

The minimum energy function $\hat{\boldsymbol{f}}$ of the above quadratic function can be obtained as follows:

$$\partial E(f) \big/ \partial f = 0 \Rightarrow \hat{\boldsymbol{f}} = \gamma\, (\gamma \boldsymbol{I} + \boldsymbol{\Omega})^{-1} \boldsymbol{y} \tag{9}$$

Because $\boldsymbol{f}^T \boldsymbol{\Omega}\, \boldsymbol{f} > 0$, $\boldsymbol{\Omega}$ is a symmetric and positive semi-definite matrix and consequently the above solution is the unique answer to our optimization problem. We normalize this vector into [-1, 1] range.

5.3 Polarity Prediction for Dongle Nodes

Given an unlabeled node, $x_i \in \mathcal{X}^u$, we utilize two methods to predict the polarity value of its corresponding d-node, d_i. The first intuitive method is based on Equation (3) that computes an initial polarity prediction for the unlabeled nodes. We refer to this prediction as CO in the experiments.

As the second prediction method, we make use of the idea proposed in [30]. In particular, we compute a positive and a negative score for each unlabeled node $x_i \in \mathcal{X}^u$. The positive score is computed as the sum over the maximum weighted path from every positive labeled node to x_i. Similarly, the negative score is computed as the sum over the maximum weighted path from every negative labeled node to x_i. The value of the corresponding d-node is then computed as the difference between the two positive and negative scores. Mathematically, for each node $x_i \in \mathcal{X}^u$, we compute the value of its d-node as follows:

$$d_i = \frac{1}{Z}\left(\sum_{x_j \in Pos} S_{ij} - \varphi \sum_{x_k \in Neg} S_{ik}\right) \quad (10)$$

where *Pos* and *Neg* are the positive and negative labeled nodes in $\mathcal{X}^l$ respectively, Z is a normalization term, S_{ij} is the value of the maximum weighted path from x_i to x_j, and φ is a constant value that accounts for the difference in the overall mass of positive and negative flow in the graph, and is computed as follows:

$$\varphi = \sum_{x_i \in \mathcal{X}^u} \sum_{x_j \in Pos} S_{ij} \Big/ \sum_{x_i \in \mathcal{X}^u} \sum_{x_j \in Neg} S_{ij} \quad (11)$$

Equation (10) assigns high positive (negative) scores to unlabeled nodes that are connected to multiple positive (negative) labeled nodes through short yet highly weighted paths [30]. If x_i has higher positive score than negative score, then its initial guess will be positive, i.e. $d_i > 0$; and $d_i < 0$ otherwise. We refer to this prediction as GP in the experiments.

Our optimization framework improves upon these two baselines by: (1) imposing the smoothness restriction over the polarity graph (see Section 4.2.), and (2) preventing label propagation through seeds with opposite polarities.

6. EXPERIMENTS

In this Section we evaluate our approach from two perspectives:

Polarity Inference: We first evaluate the ability of the optimization framework in inferring the polarity of opinion words (polarity inference). We utilize the seed opinion words for this purpose. We assume that part of the seed dataset is unlabeled and evaluate the performance of our optimization framework in predicting the correct label of such seeds.

Sentiment Classification: We then evaluate the quality of the extracted new opinion entities. For this purpose, similar to [30, 28], we consider a word-matching-based review classification task as the measure of evaluation. We expect opinion entities with higher quality result in higher performance of review classification

6.1 Data

We used the newly released Yahoo! Webscope dataset[6] as the development dataset for mining opinion entities. This dataset is collected from Yahoo! Answers cQA archives (as of 10/25/2007). We considered each question and each answer as an individual document and performed the experiments on the *Food* domain. The *Food* domain of this collection contains 244K documents and 0.5M sentences. We use these documents to detect SEs and extract co-occurrence information.

From the seed words that we compiled in Section 4.1, we only kept the seeds that occur more than once in the cQA corpus. In this way, we obtained more than 2,500 seeds (almost balanced on positive and negative categories).

For the purpose of the second evaluation, we used a restaurant review dataset crawled from *newyork.citysearch.com*[7]. In this dataset, each review has a rating star scaling from 1 (highly negative) to 5 (highly positive). We used a balanced set of positive and negative reviews for the evaluation purpose (7000 on positive and 7000 on negative reviews).

All the experiments in the subsequent Sections were performed through 10-fold cross validation and the two-tailed paired t-test $p < 0.01$ was used for significance testing. Throughout this Section, we use the asterisk mark (*) to indicate significant improvement over the best performing baseline.

6.2 Polarity Inference Performance

We use the seed dataset as the ground-truth to evaluate the performance of our optimization framework in polarity inference. For this purpose, we consider part of the seed dataset as the test data (unlabeled nodes) and the rest of the seeds as training data (labeled nodes), and evaluate the performance of the optimization framework in predicting the polarity of the unlabeled nodes. We use the following measures for the evaluation:

$$Precision = \frac{N_{correct}}{N_{tagged}}$$

$$Recall = \frac{N_{correct}}{N_{unlabeled}}$$

$$F1 = \frac{2 * Precision * Recall}{Precision + Recall}$$

where $N_{correct}$ is the number of unlabeled nodes that are assigned the correct polarities (either positive or negative), N_{tagged} is the number of unlabeled nodes that are assigned non-zero scores, and $N_{unlabeled}$ is the total number of unlabeled nodes.

We use 80% of the seed dataset for training and the rest for testing. In addition, we use 10% of the training set to tune the parameter α. For this purpose, we employ a greed search in the [0.1, 1] range with the greed step of 0.1. We analyze the effect of this parameter on the performance of polarity inference in the next Section. In addition, We treat the dongle nodes as other nodes in the graph and emperically set the value of γ to 0.5[8].

Table 1 presents the results. CO indicates the results when we use the co-occurrence information (Equation 3) to predict the polarity labels of test data. As Table 1 shows, CO produces a low F1 performance of 47.89%. This poor performance is due to the fact that CO ignores the co-occurrence among the unlabeled data. However, we should mention that the performance of CO highly depends on the amount of raw text provided for computing the co-occurrence information.

As Table 1 shows, GP produces a higher F1 performance than CO

[6] http://webscope.sandbox.yahoo.com/

[7] The restaurant review dataset has been obtained from http://www.cs.cmu.edu/~mehrbod/RR/.

[8] We also experimented with some other values of γ and observed that giving more weight to adjacent nodes improves the performance when there is no prediction available for the d-nodes.

Table 1. Performance of Polarity Assignment for Different Methods

Methods	Precision	Recall	F1
CO	47.89	47.89	47.89
GP	66.27	66.27	66.27
OPT, α:.5	69.45	65.06	**67.19**[*]
OPT-CO, α:.7	65.59	61.45	63.45
OPT-GP, α:.7	71.38	66.87	**69.05**[*]

(66.27% vs. 47.89%). This difference is significant and stems from GP's utilization of both edges (direct co-occurrence) and paths (indirect co-occurrence) of the polarity graph. We consider GP and CO as the baselines.

The results of the optimization framework are shown in the last three rows of Table 1. OPT indicates the result when there is no initial predictions for the unlabeled nodes, i.e. $\acute{y}_i = 0$ for $i=l+1 \ldots n$. As it is shown, it outperforms the CO and GP methods significantly and produces a F1 performance of 67.19%. OPT, in contrast to CO or GP, optimizes the polarity of unlabeled nodes by imposing the smoothness restriction on the polarity graph. As Table 1 shows, the value of α is 0.5 for OPT. This suggests that giving the same contribution to both labeled and unlabeled nodes produces a higher significant performance than both CO and GP when no initial prediction is available.

OPT-CO indicates the result when we use CO as the initial predictions for the unlabeled nodes. As it is shown in Table 1, this prediction decreases the F1 performance of OPT from 67.19% to 63.45%. This reduction is expected because the optimization framework has to optimize toward the polarity of both adjacent and d-nodes. Since CO produces poor performance in predicting the polarity of d-nodes, adding it to OPT reduces OPTS's performance.

Finally, OPT-GP gives the result when we use GP (see Equation 15) as the initial predictions for the unlabeled nodes. It outperforms both CO and GP by 21.16% and 2.78% in F1 score and the improvements are significant. OPT-GP also outperforms OPT by 1.86%. This result suggests that when we have better initial predictions, the performance of the optimization framework increases. Here the value of parameter α is set to 0.7 which emphasizes the important role of the labeled data (seeds) in the learning process. We study the effect of this parameter in the next Section.

6.2.1 Parameter Analysis

In this section we study the effect of parameter α on our optimization framework. As we mentioned before, this parameter has been tuned over 10% of the training data by a greed search in the [0.1, 1] range. We plot the F1 performance of different approaches (discussed in Table 1) on the test set with respect to parameter α. Note that in case of OPT the value of the d-nodes is 0 and therefore the parameter α has to be greater than 0, otherwise $f(x_i) = 0$ for $i=l+1 \ldots n$ (See Equation 4).

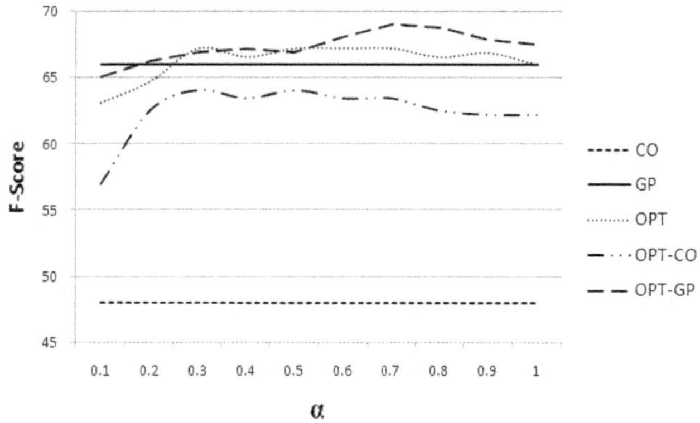

Figure 2. The Effect of α on Polarity Inference

The results are shown in Figure 2. As it is clear, the best performance is obtained when we use the optimization framework in conjunction with the GP predictions, OPT-GP, and the worst performance belongs to CO. In addition, both OPT and OPT-GP perform better than both baselines for any ≥ 0.3 .

As expected, learning the predictions from GP, i.e. OPT-GP, improves the performance of OPT for all the values of α except when $\alpha = 0.3$ and $\alpha = 0.5$ where the performance of OPT is slightly higher than OPT-GP. This small reduction could be because of the noise in the unlabeled data. Figure 2 also shows that OPT and OPT-GP outperform OPT-CO independent from the value of α.

As expected, the smaller values of α produce lower performances. This shows that the labeled data play a crutial role in the learning process. However, Figure 2 shows that, to a lesser extent, learning from unlabeled data is also important. This is because when the optimization framework only learns from the labeled data, i.e. when α=1, the performance of both OPT and OPT-GP decreases. This indicates the importance of the unlabeled data in the learning process.

6.3 Sentiment Classification Performance

The aim of SC is to assign a polarity label (positive or negative) to any given review. We expect that the performance of SC to be higher when we use an opinion lexicon with higher quality.

As the ground truth, we treated all the reviews with 1 or 2 stars as negative reviews, and the reviews with 4 or 5 stars as positive reviews. We obtained a total number of 14K reviews (balance on positive and negative classes) from the review dataset. To perform the SC experiments, we learned new opinion entities (SEs) from the cQA dataset and tested their SC performance on the 14K reviews.

We performed the word-matching-based SC as follows: given a review, the sentiment score of the review was computed as the sum of the polarity scores of the SEs that appear in the review. An overall positive sentiment score indicates a positive review; and negative otherwise. We also considered negations and disjunctive clauses as we explained in Section 4.1. Here we do not use any classifier in order to emphasize the quality of the lexicons. A higher performance can be obtained if we use an appropriate classifier.

We constructed separate polarity graphs for each value of N-Gram (N=1, 2, 3) and learned the *Top 1000* SEs that have sufficiently

Table 2. SC Performance on Positive Reviews

Lexicon	Precision	Recall	F1	imp
Seed_Lexicon	69.59	96.68	80.93	-
cQA_OPT	71.85	96.58	82.40*	+1.47
cQA_OPT-GP	72.34	96.59	**82.72***	+1.79

Table 3. SC Performance on Negative Reviews

Lexicon	Precision	Recall	F1	imp
Seed_Lexicon	97.36	42.88	59.54	-
cQA_OPT	96.57	56.16	71.02*	+11.5
cQA_OPT-GP	96.45	58.80	**73.06***	+13.5

Table 4. SC Performance Using on All the Reviews

Lexicon	Precision	Recall	F1	imp
Seed_Lexicon	76.28	69.78	72.89	-
cQA_OPT	79.32	76.37	77.82*	+4.93
cQA_OPT-GP	**79.90**	**77.70**	**78.78***	+5.89

high confidence, i.e. $|f(x_i)| \geq 0.5$, for each set[9]. We then stored all these SEs into a lexicon to perform SC. Here, we only perform the experiments with the OPT and OPT-GP methods as they are the best performing methods based on the results of the previous Section. All the other parameters are set as reported in the previous Section, i.e. $\gamma = 0.5$ and $\alpha = 0.5$ for OPT, and $\gamma = 0.5$ and $\alpha = 0.7$ for OPT-GP.

Tables 2-4 show the performance of SC using different opinion lexicons and for different types of reviews (positive, negative, and all reviews respectively). The *Seed_Lexicon* only contains the seeds, while the other lexicons, namely *cQA-OPT* and *cQA-OPT-GP*, contain the combination of seeds and SEs (mined from the cQA dataset) where OPT and OPT-GP were used for polarity inference respectively. The "*imp*" column shows the amount of F1 improvement over the *Seed_Lexicon.*

As Tables 2 and 3 show *Seed_Lexicon* produces a high F1 performance of 80.93% for the positive class, but a poor F1 performance of 59.54% for the negative class. We expected the *Seed_Lexicon* to have high precision but low recall for SC. But this is only the case for the negative class.

To find the reason, we count the number of times that seeds occur in positive and negative reviews and it turns out that the positive seeds occur more frequently than negative ones. This affects the performance of our word-matching-based sentiment classifier. Table 5 shows the statistics. The "*w negation*" column means we take into account the negation words/rules as well, i.e. a negated positive (negative) seed increases the count of negative (positive) seeds. The "*w/o negation*" column reports the statistics without considering negation rules/words.

[9] We observed the same trend of performances with different values of K. Due to space limitation we omit the related curve.

Table 5. Occurrences of Seeds in Reviews

	Pos Reviews		Neg Reviews	
	w negation	w/o negation	w negation	w/o negation
Pos Seeds	48,704	49,135	26,183	29,007
Neg Seeds	6,855	6,424	25,234	22,410
Pos/Neg Ratio	7.10	7.65	1.04	1.29

As Table 5 shows, the occurrence of positive seeds is much greater than the negative seeds in the positive reviews (7.10 and 7.65 times greater than with and without considering negation words/rules respectively)[10]. As such, the word-matching-based sentiment classifier is able to correctly label many of the positive reviews as positive. This justifies the high recall of *Seed_Lexicon* for the positive class (96.68%). On the other hand, we found that the occurrence of positive seeds is slightly higher than the negative seeds in the negative reviews (1.04 and 1.29 times greater respectively). This seems to indicate that people tend not to use many negative words even in negative reviews. This causes some of the negative reviews to be wrongly labeled as positive by the word-matching-based sentiment classifier. This in turn results in the relatively low precision of the *Seed_Lexicon* for the positive class (69.59%).

As shown in Table 5, the occurrence of positive seeds is slightly greater than the negative seeds in negative reviews (1.29 times greater). At the same time the occurrence of negation words/rules in negative reviews is greater than positive reviews. The above two indicators show that, in the negative reviews, users usually use negated positive seeds to express their negative opinions. This is consistent with the *positive encouragement principle* of critique, i.e. the shortcomings can be pointed out in a positive manner.

Table 2 and Table 3 show that the *cQA_OPT* and *cQA_OPT-GP* lexicons result in significant improvement over *Seed_Lexicon* for both positive and negative classes, with a greater improvement on the negative class.

Table 4 shows the overall SC performance on all the reviews. The results show that both cQA lexicons significantly outperform the *Seed_Lexicon.* Overall *cQA_OPT* results in 4.93% improvement over the *Seed_Lexicon* (77.82% vs. 72.89%) while the *cQA_OPT-GP* result in 5.89% improvement over the *Seed_Lexicon* (78.78% vs. 72.89%).

7. CONCLUSION

In this paper we focused on mining slang and urban opinion words and phrases from community-based question answering (cQA) archives. In the cQA context, such opinion entities can be used for discriminating opinion from factual questions, and answer summarization. The opinion entities are also useful for different tasks of sentiment analysis like review mining and sentiment classification. In this paper, we first utilized the opinion words with already known polarities (seeds) to extract a set of candidate opinion entities (or significant entities) from the community questions. We then formulated the polarity inference

[10] The number of negation words is 4,777 and 13,040 in positive and negative reviews respectively.

task as a semi-supervised learning task in the graph context where the seeds and significant entities were modeled as the graph nodes. The graph connectivity information was then used to infer the polarity of significant entities. Our method is able to utilize both labeled and unlabeled data to learn the polarity of the entities and do not require dictionary-based relations (such as *synonym*, *antonym*, or *hyponym*) to construct the graph. We experimentally showed that our approach is effective in detecting new opinion entities and inferring their polarities. Furthermore, we showed that learning from both labeled and unlabeled data play a crucial role in inferring the polarity of candidate opinion entities.

In the future we aim to improve the performance of our approach and utilize the constructed lexicon for opinion question analysis in the context of community question services.

8. REFERENCES

[1] Agichtein, E., Y. Liu, et al. (2009). "Modeling information-seeker satisfaction in community question answering." ACM Trans. Knowl. Discov. Data 3(2): 1-27.

[2] Balahur, A., E. Boldrini, et al. (2009). Opinion and generic question answering systems: a performance analysis. In Proceedings of the ACL-IJCNLP 2009.

[3] Balahur, A., E. Boldrini, et al. (2009). Towards the definition of requirements for mixed fact and opinion question answering systems. Proceeding of the 1st international CIKM workshop on Topic-sentiment analysis for mass opinion. Hong Kong, China, ACM: 25-28.

[4] Gamon, M. and A. Aue (2005). Automatic identification of sentiment vocabulary: exploiting low association with known sentiment terms. Proceedings of the ACL Workshop on Feature Engineering for Machine Learning in Natural Language Processing. Ann Arbor, Michigan, Association for Computational Linguistics: 57-64.

[5] Ghahramani, X. Z. a. Z. (2002). Learning from labeled and unlabeled data with label propagation. Technical Report CMU-CALD-02-107, Carnegie Mellon University.

[6] Hassan, A. and D. Radev (2010). Identifying text polarity using random walks. Proceedings of the 48th Annual Meeting of the Association for Computational Linguistics. Uppsala, Sweden, Association for Computational Linguistics: 395-403.

[7] Hatzivassiloglou, V. and K. R. McKeown (1997). Predicting the semantic orientation of adjectives. Proceedings of the 35th Annual Meeting of the Association for Computational Linguistics and Eighth Conference of the European Chapter of the Association for Computational Linguistics. Madrid, Spain, Association for Computational Linguistics: 174-181.

[8] Hu, M. and B. Liu (2004). Mining and summarizing customer reviews. Proceedings of the tenth ACM SIGKDD international conference on Knowledge discovery and data mining. Seattle, WA, USA, ACM: 168-177.

[9] Iadh Ounis, M. d. R., Craig Macdonald, Gilad Mishne, and Ian Soboroff (2006). Overview of the TREC 2006 blog track. Proceedings of the 15th Text Retrieval Conference (TREC).

[10] Jaap Kamps, M. M., Robert J. Mokken, and Maarten de Rijke (2004). Using wordnet to measure semantic orientation of adjectives. Proceedings of the 4th International Conference on Language Resources and Evaluation (LREC 2004). IV: 1115-1118.

[11] Kanayama, H. and T. Nasukawa (2006). Fully automatic lexicon expansion for domain-oriented sentiment analysis. Proceedings of the 2006 Conference on Empirical Methods in Natural Language Processing. Sydney, Australia, Association for Computational Linguistics: 355-363.

[12] Kim, S.-M. and E. Hovy (2004). Determining the sentiment of opinions. Proceedings of the 20th international conference on Computational Linguistics. Geneva, Switzerland, Association for Computational Linguistics: 1367.

[13] Li, B., Y. Liu, et al. (2008). Exploring question subjectivity prediction in community QA. Proceedings of the 31st annual international ACM SIGIR conference on Research and development in information retrieval. Singapore, Singapore, ACM: 735-736.

[14] Li, F., Y. Tang, et al. (2009). Answering opinion questions with random walks on graphs. Proceedings of the Joint Conference of the 47th Annual Meeting of the ACL and the 4th International Joint Conference on Natural Language Processing of the AFNLP: Volume 2 - Volume 2. Suntec, Singapore, Association for Computational Linguistics: 737-745.

[15] Liu, B. (2010). Sentiment Analysis and Subjectivity, Handbook of Natural Language Processing, Second Edition.

[16] Luxburg, U. (2007). "A tutorial on spectral clustering." Statistics and Computing 17(4): 395-416.

[17] Mohammad, S., C. Dunne, et al. (2009). Generating high-coverage semantic orientation lexicons from overtly marked words and a thesaurus. Proceedings of the 2009 Conference on Empirical Methods in Natural Language Processing: Volume 2 - Volume 2. Singapore, Association for Computational Linguistics: 599-608.

[18] Nobuhiro Kaji , M. K. (2007). Building Lexicon for Sentiment Analysis from Massive Collection of HTML Documents Proceedings of the 2007 Joint Conference on Empirical Methods in Natural Language Processing and Computational Natural Language Learning (EMNLP-CoNLL).

[19] Pang, B. and L. Lee (2008). "Opinion Mining and Sentiment Analysis." Found. Trends Inf. Retr. 2(1-2): 1-135.

[20] Popescu, A.-M. and O. Etzioni (2005). Extracting product features and opinions from reviews. Proceedings of the conference on Human Language Technology and Empirical Methods in Natural Language Processing. Vancouver, British Columbia, Canada, Association for Computational Linguistics: 339-346.

[21] Qiu, G., B. Liu, et al. (2009). Expanding domain sentiment lexicon through double propagation. Proceedings of the 21st international jont conference on Artifical intelligence. Pasadena, California, USA, Morgan Kaufmann Publishers Inc.: 1199-1204.

[22] Rao, D. and D. Ravichandran (2009). Semi-supervised polarity lexicon induction. Proceedings of the 12th Conference of the European Chapter of the Association for Computational Linguistics. Athens, Greece, Association for Computational Linguistics: 675-682.

[23] Sakai, T., D. Ishikawa, et al. (2011). Using graded-relevance metrics for evaluating community QA answer selection. Proceedings of the fourth ACM international conference on

Web search and data mining. Hong Kong, China, ACM: 187-196.

[24] Sebastiani, A. E. a. F. (2006). SentiWordNet: A publicly available lexical resource for opinion mining. P. o. L. R. a. E. (LREC).

[25] Stone, P. J. and E. B. Hunt (1963). A computer approach to content analysis: studies using the General Inquirer system. Proceedings of the May 21-23, 1963, spring joint computer conference. Detroit, Michigan, ACM: 241-256.

[26] Takamura, H., T. Inui, et al. (2005). Extracting semantic orientations of words using spin model. Proceedings of the 43rd Annual Meeting on Association for Computational Linguistics. Ann Arbor, Michigan, Association for Computational Linguistics: 133-140.

[27] Tomasoni, M. and M. Huang (2010). Metadata-aware measures for answer summarization in community Question Answering. Proceedings of the 48th Annual Meeting of the Association for Computational Linguistics. Uppsala, Sweden, Association for Computational Linguistics: 760-769.

[28] Turney, P. D. (2002). Thumbs up or thumbs down?: semantic orientation applied to unsupervised classification of reviews. Proceedings of the 40th Annual Meeting on Association for Computational Linguistics. Philadelphia, Pennsylvania, Association for Computational Linguistics: 417-424.

[29] Turney, P. D. and M. L. Littman (2003). "Measuring praise and criticism: Inference of semantic orientation from association." ACM Trans. Inf. Syst. 21(4): 315-346.

[30] Velikovich, L., S. Blair-Goldensohn, et al. (2010). The viability of web-derived polarity lexicons. Human Language Technologies: The 2010 Annual Conference of the North American Chapter of the Association for Computational Linguistics. Los Angeles, California, Association for Computational Linguistics: 777-785.

[31] Wang, F. and C. Zhang (2006). Label propagation through linear neighborhoods. Proceedings of the 23rd international conference on Machine learning. Pittsburgh, Pennsylvania, ACM: 985-992.

[32] Wang, K., Z. Ming, et al. (2009). A syntactic tree matching approach to finding similar questions in community-based qa services. Proceedings of the 32nd international ACM SIGIR conference on Research and development in information retrieval. Boston, MA, USA, ACM: 187-194.

[33] Wilson, T., J. Wiebe, et al. (2005). Recognizing contextual polarity in phrase-level sentiment analysis. Proceedings of the conference on Human Language Technology and Empirical Methods in Natural Language Processing. Vancouver, British Columbia, Canada, Association for Computational Linguistics: 347-354.

[34] Zhu, X., Ghahramani, Z., & Lafferty, J. (2003). Semi-supervised learning using Gaussian fields and harmonic functions. The 20th International Conference on Machine Learning (ICML).

[35] Islam, A. and D. Inkpen (2008). "Semantic text similarity using corpus-based word similarity and string similarity." ACM Trans. Knowl. Discov. Data 2(2): 1-25.

.APPENDIX

A. DERIVATION FOR THE ENERGY FUNCTION *E(F)*

Since $f(x_i) = y_i \; \forall \; i = 1 \dots l$, clearly:

$$\gamma(\boldsymbol{f}-\boldsymbol{y})^T \boldsymbol{I}\,(\boldsymbol{f}-\boldsymbol{y}) = \gamma \sum_{i=l+1}^{n} (f_i - \acute{y}_i)^2$$

Now we need to show that:

$$\boldsymbol{f}^T \boldsymbol{\Omega}\, \boldsymbol{f} = (1-\gamma) \sum_{i=l+1}^{n} \left(\sum_{j=1}^{l} \alpha w_{ij} \left(f_i - f_j\right)^2 + \sum_{j=l+1}^{n} (1-\alpha) w_{ij} \left(f_i - f_j\right)^2 \right)$$

By definition$\boldsymbol{\Omega} = \boldsymbol{D} - \boldsymbol{T}$, so we have:

$$\boldsymbol{f}^T \boldsymbol{\Omega}\, \boldsymbol{f} = \boldsymbol{f}^T \mathbf{D}\, \boldsymbol{f} - \boldsymbol{f}^T \mathbf{T}\, \boldsymbol{f} = \sum_{i=1}^{n} d_{ii} f_i^2 - \sum_{i=1}^{n} \sum_{j=1}^{n} T_{ij} f_i f_j = \frac{1}{2}\left(\sum_{i=1}^{n} d_{ii} f_i^2 - 2 \sum_{i=1}^{n} \sum_{j=1}^{n} T_{ij} f_i f_j + \sum_{j=1}^{n} d_{jj} f_j^2 \right) = \frac{1}{2}\left(\sum_{i=1}^{n} \sum_{j=1}^{n} T_{ij} (f_i - f_j)^2 \right)$$

Considering the symmetric matrix T defined in Equation (6), we have:

$$\begin{aligned}
\boldsymbol{f}^T \boldsymbol{\Omega}\, \boldsymbol{f} &= \frac{1}{2}\left(\sum_{i=1}^{l} \sum_{j=l+1}^{n} T_{ij} \left(f_i - f_j\right)^2 \right) + \frac{1}{2}\left(\sum_{i=l+1}^{n} \sum_{j=1}^{l} T_{ij} \left(f_i - f_j\right)^2 \right) + \frac{1}{2}\left(\sum_{i=l+1}^{n} \sum_{j=l+1}^{n} T_{ij} \left(f_i - f_j\right)^2 \right) \\
&= \sum_{i=l+1}^{n} \sum_{j=1}^{l} T_{ij} \left(f_i - f_j\right)^2 + \frac{1}{2}\left(\sum_{i=l+1}^{n} \sum_{j=l+1}^{n} T_{ij} \left(f_i - f_j\right)^2 \right) \\
&= \sum_{i=l+1}^{n} \sum_{j=1}^{l} \alpha(1-\gamma) w_{ij} \left(f_i - f_j\right)^2 + \frac{1}{2}\left(\sum_{i=l+1}^{n} \sum_{j=l+1}^{n} 2(1-\alpha)(1-\gamma) w_{ij} \left(f_i - f_j\right)^2 \right) \\
&= (1-\gamma) \sum_{i=l+1}^{n} \left(\sum_{j=1}^{l} \alpha w_{ij} \left(f_i - f_j\right)^2 + \sum_{j=l+1}^{n} (1-\alpha) w_{ij} \left(f_i - f_j\right)^2 \right) \blacksquare
\end{aligned}$$

No Search Result Left Behind: Branching Behavior with Browser Tabs

Jeff Huang
University of Washington
Seattle, WA 98195
wsdm@jeffhuang.com

Thomas Lin
University of Washington
Seattle, WA 98195
tlin@cs.washington.edu

Ryen W. White
Microsoft Research
Redmond, WA 98052
ryenw@microsoft.com

ABSTRACT

Today's Web browsers allow users to open links in new windows or tabs. This action, which we call 'branching', is sometimes performed on search results when the user plans to eventually visit multiple results. We detect branching behavior on a large commercial search engine with a client-side script on the results page. Two-fifths of all users spawned new tabs on search results in the timeframe of our study; branching usage varied with different query types and vertical. Both branching and backtracking are viable methods for visiting multiple search results. To understand user search strategies, we treat multiple result clicks following a query as ordered events to understand user search strategies. Users branching in a query are more likely to click search results from top to bottom, while users who backtrack are less likely to do so; this is especially true for queries involving more than two clicks. These findings inform an experiment in which we take a popular click model and modify it to account for the differing user behavior when branching. By understanding that users continue examining search results before viewing a branched result, we can improve the click model for branching queries.

Categories and Subject Descriptors

H.5.4 [**Information interfaces and presentation**]: Hypertext/Hypermedia—*Navigation*

General Terms

Human Factors, Measurement, Experimentation, Design

Keywords

browser tabs, examining search results, click models

1. INTRODUCTION

Every Web browser of today supports tabbed browsing, allowing people to comfortably navigate multiple Web pages simultaneously. Browsing flow within a single tab or window

Permission to make digital or hard copies of all or part of this work for personal or classroom use is granted without fee provided that copies are not made or distributed for profit or commercial advantage and that copies bear this notice and the full citation on the first page. To copy otherwise, to republish, to post on servers or to redistribute to lists, requires prior specific permission and/or a fee.
WSDM'12, February 8–12, 2012, Seattle, Washington, USA.
Copyright 2012 ACM 978-1-4503-0747-5/12/02 ...$10.00.

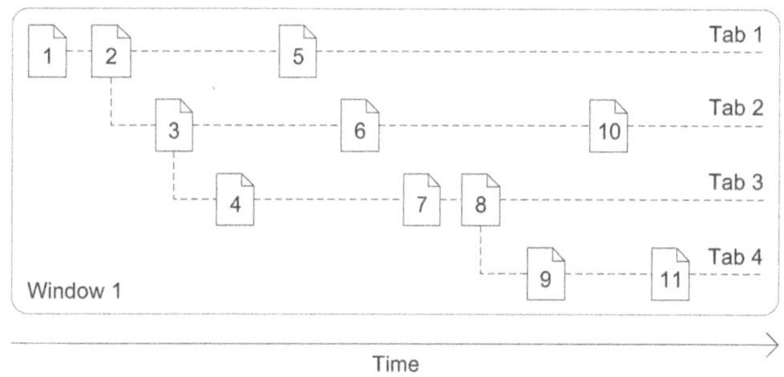

Figure 1: An example Web browsing session with multiple tabs over time. The user starts by viewing a single page and ultimately navigates to 11 pages across 4 browser tabs.

may be interrupted by switching to pages in other tabs and windows. This can be initiated by opening one or more pages from a single page; specifically, opening multiple links on a page in new windows or tabs. We call this 'branching'[1] since the user is spawning a new browsing thread and can continue browsing on either thread. Branching occurs when a user opens a link in a new tab or window, typically achieved with the right-click menu, a middle-mouse click, or by holding the CTRL key before clicking a link. Figure 1 shows the transitions between up to four tabs within a single browser window; the transition from page 2 to page 3 is an example of branching.

Branching can substitute for a classic browser feature—the Back button—which enables backtracking. Rather than sequentially viewing the interesting links on a page by clicking then tapping the Back button to return to the original page, users can simply open all the attractive links on a page in tabs to view later one by one. There are multiple benefits to this approach: opened pages will pre-load, shortening the wait time between viewing pages; there is no risk of being unable to return to the originating page (due to a Web page disabling the Back button or the originating page being inaccessible); and the user may spend as much time on the originating page as desired without having to remember all the links they were planning to view. Indeed, Weinreich et al. [22] note "the usage of multiple windows and tabs has

[1]Different authors have used alternate terminology: Chierichetti et al. [3] call this 'control-click' since this action can be performed by holding the CTRL key and clicking; the word 'branching' in Meiss et al. [15] also includes Back button usage (which we distinguish as *backtracking*); Huang and White [10] use the same terminology that we use here.

partly replaced back button usage".

This behavior affects the analysis of Web search, in which a holistic understanding of search interfaces and browser usability is important. In interviews with users who frequently use tabs in the Firefox browser [5], one user commented, *"If I search for something on Google, I just go 'right-click, right-click, right-click'—you know, opening all the tabs. And then I would look at them later."* Another explained, *"most links that I click [...] like when I do a Google search, I hold on ctrl and click on links."*

On the search engine results page (SERP), browsing behavior is deliberate rather than forced by popups or links that always open in new windows. When studying branching outside of the SERP, these popups and 'forced branches' are difficult to differentiate from user initiated branches, which make the findings less meaningful. Branching in Web search is inadequately studied, partly because capturing the required data at scale requires additional effort; they are not captured in typical query logs [11]. However, the prevalence of branching as a new search strategy has prompted our study of branching behavior on search results.

Since Web servers are agnostic to which tab or window is active, they only record clicks and queries in the order they were received. Therefore, switching to a different page to click or opening multiple tabs from a single search result page confuses algorithms that process query logs [19]. Essentially, there are two problems: 1) the challenge of understanding interleaved sessions and 2) loss of detail about branching behavior (when users open links in new tabs or windows). Also, branching has not been captured in click models (e.g., [2, 6, 7, 20]) that treat user clicks as implicit relevance feedback; thus, we evaluate the effectiveness of adapting a click model that understands branching.

Our guiding research questions are 1) which users are branching, when they do it, and to what extent does branching occur on search results? 2) How does branching compare to backtracking in user search strategies, specifically in queries with multiple result clicks? 3) Can we modify an existing click model that predicts clicks on SERPs based on a better understanding of branching behavior?

In our paper, we explore these questions to gain insight about searcher activity, unpack branching behavior as a key interaction in search, and—enabled by better understanding of branching—propose modifications to a click model.

2. RELATED WORK

Several qualitative studies have reported on the use of multiple windows and tabs in Web search. Thatcher et al. [18] observed users opening multiple browser windows to simultaneously conduct multiple searches. A survey of experienced Web users by Aula et al. [1] found that multiple windows and tabs were used to support backtracking or multitasking while one page was loading. To backtrack, they observed users branching and eventually switching back to the originating tab rather than using the Back button in the browser. For multitasking, they observed users interacting with another tab while waiting for the original one to load, i.e., tab switching. More recently, a Web navigation study by Weinreich et al. [21] found that their participants frequently used multiple windows, enabling them to compare search results side-by-side, load pages in the background while they continued browsing, and retain important pages in their sessions for backtracking. Weinreich et al. also found that the participants who used tabs backtracked less than those who did not. Similarly, those who created more windows tended to backtrack less. Dubroy and Balakrishnan [5] conducted a study on 21 users of the Firefox browser to investigate why tabs were popular when similar functionality is available by using multiple windows. They found that users preferred tabs because they are less cluttered and easier to switch between. Dubroy and Balakrishnan also looked at revisitation and their findings agree with Weinreich et al. that tab usage decreased use of other revisitation methods, especially the Back button. We extend this work by studying *when* and *how often* this behavior occurs in Web search.

Human editors from Jones and Klinkner's study [13] found that 17% of search tasks are interleaved, potentially from users switching between tabs when browsing. Spink et al. [17] discussed multitasking in Web search, which they defined as searching for multiple topics in a single session. They concluded that users frequently multitasked searches, according to this definition. However, parallel browsing, a user's use of simultaneous tab sessions [10], better resembles the classical definition of multitasking. MacKay and Watters [14] find in their diary and field studies that certain tasks required multiple sessions to complete. From a cognitive psychology perspective, Miyata and Norman [16] explained that humans have foreground and background tasks: they focus on the former and do not give conscious supervision to the latter. Parallel browsing follows this model because the user does not interact with multiple tabs simultaneously. Instead, the active tab is the foreground task and has the user's attention while other tabs may be loading in the background or contain information that is not yet needed. Indeed, Zhang and Zhao [23] found a significant difference between revisitation rates measured by pageloads, compared to revisitation rates measured by tab focus.

Viermetz et al. [19] studied the effect of tabbed browsing on the validity of search log studies. They analyzed query logs which did not directly contain information about tabs or windows since they only recorded incoming network traffic. Using this data, they constructed a 'clicktree' of possible paths from the pageviews in the logs. They found that parallel browsing occurred 4–85% of the time. In contrast, our search logs directly contained information about branching activity involving tabs on the search engine results page.

Most related to our work is a study of parallel browsing behavior on the Web conducted by Huang and White [10]. They performed a preliminary study of tabbed browsing on logs gathered through a browser plug-in in June 2009. One part of this study included branching in search results, which we believe to be the first large-scale study of branching. They found that while a small percentage of users branched frequently, the majority always clicked results directly. These users only branched 6–15% of the time for queries that were the most likely candidates for branching: non-navigational queries. In this paper, we extend the exploration of branching by delving deeper. Our study examines branching behavior using a pageload event instrumented on the search results page, whereas the previous study by Huang and White used a browser-specific plug-in. We also examine queries involving multiple clicks in order to compare branching with backtracking, which informs our experiment on accounting for branching in a click model.

Some work has improved Web browsing models by incorporating tabbed browsing data. Chierichetti et al. [3] de-

Sequence	Percent	Notes
pageload click	57.4%	click
pageload	19.7%	no clicks
pageload click pageload	5.1%	click, back
pageload click pageload click	5.0%	click, back, click
	3.9%	events lost
pageload click pageload click pageload click	1.4%	3 clicks, back each time
pageload click pageload click pageload	1.3%	click, back, click, back
pageload click click	0.7%	branch or double click
click pageload	0.7%	delayed javascript
pageload pageload	0.7%	page refresh without click

Table 1: Top 10 most common recorded event sequences

Expression	Percent	Notes
^pageload	95.2%	sequence begins with pageload
^click	0.93%	sequence begins with click
^click ∩ (pageload)	0.84%	click recorded before any pageload, events out of sync
^click ∩ ¬ (pageload)	0.1%	see click but not pageload (i.e., JavaScript off)
(click click)	1.5%	has branching or double click
^pageload.*click.*click.*	11.7%	JavaScript on, in sync, $\geq$ 2 clicks
^pageload ∩ click$	66.7%	begins with pageload, ends with click
(click pageload) ∩ (click click)	0.5%	(branch or double click), backtrack on same SERP

Table 2: Some interesting regular expressions on click sequences

veloped a new model of browsing based off Pagerank, but allowed tabs to be spawned from a page. Unfortunately, the toolbar logs they used could not distinguish between branching and backtracking, but they found that adding branching and backtracking data made the model better at predicting user browsing data. Meiss et al. [15] incorporated bookmarks, Back button usage, and tabbed browsing to develop a model that predicted user entropy, session size, and session depth better than the BookRank baseline. Our work focuses on the search domain and understanding branching behavior on the SERP, applying the findings to click models.

3. METHOD

Our method is based around collecting search logs with the necessary data for analyzing branching behavior. Studying branching behavior at scale through logs allows us to make generalizations and observe uncommon phenomena, which may not surface in small-scale studies. Search logs possess statistical power in the diversity of tasks and users, and realism which is particularly important for studying search strategies because artificial tasks and environments may alter how users search. But they cannot explain *why* a user is performing an action, or understand the user's thought process as they search; the data may be noisy, containing interactions from spammers or bots.

Since data from tabbed browsing interactions are not typically recorded, we instrument a client-side script that records user behavior on the search results page. The script allows us to study branching at scale, a user behavior that has not received attention corresponding to its impact. Our logs span 3 weeks of searches from the Bing search engine (from June 10, 2011 to June 30, 2011), comprising standard query logs supplemented by interaction logs consisting of pageload events and page information. The searches took place in the Web vertical of the search engine unless otherwise specified. We excluded the zh-CN (China) region in our study, since the branching behavior there was completely different from other regions, as we find in Section 5.1. Collecting data through the search results page makes our findings browser agnostic, differing from a previous study on branching [10]; however, this methodology prevents us from knowing whether the user branched in a new *tab* or new *window*, which slightly differ in function. In total, our data comprised over 3 billion query sessions from an estimated 390 million searchers on the first page of search results.

We develop a scalable approach to studying branching behavior that enables us to analyze real user activity in a natural setting. A small piece of JavaScript code notifies the server whenever the SERP is loaded, and the SERP's initial load sends a pageload event. When a user backtracks by clicking and using the Back button, a second pageload event is sent to the server. But when a user branches by opening links in new tabs or windows, the page is not reloaded and no pageload event is sent. In other words, when a user branches on the SERP, there is only one pageload event followed by clicks representing branches; when a user backtracks on the SERP, there is one pageload event preceding each click. This allows us to distinguish between branching and backtracking.

Errors in logging may occur, as pageload and click events may be lost due to problems with the user's computer or network connection or with JavaScript being unavailable. We noticed that 0.84% of queries had events that were obviously out of sync (a click before the first pageload); we discard these because they are temporally illogical and because given their rarity, we believe that removing them does not significantly alter the results. Over 96% of queries had a pageload event sent by the JavaScript, but only 0.1% of query sessions had a click and no pageload.

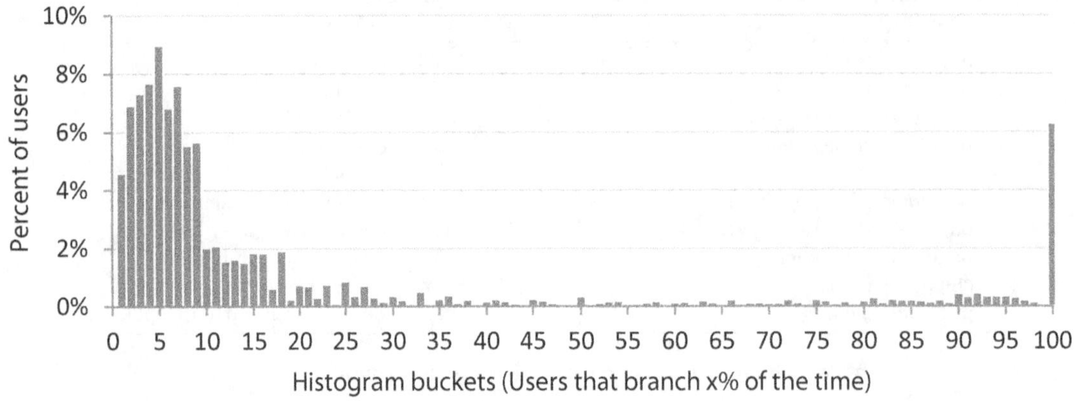

Figure 2: On Web search results, the users who exhibited any branching behavior at all tended to do so between 1–9% of the time that they clicked two results in the same page, with a peak at 5%. Over 6% of these users branched on every query session involving multiple clicks.

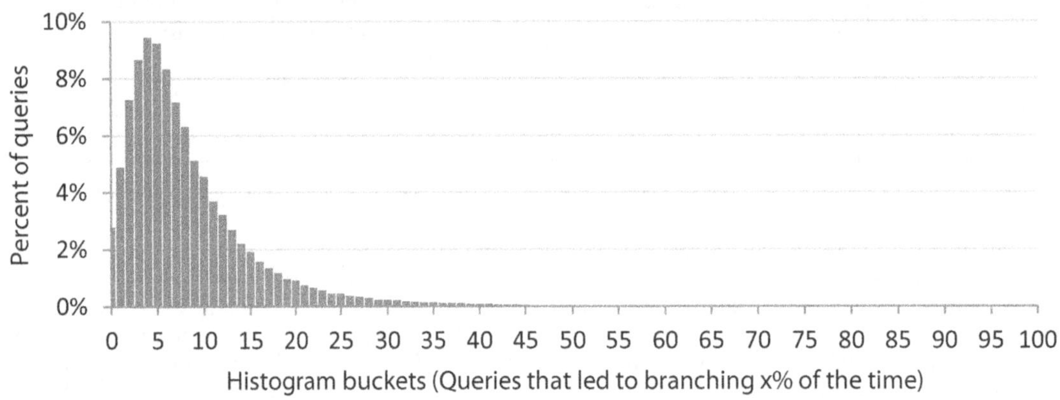

Figure 3: 56.4% of the queries (that $\geq$ 50 users issued and clicked multiple results) led to branching between 2–9% of the time (with a peak at 4–5%). Queries that had no branching or $\geq$ 40% branching were rare.

4. CHARACTERISTICS OF BRANCHING

In this section, we examine some basic characteristics of branching behavior in order to understand how frequently users branch and the general characteristics of branching.

Table 1 shows the most common pageload and click sequences that we observed. 57.4% of queries have one click and end, 19.7% have one pageload and end, and 3.9% have missing events. 'pageload click' occurred more often than 'pageload', indicating that people are more likely to click one link than none. 'pageload, click, pageload, click' (2 clicks via backtracking) occurred 5% of the time, while 'pageload, click, click' (2 clicks via branching) occurred 0.7% of the time. Backtracking remains more popular than branching on the SERP.

Table 2 presents the event sequences matching several hand-picked regular expressions. Only 0.93% of the data started with 'click'; a sequence that contains a 'click' event but no 'pageload' event happens when that JavaScript is disabled or not supported by the browser. This sequence occurred in 0.09% of query sessions, and had no clear association with the geographic region. Overall, 12.9% of queries with multiple clicks could potentially involve branching. However, some of these were actually double clicks, wherein the user clicks the same link twice before the browser navigates to the next Web page. We filter out double clicks hereafter by discarding consecutive clicks on the same result link. After removing double clicks, we find that branching occurs in 9.1% of each consecutive pair of clicks in the same query sessions.

One surprise was that queries involving both branching and backtracking were quite common. For queries with at least 3 clicks, there were almost as many queries where a user branched and backtracked in the same session, as there were queries where a user only branched. For example, a user may click a link and be unsatisfied, return to the search results page using the Back button, then open 3 other links in new tabs. We mostly observed users branching after backtracking, indicating that perhaps the first clicked link was not what they expected. This represents a shift in the user's strategy as they are clicking on search results; perhaps after realizing their first click was unsatisfying, they branched multiple results to retrieve more options.

4.1 Branching Users

Is branching caused by particular users being more prone to branch due to personal preference, or by certain classes of queries being more amenable to branching behavior (e.g., for certain classes of queries, people will know beforehand that they want to read multiple pages)? Or perhaps a particular Web browser always causes branching activity. To pin down the causes of branching behavior, we analyzed the number of users who never branch, always branch, or branch 1%, 2%, ..., 99% of the time. To avoid clusters at values like 1, $\frac{1}{2}$, $\frac{1}{3}$, $\frac{1}{4}$, and $\frac{1}{5}$ due to users with few queries in our dataset, we only included users who clicked on multiple search results on the SERP at least 10 times over the 3 weeks. We also only included click sequences beginning with a 'pageload' event to remove users without JavaScript.

When visiting two results in the same SERP, we found that 60.9% of the users always used backtracking and 2.5% of the users always used branching. Figure 2 shows the distribution of users who branched by how often they branched. Because this graph excludes all the users who never branched, the proportion that always branched increases from 2.5% to 6.3%. The United States distribution closely resembles the distribution of all non-China regions combined. It is possible that the users who always exhibited branching behavior strongly preferred branching or were using some particular software configuration that always caused branching.

The data indicates that branching is not always performed by frequently branching users, but from those who occasionally use it (e.g., 3–7% of the time). This suggests that certain queries or circumstances besides user habits increase the likelihood of user branching.

4.2 Branching Queries

To further test this hypothesis, we analyzed all the queries in our log to observe the specific queries from which users tended to branch. To avoid artifacts caused by data sparseness, we restricted the set to only queries issued by at least 50 distinct users (who then clicked two search results on the first page of results). The histogram in Figure 3 illustrates that the most common amount of branching for a query was between 2–9% of the time (with a peak at 4–5%). Queries rarely had either no branching or over 40% of the query sessions branched.

Out of the 91,545 distinct queries that matched our filtering criteria, the specific query with the highest proportion of branching was "no strings attached torrent". In our log, 121 users issued this query and then clicked on two or more results in the results page. For results loaded beyond the first, 258 were loaded via branching and 25 were loaded via backtracking: for a branching ratio of 91%. "No Strings Attached" is a film; users who query for the torrent are looking to illegally download it. However, each of the top results is a page where the user has some small chance of successfully downloading the movie. It seems logical that the large majority of users in this scenario will branch to open many of these links at once rather than checking them one by one to see if they work. Of the 69 queries that contained the word "torrent", the average branching-to-backtracking ratio was 51%.

Another indicative pattern of branching was the phrase "file extension". For example, a query for "file extension trp" means the user is wondering what the "trp" extension means and is likely to read through multiple results to learn more. Of the 399 queries that contained "file extension", the average branching ratio was 22.5%. Other examples of indicative words are "lottery" (66 queries, average branch ratio of 15.6%) and "Facebook" (104 queries, average branch ratio of 14.9%). Queries containing "lottery" generally come from people looking to check their lottery numbers; multiple candidate sites could post the numbers, and the user may

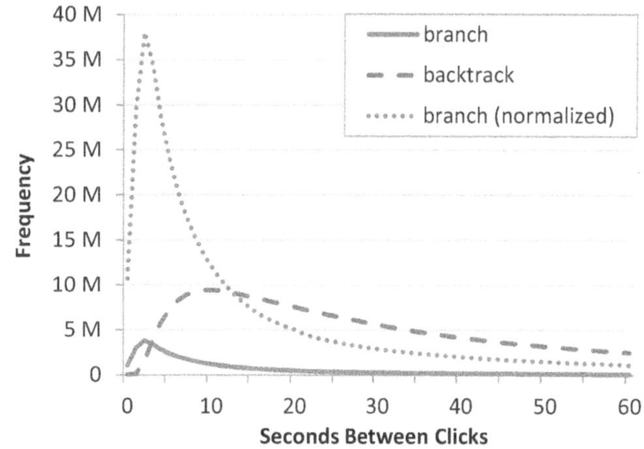

Figure 4: When users branch, the time between successive result clicks is significantly lower than when they backtrack.

not be sure which of those sites has the latest numbers, so they open multiple results. Queries containing "Facebook" are from users looking for their friends but the search engine returns Facebook pages for several people sharing that same name. The user will then open several of these result pages and examine them to find the right person.

The primary word that correlated to low branching was "trailer". Users searching for movie trailers are unlikely to open multiple results in tabs because each result is likely to play the trailer video, and the audio from multiple videos playing at once would overlap. Of the 54 queries containing "trailer", the average branching ratio was 3.9%. Most other words did not correlate with low branching by themselves. Low branching tended to be specific to the individual queries where the search engine returned a top result that clearly met the users' needs so there was no reason for the user to branch multiple results.

5. CLICK INTERVALS

We expect to see different lengths of time between clicks if the underlying user behavior is different in branching and backtracking. Figure 4 examines the Web vertical (for all regions) and displays the frequency of branching (solid line) compared to backtracking (dashed line) in situations in which the user clicked on two links in the same results page. The x-axis indicates the time elapsed between the two clicks. Branching comprises a smaller (but still substantial) proportion of the clicks compared to backtracking, as illustrated by backtracking line covering a much greater area than the branching line. By total frequency, when a user clicked on two links in the same results page, 9.1% of the clicks came from branching activity (over the 3 week period, Web vertical, excluding China). If data from China is included, then 13.4% of all clicks came from branching activity.

The dotted line in Figure 4 normalizes the branching values to have the same total frequency as backtracking, in order to better distinguish the different peak time between clicks. For branching, the peak time between clicks was 2–3 seconds. For backtracking, the peak time between clicks was 10–11 seconds. The time between clicks fell under 30 seconds about 69% of the time with branching but only 41% of the

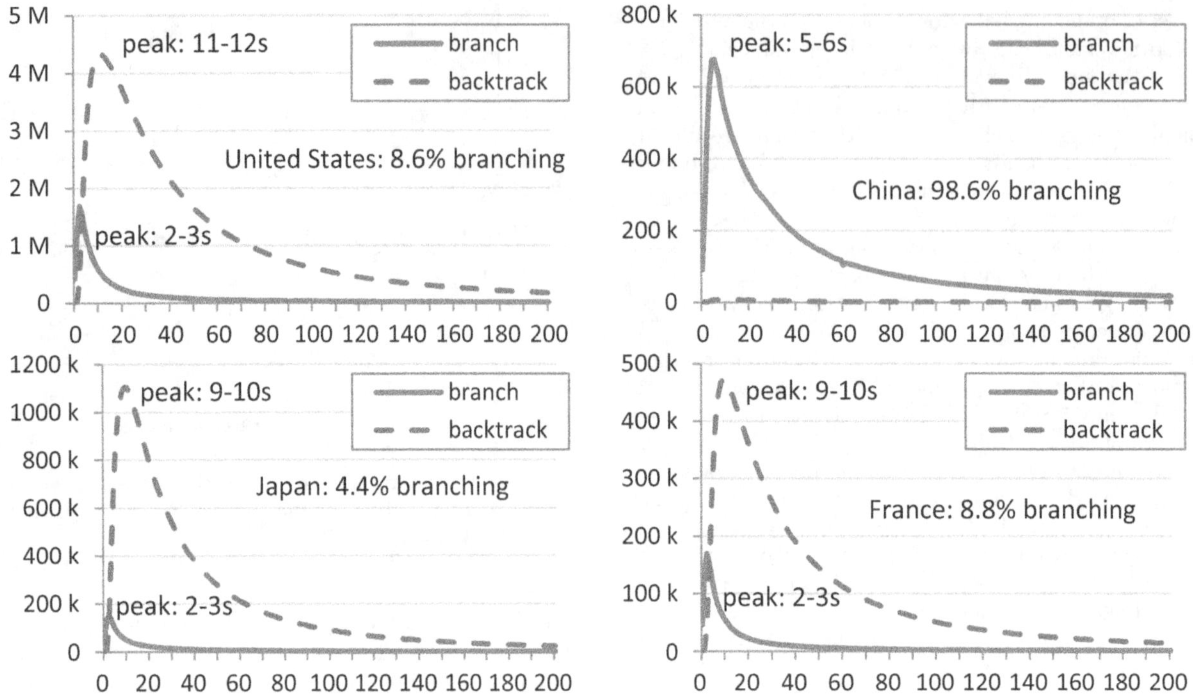

Figure 5: Seconds Between Clicks vs Frequency graph for: United States Web vertical (top left), China Web (top right), Japan Web (bottom left), France Web (bottom right). Most regions had similar branching frequencies, except China, where branching behavior is the default action.

time with backtracking. The time between clicks is sometimes used to judge user satisfaction with the initial clicked results (e.g., [8, 9]). Our findings indicate that branching activity needs to be filtered out or otherwise accounted for with this metric in order to avoid unfair penalization of branched results.

The normalized branching line illustrates that branching had a much sharper and earlier peak, indicating that compared to backtracking, branching has a much larger proportion of clicks that happen quickly. Perhaps when users branch, they often continue looking for more search results to click rather than reading the page that they opened in the new tab before coming back and selecting more links.

5.1 Regions

When we separate the Web vertical branching data by geographic region, we find that United States (8.6% branching) and France (8.8% branching) are similar. However, some regions are outliers: Japan only has 4.4% branching and China has 98.6% branching.

Japan is interesting in that branching occurs less frequently. Also, as shown in Figure 5, the branching distribution is noticeably less sharp around the 2–3 second spike than in other markets. This suggests that people are less likely to branch, and when they do, they are more likely to read the opened page before selecting another.

In China, the default action for popular search engines is to branch when users click on search results. As a result, 98.6% of our data from the Chinese market demonstrated branching behavior. The remaining 1.4% may have been due to users who found a way to disable this behavior, or people using browsers that do not support opening multiple windows. The branching distribution for China has a sharp curve, but not as sharp as most other branching curves. Most markets have branching distributions that peak in the 2–3 second range, but China's peak is at 4–5 seconds. Without backtracking, users may prefer taking the time to look at the open result in the new tab before returning to the results page to open another result.

The ubiquity of branching in China suggests that branching may become more significant as the Internet user base in China increases, and for users accustomed to this habit in China that migrate to other countries. However, to avoid confounding the data with other factors that may differ in Chinese Web search, most of our comparisons and analyses in this paper exclude data from China.

5.2 Verticals

We found that the News and Web verticals had similar branching rates. Intuitively, there are news topics for which people will want to seek out as much information as possible, which may mean reading multiple articles. However, news may not possess an equivalent to queries like "torrent" and "Facebook" where the user knows ahead of time that they need to screen multiple candidate Web results to find what they want. In terms of time between clicks, we found that when users backtrack with news, they spend more time on the page (17–18 second peak) before clicking Back. When users branch with news, the time still peaks at 2–3 seconds. These times support our hypothesis that users read the clicked page before clicking Back, but not before branching. Users are likely to spend more time reading a news article (compared to a general Web result) before deciding that they want another.

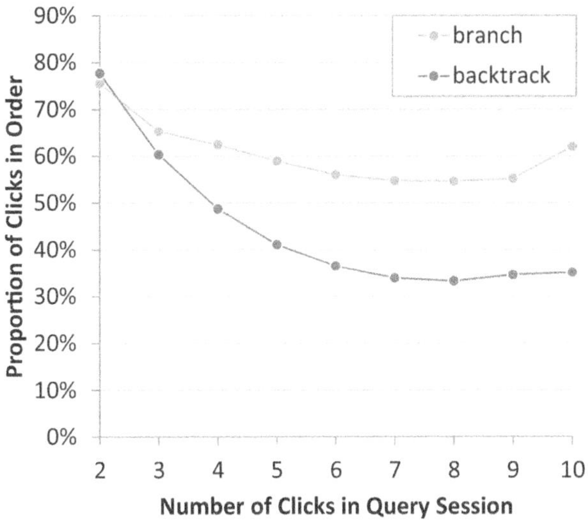

Figure 6: The effect of branching vs. backtracking on click order for multi-click queries, controlling for user. Users are more likely to click search results from top to bottom when they are branching.

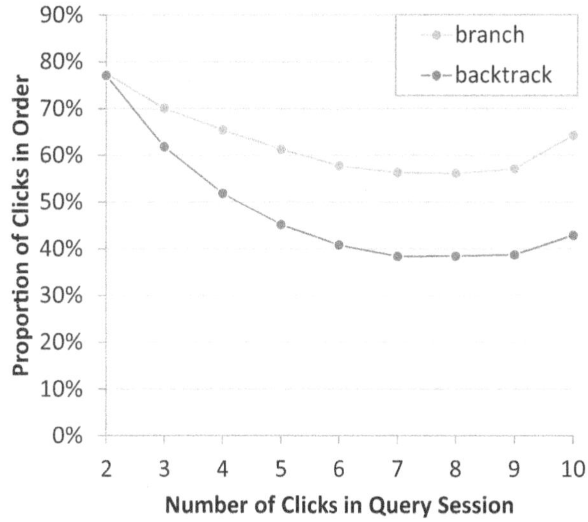

Figure 7: The effect of branching vs. backtracking on click order for multi-click queries, controlling for query. Users are more likely to click search results from top to bottom when they are branching.

We also looked at branching on the Images and Videos verticals, but our method for detecting branching was invalid in these verticals due to interface differences compared to the Web and News verticals.

6. LINEAR TRAVERSAL HYPOTHESIS

Queries with multiple clicks are interesting because they represent cases in which the user is not finished after selecting one link. In these situations, the user may have not been sufficiently satisfied, or was interested in viewing more diverse sources of information. In our data, 11.7% of queries with JavaScript enabled have at least 2 clicks.

Users can open multiple links using branching, as we have seen, they usually use the Back button after viewing each link. Here we investigate the examination pattern for the two behaviors: how often do users satisfy the *linear traversal hypothesis* [12] in each case? We want to revisit this common assumption through the lens of multiple clicks. This hypothesis suggests that users review search results from top to bottom and do not return to any previously viewed result after they have skipped it. It has been a basic assumption in several search interaction models [2, 4, 7] and is intuitive since search results are sorted in order of relevance. However, whether this hypothesis is true is a particularly tricky question to answer because it can be confounded by the effects of user style and query type and because examination behavior is difficult to observe at scale. We analyze a related question: are users *clicking* search results from top to bottom?

From this point we will refer to click sequences satisfying the linear traversal hypothesis as LTH and denote click sequences that contradict the linear traversal hypothesis as ¬LTH. While the linear traversal hypothesis does not directly tell us how users are *examining* search results, a LTH click sequence says that either users are examining search results from top to bottom, or that they are returning to a previously examined search result to click.

The search models cited above cannot account for ¬LTH behavior; Chapelle and Zhang remark, *"Sessions for which the clicks are not in the same order as the ranking have zero probability under our model. On average, roughly 3% of the sessions contain one or more out-of-the-order clicks. We could have decided to swap the click order for these sessions, but we simply discarded them."* However, most queries have only one click—one click cannot be out of order. When we look at queries featuring two or more clicks, 30% are ¬LTH. Moreover, for queries featuring three or more clicks, 44% are ¬LTH. Thus, while Chapelle and Zhang have found that only 3% of queries have ¬LTH clicks, this number is significantly higher for queries with multiple clicks. We believe these query sessions with ¬LTH clicks may encapsulate information that should not be discarded.

To deliver meaningful results, we need to control for the *user* effect, as differences in click order in branching and backtracking behavior may result from those users having a particular style of clicking. Additionally, the uneven distribution of the number of clicks by each user may skew the results. To control for these factors, we only select query sessions from users who have engaged in both branching and backtracking; additionally, for each user we only sample one query session that involves branching and one query session that involves backtracking. This method ensures that we know whether the LTH clicks are related to whether they are branched, not because of user differences.

We control for the potential effect of a query on multi-click behavior in the same way as for a user, by replacing 'user' with 'query' in the above steps. Similarly, we know that query differences are not why the clicks are LTH. Thus, our analysis distinguishes between the effect of branching or backtracking behavior on click order in queries with multiple clicks. Note that controlling for both user and query at the same time (the interaction effect) in the same manner interferes with user behavior: a user that issues the same query twice may have different click behavior the second time simply because they already issued the same query.

Figures 6 and 7 both show that ¬LTH is more common when there are more clicks. This is intuitive considering there are more permutations for the click order when there are more clicks. More interestingly, when branching, users are more likely to click as LTH when there are more than two clicks, even when controlling for user or query. LTH clicks remain at around 54–61% of occurrences when branching with 5 or more clicks. However, for queries with exactly two clicks, there is little difference in click order between branching and backtracking; in fact, when controlling for user, users who are backtracking are slightly more likely to do LTH clicks.

7. BRANCHING IN CLICK MODELS

The data that describes the user's branching behavior can also be used to better model their search result examination behavior. Several click models (e.g., [2, 6, 7, 20]) use hidden states to represent whether a user continued examining search results after clicking. Having accurate information about a user's focus can improve these models. Additionally, knowing whether a user opened a search result in new tabs or windows (i.e., branching) can provide a different signal than if they simply clicked and returned (i.e., backtracking). For example, branching may cause users to click results in a sequential top-to-bottom order, opening any attractive result, but backtracking may entail a different strategy of finding the most potentially satisfying search result.

Here we will describe a click model that we will modify using our understanding of user branching behavior. We will describe the Perplexity metric used to evaluate the model. Finally, we will report the experiment and results.

7.1 Click Model

We will replicate the Dynamic Bayesian Network (DBN) model [2], the most cited click model since the Cascade Model (which compared favorably to all models before it). The DBN model compares favorably to the Cascade Model [2, 24], and fares well compared to other models (e.g., [24, 25]), making it a solid baseline for our purposes.

The DBN model is a graphical model where the nodes represent states of the user examining the search results; the model is represented formally as follows:

- E_i: the user examined the search result
- C_i: the user clicked the search result
- A_i: the search result attracted the user
- S_i: the landing page satisfied the user

$$\begin{aligned} A_i = 1, E_1 = 1 &\Leftrightarrow C_i = 1 \\ P(A_i = 1) &= a_u \\ P(S_i = 1 | C_i = 1) &= s_u \\ C_i = 0 &\Rightarrow S_i = 0 \\ S_i = 1 &\Rightarrow E_{i+1} = 1 \\ P(E_{i+1} = 1 | E_i = 1, S_i = 0) &= \lambda \\ E_i = 0 &\Rightarrow E_{i+1} = 0 \end{aligned}$$

In this model, a user examines search results from top to bottom, assessing each result for whether or not it is attractive enough to click, a decision that depends only on the attractiveness of the link a_u. If they click, there is some probability s_u they will be satisfied and stop the search process. If they are not satisfied, they either return to the search results page to examine the next search result with probability λ, or abandon the search.

We implement the DBN model with $\lambda = 1$, labeled *Algorithm 1* in [2], to simplify the inference of latent variables.

7.2 Click Perplexity

Though we cannot evaluate unobserved events in a click model such as which results the user examined, we can test how well it predicts clicks, the observable events. Several click model studies [6, 7, 24, 25] have evaluated click perplexity as a measure of predicting click-through rates. In those studies, query sessions were divided evenly into training and test sets, each comprising at least 5 query sessions with clicks on search results. The click perplexity quantifies how much the test data surprises the trained model; it is computed for each combination of query and position as,

$$p_i = 2^{-\frac{1}{N}\sum_{n=1}^{N}(C_i^n log_2 q_i^n + (1-C_i^n) log_2(1-q_i^n))}$$

where p_i is the perplexity in the ith position, N the number of links, and q_i^n the predicted click probability for the nth query session. The exponent represents the cross-entropy estimated from a probability distribution. If the perplexity is 1, the trained model perfectly predicted the test data. A lower perplexity means the model was more accurate in predicting the test data. Because the lower bound of the perplexity depends on the click-through rate of the query, the perplexity varies substantially depending on the position of the search result. Therefore, we computed a separate perplexity value for every search result position and report perplexity values for each of the top ten rank positions.

7.3 Experiment

Zhang and Zhao remarked that a page loading from a clicked link does not necessarily mean the user has examined that page [23], since it may have opened in a background tab. Thus, a user branching on a link does not determine at that time whether that link has satisfied their search need. Our experiment exploits the following insight: when users branch, they are likely to click multiple search results even if one of the clicked search results is satisfying, i.e.,

$$P(E_{i+1} | E_i = 1, C_i, S_i) = P(E_{i+1} | P(E_i)) = \gamma$$

We use γ as the probability that the user stops examining search results at each point. Once this happens, the user will go through the opened links. Our tests showed that $\gamma = 0.9$ performed best, indicating that at each search result, users have a 90% chance of examining another search result snippet or a 10% chance of going to review the opened tabs. For the original model, we used new s_u priors for these branching queries (which helps the original model) since the probability of continuing to examine search results is higher than across all queries.

We conduct an experiment by running this 'branching model' alongside the original model for comparison. As in prior work, query sessions were divided evenly into training and test sets, each comprising at least 5 query sessions with clicks on search results. We computed the perplexity for each position and averaged the scores across a total of 1,178,176 unique queries. Figure 8 shows the perplexity for the two models across different positions. The original model poorly predicts click-through rates for query sessions

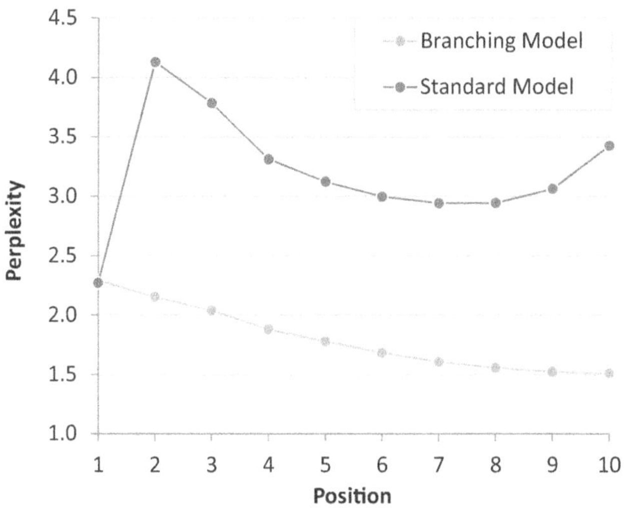

Figure 8: Perplexity for the standard DBN model with $\lambda = 1$ computed for queries where the user branched multiple clicks (lower Perplexity is better). The branching model (where users are assumed to branch all the links before examining them) compared favorably to the standard model.

involving branching, while the branching model performs better.

For positions 2–10, the original performs worse than for position 1; this is because the original model assumes the user will stop if the first result is satisfying. We believe this assumption is not true when the user is branching because they do not review the opened link until after all the clicks. Therefore, it is hard to predict multiple clicks in branching since there are more unexpected clicks on lower-ranked search results. The Perplexity will generally be high because clicks on lower-ranked results are unexpected, but this occurs frequently in queries featuring branching by definition. In practice, the branching model can be used to improve the overall click model, since the search engine can apply the branching model whenever it determines using pageload events that a user has branched.

8. DISCUSSION

Tabbed browsing is popular and has changed peoples' search behaviors by allowing them to simultaneously load multiple search results to view later. We know that users who open links in tabs behave differently based on evidence that they are more likely to click search results from top to bottom. This has an impact on click models, which should be careful about how they process query logs. It would be prudent for click models to consider that users may not be going from top to bottom, as many models assume, especially when users are backtracking.

Recent work in information retrieval has used the time between clicks as a feature to model user behavior [8, 9]. We find that when users branch, this duration is often 2–3 seconds, even across different regions and verticals. This is shorter than the approximately 10 seconds between clicks when users are backtracking. The peak also has a noticeably smaller variance when users branch. Since we would imagine that the reading time for different Web pages varies, a consistent click interval suggests that users are reading the page when they backtrack but not when they branch. This evidence suggests that the 'time between clicks' feature is not useful for determining the relevance of the clicked link when branching; it instead represents the time spent examining each search result to determine whether to branch. The anomaly in the Chinese region in which links are branched by default presents additional evidence. There, the most common dwell time is 5–6 seconds instead of 2–3 seconds, confirming our belief that users do not review the opened link when they choose to branch, but will sometimes review the opened link when they are forced to branch. Our findings show that the time between clicks is only a useful feature when the user is backtracking.

Our study differs from a previous one [10] because it infers the branch or backtrack action by checking for pageload events between clicks, rather than through a Web browser plug-in. While we are able to capture behavior across all Web browsers rather than just one, we are thus limited to a single search engine. It is possible that user interaction behavior may differ across search engines, or users of different search engines possess different branching patterns. Furthermore, we do not collect data about tab switching, which can track the user's focus in the browser. Data on anomalies due to different search engines or tab switching can be measured with a different data collection method.

Although we attempt to detect instances of branching and backtracking when possible, this is sometimes impossible given the available data. When the last recorded event is a click in a query session, we cannot tell whether this is a branch or regular click. One fewer click is required to detect backtracking since it is defined as a click followed by a pageload, whereas two consecutive clicks are required to detect branching. Finally, though we believe manual Reload actions are uncommon in the middle of a query session, they can send 'pageload' events, leading us to incorrectly classify a branch as a backtrack. Overall, our technique for distinguishing branching from backtracking may have overcounted backtracking, resulting in estimates of branching more conservative than the true proportion. However, the fraction of clicks that were branched did align closely with those reported in previous work on a browser-based data set [10].

Users in the Chinese market nearly always branch, a behavior forced by their search engines' default settings. Some people speculate[2] that this default started because Internet access is slower in China and so branching enables Web pages to load in the background. Others believe default branching is economically motivated as it allows a search engine to keep users on its site longer. However, a qualitative study of how Chinese users perceive branching versus backtracking would be interesting since their default action is opposite of that for the American and European users, who have been previously studied [1, 5, 18, 22].

Because branching queries have shorter time intervals between clicks (2–3 seconds compared to 5–30 seconds when backtracking), and *because* their clicks more often move from top to bottom, branching compels a different examination strategy. The improved branching model provides further evidence of our belief that users are not examining the search result landing pages following every click when they branch.

[2] http://www.quora.com/China/Why-do-most-hyperlinks-on-Chinese-websites-open-a-new-window-tab

9. CONCLUSIONS

Branching is a core feature of tabbed browsing. We develop a technique to differentiate between branching and backtracking, i.e., when users open links in new tabs versus when users click and use the Back button to return to the search results page. Users branch for 9.1% of clicks, although some users and queries tend to have more branches than others.

Due to a number of usability advantages, in some cases branching is replacing backtracking. Search examination behavior differs for queries requiring more than two clicks, which are likely to represent informational or difficult queries: users click on search results from top to bottom more often when they branch than when they backtrack. The time between clicks is substantially shorter for branching than backtracking. A large portion of these clicks are 2–3 seconds apart whereas backtracking queries possess a wider range of click intervals.

This set of differing branching behaviors led us to our click model experiment. We find that a modified click model performs better for branching by knowing that users do not examine the linked search result when they click, a previously held assumption in existing click models. This behavior means that the user continues examining even when they have clicked a potentially satisfying result. Better accounting for user search strategies can improve click models for query sessions in which branching occurs.

This work can be fruitful beyond search result pages. Search engines can distinguish between branching and backtracking by adding pageload events to the SERP, an event that can be implemented in other websites with hyperlinks like social news or photos sharing sites. Many sites can also use branching information to build user models and help rank their items.

10. ACKNOWLEDGMENTS

The authors thank Susan Dumais and Yu Chen for insightful discussions about the work, and Katherine Ye for editing earlier drafts of the paper.

11. REFERENCES

[1] A. Aula, N. Jhaveri, and M. Käki. Information search and re-access strategies of experienced web users. In *Proceedings of WWW*, pp. 583–592, 2005.

[2] O. Chapelle and Y. Zhang. A dynamic bayesian network click model for web search ranking. In *Proceedings of WWW*, pp. 1–10, 2009.

[3] F. Chierichetti, R. Kumar, and A. Tomkins. Stochastic models for tabbed browsing. In *Proceedings of WWW*, pp. 241–250, 2010.

[4] N. Craswell, O. Zoeter, M. Taylor, and B. Ramsey. An experimental comparison of click position-bias models. In *Proceedings of WSDM*, pp. 87–94, 2008.

[5] P. Dubroy and R. Balakrishnan. A study of tabbed browsing among mozilla firefox users. In *Proceedings of CHI*, pp. 673–682, 2010.

[6] G. E. Dupret and B. Piwowarski. A user browsing model to predict search engine click data from past observations. In *Proceedings of SIGIR*, pp. 331–338, 2008.

[7] F. Guo, C. Liu, A. Kannan, T. Minka, M. Taylor, Y.-M. Wang, and C. Faloutsos. Click chain model in web search. In *Proceedings of WWW*, pp. 11–20, 2009.

[8] A. Hassan, R. Jones, and K. L. Klinkner. Beyond dcg: user behavior as a predictor of a successful search. In *Proceedings of WSDM*, pp. 221–230, 2010.

[9] Y. He and K. Wang. Inferring search behaviors using partially observable markov model with duration (pomd). In *Proceedings of WSDM*, pp. 415–424, 2011.

[10] J. Huang and R. W. White. Parallel browsing behavior on the web. In *Proceedings of Hypertext*, pp. 13–18, 2010.

[11] B. J. Jansen and A. Spink. How are we searching the world wide web?: a comparison of nine search engine transaction logs. *Information Processing & Management*, 42(1):248–263, 2006.

[12] T. Joachims, L. Granka, B. Pan, H. Hembrooke, and G. Gay. Accurately interpreting clickthrough data as implicit feedback. In *Proceedings of SIGIR*, pp. 154–161, 2005.

[13] R. Jones and K. L. Klinkner. Beyond the session timeout: automatic hierarchical segmentation of search topics in query logs. In *Proceedings of CIKM*, pp. 699–708, 2008.

[14] B. MacKay and C. Watters. Exploring multi-session web tasks. In *Proceedings of CHI*, pp. 1187–1196, 2008.

[15] M. R. Meiss, B. Gonçalves, J. J. Ramasco, A. Flammini, and F. Menczer. Agents, bookmarks and clicks: a topical model of web navigation. In *Proceedings of Hypertext*, pp. 229–234, 2010.

[16] Y. Miyata and D. Norman. *Psychological issues in support of multiple activities*. 1986.

[17] A. Spink, M. Park, B. J. Jansen, and J. Pedersen. Multitasking during web search sessions. *Information Processing & Management*, 42:264–275, January 2006.

[18] A. Thatcher. Web search strategies: The influence of web experience and task type. *Information Processing & Management*, 44(3):1308–1329, May 2008.

[19] M. Viermetz, C. Stolz, V. Gedov, and M. Skubacz. Relevance and impact of tabbed browsing behavior on web usage mining. In *Proceedings of Web Intelligence*, pp. 262–269, 2006.

[20] K. Wang, N. Gloy, and X. Li. Inferring search behaviors using partially observable markov (pom) model. In *Proceedings of WSDM*, pp. 211–220, 2010.

[21] H. Weinreich, H. Obendorf, E. Herder, and M. Mayer. Off the beaten tracks: exploring three aspects of web navigation. In *Proceedings of WWW*, pp. 133–142, 2006.

[22] H. Weinreich, H. Obendorf, E. Herder, and M. Mayer. Not quite the average: An empirical study of web use. *ACM Transactions on the Web*, 2:1–31, March 2008.

[23] H. Zhang and S. Zhao. Measuring web page revisitation in tabbed browsing. In *Proceedings of CHI*, pp. 1831–1834, 2011.

[24] Y. Zhang, D. Wang, G. Wang, W. Chen, Z. Zhang, B. Hu, and L. Zhang. Learning click models via probit bayesian inference. In *Proceedings of CIKM*, pp. 439–448, 2010.

[25] F. Zhong, D. Wang, G. Wang, W. Chen, Y. Zhang, Z. Chen, and H. Wang. Incorporating post-click behaviors into a click model. In *Proceedings of SIGIR*, pp. 355–362, 2010.

Characterizing Web Content, User Interests, and Search Behavior by Reading Level and Topic

Jin Young Kim
University of Massachusetts, Amherst
140 Governors Drive
Amherst, MA U.S.A. 01003
jykim@cs.umass.edu

Kevyn Collins-Thompson
Paul N. Bennett, Susan T. Dumais
Microsoft Research
One Microsoft Way, Redmond, WA 98052
{kevynct, pauben, sdumais}@microsoft.com

ABSTRACT

A user's expertise or ability to understand a document on a given topic is an important aspect of that document's relevance. However, this aspect has not been well-explored in information retrieval systems, especially those at Web scale where the great diversity of content, users, and tasks presents an especially challenging search problem. To help improve our modeling and understanding of this diversity, we apply automatic text classifiers, based on reading difficulty and topic prediction, to estimate a novel type of profile for important entities in Web search – users, websites, and queries. These profiles capture topic and reading level distributions, which we then use in conjunction with search log data to characterize and compare different entities.

We find that reading level and topic distributions provide an important new representation of Web content and user interests, and that using both together is more effective than using either one separately. In particular we find that: 1) the reading level of Web content and the diversity of visitors to a website can vary greatly by topic; 2) the degree to which a user's profile matches with a site's profile is closely correlated with the user's preference of the website in search results, and 3) site or URL profiles can be used to predict 'expertness'— whether a given site or URL is oriented toward expert vs. non-expert users. Our findings provide strong evidence in favor of *jointly* incorporating reading level and topic distribution metadata into a variety of critical tasks in Web information systems.

Categories and Subject Descriptors:
H.3.3 [**Information Storage and Retrieval**]: Information Search and Retrieval.

General Terms: Experimentation, Human Factors, Measurement.

Keywords: Web search, log analysis, domain expertise, reading level prediction, topic prediction.

Permission to make digital or hard copies of all or part of this work for personal or classroom use is granted without fee provided that copies are not made or distributed for profit or commercial advantage and that copies bear this notice and the full citation on the first page. To copy otherwise, or republish, to post on servers or to redistribute to lists, requires prior specific permission and/or a fee.

WSDM'12, February 8–12, 2012, Seattle, Washington, USA.

Copyright 2012 ACM 978-1-4503-0747-5/12/02...$10.00.

1. INTRODUCTION

The World Wide Web is a diverse source of information for billions of Web users. This variety provides a significant challenge in enabling a user's access to information because large portions of the Web may fall outside of a particular user's overall interests, comprehension level, or comprehension within a particular domain. Specifically, an expert user in a given domain would likely be interested in different types of content than novice users. Furthermore, this expertise or comprehension level may vary for a particular user across domains. For example, a person might be an attorney by profession and have high proficiency in understanding content in the legal domain, but have much more limited knowledge in the medical domain, and thus prefer less technical material when searching for symptoms or remedies on health topics.

In this work, we aim to model this diversity for information retrieval systems by defining a novel form of probabilistic profile that can be used to describe users, queries, or websites – major entities of Web search. Our profile is a *probability distribution* of *reading level and topic* that we call an *RLT profile*. To compute a RLT profile for any entity, such as a website, user, or query, we first get a set of one or more URLs associated with that entity using sources such as click data or Web domain relationships. For example, a user profile might be associated with the URLs of previously clicked search results, or a website profile might be associated with the URLs making up the website content. We use automatic text classifiers to compute the RLT profiles (distributions over reading level and topic) for each URL in the set. Finally, we aggregate the distributions of the individual URL profiles to obtain the combined RLT profile of the entity. The resulting distribution is a compact yet general representation that enables novel characterizations of users, queries and websites and the interactions between them. We can then derive further useful properties of the profile's distribution, such as the expectation and entropy, to characterize interesting properties such as the diversity of topics available at a website.

Because our probabilistic profile is a distribution, this also enables a principled comparison between any two entities, by comparing their RLT distributions using information theoretic divergence metrics. Finally, using the relationship between users, queries and websites extracted from session logs, we can characterize each entity in terms of related entities. For instance, we can build a profile of a given website based on the profiles of its visitors to compare/contrast characteristics of the content of a site and its target audience.

Using search log data of 7,600 users over a 10-week period, and millions of URLs, we show how these profiles can be built and used to gain new insights into content and behavior on the Web. Specifically, we provide a new characterization of important search tasks, assess new features for personalization, and distinguish between websites oriented toward expert or non-expert users.

2. RELATED WORK

To our knowledge, this is the first study that characterizes Web content and user behavior in Web search in terms of both reading level and topic prediction at Web scale. Previous work can be divided into three main areas: using topic and reading difficulty prediction independently to improve Web search, modeling user and content familiarity, and characterizing domain expertise.

In Web retrieval, previous work tried to address the diversity among users by personalizing search results using either a user's topical interests or their desired reading level [6] [2] [8], but not both together. For example, topic predictions based on the Open Directory Project (ODP, dmoz.org) have previously been used as metadata to improve Web search effectiveness. Bennett *et al.* [2] derived an ODP class distribution for a query based on clicks and used this in combination with ODP class distributions computed for Web pages, to obtain new ranking features. Song *et al.* [15] used the entropy of the ODP category distribution as a site characteristic, analyzing the specialization of the search content at that site. Web sites with low entropies were considered to have higher search focus. The topic entropy of a site was a weak feature for predicting accurate site recommendations. White *et al.* [18] also used topic predictions to model users' short-term interests. They computed ODP labels for the top 10 search results, for clicks on the search engine result page (SERP), and for pages visited following SERP clicks. A user's short-term topic profile was the aggregate of these ODP page categories, weighted by dwell time and the length of time between a click and the current query. They found that topic-based short-term profiles helped for ambiguous queries, and that per-query optimal weights gave better improvement than globally optimal weights. Our work is different in that we used the reading level information together with the topic prediction results, and used long-term search session logs to estimate profiles and analyze user behavior.

Previously, Collins-Thompson *et al.* [6] used reading level metadata to perform Web search personalization. They computed reading level features for search result captions and the underlying full pages. Tan *et al.* [16] have also recently explored personalized content selection by modeling text comprehensibility. In contrast, our focus in this study is on general characteristics of pages, websites, users, and their relationships in Web search, as measured in terms of reading level and topic. We do not perform re-ranking or personalization as a task, although some of our results could be applied to obtain new features for personalization or contextual search tasks.

The use of reading level and topic metadata together for Web content retrieval was previously used in an intelligent tutoring application by Collins-Thompson and Callan [4]. About 20 million Web pages were tagged with both ODP topic category and reading level distributions in order to provide personalized material for improving vocabulary acquisition. However, this was a specialized retrieval application, not general Web search, and no analysis was provided on how topic and reading level interacted in pages, sites, or with users.

Previous work has also studied the relationship between a user's *topic familiarity* and search behavior and effectiveness. Kelly and Cool [10] found that with increased familiarity, document reading time decreases while search efficacy improves. Freund, Toms and Waterhouse [9] compared search behavior of work-related Web search to general search and found that work-related sessions used longer queries with a higher proportion of technical terms. The TREC Hard Track in 2003 [1] included a "familiarity" feature of a query, defined as user background knowledge on topic.

In contrast, Kumaran *et al.* [12] defined familiarity as a property of a document independent of user or query. They trained a classifier to label documents as either Introductory or Advanced, using features that included stopwords, reading level estimates, and various page-based features such as the amount of non-anchor text. Unlike their representation of a page, we use the entire vocabulary of the page, not just stopwords, and we explicitly model the interaction of reading level and topic predictions. Moreover, we consider the user's interests and background profile as critical to the nature of content difficulty – not as a static, user-independent property of documents.

Domain expertise on the Web is another closely connected area of research. White, Dumais and Teevan [17] characterized expert *vs.* non-experts according to their Web search behavior, across four domains: Computer Science, Legal, Medicine, and Finance. They also used interaction features from queries and sessions to predict whether a user was a domain expert. The expert and non-expert websites used in their study were labeled by human judges, whereas we learn to identify expert *vs.* non-expert websites automatically for a given domain.

This work extends existing research in the following ways. We introduce a novel probabilistic RLT profile and present a large-scale analysis on the interaction between reading level and topic profile on the web, particularly for content appearing in search results. We also demonstrate the value of building a profile using both reading level and topic, whereas existing work [6] [2] [8] considered them separately in building a profile. Finally, we introduce a technique for classifying expert vs. non-expert content, whereas existing work [17] focused on identifying domain experts.

3. READING LEVEL & TOPIC PROFILES

In this section, we present our methodology for building reading level and topic (RLT)-based profiles for important entities of Web search – users, websites and queries. We first describe how we obtain reading level and topic distributions for the content of individual URLs (Web pages), and how these are aggregated to form distributions that are the RLT profiles for entities such as website, queries, and users. We then define measures of the difference between profiles of individual entities, and the ambiguity or coherence of profiles for *groups* of entities. With these measures, we then explore interesting connections across entity types, or between entities and user search behavior.

3.1 Predicting Reading Level and Topic

We begin by describing how we characterize the content of a URL based on its reading level and topic distributions.

3.1.1 *Predicting Reading Level Distribution of Text*

We represent the reading difficulty of a document or text as a random variable R_d taking values in the range 1-12. These values correspond to American school grade levels, although they could easily be modified for finer or coarser distinctions in level, or for different tasks or populations. We computed reading level predictions for the full body text extracted from the underlying Web pages.

The reading difficulty prediction method that we use is a variant of an existing statistical language modeling approach that has been extensively evaluated on Web content and shown to be effective for both short, noisy texts, and full-page Web texts [4]. Unlike traditional measures that compute a single numeric score, this approach provides extra information about score reliability by computing the likely *distribution* over levels. We show later that having the entire distribution is important for higher-quality predictions. Moreover, language models are vocabulary-centric and can capture fine-grained patterns in individual word behavior across levels. Thus, they are ideal for the noisy, short, fragmented text that occurs on the Web in queries, titles, result snippets, image or table captions. Our variant incorporates feature weight estimation similar to that used in a second, recently introduced reading difficulty prediction model that computes a word's estimated age of word acquisition from a corpus of labeled examples. Evaluated on a test corpus, our classifier has a Root Mean Squared Error of approximately 1.7 grade levels (see [11] for more details).

3.1.2 *Predicting Topic Distributions from Text*

We chose to use the Open Directory Project (ODP) for topic classification because of its broad, general purpose topic coverage and availability of reasonably high-quality training data. For the experiments reported in this study we used 219 topical categories from the top two levels of the ODP.

To train topic classifiers, we used a crawl of ODP from early 2008. We first split the data into a train (70%) and validation (30%) set, then identified the topic categories (some categories like Regional are not topical and were discarded) that had at least 1K documents. This resulted in 219 categories at the top two levels of the hierarchy. To simplify the prediction-phase of the classification model, we simply flattened the two levels to an *m*-of-*N* (where $N = 219$) prediction task. A logistic regression classifier using an L_2 regularizer was trained over each of the ODP topics identified. When optimized for the F_1 score in each ODP category, the classifier has a micro-average F_1 of 0.60 (see [2] for more details).

3.2 Building Reading Level & Topic Profiles for Websites, Users, and Queries

We use the term *entity* (e) to refer to a website (s), a user (u) or a query (q). We use capital letters (S, U, Q) to denote a group of each entity type. We now define our novel reading-level and topic-based *profile* of an entity as the *probability distributions* of the given entity's reading level (R), and topic (T), or the combination of reading level and topic (RT). For example, a reading level and topic profile of a user or a query can be written as $P(RT|u)$ and $(RT|q)$, respectively.

Figure 1 summarizes typical relationships between entities in a Web search session, where a user issues a query, the query surfaces a website, and a user visits the website. The arrows here are bi-directional because a profile for any entity can be constructed from data describing any of the other entities. For instance, user information from site visits can be used to create a site profile, and site visits can be used to create user profiles.

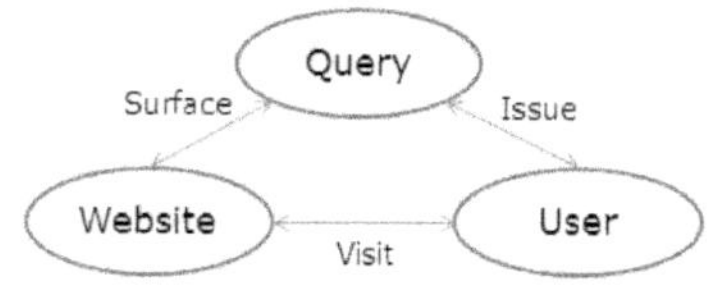

Figure 1: Relationship between entities in a search session.

One motivation for modeling the profile as a distribution, as opposed to a summary statistic, is to capture *focus effects* that allow us to distinguish between, for example, two websites or two users with identical average reading level but very different diversity in the topics or range of difficulty levels they cover.

Table 1 lists the entities used in this paper and potential sources of information for building them. We can use the information associated with the entity itself or the information aggregated from related entities to build a profile of each entity. We next describe how an entity-specific profile can be estimated.

3.2.1 *Profiles based on the Entity Itself*

Here we describe how we can build profiles of important entities based on the entity itself. Given a set of URLs associated with each entity, the joint distribution of reading level and topic is built by aggregating the distributions of the individual URLs computed by URL-level classifiers. To prevent the bias arising from the imbalance in the number of samples used, we used a fixed number of URLs (see below) to estimate the profile of each type.

Table 1: Summary of profile types used in this paper and sources used to build them.

Profile Type		Built From	Source	Weighting	Section where we use					
Page		Text classifiers	*Page text/content*	-	**4.2**				**5.1**	**5.2**
User		Aggregate	*Page profiles of visited URLs*	Num. of visits			**4.4**		**5.1**	
Session		Aggregate	*Page profiles of visited URLs in session*	Num. of visits			**4.4.2**			
Query		Aggregate	*Page profiles of top-ranked URLs*	Uniform				**4.5**		
Website	Content view	Aggregate	*Page profiles*	Uniform					**5.1**	**5.2**
	Usage view	Aggregate	*Page profiles, user-viewed*	Num. of visits		**4.3**				**5.2**
	Demographic /visitor view	Aggregate	*User profiles of visitors to site*	Uniform						**5.2**
	Surfacing queries	Aggregate	*Profiles of surfacing queries*	Uniform						**5.2**

We consider a website (or 'site') to be a set of URLs within a full URL domain. Site profiles can be built using one of two sources – site content, or user interaction with the site. In the *content view* of a site, we simply examine a sample of representative content without regard to user interaction with the site. In the *user view* of a site, we focus on the subset of URLs that users actually viewed on the site. This we call a *search-biased* user view – that is, we filter URLs that were clicked in search results.

To estimate the profile of a user, we use the URLs visited by a user during Web search sessions. In this work, we randomly choose 25 URLs to estimate the site-level or user-level profiles (we chose one fixed number to control for the amount of data used to estimate a profile).

For the case of queries, we use the top 10 URLs as of the profile for the query. When past click data is available for the query, one can use the list of clicked URLs with associated frequency, as was done in Bennett *et al.* [2].

3.2.2 Profiles based on Entity Relationships

Profiles can also be constructed from other profiles: a user's profile could be computed not only based on the webpages visited by the user, but alternatively using the profiles of websites visited by the user, or the profiles of queries issued by the user.

This is an important source of information because related entities provide a rich context by which we can make more accurate judgments on each entity. For instance, since a profile of a website is built using many webpages, it can be a more reliable source of information than using individual webpages.

In theory, relationship-based profile construction could be done in a way that introduced circular dependencies – for example, by having user profiles computed from site profiles of visits, which themselves were created from user profiles. We avoid such circularity issues here by using profiles based only on the entity itself, and not based on summaries of other entities, when building a profile based on entity relationships. In general, this type of aggregation is commonly used as an approximate way to infer properties of related entities in relational learning.

3.3 Characterizing and Comparing Profiles

Given the entity-specific profile built as above, now we define the measures used to characterize and compare entities and groups of entities.

3.3.1 Characteristics of an Individual Entity

We first describe the measures we use to characterize an individual entity. Since each profile is a probability distribution, we use the expectation and entropy to summarize the distribution. We denote expectation of reading level for a given entity e as $E[R|e]$, the expectation of topic distribution as $E[T|e]$, and the expectation of the joint distribution as $E[RT|e]$.

As a measure of variation, we use the entropy of reading level, topic and the joint distribution of reading level and topic. If we denote the probability that an entity e has a specific reading level $R_d \epsilon R$ as $P(r|e)$, the reading level entropy of the entity $H(R|e)$ can be derived as follows:

$$H(R|e) = \sum_{R_d \epsilon R} P(R_d|e) \times \log_2 P(R_d|e)$$

We can similarly define topical entropy $H(T|e)$ and joint entropy $H(RT|e)$.

3.3.2 Characteristics of a Group of Entities

In addition to summarizing the characteristics of each entity, we need to represent groups of entities. We build the profile of an entity group by aggregating the distributions of individual entities. Here, we aggregate using what may be considered a weighted centroid of the individual distributions, which for brevity we call a 'group centroid'. For instance, if we represent the probability that we observe a user u in a user group U as $P(u|U)$, we build the reading level profile for U as follows:

$$P(R|U) = \sum_{u \epsilon U} P(u|U) \times P(R|u)$$

In building a site profile based on its visitors, we estimate $P(u|U)$ based on the frequency of a user's visitation over sites. Once we have this aggregated representation, we can use the same metrics as in the case of individual entities.

In addition to using the group centroid to characterize the group profile, we can represent the diversity of the group in terms of its members. Here, we measure the diversity of a group using the average distance of members from the group centroid. In the case of reading level this is:

$$Div_R(U) = \sum_{u \epsilon U} P(u|U) \times D_R(U,u)$$

We use several metrics of comparison between an entity and a group to measure the distance, $D_R(U,u)$, which we explain in detail in the next section.

3.3.3 Comparisons between Entities or Groups

In many applications, we need to compute the profile similarity (or distance) between two entities, or between an entity and an entity group.

For the case of reading level, the simplest metric of comparison is the difference in the expectation of reading level between entities e_1 and e_2 as follows:

$$Diff_R(e_1||e_2) = E[R|e_1] - E[R|e_2]$$

However, it is not clear how we can define such difference metric for the case of topical category or the joint distribution of both. Also, the difference metrics captures only the mean of the distribution.

As an alternative, we use the Kullback-Leibler (KL) Divergence and Jensen-Shannon (JS) Divergence [7] to compare the similarity or distance between the full probability distributions of two entities. For reading level distribution between entities e_1 and e_2 these measures are defined as:

$$KL_R(e_1||e_2) = \sum_{R_d \epsilon R} P(R_d|e_1) \times \log_2 \frac{P(R_d|e_2)}{P(R_d|e_1)}$$

and

$$JS_R(e_1||e_2) = KL_R(e_1||\tfrac{e_1+e_2}{2}) + KL_R(e_1||\tfrac{e_1+e_2}{2}).$$

KL-divergence and JS-divergence for topic and joint distributions are defined similarly. To handle the zero frequency problem in calculating KL divergence, we used absolute discounting with ε = 0.001.

Category	Count	R_1	R_2	R_3	R_4	R_5	R_6	R_7	R_8	R_9	R_{10}	R_{11}	R_{12}	E[R|T]	SD[R|T]
Reference	20,959	0.00	0.00	0.00	0.02	0.17	0.10	0.15	0.04	0.02	0.03	0.20	0.27	8.80	2.86
Health	42,145	0.00	0.00	0.00	0.03	0.18	0.08	0.13	0.04	0.04	0.10	0.27	0.11	8.53	2.65
Science	19,816	0.00	0.00	0.00	0.06	0.23	0.09	0.07	0.02	0.01	0.08	0.27	0.17	8.44	2.97
Computers	93,204	0.00	0.00	0.00	0.06	0.24	0.19	0.03	0.01	0.01	0.02	0.32	0.12	8.11	3.00
Business	113,122	0.00	0.00	0.00	0.05	0.22	0.16	0.09	0.03	0.02	0.04	0.26	0.12	8.08	2.86
Society	232,791	0.00	0.00	0.00	0.02	0.23	0.07	0.35	0.03	0.01	0.01	0.22	0.06	7.62	2.42
Adult	31,044	0.00	0.00	0.00	0.05	0.28	0.26	0.14	0.05	0.02	0.01	0.13	0.06	6.98	2.41
Kids_and_Teens	10,253	0.00	0.00	0.02	0.23	0.26	0.13	0.09	0.02	0.01	0.02	0.15	0.08	6.60	2.81
Games	27,528	0.00	0.00	0.00	0.19	0.36	0.10	0.11	0.02	0.02	0.03	0.12	0.03	6.39	2.44
Recreation	48,619	0.00	0.00	0.00	0.11	0.44	0.19	0.08	0.02	0.02	0.02	0.09	0.02	6.18	2.15
Arts	162,762	0.00	0.00	0.00	0.08	0.40	0.27	0.10	0.05	0.01	0.01	0.06	0.02	6.18	1.94
Home	20,577	0.00	0.00	0.02	0.19	0.41	0.14	0.04	0.03	0.01	0.03	0.09	0.04	6.08	2.40
News	19,370	0.00	0.00	0.00	0.04	0.41	0.33	0.14	0.02	0.02	0.01	0.03	0.01	5.99	1.45
Shopping	109,875	0.00	0.00	0.01	0.22	0.29	0.24	0.09	0.03	0.01	0.02	0.07	0.02	5.98	2.09
Sports	31,942	0.00	0.00	0.00	0.09	0.56	0.11	0.10	0.03	0.03	0.02	0.06	0.02	5.94	1.93

Table 2: Reading level distribution and the average reading level for top ODP categories. Rows are ordered by the expectation of reading level. Cells are shaded according to their probability mass.

4. CHARACTERIZING THE WEB USING READING LEVEL & TOPIC PROFILES

We now show how assigning a RLT profile to websites, users, and queries reveals interesting new relationships and task characterizations that have implications for improving search.

We first provide a description of the datasets used in this study, and an analysis of Web content and websites with respect to topic and reading level. We then examine how we can characterize Web users, websites and queries using profiles.

4.1 Data Set

The primary source of data for this study is a proprietary data set containing the anonymized logs of URLs visited by users who consented to provide interaction data through a widely-distributed browser plug-in. The data set contained browser-based logs with both searching and browsing episodes from which we extract search-related data. Log entries include a browser identifier, a timestamp for each page view, and the URL of the Web page visited. To remove variability caused by geographic and linguistic variation in search behavior, we only include log entries generated in the English-speaking United States locale.

The results described in this paper are based on URL visits during 10 weeks from August through early October 2010, representing millions of Web page visits from thousands of unique users who visited at least 25 pages during the period. From these data we extracted search sessions from Bing, using a session extraction methodology similar to White et al. [18]. Search sessions begin with a query, occur within the same browser and tab instance (to lessen the effect of any multi-tasking that users may perform), and terminate following 30 minutes of user inactivity.

From these search sessions we extracted search queries and for each query, we obtained the top ten search results retrieved by Bing and the titles and the snippets for each result. In total, we built long-term profiles for 7,613 users based on more than 2 million clicks. For websites, we built both content-view and user-view profiles for 4,715 websites which had more than 25 clicked URLs during the period. Finally, we created profiles for 141,325 unique queries in our data set.

A second dataset, which we call the 'web content' dataset, comprised reading level and ODP topic predictions for a snapshot of 8 billion Web documents from April 18, 2011. Each page was tagged with a reading level distribution over American grade levels 1-12, and top-3 most likely ODP categories as described previously.

4.2 Characterizing Web Content

We start by examining the properties of Web content in terms of reading level and topic, using the 2 million URLs visited by Web users as described in the previous section. While this dataset is a search-biased subset of the Web, it represents a significant sample of content that is both broad in topic coverage and of explicit interest to users.

Table 2 summarizes the reading level distribution and the mean and standard deviation of reading levels for the 15 top-level ODP categories. Topics are sorted by descending mean reading difficulty $E[R|T]$. The resulting ordering fits with our general expectation: the categories with highest average reading difficulty have aspects that were more technically oriented, namely Reference, Health, Science, Computers, and Business. The lowest-difficulty categories were more broadly-oriented topics: Sports, Shopping, News, Home, and Arts. In addition, especially for the more technical topics, there is noticeable bi-modality in reading level distribution, with one mode in the grade 4-7 range and a second in the grade 10-12 range, perhaps reflecting the co-existence of 'layperson' and 'expert' content respectively for these topics. The standard deviation of per-topic reading level $SD[R|T]$ also varies considerably across topics. Computers, Science, Reference, and Business have the highest standard deviations in reading level. Kids & Teens also has high variance, perhaps due to its goal of providing content to a broad age range of children. Lowest variance in reading level

Table 3: The correlation between site profile entropy and site visitors' group-level profile diversity, for different entropy and group-level diversity measures.

	Visitor Group-Level Diversity		
Website Content Entropy	$Div_R(U\|s)$	$Div_T(U\|s)$	$Div_{RT}(U\|s)$
E[R|s]	0.052	0.081	0.095
H[R|s]	0.025	0.127	0.143
H[T|s]	0.094	0.336	0.324
H[RT|s]	0.057	0.260	0.264

were News, Sports, Arts, Shopping, and Recreation. The low variation among News pages in particular suggests that news content tends to be more consistent and homogeneous in style than generic Web content.

We next summarize reading level and topic distributions for the three entities of interest – websites, user and queries, and then show how these characterizations can be used to model the selection of search results.

4.3 Characterizing Websites

Here we move from individual page properties to website profiles built by aggregating reading level and topic distribution predictions over many individual pages from the website. Website-level properties help capture the overall scope of content at the site, and they provide a useful background model for dealing with previously unseen pages from the site.

4.3.1 Topic-specific Analysis

We first look at the distribution of websites in terms of the expectation of reading level and the probability that they belong to a specific topic, where we used content-based profiles. Figure 2 shows results for two topics, Kids & Teens (left) and Computers (right). Each point corresponds to a website. The *x*-axis shows the probability $P(T|s)$ of the example topic given the site while the *y*-axis shows the expected reading level over all pages for that site. For the Kids & Teens topic, there is a clear negative correlation between the predicted 'Kids' nature of a site and the average reading level of its pages: the more strongly predicted the Kids & Teens topic is for a site, the lower the site's overall reading level. The Computers topic, on the other hand, exhibits the opposite trend: the more computer-focused a website, the higher its overall reading level is likely to be.

4.3.2 Site Content Profile by User Profiles

In this section we examine the relationship between a site's profile and its visitors' profiles. Table 3 shows the correlation between entropy for site's profile (based on content) and the divergence among site visitors' profiles (based on a sample of site URLs visited). The divergences are based on topic, reading level, and the joint distribution of topic and reading level. The results show that the entropy in a given site's topic content profile is positively correlated with the topic diversity in profiles among its visitors. This means that sites with topically diverse contents attract diverse visitors. However, the correlations are lower in the case of sites' reading level profile.

The overall correlation between reading level and site diversity is low ($corr(E[R|s], Div_{RT}(U|s)) = 0.095$) in the top right cell of Table 3. However, when we analyzed this further by breaking down the results across topics, as shown in Figure 3, we discovered significant variation, with much higher correlation for some topics. This is an excellent example of how the joint analysis of reading level and topic can reveal new insights.

For example, Figure 3 shows that for the Computers and Reference categories, higher reading level of the site led to more coherent visitors. For the Kids and Teens category, however, higher reading level meant more diverse visitors. One possible interpretation of this result is that the range of users is more restricted for technical categories like computers, whereas a site for children may have content that can bring interests from more diverse user groups (e.g., parents and teachers) if it has a high reading level.

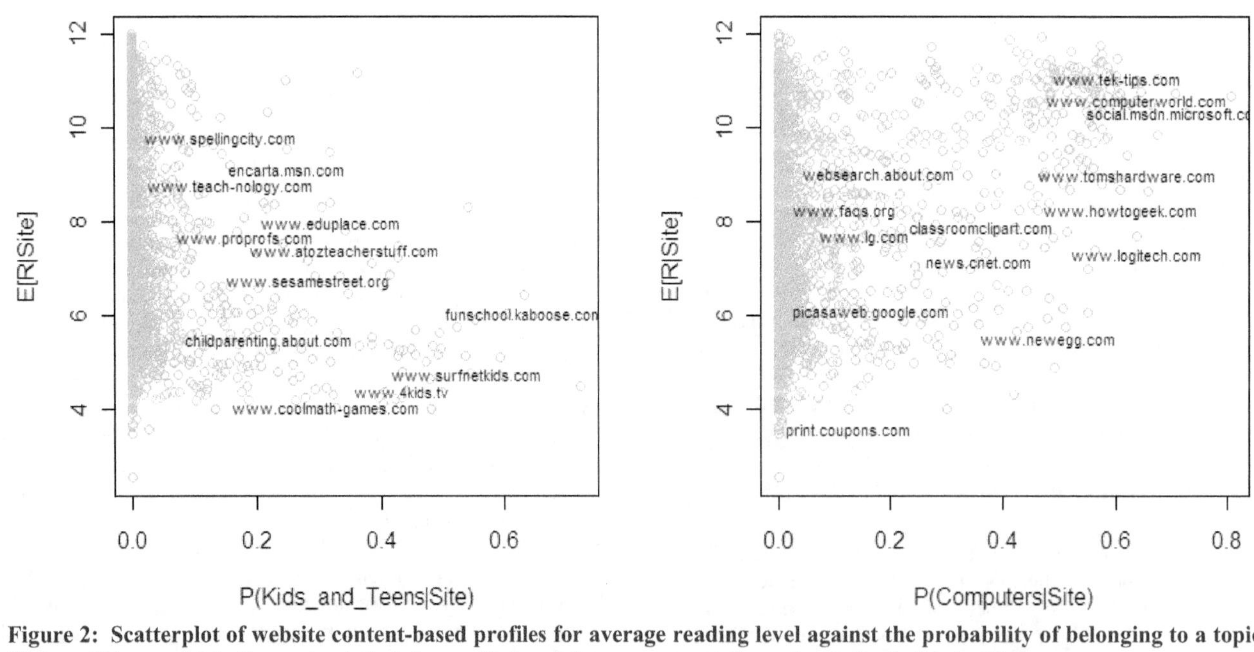

Figure 2: Scatterplot of website content-based profiles for average reading level against the probability of belonging to a topic (left: Kids and Teens, right: Computers). Labels are displayed for a representative subset of websites in this space.

4.4 Characterizing Web Users

We next look at the profile characteristics of Web users, similarly to Section 4.3, in terms of the expectation of reading level and the probability that they belong to a specific topic.

4.4.1 Topic-specific Analysis

We investigated the correlation between a user's reading level and the probability of the user belonging to a category, as estimated from their profile over a 10-week period. Figure 4 shows the results for two categories – Kids and Teens (left) and Computers (right). Each point represents a single user profile plotted as a function of dominant topic probability (x-axis) and expected reading level (y-axis). The results show that for some classes, such as the Computers topic (right), there is a clear separation into readers in terms of user preference for higher- vs. lower-level content, as the probability of a user belonging to that topic increases. Other topics, such as Kids and Teens (left) do not exhibit this behavior.

4.4.2 Users' Deviation from Their Own Profiles

Most previous work that has applied reading level or topic categories to search tasks has assumed that users want material matching their profile as closely as possible. In this section we provide a characterization of key tasks for which users *deviate* significantly from their typical profile during a search session. Our hypothesis was that users demonstrate *higher motivation to obtain information* when they exhibit *stretch reading* behavior – spending significant time reading material that involves a higher cognitive effort.

With the introduction of reading level metadata, we now have a way to measure approximate cognitive load of the search results a user sees. If we could identify such situations automatically, the search engine might customize its retrieval or interface to support such high-motivation needs. To our knowledge this is the first such estimate of cognitive load that does not require specialized client hardware such as eye-tracking [3] and thus can be widely used on a very large scale.

To perform our analysis we built a unigram language model for the titles of all 'stretch pages' that were at least four grade levels above the average reading level for a given user's profile, and

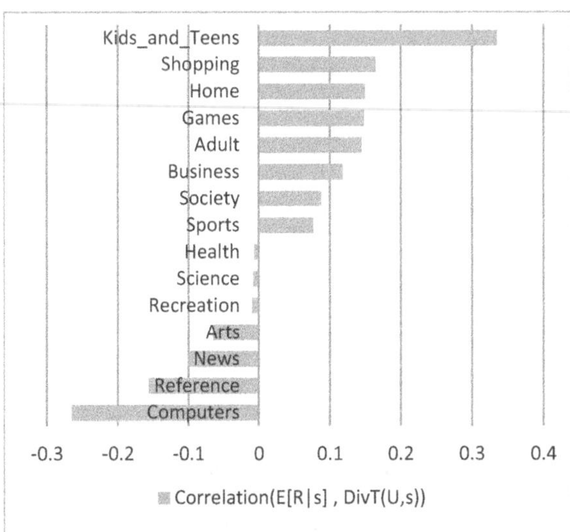

Figure 3: The correlation between a website's expected reading level and the profile diversity of its visitors, varies greatly depending on the topic of the website.

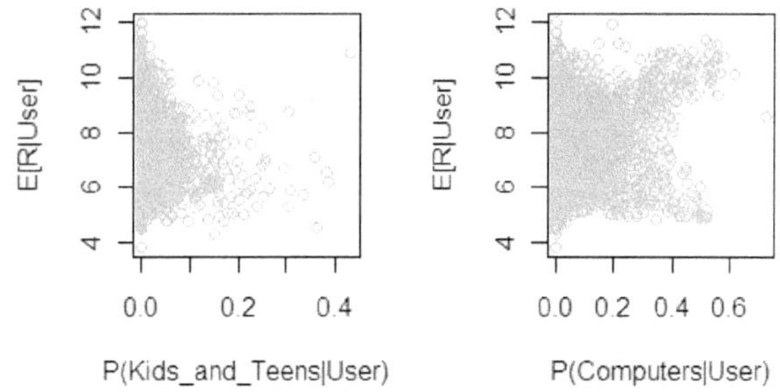

Figure 4: Scatterplot of user profiles plotted by average reading level against the probability of belonging to a topic (left: Kids and Teens, right: Computers).

which had clicks indicating that they were satisfied with the result. Based on models developed by [14], we use dwell times of 30 sec. or more to denote satisfaction. We compared this 'stretch reading' title language model to a background language model based on the titles of all clicked content. To ensure that we identified terms of interest to a broader set of users we restricted the language models to only consider words that were associated with clicks from at least ten unique users. For each word, we then computed a score using the log ratio of its probability in the 'stretch' model, to its probability in the background model. Words with log-ratio score much greater than zero are much more likely in the 'stretch reading' model than the background model.

The highest- and lowest-scoring stretch words are shown in Table 4. The top terms are 'test' and 'tests' – and looking at more detailed search context, we found the main topic areas of the corresponding queries to be a combination of education and medical tests. Other education-related terms also appear in the top set, including 'education' and 'learning'.

In general, we found the great majority of stretch reading could be classified into five main areas that correspond to important but sometimes challenging activities required in everyday life: education-related reading such as test preparation and fact-finding about schools; government-related material such as

Table 4: The strongest and weakest words associated with stretch reading, as estimated from titles of pages with a satisfied SERP click, and computed log ratio against a background model of all SAT click titles.

Highest association with stretch reading		Lowest association with stretch reading	
Title word	Log ratio	Title word	Log ratio
tests	2.22	best	-0.42
test	1.99	football	-0.45
sample	1.94	store	-0.46
digital	1.88	great (deals)	-0.47
(tuition) options	1.87	items	-0.52
(financial) aid	1.87	new	-0.53
(medication) effects	1.84	sale	-0.61
education	1.77	games	-0.65
forms	1.76	sports	-0.78
plan	1.74	food	-0.81
pay	1.71	news	-0.82
medical	1.69	music	-1.02
learning	1.62	all	-1.35

Table 5: The effectiveness of different user profile-based metrics for predicting users' preference between clicked and skipped items in search results, as measured by proportion of clicked items with a correct preference prediction. Results are subdivided by degree of user profile focus based on profile distribution entropy. Prediction generally improved for users with more focused profiles, and when reading level and topic were used together.

User data		*Page-based measures*			*Site-based measures*		
User Group	*# Clicks*	*$Diff_R(u,d)$*	*$KL_R(u,d)$*	*$KL_T(u,d)$*	*$KL_R(u,s)$*	*$KL_T(u,s)$*	*$KL_{RT}(u,s)$*
↑Focused Profile	5,960	55.03%	60.15%	69.16%	59.23%	60.79%	65.27%
	147,195	51.08%	50.43%	55.78%	52.25%	54.20%	54.41%
	197,733	49.74%	50.84%	54.20%	52.75%	53.36%	53.63%
↓Diverse Profile	15,610	49.05%	50.90%	54.54%	53.81%	53.40%	52.90%
Total	366,498	50.33%	50.83%	55.10%	52.70%	53.82%	54.10%

instructions for filling out forms, or legal/judicial information; medical content on the effects of prescriptions, diseases, and tests and procedures; financial aid and planning materials; and job-seeking. All of these scenarios are ones where it is more likely the user is highly motivated to obtain information and thus more willing to spend time outside of their typical topic and reading-level zone.

The least-likely stretch terms gives indications of very different topical content that match with our other findings, that topics such as sports, games, shopping have lower average reading level, while also being popular. The predominance of these topics could suggest that people either don't read above their reading level in these areas, or that there don't typically exist pages with high reading levels that cover those topics. This is the subject of future work.

Being able to automatically identify tasks where the user is highly motivated to learn or require help has important implications for search engines. It means that, on detecting such scenarios, a search engine could automatically suggest easier website or page alternatives if available, or provide support in other ways, such as vocabulary assistance, specialized vertical search, or enhanced suggestions through a social network of friends or people with related goals.

4.5 Characterizing Web Queries

In Section 3 we introduced the definition of a 'query profile' based on the combined reading level and topic distribution of the top-10 results returned for the query. Similar to the cases of websites and users, we investigated the correlation between a query's reading level and the probability of the query belonging to a topic category. Figure 5 shows results for two categories: Kids and Teens (left) and Computers (right). Each point represents a single user profile plotted as a function of dominant topic probability (x-axis) and expected reading level (y-axis).

The results show similar trends to those for websites: queries with higher probability for the Kids and Teens category had lower reading levels, and those with higher chance of belonging to the Computers category had higher reading levels. Again, this result shows that there exist significant correlations between reading level and topic probability within an entity profile.

We also compared the topical coherence of query profiles, as measured by the profile's topic entropy $H[T]$ over a query's results, between navigational and non-navigational queries. We found that on average, navigational queries had profiles with higher topic entropy (1.460) than non-navigational queries (1.397). This may be due to navigational queries having many minority intents after the first or second result, or results covering varied aspects of the navigational entity after the direct links. This is an area for further analysis.

5. APPLICATIONS

In this section we describe two initial applications of RLT profiles to search-related problems: using profile-based metrics to predict user preferences on Web search results, and classifying expert vs. novice content on the Web.

5.1 Analyzing the Impact of Profile Match on Search Results Clicks

We analyzed how users' preferences on search results can be predicted using their profiles. Specifically, we compared the profile divergence between a user and each clicked document in the top 10 search results, and between the user and each skipped document right above the clicked document.

We used the same 10-week session data for the experiments described in this section, with two important differences. First, since we are interested only in search behavior, we used the users' clicks only on the top 10 search results. Also, to estimate user profiles in a data set different from the search log data we are analyzing, we split the data set by time period. We used the user profile estimated from the first five-week period for analyzing the search behavior of the second five-week period.

Table 5 summarizes the results. Each cell represents the percentage of cases where clicked documents have a higher profile matching score than the corresponding skipped document. Each column represents different metrics of divergence between a user and a document (or a corresponding

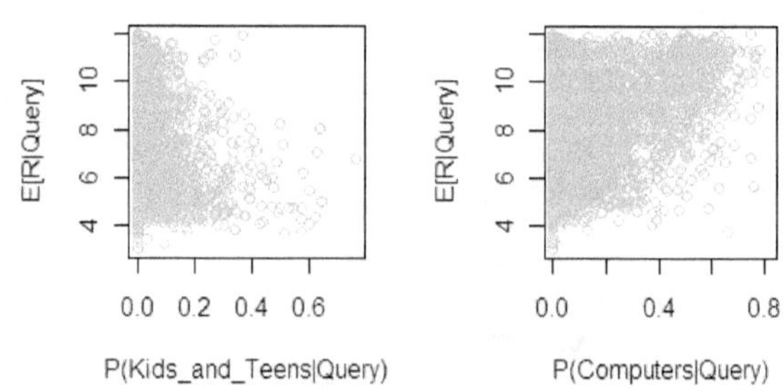

Figure 5: Scatterplot of query profiles plotted by average reading level against the probability of belonging to a topic (left: Kids &Teens, right: Computers).

Table 6: Summary of accuracy, precision and recall for expert site-finding classification task compared to the baseline accuracy of random selection.

Baseline (predict most likely class)	0.659
Classifier accuracy	0.822
Precision for expert sites	0.769
Recall for expert sites	0.683
Precision for non-expert sites	0.847
Recall for non-expert sites	0.893

website). We broke down our results by the degree of 'focus' in a user's profile, as measured by the entropy of the joint reading level and topic distribution . For instance, the data in the top-most ('Focused') row of Table 5 are from users with relatively low profile entropy and thus with very focused search behavior in terms of both reading level and topic. Users in the 'Diverse' group, on the other hand, had broader reading level and topic profiles with relatively high entropy. First, we note that in general, all KL-divergence-based measures show accuracy higher than 50% overall, indicating that the profile does give some signal about users' click preferences.

Sorted by prediction effectiveness on the total user group, each metric's gain was significantly higher than the other metrics below it, as well as the random predictions, using a paired t-test with p-value < 0.01.

Our main observations are that preference prediction was stronger for users with more focused profiles across all metrics, and that for site-level profiles, the joint distribution gives better results than using either reading level or topic distribution alone. Furthermore, site-based measures, which use the aggregated topic and reading level distribution of a page's website, performed almost as well as the measures that used the individual page, while requiring orders of magnitude less storage. The page-level KL divergence in topic between a user and a document did indeed perform better than the divergence in joint distribution between a user and a site This is understandable, in that URL-level information is more fine-grained than site-level information.

Finally, within page-based measures, the feature based on the entire distribution showed better performance than using only the expectation of the same distribution $Diff_R(u, d)$, illustrating the benefit of having more information by modeling the profile as a distribution.

5.2 Predicting Domain Expertise Using Reading Level & Topic Profiles

In this section we apply RLT profiles to data from a previous study on domain expertise. We then describe and evaluate a classification model for distinguishing expert from non-expert websites using features of reading level and topic profiles.

5.2.1 Comparing Expert vs. Non-expert URLs

White *et al.* [17] used manually annotated expert vs. novice URLs to characterize the behavior of domain experts and non-experts, comprising the 150 most popular URLs within each of four domains: Medical, Computer Science, Legal, and Finance. We computed reading level and topic distributions for each URL in their data set. With these distributions, for each URL we

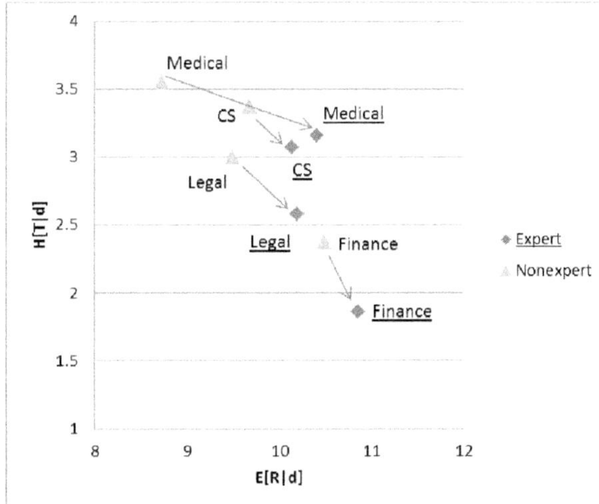

Figure 6: Expert-oriented pages had higher average reading difficulty and higher average topic focus (lower topic entropy) than non-expert pages in the same domain.

computed expected reading level and the joint entropy of reading level and topic, Figure 6 illustrates this, showing that pages labeled as 'expert' have higher reading level and higher topic focus (lower entropy) than the 'non-expert' sites. The differences in both variables varied across domains, with medical domain pages showing highest difference in reading level between expert and non-expert Web pages.

5.2.2 Predicting Expert Websites

Based on the observations in the previous section we developed a method to predict expert websites using reading level and topic profiles. We predict expertise at the site level rather than the

Feature	*Correl.*	*Description*
$KL_{RT}(s,U)$	-0.56	Divergence of average user's RLT profile from site's profile.
$KL_{T}(s,U)$	-0.55	Divergence of average user's topic profile from site's profile.
$Div_{RT}(U\|s)$	-0.45	Average divergence of user's RLT profile from its centroid.
$Div_{T}(U\|s)$	-0.41	Average divergence of user's topic profile from its centroid.
$Diff_{T}(s,U)$	-0.40	% of users whose top ODP category differs from that of site.
$Div_{R}(U\|s)$	-0.29	Divergence of average user's reading level profile from site's profile.
$Diff_{T}(s,Q)$	-0.28	% of queries whose top ODP category differs from that of site.
$H_{RT}(U\|s)$	-0.21	Average RLT entropy of site visitors.
$H(T\|s)$	-0.13	Site topical entropy (user-viewed URLs).
$E(R\|s)$	+0.23	Site reading level (user-viewed URLs).
$E(R\|Q)$	+0.34	Expectation of surfacing queries' reading level.
$E(R\|U)$	+0.44	Expectation of visitor's reading level.

Table 7: Features used for expert site prediction task, sorted by their correlation with expert/non-expert label.

URL level because sites tend to have a coherent profile in many cases, and much more data can be aggregated at the site level. We focused on predicting expertise of sites within the Computers topic. We selected websites occurring 25 or more times in our session log.

To create a site profile we used both 100 randomly chosen URLs on the site and 25 user-viewed URLs on the site. In other words, we extracted features from both content-based and user-viewed profiles of given website. We also used the aggregate profiles of site visitors and queries used to visit the website. To capture the diversity of visitors' profiles from the site profile, we used the divergence of the average user's profile from the site profile, i.e. how different site visitors were from the site profile itself, as well as the average divergence of a user's profile from the user profile group centroid, i.e. how different site visitors are among themselves.

Our prediction experiment is based on 10-fold cross validation, using a gradient boosted decision tree classifier [19]. The results in Table 6 show 82% overall accuracy. This accuracy is significantly better than the baseline accuracy of 65.9% across all 10 folds. Table 7 lists the classifier features and their correlation with the binary Expert/Non-expert label, showing that features based on profiles of visitors and queries provide strong signals for the 'expertness' of websites. The divergence of visitor's profiles shows highest negative correlation, indicating that users for expert sites have coherent profiles with the site and with each other. Also, the expectation of reading level for queries and visitors shows stronger positive correlation (+0.34, +0.44) with the 'expertness' of a site than the expected reading level of the site itself (+0.23) based on visited URLs.

6. SUMMARY AND CONCLUSIONS

We introduced a novel form of probabilistic profile, the RLT profile, which can be used to describe major entities of Web search such as users, queries, or websites – based on reading level and topic metadata produced by automatic text classifiers. Based on these profiles, we performed a large-scale analysis of Web content and search interactions. Our findings show that RLT profiles are effective for a variety of analysis and prediction purposes: they provide novel characterizations for websites, users and queries by combining distributional statistics of both topic and reading level distributions as well as their joint distribution. These representations can be used for a variety of search-related tasks such as understanding search result preferences, and predicting whether the content of a URL or site is targeted at domain experts or non-experts.

Our main finding is that reading level and topic metadata used together were more effective than either one used alone. We analyzed how reading level distribution of content on the Web varies across topics. Then, using features derived from RLT profiles, we found these features provided effective personalization signals, predicting a user's preference for Web pages and sites in search results. With these RLT profiles we characterized a user's behavior when they deviated from their profile to perform 'stretch' tasks. Finally, we applied RLT profiles of Web sites to analyze and predict the 'expertness' of these sites.

Future directions include applying these findings to various end-user tasks. The divergence metrics developed in this paper could be evaluated for their effectiveness as features for personalized re-ranking. We also plan to investigate users' stretch behavior further, so that we can detect and assist these patterns of behavior more effectively. Finally, the techniques developed for expert *vs.* novice site classification can be applied both for recommendation and ranking purposes.

Acknowledgments

We thank Ryen White for providing and assisting with the expertise URL dataset.

REFERENCES

[1] J. Allan. HARD Track Overview in TREC 2003: High accuracy retrieval from documents. In *Proceedings of TREC 2003*. NIST Special Publication.

[2] P. Bennett, K. Svore, and S.T. Dumais. Classification-enhanced ranking. In *Proceedings of WWW 2010*.

[3] M. J. Cole, J. Gwizdka, C. Liu, R. Bierig, N. Belkin, X. Zhang. Task and user effects on reading patterns in information search. *Interacting with Computers* (2011).

[4] K. Collins-Thompson and J. Callan. A language modeling approach to predicting reading difficulty. In *Proceedings of HLT 2004*.

[5] K. Collins-Thompson and J. Callan. Information retrieval for language tutoring: an overview of the REAP project. In *Proceedings of SIGIR 2004*. ACM, New York, USA.

[6] K. Collins-Thompson, P.N. Bennett, R.W. White, S. de la Chica, D. Sontag. Personalizing web search results by reading level. In *Proceedings of CIKM 2011*. ACM, New York, USA.

[7] I. Dagan, L. Lee, and F. Pereira. 1997. Similarity-based methods for word sense disambiguation. In *Proceedings of EACL 1997*. Association for Computational Linguistics, Stroudsburg, USA.

[8] Z. Dou, R.Song, J. R. Wen. A large-scale evaluation and analysis of personalized search strategies. In *Proceedings of WWW 2007*.

[9] Freund, L., Toms, E.G., & Waterhouse, J. Modeling the information behaviour of software engineers using a work-task framework. In *Proceedings of ASIST 2005*, Charlotte, NC, USA.

[10] D. Kelly and C. Cool. The effects of topic familiarity on information search and use behaviors. In *Proceedings of JCDL 2002*.

[11] P. Kidwell, G. Lebanon, K. Collins-Thompson. Statistical estimation of word acquisition with application to readability prediction. In *Proceedings of EMNLP 2009*, Singapore.

[12] G. Kumaran, R. Jones. Biasing web search results for topic familiarity. In *Proceedings of CIKM 2005*. ACM New York, USA.

[13] F. Peng, N. Ahmed, X. Li, Y. Lu. Context sensitive stemming for web search. In *Proceedings of SIGIR 2007*. ACM New York, USA.

[14] K. Wang, T. Walker, Z. Zheng. Estimating relevance ranking quality from web search clickthrough data. In *Proceedings of SIGKDD 2009*, 1355—1364.

[15] Y. Song, N. Nguyen, L. He, S. Imig, and R. Rounthwaite. 2011. Searchable web sites recommendation. In *Proceedings of WSDM 2011*.

[16] C. Tan, E. Gabrilovich, and B. Pang. To each his own: personalized content selection based on text comprehensibility. In *Proceedings of WSDM 2012*. ACM, New York, USA.

[17] R. W. White, S. Dumais, J. Teevan. Characterizing the influence of domain expertise on Web search behavior. In *Proceedings of WSDM 2009*. ACM, New York, USA.

[18] R. W. White, P. N. Bennett, S. Dumais. Predicting short-term interests using activity-based search context. In *Proceedings of CIKM 2010*. ACM, New York, USA.

[19] Q. Wu, C.J.C. Burges, K. Svore, and J. Gao. Adapting boosting for information retrieval measures. *Information Retrieval*, 2009.

Topical Clustering of Search Results

Ugo Scaiella
Dipartimento di Informatica
University of Pisa, Italy
scaiella@di.unipi.it

Paolo Ferragina
Dipartimento di Informatica
University of Pisa, Italy
ferragina@di.unipi.it

Andrea Marino
Dip. di Sistemi e Informatica
University of Florence, Italy
andrea.marino@unifi.it

Massimiliano Ciaramita
Google Research
Zürich, Switzerland
massi@google.com

ABSTRACT

Search results clustering (SRC) is a challenging algorithmic problem that requires grouping together the results returned by one or more search engines in topically coherent clusters, and labeling the clusters with meaningful phrases describing the topics of the results included in them.

In this paper we propose to solve SRC via an innovative approach that consists of modeling the problem as the *labeled clustering* of the nodes of a newly introduced *graph of topics*. The topics are Wikipedia-pages identified by means of recently proposed topic annotators [9, 11, 16, 20] applied to the search results, and the edges denote the relatedness among these topics computed by taking into account the linkage of the Wikipedia-graph.

We tackle this problem by designing a novel algorithm that exploits the spectral properties and the labels of that graph of topics. We show the superiority of our approach with respect to academic state-of-the-art work [6] and well-known commercial systems (CLUSTY and LINGO3G) by performing an extensive set of experiments on standard datasets and user studies via Amazon Mechanical Turk. We test several standard measures for evaluating the performance of all systems and show a relative improvement of up to 20%.

Categories and Subject Descriptors

H.3.3 [**Information Storage and Retrieval**]: Information Search and Retrieval—*Clustering*; I.2.7 [**Artificial Intelligence**]: Natural Language Processing—*Text analysis*

General Terms

Algorithms, Experimentation.

1. INTRODUCTION

Search Results Clustering (referred to as SRC) is a well-known approach to help users search the web [5]. It consists of clustering the short text fragments (aka snippets), returned by search engines to summarize the context of the searched keywords within the result pages, into a list of folders. Each folder is labeled with a variable-length phrase that should capture the "topic" of the clustered result pages. This labeled clustering offers a complementary view to the flat-ranked list of results commonly returned by search engines, and users can exploit this new view to acquire new knowledge about the issued query, or to refine their search results by navigating through the labeled folders, driven by their search needs. See Fig. 1 for an example.

This technique can be particularly useful for polysemous queries, but it is hard to implement efficiently and effectively [5]. This is due to many reasons. Efficiency imposes that the clustering must use only the short text of each snippet -otherwise the download of the result pages would take too long. Efficacy requires that the size of the clusters should be reasonable -otherwise too large or too small clusters would be useless for users-, the number of clusters should be limited, e.g., to 10 -to allow a fast and simple glance of the topics of the underlying search results-, the composition of the clusters should be diversified and ensure the coverage of the topics expressed by the search results, and the labels of the clusters should be meaningful and intelligible -to allow the users an efficient and effective browsing of the search results via the folder labels.

Figure 1: The web interface of LINGO3G, the commercial SRC system by CARROTSEARCH.

Permission to make digital or hard copies of all or part of this work for personal or classroom use is granted without fee provided that copies are not made or distributed for profit or commercial advantage and that copies bear this notice and the full citation on the first page. To copy otherwise, to republish, to post on servers or to redistribute to lists, requires prior specific permission and/or a fee.
WSDM'12, February 8–12, 2012, Seattle, Washington, USA.
Copyright 2012 ACM 978-1-4503-0747-5/12/02 ...$10.00.

These specific requirements cannot be addressed by traditional clustering algorithms. Numerous approaches have been proposed in the recent past to solve this problem both as commercial systems, CLUSTY and LINGO3G are the most representative examples, and as academic prototypes (see [5] for a survey). All of them rely on the (syntactic) *bag of words* paradigm applied to the short texts of the search-result snippets. This inevitably leads to two main limitations:

(a) the shortness and the fragmentation of the textual snippets makes it particularly difficult, if not impossible, to select meaningful and intelligible cluster labels. This problem is made today more significant by the diversification techniques applied by modern search-engines to their top-ranked results, which further reduces the applicability of statistically significant indicators;

(b) the polysemy or synonymy of terms often defeats the classical clustering approaches when they are applied onto the short snippets, because they are based on similarity measures that deploy just syntactic matches and/or *tf-idf* schemes.

1.1 Topic annotators

A recent line of research [9, 11, 16, 20] has started to successfully address the problem of detecting short and meaningful sequences of terms which are linked to relevant Wikipedia pages. These hyper-links constitute a sort of *topic annotation* for the input text and often solve synonymy and polysemy issues, because the identified Wikipedia pages can be seen as representation of specific and unambiguous topics. As an example, let us consider the following text fragment:

(1) US president issues Libya ultimatum

These topic-annotators are able to detect "US president", "Libya" and "ultimatum" as meaningful phrases to be hyperlinked with the topics represented by the Wikipedia pages dealing with the President of the United States, the nation of Libya and the threat to declare war, respectively.

We argue in the present paper that this contextualization of the input text might be very powerful in helping to detect the semantic similarity of syntactically different phrases, which is actually one of the limitations of the classical similarity measures. Indeed, consider the following text fragment:

(2) Barack Obama says Gaddafi may wait out military assault

It would be difficult to detect the tight relationship between phrases (1) and (2) by using classical similarity measures based on word matches, *tf-idf* or co-occurrences. On the contrary, the topics attached to the input texts by topic-annotators might allow one to discover easily this connection by taking into account the Wikipedia link-structure.

In addition, the disambiguation task performed by these annotators could allow to prevent correlation errors due to ambiguous words. As an example consider the following two fragments which are syntactically very similar:

(3) the paparazzi photographed the star

(4) the astronomer photographed the star

By considering just their one-word difference it would be hard to figure out the wide *topic distance* between the two fragments. On the contrary, the topic annotators would link the word "star" in the first fragment to the Wikipedia page entitled "Celebrity" and, in the second fragment, to the page that deals with the astronomical object. And since these two pages (topics) are far in the Wikipedia graph, an algorithm could easily spot the semantic distance between the two phrases.

1.2 Topical clustering of snippets

A first application of topic-annotators was presented in [14], where the authors used the annotated topics to extend the classical cosine-similarity measure in order to cluster long and well-formed texts. Apart from this result, to the best of our knowledge, no result is known in the literature that relies uniquely onto this novel annotation process in terms of both text representation and similarity measures.

In this paper we propose to move away from the classic *bag-of-words* paradigm towards a more ambitious *graph-of-topics* paradigm derived by using the above topic-annotators, and develop a novel labeled-clustering algorithm based on the spectral properties of that graph. Our solution to the SRC problem then consists of four main steps:

1. We deploy TAGME[1] [9], a state-of-the-art topic annotator for short texts, to process on-the-fly and with high accuracy the snippets returned by a search engine.
2. We represent each snippet as a richly structured *graph of topics*, in which the nodes are the topics annotated by TAGME, and the edges between topics are weighted via the relatedness measure introduced in [19].
3. Then we model SRC as a labeled clustering problem over a graph consisting of two types of nodes: topics and snippets. Edges in this graph are weighted to denote either topic-to-topic similarities or topic-to-snippet memberships. The former are computed via the Wikipedia linked-structure, the latter are discovered by TAGME and weighted via proper statistics.
4. Finally, we design a novel algorithm that exploits the spectral properties of the above graph to construct a *good* labeled clustering in terms of diversification and coverage of the snippet topics, coherence of clusters content, meaningfulness of the cluster labels, and small number of balanced clusters.

The final result will be a *topical decomposition* of the search results returned for a user query by one or more search engines. We have tested our approach on publicly available datasets using some standard measures plus a specific measure recently introduced in [6] that estimates the search-length time for a user query. Our experiments show that our approach achieves a relative improvement of up to 20% with respect to current state-of-the-art work [6]. We also complemented these experiments with a *user study* based on Mechanical Turk[2] aimed at comparing the quality of our cluster labels against two well-known commercial SRC systems: CLUSTY and LINGO3G. In this case our system is the best in producing semantically diversified labels over a public dataset of TREC queries, and it is the second best in terms of topics coverage compared to the gold standard sub-topics provided with the queries.

[1] `http://tagme.di.unipi.it`

[2] The crowd-sourcing service hosted by Amazon. `http://mturk.com`

Summarizing, the main contributions of this work are:

- the new *graph of topics* representation for short texts, based on the annotation by TAGME, that replaces the traditional *bag of words* paradigm (see Section 3);
- a new modeling of the SRC problem as the labeled clustering of a weighted graph consisting of topics and snippets (see Section 4);
- a novel algorithm for the labeled clustering of the above graph that exploits its spectral properties and its labeling (see Section 4);
- a wide set of experiments aimed at validating our algorithmic choices, optimizing the parameter settings and comparing our approach against several state-of-the-art systems over standard datasets [6]. The result is a relative improvement up to 20% for several standard measures (see Section 5);
- a large user study conducted on Amazon Mechanical Turk, which is aimed at ascertain the quality of the cluster labels produced by our approach against two commercial systems, namely CLUSTY and LINGO3G, based on 100 queries drawn from the TREC Web Track. This provides evidence that our system is the best in producing diversified labels, and it is competitive in terms of topics coverage (see Section 5.5).

We argue that the breakthrough performance of our approach over this "difficult problem and hard datasets" [6] is due to the successful resolution of the synonymy and polysemy issues which inevitably arise when dealing with the short and sparse snippets, and constitute the main limitation of known systems [5] which rely on syntactically-based techniques.

2. RELATED WORK

An in-depth survey of SRC algorithms is available in [5]. It is worth noting that most previous works exploit just simple syntactic features extracted from the input texts. They differ from each other by the way these features are extracted and by the way the clustering algorithms exploit them. Many approaches derive single words as features, which however are not always useful in discriminating topics and not always effective in describing clusters. Other approaches extract phrases [8], or build a different representation of the input texts through a decomposition of the vector space [21], or by mining a query-log [25]. Liu et al. [17] presented an approach that exploits spectral geometry for clustering search results: the nodes of the graph they considered are the documents returned by the underlying search engine and they use cosine similarity over traditional *tf-idf* representation of texts as weights for the edges. Even this technique relies on syntactic features and it has been evaluated over datasets composed of a few thousands long documents, i.e., not just snippets, which is obviously very different from our setting where we wish to cluster on-the-fly a few hundreds of short text fragments.

Recently Carpineto et al. [6] presented a (meta-)SRC system that clusters snippets by merging partitions from three state-of-the-art text clustering algorithms such as singular value decomposition, non-negative matrix factorization and generalized suffix trees. They also introduced a new, more realistic, measure for evaluating SRC algorithms that properly models the user behavior (called SSL_k) and takes into account the time a user spends to satisfy his/her search needs. Several experiments showed that this meta-SRC system yields considerable improvements with respect to previous work on datasets specifically built for this task. Again, these approaches rely on syntactic matches and *tf-idf* features (the term-document matrix), so they suffer from the sparsity of the short texts and the polysemy/synonymy of their terms, as argued above.

The clustering of our *graph of topics* might recall to the reader the Topical Query Decomposition problem introduced in [4]. However that setting is different from ours because it deals with query-logs and tries to decompose a query into other queries by exploiting valuable, but not easily available, information about past queries and users behavior. Conversely we try to cluster search results according to their topics detected by TAGME and deploying the "semantics" underlying the link-structure of Wikipedia.

Finally we mention that from a certain point of view our work could be considered somewhat related to similarity measures for short texts such as those proposed in [10, 22], or to approaches in which the document representation is enriched with features extracted from external knowledge-bases such as [2, 12, 13, 14]. However, all these approaches are either not designed for short texts or cannot be executed on-the-fly, which are two key requirements of our scenario.

3. THE GRAPH OF TOPICS

The traditional approach to IR tasks is to represent a text as a bag of words in which purely statistical and syntactic measures of similarity are applied. In this work we propose to move away from the classic bag-of-words paradigm towards a more ambitious *graph-of-topics* paradigm derived by using the TAGME annotator [9].

The idea is to deploy TAGME to process on-the-fly and with high accuracy the snippets returned by search engines. Every snippet is thus annotated with a few topics, which are represented by means of Wikipedia pages. We then build a graph consisting of two types of nodes: the topics annotated by TAGME, and the snippets returned by the queried search engines. Edges in this graph are weighted to denote either topic-to-topic similarities, computed via the Wikipedia linked-structure, or topic-to-snippet memberships, weighted by using proper statistics derived by TAGME.

This new representation provides a stunning contextualization for the input snippets because it helps to relate them even though they are short and fragmented. Figure 2 provides an illustrative example over the query `jaguar`: on the left-hand side are shown some snippets returned by a search engine for that query, on the right-hand side are shown some of the topics identified in those snippets by TAGME. The dashed edges represent the topic-to-snippet annotations, weighted with a score (called ρ-score in [9]) that denotes the reliability/importance of that annotation for the input text. The solid edges represent the topic-to-topic similarities, weighted by the relatedness measure introduced in [19] and recalled in the following Section 4 (here, the thickness of these edges is proportional to that measure).

This graph enhances the traditional term-document matrix deployed in most previous works [5]. In fact, that matrix would be very sparse for our input snippets which are very short and fragmented, and thus difficult to be related by means of statistics or terms co-occurrences.

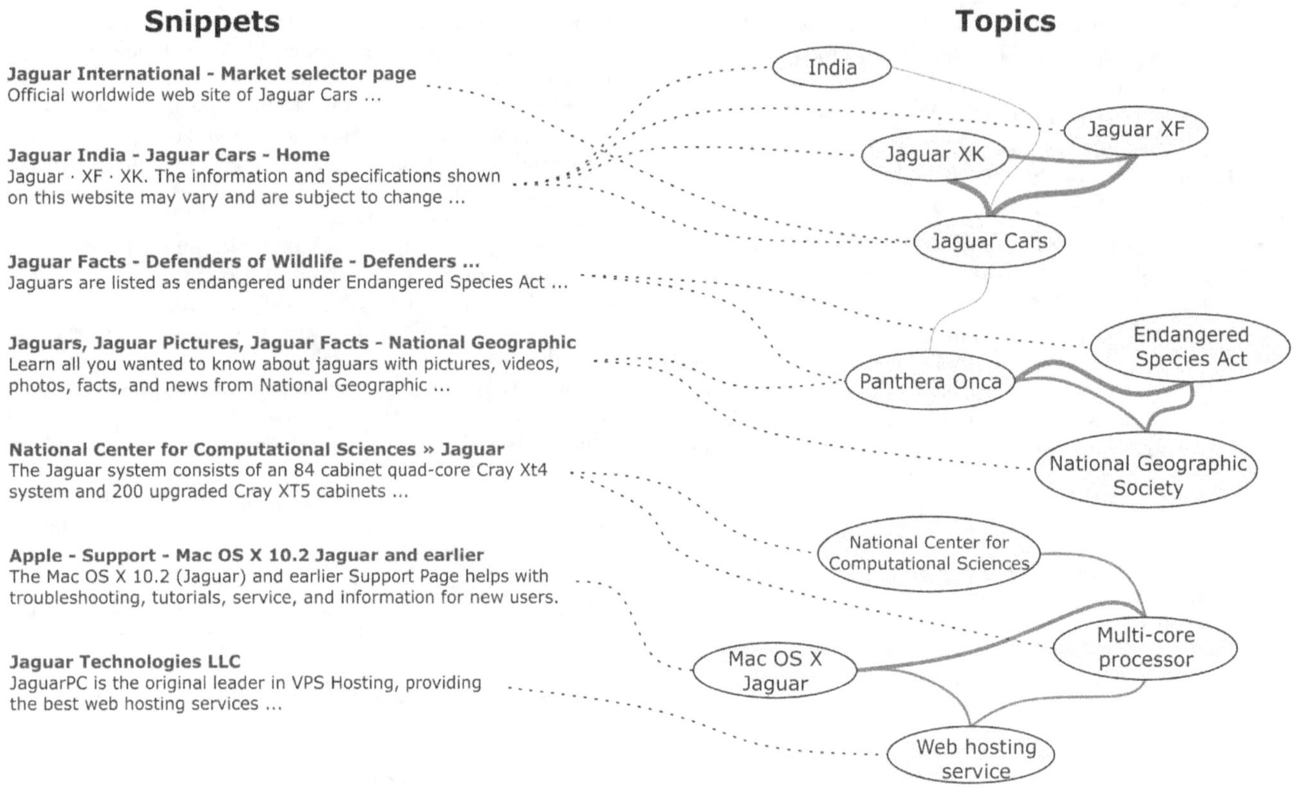

Figure 2: The *graph of topics* representation for texts.

The snapshot of the graph of topics in Fig. 2 shows the potential of this novel text representation. By looking at the graph structure one can quickly identify three main themes for the input snippets: automobiles, animals and IT. Note that the last theme is easily identifiable even though the last three snippets do not share any significant term; the second theme is identifiable even if the third and the forth snippets share just the term "jaguar", which is the query and thus obviously occurs everywhere. We finally point out that the snippet-to-topic edges could be deployed to discard some un-meaningful topics, e.g. the topic `India`, that are unrelated to the main themes of the query and are clearly "disconnected" from the rest of the graph.

It goes without saying that this graph depends strongly on the annotation of TAGME and on the content and linked-structure of Wikipedia. Moreover it does not represent a perfect ontology for the input snippets; e.g., the topic `Panthera Onca` is slightly related to `Jaguar Cars`, and more in general some relations could be missing. Nevertheless, as our wide set of experiments will show in Section 5, the coverage and the quality of our labeled-clustering algorithm proved superior to all known SRC-systems.

4. THE ALGORITHM

According to the previous section an instance of our problem consists of a graph whose nodes are n snippets $\mathcal{S} = \{s_1, ..., s_n\}$ and r topics $\mathcal{T} = \{t_1, ..., t_r\}$ that are identified by TAGME in $\mathcal{S}$.

Given a snippet s and a topic t, we denote by $\rho(s,t)$ the score assigned by TAGME to the annotation of s with topic t. This score is computed by TAGME taking into account the coherence of the disambiguated topic with respect to the other topics in the text plus some other statistical features drawn from the text corpus of Wikipedia. Indeed $\rho(s,t)$ represents the reliability/importance of the topic t with respect to the text s (for details about this score see [9]) and it is used to weight the edge (s,t) in the graph.

Given two topics t_a and t_b (i.e. Wikipedia pages), we can measure their relatedness $rel(t_a, t_b)$ by using the scoring function of [19],[3] which is mainly based on the number of citations and co-citations of the corresponding pages of Wikipedia:

$$rel(t_a, t_b) = \frac{\log(|in(t_a)|) - \log(|in(t_a) \cap in(t_b)|)}{\log(W) - \log(|in(t_b)|)} \quad (5)$$

where $in(t)$ is the set of in-links of the page t, and W is the number of all pages in Wikipedia. We make the assumption that $|in(t_a)| \geq |in(t_b)|$ and thus this measure is symmetric.

For the sake of presentation, we denote by G_t the weighted graph restricted to the topics $\mathcal{T}$ detected in the input snippets, and appearing on the right-hand side of Fig. 2. Moreover we denote by $S(t) \subseteq \mathcal{S}$ the subset of snippets which are annotated with topic t, so the snippets s such that $\rho(s,t) > 0$; and for any set of topics T, we use $S(T) = \cup_{t \in T} S(t)$ as the set of snippets annotated with at least one topic of T.

Given an integer m, we solve the SRC problem by addressing three main tasks:

(a) create a *topical decomposition* for G_t consisting of a set $\mathcal{C} = \{T_1, ..., T_m\}$ of disjoint subsets of $\mathcal{T}$;

(b) identify a labeling function $h(T_i)$ that associates to each

[3]Other measures could be considered, this is however beyond the scope of the current paper.

set of topics $T_i \in \mathcal{C}$ the one that defines its general theme.

(c) derive from the topical decomposition $\mathcal{C}$ and from the labeling function $h(\cdot)$, a labeled clustering of the snippets into m groups. For each set of topics T_i, we create a cluster consisting of the snippets $S(T_i)$, and then label it with $h(T_i)$.

Such a topical decomposition has to exhibit some suitable properties, which will be experimentally evaluated:

- High *snippet coverage*, i.e. maximize the number of snippets belonging to one of the m clusters.
- High *topic relevance*, i.e. maximize the ρ scores of the topics selected in $\mathcal{C}$, namely $\sum_{s \in \mathcal{S}} \max_{t \in T_1 \cup \ldots \cup T_m} \rho(s,t)$.
- High *coherence* among the topics contained in each cluster $T_i \in \mathcal{C}$, that is maximize $\sum_{t_j, t_z \in T_i} rel(t_j, t_z)$.
- Enforce *diversity* between topics contained in different clusters, namely, for each pair $T_1, T_2 \in \mathcal{C}$, minimize the value of $\sum_{t_i \in T_1, t_j \in T_2} rel(t_i, t_j)$.
- Enforce *balancing* over the sizes of the clusters induced by the topical decomposition, namely maximize $\min_{T_i \in \mathcal{C}} |S(T_i)|$ and minimize $\max_{T_i \in \mathcal{C}} |S(T_i)|$.

As in most previous work, we will aim at forming 10 clusters in order to ease the reading of their labels. Our experiments will show that it is preferable to set $m > 10$ and then merge the smallest $m - 10$ clusters into a new one that represents a sort of *container* for rare or not so trasparently meaningful topics of the query (typically labeled with "`Other topics`"). Section 5.1 will evaluate the impact of the value of m onto the clustering quality.

Finally, we note that there could be snippets in which TAGME is not able to identify any topic so that they are not represented in our graph. We limit the set $\mathcal{S}$ to the snippets that obtained at least one annotation from TAGME. Section 5.2 will experimentally evaluate the coverage of $\mathcal{S}$ with respect to the total set of snippets returned by the queried search engine, showing that $\mathcal{S}$ covers the 98% of them on average.

4.1 Pre-processing

First we remove from $\mathcal{T}$ the topics that cover more than 50% of the snippets, because we argue that very generic topics are not useful for clustering. Then we select from the remaining topics the most significant ones by *greedily* solving a set-cover problem in which the universe U to be covered is formed by the input snippets $\mathcal{S}$, and the collection B of covering-sets is given by the topics of $\mathcal{T}$.

We recall that the goal of the set-covering problem is to find a minimum-cardinality set cover $C \subseteq B$ whose union gives U. The particularity of our set-covering problem is that the membership of each element s (snippet) in a set t (topic) is weighted by the value $\rho(s,t)$ computed by TAGME.[4] Hence we design a special greedy algorithm that selects the next set (topic) t not based on the number of yet-uncovered elements (snippets) it contains, as in the classic greedy-approach to set covering [7], but based on the *volume* of the edges incident to t and measured as the sum of their ρ-values. The (relevant) topics selected via this greedy approach will be the nodes eventually constituting the graph G_t whose edges are weighted according to the relatedness formula in (5).

[4] A score $\rho(s,t) = 0$ indicates that s is not annotated with t.

4.2 Topical decomposition

Given the weighted graph G_t, we aim at constructing a *good* labeled clustering via spectral geometry. The goal is to find a partition of the nodes of G_t in groups such that the edges between groups are few and have low total weight, whereas edges within a group are many and have high total weight. The interpretation in terms of *topic similarity* is straightforward since the edge weights in G_t measure the relatedness between its nodes (topics), therefore the clusters produced by the spectral approach should show high intra-cluster relatedness and low inter-cluster relatedness.

In our problem, however, we cannot rely on G_t only because of the strict interplay that exists between topics and snippets, and because of the properties we wish to guarantee with our final clustering (see Section 4). Thus we propose to operate on the entire graph of topics-and-snippets of Section 3, and design a clustering algorithm that selects the next cluster of topics to be split according to the number of contained snippets and to its spectral properties over the linked structure of G_t. This selected cluster is then split into two parts which aim at minimizing intra-similarity and maximizing inter-similarity among their topics in G_t.

This is different from traditional spectral clustering techniques which deploy the spectral properties of the input graph to map its nodes in a reduced space and then apply simple clustering algorithms, such as k-means [24].

Technically speaking, our clustering algorithm deploys the normalized Laplacian matrix L_{rw}, as defined in [24]. This way the spectral decomposition induced by L_{rw} solves a relaxed version of the *normalized cut* (Ncut) objective function introduced in [18] and defined as:

$$\sum_{i=1}^{k} \frac{cut(T_i, \mathcal{T} \setminus T_i)}{vol(T_i)} \tag{6}$$

where

$$cut(T_i, T_j) = \sum_{t_a \in T_i, t_b \in T_j} rel(t_a, t_b), \tag{7}$$

$$vol(T_i) = \sum_{t_c, t_d \in T_i} rel(t_c, t_d). \tag{8}$$

L_{rw} is tightly related to the transition matrix of the weighted random walk in G_t: it is shown that minimizing Ncut means finding a cut through the graph such that a random walk seldom transitions from a group to the other one [24].

Our clustering algorithm proceeds iteratively, starting with a single large cluster (the whole G_t), and then bi-sectioning one cluster at each iteration. We concentrate our attention over the *big* clusters, namely the ones that cover more than $\delta_{\max}$ snippets, where $\delta_{\max}$ is a parameter whose value has been evaluated in our experiments and that represents the desirable maximum number of elements contained in a cluster. Among these *big* clusters, we bi-section the one that has the lowest second eigenvalue λ_2 of its L_{rw}, i.e. the normalized Laplacian matrix computed upon the sub-graph induced by that cluster. Recall that λ_2 encodes the *sparseness* of that sub-graph: so we argue that the sparser cluster is the more appropriate to be cut in order to diversify its sub-topics. The nodes of this cluster are then sorted according to their projection onto the second eigenvector of L_{rw}, and the cut point is finally found by scanning that sorted sequence and searching for the minimum of the Ncut function defined above.

As commented above, Section 4.1, the algorithm stops when it creates approximately 10 clusters or there is no more clusters to be cut. Section 5.1 will evaluate the impact of this number onto quality of the final clustering.

4.3 Snippets clustering and labeling

The final clustering of the snippets is derived from the topical decomposition of $\mathcal{T}$: each snippet is assigned to (possibly many) clusters in accordance with the snippet-to-topic annotations discovered by TAGME. These clusters of snippets could overlap: in fact, if the snippet s has been annotated with two topics t_a and t_b, and these topics belong to distinct clusters T_1 and T_2, respectively, then we will have $s \in S(T_1)$ and $s \in S(T_2)$. This is a desirable behavior because a snippet can deal with several topics [5].

The final step is then to label these clusters of snippets. This labeling plays an important role, possibly more important than the clustering itself. In fact even a perfect clustering becomes useless if the cluster labels do not clearly identify the cluster topics. This is a very difficult task since it must be executed on-the-fly and processing only the poorly composed snippets. All previous approaches tried to address this problem by exploiting different syntactic features to extract meaningful and intelligible labels [5]. Our innovative topical decomposition allows to label easily the topical clusters thanks to the topics annotated by TAGME.

Let us define the main topic $h(T_i)$ of a topical cluster T_i as the topic $t \in T_i$ that maximizes the sum of the ρ-scores between t and its covered snippets, namely

$$h(T_i) = \arg\max_{t \in T_i} \sum_{s \in S(t)} \rho(s,t)$$

Since each topic corresponds to a Wikipedia page, we finally derive the label for the cluster of snippets $S(T_i)$ by using the title of its main topic $h(T_i)$. It could be the case that the title of the page is the same as the query string, thus limiting its utility. In this case, we append to the title the most frequent anchor text that was used in Wikipedia to refer page $h(T_i)$.

As an example consider the term `jaguar`: it is an ambiguous term, and the Wikipedia page dealing with the animal is entitled `Jaguar` (hence identical to the query). If the user submits `jaguar` as a query, the cluster related to the animal will be labeled as `Jaguar panthera onca`, since `panthera onca` is the most frequent anchor text, different from the title, used to refer the `Jaguar` page in Wikipedia.

5. EXPERIMENTAL EVALUATION

The experimental validation of our approach to SRC relies on two publicly available datasets specifically created for this context by [6]. The former dataset is called AMBIENT (AMBIguos ENTitities) and consists of a collection of 44 ambiguous queries and a list of 100 result snippets for each of them, gathered from Yahoo!'s search engine. This dataset also offers a set of sub-topics for each query and a manual association between each snippet and (possibly many, one or none) related subtopics. The second (and larger) dataset is called ODP-239 and is built from the top levels of DMOZ directory. It includes 239 topics, each with 10 subtopics and about 100 documents (about 10 per subtopic), for a total number of 25580 documents. Each document is composed by a title and a brief description, even shorter than the typical snippet-length as returned by modern search engines.

Top-5			Bottom-5		
m	$\delta_{\max}$	F_1 measure	m	$\delta_{\max}$	F_1 measure
12	10	0.4136	5	8	0.3961
12	13	0.4134	5	7	0.3960
12	12	0.4132	5	11	0.3960
10	14	0.4131	5	9	0.3959
10	8	0.4129	5	10	0.3957

Table 1: Top-5 and bottom-5 settings over the ODP-239 dataset according to the F_1 measure.

We complemented these two experiments with a large user study comparing the quality of the cluster labels attached by our approach or by two well-known commercial systems: CLUSTY and LINGO3G. This user study was executed through Amazon Mechanical Turk and used the queries specified as "Web Track 2009 and 2010" in the TREC competition[5]. This dataset (TREC-100) is composed by 100 queries and for each of them is given a list (possibly incomplete) of descriptions of user intents behind these queries.

5.1 Tuning of our system parameters

Recall that our algorithm relies on two parameters (see Section 4.2):

m is the maximum number of clusters created by the topical decomposition;

$\delta_{\max}$ is the lower bound to the number of snippets contained in the topic-clusters that must be cut.

We evaluated the impact of these parameters by deploying the ODP-239 dataset. In this tuning phase, we make m range within $[5, 20]$ since in our context we are aiming at display at most 10 cluster labels (see Section 4). Similarly, since the main goal of a SRC-system is to improve the retrieval performance, we aim at displaying at most 10 snippets per cluster, so we make $\delta_{\max}$ ranging from 5 to 15.

We tested all $15 \times 10 = 150$ combinations evaluating the F_1 measure. The top-5 and bottom-5 combinations are reported in Table 1: the maximum gap is less than 0.02 (2%), that shows the robustness of our algorithm to these parameter settings. The best setting is $m = 12$ and $\delta_{\max} = 10$, which validates the necessity to set $m > 10$ as argued in Section 4. This setting will be used in all the following experiments.

5.2 Coverage analysis

We experimentally assessed the suitability of using TAGME in the SRC context by measuring the number of its annotations per input snippet. Results confirmed our choice: more than 98% of snippets are covered by at least one TAGME's annotation, and 5 is the average number of annotations per snippet attached by TAGME for both datasets, AMBIENT and ODP-239, as shown in Figure 3.

We also evaluated the impact of the pruning executed by the pre-processing phase over the total set of topics extracted by TAGME (Section 4.1). It could be the case that some snippets remain orphan of topics, because their annotated topics have been pruned, and thus they are not assigned to any topical cluster. Our experiments show that less than 4% orphan snippets are generated (namely, less than 2.4% and 3.9% on average for the AMBIENT and ODP-239 dataset, respectively).

[5] `http://trec.nist.gov/`

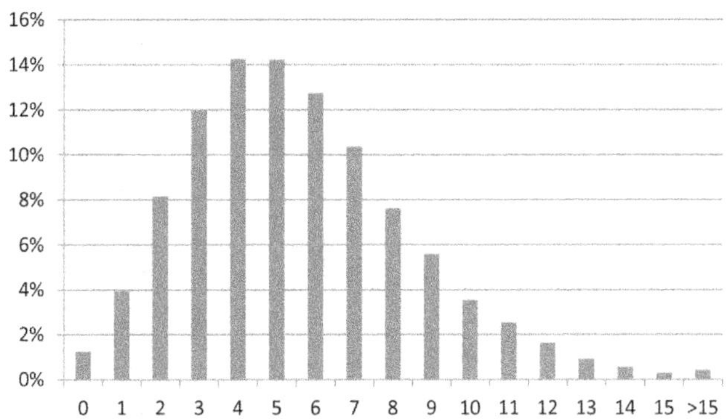

Figure 3: The distribution of the number of topic annotations per snippet, over AMBIENT and ODP-239. Column 0 corresponds to the percentage of snippets that did not get annotated by TAGME.

5.3 Subtopic retrieval

The main goal of an SRC system is to improve the retrieval performance when the user is interested in finding multiple documents of any subtopic of the query he/she issued. To this aim, [6] defined a new evaluation measure which was called the *Subtopic Search Length under k document sufficiency* (SSL_k). Basically it computes the "average number of items (cluster labels or snippets) that must be examined before finding a sufficient number (k) of documents relevant to any of the query's subtopics, assuming that both cluster labels and search results are read sequentially from top to bottom, and that only clusters with labels relevant to the subtopic at hand are opened". Moreover, if it is not possible to find the sufficient number of documents (k) via the clustering –e.g. because the clusters with an appropriate label are not enough or do not exist– then the user has to switch to the full ranked result-list and thus the search length is further increased by the number of results that the user must read in that list to retrieve the missing relevant documents.

This measure models in a realistic manner the time users need to satisfy their search needs by deploying the labeled clusters. In addition, this measure integrates the evaluation of clusters accuracy with the relevance of labels because, in order to minimize SSL_k, a system must create few but accurate clusters and their labels must be related to the topic which the contained snippets deal with. Also, the order of clusters affects the SSL_k measure: in this experiment we order our clusters according to their size (i.e. the biggest clusters are ranked first), as most of our competitors do[6].

However, the computation of this measure requires an expensive and intensive human work because for each query three kinds of assessments are needed: (a) it needs to create a list of sub-topics of the query; (b) it needs to relate each snippet with any (none, one or more) of the sub-topics of the query; (c) for each label produced by an SRC system to be evaluated, it needs to assess which sub-topic(s) the label is related with (if any). Thus we use the AMBIENT dataset that offers this manual annotation[7] and has been the testbed for the state-of-the-art algorithms evaluated in [6].

[6]Other rankings could be considered and this issue will be addressed in future works.

[7]We complemented the AMBIENT dataset with the assessment (c) for our system.

System	SSL_1	SSL_2	SSL_3	SSL_4
Baseline	22.47	34.66	41.96	47.55
LINGO	24.40	30.64	36.57	40.69
LINGO3G	24.00	32.37	39.55	42.97
OPTIMSRC	20.56	28.93	34.05	38.94
TOPICAL	**17.10**	**24.02**	**27.41**	**30.79**
Improv.	16.8%	17.0%	19.5%	20.9%

Table 2: Evaluation of SRC systems over the AMBIENT dataset using the SSL_k measure. The lowest the values of SSL_k, the more effective a system is. Our system is called TOPICAL.

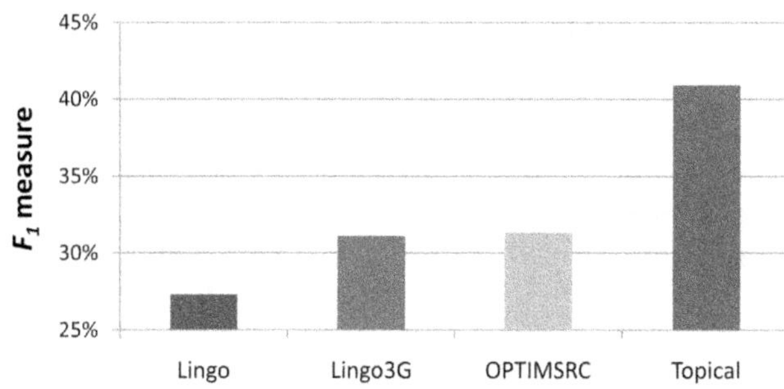

Figure 4: Evaluation of different SRC systems over the ODP-239 dataset.

Table 2 summarizes the results of our algorithm (called TOPICAL) and the main competitors on the AMBIENT dataset. LINGO [21] and OPTIMSRC [6] are two of the most recent systems appeared in the literature, and LINGO3G is a commercial system by CarrotSearch[8]. Unfortunately, to our knowledge, there is no publicly available evaluation of CLUSTY neither over this dataset nor over ODP-239.

Since the principle of the search-length can be applied also to ranked lists, we evaluated SSL_k for the flat ranked list provided by the search engine from which search results were gathered. This is used as the baseline. The experiment clearly shows that our algorithm TOPICAL outperforms the other approaches improving the SSL_k measure of about 20% on average for different values of k. The last line of Table 2 shows the relative improvement of TOPICAL over the best known approach, i.e. OPTIMSRC.

5.4 Clustering evaluation

This experiment aims at evaluating the cluster accuracy, disregarding the quality of the cluster labels. This way we can use bigger datasets because a manual assessment for each label of each algorithm is not needed. Following [6], we use the ODP-239 dataset and we use common precision and recall measures considering the subtopic memberships of DMOZ as class assignments of the ground-truth. Namely, precision P and recall R are defined as $P = \frac{TP}{TP+FP}$ $R = \frac{TP}{TP+FN}$ where True-Positives (TP) are the couples of documents of the same class assigned to the same cluster, False-Positives (FP) are the couples of documents of different classes assigned to the same cluster and False-Negatives (FN) are the couples of documents of the same class assigned to different clusters.

[8]`http://carrotsearch.com/lingo3g`

Figure 4 reports the micro-average F_1 of precision and recall over the set of queries of the ODP-239 dataset. Our approach, TOPICAL, yields an F_1 measure of 0.413 and it outperforms the previous best algorithm (OPTIMSRC) of more than 20%. This result, together with the one reported for the SSL_k in the previous section, is particularly interesting because OPTIMSRC is taking the best from three state-of-the-art clustering algorithms such as singular value decomposition, non-negative matrix factorization and generalized suffix trees.

On the other hand, the value of 0.413 for the F_1 measure could appear low in an absolute scale. However such relatively small F_1 values have been already discussed in [6], where the authors observed that the clustering task over ODP-239 is particularly hard because sub-topics are very similar to each other and textual fragments are very short.

5.5 User study

To evaluate the quality and usefulness of the labels generated by our algorithm, we devised a *user study* based on a set of 100 queries drawn from the TREC-100 dataset. To the best of our knowledge, there is no publicly available prototype for OPTIMSRC, thus we performed a comparison of our system against CLUSTY and LINGO3G.

For each system and for each query of the TREC-100 dataset, we gathered the cluster labels computed over the top-100 results returned by Yahoo!. Since CLUSTY and LINGO3G produce a hierarchical clustering, we take as cluster labels the ones assigned to the first level of the hierarchy.

To generate human ratings we used Mechanical Turk (AMT)[9]. AMT is increasingly popular as a source of human feedback for scientific evaluations (e.g., see [15]), or *artificial artificial intelligence* [3]. The evaluation task proposed to the raters needs to be designed properly; i.e., it should resemble as much as possible a natural task and it should be as simple as possible, in order to avoid unpredictable biasing and distractor effects.

We set up two evaluation tasks. The first concerns the diversification of the cluster labels. We created a survey (the *unit* of the task) for each query of the TREC-100 dataset and for each tested clustering system, by considering pairs of labels generated by each individual system. For practical reasons we limited this evaluation to the top-5 labels of each system, thus creating $\binom{5}{2} = 10$ pairs of labels per query and per system. Overall, we created about 3K units for this evaluation task. In each unit, the evaluator is given a pair of labels and we ask him/her how related they are in terms of meaning. The evaluator has to pick his/her answer from a set of four pre-defined choices: (1) unrelated; (2) slightly related; (3) very related; (4) same meaning. We required at least five different evaluators to answer each unit and we provided answers for several units (about 5%, and, obviously, they were hidden to the evaluators) as a sort of *gold standard* used to automatically discard answers from not reliable evaluators. Overall, the raters obtained about 67% total agreement and an average distance from the answer returned by AMT equals to 0.38[10].

The task breaks down the evaluation of redundancy into smaller atomic tasks where raters answer a simple question

[9]Via the `crowdflower.com` interface to AMT.

[10]Please refer to `http://crowdflower.com/self-service/faq` to read about the way answers are aggregated by `crowdflower.com`.

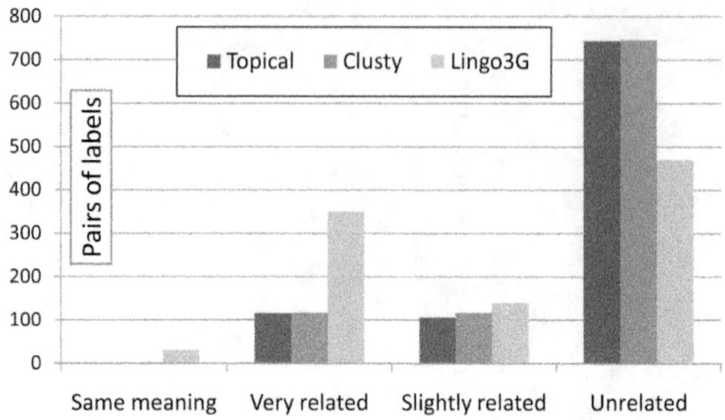

Figure 5: Evaluation of diversification of labeling produced for all queries of the TREC-100 dataset by our tested systems.

with respect to pairs of phrases. The basic assumption is that the more redundant the labels of a system the more similar they will look to the raters.

Results of this tasks are summarized in Figure 5 which clearly shows that our system TOPICAL and CLUSTY produces better diversified and less redundant labels. If we assign a rating value for each answer, starting from 0 (Unrelated) to 3 (Same meaning), we can compute a sort of "redundancy" factor for each system and it results that our system TOPICAL yields a score of 0.34, CLUSTY 0.36 and LINGO3G 0.93, where smaller means better.

The second evaluation task concerns the effectiveness of the cluster labels in *matching* the potential user intent behind the query. We created one task unit for each sub-topic, for each query of the TREC-100 dataset and for each tested system. The sub-topics are given in the TREC-100 dataset. Thus we created about 1300 units, since each query has less than 5 sub-topics on average. In each unit the evaluator is given the query, the description of the sub-topic (user intent) and the list of top-5 labels of the system to be checked, and he/she is asked to assess if the intent provided matches with at least one label provided by the system. The answer has to be taken from the list: (1) there is a label with the same meaning of the topic described by the user intent; (2) there is at least one label that is very related; (3) there is at least one label that is slightly related; (4) none of the labels are related. Thus this task intuitively aims at capturing, at least partially, the coverage guaranteed by each system with respect to a set, possibly non-exhaustive, of sub-topics which can be assumed being relevant. For this task, the rates obtained about 50% total agreement and an average distance from the answer returned by AMT equals to 0.61.

Figure 6 summarizes the results for this task[11]. In this evaluation, LINGO3G yields the best performance overall, slightly better than our approach (TOPICAL). However some comments are in order on these figures.

It is worth noticing that the top-5 labels of LINGO3G are shorter than the ones produced by our system: 1.73 versus 1.95 words per label on average. Thus they result more general and therefore might be more likely to partially match

[11]We deployed the same kind of checks to avoid unreliable evaluators and we required at least ten different evaluators to answer to each unit because we argue that this task was more subjective with respect to the previous one.

TREC's sub-topics	LINGO3G	TOPICAL
• AVP, sponsor of professional beach volleyball events. • AVP antivirus software. • Avon Products (AVP) company. • "Alien vs. Predator" movie. • Wilkes-Barre Scranton Airport in Pennsylvania (airport code AVP).	Alternatives to Violence Project Alien Avon Products Video Volleyball Equipment Definition of AVP LCD Projectors Group Anti-Violence	Alien vs. Predator Association of Volleyball Professionals Alternatives to Violence Project Sales Avon Products Leggings NEU2 Category 5 cable LCD projector The Academical Village People

Table 3: The list of sub-topics for the query avp of the TREC-100 dataset and the top-ten labels produced for that query by LINGO3G algorithm and our proposed approach TOPICAL.

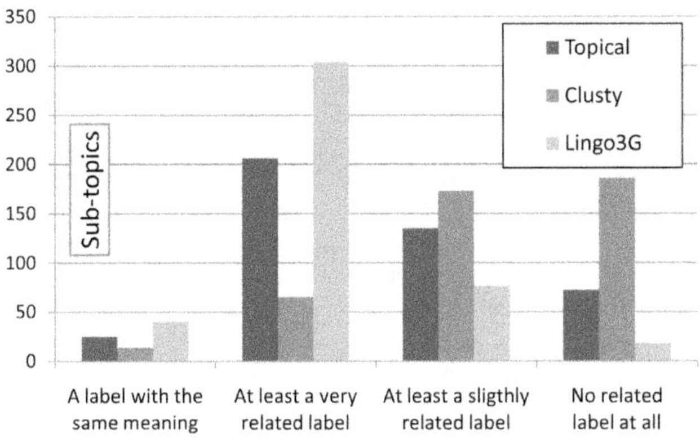

Figure 6: Evaluation of the effectiveness of the cluster labeling produced for all queries of the TREC-100 dataset by our tested systems.

one of the identified user intents. On the other hand, being more general, the labels in each set might be more likely to overlap to some extent, which seems consistent with the worse results obtained by LINGO3G in the previous redundancy evaluation.

Another potential issue to be considered is that the list of sub-topics for each query is partial and thus we are not taking into account all possible intents of the query, thus possibly giving an advantage to LINGO3G and, conversely, penalizing our system which instead offers better diversification. As an example consider the data for the query **avp** of the TREC-100 dataset showed in Table 3. The list of sub-topics is incomplete: AVP is also the name of a company that produces networking cables, the acronym of "Alternatives to Violence Project", the name of a LCD projectors manufacturer, the name of a vocal group The Academical Village People, the name of a gene that produces the NEU2 proteins. If we would have checked also these missing sub-topics, our system would have been successful whereas LINGO3G would have missed these three topics.

Even for the labels, our system is more precise and less redundant: the label *Alien* of LINGO3G corresponds to our label *Alien vs. Predator*, *Volleyball* to *Association of Volleyball Professionals*, *Group* to *The Academical Village People*. However evaluators assessed for this query **avp** that our system is the best for just one sub-topic, while for other sub-topics the outcome was a "draw".

5.6 Time efficiency

Time efficiency is another important issue in the context of SRC because the whole clustering process has to be performed on-the-fly to be useful to a user of a search engine. All figures are computed and averaged over the ODP-239 dataset and carried out on a commodity PC.

The set-covering problem, executed in the pre-processing step (Section 4.1), can be solved in $O(|\mathcal{S}| \cdot |\mathcal{T}|)$ time, where these two cardinalities are about 100 and 350, respectively, in practice. This means about 30ms.

The clustering algorithm (Section 4.2) mainly depends on the number of topics in $\mathcal{T}$, hence the number of nodes in the graph G_t. However, thanks to the pruning performed by the set-covering algorithm, this number is very small, 40 on average. Thus our spectral clustering is fast because the Laplacian matrix has a dimension of about 40. The final result is that the spectral approach takes about 350ms.

The most time consuming step in our approach is the computation of the relatedness measure defined in Section 4 that is based on the Wikipedia link-structure. Nonetheless, since we keep the whole graph indexed in internal-memory[12], the above computations are affordable in the indicated time constraints.

It goes without saying that we have to add the cost of annotating the short texts with TAGME. Although not yet engineered, TAGME is the fastest in the literature being able to annotate a snippet in about 18 ms on average with a commodity PC [9]. If the snippets to be clustered are about 100 per query (as for the datasets in our experiments), we have to add less than 2 seconds to the overall processing time. Of course, we could drop this time cost by assuming that the underlying search engine, which produces the snippets, has pre-processed with TAGME the whole collection of its indexed documents. Such a pre-processing step might also improve the topic annotation quality since more context would be available for disambiguation.

As a final note, we suggest another improvement to our system that we plan to implement in a future release of the software. It regards the spectral-decomposition step which exploits just the second eigenvalue and the second eigenvector of the Laplacian matrix. This could be quickly approximated with the well-know power method, thus avoiding the computation of all eigenvalues and all eigenvectors as it is in the current prototype.

[12]The size of such a graph is about 700Mb.

6. CONCLUSION AND FUTURE WORK

We presented a new approach to the problem of Search Results Clustering that deploys a representation of texts as *graph of concepts* rather than *bag of words*. We then designed a novel clustering algorithm that exploits this innovative representation and its spectral properties. We finally showed with a large set of experiments over publicly available datasets and user studies that our algorithm yields (significant) improvements over state-of-the-art academic and commercial systems.

Because of the lack of space we could not discuss another clustering algorithm that we have designed and tested over all datasets of Section 5. This algorithm proceeds bottom-up by carefully combining a star-clustering approach [1] with some balancedness checks on the size of the snippet-clusters to be "merged". This approach is complementary to the spectral-approach adopted by TOPICAL but, surprisingly, their performance are very close over all measures deployed in all our experiments (although TOPICAL results are still better). We argue that this is a further indication of the robustness of our experimental results and of the potentiality of the labeled and weighted graph of topics we introduced in this paper.

We strongly believe that other IR applications could benefit from this representation, indeed we are currently investigating:

(a) the design of novel similarity measures between short texts, inspired by the Earth mover's distance but now applied on subset of nodes drawn from the topic-based graphs built upon the short texts to compare;

(b) concept-based approaches to classification of news stories, or short messages in general (like tweets) [23];

(c) the application of such representation of texts to the context of Web Advertising, in which the *bag of keywords* bidden by the advertiser could be replaced by our *graph of topics* in order to enhance ad-searches or ad-page matches.

Acknowledgements

This research has been partially funded by a Google Faculty Award and Italian MIUR grants "PRIN–MadAlgo" and "FIRB–Linguistica". The authors thank professors F. Romani and G. Del Corso for insightful discussions about Laplacian matrices.

7. REFERENCES

[1] J.A. Aslam, E. Pelekhov, and D. Rus. The star clustering algorithm for static and dynamic information organization. *J. Graph Algorithms Appl.*, 8:95–129, 2004.

[2] S. Banerjee, K. Ramanathan, and A. Gupta. Clustering short texts using Wikipedia. In *ACM SIGIR*, 787–788, 2007.

[3] J. Barr, and L.F. Cabrera. AI Gets a Brain. *ACM Queue*, 4(4):24–29, 2006.

[4] F. Bonchi, C. Castillo, D. Donato, and A. Gionis. Topical query decomposition. In *ACM KDD*, 52–60, 2008.

[5] C. Carpineto, S. Osiński, G. Romano, and D. Weiss. A survey of web clustering engines. *ACM Comput. Surv.*, 41(3):1–38, 2009.

[6] C. Carpineto and G. Romano. Optimal meta-search results clustering. In *ACM SIGIR*, 170–177, 2010.

[7] V. Chvátal. A greedy heuristic for the set-covering problem. *Mathematics of Operations Research*, 4(3):233–235, 1979.

[8] P. Ferragina and A. Gulli. A personalized search engine based on web-snippet hierarchical clustering. In *WWW*, 801–810, 2005.

[9] P. Ferragina and U. Scaiella. TAGME: On-the-fly annotation of short text fragments (by Wikipedia entities). In *ACM CIKM*, 2010.

[10] E. Gabrilovich and S. Markovitch. Wikipedia-based semantic interpretation for natural language processing. *J. Artif. Int. Res.*, 34(1):443–498, 2009.

[11] J. Hoffart, M.A., Yosef, I., Bordino, H., Fürstenau, M., Pinkal, M., Spaniol, B., Taneva, S., Thater and G., Weikum. Robust Disambiguation of Named Entities in Text. In *EMNLP*, 782–792, 2011.

[12] J. Hu, L. Fang, Y. Cao, H.-J. Zeng, H. Li, Q. Yang, and Z. Chen. Enhancing text clustering by leveraging Wikipedia semantics. In *ACM SIGIR*, 179–186, 2008.

[13] X. Hu, N. Sun, C. Zhang, and T.-S. Chua. Exploiting internal and external semantics for the clustering of short texts using world knowledge. In *ACM CIKM*, 919–928, 2009.

[14] A. Huang, D. Milne, E. Frank and I. H. Witten. Clustering documents using a Wikipedia-based concept representation. In *PAKDD*, 628–636, 2009.

[15] G. Kazai, J. Kamps, M. Koolen, M. Koolen, and N. Milic-Frayling. Crowdsourcing for book search evaluation: impact of hit design on comparative system ranking. In *ACM SIGIR*, 205–214, 2011.

[16] S. Kulkarni, A. Singh, G. Ramakrishnan, and S. Chakrabarti. Collective annotation of Wikipedia entities in web text. In *ACM KDD*, 457–466, 2009.

[17] Y. Liu, W. Li, Y. Lin, and L. Jing. Spectral geometry for simultaneously clustering and ranking query search results. In *ACM SIGIR*, 539–546, 2008.

[18] M. Meila and J. Shi. A random walks view of spectral segmentation. *International Workshop on Artificial Intelligence and Statistics (AISTATS)*, 2001.

[19] D. Milne and I. H. Witten. An effective, low-cost measure of semantic relatedness obtained from Wikipedia links. *AAAI Workshop on Wikipedia and Artificial Intelligence*, 2008.

[20] D. Milne and I. H. Witten. Learning to link with Wikipedia. In *ACM CIKM*, 509–518, 2008.

[21] S. Osinski and D. Weiss. A concept-driven algorithm for clustering search results. *IEEE Intelligent Systems*, 20(3):48–54, 2005.

[22] M. Sahami and T. Heilman. A web-based kernel function for measuring the similarity of short text snippets. In *WWW*, 377–386, 2006.

[23] D. Vitale, P. Ferragina, and U. Scaiella. Classification of Short Texts by Deploying Topical Annotations. To appear on *ECIR*, 2012.

[24] U. von Luxburg. A tutorial on spectral clustering. *Statistics and Computing*, 17(4):395–416, 2007.

[25] X. Wang and C. Zhai. Learn from web search logs to organize search results. In *ACM SIGIR*, 87–94, 2007.

To Each His Own: Personalized Content Selection based on Text Comprehensibility

Chenhao Tan[†], Evgeniy Gabrilovich[‡], Bo Pang[‡]
[†] Cornell University, Ithaca, NY 14853, USA
[‡] Yahoo! Research, 4301 Great America Parkway, Santa Clara, CA 95054, USA
chenhao@cs.cornell.edu | {gabr | bopang}@yahoo-inc.com

ABSTRACT

Imagine a physician and a patient doing a search on antibiotic resistance. Or a chess amateur and a grandmaster conducting a search on Alekhine's Defence. Although the topic is the same, arguably the two users in each case will satisfy their information needs with very different texts. Yet today search engines mostly adopt the one-size-fits-all solution, where personalization is restricted to topical preference. We found that users do not uniformly prefer simple texts, and that the text comprehensibility level should match the user's level of preparedness. Consequently, we propose to model the comprehensibility of texts as well as the users' reading proficiency in order to better explain how different users choose content for further exploration. We also model topic-specific reading proficiency, which allows us to better explain why a physician might choose to read sophisticated medical articles yet simple descriptions of SLR cameras. We explore different ways to build user profiles, and use collaborative filtering techniques to overcome data sparsity. We conducted experiments on large-scale datasets from a major Web search engine and a community question answering forum. Our findings confirm that explicitly modeling text comprehensibility can significantly improve content ranking (search results or answers, respectively).

Categories and Subject Descriptors

H.3.3 [**Information Search and Retrieval**]: Retrieval Models and Selection Process

General Terms

Algorithms, Experiments

Keywords

Personalization, text comprehensibility, user modeling, re-ranking

1. INTRODUCTION

Many factors explain users' choices in content consumption, while observable human behavior often produces a single judgment of utility (e.g., a click) that conflates different factors. Most prior studies focused on modeling users' topical preferences (either long-term or short-term). Such models, however, may not be able to explain why users prefer some items over others within the same topic. For instance, an aeronautics professor and an aspiring technology journalist writing about rocket science will likely choose to read very different texts.

We conjectured that users often choose content—consciously or unknowingly—based on its *comprehensibility*. The notion of comprehensibility is inherently user-specific, as reading more involved texts may require users to possess adequate background. It is, of course, also topic-specific; for instance, a renowned professor might also be a beginner cook, and would therefore prefer easy-to-understand cooking instructions. In this paper, we build models of text comprehensibility as well as of users' reading proficiency, and use users' past preferences to predict future content choices. It is exactly the need to disentangle users' topical and comprehensibility preferences that makes this problem difficult.

Given a text fragment, our aim is to measure its degree of sophistication, that is, how easy (or difficult) it is to read for the majority of users. To this end, we build a classifier for predicting text comprehensibility, which uses a host of text readability features motivated by research in computational linguistics (see Section 2.1). A note on terminology is in order here. The word "readability" is used in the literature in a number of different senses, ranging from the degree of grammaticality of the text, to the degree of fluency in (automatically-constructed) search summaries [19], to the degree of difficulty of text as judged by average sentence length and vocabulary size [21, 11, 24, 15]. Here, we use "readability" in the latter sense, but to avoid possible confusion we opted to use the term "comprehensibility" instead.

We model users' reading preferences by analyzing the content they chose to read in the past. One way to do so is to compute the average comprehensibility of the texts read by each user. A crucial limitation of this approach, however, is that the absolute comprehensibility scores produced by the classifier are not necessarily comparable across texts on different topics. To circumvent this limitation, we only compare comprehensibility scores of related texts (e.g., those returned in response to the same search query), and use such pairwise judgments to compute the probability that the user prefers easier texts. As one would expect, our experiments show that the improvement in personalized content ranking is larger when the user's comprehensibility preference is more pronounced (i.e., when the above probability is substantially different from 0.5).

Modeling each user's overall preference allowed us to observe that not everyone prefers easy texts (cf. Section 6.1). However, this general model is necessarily too coarse, hence we refine it by computing topic-specific comprehensibility preferences. Doing so, however, is difficult, since the more specific the model is, the more data is needed to reliably compute it, while many users might have

Permission to make digital or hard copies of all or part of this work for personal or classroom use is granted without fee provided that copies are not made or distributed for profit or commercial advantage and that copies bear this notice and the full citation on the first page. To copy otherwise, to republish, to post on servers or to redistribute to lists, requires prior specific permission and/or a fee.
WSDM'12, February 8–12, 2012, Seattle, Washington, USA.
Copyright 2012 ACM 978-1-4503-0747-5/12/02 ...$10.00.

only read a few texts in each topic, or none at all in some topics. We tackle this data sparsity by using collaborative filtering techniques.

We use the output of the comprehensibility classifier for improving the ranking of content in two different scenarios, namely, Web search and community question answering (CQA). In both cases, we use historical data (click logs for Web search, and best answer tags for CQA forums), and develop models that better explain past user behavior. It should be noted that using historical data at test time puts us at an inherent disadvantage owing to the position bias, because a highly-ranked item might have been clicked merely due to its prominent position rather than true utility. Nonetheless, using our comprehensibility classifier leads to significant ranking improvements on both datasets, despite this disadvantage.

We observe the largest ranking improvements for informational queries [5] in topics such as "Hobbies & Interests", "Arts & Entertainment", and "Real Estate". Predictably, our approach does not offer much improvement for transactional queries in topics such as "Retail", where other factors (such as product price or brand recognition) may dominate users' utility judgments.

Modeling the level of text sophistication is an under-studied area, and we proposed a principled approach to personalized content selection via modeling text comprehensibility. The contributions of this paper are threefold. We developed a comprehensibility classifier for predicting the sophistication level of a given text, and used it to build topic-specific models of users' reading proficiency. Our approach is entirely based on implicit user feedback, and we evaluated a number of strategies for extracting users' comprehensibility preferences from their historically-observed actions. Finally, our experiments on two large-scale datasets confirm the utility of quantifying text comprehensibility for improved content ranking.

2. METHODOLOGY

Our goal is to better satisfy non-topical aspects of users' information needs in a variety of content selection tasks, ranging from personalized ranking of Web search results to selecting the best answer (for the asker) in community question-answering forums. In this section, we use the Web search setting as our running example.

Here we focus on one particular type of preference in content selection, namely, comprehensibility of the relevant content. Different users may have their individual preferences for easier or more sophisticated text, and our aim is to augment relevance-based ranking with comprehensibility-based personalization. To this end, we need to be able to (a) rank texts that are related to the same narrow topic (e.g., search results for a query) by their comprehensibility level, (b) model whether a given user prefers an easier or more sophisticated content for her current information need, and (c) produce a personalized ranking. In the remainder of this section, we describe the algorithms used to address each of these tasks.

2.1 Estimating text comprehensibility

Comprehensibility classifier The simplest way to perform comprehensibility-based ranking for a set of documents is to build a classifier that assigns a comprehensibility score to any input document. Texts that are topically related to an information need can then be ranked by their comprehensibility scores to produce a comprehensibility-based ranking.

It is possible that a global, "topic-agnostic" classifier may not fully capture topic-dependent aspects of reading difficulty. For simplicity, we introduce a light-weight classifier based on data easily available online; more sophisticated topic-specific classifiers can be considered in future work.

We are not aware of existing large-scale labeled resources that are publicly available and cover a broad range of topics. Thus, we construct a labeled dataset by extracting pages from Simple English Wikipedia[1] (denoted as W_S) and English Wikipedia[2] (denoted as W_{en}). Articles in Simple Wikipedia are written using *Basic English*[3], a subset of English with a restricted vocabulary and simple grammar rules. Many articles in W_S can be aligned to corresponding articles in W_{en} with the same title. Upon discarding overly short articles, we find 40,032 aligned article pairs[4]. We label articles from W_S as *easy*, and those from W_{en} as *hard*, and then train a logistic regression classifier.

Table 1: Readability index features used in the classifier.

Flesch [21]:	$206.835 - 1.015\frac{\#\text{words}}{\#\text{sentences}} - 84.6\frac{\#\text{syllables}}{\#\text{words}}$
Flesch-Kincaid [23]:	$0.39\frac{\#\text{words}}{\#\text{sentences}} + 11.8\frac{\#\text{syllables}}{\#\text{words}} - 15.59$
Gunning FOG [15]:	$0.4(\frac{\#\text{words}}{\#\text{sentences}} + 100\frac{\#\text{polysyllables}}{\#\text{words}})$
ARI [21]:	$4.71\frac{\#\text{characters}}{\#\text{words}} + 0.5\frac{\#\text{words}}{\#\text{sentences}} - 21.43$
SMOG [24]:	$1.043\sqrt{30\frac{\#\text{polysyllables}}{\#\text{sentences}}} + 3.1291$
Coleman-Liau [11]:	$0.0588L - 0.296S - 15.8$ (L: #letters per 100 words; S: #sentences per 100 words)

Polysyllables are words with 3 or more syllables.

We use as features several standard readability indices [21, 11, 24, 23, 15] (Table 1), where word length and sentence length are used as coarse proxies of semantic difficulty and syntactic complexity. We also include the bag of words features. In order to build a classifier that is applicable to a broad range of texts, we limit our vocabulary to the "Basic English 850 word list"[5]. These unigram features are weighted by term frequency and L_2-normalized.

Comprehensibility score (S_c) The output of the classifier is the likelihood of the article being hard to read, which we refer to as the *comprehensibility score* (S_c).

We report two kinds of performance metrics. First, we compute standard classification accuracy by comparing S_c with the (global) threshold of 0.5, which amounts to a binary decision on whether the text is "easy" or "hard". However, scores computed for very different topics are not necessarily comparable, hence we also report the accuracy of pairwise score comparison for each title, that is, whether the article from W_S received a lower score than the corresponding one from W_{en}. The following table reports the above metrics using 5-fold cross-validation.[6]

	Global threshold	Per-title comparison
Accuracy	88.3%	97.4%

As we can see, while the accuracy of using a global threshold is quite high, the accuracy of pairwise comparison is even higher, as

[1] http://simple.wikipedia.org

[2] http://en.wikipedia.org

[3] http://simple.wikipedia.org/wiki/Basic_English

[4] When extracting textual content from HTML, we discard <div> segments with fewer than 100 characters, and then discard documents with fewer than 50 words.

[5] http://simple.wikipedia.org/wiki/Wikipedia:Basic_English_ordered_wordlist

[6] We also conducted a small-scale evaluation of S_c scores in the Web search scenario, where one of the authors judged the relative difficulty of a pair of search results for 20 queries. 4 of the 20 document pairs were found difficult to judge; on the remaining cases the agreement between the annotator and the classifier was 81.25%.

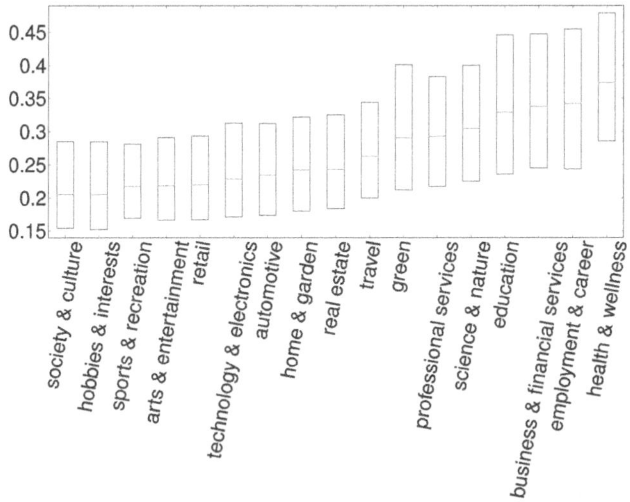

Figure 1: Comprehensibility score (S_c) distribution for different topics. Blue bars indicate 25% and 75% percentiles; red lines indicate 50% percentile (median).

we get the correct "order" over 97% of the time. This indicates that S_c is more reliable for comparing comprehensibility of texts on the same narrow topic than for texts on different topics. To verify this point, we examine the topical variance of S_c in more details.

Topical variance of S_c Figure 1 shows the topical distribution of S_c scores for 154 million Web pages (see Section 3.1 for more details on this dataset). As we can see, a relatively easy article in the "health & wellness" category might receive a higher S_c score than a relatively hard article in "hobbies & interests". This is consistent with our previous observation that it is more meaningful to use S_c for comparing documents within the same topic.

2.2 Comprehensibility-based content selection

Intuitively, different users may have different comprehensibility preferences, which can further vary on a per-topic basis. We capture such preferences by building user profiles, which are then used to modify the relevance-based ranking of available content. We now describe these two steps in turn.

2.2.1 *Modeling user comprehensibility preferences*

We describe three methods for building user profiles. We begin with a coarse model that captures a user's general (topic-independent) comprehensibility preference, that is, whether the user tends to prefer easier or more sophisticated content among search results returned for their queries.

Topic-independent profile (basic model)

For a user u, let $a >_u b$ denote the user's preference of content item a over b. Suppose we have a method (which we describe in Section 2.3) to obtain a set of n preference pairs for each user:

$$\Omega_u^{pref} = \{(< a_i, b_i >, w_i) \mid a_i >_u b_i, \text{with weight } w_i\}.$$

We start with the simple case with equal weights ($w_i = 1$) for all pairs. Consider a random variable X with a Bernoulli distribution parameterized by p, which takes value 1 if the user prefers the harder content. Assume we have a sample of size n ($X_1 = x_1, ..., X_n = x_n$), corresponding to n preference pairs of content items, where

$$x_i = \begin{cases} 1, & S_c(a_i) > S_c(b_i) \\ 0 & S_c(a_i) < S_c(b_i) \end{cases}$$

(remember the pairs are ordered to reflect the user's preference for a_i over b_i, i.e., $a_i >_u b_i$). We now estimate p, the probability of user u preferring harder content (we denote this estimator as P_u). Let $k = \sum_i x_i$. Since for most users we are dealing with relatively small n, the maximum likelihood estimator (k/n) is undesirable. Instead, we take the Laplace estimator of p, which uses Uniform$(0, 1)$ as the prior distribution. The posterior estimation of P_u is thus a function over Ω_u^{pref}:

$$P_u = f(\Omega_u^{pref}) = \frac{k+1}{n+2}$$

Again, in the simplest case, we select content for each user according to her estimated P_u, regardless of the topic. We denote this topic-independent user model as BASIC.

To incorporate weights over the pairs, we can compute a weighted version:

$$P_u^{(w)} = f^{(w)}(\Omega_u^{pref}) = \frac{k^{(w)}+1}{n^{(w)}+2},$$

where $k^{(w)} = \sum_i w_i x_i$, $n^{(w)} = \sum_i w_i$. Clearly this reduces to P_u when $\forall i, w_i = 1$. Each of the models described in the remainder of this section can be similarly modified to have a weighted and an unweighted version.

Topic-dependent profile

Suppose a set of candidate documents (e.g., top results for a search query) can be classified into an existing topic hierarchy, where the node "default" is the root. For each user, we construct a set of pairwise preferences for each topic $\Omega_{u,t}^{pref}$ from Ω_u^{pref}.

We define an order relationship between two topic nodes in this hierarchy as follows:

$$t_2 <_h t_1 \Leftrightarrow t_2 \text{ is a descendant of } t_1$$

For each preference pair $pp_i \in \Omega_u^{pref}$, let t_i be its topic (e.g., the topic of the query associated with the pair), and let

$$\Omega_{u,t}^{pref} = \{pp_i \in \Omega_u^{pref} | t_i \leq_h t\}.$$

For any reasonably sized $\Omega_{u,t}^{pref}$ (i.e., $|\Omega_{u,t}^{pref}| > \theta$), we compute $P_{u,t} = f(\Omega_{u,t}^{pref})$ similarly to the BASIC model above.

Clearly, we will not obtain enough observations for every possible (u, t) pair to reliably compute $P_{u,t}$, especially for the topics residing deep down in the hierarchy. As a coarse approximation, we can fall back to using the topic-independent (BASIC) model if necessary. For an incoming query, we consider the top-level topic node t corresponding to the topic predicted for this query. If $P_{u,t}$ can be estimated, we use $P_{u,t}$ for personalized content selection; otherwise, we fall back to P_u. We refer to this model as TOPICAL.

Collaborative Filtering

In order to alleviate this data sparseness problem (i.e., lack of topic-specific preferences) in a more principled manner, we build upon the work in collaborative filtering. That is, if there exist certain correlations between the comprehensibility preferences for some topics, then we can analyze the observed comprehensibility preferences over all (user, topic) pairs, and predict comprehensibility preferences for unseen ones.

Formally, let n_u be the number of users, and n_t be the number of topics. We construct a matrix $G^{n_u \times n_t}$, where G_{ij} is the likelihood of user i preferring harder content in topic j as estimated from observed data. Note that for cells (i, j) with no observed data, $G_{i,j}$

should receive the same value as an "average" user. We achieve this by computing the global mean of all $P_{u,t}$ values (estimated from observed data) as $g = \frac{1}{\sum_u \sum_t I(P_{u,t} \neq 0)} \sum_u \sum_t P_{u,t}$, and let

$$G_{ut} = \begin{cases} P_{u,t} - g, & \Omega^{pref}_{u,t} \neq \emptyset \\ 0, & \text{otherwise.} \end{cases}$$

This way, the cells with no observations and the cells corresponding to the "average" user receive the value of 0.

Note that this formulation is slightly different from the standard collaborative filtering setting, where the non-zero entries in the matrix are actual observations (e.g., ratings given by a user to an item). In our case, we manipulate estimates ($P_{u,t}$) rather than actually observed values, and the estimates are for a small number of topics rather actual observations over a much larger set of "items", as in the standard setting.

We adopt the maximum-margin matrix factorization approach from the collaborative filtering literature, where we compute an approximation of G with a low-rank decomposition $U^T V$. That is, we want to minimize the following objective function:

$$\sum_{i,j,G_{ij} \neq 0} ||U^T V_{(ij)} - G_{ij}||^2 + ||U||_F + ||V||_F$$

We use CofiRank [36] to solve this optimization problem. Once we obtain the optimal U and V, we compute

$$G^{cf} = U^T V + g.$$

For test queries, we first proceed as in TOPICAL, but when $P_{u,t}$ cannot be reliably estimated, we fall back to G^{cf}_{ut} computed using the above collaborative filtering approach. The default P_u is only used when the topic of the content can not be determined (e.g., a query receiving the "default" category). We denote this user model as COLLABORATIVE.

2.2.2 Combining the Rankings

We cast the content selection problem as a ranking problem. In the Web search scenario, we have an initial relevance-based ranking (as returned by the search engine), and we want to adjust it to better satisfy users' comprehensibility preferences. In the community question-answering scenario, our task is to rank answers so that the answer chosen as the best one by the asker ranks at the top. In the latter case, there might not exist any native ranking of answers on the site, and we can either produce a ranking purely based on comprehensibility preferences or implement quality-based measures to produce an initial ranking.

Here, we consider the general case where we have an original topic-relevance-based ranking R over a set of documents D. Previous work in the personalized search literature has combined topical relevance with (topical) personal preferences by simply computing the sum of the global relevance score (R) and the personalized ranking score. Our approach differs in several aspects.

Let $R(d)$ be the rank of $d \in D$ given by R. Let R_u be the ranking over D in descending order of the comprehensibility score S_c. Here, we slightly abuse the notation and use P_u to denote a user profile built using any of the three models introduced in Section 2.2.1. We then produce the combined ranking by ordering items in ascending order of the following value

$$R(d) + \beta * (2 * P_u - 1) * R_u(d) \quad (1)$$

First, we have a global parameter β, which controls the relative importance of comprehensibility (R_u). We also vary the importance of R_u depending on how pronounced the user's comprehensibility preference is, that is, how much P_u deviates from 0.5. Furthermore, we need to reverse R_u if the user prefers easier content ($P_u < 0.5$). Thus, we multiply the second term by $(2 * P_u - 1)$ to incorporate personalized adjustment over the global β.

2.3 Generating pairwise preferences

We now describe corpus-dependent methods for generating pairwise comprehensibility preferences for two different types of datasets, Web search click logs and best answers in CQA sites.

2.3.1 Web search click log

As discussed in Section 7, click logs are often used for extracting user preferences. Using different models of how users browse search result pages, prior work has examined different ways of reconstructing user preferences that account for position bias [17, 18, 27, 10]. We considered three methods for extracting pairwise preferences: two as proposed by Joachims et al. [18], and a variation over the second method (which is new to the best of our knowledge).

Let's consider a toy example to examine the differences between the three methods. Suppose we have a search result page with 5 results $(l_1, l_2, ..., l_5)$. Suppose the user clicked on l_2 and l_4.

The first method is the classical Click > Skip above. Here the assumption is that users browse results in the order of presentation, and each clicked result is "better" than those presented earlier (i.e., viewed) and not clicked. For our toy example, this yields three preference pairs: $l_2 >_u l_1$, $l_4 >_u l_1$, and $l_4 >_u l_3$.

DEFINITION 1. *Click > Skip above* (CSA)
For a ranked list $(l_1, l_2, l_3, \dots)$ *and clicked position set* C *for user* u*, we define*

$$l_j >_u l_i, \quad \textbf{if } i < j, i \notin C \textit{ and } j \in C.$$

The second method accounts for the noise in click data, and only trusts the last clicked item to be "better" than those skipped. For our toy example, this yields $l_4 >_u l_1$ and $l_4 >_u l_3$.

DEFINITION 2. *Last click > Skip above* (LCSA)
For a ranked list $(l_1, l_2, l_3, \dots)$*, a clicked position set* C *for user* u*, and the position of the (temporally) last clicked item* LC*, we define*

$$l_j >_u l_i, \quad \textbf{if } i < j, i \notin C \textit{ and } j = LC.$$

The third method makes a stronger assumption that the last item the user clicked is the one that finally satisfied the user's information need, while all the items above it, including those clicked, are inferior. For our toy example: $l_4 >_u l_1$, $l_4 >_u l_2$, and $l_4 >_u l_3$.

DEFINITION 3. *Last click > All above* (LCAA)
For a ranked list $(l_1, l_2, l_3, \dots)$*, a clicked position set* C *for user* u*, and the position of the last temporally clicked item* LC*, we define*

$$l_j >_u l_i, \quad \textbf{if } i < j \textit{ and } j = LC.$$

Preference weighting Traditionally, when pairwise preferences are used in learning to rank, each pair carries the same weight. Intuitively, the closer in position two results are, the more likely they are similar in their topical relevance, and the more confidence we have that the implied preference is due to non-topical (i.e., comprehensibility) reasons. Thus, for each pairwise preference $l_j >_u l_i$, we compute a weight as a function of their distance $w = 2^{-(j-i-1)}$. For example, using LCSA, we would obtain $(l_4, l_1, 0.25)$ and $(l_4, l_3, 1)$.

2.3.2 Best answers in CQA forums

Consider a community-based Q&A site such as Yahoo! Answers, where the asker can label one of the answers as the best answer. If there are n answers for a question, we can simply form a preference pair between the best answer and all the other $n - 1$ answers.

Since n can vary greatly from question to question, and we want the asker's preference on each question to carry roughly the same weight, we take each preference pair with weight $1/n$.

3. DATA

3.1 Search dataset

Our search dataset was sampled from one month (May, 2011) of Yahoo! Web Search query logs. After filtering adult content, the dataset underwent the following pre-processing steps.

In order to focus on search intents that are meaningful for comprehensibility-based personalized search, we filtered out navigational queries using an automatic navigational query classifier, as well as all search sessions that only resulted in one click on the first result, which are also highly likely to have navigational intents.

We then crawled the content of all Web pages returned as one of the top 10 results for queries in our data[7], and applied our comprehensibility classifier to these pages. It should be noted that the user's decision to click on a search result is based on the snippet presented on the search result page, before they view the content of the chosen URL. However, applying the comprehensibility classifier to the search snippets is problematic since most snippets are broken text segments, and those that happen to have longer "sentences" (in order to include search terms) will have higher S_c. Instead, we aggregated all Web pages at the domain level, and used the domain-averaged S_c as the smoothed S_c for each page. Intuitively, this captures the comprehensibility reputation of a domain, which can influence users' clicking decisions. Indeed, previous work has found aggregation of information at the domain level to be beneficial [25, 7].

Each page in our dataset was classified into a proprietary class hierarchy, which had 17 top-level nodes (cf. Figure 1), and 216 nodes in total; "default" was assigned to pages when the classifier had low confidence. The statistics shown in Figure 1 were computed over the 154,650,334 pages with non-default class assignments. Similarly, a class label from the same topic hierarchy was assigned to each query based on its search results [6].

The processed data was then split into three parts chronologically: the first 20 days were used as training data, the next 5 days as development data, and the last 5 days as test data.

Clearly, we cannot expect to produce reasonable personalization for users who have barely clicked on any results before. Thus, we limited our study to users with at least 10 queries and at least one click logged in the training data. We randomly selected 424,566 users to form our search dataset.

3.2 Answers dataset

Yahoo! Answers is a community question-answering site. An *asker* posts a question, which may receive multiple answers from other users. The asker has an option of choosing one of the answers as the best answer.[8] We focused on questions with more than one answer, among which a best answer was chosen by the asker. We obtained a dump of Yahoo! Answers data between January, 2010 and April, 2011, where all questions (and answers) in 2010 were used as the training data, and the 4 months in 2011 were used as the test data (development data was not needed here, as there are no parameters to tune for this dataset). We randomly selected 85,172 users who have posted at least 10 questions in the training data, and restricted the test set to these users. Our dataset consists of a total of 4.9 million questions and 39.5 million answers. Each answer in the dataset received an S_c score from the comprehensibility classifier.

[7] Queries with fewer than 8 results were removed from the dataset.
[8] If the asker does not pick the best answer, a community vote is opened to choose the best answer. We disregarded such cases.

Table 2: 18 configurations: 3 methods to generate pairwise preferences × weighted / unweighted × 3 user profile models

Preference generation methods		Weighting	User profile models
CSA	(Click > Skip above)	Weighted	BASIC
LCSA	(Last click > Skip above)	Unweighted	TOPICAL
LCAA	(Last click > All above)		COLLABORATIVE

4. EXPERIMENTS ON SEARCH DATA

We now evaluate the effectiveness of our approach in Web search.

4.1 Evaluation Measures

Following Dou et al. [14], we employ two measures to evaluate our approach to personalized search.

Average Clicked Rank In Web search, average clicked rank for query s is defined as

$$AvgRank_s = \frac{1}{|C_s|} \sum_{p \in C_s} R(p),$$

where C_s denotes the set of clicked Web pages for query s, and $R(p)$ denotes the rank of page p. The final average rank for the entire test query set S is the average of $AvgRank_s$ values:

$$AvgRank = \frac{1}{|S|} \sum_{s \in S} AvgRank_s$$

Lower *average clicked rank* values indicate better performance.

Rank Scoring The score of a ranked list of Web pages is defined as

$$R_s = \sum_j \frac{\delta(s,j)}{2^{(j-1)/(\alpha-1)}},$$

where j is the rank of a page in the list, $\delta(s,j)$ is 1 if page j is clicked for the test query s and 0 otherwise, and α is set to 5 [14, 31, 4]. The final rank scoring is aggregated over all test queries as follows:

$$R = 100 \frac{\sum_s R_s}{\sum_s R_s^{Max}}$$

R_s^{Max} is the maximum possible score when all clicked pages appear at the top of the ranked list. **Larger** *rank scoring* value indicates better performance.

4.2 Experimental setup

We report performance for the following systems:

- Baseline: The original ranking in which the search engine presented results to the users. Only the top 10 results from the original ranking were passed to our methods to compute personalized re-ranking.
- Our approach: We presented three different ways to generate pairwise preferences from click logs (Section 2.3.1), which can be either weighted or unweighted, and three user profile models (Section 2.2.1). In total, we have $3 * 2 * 3 = 18$ configurations of our methods (summarized in Table 2). The threshold θ (described in Section 2.2.1) was set to 5.

Under the evaluation measures defined in Section 4.1, our method is at a disadvantage compared to the baseline owing to the position bias: if we re-rank a result that was previously displayed at position 10 (with no clicks observed) to a position higher in the page, this penalizes our performance, but it could be that the user would have liked this result had they viewed it. One might want to restrict the re-ranking to only position 1 through the lowest clicked position. This avoids penalizing us unfairly by excluding results that might not have been viewed by the user; however, this would also give us an unfair advantage: a random re-ranking within this set is very likely to improve over the baseline (according to the above metrics). Consequently, in our experiments we report the former comparison, which is to our disadvantage: re-ranking top 10 results and comparing against the original ranking using the metrics described in Section 4.1.

User saliency For ease of presentation, we also define the notion of user preference *saliency* as

$$Q_u = |P_u - 0.5|,$$

where for each given configuration, P_u is the user preference computed under that particular combination of parameters. We expect that for users with higher saliency, the improvement of comprehensibility-based personalization would also be more pronounced, and we would be interested in the improvements obtained in each bucket of user saliency. To this end, for each configuration of our method, we rank users according to Q_u, and report improvement over the baseline for top $k\%$ users, for different values of k.[9]

We tuned the β parameter (Eq. 1, Section 2.2.2) on the development set, and obtained the best performance with $\beta = 0.4$. Thus, the importance of comprehensibility-based ranking is roughly between 20% and 30% compared to the original topical-relevance-based ranking, for users with extremely pronounced preferences.

4.3 Results

First, we take one of the configurations (WEIGHTED-LCAA +COLLABORATIVE) to make a few high-level observations. Figure 2 plots the improvement measured in both average clicked rank and ranking score. We observe that the improvement is indeed more pronounced for users with higher saliency. Computed over all queries for the top 0.1% most salient users, the average improvement is more than 0.5 in averaged clicked rank, and close to 7.0 in ranking score. While the improvement is smaller for less salient users, we do obtain a significant improvement for all users,

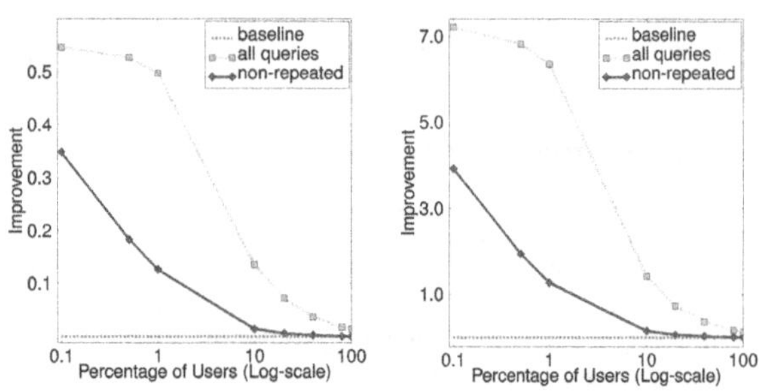

(a) Average Clicked Rank (b) Ranking Score

Figure 2: Improvement over baseline: computed on all queries and on non-repeated queries only.

[9]Note that since the top $k\%$ users are different for different configurations of our method, the corresponding baseline for that subset of the users can also be different. Instead of comparing raw performance numbers across different methods, we only report the improvement over the corresponding baseline performance, which is more comparable across different methods.

Note, however, that a significant portion of queries submitted by users are *repeated* queries [14, 33]. Previous work has shown that using a memory-based method can be highly effective for repeated queries [14]. While our method is not directly "remembering" the actual URLs clicked by the user in the past for repeated queries, it can indirectly promote the previously clicked URLs.[10] Thus, performance improvement over repeated queries may not reflect the utility of comprehensibility preferences, and for the rest of Section 4, we focus our analysis on **non-repeated** queries.

As shown in Figure 2, while the improvement over non-repeated queries is less pronounced, we do obtain a similar trend, which is consistent in both measures. As discussed in Section 4.2, we focus on the improvement over the baseline. To provide a reference point, the performance of the baseline system is 3.6 using average clicked rank, and 74.4 using ranking score for the entire test set.

Next, we examine the improvements achieved by different configurations (on non-repeated queries) in more details.

4.3.1 Overall analysis over non-repeated queries

Table 3 shows paired t-test results (using average clicked rank) for different configurations of our method versus the baseline, for top 10% and 50% (ranked by Q_u), and all users.

First, for the top 10% most salient users, all configurations significantly outperform the baseline. All improvements are statistically significant; many are highly significant with $P < 0.001$. Even when we consider the entire set of users, several variations yield highly significant improvements. That is, modeling user preferences in text comprehensibility does help achieve better content ranking in Web search, despite the adversarial experimental setup as explained in Section 4.2.

The effect of weighting the preference pairs also turns out to be quite prominent. Visually, we can readily notice there are more stars in the WEIGHTED section of the table than in the UNWEIGHTED section. Compared over 50% of all users, the UNWEIGHTED versions tend to be less effective in beating the baseline than their WEIGHTED counterparts. This conforms to our intuition that preferences based on search results that are closer in position are more useful in modeling comprehensibility.

Among different user profile models, BASIC is more robust than COLLABORATIVE when we consider less salient users. If we fix the user profile model to be BASIC, and compare different pair-generation methods, CSA and LCAA beat the baseline more significantly than LCSA.

4.3.2 Improvements for high-saliency users

One reasonable setting is to enable comprehensibility-based personalization only for users with higher Q_u. The method (e.g., BASIC) that consistently beats the baseline for all users does not necessarily achieve the best performance for the high-saliency ones. Indeed, if we focus on the top 10% most salient users, WEIGHTED-LCAA +COLLABORATIVE achieves the biggest improvement over the baseline. We now examine this in more details.

Figure 3 summarizes the improvements in both average clicked rank and ranking score for a variety of settings. Figures 3(a) and 3(d) show the performance of WEIGHTED-LCAA +COLLABORATIVE. For the top 0.1% users, the improvement reaches 0.35 in average clicked rank, and almost 4.0 in ranking score. (Recall the performance of the strong baseline is around 3.6 in average clicked

[10]Note that a memory-based method will need to record all (user, query, clicked URL) pairs, and our method uses a much more compact representation. But an in-depth exploration of the performance tradeoff for this purpose is beyond the scope of this paper.

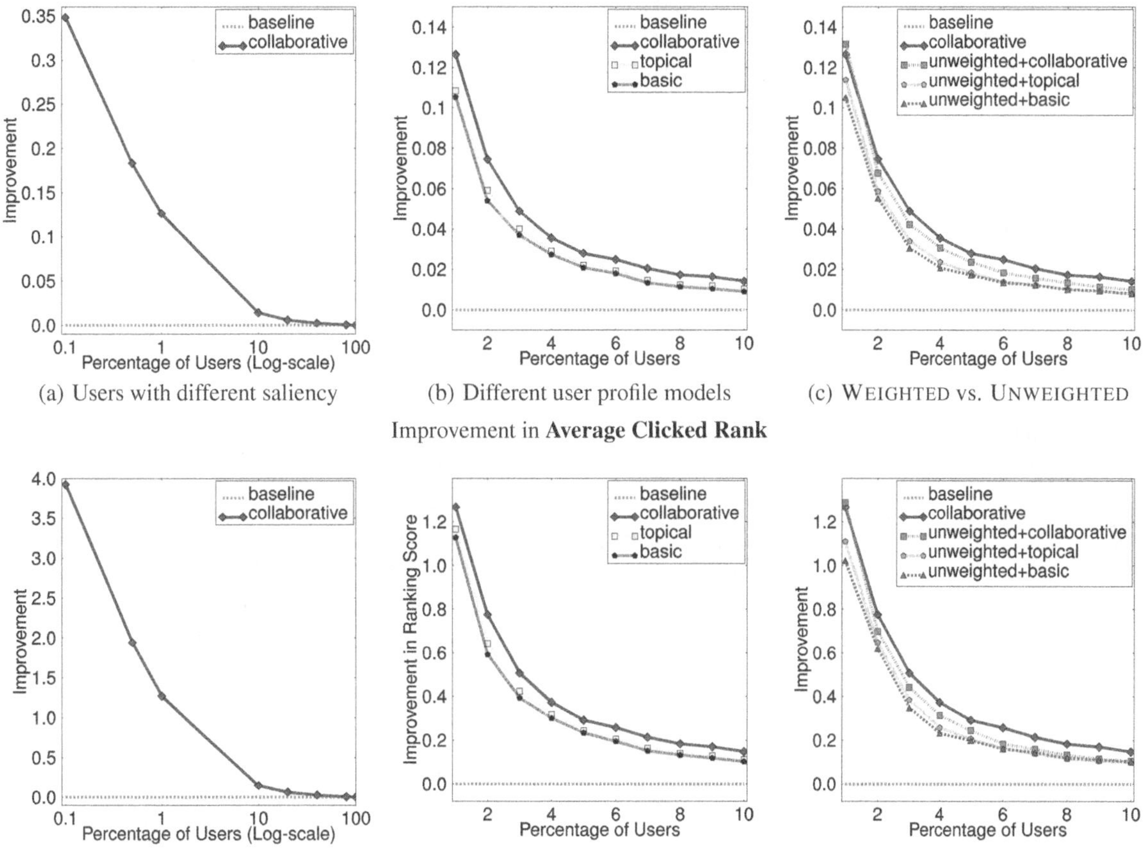

(a) Users with different saliency (b) Different user profile models (c) WEIGHTED VS. UNWEIGHTED

Improvement in **Average Clicked Rank**

(d) Users with different saliency (e) Different user profile models (f) WEIGHTED VS. UNWEIGHTED

Improvement in **Ranking Score**

Figure 3: Performance analysis focusing on high-Q_u users: comparing WEIGHTED-LCAA +COLLABORATIVE **with its variations.**

Table 3: Paired-t test for different methods against the baseline, computed for top 10%, 50%, and all users. We mark t-test results as follows: *($p < 0.05$), **($p < 0.01$), ***($p < 0.001$)

Method			10%	50%	100%
WEIGHTED	CSA	BASIC	***	***	***
		TOPICAL	***	***	***
		COLLABORATIVE	***	***	
	LCSA	BASIC	**	*	*
		TOPICAL	***	**	**
		COLLABORATIVE	***	***	
	LCAA	BASIC	***	***	***
		TOPICAL	***	***	***
		COLLABORATIVE	***	***	
UNWEIGHTED	CSA	BASIC	***	***	***
		TOPICAL	***		
		COLLABORATIVE	***		
	LCSA	BASIC	**		
		TOPICAL	**		
		COLLABORATIVE	***		
	LCAA	BASIC	***	**	**
		TOPICAL	***		
		COLLABORATIVE	***		

rank and about 74.4 in ranking score.) As expected and observed previously, performance degrades as we include less salient users.

We compared the improvement achieved by this configuration against other configurations using t-test. Keeping the same pair-generation technique (LCAA), it statistically significantly ($P < 0.05$) outperforms all other variations. However, its differences compared with WEIGHTED-CSA +COLLABORATIVE and WEIGHTED-LCSA +COLLABORATIVE are not statistically significant. At least for the top 10% users, different user profile models and the weighting scheme have more impact on the performance.

We now examine the effect of varying only the user profile model and only the weighting scheme over the best model, for the most salient 1% to 10% users.

Different user profile models

In contrast to our observations in Section 4.3.1 (where COLLABORATIVE was found to be less robust than BASIC when compared to the baseline for all the users), for the top 1%-10% users, COLLABORATIVE outperforms both BASIC and TOPICAL. Fixing the other parameters to WEIGHTED-LCAA, we plot the improvement achieved by using different user models (Figures 3(b) and 3(e)). While TOPICAL performs only slightly better than BASIC, COLLABORATIVE consistently outperforms both (statistically significant at $P < 0.05$ using t-test for top 10% users). This validates the effectiveness of modeling topic-specific comprehensibility preferences, as well as the necessity to employ collaborative filtering techniques to combat the sparseness in historical observations.

Different weighting schemes

Here we perform a direct comparison between WEIGHTED and UNWEIGHTED, and our findings reinforce the observations made in Section 4.3.1. As shown in Figures 3(c) and 3(f), our best configuration outperforms all other UNWEIGHTED variations using LCAA (statistically significant at $P < 0.05$ using the t-test for top 10% users). Interestingly, the difference between COLLABORATIVE and BASIC in the UNWEIGHTED setting is also less pronounced when more low-Q_u users are included (e.g., compare Figures 3(b) and 3(c) at the higher percentage of users).

4.4 Further analysis

In Section 4.3, we focused on performance break-down by user saliency. In this section, we examine the performance observed when using other ways to partition the data (measured at top 10% users using WEIGHTED-LCAA +COLLABORATIVE).

Improvement by topics The following table shows the improvements over the baseline in different topics.

Topic	Ranking Score	Average Rank
hobbies & interests	0.3550	0.0325
arts & entertainment	0.3517	0.0327
real_estate	0.2868	0.0302
society & culture	0.2094	0.0181
business & financial_services	0.1845	0.0195
technology & electronics	0.1519	0.0153
sports & recreation	0.1375	0.0155
employment & career	0.1038	0.0088
health & wellness	0.0778	0.0073
professional_services	0.0744	0.0059
education	0.0512	0.0065
retail	0.0426	0.0021
automotive	0.0362	0.0063
science & nature	0.0338	-0.0003
green	0.0336	-0.0000
home & garden	0.0258	0.0019
travel	-0.0521	-0.0008

In general, the topics with larger improments tend to be informational in nature (e.g., real estate, society & culture, business & financial services, and technology & electronics). On the other hand, for topics that are more transactional in nature (e.g., travel, home & garden), where comprehensibility may have less importance for users' information needs, we did not achieve similar improvements.

Per-query content variance For search results of a query, we can compute the variance in S_c. Figure 4 shows the improvement for different buckets of variance values. Most of the pages have a variance smaller than 0.3, and the plot focused on 3 buckets. The improvement increases as the variance increases from 0.1 to 0.2. This conforms to our intuition that comprehensibility-based personalization is more effective when the search results actually vary a lot in their comprehensibility. Interestingly, as the variance further increases to 0.3, the improvement decreases. This could happen because the higher variance in S_c can be partially attributed to topical differences, where the topical-relevance-based ranking needs to play a bigger role.

In our future work, we plan to incorporate both the query topic and the content variance in S_c to further improve our model.

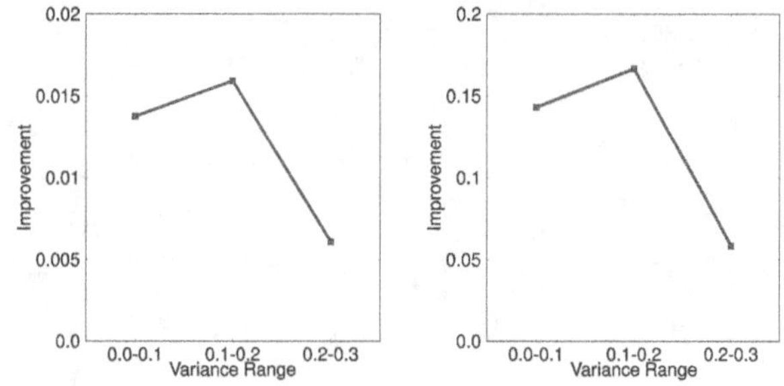

(a) Average Click Rank (b) Ranking Score

Figure 4: Improvement vs. variance in S_c.

5. EXPERIMENTS ON ANSWERS

We conducted a preliminary study on the Yahoo! Answers dataset. The goal here is to rank the answers posted to a question, based on the asker's personal comprehensibility preference.

Experimental setup To evaluate a given ranking, we simply measure the position of the best answer chosen by the asker in that ranking. Unlike the search data, there is no native ranking provided on Yahoo! Answers to use as a baseline or in rank combination.

We experimented with the following systems:

- Random baseline: answers were ranked in random order. This baseline allows us to study whether comprehensibility preferences have any signal in predicting the best answer.
- Majority baseline: we take the preference of the majority of askers and does not allow personalization. On answers data, we observed $P_u > 0.5$ for an average user (i.e., a preference for harder content), thus we rank answers in decreasing S_c for all askers. This can be viewed as a proxy of a quality-based ranking since very low S_c could correlate with low-quality content in this domain.
- Our model: for answers data, we only have one pair-generation technique. We used the BASIC user profile that takes WEIGHTED preference pairs. As there is no native ranking to combine with, we simply rank the answers by increasing S_c if $P_u < 0.5$, and by decreasing S_c otherwise.

Results The table below summarizes the performance. We show the rank of the gold-standard best answer for different percentage of users (sorted in decreasing order by Q_u). That is, **lower** values indicate **better** performance. Shown in brackets are paired t-test results versus the random and the majority baseline, respectively: *($p < 0.05$), **($p < 0.01$), ***($p < 0.001$).

Fraction of users	Random	Majority	Our model
5%	3.375	2.947	2.895 (***, ***)
10%	3.596	3.096	3.079 (***, ***)
100%	4.525	4.093	4.149 (***,)

Both the majority baseline and our model beat the random baseline, and the improvements are highly significant. For users with lower saliency (i.e., 100%), the majority baseline, which may partially approximate answer quality, performs better. But for the top 5% and top 10% most salient users, our model is significantly better than the majority baseline. This indicates that modeling *personalized* comprehensibility preferences is helpful in identifying the best answers for different users.

6. DISCUSSION

6.1 User Preference in Search Data

Across all users, P_u averages at 0.493 (using the BASIC method).[11] That is, among the search results returned to their queries, on average users have a slight preference towards easier content. We now

[11] Through out this study, we use LCAA unless specified otherwise.

address the following question: if we partition the data in different ways, will we consistently observe more users preferring easier content?

In what follows, we partition the users by their interests in different topics, as well as by gender and age. We rank the users by Q_u, and focus on the 60% most salient users (whose comprehensibility preferences are most pronounced). For each data partition, we report the percentage of users with $P_u > 0.5$ (denoted as R_h). The higher R_h is, the higher percentage of users prefer harder content. (Recall that the preference encoded in P_u is relative to the results returned for a given query, rather than an absolute preference for easy or hard content.)

The figure below shows R_h for different topics. We observed a smaller percentage of users who prefer harder content in "technology & electronics", compared to topics like "health & wellness". We conjecture that for personally more important health-related content such as in "health & wellness", more people are willing to put in the effort to read more sophisticated content. (Alternatively, it could be due to search engine returning overly complicated results in "technology & electronics".)

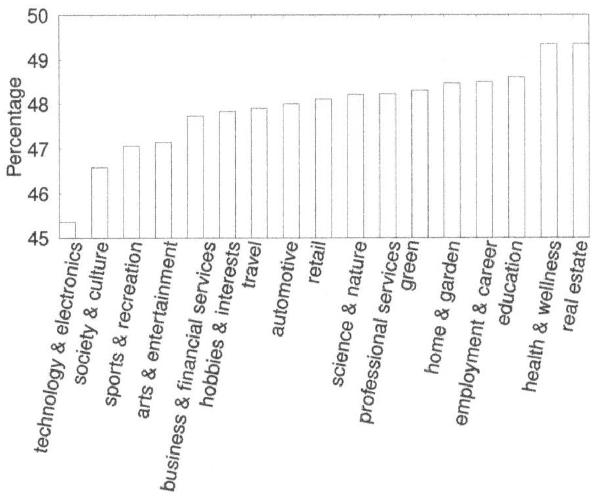

We also conducted a study on users whose demographical information is available. The figure below shows how R_h changes with gender and age. There is a slightly larger percentage of female users who prefer more sophisticated content (which could be partially correlated with different topical interests between the two genders). For different age groups (binned at 5 year increments), R_h peaks around the age of 25. In comparison, there is a smaller percentage of users preferring harder content among teenagers and seniors. In future work, such demographic information can be used to provide a better prior for users with insufficient data.

6.2 Discussion of design choices

In this work, we build user profiles using pairwise preferences (Section 2.2.1). In a preliminary study on search data, we experimented with an alternative approach, where we estimated the user's reading proficiency based on the average comprehensibility score of the (search result) pages she clicked on. We trained a variety of classifiers on a smaller-scale dataset, but did not observe any improvement over the baseline. We believe the model based on preference pairs is better suited for extracting comprehensibility-related signals from a search click log, where topical preferences and comprehensibility preferences may be conflated. Note that our framework allows us to build user profiles while accounting for

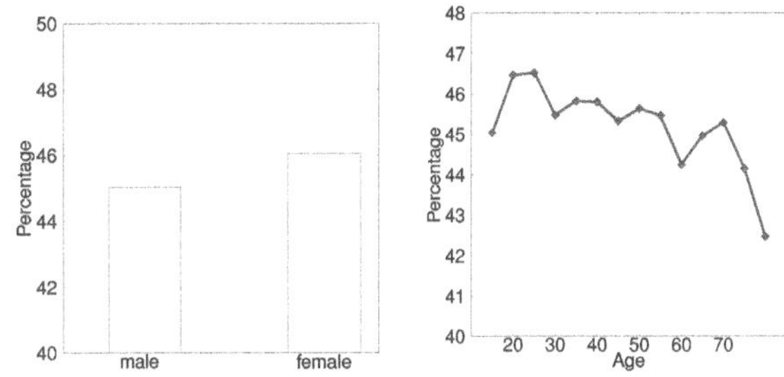

(a) Gender Study (b) Age Study

position bias (Section 2.3). It also assigns different weights to preference pairs to focus more on pairs with a smaller difference in topical relevance. Perhaps more subtly, P_u captures user preferences relative to the search results for a given query, and does not compare comprehensibility scores of results from different topics, which may differ widely (Figure 1). Thus, if a user tends to formulate queries that trigger easier content than what he needs, he would tend to click on the harder results, which would lead to a higher P_u, even if the results clicked by the user do not necessarily receive a high S_c in terms of absolute value.

7. RELATED WORK

There are several bodies of prior research that are relevant to our study, namely, those focusing on text readability, personalized content selection, and collaborative filtering.

Text readability has been long studied in linguistics, and a number of (manually-tuned) readability indices have been proposed, such as the Gunning FOG Index [15], Flesch-Kincaid Index [23], Coleman-Liau Index [11], and others [21, 24]. Recent research employed statistical methods to quantify text readability. Collins-Thompson and Callan [13] predicted reading difficulty using statistical language modeling, which they showed to be superior to classical readability indices on a Web corpus. Schwarm and Ostendorf [29] used Support Vector Machines and statistical language models. Heilman et al. [16] combined lexical and grammatical features to quantify readability of first and second language texts. Pitler and Nenkova [26] employed readability measures to predict text quality. Bendersky et al. [3] formulated the notion of document quality, which captures text readability, layout, and ease of navigation, and showed it to be beneficial for document ranking. Several studies proposed ways to quantify answer quality in CQA forums [1, 32].

Personalized search was the focus of many studies that modeled users' interests in terms of topical relevance [34, 22, 9]. Dou et al. [14] studied different personalized search methods using click logs, and found the memory-based method to perform best. Teevan et al. [35] explored the utility of personalization for different types of queries. Recently, White et al. [37] argued that search experience can be improved by modeling user's domain expertise.

Arguably, the most related prior work is that by Collins-Thompson et al. [12], who studied personalization of Web search results by reading level. One key difference between our work and theirs is that they explicitly modeled 12 reading levels corresponding to the 12 US school grades. In contrast, we devised a supervised comprehensibility classifier based on the comparison between Simple English and regular English Wikipedia, as explained in Section 2.1. Our experiments also go beyond Web search, as we include results on Yahoo Answers as well. Finally, we employ collaborative filtering techniques to alleviate data sparsity. In their follow-up work, Kim et al. [20] jointly model reading level and topic distribution.

Collaborative Filtering There is a vast body of work in collaborative filtering, and a comprehensive survey is not possible here. Most relevant to our work is the Maximum-Margin Matrix Factorization approach, which has been shown to be highly effective in recent work [28, 30, 2]. Cao et al. [8] formulated a collaborative ranking model for analyzing search click logs in a way that accounts for the position bias and alleviates data sparsity. Sun et al. [31] employed the (user, query, page) tensor built from click logs to improve personalized search.

8. CONCLUSION

We developed a unified framework for personalized content selection using text comprehensibility. We showed that modeling text comprehensibility can significantly improve content ranking, in both Web search and a CQA forum. We built a comprehensibility classifier to predict the sophistication level of a given text, and used it to construct topic-specific models of users' reading proficiency. Our approach is based on implicit user feedback, using search click logs or best answer tagging in CQA forums. We evaluated a number of strategies for extracting users' comprehensibility preferences from their historically-observed clicks, and found that manipulating pairwise preferences is far superior to merely averaging absolute comprehensibility scores across different topics. We also found that weighting preference pairs by position distance is beneficial, and also validated the effectiveness of collaborative filtering techniques in tackling data sparsity, which is inherent in modeling users' topic-specific preferences.

We believe that modeling text comprehensibility holds a lot of promise for personalizing content selection beyond topical relevance. Here we developed a text comprehensibility classifier by comparing pairs of Web pages. An immediate extension to this work would be to develop a comprehensibility-aware classifier of answers quality. In our future work, we plan to develop more sophisticated comprehensibility classifiers, as well as incorporate the difficulty of queries and questions into our framework.

Acknowledgment

We thank Oliver Chapelle, Fernando Diaz, and Lihong Li for discussions on evaluation metrics. We thank the anonymous reviewers for helpful suggestions.

9. REFERENCES

[1] L. A. Adamic, J. Zhang, E. Bakshy, and M. S. Ackerman. Knowledge sharing and Yahoo Answers: everyone knows something. In *WWW*, 2008.

[2] D. Agarwal and B.-C. Chen. Regression-based latent factor models. In *KDD*, pages 19–28, 2009.

[3] M. Bendersky, W. B. Croft, and Y. Diao. Quality-biased ranking of web documents. In *WSDM*, 2011.

[4] J. S. Breese, D. Heckerman, and C. Kadie. Empirical analysis of predictive algorithms for collaborative filtering. In *UAI*, 1998.

[5] A. Broder. A taxonomy of web search. *SIGIR Forum*, 36(2):3–10, 2002.

[6] A. Broder, M. Fontoura, E. Gabrilovich, A. Joshi, V. Josifovski, and T. Zhang. Robust classification of rare queries using web knowledge. In *SIGIR*, 2007.

[7] A. Broder, E. Gabrilovich, V. Josifovski, G. Mavromatis, D. Metzler, and J. Wang. Exploiting site-level information to improve web search. In *CIKM*, 2010.

[8] B. Cao, D. Shen, K. Wang, and Q. Yang. Clickthrough log analysis by collaborative ranking. In *AAAI*, 2010.

[9] M. J. Carman, F. Crestani, M. Harvey, and M. Baillie. Towards query log based personalization using topic models. In *CIKM*, 2010.

[10] O. Chapelle and Y. Zhang. A dynamic bayesian network click model for web search ranking. In *WWW*, pages 1–10, 2009.

[11] M. Coleman and T. L. Liau. A computer readability formula designed for machine scoring. *Journal of Applied Psychology*, 60:283–284, 1975.

[12] K. Collins-Thompson, P. N. Bennett, R. W. White, S. de la Chica, and D. Sontag. Personalizing web search results by reading level. In *CIKM*, pages 403–412, 2011.

[13] K. Collins-Thompson and J. P. Callan. A language modeling approach to predicting reading difficulty. In *HLT-NAACL*, pages 193–200, 2004.

[14] Z. Dou, R. Song, and J.-R. Wen. A large-scale evaluation and analysis of personalized search strategies. In *WWW*, 2007.

[15] R. Gunning. *The Technique of Clear Writing*. McGraw-Hill, 1952.

[16] M. J. Heilman, K. Collins-Thompson, and J. Callan. Combining lexical and grammatical features to improve readability measures for first and second language texts. In *HLT-NAACL*, 2007.

[17] T. Joachims. Optimizing search engines using clickthrough data. In *KDD*, 2002.

[18] T. Joachims, L. Granka, B. Pang, H. Hembrooke, and G. Gay. Accurately interpreting clickthrough data as implicit feedback. In *SIGIR*, pages 154–161, 2005.

[19] T. Kanungo and D. Orr. Predicting the readability of short web summaries. In *WSDM*, pages 202–211, 2009.

[20] J. Y. Kim, K. Collins-Thompson, P. Bennett, and S. Dumais. Characterizing web content, user interests, and search behavior by reading level and topic. In *WSDM*, 2012 (forthcoming).

[21] J. P. Kincaid, R. P. Fishburne, R. L. Rogers, and B. S. Chissom. Derivation of New Readability Formulas for Navy Enlisted Personnel. Technical report, NTIS, Feb. 1975.

[22] N. Matthijs and F. Radlinski. Personalizing web search using long term browsing history. In *WSDM*, pages 25–34, 2011.

[23] G. McClure. Readability formulas: Useful or useless. *IEEE Transactions on Professional Communications*, 30:12–15, 1987.

[24] G. H. McLaughlin. SMOG grading—a new readability formula. *Journal of Reading*, 12(8):639–646, 1969.

[25] D. Metzler, J. Novak, H. Cui, and S. Reddy. Building enriched document representations using aggregated anchor text. In *SIGIR*, 2009.

[26] E. Pitler and A. Nenkova. Revisiting readability: a unified framework for predicting text quality. In *EMNLP*, 2008.

[27] F. Radlinski and T. Joachims. Query chains: Learning to rank from implicit feedback. In *KDD*, 2005.

[28] J. D. M. Rennie and N. Srebro. Fast maximum margin matrix factorization for collaborative prediction. In *ICML*, 2005.

[29] S. E. Schwarm and M. Ostendorf. Reading level assessment using support vector machines and statistical language models. In *ACL*, pages 523–530, 2005.

[30] N. Srebro, J. D. M. Rennie, and T. S. Jaakola. Maximum-margin matrix factorization. In *NIPS*, 2005.

[31] J.-T. Sun, H.-J. Zeng, H. Liu, Y. Lu, and Z. Chen. CubeSVD: a novel approach to personalized web search. In *WWW*, 2005.

[32] M. Surdeanu, M. Ciaramita, and H. Zaragoza. Learning to rank answers on large online QA collections. In *ACL*, 2008.

[33] J. Teevan, E. Adar, R. Jones, and M. A. S. Potts. Information re-retrieval: repeat queries in yahoo's logs. In *SIGIR*, 2007.

[34] J. Teevan, S. T. Dumais, and E. Horvitz. Personalizing search via automated analysis of interests and activities. In *SIGIR*, 2005.

[35] J. Teevan, S. T. Dumais, and D. J. Liebling. To personalize or not to personalize: modeling queries with variation in user intent. In *SIGIR*, pages 163–170, 2008.

[36] M. Weimer, A. Karatzoglou, Q. V. Le, and A. Smola. CoFiRank, Maximum Margin Matrix Factorization for Collaborative Ranking. In *NIPS*, 2007.

[37] R. W. White, S. T. Dumais, and J. Teevan. Characterizing the influence of domain expertise on web search behavior. In *WSDM*, 2009.

WebSets: Extracting Sets of Entities from the Web Using Unsupervised Information Extraction

Bhavana Dalvi
School of Computer Science
Carnegie Mellon University
Pittsburgh, PA 15213
bbd@cs.cmu.edu

William W. Cohen
School of Computer Science
Carnegie Mellon University
Pittsburgh, PA 15213
wcohen@cs.cmu.edu

Jamie Callan
School of Computer Science
Carnegie Mellon University
Pittsburgh, PA 15213
callan@cs.cmu.edu

ABSTRACT

We describe a open-domain information extraction method for extracting concept-instance pairs from an HTML corpus. Most earlier approaches to this problem rely on combining clusters of distributionally similar terms and concept-instance pairs obtained with Hearst patterns. In contrast, our method relies on a novel approach for clustering terms found in HTML tables, and then assigning concept names to these clusters using Hearst patterns. The method can be efficiently applied to a large corpus, and experimental results on several datasets show that our method can accurately extract large numbers of concept-instance pairs.

Categories and Subject Descriptors: I.2.6[Artificial Intelligence]: Learning - Knowledge acquisition

General Terms: Algorithms, Experimentation.

Keywords: Web Mining, Clustering, Hyponymy Relation Acquisition.

1. INTRODUCTION

Many NLP tasks—include summarization, co-reference resolution, and named entity extraction—are made easier by acquiring large sets of concept-instance pairs (such as "goddess,Venus" and "US President","Bill Clinton"). Ontologies that include many such pairs (e.g., FreeBase and WordNet) exist, but are often incomplete. Here we consider the problem of automatically harvesting concept-instance pairs from a large corpus of HTML tables.

Past approaches to this problem have primarily been based detecting *coordinate terms* and *hyponym patterns*. *Hyponym patterns*, sometimes called Hearst patterns [11], are surface patterns (like "Xs such as Y") indicating that X,Y are a concept-instance pair. Two terms i and j are *coordinate terms* if i and j are instances of the same concept: for instance, "Bill Clinton" and "Richard Nixon" are coordinate terms, since both are instances of the concept "US President". Coordinate terms are most frequently detected by clustering terms based on distributional similarity [15]—i.e., the similarity of their contexts in free text. Various techniques can be used to combine these coordinate-term and hyponym information to generate additional concept-instance pairs [26, 22].

Our approach is novel in that it relies solely on HTML tables to detect coordinate terms. We present a novel clustering method that finds extremely precise coordinate-term clusters by merging table columns that contain overlapping *triplets* of instances, and show that this clustering method outperforms k-means, while still being scalable enough to apply to large corpora. We also present a new method for combining hyponym and coordinate-term information, and show that on table-rich corpora, this method improves on previously-published techniques [26], obtaining higher accuracy while generating nearly hundred times the number of concept-instance pairs. In a final set of experiments, we show that allowing a small amount of user input for each coordinate-term cluster can produce concept-instance pairs with accuracy in the high 90's for four different corpora.

The experiments in this paper are conducted on several different HTML corpora and a collection of Hearst pattern [11] instances that have been extracted from ClueWeb09, all of which are made available for future researchers.

The rest of this paper is organized as follows. Section 2 presents a more detailed overview of the related work. Section 3 describes our unsupervised IE technique, which we call WebSets. Section 4 describes the evaluation methodology and experimental results, and section 6 concludes.

2. RELATED WORK

Information extraction from unstructured and semi-structured information sources on the Web is an active area of research in recent years. In this section we summarize the existing techniques after categorizing them, by the inputs they are using and the goals they are trying to reach.

2.1 Exploiting Tables on the Web

Gatterbauer et al. [8] focus on extracting tabular data from various kinds of pages that have table-like visual representations when rendered in a browser. Although we do not make use of these techniques, they could be employed by WebSets to collect more tabular information from a corpus.

The WebTables [2] system extracted schema information from a huge corpus of 14.1 billion HTML tables from Google's general-purpose web crawl. They built an attribute correlation statistics database (AcsDB), which can be used to create an attribute name thesaurus and a schema auto-completion system. Unfortunately the WebTables corpora is not publi-

Permission to make digital or hard copies of all or part of this work for personal or classroom use is granted without fee provided that copies are not made or distributed for profit or commercial advantage and that copies bear this notice and the full citation on the first page. To copy otherwise, to republish, to post on servers or to redistribute to lists, requires prior specific permission and/or a fee.
WSDM'12, February 8–12, 2012, Seattle, Washington, USA.
Copyright 2012 ACM 978-1-4503-0747-5/12/02 ...$10.00.

cally available; it would be an interesting project to apply WebSets to a corpus of this size.

Gupta et al. [9] focuses on the task of extending a table given a few seed rows. Their technique consolidates HTML lists relevant to the example rows to build a result table. Similarly, SEAL (Set Expansion for Any Language) [28] is a set expansion system which starts with a few seed examples and extends them using lists detected using character-based heuristics. Unlike these systems, WebSets does not require seed examples, but instead extracts concept-instance pairs in an unsupervised manner from a corpus.

Gupta and Sarawagi [10] consider jointly training structured extraction models from overlapping web source (primarily in tables), thus avoiding the need for labeled data. WebSets also depends on content overlap across table columns and domains, but generates concept-instance pairs instead of building an extractor.

Limaye et al. [14] proposed a system to use an existing catalog and type hierarchy for annotating table columns and cells. They also propose better indexing techniques to improve the search engine response to table queries. WebSets differs in that the Hearst-pattern data it uses is noisier than a catalog or type hierarchy.

2.2 Information Extraction Systems

Many systems perform semi-supervised information extraction from free text on the web, using only a few seed examples or seed rules. These systems include KnowItAll [6, 7], ASIA [27], and Coupled Pattern Learning (CPL) [4]. Along similar lines, Parameswaran et al. [18] propose a concept extraction algorithm which can identify a canonical form of a concept, filtering out sub-concepts or super-concepts; and Ritter et al. [20] describe a scheme for filtering concept-instance pairs, using a SVM classifier which uses as features frequency statistics for several Hearst patterns on a large corpus. Given a training set of text containing known concept-instance pairs, Snow et al. [22] learns "dependency path" features, which can further expand the set of concept-instance pairs. WebSets is different from most of these approaches in that it builds all sets of entities from a given corpus, and does not require seed sets, a starting ontology, or a set of target concept names.

TextRunner [30] is an open-domain IE system which makes a single pass over the corpus of unstructured text and extracts a large set of relational tuples, without requiring any human input. Unlike WebSets, however, it does not build coherent sets of category or relation instances. Pantel and Ravichandran [17] proposes a method to automatically label distributional term clusters using Hearst-like patterns, and Van Durme and Pasca [26] proposed an alternative approach method to extract labeled classes of instances from unstructured text. All of these approaches use only unstructured text to find coordinate terms and assigning hypernyms, whereas WebSets uses HTML tables. As we show in the experimental results, WebSets uses a novel method for combining coordinate-term clusters and hypernyms data that quantitatively improves over Van Durme and Pasca's method for combining coordinate-term clusters and hypernym data.

There also exist some systems that use both free-text and tabular information. Talukdar et al. [24] proposed a graph random walk based semi-supervised label propagation technique for open domain class instance extractions, which extends the system of Van Durme and Pasca by using table data (from WebTables) as well as free-text distributional clusters. However, unlike Talukdar et al.'s system, WebSets does not require distributional clusters. Coupled SEAL (CSEAL) [4] use of mutual exclusion, containment and type checking relationships to extend SEAL, and CPL [4] and CSEAL are the two components of NELL [25], a multi-strategy semi-supervised learning system. However, unlike NELL, WebSets does not require seed instances or an ontology as input.

Shinzato and Torisawa [21] showed that coordinate terms can be extracted from itemizations in structured web documents. Their method finds concept-instance pairs pertaining to a single query list, and finds candidate hypernyms by querying the web on-the-fly to collect documents. In contrast, WebSets processes all lists in a corpora simultaneously, and makes no web queries.

3. WEBSETS

In this section we describe an unsupervised information extraction technique named WebSets which extracts concept-instance pairs from HTML tables in a given corpus. It builds coordinate term clusters using co-occurrence in table columns and assigns hypernyms to these clusters using Hearst pattern data extracted form text corpus. To build term clusters, system should first extract tables by parsing HTML pages, then decide which tables have useful relational data. Following the hypothesis that entities appearing in a table column possibly belong to the same concept, each table column in this extracted data is a candidate entity set; the system hence needs to have a mechanism to cluster those table columns. Clustering the table columns will yield sets of entities, each of which potentially belongs to a coherent concept. These sets will become more useful if they are labeled with appropriate concept-names. To summarize, the technique we develop needs to solve following sub-problems:

1. ***Table Identification:*** Extracting tables from the corpus that are likely to have relational data.
2. ***Entity Clustering:*** Efficiently clustering the extracted table cells to generate coherent sets of entities.
3. ***Hypernym Recommendation:*** Labeling each cluster with an appropriate concept-name (hyperym).

In this section, we describe our approach, WebSets, which solves each of the above mentioned sub-problems in an effective way.

3.1 Table Identification

Currently WebSets parses tables defined by <table> tags[1]. This is only a fraction of structured data available on the Web. Use of other techniques like Gatterbauer et al. [8] can provide more input data to learn sets from.

Further only a small fraction of HTML tables actually contain useful relational data(see Section 4). Remaining tables are used for formatting or rendering purposes rather than to present relational data. To filter out useful tables, WebSets uses the following set of features: (1) the number of rows (2)

[1]We found that large number of HTML pages have broken syntax. We use the HTML syntax cleaning software Tidy [1] to fix the syntax in these pages.

the number of non-link columns (3) the length of cells after removing formatting tags (4) whether table contains other HTML tables. The thresholds set for our experiments are explained in Section 4.

3.2 Entity Clustering

At the end of the table identification step, we have a collection of HTML tables which are likely to contain relational data. Each of the table-cells is a candidate entity and each table-column is a candidate set of entities. However many columns have information that is useful only within a site (e.g., navigational links) and many are overlapping. To solve this problem we use the redundancy of information on the Web. If a set of entities co-occur in multiple table-columns across the Web, then it is more likely to be an important entity set. Since these tables come from different domains and are created by different authors, they will typically only partially overlap. To cluster the entities in these columns into coherent sets, the first essential step will be to represent this data in a way that reveals the co-occurrence of entities across multiple table columns. In this section, we will first discuss the data representation, and then algorithms for entity clustering.

3.2.1 Data Representation

We considered two ways to represent table data. With the "Entity record representation", one record per entity is created, and it contains information about which table-columns and URL domains the entity was mentioned in. These entity records can then be clustered, based on the overlap of table-columns and domains, to yield sets of entities. One advantage of this representation is that it is compact. Another advantage is that the number of distinct domains an entity occurred in can be used as an indicator of how "important" it is. A disadvantage of this representation is that if some entity-name is ambiguous (has multiple senses), it will collapse all senses of the entity into one record. E.g., consider a corpus which contains mentions of the entity "Apple" in two senses, "Apple as a fruit" and "Apple as a company". This representation will create a single record for the entity "Apple" with its occurrence as a fruit and as a company confounded. An unsupervised IE system might find it difficult to decompose multiple senses from this single record.

To solve this problem, we propose a novel representation of the table data called "Entity-Triplet records". In this representation, there is a record for each triplet of adjacent entities instead of for individual entities. Each record contains information about which table-columns and URL domains the triplet occurred in. Hence in case of an ambiguous entity like "Apple", its occurrences as a fruit will be separate from its occurrences as a company, e.g., {Apple, Avocado, Banana} will be one triplet record and {Apple, Microsoft, DELL} will be another triplet record. Thus entities within a triplet disambiguate each other. Since we have a list of all domains a triplet occurred in, only those triplets which appear in enough domains can be considered as important.

In this way, we represent the table data as a triplet store, which contains a record for each entity triplet. The triplet store can be built in one single pass over the corpus. If the system considers all possible triplets that can be created from each table column, then number of triplet records will be quadratic in the total size of all tables. This can be a serious concern for a web-scale dataset. Hence our system constructs onlty those triplets which are adjacent i.e. subsequences of entities in a table-column. This ensures that number of triplet records are linear in total size of all tables, making the system scalable. The system keeps track of all table-columns a triplet occurred in, which makes it possible to reconstruct a column by joining triplets on columnId. Hence this storage method does not result in any loss of information.

Country	Capital City
India	Delhi
China	Beijing
Canada	Ottawa
France	Paris

Table 1: TableId= 21, domain= "www.dom1.com"

Country	Capital City
China	Beijing
Canada	Ottawa
France	Paris
England	London

Table 2: TableId= 34, URL= "www.dom2.com"

Consider an example of tables containing countries and their capitals. Original tables are shown in Table 1, 2 and the triplet records created by WebSets are shown in Table 3. Second row in Table 3, indicates that the triplet (China, Canada, France) occurred in column 1 of tableId 21 and column 1 of tableId 34. Also these entities are retrieved from webpages which reside in the domains "www.dom1.com" and "www.dom2.com".

These triplets are canonicalized by converting entity strings to lower case and arranging the constituent entities in alphabetical order. The triplets are then ranked in descending order of number of domains.

We create $O(n)$ triplets from a table column of size n. Adding each triplet to the Triplet Store using hashmap takes $O(1)$ time. Given a set of T HTML tables with a total of N entities in them, the Triplet Store can be created in $O(N)$ time. Ranking the triplets using any common sorting technique will take $O(N*logN)$ time. Hence the total complexity of building the Triplet Store is $O(N * logN)$.

3.2.2 Building entity clusters

The next task is to cluster these triplet records into meaningful sets. The system does not know how many clusters are present in the underlying dataset; and since our dataset will be constructed from a huge HTML web corpus, the clustering algorithm needs to be very efficient. Given these requirements, it can be easily seen that parametric clustering algorithms like K-means may not be effective due to the unknown number of clusters. Non-parametric algorithms like agglomerative clustering [5] fit most of our requirements. The most efficient agglomerative clustering al-

Entities	Tid:Cids	Domains
India,China,Canada	21:1	www.dom1.com
China, Canada, France	21:1, 34:1	www.dom1.com, www.dom2.com
Delhi, Beijing, Ottawa	21:2	www.dom1.com
Beijing, Ottawa, Paris	21:2, 34:2	www.dom1.com, www.dom2.com
Canada, England, France	34:1	www.dom2.com
London, Ottawa, Paris	34:2	www.dom2.com

Table 3: Triplet records created by WebSets

gorithm is the single-link clustering algorithm, but even that would require computing the similarity of every pair of entity triplets returned. This will be very expensive for the web scale datasets we are aiming to handle. Hence we develop a new bottom-up clustering algorithm which is efficient in terms of both space and time. Experiments to compare our algorithm with a standard K-means clustering algorithm are described in Section 4.

3.2.3 Bottom-Up Clustering Algorithm

The clustering algorithm (named *"Bottom-Up Clusterer"*) is described formally in Algorithm 1. The clusterer scans through each triplet record t which has occurred in at least $minUniqueDomain$ distinct domains. A triplet and a cluster are represented with the same data-structure: (1) a set of entities, (2) a set of columnIds in which the entities co-occurred and (3) a set of domains in which the entities occurred.

The clusterer compares the overlap of triplet t against each cluster C_i. The triplet t is added to the first C_i so that either of the following two cases is true:
(1) at least 2 entities from t appear in cluster C_i .
(2) at least 2 columnIds from t appear in cluster C_i.
(i.e. $minEntityOverlap = 2$ and $minColumnOverlap = 2$)
In both these cases, intuitively there is a high probability that t belongs to the same category as cluster C_i. If no such overlap is found with existing clusters, the algorithm creates a new cluster and initializes it with the triplet t.

This clustering algorithm is order dependent, i.e., if the order in which records are processed changes, it might return a different set of clusters. Finding the optimal ordering of triplets is a hard problem, but a reasonably good ordering can be easily generated by ordering the triplets in the descending order of number of distinct domains. We discard triplets that appear in less than $minUniqueDomain$ domains.

Algorithm 1 Bottom-Up Clustering Algorithm

function Bottom-Up-Clusterer($TripletStore$):$Clusters$
  {Triplet records are ordered in descending order of number of distinct domain.}
  Initialize $Clusters = \phi$; $max = 0$
  for (every $t \in TripletStore$: such that $|t.domains| >= minUniqueDomain$) **do**
    assigned = false
    for every $C_i \in Clusters$ **do**
      if $|t.entities \cap C_i.entities| >= minEntityOverlap$ OR $|t.col \cap C_i.col| >= minColumnOverlap$ **then**
        $C_i = C_i \cup t$
        $assigned = true$
        break;
      end if
    end for
    if not assigned **then**
      increment max
      Create new cluster $C_{max} = t$
      $Clusters = Clusters \cup C_{max}$
    end if
  end for
end function

3.2.4 Computational complexity

Suppose that our dataset has total T tables. Let these tables have in total N cells. For each triplet t, Algorithm 1 finds entity and column overlap with all existing clusters. This operation can be implemented efficiently by keeping two inverted indices: (1) from each entity to all clusterIds it belongs to and (2) from each columnId to all clusterIds it belongs to. ClusterIds in each "postings list "[4] will be kept in sorted order.

Merging k sorted lists, with resultant list size of n takes $O(n * logk)$ time. Now let us compute worst case time complexity of Algorithm 1. To compute entity overlap of each triplet, the algorithm merges 3 postings lists with total size of $O(N)$. This step will take $O(N)$ time. To compute TableId:ColumnId overlap of each triplet, it merges $O(T)$ postings lists with total size of $O(N)$. This step will take $O(N * logT)$ time. Hence for each triplet, finding a clusterId to merge the triplet with takes $O(N * logT)$ time. There are $O(N)$ triplets. So the *Bottom-Up Clusterer* will have worst case time complexity of $O(N^2 * logT)$. In practice, it is much less than this. If N is total number of table-cells in the corpus then the total number of triplet occurrences is also $O(N)$. Hence all the postings list merges can be amortized to be $O(N)$. Hence amortized complexity of this clustering algorithm is $O(N * logT)$. Considering the time complexity to sort the triplet store, total time complexity is $O(N * logN)$, which is much better than the complexity of a naive single-link clustering algorithm, which is $O(N^2 * logN)$.

3.3 Hypernym Recommendation

Previous sections described how do we obtain coordinate term clusters using co-occurrence of terms in the table columns. In this section we label these term clusters with the help of Hyponym Concept dataset.

3.3.1 Building The Hyponym-Concept Dataset

The *Hyponym Concept Dataset* is built by acquiring concept-instance pairs from unstructured text using Hearst patterns. For this task we used the data extracted from the ClueWeb09 corpus [3] by the developers of the NELL KB [25]. They used heuristics to identify and then shallow-parse approximately 2 billion sentences, and then extracted from this all patterns of the form "_ $word_1$ .. $word_k$ _" where the 'filler' $word_1$ .. $word_k$ is between one and five tokens long, and this filler appears at least once between two base noun phrases in the corpus. Each filler is paired with all pairs of noun phrases that bracket it, together with the count of the total number of times this sequence occurred. For instance, the filler '_ and vacations in _' occurs with the pair 'Holidays, Thailand' with a count of one and 'Hotels,Italy' with a count of six, indicating that the phrase "Hotels and vacations in Italy" occurred six times in the corpus . The hyponym dataset was constructed by finding all fillers that match one of the regular expressions in Table 4. These correspond to a subset of the Hearst patterns used in ASIA [27] together with some "doubly anchored" versions of these patterns [13].

Each record in the Hyponym Concept Dataset contains an entity and all concepts it co-occurred with. Table 5 shows an example of records in this dataset. According to this table, entity "USA" appeared with the concept "country" 1000

[4]In the information retrieval terminology, an inverted index has a record per word that contains the list of all document-ids the word occurred in. This list is referred to as the "postings list". In this paper, a "postings list" refers to the list of all clusterIds that a triplet or a columnId belongs to.

Id	Regular expression
1	arg1 such as (w+ (and|or))? arg2
2	arg1 (w+)? (and|or) other arg2
3	arg1 include (w+ (and|or))? arg2
4	arg1 including (w+ (and|or))? arg2

Table 4: Regular expressions used to create Hyponym Concept Dataset

Hyponym	Concepts
USA	country:1000
India	country:200
Paris	city:100, tourist_place:50
Monkey	animal:100, mammal:60
Sparrow	bird:33

Table 5: An example of Hyponym Concept Dataset

times. Similarly, "Monkey" appeared with two different concepts, 100 times with "animal" and 60 times with "mammal".

3.3.2 *Assigning Hypernyms to Clusters*

Assigning a meaningful concept-name to each entity set is important for two reasons. It enables us to systematically evaluate entity sets; e.g., it is easier for an evaluator to answer the question: "Is Boston a city?" than "Is Boston a member of set #37?") It also makes the system more useful for summarizing the data in a corpus (see Section 4.3.5). This section describes how WebSets recommends candidate hypernyms for each entity set produced by Algorithm 1.

For this task, we use the coordinate term clusters extracted from tables and *Hyponym Concept Dataset* extracted using Hearst patterns. Note that this part of the system uses information extracted from unstructured text from the Web, to recommend category names to sets extracted from tables on the Web.

Algorithm 2 Hypernym Recommendation Algorithm

function GenerateHypernyms
Given: c: An entity cluster generated by Algorithm 1,
  I: Set of all entities ,
  L: Set of all labels,
  $H \subseteq L \times I$: Hyponym-concept dataset,
Returns: RL_c : Ranked list of hypernyms for c.
Algorithm:
$RL_c = \phi$
for every label $l \in L$ **do**
  H_l = Set of entities which co-occurred with l in H
  $Score(l) = |H_l \cap c|$
  $RL_c = RL_c \cup < l, Score(l) >$
end for
Sort RL_c in descending order of $Score(l)$
Output RL_c
end function

The algorithm is formally described in Algorithm 2. For each set produced at the end of clustering, we find which entities from the set belong to *Hyponym Concept Dataset* and collect all concepts they co-occur with. Then these concepts are ranked by number of unique entities in the set it co-occurred with. This ranked list serves as hypernym recommendations for the set. The output of this stage can be used in two ways. We can assign the topmost hypernym in the rank list as the class label for a cluster (used in Section 4.2.4). Another possibility is to present a ranked list of hypernyms for each cluster to a user, who can then select the one which is the best for a given entity cluster (refer to Section 4.3.2).

Our method scores labels differently from Van Durme and Pasca method [26] It is also different in the sense that they output a concept-instance pair $< x, y >$ only when $< x, y >$ appears in the set of candidate concept-instance pairs, whereas we extend the labels to the whole cluster. Hence even if some pair $< x, y >$ is not present in the Hyponym Concept dataset, it can be produced as output.

4. EXPERIMENTAL EVALUATION

In this section we first discuss the datasets we worked on. Then we evaluate each step of our extraction process separately. These experiments assume that our method extracts a list of concept-instance pairs from the HTML corpus. Later part of this section discusses how well WebSets perform end to end, as a tool to process a large HTML corpus, and build coherent sets of entities along with labeling each of them. The datasets and evaluations done for these experiments are posted online at `http://rtw.ml.cmu.edu/wk/WebSets/wsdm_2012_online/index.html`.

4.1 Datasets

To test the performance of WebSets, we created several webpage datasets that are likely to have coherent sets of entities. An evaluation can then be done to check whether the system extracts expected entity sets from those datasets. Some of these datasets are created using SEAL, CSEAL and ASIA systems (refer to Section 2) that extract information from semi-structured pages on the Web. Each of these systems, takes a name or seed examples of a category as input and finds possible instances of that category using set expansion techniques. It queries a web search engine during this process and stores all the pages downloaded from the Web in a cache, so that they can be reused for any similar queries in the future. The cache contents generated by these systems help us build reasonable sized datasets for our experiments. We expect that WebSets will find reasonable number of HTML tables in these datasets.

1. **Toy_Apple:** This is a small toy dataset created with the help of multiple SEAL queries with "Apple" as a fruit and as a company. It is created to demonstrate the entity disambiguation effect of using triplet records and to compare various clustering algorithms.
2. **Delicious_Sports:** This dataset is a subset of DAI-Labor Delicious corpus [29], created by taking only those URLs which are tagged as "sports".
3. **Delicious_Music:** This dataset is a subset of DAI-Labor Delicious corpus [29], created by taking only those URLs which are tagged as "music".
4. **CSEAL_Useful:** CSEAL is one of the methods which suggest new category and relation instances to NELL KB. CSEAL mostly extracts entities out of semi-structured information on the Web. For each instance in the KB, we can retrieve the information about which methods supported the existence of the instance. The webpages from which these methods derived the support are also recorded. CSEAL_Useful dataset is a collection of those HTML pages from which CSEAL gathered information about entities in the NELL KB.

Dataset	#HTML pages	#tables
Toy_Apple	574	2.6K
Delicious_Sports	21K	146.3K
Delicious_Music	183K	643.3K
CSEAL_Useful	30K	322.8K
ASIA_NELL	112K	676.9K
ASIA_INT	121K	621.3K
Clueweb_HPR	100K	586.9K

Table 6: Dataset Statistics

Dataset	#Tables	%Rela-tional	#Filtered tables	%Rela-tional filtered	#Triplets
Toy_Apple	2.6K	50	762	75	15K
Delicious_Sports	146.3K	15	57.0K	55	63K
Delicious_Music	643.3K	20	201.8K	75	93K
CSEAL_Useful	322.8K	30	116.2K	80	1148K
ASIA_NELL	676.9K	20	233.0K	55	421K
ASIA_INT	621.3K	15	216.0K	60	374K
Clueweb_HPR	586.9K	10	176.0K	35	78K

Table 7: Table Identification Statistics

5. **ASIA_NELL:** This dataset is collected using hypernyms associated with entities in the NELL KB as queries for ASIA. Examples of such hypernyms are "City", "Bird", "Sports team" etc.

6. **ASIA_INT:** This dataset is also collected using the ASIA system but with another set of category names as input. These category names come from "Intelligence domain". Examples of categories in this domain are "government types", "international organizations", "federal agencies", "religions" etc.

7. **Clueweb_HPR:** This dataset is collected by randomly sampling high pagerank pages in the Clueweb dataset [3]. For this purpose we used the Fusion spam scores[12] provided by Waterloo university and used pages with spam-rank score higher than 60%.

Table 6 shows the number of HTML pages and tables present in each of the above mentioned datasets. Note that Clueweb_HPR contains random sample of the Clueweb dataset, and hence does not contain large number of tables like other datasets. Datasets derived using SEAL or ASIA are expected to have higher concentration of semi-structured data in them. Toy_Apple and both Delicious datasets are specifically designed for certain domains, whereas CSEAL_Useful and ASIA_NELL are relatively heterogeneous, Clueweb_HPR being the most heterogeneous dataset among all. In each of the following experiments, we work on one or more of these datasets to evaluate different aspects of WebSets.

4.2 Evaluation of Individual Stages

In this section we evaluate each stage of WebSets system and measure the performance. Here we consider WebSets as a technique to generate large number of concept-instance pairs given a HTML corpus.

4.2.1 Evaluation: Table Identification

Table 7 shows the statistics of table identification for each dataset. Based on the features described in Section 3.1, we filter out only those tables as useful which cross some predefined thresholds. These thresholds were derived from the intuitions after manually going through some samples of data, and are kept constant for all datasets and experiments described in this paper. When we evaluated a random sample of recursive tables, 93% of them were useless for our purposes, and only 7% tables contained relational data. Hence we decide to ignore the recursive tables. We construct triplets of entities in a table column, hence a table should have at least 3 rows. As we are not using any link data in our system, we consider only those columns which do not have links. WebSets is looking for tables containing relational data, hence if a table has at least 2 non-link columns, probability of it having relational data increases. While counting these rows and columns, we are looking for named entities. So from each cell, all HTML tags and links are removed. A very coarse filtering by length is then applied. We consider only those table cells which are 2-50 characters in length. Table 7 shows that percentage of relational tables increases by orders of magnitude due to this filtering step.

4.2.2 Evaluation: Clustering Algorithm

In these set of experiments we first compare WebSets with baseline K-means clustering algorithm. Later we see how "Entity-Triplet record" representation is better than "Entity record" representation. We compare the clustering algorithms in terms of commonly used clustering metrics: cluster purity (Purity), normalized mutual information (NMI), rand index (RI) [16] and Fowlkes-Mallows index (FM) which are defined as follows:

- **Cluster Purity:** To compute cluster purity, for each cluster the class which is most frequent in it gets assigned. The accuracy of this assignment is then measured by counting the number of correctly assigned documents and dividing by total number of documents. $purity(\Omega, C) = \frac{1}{N}\sum_k \max_j |\omega_k \bigcap c_j|$ where N is total number of documents, $\Omega = \omega_1, \omega_2, ..., \omega_K$ is the set of clusters and $C = c_1, c_2, ..., c_J$ is the set of classes. We interpret ω_k as the set of documents in cluster ω_k and c_j as the set of documents in cluster c_j.

- **Normalized Mutual Information:** High purity is easy to achieve when the number of clusters is large, hence purity cannot be used to trade off the quality of the clustering against the number of clusters. NMI is a measure that allows us to make such tradeoff. $NMI(\Omega, C) = \frac{I(\Omega;C)}{[H(\Omega)+H(C)]/2}$ where maximum likelihood estimates for mutual information and entropy are computed as follows: $I(\Omega, C) = \sum_k \sum_j \frac{|\omega_k \bigcap c_j|}{N}$, $H(\Omega) = -\sum_k \frac{|\omega_k|}{N} * log\frac{|\omega_k|}{N}$.

- **Rand Index:** This metric is based on information-theoretic interpretation of clustering. Clustering is a series of decisions, one for each of the $N(N-1)/2$ pairs of documents in the collection. True label denotes the pair belongs to same class or not. Predicted label denotes whether the pair belongs to same cluster or not. This way we can count True Positive(TP), False positive (FP), True Negative (TN) and False Negative (FN) score for the clustering. Rand Index is then defined as follows: $RI = \frac{TP+TN}{TP+FP+FN+TN}$.

- **Fowlkes-Mallows index:** While the previous three metrics are applicable only for hard-clustering, this metric is defined for soft clustering of data where clusters can be overlapping but classes are non-overlapping.

Dataset	Method	K	Purity	NMI	RI	FM
Toy_Apple	K-means	40	0.96	0.71	0.98	0.41
	WebSets	25	0.99	0.99	1.00	0.99
Delicious_Sports	K-means	50	0.72	0.68	0.98	0.47
	WebSets	32	0.83	0.64	1.00	0.85

Table 8: Comparison of WebSets vs. K-means

Method	K	FM w/ Entity records	FM w/ Triplet records
WebSets		0.11 (K=25)	0.85 (K=34)
K-Means	30	0.09	0.35
	25	0.08	0.38

Table 9: Comparison of performance on Entity vs. Triplet record representation (Toy_Apple dataset)

Let n_{ij} be the size of intersection of cluster ω_i and class c_j, $n_{i*} = \sum_j n_{ij}$ and $n_{*j} = \sum_i n_{ij}$.

$$FM = (\sum_{ij} \binom{n_{ij}}{2}) / \sqrt{\sum_i \binom{n_{i*}}{2} \sum_j \binom{n_{*j}}{2}}$$

The derivation of this formula can be found in Ramirez et al. [19].

Here each triplet is considered as a document. Ω refers to clusters of these triplets generated by WebSets or K-means. C refers to actual classes these triplets belong to. To compare quality of clusters across algorithms, we manually labeled each table-column of Toy_Apple and Delicious_Sports datasets. These labels are then extended to triplets within the table column. This experiment is not repeated for remaining datasets because manual labeling of the whole dataset is very expensive.

The performance of K-means depends on the input parameter K and random initialization of cluster centroids to start the clustering process. We run K-means with cosine distance function, a range of values of K and multiple starting points for each value of K. Figure 1 shows the plot of various runs of K-means vs. WebSets on Delicious_Sports dataset. Table 8 shows the comparison of WebSets vs. best run of K-means on Toy_Apple and Delicious_Sports datasets. We can see that WebSets performs better or comparable to K-means in terms of purity, NMI, RI, and FM. Through manual labeling we found that there are 27 and 29 distinct category sets in Toy_Apple and Delicious_Sports datasets respectively. We can see that WebSets defined 25 and 32 distinct clusters which are very close to actual number of meaningful sets, compared to 40 and 50 clusters defined by K-means.

Standard K-means algorithm has time complexity of $O(I * K * N * T)$, where I is the number of iterations, K is the number of clusters, N is the number of table-cells and T is the number of dimensions (here number of table-columns). As seen in Section 3, WebSets has time complexity of $O(N * logN)$. Hence our bottom-up clustering algorithm is more efficient than K-means in terms of time-complexity.

To study entity disambiguation effect of triplet records, we generated both "Entity record" and "Entity-Triplet record" representations of Toy_Apple dataset. When we ran our clustering algorithm on "Entity-Triplet record" dataset, we found "Apple" in two different clusters, one in which it was clustered with other fruits and had supporting evidence from table-columns talking about fruits; other cluster contained companies and evidence from related table-columns. Running the same clustering algorithm on "Entity record" dataset, resulted in a huge cluster containing "Apple", fruits and companies all combined. Thus we can say that entity triplets do help WebSets to disambiguate multiple senses of the same entity-string.

Now we compare the performance of clustering algorithms on entity record vs. triplet record representation. In this experiment we use Toy_Apple dataset. A table-column is considered as document and clusters produced are soft-clustering of this document set. Hence each table-column can be present in multiple clusters, but belongs to only one class. Purity, NMI and RI metrics are not applicable for soft clustering, however FM metric is valid. We run K-Means algorithm for different values of K. Table 9 shows the best performing results of K-Means. WebSets produced 25 clusters on entity record representation and 34 clusters using triplet representation. In terms of FM index, each method gives better performance on triplet record representation when compared to entity record representation. Hence triplet record representation does improve these clustering methods.

4.2.3 Evaluation: Hyponym-Concept Dataset

Note that the Hyponym-concept dataset is created in an unsupervised way, hence we cannot guarantee that the concept-instance pairs in this dataset are accurate. To get an idea of quality of concept-instance pairs in this dataset, we randomly sampled 100 pairs. 55% of them were accurate. Hence hypernym recommendation step is dealing with noisy concept-instance pairs as input.

4.2.4 Evaluation: Hypernym Recommendation

We compare our hypernym recommendation technique with Van Durme and Pasca technique [26]. Our method is different from Van Durme and Pasca Method (DPM) in the sense that, they output a concept-instance pair only when it appears in a set of candidate concept-instance pairs i.e. it exists in Hyponym-concept dataset. In our method, based on overlap of coordinate term cluster with the Hyponym Concept dataset, we extend the labels to whole cluster. Another difference is the coordinate term clusters we are dealing with. DPM assumes term clusters are semantic partitions of terms present in the text corpus. The clusters generated by WebSets are clusters of table columns. There is higher possibility of having multiple small size clusters which all belong to same semantic class, but were not merged due to our single pass bottom-up clusterer. Hence the same method may not work equally well on these clusters.

We sample 100 concept-instance pairs randomly from output of each method to measure accuracy. The results of different methods are presented in Table 10. As we can see, DPM generates concept-instance pairs with 50% accuracy even when run with conservative thresholds like $K = 5$ and $J = 0.2$. We also tried an extension of DPM called DPMExt which outputs a label for each entity in the cluster, when the label satisfies thresholds defined by J and K. This extension increases coverage of concept-instance pairs orders of magnitude (0.4K to 1.2K) at the cost of slight decrease in accuracy (50% to 44%). Hypernym recommendation of WebSets (WS) is described in Algorithm 2, and only topmost hypernym in the ranked list is produced for each cluster. Table 10 shows that WS has a reasonable accuracy (62.2%) and yield compared to DPM and DPMExt. As discussed in Section

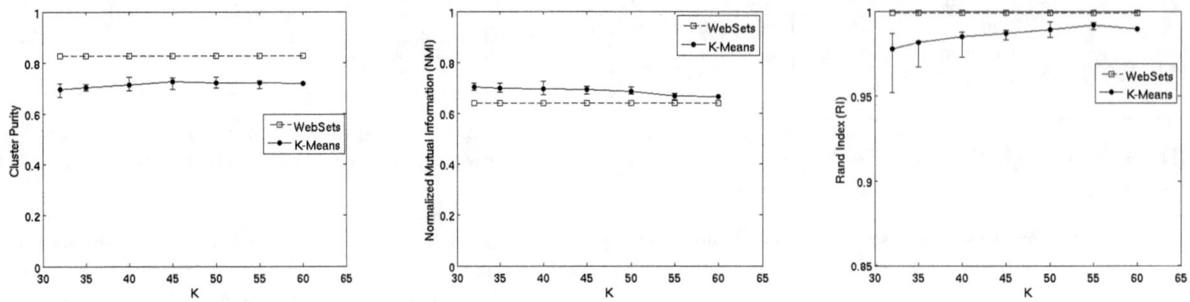

(a) Cluster Purity (b) Normalized Mutual Information (c) Rand Index

Figure 1: Comparison of WebSets and K-Means algorithms on Delicious_Sports

Method	K	J	%Accuracy	yield (#pairs produced)	#correct pairs (predicted)
DPM	inf	0.0	34.6	88.6K	30.7K
DPM	5	0.2	50.0	0.8K	0.4K
DPMExt	inf	0	21.9	100,828.0K	22,081.3K
DPMExt	5	0.2	44.0	2.8K	1.2K
WS	-	-	67.7	73.7K	45.8K
WSExt	-	-	78.8	64.8K	51.1K

Table 10: Comparison of various methods in terms of accuracy and yield on CSEAL_Useful dataset

4.2.3, Hyponym-concept dataset has noisy pairs. We also tried an extension of WebSets called WSExt which overcomes this problem by considering only those class-instance pairs which have occurred at least 5 times in the corpus. Adding this simple constraint, improves accuracy from 67% to 78% and correct pairs yield from 45K to 51K.

4.3 WebSets as an IE technique

In this section, we evaluate the whole WebSets system as an IE technique, which generates coherent sets of entities and labels each set with appropriate hypernym. At the end we demonstrate how these entity clusters can summarize the corpus.

4.3.1 Experimental Methodology

Its very expensive to label every table-column of each dataset. Here we present a sampling based evaluation method to evaluate WebSets on datasets: CSEAL_Useful, ASIA_NELL, ASIA_INT and Clueweb_HPR. We chose these four datasets to cover the different types i.e., domain-specific, open-domain and completely heterogeneous datasets. There are two parts of the evaluation: evaluating labels of each cluster and checking whether each entity of that cluster is coherent with the assigned label.

The subjective evaluation is of the form "deciding whether a cluster is meaningful or noisy", "assigning label to an unlabeled cluster". This is done by us (referred to as evaluators). The objective evaluation of the kind "whether X belongs to category Y" is done using Amazon Mechanical Turk [23]. We created yes/no questions of the form "Is X of type Y?".

To evaluate precision of clusters created by WebSets, we uniformly sampled maximum 100 clusters per dataset, with maximum of 100 samples per cluster and gave them to the Mechanical Turk in the form of yes/no questions. Each question was answered by three different individuals. The majority vote for each question was considered as a decision for that question. To evaluate quality of Mechanical Turk labels, we sampled 100 questions at random, and manually answered the questions. Then we checked whether majority vote by the Mechanical Turk matches with our answers. We specifically checked majority votes for some confusing questions which were likely to get labeled wrong. We found that majority vote of three individuals was correct more than 90% times and in case of ambiguous questions precision estimates are biased low.

We evaluate WebSets using three criteria: (1) Are the clusters generated by WebSets meaningful? (2) How good are the recommended hypernyms? (3) What is precision of the meaningful clusters? Subsequent sections discuss these experiments in detail.

4.3.2 Meaningfulness of Clusters

In this experiment, we did manual evaluation of meaningfulness of clusters, with the help of evaluators. We uniformly sampled maximum 100 clusters from each dataset. We showed following details of each cluster to the evaluator: (1) top 5 hypernyms per cluster (2) maximum 100 entities sampled uniformly from the cluster.

An evaluator was asked to look at the entities and check whether any of the hypernyms suggested by the system is correct. If any one of them is correct then he labels the cluster with that hypernym. If none of the hypernym is correct, he can label cluster with any other hypernym that represents the cluster. If entities in a cluster are noisy or do not form any meaningful set, then the cluster is marked as "noisy". If the evaluator picks any of the candidate hypernyms as label or gives his own label then the cluster is considered as meaningful, else it is considered as noisy.

Table 11 shows that 63-73% of the clusters were labeled as meaningful. Note that number of triplets used by the clustering algorithm (Table 11) is different from total number of triplets in the triplet store (Table 6), because only those triplets that occur in at least *minUniqueDomain* (set to 2 for all experiments) distinct domains are clustered.

4.3.3 Performance of Hypernym Recommendation

In this experiment, we evaluate the performance of the hypernym recommendation using following criterion:
(1) What fraction of total clusters were assigned some hypernym?: This can be directly computed by looking at the outputs generated by hypernym recommendation.
(2) For what fraction of clusters evaluator chose the label

	#Triplets	#Clusters	#clusters with Hypernyms	% meaningful
CSEAL_Useful	165.2K	1090	312	69.0%
ASIA_NELL	11.4K	448	266	73.0%
ASIA_INT	15.1K	395	218	63.0%
Clueweb_HPR	561.0	47	34	70.5%

Table 11: Meaningfulness of generated clusters

	#Clusters Evaluated	#Meaningful Clusters	#Hypernyms correct	MRR (meaningful)
CSEAL_Useful	100	69	57	0.56
ASIA_NELL	100	73	66	0.59
ASIA_INT	100	63	50	0.58
Clueweb_HPR	34	24	20	0.56

Table 12: Evaluation of Hypernym Recommender

from the recommended hypernyms?: This can be computed by checking whether each of the manually assigned labels was one of the recommended labels.

(3) What is Mean Reciprocal Rank (MRR) of the hypernym ranking?: The evaluator gets to see ranked list of top 5 labels suggested by the hypernym recommender. We compute MRR based on rank of the label selected by the evaluator. While calculating MRR, we consider all meaningful clusters(including the ones for which label does not come from the recommended hypernyms).

Table 12 shows the results of this evaluation. Out of the random sample of clusters evaluated, hypernym recommendation could label 50-60% of them correctly. The MRR of labels is 0.56-0.59 for all the datasets.

4.3.4 Precision of Meaningful Clusters

In this experiment we want to evaluate the coherency of the clusters; i.e., whether all entities in a cluster are coherent with the label assigned to the cluster. To verify this, we evaluated the meaningful clusters found in previous experiment, using the Mechanical Turk. This evaluation procedure is already discussed in Section 4.3.1. Table 13 shows that the meaningful clusters[6] have precision in the range 97-99%. This indicates that WebSets generates coherent entity clusters and hypernym assignment is reasonable.

4.3.5 Application: Summary of the Corpus

The sets of entities produced by Websets can be considered as a summary of the HTML corpus in terms of what concepts and entities are discussed in the corpus. Tables 14 and 15 show such summaries for the datasets ASIA_INT and Delicious_Music respectively. We choose these datasets because they are domain-specific and hence we have some idea of what entity sets are expected to be found. Looking at the summary we can verify if those expectations are met. Due to space constraints only few clusters with ten entities from each of them are presented here. The labels shown here are generated by Algorithm 2.

[6]First three values in column 2 of Table 13 are same as percentage values in column 5 of Table 11. This is because we sample maximum 100 clusters per dataset for the evaluation, hence percentage of meaningful clusters equals the actual number. For the Clueweb_HPR dataset, there are only 47 clusters in total, so all are evaluated.

Dataset	#Meaningful clusters evaluated	% Precision
CSEAL_Useful	69	98.6%
ASIA_NELL	73	98.5%
ASIA_INT	63	97.4%
Clueweb_HPR	24	99.0%

Table 13: Average precision of meaningful clusters

Clusters
Religions: Buddhism, Christianity, Islam, Sikhism, Taoism, Zoroastrianism, Jainism, Bahai, Judaism, Hinduism, Confucianism
Government: Monarchy, Limited Democracy, Islamic Republic, Parliamentary Self Governing Territory, Parliamentary Republic, Constitutional Republic, Republic Presidential Multiparty System, Constitutional Democracy, Democratic Republic, Parliamentary Democracy
International Organizations: United Nations Children Fund UNICEF, Southeast European Cooperative Initiative SECI, World Trade Organization WTO, Indian Ocean Commission INOC, Economic and Social Council ECOSOC, Caribbean Community and Common Market CARICOM, Western European Union WEU, Black Sea Economic Cooperation Zone BSEC, Nuclear Energy Agency NEA, World Confederation of Labor WCL
Languages: Hebrew, Portuguese, Danish, Anzanian, Croatian, Phoenician, Brazilian, Surinamese, Burkinabe, Barbadian, Cuban

Table 14: Example Clusters from ASIA_INT

Clusters
Instruments: Flute, Tuba , String Orchestra, Chimes, Harmonium, Bassoon, Woodwinds, Glockenspiel, French horn, Timpani, Piano
Intervals: Whole tone, Major sixth, Fifth, Perfect fifth, Seventh, Third, Diminished fifth, Whole step, Fourth, Minor seventh, Major third, Minor third
Genres: Smooth jazz, Gothic, Metal rock, Rock, Pop, Hip hop, Rock n roll, Country, Folk, Punk rock
Audio Equipments: Audio editor , General midi synthesizer , Audio recorder , Multichannel digital audio workstation , Drum sequencer , Mixers , Music engraving system , Audio server , Mastering software , Soundfont sample player

Table 15: Example Clusters from Delicious_Music

ASIA_INT is a dataset from Intelligence domain, and the sets shown in Table 14 indicate that corpus contains frequent mentions of officer ranks, international organizations, government types, religions etc. These clusters are related to Intelligence domain and give an idea of what the corpus is about. Similarly Table 14 shows the sets of entities discussed very frequently in Delicious_Music i.e., music domain. All of them are important concepts in the music domain. Furthermore our tool generates links to tables and domains from which this data was gathered. While looking at these sets one can click and browse the tables and pages which mention these entities. Hence it can serve as a good exploratory tool for individuals who analyze large datasets.

5. ACKNOWLEDGMENTS

This work is supported in part by the Intelligence Advanced Research Projects Activity (IARPA) via Air Force Research Laboratory (AFRL) contract number FA8650-10-C-7058. The U.S. Government is authorized to reproduce and distribute reprints for Governmental purposes notwithstanding any copyright annotation thereon. This work is also partially supported by the Google Research Grant.

The views and conclusions contained herein are those of the authors and should not be interpreted as necessarily representing the official policies or endorsements, either expressed or implied, of Google, IARPA, AFRL, or the U.S. Government.

6. CONCLUSION

We described a open-domain information extraction technique for extracting concept-instance pairs from an HTML corpus. Our approach is novel in that it relies solely on HTML tables to detect coordinate terms. We presented a novel clustering method that finds extremely precise (cluster purity 83-99%) coordinate-term clusters by merging table columns that contain overlapping *triplets* of instances. This clustering method outperforms k-means in terms of Purity, Rand Index and FM index. We showed that the time complexity of our clustering algorithm is $O(N * logN)$, making it more efficient than K-means or agglomerative clustering algorithms. We also presented a new method for combining candidate concept-instance pairs and coordinate-term clusters, and showed that on table-rich corpora, this method improved on Van Durme and Pasca method [26]. Our method increased the accuracy from 50% to 78% while generating nearly hundred times the number of concept-instance pairs.

We also showed that allowing a small amount of user input for labeling each coordinate-term cluster can produce concept-instance pairs with accuracy in the range 97-99% for four different corpora. Finally we demonstrated that the labeled entity sets produced by WebSets can act as summary of a HTML corpus. The datasets and manual evaluations generated by this work will be made available for future researchers. An interesting direction for future research can be to extend this technique to extract the relations between the entity sets and naming them.

7. REFERENCES

[1] Html TIDY project. `http://tidy.sourceforge.net/`.

[2] M. J. Cafarella, E. Wu, A. Halevy, Y. Zhang, and D. Z. Wang. Webtables: Exploring the power of tables on the web. *PVLDB*, 2008.

[3] J. Callan. The clueweb09 dataset. `http://boston.lti.cs.cmu.edu/Data/clueweb09/`.

[4] A. Carlson, J. Betteridge, R. C. Wang, E. R. Hruschka, Jr., and T. M. Mitchell. Coupled semi-supervised learning for information extraction. In *WSDM*, 2010.

[5] W. H. E. Day and H. Edelsbrunner. Efficient algorithms for agglomerative hierarchical clustering methods. In *Journal of Classification*, 1984.

[6] O. Etzioni, M. Cafarella, D. Downey, S. Kok, A.-M. Popescu, T. Shaked, S. Soderland, D. S. Weld, and A. Yates. Web-scale information extraction in knowitall: (preliminary results). In *WWW*, 2004.

[7] O. Etzioni, M. Cafarella, D. Downey, A.-M. Popescu, T. Shaked, S. Soderland, D. S. Weld, and A. Yate. Unsupervised named-entity extraction from the web: An experimental study. In *AI*, 2005.

[8] W. Gatterbauer, P. Bohunsky, M. Herzog, B. Krüpl, and B. Pollak. Towards domain-independent information extraction from web tables. In *WWW*, 2007.

[9] R. Gupta and S. Sarawagi. Answering table augmentation queries from unstructured lists on the web. In *VLDB*, 2009.

[10] R. Gupta and S. Sarawagi. Joint training for open-domain extraction on the web: exploiting overlap when supervision is limited. In *WSDM*, 2011.

[11] M. A. Hearst. Automatic acquisition of hyponyms from large text corpora. In *ACL*, 1992.

[12] J. Kamps, R. Kaptein, and M. Koolen. Using anchor text, spam filtering and wikipedia for web search and entity ranking. *TREC*, 2010.

[13] Z. Kozareva and E. Hovy. A semi-supervised method to learn and construct taxonomies using the web. In *EMNLP*, 2010.

[14] G. Limaye, S. Sarawagi, and S. Chakrabarti. Annotating and searching web tables using entities, types and relationships. *PVLDB*, 2010.

[15] D. Lin and P. Pantel. Concept discovery from text. In *COLING*, 2002.

[16] C. D. Manning, P. Raghavan, and H. Schtze. Introduction to information retrieval. In *Cambridge University Press*, 2008.

[17] P. Pantel and D. Ravichandran. Automatically labeling semantic classes. In *HLT-NAACL*, 2004.

[18] A. Parameswaran, H. Garcia-Molina, and A. Rajaraman. Towards the web of concepts: Extracting concepts from large datasets. In *VLDB*, 2010.

[19] E. Ramirez, R. Brena, D. Magatti, and F. Stella. Probabilistic metrics for soft-clustering and topic model validation. In *Web Intelligence and Intelligent Agent Technology (WI-IAT)*, 2010.

[20] A. Ritter, S. Soderland, and O. Etzioni. What is this, anyway: Automatic hypernym discovery. In *AAAI*, 2009.

[21] K. Shinzato and K. Torisawa. Acquiring hyponymy relations from web documents. In *HLT-NAACL*, 2004.

[22] R. Snow, D. Jurafsky, and A. Y. Ng. Learning syntactic patterns for automatic hypernym discovery. In *NIPS*, 2004.

[23] R. Snow, B. O'Connor, D. Jurafsky, and A. Y. Ng. Cheap and fast - but is it good? evaluating non-expert annotations for natural language tasks. In *EMNLP*, 2008.

[24] P. P. Talukdar, J. Reisinger, M. Paşca, D. Ravichandran, R. Bhagat, and F. Pereira. Weakly-supervised acquisition of labeled class instances using graph random walks. In *EMNLP*, 2008.

[25] M. Tom. Nell: Never-ending language learning. `http://rtw.ml.cmu.edu/rtw/`.

[26] B. Van Durme and M. Pasca. Finding cars, goddesses and enzymes: parametrizable acquisition of labeled instances for open-domain information extraction. In *AAAI*, 2008.

[27] R. C. Wang and W. W. Cohen. Automatic set instance extraction using the web. In *ACL*, 2009.

[28] R. C. Wang and W. W. Cohen. Character-level analysis of semi-structured documents for set expansion. In *EMNLP*, 2009.

[29] R. Wetzker, C. Zimmermann, and C. Bauckhage. Analyzing social bookmarking systems: A del.icio.us cookbook. *Mining Social Data (MSoDa) Workshop Proceedings, ECAI*, 2008. `http://www.dai-labor.de/en/competence_centers/irml/datasets/`.

[30] A. Yates, M. Cafarella, M. Banko, O. Etzioni, M. Broadhead, and S. Soderland. Textrunner: Open information extraction on the web. In *NAACL*, 2007.

Selecting Actions for Resource-bounded Information Extraction using Reinforcement Learning

Pallika Kanani
Department of Computer Science
University of Massachusetts, Amherst
Amherst, MA, USA
pallika@cs.umass.edu

Andrew McCallum
Department of Computer Science
University of Massachusetts, Amherst
Amherst, MA, USA
mccallum@cs.umass.edu

ABSTRACT

Given a database with missing or uncertain content, our goal is to correct and fill the database by extracting specific information from a large corpus such as the Web, and to do so under resource limitations. We formulate the information gathering task as a series of choices among alternative, resource-consuming actions and use reinforcement learning to select the best action at each time step. We use temporal difference q-learning method to train the function that selects these actions, and compare it to an online, error-driven algorithm called SampleRank. We present a system that finds information such as email, job title and department affiliation for the faculty at our university, and show that the learning-based approach accomplishes this task efficiently under a limited action budget. Our evaluations show that we can obtain 92.4% of the final F1, by only using 14.3% of all possible actions.

Categories and Subject Descriptors

I.2.6 [**Computing Methodologies**]: Artificial Intelligence—*Learning*

General Terms

Algorithms

Keywords

Resource-bounded Information Extraction, Active Information Acquisition, Reinforcement Learning, Web Mining

1. INTRODUCTION

Resource-bounded Information Extraction (RBIE) is the process of searching for and extracting specific pieces of information from an external information source under a limited budget of resources, such as computation time, network bandwidth, and storage space [5]. The problem of missing information in databases is ubiquitous. However, in many cases, this information is available on some external source, such as the Web. In order to fill in the missing slots, we need a mechanism to automatically extract the required information. In such settings, it is undesirable, infeasible, or even computationally intractable to use traditional information extraction pipelines on the entirety of a vast, external, unstructured or semistructured corpus in order to obtain a relatively small amount of information. Under the RBIE framework, we obtain the required information by issuing appropriate queries to the external source, such as a web search API, downloading only a small fraction of documents from the search results, and processing even fewer of them to extract the specified field.

Consider a real world example. We are building a database of all faculty at a university as shown in Table 1. We have the names, but some of the other information such as contact details, job titles and department affiliations are missing. Surprisingly, in some cases, the university administration does not have such a comprehensive, university-wide database. This may be due to the lack of data exchange, joint appointments across departments, changing contact details, etc. Building such a database would be extremely useful, since it maintains up-to-date records of the faculty, and fosters collaboration across departments. A large portion of this information exists on the Web, but it may not always be found on faculty home pages. Lecturers and faculty in some of the departments do not have home pages, and their information is sometimes scattered around the Web. Finding this information can be challenging, since it is not available in a uniform, structured manner. There are other problems such as name ambiguities and incorrect or incomplete data.

One way to obtain this information is by crawling all the websites under the university domain. This, by itself is a resource-intensive task, since most university websites are large and complex, and we would need to use a lot of computational power to crawl and download the pages, along with the corresponding network bandwidth, and disk space for storing them. We would also lose out on all the information that is scattered on the Web, outside the university domain. Can we accomplish the same task using a much smaller fraction of these resources?

We know that the information missing in the database is available on some relatively small number of pages on the Web. We need to run some extraction algorithms on those pages in order to obtain the required information. But before we can run extraction, we need to download them to our computing infrastructure, and before we can download them, we need to know where they are located on the Web.

Permission to make digital or hard copies of all or part of this work for personal or classroom use is granted without fee provided that copies are not made or distributed for profit or commercial advantage and that copies bear this notice and the full citation on the first page. To copy otherwise, to republish, to post on servers or to redistribute to lists, requires prior specific permission and/or a fee.
WSDM'12, February 8–12, 2012, Seattle, Washington, USA.
Copyright 2012 ACM 978-1-4503-0747-5/12/02 ...$10.00.

Faculty Name	Phone	Email	Job Title	Department Name
Andrew McCallum	(413) 545-1323	mccallum@cs.umass.edu	Professor	Computer Science
Jerrold S. Levinsky	?	?	Lecturer	Legal Studies
Edward G. Voigtman	?	?	?	?
Robert W. Paynter	?	?	?	Anthropology

Table 1: Example Database of University Faculty

A search engine API, such as Google can help us retrieve these web pages. We first formulate queries driven by information that is already available in the database, issue them to the search interface, obtain the location of the web pages, and download them. Then we can run the necessary algorithms to extract information, and use it to fill missing entries in the database. This process is more efficient than indiscriminate processing, and would use relatively smaller amounts of resources.

The problem of Resource-bounded Information Extraction (RBIE) was first introduced in our previous work [5]. Queries are formed by combining existing, relevant information in the database with user defined keywords. All such queries are issued to the search API, and all of the result documents are downloaded. The resource savings come from selecting a subset of the web documents to process by exploiting the network structure in the data. In general, we may need multiple queries to obtain information about a single entry in the database, and some queries work better than others. In our university faculty example, we may form different queries with keywords such as "curriculum vitae" or "home page", and it may be the case that one of them is often more successful than the other in finding the information we need. In some cases, the information in different fields may be interdependent, and finding one before another may be more efficient. In order to make the best use of available resources, we need to issue the most effective queries first.

In most scenarios, one only need process a subset of the documents returned by the queries. We need to know which of the search results are most likely to contain the information we are looking for. Information returned in the search result snippet can be exploited to decide if a web page is worth downloading. Similarly, some preliminary observation of the downloaded document can be useful to decide if it is worth passing through an expensive extraction pipeline. Hence, instead of viewing RBIE as selecting a subset of documents to process, we cast the information-gathering task as a series of resource-consuming actions, along with a mechanism to select the best action to perform at each time step.

In this paper, we formulate the RBIE problem formally as a Markov Decision Process (MDP), and propose the use of reinforcement learning techniques for solving it. The *state* of this MDP is the state of the database at each time step, and *action* is any act that leads to obtaining the required information, such that performing the action in one state leads to a different state. RBIE process is then finding the optimal policy in this MDP, so as to obtain most information with the given budget of actions, since we assume that actions consume resources. In RBIE from the Web context, actions are *query*, which is issuing a query to a search API, *download*, which is downloading a web document, and *extract*, which runs an actual extraction algorithm on a document. We assume uniform cost for each type of action in this paper, but the proposed framework can easily be extended by incorporating a specific cost model for the actions and assigning the budget accordingly. By formulating RBIE for the Web as an MDP, we can explore the rich methods of optimal action selection offered by reinforcement learning.

In the RBIE for the web setting, query actions might not lead to immediate reward, but they are necessary to perform before download and extract actions, which may lead to positive rewards. Hence, we need a method that models delayed rewards effectively. We propose the use of temporal difference q-learning to learn the value function for selecting the best action from a set of alternative actions, given a certain state of the database. In our preliminary work [4], we explored a fast, online, error driven algorithm, called SampleRank to learn this value function. Since both SampleRank and q-learning are novel approaches for the RBIE framework, we compare their relative performance on the task of finding emails, job titles and department affiliation for faculty in our university.

In general, we can use any model of choice for information extraction in our framework that can extract the required information from a web page, and provide a confidence score for the extracted value. This score can be used to choose the best among the potential candidate values, and to determine whether or not an existing entry in the database should be updated by the newly extracted value. We present a simple, but novel information extraction method that can easily scale to large problem domains. The basic idea is to generate a list of potential candidate values from the web page, and using a binary classifier, such as maximum entropy, to classify them as being correct values or not, by observing features of the context in which they are found. The candidate with the maximum probability of being correct is used to fill the entry in the database.

Our experiments show that the q-learning strategy performs better than the baseline action selection strategies, as well as SampleRank based approach to learning a value function. Given the large number of actions to choose from at each time step, and the size of the corresponding state space, the policy learned is impressive. The q-learning based approach is able to obtain 92.4% of the final F1, by only using 14.3% of all possible actions, demonstrating the effectiveness of our method.

2. RESOURCE-BOUNDED INFORMATION EXTRACTION

2.1 General Problem Definition

The general problem of Resource-bounded Information Extraction (RBIE) is defined as follows. We are given a database with missing values in some of the entries, and a set of possible actions to help acquire that information from an external source, such as the Web. Select the best action from the set of alternative actions available at each time point, so as to acquire most information with the given budget on the number of actions.

2.2 Resource-bounded Information Extraction From the Web

For RBIE from the Web, we consider three different types of actions - *query*, *download*, and *extract*. A *query* action consists of issuing a single query to a web search API and obtaining a set of search results. In order to form the query, we need to use some existing information from an input record in the database and a set of keywords. A *download* action consists of downloading the web page corresponding to a single search result. Finally, an *extract* action consists of performing extraction on the downloaded webpage to obtain the required piece of information and using it to fill the slot in the original database. Note that each instantiated 'action' consists of the type of action as well as its corresponding argument, namely, what query to send for which instance, which URL to download, or what page to extract.

In the case of RBIE from the Web, the *query* actions can be initialized at the beginning of the task because we know which instances have missing fields, and the types of queries that can be used; but *download* actions and *extract* actions are generated dynamically and added to the list of available actions. That is, after a *query* action is performed, the *download* action corresponding to each of the search results is generated. Similarly, after a web page is downloaded, the corresponding *extract* action is generated. At each time point, only the actions that are instantiated can be considered as alternative valid actions to be performed. The RBIE task is to select the "best" action at each time point from a set of all valid actions.

Before selecting an action to perform at each time step, we need to consider several factors. We need to take into account the current state of the database, such as the number of slots filled and the uncertainty about them. We need to take into account the context provided by the intermediate results of all the actions so far, such as the results of the queries, pages that are not yet downloaded and processed. Even if this context is not yet in the database, these intermediate results can provide valuable information for deciding which action to select. Finally, we also need to consider the properties of the candidate action itself, before selecting it.

We assume that we are given an existing model, M_e for extracting the required pieces of information from a single web page. We also assume that this model provides a confidence score for each value predicted. This score can be used to choose the best among the potential candidate values, and to determine whether or not an existing entry in the database should be updated by the newly extracted value.

2.3 Markov Decision Process Formulation

In this paper, we cast the Resource-bounded Information Extraction problem as solving a Markov Decision Process (MDP), M, where the states represent the state of the database at a given time, along with any intermediate results obtained from the Web, and actions represent the *query*, *download*, and *extract* actions as described in the previous section. We represent state as a tuple $S_t\langle DB_t, I_t, I'_t\rangle$, where DB_t is the state of the database at time t, I_t is the list of intermediate URL results and I'_t is the list of intermediate page results obtained till time t. The MDP for RBIE is described as a tuple, $M\langle S_0, \gamma, T(S,a,S'), R(S)\rangle$, where S_0 is the initial state of the database, γ is the discount factor, $T(S,a,S')$ is the state transition probability, or the probability that action a in state S at time t will lead to state S' at time $t+1$, and $R(S)$ is the reward function for being in state S.

One of the standard ways of solving an MDP is q-learning[15], which provides a way to learn to select the best action at each time step. The Q-function, $Q(a,S)$ is the expected utility of taking action a in state, S. Hence, the best action to select at each step is:

$$a_{t+1} = \arg\max_a Q(a,S) \tag{1}$$

Algorithm 1 summarizes the RBIE for Web framework for filling missing information in a database using Q-function.

Algorithm 1 Resource-bounded Information Extraction for the Web Using Q-function

```
Input:
   Database DB with missing entries, E_i
   Learned Q-function Q(a, S)
   Learned extraction model, M_e
   Time budget, b
Initialize all queries using keywords
t = 0
while t <= b do
  a_{t+1} = arg max_a Q(a, S)
  if a_{t+1} is a query action then
    Issue query to a web search API
    Enqueue corresponding download actions
  else if a_{t+1} is a download action then
    Download the web page
    Enqueue corresponding extract action
  else if a_{t+1} is an extract action then
    Extract all candidate values from the web page
    Score each candidate using the model, M_e
    Fill the value of the best candidate in E_i
  end if
  t = t + 1
end while
```

2.4 Learning Q-function

At the heart of solving an MDP for RBIE is the Q-function, $Q(a,S)$. We now discuss a method to learn it from real data. Much of the material in this section follows from [12, 14].

We know that Q-function obeys the following constraints:

$$Q(a,S) = R(S) + \gamma \sum_{S'} T(S,a,S') \max_{a'} Q(a',S') \tag{2}$$

To use this update equation, we need to learn the transition probability model, $T(S,a,S')$, which is difficult in our setup. Hence, we use the temporal-difference, or TD q-learning approach, which is also called model-free, because it lets us learn the Q-function without using the transition probability model. The update equation for TD q-learning is [1]:

$$Q(a,S) \leftarrow Q(a,S) + \alpha(R(S') + \gamma \max_{a'} Q(a',S') - Q(a,S)) \tag{3}$$

[1]There is some disagreement amongst q-learning experts about which form of reward function to use. We choose to use $R(S')$.

Algorithm 2 Temporal difference q-learning for RBIE, with ϵ-greedy exploration

Input:
Training database, DB
Initial parameters, θ
Q Function, $Q_\theta(a,S) = \sum_i \theta_i \phi_i(a,S)$
Reward Function, $R(S)$
Learning Rate, α
Discount factor, γ
$S_0 \leftarrow$ Initial State of DB
for $t \leftarrow 0$ to number of iterations T **do**
$\epsilon = 1 - \frac{1}{T}$
With probability ϵ, pick a random action, a_t
With probability $1-\epsilon$, pick $a_t = \arg\max_a Q_{\theta_t}(a, S_t)$
$S_{t+1} = a_t(S_t)$ //perform a_t
Let a' be all the valid actions from state, S_{t+1}
for $i = 0$ to number of features **do**
$\theta^i_{t+1} = \theta^i_t + \alpha[R(S_{t+1}) + \gamma \max_{a'} Q_{\theta_t}(a', S_{t+1}) - Q_{\theta_t}(a_t, S_t)]\phi_i(a_t, S_t)$
end for
end for

Where, α is the learning rate. For any real-world RBIE task, the state space for the corresponding MDP is large enough to make it very difficult to learn this function accurately. Hence, we use function approximation. We represent the Q-function as a weighted combination of a set of features as follows:

$$Q_\theta(a,S) = \sum_i \theta_i \phi_i(a,S) \tag{4}$$

Where $\phi_i(a,S)$ are the features of the state S and action a, and θ_i are the weights on those features that we wish to learn. We now use the following equation [12, 14] for updating the values of θ_i to try to reduce the temporal difference between successive states.

$$\theta_i \leftarrow \theta_i + \alpha\left[R(S') + \gamma \max_{a'} \hat{Q}_\theta(a', S') - \hat{Q}_\theta(a,S)\right]\frac{\partial \hat{Q}_\theta(a,S)}{\partial \theta_i} \tag{5}$$

We can now use this update equation to learn the parameters of our Q-function from training data. The TD-q-learning algorithm for RBIE is described in Algorithm 2. Note that we use ϵ-greedy approach for exploring the state space, where ϵ decreases in proportion to the number of training iterations.

We also need to design a custom reward function, $R(S)$ for using this algorithm. Under the RBIE from the Web setting, we can compute value of the reward function after performing action a_{t+1} on $S_t = \langle DB_t, I_t, I'_t \rangle$ as a weighted sum of correct, incorrect and total number of filled values, number of correct candidates found, and some properties of the intermediate results.

2.5 Building the Extraction Model

In general, we can use any model of choice for information extraction in our framework that can extract the required information from a web page, and provide a confidence score for the extracted value. In this section, we present a simple, but novel information extraction method that can easily scale to large problem domains. The basic idea is to generate a list of potential candidate values from the web page, and using a binary classifier, such as Maximum Entropy, to classify them as being correct values or not, by observing features of the context in which they are found. Algorithm 3 describes how we train the model.

Let E be the set of entries with missing values in the database. We use patterns and lexicons to generate a list of candidates, C_{E_i} for each entry, $E_i \in E$. A *candidate* is a unique string that is a potentially correct value for an entry in the database. Each candidate, $c_j \in C_{E_i}$, consists of a list of *mentions*, M_j, which represent the actual occurrence of the candidate string in the web documents. Each candidate may have multiple mentions, across different web pages. Corresponding to each mention, $m_k \in M_j$, we have a list of properties, or features, $f(m_k)$ which describe the context in which it was found. Since we are interested in classifying the single, canonical value of these mentions, i.e, the candidate, we collapse the properties of different mentions for a candidate c_j into a single feature function, $f(c_j)$.

Let y_{ij} be a binary variable that represents whether c_j is the correct value for entry E_i. We can then represent the probability of c_j being the correct candidate as:

$$P(y_{ij}|c_j) = \frac{1}{Z}\exp(\sum_l \lambda_l f_l(c_j, y_{ij})) \tag{6}$$

Where, λ_l are the weights on the features, and Z, the normalization factor is given by:

$$Z = \sum_y \exp(\sum_l \lambda_l f_l(c_j, y_{ij})) \tag{7}$$

Since this is a supervised approach, our training data consists of the true values of E, which can be used to train the classifier. At test time, during an extract action, we classify each $c_j \in C_{E_i}$ at that time point, and select the one with the maximum posterior probability, $P(y_{ij}|c_j)$, as the "best" candidate to fill the slot.

3. SAMPLERANK FOR RBIE

In our preliminary work, we explored a different approach to learning a value function for selecting actions for a different problem domain[4]. We use a fast, online, error driven learning algorithm, called SampleRank [1, 16]. Since, we are also interested in investigating the effectiveness of the SampleRank approach in our current problem domain, we give its brief introduction here. For further details on training SampleRank for RBIE, refer to [4].

Remember that we represent a state as, $S_t\langle DB_t, I_t, I'_t\rangle$. Our goal is to learn a value function similar to the Q-function, called $V(DB_t, I_t, I'_t, a)$, which is used to select the best action in a given state. In order to learn this function from training data, we first assume that its functional form is as follows:

$$V(DB_t, I_t, I'_t, a) = \exp(\sum_k \lambda_k \phi_k(DB_t, I_t, I'_t, a)) \tag{8}$$

Where, λ_k are model parameters and ϕ_k are feature functions, defined over the database context, the current action, and the results of all previous actions.

We start training with state S_0, that represents the original state of the database. We consider all available actions at this point, and sample from states that result from these actions. We choose the state S^*, which is the result of the best action $a*$, predicted by V, and the state S', which is the best state predicted by the objective, or reward function, $R(S)$. SampleRank is an error driven learning algorithm, which

Algorithm 3 Building Extraction Model, M_e

Input:
Training Database DB with entries, E
Pattern or Lexicon Matcher, $L(w)$ that returns a set of matches, M_w from a Web Page, w
Feature functions, $f(.)$ describing context of M_w
A Supervised Learning algorithm, such as Max Ent
Initialize all queries using keywords
Initialize set of potential candidates per entry, $C_{E_i} = \{\}$
Initialize set of candidates for training, $C_t = \{\}$
while Any more actions remain **do**
  Pick a random action, a to perform
  if a is a *query action*, or a *download action* **then**
    Perform a and enqueue corresponding *download* or *extract actions*
  else if a is an *extract action* for Web Page, w **then**
    $M_w \leftarrow L(w)$
    for Each match, $m_k \in M_w$ **do**
      if String value (m_k) matches $c_j \in C_{E_i}$ **then**
        Add m_k as a mention of c_j
        Merge the features, $f(m_k)$ with $f(c_j)$
      else
        Create a new candidate, c_j, and add to C_{E_i}
        $label(c_j) \leftarrow$ string value $(c_j) =$ true value (E_i)?
        Add m_k as a mention of c_j
        Set $f(c_j) \leftarrow f(m_k)$
      end if
    end for
  end if
end while
for all C_{E_i} **do**
  $C_t \leftarrow C_t \cup C_{E_i}$
end for
$M_e \leftarrow$ Train a Max Ent classifier with $f(c_t)$, for $c_t \in C_t$

lets us update parameters when the function learned up to a given point makes a mistake. We say the ranking is *in error* if the function learned so far assigns a higher score to the sample with the lower objective, or reward value, $R(S)$, i.e.:

$$[(V_\Lambda(S^*) > V_\Lambda(S')) \wedge (R(S^*) < R(S'))] \vee$$
$$[(V_\Lambda(S^*) < V_\Lambda(S')) \wedge (R(S^*) > R(S'))] \quad (9)$$

When this condition is true, we update the parameters, Λ using perceptron update as follows:

$$\Lambda^t \Leftarrow \Lambda^{t-1} + \alpha(\phi(S'_t, a'_t) - \phi(S^*_t, a^*_t)) \quad (10)$$

where α is the learning rate used to temper the parameter updates. Note that SampleRank is a special case of reinforcement learning, which makes the comparison between the two approaches very interesting.

4. RELATED WORK

4.1 Resource-bounded Reasoning

Knoblock et al. [7] introduced the idea of using planning for information gathering, followed by the development of resource-bounded reasoning techniques by Zilberstein et al. [18]. Elliasi-Rad [2] explored the problem of building an information extraction agent, but did not address the problem of acquiring specific missing pieces of information on demand. The problem of Resource-bounded Information Extraction (RBIE) was first introduced in our previous work [5], in which the main idea was to select a subset of the web documents to process by exploiting the network structure in the data. The example task in [5] is to find a missing year of publication in citation data. All available queries are issued, and all the search results are downloaded, which are then filtered using a simple heuristic. The number of documents that need to be processed for extraction is reduced by propagating information obtained from the Web through the underlying citation graph structure. In our preliminary work[4], we explored the task of finding URLs of the faculty directory pages of top Computer Science departments in the U.S., and used SampleRank for learning the value function.

4.2 Information Extraction From the Web

In the traditional information extraction settings, we are usually given a database schema, and a set of unstructured or semi-structured documents. The goal of the system is to automatically extract records from these documents, and fill in the values in the given database. These databases are then used for search, decision support and data mining. In recent years, there has been much work in developing sophisticated methods for performing information extraction over a closed collection of documents. Several different approaches have been proposed for different phases of information extraction task, such as segmentation, classification, association and coreference. Most of these proposed approaches make extensive use of statistical machine learning algorithms, which have improved significantly over the years. However, only some of these methods remain computationally tractable as the size of the document corpus grows. In fact, very few systems are designed to scale over a corpus as large as, say, the Web [3].

Among the large scale systems that extract information from the Web are KnowItAll [3], InfoSleuth [11] and Kylin [17]. The goal of the KnowItAll system is a related, but different task called, "Open Information Extraction." In Open IE, the relations of interest are not known in advance, and the emphasis is on discovering new relations and new records through extensive web access. In contrast, in our task, we are looking for specific information and the corresponding schema is known. The emphasis is mostly on filling the missing fields in known records, using resource-bounded web querying. InfoSleuth focuses on gathering information from given sources, and Kylin focuses only on Wikipedia articles.

The Information Retrieval community is rich with work in document relevance (TREC). However, traditional information retrieval solutions can not directly be used, since we first need to automate the query formulation for our task. Also, most search engine APIs return full documents or text snippets, rather than specific values. A closely related family of methods is question answering systems. These systems do retrieve a subset of relevant documents from the Web, along with extracting a specific piece of information. However, they target a single piece of information requested by the user, whereas we target multiple, interdependent fields of a relational database. QA usually interprets natural language question, whereas we need a keywords based mechanism for formulating queries. Most QA systems do not focus on prioritizing information acquisition actions, and the ideas in this paper could prove useful in building them. The semantic web community has been working on similar problems, but their focus is not targeted information extraction.

4.3 Active Information Acquisition

Learning and acquiring information under resource constraints has been studied in various forms. *Active learning* selects the best instances to label from a set of unlabeled instances; *active feature acquisition* [10] explores the problem of learning models from incomplete instances by acquiring additional features; *budgeted learning* [8] identifies the best set of acquisitions, given a fixed cost for acquisitions. At test time, the two common scenarios are selecting a subset of features to acquire, e.g. [13], and selecting the subset of instances for which to acquire features [6]. In our work, the resource-constraints are only applied at test time, and availability of unlimited resources is assumed at training time.

5. EXPERIMENTS

5.1 Extracting Faculty Information

Given a list of names of university faculty, our goal is to extract their email address, job title and department affiliation from the Web. In this section, we describe how we apply the RBIE framework to build a system that can efficiently acquire this information. We also describe experiments testing the effectiveness of SampleRank and q-learning algorithms in selecting the most effective actions at each time step.

This is a challenging task due to several factors. In some cases, this information is readily available on faculty home pages, which are semi-structured. However, lecturers and faculty in many departments do not have home pages. Their information is scattered around the Web, without a uniform structure. Web pages are noisy, and may lead to unexpected errors while performing extraction. Name ambiguity is another challenge, since many of the faculty have common names they share with other famous personalities. Some information on the Web is stale, or contradicting. For example, a faculty member can be listed on one page as "assistant professor", while on another as "associate professor", reflecting a recent change of title. Finally, some information is not available on the Web at all.

5.2 Dataset Description

We start with a list of faculty from University of Massachusetts at Amherst. We randomly choose 100 of these records as our dataset. The fields contain the first, middle and last name of the faculty, their email address, a list of job titles, and a list of department affiliations. Joint appointments lead to multiple job titles and department affiliations. The dataset we received contains several inaccuracies and is cleaned for better evaluation of our methods. For example, in some cases, a single column contains names of different departments. These are split into multiple columns. Punctuation and abbreviations, such as "Assoc. Prof." are cleaned and expanded. Despite the cleaning effort, the dataset we use is incomplete and contains errors. For example, the most current job titles are not reflected, and only one email address is included in the dataset, which may not be the one used by the person, or published on the Web. These imperfections in the data make both training and evaluation of our system challenging. Another problem in evaluating the accuracy of our system is the "generic-specific" problem in department names. For e.g., our system might predict the department affiliation for a faculty as "finance", while it might be listed as "management" in the ground truth dataset, or vice-versa. Since we use exact string match, we may even miss a match such as "school of management". Despite the difficulties, it is an interesting real world task for RBIE.

Dataset	# Faculty	# Queries	# Docs	Total Actions
Training	70	1400	13686	28772
Testing	30	600	6065	12730
Total	100	2000	19751	41502

Table 2: Datasets

Name	Name + Univ
Name in quotes	Name in quotes + Univ
Name In Univ	Name in quotes In Univ
Name w/ middle In Univ	Name w/ middle + Univ
Name + CV	Name + Univ + CV
Name + "Resume"	Name + Univ + "Resume"
Name + "Profile"	Name + Univ + "Profile"
Name + "Bio"	Name + Univ + "Bio"
Name + HomePage	Name + HomePage In Univ
Name + "Contact"	Name + "Contact" In Univ

Table 3: Types of Queries. 'Name' : first and last name, 'CV' : "curriculum vitae", 'Univ' : "university of massachusetts at amherst" and 'In Univ' : "site:umass.edu"

We use the Google search API for our experiments. In our task, the three fields that we extract are related to each other and often found in the proximity of each other on the same web pages. Hence, our query actions correspond to the entire record in the database, as opposed to a single 'entry', or cell. We formulate 20 different types of queries per faculty, as shown in Table 5.2, and consider top 20 hits returned by the search API. Assuming that we are not operating under resource-constraints, i.e., we perform all possible actions available, we get the dataset as described by Table 2. This table also helps estimate the size of the state space for our problem.

5.3 Training the Extraction Models

Before we move to the action selection experiments, we must build a model for extracting the relevant fields from individual web pages. Section 2.5 describes the algorithm we use for training the model. We use the MALLET [9] toolkit's implementation of the maximum entropy classifier. The available data is first split by 70%-30% for training and testing. The training phase for the extraction model is not resource-constrained, i.e., we use all possible query, download and extract actions.

The algorithm described in section 2.5 uses a pattern or lexicon matcher that returns a set of matches from a web page. These matches are added as a list of candidates to be filled in the database entry. For emails, we use a regular expression to match all the emails found in the web document. For job titles and department affiliations, we first build N-grams from body of the web page, where $N = 1, 2, 3, 4$. These N-grams are matched against lexicons to find candidate mentions in the web page. The features used to describe the context of these matches are shown in Table 5.3. The features across a mention are collapsed by using an 'OR' operator, since they are mostly binary. That is, if any feature is turned on in one of the mentions, it would be turned on

Features for Email Extractor
Type of query used
Email domain is from UMass
Web page domain name from UMass
Email host and web page URL host match
Relative position of faculty name and email
Match between faculty name and email username
Similarity between faculty sname and email username
Features for Job Title Extractor
Too many matches found on page
Web page domain name from UMass
Web page URL contains faculty name
Position of match on the document
The words "Assistant" or "Associate" preceds match
Relative position of faculty name and job title
Features for Department Extractor
Too many matches found on page
Web page domain name from UMass
Web page URL contains faculty name
Position of match on the document
The word "Department" precedes match
Relative position of faculty name and department name

Table 4: Features of the Extraction Models

Measure	Email	JobTitle	Department
Accuracy	97.97	92.50	96.94
Yes Precision	77.78	36.36	54.54
Yes Recall	87.50	15.38	44.44
Yes F1	82.23	21.62	48.97
No Precision	99.28	94.15	98.11
No Recall	98.57	98.06	98.73
No F1	98.93	96.06	98.42

Table 5: Performance of the Extraction Models

for the candidate. In our early experiments, we found this method perform better than other merging operations, however, in future, we can build a more sophisticated method.

Let us first study the performance of the candidate classifier, in isolation of the resource-bounded information extraction task. Any inaccuracy in this model, will not only result in poor accuracy during the RBIE process, but also misguide it due to inaccurate confidence prediction. Table 5 shows the classification performance of M_e. Note that F1 is the harmonic mean of precision and recall. The main reasons for relatively lower F1 values on this model are inaccuracy of training data as described above, as well as the noisy nature of the web data. The advantage of using this model is that it is easy to build, and is scaleable for very large scale problems. In the future, we would like to experiment with a more sophisticated extraction model, in order to facilitate better accuracy of the classifier, as well as the RBIE process.

5.4 Evaluation

At test time, we start with the database that contains names of faculty. All other columns are empty. We consider this as time, $t = 0$. We assume that each action takes one time unit. The action selection scheme that we are testing selects one of the available actions, which is performed as described in Algorithm 1. The action is then marked as completed and removed from all available actions. If an extraction action is selected, it may affect the database by filling a slot and altering the confidence value associated with that slot. We evaluate the results on the database at the end of a given budget, b, or if we run out of actions.

We are interested in finding the email address, job title and department affiliation, all of which can have multiple true values. Note that this also includes minor variations. Throughout our evaluations, we compare against the multiple values of a column, and declare a match if the predicted value matches at least one of them. We use the following evaluation metrics to measure our system's performance. Since our task is slightly different from a traditional information extraction task, we use the following definitions of evaluation metrics. Note that extraction recall measures the proportion of entries for which a true candidate value has been extracted from the web page. It may or may not get ranked as the "best" candidate. However, for the purpose of evaluating the order of selecting the query, download and extract actions, this is a very important metric. Even though at test time, it is independent of the performance of the underlying extraction model, M_e, it is still influenced indirectly by M_e through training.

$$\text{Precision} = \frac{\text{No. of Correctly Filled Entries in the Database}}{\text{No. of Filled Entries in the Database}}$$

$$\text{Recall} = \frac{\text{No. of Correctly Filled Entries in the Database}}{\text{No. of Test Entries in the Database}}$$

$$\text{Extraction Recall} = \frac{\text{No. of Correct Candidates Extracted}}{\text{No. of Test Entries in the Database}}$$

$$\text{F1} = \frac{2 * \text{Precision} * \text{Recall}}{(\text{Precision} + \text{Recall})}$$

5.5 Baselines

We use two baselines for our experiments : random, and straw-man. At each time step, the random approach selects an action randomly from all available actions. The straw-man approach is actually an extremely strong competitor and works as follows. The first query in the list is issued for each test instance. Next, the first hit from the search result for each test instance is downloaded and processed for extraction. Then, subsequent hits from the search result for each test instance are downloaded and processed. Finally, subsequent queries are issued in the descending order, followed by their corresponding download and extract actions. Note that this approach quickly fills up the slots with the top hits of the queries, making it a very difficult baseline to beat.

5.6 Learning Q-function from Data

We now describe how parameters θ for Q-function $Q_\theta(a, S)$ are learned using training data. Table 5.6 shows the features used. Note that at train time, we do not impose resource constraints. That is, training is performed till more actions are available. However, we only run Q-function parameter updates for a given number of iterations, which acts as a type of budget. We determine the number of iterations and learning rate empirically.

Similar to the test time, we start with a database with the email, job title and department name columns empty. The true values of these columns are used only to calculate the reward function. We initialize the parameters to zero. At each time step, we explore all possible actions, and update the parameters as described in Algorithm 2. We then choose the next action to perform as per the updated parameters and proceed similarly for the specified number of iterations.

Features related to query, download and extract actions
Type of query
Features related to download and extract actions
Hit value in the search result URL is from UMass Webpage is HTML Title contains keywords Title contains faculty name
Features related to extract actions
Appropriate Size Bad request code found

Table 6: Features for learning using SampleRank and Q-function

Frac. of Action Budget	Frac. of Best Extraction Recall
00.00%	00.00%
14.29%	77.78%
28.57%	93.65%
42.86%	96.83%
57.14%	96.83%
71.43%	100.00%
85.71%	100.00%
100.00%	100.00%

Table 7: Effectiveness of Biased-Q-learning in obtaining extraction recall over total entries using an oracle

We use the following reward function for training. Here, n is the number of slots filled in the database, d is the number of slots filled correctly, $\bar{d}$ is the number of slots filled incorrectly, m is the number of correct candidates found, and C_n, C_d, $C_{\bar{d}}$, and C_m are the corresponding coefficients. In our initial experiments, using intermediate results was not helpful.

$$R(S_{t+1}) = C_n * n + C_d * d + C_{\bar{d}} * \bar{d} + C_m * m \quad (11)$$

Since we are interested in comparing the SampleRank approach, we use the same features and reward function as q-learning. We also introduce a variation of q-learning, where the policy is initialized using the straw-man approach, followed by the normal q-learning. In this case, a bias value proportional to the rank of actions proposed by the straw-man method is added to the q-function value for each state-action pair. We call this method 'biased-q-learning' in our experiments.

5.7 Results and Discussion

We now compare the test-time performance of the two baselines, the value function learned using SampleRank, and the Q-function on their ability to select good actions at each time step. Note that we have already evaluated performance of the extraction method, and we are now focussing on quality of the action selection strategy. We evaluate performance after each 2000 actions from 0 to 14000 (since the total number of actions at test time is 12730). The most effective action selection scheme is the one that is fastest in achieving high values of evaluation metrics.

5.7.1 RBIE Using an Oracle

We first evaluate performance of the four action selection schemes in the presence of an oracle that perfectly classifies each candidate as the correct value for an entry or not with infinite confidence. We do this to isolate the effect of inaccuracies in the extraction model, M_e, which can severely misguide the RBIE system with wrong confidence values. For e.g., even if the action selection scheme selects a good web page for extraction, M_e can choose the wrong candidate for updating the value in the corresponding slot. While training the Q-function, this translates to incorrect reward values, which can severely impede learning. Table 5 shows that the F1 value for 'yes' label for each of the extractors are not high enough to avoid these problems.

Figure 1 shows the extraction recall values during the RBIE process for different fields, and the total number of entries. Note that in the presence of an Oracle, other evaluation metrics are not useful, since the precision is always 1, and the recall is the same as the extraction recall. We ran 2000 training iterations of SampleRank, q-learning, and biased-q-learning, with learning rate, $\alpha = 0.005$, $C_n = 0.01$, $C_m = 1$, $C_d = 0.1$, $C_{\bar{d}} = -0.05$, and a discount factor, $\gamma = 0.9$ for this experiment.

As we can see, the straw-man method is extremely effective, because it knows to process the top hits for a good query for each entry first. Given the complexity of the action domain, and the size of the state space, this policy is very difficult for a Q-learner to learn. It does, however, learn to beat the random action selection, as well as the value function learned by SampleRank. As expected, both q-learning and biased-q-learning perform better than SampleRank due to their modeling of delayed rewards, despite the use of exactly the same features and reward functions. In the example of extracting emails, biased-q-learning outperforms all other methods, while q-learning outperforms other methods over total entries.

To gain some intuition about the policy learned by q-learning, let us look at a few top features for each action type. For *query* actions : query type with just the name of the faculty, query type with the name of the faculty and the keyword, 'Homepage'. For *download* and *extract* actions : the URL is html, URL is from a umass.edu domain, the title contains faculty name, and combinations of the corresponding query type and range of hit values. For *extract* actions, it also learned high weights for features that looked at the size of the documents. Hence, even though the straw-man method has the advantage of background human knowledge, such as the importance of hit value in the search engine results, the learning-based methods learn new and more elaborate patterns that show relative usefulness of different types of queries and help identify promising documents to process by 'examining' them.

Table 7 presents the percentage of the best extraction recall obtained over total entries for the fraction of the action budget. For example, 77.78% of the best achievable extraction recall (using all available actions) is obtained using only 14.29% and so on. This shows that the proposed RBIE methods can be effective in obtaining most of the useful information using only a fraction of the resources. One thing to note here is that even with using oracle we are not able to achieve perfect extraction recall at the end of al available actions. This illustrates how challenging the problem of finding information about people online is.

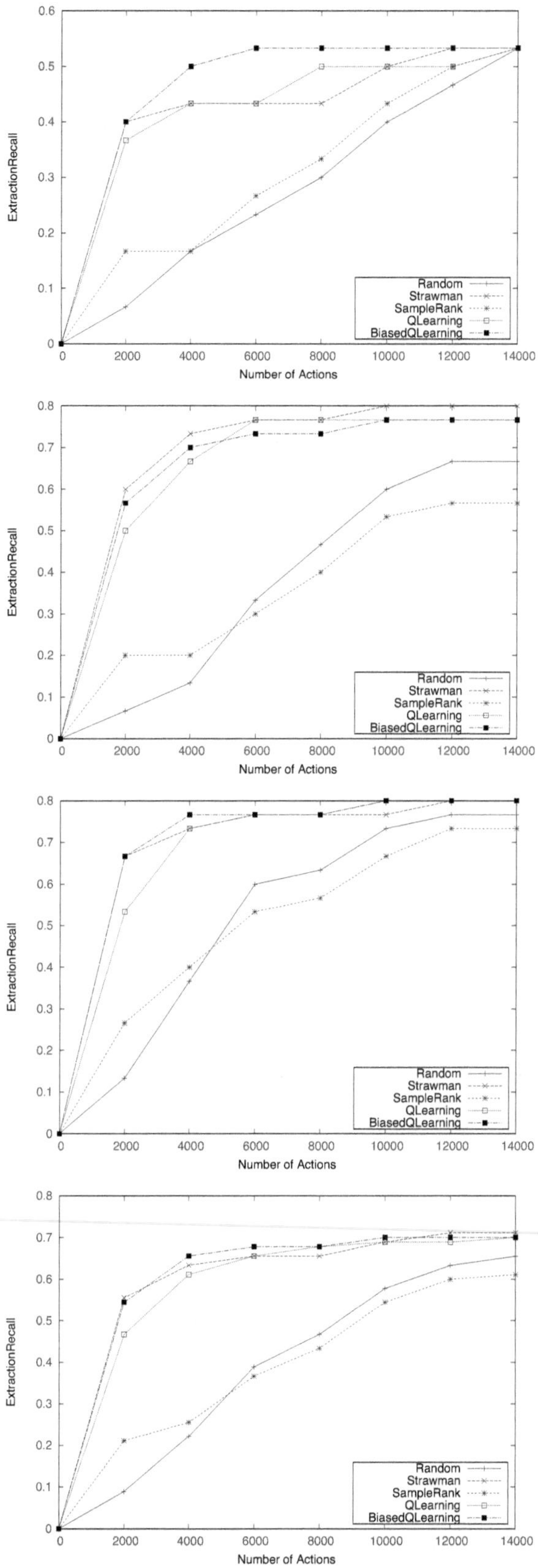

Figure 1: RBIE Using the Oracle. The graphs from top to bottom are : Email, Job Title, Department Name and Total Entries

5.7.2 RBIE Using Extraction Model

We now study the performance of our proposed method using an actual extraction model, M_e. In this case, each action selection strategy needs to balance both precision and recall. We ran 1000 training iterations of SampleRank ($C_n = 1000$, $C_m = 10$, $C_d = 100$, $C_{\bar{d}} = -50$), q-learning ($C_n = 1000$, $C_m = 10$, $C_d = 100$, $C_{\bar{d}} = -50$), and biased-q-learning ($C_n = 0.01$, $C_m = 1$, $C_d = 0.1$, $C_{\bar{d}} = -0.05$) with learning rate, $\alpha = 0.005$, and discount factor, $\gamma = 0.9$ for this experiment. Figure 2 shows the extraction recall, precision, recall and F1 values for total number of entries in the database. In these methods, precision and recall curves go down towards the end of information gathering process due to noise in the web data, and the extraction process. As before, we see that the straw-man method performs better initially. However, its precision and recall drops mid-way through the information acquisition process, and q-learning method performs better. q-learning also comfortably out-performs random and SampleRank approaches. It achieves 92.4% of the final F1, by only using 14.3% of the total actions. This demonstrates the effectiveness of the policy learned by the Q-learner for selecting good actions for information gathering task. We believe that with more accurate labeling and a better extractor, q-learning method can be shown to be even more efficient. Since SampleRank provides a faster learning approach, we would like to further investigate its applicability for this problem domain. A potential improvement on this front could be achieved by defining macro-actions that span multiple actions to better model the delayed reward.

6. CONCLUSION AND FUTURE WORK

In this paper, we formulated the problem of RBIE for the Web as a Markov Decision Process, and proposed the use of temporal difference q-learning to solve it. We learn a policy for effectively selecting information-gathering actions, leading to significant reduction in resource-usage. On our example task of extracting faculty email, job titles and department names, the q-learning based approach is able to achieve 92.4% of the final F1, by only using 14.3% of the total actions. We also compare it to a fast, online, error-driven algorithm called SampleRank [16], and found that q-learning performs better due to it's ability to model delayed reward. We would like to further investigate the use of SampleRank. We also presented a novel extraction technique that can scale well for large scale, information gathering tasks.

The basic formulation of RBIE as an MDP opens up many interesting avenues of research. Use of TD q-learning is one of the first attempts to learn general information gathering policies. More advanced techniques from the reinforcement learning literature, such as SARSA or least-square policy iteration can be explored. This framework is extendable in many ways. We can easily replace the candidate-mention scheme described in the paper with a more sophisticated extraction algorithm. We can also extend the set of information gathering actions defined here to suit the specific needs of a problem, and still use the general MDP framework. Another dimension to explore is the possibility for information acquisition in parallel, which may lead to interesting new methods. The success of such a learning based approach can lead to its application in many resource-conscious, real-world domains.

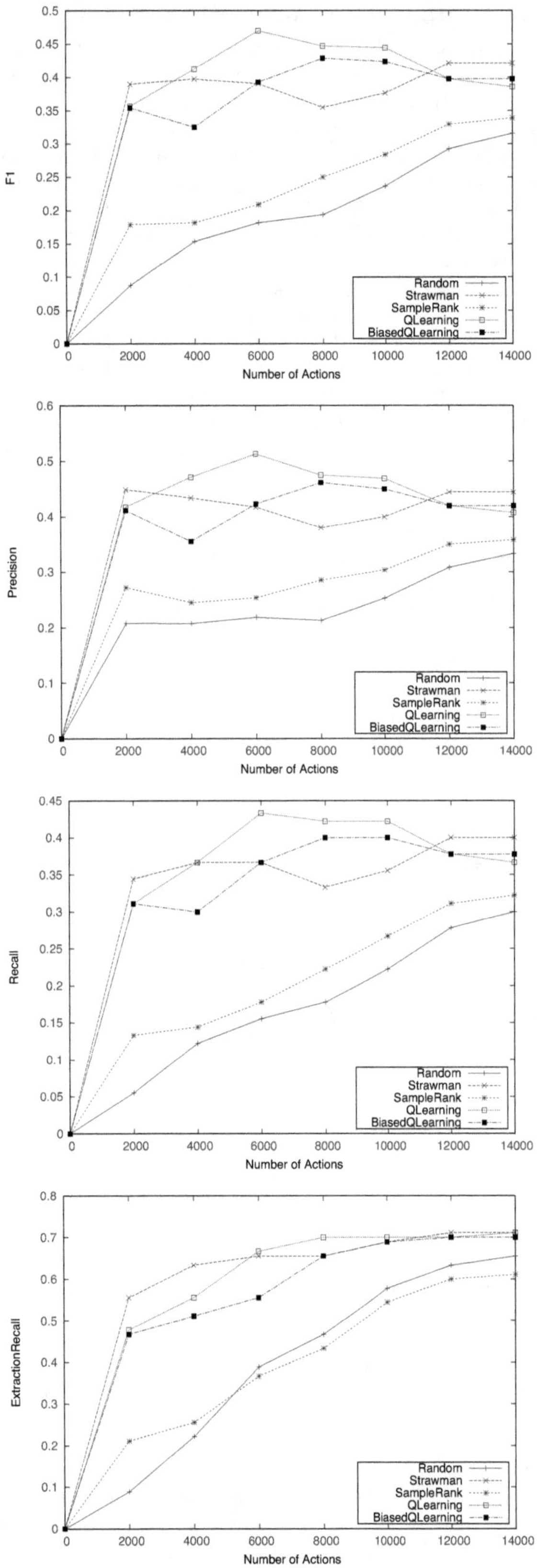

Figure 2: RBIE Using Extraction Model On Total Entries. The graphs from top to bottom are : F1, Precision, Recall and Extraction Recall

7. ACKNOWLEDGMENTS

This research draws on data provided by the University Research Program for Google Search, a service provided by Google to promote a greater common understanding of the web. We thank Michael Wick and anonymous reviewers for useful suggestions. This work was supported in part by the CIIR and in part by the CIA, the NSA, and NSF under NSF grant IIS-0326249 and NSF medium IIS-0803847. Any opinions, findings and conclusions or recommendations expressed in this material are those of the author and do not necessarily reflect those of the sponsor.

8. REFERENCES

[1] A. Culotta. *Learning and inference in weighted logic with application to natural language processing.* PhD thesis, University of Massachusetts, 2008.

[2] T. Eliassi-Rad. *Building Intelligent Agents that Learn to Retrieve and Extract Information.* PhD thesis, University of Wisconsin, Madison, 2001.

[3] O. Etzioni, M. Cafarella, D. Downey, S. Kok, A. Popescu, T. Shaked, S. Soderland, D. Weld, and A. Yates. Web-scale information extraction in knowitall. In *WWW*, 2004.

[4] P. Kanani and A. McCallum. Learning to select actions for resource-bounded information extraction. *UMass CS Tech. Report UM-CS-2011-042*, 2011.

[5] P. Kanani, A. McCallum, and S. Hu. Resource-bounded information extraction: Acquiring missing feature values on demand. In *PAKDD*, 2010.

[6] P. Kanani and P. Melville. Prediction-time active feature-value acquisition for customer targeting. In *Workshop on Cost Sensitive Learning, NIPS*, 2008.

[7] C. A. Knoblock. Planning executing, sensing and replanning for information gathering. In *IJCAI*, 1995.

[8] D. J. Lizotte, O. Madani, and R. Greiner. Budgeted learning of naive-bayes classifiers. In *UAI*, 2003.

[9] A. K. McCallum. Mallet: A machine learning for language toolkit. http://mallet.cs.umass.edu, 2002.

[10] P. Melville, M. Saar-Tsechansky, F. Provost, and R. Mooney. An expected utility approach to active feature-value acquisition. In *ICDM*, 2005.

[11] M. H. Nodine, J. Fowler, T. Ksiezyk, B. Perry, M. Taylor, and A. Unruh. Active information gathering in infosleuth. *IJCIS*, 9(1-2):3–28, 2000.

[12] S. Russell and P. Norvig. *Artificial Intelligence: A Modern Approach (2nd Edition).* Prentice Hall, 2003.

[13] V. Sheng and C. Ling. Feature value acquisition in testing: a sequential batch test algorithm. In *ICML'06.*

[14] R. S. Sutton and A. G. Barto. *Reinforcement Learning: An Introduction.* MIT Press, 1998.

[15] C. J. C. H. Watkins and P. Dayan. Q-learning. *Machine Learning*, 8(3-4):279–292, 1992.

[16] M. Wick, K. Rohanimanesh, K. Bellare, A. Culotta, and A. McCallum. Samplerank: Training factor graphs with atomic gradients. In *ICML*, 2011.

[17] F. Wu, R. Hoffmann, and D. S. Weld. Information extraction from wikipedia: moving down the long tail. In *SIGKDD*, 2008.

[18] S. Zilberstein. Resource-bounded reasoning in intelligent systems. *ACM Comput. Surv*, 28, 1996.

Online Selection of Diverse Results

Debmalya Panigrahi[*]
CSAIL, MIT
Cambridge, MA
debmalya@mit.edu

Atish Das Sarma, Gagan Aggarwal, Andrew Tomkins
Google Research
Mountain View, CA
{dassarma, gagana, tomkins}@google.com

ABSTRACT

The phenomenal growth in the volume of easily accessible information via various web-based services has made it essential for service providers to provide users with personalized representative summaries of such information. Further, online commercial services including social networking and micro-blogging websites, e-commerce portals, leisure and entertainment websites, etc. recommend interesting content to users that is simultaneously diverse on many different axes such as topic, geographic specificity, etc. The key algorithmic question in all these applications is the generation of a succinct, representative, and relevant summary from a large stream of data coming from a variety of sources. In this paper, we formally model this optimization problem, identify its key structural characteristics, and use these observations to design an extremely scalable and efficient algorithm. We analyze the algorithm using theoretical techniques to show that it always produces a nearly optimal solution. In addition, we perform large-scale experiments on both real-world and synthetically generated datasets, which confirm that our algorithm performs even better than its analytical guarantees in practice, and also outperforms other candidate algorithms for the problem by a wide margin.

Categories and Subject Descriptors

H.3 [**Information Systems**]: Information Storage and Retrieval

General Terms

Algorithms, Performance

Keywords

Result Diversity, Online Algorithm

1. INTRODUCTION

The problem of result-set diversity has been studied in multiple domains, but perhaps the most robust literature exists in web search. In search, it is common to introduce diversity by mixing in different interpretations of a query, as in [11], or by attempting to construct result sets to be pairwise distant, as in [3]. The goal in these instances is largely to cater to the needs of multiple distinct user types, each of whom enter the same query, but with different goals. The system may provide a diverse result set to meet the needs of different types simultaneously, even though a single user might be happiest with a non-diverse result set. An alternate form of the diversity problem, in which each individual user prefers a diverse result set, presents itself in applications such as providing ongoing novelty in a series of entertaining items, or a balance of opinions on a sensitive topic.

Specifically, we consider the problem of selecting subsets of items that are simultaneously diverse in multiple dimensions. This problem arises in a variety of contexts. As a toy example, consider the task of selecting the program committee for this conference. The chairs were faced with the task of producing a committee that offers sufficient expertise in all important topics of the conference, while simultaneously covering different regions of the world, providing a good mix of gender, seniority, industry versus academia, and so forth.

Many other examples exist in natural settings. An e-commerce website may wish to show televisions covering multiple technologies, screen dimensions, manufacturers, and price points. Or a website offering pre-packaged vacation travel may be interested in showing customers a small set of options that cover a wide range of alternatives: domestic or international; cheap or expensive; family-friendly or romantic; and so on. Similarly, as an example we will consider more closely below, consider a system recommending interesting content to a user. The system aims to provide content that is simultaneously diverse along a variety of axes including topic (sports vs. politics vs. technology), geographic specificity (world news vs. national news), voice (humorous, scandalous, contrapuntal), and media type (videos vs. blog articles).

In some of these applications, the itemset presented to a user must be personalized to cater to her individual tastes and preferences. Selecting a distinct itemset for each individual user from a very large corpus of items is particularly challenging from a computational perspective. To alleviate this computational bottleneck, we suggest the following natural two-step process: use a very efficient algorithm to select a single representative itemset of intermediate size that caters to the tastes of all users, and then generate individual (smaller) user summaries from this representative set using more resource-intensive techniques. Since user preferences are typically very diverse, it is important that the intermediate itemset contains a diverse set of items covering the entire range of user interests. Therefore, our techniques for selecting a diverse itemset

[*]Part of this work was done while the author was an intern at Google Research, Mountain View, CA.

Permission to make digital or hard copies of all or part of this work for personal or classroom use is granted without fee provided that copies are not made or distributed for profit or commercial advantage and that copies bear this notice and the full citation on the first page. To copy otherwise, to republish, to post on servers or to redistribute to lists, requires prior specific permission and/or a fee.
WSDM'12, February 8–12, 2012, Seattle, Washington, USA.
Copyright 2012 ACM 978-1-4503-0747-5/12/02 ...$10.00.

are useful even for applications such as news feeds in social networking websites that involve a high degree of personalization.

Note that it is important to be simultaneously diverse in all dimensions; in our program committee example, for instance, no amount of diversity in national origin will rescue the hapless committee constituted entirely of experts in itemset discovery. Similarly, geographical diversity of news feeds in a news aggregator website will not compensate for lack of diversity in the topics spanned by the articles. Hence, while we will discuss other metrics, our results will focus on maximizing the worst-case coverage over all features.

Further, in most web/internet based applications, the system must make a commitment to certain items before other items are available for consideration. This may occur because candidates truly arrive in an online manner over time, or because a large dataset is to be processed in a streaming manner, or more commonly, because each page of results must be produced at the lowest possible latency. A user should be provided with a diverse experience over many pageviews, and perhaps even many sessions, but the first response must be committed before future requests are known. Hence, an algorithm that operates purely in an offline context may not extend naturally to each successive request.

This variant of the problem arises in content recommendation, news feeds applications on news websites, search-type interfaces for web search, e-commerce search (as at `amazon.com`), item search (as at `ebay.com`), and so forth. We are primarily motivated by the problem of providing a stream of interesting content, where the items need to be presented in a timely manner with consideration for a variety of attribute features, each of which could have varying ranges and densities. Therefore (irrevocable) decisions on whether new items should be shown or skipped need to be made in an online manner.

We abstract this problem as follows. A stream of items, each decorated with features, arrives over time. As each item arrives, the algorithm must accept or decline it. The algorithm must select as many items as specified by a budget, and its score is the coverage of the least populous feature in the final set.

The content recommendation problem by which we are motivated differs from the abstract formulation in few key ways; we recap these differences here. First, the diversifier will typically have access to constant-size batches of input, rather than individual items. However, the asymptotic behavior of our problem is unchanged in this case, so we may focus our attention on the simpler variant. Next, the diversifier is required to "trade off" diversity with the quality of items selected into the result set. There are several natural mechanisms to incorporate item quality into the formulation, which we describe later. Finally, we study coverage of the worst feature, but in certain settings it may be important to study other variants, such as the average feature. We survey the results for other norms, and also present empirical results analyzing our algorithms with respect to low-performing features other than the worst.

Our Contributions. We now give a high-level overview of the contributions of this paper.

1. We formalize the problem of online diversification on multidimensional featured items. In our problem formulation, the objective is to maximize the minimum coverage over all features, but we also present simple results for other variants of this formulation, both in the offline and the online settings (cf. Sections 2 and 3).

2. We theoretically analyze our problem formulation by showing hardness results for specific small-coverage and adversarial input instances. We then present a novel algorithm for the diversification problem. As the main theoretical result of our paper (Theorem 6), we prove that the algorithm achieves an approximation ratio of 50% on the objective function, provided the optimum coverage is large enough, and the items are drawn *independently* and *identically* (i.i.d.) from some probability distribution (that is unknown to the algorithm). The theoretical analysis and techniques presented here are novel, and the main algorithm is simple, easy to implement, and lightweight, and therefore potentially applicable to a very wide range of scenarios (cf. Section 4).

3. We perform comprehensive experimental evaluation on real-world data obtained from a commercial news feed generator, as well as several synthetically generated data sets. The experimental results not only conclusively corroborate our theoretical findings but also show that our algorithm performs significantly better than its analytical guarantees on all data sets. In fact, the performance of the algorithm is close to optimal for the minimum coverage feature and very good even for subsequent low-coverage features (cf. Section 5). Further, the algorithm outperforms a set of natural and intuitive algorithms for the diversification problem by a wide margin.

2. DIVERSIFICATION FUNCTIONS

As described in the introduction, our high-level objective is to select a small collection of items that are diverse with respect to their constituent features or dimensions, from a large corpus of multi-dimensional items. In this section, we discuss multiple variants of the problem, all of which represent the high-level goal of diversification, and ultimately converge to a particular problem formulation that we focus on for the rest of the paper.

First, we establish some notation that we will use throughout the paper. Let F be the set of n features. As described in the introduction, the input consists of a set U of m items, where each item $j \in U$ consists of a subset of features $F_j \subseteq F$. The diversification algorithm needs to select a representative subset S of at most B items, where B is a given budget, from the input set U. The *coverage* of feature $i \in F$ in the selected subset S, denoted by C_i, is defined as the number of items in S that have feature i. Each feature also has a *target* T_i which is the desired coverage for the feature. The *fractional coverage* of feature i is the fraction of its target coverage that has been achieved by the selected set of items, i.e. $c_i = C_i/T_i$. Let $\mathbf{c}$ be the vector of fractional coverages, i.e. $\mathbf{c} = (c_i : i \in F)$; then the objective is to select a subset S that maximizes the value of $D(\mathbf{c})$, where D is the diversification function of interest.

We consider two versions of the diversification problem depending on whether the entire set U is available to the algorithm before it starts selecting the items in S. For example, in selecting a program committee from a set of researchers, the entire set of researchers is known to the program committee chairs before any selection decision is taken. We call this the *offline* version of the problem. On the other hand, consider the diversification problem in generating news feeds. In this case, the diversification algorithm needs to select news items as they arrive, i.e. without having access to the entire input set of items. We call this the *online* version of the problem. Thus, in the online model, on the arrival of an item j, the algorithm must immediately either select or discard it, subject to the constraint that the total number of selected items cannot exceed B. We assume that each item in the online input stream is drawn i.i.d. from some probability distribution on a set of features that is *unknown* to the algorithm.

Perhaps the simplest objective function D that one can aim for while selecting a representative subset from a large set of items is to maximize the sum of fractional coverages of all the features, i.e.

$$D(\mathbf{c}) = \sum_{i \in F} c_i.$$

However, observe that this function fails to distinguish between a subset of items that achieves large coverage on a few features but very small coverage on the remaining features, and a different subset of items that achieves uniform moderate coverage on all features. Intuitively, the second subset is clearly more diverse, and hence should be preferred. A diversification function that reflects this intuition is

$$D(\mathbf{c}) = \sum_{i \in F} p_i,$$

where $p_i = 1$ if $c_i > 0$, and $p_i = 0$ otherwise. This function clearly distinguishes between the two subsets of items described above, but has the shortcoming that it treats all non-zero coverage values identically. In fact, these two functions are the extreme ends of a continuum of candidate functions

$$D_\alpha(\mathbf{c}) = \sum_{i \in F} c_i^\alpha, \quad 0 \leq \alpha \leq 1$$

that represents the classical trade-off between maximizing *magnitude* (cf. the first function, i.e. $\alpha = 1$) and ensuring *fairness* (cf. the second function, i.e. $\alpha = 0$).

By a slight abuse of notation, let us also denote the value of the function D_α on the coverage achieved by a set of selected items S as $D_\alpha(S)$. It can be shown that all such functions $D_\alpha(S)$ (for $0 \leq \alpha \leq 1$) are *monotonically increasing submodular*[1] functions. Consider a *greedy* algorithm that repeatedly selects the item that yields the maximum increase in the value of the objective until the entire budget has been used up. It is well-known that this algorithm has an approximation factor of $(1 - 1/e)$ for the problem of maximizing any monotonically increasing submodular function.

THEOREM 1. *For any α between 0 and 1, the greedy algorithm has an approximation factor of $(1-1/e)$ for maximizing D_α in the offline setting.*

In the online setting, if the optimal value of objective function is known, then a standard thresholding technique yields an algorithm with a constant competitive ratio[2]. On the other hand, if the optimum is unknown, then we can guess its value using a standard doubling technique. The key property that we exploit in this guessing scheme is that the input stream is drawn i.i.d., and therefore only a small fraction of the budget is used in obtaining a good estimate of the optimum. (The proof of this theorem is deferred to the full version of the paper.)

THEOREM 2. *For any α between 0 and 1, there exists an algorithm that has a constant competitive ratio for maximizing D_α in the online setting, if the input is drawn i.i.d.*

[1]A function f defined on all subsets of a ground set X is said to be *monotonically increasing* if for any $A \subseteq B$,

$$f(A) \leq f(B),$$

and is said to be *submodular* if for any $A \subseteq B$ and for any $x \in X$,

$$f(A \cup \{x\}) - f(A) \geq f(B \cup \{x\}) - f(B).$$

[2]For a maximization problem, an online algorithm has a competitive ratio of β if the objective value in the solution produced by the algorithm is at least β-times the offline optimum.

We now focus on another natural candidate function for diversification, where the objective is to maximize the minimum fractional coverage all features. That is,

$$D(\mathbf{c}) = \min_{i \in F} c_i$$

Observe that this function achieves the twin objectives of *magnitude* and *fairness* of feature coverage. This function is **not** submodular, and therefore, the techniques described above cannot be used to solve this problem.

Let c_{OPT} be the optimal value of D and

$$\rho_{\text{OPT}} = c_{\text{OPT}} \min_{i \in F} T_i.$$

The next theorem (proof deferred to the full version) shows that the problem does not admit an algorithm with a finite approximation ratio even in the offline setting, if $\rho_{\text{OPT}} = o(\log n)$.

THEOREM 3. *Under standard complexity-theoretic assumptions, there exists no algorithm that obtains a finite approximation ratio for offline instances of the diversification problem where $\rho_{\text{OPT}} = o(\log n)$.*

The above theorem implies that we need to assume that the optimal solution satisfies $\rho_{\text{OPT}} = \Omega(\log n)$, in order to obtain a finite approximation ratio. (In fact, this assumption holds for most real data sets, as verified later in the experimental section.) If this property is satisfied by an offline instance of the problem, then a simple algorithm that employs randomized rounding of the natural linear programming formulation of the problem gives the following theorem. (The proof of this theorem is deferred to the full version of the paper.)

THEOREM 4. *For the problem of maximizing D in the offline setting, there is a PTAS[3] if the optimum is $\Omega(\log n)$.*

Now, we focus on the online version of the problem. The next theorem (proof deferred to the full version) shows that we need to assume that the input stream is not adversarial in order to obtain a sub-polynomial competitive ratio for this problem.

THEOREM 5. *For an adversarial input stream, the competitive ratio of any algorithm for maximizing D in the online setting is $\Omega(n)$.*

To overcome the barrier imposed by the above theorem, we assume that the input is drawn i.i.d. from a probability distribution that is unknown to the algorithm.

3. PROBLEM FORMULATION

As described in the previous section, we focus on the following problem formulation, which we call the DIVERSIFIER problem.

> Let F be a set of features and T_i be the target coverage for feature $i \in F$. An input set U of m items arrives online, where the set of features $F_j \subseteq F$ in each item $j \in U$ is drawn i.i.d. from a probability distribution on subsets of F that is unknown to the algorithm. The algorithm must decide, on the arrival of item j, whether to select or discard it. The overall goal is to select a subset S of at most B items that maximizes $\min_{i \in F} c_i = \min_{i \in F} \frac{C_i}{T_i}$, where C_i is the number of items in S that contain feature i.

[3]A *Polynomial-time Approximation Scheme* (or PTAS) for a maximization problem is an algorithm that has an approximation factor of $(1 - \epsilon)$ for any arbitrarily small constant $\epsilon > 0$. (The running time of the algorithm depends on the choice of ϵ.)

Main Result. We give an online algorithm for the DIVERSIFIER problem which proves the next theorem.

THEOREM 6. *There is a deterministic online algorithm for the* DIVERSIFIER *problem that has a competitive ratio of $\frac{1}{2} - \delta$ for any $\delta > 0$ with probability (over the input distribution) at least $1 - 1/n$, provided the input is drawn i.i.d. from an (unknown) probability distribution on feature sets satisfying the property that the expected value of $\rho_{\text{OPT}} \geq \frac{24 \ln n}{\delta^2}$.*

Our Techniques. Consider the special case where all targets T_i are equal to the budget B. Further, assume that we have the guarantee that the expected value of $\rho_{\text{OPT}} = c_{\text{OPT}} B = \Omega(\log^2 n)$ (which is stronger than that required by Theorem 6). Then, we can partition the input into $\log n$ *epochs*, where in each epoch, the algorithm selects at most $B/\log n$ subsets from an input stream containing $m/\log n$ items, and aims at achieving an expected minimum coverage of $\lambda = \Omega(\frac{\rho_{\text{OPT}}}{\log n})$.

Now, instead of achieving a coverage of λ for each feature, let us change our goal in any epoch to achieving a cumulative coverage of $\Omega(n\lambda)$ over all features, where the contribution of any single feature to this sum is at most λ, i.e. $\sum_{i \in F} \min(C_i, \lambda) = \Omega(n\lambda)$. This can be achieved by using a thresholding algorithm that selects an item *if and only if* it contains at least $\Omega\left(\frac{n\lambda \log n}{B}\right)$ features $i \in F$ with current coverage $C_i < \lambda$. This immediately implies, via an averaging argument, that some constant fraction of features have achieved a coverage of $\Omega(\lambda)$. We discard these features in the next epoch and recurse. Since the number of retained features decreases by a constant factor in every epoch, the coverage on every feature is $\Omega(\lambda)$ at the end of $\log n$ epochs. Therefore, this algorithm yields a competitive ratio of $O(\log n)$.

To transform the algorithm described above to an algorithm that proves Theorem 6, we need to make the following improvements:

- Improve the competitive ratio of the algorithm to a constant.
- Generalize the algorithm to handle arbitrary targets T_i.
- Relax the constraint on the expected value of ρ_{OPT} from $\Omega(\log^2 n)$ to $\Omega(\log n)$.

The previous algorithm can be interpreted in terms of a reward function which gives a reward of 1 every time a feature is covered until the feature has been covered λ times, at which point the reward on covering the feature drops to 0. The algorithm then essentially sets a threshold proportional to the ratio of the remaining rewards to the remaining budget, and selects an item if it meets this reward threshold. However, observe that the algorithm fails to differentiate between covering a feature that already has a large coverage (but less than λ), and a feature that has smaller coverage. To make this distinction, we introduce a smoother reward function in the next section, and show that this simple thresholding algorithm for the new reward function achieves all the three goals outlined above.

4. THE DIVERSIFICATION ALGORITHM

In this section, we describe the diversification algorithm, and use analytical techniques to show that it proves Theorem 6. The algorithm uses the expected optimal value of the objective function denoted by c_{OPT}. If c_{OPT} is not known, we can guess c_{OPT}, and update our guess repeatedly by doubling, as outlined in the previous section. Since the input stream of items is drawn i.i.d. from some (unknown) probability distribution, it can be shown that the competitive ratio of the algorithm remains a constant even if the expected optimal value of the objective function is not known to the algorithm. However, for the sake of simplicity, we assume throughout that we know c_{OPT}.

$$\begin{aligned} \sum_{S \subseteq F: i \in S} w_S p_S &\geq \frac{c_{\text{OPT}} T_i}{m} \quad \forall i \in F \\ \sum_{S \subseteq F} w_S p_S &\leq \frac{B}{m} \\ 0 \leq w_S &\leq 1 \quad \forall S \subseteq F \end{aligned}$$

Figure 1: A linear program for the DIVERSIFIER problem.

As sketched in the previous section, our algorithm uses a reward function ϕ defined as

$$\phi(k) = n^{-\alpha(k/c_{\text{OPT}})},$$

where α is a constant that we will fix later. We also define

$$\bar{\Phi}(k) = \int_{j=k}^{\infty} \phi(j) dj.$$

If the current collection of selected items has fractional coverage c_i for some feature $i \in F_j$ for the current item j, then the reward r_{ij} of item j due to feature i is defined as $\phi(c_i)$. The overall reward r_j of item j is defined as the sum of rewards of its constituent features, i.e. $r_j = \sum_{i \in F_j} r_{ij}$. At any stage of the algorithm, the remaining reward for feature i is

$$\bar{\Phi}_i = \bar{\Phi}(c_i),$$

and the overall remaining reward is

$$\bar{\Phi} = \sum_{i \in F} \bar{\Phi}_i.$$

The online algorithm selects the current item j *if and only if*

$$r_j \geq \frac{\bar{\Phi} \ln n}{\gamma B},$$

where γ is a constant we will fix later. The algorithm terminates when either the input stream has been exhausted or the algorithm has already selected B items.

Analysis. First, we state a property of the reward function that we will use later in the analysis of the algorithm.

FACT 1. *For any $k \geq 0$, $\bar{\Phi}(k) = \left(\frac{c_{\text{OPT}}}{\alpha \ln n}\right) \phi(k)$.*

Now, consider the linear program (LP) for the DIVERSIFIER problem in Fig. 1. Here, p_S denotes the probability of item j in the input stream having $F_j = S$ for any j, and w_s is the fraction to which such an item is chosen in the optimal fractional (offline) solution. Since the expected optimal value of the objective is c_{OPT}, this LP is feasible.

Recall that $\rho_{\text{OPT}} = c_{\text{OPT}} \min_{i \in F} T_i$. For simplicity of notation, let us also denote the expected value of ρ_{OPT} by ρ_{OPT} itself in the rest of this section. The next lemma lower bounds the probability that an item is chosen by our algorithm if it has not already exhausted its budget.

LEMMA 1. *At any stage of the algorithm, the expected decrease in $\bar{\Phi}$ for the next item in the input stream is at least $\left(\alpha - \frac{1}{\gamma}\right) \frac{\bar{\Phi} \ln n}{m}$. Further, the probability that the next item in the input stream is selected by the algorithm is at least $\left(1 - \frac{1}{\alpha\gamma}\right) \frac{\rho_{\text{OPT}}}{m}$.*

PROOF. Consider a hypothetical algorithm that chooses item j having a feature set $F_j = S$ with probability w_S. The expected decrease of $\bar{\Phi}$ for this algorithm at any stage is

$$\begin{aligned}
&\sum_{S\subseteq F} p_S w_S \sum_{i\in S} \frac{\phi(c_i)}{T_i} \\
&= \left(\frac{\alpha \ln n}{C_{\text{OPT}}}\right) \sum_{i\in F} \frac{\bar{\Phi}_i}{T_i} \sum_{S\subseteq F: i\in S} w_S p_S \\
&\geq \left(\frac{\alpha \ln n}{C_{\text{OPT}}}\right) \sum_{i\in F} \frac{\bar{\Phi}_i}{T_i} \left(\frac{C_{\text{OPT}} T_i}{m}\right) \\
&= \left(\frac{\alpha \ln n}{m}\right) \sum_{i\in F} \bar{\Phi}_i \\
&= \left(\frac{\alpha \ln n}{m}\right) \bar{\Phi}.
\end{aligned}$$

Let

$$y_S = \sum_{i\in S} \frac{\phi(c_i)}{T_i}$$

and

$$z_S = p_S w_S (m/B).$$

Then, we have

$$\begin{aligned}
\sum_{S\subseteq F} y_S z_S &\geq \left(\frac{\alpha \ln n}{B}\right) \bar{\Phi} \\
\sum_{S\subseteq F} z_S &\leq 1.
\end{aligned}$$

By standard convexity arguments, we can conclude that

$$\sum_{S\subseteq F: y_S \geq \frac{\bar{\Phi}\ln n}{\gamma B}} y_S z_S \geq \left(\alpha - \frac{1}{\gamma}\right) \frac{\bar{\Phi} \ln n}{B},$$

which implies that the expected decrease in $\bar{\Phi}$ due to the next item in the input stream is

$$\sum_{S\subseteq F: y_S \geq \frac{\bar{\Phi}\ln n}{\gamma B}} w_S p_S y_S \geq \left(\alpha - \frac{1}{\gamma}\right) \frac{\bar{\Phi} \ln n}{m}.$$

Further, the maximum decrease in $\bar{\Phi}$ due to a single item is

$$\max_{S\subseteq F} \sum_{i\in S} \frac{\phi(c_i)}{T_i} \leq \sum_{i\in F} \frac{\phi(c_i)}{T_i} = \left(\frac{\alpha \ln n}{C_{\text{OPT}}}\right) \sum_{i\in F} \frac{\bar{\Phi}_i}{T_i} \leq \left(\frac{\alpha \ln n}{\rho_{\text{OPT}}}\right) \bar{\Phi}.$$

Since $w_S \leq 1$ for all $S \subseteq F$,

$$\sum_{S\subseteq F: y_S \geq \frac{\bar{\Phi}\ln n}{\gamma B}} p_S \geq \sum_{S\subseteq F: y_S \geq \frac{\bar{\Phi}\ln n}{\gamma B}} p_S w_S \geq \left(1 - \frac{1}{\alpha\gamma}\right) \frac{\rho_{\text{OPT}}}{m}.$$

□

The above lemma implies that if the algorithm has not selected B items already, then the next item in the input stream is selected with probability

$$p \geq \left(1 - \frac{1}{\alpha\gamma}\right) \frac{\rho_{\text{OPT}}}{m},$$

and if the next item is selected, then the value of $\bar{\Phi}$ decreases to at most

$$\left(1 - \frac{1}{p}\left(\alpha - \frac{1}{\gamma}\right) \frac{\ln n}{m}\right) \bar{\Phi} \leq n^{-\frac{\alpha - \frac{1}{\gamma}}{pm}} \bar{\Phi}.$$

The next lemma asserts that if $\rho_{\text{OPT}} = \Omega(\ln n)$ and the algorithm does not select B items, then the value of $\bar{\Phi}$ when the algorithm terminates is small.

LEMMA 2. *Suppose the algorithm does not select B items. Further, let $\rho_{\text{OPT}} \geq \frac{3 \ln n}{\epsilon^2 \left(1 - \frac{1}{\alpha\gamma}\right)}$. Then, the value of $\bar{\Phi}$ when the algorithm terminates is at most $n^{1-(1-\epsilon)\left(\alpha - \frac{1}{\gamma}\right)}$ with probability at least $1 - 1/n$.*

PROOF. The expected number of items selected by the algorithm is

$$pm \geq \left(1 - \frac{1}{\alpha\gamma}\right) \rho_{\text{OPT}} \geq \frac{3 \ln n}{\epsilon^2}.$$

Therefore, by Chernoff bounds [10], the value of $\bar{\Phi}$ when the algorithm terminates is at most

$$n^{-\left(\frac{\alpha - \frac{1}{\gamma}}{pm}\right)(1-\epsilon) pm} \cdot n = n^{1-(1-\epsilon)\left(\alpha - \frac{1}{\gamma}\right)}$$

with probability at least $1 - 1/n$. □

Finally, we consider the case when the algorithm uses up its entire budget, i.e. selects B items.

LEMMA 3. *If the algorithm selects B items, then the value of $\bar{\Phi}$ when the algorithm terminates is at most $n^{1-\frac{1}{\gamma}}$.*

PROOF. When the algorithm selects an item, the value of $\bar{\Phi}$ decreases to at most

$$\left(1 - \frac{\ln n}{\gamma B}\right) \bar{\Phi} \leq n^{-\frac{1}{\gamma B}}.$$

Therefore, the value of $\bar{\Phi}$ when the algorithm terminates after selecting B items is at most

$$n^{-1/\gamma} \cdot n = n^{1-\frac{1}{\gamma}}.$$

□

We now set $\gamma = \frac{2-\epsilon}{(1-\epsilon)\alpha}$ which lets us summarize the above two lemmas in the following lemma.

LEMMA 4. *If $\rho_{\text{OPT}} \geq \frac{3(2-\epsilon)\ln n}{\epsilon^2}$, then the value of $\bar{\Phi}$ when the algorithm terminates is at most $n^{1-\alpha\left(\frac{1-\epsilon}{2-\epsilon}\right)}$ with probability at least $1 - 1/n$.*

The next lemma bounds the competitive ratio of the algorithm.

LEMMA 5. *If $\rho_{\text{OPT}} \geq \frac{3(2-\epsilon)\ln n}{\epsilon^2}$, then the competitive ratio of the algorithm is at most $\left(\frac{1-\epsilon}{2-\epsilon}\right) - \frac{1}{\alpha}$ with probability at least $1 - 1/n$.*

PROOF. Suppose not, and let $i_{\min}$ be the feature with the minimum fractional coverage at the end of the algorithm. Then,

$$\bar{\Phi} \geq \bar{\Phi}_{i_{\min}} = n^{-\alpha\left(\frac{1-\epsilon}{2-\epsilon} - \frac{1}{\alpha}\right)} > n^{1-\alpha\left(\frac{1-\epsilon}{2-\epsilon}\right)},$$

which violates Lemma 4. □

Observe that since $\epsilon < 1$,

$$\frac{1-\epsilon}{2-\epsilon} > \frac{1}{2} - \epsilon.$$

We now obtain Theorem 6 by setting $\epsilon = \delta/2$ and $\alpha = 2/\delta$.

5. EXPERIMENTS

We perform experiments on both real-world and synthetically generated data sets and compare our diversification algorithm with several natural and intuitive alternative algorithms for the problem. Our experimental evaluation compares the performance of these algorithms measured in terms of feature coverage by varying multiple parameters. We first describe the data sets used in our experiments; next we describe the alternative algorithms we compare our algorithm against; and finally we describe the experiments that we perform and interpret the results we obtain in these experiments.

5.1 Description of Data Sets

Real-world news feeds. This dataset is obtained from the stream of items received by a commercial news feed generator, from which it selects a news feed for individual users. Each item considered has several features associated with it, such as the source of the item, the broad category it belongs to, the types of contents in it etc. We extracted 18 features such that each item has a binary value associated with each feature (that is, either has or does not have the feature). This feature set includes a variety of dense (i.e. present in a large fraction of items) as well as sparse features such as whether the item has an embedded video, is in English language, is about Politics or Sports, and so on. The selection of these 18 features was aimed at capturing multiple kinds of dependencies: e.g., hierarchical dependency (i.e. a feature occurs always with another feature), exclusivity (an item can have only one of a set of features), dense features, or very sparse features. These features were chosen in a careful manner so as to test the performance of the diversification algorithm on dependencies, on sparse features (i.e. even when the optimum is small), on very commonly occurring features, etc. We ran our experiments on 100 such different data sets, each containing about a million items with feature vectors along these 18 dimensions.

Synthetically generated data. In addition to the real data set, we also test our algorithm on various carefully chosen synthetically generated data sets. In each of these data sets, we again generated items with 18 features and tested the algorithms on data sets of one million items each. The synthetic data sets we tested on are the following.

- **Independent.** In this data set, each entry (that is each feature for every item) is independently set to 1 or 0 (that is item either has or does not have the feature) with probability half each. Notice that this generates a data set where, in expectation, each item has nine features. Further, in expectation, each feature is contained in half of all the items.

- **Parity.** In this data set, initially we fix a bit vector of length 18 (where each bit is set to 1 or 0 independently and with equal probability) and then for each item, we pick a 1 or 0 independently and with equal probability, and XOR it with the bit vector. Observe that this results in a very strong dependence between different features, and the whole data set contains only two kinds of items.

- **Dependent Mixed.** This data set is generated in a manner very similar to parity, but in addition, after each item has been generated, each of the feature bits is flipped independently and with a small probability (set to 0.1). This results in a milder dependence between the item features.

- **Dependent.** The dependent data set is similar to the dependent mixed data set. The only difference is that the initial bit vector is set to all 1's. Therefore, there is uniform correlation between all item features.

5.2 Algorithms

We now describe all the algorithms that we compare in our experiments.

Diversifier. This is the diversification algorithm in Section 4.

Diversifier (Uniform Coverage). This algorithm is the same as the diversifier presented previously with a small difference that the reward function ϕ is not decreasing; in particular, the reward function is fixed at $\phi(k) = 1$. Comparing with this algorithm highlights the importance of the decreasing reward function in the diversification algorithm.

Fixed Threshold. The fixed threshold algorithm is a naïve baseline algorithm where a specific threshold is fixed at the beginning (between 1 and 18, the number of features). Subsequently, when items arrive online, every item that has at least as many features as the threshold is picked, until the budget is exhausted. We compare our diversification algorithm against this fixed threshold algorithm for different thresholds. We performed experiments with all possible thresholds between 1 and 18 but present only a representative set of results, for thresholds $3, 6, 9, 12, 15$. The performance of the fixed threshold algorithm with other thresholds is similar to the ones we show.

Simple Random. In this algorithm, items are selected randomly based on the number of features they contain, in such a way that the expected number selected items equals the budget B. The probability that an item containing k features is picked is determined by optimally solving a linear program that aims to maximize the coverage on every feature. This algorithm performs two passes over the input stream of items: in the first pass, it computes frequency counts of features and uses them to obtain the probability of selecting an item with k features. In the second pass, it uses these probabilities to actually select the items.

5.3 Description of the Experiments

Sorted Coverage. In this experiment, we evaluate the performance of each of the algorithms on the coverage achieved on the features. Recall that our objective is to maximize the minimum coverage over all features. In addition to the minimum coverage, we also look at the performance of the algorithms on the 2nd to 6th least covered features as well. The specific goal of the diversifier is to maximize minimum coverage, but at the same time, it is desirable that the coverage be substantial on other features as well. This experiment highlights that even though the specific goal of the diversification algorithm is to maximize minimum coverage, it achieves substantial coverage on other features as well (particularly for features where a larger coverage is attainable without compromising on the minimum coverage achieved).

Varying Budgets. We perform a series of experiments by varying the available budget to the algorithms, to see if the performance of the diversification algorithm scales with larger budgets. We also perform experiments for low budgets to test whether the algorithm is able to achieve reasonable coverage on each of the features (even on the sparse ones). These experiments show that the diversification algorithm performs admirably for a variety of budgets.

In all our experiments, the total number of features is 18 and the number of items in each data set is around $1M$. Also, when we plot sorted coverage, the default value of the budget is set to $20K$ (which is roughly 2% of the data set), and the targets for all the features are set to the budget itself. For the plots where we

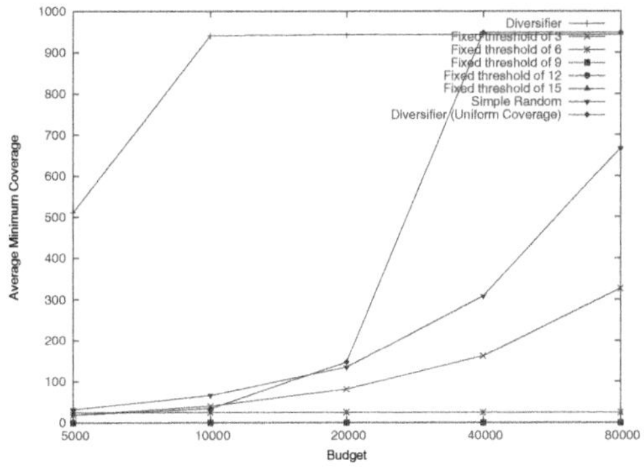

(a) Higher range of budgets between 0.5% and 8%

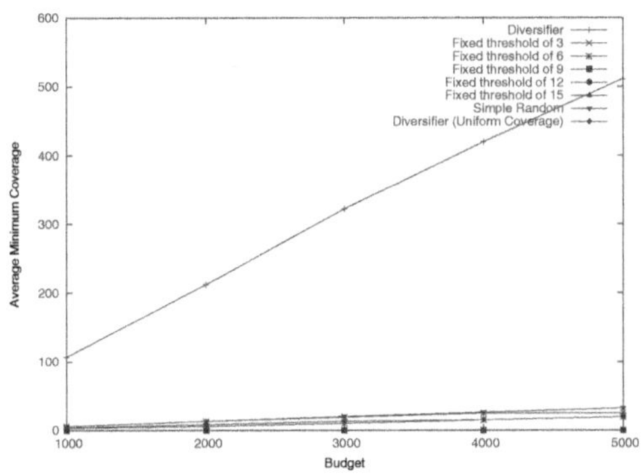

(b) Lower range of budgets between 0.1% and 0.5%

Figure 2: The average minimum coverage achieved by various algorithms over 100 real world data sets of $1M$ items each.

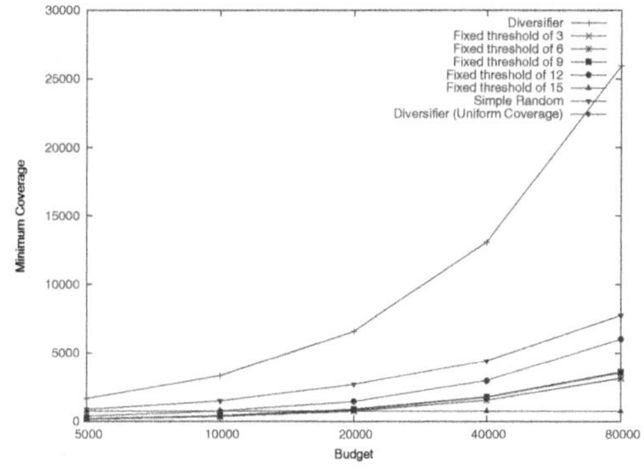

(a) Minimum coverage with varying budgets

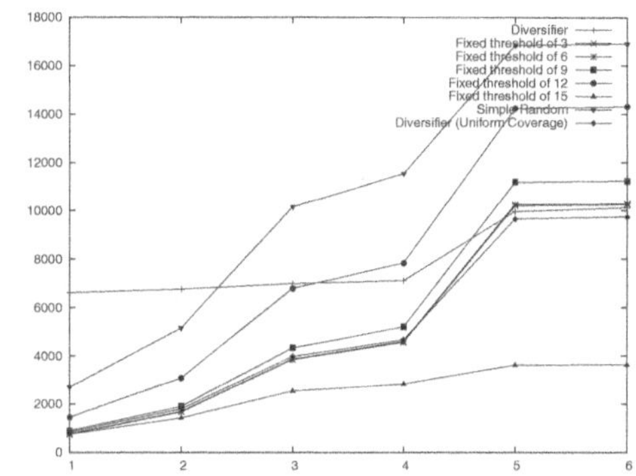

(b) Coverage on the least covered features

Figure 4: Experimental results for the Independent data set

vary budgets on the x-axis, the coverage plotted on the y-axis is the minimum over all the 18 features (which is the objective function of the diversification algorithm).

Note that the budgets are too large for individual news feeds. However, as we noted earlier, our algorithm is useful for generating a single itemset of intermediate size that contains relevant items for all users, from which individual personalized news feeds can be generated using more resource-intensive techniques. Our experiments can be viewed as generating these intermediate itemsets.

As stated in Theorem 6, our diversification algorithm achieves a $\frac{1}{2} - \delta$-approximation ratio as long as the expected optimum coverage is at least $\frac{24 \ln n}{\delta^2}$. In all our experiments, the minimum coverage on any feature (for both real and synthetic data sets) is at least 900, out of around $1M$ items. Further, since we are dealing with $n = 18$ features, $\ln n \approx 2.89$. Note that $900 \geq \frac{24 \ln n}{\delta^2}$ for values of $\delta \geq 0.28$. As we note in the experiments shortly, the performance of the diversification algorithm is significantly better than the theoretical guarantee.

5.4 Description of plots

Our first set of plots (Figure 2) compare the minimum coverage achieved by various algorithms, averaged over the 100 real data sets of $1M$ items each, with budgets varying from 0.1% to 8% of the input. Observe that the Diversifier significantly outperforms all the other algorithms for any budget between 0.1% and 4%. The minimum coverage achieved by the Diversifier levels off at a value between 900 and 1000 beyond a budget of 1% since there are features in our dataset that occur in fewer than 1000 items (and therefore the Diversifier has already achieved an almost optimal solution). Once the budget reaches 4%, the Diversifier (Uniform Coverage) also achieves optimal performance. All the other algorithms fair significantly worse, especially for smaller budgets. Notice that the other algorithms however require a budget of at least $40K$ to achieve any reasonable performance. In fact the minimum coverage achieved by the Diversifier increases linearly with the budget thereby confirming scalability of the algorithm.

For our next set of plots (Figure 3) we show the coverage achieved by the various algorithms on the least covered features. These experiments are performed on the real data set for six fixed budgets varying from 0.1% to 4%. Throughout these plots, we see a consistent trend of the Diversifier performing extremely well for the lesser covered features while the other algorithms are able to perform well only on the features that get higher coverage. In other words, these algorithms fail to perform well at the specific task of diversification which requires spreading out the coverage uniformly. Observe that in the plot for the comparatively high budget of 4%, the other algorithms also perform well for features that receive lesser coverage. This is because even the optimal solution can only attain a coverage of about as much obtained by these algorithms. However, for small budgets, the diversifier significantly outperforms all other algorithms.

Now, we describe the experimental results obtained for synthetically generated data sets. The plots for the experiments described above performed on the independent data set are given in Figure 4. In Figure 4 part (a), we see that the performance of the Diversifier rapidly improves with increasing budget while the other algorithms do not scale as well. This highlights that our algorithm is able to quickly adapt to varying coverages across features and assign importance to features that suffer from low coverage. On the

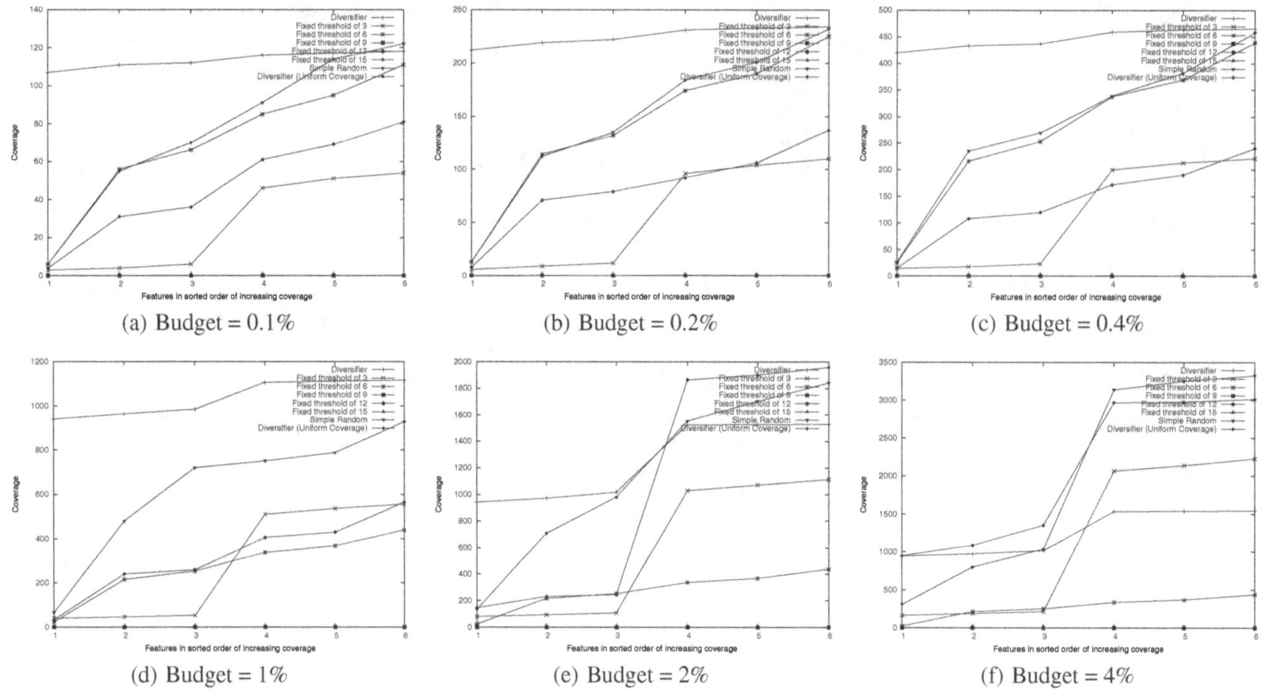

(a) Budget = 0.1% (b) Budget = 0.2% (c) Budget = 0.4%

(d) Budget = 1% (e) Budget = 2% (f) Budget = 4%

Figure 3: The coverage achieved on the least covered features on the real world data set by various algorithms.

other hand, the other algorithms continue to select items oblivious to previously selected items and therefore suffer from lower values of minimum coverage. In Figure 4 part (b), we again observe that the Diversifier performs well on the features with low coverage, i.e. it is able to balance out the coverage along different features and obtain a large minimum coverage, while other algorithms fail to do so.

Very similar trends are seen for the same experiments performed on the parity data set Figure 5 part (a). The diversifier does significantly better throughout, and the contrast is particularly noticeable as the budgets are increased. Observe that in the plot for sorted coverage in the parity data set (Figure 5 part (b)), the Diversifier does significantly better than all other algorithms. In fact, the Diversifier is very close to the optimum in this case as well, and therefore performs much better than guaranteed by Theorem 6. All these plots are horizontal because the data set contains only two kinds of items.

Finally, we show plots for the minimum coverage achieved for the different algorithms on the dependent and dependent-mixed data sets for varying budgets (Figure 6). In these plots, we notice that some of the other algorithms also perform well; in fact the randomized algorithm even outperforms the Diversifier for the dependent data set. Further, we observe that some of the fixed threshold algorithms perform well for large budgets. This is not surprising given that the features are very rigidly dependent on each other - therefore an algorithm that chooses the right threshold performs well on all features. Of course, note that we are comparing against an algorithm that somehow knows this threshold value, which is not feasible in practice. The takeaway here therefore is that the diversifier loses a bit in learning what threshold to use in an online fashion, but is then able to adapt and obtain a good coverage.

5.5 Summary

To summarize the experiments, we have seen that the diversifier performs extremely well on a wide range of parameters, and in particular, does significantly better than all the other algorithms we implemented on the real data set. The real data set comprised of several kinds of features with varying densities among items, hierarchical dependence, exclusive dependence etc., and yet the diversifier performs really well on the coverage for all budget ranges. The algorithm is fairly general, extremely simple to implement, low cost and efficient, provably approximate, and performs near-optimally even at large scales. Therefore these ideas and techniques may be useful in a wide range of other settings and applications.

6. RELATED WORK

Diversification has been studied in a variety of different contexts so we only mention some of the references here. Among them search result diversification has arguably received the most attention (e.g. [11, 8, 16, 15, 14, 13, 12]). In particular, Gollapudi and Sharma [8] adopt an axiomatic approach and specify a set of rules that must be adhered to in any reasonable definition of diversification in the context of search results. A different approach is adopted by Slivkins *et al* [16] who employ learning theoretic techniques for diversification of rankings. For some recent work in diversification, the reader is referred to [15, 14].

Search diversification is different from our context in a couple of fundamental ways. First, the primary motivation for search result diversification is keyword disambiguation, and the intent is usually to provide the user with a set of result webpages such that includes at least one s/he is looking for. However, in our context, the goal is to ensure that the user is presented with a set of items that satisfies her cumulatively. Second, in the search architecture, one normally has access to all the (meta data related to) webpages stored on disk, and for efficiency reasons, one may need to perform online/streaming decisions on the documents, or quickly prune them to a candidate set; however, making irrevocable online decisions is not a necessity. This consideration makes our context a significantly harder one.

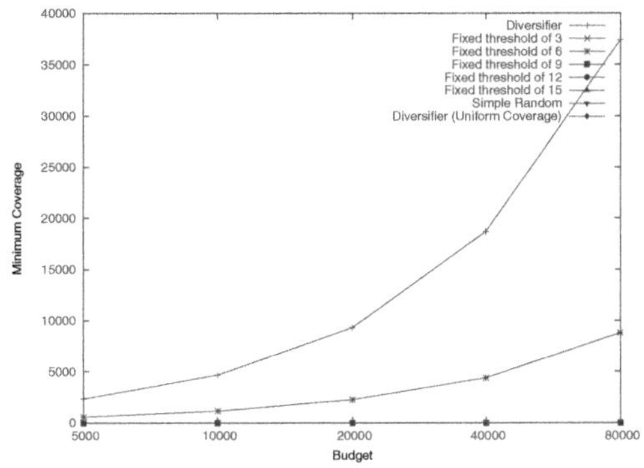

(a) Minimum coverage with varying budgets

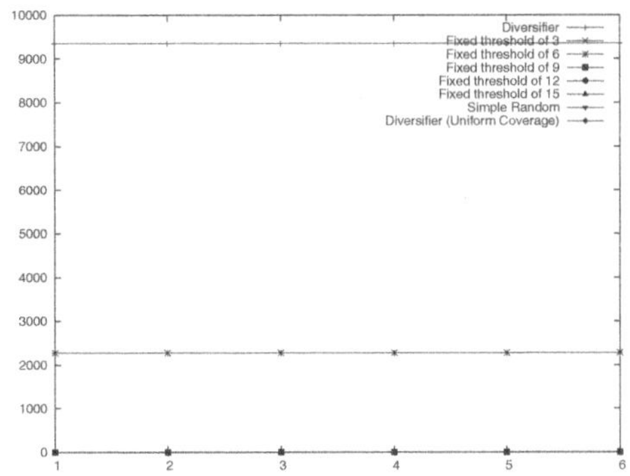

(b) Coverage on the least covered features

Figure 5: Experimental results for the Parity data set

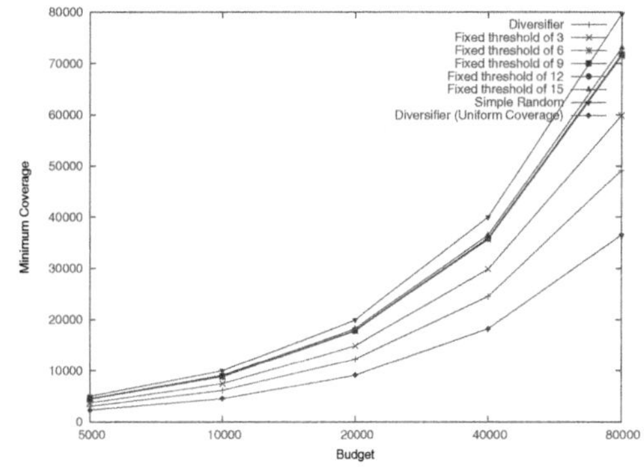

(a) Dependent data set

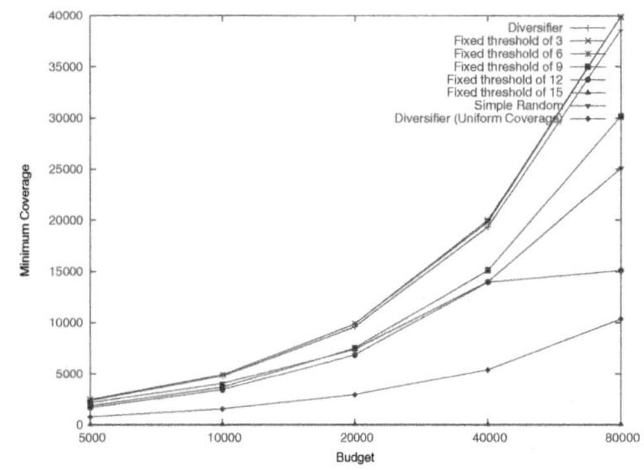

(b) Dependent Mixed data set

Figure 6: The coverage achieved on the least covered features for various budgets by all algorithms on the Dependent and Dependent Mixed data sets.

The diversification problem has also been considered extensively in the context of recommender systems (see e.g. [19, 18, 9]). Several other works on diversification have been undertaken. For example, Agrawal *et al* [1] propose a maximum likelihood based diversification objective for finding relevant documents given the categorical information of queries and documents. Other papers on topical diversification and information retrieval include [21, 20]. Vee *et al* [17] consider diversification for online shopping, while Drosou and Pitoura [5, 6] have done work on diversity over continuous data such as in the context of publish/subscribe systems. Diversification for re-ranking documents and producing summaries has been considered by Carbonell and Goldstein [3]. The problem of selecting a diverse, representative set of posts in the blogosphere was considered by El-Arini *et al* [7]. Their approach is similar to ours in that they model the task of selecting a representative set as a covering problem. However, one key difference with our problem is that the entire set of blog posts is available to the algorithm before it makes any selection, i.e. their problem is offline. In addition, they consider a linear objective function, which is submodular unlike our objective function of minimum coverage. We also refer the reader to the references of these papers for further work in any specific context.

Significant algorithmic research has previously focused on *resource allocation* problems, where the goal is to allocate a set of resources in a manner that maximizes rewards. Our algorithm also falls in this broad framework, where we have B resources in the form of the items that we can opt to select, and the reward for a set of selected items is given by the minimum coverage on any feature. However, while we have a single-dimensional budget and multi-dimensional profit, recent work on this problem (see [4] and references therein) has largely focused on the scenario where the profit function is single-dimensional but the budgets are multi-dimensional. Another related set of resource allocation problems that have a multi-dimensional profit function are the *Santa Claus problems* (see [2] and subsequent work), where the goal is to allocate a set of items among a set of agents so as to maximize the reward of the least satisfied agent. However, this problem typically differs from our problem in two ways: first, each item can be allocated to only one agent and therefore earns rewards in only one dimension; and second, this problem is typically considered in the offline setting where all the items and their valuations by the agents are known to the algorithm.

7. DISCUSSIONS

In this paper, we considered the problem of selecting a diverse and representative subset from a large corpus of items. We modeled each item as being decorated by a set of features, and the goal was to ensure that the selected subset of items achieved large coverage on all features. We discussed various problem formulations representing this goal, and studied both the online and offline versions of the problem. Our key technical contribution was an easily implementable and scalable online algorithm for this problem. We analyzed this algorithm using theoretical techniques and showed that it achieves an approximation ratio of (roughly) 50%. We also performed wide-scale experiments on a variety of real-world and synthetically generated data sets and concluded that the algorithm performs even better than its theoretical guarantees in practice, and also confirmed that it outperforms several natural and intuitive algorithms for this problem by a wide margin.

In fact, our algorithm adapts well to several real-world complications. For example, consider a data set that has *outliers*, i.e. some features that are very sparse. Our experimental results on the sorted coverage values show that in such cases, not only is the algorithm able to obtain near-optimal minimum coverage, but also does well on all features that have low coverage. This is crucial in situations where we do not want to maximize minimum coverage only, but also want to ensure that the algorithm performs well with respect to more relaxed notions of diversity, e.g. the coverage on the bottom 10% of features. This was in fact the case with our real data set, and here the diversifier algorithm performed particularly well. The algorithm is also extremely efficient and at each online stage, it only needs time proportional to the number of features to compute if a threshold is satisfied by the new arriving item; since it is very efficient, we do not plot graphs with running times, but the algorithm clearly scales to extremely large data sets as shown in our experiments.

In real-world applications, it is often the case that all items are not of identical *quality*, and while we wish to select a set of items that are diverse in terms of their feature coverage, we would also like to ensure that that these selected items have high overall quality. In such situations, we may interpret the quality of items as an additional feature on which we also want to meet a given quality target. Alternatively, we may opt to set a quality threshold on items and not select any item that does not meet this threshold irrespective of the coverage it achieves on the set of features. Other applications may have more complicated quality requirements, and an interesting direction of future research is to investigate the impact of item quality on the diversification problem.

In some other situations, items cover their constituent features to different degrees that may be represented by *coverage weights* (typically in the range $[0, 1]$). It can be shown that the same approximation guarantees hold from a theoretical perspective for this more general situation by using a slightly modified algorithm (for simplicity we omit these details). Even from an experimental standpoint, since the algorithm does well on features that are sparsely populated, it is expected to handle data sets with weighted coverages without a significant degradation in performance. However, further experimental work in this direction is desirable.

Yet another possibility is that features not only have a target coverage that we would like to achieve, but also an upper limit on coverage. Such two-sided errors can be handled by pretending to duplicate each feature by adding a compliment with the corresponding complemented coverage target.

Finally, in certain situations, the coverage function on a feature may not be additive, i.e. the overall coverage obtained by a set of items on a feature may be different from the sum of their individual coverage weights for the feature. An open problem is to design algorithms that are capable of handling such general coverage functions.

Acknowledgement. We would like to thank Vahab S. Mirrokni for useful discussions in the early stages of this work. We are also grateful to the anonymous reviewers, whose comments helped to improve the presentation of this paper.

8. REFERENCES

[1] Rakesh Agrawal, Sreenivas Gollapudi, Alan Halverson, and Samuel Ieong. Diversifying search results. In *WSDM*, pages 5–14, 2009.

[2] Nikhil Bansal and Maxim Sviridenko. The Santa Claus problem. In *STOC*, pages 31–40, 2006.

[3] Jaime G. Carbonell and Jade Goldstein. The use of mmr, diversity-based reranking for reordering documents and producing summaries. In *SIGIR*, pages 335–336, 1998.

[4] Nikhil R. Devanur, Kamal Jain, Balasubramanian Sivan, and Christopher A. Wilkens. Near optimal online algorithms and fast approximation algorithms for resource allocation problems. In *ACM Conference on Electronic Commerce*, pages 29–38, 2011.

[5] Marina Drosou and Evaggelia Pitoura. Diversity over continuous data. *IEEE Data Eng. Bull.*, 32(4):49–56, 2009.

[6] Marina Drosou and Evaggelia Pitoura. Search result diversification. *SIGMOD Record*, 39(1):41–47, 2010.

[7] Khalid El-Arini, Gaurav Veda, Dafna Shahaf, and Carlos Guestrin. Turning down the noise in the blogosphere. In *KDD*, pages 289–298, 2009.

[8] Sreenivas Gollapudi and Aneesh Sharma. An axiomatic approach for result diversification. In *WWW*, pages 381–390, 2009.

[9] Sean M. McNee, John Riedl, and Joseph A. Konstan. Being accurate is not enough: how accuracy metrics have hurt recommender systems. In *CHI Extended Abstracts*, pages 1097–1101, 2006.

[10] R. Motwani and P. Raghavan. *Randomized Algorithms*. Cambridge University Press, 1997.

[11] Filip Radlinski, Paul N. Bennett, Ben Carterette, and Thorsten Joachims. Redundancy, diversity and interdependent document relevance. *SIGIR Forum*, 43(2):46–52, 2009.

[12] Rodrygo L. T. Santos, Craig Macdonald, and Iadh Ounis. Exploiting query reformulations for web search result diversification. In *WWW*, pages 881–890, 2010.

[13] Rodrygo L. T. Santos, Craig Macdonald, and Iadh Ounis. Selectively diversifying web search results. In *CIKM*, pages 1179–1188, 2010.

[14] Rodrygo L. T. Santos, Craig Macdonald, and Iadh Ounis. How diverse are web search results? In *SIGIR*, pages 1187–1188, 2011.

[15] Rodrygo L. T. Santos, Craig Macdonald, and Iadh Ounis. Intent-aware search result diversification. In *SIGIR*, pages 595–604, 2011.

[16] Aleksandrs Slivkins, Filip Radlinski, and Sreenivas Gollapudi. Learning optimally diverse rankings over large document collections. In *ICML*, pages 983–990, 2010.

[17] Erik Vee, Utkarsh Srivastava, Jayavel Shanmugasundaram, Prashant Bhat, and Sihem Amer-Yahia. Efficient computation of diverse query results. In *ICDE*, 2008.

[18] Cong Yu, Laks V. S. Lakshmanan, and Sihem Amer-Yahia. It takes variety to make a world: diversification in recommender systems. In *EDBT*, pages 368–378, 2009.

[19] Cong Yu, Laks V. S. Lakshmanan, and Sihem Amer-Yahia. Recommendation diversification using explanations. In *ICDE*, pages 1299–1302, 2009.

[20] ChengXiang Zhai and John D. Lafferty. A risk minimization framework for information retrieval. *Inf. Process. Manage.*, 42(1):31–55, 2006.

[21] Cai-Nicolas Ziegler, Sean M. McNee, Joseph A. Konstan, and Georg Lausen. Improving recommendation lists through topic diversification. In *WWW*, pages 22–32, 2005.

Overlapping Clusters for Distributed Computation

Reid Andersen
Microsoft Corporation
Redmond, WA
reidan@microsoft.com

David F. Gleich
Purdue University
West Lafayette, IN
dgleich@purdue.edu

Vahab Mirrokni
Google Research
New York, NY
mirrokni@google.com

ABSTRACT

Most graph decomposition procedures seek to partition a graph into disjoint sets of vertices. Motivated by applications of clustering in distributed computation, we describe a graph decomposition algorithm for the paradigm where the partitions intersect. This algorithm covers the vertex set with a collection of overlapping clusters. Each vertex in the graph is well-contained within some cluster in the collection. We then describe a framework for distributed computation across a collection of overlapping clusters and describe how this framework can be used in various algorithms based on the graph diffusion process. In particular, we focus on two illustrative examples: (i) the simulation of a randomly walking particle and (ii) the solution of a linear system, e.g. PageRank. Our simulation results for these two cases show a significant reduction in swapping between clusters in a random walk, a significant decrease in communication volume during a linear system solve in a geometric mesh, and some ability to reduce the communication volume during a linear system solve in an information network.

Categories and Subject Descriptors

G.2.2 [**Discrete Mathematics**]: Graph Theory—*network problems*; H.3.3 [**Information Systems**]: Information Search and Retrieval—*clustering*

General Terms

Algorithms, Performance, Theory

Keywords

conductance, diffusion, PageRank, leave-time, covering

Permission to make digital or hard copies of all or part of this work for personal or classroom use is granted without fee provided that copies are not made or distributed for profit or commercial advantage and that copies bear this notice and the full citation on the first page. To copy otherwise, to republish, to post on servers or to redistribute to lists, requires prior specific permission and/or a fee.
WSDM'12, February 8–12, 2012, Seattle, Washington, USA.
Copyright 2012 ACM 978-1-4503-0747-5/12/02 ...$10.00.

1. INTRODUCTION

Graph partitioning is a broad term for processes that take a graph and break it into pieces. These processes are applied throughout scientific computation because they model the conundrum of distributed computations, namely, how to balance local work and communication. In a typical application, a graph serves as a surrogate for the computational domain [14]. Each vertex denotes a piece of information and each edge denotes dependencies between information. Usually, the goal is a partition of the vertices where no piece is too large, and the number of edges crossing between partitions is small. Such a partition implies that most of the work is within a piece and only minimal work takes place between pieces. Thus, a good partitioning minimizes the amount of communication during a distributed computation.

But why partition the *vertices*? Alternatives such as hypergraph partitioning or partitioning the edges often show better results [38, 18, 9]. These models minimize the total number of communication messages and their volume by constructing a hyper-graph to model the actual computation structure more accurately. A concern with such methods is that they make distributed computations more difficult to implement.

We tackle the problem from a different angle. In light of the plethora of local resources available on modern computers and the paucity of communication bandwidth and latency [17], we ask why *partition* at all? Partitioning minimizes the total amount of storage under the constraint of minimizing communication volume. In this paper, we want to design scalable algorithms that address communication problems using a set of *overlapping clusters*, or vertex partitions that intersect. With overlapping clusters, we store more of the graph than required. The framework then affords the ease of implementation of vertex partitioning, and by removing the minimum storage constraint, our hope is that this technique allows us to reduce communication in a distributed computation. As we shall see in the results section, such an idea is a simple means to improve a distributed computation. For a standard test problem – computing the PageRank vector – we observe a drastic reduction in communication volume for geometric graphs and a modest reduction in communication volume for some information networks.

Our main application for this procedure is a distributed diffusive process on a graph. This differs from the goal of much of the overlapping clustering work in the statistical physics communities (see ref. [15] for a survey). There, the goal is to use the clusters to extract information from the network. Many of the methods employed are also rather expensive for a large graph, for example, building overlapping clusters by finding large cliques. As mentioned above, we use a particularly well known diffusion process as our test problem: the PageRank random surfer [32]. Diffuse processes such as PageRank often become linear systems, and our overlapping clustering computation framework also applies to solving a linear system. This lets us compute Katz indices [22], hitting times, commute times, and semi-supervised learning on graphs [40]. We discuss linear systems further in Sections 3 and 6 Our goal is to have a single set of overlapping clusters that will make all of these diffusive graph processes fast, not just PageRank. Thus, much of this paper is spent analyzing random walks on overlapping clusters. This metric is indicative of the performance of any diffusive process. Random walks are, themselves, a key enabling routine for many approximate graph computations (e.g. nearest tree [11] and *MaxCut* [19]) and distributed graph computations (e.g. random spanning tree [34]).

In the remainder of the paper, we explore overlapping clusters. We first review existing work on overlapping clustering in matrix computations and graph computations (Section 3). Next we formally define overlapping covers and specify how we use them in distributed computation of a random walk (Section 4). For a concrete example, we study a random walk process on a cycle graph. For this graph, we prove that overlapping clusters need fewer communication steps than do partitions (Theorem 1). This proof uses an optimal set of overlapping clusters for the graph. In the remainder of the paper, we provide a scheme to find a good set of overlapping clusters for the purpose of distributed computation (Section 5). Our algorithm combines several primitive operations: (i) determining a good set of clusters, (ii) computing a containment score for these clusters to find good vertices, (iii) covering the graph with highly contained vertices, and (iv) combining clusters to optimize performance. These steps involve a few interesting sub-algorithms. For example, we use a personalized PageRank clustering algorithm [3] to determine a good set of clusters in a local graph computation framework. Also, we use an approximate set covering algorithm to cover the vertices with a small set of clusters.

With a computational algorithm in hand, we investigate its performance in the final section. These experiments evaluate the clusters from our algorithm in terms of total storage and communication. We compare against the METIS graph partitioner [21] and the GRACLUS graph partitioner [13]. To evaluate the clusters in a computational setting, we simulate random walks and measure the number of times these walks switch between clusters. We use this as a proxy for the performance of a diffusion process on a graph. Again, we compare against METIS and GRACLUS. These comparisons show that our procedure reduces the probability of swapping between clusters by a factor of between 1.15 to 100.

Let us explicitly note that this paper is intended as a proof of concept demonstration that overlap can help. We do *not* evaluate our procedures in a true distributed environment. Instead, we simulate what communication would have occurred in such an environment. Because of this nature and that many of our results appear to depend strongly on the individual properties of the graph, we make our codes and experiments available for others to use and reproduce: `http://www.cs.purdue.edu/homes/dgleich/codes/overlapping`

2. NOTATION

Throughout the paper, we are concerned with graphs. Thus, we adopt standard graph theoretic notation. A graph $G = (V, E)$ consists of its vertex set V and edge set E. We use $\deg(v)$ to denote the degree of a vertex. Sets are denoted with a capital letter. For a set of vertices S, then the *volume* of the set measures the degree of all vertices in the set:

$$\mathrm{Vol}(S) = \textstyle\sum_{v \in S} \deg(v).$$

Just like a physical volume quantifies space, the volume of a set of vertices is the amount of storage space they require. Another useful measure is the boundary of a set $\partial(S)$:

$$\partial(S) = \{(u, v) \in E : u \in S, v \in \bar{S}\}.$$

In this definition, we denote the complement of a set S by $\bar{S}$. The complement is respect to the set vertices for the entire graph, thus $\bar{S} = \{v \in V : v \notin S\}$. Finally, let $\mathrm{cut}(S, T) = |\{(u, v) \in E : u \in S, v \in T\}|$ be the generalization of the size of a boundary to the size of a particular boundary. Notice that these definitions are related by: $\deg(v) = \mathrm{Vol}(\{v\}) = |\partial(\{v\})| = \mathrm{cut}(\{v\}, V - \{v\})$. Also, $|\partial(S)| = \mathrm{cut}(S, \bar{S})$.

Our final definition is the conductance of a set:

$$\mathrm{Cond}(S) = \frac{|\partial S|}{\min\big(\mathrm{Vol}(S), \mathrm{Vol}(\bar{S})\big)}.$$

Conductance is a useful metric for graph partitioning because it is small when there are few edges leaving a big group of vertices and large elsewhere.

3. RELATED WORK

Our proposal for overlapping clusters is novel in its implementation, but not so in concept. As always seems to be the case with clustering algorithms, statisticians studied the problem of overlap in the 1970s [10]. These have also been studied for a long time in the field of domain decomposition. There, overlapping domains are used to solve a partial differential equation (PDE) using a Schwarz method. Given a domain that is decomposed into overlapping pieces, Schwarz methods solve the PDE by iterative solving the PDE on each piece and communicating between the domains via the overlapping boundary. Within the numerical linear algebra community, these ideas have been generalized to solve many linear systems $Ax = b$ in either an *additive* or *multiplicative* Schwarz method [37, 6, 28]. The difference between the methods is not important for this paper, but suffice it to say that our distributed PageRank technique discussed in Section 6 is equivalent to an additive method. These techniques have been applied to solving PageRank [7] and recently this community began studying techniques to generate overlap from an existing graph partition [16]. Yet another recent and related idea from numerical linear algebra is the notion of a communication avoiding algorithm, see, for example, ref. [31]. A communication avoiding algorithm substitutes local computation instead of communication. In ref. [31]., they design a matrix-power kernel to reduce the communication required for k consecutive sparse matrix-vector products. The matrix-power kernel will create overlap among the vertices managed by each processor. A key difference between our work and the two previous projects is that they start with a partitioning and add overlap; instead, we build a set of overlapping clusters and then add a mapping from vertices to clusters.

Others recognized the benefits of overlapping clusterings too. These have also been studied in social network analysis [30, 1], and inherent multi-assignment clustering [36]. In some settings, like discovering communities in social networks, the clusters are naturally overlapping and by restricting our attention to non-overlapping clustering, we may lose valuable information about the structure of communities in a social network. This fact have been formally observed in the context of social networks [30] and information networks [1].

Graph partitioning and finding sets with small conductance are important problems that have also been attacked theoretically. Several approximation algorithms exist for them [35, 4, 25, 2, 3]. One of the authors has recently studied the analogous problems with overlapping clusters and established both complexity results and new polylogarithmic approximation algorithms for these problems [23].

Many decentralized or distributed graph computations also use overlap among a partition. For example, ref. [33] proposes a PageRank algorithm for a peer-to-peer environment, and ref. [20] uses a specific type of overlap to compute minimum spanning trees in a MapReduce environment.

4. DISTRIBUTED COMPUTATION WITH OVERLAPPING CLUSTERS

In this section, we formally define an overlapping cover for a graph and specify how to use it in a distributed random walk. The number of swaps between clusters will be one of our distributed computation metrics. We then show the relationship between our overlapping clusters and partitioning. This will let us formally show an instance where overlapping clusters minimize swaps compared to a partitioning.

4.1 Overlapping covers

An overlapping cover $(\mathcal{C}, \tau)$ consists of a collection $\mathcal{C}$ of *clusters*, which are subsets of V, and a *mapping* $\tau : V \to \mathcal{C}$ that associates each vertex $v \in V$ with a single cluster $\tau(v) \in \mathcal{C}$. We require that the collection $\mathcal{C}$ cover the graph, and that each vertex v be contained in its associated cluster $\tau(v)$. For this reason, τ will define a partition of the vertices. As further explained below, the idea is that τ will give the *best* cluster for a given overlapped vertex.

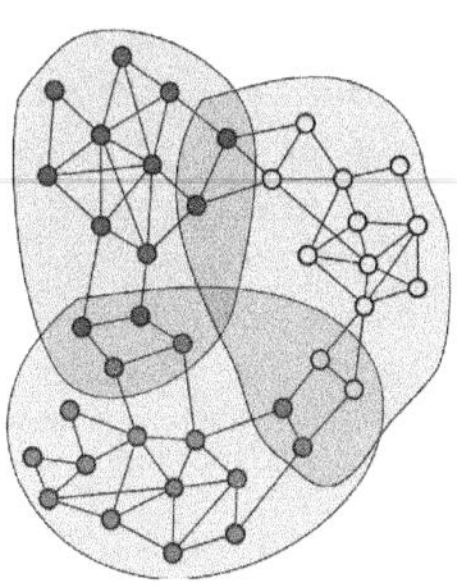

At left, we illustrate an overlapping cover with three clusters denoted by the red, blue, and gray regions. The function τ is given by the color of the vertices themselves, not the regions. For instance, the gray cluster contains two vertices from the whose associated cluster is the blue cluster; but the blue cluster contains no vertices whose associated cluster is the gray one. These two "blue" vertices are stored in both blue and gray clusters, providing an instance of overlap. In our model, the adjacency information for the graph G is distributed among the clusters in $\mathcal{C}$. Each cluster stores the adjacency list of its member vertices, but not the adjacency lists of other vertices in the graph. Thus, $\mathrm{Vol}(C)$ is a proxy for the space required to store the cluster C, since $\mathrm{Vol}(C)$ is the total size of the adjacency lists of vertices in C. We define $\mathrm{MaxVol}(\mathcal{C})$ to be the maximum volume of any cluster in $\mathcal{C}$, and define $\mathrm{TotalVol}(\mathcal{C})$ to be the sum of the volumes of all clusters in the collection. We will also commonly refer to the volume ratio of a collection: $\mathrm{TotalVol}(\mathcal{C})/\mathrm{Vol}(V)$.

4.2 A random walk in overlapping clusters

Given a maximum volume MaxVol as an upper bound for the volume of a graph on each machine, we need to divide a large graph into several clusters and store each cluster on one machine. The main drawback of this process is that any type of distributed computation or random walk incurs some communication cost or swapping probability among clusters. To model that cost, the random walk process is defined in the usual way. Given a starting vertex X_0, a sequence of vertices $X_0 \dots X_T$ is obtained by choosing X_{t+1} uniformly at random from the neighbors of X_t.

We can simulate the random walk process in G using a collection $(\mathcal{C}, \tau)$ of overlapping clusters. For each time step t let Y_t be the current vertex and C_t be the current active cluster. The current vertex Y_t is some vertex in V, and the current active cluster C_t is some cluster in $\mathcal{C}$ that contains Y_t. Initially, Y_0 is a specified starting vertex, and $C_0 = \tau(Y_0)$. To advance to the next time step, the active cluster C_t chooses the next vertex Y_{t+1} uniformly at random from the neighbors of Y_t. If the new vertex Y_{t+1} is contained in C_t, then the current cluster remains the active cluster. If the new vertex Y_{t+1} is not contained in C_t, then the cluster $\tau(Y_{t+1})$ becomes the active cluster. The sequence of active clusters $\{C_i\}$ is completely determined by the sequence of vertices $\{Y_i\}$,

$$C_{t+1} = \begin{cases} \tau(Y_{t+1}) & \text{if } Y_{t+1} \notin C_t, \\ C_t & \text{otherwise.} \end{cases}$$

Also, the state of the walk simulation at time t is completely described by the pair (Y_t, C_t).

4.3 The frequency of cluster swapping

Our goal is to minimize the number of times the active cluster C_t must be changed during the simulation of the walk. A good collection $\mathcal{C}$ will allow us to simulate a random walk without constantly switching between clusters.

We define $\mathrm{Swaps}(X_0, \dots, X_T)$ to be the number of times the active cluster C_t changes during the walk $X_0, \dots, X_T$. We also define $\rho(X_0, \dots, X_T) = \mathrm{Swaps}(X_0, \dots, X_T)/T$ to be the fraction of steps where the active cluster changes during the walk. For a given vertex v, we define

$$\rho_T(v) = E\left[(1/T)\,\mathrm{Swaps}(X_0, \dots, X_T) \mid X_0 = v\right]$$

to be the expected number of swaps in a walk starting from v. We also define

$$\rho_T = \frac{1}{n} \sum_{v \in V} \rho_T(v)$$

to be the average number swaps in a walk from a starting vertex chosen uniformly at random. Finally, we define ρ_∞ to be the limit of $\rho_T(G)$ as $T \to \infty$.

We can easily estimate these quantities by repeatedly simulating a random walk. However, we can also compute ρ_∞ exactly. To do so, define a directed graph $G(\mathcal{C}, \tau)$ that describes the transition between the pairs (Y_t, C_t). Presuming that a random walk on $G(\mathcal{C}, \tau)$ has a single ergodic class – which it will if the initial graph is connected and undirected – then let $\hat{\pi}$ be the stationary distribution. The swapping

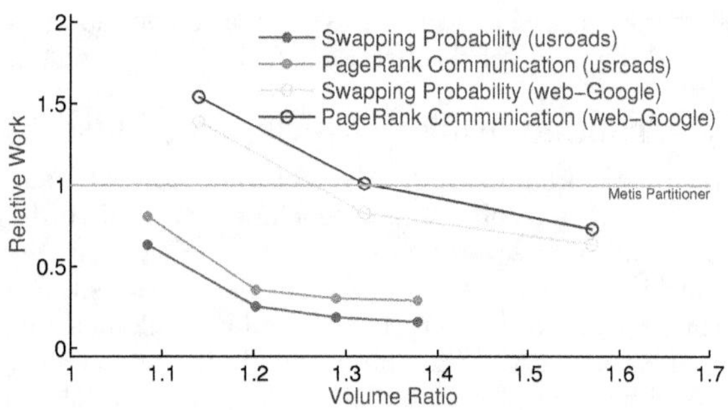

Figure 1: Overlap improves performance for the US road network and a WWW network; see §7.1.

probability ρ_∞ is then

$$\rho_\infty = \sum_C \sum_{u \in C} \hat{\pi}(u, C) \frac{\text{cut}(u, \bar{C})}{\deg(u)}.$$

4.4 Relationship with partitioning

Recall, the traditional way to find such clusters is to partition the graph into several non-overlapping parts. Based on a partitioning $\mathcal{P} = (P_1, \ldots, P_m)$, we can define an overlapping cover $(\mathcal{P}, \tau)$ where $\tau(v) = P_i$ if $v \in P_i$. In this case, the stationary distribution of $(\mathcal{P}, \tau)$ is the standard stationary distribution of a random walk on an undirected graph: $\hat{\pi}(u) = \deg(u)/\operatorname{Vol}(G)$. The swapping probability of $(\mathcal{P}, \tau)$ is then

$$\rho_\infty = \sum_{C \in \mathcal{P}} \sum_{u \in C} \hat{\pi}(u) \frac{\text{cut}(u, \bar{C})}{\deg(u)} = \frac{1}{\operatorname{Vol}(G)} \sum_{C \in \mathcal{P}} |\partial(C)|.$$

Therefore, the goal for partitioning is to minimize the the number of edges among clusters: $\sum_{C \in \mathcal{P}} |\partial(C)|$. The advantages of partitioning the graph are that it is simple and uses the minimal storage to store the whole graph, since each node in the original graph corresponds to only one node on exactly one machine. On the other hand, this advantage may result in large communication or swapping probability among clusters. Using overlapping covers may improve the communication cost and the switching cost of the clustering by a large factor. See Figure 1 for an example of this phenomenon. For the graph of the US road network and a web-graph, adding overlap improves the performance of a distributed PageRank computation and the swapping probability of a random walk considerably compared to a partition from the METIS partitioner. The vertical axis is the relative work compared to METIS, and the horizontal axis is the overlap expressed as a volume ratio. Of course, storing overlapping clusters take more space. It is not hard to see that there is a trade-off between the total volume of the clusters TotalVol, and the swapping probability ρ_∞. Next, we show that for cycle graphs, storing overlapping clusters with TotalVol $= 2\operatorname{Vol}(G)$ improves the cost function ρ_∞ significantly.

4.5 A clear win for overlap

THEOREM 1. *Consider a large cycle C_n of $n = M\ell$ nodes for a large number $M > 0$, and let the maximum volume of a cluster* MaxVol *be ℓ. Let P be the optimal partitioning of G to non-overlapping clusters of size at most* MaxVol *and ρ^*_∞ be the swapping probability of P. There exists an overlapping cover with* TotalVol *of* 2Vol(G) *whose swapping probability ρ'_∞ is less than $\frac{\rho^*_\infty}{\Omega(\text{MaxVol})}$.*

PROOF. In a cycle of size n, any cluster of size at most ℓ nodes has a cut size of at least 2. We know that partition $\mathcal{P}$ is at least M clusters. Thus, the size of the cut $\partial(\mathcal{P})$ is at least $2M$. Therefore, the optimal partition $\mathcal{P}$ is to divide the cycle into M paths of consecutive nodes each of which have ℓ nodes, Thus, the swapping probability $\rho^*_\infty = \frac{\partial(\mathcal{P})}{\operatorname{Vol}(C_n)} = \frac{2M}{n} = \frac{2}{\ell}$.

We now illustrate an overlapping cover $(\mathcal{C}, \tau)$ of TotalVol $= 2\operatorname{Vol}(G)$ with swapping probability $\rho_\infty \leq \frac{4}{\ell^2}$: $\mathcal{C}$ has $2M$ clusters $(C_1, \ldots, C_M, C'_1, \ldots, C'_M)$, where $C_i = \{v | i\ell - \ell + 1 \leq v \leq i\ell\}$ for $1 \leq i \leq M$, and $C'_i = \{v | i\ell - \frac{\ell}{2} + 1 \leq v \leq i\ell + \frac{\ell}{2}\}$ for $1 \leq i \leq M-1$, and $C'_M = \{v | 1 \leq v \leq \frac{\ell}{2}\} \cup \{v | M\ell - \frac{\ell}{2} \leq v \leq M\ell\}$. Let *centers* of clusters C_i and C'_i be the two middle nodes of each cluster, e.g., centers of C_i are $i\ell - \frac{\ell}{2}$ and $i\ell - \frac{\ell}{2} + 1$. center of a cluster C is denoted by center(C). For any node $v \in V(G)$, let $\tau(v)$ the cluster whose center is the closest center to v. In particular, $\tau(\text{center}(C)) = C$.

Consider a long enough random walk W. Note that centers of C_i are borders of C'_{i-1} and C'_{i+1}. In particular, on walk W whenever we swap to a new cluster, we go to the center of another cluster. As a result, the expected number of steps between two swaps on walk W is the expected time that a random walk starting at the center of a cluster leaving that cluster. Consider cluster C_1, and let a_i be the expected number of steps before a uniform random walk leaves cluster C_1 starting from node i. Also let $a_0 = a_{\ell+1} = 0$. Since the random walk is uniform, we know that for $1 \leq i \leq \ell$, $a_i = 1 + \frac{1}{2}(a_{i+1} + a_{i-1})$. Solving this recurrence relation, we get $a_i = i(\ell - i)$. Thus, $a_{\text{center}(C_1)} = \frac{\ell(\ell+2)}{4}$. As a result, starting from any cluster in $\mathcal{C}$, the expected time to leave the cluster and swap to another cluster is $\frac{\ell(\ell+2)}{4}$. As discussed before, after swapping to a new cluster, we start from the center of another cluster. Therefore, in average, after $\frac{\ell(\ell+2)}{4}$ steps of the random walk, a swapping occur. Thus, the swapping probability $\rho'_\infty = \frac{4}{\Omega(\ell^2)}$. □

4.6 Hardness of optimality

Before stating the heuristic algorithms to identify the clusters, let us remark that the corresponding optimization problems are NP-hard *and*, most likely, hard to approximate as well. To be formal, consider the following optimization problem: *Given a graph $G(V, E)$, an upper bound for the volume each cluster ℓ, and an upper bound on total volume of T. Find an overlapping cover of G with clusters of volume at most ℓ and total volume of at most T with the minimum swapping probability ρ_∞.* This problem is NP-hard and we sketch a proof of this hardness result.

To do so, we use a hardness result for the minimum bisection problem. *Given a graph, the goal of the minimize bisection problem is to find a minimize size edge set whose deletion splits the graph into two parts with an (almost)-equal number of nodes.* Consider our problem with $\ell = \operatorname{Vol}(G)/2$ and $T = \operatorname{Vol}(G)$, i.e., the total volume of clusters in the overlapping cluster is the same as the volume of G. In this special case, the goal is really to partition the graph into two equal volume clusters and our solution will minimize the edge set between these clusters – thus in the minimize bisection problem. Hence, the hardness of the minimum bisection problem translates to our problem as well [8]. Other than the NP-hardness, we think that combining inapproximability results for minimum bisection [5, 24] shows the hardness of approximation of our problem. We leave a formal proof of this to the longer version of this manuscript, and proceed to develop a multi-stage scalable heuristic clustering algorithm for the purpose of efficient distributed computation

5. FINDING OVERLAPPING CLUSTERS

In this section, we give an overview of the algorithm for computing the overlapping cover. Given a graph and an upper bound of MaxVol for the volume of the graph stored on each machine, we need find such an overlapping cover that results in a small ρ_∞. The algorithm has 4 main parts:

Identify candidate clusters In the first stage, we want to find clusters with maximum volume MaxVol and small conductance. The idea is to produce a bag of *good* clusters that we'll wheedle down and combine.

Compute well-contained sets For each cluster, we compute a containment score for each vertex. The vertices with highest containment are assigned as *cores* of the cluster. A random walk from a core vertex should take a while to leave the cluster.

Cover with cluster cores We now find a subset of the candidates based on three measures: (i) the total volume should not be too large; (ii) the sum of the cut sizes should be small; and (iii) for each node v, we should pick a cluster C such that v is in the core of C. This is a set-cover problem.

Combine clusters Finally, we combine any small clusters until the final size of each is about MaxVol.

5.1 Candidate clusters

As previously mentioned, we desire a large set of clusters with "high" containment. This implies that we want a small cutsize. We use two procedures to generate candidate clusters. The first is a local clustering algorithm based on personalized PageRank [3]. The second is repeatedly running the METIS algorithm with randomization enabled.

In the first, we compute personalized PageRank vectors with a local algorithm (one that does not access the entire graph) and then generate clusters by sweeping through the ordering induced by the personalized PageRank vector rescaled by inverse degree. In the sweep, we pick the cluster with minimum conductance less than MaxVol. A parameter ε controls the accuracy of the PageRank vector and affects the final size of the cluster. We proceed through all vertices of the graph and compute a PageRank vector from each vertex with a random value of ε chosen to give a cluster with volume between 10 and MaxVol. We will skip looking for a cluster at vertex if that vertex is already in k clusters. This helps keep the work down. The value of α controls the size of the clusters, and $\alpha = 0.99$ produces clusters of a reasonable size. (In this case, α is the link-following probability. This is different from the convention in [3].)

In the second, we repeatedly run METIS with different random seeds and different partition sizes to generate a range of partitions. Each partition is considered a cluster, and thus running this procedure at least twice yields a set of overlapping clusters.

5.2 Core vertices

Given a cluster C, we want to find the vertices that are the most central in C in the sense that a random walk takes a long time to exit the cluster when started from those vertices. We quantify this with the expected leave time for a random walk in a cluster. This derivation is just an application of first-transition analysis in the random walk to the non-cluster vertices. Let $X_0, \dots$ be the random walk. Also let $u(v) = E[\min(T) \mid X_0 = v, \dots, X_T \notin C]$ be the expected exit time from the cluster. Trivially, $u(v) = 0$ if $v \notin C$. Applying the memory-less hypothesis and note about $v \notin C$, we have

$$u(v) = 1 + \sum_{(v,r)\in E} \frac{u(r)}{\deg(v)} = 1 + \sum_{\substack{(v,r)\in E\\ r\in C}} \frac{u(r)}{\deg(v)}.$$

Now let $\mathbf{u}$ be a vector of these leavetimes for each vertex in C and let B be the random walk transition matrix restricted to vertices in C. This second equation states $\mathbf{u} = \mathbf{e} + B\mathbf{u}$ where $\mathbf{e}$ is a vector of all ones. Assuming that there is at least one vertex not in C, then this equation is a non-singular linear system. We can quickly approximate its solution using the Neumann series:

$$\mathbf{u} \approx \mathbf{u}_k = B\mathbf{u}_k + \mathbf{e} = \textstyle\sum_{j=0}^{k} B^j\mathbf{e} \qquad \mathbf{u}_0 = \mathbf{e}.$$

This formulation has the attractive property that $\mathbf{u}_k$ is related to the expected leavetime in walks of length at most k. Thus, we can quickly compute expected leavetimes in time $k\,\mathrm{Vol}(C)$, where k is a large but finite random walk time. We use $k = 150$ and additionally modify B to be a PageRank Markov chain with $\alpha = 0.99$. This latter modification changes the answer only slightly, but avoids a few convergence problems when the random walks are slow to exit the cluster. Let $\mathsf{leavetime}(C, v) = u(v)$ which we treat as our containment score. Vertices in a cluster with high leavetime are considered core vertices, which we describe further next.

5.3 Covering the graph

Consider a set of clusters $\mathcal{B} = (C_1, C_2, \dots, C_m)$. For any cluster C, let $\mathsf{Core}(C)$ be the well-contained set of vertices in C. (These nodes should have long leavetimes.) From $\mathcal{B}$, our goal is to find a minimum cost overlapping cover $(\mathcal{C}, \tau)$ such that for each node $v \in V(G)$, there exists a cluster $C \in \mathcal{C}$ whose core include v, i.e., $v \in V(C)$. Also, it is required that for each node v, $v \in \mathsf{Core}(\tau(v))$. Two parameters are important in determining the cost of the overlapping cover. One parameter is $\mathrm{TotalVol}(\mathcal{C})$, and the other parameter is the total number of edges outgoing from clusters in $\mathcal{C}$. As a heuristic solution, we can formalize this problem as a set cover problem as follows. Each cluster C has some cost $\mathsf{Cost}(C) = \mathrm{Vol}(C) + \gamma|\partial(C)|$, where γ is an appropriate scaling factor. We find it isn't particularly sensitive to this choice and use γ of 0.2.

To find a minimum-cost overlapping cover, we need to find a set of clusters that cover all the nodes of the network. This can be formalized as a set cover problem. In an instance of the set cover problem, we are given a family of sets $S_1, \dots, S_m$ of a ground set V, each with a cost $c(S_i)$, we need to pick a minimum-cost subfamily of S_i's that cover all elements of V. Given a set of clusters $\mathcal{B}$, we construct a set cover instance as follows: we set S_i in the set cover problem to be $\mathsf{Core}(C_i)$, and the cost $c(S_i)$ to be $\mathsf{Cost}(C)$ as defined above.

The set cover problem is NP-hard, and not approximable better than a factor of $\Omega(\log n)$. Nevertheless, the following simple greedy algorithm gives an $O(\log n)$-approximation algorithm for this problem. It also assigns core vertices in the final step.

1. Let $\mathcal{C} = \emptyset$, and $T = V(G)$.
2. While some nodes of $V(G)$ are uncovered,
   (a) Find a cluster $C \notin \mathcal{B}\backslash\mathcal{C}$ that maximizes $\frac{|\mathsf{Core}(C)\cap T|}{\mathsf{Cost}(C)}$.
   (b) Add C to $\mathcal{C}$, and let $T = T\backslash\mathsf{Core}(C)$.
3. For all nodes v,
   (a) Find a cluster $C' \in \mathcal{C}$ such that $v \in C'$, and $\mathsf{leavetime}(v, C')$ is maximized,
   (b) Set $\tau(v) = C'$.

5.4 Combining the Clusters

We take into account the maximum allowed volume of the cluster MaxVol while computing the candidate clusters, but we did not use the parameter MaxVol while selecting the final set of clusters C using the set cover greedy algorithm. In this section, we show that we can combine the clusters resulting from the set cover algorithm, and only improve the the total volume, the total cost, and the parameter ρ_∞. Then, we give a heuristic to combine a set of clusters given a maximum volume constraint on each combined cluster.

In order to prove that various cost functions only improve by combining the clusters, we need to prove that these cost functions are subadditive. A function f is subadditive if for any two cluster $A, B \subset V(G)$, $f(A \cup B) \leq f(A) + f(B)$. We first observe this for Vol and ∂ cost functions.

REMARK 1. *For any two clusters C_1 and C_2:*

1. $\mathrm{Vol}(C_1 \cup C_2) \leq \mathrm{Vol}(C_1) + \mathrm{Vol}(C_2)$,

2. $\partial(C_1 \cup C_2) \leq \partial(C_1) + \partial(C_2)$,

The above remark implies that after combining any set of clusters, the cost function Vol, function ∂, and as a result function Cost will not increase. Now, we show that combining clusters only improve the cost function ρ_∞. Consider an overlapping cover $(\mathcal{C}, \tau)$, and two cluster $C_1, C_2 \in \mathcal{C}$. Let $\mathcal{C}' = \mathcal{C}\backslash\{C_1, C_2\} \cup \{C_1 \cup C_2\}$, i.e, $\mathcal{C}'$ is $\mathcal{C}$ after removing clusters C_1 and C_2 and adding the cluster $C_1 \cup C_2$. Also, construct the mapping τ' as follows: if $\tau(v)$ is C_1 or C_2, then $\tau(v) = C_1 \cup C_2$; otherwise, $\tau'(v) = \tau(v)$. While performing a (random) walk W on the overlapping cover $(\mathcal{C}', \tau')$, we know that whenever we switch from $C_1 \cup C_2$, the same change has to happen in the overlapping cover $(\mathcal{C}, \tau)$. This fact proves that cost function ρ_∞ is not larger for $(\mathcal{C}', \tau')$ compared to $(\mathcal{C}, \tau)$.

The above discussion shows that combining the cluster can only decrease all cost functions that we have considered so far. Here, we give a heuristic for combining the clusters that attempts to maximize such decrease in the cost. The algorithm reads an overlapping cluster $(\mathcal{C}, \tau)$, and a parameter MaxVol and runs the following algorithm:

1. Let $\mathcal{C}' = \emptyset$, $\mathcal{B} = \mathcal{C}$, and $T = \emptyset$.
2. While $\mathcal{B}$ is nonempty
   (a) Find $C \in \mathcal{B}$ that minimizes $\mathrm{Vol}(C \cap T)$.
   (b) Let $C' = C$, $\mathcal{B} = \mathcal{B} - \{C\}$, $T = T \cup C$.
   (c) While $\mathcal{B}$ is nonempty
      i. Find $C \in \mathcal{B}$ with $\mathrm{Vol}(C \cup C') \leq$ MaxVol and maximum $\mathrm{Vol}(C \cap C')/\mathrm{Vol}(C)$.
      ii. Break if no such C exists, otherwise let $C' = C' \cup C$, $\mathcal{B} = \mathcal{B} - \{C\}$, $T = T \cup C$.
   (d) Add cluster C' to $\mathcal{C}'$ and update τ to C' for all agglomerated clusters.

6. SOLVING LINEAR SYSTEMS WITH OVERLAPPING CLUSTERS

We now describe how to solve a certain class of linear systems using overlapping clusters. The convergence analysis of this algorithm places some restriction on where it may be applied, but these are not too restrictive. Many linear systems, including the PageRank linear system [32] and the linear system for Katz scores [22], satisfy these restrictions. Note that this algorithm for PageRank is not new. McSherry discussed its essence in ref. [29].

We first describe the algorithm in general, and then discuss how it applies to the PageRank linear system. Consider a linear system $A\mathbf{x} = \mathbf{b}$. Each row and column of A corresponds to a vertex in our graph. For each cluster, assign that cluster to a processor. The processor holds the columns of the linear system associated with the vertices in its cluster. For a cluster/processor, we allocate a solution vector $\mathbf{x}_C$ and a residual vector $\mathbf{r}_C$. These vectors store information about the solution and residual for all vertices in the cluster. If it helps, think about them as sparse vectors defined only on the vertices of the cluster. Our goal is to compute a sequence of $\mathbf{x}_C^{(k)}$ and $\mathbf{r}_C^{(k)}$ on each processor such that

$$\mathbf{x} \approx \sum_C \mathbf{x}_C^{(k)} \qquad \mathbf{r} \approx \sum_C \mathbf{r}_C^{(k)}$$

where $A\mathbf{x} \approx \mathbf{b}$ and $\mathbf{b} - A\mathbf{x} = \mathbf{r}$ is small. On each processor, we only store a non-zero value in the vector $\mathbf{x}_C$ for the vertices in the cluster, however, we store a non-zero value the vector $\mathbf{r}_C$ for the vertices in the cluster *and* the vertices on the boundary of the cluster. We call the latter $\mathbf{f}_C$ when we refer only to these vertices. Let A_C be the local matrix among vertices in C and let B_C be the matrix from vertices in C to the boundary. In each iteration, we compute

$$\mathbf{x}_C^{(k+1)} = \mathbf{x}_C^{(k)} + A_C^{-1}\mathbf{r}_C(k).$$

This is, we locally solve the linear system. This has the effect of making $\mathbf{r}_C^{(k+1)} = 0$ for all vertices in the cluster. However, we then must update the residual for all boundary vertices. Recall that we use $\mathbf{f}_C$ to denote the "foreign" residual: $\mathbf{f}_C = B_C A_C^{-1}\mathbf{r}_C^{(k)}$. After performing this update, we communicate $\mathbf{f}_C(v)$ to the processor with $\tau(v)$. The remote processor, say C', adds this element into $\mathbf{r}_{C'}^{(k+1)}$. The local processor subsequently sets $\mathbf{f}_C(v) = 0$. Thus, at the end of an iteration $\mathbf{f}_C = 0$ (all the foreign residual was communicated elsewhere), and $\mathbf{r}_C^{(k+1)}$ is only non-zero where other processors communicated their values to C. Take note that *all communication occurs via residuals.* This property is a hallmark of additive Schwarz methods, which locally solve for the residual. Consequently, this algorithm *is* an additive Schwarz method. Also note that $\mathbf{b}$ does not appear in the above iteration. Each solution vector $\mathbf{x}_C$ is set to 0 initially, and thus $\mathbf{r}_C(v)$ is initially set to $\mathbf{b}(v)$ when $\tau(v) = C$. Put another way, the residual is assigned to the "core" vertices. The relationship with the additive Schwarz method lets us conclude that this approach will converge for linear systems with M-matrices and symmetric positive definite systems [37].

When we apply this algorithm, we do not always communicate the foreign residual as described above. Instead, we only communicate elements of the foreign residual if they exceed a solution dependent tolerance. This further reduces communication. *The final communication volume metric is the number of foreign residual elements communicated during the course of the linear system solve.*

PageRank as a linear system is $(I - \alpha P^T)\mathbf{x} = \mathbf{e}$, where P is the random walk normalization of an adjacency matrix and α is the link-following probability in PageRank. This "A" is an M-matrix and thus the above procedure will converge – although PageRank admits a much simpler convergence analysis, which we omit due to space. For PageRank, we solve each local system using the PageRank push algorithm proposed by McSherry [29], using a queue as described by Andersen et al. [3]. This algorithm updates the foreign residuals along with the local residuals. At each iteration, it "pushes" the residual rank to the boundary of the cluster, updating the solution $\mathbf{x}_C$ within the current cluster. After completing all of these push operations, it communicates the residuals to the core vertices as above.

There is no closed form solution for the PageRank vector of an undirected graph, although it is usually nearby the standard normalized degree stationary distribution. Nonetheless, using this approach, it is actually possible to solve a PageRank system with *zero* communication. This occurs when the core vertices are sufficiently far from the boundary, so that the residual rank arriving at the boundary is negligible. In a real implementation, there would be a few small communication steps in aggregating the solution vector $\mathbf{x}$ and checking the residual $\mathbf{r}$; however, we do not model those communication steps in our PageRank communication metric. This result cannot occur in a partitioning because there no boundary around the cluster.

To summarize, when solving a problem with overlapping clusters, solve locally within each cluster and communicate the residual on the boundary to the core vertices identified by the map τ.

7. EXPERIMENTAL RESULTS

At this point, we provide experimental evidence for the ability of our heuristic technique to (i) reduce the swapping probability (Table 2) and (ii) reduce the communication in a distributed PageRank solve (Table 3). Before getting to that demonstration, we first discuss the datasets we utilize for our experiments.

7.1 Data Sets

The data we use to evaluate our techniques comes in two classes: geometric networks and information networks. (We include social networks within information networks.) Our technique is extremely effective at the geometric networks, whereas it is less effective at information networks. Thus, we focus more on the latter. All of our experimental data comes from the following public sources: the University of Florida Sparse Matrix collection [12], the Stanford SNAP collection [26], the Library of Congress subject headings (`lcsh` graph) [39], and the National Highway Planning Network (`usroads` graph – `http://www.fhwa.dot.gov/planning/nhpn/`). The `annulus` graph is a random triangulation of points in an large annulus. Please see Table 1 for information about the size of the networks. We removed the direction of any edges and only consider the largest connected component of the network.

7.2 Cluster performance

The first stage of our algorithm is to generate a set of clusters with small conductance using a local personalized PageRank algorithm [3]. This algorithm has well known properties and has been used in other experimental probes of graph clusters [27]. This algorithm has a few parameters we can control. Although our final goal may be to have clusters of the network with a MaxVol of 10% of the total graph volume, we often found it effective to find smaller clusters and combine these together. We investigate three regimes. The first, called *small*, seeks clusters up to MaxVol of 10000 with a small average volume. The second, called *med*, seeks clusters up to MaxVol of 10000 with a large average volume. The third, called *big*, seeks clusters up to MaxVol of 10% of the total graph volume with a average volume comparable to the medium set. The conductance of the sets generated by these algorithms is plotted in Figure 2 for the graph `lcsh`.

Table 1: All graphs are undirected and connected. Edges are counted twice and some graphs have self-loops. The first group are geometric networks and the second are information networks.

Graph	$\|V\|$	$\|E\|$	max deg	$\|E\|/\|V\|$
`onera`	85567	419201	5	4.9
`usroads`	126146	323900	7	2.6
`annulus`	500000	2999258	19	6.0
`email-Enron`	33696	361622	1383	10.7
`soc-Slashdot`	77360	1015667	2540	13.1
`dico`	111982	2750576	68191	24.6
`lcsh`	144791	394186	1025	2.7
`web-Google`	855802	8582704	6332	10.0
`as-skitter`	1694616	22188418	35455	13.1
`cit-Patents`	3764117	33023481	793	8.8

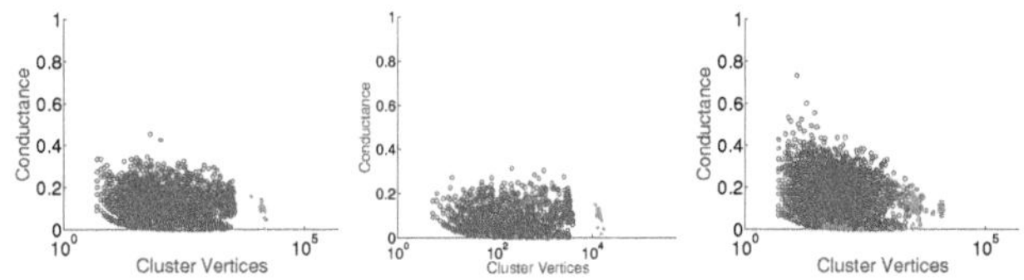

Figure 2: Cluster conductance for three different regimes on the graph lcsh. From left: small, medium, and big. The red dots are the results with the final set of combined clusters.

7.3 Combine performance

We now show that we can effectively combine clusters. See Figure 3 for relationships between the input to the cluster combination process and the output in three measures. This experiment summarizes the result of all the cluster combination experiments we performed on the information networks during the sweep experiment discussed in the next section. The first measure is the number of clusters. In this measure, the algorithm effectively combines up to 1,000,000 initial clusters down to a few hundred or thousand. The second measure is the volume ratio of the input clusters to the volume ratio of the output clusters. This ratio always decreases, though not always by a large margin. The final measure is the average conductance of the input clusters to the average conductance of the output clusters. Here, we find the average conductance *can* increase, although it most often decreases.

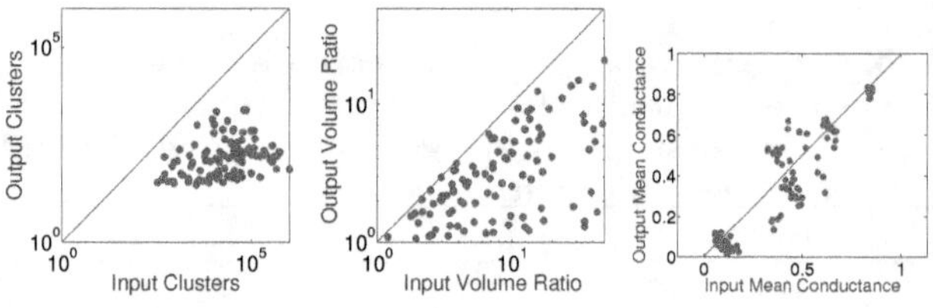

Figure 3: Cluster combinations. See §7.3 for details.

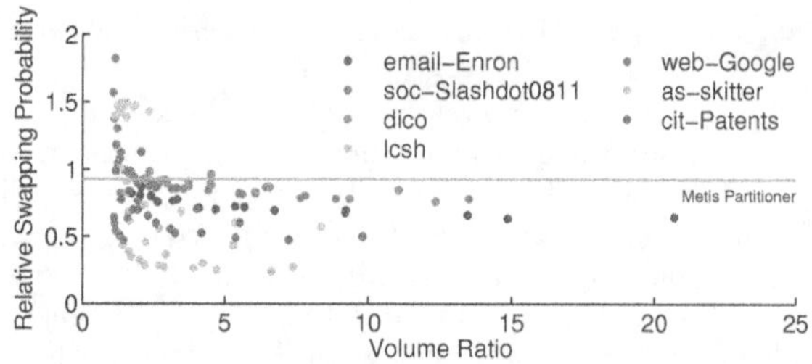

Figure 4: Swapping probability relative to METIS for all our overlapping experiments.

7.4 Distributed computation measures

At last we come to our experiment demonstrating the benefit of overlapping clusters. In this experiment, MaxVol is 10% of the edges in the graph. For each graph in Table 1, we then compute two partitions: one with METIS and one with GRACLUS. We asked for more than 10 partitions when the algorithms returned partitions exceeding MaxVol; and then combined small partitions using a heuristic based on the intersection in boundary vertices until all partitions were about size MaxVol.

Tables For the overlapping experiments, we ran our cluster identification algorithm in the *small*, *med*, and *big* regimes described in Section 7.2. We examined these cases with a target overlap T of 1, 2, 5, 10, and 30. Recall that the PageRank clustering algorithm looks for a cluster around a starting vertex. We sequentially iterate through all the vertices of the graph and start a cluster from that vertex if it is not already in T clusters. This setup has 15 different experiments for each graph. In the tables, we label each method by the combination of regime and overlap, i.e. "med.5" is the med regime with an overlap of 5. We also use METIS to generate overlapping clusters. We do so by running it 2, 4, or 10 times to generate the same number of partitions. Each run uses a different seed and a different number of partitions designed to produce clusters with volume of 1000 and 10000. This gives us the methods "metis.2", "metis.4", and "metis.10".

After generating the clusters, we combine them into a set of clusters with MaxVol up to 10% of the edges in the graph. Given the resulting partitions and overlapping clusterings, we estimate the swapping probability via sampling and measure the communication volume of solving PageRank on the overlapping clusters using the procedure from Section 6. The results for swapping probability are shown in Table 2. Each row of the table shows the swapping probability for the best partition result, along with the average conductance of the clusters in that partition. When the partitioning results from GRACLUS are superior to those of METIS, we show them in the table and denote them with a $*$. The next set of columns shows the best swapping probability from any of the overlapping clustering experiments. We also list the performance ratio (overlap / partition), volume ratio, average conductance, and method for the best overlap result as well. In Table 3 we see the same data, but for PageRank communication volume instead. The PageRank problem used $\alpha = 0.85$ and a relative tolerance of $1/n$ where n is the number of vertices in the graph.

Table 2: Swapping probability results. See §7.4, *Tables* paragraph for more information.

Graph	Swap. Prob. of Partition	Avg. Cond.	Swap. Prob. of Overlap	Perf. Ratio	Vol. Ratio	Avg. Cond.	Method
onera	7.6×10^{-4}	0.02	1×10^{-4}	0.129	2.82	0.03	Med.30
usroads	$1.3 \times 10^{-4}*$	<0.01	1×10^{-6}	0.008	1.49	0.01	Med.30
annulus	1×10^{-4}	<0.01	5×10^{-6}	0.049	1.17	<0.01	Med.10
email-Enron	0.02	0.39	0.013	0.650	14.86	0.47	Big.30
soc-Slashdot	0.03	0.66	0.026	0.867	13.52	0.65	Med.30
dico	0.04	0.82	0.03	0.750	12.35	0.82	Big.30
lcsh	0.003*	0.06	0.0007	0.233	6.63	0.12	Med.30
web-Google	$7.8 \times 10^{-4}*$	0.02	4.6×10^{-4}	0.592	1.43	0.02	Big.30
as-skitter	0.005	0.1	0.004	0.549	8.36	0.2	Big.30
cit-Patents	0.0064	0.13	0.0034	0.524	3.25	0.42	Small.10

Table 3: PageRank computation volume. See §7.4, *Tables* paragraph for more information.

Graph	Comm. of Partition	Avg. Cond.	Comm. of Overlap	Perf. Ratio	Vol. Ratio	Avg. Cond.	Method
onera	18654	0.02	48	0.003	2.82	0.03	Med.30
usroads	3256*	<0.01	0	0.000	1.49	0.01	Med.30
annulus	12074	<0.01	2	0.000	0.01	<0.01	Med.10
email-Enron	194536*	0.4	235316	1.210	1.7	0.46	Metis.2
soc-Slashdot	875435*	0.68	1.3×10^{6}	1.480	1.78	0.74	Metis.2
dico	$1.5 \times 10^{6}*$	0.79	2.0×10^{6}	1.320	1.53	0.84	Metis.2
lcsh	73000*	0.06	48777	0.668	2.17	0.08	Small.5
web-Google	201159*	0.02	167609	0.833	1.57	0.04	Metis.10
as-skitter	2.4×10^{6}	0.1	3.9×10^{6}	1.645	1.93	0.24	Metis.10
cit-Patents	8.7×10^{6}	0.13	7.3×10^{6}	0.845	1.34	0.16	Metis.4

The results for swapping probability show that our overlapping cluster method reduces it by a factor of 10 to 100 on geometric networks and 1-2 for information networks. The results for PageRank communication are perhaps more compelling for geometric networks. In all cases, we only needed a trivial amount of communication compared to the partitioning approach. (The zero result is not an error, see §6.) For information networks, they are much less compelling. We reduce the communication for three graphs: `lcsh`, `web-Google`, and `cit-Patents`. These graphs have the lowest average conductance scores among the information networks, suggesting a possible a priori performance estimate.

Finally, Figure 4 shows the reduction in swapping probability occurred in almost every experiment we performed with the overlapping clusters. The figure also shows that slightly smaller swapping probabilities may be obtained for significantly less total volume.

8. CONCLUSION AND FUTURE WORK

Minimizing communication in a distributed computation with an information network is a challenging problem. Here, we have tried to address the issue of whether careful use of *overlap* or redundancy of the distributed data can help reduce the communication. Towards that end, we proposed a computational framework with overlapping clusters. These overlapping groups of vertices are simple to use, and we propose a procedure to find a good set of them. The results on our large information networks are encouraging as preliminary support for the use of overlapping clusters. We are consistently able to reduce the swapping probability of a random walk in a network with only a moderate amount of overlap. Typically, this metric decreases almost monotonically with increasing overlap. For such applications: *overlap*, do not *divide*. In the future, we plan to investigate how caching small blocks of vertex information would compare against our centralized heuristic approach.

The results in our second metric – the communication volume of a distributed linear system solve – are more murky. Our heuristic algorithm to identify good overlapping clusters is able to find a good set in geometric meshes. In large information networks, using a set of overlapping partitions by repeatedly running METIS and using our cluster combination algorithm seems to perform better. In a few cases, these clusters actually reduce the communication. For the communication problem on an information network, there seems to be a tension between large overlap and total communication volume. We are most successful when we find a set of clusters that does not increase the total volume stored too much. Currently, our bag of clusters from the local PageRank algorithm does not appear to identify a good set for this task. We plan to study variations on this heuristic to identify better sets of clusters from the algorithm. Also, we plan to investigate some of the overlapping community detection algorithms from the statistical physics community.

Our goal is to highlight possible advantages of overlapping clustering over partitioning in the context of distributed computing. We believe that our evaluation of overlapping clustering for two related objective functions along with our preliminary theoretical analysis have shown the effectiveness of this idea. Evaluating these ideas in a true distributed setting is an interesting subject of future research.

9. REFERENCES

[1] Y.-Y. Ahn, J. P. Bagrow, and S. Lehmann. Link communities reveal multiscale complexity in networks. *Nature*, 466:761–764, 2009.

[2] R. Andersen. A local algorithm for finding dense subgraphs. In *SODA*, pages 1003–1009, 2008.

[3] R. Andersen, F. Chung, and K. Lang. Local graph partitioning using PageRank vectors. In *FOCS*, 2006.

[4] S. Arora, S. Rao, and U. V. Vazirani. Expander flows, geometric embeddings and graph partitioning. *J. ACM*, 56(2), 2009.

[5] P. Berman and M. Karpinski. Approximation hardness of bounded degree min-csp and min-bisection. In *Automata, Languages and Programming*, volume 2380 of *LNCS*, pages 782–782. Springer Berlin / Heidelberg, 2002.

[6] R. Bru, F. Pedroche, and D. B. Szyld. Additive Schwarz iterations for Markov chains. *SIAM J. Matrix Anal. Appl.*, 27(2):445–458, 2005.

[7] R. Bru, F. Pedroche, and D. B. Szyld. Cálculo del vector PageRank de Google mediante el método iterativo de Schwarz. In J. P. A. et al., editor, *Congreso de Métodos Numéricos en Ingeniería*, Granada, Spain, 2005. In Spanish.

[8] T. N. Bui and C. Jones. Finding good approximate vertex and edge partitions is NP-hard. *Inf. Process. Lett.*, 42(3):153–159, 1992.

[9] U. V. Çatalyürek and C. Aykanat. Hypergraph-partitioning-based decomposition for parallel sparse-matrix vector multiplication. *IEEE Trans. Parallel Distrib. Syst.*, 10(7):673–693, 1999.

[10] A. J. Cole and D. Wishart. An improved algorithm for the Jardine-Sibson method of generating overlapping clusters. *The Computer Journal*, 13(2):156–163, 1970.

[11] A. Czumaj, O. Goldreich, D. Ron, C. Seshadhri, A. Shapira, and C. Sohler. Finding cycles and trees in sublinear time. *arXiv*, cs.DM:1007.4230, 2010.

[12] T. A. Davis and Y. Hu. The University of Florida Sparse Matrix Collection. Submitted., 2010.

[13] I. S. Dhillon, Y. Guan, and B. Kulis. Weighted graph cuts without eigenvectors a multilevel approach. *IEEE Trans. Pattern Anal. Mach. Intell.*, 29(11):1944–1957, November 2007.

[14] J. Dongarra, I. Foster, G. Fox, W. Gropp, K. Kennedy, L. Torczon, and A. White. *The Sourcebook of Parallel Computing*. Morgan Kaufmann Publishers Inc., San Francisco, CA, USA, 2003.

[15] S. Fortunato. Community detection in graphs. *arXiv*, physics.soc-ph:0906.0612v2, 2010.

[16] D. Fritzsche, A. Frommer, and D. B. Szyld. Overlapping blocks by growing a partition with applications to preconditioning. Technical Report 10-07-26, Department of Mathematics, Temple University, October 2011.

[17] S. L. Graham, M. Snir, and C. A. Patterson, editors. *Getting up to Speed: The Future of Supercomputing*. National Academies Press, 2005.

[18] B. Hendrickson and T. G. Kolda. Graph partitioning models for parallel computing. *Parallel Comput.*, 26(12):1519–1534, November 2000.

[19] S. Kale and C. Seshadhri. Combinatorial approximation algorithms for maxcut using random walks. In *Innovations in Computer Science*, pages 367–388, 2011.

[20] H. Karloff, S. Suri, and S. Vassilvitskii. A model of computation for mapreduce. In *Proceedings of the Twenty-First Annual ACM-SIAM Symposium on Discrete Algorithms*, SODA '10, pages 938–948, Philadelphia, PA, USA, 2010. Society for Industrial and Applied Mathematics.

[21] G. Karypis and V. Kumar. A fast and high quality multilevel scheme for partitioning irregular graphs. *SIAM J. Sci. Comput.*, 20(1):359–392, 1998.

[22] L. Katz. A new status index derived from sociometric analysis. *Psychometrika*, 18(1):39–43, March 1953.

[23] R. Khandekar, G. Kortsarz, and V. Mirrokni. On the advantage of overlapping clusters for minimizing conductance. In *LATIN*, 2012.

[24] S. Khot. Ruling out ptas for graph min-bisection, densest subgraph and bipartite clique. In *FOCS*, pages 136–145, Washington, DC, USA, 2004. IEEE Computer Society.

[25] F. T. Leighton and S. Rao. Multicommodity max-flow min-cut theorems and their use in designing approximation algorithms. *J. ACM*, 46(6):787–832, 1999.

[26] J. Leskovec. The Stanford large network dataset collection. `http://snap.stanford.edu/data/index.html`, 2010.

[27] J. Leskovec, K. J. Lang, A. Dasgupta, and M. W. Mahoney. Statistical properties of community structure in large social and information networks. In *WWW*, pages 695–704, New York, NY, USA, 2008. ACM.

[28] A. A. Maleev. On the SOR method with overlapping subsystems. *Comp. Math. and Math. Phys.*, 46(6):919–929, June 2006.

[29] F. McSherry. A uniform approach to accelerated PageRank computation. In *WWW*, pages 575–582, 2005.

[30] N. Mishra, R. Schreiber, I. Stanton, and R. E. Tarjan. Clustering social networks. In *WAW2007*, pages 56–67, 2007.

[31] M. Mohiyuddin, M. Hoemmen, J. Demmel, and K. Yelick. Minimizing communication in sparse matrix solvers. In *SC09*, pages 1–12, New York, NY, USA, November 2009. ACM.

[32] L. Page, S. Brin, R. Motwani, and T. Winograd. The PageRank citation ranking: Bringing order to the web. Technical Report 1999-66, Stanford University, November 1999.

[33] J. X. Parreira, C. Castillo, D. Donato, S. Michel, and G. Weikum. The juxtaposed approximate PageRank method for robust PageRank approximation in a peer-to-peer web search network. *The VLDB Jour.*, 17(2):291–313, March 2008.

[34] A. D. Sarma, D. Nanongkai, G. Pandurangan, and P. Tetali. Near-optimal sublinear time bounds for distributed random walks. *arXiv*, cs.DS:0911.3195, 2009.

[35] D. A. Spielman and S.-H. Teng. Spectral partitioning works: Planar graphs and finite element meshes. In *FOCS*, pages 96–105, 1996.

[36] A. P. Streich, M. Frank, D. Basin, and J. M. Buhmann. Multi-assignment clustering for boolean data. In *ICML*, 2009.

[37] D. B. Szyld and A. Frommer. Weighted max norms, splittings, and overlapping additive schwarz iterations. *Numerische Mathematik*, 83:259–278, 1999.

[38] Ümit V. Çatalyürek and C. Aykanat. A fine-grain hypergraph model for 2d decomposition of sparse matrices. In *PDPS*, pages 1199–1204, April 2001.

[39] Various. The Library of Congress subject headings. `http://id.loc.gov`, 2009. Accessed in September 2009.

[40] D. Zhou, J. Huang, and B. Schölkopf. Learning from labeled and unlabeled data on a directed graph. In *ICML '05: Proceedings of the 22nd International Conference on Machine Learning*, pages 1036–1043, New York, NY, USA, 2005. ACM Press.

Sponsored Search Auctions with Conflict Constraints

Panagiotis Papadimitriou
Stanford University
Stanford, CA, USA
papadimitriou@stanford.edu

Hector Garcia-Molina
Stanford University
Stanford, CA, USA
hector@cs.stanford.edu

ABSTRACT

In sponsored search auctions (SSA) advertisers compete for ad slots in the search engine results page, by bidding on keywords of interest. To improve advertiser expressiveness, we augment the bidding process with *conflict* constraints. With such constraints, advertisers can condition their bids on the non-appearance of certain undesired ads on the results page. We study the complexity of the *allocation* problem in these augmented SSA and we introduce an algorithm that can efficiently allocate the ad slots to advertisers. We evaluate the algorithm run time in simulated conflict scenarios and we study the implications of the conflict constraints on search engine revenue. Our results show that the allocation problem can be solved within few tens of milliseconds and that the adoption of conflict constraints can potentially increase search engine revenue.

Categories and Subject Descriptors

H.3.3 [**Information Storage and Retrieval**]: Information Search and Retrieval—*search*; J.4 [**Social and Behavioral Sciences**]: Economics

General Terms

Algorithms, Design, Experimentation

Keywords

sponsored search, auction design, conflicts, branch-and-bound

1. INTRODUCTION

In sponsored search auctions advertisers compete for m ad slots next to the organic search results. The participation of each advertiser in the auction is determined by the relevance of the submitted query to the advertiser interests. These interests are expressed through keywords that should match the submitted queries. For example, an advertiser with an online movies web site may specify that he is interested in queries that contain the word "movie". The advertiser also provides a *bid*, the maximum amount the he is willing to pay for a click on his ad.

Permission to make digital or hard copies of all or part of this work for personal or classroom use is granted without fee provided that copies are not made or distributed for profit or commercial advantage and that copies bear this notice and the full citation on the first page. To copy otherwise, to republish, to post on servers or to redistribute to lists, requires prior specific permission and/or a fee.
WSDM'12, February 8–12, 2012, Seattle, Washington, USA.
Copyright 2012 ACM 978-1-4503-0747-5/12/02 ...$10.00.

Although this auction model is simple, it lacks some necessary expressiveness. For example, there is no way for an advertiser to express that his value for a click, and consequently his bid, depends on the identity of other advertisers that appear in the m slots. In the movie advertiser example, he may not want his ad to appear when other slots advertise adult movies or when certain competitors appear.

To improve expressiveness in SSA, we allow an advertiser to specify, in addition to keywords of interest, a set of *conflict* advertisers, i.e., advertisers that should not appear in the top m slots when his ad is displayed. The advertiser can express a different valuation for a click if his conflict constraints are satisfied and a different bid if his conflict constraints are violated.

What makes the adoption of conflicts attractive is that they can benefit all parties of sponsored search. The advertisers who declare conflicts can more effectively control the context where their ads get clicked and avoid the cost of "undesired" advertising. The search engines can potentially increase their revenues from the new service (as we will show) and users may enjoy benefits such as the decrease of scam ads. The only concern about the support of conflicts comes from its computational cost. However, we believe that this papers addresses effectively this concern.

The paper is organized as follows. In Section 2 we introduce our formal model and describe the problems that need to be solved to support conflict constraints: (a) the *allocation problem*, i.e., how will the ad slots be allocated to advertisers in the new auction mechanism, and (b) the *payment problem*, i.e., how will advertisers be charged. Then, in Section 3 we provide two solutions to the allocation problem. The first solution uses a depth-first-search (DFS) branch-and-bound algorithm and the second solution (just summarized due to space constraints) uses the combinatorial auctions framework. In the same section we provide a solution for the payment problem using the *Vickrey-Clarke-Groves* mechanism. In Section 4 we evaluate the run time performance of the proposed solutions and we quantify the impact of conflicts on the search engine revenue. We present the related work in Section 5 and we conclude in Section 6.

2. PROBLEM DEFINITION

In a sponsored search auction the *search engine* is the auctioneer, the *advertisers* are the bidders and the ad *slots* are the auctioned items.

Let $A = \{a_1, \dots, a_j, \dots, a_n\}$ denote the set of n advertisers that participate in a sponsored search auction. Without loss of generality we assume that each advertiser participates in the auction with a single ad. Thus, in the rest of the paper we will use the terms "advertiser" and "ad" interchangeably. The advertisers participate in the auction to get their ads clicked by the users. Advertiser a_j participates in the auction with:

- the private valuation v_j for a click;
- the bid b_j, i.e., the maximum that he is willing to pay for a click; and
- the set of *conflict* advertisers $C_j \subseteq A$. Advertiser a_j's bid is conditioned upon the constraint that none of his conflict advertisers C_j wins a slot.

Note that in our model each advertiser specifies his conflicts explicitly. Although this convention simplifies the presentation, it does not restrict the generality of our model. In practice, we expect advertisers to specify their conflicts by describing conflict advertiser properties. For example, an advertiser can declare conflicts against advertisers that use certain keywords in their ad messages or against advertisers whose landing pages belong to a certain domain. In any case the advertiser preferences can eventually be translated to specific conflicts at the auction time.

Although the advertisers are interested in user clicks, the search engine cannot auction such clicks directly. The search engine auctions instead m ad slots $S = \{s_1, \ldots, s_i, \ldots, s_m\}$, where the ads can be displayed and potentially get clicked by users. These slots are not identical, because each slot s_i has its own click probability ρ_i. The click probabilities are estimated through historic click through rates (CTRs) and they are presumed to drop as the slot index i increases [9], i.e., $\rho_i \geq \rho_{i+1}, \forall s_i \in S$. The click probability decrease is a consequence of the slot placement in the search results page, where the slots span a vertical column with one slot per row. The closer a slot is to the top, the more it attracts user's attention and the more likely it is to be clicked.

Note that the click probability of an ad does not depend only on the hosting slot but also on the ad itself. However, the most popular search engines such as Google[1] and Bing[2] take the advertiser impact into account through a multiplicative factor that is applied to the advertiser bid[3][9]. We follow this convention and in the rest of the paper we assume ad independent click probabilities. However, the algorithms that we present could be applied to ad-dependent click probabilities with minor changes. Given the click valuation v_j and the click probabilities ρ_i, the expected *utility* of advertiser a_j who wins slot s_i is

$$v_j \rho_i.$$

If advertiser j does not win any slot, then his utility is 0.

The auctioneer, i.e., the search engine, has to allocate the auctioned slots to the advertisers and charge them accordingly. Thus, the auctioneer needs to define an *allocation rule* and a *payment rule*. In the following paragraph we discuss the desired properties of these rules.

The objective of the allocation rule is to maximize the *social welfare* [12], i.e., to maximize the sum of the advertisers' utilities. If the binary variable $x_{ij} \in \{0, 1\}$ indicates whether advertiser a_j wins slot s_i, then the social welfare is:

$$\sum_{j=1}^{n} \sum_{i=1}^{m} v_j \rho_i x_{ij}. \tag{1}$$

[1]`http://www.google.com`

[2]`http://www.bing.com`

[3]Each bid is multiplied by a "quality score" and the advertiser participates in the auction with a virtually increased or decreased bid.

Apart from maximizing the social welfare, the allocation rule must also satisfy a series of constraints that we show in the following Integer Linear Program (ILP):

$$\text{max.} \quad \sum_{j=1}^{n} \sum_{i=1}^{m} v_j \rho_i x_{ij} \tag{2a}$$

$$\text{s.t.} \quad \sum_{j=1}^{n} x_{ij} \leq 1, \qquad \forall s_i \in S \tag{2b}$$

$$\sum_{i=1}^{m} x_{ij} \leq 1, \qquad \forall a_j \in A \tag{2c}$$

$$\sum_{i=1}^{m} (x_{ij} + x_{ik}) \leq 1, \quad \forall a_j \in A \wedge a_k \in C_j \tag{2d}$$

$$x_{ij} \in \{0, 1\}$$

We refer to this ILP as the *allocation problem*. Note that the objective contains the secret valuations v_j instead of the known bids b_j, since the search engine desires to maximize the actual welfare. With the appropriate allocations scheme (to be discussed), advertisers will use their v_j values as their bids. Therefore, we will assume that the b_j are indeed the v_j values, and we can use the known b_j values to compute utility in our allocation scheme.

The constraints of Equation 2b guarantee that every slot is allocated to at most one advertiser. The constraints of Equation 2c guarantee that every advertiser wins at most one slot. Finally, the constraints of Equation 2d guarantee that the conflict constraints of the advertisers are also satisfied. A *feasible allocation* is an allocation of slots to advertisers that satisfies all the constraints of the ILP. The *optimal allocation* x^* is a feasible allocation that maximizes the objective.

For example, say that there are three advertisers a_1, a_2 and a_3 with conflicts $C_1 = C_3 = \emptyset$ and $C_2 = \{a_1\}$ and two ad slots. If we denote the allocation of advertisers to slots as an ordered advertiser list, the allocation $[a_1]$, i.e., advertiser a_1 wins the first slot, or the allocation $[a_2, a_3]$, i.e., advertiser a_2 wins the first slot and advertiser a_3 wins the second slot, are feasible allocations. However, the allocation $[a_1, a_2]$ is not feasible because the advertiser a_2 has a conflict with advertiser a_1 and the constraint of Equation 2d is violated.

Note that in our formulation each advertiser bids only upon the condition that his conflict constraints are satisfied. However, an advertiser may want to specify two different bids: one for the case that his conflict constraints are satisfied and a different one for the case that his constraints are violated. Althouh we do not dicuss such bids in the rest of the paper, our formulation can support them in the following way. For advertiser a_j that wants to submit two bids we create a virtual advertiser a'_j and we make sure that $a_j \in C'_j$ and $a'_j \in C_j$ (so that the advertiser does not win two slots). Then, the advertiser can submit two different bids with different conflict sets.

Given the allocations $x = \{x_{ij}\}$ and the bid vector $b = \{b_j\}$, the payment rule defines the price $p_j(b, x)$ that advertiser j has to pay. A desired property of the payment rule is to motivate *truthful bidding*, i.e., to motivate advertisers to report their real click valuations ($b_j = v_j$). An advertiser has such an incentive, if his *payoff* is maximized when $b_j = v_j$, regardless of the other advertisers' valuations, and regardless of how they decide to bid [12]. The payoff of an advertiser is defined as his utility minus his payment: $\sum_{i=1}^{m} v_j \rho_i x_{ij} - p_j(b, x)$. Thus, if $b, \hat{b}$ are two bid vectors that differ only in the j-th position with $b_j = v_j$ and $\hat{b}_j \neq v_j$, and x^*, $\hat{x}^*$ are the respective allocations by some allocation rule, then the payment rule ensures truthful bidding if and only if for all $b_1, \dots, b_{j-1}, b_{j+1}, \dots, b_n$:

$$\sum_{i=1}^{m} v_j \rho_{ij} x^*_{ij} - p_j(b, x^*) \geq \sum_{i=1}^{m} v_j \rho_{ij} \hat{x}^*_{ij} - p_j(\hat{b}, \hat{x}^*).$$

Without truthful bidding the advertisers have incentive to report untrue evaluations that may result in inefficient allocations [12, 5].

In the next sections of the paper we address the following questions: (a) how can we efficiently solve the allocation problem, (b) which payment rule ensures truthful bidding, and (c) how are the advertiser utilities and consequently the search engine revenue affected by the ability to declare conflicts.

3. SSA WITH CONFLICTS

In this section we study the allocation and the payment rules in SSA with conflict constraints. In Section 3.1 we provide a proof that the allocation problem is NP-hard to solve. Then, in Section 3.2 we present Debbassac, a DFS algorithm that can solve the allocation problem efficiently by reducing the search space with branch-and-bound pruning. In Section 3.3 we provide an alternative formulation of the allocation problem in the context of combinatorial auctions. Then, in Section 3.4 we present a payment rule that ensures truthful bidding. Finally, in Section 3.5 we study the implications of the ability to specify conflicts on the advertiser utilities and bids.

Throughout the section we use the following auction as an example: there are four advertisers $A = \{a_1, a_2, a_3, a_4\}$ with click valuations $v_1 = \$10$, $v_2 = \$8$, $v_3 = \$5$ and $v_4 = \$2$ that have the following conflicts: $C_1 = C_4 = \emptyset$ and $C_2 = C_3 = \{a_1\}$. The auctioned slots are $S = \{s_1, s_2\}$ and their click probabilities are $\rho_1 = 0.2$ and $\rho_2 = 0.1$.

3.1 Problem hardness

We represent the advertiser conflicts and click valuations with the weighted *undirected conflict graph* $G = (V, E)$. Each node $a_j \in V$ corresponds to advertiser a_j and weight of the node is equal to the advertiser click valuation v_j. The graph has an edge (a_j, a_k) if $a_k \in C_j$ or $a_j \in C_k$. Note that the graph is undirected, since no matter whether $a_k \in C_j$ or $a_j \in C_k$, the advertisers a_j and a_k cannot appear in the ad slots together. For example, in Figure 1 we show the conflict graph for our running example.

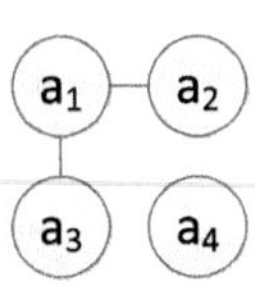

Figure 1: Conflict Graph.

In our NP-hardness proof we use a reduction from the *Maximum Weight Independent Set* or MWIS problem. An *independent set* is set of nodes in a graph, no two of which are adjacent. The MWIS in a weighted graph is the independent set with the maximum sum of node weights. The problem of finding the MWIS in a weighted graph is NP-hard.

THEOREM 1. *It is NP-hard to solve the allocation problem of Equation 2.*

PROOF. Sketch: Use reduction from the MWIS. Take any instance of the MWIS problem on a graph $G = (V, E)$ and create an allocation problem with one advertiser per node of V and one conflict per edge of E. Then say that there are $m = |V|$ slots with equal click probabilities $\rho_1 = \rho_2 = \dots = \rho_n$. The set of nodes that correspond to the advertisers of the optimal allocation is the MWIS of graph G. □

Algorithm 1 Debbassac: **De**pth-first-search **b**ranch-and-**b**ound **a**lgorithm for **s**ponsored **s**earch **a**uctions with **c**onflict constraints.

Input: set of advertisers A with conflict set C_j and valuations $v_j, \forall a_j \in A$, slots S with click probabilities $\rho_i, \forall s_i \in S$.
Output: optimal allocation x^* and social welfare w^*.

```
Global variable w* ← 0                          ▷ Optimal welfare
Global variable X* ← ∅        ▷ Sparse representation of the optimal allocation
ALLOCREM(∅, 0, A)
x*_ij ← 0, ∀a_j ∈ A, s_i ∈ S
for all (s_i, a_j) ∈ X* do
    x*_ij ← 1
return x*, w*

procedure ALLOCREM(X_in, w_in, A_rem)
Input invariants: {a_j | (s_i, a_j) ∈ X_in} ∩ A_rem = ∅
    i ← |X_in| + 1
                                   ▷ Check for the end of recursion.
    if i = m + 1 ∨ A_rem = ∅ then
        if w_in > w* then
            w* ← w_in
            X* ← X_in
        return
                         ▷ Calculate w_j, h_j and A_j,rem for a_j ∈ A_rem.
    for all a_j ∈ A_rem do             ▷ A_rem sorted by v_j desc.
        w_j ← w_in + ρ_i v_j
        C'_j ← {a_k | a_k ∈ A_rem ∧ a_j ∈ C_k}
        L_j ← {a_k | a_k ∈ A_rem ∧ v_k > v_j}
        A_j,rem ← A_rem − ({a_j} ∪ C_j ∪ C'_j ∪ L_j)
        h_j ← UPPERBOUND(m − i, A_j,rem)
        if (C_j ∪ C'_j) ∩ A_rem = ∅ then
            break
                                    ▷ Explore allocations recursively.
    Remove un-examined advertisers from A_rem.
    Sort A_rem by w_j + h_j desc.
    for all a_j ∈ A_rem do
        if w_j + h_j ≤ w* then                ▷ Pruning condition
            break
        else
            ALLOCREM(X_in ∪ {(s_i, a_j)}, w_j, A_j,rem)

function UPPERBOUND(m_rem, A_rem)
    h ← 0
    while m_rem > 0 ∧ A_rem ≠ ∅ do
        i ← m − m_rem + 1
        a_j ← arg max_{a_k ∈ A_rem} v_k
        h ← h + ρ_i v_j
        m_rem ← m_rem − 1
        A_rem ← A_rem − {a_j}
    return h
```

3.2 Debbassac algorithm

The allocation problem can be solved as follows:

1. Enumerate all the possible allocations of advertisers to ad slots. Note that we can consider only the allocations that ei-

ther fill all the slots or they leave some bottom slots empty. Allocations that leave a top slot empty can be discarded, since we can always shift the advertisers up-wards to fill the slot and improve the social welfare. The number of possible allocations is $n + \binom{n}{2} + \cdots + \binom{n}{m}$, since n is the number of allocations that fill just the top slot, $\binom{n}{2}$ is the number of allocations that fill the two top slots, and so on.

2. Remove allocations that are not feasible, i.e., allocations that contain advertisers with conflicts among them.

3. Find among the remaining allocations the one that yields the maximum social welfare.

Such an algorithm is exhaustive and it finds the optimal allocation. However, the algorithm is expensive, since it examines all possible allocations.

We can substantially improve upon the brute-force algorithm with a more "careful" search in the space of possible advertiser allocations. In the Debbassac algorithm that we present in Algorithm 1 we show (a) how we can restrict the search within the space of feasible allocations, and (b) how we can prune allocations that have no way beating allocations that have already been explored.

The algorithm input consists of the advertisers A (along with their click valuations and their conflict sets) and the ad slots S (along with their click probabilities). The algorithm explores the space of feasible allocations in a DFS fashion and uses a branch-and-bound approach to prune the search space. The algorithm returns the optimal allocation x^* and the corresponding social welfare w^*. In the pseudo-code we also use variable X^* as a sparse representation of the optimal allocation. X^* is a set of pairs such as (s_i, a_j) that indicates that advertiser a_j wins the slot s_i.

The search in the allocation space is performed in the procedure $\text{ALLOCREM}(X_{in}, w_{in}, A_{rem})$. The input of the procedure is the allocation of advertisers to the first $i-1$ slots X_{in}, the corresponding social welfare w_{in} and the set of advertisers A_{rem} that can fill the remaining $m-(i-1)$ slots. The procedure tries to fill the i-th slot with one of the A_{rem} advertisers and then it calls itself recursively to fill the remaining $m-i$ slots. The procedure does not have a return value, but it updates the global variables w^* and X^* when it finds an allocation that yields higher social welfare than the current maximum.

In lines 2-7 the procedure checks whether the input allocation is *complete*, i.e., checks if all m slots are filled or if there are no advertisers left. If the allocation is complete, the procedure compares the input social welfare with the current maximum and updates the global variables.

If the input allocation is not complete, then the algorithm evaluates the allocations that augment X_{in} with an advertiser $a_j \in A_{rem}$ in the slot s_i (lines 8-15). In particular, for each such allocation the algorithm calculates (a) the new social welfare w_j, (b) the advertisers $A_{j,rem}$ that will be considered to fill the remaining $m-i$ slots, and (c) an upper bound h_j of the social welfare that the remaining slots can contribute. The calculation for w_j in (a) is straight-forward. For $A_{j,rem}$ in (b) the algorithm removes from A_{rem} the advertiser a_j himself, his conflicts C_j, the advertisers C'_j that have a_j in their conflicts, and the advertisers L_j that have a higher valuation than a_j. The first three removals ensure that the algorithm will explore only feasible allocations while trying to fill the remaining $m-i$ slots. The L_j advertisers are removed, because we do not need to consider an advertiser a_k with higher valuation than a_j for the remaining slots. At some other point in search the algorithm will consider a scenario with a_j and a_k roles reversed and that alternative scenario dominates the one where a_j wins slot

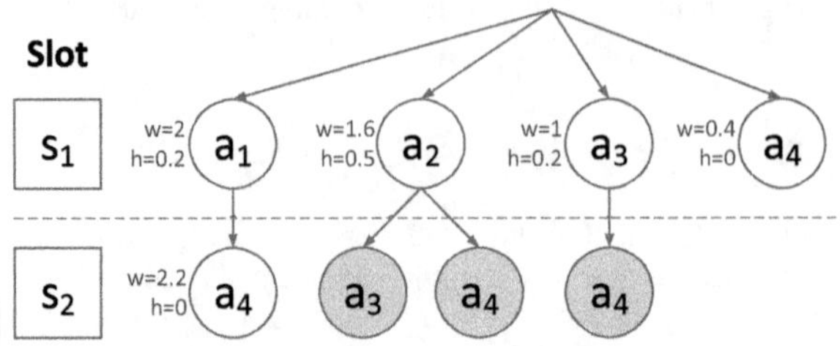

Figure 2: The search space that corresponds to the running example.

s_i and a_k wins a lower slot s'_i with $i < i'$. To obtain an upper bound in (c) we can assume that the advertisers with the top $m-i$ click valuations in $A_{j,rem}$ will win the remaining $m-i$ slots (ignoring possible conflicts). This calculation yields an upper bound, because it ignores possible conflicts within these $m-i$ advertisers.

The algorithm stops the loop execution in lines 14-15 if the current advertiser a_j has no conflicts with the remaining advertisers. The lack of conflicts ensures that no restriction is imposed on the allocation of the remaining slots. Moreover, since the advertisers are examined in descending order of click valuation, the allocation of slot s_i to a_j dominates the allocation of this slot to any of the un-examined advertisers.

In lines 16-22, the algorithm attempts to allocate slot s_i to advertiser a_j and then recursively allocate the rest of the slots. First, the algorithm sorts the advertisers A_{rem} by the sum $w_j + h_j$ to explore the most promising allocations first. In lines 18-22 the procedure calls itself to explore the allocation with the slot s_i to advertiser a_j, only if such an allocation can yield a higher social welfare than the current maximum (line 19). If this condition does not hold the procedure breaks the loop and returns. Note that it does not need to consider the remaining advertisers, since they are sorted in decreasing values of $w_j + h_j$. If the condition holds, the procedure calls recursively itself with an updated input allocation $X_{in} \cup \{(s_i, a_j)\}$, social welfare w_j and remaining advertisers $A_{j,rem}$.

In Figure 3.2 we illustrate how the algorithm would be applied in the auction of our running example. Each path in the figure (from root to leaf) represents a possible allocation, e.g., the $a_1 \rightarrow a_4$ path represents the allocation of the slot s_1 to a_1 and the slot s_2 to a_4. Note that the algorithm considers all four advertisers as candidates to fill the first slot. If advertiser a_1 is selected, then the algorithm will consider only advertiser a_4 for the second slot, because advertisers a_2 and a_3 have a_1 in their conflict sets. If advertiser a_2 is selected, then the algorithm will consider only a_3 and a_4 for the second slot, since a_2 has advertiser a_1 in his conflict set. If the advertiser a_3 is selected, then the algorithm will consider only a_4 for the second slot, since a_4 has advertiser a_1 in his conflict set and a_2 has a higher click valuation than a_3. Finally, if advertiser a_4 is selected there will be no advertiser to consider for the second slot, since the rest of the advertisers have higher click valuations than him. The algorithm also calculates the w and h values for each node. For example, if advertiser a_1 is selected for the first slot, then $w = v_1\rho_1 = \$10 \times 0.2 = \$2$ and $h = v_4\rho_2 = \$2 \times 0.1 = \$0.2$. Based on the social welfare upper bound $w + h$, the algorithm will choose to explore first the allocation with advertiser a_1 in the first slot. Then the algorithm allocates the second slot to advertiser a_4 and updates the maximum welfare $w^* = \$2.2$. Since none of the upper bound values is higher than $\$2.2$ the algorithm will terminate and it will never explore the gray nodes of the search tree.

3.3 Combinatorial auction formulation

In this section we briefly describe how to formulate the sponsored search auctions with conflicts in the combinatorial auctions framework [3] (due to space constraints, the formulation is presented in detail only in [13]). A bidder in a combinatorial auction can place his bid on a *bundle*, i.e., a combination of the auctioned items, and he wins either all or none of the bundle items. For example, if the auctioned items are $\{\alpha, \beta, \gamma\}$ then a bidder can place a bid on the bundle $\{\alpha, \beta\}$ and another bidder on the bundle $\{\beta, \gamma\}$. Since the two bundles have item β in common, only one of the bidders can win. If the first bidder wins, then the item γ will be unassigned and if the second bidder wins, then the item α will be unassigned.

We use the notion of shared items to represent the conflicts between advertisers. In paricular, we introduce a set of *dummy* slots, one for each conflict, and we have the two advertisers involved in a conflict to include the dummy slot in their bids. After we transform the auction with conflicts to a combinatorial auction, we can use off-the-shelf tools to solve the allocation problem. In our experiments we evaluate CABOB [15], the state-of-the-art search algorithm for the winner determination problem in combinatorial auction, as the solver of the allocation problem in the sponsored search auctions with conflicts.

3.4 Payment rule

In traditional SSA the most popular payment rule requires from the advertiser who wins slot s_i to pay the bid of the advertiser who wins s_{i+1}. The rationale of this rule is that each advertiser pays the minimum bid that would be required to win his slot. We cannot apply this rule to SSA with conflicts, because an advertiser does not only have to outbid the advertiser with next highest bid, but also he has to outbid his conflicts.

To determine the prices for the advertisers that win the available slots we use the Vickrey-Clarke-Groves (VCG) mechanism. The VCG mechanism is a generalization of the Vickrey auction[4] and similarly to the Vickrey auction it gives the bidders incentive to bid truthfully. The idea in VCG is that items are assigned to maximize the social welfare; then each advertiser pays the "opportunity cost" that his presence introduces to all the other advertisers. In the following paragraph we provide the explicit formula for the price charged to each advertiser.

Let $u_j^*(A, S)$ denote the utility of the advertiser a_j in the optimal allocation x^* (optimal with respect to social welfare maximization) of slots S to advertisers A:

$$u_j^*(A, S) = \sum_{i=1}^{m} v_j \rho_i x_{ij}^*. \tag{3}$$

Then, the price for the advertiser a_j equals the difference of the total utility that the other advertisers receive when a_j does not participate and when a_j participates in the auction:

$$p_j = \frac{\sum_{k \neq j} u_k^*(A - \{j\}, S) - \sum_{k \neq j} u_k^*(A, S)}{\rho_i} \tag{4}$$

The difference is divided by ρ_i, the click probability of the slot assigned to a_j in the optimal allocation, to obtain the price per click.

To illustrate, we calculate the advertiser payments in our running example. Recall that in the optimal solution advertiser a_1 wins s_1 and advertiser a_4 wins s_2. If advertiser a_1 does not participate in the auction, then the winners of the auction will be advertiser a_2 (s_1) and advertiser a_3 (s_2). Thus, the payment of advertiser a_1 is:

$$p_1 = \frac{v_2\rho_1 + v_3\rho_2 - (v_4\rho_2)}{\rho_1} = \frac{\$1.9}{0.2} = \$9.5$$

Note that the advertiser a_1 is mostly charged for depriving advertisers a_2 and a_3 of ad slots rather than for "pushing" advertiser a_4 to the second slot. With similar calculations the payment for a_4 is $p_4 = [v_2\rho_1 + v_3\rho_2 - (v_1\rho_1)]/\rho_2 = \$1$.

The main criticism against the VCG mechanism is its computational inefficiency, since it requires solving the allocation problem n times to find the payment for each bidder. In our setting the number of bidders/advertisers that can win a slot is limited by the number m of slots and the advertisers that do not win any slot have zero payment. Thus, to determine the prices for the winners we need to the allocation problem at most m times no matter what the number of advertisers is.

3.5 Implications on utilities and bids

A natural question that arises with conflict constraints is whether the search engine is likely to make more or less money with this feature. In particular, constraints rule out certain combinations of ads, so shouldn't search engine revenue drop as a consequence? The first step in answering this question is to consider whether advertisers will bid differently on a search engine that offers conflicts as opposed to one that does not.

To illustrate, consider an advertiser a_j that wishes to display ads on two search engines, T (traditional) and K (conflicts supported). The search engines and their advertisers are identical, except that K supports conflict constraints while T does not. Say that a_j submits an ad to K with a valuation $v_j = 100$ and a conflict with another advertiser a_k. What is the valuation of this same ad at T? Since T does not support conflicts, sometimes it will display the ad together with the undesired a_k ad, and sometimes it will be shown without a_k. Say that the former case (a_j and a_k appear) occurs with probability β.

We can estimate this probability as the fraction of auctions where both a_j and a_k win a slot versus all the auctions where a_j wins a slot. Say that $\beta = 0.5$ and for simplicity say that the click probability of the slot that a_j wins is 1. Then the expected utility of advertiser a_j at K is $(1 - \beta)\rho_i v_j = 0.5 \times \$10 = \$5$. Note that we have to discount his raw utility $\rho_i v_j$ by $1 - \beta$ because of the advertiser conflict with a_k. Since the advertiser utility is $\$5$, the advertiser has to bid $\$5$ at T instead of the $\$10$ he bid at K to avoid paying more than his utility. So if the advertiser bids truthfully and we know the value of β, we can estimate the value v_j at T as

$$v_j = b_j/(1 - \beta).$$

We can generalize this example to an advertiser a_j with $d = |C_j|$ conflicts. If advertiser a_j wins a slot along with one of his conflicts with probability β, and the probability for each conflict is independent from the others, then he will win a slot next to none of his conflicts with probability $(1 - \beta)^d$. Assuming truthful bidding, we can estimate the advertiser's click valuation v_j at T from his K bid b_j as:

$$v_j = b_j/(1 - \beta)^d. \tag{5}$$

The formula shows that an advertiser will bid *more* at a site that supports conflict constraints, as opposed to one that does not. We take this fact into account in Section 4.4 when we compare the revenue at a search engine like K, as compared to one like T.

[4] A Vickrey or second-price auction is a type of sealed-bid auction, where bidders submit written bids without knowing the bid of the other people in the auction, and in which the highest bidder wins, but the price paid is the second-highest bid. The Vickrey auctions provides the bidders with incentive for truthful bidding.

4. EXPERIMENTS

In this section we evaluate the performance of the Debbassac algorithm and we study the properties of sponsored search auctions with conflicts through a series of experiments. To goals of these experiments are the following: (a) to evaluate the run time efficiency of Debbassac and understand the factors that affect its performance, e.g., the number of advertisers that participate in the auction, the number of conflicts among them and the click probabilities distribution (Section 4.2); (b) to compare the run time of Debbassac against the state-of-the-art algorithm that solves the allocation problem in the combinatorial auction formulation presented briefly in Section 3.3 (Section 4.3); and (c) to assess the impact of the conflict constraints on the search engine revenue (Section 4.4).

4.1 Experimental Setup

4.1.1 Dataset

We use the Yahoo! Search Marketing Advertiser Bidding Data from the Yahoo! Webscope [5] dataset collection. The dataset contains the advertiser bids for the top 1,000 keywords by volume during the time period from Jun 15, 2002 to Jun 14, 2003. Each dataset record includes an advertiser identifier, a keyword identifier, the bid amount and the time. These records contain 10,475 distinct advertiser identifiers.

Since we focus on a single auction we ignore the time aspect of the bids and we construct 1,000 auctions, one for each keyword. The participants in the auction for a certain keyword are all the advertisers with at least one bid on the keyword in the dataset. The bid of each advertiser is considered to be equal to the mean value of his bids on the auction keyword.

In Figure 3 we report some interesting statistics about the 1,000 auctions of our dataset. In Figure 3(a) we plot the distribution of the number of advertisers over the 1,000 keyword auctions in double logarithmic axes. Note that the distribution is skewed: there are few auctions with many advertisers and many auctions with few advertisers. As we discuss later in Section 4.2, such a distribution has implications on the reported mean run times of Debbassac over the auction instances of our dataset. In Figure 3(b) we plot the distribution of the advertiser bids in the auction for the keyword with identifier 122 (the distribution for other auctions look similar). Note that the distribution of bids is also skewed. Thus, although the number of advertisers that participate in an auction is large there are actually few who have realistic chances to get one of the $m(=10)$ auctioned slots. As we discuss later such a bid distribution paired with the smart search space pruning of Debbassac makes the NP-hard allocation problem efficiently solvable in practical cases.

4.1.2 Conflicts

Our dataset auction instances come from real data and they do not contain conflicts. We introduce conflicts in these instances by simulating two scenarios that we discuss in the following paragraphs.

Competing advertisers.

The motivation for the competing advertisers or simply "competitors" scenario is that advertisers may introduce conflicts with their competitors to ensure exclusivity in the ad section of the results page. For example, Hertz may introduce conflicts against ads from Enterprise to get a greater market share. Recall that an advertiser can also place a bid without conflicts (as discussed in Section 2) to ensure that he is not deprived of a winning slot because of his own conflicts.

[5] http://webscope.sandbox.yahoo.com

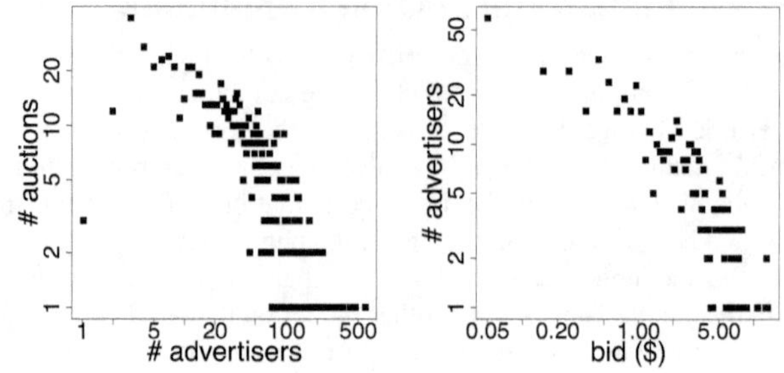

(a) Advertisers per auction (b) Bid distribution (single auction)

Figure 3: Dataset statistics.

To implement this scenario we need to identify advertisers that can be considered as competitors. Although there are many ways to identify such advertisers, we picked competitors through their bids' similarity. In particular, we define the similarity $sim(a_j, a_k)$ between advertisers a_j and a_k as the Jaccard index between their keyword bids:

$$sim(a_j, a_k) = \frac{\#\text{ keywords with bids from } a_j \text{ AND } a_k}{\#\text{ keywords with bids from } a_j \text{ OR } a_k} \quad (6)$$

Then, we consider the advertisers a_j and a_k as competitors if they have at least 2 keywords in common and $sim(a_j, a_k) \geq 0.5$.

Given that advertisers a_j and a_k are competitors, we introduce a conflict between them with probability ψ. The direction of the conflict, i.e., $a_j \in C_k$ or $a_k \in C_j$, is determined by an unbiased coin. We generated conflicts for the following 10 values of the conflict probability ψ: $0.1, 0.2, \ldots, 1$ and for every value of ψ we created 20 instances of the conflict graph. Finally, we obtain $1,000 \times 10 \times 20 = 200,000$ instances of auctions with conflicts among competing advertisers.

After manual inspection of the conflict graphs that we obtained, we noticed that they are quite dense even for $\psi = 0.3$ (see [13] for more details). Thus, we believe that the auction instances that we study in this paper are more demanding than expected in practice and our run time results can be considered upper bounds of real-world performance.

Conflict-breeding advertisers.

The motivation for the conflict-breeding advertisers or simply "conflict-breeders" scenario is a set of advertisers may attract conflicts from the rest of advertisers. For example, the ads of scammers may appear in the conflict sets of many non-scammer advertisers.

To implement this scenario we first select a set of κ conflict-breeding advertisers with weighted sampling. The weight of each advertiser is the sum of his bids. We use such a weight to select the conflict-breeders among the advertisers with either bids to many (and possibly unrelated) keywords or advertisers with high bids. The former advertisers include spammers who try to win slots independent of the submitted queries, while the latter advertisers include scammers, who have high valuations for clicks because of the potential high returns.

The values that we used for the parameters κ and ψ are $\kappa = 50, 100, \ldots, 300$ and $\psi = 0.1, 0.2, \ldots, 1$. We selected the conflict-breeding advertisers once for each value of κ and then we generated conflicts 20 times for each value of ψ. Finally we obtain $1,000 \times 6 \times 20 = 120,000$ auction instances with conflict-breeding advertisers.

The generated conflict graphs are bipartite with conflict-breeders in one part and the rest of the advertisers in the other. Note also that the graphs are quite dense, since the expected in-degree of a conflict-breeding advertiser is $(n - \kappa)\psi$, while the expected out-degree of a regular advertiser is $\kappa\psi$. The conflict graph densities of our dataset auctions make the allocation problem more challenging than what is expected in practice.

4.1.3 *Click probabilities*

Our dataset does not contain information about the click probabilities of ad slots. However, various other studies [7, 14] indicate that the click probabilities follow a Zipfian distribution. Thus, we assume that the click probability of slot s_i is $\rho_i \propto 1/i^{\sigma}$. Since the objective of the allocation problem (Equation 2) is a linear combination of the click probabilities, the solution to the problem is indifferent to the proportionality constant between ρ_i and $1/i^{\sigma}$. However, the parameter σ affects the solution and in Section 4.2.3 we show that it also affects the run time of Debbassac. Outside of Section 4.2.3 we use $\sigma = 0.5$.

4.1.4 *Implementation*

We implemented the Debbassac and the CABOB algorithm in Python and we have made our implementation available online[6]. We ran our code on a CentOS Linux server with two Xeon X5680 processors and 196GB of memory. Despite the large amount of available memory, our code uses only few tens of megabytes for each auction instance.

4.2 Debbassac run time analysis

In this section we study the run time of Debbassac. We are interested to see whether the Debbassac run time is acceptable in practice, where the allocation problem must be solved in few hundreds of milliseconds. This time is required by the search engine to compute the organic search results and the allocation problem should be solved concurrently in the same amount of time.

We perform the run time analysis with respect to the following parameters:

(i) the number of the auction advertisers n,

(ii) the density of the conflict graph that is controlled by the parameter ψ in the competitors scenario and by the parameters ψ and κ in the conflict-breeders scenario, and

(iii) the distribution of the click probabilities that is controlled by the parameter σ of the Zipfian distribution.

Note that the reported run times do not include the time to calculate the prices for the winners. We study the overhead of pricing in Section 4.2.4.

We run the Debbassac algorithm on all auction instances from both the competitors and the conflict-breeders scenario. We discuss the results in the following paragraphs.

4.2.1 *Number of advertisers*

In Figure 4 we plot the run time of Debbassac with respect to the number of advertisers in an auction n. Sub-figure 4(a) focuses on auction instances from the competitors scenario with $\psi = 0.3$. The vertical axis shows the run time and the horizontal axis shows the number of advertisers. Each point of the plot corresponds to an auction instance. The maximum run time is below 30 milliseconds which is considered acceptable. Note that the run time increases as n increases, but the increase is diminishing for large values of

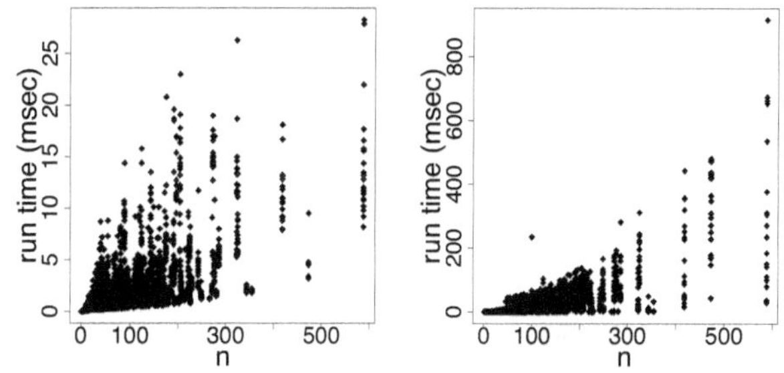

(a) Competitors (b) Conflict-Breeders

Figure 4: Debbassac run time vs number of advertisers.

n. This trend is a consequence of the skewed bid distribution that we showed in Figure 3(b). If n is large, then there are enough advertisers with high bids to win all of the available slots and the tail advertisers are ignored by the Debbassac pruning. In such cases the run time of the algorithm is determined by the number of advertisers with high bids rather than the total number of advertisers n.

Sub-figure 4(b) focuses on auction instances from the conflict-breeders scenario with $\psi = 0.3$ and $\kappa = 200$. Note here that the run time increases with n and the increase seems to be quadratic on n. Thus, in the conflict-breeders scenarios there are run times for $n \approx 600$ that are not acceptable. The reason for the quadratic increase in the run time is not the number of advertisers but the number of conflicts that increase quadratically because of the scenario design. Since κ is constant, the probability that a conflict-breeder will participate in an auction grows linearly with the number of advertisers n. Every conflict-breeder attracts $n\psi$ conflicts and consequently the number of conflicts in the auction increases quadratically with n. We further discuss the impact of conflicts on the run time of Debbassac in the following subsection.

4.2.2 *Conflict graph density*

The conflict graph density is another factor that affects the run time of Debbassac, because conflicts increase the number of alternatives that the algorithm has to explore to allocate a slot. We show the effect of conflicts in Figure 5(a) for the competitors scenario and in Figures 6(a) and 6(b) for the conflict-breeders scenario (Figures 5(b) is discussed later on).

In Figure 5(a) we plot the mean running time of Debbassac as a function of ψ for the competitors scenario auctions. Recall that for every value of ψ we generated 20 different conflict graphs and for each conflict graph we solved the allocation problem for all $1,000$ auction instances. First we compute the mean run time over these $1,000$ instances and then we compute the mean of 20 means for each value of ψ. Each point in the plot shows the mean of the means for a particular value of ψ and the error bars indicate 95% confidence intervals. Note that the mean time is less than 1 millisecond for all values of ψ and this result shows that Debbassac can handle conflicts efficiently. Note also that the curve has a steep increase in the $0 - 0.3$ range of ψ and the increase slows down for larger value of ψ. The reason for the initial steep increase is that as ψ increases advertisers without conflicts obtain at least one conflict and Debbassac cannot take advantage of the pruning condition of lines 14-16 (Algorithm 1) in the top level of the search tree. To illustrate, say that an advertiser a_j has four competitors. The probability that there is at least one conflict between him and one of his competitors is $1 - (1 - \psi)^4$. This probability increases from 0 for

[6]http://infolab.stanford.edu/~ppapadim

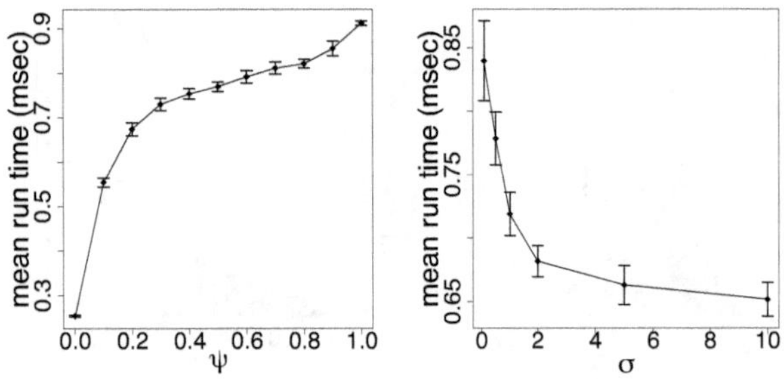

(a) $\sigma = 0.5$ (b) $\psi = 0.3$

Figure 5: Debbassac mean run time vs (a) the conflict probability ψ, and (b) the Zipfian distribution exponent σ in the competitors scenario auctions.

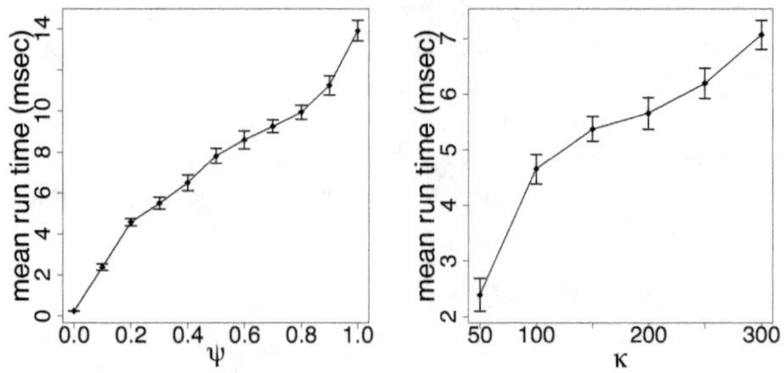

(a) $\kappa = 200$ (b) $\psi = 0.3$

Figure 6: Debbassac mean run time vs (a) the conflict probability ψ, (b) the number of conflict-breeders κ in the conflict-breeders scenario auctions.

$\psi = 0$ to 0.76 for $\psi = 0.3$ and it reaches 1 for $\psi = 1$. Thus, for $\psi = 0.3$ the probability that Debbassac does not explore the advertisers $\{a_k \mid v_k < v_j\}$ at the top level of the search tree drops to 0.24 for $\psi = 0.3$ from 1 for $\psi = 0$.

In Figure 6(a) we plot the mean run time of Debbassac as a function of ψ for the conflict-breeders scenario auctions and in Figure 6(b) we plot the mean run time as a function of κ. We restrict our study to auctions with $\kappa = 200$ for the former figure and to auctions with $\psi = 0.3$ for the latter figure. Recall that for each combination of κ and ψ we generated 20 conflict graphs and the reported run times are the means of the means similarly to Figure 5(a). The two curves have similar trends because increasing either ψ or κ has similar impact on the number of conflicts. The maximum run times are 14 milliseconds in Figure 6(a) is 7 milliseconds in Figure 6(b). Both these numbers are low and they confirm that Debbassac can handle conflicts efficiently.

4.2.3 *Click probabilities*

The distribution of the click probabilities proved also to be an important factor for the run time of Debbassac. As mentioned above we assume that the click probabilities follow a Zipfian distribution and we study the impact of the exponent σ. We used the following values of σ: 0.1, 0.5, 1, 2, 5 and 10. For each value of σ we derived the slot click probabilities and we solved the allocation problem for all auction instances in our dataset. In Figure 5(b) we present the results for the competitors scenario auctions. The results for the conflict-breeders scenario are similar and we report them in [13].

In Figure 5(b) we plot the mean running time of Debbassac as a function of σ. The plot looks only at the $20 \times 1{,}000$ auction instances whose conflict graphs were generated with $\psi = 0.3$ (plots for other ψ values are similar). As discussed above, for each conflict graph we calculate the mean run time over the $1{,}000$ auctions and the plot shows the mean of the 20 means that we obtain. The error bars indicate 95% confidence intervals. Note that the mean run time drops from 6.5 milliseconds for $\sigma = 0.1$ to less than 5 milliseconds for $\sigma = 10$. The reason why the run time decreases is that high values of σ increase the relative difference among the slot click probabilities. For example, for $\sigma = 10$ the ratio of the click probabilities between the first and the second slot is $\frac{1/1^{10}}{1/2^{10}} = 2^{10}$. With such a big ratio, it is preferable to allocate the first slot to the advertiser with the highest bid while ignoring his many conflicts rather than allocating the first slot to another advertiser with lower bid and no conflicts. The allocation of the first slot to the highest bid is more beneficial for the the social welfare rather than the more efficient allocation of the rest of the slots. For smaller values of σ the algorithm has to estimate more carefully the trade-off of allocating a slot to an advertiser versus allocating the same slot or others to his conflicts. However, it is important that Debbassac can take advantage of certain click probability distributions and decrease its run time.

4.2.4 *Pricing overhead*

The reported run times so far do not include the time to assign prices to the winning advertisers. Although the search engine needs to find the slot winners by the time it displays the search results to users, it can determine the slot prices even beyond this time point. So the time constraint of few hundred milliseconds does not apply to the price determination time.

Even if the time contraint was applied to the price determination, note that the total run time to determine the prices is not equal to the minimum possible latency to learn these prices. Recall that the price determination requires solving up to m allocation problems. However, if the search engine needs to have the prices as early as possible, it can solve the m allocation problems in parallel, since they are independent. So even if the computational cost of pricing is m times the cost of solving the allocation problem, the minimum latency to calculate the prices is equal to the run time of a single allocation problem.

We measured the run time to determine the slot prices for all the auctions of our dataset. Our code solved the m allocation problems in a serial fashion. In Figure 7 we plot the empirical CDF of the ratio

$$\alpha = \frac{\text{pricing run time}}{\text{allocation run time}}$$

for the auctions of the competitors scenario with $\psi = 0.3$. The x-axis shows the value of α and the y-axis shows the percentage of auctions whose ratio of price to allocation run time is less than α. Since there are $m = 10$ slots, the expected value for α is 10. However, the value of α is not always exactly 10 because the m problems that need to be solved are not identical with the original allocation problem. Note that α is less or equal to 10 for approximately 60% of the auctions and more than 10 for the rest 40%. This was expected because an allocation problem is expected to be simpler to solve after we remove one advertiser. However, there are some rare cases where pruning cannot be efficient in the resulting problems and the pricing run time is 30 times greater than the allocation time. The results for the conflict-breeders sceario are similar and we do not report them here. In both cases the time overhead of price determination is on average slightly less than m times the run time of the winner determination problem.

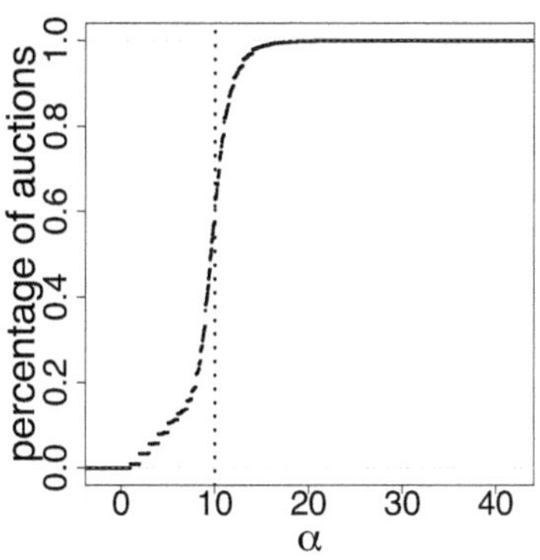

Figure 7: Empirical CDF of the α ratio ($\psi = 0.3$).

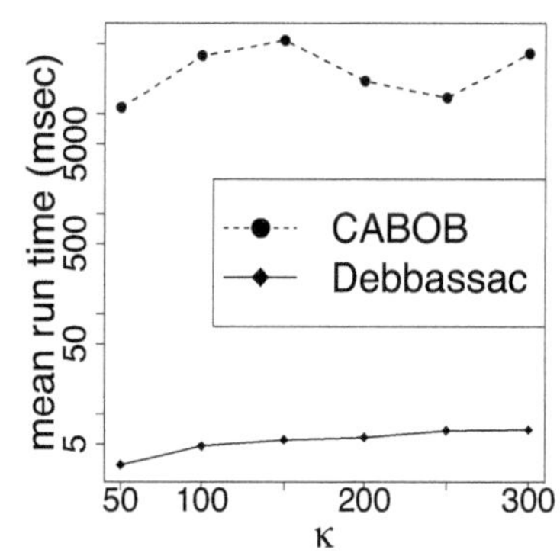

Figure 8: Mean run time comparison of Debbassac and CABOB in auctions with conflict-breeding advertisers.

4.3 Comparison with CABOB

In this section we compare Debbassac with CABOB [15], the state-of-the-art algorithm for the allocation problem in combinatorial auctions. Despite the different formulations, recall that both algorithms provide an exact solution to the same problem. So their solutions are the same and our comparison refers only to the algorithms' run times.

We implemented CABOB and a program to transform a sponsored search auction with conflicts to a combinatorial auction. Note that the run times we provide for CABOB do not include the run time of the transformation. Since the difference in the run times between Debbassac and CABOB exceed the three orders of magnitude, we provide here only one figure with numerical results and we discuss the differences of the two algorithms qualitatively. In Figure 8 we plot the mean run time of the two algorithms as a function of κ. The mean is computed over $1,000$ auctions with conflicts from one conflict graph with $\psi = 0.3$ and the κ indicated in the plot. We did not use all of the 20 conflict graphs that we have generated for every combination of κ and $\psi = 0.3$ because of the high cost of running CABOB. The dashed line in the plot looks at the CABOB running times and the solid line looks at the Debbassac run times. Note that the maximum time for Debbassac is below 10 milliseconds, while the minimum run time of CABOB exceeds the $10,000$ milliseconds.

Although both algorithms use DFS with branch-and-bound pruning, there is a huge performance gap between them. The main reasons for this gap are the following: (a) CABOB solves an LP problem in every node of the search tree. The time to solve one LP is usually more than the run time required by Debbassac to solve the allocation problem. (b) One of the main optimizations of CABOB is that it tries to allocate early the items that have bids from many bidders. The hope is that after allocating such items, there will be only items with bids by a single advertiser and the allocation problem will become trivial. However, in the combinatorial auction formulation of the sponsored search auctions with conflicts all advertisers bids include the same items, i.e., the real slots, and the CABOB optimization cannot yield any benefit. (c) Debbassac is tailored to the allocation problem of sponsored search auctions with conflicts and it uses various problem properties to prune the search space. For example, Debbassac considers allocating slots with lower click probabilities only to advertisers with lower bids and it prunes the search space when a an advertiser without conflicts is encountered. Such pruning decisions reduce dramatically the number of nodes in the search tree and the running time of the algorithm.

Although CABOB is a general purpose algorithm, it is still the state-of-the-art approach for solving the allocation problem in combinatorial auctions. The fact that Debbassac greatly improves the run time with respect to CABOB shows that Debbassac does efficiently take advantage of the problem specific properties. However, the combinatorial auction formulation is still useful, since it can benefit from any progress in the allocation or pricing methods for combinatorial auctions.

4.4 Revenue Implications

In this section we study the implications of conflicts on search engine revenue. As in Section 3.5, we consider a traditional search engine T that does not support conflict constraints with an engine K that does support conflicts. Then we address the question: Under otherwise equal circumstances, will K make more or less money than T?

There are two competing factors in this comparison. On the positive side (for K), advertisers will bid more at K than at T (see Equation 5). On the negative side, due to conflicts K will have fewer display choices than T so may "lose out on some opportunities." Which factor is more important depends on the value of β (defined in Section 3.5).

While we could estimate the value of β in our two specific conflict scenarios, we believe it is more instructive to study search engine revenue as β varies. In other words, we will answer the question: How large does β have to be so that the search engine K does not make less money than T? To find the answer, we assume that the bids in our data sets are for engine T, and we calculate the K bids for $\beta = 0$ to $\beta = 0.02$ with 0.01 increments. In the calculation of the new bids, we take into account only the conflicts within each auction to avoid bid inflation. Then we solve the allocation problem using the new bids for all auctions in our dataset and we calculate the K search engine revenue. We plot the results for the auctions of the competitors scenario in Figure 9. The results for the conflict-breeders are almost identical and we do not plot them here. The x-axis shows the value of β and the y-axis shows the K revenue. There are three lines in the plot and each line looks at auctions with different value of ψ. The flat solid line shows the mean T revenue in the $1,000$ auctions without conflicts. The line is flat, since at K the advertisers report no conflicts and the change of β does not affect the advertiser bids. The dotted line looks at auctions with $\psi = 0.1$, the dashed line looks at auctions with $\psi = 0.2$ and the solid line looks at auctions with $\psi = 0.3$. Each point in any line shows the mean revenue among all auctions with the corresponding ψ value. Note that all lines are increasing because the K advertiser

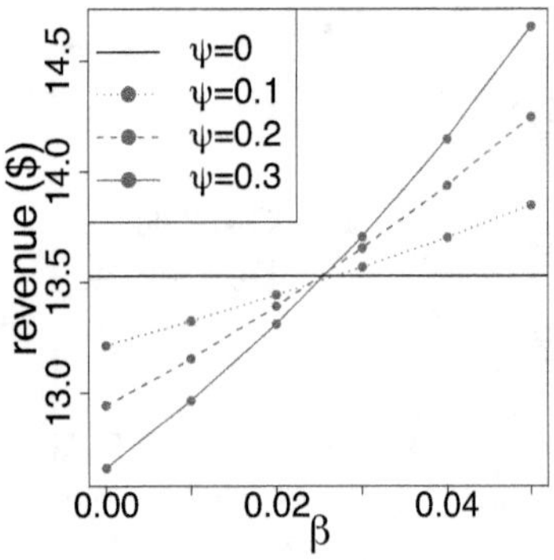

Figure 9: Search engine revenue versus probability β.

bids increase with β. Note also that the higher the ψ the higher the slope of the curves, because higher ψ results into more conflicts and higher bid increases. The most important conclusion from this graph is that all three blue lines cross the $\psi = 0$ line between the relatively low values of $\beta = 0.02$ and $\beta = 0.03$. Thus, if we expect that in traditional sponsored search auctions the advertisers win a slot next to a potential conflict, i.e., either a competitor or a spammer, with probability more than 0.02, then the search engine could increase its revenue by supporting conflicts.

5. RELATED WORK

Sponsored search auctions are studied in the two seminal papers by Varian [16] and Edelman et al. [5]. A book chapter by Lahaie et al. [9] provides also a good overview about the work on the field.

The work of Ghosh et al. [6] and the work of Muthukrishnan [11] are the most relevant to our work. Ghosh et al. [6] study auctions where the advertiser bids are conditioned upon *exclusivity* on the sponsored search results, i.e., one advertiser wins the first slot and the rest of the slots remain empty. Our auction is more expressive, since an advertiser can achieve exclusivity by declaring conflicts against the rest of the advertisers. However, their limited setting allows them to present strong theoretical results about the payment rule and the search engine revenue. Muthukrishnan [11] studies auctions where the bid of advertiser a_j is conditioned on the ad appearing at the top-k_j positions. Such a constraint relies on the ad ranking and cannot be expressed through conflicts.

Our work is also related to various other works [1, 8] that study *externalities* in sponsored search or more expressive sponsored search auctions [10, 2, 4]. An externality refers to the dependence of a click valuation on the context where an ad is displayed. The works on externalities focus on the study of such dependences rather than on allowing advertisers to condition their bids upon them. The works on expressive sponsored search auctions study alternative utility functions that take into account clicks, impressions and may be discontinuous.

6. CONCLUSIONS

In this paper we introduced a variation of sponsored search auctions where advertisers are allowed to declare conflicts against their peers. The main focus of our study is the computational feasibility of the new auctions. Despite the NP-hardness result for the slot allocation problem, we have presented Debbassac, a DFS branch-and-bound algorithm, that can efficiently allocate the auctioned slots to advertisers in practical cases. Our experiments showed that Debbassac can solve the allocation problem of an auction with hundreds of advertisers and thousands of conflicts in tens to hundreds of milliseconds.

We have studied the implications of the new auction on search engine revenue using a VCG payment rule to determine prices. Our results show that a search engine can under certain circumstances increase its revenue by introducing conflicts. The increase of the revenue is not at the expense of the advertisers. The advertisers enjoy actually higher utility per auction, since they have greater control over the context where their ads get clicked.

In our future work we plan to explore alternative approaches for the payment rule of the new auction. Although the VCG mechanism provides truthful bidding, a simpler GSP-like payment rule might be more appealing to search engines. Another promising direction for future work is the introduction of additional interaction among advertisers. For example, advertisers may want to "follow" other advertisers and have their ads appear next to them. We plan to study such interactions in our future work.

7. REFERENCES

[1] G. Aggarwal, J. Feldman, S. Muthukrishnan, and M. Pal. Sponsored search auctions with markovian users. In *Internet and Network Economics, LNCS* 5385: 621–628. Springer Berlin / Heidelberg, 2008.

[2] G. Aggarwal, S. Muthukrishnan, D. Pál, and M. Pál. General auction mechanism for search advertising. In WWW, 2009.

[3] P. Cramton, Y. Shoham, and R. Steinberg. *Combinatorial Auctions*. The MIT Press, 2006.

[4] P. Dütting, M. Henzinger, and I. Weber. An expressive mechanism for auctions on the web. In WWW, 2011.

[5] B. Edelman, M. Ostrovsky, and M. Schwarz. Internet advertising and the generalized second-price auction: Selling billions of dollars worth of keywords. *American Economic Review*, 97(1):242–259, March 2007.

[6] A. Ghosh and A. Sayedi. Expressive auctions for externalities in online advertising. In WWW, 2010.

[7] D. Kempe and M. Mahdian. A cascade model for externalities in sponsored search. In WINE, 2008.

[8] D. Kempe and M. Mahdian. A cascade model for externalities in sponsored search. In *Internet and Network Economics, LNCS* 5385: 585–596. Springer Berlin / Heidelberg, 2008.

[9] S. Lahaie, D. M. Pennock, A. Saberi, and R. V. Vohra. Sponsored search auctions. In *Algorithmic Game Theory*. Cambridge University Press, 2007.

[10] D. J. Martin, J. Gehrke, and J. Y. Halpern. Toward expressive and scalable sponsored search auctions. In ICDE, 2008.

[11] S. Muthukrishnan. Bidding on configurations in internet ad auctions. In COCOON, 2009.

[12] N. Nisan, T. Roughgarden, E. Tardos, and V. V. Vazirani. *Algorithmic Game Theory*. Cambridge University Press, New York, NY, USA, 2007.

[13] P. Papadimitriou and H. Garcia-Molina. Sponsored search auctions with conflict constraints. Technical report 1010, Stanford InfoLab, 2011. URL: `http://ilpubs.stanford.edu:8090/1010/`

[14] D. H. Reiley, S.-M. Li, and R. A. Lewis. Northern exposure: a field experiment measuring externalities between search advertisements. In EC, 2010.

[15] T. Sandholm, S. Suri, A. Gilpin, and D. Levine. Cabob: a fast optimal algorithm for combinatorial auctions. In IJCAI, 2001.

[16] H. R. Varian. Position auctions. *International Journal of Industrial Organization*, 25(6):1163 – 1178, 2007.

Post-Click Conversion Modeling and Analysis for Non-Guaranteed Delivery Display Advertising

Rómer Rosales
Yahoo! Labs
4401 Great America Parkway
Santa Clara, CA
romerr@yahoo-inc.com

Haibin Cheng
Yahoo! Labs
4401 Great America Parkway
Santa Clara, CA
hcheng@yahoo-inc.com

Eren Manavoglu
Yahoo! Labs
4401 Great America Parkway
Santa Clara, CA
erenm@yahoo-inc.com

ABSTRACT

In on-line search and display advertising, the click-trough rate (CTR) has been traditionally a key measure of ad/ campaign effectiveness. More recently, the market has gained interest in more direct measures of profitability, one early alternative is the conversion rate (CVR). CVRs measure the proportion of certain users who take a predefined, desirable action, such as a purchase, registration, download, etc.; as compared to simply page browsing. We provide a detailed analysis of conversion rates in the context of non-guaranteed delivery targeted advertising. In particular we focus on the post-click conversion (PCC) problem or the analysis of conversions after a user click on a referring ad. The key elements we study are the probability of a conversion given a click in a user/page context, P(conversion | click, context). We provide various fundamental properties of this process based on contextual information, formalize the problem of predicting PCC, and propose an approach for measuring attribute relevance when the underlying attribute distribution is non-stationary. We provide experimental analyses based on logged events from a large-scale advertising platform.

Categories and Subject Descriptors

H.3.5 [**Online Information Services**]: Commercial Services; H.4.m [**Information Systems**]: Miscellaneous; I.5.2 [**Design Methodology**]: Classifier Design and Evaluation

General Terms

Algorithms, Design, Experimentation

Keywords

Display Advertising, Non-Guaranteed Delivery, Conversion Rate, Conversion Modeling, Post-click Conversion

1. INTRODUCTION

Display advertising is a fast growing on-line advertising medium where advertisers pay publishers to place graphical ads on their web pages. There are two ad purchasing and delivery mechanisms that are commonly used today. Guaranteed Delivery (GD) is the traditional mechanism where an advertiser buys a predetermined number of impressions (5 million) at a fixed price (10 cents per impression) for a fixed time period (August 2011) from the publisher. In this model, the publisher is obligated to deliver the agreed upon number of impressions that satisfy the advertiser's targeting requirements (*e.g.*, females, between the age of 25-30, in California). The second mechanism, Non-Guaranteed Delivery (NGD), is a spot market where the advertisers can buy ad impressions one at a time. Under this mechanism every time a user loads a web page with an ad slot, an auction is run among the ads that match the targeting specifications of that particular opportunity and an ad is chosen for display.

Guaranteed delivery is preferred by risk-averse publishers and advertisers as it provides one with a steady and predictable source of income, and the other with an exact exposure rate. Spot markets, on the other hand, allow the advertisers to change their bids based on highly granular targeting profiles, and let them adapt to varying trends in traffic patterns quickly.

Spot markets also offer advertisers a wider range of payment models. Like in guaranteed display, advertisers can choose to pay per impression (CPM). This model works well for the advertisers who are trying to build brand awareness where getting the message out is the goal. However, for many advertisers, an ad impression that does not ultimately lead to a visit to their website or to a product purchase is not worth paying for. To address this concern many non-guaranteed display exchanges provide performance-dependent payment methods such as pay per click (CPC) and pay per conversion/action (CPA) [21]. In the pay per click model, an advertiser will not be charged unless the user clicks on their ad. Pay per conversion/action model reduces the risk for the advertisers even further by allowing them to pay only when the user takes an action that is of interest to them. Advertisers have complete control over the definition of these conversion actions. Example actions include but are not limited to: subscribing to an email list, adding an item to the shopping cart, or making a purchase.

In a marketplace where advertisers with different payment types will be competing for the same ad slot, the auction mechanism needs to convert these bids that are in different currencies to a common base, such as a monetary unit. *Expected* price per impression (eCPM) is a natural choice for such a common unit. For CPM ads, the expected price per impression (eCPM) would be the same as their bid for

Permission to make digital or hard copies of all or part of this work for personal or classroom use is granted without fee provided that copies are not made or distributed for profit or commercial advantage and that copies bear this notice and the full citation on the first page. To copy otherwise, to republish, to post on servers or to redistribute to lists, requires prior specific permission and/or a fee.
WSDM'12, February 8–12, 2012, Seattle, Washington, USA.
Copyright 2012 ACM 978-1-4503-0747-5/12/02 ...$10.00.

that impression. For ads that are defined as pay per click (CPC) or pay per conversion (CPA), their eCPM will depend on the expected click or conversion rate of the given impression. More precisely, $eCPM(CPC) = p(click) * bid$ and $eCPM(CPA) = p(conversion) * bid$, where $p(click)$ is the probability that an impression will result in a click, and $p(conversion)$ is the probability that an impression will lead the user to take the actions that constitute a conversion for that advertiser.

Accurate estimations of these probabilities are critical for the efficiency of an exchange [22]. While the problem of estimating click probabilities have been studied extensively in the context of both search [17, 27, 11, 25, 2, 29, 16], contextual [24, 9] and display advertising [10, 14], literature on conversion prediction is much sparser. In this paper we try to address precisely this issue by providing empirical answers to practical questions that arise in conversion prediction and its application to NGD: How different is conversion modeling from click modeling, can we apply lessons learned from clicks directly to conversions? Previous studies suggest that the delay between a click and a conversion event could be quite long, what does the data tell us? How tolerant are our models to temporal changes? How important are user and publisher attributes in predicting conversions?

The focus of our analysis is the conversion probability for clicked ads. While a click is not necessary for a conversion event to happen, most CPA advertisers do not give credit to publishers unless they can trace the conversion event back to an impression on the publisher's page via a click event; thus making the click a prerequisite for a conversion action (hence, this is often called a post-click conversion or PCC).

The rest of the paper is organized as follows. In Section 2 we discuss related work and in Section 3 we describe the data that will be used in the rest of the paper. In Section 4 we present the results of our analysis on the various aspects of post click conversion problem. Section 5 follows by introducing our baseline model and feature selection algorithm. Then in Section 6 we present our experimental results. We finally conclude in Section 7 by summarizing our findings.

2. RELATED WORK

Although the importance of conversion modeling is widely recognized in the computational advertising community [7] the published literature on the subject has only recently begun to accumulate. Becker et al. [4] analyze the impact of landing page on the user's conversion behavior in the context of sponsored search. They first provide a taxonomy for the advertiser landing pages and then show that the conversion rates varies significantly from category to category. Our paper is complementary to this work because we identify what other factors could be playing a role in the user's conversion behavior. In [3], the authors propose a new model that optimizes the conversion funnel even for CPC campaigns. Since the authors evaluate their model for contextual advertising their analysis of conversion prediction is heavily focused on keyword matches. While the auction model proposed in that study could easily be applied to display advertising, their results on conversion modeling would not be directly applicable to graphical ads. In [28] Shi et al. propose the use of Kullback-Leibler divergence between the default distribution of user attributes and the user specific distribution as a feature selection mechanism to build compact user profiles. They show that these compact user profiles improve the performance of conversion models that are used for behavioral targeting.

The work by Agarwal et al. [1] is perhaps the closest to our paper in terms of domain. The authors propose a log-linear model to estimate click and conversion rates, which exploits the correlations in aggregates at multiple resolutions. Their results show that this model performs better than vanilla models that do not make use of the hierarchy that's found naturally in the ad data. While the focus of their paper is purely the modeling aspect, the authors also report observing differences in relative model performances on PCC vs click prediction.

While display advertising has been used from the early days of Internet, data driven research and analysis on the economic impact of it has been relatively sparse. Results published by Reiley and Lewis [26] provide the strongest quantitative analysis to the best of our knowledge. The authors ran a controlled experiment on over a million users who could also be linked with their offline activities and reported that the users who were exposed to the ads showed a statistically significant increase in both in store and online sales. Lewis was also able to show that exposing the same ad to the same user over and over again has diminishing returns [20] and that display advertising has a bigger impact on older users [19].

3. DATA DESCRIPTION

We collected live traffic logs from Yahoo!'s Right Media Exchange (RMX), one of the largest ad exchanges in the world, which serves around ten billion impressions every day. RMX follows a "network-of-networks" model where the connections between advertisers and publishers are facilitated by intermediaries called networks. Networks can have either only publishers or advertisers, or both. Every entity in the exchange (networks, publishers and advertisers) has a unique identifier.

Publishers label their web-pages with site id's. They can also tag different parts of the same page with a different section id. While the exchange does not enforce any rules on the semantics of section id's, publishers often use a different section id for different ad slots on the same page.

An insertion order represents the contractual relationship between a network and an advertiser or a publisher, or between any two entities on the Exchange. A line item is an element of an insertion order. An insertion order can have one or more line items, each with a different pricing type, budget and targeting profile. Advertisers can have multiple ad groups within a line item, each with a custom target profile, and different budget settings. In RMX one ad group can also be associated with multiple line items. In this paper we represent each {line item, ad group} pair as a campaign. In RMX, the relationship between campaigns and ad creatives are not necessarily hierarchical. Advertisers can use the same creative in multiple campaigns.

For CPA campaigns advertisers also need to select the type of conversion (post-click or post-view), and set the time out period for a conversion to be valid after the preceding event. Advertisers can also specify how frequently a conversion is allowed to repeat (*e.g.*, no consecutive conversions can trigger within one hour of the last conversion). Conversions are tracked using pixels, and each distinct conversion action is assigned a pixel id. Advertisers are allowed to reuse existing conversion pixel ids (conversion ids).

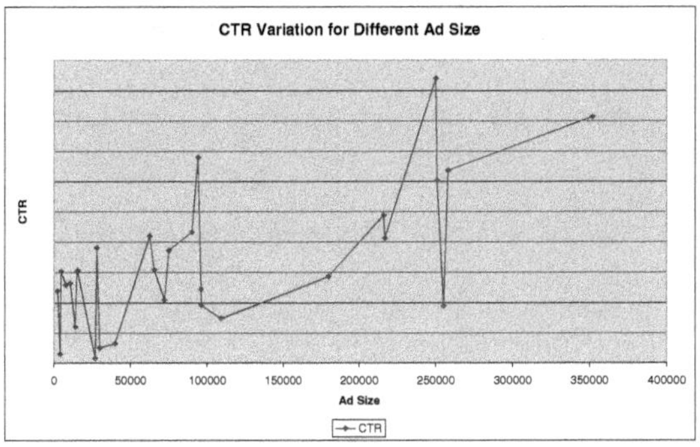

Figure 1: Relative CTR variation for different ad sizes (measured in pixels).

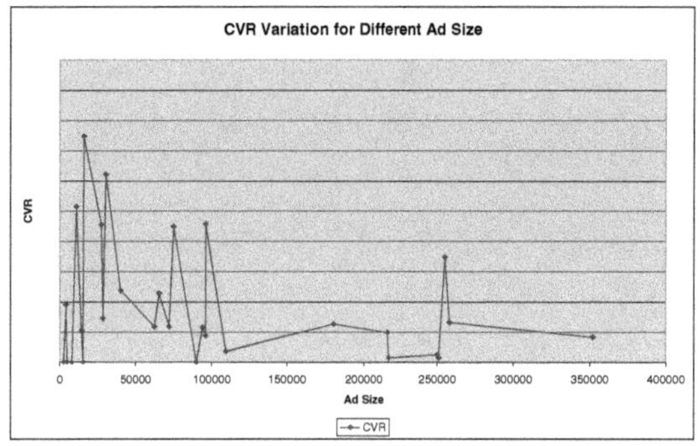

Figure 2: Relative CVR variation for different ad sizes (measured in pixels).

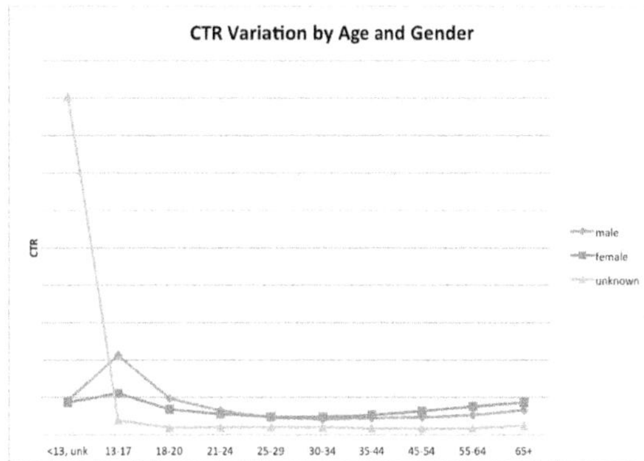

Figure 3: Relative CTR variation for different age and gender categories.

4. POST-CLICK CONVERSION ANALYSIS

In this section we provide an analysis of the post-click conversion problem using a large collection of logged events. The goal of this analysis is to help us uncover special problem properties and patterns of user behavior to guide the modeling tasks discussed later. For this we use data collected for a period of one month containing approximately 1 billion user events involving an ad click.

4.1 Contrasting CTR and CVR

We are interested in uncovering the fundamental properties of the post-click conversion (PCC) event. PCC occurs after a user has clicked on a relevant ad. Thus, a basic question is whether there is evidence that elements of importance in modeling click-through rate (CTR)[1] are also relevant in modeling PCC conversion rate (CVR). We investigate this by exploring three important attributes in click modeling, the user age, the user gender and the ad size.

In click modeling, ad size is strongly correlated with CTR. This makes intuitive sense likely because large ads are on average more attractive and more attention-grabbing to users than small ads, resulting in measurably higher CTR. This has been confirmed in the present data. Figure 1 shows the CTR variation (y-axis) with respect to different ad sizes in terms of number of pixels (x-axis). The absolute CTR value in the Figure is removed to comply with company policy. Due that ad sizes have been predefined (to a large extent) in the on-line advertising industry, only a few points in the x-axis can be measured. Figure 1 clearly indicates that the CTR of ads increase approximately linearly with the ad size. Using the conversion logs for the same period, the post-click conversion rate for different ad sizes is calculated and plotted in Figure 2. In contrast with the trend observed in CTR with regard to the ad size, the CVR for users does not increase when the ad size increases. The size of the ad appears to have no effect on the user's decision on converting or not likely because the user has been directed to a different page (the ad landing page) and has lost the visual perception of the ad on the initial page view. In summary, this provides evidence that the ad size may not be an informative element for PCC modeling, particularly when compared with click modeling.

A similar analysis was extended to user profile attributes such as age and gender. Using the same click logs, Figure 3 shows the variation of click through rates for different age groups and genders (male, female and unknown). There is an unexpected high CTR rate for users with (mostly) unknown age and unknown gender, otherwise we did not see a strong trend in terms of CTR with respect to age groups. However, male users seem to click more often than female users at a younger age, with the trend reversing (to a small extent) for older users. Figure 4 shows the variation of post-click conversion rates for different age groups and genders. We can observe that female users tend to convert more often than male users. Also there is strong linear trend in terms of conversion rate with respect to the age groups. Older users seems to covert more often than younger users. Thus, unlike our observation for ad sizes, the age and gender can clearly play a more important role in post-click conversion modeling.

[1]The probability that a user clicks on a given ad.

4.2 Analysis of the Click→Conversion Delay

A critical aspect in PCC modeling is the association or attribution of a conversion event to the corresponding click event. In order to build a conversion model, we need to attribute the conversion event to the correct click event as this represents a positive PCC example (vs. a click event without any associated conversion event). A conversion event can happen minutes, hours or even days after a click event. The proper attribution of the conversion event to the right click event, which can done by properly matching the click and conversion event attributes, is essential not only for PCC but also for payment processing.

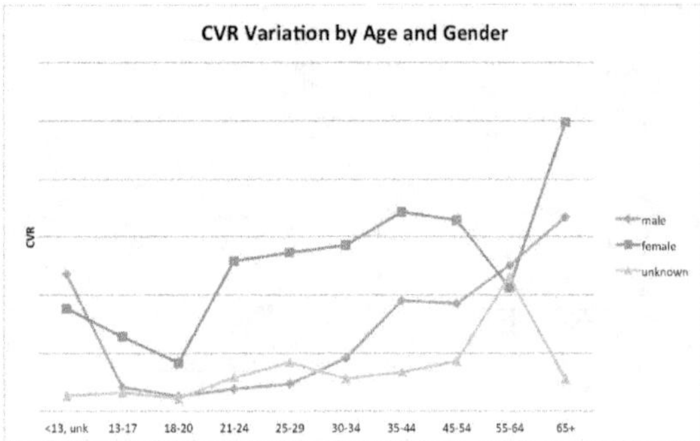

Figure 4: Relative CVR variation for different age and gender categories.

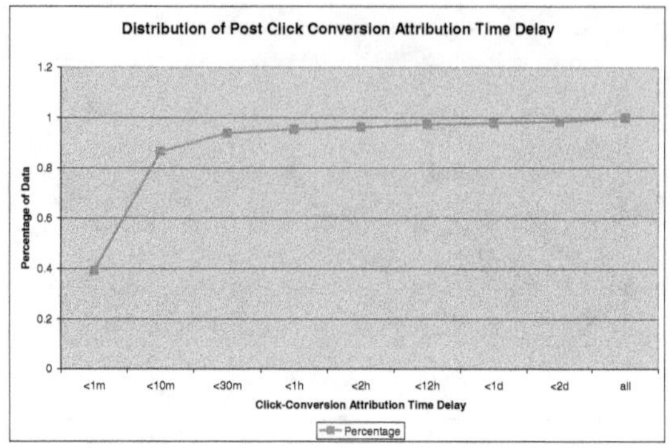

Figure 5: Distribution of click conversion attribution time delay.

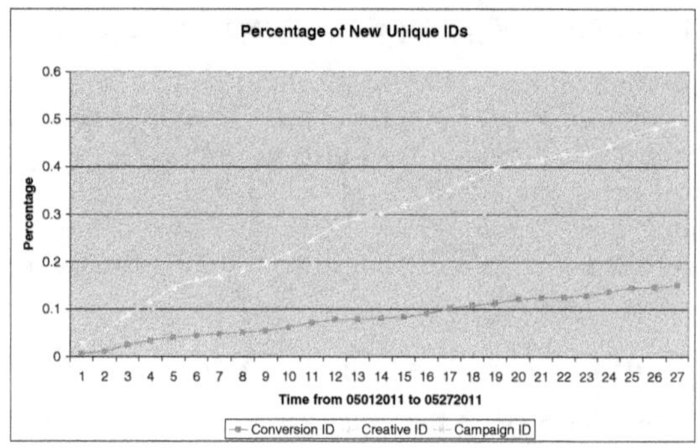

Figure 6: Percentage of new unique conversion identifiers, creatives and campaigns emerging for each day in one month (relative to those existing in the previous month).

In general several conversion events could be associated with the same click, as advertisers may show a sequence of conversion-generating pages to the user after a click on the relevant ad. On the other hand, a conversion event may not necessarily be associated with any ad click[2]. This association process faces certain practical limitations as the longer the time elapsed between click and conversion the more logged events that need to be maintained and matched. In order to get a better picture of the click-conversion process and to answer the question of how much data needs to be utilized for matching conversions with their corresponding click events, we analyzed the properties of the time delay for conversion events.

We calculated the percentage of conversion events with different attribution time intervals as shown in Figure 5. From the graph, we can observe that a large majority (86.7%) of conversion events are triggered within 10 minutes of the click events. Approximately half of these conversion events (39.2%) occur within 1 minute of the corresponding click event. If we look further, we observed that we can match 95.5% of the conversion events within one hour of the clicks. As we are interested in achieving the largest possible recall within practical boundaries, we decided to consider various days of delay. Within two days of the click, 98.5% of the conversions can be recovered. Thus, we would be ignoring approximately 1.5% of the conversion events and as a consequence incorrectly labeling a click event as referring to a negative conversion (no conversion) if the time frame set for post click conversion attribution is limited to 2 days. This was believed to be sufficient given the practical cost of looking further in time; and thus, we utilize this limit throughout the paper.

4.3 Ad Emergence Rate Analysis

Post-click conversion models are built based on data collected in the historical logs, using performance information of ads that have been in the advertising system for some time. When completely new ads are added to the advertising system, models built in the past may not perform well particularly for those new ads (this clearly depends on the generalization power of the attributes utilized for modeling). This property of the system raises some challenges regarding how to keep a conversion prediction model up-to-date. One strategy is to constantly update the model using the latest data[3]. However, this could be too expensive for practical purposes and potentially unnecessary.

In order to design a model updating mechanism (that is able to cope with the dynamic nature of campaign generation) with reasonable trade off between performance and latency, it is important to investigate the ratio of new ads emergence with respect to time. In this section, we calculate the percentage of new ads arising daily for a period of one month relative to ads already existing in the previous month. Three representation levels of the ads are investigated: conversion, creative, and campaign level (these also turned out to be the most informative advertiser-based features in the conversion models studied).

Figure 6 plots the percentage of new unique ads for each day. It is clear from the figure that the percentage of unique new ads in the data is increasing steadily day by day in terms of all the three representations. There is a difference in terms of the emerging rate. Creatives are observed to change most frequently. There are 19.7% new creatives after 10 days and 39.8% after 20 days. Ad campaigns also increase steadily, but at a slower rate, with approximately 16% increase after 10 days and 31% after 20 days. Conversion identifiers are the most stable of the three, with only 5.4% of new unique ids

[2]This can be analyzed in the context of post-view conversion, a process complementary to post-click conversion

[3]There are other phenomena that motivates frequent model updates, including the dynamic nature of on-line information as changes in page-viewing behavior in intrinsically related to ad effectiveness

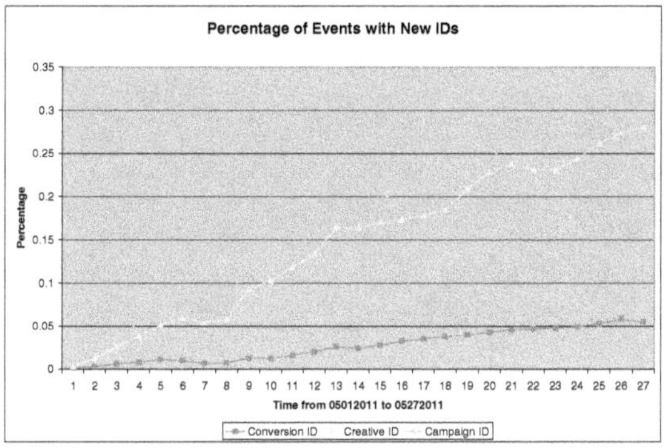

Figure 7: Percentage of events with new conversion identifiers, creatives, and campaigns for each day in one month (relative to those existing in the previous month).

after 10 days and 11.2% after 20 days. This indicates that advertisers tend to use the same conversion identifiers to track the respective conversion events even after they create new ad creatives and campaigns.

This is beneficial to some extent to PCC modeling since a model relying on conversion identifiers should be relative stable with respect to changes in time. Furthermore, the linear trend of the emerging rate in campaigns and creatives may indicate that the performance dependence of the model with respect to those features is linearly related to its updating frequency.

Similar conclusions can be reached by looking at the percentage of events with new campaign, creatives, and conversion identifiers with regard to the total number of daily events using the same time period as before. This is shown in Figure 7. A proportion of 1.3% of the events contain new conversion identifiers after 10 days and 4.3% after 20 days respectively. This is considered to be a relatively small increase for practical purposes as a model not updated for a very large period (*e.g.,* 10 days) will still consider all the available conversion identifiers in the system.

4.4 Ad Life-time Analysis

The previous section indicates that there are new ads emerging day by day. However, it does not tell their actual lifetime, another relevant property. Figure 8 plots the distribution of the actual lifetime of ads at three levels: conversion id, campaign, and creative levels. 37.4% of conversion ids lives longer than 2 months, which is quite significant compared to 8% for creative ids and 14.9% for campaign ids. 23.6% of creative ids and 18.7% of campaign ids have a lifetime shorter than 3 days, while this number for conversion id is only 7.4%. It is notable that conversion id lives much longer than the creative id and campaign id, which is consistent with the conclusion reached in Section 4.3.

5. POST-CLICK CONVERSION MODELS

In this section we focus on PCC prediction modeling, including various types of feature definitions, and the problem of feature selection given the properties of the attribute distributions in PCC (in particular their non-stationary nature).

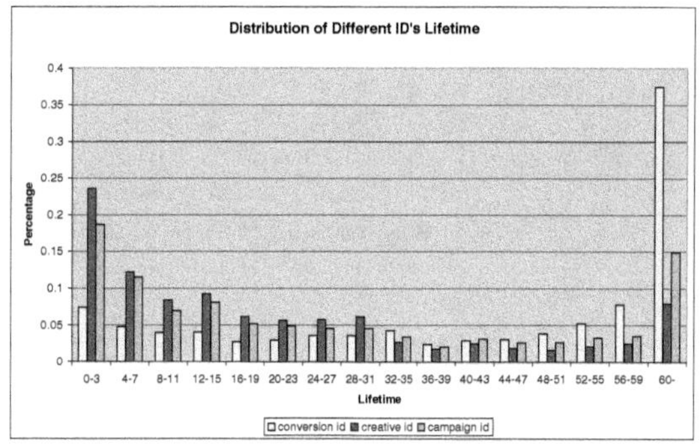

Figure 8: Distribution of lifetime for different IDs.

5.1 Predicting Conversions after a Click

Non-guaranteed delivery (NGD) advertisement is a large and complex subsystem of the more general on-line display advertisement market. In NGD, multiple market players including publishers, advertisers, ad networks, and ad exchanges, try to optimize ad placement in a distributed manner. Various elements are fundamental in this large ecosystem, including prices, inventories, and (crucially) expected user behavior. The details of this overall system are beyond the scope of this paper. However, the latter element is of particular importance as revenue for a large sub-class of advertisement is tied to user actions as related to ads. One class of such actions is generally referred to as a conversion: a predefined user transaction such as a purchase, registration, download, referral, etc. The focus of this section is on estimating a crucial quantity in this system, that is the probability that an on-line user (*e.g.,* page visitor) will trigger a conversion after clicking on a specific advertisement. We call this the post-click conversion (PCC) prediction problem.

We characterize and formalize PCC prediction as a machine learning problem. For this, we utilize the logs from a large-scale advertising platform to identify the conversions and associate them with their corresponding ad clicks. More specifically, we are interested in modeling the conditional probability of a conversion given that a user clicked on a relevant ad. Two classes of events are of interest in order to approach this problem: 1) events where a user clicked on an ad but did not convert are considered negative conversion instances, whereas 2) events where a user clicked and subsequently converted are considered positive conversion instances.

Given these definitions, let a set of events be represented by $\mathcal{D} = \{\mathbf{x}(b_i, a_i, u_i), y_i\}$ where $\mathbf{x}(b_i, a_i, u_i) \in \Re^d$ is a representation of the information available about the event, normally associated to a publisher b_i, advertisement a_i and user u_i; whereas $y_i \in \{0, +1\}$ is an indicator of whether a conversion was associated to the event. Thus, given some or all event information, the goal is to produce a probability of a conversion $p(y|b, a, u)$, or more succinctly $p(y|\mathbf{x})$.

Throughout this paper we utilize a maximum entropy model of the above distribution. This, also referred to as logistic regression in statistics[13], is a log-linear model that combines the individual contributions of each element of the feature vector representation through a weighting $\mathbf{w} = (w_1, ..., w_d)$. Formally:

Table 1: Summary of basic features considered divided into feature families

Feature family	Feature members
Advertiser	advertiser (id), advertiser network, campaign, creative, conversion id, ad group, ad size, creative type, offer type
Publisher	publisher (id), publisher network, site, section, url, page referrer
User (when avail.)	gender, age, region, network speed, accept cookies, geo, user segments
Other	serve time

$$p(y = 1|b, a, u) = \frac{1}{1 + \exp(-\sum_{i=1}^{d} w_i \mathbf{x}_i(b, a, u))}, \quad (1)$$

where $w_i \in \Re$ weighs the feature specific contributions.

We find the optimal values for w_i by employing the maximum-a-posteriori probability criterion: $\mathbf{w}^* = \text{argmax} p(\mathbf{w}|\mathcal{D})$. We attach a Gaussian prior $p(\mathbf{w}) = \mathcal{N}(\mathbf{w}; \mathbf{0}, \Sigma)$ to $\mathbf{w}$ and solve:

$$\mathbf{w}^* = \arg\max_{\mathbf{w} \in \Re^d} \sum_{i=i}^{N} \log(p(y_i|b_i, a_i, u_i)) + \log p(\mathbf{w}). \quad (2)$$

The problem given by formulation (2) is a convex optimization problem and therefore has an unique maximum [6]. It can be solved using a variety of techniques [23]; however, for large-dimensional representations (large d) most approaches face practical limitations related to computing and storing the second-order information of the objective function. Non-linear conjugate methods are a feasible alternative due that they rely on computing the function gradient and only an estimate of its Hessian. We utilize a distributed conjugate gradient algorithm with a pre-conditioner to accelerate convergence [5].

5.2 Features

When building personalized conversion models, it is fundamental to gather the appropriate information about the different axes of personalization. We consider four sets of attributes or features available in most on-line advertisement systems as depicted in Table 1. These attributes are obtained at the event level, that is every time a user clicks and (potentially) makes a conversion on a corresponding ad-publisher pair. However various forms of feature aggregations are utilized and explained below. The first set is represented by advertiser-dependent attributes such as its identifier and ad-specific information for the click event in consideration. The second set correspond to publisher information where the event (click or conversion) took place. The third set includes some pieces of available user information. It is worth mentioning that the availability of these attributes varies across events. The last set includes other information such as the time of the transaction. Because of their *fine-grained nature*, some of the above features carry very little information in their original form (*e.g.,* user age and the event times); thus, these have been quantized appropriately.

The use of feedback features in conversion modeling relies on the simple observation that ads performing better in the past will likely perform better in the future. In PCC modeling, statistics such as the total number of clicks and the conversion rate (conversions/clicks) are often utilized to measure the performance of ads. Feedback features are derived from these statistics by aggregating the historical data for ads at different levels such as advertiser, campaign, creative, and conversion id organized by advertisers as described in Table 1. To capture the variation of ad performance for different publishers, similar features can also be obtained by paring the advertisers at different levels with publishers, *e.g.,* . the publisher-creative pair, the site id-creative pair, etc. Similarly, aggregations such as age- creative, gender-creative, and geo-creative are expected to be good feedback features because they can capture the variation of past ad performance for different users. Feedback features are quantized using a simple k-means clustering algorithm [8] before they are fed to the maximum entropy optimization algorithm. Note that feedback features are often refreshed regularly by updating the statistics with the latest historical information available.

5.3 Automated Feature Analysis

As seen in the analyses of Section 4, post-click conversion (PCC) events have the property that the distribution of certain attributes (*e.g.,* campaign, creative, conversion identifiers) evolve considerably with time. From a machine learning perspective, this raises some difficulties as the underlying attribute distribution is non-stationary. A feature value occurring with some regularity in the training data may not necessarily occur in the same manner on-line (at inference/classification time) and thus a machine learning model would likely learn from values that are not as representative of the test data as expected[4] Two reasons for the above phenomenon include a) the underlying dynamic nature of the attribute distribution (as seen in Figures 6-8) b) the fact that some attribute values are relatively unique to the data point (*i.e.,* logged event) and cannot be used to generalize in a machine learning sense. The latter is an extreme case of the former and includes features such as event identifiers, non-processed time-stamps, etc. Our goal is to automatically discover the relevant/non-relevant attributes with as little human involvement as possible. This is of clear importance when building/updating models regularly in a live system.

This problem can be studied in the context of the mutual information (MI) score, an information theoretic quantity employed to measure the degree of dependence between random variables[18, 12]. In our particular context, let $I(X_j, Y)$ represent the information in feature X_j about Y. A widely used feature selection method consists of selecting the features X_j such that $I(X_j, Y)$ is *high*, with Y the target attribute (*e.g.,* whether a conversion occurred). For example, select the top ranked features [15].

For features with a dynamic distribution as in our case, the MI calculated on a training set fails to provide a good measure of feature relevance. This can be illustrated as follows: Let X_u be a random variable taking unique values (X_u can for instance be an event identifier), then $I(X_u, Y) = H(Y)$ since the values of X_u can fully identify the data point and therefore its label. Formally:

[4]The degree to which this distribution is non-stationary depends on the choice of features.

$$I(X_u, Y) = \sum_{x,y} p(x_u, y) \log p(y|x_u)/p(y) \quad (3)$$

$$= \sum_{y} p(y) \log 1/p(y) = H(Y), \quad (4)$$

since $p(y^*|x_u) = 1$ for some $y = y^*$ (zero otherwise). However, X_u is useless as an attribute for predicting y since its values are unique and not observed in any test set.

In order to address this problem we propose using a related function that explicitly considers a reference distribution. Let the reference distribution be given by $\tilde{p}(x, y)$, then define the MI with respect to the reference distribution by:

$$I_{\tilde{p}}(X_i, Y) = \sum_{x_i,y} \tilde{p}(x_i, y) \log \frac{p(x_i, y)}{p(x_i)p(y)}, \quad (5)$$

where the difference compared with the standard mutual information function lies in calculating the expectation with respect to the reference (not training) distribution.

This definition has the problem that the log ratio is undefined for cases when $p(x_i) = 0$. This happens when an attribute value has been seen in the reference distribution $\tilde{p}$ but not in the training set distribution p. Thus, we utilize a smoothing of the training data distribution of the form:

$$p_r(x_i, y) = \frac{Np(x_i, y) + p(y)}{N + |X_i|}, \quad (6)$$

guaranteeing $p_r(x_i) > 0$, where $|X_i|$ is the number of states taken by X_i. It is possible to show that, if $(\forall y)p(y) > 0$, this does not affect the target distribution, that is: $p_r(y) = p(y)$. In the critical case where X_j does not appear in the training data distribution, we can show that $p_r(y|x_i) = p(y)$. In the latter case we have that the log ratio above becomes 0.

The main relevant property of the new information quantity is that as attributes are evaluated on a reference distribution, spurious relationships (such as those seen above) found in a specific data set and that do not generalize to the test data set are mostly ignored. Consider the same illustrative example above: the values of X_u do not appear in the test distribution (as these values are unique to a data point); thus, the test distribution will place no mass on these values, and X_u will have no measured information about the target variable of interest. More formally:

$$I_{\tilde{p}}(X_u, Y) = \sum_{x_u,y} \tilde{p}(x_u, y) \log \frac{p_r(x_u, y)}{p_r(x_u)p_r(y)} = 0. \quad (7)$$

We note that in many instances, any reference distribution $\tilde{p}$ computed on a valid sample (not necessarily the test data) different than the training distribution will allow the proposed measure to avoid spurious relationships particular to the training data. However, a reference distribution closer to the test distribution is preferred as test-specific dependencies will be better captured by the new MI definition.

6. MODELING EXPERIMENTS

In this section we further provide experimental evaluations involving conversion modeling. In particular, we study the importance of publisher information, the impact of model update frequency and methodology prediction accuracy, and the use of more automated feature selection methods in both model interpretability and accuracy. All of these experiments optimize formulation (2) using $\Sigma = \lambda^{-1}\mathbf{I}$, with $\lambda \in \Re$ and employ a Map-Reduce implementation of the pre-conditioned conjugate gradient method referred in Section 5.1.

Except where noted, for all of our modeling experiments we utilize one full month as training data and the following month as test data, as highlighted in Section 4.

Table 2: Impact of publisher information on post-click conversion prediction accuracy (in terms of area under precision-recall curve

Model	AUC (PR)	Lift
Base (No pub info)	0.13432	–
Base + pub	0.14187	5.62%
Base + pub + pub nwrk	0.14239	6.01%
Base + pub + pub nwrk + site	0.14260	6.15%
Base + pub + pub nwrk + site + sect.	0.14298	6.45%

6.1 Relevance of Publisher-Side Information

We now provide an analysis of the relevance of publisher information in the task of post-click conversion prediction. Our motivation for this experiment was to understand whether knowing the publisher would improve prediction at all when the advertiser and the user are known. It seems plausible that once the user clicks on the ad, the publisher's page should not have an impact on that user's conversion behavior. If this were the case, then PCC models could be considerably simplified as no publisher-side information would be needed.

For this we built models that include no publisher information and then models that progressively add more detailed information from the publisher side. We considered the attributes: publisher, publisher network, publisher site, and publisher section. The results are shown in Table 2.

The results indicate that knowledge of the publisher identity benefits conversion predictive accuracy to some extent (5.62% improvement). Additional information helps but to a smaller degree. Thus, while the contribution is not large, the models utilized in the following sections do utilize publisher-side information.

6.2 Model Evaluation with Respect to Update Frequency

The results in Section 4.3 and 4.4 indicate that there is a non-trivial percentage of new ads entering the system every day. In this section, we first evaluate the actual impact of the new ads on post-click conversion modeling and then develop two solutions to address this problem. A single model, called the ID model due to its reliance on identifier attributes (Table 1) is trained using data collected for one entire month, with post-click conversion events as positive examples and clicks without conversions as negative examples (as before). These attributes have been converted into indicator features (one for each attribute-value pair) resulting in approximately $368K$ features. The data collected from the following month is used as test data. The data utilized contained two types of ad campaigns: cost per action (CPA) and dynamic cost-per-mille (dCPM) campaigns. The performance of the model is evaluated using the AUC (area under the receiver operating characteristic or ROC) curve.

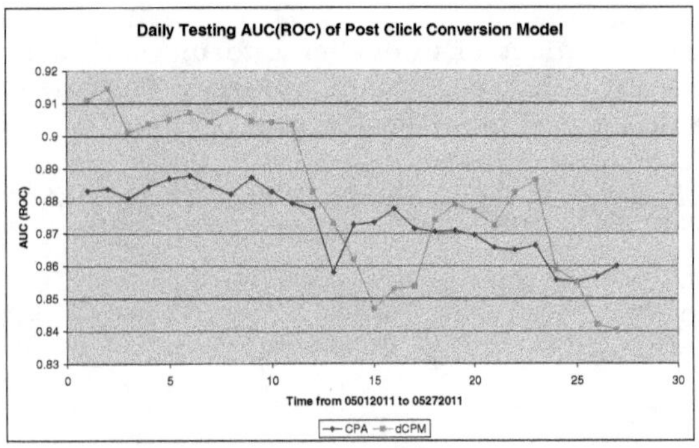

Figure 9: The performance (AUC) of the single ID model degrades with time for both CPA and dCPM campaigns.

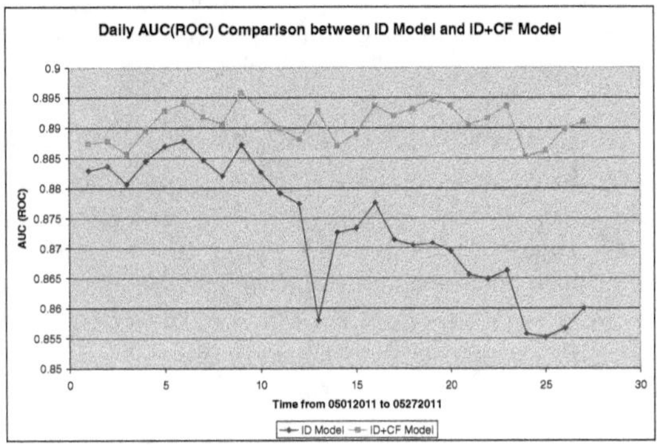

Figure 10: The Performance (AUC) of the ID+CF model is considerably more stable than the that of the ID model.

In order to evaluate the impact of the new ads on the performance of the single model, we divided the test data into separate slices. Each slice of the data represents one day test data of each campaign type. In Figure 9 we plot the AUC calculated based on different slices of the test data using the learned model. The x-axis represents each day in the test data and the y-axis indicates the AUC for each slice of data. We can see from Figure 9 that the performance of the model degrades almost linearly with respect to time for both CPA and dCPM campaigns. It seems clear that the degrading performance is closely related to the new ads emerging in the test data, as elucidated in previous analyses (Sections 4.3-4.4).

We experimented with one way to address the problem of performance degradation above (when using a single model for the entire test period). For this, we use the feedback features introduced in Section 6 and refresh the statistics captured by these features regularly to include information about new ads (on a daily basis). Feedback features capture the current performance of different ads, publishers and users by updating the number of clicks and conversion rates to the reflect their most up-to-date rates. A second approach (not tested) would be to adapt the model parameters to the latest data. In this second approach, the model is simply retrained regularly using Table 1 features, thus including the emerging advertisement-publisher information directly. Note that the first method is considerably less expensive because there is no need to update (re-train) the conversion model *per se*, but only to update the feedback statistics.

Figure 10 shows the performance of a model that utilizes feedback features refreshed every day (ID+CF model) compared with the single ID model. The feedback features included are the number of clicks and the conversion rates for each campaign, conversion identifier, creative, and publisher. In addition we compute the click and conversion rates for every pair of (publisher, creative), (publisher, campaign), (creative, conversion id), (user age, creative), (user age, conversion id), (user gender, creative), (user gender, conversion id), (geo, creative), (geo, campaign) and the triplet (publisher, creative, conversion id) . After quantization, there are approximately $1K$ new features added and refreshed every day, which is quite small compared to the size of the ID features above. From 10, we can see that the ID+CF model clearly outperforms the ID model for every daily slice of testing data. More importantly, the performance of ID+CF is quite stable compared with the ID model, which degrades linearly along time. Thus, we conclude that adding feedback features improves the performance of the post click conversion model and refreshing the features with sufficient regularity (*i.e.*, daily) will maintain these improvements.

6.3 Automated Feature Selection

We utilized the method described in Section 5.3 for determining feature relevance. Our main motivations were not only increasing automation in cases were the underlying data distribution is non-stationary but also decreasing model complexity as the available number of possible features is too large to be used in their entirety during prediction/modeling. Practical considerations, such as memory, latency, and training time constraints, make attribute selection a clear requirement in this task. Non-informative attributes can introduce noise and reduce the predictive accuracy of the system.

We used events for a period of 5 days (training), 1 day (reference), and 2 days (testing). The statistics of this data set were: 125M events for training, 25M for reference, and 50M for testing. The conversion rate varies considerable for different advertisers/publishers/users but rarely exceeds 5%; thus the data set is to a large extent unbalanced.

Our goal is to identify predictive features in the most automated manner possible (reducing time spent by people on this task). Thus, practically all the raw (unprocessed) data attributes available were included in the analysis. These attributes are a super-set of those in Table 1 and include identifiers for the actual (serve/click/conversion) event, advertiser, publisher, campaign, bcookies, timestamps, advertiser/publisher specific attributes, related urls, demographics, user-specific attributes (identifiers, assigned segments), etc. We consider conjunctions of any of these attributes, giving rise to about 5000 possible compound features in practice. Each feature in turn can take from two to millions of possible values.

The important element to consider is that without time-consuming research into attribute definitions, it is extremely tedious to apply most machine learning or data mining/ analysis algorithms. Thus, requiring considerable effort from *e.g.,* machine learning scientists or domain experts. Wrapper methods are not appropriate in this setting as they require training using a large set of variables; this is usually impractical except for some simple models. It is in this set-

Table 3: Top features for conversion prediction along with their mutual information. Top: standard mutual information; Middle and Bottom: modified mutual information. Bottom table contains the top conjunction features.

Single feature	SMI (bits)
event_guid	0.03102
receive_time	0.03059
query_string	0.02963
xcookie	0.02925
user_identifier	0.02923
Single feature	**RMI (bits)**
conversion_id	0.02338
campaign_id	0.02207
ad_group_id	0.02136
line_item_id	0.02090
advertiser_id	0.02082
Conjunction feature	**RMI (bits)**
conversion_id x offer_type_id	0.02379
conversion_id x pop_type_id	0.02369
conversion_id x campaign_id	0.02347
campaign_id x offer_type_id	0.02267
campaign_id x bid_type	0.02235
advertiser_id x pop_type_id	0.02120
advertiser_id x offer_type_id	0.02108
advertiser_network_id x offer_type_id	0.00993
publisher_network_id x advertiser_network_id	0.00770

ting where filter methods, such as the MI methods described here, can be more advantageous.

6.3.1 Attribute Selection Results

We applied the standard MI (SMI) ranking algorithm for feature selection. The results, summarized in Table 3(top) reflect our main concern. In the presence of spurious features, or features that are informative about the data point *per se* rank substantially high. The calculated MI score is correct in that it reflects the information content of these features; however, these features are too specific to the training data distribution.

The proposed extension of the MI score utilizing a reference distribution (RMI) provides a more appropriate ranking as shown in Tables 3(mid-bottom). The reason for this is that the information content is calculated with respect to (expectations on) the reference distribution and thus feature values that are not seen in the new distribution are basically considered less important and their impact on the information score is reduced.

More specifically, attributes such as `event_guid` that identifies the data point have maximal information content according to the training distribution (SMI), but near zero information content when calculated with a reference distribution (RMI) (*c.f.*; Section 5.3). A similar effect was observed for other features that have low relevance for prediction such as `query_string` and `receive_time` which unless parsed are too specific, `xcookie` and `user_identifier` which clearly do not generalize across users (but could be quite informative about a small fraction of the test data), and `user_segments` which is encoded as a string with a list of segments. The results for other features are more subtle but follow the same underlying principle where a reference distribution is utilized to avoid spurious dependencies often found when utilizing empirical distributions.

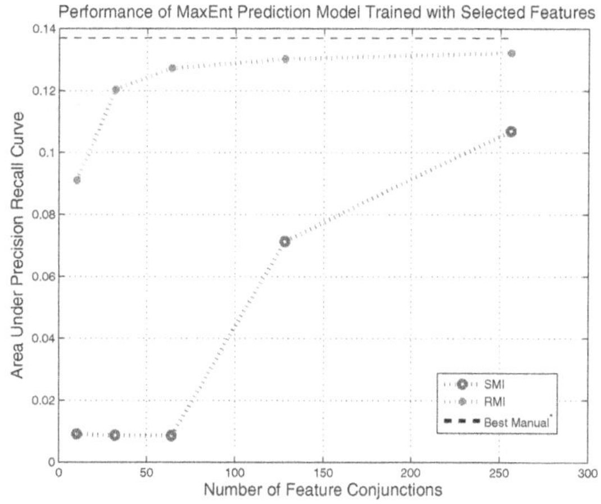

Figure 11: Performance of Logistic Regression Models trained with the top K features given by SMI and RMI

6.3.2 Learning Performance Results

Here we explore the question of whether the new feature rankings actually offer any performance gains. For this, we ranked all the feature conjunctions provided by SMI/RMI and trained a Maximum Entropy (Logistic Regression) model using the top K conjunctions given by each method. The results for conversion prediction are shown in Fig. 11 for various values of K.

The graph shows performance in terms of Area Under the Precision-Recall curve (similar results were obtained when measuring the Area Under the ROC curve and percentage of correct predictions). The results indicate that SMI ranks very irrelevant features on top. After more than 100 conjunctions, more relevant features start to be included in the model as evidenced by the performance gains. On the contrary, RMI captures relevant features much earlier, as only the top 10 features are sufficient to perform better than SMI with 128 features. The performance increases considerably at 32 features, and appears to stabilize after 64 features. One interesting question is whether after a large K the performance of both methods will be comparable. As seen at the end of both curves, when 256 features are utilized, still the difference is considerable. We believe the performance of SMI will remain affected by the various irrelevant feature included early on, depending on how much the model is susceptible to the noise introduced by these. Finally, the top line in the graph represents the current best model[5], using the features described in Table 1, after considerable feature engineering (*e.g.*, where features such as `receive_time` and `query_string` have been parsed and transformed into a suitable quantized representation), manual feature selection, grouping, and train/test exploration experiments. Thus, the proposed selection method produced quantitatively comparable results but is much more resource-efficient.

7. CONCLUSIONS

The accurate estimation of click and conversion probabilities is critical for the efficiency of on-line advertisement exchanges. While click-trough rate (CTR) analyses have been

[5]for the train/test period utilized in this experiment

the subject of much attention, post-click conversion (PCC) analysis studies are much more limited in scope and data coverage. As advertisers gain interest in more direct measures of profitability such as conversion rates, PCC becomes more important.

This paper provided a detailed analysis of conversion rates in the context of non-guaranteed delivery (NGD) for display advertising. We provided fundamental properties of the PCC process based on contextual information including a comparison between CTR and CVR for some relevant data attributes, an analysis of click-to-conversion delay, various properties about how rapidly new advertisements appear and stay in the system. We formalized the problem of conversion modeling along with the problem of determining attribute relevance in the specific setting of CVR optimization where the underlying data distribution is non-stationary. We also provided PCC modeling experimental results including measuring relevance of publisher information, measuring the effect of model update frequency (relevant for evolving attribute distributions), and the effect of automated feature analysis in this scenario. All this was done using data from a large-scale advertising platform. We believe this can provide a more thorough understanding of the PCC process and its modeling challenges.

Acknowledgments

We thank our colleagues for their assistance with data collection, model evaluation, and discussions on the RMI idea.

8. REFERENCES

[1] D. Agarwal, R. Agrawal, R. Khanna, and N. Kota. Estimating rates of rare events with multiple hierarchies through scalable log-linear models. In *KDD*, 2010.

[2] A. Ashkan, C. L. A. Clarke, E. Agichtein, and Q. Guo. Estimating ad clickthrough rate through query intent analysis. In *WI-IAT*, Washington, DC, USA, 2009.

[3] A. Bagherjeiran, A. O. Hatch, and A. Ratnaparkhi. Ranking for the conversion funnel. In *SIGIR*, 2010.

[4] H. Becker, A. Broder, E. Gabrilovich, V. Josifovski, and B. Pang. What happens after an ad click?: quantifying the impact of landing pages in web advertising. In *CIKM*, 2009.

[5] D. Bertsekas. *Nonlinear Programming*. Athena Scientific, 1999.

[6] S. Boyd and L. Vandenberghe. *Convex Optimization*. Cambridge University Press, 2004.

[7] A. Broder and V. Josifovski. Introduction to Computational Advertising, 2010.

[8] D. Chakrabarti, D. Agarwal, and V. Josifovski. Some methods for classification and analysis of multivariate observations. In *Proceedings of 5th Berkeley Symposium on Mathematical Statistics and Probability*, pages 281–297, Berkeley, CA, 1967. University of California Press.

[9] D. Chakrabarti, D. Agarwal, and V. Josifovski. Contextual advertising by combining relevance with click feedback. In *WWW*, 2008.

[10] Y. Chen, D. Pavlov, M. Kapralov, and J. F. Canny. Factor modeling for advertisement targeting. In *NIPS*, 2009.

[11] M. Ciaramita, V. Murdock, and V. Plachouras. Online learning from click data for sponsored search. In *WWW*, 2008.

[12] T. Cover and J. A. Thomas. *Elements of Information Theory*. Wiley Interscience, New York, NY, USA, 1991.

[13] D. Cox and E. Snell. *The analysis of binary data*. Chapman and Hall, 1970.

[14] N. Gupta, U. Khurana, T. Lee, and S. Nawathe. Optimizing display advertisements based on historic user trails. In *SIGIR Workshop on Internet Advertising*, 2011.

[15] I. Guyon and A. Elisseeff, editors. *JMLR Special Issue on Variable and Feature Selection*. Journal of Machine Learning Research, 2003.

[16] D. Hillard, E. Manavoglu, H. Raghavan, C. Leggetter, E. Cantú-Paz, and R. Iyer. The sum of its parts: reducing sparsity in click estimation with query segments. *Information Retrieval*, pages 1–22, 2011.

[17] T. Joachims, L. Granka, B. Pan, H. Hembrooke, and G. Gay. Accurately interpreting clickthrough data as implicit feedback. In *SIGIR*, 2005.

[18] S. Kullback. *Information Theory and Statistics*. Dover, 1968.

[19] R. A. Lewis. Advertising especially influences older users: A yahoo! experiment measuring retail sales. In *Measuring the effects of online advertising on human behavior using natural and field experiments*. Massachusetts Institute of Technology, 2010.

[20] R. A. Lewis. Where is the Wear-Out? Online Display Ads and the Impact of Frequency. In *Measuring the effects of online advertising on human behavior using natural and field experiments*. Massachusetts Institute of Technology, 2010.

[21] M. Mahdian and K. Tomak. Pay-per-action model for online advertising. In *ADKDD*, 2007.

[22] R. McAfee. The design of advertising exchanges. *Review of Industrial Organization*, pages 1–17, 2011.

[23] T. Minka. A comparison of numerical optimizers for logistic regression. http://research.microsoft.com/en-us/um/people/minka/papers/logreg.

[24] V. Murdock, M. Ciaramita, and V. Plachouras. A noisy-channel approach to contextual advertising. In *ADKDD*, 2007.

[25] M. Regelson and D. C. Fain. Predicting click-through rate using keyword clusters. In *In Electronic Commerce (EC)*. ACM, 2007.

[26] D. Reiley and R. A. Lewis. Does Retail Advertising Work? Measuring the Effects of Advertising on Sales via a Controlled Experiment on Yahoo! . Technical report, Yahoo! Labs, 2011.

[27] M. Richardson, E. Dominowska, and R. Ragno. Predicting clicks: estimating the click-through rate for new ads. In *WWW*, 2007.

[28] X. Shi, K. Chang, V. Narayanan, V. Josifovski, and A. Smola. A compression framework for generating user profiles. In *SIGIR Workshop on Feature Generation and Selection for Information Retrieval*, 2010.

[29] W. Xu, E. Manavoglu, and E. Cantú-Paz. Temporal click model for sponsored search. In *SIGIR*, 2010.

Incorporating Revisiting Behaviors into Click Models [*]

Danqing Xu, Yiqun Liu, Min Zhang, Shaoping Ma,Liyun Ru
State Key Lab of Intelligence Technology and Systems
Tsinghua National Laboratory for Information Science and Technology
Department of Computer Science and Technology, Tsinghua University, Beijing, 100084, China P.R.
xudanqing06@gmail.com, {yiqunliu,z-m, msp}@tsinghua.edu.cn, lyru@vip.sohu.com

ABSTRACT

Click-through behaviors are treated as invaluable sources of user feedback and they have been leveraged in several commercial search engines in recent years. However, estimating unbiased relevance is always a challenging task because of position bias. To solve this problem, many researchers have proposed a variety of assumptions to model click-through behaviors. Most of these models share the sequential examination hypothesis, which is that users examine search results from the top to the bottom. Nevertheless, this model cannot draw a complete picture of information-seeking behaviors. Many eye-tracking studies find that user interactions are not sequential but contain revisiting patterns. If a user clicks on a higher ranked document after having clicked on a lower-ranked one, we call this scenario a revisiting pattern, and we believe that the revisiting patterns are important signals regarding a user's click preferences. This paper incorporates revisiting behaviors into click models and introduces a novel click model named Temporal Hidden Click Model (THCM). This model dynamically models users' click behaviors with a temporal order. In our experiment, we collect over 115 million query sessions from a widely-used commercial search engine and then conduct a comparative analysis between our model and several state-of-the-art click models. The experimental results show that the THCM model achieves a significant improvement in the Normalized Discounted Cumulative Gain (NDCG), the click perplexity and click distributions metrics.

Categories and Subject Descriptors

H.3.3 [**Information Search and Retrieval**]:

*This work was supported by Natural Science Foundation (60903107, 61073071), National High Technology Research and Development (863) Program (2011AA01A205) and Research Fund for the Doctoral Program of Higher Education of China (20090002120005)

Permission to make digital or hard copies of all or part of this work for personal or classroom use is granted without fee provided that copies are not made or distributed for profit or commercial advantage and that copies bear this notice and the full citation on the first page. To copy otherwise, to republish, to post on servers or to redistribute to lists, requires prior specific permission and/or a fee.
WSDM'12, February 8–12,2012,Seattle,Washington,USA.
Copyright 2012 ACM 978-1-4503-0747-5/12/02 ...$10.00.

General Terms

Experimentation, Algorithms, Performance

Keywords

Click-through Behaviors, Revisiting Patterns, Temporal Hidden Click Model, Document Relevance

1. INTRODUCTION

With the explosive growth of information on the Web, search engines have become indispensable information acquisition tools for users. How to obtain an ideal ranking is always a challenging task with respect to search engines. Previous studies [5, 10, 20] have developed a number of ranking optimization algorithms for manually labeled data. However, the manual labeling process is both expensive and time-consuming, especially for updating some labels. Updating these labels is a necessary yet difficult job because some queries require the up-to-date results. For example, if a user submits "WSDM" as a query, results related to WSDM2012 are more likely to be expected documents than results related to WSDM2011. Click-through logs record user interactions with search engines and can be collected at a low cost. In addition, click-through data is treated as an important signal of users' click preferences [1, 2] because click-through data can provide fresh and timely information. As a result, click-through logs are widely adopted in both sponsored searches [6, 21] and Web searches [5, 7, 8, 9, 12, 13, 18].

Previous studies [5, 7, 8, 9, 12, 13, 18] show that click logs are informative but biased. This phenomenon is represented as follows: a higher ranked document has a higher probability to be examined and clicked even if it is not as relevant as lower ones. Based on position bias problem, researchers have proposed many click models to obtain an unbiased estimation of document relevance. The cascade model [8] assumes that each user examines the results from top to bottom sequentially. A strong assumption is that a user will end the current search session as soon as he clicks a document; therefore, this model is only suitable for single-click situations and cannot draw a whole picture of multi-click sessions. To solve this problem, the DCM model [13] proposes the following assumption: a user who clicks a document has a λ probability of continuing and 1-λ of abandoning the search. Here λ depends on the rank of this document. Thus, the DCM model [13] extends the cascade model to multi-click situation. Guo et al. [12] introduce the skipping behavior into the CCM model by assuming that user can choose to click or skip according to the current relevance.

Eye-tracking studies [11, 17, 19] are used as direct microcosmic evidences for user behaviors. According to [17], the eye-tracking processing is categorized into two parts: the depth-first strategy and the breadth-first strategy. The depth-first model assumes that the user examines the result list from top to bottom and decides immediately whether to click. The breadth-first strategy is described as follows: the user looks ahead at a series of results and then revisits the most relevant results to click on. Most of previous click models [7, 8, 9, 12, 13] are rooted in the depth-first model. Lorigo et al. [19] performed a series of eye-tracking experiments and used scan path to characterize users' browsing behaviors. They found that only 34 percent of the scan paths are linear while over 50 percent of sessions contain revisiting (also named as regression behaviors in [19]) or skipping behaviors which cannot be covered by the depth-first model. Their experimental results indicated that a majority of users may not, in general, follow the presentation order. According to their findings, empirical seeking behavior is very complex, and the depth-first model is a simplification. The revisiting behaviors are acceptable supplements to the depth-first model. However, little work has been done for incorporating revisiting behavior into recent click models.

According to our analysis of click-through data containing over 115 million user sessions (described in Section 3.1), we discover that 24.1% of multi-click sessions contain revisiting behaviors. This result coincides with the eye-tracking study performed by [19]. Based on these findings, we can see that the revisiting behaviors cover a large number of search sessions and should not be ignored in the construction of a practical click model. As a result, we will introduce revisiting behaviors to solve the position bias problem. To the best of our knowledge, this study is the first attempt to incorporate revisiting behaviors into click models. For each position on a search engine results page (SERP), a user may move down for lower results, may stop and abandon the search or may review the higher ranked results. Previous models only estimate the probability of going down for lower results and the probability of stopping or abandoning the search. In our model, we will determine the probability of revisiting higher results. Thus, our model provides a more complete simulation of a user's information-seeking behaviors. Given M results in a SERP, the i-th result is accessed from two perspectives: going down from the higher ranked results and revisiting from the lower ones. In other words, the probability of being examined is estimated based on both the higher ranked (from 1 to i-1) and the lower-ranked (from i+1 to M) results. To make our model generative, we build up a new model with a dynamic temporal order. Our model is named Temporal Hidden Click Model (THCM), and it differs from previous models in two respects: 1. revisiting behaviors are taken into consideration; 2. user interaction is organized in a temporal order instead of ranking order.

The main contributions of our work are as follows:

i. A novel click model THCM is proposed to incorporate revisiting behaviors in the whole search process and improves the performance of the click models.

ii. The users' interactions are organized in a temporal order. This order is more reasonable than the ranking order because users do not always follow the ranking order.

iii. A practical method based on the THCM model is also proposed to solve the relevance inference and parameter estimation problems with an acceptable scalability in both time and space.

The remainder of this paper is organized as follows. We first present some important hypotheses and existing click models in Section 2. After providing a detailed description of our model in Section 3, the process of relevance inference and parameter estimation are represented in Section 4. In Section 5, we conduct experimental studies and evaluation, and we discuss and conclude our work in Section 6.

2. PRELIMINARIES

Algichtein et al. [2] were among the first researchers to utilize click-through logs to improve Web search rankings. They aggregated useful implicit feedback from the "noisy" user behaviors and found that incorporating the implicit feedback can help improve Web search performance. Baeza-Yates et al. [3] analyzed into users' Web searching process and modeled users' behaviors on user clicks, query formulations and page visited and other related features. Their experimental results showed that the aggregation of these features provided a valuable indicator of relevance preference. Joachims et al. [16] conducted eye-tracking experiments to track users' information-seeking behaviors. Their studies showed that clicks are informative but biased. In addition, to address the position bias problem, many researchers attempted to model the relationship between document relevance and click-through behaviors. In this section, we first give a general description of some important hypotheses and click models.

Basic Hypothesis: A document being clicked ($C_i = 1$) accords with($\rightarrow$) two conditions: it is examined ($E_i = 1$) and it is relevant ($R_i = 1$), and these two conditions are independent of each other.

$$C_i = 1 \rightarrow E_i = 1, R_i = 1 \quad (1)$$

$$E_i = 0 \rightarrow C_i = 0 \quad (2)$$

$$R_i = 0 \rightarrow C_i = 0 \quad (3)$$

Therefore,

$$P(C_i = 1) = P(E_i = 1)P(R_i = 1) \quad (4)$$

Examination Hypothesis: Each document at a given position has a certain probability of being examined, and this probability depends on its ranking position. A higher rank usually leads to a bigger examination probability. Taking this factor into the basic hypothesis, Equation 4 is rewritten as follows:

$$p(c|p,u,q) = p(e|p)p(r|u,q) \quad (5)$$

where $p(c|p,u,q)$ represents the click probability of document u at position p for a query q, $p(e|p)$ stands for the examination probability of the ranking position p and $p(r|u,q)$ is the probability of this (query,document) pair being relevant. Hence, if the result is relevant, a higher examination probability will bring more clicks. For click-through logs, only the click events are observed, while examination and relevance events are not. Therefore, estimating the examination probability is usually an important step for most click models to obtain unbiased document relevance estimations.

The cascade model [8] assumes that the first document is always examined and a user will end the search when he clicks on a result. The corresponding examination hypothesis is as follows.

$$P(E_1) = 1 \tag{6}$$

$$P(E_{i+1} = 1|E_i = 1, C_i) = 1 - C_i \tag{7}$$

Here the (i+1)-th result being examined indicates the i-th result being examined yet not clicked. Although the cascade model has a good performance in predicting the click-through rates, this model is only suited for a single-click scenario.

Grounded in the cascade model, the DCM model [13] extends to model user interactions with multi-click sessions. Compared to the cascade model [8], the DCM model [13] assumes that a user may have a certain probability of examining the next one even if the current document is already clicked, and this probability is associated with the ranking position of the result. The DCM model is characterized as follows:

$$P(E_{i+1} = 1|E_i = 1, C_i = 0) = 1 \tag{8}$$

$$P(E_{i+1} = 1|E_i = 1, C_i = 1) = \lambda_i \tag{9}$$

where λ_i represents the preservation probability[1] of the position i and can be obtained through Equation 10 as follows.

$$\lambda_i = 1 - \frac{\#Query\, sessions\, when\, (last\, clicked\, position = i)}{\#Query\, sessions\, when\, position\, i\, is\, clicked} \tag{10}$$

Subsequently, the UBM model [9] makes further effort on the examination hypothesis. It is modified as Equation 11, where the event of the current document being examined depends on both the preceding click position and their corresponding distance.

$$P(E_i = 1|C_{1...i-1}) = \lambda_{r_i, d_i} \tag{11}$$

where r_i represents the preceding click position and d_i is the distance between the current rank and r_i. A total of $M * (M + 1)/2$(There exist M document in a SERP) global parameters need to be estimated, which makes the UBM model unfeasible for large-scale data. The BBM model [18] inherits the assumptions proposed by the UBM model and makes this model fit at the scalability of terabyte-scale data. This model is designed to estimate global parameters with a single pass of the large-scale data.

In contrast to the above models, the DBM model [7] is the first model to take presentation bias[2] into consideration. This model distinguishes the actual relevance(S_i) from the perceived relevance(R_i), where the perceived relevance indicates the relevance represented by abstracts or snippets in SERPs and the actual relevance is the relevance of the landing page. The user satisfaction is determined by the actual relevance, but the click events depend on its perceived relevance. The DBM model can be represented as follows:

$$R_i = 1, E_i = 1 \rightarrow C_i = 1 \tag{12}$$

$$P(R_i = 1) = r_u \tag{13}$$

$$P(S_i = 1|C_i = 1) = s_u \tag{14}$$

$$P(E_{i+1}|E_i = 1, S_i = 0) = \lambda \tag{15}$$

where S_i represents that whether or not the user is satisfied with the i-th document, s_u is the probability of this event, r_u is the probability of the perceived relevance(R_i), and λ represents the preservation probability.

Subsequently, the CCM model [12] presents a Bayesian inference to obtain the posterior distribution of the relevance. In contrast to other existing models, this model introduces skipping behaviors. According to [12], the CCM model is scalable for large scale click-through data. Moreover, the experimental results show that the CCM model is effective for low frequency(also known as long-tail) queries. Both the DBM model and the CCM model are two present common click models, and we analyze the performance of our model compared to these two ones in our experiments.

3. TEMPORAL HIDDEN CLICK MODEL

3.1 Revisiting Behaviors

Lorigo et al. [19] point out that different user groups have different information-seeking behaviors and that the majority of users have skipping or revisiting behaviors. In this section, we perform an experiment to analyze revisiting behaviors. First, a revisiting pattern can be defined as follows: a user clicks on another higher ranked result after having clicked on a lower result. With the help of a widely-used commercial Chinese search engine, we collect click-through logs from November 1st, 2010 to November 10th, 2010. The data set contains over 115 million query sessions. A query session is initialized when a user submits a query to a search engine, and query reformulations, re-submissions or a session lasting over 30 minutes will be regarded as a new session. For simplicity, we only record user interactions in Web organic results lists; other actions, such as ad clicks, are discarded in our experiments.

To have clearer statistics on revisiting behaviors, click-through logs were divided into 5 groups in terms to their own query frequencies. The statistics on revisiting behaviors of different query frequencies are shown in Table 1. The proportions of multi-click sessions are roughly equal among different query frequencies. On average, 24.1% of multi-click sessions contain the revisiting behaviors. This result is in accordance with the eye-tracking studies in [19], and indicates that revisiting behaviors are important parts of user interactions. Users may not follow the ranking order of a SERP in some cases.

In addition, we conduct a position-based analysis of revisiting behaviors. For each position, the corresponding document may be revisited from the lower ranked results and also has a certain probability of being skipped from the higher ranked ones. Conducted on the collected click-through data, the revisiting behaviors related probabilities on different positions are shown in Figure 1. The result shows that the top positions have a higher probability of being revisited, while the lower positions are more likely to be revisited from. In Figure 1, the first ranked documents are revisited from the lower ranked ones in 60.2% of all multi-click sessions, and the users who have clicked on the 10th result will perform revisiting behaviors in 34.7% multi-click sessions.

To examine the relevance influence from the revisited results, according to the time-series click events, we extract

[1]The probability of the (i+1)-th result being examined when the i-th document is clicked

[2]Different from the position bias, the presentation bias is a bias caused by the presentation form of the results list, such as the abstract, the snippet and so on

Table 1: Revisiting Features over Different Query Frequencies

Query Frequency	[1,9]	[10,30]	[31,99]	[100,499]	[500,∞)
Total query sessions	40,036,796	9,369,628	9,619,008	13,520,812	42,835,848
Single-click sessions	31,024,348	8,021,876	8,301,504	11,766,600	36,976,904
Multi-click sessions without revisiting behaviors	6,859,335	1,030,918	1,017,741	1,304,911	4,402,210
Multi-click sessions with revisiting behaviors	2,153,113	316,834	299,763	449,301	1,456,734
The proportion of sessions with revisiting behaviors	0.239	0.235	0.228	0.256	0.249

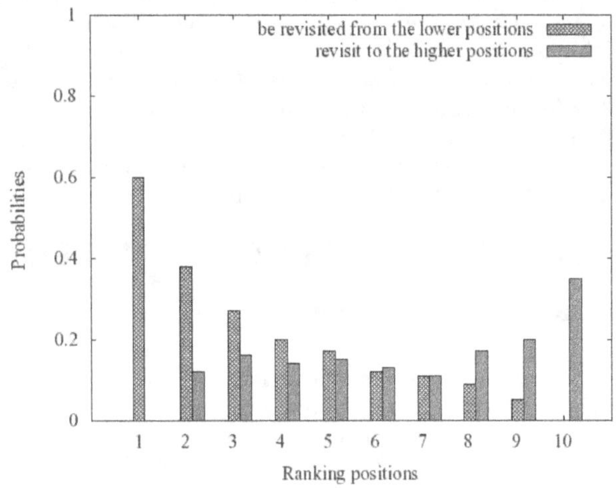

Figure 1: Revisiting behaviors related probabilities on different positions in a SERP

10,450 revisited items from the collected click-through data. Each item is presented in the form: (query, URL, relevance), where the relevance is manually labeled by three professional assessors. The details of labeling rules are available in Section 5.1. These relevance labels are divided into 5 levels(bad, fair, good, excellent, perfect). Through our statistics, 50.2% of these revisited items have a high relevance(excellent or perfect) with the original query, and only 14.5% items show bad performance in relevance(bad).

Summarizing the above studies, we find that revisiting behaviors are relatively common, and have a strong correlation with the relevance. As a result, revisiting behaviors may be important signals of click preferences. Based on this fact, we will incorporate revisiting behaviors into our click models.

3.2 Model Specification

We first introduce some definitions and notations. Here a session is treated as a unit in our model, and it records the whole user interaction with top-M results (usually M=10). In our model, all of our variable sets can be represented as the sequences. The presented results are represented as an impression sequence: $A =< a_1, a_2, ..., a_i, ..., a_M >$, i corresponds to the ranking position and a_i is ranked higher than a_j if $i < j$. According to the timestamps, clicks can also be re-organized as a temporal click sequence: $C =< C_1, C_2, ..., C_t, ..., C_T >$, where t is a discrete time variable and C_t represents the corresponding ranking of the result being clicked at time t. In addition, we introduce another variable sequence: $U =< U_1, U_2, ..., U_t, ..., U_T >$, where U_t represents the ranking position of the preceding click, i.e, $U_t = C_{t-1}$. The examination sequence $E =< E_1, E_2, ..., E_t, ..., E_T >$, where E_t is an M dimensional vector. $E_t = (E_{t1}, E_{t2}, ..., E_{ti}, ..., E_{tM})$ is used to represent examination events at time t.

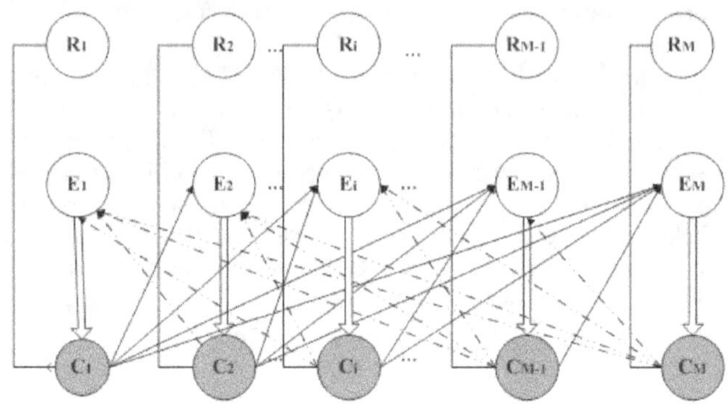

Figure 2: The graphical model by introducing revisiting behaviors. Here the solid line represents the forward event and the dotted line stands for the backward event(revisit). Observed click variables C_i are shaded.

Figure 2 shows the graphic model by incorporating revisiting behaviors. The whole user interactions are no longer strictly from top to bottom. In a SERP, a user examines the i-th document, followed by examining the j-th document. If $i < j$, we will define this event as the forward event; otherwise, we call it as the backward event. In Figure 2, both forward examination probability and backward examination probability constitute the whole examination probability. Given a position i, it may be examined from the (i-1)-th document, and also be revisited from lower documents. We can see that there can be some loops in Figure 2, and previous approaches will be difficult for solving generative process. Hence we need to provide a temporal generative process which is illustrated in Figure 3. We call it Temporal Hidden Click Model(THCM) and the corresponding hypotheses are as follows.

$$p(E_{t(i+1)} = 1 | E_{ti} = 1) = \alpha \quad (16)$$

$$p(E_{t(i-1)} = 1 | E_{ti} = 1) = \gamma \quad (17)$$

$$0 \leq \alpha + \gamma \leq 1, \alpha \geq 0, \gamma \geq 0 \quad (18)$$

$$p(C_t | C_1, C_2, ..., C_{t-1}) = p(C_t | C_{t-1}) \quad (19)$$

$$p(C_t = i) = p(E_{ti} = 1).p(R_i = 1) \quad (20)$$

For the THCM model, if a user examines a document, then he will have a α probability to examines the next one(Equation 16). Different from previous models, we introduce the revisiting probability γ: if the user examines a result, he may

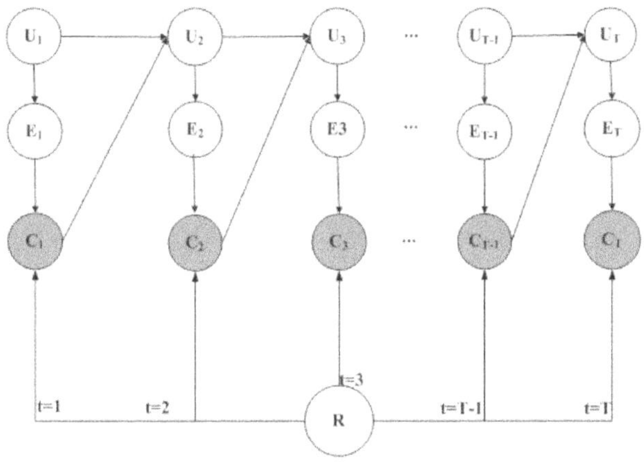

Figure 3: The graphical model on the temporal order. C_i represents the observed click events at time t, while E_t implies the examination vector for M results at time t, and U_t represents the rank of the click events at time $t-1$.

also have a γ probability of revisiting the preceding rank result(Equation 17). The relationship between α and γ needs to satisfy Equation 18. To make our model simple, we introduce the **First-order Click Hypothesis**: the click event at time t are determined by that at time $t-1$(Equation 19). Similar with previous models, if a result is both examined and relevant, the user will click this result(Equation 20). Thus, the probability of the event that the results ranked lower than C_{t-1} is examined can be calculated as follows:

$$\begin{aligned} & p(E_{ti} = 1 | C_{t-1} < i) \\ & = \prod_{j=U_t}^{i-1} p(E_{t(j+1)} = 1 | E_{tj} = 1) = \alpha^{i-C_{t-1}} \end{aligned} \tag{21}$$

In Equation 21, the probability of a lower result being examined is determined by both the forward probability α and the distance between current rank and the previous clicked position. In our model, we assume that the relevance event(R_i) is a binary variable. If there exist follow-up clicks for a clicked result a_m, the user may not be satisfied with this result, i.e., $R_{a_m} = 0$. Thus, given a position i at time t, if the preceding clicked position C_{t-1} is ranked higher than i, this document is clicked by forward examination events(Equation 22); otherwise, the i-th document is revisited by backwards examination events(Equation 23).

$$\begin{aligned} & p(C_t = i | C_{t-1} < i) \\ & = p(R_{C_{t-1}} = 0).\underbrace{p(C_t = i | E_{ti} = 1)}_{R_i}.\underbrace{p(E_{ti} = 1 | C_{t-1} < i)}_{\alpha^{i-C_{t-1}}} \\ & = (1 - R_{C_{t-1}}).R_i.\alpha^{i-C_{t-1}} \end{aligned} \tag{22}$$

$$\begin{aligned} & p(C_t = i | C_{t-1} >= i) \\ & = p(R_{C_{t-1}} = 0).\underbrace{p(C_t = i | E_{ti} = 1)}_{R_i}.\underbrace{p(E_{ti} = 1 | C_{t-1} >= i)}_{\gamma^{C_{t-1}-i}} \\ & = (1 - R_{C_{t-1}}).R_i.\gamma^{C_{t-1}-i} \end{aligned} \tag{23}$$

In our model, α and γ are global parameters for each query session, and represent the forward and backward examination probabilities, respectively. In the next section, we will assume that the document relevance $\mathbf{R}$ and the click events of different sessions are independent of each other. Based on this assumption, we will discuss the inference of document relevance and introduce a feasible algorithm that has a acceptable scalability with using a large volume of click logs.

4. ALGORITHMS

4.1 Relevance Inference

The goal of the click models is to obtain an unbiased estimation of the relevance for each query-document pair. Previous click models all require the following assumption: users examine a document and decide to click or skip, but they cannot revisit previous documents. According to our statistics on revisiting behaviors in Section 3.1, revisiting behaviors may be an important feedback for Web search performance. Given the click-through data $C^{1...n}$, incorporating revisiting behaviors into previous models will increase the computational complexity of the posterior probability over $\mathbf{R}$. To address this problem, our THCM model re-organizes the click sequences into a dynamical temporal order.

Given a query with N sessions, $A =< A^1, A^2, ..., A^N >$ and $C =< C^1, C^2, ..., C^N >$ represent the corresponding impression and temporal click sequences, respectively. We assume that the click sequences of different sessions are independent of each other. Thus, according to the Bayes principle, the posterior probability is calculated as follows.

$$p(\mathbf{R} | C^{1,...,N}) \propto p(\mathbf{R}) p(C^{1,...,N} | \mathbf{R}) \tag{24}$$

Because $p(\mathbf{R})$ is a known prior, we assume that $p(\mathbf{R})$ follows the prior beta distribution, thus we need to compute $p(C^{1,...,N}|\mathbf{R})$. Since click sequences of different sessions are treated as conditionally independent variables for each query session given $\mathbf{R}$, we obtain the following equation:

$$p(C^{1,...,N} | \mathbf{R}) \propto \prod_{n=1}^{N} p(C^n | \mathbf{R}) \tag{25}$$

where C^n represents the click sequence of the n-th session. In the following steps, we assume that the user clicks the m-th document at time t, i.e, $C_t = a_m$. According to the First-order Click Hypothesis, the relevance of the t-th clicked document is related to both the preceding clicked document(C_{t-1}) and next clicked document(C_{t+1}), and is independent of the remaining documents. Therefore, we obtain Equation 26 as follows.

$$\begin{aligned} & p(C^n =< C_1, C_2, ..., C_t, ..., C_T > | R_m, A^n) \\ & = p(C^n =< C_1, C_2, ..., C_t = a_m, ..., C_T > | R_m, A^n) \\ & = \prod_{t=1}^{T-1} p(< C_{t-1}, C_t = a_m, C_{t+1} >) | R_m, A^n) \end{aligned} \tag{26}$$

Here we will use the symbol $\square$ to represent no click and the symbol $\times$ to represent any click. According to the rankings of different times, a click sequence $C =< C_{t-1}, C_t = a_m, C_{t+1} >$ can be categorized into different behavior patterns. Table 2 lists the set of these behavior patterns, and we only present the derivation of Cases 1-3 due to space limitations.

Table 2: Different Cases for Computing $p(C|R_m, A)$ on Different Click Sequences

Cases	Sequences	Results
1	$< \square, a_m, \square >$	$R_m\alpha^m$
2	$< \square, a_m, a_j >, j > m$	$\frac{R_m.(1-R_m)(\alpha^{m+1}-\alpha^{M+1})}{2(1-\alpha)}$
3	$< \square, a_m, a_j >, j < m$	$\frac{R_m.(1-R_m)(\gamma-\gamma^m)}{2(1-\gamma)}$
4	$< a_j, a_m, \times >, j < m$	$\frac{R_m.(\alpha-\alpha^m)}{6(1-\alpha)}$
5	$< a_j, a_m, \times >, j > m$	$\frac{R_m.(\gamma-\gamma^{M-m+1})}{6(1-\gamma)}$

Case 1: $t = 1$, $T = 1$, $C =< \square, a_m, \square >$, $C_0 = 0$, that is, the m-th document is the first and only click in this session. $C_1 = a_m$, According to Equations 22, $p(C =< \square, a_m, \square >) = p(C_1 = a_m|C_0 = 0)$, and the document a_m is examined through the forward event.

$$\begin{aligned} &p(C =< \square, a_m, \square > |R_m, A) \\ &= p(C_1 = m|E_{1m} = 1)p(E_{1m} = 1|U_1 = C_0 = 0) = R_m\alpha^m \end{aligned} \tag{27}$$

Case 2: $t = 1$, $T > 1$, $C =< \square, a_m, a_j >$, $j > m$, $C_0 = 0$, that is, the m-th document is the first click and the next clicked document is ranked lower than m. This event can be explained by Equations 19 and 22, $C_1 = a_m$, $C_2 = a_j$. This sequence is divided into two parts: $< \square, a_m >$ and $< a_m, a_j >$. The probability of this case can be described as follows:

$$\begin{aligned} &p(C =< \square, a_m, a_j > |R_m, A) \\ &= \underbrace{p(< \square, a_m > |R_m, A)}_{R_m.\alpha^m}\underbrace{p(< a_m, a_j > |R_m, A)}_{(1-R_m)R_j\alpha^{j-m}} \\ &= R_m(1 - R_m)R_j\alpha^m\alpha^{j-m} = R_m(1 - R_m)R_j\alpha^j \end{aligned} \tag{28}$$

To calculate $p(C|R_m, A)$, other hidden random variables, such as R_j, need to be integrated out in Equation 29.

$$\begin{aligned} &p(C =< \square, a_m, a_j >, j > m|R_m, A) \\ &= \sum_{j=m+1}^{M} p(C =< \square, a_m, a_j > |R_m, A) \\ &= \sum_{j=m+1}^{M} \int_{R_j=0}^{1} R_m(1 - R_m)R_j\alpha^j \\ &= \frac{R_m(1 - R_m)(\alpha^{m+1} - \alpha^{M+1})}{2(1 - \alpha)} \end{aligned} \tag{29}$$

Case 3: $t = 1$, $T > 1$, $C =< \square, a_m, a_j >$, $j < m$, that is, the m-th document is the first click and the next clicked document is ranked higher than m. This click event comes from the revisiting events. According to Equations 19,22 and 23, this sequence can also be divided into two parts: $< \square, a_m >$ and $< a_m, a_j >$.

$$\begin{aligned} &p(C =< \square, a_m, a_j > |R_m, A) \\ &= \underbrace{p(< \square, a_m > |R_m, A)}_{R_m\alpha^m}\underbrace{p(< a_m, a_j > |R_m, A)}_{(1-R_m)R_j\gamma^{m-j}} \\ &= R_m(1 - R_m)R_j\alpha^m\gamma^{m-j} \end{aligned} \tag{30}$$

By integrating and summing the hidden random variable R_j, the probability can be represented as follows.

$$\begin{aligned} &p(C =< \square, a_m, a_j >, j < m|R_m, A) \\ &= \sum_{j=1}^{m-1} p(C =< \square, a_m, a_j > |R_m, A) \\ &= R_m(1 - R_m)\alpha^m \sum_{j=1}^{m-1} \int_{R_j=0}^{1} R_j\gamma^{m-j} \\ &= \frac{R_m(1 - R_m)(\gamma - \gamma^m)}{2(1 - \gamma)} \end{aligned} \tag{31}$$

Cases 4 and 5 are also obtained by taking a summing and integrating over the corresponding hidden random variables. In addition, different sessions of a given query are independent of each other. Thus, the posterior of R_m has the following un-normalized form:

$$p(R_m|C, A) \propto \prod_{i=1}^{5} O_i(R_m)^{N_i^m} \tag{32}$$

where O_i is the closed form of $p(C|R_m, A)$ for i-th kind of click sequence in Table 2.

4.2 Parameter Estimation

In this section, we adopt the maximum-likelihood (ML) algorithm to estimate the global parameters α and γ. By integrating the hidden random variable R_m and summing the log likelihood of all of the click sequences, the whole log-likelihood function is illustrated in Equation 33.

$$\begin{aligned} L(\alpha, \gamma) = &\sum_{m=1}^{M} \{N_1^m log[\frac{\alpha^m}{2}] + N_2^m log[\frac{\alpha^{m+1} - \alpha^{M+1}}{12(1 - \alpha)}] \\ &+ N_3^m log[\frac{\gamma - \gamma^m}{12(1 - \gamma)}] + N_4^m log[\frac{\alpha - \alpha_m}{12(1 - \alpha)}] \\ &+ N_5^m log[\frac{\gamma - \gamma^{M-m+1}}{1}]\} \end{aligned} \tag{33}$$

Through taking the derivation of the above likelihood function on α, we get the following equation:

$$\begin{aligned} &N_1^m \frac{2m}{\alpha} + (N_2^m + N_4^m)\frac{1}{1 - \alpha} + N_4^m \frac{1 - m\alpha^{m-1}}{\alpha - \alpha^m} \\ &+ N_2^m \frac{(m + 1)\alpha^m - (M + 1)\alpha^M}{\alpha^{m+1} - \alpha^{M+1}} = 0 \end{aligned} \tag{34}$$

The equation about γ can be obtained through the same approach. However, we find that there exists no closed form for our global parameters α and γ. Thus, we need to seek for an approximate solution. According to Equation 18, the feasible zone is convex and the log likelihood is a concave function; hence, solving for the parameters is a convex optimization problem. In our experiment, we use the primal-dual interior-point method [4] to obtain approximate values for parameters α and γ.

5. EXPERIMENTS

5.1 Experiment Setup

As described in Section 3.1, we collect click-through logs from November 1, 2010 to November 10, 2010, including 93 million queries with 115 million query sessions. Taking the users' privacy into consideration, we only collect the following information for each session: the original query, the top

10 documents in the first SERP, the timestamps and the list of which documents are clicked. In our experiments, 2,000 queries and 47,891 related documents are randomly sampled as our data set. 10,450 items are revisited among these query-document pairs, and they are selected as the data set of revisiting behaviors in Section 3.1. The frequency distribution of these randomly selected queries is shown in Figure 4. The frequency range is from 1 to 62,688, indicating that our data set contains different queries of high, middle and low frequencies. Three professional assessors took two weeks to label the relevance of these sampled query-document pairs. Each of them labeled 1,335 queries and their corresponding results, and the average Kappa coefficient is 0.68.

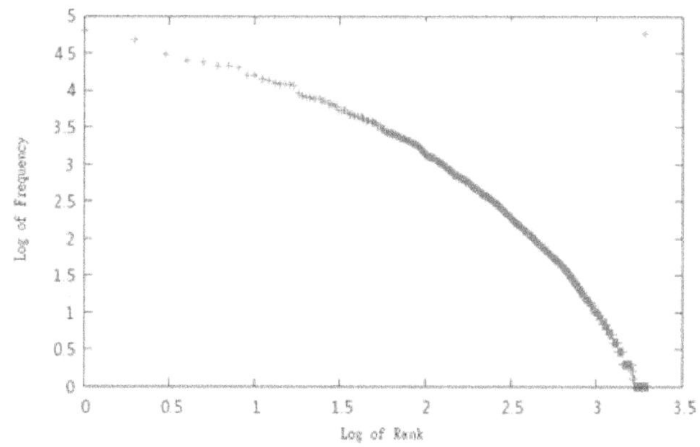

Figure 4: Frequency distribution of randomly sampled queries

According to our statistics in Section 3.1, revisiting behaviors may be important signals to reflect click preferences. Previous models usually discard sessions that contain revisiting behaviors because these sessions cannot satisfy the depth-first examination hypotheses. However, these sessions are preserved in our experiments, and our model can explain revisiting behaviors well. What's more, the method of 5-fold cross-validation is used in our experiments. Compared to the DBM model [7] and the CCM model [12], the performance of our model is evaluated in different aspects, including the NDCG values, the click perplexity and the click distribution of position-bias.

5.2 Evaluation on NDCG

The Normalized Discounted Cumulative Gain (NDCG, [15]) is always an important metric to measure the relevance of ranking functions. The NDCG at position $p(NDCG_p)$ is computed as:

$$DCG_p = \sum_{i=1}^{p} \frac{2^{rel_i} - 1}{log_2(1+i)} \tag{35}$$

$$NDCG_p = \frac{DCG_p}{IDCG_p} \tag{36}$$

where rel_i is the manual label of the i-th document, and $IDCG_p$ represents an ideal DCG value obtained when sorting the documents by relevance. The NDCG metric indicates that the rankings of higher relevance results play more important roles than that of the lower relevance ones. For example, if a high relevance document is ranked low, the NDCG value becomes relatively small and then the performance of this ranking function will become relatively poor. The NDCG value measures the distance between the current ranking and an ideal ranking, and this value of an ideal ranking is 1.0. First, we report on the changes of the NDCG values of the THCM, DBM and CCM models.

Table 3: P-values on Different Positions

$NDCG_{pos}$	THCM over DBM	THCM over CCM
$NDCG_1$	$1.30 * 10^{-2}$	$5.20 * 10^{-3}$
$NDCG_3$	$4.00 * 10^{-4}$	$7.00 * 10^{-4}$
$NDCG_5$	$8.00 * 10^{-4}$	$2.30 * 10^{-3}$
$NDCG_{10}$	$1.02 * 10^{-2}$	$4.00 * 10^{-3}$

Table 4: P-values on Different Query Frequencies

$frequency_q$	THCM over DBM	THCM over CCM
[1,9]	$\mathbf{9.00 * 10^{-6}}$	$\mathbf{4.00 * 10^{-3}}$
[10,30]	$\mathbf{5.00 * 10^{-2}}$	$\mathbf{2.70 * 10^{-2}}$
[31,100]	$\mathbf{2.00 * 10^{-2}}$	$\mathbf{1.20 * 10^{-2}}$
[100,499]	$8.90 * 10^{-1}$	$5.00 * 10^{-3}$
[500,∞)	$3.30 * 10^{-1}$	$3.00 * 10^{-5}$

Given each query, we estimate the relevances of all corresponding documents based on these three models. For the THCM model, on the training set, we learn the model parameters by the method of Section 4.2, and then obtain estimated relevances on the test set. The implementations of the DBM and CCM models are available in [7, 12]. Figures 5 and 6 show the performance on the NDCG values of different positions and different query frequencies, respectively. Figure 5 shows that all of $NDCG_1$, $NDCG_3$, $NDCG_5$ and $NDCG_{10}$ of our model show more improvement than that of the other two models. The $NDCG_1$ value of our model is 0.841, with 8.52% and 25.0% improvement over DBM and CCM, respectively. Figure 6 shows that our model improves the performance on long-tail queries. As described in [12], the CCM model has a commendable performance on the tail queries, which can also be seen in Figure 6. Compared to the CCM model, our model attains a 1.50% improvement of $NDCG_5$. For tail queries, related click-through behaviors are also sparse, and the user interaction may be fairly complex. Thus, revisiting behaviors may provide a key evidence for predicting click preference for long-tail queries. However, our model shows relatively poor performance for high frequency queries. For high frequency queries, compared to enough click-through data, different types of revisiting behaviors may be "noisy" for estimating document relevance.

In addition, we use the t-test to quantify whether our model is better than the others. Having no significant difference is denoted as the null hypothesis, with a significant difference as the alternative hypothesis. If the p-value is less than $5.0 * 10^{-2}(5.0 * 10^{-2}$ is usually set as the critical level), the null hypothesis will be rejected and the alternative hypothesis will suffice. The testing values for NDCGs on different positions and query frequencies are illustrated in Tables 3 and 4. The result shows that our model may be no significant improvement for high frequency queries, but the improvement is relatively sharp for moderate frequency and rare frequency queries.

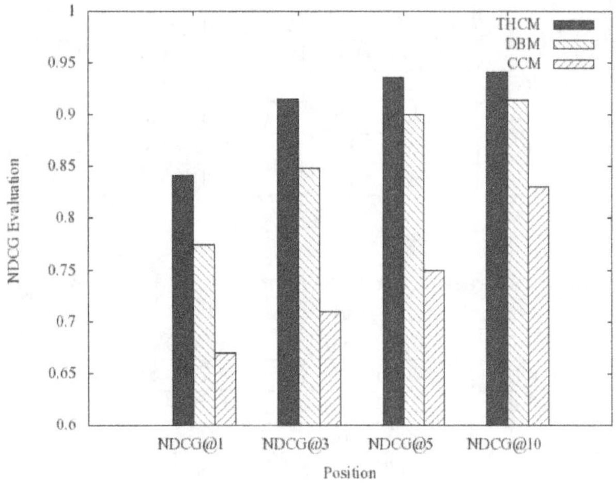

Figure 5: Performance comparison of THCM, DBM and CCM with $NDCG_n$

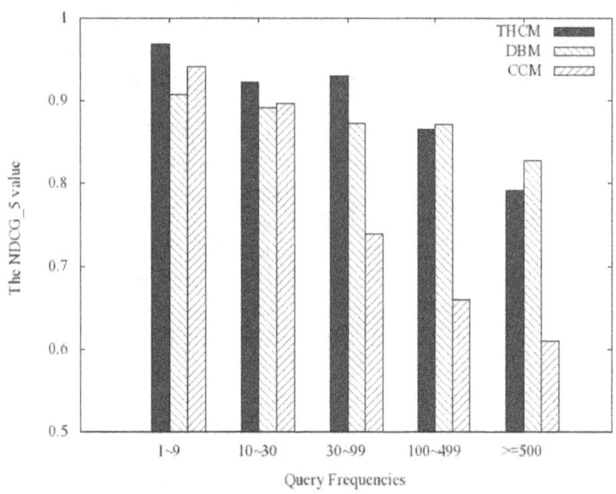

Figure 6: Performance comparison of THCM, DBM and CCM for queries with different frequencies

5.3 Evaluation on Click Perplexity

In addition to the NDCG value, the click perplexity [12] is another metric to evaluate the performance of each position. A smaller perplexity value indicates a better performance, and the value reaches 1 in an ideal case. In our experiment, the click-through logs are organized into a temporal order for each query session. The click perplexity at a given position is computed as the following equation.

$$CP_i = 2^{-\frac{1}{U}\cdot\sum_{u=1}^{U}(C_i^U.log_2 p_i^u+(1-C_i^U.log_2(1-p_i^u)))} \quad (37)$$

where CP_i is the click perplexity of position i, U is the total number of sessions for a given query. C_i^U represents the click event of the i-th document, and p_i^u is the corresponding probability. The improvement of click perplexity CP_1 over CP_2 is calculated through $\frac{CP_2-CP_1}{CP_2-1} * 100\%$, and the average click perplexity is obtained using the arithmetic mean. Based on our experimental data, the average perplexities on different positions are illustrated in Figure 7.

In Figure 7, we can see that our THCM model performs best for all of the positions. The average perplexity of all positions is 1.1402 for THCM, 1.28 for DBM and 1.237 for CCM. What's more, the perplexities have a varying degree of improvement, with an 18% improvement over the DBM model and a 7.8% improvement over the CCM model for the first position. The click perplexity of the THCM model indicates that temporal click sequences will obtain a better click prediction.

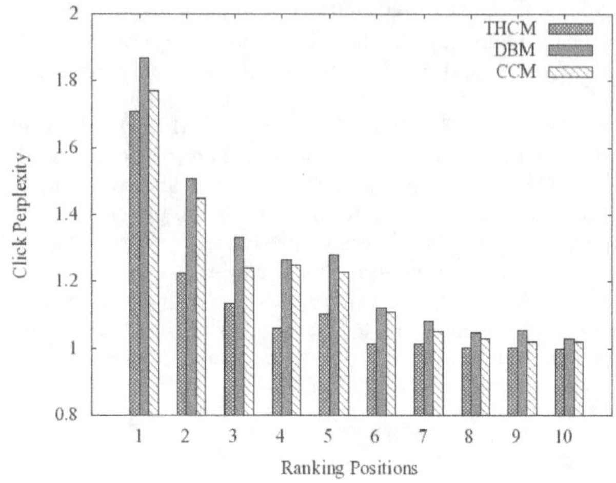

Figure 7: Performance comparison of THCM, DBM and CCM with click perplexity of different positions

5.4 Results on Position Bias

To address the position bias problem, the click distributions of different positions are also introduced to evaluate the effect of click models [12]. Given a position, the click distribution metric is quantified as follows: collect all of the sessions on the test set, calculate the click events (which documents will be clicked) according to learned model parameters in Section 4 and count the total number of the document at the given position being clicked. The click probabilities of a given position can be estimated through the total number of the position being clicked divided by the total number of the test set. Different click models can estimate different click distributions, and empirical click distributions can be obtained using actual click behaviors. Thus, the distance between the estimated click distributions of click models and that of empirical clicks can measure the prediction effect, and the smaller distance indicates more accurate click predictions.

Figure 8 illustrates that the click distributions derived from THCM, DBM and empirical click on the test set. We can see that all of the click distributions have a position bias, with a document that is ranked higher having a higher click probability compared to the lower documents. In Figure 8, the THCM model has a closer match with empirical clicks than the DBM model has on different positions, and their correlation coefficient reaches 0.99. The THCM model provides a temporal perspective on users interactions, which is closer to actual user's information-seeking behaviors. The results on the click distribution of position-bias further verifies that the THCM model may produce a better click prediction.

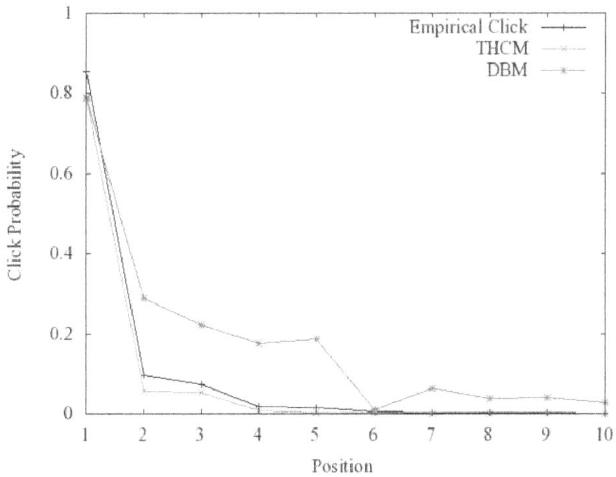

Figure 8: Click probability distribution of THCM and DBM on the top 10 positions

6. CONCLUSIONS AND DISCUSSIONS

In this paper, a statistical investigation on large-scale click-through data was presented, indicating that revisiting behaviors are important aspects of user interaction. Based on this finding, we proposed the novel THCM model, which models the temporal click sequences and incorporates revisiting behaviors. This paper also provides a solution to the estimation of document relevance and other relevant parameters. The experimental results on huge-volume click-through data show that our model outperforms existing models in a number metrics, including the NDCG value, the click perplexity and the click distributions of different positions.

Despite these successes, several assumptions of the THCM model need to be further discussed. In our experiment, we introduce the First-order Click Hypothesis, which indicates that the current state only depends on the preceding state. However, empirical click events may not be independent of each other. To facilitate describing and solving problems, we simplify this process to a first-order model. In the future, we will move forward to multi-order models.

According to [14], information needs are classified into three categories: navigational, informational and transactional. Different informational needs tend to generate different types of user interactions. For a navigational query, the information demand is relatively concentrated, so the corresponding behaviors may be simple. However, for informational queries, the relatively dispersed resources may lead to more clicks, and it is more likely that revisiting behaviors occur. In our model, the method for calculating the global parameters α and γ is a globally optimal solution, but it may be not efficient for all individual users. In the future, we will distinguish the global parameters from different categorizations of user behaviors; this development will be a new direction that we will explore in the future.

7. REFERENCES

[1] E. Agichtein, E.Brill, and D.Susan. Improving web search ranking by incorporating user behavior information. *In proceeding of SIGIR06*, 2006.

[2] E. Agichtein, E.Brill, S.Dumais, and R.Ragno. Learning user interaction models for predicting web search result preferences. *In proceeding of SIGIR06*, 2006.

[3] R. Baeza-Yates, C. Hurtado, M. Mendoza, and G. Dupret. Modeling user search behavior. *In LA-WEB 2005*, 2005.

[4] S. Boyd and L. Vandenberghe. *Convex Optimization.* Cambridge University Press, 2004.

[5] B. Carterette and R. Jones. Evaluating search engines by modeling the relationship between relevance and clicks. *Advances in Neural Information Processing Systems*, 2008.

[6] D. Chakrabarti, D. Agarwal, and V. Josifovski. Contextual advertising by combining relevance with click feedback. *In proceeding of WWW08*, 2008.

[7] O. Chapelle and Y. Zhang. A dynamic bayesian network click model for web search ranking. *In proceedings of WWW2009*, 2009.

[8] N. Craswell, O. Zoeter, M. Taylor, and B. Ramsey. An experimental comparison of click position-bias models. *In proceedings of WSDM2008*, 2008.

[9] G. Durpret and B. Piwowarski. A user browsing model to predict search engine click data from past observations. *In proceedings of SIGIR2008*, 2008.

[10] Y. Freund, R. Iyer, R. Schapire, and Y. Singer. An efficient boosting algorithm for combining preferences. *The Journal of Machine Learning Research*, 2003.

[11] L. Granka, T. Joachims, and G. Gay. Eye-tracking analysis of user behavior in www search. *In proceeding of SIGIR04*, 2004.

[12] F. Guo, C. Liu, A. Kannan, T. Minka, M.Taylor, Y.Wang, and C. Faloutos. Click chain model in web search. *In proceedings of WWW2009*, 2009.

[13] F. Guo, C. Liu, and Y. Wang. Efficient multiple-click models in web search. *In proceedings of WSDM09*, 2009.

[14] B. J. Jansen and D. Booth. Classifying web queries by topic and user intent. *In the proceeding of CHI2010*, 2010.

[15] K. Jarvelin and J. Kelalainen. Cumulated gain-based evaluation of ir techniques. *ACM Transactions on Information System*, 2002.

[16] T. Joachims, L. Granka, B. Pan, H.Hembrooke, and G. Gay. Accurately interpreting clickthrough data as implicit feedback. *In proceeding of SIGIR05*, 2005.

[17] K. Klockner, N. Wirschum, and A. Jameson. Depth-and breadth-first processing of seach result lists. *In proceeding of CHI04*, 2004.

[18] C. Liu, F. Guo, and C. Faloutsos. Bbm: Beyesian browsing model from petabyte-scale data. *In proceedings of KDD09*, 2009.

[19] L. Lorigo, B. Pan, H. Kembrooke, T. Joachims, L. Granka, and G. Gay. The influence of task and gender on search and evaluation behavior using google. *Information Processing and Management*, 2005.

[20] F. Radlinski and T. Joachims. Query chains: learning to rank from implicit feedback. *In proceeding of KDD2005*, 2005.

[21] M. Richardson, E. Dominowska, and R.Rango. Predicting clicks: estimating the click-through rate for news ads. *In proceeding of WWW07*, 2007.

A Noise-aware Click Model for Web Search

Weizhu Chen
Microsoft Research Asia
wzchen@microsoft.com

Dong Wang
Microsoft Research Asia
dongw89@gmail.com

Yuchen Zhang
Microsoft Research Asia
zhangyuc@gmail.com

Zheng Chen
Microsoft Research Asia
zhengc@microsoft.com

Adish Singla
Microsoft BING Bellevue
adishs@microsoft.com

Qiang Yang
Hong Kong University of Science & Technolgy
qyang@cse.ust.hk

ABSTRACT

Recent advances in click model have established it as an attractive approach to infer document relevance. Most of these advances consider the user click/skip behavior as binary events but neglect the context in which a click happens. We show that real click behavior in industrial search engines is often noisy and not always a good indication of relevance. For a considerable percentage of clicks, users select what turn out to be irrelevant documents and these clicks should not be directly used as evidence for relevance inference. Thus in this paper, we put forward an observation that the relevance indication degree of a click is not a constant, but can be differentiated by user preferences and the context in which the user makes her click decision. In particular, to interpret the click behavior discriminatingly, we propose a Noise-aware Click Model (NCM) by characterizing the noise degree of a click, which indicates the quality of the click for inferring relevance. Specifically, the lower the click noise is, the more important the click is in its role for relevance inference. To verify the necessity of explicitly accounting for the uninformative noise in a user click, we conducted experiments on a billion-scale dataset. Extensive experimental results demonstrate that as compared with two state-of-the-art click models in Web Search, NCM can better interpret user click behavior and achieve significant improvements in terms of both perplexity and NDCG.

Categories and Subject Descriptors

H.3.3 [**Information Storage and Retrieval**]: Information Search and Retrieval

General Terms

Algorithms, Measurement, Experimentation

Keywords

click model, click noise, log analysis

Permission to make digital or hard copies of all or part of this work for personal or classroom use is granted without fee provided that copies are not made or distributed for profit or commercial advantage and that copies bear this notice and the full citation on the first page. To copy otherwise, to republish, to post on servers or to redistribute to lists, requires prior specific permission and/or a fee.
WSDM'12, February 8–12, 2012, Seattle, Washington, USA.
Copyright 2012 ACM 978-1-4503-0747-5/12/02 ...$10.00.

1. INTRODUCTION

Modeling user behavior recorded in search engine click-through logs is attracting more and more attention in information retrieval research, since user click behavior seems to be an excellent source of encoding user preferences to search results. Furthermore, in industrial search engines, click-through logs can be collected at a very low cost. This makes the modeling scalable and practical to better understand user favorites. Consequently, many attempts have already positioned it as an appealing area and formalized this issue of learning document relevance from click-through logs as a click modeling problem.

Although click-through logs are very informative, a well-known challenge for click modeling is position bias, where it states that a document appearing in a higher position is more likely to attract more user clicks even though it is not as relevant as other documents appearing in lower positions. Thus, the often used metric click-through rate (CTR) is not an exact measure of document relevance. An effective click model needs to alleviate position bias. This bias was firstly noticed by Granka et al. [11] in their eye-tracking experiments and a lot of research since then has proposed to correct it and infer an unbiased relevance. Thereafter, Richardson et al. [18] proposed to increase the relevance of documents in lower positions by a multiplicative factor; Craswell et al. [8] later formalized this idea as the examination hypothesis which states that a document is clicked if and only if it is both examined and relevant.

Under the examination hypothesis, given a document that has been examined, its relevance is exclusively determined by its CTR. Thus, for each click in the logs, it contributes to the CTR and directly plays a positive impact on increasing the relevance of a clicked document. Perversely, after carefully examining the real user click behavior in an industrial search engine, we observed that user click behavior is often complex and noisy. It is far from ideal that every click is informative and can be a good indication of relevance. Rather, we show that there is a considerable amount of noise in clicks and some clicked documents turn out to be irrelevant documents. Obviously, the existence of click noise may hinder click models to infer an accurate document relevance. Yet, most of the existing works on click model only treat each click as a binary event (click or not) but disregard the noise or quality born with it. This may result in their research being based on unreliable user click signals for relevance inference.

In this paper, we put forward an observation that not

all clicks are equal and not all clicks are good indications of relevance. Rather, we illustrate the complex causes of a click and the necessity to characterize the noise in each click. To capture the click noise, we propose a Bayesian model called Noise-aware Click Model (NCM). NCM is designed to complement the click data with the human judged data so as to learn a predictor to characterize click noise. NCM is also capable of predicting the noise of large-scale clicks without human judged data by exploiting the user preferences and the context in which a user makes her click decision. Different from previous research in click modeling, NCM assesses the noise of each click and encourages the high quality clicks with less noise to play an important role in relevance inference. In addition, NCM is the first attempt to incorporate both click data and human labeled data together in learning a click model thus can be regarded as a semi-supervised model. We developed NCM as a general model which makes it capable of embracing the assumptions of most existing click models. Especially, we successfully extended NCM to embrace the assumptions of two state-of-the-art models in Web search. To verify the effectiveness of NCM, we conducted experiments on a billion-scale industrial dataset. Extensive experimental results demonstrated that NCM can achieve consistent and significant improvements in terms of both perplexity and NDCG.

The rest of the paper is organized as follows. In Section 2, we briefly introduce the preliminaries of click models and summarize the related work. We introduce the methodology in Section 3 and the NCM in Section 4. Finally, we conduct comparison experiments in Section 5 and conclude the paper in Section 6.

2. PRELIMINARIES & RELATED WORKS

Before delving into hypothesis details, we begin by introducing some definitions and background that will be used throughout the paper. A user starts a *query session* by issuing a *query* to a search engine, the search engine returns M (usually $M = 10$) ranked *documents* in a *Search Engine Result Page* (SERP). We use $d_{\phi(i)}$ to indicate the document ranked at the position i. We assume all documents are indexed and d_i is the i-th document. Here we use a mapping function ϕ to represent the document at position i. The user then examines the SERP and clicks on some or none of the documents. Clicks on sponsored ads or other web elements such as query suggestion results are not considered in our query session. Any subsequent query re-submission or re-formulation will be regarded as initiating a new query session. It is worth noting that there exist different definitions of a user session in prominent literature. Thus in this paper, we differentiate them by query session and search session, where a query session only contains the actions related to a single query, while a search session includes all the actions a user undertakes to perform a search task, which may include one or more query sessions, multiple query reformulations and clicks under different queries.

In click models, examinations and clicks are treated as probabilistic events. For a particular query session, we use a binary random variable $E_i = 1$ to indicate that the document at position i is examined and otherwise $E_i = 0$. Similarly, we use $C_i = 1$ to indicate the document at position i is clicked and otherwise $C_i = 0$. Therefore, $P(E_i = 1)$ indicates the examination probability for position i and $P(C_i = 1)$ is the corresponding click probability.

2.1 Examination Hypothesis

The *examination hypothesis* assumes that a displayed document is clicked if and only if this document is both *examined* and *relevant*. In the literature[6, 20, 25], if the document is examined, the perceived relevance of a document is a query-specific variable which directly measures the likelihood that a user will click this document. More precisely, given a query q and a document $d_{\phi(i)}$ at the position i, the examination hypothesis assumes the probability of the binary click event C_i as follows:

$$P(C_i = 1|E_i = 0) = 0 \tag{1}$$
$$P(C_i = 1|E_i = 1, q, d_{\phi(i)}) = a_{\phi(i)} \tag{2}$$

where $a_{\phi(i)}$ measures the degree of relevance between query q and document $d_\phi(i)$. Obviously, $a_{\phi(i)}$ is the conditional probability of a click after examination. Thus, the Click-Through Rate (CTR) is represented as

$$P(C_i = 1) = \underbrace{P(E_i = 1)}_{position\ bias}\ \underbrace{P(C_i = 1|E_i = 1)}_{document\ relevance} \tag{3}$$

where CTR is decomposed into position bias and document relevance.

Following the examination hypothesis, given the condition $P(E_i = 1)$, the relevance of the document is a constant value. However, a challenge in this decomposition is that whether a document is examined or not is not observable from click-through logs, so subsequent click models try to formalize this examination event as a hidden variable and make different assumptions to deduce its probability.

An important extension of the examination hypothesis is the user browsing model (UBM). It assumes that the examination event E_i depends not only on the position i but also on latest clicked position l_i in the same query session, where $l_i = \max\{j \in \{1, \cdots, i-1\} \mid C_j = 1\}$. It introduces a series of global parameters $\beta_{l_i,i}$ to measure the transition probability from position l_i to position i. Formally, the UBM is characterized by the following equations:

$$P(E_i = 1|C_{1:i-1} = 0) = \beta_{0,i} \tag{4}$$
$$P(E_i = 1|C_{l_i} = 1, C_{l_i+1:i-1} = 0) = \beta_{l_i,i} \tag{5}$$
$$P(C_i = 1|E_i = 0) = 0 \tag{6}$$
$$P(C_i = 1|E_i = 1) = a_{\phi(i)} \tag{7}$$

Here $l_i = 0$ if there are no preceding clicks. The term $C_{i:j} = 0$ is an abbreviation for $C_i = C_{i+1} = \cdots = C_j = 0$.

A similar work to UBM is Bayesian browsing model (BBM) [17], which adopts a Bayesian approach for inference with each random variable as a probability distribution. This is similar to the work on the General Click Model (GCM)[28]. It extends the model to consider multiple biases and shows that previous models are special cases of GCM.

2.2 Cascade Model

The *cascade model* assumes that users always examine documents from top to bottom without skipping. Therefore, a document is examined only if all previous documents are examined. For an examined document, whether it is clicked or not still depends on its relevance. But the click events depend on the relevance of all the documents shown above. Formally, the cascade model can be formalized as:

$$P(E_1 = 1) = 1 \tag{8}$$
$$P(E_{i+1} = 1|E_i = 0) = 0 \tag{9}$$
$$P(C_i = 1|E_i = 1) = a_{\phi(i)} \tag{10}$$
$$P(E_{i+1} = 1|E_i = 1, C_i) = 1 - C_i \tag{11}$$

Eq.11 implies that a user will abandon the query session if she finds a desired search result; otherwise she always continues the examination. This simultaneously reveals that it can only be applied to query sessions with one click at most. Yet this is too strict for real logs with multiple clicks in a query session.

Subsequently, the DCM, CCM and DBN are introduced to deal with the multiple clicks within a query session. The *dependent click model* (DCM) [13] introduces a set of global position-dependent parameters to represent the probability of examining the next document after a click. *Click Chain Model*(CCM) [12] continues to model the relationship between the examination probability and the relevance of previous documents. The *Dynamic Bayesian Network* (DBN) [6] model emphasizes that a click does not necessarily indicate user's satisfaction with the document. Instead, the user may have been attracted by some misleading snippets, including the title and summary, to trigger a click. Hence, it distinguishes document relevance as *perceived relevance* a_i and *actual relevance* s_i. Whether a user clicks a document or not depends on its perceived relevance and whether the user is satisfied with the document or not depends on the actual relevance. If the user is satisfied with the clicked document, she will not examine the next document. Otherwise, there is a probability $1 - \gamma$ that the user abandons her query session and a probability γ that the user continues her search. Thus, DBN replaces Eq.11 as follows:

$$P(S_i = 1|C_i = 0) = 0 \tag{12}$$
$$P(S_i = 1|C_i = 1) = s_{\phi(i)} \tag{13}$$
$$P(E_{i+1} = 1|S_i = 1) = 0 \tag{14}$$
$$P(E_{i+1} = 1|E_i = 1, S_i = 0) = \gamma \tag{15}$$

Where S_i is a hidden event indicating whether a user is satisfied with the document $d_{\phi(i)}$. The values a_i and s_i are estimated by applying the expectation-maximization algorithm in the original paper, while there exists a probit approach to infer the model introduced in [26].

2.3 Externalities and Others

Unlike the UBM model and the other models following the cascade assumption, which assumes that the examination event will only be affected by the documents shown above, externalities consider that the click behavior in a position will be simultaneously affected by the documents below. Two recent works [20][24] have conducted good experiments to demonstrate this phenomenon in online advertising and developed models to characterize it. [24] verified the existing of externalities based on two advertisements and modeled their competitive property as attracting a user for a click. Work[20] studied the externalities in online advertisements with respect to the clicks in other below positions and stated that the relevance of a document is not a constant but affected by clicks in other positions. This factor was also observed in an experimental finding in a previous work [4]. It is pointed out that the CTR of an advertisement can be affected by the quality of other advertisements shown together. It is obvious that externalities exist in online advertising and most of the previous works are motivated by observations from the advertisement instead of general Web Search. As compared with the general Web Search, the number of advertisements in a SERP is smaller and users may have a more commercial intent when clicking on an advertisement. This may encourage users to conduct more comparison between advertisements.

There are four other models that are not part of previous assumptions. The whole page click model (WPC)[7] interprets user click behavior in the whole page, including both the search and ads. The post-click click model (PCC)[27] captures user post-click behavior after the click. The Session Utility Model (SUM) [10], given a single query, measures the relevance of a set of clicked documents as the probability that a user stops the query session. The intent-bias model [14] demonstrates the existence of multiple intents for a same query and extends UBM and DBN to characterize the diversity of search intents in click models.

2.4 Modeling Context

Contextual information has been utilized by many applications and previous works have already demonstrated its usefulness in understanding user behavior. [1] used the contextual information as features to improve Web Search ranking. [22] represented the contextual information as ODP categories and used them to predict user short-term interests. [23] considered how users reformulate queries and used this information for Web search ranking. [3] leveraged the contextual information to better model query completion. [9] utilized the contextual user behavior in organic search to characterize the user behavior in sponsored search. [19] used the contextual information for recommendation systems and showed its effectiveness in collaborating filtering problem. Our work differs from these studies. First, we are working on a click model problem to automatically infer document relevance based on user click behavior. Second, we focus on utilizing the contextual behavior and user preference to understand click noise and then qualify a click for inferring a more accurate relevance.

3. THE DATA & METHODOLOGY

Previous works have already illustrated the complexity of user behavior and the challenges to interpret click data [22, 19], since the cause for a user to perform a click may be complex and varied. She may be attracted by a snippet, or just want to explore some information need with a strong uncertainty. Whenever we are aiming to interpret the complex user click data in a commercial search engine, there is no doubts that click data are not extremely clean. To let the real data speak for this, we first collect a human judged dataset containing 474,185 judged documents and collect 16.18 million clicks on these documents. We then classify all these clicks based on the relevance rating of judged documents, from *Bad, Fair, Good, Excellent* to *Perfect*. We present the relationship between the number of clicks and each corresponding rating in Figure 1. The x-axis indicates the relevance degree from irrelevant to the most relevant and the y-axis illustrates the density distribution of this click data. It clearly shows that there are less than 35% clicks on perfect documents. If we treat *Bad* and *Fair* in judged ratings as irrelevant, there are more than 28% of

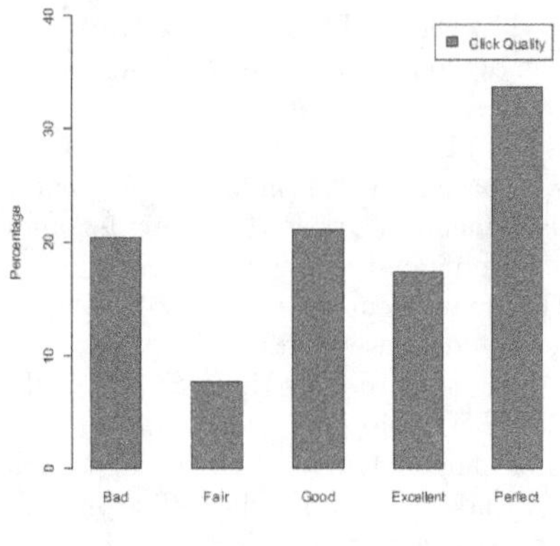

Figure 1: The distribution of click quality.

clicks on irrelevant documents. This clearly shows that there exists a considerable amount of noise in click data, i.e, not all clicks are good indications of document relevance.

To characterize the noise of a click, we complement click data with human judged data. The human judged dataset is collected from a commercial human relevance system (HRS), where it randomly picks up a set of representative queries and requires judges to give a rating denoting the relevance between a query and each of its corresponding documents. If we treat this human judged data as ground-truth, we may classify all the clicks on judged documents into two categories. For a click on a document which is judged as relevant in the HRS system, we define it as a noise-free click; otherwise it could be a noisy click since the click might not bring a good indication of relevance. If we can have the judged rating for each clicked document, we can identify the noise of each click easily. However, the size of the queries in the HRS system is very limited due to the high cost of manual judgement. Even if we are using a HRS set which is used to evaluate the performance of a commercial search engine, it only contains 12,590 queries. While in the click through data for one month, there are billions of queries and clicks. Apparently, compared with the HRS data, click data are much larger in scale and can be collected with a much lower cost. Given the HRS data as the ground-truth, this can be vividly represented as a semi-supervised learning problem where small portion of click data are labeled but most data are unlabeled. Hence, a big challenge is to generalize the limited HRS labeled data to understand the noise in each click, and then we may use it to infer a more accurate relevance via click models for large-scale unlabeled queries.

Our methodology is to design a model to leverage the user preference and contextual information as features for this generalization. We list them in Table 1, which can be classified into two categories. The *Context* class specifies the contextual information in which users make the click decision, such as its previous queries and click information in these queries. The *User* class characterizes the historical behavior of a user, such as her average click or skip behavior for documents in other search sessions. Based on the limited labeled documents in HRS, we classify all the clicks on them into two categories: noise-free click and noisy click. The task in the training is to learn a predictor to characterize the relationship between values of the features mentioned above and the degree of a noise. With this predictor learnt in the training phrase, we may predict the noisy degree for large-scale unlabeled click data. The challenge lies in how to learn this predictor effectively with consideration of the assumptions in click models. The details will be presented in next section.

An interesting analysis is to understand the cause of the noise although it may be complex and varied. A well known explanation is the difference between perceived relevance and intrinsic relevance[10] , where perceived relevance corresponds to a snippet while intrinsic relevance relates to a document. While a user performs a click, she is mostly attracted by a snippet but is generally not aware of whether the corresponding document is relevant or not. Similarly, as demonstrated in [21], there is a strong disagreement between the judgement of snippet and that of the document itself. A snippet may make an irrelevant document appear relevant, or a relevant document appear irrelevant. However, a click happens before a user examines the document thus it may have some disagreement with the intrinsic relevance. This disagreement will be characterized in our Noise-aware click model.

Based on the data we use, one other cause of the noise may be the difference between general search users' conception of relevance and the judges', especially when search users have multiple intents for the same query, such as an informational query with an ambiguous meaning. However, it is very hard to ask a judge to understand each intent for each query. We are aware of this possible cause and that numerous studies have documented this difference [5]. Thus in a commercial HRS system, it adopts a multiple-judges approach to alleviate this for ambiguous queries. For each ambiguous query, it asks about three judges to give ratings for all its corresponding documents based on as many intents as they can be aware of. This approach may most likely reduce the inconsistency and cover most intents from general users. Another issue caused by the multiple judges is their mutual disagreement. We studied a dataset and found that if we calculate from the 5-level ratings:*Bad, Fair, Good, Excellent* and *Perfect* respectively, the pair-wise consistency is about 70%. However, if we only separate the ratings into binary categories with *Bad, Fair* as irrelevant while the others as relevant, the pair-wise consistency value increases to more than 90%. This mean that, in most of the data, judges can agree with each other; for the remaining small portion of data with inconsistent ratings, we may use the majority of this binary rating as the final rating.

Another cause of this noise may be related to the type of queries. Given a set of navigational queries, users may have a fairly consistent and clear idea of what they are looking for, so the clicks among different users may be consistent and informative for relevance inference. While for a navigational query, users might represent more exploratory information needs or situations where there is an uncertainty and lack of domain knowledge. This may lead to more inconsistent click behavior among users and more clicks on irrelevant documents. This query type difference will be modeled by our noise-aware click model via a query specific parameter.

4. NOISE-AWARE CLICK MODEL

In this section, we first present the model specifications of NCM and then illustrate its extension to embrace the assumptions of two state-of-the-art click models in Web Search. Following this we introduce the inference of NCM to make

Feature Name	Feature description
	User class
AvgDwellTime	The average dwell time of clicks for this user.
IntervalTime	The average interval time between two clicks for this user.
UserSkip	True if the user skips this document before.
UserClick	True if the user clicks this document before.
UserFirstClick	True if the user first clicks this document before.
UserLastClick	True if the user last clicks this document before.
UserOnlyClick	True if the user only clicks this document before.
FracQueryNoClick	Fraction of queries with no clicks for this user.
FracQueryOneClick	Fraction of queries with one click for this user.
FracQueryMultiClicks	Fraction of queries with more than one clicks for this user.
	Context class
SubmitTime	The issued time of current query.
QuerySubsetPre	True if current query is a subset of previous query.
QuerySupsersetPre	True if current query is a superset of previous query.
QueryDistPre	Edit distance between current query and previous query.
ClickInLastSession	Whether there is a click in previous query session.
DwellTimeInLastSession	The dwell time the user spends on last session (in seconds).
FirstQuery	True if it is the first query in the search session.
TimeInSearch	Time spent on the search engine so far (in seconds).
URLInSearch	Number of URL in the search session so far.
QueryInSession	Number of queries in the search session so far.
ClickInSession	Number of clicks in the search session so far.
AvgTimeBetQueries	Average interval time between two issued queries.
TimeToLastAction	Time to last action such as submit a query or click.

Table 1: Features used in NCM.

it capable of learning from large-scale data and present its prediction formula.

4.1 Model

The Noise-aware click model (NCM) introduces a random variable N to characterize the noise degree of a click. There are two extreme contexts for a click. In an extremely noisy context with $N = 1$, users may click on irrelevant documents. While in a noise-free context, users tend to click on relevant documents. With the limited HRS data as ground-truth to represent a relevant or irrelevant rating of a document, we may make the following two observations on this noise factor:

- In a noise-free context with $N = 0$, users tend to skip (i.e., not click) a document with a *Bad* or *Fair* rating.
- In an extremely noisy context with $N = 1$, a click tends to be a noisy event that is not fully dependent on document relevance.

Figure 2 is a NCM flow chart that illustrates the user behavior when examining a document at position i. It characterizes two extreme contexts: The extremely noisy context with $N_i = 1$ and the noise-free context with $N_i = 0$. Suppose document $d_{\phi(i)}$ is relevant to query q according to the HRS rating. In a noise-free context, a user will examine it and then click it with probability $r_{\phi(i)}$. Here we do not assume $r_{\phi(i)} = 1$ because this value is to be learnt via click models. Also, if the document is irrelevant according to the HRS rating, a user in a noise-free context tends to skip it. On the other hand, in an extremely noisy context, the user may be attracted by its snippet but click it according to a parameter b no matter whether the document is relevant or not, where b is a query-specific parameter. In either way,

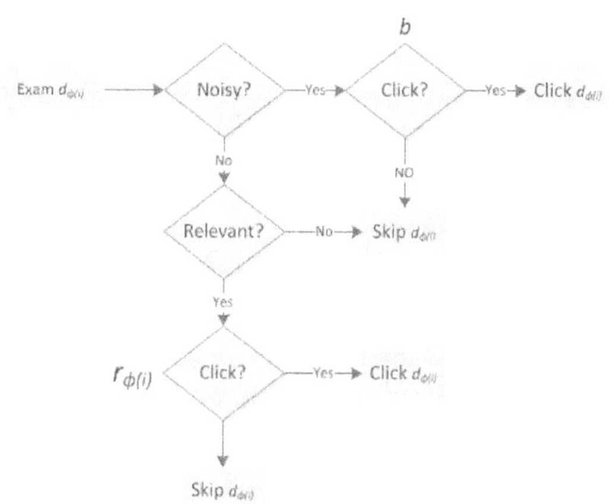

Figure 2: The user click behavior of NCM

after the user makes her decision, she can choose to continue the examination of other documents or abandon the current query session according to the assumptions defined in traditional click models. It is worth noting that these two extreme contexts are only formalized for the limited clicks with HRS ratings. Meanwhile, we are to learn the noise degree predictor by using the labeled documents in HRS with features extracted from their corresponding clicks as the training data. Thereafter, for the unlabeled clicks without HRS ratings, the degree of noise will be predicted using the predictor, i.e, calculating $P(N_i = 1)$ according to the contextual feature values.

To represent our assumptions in a probabilistic way, we use a symbol L_i to represent the binary rating of the i−th document. $L_i = 1$ indicates that the document at position

i has a relevant HRS rating to the query otherwise $L_i = 0$. We use N_i to represent the degree of noise in the context when a user is examining the document at position i. $N_i = 0$ indicates that the click happens in a noise-free context while $N_i = 1$ indicates that the context is extremely noisy. Under these definitions, we use the following equations to represent the above flow chart.

$$P(N_i = 1) = g(f_1, f_2, \cdots, f_n) \quad (16)$$
$$P(C_i = 1|E_i = 0) = 0 \quad (17)$$
$$P(C_i = 1|E_i = 1, L_i = 1, N_i = 0) = r_{\phi(i)} \quad (18)$$
$$P(C_i = 1|E_i = 1, L_i = 0, N_i = 0) = 0 \quad (19)$$
$$P(C_i = 1|E_i = 1, N_i = 1) = b \quad (20)$$

In the above, $r_{\phi(i)}$ indicates the click probability when a user in a noise-free context examining the document at position i and this document has a relevant HRS rating with $L_i = 1$. The f_i represents each user behavior feature defined in Table 1 and $g : R^n \to R$ is a function that maps features to a value indicating how noisy a context is. There are many kinds of functions such as the logistic function and sigmoid function which can be used to represent g. In our work, we define $g(f_i) = \Phi(\sum w_i f_i)$, where w_i is the feature weight. $\Phi(x) = \int_{-\infty}^{x} N(t; 0, 1)dt$ is the cumulative distribution function of the standard normal distribution. It is also referred to as the probit link [2]. We use it for convenience of inference and to assure the probability value within an interval of $[0, 1]$. We divide continuous feature f_i into several buckets so that we only need to consider binary features in the inference step. Generally, the estimated relevance in our model is defined as the probability of a click in a noise-free context given the document has been examined.

The NCM model is general and can function under many click models. Since it does not make any assumptions or constraints in estimating the probability of examination, it can be used with existing models based on the examination hypothesis. In this paper, we apply it to two typical click models, UBM and DBN, and adopt a Bayesian inference method to learn the parameters.

4.2 Noise-aware UBM

Same as the NCM specifications, the Noise-aware UBM model will introduce a random variable N_i to characterize the noise of the context where a click happens. We denote the noise-aware UBM as N-UBM with the following equations:

$$P(E_i = 1|C_{1:i-1} = 0) = \beta_{0,i} \quad (21)$$
$$P(E_i = 1|C_{l_i} = 1, C_{l_i+1:i-1} = 0) = \beta_{l_i,i} \quad (22)$$
$$P(N_i = 1) = \Phi(\sum w_i f_i) \quad (23)$$
$$P(C_i = 1|E_i = 0) = 0 \quad (24)$$
$$P(C_i = 1|E_i = 1, L_i = 1, N_i = 0) = r_{\phi(i)} \quad (25)$$
$$P(C_i = 1|E_i = 1, L_i = 0, N_i = 0) = 0 \quad (26)$$
$$P(C_i = 1|E_i = 1, N_i = 1) = b \quad (27)$$

In N-UBM, the probability of $N_i = 1$ is calculated from the probit function based on the feature values related with the context. If a user is in a noise-free context where $N_i = 0$ and the document is with a relevant rating with $L_i = 1$, the click probability is determined by the examination probability $P(E_i = 1)$ and a relevance parameter $r_{\phi(i)}$. But if the document has an irrelevant rating where $L_i = 0$ under a noisy-free context where $N_i = 0$, the click probability is assumed to be 0. On the other hand, in an extremely noisy context with $N_i = 1$, N-UBM assumes that a user will click the document according to a query specific parameter b, which is not characterized in traditional UBM assumptions. For the value of $P(N_i = 1)$, it will be calculated based on the contextual feature values f_i and the learnt weights w_i, which will be discussed in Section 4.4. After the user finishes her action in this position, she will continue to examine the following documents with probabilities related to β.

4.3 Noise-aware DBN

Similar to N-UBM model, the N-DBN model introduces a random variable N_i to characterize the noise of a context. When a user is in a noisy-free context, she will click the relevant document ($L_i = 1$) and skip the irrelevant document ($L_i = 0$) given that the document has been examined. If the user is in an extremely noisy context, there is a query-specific probability b that the document will be clicked, but this click event is not dependent on the document relevance. If the document is not clicked, there is a probability γ to examine the next document and $1 - \gamma$ to abandon the search. We can formalize the N-DBN model by following equations:

$$P(E_1 = 1) = 1 \quad (28)$$
$$P(C_i = 1|E_i = 0) = 0 \quad (29)$$
$$P(N_i = 1) = \Phi(\sum w_i f_i) \quad (30)$$
$$P(C_i = 1|E_i = 1, L_i = 1, N_i = 0) = r_{\phi(i)} \quad (31)$$
$$P(C_i = 1|E_i = 1, L_i = 0, N_i = 0) = 0 \quad (32)$$
$$P(C_i = 1|E_i = 1, N_i = 1) = b \quad (33)$$
$$P(S_i = 1|C_i = 0) = 0 \quad (34)$$
$$P(S_i = 1|C_i = 1) = s_{\phi(i)} \quad (35)$$
$$P(E_{i+1} = 1|E_i = 0) = 0 \quad (36)$$
$$P(E_{i+1} = 1|S_i = 1) = 0 \quad (37)$$
$$P(E_{i+1} = 1|E_i = 1, S_i = 0) = \gamma \quad (38)$$

4.4 Inference and Implementation

The parameter estimation of NCM is a two-stage procedure due to the existance of HRS data. In the first stage, we use the HRS data and the limited click data on the labeled documents to train a noise predictor to characterize the degree of noise for a click, i.e. we estimate the value of w_i $(i = 1, \cdots, n)$. The predictor takes a feature vector $\mathbf{f}$ and outputs a noise probability, i.e. $\Phi(\mathbf{w}^T\mathbf{f})$. Note that the inference in this stage only involves the sessions for a limited number of queries whose corresponding documents have been judged in the HRS system.

In the second stage, we infer the click model on all search sessions in the click-through logs. The training no longer depends on the HRS judgements but moves on to all unlabeled queries. We use the noise predictor obtained in the previous stage and the contextual feature values to estimate the noise degree of a context in which a click happens. This allows us to more accurately simulate real user behavior and learn the model parameters accordingly, such as the relevance parameters for each query-document pair. When the training is completed, we are able to predict the noise degree of clicks in future sessions based on both w_i and related contextual feature values f_i $(i = 1, \cdots, n)$. Next, we illustrate the im-

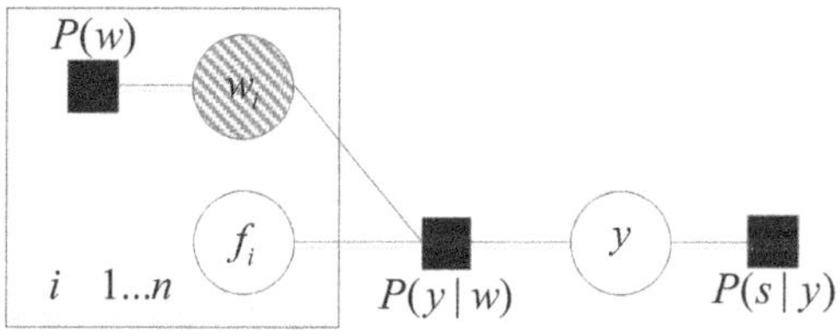

Figure 3: Factor graph for updating parameters w_i.

plementation of the two inference stages and the prediction formula.

4.4.1 Stage 1: Training with HRS

In the first stage, the training data is the intersection of click-through logs and HRS judgements. In other words, we consider only the queries and documents for which the relevance is judged. Given the noise-aware click model defined in Section 4.1, let $\mathbf{w}$ and $\mathbf{\Theta}$ be the parameters of the model: $\mathbf{w} = (w_1, \cdots, w_n)$ are coefficients of the noise predictor and $\mathbf{\Theta} = (\theta_1, \cdots, \theta_m)$ are other probability parameters, including the relevance of each query-document pair and the parameters with respect to model assumptions. We employ an approximate Bayesian inference to estimate $\mathbf{w}$ and $\mathbf{\Theta}$. The learning process is incremental: We load and process search sessions one by one, and the data for each session is discarded after they have been processed. Given a new incoming session s, we update the distribution of each parameter based on the session data and the click model. Before the update, $\mathbf{w}$ and $\mathbf{\Theta}$ have prior distributions $p(\mathbf{w})$ and $p(\mathbf{\Theta})$. We compute the likelihood function $P(s|w_i)$ and $P(s|\theta_j)$, multiply each to the prior distribution and then derive the posterior distribution $p(w_i|s)$ and $p(\theta_j|s)$. Finally, these posteriors are used as priors in the processing of next session.

With the Probit Bayesian Inference (PBI) technique invented by Zhang et. al [26], we can smoothly update the distribution of each θ_j. The update of each w_i is somewhat complicated because w_i is a real number instead of a probability, which is incompatible with the PBI's input format. However, the problem can be solved by introducing an auxiliary variable $y = \mathbf{w}^T\mathbf{f}$. Since $\Phi(y)$ is a probability, we first apply PBI to derive the posterior distribution $p(\Phi(y)|s)$, and then calculate $p(y|s)$. Actually, PBI guarantees that $p(y|s)$ is always a Gaussian density. Furthermore, each $p(w_i|s)$ is the marginal of the joint distribution $p(y, \mathbf{w}|s)$ after integrating y and all other variables in $\mathbf{w}$, denoted as $\mathbf{w}^{\setminus i}$, so we can calculate it by the following integration:

$$p(w_i|s) \propto \int (\prod_{i=1}^{n} p(w_i))p(y|\mathbf{w})p(s|y)\mathrm{d}\mathbf{w}^{\setminus i}\mathrm{d}y; \quad (39)$$

$$p(s|y) \propto \frac{p(y|s)}{p(y)} = \frac{p(y|s)}{\int (\prod_{i=1}^{n} p(w_i))p(y|\mathbf{w})\mathrm{d}\mathbf{w}} \quad (40)$$

The Eq. (39) and Eq.(40) can be efficiently computed by the sum-product message passing algorithm on the factor graph (Figure 3), where (39) represents the leftward message passing and (40) represents the rightward message passing. A more detailed illustration of the message passing algorithm can be found in [16].

When the training is completed, we can get a distribution for each w_i. The inference procedure ensures that all distributions are Gaussian, so we can assume that $p(w_i) = \mathcal{N}(w_i; \mu_i, \sigma_i^2)$. Thus, given an arbitrary feature vector $\mathbf{f}$, we can predict the probability of noise by the expectation of $\Phi(\mathbf{w}^T\mathbf{f})$:

$$P(N=1) = E(\Phi(\mathbf{w}^T\mathbf{f})) = \Phi\Big(\frac{\sum_{i=1}^{n}\mu_i f_i}{\sqrt{1+\sum_{i=1}^{n}\sigma_i^2 f_i^2}}\Big).$$

4.4.2 Stage 2: Training without HRS

In the second stage, the training data are the entire click-through logs that mostly consist of unlabeled queries and their corresponding documents. For the unlabeled click data with L_i unknown in this stage, we formulate the noise-aware click probability as:

$$P(C_i = 1|E_i = 0) = 0; \quad (41)$$

$$P(C_i = 1|E_i = 1) = P(N_i = 0)r_{\phi(i)} + P(N_i = 1)b; \quad (42)$$

Here, $P(N_i = 0) = 1 - P(N_i = 1)$ is given by the predictor trained in Stage 1. Since parameter $r_{\phi(i)}$ is exactly the click-through rate of $d_{\phi(i)}$ after examined by a user in a noise-free context, it is the value of the document relevance and will be used for predicting future clicks in Section 4.5

Again, we employ the Probit Bayesian Inference (PBI) to perform parameter estimation. The inference is simpler than that in Stage 1 since w_i are constant values at this stage, and all other parameters are probability values. Thus, we use PBI to go through the whole data set and derive the probability distribution for each parameter. In most cases, the variance of such distribution converges to zero, so we get a numerical estimation after the training. If the variance is still large, we compute the expectation of the parameter to achieve a numerical estimation. The detailed formulas are also given in [26].

4.5 Prediction

Given a test session, the probability distribution of a click event in this session at position i can be calculated by the formula below:

$$P(C_i = 1) = P(E_i = 1)((1 - \Phi(\sum w_i f_i))r_{\phi(i)} + \Phi(\sum w_i f_i)b)$$

In N-DBN, $P(E_i = 1)$ is calculated as the below equations:

$$P(E_1 = 1) = 1 \quad (43)$$

$$P(E_{i+1} = 1) = (1 - P(C_i = 1)s_{\phi(i)})\gamma \quad (44)$$

In calculating $P(E_i = 1)$ for N-UBM, we need to consider the probability of clicks in each position above it. If there exists at least one click above, it enumerates the latest click position j above the position i. Then, we can calculate it by the equation below:

$$P(E_i = 1) = P(C_{1:(i-1)} = 0)\beta_{0,i} + \sum_{j=1}^{i-1} P(C_j = 1)P(C_{(j+1):(i-1)} = 0)\beta_{j,i} \quad (45)$$

5. EXPERIMENTAL RESULTS

In this section, we evaluate the NCM model by comparing it with two state-of-the-art click models in Web search. As we implement our NCM to embrace the assumptions of these two models, the reformulated models, i.e., the Noise-aware DBN and the Noise-aware UBM, are denoted as N-DBN and N-UBM respectively. We use *perplexity* and *normalized discounted cumulative gains (NDCG)* [15] to evaluate the performance of different click models.

5.1 Experimental Data

Click log data: The query sessions used to train and evaluate the click models are collected from a commercial search engine in the U.S. market in English from January 1st to January 31st in 2011. Several query sessions from one user may belong to the same search session, thus we uses a 30 minutes inactivity time interval to separate any two search sessions. For each query session, we extract contextual information from other query sessions appearing before and in the same search session. We collect the values for each feature in Table 1. In order to prevent the whole dataset being dominated by some extremely frequent queries, we limit the number of query sessions for each query to 10^4. When calculating perplexity, we use the first 15 days of data as the training data and the rest 16 days of data as the test data. In total, we collect approximately 380 million distinct queries and 1.17 billion query sessions. The detailed information about the dataset is summarized in Table 2.

HRS data: The details of the HRS data have already been introduced in Section 3. We provide its distribution over query frequency in table 2. Overall, there are 12,150 queries which appear in both the HRS data and the click data. For each query, there are 39 judged documents on average. While we are training the NCM in the stage 1, we treat the rating of *Bad* or *Fair* as irrelevant, and the other three ratings (*Good, Excellent* and *Perfect*) as relevant.

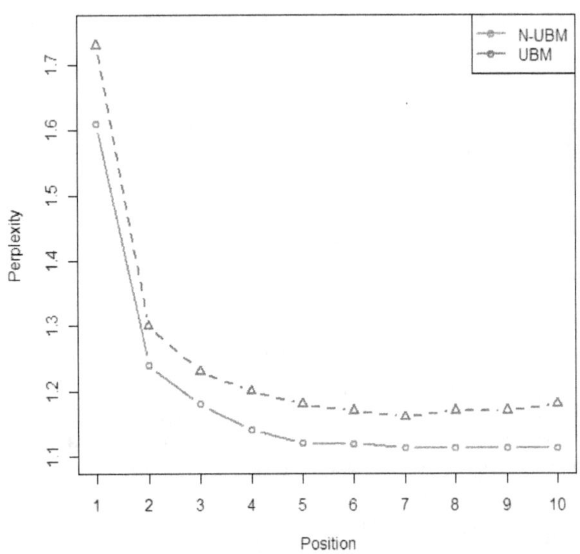

Figure 4: N-UBM & UBM perplexity Over Position

5.2 Perplexity

After the click model estimates its parameters while in training, as illustrated in Section 4.5, we can predict the click probabilities in the test query sessions. We evaluate the prediction accuracy by click perplexity, which has been widely used to measure the quality of click models[8, 12, 28]. A smaller perplexity indicates a better prediction accuracy and the optimal value is 1.0. For a given position i and a set of query sessions $s_1, s_2, \cdots, s_n$, we use $c_1, c_2, \cdots, c_n$ to denote the binary click events of the i-th document in each query session. Let $q_1, q_2, \cdots, q_n$ denote the predicted click probability by the click model. The perplexity p_i for the

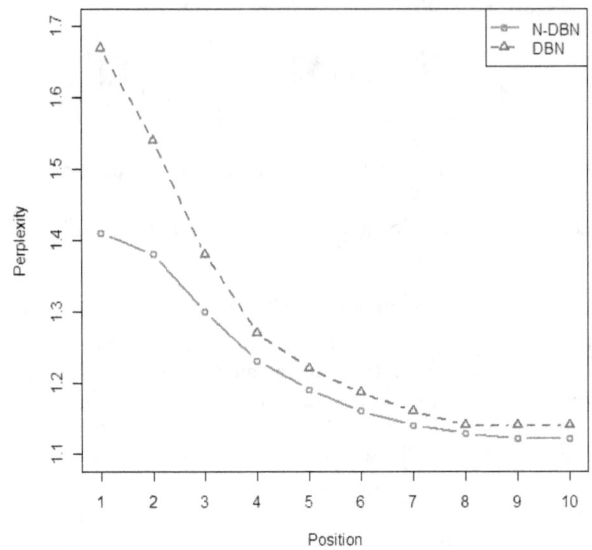

Figure 5: N-DBN & DBN perplexity Over Position

position i is:

$$p_i = 2^{-\frac{1}{n}\sum_{i=1}^{n}(c_i \log_2 q_i + (1-c_i)\log_2 q_i)} \quad (46)$$

The perplexity of the entire dataset is averaged over all positions, and the improvement of perplexity value p_a over p_b is calculated as $(p_b - p_a)/(p_b - 1) \times 100\%$ [12].

In Figure 4 and 5, we report the perplexity of N-DBN vs. DBN, and N-UBM vs. UBM on the testing dataset over different positions. The experimental results clearly show that N-UBM and N-DBN consistently outperform the original UBM and DBN respectively. We also provide the overall results in Table 3. The overall relative improvements of N-DBN over DBN and N-UBM over UBM are 30.4% and 33.9% respectively. This is particularly notable given that the dataset we used is a billion-scale one from a commercial search engine. Next, we separate queries into six groups as Table 2 based on the number of times that each query appears in the training sessions, calculate the overall perplexity for each group, and show the results in Figure 6. If we look at the two solid lines, it clearly shows that the N-DBN consistently outperforms DBN at all frequency level. Meanwhile, if we look at the two dash lines, N-UBM also consistently performs better than UBM. It is worth noting that the relative improvement of the high frequency group is much larger than that of the low frequency group due to a difference in dominator in the calculation. For example, the relative improvement of N-DBN over DBN in the first group with the lowest frequency is 20.4% while that of the last group with the highest frequency is 48.9%.

5.3 Ranking Performance

In this part of experiments, we sort the documents with respect to the estimated relevance given by a click model, and compare the ranking result with the ideal ranking in the HRS judgement data. In this case, the relative order of estimated relevance is more important than value.

We use NDCG to evaluate our ranking results. NDCG is a well-known metric which measures the gap between the currently available ranking and the theoretically ideal ranking.

Query Frequency	#HRS Query	#HRS Rating	#Query in Train	#Session in Train	#Query in Test	#Session in Test
$1 \sim 3$	1,726	33,079	157,202,923	179,610,940	181,477,994	207,287,519
$3 \sim 10^1$	2,329	57,201	18,777,342	84,904,526	21,617,259	97,766,874
$10^1 \sim 10^2$	3,858	106,082	3,688,839	93,883,180	4,275,037	109,035,850
$10^2 \sim 10^3$	2,439	118,224	332,590	84,461,513	386,995	97,924,566
$10^3 \sim 10^4$	1,089	86,970	30,794	76,442,296	35,363	87,544,334
$> 10^4$	719	72,629	2729	27,290,000	2985	29,850,000
Total	12,150	474,185	180,032,217	546,592,455	207,795,633	629,409,143

Table 2: The summary of the data set collected from one month in Jan 2011.

Model		Perplexity	NDCG@1	NDCG@2	NDCG@3	NDCG@4	NDCG@5
DBN	N-DBN	1.2182	0.738	0.724	0.727	0.740	0.753
	DBN	1.2846	0.651	0.641	0.648	0.656	0.663
	Improvement	30.4%	13.2%	12.9%	12.3%	12.6%	13.5%
UBM	N-UBM	1.1859	0.700	0.698	0.707	0.714	0.718
	UBM	1.2490	0.609	0.618	0.631	0.643	0.650
	Improvement	33.9%	14.9%	13.0%	12.0%	11.1%	10.5%

Table 3: Detailed experimental results for different click models.

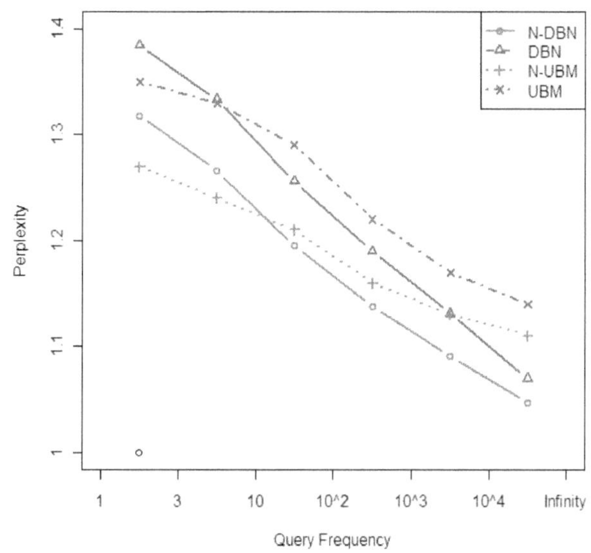

Figure 6: Perplexity Over Frequency

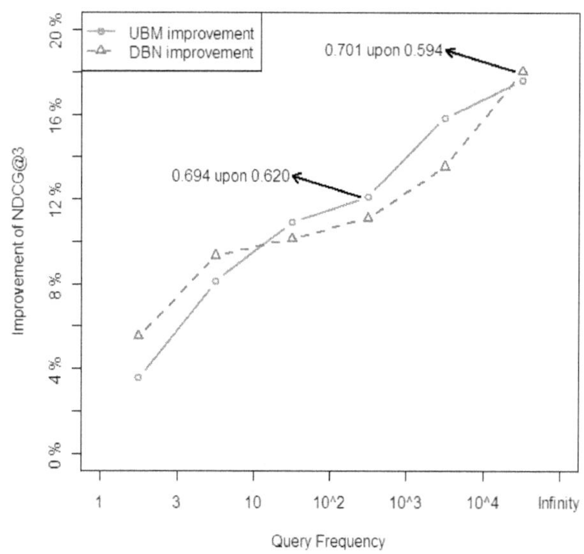

Figure 7: Imp of NDCG@3 over query frequency.

For a given query q, the results are sorted by the decreasing order of estimated relevance, and then the NDCG is calculated as

$$NDCG@i = \frac{1}{IdealDCG@i} \sum_{j=1}^{i} \frac{2^{g_i} - 1}{\log 1 + j}, \quad (47)$$

where $IdealDCG@i$ is the maximum DCG over all possible rankings. g_i is the HRS judgement of the i-th document. It represents judges' rating on the relevance of the document to q. Note that for those documents which have no rating, we treat them as $g_i = 0$. For the whole HRS data, we randomly pick half of the queries into the training of the stage 1 and leave the other half of the queries as the evaluation queries to calculate the NDCG.

We show the detailed NDCG results (at different positions) for DBN, N-DBN, UBM and N-UBM in Table 3. The results show that the noise-aware models have significant improvements over the original models in terms of NDCG. The improvements at all positions are over 10%. These results demonstrate that after taking click noise into consideration by the NCM model, clicks models can infer a more accurate document relevance. We perform a t-test to verify the significance. The result shows that the P-values of t-test are all less than 0.01, which confirms that the estimated relevance from N-DBN and N-UBM is consistently and significantly better than that from DBN and UBM respectively.

To investigate the variance of NDCG over different query frequencies, we recalculate the NDCG@3 improvements over frequency. The results are shown in Figure 7. This experiment continues to verify the consistent improvements over different frequency. The improvement of high frequency group is more significant than that of the low frequency group. This may be attributed to the property that high-frequency queries can usually provide more sufficient information for the NCM model to better understand click noise.

6. CONCLUSION

In this paper, we have introduced a noise-aware model to capture the noisiness of a click which causes the learning model to weight differently the user click observation. We design the NCM by complementing click data with the HRS data and characterizing the context in which a user performs her click decision. NCM is a general model to embrace the assumptions in most existing click models. We have successfully extended it to embrace the assumptions of two typical click models and formalized the new models as N-UBM and N-DBN. We have designed a Bayesian inference approach to make NCM capable of processing large-scale click data. The billion-scale experimental results demonstrate the necessity to account for uninformative click noise and identify good click data in learning a click model.

NCM is initially designed as a semi-supervised model to learn the click data with limited human labeled data. It is actually a very general model to learn for two inconsistent objectives, like the HRS based objective and click likelihood based objective in this paper. This two-stage approach in NCM is also suitable for addressing the problem of a limited number of samples for one objective, like the HRS based objective with a limited size.

7. ACKNOWLEDGMENTS

We thank the support of Hong Kong RGC GRF Grant 621010. We thank Si Shen and Nan Liu from HKUST and the anonymous reviewers for their help and comments.

8. REFERENCES

[1] E. Agichtein, E. Brill, and S. Dumais. Improving web search ranking by incorporating user behavior information. SIGIR '06, pages 19–26.

[2] J. H. Albert and S. Chib. Bayesian analysis of binary and polychotomous response data. *Journal of the American Statistical Association*, 88(422):669–679, 1993.

[3] Z. Bar-Yossef and N. Kraus. Context-sensitive query auto-completion. WWW '11, pages 107–116. ACM.

[4] H. Becker, C. Meek, and D. Chickering. Modeling contextual factors of click rates. AAAI '07, pages 1310–1315.

[5] P. Borlund. The concept of relevance in IR. *Journal of the American Society for information Science and Technology*, 54(10):913–925, 2003.

[6] O. Chapelle and Y. Zhang. A dynamic bayesian network click model for web search ranking. WWW '09, pages 1–10.

[7] W. Chen, Z. Ji, S. Shen, and Q. Yang. A whole page click model to better interpret search engine click data. In *AAAI*, 2011.

[8] N. Craswell, O. Zoeter, M. Taylor, and B. Ramsey. An experimental comparison of click position-bias models. WSDM '08, pages 87–94.

[9] C. Danescu-Niculescu-Mizil, A. Broder, E. Gabrilovich, V. Josifovski, and B. Pang. Competing for users' attention: on the interplay between organic and sponsored search results. WWW '10, pages 291–300.

[10] G. Dupret and C. Liao. A model to estimate intrinsic document relevance from the clickthrough logs of a web search engine. WSDM '10, pages 181–190.

[11] L. A. Granka, T. Joachims, and G. Gay. Eye-tracking analysis of user behavior in www search. SIGIR '04, pages 478–479.

[12] F. Guo, C. Liu, A. Kannan, T. Minka, M. Taylor, Y.-M. Wang, and C. Faloutsos. Click chain model in web search. WWW '09, pages 11–20.

[13] F. Guo, C. Liu, and Y. M. Wang. Efficient multiple-click models in web search. WSDM '09, pages 124–131.

[14] B. Hu, Y. Zhang, W. Chen, G. Wang, and Q. Yang. Characterize Search Intent Diversity into Click Models. WWW '11, pages 17–26.

[15] K. Järvelin and J. Kekäläinen. Cumulated gain-based evaluation of ir techniques. *ACM Trans. Inf. Syst.*, 20:422–446, October.

[16] F. R. Kschischang, B. J. Frey, and H.-A. Loeliger. Factor graphs and the sum-product algorithm. *IEEE Transactions on Information Throry*, (498-519), 1998.

[17] C. Liu, F. Guo, and C. Faloutsos. BBM: Bayesian browsing model from petabyte-scale data. SIGKDD '09, pages 537–546. ACM.

[18] M. Richardson, E. Dominowska, and R. Ragno. Predicting clicks: estimating the click-through rate for new ads. WWW '07, pages 521–530.

[19] H. Z. S.H. Yang, B. Long, A. Smola and Z. Zheng. Collaborative Competitive Filtering : Learning Recommender Using Context of User Choice. SIGIR '11.

[20] R. Srikant, S. Basu, N. Wang, and D. Pregibon. User browsing models: Relevance versus examination. KDD '10, pages 223–232.

[21] A. Turpin, F. Scholer, K. Jarvelin, M. Wu, and J. Culpepper. Including summaries in system evaluation. SIGIR '09, pages 508–515. ACM.

[22] R. W. White, P. N. Bennett, and S. T. Dumais. Predicting short-term interests using activity-based search context. CIKM '10, pages 1009–1018.

[23] B. Xiang, D. Jiang, J. Pei, X. Sun, E. Chen, and H. Li. Context-aware ranking in web search. SIGIR '10, pages 451–458.

[24] W. Xu, E. Manavoglu, and E. Cantu-Paz. Temporal click model for sponsored search. In *SIGIR*, pages 106–113. ACM, 2010.

[25] Y. Zhang, W. Chen, D. Wang, and Q. Yang. User-click modeling for understanding and predicting search-behavior. In *KDD*, 2011.

[26] Y. Zhang, D. Wang, G. Wang, W. Chen, Z. Zhang, B. Hu, and L. Zhang. Learning click models via probit bayesian inference. CIKM '10, pages 439–448.

[27] F. Zhong, D. Wang, G. Wang, W. Chen, Y. Zhang, Z. Chen, and H. Wang. Incorporating post-click behaviors into a click model. In *SIGIR*, 2010.

[28] Z. A. Zhu, W. Chen, T. Minka, C. Zhu, and Z. Chen. A novel click model and its applications to online advertising. WSDM '10, pages 321–330.

Personalized Click Model through Collaborative Filtering

Si Shen *
Hong Kong University of Science and Technology
shensi@ust.hk

Botao Hu
Institute for Interdisciplinary Information Sciences
Tsinghua University
botao.a.hu@gmail.com

Weizhu Chen
Microsoft Research Asia
wzchen@microsoft.com

Qiang Yang
Hong Kong University of Science and Technology
qyang@cse.ust.hk

ABSTRACT

Click modeling aims to interpret the users' search click data in order to predict their clicking behavior. Existing models can well characterize the position bias of documents and snippets in relation to users' mainstream click behavior. Yet, current advances depict users' search actions only in a general setting by implicitly assuming that all users act in the same way, regardless of the fact that anyone, motivated with some individual interest, is more likely to click on a link than others. It is in light of this that we put forward a novel *personalized click model* to describe the user-oriented click preferences, which applies and extends matrix / tensor factorization from the view of collaborative filtering to connect users, queries and documents together. Our model serves as a generalized personalization framework that can be incorporated to the previously proposed click models and, in many cases, to their future extensions. Despite the sparsity of search click data, our personalized model demonstrates its advantage over the best click models previously discussed in the Web-search literature, supported by our large-scale experiments on a real dataset. A delightful bonus is the model's ability to gain insights into queries and documents through latent feature vectors, and hence to handle rare and even new query-document pairs much better than previous click models.

Categories and Subject Descriptors

H.3.3 [**Information Storage and Retrieval**]: Retrieval Models

*This work is done during the author's internship at Microsoft Research Asia

Permission to make digital or hard copies of all or part of this work for personal or classroom use is granted without fee provided that copies are not made or distributed for profit or commercial advantage and that copies bear this notice and the full citation on the first page. To copy otherwise, to republish, to post on servers or to redistribute to lists, requires prior specific permission and/or a fee.
WSDM'12, February 8–12, 2012, Seattle, Washington,USA.
Copyright 2012 ACM 978-1-4503-0747-5/12/02 ...$10.00.

General Terms

Algorithms

Keywords

Click Model, Click Log Analysis, Personalization, Search Engine, User Behavior

1. INTRODUCTION

Click-through logs in search engines are a valuable resource for learning user preferences for search or advertisement (ads) results. The analysis of these log data can facilitate a number of search-related applications, such as Web search ranking, ads click-through rate (CTR) prediction and optimization, and user satisfaction estimation. The relevant research can not only enhance user search experience, but also make an impact on search revenue as well.

Click prediction aims at computing the probability that a given document in a search-result list is clicked on after a user enters some query. To accurately predict user clicks, a central question is to resolve the user-perceived relevance between query-document pairs. Having learnt this relevance from massive search click data, a commercial search engine can improve its understanding of search users and therefore polish its search results. Recently, the problem of learning user-perceived document relevance from click-through data has been formalized as a problem of click model learning, and has become an attractive research topic. Many studies have been attempted to mine the general user preferences from click-through logs to improve the overall relevance of search results [14, 13, 2].

Since click data are informative and can be easily collected, they offer a promising approach to optimize search engine performance with low cost. However, a well-known challenge of using such data is the position bias, whereby a document at a higher position on a Web page tends to attract more user clicks even when in the case of low document relevance. This bias was firstly mentioned by [9] in their eye-tracking experiment, which pointed out that the frequently used CTR may not be appropriate as an estimator of document relevance. Prior work [19] in sponsored advertisement search attempted to exploit the position bias by imposing a multiplicative factor on documents at lower positions to infer their true relevance scores. This idea was further explored in organic searches [5], and was formalized as the so-called *Examination Hypothesis*, a fundamental assumption for many following important models. For example, these models include the User Browsing Model (UBM) [8], Dynamic Bayesian Network (DBN) model [3], Click Chain Model (CCM) [10], Bayesian Browsing Model (BBM) [17], General Click Model (GCM) [24] and the Session Utility Model (SUM) [7].

In spite of their merits, these previous developments in click modeling are limited by their assumption that the query-document relevance model is identical for all search engine users. However, we observe that there are a large number of similar queries submitted by different users that resulted in very different information needs and search preferences [12]. In response, in this paper, we argue that a single global query-document relevance is not sufficient to truly reflect the interest of every individual user. Therefore, we must develop a new method for building personalized relevance models to fully capture diversified user interests.

To further illustrate our motivation, take a query "opera" as an example. This query may come from an engineer, who expects results that present the web browser Opera at `opera.com`. In contrast, a music lover who submits the same query may look for some vocal concert performance. In this situation, search results like `sfopera.com` and other opera houses are more likely to be clicked. This example indicates that the attractiveness of a search result is not only influenced by its relevance but also determined by the user's intrinsic search need for the query. Furthermore, notice that the engineer might have searched for technological software for a couple of times previously, and that the music lover could be a regular visitor to music Web sites. In this paper, we show that those activities that are embedded in the search history logs can be exploited to imply users' personal search preferences. Thus, we can analyze this history data to provide personalized search results to meet user's interests.

An intuitive approach to solve the personalization problem is to utilize the user's historical search data to learn personalized document relevance models. However, a major challenge is that user click data for a query-document pair are often grossly insufficient and sparse. Existing click models consider query-document as an integrated pair, but do not have the ability to handle such sparse data. This limitation leads us to a different approach, in which we capture user preferences from click logs *collaboratively*. In particular, we propose a collaborative-filtering based click-model framework. In this framework, we factorize the user-query-document relations as latent vectors, which reflect the diversity of user's intrinsic preferences and the inter- and intra-relationships of queries and documents. In the process, we take the personalized click model under a general framework user modeling, for which we pay attention to personalize document relevance and leave position biases intact. Note that the two parts of Examination Hypothesis remain relatively independent, so that not only different depictions of position bias from previous click models can be replaced in the model, but various collaborative filtering models may substitute one another as well.

The contribution of this paper is two-fold.

- We address the issue of personalization for click models by introducing collaborative filtering to the literature of web search. Our model is able to handle low frequency and even new query-document combinations that preceding click models cannot manage, for we introduce matrix factorization, and its extension tensor factorization, as a mature and highly scalable model. Queries and documents are then implicitly connected through their latent feature vectors and further through users. As a result, new query-document pairs that are not present in training data may still be inferred, and informational queries with complex click logs can be predicted more precisely. We believe that this is the first time for this to be done.
- We conduct extensive experiments on large-scale real-world click log data to evaluate our model and algorithm. Our results show that the personalization of click model is a highly promising direction for click-modeling research.

In the rest of this paper, we first introduce some of the existing click models and related theories in Section 2. We then explain our factorization models, as well as the inference method in details in Section 3. We perform experiments on the personalized click models based on real dataset and present our results and insights in Section 4 and Section 5, respectively. We share our thoughts of possible future work and conclude the paper in Section 6.

2. BACKGROUND

In this section, we first introduce the basic Position Model and then explore its extensions to various existing click models.

Before delving into the detailed introduction of click models, we describe some relevant concepts when a user submits a search query and the notations used throughout the paper. A user u first makes an inquiry by sending query q. After fetching Search Engine Result Page (SERP), one scrutinizes the provided documents, or referred as urls in some work [5], in a particular order and decides to either click or skip a document d. The widely accepted assumption is that the decision is made according to the user-perceived relevance between document and query. In general, the prediction of user click behavior is modeled in a probabilistic setting. It should be noted that SERP returns not only the organic search results mentioned above, but also other links like ads and related queries that a user might perform a click [4]. To simplify the problem, such links are out of the scope of this paper.

We introduce notations used in the paper. Each observation of click contains a vector $\{C, u, q, d, i\}$, where $C = 1$ means a click and i is the document position. The data set $\mathbf{S}$ in query logs are partitioned into $\mathbf{S}^{\bullet}$, the subset that contains all the clicked items where $C = 1$, and its complement $\mathbf{S}^{\circ}$, the subset of observations that are not clicked. Within our paper, we follow the notations in [8] where a dot denotes a click and a hallow circle a skip. The index of $\mathbf{S}$ denotes the requirement that the observations need to meet to be in the set. For example, $\mathbf{S}^{\bullet}_{qd,i}$ refers to all the observations such that document d at position i for the given query q is clicked. Similarly, $\mathbf{S}^{\circ}_{i}$ represents all the observations such that a document at position i is neglected. Additionally, we designate $S^{\bullet}$ and S° the cardinalities of the corresponding sets.

2.1 Position Model

The Position Model [19] is a broadly accepted basic click model. It incorporates position bias by assuming that a user makes the click decision only after examining the document's title and snippet. Whether the user examines a document item or not depends on the position of the document. This is referred as the *Examination Hypothesis*.

If we let $C = 1$ denote the event of click and value 0 the absence of the event, then the probability to click a document d at position i given query q can be expressed as $P(C_i = 1|q, d)$.

Now let $E = 1$ denote the event of examination and value 0 disregard for the document, and the probability of click under Examination Hypothesis can be formulated as

$$\begin{aligned} P(C_i = 1|q, d) &= \sum_{E_i} P(C_i = 1|E_i, q, d)P(E_i) \\ &= \underbrace{P(C_i = 1|E_i = 1, q, d)}_{document\ relevance}\ \underbrace{P(E_i = 1)}_{position\ bias} \end{aligned}$$

Define

$$\alpha_{qd} = P(C_i = 1|E_i = 1, q, d) \text{ and } \beta_i = P(E_i = 1) \ ,$$

then

$$\begin{aligned} P(C_i = 1|q, d) &= \alpha_{qd}\beta_i \\ P(C_i = 0|q, d) &= \sum_{E} P(C = 0|E, q, d)P(E_i) \\ &= 1 - \alpha_{qd}\beta_i \end{aligned}$$

From the above, the click event follows a simple Bernoulli distribution. When the parameter set $\boldsymbol{\beta}$ are set as ones, the model degrades to a baseline model that a click depends solely on the user-perceived relevance of the document to a given query. The joint likelihood under our notations is then

$$\mathcal{L}(\boldsymbol{\alpha}, \boldsymbol{\beta}|\mathbf{S}) = \prod_{q,d,i} (\alpha_{qd}\beta_i)^{S^{\bullet}_{qd,i}} (1 - \alpha_{qd}\beta_i)^{S^{\circ}_{qd,i}}$$

In this model, the hidden variable is the event of examination E. One can apply Expectation Maximization (EM) algorithm to estimate $\boldsymbol{\alpha}$ and $\boldsymbol{\beta}$ in an alternation fashion [6]. This method can also avoid the possible situations when $\alpha > 1$.

2.2 Cascade Model

The pure Position Model copes only with different positions that are independent of each other. Many extensions were subsequently proposed to take the whole-session interactions into consideration. One session here is defined as all the search results returned for one requested query. The number of relevant documents within a session is normally set as 10. More hypotheses were raised to interpret hidden information in a session.

A prominent hypothesis is that users tend to examine documents one by one from top of the page. A document can be examined only if its upper neighbor is examined. An additional condition that a user stops the session when a document is clicked gives Cascade Model [15]. Under these requirements, a click on the document indicates that: (1) the user has examined all the documents above and regarded them as irrelevant; (2) all the documents below will not be examined and the session is terminated. Again, it is quite clear that whether a user submits a click depends on the user-perceived document relevance just as in Position Model.

Following prior notations, Cascade Model can be formalized.

$$\begin{aligned} &P(E_i = 1) = 1 \\ &P(E_{i+1} = 1|E_i = 0) = 0 \\ &P(C_i = 1|E_i = 1) = \alpha_{qd_i} \\ &P(E_{i+1} = 1|E_i = 1, C_i) = 1 - C_i \end{aligned}$$

Then the probability of click can be computed as

$$P(C_i = 1) = \alpha_{qd_i} \prod_{j=1}^{i-1} (1 - \alpha_{qd_j})$$

While the Position Model focuses on depicting position bias as precisely as possible, the Cascade Hypothesis was proposed to view user search behavior as an action chain. One drawback of the Cascade Model is that the assumption is so strict that sessions with more than one click are to be discarded. This restriction gives rise to some subsequent extensions, which we review below.

2.3 User Browsing Model

The hypothesis raised by the User Browsing Model (UBM) [8] aims at arriving at a better estimation of position bias by relaxing it from the limitation of constant multipliers. It also overcomes the constraint of Cascade Model that only one-click sessions can be handled. The model says that position bias depends not only on current position i, but also on the distance to the position of the latest clicked document r. β_i is hence extended to β_{ir}.

We set $r = 0$ if there is no preceding clicks. If we let α_{qd_i} denote the user-perceived relevance of document d at position i for a given query q, then UBM can be formally illustrated as follows.

$$\begin{aligned} &P(C_i = 1|E_i = 1) = \alpha_{qd_i} \\ &P(C_i = 1|E_i = 0) = 0 \\ &P(E_i = 1|C_{i-r} = 1, C_{i-r+1} = \cdots = C_{i-1} = 0) = \beta_{ir} \\ &P(E_i = 1|C_1 = \cdots = C_{i-1} = 0) = \beta_{i0} \end{aligned}$$

The joint likelihood bears a form similar to Position Model.

$$\mathcal{L}(\boldsymbol{\alpha}, \boldsymbol{\beta}|\mathbf{S}) = \prod_{i,r}\prod_{q,d} (\alpha_{qd}\beta_{ir})^{S^{\bullet}_{qd,ir}} (1 - \alpha_{qd}\beta_{ir})^{S^{\circ}_{qd,ir}}$$

Similarly, we can also use Expectation Maximization (EM) algorithm to complete model inference [8].

3. PERSONALIZED CLICK MODEL

In this section, we present our main approach for personalized click models. We first analyze the drawbacks of current click models and then introduce collaborative filtering to the click-through-rate prediction problem. We then consider three different matrix or tensor factorization set-ups. The first one is a matrix factorization model on queries and documents only to compare with preceding click models to show the capability of our decomposition method. The model has self-explanatory probability meanings. The second one is a direct incorporation of probabilistic tensor factorization on users, queries and documents to illustrate the framework of personalized click model. The last one is a hybrid factorization model that emphasizes on queries and documents interaction and characterizes user preference through user's deviation from average. We give reasons for why the hybrid model is superior to the other two, and the inference is given after the models.

3.1 Limitation of Previous Works

When looking back at the preceding click models, we notice two main drawbacks. It was these two limitations that inspires our new models. Firstly, while existing models put quite some efforts to depict position bias, the complexity of document relevance has been largely neglected. Individual characteristics of queries and documents were not thoroughly considered. A query and a document has been simply treated as an integrated pair. Hence, a new query-document combination in testing data cannot be effectively handled.

Another problem is that previous click models regard document relevance as a global parameter and overlook any possible disparity due to user personal behavior. However, user u may have personal interest in or preference to a particular url entry d of query q, and consequently, CTR of this query-document pair by u can be relatively higher than average.

To relax the limitation of query-document pair perspective and to incorporate personalization to click models, our novel approach adopts some ideas from recommender systems [20, 16, 18].

The general setting of a recommender system consists of two main components, users and items. A user u may have rated an item i, with score r_{ui}. The score associated with that user-item pair can be a numerical value, or a 0/1 indicator. Yet, there are also many unrated user-item pairs. The goal of a recommender system is to use existing rated values $\{r_{ui}\}$ to predict scores for requisite user-item pairs with missing values.

Collaborative filtering is an important technique that explores user similarity to compute new ratings for products in recommender systems. Among many of the models of collaborative filtering, we use matrix factorization, and its tensor extension, in our work for two reasons: (1) matrix factorization characterizes latent factors of both items and users implied from feedback log; (2) matrix factorization is scalable and flexible with high accuracy. By using matrix factorization, we can not only handle new query-document pairs from latent factors and implicit connections, but effectively and efficiently solve the problem of personalization as well.

3.2 Matrix Factorization Click Model

As introduced in Section 3.1, one limitation of previous work neglects interactions between queries and documents, which are simply modeled as pairs. We now propose a matrix factorization click model (MFCM) to focus on queries and documents interactions through their latent feature vectors. Suppose that a query q is submitted in a session and N documents are fetched, the i-th document being d_i. If there are in total M_q queries and M_d documents, then we let $Q \subset \mathbb{R}^{F \times M_q}$, where the set consists of all possible real-valued matrices with size $F \times M_q$, and $D \subset \mathbb{R}^{F \times M_d}$ represents the latent factors of queries and documents, respectively. In this equation, F is the number of factors. Let $\mathcal{N}(\mu, \sigma^2)$ be the probability density function of Gaussian distribution with mean μ and variance σ^2.

We adopt a probabilistic linear model with Gaussian observation noise, and place zero-mean spherical Gaussian priors on queries and documents latent factors. MFCM is constructed as

$$
\begin{aligned}
&P(C_i = 1) = P(C_i = 1|E_i = 1)P(E_i = 1) \\
&P(C_i = 1|E_i = 1) = \alpha_{qd_i} \\
&P(\alpha_{qd_i}|Q_q, D_d, \sigma) \sim \mathcal{N}((Q_q \circ D_{d_i}), \sigma^2) \\
&P(Q_q|\sigma_Q) \sim \mathcal{N}(0, \sigma_Q^2 I) \\
&P(D_d|\sigma_D) \sim \mathcal{N}(0, \sigma_D^2 I)
\end{aligned}
$$

Although MFCM collaboratively solves the first limitation of previous works, it does not introduce personalization to click models. Hence, a tensor factorization click model with users as another dimension is presented next.

3.3 Tensor Factorization Click Model

To include personalization in our click models, we introduce a Personalized Click Model (PCM) in this section to extend MFCM to the user domain. Suppose that there are M_u users. Let $U \subset \mathbb{R}^{F \times M_u}$ denote the latent factors of user domain. The event of user being personally interested in the i-th document is indicated by N_i. Let α_{uqd_i} denote the probability of event N_i.

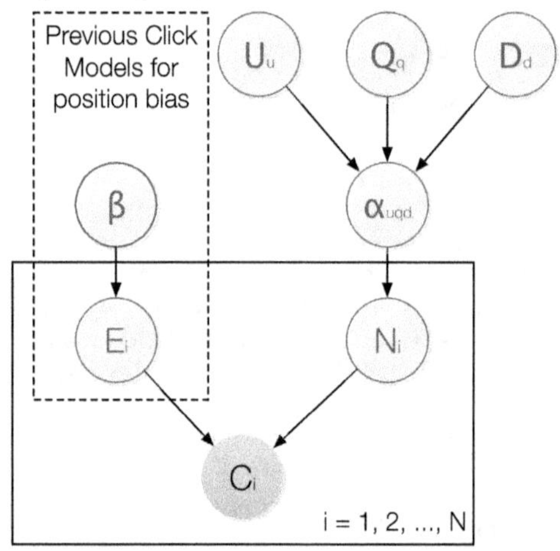

Figure 1: Graphic representation of Personalized Click Model

We impose again zero-mean spherical Gaussian priors on user latent factors, and extend matrix factorization to tensor decomposition, which naturally produces personalized click predictions. Our PCM can be characterized by the following group of equations.

$$
\begin{aligned}
&C_i = 1 \Leftrightarrow E_i = 1, N_i = 1 && (1) \\
&P(N_i = 1) = \alpha_{uqd_i} && (2) \\
&P(\alpha_{uqd_i}|U_u, Q_q, D_d, \sigma) \sim \mathcal{N}((U_u \circ Q_q \circ D_{d_i}), \sigma^2) && (3) \\
&P(U_u|\sigma_U) \sim \mathcal{N}(0, \sigma_U^2 I) && (4) \\
&P(Q_q|\sigma_Q) \sim \mathcal{N}(0, \sigma_Q^2 I) && (5) \\
&P(D_d|\sigma_D) \sim \mathcal{N}(0, \sigma_D^2 I) && (6)
\end{aligned}
$$

Note that $U_u \circ Q_q \circ D_{d_i} = \sum_{f=1}^{F} U_{fu} Q_{fq} D_{fd_i}$ as a traditional canonical tensor factorization.

Figure 1 gives a graphic representation of PCM, showing the connections of parameters. Gaussian priors are omitted from the graph model. As Examination Hypothesis suggested, the event of click at position i is dependent on the event of user examination and an individual document interest from user u. The examination of a document can still follow various assumptions of previous click models, while the personal document interest is modeled as a probability based on the latent factors of users, queries and documents themselves.

PCM is promising intuitively by considering the implicit interactions among users, queries and documents. However, for a number of navigational queries, personal differentiation is relatively insignificant. A fully personalized click model may occasionally suffer from over-fit problem.

3.4 Hybrid Personalized Model

In light of the capabilities and limitations of both MFCM and PCM, in this section, we put forward a hybrid personalized click model (HPCM). Instead of performing a direct canonical tensor factorization, we place our emphasis on the interactions between queries and documents, which have been believed to be the dominant part for relevance determination. Then to solve the problem of personalization, only the residuals are factorized using user latent factors to describe personal deviations from the global query-document factor model. That is, HPCM is a combination of PCM and MFCM. The conditional distribution of α_{uqd_i} can be modeled as

$$P(\alpha_{uqd_i}|\tilde{Q}_q, \tilde{D}_d, U_u, Q_q, D_d, \sigma) \sim \mathcal{N}(\underbrace{\tilde{Q}_q \circ \tilde{D}_{d_i}}_{query-doc\ bias} + \underbrace{U_u \circ Q_q \circ D_{d_i}}_{user\ diversity}, \sigma^2)$$

Gaussian priors are

$$P(\tilde{Q}_q|\sigma_{\tilde{Q}}) \sim \mathcal{N}(0, \sigma_{\tilde{Q}}^2 I)$$
$$P(\tilde{D}_d|\sigma_{\tilde{D}}) \sim \mathcal{N}(0, \sigma_{\tilde{D}}^2 I)$$
$$P(U_u|\sigma_U) \sim \mathcal{N}(0, \sigma_U^2 I)$$
$$P(Q_q|\sigma_Q) \sim \mathcal{N}(0, \sigma_Q^2 I)$$
$$P(D_d|\sigma_D) \sim \mathcal{N}(0, \sigma_D^2 I)$$

The interactions between queries and documents can be viewed as a relevance bias, while the user-query-document relationship may be viewed as user preference variations. Personalization is implemented after a global inference of query-document relevance. This combined factor model can therefore outperform MFCM and PCM, illustrated in Section 4. The graphic model of HPCM can be found in Figure 2.

3.5 Inference

Due to space limitation, we present inference process using Position Model describing position bias, that is, β_i. Inference for other position bias models are very similar and can be derived accordingly. Taking PCM as an example, the parameters to be inferred are

$$\boldsymbol{\Theta} = \{\boldsymbol{\alpha}, \boldsymbol{\beta}, U, Q, D\}$$

Define

$$R_{uqd} \equiv \exp\{-\frac{(\alpha_{uqd} - U_u \circ Q_q \circ D_d)^2}{2\sigma^2} - \frac{U_u^T U_u}{2\sigma_U^2} - \frac{Q_q^T Q_q}{2\sigma_Q^2} - \frac{D_d^T D_d}{2\sigma_D^2}\}$$

The conditional joint probability of observed data is then

$$P(\mathbf{S}|\boldsymbol{\Theta}) \propto \prod_{u,q,d,i} (\alpha_{uqd}\beta_i)^{C_i}(1-\alpha_{uqd}\beta_i)^{1-C_i} R_{uqd}$$

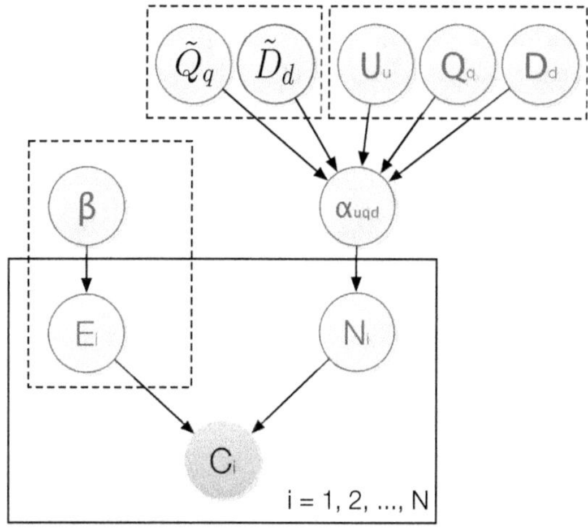

Figure 2: Graphic representation of Hybrid Personalized Click Model

The log-likelihood can be computed as

$$\begin{aligned}
&\log \mathcal{L}(\boldsymbol{\Theta}|\mathbf{S}, \sigma^2, \sigma_U^2, \sigma_Q^2, \sigma_D^2) \\
&= \sum_{u,q,d,i} S^{\bullet}_{uqd,i}(\alpha_{uqd}\beta_i) + \sum_{u,q,d,i} S^{\circ}_{uqd,i}(1-\alpha_{uqd}\beta_i) \\
&- \frac{1}{2\sigma^2}\sum_{u,q,d} S_{uqd}(\alpha_{uqd} - U_u \circ Q_q \circ D_d)^2 \\
&- \frac{1}{2\sigma_U^2}\sum_u S_u U_u^T U_u - \frac{1}{2\sigma_Q^2}\sum_q S_q Q_q^T Q_q \\
&- \frac{1}{2\sigma_D^2}\sum_d S_d D_d^T D_d + \text{constant}
\end{aligned}$$

EM algorithm is utilized, with the event of examination as hidden variable, to estimate the parameters maximizing the above log likelihood. A more detailed inference procedure can be found in Appendix.

Three observations can be made from the inference process.

- Position bias $\boldsymbol{\beta}$ has a rather independent inference process, which implies that previous click models portraying this bias can be substituted into the framework.
- The inference of latent vectors can also be implemented independently to some extent, allowing various factor models to be included. In our case, PCM, MFCM, and HPCM.
- Since the updating formulas for latent factors of users, queries and documents are dependent on one another, we could apply Stochastic Gradient Descent (SGD) algorithm to learn hidden factors during each EM iteration after α_{uqd} is updated, instead of direct Least Squared estimation.

So far, we have illustrated our model as a general personalization framework for click models with probabilistic implications and explained its ability to connect the domains of users, queries and documents through latent factors.

4. EXPERIMENTS

To illustrate our experiments in this section, we begin with our data preparation and experiment set-up. We then discuss our evaluation metric. Finally, we compare our models to a baseline model, where we study the impact of varying variables such as the number of factors and the number of iterations.

4.1 Experiment Setting

We sampled the search sessions used to train and evaluate click models from a commercial search engine in the U.S. market in English language in the first half of May 2011. A session consists of a input query, a list of returned documents on the search result page, a list of clicked positions, and a cookie ID to implicitly represent a user. We collected sessions subject to the following constraints: (1) the search session is on the first result page returned by the search engine; (2) all clicks in the session are on the search results, neither on sponsored ads nor on other web elements. We sort search sessions according to time stamps when the query is sent to the search engine and split them into training and the testing sets by a ratio of 1:1. In total, we collected approximately 66 million sessions over $2,264,889$ distinct queries submitted by $2,975,306$ different users. The total number of documents returned is $24,864,764$. We filtered high-frequency queries and spam users that may dominate the training process. The average number of users per query is 4.253, and the average number of queries submitted by one user is 2.228. The detailed distribution of our data is presented in Table 1.

The column of "Percentage of New Query-User-Doc Tuple" denotes the percentage of the query-user-doc tuples that occur in testing dataset but are absent in training dataset. So does the last column for new query-doc pairs. As Table 1 shows, the percentage of these new pairs or tuples is rather high in real log data (28.90% for pairs and 67.75% for tuples). However, the baseline model can not predict well on these new pairs/tuples that it never meets in training dataset. We expect that our proposed model can boost up the performance on these pairs/tuples with help of collaborative filtering technology.

The baseline click model used in this paper for comparison is UBM (Section 2.3). We adopted EM inference process for parameters $\boldsymbol{\alpha}$ and $\boldsymbol{\beta}$ [8]. To avoid in-finite values in log-likelihood, a lower bound of 0.01 and a upper bound of 0.99 are applied to document relevance estimators for UBM. The number of iterations for EM algorithm is set as 100. To compare with UBM, we setup our factorization framework by using UBM to depict the part of position bias (Figure 1).

All experiments were carried out with HPC cluster of 144 machines, each with eight 2.4GHz cores and 16GB RAM.

4.2 Evaluation of Performance

To define and quantify the performance of a model, as well as to compare the soundness of different models, we introduce log-likelihood and perplexity as evaluation metrics in this section. These widely adopted metrics ([24, 3, 11, 12, 5, 23]) are used throughout our experiments. We then report the performance of our models, along with UBM baseline, under the according evaluation measurement.

4.2.1 *Log Likelihood*

Log Likelihood (LL) is widely utilized in CTR prediction. One natural reason is that models often try to maximize the log likelihood of the joint distribution of click events in the course of inference. Therefore, LL becomes a direct measurement of the effectiveness of the estimators. For a single document, the LL value is the log of the predicted clicking probability if there is a click on the document. The value is the log of the predicted non-clicking probability, otherwise. Take the Position Model as an example. $LL_{\Theta}(\mathbf{S})$ is calculated as

$$\frac{1}{S}\sum_{q,d,i}[S^{\bullet}_{qd,i}\log_2(\alpha_{qd}\beta_i) + S^{\circ}_{qd,i}\log_2(1-\alpha_{qd}\beta_i)]$$

It is clear that a perfectly-fit set of estimators has a LL of value 0, and the smaller this value, the worse fit of the estimators. Also noteworthy is that when two models, or two sets of estimators, are to be compared, the improvement of LL_{Θ} over $LL_{\Theta'}$ is calculated up to an exponential transformation, $(2^{LL_{\Theta}-LL_{\Theta'}}-1)\times 100\%$.

Model	Log-Likelihood	Improvement over UBM
UBM	−0.4236	-
MFCM	−0.3055	8.53%
PCM	−0.2577	12.18%
HPCM	−0.2448	13.20%

Table 2: Performance of models measured by log-likelihood.

We present our experiment results on all three proposed models (MFCM, PCM, and HPCM) and baseline UBM in Table 2. The average LL is −0.4236 for UBM over all query sessions. Thanks to latent factor analysis, MFCM has a LL of −0.3055 and scores a 8.53% improvement. With LL at −0.2577 and −0.2448, our two personalized click model, PCM and HPCM, show improvements of 12.18% and 13.20% respectively. As expected, our HPCM leads to the most advance over UBM compared with other proposed models in our paper.

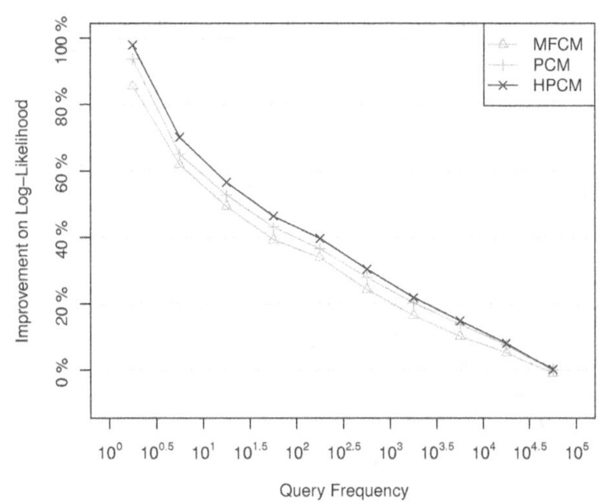

Figure 3: Log-likelihood on test dataset with respect to different query frequencies. The factor models have more significant improvement ratios for tail queries.

It has long been known that previous click models suffer from the so-called *tail problem*, whereby the click-through-rate prediction is far from satisfactory for infrequent queries.

Query Frequency	#Session	# Query	# User	# Document	Percentage of New Query-User-Doc Tuple	Percentage of New Query-Doc Pair
10^0 to $10^{0.5}$	14,935,135	1,077,691	2,211,723	11,747,545	83.47%	36.49%
$10^{0.5}$ to 10^1	9,480,325	586,620	2,186,747	7,382,319	59.34%	22.12%
10^1 to $10^{1.5}$	9,030,565	283,449	290,581	4,171,647	50.79%	20.33%
$10^{1.5}$ to 10^2	9,653,622	191,555	299,268	3,674,129	45.25%	23.21%
10^2 to $10^{2.5}$	7,573,039	64,186	142,140	1,708,899	46.00%	26.43%
$10^{2.5}$ to 10^3	7,953,625	45,320	97,588	1,637,040	44.47%	21.31%
10^3 to 10^4	4,958,208	13,644	86,969	637,606	40.36%	18.52%
10^4 to $10^{4.5}$	1,937,258	2,223	31,403	112,575	37.45%	11.20%
Total	66,547,897	2,264,889	2,975,306	24,864,764	67.75%	28.90%

Table 1: Summary of the dataset sampled from half month of click logs.

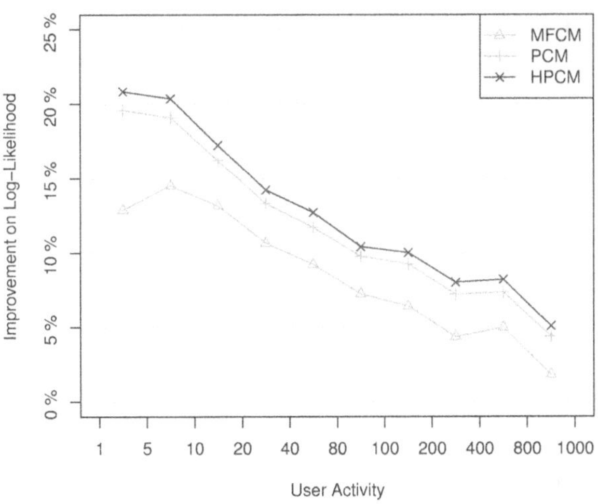

Figure 4: Log-likelihood on test dataset for various degree of user activeness. Our models have larger enhancement for infrequent users.

Our factor models solve the tail problem collaboratively. In Figure 3, we present the model improvement over baseline versus query frequency. The horizontal axis shows the log-scale of query frequency in training dataset. The improvement for rare queries boosts up to 80% to 100%. Similar phenomenon can be observed in Figure 4, where horizontal axis becomes the degree of user activeness characterized by user frequency. When both query frequency and user activeness decrease, the enhancement of our factor models shrinks, for UBM baseline can handle recurring training data well and leaves extremely limited space for other models to build up.

4.2.2 *Click Perplexity*

Perplexity of click events is defined at each position independently rather than on the whole set. The metric is related to log-likelihood by putting negative of the latter to the exponent. In Position Model, for instance, click Perplexity (p) at position i is defined as $p^i_\Theta(\mathbf{S}) =$

$$2^{-\frac{1}{S_i}\sum_{q,d}[S^\bullet_{qd,i}\log_2(\alpha_{qd}\beta_i)+S^\circ_{qd,i}\log_2(1-\alpha_{qd}\beta_i)]}$$

Smaller perplexity indicates higher prediction quality, and the optimal value is 1. When comparing two models, the improvement of perplexity value p^i_Θ over $p^i_{\Theta'}$ is given by

$$\frac{p^i_{\Theta'}-p^i_\Theta}{p^i_{\Theta'}-1}\times 100\%$$

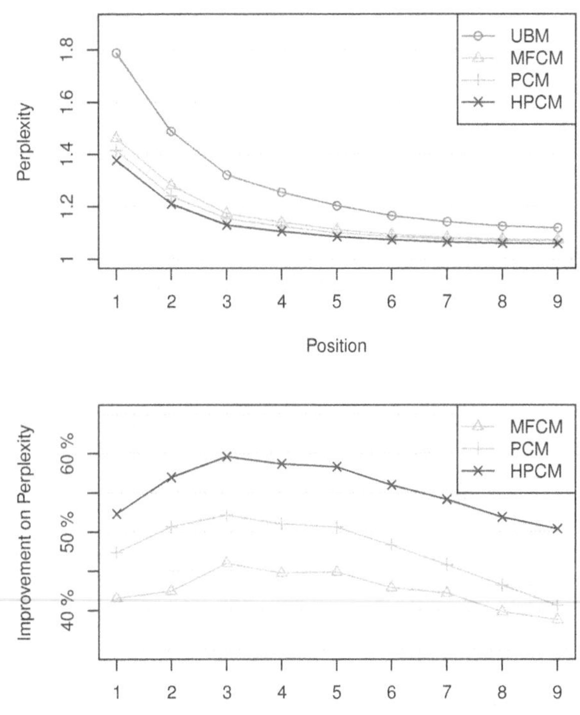

Figure 5: (a) upper. Model performance measured by perplexity at each position. (b) lower. Model improvement ratios over UBM at each position.

The experiment results of all three factor models and the baseline are summarized in Figure 5(a). The average click perplexity over all query sessions and positions is 1.1659 for MFCM and 1.1488 for PCM, 42.74% and 48.65% improvements per position over UBM (1.2898) respectively. Again, HPCM outperforms the other two factor models significantly, scoring an average click perplexity of 1.1293, which enhances 55.39% of UBM. As shown in Figure 5(a), the improvement ratios of all proposed models in this paper does not suffer greatly when going down the SERP. The improvement of HPCM over UBM even hits to 50% for the lowest position. The figure also demonstrates that click prediction quality of HPCM is better than other models at every position. MFCM cannot compete with PCM or HPCM because of its lack of personalization, while PCM can be too overfit and sacrifice performance at higher positions where user diversity is not that dominant. These results are consistent with our reasoning in Section 3.

4.3 Impact of Model Parameters

The three factor models we proposed in Section 3 have two model parameters, the number of factors and the number of iterations for SGD algorithm to well converge. We discuss the influence of these two parameters on model performance.

4.3.1 Number of Factors

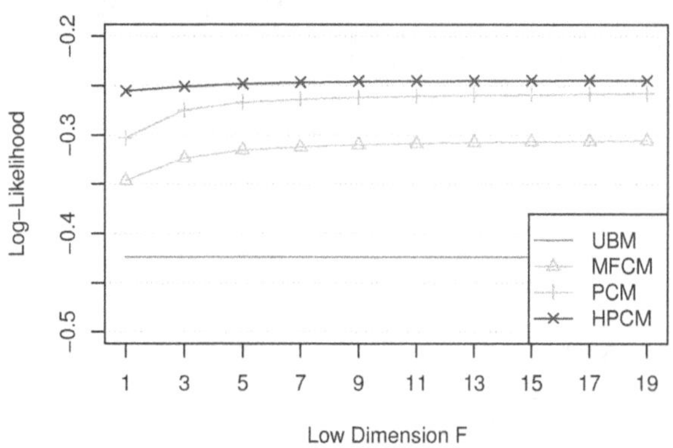

Figure 6: The influence of the number of factors on performance under log-likelihood. A few number of factors are adequate for stable performance.

We study the influence of the number of factors on all of our three proposed models, MFCM, PCM and HPCM, and present the experiment results in Figure 6. MFCM needs more than 10 factors to achieve a relatively stable performance, while PCM needs around 8, for PCM has one more domain of user than MFCM and the number of parameters to be estimated is greater. This also explains the reason why HPCM requires fewer number of factors to stabilize than PCM. Despite of the disparity among the models, the number of factors needed is rather low in general, implying that a few latent factors are adequate to catch most features of users, queries and documents.

4.3.2 Number of Iterations

To infer the factor models, we need to run SGD algorithm iteratively in one EM iteration. We study whether our inference procedures converge and how fast they converge on our datasets. Figure 7 gives the curve showing the relationship between model performance and the number of iterations for factor models. All of our factor models converge. It is presented that more than 9 iterations of factorization are needed for MFCM to catch up with the performance of our baseline UBM. The tensor models, PCM and HPCM, become stable after around 20 iterations, while outperforming UBM from the beginning of iterations.

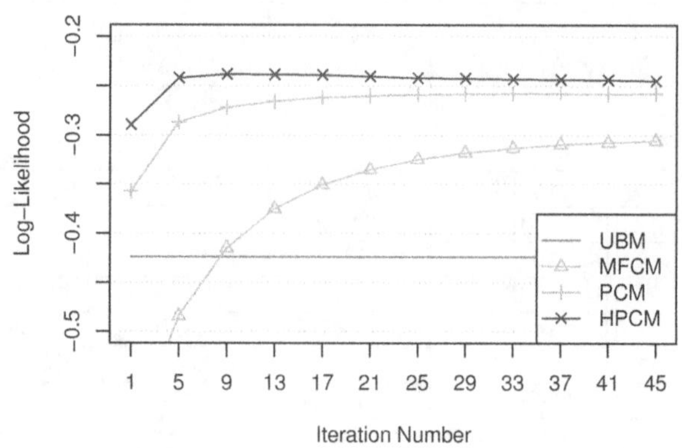

Figure 7: The influence of the number of iterations on performance under log-likelihood. All our models converge as the number of iterations goes up.

5. DISCUSSION

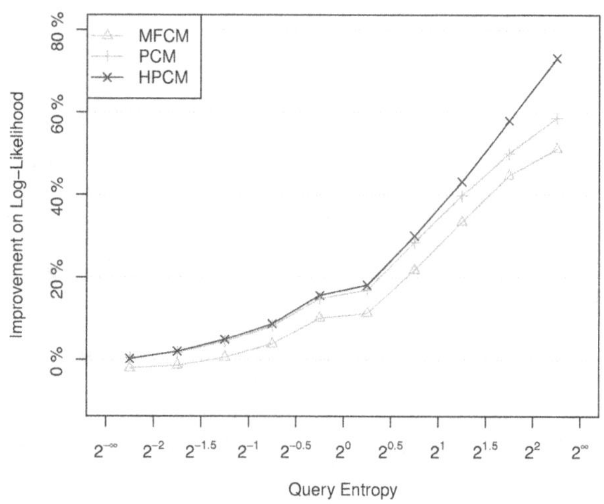

Figure 8: Perplexity on the test data for different query entropies. Factor models advance more when query entropy is higher, signaling supremacy on informational queries

We have demonstrated the sound performances of three factor models, MFCM, PCM and HPCM, in previous section, we then look into the enhancement and discuss our insights during the experiments.

Define query entropy of query q as

$$H(q) = -\sum_{d} CTR_{q,d} \log_2 CTR_{q,d}$$

where $CTR_{q,d}$ is the predicted click-through-rate for document d under query q.

A high entropy signals a higher degree of complexity, or more precisely unpredictability. We present model improvement on Log-likelihood as query entropy varies in Figure 8. The horizontal axis is query entropy in log-scale. Although it is clear that the improvement is insignificant for low entropy queries, which mainly consist of navigational queries like `amazon.com` and user diversity is negligible, the enhancement on performance impressively boosts up for more than 60% as query entropy rises. The reason is that high entropy queries possess complicated click logs that existing models cannot effectively deal with, whereas collaborative filtering can solve complex and diverse clicks efficiently. This matches our motivations and expectations of our factor models.

6. CONCLUSION

In this paper, we propose three factorization click models, which include: (1) a matrix factorization click model (MFCM) that relates queries and documents collaboratively; (2) a personalized click model (PCM) that uses indiscriminate tensor factorization to exploit the latent relationships of users, queries and documents; (3) a hybrid personalized click model (HPCM) with an emphasis on query-document interactions while characterizing user variations simultaneously.

We carry out a set of extensive experiments with two evaluation metrics on a real-world dataset. Our results clearly show the enhancement over state-of-the-art results. We see that MFCM performs well for capturing latent feature vectors of queries and documents, while PCM is better for the capability of personalization. Furthermore, HPCM achieves the greatest improvement by combining the strengths of previous two models. In addition, we show that our models are able to handle tail queries and informational queries, both of which are limitations in previously existing click models.

Through factor models, we address the personalization issues by characterizing user preferences toward documents. To simplify the model, however, we assume constant user preferences that are not varying with time. A future direction is to extend our models to a temporal click model to incorporate user preference dynamics to click models.

7. ACKNOWLEDGMENTS

The authors would like to thank Zhepeng Yan, Nan Liu, Bin Cao and Wenchen Zheng for their help and efforts.

This work was supported by Hong Kong RGC GRF project 621010, the National Basic Research Program of China Grant 2011CBA00300, 2011CBA00301, and the National Natural Science Foundation of China Grant 61033001, 61061130540, 61073174.

8. REFERENCES

[1] D. Agarwal, R. Agrawal, R. Khanna, and N. Kota. Estimating rates of rare events with multiple hierarchies through scalable log-linear models. In *KDD*, 2010.

[2] E. Agichtein, E. Brill, and S. Dumais. Improving web search ranking by incorporating user behavior information. In *SIGIR*, 2006.

[3] O. Chapelle and Y. Zhang. A dynamic bayesian network click model for web search ranking. In *WWW*, 2009.

[4] W. Chen, Z. Ji, S. Shen, and Q. Yang. A whole page click model to better interpret search engine click data. In *AAAI*, 2011.

[5] N. Craswell, O. Zoeter, M. Taylor, and B. Ramsey. An experimental comparison of click position-bias models. In *WSDM*, 2008.

[6] A. P. Dempster, N. M. Laird, and D. B. Rubin. Maximum likelihood from incomplete data via the em algorithm. *Journal of the Royal Statistical Society, Series B*, 39(1), 1977.

[7] G. Dupret and C. Liao. A model to estimate intrinsic document relevance from the clickthrough logs of a web search engine. In *WSDM*, 2010.

[8] G. E. Dupret and B. Piwowarski. A user browsing model to predict search engine click data from past observations. In *SIGIR*, 2008.

[9] L. A. Granka, T. Joachims, and G. Gay. Eye-tracking analysis of user behavior in www search. In *SIGIR*, 2004.

[10] F. Guo, C. Liu, A. Kannan, T. Minka, M. Taylor, Y.-M. Wang, and C. Faloutsos. Click chain model in web search. In *WWW*, 2009.

[11] F. Guo, C. Liu, and Y. M. Wang. Efficient multiple-click models in web search. In *WSDM*, 2009.

[12] B. Hu, Y. Zhang, W. Chen, G. Wang, and Q. Yang. Characterizing search intent diversity into click models. In *WWW*, 2011.

[13] T. Joachims. Optimizing search engines using clickthrough data. In *KDD*, 2002.

[14] T. Joachims, L. Granka, B. Pan, H. Hembrooke, and G. Gay. Accurately interpreting clickthrough data as implicit feedback. In *SIGIR*, 2005.

[15] D. Kempe and M. Mahdian. A cascade model for externalities in sponsored search. Springer-Verlag.

[16] Y. Koren, R. Bell, and C. Volinsky. Matrix factorization techniques for recommender systems. *Computer*, August 2009.

[17] C. Liu, F. Guo, and C. Faloutsos. Bbm: bayesian browsing model from petabyte-scale data. In *KDD*, 2009.

[18] S. Rendle and S.-T. Lars. Pairwise interaction tensor factorization for personalized tag recommendation. In *WSDM*, 2010.

[19] M. Richardson, E. Dominowska, and R. Ragno. Predicting clicks: estimating the click-through rate for new ads. In *WWW*, 2007.

[20] R. Salakhutdinov and A. Mnih. Probabilistic matrix factorization. In *NIPS*, 2008.

[21] W. Xu, E. Manavoglu, and E. Cantu-Paz. Temporal click model for sponsored search. In *SIGIR*, 2010.

[22] Y. Zhang, W. Chen, D. Wang, and Q. Yang. User-click modeling for understanding and predicting search-behavior. In *KDD*, 2011.

[23] Y. Zhang, D. Wang, G. Wang, W. Chen, Z. Zhang, B. Hu, and L. Zhang. Learning click models via probit bayesian inference. In *CIKM*, 2010.

[24] Z. A. Zhu, W. Chen, T. Minka, C. Zhu, and Z. Chen. A novel click model and its applications to online advertising. In *WSDM*, 2010.

APPENDIX

The resemblance of the log-likelihood of PCM and previous click models can be easily observed, so similar EM algorithm can be used to infer our new model. We explain the two steps separately and give the updating equations for a simpler case, where the number of latent vectors is one for all users, queries and documents.

E Step

Let us define $\mathbf{E}$ as the unobserved events of examination. EM algorithm first finds the expected value of the log likelihood $\log P(\mathbf{S}, \mathbf{E}|\mathbf{\Theta})$ with respect to unobserved $\mathbf{E}$ given observed $\mathbf{S}$ and current parameters $\mathbf{\Theta}$. That is,

$$\begin{aligned}
Q(\mathbf{\Theta}, \mathbf{\Theta}^{t-1}) &= E[\log P(\mathbf{S}, \mathbf{E}|\mathbf{\Theta})|\mathbf{S}, \mathbf{\Theta}^{t-1}] \\
&= \sum_{E} \log P(\mathbf{S}, E|\mathbf{\Theta}) \times P(E|\mathbf{S}, \mathbf{\Theta}^{t-1}) \\
&= \sum_{u,q,d,i} \sum_{C,E} [\log P(C, E|u,q,d,i,\mathbf{\Theta}) \\
&\times P(E|C,u,q,d,i,\mathbf{\Theta}^{t-1})] \\
&= \sum_{u,q,d,i} \sum_{C,E} [\log P(C,E|\mathbf{\Theta}) P(E|C, \mathbf{\Theta}^{t-1})]
\end{aligned}$$

where $\mathbf{\Theta}$ is the set of parameters following the tradition. We drop $\{u, q, d, i\}$ temporarily for notation convenience.

Note that when the number of factors is one, U_u, Q_q and D_d all become real numbers. By the assumption of the Position Model, the probability $P(E|\mathbf{S}, \mathbf{\Theta}^{t-1})$ mentioned above can be simplified to different cases.

$$\begin{aligned}
P(E=1|C=1, \mathbf{\Theta}^{t-1}) &= 1 \\
P(E=0|C=1, \mathbf{\Theta}^{t-1}) &= 0 \\
P(E=1|C=0, \mathbf{\Theta}^{t-1}) &= \frac{\beta_i^{t-1}(1-U_u^{t-1}Q_q^{t-1}D_d^{t-1})}{1-U_u^{t-1}Q_q^{t-1}D_d^{t-1}\beta_i^{t-1}} \\
&\doteq \tilde{C}_{uqd,i}^{t-1} \\
P(E=0|C=0, \mathbf{\Theta}^{t-1}) &= 1 - \tilde{C}_{uqd,i}^{t-1}
\end{aligned}$$

where $\tilde{C}_{uqd,i}^{t-1}$ can be interpreted as the probability of document d being *irrelevant* of query q judged by certain user u.

$P(C, E|\mathbf{\Theta})$ is even more straight-forward, hence omitted. Then $Q(\mathbf{\Theta}, \mathbf{\Theta}^{t-1})$ can be computed as

$$\begin{aligned}
Q(\mathbf{\Theta}, \mathbf{\Theta}^{i-1}) = &\sum_{\mathbf{S}^\bullet} \{\log(\alpha_{uqd}\beta_i) - \frac{1}{2\sigma^2}(\alpha - U_u Q_q D_{d_i})^2 \\
&- \frac{1}{2\sigma_U^2} U_u^2 - \frac{1}{2\sigma_Q^2} Q_q^2 - \frac{1}{2\sigma_D^2} D_{d_i}^2\} \\
&+ \sum_{\mathbf{S}^\circ} \{[\log((1-\alpha_{uqd})\beta_i) \\
&- \frac{1}{2\sigma^2}(\alpha - U_u Q_q D_{d_i})^2 - \frac{1}{2\sigma_U^2} U_u^2 \\
&- \frac{1}{2\sigma_Q^2} Q_q^2 - \frac{1}{2\sigma_D^2} D_{d_i}^2] \tilde{C}_{uqd,i}^{t-1} \\
&+ \log(1-\beta_i)(1-\tilde{C}_{uqd,i}^{t-1})\}
\end{aligned}$$

This completes the Expectation step.

M Step

The M step of EM iteration tries to maximize the expectation computed above, that is, to find

$$\mathbf{\Theta}^t = argmax_{\mathbf{\Theta}} Q(\mathbf{\Theta}, \mathbf{\Theta}^{t-1})$$

Taking derivatives of $Q(\mathbf{\Theta}, \mathbf{\Theta}^{i-1})$ in respect to $\mathbf{\Theta}$ produces the updating formulas for parameters.

$$\begin{aligned}
\beta_i^t &= \frac{S_i^\bullet + \sum_{uqd}(S_{uqd,i}^\circ \tilde{C}_{uqd,i}^{t-1})}{S_i} \\
U_u^t &= \frac{\frac{1}{\sigma^2}\sum_{q,d}(\alpha_{uqd} Q_q D_d W_{uqd}^{t-1})}{\frac{1}{\sigma^2}\sum_{q,d} Q_q^2 D_d^2 W_{uqd}^{t-1} + \frac{1}{\sigma_U^2}\sum_{q,d} W_{uqd}^{t-1}} \\
Q_q^t &= \frac{\frac{1}{\sigma^2}\sum_{u,d}(\alpha_{uqd} U_u D_d W_{uqd}^{t-1})}{\frac{1}{\sigma^2}\sum_{u,d} U_u^2 D_d^2 W_{uqd}^{t-1} + \frac{1}{\sigma_Q^2}\sum_{u,d} W_{uqd}^{t-1}} \\
D_d^t &= \frac{\frac{1}{\sigma^2}\sum_{u,q}(\alpha_{uqd} U_u Q_q W_{uqd}^{t-1})}{\frac{1}{\sigma^2}\sum_{u,q} U_u^2 Q_q^2 W_{uqd}^{t-1} + \frac{1}{\sigma_D^2}\sum_{u,q} W_{uqd}^{t-1}}
\end{aligned}$$

where

$$W_{uqd}^{t-1} = \sum_{\mathbf{S}_{uqd}^\bullet} 1 + \sum_{\mathbf{S}_{uqd}^\circ} \tilde{C}_{uqd,i}^{t-1}$$

can be viewed as a fixed weighting term for each element in tensor. $\boldsymbol{\alpha}$, however, does not have a close form calculation, but an equation to be solved numerically. The inference of EM algorithm completes. Each iteration is sure to increase log likelihood and the process is bound to converge to a local maximum of the joint likelihood function.

Fair and Balanced: Learning to Present News Stories

Amr Ahmed[*1], Choon Hui Teo[*1], S.V. N. Vishwanathan[2], Alex Smola[1]
[1]Yahoo! Research, Santa Clara, CA 95053, USA
[2]Purdue University, West Lafayette, IN 47907, USA
[*] Co-first authors.
{amahmed,choonhui,smola}@yahoo-inc.com, vishy@stat.purdue.edu

ABSTRACT

Relevance, diversity and personalization are key issues when presenting content which is apt to pique a user's interest. This is particularly true when presenting an engaging set of news stories. In this paper we propose an efficient algorithm for selecting a small subset of relevant articles from a streaming news corpus. It offers three key pieces of improvement over past work: 1) It is based on a detailed model of a user's viewing behavior which does not require explicit feedback. 2) We use the notion of submodularity to estimate the propensity of interacting with content. This improves over the classical context independent relevance ranking algorithms. Unlike existing methods, we learn the submodular function from the data. 3) We present an efficient online algorithm which can be adapted for personalization, story adaptation, and factorization models. Experiments show that our system yields a significant improvement over a retrieval system deployed in production.

Categories and Subject Descriptors

I.2.6 [**Computing Methodologies**]: Artificial Intelligence-Learning

General Terms

Algorithms, Experimentation

Keywords

Submodularity, Personalization, Online Learning, Graphical Models

1. INTRODUCTION

As global events unfold (e.g. the debt crisis, the BP oil spill, or the Japan earthquake) a large number of newspapers, blogs and other online news sources report developments. Selecting a personalized subset of articles from this large, ever-changing corpus of news articles is vital for dealing with information overload. In this context, the goal is to provide a comprehensive yet personalized subset of articles which cover all relevant aspects of the events of any given day. Moreover, the selection algorithm we develop should be able to adapt to the users' tastes. For instance, a user may have specific interest in news that relates to a certain topic (e.g. politics, sports) or might favor a specific news source (e.g. Fox news, New York Times). Building such a system entails addressing the following challenges:

Relevance: Clearly we want to ensure that we retrieve the articles that have the highest quality score, i.e. which are obtained from high quality sources, attract a large number of clicks, that are relevant for a given user, and which satisfy other commercial motives (e.g. traffic shaping).

Coverage: We also would like to ensure that information is not only relevant but also complete in the sense that it covers all aspects of the event, e.g. in terms of content, time and with regard to the sources of information.

Key Events: When displaying news with respect to a timeline it is desirable to detect the *key events* in the thread. This means that we generally want to get the article which describes the outbreak of an earthquake rather than the summary recap written one month later (unless the latter is extremely well written and the article occurred a long time ago). In other words, we want summaries which are attached to key events but whose temporal attachment to events decreases with the age of the event.

Recency: Users are generally more interested in the present rather than the past. This means that when displaying content we should focus preferably on recent events more than events that occurred a long time in the past (unless they are very important). This is also relevant when invoking the system in an online fashion. In this case we would like to obtain novel articles as part of an ongoing news stream.

Personalization: Given that users' preferences may vary widely we need to adjust any relevance scores by the source, topical, and page quality interests of a user. In particular, we want to learn which results are preferred by which user, and which pages on a site are of most interest to the visitors of that site.

Storyline Adjustment: A complementary aspect to personalization is the ability to adjust to coverage of stories. That is, we want to be able to learn from user interactions

Permission to make digital or hard copies of all or part of this work for personal or classroom use is granted without fee provided that copies are not made or distributed for profit or commercial advantage and that copies bear this notice and the full citation on the first page. To copy otherwise, to republish, to post on servers or to redistribute to lists, requires prior specific permission and/or a fee.
WSDM'12 February 8–12, 2012, Seattle, Washington USA
Copyright 2012 ACM 978-1-4503-0747-5/12/02 ...$10.00.

which aspects of a story are relevant. For instance, some users might be more interested in the political aspects of the debt crisis while the others might be more interested in its economic implications.

Deduplication: While implicit in the above discussion, deduplication is absolutely necessary since duplicates create a rather unpleasant user experience. It is desirable to deal with this problem in an *integrated* fashion.

Of course, the above desiderata are not just limited to presenting news stories. More generally, one can consider the scenario of a user interacting with a source of information. This may be a search results page where users where users would like to obtain relevant and diverse answers. Likewise it might be a set of articles related to a security on a finance page, or we might consider aggregating feeds from various social networks. Selecting a personalized subset of documents from such corpora remains an important problem.

Contributions

We argue in this paper that all the above aspects of the problem can be addressed by a model that

1. takes implicit user feedback into account,
2. uses a submodular rather than modular objective for estimating item relevance, and
3. uses a composite model for personalization.

Specifically, we build a detailed and adaptive user interaction model that accurately captures the way a user traverses a list of items. Towards this end we use a graphical model to describe both the click and viewing behavior of a user in a fully adaptive fashion through a latent variable model, thereby extending the work of [5].

Secondly, we propose an information gain score for *estimating* the click propensity of a user. This is a departure from two lines of research: the classical relevance ranking approach, which views relevance as an aggregate of the relevance of individual objects [17] and a combinatorial optimization driven approach, which tries to approximate the problem of selecting a relevant and diverse subset by crafting a suitable submodular objective function, possibly subject to side constraints [9, 1]. That is, we first and foremost attempt to model the problem accurately rather than approximating it by a mathematically simpler object.

Finally, we discuss effective optimization algorithms and parametrizations of user interest and article relevance which are well suited to composite weights (e.g. for personalization, storyline adjustment, categorical preferences, etc.). They arise naturally from the information-gain objective used to characterize user interest. A side-effect of the proposed model is that it provides effective cold-start customization for new stories and new users alike. Moreover, this yields an algorithm which is capable of selecting from a parametric set of submodular objectives. This is different from prior work [1, 9, 15] who posit the existence of a particular submodular gain function which is supposed to describe user interest accurately. Instead, our framework can *learn* the degree of submodularity for each attribute individually.

We show that our system improves the quality of estimates considerably. In aggregate, we find that our system shows a lift of over 20% over the currently deployed system in Yahoo!. Furthermore, it outperforms a number of recent related work including Turning down the Noise (TDN) algorithm of [9], the Session Utility Model (SUM) of [7], and the Cascade Click Model (CCM) of [6] significantly.

2. MODEL DESCRIPTION

In what follows, we assume that we have access to an algorithm which aggregates articles into storylines, such as described by [2] or a low-level search engine to find articles relevant for a query. This yields sets of articles which are largely coherent in accordance. Given that, we describe our model by tackling each of the following aspects: building a detailed user interaction model by using implicit user feedback (Section 2.1), modeling article relevance (Section 2.2), personalization by using a composite set of weights (Section 2.3), online optimization of the model parameters (Section 2.4) and finally article recommendation (Section 2.5).

2.1 Sequential View Click Model

Our Sequential View Click Model (SVCM) for user interaction draws on the view-click model of [5]. That is, we assume that a user traverses a list of results (URLs) from top to bottom in *sequential* order. At any given point a user can perform one of four possible actions:

1. follow a link and leave,
2. follow a link and return to examine the remainder of the results afterwards,
3. skip forward to the next result,
4. abandon the task.

Unfortunately, by using click data we have no way of knowing whether the user continued examining the list of results or whether he simply abandoned inspection, *unless* we observe further clicks by the user. In other words, we are dealing with a model in which some of the variables are latent. This can be addressed by a proper probabilistic description.

The above conditions of state transition provide us with a rather nice grammar which restricts which observations are admissible. In particular, they imply that the user will abandon examining the presented results at some point in time (this could be anywhere between the first and the last position) and after he does so, there is no chance of any further interaction with the result list. Note that this model makes a rather drastic approximation, namely that users always examine results *in order* rather than in some other (possibly nondeterministic) scheme. While not quite true in practice, we found by inspecting click logs that the approximation is fairly accurate.[1] Our model extends [5] in a number of ways:

- We allow for different transition and baseline click probabilities per position rather than assuming that these coefficients are identical.
- We assume that the click propensity depends on
  - the number of previous clicks, and
  - the set of previously displayed articles.
- We allow for the user to potentially not examine the displayed results at all.

This additional set of parameters is acceptable since it is minuscule relative to the total set of parameters used in

[1]We are unable to provide specific figures since this is commercially sensitive data.

modeling user behavior, hence we can assume that the estimates are statistically reliable. In order to make matters more specific we now describe the probabilistic model associated with the above assumptions. We use $v^t := (v_1, \ldots, v_t)$ as a shorthand to denote vectors of length t consisting of the first t elements in an array.

In the following we denote by $v_i \in \{0, 1\}$ a variable which indicates whether a user examined result i and by $c_i \in \{0, 1\}$ whether he clicked on result i. We use standard directed graphical models syntax, that is, arrows indicate statistical dependencies from parent to child. Shaded vertices are considered observed, blank ones are considered latent. Extending [5] we obtain the following model. Note that we omitted some edges not pertaining to vertex c_i for readability. Furthermore, we define $v_0 = 1$ and $c_0 = 0$ as auxiliary constants to keep the notation simple.

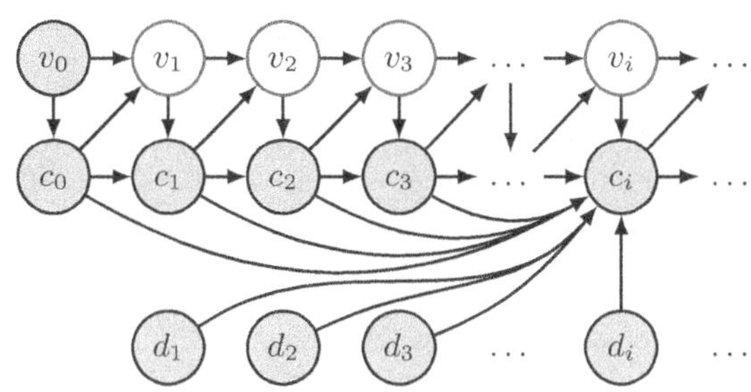

Note that here c_i is determined by a multitude of random variables, in particular *all* previously shown articles d^{i-1} and the current article d_i. The equivalent joint probability distribution of $p(v, c|d)$ is given by

$$p(v, c|d) = \prod_{i=1}^{n} \left[p(v_i|v_{i-1}, c_{i-1}) p(c_i|v_i, c^{i-1}, d^i) \right] \quad (1)$$

We use a logistic transfer function to model the binary conditional probabilities, and defer specifying the functional form of the scores until Section 2.2 because it requires us to introduce submodular gains first.

Examination probability: We distinguish two cases: the examination probability whenever a user clicked on a previous item and the examination probability when the previous item was not clicked.

$$p(v_i = 1|v_{i-1} = 0) = 0 \quad (2)$$

$$p(v_i = 1|v_{i-1} = 1, c_{i-1} = 0) = \frac{1}{1 + e^{-\alpha_i}} \quad (3)$$

$$p(v_i = 1|v_{i-1} = 1, c_{i-1} = 1) = \frac{1}{1 + e^{-\beta_i}} \quad (4)$$

In other words, provided that the user examined the previous link, we allow for a logistic dependence which differs according to whether the user returns after having clicked a link or whether he is already on the page. Choosing different coefficients α_i, β_i makes sense since the propensity to click on a result varies in accordance to the location on the results page (e.g. whether a user will be required to scroll).

Click probability: The key aim of our user interaction model is to obtain good estimate of the click probability. As described in the graphical model above, it depends on $c_i|v_i, c^{i-1}, d^i$. In this context we stratify by the value of v_i by setting

$$p(c_i = 1|v_i = 0) = 0,$$

that is, if a user did not examine a result then he will not click on it. Furthermore, we assume that the click probability for a given article is characterized by 1) the *number* of previous clicks, as denoted by $|c^{i-1}|$ and 2) by the relevance of the current article d_i given the previously displayed articles d^{i-1} where the particular order of the latter is irrelevant. These simplifying assumptions lead to the following functional form:

$$p(c_i = 1|v_i = 1, c^{i-1}, d^i) = \frac{1}{1 + e^{-f(|c^{i-1}|, d_i, d^{i-1})}}$$

The specific functional form of f will be described as part of the relevance model next.

2.2 Relevance Model

A key component in our model is a score to capture notion of information gain based on a set of articles presented to the user. The intuition behind our approach is that two articles which might be equally relevant might attract considerably different number of clicks depending on which of them is displayed above the other. We model this effect via a submodular coverage function. There is plenty of evidence that submodular functions capture the effects of diversity fairly accurately both in terms of user satisfaction and in terms of their mathematical properties (see e.g. [9] and references therein).

Here we present key results about submodular functions necessary for the development of our relevance models, for more details, please see Appendix A. In a nutshell, submodularity is characterized by its diminishing returns property. That is, for a set S, a subset $A \subseteq S$, elements $x, y \in S$, and a submodular function $f : \{0, 1\}^S \to \mathbb{R}$ we have

$$f(A \cup \{x\}) - f(A) \geq f(A \cup \{x, y\}) - f(A \cup \{y\}) \quad (5)$$

and the improvement decreases as we add more elements to the set A. Moreover, the set of submodular functions forms a convex cone. One of the main reasons for the popularity of submodular functions is the fact that constrained submodular maximization can be carried out efficiently through a greedy procedure, as described in the celebrated paper of [16] which can be accelerated even further by a lazy evaluation procedure as described in [14].

Consider two sets of articles: a set S of "source" articles to be covered and a set D of articles chosen to represent the content described in S. Given those sets we may define a coverage score via

$$\rho(S, D) := \sum_{s \in S} \sum_j [s]_j \rho_j(D), \quad (6)$$

where $[s]_j$ is a real value describing the extent to which feature j is present in s, and $\rho_j(D)$ a monotonically nondecreasing submodular function capturing how well the feature j of article collection D covers the same feature in article s. We assume that S is generated, e.g. by a set of search results or a storyline clustering module (e.g. articles about the debt crisis).

Next we need to define the properties of ρ. For this we introduce the notion of a generating function to deal with a large family of submodular functions abstractly.

Definition 1 *A monotonic, concave and nonnegative function $\sigma : [0, \infty) \to [0, 1]$ is a cover generator.*

Lemma 2 *Given a domain X and coefficients $c_x \geq 0$ for all $x \in X$, and $A \subseteq X$, the function $\rho(A) := \sigma(\sum_{x \in A} c_x)$ is submodular whenever σ is a cover generator.*

PROOF. Clearly ρ is monotonic with respect to addition to A. The diminishing returns property follows immediately from concavity in σ and the fact that $c_x \geq 0$ for all $x \in X$. Hence ρ is submodular. □

Our definition covers a number of popular submodular coverage scores as special case:

$$\sigma(z) = \begin{cases} 0 & \text{if } z = 0 \\ 1 & \text{if } z > 0 \end{cases} \qquad \text{(set cover)} \tag{7}$$

Here we simply assume that once we discussed a subject even once it is considered covered.

$$\sigma(z) = 1 - e^{-\theta z} \text{ for } \theta > 0 \qquad \text{(probabilistic cover)} \tag{8}$$

This equation can be seen, e.g. from [9], where one chooses the probability of not finding what is required, i.e. $1 - \prod_{x \in A}(1 - \pi_x)$ to be the coverage score, where π_x is the probability of the features in x. By setting $c_x := -\log(1 - \pi_x)$ and $\theta = 1$ we obtain this case.

$$\sigma(z) = \log(\theta z + 1) \text{ for } \theta > 0 \qquad \text{(logarithmic cover)} \tag{9}$$

Recall that modular function is a special case of submodular function and that submodular functions form a convex cone. Hence, $a \sum_{d \in D} [d]_j + b\rho_j(D)$ is submodular for $a, b \geq 0$. By plugging this generalization into (6), it leads to a powerful parametrization of $\rho(S, D)$ as follows:

$$\rho(S, D|a, b) := \sum_{s \in S} \sum_j [s]_j \Big(a_j \sum_{d \in D} [d]_j + b_j \rho_j(D) \Big). \tag{10}$$

The significance of the expansion is that it combines both modular and submodular scores into a unified formula and allows us to learn the weights of the modularity a_j and submodularity b_j of a each feature j. Covering a modular feature always increases the coverage score, but covering a submodular feature has a diminishing return effect.

Given this definition of coverage, we now convert it into a relevance score to be used in the model of Section 2.1 by defining:

$$\begin{aligned} & f(|c^{i-1}|, d_i, d^{i-1}) \\ :=& \rho(S, d^i|a, b) - \rho(S, d^{i-1}|a, b) + \gamma_{|c^{i-1}|} + \delta_i \\ :=& \sum_{s \in S} \sum_j [s]_j \left(a_j \sum_{d \in d^i} [d]_j + b_j \left(\rho_j(d^i) - \rho_j(d^{i-1}) \right) \right) \\ & + \gamma_{|c^{i-1}|} + \delta_i \end{aligned} \tag{11}$$

Here $\gamma_{|c^{i-1}|}$ is a correction coefficient which captures the effect of having visited $|c^{i-1}|$ links previously. δ_i captures the position specific effect, i.e. how clickable different positions in the result set are. Furthermore note that for $b = 0$ we are back to a modular relevance ranking model where each article is considered regardless of previously shown content. In other words, we recover the vector space model as a special case [18]. Moreover, setting $a = 0$, we recover the submodular score in [9] as another special case.

2.3 Composite Weights

Let $\Psi = (\alpha, \beta, a, b, \gamma, \delta)$ denotes the parameter set of our model. This parameter set is shared across all stories and users. A significant advantage of our parametrization is that the expected negative log-likelihood of the model is convex in the Ψ. This allows us to perform the following personalization extensions rather easily:

User Personalization: Different users have different preferences. It is therefore desirable that we learn from such interactions and personalize the results. We resort to an additive model along the lines of [20], i.e. we assume that the parameters Ψ are given by $\Psi_0 + \Psi_u$ where the latter are user-specific terms and the former are common parameters which ensure that we obtain a generally relevant set of articles. In other words, the latter pair allows us to personalize results to a user's preferences whereas the former pair ensures good coldstart behavior.

Storyline Adjustment: It is unlikely that all stories would be characterized by the same set of attributes. Hence, it is equally desirable to learn how to adjust the summaries to the stories at hand. Based on the amount of interaction with users we hope to improve the estimates after recording sufficient amounts of user feedback. Our model is flexible, for instance, one can have a weight for each storyline (Ψ_s) and also group stories based on their category and learn corresponding category weights (Ψ_c). We can address all of this by an additive decomposition. In conjunction with user personalization this leads to

$$\Psi = \Psi_0 + \Psi_u + \Psi_s + \Psi_c. \tag{12}$$

Our experiments show that personalization and storyline adjustment can significantly improve retrieval quality.

2.4 Online Learning

Our goal of learning is to find a weigh vector Ψ^* that fits our proposed probabilistic click models (1) on an observed data set of presumably independent examples. We formulate this learning process as a (regularized) maximum likelihood estimation problem which can be written as the following convex minimization problem:

$$\Psi^* = \lambda\Omega(\Psi) + \operatorname*{argmin}_{\Psi} \sum_{(c,d)} -\log p(c|\Psi, d). \tag{13}$$

Here, $-\log p(c|\Psi, d)$ is the marginal log-likelihood of the observed click behavior i.e., (1)). $\Omega(\Psi)$ is a regularizer defined as:

$$\Omega(\Psi) = \|\Psi_0\|_2^2 + \sum_u \|\Psi_u\|_2^2 + \sum_s \|\Psi_s\|_2^2 + \sum_c \|\Psi_c\|_2^2. \tag{14}$$

The regularizer helps prevent overfitting and the regularization constant λ determines the extent to which we prefer smooth solutions to solutions which maximize the likelihood.

The key challenge in solving the problem (13) lies in the facts that $p(c|\Psi, d)$ is the marginal of (1) with respect to v and that v's after the last clicked position are unobserved (without the use of more advanced tracking mechanism for user browsing behavior). Thus we resort to an Expectation Maximization (EM) algorithm and use an variational upper bound on the negative log likelihood on observed data as follows:

$$\begin{aligned} -\log p(c) &\leq -\log p(c) + D(q(v)\|p(v|c)) \\ &= \mathbf{E}_{v\sim q(v)}\left[-\log p(c) + \log q(v) - \log p(v|c)\right] \\ &= \mathbf{E}_{v\sim q(v)}\left[-\log p(c,v)\right] - H(q(v)). \end{aligned}$$

Here $q(v)$ is a distribution over the latent variables, $H(q)$ is the entropy of the distribution q, and $D(p\|q)$ is the Kullback-Leibler divergence between p and q. Putting everything together, we have the following optimization problem:

$$\min_{q(v),\Psi} \lambda\Omega(\Psi) + \sum_{(c,d)} \mathbf{E}_{v\sim q(v)}\left[-\log p(c,v|d,\Psi)\right] - H(q(v)). \tag{15}$$

The standard EM algorithm that runs in batch mode and require all data to be available at hand is not appropriate in our case as a successful and efficient deployment of our system must process data in near real-time as we observe them in a streaming fashion. To meet the system requirement, we employ an online EM [4] that performs an approximate yet complete EM step on a example-by-example basis. We describe these two steps in more details below.

E-step: Expected Log-Likelihood

In the E-step, we need to compute $q(v)$, however, we note that the bound on the marginal log-likelihood is tight when $q = p(v|c,d)$, which is the minimizer of Eq (15). In this Section we show how to compute $p(v|c,d)$, i.e. the probability distribution over views, given the observed clicks c and the presented set of articles d.

While the graphical model in Section 2.1 suggests that dynamic programming might be needed, computing $p(v|c,d)$ is, in fact, considerably simpler as we may exploit the fact that v_i is a monotonically decreasing sequence, that is, it is fully specified by counting how many views there are. In other words, since $p(v_i = 1|v_{i-1} = 0) = 0$ and $p(v_i = 0|v_{i-1} = 0) = 1$, the only admissible values for v are those which consists of a sequence of 1s followed by a sequence of zeros and as such v is completely defined by counting the number of 1s in v. Hence we denote by $\bar{v} := |v|$ the view count. Next denote by π_l the unnormalized likelihood scores for the user viewing l results.

$$\begin{aligned} \pi_l :=& p(\bar{v} = l, c, d) \\ =& \prod_{i=1}^{l}\left[p(v_i = 1|v_{i-1} = 1, c_{i-1})p(c_i|v_i = 1, c^{i-1}, d^i)\right] \cdot \\ & p(v_{l+1} = 0|v_l = 1, c_l) \cdot \begin{cases} 1 & \text{if } c_j = 0 \text{ for } j > l \\ 0 & \text{otherwise} \end{cases} \end{aligned} \tag{16}$$

It is easy to see that (16) can be computed for all values of l in linear time. This yields

$$q_l := p(\bar{v} = l|c,d) = \frac{\pi_l}{\sum_i \pi_i} \text{ and } r_l := p(\bar{v} \geq l|c,d) = \sum_{i=l}^{n} q_i \tag{17}$$

Here q_l, r_l are the coefficients of the variational distribution to be used in the M-step as described below.

M-step: Stochastic Gradient Descent

In the M-step we optimize over Ψ. First, we plug $q(v)$ derived in Section 2.4 and specified in (17) into the negative log-likelihood of the click and view probability in (15) (ignoring the last term $H(q(v))$ as it does not depend on Ψ). We have that $\mathbf{E}_{\bar{v}\sim q}\left[\log p(v,c|d,\Psi)\right]$ is given by:

$$\begin{aligned} &\sum_{i=1}^{n} \mathbf{E}_{\bar{v}\sim q}\left[\log p(v_i|v_{i-1}, c_{i-1}, \Psi)\right] + \mathbf{E}_{\bar{v}\sim q}\left[\log p(c_i|v_i, c^{i-1}, d^i, \Psi)\right] \\ =& \sum_{i=1}^{n} r_i \log p(v_i = 1|v_{i-1} = 1, c_{i-1}, \Psi) + \\ & \sum_{i=1}^{n} q_{i-1} \log p(v_i = 1|v_{i-1} = 0, c_{i-1}, \Psi) + \\ & \sum_{i=1}^{n} q_i \log p(c_i|v_i = 1, c^{i-1}, d^i, \Psi). \end{aligned} \tag{18}$$

The remaining terms all vanish from the above expansion. For instance, $\log p(v_i = 0|v_{i-1} = 0) = 0$. The regularized expected log-likelihood is now amenable to convex optimization with respect to the parameters Ψ. Since our goal is to learn the weight vector Ψ online, we use the SVMSGD2 algorithm described in [3] to update Ψ. The update procedure at example $t+1$ is as follows:

$$g := \frac{\partial}{\partial\Psi}\mathbf{E}_{\bar{v}\sim q}\left[\log p(v,c|d,\Psi^t)\right] \tag{19}$$

$$\Psi^{t+1} := \Psi^t - \frac{1}{\lambda(t+t_0)}g \tag{20}$$

$$\Psi^{t+1} := \Psi^{t+1} - \frac{\texttt{skip}}{t+t_0}\Psi^{t+1} \quad [\text{if } (\texttt{skip} \bmod t) = 0] \tag{21}$$

where t_0 and `skip` are predefined hyperparameters. To maintain submodularity, we project (i.e. truncate) the a, b part of Ψ so that they remain nonnegative. The average regret (with respect to the best parameters learned in hindsight if we observe all the clicks at once, i.e. as in batch settings) vanishes at rate $O(t^{-\frac{1}{2}})$ for the above projected gradient algorithm, where t is the number of examples seen [22].

Online Model Selection

The hyper-parameters in our model that we need to specify are the scale *theta* in the cover function (8), regularization constant λ, and SGD parameters t_0 and `skip`. In batch setting one can select these hyper-parameters using cross-validation, however this is not feasible in our online setting. We adopt an online approach to tune these hyper-parameters as learning progresses by learning a set of K candidate models, each of which corresponds to a specific value of these hyper-parameters. After we receive an example, we ask each model to first predict which documents the user clicked on, and we keep track of the accuracy of each model. The best model is determined periodically based on its accumulated accuracy. Recommendation of articles (see Section 2.5) will be made using the best model until the next model selection. We note that the user's interaction is used to update all candidate models and this setup is similar is spirit to the mixture of expert framework, where each model is treated as an expert. Experimentally, we found that this strategy works well. In our experiments we start with $K = 48$ and we then shrink K to 5 after observing the first 10000 sessions for efficiency.

2.5 Recommendation

An important aspect to be addressed is the issue of display optimization. That is, we are not learning the user and relevance model for its own sake. Instead, this is done in order to increase the amount of engagement a user displays with respect to the website. It follows from our model (1) that the amount of interaction is maximized whenever the score functions $f(|c^{i-1}|, d_i, d^{i-1})$ are as large as possible. While it is difficult to find an optimal strategy, we may at least strive to achieve two goals:

- Find a set of articles such that $\sum_{i=1}^{m} f(|c^{i-1}|, d_i, d^{i-1})$ is maximized. This goal is identical to maximizing a submodular objective as can be seen easily from the fact that f is given by the difference between two submodular functions and from the fact that the sum telescopes. Hence the greedy procedure at least guarantees that we will obtain a near optimal solution of this problem, as stated in Theorem 4.
- Choose articles with the largest contributions in f at the beginning of the list. Due to the diminishing returns property of submodular functions we are guaranteed that the value of the score function is monotonically decreasing, the more articles have already been selected. Combining this with a greedy selection procedure guarantees that the values $f(|c^{i-1}|, d_i, d^{i-1})$ are monotonically decreasing in i.

We use the second strategy in selecting and ordering articles in our experiments.

3. RELATED WORK

Probably closest to the present work is the Turning Down the Noise (TDN) algorithm of [9]. It uses a submodular score function to estimate the relevance of a retrieved set. This allows the use of a greedy algorithm for obtaining a summary of the current set of events. To deal with user interaction data it requires users to respond explicitly with a preference rating for articles. The latter is then used to ensure that the articles preferred by a user are retrieved in the order of preference — it treats each stage of the greedy procedure as a classification problem where the preferred articles are to be selected over the ones a user dislikes. Optimization is carried out by means of an exponentiated gradient (EG) algorithm.

While theoretically elegant, the TDN algorithm suffers from a number of drawbacks. It requires explicit feedback from the users, that is, a user has to indicate if she is interested/not interested/indifferent to a presented article. This is unrealistic in a real-world setting. Instead, we need systems which are capable of exploiting the implicit feedback inherent in the interaction of a user with an application. In particular, we would like to decouple the user model from the relevance score to some extent. This is desirable since results can be presented in different modalities (desktop vs. mobile application, push vs. pull), yet we would like to use all data to improve our estimates.

Secondly, while the notion of submodularity is desirable in general for proving approximation guarantees for otherwise NP hard problems, it somewhat obscures the (more generally applicable) property of diminishing returns in the context of relevance ranking. More to the point, while several simple problems can be modelled quite conveniently as submodular maximization problems, this is not necessarily the case for general user interaction models. For instance, to deal with the relatively simple addition of position bias in ranking one needs to add matroid constraints to the optimization problem. This, in turn, leads to considerably weaker approximation guarantees than the greedy approach of [16], thus negating some benefits of a pure submodular maximization strategy. In summary, we consider the fixation to submodular objectives rather harmful, yet the notion of diminishing returns in user-modeling is valuable.

Thirdly, since the EG algorithm converges rather rapidly to a sparse solution placing emphasis on a small number of features, it is prone to focusing on a very small number of terms [10], thus potentially leading to the 'filter bubble' of many recommendation algorithms (also see our experiments in Section 4). We conjecture that this effect did not manifest itself in [9] due to the short length of the feedback sessions (only up to 5 interactions per user). Moreover, exponentiated gradient algorithms are not quite so easily amenable to composite weights and bilinear recommendation algorithms, such as those by [11].

The present paper addresses all these concerns by learning the submodular score, via a dedicated user model, and by employing a stochastic gradient descent procedure. The key differences between TDN and our algorithm can be summarized as follows:

	optimization	objective	usermodel
TDN	EG	submod.	explicit
This paper	SGD	submod. + mod.	sequence

Another relevant work is the Cascade Click Model (CCM) originally proposed by [6] to explain the effect of position bias in web search results. This model assumes that users examine the documents in sequential order and click on one document and then abandon the session.

Finally, [7] use the metaphor of user satisfaction in their Session Utility Model (SUM) to capture the effect of diversity and satisfaction in a session. This leads to a (slightly nonstandard) objective function which characterizes the stopping probability of a user. While exciting, we found it not to be an ideal fit to our datastream. More to the point, for news-search drill down clicklogs we observed that often $\Pr(c > n+1 | c \geq n+1) > \Pr(c > n | c \geq n)$ holds. Here c denotes the number of clicks and $n \in \mathbb{N}$. In other words, the user is often *more* likely to click at least one more time given that he already clicked once than clicking at least once. This is contrary to what the model of [7] describes. This insight is matched in our experiments.

4. EXPERIMENTS

We perform extensive experimental evaluation to compare our method with existing algorithms, and to answer the following natural questions:

- What is the effect of the user interaction model on the overall performance of the system?
- Does the coverage function (10) which combines modular and submodular coverage scores work better than the submodular only score proposed in [9]?
- How does changing the optimizer impact the overall performance of the system?
- What is the effect of the composite weights on the performance of the model, especially in the context of personalization.
- Does our system personalize to a user and therefore lead to improved user satisfaction?

In order to answer these questions we collected data from logs of user interaction with news content. The user provides implicit feedback by clicking or skipping over the displayed articles, and this is used to adjust our model. The goal is to learn to present articles so as to maximize the positions of clicked articles (i.e. places more relevant and diverse articles at the top).

As our performance metrics we use the Precision at One (Prec@1) and Precision at Full Click (Prec@FC). Prec@1 measures the fraction of times a user clicks on the first displayed article. On the other hand, if k denotes the number of clicks in a session then Prec@FC measures the fraction of the top k articles that were clicked. For instance, if the user clicked on positions 1, 3, and 5 then the Prec@FC is 3/5. All results are relative to the performance of the deployed system which is computed as follows: $100 \times \frac{a-b}{b}$ where a is the performance of our system and b is the performance of the deployed system.

We perform online evaluation. At every iteration, the algorithm receives a set of articles from a given story out of which it selects 10 articles and presents them to the user. Feedback is provided by the user in the form of clicks. This is used to compute the performance metrics and to update the model. The data set used in the experiments consists of user sessions collected over a period of 10 weeks between May and July, 2011. A random subset of around 140K sessions with user feedback was chosen for reporting results.

4.1 Features

We use the following features which adequately capture the essence of news stories.

Entities and Concepts: We used Yahoo!'s *Spectrum* named entity detection and resolution tools to determine key and relevant tokens in the article [21]. Particular importance was given to terms in headlines and abstracts of an article and terms were weighted according to their term frequency. This ensures that we retrieve articles that are relevant in terms of their content with respect to the ground set of articles.

Recency: Another set of attributes is the distribution of time stamps of articles. To be independent of the absolute time of the event we use the most recent article in the source collection of articles S as reference. The count distribution is then aggregated in a histogram. This approach automatically selects the key events of a set of articles. After all, we expect that news intensity should correlate with the relevance of an event. If we were to use this in the context of financial news we could simply reweight events with a measure of volatility in the price of the security under consideration. A secondary effect is that due to the modular part of the relevance score we are able to learn the relative relevance of recent articles with respect to older articles.

Source: Clearly news sources are highly relevant for customizing results to the tastes of individual users. Consequently we want to ensure that the identity of a source is used as a feature. Quite interestingly, its use in the modular vs. submodular part has different effects: a contribution to the modular part via a_j means that we prefer articles predominantly originating from a particular news source. On the other hand, their use in the submodular part ensures that we faithfully represent the article distribution found in the source set S.

4.2 Results

User Interaction Models

For a fair comparison we use the same set of features and the same optimizer (SGD) for each user model. In other words, everything else is held equal and therefore the difference in performance observed in Figure 1 is solely due to the use of different user models. The click aggregation model used by TDN requires explicit feedback from the user to each displayed item as either: like, dislike or indifferent. To cast click feedback into the TDN setting, we assign a *like* label to all articles clicked by the user, *dislike* label to all articles that appear before the last clicked article but were not clicked, and *indifferent* label to remaining articles. We can see that TDN's performance is sub-optimal here as it cannot handle the implicit feedback adequately[2]. We use enhanced versions of the Session Utility Model (SUM) and Cascade Click Model (CCM) which use the submodular selection strategy. We call them SUM+ and CCM+ in Figure 1.

Even though SUM+ takes into account the sequential nature of the interaction, it is not well suited for our application as it was originally proposed for web search with a different assumption on the way user consume information. CCM+ does not incorporate articles after the first clicked article and hence is not able to perform well. In contrast to all the aforementioned models, our Sequential View Click Model (SVCM) is able to faithfully capture user interaction and therefore comprehensively outperforms the other models including the deployed system.

Coverage Scores

We now shift our focus to comparing the performance of the combined coverage score (10) to that of the submodular only scores [9]. The results can be found in Figure 2. For this experiment we used SVCM for the user interaction model and SGD as the optimizer. Clearly, the combination of modular and submodular scores comprehensively outperforms the submodular only score in terms of both Prec@1 and Prec@FC. This is because the model with combined coverage score is more powerful in learning the shape of the submodular function and is able to compensate the potential unnecessary penalization due to submodular score with the gain from the modular score. In other words, this combined score can learn the degree of modularity and submodularity for each feature separately.

Optimization Procedure

Next we study the impact of the optimization procedure on the overall performance. Results for Prec@1 and Prec@FC are shown in Figure 3. Clearly, stochastic gradient descent (SGD) outperforms Exponentiated Gradient (EG) in our setting. To understand this result further we examined the distribution of the final weights obtained by the two methods. Because of the multiplicative nature of EG, once a weight is set to zero (e.g. because it falls below machine precision) it can never recover. Consequently, the final weight vector of EG is sparse e.g. the sparsity of the best EG model

[2] we even obtained worse results if we don't use negative feedback at all, i.e. only positive (for clicked articles) and indifferent feedback for all other articles

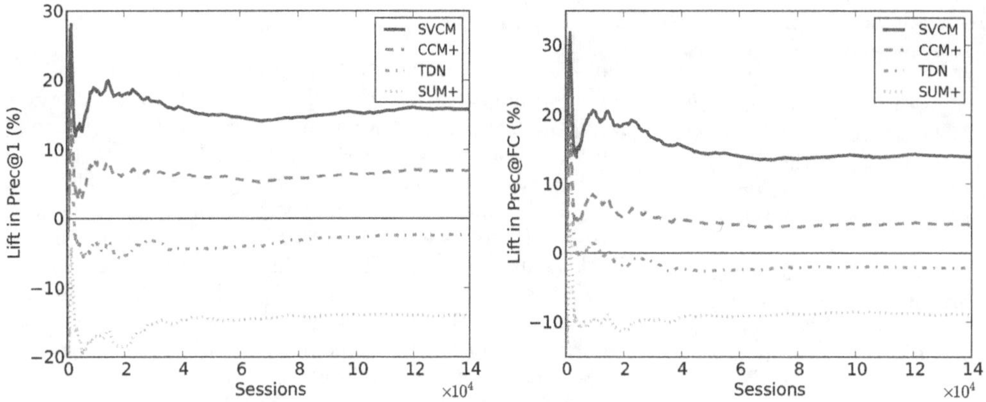

Figure 1: Prec@1 (left) and Prec@FC (right) of various user models relative to the deployed model. SVCM is the Sequential View Click Model, TDN is the model in [9], SUM is the Session Utility Model of [7], CCM is the Cascade Click Model of [6]. All models were trained using SGD (See Figure 3).

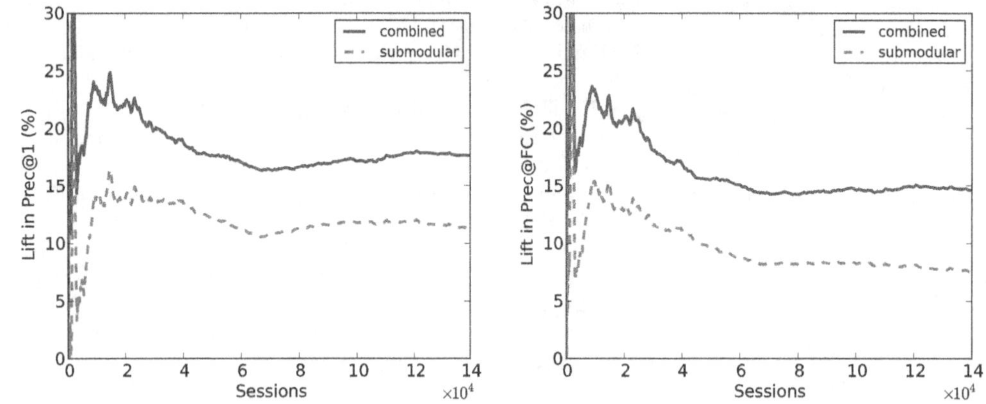

Figure 2: Prec@1 (left) and Prec@FC (right) of the combined (10) and submodular only coverage scores, relative to the deployed model.

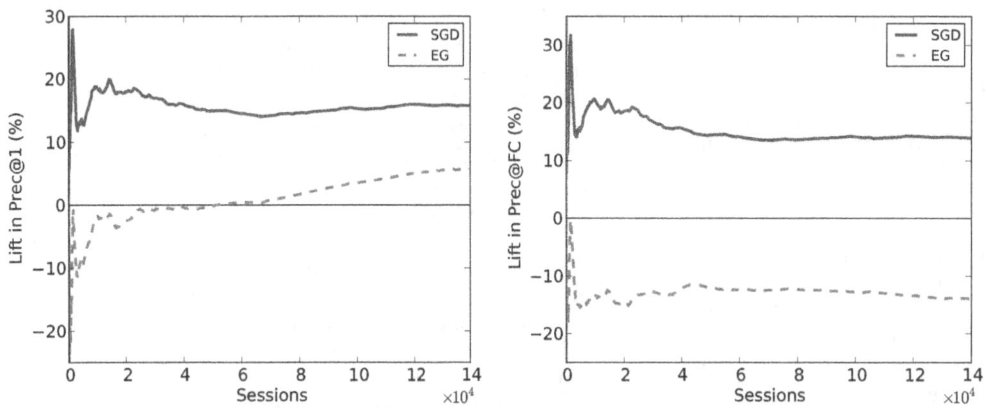

Figure 3: Prec@1 (left) and Prec@FC (right) of stochastic gradient descent (SGD) vs exponentiated gradient (EG) relative to the deployed model.

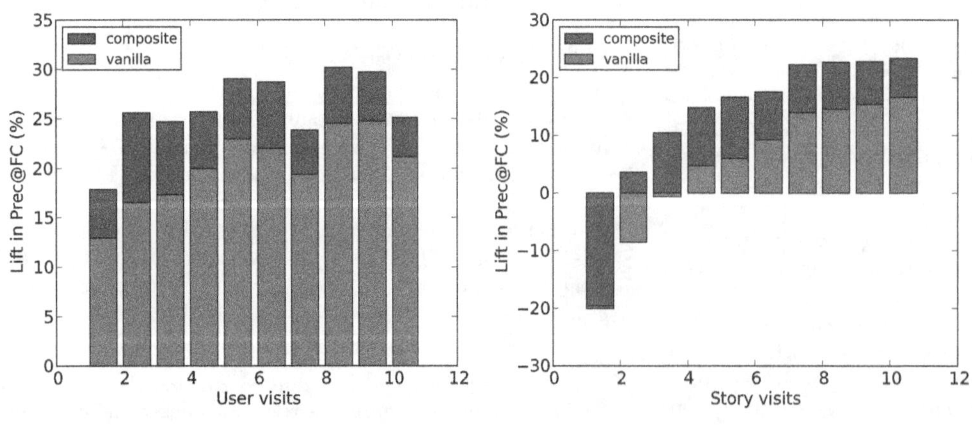

Figure 4: Lift in Prec@FC achieved by SVCM over deployed system vs number of user visits (right) and vs the number of times a story was displayed (left).

is 85% whereas the best SGD model is 0.5%. However, because of the temporal nature of news, aggressively switching off features tends to adversely affect performance.

Composite Weights

Next, in Figure 5 we examine the contribution of each component of the composite weight vector. We restrict this figure to storylines that the user has visited at least twice (i.e. examining the effect of the model in the story following task – when the user returns to examine the development of a given story). We see that more refined composite weights vectors give higher performance lift. We also observed that the contribution of the category weight over the story weight is marginal. There are two reasons for that: 1) the categories of the stories in this experiment are automatically generated using a classifier, thus there are some errors and 2) the assumption that each story belongs to a single category is restrictive since for instance a story about "Occupy Wall Street" belongs to both politics and finance categories. Models like [2] can remedy both of these deficiencies.

In Figure 4 we show how the performance improves as we observe more interactions with the user and as the number of times we display a story (possibly to different users) increases. We show the performance improvement over the deployed system with and without the story and user part of the weights turned on. The numbers in the figure are aggregated over all users (left) and stories (right). Two observations are in order. First, using the composite weighing scheme improves performance as compared to a Vanilla system which does not use composite weights. Second, our system adapts to each user and story preferences and learns to present interesting stories at the top of the list. Our composite scheme is worser than the deployed system the first time a story is displayed. This happens because a new story brings new features which might not have been seen before. This problem can be addressed by using an explore-exploit strategy by first encouraging more exploration about how to present a new story and then exploiting the learned weights to present the story. As can be observed, it only takes 1 to 3 visits before the composite weight shows improvement.

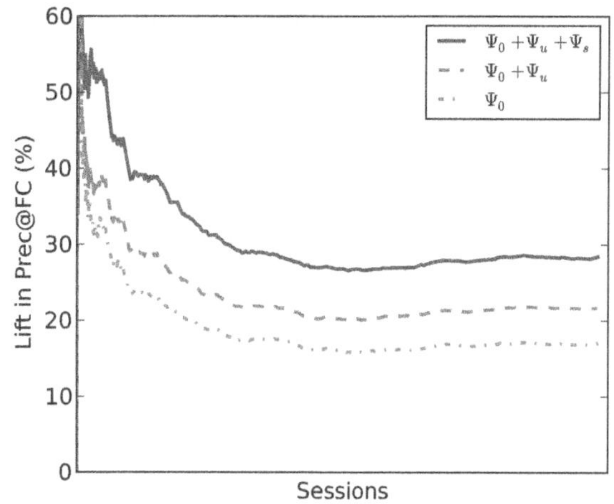

Figure 5: Lift in Prec@FC achieved by SVCM with various combinations of composite weights. The data used here are restricted to the sessions where users have visited a story at least once (we are unable to provide the number of session in the X-axis under this restriction since this is a commercially sensitive data). Here, Ψ_0 denotes the global weights, Ψ_c denotes category specific weights, Ψ_s denotes story specific weights, and Ψ_u denotes user specific weights.

5. SUMMARY

In this paper we proposed a new integrated algorithm for capturing nontrivial interaction effects between articles when presented to a user. We demonstrated that our method is significantly better than both Yahoo's deployed system and recent algorithms which aim to solve the same problem, most notably [9, 7]. Nonetheless, there remains a significant number of problems to be addressed:

- First and foremost we need to combine the user model with an exploration / exploitation algorithm to make it well suited for large scale user interaction problems. Fortunately methods such as Thompson sampling appear to be well suited to the problem.
- While rather more sophisticated than the average user model, the SVCM user interaction model still falls short of the much more detailed representations of user behavior reported by [13]. It is quite natural to attempt to learn the *structure* of such a model directly from users and to supplement this by using parameter fitting from live traffic.
- We only discussed a pull model in the current context. However, it is fairly straightfoward to adapt the relevance score to a push model where the user is provided with additional information whenever a new event occurs. This can be achieved, e.g. by an adjusted submodular information gain measure relative to messages previously sent to the user.
- When showing headlines repeatedly to the same user, it is quite likely that he will experience display fatigue. That is, even if we were to choose the most relevant link, displaying it ten times is unlikely to increase the probability of interaction tenfold. It is common to resort to display rotation to combat this effect. We conjecture that the latter could also be captured quite well through submodularity in a much less heuristic fashion.
- Diminishing returns effects and result interactions are also quite likely in the context of advertising (e.g. three chocolate ads on the same page are probably an undesirable outcome of an auction for the keyword 'sweets'). This implies that the commonly used Generalized Second Price strategy [8] is likely not perfectly adequate for pricing interacting advertisements.

In summary, we believe that the present paper is but a first step towards a more realistic user model capable of capturing the *interaction* between individual results and we are excited about the new avenues of research listed above.

6. REFERENCES

[1] R. Agrawal, S. Gollapudi, A. Halverson, and S. Ieong. Diversifying search results. In R.A. Baeza-Yates, P. Boldi, B.A. Ribeiro-Neto, and B.B. Cambazoglu, editors, *WSDM*, pages 5–14. ACM, 2009.

[2] A. Ahmed, Q. Ho, C. H. Teo, J. Eisenstein, A. J. Smola and E. P. Xing. Online inference for the Infinite topic-cluster model: storylines from streaming text In *AISTATS*, 2011.

[3] A. Bordes, L. Bottou, and P. Gallinari. SGD-QN: Careful quasi-Newton stochastic gradient descent. *JMLR*, 10:1737–1754, 2009.

[4] O. Cappé and E. Moulines. Online expectation-maximization algorithm for latent data models. *Journal of the Royal Statistics Society: Series B (Statistical Methodology)*, 71, 2009.

[5] O. Chapelle and Y. Zhang. A dynamic bayesian network click model for web search ranking. In J. Quemada, G. León, Y.S. Maarek, and W. Nejdl, editors, *WWW*, pages 1–10. ACM, 2009.

[6] N. Craswell, O. Zoeter, M. Taylor, and B. Ramsey. An experimental comparison of click position-bias models. In *WSDM*, pages 87–94, NY, USA, 2008. ACM.

[7] G. Dupret and C. Liao. A model to estimate intrinsic document relevance from the clickthrough logs of a web search engine. In B. D. Davison, T. Suel, N. Craswell, and B. Liu, editors, *WSDM*, pages 181–190. ACM, 2010.

[8] B. Edelman, M. Ostrovsky, and M. Schwarz. Internet advertising and the generalized second price auction: Selling billions of dollars worth of keywords. *American Economic Review*, 97(1):242–259, 2007.

[9] K. El-Arini, G. Veda, D. Shahaf, and C. Guestrin. Turning down the noise in the blogosphere. In J. F. Elder IV, F. Fogelman-Soulié, P. A. Flach, and M. J. Zaki, editors, *KDD*, pages 289–298. ACM, 2009.

[10] J. Kivinen and M. K. Warmuth. Exponentiated gradient versus gradient descent for linear predictors. *Information and Computation*, 132(1):1–64, 1997.

[11] Y. Koren, R.M. Bell, and C. Volinsky. Matrix factorization techniques for recommender systems. *IEEE Computer*, 42(8):30–37, 2009.

[12] A. Krause and C. Guestrin. A note on the budgeted maximization of submodular functions. CMU-CALD 05-103, CMU, 2005.

[13] D. Lagun and E. Agichtein. Viewser: Enabling large-scale remote user studies of web search examination and interaction. In *ACM SIGIR*, 2011.

[14] J. Leskovec, A. Krause, C. Guestrin, C. Faloutsos, J.M. VanBriesen, and N.S. Glance. Cost-effective outbreak detection in networks. In *KDD*, pages 420–429. ACM, 2007.

[15] H. Lin and J. Bilmes. Multi-document summarization via budgeted maximization of submodular functions. In *NAACL*, pages 912–920. ACL, 2010.

[16] G. Nemhauser, L. Wolsey, and M. Fisher. An analysis of the approximations for maximizing submodular set functions. *Math. Programming*, 14:265–294, 1978.

[17] M. Richardson, A. Prakash, and E. Brill. Beyond pagerank: machine learning for static ranking. In L. Carr, D. De Roure, A. Iyengar, C.A. Goble, and M. Dahlin, editors, *WWW*, pages 707–715. 2006.

[18] G. Salton. *Automatic Text Processing*. Addison-Wesley, Massachusetts, 1989.

[19] A. Schrijver. *Combinatorial Optimization*, volume 24 of *Algorithms and Combinatorics*. Springer, 2003.

[20] K. Weinberger, A. Dasgupta, J. Attenberg, J. Langford, and A.J. Smola. Feature hashing for large scale multitask learning. In L. Bottou and M. Littman, editors, *ICML*, 2009.

[21] Y. Zhou, L. Nie, O. Rouhani-Kalleh, F. Vasile, and S. Gaffney. Resolving surface forms to wikipedia topics. In *COLING*, pages 1335–1343, 2010.

[22] M. Zinkevich. Online convex programming and generalised infinitesimal gradient ascent. In *ICML*, pages 928–936, 2003.

APPENDIX

A. SUBMODULAR FUNCTIONS

In a nutshell submodularity is characterized by its diminishing returns property. That is, for a set S, subsets $A, B \subseteq S$, and a function $f : \{0,1\}^S \to \mathbb{R}$ we have

$$f(A) + f(B) \geq f(A \cup B) + f(A \cap B). \tag{22}$$

An equivalent formulation is that $f(A \cup \{x\}) - f(A) \geq f(A \cup \{x, y\}) - f(A \cup \{y\})$ holds, that is, the improvement decreases as we obtain more instances. Functions for which the comparison holds with *equality* are referred to as *modular*. A particularly useful fact is the following:

Theorem 3 *The set of submodular functions on some domain X forms a convex cone.*

This follows immediately from the fact that (22) remains valid under addition and multiplication with nonnegative numbers. This means that we may add and rescale such functions while the result retains submodular properties. It also makes optimization over the family of such functions easier. One of the main reasons for the popularity of submodular functions is the fact that constrained submodular maximization can be carried out efficiently through a greedy procedure, as described in the celebrated paper of [16].

Theorem 4 *Assume that we are given a monotonically increasing submodular function f defined on a domain X. Denote by $A_k^* := \operatorname{argmax}_{A \subset X \text{ and } |A| \leq k} f(A)$ the optimal set of size bounded by k maximizing f. Then the greedy procedure*

$$A_0 := \emptyset \text{ and } A_{i+1} := A_i \cup \left\{ \operatorname*{argmax}_{x \in X} f(A_i \cup \{x\}) \right\} \tag{23}$$

achieves a solution that satisfies $f(A_k) \geq (1 - e^{-1}) f(A_k^*)$.

Cost-weighted variants of the greedy algorithm exist [12]. Note also that while invoking the algorithm given in (23) appears to require $O(|X|)$ operations per iteration, i.e. a total of $O(k|X|)$ computations, we can accelerate it significantly by lazy evaluation [14]. The idea is as follows:

We know that the gains achievable by adding elements to A can only decrease through the addition of further elements. This is, after all, a submodular function. Hence, after an initial pass which computes

$$\delta_x := f(\{x\}) - f(\emptyset) \tag{24}$$

for all $x \in X$ we can simply exploit the fact that $\delta_x^{\text{old}} \geq \delta_x^{\text{new}} := f(A \cup x) - f(A)$ and select from the list of upper bounds. Each re-evaluation is then cached. This way we need not check every time on instances $x \in X$ that turned out to be useless already before. Empirically [14] this algorithm requires only $\log m$ operations per search once the initial scores are computed thus reducing computation to $O(|X| + k \log |X|)$. This is due to the fact that we are able to rule out a significant number of objects that are simply not promising enough after an initial inspection.

Extracting Search-Focused Key N-Grams for Relevance Ranking in Web Search*

Chen Wang
Fudan University
Shanghai, P.R.China
chen.wang0517@gmail.com

Keping Bi
Peking University
Beijing, P.R.China
bikeping@pku.edu.cn

Yunhua Hu
Microsoft Research Asia
Beijing, P.R.China
yuhu@microsoft.com

Hang Li
Microsoft Research Asia
Beijing, P.R.China
hangli@microsoft.com

Guihong Cao
Microsoft Corporation
Redmond, WA USA
gucao@microsoft.com

ABSTRACT

In web search, relevance ranking of popular pages is relatively easy, because of the inclusion of strong signals such as anchor text and search log data. In contrast, with less popular pages, relevance ranking becomes very challenging due to a lack of information. In this paper the former is referred to as head pages, and the latter tail pages. We address the challenge by learning a model that can extract search-focused key n-grams from web pages, and using the key n-grams for searches of the pages, particularly, the tail pages. To the best of our knowledge, this problem has not been previously studied. Our approach has four characteristics. First, key n-grams are search-focused in the sense that they are defined as those which can compose "good queries" for searching the page. Second, key n-grams are learned in a relative sense using learning to rank techniques. Third, key n-grams are learned using search log data, such that the characteristics of key n-grams in the search log data, particularly in the heads; can be applied to the other data, particularly to the tails. Fourth, the extracted key n-grams are used as features of the relevance ranking model also trained with learning to rank techniques. Experiments validate the effectiveness of the proposed approach with large-scale web search datasets. The results show that our approach can significantly improve relevance ranking performance on both heads and tails; and particularly tails, compared with baseline approaches. Characteristics of our approach have also been fully investigated through comprehensive experiments.

Categories and Subject Descriptors

H.3.3 [**Information Storage and Retrieval**]: Information Search and Retrieval

*This work was conducted at Microsoft Research Asia when the first two authors were interns there.

Permission to make digital or hard copies of all or part of this work for personal or classroom use is granted without fee provided that copies are not made or distributed for profit or commercial advantage and that copies bear this notice and the full citation on the first page. To copy otherwise, to republish, to post on servers or to redistribute to lists, requires prior specific permission and/or a fee.
WSDM'12, February 8–12, 2012, Seattle, Washington, USA.
Copyright 2012 ACM 978-1-4503-0747-5/12/02 ...$10.00.

General Terms

Algorithms, Experimentation, Performance

Keywords

Search Relevance, Ranking, Tail page, Key N-Gram Extraction, Learning to Rank

1. INTRODUCTION

In web search, the relevance ranking model, which can be either manually created or automatically learned, assigns scores representing degree of web page relevance in respect to the query, and ranks pages according to score. The ranking model utilizes information such as the frequency of query words in the title, body, URL, anchor text and search log data in determining the relevance.

There are popular web pages that include rich information such as anchor text and search log data. For these pages, it is easy for the ranking model to predict relevance with respect to a query and thereby assign reliable relevance scores. In contrast, there are also less popular web pages that lack sufficient information. In these instances, it is challenging to accurately calculate the relevance.

In this paper, we refer to web pages with a lot of anchor text and associated queries in search log data, as head pages. Web pages with less anchor text and associated queries are called tail pages. If there is a distribution of web page visits, then the head pages should have high visit frequencies, while the tail pages should have low visit frequencies. In this paper, we aim to solve the problem of improving tail page relevance, currently one of the most challenging problems in web search.

Our approach has the following characteristics: 1) Extracting search-focused information from web pages. 2) Taking key n-grams as the representations of search-focused information. 3) Employing learning to rank to train the extraction model using search log data. 4) Employing learning to rank to train a model for relevance ranking using search-focused key n-grams as features.

We deal with tail page relevance by extracting "good queries". These are most suitable for searching the page, assuming that the data sources for the extraction only include the title, URL, and page body (A more difficult question is how to automatically *generate* good queries instead of extracting good queries and we will leave this problem for future work). Such information is available for any page, including tail pages. When searching with a page's good queries, both the page and queries should be highly relevant. We refer to this as *search-focused extraction.*

We extract search-focused *key n-grams* from web pages and use them to improve relevance, particularly tail page relevance. The key n-grams should compose good queries for searching the pages. There are two reasons why we chose key n-gram extraction rather than keyphrase extraction. First, conventional relevance models, whether or not they are created by machine learning, usually only employ n-grams from queries and documents. Therefore, the extraction of key n-grams is more than adequate for the purpose of enhancing ranking model performance. Second, the use of n-grams eliminates the need to segment queries and documents, and thus frees us from segmentation errors.

We further employ a learning to rank approach to the extraction of key n-grams. The problem is formalized as ranking key n-grams from a given web page. The importance of key n-grams is only meaningful in a relative sense, and thus one does not need to make hard categorization decisions regarding important n-grams vs. unimportant n-grams, as we proposed earlier in [14]. We use n-gram positions and web page html tags, as well as term frequencies as features in the learning to rank model. We take search log data as training data for learning the model of extraction (one can also consider taking anchor text data as training data). The premise is that the statistical properties of a page's good queries can be learned and applied across different web pages. The objective of learning is an exact and accurate extraction of search-focused key n-grams, because the page-associated queries are sets of *key n-grams for search*. The abundance of search log data available for head pages facilitates the actual learning of the model of extraction primarily from those pages. In this way, we can extend the knowledge we acquire from head pages and apply it to the tail pages, thereby effectively addressing the challenge of determining tail page relevance. Note that the learned model can also help improve the relevance of head pages.

The extracted key n-grams include scores representing the strength of key n-grams on a given page. We further take a learning to rank approach to train the relevance ranking model, using the key n-grams and their scores as additional ranking model features. Those n-grams are also utilized in the original ranking model, as they are from the same page, and thus their contributions to the ranking model are further enhanced by our approach.

We have conducted experiments with two large-scale web search datasets to validate the effectiveness of the proposed approach. Each dataset contains more than 10,000 queries and approximately 1,000,000 documents. There are, on average, 65 documents for each query that includes relevance judgments. All the evaluations are conducted on search relevance ranking in terms of MAP and NDCG.

Results show that our approach can significantly improve search relevance on both head and tail pages, with the particularly greater improvement on tail pages. Our method also works better than a conventional keyphrase extraction method, indicating it is better to employ a search-focused approach.

We studied several important characteristics in our approach to both the key n-gram extraction phase and relevance ranking phase. The results show that it is better to formalize the key n-gram extraction as a ranking problem rather than a classification problem. The results also show that our approach with search log data is comparable to human-labeled data. Moreover, the performances of our approach trained with search log data will saturate when the size of search log data increases. These results suggest that head page search log data, which is of low cost, can be effectively leveraged to train a model for improving search relevance.

We have found that considerably good relevance ranking results can be achieved with just unigrams, and that performance can be further improved when bigrams and trigrams are also included. Furthermore, we have found that extracting the top 20 key n-grams achieves the best performance in relevance ranking. In addition, it has been observed that the use of key n-gram scores can further enhance relevance ranking.

The contributions in this paper are as follows.

- We have proposed conducting a search-focused key n-gram extraction from web pages to enhance search relevance, particularly tail page relevance. (To the best of our knowledge, this problem has not been studied before.)
- We have developed a method for extracting search-focused key n-grams, using learning to rank and search log data.
- We have significantly improved search relevance using the extracted key n-grams, particularly for the tail pages. We have also conducted comprehensive studies to investigate the characteristics of our approach.

The rest of the paper is organized as follows. Sec. 2 introduces related work. Sec. 3 gives the motivation of the problem. We introduce our proposed approach in Sec. 4 and present experimental results in Sec. 5. We also offer discussion in Sec. 6. Sec. 7 concludes the paper and provides suggestions for further work.

2. RELATED WORK

2.1 Relevance Ranking

Relevance ranking, one of the most important search engine components, assigns scores representing a document's relevance degree with respect to the query and ranks the documents according to their scores. Many methods have been proposed as a basis for constructing a relevance ranking model. Traditionally, the ranking model is manually created with a few fine-tuned parameters. Recently, machine learning techniques, called learning to rank, have also been applied to ranking model construction. Traditional models such as the Vector Space Model [26], BM25 [25], Language Model for IR [18, 23], Markov Random Field [21], and the learning to rank models [19, 20] make use of the n-grams that exist as features of the queries and documents. In fact, with all of these methods, the queries and documents are viewed as vectors of n-grams. Intuitively, if query-based n-grams occur a number of times in the document, then it is likely that the document is relevant to the query.

More information about web pages can be utilized in web search; for example, the body, URL, anchor texts and associated search log data queries. Previous work has shown that the use of web page (HTML documents) titles, anchor texts and URLs can enhance relevance ranking accuracy in web search. For example, Cutler et al. [5] proposed using the structures of HTML documents to improve document retrieval. They linearly combined term frequencies in several fields extracted from an HTML document. In TREC-2003, for example, more than half of the participants considered the use of richer representations of web pages [4]. Hu et al. [11] proposed extracting titles from the bodies of web pages and using the extracted titles as new metadata fields for web search. Search log data is also a useful resource for improving relevance ranking performance. Agichtein et al. [1], for example, showed that using a web page's associated queries in search log data can enhance the accuracy of the page's relevance ranking. Wang et al. [31] indicated that the different web page fields usually have different characteristics, and should be represented by different language models. Bendersky et al. [2] proposed employing a discriminative method for extracting and weighting terms or phrases in pseudo relevance feedback and then exploiting the weighted terms in relevance ranking. They focused on term weighting from the query side and did not make use of information from the document side. Carvalho et al. [6] proposed finding phrasal terms from documents to enhance relevance ranking. To extract phrasal terms, they utilized statistical features and an SVM classifier.

To the best of our knowledge, there was no previous work that studies the problem of extracting and using key n-grams from web pages for relevance ranking.

2.2 Keyphrase Extraction

Our work is also related to keyphrase extraction, given that n-grams represent phrase fragments. A number of authors such as Frank et al., Witten et al., and Turney [7, 28, 29, 32] propose keyphrase extraction is a problem of classification. In this approach, document phrases are labeled as keyphrases or non-keyphrases. A classifier is then trained using the labeled data. The classifier is used to categorize phrases within a new document as keyphrases or non-keyphrases. Several learning methods were applied into the classifier's learning, including naive Bayes [7, 32], decision tree [28, 29], rule-induction [12], and neural network [27]. The KEA tool based on naive Bayes is publically available for use in keyphrase extraction studies. Recently, we [14] proposed formalizing keyphrase extraction as a ranking problem, and learning a ranker to rank phrases based on the degree that they are keyphrases. The learning to rank method, Ranking SVM, is employed in the construction of ranker.

Another method proposes the use of log data as training data for keyphrase extraction. Irmak et al. extracted key terms from user log data in a user-centric entity detection system [13] and used learning to rank to learn the extraction model. Paranjpe proposed a similar method [22] which utilizes search log data to learn the aboutness of a document represented by words and phrases. A regression model was used. The evaluation of the extracted keyphrases in both studies was limited to browsing scenarios.

Our work differs from existing work in the following points: 1) Our goal is to enhance search relevance ranking. 2) We extract key n-grams instead of keyphrases.

2.3 Search Log Mining for Ranking

Search log data contains queries and clicked URLs. Each web page's URL is associated with a number of queries, as well as with the number of times the page is clicked as the query's searches are also recorded.

Search log data has been used for relevance ranking in web search; for example, as training data for creating a ranking model [15, 24], and as features of a relevance ranking model [1]. Search log data is usually only available for popular queries and pages. Gao et al. proposed two smoothing methods to propagate click numbers along the click-through graph [8]. In this paper, we use search log data as training data for key n-gram extraction. The model learned by our method can even be applied to web pages (tail pages) without any click or anchor text.

3. MOTIVATION

Head pages usually have a lot of anchor text and associated queries in search log data, and they can become strong signals for judging page relevance with respect to queries. Modern search engines can effectively leverage these signals and perform very well in head page searches. In contrast, tail pages are usually limited to just a few anchor texts and associated queries, or even none at all. As a result, searching such pages tends to be difficult.

Tail pages - including new pages, personal homepages, and discussion pages - are of high value to users. These pages need to be easily found for those who want to search them.

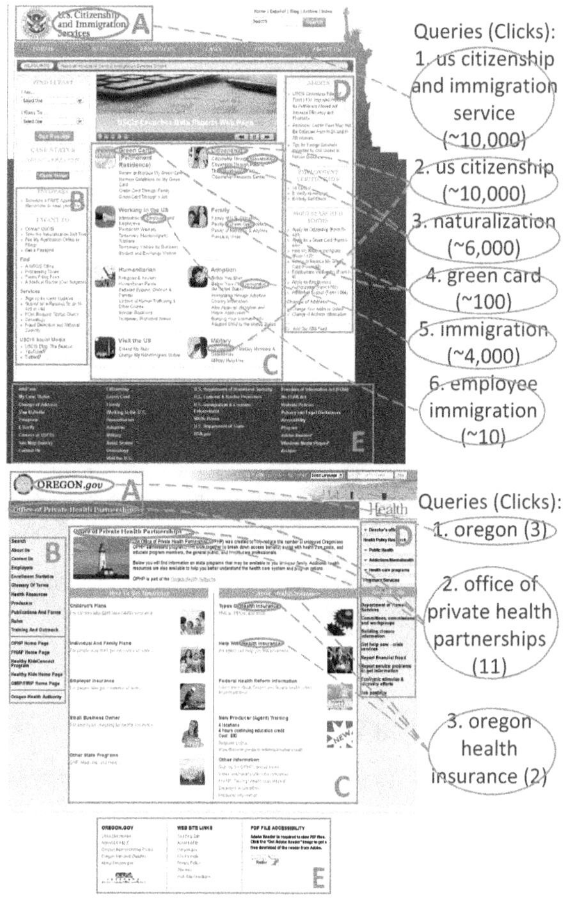

Figure 1: Similar appearances of queries in example head page (top) and tail page (bottom)

According to a study by Goel et al. [9], search of tail pages is an important element in enhancing user satisfaction, and good search results on tail pages can play a central role in winning users' loyalty to a particular search engine. If, for example, a user wants to find his friend's homepage, his satisfaction will be quite high if it can be found immediately by the search engine. Our statistics on a collection of web pages show that more than 75% are tail pages with less than one anchor text and associated query. This effectively illustrates how tail page relevance becomes one of the most challenging issues in web search.

Our proposal is to extract or generate good queries for each page, including tail pages, which should be more suitable for searching the page. The extraction or generation uses the page title, URL and body, all of which are available for tail pages. When searched with good queries, the page should rank highly. Berger et al. [3] proposed taking a translation approach to document retrieval. The generation or extraction can be viewed as 'translating' a web page into a number of keyphrases. We refer to this task *search focused keyphrase extraction or generation.* In this paper, we focus on extraction.

We accomplish our task with two means; namely, learning from search log data and key n-gram extraction.

First, we take search log data as training data for the extraction. A web page's associated queries can be viewed as good queries for searching the page. The data can be used to train a model. Since the head pages have more click data, we end up with learning the model from head pages and apply the learned model to tail pages.

Second, we consider key n-gram extraction an approximation of keyphrase extraction. Queries, particularly long queries such as "star wars anniversary edition lego darth vader fighter," are difficult to segment. If the query is associated with a page in the search log data, then we take all of the query's n-grams as key n-grams of the page. In this way, we can skip query segmentation, which is difficult to do with a high degree of accuracy. Actually, all current ranking models, even those based on machine learning, usually use n-grams only as features, meaning that key n-gram extraction sufficiently enhances the model's performance.

We assume that key n-grams share the same patterns across different pages, and that we can successfully learn an extraction model from the head and apply it to the tail. Fig. 1 gives an example to illustrate this. The page on the top is a head page with more than 600,000 clicks in the search engine's search log data within one year. The page on the bottom is a tail page with just 23 clicks. Despite this difference, the queries in the two pages have similar patterns and appearances. In both pages, the queries are located in region A and region C. Specifically, region A includes the page's title and subtitle. Regions B and D include website navigation links. R The page's main content is in region C. Region E consists of outer links.

We can use the formatting, term frequency and position information to identify whether an n-gram is likely to be a key n-gram.

4. OUR APPROACH

Our approach consists of two parts: Key n-gram extraction and relevance ranking. Fig. 2 shows an overview.

4.1 Key N-Gram Extraction

4.1.1 Pre-Processing

We assume that the objects to be searched and ranked by the search engine are web pages. During pre-processing, a web page in HTML format is parsed and represented as a sequence of tags/words. Then all the words are converted into lower case, and stop words into a list[1] are removed.

In our approach, we define an n-gram as n successive words within a short text separated by punctuation symbols and special HTML tags. Note that some HTML tags provide a natural separation of text, e.g., "<h1>Experimental Result</h1>" indicates that "Experimental Result" is a short text. Some tags do not mean a separation, e.g., "<font color="red">significant</font> improvement."

4.1.2 Training Data Generation

We propose using search log data for training a key n-gram extraction model, because search log data represents users' implicit judgments on the relevance between queries and documents. More specifically, if users search with a query and click a page afterward, and this occurs many times (e.g., beyond a threshold), then it is very likely that the query and the page are relevant. We can consider automatically extracting queries from the page. Head pages generally include a number of associated queries in the search log data. Such data can naturally be used as training data for the automatic extraction of queries, particularly for tail pages.

Instead of extracting queries or keyphrases, we extract key n-grams. We treat the n-grams in each of the document's queries as its labeled key n-grams. For example, when a document is "ABDC" associated with the query "ABC", we consider unigrams "A", "B", "C", and bigrams "AB" are key n-grams with the assumption that they should be ranked higher than unigram "D", and bigrams "BD" and "DC", by the extraction model. Features for each n-gram are then extracted, as described in Sec. 4.1.3, and then an extraction model is trained. The advantage of taking this approach is that no segmentation on queries and documents is necessary, which is difficult to accurately carry out. In fact, existing ranking models usually make use of n-grams only as features, and thus extraction of key n-grams is sufficient for enhancing search relevance.

Deriving training data from search log data is an approach with the benefit of low cost. An alternative would allow human labelers to assign relevant queries to selected web pages. However, this suffers from two problems: 1) Cost is high. 2) Human labelers are not query owners, making it difficult for them to come up with relevant page queries. An approximation of such a method uses conventional relevance judgment data created from queries whereby each page is associated with a small number of queries, or even just one query. As will be seen in our experiment, such an approximation does not work better than our method using search log data. Given that human labeling is expensive and log data is very low cost, the use of log data for training data creation is definitely a good practice.

4.1.3 N-Gram Features Generation

Web pages contain rich formatting information compared to plain text. We utilize both textual and formatting information to create features in the extraction (ranking) model in order to accurately extract key n-grams. We have conducted a comprehensive study on the features for the task. Below is a list of features which were found to be useful from an empirical study of 500 randomly selected pages and the key n-grams associated with them.

N-grams may be highlighted with different HTML formatting information, and the formatting information is useful in identifying the importance of n-grams.

1. Frequency Features

The original/normalized term frequencies of an n-gram within several fields, tags and attributes are utilized.

a) **Frequency in Fields:** The n-gram frequencies in four web page fields, including URL, page title, meta-keyword and meta-description.

b) **Frequency within Structure Tags:** The frequencies of n-gram in texts within a header, table or list indicated by HTML tags including <h1>, ..., <h6>, <table>, <li> and <dd>.

c) **Frequency within Highlight Tags:** The frequencies of n-gram in texts highlighted or emphasized by HTML tags including <a>, <b>, <i>, <em> and <strong>.

d) **Frequency within Attributes of Tags:** The frequencies of n-gram in web page tag attributes. These are hidden texts which are not visible to users. We found, however, that they are still valuable for key n-gram extraction; for example, the title of an image <img title="Still Life: Vase with Fifteen Sunflowers" .../>. Specifically, title, alt, href and src tag attributes are used.

e) **Frequencies in Other Contexts:** The frequencies of n-gram in other contexts including 1) The page headers, which means n-gram frequency within any of <h1>, ..., <h6> tags. 2) The page meta-data field. 3) The page body. 4) The whole HTML file.

2. Appearance Features

The appearances of n-grams are also important indicators of their importance.

a) **Position:** The n-gram's position when it first appears in the title, paragraph and document.

b) **Coverage:** The coverage of an n-gram in the title or a header, e.g., whether an n-gram covers more than 50% of the title.

c) **Distribution:** The n-gram's distribution across different parts

[1]ftp://ftp.cs.cornell.edu/pub/smart/english.stop

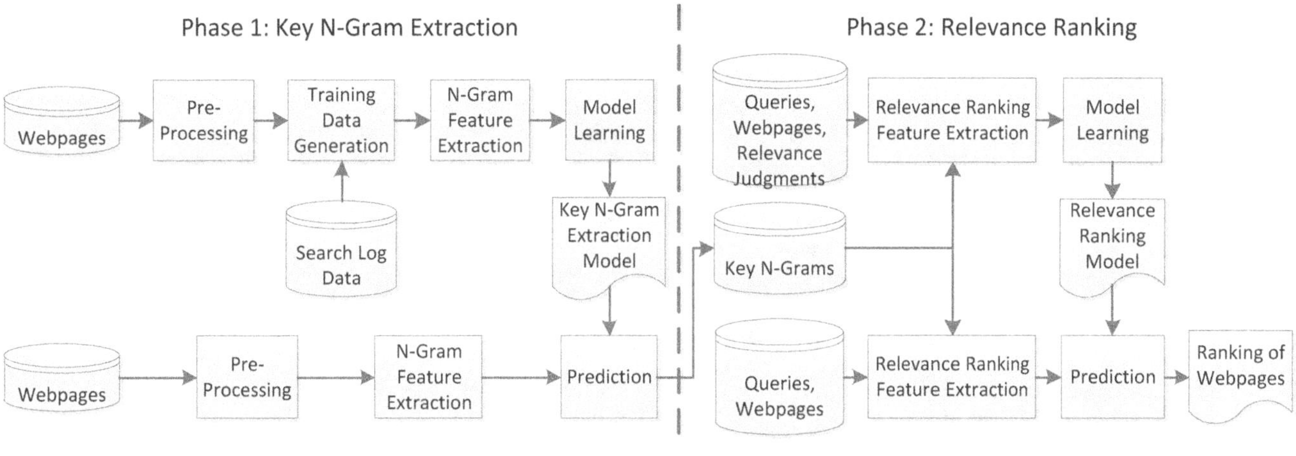

Figure 2: Framework of our approach

of a page. The page is separated into several parts and the entropy of the n-gram across the parts is used.

4.1.4 *Key N-Gram Extraction*

Key n-gram extraction is formalized as a learning to rank problem. In learning, a ranking model is trained which can rank n-grams according to their relative importance as key n-grams associated with a given web page. Features are defined and utilized for the ranking of n-grams. In extraction, given a new page and the trained model, the n-grams in the page are ranked with the model. Top K n-grams are selected as key n-grams of the page.

We give a formalization of the learning task. Let $X \in \mathbb{R}^p$ is the space of features of n-grams, while $Y = \{r_1, r_2, \ldots, r_m\}$ is the space of ranks. There exists a total order among the ranks: $r_m \succ r_{m-1} \succ \ldots \succ r_1$. Here, $m = 2$, representing key n-grams and non key n-grams. The goal is to learn a ranking function $f(\mathbf{x})$ such that for any pair of n-grams $(\mathbf{x}_i, y_i)$ and $(\mathbf{x}_j, y_j)$, the following condition holds:

$$f(\mathbf{x}_i) > f(\mathbf{x}_j) \Leftrightarrow y_i \succ y_j \quad (1)$$

Here $\mathbf{x}_i$ and $\mathbf{x}_j$ are elements of X, and y_i and y_j are elements of Y representing the ranks of $\mathbf{x}_i$ and $\mathbf{x}_j$.

We employ Ranking SVM [10] to learn the ranking function $f(\mathbf{x})$, and we specifically use the SVM^{Rank} tool [16] [2]. We assume that $f(\mathbf{x}) = \mathbf{w}^T\mathbf{x}$ is a linear function on $\mathbf{x}$.

Given a training set, we first convert it to ordered pairs of n-grams: $P = \{(i, j)|(\mathbf{x}_i, \mathbf{x}_j), y_i \succ y_j\}$. $f(\mathbf{x})$ is learned by the following optimization:

$$\hat{\mathbf{w}} = \arg\min_{\mathbf{w}} \frac{1}{2}\mathbf{w}^T\mathbf{w} + \frac{c}{|P|}\sum_{(i,j)\in P}\xi_{ij} \quad (2)$$
$$s.t.\ \forall(i, j) \in P : \mathbf{w}^T\mathbf{x}_i - \mathbf{w}^T\mathbf{x}_j \geq 1 - \xi_{ij},\ \xi_{ij} \geq 0$$

where ξ_{ij} denotes slack variables and c is a parameter.

4.2 Relevance Ranking

4.2.1 *Relevance Ranking Features Generation*

In web search, web pages are represented in several fields, also referred to as meta-streams. In this paper, we consider the following meta-streams: URL, page title, page body, meta-keywords, meta-description, anchor texts, search log data associated queries and the key n-gram stream created by our method. The first five meta-streams are extracted from the web page itself, and they reflect the web designer's view. Anchor texts are extracted from other pages and they represent other web designers' summaries. The query meta-stream consists of users' queries leading to clicks on the page. It provides the search users' view. The key n-gram meta-stream created by our method also provides a web page summary. Note that the key n-grams are extracted based solely on the information from the first five meta-streams. The model for extraction is trained primarily from head pages using a number of associated queries as training data; and is applied to tail pages, which may not include anchor texts and associated queries.

A ranking model includes query-document matching features that represent the relevance of the document with respect to the query. Popular features include tf-idf, BM25 and minimal span. All can be defined on the meta-streams. Document features which describe the importance of the document itself, such as PageRank and Spam Score, are also used.

Given a query and a document, we derive the following query-document matching features from each meta-stream:

a) **Unigram/Bigram/Trigram BM25**: N-gram BM25 [33] is an extension of traditional unigram-based BM25

b) **Original/Normalized PerfectMatch**: Number of exact matches between query and text in the stream

c) **Original/Normalized OrderedMatch**: Number of continuous words in the stream which can be matched with the words in the query in the same order

d) **Original/Normalized PartiallyMatch**: Number of continuous words in the stream which are all contained in the query

e) **Original/Normalized QueryWordFound**: Number of words in the query which are also in the stream

In addition, PageRank and domain rank scores are also used as document features in our model.

4.2.2 *Ranking Model Learning and Prediction*

We employ learning to rank techniques to automatically construct the ranking model from labeled training data for relevance ranking. Again, we use Ranking SVM as the learning algorithm. In search, given a new query and retrieved web pages, we generate the query-document matching features between the query and each page's meta-streams, and calculate ranking scores using the learned ranking model. Next, we rank all of the web pages in descending order of their ranking model scores.

[2]http://svmlight.joachims.org/

5. EXPERIMENTS

5.1 Experiment Settings

5.1.1 Dataset

We conducted experiments on a large search log dataset and three large-scale relevance ranking datasets.

We used a search log collected from a commercial search engine over the course of one year. It contains 76,882,604 distinct URLs and 121,100,491 distinct queries with 10,280,590,031 clicks. To derive training data for key n-gram extraction, the query-document pairs with at least $click_{min} = 2$ clicks were kept and the others were discarded. Then $N_{train} = 2,000$ HTML pages were randomly selected from the search log data, which had a minimum of $query_{min} = 5$ associated queries. Some data statistics are given in Tab. 1.

Table 1: Dataset used for training of key n-gram extraction

# of HTML Pages	2,000
Average # of queries per page	15.64
Average # of words per query	3.47

The relevance ranking experiments were conducted on three large-scale datasets which contained queries, documents, and their relevance judgments. The first two sets are comprised of general queries (queries randomly sampled from the search log), and the last set of tail queries (queries randomly sampled from the search log's low frequency queries), referred to as Training (Training Set), Test1 (Test Set with General Queries) and Test2 (Test Set with Tail Queries). We use Training Set to learn a relevance ranking model and use Test1 and Test2 evaluate the model. Each set includes 10,000 queries and about 1,000,000 web pages. The relevance judgments are represented at five levels including "Perfect", "Excellent", "Good", "Fair" and "Bad". Some statistics about the three datasets are given in Tab. 2.

Table 2: Datasets used for relevance ranking

Dataset	Training	Test1 (General Queries)	Test2 (Tail Queries)
# of queries	20,429	12,705	10,991
# of HTML pages	1,008,480	1,131,367	708,768
Avg. # of pages/query	49.37	89.05	64.49
Avg. # of perfect/query	0.26	0.59	0.15
Avg. # of excellent/query	0.75	1.41	0.30
Avg. # of good/query	6.44	15.70	6.00
Avg. # of fair/query	15.86	33.98	16.63
Avg. # of bad/query	26.14	37.37	41.41
Avg. # of words/query	3.65	3.27	4.48

5.1.2 Parameters and Evaluation Measures

We first set the ranges for our method's parameters, and then created extraction and ranking models under all possible parameter settings, and tested the our method's relevance ranking performance on the Test1 and Test2 datasets. We report the best performance on the two test datasets at the best parameter setting. (It turns out that the best parameter settings are the same.) As we later describe in detail, we started from the best parameter setting, changed one parameter, and fixed the other parameters.

In key n-gram extraction, there are three parameters: number of training pages N_{train}, minimum number of clicks between a query and a page $click_{min}$, and minimum number of queries associated with a page $query_{min}$. We set the ranges of N_{train} as $\{100, 200, 500, 1000, 2000\}$, $click_{min}$ as $\{1, 2, 5\}$, $query_{min}$ as $\{2, 5, 10\}$. The best setting is as follows: $N_{train} = 2,000$, $click_{min} = 2$, and $query_{min} = 5$.

In relevance ranking, there are two parameters: Number of top K n-grams selected, and number of words in n-grams n. We set the ranges of K as $\{5, 10, 20, 30\}$ and n as $\{1, 2, 3\}$. The best setting is as follows: $K = 20$ and $n = 3$.

There is a parameter c for Ranking SVM which is used in both key n-gram extraction and relevance ranking. In extraction, c is chosen among $\{0.001, 0.01, 0.1, 1, 10, 100, 1000\}$. In ranking, c is selected from $\{0.01, 0.1, 1, 10, 100, 1000, 10000, 100000\}$. Note that the ranges of c in the two phases are quite different because the tasks in the two phases are quite different. The best parameter setting is $c = 0.1$ and $c = 1,000$.

Mean Average Precision (MAP) [30] and Normalized Discounted Cumulative Gain (NDCG) [17] are used as evaluation measures in relevance ranking.

5.2 Experiments on Relevance Ranking

We evaluated our proposed approach for relevance ranking. First, we evaluated performance to see whether our method can enhance relevance ranking. Then, we compared our method against a popular keyphrase extraction method KEA [32] used in relevance ranking. We particularly examined how our approach performed on head and tail pages.

5.2.1 Relevance Ranking with Extracted Key N-Grams

We tested the effectiveness of our method using extracted key n-grams in relevance ranking. One baseline used the ranking model trained with features derived from several meta-streams (see Sec. 4.2 for details) without using extracted n-grams, referred to as "baseline". Note that both our method and the baseline were built with the same web page information. Our method further extracts and utilizes information, namely search-focused key n-grams, for page ranking. The parameters of our method were at the best setting as explained in Sec. 5.1.2. The experimental results are presented in Fig. 3.

The experimental results indicate that relevance ranking performance can be significantly enhanced by adding extracted key n-grams into the ranking model. More specifically, our method can improve NDCG@1 by 1.92 and 1.94 points on Test1 and Test2 datasets respectively. The improvements of MAP on Test1 and Test2 are 0.87 and 1.28 points respectively. T-test shows that the improvements are all statistically significant ($p < 0.001$).

5.2.2 Ranking Performance Comparison with KEA

Another baseline used KEA [32] for relevance ranking, which takes web pages as input but extracts keyphrases from the pages. The keyphrases are used as a page meta-stream, and a ranking model with additional features from the meta-stream is trained. There are differences between our method and KEA. Our method learns the model from search log data while KEA learns from human-labeled keyphrases, and our method is search focused while KEA is for general purposes. The KEA model was trained using the data in Jiang et al.'s work [14], which has 300 web pages adopted with human-labeled keyphrases. To make the comparison fair, we took the same set of web pages and their associated queries as training data for our method. The other parameters of our method were set the same as those in the best parameter setting. Note that our approach performance is slightly worse than Sec. 5.2.1. The parameters of KEA, such as the number of output keyphrases, were tuned and here we report the best KEA results.

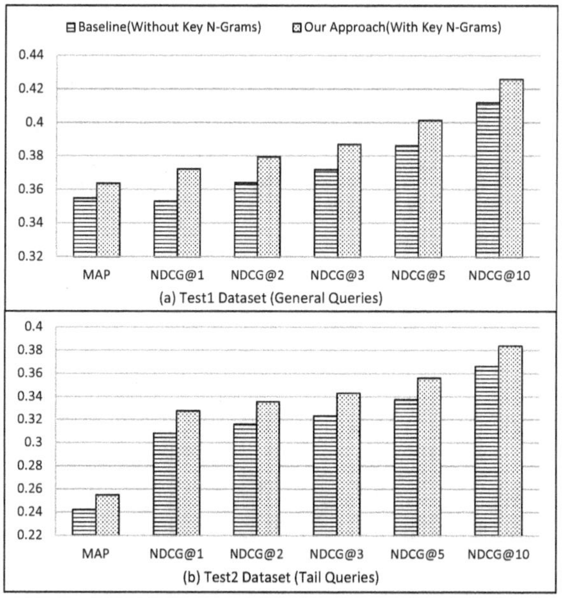

Figure 3: Ranking performance comparison between baseline (without key n-grams) and our approach (with key n-grams)

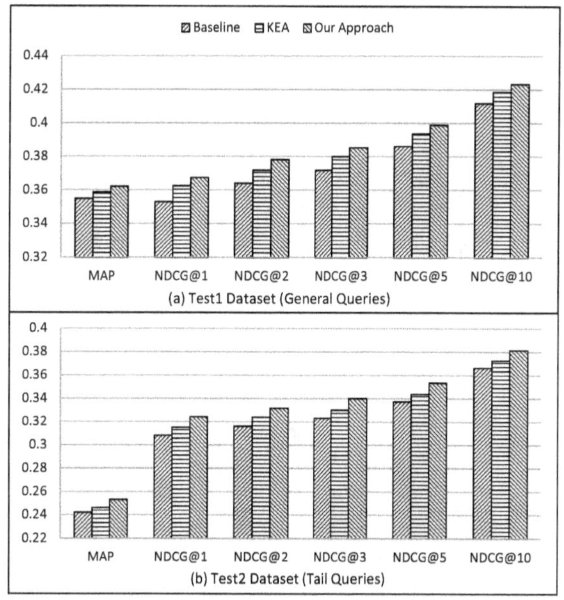

Figure 4: Ranking performance comparison between KEA and our approach

From the result shown in Fig. 4, we can see that KEA can work better than the baseline, but performs worse than our method. The results indicate that relevance ranking can be enhanced by both keyphrase and key n-gram extraction. Moreover, it is better to employ search-focused key n-gram extraction than general keyphrase extraction.

5.2.3 Ranking Performance on Head and Tail Pages

Our method is trained mainly with head page data, because head pages have more associated queries with higher click frequencies. It is potentially more useful for relevance ranking of tail pages, because tail pages usually have less anchor text and associated queries. We evaluated our method's performance on head pages and tail pages respectively.

We respectively split both Test1 Dataset and Test2 Dataset into a Head Page Subset and Tail Page Subset. When more than 75% a query's relevant pages - which were rated as perfect, excellent or good - did not have other associated queries and anchor texts, we classified the query and its associated pages into a Tail Page Subset, otherwise Head Page Subset. The ratio of of Head Page Subsets and Tail Page Subsets was about 3:1 for both Test1 and Test2.

The results are shown in Fig. 5. We can see that: 1) Our proposed method significantly improves the Tail Page Subset vs. the Head Page Subset for both datasets. 2) The improvements made by our method remain statistically significant even for Head Page Subsets ($p < 0.001$). 3) We can also observe that the improvements on Test2 Dataset are slightly greater than on Test1 Dataset, indicating that our approach can be more effective on tail queries than general queries.

Similar conclusions were drawn when we tested other split ratios such as 50%, 60%, 70%, 80% and 90%.

5.3 Studies on Key N-Gram Extraction

We studied the alternatives to our approach with key n-gram extraction.

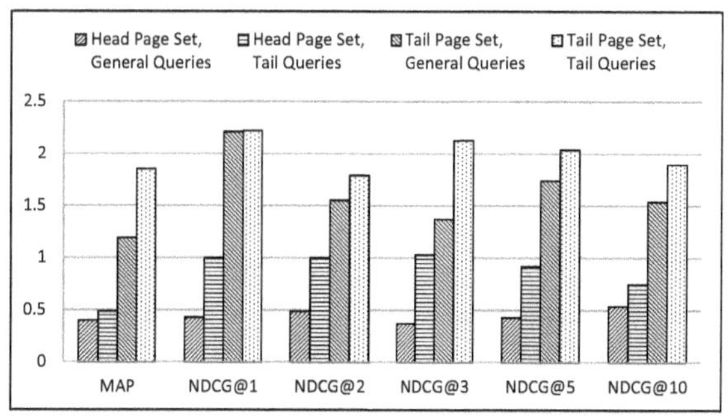

Figure 5: Ranking performance improvement comparison between head pages and tail pages

5.3.1 Classification vs. Ranking

In our approach, we formalize the extraction problem as one of ranking instead of alternatively viewing it as one of classification. We compared the two options based on Ranking SVM and SVM. Results are shown in Fig. 6.

The results indicate that using Ranking SVM is more effective than using SVM. T-test shows that Ranking SVM's improvement over SVM is statistically significant ($p < 0.001$). The result validates the correctness of the assumption that it is better to formalize the key n-gram extraction problem as one of ranking rather than classification. This is because it is hard to detect key n-grams in an absolute manner, but easy to judge whether one n-gram is more important than another.

5.3.2 Training Data Generation

In our approach, we derive training data from search log data. We assume that the document is relevant to the query if the document is searched and clicked by the query at least $click_{min}$ times.

We evaluated the data creation method effectiveness by comparing training with search log data vs. training with human-labeled data.

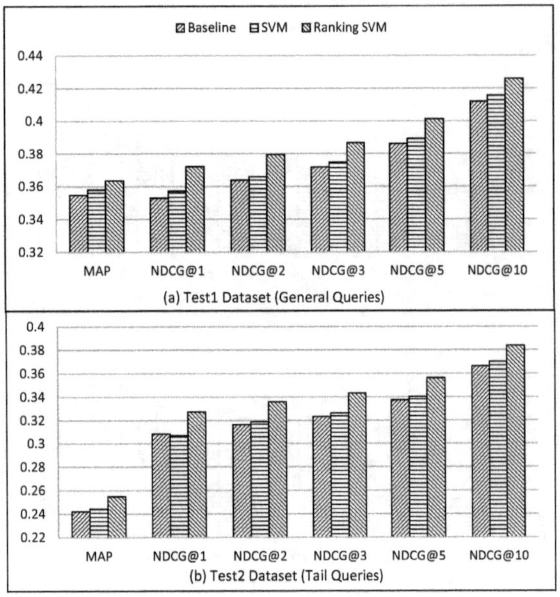

Figure 6: Ranking performance comparison between SVM (classification) and Ranking SVM (ranking) for key n-gram extraction

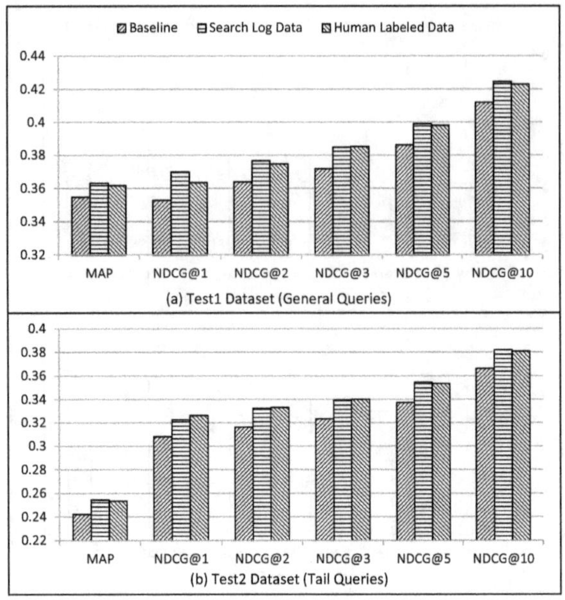

Figure 7: Ranking performance comparison between different training data generation methods in the extraction phase

We randomly selected $N_{train} = 2,000$ web pages which included both search log data and human judgments in data collection. The data did not overlap with the test data in Test1 and Test2. The pages labeled by search log data and the pages labeled by human judgments were used to train the key n-gram extraction models respectively. For the human-labeled data, the queries with the original judgments "perfect", "excellent", and "good" were viewed as the labeled data. Results are shown in Fig. 7.

We can see that: 1) These two options both perform better than the baseline, suggesting that it is better to take a search-focused key n-gram extraction approach. 2) It appears that the model trained by the search log data offers slightly better performance than the model trained by the human-labeled data, indicating that the use of search log data is adequate for the accurate extraction of key n-grams. Given the cost advantages, it is definitely better to exploit search log data as training data.

5.3.3 Training Data Size

We studied different values of N_{train}, training data size. We randomly selected 100, 200, 500, 1,000 and 2,000 web pages leveraging associated queries as training data for key n-gram extraction. The results in Fig. 8 indicate that the differences among different training data sizes are quite small. The performance may increase slightly as more training data becomes available. It appears that $N_{train} = 2,000$ is enough to train a good model for key n-gram extraction.

5.4 Studies on Relevance Ranking

We investigated alternatives to our relevance ranking approach.

5.4.1 Unigram, Bigram and Trigram

We studied the effect of different n's of n-gram in relevance ranking. Specifically, we considered three options: 1) Using unigrams. 2) Using both unigrams and bigrams. 3) Using unigrams, bigram, and trigrams. We did not consider four-grams or higher order grams because the average word number within a query is approximately three.

Fig. 9 shows the relevance ranking results. It can be seen that the use of unigrams outperforms the baseline. When bigrams and trigrams are included, the performance further improves. However, the amount of improvement becomes smaller as n increases. Thus, we can conclude that unigrams play the most important role in the results. Bigrams and trigrams add more value.

5.4.2 Top K

We studied the impact of using different K's for top K n-grams selection. We tried different values for K, i.e., 5, 10, 20, and 30. The result is given in Fig. 10. We can see that the ranking performance initially increases and then decreases when K increases. When $K = 20$, it achieves the best result.

5.4.3 N-Gram Extraction Score

Our approach uses extracted key n-grams as a new meta-stream and creates ranking model features. In other words, we ignore key n-grams' extraction scores. An alternative also utilizes the extraction scores as features in the ranking model.

We considered three ways to use the scores: 1) The scores are used to weigh the n-grams in our key n-gram meta-stream (Score as Weight). 2) The scores of all the key n-grams in the query are summed up and used as features (Score Sum). 3) The above two strategies are combined (All).

The experimental results are shown in Fig. 11. We can see the change in performance is quite small when using "Score as Weight." However, "Score Sum" further improves the ranking performance in both datasets. Moreover, the best performance is achieved when both strategies are combined. It further improves our method's NDCG@1 by 1.04 and 1.24 points on Test1 and Test2 Datasets. (Compared with the baseline, the improvements are 2.96 and 3.18 points respectively)

This experiment shows that key n-gram scores can also benefit relevance ranking even when very simple strategies are utilized.

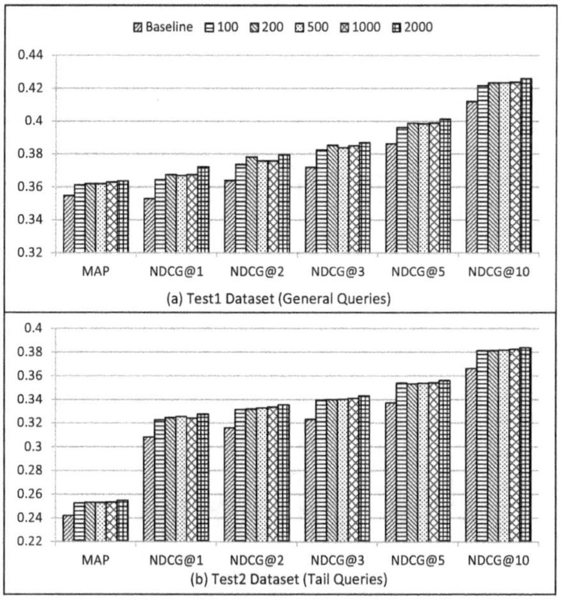

Figure 8: Ranking performance with different training data size in the extraction phase

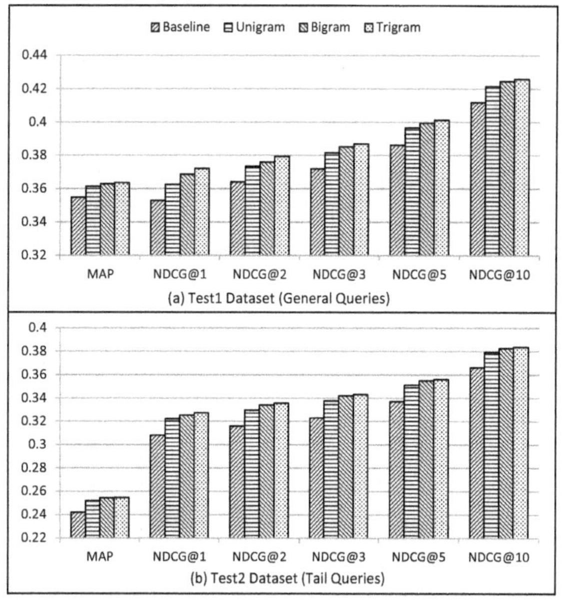

Figure 9: Ranking performance comparison between unigram, bigram and trigram

6. DISCUSSION

Our analysis of the results investigated why our approach resulted in performance that was better than the baseline and its limitations.

Table 3: Examples of extracted key n-grams

URL	http://www.idownloadblog.com/2008/11/13/transformer-app-makes-your-ipod-touch-look-like-an-iphone/
Queries	cydia app to make itouch in to an iphone
Search Log	(none)
Key N-Grams	transformer, **ipod**, **iphone**, ipod touch look, touch look like, look like, like iphone, **ipod touch**, **transformer app**, app makes
URL	http://www2.scnow.com/news/2010/may/14/cbs_early_show_crowd_celebrates_myrtle_beach_board-ar-356151/
Queries	myrtle beach boardwalk grand opening
Search Log	myrtle beach, myrtle beach boardwalk
Key N-Grams	myrtle beach, beach, myrtle, **grand opening**, cbs, show, cbs early show, early show, crowd celebrate, myrtle beach boardwalk

By checking those cases in which our method worked better than the baseline, we found that our approach extracted "good" page n-grams that matched against a query when they did not appear in anchor texts and associated page queries. Tab. 3 shows examples. In the first example, there is no search log data associated with the page. In contrast, our approach can extract key n-grams contributing to ranking. In the second example, our approach can further extract a "grand opening" which does not occur in the log data regardless of the search log data associated with the page. Indeed, our method adds a good representation of a web page and enhances its relevance ranking.

We examined the erroneous cases generated by our approach, and found that the ranking performance can be further improved with representations that are better than n-grams. Occasionally, n-grams do not suffice as representatives for the matches between queries and documents. Obviously there are some matches based on linguistic structures which cannot be represented well by n-grams. For example, "ipod touch look" in Tab. 3 is extracted by our approach but its linguistic structure is not captured. If the query is "Abraaj Capital" and the web page is the home page of "Abraaj Capital Art Prize", our method still assigns a high score to the page, because of the match through bigram "Abraaj Capital". This means that a fundamental change to relevance models allowing the use of more complicated data might be necessary.

7. CONCLUSIONS

This paper studies the problem of extracting search-focused key n-grams from web pages and utilizing these key n-grams, as well as their weights, as features to enhance search relevance ranking. We use search log data to generate training data and employ learning to rank to learn the model of key n-grams extraction mainly from head pages, and we apply the learned model to all web pages, particularly tail pages. The extracted key n-grams provide another description of the web page, in addition to search log data anchor texts and queries. Results validate the effectiveness of the proposed web search approach on several large datasets. The proposed approach significantly improves relevance ranking. The improvements on tail pages are particularly great.

We plan to apply our method of key n-gram extraction to other datasets and to other tasks such as index compression in future work. We also want to study the problem of web page key n-grams *generation*.

8. REFERENCES

[1] E. Agichtein, E. Brill, and S. Dumais. Improving web search ranking by incorporating user behavior information. In *Proc. of SIGIR'06*, pages 19–26, 2006.

[2] M. Bendersky, D. Metzler, and W. B. Croft. Parameterized concept weighting in verbose queries. In *Proc. of SIGIR'11*, pages 605–614, 2011.

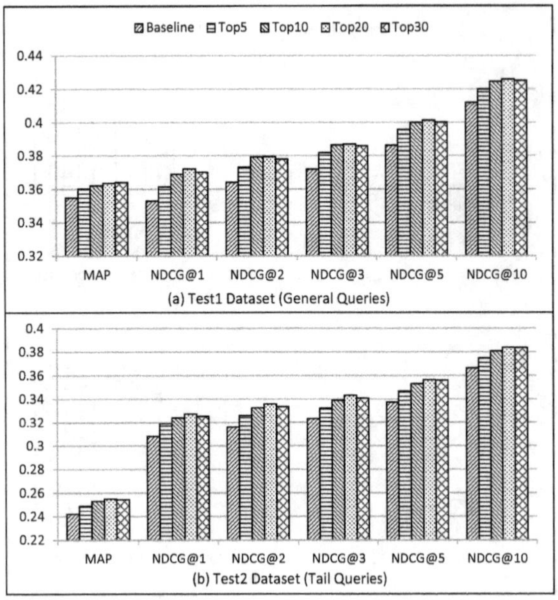

Figure 10: Ranking performance with different K in top K n-grams selection

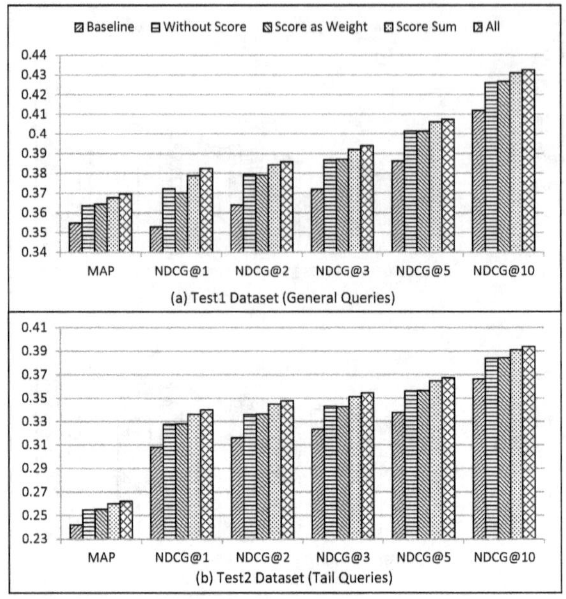

Figure 11: Ranking performance with extraction scores of key n-grams as features in relevance ranking

[3] A. Berger and J. Lafferty. Information retrieval as statistical translation. In *Proc. of SIGIR'99*, pages 222–229, 1999.

[4] N. Craswell, D. Hawking, R. Wilkinson, and M. Wu. Overview of the trec 2003 web track. In *Proc. of TREC'03*, pages 78–92, 2003.

[5] M. Cutler, Y. Shih, and W. Meng. Using the structure of html documents to improve retrieval. In *Proc. of USITS'97*, pages 241–251, 1997.

[6] A. L. da Costa Carvalho, E. S. de Moura, and P. Calado. Using statistical features to find phrasal terms in text collections. *Journal of Information and Data Management*, 1(3):583–597, 2010.

[7] E. Frank, G. W. Paynter, I. H. Witten, C. Gutwin, and C. G. Nevill-Manning. Domain-specific keyphrase extraction. In *Proc. of IJCAI'99*, pages 668–673, 1999.

[8] J. Gao, W. Yuan, X. Li, K. Deng, and J.-Y. Nie. Smoothing clickthrough data for web search ranking. In *Proc. of SIGIR'09*, pages 355–362, 2009.

[9] S. Goel, A. Broder, E. Gabrilovich, and B. Pang. Anatomy of the long tail: ordinary people with extraordinary tastes. In *Proc. of WSDM'10*, pages 201–210, 2010.

[10] R. Herbrich, T. Graepel, and K. Obermayer. Large margin rank boundaries for ordinal regression. *Advances in Large Margin Classifiers*, 2000.

[11] Y. Hu, G. Xin, R. Song, G. Hu, S. Shi, Y. Cao, and H. Li. Title extraction from bodies of html documents and its application to web page retrieval. In *Proc. of SIGIR'05*, pages 250–257, 2005.

[12] A. Hulth. Improved automatic keyword extraction given more linguistic knowledge. In *Proc. of EMNLP'03*, pages 216–223, 2003.

[13] U. Irmak, V. V. Brzeski, and R. Kraft. Contextual ranking of keywords using click data. In *Proc. of ICDE'09*, pages 457–468, 2009.

[14] X. Jiang, Y. Hu, and H. Li. A ranking approach to keyphrase extraction. In *Proc. of SIGIR'09*, pages 756–757, 2009.

[15] T. Joachims. Optimizing search engines using clickthrough data. In *Proc. of KDD'02*, pages 133–142, 2002.

[16] T. Joachims. Training linear svms in linear time. In *Proc. of KDD'06*, pages 217–226, 2006.

[17] K. Järvelin and J. Kekäläinen. Ir evaluation methods for retrieving highly relevant documents. In *Proc. of SIGIR'00*, pages 41–48, 2000.

[18] J. Lafferty and C. Zhai. Document language models, query models, and risk minimization for information retrieval. In *Proc. of SIGIR'01*, pages 111–119, 2001.

[19] H. Li. Learning to rank for information retrieval and natural language processing. *Synthesis Lectures on Human Language Technologies*, 4(1):1–113, 2011.

[20] T. Liu. Learning to rank for information retrieval. *Foundations and Trends in Information Retrieval*, 3(3):225–331, 2009.

[21] D. Metzler and W. Croft. A markov random field model for term dependencies. In *Proc. of SIGIR'05*, pages 472–479, 2005.

[22] D. Paranjpe. Learning document aboutness from implicit user feedback and document structure. In *Proc. of CIKM'09*, pages 365–374, 2009.

[23] J. Ponte and W. Croft. A language modeling approach to information retrieval. In *Proc. of SIGIR'98*, pages 275–281, 1998.

[24] F. Radlinski and T. Joachims. Query chains: learning to rank from implicit feedback. In *Proc. of KDD'05*, pages 239–248, 2005.

[25] S. E. Robertson and S. J. Walker. Some simple effective approximations to the 2-poisson model for probabilistic weighted retrieval. In *Proc. of SIGIR'94*, pages 232–241, 1994.

[26] G. Salton, A. Wong, and C. S. Yang. A vector space model for automatic indexing. *Communications of the ACM*, 18:613–620, 1975.

[27] K. Sarkar, M. Nasipuri, and S. Ghoser. A new approach to keyphrase extraction using neural networks. *International Journal of Computer Science*, 7:16–25, 2010.

[28] P. D. Turney. Learning algorithms for keyphrase extraction. *Information Retrieval*, 2(4):303–336, 2000.

[29] P. D. Turney. Mining the web for lexical knowledge to improve keyphrase extraction: Learning from labeled and unlabeled data. Technical Report ERB-1096, National Research Council, Institute for Information Technology, 2002.

[30] E. Voorhees and D. Harman. Trec: Experiment and evaluation in information retrieval. *Computational Linguistics*, 32(4):563–567, 2005.

[31] K. Wang, X. Li, and J. Gao. Multi-style language model for web scale information retrieval. In *Proc. of SIGIR'10*, pages 467–474, 2010.

[32] I. H. Witten, G. W. Paynter, E. Frank, C. Gutwin, and C. G. Nevill-Manning. Kea: practical automatic keyphrase extraction. In *Proc. of DL'99*, pages 254–255, 1999.

[33] J. Xu, H. Li, and C. Zhong. Relevance ranking using kernels. In *Proc. of AIRS'10*, pages 1–12, 2010.

Query Suggestion by Constructing Term-Transition Graphs

Yang Song, Dengyong Zhou, Li-wei He

Microsoft Research,
One Microsoft Way,
Redmond, WA 98052, USA
{yangsong, denzho, lhe}@microsoft.com

ABSTRACT

Query suggestion is an interactive approach for search engines to better understand users information need. In this paper, we propose a novel query suggestion framework which leverages user re-query feedbacks from search engine logs. Specifically, we mined user query reformulation activities where the user only modifies part of the query by (1) adding terms after the query, (2) deleting terms within the query, or (3) modifying terms to new terms. We build a term-transition graph based on the mined data. Two models are proposed which address topic-level and term-level query suggestions, respectively. In the first topic-based unsupervised Pagerank model, we perform random walk on each of the topic-based term-transition graph and calculate the Pagerank for each term within a topic. Given a new query, we suggest relevant queries based on its topic distribution and term-transition probability within each topic. Our second model resembles the supervised learning-to-rank (LTR) framework, in which term modifications are treated as documents so that each query reformulation is treated as a training instance. A rich set of features are constructed for each (query, document) pair from Pagerank, Wikipedia, N-gram, ODP and so on. This supervised model is capable of suggesting new queries on a term level which addresses the limitation of previous methods. Experiments are conducted on a large data set from a commercial search engine. By comparing the with state-of-the-art query suggestion methods [4, 2], our proposals exhibit significant performance increase for all categories of queries.

Categories and Subject Descriptors

H.3.3 [**Information Storage and Retrieval**]: Information Search and Retrieval - Search process

General Terms

Algorithms, Experimentation

Permission to make digital or hard copies of all or part of this work for personal or classroom use is granted without fee provided that copies are not made or distributed for profit or commercial advantage and that copies bear this notice and the full citation on the first page. To copy otherwise, to republish, to post on servers or to redistribute to lists, requires prior specific permission and/or a fee.
WSDM'12, February 8–12, 2012, Seattle, Washington, USA.
Copyright 2012 ACM 978-1-4503-0747-5/12/02 ...$10.00.

Keywords

query suggestion, page rank, learning to rank

1. INTRODUCTION

While more and more sophisticated algorithms have been applied to web search engines to increase user search experiences, it is still admittedly difficult for search engines to fully understand user's search intent in many scenarios. Consequently, many researches have been focused on interaction with users to find out what the users really want [12, 13]. Among all, query suggestion [5, 23] has established as one of the most promising interactive techniques as we have witnessed its wide usage in most commercial web search engines. Generally speaking, query suggestion techniques aim at recommending a list of relevant queries to user's input, by mining correlated queries from previous knowledge, e.g., search engine logs. Indeed, the quality of query suggestion can be affected by many factors. For example, depending on the underlying algorithms, query suggestion techniques can be categorized into graph-based models (e.g., random walk on click graphs)[16, 7] and probabilistic models (e.g., language models)[24, 11]. Moreover, depending on the length of suggested queries, we can further divide existing query suggestion techniques into query expansion [17, 6], query reduction [12] and query reformulation [24, 8].

Among all existing techniques, random walk-based models [16, 7, 23] have exhibited their superiority over others on both efficiency and effectiveness. Due to its simplicity and mathematically-proven fast convergence, random walk-based query suggestion models are capable of scaling up to large data sets for commercial search engines. Essentially, most models in this category construct a bipartite graph of queries and clicked URLs by assuming the goodness of clicked URLs. Queries are treated relevant to each other if they share common clicks. While both theoretically sound and empirically usable, this approach appears to have a drawback that needs attention. To be specific, random walk models only focus on query and clicks but ignore the rich information which is embedded in the entire user session. For example, considering four user activities in a session: $\{q_1, URL_1, q_2, URL_2\}$. The user clicked URL_1 after issuing q_1. Not satisfied by the result, the user immediately reformulates the query to q_2 and clicked URL_2. Apparently, URL_1 is not as a good click as URL_2, which is unfortunately treated equally in random walk models.

In this paper, we try to address two fundamental questions in query suggestion research. (1) How to extract high-quality user clicks in the user session and use the clicks properly? Since the quality of the clicks directly affects the recommendation performance of models which leverage clicks as signals, it is critical to accurately infer user intent by examining the entire user search session. (2) Given a specific query, which query suggestion method should be used? e.g., can query reduction method be applied to short queries? Is query expansion always better than query reformulation? In our opinion, answers to these questions are non-trivial. And in practice, it usually depends on each individual queries as well as the user intent at that moment.

To briefly answer these questions, we first derive high-quality user clicks by extracting specific user activity patterns which conveys implicit user preferences. Secondly, instead of using the clicks directly, we construct a term-transition graph model from the data. We use random walk as a guideline to find user preferences within each topic and choose the best suggestion method according to our model.

To be concrete, we propose a framework that combines the strength of graph-based models and probabilistic models. Our model naturally unifies the advantages of query expansion, reduction and reformulation techniques while successfully avoids their relative shortcomings. More specifically, we make the following contributions in this paper:

- From the search engine session logs, we mine a large amount of user preference data. We consider the following tuple $\{q_1, q_2, u\}$ where a user abandoned a query q_1 and immediately reformulated it into q_2 then made a click on URL u, during the same session. These activities strongly indicate a user's preference on query q_2 over q_1, which often differs by only a few terms.
- We construct a term-preference graph from the above data where each node is a term in the query and each directed edge a preference. We then train a topic-biased Pagerank model for each of the query topics by extracting topics from clicked URLs. Given a query, this model guides the decision of (1) expanding relevant terms to the original query, (2) removing terms from the original query, or (3) replacing existing terms with relevant terms. This unsupervised model learns the user preference from the log which does not require any specific user labels.
- We further propose a supervised learning-to-rank model to interpret user preference at term level. This model leverages a set of rich features, which includes N-gram features, external knowledge (e.g., Wikipedia, ODP) as well as the topic-biased Pagerank features learnt in the previous model. No human labeling was conducted. Instead, we automatically infer the training labels from the logs by leveraging a sophisticated probabilistic preference model.

To summarize, our system provides a principled formulation that is capable of addressing both topic and term-level suggestions. Both of our methods exhibit much better recommendation performance than the state-of-the-art methods [16, 7] on a real-world large data set mined from a commercial search engine.

2. RELATED WORK

The complexity of dealing with query suggestion related problems has led to a myriad of proposals of methods in literature. In general, this problem has been addressed by different techniques including query reduction, query expansion, query reformulation and query suggestion using search engine logs [22, 12, 17, 4, 19].

In [12], the authors proposed to reduce long queries into shorter ones by removing redundant terms and extract key phrases. Three methods for selecting sub-queries were introduced: mutual information, maximum spanning tree and extracting named entities. Results indicated that with user interaction, the precision of retrieval improved. However, this method is only useful for long queries. When applying to short queries, it only exhibits marginal improvement.

Automatic query expansion was first proposed in [17], where the authors leveraged term correlations in documents as a metric to recommend similar terms. Similarly, authors in [6] measured the difference between the distribution of terms in relevant documents and in collections to score similar terms. In general, query expansion techniques were able to introduce useful terms while also bring in unhelpful terms.

Differing from the above two approaches, query reformulation replaces the existing terms in the query by more relevant ones. Essentially, it tries to map the query language model into document language model with term replacement. In [24], the authors used context distribution to extract term associations from the logs. Given a new query, their method replaced the terms with new terms of higher matching probability in the context. Similarly, using anchor text as the context for reformulation was recently studied [8].

The three approaches mentioned above primarily focused on improving retrieval relevance. On the other hand, query suggestion aims at interaction with users to improve search experience by showing relevant queries on the search engine result pages (SERP) and allowing users to decide whether to click or not. Among all related techniques for query suggestion, log-based random walk methods have shown good results [7, 16, 9]. Most random walk models are performed on query-document bipartite graphs. For example, in [7], the authors introduced a backward random walk model which alleviates the bias towards documents with more clicks. The model normalizes the correlation matrix on the document clicks rather than query counts, which is why the transition from a document to query is not biased to popular queries. In [16], a parameter-free random walk model is proposed which addressed the efficiency of random walk. The model constructed a subset of query-url nodes in the bipartite graph and performed depth-first search for relevant queries. By estimating the transition probabilities between queries using similarity-based method, this model was capable of suggesting semantically related queries. In [4], the authors proposed a query-flow graph that calculates the probability of going from one query to another, by leveraging a set of features. This approach can be treated a special case of random walk on the query-URL graph where the URLs are removed but used to calculate the transition probability. Although looks similar to our method, it only considered query-level transition while our model deals with much finer granularity by addressing term level transitions.

Recently, the authors in [23] introduced an optimal way of query suggestion using random walk. The authors addressed two important factors in the paper. First, how to tune the jumping parameter in the random walk model and second, how to optimally combine the clicked and skipped URLs in the log for relevance estimation. The authors proposed to perform two random walks on click graph and skip graph respectively, and optimally combine the results by minimizing the categorization error on the URL correlations, which was estimated using ODP data. Experimental results indicated a significant improvement over previous random walk models.

3. GET USER PREFERENCE FROM LOG

In this section we describe how we acquire a large collection of user preference data from the logs. The primary source of data used in this paper is from logs of a widely-distributed browser toolbar, where a large sample of users opted-in for providing their online browsing activities. The logs are anonymized so that no user personal information is recorded. A typical log entry contains the following fields: a unique user identification number generated by a one-way hash function, the URL that the user visited, the timestamp of the visit, and the total dwell time on that URL. Since we are interested in the user queries when visiting search engines, we also post-processed the data to generate the user queries and the name of the search engine. The logs are organized based on sessions, where each session contains a series of URL visits from a particular user, ordered by the timestamp. If the user becomes inactive for more than 30 minutes, that session ends.

We are particularly interested in spontaneous query refinement behaviors by the users, which can be summarized in a sequence of three activities:

1. A user enters a query q_1 to a search engine.
2. After examining the search result page, the user did not get the right information, so he/she refines the query to be q_2.
3. This time the user is satisfied with the results and clicked one of the URLs, therefore ends the search session.

For example, the user first issued "nyc traffic cameras" and refined the query by adding one term at the end "nyc traffic cameras live", followed by a click on the satisfied result. This sequence of activities conveys two important pieces of information: first, the user prefers the query q_2 to q_1 since he performed no click after issuing q_1 but then becomes positive about the results after q_2. Second, the user chooses to refine the query rather than clicking the suggested queries by the search engine, which may indicate poor suggestion quality for that particular query.

Although the users may refine the queries in whatever way they want, our statistics have shown that more than 76% of times users only modify one of the terms in the queries. It has also shown the users are much more likely to revise the last term in the query, which covers more than 80% of all cases[1]. Consequently, we only focus on mining user preferences that fall into these two categories in this paper, although the proposed methods can be easily generalized to handle more complex scenarios.

Formally, given a word vocabulary $W = \{\epsilon, w_1, ...w_n\}$ where ϵ is used to denote the empty string, we define three cases of user query refinements as follows:

[1]These statistics are drawn from one month search logs from a commercial search engine with over 100 million queries

Type	User Activity	Pattern
Modification	1. q:{single ladies song} 2. q:{single ladies lyrics} 3. URL click	song→lyrics
Expansion	1. q:{sports illustrated} 2. q:{sports illustrated 2010} 3. URL click	ϵ→2010
Deletion	1. q:{ebay auction} 2. q:{ebay} 3. URL click	auction → ϵ

Table 1: Three types of user refinement examples.

- Modification: user modifies the last term of the query: $\{w_{i1}, ...w_{im}\} \rightarrow \{w_{i1}, ...w'_{im}\}$, e.g., "single ladies song" → "single ladies lyrics".
- Expansion: user adds one term to the end of the query: $\{w_{i1}, ...w_{im}\} \rightarrow \{w_{i1}, ...w_{im}, w_{i(m+1)}\}$, e.g., "sports illustrated" → "sports illustrated 2010".
- Deletion: user removes the last term of the query: $\{w_{i1}, ...w_{i(m-1)}, w_{im}\} \rightarrow \{w_{i1}, ...w_{i(m-1)}\}$, e.g., "ebay auction" → "ebay".

Table 1 summarizes the three types of refinements used in this paper. Overall, we extracted the aforementioned information from 3-month Toolbar logs between May 2010 and August 2010. In total, over 4 million user refinement activities were discovered in the log. By aggregating the refinements, a total of 350,000 pairs of refinements were found. Table 2 summarizes the top user refinements in each case.

Next, we show how these implicit user feedbacks can be leveraged for query suggestion in our models.

4. MODEL 1: AN UNSUPERVISED APPROACH

Given the pair-wise transition between each pair of terms, we represent the transitions between all terms into a directed graph. Since every transition from t_i to t_j indicates a preference of t_j over t_i, we assume this is an analogy of webpage inlinks and outlinks, where in general the more inlinks a webpage has, the higher its authority score is. The most famous algorithm for calculating such kind of score is the Pagerank algorithm [18], which is widely used in commercial search engines for webpage static rank estimation. In

Modification	Expansion	Deletion
login→home	ϵ→free	the→ϵ
2009→2010	ϵ→2010	search→ϵ
facebook→myspace	ϵ→online	mail→ϵ
lyrics→video	ϵ→download	2→ϵ
google→yahoo	ϵ→lyrics	facebook→ϵ
music→songs	ϵ→video	scam→ϵ
earth→maps	ϵ→login	best→ϵ
check→access	ϵ→pictures	cheats→ϵ
jobs→employment	ϵ→games	cheap→ϵ
depot→max	ϵ→reviews	wiki→ϵ

Table 2: Summary of top user query refined queries in each category.

our scenario, we assume that terms exhibit different level of importance in a set of pre-defined topics. In what follows, we describe a topic-based Pagerank approach which is inspired by [10].

The Pagerank is a random walk-like algorithm where higher Pagerank is assigned to pages with greater importance. In the Pagerank algorithm, the rank of each page can be estimated iteratively. Specifically, at the $t+1$ step, the Pagerank is updated as follows:

$$Rank^{(t+1)} = (1-\alpha)M \times Rank^{(t)} + \alpha p, \quad (1)$$

where M is a stochastic matrix where $M_{ij} = 1/N(j)$ if there is a transition from node j to node i, with $N(j)$ being the total number of outlinks of node j. At each step, the random walk has a probability of $\alpha \in (0,1)$ that jumps to an arbitrary node. In the original Pagerank algorithm, $p = [\frac{1}{N}]N \times 1$ so that the probability of jumping to any node is the same.

In our topic-based Pagerank model, for each topic t_j, the jumping vector p is calculated as follows:

$$p_{ji} = \begin{cases} \frac{1}{|U_j|} & \text{if } i \in U_j \\ 0 & \text{otherwise} \end{cases}$$

where U_j is the set of terms belonging to topic j. Given t topics, this approach essentially constructs t topic graphs where each graph G_j only contains nodes which is categorized in topic j.

Figure 1 illustrates an example of such graph that contains 9 nodes (our actual graph is much bigger). After Pagerank algorithm converges, each term w is assigned with a vector of scores denoting its Pagerank score in all t topics.

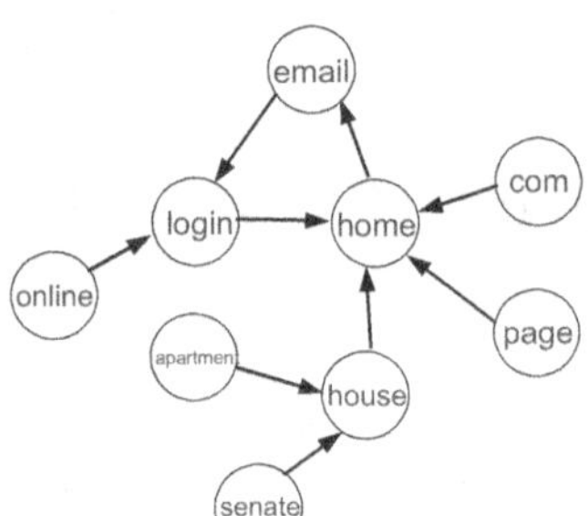

Figure 1: An illustration of graph construction from the term transition data. Each arrow indicates a user preference, e.g., page → home.

4.1 Extracting Topics from Clicks

Recall that in our definition, a query refinement essentially contains three elements: $\{q_1, q_2, click_{url}\}$. Since getting the topics directly from query is difficult, we propose to infer the topics from the clicked webpage which naturally reflects the query intent. In this paper, we leverage a sophisticated content-based classifier that categorizes webpages into ODP categories [3]. The ODP categories are organized hierarchically where higher level topics are more abstract. For example, www.microsoft.com belongs to "Computers"→"Companies" category. We leverage the 14 top-level categories from ODP and construct 14 topic graphs in our models. Note that it is common for a transition to appear in more than one category according to the URLs clicked. For example, coupon→free happens very often in both Computers and Shopping categories. Table 3 shows the top-ranked terms in several categories after running the topic-based Pagerank model.

4.2 Query Suggestion

After calculating topic-based Pagerank, the next step is to suggest query-dependent terms when a new query comes. Given a query q_i with m terms $\{w_{i1}, ..., w_{ij}, ..., w_{im}\}$, we want to suggest a set of related queries by reformulating the query using modification, expansion or deletion methods. Although for training we only consider the modification of the last term in the query, it should be noted that at query suggestion time, our model can be adapted to make modifications for any terms in the query.

Overall, any term can be either modified or deleted from the query. The query itself in the meanwhile can be expanded where the expanded term is considered to be appended at the end. Specifically, for any term w_{ij}, the term refinement probability is defined as

$$P(w_{ij} \to w'_{ij}|q_i) = \sum_k P(w_{ij} \to w'_{ij}|T_k)P(T_k|q_i),$$
$$w'_{ij} \in W = \{\epsilon, w_1, ...w_n\}, j \in 1, ..., m. \quad (2)$$

Here $P(w_{ij} \to w'_{ij}|T_k)$ is a query-dependent score, i.e., the most likely transition in topic T_k given w_{ij}, which is estimated by controlling the jumping factor in Pagerank:

$$p_{ji} = \begin{cases} 1 & \text{if } i \in U_j \\ 0 & \text{otherwise} \end{cases}$$

Meanwhile, $P(T_k|q_i)$ denotes the topic distribution of the new query. For simplicity, we leverage the pseudo-relevance feedback from the search engine [21, 25] which assumes that the top-returned results are usually relevant. We thus classify the top-10 URLs returned by a search engine into ODP categories and treat it as the topic distribution of q_i. Table 5 shows examples of the most possible transitions.

To choose the best candidates among all refinements for all terms in the query, we leverage the Pagerank of the terms to rank the refinements:

$$P(q'_i|q_i) = \arg\max P(w_{ij})P(w_{ij} \to w'_{ij}|q_i), \quad (3)$$

where q'_i equals to q_i except for term j being replaced: $w_{ij} \to w'_{ij}$.

In addition, query q_i has the following probability to be expanded by adding a new term w', according to our model,

$$P(w'|q_i) = \sum_k P(w'|T_k)P(T_k|q_i), \quad (4)$$

where $P(w'|T_k)$ is the static Pagerank of term w' in topic T_j.

The results from term refinement and query expansion are then combined to suggest new queries based on the descending order of their probabilities. Table 4 shows a concrete example for the query "stanford university map". The final winners are "stanford university location", "stanford university address", "stanford university", "harvard university map" and "yale university map". In this case, suggestions from using expansion gets a very low score hence are not suggested, indicate that our model is capable of suggesting queries that are different from a syntactic point of view.

Computers	Health	Home	Science	Shopping	Sports	Business
download	symptoms	recipes	channel	walmart	sports	jobs
free	hospital	recipe	zoo	parts	espn	bank
verizon	treatment	coupons	salary	furniture	games	ashley
wireless	pain	cooking	coupons	store	results	dmv
software	diet	food	weather	buy	schedule	locations
iphone	health	baby	ohio	accessories	news	free
email	calculator	network	calculator	shoes	soccer	calculator
microsoft	surgery	easy	craigslist	supplies	cup	continental
windows	doctor	reviews	toyota	target	rumors	america
support	dosage	grilled	jetblue	clothing	nba	chase

Table 3: Top-ranked terms in each category by the topic-biased Pagerank method. A total of 14 ODP categories are assigned to queries.

Query		Prob(expansion)	
stanford university map		stanford university map online (0.0005) stanford university map download (0.0003) stanford university map printable (0.0001)	
Term	**Pagerank Score**	**Prob(replacement)**	**Prob(deletion)**
stanford	0.04	harvard (0.03), yale (0.02), columbia (0.02)	0.005
university	0.04	college (0.02), school (0.01), institute (0.002)	0.01
map	0.05	location (0.04), address (0.03), history (0.005)	0.015
Final Suggestions		**Source**	**Score**
stanford university location		replacement	0.04
stanford university address		replacement	0.03
stanford university		deletion	0.015
harvard university map		replacement	0.03
~~stanford university map online~~		expansion	0.0005
~~stanford university map download~~		expansion	0.0003

Table 4: Examples of query suggestion for "stanford university map". Top: query level expansion probability. Bottom: term level replacement and deletion probabilities for each term in the query. The final suggestion is the highest-scored queries from both models. Candidates from expansion are not suggested in this case.

Walmart	Microsoft	Steelers	Weather
target	msn	penguins	hurricane
sears	office	pirates	radar
costco	hp	panthers	zoo
wal-mart	microsoft.com	hurricanes	news
walgreens	live	ravens	earthquake

Table 5: Some examples of the most relevant terms given specific terms. Calculated using term-specific Pagerank algorithm.

5. MODEL 2: A SUPERVISED APPROACH

The Pagerank-based query suggestion model presents a novel way to efficiently reformulate queries on the topic level. Nevertheless, the model ignores the underlying relationship between the query and the suggested term after it aggregates the term transitions into topics. Indeed, within the same topic the term transition probability still varies from queries. In this section, we propose a query-level learning-to-rank approach which leverages a set of language-modeling features to address the limitation of the previous model.

We briefly introduce the idea of learning-to-rank here. For a better understanding of learning-to-rank, we refer readers to [15]. Given a set of queries and URLs as well as labeled relevance score (usually in 5-scale) for each query-URL pair, learning-to-rank tries to optimize for the ranking loss for all queries in the training set. Generally, three sets of features are often used during training, (1) query features (e.g., query frequency), (2) URL features (e.g., the Pagerank score of the URL), and (3) query-URL features (e.g., BM25 [20]). In our model, we mimic these principles and construct three sets of features for each triplet of transition: $\{q_1, q_2, click\}$. To be specific, the common part of q_1 and q_2 are extracted to represent the query part, whereas the refinement is treated similar as the URL role. For example, for the first example shown in Table 1, "single ladies" is the query, while "song" and "lyrics" are treated as refinements.

5.1 Feature Construction

For each of the query-refinement pair, we construct three sets of features as shown in Table 7.

The query features generally fall into two categories. The first category is related to Wikipedia. We dumped over 8 million Wikipedia articles in English, which contains the Title, Body content and Category information. In total, the corpus contains 7,181,315 titles and 10,170,187 articles. We match the query to the Title, Body and Category to estimate its popularity in the Wikipedia corpus. Secondly, we construct N-gram language modeling features from a publicly available N-gram services built from Billions of documents [1]. The N-gram contains four streams: title, body, anchor and query streams, available in unigram, bigram, trigram, N-gram with $N = 4, 5$. For each query, each stream returns an N-gram probability for the query within that stream.

The term features are quite similar to URL/document features in information retrieval systems. The Pagerank scores of the terms are directly calculated from previous model with different jumping rates from 0.55 to 0.85. The entropy of the Pagerank score is calculated as $-\sum_i P(t_i) \log P(t_i)$ for term t_i, which estimates the term's specificity across all topics. In addition, a good indicator of term importance is the number of times users expand the original query by adding the term, which is specified as "# of times derived from _EMPTY_ node".

Finally, the query-term features consist of Wikipedia, N-gram and several other features. The N-gram conditional probability measures $P(term|\text{N-gram})$ where the N-gram equals to all phrases (N up to 5) in the original query. e.g., for query "stanford university map" and term "online", there are three probability scores: $P(\text{online}|\text{stanford university map})$, $P(\text{online}|\text{university map})$ and $P(\text{online}|\text{map})$. Meanwhile, the KL Divergence score measures the closeness of two probability distributions: ODP-topic distribution for the query and for the term. Additionally, the inverted query frequency also measures the specificity of the term given a query, defined as $\log N(t_i)/N(t_i|q_j)$, where $N(t_i)$ is the total number of appearances of term t_i and $N(t_i|q_j)$ measures how many times t_i is used to modify query q_j.

Overall, we constructed 30 features for each training instance. The importance of individual features will be discussed in the experiment section.

5.2 Inferring Training Labels from Log

The next step is to generate ranking labels for each group of query refinements. Instead of asking human judgers to manually label a large set of training data, we infer training labels automatically from implicit user feedbacks in the log. For each of the training instance, we extract its total number of appearances (impressions) and total number of user clicks from the log. In literature, it is quite common to use either the total clicks or the click through rate (defined as clicks/impressions) to approximate the labels. Nevertheless, these two metrics sometimes conflict with each other (as shown in the following examples). Instead, we use a more principled way to derive rankings. Since in our training tuple $\{q_1, q_2, click_{url}\}$, we consider both clicks and skips (impressions-clicks) as good signals, it is important to find a model that takes both numbers into consideration. Specifically, given a refined query q' for the original query q, we model its probability of click distribution using a function $\Phi(\alpha, \beta)$ where α corresponds to the total clicks and β is the total skips. In our model, we fit this distribution using a *Beta* function by following [14], i.e., $Beta(\alpha, \beta)$. Consequently, to compare two query refinements q_i and q_j, it has been shown in [14] that the probability of q_j better than q_i can be computed as

$$P(q_j \succ q_i) = \int_0^1 Beta_j(R_j)\Phi_i(R_j)dR_j, \quad (5)$$

where R_i and R_j corresponds to the ranking of q_i and q_j respectively, Φ_i the cumulative distribution function of R_i. Numerical integration is used to estimate the solution. The rankings of the refined queries are then derived directly from the probabilities which show the pair-wise comparison results. Figure 2 shows an example of comparing two cases.

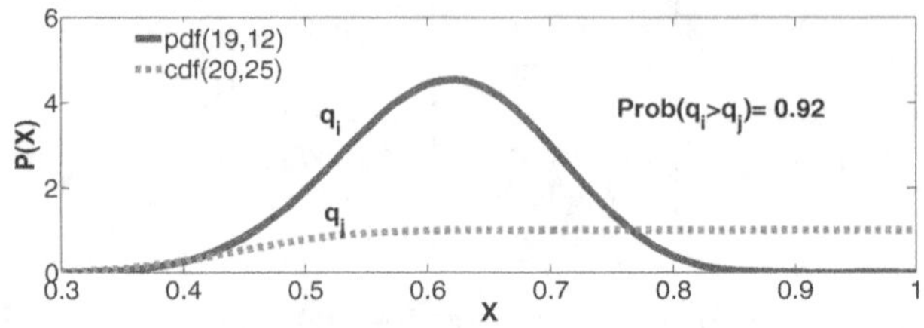

Figure 2: An example of compare two query refinements q_i:(19, 12) and q_j:(20, 25). Although q_i has less clicks than q_j (19 vs. 20), it has a very high probability (0.92) of being a better refinement due to its significantly less number of skips (12 vs. 25).

More specifically, table 6 shows two examples from our log. Using our model, we show that

$$P(\text{stanford admission} > \text{stanford map}) = 0.61$$
$$P(\text{stanford map} > \text{stanford history}) = 0.08$$

The query "stanford admission" is a clear winner over "stanford map" with higher number of clicks and relative less number of skips. On the other hand, "stanford map" is ranked lower than "stanford history". According to our method, the former query has more clicks but also significantly more skips that the latter, thus "map" should be treated as a less relevant term than "history" for the query "stanford".

Query	Term	# of clicks	# of skips	rank
stanford	admission	1913	1235	1
	map	568	438	4
	history	324	148	2
	employment	1273	934	3
microsoft	career	2274	1589	2
	office	1089	222	1
	jobs	1748	1733	3
	games	523	670	4

Table 6: Two examples of constructing query-term training data. Each query consists of a list of terms with their statistics. Labels are assigned according to the probability from eq.(5).

5.2.1 *Online Query Suggestion*

Given a new query q that contains k terms: $\{t_1, ..., t_k\}$, we first create a candidate set of queries by removing one terms from the original query. e.g., for query with terms $\{t_1, t_2, t_3\}$, the candidate set contains $\{t_1, t_2\}$, $\{t_1, t_3\}$ and $\{t_2, t_3\}$, as well as the query itself. Then for each query in the candidate set, we construct features for all terms available in our training set and calculate its score using our model. The highest scored terms are suggested for the query. In practice, since the potential number of candidate suggestions is quite big (n suggested terms for each candidate, where n is the number of unique terms in the training data), we pre-filtered candidates by using ODP categories, where only the

Query Features	Is the query a Wikipedia title? $\in \{0,1\}$ Is the query a Wikipedia category? $\in \{0,1\}$ # of times query contains in Wikipedia title $\in \mathbb{R}$ # of times query contains in Wikipedia body $\in \mathbb{R}$ N-gram probabilities in the title, body, anchor and query streams $\in \{0 \sim 1\}$
Term Features	Pagerank score of the term # of inlinks & outlinks entropy of Pagerank score in 16 ODP topics: $-\sum_i P(t_i)\log P(t_i)$ # of times derived from _EMPTY_ node
Query-Term Features	All Wikipedia features from query features N-gram conditional probabilities, $p(w_n \mid w_{n-m+1}, ..., w_{n-1})$ KL Divergence of query and term probability distributions Inverted Query Frequency: $\log N(t_i)/N(t_i \mid q_j)$

Table 7: Some of the features used in the learning-to-rank method.

terms within the same category as the candidate query are considered.

6. EXPERIMENTS

In this section, we describe the evaluation methods. Our experiments consist of primarily two steps. During the first step, we compare the performance of the two proposed models based on the labels we derived from the log. We also calibrate the parameters of our methods according to the labels. During the second step, we conduct user study and ask judgers to evaluate the query suggestion performance of our proposals as well as several state-of-the-art methods.

6.1 Parameter Tuning

This section describes how to calibrate the parameters in our algorithms. For the Pagerank algorithm, we only need to tune one parameter which is the jumping rate α. Since we use the SVM-rank package[2] for our learning-to-rank approach, we calibrate the c parameter which specifies the trade-off between training error and the margin[3].

For evaluation, we use two well-known metrics: normalized discounted cumulative gain (NDCG) and zero/one-error.

NDCG is widely used in information retrieval systems. In our study, we treat the training labels as the golden standard. We use the top-5 suggested queries for evaluation. From the training label, we use a five-scale relevance score (rel): Perfect (5), Excellent (4), Good (3), Fair (2) and Poor (1). The Ideal DCG (IDCG) is calculated from the training set itself. For the suggestions, if the query is in top 5 of the training data, we assign the score according to its original position or 0 otherwise. The NDCG is calculated as:

$$NDCG(q) = \frac{\sum_i (rel_i)/\log(i+1)}{IDCG(q)}. \quad (6)$$

The NDCG of the test set is averaged over all queries.

The zero/one-error metric, on the other hand, is a more rigorous metric. It calculates the fraction of perfectly correct rankings between training set and test result. The output is binary for each ranking and averaged over all queries.

Figure 3 depicts the results of two metric according to different jumping rates of Pagerank algorithm. The two horizontal lines correspond to the learning-to-rank approach which is not affected by α. It can be noticed that when $(1-\alpha)$ increases, Pagerank generally performs better and better. The best NDCG score is achieved at 0.85 for Pagerank with the value of 0.61, whereas learning-to-rank achieves 0.82 NDCG — a 25% better performance. Similarly, Pagerank has the best zero/one loss score of 0.52, comparing to 0.75 for learning-to-rank algorithm.

In Figure 4, we show the results of the Pagerank algorithm across 14 ODP topics. Comparatively, our algorithm achieves the best performance in the business category, a 0.7 NDCG score. The news category, on the other hand, exhibits the worst performance, which has only 0.47 NDCG and 0.35 zero/one loss scores.

Next, we split the training data into different proportions and examine the performance of the learning-to-rank approach. Figure 5 shows the results of two metrics with training data ranging from 20% to 90%. Even with only 20% of training data, the learning-to-rank method is capable of achieving 0.63 NDCG score. The highest NDCG score is around 0.82 when most of the data is used for training.

Finally, we performed a 5-fold cross validation to select the optimal parameter c in SVM-rank in the range of [-3, 3]. The performance generally increases when c becomes larger. The optimal performance was found when c equals 2.8.

Figure 6 lists the top-weighted features used in learning-to-rank model. The Wikipedia title feature indicates critical importance which is top-ranked. The Pagerank score with 0.85 jumping rate also shows superiority which predicts the term relevance well. 4 of the N-gram features made to the top-10 feature list where the uni-gram feature ranks the highest among them.

6.2 User Study

After calibrating the parameters for our models, we conducted a user study by comparing our methods to others. Since the user study is unable to cover all queries in our data set, we applied a similar approach as in [7, 23] by randomly selecting 450 queries from the search log for judgment.

To compare with state-of-the-art algorithms, we implemented two random walk algorithms which have shown good performance in literature. The first algorithm involves using pseudo relevance feedback [23] which builds the query-url bipartite graph by considering all top URLs returned by a search engine as relevant (RW-Pseudo). This algorithm has shown significantly better performance than the traditional random walk method. The second algorithm considered

[2]http://www.cs.cornell.edu/People/tj/svm_light/svm_rank.html
[3]We used linear kernel in our experiments. Due to the data size, all other kernels reported out-of-memory errors.

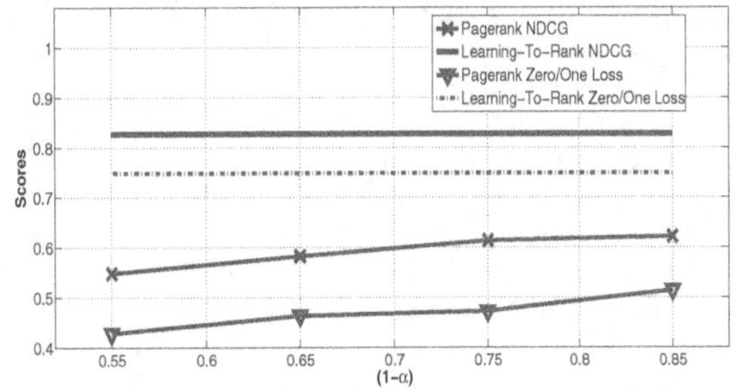

Figure 3: The NDCG & zero/one loss scores affected by the jumping rate α.

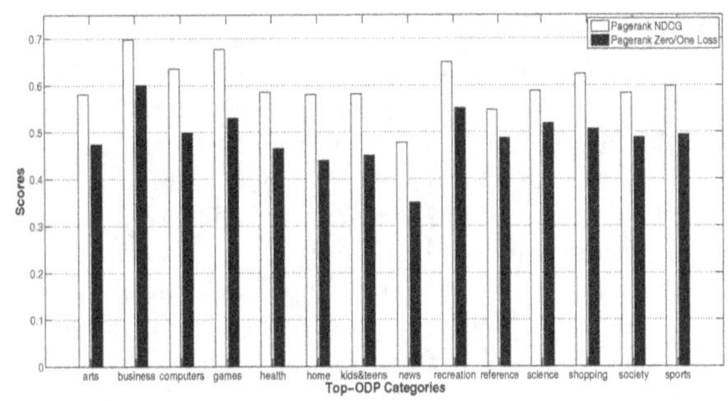

Figure 4: The performance of Pagerank algorithm in all top-14 ODP categories in the training set.

is a backward random walk model [7](RW-Back), which addresses the bias towards URLs with more clicks in traditional forward walk models. This model assumes a uniform prior on all URLs by normalizing the graph on URL clicks instead of query counts, which turns out to be much more efficient in retrieval relevant queries and URLs.

To be more convincing, we also compare with a recently developed query-flow approach [4] that represents the transition between queries into directed graphs and learns the edge weight from a set of features. For query suggestion, we use one of their methods which also leveraged random walk that shown better performance than maximum weight and history-based methods. Furthermore, we compare with an optimized model of the query-flow approach that is de-

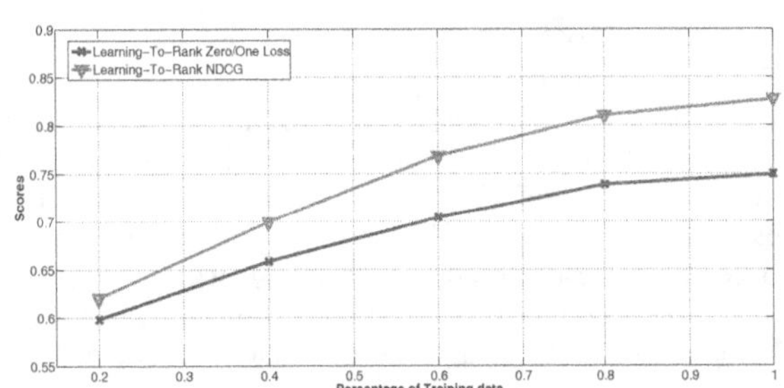

Figure 5: The performance of learning-to-rank algorithm given different portion of training data.

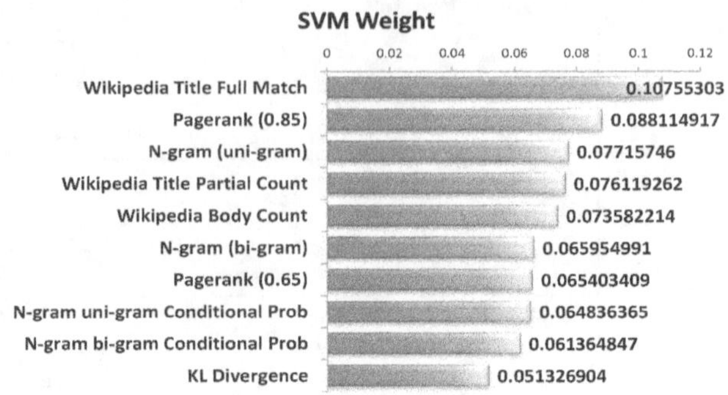

Figure 6: Top-ranked features from SVM-rank used in learning-to-rank model.

scribed in [2], which introduced query-recommendation links that improve the quality of the random walk model.

Finally, we implemented a baseline model. This simplified model only takes query frequency into consideration. Specifically, for any query q, this model recommends q' which appears most frequently after users issued q, and leads to a successful click in the session.

Following [7, 23], we conducted the user study approach as follows. For each sampled query, the four algorithms in comparison independently generate top-5 suggested queries. We then mixed the suggestions by removing the duplicates and randomly sort the remaining, which helps eliminating the positional bias during user study. The suggestions, along with the original query, are given to judgers to evaluation. We asked the judgers to evaluate whether each suggestion is (1) relevant, (2) irrelevant or (3) no opinion (hard to judge). Every query is triple-judged by three different judgers and the majority vote is used as the final label. During the user study, we also give the judgers some context by showing the results from search engine besides the queries, for a better understanding of what the query means.

Since the responses from judgers are binary, the NDCG metric used in previous section no longer applies. Instead, we evaluate by using Precision at rank N (P@N) and Mean Average Precision (MAP). The precision at rank N for a specific query is defined as the percentage of relevant queries:

$$P(N) = \frac{\#\ rel.\ queries}{N}. \qquad (7)$$

P@N is defined as the aggregated precision for all queries,

$$P@N = \frac{\sum P(N)}{\#\ total\ queries}. \qquad (8)$$

While P@N addresses the precision, MAP takes both precision and recall into consideration. Specifically, for each query q_i

$$AverageP(q_i) = \frac{\sum_j (P(j) \cdot \mathcal{I}(j))}{\#\ rel.\ queries},$$
$$MAP = \frac{1}{K} \sum_k AverageP(q_k), \qquad (9)$$

where $P(j)$ is the precision at rank j as defined in eq.(7) and $\mathcal{I}$ equals 1 when query at j is relevant and 0 otherwise.

Query	Pagerank	Learning-to-Rank
battlefield bad company 2	battlefield bad company 1 battlefield bad company 2 ringtones battlefield bad company 2 slots battlefield bad company 2 realms battlefield bad company 2 games	battlefield bad company 2 price battlefield bad company 1 battlefield bad company 2 download battlefield bad company 2 walkthrough battlefield bad company 2 games
best exercise for abs	best exercise for abs workout best exercise for abs exercise best exercise for abs lower best exercise for abs exercises best exercise for abs workouts	best exercise for abs home best exercise for abs six best exercise for abs workouts best exercise for abs cardio best exercise for abs diet
dante's inferno xbox360	dante's inferno xbox360 wiki dante's inferno ps3 dante's inferno xbox360 cheats dante's inferno xbox360 walkthrough dante's inferno	dante's inferno xbox360 wiki dante's inferno xbox360 video dante's inferno xbox360 walkthrough dante's inferno xbox360 cheats dante's inferno xbox360 guide

Table 8: Examples of query suggestions by Pagerank and learning-to-rank methods. Our methods work best for short and medium queries in most scenarios.

Algorithm	MAP	P@5	P@1
LTR	0.6709452	0.6346841	0.668909
Pagerank	0.6483460	0.600000	0.630982
RW-Back [7]	0.5805054	0.5480981	0.57902
RW-Pseudo [23]	0.5789023	0.5408738	0.573906
Baseline	0.458293	0.428911	0.452865
Query-Flow [4]	0.570428	0.539200	0.609072
Query-Flow-Opt [2]	0.583297	0.543886	0.570965

Table 9: Overall scores of the seven algorithms in MAP, P@5 and P@1. LTR performs the best in all metrics. Query-Flow is the second worst for $P@5$ after the Baseline. Query-Flow-Opt shows marginal improvement over Query-Flow but not significantly.

6.2.1 The Results

Table 9 summarizes the overall performance of the four algorithms in terms of MAP, P@5 and P@1. The learning-to-rank and Pagerank approaches significantly outperformed random walk methods in all three metrics. Comparatively, LTR improves 2.2% of MAP, 2.4 % P@5 and 3.8% P@1 upon the Pagerank algorithm, which shows the usefulness of the Wikipedia and N-gram features in addition to the Pagerank features. Note the query-flow approach performs better than both random walk models (but worse than both of ours) for $P@1$, but the performance significantly decreased for precision at 5. We looked into the data and figured out the reason. Since the query-flow method aggregates node at query level, the graph loses the power of distinguishing ambiguous queries with different user intent. Therefore lots of noises are introduced to random walk which also gradually increases with the length of the walk. On the other hand, the optimization framework proposed in [2] only achieves marginal improvement over the query-flow method. Both query-flow approaches are significantly worse than our proposals, which supports the importance of topical-level term-transition graph.

Figure 7 presents the P@5 scores in different ODP categories. Learning-to-rank outperforms other approaches in almost all categories except for the business and games categories. On the other hand, Pagerank exhibits better performance than random walks and query-flow graphs in 8 out of 13 categories. In general, the home and kids&teens are the most difficult categories to make query suggestions, while games and computers are relatively easier than others.

	Deletion		Modification		Expansion	
	Pagerank	LTR	Pagerank	LTR	Pagerank	LTR
S	0.47	0.56	0.59	0.62	0.64	0.68
M	0.54	0.61	0.57	0.6	0.63	0.66
L	0.47	0.57	0.54	0.56	0.63	0.67
Avg	0.5	0.58	0.58	0.6	0.63	0.67

Table 10: Comparison of Pagerank and LTR in terms of suggested methods: deletion, modification and expansion. Results are broken down into query lengths. Short: ≤ 2, medium: $[3,5]$ and long: ≥ 6.

Furthermore, we analysis the effectiveness of our algorithms by breaking down the queries into different query lengths as well as the three techniques (term deletion, modification and expansion) in terms of P@5. As shown in Table 10, long queries are generally the most difficult to make suggestions. While for short and medium queries, the expansion technique indicates better suggestion performance than deletion and modification. The Pagerank algorithm exhibits relatively poor performance for long queries since it is usually harder to accurately infer the topics from long queries, which justifies the superiority of term-level suggestion method over the topic-level method.

Table 8 shows four randomly-selected queries and the suggestions by our algorithms. As it can be seen, most of the suggestions are quite relevant to the query itself yet some of the irrelevant ones are suggested due to the ambiguity of the query itself (e.g., "eclipse" in the query "eclipse 2010").

7. CONCLUSION AND FUTURE WORK

In this paper, we presented a novel query suggestion framework which extracted user preference data from user sessions in search engine logs. We then used the user pat-

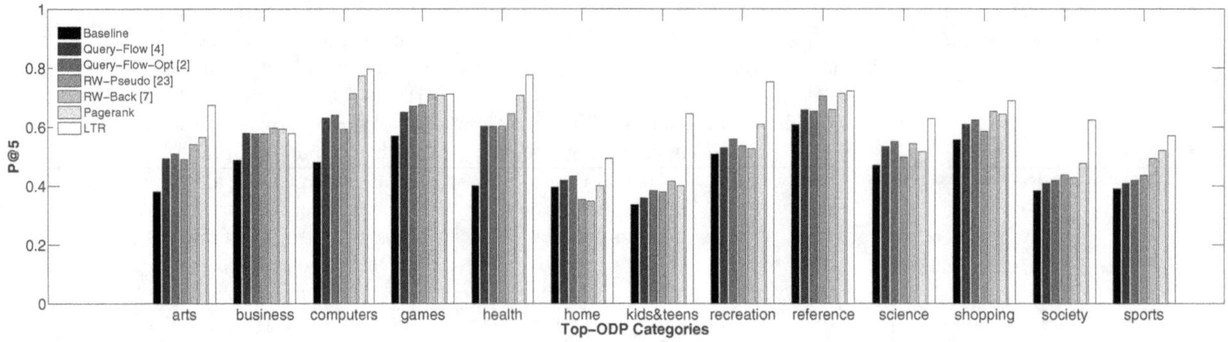

Figure 7: Breakdown of P@5 for 13-ODP categories in the testing set consisting of 450 queries.

terns to build two suggestion models. The first model was a topic-based Pagerank model where the suggested terms were treated as nodes in directed graphs. Pagerank algorithm was used to calculate the relative importance of each term within a topic. The model suggested new queries to the original query by using one of the three techniques: term deletion, term expansion and term modification. The second model was meant to address the limitation of the topic-based model, which constructed features from Wikipedia, N-gram, Pagerank and other resources, and performed query-level suggestions by training a learning-to-rank model.

Our models were compared with two state-of-the-art random walk methods and query-flow models on randomly-sampled queries. A rigorous user study was conducted where all queries are triple-judged by human judgers. Experimental results indicated significant improvement on our models. We also broke down the queries into different ODP categories as well as query lengths. It was shown that our models worked the best for short and medium-length queries.

There is a rich body of work to be extended. As a preliminary study, our model only considered changing one term from the queries. It would be interesting to see how the performance will increase/decrease by leveraging a more sophisticated user preference extraction model which could consider multi-term alteration. In our topic-biased Pagerank model, only the first-level ODP categories are used to classify queries, while suggesting queries in a lower-level of category which further narrows down user intent, might be more relevant than queries on the same topic category.

8. REFERENCES

[1] Microsoft web n-gram services. http://research.microsoft.com/en-us/collaboration/focus/cs/web-ngram.aspx.

[2] A. Anagnostopoulos, L. Becchetti, C. Castillo, and A. Gionis. An optimization framework for query recommendation. In WSDM '10, pages 161–170, 2010.

[3] P. N. Bennett and N. Nguyen. Refined experts: improving classification in large taxonomies. In SIGIR '09, pages 11–18, New York, NY, USA, 2009. ACM.

[4] P. Boldi, F. Bonchi, C. Castillo, D. Donato, A. Gionis, and S. Vigna. The query-flow graph: model and applications. In Procs of CIKM, 2008.

[5] H. Cao, D. Jiang, J. Pei, Q. He, Z. Liao, E. Chen, and H. Li. Context-aware query suggestion by mining click-through and session data. In KDD '08, 2008.

[6] K. Collins-Thompson and J. Callan. Query expansion using random walk models. In CIKM '05, pages 704–711.

[7] N. Craswell and M. Szummer. Random walks on the click graph. In SIGIR '07, pages 239–246, 2007.

[8] V. Dang and B. W. Croft. Query reformulation using anchor text. In WSDM '10, pages 41–50, 2010.

[9] H. Deng, I. King, and M. R. Lyu. Entropy-biased models for query representation on the click graph. In SIGIR '09, pages 339–346, 2009.

[10] T. H. Haveliwala. Topic-sensitive pagerank. In WWW '02, pages 517–526, 2002.

[11] R. Jones, B. Rey, O. Madani, and W. Greiner. Generating query substitutions. In WWW '06, pages 387–396, 2006.

[12] G. Kumaran and J. Allan. A case for shorter queries, and helping users create them. In Human Language Technologies 2007, pages 220–227, April 2007.

[13] G. Kumaran and J. Allan. Effective and efficient user interaction for long queries. In SIGIR '08, pages 11–18, New York, NY, USA, 2008. ACM.

[14] C. Liu, M. Li, and Y.-M. Wang. Post-rank reordering: resolving preference misalignments between search engines and end users. In CIKM '09, pages 641–650, 2009.

[15] T.-Y. Liu. Learning to Rank for Information Retrieval. Now Publisher, 2009.

[16] Q. Mei, D. Zhou, and K. Church. Query suggestion using hitting time. In CIKM '08, pages 469–478, 2008.

[17] M. Mitra, A. Singhal, and C. Buckley. Improving automatic query expansion. In SIGIR '98, pages 206–214, 1998.

[18] L. Page, S. Brin, R. Motwani, and T. Winograd. The pagerank citation ranking: Bringing order to the web. Technical Report 1999-66, Stanford InfoLab, 1999.

[19] F. Radlinski and T. Joachims. Query chains: learning to rank from implicit feedback. In KDD '05, pages 239–248.

[20] S. Robertson, S. Walker, S. Jones, M. Hancock-Beaulieu, and M. Gatford. Okapi at trec-3. pages 109–126, 1996.

[21] J. Rocchio. Relevance Feedback in Information Retrieval, pages 313–323. 1971.

[22] F. Silvestri. Mining query logs: Turning search usage data into knowledge. Foundations and Trends in Information Retrieval, 4(1-2):1–174, 2010.

[23] Y. Song and L. He. Optimal rare query suggestion with implicit user feedback. In WWW '10, pages 901–910.

[24] X. Wang and C. Zhai. Mining term association patterns from search logs for effective query reformulation. In CIKM '08, pages 479–488, 2008.

[25] C. Zhai and J. Lafferty. Model-based feedback in the language modeling approach to information retrieval. In CIKM '01, pages 403–410. ACM, 2001.

Language Models for Keyword Search over Data Graphs*

Yosi Mass†‡ and Yehoshua Sagiv‡
†IBM Haifa Research Lab, Haifa 31905, Israel
yosimass@il.ibm.com
‡The Hebrew University, Jerusalem 91904, Israel
sagiv@cs.huji.ac.il

ABSTRACT

In keyword search over data graphs, an answer is a non-redundant subtree that includes the given keywords. This paper focuses on improving the effectiveness of that type of search. A novel approach that combines language models with structural relevance is described. The proposed approach consists of three steps. First, language models are used to assign dynamic, query-dependent weights to the graph. Those weights complement static weights that are pre-assigned to the graph. Second, an existing algorithm returns candidate answers based on their weights. Third, the candidate answers are re-ranked by creating a language model for each one. The effectiveness of the proposed approach is verified on a benchmark of three datasets: IMDB, Wikipedia and Mondial. The proposed approach outperforms all existing systems on the three datasets, which is a testament to its robustness. It is also shown that the effectiveness can be further improved by augmenting keyword queries with very basic knowledge about the structure.

Categories and Subject Descriptors

H.3.3 [**Information Storage and Retrieval**]: Information Search and Retrieval—*Search processes*

General Terms

Algorithms, Experimentation, Performance

Keywords

Data graphs, language models, semantic weights, ranking

1. INTRODUCTION

Keyword search over free text is a very common and important tool. However, the emergence of large knowledge bases, such as DBPedia,[1] Yago,[2] Freebase,[3] the CIA World-Factbook,[4] to name just a few, enables a different type of search, where a user can get precise and focused answers to her information need. This is much preferable to keyword search that can only provide the user with a list of relevant documents that might contain the answers somewhere.

In general, knowledge bases contain information about entities and their relationships. In practice, they are typically represented as RDF triples consisting of a *subject* and an *object* that are entities connected through a *property*. Knowledge bases can also be stored in relational databases, which represent entities and their relationships by means of tuples and foreign keys.

Those representations can be transformed to data graphs, where nodes represent entities and edges correspond to relationships. Additional free text can be added to each entity or relationship, resulting in a richer representation. That is, the graph structure represents the semantics of entities and of the relationships among them, while the free text helps in deciding the relevancy of a particular entity or relationship to a given query.

Such data graphs enable a shift in the paradigm of search, from a document as the basic returned unit to a finer granularity of entities. An answer can be a single entity or a set of entities connected through some relationships. There are already TREC and INEX tracks for returning entities instead of full documents.

Consider, for example, a user who needs to find the language spoken in Poland. A traditional search engine returns documents about Poland that might contain the needed information. But if we have both Poland and Polish as entities of the types *country* and *language*, respectively, and these two entities are connected by an edge, then we can return Polish as the spoken language of Poland.

The main drawback is that querying data graphs requires a nontrivial understanding of their underlying schemas. Even RDF, which is regarded as having no schema, requires a nontrivial query language, such as SPARQL. For databases, we need to use SQL as the query language. Both SPARQL and SQL are too difficult for end users.

To overcome this problem, a lot of research has been conducted in recent years on efficient and effective methods for keyword search over data graphs. The idea is that users

*This work was partially supported by The German-Israeli Foundation for Scientific Research & Development (Grant 973-150.6/2007).

Permission to make digital or hard copies of all or part of this work for personal or classroom use is granted without fee provided that copies are not made or distributed for profit or commercial advantage and that copies bear this notice and the full citation on the first page. To copy otherwise, to republish, to post on servers or to redistribute to lists, requires prior specific permission and/or a fee.
WSDM'12, February 8–12, 2012, Seattle, Washingtion, USA.
Copyright 2012 ACM 978-1-4503-0747-5/12/02 ...$10.00.

[1]`http://dbpedia.org`
[2]`http://www.mpi-inf.mpg.de/yago-naga/yago/`
[3]`http://freebase.com`
[4]`https://www.cia.gov/library/publications/the-world-factbook/index.html`

can still pose queries consisting merely of keywords, and the system exploits the semantics encoded in the data graph in order to return entities and relationships as answers.

In keyword search over data graphs, an answer is a non-redundant subtree that includes the given keywords. Non-redundancy means that an answer does not have a proper subtree that also contains all the keywords. There are two main challenges. The first is to develop an algorithm for efficiently generating answers. In this paper, we use the algorithm of [9]. To apply this algorithm, we first have to create a node for each keyword q_i of the given query, and then add edges from q_i to all the nodes of the data graph that contain q_i.

The second challenge is to find methods for effectively ranking the generated answers according to their relevance to the user. This challenge is the focus of our work. There are two main approaches regarding how to rank answers: IR methods and proximity search. In the former, IR techniques are used, whereas in the latter the idea is to minimize the structural (i.e., semantic) weights of answers. Some papers have tried to combine IR methods with structural weights into a unified approach to the task of ranking answers.

In this paper, we propose a novel ranking method that is based on language models as well as structural weights. Our approach consists of the following steps. First, we assign structural weights to the nodes and edges of the data graph. These weights are derived only from semantic considerations and are *static*, namely, they are independent of any particular query. Second, language models are used to assign weights to the edges that connect the keywords of a given query to the nodes that contain them. These weights are *dynamic*, that is, they depend on the given query. Third, an existing algorithm [9] returns candidate answers based on their weights. Finally, the candidate answers are re-ranked by creating a language model for each one.

The contributions of this paper are the following. First, we describe a novel and effective ranking technique that combines language models with structural weights. Second, we show that our ranking model is robust by testing it on the first (and only) standard benchmark for keyword search over data graphs, which was recently developed by [4]. This benchmark consists of three datasets: IMDB, Wikipedia and Mondial, as well as fifty queries for each one. On each of these datasets, our approach outperforms in terms of MAP (mean average precision) all the existing systems that have been tested so far on this benchmark. Additional tests, using other metrics, also support the robustness of our approach. Finally, we show that the effectiveness can be further improved by augmenting keyword queries with very basic knowledge about the structure of the data graph.

The rest of the paper is organized as follows. In Section 2, we discuss related work. In Section 3, we describe the data model. In Section 4, we describe how to rank answers (which are subtrees) based on a combination of language models and semantic considerations. Section 5 describes the implementation and experiments that verify the effectiveness of our approach. We conclude in Section 6.

2. RELATED WORK

A survey of systems for keywords search over data graphs is given in [4]. There are two main approaches for ranking answers: IR methods and proximity search. In the former IR techniques are used, whereas in the latter the idea is to minimize the weights of trees that contain the keywords of the query. In this paper, we focus on the effectiveness of the search. Thus, we discuss that aspect of the state-of-the-art, and ignore considerations related to efficiency.

The systems of [2, 12] were the first to introduce keyword search over databases. An answer in both systems consists of tuples that contain all the keywords of the query. In [12], they construct an execution plan for generating networks of tuples that together contain all the query keywords. Both [2, 12] use a very simple ranking model that counts the number of tuples in an answer (the fewer, the better).

The systems that rank answers by means of IR methods are [11, 15, 5, 16]. The work of [11] extends the scoring model of [12] as follows. Each tuple in an answer gets an IR score that is produced by some underlying inverted index on columns that contain text attributes. That index could be provided, for example, by an RDBMS. The IR score of a set of tuples is defined as the sum of the IR scores of the individual tuples divided by the number of tuples. Thus, it is the average IR score per tuple of an answer. The work of [15] extends the work of [11] by introducing several normalization factors that are used for combining the individual IR scores into an IR score of an answer. The work of [5] uses a cover density ranking. In [16], instead of combining individual tuple scores as in [11], they view a whole answer as a *virtual document* and use IR methods, such as *tf* and *idf*, to assign a relevance score. They also apply some normalization factors; for example, a *size normalization factor* that depends on the number of tuples in an answer (the fewer tuples, the better). In this work, we assign IR scores to nodes and edges as well as to full answers. We combine the IR scores with structural weights that reflect the semantic strength of answers.

The systems of [3, 13, 7, 10, 9] employ the second approach that assigns weights to the nodes and edges of the data graph, and then ranks answers by increasing weight. In [3], they find answers by starting instances of Dijkstra shortest-path algorithm from several nodes that (between them) contain the keywords of the query. When all these instances meet in a node r, they find an answer (having r as its root). In [3], weights are assigned to nodes based on their *prestige*. The work of [13] improves the efficiency of [3] by allowing forward search from potential roots toward leaves, in addition to the backward search of [3]. In [7], they produce answers based on an algorithm for finding the minimum group Steiner tree. They extend this algorithm so that it can find some more trees, in additional to the minimal one. In [9], the emphasis is on provable properties. Their algorithm enumerates answers with polynomial delay in a 2-approximate order by increasing height. That algorithm can provably find all the non-redundant subtrees (of the data graph) that contain the keywords of the query. In [10], the focus is on efficiency which is achieved by keeping, in a bi-level index, some of the shortest paths that have already been computed. They mention that their scoring function for answers combines both the graph structure and content scoring using IR methods. However, since their focus is on efficiency, they do not give details on their scoring function. In this paper, we present a ranking method that uses structural weights and combines them in a novel way with IR scores that are derived by means of language models.

The work of [8] has developed a language-model approach to SPARQL queries that are augmented with keywords. (The evaluation is, of course, over RDF graphs). They use a *wit-*

ness count for each triplet to indicate the number of times that the triplet was extracted from some text. Then they build a language model for a given query as well as a language model for each answer. Ranking is done according to the Kullback-Leibler (KL) divergence between the language models of the query and each answer. This work requires queries to be formulated in SPARQL, so it does not fall under the category of keyword search over data graphs.

Keyword search is attractive, since it does not require any knowledge of the underlying schema of the data graph. However, it still has its limitations, because the user cannot precisely define her information need. Several papers [17, 6, 14, 18] have tried to bridge the gap between fully structured queries and keyword search by letting the user refine her query. The work of [17] suggests an interactive framework, where the user starts with keyword search and then, through an exploration phase, she can focus her query by refining and filtering. Finally, she can also aggregate results that are either similar or complementary. The work of [6] suggests a UI, where the user starts with keyword search and the system presents several interpretations for the query. The user can select an interpretation and the system then formulates a more structured query. Similarly, the work of [14] allows the user to start with keyword search, and then it selects the best interpretation and presents the results to the user. The work of [18] suggests a new query language that is based on keyword search, but with a simple notation for structural constraints using conjunctions and nesting with relations. In this paper, we show that the effectiveness of keyword search can be increased significantly by using very simple syntax that expresses basic knowledge about the schema of the data graph.

3. THE DATA MODEL

Data is stored in a directed graph. Each *node* and *edge* has a set of attribute-value pairs. Some values are short (e.g., an integer or a character string) while others comprise free text. Two special attributes are *name* and *type*. The name is a short string that serves as a not-necessarily-unique identifier; for example, the name could be the title of an article or the name of a country. The type denotes the class to which the given node or edge belongs; for example, the type could be article or country. There can be several edges between a pair of nodes. For example, the graph can represent a social network, where nodes are people and the edges correspond to relationships between people, such as friendship, business associations, etc. In summary, a node or an edge can have any number of attributes, and each one has a value.

The attributes of a node or an edge describe semantic information. We group the attributes into three semantic *fields* (that could overlap). The *title* field comprises the values of the name and type attributes. The *content* field of either a node or an edge consists of all its attributes and their values. Finally, the *structure* field captures the structural semantics of the given node or edge. It contains the value of the type attribute as well as all the other attributes, but without their values.

The title and content fields (of a node or an edge) contain textual descriptions that we use to assign IR scores. We distinguish between these two fields in order to control the relative importance of an occurrence (of a query keyword) in the title compared with an occurrence only in the content field. The structure field does not carry a textual description. Typically, terms that appear in the structure field are repeated in many nodes or edges. For example, in the IMDB dataset, "movie" is the value of the type of all the movie nodes; hence, it appears in all them. We use the structure field to improve efficiency. In particular, occurrences of query keywords in the structure field are handled differently, as we explain in Section 4.4.

A data graph is usually derived from a database or an XML file. For example, when creating a data graph from a relational database, each tuple t becomes a node v_t. The value of the type attribute of v_t is the relation name to which t belongs. The attribute-value pairs of the node v_t are those of the tuple t, excluding foreign keys. That is, a foreign key is represented in the data graph by an edge (hence, the corresponding attribute-value pair is not included in the node).

A query $Q = (q_1, ..., q_n)$ on the data graph is given as a set of keywords. Each q_i should match a term in the content field of some node or edge (i.e., we use the AND semantics).

An *answer* to a query $Q = (q_1, ..., q_n)$ is a *non-redundant* subtree A of the data graph, such that A contains all the keywords of Q. Containment means that each keyword appears in the content field of some node or edge. Non-redundancy means that an answer does not have a proper subtree that also contains all the keywords of the query. Note that non-redundancy does *not* imply minimality, and a query could have a large number of answers. As an example, consider the query "movie, love." An answer to this query is not necessarily a single node. There could be a subtree with one node that has "movie" in its structure field (e.g., as the value of its type) and with another node that contains "love" in its content field.

We use a system [9] that handles attribute-value pairs in edges by adding nodes that are called *connectors* [1]. Due to a lack of space, we omit the technical details and simply assume that only nodes have attribute-value pairs.

4. RANKING ANSWERS

Two principles guide us when ranking answers by their relevance to the query. First, a smaller subtree typically represents a stronger semantic connection between its nodes. Second, the relevance of an individual node or edge depends on its text; in particular, to be relevant, the text should include (at least some of) the keywords of the query. Thus, we would prefer subtrees that are small, and have nodes and edges that are highly relevant to the keywords of the query. These two requirements are not congruent. In other words, even in a highly relevant subtree, some nodes and edges may not contain any keyword of the query. Similarly, a relevant subtree is not necessarily small. In this section, we describe how to rank subtrees based on a combination of language models and structural weights.

4.1 Language Models

Language models (abbr. LM) for IR define a probability space for each document d of a given collection. The probability space of d, called the *document model*, measures the probability to generate a term t given the document d. Sometimes a document has multiple *fields*, that is, it can be viewed in different ways. For example, we may consider just the title of each document, or alternatively, take the whole document into account. For a given field f, we use d_f to denote that only the text of field f is taken into account when referring to the document d. For example, d_{title} means that only the text in the title of d is considered. The field *content* means that all of the text (including the title) is considered.

We assume that query terms are independent of one another and use the Jelinek-Mercer smoothing [19]. Thus, for a query $Q = (q_1, ..., q_n)$ and field f of document d, we get

$$P(Q|d_f) = \prod_i ((1-\lambda)P(q_i|d_f) + \lambda P(q_i|C)) \quad (1)$$

where C is the whole collection and $0 \leq \lambda \leq 1$ is a smoothing parameter. The smoothing is done over the whole collection C, rather than just its field f (i.e., C_f), because some fields (e.g., title) may not have enough text to make the smoothing effective. Typically, the probabilities on the right side of Equation (1) are determined by the maximum-likelihood estimate, namely,

$$P(q_i|X) = \frac{tf(q_i, X)}{\sum_{t \in X} tf(t, X)}, \quad (2)$$

where X is either d_f or C, and $tf(t, X)$ is the term frequency of t in X.

4.2 Language Models for Data Graphs

Recall that an answer A is a subtree of a given data graph G. We now describe how to extend the above language model to answers that are graphs rather than documents. In doing so, there is no need to assume that A is a subtree of G; rather, A could be any subgraph of G.

Consider an answer $A = (V, E)$, where V is the set of nodes and E is the set of edges. The text associated with A, denoted by text(A), is obtained by concatenating the texts of all the nodes and edges of A. Similarly to documents, A can have multiple fields. For example, the title field of A, denoted by A_{title}, is the graph A under the restriction that in each node and edge, only the title field of the text is considered. Thus, text(A_{title}) is the result of concatenating the title fields of all the nodes and edges of A.

Analogously to Equation (1), the following is the probability that a query $Q = (q_1, ..., q_n)$ is generated by a field f of an answer A (i.e., by A_f).

$$P(Q|A_f) = \prod_i ((1-\lambda)P(q_i|A_f) + \lambda P(q_i|G)) \quad (3)$$

As explained earlier, the smoothing term considers the whole collection, which in this case is the data graph G.

We need to estimate the probability $P(q_i|X)$, where X is either A_f or G. Ideally, both the graph structure and the text of X should be taken into account. However, developing language models that consider the graph structure is beyond the scope of this paper, and is left for future research. In this section, we only deal with the text, and the graph structure is handled in Section 4.4. Thus, we estimate the probabilities on the right side of Equation (3) similarly to Equation (2), that is,

$$P(q_i|X) = \frac{tf(q_i, \text{text}(X))}{\sum_{t \in \text{text}(X)} tf(t, \text{text}(X))}, \quad (4)$$

where X is either A_f or G, and $tf(t, \text{text}(X))$ is the term frequency of t in text(X).

4.3 Normalization

In this work, language models are used for ranking nodes and answers (which are subtrees of the data graph). The former are just a special case of the latter, because a node is a subtree. Alternatively, a node v can be viewed just as a document that consists of the text in v. Thus, Equations (1) and (3) apply equally to nodes. In order to deal uniformly with nodes and answers, we will use Equation (3) for both.

As explained later, we combine probabilities of language models with weights of semantic connections. A higher probability means that the answer is more relevant, whereas a lower weight indicates a stronger semantic connection. Therefore, to combine probabilities with weights, we need to normalize them to the interval $[0, 1]$; and in the case of probabilities, we should also invert them. Consequently, for both of them, lower normalized values are preferable (i.e., indicate higher relevance). This section describes how we process probabilities. Weights are discussed later.

When using Equation (3) for ranking, we actually apply it twice: once with *title* as the field f and then with *content* as f. Sometimes, the former probability is considerably higher than the latter. Thus, we normalize each of these two probabilities before taking their linear combination. Another consideration is to avoid underflow when taking the product of many probabilities. We do it by applying logarithm to Equation (3), thereby summing instead of multiplying. Note that taking the logarithm does not effect the ranking order of relevant nodes or answers. Next, we describe in detail how the normalization is done.

As already noted, we start by applying logarithm to Equation (3). The result is called the *IR relevance* of A_f with respect to the query Q, denoted by $R(Q, A_f)$. Thus,

$$R(Q, A_f) = \sum_i (\ln((1-\lambda)P(q_i|A_f) + \lambda P(q_i|G))), \quad (5)$$

where f is either *content* or *title*, and A is either a single node or a whole subtree, depending on what we rank.

As explained later, we apply Equation (5) to some elements (which are either nodes or answers) and choose the top-K. Let Γ be the set of those top-K elements. Suppose that $R_{\max}$ is the maximum of Equation (5) over all the elements of Γ, namely, $R_{\max} = \max_{A \in \Gamma}\{R(Q, A_f)\}$. Note that $R_{\max} \leq 0$, because the $R(Q, A_f)$ are obtained by taking logarithm of probabilities. The values obtained for the elements of Γ are in the interval $(-\infty, R_{\max}]$, where $R_{\max} \leq 0$. We need to normalize those values to the interval $[0, 1]$; and since we want lower values to be preferable, $R_{\max}$ should become 0 and $-\infty$ should become 1. So, we apply the following transformation that computes the *IR l-score*[5] of A_f with respect to the query Q, denoted by $lscr^{ir}(Q, A_f)$.

$$lscr^{ir}(Q, A_f) = 1 - \frac{1}{\ln(-R(Q, A_f) + R_{\max} + 2.718)} \quad (6)$$

We use logarithm in the above equation so that $lscr^{ir}(Q, A_f)$ will not grow too fast as $R(Q, A_f)$ gets smaller (i.e., more negative). Note that the values of $lscr^{ir}(Q, A_f)$ are in the interval $[0, 1]$. Furthermore, smaller values of $lscr^{ir}(Q, A_f)$ are better, namely, more relevant.

By using Equation (6), we obtain two normalized scores: $lscr^{ir}(Q, A_{content})$ and $lscr^{ir}(Q, A_{title})$ for the fields *content* and *title*, respectively. The next equation computes the IR l-score of A with respect to the query Q as a linear combi-

[5]The name *l-score* emphasizes that lower scores are better.

nation of the two, where $0 \leq \alpha \leq 1$.

$$lscr^{ir}(Q, A) = \alpha \cdot lscr^{ir}(Q, A_{title}) + (1-\alpha) lscr^{ir}(Q, A_{content}) \quad (7)$$

The above equation enables us to control the weight we give to the title field compared with that of the content field.

The normalization of Equation (6) depends only on $R_{\max}$ (but not on the minimum in the set of values that is normalized). Therefore, we can efficiently find the top-K elements (answers or nodes) according to Equation (7), even though each of $lscr^{ir}(Q, A_{title})$ and $lscr^{ir}(Q, A_{content})$ is normalized before it is used in Equation (7).

4.4 Graph Weights

We assign weights to the nodes and edges of a data graph based on two criteria: semantic strength and relevance to the given query. The former induces static weights (i.e., they do not depend on the query), whereas the latter determines dynamic weights.

The static weights are assigned to the graph that is generated from the original data, as explained in Section 3. These weights reflect the semantic strength of the nodes and edges. In this context, lower weights are better, because a smaller answer (i.e., subtree) is deemed more meaningful.

When processing a given query Q, nodes for the keywords of Q are created and connected to nodes of the graph that are relevant to Q. The edges that emanate from (the nodes for) those keywords get dynamic weights that are obtained from the IR l-scores of Equation (7). Recall that IR l-scores, just like weights, are better when they are smaller.

We start by discussing the static weights. The naive approach of assigning equal weights to all the nodes and edges is not effective [4]. We assign static weights as follows.

Static weights of nodes. The weight of a node v, denoted by $w(v)$, is static and depends on its incoming edges. Intuitively, nodes with many incoming edges are more important and, hence, should be assigned lower weights (which are better than higher ones).

Formally, $w(v)$ is defined as follows. Let $idg(v)$ be the in-degree of node v. If $idg(v) > 0$, then

$$w(v) = \frac{1}{\ln(1.718 + idg(v))}. \quad (8)$$

Otherwise (for isolated nodes or nodes with no incoming edges), we set $w(v) = 1$ which is the largest weight.

The weight of a node v depends inversely on the number of edges that point to v. The more incoming edges there are, the lower the weight is, which means that nodes with many incoming edges are more important. We use logarithm in the above formula so that the weight will not decay too fast as the number of edges increases. Due to the constant 1.718, the value $w(v)$ is in the interval $[0, 1]$. Nodes with a single incoming edge have weight 1 (namely, they are the least important). Our way of assigning weights to nodes is similar to *node prestige* [3]; however, they use some normalization while our weights are already in the interval $[0, 1]$.

Static weights of edges. When creating a graph from the original data source (see Section 3), each edge $e = (u, v)$ is assigned a static weight $w(e)$ that depends on the number of similar edges [9]. By definition, an edge e' is *similar* to e if at one end they have the same node and at the other end they have the same type. Intuitively, an edge with fewer similar edges is more unique and, hence, describes a stronger semantic relationship between its nodes.

Formally, let $fdg(e)$ be the number of edges that have the same type as e and are from u to nodes with the same type as v. Similarly, let $tdg(e)$ be the number of edges that have the same type as e, emanate from nodes with the same type as u and point to v. Note that e itself is counted in both $fdg(e)$ and $tdg(e)$. Then,

$$w(e) = 1 - \frac{1}{\ln(0.718 + fdg(e) + tdg(e))}. \quad (9)$$

The larger the number of edges that are similar to e, the higher the weight of e. Thus, an edge is more important if it has only a few similar edges. The logarithm is used so that the weight will not grow too fast as the number of similar edges increases. The constant 0.718 guarantees that $w(e)$ is in the interval $[0, 1]$. In particular, $w(e) = 0$ when e has no similar edges (other than itself), because in this case, $fdg(e) = 1$ and $tdg(e) = 1$.

Dynamic weights of edges. In search over data graphs, some keywords target the structure field while others are aimed at the content field. For example, a user who wants to find Wikipedia pages that were modified by AlleborgoBot would pose the query "page AlleborgoBot." The keyword "page" targets the type of a relevant node (which is in the structure field) while "AlleborgoBot" is aimed at the title or content of (possibly) another node. When a keyword (e.g., "page") may appear either in the structure field or only in the content field, we prefer occurrences in the former.

To generate answers for a query $Q = (q_1, ..., q_n)$, a node is created for each q_i and connected to all nodes v that contain q_i. The node for q_i has weight 1 (which is actually equivalent to the rule for static weights, because that node does not have any incoming edges). The weight of the edge from (the node for) q_i to v depends on whether q_i appears in the structure field or not; the aforementioned example is a motivation for doing so. If q_i appears in the structure field of v, then the weight is 0 (i.e., the best). If q_i appears in the content field of v but not in its structure field, the weight of the edge e from q_i to v is the IR l-score of v with respect to the whole query Q (rather than just q_i), as given by Equation (7).

For efficiency reasons, we do not connect q_i to all the nodes containing it, but only to those that are most relevant. We apply a two-step process as follows. First, for each keyword q_i, we use Equation (7) to select the top-K nodes among those having q_i in the content (which includes the title) field, but not in the structure field. (K is a parameter of the system.) We connect q_i to each of the selected nodes. The weight of the connecting edge is the IR l-score of Equation (7). We say that a node is *relevant* if it is connected to some keywords in the first step.

In the second step, we connect each q_i to all nodes v, such that v contains q_i in its structure field and is in the vicinity of some relevant node, namely, within a distance[6] r. We call r the *distance parameter*. The connecting edge has weight 0. It could be (e.g., the query "movie" over IMDB) that there are no relevant nodes at the end of the first step (that is, whenever a keyword appears in a node, it is also included in the structure field). In this case, we connect every q_i to the top-K nodes (according to Equation (7)) that contain q_i. The connecting edges have weight 0. Note that the structure field is a subset of the content field, so q_i appears

[6]The *distance* between two nodes is defined as the number of edges on the shortest path that connects them.

in the content field of the nodes to which it is connected, and it could also be in the title field of some of those nodes.

4.5 Scoring Answers

We now describe how to rank answers by combining the IR l-scores of Equation (7) with the graph weights of the previous section. First, we define the *structural weight* of an answer $A = (V, E)$, denoted by[7] $W(Q, A)$, as the sum of weights of all its nodes and edges, that is,

$$W(Q,A) = \sum_{v \in V} w(v) + \sum_{e \in E} w(e) \,. \qquad (10)$$

Before combining IR l-scores with structural weights, we need to normalize the latter (the former were already normalized in Section 4.3). Let $W_{\min} = \min_{A \in \Gamma}\{W(Q, A)\}$ be the minimum structural weight over all the generated answers. The structural weights are in the interval $[W_{\min}, \infty)$, where $W_{\min} \geq 0$. We need to normalize those weights to the interval $[0, 1]$. As a result, $W_{\min}$ will become 0 and ∞ will become 1. We do it by applying the following transformation that computes the *structural l-score* of an answer A with respect to the query Q, denoted by $lscr^s(Q, A)$.

$$lscr^s(Q,A) = 1 - \frac{1}{\ln(W(Q,A) - W_{\min} + 2.718)} \qquad (11)$$

We use logarithm in the above equation so that the structural l-score will not grow too fast as $W(Q, A)$ gets larger. Note that lower structural l-scores are preferable. Clearly, the values of $lscr^s(Q, A)$ are in the interval $[0, 1]$.

Now, we combine the IR l-score of Equation (7) with the structural l-score of Equation (11) as follows. The *l-score* of an answer A with respect to a query Q, denoted by $lscr(Q, A)$, is given by the linear combination

$$lscr(Q,A) = \beta \cdot lscr^s(Q,A) + (1-\beta) \cdot lscr^{ir}(Q,A)\,, \quad (12)$$

where $0 \leq \beta \leq 1$ controls the importance we give to the structural l-score compared to the IR l-score.

5. EXPERIMENTS

5.1 Datasets

In information retrieval, TREC[8] is an established methodology for evaluating search algorithms over free text. INEX[9] is a similar effort aimed at information retrieval from XML documents. However, only recently has an evaluation framework been developed by Coffman and Weaver [4] for testing the effectiveness of systems for keyword search over data graphs. The framework consists of three datasets: IMDB, Wikipedia and Mondial. For each data set, there are fifty queries and their assessment.

The datasets are given as relations. Each tuple of those relations has a unique id and may have some foreign keys pointing to other tuples. IMDB and Wikipedia contain six relations each, and Mondial contains twenty four relations. Table 1 describes all the relations of IMDB and Wikipedia, as well as some of the main relations of Mondial.

IMDB and Wikipedia contain relatively large chunks of text, while Mondial has only short strings, such as names of countries and cities, etc. Specifically, the relations that have large amounts of text are *MovieInfo* from IMDB, which contains quotes from movies, and *PageContent* from Wikipedia, which comprises the actual content of pages. On the other hand, the Mondial data graph has a complex structure with a large number of edges, compared to the other two datasets.

Table 1: The three datasets

Dataset	Tuples
IMDB (6 relations)	1,673,074
Movie (id, title, year)	181,706
Person (id, name)	273,034
Character (id, name)	206,951
Role (id, type)	11
MovieInfo (id, movieId, info)	198,678
Cast (id, **movieId, roleId, personId, characterId**)	812,694
Wikipedia (6 relations)	206,318
Page (id, title)	5,540
PageContent (id, text)	5,540
User (id, name)	1,745
Revision (id, **pageId, pageContentId,userid**)	5,540
PageLinks (id, **pageId1, pageId2**)	187,951
UserGroups (id, group)	2
Mondial (24 relations)	17,115
Country (id, name)	195
Province (id, name, **countryId**)	1382
City (id, **countryId, provinceId**)	3,051
Organization (id, name, **countryId, provinceId, cityId**)	168
Language/Economy/Politcs (id, **countryId**)	711
Is_member(id,**countryId,organizationId**)	7,766
Borders(id,**countryId1,countryId1**)	305

5.2 Queries

For each dataset, the benchmark of [4] has fifty queries and their qrels (i.e., query relevance judgments). The average number of keywords per query is 2.91. This average excludes five queries of IMDB that consist of very long citations from movies. The average number of answers per query is 4.49.

For some queries, each answer is just a single tuple, while for others, an answer is a subtree consisting of several tuples and the edges connecting them. For example, the IMDB query #1, which is "denzel washington," should return the tuple of that actor. As another example, for the Wikipedia query #24, which is "lance armstrong tour de france," an answer is a subtree consisting of three tuples. For this particular query, there is just one relevant answer comprising the tuples: Page(id=183266, title="lance armstrong"), PageContent(id=188071, text="tour de france"), and Revision(id=1507622, pageId=183266, pageContentId=188071). The two edges of this answer connect the last tuple with the first and second ones.

5.3 System Implementation

We have translated each dataset into a data graph, where tuples are nodes and foriegn keys (shown in bold in Table 1) are edges. Thus, text is associated only with nodes but not with edges.

Each data graph is indexed into two data structures. First, the skeleton of the graph (i.e., the nodes and edges with their ids only) is built as required by the system [9] that we have used. We refer to this data structure as the *graph index*. The second data structure is an Apache Lucene[10] inverted index,

[7]We denote it by $W(Q, A)$, rather than $W(A)$, because some weights are dynamic, i.e., depend on the query Q.

[8]http://trec.nist.gov/

[9]http://inex.is.informatik.uni-duisburg.de/

[10]http://lucene.apache.org/

where each node appears as a separate document consisting of three fields: content, title and structure, as described in Section 3. We use the Lucene *Document* and *Field* classes to implement those three fields. We have applied stemming and stop-word removal to the three fields of each node.

When given a query $Q = (q_1, \ldots, q_n)$, we need to connect each q_i to the data graph according to the two-step process of Section 4.4. Lucene enables us to do the first step efficiently (without having to implement it from scratch). For the second step, we use the graph index.

After attaching the keywords and assigning the dynamic weights to their edges, as describe in Section 4.4, we need to generate the top-k subtrees according to Equation (12). However, there is no practical algorithm for doing that. Thus, we apply the algorithm of [9] that produces answers based on the structural weight of Equation (10). As done in the benchmark of [4], we generate k answers (where k is a parameter) and re-rank them by the score of Equation (12). These answers do not include the nodes of the keywords.

5.4 The Setup of the Experiments

We ran our system on the benchmark of [4]. We show the results in the same manner as in [4], and include a comparison with all the systems that they tested. The experimental results for those systems were taken from [4]. The following systems were evaluated in [4]: BANKS [3], DISCOVER [12], Efficient [11], Bidirectional [13], Effective [15], DPBF [7], BLINKS [10], SPARK [16], and CD [5]. Our system is called GraphLM.

There are several parameters that should be learned in our algorithm. Those are the title weight α in Equation (7), the structure weight β in Equation (12), the collection-smoothing parameter λ in Equation (5), the parameter K that controls the number of nodes retrieved for each keyword of the query, and the distance parameter r. (The last two parameters are discussed in Sections 4.4.) Section 5.6 describes how we have empirically learned the first two parameters α and β. For λ we have selected the common value 0.1 [19]. Learning the optimal values of K and r is left for future work. We have selected $K = 10,000$ and $r = 4$. Finally, as in [4], our system produced $k = 1,000$ answers for each query.

We use the same four IR metrics as in [4], namely, *MAP* (mean average precision), *top*-1 (which counts how many queries returned the correct top result), *MRR* (mean reciprocal rank) and *11-point interpolated precision*. To compute the mean reciprocal rank, we take for each query, the inverse of the rank of the first correct answer (i.e., $1/rank$), and then average over all queries. The 11-point interpolated precision computes the precision at 11 recall points (from 0.0 to 1.0), and it is the average over all queries.

5.5 GraphLM Compared to State-of-the-Art

Figure 1 shows the MAP of GraphLM in comparison with all the other systems. For the GraphLM runs, we have used $\alpha = 0.7$ and $\beta = 0.8$ which are the optimal values for all of the three collections (see Section 5.6).

GraphLM outperforms all the other systems on each of the three datasets. On IMDB, it gets MAP=0.623, while for BANKS [3] (the second-best system) the MAP is 0.5. This is an improvement of about 25%. On Mondial, GraphLM has MAP=0.828 compared with MAP=0.82 for DPBF [7] (the second-best system). On Wikipedia, GraphLM gets MAP=0.626, whereas CD [5] (the second-best system) has MAP=0.57. The fact that our system is the best on all three datasets is a testament to its robustness.

Overall, the MAP values for Mondial are much higher than for the other two datasets. This is quite expected, because Mondial does not have a lot of free text attached to its data graph.

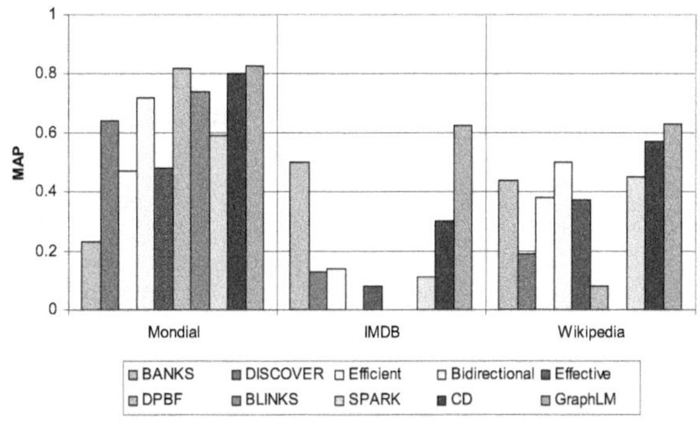

Figure 1: MAP of GraphLM compared with state-of-the-art systems ($\alpha = 0.7$, $\beta = 0.8$)

Figure 2 shows the MRR of all the systems, for the three datasets, when running a subset of the queries where exactly one database tuple is relevant (20, 20, and 15 queries for the Mondial, IMDB and Wikipedia datasets respectively).

On IMDB, GraphLM outperforms all the other systems, having MRR = 0.925 compared with 0.86 for BANKS [3], which is the second. GraphLM is also the best on Wikipedia, having MRR = 1.0 compared with 0.94 for CD [5], which is the second. On Mondial, GraphLM is the second with MRR = 0.891, whereas Bidirectional [13] is the best with MRR = 0.97. Once again, these results confirm the robustness of our system.

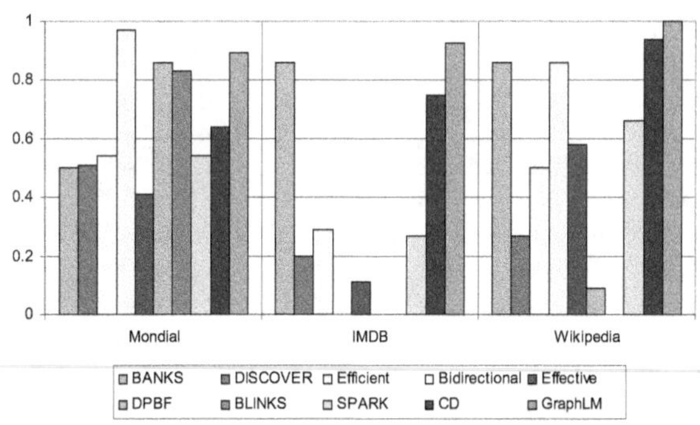

Figure 2: Mean reciprocal rank of GraphLM compared with state-of-the-art systems for the queries where exactly one tuple is relevant ($\alpha = 0.7$, $\beta = 0.8$)

Table 2 shows the top-1 and MRR for the fifty queries of Mondial. Our system achieves top-1 = 37 and MRR = 0.8 compared with 37 and 0.823, respectively, for DPBF [7]. The fact that our system has the second highest MRR on Mondial is consist with the observation that on this dataset, its MAP is just slightly higher than the best state-of-the-art. The values of top-1 and MRR are not given in [4] for the other two datasets. Our values are shown in Table 3.

Figure 3 shows the MAP for the three datasets as a function of k, which is the number of answers returned by the

Table 2: Top-1 and reciprocal rank for Mondial

	top-1	MRR
BANKS	16	0.358
DISCOVER	31	0.671
Efficient	21	0.514
Bidirectional	34	0.730
Effective	22	0.495
DPBF	37	0.823
BLINKS	36	0.770
SPARK	27	0.607
CD	36	0.804
GraphLM	37	0.800

Table 3: Top-1 and reciprocal rank of GraphLM for all the three datasets

	top-1	MRR
Mondial	37	0.800
IMDB	28	0.615
Wikipedia	32	0.716

system. We see that the top-50 answers have almost the same MAP as the top-1,000. Even for the top-20, the MAP is close to that of the top-1,000. These results are due to the fact that many queries of the benchmark have only a small number of correct answers. When $k \leq 10$, the largest drop of the MAP is for Mondial, because this dataset has the largest average number (5.9) of answers per query. The results of Figure 3 indicate that our system could perform well as a fact-retrieval engine.

Figure 4 shows the 11-point interpolated precision of all the systems for a subset of 10 Trec-style queries (#36–#45) of Wikipedia. GraphLM has a MAP of 0.276 for these 10 queries compared with 0.518 for Efficient [11], which is the best in this test. Although the MAP of our system is low, for the top-1 metric, we get 6 out of 10. (The top-1 results of this test are not reported in [4].) The cause of the poor performance of our system is probably the AND semantics, which we use. The qrels of the 10 Trec-style queries have answers that do not contain all the keywords. For example, query #36 is "soviet casualties world war ii" and its qrel includes the tuple "world war ii" of the relation Page, although that tuple does not have the rest of the keywords. The tuple "world war ii" of the relation PageContent is also in the qrel, and so is the subtree comprising these two tuples as well as their connecting tuple of the relation Revision. Since all the keywords appear in the tuple of the relation PageConent, our system returns two out of

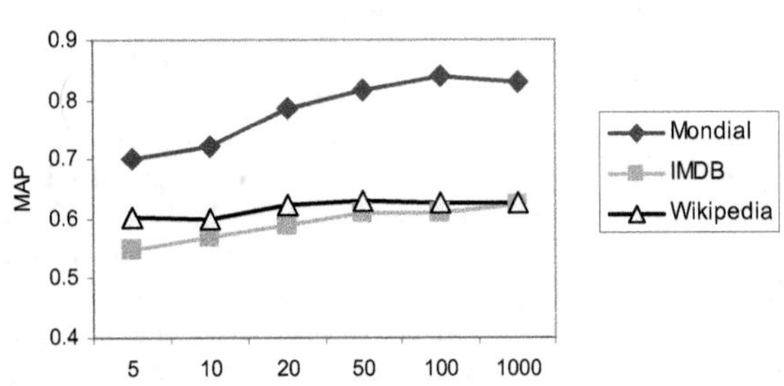

Figure 3: Varying the value of k ($\alpha = 0.7$, $\beta = 0.8$)

these three answers. A similar situation occurs with the tuple "Eastern_Front_(World_War_II)" of the relation Page and its corresponding tuples of the relations PageContent and Revision. We plan to extend our system so that it will support the OR semantics.

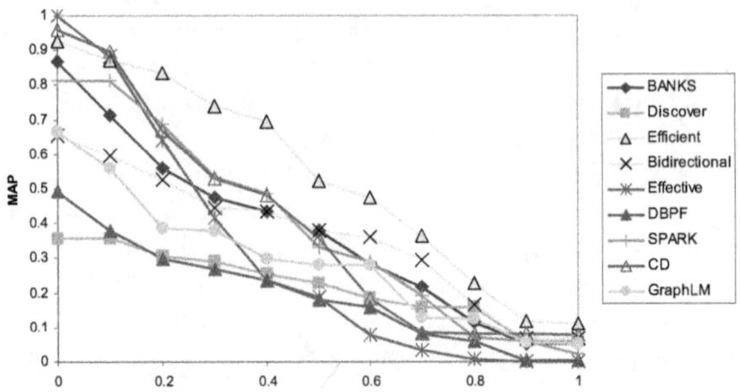

Figure 4: 11-point interpolated precision for the 10 Trec-style queries (#36–#45) of Wikipedia

5.6 Tuning the Parameters

We now describe experiments with different values for the parameters. Our goal is to determine the optimal setup. In particular, we have tried different values for the title weight α of Equation (7) and the structure weight β of Equation (12). Figure 5(a,b,c) shows the MAP when varying β for $\alpha = 0.5$, $\alpha = 0.7$ and $\alpha = 0.9$. We can see that the best MAP for each of the three datasets is achieved for $\beta \geq 0.6$, regardless of the value of α. For $\beta < 0.6$, the MAP starts dropping. Generally, the drop for $\alpha = 0.9$ is gentler whereas the drop for $\alpha = 0.5$ is sharper. Furthermore, we can see that in Wikipedia the drop is very fast, in Mondial there is a moderate drop, and in IMDB the MAP is the stablest across all values of β.

A closer look at the queries of the three datasets can explain this phenomenon. Wikipedia has 15 queries whose only correct answer is a single Page node that contains all the query keywords in its title. In addition, Wikipedia has a large number of nodes of type PageLinks (i.e., they represent hyperlinks), such that the name attribute of their title has the same value as in the Page nodes they link to. Thus, the probability $P(Q|v_{title})$ is the same for both the PageLinks nodes and the Page nodes they point to. But $P(Q|v_{content})$ is a little bit better for the PageLinks nodes than for the Page nodes, because the Page nodes have some more attributes. When β is large, most of the score of the nodes comes from their structural weight, which is a function of the number of incoming edges. Hence, Page nodes have a better score, because they have several incoming edges while PageLinks nodes have none. When β is small, the IR l-score is more dominant. Therefore, if α is also small, PageLinks nodes get a better IR l-score (and, hence, also an overall better score) and they are returned before the Page nodes (even though the latter are the desired answers).

A similar phenomenon exists (albeit less strongly) for Mondial, which has five queries with a single Country node as the only answer. Some of those countries have a province with the same name. In addition, a Province node has an attribute with the name of its country. Hence, when a keyword is a country name and there is also a province with that name, $P(Q|v_{content})$ is better for the Province node than for the Country node. So, when β and α are small, the Province

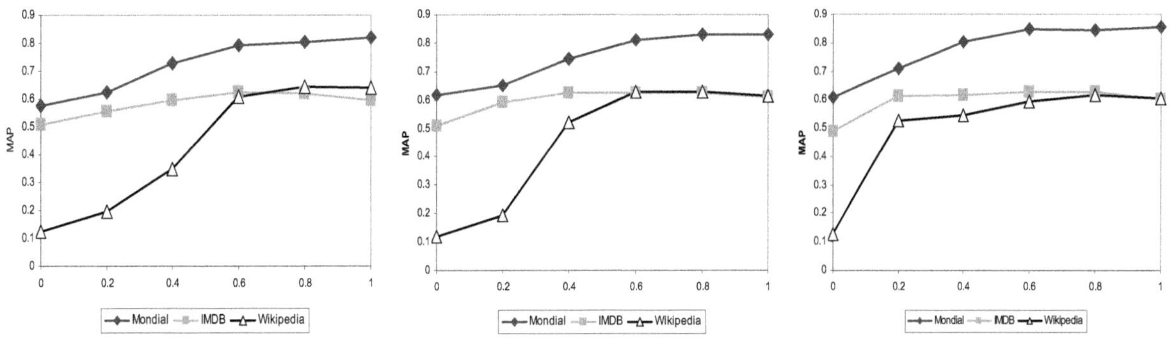

(a) Title weight $\alpha = 0.5$ (b) Title weight $\alpha = 0.7$ (c) Title weight $\alpha = 0.9$

Figure 5: Varying the structure weight β for different values of the title weight α

node is returned before the Country node (even though the latter is the desired answer). When β is large, the Country node is returned first, because it has more incoming edges than the Province node, so its structural l-score is better.

In IMDB, there are fewer nodes with the above characteristics and, so, it is less sensitive to changes in β and α.

Interestingly, for each of the three datasets, the MAP is almost unchanged when β ranges between 0.6 and 1.0. For example, consider $\beta = 0.8$ and $\beta = 1.0$ in Figure 5(b), where $\alpha = 0.7$. The MAP for IMDB is 0.623 and 0.609 for these two values of β, respectively. For Wikipedia, the MAP is 0.626 and 0.613, respectively. For Mondial, the MAP is 0.828 and 0.83, respectively. When $\beta = 1.0$, the final ranking by Equation (12) depends only on the structural score, whereas the IR l-score is ignored. However, the language models still determine the dynamic weights (of the edges connecting query keywords to the graph), which are part the structural l-score (see Equations (10) and (11)). It is important to take $\beta < 1.0$ when computing the final score (Equation (12)) if answers have internal[11] nodes that contain some of the query keywords. In the benchmark, there are not many queries with such answers.

Another interesting observation is that for a large β, Mondial has a higher MAP for $\alpha = 0.9$ whereas Wikipedia has a higher MAP for $\alpha = 0.5$. For example, when $\beta = 0.8$, Mondial has a MAP of 0.806 and 0.845 for $\alpha = 0.5$ and $\alpha = 0.9$, respectively, while the values for Wikipedia are 0.643 and 0.617, respectively. This can be explained by the fact that Wikipedia has more than 20 queries that return subtrees with multiple tuples, where some of the keywords appear in the content filed of nodes but not in the title field. For example, there are 10 queries whose relevant answers consist of three tuples: $Page \leftarrow Revision \rightarrow PageContent$. Two such queries are "lance armstrong tour de france" and "european hawfinch." In addition, there are 10 TREC-style queries, such as "soviet casualties world war ii" and "einstein special relativity," that return subtrees with more than one tuple where some of the keywords appear in the content field but in the title field. For those queries, a smaller α is better, because relevant answers have the query keywords in the content field but not in the title field. For example, when $\beta = 0.8$, the MAP of the above 20 queries is 0.323 and 0.194 for $\alpha = 0.5$ and $\alpha = 0.9$, respectively. For Mondial, the content and title fields are almost the same (except for some additional attributes with short values in the content field) and, therefore, a larger α is better.

Figure 6 shows the MAP for $\beta = 0.8$, when varying the value of α in Equation (7). For the three datasets, the MAP drops moderately for smaller values of α. For Mondial, the MAP drops from 0.845 when $\alpha = 0.9$ to 0.74 when $\alpha = 0$ (i.e., only the content field is taken into account). For Wikipedia, the MAP drops from 0.643 when $\alpha = 0.5$ to 0.415 when $\alpha = 0$.

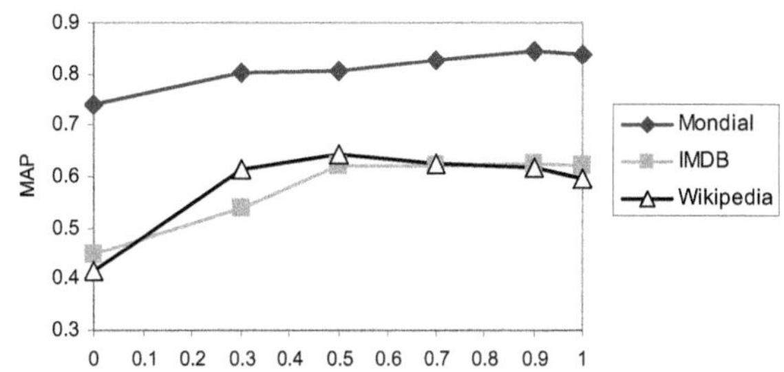

Figure 6: Varying the title weight α for the structure weight $\beta = 0.8$

To summarize, a larger value of β is preferred across all datasets. Regarding α, it depends on whether there are relevant answers where some query keywords appear only in the content (but not in the title) field. If so, a smaller α is preferred; otherwise, a larger α is better. Overall, $\alpha = 0.7$ is a good choice (i.e., close to the optimum). In practice, query logs can be used to determine the optimal value of α. If most queries target entities through their name, a larger α should be used, whereas if most queries target the content, a smaller value of α is better.

5.7 Advanced Options: Query Rewriting

We now describe how to manually rewrite queries so that they better reflect the intended meaning, as defined in the benchmark. This type of rewriting is straightforward and can be easily done by naive users. It utilizes two extensions to pure keyword search over data graphs [1]. The first enables a user to explicitly specify that a keyword should match only the structure by adding ? as a suffix. The second is grouping of several keywords by enclosing them inside curly brackets, which means that they all must appear

[11] Recall that after generating an answer, and before computing its score, we remove the nodes for the query keywords. A node is *internal* if it is not a leaf after that removal.

in the same node or edge. For example, consider again the Wikipedia query #24, which is "lance armstrong tour de france." According to its information need, we formulate the query as "{Page? lance armstrong} {PageContent? tour de france}." In this particular case, our system returns the only relevant result as the top answer.

To do the rewriting, some elementary knowledge about the structure of the data graph is required. The user may obtain that knowledge before she begins to submit queries to the system (e.g., by browsing some help files). Alternatively, the user can derive that knowledge by doing some exploratory search, as enunciated in [17]. Once that knowledge is obtained, the rewriting itself is straightforward.

We now describe how to connect the query keywords to the data graph. For ordinary keywords (i.e., that are neither inside curly brackets nor with ?), we apply the two steps as described in Section 4.4. Next, suppose that the query has a group of keywords inside curly brackets, such that at least one of them is without ? as a suffix.[12] A single node g is created for the whole group (rather than a node for each keyword of that group). We connect g to the top-K nodes that contain all the keywords of the group, but require that keywords with ? as a suffix would appear in the structure field of the connected nodes. The weight of an edge from g to a node v is determined as before using Equation (7), except that it is multiplied by the number of keywords in g that do not have ? as a suffix. We multiply the weight in order to achieve the same effect as when connecting each keyword of the group by a separate edge. For single keywords (i.e., not inside curly brackets) that have ? as a suffix, we apply just the second step that is described in Section 4.4.

We did the rewriting manually, but in strict adherence to the information need of each query, as specified in [4]. The numbers of rewritten queries (out of a total of 50 in each dataset) are: 23 in Mondial, 50 in IMDB and 25 in Wikipedia. Table 4 compares the MAP values before and after the rewriting (for all 50 queries of each dataset).

Table 4: MAP before and after query rewriting for all the three datasets ($\alpha = 0.7$, $\beta = 0.8$)

	Original Queries	After Rewriting
Mondial	0.828	0.856
IMDB	0.623	0.711
Wikipedia	0.626	0.847

There is a significant improvement for all three datasets. Moreover for Wikipedia, the rewriting increased the number of top-1 queries from 32 to 47.

6. CONCLUSIONS AND FUTURE WORK

We presented a novel and effective ranking technique for keyword search over data graphs. Our method combines language models with structural weights. The language models are used twice. First, they determine the dynamic weights that are assigned to the edges that connect query keywords to the data graph. Second, they are a part of the scoring function used in the final ranking of answers. The other part of that function incorporates the structural weights that encode the semantic strength of nodes and edges. We showed empirically how to tune the parameters of our system so as to achieve an optimal effectiveness over different types of data graphs and various types of queries.

We compared our approach with other systems on a standard benchmark of three datasets: IMDB, Wikipedia and Mondial. In terms of MAP, our system is the best on each of these datasets. For example on IMDB, it achieved an improvement of about 25% in the MAP compared with the second-best system. We further showed that by a simple rewriting of the queries, we can improve the performance of our system. For example, after query rewriting of some of the Wikipedia queries, we achieved an improvement of more than 35% in the MAP, and the top-1 value was increased from 32 to 47.

We conclude that systems for keyword search can also be used as effective fact-retrieval engines. However, there could still be limitations in interpreting correctly the user needs. Hence, a minimal user intervention may be needed in some cases, in order to get better results.

For future work, we plan to study how language models can also take the graph structure of an answer into account, and to incorporate support for disjunctive queries.

[12]We do not allow groups in which all the keywords have ? as a suffix.

7. REFERENCES

[1] H. Achiezra, K. Golenberg, B. Kimelfeld, and Y. Sagiv. Exploratory keyword search on data graphs. In *SIGMOD*, 2010.

[2] S. Agrawal, S. Chaudhuri, and G. Das. Dbxplorer: A system for keyword-based search over relational databases. In *ICDE*, 2002.

[3] G. Bhalotia, A. Hulgeri, C. Nakhe, and S. Chakrabarti. Keyword searching and browsing in databases using banks. In *ICDE*, pages 431–440, 2002.

[4] J. Coffman and A. C. Weaver. A framework for evaluating database keyword search strategies. In *CIKM*, 2010.

[5] J. Coffman and A. C. Weaver. Structured data retrieval using cover density ranking. In *KEYS*, pages 115–126, 2010.

[6] E. Demidova, X. Zhou, and W. Nejdl. Iqp: Incremental query construction, a probabilistic approach. In *ICDE*, 2010.

[7] B. Ding, J. X. Yu, S. Wang, L. Qin, X. Zhang, and X. Lin. Finding top-k min-cost connected trees in databases. In *ICDE*, pages 836–845, 2007.

[8] S. Elbassuoni1, M. Ramanath, R. Schenkel, M. Sydow, and G. Weikum1. Language-model-based ranking for queries on rdf-graphs. In *CIKM*, 2009.

[9] K. Golenberg, B. Kimelfeld, and Y. Sagiv. Keyword proximity search in complex data graphs. In *SIGMOD*, 2008.

[10] H. He, H. Wang, J. Yang, and P. S. Yu. Blinks: Ranked keyword searches on graphs. In *SIGMOD*, 2007.

[11] V. Hristidis, L. Gravano, and Y. Papakonstantinou. Efficient ir-style keyword search over relational databases. In *VLDB*, pages 850–861, 2003.

[12] V. Hristidis and Y. Papakonstantinou. Discover: Keyword search in relational databases. In *VLDB*, 2002.

[13] V. Kacholia, S. Pandit, S. Chakrabarti, S. Sudarshan, and R. Desai. Bidirectional expansion for keyword search on graph databases. In *VLDB*, pages 505–516, 2005.

[14] E. Kandogan, R. Krishnamurthy, S. Raghavan, S. Vaithyanathan, and H. Zhu. Avatar semantic search: a database approach to information retrieval. In *SIGMOD*, 2006.

[15] F. Liu, C. Yu, W. Meng, and A. Chowdhury. Effective keyword search in relational databases. In *SIGMOD*, pages 563–574, 2006.

[16] Y. Luo, X. Lin, W. Wang, and X. Zhou. SPARK: top-k keyword query in relational databases. In *SIGMOD*, pages 115–126, 2007.

[17] Y. Mass, M. Ramanath, Y. Sagiv, and G. Weikum. Iq: The case for iterative querying for knowledge. In *CIDR*, 2011.

[18] J. Pound, I. F. Ilyas, and G. Weddell. Expressive and flexible access to web-extracted data: A keyword-based structured query languag. In *SIGMOD*, 2010.

[19] C. Zhai and J. Lafferty. A study of smoothing methods for language models applied to information retrieval. *ACM Trans. Inf. Syst.*, 22(2):179–214, 2004.

Large-Scale Analysis of Individual and Task Differences in Search Result Page Examination Strategies

Georg Buscher
Microsoft Bing
Bellevue, WA 98004
georgbu@microsoft.com

Ryen W. White and Susan T. Dumais
Microsoft Research
Redmond, WA 98052
{ryenw, sdumais}@microsoft.com

Jeff Huang
University of Washington
Seattle, WA 98195
wsdm@jeffhuang.com

ABSTRACT

Understanding the impact of individual and task differences on search result page examination strategies is important in developing improved search engines. Characterizing these effects using query and click data alone is common but insufficient since they provide an incomplete picture of result examination behavior. Cursor- or gaze-tracking studies reveal richer interaction patterns but are often done in small-scale laboratory settings. In this paper we leverage large-scale rich behavioral log data in a naturalistic setting. We examine queries, clicks, cursor movements, scrolling, and text highlighting for millions of queries on the Bing commercial search engine to better understand the impact of user, task, and user-task interactions on user behavior on search result pages (SERPs). By clustering users based on cursor features, we identify individual, task, and user-task differences in how users examine results which are similar to those observed in small-scale studies. Our findings have implications for developing search support for behaviorally-similar searcher cohorts, modeling search behavior, and designing search systems that leverage implicit feedback.

Categories and Subject Descriptors

H.3.3 [**Information Storage and Retrieval**]: Information Search and Retrieval–*search process, selection process.*

General Terms

Experimentation, Human Factors.

Keywords

Rich interaction logging, individual differences, task differences

1. INTRODUCTION

Better understanding how users interact with Web search engines is important for improving the search experience. The information science community has studied individual differences in search strategies, tactics, and performance, and identified important factors such as prior experience, gender, age, cognitive styles, interface design, and domain expertise [1][4][30] that influence search strategies and task performance. Most of these studies are conducted in a controlled laboratory setting which limits the number of participants and the naturalness of the tasks selected for study. Thus it is unclear the extent to which these findings generalize to the wide diversity of searchers' tasks seen in Web search settings.

Permission to make digital or hard copies of all or part of this work for personal or classroom use is granted without fee provided that copies are not made or distributed for profit or commercial advantage and that copies bear this notice and the full citation on the first page. To copy otherwise, or republish, to post on servers or to redistribute to lists, requires prior specific permission and/or a fee.

WSDM'12, February 8–12, 2012, Seattle, Washington, USA.

Copyright 2012 ACM 978-1-4503-0747-5/12/02...$10.00.

The Web provides unprecedented opportunities to evaluate alternative design, interaction, and algorithmic methods at scale and *in situ* with actual people doing their own tasks in their own environments [22]. Studies of searcher engagement with search engine result pages (SERPs) focus primarily on search result clickthrough behavior. These studies provide insights regarding the order in which results are clicked. However, they fail to capture behaviors that do not lead to clicks (e.g., which items are attended to, in what order, etc.) or subjective impressions.

There are two main ways to capture detailed behavioral patterns in search: gaze tracking and mouse cursor logging. Gaze tracking studies can provide more detailed insights about how visual attention is distributed on the SERP (and subsequent pages). However these studies are typically conducted in laboratories using a small number of participants with assigned tasks (e.g., [9][15]), with summaries of gaze behavior aggregated across participants and tasks. Some studies examined individual and task differences in gaze patterns, and found individual differences in the strategies with which users inspect results [12], and different clusters of users who exhibit similar result examination behaviors [3][12]. Others found that the type of search task (informational vs. navigational) influenced task completion time and time spent reviewing documents [9][27]. Gaze tracking can provide valuable insights but the technology is expensive and needs calibration, meaning that it does not scale well to non-laboratory settings. A new technique, *ViewSer,* allows for approximate tracking of gaze at much larger scale. It does so by blurring the SERP and only revealing the region proximal to the mouse pointer in more detail [23]. However, this method influences the SERP's visual presentation which likely also affects users' SERP examination strategies.

An alternative to gaze tracking is mouse cursor tracking. Recent research has shown that cursor movements correlate with eye gaze [5][17][28][29], and may therefore be an effective indicator of user attention. Small-scale laboratory studies have observed participants making many uses of the cursor on SERPs beyond hyperlink clicking [2][25]. These uses include moving the cursor as a reading aid, using it to mark interesting results, using it to interact with controls on the screen (e.g., buttons, scroll bars), or simply positioning the cursor so that it does not occlude Web page content. However, these studies were in small-scale laboratory settings which limit what inferences can be made about more naturalistic search behavior. Cursor tracking provides an efficient and unobtrusive way to track mouse movement behavior and can be deployed at scale [18]. We believe that rich cursor tracking data affords a detailed analysis of user, task and user-task differences that is not possible with current evaluation methodologies.

In the research reported in this paper, we use rich cursor logs gathered from a deployment on the Bing commercial Web search engine to better understand individual and task effects on SERP interaction. In addition to tracking mouse behaviors such as cursor movements and clicks, we also logged the location of all areas of interest (to enable accurate assignment of movements to SERP elements), viewport size, scrolling activity, and text selections. Rich data of this type were captured for over 1.8 million queries using a methodology similar to that proposed by Huang *et al.* [18]. This provides sufficient data to allow us to investigate the effects of user and task differences, and interactions between them, and reach conclusions which are potentially generalizable. As we show in our analysis there are distinct user clusters exhibiting specific SERP interaction strategies that can be observed from these data, and are particularly apparent when we also consider the effect of search task on users' SERP examination behaviors.

We make the following contributions with this research:

- Gather and use rich cursor interaction log data on a Web scale;
- Automatically identify distinct users clusters at scale based on SERP examination behaviors, and relate these clusters to findings from previous smaller-scale user studies;
- Study the effect of task type (navigational vs. non-navigational) and consider their impact on the user clustering, and;
- Propose design implications based on our behavioral clustering.

The remainder of this paper is structured as follows. Section 2 describes related work on individual differences in search behaviors, past work on the effect of search task on search behavior, and previous work on gaze- and cursor-tracking. Section 3 describes the large scale cursor tracking data, including the methodology used to gather the data and summary statistics on SERP interaction. Section 4 describes the features that we extracted from the data, the findings of our analysis of user differences, task differences, and any interactions between them. We discuss findings and their implications in Section 5, and conclude in Section 6.

2. RELATED WORK

Three lines of prior research are related to the work described in this paper: (i) examining individual differences in search behaviors and strategies, (ii) studying the relationship between search task and search behavior, and (iii) characterizing how people interact with SERPs using gaze- and cursor-tracking studies.

Saracevic summarized the long history in information science of understanding how individual differences influence search strategies and task performance [30]. Allen [1] showed that cognitive styles, specifically field dependence, influences search task performance. Ford *et al.* [13] showed that a variety of individual differences including cognitive style, search experience and age influence both search strategies and task outcome. Bhavnani [4] and Thatcher [33] examined how search behavior varies with domain and search expertise. Bhavnani showed that domain knowledge influences the choice of search strategies and search success. Thatcher observed search differences related to Web experience with experts using more known URL addresses and parallel strategies. These studies provided very detailed modeling of searcher behaviors, often coupled with survey data to better understand motivations, but are laboratory studies involving small numbers of searchers and tasks. At the other end of the spectrum, large-scale log analyses examined the relationship between search expertise (White and Morris [34]) and domain expertise (White *et al.* [36]) on Web search behaviors. White *et al.* found that domain experts are more successful than novices (in the domain of their expertise) and achieve this success using different vocabulary, sites and broader search strategies. Using a different strategy of clustering users with similar behavioral patterns (rather than using known cognitive, skill or demographic differences), White and Drucker [35] identified two general types of Web searchers: navigators (with very consistent search and browsing patterns) and explorers (with much more varied search and browsing patterns).

There has also been research on the relationship between search tasks and search behavior. Using a diary study, Byström and Järvelin [6] looked directly at the impact of task complexity on user search behavior, examining the relationships between task complexity, information types, and information sources. They showed that as task complexity increased, users needed more sources of information, more domain information and more problem solving information, were less likely to predict the types of information they needed, and were more dependent upon experts to provide useful information. Kellar *et al.* [21] used a field study to examine four task types: fact-finding, information gathering, browsing, and transactions, and examined how users interacted across them as they navigated the Web. They showed that the information gathering task was most complex: participants spent the most time completing it, viewed more pages, and used browser functionality most heavily. Liu *et al.* [26] investigated user behaviors associated with different task types in a controlled laboratory experiment. They varied tasks on different dimensions: complexity, product, goal, and level. Their results indicate differences in search behaviors associated with different task characteristics, including task completion time, the time to assess document utility, and eye fixations. They further suggest that these implicit behaviors could be indicative of task type.

In addition to Liu *et al.*, others have used eye-tracking to provide detailed quantitative analyses of the distribution of gaze as people perform search tasks (e.g., [5][9][15][23][27][28][29]). Since eye gaze position is highly correlated with visual attention, these studies provide rich insight into what people are attending to as they interact with SERPs. Several studies characterized how visual attention is distributed over the search results [15][23][27], or between search results and advertisements [5]. Guan and Cutrell [15] and Lorigo *et al.* [27] found differences in search time and examination patterns for informational vs. navigational tasks. Cole *et al.* [8] identified differences in reading patterns associated with different task characteristics and page types. Aula *et al.* [3] identified two general patterns that people used in examining search results: exhaustive evaluators (54% of the participants who looked at more than half of the visible results for more than half the tasks) and economic evaluators (46% of the participants). Dumais *et al.* [12] performed a similar analysis of search behavior using more complex result pages that included both organic results and advertisements. They found three general groups of searchers – exhaustive (32%), economic with a focus on results (39%), and economic with a focus on advertisements (29%). Although gaze-tracking provides detailed insight into search behavior, it requires calibration, is laboratory based, and does not scale well to the wide range of tasks and users observed in Web search.

To address these issues, cursor-tracking has recently been used to examine search behavior. Initial studies established a close correspondence between eye gaze and cursor position [5][18][28][29]. More recent studies have looked at ways in which cursor movements can be used to understand search behavior. In small-scale studies, Guo and Agichtein used cursor movement to predict query intent [16], and to predict gaze position [17]. In another small-scale study, Rodden *et al.* [29] identified four general uses of the cursor in Web search – neglecting the cursor while reading, using the cursor as a reading aid (either horizontally or vertically), and using the cursor to mark interesting results. In a larger-scale study, Huang *et al.* [18] summarized how cursor activity (including clicks on hyperlinks, clicks on non-hyperlinks, and search result snippet hover behavior) related to Web search behavior. They also showed how cursor activity could be used to estimate the relevance of search results and to differentiate between good and bad SERP abandonment. Rather than tracking the mouse cursor at scale, Lagun and Agichtein [23] presented a scalable method to estimate gaze position by blurring the SERP and only revealing a region proximal to the mouse cursor. They found that result viewing and clickthrough patterns agree closely with unrestricted viewing of results, as measured by eye-tracking.

The research presented in this paper extends the previous work presented in this section in several ways. First, we describe a large-scale analysis of cursor behavior (including clicks, hovers, text selection and cursor trails) on different regions of a search results page. Second, we use these implicit signals of user engagement with search result pages to cluster individuals with similar patterns of behavior. Finally, we examine how user, task and user × task interactions influence search behavior.

We begin by describing the interaction log data used in this study.

3. INTERACTION LOG DATA

We recorded interaction data directly on the SERP of the Bing commercial Web search engine. Log data were gathered over a period of 13 days between May 26, 2011 and June 7, 2011 during an external experiment on a small fraction of user traffic.[1] In the following, we describe our logging methods and provide an initial overview of the data gathered.

3.1 Methodology

To record user interactions with the SERP at scale without the need to install any browser plugins, we used an efficient and scalable approach similar to that developed by Huang *et al.* [18]. As such, JavaScript-based logging functions were embedded into the HTML source code of the SERP. To obtain a detailed understanding of user interactions with the SERP, we recorded information on mouse cursor movements, clicks, scrolling, text selection events, focus gain and loss events of the browser window, as well as bounding boxes of several areas of interest (AOIs) on the SERP and the browser's viewport size. Combining these data sources enabled us to develop a rich picture of how searchers engaged with the SERP, something not previously possible at scale.

When logging any additional type of user interaction data beyond clickthrough, a tradeoff has to be made between: (i) level of detail (e.g., temporal and spatial resolution), (ii) the impact of any additional JavaScript code on page load time, and therefore the user experience, which can be sensitive to even small increases in load time, and (iii) the amount of data transferred (and hence bandwidth consumed) between the client and the remote server as well as log volume created on the backend server.

We now describe in more detail the fields that are recorded in our log data and the methods used to record them.

3.1.1 Mouse Cursor Position

The JavaScript function for logging mouse cursor positions checked the cursor's x- and y-coordinates relative to the top-left corner of the SERP every 250 milliseconds. Whenever the cursor had been moved more than eight pixels away from its previously logged position, its new coordinates were sent to the remote Web server. Eight pixels correspond to approximately the height of half a line of text on the SERP. We used this approach rather than recording every cursor movement since we wanted to minimize the data gathered and transmitted so as to not adversely affect the user experience with delays associated with log data capture and data uploads to the remote server. Since cursor tracking was relative to the document, we captured cursor alignment to SERP content regardless of how the user reached that position (e.g., by scrolling or keyboard). Therefore this approach did not constrain other behaviors such as scrolling or keyboard input.

3.1.2 Mouse Clicks

Mouse clicks were recorded using the JavaScript *onMouseDown* event handling method. Thus, the backend server received log entries with location coordinates for *every* mouse click, including clicks that occurred on a hyperlink as well as those that occurred elsewhere on the page (even on white space containing no content). To identify clicks on hyperlinks and differentiate them from clicks on inactive page elements, we also logged unique hyperlink identifiers embedded in the SERP.

3.1.3 Scrolling

We also recorded the current scroll position, i.e., the y-coordinate of the uppermost visible pixel of the SERP in the browser viewport. This coordinate was checked three times per second and was recorded whenever it had changed by more than 40 pixels compared to the last logged scrolling position. Forty pixels correspond to the height of about two lines of text. From this coordinate we gain a number of insights into scrolling behavior, including whether the user scrolled up or down, and the maximum scroll depth, to understand how far down the SERP the user scrolled.

3.1.4 Text Selections

Searchers may select text for a number of reasons, including to copy-and-paste to another application or to issue a new query to a search engine. Using browser-specific JavaScript functionality, we could identify when text selections occurred and could also determine the bounding box of the immediately surrounding HTML element inside which the selection occurred. For every text selection we recorded the coordinates of the upper left corner of the determined element's bounding box. The actual contents or the exact position of the selected text were not recorded.

3.1.5 Viewport Size

The width and height of the browser viewport in pixels at SERP load time were also logged. Cases where the browser window was resized during interaction with the SERP were not accounted for.

3.1.6 AOI Positions

Simply logging the text of what was displayed on the SERP is insufficient for reconstructing its layout since SERPs vary per query (depending on whether answers are shown, etc.), font sizes, and other browser preferences. To reconstruct the exact SERP layout as it was rendered in the user's browser, we recorded the positions and sizes of AOIs. The specific AOIs that we were interested in were: (i) top and bottom search boxes, (ii) left rail and its contained related searches, search history, and query refinement areas, (iii) mainline results area and its contained result entries, including advertisements and answers, and (iv) right rail. Some of these AOIs are visualized overleaf in Figure 1.

For each AOI bounding box, we determined and logged the coordinates of its upper left corner as well as its width and height in pixels. Using this information, we could later map cursor positions, clicks, and text selections to specific AOIs.

Before describing our analysis of user and task differences, we first provide some summary statistics on the data set gathered.

[1] Note that these data differ from those used by Huang *et al.* [18], in that they are from external users and not Microsoft employees.

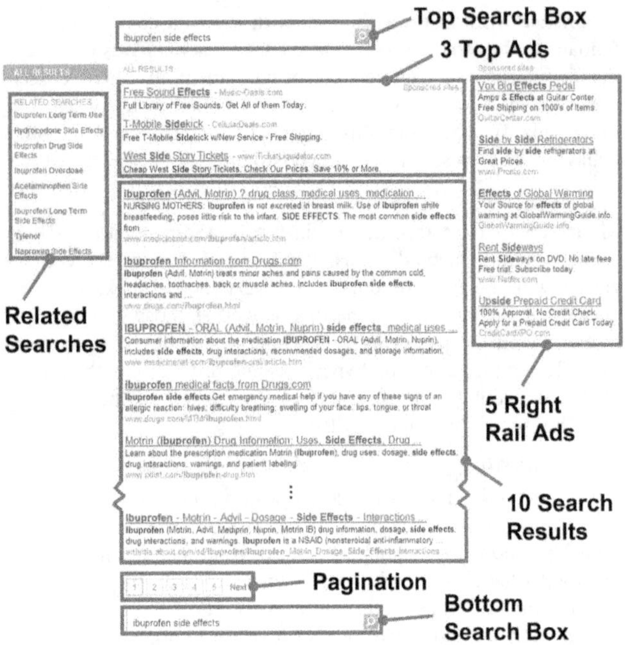

Figure 1. Recorded AOIs on an example SERP.

3.2 Summary Statistics

As described in the previous subsection, the raw interaction events comprised cursor positions, clicks, window scrolls, and text selection events. In total, our data set contained over 1.8 million queries. The average amount of time on the SERP was 47.2 seconds (median=5 seconds). Other summary measures specific to the different types of data logged include:

Cursor: The average speed of the cursor was 172.3 pixels (px) per second (median=123.9 px/sec). The total length of the cursor trail depicting the path that the trail follows on the SERP is 1467.3 px (median=630.7 px), and the trail changes direction (defined in terms of the compass directions North, South, East, and West) almost four times in the course of the trail (mean=3.8, median=1). Finally, users hover over multiple result captions (mean=2.6, median=2), even for navigational queries when a single search result will suffice. This behavior pattern has been observed in studies of eye tracking [9], as well as previous work on cursor tracking [18].

Clicks and text selections: Mouse clicks were collected regardless of whether they were on a hyperlink or on other regions of the page. 64.7% of all clicks were hyperlink clicks and 35.2% were non-hyperlink clicks, which are missed by traditional click-based instrumentation methods. Non-hyperlink clicks were on empty regions of the page (58.1% of all SERPs), on controls (38.8% of all SERPs), and on the upper or lower search boxes (11.4% of all SERPs). Text selections occurred on 1.9% of all SERPs.

Scrolling: Window scrolling is a client-side interaction that is rarely captured in the context of Web search. Of the queries in our set, 29.7% contained at least one scroll event. 61.8% of logged interaction sequences for a query ended on a downwards scroll. As expected, there were more downward scrolls than upward scrolls, and the majority of scrolled queries (54.8%) comprised only downward scrolls. This suggests that most queries do not result in the user returning to the top of the SERP to examine search results that may be hidden following scrolling.

We now extract features from the events and cluster them to analyze the relationships between search behavior, users, and tasks.

4. USER AND TASK DIFFERENCES

The data that we gathered allows us to study how user and task differences impact search result page examination behavior. This is important for better understanding how users engage with search engines and informing the design of new kinds of search support tailored to observed strategies. Using the cursor data described in Section 3.1, we developed summary and composite features to characterize search behavior.

4.1 Feature Extraction

There were four main classes of SERP interaction features: (i) cursor, describing features related to movement of the mouse cursor; (ii) click, related to clicks (both hyperlink and otherwise); (iii) scrolling, describing scrolling behavior (using scrollbar, scroll wheel on mouse, or keyboard commands); and (iv) other features such text selections and interactions with specific SERP features particular to the search engine on which this study was performed. These features are aggregated at the level of a single SERP.

4.1.1 Cursor

We computed a number of cursor-related features based on cursor movements, positions, and dwells, which fall into four groups:

Trails: These features are derived from the recorded cursor movement trails on the SERP and include trail length, trail speed, trail time, total number of cursor movements, and summary values (average, median, standard deviation) for single cursor movement distances and cursor dwell times in the same position, etc. We also created features for the total number of mouse movements and the total number of times that the cursor changed direction in the trail.

Hovers: We recorded total hover time on the SERP. Since we recorded the coordinates of the AOIs we were also able to associate cursor movements with particular SERP elements (see Figure 1). This allowed us to represent the total hover time on inline answers (e.g., stock quotes, news headlines, etc.), in the lower and upper search box on the result page, in the left rail (where search support such as query suggestions and search history would usually be shown), in the right rail (where advertisements would usually be shown), and in the algorithmic results. We also computed the total amount of time that the mouse cursor was idle on the SERP.

Result Inspection Patterns: We computed features summarizing how users inspected the search results, including the total number of search results that users hovered over, the average result hover position, and the fraction of the top ten results that were hovered. We also created features of the linearity of scanning over search results using the same basic definitions introduced by Lorigo *et al.* [27]. We obtain a numbered *scan sequence* by assigning numbers to all top ads (i.e., -2, -1, 0) and organic results (i.e., 1, 2, …, 10) and using these numbers to describe the scan path. The *minimal scan sequence* is obtained by removing repeat visits to a result entry. We had binary features describing whether the scan sequence and the minimal scan sequence were strictly linearly increasing (e.g., 1, 2, 3, …) meaning that users were traversing the search results linearly, as has been suggested previously [19].

Reading Patterns: We used sequences of cursor actions to identify reading-with-mouse behavior (frequent left-right-left movements) which is one of the behaviors identified by Rodden *et al.* [29]. We encoded mouse moves (specified by two adjacent cursor movement events) with the symbols "N", "E", "S", "W" corresponding to the four capital movement directions. All other events (such as scrolling, clicking, text selections) were encoded with "X". Encoding all mouse moves for one SERP interaction pattern such as this resulted in a character sequence. Symbols that occurred contiguously at multiple times were collapsed (e.g., "WEEEWX" →

"WEWX"). The feature "EWEW" encodes whether the user moved the cursor in a right-left-right-left pattern without moving it vertically in between, which is indicative of reading with the mouse (as suggested in Rodden *et al.* [29]). In addition to horizontal reading patterns, we also encoded a number of common sequences (20 in total) that were suggestive of a variety of different SERP engagement strategies (e.g., scrolling vertically with the scroll wheel). Substring searches were performed to determine whether SERP interaction contained the sequence of interest.

4.1.2 Clicks

We computed a range of different features of the clickthrough behavior of users, including the total number of search results that were clicked, the time between the SERP loading and a result click, and the fraction of queries that were abandoned.[2] In a similar way to the featurization of cursor movements, we also computed the total number of hyperlink and non-hyperlink clicks in various AOIs on the SERP, including the number of clicks in the upper and lower search box, the left and right rails, the algorithmic results, and overall across all regions of the SERP.

4.1.3 Scrolling

We also computed features of users' scrolling behavior. These included the total number of scroll events, the number of times they scrolled up, the number of times they scrolled down, the total scroll distance (in pixels), the maximum scroll height (in pixels) referring to the y-coordinate at the top of the viewport relative to the SERP, and the time between SERP load and scroll activity.

4.1.4 Other Features

There were also several other features that were used in this analysis. These include whether the user clicked on the search box (suggesting that they were going to re-query), the number of text selections (total and unique results), and the number of hover previews (total and unique results) requested. Hover previews are a Bing interface feature that provides more information about a search result when requested by a hover over its caption.

Over 80 features are generated for each SERP. We use these features in the analysis presented in the remainder of the paper.

4.2 Individual Differences

To analyze the effects of individual differences we aggregate (average) features per user and cluster users based on those features to identify different patterns of search interaction and groups of users who exhibit those patterns when interacting with SERPs.

Users were identified by an ID stored in a browser cookie. To give us sufficient data from which to base aggregation for each user, we selected all users who had issued at least 20 queries in the time period during which we captured logs. This resulted in a set of 22,084 users whose SERP behavior we analyzed further. Each user in this set issued an average of 39.6 queries (median=31).

4.2.1 Clustering

For each user and for each feature described in Section 4.1, we averaged the feature values across all queries issued by that user in the course of the study. Missing values were properly considered during averaging, e.g., SERPs with no clicks were excluded from the calculation of time-to-first-click.

[2] Note that we had two definitions of SERP abandonment in our analysis: one where there were no clicks anywhere on the page and one where there were no hyperlink clicks. The latter is more traditionally associated with abandonment (e.g., [24]) although we find that the former is more discriminative for clustering.

We used the CLUTO clustering package [20] to identify groups of users who shared similar SERP interaction behaviors. Specifically, we used repeated-bisection clustering with a cosine similarity metric and the ratio of intra- to extra-cluster similarity as the objective function. We found that clusters are fairly stable regardless of the specific clustering or similarity metric. We varied the number of clusters (k) from 2 to 100 and tested within- and between-cluster similarity. We found that the objective function leveled off at k=45, meaning 45 distinct user clusters in our set.

Outlier users were identified and removed by looking for very small clusters (where the number of users was less than ten) with very low extra-cluster similarity at high levels of k. We removed 16 users from the set, leaving us 22,068 users to cluster. To facilitate interpretation of the clusters, we chose a representative set of the 12 most descriptive and discriminative features based on CLUTO output. The following features were selected based on their descriptive value and discriminative power:

- *Time on SERP* (TrailTime): Total time spent on SERP.
- *Clicks*:
  - *HyperlinkResultClickCount*: Number of result clicks.
  - *NonHyperlinkClickCount*: Number of non-link clicks anywhere on the SERP.
  - *TimetoFirstResultClick*: Time between the SERP loading and the first click on a search result.
  - *NoClick*: Whether there was a click (hyperlink or non-hyperlink) on the SERP. We call this abandonment.
- *Re-Query* (ClickInSearchBox): Whether the search box is clicked with the mouse cursor.
- *Scrolling* (Scroll): Whether users scroll (using scrollbar, mouse scroll wheel, or keyboard commands such as Page Down).
- *Cursor*:
  - *FractionTopTenHovered*: Fraction of the top ten result captions (titles/snippets/URLs) that users hover over.
  - *TrailSpeed*: Average speed with which the mouse is moved, in pixels per second.
  - *MedianMouseMovementDistance*: Median distance of individual mouse movements without pauses, in pixels. This helps us understand the degree of focus in the movement. A long distance suggests that the movement is directed.
  - *Reading*: Whether reading pattern is present (Section 4.1.1).
  - *CursorIdle*: Average time the cursor is not moving.

We used these 12 features in a second run of CLUTO, clustering all users based only on this subset. This time, the ratio of within- and between-cluster similarity leveled off at k=6 clusters. We grouped all users in the same cluster together and averaged the feature values. Note that a feature value for a cluster is an average of user averages, thus, every user contributes equally to the cluster average independent of the number of queries they issued.

4.2.2 Cluster Characteristics

Table 1 shows the average values for each feature in each of the six clusters identified. Green (dark) indicates high feature values and yellow (light) low feature values. Labels (e.g., "Long time on SERP") are added to improve interpretability of the clusters. The six clusters are different along a number of dimensions.

Closer inspection of the table reveals three distinct meta-clusters centered on the amount of time and detail with which users spend inspecting the search result page. The three meta-clusters that we identified are: (i) *long (clusters 0 and 1, 11% of users):* careful and detailed SERP examination, many search results hovered on and clicked, lots of scrolling, and signs of reading behavior with the mouse cursor; (ii) *medium (clusters 3 and 4, 15% of users):*

Table 1. Mean average feature values for each of the six user clusters. Green/dark = high values, yellow/light = low values.

	Meta-cluster Name	*Long*		*Medium*		*Short*	
	Cluster	**#0**	**#1**	**#4**	**#3**	**#5**	**#2**
	Number of Users	1178	1283	2240	1167	5645	10555
	Feature						
Time		Long time on SERP				Short time on SERP	
	TrailTime	617.56	342.74	102.83	186.90	55.89	17.51
Clicks			Many R clicks				Few R clicks
	HyperlinkResultClickCount	1.11	1.23	1.17	0.95	0.99	0.88
		Many NH clicks					Few NH clicks
	NonHyperlinkClickCount	0.91	0.92	0.81	0.66	0.58	0.32
			Late first R click				Early first R click
	TimeToFirstResultClick	95.09	325.54	90.91	31.56	38.58	13.52
				Less abandons	More abandons		
	NoClick	0.13	0.12	0.11	0.15	0.14	0.14
Re-Query		More search box					Less search box
	ClickInSearchBox	0.10	0.08	0.07	0.09	0.06	0.04
Scrolling		More scrolling					Less scrolling
	Scroll	0.19	0.21	0.20	0.16	0.14	0.09
Cursor		More hover results					Less hover results
	FractionTopTenHovered	0.30	0.31	0.30	0.28	0.26	0.22
		Slow mouse movements					Fast mouse move
	TrailSpeed	119.07	116.73	127.58	152.52	159.69	230.59
		Short mouse movements					Long mouse move
	MedianMouseMovementDistance	76.91	75.85	77.42	84.05	85.61	90.86
		More reading w/ mouse					Less reading w/ mouse
	Reading	0.06	0.06	0.06	0.06	0.05	0.03
		More cursor idle				Less cursor idle	
	Cursor Idle	54.59	39.85	8.42	18.79	5.36	2.10

intermediate time spent on the SERP and distinguished from other clusters primarily by the amount of abandonment; and *short (clusters 2 and 5, 73% of users):* short time on SERPs, mouse moved quickly and in a focused way, and only a few results inspected.

It is clear that there are differences in how users engage with SERPs. However, it is difficult to isolate user from task differences since most users engage in a variety of tasks during a 13-day time period. Previous work has shown that task and query characteristics impact search behavior. Cole *et al.* [8] found significant differences in how users read results depending on the task. Downey *et al.* [11] showed that user behavior following a query varied significantly with popularity. And, Buscher *et al.* [5] and Cutrell and Guan [9] showed large differences in behavior for navigational vs. informational queries. We now study the impact of task on SERP examination strategies.

4.3 Task Differences

To study task effects, we needed a way to identify different task types at scale. To simplify our analysis we examine individual queries rather than complete search tasks. We focused on navigational and non-navigational queries, which are easy to identify and have been shown to yield different search behaviors in previous work [5][9]. There are other ways to identify queries of different task types, such as if advertisements were shown (commercial queries), the type of inline answer shown (queries with clear intent), etc. We leave such detailed analysis to future work.

To distinguish between navigational and non-navigational queries, we use click entropy [10], which measures the variability in clicked results across users. Click entropy (CE) is calculated as:

$$CE(q) = -\sum_{URL\ u} p(c_u|q) \cdot log_2(p(c_u|q))$$

where $p(c_u|q)$ is the probability that URL u was clicked following query q. A large click entropy means many pages were clicked for the query, while a small click entropy means only a few were clicked. To divide queries into navigational and non-navigational, we adopted thresholds used by Teevan *et al.* [31] when identifying queries of low and high click entropy: navigational queries < 1.25 click entropy and non-navigational queries > 1.75 click entropy. Click entropy values for all queries in our set were computed across a held out set of one year of Bing query logs. This yielded a set of 514,989 navigational queries and 226,348 non-navigational queries, issued by a total of 22,056 users.

For consistency, we used the same set of 12 features we used in the user clustering analysis and describe how they differ between navigational and non-navigational queries. Table 2 presents the average feature values for each of the two task types.

Table 2. Differences in interaction behavior for different tasks.

Feature		Task Type: *Nav.*	Task Type: *Non-nav.*
TrailTime (secs)		49.59	62.93
Clicks	HyperlinkResultClickCount	0.91	1.02
	NonHyperlinkClickCount	0.49	0.57
	TimetoFirstResultClick (secs)	21.24	29.31
	NoClick	0.13	0.16
ClickInSearchBox		0.11	0.16
Scroll		0.12	0.17
Cursor	FractionTopTenHovered	0.19	0.22
	TrailSpeed (px/second)	180.21	167.43
	MovementDistance (px/move)	80.92	82.94
	Reading	0.04	0.05
	Cursor Idle (secs)	4.31	3.74

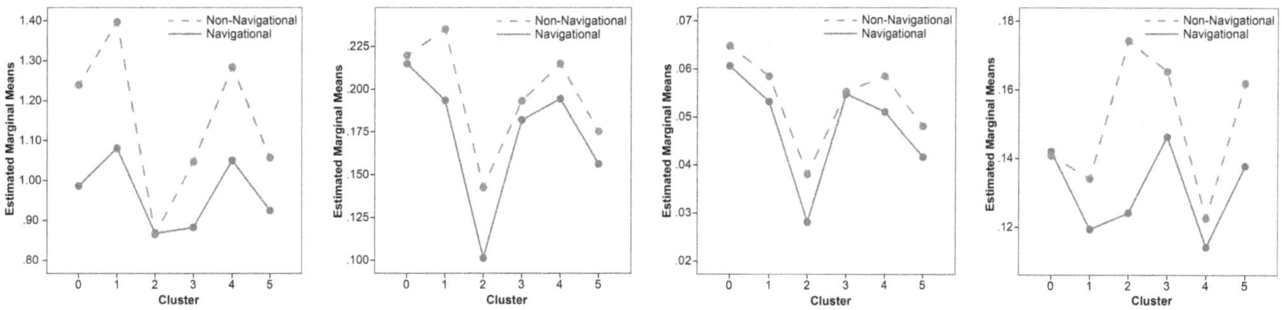

(a) HyperlinkResultClickCount *(b) FractionTopTenHovered* *(c) Reading* *(d) NoClick (Abandonment)*

Figure 2. Marginal means for user and task interactions for several features of interest.

Table 2 shows substantial differences in search result page examination behavior between navigational and non-navigational search queries. Given the large sample sizes, all differences across all variables were found to be significant using a multivariate analysis of variance (MANOVA) ($F(12,741314) = 632.54$, $p < .001$). All paired differences for each variable between the task types for each variable were also significant at $p < .002$ using Tukey post-hoc testing. We also computed the effect size of the differences between task types using *partial eta squared* (η_p^2), a commonly used measure of effect size in analyses of variance. The features with the largest effect sizes were the time spent on the SERP (more for non-navigational, η_p^2=.04), the time to first search result click (longer for non-navigational, η_p^2=.02), whether they scrolled on the SERP (more for non-navigational, η_p^2=.01), and the speed with which the mouse was moved (faster for navigational, η_p^2=.01). As expected, users engaged in non-navigational tasks interacted more with the SERP, likely because there may not be a single result to satisfy their needs or they may need to consider many results before selecting a result.

It is clear from the analysis presented in this subsection that there are strong task effects which appear to have a consistent impact on SERP interaction behaviors. So far we have focused on differences in search behavior related to the individual searcher and to the type of search task being attempted. However, there may also be effects attributable to the interaction between users' personal traits and interaction styles and task type which may lead users to examine the SERP differently.

4.4 User × Task Interactions

An important initial step in studying user × task interactions was to compute the fraction of queries for each task type in each of the six user clusters identified in the earlier analysis. Large differences in the distribution of task types found in each user cluster could influence the behavior in each cluster to relate to that task. Analysis of the distribution across navigational and non-navigational queries in each of the user clusters showed that it is approximately similar, with 67–71% of queries labeled navigational in all clusters. This suggests that there is at least a consistent distribution of task types in each user cluster, but says little about the relationship between task and user cluster behavior.

To test for interactions between user and task, we performed a 6 (cluster) × 2 (task type) MANOVA over the 12 dependent variables of interest. The main effects of user and task were both significantly different at $p < .001$ (all $F_{\text{User}}(5,741335) \geq 120.92$, all $F_{\text{Task}}(1,741335) \geq 2.44$). In addition, the user-task interaction was significant for all dependent variables ($F_{\text{User}\times\text{Task}}(60,3706562) = 88.42$, $p < .001$; Tukey post-hoc testing: all $p < .001$). This was expected given the large sample sizes, but many of the interaction effects were small in magnitude. There were some cases where interaction effects size was greater than slight (i.e., $\eta_p^2 \geq 0.04$).

Figure 2 shows examples of the marginal means for four of the dependent variables where there were larger interaction effects between user and task. Non-navigational tasks are represented as red dashed lines and navigational tasks are shown as blue solid lines for each of the six clusters. In each case, most clusters show task-type differences, as often reported in the literature; however one cluster shows little or no task type effects:

1. In Figure 2a, cluster 2 shows no differences in the total number of result clicks per task type, where other clusters of users show a difference of approximately 20%.
2. Figure 2b shows that members of user clusters 1 and 2 explore the results even relatively more deeply for non-navigational queries. Those in user cluster 0 explore search results to the same depth regardless of task type.
3. The reading behavior of members of user cluster 3 is not affected by task type (Figure 2c).
4. The abandonment rate for user cluster 0 is similar regardless of task type and, for cluster 2 abandonment is much higher for non-navigational tasks (Figure 2d).

A better understanding of the nature of the interactions between users and search tasks is important for accurately modeling users and tasks. One way to control for search task is as part of an experiment. Laboratory studies of information seeking behavior (e.g., [5][9]) often control for task type at experiment time. In our case, we must consider the impact of task type retrospectively, by only focusing on user behavior for a particular type of search task. To that end, we now report a new cluster analysis that is restricted to non-navigational tasks to better understand user search patterns for that task type.

4.5 User Clusters for Non-Navigational Tasks

Re-clustering the user data for just non-navigational tasks allowed us to focus our analysis of patterns in the user interaction behavior. We targeted non-navigational tasks rather than navigational since there may be a broader range of information seeking behaviors for those tasks. Given space constraints we cannot share detailed findings for navigational tasks, but as expected there was much more consistency in users' SERP behaviors for those tasks.

We used a similar procedure to that described in Section 4.2.1 to identify the user clusters. However, in this case we extracted only non-navigational queries for each user, and filtered out users who had fewer than 20 non-navigational queries. We clustered these users into k=50 clusters to identify outlier users, i.e., very small clusters with low between cluster similarity. We identified and re-

Table 3. Mean average feature values for each non-navigational user cluster. Green/dark = high values, yellow/light = low values.

	Cluster	*Exhaustive-Passive*	*Exhaustive-Active*	*Economic*
	Number of Users	232	408	1905
	Feature			
Time		Long time on SERP		Short time on SERP
	TrailTime	446.00	156.14	28.03
Clicks		Many R clicks		Few R clicks
	HyperlinkResultClickCount	1.10	1.30	0.85
		Many NH clicks		Few NH clicks
	NonHyperlinkClickCount	0.70	0.85	0.40
			Late first R click	Early first R click
	TimeToFirstResultClick	88.74	144.56	21.05
			Less abandons	More abandons
	NoClick	0.17	0.13	0.20
Re-Query		More search box		Less search box
	ClickInSearchBox	0.08	0.06	0.04
Scrolling		More scrolls		Less scrolls
	Scroll	0.19	0.21	0.13
Cursor		More hover results		Less hover results
	FractionTopTenHovered	0.28	0.29	0.22
		Slow mouse move		Fast mouse move
	TrailSpeed	130.70	118.31	209.11
		Short mouse move		Long mouse move
	MedianMouseMovementDistance	83.75	80.34	94.79
		More reading w/ mouse		Less reading w/ mouse
	Reading	0.05	0.05	0.04
		More cursor idle		Less cursor idle
	Cursor Idle	34.40	9.68	2.21
	Dominant user cluster (% queries from user cluster, meta-cluster)	#0 (30.7%, Lots)	#4 (55.7%, Medium)	#2 (67.8%, Little)

moved one outlier user leaving us with 2,545 users. Next, we reran CLUTO with the same 12 representative features (see above) for the non-navigational tasks for those users, and used the intra- and extra-similarity ratio as the objective function. The ratio between intra- and extra-similarity was maximized at three clusters.

Table 3 shows three distinct emergent clusters of search behavior:

1. *Economic* (75% of users): Users spend little time on the SERP, have focused and fast mouse movements, click quickly, and click on average less than one result per query. Behaviorally, these users are similar to the "economic" users identified in previous work on gaze tracking research [3][12].

2. *Exhaustive-Active* (16% of users): Users who examine the SERP in detail, click a lot (both on hyperlinks and elsewhere), have little cursor idle time, and infrequently abandon. These users are similar to the "exhaustive" users identified previously [3][12].

3. *Exhaustive-Passive* (9% of users): Users who exhibit many of the characteristics as Exhaustive-Active, but spend more time on the SERP, have the cursor idle for a long time, and abandon often.

Interestingly, if we compute the dominant user cluster from which members of each these non-navigational task-related user clusters originated, we see that each cluster in Table 3 corresponds to exactly one of the three meta-clusters in Table 1. The dominant user cluster, the percentage of users from that cluster, and the meta-cluster label are shown in the last row of Table 3. One possible explanation for this finding is that by partitioning by task type, we were able to identify user groupings that were present in Table 1, but were partially hidden due to task effects. In addition to characterizing search behavior using detailed numerical feature values, we also created heat maps of search behavior to determine whether there were any qualitative visual differences in the way that users in each of the clusters inspected the SERPs.

4.5.1 Cluster Heat Maps

To create these clusters, we randomly selected 100 users from each cluster, and then randomly selected a single query for each of the users. We used these 100 queries to generate the aggregated heat map for each cluster. Figure 3 contains the heat maps for all users (left) and for the three user clusters separately. The spottiness of the heatmap relates to the cursor data sampling rate.

4.5.1.1 Interpreting the Heat Maps

In the heat maps in Figure 3, color represents hover time of the mouse cursor anywhere on the page. For each heatmap this is normalized with respect to the longest existing hover time so that the longest hover time is displayed in dark red. Although small in the figure, clicks are displayed with crosses (×). Green crosses represent hyperlink clicks, red crosses represent non-hyperlink clicks. The image of the SERP in the background is just included as an example for reference. The aggregated impressions come from a large variety of different queries with a variety of SERP layouts, depending on the query. Adjacent to each of the heat maps is a box-and-whisker plot depicting the maximum scroll height reached for each of the clusters. As noted earlier, the scroll position is measured with respect to the uppermost visible pixel in the viewport. Since the average viewport height across all Web browsers in our study was 1142 px (median=743 px), users often had to scroll, but generally only up to one third of the total height of the SERP to see its full contents.

4.5.1.2 Differences in Clusters

The cluster heat maps show fairly consistent differences between the three user clusters that align well with the numeric features reported in Table 3. It is clear from the figures that users in the Economic cluster inspect less of the result page. The deeper examination of Exhaustive-Active and Exhaustive-Passive users is evident in the amount of scrolling that they do, the number of

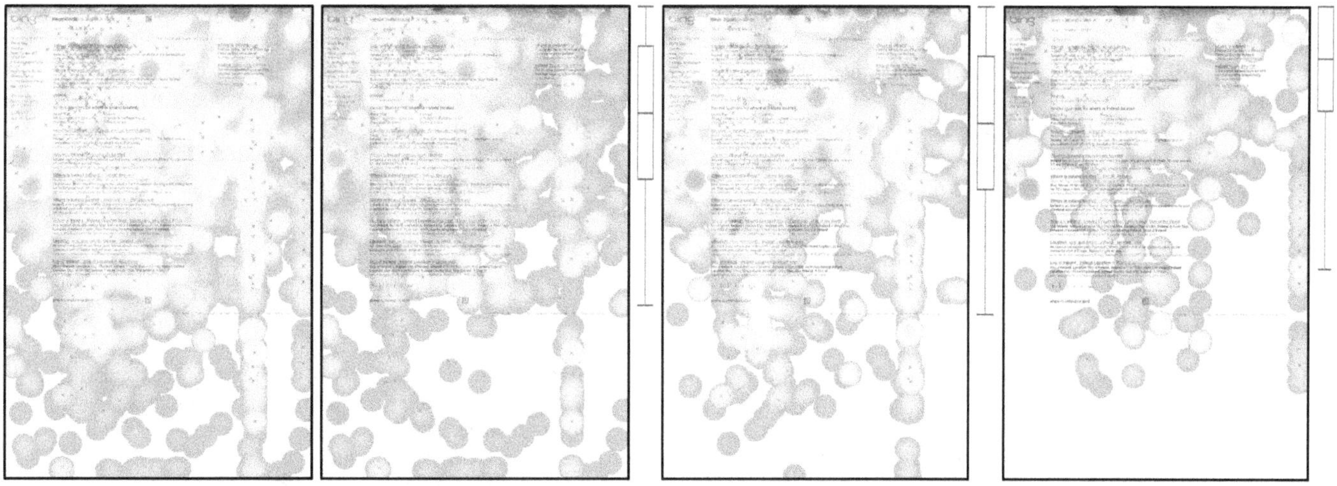

All *Exhaustive-Active* *Exhaustive-Passive* *Economic*

Figure 3. User cluster heat maps. Box and whisker diagrams show the median, first/third quartiles, and min/max scroll depth.

results hovered over, and the total trail time. The difference between Exhaustive-Active and Exhaustive-Passive users is that Exhaustive-Passive users spend more time over the full result page, as shown by the high *CursorIdle* times in Table 3 and by the more intensely colored heatmap in Figure 3.

Overall, it seems that when we focus on one task type, there are three distinct clusters of search behavior that emerge. These clusters share strong similarities with those identified in previous small-scale gaze tracking studies [3][12]. However, demonstrating the capability to identify similar patterns at scale in more naturalistic cursor tracking logs with more variable tasks is promising.

5. DISCUSSION AND IMPLICATIONS

We have presented a study of individual differences in search result page examination behavior. To our knowledge, this is the first large-scale study of SERP interaction behavior that moves beyond search result click-through. Our findings show that there are cohorts of users who examine search results in a similar way, and that the grouping becomes clearer when we consider task effects. We also showed that there are pronounced task effects that impact how users engage with the SERP and that can interact with users' typical search behaviors. Identifying users with consistent search strategies and patterns is important to understanding how systems are currently being used and create search support.

Our initial analysis revealed six user clusters. However, we also showed that there are strong effects from the type of search task on users' search behavior, as well as strong interaction effects between task and user. When we focused on non-navigational tasks, we found three distinct user clusters who exhibited different result examination behaviors. Promisingly, users exhibited behavioral patterns similar to those found in previous gaze tracking research [3][12], especially the presence of exhaustive and economic groups. Not only do we confirm the existence of these clusters in a naturalistic search setting, but also demonstrate that we can automatically generate them via search engine log analysis.

There are some limitations that we should acknowledge. Since the study was conducted in a naturalistic setting, we do not have control over the search tasks being attempted. Although we automatically labeled task types as navigational or non-navigational, this is a very general task division and it does not incorporate many task nuances that may affect search behavior. The non-navigational tasks in particular are likely to be heterogeneous, and encompass tasks ranging from fact finding to browsing. It would also be possible to identify tasks in other ways based on attributes of the query such as length or popularity, or attributes of the search results such as whether inline answers or advertisements were shown. Developing a finer-grained analysis of task differences is an important direction for future work. We also do not consider the impact of different SERP presentations, as well as users who often issue the same query types (e.g., many queries that return answers, lessening the likelihood that they would click). Future work could address these shortcomings using in-situ methods, where tasks could be assigned and interaction data and user feedback gathered remotely from willing participants. Such methods have been used effectively in previous studies (e.g., [14]).

The cursor-based methods that we have described have the advantage over gaze tracking in that they can be applied on a Web scale, allowing many different types of search behavior to be mined from log data, and significant user cohorts identified. In addition, they provide valuable information about the distribution of visual attention on the SERP that is not available with just hyperlink clicks. This could help improve the search support offered by search engines. For example, we can support the three user groups identified in our analysis in a number of different ways:

Economic users do not spend much time exploring the SERP, have more directed mouse movements, and abandon SERPs often. These users may have clear information needs (that could perhaps be satisfied by a tailored answer on the result page) or are revisiting specific sites. These users could be helped by offering richer answers directly on the result page or direct support for re-finding (as proposed by Teevan *et al.* [32]).

Exhaustive-Active users explore search results in detail and ultimately click on a result. They could benefit from richer summaries that would facilitate decisions about result selection and comparisons between results, as well as an ability to re-rank and explore results based different meta-data (time, topic, author, etc.).

Exhaustive-Passive users explore the results, but are less likely to click on a search result. We could show these users more results or more diverse results to increase the likelihood that they will find something that matches their needs. In addition, we could offer them support for query refinement, since they are also more likely to re-query than other groups.

In addition to supporting users directly, search engines could also use archetypal behaviors for each cohort as additional input to train and evaluate click prediction models (e.g., [7]). Similarly, since cursor tracking provides detailed evidence about the distribution of visual attention to SERP elements, it could be used to evaluate "good abandonment" (where no clicks on the SERP are a good thing [24]), or to measure the impact of new SERP features.

More research is also needed to identify sub-clusters of behavior given more data about each user's SERP interactions, more interaction features for clustering, and more nuanced search task definitions, perhaps spanning multiple queries or sessions.

6. CONCLUSIONS

We have presented the findings of a study on individual and task effects on SERP examination behavior. We analyzed logs containing detailed data on user interactions including clicks, scrolls, and cursor movements for millions of search queries. By clustering the data using these interaction features, we identify individual differences in search behavior, and strong effects of user, task and user-task interaction. When we consider task type (by focusing on non-navigational queries), three distinct user clusters emerge. These clusters share behavioral traits with those identified in laboratory studies, but we observe these without gaze tracking technology and at scale on the Web, opening up a wealth of opportunity for adaptation of the search experience based on individuals' searching behaviors. Future work will expand the feature set and task definitions, explore the use of behavioral patterns to create tailored search experiences, and leverage these rich data for tasks such as click prediction and search result ranking.

REFERENCES

[1] Allen, B. (2000). Individual differences and conundrums of user-centered design. *JASIS*, 51(6): 508–520.

[2] Arroyo, E., Selker, T., and Wei, W. (2006). Usability tool for analysis of web designs using mouse tracks. *Ext. Abstracts CHI*, 484–489.

[3] Aula, A., Majaranta, P., and Raiha, K.-J. (2005). Eye-tracking reveals personal styles for search result evaluation. *INTERACT*, 1058–1061.

[4] Bhavnani, S. (2001). Important cognitive components of domain-specific search knowledge. *TREC*, 571–578.

[5] Buscher, G., Dumais, S., and Cutrell, E. (2010). The good, the bad and the random: An eye-tracking study of ad quality in Web search. *SIGIR*, 42–49.

[6] Byström, K. and Järvelin, K. (1995). Task complexity affects information seeking and use. *IP&M*, 31(2), 191–213.

[7] Chapelle, O. and Zhang, Y. (2009). A dynamic Bayesian click network click model for Web search ranking. *WWW*, 1–10.

[8] Cole, M., Gwizdka, J., Liu, C., Bierig, R., Belkin, N.J., and Zhang, X. (2011). Task and user effects on reading patterns in information search. *Inter. with Comp.*, 23: 346–362.

[9] Cutrell, E. and Guan, Z. (2007). What are you looking for? An eye-tracking study of information usage in Web search. *CHI*, 407–416.

[10] Dou, Z., Song, R., and Wen, J.R. (2007). A large-scale evaluation and analysis of personalized search strategies. *WWW*, 581–590.

[11] Downey, D., Dumais, S., Liebling, D., and Horvitz, E. (2008). Understanding the relationship between searchers' queries and information goals. *CIKM*, 449–458.

[12] Dumais, S., Buscher, G., and Cutrell, E. (2010). Individual differences in gaze patterns for Web search. *IIiX*, 185–194.

[13] Ford, N., Miller, D., and Moss, N. (2005). Web search strategies and human individual differences. *JASIST*, 56(7): 741–756.

[14] Fox, S., Karnawat, K., Mydland, M., Dumais, S., and White, T. (2005). Evaluating implicit measures to improve the search experience. *ACM TOIS*, 23(2): 147–168.

[15] Guan, Z. and Cutrell, E. (2007). An eye tracking study of the effect of target rank on web search. *CHI*, 417–420.

[16] Guo, Q. and Agichtein, E. (2008). Exploring mouse movements for inferring query intent. *SIGIR*, 707–708.

[17] Guo, Q. and Agichtein, E. (2010). Towards predicting Web searcher gaze position from mouse movements. *Ext. Abstracts CHI*, 3601–3606.

[18] Huang, J., White, R.W., and Dumais, S.T. (2011). No clicks, no problem: Using cursor movements to understand and improve search. *CHI*, 1225–1234.

[19] Joachims, T., Granka, L., Pan, B., Hembrooke, H., and Gay, G. (2005). Accurately interpreting clickthrough data as implicit feedback. *SIGIR*, 154–161.

[20] Karypis, G. Cluto: A clustering toolkit. www.cs.umn.edu/~cluto. Retrieved July 2011.

[21] Kellar, M., Watters, C., and Shepherd, M. (2007). A field study characterizing Web-based information-seeking tasks. *JASIST*, 58(7): 999–1018.

[22] Kohavi, R., Longbotham, R., Sommerfield, D., and Henne, R.M. (2009). Controlled experiments on the Web: Survey and practical guide. *Data Min. Know. Disc.*, 18(1): 140–181.

[23] Lagun, D. and Agichtein, E. (2011). ViewSer: Enabling large-scale remote user studies of Web search examination and interaction. *SIGIR*, 365–374.

[24] Li, J., Huffman, S.B., and Tokuda, A. (2009). Good abandonment in mobile and PC internet search. *SIGIR*, 43–50.

[25] Liu, C. and Chung, C. (2007). Detecting mouse movement with repeated visit patterns for retrieving noticed knowledge components on web pages. *IEICE Trans. Inform. & Syst.*, E90-D(10): 1687–1696.

[26] Liu., J., Cole., M.J., Liu, C., Bierig, R., Gwizdka, J., Belkin, N.J., Zhang, J., and Zhang, X. (2010). Search behaviors in different task types. *JCDL*, 69–78.

[27] Lorigo, L., Pan, B., Hembrooke, H., Joachims, T., Granka, L., and Gay, G. (2006). The influence of task and gender on search evaluation and behavior using Google. *IP&M*, 42(4): 1123–1131.

[28] Rodden, K. and Fu, X. (2007). Exploring how mouse movements relate to eye movements on web search results pages. *SIGIR Workshop on Web Info. Seek. and Interact.*, 29–32.

[29] Rodden, K., Fu, X., Aula, A., and Spiro, I. (2008). Eye-mouse coordination patterns on web search results pages. *Ext. Abstracts CHI*, 2997–3002.

[30] Saracevic, T. (1991). Individual differences in organizing, searching and retrieving information. *ASIS*, 82–86.

[31] Teevan, J., Dumais, S.T., and Liebling, D. (2008). To personalize or not to personalize: Modeling queries with variation in user intent. *SIGIR*, 163–170.

[32] Teevan, J., Liebling, D.J., and Geetha, G.R. (2011). Understanding and predicting personal navigation. *WSDM*, 85–94.

[33] Thatcher, A. (2008). Web search strategies: The influence of Web experience and task type. *IP&M*, 44(3): 1308–1329.

[34] White, R. and Morris, D. (2007). Investigating the querying and browsing behavior of advanced search engine users. *SIGIR*, 255–262.

[35] White, R. and Drucker, S. (2007). Investigating behavioral variability in Web search. *WWW*, 21–30.

[36] White, R., Dumais, S.T., and Teevan, J. (2009). Characterizing the influence of domains expertise on Web search behavior. *WSDM*, 132–141.

Sequence Clustering and Labeling for Unsupervised Query Intent Discovery

Jackie Chi Kit Cheung*
Department of Computer Science
University of Toronto
Toronto, ON Canada
jcheung@cs.toronto.edu

Xiao Li*
Facebook Inc.
Palo Alto, CA USA
xiaol@fb.com

ABSTRACT

One popular form of semantic search observed in several modern search engines is to recognize query patterns that trigger instant answers or domain-specific search, producing semantically enriched search results. This often requires understanding the query intent in addition to the meaning of the query terms in order to access structured data sources. A major challenge in intent understanding is to construct a domain-dependent schema and to annotate search queries based on such a schema, a process that to date has required much manual annotation effort. We present an unsupervised method for clustering queries with similar intent and for producing a pattern consisting of a sequence of semantic concepts and/or lexical items for each intent. Furthermore, we leverage the discovered intent patterns to automatically annotate a large number of queries beyond those used in clustering. We evaluated our method on 10 selected domains, discovering over 1400 intent patterns and automatically annotating 125K (and potentially many more) queries. We found that over 90% of patterns and 80% of instance annotations tested are judged to be correct by a majority of annotators.

Categories and Subject Descriptors

H.3.3 [**Information Storage and Retrieval**]: Information Search and Retrieval—*clustering*

General Terms

Algorithms, Experimentation

Keywords

semantic search, query intent discovery, clustering

*The work was done while both authors were with Microsoft Research, Redmond.

Permission to make digital or hard copies of all or part of this work for personal or classroom use is granted without fee provided that copies are not made or distributed for profit or commercial advantage and that copies bear this notice and the full citation on the first page. To copy otherwise, to republish, to post on servers or to redistribute to lists, requires prior specific permission and/or a fee.
WSDM'12, February 8–12, 2012, Seattle, Washington, USA.
Copyright 2012 ACM 978-1-4503-0747-5/12/02 ...$10.00.

1. INTRODUCTION

In the traditional IR model of search, a search engine is responsible for returning documents relevant to a search query. Ranking algorithms using surface-level word statistics have been developed which have made keyword search the dominant form of web search today. Modern search engines are moving beyond this paradigm by more deeply analyzing the structure and semantics of search queries. Doing so can not only improve ranking results, it can also allow domain-dependent types of semantically enriched search results to be displayed in addition to the standard ranked list of relevant documents. For example, a search query that matches the pattern "[city] weather" would trigger a weather forecast for that city, while one that matches "[movie_title] showtimes [location]" would return an appropriate list of showtimes at cinemas near the specified location. These *instant answers* understand and directly address the information need of the user, obviating the step of clicking into and searching through an external document.

A related trend is the development of structured (or vertical/specialized) search, which allows precise search within a domain. Structured search requires a query understanding component to extract structured information that is matched with a back-end database. A query may be in the form of a keyword search, which is relatively unstructured with free word order, such as "hotel seattle february". Or, a query may be in a more natural language form, as is often the case with virtual assistant applications on mobile devices. These applications take a voice command from a user, such as "Book a reservation at an Italian restaurant for 7:30 tonight", then perform the desired action, or automate a substantial portion of it, such as by filling in an online reservation form.

One key issue for these applications is to connect the surface-level query to a structured data source according to the intent of the user. Doing so requires an intent understanding system, which makes use of a *schema*. We define a schema as consisting of a *domain*, a set of domain-dependent *intents*, and *slots* or *concepts*. Slots are often assumed to be shared among different intents in the same domain.

Given a schema, an intent understanding system consists of the following: (1) domain classification, (2) intent detection, and (3) slot filling. For example, "harry potter showtimes boston" should be classified into the *Movie* domain with the intent *FindShowtimes* and slots including *Title* = "harry potter" and *Location* = "boston". The first component can be viewed as identifying a coarse semantic class of query intent to limit the hypothesis space of the following components. Next, intent detection and slot filling aim at finding more fine-grained user intents within the domain of interest and extracting the slots related to that intent. The last two components are tightly coupled and are often modeled jointly.

There have been two major approaches to doing schema discovery to enable such an intent understanding system. The first is to use a grammar-based approach, defining rules in a domain and matching queries to these predefined rules, often based on the schema of the back-end database. While such an approach may work for simple domains and intents such as accessing weather reports, it is difficult to scale up to a larger number of domains. In addition, manually crafting grammar rules imposes a high cognitive load on humans and is often imprecise. Another approach is to use statistical models to classify queries by intent and to label sequences for slot filling. While this eliminates the need to specify rules, it still requires, in addition to the predefined schema, much annotation effort in the form of labeled data to train supervised machine learning models. Although semi-supervised methods [14] have been developed to reduce this cost, a reasonably large amount of labeled data is still needed as "seeds" to bootstrap learning. Furthermore, by relying on a predefined schema, both methods are susceptible to biases which can result in a mismatch to a user's real information need. For example, in the *Products* domain, databases often contain fields like "serial number" which are rarely queried by users or used as search criteria. Human-designed schemata generally do not cover all intents and their associated slots; search engines to date know how to semantically interpret a subset of user requests that are popular or important like "[city] weather", but there are many more that are yet to be understood and answered.

The goal of this work is to discover popular user intents and their associated slots, and to annotate query instances accordingly in a completely unsupervised manner. As in [1], we define *intent* as represented by a *pattern* or *template* consisting of a sequence of semantic concepts or lexical items. Continuing the above example, a pattern that describes "harry potter showtimes boston" would be "[movie title] showtimes [city]", and other queries that would be annotated with the same pattern might include "madagascar 2 showtimes sydney" or "planet of the apes showtimes london". We present a sequence clustering method for finding such clusters of queries with similar intent, and an *intent summarization* method for labeling clusters with such an intent pattern that describes the queries in the cluster. As such, our system not only discovers the patterns and slots in a domain, it also produces annotated instances of each pattern, and allows classification of new queries not used in clustering into the discovered patterns. Figure 1 shows the components of our system.

We evaluate our methods using Mechanical Turk judgments, and find that over 90% of patterns and over 80% of instances within a pattern are correct according to a majority of judges. Our approach discovers patterns that cover up to 20% of the traffic within a domain, and this number can be easily adjusted at the cost of precision. It can thus facilitate structured search, and is an important step toward fully automating query intent understanding.

2. RELATED WORK

Query clustering has been applied to various tasks, such

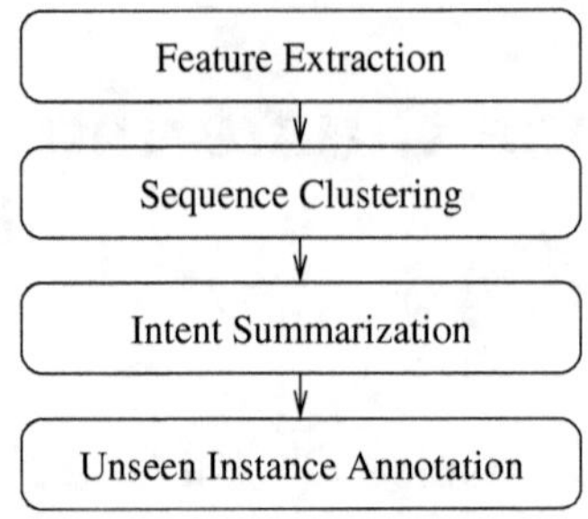

Figure 1: Components of our intent discovery system.

as to construct domains of similar documents or to find documents that may be interesting to a user [4], to semi-automatically improve identification of frequent natural language queries [28], or for query refinement and recommendation [2, 3, 24]. In contrast, this work aims to discover common query intent patterns.

There has been work on concept (slot) discovery, which aims to discover entities that belong to the same concept (according to the IS-A relation) and to label these concepts. One body of work discovers concepts by noting that they often appear in the same patterns in context [15, 17], stemming from work on hyponym and relation extraction [10, 23]. The related distributional hypothesis [9], which states that words with similar meaning appear in similar contexts, motivates other work [18, 20]. In [7], named entities in queries are classified into a list of predefined classes using a weakly supervised method. Whereas the above approaches discover flat concepts, ontology building places lexical items and named entities into a hierarchy [5, 26, 19]. Within the framework of the Semantic Web, the discovered ontologies can be used to facilitate inter-website communication [6, 12, for example].

The algorithm of Sarkas et al. [25] maps a query to a table of structured data and to attributes of the table. While they train an unsupervised model to disambiguate between possible mappings, their method requires a highly developed and structured domain schema, which may be available for some domains like the *Products* domain that they test their method on, but is not appropriate for discovering intents in new domains.

On automating sequence labeling of queries, the work most related to ours is the use of supervised or semi-supervised machine learning models for semantic annotation. In [13], a distinction is defined between intent heads, which are slot names indicative of the intent such as "movie", and intent modifiers, which are slot fillers such as *rio* or *matrix*. Discriminative classifiers are trained on labeled data to recognize the distinction. In contrast, our unsupervised technique does not require making this decision and automatically decides which words should be generalized into a slot based on the clusters discovered. Semi-supervised and supervised methods to do query tagging using conditional random fields have also been proposed [14, 29], but these methods still require a predefined schema.

The work of Agarwal et al. [1] studies the importance of query templates and structured patterns. They find that a large majority of queries follow some query template in most domains they examined, and that most queries in a domain can be covered by a small number of templates (in the hundreds). They also investigate the problem of template discovery. Starting from a seed set of in-domain queries, websites, or templates, a click graph, and at least a partial schema for a domain, their method produces a ranked list of templates relevant to that domain by an iterative graph walking method. Our work is completely unsupervised and does not require any seed annotations or schemata; while we do use a semi-supervised method to extract queries in a domain (Section 7.1), this is merely to speed up computation and facilitate analysis of the resulting clusters. Our method can be applied to the full query log, and we describe two algorithmic speed-ups to support this in Section 4.3. In addition to supporting structured search, query templates can also be used to improve query recommendations [27].

	2010	*buick*	*regal*	*review*
[car]	0	1	1	0
[episode]	1	0	0	1
[model]	0	1	1	0
[season]	1	0	0	0
[year]	1	0	0	0
...	...	...	...	...
review	0	0	0	1
test	0	0	0	0

Figure 2: Sample query representation, abbreviated. Notice that *buick* and *regal* share similar feature vectors because they are found in a surface form *buick regal* in Freebase.

3. FEATURE REPRESENTATION

At the core of our approach is the use of feature vectors to represent queries. The key advantages of a feature vector representation are that semantic and lexical information about the queries can be encoded as features, and similarity scores can be computed between queries, as we will describe.

We let $q = (w_1, w_2, \ldots, w_M)$ denote a query consisting of M word tokens. We create a feature vector of N dimensions for each word token in the query, *i.e.*, $\mathbf{x}_i = (x_{i,1}, x_{i,2}, \ldots, x_{i,N})^T$, $i = 1, 2, \ldots, M$. We will discuss the features shortly. A query, therefore, is represented by an $N \times M$ matrix denoted as $X^q = (\mathbf{x}^q_1, \ldots, \mathbf{x}^q_M)$, where N is fixed and M varies based on query length. Given a large set of queries $\{q\}$, we would like to find query clusters based on X^q. To find semantically meaningful clusters, it is crucial to construct the features in such a way that semantically similar words are close to each other in the vector space. We leverage a knowledge base to achieve this goal.

3.1 Knowledge Base

Freebase is a large knowledge base with structured data harvested from many sources such as Wikipedia. We used the Freebase "Simple Topic Dump" data which consists of over 20 million entities assigned to over 13K concepts. There can be multiple concepts associated with one entity, and multiple entities corresponding to the same surface form. We created a list of concepts for each surface form by merging the concepts of all entities for that surface form. Although the Freebase concepts are hierarchical, we do not make use of the structure of the hierarchy, because it is very flat and uninformative, and because some of the concepts serve a Freebase-internal functional purpose, such as to group together topics defined by a particular Freebase user.

We removed five concepts that each appear in more than two million entities[1], as these are too common to be informative. This results in 13647 concepts.

3.2 Feature Extraction

Our feature vector space consists of $N = N_S + N_L$ dimensions, where N_S represents the number of semantic features and N_L is that of lexical features.

We extract semantic features based on the knowledge base data: if an n-gram $w_{t:t+n}$ in q matches an entity surface form in the freebase data, then for *each* $\mathbf{x}_i$, $i = t : t + n$, we set the value 1 to all the feature dimensions represented by the Freebase concepts that contain this entity surface form.

Next, we extract domain-independent lexical features from a corpus. Specifically, we extract all the word-types in the Wall Street Journal corpus that are not predominantly proper nouns or cardinal numbers (*i.e.*, the most common part-of-speech tag for that word-type is not CD, NNP or NNPS). In other words, for each w_i in q, we assign the value 1 to the feature dimension corresponding to the word identity. We removed such words because during intent summarization, we would like our algorithm to generalize these words into an appropriate semantic concept. For example, many clusters in the *Cars* domain contain a specific model year, like "2010", and it would be more useful to generalize this to the semantic concept [year] than to produce a pattern containing the specific year "2010". Figure 2 shows an example of a query's feature representation.

3.3 Inverse Entity Frequency

In standard information retrieval, it is well known that not all words are equally important. Similarly, not all semantic features extracted from Freebase are equally important in determining query similarity. We define a measure of *inverse entity frequency* that is analogous to inverse document frequency in information retrieval. Intuitively, the importance of a shared concept in determining query similarity is inversely correlated with the number of entities contained in that concept, so that sharing a very general concept like [album] provides only weak evidence of similarity, while sharing a specific concept like [sports car] provides stronger evidence.

We experimented with several specific instantiations of this idea, and we found that using the reciprocal entity frequency worked best. That is,

$$REF(y) = 1/size(y), \tag{1}$$

where y is a Freebase concept or lexical item, and $size(y)$ is the number of surface forms that concept y contains, or 1 if y is a lexical item.

4. CLUSTERING

We now introduce our sequence clustering method to discover groups of queries with similar intents. Sequence clustering is one of the most widely used techniques for pattern discovery from sequential data, and is used in virtually every field that deals with sequences, *e.g.*, gene sequences in biology or time series in telecommunications.

[1]"/common/topic" (which appears in every entry), "music/track", "book/book_edition", "/book/written_work" and "book/book"

There are typically three strategies for clustering sequential data[2]. The first strategy relies on defining a similarity metric between a pair of sequences. Based on a similarity matrix constructed for the entire sequence collection, a good number of clustering algorithms can be applied, including agglomerative clustering such as single-link and complete-link algorithms, partitional clustering such as medoid-based method, and spectral clustering [16]. A second approach is to transform sequences into feature vectors of fixed dimensions, and then to perform any clustering algorithm that operates on feature vectors, *e.g.*, k-means. Note that since similarity can be computed from feature vectors, the algorithms mentioned above for the first strategy are applicable here as well. Finally, there is a class of methods based on generative models. Hidden Markov models, for example, are widely used for modeling sequential data. Clustering is done iteratively by alternately updating model parameters and computing the likelihood of a cluster generating a sequence. Non-parametric approaches are used to deal with the issue of the unknown number of concepts (topics). However, we expect a very large number of concepts in web queries, making such an approach infeasible.

Orthogonal to the above strategies, clustering can be performed in a bottom-up, top-down or partition-based fashion. In this work, we adopt a bottom-up approach based on a similarity metric. The reason is that the number of clusters is likely on the same scale with the number of queries, since there is a long tail of rare queries that each represent a unique intent. This prevents us from starting with K-partitions or applying a top-down approach. Specifically, we choose agglomerative clustering using a distance metric based on dynamic time warping (DTW) between a pair of sequences [21], which we will describe in more detail. While there might be other clustering strategies that could work well, but it is beyond the scope of this work to give a concise evaluation of different clustering algorithms.

4.1 Distance Metric

First, we let $d(\mathbf{x}_i, \mathbf{x}_j)$ denote a distance metric defined on a pair of static feature vectors. Let $\mathbf{r}_i$ be the REF-weighted vector for $\mathbf{x}_i$. That is,

$$\mathbf{r}_i = (REF(1) \times x_{i,1}, \ldots, REF(N) \times x_{i,N})^T. \quad (2)$$

Then, we define the distance as

$$d(\mathbf{x}_i, \mathbf{x}_j) = \log\left(1 - \frac{\mathbf{r}_i \cdot \mathbf{r}_j}{|\mathbf{r}_i||\mathbf{r}_j|}\right). \quad (3)$$

Given a query pair (q, q'), we define an *alignment* as a set of edges E connecting the two sequences of nodes such that (1) every node has at least one edge, and (2) there are no crossing edges (monotonic assumption). The optimal alignment is the one that produces the smallest total distance computed by summing over all edges, *i.e.*,

$$E^* = \underset{E}{\operatorname{argmin}} \sum_{(i,j) \in E} d(\mathbf{x}_i^q, \mathbf{x}_j^{q'}). \quad (4)$$

The DTW distance can be efficiently computed by dynamic programming (Algorithm 1). We normalize the DTW distance by the average query length to compensate for the impact of sequence lengths on distance scores. So,

Algorithm 1 Dynamic Time Warping

$DTW(0,0) = 0$
$DTW(i,0) = DTW(0,j) = \infty$, $i = 1..|q|$, $j = 1..|q'|$
for $i = 1$ to $|q|$ **do**
  for $j = 1$ to $|q'|$ **do**
    $DTW(i,j) = d(\mathbf{x}_i^q, \mathbf{x}_j^{q'}) + \mathrm{Min}(DTW(i-1,j), DTW(i,j-1), DTW(i-1,j-1))$
  end for
end for
return $DTW(|q|, |q'|)$

$$dist(X^q, X^{q'}) = \frac{\min_E \sum_{(i,j)\in E} d(\mathbf{x}_i^q, \mathbf{x}_j^{q'})}{(|q| + |q'|)/2}. \quad (5)$$

4.2 Agglomerative Clustering

Agglomerative clustering starts by treating each data point (a sequence in our case) as a cluster, and then iteratively merging pairs of clusters with the lowest distance (equivalently, highest similarity) until a stopping criterion is satisfied. After each merging step, the cluster distances are recalculated as necessary.

Different versions of agglomerative clustering exist depending on their definition of cluster distance. In single-link clustering,

$$dist(C, C') = \min_{q \in C, q' \in C'} dist(X^q, X^{q'}), \quad (6)$$

while in complete-link clustering,

$$dist(C, C') = \max_{q \in C, q' \in C'} dist(X^q, X^{q'}). \quad (7)$$

If D is the number of input data-points (sequences), single-link clustering has time complexity $O(D^2)$, whereas complete-link clustering has time complexity $O(D^2 \log D)$ [16]. In practice, single-link clustering is faster as well. In our experiments, we evaluated both single- and complete-link agglomerative clustering. Figure 3 shows a sample output cluster in the *Cars* domain using single-link clustering.

There also exists average-link agglomerative clustering, which takes the average distance between cluster instances to be the cluster distance, but it is computationally more expensive and its behavior would simply be intermediate between single- and complete-link, so we did not use it in our experiments.

The stopping criterion can be determined in several ways. Two popular options are to threshold the minimum inter-cluster distance of the remaining clusters, or to set a fixed number of merging iterations. We opt for the former, because the number of queries with similar intent that should be merged is unknown, and this number is different for each domain. At this point, all singleton clusters are removed, and the remaining non-singleton clusters are passed to intent summarization. After the sequence clustering step, when we say cluster we refer to non-singleton clusters.

4.3 Speed-up and Distributed Computation

The main computation bottleneck is to compute the similarity matrix between sequences, which is quadratic in the number of sequences. Since each similarity calculation is

[2]See [11] for a general overview of clustering algorithms, and [8] for one specific to clustering sequential data.

Queries			
2007	audi rs4	review	
2007	infiniti m45	review	
2004	audi s4	review	
2010	jaguar xj	review	
2011	jaguar xj	review	
1987	bmw m6	review	
2010	pontiac gto	review	
09	acura rl	review	
2010	audi tt	review	video
2010	buick regal	review	
2010	mazdaspeed 3	review	
2010	acura zdx	review	
Pattern			
[year]	[model]	**review**	

Figure 3: Sample query cluster, with alignment and pattern produced by intent summarization.

independent of other calculations, the matrix computation can be naturally parallelized across the cells of the matrix.

Another possible algorithmic speed-up is to use the inverted index trick to filter out calculations for cells which have no common features. To do so, an inverted index is first constructed from the dimensions of the feature vectors to the queries for which this dimension is non-zero. Then, to compute the similarity between a query q and all of the other queries, the inverted index is consulted for each non-zero dimension in q to obtain a set of queries with at least one overlapping feature. The similarity score calculation is then only performed on this subset of queries, as the similarity scores for the other queries are zero. We did not implement this method, as we found computing the entire similarity matrix to be feasible, but we mention this method to show that our method can be scaled to many more query instances if so desired.

5. INTENT SUMMARIZATION

After clustering, groups of queries with similar intent are constructed. The next step is to produce a pattern (*i.e.*, a label sequence of slots and lexical items) that describes the intent of the cluster, which we call *intent summarization.* We denote a pattern by $p = (y_1, y_2, \ldots, y_L)$, where L is the length of the label sequence. This length is less than or equal to the lengths of the queries being summarized, because one semantic concept may consume multiple query words.

Intent summarization is useful for several reasons. First, if these automatically discovered intents are to inform development of structured search, a human-readable and interpretable pattern would be highly useful to connect the intents to a structured database, or to construct new knowledge bases or tools based on the pattern. Second, the patterns produced by intent summarization would allow generalization of the intents to new query instances, as we will demonstrate in Section 6.

In this work, we use Freebase concepts as slots. Doing so allows us to avoid manually building domain-dependent lists of slots. We use the head word of the name of the Freebase concept as the slot name, unless it is the generic word "topic", in which case we use the concept's parent concept in the Freebase hierarchy. The head word is found by using an in-house chunker with head-finding heuristics. So, "[city with dogs]" would become "[city]".

Intent summarization consists of the following steps. First, the queries are segmented and aligned. Each alignment represents one slot in the pattern. Then, for each position in the pattern, we select a Freebase concept or lexical item to represent the segments at that position. We now describe these steps in more detail.

5.1 Segmentation and Alignment

We segment each query based on the feature vector representation of the words in the query. As a result of the feature extraction procedure discussed in Section 3.2, words that belong to the same entity in Freebase have very similar feature vector representations; *e.g.*, "san" and "francisco" because of the city name "san francisco". We thus segment the query greedily by considering the cosine similarity of adjacent feature vectors, merging words into a segment if the similarity is below a low threshold.

After segmentation, all segments at the same absolute position are aligned and passed on to the concept selection step. There may be errors in clustering or segmentation that lead to some queries having more segments than others, in which case we take the floor of the median to be the length of the pattern. This is, however, rare, because the dynamic time warping algorithm in the clustering step usually results in low similarity in these cases. Also, our concept selection method is robust to many such errors, as we will describe.

5.2 Concept Selection

Suppose we have a cluster of K queries. We define a function, $y_i = generalize(\mathcal{S}_i = s_i^1, \ldots, s_i^K)$, which, given a multiset of segments $\mathcal{S}_i$ at a fixed position i, returns a Freebase concept or lexical item y_i that summarizes the input segments. Note that an arbitrary order is assigned to $\mathcal{S}_i$ so that all of its segments can be enumerated (as indexed by the superscript), and that each segment comes from a different query in the cluster. We assume that the function is independent of the position, so for clarity, we will omit the subscript i in this section.

One natural way to do generalization is to pick the concept that contains the most input segments according to Freebase. This approach, however, turns out not to be robust. Noise, whether from the clustering procedure, or, more commonly, from the Freebase concept omissions and ambiguity of the segments can lead to incorrect generalizations.

For example, suppose we would like to generalize the first position of the queries "2004 audi s4 review", "2010 buick regal review", and "09 acura rl review" . The Freebase concept for [year] contains "2004" and "2010", but not "09". On the other hand, all three segments belong to the concept [tv series episode], so this simple approach would incorrectly select this concept to be the generalization. Furthermore, there is usually no unique concept that maximizes the number of contained segments, and a procedure is needed to select among these features.

To solve these problems, we use a generative model to implement the generalization function with REF scores to initialize the parameters to the model. The intuition for choosing this approach is that we want to prefer the most specific concept (*i.e.*, the concept with the highest REF score) that contains all of the segments according to Freebase, but we want to be flexible and account for the fact that Freebase concepts are noisy and may contain omissions.

Assuming that each of the segments in the cluster can be modeled independently of the others, the following model gives the joint probability of the segments and the concept:

$$P(\mathcal{S}, y) = P(y) \prod_{k=1}^{K} P(s^k|y). \tag{8}$$

The parameters of the model $P(s|y)$ are initialized using REF scores with linear discounting for smoothing purposes:

$$P(s|y) = \begin{cases} \gamma * REF(y) & \text{if concept } y \text{ contains } s \\ \dfrac{1-\gamma}{F - size(y)} & \text{otherwise.} \end{cases} \tag{9}$$

F represents the total number of surface forms in Freebase. This initialization corresponds to the following scenario for generating a segment from a concept. With probability γ, we randomly select a segment from the concept using a uniform multinomial distribution according to Freebase. With probability $1-\gamma$, we select a segment not contained by that concept according to Freebase (of which there are $F - size(y)$). We set γ to be 0.5. The prior probabilities are initialized uniformly. Inference means finding

$$\begin{aligned} y^* &= \operatorname*{argmax}_y \log P(\mathcal{S}|y) + \log P(y) \\ &= \operatorname*{argmax}_y \sum_{k=1}^{K} \log P(s^k|y) + \log P(y). \end{aligned} \tag{10}$$

Given the parameters, the maximized expression is simple to calculate for each concept and lexical item. It can be sped up by considering only those concepts which contain at least one of the input segments.

While this initialization prefers concepts with higher REF scores and lexical items, it is not ideal because it is susceptible to overly-specific concepts. For example, different subsets of countries would generalize to different concepts, such as [breed origin] or [olympic participating country], whereas in most domains, the desired generalization is simply the more natural [country] concept. To refine the parameters to prefer such "natural" features, we reestimate the prior probabilities using hard EM.

In the E-step, we use the above model to infer y^* for each aligned segment in the cluster. Then in the M-step, we reestimate model parameters, *i.e.*, the prior probabilities, in the maximum likelihood sense:

$$P(y) = \frac{count(y)}{\sum_{j=1}^{N} count(j)}, \tag{11}$$

where $count(y)$ is the number of times y appeared in the E-step's classification, and the denominator is the total number of classifications made. These two steps are alternated until convergence. In our experiments, we simply conduct one iteration of the algorithm and empirically found the results satisfactory, as will be shown in Section 7.2.

Finally, as a further refinement, any clusters that have the same pattern after intent summarization are merged. Figure 3 shows the output of intent summarization on the example query cluster. We could further merge clusters based on semantic intent, as an intent may be expressed by several different, but related patterns, such as "[city] map" and "map of [city]", but we leave this to future work.

	[year]	*[model]*	*review*
[car]	0	0	0
[episode]	0	0	0
[model]	0	1	0
[season]	0	0	0
[year]	1	0	0
...	...	...	...
review	0	0	1
test	0	0	0

Figure 4: Pattern representation for instance annotation.

6. INSTANCE ANNOTATION

The procedure above produces a set of patterns within a domain and classifies query instances into these patterns. When encountering new query instances, we would like an efficient method to classify them into one of the existing patterns without having to perform clustering again, which is expensive and would not yield substantially different results. Fortunately, the feature representation in our method suggests a natural way to do this.

For each discovered pattern $p = (y_1, y_2, \ldots, y_L)$, we define $\mathbf{z}_i$ to be a feature vector in the same space as the word tokens that represents the ith element in the pattern. It thus has dimension N, and the interpretation of the dimensions is the same as before. Each $\mathbf{z}_i$ is defined to be a zero vector, except at the dimension corresponding to y_i, where it has value one. So,

$$\begin{aligned} \mathbf{z}_i &= (z_{i,1}, z_{i,2}, \ldots, z_{i,N})^T \\ z_{i,j} &= \begin{cases} 1 & \text{if } y_i = j \\ 0 & \text{otherwise.} \end{cases} \end{aligned} \tag{12}$$

A pattern is then represented by a matrix of size $N \times L$, $Z = (\mathbf{z}_1, \ldots, \mathbf{z}_L)$. See Figure 4 for a sample pattern representation.

Given this representation of a pattern, a new instance can be classified into one of the existing patterns, Z^*, by finding the pattern that is the most similar to the new query, using the same log REF-weighted cosine and DTW algorithm as before to calculate similarity:

$$Z^* = \begin{cases} \operatorname*{argmin}_Z dist(X^q, Z) & \text{if } dist(X^q, Z) < \tau \\ \text{undefined} & \text{otherwise.} \end{cases} \tag{13}$$

If the minimum distance is above a threshold τ, the query is judged to be not similar enough to any of the existing patterns and not classified into one. We set this threshold to be the same as the termination threshold in agglomerative clustering. Note that the inverted index speed-up applies here as well, and would likely result in a great speed-up because the pattern representations are very sparse.

7. EXPERIMENTS

Evaluating unsupervised methods is a challenging problem, especially if there is little labeled data available, as is the case here. As a first evaluation, we elicited human judgments on the output of the algorithms (Evaluations 1 and 2). We also measured the domain coverage of the extracted patterns (Evaluation 3).

Domains		10
Sampled queries		~101K
Single-link clusters	*total*	1069
	min	13
	max	203
	std	63.5
	avg. size	4.22
Complete-link clusters	*total*	1466
	min	18
	max	279
	std	85.4
	avg. size	2.68

Table 1: Data and cluster characteristics. The attributes *min*, *max* and *std* refer to the number of non-singleton clusters discovered over the domains. *avg. size* is the average number of queries in non-singleton clusters.

G	N	B	*Single*		*Complete*	
3	0	0	497	(70.7%)	579	(62.6%)
2	1	0	26	(23.3%)	35	(28.6%)
2	0	1	138		230	
1	2	0	2		3	
1	1	1	10	(5.0%)	18	(8.0%)
1	0	2	23		53	
0	2	1	0		2	
0	1	2	3	(1.0%)	1	(0.8%)
0	0	3	4		4	
		Total:	**703**		**925**	

Table 2: Evaluation 1 results in terms of annotator judgments, separated by agglomerative clustering algorithm. G: Good, N: Not sure, B: Bad.

G	N	B	*Before*		*After*	
3	0	0	331	(43.2%)	184	(69.7%)
2	1	0	23	(32.1%)	8	(20.5%)
2	0	1	223		46	
1	2	0	3		2	
1	1	1	32	(22.3%)	5	(9.5%)
1	0	2	136		18	
0	2	1	2		0	
0	1	2	7	(2.3%)	0	(0.4%)
0	0	3	9		1	
		Total:	**766**		**264**	

Table 3: Comparison of the subset of both single- and complete-link clusters changed by EM prior reestimation. The cases in the *After* column are a subset of the cases shown in Table 2

We are interested in evaluating two aspects of our system: the patterns that result from intent summarization and the query instances that are classified into each cluster. For each aspect, we can measure the precision; *i.e.*, the quality of the output of our system, or the recall; *i.e.*, whether we have extracted all of the useful patterns and instances that fit a pattern. Naturally, recall is much harder to evaluate in this case because there is no clear way to obtain all of the possible patterns in a domain or query instances that belong to a certain pattern. While one could approximate pattern recall evaluation by comparing to the patterns in a human-labeled dataset, no such labels are available for our dataset, and the labeled datasets that are available, even in related domains, are not appropriate due to differences in schema and data creation. In particular, the schema in a domain is often manually predefined, and queries that do not follow the schema are not included, thus not being representative of actual user needs in a domain.

7.1 Data set

We extracted search queries and segmented them into domains using a click graph. The nodes in the click graph are queries and URLs, while the edges connect queries to URLs based on search engine click-through data. We extracted queries belonging to a particular domain by specifying a number of seed URLs from each domain, and taking the queries that are linked to these URLs. We created ten domains in this manner: *Cars*, *Celebrities*, *Gaming*, *Health*, *Real estate*, *Sports*, *Travel*, *Jobs*, *Movies*, and *Education*.

We sampled at least 10K queries[3] from each domain and ran our sequence clustering and intent summarization algorithms on these samples as described above. When calculating the similarity matrix for sequence clustering, we split computation into fifteen processes, finishing all calculations within ten minutes, and we set the stopping criterion for agglomerative clustering to be a threshold of 2.0 on the minimum cluster distance. While we could have compared our methods to a a bag-of-words baseline, we did not do so because the outcome of our work is to produce grammar rules in which word order is important. We cannot group queries by a bag-of-words approach because it would be hard to express the resulting clusters in this format.

[3]The *Education* domain contained less than 20K queries overall, so we used all of the queries in that domain.

The remaining queries from each domain were treated as unseen queries and annotated using the method described in Section 6. The only exceptions to the input to instance annotation were that we did not run instance annotation on the *Gaming* or *Health* domains, because we found relatively few patterns in these domains. Overall, ~7.8M unseen queries were processed using the output of both clustering algorithms, resulting in over 15M classification decisions. Of this, ~125K were classified into a pattern that was discovered. Some other basic statistics on the data and the results of the algorithms are presented in Table 1.

7.2 Evaluation 1: Cluster Pattern Precision

We first evaluated the quality of the cluster patterns that are produced by sequence clustering and intent summarization. For each pattern, we selected between two to three compatible instances arbitrarily, and displayed these to judges along with the pattern. Annotators were given instructions and examples of what good and bad patterns are, then asked to judge whether the pattern describes the instances displayed. We asked annotators to consider the order of the items and whether they fit the concepts in the pattern, as well as the granularity of the concepts, but not the spelling, punctuation, or capitalization. See Appendix A.1 for the complete guidelines. For each pattern, annotators could indicate that the pattern was "good", "bad", or that they were "not sure". Each case was assigned to three different annotators to judge using Mechanical Turk, with a

G	N	B	*Single*		*Complete*	
3	0	0	1282	(65.4%)	1286	(74.5%)
2	1	0	66	(16.3%)	93	(13.2%)
2	0	1	254		134	
1	2	0	3		5	
1	1	1	54	(14.9%)	30	(9.6%)
1	0	2	236		131	
0	3	0	2		0	
0	2	1	6	(3.4%)	1	(2.7%)
0	1	2	10		7	
0	0	3	48		39	
		Total:	**1961**		**1726**	

(a) Original queries

G	N	B	*Single*		*Complete*	
3	0	0	1059	(64.1%)	1012	(68.7%)
2	1	0	63	(20.3%)	76	(17.1%)
2	0	1	272		176	
1	2	0	8		8	
1	1	1	46	(11.0%)	49	(11.7%)
1	0	2	128		116	
0	3	0	1		0	
0	2	1	12	(4.5%)	1	(2.5%)
0	1	2	13		9	
0	0	3	49		27	
		Total:	**1651**		**1474**	

(b) Unseen queries

Table 4: Evaluation 2 results.

resulting free-marginal kappa [22] of 0.657. Table 2 shows the results of this evaluation.

Overall, more than 60% clusters were judged to be correct by all three annotators, and over 90% were correct by at least two annotators. The single-link clusters were more precise than the complete-link ones (Mann-Whitney U $p < 0.001$), but the complete-link algorithm discovered more clusters. Intuitively, complete-link clustering prefers more coherent clusters, which means that the average cluster size will tend to be small, resulting in more non-singleton clusters.

To measure the impact of the EM prior reestimation, we ran the same study on the subset of the clusters where EM reestimation changed the pattern output, before EM reestimation was done. We compared this subset to the analogous subset after EM reestimation (Table 3). Because we filtered out patterns with fewer than two compatible query instances, a different number of patterns qualified before EM reestimation (766 across both clustering algorithms compared to 264). The results show that the hard EM procedure was able to produce substantially more precise patterns (Mann-Whitney U $p < 1^{-14}$), at the cost of having fewer patterns with at least two compatible instances according to Freebase. Notice, however, that this is to be expected, since the point of the prior reestimation is precisely to overcome Freebase annotation errors and omissions.

7.3 Evaluation 2: Query Labeling Precision

In the second evaluation, we asked annotators to judge the correctness of each query instance in a pattern, assuming that the pattern itself is correct. For each case, annotators were given one query (rather than several as in the previous evaluation) and the pattern that describes it, and asked to judge whether the query fits the pattern, does not fit, or whether they are not sure. See Appendix A.2 for the guidelines given to the annotators. We filtered out the patterns that were not judged to be correct by all three annotators from Evaluation 1, as this evaluation is meaningless if the pattern is not correct.

We performed this evaluation not only on the original 10K samples as in Evaluation 1, but also on the classified unseen queries from Section 6, to check the precision of instance annotation. To ensure that the sample sizes and distribution between domains are comparable, we sampled from each domain the same number of unseen queries as were put into a cluster in the original data.

G	N	B	*Incompatible*	
3	0	0	379	(57.3%)
2	1	0	29	(19.2%)
2	0	1	98	
1	2	0	1	
1	1	1	25	(19.0%)
1	0	2	100	
0	3	0	2	
0	2	1	5	(4.5%)
0	1	2	6	
0	0	3	17	
		Total:	**662**	

Table 5: Evaluation of query labeling on subset not compatible with the intent pattern according to Freebase.

The results of the second evaluation are presented in Table 4. The inter-annotator agreement by kappa was 0.692. In contrast to Evaluation 1, the precision of the instances in complete-link clusters was greater (Mann-Whitney U $p < 1^{-10}$). Complete-link clustering is known to produce more coherent clusters than single-link clustering in general, which likely explains this result.

Since query labeling correctness and pattern correctness are highly interconnected, we would expect the original queries to be very precise, since we filtered out the patterns not judged to be correct by all three annotators in Evaluation 1. This is seen in the results, as the precision of the original queries is slightly higher. However, instance annotation results are only slightly lower, despite not being used in the original clustering algorithm. The difference in precision between the original and the unseen cases was statistically significant (Mann-Whitney U $p < 0.01$). Note, however, that the large sample size means that even very small differences in magnitude would be significant.

One interesting point to note is that our algorithms are tolerant of Freebase omissions. For example, the pattern "who is [celebrity] married to" contains many celebrities that are not listed in this concept in Freebase, such as "alanis morissette" and "julie berman". Table 5 shows the results on the subset of instances that do not fit the pattern according to Freebase. As expected, the precision on this subset is lower than the overall precision, but even so, the majority of such instances do actually fit the discovered pattern

Domain	*Single*	*Complete*
cars	5.4%	5.9%
celebrities	1.2%	1.7%
real estate	0.31%	0.45%
sports	0.84%	9.4%
travel	20.2%	21.2 %
jobs	1.2%	1.2 %
movies	2.3%	9.2%
Average:	**4.5%**	**7.0%**

Table 6: Traffic-weighted domain coverage.

according to annotators. Thus, our algorithm can be used to discover new intent-specific slot-fillers that cannot be directly predicted from the knowledge base.

7.4 Evaluation 3: Domain Coverage

Another measure of performance is the domain coverage of the patterns that are extracted; *i.e.*, the proportion of the traffic in a particular domain that is described by one of the patterns that are extracted. We approximate this by calculating the proportion of unseen queries in each domain that are classified into a cluster pattern, weighted by the traffic of the queries. Table 6 shows the coverage results by domain and clustering method. Complete-link clustering results in higher domain coverage than single-link. There is substantial variation in coverage between domains, ranging from less than 0.4% in the *Real estate* domain to more than 20% in the *Travel* domain. This variation is likely due to the Freebase coverage of the entities in that domain. For example, the *Real estate* domain contains many queries that are specific addresses in real estate listings, and many of the local street names are not recognized in Freebase as such. On the other hand, the *Travel* domain contains countries and cities that are correctly recognized.

8. CONCLUSION

We have presented an unsupervised method to find clusters of queries with similar intent, induce patterns to describe these clusters, and classify new queries into the cluster that are discovered, all using only domain-independent resources. Judgments by human annotators indicate that the patterns and the instance annotations are done precisely, and the domain coverage of the patterns that our algorithms found reach up to 20% of traffic in certain domains. Our work can facilitate structured search development by reducing the amount of manual labour needed to extend structured search into a new domain.

There are many avenues of future research. Besides refining the sequence clustering and intent summarization algorithms, it remains to merge patterns with the same intent. For example, word order sometimes (but not always) does not matter, as in "[movie] showtimes" and "showtimes [movie]", and there may be minor variations in the lexical items, such as "[movie] review" and "[movie] reviews" which convey the same intent. Another future direction is to automate the process of matching the slots discovered by our method to a structured database. A modified version of our algorithms could also be applied to match patterns to URLs and website, which often contain structure that can be exploited. Doing so could further automate instant answer generation for many more patterns and domains.

9. ACKNOWLEDGMENTS

The authors would like to thank Alex Acero and Ye-Yi Wang for useful discussions.

References

[1] G. Agarwal, G. Kabra, and K. Chang. Towards rich query interpretation: Walking back and forth for mining query templates. In *Proceedings of the 19th international conference on World wide web*, pages 1–10. ACM, 2010.

[2] R. Baeza-Yates, C. Hurtado, and M. Mendoza. Query recommendation using query logs in search engines. In *Current Trends in Database Technology-EDBT 2004 Workshops*, pages 395–397. Springer, 2005.

[3] R. Baeza-Yates, C. Hurtado, and M. Mendoza. Improving search engines by query clustering. *Journal of the American Society for Information Science and Technology*, 58(12):1793–1804, 2007.

[4] D. Beeferman and A. Berger. Agglomerative clustering of a search engine query log. In *Proceedings of the Sixth ACM SIGKDD International Conference on Knowledge Discovery and Data Mining*, pages 407–416. ACM, 2000.

[5] S. Chuang and L. Chien. Enriching web taxonomies through subject categorization of query terms from search engine logs. *Decision Support Systems*, 35(1): 113–127, 2003.

[6] P. Clerkin, P. Cunningham, and C. Hayes. Ontology discovery for the semantic web using hierarchical clustering. *Semantic Web Mining*, page 27, 2001.

[7] J. Guo, G. Xu, X. Cheng, and H. Li. Named entity recognition in query. In *Proceedings of the 32nd International ACM SIGIR Conference on Research and Development in Information Retrieval*, pages 267–274. ACM, 2009.

[8] V. Guralnik and G. Karypis. A scalable algorithm for clustering sequential data. In *Proceedings of the IEEE International Conference on Data Mining*, pages 179–186. Published by the IEEE Computer Society, 2001.

[9] Z. Harris. Distributional structure. *Word*, 1954.

[10] M. A. Hearst. Automatic acquisition of hyponyms from large text corpora. In *Proceedings of the 14th Conference on Computational Linguistics*, pages 539–545, 1992.

[11] A. Jain, M. Murty, and P. Flynn. Data clustering: a review. *ACM Computing Surveys (CSUR)*, 31(3):264–323, 1999.

[12] L. Karoui, M. Aufaure, and N. Bennacer. Ontology discovery from web pages: Application to tourism. In *In the Workshop of Knowledge Discovery and Ontologies*. Citeseer, 2004.

[13] X. Li. Understanding the semantic structure of noun phrase queries. In *Proceedings of the 48th Annual Meeting of the Association for Computational Linguistics*, pages 1337–1345. Association for Computational Linguistics, 2010.

[14] X. Li, Y.-Y. Wang, and A. Acero. Extracting structured information from user queries with semi-supervised conditional random fields. In *Proceedings of the 32nd International ACM SIGIR Conference on Research and Development in Information Retrieval*, pages 572–579. ACM, 2009.

[15] D. Lin and P. Pantel. Concept discovery from text. In *Proceedings of the 19th International Conference on Computational Linguistics*, pages 1–7, 2002.

[16] C. Manning, P. Raghavan, and H. Schütze. *Introduction to information retrieval*, chapter 17. Cambridge University Press, 2008.

[17] P. Pantel and D. Ravichandran. Automatically labeling semantic classes. In *Proceedings of HLT/NAACL*, volume 4, pages 321–328, 2004.

[18] M. Pasca, D. Lin, J. Bigham, A. Lifchits, and A. Jain. Organizing and searching the world wide web of facts-step one: the one-million fact extraction challenge. In *Proceedings of the National Conference on Artificial Intelligence*, volume 21, pages 1400–1405, 2006.

[19] M. Pennacchiotti and P. Pantel. Ontologizing semantic relations. In *Proceedings of the 21st International Conference on Computational Linguistics and the 44th annual meeting of the Association for Computational Linguistics*, pages 793–800. Association for Computational Linguistics, 2006.

[20] M. Pennacchiotti and P. Pantel. Entity extraction via ensemble semantics. In *Proceedings of the 2009 Conference on Empirical Methods in Natural Language Processing*, pages 238–247. Association for Computational Linguistics, 2009.

[21] L. Rabiner and B. Juang. *Fundamentals of Speech Recognition*, chapter 4. Prentice Hall, 1993.

[22] J. Randolph. Free-marginal multirater kappa (multirater κfree): An alternative to fleiss fixed-marginal multirater kappa. In *Joensuu Learning and Instruction Symposium*, 2005.

[23] E. Riloff. Automatically generating extraction patterns from untagged text. In *Proceedings of the National Conference on Artificial Intelligence*, pages 1044–1049, 1996.

[24] E. Sadikov, J. Madhavan, L. Wang, and A. Halevy. Clustering query refinements by user intent. In *Proceedings of the 19th International Conference on World Wide Web*. ACM, 2010.

[25] N. Sarkas, S. Paparizos, and P. Tsaparas. Structured annotations of web queries. In *Proceedings of the 2010 International Conference on Management of Data*, pages 771–782. ACM, 2010.

[26] R. Snow, D. Jurafsky, and A. Ng. Semantic taxonomy induction from heterogenous evidence. In *Proceedings of the 21st International Conference on Computational Linguistics and the 44th Annual Meeting of the Association for Computational Linguistics*, pages 801–808. Association for Computational Linguistics, 2006.

[27] I. Szpektor, A. Gionis, and Y. Maarek. Improving recommendation for long-tail queries via templates. In *Proceedings of the 20th international conference on World wide web*, pages 47–56. ACM, 2011.

[28] J. Wen, J. Nie, and H. Zhang. Clustering user queries of a search engine. In *Proceedings of the 10th International Conference on World Wide Web*, pages 162–168. ACM, 2001.

[29] D. Yu, S. Wang, and L. Deng. Sequential labeling using deep-structured conditional random fields. *IEEE Journal of Selected Topics in Signal Processing*, 4(6): 965–973, 2010.

APPENDIX

A. ANNOTATOR GUIDELINES

A.1 Evaluation 1 Guidelines

Do the phrases fit the pattern?
— A pattern contains category names in square brackets (e.g., [movie]) and/or words or abbreviations (e.g. vs).
— Ignore misspellings or capitalization mistakes and treat words as if they were spelled correctly.
— A good pattern fits the words in the phrases in the correct order.
— A good pattern has categories that are neither too general nor too specific.

Example.
1. kung fu panda 2 showtimes
2. pirates of the caribbean showtimes
GOOD: [movie] showtimes
BAD: [martial arts] 2 showtimes (doesnt́ generalize correctly)
BAD: [location] [artist] (irrelevant patterns)
BAD: [art] showtimes (too general)
BAD: [movies that i have watched] showtimes (too specific)

A.2 Evaluation 2 Guidelines

Does the phrase fit the pattern?
— A pattern contains category names in square brackets (e.g. [movie]) and/or words or abbreviations (e.g. vs). It will be italicized.
— Order matters; a phrase that fits the pattern should fit it in the correct order.
— Think about whether the entire phrase fits in context; not just whether each individual part fits.
— Ignore misspellings or capitalization mistakes and treat words as if they were spelled correctly.
— Ignore any blank cases.

Examples.
1. "kung fu panda 2 showtimes" fits [movie] showtimes, because kung fu panda 2 is a movie and the word showtimes matches and comes after the movie title.
2. "houses for sale in chicago" does not fit houses for sale in [musical], because in this context, Chicago refers to the city, not the musical.
3. "honda 2012" does not fit [year] [model], because the order of the elements is reversed.

IR System Evaluation using Nugget-based Test Collections

Virgil Pavlu Shahzad Rajput Peter B. Golbus Javed A. Aslam
College of Computer and Information Science, Northeastern University
{vip, rajput, pgolbus, jaa}@ccs.neu.edu*

ABSTRACT

The development of information retrieval systems such as search engines relies on good test collections, including assessments of retrieved content. The widely employed "Cranfield paradigm" dictates that the information relevant to a topic be encoded at the level of documents, therefore requiring effectively complete document relevance assessments. As this is no longer practical for modern corpora, numerous problems arise, including *scalability*, *reusability*, and *applicability*. We propose a new method for relevance assessment based on relevant *information*, not relevant *documents*. Once the relevant "nuggets" are collected, our matching method [23] can assess any document for relevance with high accuracy, and so any retrieved list of documents can be assessed for performance. In this paper we analyze the performance of the matching function by looking at specific cases and by comparing with other methods. We then show how these inferred relevance assessments can be used to perform IR system evaluation, and we discuss in particular reusability and scalability. Our main contribution is a methodology for producing test collections that are highly accurate, more complete, scalable, reusable, and can be generated with similar amounts of effort as existing methods, with great potential for future applications.

Categories and Subject Descriptors

H.3 [**Information Systems**]: Information Storage and Retrieval; H.3.4 [**Systems and Software**]: Performance Evaluation

General Terms

Measurement, Performance

1. INTRODUCTION

Much thought and research has been devoted to each of the steps of evaluation of IR systems: constructing a test collection of documents and queries, judging the relevance of the documents to each query, and assessing the quality of the ranked lists. The annual text retrieval conference TREC [17] is central to the standardization of these tasks.

For large collections of documents and/or topics, it is impractical to assess the relevance of each document to each topic. Instead, only a small subset of the documents is assessed. When evaluating the performance of a collection of retrieval systems, as in the annual TREC conference, this judged "pool" of documents is typically constructed by taking the union of the top c documents returned by each system in response to a given query. In TREC, $c = 100$ has been shown to be an effective cutoff in evaluating the relative performance of retrieval systems. Shallower and deeper pools have been studied [32, 17] for TREC and within the greater context of the generation of large test collections. Pooling is an effective technique since many of the documents relevant to a topic will appear near the top of the lists returned by (quality) retrieval systems; thus, these relevant documents will be judged and used to effectively assess the performance of the collected systems; unjudged documents are assumed to be non-relevant.

This process, often referred to as the "Cranfield paradigm" for information retrieval evaluation, essentially operates in two phases: In Phase 1, "Collection Construction", documents, topics, and relevance assessments are all gathered. Following Phase 1, we have a *test collection* that can be used to evaluate the performance of systems in Phase 2, "Evaluation". Note that evaluation can be performed on the systems that contributed to the pool, and perhaps even more importantly, it can be performed on new systems that did not originally contribute to the pool. A test collection is *accurate* if it correctly assesses the performance of systems that contributed to the pool, and it is *reusable* if it correctly assesses the performance of new systems that did not originally contribute to the pool. That a test collection must be accurate is a given, but for a test collection to be truly useful, it must also be reusable: New information retrieval technologies will be tested against existing test collections, as happens continually with the various TREC collections, and for those assessments to be meaningful, these test collections must be reusable. In order for a Cranfield paradigm test collection to be both *accurate* and *reusable*, the relevance assessments must be *effectively complete*. In other words, the vast majority of relevant documents must be found and judged; otherwise, a novel retrieval system could return unseen relevant documents, and the assessment of this system with respect to the test collection will be highly

*We gratefully acknowledge the support provided by the NSF grant IIS-1017903.

Permission to make digital or hard copies of all or part of this work for personal or classroom use is granted without fee provided that copies are not made or distributed for profit or commercial advantage and that copies bear this notice and the full citation on the first page. To copy otherwise, to republish, to post on servers or to redistribute to lists, requires prior specific permission and/or a fee.
WSDM'12, February 8–12, 2012, Seattle, Washington, USA.
Copyright 2012 ACM 978-1-4503-0747-5/12/02 ...$10.00.

inaccurate. Unfortunately, the burden of effectively complete assessments is quite large; in TREC 8, for example, 86,830 relevance judgments were collected in order to build a test collection over a relatively small document collection for just 50 topics.

1.1 Limitations of the Cranfield Paradigm

The key limitation of the Cranfield paradigm is that (1) during collection construction *the information relevant to a topic is encoded by documents* and (2) during evaluation *the information retrieved by a system is encoded by documents.* Thus, in order to assess the performance of a system, one must determine which relevant documents are retrieved (and how), and this necessitates effectively complete relevance judgments.

Other retrieval tasks engender variants on the Cranfield paradigm, but they all tend to retain the central feature above, that the *information* relevant to a topic is *encoded* by documents. The difference is that other metadata is often collected which is specific to the retrieval task. For example, *Graded Relevance* was introduced in web search; instead of documents being "relevant" or "non-relevant", they can be "highly relevant", "relevant", "marginally relevant", or "non-relevant". However, the information relevant to a topic is still encoded by documents (together with their relevance grades), and the information retrieved by a system is also encoded by documents. For *Novelty and Diversity* measurements, the information relevant to a query is encoded by documents and associated "subtopics" [13], and the information retrieved by a system is encoded by documents and either their "marginal utility" with respect to previously retrieved documents or some measure of the coverage of those documents over the associated subtopics.

The central issue with the Cranfield paradigm and with its variants described above is that the information relevant to a topic is encoded by *documents*, and in the presence of large topic sets or large and/or dynamic collections, it is difficult or impossible to find and judge all relevant documents. Hundred of thousands of documents were analyzed, both by governmental organizations (TREC, NTCIR) and large corporations (Google, Microsoft). Even so, and critical to evaluation, many relevant documents are missed; ultimately, it gives rise to several related problems:

1. **Scalability:** Given that the information relevant to a topic is encoded by documents, and given the necessity of effectively complete relevance assessments that this entails for accurate and reusable evaluation, the Cranfield paradigm and its variants cannot scale to large collections and/or topic sets. For example, the query "Barack Obama" yields 233 million results on Google as of August 2011, and it would be impossible to judge all at any reasonable cost or in any reasonable time.
2. **Reusability:** The problem of scale directly gives rise to problems of reusability: (1) For a static collection, novel systems will retrieve unjudged but relevant documents, and the assessments of these systems will be inaccurate. (2) For dynamic collections (such as the World Wide Web), new documents will be added and old documents removed, rendering even statically constructed "effectively complete" relevance assessments incomplete over time, with an attendant loss in reusability.
3. **Applicability:** It can be difficult to apply a test collection designed for one retrieval task and evaluation to another retrieval task or evaluation, especially for test collections that are designed to "address" the scalability and reusability issues described above using current methodologies. This issue is discussed below.

In order to address the inherent limitations of the Cranfield paradigm and variants thereof described above, we propose a test collection construction methodology based on *information nuggets.* We refer to minimal, atomic units of relevant information as "nuggets". Our thesis is that while the number of *documents* potentially relevant to a topic can be enormous, the amount of *information* relevant to a topic, the nuggets, is far, far smaller. Nuggets can range from simple answers such as people's names to full sentences or paragraphs. In this model, assessors indicate as relevant only the relevant portions of documents. This relevant *information* is used to automatically assign relevance judgments to documents and/or evaluate retrieval systems.

1.2 Related Work

Various attempts to address the issues described above have been proposed. (1) Sampling techniques such as infAP [31], statAP [12], and their variants have been used extensively in various TREC tracks, including the Million Query Track, the Web Track, the Relevance Feedback Track, the Enterprise Track, the Terabyte Track, the Video Track, and the Legal Track. These techniques are designed to directly address the *scale* issue described above. A carefully chosen sample of documents is drawn from the pool, these documents are judged, and a *statistical estimate* of the true value of a performance measure over that pool is derived. Given that accurate estimates can be derived using samples as small as roughly 5% of the entire pool, these methods permit the use of pools roughly 20 times the size of standard fully-judged pools. This increases reusability, for example; however, it is only a stop-gap measure. These methods cannot scale to collections the size of the web (where potentially 233 million documents are relevant to a query such as "Barack Obama"), they only partially address the issue of dynamic collections such as the web, and they reduce applicability in that the samples drawn and estimates obtained are typically tailored to specific evaluation measures such as average precision. (2) The Minimal Test Collection methodology [11] also employed in the TREC Million Query Track has generally similar benefits and drawbacks, as described above. (3) Crowd-sourcing relevance judgments, via Mechanical Turk, for example, has also been proposed to alleviate the scale issue [2]. However, this too is only a stop-gap measure, in roughly direct proportion to the relative ease (in time or cost) of crowd-sourced judgments vs. assessor judgments: If 10 to 100 crowd-sourced judgments can be obtained in the same time or at the same cost as 1 assessor judgment, then pools one to two orders of magnitude larger than standard pools can be contemplated, but this still does not scale to the web or address the issue of dynamic collections, as described above. The use of click-through data has also been proposed [22], but this is only applicable to the web and only for those queries and documents with sufficient "clicks". Evaluating IR systems without relevance assessments has also been the subject of research [25, 26, 24]; however, these methods tend to lack the capability of inferring the relevance of arbitrary documents outside the pool, limiting reusability. Quite similar to our work, [4] proposes using "Trels", sets of relevant and non-relevant keywords, to assess arbitrary documents. We believe nuggets can capture more information than simple keywords.

Finally, we note that nuggets of a somewhat different kind are widely used in other contexts. For example, the evaluation of question answering systems [19, 20, 15, 28, 21] uses nuggets, which in this context tend to be very short and specific answers to "who", "when", and "where" type questions. Nuggets have also been used as a form of user feedback in multi-session information distillation tasks [30, 29]. Conceptual nuggets are currently used in novelty and diversity evaluation: subtopics can be thought of as nuggets [14], or systems can be evaluated on coverage of both subtopics and nuggets [6]. However, in none of these contexts are nuggets used to infer relevance automatically. In an effort to improve retrieval under resource restricted conditions (e.g. small screen mobile devices) INEX focuses on retrieving relevant elements/passages from XML documents. However, properly evaluating the effectiveness in XML-IR remains an ongoing research question at INEX [5]. Additionally, the collection used is a set of documents from Wikipedia, which is much cleaner and more structured than arbitrary HTML document on the web. All of the above are still susceptible to the limitations of the Cranfield paradigm.

To address the limitations of the Cranfield paradigm and to achieve test collection scalability, reusability, and applicability, we propose a test collection construction methodology based on nuggets. In previous work [23], we describe a methodology for collecting nuggets, a technique for assessing the relevance of documents given these nuggets, and a preliminary analysis of the quality of these relevance assessments. These results are summarized in Section 2 and parts of Section 3 below. In this work, we provide a detailed exposition of our methodology, a thorough analysis of the quality of our inferred relevance assessments, and a demonstration that these relevance assessments and the test collection thus inferred addresses the issues of scalability, reusability, and applicability for information retrieval evaluation.

2. METHODOLOGY

Consider for example the web query "Barack Obama". The vast majority of the potentially 233 million documents relevant to this topic probably do not contain any information that could not be found in his biography, or even just his Wikipedia page. Furthermore, relevant documents are constantly being created and destroyed, whereas major changes to the set of relevant information are much less frequent. Thus, collecting and encoding the relatively small set of relevant nuggets, as opposed to the dynamically changing and effectively infinite set of *documents* relevant to a topic, will enable us to address the issues of scalability, reusability, and applicability described above.

Figure 1 graphically illustrates the differences between the traditional Cranfield-style evaluation methodology (left) and the nugget-based methodology proposed (right). The nuggets themselves are the relevant and useful pieces of information for a given topic—the information that the user seeks. As a set, they yield a natural encoding of the information relevant to a topic. In principle, if this set is complete,

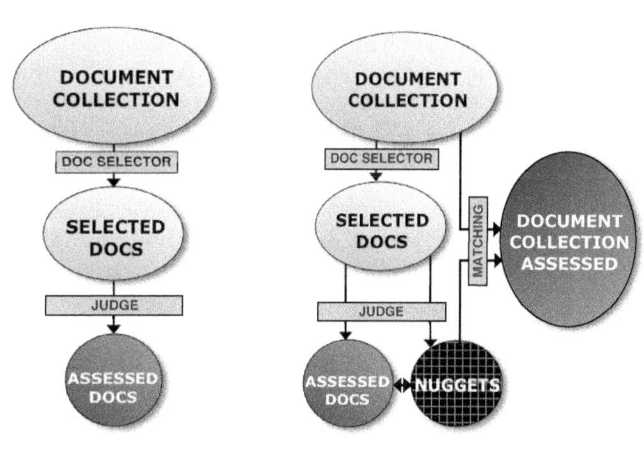

Figure 1: For a given query, selected documents are evaluated as "relevant/nonrelevant". Left: Traditional TREC strategy for relevance. Right: Proposed nuggets method.

we can use the nuggets to infer the relevance of any document.

To build our test collection, we ask assessors to view documents as before. However, rather than providing binary or graded "relevance judgments", we instead ask the assessor to extract nuggets. Our thesis is that while collecting effectively complete document relevance judgment sets is impractical (on a large scale) or impossible (in a dynamic environment), collecting effectively complete nugget sets is much more tractable. Certainly the problem of collecting effectively complete nugget sets is no harder than the problem of collecting effectively complete relevance judgment sets: any effectively complete set of relevant documents must collectively contain an effectively complete set of nuggets, by definition, and the judges would find these nuggets at the time of assessment. However, an effectively complete set of relevant documents will contain vast quantities of highly redundant information (nuggets or their variants), and thus the effectively complete set of nuggets will likely be vastly smaller, more tractable, and more easily found with far fewer total judgments.

In Phase 2 of our nugget-based evaluation paradigm ("Evaluation"), we dynamically assess the relevance of documents retrieved by a system under evaluation, using the nuggets collected. This is accomplished, in principle, by matching the information relevant to a topic (as encoded by the nuggets) with the documents in question. Once documents are automatically assessed, all standard measures of retrieval performance (such as Average Precision) can be computed for any ranked list. In Section 4 we demonstrate that runs submitted to TREC can be effectively evaluated using collected nuggets.

We further note that this nugget-based evaluation paradigm can be easily extended to accommodate other retrieval tasks:

- **Graded Relevance:** Nuggets can be graded at the time of extraction, in much the same manner that documents are graded, and the matching function can take these nugget grades into account when assigning grades to documents: the "stronger" the match with more "relevant" nuggets, the "higher" the overall grade.
- **Novelty:** Nuggets could be clustered or categorized, either automatically or by the assessor. A document

could then be judged relevant if it contains relevant information (as above), but its *marginal utility* will only be high if it contains relevant information not already seen in the output list, i.e., information from previously unseen nugget clusters or categories.

- **Diversity:** Nuggets can be assigned to aspects or subtopics by the assessor. Then the *coverage* of a document or list can be determined by matching information across nugget aspect or subtopic classes, thus permitting diversity-based evaluation.

2.1 Implementation

Building a test collection in our framework consists of three distinct tasks: (1) selecting documents from which to extract nuggets, (2) extracting nuggets from those documents, and (3) using the extracted nuggets to algorithmically create relevance judgments for any desired subset of the corpus. Each of these tasks could be performed in various ways; in this section, we document the decisions we made in implementing our particular methodology, previously summarized in [23].

Document Selection. Any human assessment of documents must use a selection procedure, e.g. sampling or pooling. Typically for this selection, documents retrieved by many systems and/or at higher ranks are preferred to documents retrieved by fewer systems and/or at lower ranks. While virtually all known selection mechanisms can be used, we preferred in our implementation one that balances preference for top/consensus documents with coverage (or depth) of the sample; we used the statAP selection mechanism because it is designed specifically on this principle applied to Average Precision measure, and it has been shown to be an effective document selection procedure in previous TREC ad hoc tracks for system evaluation [12].

Nugget Extraction. Nugget extraction was performed by our internal assessors (primarily graduate students working on IR research). For each *relevant* document in the sample, the assessors were asked to extract the relevant nuggets. They were instructed to find the smallest portion of text that constitutes relevant information in and of itself; however nuggets are not restricted to text as it appears in the document: slight modifications of the text, e.g. co-reference disambiguation, deleting contextual stopwords, etc. were encouraged. In the end, the vast majority of nuggets are information encoded in the form of verbatim text, e.g. "A healthy diet with enough calcium helps reduce high risk of osteoporosis".

Assessors were also given the option of adding query keywords, which would be used later as a retrieval filter. If a query has keywords associated with it, a document must contain at least one keyword to be considered relevant for that query. For example, for the topic "JFK assassination", an assessor might add the keyword "`Kennedy`": if a document does not contain this term, it is promptly not relevant.

Inferred Relevance Judgements. According to the typical TREC definition of relevance for ad hoc retrieval, a document is considered relevant if it contains at least one relevant piece of information. Thus if a document contains a known relevant information nugget, then it is necessarily relevant. However, a document may "match" the *information* or *meaning* of a nugget, without matching verbatim the nugget text; the matching strategy has to account for possible mismatches of *text* that are in fact matches of *information.* There are some simple approaches one could use for such a matching strategy, e.g. matching based only on text, like our own implementation below; there are also more sophisticated approaches to this problem: NLP-based, thesaurus-synonyms-ontology, statistical clustering including mutual information techniques, language dependence learning like CRF, machine learning, etc.

To test our methodolgy, we implemented a text-based matching algorithm that automatically infers the relevance of documents given the nuggets extracted. Each document received a relevance score after matching with all nuggets. The matching algorithm is based on a variant of *shingle matching*, which is often used in near-duplicate detection [9, 10]. A shingle is a sequence of k consecutive words in a piece of text. For example, after stopwording, the nugget "`John Kennedy was elected president in 1960`" has the following shingles for $k = 3$: (`John Kennedy elected`), (`Kennedy elected president`), and (`elected president 1960`).

Given the set of nuggets, we computed a relevance score for each document by (1) computing a score for each shingle, (2) combining these shingle scores to obtain a score for each nugget, and (3) combining these nugget scores to obtain a score for the document:

- **Shingle score:** For any nugget and each shingle of size k, let S be the minimum *span* of words in the document that contains all shingle words in any order. A shingle matches well if it is contained in a small span. We used the algorithm presented in [18] to find the shortest span of shingle words in a text document in linear time. We define the shingle score as follows

$$shingleScore = \lambda^{(S-k)/k}.$$

where λ is a fixed decay parameter. We found $\lambda = 0.95$ to be an effective value. A shingle that matches "perfectly" will have a score of 1. Note that, in contrast to standard *shingle matching* used for duplicate detection, we do not require all shingle words to be present in the matching document in the same order or contiguously.

Our method is inspired by near-duplicate detection, but is in fact quite different. High scores indicate a match of known relevant information, not necessarily of redundant or duplicate text. Furthermore, while a known nugget is required to be present in a document for a good match, the document often contains new/unknown relevant information as well.

- **Nugget score:** To obtain a score for each nugget, we average the scores for each of its shingles.

$$nuggetScore = \frac{1}{\#shingles} \sum_{s \in shingles} shingleScore(s)$$

- **Document score:** Each document gets a relevance score equal to the maximum matching score with any nugget:

$$docScore = \max_{n \in nuggets} nuggetScore(n)$$

Sample	Docs/Relev	Assess time	Nuggets	Extract time
AdHoc	200/34	3.3 hours	86.98	1.7 hours
Web	200/25.18	3.2 hours	61.82	1.3 hours

Table 1: Sample statistics (query average)

We note briefly that we have explored learning algorithms for the combination of nugget scores into a document score, using the sample as a training set of documents. So far our conclusion is that the improvement (if any) in performance of such techniques like Regression or Boosting does not justify the increase in complexity compared to simple functions like "`max`".

- **Inferred relevance judgment:** We convert a document relevance score to an inferred relevance score by performing a simple thresholding, i.e., if a document score is above the threshold $\theta = 0.8$, then the document is inferred to be relevant. This threshold is optimized empirically, but it is constrained to be a constant across all experiments; better performance can be obtained by setting the threshold differently for each query or experiment. Such variable thresholds could be learned from data.

3. EXPERIMENTS

In this section, we validate the performance of our method, show that our method requires far less human effort while producing many more assessments than the traditional procedure, and analyze the causes of disagreement between inferred judgements and TREC assessments. To this end, we constructed two separate test collections based on well-studied collections produced by previous TREC tracks.

The first experiment uses ad hoc retrieval data from the TREC 8 ad hoc task [1]: a collection of about half million newswire articles (in clean text) considered to have effectively complete assessments (depth-100 pool), with an average of about 1,736 assessed documents for each of 50 queries. There were 129 IR systems submitted to the TREC 8 ad hoc task; we refer to this data collectively (documents, judgments, queries, systems) as "ad hoc".

The second experiment is based on data from the TREC09 web track [13], which uses the ClueWeb09 html collection of about one billion documents; it contains an average of only about 528 documents assessed per query; it is considered to have incomplete assessments. Queries are shorter, but have specific subtopics. About 120 IR systems were submitted to TREC for this task. This data is referred to as "web".

Using statAP sampling, we selected 200 documents for each query from each collection. Of these documents, we extracted nuggets from only those that had been judged *relevant* by TREC assessors (we did not assess relevance at this stage; we did assess relevance on new documents for web data, later, as validation). The TREC 8 ad hoc collection sample, denoted "SampleAdHoc", was approximately 11% of the full pool assessed by TREC. The TREC09 web sample, denoted "SampleWeb", contains approximately 38% of the full pool assessed by TREC.

On average, about 87 nuggets were extracted per query for the ad hoc sample and about 62 nuggets were extracted per query for the web sample (Table 1).

The notion of correctness of relevance judgments is somewhat problematic. Inter-assessor disagreement [8, 27] is a well known phenomenon — the question of relevance is ambiguous for many documents. Bearing this in mind, we next analyze the quality of our inferred relevance judgments in several ways: (1) sort documents by their document relevance scores and measure Mean Average Precision (MAP) of the induced retrieval performance, (2) threshold relevance scores to create a qrel file and compare directly with TREC qrel file in terms of precision, recall, F1; (3) human verification of documents inferred relevant but not judged by TREC, and (4) use our inferred qrel to evaluate retrieval systems and compare system ranking with published TREC rankings in terms of Kendall's τ.

3.1 Performance: Finding Relevant Documents

Treating the relevances inferences as a retrieval function, and restricting to only those documents judged by TREC, we compute an average precision of AP=0.75 (Table 2) or better for our ranked list, which implies the vast majority of relevant documents are ranked higher than non-relevant ones. To our knowledge MAP=0.75 compares very favorably to any previous adhoc/web retrieval method, including machine learning and relevance feedback mechanisms (see 3.2). Some of these results we stated in a previous work [23].

Next, we use a threshold derived by trial and error to infer binary relevance for all documents retrieved by any system. For a fair comparison, we produce our own nuggets-based qrel as the inferred relevance assessments on TREC judged documents, and refer to it based on the sample of documents from which nuggets were extracted; e.g., "SampleAdHoc+InfRel(Nuggets)" refers to the judgments by TREC assessors of documents in the ad hoc sample, plus the judgments inferred for the other documents.

After thresholding ($\theta = 0.8$), we can compare our obtained qrel against the published TREC qrel in terms of precision, recall, F1, etc (see Table 2). This process is sometimes referred to as qrel inference. For comparison, a previously published result on qrel inference [7] achieves an F1 of 0.68 (compared with our F1=0.75), and uses significant extra ranking information which is highly contextual and may not be available.

	Judged Rel	Judged NonRel	Total	Agreement
AdHoc	2464	337	2801	87.96%
Web	2969	411	3380	87.84%

Truncated Result List	MAP	Precision	Recall	F1
SampleAdHoc	n/a	0.18	0.47	0.26
SampleAdHoc+InfRel	0.76	0.88	0.65	0.75
SampleWeb	n/a	0.23	0.25	0.24
SampleWeb+InfRel	0.75	0.88	0.60	0.71

Table 2: Documents inferred relevant from TREC qrel, compared to TREC assessments.

3.2 Comparison with Learning and Relevance Feedback Methods

In Table 3, we show comparison with other approaches that also use manual intervention. The training or relevance feedback set used by these methods is the same as that used by the Nuggets method. For reference we include basic results without relevance feedback (BM25, Language Model with Dirichlet smoothing). The learning algorithms (Linear regression, SVM, and RankBoost) use for each query the sampled documents as training; note that this is training per query, as opposed to the traditional learning-to-rank setup where different sets of queries are used for training and testing. RankBoost achieves the best result of the comparison methods (MAP=0.484 for ad hoc, MAP=0.661 for web) but still significantly lower than our Nuggets method.

Method	Ad Hoc	Web
Boolean Retrieval (Keyword Filtering)	0.111	0.219
BM25	0.204	0.293
BM25 + Keyword Filtering	0.198	0.292
BM25 + Relevance Feedback	0.387	0.428
LM Dirichlet	0.152	0.266
LM Dirichlet + Keyword Filtering	0.151	0.266
LM Dirichlet + Relevance Feedback	0.272	0.418
TFIDF	0.204	0.293
TFIDF + Keyword Filtering	0.199	0.292
TFIDF + Relevance Feedback	0.390	0.428
Learning(per query) Regression	0.311	0.466
Learning(per query) SVM+RBF kernel	0.476	0.632
Learning(per query) RankBoost	0.484	0.661
Nuggets Method	0.746	0.754
Nuggets Method + Keyword Filtering	**0.755**	**0.755**

Table 3: MAP Comparison with Learning Methods.

3.3 Failure Analysis

	Sources of Errors	Ad Hoc(%)	Web(%)
1	Assessor disagreement	46 (-)	71 (-)
2	Spam filter [16]	N/A	45 (-)
3	Missing information	64 (50.3%)	47 (55.9%)
4	Textual ambiguity	12 (9.5%)	2 (2.4%)
5	Overly general nuggets	39 (30.7%)	4 (4.7%)
6	Non-atomic nuggets	7 (5.5%)	14 (16.7%)
7	Text string	5 (3.9%)	11 (13.1%)
8	HTML parsing	N/A	6 (7.1%)

Table 4: Failure Analysis. Percentages are computed out of total count excluding disagreement and spam.

While it is sometimes difficult to decide which of two conflicting relevance judgments is correct, it is often easy to determine that one of them is wrong. In Table 4, we categorize about 400 instances of conflicting relevance judgments between TREC assessors and our inferred judgments. The analyzed documents represent the most significant disparities in terms of document score and TREC relevance assessment. We describe the main eight reasons below:

1. Assessor disagreement: Upon visual inspection, either we agreed with our inferred judgment and disagreed with the TREC judgment, or else we felt that either could be considered correct.
2. Relevant document marked as spam: We did not apply our matching algorithm to documents in the ClueWeb09 corpus that were marked as spam by the Waterloo spam filter [16]. Our method does not address the spam problem in any way; the filter used is totally independent of our matching method and can be used, or not, or replaced with any other filter.
3. Missing information: There may be relevant information not present in the collected nuggets. Documents that only discuss this unrepresented information will not be found. This can be addressed by extracting nuggets from more documents.
4. Textual ambiguity: Either the match is not exact due to limitations of our particular matching function (for example not recognizing synonyms or coreferences) or the text is inherently ambiguous. Solution: improved NLP into the matching function.
5. Overly general nuggets: A nugget could be rendered meaningless by stopping and stemming, or it could be so vague as to apply to many topics. This can be eliminated with proper assessor training and keyword filtering.
6. Non-atomic nuggets: Some nuggets as collected actually contained several nuggets. A document might match some part of these nuggets, but this was not enough for our algorithm to consider it a good match. Again, proper training of assessors can address this issue.
7. Relevance cannot be captured by a text string: It is not always possible to capture relevance with just a string. For example, a query might ask for specific images or home pages, in which case image data or URLs might be a more appropriate choices for nuggets.
8. Nugget does not match due to HTML parsing: The HTML structure of some web pages was complicated enough to foil our nugget matching algorithm.

Our analysis shows that our largest cause of error is missing information, which can be addressed by using a more diverse document sample. Some of our errors are perhaps unavoidable, e.g. spam, or not really errors, e.g. disagreement. Many of the remaining errors can be corrected simply with technical fixes such as keyword filters and better HTML parsing, or the proper training of assessors.

3.4 Effort vs. Nuggets vs. Information

Since our samples are small compared to those judged by TREC, our methodology requires significantly less human effort. We found that extracting nuggets from a relevant document took roughly four times longer than providing a binary relevance judgment for that document. No nuggets are extracted from non-relevant documents.

TREC assessors judge between 50 and 100 documents an hour.[1] For the sake of comparison, assume that it requires one minute to assess each document. At that rate, the entire TREC 8 ad hoc qrel took about 36 man-weeks to produce. SampleAdHoc required about 4 man-weeks for binary relevance assessments. For the relevant documents found in the sample, we spent an additional 2.1 man-weeks on extracting nuggets; thus the total human effort required for our method on SampleAdhoc is about 6.2 man-weeks.

Under the same assumption, TREC spent about 11 man-weeks creating the full web qrel of about 26,000 documents. SampleWeb, which is about 38% the size of entire full qrel, required about 4 man-weeks. Nugget extraction from relevant documents in the sample took another 1.6 man-weeks, for a total human effort on SampleWeb of about 5.6 man-weeks.

In Figure 2, the solid blue curve shows the rate of finding nuggets per unit of human effort (including assessment for relevance and nugget extraction from relevant documents). Since the order of processing documents reflected on the x-

[1]Private communication with TREC organizer.

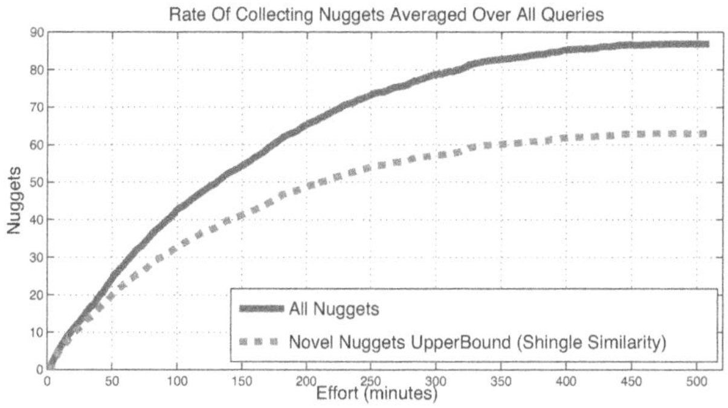

Figure 2: Rate of collecting (all and novel) nuggets averaged over all queries compared with the effort spent over the documents in the SampleAdHoc.

axis is "most likely relevant first", the curve is initially steep for the first few hours of effort and then it starts to flatten, ultimately asymptoting at approximatley 90 nuggets on average per query. This in part validates our hypothesis that while there may be vast numbers of relevant documents, there are likely far fewer relevant pieces of information. In fact, there are likely even fewer relevant pieces of information than indicated by the solid blue curve in Figure 2, since multiple nuggets may encode the same underlying information. To assess this phenomenon, we employed shingle matching on the extracted nuggets with a conservative threshold of $\theta = 0.3$ that yields virtually no false positive similarity mistakes, as validated on a separate entailment data set [3]. The resulting dashed red curve is an *upper bound* on the number of novel (semantically distinct) nuggets found, asymptoting at just over 60 novel nuggets per query on average. (In further analyzing the nuggets manually, we believe that the true value is closer to 40.) In short, this plot confirms our thesis that after relatively few documents selected well (or at least not selected badly), an assessor sees most of relevant information.

3.5 Many More Relevant Documents

To test the hypothesis that our method finds many additional relevant documents, as well as to further test the correctness of our inferred relevance judgments, we also used the nuggets extracted from SampleWeb to infer the relevance of documents retrieved within the top 300 ranks by any web system (depth-300 pool) — about 5891 documents per query. About 460 documents were marked relevant per query; on average 400 of these were unjudged by TREC.

Validation of the inferred relevance assessments outside the TREC qrel was performed by taking a uniform random sample of about 80 out of the 400 inferred-relevant, TREC-unjudged, documents per query, and having them assessed for relevance by humans using Amazon's Mechanical Turk service.[2] (Note that this test is not part of the nugget-based methodology, but is instead intended as a validation of our hypothesis and implementation.) If a document had multiple assessments for a given query, the majority vote was used. In case of a tie, the document was discarded from measurement. The results of this experiment showed an agreement of 73.29% between the Mechanical Turk judges and our inferred assessments on unjudged documents (outside TREC qrel).

[2]mturk.com. Each Mechanical Turk job was verified for quality: Each job consisted of 30 documents out of which 10 were verification documents with known TREC assessments, and they were required to correctly assess 70% of these 10 documents; if below 70% threshold on verification documents, the job was not accepted.

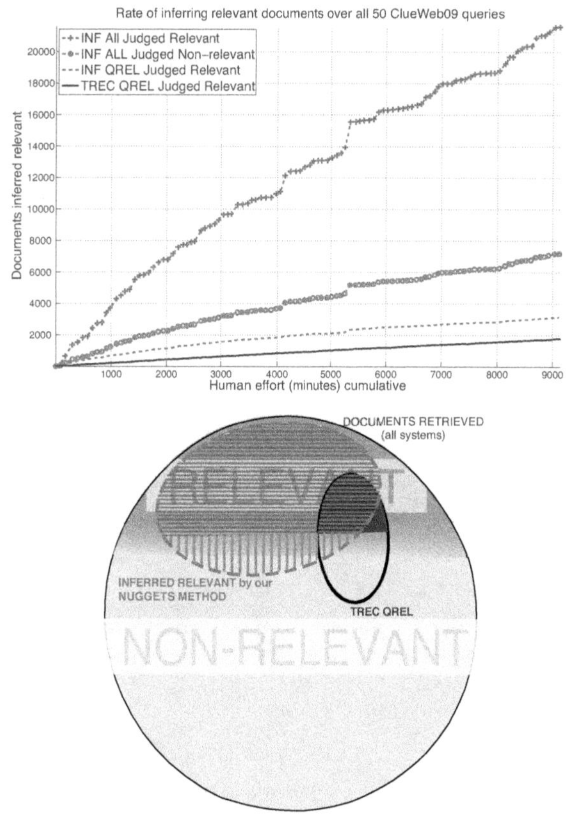

Figure 3: The top plot shows the rate of finding relevant documents per unit of time: TREC qrel (black), nuggets inferred from TREC qrel (blue), nuggets inferred–assessor disagreement (pink) and nugget inferred–assessor agreement (green). The result of this process is shown in the bottom diagram, which illustrates the vast number of inferred relevant documents our method finds.

	Judged Rel*	Judged NonRel*	Total	Agreement
Web	14624	5329	19953	73.29%

(* denotes the extrapolation from about 4000 documents assessed by Turks to all 19953 documents inferred relevant.)

Given the sample size of about 4000 documents, there is a 99.9% statistical confidence that the number of relevant documents outside the TREC qrel is at least 14,049, or about 281 per query (maximum likelihood estimate is 14,624, or 292 per query, on average).

Overall, using nuggets extracted from a small sample of assessed documents, our method created relevance judgments that were both highly correlated with existing qrels and validated by human assessors with very high accuracy (precision), and also found many relevant documents not found by TREC (recall). Figure 3 shows of grand overview of the documents inferred relevant vs. the ones marked relevant by TREC (bottom diagram), for the Web collection. Note

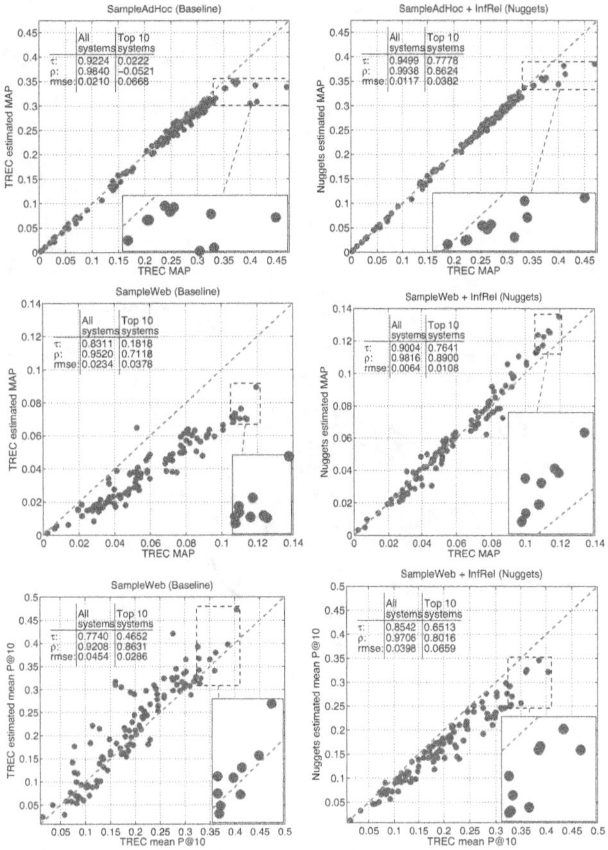

Figure 4: Evaluation comparison. Left: evaluations obtained using only the assessed sample; Right: evaluations obtained using the assessed sample and the inferred documents. Top: evaluations obtained using SampleAdHoc; Middle: evaluations (MAP) obtained using SampleWeb; Bottom: evaluations (P@10) obtained using SampleWeb. Top 10 systems are zoomed in the same plot.

also the vast number of documents inferred relevant outside the TREC qrel (green). On the top plot, the number of documents inferred total (green) and incorrectly (pink) is compared with the TREC qrel size (black) per unit of human effort of assessment/extraction.

4. IR SYSTEM EVALUATION

Notwithstanding the incompleteness of the published TREC qrels (see previous section), we will treat them as the "ground truth" for the purpose of demonstrating the utility of our test collection methodology to IR system evaluation. We produce two separate qrels based on our sample, one containing the TREC assessments of documents in our sample, denoted "Sample (Baseline)", and the other containing those judgments as well as the judgments inferred using the extracted nuggets, denoted "Sample + InfRel (Nuggets)". Using these qrels, we evaluated all systems submitted to the TREC 8 adhoc track over all 50 queries, and separately all systems submitted to the TREC 09 web track, also over all 50 queries. The results of this experiment are shown in Figure 4, with each data point representing an IR system. Perfect performance would be indicated by all data points coinciding with the line $y = x$.

While the scatter plots are largely qualitative, we also compute several statistics. Kendall's τ is a measurement of rank agreement. The linear correlation coefficient ρ measures linear agreement, i.e. the goodness of fit to some straight line, which implies rank correlation. We also compute the root mean square error, the difference of our scores compared to the actual scores, which implies both linear and rank correlation.

While the baseline evaluation using the relevance judgments of the sample already performs very well, our methodology using nuggets and inferred relevance judgments shows definite improvement. For the ad hoc experiment, using inferred relevance increases Kendall's τ from 0.92 to 0.95, linear correlation from 0.98 to 0.99, and decreases RMS error from 0.02 to 0.01. For web, MAP evaluation with inferred relevance increases Kendall's τ from 0.83 to 0.90, linear correlation from 0.95 to 0.98, and decreases RMS error from 0.02 to 0.01. Also for web, P@10 evaluation with inferred relevance increases Kendall's τ from 0.77 to 0.85, linear correlation from 0.92 to 0.97, and decreases RMS error from 0.05 to 0.04.

In most circumstances, evaluation accuracy matters most for the top systems. For this reason, it is important to note that the baseline evaluation significantly under-evaluates the top 10 systems. To make this point clear, we zoom in on the top 10 systems in each plot. Also of interest is the fact that, for ad hoc runs, the nugget-based evaluation of the top systems is much better than the baseline evaluation of the same systems. This is significant since the TREC ad hoc assessments (based on depth-100 pooling) are far more complete than the web ones (based on depth-10 pooling): using the SampleAdHoc and the inferred relevant documents and limiting our analysis to the top 10 systems, we obtain a dramatic increase of Kendall's τ from 0.02 to 0.78, linear correlation from -0.05 to 0.87, and a decrease of RMS error from 0.07 to 0.04. MAP evaluations of the top 10 systems using the SampleWeb and the inferred relevant documents shows similar results. However, for P@10 on web runs, the Kendall's τ is not much better than the baseline evaluation; we believe this is due to the following factors: (1) P@10 is more sensitive to judging disagreements than MAP, and many such cases exist in the web qrel, (2) web text matching is more difficult, and (3) in general, the nuggets-based framework shows the most dramatic gains for recall-oriented tasks and metrics. Table 5 shows the comparison of the rankings of the top 10 systems in the various systems. Rankings based on nugget-inferred relevance are generally more consistent with the TREC rankings than their baseline counterparts. For ad hoc systems, using inferred relevance reduced the total absolute rank difference for top the 10 systems from 36 to 8. For MAP on web runs, we reduced the total absolute rank difference for top the 10 systems from 28 to 10. For P@10 on web runs, we reduced the total absolute rank difference for top the 10 systems from 22 to 18.

4.1 Reusability: Systems Not Part of the Pool

The reusability of a test collection is its ability to accurately assess the performance of *unseen* systems that did not contribute to its own construction. Reusability can be estimated by holding out a set of *seen* systems—eliminating their contribution to the test collection—and assessing the ability of the modified test collection to accurately assess both the held-out systems and the systems that yet remain.

TREC Rank (qrel)	SampleAdHoc			SampleWeb (MAP)			SampleWeb (P@10)		
	System Name	Rank (Baseline)	Rank (Nuggets)	System Name	Rank (Baseline)	Rank (Nuggets)	System Name	Rank (Baseline)	Rank (Nuggets)
1	READWARE2	5(-4)	1(0)	NeuDiv1	1(0)	1(0)	uwgym	1(0)	4(-3)
2	orcl99man	9(-7)	3(-1)	uogTrDYCcsB	9(-7)	3(-1)	uogTrDPCQcdB	2(0)	1(1)
3	iit99ma1	4(-1)	2(+1)	udelIndDRSP	5(-2)	2(1)	NeuDiv1	3(0)	2(1)
4	READWARE	10(-6)	7(-3)	uogTrDPCQcdB	2(2)	5(-1)	uogTrDYCcsB	8(-4)	3(1)
5	CL99XTopt	2(+3)	4(+1)	UMHOOsd	8(-3)	7(-2)	MSDiv3	6(-1)	8(-3)
6	CL99XT	3(+3)	6(0)	UMHOOsdp	7(-1)	6(0)	MSRACS	9(-3)	7(-1)
7	CL99SDopt1	1(+6)	5(+2)	NeuLMWeb600	4(3)	8(-1)	MSRAACSF	10(-3)	9(-2)
8	CL99SD	6(+2)	8(0)	NeuDivW75	3(5)	4(4)	UCDSIFTslide	4(4)	5(3)
9	CL99SDopt2	7(+2)	9(0)	udelIndDMRM	10(-1)	9(0)	UCDSIFTdiv	5(4)	6(3)
10	8manexT3D1N	8(+2)	10(0)	NeuLMWeb300	6(4)	10(0)	MSDiv2	7(3)	10(0)
	Total absolute difference	**(36)**	**(8)**		**(28)**	**(10)**		**(22)**	**(18)**

Table 5: TREC top 10 systems ranking (ranking difference in parenthesis)

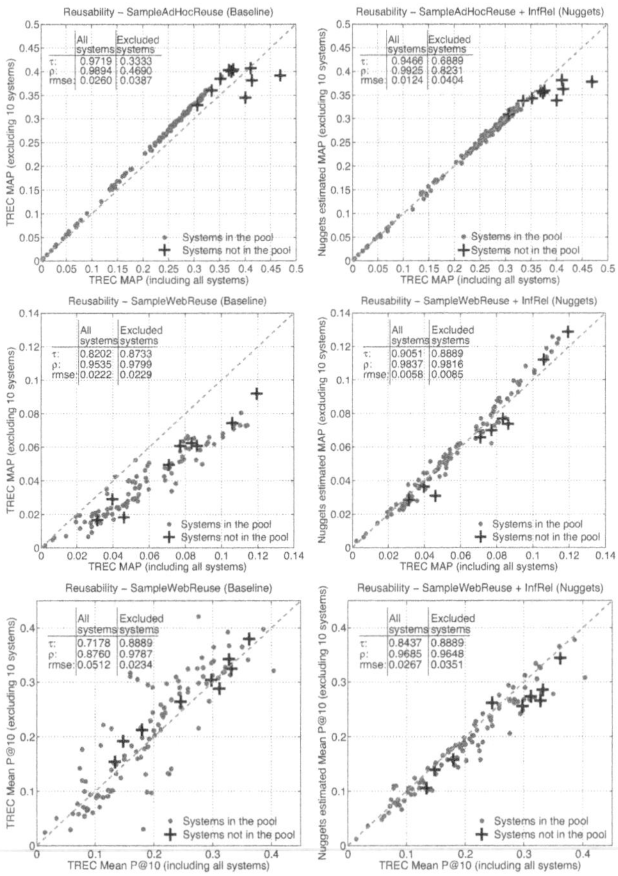

Figure 5: Reusability comparison; "+" denotes systems not contributing to selection of documents. Left: evaluations obtained using only the assessed sample - self-stability of TREC evaluations; Right: evaluations obtained using the assessed sample and the inferred documents - stability of Nuggets evaluations with respect to TREC; Top: evaluations obtained using SampleAdHocReuse; Middle: evaluations (MAP) obtained using SampleWebReuse; Bottom: evaluations (P@10) obtained using SampleWebReuse.

In order to test the reusability of the inferred relevance assessments, we remove the nuggets extracted from several systems, as well as any relevance assessments for documents only returned by these systems. We pick 10 systems greedily based on their high number of unique relevant documents not retrieved by other systems. Together the removed systems contributed 1306 unique relevant documents to the full ad hoc qrel of 4728 relevant documents; the removed systems contributed 72 out of 1701 relevant documents to SampleAdHoc. We call the new sample, with the corresponding documents and nuggets removed, "SampleAdHocReuse". Similarly, 126 out 1260 relevant documents were removed from SampleWeb, producing "SampleWebReuse".

The results of removing these relevant documents and their nuggets from the samples are shown in Figure 5. In order to make an analysis, we need to compare the reusability plots with corresponding evaluation plot. The effect can be seen for systems having higher MAP values (higher than 0.15). Note that the baseline evaluation over-evaluates the majority of the systems. These systems were penalized in the original TREC assessment for not retrieving these unique relevant documents now removed from the qrel. The baseline also significantly under-evaluates the top removed systems (black pluses), because of the unique relevant documents these systems retrieve, which are considered not relevant since they are not assessed. However, the nuggets-based evaluations (right plot) are very stable. This is due to the ability of our method to infer relevance on most missing documents. P@10 on web runs shows similar effects.

5. CONCLUSIONS AND FUTURE WORK

We showed that starting with a few relevant documents, by carefully collecting relevant facts, a simple matching function can recover the vast majority of assessed relevant documents and a great many other unassessed yet relevant documents. We also showed that these inferred-relevant documents can be successfully used for IR system evaluation. While the documents retrieved by our system are necessarily similar to those in our sample, our method still demonstrates that a large number of relevant documents will not be assessed by the Cranfield paradigm.

Pool Bias. All test collection methodologies, including ours, are biased towards documents rich in query terms. We believe that nuggets-based test collections will in the future be able to find many more non-obvious documents.

Learning-to-rank. Recently, much effort has been devoted to applying machine learning techniques to creating ranking functions via training on assessed (query, document) pairs. Using the inferred relevance, we can create much, much larger training sets. Even if the inferred relevance is not 100% accurate, larger training sets are likely to improve both quantitative learning (e.g. regression) and discriminative learning (e.g. boosting or support vector machines).

Performance measure. Most current performance measures assume that the document is an atomic unit: it is either relevant or non-relevant (or relevant to some degree), and it is effectively assumed to take a fixed constant effort to read and understand. This is, of course, incorrect in practice: short documents that contain large fractions of relevant information are far superior to long documents containing relatively small fractions of relevant information, though both may equally be assessed "relevant". Given relevant information encoded as nuggets, we could potentially assess the fraction of a document that is relevant and the fraction of the relevant information that it contains (information precision and information recall), thus obtaining an overall measure of performance much more closely matching user utility.

Summarization and canonical document evaluation. Finally, one can envision entirely new evaluation tasks and methodologies using the techniques that underly the nugget-based evaluation proposed above. For example, how could one evaluate the quality of the canonical Wikipedia page on Barack Obama or the output of a "knowledge engine" such as Wolfram Alpha? Given the information relevant to a query, as encoded by nuggets, one could potentially assess the fraction of relevant information found in the output (information recall) and the fraction of information in the output that is relevant (information precision).

6. REFERENCES

[1] *The Eighth Text REtrieval Conference (TREC-8)*. U.S. Government Printing Office, 2000.

[2] *33rd ACM SIGIR Workshop on Crowdsourcing for Search Evaluation*, Geneva, Switzerland, 2010.

[3] P. Achananuparp, X. Hu, and X. Shen. The evaluation of sentence similarity measures. DaWaK '08, Berlin, Heidelberg, 2008.

[4] E. Amitay, D. Carmel, R. Lempel, and A. Soffer. Scaling IR-system evaluation using term relevance sets. SIGIR '04, New York, NY, USA, 2004.

[5] P. Arvola, S. Geva, J. Kamps, R. Schenkel, A. Trotman, and J. Vainio. Overview of the INEX 2010 ad hoc track. In *Preproceedings of the INEX 2010 Workshop*, Vught, The Netherlands, 2010.

[6] A. Ashkan and C. L. Clarke. On the informativeness of cascade and intent-aware effectiveness measures. WWW '11, 2011.

[7] J. A. Aslam and E. Yilmaz. Inferring document relevance via average precision. SIGIR '06, 2006.

[8] P. Bailey, N. Craswell, I. Soboroff, P. Thomas, A. P. de Vries, and E. Yilmaz. Relevance assessment: Are judges exchangeable and does it matter? SIGIR '08, New York, NY, USA, 2008.

[9] A. Z. Broder. Identifying and filtering near-duplicate documents. COM '00, London, UK, 2000.

[10] A. Z. Broder, S. C. Glassman, M. S. Manasse, and G. Zweig. Syntactic clustering of the web. WWW'97.

[11] B. Carterette, J. Allan, and R. K. Sitaraman. Minimal test collections for retrieval evaluation. SIGIR'06.

[12] B. Carterette, V. Pavlu, E. Kanoulas, J. A. Aslam, and J. Allan. Evaluation over thousands of queries. SIGIR'08, 2008.

[13] C. L. A. Clarke, N. Craswell, and I. Soboroff. Overview of the trec 2009 web track, 2009.

[14] C. L. A. Clarke, M. Kolla, G. V. Cormack, O. Vechtomova, A. Ashkan, S. Büttcher, and I. MacKinnon. Novelty and diversity in information retrieval evaluation. SIGIR'08, 2008.

[15] H. T. Dang, J. J. Lin, and D. Kelly. Overview of the TREC 2006 question answering track 99. In *TREC*, 2006.

[16] C. L. A. C. Gordon V. Cormack, Mark D. Smucker. Efficient and effective spam filtering and re-ranking for large web datasets. University of Waterloo, 2010.

[17] D. Harman. Overview of the third text REtreival conference (TREC-3). In *Overview of the Third Text REtrieval Conference (TREC-3)*. U.S. Government Printing Office, Apr. 1995.

[18] S. Krenzel. Finding blurbs. Website. http://www.stevekrenzel.com/articles/blurbs.

[19] J. Lin and D. Demner-Fushman. Automatically evaluating answers to definition questions. HLT '05, Morristown, NJ, USA, 2005.

[20] J. Lin and D. Demner-Fushman. Will pyramids built of nuggets topple over? HLT'06, Morristown, NJ, USA, 2006.

[21] G. Marton and A. Radul. Nuggeteer: Automatic nugget-based evaluation using descriptions and judgements. In *Proceedings of NAACL/HLT*, 2006.

[22] F. Radlinski, M. Kurup, and T. Joachims. How does clickthrough data reflect retrieval quality? CIKM '08, New York, NY, USA, 2008.

[23] S. Rajput, V. Pavlu, P. B. Golbus, and J. A. Aslam. A nugget-based test collection construction paradigm. CIKM '11, New York, NY, USA, 2011.

[24] T. Sakai and C.-Y. Lin. Ranking Retrieval Systems without Relevance Assessments — Revisited. In *the 3rd International Workshop on Evaluating Information Access (EVIA) — A Satellite Workshop of NTCIR-8*, Tokyo, Japan, 2010.

[25] I. Soboroff, C. Nicholas, and P. Cahan. Ranking retrieval systems without relevance judgments. SIGIR '01, New York, NY, USA, 2001.

[26] A. Spoerri. Using the structure of overlap between search results to rank retrieval systems without relevance judgments. *Inf. Process. Manage.*, 43, 2007.

[27] E. M. Voorhees. Variations in relevance judgments and the measurement of retrieval effectiveness. *Inf. Process. Manage.*, 36, 2000.

[28] E. M. Voorhees. Question answering in TREC. CIKM '01, New York, NY, USA, 2001.

[29] Y. Yang and A. Lad. Modeling expected utility of multi-session information distillation. ITCIR'09, 2009.

[30] Y. Yang, A. Lad, N. Lao, A. Harpale, B. Kisiel, and M. Rogati. Utility-based information distillation over termporally sequenced documents. SIGIR'07, 2007.

[31] E. Yilmaz and J. A. Aslam. Estimating average precision when judgments are incomplete. *Knowledge and Information Systems*, 16(2), 2008.

[32] J. Zobel. How reliable are the results of large-scale retrieval experiments? SIGIR'98, Aug. 1998.

Tapping into Knowledge Base for Concept Feedback: Leveraging ConceptNet to Improve Search Results for Difficult Queries

Alexander Kotov
akotov2@illinois.edu

ChengXiang Zhai
czhai@illinois.edu

Department of Computer Science
University of Illinois at Urbana-Champaign
201 N Goodwin Ave, Urbana, IL, 61801, USA

ABSTRACT

Query expansion is an important and commonly used technique for improving Web search results. Existing methods for query expansion have mostly relied on global or local analysis of document collection, click-through data, or simple ontologies such as WordNet. In this paper, we present the results of a systematic study of the methods leveraging the ConceptNet knowledge base, an emerging new Web resource, for query expansion. Specifically, we focus on the methods leveraging ConceptNet to improve the search results for poorly performing (or difficult) queries. Unlike other lexico-semantic resources, such as WordNet and Wikipedia, which have been extensively studied in the past, ConceptNet features a graph-based representation model of commonsense knowledge, in which the terms are conceptually related through rich relational ontology. Such representation structure enables complex, multi-step inferences between the concepts, which can be applied to query expansion. We first demonstrate through simulation experiments that expanding queries with the related concepts from ConceptNet has great potential for improving the search results for difficult queries. We then propose and study several supervised and unsupervised methods for selecting the concepts from ConceptNet for automatic query expansion. The experimental results on multiple data sets indicate that the proposed methods can effectively leverage ConceptNet to improve the retrieval performance of difficult queries both when used in isolation as well as in combination with pseudo-relevance feedback.

Categories and Subject Descriptors

H.3.3 [**Information Storage and Retrieval**]: Information Search and Retrieval—*search process, query formulation, relevance feedback*

Permission to make digital or hard copies of all or part of this work for personal or classroom use is granted without fee provided that copies are not made or distributed for profit or commercial advantage and that copies bear this notice and the full citation on the first page. To copy otherwise, to republish, to post on servers or to redistribute to lists, requires prior specific permission and/or a fee.
WSDM'12, February 8–12, 2012, Seattle, Washington, USA.
Copyright 2012 ACM 978-1-4503-0747-5/12/02 ...$10.00.

General Terms

Algorithms, Experimentation

Keywords

Query Analysis, Query Expansion, Knowledge Bases, ConceptNet

1. INTRODUCTION

The information needs of the searchers, concisely formulated as keyword queries, can greatly vary in complexity, which is determined by the number of concepts that constitute the need. For this reason, the quality of search results largely depends on how completely and accurately all the concepts constituting the information need are translated into the query terms. It is often the case that the users of Web search systems tend to minimize their effort by intentionally posing very short, under-specified queries. As a result, many documents representing certain aspects of the information need will be missing in the search results. In addition to that, synonymy gives rise to the problem of *vocabulary mismatch*, which occurs when the authors of relevant documents and the searchers use different terms to designate the same concepts. This problem arises particularly often when non-professional users perform domain-specific searches and are not closely familiar with the vocabulary of the domain of the search problem. The most common examples of such domains are legal and medical.

Query expansion is a standard technique allowing to mitigate the problems of differing vocabularies and partially specified information needs by selecting and adding the related terms and phrases to the initial query. The main difficulty in effective application of automatic query expansion lies in correct identification of underrepresented aspects of the information need and selecting the right expansion terms with the right weights. Typical sources of term associations for query expansion can be either static and exist at the time of query (such as the search logs, ontologies, encyclopedias, manual or statistical thesauri constructed from the corpus) or dynamic, such as the top-ranked initially retrieved documents, from which the expansion terms can either be selected automatically by the system through pseudo-relevance feedback (PRF) or by asking the users to designate the relevant documents through explicit relevance feedback. All approaches using the dynamic sources of expansion terms rely on the assumption that the initially retrieved results include some relevant documents, which can be used as a source of expansion terms. It is often the case, however, that the top-ranked search results for a query include very few or no relevant documents and neither the search systems nor the users can communicate the positive relevance signals back to the search system through feedback mechanisms. Such queries are often referred to as *difficult* for a particular search system and underspecified queries as well as vocabulary mismatch are some of the main reasons for search systems failures. In most cases, the users are unaware of the underlying problems of poorly performing queries, the search systems currently offer no support to them in trying to improve the search results. Although many users are aware that the quality of search results can be improved by reformulating a query, finding the right query formulation can be a fairly difficult and time consuming process. While some of the static sources of expansion terms, such as the query logs and statistical co-occurrence thesauri constructed through the global collection analysis, allow to avoid the dependence on the quality of initial results, the coverage of these resources is limited and they may simply not contain effective expansion terms, which are broadly or conceptually related to a particular query.

In this work, we systematically and comprehensively explore the potential of *concept feedback*, a set of different strategies for leveraging ConceptNet [22] [1] as a source of expansion terms for difficult queries. ConceptNet is presently the largest commonsense knowledge base, consisting of more than 1.6 million assertions about the world. Similar to Wikipedia, ConceptNet reflects the "wisdom of the crowds" and was constructed by gathering a large number of sentence-like assertions about the real world from a large number of on-line collaborators. ConceptNet uses semantic network as a knowledge representation model. The nodes in its semantic network correspond to semi-structured natural language fragments (e.g., "food", "grocery store", "buy food", "at home") and represent the real world concepts. An edge between the two nodes represents a semantic relationship between the two concepts. A fragment of the concept graph of ConceptNet is shown in Figure 1. As opposed to ontologies, such as WordNet, ConceptNet is not limited to hyponym/hypernym relations and features a more diverse relational ontology of twenty relationship types, such as causal, spatial and functional. As opposed to on-line encyclopedias, such as Wikipedia, the network structure of ConceptNet does not require any additional analysis to establish the relations between the concepts.

The network-based structure of ConceptNet in combination with its rich relational ontology opens up possibilities for making more complex, multi-step inferences. For example, from Figure 1 it follows that the concepts "morning" and "stomach" are related via the following chain of inferences: "wake up in the morning"→"eat breakfast"→"full stomach". The key idea behind this work is that the network-based structure of ConceptNet can be leveraged to make similar complex inferences to identify the effective expansion terms that are *broadly* related to the query, when the initially retrieved results are of poor quality and, consequently, cannot be used as a source of expansion terms. Although other lexico-semantic resources, such as WordNet, can be used

[1] `http://conceptnet5.media.mit.edu/`

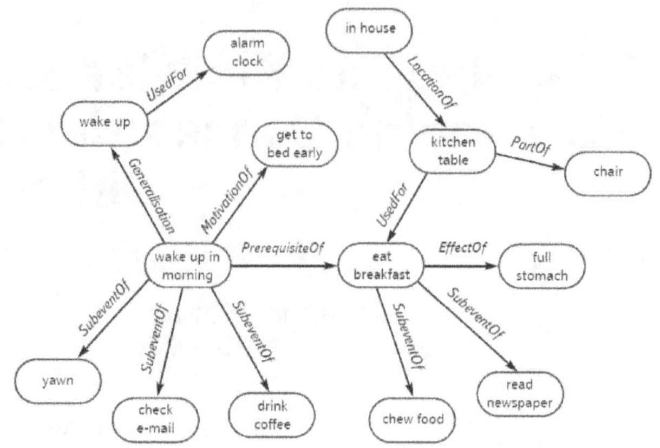

Figure 1: Fragment of the concept graph of ConceptNet (adopted from [22])

[23] [29] to help address the issue of vocabulary divergence between the queries and relevant documents, effective expansion terms may have much broader conceptual relations to the query terms than the tight semantic coherence of WordNet synsets may allow.

Concept	AP
target	0.2011
threat	0.1864
machine	0.1698
explosive	0.1684
tighten	0.1564
afghanistan	0.1559
worldwide	0.1495
chain	0.1464
measure	0.1462
link	0.1450

Table 1: Top 10 expansion concepts from ConceptNet for the TREC query 341 "airport security" along with the average precision (AP) of the query expanded with each of the concepts, when the expanded queries are run on the AQUAINT dataset. AP of the original query is 0.0657.

Figure 1 provides an example of the expansion concepts from ConceptNet identified using the simulation experiment presented in Section 4.2. As can be seen from this example, some effective expansion concepts have very broad and complex semantic relationships with the original query terms. Establishing such relationships may require making several inference steps, for which the graph-based knowledge representation model of ConceptNet is particularly well-suited. On the other hand, the hierarchical structure of WordNet and vector-space knowledge representation models for Wikipedia [14] present certain difficulties for making complex and multi-step inferences.

In this work, we explore different methods of leveraging the semantic network of ConceptNet to select a *small set of highly effective expansion concepts* to improve the performance of difficult queries. In particular, we address the following two research questions. The first question is whether ConceptNet can in principle be leveraged to improve the retrieval results of *difficult queries*? To answer this question, we conducted a simulation experiment, in which for each query we measured the retrieval performance of that query extended with each single concept within a certain distance from its terms. The retrieval results of the best performing expansion concept for each query were used to determine the overall upper bound for the potential retrieval effectiveness of concept feedback on each data set. The results of this experiment are presented in Section 4.2. The second question is how to design the methods to automatically select a small number of effective expansion concepts? To answer this question, in Sections 3.1 and 3.2 we propose the heuristic and machine learning-based methods for selecting expansion concepts and present the results of an experimental evaluation of those methods in Section 4.

The main contribution of the present work is in systematic and comprehensive exploration of the heuristic and machine learning-based methods for selecting the query expansion terms from ConceptNet and comparing the effectiveness of those methods with the effectiveness of automatic query expansion based on pseudo-relevance feedback.

2. RELATED WORK

The problem of vocabulary mismatch is a fundamental problem in information retrieval. It has long been recognized that capturing lexico-semantic relationships can reduce the negative impact of this problem on the quality of retrieval results. Early attempts to utilize lexico-semantic relationships include introduction of the concept of associative retrieval. Associative retrieval is based on the association hypothesis formulated by van Rijsbergen [28], which states that "if an index term is good at discriminating relevant from irrelevant documents, then any closely associated index term is also likely to be good at this". In associative retrieval, knowledge about associations among information items (terms, concepts or documents) is represented as a network, in which the information items correspond to the nodes and associations between them to the links connecting the nodes. Constrained spreading activation [12] [26] [9] is a typical processing paradigm used in associative retrieval. The main difficulty faced by the early attempts to apply associative retrieval was a labor-intensive process of manual construction of the association network between the documents and concepts. As a result, the focus of query expansion research has shifted to using local and global document analysis to automatically extract the expansion terms. Early global expansion techniques [15] [33] [30] aim to determine the strength of semantic relatedness between the terms based on the term co-occurrence statistics obtained through the analysis of the entire document collection and use the terms that are strongly associated with the initial query terms for expansion. More complicated global-analysis models than those involving simple term co-occurrence statistics have been proposed later [5]. In our previous work [20] [19], we proposed *sense feedback* and *question-based feedback*, two complimentary collection analysis-based methods to interactively improve the performance of difficult queries, when the poor retrieval performance is caused by underspecified and ambiguous queries. Local collection expansion techniques [31] generally follow a two-stage process often called pseudo-relevance feedback. First, a query is issued to retrieve the initial set of results and then a certain number of the top-ranked documents is used to extract the expansion terms. Xu and Croft [30] proposed a local analysis method, in which the candidate expansion terms are ranked by their co-occurrence with the original query terms and weighted by a constant according to their rank. They also compared the performance of the local and global document analysis and concluded that the local analysis is generally more effective than the global analysis. However, a major deficiency of the local analysis is that it is based on the assumption that the initially retrieved results include at least some relevant documents, which is violated in case of difficult queries.

The emergence of the Web and hand-crafted general purpose or domain-specific ontologies provided access to the new sources of high quality term associations for query expansion. In particular, three major types of external resources have been explored: external corpora (including the Web), general-purpose and domain-specific ontologies and Wikipedia. For example, Diaz and Metzler [13] demonstrated in the context of relevance models that using a high quality external corpus that is comparable to the target corpus can be as, if not more, effective than using the Web for pseudo-relevance feedback. Yin et al. [32] proposed an expansion method based on using random walk on the query-URL graph generated from the web query logs and snippets provided by an external search engine. Their main assumption is that users submit various queries to express the same information need and, therefore, the query can be expanded using related query formulations. Several researchers have experimented with heuristic methods based on WordNet and mixed results have been reported. Voorhees [29] experimentally determined the upper bound for the effectiveness of different WordNet-based query expansion strategies by manually choosing the query terms for expansion and annotating the query topics with the WordNet synsets. The reported results indicate that while query expansion makes little difference in the retrieval effectiveness, if the original queries are relatively complete descriptions of the information need, lexico-semantic relations have the potential to significantly improve less well-formulated initial queries. Liu et al. [23] proposed several heuristic methods for disambiguating and selecting the candidate expansion terms using adjacent query terms and WordNet. Only the candidate terms that are globally correlated with the query terms were used for expansion. Shah and Croft [27] proposed heuristic methods for query term re-weighting and locating the query terms to expand with WordNet synonyms with the goal of improving precision in the top document ranks. Meij et al. [25] showed that discriminative semantic annotations of documents using domain-specific ontologies, such as MeSH, can be effectively used to improve retrieval. Li et al. [21] experimented with using Wikipedia articles retrieved with the original query as a source of the expansion terms for PRF and observed that the queries, for which the standard PRF failed and which were improved using Wikipedia-based PRF, were the ones that did not perform well after the initial retrieval. Hsu and Chen [16] investigated the utility of commonsense knowledge in ConceptNet for image retrieval by focusing on finding concepts related to the original query through a set of spatial relationships and found that commonsense knowledge is deeply context-sensitive and effective for precision-oriented tasks.

In addition to experimenting with individual lexico-semantic resources for query expansion, several methods combining multiple resources to overcome the problem of data sparsity have also been proposed for both the vector-space and language modeling-based retrieval models. In the context of vector-space models, Mandala et al. [24] proposed a method to combine three different thesaurus types for query expansion: manually constructed (WordNet), automatically constructed based on term co-occurrence, automatically constructed based on head-modifier relations and found out that improvements in retrieval performance can be achieved by combining all three types of lexical resources. Bodner et al. [4] conducted similar experiments by combining WordNet and co-occurrence based thesauri for query expansion. In the context of language modeling approach, Bai et al. [3] proposed a method for query expansion by integrating term relationships (documents co-occurrence, HAL scores, globally and locally computed information flows) explicitly into the query language model. In Cao et al. [7] term relationships from co-occurrence statistics and WordNet were used to smooth the document language model, so that the probabilities of the related terms in the document model are increased. Collins-Thompson and Callan [10] proposed a Markov chain framework for query expansion, combining multiple sources of knowledge on term associations, such as synonyms from WordNet, terms that share the same prefix when stemmed to the same root, terms co-occurring in a large Web corpus and terms co-occurring in the top retrieved documents. Given a small set of initial query terms, they constructed a term network and used a random walk to estimate the likelihood of relevance for potential expansion terms. Hsu et al. [17] compared the effectiveness of using WordNet and ConceptNet for query expansion. The experimental results indicated that WordNet and ConceptNet can complement each other, since the queries expanded using WordNet have higher discrimination ability (i.e., expansion concepts from WordNet are usually more specific than those from ConceptNet), whereas the queries expanded using ConceptNet have higher concept diversity (i.e., expansion concepts from ConceptNet usually co-occur with the topical terms in relevant documents). They also demonstrated that the retrieval performance improves when the expansion concepts are manually filtered to remove noise, but did not propose any algorithm for that. In general, to the best of our knowledge, an extensive and systematic study of the feasibility of using ConceptNet for query expansion has not yet been conducted.

3. CONCEPT FEEDBACK

This work follows the language modeling approach to information retrieval, specifically the KL-divergence retrieval model [34], according to which the retrieval task involves estimating a query language model, Θ_q, for a given keyword-based query q and the document language models Θ_{D_i} for each document D_i in the collection $\mathcal{C} = \{D_1, \dots, D_m\}$. The documents in the collection are scored and ranked according to the Kullback-Leibler divergence:

$$\mathrm{KL}(\Theta_q||\Theta_D) = \sum_{w \in V} p(w|\Theta_q) \log \frac{p(w|\Theta_q)}{p(w|\Theta_D)}$$

Within the KL-divergence retrieval model, relevance feedback [35] is considered as the process of updating the query language model Θ_q, given the feedback obtained after the initial retrieval results are presented to the users. Such feedback may be explicitly provided by the users or implicitly derived from the top-ranked retrieval results. Following this approach, a concept expansion language model, $\hat{\Theta}_q$, derived for a given query q from ConceptNet can be used for updating the original query language model Θ_q through linear interpolation:

$$p(w|\tilde{\Theta}_q) = \alpha p(w|\Theta_q) + (1-\alpha) p(w|\hat{\Theta}_q)$$

where α is the interpolation coefficient between the concept expansion language model and the original query model.

The two major challenges for query expansion methods are in identifying as many effective expansion terms as possible and adding those terms to the original query with the weights that would accurately reflect the degree of their effectiveness for improving the quality of retrieval results. If a limited number of automatically identified expansion terms are added to the query, there is a possibility that effective expansion terms will be missed and the results are unlikely to be substantially improved. On the other hand, when the query vocabulary is substantially altered, the advantages gained from effective expansion terms may be lost due to the query topic drift. Within the language modeling context, selecting the right number of terms becomes less important than the right allocation of weights. In this section, we propose heuristic and learning-based approaches for selecting the expansion concepts from ConceptNet and assigning the weights to them. Both methods utilize the concept relations graph of ConceptNet. The main idea behind the first method is that effective expansion concepts should be along the paths connecting the original query terms in the concept relations graph. The second method is based on a finite-step random walk on the concept relations graph, which starts from the query terms. Before discussing the proposed methods in more detail, we need to provide several important definitions.

DEFINITION 1. QUERY TERM CONTEXT C_q^r *of radius* r *for a given query term* q *includes all the concepts in ConceptNet that are at most* r *edges away from* q.

For example, the query term context of radius 2 includes all the concepts that are connected with the given query term (query term neighbors) and all the concepts that are connected with query term neighbors.

DEFINITION 2. QUERY CONCEPT GRAPH $G_q^r = (V, E)$ *of radius* r *for a given query* $q = \{q_1, q_2, \dots, q_n\}$ *is a weighted sub-graph of the entire concept relations graph of ConceptNet* $\mathcal{C} = (\mathcal{V}, \mathcal{E})$*, such that* $V = \bigcup_{i=1}^{n} C_{q_i}^r, V \subseteq \mathcal{V}$ *and* $E = \{(c_1, c_k, w_{1k}), \dots, (c_m, c_n, w_{mn})\}, \forall i,j : (c_i, c_j) \in \mathcal{E}$.

When constructing a query concept graph, all the concepts represented by a phrase were split into concept terms. For example, given a pair of concepts "telescope" and "astronomical tool" and a relation "IsA" between them, the concept "telescope" in the resulting query concept graph will be connected with weighted edges to two separate concept nodes (concept terms) "astronomical" and "tool". In addition to that, at most 100 neighboring concept terms with the highest IDF ($IDF(t) = N/log(c(t,d))$, where N is the total number of documents in the collection and $c(t,d)$ is the number of documents containing the concept term t) were considered for each concept term, excluding very common concept terms (that occur in more than 10% of the documents in the collection).

Since the relations between the concepts in ConceptNet do not have explicit weights, we designed an empirical procedure to calculate them, which is presented in detail in Section 4.3.

3.1 Heuristic methods

3.1.1 Path finding

DEFINITION 3. PATH $\rho(c_i \rightarrow c_j)$ *between the two concepts* c_i *and* c_j *in the query concept graph* G_q^r *of radius* r *corresponds to a set of concepts and their associated weights* $\{(c_n, w_n), \ldots, (c_m, w_m)\}$ *along any non-repetitive sequence of edges* $((c_i, c_n), \ldots, (c_m, c_j))$ *connecting* c_i *and* c_j.

Given a query $q = \{q_1, q_2, \ldots, q_n\}$ and a query concept graph G_q^r of radius r, this method determines all possible unique paths between the query terms and uses a set of concepts $\bigcup_{i=1}^{n} \bigcup_{j=i}^{n} \rho(c_i \rightarrow c_j)$ corresponding to those paths as expansion concepts.

3.1.2 Random walk

Given a query $q = \{q_1, q_2, \ldots, q_n\}$ and a query concept graph G_q^r of radius r, this method first constructs the concept matrix $\mathbf{C}$ (i.e., adjacency matrix of G_q^r) and performs a k-step random walk on that matrix. The weight of the expansion concept c for a query term q_i is determined as follows:

$$p(c|q_i) = (1 - \beta)\beta^k \mathbf{C}_{c,q_i}^k$$

where β is the probability of continuing the random walk.

3.2 Learning-based method

The learning-based expansion method is based on training a regression model, in which the independent variables are the features of an expansion concept and the response variable is a measure of performance (we used mean average precision or MAP) of an original query expanded with the given concept. After estimating the parameters of a regression model based on the actual MAP values of the queries expanded with the concept terms in the training data set, new expansion concepts can be ranked based on the MAP values predicted by the model and a certain number of the highest ranked concepts can then be used to expand the query. The expanded query can then be used to retrieve a new improved set of results, which can be either presented to the users or used for pseudo-relevance feedback to further improve the performance of the query. The learning-based expansion method is further referred to as LR and the combined leaning-based expansion and pseudo-feedback method as LR-PF.

3.3 Model

Due to its computational efficiency, we used the generalized linear regression model (GLM) as the learning algorithm. We also experimented with logistic regression and found it to be consistently worse than the GLM. Since both models are very similar, due to space limitations, we do not provide the experimental results for logistic regression. We also leave experimentation with other methods (e.g., learning-to-rank, such as ListNet [8]) as future work. Given a vector of features $\bar{x}$, the GLM estimates a vector of feature weights $\bar{w}$ during training, and generates the output as a linear combination of the feature and weight vectors, $f(\bar{x}) = \bar{x}\bar{w}$, during testing. Another advantage of GLM over other methods is that it allows to easily interpret the feature weights in order to determine the important properties of effective expansion concepts.

3.4 Features

The set of features used in the experiments is presented in Table 2. This feature set reflects the properties of queries, expansion concepts and expansion concepts with respect to queries. It extends the set of features used in [18] (designated by bullets in the BL column) and includes 7 new features, focused on the structural properties of the expansion concepts with respect to the query terms in the query concept graph: CONFANOUT, RNDWALKSCORE, PATHFINDSCORE, AVGQDIST, MAXQDIST, AVGPWEIGHT, MAXPWEIGHT. Since PATHFINDSCORE and RNDWALKSCORE correspond to the score of an expansion term using the heuristic methods presented in Sections 3.1.1 and 3.1.2 respectively, learning-based method unifies and extends the heuristic methods.

4. EXPERIMENTS

In this section, we present the results of an experimental evaluation of unsupervised and supervised methods for query expansion with concepts from ConceptNet. We first discuss our experimental setup and datasets.

4.1 Experimental setup and datasets

All experiments in this work were conducted on three standard TREC collections: ROBUST04, which was used in TREC 2004 Robust Track [1]; AQUAINT, which was used in TREC 2005 HARD [2] and Robust Tracks; and GOV, which was used in TREC 2004 Web Track [11]. AQUAINT and ROBUST04 datasets consist of the newswire documents, while GOV consists of the Web documents. Various statistics for experimental datasets are summarized in Table 3.

Corpus	#Docs	Size(Mb)	#Topics	Avg. topic
AQUAINT	1,033,461	3042	50	2.56
ROBUST04	528,155	1910	250	2.65
GOV	1,247,753	18554	225	3.04

Table 3: Statistics of the datasets used for experiments.

In this work, we focus on studying the effectiveness of expansion using ConceptNet with respect to difficult queries. We define a difficult query as a query, for which either the average precision of the retrieved results is less than 0.1 or the top 10 results are non-relevant (i.e. $Pr@10 = 0$). In all the experiments in this work, we used the same suggested settings of Dirichlet priors for both the baselines (KL-divergence retrieval model and model-based pseudo-relevance feedback) and concept feedback methods: 2000 for AQUAINT and ROBUST04 and 500 for GOV.

4.2 Upper-bound performance

In order to determine the upper bound for the potential effectiveness of using ConceptNet for query expansion, we conducted a simulation experiment, in which for each query term it was first checked if there exists a concept in ConceptNet that matches it. If such node was found, then all the concepts within the query term context of certain radius were identified. We experimented with the contexts of one, two and three edges from the query terms. If a concept was

Feature	BL	Description
		Features of the query
NUMQRYTERMS	•	number of query terms
TOPDOCSCORE	•	retrieval score of the top-ranked document for the initial query
		Features of the expansion concept
EXPTDOCSCORE	•	retrieval score of the top-ranked document for the initial query expanded with the concept
TOPTERMFRAC	•	ratio of the number of occurrences of the expansion concept over all the terms in the top 10 retrieved documents
NUMCANDOCS	•	number of the top 10 documents containing the expansion concept
AVGCDOCSCORE	•	average retrieval score of the documents containing the expansion concept
MAXCDOCSCORE	•	maximum retrieval score of the documents containing the expansion concept
CONIDF	•	IDF of the expansion concept
CONFANOUT		number of nodes adjacent to the expansion concept node in the query concept graph
SPACTSCORE	•	spreading activation score of the expansion concept in the query concept graph
SPACTRANK	•	rank of the expansion concept after spreading activation in the query concept graph
RNDWALKSCORE		weight of the expansion concept by using the Finite Random Walk method (Section 3.1.2)
PATHFINDSCORE		weight of the expansion concept by using the Path Finding method (Section 3.1.1)
		Features of the expansion concept with respect to the query terms
AVGCOLCOR	•	average co-occurrence of the expansion concept with the query terms in the collection
MAXCOLCOR	•	maximum co-occurrence of the expansion concept with the query terms in the collection
AVGTOPCOR	•	average co-occurrence of the expansion concept with the query terms in the top 10 retrieved documents
MAXTOPCOR	•	maximum co-occurrence of the expansion concept with the query terms in the top 10 retrieved documents
AVGTOPPCOR	•	average co-occurrence of the expansion concept with pairs of query terms in the top 10 retrieved documents
MAXTOPPCOR	•	maximum co-occurrence of the expansion concept with pairs of query terms in the top 10 retrieved documents
AVGQDIST		average distance of the expansion concept to the query terms in the query concept graph
MAXQDIST		maximum distance of the expansion concept to the query terms in the query concept graph
AVGPWEIGHT		average weight of the paths to the expansion concept from the query terms in the query concept graph
MAXPWEIGHT		maximum weight of the paths to the expansion concept from the query terms in the query concept graph

Table 2: Features for ranking the expansion terms. Baseline feature set is designated in the BL column with a bullet (•).

designated by a phrase, it was split into individual concept terms and very popular concept terms (the ones that occur in more than 10% of the documents in the collection) were not considered.

First, each query was expanded with each of the neighboring concepts (expansion context of size one) of the query terms by simply adding each concept term to the query with equal weight $1/|q|$ (where $|q|$ is the length of an expanded query) and comparing the average precision of the original query with the average precision of the expanded query. Then in each dataset we counted the number of queries, for which there was at least one expansion concept that improved the query performance (Improved), the number of queries for which all expansion concepts degraded the query performance (Hurt) and the number of queries, for which none of the expansion concepts worsened or improved the query performance (Neutral). The results for this experiment along with the total number of queries and difficult queries in each dataset are presented in Table 4.

	Total	Diff	Improved	Hurt	Neutral
AQUAINT	50	17	42	8	0
ROBUST04	250	75	232	14	4
GOV	225	147	161	8	56

Table 4: Number of improved, hurt and neutral queries when simulating expansion using the expansion context of size one.

As follows from Table 4, for most queries (not only the difficult ones) in all datasets there exists at least one effective expansion concept among the immediate context of the query terms. For difficult queries in each dataset, we also determined the upper-bound effectiveness of concept expansion with respect to the mean average precision (MAP), geometric mean average precision (GMAP), the total number of relevant documents retrieved (RR) and precision at top 10 retrieved documents (P@10) by varying the radius of the expansion context. The results of this experiment are presented in Table 5.

As follows from Table 5, in the upper bound, concept feedback (CF) significantly improves the performance of the KL-divergence retrieval model and also outperforms the baseline (model-based pseudo-relevance feedback), even when the context of size 1 (column CF-1) is used for expansion. In other words, *for each difficult query there exists at least one highly effective expansion concept.* Using the most effective concept within the context of radius one on average doubles the performance of the baseline KL-divergence retrieval for difficult queries on all datasets. Using the contexts of larger radius improves the performance even more, with the context of radius 3 (column CF-3) having about *triple* (for the newswire datasets) and *six times* (for the Web dataset) the performance of the KL-divergence retrieval model without feedback. This simulation experiment clearly illustrates that using conceptually related terms for query expansion has a tremendous potential for improving the performance

		KL	KL-PF	CF-1	CF-2	CF-3
AQUAINT	MAP	0.0521	0.0429	0.1247	0.1622	0.1880
	GMAP	0.0414	0.0214	0.1033	0.1438	0.1707
	RR	567	519	671	730	772
	P@10	0.1176	0.1000	0.3765	0.5412	0.6059
ROBUST04	MAP	0.0509	0.0788	0.1061	0.1539	0.1823
	GMAP	0.0268	0.0225	0.0718	0.1162	0.1464
	RR	2078	2573	2560	2826	3102
	P@10	0.1467	0.1587	0.2893	0.3973	0.4280
GOV	MAP	0.0748	0.0447	0.1830	0.3481	0.4326
	GMAP	0.0243	0.0166	0.0668	0.1627	0.2403
	RR	760	742	811	793	800
	P@10	0.0347	0.0197	0.0823	0.1190	0.1558

Table 5: Comparison of the upper-bound performance of concept feedback (CF) with KL-divergence retrieval model (KL) and model-based pseudo-relevance feedback (KL-PF) on difficult topics by varying the the radius of the expansion context.

of difficult queries. However, how to automatically identify those few highly effective expansion concepts is unclear. In the rest of this work, we propose and study heuristic and learning-based methods for selecting and assigning the importance weights to the expansion concepts.

4.3 Edge weighting

Since our automatic query expansion procedure selects many expansion terms, we need to design a method to allocate the importance weights to them. In particular, for this task we can use several properties of the expansion terms, such as the length of the paths, as well as the types and weights of ConceptNet relations connecting them to the query terms. Given a concept graph constructed from ConceptNet for a particular query, we used the following empirical procedure to assign the weights to its edges:
1. First, before query processing we used the results of simulation experiment presented in Section 4.2 on the dataset with the largest number of queries (ROBUST04) to count the number of times the best expansion concept was connected to the original query term with the ConceptNet relation of each type.

Relation	Count	Group
IsA	132	1
HasProperty	72	1
CapableOf	65	1
AtLocation	40	1
ConceptuallyRelatedTo	35	1
UsedFor	35	1
HasA	27	2
DefinedAs	26	2
ReceivesAction	21	2
PartOf	15	2
CausesDesire	8	2
LocatedNear	5	2
Causes	5	2
HasPrerequisite	2	3
Desires	2	3
InstanceOf	2	3
MadeOf	2	3
MotivatedByGoal	2	3
HasFirstSubevent	1	3
SimilarSize	1	3

Table 6: Number of times the best expansion term was connected to the expanded query term with the relation of each type.

We then sorted the relations according to those counts and divided them into three groups of the same size, which are presented in Table 6.
2. Second, we constructed a term relationship graph for all the terms in the vocabulary of the collection. Term relationship graph is a weighted graph, in which the set of vertices corresponds to the terms in the collection and the edges correspond to the semantic relationships between the terms. The weight of an edge represents the degree of semantic relatedness of between the two terms measured by the Hyperspace Analog to Language (HAL) model [6]. Constructing HAL space for an n-term vocabulary involves traversing a sliding window of width w over each word in the corpus, ignoring punctuation, sentence and paragraph boundaries. All the words within the sliding window are considered as the local context of the term, over which the sliding window is centered. Each word in the local context receives a score, according to its distance from the center of the sliding window (words that are closer to the center receive higher scores). After traversing the entire corpus, an $n \times n$ HAL space matrix $\mathbf{H}$, which aggregates the local contexts for all the terms in the vocabulary is produced. In this matrix, the row vectors encode the preceding word order and the column vectors encode the posterior word order. An example of the HAL space for the sentence "the effects of pollution on the population" constructed using the sliding window of size 10 (5 words before and after the center word) is shown in Table 7.

	the	eff	of	poll	on	pop
the	1	2	3	4	5	
eff	5					
of	4	5				
poll	4	5				
on	2	3	4	5		
pop	5	1	2	3	4	

Table 7: HAL space for the sentence "the effects of pollution on the population".

The final HAL weights are produced by merging the row and column corresponding to each term in the HAL space matrix. Each term t in the vocabulary $V, |V| = n$ corresponds to a row in the HAL space matrix:

$$\mathbf{H}_t = \{(t_1, c_1), \ldots, (t_n, c_n)\}$$

where each $c_1, \ldots, c_n$ is the number of co-occurrences of the term t with other terms in the vocabulary V. After the merge, each element in the HAL matrix $\mathbf{H}$ is normalized to estimate the strength of semantic relatedness between the terms $\mathbf{H}_{ti} = c_i / \sum_{j=1}^{n} c_j$. Unlike the mutual information, in which the entire document is used as the context to calculate the number of co-occurrences between the terms, HAL uses the contexts of smaller size (we used a sliding window of 10 words before and after the center word) and has been shown in our previous work [20] to produce less noisy term relationship graphs.

3. Third, for each query we constructed the query concept graph and performed two passes over its edges. In the first pass, if an edge between the concept terms in the query concept graph also existed between the same terms in the term relationship graph, its ConceptNet relation type and weight in the term relationship graph was used to calculate the average weight of all relations in the query concept graph, which belong to the same relation group according to Table 6. In the second pass, the weight of an edge between the concept terms in the query concept graph was set to the weight of an edge between the same terms in the term relationship graph, if such an edge existed. Otherwise, its weight was set to the average weight of relations in the same relation group, determined in the previous pass. Given the weighted query concept graph, the weight of a concept within the context of a certain radius from the query term was determined as the product of the weights of all the edges and IDFs of all the concepts (including the target one) along the shortest path from the query term.

4.4 Learning-based expansion

We used 5-fold cross validation to train and test the linear regression model. During testing we selected 100 top-scoring concepts and used them for expansion. In order to determine the optimal setting for learning-based concept expansion (LR) and the combined method (LR-PF), we experimented with different feature sets and contexts of different size (2 and 3). Performance of different configurations of the learning-based expansion method on different datasets is presented in Figure 2.

Several interesting observations can be made based on the analysis of Figure 2. First, for both the learning-based concept expansion and the combined method, using the extended feature set (FULL) generally results in better performance than using the baseline (BASE) feature set, which empirically demonstrates the benefits of exploiting the graph-based properties of the expansion concepts with respect to the query terms. Second, selecting candidate concept terms from the query concept graph of larger radius generally results in better performance for both feature sets, which is consistent with the results of the simulation experiment presented in Section 4.2. Similar conclusions can also be drawn by analyzing the behavior of different configurations of the learning-based (LR) and the combined (LR-PF) methods on the ROBUST04 and GOV datasets, although on those datasets the different methods within each group behaved very similar to each other. In addition to that, applying pseudo-feedback on top of the learning-based method not only did not further improve its performance on GOV (as opposed to both ROBUST04 and AQUAINT), but even significantly decreased it. This can be attributed to the fact that GOV queries are highly focused and have fewer relevant documents associated with them, thus applying pseudo-feedback on top of concept-feedback may cause the query drift.

In order to better understand the properties of effective expansion concepts, we averaged across the splits the feature weights from the model learned on the ROBUST04 dataset when the size of the expansion context is 3. Table 8 shows the weights of some of the features of the expansion concepts.

Feature	Weight
TopDocScore	0.0944
AvgTopCor	0.0518
TopTermFrac	0.0119
AvgColCor	0.0078
FanOut	0.0052
AvgPWeight	-0.0012
SpActRank	-0.0087
AvgQDist	-0.0267
ConIDF	-0.1004

Table 8: Feature weights for the expansion concepts.

As follows from Table 8, effective expansion concepts are those concepts, which both frequently occur in the top 10 retrieved documents (as follows from the high positive weight of the TopTermFrac feature) and frequently co-occur with the query terms in the entire collection and in the top 10 retrieved documents (AvgColCor and AvgTopCor). The high negative weight for the ConIDF feature indicates that effective expansion concepts are not rare in the collection (can't have high IDF). Positive weight for the FanOut and negative weight for the SpActRank features both indicate that effective expansion concepts are typically connected with edges of high weight to many other concepts in ConceptNet and are not far from the query terms (as evidenced by the negative weights for AvgQDist and AvgPWeight).

4.5 Comparison of methods

Having determined the best performing configuration of the learning-based methods, we compare them with the heuristic methods and the baselines in Figure 3 and Table 9.

As follows from Figure 3, the learning-based method predictably outperforms both heuristic methods on all datasets, since it uses the weights of expansion concepts generated by both heuristic methods as features. Moreover, as the weight of the original query language model in the mixture increases, the performance of the learning-based and the combined methods drops, which clearly illustrates the effectiveness of expansion concepts. The best performance of heuristic, learning-based and combined methods is summarized in Table 9

Several important conclusions can be drawn based on the analysis of Table 9. First, heuristic, learning-based and combined methods all improve over the KL-divergence baseline (KL) on all datasets. Secondly, the combined method (LR-PF) consistently outperforms pseudo-feedback (KL-PF) on all datasets. Moreover, as opposed to pseudo-feedback (KL-PF), the combined method actually improves the performance relative to the KL baseline for both expansion contexts of radius 2 and 3 on AQUAINT and GOV datasets. Consequently, we can conclude that learning-based method is an effective strategy to combine multiple signals for robust query expansion and pseudo-feedback in case of difficult queries, when the initially retrieved documents cannot be considered as a reliable source of effective expansion terms.

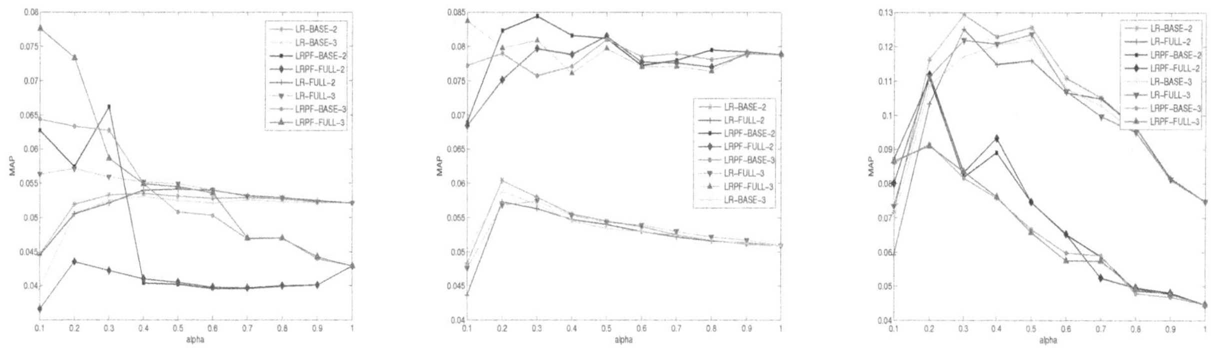

(a) **AQUAINT dataset** (b) **ROBUST04 dataset** (c) **GOV dataset**

Figure 2: Comparison of performance of learning-based concept feedback methods with different feature sets and different values of context radius by varying the interpolation coefficient α.

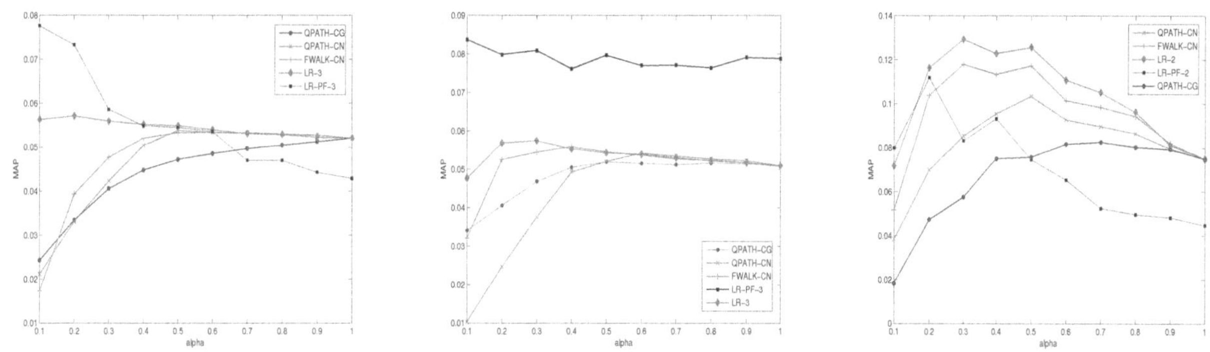

(a) **AQUAINT dataset** (b) **ROBUST04 dataset** (c) **GOV dataset**

Figure 3: Comparison of performance of heuristic to learning-based methods by varying the interpolation coefficient α

		KL	KL-PF	QPATH	RWALK	LR-2	LR-PF-2	LR-3	LR-PF-3
AQUAINT	MAP	0.0521	0.0429	0.0538	0.0534	0.0535	0.0662	0.0571*	0.0776*†
	P@10	0.1176	0.1	0.1353	0.1118	0.0941	0.1059	0.1294	0.1471
ROBUST04	MAP	0.0509	0.0788	0.0542	0.0559	0.0604$^+$	0.0844	0.0588$^+$	0.0837
	P@10	0.1467	0.1587	0.1413	0.1707	0.1747	0.1747	0.1707	0.1627
GOV	MAP	0.0748	0.0447	0.1034	0.1179	0.1293*	0.1119*†	0.1236*	0.0914*†
	P@10	0.0347	0.0197	0.0401	0.0673	0.066	0.0517	0.0551	0.049

Table 9: Comparison of the best performance of heuristic (QPATH and RWALK), learning-based (LR-2 and LR-3) and the combined (LR-PF-2 and LR-PF-3) methods with the KL-divergence retrieval model (KL) and model-based pseudo-relevance feedback (KL-PF) on difficult topics. $^+$ and * indicate statistical significance relative to KL (95% and 99% confidence levels, respectively) according to the Wilcoxon signed-rank test. † indicates statistical significance relative to KL-PF (99% confidence level) according to the Wilcoxon signed-rank test. Significance testing was performed on the results of the learning-based and combined methods only.

5. SUMMARY AND CONCLUSIONS

In this work, we presented the results of the first systematic exploration of the potential for utilizing the knowledge base of ConceptNet to improve the retrieval results of *difficult queries* and overcome the problem of the lack of relevant documents for such queries in the initial search results. In particular, we:

1. conducted a simulation experiment to determine the upper bound for the effectiveness of query expansion with the related concepts from ConceptNet, which demonstrated that there exists a small number of highly effective expansion concepts for difficult queries;
2. proposed several heuristic and learning-based methods for automatically selecting effective expansion concepts, which leverage the graph-based knowledge representation structure of ConceptNet, and empirically compared the proposed methods on different datasets. Our results indicate

that learning-based expansion methods can effectively leverage the common sense knowledge in ConceptNet to improve the search results of difficult queries both through query expansion alone and in combination with the traditional model-based pseudo-relevance feedback;

3. analyzed the obtained learning-based expansion models to determine the properties of effective expansion terms.

Designing the methods to improve the search results of difficult queries is a challenging and very important practical and theoretical information retrieval problem. Our results and findings indicate that ConceptNet has a great potential to be effectively used as an external source of expansion terms, when the initial search results are of very bad quality and other techniques such as relevance feedback and pseudo-relevance feedback become ineffective.

6. ACKNOWLEDGEMENTS

This material is based upon work supported by the National Science Foundation under Grant Number NSF-1027965, AFOSR MURI Grant FA9550-08-1-0265, and a gift grant from Microsoft. We would like to thank the anonymous reviewers for their helpful comments.

7. REFERENCES

[1] J. Allan. Overview of the trec 2004 robust retrieval track. In *Proceedings of TREC 13*, 2004.

[2] J. Allan. Hard track overview in trec 2005 - high accuracy retrieval from documents. In *Proceedings of TREC 14*, 2005.

[3] J. Bai, D. Song, P. Bruza, J.-Y. Nie, and G. Cao. Query expansion using term relationships in language models for information retrieval. In *Proceedings of CIKM*, pages 688–695, Bremen, Germany, 2005.

[4] R. C. Bodner and F. Song. Knowledge-based approaches to query expansion in information retrieval. *Advances in Artificial Intelligence*, pages 146–158.

[5] P. Bruza and D. Song. Inferring query models by computing information flow. In *Proceedings of CIKM*, pages 260–269, 2002.

[6] C. Burgess, K. Livesay, and K. Lund. Explorations in context space: Words, sentences and discourse. *Discourse Processes*, 25:211–257, 1998.

[7] G. Cao, J.-Y. Nie, and J. Bai. Integrating word relationships into language models. In *Proceedings of SIGIR*, pages 298–305, 2005.

[8] Z. Cao, T. Qin, T.-Y. Liu, M.-F. Tsai, and H. Li. Learning to rank: from pairwise approach to listwise approach. In *Proceedings of ICML*, pages 129–136, 2007.

[9] P. R. Cohen and R. Kjeldsen. Information retrieval by constrained spreading activation in semantic networks. *Information Processing and Management*, 23(4):255–268, 1987.

[10] K. Collins-Thompson and J. Callan. Query expansion using random walk models. In *Proceedings of CIKM*, pages 704–711, 2005.

[11] N. Craswell and D. Hawking. Overview of the trec 2004 web track. In *Proceedings of TREC 13*, 2004.

[12] F. Crestani. Application of spreading activation techniques in information retrieval. *Artificial Intelligence Review*, 11(6):453–482, 1997.

[13] F. Diaz and D. Metzler. Improving the estimation of relevance models using large external corpora. In *Proceedings of SIGIR*, pages 154–161, 2006.

[14] E. Gabrilovich and S. Markovitch. Computing semantic relatedness using wikipedia-based explicit semantic analysis. In *Proceedings of IJCAI*, pages 1606–16011, 2007.

[15] S. Gauch and J. Wang. A corpus analysis approach for automatic query expansion. In *Proceedings of CIKM*, pages 278–284, 1997.

[16] M.-H. Hsu and H.-H. Chen. Information retrieval with commonsense knowledge. In *Proceedings of SIGIR'06*, pages 651–652, 2006.

[17] M.-H. Hsu, M.-F. Tsai, and H.-H. Chen. Query expansion with conceptnet and wordnet: An intrinsic comparison. In *Proceedings of AIRS*, pages 1–13, 2006.

[18] M.-H. Hsu, M.-F. Tsai, and H.-H. Chen. Combining wordnet and conceptnet for automatic query expansion: A learning approach. In *Proceedings of AIRS*, pages 213–224, 2008.

[19] A. Kotov and C. Zhai. Towards natural question-guided search. In *Proceedings of WWW*, pages 541–550, 2010.

[20] A. Kotov and C. Zhai. Interactive sense feedback for difficult queries. In *Proceedings of CIKM*, pages 163–172, 2011.

[21] Y. Li, W. P. R. Luk, K. S. E. Ho, and F. L. K. Chung. Improving weak ad-hoc queries using wikipedia as external corpus. In *Proceedings of SIGIR*, pages 797–798, 2007.

[22] H. Liu and P. Singh. Conceptnet-a practical commonsense reasoning tool-kit. *BT Technology Journal*, 22(4):146–158.

[23] S. Liu, F. Liu, C. Yu, and W. Meng. An effective approach to document retrieval via utilizing wordnet and recognizing phrases. In *Proceedings of ACM SIGIR'04*, pages 266–272, 2004.

[24] R. Mandala, T. Tokunaga, and H. Tanaka. Combining multiple evidence from different types of thesaurus for query expansion. In *Proceedings of ACM SIGIR'99*, pages 191–197, 1999.

[25] E. Meij, D. Trieschnigg, M. de Rijke, and W. Kraaij. Conceptual language models for domain-specific retrieval. *Information Processing and Management*, 2:25–45, 2000.

[26] G. Salton and C. Buckley. On the use of spreading activation methods in automatic information retrieval. In *Proceedings of SIGIR*, pages 147–160, 1988.

[27] C. Shah and W. B. Croft. Evaluating high accuracy retrieval techniques. In *Proceedings of SIGIR*, pages 2–9, 2004.

[28] C. van Rijsbergen. *Information Retrieval.* Butterworths, London, UK, 1979.

[29] E. M. Voorhees. Query expansion using lexical-semantic relations. In *Proceedings of ACM SIGIR'93*, pages 61–69, 1994.

[30] J. Xu and W. B. Croft. Query expansion using local and global document analysis. In *Proceedings of ACM SIGIR'96*, pages 4–11, 1996.

[31] J. Xu and W. B. Croft. Improving the effectiveness of information retrieval with local context analysis. *ACM Transactions on Information Systems*, 18:79–112, 2000.

[32] Z. Yin, M. Shokouhi, and N. Craswell. Query expansion using external evidence. In *Proceedings of ECIR*, pages 362–374, 2009.

[33] J. Yufeng and W. B. Croft. An association thesaurus for information retrieval. In *Proceedings of RIAO*, pages 146–160, 1994.

[34] C. Zhai and J. Lafferty. Document language models, query models, and risk minimization for information retrieval. In *Proceedings of SIGIR'01*, pages 111–119, 2001.

[35] C. Zhai and J. Lafferty. Model-based feedback in the language modeling approach to information retrieval. In *Proceedings of CIKM'01*, pages 403–410, 2001.

Domain Bias in Web Search

Samuel Ieong
Microsoft Research
samuel.ieong@microsoft.com

Nina Mishra
Microsoft Research
ninam@microsoft.com

Eldar Sadikov*
Stanford University
eldar@cs.stanford.edu

Li Zhang
Microsoft Research
lzha@microsoft.com

ABSTRACT

This paper uncovers a new phenomenon in web search that we call *domain bias* — a user's propensity to believe that a page is more relevant just because it comes from a particular domain. We provide evidence of the existence of domain bias in click activity as well as in human judgments via a comprehensive collection of experiments. We begin by studying the difference between domains that a search engine surfaces and that users click. Surprisingly, we find that despite changes in the overall distribution of surfaced domains, there has not been a comparable shift in the distribution of clicked domains. Users seem to have learned the landscape of the internet and their click behavior has thus become more predictable over time. Next, we run a blind domain test, akin to a Pepsi/Coke taste test, to determine whether domains can shift a user's opinion of which page is more relevant. We find that domains can actually flip a user's preference about 25% of the time. Finally, we demonstrate the existence of systematic domain preferences, even after factoring out confounding issues such as position bias and relevance, two factors that have been used extensively in past work to explain user behavior. The existence of domain bias has numerous consequences including, for example, the importance of discounting click activity from reputable domains.

Categories and Subject Descriptors

H.1 [**Information Systems**]: Models and Principles

General Terms

Experimentation, Human factors, Measurement

Keywords

domain bias, user behavior, web search

*The work is done while the author was at Microsoft Research.

Permission to make digital or hard copies of all or part of this work for personal or classroom use is granted without fee provided that copies are not made or distributed for profit or commercial advantage and that copies bear this notice and the full citation on the first page. To copy otherwise, to republish, to post on servers or to redistribute to lists, requires prior specific permission and/or a fee.
WSDM'12, February 8–12, 2012, Seattle, Washington, USA.
Copyright 2012 ACM 978-1-4503-0747-5/12/02 ...$10.00.

1. INTRODUCTION

Obtaining high quality labeled data is important for a search engine since it can be used both for creating a better ranking function, as well as assessing the quality of search results. Human judgments are commonly used for both purposes. However, over time it has become evident that human judgments will not scale. Specifically, obtaining human judgments for every country/language as well as specific verticals such as commerce and health will be challenging in terms of cost and efficiency.

As a result, the click logs have been proposed as a substitute for human judgments. Clicks are a relatively free, implicit source of user feedback. Finding the right way to exploit clicks is crucial to designing an improved search engine.

However, clicks are fraught with biases. The most widely studied bias is position bias [12, 13], a user's propensity to click on a search result just because it appears closer to the top of a search results page. Much work has been invested in both establishing the existence of position bias [8, 18], as well as understanding how to remove position bias from click activity [2, 3, 7]. Other biases are also known to exist, for example, snippet attractiveness bias, a user's propensity to click on a result because the query terms appear in bold in the title multiple times [23].

In this paper, we uncover a new phenomenon in click activity that we call *domain bias*—a user's propensity to click on a search result because it comes from a reputable domain, as well as their disinclination to click on a result from a domain of unknown or distrustful reputation. The propensity constitutes a bias as it cannot be explained by relevance or positioning of search results.

Our goal is to provide incontrovertible proof of the existence of domain bias. We do so via a series of carefully designed experiments. We ask if a search engine drastically changes the surfaced domains, do domain clicks also change accordingly? Amazingly, the answer turns out to be no. Instead, we find that users click on the same domains despite changes in surfaced content. In a similar vein, if we take two search engines of wildly different relevance, we ask if domain clicks also swing wildly. Again, to our surprise, the answer is no. We observe that the top domains garner a larger and larger fraction of the clicks and it is not because search engines are surfacing a smaller number of domains. On the contrary, search engines are changing the domains they show. It is users who have decided to visit a smaller number of domains.

It should not be surprising that users have learned to trust some domains over others. Indeed, past work such as TrustRank measures user trust at a domain level [10]. A recent eye-tracking study also confirms that users pay attention to the displayed URL[1]. One could argue that search engines already know this and exploit it by using the PageRank of a domain in their scoring functions so as to boost documents from domains of high reputation.

What is surprising is that users click on results from reputable domains even when more relevant search results are available. Our experiments are geared towards proving that domains can so drastically influence perceived relevance that users will favor some domains, regardless of content. Viewing content on the Internet as products, domains have emerged as brands. And users have developed such fierce brand loyalty that their clicks are tainted by domains.

We establish the existence of domain bias via a Pepsi/Coke style blind taste test. In our experiment, we request relevance feedback from different users where each is shown a query and two search results in three scenarios: with the snippet only (i.e., absent domain), with the snippet and true URL, and with the snippet and swapped URL. We find that in 25% of the cases, the behavior of users resembles a blind following to domains. For example, for the query {one of the most common types of heart disease}, there are two snippets and two domains, one from `webmd.com` and another from `genetichealth.com`. Absent domain, users prefer the snippet from `genetichealth`. When domains are revealed, users prefer the snippet of `webmd`. More interestingly, when we paired the `genetichealth` snippet with the `webmd` URL, users flip their preference and go back to preferring the snippet from `genetichealth` (now paired with the domain `webmd`). The experiment demonstrates that users have become reliant on domains in assessing the relevance of search results, and may in some cases blindly trust content from reputable domains.

Next, we design an experiment to demonstrate a systematic bias towards certain domains that spans across search queries. Designing an experiment to tease out the existence of domain trust is a non-trivial task. One confounding factor is relevance—perhaps the reason why certain domains attract the majority of clicks is that content from the domain appears to be more relevant to the user. Another confounding factor is position bias—perhaps the search engine tends to rank some domains higher than others and that is what leads to the observed domain preference. We design an experiment that removes the relevance factor by focusing on query, URL1, URL2 combinations that are labeled equally relevant by a strong majority of a panel of human judges. Further, the experiment removes position bias by only drawing inferences about domain A being preferred to domain B when A is ranked below B and yet still A is clicked more often. By accumulating these preferences, we find that we can construct an ordering of domains that agrees well with user preferences. Such an ordering with strong agreement would have been impossible in the absence of domain trust, thus confirming its presence.

The existence of domain trust has important consequences for several areas of web search research. For example, it influences the design of user click models [3, 6, 7, 9], which have focused on relevance and position of the search results as the principal factors that influence user clicks. Domain bias introduces a new factor that needs to be considered. It also influences the large body of literature of learning relevance from clicks. While many studies have considered ways to remove position bias [2, 7, 11], we must now consider how to remove domain bias. Domain bias also affects how queries are categorized as navigational vs. informational. As user visits concentrate on fewer domains, former informational queries may now appear navigational, and semantic approaches may be needed to distinguish between the two types.

The goal of this paper is to provide indisputable proof of the existence of domain bias. We believe this is an important phenomenon and we take careful steps in establishing that it exists beyond reasonable doubt. We also take first steps in quantifying the amount of bias as it can help with the aforementioned applications. Nonetheless, our approach is limited in scale due to the reliance of human labels. The quantification of domain bias at web scale remains a deep challenge and we leave it as a great question for future work.

[1]"Eye-tracking studies: More than meets the eye", published at `http://googleblog.blogspot.com/2009/02/eye-tracking-studies-more-than-meets.html`, 2009.

2. RELATED WORK

The bias of user clicks on search engines has been studied before. Joachims *et. al.* found user clicks to be good signals for implicit relevance judgments but observed via an eye-tracking study that there is considerable position bias [12]. Later, Craswell *et. al.* carried out ranking perturbation experiments and proposed a cascade model: users scan results from top to bottom and make click decisions based on relevance [6]. Similar to our study, Craswell *et. al.* found that users did not blindly trust search engines. Unlike the study by Craswell *et. al.*, however, our findings are at the aggregate level of page domains and explain clicks beyond pure relevance. In [23], the authors show that users are biased towards "attractively" formatted snippets. Our experiments are geared towards establishing a different bias, by pairing snippets with swapped URLs.

User browsing models for search engine results, both organic and sponsored, have attracted considerable attention in recent years [1, 3, 6, 9, 21, 22, 23]. These models aim to estimate the click-through rate (CTR) of a result (i.e., the probability that a result is clicked), given the result's position and previous clicks in the user session. The CTR is commonly modeled as the product of the examination probability and the perceived relevance of the result (probability of a click given examination). The models vary in the examination probability and perceived relevance functions, but all agree that these functions depend only on the current state of the results (i.e., pages) and the current user's session clicks. On the other hand, our work shows that CTR is not only influenced by relevance and examination but also by domain preference.

It is well known that page quality is correlated with its hosting domain. There is related work on domain trust in the context of spam. For example, Gyöngyi *et. al.* proposed TrustRank – PageRank like ranking of domains based on a seed set of trusted reputable sites [10]. It is common practice for search engines to use domain as a feature in ranking. For example, PageRank [17] can be applied to the hyperlink structure on domains to obtain domain rank scores. Alternatively, domains that garner many clicks may be boosted higher in the ranking. Our work shows that if clicks are used to boost pages in the ranking, that domain bias must first be discounted.

A related line of research is on the bias of search engines on page popularity. Cho and Roy observed that search engines penalized newly created pages by giving higher ranking to the current popular pages [4]. A number of solutions were proposed including using the change in popularity as a signal of page quality [5] and partial randomization of ranking [19]. Although this line of work is related to ours in that we look at the influence of search engines on users, our focus is different: we aim to understand and model user's long-term preference for specific domains.

There are a number of macro-level user behavior studies that we will present in Section 3. For example, [20, 14, 15] analyze user traffic from search engines to individual sites and characterize search and browsing behavior. Unlike previous studies that characterize search behavior at a particular time point, our work emphasizes longitudinal search behavior. Mei and Church [15] conducted a related study where they showed that the visited web at a particular point in time has low entropy. Our work is different in that we look at the visited web over time. We similarly confirm that user visits are predictable, but we also point out that user visits are slow to change. Users are consistent about the domains they visit and are less influenced by changes in the displayed results.

3. SEARCH ENGINE INFLUENCE

We set out to study user domain bias by examining user behavior from search engines at the aggregate level. Our goal is to check whether users simply follow search engines and click on the top returned results without giving them much scrutiny. So we start by comparing the changes in the top displayed results to the changes in the clicked results. Intuitively, if users have little preference for domains, we expect the changes in the displayed results to trigger equivalent changes in the clicked results. Surprisingly, however, in spite of the changes in the displayed results we find that clicks tend to be rather stable with respect to domains.

Our experiments also reveal that search results concentrate over time on fewer domains with increasingly larger share of results pointing to the top domains. This trend is accompanied by an increase in click-through rates (even after factoring out query distribution changes) and is in contrast to the growing size of the web content and the number of registered domains.

Although the evidence we present in this section alone does not definitively prove the existence of domain bias (we provide more rigorous experiments in the subsequent sections), the results are likely to be potential consequences of the phenomenon. By pointing out the potential consequences up front, we motivate careful examination of domain bias in web search.

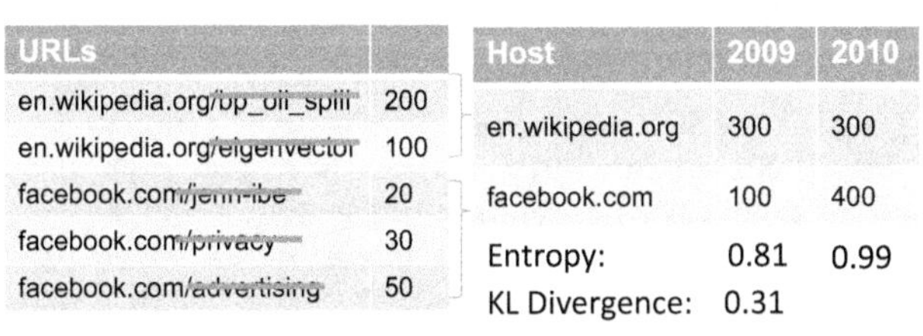

Figure 1: Methodology.

Why Domains? We study user visit patterns in terms of the aggregate distribution of page views over their hosting domains. Although technically we aggregate at the level of hosts, we use the term "domains" throughout the paper. Consider Figure 1. This is a sample of URLs clicked by search engine users with the total number of clicks each URL received, irrespective of queries. We aggregate clicks on pages from the same host to obtain a distribution of clicks over the host names. We look at hosts and not the individual pages because studying visits with respect to pages over a long time period becomes impractical: after one year nearly 60% of the pages are replaced by new ones [16]. More importantly, aggregating visits over hosts makes sense because hosts roughly correspond to individual publishers on the web, e.g., each sub-domain of `wordpress.com` corresponds to an individual blog. We also performed experiments on top level domains and obtained similar results to the ones presented here.

Data. Our findings are based on data derived from search logs. We study user visit patterns over a seven-day period at two different time points: July 2009 and July 2010. Looking at the same period in 2009 and 2010 minimizes the temporal bias. To remove variance due to geographic and linguistic differences in search behavior, we only consider queries issued in the English speaking United States locale.

Method. We use Shannon entropy to measure the display and visit distribution of domains. Compared to other measures such as power-law exponent, Shannon entropy has an intuitive meaning: it is the average number of bits required to encode the destination domain of each visit. Increasing entropy is a sign of user visits becoming more diverse, while decreasing entropy is a sign of user visits becoming more predictable and suggests the formation of domain preferences.

We use KL(Kullback-Leibler) divergence to measure the difference between two distributions. Recall that KL divergence is defined as $D_{KL}(p||q) = \sum_{d \in \mathcal{D}} p(d) \log \frac{p(d)}{q(d)}$ for two distributions $p = \{p(d)\}$ and $q = \{q(d)\}$. KL divergence measures the average number of extra bits required to encode the distribution of p using the optimal encoding of q. Together with Shannon entropy, it provides an intuition of the magnitude of distribution changes. One problem with the use of KL divergence is that it is undefined when there is a domain d such that $p(d) > 0$ and $q(d) = 0$. To address this issue, we employ the standard add-one smoothing: before computing the distribution, we add one to the count of each domain.

3.1 Displayed vs. Clicked Results

We compare the search displays and user visits from the same search engine in two time periods: July 2009 and July 2010. We refer to these data sets as 2009 and 2010 data, respectively. We only consider the top 5 results returned by the search engine for each query. By focusing on the top results, we aim to reduce the influence of examination bias: users scan results from the top to bottom, so the top results are more likely to be examined [12]. We also analyzed the top 1 result and top 10 result distributions and found similar insights to the ones we present here.

Table 1 shows the ten most frequently displayed domains in 2009. We show the display and visit shares[2] point-wise for each domain in 2009 and 2010. Observe the drastic change

[2]The display (visit) share of a domain is the number of times the domain is displayed (visited) over the total number of displays (visits).

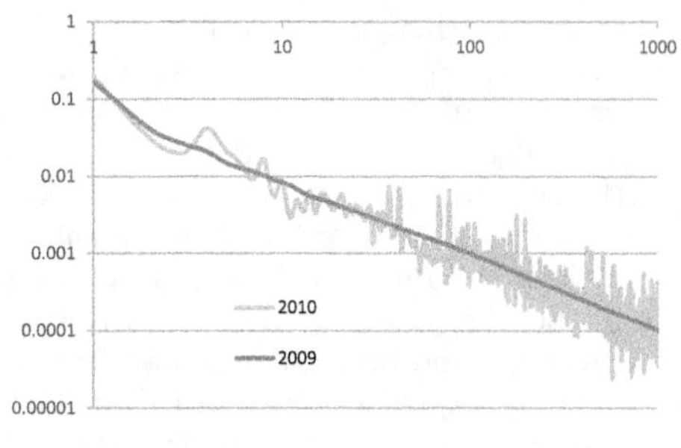

(a) Display Distribution Changes

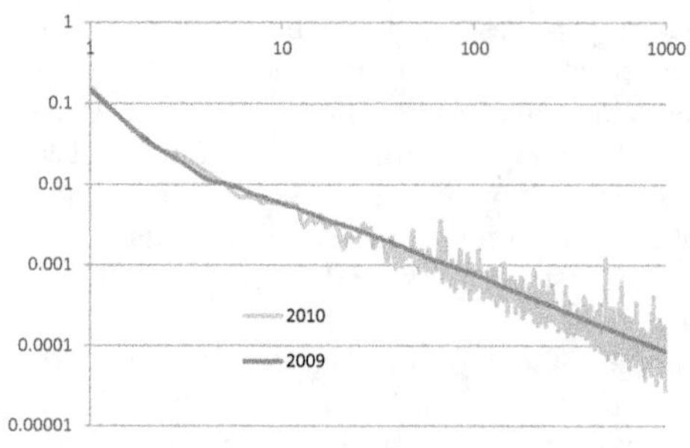

(b) Click Distribution Changes

Figure 2: Display and click distributions point-wise for 2009 and 2010. Both (a) and (b) plots are on log-log scale. The points are connected in a line for better exhibition of the distribution differences.

Domains	2009 display	2010 display	2009 visit	2010 visit
`en.wikipedia.org`	0.0750	0.0923	0.0274	0.0279
`www.facebook.com`	0.0119	0.0251	0.0233	0.0497
`www.youtube.com`	0.0098	0.0104	0.0177	0.0197
`www.google.com`	0.0085	0.0087	0.0276	0.0236
`groups.google.com`	0.0053	0.0002	0.0001	0.0001
`checkout.google.com`	0.0043	0.0000	0.0000	0.0000
`mail.yahoo.com`	0.0044	0.0030	0.0067	0.0069
`www.yahoo.com`	0.0044	0.0034	0.0137	0.0110
`www.imdb.com`	0.0042	0.0035	0.0038	0.0036
`blog.facebook.com`	0.0042	0.0001	0.0000	0.0000

Table 1: Display and visit share for a sample of domains in 2009 and 2010. The ten domains are the most displayed domains in 2009.

in the display shares in contrast to the more modest change in the visit shares. The entropy, as well as the KL divergence, of the distribution of displayed and visited domains are shown in Table 2.

	displays	visits
2009 entropy	15.24	15.07
2010 entropy	14.24	14.72
KL divergence	1.33	0.76

Table 2: Summary of the changes to the distribution of displayed and visited domains from 2009 to 2010.

From Table 2, we can see that while the distribution of displayed domains undergoes significant changes, there is no comparable shift in the distribution of visited domains. To provide a visual illustration of the scale of changes behind the numbers, we plot in Figure 2 (a) and (b) the distributions from the two time periods point-to-point for displayed and visited domains, respectively. In both figures, we use 2009 data as the baseline, sorting all domains in decreasing order of their frequencies in 2009. We then bin every 10 domains and plot the cumulative frequency for each bin as the dark curve. Since we order by the frequencies in 2009, the dark curve monotonically decreases. With the light curve, we plot the corresponding frequency for 2010 data, keeping the same binning of domains as for 2009. As a result, the curve need not be monotonic. This presentation allows one to visually observe the difference between the two distributions. From Figure 2(a) and (b), we can see that the displayed results have undergone a larger change compared to the visits. This effect is especially prominent in the head of the distributions. Furthermore, the discrepancy between the changes in the displays and the visits are prominent even when looking at the distributions for the top result only.

3.2 Nature of the Displayed Result Changes

We next look at the nature of the changes in the surfaced results between 2009 and 2010 (by the same search engine).

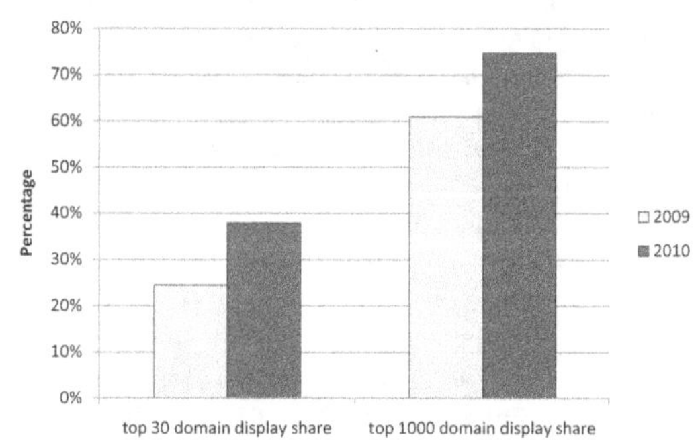

Figure 3: Cumulative share of displays attributed to the 30 and 1000 most popular domains in 2009 and 2010, respectively.

Figure 3 shows the cumulative share of search displays attributed to the 30 most popular domains in the time periods of July 2009 and July 2010. As seen from the graph, 2010 share of search results pointing to the top 30 domains increases from 25% to 38% and to the top 1000 domains from 61% to 74%. Note that the increase is not limited to particular few domains, e.g., `facebook.com`, but rather applies to a large set of domains beyond the topmost few. Further, the observed trend cannot be explained by the increasing share of navigational queries, as the increase in the share of search results pointing to the top 1000 domains persists after re-normalizing for the query distribution changes.

The shift of the search results towards popular domains is also demonstrated by the entropy of the distribution of search displays over domains in Table 2. There is a 1-bit drop in the entropy, which is quite drastic when viewed in the context of the vast growth of the web. While there is an increasing volume of content on the web and an increasing number of sites, search engine results tend to concentrate on increasingly fewer domains!

Both the increasing share of search displays attributed to the top domains and the drop in the overall entropy indicate that the search engines show increasingly less diverse domains. The logical question is whether this trend aligns with the user preferences. It turns out that the answer is yes: for the particular search engine we study, the click-through rate in 2010 compared to 2009 has increased dramatically; so does the click-through rate on the top position of search results. The trend can be verified even after re-normalizing for the query distribution changes, which may suggest (although not definitively yet) that increasing number of users develop preference for specific domains that cannot be explained by the increasing share of navigational queries alone.

3.3 Clicks of Different Search Engines

Our analysis has so far focused on a particular search engine. Next, we compare the distribution of clicks from two different search engines side by side observed in the same time period in July 2010. Search engine A is a major search engine with a large market share, while search engine B is a niche search engine with a tiny market share. Given differences in the two search engines' target audiences, we hypothesize a large difference in their displayed results (we verified this hypothesis with a limited sample of queries). If users have an intrinsic preference for specific domains, their clicks should be similar independently of the search engine they use and the results surfaced.

Indeed, comparing the two search engines' distributions of the visited domains, we find them to be fairly close. The KL divergence between the click distributions of the two search engines is only 0.92 bits. This number is quite low considering that the entropy of the click distributions for the two search engines are 16.72 and 14.7 bits, respectively for search engine A and B. Although the two search engines are likely to be using different ranking functions and, hence, displaying different results for the same queries, the click distributions are quite similar.

To put the KL divergence value of 0.92 bits in perspective, contrast it against the KL divergence numbers in Table 2. The displayed results of the same search engine from two different time periods already differ by 1.33 bits, we expect the displayed results of two different search engines to diverge even more. Nonetheless, the 0.92 bits is only slightly higher than the 0.76 bits of divergence in that table.

To summarize, our experiments suggest that users do not blindly visit results surfaced by search engines, instead they show preference for the domains they visit. The concentration of search results on fewer domains is accompanied by an increase in click-through rates. Such a trend may suggest that users have intrinsic preferences for certain domains. However, to understand whether this preference constitutes a bias, we need to conduct more careful experiments since domains are likely to be correlated with relevance. In what follows, we will address this concern, and find out to what extent domains can influence perceived relevance of search results, and verify that even after removing confounding factors such as relevance and position bias, there still remains a systematic domain bias.

4. PEPSI/COKE TEST FOR DOMAINS

We are interested in determining if URL influences perceived relevance. We answer this question via an experiment similar in spirit to the Pepsi/Coke taste test. In our experiment, the products under question correspond to the snippets[3] shown to the user. In the taste test analogy, we are interested in whether simply labeling a product "Pepsi" or "Coke" can make a product taste better.

We measure a user's preference under three different conditions: (1) only the snippets are shown, i.e., URLs are hidden, (2) the snippet and true URLs are shown and (3) the snippet and swapped URLs are shown. The first test is a blind taste test that establishes the baseline. An example is given in Figure 4. The second gives the true labels and the third labels "Coke" as "Pepsi" and vice versa. An example of the second and third experimental conditions is given in Figure 5.

In our experiments, we present these three modes to different human judges and ask them to choose the result with higher relevance. This step is done by creating human intelligence tasks (HITs) on the Amazon Mechanical Turk platform. We describe the details next.

4.1 Setup

We obtain human judgments of the relevance of about 30 URLs each for $14K$ queries sampled from the search log of a commercial search engine. We select queries for which at least two URLs from different domains are judged to be equally and highly relevant to the query. This selection step effectively removes navigational queries for which domains are unlikely to introduce a bias to the perceived relevance of the URLs. Next, we sort the domains by popularity as measured by the frequency with which they appear in the judged URLs. We keep ⟨query, URL1, URL2⟩ tuples for which URL1 belongs to one of the top 50 most popular domains while URL2 belongs to a domain outside of the top 200 most popular domains. This helps to selects tuples for which both URLs are considered equally relevant by a human expert, but one URL belongs to a highly recognizable domain while the other belongs to a more obscure domain. Finally, we sample $1K$ instances from the tuples for which we have successfully obtained snippets for both URLs. The snippets are obtained from a major commercial search engine and anonymized algorithmically based on a set of handcrafted rules so that the content of snippet does not reveal the domain it comes from. This is important as we subsequently paired each snippet with both URLs, and anonymization is needed to avoid creating confusion to the users when a snippet is paired with a different URL.

Using this dataset, we generate HITs to verify the existence of domain bias. Each HIT requires the worker to decide whether one snippet or the other is more relevant to the query. To reduce the effect of presentation bias, we present the two snippets side-by-side, and randomly flip the ordering of the snippets. To mimic the conditions of a search engine,

[3]A snippet is the short summary of a page presented to the user by the search engine. It does not include the URL in our definition.

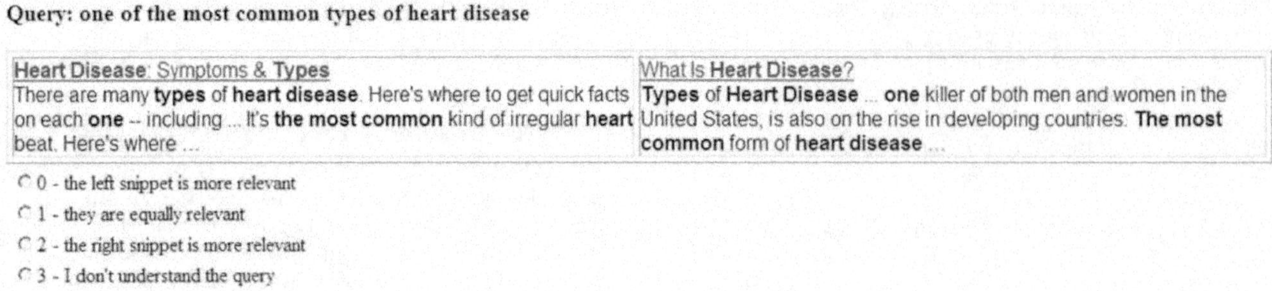

Figure 4: The design of the HIT for Mechanical Turks under the first condition—hidden URLs.

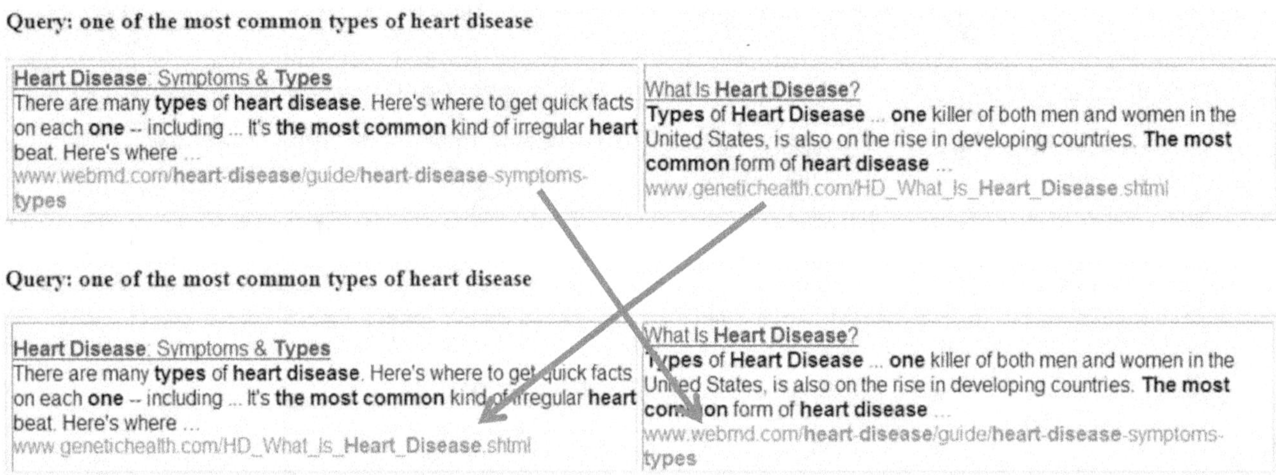

Figure 5: The second and third experimental conditions—pairing URLs with snippets. The pairing above corresponds to the correct labeling of the snippet with the URL. The one below swaps the two URLs.

we format the snippets and the URLs in exactly the same manner as a search engine would, together with in-context highlighting. The worker is given four choices: "the left snippet is more relevant", "they are equally relevant", "the right snippet is more relevant", and "I don't understand the query". For each instance ⟨query, URL1, URL2⟩, we generated three different types of tasks corresponding to different experimental conditions, as discussed before. An illustration of the HIT interface is given in Figure 4.

To root out workers who may randomly select answers, we introduce and scatter honeypots into the tasks, and exclude in our results the judgments provided by any workers who have failed the honeypot tests (which is about 10% in the received results). Each instance for each of the experimental conditions is repeated six times, three each for the two different ordering of the snippets.

4.2 Results

For each pair of results (R_1, R_2) presented to the worker i, we assign a rating $q^{(i)}(R_1 : R_2) \in \{1, 0, -1\}$ to R_1 according to the worker's response. The rating indicates whether the worker thinks R_1 is more (1), equally (0), or less (-1) relevant than R_2 for the given query. Averaging over the ratings from the six trials for each of the experimental conditions, we obtain an overall rating $q(R_1 : R_2) \in [-1, 1]$ for each pair of results, with the sign of q indicating the preferences of the workers. We also compute the standard deviation of the ratings and use it to compute confidence intervals of the ratings.

We write a result R as sd if it consists of the snippet s and the URL with domain d, or s if the URL is not shown to the worker. By the three types of tasks we designed, for each pair $(R_1 = s_1d_1, R_2 = s_2d_2)$, we obtain three ratings $q_0 = q(s_1 : s_2)$, $q_1 = q(s_1d_1 : s_2d_2)$, and $q_2 = q(s_1d_2 : s_2d_1)$. We will use q_0 as the baseline and q_1, q_2 to verify to what extent URL influences preference.

If there is no domain bias, then the sign of q_1 and q_2 should be the same as that of q_0's, indicating that the user has the same preference regardless of whether the URL is presented. On the other hand, if $q_1 > 0$ but $q_2 < 0$, it means that users prefer both s_1d_1 to s_2d_2 and s_2d_1 to s_1d_2. This indicates that the user follows the domain d_1 in his preference. Similarly $q_1 < 0$ and $q_2 > 0$ indicates that d_2 is preferred.

Consider the example presented in Figures 4 and 5. When the URLs are not presented, users prefer the *right* snippet. However, when the URLs are presented correctly, they change their preference to the *left* snippet. When the URLs are swapped, their preference flips once again to the *right* snippet. In both the second and third conditions, their preference follows `webmd`. This provides strong evidence that `www.webmd.com` is preferred to `www.genetichealth.com`.

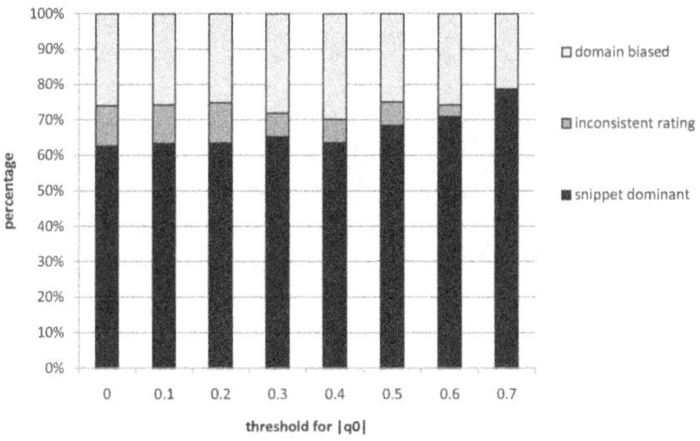

Figure 6: Distribution of three preference patterns with different minimum value of $|q_0|$.

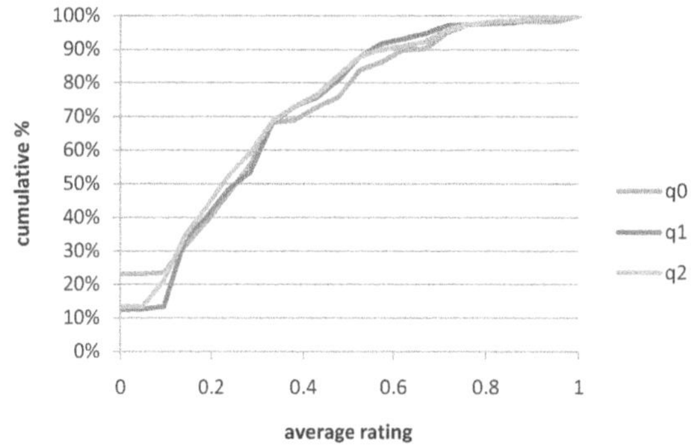

Figure 7: Cumulative distribution of user ratings.

We use this intuition to consider how user preferences are influenced by domains. To do so, we focus on only the ratings for which the workers are "confidently" positive or negative, i.e., we consider only the ratings whose 70% confidence interval is entirely positive or entirely negative. For each pair, according to the sign of q_0, q_1, q_2, we distinguish three cases

- **Snippet dominant.** q_0, q_1, q_2 all have the same sign. In this case, user preferences follow the snippet.
- **Domain biased.** q_1 and q_2 have opposite sign. In this case, user preferences follow the domain.
- **Inconsistent ratings.** q_1 and q_2 have the same sign but opposite to q_0's. This is an inconsistent outcome that cannot be explained by either the snippet or the domain. Such inconsistency is likely due to randomness in human judgments.

Figure 6 shows the distribution of the three cases for different minimum values of $|q_0|$ (non-inclusive). For example, the distribution of cases for the case of $|q_0| = 0.1$ includes all cases for which $|q_0| > 0.1$. As we can see from the graph, a majority of the cases are dominated by the snippet. This is as expected as the snippet contains rich contextual information to help users determine its relevance. However, we see that in a substantial fraction (about 25%) of the cases, user preferences are driven by domains. More importantly, domain bias persists for different values of $|q_0|$. That is, for 25% of cases users follow the URL even when there is a large difference between the perceived relevance of snippets in the absence of URLs! On the other hand, the fraction of inconsistent cases diminishes to 0% as the baseline preferences $|q_0|$ increases, providing evidence that the inconsistent cases are due to randomness in human judgments and they happen only when the users do not have strong preferences between the two snippets by themselves.

A reasonable question is whether users react differently to the three different modes. For example, if the snippet itself contains some domain information, when presented with swapped URLs, the user might get confused by the combination and provide inconsistent feedback. Our results suggest that users are not confused. Consider the distribution of ratings for the three different types of tasks. Figure 7 shows the cumulative distribution of the absolute value of the ratings[4]. First, we note that even though the content of the URLs are judged by human experts to be equally relevant to the query, the workers do not rate the snippets to be equally relevant. Further, comparing the distribution of q_0 and q_1 (and likewise q_0 and q_2), we observe a 10% difference in distribution in the ratings region of $(0, 0.1)$. This difference suggests that users are more inclined to prefer one URL to another when they learn of the URL and its domain. Second, comparing the distribution of q_1 and q_2, we notice that the distribution is almost identical as the two lines overlap one another. This suggests that the pairing of the snippets with both the correct URL and the opposite URL does not introduce systematic bias in the ratings, and alleviates the concern of whether pairing a snippet with an incorrect URL will confuse users.

In summary, the results from the experiments on Amazon Mechanical Turk platform show that while the perceived relevance of a URL is primarily determined by the snippet, which we view as an approximation of the relevance of its content, the exact URL contributes substantively to its perceived relevance. We believe the URL influences perceived relevance through its domain. We verify this in the following section.

5. SYSTEMATIC DOMAIN BIAS

Our previous experiment has demonstrated that the perceived relevance of search results can be swayed by domains. But could this phenomenon be query specific, hence hard to predict for each particular query? In this section, we design experiments to show that domain bias is actually consistent across different queries. Further, based on our experimental data, there exists an ordering of the domains that is highly consistent with the outcome of "head-to-head preference" between two domains as exhibited by users.

[4]Since $q(R_1; R_2) = -q(R_2; R_1)$, the distribution is symmetric, and it suffices to show the distribution of the absolute value.

5.1 Methodology

Designing an experiment to single out the influence of domain turns out to be challenging, as we need to carefully factor out relevance and position bias, two well studied factors that may influence user click behavior [3, 6, 7].

Our strategy is to first identify pairs of webpages in which one is clearly preferred to the other by the users after relevance and position bias is controlled for. We then verify that user preferences are strongly correlated with the domains of the pages and they exhibit a consistent bias across queries. Our experiment consists of three steps.

First, we identify pairs of URLs p_1 and p_2 that are deemed to be equally relevant to a query q, denoted by $p_1 \sim_q p_2$. The relevance of the URLs for the query are determined by human judges.

Next, we identify user preferences between two URLs that cannot be explained by position bias. For each pair of equally relevant URLs, we examine the search logs for instances where both appeared in the search results. We then count the number of times p_1 preceding p_2 and vice versa. We also count the number of clicks both URLs received. We say that p_1 is preferred to p_2 under q, $p_1 \rightarrow_q p_2$, if p_1 receives more clicks *and* p_2 appears before p_1 *more* often than p_1 before p_2. The latter requirement is there to ensure that the preference is not explicable by position bias.

Finally, we aggregate these preferences at the domain level and determine if the users exhibit a systematic bias based on hypothesis testing. This is a complex step that involves a number of sub-steps. First, we construct a *domain preference graph* based on user preferences from the last step. The domain preference graph, $G = \langle V, E\rangle$, is a unweighted directed multi-graph. The nodes V in the graph represent domains. For each preference $p_1 \rightarrow_q p_2$ we add a directed edge from the domain of p_1 to the domain of p_2 (we ignore the pair if p_1, p_2 are from the same domain). The graph can be viewed as a summary of the preference the users exhibit over the domain.

We show an example taken from a domain preference graph constructed in our experiments in Figure 8. The data behind this graph is discussed further in the next section. The nodes in this sub-graph are domains related to exchange rates. For presentation, we drew only a single edge between each pair of domains (u, v). The two numbers on the edge, x/y, represent the number of the edges that go with the indicated direction (x) and those that go backwards (y). Recall that this graph is actually an unweighted multi-graph.

An important statistic that we compute over the domain preference graph G is the *maximum agreement rate*, $\mathrm{A}(G)$. Given a linear order L over the nodes V, $(v_1 > v_2 > \cdots > v_n)$, we say that an edge $e = (v_i, v_j)$ *agrees* with the order, $L \Rightarrow e$, if $v_i > v_j$ according to L. The *agreement rate* between graph G and order L, $\mathrm{A}(G, L)$, is defined as the fraction of edges E in G that agrees with L, i.e., $|\{e \mid L \Rightarrow e\}|/|E|$. The maximum agreement rate, $\mathrm{A}(G)$, is defined as the agreement rate achieved by the best linear order, $\mathrm{A}(G) = \max_L \mathrm{A}(G, L)$. As an example, consider the sub-graph in Figure 8. The best linear order over the nodes is (`xe.com` > `oanda.com` > `x-rates.com` > `finance.yahoo.com`). Under this order, $\mathrm{A}(G, L) = (32+23+48+21+51+8)/(32+13+23+4+48+5+21+6+51+3+8+3) \approx 0.84$, the ratio between the number of forward edges and the total number of edges.

But does the value 0.84 confirm the existence of a systematic bias? To answer, we use statistical hypothesis testing. Our null hypothesis, H_0, is that there is *no* systematic bias. If so, the observed preference relationship would have been arisen from a random process, and that for each preference $p_1 \rightarrow_q p_2$, we would have equally likely observe $p_2 \rightarrow_q p_1$, since the preference is random. Hence, our statistical experiment consists of the following. For each preference relationship, we flip a fair coin to decide whether p_1 is preferred to p_2 or vice versa. We then construct the corresponding domain preference graph G', and compute $\mathrm{A}(G')$. If the observed value of $\mathrm{A}(G)$ is significantly larger than the mean value of $\mathrm{A}(G')$, we reject H_0, thus confirming the existence of domain preference. Note that one cannot simply confirm the existence of domain preference by the maximum agreement rate alone. This is because for very sparse graphs, $\mathrm{A}(\cdot)$ will be close to one regardless of the direction of the edges. Hence, it is important to consider the statistical hypothesis testing explained above.

There are practical reasons we choose to test according to $\mathrm{A}(G)$. If we are to assign a number to each domain as a measure for the domain preference, it necessarily imposes a linear order on the domains. By definition, $\mathrm{A}(G)$ is the maximum agreement of any linear order with the preference graph. Therefore, it represents the best we can achieve if we are to preserve the preference order faithfully.

To close this section, we note that computing $\mathrm{A}(G)$ exactly is equivalent to solving the *minimum feedback-arc set*, an NP-hard problem. In our experiments, we use a local search algorithm that starts from an arbitrary linear order and swaps two vertices until no improvement can be made. This is repeated many times and the best linear order is selected. While there is no direct performance guarantee on the algorithm, we found that it works well as it typically finds solution with maximum agreement rate close to an upper-bound estimated by summing over all pairs of nodes v_i and v_j the larger of the size of the two sets of edges $|(v_i, v_j)|$ and $|(v_j, v_i)|$. The value is a valid upper bound

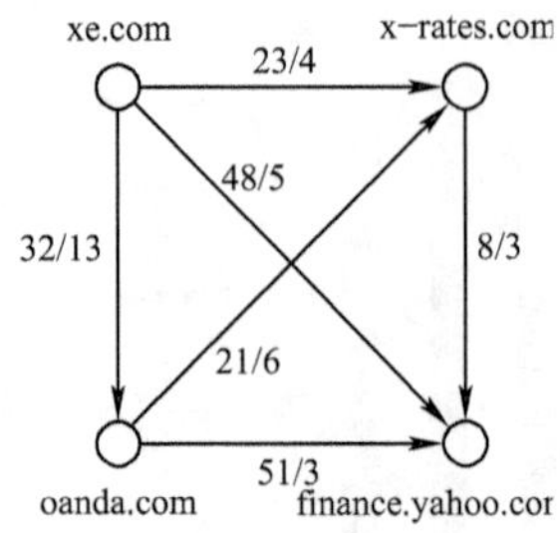

queries
foreign currency converter
currency exchange rates
foreign exchange rates
foreign money converter
euro currency converter
currency rates
currency converter
conversion dollars
convert to us dollars
convert currency
world currency rates

Figure 8: A sub-graph of the domain preference graph. In the left figure, each node corresponds to a domain, and each (super)edge represents the set of multi-edges between the two nodes. The two numbers on each super-edge represent the number of forward and backward multi-edges with respect to the direction of the arrow. For example, there are 32 multi-edges from `xe.com` to `oanda.com` and 13 multi-edges from `oanda.com` to `xe.com`. On the right is the list of top 10 queries that contribute to the multi-edges of the graph.

	G_0	G_q	G_p	$G_{q,p}$
`# of vertices`	60	287	282	1020
`# of edges`	33	308	575	7519

Table 3: The size of preference graphs.

	G_q	G_p	$G_{q,p}$
A(·)	0.90	0.85	0.76
A(·) under H_0	0.83 ± 0.008	0.71 ± 0.007	0.60 ± 0.005

Table 4: The maximum agreement rate A(·) on graph G_q, G_p, $G_{q,p}$ and under the null hypothesis that randomly flips the direction of the preference, with its 0.99 confidence interval.

since no linear order can agree with both (v_i, v_j) and (v_j, v_i) simultaneously.

5.2 Results

To instantiate the framework, for step 1, we obtain human judgment for about $2K$ queries (mostly informational queries) and $770K$ pairs of URLs, each judged by a panel of 11 judges. We keep only those pairs for which at least 8 out of 11 judges deemed the two URLs to be equally relevant to the query, resulting in about $130K$ pairs. For step 2, we examine 6 months of search logs from July 2010 to December 2010 and keep the preference relationship in cases where there are at least 5 clicks in total for both results. We then construct the domain preference graph G_0. Unfortunately, due to index churn between the time when the URLs are judged and the collection of the log data, we found very few pairs of the judged URLs appearing together in the log, and the number of directed edges is further reduced due to the stringent requirement in step 2 that corrects for position bias, giving rise to a very sparse graph. The graph is unsuitable for the hypothesis testing framework as most random instantiation of it will be perfectly consistent with some linear ordering of the domains.

To remedy this situation, we relax the definition of equivalent pairs in the first step. We consider three approaches for each pair $p_1 \sim_q p_2$. Under *query relaxation*, we include a pair $p_1 \sim_{q'} p_2$ if q' is a super-string of q. Under *page relaxation*, we include a pair $p_1' \sim_q p_2'$ if pages p_1' and p_2' are from the same domain as p_1 and p_2 respectively. Under the *query-page relaxation*, we allow both query and page relaxations. The domain preference graphs based on these three relaxations are denoted G_q, G_p, and $G_{q,p}$ respectively. We summarize the statistics of all four graphs in Table 3.

While it is possible that the relaxation we performed may introduce noise in the results, by requiring that both p_1 and p_2 have surfaced in response to a query, and that the user clicks on at least one of the results, the drift in query intent is limited. Hence the relevance judgments still apply to the expanded set of results. This is demonstrated by the set of queries related to *exchange* and *currency* that appeared in Figure 8. For example, even though "microsoft exchange" is a super-string of "exchange", it was not included because the domains surfaced do not match the exchange currency domains in the human judgment data set. To further ensure the safety of this relaxation step, we also manually check a random sample of the data and find that the relaxation does indeed produce coherent sets of queries and results.

The values of A(·) for preference graphs G_q, G_p, and $G_{q,p}$ are shown in Table 4, along with the sample mean and confidence interval at $p = 0.99$ under the null hypothesis H_0. For all three graphs, the value A(·) for the actual graph lies outside the confidence interval of the null hypothesis, hence we can reject the null hypothesis and confirm that users do indeed exhibit a systematic and consistent bias over domains.

6. DISCUSSION AND FUTURE WORK

The phenomenon that Internet users favor certain domains over others in their visits is not a new discovery. Indeed, past work has recognized the importance of domains in web search [10]. One explanation of why this happens is that documents belonging to a domain are typically written by the same author, as in the case of a blog, or are subject to the same quality control, as in the case of a wiki or a news organization, and therefore good documents are often clustered at the domain level. Our experiment in Section 3 confirms that users indeed have discovered the good domains, and their visits are increasingly concentrated on these domains.

The new phenomenon discovered in this paper is that user preferences of certain domains to others is beyond what can be explained due to relevance, and creates a bias similar in spirit to position bias [11] and snippet bias [23]. The bias manifests itself as leading a user to perceive the same document as being more relevant when it is attached to a more reputable domain than a less reputable one. Its existence is established beyond reasonable doubt through a series of carefully controlled experiments in Sections 4 and 5.

Why is domain bias an important concept and how does it influence search today? First, it has important consequences for click prediction, a central problem for both web search and sponsored search. Many click models have been proposed in the web literature over the past few years [3, 6, 7, 9]. While these models differ in how they capture user behavior, a common theme is that they focus on three factors that influence how users click—the user queries, the positions of the results, and the relevance of the results. The existence of domain bias implies that the precision of these models can be improved, and the design of click models should be revisited in light of the findings in this paper.

Second, domain bias has important consequences on learning relevance from clicks, the dual problem to click prediction. The web community has long recognized the importance of clicks as a source of signal for learning relevance, and there are many studies on how to learn relevance in the presence of position bias [2, 7, 11]. As domain bias becomes stronger, we need new learning algorithms that can account for domain bias. This is a challenging problem as domain bias exists partly due to difference in relevance across different domains, and therefore it cannot be easily teased out as a component separate from relevance. Further, users may exhibit different bias depending on the class of queries. For example, while users may strongly prefer `wikipedia.org` for queries about world geography, users may prefer `amazon.com` for queries about digital cameras. Whether we should consider bias at a query level or at a category level (and if so, which degree of categorization) will influence the success of the learning algorithm.

Finally, domain bias also affects existing approaches for classifying queries into navigational vs. informational ones. One common approach for determining whether a query is navigational is based on the entropy of its clicks. As domain bias becomes stronger, user visits are concentrated on fewer domains, even for informational queries. Algorithms for distinguishing between informational and navigational queries may have to be revisited in the presence of domain bias.

In view of the important consequences of domain bias, how does one go about measuring this bias? This is a fundamental and challenging question to which we only have a partial answer. The main obstacle to successfully measuring domain bias is the need to control for other factors that may lead a user to prefer one domain to another, chief among which is relevance, although other forms of confounding bias such as position bias also play a role. The experiment in Section 5 offers our best effort in isolating domain bias in a controlled setting. We believe it is a sound approach to both establishing and estimating domain bias. Nonetheless, it only constitutes a partial answer to the measurement question, as the methodology cannot be easily scaled up due to the need for a large quantity of human labels. Our limited data-set has forced us to use various heuristics to expand our coverage of domains; to scale to all domains is out of reach today. We believe that as user visits become increasingly concentrated on certain domains, domain bias will become an even more important issue, and measuring domain bias will be an important future research topic. Progress in this area will also have important implications on how to measure other forms of bias in web search.

Domain bias has led users to concentrate their web visits on fewer and fewer domains. It is debatable whether this trend is conducive to the health and growth of the web in the long run. Will users be better off if only a handful of reputable domains remain? We leave it as a tantalizing question for the reader.

7. REFERENCES

[1] E. Agichtein, E. Brill, S. T. Dumais, and R. Ragno. Learning user interaction models for predicting web search result preferences. In *Proceedings of SIGIR*, pages 3–10, 2006.

[2] R. Agrawal, A. Halverson, K. Kenthapadi, N. Mishra, and P. Tsaparas. Generating labels from clicks. In *WSDM*, pages 172–181, 2009.

[3] O. Chapelle and Y. Zhang. A dynamic bayesian network click model for web search ranking. In *WWW*, pages 1–10, 2009.

[4] J. Cho and S. Roy. Impact of search engines on page popularity. In *WWW*, pages 20–29, 2004.

[5] J. Cho, S. Roy, and R. Adams. Page quality: In search of an unbiased web ranking. In *SIGMOD*, pages 551–562, 2005.

[6] N. Craswell, O. Zoeter, M. Taylor, and B. Ramsey. An experimental comparison of click position-bias models. In *WSDM*, pages 87–94, 2008.

[7] G. Dupret and B. Piwowarski. A user browsing model to predict search engine click data from past observations. In *SIGIR*, pages 331–338, 2008.

[8] Z. Guan and E. Cutrell. An eye tracking study of the effect of target rank on web search. In *CHI*, pages 417–420, 2007.

[9] F. Guo, C. Liu, A. Kannan, T. Minka, M. Taylor, Y.-M. Wang, and C. Faloutsos. Click chain model in web search. In *WWW*, pages 11–20, 2009.

[10] Z. Gyöngyi, H. Garcia-Molina, and J. Pedersen. Combating web spam with trustrank. In *VLDB*, pages 576–587, 2004.

[11] T. Joachims. Optimizing search engines using clickthrough data. In *KDD*, pages 133–142, 2002.

[12] T. Joachims, L. Granka, B. Pan, H. Hembrooke, and G. Gay. Accurately interpreting clickthrough data as implicit feedback. In *SIGIR*, pages 154–161, 2005.

[13] T. Joachims, L. Granka, B. Pan, H. Hembrooke, F. Radlinski, and G. Gay. Evaluating the accuracy of implicit feedback from clicks and query reformulations in Web search. *ACM Transactions on Information Systems*, 25(2), Apr. 2007.

[14] R. Kumar and A. Tomkins. A characterization of online browsing behavior. In *WWW*, pages 561–570, 2010.

[15] Q. Mei and K. Church. Entropy of search logs: how hard is search? with personalization? with backoff? In *WSDM*, pages 45–54, 2008.

[16] A. Ntoulas, J. Cho, and C. Olston. What's new on the web?: the evolution of the web from a search engine perspective. In *WWW*, pages 1–12, 2004.

[17] L. Page, S. Brin, R. Motwani, and T. Winograd. The pagerank citation ranking: Bringing order to the web. Technical Report 1999-66, Stanford InfoLab, November 1999. Previous number = SIDL-WP-1999-0120.

[18] B. Pan, H. Hembrooke, T. Joachims, L. Lorigo, G. Gay, and L. A. Granka. In google we trust: Users' decisions on rank, position, and relevance. *Journal of Computer-mediated Communication*, 12:801–823, 2007.

[19] S. Pandey, S. Roy, C. Olston, J. Cho, and S. Chakrabarti. Shuffling a stacked deck: the case for partially randomized ranking of search engine results. In *VLDB*, pages 781–792, 2005.

[20] F. Qiu, Z. Liu, and J. Cho. Analysis of user web traffic with a focus on search activities. In *WebDB*, pages 103–108, 2005.

[21] M. Richardson, E. Dominowska, and R. Ragno. Predicting clicks: estimating the click-through rate for new ads. In *WWW*, pages 521–530, 2007.

[22] R. Srikant, S. Basu, N. Wang, and D. Pregibon. User browsing models: relevance versus examination. In *KDD*, pages 223–232, 2010.

[23] Y. Yue, R. Patel, and H. Roehrig. Beyond position bias: Examining result attractiveness as a source of presentation bias in clickthrough data. In *WWW*, pages 1011–1018, 2010.

Optimized Top-K Processing with Global Page Scores on Block-Max Indexes

Dongdong Shan[1] Shuai Ding[2] Jing He[1] Hongfei Yan[1] Xiaoming Li[1]
Peking University, Beijing, China[1]
Polytechnic Institute of NYU, Brooklyn, New York, USA[2]
{sdd, hejing, yhf }@net.pku.edu.cn[1] sding@cis.poly.edu[2] lxm@pku.edu.cn[1]

ABSTRACT

Large web search engines are facing formidable performance challenges because they have to process thousands of queries per second on tens of billions of documents, within interactive response time. Among many others, Top-k query processing (also called early termination or dynamic pruning) is an important class of optimization techniques that can improve the search efficiency and achieve faster query processing by avoiding the scoring of documents that are unlikely to be in the top results. One recent technique is using Block-Max index. In the Block-Max index, the posting lists are organized as blocks and the maximum score for each block is stored to improve the query efficiency.

Although query processing speedup is achieved with Block-Max index, the ranking function for the Top-k results is the term-based approach. It is well known that documents' static scores are also important for a good ranking function. In this paper, we show that the performance of the state-of-the-art algorithms with the Block-Max index is degraded when the static score is added in the ranking function. Then we study efficient techniques for Top-k query processing in the case where a page's static score is given, such as PageRank, in addition to the term-based approach. In particular, we propose a set of new algorithms based on the WAND and MaxScore with Block-Max index using local score, which outperform the existing ones. Then we propose new techniques to estimate a better score upper bound for each block. We also study the search efficiency on different index structures where the document identifiers are assigned by URL sorting or by static document scores. Experiments on TREC *GOV2* and *ClueWeb09B* show that considerable performance gains are achieved.

Categories and Subject Descriptors

H.3.3 [**INFORMATION STORAGE AND RETRIEVAL**]: Information Search and Retrieval.

General Terms

Algorithms, Performance.

Keywords

top-k query processing, early termination, block-max inverted index.

Permission to make digital or hard copies of all or part of this work for personal or classroom use is granted without fee provided that copies are not made or distributed for profit or commercial advantage and that copies bear this notice and the full citation on the first page. To copy otherwise, or republish, to post on servers or to redistribute to lists, requires prior specific permission and/or a fee.
WSDM'12, February 8-12, 2012, Seattle, Washington, USA.
Copyright 2012 ACM 978-1-4503-0747-5/12/02...$10.00.

1. INTRODUCTION

Modern commercial web search engines are facing formidable performance challenges due to the data sizes and query loads. The major engines have to process many thousands of queries per second over tens of billions of documents. To deal with this heavy workload, all the engines employ massively parallel systems consisting of thousands of machines. The significant cost of operating these systems has motivated a lot of research into more efficient query processing mechanism.

One major bottleneck in query processing is the length of the inverted list index structure, which could easily grow to hundreds of MBs or even GBs for common search terms (roughly linear with the size of the collection). Given that the modern search systems need to answer queries within fractions of a second, the naïve way to traverse this basic index structure, which could take hundreds of milliseconds for common terms, is impractical.

This problem has long been recognized by researchers, and has motivated a lot of work on optimization techniques, including parallel computation, caching, index compression and Top-k document retrieval (also called early termination or dynamic pruning). In this paper we focus on early termination techniques [1, 3, 5, 10, 12, 15-17, 22, 23, 30, 31, 33, 34]. In a nutshell, early termination techniques speed up the query processing by avoiding the scoring of the documents which are not likely to be in the Top-k results.

The existing techniques for early termination could be roughly divided into two groups: The first group of techniques [1, 3, 16, 17, 22, 23, 30, 31, 33, 34] usually require the inverted lists organized in a way that the most promising documents could be accessed first. Then after processing a certain amount of the most promising documents, the Top-k documents are returned without processing the rest of the less promising documents. In other words, this group of techniques try to "stop early" compared with the naive traversal of the complete lists. The early stop usually happens when the following condition is met: the minimum score in the current Top-k results is larger than the maximal possible score of the unprocessed documents (and sometimes also the rank order of the current Top-k results will not be changed). Thus, for this group of techniques, the way to organize the inverted lists plays a vital role. It decides the number of documents to be processed. Also for this group of techniques, an accumulator table is used to keep track of the most promising documents.

Instead of trying to "stop early", the other group of techniques [5, 10, 12, 15] organize the inverted index lists by document identifier (docID) sorted order and try to "skip" the less promising documents. In practice, the inverted lists are usually stored in blocks (e.g., a block consists of 64 or 128 postings), so each block could be compressed and decompressed separately. To access each single block without decompressing the whole list, one skipping pointer is stored separately for each block, in the form of *<d,*

p>, which indicates that the offset for the particular block is *p* and the minimal (or maximal) docID of that block is *d*. Recent works [12] propose to use the Block-Max index to speed up the query processing. Similar idea also appears in [10]. In the Block-Max index, the maximum score information (e.g., maximum BM25 score) for each block is also stored in the skipping pointer. It is shown in [10, 12] that using block level maximum information would enable us to estimate the score upper bound for one particular document much more accurately, and thus lead to a much better skipping behavior in query processing.

It has some advantages to organize the inverted index by a document sorted order. It gives better inverted index compression and easier conjunctive query processing (described later). Moreover, it is shown in [12] that faster query processing could be achieved. However, they only investigated the ranking function for the Top-k results with term-based score function [10, 12], and it is well known that the documents' static scores such as PageRank are also essential for a good ranking function.

In this paper, we study the methods for efficient query processing on Block-Max indexes when the ranking function consists of documents' static scores such as PageRank, in addition to the term-based scores. We show that the state-of-the-art algorithm BMW in [12] has performance degradation when static scores are added into the ranking function. We propose a new version of BMW called LBMW using local maximum score which outperform the existing ones. Beside this, we also modify the MaxScore algorithm with Block-Max index (called BMM) which has comparable performance with BMW. Basically our improved algorithms can estimate the upper bound score more accurate and find a better candidate document to process. In addition, we also study different methods to dynamically estimate a better score upper bound for each block, compared with the naive way to store both the maximum term-based score and the maximum static score for each block. Essentially, we store the maximum term-based score plus static score, which makes the estimated document upper bound score more accurately. We also empirically study the search efficiency on different index structures where the document identifiers are assigned by URL sorting or by static document scores. The experiments show that our algorithms, combined with our improved score upper bound estimation technique; give the best query processing performance.

2. BACKGROUND

2.1 Index Organization

Modern search engines usually use the inverted index structure to support fast query processing. According to the way of the document identifiers are assigned, there are mainly two types of index organization:

Document-sorted index: In the *document-sorted* index [2, 35], the postings in each inverted list are stored in increasing order of the document identifiers (docIDs). This allows the consecutive docIDs to be stored as *d-gaps* (e.g., d_i is stored as d_i-d_{i-1}-1). With the *d-gap* operation, the list of numbers are changed into a list of smaller gaps and thus we can get a much smaller compressed index, since most of the compression algorithms will benefit from smaller numbers.

Frequency-sorted or **impact-sorted index**: In the frequency-sorted index [17], each inverted list is ordered in decreasing order of the term's frequencies in its corresponding documents (TF). In the impact-sorted index [1, 3] the postings are ordered according to their impact values. Impact value is one small integer indicating the overall contribution of one term to the document's relevance score. In both arrangements, one index list consists of a sequence of groups, within which the postings are equally weighted. Within each group the postings are sorted by docIDs, and then again stored as *d-gaps* to achieve better compression ratio.

With the *d-gaps* representation of the docIDs, the most efficient way to restore the docIDs is to do a sequential scan. In practical, we hope that the inverted list can be accessed randomly to support fast query processing (e.g., conjunctive query). Therefore, the inverted lists are usually divided into blocks [32] (e.g., a block consists of 64 or 128 postings). Usually within each posting list, one skipping pointer is stored for each block at the beginning of the list [6, 10, 12, 35].

2.2 Query Processing

Many query processing methods [1, 5, 10, 16, 17, 22, 23, 27, 29, 35] have been proposed in the IR and Web search areas. Roughly they can be divided into three categories:

Document-at-a-time (DAAT): In the DAAT query processing [4, 5, 10, 12, 16, 35], all relevant inverted lists are simultaneously processed, and the score of a document is fully computed before moving to the next document.

Term-at-a-time (TAAT): In the TAAT query processing [27, 35], only one inverted list is processed at any given time, and the document scores are partial computed in a term-by-term manner. The partial document scores are usually stored in an accumulator table. The complete score of a document is unknown until all query terms are processed.

Score-at-a-time (SAAT): SAAT method [1, 3, 22] is only applicable for the impact-sorted index. It processes one impact block at a time. This method also requires an accumulator table to store documents' partial scores.

For a large collection or for term-dependent queries (e.g. phrase query) [5], DAAT strategies have two advantages compared with TAAT and SAAT methods: (1) DAAT only requires a small-size priority queue to store current Top-k (e.g., 10) results while TAAT or DAAT needs a much larger accumulator table, which is usually expensive to maintain. (2) DAAT methods can easily identify whether query terms satisfy some given conditions in a document (e.g., phrase). In contrast, TAAT and SAAT strategies need keep the occurrences of the first term within the document in the intermediate results, in order to verify whether the second term satisfies the constraint. Please refer to [1, 5, 35] for more detailed comparison among those strategies.

2.3 Pruning Methods

Index pruning is a popular technique for efficient query processing. It can be divided into two categories: **static pruning** and **dynamic pruning** (also called Top-k processing or early termination). For **static pruning** methods [6, 9], the goal is to predict and discard the less important information during the offline index construction, so that the size of the pruned index is much smaller than original full index. The pruned index is usually small enough to be fit into the main memory. Note that static pruning methods usually boost the search efficiency at the cost of search result quality. On the other hand, the **dynamic pruning** methods speed up the query processing by avoiding scoring all documents in the inverted lists during the online search phase.

Various dynamic pruning methods are used for different query processing modes. Those methods could be roughly divided into two groups. One is "stop early", which often requires the inverted list to be organized in such a way that the most promising documents can be evaluated first. The other is "skip", which adapts the skipping pointers into inverted lists and uses some strategies to skip less important documents. Usually, "stop early" methods [1, 3, 16, 17, 22, 23, 30, 31, 33, 34] are used in TAAT or SAAT query processing mode, while "skip" methods [5, 10, 12, 15] are used in DAAT mode. Another dimension for categorizing the dynamic pruning methods is its safety, indicating whether the results are in the exactly same order as the results from the exhaustive query processing. In this paper, we focus on the safe pruning techniques in DAAT query processing. Furthermore, we focus on disjunctive (OR) queries, which does not disqualify one document when it misses some of the search terms.

2.4 State-of-the-art DAAT pruning methods

As mentioned above, DAAT has many advantages compared with TAAT or SAAT and is shown to be faster in [12] with the Block-Max index structure. Also in the major commercial search engines DAAT is more adapted [5]. Thus in this paper, we focus on query processing with DAAT index traversal. There are two basic state-of-the-art dynamic pruning strategy with DAAT, namely WAND strategy [5, 12, 25] and MaxScore strategy [15, 23, 25, 27].

The original description of the MaxScore [27] strategy does not contain enough details, and it is different from a later implementation by Strohman [23]. Jonassen and Bratsberg [15] presented a more detailed MaxScore algorithm which combines the advantage of both Strohman's and Turtle's implementations. In the MaxScore strategy, it sorts the inverted lists by theirs maximum term scores in the decreasing order before query processing. And during the query processing phase this order is always fixed. After scoring some documents, the current minimum score of the Top-k results is known and it is used as a threshold. With this threshold, the MaxScore algorithm calculates a required term set *T* based on the sorted inverted lists. Thus, any document in the final Top-k results has to contain at least one term in the set *T*. Therefore, we only need to evaluate the documents containing terms in the set *T*. For the terms not in the required set *T*, we only need to move the pointer of their corresponding posting list to the current document candidate chosen from the posting lists in set *T*. In other words, we never use the document candidates from the non-required set *T* to "drive" the query processing. Besides, we can terminate the processing of one particular document when its partial score plus the upper bound score of terms yet to be scored is less than the threshold. Figure 1 gives an example of the MaxScore algorithm. Assume that we are given a query with terms "T_1, T_2, T_3", and their current docIDs are 12, 11 and 5 respectively. Recall that we will store the maximum scores for each list, as 5, 3 and 2 respectively in this example. The current Top-k threshold is 4. So we will know that the required term set *T* is {T_1, T_2}, because the score of a document containing term T_3 only would not exceed the threshold. The MaxScore method selects the current minimum docID 11 in T_2 to calculate its full score. In this case, for term T3, it will skip to docID 11, so the documents with the docID 5 and 10 would not be scored.

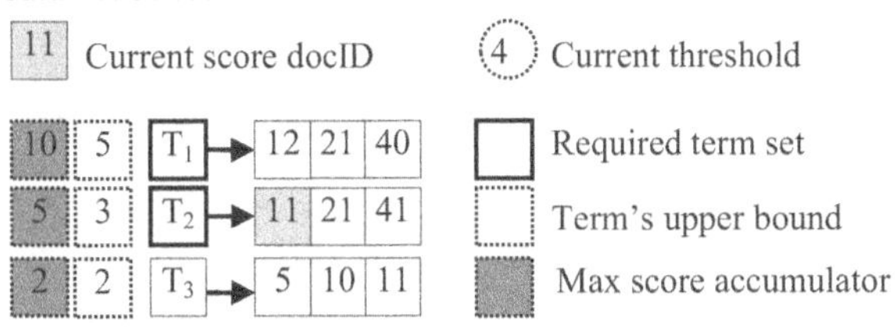

Figure 1. A scenario of processing a 3-term query, where the current pointers in the lists point to docID 12, 11 and 5 (note that lists are sorted by theirs upper bound scores). The MaxScore strategy calculates required term set as T1 and T2, and selects minimum docID 11 from required set. T_3 will skip to docID 11.

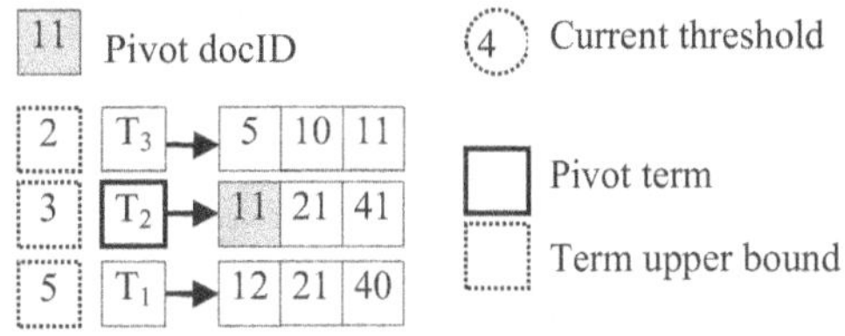

Figure 2. A scenario of processing a 3-term query, where the current pointers in the lists point to docID 5, 11 and 12 (note that lists are sorted by their current docIDs). The WAND strategy will select T_2 as the pivot term and 11 as the pivot docID. If the first term's current docID is identical to the pivot docID, it will calculate a full score for the pivot docID. Otherwise, it moves all earlier posting lists' pointer to the pivot docID 11. In this case, T_3 will skip to docID 11.

In contrast to MaxScore, the WAND [5, 25] strategy sorts the inverted lists by their current docIDs ascending during the query processing phase, which means the order of the posting lists are not fixed. It needs to calculate a pivot term, with the property that the accumulated term's maximum scores from the first term to the pivot term is the first one with a larger score than the threshold. Then it uses the pivot term's current docID as the pivot docID, and compares it with the first terms' current docIDs. If the docIDs are identical, the pivot document is fully scored. Otherwise, it moves all earlier posting lists' pointer to the pivot docID, achieving skipping within these lists. Figure 2 gives a scenario during the processing of query "T1, T2, T3". The reader may refer to the more detail example in the appendix in [25].

2.5 Ranking Function

In this work, we assume that the ranking function consists of: query-independent features, e.g., PageRank, and query-dependent features, e.g., BM25. A similar ranking function has been used in [16, 31]. For the query-dependent IR score, we are not considering the features such as term proximity [7]. Efficient query processing with term proximity will be left for future work. So the ranking function is in the following form:

$$S(d,q) = \alpha \cdot G(d) + \beta \cdot IR(d,q) \qquad (2.1)$$

where *S(d, q)* is the overall score for the document *d* with respect to the query *q*, *G(d)* is the global or static score of *d*, *IR(d, q)* is the query-dependent IR score for the document *d* with respect to the query *q*, α and β are parameters satisfying $\alpha + \beta = 1$. Static score and IR scores are usually normalized into a specific range, e.g., [0, 1] [19, 28]. Craswell et al. [11] proposes another way to combine the static score and IR score. They use a sigmoid function to translate static score then combine IR score without normalization. In this paper, we use the normalized version which is shown to give the best search quality [21, 33]. Our technique could also be applied on Craswell's method and many others.

As shown later, when the above ranking function is used, the state-of-the-art pruning methods will face performance degradation. The reason is that both of the WAND algorithm and the MaxScore algorithm use the maximum IR score (*IR*) and global score (*G*) to select the candidate documents to evaluate. And it is very likely that a posting list contains a document with a high *G* or with a large *IR*, thus the upper bound score of the inverted list would be very large. Could we use the Block-Max index to solve this problem? Does simply storing the maximum IR and maximum *G(d)* for each block give the best performance? Will different document ID assignment techniques play a role? The rest of the paper will focus on these questions.

2.6 Pruning Strategies with Static Scores

When a ranking function has static scores, usually the inverted index is organized in the following ways:

Single segment sorted by static scores [16, 31, 33]**:** When organized in this way, the document identifier is reassigned by their static score, and the promising documents with high static scores are placed at the beginning of the inverted lists. As a result, it is possible to stop early since we will evaluate the documents with high static score first.

Multi-segment divided by impact score [16, 33]: In this structure, the inverted list is divided into multiple segments by one specific kind of term impact scores (e.g., Impact value, term IR score, etc.), and in each segment, the document is sorted by static score or by docID. For one document, its information corresponding to different query terms may appear in different segments. So we still need document score accumulators to maintain the document partial scores

3. OUR CONTRIBUITION

In this paper, we focus on the efficient Top-k document retrieval where the ranking function consists of both documents' static scores and IR scores. We make the following contributions:

(1) We study the performance of the state-of-the-art DAAT strategies (WAND and MaxScore) on the Block-MAX index, considering both the IR score and the static score.
(2) We propose several modified algorithms based on MaxScore and WAND, which make the Top-k document retrieval on the Block-Max index more efficient.
(3) We propose a method to combine the static score and the IR score into one score. We then show how to dynamically use the combined score to give a correct and better estimation of the document's upper bound score.
(4) We evaluate our techniques on the TREC GOV2 and Clue-Web09B datasets. The results show that our algorithms outperform the state-of-the-art techniques.

4. RELATED WORK

We now briefly summarize some previous work. Note that early termination techniques differ in terms of their assumptions about result quality. In this work we only focus on safe (or reliable) early termination techniques that return exactly the same Top-k results in same order as the baseline. Based on the different ranking techniques, previous work on early termination (ET) can be divided into four sets.

In the first set, it is assumed that the ranking function only consists of the IR scores [1, 5, 13, 17, 27], e.g., BM25. In this set there has been a lot of work in both database and IR community. In the database literatures, most of the works assume that the posting lists are sorted by the term scores, and the basic operation in the query processing includes the sequential access and random access. Then optimized algorithms are proposed to minimize the cost, which is measured by the number of sequential access and random access. See [13, 14] for more details. In the IR literatures, some [1, 17] assume that the posting lists are sorted by impact or frequency, and then SAAT index traversal is used to speed up the query processing with the idea of stopping early. Whereas the others assume the posting lists are sorted by docIDs, and usually the maximum IR scores for the posting lists are stored to skip the less promising postings. See [1, 5, 15, 22, 27] for more details. Recently the Block-Max index is used to speed up query processing. In the Block-Max index, the posting lists are sorted by docIDs and the maximum IR score of each block is stored in the skipping pointer. The BMW algorithm is used in [12], and they find it is much faster than the state-of-the-art algorithms SC in [22] when processing disjunctive queries. A block interval based method is used in [10]. It splits blocks into intervals with aligned boundaries, and then it discards the intervals which cannot contain any top results.

In the second set, it is assumed that the ranking function consists of both IR scores and documents' static scores. Long et al. first study this problem in [16] and propose to use the "fancy list" to achieve the goal of stopping early. Fancy list is a 2-segment index, which contains the document with high IR score in fancy part, and in each segment, the docID is sorted by static score. Zhang et al. [31] propose some methods to organize inverted list by the global information combines the static score and the upper bound of its IR scores for all terms contained in document.

In the third set, the term proximity scores are considered in the ranking function [25, 30, 34]. Usually, an auxiliary structure such as phrase index or term pair's index is employed to calculate the term proximity scores. Then it uses the method of the second set to evaluate the documents.

In the fourth set, hundreds of features are considered in the ranking function which learned from machine learning methods. In practice, it is not possible to score every document using expensive machine learned ranking function. Thus, there are several works to solve the efficient problem in this field, such as multi-stages ranking [8], cascade ranking model [28] and so on. Usually, those methods view retrieval as a multi-stage progressive refinement problem. Each stage uses a more complex ranking model in a smaller candidate document set. Ours describe methods below can be used as a first stage ranking model. Note that those methods are not safe pruning techniques.

Independent of what is mentioned above, another idea in IR query processing, namely, docID reordering, is also relevant to our work. Generally, there are two kinds of docID reordering methods: one is to minimize the index size and the other is to optimize the dynamic query pruning. In the first case, a number of recent works [19, 20] show that inverted index size can be reduced a lot by reordering the docIDs. Intuitively, if we assign similar pages with close docIDs, the *d-gaps* between the consecutive documents in the inverted lists are much smaller, and the required space for the *d-gaps* is reduced. Moreover, as shown in [12, 29], docID reordering in this way can significantly increases the speed of processing both conjunctive and disjunctive queries. The most commonly used method for reordering docIDs in this way is to sort the documents by their URLs, and then assign the docIDs sequentially. In the second case, documents are sorted descending by their static scores, and then the docIDs are assigned sequentially. This reordering technique would place the documents with larger static scores at the beginning of inverted lists, so the important documents can be scored first, and then it is more likely that we will stop the query processing when the early termination condition is reached. It has been shown by experiments [16, 33, 34] that the static score ordered index do not perform well in early termination when the weight of static score in the ranking function is assigned small, e.g., α =0.2. Our work here shows that it can enhance the query processing speed a lot based on Block-Max index even when the weight of the static score is small.

5. OUR ALGORITHM

Query processing on the Block-Max index mainly has three steps:

Step 1: Select a candidate document to be scored. In this step, both WAND and MaxScore strategies can be used.

Step 2: Estimate the upper bound score for the candidate document using the block maximum information.

Step 3: Score the document if its estimated upper bound score is larger than the current top-k threshold score, otherwise select the next candidate document.

There are three important problems in this framework:

1) What is the best way to find a candidate document?
2) How the upper bound score of a candidate document can be estimated accurately?
3) When shall we score a document, and how can we terminate earlier after acquiring some partial score information?

5.1 Ranking Function

Our ranking function is based on the formula (2.1) discussed in Section 2. We use PageRank as the document static score *G(d)*, and normalize it with formula (5.1) [21, 33]:

$$G_{PR\_norm} = \frac{\log(1 + G_{PR})}{\log(1 + G_{\max\_PR})} \quad (5.1)$$

We use BM25 formula [6, 18] to calculate the IR score, and we set parameter k_2 and k_3 to zero for convenience [6, 21].

$$S_{bm25} = \sum_{t \in q} w^i \cdot \frac{tf_{(t,d)} \cdot (k_1 + 1)}{tf_{(t,d)} + K} \quad (5.2)$$

where w^i is the query term i's IDF value. $tf_{(t,d)}$ is term frequency in document d. Maximum BM25 score can be calculated when $tf_{(t,d)}$ is set large enough [21, 33] . The maximum BM25 score is:

$$S_{\max\_bm25} = \sum_{t \in q} w^t \cdot (k_1 + 1) \quad (5.3)$$

We can calculate a normalized BM25 score by formula 5.4:

$$S_{bm25\_norm} = \frac{S_{bm25}}{S_{\max\_bm25}} \quad (5.4)$$

In [16] the BM25 score is normalized using the local maximum score in the inverted lists as S_{bm25_norm}, and all our techniques could be applied using that normalization.

5.2 Local Block-Max WAND (LBMW)

The basic BMW algorithm is proposed in [12]. Our LBMW algorithm improves it in the pivot term selecting phase. In our method, we use the local block upper bound score to select the pivot term while the BMW algorithm still uses the global term upper bound score as in [5]. Usually, the local block upper bound score is much smaller than the global one. Thus, our pivot term selection method can select a better pivot term. Figure 3 shows an example on LBMW to select the pivot term. In this example, each block consists of two docIDs. The maximum IR score of each block is represented as the superscript in "()". After sorting lists by their current docIDs, we know that T_1's current docID (90) is the current maximum docID. The LBMW method calculates a local block maximum score for each term from their current docID to the current maximum docID (90). In this scenario, T_3, T_2 and T_1's local maximum scores are 1.3, 2.5 and 3.0 respectively. So we can calculate the pivot term in LBMW is T_1, because the cumulated maximum scores for T_3(1.3) and T_2 (3.8) are both smaller than the threshold score 4. Thus the pivot docID in LBMW is 90. In the BMW, it uses global term maximum score 2(T_3), 2.8(T_2) and 3.0(T_1) to calculate the pivot term. So the pivot term in BMW is T_2 (T_2' cumulated score is 4.8) and the pivot docID is 61. So the next processing document in BMW method is 61, but its score actually cannot exceed the threshold 4. The processing on this document wastes of time. In our LBMW method, docID 61 will be skipped.

Local block upper bound score can be calculated very efficiently by recording last calculated score and its block's maximum docID. For example, T_3's list iterator can keep a temp local maximum score 1.3 and its corresponding maximum docID 111 to avoid redundant calculation. Similarly, we can also calculate its local maximum static score by this method. This idea is similar to the interval-based method in [10]. The interval-based method splits the blocks with aligned boundaries before query processing, while the LBMW method aligns document boundaries during query processing.

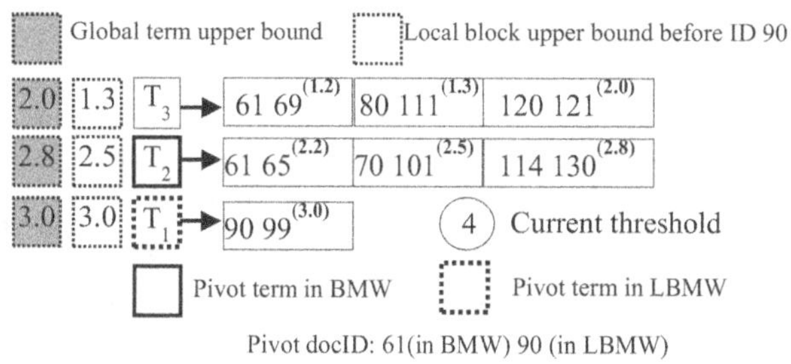

Figure 3. LBMW sorts lists by their current docIDs, and then calculates the local block maximum for each term from their current docID to current maximum docID 90. In this scenario, T_3, T_2 and T_1's local maximum scores are 1.3, 2.5, and 3.0. Then it uses these local maximum scores to calculate pivot term. In this case, pivot term in LBMW is T_1, while pivot term in BMW is T_2.

5.3 Local Block-Max MaxScore (LBMM)

The MaxScore algorithm in [15, 23, 27] can be easily extended on the Block-Max index, by adding an estimating step for the upper bound score, before scoring the candidate document. We call this extended method Block-Max MaxScore (BMM). The candidate document selecting step in BMM is similar to the example in Figure 1. It selects a minimum docID in the required term set as its candidate document. In BMM, we add an estimating step before scoring document. With this step, we can calculate document's upper bound score based on the block maximum information. If the score surpasses the threshold, we score this candidate document; otherwise, we will select the next validated candidate document.

Scoring document in MaxScore is slightly different from that in WAND. In the MaxScore (as shown in Figure 1), the inverted lists have been sorted by their maximum IR score, so the important term is scored first. While in WAND, the inverted lists are sorted by their current docID, and it is not likely that the important term would be scored first. When scoring a document, we can estimate the document's upper bound by summing its current score and the maximum scores of the unseen terms. In the MaxScore, the unseen terms upper bound score can be computed once before the query processing starts. In our implement, we use the local block upper bound score to estimate the unseen terms' upper bound score instead of the term's global upper bound score as in [15]. Usually, the local maximum score is much smaller than the global score. So we can estimate document's upper bound score more accurately. We call this method as Local Block-Max MaxScore (LBMM).

5.4 Estimate Upper Bounds More Accurately

One important operation in LBMW or LBMM algorithms is to estimate the upper bound score of the candidate document. One natural way is to store the maximum normalized PageRank score and the maximum IR score respectively in the skipping table. Then we can use those two maximums to estimate the overall upper bound score. Intuitively, this method is better than using global maximum static score and global maximum term IR score to estimate the upper bound score since the local upper bounds are much closer to the real scores than the global upper bounds. In the LBMW and LBMM, we use this method to estimate the upper bound score. However, in one block, the document with the maximum term IR score and the document with the maximum static score usually are usually not identical. Thus, the overall upper bound would be overestimated by respective maximum term IR score and maximum static score. Is there a better way to estimate the upper bound more accurately?

Our answer is yes. The main idea is to combine the static score and term IR score, and use the combined score as the block's single maximum score. But it is a little complex to combine those two scores to give the correct results, due to the normalization used in the ranking function. First, we can calculate a combined score for each document in a block by Formula 5.5. Then we can select the maximum combined score as the block maximum score.

$$\begin{aligned} S(d,q) &= \alpha \cdot G(d) + \beta \cdot IR(d,q) \\ &= \alpha \cdot G_{norm}(d) + \beta \cdot \frac{\sum_{t \in q} w^t \cdot \frac{tf_{(t,d)} \cdot (k_1+1)}{tf_{(t,d)}+K}}{\sum_{t \in q} w^t \cdot (k_1+1)} \\ &= \frac{\alpha \cdot G_{norm}(d) \cdot \sum_{t \in q} w^t + \beta \cdot \sum_{t \in q} w^t \cdot \frac{tf_{(t,d)}}{tf_{(t,d)}+K}}{\sum_{t \in q} w^t} \\ &= \frac{\sum_{t \in q} (\alpha \cdot G_{norm}(d) \cdot w^t + \beta \times w^t \cdot \frac{tf_{(t,d)}}{tf_{(t,d)}+K})}{\sum_{t \in q} w^t} \end{aligned} \tag{5.5}$$

In Formula 5.5, we note that the static score needs to multiply a maximum term score when combining with term IR score. Using this combined score, it will underestimate document's upper bound score in two cases:

1. When one list for term T_i ends up and other lists still have candidate documents. In this case, the static upper bound score of candidate documents may be underestimated, because the static scores assigned to inverted list of term T_i have not been considered.
2. One of term's block maximum combined score is lower than the current candidate document's static score. Figure 4 shows an example in this case. In the figure, each block has two docIDs, and the maximum combined score is represented as the superscript in "()". Each document's term IR score and normalized PR score is represented as the superscript in order in "<>". We assume T_1 and T_2's IDF value (w^{T_1}, w^{T_2}) are equal to 10 and α=0.3. According to formula 5.5, we can get T_1's and T_2' first block maximum combined score is 4.8 and 1.0 respectively. When using this maximum combined score to estimate a document's upper bound, it can get the upper bound score as (4.8+1.0)/(10+10)=0.29. But the document with ID 20's real score is 0.9*0.3+3*0.7/(10+10)=0.375. So this document's upper bound score is underestimated. This case happens when one document's static score is much larger than the block's combined score, here document with ID 20's static score is 0.9*0.3=0.27, T_2's first block's maximum combined score is 0.1*0.3+1.0*0.7/(10+10) = 0.1.

We have known that the underestimation happens when the document static score is larger than the other block's combined score. Thus, we need to store the maximum static score in blocks to check whether this situation actually happens. If this happens, we can use the maximum static score to estimate the upper bound score, otherwise, we will use the combined score. To the first case, we can use the similarly method.

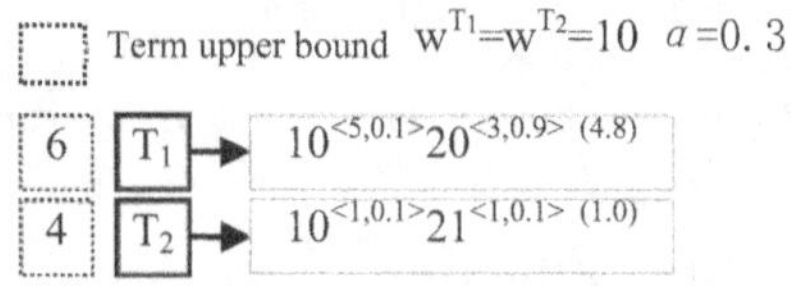

Figure 4. Document's upper bound score is underestimated in this example if only using the maximum combined score.

6. EXPERIMENTS

6.1 Experimental Setup

Datasets: We test our algorithms using two TREC collections, as illustrated in Table 1. The GOV2 collection consists of 25.2 million Web pages crawled from the .gov Internet domain in 2004 and it consumes 426GB of disk space uncompressed. The ClueWeb09B collection is a subset of the ClueWeb09 collection which consists of roughly the first 50 millions of English Web pages and it consumes 1.5TB of disk space uncompressed. We preprocess the documents by removing the html tags and index the pages' content, URL and anchor text. Each token is stemmed by a porter stemmer. For the inverted list whose length is longer than 512, we group 64 postings into one block, and use PForDelta algorithm [32] to compress its docIDs and term frequencies respectively. The compressed indexes for the GOV2 and ClueWeb09B collection consume 10.6GB and 23.4GB respectively. For each block, we can store block maximum BM25 score, maximum PageRank score, and the maximum combined version of PageRank and BM25 score. But for different dynamic pruning algorithm, we build different indexes which only store two of those scores. These scores are represented by float (4 byte) uncompressed, and each score takes about 313MB (2.8%) for the GOV2 index and 0.7GB (3%) for the ClueWeb09B index.

Table 1. The statistic information for GOV2 and ClueWeb09B index

	Documents	Text	Index size
GOV2	25M	426G	10.6G
ClueWeb09B	50M	1.5T	23.4G

Query Sets: We use **TREC 2006 Efficiency 10k Queries (GOV2#10K)** and **TREC 2009 Million Query 40k Queries (MQ09#40K)** as our test query sets for the GOV2 and ClueWeb09B datasets respectively. We use a list of 400 stopwords provided by Lemur toolkit to remove the stop words (we only remove stop words in the queries. In the inverted index, it still contains those stopwords.). Figure 5 shows the distributions of query lengths in two query sets. Note that the lengths reported here don't contain the stopwords or the terms not appearing in the collection. The average query length in GOV2#10K and MQ09#40K is 3.47 and 2.29 respectively. The average posting number of GOV2#10K and MQ09#40K queries is 5.37M and 6.56M respectively. We run all the experiments on the Dell R905 server with four Quad-Core AMD 8380 (2.5GHz) processors (but we only use one core of them) and 64GB of RAM. We load the full index into the main memory before processing the queries. Without specifying, we return top-10 results for each query.

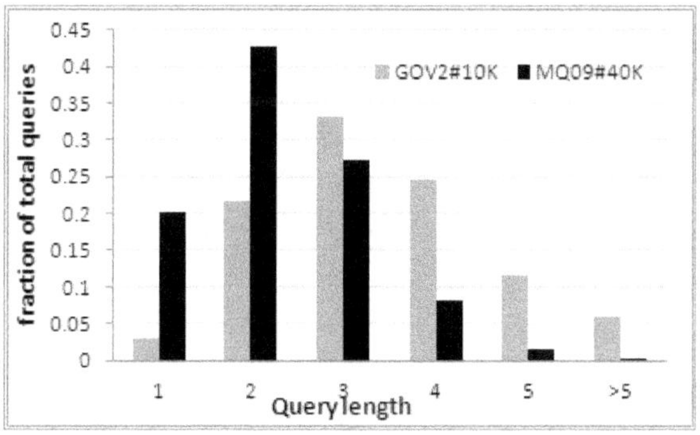

Figure 5. Query length distrubute in GOV2#10K and MQ09#40K

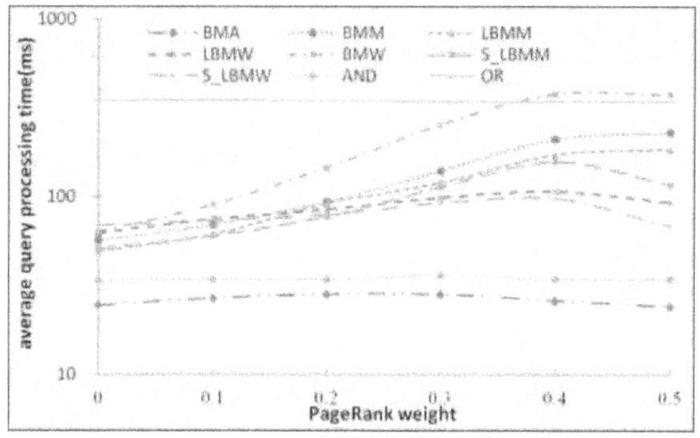

Figure 6. Average query processing time for different static score weights on the random ordered GOV2 dataset.

Index structures and pruning strategies: We compare different pruning strategies on three index organizations using DAAT query processing. Note that our pruning strategies are safe pruning methods which mean the results returned by our methods are exactly same as exhaustive query processing.

Exhaustive AND (OR): Exhaustive conjunctive or disjunctive query processing [2].

BMW: The WAND pruning strategy on Block-Max index [12] .

BMM: The MaxScore pruning strategy on Block-Max index.

LBMW: An improved version of BMW which uses the algorithm in section 5.2 to find a better pivot document in selecting document step.

LBMM: An improved version of BMM, which uses the algorithm in section 5.3 to estimate the documents' upper bound in scoring document step.

S_LBMW and S_LBMM: An improved version of LBMW and LBMM. They use the algorithm in section 5.4 to give a better document's upper bound estimation in estimating document upper bound step.

BMA: Query processed for conjunctive queries on the Block-Max index.

6.2 Basic Results

In this section, we list the performance of various pruning strategies on the index where document identifies are randomly assigned (we first randomize the documents in the dataset, and then assign docIDs sequentially.).

In the Figure 6, there are four main observations: Firstly, when the weight of PageRank (PR) is small, most of pruning strategies perform well, especially for the MaxScore based algorithms; e.g., when the weight of PR is zero, BMM and LBMM achieve 12% and 22% improvement compared with BMW and LBMW respectively. The performance of BMW drops rapidly when the weight of PR increases, and it performs even worse than naïve OR when PR's weight is large than 0.4. The main reason is that BMW (or BMM) still uses global term maximum IR score and global maximum PR score to select candidate documents. Secondly, the methods with the local maximum information (LBMM, LBMW) perform better than those using global information. One reason is that with the local maximum IR and PR score, LBMW can find a better candidate documents than BMW which uses the global maximum IR and PR score. For the LBMW, with local block maximum IR score, it can estimate the document's upper bound more accurately and for LBMM, it can terminate earlier when scoring a document. Thirdly, the methods (S_LBMM, S_LBMW) using maximum IR+PR to estimate the documents' upper bound scores also improve the query processing efficiency. Finally, we note that all the pruning methods still have a performance gap compared with BMA and Exhaustive AND on GOV2 Dataset. Though BMA and AND methods are much faster than the other pruning methods, they will lead to inferior search quality. Since relevant documents do not contain all the query words are ignored by those methods. We get similarly results on the ClueWeb09B dataset (Due to the limited of space, the results are not shown.). One interesting observation in the ClueWeb09B dataset is that all the pruning methods are better than the exhaustive AND operation when the weight of PageRank is 0. The S_LBMW method performs better than the exhaustive AND operation in a wide range of PR weight setting.

Table 2 shows the average query processing time with different query lengths. We set the weight of static score is 0.2 as in [26]. Firstly, we can find that for the queries containing more than four terms, the MaxScore based strategies are better than the WAND based strategies. The main reason is that the MaxScore based methods select candidate documents in the required term set which is likely to be composed of important terms, while the WAND based methods select candidate documents based on its docIDs without considering the terms' importance. Secondly, for the queries having fewer terms, the LBMW based methods are performing better. In this case, the LBMW and S_LBMW will use the local block maximum IR and PR scores to calculate a candidate documents. In LBMM based methods, it still uses global term maximum score and maximum PR score to select a candidate document. So the candidate document selected by LBMW based methods is likely to be better than the one selected by MaxScore based methods. We also note that when the query length is two, the pruning strategies are faster than exhaustive conjunctive (AND) query processing.

Table 2. Average query processing time in ms for different number of query terms (DataSet:GOV2, Index Type: random α=0.2)

	AVG	1	2	3	4	5	>5
OR	347	35	140	288	418	577	843
BMM	94.0	3.1	27.2	68	118	173	276
BMW	146	2.5	36.1	96	182	284	475
LBMM	91.7	3.6	27.1	69	117	165	249
LBMW	84.9	2.5	30.2	63	101	151	257
S_LBMM	**77.5**	3.0	**19.2**	56	100	**144**	**229**
S_LBMW	79.5	**2.5**	20.8	**53**	**97**	152	270
AND	34.2	34	30.6	35	36	35	33
BMA	29.1	2.8	15.8	29	36	39	37

Table 3 shows some detail statistic information for each phase of the query processing when the static score weight is set as 0.2. From Table 3, we can see that all the pruning strategies can improve the performance greatly compared to the exhaustive OR query processing. The S_LBMW only needs to score 1.1% of number of documents processed by exhaustive disjunctive (OR) operation and its number of evaluated documents are even much smaller than that of AND query processing. Note that the evaluated documents we report here contain the partial evaluated documents. The BMM based methods evaluate much more documents. One reason is that those methods need to calculate partial document scores to determine whether it can stop scoring the candidate document or not. While the WAND based methods can test if the document needs scoring by comparing the pivot docID to the first term's current docID. If they are not identical, it will skip scoring the document. As a result, the WAND based methods can perform better when the ranking function is expensive. Another interesting finding in Table 3 is that the MaxScore based methods decode fewer integers than WAND based methods. The S_LBMM algorithm only decodes 12% of integers compared with exhaustive OR. The main reason is that MaxScore based methods can skip a lots of blocks in the unimportant terms' inverted lists (usually, they are much longer than important terms' lists). Thus, MaxScore based methods are better if the decoding is the bottleneck. The document upper bound estimation times we report here is the called times for the actually estimation function. We judge if the block in each list is moved to a new block or not before we call the estimation function. If not, the latest estimated score can be used. This trick reduces the estimation time a lot. The average estimation number used by the MaxScore based methods is still fewer than the WAND based methods.

Table 3. The average number of evaluated documents, document upper bound estimation times, decoded integers and decoded blocks for different methods (DataSet:GOV2, α=0.2).

	evaluated docs (K)	estimation times (K)	decoded ints (M)	decoded blocks (K)
OR	4248.2	0	10.51	84.1
BMM	582.9	66.7	1.48	15.5
BMW	210.6	109.7	6.86	63.6
LBMM	582.9	65.4	1.25	13.8
LBMW	55.9	90.4	5.16	56.5
S_LBMM	538.4	**65.4**	**1.23**	**13.8**
S_LBMW	**48.1**	85.6	4.58	50.9
AND	53.0	0	3.28	31.1
BMA	19.9	40.2	2.61	25.5

6.3 DocID Reassignment by URL Sorting

In this section, we show the impact of document reassignment on Top-k processing. The work [12, 19, 20, 24] show that reassigning docIDs by their similarities can not only improve index compression ratio but also speed up the conjunctive and disjunctive query processing. One most commonly used method to assign docID according to the content similarities is to sort the documents in the URL order.

Figure 7 show the performance of different dynamic pruning methods on GOV2 dataset with docID reassignment strategy. We can find that the average query processing time is reduced a lot compared with random ordered index in the Figure 6. The average processing time almost decreases by half when the weight of PR is small. This docID reassignment strategy makes the documents in one block similar to each other, so the maximum score in one block is closer to the scores of the average documents. Thus it helps to skip more unimportant blocks in the inverted list. We also find that the query processing performance is improved for the exhaustive OR operation, mainly due to smaller storage size of the inverted index and thus the better CPU caching performance. One interesting finding is the LBMW and S_LBMW are faster than

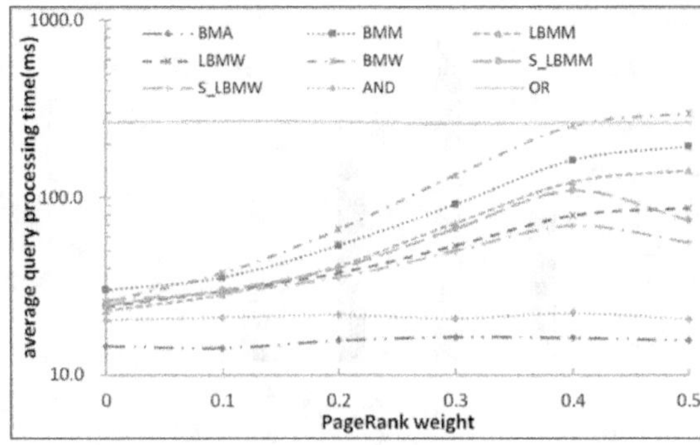

Figure 7. Average query processing time for different static score weights on the URL ordered GOV2 dataset

LBMM and S_LBMM in URL ordered index. As shown in Figure 7, the S_LBMM is better than LBMW and S_LBMW when static score weight is less than 0.2. Thus, the WAND based methods can get more benefit when the scores in one block become smoother. We also get similarly results in the ClueWeb09B dataset. One interesting finding is the ClueWeb09B dataset is the speed of S_LBMW is even faster than exhaustive AND operation in the Clueweb09B dataset. One reason is that relevant documents processed by exhaustive AND operation in the Clueweb09B dataset is about five times more than that in the GOV2 dataset. Thus, the exhaustive AND operation needs to evaluate more documents. In Table 5, we find that the number of documents evaluated by the S_LBMW is 11% of that by the exhaustive AND operation, and the decoded integers are almost half of the later.

Table 4. The average number of full evaluated docIDs, condition checked times, decoded integers and decoded blocks for different methods on URL ordered index (Dataset: GOV2, α =0.2).

	evaluated docs (K)	estimation times (K)	decoded ints (M)	decoded blocks (K)
OR	4248.2	0	10.51	84.1
BMM	498.0	36.3	1.07	12.3
BMW	186.3	47.5	3.24	29.4
LBMM	498.0	35.8	0.92	11.8
LBMW	57.0	34.0	2.19	22.7
S_LBMM	432.0	35.8	**0.91**	**11.8**
S_LBMW	**52.0**	**33.1**	1.92	20.2
AND	53.0	0	1.55	13.9
BMA	9.8	16.0	1.0	10.4

Table 5. The average number of full evaluated docIDs, condition checked times, decoded integers and decoded blocks for different methods on URL ordered index (Dataset: ClueWeb09B, α=0.2).

	evaluated docs (K)	estimation times (K)	decoded ints (M)	decoded blocks (K)
OR	5901.0	0.0	13.1	105.0
BMM	388.1	61.3	1.4	15.7
BMW	125.4	81.7	4.0	40.4
LBMM	388.1	60.1	1.1	14.2
LBMW	41.7	72.3	3.2	36.7
S_LBMM	268.7	**60.0**	**1.1**	**14.2**
S_LBMW	**28.1**	64.6	2.1	26.2
AND	262.4	0.0	5.1	46.9
BMA	20.7	32.4	2.3	25.1

From Table 4, we note that the documents' upper bound estimation time is reduced by almost a half compared with that of the random ordered index. One reason is that after document reassignment, the candidate documents are more likely to be in the same blocks. So we can get more documents with high score, if decoding one block. Thus the number of decoded integers can be reduced a lot (as shown in Table 4 and Table5). One interesting finding is that though the ClueWeb09B dataset contains double of documents of the GOV2, the number of the retrieved documents by the exhaustive OR operation only increases by 38.9% and the retrieved documents by the exhaustive AND operation almost increases five times. One reason is that the query of MQ09#40K is much shorter than those of GOV2#10K, as shown in Figure 4. Besides, the BMA method can reduce the number of evaluated documents and decoded much less integers compared with exhaustive AND, and it is the fastest processing method.

6.4 DocID Reassignment by Static Score

Figure 8 show the performance of different pruning strategies on the GOV2 dataset with PageRank ordered. In this kind of index organization, the "stop early" method can be combined to achieve fast query processing. We also run the pruning OR [16, 33, 34] which stops scoring document if it finds the maximum score of unprocessed document is smaller than current threshold. It takes about 320ms to process query when the PR weight is less than 0.3 on the GOV2 dataset. When the PR weight is larger, it performs better. It takes 265ms and 125ms to process one query when the PR weight is set as 0.4 and 0.5. Pruning OR improves about 3 times compared with the exhaustive OR when PageRank weight is set to 0.5. But things change when using the Block-Max index. We find that as the PageRank weight increases, the performance of different pruning strategies all improved a lot. It is very different from URL ordered index, whose performances decrease when PR weight increases. One interesting finding is that the MaxScore based methods are faster than WAND based methods when PR weight is less than 0.4. The main reason is that MaxScore based methods can get more benefit from PR ordered index in selecting a candidate document (In URL or Random order index, it still uses global maximum PR value to select a candidate document. In PR order index, it can use current maximum PR value). The BMW method is the fastest one when PR weight equal to 0.5. It takes only 9ms to process a query, almost 13.9 times faster compared with the Pruning OR 125ms in this case.

From the Figure 8, we find that all the pruning methods are faster than the exhaustive AND operation. One reason is that the MQ09#40K is much shorter and it has more relevant documents in the ClueWeb09B dataset (about five times of those in GOV2) when processing conjunctive queries. Another reason is that the pruning methods perform better when the length of query is shorter.

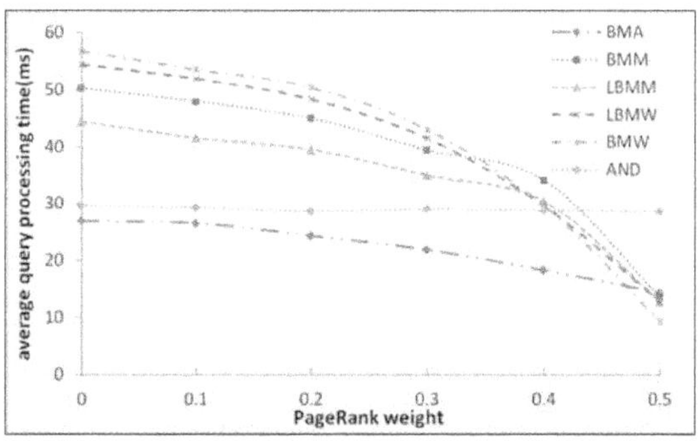

Figure 8. Average query processing time for different static score weights on the PageRank ordered GOV2 dataset

Table 6. The average number of full evaluated docIDs, condition checked times, decoded integers and decoded blocks for different methods on PageRank ordered index(Dataset: GOV2, α=0.2).

	evaluated docs (K)	estimation times (K)	decoded ints (M)	decoded blocks (K)
OR	4248.2	0.0	10.51	84.1
BMM	155.2	41.7	0.90	9.4
BMW	13.9	57.6	3.05	35.3
LBMM	155.2	**40.8**	**0.75**	**8.2**
LBMW	**10.2**	56.0	2.89	34.6
AND	53.0	0.0	2.73	25.7
BMA	7.0	31.5	1.48	15.4

From Table6, we find that the average evaluated documents is reduced more than three times for MaxScore based methods and five time for WAND based methods compared with that in URL ordered index. For the LBMM method, the number of decoded integers is also reduced by 18% compared with that in URL ordered index. The BMA method still is the fastest query processing method.

6.5 Increase K of the Top-K Processing

In this section, we show the query performance as we increase the parameter K. Figure 9 shows the experimental results on the GOV2 with URL ordered index and PR weight is set to be 0.2. As shown in the chart, the performance for the exhaustive AND operation and OR operation are quite stable as they decode and evaluate all the documents for any K. Other methods generally need more time for getting more top documents. We find that the processing time is in the scale of $\log_{10}$K. As K becomes larger, the performance gap between S_LBMM and S_LBMW becomes smaller and they both outperform the other pruning methods. The situation almost same in the Clueweb09B dataset or in other organized indexes, those results are not shown for the space constraint.

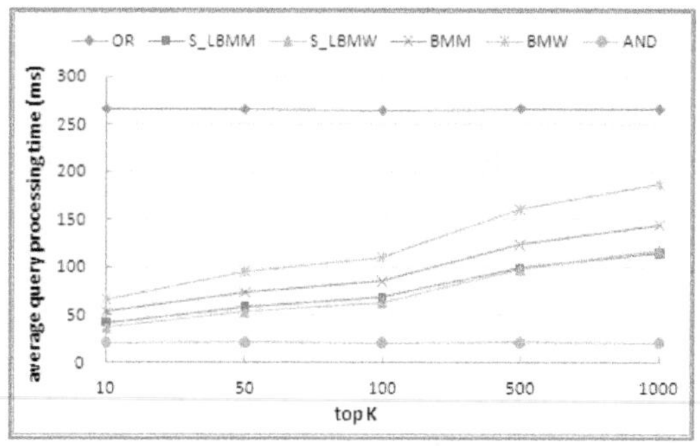

Figure 9. Average query processing time as increasing K (Dataset: GOV2, α=0.2, Index type: URL ordered)

7. CONCLUSION

To conclude, our query processing framework using Block-Max index contains three steps: 1) Select a candidate document; 2) Estimate its upper bound score; 3) Score the document if its upper bound score is larger than the threshold. Based on this framework, we study efficient query processing techniques when the ranking function consists of both the IR scores and documents' static scores. In particular, we propose the BMM pruning strategy, and it performs as well as the state-of-the-art method BMW. We also propose the LBMW and LBMM for selecting better candidate documents. Experiments show that the performances of the local based methods (LBMW, LBMM) are better than global based methods (BMW, BMM). We have studied how to dynamically estimate a better overall upper bound score for each block. We make efforts to give both correct and faster results using this improved upper bound estimation. Besides, we also study the search efficiency on different index structures where the document identifiers are assigned by URL sorting or by the static document scores. We show experimentally that our algorithms (S_LBMW and S_LBMM), combined with our improved score upper bound estimation technique, can give the best query processing performance.

Acknowledgements

This work is supported by NSFC Grant (60933004, 70903008, 61073082) and HGJ Grant 2011ZX01042-001-001. We would like to thank Torsten Suel and the anonymous reviewers for their helpful comments.

8. REFERENCES

[1] Anh, V.N. and Moffat, A. 2006. Pruned query evaluation using pre-computed impacts. *SIRGIR'06* (New York, NY, USA, Aug. 2006), 372-379.

[2] Anh, V.N. and Moffat, A. 2006. Structured Index Organizations for High-Throughput Text Querying. *SPIRE* (2006), 304-315.

[3] Anh, V.N., de Kretser, O. and Moffat, A. 2001. Vector-space ranking with effective early termination. *SIGIR'01* (New York, NY, USA, Sep. 2001), 35-42.

[4] BRIN, S. and PAGE, L. 1998. The anatomy of a large-scale hypertextual Web search engine. *Computer Networks and ISDN Systems*. 30, 1-7 (Apr. 1998), 107-117.

[5] Broder, A.Z., Carmel, D., Herscovici, M., Soffer, A. and Zien, J. 2003. Efficient query evaluation using a two-level retrieval process. *CIKM'03* (New York, NY, USA, 2003), 426-434.

[6] Büttcher, S. and Clarke, C.L.A. 2006. A document-centric approach to static index pruning in text retrieval systems. *CIKM'06* (New York, NY, USA, 2006), 182-189.

[7] Büttcher, S., Clarke, C.L.A. and Lushman, B. 2006. Term proximity scoring for ad-hoc retrieval on very large text collections. *SIGIR'06* (2006), 621-622.

[8] Cambazoglu, B.B., Zaragoza, H., Chapelle, O., Chen, J., Liao, C., Zheng, Z. and Degenhardt, J. 2010. Early exit optimizations for additive machine learned ranking systems.*WSDM'10* (New York, NY, USA, 2010), 411-420.

[9] Carmel, D., Cohen, D., Fagin, R., Farchi, E., Herscovici, M., Maarek, Y.S. and Soffer, A. 2001. Static index pruning for information retrieval systems. *SIGIR'01* (New York, NY, USA, 2001), 43-50.

[10] Chakrabarti, K., Chaudhuri, S. and Ganti, V. 2011. Interval-based pruning for top-k processing over compressed lists. *ICDE'2011*, 709-720.

[11] Craswell, N., Robertson, S., Zaragoza, H. and Taylor, M. 2005. Relevance weighting for query independent evidence. *SIGIR'05* (New York, NY, USA, 2005), 416-423.

[12] Ding, S. and Suel, T. 2011. Faster top-k document retrieval using block-max indexes. *SIGIR'11* (New York, NY, USA, 2011), 993-1002.

[13] Fagin, R. 2003. Optimal aggregation algorithms for middleware. *Journal of Computer and System Sciences*. 66, 4 (2003), 614-656.

[14] Ilyas, I.F., Beskales, G. and Soliman, M.A. 2008. A survey of top-k query processing techniques in relational database systems. *ACM Comput. Surv.* 40, 4 (2008), 11:1--11:58.

[15] Jonassen, S. and Bratsberg, S. 2011. Efficient Compressed Inverted Index Skipping for Disjunctive Text-Queries. *Advances in Information Retrieval.* (2011), 530-542.

[16] Long, X. and Suel, T. 2003. Optimized query execution in large search engines with global page ordering. *VLDB'03* (Sep. 2003), 129-140.

[17] Persin, M., Zobel, J. and Sacks-Davis, R. 1996. Filtered Document Retrieval with Frequency-Sorted Indexes. *JASIS*. 47, 10 (1996), 749-764.

[18] Robertson, S.E., Walker, S. and Hancock-Beaulieu, M. 1998. Okapi at TREC-7: Automatic Ad Hoc, Filtering, VLC and Interactive. *TREC* (1998), 199-210.

[19] Shieh, W. 2003. Inverted file compression through document identifier reassignment. *Information Processing & Management*. 39, 1 (Jan. 2003), 117-131.

[20] Silvestri, F. 2007. Sorting out the document identifier assignment problem. *Advances in Information Retrieval*. (Apr. 2007), 101-112.

[21] Song, R., Wen, J.R., Shi, S., Xin, G., Liu, T.Y., Qin, T., Zheng, X., Zhang, J., Xue, G. and Ma, W.Y. 2004. Microsoft research asia at web track and terabyte track of trec 2004. *TREC'04* (2004).

[22] Strohman, T. and Croft, W.B. 2007. Efficient document retrieval in main memory. *SIGIR'07* (New York, NY, USA, 2007), 175-182.

[23] Strohman, T., Turtle, H. and Croft, W.B. 2005. Optimization strategies for complex queries. *SIGIR'05* (New York, NY, USA, 2005), 219-225.

[24] Tonellotto, N., Macdonald, C. and Ounis, I. 2011. Effect of different docid orderings on dynamic pruning retrieval strategies. *SIGIR'11* (New York, NY, USA, 2011), 1179-1180.

[25] Tonellotto, N., Macdonald, C. and Ounis, I. 2010. Efficient dynamic pruning with proximity support. *Large-Scale Distributed Systems for Information Retrieval* (2010), 33-37.

[26] Tsai, M.-F., Liu, T.-Y., Qin, T., Chen, H.-H. and Ma, W.-Y. 2007. FRank: a ranking method with fidelity loss.*SIGIR'07* (New York, NY, USA, 2007), 383-390.

[27] Turtle, H. and Flood, J. 1995. Query evaluation: strategies and optimizations. *Inf. Process. Manage.* 31, 6 (1995), 831-850.

[28] Wang, L., Lin, J. and Metzler, D. 2011. A cascade ranking model for efficient ranked retrieval. *SIGIR'11* (New York, NY, USA, 2011), 105-114.

[29] Yan, H., Ding, S. and Suel, T. 2009. Inverted index compression and query processing with optimized document ordering. *WWW'09* (2009), 401-410.

[30] Yan, H., Shi, S., Zhang, F., Suel, T. and Wen, J.-R. 2010. Efficient term proximity search with term-pair indexes. *CIKM'10* (New York, NY, USA, Oct. 2010), 1229-1238.

[31] Zhang, F., Shi, S., Yan, H. and Wen, J.-R. 2010. Revisiting globally sorted indexes for efficient document retrieval. *WSDM'10* (New York, NY, USA, Feb. 2010), 371-380.

[32] Zhang, J., Long, X. and Suel, T. 2008. Performance of compressed inverted list caching in search engines. *WWW'08* (New York, NY, USA, 2008), 387-396.

[33] Zhu, M., Shi, S., Li, M. and Wen, J.-R. 2007. Effective top-k computation in retrieving structured documents with term-proximity support. *CIKM'07* (New York, NY, USA, 2007), 771-780.

[34] Zhu, M., Shi, S., Yu, N. and Wen, J.-R. 2008. Can phrase indexing help to process non-phrase queries? *CIKM'08* (2008), 679-688.

[35] Zobel, J. and Moffat, A. 2006. Inverted files for text search engines. *ACM Comput. Surv.* 38, 2 (2006)

Probabilistic Models for Personalizing Web Search

David Sontag
New York University
New York, USA
dsontag@cs.nyu.edu

Kevyn Collins-Thompson
Microsoft Research
Redmond, USA
kevynct@microsoft.com

Paul N. Bennett
Microsoft Research
Redmond, USA
paul.n.bennett@microsoft.com

Ryen W. White
Microsoft Research
Redmond, USA
ryenw@microsoft.com

Susan Dumais
Microsoft Research
Redmond, USA
sdumais@microsoft.com

Bodo Billerbeck
Bing, Microsoft
Melbourne, Aus
bodob@microsoft.com

ABSTRACT

We present a new approach for personalizing Web search results to a specific user. Ranking functions for Web search engines are typically trained by machine learning algorithms using either direct human relevance judgments or indirect judgments obtained from click-through data from millions of users. The rankings are thus optimized to this generic population of users, not to any specific user. We propose a generative model of relevance which can be used to infer the relevance of a document to a specific user for a search query. The user-specific parameters of this generative model constitute a compact user profile. We show how to learn these profiles from a user's long-term search history. Our algorithm for computing the personalized ranking is simple and has little computational overhead. We evaluate our personalization approach using historical search data from thousands of users of a major Web search engine. Our findings demonstrate gains in retrieval performance for queries with high ambiguity, with particularly large improvements for acronym queries.

Categories and Subject Descriptors

H.3.3 [**Information Retrieval**]: Retrieval Models

General Terms

Algorithms

Keywords

Personalization, re-ranking, probabilistic models, machine learning

1. INTRODUCTION

Search personalization typically involves tailoring the ranking of results for individual users based on models of their interests. Personalization has been shown to be useful for improving retrieval effectiveness [15, 17, 20], but there has been little work on developing robust probabilistic formalisms or in evaluating these algorithms at Web scale.

The three key problems that must be solved in any personalization approach are: representation, learning, and ranking. Specifically, for representation we need some way to compactly summarize the interests or preferences for each user into a user profile. For learning, we need an algorithm to discover these user profiles from data. Finally, we need an algorithm to combine these user profiles with other relevance signals to rank documents with respect to a query.

Our paper proposes an end-to-end system for personalization addressing each of the above challenges. We formalize the problem using a probabilistic model for predicting the relevance of a document to a specific user with respect to a query. The user representation corresponds to user-specific parameters for part of the model. Our formalization is general and assumes only that there are document-specific latent variables (i.e., document features), user-specific latent variables (i.e., information need for this query), and some way of combining them to determine whether a document's features satisfy the user's information need.

Our approach begins with the assumption that the Web search engine provides a generic estimate of the probability that a document is relevant to the query. Since relevance is subjective, different people will find different documents relevant for the same query and no single ranking can satisfy all users [19, 20]. We explicitly consider the distribution of users for which the global ranking function was trained, and identify how a specific user is different from the population as a whole. Using this, we deconvolve the relevance probability into the probability that a page is relevant given any specific query intent. Then, we recompute the probability of relevance taking into consideration the user's profile.

Although our formalization is general, in this paper we specifically consider its application to the task of personalization using topic-based profiles. We have one discrete variable for each document whose states specify the topic of the document. The state space that we use corresponds to the top two levels of the human-generated ontology provided by the Open Directory Project (ODP, dmoz.org). Some example categories are 'Sports', 'Arts/Movies', and 'Shopping'. In a pre-processing step, we use a text-based classifier, trained with logistic regression, to obtain the distribution over topics for each document in the index. This allows the personalized ranking to be computed extremely quickly at query time.

Permission to make digital or hard copies of all or part of this work for personal or classroom use is granted without fee provided that copies are not made or distributed for profit or commercial advantage and that copies bear this notice and the full citation on the first page. To copy otherwise, to republish, to post on servers or to redistribute to lists, requires prior specific permission and/or a fee.
WSDM'12, February 8–12, 2012, Seattle, Washington, USA.
Copyright 2012 ACM 978-1-4503-0747-5/12/02 ...$10.00.

In addition to having one variable per document, we have one variable for the user whose states specify the topic of the documents being searched for using the query. Even before seeing the query, the user's history provides a prior distribution for this variable. For example, if there are previous queries and clicks in this search session, these could be used to perform short-term personalization. In this paper we focus on personalization using *long-term* search histories, which have been less thoroughly investigated, especially with large numbers of users (see Section 4 for more details).

We evaluate our approach using the Bing search logs. We use the queries and search-result clicks in these logs to obtain the queries and search results, to build long-term profiles of user search interests, and to obtain personalized relevance judgments for each user-query pair based on search result clickthrough. As we will show, the methods lead to significant gains in retrieval effectiveness over competitive baselines.

The remainder of this paper is structured as follows. Section 2 describes related work in areas such as personalization and result re-ranking. Section 3 describes our personalization framework based on probabilistic models, and Section 4 describes how we learn user profiles from users' search history. Experiments to determine the performance of our models are described in Section 5, and we conclude and highlight possible areas of future work in Section 6.

2. RELATED WORK

There is a growing interest in the information retrieval and machine learning communities in moving beyond context-free search experiences, and toward examining how knowledge of a searcher's interests and search context can be used to improve various aspects of search (e.g., ranking, query suggestion, query classification). For example, there has been work on using session context, such as the previous few searches or result clicks, to personalize search results and improve retrieval performance [6, 15]. Short-term session profiles have also been used for other tasks such as predicting future interests [23], query categorization [3], query suggestion, and URL recommendation [2]. We focus on personalizing using user profiles constructed from logs comprising long-term interaction behaviors, potentially providing a richer view of searcher interests over time.

Another line of prior research uses long-term histories to directly improve retrieval effectiveness. Teevan *et al.* [18] constructed user profiles from indexed desktop documents and showed that this information could be used to re-rank search results and improve relevance for individuals. Matthijs and Radlinski [13] constructed user profiles using users' browsing history, and evaluated their approach using an interleaving methodology. Rather than using all of the previous search history, Tan *et al.* [17] focused only on the most relevant prior queries and constructed language models for this task. Personalization is not equally effective on all queries. Teevan *et al.* [19, 20] introduced a framework to identify the potential-for-personalization for different queries. In particular, the implicit measure click entropy (the number of different results that different people clicked) was highly correlated with explicit judgments of relevance by individuals. All of these approaches to personalization use word-based profiles, and ranking is done by re-weighting terms using an existing scoring method such as BM25 or TF-IDF. In contrast, our approach uses a higher-level representation. One of the key advantages of such a representation is that it allows us to naturally build on top of the probability of relevance computed by a more complex ranking function, such as that of a commercial search engine.

Various authors have considered topic-based representations for personalization, typically learning a user's profile from either browsing or search history [4, 7, 9, 12, 14, 16]. These papers suggest a variety of heuristic methods for ranking using a user's profile. Our approach differs significantly in that we propose a probabilistic framework for personalization, resulting in principled procedures for: (1) estimating the topic that a user is searching for, given the query and user profile, and (2) computing the personalized ranking by combining what we know about the user with other relevance signals. A notable exception is Zhai *et al.* [24], who studied the incorporation of novelty into search results. They propose a probabilistic approach that is similar in spirit to the first model that we present in Section 3. Our approach also differs from these earlier works in that we propose using a *background model*, explicitly taking into consideration the relative likelihood that this user, compared to a generic user, has a particular search intent. We show in the large-scale evaluation of Section 5 that the background model results in large improvements in ranking accuracy over a personalization approach that does not use the background model.

3. PROBABILISTIC MODELS FOR PERSONALIZATION

In this section we present two probabilistic models and inference algorithms for computing the probability that a document d is relevant to user u for the query q. These probabilistic models are called *generative models* because they describe the process by which a user decides whether a document is relevant to a particular query. We have a single variable for the document, T_d, and a single variable for the user, T_u. These discrete-valued variables refer to the document's topic and the topic that the user is searching for, respectively. A document about topic T_d is assumed relevant to a user looking for topic T_u if both:

1. Topic T_d satisfies a user with information need T_u, and
2. Given that the document's topic matches that of the search intent, the document is relevant to the query.

The first criterion is measured by the variable $\text{cov}_u(d,q) \in \{0,1\}$, which represents the extent to which T_d "covers" the information need T_u. The second criterion is measured by the variable $\psi(d,q) \in [0,1]$, which we call the *non-topical* relevance score, corresponding to the user-independent probability that the document is relevant to this query. This score is assumed to be comprised of a large number of user-independent signals such as the match of the query to document text or anchor text, aggregate user behavior for this query, etc.

In Model 1 we assume that $\psi(d,q)$ is observed, given to us by the search engine. This turns out to be a very strong assumption, and we relax it in Section 3.2 when we describe Model 2. We intentionally do not model how this score arises, instead choosing to take a black-box view of it. The reason for this choice is that modern Web search engines use a large number of relevance signals that are typically combined in a complex fashion, and we want our algorithms to be broadly applicable.

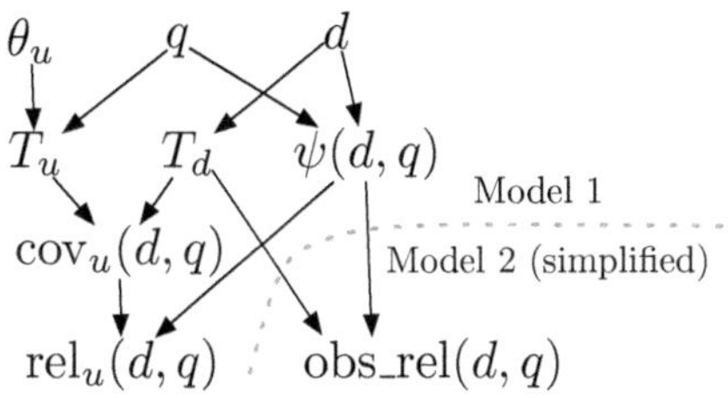

Figure 1: Graphical illustration of two probabilistic models used for personalization. Arrows denote dependencies between the variables [11]. The first approach, Model 1, is described in Section 3.1. The second, Model 2 (simplified), additionally includes the variable obs_rel(d,q), which is the expected probability of relevance with respect to the distribution of users that typically search for query q. It is equivalent to Model 2 from Fig. 2, except that the background model, i.e. the variables in the box, are integrated out.

The variable $\mathrm{rel}_u(d,q) \in \{0,1\}$ combines the two criteria, taking the value 1 when the user finds the document relevant to the query, and 0 otherwise. Specifically, we have $\Pr(\mathrm{rel}_u(d,q) = 1 \mid \mathrm{cov}_u(d,q), \psi(d,q)) = 0$ if $\mathrm{cov}_u(d,q)$ is 0, and $\psi(d,q)$ if $\mathrm{cov}_u(d,q)$ is 1. The user's personalized ranking is then obtained by sorting all of the documents by this probability.[1] In practice, this approach would be used to *re-rank* a number of top-scoring documents with respect to the user-independent ranking function.

3.1 Model 1 (no background model)

Fig. 1 shows the probabilistic model for the simplest personalization method, denoted as Model 1.

The notation θ_u refers to user-specific parameters, also called the user profile, that are learned from the user's historical data in an offline step. The user profile together with the current query q are used to come up with a *distribution* over the user's search intent (i.e. a distribution over topics), $\Pr(T_u \mid \theta_u, q)$. Our framework is modular, with many different data sources able to feed into this distribution. For example, one could do short-term personalization by conditioning on the previous queries of the session. In Section 4 we describe our approach to estimating this distribution by learning the user profiles from long-term user interaction data.

The conditional distribution $\Pr(T_d \mid d)$ specifies the topic of each document. This distribution could be estimated using a variety of techniques. In our evaluation, we use a text-based classifier, described in [1], that was trained using logistic regression to predict the ODP category for each Web page present in the Bing index.

The distribution $\Pr(\mathrm{cov}_u(d,q) \mid T_u, T_d)$ could simply be given by $1[T_u = T_d]$, the indicator function for whether T_u is the same as T_d. This choice would imply that a document is irrelevant for queries outside of its topic area. More generally, $\Pr(\mathrm{cov}_u(d,q) \mid T_u, T_d)$ can be a function of some distance between topics T_u and T_d, or it could be learned from data.

[1]There are also more sophisticated methods for personalizing the results using the probabilistic model, such as blending the personalized results with the original search results, and considering the confidence in our estimates when deciding whether to personalize.

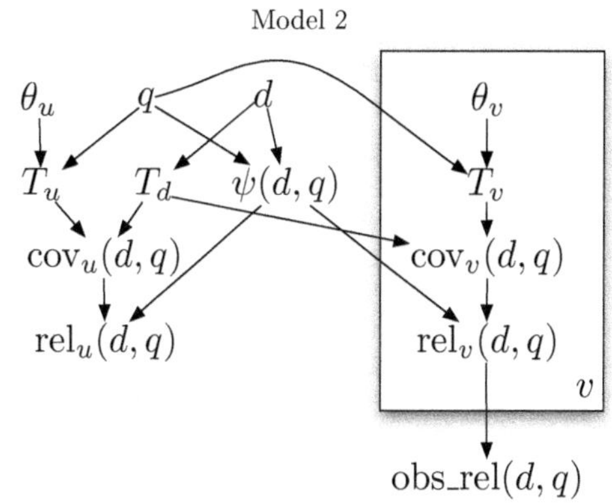

Figure 2: Graphical illustration of the probabilistic model of personalization for user u where we explicitly take into consideration the background distribution of users (denoted as v) who typically search the query q and for whom the ranking function was trained. The box notation used in this figure signifies that each of the variables inside the box should be replicated, once for each user $v \in V(q)$ (see Section 3.2). We assume that the probability of relevance reported by the search engine, obs_rel(d,q), is equal to the expectation of $\mathrm{rel}_v(d,q)$ with respect to the distribution of users that typically search on q, described by $\Pr(\theta_v \mid q)$. The only observed variables are the user-specific parameters θ_u, the query q, the document d, and obs_rel(d,q).

The variables θ_u, q, d, and $\psi(d,q)$ are observed. Integrating over all of the latent variables, we obtain the following formula to use during ranking:

$$\Pr(\mathrm{rel}_u(d,q) = 1 \mid \theta_u, q, d, \psi(q,d))$$

$$= \psi(d,q) \sum_{T_d} \Pr(T_d \mid d)\alpha(T_d) , \quad (1)$$

$$\alpha(T_d) = \sum_{T_u} \Pr(T_u \mid \theta_u, q)\Pr(\mathrm{cov}_u(d,q) = 1 \mid T_u, T_d)$$

$\alpha(T_d)$ can be computed just once for each query, regardless of the number of documents to be ranked. Furthermore, for a specific document d, $\Pr(T_d \mid d)$ typically has support on only a few categories (having close to zero probability elsewhere), and so the sum in Eq. 1 has very few terms. As a result, we can compute the personalized probabilities of relevance in linear time with respect to the number of documents to be ranked. Over time, the profile θ_u can be updated efficiently as we see additional behavior from users.

3.2 Model 2 (background model)

The approach described in the previous section assumes that the search engine provides the non-topical relevance score, $\psi(d,q)$, which is the user-independent probability that the document is relevant. However, this quantity is difficult to obtain. The ranking functions of modern search engines are trained using a combination of hand-labeled relevance judgments and implicit relevance judgments from millions of users' click-through information. Thus, the probability of relevance obtained from the ranking function is biased toward the population of users that typically search on the query using this search engine.

For example, on the query "Kevin Murphy", the top search results using Bing are about a hair stylist and an actor. This is not to say that the other results, such as that of Kevin Patrick Murphy (a researcher who frequently publishes in Computer Science) are irrelevant, just that for the generic user they are less likely to be relevant.

Suppose that we knew the set of users $V(q) = \{v\}$ that have previously searched for query q and whose relevance feedback we used to train the ranking function. The probabilistic model described in this section, shown in Fig. 2, explicitly takes these users' intended topics into consideration when interpreting the probability of relevance computed by the ranking function. In particular, we assume that, rather than $\psi(d,q)$, the search engine only provides the following quantity:

$$\text{obs\_rel}(d,q) = \frac{1}{|V(q)|} \sum_{v \in V(q)} \text{rel}_v(d,q) \ .$$

This is the *expected* relevance with respect to the distribution of users who typically search for query q (across all possible query intents). We no longer assume that $\psi(d,q)$ is observed.

Since it is unrealistic to assume that we know $V(q)$, we instead propose to use an aggregate distribution. In particular, consider a simplified version of Model 2, shown in Fig. 1, where we integrated over the variables T_v, $\text{cov}_v(d,q)$, and $\text{rel}_v(d,q)$ for all $v \in V(q)$. Now $\text{obs\_rel}(d,q)$ depends on $\psi(d,q)$, q, and T_d, and can be shown to be equal to:

$$\psi(d,q) \sum_T \Pr(\text{cov}(d,q) = 1 \mid T, T_d)\Pr_r(T \mid q), \quad (2)$$

where we define:

$$\Pr_r(T \mid q) = \frac{1}{|V(q)|} \sum_{v \in V(q)} \Pr(T \mid \theta_v, q).$$

Instead of assuming that we know $V(q)$, we assume that we know this *background distribution* $\Pr_r(T \mid q)$ (the r denotes that this is for a random, or generic user). We propose estimating $\Pr_r(T \mid q)$ using an approach similar to [23]. Assuming that the existing ranking function is targeted at the generic user, we compute this distribution by taking the weighted average of the topic distributions (as computed by our classifier) for each of the top-scoring search results. Specifically, we estimate:

$$\Pr_r(T = t \mid q) \propto \sum_{i=1}^{N} \text{obs\_rel}(d_i, q)\Pr(T_{d_i} = t \mid d_i)$$

for the N highest scoring documents according to $\text{obs\_rel}(d,q)$.

As with Model 1, we next compute the posterior marginals $\Pr(\text{rel}_u(d,q) = 1 \mid \theta_u, q, d, \text{obs\_rel}(d,q))$, and sort these to obtain the personalized rankings. From Eq. 2 we obtain

$$\psi(d,q) = \frac{\text{obs\_rel}(d,q)}{\sum_T \Pr(\text{cov}(d,q) = 1 \mid T, T_d)\Pr_r(T \mid q)} \ .$$

Note that this is a random variable because of its dependence on T_d. To simplify probabilistic inference, we assume:

ASSUMPTION 1. *$Pr(T_d \mid d, obs\_rel(d,q)) \approx Pr(T_d \mid d)$.*

That is, although the observed relevance of a document with respect to a query does provide some information about the document's topic, we assume that this is dwarfed by the information contained in the document's text. Using this, we integrate over T_u and T_d, and obtain the following for the posterior marginal:

$$\text{obs\_rel}(d,q) \sum_{T_d} \overbrace{\Pr(T_d \mid d) \frac{\sum_{T_u} \Pr(T_u \mid \theta_u, q) f(T_u, T_d)}{\sum_T \Pr_r(T \mid q) f(T, T_d)}}^{\text{Re-weighting factor}}, \quad (3)$$

where $f(T, T_d) = \Pr(\text{cov}(d,q) = 1 \mid T, T_d)$. The numerator of the fraction is $\alpha(T_d)$ (see Eq. 1) and, as before, can be computed just once per query (same for the denominator).

The personalized relevance score given by Model 2 (specified in Eq. 3) satisfies an important invariance property:

When $Pr(T_u \mid \theta_u, q)$ is the same as $Pr_r(T \mid q)$, the ranking is unchanged.

That is, given what we know about the user, if we cannot distinguish the user's query intent from that of the general population of users that search for this query, then the reweighting factor has value 1 and the personalized probability of relevance is simply given by $\text{obs\_rel}(d,q)$. We believe that this invariance property is essential to our approach's success. To our knowledge, our approach is the first personalization algorithm that explicitly uses a background distribution and satisfies this invariance property.

We conclude this section by noting that $\Pr_r(T \mid q)$ could come from a variety of different sources. For example, rather than estimating it using the approach described above, for popular queries we could simply collect statistics for the number of times that users click on results that are labeled with category T given that they have searched for query q. More broadly, our method could be used to adjust the rankings of any search engine that was trained on one set of users but is then applied to a different set of users.

4. MODELING USERS

In this section we describe how we use a user's long-term search history to compute a compact user profile. In particular, to apply the personalization approaches introduced in the previous section, we need the distribution $\Pr(T_u \mid \theta_u, q)$, the probability that when issuing a query q, a user u is seeking information on topic T_u. θ_u denotes the user-specific parameters. We propose two different approaches for obtaining this conditional distribution:

1. Learn a user-independent language model $\Pr(q \mid T)$ and a user-specific prior $\Pr(T \mid \theta_u)$, and then apply Bayes' rule:

$$\Pr(T_u \mid \theta_u, q) = \frac{\Pr(T_u \mid \theta_u)\Pr(q \mid T_u)}{\sum_{T'} \Pr(T' \mid \theta_u)\Pr(q \mid T')}. \quad (4)$$

2. Learn a user-specific way of reweighting $\Pr_r(T \mid q)$ to obtain $\Pr(T_u \mid \theta_u, q)$.

The first approach (Generative method) is based on the generative models described in the previous section. It assumes that the user first chooses a topic to search for, and then chooses a particular query from this topic. The second approach (Discriminative method) we formulate as a discriminative learning task, directly attempting to maximize the probability of the user's actual intent conditioned on the query, over their previous search history.

Both approaches have their advantages and disadvantages. The first approach gives an accurate picture of a user's typical intent distribution, but relies heavily on being able to estimate a good language model. For some infrequently searched categories, such as Computer Science, we do not observe sufficiently many queries to estimate a good language model. As a result, we may end up missing these intents for all but their most popular queries. The second approach usually does a good job of predicting a user's most likely intent, but can give very peaked distributions, underestimating the model's uncertainty in the user's intent.

We also evaluated a convex combination of the two distributions (50% each) which we call the Interpolation method. Averaging the output of the two different classifiers is a type of ensemble method, frequently used in machine learning, and results in a more stable prediction. We show in the evaluation that this results in significantly fewer queries where the personalized ranking is worse than the original ranking.

4.1 Training data

We assume that we have search history for each user consisting of the queries issued, the list of documents in the visible search results, and the list of documents clicked on by the user in response to each query. There has been a significant amount of work on interpreting click-through information as a weak relevance signal, and it is straightforward to use these approaches together with our probabilistic models. The simplest approach, for example, equates a user's click on a document with the observation $\text{rel}_u(d,q) = 1$ and, conversely, the lack of a click as $\text{rel}_u(d,q) = 0$. Then, we could estimate the user's parameters by maximizing the likelihood of the observed click-through data. Unfortunately, the resulting learning problem is computationally difficult to solve because some of the variables, e.g. the user's true intent T_u, are unknown and their values must be integrated over.

We could use expectation maximization (EM) or gradient ascent to reach a local maximum of the likelihood. However, in this paper we avoid this complexity by making a simple approximation. We assume that the user's intended topic T_u is equal to the topic of the document that they click on. Specifically, let $d_1, \ldots, d_c$ be the documents that the user clicks on for query q. Then, we let

$$\widehat{\Pr}(T)_t = \frac{1}{c}\sum_{i=1}^{c} \Pr(T \mid d_i),$$

where the documents' topic distributions are computed by our classifier and the subscript t refers to a specific query. Then, the training data for each user consists of a set of pairs, $(q_t, \widehat{\Pr}(T)_t)$.

This approximation corresponds to ignoring the negative data points (i.e., documents that a user *does not* click on), assuming that a click implies that a user thinks that the document is relevant, and assuming that $\Pr(\text{cov}_u(d,q) \mid T_u, T_d) = 0$ if $T_u \neq T_d$. The first two assumptions are often very reasonable, and become less important the more training data that we have for a user.

4.2 Language model

In this approach, we estimate the prior probability that a user u searches for topic T, independent of the query. Let N denote the number of training points, $(q_t, \widehat{\Pr}(T)_t)$. Then, our estimate is:

$$\Pr(T \mid \theta_u) = \frac{1}{N}\sum_{t=1}^{N} \widehat{\Pr}(T)_t.$$

where we ignore the queries.

To apply Eq. 4 we estimate a unigram language model, $\Pr(q \mid T) = \prod_{w \in q} \Pr(w \mid T)$ for each topic T, where w denotes a word. We calculate the required statistics using half a billion search queries sampled from a month of web search query logs, and the topic distributions of the clicked documents as computed by our classifier.

4.3 Reweighting the generic user's intent

In this section, we propose a discriminative approach to directly estimate the conditional distribution $\Pr(T_u \mid \theta_u, q)$ from training data. We begin by assuming that the conditional distribution lies in the exponential family, with the following parametric form:

$$\Pr(T \mid q; \theta) = \exp(\phi(T,q) \cdot \theta - A(\theta)), \tag{5}$$

where $A(\theta)$ denotes the log partition function. The feature vector we use is:

$$\phi(T,q) = < \log \Pr_r(T \mid q), 0, 0, \ldots, 0, 1, 0, \ldots 0 > ,$$

where the 1 is in the T'th location. That is, the parameters that we learn correspond to a user-specific reweighting of $\Pr_r(T \mid q)$, the topic distribution for a generic user who searches on query q. We learn one multiplier per topic.

We learn a different parameter vector θ for each user. Our goal during learning is to minimize

$$\sum_{t=1}^{N} \text{KL}\left(\widehat{\Pr}(T)_t, \Pr(T \mid q; \theta)\right) + C_1(\theta_0 - 1)^2 + C_2||\theta_{1:\text{end}}||^2 \tag{6}$$

where θ_0 refers to the weight which multiplies $\log \Pr_r(T \mid q)$. We also require that $\theta_0 \geq 0$.

Ignoring constant terms, $\text{KL}\left(\widehat{\Pr}(T)_t, \Pr(T \mid q; \theta)\right)$ equals

$$\begin{aligned} & -\sum_T \widehat{\Pr}(T)_t \log \Pr(T \mid q; \theta) \\ = \; & \log \sum_T \exp(\phi(T,q) \cdot \theta) - \sum_T \widehat{\Pr}(T)_t \phi(T,q) \cdot \theta. \end{aligned}$$

The objective in Eq. 6 is convex, and can be optimized using a number of standard methods.

The quadratic terms in Eq. 6 regularize the data terms to prevent the learning algorithm from overfitting. The regularization is motivated by the following generative model. Suppose that we estimate $\Pr_r(T)$, the prior distribution over topics for generic users of the search engine. We can apply Bayes' rule to "invert" $\Pr_r(T \mid q)$:

$$\Pr(q \mid T) = c\frac{\Pr_r(T \mid q)}{\Pr_r(T)}, \tag{7}$$

where c is a constant. Then, using Eq. 7 as our new language model, we do a second application of Bayes' rule as in Eq. 4 to obtain:

$$\Pr(T_u \mid \theta_u, q) \propto \Pr_r(T_u \mid q)\frac{\Pr(T_u \mid \theta_u)}{\Pr_r(T_u)}. \tag{8}$$

Setting the parameters $\theta_0 = 1$ and $\theta_T = \log \frac{\Pr(T \mid \theta_u)}{\Pr_r(T)}$ in Eq. 5 recovers Eq. 8. The regularization then says that, unless we see a lot of evidence to the contrary, we think θ_0 should be equal to 1 and θ_T should be equal to 0, where the latter corresponds to setting $\Pr(T \mid \theta_u) = \Pr_r(T)$.

5. EVALUATION

In Section 5.1 we present examples that illustrate the different components of our personalization framework and how applying personalization with topic-based user profiles affects re-ranking. Then in Section 5.2 we summarize key performance metrics for the models described above.

Our models make use of a probability of relevance that is supposed to be provided by the search engine, obs_rel(d, q). When the score provided by the ranking function cannot be easily interpreted as a probability of relevance (e.g., because it can be negative), a simple substitute is to use the inverse rank of the document. Rather than use the ranking score, we use this second alternative of inverse rank. This enables others without access to commercial search engine logs to reproduce our work as a client-side personalized re-ranking study, such as the one performed in [13].

We obtain the personalized ranking by ordering the results according to β*original score + $(1-\beta)$*personalized score. In our experiments we set $\beta = 0.3$, where β serves as a serendipity parameter. This corresponds to a generative model where with probability β the user's intent matches the generic user, ignoring the user's typical interests.

We learn the coverage function $\Pr(\text{cov}_u(d, q) = 1 \mid T_u, T_d)$, which describes the relationship between the classes and the extent to which a user's intent T_u (e.g., "Computers/Artificial Intelligence") is satisfied by a document's topic T_d (e.g., "Computers"). We used a hold-out set of one month's worth of training logs. In particular, we assume:

$$\Pr(\text{cov}_u(d, q) = 1 \mid T_u, T_d = t) = \frac{\Pr(d \text{ satisfies } u \mid u \text{ has intent } T_u, T_d = t)}{\max_c \Pr(d \text{ satisfies } u \mid u \text{ has intent } T_u, T_d = c)} \quad (9)$$

The max term normalizes with respect to the most frequently satisfying class, to account for the fact that multiple document topics may align well with a user's intent. For example, "Shopping/Vehicles" and "Recreation/Autos" may both equally satisfy queries about automobiles. This is often because how information needs are distributed across an ontology may differ in practice from how the ontology was designed. We compute an empirical estimate of the satisfaction probability as follows:

$$\Pr(d \text{ satisfies } u \mid u \text{ has intent } T_u, T_d = t) = \frac{\frac{1}{|Q|}\sum_{q \in Q} \Pr_r(T_u \mid q) \sum_{d' \in \text{results}(q)} \text{sat}(d', q) \Pr(T_{d'} = t \mid d')}{\frac{1}{|Q|}\sum_{q \in Q} \Pr_r(T_u \mid q)}$$

Here the indicator function $\text{sat}(d', q)$ is 1 if d' received the *last* satisfied result click for query q, and 0 otherwise. We define a satisfied result click (SAT) as either a click followed by no further clicks for 30 seconds or more, or the last result click in the session [17, 21]. The set Q corresponds to all queries with at least one satisfied result click.

We implemented the discriminative learning algorithm for learning the user profiles using Matlab and `CVX`, a package for specifying and solving convex programs [10]. We set the regularization parameters to be $C_1 = 25$ and $C_2 = 0.5$.

5.1 Illustrative examples

In this section, we demonstrate various aspects of our personalization approach using a demo that we implemented to re-rank the top 200 Bing search results. The user profiles used in the demo were learned from two months of search logs from one of the authors, a computer scientist, and from another volunteer, a biologist.

Fig. 3 shows the results of our algorithms for the ambiguous query `[kevin murphy]` issued by the computer science researcher. Fig. 3(a) shows the top five ODP categories from the background model, $\Pr_r(T \mid q)$, and also the top five ODP categories that our algorithms predict as the query intent for the computer science researcher, given by $\Pr(T_u \mid \theta_u, q)$. There are marked differences. The distribution over query intents for the generic user for the `[kevin murphy]` query is centered around business, society, and health, whereas for the computer science researcher, the predicted query intent involved artificial intelligence, people, and science.

Fig. 3(b) presents the search results returned for this query, issued by the computer science researcher, to: (i) Bing, (ii) the same Web search engine with results re-ranked using Eq. 1, and (iii) the same engine with results re-ranked using Eq. 3. When a computer science researcher issues this query, it is likely that the intent is to reach the website of the University of British Columbia (UBC) professor (`http://www.cs.ubc.ca/~murphyk`), and not the actor or hair stylist. As can be seen from the example, both Eq. 1 and Eq. 3 promote the UBC professor's page from outside the top 10 results.

Fig. 4 shows the results of our algorithms for the ambiguous query `[rockefeller]` issued by the biologist. We see in Fig. 4(a) that, again, there are marked differences in the query intents, with the dominant categories for the generic user centering on business, society, and health, whereas for the biologist they center on biology, science, and health. Fig. 4(b) shows the results returned for the query `[rockefeller]` issued by the biologist to: (i) Bing, (ii) the same Web search engine with results re-ranked using Eq. 1, and (iii) the same engine with results re-ranked with Eq. 3.

We observed across a large number of ambiguous queries that Eq. 3 (Model 2) performs significantly better than Eq. 1 (Model 1), typically promoting the desired result directly to the top position. The algorithms appear to work particularly well for name queries (e.g., on the query `[Michael Jordan]`, promoting the website of the statistician to position 1 from position 198 when queried by the computer scientist) and acronyms (e.g., `[sigir]`).

5.2 Large-scale evaluation

The primary source of data for this study is a proprietary data set comprising the search logs (queries and result clicks) for the Bing Web search engine. The data set consists of tuples including a random unique user identifier (stored in a browser cookie), the date and time, and the query issued. For each of the queries, we also know the top-10 search results that were shown to users at query time, the rank order in which they were presented, and which results were clicked on. These data provide us with examples of real-world searching behavior that are useful for evaluating the performance of our personalized search algorithms. To isolate the impact of long-term personalization, we did not use any other form of personalization from the Bing search engine over the time period for which the data were collected. To remove variability caused by cultural and linguistic variation in search behavior, we only include log entries generated in the English-speaking United States locale.

The evaluation results described in this paper are based on queries and result clicks in this data during September

Pr(topic | query) for generic user
Business: 0.213
Society: 0.107
Shopping/Health: 0.096
Business/Consumer Goods+Services: 0.077
Arts: 0.062

Pr(topic | query) for CS researcher
Computers/Artificial Intelligence: 0.663
Arts/People: 0.098
Science: 0.044
Computers: 0.042
Arts/Performing Arts: 0.036

(a)

Web search engine results		Categories
1. http://www.kevinmurphy.com.au		Business, Shopping
2. http://en.wikipedia.org/wiki/Kevin_Murphy_(actor)		Arts
3. http://www.kevinmurphystore.com		Health, Shopping

Personalized re-ranking results (using Model 1)		Categories
1. http://en.wikipedia.org/wiki/Kevin_Murphy_(actor)	(2)	Arts
2. http://www.kevinmurphy.com.au	(1)	Business, Shopping
3. http://www.cs.ubc.ca/~murphyk	(13)	Reference, Computers

Personalized re-ranking results (using Model 2)		Categories
1. http://www.cs.ubc.ca/~murphyk	(13)	Reference, Computers
2. http://en.wikipedia.org/wiki/Kevin_Murphy_(actor)	(2)	Arts
3. http://www.kevinmurphystore.com	(3)	Health, Shopping

(b)

Figure 3: (a) Top categories based on Pr(topic | query) for a generic user and a computer science researcher for the query [kevin murphy]. (b) The original top three results from a Web search engine for query [kevin murphy], and re-ranked results using Models 1 and 2. Also shown to the right of each result is the original rank in parentheses and the top-level ODP categories, as predicted by the text classifier used throughout this paper.

2010. 20 days of search logs from Sept. 1-20 were used to construct users' long-term profiles. The queries in five days of search logs from Sept. 21-25 were used to evaluate the performance of our personalization algorithms. We selected users from the 5-day test period who had at least 100 satisfied result clicks in the 20-day profile building period (see Table 1). For this subset of users, we also identified search sessions using a session extraction methodology similar to [22]. Search sessions begin with a query and contain result clicks and any subsequent queries and clicks that occurred. Sessions terminated following 30 minutes of inactivity. We used these sessions to obtain personalized relevance judgments for each query (see below for more details).

Table 1: Descriptive statistics about our users, after filtering for those who had at least 100 SAT clicks, computed on the 20 days of search history.

	average	stdev	median
num days	16.21	3.72	17
num queries	229.60	112.28	204
num SAT clicks	143.82	52.80	128

To explore parameter choices, we use a set of five weeks of hold-out log-data from the same search engine and of a similar type to our evaluation data described above but non-overlapping with it. In particular, this hold-out data was used to explore the parameter choices mentioned in this section (e.g., β), learn the coverage function as described earlier, and set a threshold for the entropy criteria used to identify ambiguous queries, described later.

To focus on underspecified queries which [20] have found especially amenable to personalization, we filtered the test queries to only include one word queries. We also filtered out the one word queries that we have not seen sufficiently many times in the historical query logs to reliably estimate the language model.[2]

This resulted in 571598 queries from 195108 users. In our primary experiments, to further emphasize ambiguity, we retained only non-navigational queries (using a classifier) and queries where the entropy of the ODP topics of the top 10 URLs (*i.e.*, the entropy of $\Pr_r(T_d \mid q)$) is above a threshold. We refer to the queries that have passed the entropy filter as "ambiguous" in our results below. After these filters, our test set consisted of 54581 users with at least one query, and 102417 queries in total.

Evaluation of our personalized ranking algorithms required a personalized relevance judgment for each result. Obtaining relevance judgments from a large number of real users is impractical, and there is no known approach to train expert judges to provide reliable personalized judgments that reflect real user preferences. Instead, we obtained these judgments using a log-based methodology inspired by [8]. Specifically, we assign a positive judgment to one of the top 10 URLs if it is the last satisfied result click in the session (Last SAT). The remaining top-ranked URLs receive a negative judgment. This gives us one positive judgment and nine negative judgments for each of the top-10 URLs for each session.

One consequence of evaluating on retrospective data is that we can only evaluate based on the search results which were shown. Since items below the last clicked item may have been unexamined by the user and actually be relevant, treating them as irrelevant serves as a lower bound on the performance of our algorithms.

The rank position of the single positive judgment is used to evaluate retrieval performance before and after re-ranking. Specifically, we measure our performance using the inverse

[2]In particular, we considered words w that had at least one category c such that w was part of at least 50 queries leading to a click on a document with category c.

Pr(topic | query) for generic user
Business: 0.213
Society: 0.107
Shopping/Health: 0.096
Business/Consumer Goods+Services: 0.077
Arts: 0.062

Pr(topic | query) for biologist
Science/Biology: 0.402
Science: 0.228
Society: 0.052
Reference: 0.040
Health: 0.031

(a)

Web search engine results		Categories
1. http://en.wikipedia.org/wiki/John_D._Rockefeller		Society
2. http://en.wikipedia.org/wiki/Rockefeller_family		Science, Society
3. http://www.rockefeller.edu		Reference, Science

Personalized re-ranking results (using Model 1)		Categories
1. http://en.wikipedia.org/wiki/Rockefeller_family	(2)	Science, Society
2. http://www.rockefeller.edu	(3)	Reference, Science
3. http://en.wikipedia.org/wiki/John_D._Rockefeller	(1)	Society

Personalized re-ranking results (using Model 2)		Categories
1. http://www.rockefeller.edu	(3)	Reference, Science
2. http://en.wikipedia.org/wiki/Rockefeller_family	(2)	Science, Society
3. http://bridges.rockefeller.edu/?page=news	(12)	Science, Health

(b)

Figure 4: (a) Top categories based on Pr(topic | query) for a generic user and a biologist for the query [rockefeller]. (b) Top three results from a Web search engine for query [rockefeller], and re-ranked search results using Models 1 and 2. Also shown to the right of each result is the original rank in parentheses and the top-level ODP categories assigned to that result.

of the rank of the relevant document, otherwise known as the mean reciprocal rank (MRR). Queries for which we cannot assign a positive judgment to any top-10 URL are excluded from the evaluation dataset.

We labeled each of top-10 results with ODP categories using a text-based classifier, described in [1] and mentioned earlier in the paper. The text-based classifier has a micro-averaged F1 value of 0.60. The coverage of the classifier across all result URLs was 86.2%; classifier coverage was not 100% due to index churn over time. When producing the personalized search results, we do not change the position of any URL for which we do not have ODP classifications.

5.2.1 *Retrieval performance*

Table 2 shows the change in MRR of the queries in the test set for each of the three methods of predicting the user's query intent, $\Pr(T_u \mid \theta_u, q)$, and for both Models 1 and 2. The generative method refers to the language modeling approach described in Section 4.2, the discriminative method refers to the user-specific re-weighting of $\Pr_r(T \mid q)$, described in Section 4.3, and the interpolation method refers to using the convex combination of the distributions predicted by the generative and discriminative methods.

The baseline for these experiments is the original ranking provided by the Bing Web search engine. The results are shown relative to the MRR of the baseline.[3] The first column summarizes the proportion of queries in which the method moves the last SAT click, which reflects the coverage of the method. The second column shows the MRR for this subset of queries. The final column shows the overall effect of this method, obtained by multiplying the first and second columns. All of the methods improve on the baseline, with the best results achieved by using the background model (Model 2) together with the interpolation method.

[3]To help interpret MRR Δ, if the last satisfied clicked document was always returned in the fourth position by the baseline and the personalized ranking always returned it in the third position, then this would be an MRR Δ of 0.0833. Moving from third to second would yield a Δ of 0.1667.

Table 2: Performance on ambiguous, one word non-navigational queries. MRR Δ is improvement over the baseline commercial search engine's ranking. Bold face indicates significant ($p = 0.05$, Bonferroni correction) improvement over the baseline according to a sign test.

Model	Last SAT Moved	Moved MRR Δ	MRR Δ
Generative, Model 1	8.93%	**0.0753**	**0.0067**
Generative, Model 2	18.41%	0.0187	0.0034
Discriminative, Model 1	4.22%	**0.0732**	**0.0031**
Discriminative, Model 2	7.96%	**0.1808**	**0.0144**
Interpolated, Model 1	5.23%	**0.0957**	**0.0050**
Interpolated, Model 2	11.18%	**0.1686**	**0.0189**

In general, Model 2 appears to be more aggressive than Model 1, re-ranking more often (as can be seen in the first column). This is because while Model 1 may change scores, it often does not change scores enough to change the ranking. Because Model 2 normalizes by the background model, a document whose topic is substantially more likely to be the intent of the user than of the generic user has its score dramatically amplified, even if the absolute probability of this topic being the user intent is small. It is thus essential that we correctly predict the user's query intent. For the generative method, this aggressiveness results in lower performance (as seen in the third column), while the discriminative method is much more reliable and actually gains in performance. The interpolation method provides the best overall estimate of the user's query intent: when applied together with Model 2 it achieves good performance with high coverage, yielding the highest total gain of 0.0189, much higher than the next best method.

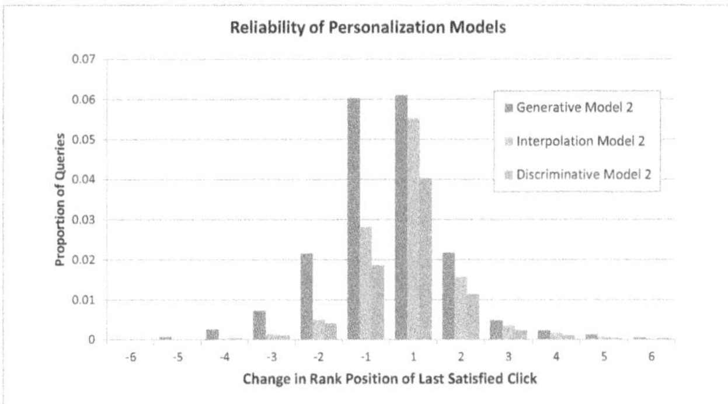

Figure 5: Histogram showing the variance of rank position gains and losses for personalization. The loss or gain in rank position of the last satisfied click is given on the x-axis. The y-axis denotes the fraction of queries in that bucket.

5.2.2 *The risk of personalization*

While achieving good average retrieval gains across queries is important, in the case of re-ranking an existing set of results, the *variance* of relative gains and losses compared to the initial ranking is also critical to measure. For example, two algorithms may appear identical with respect to their MRR performance, but one algorithm may have significantly higher variance in the magnitude of gains and losses it achieves compared to the initial ranking. Thus, we include a brief analysis of the variability in gains and losses.

Fig. 5 compares the distribution of gains and losses across queries using Model 2 for each of the three methods of predicting the user's query intent, $\Pr(T_u \mid \theta_u, q)$, as measured by the gain/loss in rank position of the last satisfied click. The x-axis shows the change in rank position of the last satisfied click, and the y-axis shows the fraction of queries with this change. Larger positive changes in rank positions are better. As shown in Table 2, the ensemble interpolation method reranks more frequently than the discriminative model though at a lower precision yielding a higher total gain. Fig. 5 shows that this gain results from having significantly fewer hurt queries (31%) than the generative model (50%) while being as reliable as the discriminative (30%) model. Thus, the ensemble effectively combines the greatly reduced downside risk of the discriminative model with the majority of upside gains achieved by the generative model.

Out of the total 102417 ambiguous, non-navigational queries in the test set, for the interpolation method, 11448 queries (11%) had a change in position of the relevant item, with 7881 (69%) of these queries helped – significantly higher than the null hypothesis of 50%.[4]

5.2.3 *Filter Analysis*

As research has indicated, when to personalize is as important as how to personalize [19]. Therefore, we evaluated the impact of the filtering conditions we used (non-navigational and ambiguous queries). Additionally, having noticed over the hold-out data that acronyms were a large class of ambiguous queries, we also explored acronyms as an alternative filter for identifying ambiguous queries.

We therefore extracted acronyms from a bipartite graph of co-clicked queries [5] and clicked page titles. The queries and clicked pages were taken from Bing search logs, pruning edges with less than two clicks. We only used query pairs connected directly to co-clicked pages (i.e., a two-step walk); we also related queries with clicked page titles and vice versa. An acronym was added for each case-folded pair of queries and/or titles where one of these expanded to the other following these rules: expansions may contain additional stopwords (we used 114 common stopwords), acronyms only contain alphanumerical characters (0-9, a-z).

Table 3 presents the results of our filter analysis. For all results in this table, we consider only the set of queries where the last satisfied clicked document moves position, using Interpolation and Model 2. The first column shows the proportion of single word queries covered by the filter. The second column shows MRR on this subset of queries, and the final column shows the overall effect on this subset of one word queries (obtained by multiplying the first and second column). As the MRR gains in the table illustrate, filtering to both ambiguous and non-navigational queries identifies segments of queries that have larger potential for personalization (gain on this segment in "Filter Set MRR Δ" column) than either filter alone. Also, as can be seen in the table, filtering to acronyms alone yields a segment which has high potential for personalization and therefore is an interesting class for study. Adding the ambiguity or non-navigational filter increases the gains that personalization can yield by a large amount (up to 0.2269). However, since acronyms make up a small proportion of queries, the total gain seen (far right column) is lower than for other segments. The highest total gain was achieved over all one-word queries. Nonetheless, the use of filtering allows higher precision groups of queries to be identified, with acronyms providing one such high-potential segment for personalization.

Table 3: Performance of filtering conditions on one word queries where the last satisfied clicked document moves position. MRR Δ is improvement over the baseline commercial search engine's ranking. Bold face indicates statistically significant ($p = 0.05$, Bonferroni correction) improvement over the baseline according to a sign test.

Filter Conditions	Set Size	Filter Set MRR Δ	MRR Δ
One Word	100.00%	**0.1213**	**0.1213**
One Word, Ambig.	68.21%	**0.1361**	**0.0928**
One Word, non-Nav	73.82%	**0.1442**	**0.1064**
One Word, Ambig., non-Nav	54.81%	**0.1686**	**0.0924**
Acronym	31.73%	**0.1745**	**0.0554**
Acronym, Ambig.	25.05%	**0.1988**	**0.0498**
Acronym, non-Nav	25.55%	**0.2052**	**0.0524**
Acronym, Ambig., non-Nav	21.08%	**0.2269**	**0.0478**

6. CONCLUSION

We presented a general framework for personalization based on probabilistic models. We showed that we could achieve gains over a competitive baseline for one-word queries, and

[4]For a competitive baseline this is a conservative estimate; assuming a random method is equally likely to move the result to any position, there are far fewer positions on average above a result than below.

especially for queries comprising acronyms, which represent a query segment that seems particularly amenable to our long-term personalization approach. Importantly, acronyms can easily be identified by practitioners who may lack access to search engine log data needed to identify ambiguous and non-navigational queries.

Although in this paper we specifically applied the framework to the problem of single topic-based personalization, the same ranking formula can be directly applied to a number of different types of personalization criteria such as multiple topics, geographic location, and reading proficiency. The ranking approach can also be used for personalizing based on short-term user profiles, by simply plugging in a different distribution for $\Pr(T_u \mid q, \theta_u)$.

Our approach can be extended in a number of directions. In this paper we describe personalization based on a single criterion using an ODP topic distribution. In future work, it would be interesting to explore personalization based on a variety of different criteria. Although the same probabilistic model can naively be used by simply using a larger state space for the user and document latent variables, it would be better to consider the structure underlying the various personalization criteria. We would likely need to resort to approximate inference methods to maintain low ranking latency. Learning user profiles also becomes more difficult in this setting, as we mentioned in Section 4.

The objective functions that we optimize to learn the user profiles are convex, making it straightforward to design online learning algorithms for the user profiles. This would give a simple update to use for θ_u after observing each new search query, and would guarantee low regret relative to the best possible θ_u chosen in hindsight. We can also consider smoothing across similar users, in contrast to our current approach which only uses a single user's data when learning the parameter vector θ_u.

Acknowledgements

Thanks to Dan Liebling and Josh Feng for assistance with data collection and classification.

References

[1] P. Bennett, K. Svore, and S. Dumais. Classification-enhanced ranking. In *WWW '10*, pages 111–120, 2010.

[2] H. Cao, D. Hu, D. Shen, D. Jiang, J.-T. Sun, E. Chen, and Q. Yang. Context-aware query classification. In *SIGIR '09*, pages 3–10, 2009.

[3] H. Cao, D. Jiang, J. Pei, Q. He, Z. Liao, E. Chen, and H. Li. Context-aware query suggestion by mining click-through and session data. In *KDD '08*, pages 875–883, 2008.

[4] P. Chirita, W. Nejdl, R. Paiu, and C. Kohlschutter. Using ODP metadata to personalize search. In *SIGIR '05*, pages 178–185, 2005.

[5] N. Craswell and M. Szummer. Random walks on the click graph. In *SIGIR '07*, pages 239–246, 2007.

[6] M. Daoud, L. Tamine-Lechani, M. Boughanem, and B. Chebaro. A session based personalized search using an ontological user profile. In *SOC '09*, 2009.

[7] Z. Dou, R. Song, and J. Wen. A large-scale evaluation and analysis of personalized search strategies. In *WWW '07*, pages 581–590, New York, NY, USA, 2007. ACM.

[8] J. Gao, W. Yuan, X. Li, K. Deng, and J.-Y. Nie. Smoothing clickthrough data for web search ranking. In *SIGIR '09*, pages 355–362, 2009.

[9] S. Gauch, J. Chaffee, and A. Pretschner. Ontology-based user profiles for search and browsing. In *WIAS '03*, pages 219–234, 2003.

[10] M. Grant and S. Boyd. CVX: Matlab software for disciplined convex programming, version 1.21. http://cvxr.com/cvx, Apr. 2011.

[11] M. Jordan. Graphical models. *Statistical Science (Special Issue on Bayesian Statistics)*, 19:140–155, 2004.

[12] F. Liu, C. Yu, and W. Meng. Personalized web search for improving retrieval effectiveness. *IEEE Transactions on Knowledge and Data Engineering*, 16(1):28–40, 2004.

[13] N. Matthijs and F. Radlinski. Personalizing web search using long term browsing history. In *Proceedings of the fourth ACM international conference on Web Search and Data Mining*, WSDM '11, pages 25–34, New York, NY, USA, 2011. ACM.

[14] J. Pitkow, H. Schütze, T. Cass, R. Cooley, D. Turnbull, A. Edmonds, E. Adar, and T. Breuel. Personalized search. *CACM*, 45(9):50–55, 2002.

[15] X. Shen, B. Tan, and C. Zhai. Context-sensitive information retrieval using implicit feedback. In *SIGIR '05*, pages 43–50, 2005.

[16] M. Speretta and S. Gauch. Personalizing search based on user search histories. In *WI '05*, pages 622–628, 2005.

[17] B. Tan, X. Shen, and C. Zhai. Mining long-term search history to improve search accuracy. In *SIGKDD '06*, pages 718–723, 2006.

[18] J. Teevan, S. Dumais, and E. Horvitz. Personalizing search via automated analysis of interests and activities. In *SIGIR '05*, pages 449–456, 2005.

[19] J. Teevan, S. Dumais, and E. Horvitz. Potential for personalization. *ACM TOCHI*, 17(1), 2010.

[20] J. Teevan, S. Dumais, and D. Liebling. To personalize or not to personalize: modeling queries with variation in user intent. In *SIGIR '08*, pages 163–170, 2008.

[21] K. Wang, T. Walker, and Z. Zheng. Pskip: Estimating relevant ranking quality from web search clickthrough data. In *SIGKDD '09*, pages 1355–1364, 2009.

[22] R. White and S. Drucker. Investigating behavioral variability in web search. In *WWW '07*, pages 21–30, 2007.

[23] R. W. White, P. N. Bennett, and S. T. Dumais. Predicting short-term interests using activity-based search context. In *CIKM '10*, pages 1009–1018, 2010.

[24] C. X. Zhai, W. W. Cohen, and J. Lafferty. Beyond independent relevance: methods and evaluation metrics for subtopic retrieval. In *SIGIR '03*, pages 10–17, 2003.

Effective Query Formulation with Multiple Information Sources

Michael Bendersky
Dept. of Computer Science
U. of Massachusetts
Amherst, MA
bemike@cs.umass.edu

Donald Metzler
Information Sciences Institute
U. of Southern California
Marina del Rey, CA
metzler@isi.edu

W. Bruce Croft
Dept. of Computer Science
U. of Massachusetts
Amherst, MA
croft@cs.umass.edu

ABSTRACT

Most standard information retrieval models use a single source of information (e.g., the retrieval corpus) for query formulation tasks such as term and phrase weighting and query expansion. In contrast, in this paper, we present a unified framework that automatically optimizes the combination of information sources used for effective query formulation. The proposed framework produces fully weighted and expanded queries that are both more effective and more compact than those produced by the current state-of-the-art query expansion and weighting methods. We conduct an empirical evaluation of our framework for both newswire and web corpora. In all cases, our combination of multiple information sources for query formulation is found to be more effective than using any single source. The proposed query formulations are especially advantageous for large scale web corpora, where they also reduce the number of terms required for effective query expansion, and improve the diversity of the retrieved results.

Categories and Subject Descriptors

H.3.3 [**Information Storage and Retrieval**]: Information Search and Retrieval

General Terms

Algorithms, Experimentation

Keywords

Query formulation, query expansion, external sources

1. INTRODUCTION

Most of today's commercial web search engines heavily rely on sophisticated machine learned ranking functions to produce high quality results. Such ranking functions typically combine evidence from hundreds, or even thousands, of different features[1]. Amongst the most basic and essential of these features are those that match the text of the query to the text of the document, which are often referred to as *text matching features*. The quality of text matching features can often be a key factor in the success of the learned ranking function [21].

The derivation of text matching features depends on the process of *query formulation* – a process during which the original keyword query issued by the user is transformed into a structured query representation that is consumed by the search engine. A standard query formulation process usually involves query segmentation into atomic concepts, weighting of these concepts and query expansion with related concepts, among other possible transformations.

Up until now, most of the research that has gone into improving the process of query formulation has been fragmented, and has not produced a unified query formulation framework. Without such a framework, it is difficult for researchers and practitioners to systematically and monotonically improve the effectiveness of the text matching capabilities of their retrieval systems. Instead, to achieve a high level of effectiveness, it is often necessary to mix and match ideas from multiple, competing methodologies or techniques in ways that are often heuristic, inefficient, or sub-optimal.

Nearly all of the recent advances in query formulation have been a result of research on improving one of the following types of query transformation: identification and matching of atomic query concepts, concept weighting and query expansion. For effective concept identification and matching, researchers employed retrieval methods based on the Markov random field (MRF) model [6, 28] and the positional language models [24, 25]. For improved term weighting, researchers proposed unsupervised methods such as term frequency saturation, document length normalization, and field weighting (e.g., BM25F [34]), as well as supervised methods that estimate the global term importance based on a variety of external sources (e.g., number of times a term occurs in a query log or a title of a Wikipedia article) [20, 19, 6, 7]. Finally, best practice query expansion techniques include, among others, positional relevance models [25], latent concept expansion (LCE) [29], parameterized query expansion (PQE) [7], and expansion using external corpora [12, 45].

While there has been some synergistic research across these types of query transformations (e.g., positional language models giving rise to positional relevance models [25]),

[1]For instance, a recently released dataset by Yahoo! (`http://learningtorankchallenge.yahoo.com/`) includes approximately 700 features.

Permission to make digital or hard copies of all or part of this work for personal or classroom use is granted without fee provided that copies are not made or distributed for profit or commercial advantage and that copies bear this notice and the full citation on the first page. To copy otherwise, to republish, to post on servers or to redistribute to lists, requires prior specific permission and/or a fee.
WSDM'12, February 8–12, 2012, Seattle, Washington, USA.
Copyright 2012 ACM 978-1-4503-0747-5/12/02 ...$10.00.

Latent Concept Expansion *(Retrieval Corpus)* Query	Expansion Terms
0.479 er	0.145 tv
0.479 tv	0.112 er
0.479 show	0.055 folge
0.120 er tv	0.054 selbst
0.120 tv show	0.034 show
	...

Mean Average Precision 12.29

Latent Concept Expansion *(Wikipedia)* Query	Expansion Terms
0.464 er	0.156 tv
0.464 tv	0.074 bisexual
0.464 show	0.066 film
0.116 er tv	0.064 season
0.116 tv show	0.059 series
	...

Mean Average Precision 25.68

Query Formulation *(Multiple Sources)* Query	Expansion Terms
0.297 er	0.085 season
0.168 tv	0.065 episode
0.192 show	0.051 dr
0.051 er tv	0.043 drama
0.012 tv show	0.036 series
	...

Mean Average Precision 38.31

Table 1: Comparison of the performance of the latent concept expansion with retrieval corpus or Wikipedia to the performance of the query formulation using multiple information sources for the query *"ER TV Show"*.

there does not exist a robust, unified framework capable of encompassing the current state-of-the-art across all transformation types. Accordingly, in this paper, we propose a novel *query formulation framework* that combines the best aspects of each of these transformations in a highly robust and effective manner and produces a richly structured representation of a keyword query.

As an example, Table 1 compares the output of the proposed query formulation method for the keyword query *"ER TV Show"* to the output of the latent concept expansion (LCE) method [29] that uses either the retrieval corpus or the Wikipedia corpus for query expansion. Both of these expansion strategies have been shown to be highly effective strategies in previous work [29, 16, 26, 45]. It is clear from Table 1 that there are two main advantages of our query formulation approach compared to the LCE method.

First, LCE assumes equal importance among query terms and query phrases by assigning them fixed weights. On the other hand, our query formulation assigns relative importance weights, based on evidence from multiple information sources, to explicit query terms and phrases. For instance, in the context of the query *"ER TV Show"*, the most important term is *"er"* and the phrase *"er tv"* is more important than the phrase *"tv show"*.

Second, LCE uses a single source for expansion, which can sometimes lead to topic drift. As a case in point, in Table 1, LCE with the retrieval corpus expands the query with non-English terms *folge* and *selbst*, and LCE with Wikipedia expands the query with non-helpful terms *bisexual* and *film*. To combat topic drift, the proposed query formulation method combines evidence from multiple sources (including, among others, the retrieval corpus and Wikipedia) to derive a relevant and diverse list of expansion terms.

Due to these advantages, we hypothesize that a unified query formulation approach that uses multiple information sources will yield better results than any of the previously proposed query transformation methods in isolation. In fact, for the query in Table 1, our query formulation improves the retrieval performance by 50% compared to the best performing LCE-based method.

The query formulation method presented in this paper synthesizes three main research directions. First, it incorporates the highly effective term proximity matching of the sequential dependence model, which was first proposed by Metzler and Croft [28]. Second, it incorporates the state-of-the-art parameterized concept weighting framework recently proposed by Bendersky et al. [7]. Finally, it is inspired by previous work that demonstrates that query expansion using external corpora is highly effective [12, 23, 45].

The end result of this synthesis is a unified framework, which distills effective and compact query formulations, such as the one shown in Table 1. Empirical results show that these query formulations are significantly more effective than many of the current state-of-the-art text matching methods used as baselines.

This work has three primary contributions. First, we develop a novel unified query formulation framework that (a) supports arbitrary query concepts (e.g., unigrams, bigrams, expansion terms, etc.); (b) supports explicit query concept weighting; and (c) extracts and weights expansion terms using a parameterized approach that leverages evidence from external information sources. All of the weighting and expansion models are learned using a simple, yet effective learning to rank approach.

Second, the proposed query formulation framework naturally gives rise to a text matching function that scores a query formulation with respect to a document. This matching function can be used alone as a (text-only) retrieval model or within a machine learned ranking function as a highly effective text matching feature.

Finally, we carry out a detailed experimental evaluation of the proposed framework. Our results demonstrate that the proposed approach achieves state-of-the-art effectiveness compared to a number of highly competitive baseline systems. Our experimental evaluation also shows that our proposed approach has desirable efficiency and robustness properties, and also achieves strong performance in terms of a number of diversity metrics.

The remainder of this paper is laid out as follows. First, Section 2 describes the theoretical underpinnings of the proposed query formulation framework. Next, Section 3 discusses the external sources of evidence that we use to formulate highly effective queries. Section 4 highlights related work, while Section 5 presents the findings of our experimental evaluation. Finally, Section 6 concludes the paper.

2. QUERY FORMULATION

The process of *query formulation* (also referred to as *query rewriting* or *query transformation* [11]) modifies the original keyword query submitted by the user to the search engine in order to better represent the underlying intent of the query. The formulated query is then used as an input to the search engine's ranking algorithm. Thus, the primary goal of query formulation is to improve the overall quality of the ranking presented to the user in response to her query [11].

Query formulation is usually divided into two main processing stages. The first processing stage, which is usually referred to as *query refinement* [13], alters the query on the morphological level (e.g., tokenization, spelling corrections, stemming, etc.).

After the query refinement stage is completed, the second processing stage alters the query on the structural level. Such structural alterations may include, among other actions, segmenting the query into atomic concepts (i.e., combinations of terms), assigning weights to these concepts, or expanding the query with related weighted concepts.

In this work, our focus is on the structural stage of query formulation. Hence, we assume that all the input queries are either spelled and tokenized correctly, or have undergone the query refinement process.

Accordingly, given an input keyword query Q, we assume that we can identify a weighted set of concepts $\mathcal{K}_Q$, which can be associated with the user intent underlying this query. Note that the concepts in the set $\mathcal{K}_Q$ can be either explicitly present in the query Q, or associated with it via some process of query expansion (e.g., pseudo-relevance feedback [44]).

Once the set of concepts $\mathcal{K}_Q$ is identified, and the concept weights are determined, we can score the documents in the collection using a linear weighted combination of the matches of concepts in the set $\mathcal{K}_Q$, and rank the documents based on this score. Formally, the score of document D in the collection can be written as

$$sc(Q, D) \triangleq \sum_{\kappa \in \mathcal{K}_Q} \lambda(\kappa, Q) f(\kappa, D) \quad (1)$$

The ranking function in Equation 1 consists of two components. First, a concept matching function $f(\kappa, D)$ measures the relatedness between the document D and the concept κ. Second, a concept weighting function $\lambda(\kappa, Q)$ measures the importance of the concept κ for query Q. Intuitively, Equation 1 assigns higher scores to documents that match more of the important concepts related to the query. In the remainder of this section, we detail the modeling and the estimation of the concept matching function and the concept weighting function.

2.1 Concept Matching Function

The concept matching function $f(\kappa, D)$ assigns a score to the matches of concept κ in the document D. This function may take various forms, however in information retrieval applications it is commonly a monotonic function, i.e., its value increases with the number of times concept κ matches document D.

In this paper, we assume that the matching function $f(\kappa,D)$ is estimated using the log of the probability of concept κ given document D with Dirichlet smoothing [46], i.e.,

$$f(\kappa, D) = \log \frac{tf_{\kappa,D} + \mu \frac{tf_{\kappa,\mathcal{C}}}{|\mathcal{C}|}}{|D| + \mu}, \quad (2)$$

where $tf_{\kappa,D}$ and $tf_{\kappa,\mathcal{C}}$ are the number of concept occurrences in the document and the collection, respectively; μ is a free parameter; $|D|$ is the number of terms in D, and $|\mathcal{C}|$ is the total number of terms in the collection.

We use this probabilistic estimate as a concept matching function since it is convenient and efficient to compute and exhibits state-of-the-art retrieval performance in other concept-based retrieval models [7, 28, 29]. However, other commonly used matching functions (such as BM25 [35] or DFR [2]) can be substituted in Equation 1 without loss of generality.

2.2 Concept Weighting Function

The concept importance function $\lambda(\kappa, Q)$ measures the importance of concept κ for conveying the user intent underlying the query Q. In its simplest form, the concept importance function may be a single collection statistic associated with the concept κ such as inverse document frequency [40].

Recently, researchers have found that supervised models of concept weighting that leverage statistics from external information sources (e.g., query logs, Wikipedia, large n-gram repositories, large newswire collections, etc.) can significantly improve the retrieval performance [20, 19, 6, 7]. Thus far, however, these models were mainly used for weighting the explicit query concepts [20, 6] or re-weighting the expansion terms that were associated with the query via pseudo-relevance feedback using the retrieval corpus [7, 8].

In contrast, in this section we show that external information sources can also be used, in addition to concept weighting, to select and weight related and helpful terms with which the original query can be expanded. As the example in Table 1 demonstrates, such terms can be more relevant and diverse than the expansion terms that are obtained through the standard process of pseudo-relevance feedback on the retrieval corpus [17, 29].

To this end, we define a set of external information sources $\mathcal{S}$, which we use as a basis for deriving features for either concept weighting or query expansion. To make our approach as widely applicable as possible, we make no assumptions about the internal structure of these sources, and treat them as standard unstructured textual corpora.

In Section 2.2.1 we explain how to use the set of external sources $\mathcal{S}$ for weighting the explicit query concepts. Then, in Section 2.2.2, we describe how the set of external sources $\mathcal{S}$ is used to expand the original query with new related terms. We defer the precise definition of the external information sources in the set $\mathcal{S}$ used for weighting and expansion to Section 3.

2.2.1 Explicit Query Concepts

Following previous work, we define an explicit query concept as any combination of terms that appears in the query and can be matched within a document in the retrieval corpus [6, 7]. In particular, we use a subset of concepts first proposed by Metzler and Croft [28], and restrict our attention to single terms and adjacent bigram phrases and proximities. This provides a set of explicit query concepts, which we refer to as $\mathcal{X}_Q$. The set of concepts $\mathcal{X}_Q$ is compact (it is linear in the number of query terms), and has been shown to attain highly effective retrieval performance [6, 7, 28, 29, 16].

To weight a concept $\kappa_x \in \mathcal{X}_Q$, we use the *parameterized weighting* approach, proposed by Bendersky et al. [6, 7], which leverages the statistics from external information sources to assign reliable weights to the concepts in the query. Formally, the concept weight of κ_x is modeled as

$$\lambda(\kappa_x, Q) = \sum_{\varphi \in \Phi_\mathcal{S}} w_\varphi \varphi(\kappa_x, Q, \sigma). \quad (3)$$

As can be seen from Equation 3, the weight $\lambda(\kappa_x, Q)$ of the concept $\kappa_x \in \mathcal{X}_Q$ is expressed by a weighted combination of *importance features* $\Phi_\mathcal{S}$, which are defined over a set of sources $\mathcal{S}$. Each importance feature $\varphi \in \Phi_\mathcal{S}$ is associated with an explicit query concept κ_x and is computed over a source $\sigma \in \mathcal{S}$.

2.2.2 Expansion Terms

A key observation from Equation 1 is that the proposed ranking function is not limited to the set of explicit query concepts $\mathcal{X}_Q$ defined in the previous section. Instead, the ranking function may include expansion concepts from sources other than the search query or the retrieval corpus, which has been the standard practice in previous work [6, 7, 8, 28, 29]. While any combination of terms can serve as an expansion concept, in this work we focus on expansion with single terms, mainly for ensuring the efficiency of the expansion concept selection process.

To incorporate expansion terms from external sources in the set $\mathcal{S}$, we first obtain a large pool of potential expansion terms associated with an information source $\sigma \in \mathcal{S}$ using pseudo-relevance feedback. To this end, we first rank documents in the source σ using the ranking function

$$sc(Q,D) \triangleq \sum_{\kappa_x \in \mathcal{X}_Q} \lambda(\kappa_x, Q) f(\kappa_x, D), \quad (4)$$

which utilizes only explicit query concepts and their corresponding weights. Then, each term in the pseudo-relevant set of documents $\mathcal{R}_\sigma$ (top ranked documents in source σ) is assigned an *expansion score*

$$\psi(\kappa, Q, \sigma) = \sum_{D \in \mathcal{R}_\sigma} \exp\left(\gamma_1 sc(Q,D) + \gamma_2 f(\kappa, D) - \gamma_3 \log \frac{tf_{\kappa,\sigma}}{|\sigma|}\right), \quad (5)$$

where γ_i's are free parameters.

Note that Equation 5 uses the same concept expansion weighting scheme used by Latent Concept Expansion [29]. The score $\psi(\kappa, Q, \sigma)$ is a linear combination of three key components: document relevance (manifested by the document score $sc(Q,D)$), weight of the term in the pseudo-relevant set $\mathcal{R}_\sigma$ (manifested by the matching function $f(\kappa,D)$), and the inverse of the frequency of the term in the source σ ($-\log \frac{tf_{\kappa,\sigma}}{|\sigma|}$), which dampens the scores of very common terms, thereby improving the quality of the initial pool $\mathcal{E}_Q^{init}$.

Finally, at most M terms with the highest value of $\psi(\kappa, Q, \sigma)$ per source σ are added to $\mathcal{E}_Q^{init}$, the initial pool of expansion terms[2]. This ensures that the size of the initial pool $\mathcal{E}_Q^{init}$ is bounded by $|\mathcal{E}_Q^{init}| \leq M|\mathcal{S}|$.

Once the initial pool $\mathcal{E}_Q^{init}$ is obtained, we assign a weight to each unique term $\kappa_e \in \mathcal{E}_Q^{init}$, using the weighted combination of expansion scores

$$\lambda(\kappa_e, Q) = \sum_{\psi \in \Psi_\mathcal{S}} w_\psi \psi(\kappa_e, Q, \sigma). \quad (6)$$

According to Equation 6, the weight $\lambda(\kappa_e, Q)$ of the term $\kappa_e \in \mathcal{E}_Q^{init}$ is expressed by a weighted combination of *expansion scores* $\Psi_\mathcal{S}$, which is defined over a set of sources $\mathcal{S}$. Each expansion score $\psi \in \Psi_\mathcal{S}$ is associated with an expansion term κ_e and query Q, and is computed over a source $\sigma \in \mathcal{S}$. To handle missing terms, if κ_e is not one of the top M terms selected per source σ, we set $\psi(\kappa_e, Q, \sigma) = 0$.

To ensure efficient query expansion, we retain only the top K terms[3] from the initial pool $\mathcal{E}_Q^{init}$, based on Equation 6. We refer to this small set of expansion terms as $\mathcal{E}_Q$.

[2]To ensure that the initial pool $\mathcal{E}_Q^{init}$ is large enough for selecting diverse expansion terms, we set $M = 100$.

[3]In all the experiments in this paper, $K \leq 10$.

2.3 Parameter Estimation

To better illustrate the free parameters that need to be estimated in order to complete the query formulation derivation, we substitute the weighting function $\lambda(\kappa, Q)$ in Equation 1 with its derivations in Equation 3 and Equation 6, which yields

$$sc(Q,D) \triangleq \sum_{\kappa \in \mathcal{K}_Q} \lambda(\kappa, Q) f(\kappa, D) =$$
$$\sum_{\varphi \in \Phi_\mathcal{S}} w_\varphi \sum_{\kappa_x \in \mathcal{X}_Q} \varphi(\kappa_x, Q, \sigma) f(\kappa_x, D) +$$
$$\sum_{\psi \in \Psi_\mathcal{S}} w_\psi \sum_{\kappa_e \in \mathcal{E}_Q} \psi(\kappa_e, Q, \sigma) f(\kappa_e, D). \quad (7)$$

Equation 7 demonstrates that the final document score is determined by the combination of explicit query concept matches (matches in the set $\mathcal{X}_Q$), and the expansion term matches (matches in the set $\mathcal{E}_Q$). Accordingly, the free parameters in Equation 7 are: (a) the parameters that combine the importance features (w_φ), and (b) the parameters that combine the expansion scores (w_ψ).

To estimate these two sets of parameters, we use a three-stage optimization approach, which leverages the available relevance data as a training set. We use this three-stage optimization approach due to the fact that the setting of the parameters w_φ will influence the choice of the set of expansion terms in the initial set $\mathcal{E}_Q^{init}$, which will consequently influence the setting of the parameters w_ψ (as described in Section 2.2.2) that control the choice of terms in the expansion set $\mathcal{E}_Q$.

Stage I First, we optimize the set of parameters that combine the importance features

$$\{w_\varphi | \varphi \in \Phi_\mathcal{S}\}.$$

This determines the weights assigned to the explicit query concepts in the set $\mathcal{X}_Q$ (see Equation 3).

Stage II We then obtain an initial set of expansion terms $\mathcal{E}_Q^{init}$, by using the parameters w_φ (obtained at Stage I) in Equation 4.

Stage III Finally, we optimize the set of parameters that combine the expansion scores

$$\{w_\psi | \psi \in \Psi_\mathcal{S}\}.$$

This determines the choice of top K expansion terms in the set $\mathcal{E}_Q$ used for query formulation and their weights (see Equation 6).

For parameter optimization at Stage I and Stage III, we use the coordinate ascent (CA) algorithm proposed by Metzler and Croft [30]. The CA algorithm iteratively optimizes a target metric on a given training set of query-document relevance judgments (in our case, retrieval metric such as MAP) by performing a series of one-dimensional line searches. It repeatedly cycles through each of the parameters w, holding all other parameters fixed while optimizing it. This process is performed iteratively over all parameters until the gain in the target metric is below a certain threshold. Although we use the CA algorithm primarily for its simplicity, efficiency and effectiveness, any other learning to rank approach that optimizes the parameters for linear models (see Li [21] for a survey on learning to rank techniques) can be adopted as well.

Sources used for concept weighting		Sources used for query expansion	
Source	*Extracted Importance Features*	*Source*	*Unit of Retrieval*
Google N-grams	Frequency of concept κ	ClueWeb Heading Text	Single line of heading text (as defined by the <h1> – <h6> tags)
MSN Query Log	Frequency of concept κ	ClueWeb Anchor Text	Single line of anchor text (as defined by the <a> tag)
Wikipedia Titles	Frequency of concept κ	Wikipedia Corpus	Single article
Retrieval Corpus	Document frequency of concept κ Collection frequency of concept κ	Retrieval Corpus	Single document

Table 2: External information sources used for concept importance weighting (Section 2.2.1) and query expansion (Section 2.2.2). All the frequency features are log-scaled.

Retrieval Corpus	Wikipedia	Anchor Text	Heading Text	*Combined*
chemical, weapon, toxic, convention, substance, gas, destruction, product, plant, mirzayanov, ...	chemical, agent, gas, weapon, warfare, war, poison, mustard, disseminate, nerve, ...	toxic, chemical, cigarette, tobacco, terrorist, tts, weapon, leach, terror, wwf, ...	toxic, chemical, weapon, terrorist, terror, assess, biology, behavior, incinerate, emission, ...	*weapon, agent, gas, russia, convention, mustard, warfare, substance, destruction, product, ...*

Table 3: Comparison between the lists of expansion terms derived from the individual external information sources for the query *"toxic chemical weapon"* and the combined list produced by our query formulation method.

3. INFORMATION SOURCES

In this section, we provide a detailed description of the set of external information sources $\mathcal{S}$ used for query formulation. As described in Section 2.2, we make no assumptions about the internal structure of these sources, and treat them as unstructured textual corpora. We either extract some collection-based statistics from the sources in the set $\mathcal{S}$ (for computing the importance features associated with the explicit query concepts in the set $\mathcal{X}_Q$ — see Section 2.2.1), or use them to perform pseudo-relevance feedback (for computing the expansion scores associated with the expansion terms in the set $\mathcal{E}_Q^{init}$ — see Section 2.2.2).

It is theoretically possible to use the same information sources for deriving both the importance features and the expansion scores. In practice, however, a single external source is commonly better suited for only one of these tasks. For instance, the Google N-grams source (a large collection of web n-gram counts) is useful for concept weighting, but not for query expansion. On the other hand, an entire external document collection such as Wikipedia is more suitable for query expansion.

Accordingly, in Table 2 we provide a list of external information sources along with their usage. For sources used for concept weighting, Table 2 defines the extracted importance features, which are similar to features used in previous work [4, 6, 7, 20, 43]. For sources used for query expansion, Table 2 defines a unit of retrieval, which is used for pseudo-relevance feedback from the source. As external sources for query expansion, we use, in addition to the retrieval corpus, the heading text and the anchor text extracted from ClueWeb09, a large, publicly available web collection[4], as well as an English Wikipedia corpus.

As an example of the role that the external sources may play in query formulation, Table 3 demonstrates the expansion terms derived from the external information sources for the query *"toxic chemical weapon"*. Note that the *Combined* column in Table 3, which is the output of the process described in Section 2.2, includes expansion terms which are more relevant and address more of the query aspects than those produced by any individual source. For instance, it includes the terms *russia*, *agent*, *mustard* and *warfare*, which do not appear in the top terms obtained via pseudo-relevance feedback on the retrieval corpus. As a result, in this case, our query formulation approach improves the retrieval effectiveness by 33% over a method that uses pseudo-relevance feedback with the retrieval corpus, and by 14% over a method that uses pseudo-relevance feedback with Wikipedia.

4. RELATED WORK

The work presented in this paper integrates insights from several research areas into a unified and principled query formulation framework. In this section, we provide a brief overview of these research areas, and their relation to our work.

First, our framework is based on concept matching, rather than simple term matching used in the standard bag-of-words retrieval models [33, 35]. As such, it draws on the current research that goes beyond terms and utilizes phrases, proximities and term spans for information retrieval [28, 24, 31, 39]. Specifically, we adopt the *sequential dependence model* first proposed by Metzler and Croft [28], which incorporates single terms, adjacent bigram phrases and proximities.

Second, our framework is inspired by the recent research that leverages external information sources for supervised term and concept weighting [4, 6, 7, 20, 18, 14, 27, 42]. This research is mainly motivated by the need to address the challenge of retrieval with verbose queries, which often mix important and redundant concepts [3, 4, 20, 42]. The novelty of our work compared to this previous research is that, in addition to concept weighting, we use the external information sources for selecting helpful and diverse expansion terms.

Finally, our method uses pseudo-relevance feedback for query expansion, a practice which has a long and successful history in information retrieval (e.g., [8, 17, 25, 29, 44] to name just a few). Most of this research, however, has not been applied on the scale of web corpora, and only uses the retrieval corpora as a source for pseudo-relevance feedback. More recently, researchers started to examine the benefits

[4]http://boston.lti.cs.cmu.edu/clueweb09/

⟨*title*⟩	*Robust04*		*Gov2*		*ClueWeb-B*	
	nDCG@20	MAP	nDCG@20	MAP	nDCG@20	MAP
SD	41.78	25.85	43.24	30.90	21.36	19.37
WSD	42.02	26.10	44.06	31.68	22.20	20.23
MSF[10]	**44.13**$_s^w$	**30.49**$_s^w$ *(+17.9/+16.9)*	**44.91**	**34.35**$_s^w$ *(+11.2/+8.4)*	**25.76**$_s^w$	**23.96**$_s^w$ *(+23.7/+18.4)*

⟨*desc*⟩	*Robust04*		*Gov2*		*ClueWeb-B*	
	nDCG@20	MAP	nDCG@20	MAP	nDCG@20	MAP
SD	40.85	25.70	40.69	27.23	17.47	12.90
WSD	43.16	27.82	41.74	28.53	18.78	13.81
MSF[10]	**44.86**$_s^w$	**30.68**$_s^w$ *(+19.4/+10.3)*	**43.13**$_s$	**31.10**$_s^w$ *(+14.2/+9.0)*	**20.32**$_s$	**15.23**$_s^w$ *(+18.0/+10.3)*

Table 4: Comparison with the query weighting methods. Statistically significant difference of MSF over the baselines are marked using s and w, for SD and WSD baselines, respectively. Best result per column is marked by boldface. The numbers in parenthesis indicate improvement over SD and WSD baselines, respectively.

of external information sources for pseudo-relevance feedback. Diverse sources such as Wikipedia [5, 26, 22, 45], large web and news corpora [12] and social bookmarking data [23] were found to be beneficial for document retrieval on both newswire and web corpora.

While each of the above parts of query formulation process (namely, concept detection, concept weighting and query expansion) has been extensively studied, there is still a lack of holistic approaches to query formulation framework, which integrate the above areas of research. Developing such an approach is our goal in this paper.

5. EVALUATION

In this section, we describe the details of our experimental evaluation. First, in Section 5.1 we explain the experimental setup used for our experiments. In Section 5.2 and Section 5.3 we compare the proposed query formulation framework to several baselines that use query weighting and/or query expansion. In Section 5.4 and Section 5.5 we further analyze our method, and explore its sensitivity to the number of expansion terms and its robustness. Finally, in Section 5.6 we examine the impact of query formulation with multiple information sources on the diversity of the retrieved results.

5.1 Experimental Setup

The retrieval experiments described in this section are implemented using Indri, an open-source search engine [41]. The structured query language implemented by Indri natively supports multiple concept types, including exact phrases and proximity matches, as well as custom term weighting schemes. As a result, Indri provides a flexible and convenient platform for evaluating the performance of the proposed query formulation method.

Table 5 presents a summary of the TREC corpora[5] used in our experiments. The corpora vary both by type (*Robust04* is a newswire collection, *Gov2* is a crawl of the .gov domain, and *ClueWeb-B* is a set of pages with the highest crawl priority derived from a large web corpus), number of documents, and number of available topics, thereby providing a diverse experimental setup for assessing the robustness of our query formulation method.

During indexing and retrieval, both documents and queries are stemmed using the Krovetz stemmer, which is a "light" stemmer, as it makes use of inflectional linguistic morphology [15]. The Krovetz stemmer is especially suitable for web collections (e.g., *ClueWeb-B*) where aggressive stemming can decrease precision at top ranks [32]. Stopword removal is performed on both documents and queries using the standard INQUERY stopword list. The free parameter μ in the concept matching function $f(\kappa,D)$ (see Equation 2) is set to 2500, according to the default Indri configuration of the Dirichlet smoothing parameter.

[5] `http://trec.nist.gov/`

Name	# Docs	Topic Numbers
Robust04	528,155	301-450, 601-700
Gov2	25,205,179	701-850
ClueWeb-B	50,220,423	1-100

Table 5: Summary of TREC collections and topics used for evaluation.

⟨*title*⟩	discovery channel store
⟨*desc*⟩	Find locations and information about Discovery Channel stores and types of products they sell.

Figure 1: An example of ⟨*title*⟩ and ⟨*desc*⟩ portions of a TREC topic.

The performance of our query formulation method is compared to a number of state-of-the-art retrieval methods that perform concept weighting, query expansion or both. In all the comparisons, our query formulation method is denoted `MSF[N]` (*Multiple Source Formulation*), where N is the number of terms used for query expansion. As comparison metrics, we use both the mean average precision (*MAP*) of the entire ranked list, and the normalized discounted cumulative gain at the top ranks (*nDCG@20*).

The optimization of the free parameters for both the proposed query formulation method and all the baseline methods is done using 3-fold cross-validation with mean average precision (*MAP*) as the target metric. The statistical significance of differences in the performance of the `MSF` method with respect to other baselines is determined using a two-sided Fisher's randomization test [38] with 25,000 permutations and $\alpha < 0.05$.

As was shown in previous work [3, 4, 6, 7, 18], the impact of query formulation techniques varies significantly across queries of different length. In general, more verbose queries are expected to benefit more from effective weighting of both explicit query concepts and expansion terms, since they are more likely to contain concepts of varying importance.

⟨*title*⟩	*Robust04*		*Gov2*		*ClueWeb-B*	
	nDCG@20	MAP	nDCG@20	MAP	nDCG@20	MAP
LCE[10]	43.77	28.89	43.26	32.59	21.95	20.90
LCE-WP[10]	**44.63**	28.93	43.98	31.90	25.43	23.47
PQE[10]	44.23	29.06	44.58	33.64	21.94	20.82
MSF[10]	44.13	$\mathbf{30.49}^{p}_{l,lw}$ *(+4.9)*	$\mathbf{44.91}_{l}$	$\mathbf{34.35}^{p}_{l,lw}$ *(+2.1)*	$\mathbf{25.76}^{p}_{l}$	$\mathbf{23.96}^{p}_{l}$ *(+2.1)*

⟨*desc*⟩	*Robust04*		*Gov2*		*ClueWeb-B*	
	nDCG@20	MAP	nDCG@20	MAP	nDCG@20	MAP
LCE[10]	42.24	28.05	41.10	30.14	18.17	14.00
LCE-WP[10]	44,38	29.08	41.45	28.70	19.90	14.52
PQE[10]	44.32	29.56	42.86	30.96	18.35	14.10
MSF[10]	$\mathbf{44.86}_{l}$	$\mathbf{30.68}^{p}_{l,lw}$ *(+3.8)*	$\mathbf{43.13}_{l,lw}$	$\mathbf{31.10}_{lw}$ *(+0.5)*	$\mathbf{20.32}^{p}_{l}$	$\mathbf{15.23}^{p}_{l,lw}$ *(+4.8)*

Table 6: Comparison with the query expansion methods. Statistically significant difference of MSF over the baselines are marked using l, lw, and p, for LCE, LCE-WP and PQE baselines, respectively. Best result per column is marked by boldface. The numbers in parenthesis indicate improvement over the baseline with the best performance.

Thus, to test the performance of MSF across different query types we treat the ⟨*title*⟩ and the ⟨*desc*⟩ portions of TREC topics as two separate query sets in our experiments. The ⟨*title*⟩ and the ⟨*desc*⟩ versions of each query represent the same information need, but differ in their level of verbosity. The ⟨*title*⟩ query is a short keyword query, while the ⟨*desc*⟩ query is a verbose natural language description of the information need. Figure 1 shows an example of ⟨*title*⟩ and ⟨*desc*⟩ queries for a standard TREC topic.

5.2 Comparison to Query Weighting Methods

In this section, we compare the retrieval effectiveness of our query formulation method, MSF, which performs both concept weighting and query expansion using external information sources (see Section 3 for details of the sources used), to the performance of the methods that perform query weighting alone.

Our first baseline is the sequential dependence model, which was first proposed by Metzler and Croft [28]. The sequential dependence model, denoted SD, uses the same explicit query concepts (query terms, and adjacent bigram phrases and proximities) as our query formulation method. SD assigns fixed weights $\lambda(\kappa, Q)$ to all the concepts of the same type.

Following Metzler and Croft [28] we set these weights to 0.8, 0.1 and 0.1 for query terms, phrases and proximities, respectively. This parameter setting has been found to lead to a performance that is significantly superior to that of the standard bag-of-words models such as query likelihood or BM25 [28] for both TREC collections [28, 29] and web corpora [6].

Our second baseline is a weighted variant of the sequential dependence model, first proposed by Bendersky et al. [6]. The weighted sequential dependence model, denoted WSD, uses a combination of external sources for query concept weighting, but does not perform query expansion. It has been shown to attain significant gains over the SD method, especially for verbose queries, which contain concepts of varying importance [6, 7]. WSD uses the method described in Section 2.2.1 for estimating explicit concept weights, and the same set of sources for query weighting as in Table 2. As such, WSD allows us to examine the benefit provided by the *expansion* stage of the query formulation.

Table 4 compares the performance of the above baselines (SD and WSD) and our query formulation method, MSF, with 10 expansion terms. Table 4 unequivocally demonstrates the importance of query expansion for query formulation.

MSF is always more effective than the baselines that do not perform query expansion, and in all cases its improvements are statistically significant. These improvements are consistent across retrieval metrics, corpora and query types. The largest improvements are observed for short web queries (*ClueWeb-B*, ⟨*title*⟩ queries) where our method achieves effectiveness gains over 17% at high ranks (*nDCG@20* metric) and over 18% improvement in the quality of the entire ranked list (*MAP* metric).

5.3 Comparison to Query Expansion Methods

After comparing the effectiveness of the MSF method against methods that do not perform query expansion, in this section we focus on comparing its performance to that of current state-of-the-art query expansion methods.

First, we make use of the Latent Concept Expansion (LCE) method, which was shown to be a state-of-the query expansion method that uses a single collection [29, 16, 19]. Similarly to MSF, LCE uses Equation 5 to select expansion terms from the collection on which the pseudo-relevance feedback is performed.

As baselines, we implement two variants of LCE. The first baseline is denoted LCE. It is the standard version of Latent Concept Expansion, which performs the pseudo-relevance feedback on the retrieval corpus.

The second baseline is denoted LCE-WP. LCE-WP performs the pseudo-relevance feedback on Wikipedia, rather than the retrieval corpus. LCE-WP is based on some recent work that shows that query expansion using Wikipedia corpus can be beneficial, especially for short ambiguous queries over large web collections [5, 22, 26, 45].

In addition to the LCE-based baselines, we use the Parameterized Query Expansion method [7] as a baseline. This method, denoted PQE, combines explicit concept weighting and expansion term weighting in a unified framework that uses external information sources. The main difference between the PQE and the MSF methods, is that the former uses the external sources solely for weighting purposes, while the latter uses them also for expansion term selection.

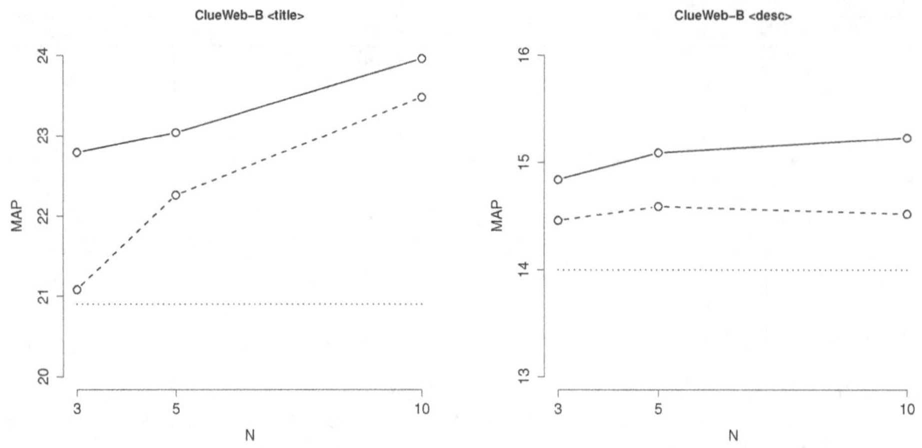

Figure 2: Varying the number of expansion terms (*ClueWeb-B* corpus). Dotted line indicates the performance of LCE[10]. Dashed and solid lines represent the performance of LCE-WP[N] and MSF[N], respectively.

Table 6 compares the effectiveness of the three baselines described above (`LCE`, `LCE-WP` and `PQE`) to the proposed `MSF` method, when 10 expansion terms are used. This comparison highlights the different positive aspects of `MSF` method.

The main observation from the Table 6 is that `MSF` is almost always more effective than any of the three baselines (except for *nDCG@20* for *Robust04*, where it is statistically indistinguishable from other methods). In contrast to the baselines, the performance of `MSF` is stable across corpora and query types. In comparison, the performance of the baselines is not as consistent. For instance, `LCE-WP` is more effective than `LCE` for *Robust04* and *ClueWeb-B*, but less effective for *Gov2*. Similarly, `PQE` outperforms LCE-based baselines for *Robust04* and *Gov2* corpora, but is not as effective for the *ClueWeb-B* corpus.

In addition, Table 6 clearly demonstrates the importance of using the external information sources for both concept weighting and expansion term selection. Compared to `PQE`, which uses the external sources solely for weighting purposes, `MSF` achieves significantly better performance on all metrics. This is especially evident in the case of the *ClueWeb-B* corpus, for which expansion using the retrieval corpus attains only marginal gains. For the *ClueWeb-B* corpus, `PQE` achieves merely a 2% gain over the `WSD` baseline for ⟨*title*⟩ queries, while `MSF` achieves over 18% gain (see Table 4). It is clear that in this case, using multiple sources for selecting the expansion terms, in addition to concept weighting, is highly beneficial.

Finally, Table 6 shows that the synergy of concept weighting and expansion term selection using external sources as performed by the `MSF` is superior to the ad-hoc approach that simply uses an external corpus (e.g., Wikipedia) for query expansion. `MSF` is more stable than `LCE-WP` across all collections, and is more effective even for the *ClueWeb-B* corpus, where expansion with Wikipedia was shown to be a highly effective strategy [5, 26].

5.4 Number of Expansion Terms

Massive query expansion with tens or even hundreds of terms, as is often done in TREC evaluation [8, 12] is not suitable for the scenario of web search, where the size of the retrieval corpus is large, and users expect low query latencies. Accordingly, in this section we explore the effect of query expansion with very few expansion terms, to demonstrate the scalability of the `MSF` method for web corpora.

In Figure 2 we plot the effectiveness (in terms of *MAP*) of query formulation methods that have the best performance for the *ClueWeb-B* corpus – `LCE-WP` and `MSF`– when using the 3, 5 and 10 highest weighted expansion terms. For comparison, we also plot the effectiveness of a standard query expansion method, `LCE` with 10 terms.

First, Figure 2 clearly demonstrates the superiority of both `LCE-WP` and `MSF` compared to `LCE`, even with fewer expansion terms. We can also see from Figure 2 that the superiority of the proposed `MSF` method over the `LCE-WP` method, which uses Wikipedia for query expansion, is not limited to the scenario in Table 6, where 10 expansion terms are used. The effectiveness gains of `MSF` over `LCE-WP` are consistent with minimal query expansion (3 or 5 additional terms) as well. For instance, when only 3 terms are used for query expansion, `MSF` achieves around 8% and 3% improvement over `LCE-WP` for ⟨*title*⟩ and ⟨*desc*⟩ queries, respectively.

Overall, the results in Figure 2 showcase the ability of the `MSF` method to produce both effective and compact query formulations, which could potentially scale to real world web search scenarios.

5.5 Robustness

In Table 6 we have shown that the `MSF` method significantly improves the overall performance compared to Latent Concept Expansion with the retrieval corpus (`LCE`) and Wikipedia (`LCE-WP`), and Parameterized Query Expansion (`PQE`). As discussed in Section 5.3, `LCE-WP` is a highly effective method for the *ClueWeb-B* corpus, while `LCE` and `PQE` are more suitable for the other two corpora. In this section, we analyze the *robustness* of `MSF`, compared to these methods. Following previous work [29], we define the robustness of the method as the number of queries improved or hurt (and by how much – in terms of *MAP*) as the result of the application of the method. A highly robust expansion technique will significantly improve many queries and only minimally hurt a few.

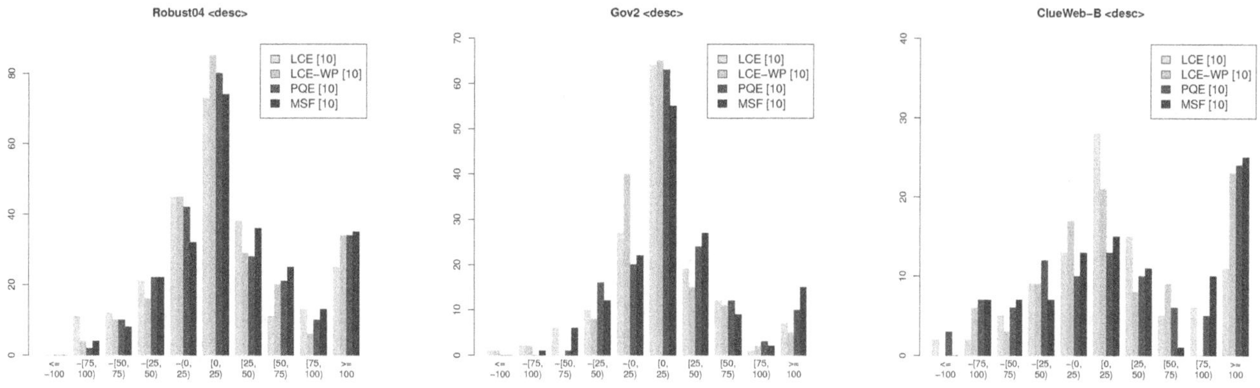

Figure 3: Robustness of the LCE, LCE-WP and MSF methods for the $\langle desc \rangle$ queries w.r.t. the SD method.

$\langle title \rangle$	α-nDCG@20	S-Recall@20	MAP-IA
WSD	22.36	46.04	9.20
PQE[10]	21.07	42.47	9.39
LCE-WP[10]	24.51	46.91	11.00
MSF[10]	$\mathbf{25.85}^{lw}_{w,p}$	$\mathbf{48.94}^{lw}_{p}$	$\mathbf{11.25}_{w,p}$

Table 7: Result diversification performance (*ClueWeb-B*). Statistically significant difference of MSF over the baselines are marked using w, p, and lw, for WSD, PQE and LCE-WP baselines, respectively. Best result per column is marked by boldface.

Figure 3 provides an analysis of the robustness of LCE, LCE-WP, PQE and MSF for the $\langle desc \rangle$ queries (which are, in general, harder than the $\langle title \rangle$ queries and benefit more from query expansion) with 10 expansion terms. The histograms in Figure 3 show, for various ranges of relative decreases or increases in *MAP*, the number of queries that were hurt or improved with respect to the SD baseline (see Table 4).

Figure 3 demonstrates that MSF is more robust compared to the other three methods. In all cases, MSF improves the performance of more queries than both LCE, LCE-WP and PQE. For instance, for the *Robust04* collection, MSF improves the performance of 72% of the queries w.r.t. SD, compared to 62%, 67% and 68% of the queries improved by LCE, LCE-WP and PQE respectively. Similar improvements are observed for the other two collections.

In addition, the MSF method is, on average, less likely to decrease the query performance, compared to the other methods. It hurts less queries than LCE and LCE-WP on all collections, and less queries than PQE on all collections except *Gov2*, where both methods hurt around 27% of the queries.

5.6 Impact on Result Diversification

Recently, result diversification in web search has become an active research topic [1, 9, 10, 36, 37]. Since web search queries are often underspecified and/or ambiguous, diversifying the search results may assist users with varying intents in finding relevant information in a single ranked list returned by the search engine. Due to the research interest in this problem, result diversification was chosen as a search task during the 2009 and 2010 TREC Web Tracks [10].

Effective result diversification is often achieved by *inter-query* approaches. These approaches combine results from queries that are found to be related to the original user query (e.g., through access to the query suggestions proposed by commercial search engines [36, 37]). However, even in the inter-query approaches, the retrieval effectiveness and diversity performance of each single query is important for obtaining the optimal diversification results [37].

Therefore, in this section we examine *intra-query* result diversification, i.e., the diversity performance that can be achieved by using the original user query alone. To this end, we compare the performance of the three best-performing baselines from Table 4 and Table 6 (WSD, PQE and LCE-WP) to that of the MSF method in terms of three standard diversity metrics. These diversity metrics include metrics that examine the diversity at the top ranks (α-nDCG and subtopic recall at rank 20) [9, 10], as well as a metric that measures the diversity of the entire ranked list (intent-aware MAP) [1].

Table 7 demonstrates the comparison of the result diversification performance of the different methods on the $\langle title \rangle$ queries for the *ClueWeb-B* collection[6]. Overall, MSF achieves the best diversity performance, especially for the diversity at the top ranks, where it achieves over 6% improvement over LCE-WP, the best-performing baseline.

In the context of search result diversification, it is interesting to note that previous work suggested that query expansion with the retrieval corpus may reduce diversity at top ranks [9]. The comparison between the WSD and the PQE baselines in Table 7 is in line with this finding. In contrast to the expansion with the retrieval corpus alone, the proposed MSF method helps to improve the diversity of the search results, since it combines expansion terms from different sources.

6. CONCLUSIONS

In this paper, we introduced a novel framework for query formulation. This framework synthesizes, in a principled and effective manner, arbitrary concept matches, concept weighting and query expansion. Our query formulation ap-

[6]We do not include the $\langle desc \rangle$ queries in our diversification performance analysis, since these are verbose and non-ambiguous queries that fully specify the user intent.

proach leverages external sources of information such as web n-gram counts, anchor and heading text extracted from a large web corpus, and articles and titles from Wikipedia for weighting the explicit query concepts as well as selecting relevant and diverse set of weighted expansion terms.

We perform a thorough empirical evaluation of our query formulation approach, MSF. Our experimental results unequivocally demonstrate the superiority of MSF to several state-of-the-art baselines that perform concept weighting, query expansion or both. Further analysis of the performance of the MSF method shows that it is highly robust across corpora and query types, enables compact query representations by reducing the number of required expansion terms, and improves the diversity of the retrieved results.

7. ACKNOWLEDGMENTS

This work was supported in part by the Center for Intelligent Information Retrieval and in part by ARRA NSF IIS-9014442. Any opinions, findings and conclusions or recommendations expressed in this material are those of the authors and do not necessarily reflect those of the sponsor.

8. REFERENCES

[1] R. Agrawal, S. Gollapudi, A. Halverson, and S. Ieong. Diversifying search results. In *Proc. of WSDM*, pages 5–14, 2009.

[2] G. Amati and C. J. Van Rijsbergen. Probabilistic models of information retrieval based on measuring the divergence from randomness. *ACM Transactions on Information Systems (TOIS)*, 20(4):357–389, October 2002.

[3] N. Balasubramanian, G. Kumaran, and V. R. Carvalho. Exploring reductions for long web queries. In *Proc. of SIGIR*, pages 571–578, 2010.

[4] M. Bendersky and W. B. Croft. Discovering key concepts in verbose queries. In *Proc. of SIGIR*, pages 491–498, 2008.

[5] M. Bendersky, D. Fisher, and W. B. Croft. UMass at TREC 2010 Web Track: Term Dependence, Spam Filtering and Quality Bias. In *Proc. of TREC-10*, 2011.

[6] M. Bendersky, D. Metzler, and W. B. Croft. Learning concept importance using a weighted dependence model. In *Proc. of WSDM*, pages 31–40, 2010.

[7] M. Bendersky, D. Metzler, and W. B. Croft. Parameterized concept weighting in verbose queries. In *Proc. of SIGIR*, 2011.

[8] G. Cao, J.-Y. Nie, J. Gao, and S. Robertson. Selecting good expansion terms for pseudo-relevance feedback. In *Proc. of SIGIR*, pages 243–250, 2008.

[9] C. L. Clarke, M. Kolla, G. V. Cormack, O. Vechtomova, A. Ashkan, S. Büttcher, and I. MacKinnon. Novelty and diversity in information retrieval evaluation. In *Proc. of SIGIR*, pages 659–666, 2008.

[10] C. L. A. Clarke, N. Craswell, and I. Soboroff. Overview of the TREC 2009 Web Track. In *Proc. of TREC-09*, 2010.

[11] W. B. Croft, M. Bendersky, H. Li, and G. Xu. Query representation and understanding workshop report. SIGIR Forum, December 2010.

[12] F. Diaz and D. Metzler. Improving the estimation of relevance models using large external corpora. In *Proc. of SIGIR*, pages 154–161, 2006.

[13] J. Guo, G. Xu, H. Li, and X. Cheng. A unified and discriminative model for query refinement. In *Proc. of SIGIR*, pages 379–386, New York, NY, USA, 2008.

[14] D. Hiemstra. Term-specific smoothing for the language modeling approach to information retrieval: the importance of a query term. In *Proc. of SIGIR*, pages 35–41, 2002.

[15] R. Krovetz. Viewing morphology as an inference process. In *Proc. of SIGIR*, pages 191–202, 1993.

[16] H. Lang, D. Metzler, B. Wang, and J.-T. Li. Improved latent concept expansion using hierarchical markov random fields. In *Proc. of CIKM*, pages 249–258, 2010.

[17] V. Lavrenko and W. B. Croft. Relevance Models in Information Retrieval. In W. B. Croft and J. Lafferty, editors, *Language modeling for Information Retrieval*, pages 11–56. Kluwer, 2003.

[18] M. Lease. An improved markov random field model for supporting verbose queries. In *Proc. of SIGIR*, pages 476–483, 2009.

[19] M. Lease. Incorporating relevance and pseudo-relevance feedback in the markov random field model. In *Proc. of TREC-08*, 2009.

[20] M. Lease, J. Allan, and W. B. Croft. Regression rank: Learning to meet the opportunity of descriptive queries. In *Proc. of ECIR*, pages 90–101, 2009.

[21] H. Li. *Learning to Rank for Information Retrieval and Natural Language Processing*. Morgan and Claypool Publishers, 2011.

[22] Y. Li, W. P. R. Luk, K. S. E. Ho, and F. L. K. Chung. Improving weak ad-hoc queries using wikipedia as external corpus. In *Proc. of SIGIR*, pages 797–798, 2007.

[23] Y. Lin, H. Lin, S. Jin, and Z. Ye. Social annotation in query expansion: a machine learning approach. In *Proc. of SIGIR*, pages 405–414, 2011.

[24] Y. Lv and C. Zhai. Positional language models for information retrieval. In *Proc. of SIGIR*, pages 299–306, 2009.

[25] Y. Lv and C. Zhai. Positional relevance model for pseudo-relevance feedback. In *Proc. of SIGIR*, pages 579–586, 2010.

[26] R. McCreadie, C. Macdonald, I. Ounis, J. Peng, and R. L. T. Santos. University of Glasgow at TREC 2009: Experiments with Terrier. In *Proc. of TREC-09*, 2010.

[27] Q. Mei, H. Fang, and C. Zhai. A study of Poisson query generation model for information retrieval. In *Proc. of SIGIR*, pages 319–326, 2007.

[28] D. Metzler and W. B. Croft. A Markov random field model for term dependencies. *Proc. of SIGIR*, pages 472–479, 2005.

[29] D. Metzler and W. B. Croft. Latent concept expansion using markov random fields. *Proc. of SIGIR*, pages 311–318, 2007.

[30] D. Metzler and W. B. Croft. Linear feature-based models for information retrieval. *Information Retrieval*, 10(3):257–274, 2007.

[31] G. Mishne and M. de Rijke. Boosting Web Retrieval Through Query Operations. In *Proc. of ECIR*, pages 502–516, 2005.

[32] F. Peng, N. Ahmed, X. Li, and Y. Lu. Context sensitive stemming for web search. In *Proc. of SIGIR*, pages 639–646, 2007.

[33] J. M. Ponte and W. B. Croft. A language modeling approach to information retrieval. In *Proc. of SIGIR*, pages 275–281, 1998.

[34] S. Robertson, H. Zaragoza, and M. Taylor. Simple bm25 extension to multiple weighted fields. In *Proc. of CIKM*, pages 42–49, 2004.

[35] S. E. Robertson and S. Walker. Some simple effective approximations to the 2-Poisson model for probabilistic weighted retrieval. In *Proc. of SIGIR*, pages 232–241, 1994.

[36] R. L. Santos, C. Macdonald, and I. Ounis. Exploiting query reformulations for web search result diversification. In *Proc. of WWW*, pages 881–890, 2010.

[37] R. L. Santos, C. Macdonald, and I. Ounis. Intent-aware search result diversification. In *Proc. of SIGIR*, pages 595–604, 2011.

[38] M. D. Smucker, J. Allan, and B. Carterette. A comparison of statistical significance tests for information retrieval evaluation. In *Proc. of CIKM*, pages 623–632, 2007.

[39] R. Song, M. Taylor, J.-R. Wen, H.-W. Hon, and Y. Yu. Viewing term proximity from a different perspective. In *Proc. of ECIR*, pages 346–357, 2008.

[40] K. Sparck Jones. *Document retrieval systems*, chapter A statistical interpretation of term specificity and its application in retrieval, pages 132–142. Taylor Graham Publishing, 1988.

[41] T. Strohman, D. Metzler, H. Turtle, and W. B. Croft. Indri: A language model-based search engine for complex queries. In *Proc. of IA*, 2004.

[42] K. M. Svore, P. H. Kanani, and N. Khan. How good is a span of terms?: exploiting proximity to improve web retrieval. In *Proc. of SIGIR*, pages 154–161, 2010.

[43] L. Wang, D. Metzler, and J. Lin. Ranking under temporal constraints. In *Proc. of CIKM*, pages 79–88, 2010.

[44] J. Xu and W. B. Croft. Query expansion using local and global document analysis. *Proc. of SIGIR*, pages 4–11, 1996.

[45] Y. Xu, G. J. F. Jones, and B. Wang. Query dependent pseudo-relevance feedback based on wikipedia. In *Proc. of SIGIR*, pages 59–66, 2009.

[46] C. Zhai and J. Lafferty. A study of smoothing methods for language models applied to information retrieval. *ACM Transactions on Information Systems*, 22(2):179–214, 2004.

Learning to Rank with Multi-Aspect Relevance for Vertical Search

Changsung Kang, Xuanhui Wang, Yi Chang, Belle Tseng
Yahoo! Labs
Sunnyvale, CA
{ckang,xhwang,yichang,belle}@yahoo-inc.com

ABSTRACT

Many vertical search tasks such as local search focus on specific domains. The meaning of relevance in these verticals is domain-specific and usually consists of multiple well-defined aspects (e.g., text matching and distance in local search). Thus the overall relevance between a query and a document is a tradeoff between multiple relevance aspects. Such a tradeoff can vary for different types of queries or in different contexts. In this paper, we explore these vertical-specific aspects in the learning to rank setting. We propose a novel formulation in which the relevance between a query and a document is assessed with respect to each aspect, forming the multi-aspect relevance. In order to compute a ranking function, we study two types of learning-based approaches to estimate the tradeoff between these relevance aspects: a label aggregation method and a model aggregation method. Since there are only a few aspects, a minimal amount of training data is needed to learn the tradeoff. We conduct both offline and online test experiments on a local search engine and the experimental results show that our proposed multi-aspect relevance formulation is very promising. The two types of aggregation methods perform more effectively than a set of baseline methods including a conventional learning to rank method.

Categories and Subject Descriptors

H.3.3 [**Information Storage and Retrieval**]: Information Search and Retrieval—*Retrieval models*

General Terms

Algorithms

Keywords

Web search, multi-aspect relevance, aggregation

Permission to make digital or hard copies of all or part of this work for personal or classroom use is granted without fee provided that copies are not made or distributed for profit or commercial advantage and that copies bear this notice and the full citation on the first page. To copy otherwise, to republish, to post on servers or to redistribute to lists, requires prior specific permission and/or a fee.
WSDM'12, February 8–12, 2012, Seattle, Washington, USA.
Copyright 2012 ACM 978-1-4503-0747-5/12/02 ...$10.00.

1. INTRODUCTION

As the popularity of search engines has grown, the information needs of end users continue being refined. One of the emerging trends is using vertical search intent. For example, a user may want to find a restaurant near her current location; another user may want to follow the recent development of a breaking event such as the earthquake in Japan. Some recent studies show that at least 20% of Web queries have some local intent [26]. As a result, vertical search engines start attracting more and more attention. For example, many search engines provide specialized vertical search results for local search [1, 3] and for real-time search [8]. Furthermore, vertical search results are often slotted into general Web search results [4, 5]. Thus, designing effective ranking functions for vertical search has become practically important to improve users' search experience.

A natural way to build a vertical search engine is to apply the existing ranking techniques on a vertical. In the TREC conference [2], several specialized tracks such as blog and chemical tracks have been introduced to provide a testbed to study retrieval tasks on these special text collections. The main focus of these tracks is on content-based relevance and most participants extend traditional IR techniques to consider a few task-specific ranking signals. Recently, learning to rank approaches [15, 7, 31] have been studied extensively and shown to be effective to combine many useful signals into a ranking function. To adapt such a technique on a vertical, an intuitive approach is to construct a training data set by collecting a set of queries and documents which belong to the vertical and asking human editors to give a single relevance label between a query and a document. A ranking function thus can be learned for the vertical.

However, we observed that in many verticals, the meaning of relevance is domain-specific and usually consists of multiple well-defined aspects. For example, in real-time search, content matching and temporal recency are both important: A stale result which matches a query perfectly is no longer interesting to end users. In local search, as shown in Figure 1, to find a "restaurant" in "Sunnyvale CA", a satisfactory search result is not only about a dining place (text matching aspect), but also requires the place to be close to the search location (distance aspect) and with good user reviews (reputation aspect). Usually, there is no result which is the best in all these aspects. Ranking the results based on a single aspect such as text matching is not optimal. The optimal ranked list of results needs to tradeoff these different aspects appropriately. In such a vertical, blindly applying the conventional learning to rank approaches by ignoring

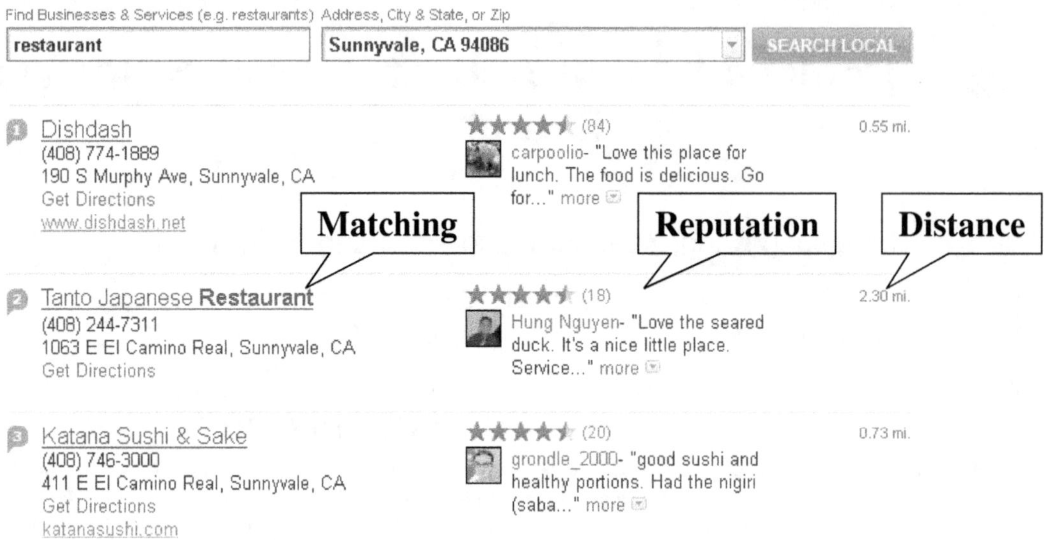

Figure 1: An example of local search results

vertical-specific domain knowledge may not be cost-effective for collecting training data: (1) Since there are several pertinent aspects in a vertical, human editors naturally need to consider and tradeoff the relevance from different aspects before making the overall relevance judgement. Thus assessing aspect relevance is a necessary step. (2) Trading off multiple aspects is not trivial since such a tradeoff can vary for different queries or in different contexts. For example, in local search, the reputation aspect can be more important for "restaurants" but the distance aspect can be more important for "banking centers". (3) For different verticals, different aspects are involved and the tradeoff among aspects is vertical-dependent. Collecting training data with overall relevance for a new vertical requires human editors learn how to appropriately tradeoff different aspects.

In this paper, we propose a novel multi-aspect relevance formulation to leverage vertical-specific knowledge in a cost-effective way. Instead of asking editors to provide the overall relevance directly, our key idea is to collect aspect relevance labels and *learn* the tradeoff among them in a *quantitative* way. Specifically, in our formulation, the relevance between a query and a document is only judged with respect to individual aspects. Intuitively, the aspect relevance is more finely specified. Thus it is less dependent on other contexts and can be presumably judged by editors with less effort. To learn a ranking function using our multi-aspect relevance formulation, we study two types of learning-based approaches to tradeoff these aspect relevancies: a label aggregation approach and a model aggregation approach.

- In the label aggregation approach, we first learn an aggregation function which predicts the overall relevance given the aspect relevance labels. After we get the overall relevance labels, conventional learning to rank algorithms can be applied to obtain a ranking function.
- In the model aggregation approach, we first train several aspect-specific ranking models based on the aspect relevance labels. The model aggregation function is then learned to combine the output of these aspect ranking models to generate the final overall relevance score.

Compared with the first approach, an advantage of the second one is that we can use different ranking models for different aspects. Since there are only a few aspects in a vertical, a minimal amount of data is needed to learn either the label aggregation function or the model aggregation function. Furthermore, in our aggregation approaches, a mapping function which assigns numerical values to editorial labels (for example, "exact match", "plausible match" and "no match" for the text match aspect) for each aspect is necessary. Such a function can be defined heuristically but we show that we can automatically learn such a function based on training data. Thus our proposed methods are completely free from heuristics.

The main advantage of our learning-based approaches is that they are vertical-independent and can be easily applied to different vertical search tasks. Specifically in this paper, we focus on learning a generic ranking function for each of the two types of queries in local search: business name queries (e.g., walmart) and category queries (e.g., restaurant). We use a training data set with relative preferences to learn the aggregation functions and study several variants on a large data set from local search. The experimental results show that our proposed methods for the multi-aspect relevance formulation is quite promising. The two types of aggregation methods perform more effectively than a set of baseline methods including a conventional learning to rank method.

The rest of the paper is organized as follows. In Section 2, we introduce related work. We define our problem in Section 3 and describe our methods to aggregate aspect relevance in Section 4. We present our experimental results in Section 5 and conclude our paper in Section 6.

2. RELATED WORK

Modeling relevance is the central topic in the information retrieval community and most of the previous work focuses on the overall relevance. In particular, almost all the evaluation methodologies are based on overall relevance. For example, in the TREC conference [2], benchmark data sets are labelled by human editors with overall relevance. The relevance labels can be either binary or graded [14]. In the past, many models have been proposed to capture the overall relevance [23, 22, 21, 29, 7]. Most of the existing work treats the overall relevance as a unit and does not study at a finer granularity.

Vertical search engines have become popular recently. For example, in the TREC conference, there are multiple tracks and some tracks such as the blog track and the legal track focus on articles from specific domains. Specific characteristics have been explored for vertical search ranking mechanisms. For example, most participants in the TREC conference designed task-specific ranking features. [11] went beyond single blog articles and studied how to rank blog feeds. [9] advocated a comparison-based ranking scheme to rank items in Twitter-like forums. [28] tried to discover implicit geographic local search intents of queries automatically. [19] proposed to use the geographic information to personalize Web search results. On the top of different verticals, [4, 5] studied how to select appropriate verticals by predicting the vertical intents of different queries based on multiple sources of evidence. Our work focuses on the learning to rank approaches for individual verticals and our multi-aspect relevance formulation is novel for vertical search.

Our work is related to multi-faceted search [27, 30]. The goal of multi-faceted search is to use facet metadata of a domain to help users narrow their search results along different dimensions. In the most recent TREC Blog track 2009 [20], a special track of "faceted blog distillation" was initiated and the task of this track is to find results relevant to a single facet of a query in the blog collection. This task is tied with multi-faceted search in that it is aimed at studying how to rank blog articles after a user selects a facet (e.g., "opinionated" or "factual") to refine the original query. While facets are usually categorical and intended to help explore search results, our definition of aspects is closely related to the notion of relevance and intended to capture partial relevance.

We note that our model aggregation technique is closely related to rank aggregation which includes score-based and rank-based methods [18, 10] and model interpolation [12]. We are not contributing any new techniques to this body of work. Rather, we show that supervised score-based aggregation techniques can be used in our multi-aspect relevance formulation. Our work is also different from multi-label learning [13] where the primary focus is to use label correlation to improve learning accuracy.

A recent related work tries to optimize multiple objectives in the learning to rank framework [25]. It considers multiple label sources and design optimization procedures based on the lambdaMART method. In their work, the priority of different label sources and the combination weights are predefined and thus it is not easy to handle a large number of label sources. In our work, the combination weights between different aspects are learned automatically and our formulation is more scalable with respect to the number of aspects. Furthermore, in our paper, we will compare with a rule-based baseline method which is similar to their *graded measure* in the sense that we predefine the aspect priority and use the labels with lower priority to break the ties of labels with a higher priority.

3. PROBLEM FORMULATION

In this section, we formally define our problem. We first describe a conventional learning to rank approach for vertical searches and then propose our multi-aspect relevance formulation.

```
Given a query and a list of documents, answer the the
following questions for each document.
```

Question 1: `How does this document match the query?`

```
[ ] Exact match
[ ] Plausible match
[ ] No match
```

Question 2: `What is the relative distance between the document location and the query location?`

```
[ ] Same location
[ ] Reasonable location
[ ] Too far
```

Question 3: `How is the rating from different raters?`

```
[ ] Excellent rating
[ ] Good rating
[ ] Bad rating
```

Question 4: Overall Relevance

Matching	Distance	Reputation	Overall
Exact	Same	Excellent	Perfect
Exact	Same	Good	Excellent
Exact	Same	Bad	Good
Exact or Plausible	Same or Reasonable	-	Fair
No	-	-	Bad

Figure 2: An example of an editorial guideline for local search. Note that the overall relevance question is NOT needed in our aggregation methods. The overall relevance is used only for the conventional method.

3.1 Learning to Rank for Vertical Search

Although vertical search involves multiple aspects such as matching, reputation and distance, we can still apply conventional learning to rank methods. Given a query q, let $\mathcal{D}_q = \{(\mathbf{x}_1, z_1), ..., (\mathbf{x}_n, z_n)\}$ be the training data of n documents where $\mathbf{x}_i \in \mathbb{R}^d$ is the feature vector and z_i is the overall relevance label of the i-th document. In a ranking problem, $\mathcal{D}_q$ is given as input and a permutation τ of $\{1, \ldots, n\}$ is returned as output. $\mathbf{x}_i$ is ranked higher than $\mathbf{x}_j$ if $\tau(\mathbf{x}_i) < \tau(\mathbf{x}_j)$ and this means $\mathbf{x}_i$ is more relevant to q than $\mathbf{x}_j$. Typically, a *ranking function* $f : \mathbb{R}^d \rightarrow \mathbb{R}$ is trained and applied to $\mathcal{D}_q$. A permutation or ranking τ is generated by ordering the $f(\mathbf{x}_i)$ in the descending order.

The overall relevance label z_i is a discrete label given by human editors. In this work, we follow a common five-grade labeling scheme: {Perfect, Excellent, Good, Fair, Bad}. To reduce disagreement among editors, it is a common practice that an *editorial guideline* is drawn up. An editorial guideline is essentially a set of rules or heuristics that specify a condition for each grade of the overall relevance label.

In this section, we use local search as an example to describe an editorial guideline. A unique characteristic of local search is that the query intents are to find some locations such as restaurants, hotels, or business centers. This also implies that the users intend to use some services provided by the local businesses. Therefore, a user would prefer a location which is close and at the same time whose reputation of services is good. For example, to find a restaurant in local search, a satisfactory search result is not only about a dining place (matching aspect), but also requires the place to be close to the user (distance aspect) and to have good user reviews (reputation aspect). Overall, we have found that three aspects, i.e., matching, distance and reputation, are the most important aspects for local information needs.

In Figure 2, we show an example of an editorial guideline for local search. We have several questions which are intended to capture the desired properties of local search. Question 1, 2, and 3 are to capture the matching, distance, and reputation aspects respectively. Each question has a graded judgement which is going to be labelled by editors. Finally, there is an aggregation guideline that specifies a rule for each grade of the overall relevance label. An aggregation guideline is important since it defines the learning targets. It is necessary for most conventional learning to rank tasks, especially which involve multiple aspects of relevance. Without a good aggregation guideline, the training data will have too much noise to train a good ranking function due to disagreement among editors regarding the overall relevance.

For example, given the query "Bank of America, Los Angeles, CA 90018", the result "Bank of America, 2907 Crenshaw Blvd, Los Angeles, CA" has a distance of 1 mile and the average rating from 2 people is 3 out of 5. In this case, the labels for these questions are Exact match, Same location, and Good rating. The overall relevance is Excellent according to the aggregation guideline.

Such a rule-based approach is similar to [25] in the sense that we predefine priorities between aspects and use the labels with a lower priority to break the ties for labels with a higher priority. The drawbacks of the conventional rule-based approach are: (1) Defining the right rules needs deep domain knowledge and thus is non-trivial; (2) The rules are very coarse and cannot capture the true preferences at a finer granularity; (3) This method will not scale well since the complexity of defining rules grows exponentially as the number of aspects increases, though it is feasible for the 3 aspects in our work.

3.2 Multi-Aspect Relevance Formulation

In the conventional learning setting, the intermediate questions regarding aspects are only used to help editors reach the final overall relevance and are usually discarded when training a ranking function. How to leverage these aspect relevance labels effectively is not well explored. In this section, we propose a new learning to rank framework for multi-aspect relevance to tackle the drawbacks of the conventional rule-based overall relevance scheme.

First,we define the following concepts:

DEFINITION 1 (ASPECT RELEVANCE). *Given a query q, a document d, and the k-th aspect, the corresponding aspect relevance is the relevance between q and d with respect to this aspect. An aspect relevance label* $\hat{l} \in L_k = \{l_{k,1} \prec, ..., \prec l_{k,n_k}\}$ *is used to represent the degree of the relevance where* $\prec$ ($\succ$) *means the left label is less (more) relevant than the right label.*

For example, in the editorial guideline shown in Figure 2, each intermediate question is to assess a single aspect relevance label. An aspect relevance label is independent of other aspect relevance labels.

DEFINITION 2 (MULTI-ASPECT RELEVANCE). *Given a vertical which has m pertinent aspects, the multi-aspect relevance between a query and a document is an m-dimensional vector with each entry corresponding to an aspect relevance label between the query and the document.*

Each entry in a multi-aspect relevance vector corresponds to an aspect relevance label. This label can be mapped to a numerical value by a mapping function as defined below.

DEFINITION 3 (MAPPING FUNCTION). *A mapping function for the k-th aspect* $\phi_k : L_k \to \mathbb{R}$ *maps an aspect relevance label to a numerical value. For example,* ϕ_1*(matching = Plausible match) = 0.5. A mapping function is consistent if* $\phi_k(l_{k,i}) > \phi_k(l_{k,j})$ *for* $l_{k,i} \succ l_{k,j}$. *We use* Φ *as the general notation of the m aspect mapping functions.*

A mapping function can be manually defined or learned. In the following, for ease of exposition, we use notation $\mathbf{y}$ to represent a multi-aspect relevance vector of either labels or values unless otherwise specified.

3.3 Label Aggregation

Given the above definitions, the basic idea of label aggregation is to train a function which can *quantitatively* aggregate the multi-aspect relevance values into an overall relevance value.

DEFINITION 4 (LABEL AGGREGATION FUNCTION). *A label aggregation function* $h : \mathbb{R}^m \to \mathbb{R}$ *is a function that maps a multi-aspect relevance vector* $\mathbf{y}$ *to an absolute overall relevance value z, i.e.,* $h(\mathbf{y}) = z$.

To learn an aggregation function h, we need training data with overall relevance signals, either *absolute* relevance labels or *relative* preferences. In this paper, we focus on the relative preferences and use $\mathcal{P} = \{(\mathbf{x}_i, \mathbf{x}_j) \mid \mathbf{x}_i \succ \mathbf{x}_j\}$ to represent the data where $\mathbf{x}_i \succ \mathbf{x}_j$ denotes that $\mathbf{x}_i$ is preferred to $\mathbf{x}_j$. Since there are only a few aspects in a vertical, training the aggregation function needs a minimal amount of data. After learning an aggregation function, we can then apply it to the large amount of multi-aspect relevance labels and thus generate a large amount of training data with overall relevance.

In summary, we have a large data set with ranking features $\mathbf{x}$ and the corresponding multi-aspect relevance vectors $\mathbf{y}$: $\mathcal{F} = \{(\mathbf{x}, \mathbf{y})\}$ and a small set of relative preference data $\mathcal{P}$. Since there is a one-to-one correspondence between $\mathbf{x}$ and $\mathbf{y}$ in our data, we use either $(\mathbf{x}_i, \mathbf{x}_j) \in \mathcal{P}$ or $(\mathbf{y}_i, \mathbf{y}_j) \in \mathcal{P}$. We have the following steps:

- Learn an aggregation function $h(\mathbf{y})$ (and a mapping function Φ if not manually defined) using $\mathcal{P}$.
- Apply $h(\mathbf{y})$ on $\mathcal{F}$ and generate data set $\hat{\mathcal{F}} = \{(\mathbf{x}, h(\mathbf{y})\}$.
- Train a ranking function f_h using $\hat{\mathcal{F}}$ based on a conventional learning to rank method.

3.4 Model Aggregation

The label aggregation method converts the problem of learning from multi-aspect relevance into a conventional learning to ranking problem. All the ranking features related to different aspects are treated uniformly in this method. The idea of model aggregation is to train an individual ranking model for each aspect. In this section, we propose a *model aggregation* method, which aggregates the output of aspect ranking functions to generate the overall relevance score.

Aspect	Label	Score
Matching	Exact Match	$y_1 = 1.0$
	Plausible Match	$y_1 = 0.5$
	No Match	$y_1 = 0$
Distance	Same Location	$y_2 = 1.0$
	Reasonable Location	$y_2 = 0.5$
	Too Far	$y_2 = 0$
Reputation	Excellent Rating	$y_3 = 1.0$
	Good Rating	$y_3 = 0.5$
	Bad Rating	$y_3 = 0$

Table 1: The aspect relevance mapping function for local search.

DEFINITION 5 (ASPECT RANKING FUNCTION). *An aspect ranking function $f_a : \mathbb{R}^k \to \mathbb{R}$ for an aspect a is a function that maps a feature vector $\mathbf{x}$ to an aspect relevance score.*

DEFINITION 6 (MODEL AGGREGATION FUNCTION). *A model aggregation function $h : \mathbb{R}^m \to \mathbb{R}$ is a function that aggregates the estimated aspect relevance scores into the final overall relevance score.*

In summary, we have the following steps for model aggregation:

- For each aspect a_i, learn an aspect ranking function f_{a_i} based on aspect relevance labels and a mapping function.
- For each $\mathbf{x}$ in $\mathcal{P}$, generate an m-dimensional vector $\mathbf{f}(\mathbf{x}) = [f_{a_1}(\mathbf{x}), ..., f_{a_m}(\mathbf{x})]$.
- Train an aggregation function h based on the feature vector $\mathbf{f}(\mathbf{x})$ and the pairs in $\mathcal{P}$.

The final ranking score is computed as $h(\mathbf{f}(\mathbf{x}))$.

Then the central question is how to learn these aggregation functions (and a mapping function Φ). We explore different formulations in the next section.

4. LEARNING AGGREGATION FUNCTIONS

In this section, we propose different methods to learn aggregation functions based on pairwise preferences.

4.1 Learning Label Aggregation

We propose 2 different approaches: a linear aggregation approach and a joint learning approach.

4.1.1 A Linear Aggregation Method

In this section, we explore a linear model for aggregation by assuming that we have a predefined mapping function. A simple mapping function for an aspect label set L_k can be constructed as

$$\phi_k(l_{k,s}) = \frac{s-1}{n_k - 1} \text{ for } s = 1, \ldots, n_k,$$

For example, a fixed mapping function is given in Table 1. We have an unknown parameter vector $\mathbf{w}$ and the linear function takes the form $h(\mathbf{y}) = \mathbf{w}^T\mathbf{y}$. We use the following loss function on the pairwise training data.

$$\mathcal{L} = \frac{1}{2} \sum_{(\mathbf{y}_i, \mathbf{y}_j) \in \mathcal{P}} \left(\max(0, 1 - \mathbf{w}^T\mathbf{y}_i + \mathbf{w}^T\mathbf{y}_j) \right)^2$$

Furthermore, to ensure the monotonicity, we have to constrain $\mathbf{w}$ to be non-negative element-wise:

$$\mathbf{w} \succeq 0.$$

We solve the above optimization problem by a simple gradient descent approach in a similar way to the joint learning model in the next section.

4.1.2 A Joint Learning Method

The above method assumes that we have a predefined mapping function and learn the aggregation function directly on the numeric values of aspect relevance. But such a mapping is in an ad-hoc fashion. In this section, we propose a joint learning model which learns a mapping function and aggregation weights simultaneously. Without loss of generality, for each aspect, we assign 0 to its lowest relevance label and 1 to its highest one, i.e., $\phi_k(l_{k,1}) = 0$ and $\phi_k(l_{k,n_k}) = 1$ for $k = 1, \ldots, m$. Our joint learning method will automatically determine the numeric values for the middle labels.

Formally, our goal is to learn the values of all the labels in $L_1, \ldots, L_m$ and weights $\mathbf{w}$ to minimize the following loss function

$$\mathcal{L} = \frac{1}{2} \sum_{(\mathbf{y}_i, \mathbf{y}_j) \in \mathcal{P}} \left(\max(0, 1 - \mathbf{w}^T\Phi(\mathbf{y}_i) + \mathbf{w}^T\Phi(\mathbf{y}_j)) \right)^2$$

Here we use $\mathbf{y}$ to specifically denote an aspect label vector. Note the following differences compared to the linear method: (1) $\Phi(\mathbf{y}_i) = [\phi_1(y_{i,1}), ..., \phi_m(y_{i,m})]^T$ is the vector after applying the mapping function. It is also unknown and needs to be optimized; (2) We have the following additional consistency constraint which ensures that a better label gets a higher score:

$$0 = \phi_k(l_{k,1}) \le \phi_k(l_{k,2}) ... \le \phi_k(l_{k,n_k}) = 1 \text{ for } k = 1, \ldots, m$$

It easy to verify that the space with the constraints is convex. However, such a problem is not easy to optimize due to the quadratic terms in the objective function. Since the dimensionality of the problem is not high, we thus propose a gradient descent approach with projection to optimize the objective function. Let $\mathcal{A}_{k,s} = \{(\mathbf{y}_i, \mathbf{y}_j) \in \mathcal{P} \mid y_{i,k} = l_{k,s}, y_{j,k} \neq l_{k,s}\}$ and $\mathcal{B}_{k,s} = \{(\mathbf{y}_i, \mathbf{y}_j) \in \mathcal{P} \mid y_{i,k} \neq l_{k,s}, y_{j,k} = l_{k,s}\}$. The gradient for each variable with respect to the objective function is:

$$\frac{\partial \mathcal{L}}{\partial w_k} = \sum_{(\mathbf{y}_i, \mathbf{y}_j) \in \mathcal{P}} \max(0, 1 - \mathbf{w}^T\Phi(\mathbf{y}_i) + \mathbf{w}^T\Phi(\mathbf{y}_j))$$

$$\cdot (-\phi_k(y_{i,k}) + \phi_k(y_{j,k}))$$

$$\frac{\partial \mathcal{L}}{\partial \phi_k(l_{k,s})} = \sum_{(\mathbf{y}_i, \mathbf{y}_j) \in \mathcal{A}_{k,s}} \max(0, 1 - \mathbf{w}^T\Phi(\mathbf{y}_i) + \mathbf{w}^T\Phi(\mathbf{y}_j))(-w_k)$$

$$+ \sum_{(\mathbf{y}_i, \mathbf{y}_j) \in \mathcal{B}_{k,s}} \max(0, 1 - \mathbf{w}^T\Phi(\mathbf{y}_i) + \mathbf{w}^T\Phi(\mathbf{y}_j)) \cdot w_k$$

We use t to denote the iteration in the gradient descent. After iteration t, we project the estimated parameters to the convex space defined by the constraints. We use the norm-2 distance for the projection

$$\min_{\mathbf{w}, \phi_k(l_{k,s})} ||\mathbf{w} - \mathbf{w}^{(t)}||^2 + \sum_{k,s} |\phi_k(l_{k,s}) - \phi_k(l_{k,s})^{(t)}|^2$$

$$\text{s.t. } 0 = \phi_k(l_{k,1}) \le \phi_k(l_{k,2}) ... \le \phi_k(l_{k,n_k}) = 1$$

$$\mathbf{w} \succeq 0$$

The projection can be efficiently solved since it is a standard quadratic programming problem [24].

4.2 Learning Model Aggregation

In this section, we propose another method for our multi-aspect relevance formulation, the model aggregation method, which is formulated in Section 3.4. In this method, we first learn an aspect ranking function f_{a_i} for each aspect a_i and use a supervised linear model as our aggregation function

$$h(\mathbf{f}(\mathbf{x})) = \mathbf{w}^T \mathbf{f}(\mathbf{x}).$$

To learn an aspect ranking function f_{a_i} using a method such as GBRank [31], we need to assign numerical values to aspect labels, e.g., by a mapping function. We have proposed to automatically learn a mapping function in the joint learning method in the previous section and thus we use the obtained mapping function Φ to convert the aspect labels.

To learn the parameter $\mathbf{w}$, we use the following loss function:

$$\mathcal{L} = \frac{1}{2} \sum_{(\mathbf{x}_i, \mathbf{x}_j) \in \mathcal{P}} \left(\max(0, 1 - \mathbf{w}^T \mathbf{f}(\mathbf{x}_i) + \mathbf{w}^T \mathbf{f}(\mathbf{x}_j)) \right)^2$$

where $\mathbf{f}(\mathbf{x}) = [f_{a_1}(\mathbf{x}), ..., f_{a_m}(\mathbf{x})]$. This model is very similar to the linear model in the label aggregation methods. The difference is that we replace the labels with the output of aspect ranking functions.

Compared to the label aggregation methods, there are two benefits of the model aggregation method. First, we can use a different type of model for each aspect ranking function. This is desirable since aspects are not necessarily homogeneous. For example, the matching aspect can be complex and thus needs a ranking function with high model complexity, but a simple regression model may be good enough for the distance aspect. In particular, we use a gradient-boosted decision tree model GBRank [31] for the matching aspect which shows excellent performance in learning such a function. On the other hand, we use linear regression models for distance and reputation aspects. Hence, the combination of various types of models for different aspects gives great flexibility to the final ranking function.

Also, in the model aggregation method, we can exploit preference data inferred from other sources such as user clicks to learn the aggregation function. Unlike the label aggregation methods, each document in $\mathcal{P}$ does not need aspect relevance labels $\mathbf{y}$ and we only need $\mathbf{f}(\mathbf{x})$, the output of aspect ranking functions, to learn the aggregation function. This provides flexibility to quickly adapt the aggregation function to different contexts. For example, this makes it possible to provide personalized search rankings: We may collect preference data $\mathcal{P}$ for a user u and use it to learn a user-specific aggregated function $\mathbf{w}_u^T \mathbf{f}(\mathbf{x})$. Note that we do not need to learn aspect ranking functions for each user since each aspect ranking function should be common among users but the tradeoff between aspects depends on personal preference. Similarly, we can provide customized search rankings for different search applications. For example, in mobile local search, the distance aspect may be more important than in desktop local search. We can easily build a separate ranking function for mobile local search using the preference data obtained from user clicks in mobile local search.

		#query	#listing
Category Queries	Training	4211	70701
	Test	1055	17675
	Total	5266	88376
Business Name Queries	Training	6966	76343
	Test	1739	18550
	Total	8705	94893

Table 2: Statistics of multi-aspect relevance data.

5. EXPERIMENTS

In this section, we present experimental results to validate our approaches. The main objective of our experiments is to study the effectiveness of our multi-aspect relevance formulation and the proposed aggregation methods for local search. We report both offline and online test results in this section.

5.1 Data Sets

The data sets we use are from a commercial local search engine where a document is called "business listing" or "listing" for short. We follow the editorial guideline similar to the guideline in Figure 2 to obtain the training data. Specifically, each query in our data has a location associated (e.g., "Target Sunnyvale CA"). For each (query, listing) pair, we consider 3 aspects: matching, distance and reputation as discussed in Section 3.1 and ask editors to provide 3 aspect relevance labels and an overall relevance label according to the editorial guideline. Note that in our aggregation methods, we do not use the overall relevance labels given by human editors. Table 2 shows the statistics of this data set. In particular, we have two types of queries: category queries and business name queries. A category query such as "Chinese restaurant Los Angeles, CA 90018" is similar to an informational query and can be broadly matched by any Chinese restaurant, while a business name query such as "Bank of America, Los Angeles, CA 90018" is more like a navigational query and can only be matched by Bank of America branches. Intuitively, the relative importance of each aspect for these two types of queries can be potentially different.

In Figure 3, we show the distribution of the labels for different types of queries and different aspects. We can see clear differences between them. The differences of the statistics regarding matching and distance aspects are due to the different densities of businesses for the two query categories: There are more matching businesses for category queries than business name queries (e.g., typically, there are more restaurants than Target stores in a city.). The high percentage of the "Bad rating" label for the reputation aspect for business name queries is due to two reasons: (1) When there is no user review, it is considered as a "Bad rating" in our guideline. (2) About 50% of the business name queries are *chain* queries such as "Walmart" and users typically do not bother review the chain stores. Indeed we will show that the reputation aspect is not particularly important for business name queries.

We obtain the overall relative preference using a side by side comparison as follows: given any query, we randomly sample a pair of documents and put them side by side. The position of the two documents are randomly shuffled to avoid

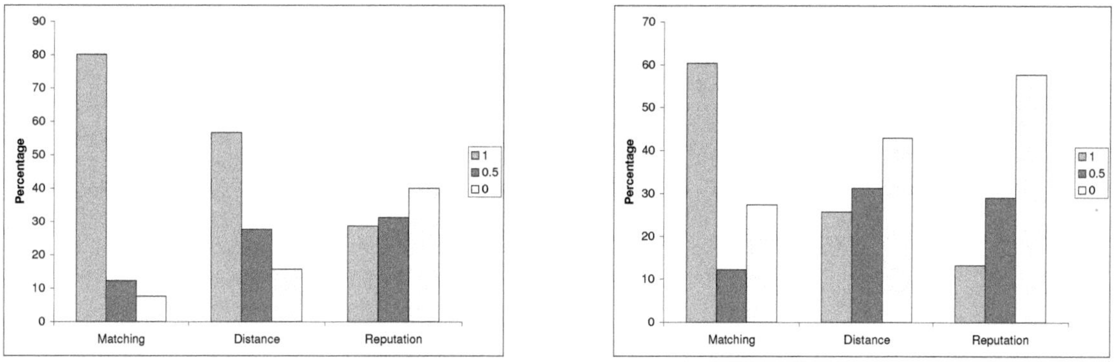

(a) Category Queries (b) Business Name Queries

Figure 3: Distribution of aspect relevance labels. 1, 0.5 and 0 correspond to the aspect labels in Table 1.

	#Training $\mathcal{P}_{train}$	#Test $\mathcal{P}_{test}$
Category Queries	549	493
Name Queries	445	457

Table 3: Statistics of overall relative preference data sets obtained by side by side comparison.

any kind of bias. We then ask editors to judge which one is better than the other. The obtained overall training signals are thus relative preferences. Previous studies have shown that relative preferences are more reliable than absolute judgements in many scenarios [6, 16]. This is very critical when the training data is small. However, it is expensive to obtain a large amount of such data. Fortunately, our experiment results show that only a small amount of such data is needed to obtain highly accurate aggregation functions. Table 3 summarizes the statistics of this data set. We split this data into training ($\mathcal{P}_{train}$) and test ($\mathcal{P}_{test}$) to evaluate our aggregation functions.

5.2 Ranking Algorithms

We compare the following ranking algorithms.

- **Rule**: A traditional one overall relevance label scheme described in Section 3.1.
- **Ed-overall**: A ranking function trained directly using editorial pairwise preference data $\mathcal{P}_{train}$.
- **Click**: A ranking function trained using pairwise preference data induced from a click model [17].
- **Linear**: The linear aggregation function described in Section 4.1.1.
- **Joint**: The joint learning model described in Section 4.1.2.
- **ModAgg**: The model aggregation method described in Section 4.2.

Rule, Ed-overall and Click serve as baselines. Rule, a traditional one overall relevance label scheme described in Section 3.1 is similar to the *graded measure* used in [25] in the sense that the secondary labels are used to break the ties of the primary labels. Ed-overall and Click are other baselines to show the benefit of our multi-aspect relevance. They do not use aspect relevance labels but only use pairwise preference data as the training data. Both are learned using the GBRank model [31]. For the Click method, we obtain *SkipAbove* and *SkipNext* [17] pairs from click logs. The click-based training data is easy to obtain but it is noisy. We have 1,441,975 and 58,782 click-based training pairs for category and business name queries respectively. In all our label aggregation methods, the final ranking functions are learned using the GBRank model [31].

5.3 Offline Experimental Results

We report our offline experiment results based on the data sets with editorial labels.

5.3.1 Evaluation Metrics

To evaluate aggregation functions, we consider two types of pair accuracy with respect to the test data set $\mathcal{P}_{test}$. (1) Label aggregation accuracy: how accurate is an aggregation function to aggregate the multi-aspect relevance to generate the overall relevance? This accuracy is only applied to label aggregation methods. (2) Ranking accuracy: how effective is a ranking function trained using either label or model aggregation methods?

Let h be a label aggregation function and f be a final ranking function trained using either label aggregation or model aggregation methods. The label aggregation accuracy of h is:

$$\frac{|\{(\mathbf{y}_i,\mathbf{y}_j) \mid h(\mathbf{y}_i) > h(\mathbf{y}_j), (\mathbf{y}_i,\mathbf{y}_j) \in \mathcal{P}_{test}\}|}{|\mathcal{P}_{test}|} \quad (1)$$

and the ranking accuracy of f is:

$$\frac{|\{(\mathbf{y}_i,\mathbf{y}_j) \mid f(\mathbf{x}_i) > f(\mathbf{x}_j), (\mathbf{y}_i,\mathbf{y}_j) \in \mathcal{P}_{test}\}|}{|\mathcal{P}_{test}|}. \quad (2)$$

Note that an NDCG-like metric seems to be possible to compare the ranking accuracy of different aggregation methods since a label aggregation function can generate absolute overall relevance values. However, different label aggregation methods can generate different overall values for the same (query, listing) pair and thus we do not have a common

	Category Queries	Business Name Queries
Rule	0.640	0.650
Linear	**0.825**	**0.926**
Joint	**0.825**	**0.932**

Table 4: Evaluation of aggregation functions on label aggregation accuracy. Linear, and Joint are significantly better than Rule (p-value < 0.01).

	Category Queries	Business Name Queries
Rule	0.614	0.788
Ed-overall	0.575	0.841
Click	0.638	0.841
Linear	**0.750**	0.879
Joint	**0.760**	0.871
ModAgg	**0.769**	**0.917**

Table 5: Evaluation of aggregation functions on ranking accuracy. Statistically significant differences (p-value < 0.01) compared to Rule are highlighted in bold.

ground to compare them. Hence, we use the pair accuracy as a more isolated and unbiased metric for evaluation.

5.3.2 Results on Label Aggregation Accuracy

Table 4 shows the comparison of different aggregation functions based on the label aggregation accuracy which is defined in Eq. (1). In this experiment, we only use the data in Table 3. We learn the aggregation functions for each type of queries separately. Table 4 shows the results on category queries and business name queries respectively. From this table, we have the following observation. (1) The Rule method performs much worse than all the learning based methods for both types of queries. For example, for category queries, the rule-based method has about 64% accuracy and all other methods have 82.5% accuracy. This shows that the rules are too coarse to capture the desired tradeoff. (2) The Linear and Joint methods perform equally well on both category and business name queries. The pair accuracy is 83% on category queries and 93% on business name queries. This demonstrates high consistency between the aggregated overall relevance and the true one. (3) Comparing the two types of queries, we can see higher accuracy for business name queries than category queries. This is expected since the relevance for category queries is naturally more complex than business name queries.

5.3.3 Results on Ranking Accuracy

Table 5 shows the comparison of the ranking accuracy for both label and model aggregation methods. For a label aggregation method, we first use the training data in Table 3 to learn the label aggregation function and then apply it to obtain the overall relevance for the set of training queries in Table 2. We then test the ranking function using $\mathcal{P}_{test}$. The pair ranking accuracy is defined in Eq. (2). For the model aggregation method, we use the training data with aspect relevance label data in Table 2 to learn the aspect ranking functions $\mathbf{f}$ and then use the training data in Table 3 to learn the model aggregation function h. We then apply the overall ranking function $h(\mathbf{f}(\mathbf{x}))$ on the test data. We have the following observations: (1) For category queries, all the learning based methods are significantly better than the Rule method. The ModAgg method is slightly better than all other methods. (2) However, for business name queries, only the ModAgg method is significantly better than the Rule method, while the improvement of the Linear and Joint methods over the Rule method is not significant with respect to p-value < 0.01. One possible reason is that business name queries are relative easy and all the methods have achieved high accuracy.

Overall, we can see that our learning methods are quite effective and the model aggregation method is the most stable one for both classes of queries.

Our learning methods improve not only ranking accuracy but also the efficiency of the training procedure compared to the Rule method. In our learning methods, training data collection can be done more efficiently since we do not need overall relevance labels but only need aspect relevance labels and a small amount of data $\mathcal{P}_{train}$.

5.3.4 Benefit of Multi-Aspect Relevance

Table 5 also shows the benefit of our multi-aspect relevance formulation compared to approaches that do not leverage aspect relevance in the learning process. Both Ed-overall and Click only use pairwise preference data as the training data ignoring aspect relevance. We can see that Ed-overall performs much worse compared to the ModAgg method. The reason why Ed-overall performs worse is mainly due to the limited amount of the training data. The Click method performs worse mainly because it is noisy. Our method leverages the aspect relevance and thus can utilize the small amount of Ed-overall data ($\mathcal{P}_{train}$) more effectively.

5.3.5 Comparison of Aspect Importance

The Linear, Joint and ModAgg methods generate a weight vector $(w_{Matching}, w_{Distance}, w_{Reputation})$ for aspects as output. These weights indicate the relative importance of aspects in the overall relevance. For category queries, we have

$$w_{Matching} \gg w_{Reputation} \gg w_{Distance}.$$

For business name queries, we have

$$w_{Matching} \gg w_{Distance} > w_{Reputation}.$$

This result confirms our intuition that the reputation aspect is more important than the distance aspect for category queries and vice versa for business name queries. This shows that different types of queries work best with different aggregation functions.

In our current work, we mainly focus on two broad types of queries. This results show that there is probably a large room for improvement if we can make our aggregation functions query-dependent or personalized. We leave this as future work.

5.4 Online Experimental Results

Ranking functions can be compared in terms of pair accuracy in the offline setting, but they can also be compared on how users interact with the search results in the online setting. In this section, we report our online results.

5.4.1 Experiment Design

In our online experiments, we conduct "bucket tests" during a certain period to compare different ranking algorithms in a commercial local search engine. The bucket is created based on user cookies. A cookie is assigned to a fixed bucket in our test period. Each bucket corresponds to a small percentage of user population who use the local search engine. In different buckets, we show search results of different ranking algorithms. If a ranking algorithm is better than another, we would expect that the user experience metric is better.

It can be seen that online experiments are expensive and we cannot test many different algorithms. In our experiments, we were able to test only two functions during the same time period in the commercial local search engine. During two weeks, we compared Rule and Linear. During another two weeks, we compared Linear and ModAgg. To compare two functions, we use the click-through rate (CTR) as our user experience metric. Specifically, we use CTR for top i positions and denote it as CTRi:

$$\text{CTR}i = \frac{\sum_{k=1}^{k=i} \text{clicks at position } k}{\sum_{k=1}^{k=i} \text{views at position } k}$$

Due to confidential reasons, we do not report the exact CTR but report a normalized CTR over a fixed number.

5.4.2 Results

In Figure 4, we report the daily trends of the click-through rate (CTR) of ranking functions. The CTRs naturally fluctuate on different days. We can see that Linear is consistently better than Rule and ModAgg outperforms Linear during the whole period. The average CTR5s of Rule and Linear during the first test period are 0.315 and 0.325 respectively. The average CTR5s of Linear and ModAgg during the second test period are 0.308 and 0.314 respectively. These differences are statistically significant (p-value < 0.01).

This result is consistent with our offline experimental results and shows that our multi-aspect relevance framework outperforms the traditional one overall relevance scheme. Also, it demonstrates that the model aggregation method is more effective than the label aggregation methods. Thus, using different ranking models for different aspects is more suitable for multi-aspect relevance aggregation.

6. CONCLUSIONS AND FUTURE WORK

The meaning of relevance in vertical search is domain-specific and usually consists of multiple aspects. In this paper, we proposed a multi-aspect relevance formulation for vertical search in the learning to rank setting. In our formulation, the relevance between a query and a document is assessed with respect to each aspect, forming multi-aspect relevance. In order to learn a ranking function, we studied two types of learning-based approaches to estimate the tradeoff between the multiple aspects, a label aggregation method and a model aggregation method. Then a ranking function is learned based on the multi-aspect relevance formulation. Since there are only a few aspects, a minimal amount of training data is needed to learn the tradeoff. We studied several methods to learn aggregation functions and conducted experiments on local search engine data. Our experimental results show our multi-aspect relevance formulation is promising. The proposed aggregation approaches are very effective to learn the tradeoff between different aspects.

Our work can be extended as follows. First, we proposed to learn the ranking functions and aggregation functions separately in this paper. How to learn them jointly is a promising direction. Second, our methods rely on manually identified aspects and thus how to automatically discover all important aspects given a vertical is worth studying. Third, our multi-aspect relevance formulation provides a new base for studying how to learn context sensitive or personalized ranking functions. For example, it is possible to dynamically update our aggregation function based on the short-term user interaction history.

7. REFERENCES

[1] Google Local. http://local.google.com/.

[2] TREC. http://trec.nist.gov/.

[3] Yahoo Local. http://local.yahoo.com/.

[4] J. Arguello, F. Diaz, J. Callan, and J.-F. Crespo. Sources of evidence for vertical selection. In *SIGIR*, pages 315–322, 2009.

[5] J. Arguello, F. Diaz, and J.-F. Paiement. Vertical selection in the presence of unlabeled verticals. In *SIGIR*, pages 691–698, 2010.

[6] R. K. Belew. *Finding Out About*. Cambridge Univ. Press, 2000.

[7] C. Burges, T. Shaked, E. Renshaw, A. Lazier, M. Deeds, N. Hamilton, and G. Hullender. Learning to rank using gradient descent. In *Proceedings of the 22nd international conference on Machine learning*, pages 89–96, 2005.

[8] N. Carr. Real-time search. *Communication of ACM*, 2010. http://www.technologyreview.com/computing/25079/.

[9] A. Das Sarma, A. Das Sarma, S. Gollapudi, and R. Panigrahy. Ranking mechanisms in twitter-like forums. In *Proceedings of the third ACM international conference on Web search and data mining*, WSDM, pages 21–30, 2010.

[10] C. Dwork, R. Kumar, M. Naor, and D. Sivakumar. Rank aggregation methods for the web. In *Proceedings of the 10th international conference on World Wide Web*, WWW '01, pages 613–622, 2001.

[11] J. L. Elsas, J. Arguello, J. Callan, and J. G. Carbonell. Retrieval and feedback models for blog feed search. In *Proceedings of the 31st annual international ACM SIGIR conference on Research and development in information retrieval*, pages 347–354, 2008.

[12] J. Gao, Q. Wu, C. Burges, K. Svore, Y. Su, N. Khan, S. Shah, and H. Zhou. Model adaptation via model interpolation and boosting for Web search ranking. In *Proceedings of the 2009 Conference on Empirical Methods in Natural Language Processing*, pages 505–513, August 2009.

[13] N. Ghamrawi and A. McCallum. Collective multi-label classification. In *CIKM*, pages 195–200, 2005.

[14] K. Järvelin and J. Kekäläinen. Cumulated gain-based evaluation of ir techniques. *ACM Trans. Inf. Syst.*, 20:422–446, October 2002.

[15] T. Joachims. Optimizing search engines using clickthrough data. In *KDD '02: Proceedings of the eighth ACM SIGKDD*, pages 133–142, New York, NY, USA, 2002. ACM Press.

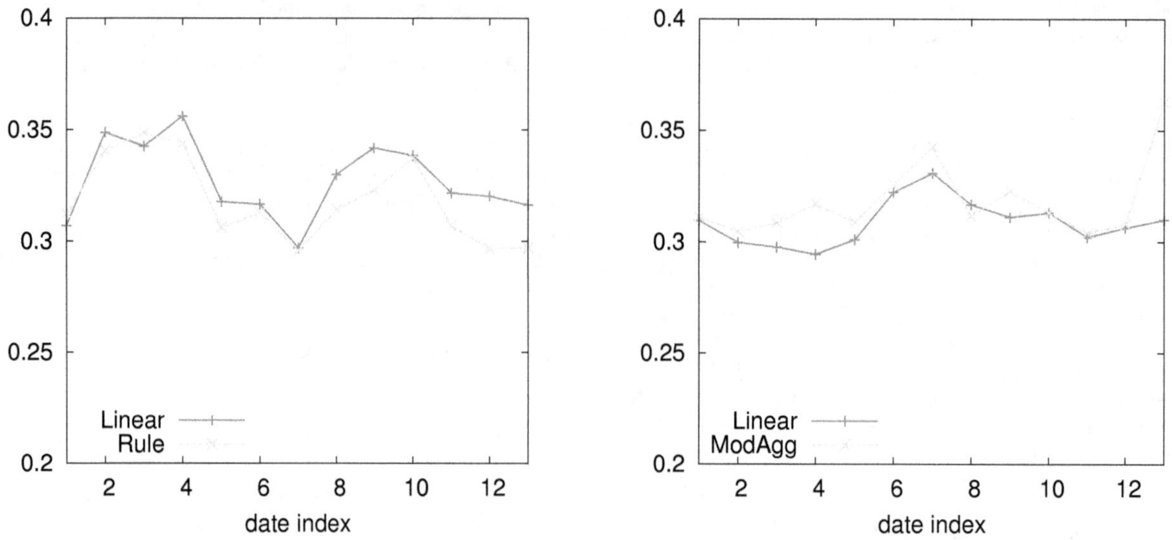

(a) CTR5 comparison of Rule and Linear

(b) CTR5 comparison of Linear and ModAgg

Figure 4: The click-through rate (CTR) comparisons based on online experiments for a commercial local search engine. CTRs are normalized not to show absolute values. Each comparison is done for a different test period due to online experiment constraints.

[16] T. Joachims, L. Granka, B. Pan, H. Hembrooke, and G. Gay. Accurately interpreting clickthrough data as implicit feedback. In *Proceedings of ACM SIGIR 2005*, pages 154–161, New York, NY, USA, 2005. ACM Press.

[17] T. Joachims, L. Granka, B. Pan, H. Hembrooke, F. Radlinski, and G. Gay. Evaluating the accuracy of implicit feedback from clicks and query reformulations in web search. *ACM Transactions on Information Systems (TOIS)*, 25(2), 2007.

[18] Y.-T. Liu, T.-Y. Liu, T. Qin, Z.-M. Ma, and H. Li. Supervised rank aggregation. In *Proceedings of the 16th international conference on World Wide Web*, WWW, pages 481–490, 2007.

[19] Y. Lu, F. Peng, X. Wei, and B. Dumoulin. Personalize web search results with user's location. In *SIGIR*, pages 763–764, 2010.

[20] C. Macdonald, I. Ounis, and I. Soboroff. Overview of the trec 2009 blog track. 2009.

[21] J. M. Ponte and W. B. Croft. A language modeling approach to information retrieval. In *Proceedings of the 21st annual international ACM SIGIR conference on Research and development in information retrieval*, pages 275–281, 1998.

[22] S. E. Robertson and S. Walker. Some simple effective approximations to the 2-poisson model for probabilistic weighted retrieval. In *SIGIR*, pages 232–241, 1994.

[23] G. Salton, A. Wong, and C. S. Yang. A vector space model for automatic indexing. *Commun. ACM*, 18(11):613–620, 1975.

[24] S.Boyd and L.Vandenberghe. *Convex Optimization*. Cambridge University Press, 2004.

[25] K. M. Svore, M. Volkovs, and C. J. C. Burges. Learning to rank with multiple objective functions. In *WWW*, pages 367–376, 2011.

[26] P. Venetis, H. Gonzalez, C. S. Jensen, and A. Y. Halevy. Hyper-local, directions-based ranking of places. *PVLDB*, 4(5):290–301, 2011.

[27] K.-P. Yee, K. Swearingen, K. Li, and M. Hearst. Faceted metadata for image search and browsing. In *CHI*, pages 401–408, 2003.

[28] X. Yi, H. Raghavan, and C. Leggetter. Discovering users' specific geo intention in web search. In *WWW*, pages 481–490, 2009.

[29] C. Zhai and J. Lafferty. A study of smoothing methods for language models applied to ad hoc information retrieval. In *Proceedings of ACM SIGIR 2001*, pages 334–342, 2001.

[30] L. Zhang and Y. Zhang. Interactive retrieval based on faceted feedback. In *Proceeding of the 33rd international ACM SIGIR*, pages 363–370, 2010.

[31] Z. Zheng, H. Zha, T. Zhang, O. Chapelle, K. Chen, and G. Sun. A general boosting method and its application to learning ranking functions for web search. In *Advances in Neural Information Processing Systems 20*, pages 1697–1704. MIT Press, 2008.

Beyond Ten Blue Links: Enabling User Click Modeling in Federated Web Search

Danqi Chen *
Institute for Interdisciplinary Information Sciences
Tsinghua University, China
cdq10131@gmail.com

Weizhu Chen
Microsoft Research Asia
Beijing, China
wzchen@microsoft.com

Haixun Wang
Microsoft Research Asia
Beijing, China
haixunw@microsoft.com

Zheng Chen
Microsoft Research Asia
Beijing, China
zhengc@microsoft.com

Qiang Yang
Hong Kong University of Science & Technolgy
Hong Kong
qyang@cse.ust.hk

ABSTRACT

Click models have been positioned as an effective approach to interpret user click behavior in search engines. Existing click models mostly focus on traditional Web search that considers only ten homogeneous Web HTML documents that appear on the first search-result page. However, in modern commercial search engines, more and more Web search results are federated from multiple sources and contain non-HTML results returned by other heterogeneous vertical engines, such as video or image search engines. In this paper, we study user click behavior in federated search. We observed that user click behavior in federated search is highly different from that in traditional Web search, making it difficult to interpret using existing click models. In response, we propose a novel federated click model (FCM) to interpret user click behavior in federated search. In particular, we take into considerations two new biases in FCM. The first comes from the observation that users tend to be attracted by vertical results and their visual attention on them may increase the examination probability of other nearby web results. The other illustrates that user click behavior on vertical results may lead to more clues of search relevance due to their presentation style in federated search. With these biases and an effective model to correct them, FCM is more accurate in characterizing user click behavior in federated search. Our extensive experimental results show that FCM can outperform other click models in interpreting user click behavior in federated search and achieve significant improvements in terms of both perplexity and log-likelihood.

*This work was done when the author was an intern at Microsoft Research Asia.

Permission to make digital or hard copies of all or part of this work for personal or classroom use is granted without fee provided that copies are not made or distributed for profit or commercial advantage and that copies bear this notice and the full citation on the first page. To copy otherwise, to republish, to post on servers or to redistribute to lists, requires prior specific permission and/or a fee.

WSDM'12, February 8–12, 2012, Seattle, Washington, USA.
Copyright 2012 ACM 978-1-4503-0747-5/12/02 ...$10.00.

Categories and Subject Descriptors

H.3.3 [**Information Storage and Retrieval**]: Information Search and Retrieval

General Terms

Algorithms, Measurement, Experimentation

Keywords

click model, federated search, log analysis

1. INTRODUCTION

Utilizing user click behavior in log data to understand user preference of search results is one of the most essential techniques for commercial search engines. Log data contains valuable information about user preference and can be collected at a low cost in most commercial search engines. This may in turn help search engines better entertain their users or deliver user-preferable advertisements. However, user click behavior in a commercial search engine may contain noise and biases. Many attempts have been made to address these challenges and most of them formalized the problem of learning an unbiased document relevance from user click data as the click model problem.

A well-known bias that needs to be corrected in learning an effective click model is the position bias, where a document appearing in a higher position will attract more user clicks even it is not as relevant as other documents appearing in lower positions. As a result, the often used metric click-through rate (CTR) is not an ideal measure of document relevance. Granka et al. [12] firstly observed this bias in their eye-tracking experiments and a lot of research has been done since then with the goal of inferring an unbiased relevance. Richardson et al. [20] proposed to increase the relevance of documents in lower positions by a multiplicative factor. Craswell et al. [7] later formalized this idea as the examination hypothesis, which states that a document is clicked if and only if it is both examined and relevant. More recent work extended these methods to better interpret user click data in either organic Web search [5, 11, 13] or online advertising in sponsored search [26, 23, 21].

Despite their success, existing click models in organic Web search mostly focus on traditional Web search that returns ten homogeneous HTML documents, which are often referred to as ten blue links in prominent literature. In modern commercial search engines, more and more Web search results are federated from multiple sources and contain non-HTML results returned by other heterogeneous vertical engines. For example, the result of the query 'Michael Jordan' in Bing is shown in Figure 1. Besides the traditional HTML documents, it also contains results from vertical search engines such as *image, video* and *news*. It is clear that the vertical results differ from traditional HTML documents due to the difference in presentation, layout, attractiveness, etc, which may in turn affect users' browsing behavior and their decision to perform clicks. However, previous click models are unable to address this issue since they assume only the availability of the ten blue links. As a result, modeling user click behavior in the federated search is an important but under-explored research problem.

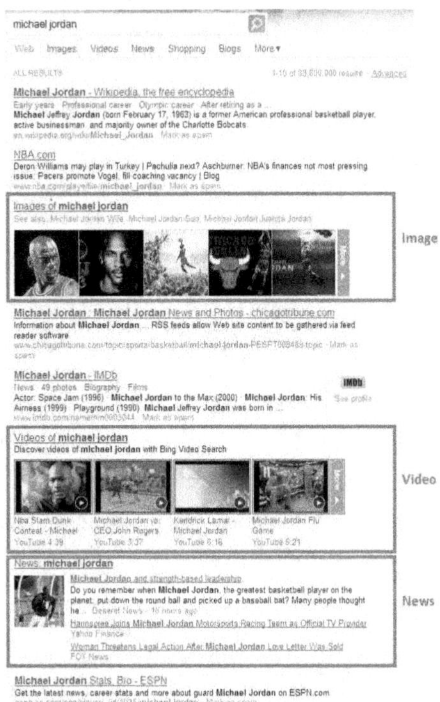

Figure 1: Screenshot of the Bing SERP page showing vertical search results at different slots.

In this paper, we first study user behavior in federated search and then put forward an observation that user behavior in federated search is highly different from that in traditional Web search. To better characterize user behavior in federated search, we propose a novel Bayesian model called Federated Click Model (FCM), which introduces two new biases in order to capture the distinctive user behavior in federated search. The first illustrates that users tend to be attracted by vertical results and the visual attention on these vertical results will increase the examination probability of other nearby web results. This motivates us to reconsider the examination probability of each document in federated search and develop an attention model beyond the cascade hypothesis [7]. The other bias is due to the fact that vertial results have a special presentation style in federated search, user clicks are more highly correlated with the relevance of the results, which may impact the examination probability of the other Web documents. FCM takes these biases into account, leading to better characterizations of user click behavior in federated search. We conduct extensive experiments on a large-scale commercial dataset to evaluate the effectiveness of FCM in federated search. Experimental results demonstrate that FCM outperforms other existing click models and achieves significant improvements in terms of both perplexity and log-likelihood.

2. BACKGROUND & RELATED WORKS

In this section, we present the background and related works of click model, as well as works more closely related to federated search.

2.1 Click Model

We begin by stating some definitions and notations of the click model. When a user submits a *query* q, the search engine returns a list of ranked documents as *search results*. A search session within the same query is called a *session*, denoted by s. The user *examines* some search results and *clicks* some or none of them. In our study, we only consider the first search result page of a session. We assume that the *search engine results page* (SERP) contains M documents, denoted by $\{d_1, d_2, \ldots, d_M\}$ where d_i is the document at position i from the top of the page. Usually, there are 10 traditional Web documents on the first page.

We use three binary random variables E_i, C_i and R_i to represent the examination, click and document relevance events of the document at position i.

- $E_i = 1$: the document at position i is examined.
- $C_i = 1$: the document at position i is clicked.
- $R_i = 1$: the document at position i is relevant.

Specifically, C_i is observable from the sessions while E_i and R_i are hidden random variables. We use the parameter r_{d_i} to represent the *document relevance*:

$$P(R_i = 1) = r_{d_i}. \tag{1}$$

Next, we introduce two important hypothesis: *examination hypothesis* and *cascade hypothesis*, which are the foundations of most existing click models.

Examination Hypothesis ([20, 7]) assumes that a document is clicked if and only if it is examined and relevant, which can be formulated as:

$$C_i = 1 \Longleftrightarrow E_i = 1, R_i = 1 \tag{2}$$

where E_i and R_i are independent. More precisely, we can represent the click-through rate as:

$$P(C_i = 1) = \underbrace{P(E_i = 1)}_{\text{position bias}} \underbrace{P(C_i = 1 | E_i = 1)}_{\text{document relavance}} \tag{3}$$

where $P(R_i = 1) = P(C_i = 1 \mid E_i = 1)$ indicates the probability of click after examination. [20] assumes that the examination probability depends solely on position i, and thus $P(C_i = 1) = \lambda_i r_{d_i}$, in which λ_i models the position bias.

An extension of the examination hypothesis is the *user browsing model* (UBM) [11]. It assumes that the examination probability $P(E_i = 1) = \gamma_{i,i-l_i}$, which depends not only on position i, but also on the distance from the last clicked position $l_i = \max\{j : j < i, C_j = 1\}$. Thus

$$P(C_i = 1) = \gamma_{i,i-l_i} \times r_{d_i} \quad (4)$$

The *Bayesian browsing model* (BBM) [17] uses exactly the same model assumptions as UBM, but adopts a Bayesian algorithm for model inference.

Cascade Hypothesis [7] assumes that the user scans linearly from top to bottom of the search result page. Thus, a document is examined only if all previous documents are examined and the first document is always examined.

$$P(E_{i+1} = 1 \mid E_i = 0) = 0 \quad (5)$$
$$P(E_1 = 1) = 1 \quad (6)$$

Based on the hypothesis, the *cascade model* [7] constrains that a user will continue the examination until the first click, and then she abandons the whole search session:

$$P(C_i = 1 \mid E_i = 1) = r_{d_i} \quad (7)$$
$$P(E_{i+1} = 1 \mid E_i = 1, C_i) = 1 - C_i \quad (8)$$

The *dependent click model* (DCM) [14] generalizes the cascade model to allow multiple clicks:

$$P(E_{i+1} = 1 \mid E_i = 1, C_i = 1) = \lambda_i. \quad (9)$$

Another two important extensions to the cascade model are the *Click Chain Model* (CCM) [13] and the *Dynamic Bayesian Network Model* (DBN) [5]. CCM assumes that the probability to continue examination after a click depends on the relevance of the clicked document and ranges between two parameters α_2 and α_3:

$$P(E_{i+1} = 1 \mid E_i = 1, C_i = 0) = \alpha_1 \quad (10)$$
$$P(E_{i+1} = 1 \mid E_i = 1, C_i = 1) = \alpha_2(1 - r_{d_i}) + \alpha_3 r_{d_i} \quad (11)$$

DBN distinguishes the "perceived" relevance and the "actual" relevance and assumes that the actual relevance decides whether the user will examine the next document:

$$P(E_{i+1} = 1 \mid E_i = 1, C_i = 0) = \zeta \quad (12)$$
$$P(E_{i+1} = 1 \mid E_i = 1, C_i = 1) = \zeta(1 - s_{d_i}) \quad (13)$$

where parameter s_{d_i} is the actual relevance (or refered to as satisfaction) of document at position i.

Most recent works on click models incorporate more factors into user modeling: The *post-click click model* (PCC) [25] incorporates post-click behaviors (dwell time, whether a user has the next click, etc) into the click modeling; [15] argues that user clicks cannot be explained only by relevance and position bias, but also the user intents; The *session utility model* (SUM) [10] measures the relevance of a set of clicked documents as the probability that a user stops the session; The *joint relevance examination model* (JRE) [21] and *temporal click model* [23] capture the externality factor. [21] states that the relevance of a document is not a constant but affected by clicks in other positions and extends the UBM model by integrating a new parameter δ_{η_i} where η_i is the total number of clicks on positions other than i; [23] verifies the existence of externalities based on two advertisements and models their competition in click prediction. The *whole page click model* (WPC) [6] considers the search result page including the organic search and sponsored search as a whole to perform the CTR prediction; The *task-centric click model* (TCM) [24] characterizes user behavior related to a task as a collective whole; The *general click model* (GCM) [26] treats all relevance and examination effects as random variables and allows multiple biases.

The main divergence of our work from previous approaches is that we focus on understanding the user click behavior in federated search which contains vertical results. To the best of our knowledge, this is the first attempt to combine click model with federated search.

2.2 Federated Search

In traditional Web search engines, a ranked list of Web documents is retrieved in response to a user's query. This old-school paradigm becomes less effective since the information sought by the user is not always contained in a single document or category. Thus, to meet users' expectation, many search portals assemble relevant contents from specific sub-collections, and place them in an interface called *verticals*. The method that integrates vertical results into Web search is known as *federated search* or *aggregated search* [18] . Figure 1 introduces 3 major kinds of vertical results: image, video, and news, which are displayed in collections of single vertical documents embedded into the search engine results page (SERP).

Heterogeneous search results are promising to enhance user searching experience to higher levels. Previous studies mainly concentrate on several aspects:

- Most prior work [8, 16, 9, 3, 4] focuses on *vertical selection* — the task of determining, for a given query, which verticals, if any, should be presented alongside Web search results.
- *Vertical composition* is another important task. The goal is to put multiple relevant verticals in the right positions relative to Web search results [19, 2, 1].
- Furthermore, several studies have been done to investigate user preference behavior. For example, Sushmita et al [22] investigates the effects of position and relevance on click-through behavior and finds a positive correlation between them.

Unlike prior works on federated search, we are working on a click model problem to automatically infer document relevance based on user click behavior. Besides the position bias in existing click models, we focus on illustrating the other biases introduced by the federated search and designing a new model to correct these biases to infer a more accurate document relevance. This is not covered by previous research.

3. USER BEHAVIOR ANALYSIS

Compared with web results, vertical results contain media types which make user behaviors vary according to different entities. In this section, we investigate the impacts of verticals on the click-through rate (CTR) of web results and present a click log analysis to reveal the essential difference between vertical and web results. From the outcome of this analysis, we got an inspiration to build up an effective click model for federated search.

As a motivational experiment, we have collected a three-day click log dataset in June 2011 from Microsoft Bing search engine, and randomly sample 20,000,000 query sessions with 4,276,432 distinct queries. In this paper, we focus on 3 major verticals: image, video and news. We only consider sessions that contain at least one image, video or news result. We treat each vertical result as a single document and a vertical is clicked if one of its internal urls is clicked. Every kind of verticals displays at most once in the SERP; therefore, including 10 traditional web results, a SERP contains at most 13 results from top to bottom. Moreover, in our observed data, image, video and news verticals account for 14.23%, 31.04% and 54.73% respectively among all verticals. Figure 2 illustrates the distribution of positions where verticals are placed, and Table 1 indicates the average CTR of web and vertical documents over different positions. It is clear to see that the verticals are mainly placed in three positions: position 1 (top), position 4 (middle) and position 11 (bottom). Also, Table 1 shows that the average CTR of vertical documents is generally lower than that of the web documents, especially at the top 2 positions.

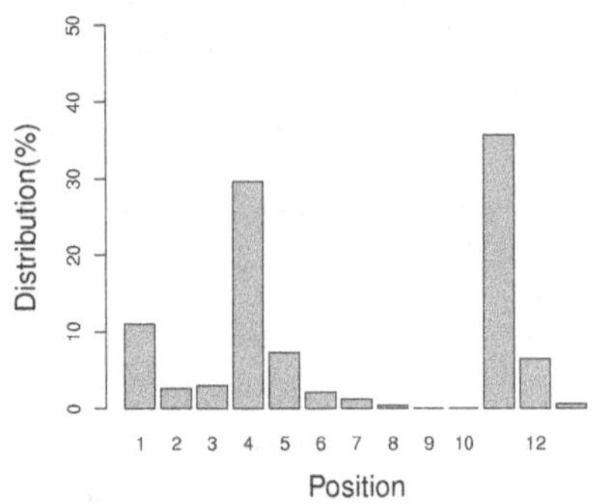

Figure 2: The distribution of positions where verticals are placed.

	@1	@2	@3	@4	@5
Web	53.71%	10.50%	5.09%	2.95%	2.27%
Vertical	19.09%	3.70%	8.35%	2.43%	1.08%

Table 1: The average click-through rate of web and vertical documents at position 1 - 5.

In the first experiment, we study the top 3 positions and explore the relationship between click patterns and types of the top results returned by the search engine. As receiving a high percentage of clicks, the top three results have a great positional advantage. Meanwhile, it is less likely that they are affected by other results underneath. We group sessions by the types of top three results, for example, "WVW" means that the top three results from top to bottom are from *web, vertical* and *web* respectively. For each group, we compute the probability distribution of 8 different click patterns (000, 001, 010, 011, 100, 101, 110, 111) where 1 means a click while 0 means a skip. We discard sessions with the top results "VVV" and "VWV" which occur only few times and report the results in Figure 3. According to the results, we attain the following observations: (1) Comparing "WWW", "WVV" with "VWW" and "VVW", if the first impression is a web result, then with a high probability, users will click the first one and perform no clicks in lower positions. On the other hand, if the top results are verticals, users tend to scan from top to bottom until reaching the first web result, thereby the positional bias among the top results diminishes. (2) The difference between the distributions of "WWW" and "WWV" shows that, if the third result is a vertical, the probability of "100" decreases significantly, whereas "010" increases. The existence of a vertical result at position 3 decreases the position bias at above positions, i.e., for the case of "WWV", users are more likely to examine the second results. (3) The group "WVW" has the highest probability of the click pattern "100" (71.50%). In the same manner, the existence of vertical will increase the CTR of the results in above positions while decrease that of the below results.

To further investigate the impact of verticals on the web documents, we perform a second experiment: In order to avoid the combinatorial effects of several verticals, we only keep those sessions with exactly one vertical (more than 85.0% of the dataset has only one vertical). We group sessions by the position and the type of the vertical, then compute the average CTR of web documents at other positions. In addition, we retrieve the sessions without any verticals from the same three days' log data and also compute the average CTR of web results at position 1 - 10. We only consider the sessions where the vertical is placed at position 1, 2, 3, 4, 5, 6 and 11 since position 7 - 10 only occupy 0.06% of the sessions in the whole dataset. The result is summarized in Table 2. The darker the color is, the more significantly the CTR increases. The average CTR at position 1 for traditional Web search is 57.27%. If there is an image vertical at position 3, the CTR of the first position decreases to 25.13%, but the CTR of the second position increases from 8.87% to 10.57%. In general, we observed that, except for position 1, either image or video vertical has an obvious influence on the CTR of web documents, especially when the web documents are placed closely with the vertical. In particular, the CTR increases 100% $\sim$ 200% in many lower positions. On the other hand, there is no apparent increase when a news vertical is placed, this may be mainly attributed to the presentation style of news since it is actually still text-based document and the font sizes are similar as web results.

In the third experiment, we focus on users' behaviors after clicking a document. We explore the probability of a click being the last click of the session in terms of the position and the type of the clicked document, since last click is believed to be informative and a good indication of user satisfaction [5]. Figure 4 illustrates that clicks on vertical results have significantly higher probability of being the last click except for position 1. For the exception of position 1 in Web, this may be driven by the high percentages of navigational queries like 'microsoft.com'. For all the other positions, given a click, a vertical result is more likely to achieve user satisfaction. Specifically, image and video verticals have a higher probability than news verticals. This observation can also be explained by introducing the notions "perceived" relevance and "actual" relevance in [5]. The decision to click is made based merely on perceived relevance but the actual relevance decides whether the user is satisfied with the result, which in turn decides whether he will continue to examine following results. For a web document, users can only see a snippet including its title, url and a short description. However, for image, video and news documents, search engine can offer an image thumbnail, a hover-to-play video thumbnail, even the news headline also delivers more

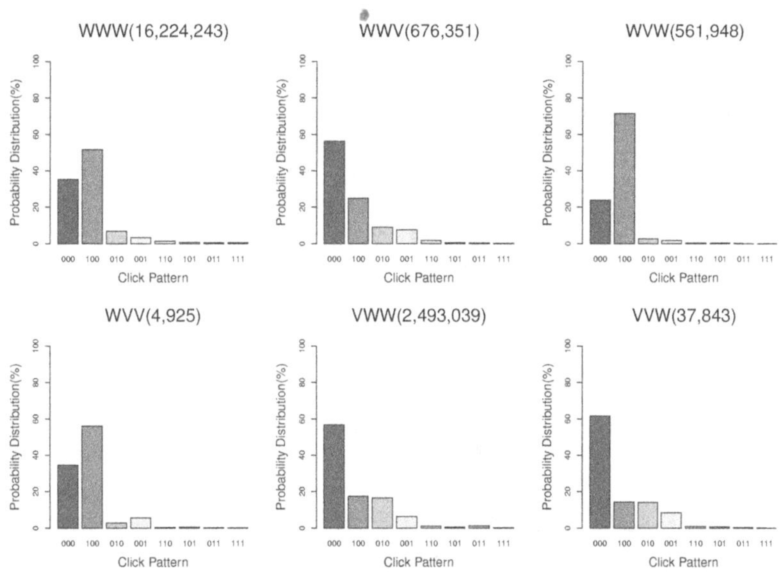

Figure 3: The probability distribution of click patterns over different results (top 3). The number in the parentheses refers to the number of sessions in the group.

information than Web. In other words, it is hard for users to examine a snippet and then judge whether it is really relevant or not. Rather, he can be aware of this from the thumbnail of an image or a video. Thus, the user will not continue to explore other results because his click on the image or the video most likely indicates his satisfaction.

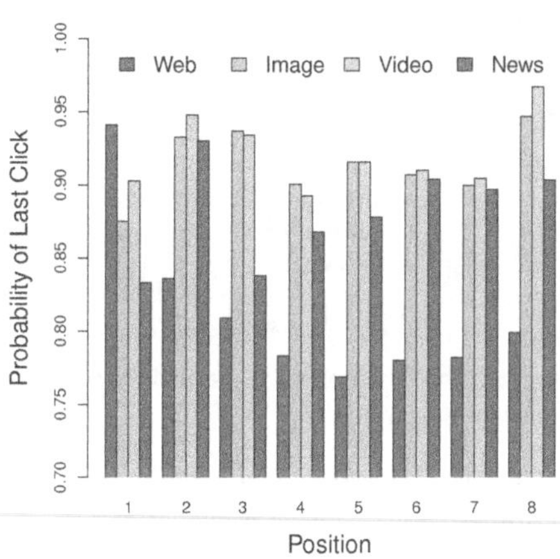

Figure 4: The probability of a click being the last click with respect to the position and the type of the clicked document.

In summary, vertical results and traditional web results mainly differ in three aspects: (1) Vertical results, especially image and video documents can attract more attentions and also make the surrounding web documents appear more prominent. (2) As a user clicks a vertical result, he is more likely to be satisfied with the document and then will not continue to examine other results. (3) For many users, they do not always seek vertical content, but may prefer the default web results instead. Therefore, web documents have a natural advantage to be trusted by users even in the federated search. (2) and (3) together explain why vertical results actually obtain more attentions but receive a lower click-through rate.

4. FEDERATED CLICK MODELS

Based on the observations and analysis in previous sections, in this section, we focus on developing an effective click model for federated search. We will propose two assumptions — *attention bias* and *exploration bias* to supervise the development of new click models.

4.1 Attention Model

According to the observations in Section 3, vertical results, especially image and video results tend to attract more attentions from users because of their visual presentation. As users' eyeballs are attracted by a vertical result, the other results close to it are more likely to receive more attention. We formalize this assumption as follows:

ASSUMPTION 1 (ATTENTION BIAS). *If there is a vertical placed in the SERP, users are more likely to examine the vertical as well as the web documents nearby. That is, vertical results play an extra role for attracting users' attention for other results around.*

To characterize the attention bias, we reconsider users' examination habits and present the new decision making flow in Figure 5. We use a binary random variable A to indicate whether there exists an attention bias in the current session s. We denote the probability of attention bias as $a(s)$ but it can vary based on the attention assumption design and incorporate many factors of verticals. If the session has no attention bias, the user will examine the document at position i with a probability ϕ_i where ϕ_i is the position bias in traditional click models. If there is an attention bias, the probability of examining a document will rise due to the effect of verticals, which is written as $\phi_i + (1 - \phi_i)\beta_{dist}$. $dist$ is an abbreviation for distance. β_{dist} is the parameter corresponding to the distance between the vertical result

Pos	1	2	3	4	5	6	7	8	9	10
No vertical										
avg	57.27	8.87	3.87	2.19	1.49	1.06	0.80	0.66	0.58	0.56
An image vertical placed at position 1, 2, 3, 4, 5, 6, 11										
1		21.58	10.07	6.19	4.04	3.01	2.31	1.89	1.58	1.38
2	46.76		6.04	2.89	1.60	1.04	0.79	0.65	0.46	0.39
3	25.13	10.57		5.75	3.96	2.60	1.86	1.48	1.16	1.02
4	26.29	11.61	7.34		4.18	3.53	2.37	1.98	1.67	1.46
5	36.47	12.54	7.66	4.97		3.12	2.46	1.98	1.54	1.38
6	28.16	14.38	10.14	6.38	4.55		3.05	2.45	1.99	1.79
11	47.28	12.10	6.63	3.99	2.78	1.94	1.45	1.10	0.88	0.70
A video vertical placed at position 1, 2, 3, 4, 5, 6, 11										
1		19.37	8.34	5.20	3.28	2.50	1.93	1.54	1.31	1.16
2	63.34		3.67	2.17	1.16	0.76	0.60	0.44	0.37	0.31
3	30.78	12.40		4.52	2.96	1.98	1.47	1.11	0.91	0.78
4	35.91	13.38	7.86		4.09	3.25	2.24	1.79	1.48	1.28
5	48.94	11.69	6.74	3.85		2.33	1.78	1.42	1.14	0.93
6	34.68	16.82	10.09	5.80	4.21		2.72	2.00	1.62	1.39
11	51.28	14.17	7.73	4.67	3.36	2.35	1.76	1.37	1.09	0.87
A news vertical placed at position 1, 2, 3, 4, 5, 6, 11										
1		23.82	8.04	4.55	2.53	1.97	1.46	1.08	0.91	0.80
2	72.55		2.88	1.32	0.69	0.48	0.36	0.28	0.20	0.19
3	58.18	6.53		2.12	0.87	0.88	0.47	0.33	0.31	0.41
4	60.50	7.57	3.35		1.06	0.99	0.70	0.52	0.43	0.36
5	74.18	4.58	1.71	0.80		0.48	0.32	0.24	0.20	0.17
6	68.31	4.98	2.18	1.00	0.86		0.35	0.33	0.25	0.23
11	54.80	6.72	3.03	1.63	1.15	0.75	0.55	0.42	0.34	0.26

Table 2: The CTR of web documents (%) at each position when there is no vertical or there is an image/video/news vertical.

and the current result i. Generally, the closer the document from a vertical, the more attentions it receives from the user. Given the document is examined, following the *examination hypothesis*, the probability of click still depends on the document relevance r_{d_i}.

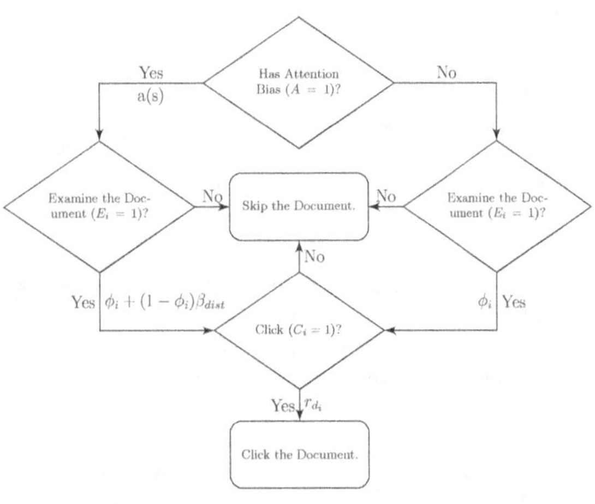

Figure 5: The Attention Model.

To formalize the model, we may summarize it as the following conditional probabilities:

$$P(A = 1) = a(s) \quad (14)$$

$$P(E_i = 1 \mid A = 0) = \phi_i \quad (15)$$

$$P(E_i = 1 \mid A = 1) = \phi_i + (1 - \phi_i)\beta_{dist} \quad (16)$$

$$P(C_i = 1 \mid E_i = 0) = 0 \quad (17)$$

$$P(C_i = 1 \mid E_i = 1) = r_{d_i} \quad (18)$$

Since the majority of sessions in a search engine contain at most one vertical, for a sound illustration, we consider single verticals in model specifications. On the other hand, it is natural to extend single verticals to multiple verticals by treating $a(s)$ as the joint impacts of all verticals, and replacing β_{dist} with the distance from the closest vertical. Thus, we consider single vertical in the following model specifications to achieve simplicity.

In particular, we use β_{dist} to characterize the position effect, where *dist* describes the distance between the web document at position i and the vertical. β_0 can be assumed as 1 with $\beta_0 = 1$, to assure the fact that if the session has an attention bias, the probability of examining the vertical itself is

$$\phi_i + (1 - \phi_i) \times 1 = 1.$$

Furthermore, the degree of web documents influenced by a vertical may differ on the distance variable *dist*. If the position of the vertical is j while the current position for a Web document is i, we calculate $dist = j - i$ and each $dist$ has a corresponding parameter β_{dist}. Note that *dist* may be a negative value and this is allowed in our model.

Another variable of the attention model is the parameter $a(s)$. We propose two different assumptions to develop $a(s)$ and call them as the *position attention model* and the *document attention model*.

4.1.1 Position Attention Model

The position attention model assumes that the attention bias of a session is decided only by the position of the vertical, where $a(s)$ is a position-specific parameter. We use pos_v to denote the position of the vertical in the SERP, then

$$P(A = 1 \mid pos_v) = h_{pos_v}.$$

$\{h\}$ is a group of global parameters and can vary according to different type of verticals.

4.1.2 Document Attention Model

Another approach is to consider $a(s)$ as a document-specific parameter for each vertical. For different vertical documents, even they are placed in the same position, their attention bias values are different. Thus for each vertical document d, along with the relevance parameter r_d, we use another intrinsic parameter u_d to characterize the degree of the attention born with this document, thus

$$P(A = 1 \mid d) = u_d$$

4.2 Exploration Model

According to the experimental findings in the third experiment of last Section, although vertical results receive a lower CTR, given a vertical result is clicked, it predominantly leads to more user satisfaction. Obviously, the increase of satisfaction may decrease the examination probability of other documents. We may formalize this as another assumption as follows:

ASSUMPTION 2 (EXPLORATION BIAS). *As a user clicks a vertical result, he is more likely to be satisfied with the result and end the whole search session.*

We introduce a binary variable D to indicate whether the session has an exploration bias and C_v to indicate whether the user clicks a vertical result. If there is a click on a vertical result ($C_v = 1$), we use a parameter $e(s)$ to characterize the degree of the exploration bias of the session. We further assume that if the session has an exploration bias ($D = 1$), the user tends to skip web results. Furthermore, the probability of click ($C_i = 1$) still obeys the examination hypothesis. To distinguish web results and vertical results, we rely on a binary variable V_i, where $V_i = 1$ denotes a vertical document and $V_i = 0$ stands for a web document. The exploration model can be formalized as below:

$$P(D=1 \mid C_v=0) = 0 \quad (19)$$
$$P(D=1 \mid C_v=1) = e(s) \quad (20)$$
$$P(E_i=1 \mid D=1, V_i=0) = 0 \quad (21)$$
$$P(E_i=1 \mid V_i=1 \vee (D=0, V_i=0)) = \phi_i \quad (22)$$
$$P(C_i=1 \mid E_i=0) = 0 \quad (23)$$
$$P(C_i=1 \mid E_i=1) = r_{d_i} \quad (24)$$

where ϕ_i is the position bias in traditional click models. Similar to the attention model, we can also estimate the exploration bias $e(s)$ in two approaches — position-specific and document-specific — which are denoted by the *position exploration model* and the *document exploration model* respectively.

4.3 Joint Vertical Model

A natural generalization of the above two models is to integrate the attention model and the exploration model into one model. We call this the *joint vertical model* (JVM). We combine the examination probability as the product of the probability relying on the attention bias and the probability relying on the exploration bias. It is written as

$$P(E_i=1 \mid A, D) = P(E_i=1 \mid A)P(E_i=1 \mid D) \quad (25)$$

where $P(E_i = 1 \mid A)$ is given in Eq.(14), (15) and (16), $P(E_i = 1 \mid D)$ is given in Eq.(19), (20), (21) and (22). And the probability of click after examination still depends on the document relevance r_{d_i}.

In particular, each session has an attention bias $a(s)$ and an exploration bias $e(s)$ in the model. Following the previous models, we can define either of them in a position-specific or a document-specific approach.

The joint vertical model incorporates the attention bias and the exploration bias together, in which a placed vertical would increase the examination probability of surrounding web results but receive a low click-through rate. Meanwhile, if the vertical is clicked, the examination probability of all the web results will drop.

4.4 Inference

The proposed federated click models FCM can embrace the assumption of most existing click models dependent on the examination hypothesis. Till now, we assume ϕ_i as the position bias in traditional click models. Next, we may extend the FCM to embrace different assumption of ϕ_i based on different models. For the examination model in [20] we have,

$$\phi_i = \lambda_i.$$

For the user browsing model (UBM) [11],

$$\phi_i = \gamma_{i,i-l_i}$$

where l_i is the last clicked document. Even for the models relying on the cascade hypothesis, such as the dynamic bayesian network model (DBN) [5], it can be also extended naturally by combining Eq.(12),(13) and designed ϕ_i as:

$$\phi_i = \prod_{j<i} (\zeta(1 - s_{d_j})^{C_j})$$

We use the Expectation-Maximization (EM) algorithm to complete the inference step. The EM algorithm is used to find the maximum likelihood estimates of parameters, including the attention bias parameters $a(s)$, the exploration bias parameters $e(s)$, the distance parameters β_{dist}, the document relevance r_d and all parameters associated with ϕ (for example, in DBN model, the parameters s_d, γ are included). To perform EM iterations, in the E-Step, we compute the marginal posterior distribution of each hidden variable. The computation is performed based on the parameter values updated in the previous iteration. In the M-Step, all posterior probabilities associated with the same parameter are averaged to update the parameters.

We take an example to illustrate the inference where $\phi_i = \gamma_{i,i-l_i}$ as in UBM, $e(s) = \alpha_{pos_v}, a(s) = \eta_{pos_v}$ where $e(s), a(s)$ are only related to the position of the vertical pos_v. Next we show how to update $\{\eta\}$, and the other parameters can be derived similarly. As shown in Algorithm.1, at each iteration, we enumerate each document of each session and compute the posterior probability of η_{pos_v} using the parameters in the previous iteration, where pos_v is the position of the vertical in the current session. Finally, we update each η_p as the average posterior probabilities.

Algorithm 1 Inference

Iteration k:
for every position p **do**
  $\eta_p^A \leftarrow 0, \eta_p^B \leftarrow 0$
for each document d of each session **do**
  $pos_v \leftarrow$ the position of the vertical
  $i \leftarrow$ the position of d
  $l_i \leftarrow$ the position of last clicked document
  $dist \leftarrow$ the distance from the vertical
  if d is a web result and $C_v = 1$ **then**
    $e \leftarrow 1 - \alpha_{pos_v}^{k-1}$ // e is the exploration bias
  else
    $e \leftarrow 1$
  if d is clicked **then**
    $\eta_{pos_v}^A \leftarrow \eta_{pos_v}^A + \frac{\eta_{pos_v}^{k-1} e(\beta_{dist}^{k-1} + (1-\beta_{dist}^{k-1})\gamma_{i,i-l_i}^{k-1})}{e(\gamma_{i,i-l_i}^{k-1} + (1-\gamma_{i,i-l_i}^{k-1})\eta_{pos_v}^{k-1}\beta_{dist}^{k-1})}$
  else
    $\eta_{pos_v}^A \leftarrow \eta_{pos_v}^A + \frac{\eta_{pos_v}^{k-1}(1-r_d^{k-1} e(\beta_{dist}^{k-1} + (1-\beta_{dist}^{k-1})\gamma_{i,i-l_i}^{k-1}))}{1-r_d^{k-1} e(\gamma_{i,i-l_i}^{k-1} + (1-\gamma_{i,i-l_i}^{k-1})\eta_{pos_v}^{k-1}\beta_{dist}^{k-1})}$
  $\eta_{pos_v}^B \leftarrow \eta_{pos_v}^B + 1$
for every position p **do**
  $\eta_p^k \leftarrow \frac{\eta_p^A}{\eta_p^B}$

5. EXPERIMENTS

In this section, we compare the federated click model with two existing click models in Web search: UBM [11] and DBN [5]. For the FCM, there are three specific models. They are attention model, exploration model and joint vertical model (JVM). For each specific model, there are two assumptions: position-specific or document-specific. We use click perplexity and log-likelihood as metrics to measure the effectiveness of a click model.

5.1 Experimental Setup

The click logs used to train and evaluate click models are collected from Microsoft Bing search engine for a week in June 2011, which comprises $998,489$ randomly sampled queries. A session consists of an input query, a list of returned results on the search result page, each of which is either a web result or a vertical result, and a list of clicked positions. We keep those sessions with at least one vertical result (image, video or news). Only query sessions with at least one click are kept for performance evaluation. In order to prevent the whole dataset from becoming dominated by the extremely frequent queries, we allow each query at most 10^4 sessions. Finally, we collect nearly 27.5 million query sessions and 11.2 million web urls, 15.02% sessions have image impressions, 33.79% sessions have video impressions and 67.53% sessions have news impressions. The detailed information about the dataset is summarized in Table 3. For each query, we sort its search sessions by the timestamp when the query is sent to the search engine and split them into the training and testing sets at a ratio of $3:1$.

To evaluate the accuracy in click-through rate prediction, we trained different click models on the same training set. For the baseline models UBM and DBN, we use the inference algorithms introduced in the original papers. The training of our models follows the algorithm given in Section 4.4. Initially, all the relevance parameters are set to 0.2 and all the other parameters are set to 0.5. For either the attention model or the exploration model, we train the models from the two approaches — position-specific and document-specific for the attention bias $a(s)$ and the exploration bias $e(s)$. The iterative training of EM algorithms will run until all parameters converge. All the parameters related to the verticals are learnt according to the vertical types respectively. As the training is completed, we use the estimated parameters to predict the click-through rate for each document of every query sessions in the testing set. Utilizing the derived click probability, we evaluate the effectiveness of click models in terms of perplexity and log-likelihood.

5.2 Perplexity Evaluation

Perplexity is widely used to evaluate the accuracy of click-through rate prediction. It measures the accuracy for individual positions instead of the whole session. For a set of query sessions $s_1, \ldots, s_N$, if q_i^n is the probability of click at position i derived from the click model and C_i^n is the observed click event, the click perplexity at position i is:

$$p_i = 2^{-\frac{1}{N}(C_i^n \log_2 q_i^n + (1-C_i^n)\log_2(1-q_i^n))}.$$

The perplexity of the entire dataset is the average of p_i over all positions. A perfect click prediction will have a perplexity of 1 and a smaller number indicates better prediction accuracy. The improvement of perplexity value p_1 over p_2 is given by $(p_2 - p_1)/(p_2 - 1) \times 100\%$.

Table 4 illustrates the perplexity over positions from 1 through 8. It also reports the relative improvement of the federated click models over UBM. It shows that there is a clear ordering that JVM > (attention model or exploration model) > (UBM or DBN). More specifically, the UBM performs slightly better than DBN on perplexity, and all the federated models are significantly better than the UBM with more than 5% improvement of overall perplexity.

We can see that the two biases introduced in our federated click models can both learn a better accuracy in CTR prediction. Meanwhile, by combining the two biases together, JVM achieves a more significant improvement especially at the top 2 positions. It is clear to see that the JVM model has a 4.13%, 3.16% improvement at position 1 and position 2 respectively, and the overall improvement reaches 6.76%. In addition, if we compare either the position attention model with the document attention model, or the position exploration model with the document exploration model, we find that the position-specific models are slightly better than the document-specific models. This may be attributed to the skewness of the data since for a lot of low frequency queries, there is no enough data to learn an accurate document-specific parameter for each document. Thus in the following experiments, we use the position-specific approach to estimate $a(s)$ and $e(s)$.

5.3 Log-likelihood Evaluation

Another common metric to evaluate the effectiveness of click models is the Log-likelihood(LL). LL is computed as the average log probability of observed click events under the trained model. For a document d under a given query, if Pr is the derived probability of click, and C is the observed binary click event, then

$$LL = C \log_2 Pr + (1-C)\log_2(1-Pr)$$

The Log-likelihood of a dataset with a number of query sessions is measured as the average LL on individual documents. A larger LL indicates a better performance, and the optimal value is 0. The improvement of LL values l_1 over l_2 is computed as $(\exp(l_1 - l_2) - 1) \times 100\%$. We compute the average LL in terms of each types of documents, including web, image, video and news results. LL is often presented over the query frequency, which represents the number of sessions for a query in the training data. We separate the testing session based on the query frequency into 7 sets as Table 3. We then present the results of each set for both Web and different verticals in Figure 6.

It is also shown that all the federated click models outperform either UBM or DBN model for Web, especially for the low-frequency queries. Web results occupy about 80% of all the predictions thus it plays a major role in the overall prediction. The improvements on Set 1 and Set 2 in Web are more than 4% and 2% respectively for JVM, as compared with DBN. For the image and video results, attention model performs the best and achieves 2.04% and 2.26% improvements respectively.

6. CONCLUSIONS

In this paper, we have shown the user behavior difference between federated search and traditional Web search. We have demonstrated the necessity to model user specific behavior in federated search. Thereafter, we propose several federated click models to characterize user behavior as

Table 3: The summary of the dataset in experiments. Image(#Queries, #Sessions) represents the number of queries and sessions with image impressions.

Set	Query Frequency	#Queries	#Sessions	Image		Video		News	
				#Queries	#Sessions	#Queries	#Sessions	#Queries	#Sessions
1	$1 \sim 10$	733,833	2,726,280	219,607	718,439	402,742	1,419,233	228,238	858,314
2	$10 \sim 10^{1.5}$	159,543	2,826,188	47,815	589,878	89,107	1,353,219	81,427	1,236,861
3	$10^{1.5} \sim 10^{2}$	67,239	3,650,037	23,059	634,601	37,272	1,490,827	45,188	2,085,483
4	$10^{2} \sim 10^{2.5}$	25,399	4,346,371	10,344	663,639	14,148	1,423,203	20,671	3,030,331
5	$10^{2.5} \sim 10^{3}$	8,489	4,550,372	3,684	611,990	4,802	1,234,566	7,561	3,571,209
6	$10^{3} \sim 10^{3.5}$	2,722	4,624,375	1,147	488,722	1,600	1,255,966	2,500	3,760,290
7	$10^{3.5} \sim 10^{4}$	882	4,738,227	377	418,657	500	1,102,033	832	4,002,307
Total		998,107	27,461,850	306,033	4,125,926	550,171	9,279,047	386,417	18,544,795

Table 4: The perplexity of comparison over ranking positions. "@n" represents the perplexity at position n.

	@1	@2	@3	@4	@5	@6	@7	@8	Overall
DBN	1.5487	1.4284	1.2758	1.1629	1.1351	1.1111	1.0902	1.0755	1.1660
UBM	1.5527	1.4253	1.2705	1.1624	1.1355	1.1118	1.0922	1.0789	1.1655
Attention(position)	1.5449	1.4197	1.2678	1.1569	1.1282	1.1027	1.0811	1.0660	1.1553
Impr.(vs. UBM)	1.42%	1.31%	0.99%	3.39%	5.36%	8.19%	12.10%	16.44%	6.11%
Attention(document)	1.5449	1.4203	1.2688	1.1571	1.1293	1.1027	1.0811	1.0659	1.1557
Impr.(vs. UBM)	1.41%	1.16%	0.62%	3.22%	4.54%	8.16%	12.07%	16.52%	5.87%
Exploration(position)	1.5469	1.4139	1.2720	1.1575	1.1280	1.1030	1.0819	1.0669	1.1559
Impr.(vs. UBM)	1.05%	2.66%	-0.56%	3.02%	5.48%	7.87%	11.19%	15.24%	5.79%
Exploration(document)	1.5518	1.4149	1.2720	1.1573	1.1278	1.1027	1.0816	1.0666	1.1564
Impr.(vs. UBM)	0.17%	2.44%	-0.56%	3.14%	5.65%	8.18%	11.53%	15.63%	5.47%
JVM	1.5299	1.4099	1.2683	1.1591	1.1286	1.1034	1.0819	1.0669	1.1543
Impr.(vs. UBM)	**4.13%**	**3.16%**	0.82%	2.01%	5.07%	7.54%	11.25%	15.30%	**6.76%**

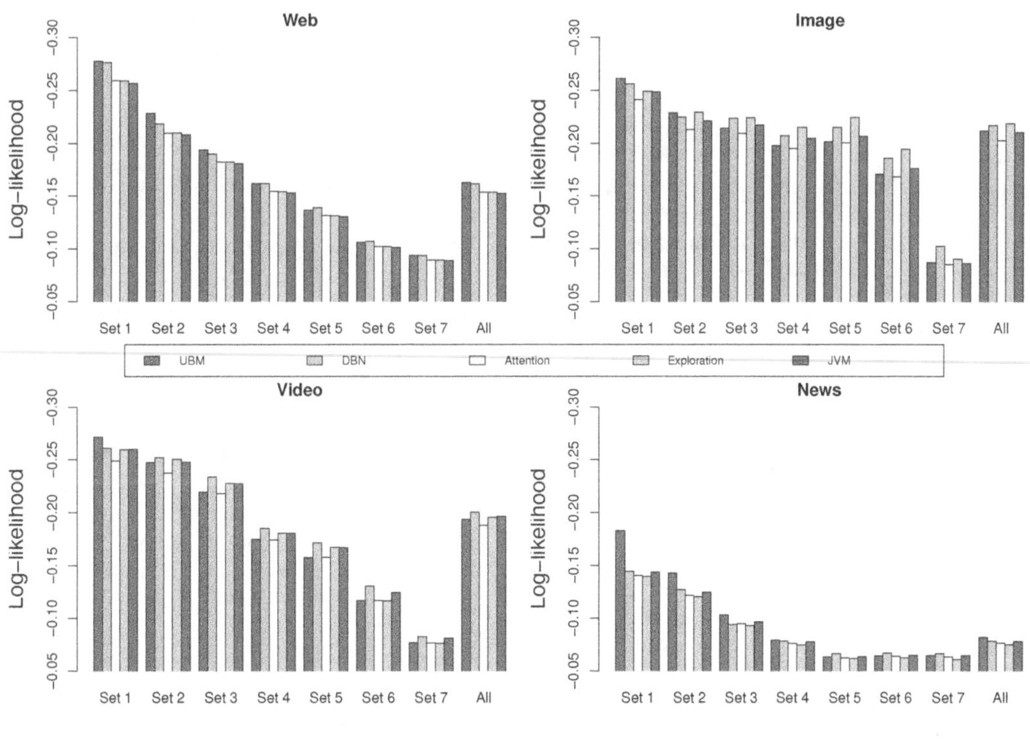

Figure 6: The log-likelihood of comparison over the web, image, video and news results.

examining and clicking on vertical results in nowadays Web search. In particular, FCM introduces two novel biases. The first indicates that users tend to be attracted by vertical results and their visual attention on them may increase the examination probability of other Web results. The other illustrates that user click behavior on vertical results may lead to more indication of relevance due to their presentation style in federated search. Taking these biases into consideration, we have designed FCM as a general model that makes it capable of embracing the assumptions in most existing click models. We have successfully extended it to embrace the assumptions of DBN and UBM, and designed an EM-based inference approach to make FCM capable of processing large-scale click data. Extensive experimental results have demonstrated that the proposed click models can better interpret user click behavior and achieve significant improvements in terms of both perplexity and log likelihood.

Designing an effective click model to better understand user click behavior is critical but challenging for any commercial search engines. One of the challenges is the layout of the vertical results. Even with the same vertical, it will have multiple layouts for different queries. We plan to further study user click behavior by changing the positions in which the vertical results are placed. Some controlled experiments may be helpful on this, such as in an eye tracking environment. Another challenge is to better understand user intents when clicking on the vertical results. Even with the same query, different intents will lead to click on different vertical results.

7. ACKNOWLEDGMENTS

This work was supported in part by Hong Kong RGC GRF Grant 621010, the National Basic Research Program of China Grant 2011CBA00300, 2011CBA00301, the National Natural Science Foundation of China Grant 61033001, 61061130540, 61073174.

We would like to thank Derek Hao Hu from HKUST and the anonymous reviewers for their helpful comments.

8. REFERENCES

[1] J. Arguello, F. Diaz, and J. Callan. Learning to aggregate vertical results into web search results. In *CIKM*, 2011.

[2] J. Arguello, F. Diaz, J. Callan, and B. Carterette. A methodology for evaluating aggregated search results. In *ECIR*, 2011.

[3] J. Arguello, F. Diaz, J. Callan, and J.-F. Crespo. Sources of evidence for vertical selection. In *SIGIR*, 2009.

[4] J. Arguello, F. Diaz, and J.-F. Paiement. Vertical selection in the presence of unlabeled verticals. In *SIGIR*, 2010.

[5] O. Chapelle and Y. Zhang. A dynamic bayesian network click model for web search ranking. In *WWW*, 2009.

[6] W. Chen, Z. Ji, S. Shen, and Q. Yang. A whole page click model to better interpret search engine click data. In *AAAI*, 2011.

[7] N. Craswell, O. Zoeter, M. Taylor, and B. Ramsey. An experimental comparison of click position-bias models. In *WSDM*, 2008.

[8] F. Diaz. Integration of news content into web results. In *WSDM*, 2009.

[9] F. Diaz and J. Arguello. Adaptation of offline vertical selection predictions in the presence of user feedback. In *SIGIR*, 2009.

[10] G. Dupret and C. Liao. A model to estimate intrinsic document relevance from the clickthrough logs of a web search engine. In *WSDM*, 2010.

[11] G. E. Dupret and B. Piwowarski. A user browsing model to predict search engine click data from past observations. In *SIGIR*, 2008.

[12] L. A. Granka, T. Joachims, and G. Gay. Eye-tracking analysis of user behavior in www search. In *SIGIR*, 2004.

[13] F. Guo, C. Liu, A. Kannan, T. Minka, M. Taylor, Y.-M. Wang, and C. Faloutsos. Click chain model in web search. In *WWW*, 2009.

[14] F. Guo, C. Liu, and Y. M. Wang. Efficient multiple-click models in web search. In *WSDM*, 2009.

[15] B. Hu, Y. Zhang, W. Chen, G. Wang, and Q. Yang. Characterizing search intent diversity into click models. In *WWW*, 2011.

[16] X. Li, Y.-Y. Wang, and A. Acero. Learning query intent from regularized click graphs. In *SIGIR*, 2008.

[17] C. Liu, F. Guo, and C. Faloutsos. Bbm: bayesian browsing model from petabyte-scale data. In *KDD*, 2009.

[18] V. Murdock and M. Lalmas. Workshop on aggregated search. *SIGIR Forum*, 2008.

[19] A. K. Ponnuswami, K. Pattabiraman, Q. Wu, R. Gilad-Bachrach, and T. Kanungo. On composition of a federated web search result page: using online users to provide pairwise preference for heterogeneous verticals. In *WSDM*, 2011.

[20] M. Richardson, E. Dominowska, and R. Ragno. Predicting clicks: estimating the click-through rate for new ads. In *WWW*, 2007.

[21] R. Srikant, S. Basu, N. Wang, and D. Pregibon. User browsing models: relevance versus examination. In *KDD*, 2010.

[22] S. Sushmita, H. Joho, M. Lalmas, and R. Villa. Factors affecting click-through behavior in aggregated search interfaces. In *CIKM*, 2010.

[23] W. Xu, E. Manavoglu, and E. Cantu-Paz. Temporal click model for sponsored search. In *SIGIR*, 2010.

[24] Y. Zhang, W. Chen, D. Wang, and Q. Yang. User-click modeling for understanding and predicting search-behavior. In *KDD*, 2011.

[25] F. Zhong, D. Wang, G. Wang, W. Chen, Y. Zhang, Z. Chen, and H. Wang. Incorporating post-click behaviors into a click model. In *SIGIR*, 2010.

[26] Z. A. Zhu, W. Chen, T. Minka, C. Zhu, and Z. Chen. A novel click model and its applications to online advertising. In *WSDM*, 2010.

Finding the Right Consumer: Optimizing for Conversion in Display Advertising Campaigns

Yandong Liu‡ *, Sandeep Pandey†, Deepak Agarwal†, Vanja Josifovski†

‡ Carnegie Mellon, 5000 Forbes Avenue, Pittsburgh, PA 15213, USA
† Yahoo! Research, 4301 Great America Parkway, Santa Clara, CA 95054, USA
yandongl@cs.cmu.edu | {spandey | dagarwal | vanjaj}@yahoo-inc.com

ABSTRACT

The ultimate goal of advertisers are *conversions* representing desired user actions on the advertisers' websites in the form of purchases and product information request. In this paper we address the problem of finding the right audience for display campaigns by finding the users that are most likely to convert. This challenging problem is at the heart of display campaign optimization and has to deal with several issues such as very small percentage of converters in the general population, high-dimensional representation of the user profiles, large churning rate of users and advertisers. To overcome these difficulties, in our approach we use two sources of information: a *seed* set of users that have converted for a campaign in the past; and a description of the campaign based on the advertiser's website. We explore the importance of the information provided by each of these two sources in a principled manner and then combine them to propose models for predicting converters. In particular, we show how seed set can be used to capture the campaign-specific targeting constraints, while the campaign metadata allows to share targeting knowledge across campaigns. We give methods for learning these models and perform experiments on real-world advertising campaigns. Our findings show that the seed set and the campaign metadata are complimentary to each other and both sources provide valuable information for conversion optimization.

Categories and Subject Descriptors

H.4.m [**Information Systems**]: Miscellaneous

General Terms

Algorithms, Performance, Experimentation

Keywords

conversions, modeling, advertising

*Work done while at Yahoo! Research

Permission to make digital or hard copies of all or part of this work for personal or classroom use is granted without fee provided that copies are not made or distributed for profit or commercial advantage and that copies bear this notice and the full citation on the first page. To copy otherwise, to republish, to post on servers or to redistribute to lists, requires prior specific permission and/or a fee.
WSDM'12, February 8–12, 2012, Seattle, Washington, USA.
Copyright 2012 ACM 978-1-4503-0747-5/12/02 ...$10.00.

1. INTRODUCTION

Businesses, small and large alike, seek to expand by reaching out to users who can be their potential customers. Online advertising is becoming one of the main advertising channels, accounting for estimated $80 billion spending in 2011 and growing at the rate of 17% annually,[1] with display advertising being a big part of it. To make their campaign effective, display advertisers target specific users based on their historical pattern of activity or behavior, i.e., *behavioral targeting*. Different advertisers target different kind of users, e.g., a cellular company would be interested in users looking to subscribe to a cell phone plan or buying a handset, an online trading/investing company looks for finance-savvy users interested in buying/selling of shares, a travel agency wants to find customers for purchasing of flight tickets and booking of hotel rooms. While in some cases targeting criteria can be specified as a simple condition/function of the past user behavior, to get the best performance, increasingly sophisticated modeling techniques are being applied to detect the behavior patterns indicative of the user interest in a particular campaign/product.

Behavioral targeting aids advertisers in finding the right audience for their campaigns by characterizing and targeting users who fit their needs. Intermediaries such as ad networks, online exchanges and demand side platforms, perform behavioral targeting by bringing in the three parties involved, users, publishers and advertisers. While the complete details of advertising ecosystem is beyond the scope of this paper, a simplified view showing the interaction between advertisers and publishers is given in Figure 1. Here we use the term *ad broker* to refer to the intermediaries that (a) facilitate the collection of user data to build profiles and (b) select the best advertising campaign to display on a given Web page being viewed (impression) by a user on the publisher site. The ad broker constructs profiles for users based on their past online activities such as Web pages viewed at the participating publishers, Web search queries, vertical searches, etc. These profiles are then leveraged to learn advertiser-specific segment/model describing the desired target audience in terms of the pattern of user behavior. The focus of this paper is on producing such effective models for display advertising.

Most prior work on building behavioral targeting models focuses on maximizing clicks [6, 22], that is, construct models to identify those users who are most likely to click on ads when shown. While clicks serve as a natural proxy for

[1]According to a study by emarketer.com.

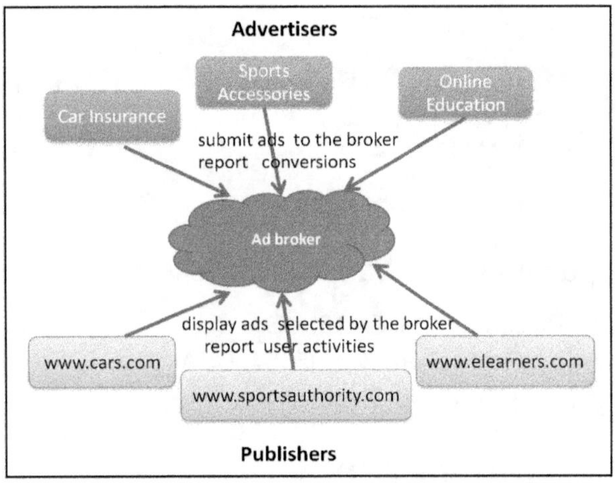

Figure 1: Behavioral Targeting.

user's interest in the advertised product, they can often be misleading, e.g., click fraud, bounce clicks [7, 12, 23]. Hence, in this work our goal is to target users for *conversions*, representing user activity on the advertisers website beyond the ad click [2, 4, 14]. Conversions are more tangible indication of user interest in the advertiser than clicks, separating the incidental and casual interest from purchasing intent.

Building conversion models is extremely challenging for many reasons. Usually, only a very small portion of the users that click eventually convert and thus, conversions are very rare events. This constrains the modeling techniques to parsimoniously work with the data. On the user side, user profiles are high dimensional consisting of several different kinds of activities, ranging from user demographics to search queries and page browsing. Dealing with such different activities in the presence of limited target/conversion information is non-trivial. To add to this, the data is highly volatile due to cookie churn, changes in campaigns, variability in user interests and other temporal effects that do not allow accumulating long-standing data and require the modeling approach to have a quick start and dynamically adapt over time as new data comes in.

Our Approach.

In view of these challenges, we propose a novel approach for conversion prediction that relies on two distinct sources of information: (a) the *metadata* associated with the advertising campaign such as ad creative, landing page etc.; and (b) *seed users* who have converted or viewed ads for the advertiser in the past. These two sources are complimentary in the way they guide the modeling process. For a new advertiser, since its ads have not been shown by the advertising network yet, the ad broker does not have any record of past converted users. As a result, initially, the ad broker must rely on using campaign's metadata to find right users for it. The campaign metadata quickly helps in understanding what the advertising campaign is about and thus identifying the potential targeting set. The metadata can be leveraged both in an unsupervised manner (e.g., target sports enthusiasts for sports related advertising) and supervised manner (e.g., pool the seed sets of campaigns using campaign metadata; more details in Section 3).

Subsequently, when the network has shown ads to enough users for the campaign, some of these users would have converted. This information can be used in refining the initial model: the converted users make the positive instances, while the unconverted users can be treated as the negatives. This can be modeled as a regression/classification task; predicting the conversion likelihood based on user profiles.

We give a principled approach to combine the two sources of information and propose a series of models. In particular, we show how seed set can be used to capture the campaign-specific targeting constraints (*local* component), while the campaign metadata allows to share targeting knowledge across campaigns (*global* component). For example, a "nike" campaign can learn/teach which users to target from/to an "adidas" campaign. Also, we give methods for learning these models in a joint manner that simultaneously optimizes for the local and global components and a two-step approach that performs this optimization in two stages.

In doing so we investigate several technical questions. For example, how do we represent users and campaign in a succinct manner? How useful are the two sources of information and how do they interact with each other? How can we combine them both in a principled manner? We answer these questions and make interesting observations through real advertising data collected from a large ad network. For example, we found that contrary to popular belief, learning models for large campaigns (in terms of number of conversions) can be more difficult compare to the smaller campaigns and the metadata can help in dealing with this issue.

Contributions.

In summary, we make the following contributions in this paper:

- We propose to predict conversions using: campaign metadata and seed users. We examine their relative value for campaigns with different characteristics (e.g., large and small, new and old).
- We give a set of modeling techniques that combine the two sources of information for optimal performance (through the local and global component). To the best of our knowledge, this is the first study on behavioral targeting to model the global component.
- Using the campaign metadata, we propose a method to bootstrap the prediction model for a campaign by exploiting information from related campaigns.
- We conduct extensive experiments and report the results from a real-life advertising dataset, to confirm the validity of our approach.

Finally, we note that, although the experiments are focused on conversion maximization for performance-based display advertisers, the principles described are applicable in a broader context as user profiles are the basis for audience selection in almost any setting of online advertising targeting and content personalization.

2. PROBLEM DEFINITION

As in traditional brand and performance advertising, display advertisers aim to *target* the users that might be interested in their products to promote their brand or get a direct response from the users. Depending on the *brand* or *performance* inclination, the advertisers can set up their campaigns using different goals. While brand advertisers are primarily interested in number of ad views (impressions) by the targeted audience, performance advertisers usually set up either click or conversions goals. In this paper we focus on performance advertisers with **conversion optimization goals.** (More details on performance-advertising and the technical difficulties of it are given in Section 5.1).

Mathematically, the conversion optimization task can be formulated as the following. Let $c \in \mathcal{C}$ denote a campaign and $\boldsymbol{z}_c$ be the feature representation of its metadata. Let $seed_c$ denote the seed set for campaign c with labeled converters and non-converters. For each campaign $c \in \mathcal{C}$, the goal is to learn a model to differentiate between converters and non-converters. Let $\boldsymbol{x}_u$ denotes the feature profile of user u. In our example this is a high dimensional vector where each co-ordinate is binary. We want to learn a function $f(\boldsymbol{x}_u, \boldsymbol{z}_c, c)$ that helps us estimate the propensity of user u to convert on campaign c.

We can achieve this through a classification approach where we learn a function f that classifies a user u as a converter for campaign c if $f(\boldsymbol{x}_u, \boldsymbol{z}_c, c) > T$, T is a threshold (could be campaign specific) that is decided based on the cost of false positive and false negative. An alternate approach could learn f as odds of user u to convert on campaign c. The output scores can then be used to perform classification.

We discuss the class of functions f in the modeling section 3. Next we discuss how to derive the user and campaigns vectors ($\boldsymbol{x}_u$ and $\boldsymbol{z}_c$) that can be used in the subsequent modeling tasks.

2.1 User Representation

As in the offline advertising, to infer user interests, user profiles are constructed from known past user activity. User activity is tracked by the advertisers, publishers and third-parties through browser cookies that uniquely identify the user. For each user, the ad broker may store the history of page visits, ad views, and search queries, and based on the content of these events compose the profile used for targeting. Most of these events have textual content that can be analyzed using established text processing techniques. For example, the text of search queries issued, ids of ads viewed, the content of the pages viewed, etc. To represent event content we employ the bag of words method, which uses unigrams and bigrams, as well as nodes of a topical taxonomy that represent more general text categories. This gives us a feature vector representing a user, $\boldsymbol{x}_u$, for modeling purposes (see Figure 2). The weight of each feature can be binary or it can be computed based on its intensity in the user activities.

2.2 Campaign Representation

As mentioned before, we employ two sources of information to represent campaigns, as shown in Figure 2. First, we derive metadata from the campaign definition. Each campaign is composed of multiple *ad creatives.* An ad creative is an image or text snippet that is displayed to the user. Upon a click on the ad, the user is taken to a web page associated with this creative, also called a *landing page.* The creatives and the landing pages give a succinct characterization of the advertising campaign, and they can be useful to infer the domain of the campaign. In our approach, we construct a campaign metadata feature vector, $\boldsymbol{z}_c$, using the creatives and landing page content. One of the challenges in creating this feature vector is that campaigns can have multiple creatives and also creatives can be associated with multiple campaigns (see Figure 2). To be able to produce reasonable campaign metadata, we considered several variants and in our experiments we adopted the approach of merging the content of all landing pages connected to a campaign as its source of features. (More details are given in the experiment section.)

The second data source that characterizes the campaign is the set of *seed* users. The seed set is composed of *positive* and *negative* examples with regard to the given campaign. The positive set is composed of users that have converted for this campaign in the past, while the negative set represents the non-converted users. We will provide more details on this in our experimental evaluation section.

For new campaigns, there is no seed set available, and thus we must rely on campaign metadata to characterize the targeting requirements of the campaign. Over time the campaign expands as it is exposed to more and more users. Note that each user in the seed set comes at the cost of allocating one or more ad impressions to her.

3. MODELING APPROACHES

Recall from Section 2 that our goal is to learn function $f(\boldsymbol{x}_u, \boldsymbol{z}_c, c)$ that helps us estimate the propensity of user u to convert on campaign c. We confine ourselves to a class of functions f that can be decomposed additively as $f(\boldsymbol{x}_u, \boldsymbol{z}_c, c) = g(\boldsymbol{x}_u, \boldsymbol{z}_c) + f_c(\boldsymbol{x}_u)$, where g is a function of user features but depends on campaign c only through metadata $\boldsymbol{z}_c$, f_c is a campaign-specific function of user features.

Function Class. We consider three choices for function class f in this paper: a) Linear Support Vector Machine (L-SVM), b) Logistic Regression (LR), and c) Naive-Bayes (NB). Both SVM and logistic regression are known to provide good performance in advertising and many other applications, Naive Bayes was chosen due to its ability to substantially reduce variance at the expense of incurring bias due to the independence assumption. In noisy conversion data, this provides a good baseline to compare other more advanced methods like Linear SVM and logistic regression.

Linear SVM. Let $y_{u,c}$ denote a binary indicator that takes value $+1$ if user u converts on campaign c, -1 otherwise. Then SVM estimates function f to minimize the hinge loss $\sum_{u,c} \max(0, 1 - y_{u,c} \cdot f(\boldsymbol{x}_u, \boldsymbol{z}_c, c))$ (call L_1 SVM), or squared squared hinge loss $\sum_{u,c} \max(0, 1 - y_{u,c} \cdot f(\boldsymbol{x}_u, \boldsymbol{z}_c, c))^2$ (called L_2 SVM). If f is too flexible, it tends to overfit the data and additional penalty term to constrain f is often used. Hence, we assume f to be linear in the known variables ($\boldsymbol{x}_u$ and $\boldsymbol{z}_c$).

Logistic Regression. The hinge loss in this case is replaced by the sigmoid loss function $\sum_{u,c} \log(1 + exp(-y_{u,c} \cdot f(\boldsymbol{x}_u, \boldsymbol{z}_c, c)))$. As in SVM, we confine ourselves to a linear function and perform appropriate regularization. One can impose either the L_1 or L_2 norm constraint on the unknown coefficients. The former also ensures sparse solutions, i.e., many irrelevant variables have zero coefficients.

Naive Bayes. Naive Bayes builds f by estimating the joint density of features (user and/or campaigns) separately in the converting and non-converting classes. By Bayes theorem,

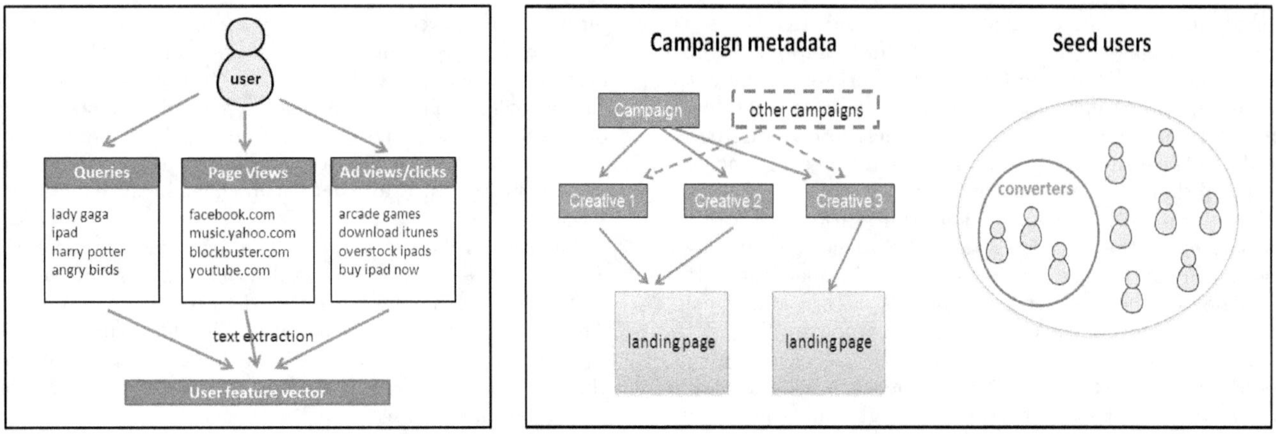

Figure 2: User and campaign representation.

the log-odds of probability of conversion is given by

$$log\frac{D_c(\boldsymbol{x}_u|y_{u,c}=1)}{D_c(\boldsymbol{x}_u|y_{u,c}=-1)} + log\frac{P(y_{u,c}=1)}{P(y_{u,c}=-1)}$$

where D_c denotes the appropriate joint density of user features in campaign c. The second term which is the prior log-odds of conversion for a campaign is constant when classifying a user as converter/non-converter on a given campaign, hence it can be ignored. Estimating the notoriously high-dimensional density is the crucial task here, Naive Bayes simplifies this through the independence assumption which ensures joint estimates as products of one dimensional marginals. Although the one dimensional marginals are estimated with precision and reduces variance, the bias incurred due to the independence assumption may degrade performance.

For a given function class f, next we describe how we use the seed set and the campaign metadata to build these models.

3.1 Local Models Using the Seed Set

Given that each campaign targets a different set of users, the first approach is to build a separate *local* model for each campaign. In particular, given the seed set, we exploit the positive and negative examples to learn a campaign-specific targeting function. In other words, we ignore $g(\boldsymbol{x}_u, \boldsymbol{z}_c)$ and assume $f(\boldsymbol{x}_u, \boldsymbol{z}_c, c) = f_c(\boldsymbol{x}_u)$. For training L-SVM and logistic regression, $f_c(\boldsymbol{x}_u) = \boldsymbol{x}'_u\,\boldsymbol{\beta}_c$, where $\boldsymbol{\beta}_c$ is an unknown vector that is to be estimated from training data. Formally stated, we obtain $\boldsymbol{\beta}_c$ as a solution to the following optimization problem.

$$\text{argmin}_{\boldsymbol{\beta}_c} \sum_{u \in \mathcal{C}} L(\boldsymbol{x}_u, y_{u,c}, \boldsymbol{\beta}_c) + \lambda_c \|\, \boldsymbol{\beta}_c \,\|_p \qquad (1)$$

where L is either the hinge $\max(0, 1 - y_{u,c} \cdot \boldsymbol{x}'_u\,\boldsymbol{\beta}_c)$ or squared hinge $\max(0, 1 - y_{u,c} \cdot \boldsymbol{x}'_u\,\boldsymbol{\beta}_c)^2$ for L-SVM, and sigmoid $log(1 + exp(-y_{u,c} \cdot \boldsymbol{x}'_u\,\boldsymbol{\beta}_c))$ for logistic regression respectively. For L-SVM, we use $p = 2$ but for logistic we use two values of p for the penalty: $p = 1$ for L_1 regularization and $p = 2$ gives L_2 regularization. The parameter $\lambda_c (\geq 0)$ determines the relative weight of the penalty term and is estimated through cross-validation. Larger values of λ_c implies more penalty on the parameters. We note that if the user vector $\boldsymbol{x}_u$ contains m features, the dimension of $\boldsymbol{\beta}_c$ is also m. This leads to too many parameters for large values of m, often the case in advertising applications. The lack of conversions per campaign further exacerbates the situation. In fact, in most settings the number of conversions could be much smaller than m. This makes penalization important to avoid over-fitting. Hence the right choice of λ_c is essential for good performance (see Section 4.3). We select this parameter by extensive cross-validation.

Expanding $\boldsymbol{x}_u = (x_{u1}, \cdots, x_{um})$, for Naive Bayes $f_c(\boldsymbol{x}_u)$ is given by

$$f_c(\boldsymbol{x}_u) = \sum_{i=1}^{m} log\frac{D_i(x_{ui}|y_{uc}=1)}{D_i(x_{ui}|y_{uc}=-1)} \qquad (2)$$

where $D_i(x_{ui}|y_{uc})$ is the conditional marginal density of the ith user feature in class y_{uc}. The estimation of marginal density $D_i(.|.)$ depends on the nature of the feature. In this paper, since all our user features are binary, this density is obtained simply by counting. For instance, $D_i(x_{ui} = 1|y_{uc} = 1)$ is simply the fraction of converters on campaign c who possess feature i. To avoid unreliable estimates for campaigns with small number of conversions and/or features that occur rarely, we perform mild smoothing. In particular, we estimate $D_i(x_{ui} = 1|y_{uc} = 1)$ as $\frac{|u:x_{ui}=1, y_{uc}=1| + (a \cdot p_{ic})}{|u:y_{uc}=1| + a}$, where a is a positive smoothing constant that could be interpreted as pseudo number of conversions, p_{ic} is the fraction of users who possess feature i in campaign c. We choose small values of a (e.g $a \in [1, 5]$). Our experiments showed that Naive-Bayes is very robust and it showed little sensitivity in performance with respect to the choice of a.

We also note that learning local models is computationally efficient since the computation can be done separately for each campaign in parallel. All our computations with SVM and logistic regression were done with LIBLINEAR [19].

3.2 Global Models Using the Campaign Metadata

Per campaign local models work well for campaigns with large seed set, i.e., large number of conversions. For new campaigns or those with little training data, the performance is not satisfactory due to data sparsity. To mitigate this, we employ the campaign metadata information ($\boldsymbol{z}_c$). One option is to obtain user and campaign similarity using their features as in traditional information retrieval. However, this does not work in our case since user and campaign features are not mapped to the same semantic space. The other idea is to exploit campaign metadata to correlate learning across campaigns and perform better prediction for those campaigns that lack enough data.

We explore several different ways of performing learning across campaigns in this paper. The first approach shares the model coefficients β_c for user features across campaigns. We call this the **Merge-based Global** model. The second approach extends the merge model to include an additional component that models user and campaign interaction through user features and campaign metadata. We call this the **Interaction-based Global** model. Finally, we explore our most complex model that extends the interaction model to include a campaign-specific local model, we call this the **Global+Local** model.

3.2.1 Merge-based Global Model

Here, we merge the seed users from all campaigns to learn a global model. In other words, $f_c(\boldsymbol{x}_u) = \boldsymbol{x}'\boldsymbol{\beta}$ for all campaigns c where $\boldsymbol{\beta}$ is the global weight vector. Thus, one single set of coefficients is estimated for all campaigns. This reduces the number of parameters dramatically and allows us to derive more precise estimates of the global coefficients. However, this model does not capture any user and campaign specific interactions. Instead, it captures the user's propensity to convert in general, which can be useful in many real scenarios. For example, the willingness of a user to conduct online transactions affects each campaign in the same way and can be learned/exploited globally.

To build this global model, we put together the seed sets of all campaigns. Even if the goal is to learn user's global propensity to convert, one has to be careful in training this model. For example, campaigns with large seed sets can easily dominate the global model and bias the model estimates. This is counter-effective since such a global model would not perform well on campaigns with small seed set, which are the ones that should benefit the most from such a collapsed model. We address this by weighing each campaign's seed set equally, both in the positive and negative classes.

3.2.2 Interaction-based Global Model

Merge model estimates the global propensity of a user to convert. However, it does not capture any affinity of campaigns to each other. For instance, if a kind of users has high propensity to convert on travel campaigns, we can perhaps use this information to recommend these users to a new travel campaign. One way to perform such cross campaign learning is by positing a linear model that is a function of both user and campaign features. We accomplish this through our **interaction** model by assuming $g(\boldsymbol{x}_u, \boldsymbol{z}_c) = \boldsymbol{x}'_u D \boldsymbol{z}_c$, where D is a matrix of unknowns to be estimated by pooling data across all campaigns. Hence, $f(\boldsymbol{x}_u, \boldsymbol{z}_c, c) = \boldsymbol{x}'_u D \boldsymbol{z}_c + \boldsymbol{x}'_u \boldsymbol{\beta}$. Mathematically, we obtain D by solving the following optimization problem.

$$\min_D \sum_{u,c} L(y_{u,c}, \boldsymbol{x}'_u D \boldsymbol{z}_c + \boldsymbol{x}'_u \boldsymbol{\beta}) + \lambda(\|D\|_p + \|\boldsymbol{\beta}\|_p) \quad (3)$$

Note that this optimization is performed by pooling data across all campaigns. Also, the number of parameters to be estimated in (D,$\boldsymbol{\beta}$) is $(m+1) \cdot n$, where m and n are the number of user and campaign features respectively. When m and/or n is large, this can lead to a high dimensional optimization problem that is difficult to solve. For instance, in our experiments we deal with $m = 70k$ and $n = 500$, this leads to an optimization problem consisting of $35M$ parameters. Also, the computations are not separable by campaigns (unlike Section 3.1). Further, several user and campaign features are non-informative and noisy. To keep the interaction matrix manageable, we use a simple a-priori feature filtering procedure that removes irrelevant user features (since the number of campaign features is relatively small, we do not perform any such filtering there). This filtering is performed through a Kullback-Liebler divergence measure, as described below.

Variable filtering. We describe a variable importance score for a user feature i. Let $q_{i,c}$ denote the conversion probability for feature i on campaign c and $q_{i.}$ denote the overall conversion probability for feature i. We compute the values of $q_{i,c}$ and $q_{i.}$ using their maximum-likelihood estimates, and to avoid unreliable estimates, we perform mild smoothing similar in spirit to that described in the context of Naive Bayes. The variable score for i is then given by the Kullback-Liebler divergence $\sum_c q_{i,c} \cdot log(\frac{q_{i,c}}{q_{i.}})$. Note that a value of 0 implies no interaction of feature i with campaigns and hence this feature is not important to be included in our model.

3.3 Global + Local Model

Local models have the advantage that they capture the campaign-specific effect. Global models capture the global targeting constraints and have the advantage that they can generalize well even when there is lack of campaign-specific data. To get the best of both worlds, we build models that include both the global and local components. More specifically, we assume $f(\boldsymbol{x}_u, \boldsymbol{z}_c, c) = \boldsymbol{x}'_u D \boldsymbol{z}_c + \boldsymbol{x}'_u \boldsymbol{\beta}_g + \boldsymbol{x}'_u \boldsymbol{\beta}_c$ and solve for $(D, \boldsymbol{\beta}_g, \boldsymbol{\beta}_{c:c \in \mathcal{C}})$ by solving an appropriate L-SVM or logistic regression task. Mathematically, we obtain the parameters by solving the following optimization problem:

$$\min_D \sum_{u,c} L(y_{u,c}, \boldsymbol{X}'_u D \boldsymbol{z}_c + \boldsymbol{x}'_u \boldsymbol{\beta}_g + \boldsymbol{x}'_u \boldsymbol{\beta}_c)$$
$$+ \lambda \|D\|_p + \lambda \|\boldsymbol{\beta}_g\|_p + \sum_c \lambda_c \|\boldsymbol{\beta}_c\|_p$$

Here $\boldsymbol{X}_u$ are user features used for the interaction component after a-priori filtering, and so $\boldsymbol{x}_u$ can be different from $\boldsymbol{X}_u$. Note that this equation involves separate λs for each campaign and another λ for the transfer learning parameters. Obtaining so many tuning parameters when jointly optimizing $(D, \boldsymbol{\beta}_g, \boldsymbol{\beta}_{c:c \in \mathcal{C}})$ by pooling data across all campaigns is difficult in practice and computationally challenging.

We address the computational challenges by using two different approaches

- simultaneously learn the global and local components (i.e., *joint approach*) but assume $\lambda_c = \lambda$.
- learn the global component first, then fit a separate campaign-specific local model using $\boldsymbol{X}'_u \hat{D} \boldsymbol{z}_c + \boldsymbol{x}'_u \hat{\boldsymbol{\beta}}_g$ as a known constant where $\hat{D}$ and $\hat{\boldsymbol{\beta}}_g$ are the global component estimates (i.e., *offset approach*). This entails changing $L(\boldsymbol{x}_u, y_{u,c}, \boldsymbol{\beta}_c)$ to $L(\boldsymbol{x}_u, y_{u,c}, \boldsymbol{X}'_u \hat{D} \boldsymbol{z}_c + \boldsymbol{x}'_u \hat{\boldsymbol{\beta}}_g + \boldsymbol{\beta}_c)$ in Equation 1.

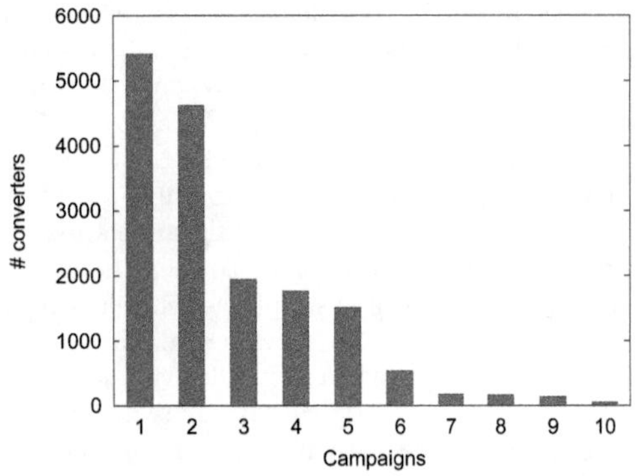

Figure 3: Campaign sizes in terms of the number of conversions.

This model performs well on both mature and new campaigns. For the latter, the transfer learning component based on campaign features plays an important role, while for the former the additional local term adds a correction that helps it converge to the local campaign models.

4. EXPERIMENTS

Next we evaluate our proposed models on a real dataset collected from a large advertising network.

4.1 Dataset

We constructed a dataset of user profiles, which are labeled as positive or negative depending on whether the user converted on a given campaign. Any potentially personally identifiable information was removed, and all the data was anonymized. All datasets were compliant with the company privacy policy. The users were drawn from 10 randomly selected display ad campaigns, which were registered on a major US advertising network in 2011. The dataset spans more than 300,000 users allowing us to draw meaningful conclusions from these experiments. All these campaigns are performance-based, i.e., advertisers only pay to the advertising network for actual conversions. Of the 10 campaigns, some are fairly small in terms of number of conversions (with 10 to 20 conversions per week, on average), while others are large and receive many thousands of conversions every week, as shown in Figure 3. For these campaigns we obtained a log of ad activity for the four weeks period from 03/18/2011 to 04/15/2011. The log contains fully anonymized ids of users who viewed, clicked, or converted on the ads from these campaigns.

For each campaign c we construct a dataset with those users that were shown one or more ads from the campaign during the study period. Using the conversion data described above we give binary labels to these user profiles as either positive or negative. Users who converted make the positive instances, while the rest make the negative examples. Since the number of negative examples can be huge (many millions) for large campaigns, we down-sample them to keep about 30,000 examples per campaign. We perform 3-fold cross validation on this dataset in our experiments and report the performance averaged over the 3 folds.

User profiles.

For each user observed in the period above, we take the four weeks of her online activity *preceding the conversion* to construct the user profile, as described in Section 2. These activities include page visits, ad views, and search queries. Note that while predicting a test instance, say on day t, we allow the prediction models to access user history up to day $t-1$. Hence, the prediction method is not using any future information.

Campaign metadata.

For the 10 campaigns in our experiments we collected the ad creatives associated with them (see Figure 2). This gives us about 15,000 creatives, of which most are images and do not have associated text. However, each creative contains a landing page that denotes the URL of the page which the user is directed to after clicking on the ad. We crawl each landing page, parse, and attribute the extracted content to its corresponding creative(s).

Since the relationship between campaigns and creatives is many-to-many, it is not clear how to propagate creative's content to a campaign. The experiments reported in this paper use a simple approach where, for a given campaign, we weigh all the connected creatives equally and put their content together. Another alternative is to differentiate the creatives and their contributions to a given campaign using the creative-campaign graph, e.g., give less weight to those creatives which are shared by more campaigns and vice-versa. We leave this exploration as a part of our future work. Finally, we perform some feature selection over campaign features using the number of landing pages a feature appears in.

Seed set.

We compose the seed set with positive and negative examples as described earlier in this section. Recall that the seed set denotes the labeled users that are available for training for a campaign at a given time. In our experiments we explore how the prediction power of the models depends on the size of the seed set. Thus, we simulate different sizes of the seed set by sampling the data from the full training seed set of a campaign. To explain further, say $local(c, x)$ denotes the local model built for campaign c using x number of positive examples (since negative examples are easy to acquire, even for a new campaign, we do not vary them). This allows us to simulate a campaign at different stages of its life. For example, to simulate a new campaign we set x to 0. To simulate slightly more mature campaigns, we can set x to 30 or 70 conversions. For the long-standing campaigns we set x to a large value which means that all the positives examples for this campaign in the training folds are used.

4.2 Evaluation Metric

We use the Receiver Operating Characteristic (ROC) curve to evaluate the ranked list of users produced by the different targeting models. A ROC curve plots true positives versus false positives for different classification thresholds. The area under the ROC curve is particularly interesting due to its probabilistic interpretation. The Area Under Curve (AUC) gives the probability that the audience selection method assigns a higher score to a random positive example than a random negative example (i.e., probability of concordance) [8, 10]. So, a purely random selection method will have an area under the curve of exactly 0.5. An algorithm that achieves AUC of 0.6 can distinguish a positive

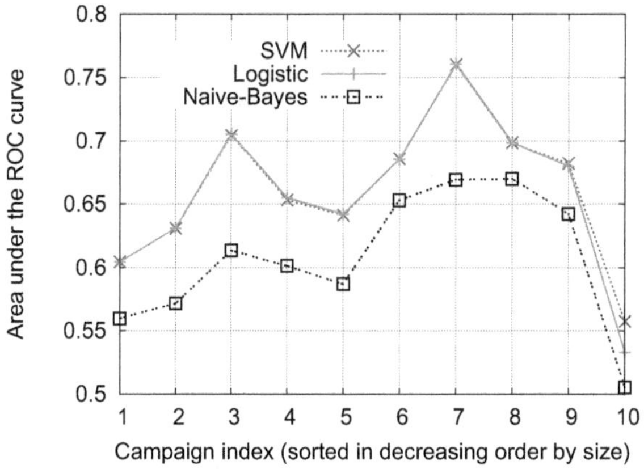

Figure 4: Performance comparison of SVM, Logistic and Naive-Bayes based local models.

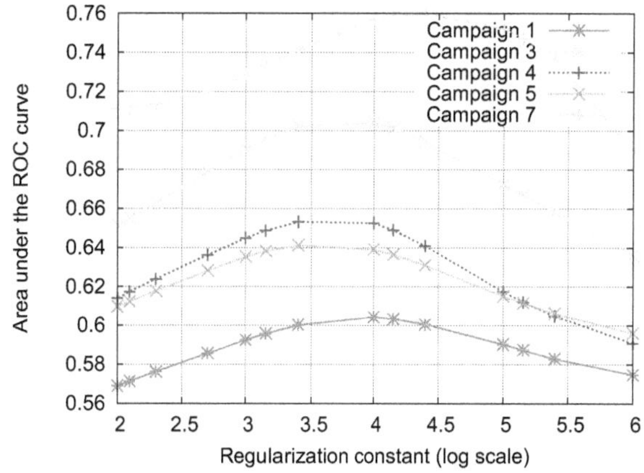

Figure 5: Effect of the regularization constant on SVM models.

user from a negative user with 60% probability, and is thus better than the random method by 20%.

An alternative metric could be to measure precision/recall at a certain rank in the list. Note that different campaigns may have different requirements in terms of precision and recall. For example, a small campaign whose reach is limited would prefer higher recall, while a large campaign that reaches out to many users might prefer higher precision). Consequently, selecting a rank at which to evaluate precision such that it would be suitable for all campaigns, is not possible. Instead, we use AUC since it combines the prediction performance over all ranks into a single number.

4.3 Local models using the seed set

For this experiment we build a separate model for each campaign using all the positive examples from the training folds. Hence, large campaigns will get to use more than 5000 conversions, while the small campaigns learn from some 500 conversions. First, in Figure 4 we show the performance comparison of SVM, Logistic (with L2 regularization) and Naive-Bayes models. The x-axis is the campaign index where the campaigns have been sorted in the decreasing order by the number of conversions (i.e., smaller indices denote larger campaigns). On the y-axis we plot the best AUC performance obtained for each campaign averaged over 3 folds after varying the model parameters. For SVM and Logistic we vary the regularization constant and for Naive-Bayes the smoothing constant was varied. We note that Logistic and SVM perform very similar, while Naive-bayes is slightly worse. However, we observed that Naive-Bayes was not too sensitive to any learning parameters (such as smoothing constant). The same is not true for SVM and Logistic. In Figure 5 we show the performance of the SVM models for 5 different campaigns (of the 10 campaigns in our dataset). Here the x-axis denotes the value of the regularization constant. As we can see that the performance depends quite significantly on the regularization constant. When the constant is too small, many useful features get eliminated due to severe penalization. On the other hand, when the constant is too large, the model starts overfitting and does not perform well on the test folds. For brevity we will use SVM to report the results for the remaining experiments.

Impact of the number of conversions in the training set.

We also note that the best performance for different campaigns can be quite different; AUC varies from 0.55 to 0.75 in Figure 4. To analyze this further we performed the following experiment. We varied the number of positive examples that were allowed for training while learning the model for a campaign. We call this $local(c, x)$ where c denotes the campaign and x denotes the *allowed* number of positive examples in the seed/training set. We note here that x is the upper-bound; we vary x up to 5000 but for small campaigns the seed set does not change beyond $x = 540$ since these are the maximum number of conversions we have for the small campaigns in our dataset. As mentioned earlier, in this experiment we aim to simulate a campaign at different stages of its life cycle. For new campaign x is close to 0, while for a mature campaign x can be in a range of a couple of hundreds depending on the size of the campaign. The results of this experiment are shown in in Figure 6. To avoid cluttering, we grouped campaigns by their sizes in the figure – the largest 2 campaigns in terms of the number of conversions were put into the "large" category, the middle 3 campaigns into the "medium" and the bottom 5 into "small" category.

On the first inspection the results look contrary to what one might expect: we see that the small campaigns not only outperform the large campaigns when x is small, but they also perform better for large values of x. For example, when $x = 5000$ large campaigns use all their 5000 conversions as positive examples for training, while small campaigns use $x = 540$ positive examples only and they still perform better. From a careful investigation of the data, we identified the following reason behind this. The small campaigns are quite restrictive in their definition of conversion (which is partly the reason behind them being small), e.g., they require email sign-up, click on the ad and order completion page for conversions. On the other hand, the large campaigns have more relaxed definition of conversion, e.g., conversions defined as a view of the ad followed by some kind of positive activity on the website. The converters for such large campaigns are very heterogeneous and noisy. As a result, even for large values of x (i.e., large number of positive examples in the training set) it is difficult to discriminate between converters and non-converters. Small campaigns, due

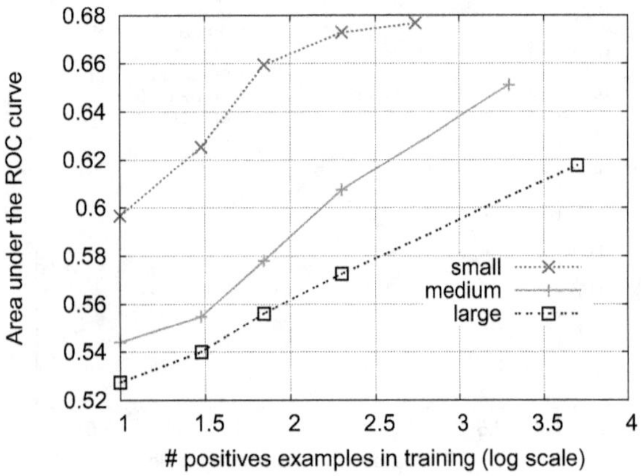

Figure 6: Performance evaluation of the local models for different number of positives (x) in the seed set. Note that for the small campaigns the maximum number of conversions is $x = 540$ in our dataset.

to their restrictive conversion definition and specific targeting segment, are easier to learn and have a quick start, i.e., even with a few positive examples the models can be learned significantly well.

4.4 Global Models

We start the evaluation of global models by studying the merge-based model. Recall from Section 3.2.1, merge model pools the seed sets from all campaigns while learning the model for a given campaign. In particular, let $merge(c, x)$ denote the merge model for campaign c when the seed set is of size x. To learn $merge(c, x)$, we employ all the data from the other campaigns, $\{\mathcal{C} - c\}$, and from campaign c we use x positive examples. This simulates the setting where campaign c is new and $\mathcal{C} - c$ are old/mature campaigns that the ad matching platform has run in the past.

The results are shown in Figure 7. We compare $merge(c, x)$ with $local(c, x)$ in the figure for small, medium and large campaign sizes. We note that for large campaigns the merge model performs better than the local model for small x values. In particular, till $x = 200$ conversions the merge model achieves higher AUC than the local model. This is expected in view of the previous section since we observed there that the large campaigns have slow start. Hence, using the seed sets of other campaigns allows the merge-based approach to learn more robust models. For small/medium campaigns the local models get better quite quickly (after 30 to 50 conversions). However, note that collecting 50 conversions may take a couple of days (if not week) for small vertically focused campaigns in a real-world environment where multiple advertisers compete for the attention of a relatively small set of targeted users.

Interaction-based global model.

Next we study the interaction-based global model from Section 3.2.2. We performed feature selection using KL-divergence to keep 3000 user features. On the campaign side, we kept 50 features per campaign by selecting the most frequent words in landing pages. In Table 1 we compare the interaction-based and merge-based global models. We note that overall the interaction approach is better, as expected.

Campaign size	Interaction-based model
Small	6.06%
Medium	0.4%
Large	3.93%

Table 1: Performance improvement achieved by the interaction-based model over merge-based.

Campaign size	Global	Global+Local
Small	-10.5%	**-8.5%**
Medium	**6.4%**	6.1%
Large	70%	**78.6%**

Table 2: Performance improvement of the global and global+local models over the local models for different campaign sizes.

We expect the improvement to increase with the number of campaigns pooled together, as that allows better learning of the weights for the user-campaign interaction features.

As shown in the table, the most gain comes for the small campaigns. Compare to the large campaigns which can have many thousand creatives and landing pages, the small campaigns have few creatives providing us with a high-quality homogeneous set of campaign features.

4.5 Global + Local Models

In this experiment we study the global+local models from Section 3.3. For brevity, we only focus on the joint optimization approach. In Table 2 we compare the joint model against the $local(c, x)$ and $merge(c, x)$ for $x = 30$. As discussed in Section 3.3, global+local model, in theory, subsumes both the local and global model and is a strict generalization over these models. In practice, this seems to hold true except for the small campaigns where the joint global+local model is slightly worse than the local model. We believe that this is due to the fact that the regularization constant is shared across all campaigns in the joint approach, while the local models have per-campaign tuning of regularization constant. In fact, we observed that if we force the local models to share the same regularization constant, then the performance difference between the local and joint models on the small campaigns is marginal.

More importantly, we observe that the global+local approach brings a large improvement (about 78%) over the local models on large campaigns. Recall that large campaigns suffer from slow start and so this is greatly beneficial to these campaigns. This demonstrates how the campaign metadata can be useful in sharing targeting knowledge across campaigns.

5. BACKGROUND AND RELATED WORK

First, we give some background on conversion optimization in display advertising. Then we compare our work against the existing literature.

5.1 Conversion Optimization in Display Advertising

Display advertising takes the form of graphical ads displayed on web pages alongside the original content. From

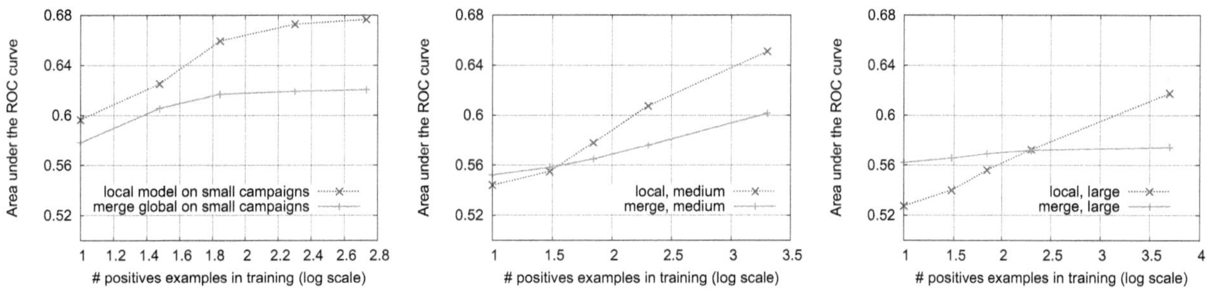

Figure 7: Performance comparison of local model with merge-based model for different number of positives (x) in the training set. The three figures are for the three different campaign groups (based on size).

its meager beginnings in the 1990's, display advertising has grown to an estimated $12.33 billion industry in 2011, according to the latest IDC report [21]. Display ads today are standardized in size, and created, sold, traded, and placed by an industry composed of hundreds of companies that include publishers, publisher optimizers, ad agencies, ad exchanges, ad networks, advertisers, and others.

Conversions are user actions that indicate the ad was successfully perceived by users such as making a purchase, requesting a price quote, signing up for an account, etc. Maximizing conversions is one of the key challenges for today's display ad brokers, posing several technical difficulties. First, conversions are very rare events. Only a small percentage of users who see an ad will click on the ad, and only a small percentage of those users convert. Conversions often occur in the range of one out of $10^5 - 10^6$ ad views. Furthermore, the conversions represent a diverse set of events and there is no single definition for conversions as it varies among the advertisers. For example, certain advertisers define conversion as the event when a user purchases a product, while others may call a subscription to mails/alerts or the filling of a form as conversion. Thus the conversion rate can vary significantly across different advertisers.

Lastly, conversions are tracked through *conversion pixel* which is a javascript code embedded in the advertiser's conversion page (e.g., order completion page). The code gets triggered to notify the advertising network when a user who was shown ads by the advertising network reaches the conversion page. A campaign can encompass multiple conversion pixels in the creative landing pages. Conceptually, the conversions pixels represent *goals* of the campaign while creatives are the *means* of achieving those goals. There could be multiple means to achieve the same goal as well as the same mean can lead to multiple goals. This further complicates the issue making the task of predicting conversions even harder.

5.2 Prior Work

Our work is related to modeling of user behavior and targeting based on observed past events. User behavior has been studied to understand user's querying pattern [20], news browsing behavior [11], interests inferencing [17] and personalized search [18]. In contrast, our focus is on online advertising and behavioral targeting in particular. Initial behavioral targeting studies mostly focused on predicting clicks on ads [6, 22]. Clicks are used simply because they are available and other information is not available at a large scale. While clicks do represent user intent, they are known to suffer with fraud issues [7, 12, 23]. Recently, however, advertisers have been willing to share feedback (through conversion pixeling) at the level of individual users, telling publishers which of the users who saw the ad have actually purchased the product [2, 3, 4, 14]. Since conversions are the ultimate goal of advertisers, we focus on conversion optimization in this study.

Previous work on conversion optimization uses only the seed set and learns local models [2, 3, 4], but as we showed in our experiments that the model performance depends significantly on the size of the seed set. Hence, we employ campaign metadata along with the seed set and propose a series of global models that pool campaigns together using their metadata. When the campaigns are new and the seed set is small or unavailable, we show that the metadata can be significantly useful. To the best of our knowledge, this is the first study in behavioral targeting framework which employs such collaborative modeling. Our work is also related to the cold-start problem in collaborative filtering literature where movies/items play the role of campaigns [1, 9, 15, 16]. However, there are a couple of major differences: (a) users interact with and give thumbs up to many movies/items, while they do not convert on that many campaigns, (b) the number of campaigns is not of the order of the number of items. Both these limitations restrict the factor models in our setting [1, 15].

Another area of online advertising is social targeting where the goal is to identify users having strong influence over others [5]. Since brand affinity is likely to be shared between socially connected users, Provost et al. [13] identified regions of the social network that may be more susceptible to a given brand message. This approach relies on the existence of a social network, although in their work [13] the network was approximated using co-visitations.

6. CONCLUSIONS

Advertisers want more bang per buck and as a result, conversion optimization in display campaigns is getting increasingly more attention. The task is very challenging for several reasons such as very low conversion rate, high variance in number of conversions across campaigns, and diverse set of events logged as conversions. In addition, on the user side we also have sparse and noisy profile activities. In this paper we proposed a two-pronged approach for conversion optimization whereby we use a seed set of converters to capture the campaign-specific or local targeting criteria (e.g., interests in finance, shares, mortgage), and the campaign metadata to share targeting knowledge across campaigns (i.e., global component). To learn the local models we experimented with SVM, Logistic and Naive-Bayes models. We showed that SVM and Logistic perform better than Naive-Bayes, however they are sensitive with respect to the setting of model parameters while Naive-bayes is fairly resilient. We found it surprising that campaigns with higher number of conversions are actually harder to model, due to the heterogeneity among the converted users.

To investigate the global models we proposed merge-based and interaction-based models for pooling together the information from different campaigns. We showed how global models improve the prediction performance for large campaigns which suffer from slow learning rate during the initial phase. Next we showed how our global+local models capture the best of both worlds. They include the campaign-specific weight vector for user features (local), the shared weight vector for user features (merge-based) and the interaction of user and campaign features (interaction-based). Also, to learn these models we give a joint optimization approach which simultaneously accounts for both the local and global components. The offset approach, on the other hand, performs optimization in two steps, but it allows per-campaign regularization which is beneficial.

While in this work we focused on advertising, user profiling and targeting are required in a wide range of web applications beyond advertising, such as content recommendation and search personalization. The principles of user profile generation and two-pronged targeting described in this paper are not specific to advertising, and are therefore applicable to these other applications.

7. REFERENCES

[1] D. Agarwal and B. chung Chen. Regression-based latent factor models. In *Proceedings of the 13th ACM SIGKDD International Conference on Knowledge Discovery and Data Mining*, 2009.

[2] N. Archak, V. S. Mirrokni, and S. Muthukrishnan. Mining advertiser-specific user behavior using adfactors. In *Proceedings of the Nineteenth International World Wide Web Conference*, 2010.

[3] A. Bagherjeiran, A. O. Hatch, and A. Ratnaparkhi. Ranking for the conversion funnel. In *Proceeding of the 33rd international ACM SIGIR conference on Research and development in information retrieval*, pages 146–153, 2010.

[4] A. Bagherjeiran, A. O. Hatch, A. Ratnaparkhi, and R. Parekh. Large-scale customized models for advertisers. In *Proceedings of the IEEE International Conference on Data Mining Workshops*, 2010.

[5] R. Bhatt, V. Chaoji, and R. Parekh. Predicting product adoption in large-scale social networks. In *Proceedings of the 19th ACM International Conference on Information and Knowledge Management*, 2010.

[6] Y. Chen, D. Pavlov, and J. Canny. Large-scale behavioral targeting. In *Proceedings of the 15th ACM SIGKDD International Conference on Knowledge Discovery and Data Mining*, 2009.

[7] I. Click Forensics. Click fraud index. `http://www.clickforensics.com/resources/click-fraud-index.html`, 2010.

[8] M. Gonen. Receiver operating characteristic (ROC) curves. *SAS Users Group International (SUGI)*, 31:210–231, 2006.

[9] N. Good, J. B. Schafer, J. A. Konstan, A. Borchers, B. Sarwar, J. Herlocker, and J. Riedl. Combining collaborative filtering with personal agents for better recommendations. In *Proceedings of the Sixteenth National Conference on Artificial Intelligence*, 1999.

[10] M. Greiner, D. Pfeiffer, and R. D. Smith. Receiver operating characteristic (roc) curves. *Preventive Veterinary Medicine*, 45:23–41, 2000.

[11] J. Liu, P. Dolan, and E. R. Pedersen. Personalized news recommendation based on click behavior. In *Proceedings of the 15th International Conference on Intelligent User Interfaces*, 2010.

[12] Y. Peng, L. Zhang, M. Chang, and Y. Guan. An effective method for combating malicious scripts clickbots. In *Proceedings of the 14th European Symposium on Research in Computer Security (ESORICS)*, 2009.

[13] F. Provost, B. Dalessandro, R. Hook, X. Zhang, and A. Murray. Audience selection for on-line brand advertising: privacy-friendly social network targeting. In *Proceedings KDD*, 2009.

[14] B. Rey and A. Kannan. Conversion rate based bid adjustment for sponsored search auctions. In *Proceedings of the Nineteenth International World Wide Web Conference*, 2010.

[15] R. Salakhutdinov and A. Mnih. Probabilistic matrix factorization. In *Advances in Neural Information Processing Systems*, 2008.

[16] A. I. Schein, A. Popescul, L. H., R. Popescul, L. H. Ungar, and D. M. Pennock. Methods and metrics for cold-start recommendations. In *Proceedings of the 25th International ACM SIGIR Conference on Research and Development in Information Retrieval*, 2002.

[17] M. Shmueli-Scheuer, H. Roitman, D. Carmel, Y. Mass, and D. Konopnicki. Extracting user profiles from large scale data. In *Proceedings MDAC*, 2010.

[18] K. Sugiyama, K. Hatano, and M. Yoshikawa. Adaptive web search based on user profile constructed without any effort from users. In *Proceedings WWW*, 2004.

[19] X.-R. Wang, K.-W. Chang, C.-J. Hsieh, R.-E. Fan, G.-X. Yuan, H.-F. Yu, F.-L. Huang, and C.-J. Lin. Liblinear – a library for large linear classification. `http://www.csie.ntu.edu.tw/~cjlin/liblinear/`.

[20] S. Wedig and O. Madani. A large-scale analysis of query logs for assessing personalization opportunities. In *Proceedings KDD*, 2006.

[21] K. Weide. Worldwide and U.S. internet ad spend report: Growth accelerates, but dark clouds gather. http://www.idc.com/getdoc.jsp?containerId=224593 (visited on 10/19/2010), 2010.

[22] J. Yan, N. Liu, G. Wang, W. Zhang, Y. Jiang, and Z. Chen. How much can behavioral targeting help online advertising? In *Proceedings of the 18th International Conference on World Wide Web*, 2009.

[23] L. Zhang and Y. Guan. Detecting click fraud in pay-per-click streams of online advertising networks. In *Proceedings of the 28th IEEE International Conference on Distributed Computing Systems*, 2008.

Fast Top-k Retrieval for Model Based Recommendation

Deepak Agarwal
Yahoo! Research
Santa Clara, CA
dagarwal@yahoo-inc.com

Maxim Gurevich
Yahoo! Research
Santa Clara, CA
maximg@yahoo-inc.com

ABSTRACT

A crucial task in many recommender problems like computational advertising, content optimization, and others is to retrieve a small set of items by scoring a large item inventory through some elaborate statistical/machine-learned model. This is challenging since the retrieval has to be fast (few milliseconds) to load the page quickly. Fast retrieval is well studied in the information retrieval (IR) literature, especially in the context of document retrieval for queries. When queries and documents have sparse representation and relevance is measured through cosine similarity (or some variant thereof), one could build highly efficient retrieval algorithms that scale gracefully to increasing item inventory. The key components exploited by such algorithms is sparse query-document representation and the special form of the relevance function. Many machine-learned models used in modern recommender problems do not satisfy these properties and since brute force evaluation is not an option with large item inventory, heuristics that filter out some items are often employed to reduce model computations at runtime.

In this paper, we take a two-stage approach where the first stage retrieves top-K items using our approximate procedures and the second stage selects the desired top-k using brute force model evaluation on the K retrieved items. The main idea of our approach is to reduce the first stage to a standard IR problem, where each item is represented by a sparse feature vector (a.k.a. the vector-space representation) and the query-item relevance score is given by vector dot product. The sparse item representation is learnt to closely approximate the original machine-learned score by using retrospective data. Such a reduction allows leveraging extensive work in IR that resulted in highly efficient retrieval systems. Our approach is model-agnostic, relying only on data generated from the machine-learned model. We obtain significant improvements in the computational cost vs. accuracy tradeoff compared to several baselines in our empirical evaluation on both synthetic models and on a click-through (CTR) model used in online advertising.

Permission to make digital or hard copies of all or part of this work for personal or classroom use is granted without fee provided that copies are not made or distributed for profit or commercial advantage and that copies bear this notice and the full citation on the first page. To copy otherwise, to republish, to post on servers or to redistribute to lists, requires prior specific permission and/or a fee.
WSDM'12, February 8–12, 2012, Seattle, Washington, USA.
Copyright 2012 ACM 978-1-4503-0747-5/12/02 ...$10.00.

Categories and Subject Descriptors

H.3.3 [**Information Search and Retrieval**]: Selection process

General Terms

Algorithms, Measurement

Keywords

Inverted index, top-k retrieval, machine learning, LASSO, support vector machines

1. INTRODUCTION

Recommender systems serve items to users in some given context in an automated fashion. Examples of such systems broadly include content recommendation [7, 1, 5] that serves articles to user visits on a webpage, computational advertising [2, 13] that serves ads to users in the context of a search query or visit some particular page, web search that serves documents to a user in the context of a query, and many others [6]. Since the number of user visits is large, automated serving ensures low marginal cost per serve and leads to profitable systems. Typically, the goal of such systems is to maximize some business objectives like click-rates, advertising revenue, relevance, and so on. Classical techniques based on Information Retrieval (IR) that map context and items to a common semantic space and measure goodness through some relevance function like cosine similarity are not sufficient for such problems. For instance, items and contexts may have orthogonal sets of features, with no direct mapping between them. Additional feedback from users in the form of clicks, buys, etc., provides valuable information on the appropriateness of items for different (user, context) pairs that is not captured through pure IR techniques. One attractive approach that has been pursued to incorporate such information is through machine-learned or statistical models that directly optimize for the measure of interest like click rate, buy rate, etc. Such models leverage retrospective data and build functions that are predictive of the value of this measure for different user-item pairs in various contexts. Ranking of items for a given visit in a given context is then based on predicted values from the model.

While machine-learned models are in general more accurate, they present additional challenges in terms of retrieval at serve time, especially when working with large item inventory. For most recommender systems, the top results have to be retrieved in a few milliseconds to ensure that webpage loads quickly. As brute force evaluation of scores on all items is not feasible, fast retrieval techniques that scale gracefully to a large number of items are imperative.

Research on machine-learned models on the other hand have focused mostly on accuracy without much attention to retrieval. Often the structure of state-of-the-art models is not amenable to standard IR indexing and retrieval approaches that power many large-scale serving systems. Hence, despite their accuracy, the potential of such models cannot be fully realized for applications with a large number of items. Heuristics are mostly used to address the issue of scale. For instance, it is common to take a filtering approach where a simple IR system retrieves a small number of items that are further re-ranked using a more accurate machine-learned model. An alternate approach is to restrict to models that are amenable to efficient indexing and hence scalable to large itemsets.

In this paper we take a two stage approach where the first stage retrieves the top-K candidates efficiently by approximating the original scoring function. To perform such approximation, we use a function class that is similar to the classical IR score and hence allows efficient indexing and retrieval using off-the-shelf IR systems. The second stage does a brute force evaluation on the K candidates returned by the first stage using the original machine-learned scoring function. We show that our first stage approximation makes the retrieval scalable without losing too much accuracy. In particular, our approximate model has sparse vector space structure as in the classical IR, and hence classical algorithms for inverted indices can be used for efficient retrieval.

The main idea of our technique is to approximate the true model scores of items on a representative sample of (user, context) queries using a simple linear function amenable to indexing — the vector dot product between the query features and the (learnt) item vectors. We obtain item vectors by solving an optimization problem that minimizes the discrepancy between the true and the approximate scores. Furthermore, to prevent index blow-up, we enforce sparsity on the item vectors through standard techniques used in regression and classification literature. One variant of our formulation based on regression achieves sparsity through the LASSO procedure [15] with L_1 regularization, another rank based variant does so by using L_1 regularized Support Vector Classification (SVC) [12]. Learning item vectors is independent for different items and thus can be done in parallel, ensuring scalability even for a large number of items. We treat the original model as a black-box, requiring only the ability to compute scores on concrete query-item examples, and thus do not assume any particular structure of the model. We note that approximating the model scores is better than learning the approximate model from original data since model scores can be generated for any number of query-item pairs, and hence are not prone to sparsity problem that is typically present in the original data. We show that our vector-space representation is flexible enough to provide a good approximation for a rich class of machine-learned models.

To the best of our knowledge, there is little prior work along these lines, with the only exception of [11]. Empirical evaluation on synthetic and real-world datasets reduces approximation error by up to 85% for a fixed budget of model evaluations, compared to this prior work. The overall query latency of our two-stage approach is two orders of magnitude lower than that of the brute force evaluation.

Our **contributions** are thus threefold: (1) Formulating the problem of model approximation for indexing as an optimization problem, (2) Proposing effective and scalable algorithms for solving this problem, and finally (3) Evaluating the proposed technique, along with several baselines, on synthetic and real-world datasets and showing significant advantages compared to the baselines.

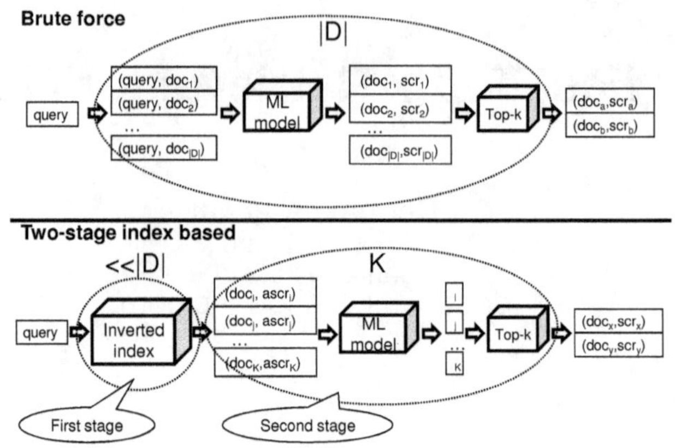

Figure 1: Brute force (top) vs. our two-stage (bottom) approaches.

2. MOTIVATION AND PROBLEM DEFINITION

To be consistent with the IR terminology, we shall refer to the (user,context) pair as a query and to items as documents. Given a document collection $\mathcal{D}$ and a query space $\mathcal{Q}$, the goodness of a document $d \in \mathcal{D}$ to a query $q \in \mathcal{Q}$ is given by a score function $\texttt{scr}(d,q)$ that is obtained through a machine-learned model. At the serve time, one has to retrieve the top-k scoring documents in response to an incoming query q. Typically, k is small (in many cases $k = 1$). If the candidate document set is large and the machine-learned score is complex, brute force evaluation to retrieve the top-k documents is not feasible under latency constraints. We take recourse to a two-stage approach, illustrated in Figure 1, where top-K, $K \geq k$, documents are retrieved efficiently by the first stage, followed by the second stage that finds the top-k out of K candidates using brute force model evaluation. The main saving comes from reducing the number of model evaluations from $|\mathcal{D}|$ to K. Obviously the first stage procedure has to be very efficient (i.e., much faster than $|\mathcal{D}|$ model evaluations) and the value of K should be small relative to $|\mathcal{D}|$. Ideally, given the cost of computing $\texttt{scr}(d,q)$ we would like to choose the maximum permissible K according to latency budget and then select a first stage retrieval procedure that minimizes error incurred when some (or all) true top-k documents are missed in the retrieved top-K. We formalize this notion below.

Given query q, let the set of top-k documents from a subset $X \subseteq \mathcal{D}$ with highest scores on q be

$$T_X^k(q) \triangleq \arg\max_{d \in X}^{k} \texttt{scr}(d,q),$$

where ties are broken arbitrarily. Let the approximate top-K set retrieved by the first stage using an approximate first stage score function $\texttt{ascr}(d,q)$ be

$$tK(q) \triangleq \arg\max_{d \in \mathcal{D}}^{K} \texttt{ascr}(d,q).$$

A natural objective function, given k, K, and a query distribution $\tilde{\mathcal{Q}}$, is minimizing the score loss of choosing top-k from $tK(q)$ instead of from the whole set $\mathcal{D}$. That is, for $1 \le i \le k$, we want to minimize the gap between the score of the i-th document in the true ranking and the score of the i-th document retrieved by our two-stage approach. We now formalize this into the objective function:

$$\mathbb{E}_{q \propto \tilde{\mathcal{Q}}} \left(\sum_{d \in T^k_{\mathcal{D}}(q)} \texttt{scr}(d,q) - \sum_{d \in T^k_{tK(q)}(q)} \texttt{scr}(d,q) \right). \quad (1)$$

Our goal is to find a first stage procedure for computing $tK(q)$ that minimizes the value of the objective in equation (1) for the maximum permissible value of K that is feasible based on the computational time needed to evaluate $\texttt{scr}(d,q)$. The upper bound on the complexity of computing $tK(q)$ using $\texttt{ascr}(d,q)$ depends on the latency constraints (typically milliseconds) for large document sets. Some classes of ascr functions like cosine similarity allow efficient retrieval of the top-K candidates through precomputation of partial scores and organizing them into inverted indices. Other choice of ascr could be simple filtering rules. For instance, one such filtering rule could retrieve K documents at random out of those that contain the terms "Obama" or "White House" or "Democrat" when the query contains the term "Obama". However, such naive filtering approaches sacrifice accuracy and hence are not preferable in practice.

We consider settings where the $\texttt{scr}(d,q)$ cannot be computed using existing indexing techniques and is computationally complex enough to make brute force evaluation infeasible for large document sets. For problems where item inventory is small and/or $\texttt{scr}(d,q)$ is simple or amenable to classical IR indexing, model approximation is not needed.

3. BACKGROUND AND RELATED WORKS

In this section we provide a background on the standard IR indexing and retrieval based on the vector-space model, and discuss related works.

3.1 Top-k retrieval in the vector-space model

In the vector-space model, both queries and documents are represented by vectors in the same multidimensional space. Typically every term is a dimension, and queries and documents are sparse vectors where the magnitude of a nonzero value indicates the weight of the corresponding term in a query/document. By slight abuse of notation, let $\mathbf{q} = (q_1, \ldots, q_m)$ be the query vector of query q, where m is the number of different terms and q_i is the weight of term i in query q. Analogously, for a document d, $\mathbf{d} = (d_1, \ldots, d_m)$. The IR score of document d on query q is defined by $\sum_{i=1}^m q_i d_i$. Given a query, retrieving the top-k documents from a corpus $\mathcal{D}$ that have the highest scores on that query is a common task in IR systems.

The standard approach to the top-k retrieval is first preprocessing the corpus $\mathcal{D}$ and constructing an *inverted index* which is a collection of *posting lists* $L_1, L_2, \ldots, L_m$: a list for each term appearing in the corpus. List L_i enumerates all documents that have nonzero weights on term i. Typically, the weight is zero for most documents, thus a sparse representation is used where a posting list is a collection of postings of the form $\langle d, d_i \rangle$ (where d is document identifier) for all d-s such that $d_i \neq 0$. Given a query, retrieval algorithms consider only the lists of terms present in the query, thus significantly reducing their search space. Many algorithms (e.g., [3, 8]) further reduce retrieval time by examining only a fraction of postings in the relevant posting lists through clever branch and bound heuristics, allowing to skip large fraction of postings even in the lists of query terms. For instance, in the WAND algorithm [3], an upper bound on partial scores in each list helps skip partially evaluated candidates once it is determined that their full score will not suffice to make it into the current set of top-k candidates.

3.2 Predictive Indexing

In the most relevant prior work, Goel, Langford, and Strehl [11] proposed a "Predictive Indexing" technique which, similarly to our work, considers the problem of efficiently approximating top-k retrieval from a machine-learned model. There, the index is constructed so as to predict the most likely top-k documents under a given query workload. The main idea is to define *query sets* — possibly overlapping subsets of related queries, and for each such set to precompute the expected scores of all documents on the queries in the set, sorting the postings in each list in the descending order of their expected scores. One natural way is to define a query set for each term i, containing all the queries that contain this term, i.e., $q_i \neq 0$. At the query time, the lists corresponding to the query terms are traversed sequentially and the full model score is computed for the encountered documents, until exhausting the time budget.

Predictive indexing relies on the assumption that a document d that scores high (and is thus in the top-k) on a query q has sufficiently high expected score in at least one of the query sets of query q, and is close to the head of the corresponding list. While this assumption is plausible in some settings, it may not hold always, and depends heavily on the corpus, the query workload, and the scoring model. It is especially inaccurate in problems where the machine learned scores exhibit strong interactions among terms. The performance also depends on the construction of the query classes, we follow the one used by the authors in all our comparative studies.

In contrast to predictive indexing, our approach optimizes the partial scores in each posting list so as to approximate the true scores as accurately as possible, and at the same time require sparsity in order to obtain a small index. Indeed, as we show in our experimental results, our technique significantly reduces the score loss compared to predictive indexing for models where strong interactions exist.

3.3 Alternative approaches

A more traditional approach for scaling to large serving systems is caching. Exact match caching techniques are ineffective in the setting we consider due to the sparse domain leading to low hit rates. In [14], the authors propose to relax the notion of cache hit by allowing the cache to return results of different but similar queries. Such caching technique is complementary to our work, since even when the cache hit rate is high enough, cache misses need to be processed accurately and within latency constraints.

Another approach is to use a secondary, less computationally intensive model for the first stage retrieval. Some work has been done on developing models that are faster to evaluate while sacrificing some accuracy [4]. However, this approach is model-dependent, and, unless the secondary model is amenable to indexing, may still be unacceptable from the latency perspective for large document sets. Also, as remarked earlier in Section 1, learning a vector space model on the original data is more difficult due to data sparsity. Our approach alleviates the sparsity problem by learning on the outputs $\texttt{scr}(d, q)$ from the accurate machine-learned model that can be computed on any (d, q) pair.

4. OUR APPROACH

4.1 Vector-space representation

We now describe our approach for obtaining $\texttt{ascr}(q, d)$ that is constructed to efficiently optimize objective in Eq. (1). At a high level, we assume $\texttt{ascr}(q, d)$ is obtained from a class of functions based on the vector-space model that is widely used in IR and hence amenable to inverted index kind of precomputation. However, unlike typical IR systems where document vectors are derived directly from document content and auxiliary information (e.g., anchor text), we *learn* document vectors by minimizing the deviation from the original scores $\texttt{scr}(d, q)$ while ensuring sparsity to reduce the index size and to improve retrieval efficiency.

The $\texttt{ascr}(q, d)$ function we learn approximates $\texttt{scr}(q, d)$. We learn $\texttt{ascr}(\cdot)$ offline from $\texttt{scr}(q, d)$ computed for sufficiently many (q, d) pairs.

We now provide a detailed description of our approach. Recall that $\mathbf{q} = (q_1, \ldots, q_m)$ is an m-dimensional term (or, more generally, feature) vector corresponding to query q. These features include those of context and user and could be high dimensional. Typically in recommender applications, although m is large, only a small fraction of m features occurs (has nonzero weight) in each query. Although our solution does not depend on this assumption, inverted index approaches are efficient for such sparse queries.[1] We thus define $\texttt{ascr}(d, q)$ to be a simple linear function, that can be easily plugged into any existing IR system based on inverted indices over vector-space representation:

$$\texttt{ascr}(d, q) \quad = \quad \sum_{i=1}^{m} q_i d_i \quad = \quad \mathbf{q}^{'}\mathbf{d}, \qquad (2)$$

where $\mathbf{d}$ is the m-dimensional weight vector of document d that needs to be learned based on the machine-learned score function $\texttt{scr}(\cdot)$.

The above approach allows straightforward indexing of the corpus $\mathcal{D}$ by learning vectors $\mathbf{d}$ for all $d \in \mathcal{D}$, and indexing these vectors as if they were standard term vectors of textual documents. At the query time, the first stage issues query vector $\mathbf{q}$ to a retrieval system against the index, and it returns the top-K documents with highest $\texttt{ascr}(d, q) = \mathbf{q}^{'}\mathbf{d}$.

4.2 Special cases - exact solution

We show that the class of functions in Eq. (2) is flexible by showing optimality for the objective function in Eq. (1) in some restricted special cases. Let us consider a scenario where our query space $\mathcal{Q}$ consists of a single query q. In this case, it is trivial to find $\mathbf{d}$-s resulting in zero loss by setting the first coordinate of each vector $\mathbf{d}$ to be $\texttt{scr}(d, q)$ (and ensuring the first coordinate of every $\mathbf{q}$ is positive). In fact, for any m queries $(q^1, q^2, \ldots, q^m)$ one can solve, for each $d \in \mathcal{D}$, a linear system consisting of m equations and m variables $d_1, d_2, \ldots, d_m$: $\mathbf{q}^{i'}\mathbf{d} = \texttt{scr}(q^i, d), i = 1, \ldots, m$. The solution of such a system is a unique $\mathbf{d}$ for document d that simultaneously satisfies $\mathbf{q}^{i'}\mathbf{d} = \texttt{scr}(q^i, d), i = 1, \ldots, m$ and the objective functions is again trivially zero and the approximation lossless.

However, the total number of distinct queries is typically much larger than the number of dimensions m, hence one cannot in general obtain a solution $\mathbf{d}$ that is lossless in the entire query space. In yet another special case, if the original score function is additive in queries[2], i.e,

$$\texttt{scr}(\sum_{i=1}^{m} a_i \mathbf{q}^i, d) = \sum_{i=1}^{m} a_i\, \texttt{scr}(q^i, d),$$

then the approximation $\texttt{ascr}$ is lossless. This is true because any query vector $\mathbf{q}$ can be written as a linear combination $\sum_{i=1}^{m} a_i \mathbf{q}^i$ of queries in some basis set $\{q^1, q^2, \ldots, q^m\}$, and as we have seen earlier, the scores on a set of m queries can be encoded losslessly. Then,

$$\begin{aligned}\texttt{ascr}(q, d) \quad &= \quad \sum_{i=1}^{m} a_i\, \texttt{ascr}(q^i, d) \\ &= \quad \sum_{i=1}^{m} a_i\, \texttt{scr}(q^i, d) \quad = \quad \texttt{scr}(q, d)\end{aligned}$$

is lossless. But in general $\texttt{scr}(q, d)$ need not be additive in queries, hence one has to learn $\mathbf{d}$ by incurring some loss.

4.3 General case - approximation

Going back to the general problem, let $\mathbf{D}$ be the set of vectors $\mathbf{d}$ for all documents in $\mathcal{D}$. Based on the objective given in Eq. (1), let

$$A(q) = \text{avg}_{d \in T^k_{\mathcal{D}}(q)}\, \texttt{scr}(d, q)$$

be the true average score on query q, and

$$B(q, \mathbf{D}) = \text{avg}_{d \in T^k_{tK(q)}(q)}\, \texttt{scr}(d, q)$$

be the average retrieved score that we want to maximize (obviously, $B(q, \mathbf{D}) \leq A(q)$ for all q). Then, to estimate $\mathbf{D}$, we want to minimize the expectation of the discrepancy function

$$A(q) - B(q, \mathbf{D}),$$

over the query distribution of interest $\tilde{\mathcal{Q}}$. In practice, the theoretical expectation is replaced by the empirical average over a set of queries Q_s obtained by sampling from historical data.

We are not aware of a technique for directly optimizing the above expression, and thus resort to solving simpler variants similar to it. Before going into details, we consider the sparsity of the desired solution.

4.4 Sparsification

The main problem with the approach of obtaining $\mathbf{D}$ by minimizing some discrepancy function is the index size. The solution $\mathbf{D}$ is not guaranteed to be sparse, i.e., may result in $\mathbf{D}$ containing no or few zero elements, which leads to long

[1] If the original problem is in a low-dimensional dense domain, the numerical feature values can be binned into a discrete set of binary features, thus converting the problem to a sparse domain amenable to indexing.

[2] By slight abuse of notation we allow the $\texttt{scr}$ function to take query vector as an argument, i.e., $\texttt{scr}(\mathbf{q}, d)$.

posting lists containing all or almost all documents, which negatively affects both the index size and the retrieval performance. Ideally, we would like to obtain sparse $\mathbf{D}$ (i.e., set the majority of elements in $\mathbf{D}$ to zero), while minimizing the error given in Eq. (1), possibly by modifying some other postings. To ensure such sparsity, we minimize the discrepancy function subject to a constraint on the number of non-zero elements in $\mathbf{D}$. In other words, we estimate $\mathbf{D}$ by solving the following problem:

$$\min \sum_{q \in Q_s} A(q) - B(q, \mathbf{D}) \quad \text{s.t. } ||\mathbf{D}||_0 < c. \tag{3}$$

In practice, we relax the L_0 constraint in Eq. (3) to an L_1 constraint, this makes it easier to solve the problem analytically and still obtain a sparse solution. The relaxed problem using the Lagrangian formulation is

$$\min \ 2\lambda||\mathbf{D}||_1 + \sum_{q \in Q_s} A(q) - B(q, \mathbf{D}), \tag{4}$$

where $\lambda \geq 0$ is the Lagrange parameter that determines the amount of L_1 penalty we are imposing on $\mathbf{D}$. Higher λ ensures higher L_1 penalty and lead to sparser solutions.

We next describe two alternative relaxations of the above problem amenable to efficient numerical approximation.

4.5 Binary classifications

The first relaxation of the discrepancy function given in Eq. (4) we consider is casting the problem as a two-class classification problem, where for each document d we want to learn vector $\mathbf{d}$ that predicts whether d in among the top-k documents on a query $\mathbf{q}$ by a simple thresholding operator $\mathbf{q}'\mathbf{d} > \theta$.

Let $y_{q,d}$ be the indicator variable of whether d is among the top-k result on query q:

$$y_{q,d} = \begin{cases} 1 & d \in T^k_{\mathcal{D}}(q) \\ -1 & d \notin T^k_{\mathcal{D}}(q). \end{cases}$$

We then learn $\mathbf{D}$ by minimizing for each $d \in \mathcal{D}$

$$\min_{\mathbf{d}} \ 2\lambda||\mathbf{d}||_1 + \sum_{q \in Q_s} \max(0, 1 - y_{q,d} \cdot \mathbf{q}'\mathbf{d})^2. \tag{5}$$

There exist efficient algorithms for solving the above problem. In our experiments we used the algorithm for an equivalent problem — L1-regularized L2-loss Support Vector Classification in the Liblinear package [9].

This formulation has two advantages. First, it decomposes the large problem of finding $\mathbf{D}$ into many small independent problems, one for each document, of finding $\mathbf{d}$. This allows for efficient numerical solution as well as for parallelization. The second advantage is not relying score values, but rather only on the ranking induced by the scores. This simplifies data collection for some models that do not readily produce model scores but directly output document rankings. Furthermore, such data can be obtained from the historical logs (assuming the system served documents from $\mathcal{D}$).

On the other hand, the fine-grained information encoded in model scores is lost, potentially degrading the accuracy and/or requiring more training data. In applications where scores are available,it might be possible to do better by using the information encoded in score values. This motivates us to consider the following alternative formulation.

4.6 Score approximation

Here we approximate model scores of query-document pairs directly, assuming that if the scores are approximated well then the top-k sets will be accurate too. That is, for every $q \in \mathcal{Q}_s, d \in \mathcal{D}$ we want to minimize some score discrepancy function f and the L_1 regularization factor:

$$\min \ 2\lambda||\mathbf{D}||_1 + \sum_{q \in Q_s} \sum_{d \in \mathcal{D}} f(\mathbf{q}'\mathbf{d}, \mathtt{scr}(d, q)). \tag{6}$$

When the discrepancy function is squared-loss $f(a, b) = (a-b)^2$, the problem is the well known LASSO problem [15] that has been studied extensively. Although we use here squared error loss, other loss functions like Kullback-Leibler can easily be incorporated.

We now describe a coordinate descent algorithm for obtaining a solution to the above problem as proposed in [10]. Observe that, here too, we can decompose the problem defined in Eq. (6) into independent per-document problems:

$$\forall d \in \mathcal{D}: \quad \min_{\mathbf{d}} \ 2\lambda||\mathbf{d}||_1 + \sum_{q \in Q_s} (\mathtt{scr}(d, q) - \mathbf{q}'\mathbf{d})^2.$$

An iterative technique optimizes the above through a sequential one-at-a-time update method. Let $\mathbf{d}$ be the current document vector and our goal is to update its i-th element d_i. For simplicity, denote d_i by x. Define the partial residual as

$$r(q) = \mathtt{scr}(d, q) - \sum_{j \neq i} q_j \cdot d_j.$$

We compute the new value of x (denoted by x^*) by solving the one-dimensional problem

$$\min_x \left(2\lambda|x| + \sum_{q \in Q_s} (r(q) - q_i x)^2 \right),$$

that from elementary calculus on subgradients has a closed form solution

$$x^* = \frac{T\left(\sum_{q \in Q_s} r(q) q_i, \lambda\right)}{\sum_{q \in Q_s} q_i^2},$$

where $T(a, \lambda)$ is the soft thresholding operator:

$$T(a, \lambda) = \begin{cases} a - \lambda & a > \lambda \\ a + \lambda & a < -\lambda \\ 0 & \text{otherwise.} \end{cases}$$

A similar co-ordinate descent algorithm could be easily derived for other smooth loss functions f.

The sequential update algorithm is then as follows — (a) initialize $\mathbf{d}$ by the all-zeros vector, (b) for $i = 1, 2, \ldots, m$, update d_i, (c) Repeat (b) until convergence.

4.7 Index construction and retrieval

Here we consider several practical aspects of computing $\mathbf{D}$, constructing the index from it, and retrieving from that index.

Parallel construction. As we have shown above, both techniques for constructing $\mathbf{D}$ are decomposable by documents. This property allows us to parallelize computation so as to allow fast construction of $\mathbf{D}$ even for large document collections, using, e.g., the MapReduce framework.

Incremental updates. The decomposability by documents allows to easily add new document to the index. The optimization problem corresponding to the newly arriving document is solved independently of other document (and of the current index), and the resulting postings are added to the index. Similarly, the postings of the deleted documents are removed from the index without affecting other postings.

Accommodating changes in query distribution. Typically, query distribution (and thus the sample Q_s) gradually change over time. Thus, to keep the accuracy high, document postings have to be periodically recomputed. The cost of such recomputation can be reduced by using the current postings as warm-start; this expedites convergence of our algorithms.

Negative partial scores. Note that our formulations do not require values in vectors $\mathbf{d}$ to be non-negative. Non-negativity of partial scores is assumed (explicitly or implicitly) in some retrieval algorithms. For instance, the initial score threshold for getting added to the current set of top-k candidates is often set to 0, and the upper bound of the partial scores in a posting list is often computed as the maximum score in the list. In the presence of negative partial scores these lead to incorrect results by the algorithms.

We experimented with WAND [3] and MaxScore [16] algorithms, and found that they can be easily adapted to accommodate negative scores. We initialize score threshold with a large negative constant instead of 0. For the upper bounds, observing that the documents that do not appear in a posting list have implicitly partial score 0 in that list, we make the upper bound to be the maximum of 0 and the highest partial score that appears in the list.

In general, negative scores decrease the effectiveness of skipping and early termination in retrieval algorithms. It is possible to restrict the solution vectors $\mathbf{d}$ to be non-negative. However, such a restriction leads to higher accuracy loss, and may be more computationally expensive. Thus, and since non-negativity alone is not a sufficient condition for effective skipping, we did not further explore this direction, which would be an interesting future work. In our experiments we observed that despite negative scores, the retrieval algorithms still achieved orders of magnitude faster query response compared to the brute force model evaluation.

5. EXPERIMENTAL EVALUATION

5.1 Datasets and setup

We evaluate our method on three dataset-model combinations:

Synthetic model — simple. In this dataset we simulate a reasonable query distribution and a model with weak non-linear query-document interactions.

We used a set of 10,000 documents (with no actual content, just document IDs), and assigned unpredictable document orders unique query term (features) out of the set of 10,000 unique terms. That is, for each term we generated a random permutation of the 10,000 documents, and assigned scores to the documents according to their position in the permutation as follows: the score of a document at a position i is $(1 - 1/100)^i$. This function simulates some fitness function of each document on the term and results in a few "relevant" documents having high score and the rest having very low score, which is often the case in real scoring functions.

We then randomly generated 12,000 queries (10,000 for training and 2,000 for testing), each consisting of 3 terms. Each query term was sampled independently from a power-law distribution on the 10,000 unique terms, which is a distribution of terms/features often observed in user-generated requests. The scores of document d on different terms in query q were then summed into the final score of the document on the query, thus obtaining $\texttt{scr}(q, d)$.

The goal here is to simulate a relatively simple model where the score is simply the sum of three independent term-document scores. This is used to test the robustness of our methods. Clearly, predictive indexing approach should work well here due to the weak interaction between query terms, the goal is to study the behavior of our approach in such scenarios relative to predictive indexing.

Synthetic model — complex. This model is identical to the previous one, with the following two modifications: (1) each query consists of 5 terms, and (2) in addition to single terms, each pair and triple of query terms is associated with a random permutation of documents and the induced scores. Thus, each query-document score $\texttt{scr}(q, d)$ is a sum of 25 independent scores: 5 scores on single terms, 10 scores on pairs, and 10 scores on triples of terms. Clearly such a model is highly nonlinear and thus poses a challenge to the linear approximation function we use in equation (2).

Click probability model — CTR. To demonstrate applicability to a realistic model, we evaluated our method on a click probability model fitted to a computational advertising dataset. The model was fitted using a logistic regression model with roughly $16M$ features that were generated by using cross-product of (user,page) and ad attributes. The attribute set includes many granular features including ad-id, campaign-id, publisher-id, publisher category, user age, gender, and others. Since the total number of all possible cross-products are *astronomical*, the features are hashed into a large number ($16M$) of bins. This "hashing trick" has been shown to provide good performance, especially in applications where the features are sparse [17]. In fact, one can interpret the hashing as feature transformation using a large number of sparse random projections.

This model was trained on the real traffic obtained from an advertising system and was observed to provide accurate results. However, due to the complex non-linearity induced by taking projections of cross-product features, brute force evaluation becomes costly. The dataset contains $|\mathcal{D}| = 50,000$ documents (ads) and a sample of $|Q_s| = 50,000$ queries from a single day. Q_s was used for index construction only, and the evaluation was performed using a different sample of 50,000 queries from the following day. Query features have binary weights, query length is between 7 and 8, and the number of unique query features is 18,000. This is a highly non-linear model that is challenging to approximate.

Baselines. We compare the two techniques we propose — BINARY SVC (Section 4.5) and L_2 REGRESSION (Section 4.6) — to the three baselines: RANDOM— the first stage randomly selects K documents from $\mathcal{D}$; STATIC— the first stage returns the fixed document set, independent of the query, of K documents having the highest average score on queries in Q_s; PREDICTIVE— predictive indexing [11].

Evaluation metrics. As the main evaluation metric we use the relative score loss, i.e., our objective function given in Eq. (1), normalized by the true scores in order to bring scores of different models to the same scale. Let t_q be the ground-truth results, i.e., an array containing k documents from $T^k_{\mathcal{D}}(q)$ ordered by their true scores. Similarly, let a_q be the results of our two-stage approach, i.e., an array containing k documents from $T^k_{tK(q)}(q)$ ordered by their true scores. We then define the relative score loss as follows:

$$\text{avg}_{q \in Q_t, 1 \le i \le k} \left(\frac{\texttt{scr}(t_q[i], q) - \texttt{scr}(a_q[i], q)}{\texttt{scr}(t_q[i], q)} \right),$$

where Q_t is the set of test queries.

The goal of this metric is to measure the relative loss in the application-specific utility (e.g., CTR) as a result of our approximation. Thus, if the scores produced by a model are "raw", i.e., order-consistent but not necessarily equal to the utility function, then, at the evaluation time the raw scores are converted monotonically to the utility domain by an application-specific function. For instance, for the CTR model, we used the following sigmoid function that converts the raw model scores into click-through probabilities $g(\texttt{scr}(q,d)) = 1/(1 + e^{-\texttt{scr}(q,d)})$. The scores of the synthetic models were used as is.

An alternative metric that does not depend on the scale and the distribution of the scores can be obtained by replacing the scores with ranks of documents for queries. Let $\texttt{rank}(d, q, X)$ be the rank of d among the document from set X ordered in the descending order of the true scores $\texttt{scr}(d', q), d' \in X$. Then, the rank loss is given by

$$\text{avg}_{q \in Q_t, d \in a_q} (\texttt{rank}(d, q, \mathcal{D}) - \texttt{rank}(d, q, a_q)) =$$
$$\text{avg}_{q \in Q_t, 1 \le i \le k} (\texttt{rank}(a_q[i], q, \mathcal{D}) - i).$$

Hardware and software. The two-stage retrieval prototype was implemented as a single-threaded Java application and was run on an Intel Xeon 2.00GHz 8-core machine with 32GB RAM. We pre-loaded all the data (including the index) into the main memory, which is the dominant approach in modern large scale serving systems.

Index construction was run on a Hadoop[3] cluster consisting of thousands of machines.

5.2 Index construction

Since as we showed in Section 4.7 the regression subproblems are independent for each document, index computation is easily parallelized. In our experiments, computing model scores and solving the optimization problem for a single document in CTR (the larger dataset) took about 1/3 minutes for BINARY SVC and between 1 to 2 minutes for L_2 REGRESSION on single machine. Utilizing 2,000 machines, index construction for $|\mathcal{D}| = 50{,}000$ documents took below 10 minutes for BINARY SVC and below one hour for L_2 REGRESSION.

5.3 Accuracy

We measured the accuracy of different methods in retrieving the true top-k documents using both the score loss and the rank loss. For BINARY SVC and L_2 REGRESSION we generated several indices having different sparsity and measured the accuracy of the top-10 results when the first stage retrieves 50 results, i.e., $k = 10, K = 50$. We report the results on the index having the highest accuracy at $k = 10, K = 50$, while having no more than 350 postings per document on average (which we believe is a reasonable bound on the acceptable index size).

[3]http://hadoop.apache.org

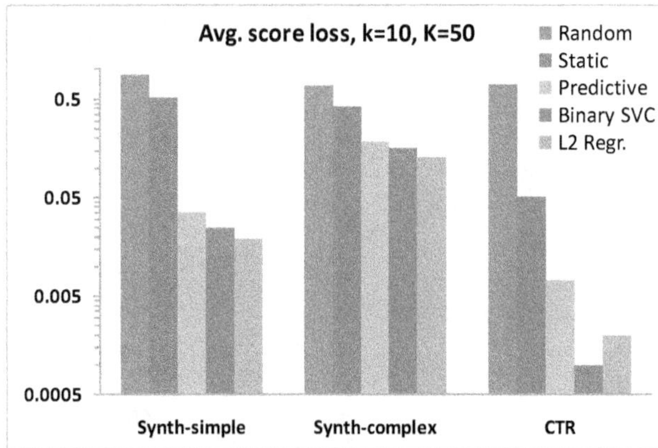

Figure 2: Average score loss.

Figure 2 summarize the accuracy of our methods compared to the baselines (note the logarithmic scale). The results clearly show the advantage of our algorithms over the baselines on all the three datasets. Observe that the random SYNTH-COMPLEX model in much harder to deal with for all the methods, which are unable to achieve score loss of below 0.1, while the loss on other models is orders of magnitude lower. The CTR dataset appears to admit much better approximation, perhaps due to the nonuniform query distribution and inherent dependencies between document scores on different query terms, that are not present in our synthetic datasets where the queries and the scores on different terms (and their combinations) are independent. This demonstrates that our approximation techniques (as well as some baselines) are able to take advantage of potential dependencies in scores across terms.

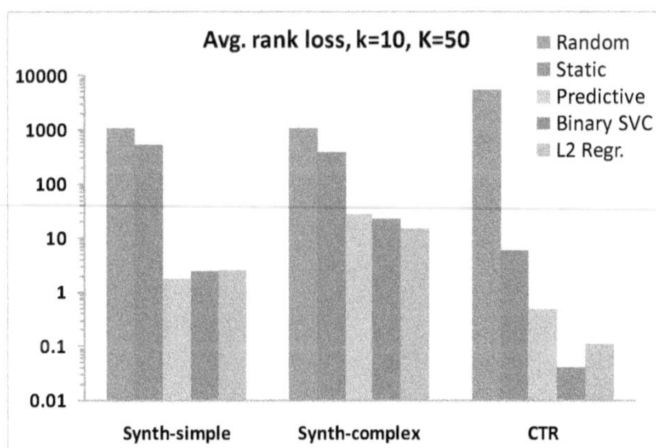

Figure 3: Average rank loss.

Figure 3 shows the rank loss on the same results shown in Figures 2. The results are mostly unchanged, except the SYNTH-SIMPLE model where the order of PREDICTIVE, BINARY SVC, and L_2 REGRESSION has reversed. This indicates that our methods make more mistakes in ranking the document when their scores are close and less mistakes when the scores are different. This is a desired property as it allows better approximating the application-specific objective reflected in scores.

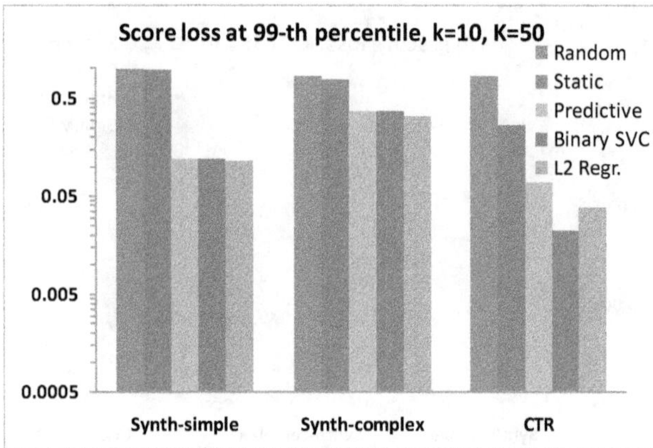

Figure 4: Score loss at 99-th percentile.

Average loss alone may not be sufficient to decide on applicability of an approximation technique since there may still be significant number of queries on which the loss is much above the average. We thus measured the score loss on 99-th percentile, i.e., the loss value such that 99% of queries have loss below that value. The results, shown in Figure 4, confirm that our techniques are more accurate, albeit with smaller gap compared to the baselines.

Since the score and the rank losses are mostly consistent, as we also observed in the following experiments, in the following results we report only the score loss. Similarly, we only show results of the PREDICTIVE baseline, as the other two baselines are consistently inferior.

5.4 Dependence on K

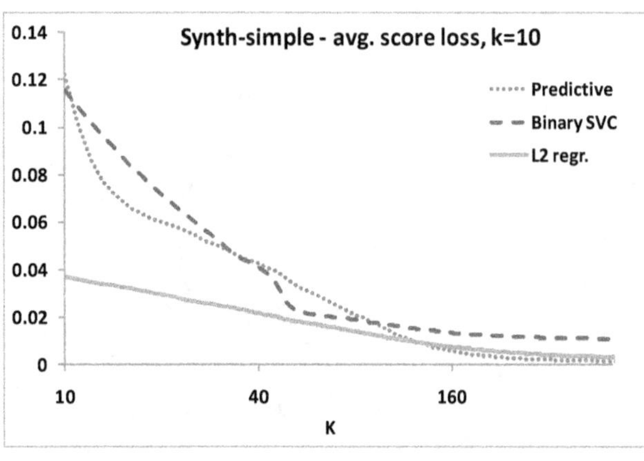

Figure 5: Average score loss as a function of K.

We next analyze the dependence of the score loss on K. Figures 5, 6, and 7 show this dependence for $k = 10$, on the SYNTH-SIMPLE, SYNTH-COMPLEX, and CTR datasets respectively.

We can see that L_2 REGRESSION method is consistently and significantly more accurate than PREDICTIVE in low K's, and the gap shrinks as K increases. Observe that the loss

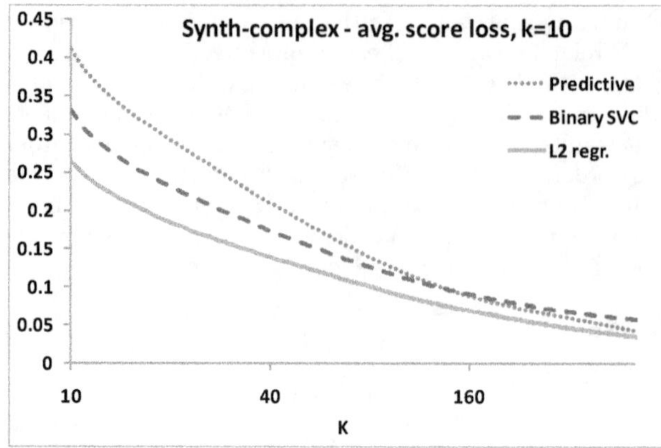

Figure 6: Average score loss as a function of K.

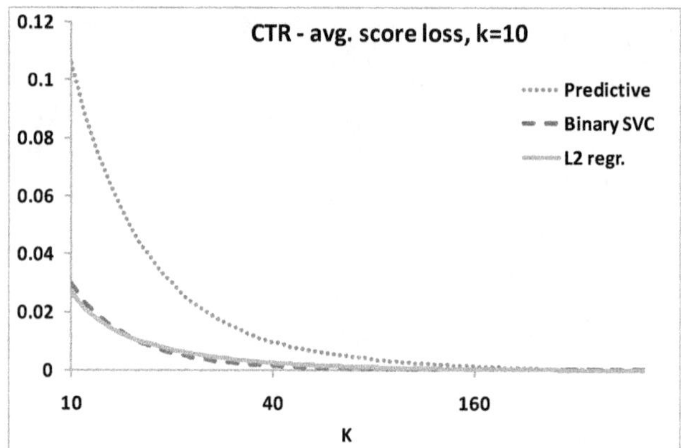

Figure 7: Average score loss as a function of K.

decays rather quickly with K on SYNTH-SIMPLE and CTR, and much slower on SYNTH-COMPLEX, which is not surprising since we intentionally designed SYNTH-COMPLEX to be harder for approximation. Note that the operating region of our proposed two-stage approach lies in the lower K's, where the number of expensive model evaluations is minimized. This is the region where the gap between our L_2 REGRESSION algorithm and the baselines is the largest. Alternatively, for achieving the same accuracy, L_2 REGRESSION requires significantly lower K compared to PREDICTIVE. The accuracy of BINARY SVC is less stable, from being close to PREDICTIVE on SYNTH-SIMPLE, through being between PREDICTIVE and L_2 REGRESSION on SYNTH-COMPLEX, to beating L_2 REGRESSION for most K's on CTR. We conclude that L_2 REGRESSION is the more accurate technique consistently achieving optimal or near-optimal accuracy among the methods we compare.

5.5 Accuracy vs. index size

We now analyze the dependence between accuracy and sparsity, which directly translates to the index size. Recall that the sparsity is controlled by the regularization parameter λ (see Section 4.4). Figures 8, 9, and 10 show the dependence of the accuracy on the average number of postings per document, at $k = 10, K = 50$ on the SYNTH-SIMPLE, SYNTH-COMPLEX, and CTR datasets respectively. Points in the plot correspond to different indices we constructed using

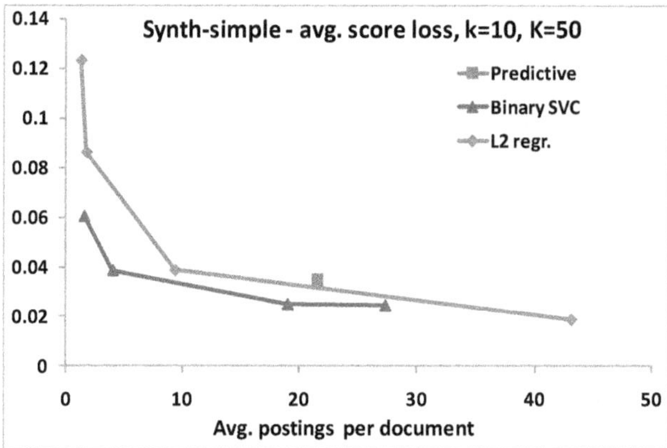

Figure 8: Average score loss as a function of postings per document.

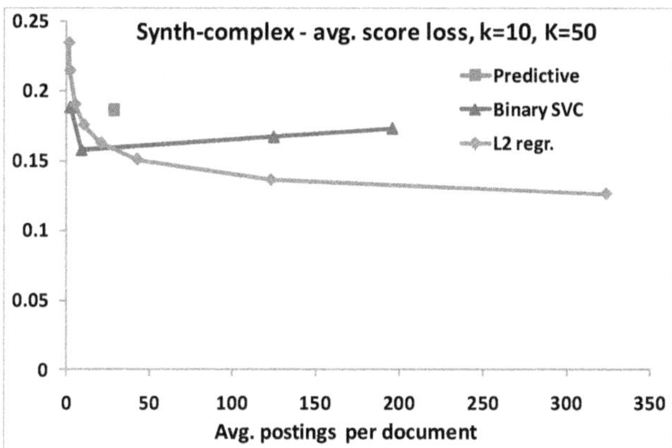

Figure 9: Average score loss as a function of postings per document.

different values of λ. For PREDICTIVE, which does not have regularization parameter and therefore has no flexibility of trading-off index size for accuracy, there is only one point in the plot, where the index size of PREDICTIVE was calculated as follows: For a given K, PREDICTIVE needs to traverse no more than the first K postings in each list, the rest can be safely pruned, i.e., all posting lists contain exactly $K = 50$ postings. Although for the majority of multi-term queries less than K postings in each list may be needed, different lists can contain duplicate documents, preventing pruning below K. Thus, we computed the average postings-per-document of PREDICTIVE as $\frac{K \cdot m}{|\mathcal{D}|}$.

The results show that in terms of the index size, BINARY SVC is a clear winner achieving near-optimal accuracy at very low cost of 10 postings per document or less on all the three datasets. Observe that on SYNTH-COMPLEX and CTR, the score loss of BINARY SVC *increases* with growing index size, possibly due to overfitting. PREDICTIVE is inferior in accuracy and index size simultaneously, to both BINARY SVC and L_2 REGRESSION on two of the three datasets. Here too, L_2 REGRESSION is the more stable method, consistently improving in accuracy with growing index. This is expected, since unlike BINARY SVC and PREDICTIVE, L_2 REGRESSION approximates model scores directly, and thus every improvement in score approximation leads to improved accuracy.

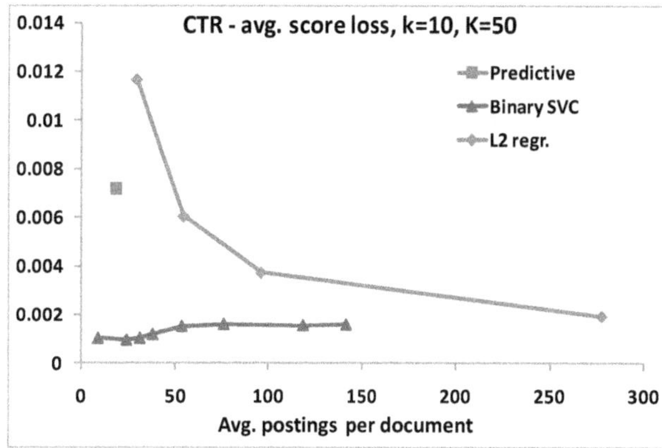

Figure 10: Average score loss as a function of postings per document.

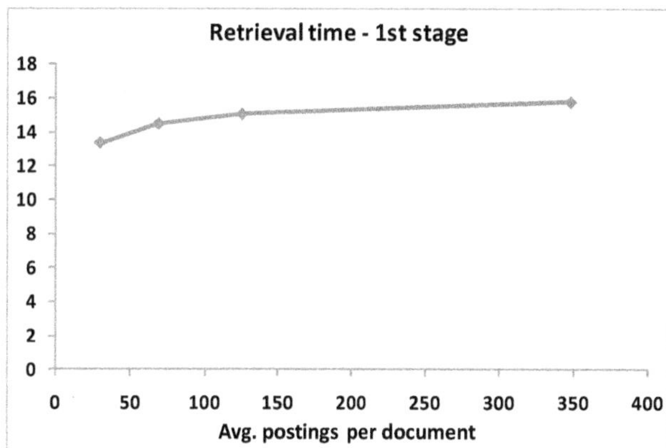

Figure 11: Latency (in ms) of the first stage retrieving $K = 100$ documents.

5.6 Retrieval performance

We evaluated the overall performance of our approach on a prototype of the two-stage system on the CTR dataset as it is larger and more realistic, and since for the CTR model we have an efficient procedure for computing $\mathtt{scr}(q, d)$. We evaluated five different indices generated by L_2 REGRESSION and containing from 30 to 350 postings per document on average. Figure 11 shows the latency (in milliseconds) of the first stage implemented by the MaxScore algorithm [16] (adapted to handle negative scores, see Section 4.7). We can see that the number of postings per document has relatively low effect on the retrieval latency, that increased only by 20% when going from 30 to 350 postings per document, and remains around $15ms$.[4]

The brute force evaluation of model scores on all the 50,000 document took 4.3 seconds per query on average, while the score evaluation on the $K = 100$ documents retrieved by the first stage took $9ms$ on average. This demonstrates two orders of magnitude reduction in the average

[4]The numbers are reported for illustrative purposes and can likely be improved. We also do not report here additional performance results using different retrieval algorithms, the dependence on K, etc., since these were studied extensively in the IR literature and are not the focus of this work.

retrieval time of the two-stage approach compared to the brute force evaluation.

Note that in this setting the first and the second stages have roughly the same latencies. Although the latency of the first-stage implemented with RANDOM, STATIC, or PREDICTIVE, that require simpler data structures and retrieval algorithms, is lower, the effect on the total latency is not as significant since the total latency becomes dominated by the second stage. We thus conclude that our two-stage approach, combined with the indices constructed with BINARY SVC and L_2 REGRESSION, provides better accuracy-latency tradeoff by approaching the accuracy of the original model while paying only a small fraction of the cost of the brute force approach.

6. CONCLUSIONS

In this work we considered the problem of top-k selection arising in a variety of modern web applications such as content recommendation or computational advertising. We explored a two-stage approach under a generic (black-box) model of query-document relevance. We show a reduction of the first stage to the standard IR problem, implementable using commodity high-performance systems, while in the second stage, the small set of candidates returned by the first stage is evaluated using the full model. We propose two principled and efficient algorithms for constructing the index, and experimentally demonstrate the advantages of our techniques over the baselines. Furthermore, we analyze the properties of each of the two algorithms and show that while one more consistently achieves high accuracy on different datasets, the second generates smaller index with only slight loss in the accuracy, and requires less detailed data for training (only the top-k sets, not score values).

In this work we proposed a principled approach and two initial algorithms for indexing machine-learned models, leaving several directions for future research. It might be possible to improve approximation accuracy by partitioning queries to several disjoint classes, e.g., by time of the day, or user location, so as to obtain higher query and top-k sets coherence in each partition, and to train a separate index for each partition. Recommender systems often improve model accuracy using the explore-exploit technique which typically randomly perturbs model scores on every query. Integrating this useful technique into our two-stage approach is an interesting future work. Another way to improve index size-accuracy tradeoff would be exploiting different confidence levels of model scores, often available along the scores themselves. Finally, as efficiency of IR algorithms used in the first stage depends on the distribution of partial score values in the index, altering this distribution could be beneficial.

Acknowledgments

We are grateful to Marcus Fontoura for useful discussions.

7. REFERENCES

[1] D. Agarwal, B.-C. Chen, P. Elango, N. Motgi, S.-T. Park, R. Ramakrishnan, S. Roy, and J. Zachariah. Online models for content optimization. In *NIPS*, pages 17–24, 2008.

[2] A. Broder. Computational advertising and recommender systems. In *Proceedings of the 2nd ACM International Conference on Recommender Systems (RecSys)*, 2008.

[3] A. Z. Broder, D. Carmel, M. Herscovici, A. Soffer, and J. Zien. Efficient query evaluation using a two-level retrieval process. In *CIKM*, 2003.

[4] B. B. Cambazoglu, H. Zaragoza, O. Chapelle, J. Chen, C. Liao, Z. Zheng, and J. Degenhardt. Early exit optimizations for additive machine learned ranking systems. In *WSDM*, pages 411–420, 2010.

[5] W. Chu and S. T. Park. Personalized recommendation on dynamic content using predictive bilinear models. In *Proceedings of the 18th international conference on World Wide Web (WWW)*, 2009.

[6] P. Cremonesi, Y. Koren, and R. Turrin. Performance of recommender algorithms on top-n recommendation tasks. In *Proceedings of the fourth ACM conference on Recommender systems*, RecSys '10, pages 39–46, New York, NY, USA, 2010. ACM.

[7] A. S. Das, M. Datar, A. Garg, and S. Rajaram. Google news personalization: scalable online collaborative filtering. In *Proceedings of the 16th international conference on World Wide Web (WWW)*, 2007.

[8] R. Fagin, A. Lotem, and M. Naor. Optimal aggregation algorithms for middleware. *J. Comput. Syst. Sci.*, 66(4):614–656, 2003.

[9] R.-E. Fan, K.-W. Chang, C.-J. Hsieh, X.-R. Wang, and C.-J. Lin. Liblinear: A library for large linear classification. *J. Mach. Learn. Res.*, 9:1871–1874, June 2008.

[10] J. Friedman, T. Hastie, H. Hoefling, and R. Tibshirani. Pathwise coordinate optimization. *Annals of Applied Statistics*, 1(2):302–332, 2007.

[11] S. Goel, J. Langford, and A. Strehl. Predictive indexing for fast search. In *NIPS*, 2008.

[12] S. R. Gunn. Support vector machines for classification and regression. Technical report, Dept. of Electronics and Computer Science, University of Southampton, 1998.

[13] V. Josifovski and A. Z. Broder. Web advertising. In *Encyclopedia of Database Systems*, pages 3457–3459. 2009.

[14] S. Pandey, A. Z. Broder, F. Chierichetti, V. Josifovski, R. Kumar, and S. Vassilvitskii. Nearest-neighbor caching for content-match applications. In *WWW*, pages 441–450, 2009.

[15] R. Tibshirani. Regression shrinkage and selection via the lasso. *Journal of the Royal Statistical Society*, 58(1):267–288, 1996.

[16] H. Turtle and J. Flood. Query evaluation: strategies and optimizations. *Inf. Process. Manage.*, 31(6), 1995.

[17] K. Q. Weinberger, A. Dasgupta, J. Langford, A. J. Smola, and J. Attenberg. Feature hashing for large scale multitask learning. In *ICML*, page 140, 2009.

Relational Click Prediction for Sponsored Search

Chenyan Xiong[1,2,*]
[2]Graduate University
Chinese Academy of Sciences
Beijing, P.R.China
xiongcy@ios.ac.cn

Taifeng Wang
Microsoft Research Asia
Beijing, P.R.China
taifengw@microsoft.com

Wenkui Ding[*]
Tsinghua University
Beijing, P.R.China
dingwenkui@gmail.com

Yidong Shen[1]
[1]Institute of Software
Chinese Academy of Sciences
Beijing, P.R.China
ydshen@ios.ac.cn

Tie-Yan Liu
Microsoft Research Asia
Beijing, P.R.China
tyliu@microsoft.com

ABSTRACT

This paper is concerned with the prediction of clicking an ad in sponsored search. The accurate prediction of user's click on an ad plays an important role in sponsored search, because it is widely used in both ranking and pricing of the ads. Previous work on click prediction usually takes a single ad as input, and ignores its relationship to the other ads shown in the same page. This independence assumption here, however, might not be valid in the real scenario. In this paper, we first perform an analysis on this issue by looking at the click-through rates (CTR) of the same ad, in the same position and for the same query, but surrounded by different ads. We found that in most cases the CTR varies largely, which suggests that the relationship between ads is really an important factor in predicting click probability. Furthermore, our investigation shows that the more similar the surrounding ads are to an ad, the lower the CTR of the ad is. Based on this observation, we design a continuous conditional random fields (CRF) based model for click prediction, which considers both the features of an ad and its similarity to the surrounding ads. We show that the model can be effectively learned using maximum likelihood estimation, and can also be efficiently inferred due to its closed form solution. Our experimental results on the click-through log from a commercial search engine show that the proposed model can predict clicks more accurately than previous independent models. To our best knowledge this is the first work that predicts ad clicks by considering the relationship between ads.

*This work was done when the first and third authors were visiting Microsoft Research Asia.

Permission to make digital or hard copies of all or part of this work for personal or classroom use is granted without fee provided that copies are not made or distributed for profit or commercial advantage and that copies bear this notice and the full citation on the first page. To copy otherwise, to republish, to post on servers or to redistribute to lists, requires prior specific permission and/or a fee.

WSDM'12, February 8–12, 2012, Seattle, Washington, USA.

Copyright 2012 ACM 978-1-4503-0747-5/12/02 ...$10.00.

Categories and Subject Descriptors

H.3.3 [**Information Storage and Retrieval**]: [Information Search and Retrieval]

General Terms

Economics, Algorithms, Experimentation

Keywords

Online Advertising, Sponsored Search, Relational Click Prediction, Continuous CRF

1. INTRODUCTION

Online advertising has been a major business model for today's commercial search engines. When search engines deliver organic search results to a user, sometimes they also show sponsored search results, i.e., advertisements (ads). These ads are usually ranked according to two kinds of information[14]: the bid price on the query keywords given by the advertiser and the probability for the user to click on the ad predicted by the search engine. As a dominant industry practice, only when a user clicks on an ad, will the search engine charge the corresponding advertiser. This is referred to as cost per click (CPC). Generalized second price auction (GSP)[10] is a widely used pricing model for CPC, in which the price that an advertiser has to pay depends on the predicted click probability of his/her own ad as well as the bid price and predicted click probability of the ad ranked in the next position.

From the above introduction, we can clearly see that the accurate prediction of click probability is very important to sponsored search, since it impacts both ranking and pricing of the ads. In the literature, there have been several pieces of work on predicting the ad click probability. In [8] and [15], the click probability of an ad is predicted based on its historical click-through data. In real systems, however, there are many ads without (sufficient) historical click-through data and therefore the above work cannot be directly applied to these ads. To tackle the challenge, in [16][19], two kinds of new features are introduced: *semantic features* (e.g., the relevance of an ad to the query and the quality of the ad) and *aggregated click features* (e.g., aggregated at the advertiser or query levels). These new features can handle many ads

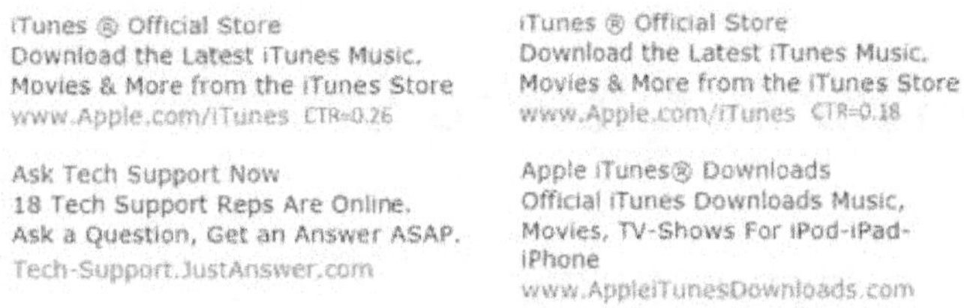

Figure 1: Two ad lists for query 'iTunes account'.

without historical data and can increase the data density of click prediction. To further improve the accuracy of click prediction, in some other work [4], the user demographic information is also used to personalize the prediction result.

Please note that all the aforementioned works predict the clicks on ads in an independent manner. That is, the click probability is computed only based on the information of a given ad, without considering the other ads shown together with it. However, our data study shows that it is inappropriate to ignore the influences of the other ads in real search scenarios. Fig. 1 shows two different ad lists from a commercial search engine triggered by the same query 'iTunes account'. We can see that ad 'iTunes Official Store' is shown in the same position of both lists. By analyzing the click-through logs, we find that its click-through rate (CTR) in the first list is 26%, while its CTR is just 18% in the second list. Actually this is not a rare phenomenon. Statistically, the CTR of the same ad, in the same position, and for the same query, can vary largely when surrounded by different ads (see Section 2.2).

We believe that the aforementioned observations will have profound impact on the accuracy of click prediction. However, it has not been well investigated in the literature. First, there are some previous studies [7, 11, 12, 21] on the mutual influence between ads. However, they are focused on mining user click behaviors or designing auction mechanisms, rather than predicting click probability. Second, there are not many attempts on understanding what kinds of factors account for the observed mutual influence between ads. Third, the experimental setting of some previous work was not specifically designed for click prediction, making their findings on the factors behind ad mutual influence not directly applicable to our scenario.

For example, in [21], the authors studied the user click behaviors on sponsored listings shown in the search results page. As part of the study, they claimed that when multiple ads are shown together, high-quality ads will influence low-quality ads in attracting user's attention (and therefore clicks). In their experiments to verify this claim, they used CTR as a surrogate of the ad quality. Given a CTR value at the first position (denoted by CTR-1), they averaged the CTR of the ads in the second position from different queries to get CTR-2, and showed that there is a strong dependency between CTR-1 and CTR-2. Please note that this dependency is observed when the query information is averaged out (and therefore unknown). However, in the context of click prediction, the query is always given and fixed. In this new setting, the conditional dependency between CTR-1 and CTR-2 may not exist any longer. Actually our experiments in Section 2 verified that the conditional dependency really does not exist. In other words, the CTR of an ad is not clearly influenced by the qualities of its surrounding ads when the query is given.

Considering the limitations of previous work, in this paper, we perform a new study on click data, with an experimental setting that targets the click prediction problems. Our study shows that the similarity between ads can explain the mutual influence much better than ad quality. Our statistics show that when the query is given, the CTR of an ad is (very well) negatively correlated with the similarity between it and the surrounding ads. Actually, this phenomenon can be intuitively explained. When the surrounding ads are similar to the given ad in their contents (or topics), it is very likely that they will distract user's attention since all these ads offer similar products or services. However, when the ads are dissimilar, they may become complementary to each other and will not distract user's attention by much. [1]

Based on our data study, we make the first proposal in the literature to predict ad click probability by considering the mutual similarity between ads. Specifically, we assume that the CTR of an ad is determined by two kinds of information. First, it is largely determined by the intrinsic properties of the ad itself, e.g., the relevance to the query, the static quality, and the historical CTR. Second, it is also affected by the similarity between this ad and the surrounding ads. We propose using a Conditional Random Fields (CRF)[20] model that can naturally leverage both kinds of information. Specifically, the feature functions on the vertices of the CRF capture the intrinsic properties of the ad, and the feature functions on the edges capture the similarity between ads. We show that this model can be effectively learned with maximum likelihood estimation and can be efficiently inferred due to its closed-form solution. We have conducted experiments using the ad click-through logs from a commercial search engine. The experimental results have shown that our proposed model can produce consistently better prediction accuracy on ad clicks than baseline models. This verifies the usefulness of leveraging the relationship between ads in click prediction.

To sum up, the contributions of our work include:

- We have performed a solid data analysis that certificates the existence of mutual influence between ads in the context of click prediction. In addition, we have found that the similarity between ads is a factor that can better explain the mutual influence than the quality of ads.
- We have proposed a CRF model to predict ad click probability by considering both the intrinsic properties of an ad and its similarity to other ads in same sponsored list. To the best of our knowledge, this is the first model that considers the relationship between ads in click prediction.

[1]Our finding is related to the diversity in organic search results [2, 9, 18, 22]. It has been shown that more diverse search results will have a higher probability of satisfying user's information needs, while similar search results will distract each other. There was some work[22] in the search space that diversifies search results by considering the similarity between web pages, however, as far as we know, there is no work in the online advertising area that considers the mutual similarity between ads when predicting their click probabilities.

The remaining parts of this paper are organized as follows. In Section 2, we present our data analysis. Before introducing our click prediction model in Section 4, we review the click prediction task and propose a new setting of click prediction called *relational click prediction* in Section 3. In Section 5, we present our experiment settings and compare our results with other baseline models. At last, we conclude the paper and discuss the future work in Section 6.

2. DATA ANALYSIS

As mentioned in the introduction, the focus of this work is to leverage the relationship between ads to improve click prediction. In this section, we will present some related data analysis. With the analysis, we would like to answer the following questions: 1) Is there mutual influence between the ads shown together that affects their CTR's, and furthermore in what manner and to what degree? 2) If the answer to the first question is yes, what kind of relationship will be the key factor behind this mutual influence?

In the remainder of this section, we will first introduce the setting of our study, and then introduce our findings with respect to the two questions.

2.1 Setting of the Study

We used the ad click-through log of one month from a commercial search engine in our study. The log contains all the ad information for each submitted query, including ad copy, displayed position, and click information. In our study, we focus on the mainline ads, which are shown above the organic search results, because the mainline ads contribute to the majority of search engines' ad clicks and revenue. We represent the data in terms of ⟨query, ad list⟩, where the ad list corresponds to the ordered group of ads shown for the query. We remove all those ⟨query, ad list⟩ with fewer than 10 occurrences in the data to make our study more reliable. After that, our data set contains over two millions of unique ⟨query, ad list⟩, about 700K unique queries, 600K unique ads, and over two hundred million impressions in total.

In order to study the mutual influence of ads on their CTR's, i.e., how the CTR of an ad is affected by its surrounding ads, we need to remove the influences of other factors, such as the different properties of ad and query. To this end, we put an ad in a specific context, i.e., a triple $T = \langle q, a, p \rangle$, where q, a, and p represent query, ad, and position respectively. In our data analysis, we select the triples T that appear in multiple ⟨query, ad list⟩ (for ease of reference, we denote these ad lists as $L = \{l_1, l_2, \cdots .l_n\}$). If we use $IMP = \{imp_1, \cdots, imp_n\}$ to denote the number of impressions, and $CLK = \{clk_1, \cdots, clk_n\}$ the number of clicks of T in these lists, we can compute the CTR of T in l_i as follows:

$$CTR_{T,l_i} = \frac{clk_i}{imp_i}.$$

And the average CTR of T will be

$$CTR_T = \frac{\sum_i imp_i \times CTR_{T,l_i}}{\sum_i imp_i}.$$

By comparing CTR_{T,l_i} for the same T but in different l_i, we will be able to examine the influence of other ads in l_i on the CTR of T.

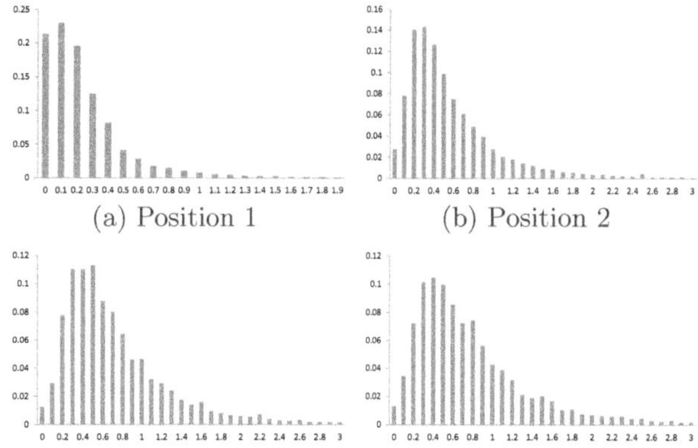

(a) Position 1 (b) Position 2

(c) Position 3 (d) Position 4

Figure 2: NSDev of $\langle q, a, p \rangle$ triple at different Positions.

2.2 Mutual Influence on CTR

Previous work on click prediction assumes that the CTR of T is independent of other ads shown together with it. That is, the CTR of T will not change (or not change by much) in different ad lists. In order to verify whether this assumption holds, we check the normalized standard deviation (NSDev) of T's CTR in different ad lists:

$$NSDev_T = \frac{SDev\{CTR_{T,l_1}, \cdots, CTR_{T,l_n}\}}{CTR_T},$$

where $SDev\{CTR_{T,l_1}, \cdots, CTR_{T,l_n}\}$ is the standard deviation of $\{CTR_{T,l_1}, \cdots, CTR_{T,l_n}\}$.

Fig. 2 shows the $NSDev_T$ with respect to different positions of the ads. The horizontal axis corresponds to the $NSDev_T$ value, and the vertical axis corresponds to the percentage of triples having this value. From the figure, we can see that the CTR of an ad varies largely among different lists, indicating that the surrounding ads will heavily influence the CTR of a given ad. Therefore, if we estimate the CTR of an ad without considering its surrounding ads, the best we can get will be the average CTR over different lists. It is clear that for most cases, the real CTR will be very different from this estimation given the large variance. This motivates us to perform deep investigation on the relationship between ads, and take the relationship into consideration when predicting click probabilities. This is exactly the focus of our paper.

2.3 Factors of Mutual Influence

In this subsection, we study two kinds of factors that may potentially account for the mutual influence: quality of ads and similarity between ads.

2.3.1 Ad Quality

Inspired by [21], we first study whether the CTR of an ad will decrease if the other ads shown together with it are of high quality. We also use the historical CTR of an ad as the surrogate of its quality. Given a triple T and an ad list l_i containing T, we test whether the CTR of T in l_i (calibrated by its average CTR on all the ad lists in order to better reflect the influence of other ads) correlates with the CTR's of the others ads in l_i. Here we use ΔCTR to

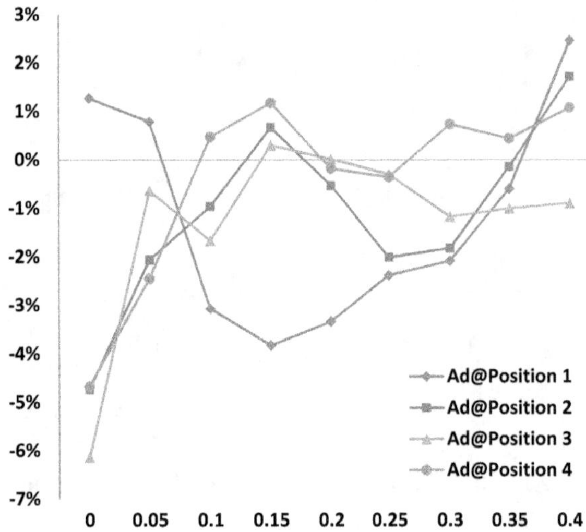

(a) Quality

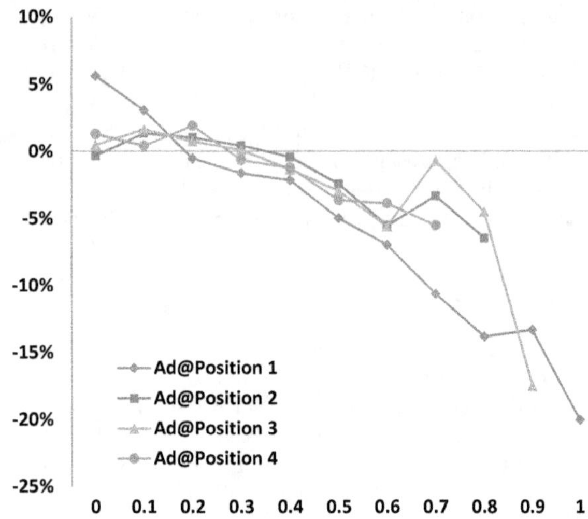

(b) Similarity

Figure 3: ΔCTR with ad quality and similarity. Y axis is ΔCTR. X axis is surrounding ads' CTR in (a) and similarity with surrounding ads in (b).

denote the calibrated CTR:

$$\Delta CTR_{l_i} = \frac{CTR_{T,l_i} - CTR_T}{CTR_T}.$$

Then we plot the ΔCTR_{l_i} for all the triples T with respect to different CTR values of their surrounding ads in Fig. 3.a. Surprisingly, as the CTR (quality) of other ads increases, the ΔCTR of the target triple T does not decrease as expected. That is, given the query, the CTR of an ad is not clearly influenced by the quality of other ads shown together with it.

At first glance, our finding seems to be contradictory to the results given in [21]. In our opinion, however, they are not opposite to each other, and the difference mainly comes from different experimental settings.

In [21], for each <query, ad list>, the CTR's of the ads ranked in position 1 and position 2 are computed. Then all the ad lists whose first ads have similar CTR (denoted as CTR-1) are put together, no matter they are from the same query or not, and the average value of the CTR's of their second ads are computed (denoted as CTR-2). They observed that when CTR-1 increases, CTR-2 drops accordingly. Actually, we have rerun their experiments on our data, and have obtained very similar results (see Fig. 4). However, please note that according to the experimental setting in [21], the dependency between CTR-1 and CTR-2 are observed when the query information is averaged out (and thus unknown). Therefore, it is unclear whether the dependency comes from CTR-1 and CTR-2 themselves, or from the unknown query. Further study is needed to make it clear. By carefully looking at the data, we find that it is the navigational queries that account for the major part of the above dependency. Specifically, a lot of ads with 20% or even higher CTR were shown for navigational queries. Usually, for navigational queries, user will only click on one ad whose display URL is from the web site created for the query. As a result, the CTR's of all the other ads will be low. In such case, CTR-2 is low not because CTR-1 is high. The true reason lies in the navigational nature of the query.

In the setting of click prediction, the mutual influence between ads is always studied when the query is given and fixed. In this setting, the conditional dependency between CTR-1 and CTR-2 may not exist any longer. This is easy to understand according to the basic principles of probability theory. That is, when two random variables are dependent, they can become conditionally independent when a third random variable is observed. In our experimental setting, we consider the query as given, and therefore our finding can be used to verify whether the CTR's of the first ad and the second ad are conditionally independent. According to our results, they seen to be independent of each other (at least, there is no clearly dependency observed).

2.3.2 Similarity between Ads

While the mutual influence between ads is not well evidenced by ad quality, we have found another factor, i.e., the similarity between ads, which seems to be more relevant to the mutual influence between ads. Our finding is based on the investigation on those triples whose CTR variances in different ad lists are relatively large among all the triples. We find that when a triple T is shown in a list l_i, its CTR_{T,l_i} will be relatively lower than its average CTR_T when the other ads in l_i have similar contents to it. Please refer to several such examples in Fig. 5.

To see whether the observations from examples are statistically reliable, we have conducted the following experiments. For simplicity and without loss of generality, we use term overlap in the title and description of two ads as the similarity measure. Denote $S(str_1, str_2)$ as the term overlap of two strings str_1, str_2, whose definition is as below:

$$S(str_1, str_2) = \frac{2\sum_{t_i \in str_1, t_j \in str_2} I(t_i, t_j)}{|str_1| + |str_2|},$$

Where t_i, t_j are terms in str_1 and str_2, $I()$ is an indicator function whose value is one only when $t_i = t_j$, and $|str_1|, |str_2|$ are the lengths of the two strings. Furthermore,

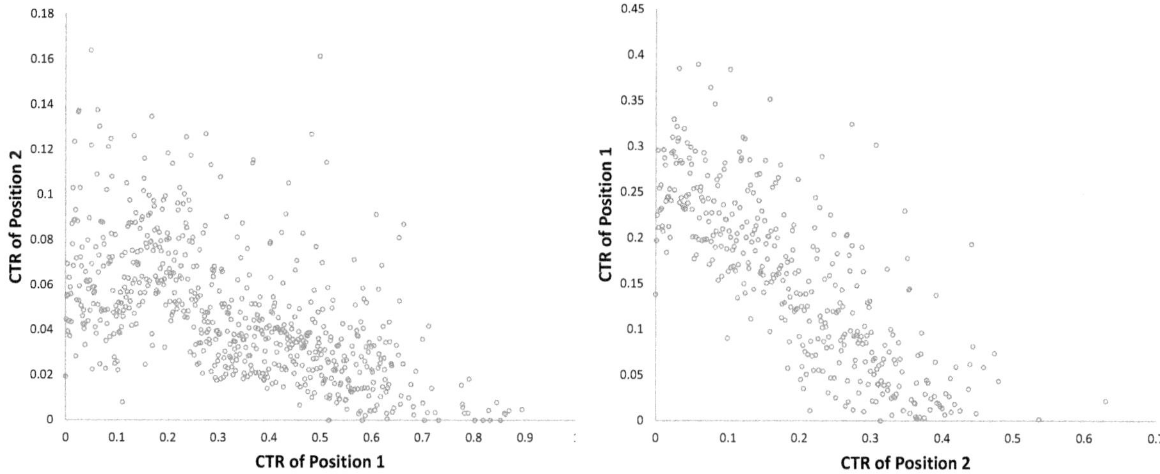

(a) Position 2 via position 1 (b) Position 1 via position 2

Figure 4: CTR pairs: The left one is CTR of ad in Position 2 bucketed by Position 1; the right one is CTR of Position 1 bucketed by Position 2.

(a) Ad lists for query 'car.com'

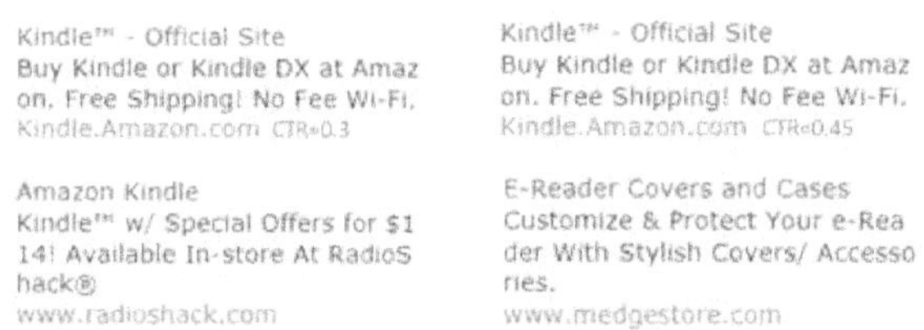

(b) Ad lists for query 'kindle'

Figure 5: Examples for ads' different CTR's with different surrounding ads.

we define the similarity between two ads a_1, a_2 as follows,

$$S(a_1, a_2) = \frac{1}{2}(S(str_{t1}, str_{t2}) + S(str_{d1}, str_{d2}))$$

where str_{ti}, str_{di} are the strings of a_i's title and description.

For a triple T, we get all the ⟨query, ad list⟩ from our data set, denoted as $L = \{l_1, l_2, \cdots, l_n\}$. We then compute the average similarity S_i between the ad in T and the other ads in l_i. After that, we check whether S_i has some correlation with $\Delta CTR_{T,l_i}$, and the result is plotted in Fig. 3.(b).

From the figure, we can clearly see that $\Delta CTR_{T,l_i}$ is negatively correlated [2] with S_i. This indicates that for a particular triple T, when it is shown in an ads list where the other ads are more similar to it, the CTR of T will become lower.

In our opinion, the above finding can be explained in the following intuitive manner. When the surrounding ads are similar to the given ad in their contents (or topics), it is very likely that they will distract user's attention since all these ads offer similar products or services. However, when the ads are dissimilar, they may become complementary to each other and will not distract user's attention by much.

Motivated by our findings, we propose a new click prediction model which takes the similarity between ads into consideration. Details will be given in the next two sections.

3. RELATIONAL CLICK PREDICTION

In this section, we first review the sponsored search system and the click prediction task. Then we propose a new setting of click prediction, which we call *relational click prediction*.

3.1 Overview of Sponsored Search System

Given a query and a user, the sponsored search system tries to find an optimal subset of ads that achieves the best expected revenue from its inventory of ads. Roughly speaking, this process can be divided into three steps:

1. Ad selection: select a set of candidate ads for a search, based on the bid keywords and the match type (e.g., exact match and broad match).

2. Ad ranking: rank the candidate ads based on their expected revenue[14]: $E(revenue) = pClick \times b$, where $pClick$ is the output of a click prediction model and b is the bid price. According to the ranking results and the expected revenue, the system also determines where to show these ads (e.g., in the mainline or sidebar of the search result page).

3. Ad pricing: charge the corresponding advertiser a certain amount of money if a user clicks on his/her ad. Usually the general second price auction (GSP) is used to determine the price. Specially, the price for ad a_i is calculated as follows: $\frac{pClick_{i+1} \times b_{i+1}}{pClick_i}$, where a_{i+1} is the

[2] The Pearson product-moment correlation coefficient r of S_i and $\Delta CTR_{T,l_i}$ at position 1 to 4 are $-0.99, -0.74, -0.73, -0.64$ ($r < -0.5$ usually means a strong correlation.)

ad displayed in the next position to a_i, and $pClick_{i+1}$, b_{i+1} are the $pClick$ and bid price of a_{i+1} respectively.

We can see that the click prediction plays a fundamental role in the above process: it determines both ranking and pricing of the ads. Previous works on click prediction [1, 4, 5, 19] usually treat each ad in an independent manner, without considering the influence of other ads shown together with the ad. However, based on the analysis in the previous section, the CTR of an ad is highly dependent on its relationship with other ads. Therefore, it would be meaningful to consider all the ads showed in the same ad list together and reformulate the click prediction problem in a relational manner.

3.2 Relational Click Prediction

Let u denote a user and q denote a query submitted by the user. Let $\{a_1, \cdots, a_n\}$ be the set of ads in the ad list l, c_i a binary variable indicating whether a click on ad a_i happens, and p_i the position of ad a_i.

Conventional click prediction models aim to predict the probability of $c_i = 1$ given user u, query q and position p_i for each individual ad a_i, in an independent manner:

$$p(c_i = 1|u, q, p_i, a_i) = f(x_i),$$

where x_i is the feature vector extracted from $\langle u, q, p, a_i \rangle$, and f is the predictive model to be learned.

In this paper, we treat the ads in a list no longer independent with each other and propose a new setting of click prediction, referred to as *relational click prediction*. Instead of predicting each $p(c_i = 1|u, q, p_i, a_i)$ individually, relational click prediction leverages the relationship between ads and predicts the CTR's of all the ads in an ad list simultaneously using a unified model:

$$(p(c = 1|u, q, p_1, a_1, l), \cdots, p(c = 1|u, q, p_n, a_n, l))^T = F(X, R)$$

where $X = \{x_1, x_2, \cdots, x_n\}$ includes all the feature vectors x_i extracted from $\langle u, q, p_i, a_i \rangle$ and R is the relationship between ads, and F is a model whose output is a n-dimension vector (the i-th dimension corresponds to the CTR of a_i). We refer to F as the relational click prediction model, and f the local model. Also, we call X the local features and R the relational information.

Specially in this paper, we choose Conditional Random Fields (CRF) as the relational click prediction model $F(X, R)$. CRF is widely used to model relationships between variables. It can capture the local features using its vertexes and the relational information using its edges. In the next section, we will present the details of the CRF model as well as its learning and inference processes.

4. CRF FOR RELATIONAL CLICK PREDICTION

In this section, we introduce our CRF model for relational click prediction. Since we require the model to output a click probability, which is a continuous value, we choose to use the continuous CRF model proposed in [17]. Fig. 6 shows the graph representation of the continuous CRF model.

4.1 Continuous CRF Model

Let $X = \{x_1, x_2, \cdots, x_n\}$ denote the input feature vectors of the ads displayed for a query, and $Y = \{y_1, y_2, \cdots, y_n\}$

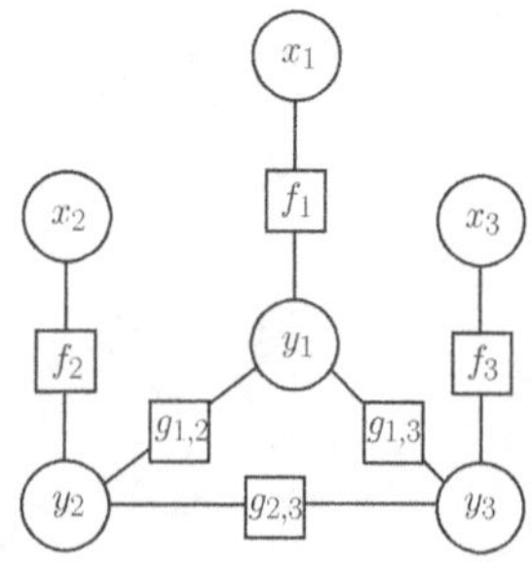

Figure 6: A continuous CRF model for relational click prediction.

denote the log mods[3] of the CTR's for the ads. The probability distribution of the output Y conditioned on the input X is defined as

$$P(Y|X) = \frac{1}{Z(X)} \exp\left\{\sum_i h(y_i, X; w) + \sum_{j>i} \beta g(y_i, y_j, X)\right\}, \tag{1}$$

where h is the vertex feature function representing the dependence of the CTR on the input vector of ads, g is the edge feature function representing pairwise relationship between ads, and $Z(X)$ is a normalization factor (also known as the partition function).

$$Z(X) = \int \left\{\sum_i h(y_i, X; w) + \sum_{j>i} \beta g(y_i, y_j, X)\right\} \mathrm{d}Y.$$

For simplicity, we define the vertex feature function as follows,

$$h(y_i, X; w) = -(y_i - f(x_i; w))^2 \tag{2}$$

where $f(x_i; w)$ can be any conventional click prediction model which only depends on the feature vector of each individual ad.

According to our findings in Section 2, we use similarity between ads as the relationship. The intuition is that if two ads are very similar to each other, their click probabilities will both become lower. To encode this intuition, we define the edge feature function as below.

$$g(y_i, y_j, X) = -s_{i,j}(y_i + y_j), \tag{3}$$

where $s_{i,j}$ is the term similarity between ads i and j: $s_{i,j} = S(a_i, a_j)$. This feature function implies a penalty imposed on the CTR's of a similar ad pair (a_i, a_j) and the penalty strength is determined by the degree of their similarity. Please note that although we only use one edge feature function here, the model allows multiple relationships by adding more edge functions.

By combining all the feature functions, we obtain the overall conditional probability distribution:

$$\begin{aligned} P(Y|X) \quad = \quad & \frac{1}{Z(X)} \exp\left\{\sum_i -(y_i - f(x_i; w))^2 \right. \\ & \left. + \sum_{j>i} -\beta s_{i,j}(y_i + y_j)\right\}, \end{aligned} \tag{4}$$

[3]We use log mods for numerical convenience in learning.

where

$$Z(X) = \int \exp\Big\{\sum_i -(y_i - f(x_i; w))^2 + \sum_{j>i} -\beta s_{i,j}(y_i + y_j)\Big\} \mathrm{d}Y.$$

It is clear that if we remove the edge feature function, this new model will reduce to the conventional click prediction model as its special case.

4.2 Learning

Given training data $\{X^q, Y^q\}_{q=1}^N$ where $X^q = \{x_1^q, x_2^q, ..., x_N^q\}$ is a set of input feature vectors of ads shown for query q, and $Y^q = \{y_1^q, y_2^q, ..., y_N^q\}$ is the set of the corresponding log mods of CTR's, we estimate the parameters of the continuous CRF model by Maximum Likelihood Estimation (MLE). Suppose the parameters of the continuous CRF model are $\theta = \{w, \beta\}$, we can write the conditional log likelihood of the training data as follows.

$$\begin{aligned} L(\theta) &= \sum_{q=1}^N \log P(Y^q|X^q;\theta) \\ &= \sum_{q=1}^N \Big(-\sum_i (y_i^q - f(x_i^q; w))^2 - \beta \sum_{j>i} s_{i,j}(y_i^q + y_j^q) \\ &\quad - \log Z(X^q) \Big). \end{aligned} \tag{5}$$

With some mathematical deduction, the normalizer $Z(X)$ becomes

$$Z(X) = \pi^{\frac{n}{2}} \exp\{-c + \frac{1}{4}\alpha^T \alpha\}, \tag{6}$$

where

$$c = \sum_i f(w, X_i)^2$$

and α is a n-dimensional vector whose ith dimension is

$$\alpha_i = 2f(w, X_i) - \beta \sum_{j \neq i} s_{i,j}.$$

We adopt the gradient ascent method to maximize this log likelihood. The gradients of $L(\theta)$ with respect to w and β can be computed as follows.

$$\begin{aligned} \frac{\partial L(\theta)}{\partial w} &= \sum_{q=1}^N \left(\sum_i 2(y_i^q - f(x_i^q; w)) \frac{\partial f(x_i^q; w)}{\partial w} \right) \\ &\quad - \sum_{q=1}^N \frac{\partial \log Z(X^q)}{\partial w} \end{aligned}$$

$$\frac{\partial L(\theta)}{\partial \beta} = -\sum_{q=1}^N \sum_{i,j} s_{i,j}(y_i^q + y_j^q) - \sum_{q=1}^N \frac{\partial \log Z(X^q)}{\partial \beta}$$

The partial derivatives $\frac{\partial \log Z(X^q)}{\partial \beta}$ and $\frac{\partial \log Z(X^q)}{\partial w}$ are computed in the following way.

$$\frac{\partial \log Z(X^q)}{\partial \beta} = \frac{1}{2}\sum_i \left(\sum_{j \neq i} s_{i,j} \right) \left(\beta \sum_{j \neq i} s_{i,j} - 2f(x_i^q; w) \right)$$

and

$$\frac{\partial \log Z(X^q)}{\partial w} = -\sum_i \beta \sum_{j \neq i} s_{i,j} \frac{\partial f(x_i; w)}{\partial w}.$$

To further speed up the learning process, we adopt the Stochastic Gradient Ascent method, which updates the parameters for each training query in an iterative manner.

4.3 Inference

In inference, given parameters θ, we choose the Y^* that maximizes the conditional probability $P(Y|X)$ as the predicted log mods of CTR.

$$\begin{aligned} Y^* &= \arg\max_Y P(Y|X;\theta) \\ &= \arg\max_Y \Big\{ -(Y - f(X;w))^T (Y - f(X;w)) \\ &\quad -\beta S^T Y \Big\} \end{aligned} \tag{7}$$

where

$$f(X; w) = (f(x_1; w), \cdots, f(x_n; w))^T$$

and

$$S = \left(\sum_{j \neq 1} s_{1,j}, \cdots, \sum_{j \neq n} s_{n,j} \right)^T.$$

Please note that the objective function in Eqn.(7) is concave with respect to Y, and therefore the optimization is easy. Actually, we can get the closed-form solution of the optimization problem, as shown below.

$$Y^* = f(X; w) - \frac{1}{2}\beta S. \tag{8}$$

Due to this closed-form solution, the time complexity of the inference is the same as the conventional click prediction models. This makes the adoption of the relational click prediction model feasible in practice.

5. EXPERIMENTS

In this section, we first describe the settings of our experiments, and then report the experimental results.

5.1 Experimental Settings

We use the same data set as in our data analysis, and split it into three parts, each containing the data of ten days. We use the first part for feature extraction, the second part for training, and the last part for testing. We remove those ad lists with only one ad since there is no need to do relational prediction for them. The detailed statistics of our data set are listed in Table 1.

	Query-list pair	query	ad	impression
Training	482,903	140,435	255,788	24,352,968
Testing	514,878	136,525	254,407	24,943,320

Table 1: Statistics of the data set.

Feature extraction is not the focus of our paper, and therefore we simply use some representative features according to previous work [4][19]: history COEC (position normalized CTR) for query-ad pair, query, and ad respectively, smoothed COEC according to query term, ad term, and advertiser's bid information; relevance of ad to query; attractiveness of ad title and description; reputation of advertiser; etc.. As for the relational information, we use the term similarity as introduced in Section 2.

5.2 Baseline Algorithms

To demonstrate the power of relational click prediction, we compare our CRF model with conventional click prediction models. Specially, we implement the logistic regression based model proposed in [4][19] as a baseline. This algorithm only uses the local features that we extracted. For ease of reference, we denote it as LOCAL. In our CRF model, we use the linear regression function as our local model, i.e., $f(x, w) = w^T x$, for simplicity and without loss of generality. We denote our method as CRF. To further examine the power of relational information, we test the performance of a variant of our CRF model with β set to 0. We treat this algorithm as another baseline, denoted as CRF-NR. Note that in CRF-NR, the CRF model has no edge feature function and reduces to a local prediction model that is very similar to logistic regression, because the Y in the model represents the log mods of CTR's.

Following [19], we use the CTR computed from the log data as the ground truth for training.[4] For evaluation, we choose the relative information gain (RIG) [15] and mean square error [19] as the metrics. For ease of discussion, we normalize the MSE of CRF and CRF-NR by the MSE of LOCAL (denoted as NMSE).

5.3 Experimental Results

5.3.1 *Overall Performance*

The parameter β learned by our CRF model from the training data is 0.6810, which is consistent with our intuition and data analysis: a positive β indicates that the CTR of an ad will decrease when the similarity increases. Fig. 7 shows the MSE and RIG of the click prediction algorithms on the test set with respect to different ad positions. Higher RIG and lower MSE mean better prediction accuracy. From the figure, we can see that for all the positions our proposed model significantly outperforms the baselines. The best result is achieved by CRF at slot 4, where it reduces MSE and increases RIG both by about 40% relatively as compared to LOCAL. Even in the worst case, CRF at position 1 still reduces MSE by 25% relatively and increases RIG by 20% relatively. These results clearly show that using relational information in click prediction does improve the prediction accuracy.

Also, the performance of CRF-NR has no significant difference from the conventional click prediction model, but is much worse than that of CRF. As the only difference between CRF-NR and CRF is that our CRF model considers the relational information in its edges, this result demonstrates that the advantage of our method does come from modeling the relational information.

Furthermore, by comparing the results in different ad slots, one could see that our model performs better in lower positions than higher positions. This result consists with the cascade assumption [23] that most users tend to examine search results and ads from top to bottom. So the influence of the ads in higher position on the ads in lower position will be stronger, and weaker vice versa. As a consequence, when predicting the CTR of ads in lower positions, the relational information will help more.

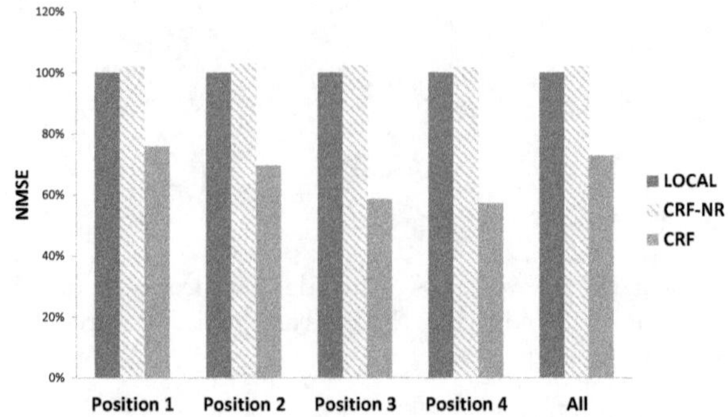

(a) NMSE

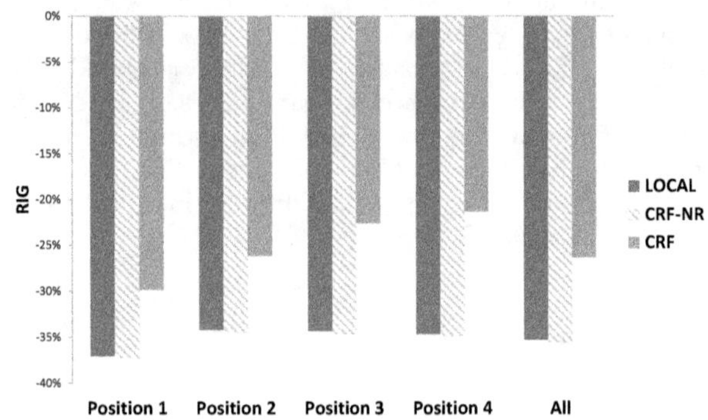

(b) RIG

Figure 7: Results of NMSE and RIG.

5.3.2 *Performance at Different Similarity Level*

We further study the performance of click prediction with respect to different levels of similarities in the ad lists. The results are shown in Fig. 8. We bucket the ads according to their similarities to others ads in the same ad lists. Then we check the prediction performance in different buckets. As we can see from Fig. 8, when the similarity between ads increases, the performance of CRF also increases, while the performance of baselines does not. This result indicates that our CRF model can effectively handle the relationship information and provide better click prediction, especially when the relationship gets stronger.

To sum up, by comparing the proposed CRF model with a local model, our experiments show that modeling the relationship between ads can significantly increase the accuracy of click prediction.

6. CONCLUSION AND FUTURE WORK

In this paper, we have studied the problem of click prediction in sponsored search. We have reported our data analysis that verifies the mutual influence between ads in their click probabilities. Based on the analysis, we have found that the similarity between ads is an important type of relationship that accounts for the mutual influence, and should be modeled in click prediction. Accordingly, we have proposed a relational click prediction model based on continuous Conditional Random Fields. Our experimental results

[4]Please note that our model is also able to deal with $0-1$ ground truth (skip or click).

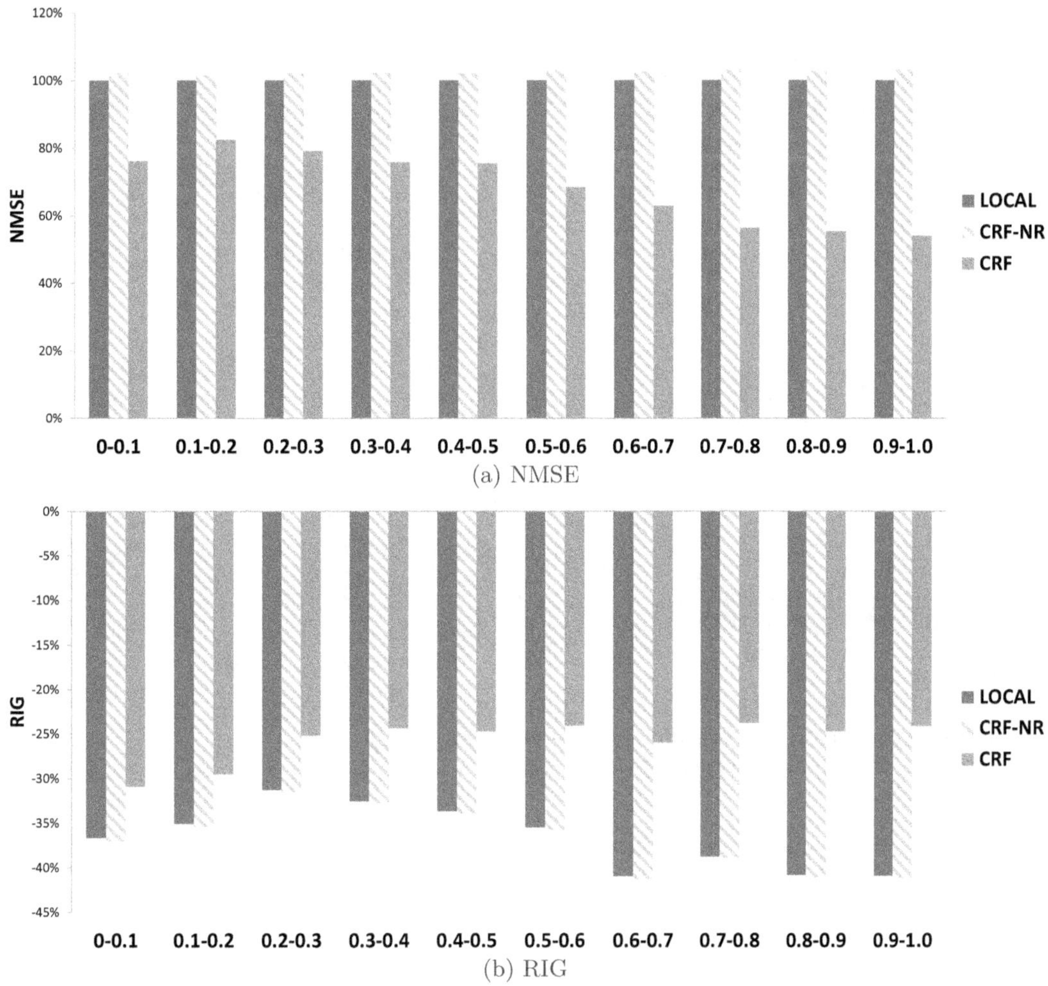

Figure 8: NMSE and RIG results at different similarity levels.

have shown that modeling the relational information can significantly increase the accuracy of click prediction.

For the future work, we plan to investigate on the following challenging but important issues.

- We will study how the mutual influence works for the sidebar ads, i.e., the ads shown in the right hand side of the search result page. The click-through rate on sidebar ads is usually much lower than that on mainline ads. It is highly possible that the mutual influence between sidebar ads will also be different from that between mainline ads. We need to perform a new data analysis to verify this assumption, and adjust our relational click prediction model accordingly.

- We will study more types of relationships. For example, in addition to the term similarity, we can also explore the similarity computed from the click-through bipartite graph. For another example, in addition to the relationship between ads, the relationship with the organic search results [3, 6, 13] should also be considered when predicting the ad click probability. In this case, the relationship will become heterogeneous, and we may need a more powerful mathematical tool to deal with it.

- We will study how to leverage the output of relational click prediction to refine the ranking and pricing components in the sponsored search system. This task turns out to be non-trivial. First, since the relational click prediction is performed at the level of ad list, it will become very time consuming to find the ranked list of ads with the largest expected revenue. Second, it is not clear how the price for each ad should be determined. We believe the solution to the aforementioned task will significantly improve the existing sponsored search systems, and we will have a careful look at it in our future work.

Acknowledgments

We would like to thank our colleagues Ying Zhang, Di He, Wei Chen, Tao Qin, and Bin Gao for their helpful discussions with us on this work.

7. REFERENCES

[1] D. Agarwal, B.C. Chen, and P. Elango. Spatio-temporal models for estimating click-through rate. In *Proceedings of the 18th international conference on World wide web*, pages 21–30. ACM, 2009.

[2] R. Agrawal, S. Gollapudi, A. Halverson, and S. Ieong. Diversifying search results. In *Proceedings of the Second ACM International Conference on Web Search and Data Mining*, pages 5–14. ACM, 2009.

[3] G. Buscher, S.T. Dumais, and E. Cutrell. The good, the bad, and the random: An eye-tracking study of ad quality in web search. In *Proceeding of the 33rd international ACM SIGIR conference on Research and development in information retrieval*, pages 42–49. ACM, 2010.

[4] H. Cheng and E. Cantú-Paz. Personalized click prediction in sponsored search. In *Proceedings of the third ACM international conference on Web search and data mining*, pages 351–360. ACM, 2010.

[5] M. Ciaramita, V. Murdock, and V. Plachouras. Online learning from click data for sponsored search. In *Proceeding of the 17th international conference on World Wide Web*, pages 227–236. ACM, 2008.

[6] C. Danescu-Niculescu-Mizil, A.Z. Broder, E. Gabrilovich, V. Josifovski, and B. Pang. Competing for users' attention: on the interplay between organic and sponsored search results. In *Proceedings of the 19th international conference on World wide web*, pages 291–300. ACM, 2010.

[7] K. David and M. Mohammad. A cascade model for externalities in sponsored search. In *Proceedings of the 4th International Workshop on Internet and Network Economics.* ACM, 2008.

[8] K. Dembczynski, W. Kotlowski, and D. Weiss. Predicting ads click-through rate with decision rules. In *Workshop on Targeting and Ranking in Online Advertising*, volume 2008. Citeseer, 2008.

[9] Z. Dou, S. Hu, K. Chen, R. Song, and J.R. Wen. Multi-dimensional search result diversification. In *Proceedings of the fourth ACM international conference on Web search and data mining*, pages 475–484. ACM, 2011.

[10] B. Edelman, M. Ostrovsky, and M. Schwarz. Internet advertising and the generalized second price auction: Selling billions of dollars worth of keywords. 2005.

[11] A. Ghosh and M. Mahdian. Externalities in online advertising. In *Proceeding of the 17th international conference on World Wide Web*, pages 161–168. ACM, 2008.

[12] A. Ghosh and A. Sayedi. Expressive auctions for externalities in online advertising. In *Proceedings of the 19th international conference on World wide web*, pages 371–380. ACM, 2010.

[13] S. Gollapudi, R. Panigrahy, and M. Goldszmidt. Inferring clickthrough rates on ads from click behavior on search results. pages 1–5, 2011.

[14] Google. How are ads ranked. In *http://www.google.com/support/grants/bin/answer.py ?hl=en&answer=98917.*

[15] T. Graepel, J.Q. Candela, T. Borchert, and R. Herbrich. Web-scale bayesian click-through rate prediction for sponsored search advertising in microsoftŠs bing search engine. In *Proc. 27th Internat. Conf. on Machine Learning. Morgan Kaufmann, San Francisco, CA*. Citeseer, 2010.

[16] Dustin Hillard, Eren Manavoglu, Hema Raghavan, Chris Leggetter, Erick Cantĺš-Paz, and Rukmini Iyer. The sum of its parts: reducing sparsity in click estimation with query segments. In *Information Retrieval Journal.* Springer, 2011.

[17] T. Qin, T.Y. Liu, X.D. Zhang, D.S. Wang, and H. Li. Global ranking using continuous conditional random fields. In *Proceedings of the Twenty-Second Annual Conference on Neural Information Processing Systems (NIPS 2008)*, 2008.

[18] D. Rafiei, K. Bharat, and A. Shukla. Diversifying web search results. In *Proceedings of the 19th international conference on World wide web*, pages 781–790. ACM, 2010.

[19] M. Richardson, E. Dominowska, and R. Ragno. Predicting clicks: estimating the click-through rate for new ads. In *Proceedings of the 16th international conference on World Wide Web*, pages 521–530. ACM, 2007.

[20] H.M Wallach. Conditional random fields: An introduction. In *Technical report MS-CIS-04-21, University of Pennsylvania*, 2004.

[21] W. Xu, E. Manavoglu, and E. Cantu-Paz. Temporal click model for sponsored search. In *Proceeding of the 33rd international ACM SIGIR conference on Research and development in information retrieval*, pages 106–113. ACM, 2010.

[22] C.X. Zhai, W.W. Cohen, and J. Lafferty. Beyond independent relevance: methods and evaluation metrics for subtopic retrieval. In *Proceedings of the 26th annual international ACM SIGIR conference on Research and development in informaion retrieval*, pages 10–17. ACM, 2003.

[23] Z.A. Zhu, W. Chen, T. Minka, C. Zhu, and Z. Chen. A novel click model and its applications to online advertising. In *Proceedings of the third ACM international conference on Web search and data mining*, pages 321–330. ACM, 2010.

"I Loan Because...": Understanding Motivations for Pro-Social Lending

Yang Liu
University of Michigan
Ann Arbor, MI, USA
owenliu@umich.com

Roy Chen
University of Michigan
Ann Arbor, MI, USA
roywchen@umich.edu

Yan Chen
University of Michigan
Ann Arbor, MI, USA
yanchen@umich.edu

Qiaozhu Mei
University of Michigan
Ann Arbor, MI, USA
qmei@umich.edu

Suzy Salib
University of Michigan
Ann Arbor, MI, USA
ssalib@umich.edu

ABSTRACT

As a new paradigm of online communities, microfinance sites such as Kiva.org have attracted much public attention. To understand lender motivations on Kiva, we classify the lenders' self-stated motivations into ten categories with human coders and machine learning based classifiers. We employ text classifiers using lexical features, along with social features based on lender activity information on Kiva, to predict the categories of lender motivation statements. Although the task appears to be much more challenging than traditional topic-based categorization, our classifiers can achieve high precision in most categories. Using the results of this classification along with Kiva teams information, we predict lending activity from lender motivation and team affiliations. Finally, we make design recommendations regarding Kiva practices which might increase pro-social lending.

Categories and Subject Descriptors

I.2.7 [**Natural Language Processing**]: text analysis

General Terms

Economics, Performance

Keywords

lending motivation, text classification, microfinance, pro-social lending, Kiva

1. INTRODUCTION

Understanding the motivation for pro-social behavior is the foundation for building a more realistic theoretical model of social preferences. Towards this end, experimental economists have used sophisticated experimental designs and econometric techniques to infer participants' motivations and social preferences in the lab [9]. While experimental data generated from the laboratory have yielded important insights into social preferences [14, 6], such results typically come from student subjects who engage in artificially-constructed games. This is necessary because social scientists rarely have the opportunity to record the self-articulated motivations of a large number of people as they engage in pro-social behavior in the real world. The growing popularity of microfinance provides a unique opportunity to explore this issue.

Globally, more than one billion people live in absolute poverty.[1] With few assets, most of these low-income households are excluded from the formal banking sector. To alleviate poverty, microfinance programs have emerged in many parts of the world to provide small loans and other financial services to the poor. Currently about 155 million households are served by microfinance programs, which help very poor households meet basic needs, improve household economic welfare, empower women, and promote entrepreneurship.[2]

Created in October 2005 as the first peer-to-peer microlending site, Kiva (kiva.org) matches citizen lenders with low-income entrepreneurs in developing countries.[3] Through Kiva's platform, anyone can make an interest-free loan of $25 or more to support an entrepreneur. As of August 2011, the total value of all loans made through Kiva was $233,051,800, 81% of which have been made to female entrepreneurs. When lenders register on the site, they have the option to fill in a field labeled "I loan because ...." About 100,000 lenders articulate these motivations on Kiva. Thus, in addition to its social impact on poverty alleviation, Kiva provides a unique data set with which we can study motivations for pro-social behavior.

This study classifies pro-social behavior outside the laboratory setting and uses the classified motivations and team affiliations to predict lending behavior, thus furthering our understanding of the motivations for such behavior. To do so, we draw on theories of social preferences and social identity to generate categories of motivation. We then train human coders to classify a randomly-selected sample of these statements. We use text classification techniques from machine learning to train classifiers on these hand-coded statements, which are then used to label the remaining state-

Permission to make digital or hard copies of all or part of this work for personal or classroom use is granted without fee provided that copies are not made or distributed for profit or commercial advantage and that copies bear this notice and the full citation on the first page. To copy otherwise, to republish, to post on servers or to redistribute to lists, requires prior specific permission and/or a fee.

WSDM'12, February 8–12, 2012, Seattle, Washington, USA.

Copyright 2012 ACM 978-1-4503-0747-5/12/02 ...$10.00.

[1]In 2008, the World Bank revised its poverty cutoff to $1.25 per day at 2005 purchasing-power parity [36].

[2]MicroBanking Bulletin, Issue #19, December, 2009, pp. 49. Microfinance Information Exchange, Inc.

[3]More recently, through the Kiva City program, small business owners in the United States also can become beneficiaries of microlending on Kiva.

ments. We then use econometrics to predict lending behavior based on motivations and team information.

Text classification of user motivations is a novel, yet well-defined natural language processing task. However, it is more challenging than traditional topic-based classification tasks due to the relatively short text lengths of stated motivations and the subjectivity and subtleness of the motivations. Our work serves as a pioneering exploration of motivation classification. Our technique is applicable to other contexts where understanding user motivations is a concern.

Using the best-performing classifiers, the motivations of the 95k unlabeled statements are classified. Along with the information of Kiva teams, we predict lending activities from lender motivation and team affiliations. Finally, we make design recommendations regarding Kiva practices which might increase pro-social lending.

2. RELATED WORK

In general, our study is related to the literature of both computer science, especially text mining, and economics.

To the best of our knowledge, the classification of user motivations is not well covered in previous literature. The most closely-related work is the classification of user intent in search queries [28, 19]. An early classification scheme categorizes the intent of Web search queries into navigational, informational, and transactional [7]. More recent work identifies the missions and tasks in search sessions [22]. The goal of such work is to better understand user intent in order to improve the quality of results of search engines. Most such classification tasks are done based on the analysis of search engine logs rather than natural language processes. Among them, Daumè and Brill [12] induce web search intent via query reformulation which does not require click through data.

The subjectivity and subtleness of user motivations have distinguished our task from traditional topic-based text classification (e.g., politics vs. sports). This links our work to sentiment classification and opinion mining [34, 33]. Indeed, sentiment classification is widely considered to be a much more challenging task than topic-based classification. While the target categories of sentiment classification are usually simple and clear (e.g., positive vs. negative, like vs. dislike), the classification scheme of user motivations is usually not pre-defined - it largely depends on context, usually involves many more categories, and is usually distributed unevenly. As a result, motivation classification appears to be even more challenging than sentiment classification.

Furthermore, our work is also related to text classification of user-generated content and social media in general (e.g., [1, 30, 38]). For example, Agichtein et al.[1] have used classification methods to extract high-quality content from question/answer forums using both content and usage metadata features such as user relationships and usage statistics. Although our goal is fundamentally different from this body of work, the selection of techniques and features is certainly related.

In recent years, the study of microfinance in economics has grown substantially [4]. While they have historically offered low rates of default and good returns and growth [25], a major problem with microfinance that has received attention from economists is that of funding. As Bogan [5] points out, the demand for microfinance services far outstrips the supply. However, much of the recent economic literature on microfinance focuses on the demand (borrower) side, investigating the factors [23] and incentive mechanisms [17] affecting loan repayment. In comparison, we study the supply (lender) side. Specifically, we investigate the effects of lender motivations and team affiliations on lending behavior, neither of which, to our knowledge, has been studied in the economics literature.

3. DATA SOURCE AND KIVA STATISTICS

Using the data API provided by Kiva, we downloaded the motivation statements, team membership, and activity history of all lenders. All data used in this study will be made available.

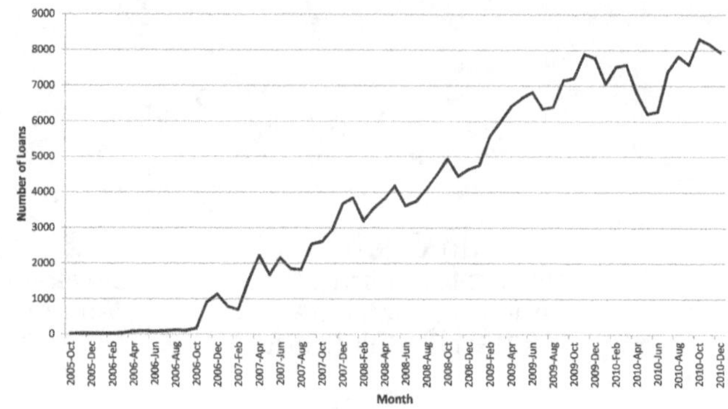

Figure 1: Number of loans funded through Kiva grows.

As of December 2010, Kiva has 660,183 registered lenders from 209 countries. The top five countries by the number of lenders are the United States, Canada, Australia, Great Britain, and Germany. Among all registered lenders, around two thirds of them have made at least one loan. Figure 1 shows the number of loans funded through Kiva each month from October 2005 to December 2010. We see that the number of loans has increased dramatically. As of December 2010, the number of loans made per month per lender is around 0.014.

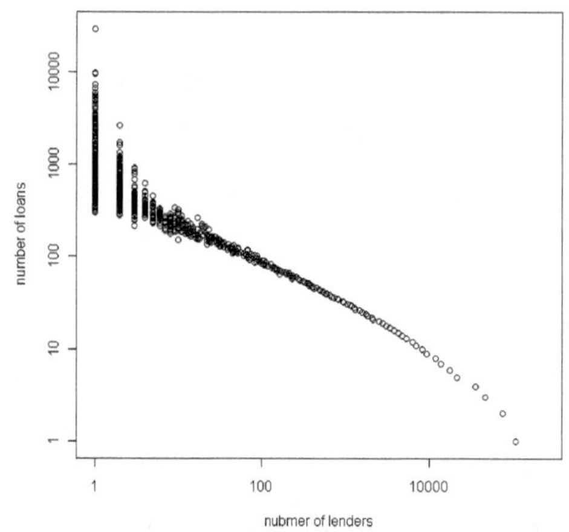

Figure 2: Distribution of lending frequency in log-log scale: few lenders made many loans; many lenders made few loans.

Figure 2 shows the distribution of the frequency of lending activity. The distribution follows a power law (characterized by a long tail). As mentioned above, one third of Kiva lenders have never made a loan. 106,511 (16.1%) lenders have only made one loan. A major problem within the Kiva community is that a large proportion of users are peripheral, contributing once or not at all, and only a few are core users who contribute frequently.

In August 2008, Kiva launched a new program supporting teams of lenders. This allowed users to join teams of other lenders, such as "Team Europe" or "Poverty2Prosperity.org - Poverty-Escape."

The teams are displayed on a leaderboard ranked by the total amount loaned by its members. A lender can join more than one team. Figure 3 show that the number of teams that a Kiva user joined also follows a power law distribution. 85% of lenders have no team affiliation and 12% of lenders joined only one team. Very few people have joined multiple teams.

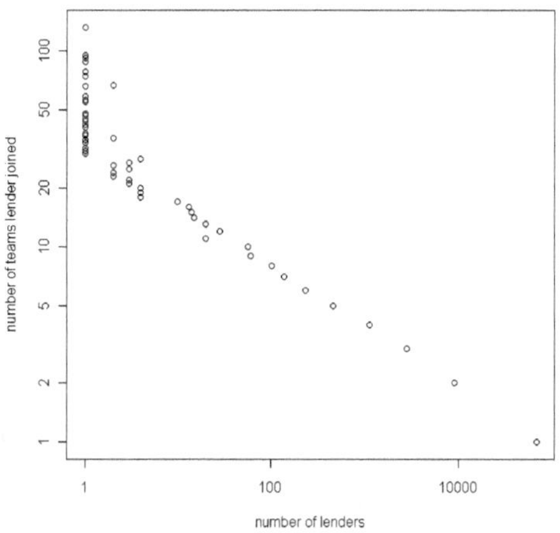

Figure 3: Distribution of lender joined teams in log-log scale: few lenders joined multiple teams; many lenders joined only one team.

At registration, Kiva allows a lender to write a short statement of her motivation for lending. It is interesting to notice that the lenders' motivations are usually closely related to the teams they join. To test whether lenders in same team have similar motivations in a quantitative way, we compute how similar the motivations of two users are, based on the the cosine similarity of the two statements. This enables us to evaluate how the motivational coherency (i.e., the average similarity of the motivation statements of every pair of team members) of each team. We then compare these intra-team similarities with a baseline computed as the average similarity of motivations among all users. The distribution of intra-team similarities is plotted in Figure 4. Among 1,185 Kiva teams having at least two members with a motivation statement, more than 1,000 of them have more coherent member motivations than the baseline (the horizontal line in Figure 4).

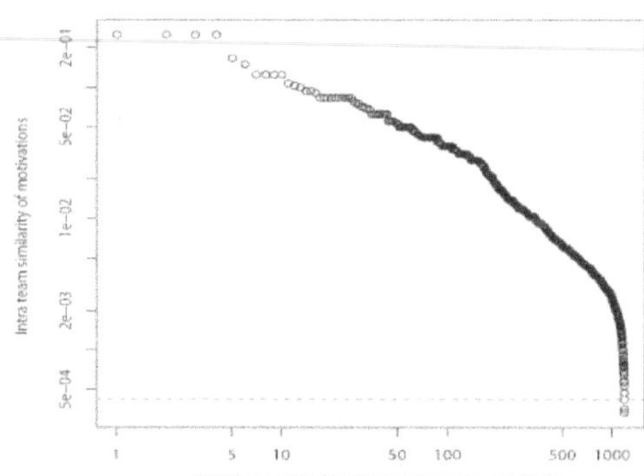

Figure 4: Distribution of intra-team similarity: most teams have more coherent motivations than the baseline.

This statistic suggests that a lender's motivation statement is likely to be correlated with her team membership, and could potentially predict her lending behavior. Is this necessarily true? We present a formal analysis to test whether lending activity is predictable from lender motivation and team affiliations.

4. METHOD

We combine research methods from text mining, experimental economics and econometrics. Our data analysis proceeds in four phases: theory-guided categorization, incentivized coding, text classification, regression analysis.

4.1 Theory-Guided Categorization

Based on theories of social preferences [14, 35] and social identity [3, 39] as well as our own understanding of the microfinance lending market, we develop an initial set of motivation categories for the individual "I loan because ..." statements. Two of the authors code a random sample of 200 individual statements independently and compare their coding assignments. They discuss any discrepancies until they agree. Based on these discussions, we revise the categories for each of the 200 statements into the following ten categories (with abbreviations in parentheses):

1. **General altruism** (Gnl. Altruism): e.g., "I believe in a global community."
2. **Group-specific altruism** (Grp. Altruism): e.g., "I want to help women succeed in business and in life."
3. **Empathy**: e.g., "I am disabled and I know what it's like to feel helpless."
4. **Reciprocity**: e.g., "I am very fortunate to have several people in my life to lend me a hand when I needed help. I hope that I can do the same for someone."
5. **Equality and social safety net** (Equity): e.g., "I want to help others who are less fortunate. Everyone deserves a fair chance."
6. **Social responsibility and social norms** (Norms): e.g., "I have the ability and I'm lucky enough to be able to."
7. **Effective development tool** (Tool): e.g., "I believe in change through bottom-up initiatives and sustainable business models."
8. **Personal satisfaction** (Satisfaction): e.g., "It makes my heart smile."
9. **Religious duty** (Religious): e.g., "I believe that sometimes God works thru people to answer prayers. What a privilege!"
10. **External reasons** (External): e.g., "It's for a community service project at my university."

4.2 Incentivized Coding Procedure

After determining our motivation categories, we have human coders code a randomly-selected sample of 5,250 statements, following the standard coding procedures in content analysis [26]. Each statement is coded by three independent coders.

To train the coders, we hold a one-hour in-person training session for 21 coders recruited from a database of University of Michigan students willing to participate in behavioral economics experiments. In this session, coders are introduced to microfinance, the Kiva web site, and the coding task at hand. We then describe the motivation categories in detail, and use a practice set of 50 random statements to train coders on the appropriate category for each of the different types of statements. Coders are encouraged to ask clarifying questions, which are answered in public. Coding instructions are available from the authors upon request. After the training session, each coder is asked to code 750 "I loan because..." statements and to log into a web interface to code the assigned statements remotely.

The computer interface used for the in-person training is the same as the remote interface used for the off-site coding by each of the human coders. Each human coder is assigned a unique login ID and a password to ensure the security of the coding sessions.

To encourage accurate coding, we employ an incentivized payment scheme. Recent experimental evidence indicates that coders are more responsive to classification criteria with incentivized payment based on correctness than with traditional piece-rate or flat-rate payment schemes [18]. Specifically, we pay coders a base rate of $0.15 per statement, for a maximum possible base rate payment of $112.50 if a coder finishes all 750 statements. To the base rate, we add the possibility of a bonus payment of up to $20, based on the percentage of coded statements which agree with the authors' categorizations[4]. If a coder correctly codes 100% of the 750 statements assigned to her, she receives the full $20 bonus. Otherwise, the bonus is calculated as the percentage of correct categorizations multiplied by $20. This bonus is added to the base rate.

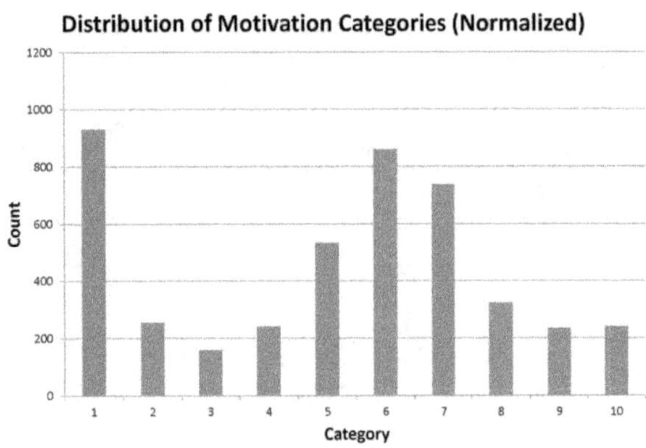

Figure 5: Distribution of Motivation Categories In Hand-Coded Sample (with normalization)

In the random sample of 5,250 statements, the distribution of motivations is presented in Figure 5. Note that this figure is normalized. Any statement can only contribute a total of 1 to the total count. If a statement is coded to two categories, for instance, then both of those categories receive a count of 0.5 for that statement.

We then examine the degree to which the coders agree with each other using interrater reliability. Interrater reliability is assessed with the intraclass correlation coefficient (ICC[3,3]),[5] which is a multi-rater generalization of Cohen's Kappa for the two-rater case.

[4]If the authors assign a statement to two or more categories, the human coder has to do the same, both in the number of categories and the specific assignments, to be considered correct.

[5]There are six main cases of intraclass correlation coefficients (ICC), distinguished by the numbers in parentheses following the letters ICC. The first number indicates the statistical model assumed. Case 3 assumes that judges are fixed and not drawn from a random population. The second number indicates the number of raters. More details on ICC computation can be found in [37].

	Rater Groups						
Category	1	2	3	4	5	6	7
1. Gnl. Altruism	0.50	0.47	0.44	0.53	0.44	0.54	0.52
2. Grp. Altruism	0.69	0.70	0.59	0.57	0.72	0.87	0.69
3. Empathy	0.61	0.76	0.64	0.64	0.48	0.82	0.55
4. Reciprocity	0.72	0.70	0.52	0.58	0.66	0.75	0.48
5. Equity	0.37	0.46	0.47	0.35	0.61	0.63	0.38
6. Norms	0.58	0.76	0.44	0.67	0.69	0.83	0.77
7. Tool	0.46	0.60	0.41	0.39	0.51	0.65	0.56
8. Satisfaction	0.73	0.69	0.52	0.54	0.74	0.77	0.59
9. Religious	0.89	0.87	0.72	0.85	0.87	0.93	0.86
10. External	0.67	0.68	0.31	0.57	0.65	0.74	0.50

Table 1: Intraclass Correlation Coefficients: ICC[3,3]

Table 1 reports the reliability statistics for the seven groups of raters. In general, values above 0.75 represent excellent reliability, values between 0.40 and 0.75 represent good reliability, and values below 0.40 represent poor reliability. We find that reliability varies across categories. Raters achieve good to excellent reliability in categories 1 (general altruism), 2 (group-specific altruism), 3 (empathy), 4 (reciprocity), 6 (social responsibility and social norms), 8 (personal satisfaction) and 9 (religious duty), and poor to good reliability among the remaining categories, indicating the challenge of classifying motivations.

4.3 Text Classification

The feasibility of human coding at a much larger scale is restricted by the availability of human and financial resources. We use the hand-coded motivations obtained through the above procedure to perform machine learning and train automatic text classifiers. We employ standard supervised and semi-supervised learning methods with different semantic, syntactic and social network features.

Since we do not obtain uniformly high inter-rater reliability across all ten categories, we conduct all experiments restricting our analysis to lender motivations for which all three coders agree on the motivation categories. Bear in mind that the purpose of our text classification is to accurately generate motivation categories for the 95k unlabeled lenders as one of the inputs for further regression analysis. The quality of the training data is critical to the the accuracy of our prediction. The restriction of the training set to unanimously coded data gives us higher confidence in the regression results. Of the original 5,250 motivations, 1,964 are unanimously coded in at least one category.

The distribution of unanimous motivations is presented in Figure 6. Note that this figure is normalized in the same way as Figure 5. From Figure 6 we see that the number of motivations in categories with low inter-rater reliability (e.g. category 1) drops more significantly than the number of motivations in categories with high inter-rater reliability (e.g. category 9).

We first process the statements stemmed by the Krovetz stemmer [27]. Stop words are not removed, as some stop words may be useful features for some classes (e.g., "I can."). We represent each document as a vector of features. By default, for each motivation statement, unigram, bigram, and parts-of-speech tags are extracted as features. These features are quantified either using a binary value or using a TF-IDF weight. No feature selection is applied.

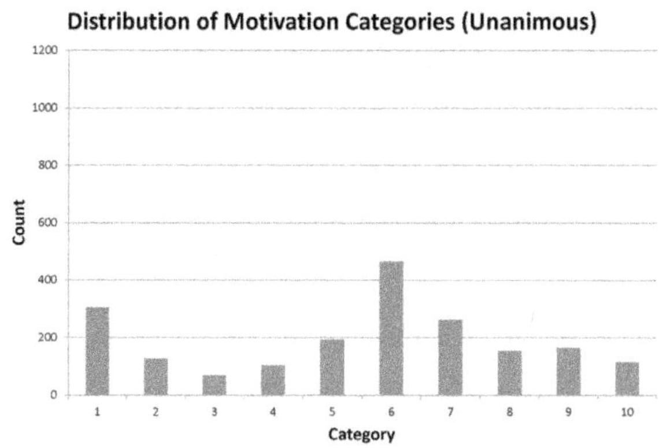

Figure 6: Distribution of Motivation Categories In Consentient Hand-Coded Sample (with normalization)

We then train a binary classifier for each category using Naïve Bayes [29], maximum entropy [31], and support vector machines (SVM) [11]. Note that we do not use multiclass classifiers directly because a statement can belong to more than one category. We adopt the the Naïve Bayes and maximum entropy classifiers from the Mallet package[6], and the SVM^{light} implementation[7] of the SVM classifiers. For the SVM classifiers, we explore different parameters, trading-off between training error and margin, and use two different kernels (i.e., a linear kernel and a RBF kernel).

Note that there are multiple interesting research issues beyond the application of a standard text classifier. First, since we are training a binary classifier for each category, the number of negative examples is far greater than the number of positive examples in the training data. This imbalance may result in the suboptimal performance of standard classification algorithms [20]. To address this issue, previous studies such as [10] have employed several approaches: cost-sensitive learning, minority-class oversampling and majority-class undersampling [40]. We use a model called "SVM-WEIGHT," which utilizes a cost-sensitive learning approach for SVM [2], implemented by libsvm. The basic idea of this algorithm is to penalize false negatives more heavily than false positives [32, 41]. We experiment with Tang et al (2009)'s approach to find the best value for the cost of a false negative.

Second, in our task there are far more unlabeled statements (i.e., 95k) than labeled statements. We therefore employ semi-supervised learning methods to utilize this unlabeled data in the classification. In particular, we use Transductive SVM [21] (also released in the SVMlight package), a typical transductive learning method, to bring unlabeled statements into the loop.

Finally, we intend to leverage the information of lender's social and lending activities in the classification tasks. The intuition here is that users' motivations are related to the teams they join and the number of loans they make. Thus the observation of such activity will in turn aid in the classification of motivations. We introduce specific features to the representation of a statement, such as the number of times a lender has loaned and the team(s) she has joined.

[6]McCallum, Andrew Kachites. "MALLET: A Machine Learning for Language Toolkit." http://mallet.cs.umass.edu. 2002.

[7]http://svmlight.joachims.org

Note that team membership may introduce many features as the number of teams is large. In our experiments, we first train a Naïve Bayes classifier using only team membership as the features, and then incorporate the output of this classifier as a meta-feature of the statement.

To train the text classifiers, we break the hand-coded data into training and test sets, and apply 5-fold cross-validation. The performance of each classifier is measured using a weighted F1 score (also referred to as the $F_{0.5}$ measure in some context [24]):

$$F_\beta = (1+\beta^2) \cdot \frac{precision \cdot recall}{\beta^2 \cdot precision + recall},$$

where β is set as 0.5. The reason we adopt the weighted F1 measure instead of the original F1 measure is that in the regression analysis, the precision of the motivation classification is a more important concern than the recall. For each category, we then apply the classifier with the highest performance on the hand-coded data to classify the rest of the 95k statements.

5. RESULTS: TEXT CLASSIFICATION

In this section, we present and discuss the performance of the text classifiers, assessed using the hand-coded statements. Note that the performances of classifiers with maximum $F_{0.5}$ measure are reported.

5.1 Standard Classifiers

We start with the performance of the standard classifiers, namely Naïve Bayes, maximum entropy, and SVM. Although we select the classifiers based on the $F_{0.5}$ measure which weights precision higher than recall, we also report the precision and recall of the classifiers.

Classifier	SVM	ME	NB
unigram presence	**72.62**	71.13	46.34
unigram tf-idf	**71.49***	55.86	23.82
bigram presence	65.13	**65.72**	36.45
bigram tf-idf	**65.84****	42.90	34.53
unigram+bigram presence	**73.17**	72.32	43.06
unigram+bigram tf-idf	**70.97*****	40.58	22.56
unigram+POS presence	**72.67**	70.62	46.45
unigram+POS tf-idf	**68.08*****	36.07	12.79

Table 2: Average $F_{0.5}$ measure of all classifiers with five-fold cross-validation, in percent. Boldface: best performance for a given row. Significant at the: * 10% level;** 5% level; *** 1% level. Note that SVM classifiers consistently outperform the other two families of classifiers

Table 2 summarizes the performance of each standard classification method averaging ten classes. Clearly, all classifiers perform significantly better than the random baseline $F_{0.5}$ measure of 10% (10% positive examples on average for ten categories). Among the three methods, we see that SVM classifiers with linear kernel consistently outperform the other two classifiers. When comparing the best performance of the SVM and maximum entropy classifiers, however, the difference between the best performers is not statistically significant (73.17 versus 72.32 with unweighted unigram and bigram features). Naïve Bayes performs significantly worse than the other two classifiers.

Table 3 presents the performance of the best SVM classifiers on each of the ten classes. The results suggest that some motivation categories lead to an easier classification task (for example, category 9: *religious duty*), while others present a greater challenge (e.g., category 5: *equality and social safety net* and category 7:

Category	$F_{0.5}$ measure (%)	Precision	Recall
Gnl. Altruism	67.87	72.15	55.20
Grp. Altruism	78.32	87.27	59.20
Empathy	74.81	82.24	55.97
Reciprocity	72.00	80.58	51.36
Equity	68.66	76.20	49.92
Norms	79.40	80.70	74.86
Tool	63.96	69.68	49.32
Satisfaction	75.51	84.54	53.45
Religious	88.21	95.60	67.63
External	62.91	74.25	39.70

Table 3: $F_{0.5}$ measure, precision, recall of classifers using unigram+bigram presence feature with 5-fold cross-validation

Category	$F_{0.5}$ measure (%)	Precision	Recall
Gnl. Altruism	**68.71**	73.06	55.92
Grp. Altruism	78.32	87.28	59.20
Empathy	74.81	82.24	55.97
Reciprocity	72.00	80.58	51.36
Equity	**71.53**	94.13	36.58
Norms	**79.88**	80.92	76.47
Tool	63.96	69.68	49.32
Satisfaction	75.51	84.54	53.45
Religious	**88.44**	95.64	68.32
External	62.91	74.25	39.70

Table 4: The results of SVM-WEIGHT classifier with 5-fold cross-validation. Boldface: improvement over SVM.

Category	$F_{0.5}$ measure (%)	Precision	Recall
Gnl. Altruism	66.72	68.91	59.59
Grp. Altruism	71.35	70.00	77.76
Empathy	65.33	65.05	70.74
Reciprocity	64.81	64.24	67.93
Equity	59.66	61.71	56.07
Norms	73.71	71.64	83.50
Tool	61.75	63.81	55.74
Satisfaction	60.7	59.42	68.12
Religious	72.44	71.20	78.05
External	61.66	61.97	61.55

Table 5: The results of Transductive SVM with 5-fold cross-validation.

effective development tool). This is anticipated. In fact, the easy categories can usually be easily distinguished from others by keywords (e.g., for *religious duty*, "god", "prayers", etc.). The corresponding classification task is thus close to traditional topic-based classification. The other categories present much more subjectiveness and subtleness, where keywords and phrases do not have significant discriminative power. Another interesting perspective is to link the performance of automatic classification to the performance of human-coding. Indeed, the categories more "friendly" to the text classifiers are also associated with a higher inter-rater reliability (e.g., above 0.85 for *religious duty*), while the "classifier-resistant" categories are associated with a low inter-rater reliability (e.g., below 0.5 for *equality and social safety net*).

Furthermore, we find that, similar to the findings in sentiment classification [34], better performance is usually achieved when the features are not weighted (e.g., quantified with presence/absence only). This is because both sentiment classification and motivation classification documents are performed on short text (sentences and short statements) rather than rich documents (e.g., news articles). We anticipate that the presence of a feature conveys a strong signal in short documents, and that repeated appearance provides only marginal improvement. The combination of unigram and bigram features generally performs better than other combinations of features. Therefore, we adopt this combination in all following experiments.

5.2 Accommodating Imbalanced Data

Beyond the standard classifiers, we investigate the problem of handling imbalanced data (i.e. many more negative examples than positive examples in training). The performance of SVM-WEIGHT classifiers are reported in Table 4.

Compared to the standard classifiers reported in Table 3, we observe improved performance in four categories (1,5,6,9). However, none of the improvements is statistically significant. This can mostly be attributed to the high baselines achieved by the SVM classifiers. Since cost-sensitive learning moves the boundary towards the negative support vectors, a higher recall rate will be achieved at the expense of precision. The results suggest that overweighting the minority class is effective in managing imbalanced datasets when precision is more important than recall.

5.3 Leveraging Unlabeled Data

Our second investigation is to leverage the unlabeled data in the classification - this is a plausible intuition behind semi-supervised learning. We incorporate an additional 19,000 randomly-selected (1/5 of the 95K available) unlabeled motivations into the training process using Transductive SVM. The results are summarized in Table 5. Surprisingly, we find that the use of transductive SVM results in a decrease of the $F_{0.5}$ measure in all ten categories.

This seems to be inconsistent with the intuition of semi-supervised learning. With a more careful analysis, we observe that despite the decreased $F_{0.5}$ measure, the recall of all ten categories are largely improved. The improvement in recall for category 10 is more than 20 percentage points. With the help of the unlabeled data, the TSVM classifiers successfully generate more conservative boundaries towards the negative examples. In our precision-emphasized context, however, this doesn't lead to an increase of the $F_{0.5}$ measures. Also, the lexical properties of unanimously coded data are slightly different from that of the unlabeled data since the unanimously coded data have more salient features and are more easily classified. Besides transductive SVM, we also employ a number of classical graph-based semi-supervised learning methods (in particular, the methods proposed in Zhu et al (2003) [43] and Zhou et al (2004) [42]). A similar effect has been observed. Interestingly, similar patterns are reported in [15], which applied semi-supervised learning methods in the context of sentiment classification.

5.4 Leveraging Activity Features

Our next investigation goes beyond the text, incorporating signals from the activities of lenders. As presented in Section 4.3, features related to team membership and lending activities are incorporated into the SVM classifiers. The results are summarized in Tables 6 and 7. The involvement of activity features improve the performance of standard SVM classifiers in some categories. Interestingly, the only statistically significant improvement appears in one of the "hard" classes (category 5, *equality and social safety net*). None of the other categories present significant improvement. The results again imply a correlation between lenders' motivation categories and their lending and team joining activities.

5.5 Discussion

We have completed a systematic exploration of a new natural language processing task - the classification of user motivations. The subtleness and subjectiveness of user motivations have made

Category	$F_{0.5}$ measure (%)	Precision	Recall
Gnl. Altruism	**70.22**	77.89	51.42
Grp. Altruism	78.31	85.79	58.54
Empathy	68.61	80.89	49.18
Reciprocity	59.19	78.88	30.14
Equity	**71.35****	86.02	43.75
Norms	78.36	80.17	71.98
Tool	61.37	70.43	41.29
Satisfaction	69.24	79.02	46.86
Religious	88.11	94.75	69.70
External	**69.01**	82.45	43.22

Table 6: The classification results with unigram+bigram pres+team feature with 5-fold cross-validation. Boldface: improvement over SVM. Significant at the: ** 5% level

Category	$F_{0.5}$ measure (%)	Precision	Recall
Gnl. Altruism	64.44	63.41	69.54
Grp. Altruism	**81.11**	88.96	61.47
Empathy	73.69	83.91	51.83
Reciprocity	57.38	57.98	56.37
Equity	**73.25**	87.37	47.73
Norms	79.19	81.47	71.63
Tool	**65.08**	74.66	43.19
Satisfaction	72.89	84.28	47.82
Religious	87.49	94.55	67.51
External	**71.98**	84.12	46.55

Table 7: The classification results with unigram+bigram pres+loan times feature with 5-fold cross-validation. Boldface: improvement over SVM.

the problem much more challenging than common text classification tasks that are based on topics (e.g., Reuters, 20 newsgroups, political vs. sports). This difficulty is not only observed in the classification results, but also in the human coding results (i.e., low inter-rater reliability). Indeed, the closer the motivation category is to a topic (e.g., "religious duty"), the more discriminative power keyword features have, and the better text classifiers perform. Despite this challenge, a standard SVM classifier with unigram and bigram features still achieves reasonable performance over most of the categories.

The most closely related classification task is perhaps sentiment classification, which also has subtle and subjective classes. Indeed, many observations similar to ours can be found in the literature of sentiment classification. The major challenge here is the lack of a natural definition of categories in user motivation (e.g., positive vs. negative). Therefore, there is little established domain knowledge that can be utilized. Keyword matching using a simple list/lexicon of sentimental words can perform reasonably well (with an accuracy up to 69% reported in [34]). Unfortunately, such a resource does not exist in the context of motivation classification. Another additional challenge comes from the imbalanced distribution of classes.

Our exploration also provides useful insights into the future development of motivation classification. Although neither the treatment of imbalanced data nor the use of unlabeled data have brought significant improvement in our precision-driven context, they may help significantly in other scenarios where recall is more of a concern. On the other hand, the incorporation of user activity information has brought considerable improvement even though it is explored in a rather simple way. This suggests a promising direction for inferring a user's motivation from her behavior rather than from a motivation statement, especially in a context where rich social activity data is available. This also strengthens our hypothesis that the lending behaviors of Kiva users are predictable from their motivations.

Please note that in the regression analysis that follows, we do not use the classification results with activity features involved. This is because such information overlaps with some of our dependent/independent variables (e.g., lending amount and team membership). We thus classify the unlabeled statements with the best performer in Table 3 and use the results in the regression analysis.

6. RESULTS: LENDING BEHAVIOR

In this section, we first report regression analysis relating motivation categories and team affiliations to lending behavior. We then discuss design implications based on our regression results.

6.1 Regression Analysis

To evaluate how lender motivations affect their lending behavior, we run several ordinary least squares (OLS) regressions. The dependent variables are either (a) the average number of loans that a lender gives per month, or (b) the amount that a lender lends per month.

Table 8 reports four OLS regressions investigating factors affecting the average number of loans a user makes per month, i.e., loan frequency. The independent variables include lender motivations and their team affiliation information. Column (1) reports the first specification where only lender motivations are included as independent variables. Columns (2) - (4) report three more regressions, where we control for the number of teams a user has joined. We do this in three different ways. In column (2), we simply control for whether or not the user has joined at least one team. In column (3), we assume that the number of teams a user has joined affects behavior linearly, and therefore include the number of teams the user has joined as a regressor. Finally, in column (4), we again control for the number of teams a user has joined, but nonlinearly (i.e. we include a dummy variable for whether the user has joined 1 team, 2 teams, etc.).

Table 8 shows robust motivation and team activity effects on lending frequency, as the significance and direction of these effects do not change between specifications. Specifically, categories 1 (general altruism), 2 (group-specific altruism), and 10 (external reasons) negatively affect lending frequency. A lender motivated by general or group-specific altruism on average makes 0.11 fewer loans per month than others. The general altruism category, e.g., "I care," can be viewed as a catch-all category, both by Kiva lenders and by our coders. Lenders in this category gave non-specific statements about why they lend, perhaps indicating a lesser degree of motivation to lend than users who gave very specific reasons for lending. Users in the group-specific altruism category, on the other hand, may be more selective regarding the projects they lent to, denoted by their naming specific groups to which they wished to lend. Finally, lenders with external reasons to lend, such as fulfilling a required school project or as a recipient of a Kiva gift card, make 0.16 fewer loans per month than others. These lenders might be less intrinsically motivated compared to others on Kiva.

By contrast, categories 7 (effective development tool) and 9 (religious duty) both positively affect lending frequency. A lender who sees Kiva as an effective development tool makes 0.17 more loans per month than others. Their motivation statements indicate that they believe Kiva to be a better way to help the poor than through other means. While other Kiva lenders might also utilize other methods of helping, such as direct charitable donation, lenders in this category might be more likely to use Kiva than other methods. Of all motivation categories, category 9 (religious duty) has by far the largest effect on lending frequency. A lender motivated

Table 8: OLS Regressions of Motivations and Team Activity on Lending Frequency

Dependent Variable: Number of Loans Per Month				
	(1)	(2)	(3)	(4)
Gnl. Altruism	-0.12***	-0.12***	-0.12***	-0.11***
	(0.044)	(0.043)	(0.043)	(0.043)
Grp. Altruism	-0.14**	-0.13**	-0.12**	-0.11**
	(0.057)	(0.057)	(0.056)	(0.056)
Empathy	-0.10	-0.08	-0.07	-0.06
	(0.086)	(0.086)	(0.085)	(0.085)
Reciprocity	-0.08	-0.05	-0.05	-0.05
	(0.071)	(0.070)	(0.070)	(0.070)
Equity	0.02	0.01	0.01	0.01
	(0.054)	(0.054)	(0.054)	(0.053)
Norms	-0.00	-0.02	-0.01	-0.01
	(0.034)	(0.033)	(0.033)	(0.033)
Tool	0.19***	0.17***	0.16***	0.17***
	(0.037)	(0.037)	(0.037)	(0.037)
Satisfaction	-0.07	-0.05	-0.06	-0.05
	(0.059)	(0.058)	(0.058)	(0.058)
Religious	0.27***	0.24***	0.25***	0.25***
	(0.061)	(0.061)	(0.060)	(0.060)
External	-0.26***	-0.18**	-0.18**	-0.16**
	(0.081)	(0.080)	(0.080)	(0.079)
$\geq$1 Team		0.78***		
		(0.025)		
# Teams			0.42***	
			(0.008)	
1 Team				0.53***
				(0.027)
2 Teams				0.82***
				(0.053)
3 Teams				1.09***
				(0.087)
4 Teams				1.71***
				(0.134)
5 Teams				2.60***
				(0.204)
6 Teams				4.09***
				(0.279)
7 Teams				4.71***
				(0.346)
8 Teams				1.43***
				(0.416)
$\geq$9 Teams				11.51***
				(0.234)
Constant	0.64***	0.43***	0.46***	0.43***
	(0.015)	(0.017)	(0.015)	(0.016)
# Obs.	100240	100240	100240	100240
R^2	0.001	0.011	0.026	0.036

Notes: Standard errors in parentheses
Significant at the: *** 1%, ** 5%, or * 10% level

by religious duty makes 0.25 more loans per month than others. Social identity research finds that a salient group identity increases contribution to public goods [13]. We argue that religious identities are made salient on Kiva through its lending teams program. Since its inception in August 2008, the top two lending teams (in total amount loaned) have consistently been the Atheists (first place) and the Kiva Christians (second place), each featured prominently on the team leaderboards. Such identity-based team competition should motivate the team members to lend more.

When controlling for team affiliation (column 2), we find that a lender belonging to any team(s) makes 0.78 more loans per month than those without any team affiliation. Furthermore, assuming linearity (column 3), belonging to an additional team is associated with 0.42 more loans per month. Lastly, column (4) separately estimates the effects of belonging to different number of teams without assuming linearity. Overall, the positive effect of team affiliation on lending frequency is consistent with the predictions of social identity theory. Ethnographic studies of Kiva teams reveal that teams communicate through the Kiva message board [16], set specific goals with deadlines, and coordinate team activities by singling out specific loans to the team with the goal of raising 100% of the money for each loan ("loan-a-thon"). Although we are not aware of any systematic investigation of the effects of teams on lending, we conjecture that the ability of teams to communicate, coordinate and compete might contribute to the increased lending activity of team members.

In addition to lending frequency, we are also interested in the effects of motivation categories and team affiliation on the amount lent. However, to protect lender privacy, individual loan amount is not available through Kiva data API. Therefore, for this analysis, we employ a proxy variable for the amount lent. We know the list of projects that each lender lends to, as well as the total amount lent to each project. We therefore assume that each lender to a project lends an equal amount. Once we apply this assumption to all projects, we have a proxy for the total amount lent by each user.

Table 9 presents four OLS regressions using the proxy lending amount as the dependent variable. Independent variables in each regression are the same as those in Table 8. While the significance and direction of motivation categories and team effects remain the same as those in Table 8, it is informative to highlight the size of some of these effects. Specifically, a lender motivated by general or group-specific altruism lends \$6 less per month than others, while those motivated by external reasons lend approximately \$7 less. By contrast, a lender who sees Kiva as an effective development tool lends \$5 more per month, while one motivated by religious duty lends \$9 more. Again, when controlling for team affiliation (column 2), we find that a lender belonging to any team(s) lends \$31 more per month than those without any team affiliation, while each additional team joined is associated with \$16 more lent per month. Overall, the effects of motivation categories and team affiliation on amount lent is consistent with those on lending frequency.

Even though team affiliation is positively correlated with both the lending frequency and lending amounts, we do not rule out the possibility of a selection issue, in that lenders who join teams are perhaps inclined to lend more in the first place. We are collecting additional data in ongoing work to account for this possibility.

It is also important to note that the reliability of these regression results depends on the effectiveness of the classifier, which in turn depends on the quality of the human coded sample. Though we attempt to minimize the disagreement between the human coders through incentivized coding procedure, these regression results are still affected by these disagreements.

Table 9: OLS Regressions of Motivations and Team Activity on Lending Amount

Dependent Variable: Average Lent Per Month (Proxy)				
	(1)	(2)	(3)	(4)
Gnl. Altruism	-5.72***	-5.93***	-5.81***	-5.66***
	(1.759)	(1.750)	(1.739)	(1.731)
Grp. Altruism	-6.28***	-5.81**	-5.70**	-5.26**
	(2.296)	(2.286)	(2.270)	(2.260)
Empathy	-4.56	-3.78	-3.52	-3.04
	(3.483)	(3.467)	(3.444)	(3.428)
Reciprocity	-3.90	-2.79	-2.80	-2.76
	(2.861)	(2.848)	(2.829)	(2.816)
Equity	0.29	-0.00	-0.12	0.01
	(2.196)	(2.186)	(2.171)	(2.161)
Norms	-1.34	-2.05	-1.78	-1.62
	(1.360)	(1.354)	(1.344)	(1.338)
Tool	6.03***	5.07***	4.93***	5.08***
	(1.503)	(1.496)	(1.486)	(1.479)
Satisfaction	-3.43	-2.65	-3.04	-2.89
	(2.373)	(2.362)	(2.346)	(2.336)
Religious	10.13***	8.76***	9.53***	9.14***
	(2.469)	(2.458)	(2.441)	(2.430)
External	-10.73***	-7.57**	-7.33**	-6.71**
	(3.265)	(3.251)	(3.229)	(3.215)
≥1 Team		30.58***		
		(0.996)		
# Teams			15.93***	
			(0.331)	
1 Team				20.94***
				(1.111)
2 Teams				32.12***
				(2.158)
3 Teams				44.05***
				(3.539)
4 Teams				64.43***
				(5.408)
5 Teams				99.57***
				(8.262)
6 Teams				154.70***
				(11.301)
7 Teams				170.42***
				(14.022)
8 Teams				54.79***
				(16.830)
≥9 Teams				439.25***
				(9.475)
Constant	26.33***	18.11***	19.54***	17.97***
	(0.615)	(0.668)	(0.624)	(0.660)
# Obs.	100240	100240	100240	100240
R^2	0.001	0.010	0.023	0.032

Notes: Standard errors in parentheses
Significant at the: *** 1%, ** 5%, or * 10% level

6.2 Design Implications

Our regression analysis of lender motivation and team affiliation on lending behavior suggests that some Kiva practices can be improved to increase participation and commitment.

We find that lenders motivated by external reasons, such as those receiving a Kiva gift card from a friend, make 0.16 fewer loans and lend $7 less per month than others. This suggests that recruiting newcomers through gift cards or social networks[8] might not be sufficient to make newcomers commit to the Kiva cause. For instance, the Kiva gift cards act as another way for existing users to lend on Kiva rather than a way to bring in new active members. Lenders recruited through such channels are likely to become peripheral users. As it stands, Kiva has a large number of peripheral users. Recall one-third of Kiva users have never made a loan and 16% have only made one loan. Socializing newcomers and motivating peripheral participants to become active contributors is a core issue facing Kiva.

Our finding that lenders belonging to any team(s) make 0.78 more loans and lend $31 more per month than those without team affiliations, combined with ethnographic studies of Kiva teams, suggest that successful teams (measured by total amount loaned) might be an effective mechanism to socialize newcomers and to motivate peripheral participants.

After a new lender joins Kiva through one of its existing channels, Kiva should encourage them to join an active and successful team. Team recommendation could be based on the similarity between the newcomer motivation and existing team member motivations.

7. CONCLUSION

Understanding user motivations in online communities helps the analysis and modeling of user behavior. In this paper, we study the novel problem of classifying user motivation statements from Kiva, a well-known online microfinance community. An incentivized coding procedure is employed to generate human-labeled datasets for this text classification task. Despite the specific challenges of this task, we find that SVM-based classifiers using unigram and bigram features work reasonably well. However, the use of primitive community-based features does not significantly improve classification performance.

It is clear that some categories of user motivations are more difficult to identify than others. In our future work, we will pursue deeper linguistic features, both syntactic and semantic, to enhance the SVM classifiers. In addition, a richer set of social-behavioral features will be explored to further improve the classification task.

We also examine which categories are associated with changes in lending behavior and found both categories that increased and decreased lending. These indicate that Kiva should reconsider policies that will create peripheral lenders and focus on those that encourage users to become core contributors. While Kiva gift cards and their more recent "Help Kiva branch out" campaign might not be very effective, further development of the Kiva lending teams may have a beneficial effect on lending. To further study this idea, the next step in this research is for us to correctly control for selection bias in users' joining of Kiva teams, thus giving us insight as to whether the act of joining teams increases lending.

[8]A more recent example is the "Help Kiva branch out" campaign from August 1, 2011 to August 13, 2011, when Kiva lenders are encouraged to invite their friends to join Kiva. Kiva provides free trial loans to the first 4,000 new users who make a loan through this campaign.

8. ACKNOWLEDGMENTS

The financial support from the National Science Foundation through grants no. SES-0720943, IIS-1054199, BCS-1111019 and a Google Research Award is gratefully acknowledged. We thank Xuan Liang for her excellent research assistance in the early phase of the project.

9. REFERENCES

[1] E. Agichtein, C. Castillo, D. Donato, A. Gionis, and G. Mishne. Finding high-quality content in social media. In *Proceedings of the international conference on Web search and web data mining*, pages 183–194. ACM, 2008.

[2] R. Akbani, S. Kwek, and N. Japkowicz. Applying support vector machines to imbalanced datasets. *Machine Learning: ECML 2004*, pages 39–50, 2004.

[3] G. A. Akerlof and R. E. Kranton. *Identity Economics: How Our Identities Shape Our Work, Wages, and Well-Being*. Princeton University Press, Princeton, New Jersey, 2010.

[4] B. Armendáriz and J. Morduch. *The Economics of Microfinance*. The MIT Press, Cambridge, Massachusetts, second edition, 2010.

[5] V. L. Bogan. Capital structure and sustainability: An empirical study of microfinance institutions. *Review of Economics and Statistics*, 2011. forthcoming.

[6] G. E. Bolton and A. Ockenfels. Erc: A theory of equity, reciprocity, and competition. *American Economic Review*, 90(1):166–193, March 2000.

[7] A. Broder. A taxonomy of web search. In *ACM Sigir forum*, volume 36, pages 3–10. ACM, 2002.

[8] C.-C. Chang and C.-J. Lin. *LIBSVM: a library for support vector machines*, 2001. Software available at `http://www.csie.ntu.edu.tw/~cjlin/libsvm`.

[9] G. Charness and M. Rabin. Understanding social preferences with simple tests. *Quarterly Journal of Economics*, 117(3):817–869, August 2002.

[10] N. V. Chawla, N. Japkowicz, and A. Kotcz. Editorial: special issue on learning from imbalanced data sets. *SIGKDD explorations*, 6(1):1, 2004.

[11] C. Cortes and V. Vapnik. Support-vector networks. *Machine learning*, 20(3):273–297, 1995.

[12] H. Daumé III and E. Brill. Web search intent induction via automatic query reformulation. In *Proceedings of HLT-NAACL 2004: Short Papers*, pages 49–52. Association for Computational Linguistics, 2004.

[13] C. C. Eckel and P. J. Grossman. Managing diversity by creating team identity. *Journal of Economic Behavior & Organization*, 58(3):371–392, November 2005.

[14] E. Fehr and K. M. Schmidt. The theory of fairness, competition, and cooperation. *Quarterly Journal of Economics*, 114(3):817–868, August 1999.

[15] A. B. Goldberg and X. Zhu. Seeing stars when there aren't many stars: graph-based semi-supervised learning for sentiment categorization. In *Proceedings of the First Workshop on Graph Based Methods for Natural Language Processing*, TextGraphs-1, pages 45–52, Stroudsburg, PA, USA, 2006. Association for Computational Linguistics.

[16] S. E. Hartley. Kiva.org: Crowd-sourced microfinance and cooperation in group lending. Harvard University Working Paper, 2010.

[17] N. Hermes and R. Lensink. The empirics of microfinance: what do we know? *The Economic Journal*, 117(517):F1–F10, 2007.

[18] D. Houser and E. Xiao. Classification of natural language messages using a coordination game. *Experimental Economics*, 14:1 – 14, 2011.

[19] B. Jansen, D. Booth, and A. Spink. Determining the informational, navigational, and transactional intent of web queries. *Information processing management*, 44(3):1251, 2008.

[20] N. Japkowicz and S. Stephen. The class imbalance problem: A systematic study. *Intelligent Data Analysis*, 6(5):429–449, 2002.

[21] T. Joachims. Transductive inference for text classification using support vector machines. In *Proceedings of ICML*, pages 200–209. ACM, 1999.

[22] R. Jones and K. Klinkner. Beyond the session timeout: automatic hierarchical segmentation of search topics in query logs. In *Proceeding of the 17th ACM conference on Information and knowledge management*, pages 699–708. ACM, 2008.

[23] D. Karlan. Using experimental economics to measure social capital and predict financial decision. *American Economic Review*, 95(5):1688–1699, December 2005.

[24] R. Klinger and C. M. Friedrich. User's choice of precision and recall in named entity recognition. In *Proceedings of the International Conference RANLP-2009*, pages 192–196, Borovets, Bulgaria, September 2009. Association for Computational Linguistics.

[25] N. A. Krauss and I. Walter. Can microfinance reduce portfolio volatility? *Economic Development and Cultural Change*, 58(1):85–110, October 2009.

[26] K. Krippendorff. *Content analysis: An introduction to its methodology*. Sage Publications, Thousand Oaks, CA, 2nd edition, 2003.

[27] R. Krovetz. Viewing morphology as an inference process. In *Proceedings of the 16th annual international ACM SIGIR conference on Research and development in information retrieval*, pages 191–202. ACM, 1993.

[28] X. Li, Y. Wang, and A. Acero. Learning query intent from regularized click graphs. In *Proceedings of the 31st annual international ACM SIGIR conference on Research and development in information retrieval*, pages 339–346. ACM, 2008.

[29] M. Maron. Automatic indexing: an experimental inquiry. *Journal of the ACM (JACM)*, 8(3):404–417, 1961.

[30] G. Mishne. Experiments with mood classification in blog posts. In *Proceedings of ACM SIGIR 2005 Workshop on Stylistic Analysis of Text for Information Access*, page 19. Citeseer, 2005.

[31] K. Nigam, J. Lafferty, and A. McCallum. Using maximum entropy for text classification. In *IJCAI-99 workshop on machine learning for information filtering*, volume 1, pages 61–67. Citeseer, 1999.

[32] E. Osuna, R. Freund, and F. Girosi. Training support vector machines: an application to face detection. In *cvpr*, page 130. Published by the IEEE Computer Society, 1997.

[33] B. Pang and L. Lee. Opinion mining and sentiment analysis. *Foundations and Trends in Information Retrieval*, 2(1-2):1–135, 2008.

[34] B. Pang, L. Lee, and S. Vaithyanathan. Thumbs up?: sentiment classification using machine learning techniques. In *Proceedings of the ACL-02 conference on Empirical methods in natural language processing-Volume 10*, pages 79–86, 2002.

[35] M. Rabin. Incorporating fairness into game theory and economics. *American Economic Review*, 83(5):1281–1302, December 1993.

[36] M. Ravallion, S. Chen, and P. Sangraula. Dollar a day revisited. *World Bank Economic Review*, 23(2):163 – 184, 2009.

[37] P. E. Shrout and J. L. Fleiss. Intraclass correlations: Uses in assessing rater reliability. *Psychological Bulletin*, 86(2):420–428, 1979.

[38] B. Sriram, D. Fuhry, E. Demir, H. Ferhatosmanoglu, and M. Demirbas. Short text classification in twitter to improve information filtering. In *Proceeding of the 33rd international ACM SIGIR conference on research and development in information retrieval*, pages 841–842. ACM, 2010.

[39] H. Tajfel and J. Turner. An integrative theory of intergroup conflict. In S. Worchel and W. Austin, editors, *The Social Psychology of Intergroup Relations*. Brooks/Cole, Monterey, CA, 1979.

[40] Y. Tang, Y. Zhang, N. Chawla, and S. Krasser. SVMs modeling for highly imbalanced classification. *Systems, Man, and Cybernetics, Part B: Cybernetics, IEEE Transactions on*, 39(1):281–288, 2009.

[41] K. Veropoulos, C. Campbell, and N. Cristianini. Controlling the sensitivity of support vector machines. In *Proceedings of the International Joint Conference on AI*, pages 55–60, 1999.

[42] D. Zhou, O. Bousquet, T. Lal, J. Weston, and B. Schölkopf. Learning with local and global consistency. In *Advances in Neural Information Processing Systems 16: Proceedings of the 2003 Conference*, pages 595–602, 2004.

[43] X. Zhu, Z. Ghahramani, and J. Lafferty. Semi-supervised learning using gaussian fields and harmonic functions. In *Proceedings of ICML*, pages 912–919. ACM, 2003.

Correlating Financial Time Series with Micro-Blogging Activity

Eduardo J. Ruiz, Vagelis Hristidis
Department of Computer Science & Engineering
University of California at Riverside
Riverside, California, USA
{eruiz009,vagelis}@cs.ucr.edu

Carlos Castillo, Aristides Gionis, Alejandro Jaimes
Yahoo! Research Barcelona
Barcelona, Spain
{chato,gionis,ajaimes}@yahoo-inc.com

ABSTRACT

We study the problem of correlating micro-blogging activity with stock-market events, defined as changes in the price and traded volume of stocks. Specifically, we collect messages related to a number of companies, and we search for correlations between stock-market events for those companies and features extracted from the micro-blogging messages. The features we extract can be categorized in two groups. Features in the first group measure the overall activity in the micro-blogging platform, such as number of posts, number of re-posts, and so on. Features in the second group measure properties of an induced *interaction graph*, for instance, the number of connected components, statistics on the degree distribution, and other graph-based properties.

We present detailed experimental results measuring the correlation of the stock market events with these features, using Twitter as a data source. Our results show that the most correlated features are the number of connected components and the number of nodes of the interaction graph. The correlation is stronger with the traded volume than with the price of the stock. However, by using a simulator we show that even relatively small correlations between price and micro-blogging features can be exploited to drive a stock trading strategy that outperforms other baseline strategies.

Categories and Subject Descriptors

H.3.4 [**Information Systems Applications-Systems and Software**]: Information networks; J.4 [**Social and Behavioral Sciences**]: Economics

General Terms

Algorithms, Experimentation

Keywords

Social Networks, Financial Time Series, Micro-Blogging

Permission to make digital or hard copies of all or part of this work for personal or classroom use is granted without fee provided that copies are not made or distributed for profit or commercial advantage and that copies bear this notice and the full citation on the first page. To copy otherwise, to republish, to post on servers or to redistribute to lists, requires prior specific permission and/or a fee.
WSDM'12, February 8–12, 2012, Seattle, Washington, U SA.
Copyright 2012 ACM 978-1-4503-0747-5/12/02 ...$10.00.

1. INTRODUCTION

As the volume of data from online social networks increases, scientists are trying to find ways to understand and extract knowledge from this data. In this paper we study how the activity in a popular micro-blogging platform (Twitter) is correlated to time series from the financial domain, specifically stock prices and traded volume. We compute a large number of features extracted from postings ("*tweets*") related to certain publicly-traded companies. Our goal is to find out which of these features are more correlated with changes in the stock of the companies.

We start by carefully creating filters to select the relevant tweets for a company. We study various filtering approaches such as using the stock symbol, the company name or variations of the two. We also evaluate the effects of expanding this set of tweets by including closely related tweets.

Next, in order to enrich the feature-extraction mechanism, we represent the tweets during a time interval as an *interaction graph*, an example of which is shown in Figure 1. The nodes in this graph are tweets, users, URLs and hash-tags. The edges express relationships among the nodes, such as authorship, re-tweeting and referencing.

On these graphs, which we call *constrained subgraphs*, we define a large number of features, divided in two groups: activity-based and graph-based features. Activity-based features measure quantities such as the number of hashtags, the number of tweets, and so on. Graph-based features capture the link-structure of the graph. We then study how these features are correlated with the price and traded volume time-series of stock.

Our first key result is that the traded volume for a stock is correlated with the number of connected components in its constrained subgraph, as well as with the number of tweets in the graph. Intuitively, we expect that the traded volume is correlated with the number of tweets. Surprisingly, it is slightly more correlated with the number of connected components. On the other hand, the stock price is not strongly correlated with any of the features we extracted, but it is only slightly correlated with the number of connected components and even less with the number of nodes in the constrained subgraph. We found that other graph-based features, such as PageRank and degree, are effective for larger constrained graphs built around groups of stocks (e.g., financial indexes).

Clearly, finding a correlation with price change has wider implications than finding a correlation with traded volume. Therefore, we test how the slight correlation of the price with the micro-blogging features can be applied to guide a stock trader. Specifically, we create a stock trading simulation, and compare various trading strategies. The second key result of this paper is that by using the Twitter constrained subgraph features of the previous days, we can develop a trading strategy that is successful when compared against several baselines.

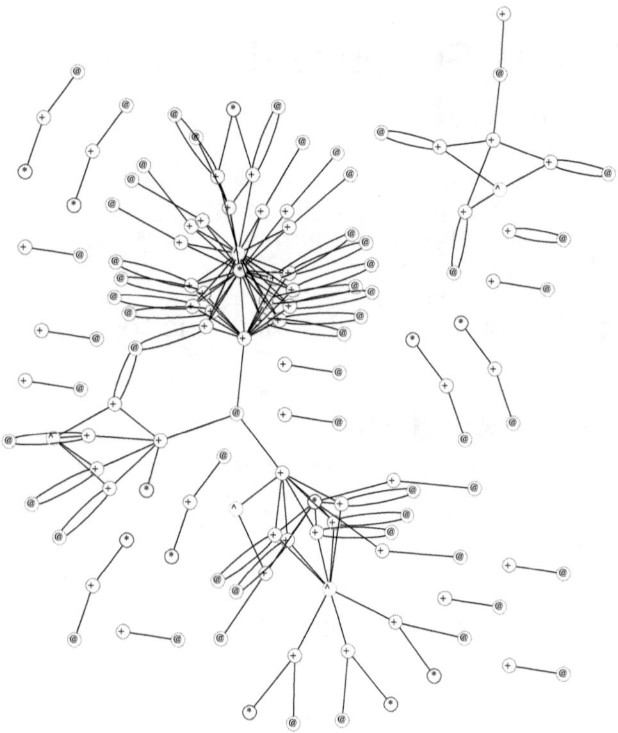

Figure 1: Example of a constrained subgraph for one day and one stock (YHOO). Tweets are presented with red color (+), users are presented with green (@), and URLs with blue (*). Light gray are the similarity nodes (∧)

Our main contributions can be summarized as follows:

- We compare alternative filtering methods to create graphs of postings about a company during a time interval (Section 2). We also present a suite of features that can be computed from these graphs (Section 3).
- We study the correlation of the proposed features with the time series of stock price and traded volume. We also show how these correlations can be stronger or weaker depending on financial indicators of companies, for instance, on their current level of debt (Section 4).
- We perform a study on the application of the correlation patterns found to guide a stock trading strategy. We show that it can lead to a strategy that is competitive when compared to other automatic trading strategies (Section 5).

Roadmap. In Section 2 we discuss the data used in our analysis and the preprocessing steps we performed in order to compute the features. A detailed description of the features we use is given in Section 3. In Section 4 we present correlation results between the proposed features for a company, and the financial time series for its stock, in terms of volume traded or change in price. In Section-5 we discuss how the correlations with price change can be used to develop a trading strategy via simulation. Finally, Section 6 outlines related work, while Section 7 presents our conclusions.

2. DATA PROCESSING

We start our presentation by describing the data used for our analysis, and the processing done in order to compute the features.

2.1 Data acquisition and pre-processing

Stock market data: We obtained stock data from Yahoo! Finance (http://finance.yahoo.com/) for 150 (randomly selected) companies in the S&P 500 index for the first half of 2010. For each stock we recorded the daily closing price and daily traded volume.

Then, we transformed the price series into its daily relative change, i.e., if the series for price is p_i, we used $\frac{p_i - p_{i-1}}{p_{i-1}}$. In the case of traded volume, we normalized by dividing the volume of each day by the mean traded volume observed for that company during the entire half of the year.

Twitter data: We set filters to obtain all the relevant tweets on the first half of 2010. By convention, Twitter in discussions about a stock usually include the stock symbol prefixed by a dollar sign (e.g., $MSFT for Microsoft Corp.). We use a series of regular expressions that find the name of the company, including the company ticker name and hash-tags associated with the company. The expressions were checked manually, looking at the output tweets, to remove those that extracted many spurious tweets. For example, the filter expression for Yahoo is: "#YHOO | $YHOO | #Yahoo".

To refine this expression we randomly selected 30 tweets from each company, and re-wrote the extraction rules for those sets that had less that 50% of tweets related to the company. To be acceptable, tweets should be related to the company, e.g., mentioning their products or their financial situation. When we determined that a rule-based approach was not feasible, we removed the company from our dataset.

For instance, consider the companies with tickers YHOO, AAPL and APOL, for which the extraction rules had to be rewritten. The short name for *Yahoo* is used in many tweets that are related with the news service provided by the same company (Yahoo! News). In the second case, *Apple* is a common noun and is also used widely for spamming purposes ("Win a free iPad" scams). The last company, *Apollo*, is also the name of a deity in Greek mythology and it appears in many context that are unrelated to the stock.

2.2 Graph representation

We represent each collection of filtered tweets as a graph containing different entities the relationships among these entities.

Figure 2 shows the graph schema, which is also described in Table 1. The nodes in this graph are: the tweets themselves, the users who tweet or who are mentioned in the tweets, and the hash-tags and URLs included in the tweets. The relations in this graph are: re-tweets (between two tweets), authorship (between a tweet and its author), hash-tag presence (between a hash-tag and the tweets that contain it), URL presence, (between a URL and the tweets that contain it), etc.

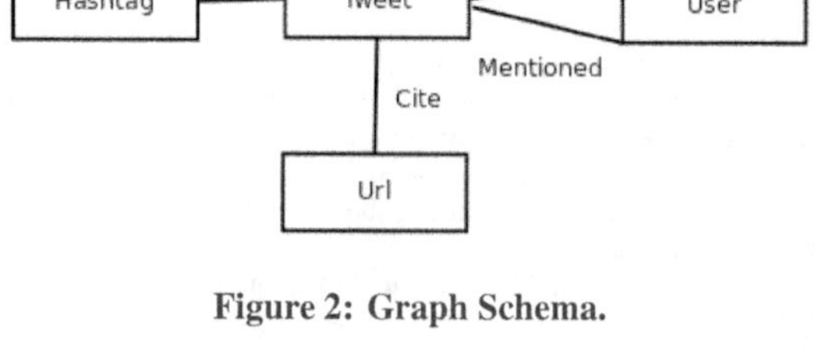

Figure 2: Graph Schema.

Table 1: Schemas.

Nodes	Schema and description
Tweet	(TweetId, Text, Company, Time) A microblog posting
User	(UserId, Name, #Followers, #Friends, Location, Time) A user that posts a tweet or is mentioned
Url	(Url, ExpandedUrl, Time) A URL included in a tweet
Hashtag	(Hashtag, Time) An annotation used in one tweet

Edges	Schema and description
Annotated	(TweetId, Hashtag, Timestamp) Relate a tweet with one hash-tag
Re-tweeted	(RTId, TweetId, Time) Represents the re-tweet action
Mentioned	(TweetId, UserId, Time) A explicit mention of another user
Cited	(TweetId,Url,Time) Connects a URL with tweets including it
Created	(TweetId, UserId, Time) Connects a tweet with its author

HASHTAG	2010-01-28	AAPL	#mkt
TWEET	2010-03-12	AAPL	1XX7XXXXX08
TWEET	2010-03-12	AAPL	1XXX1XXXX11
USER	2010-05-16	AAPL	1XX6XXX83
USER	2010-05-16	AAPL	1XX1XXX2
URL	2010-06-28	AAPL	http://bit.ly/bXXus
URL	2010-06-28	AAPL	http://bit.ly/bXX13
USRMENTION	2010-06-15	AAPL	@CNNMoney

Figure 3: Example nodes (node type, timestamp, stock symbol, node identity) on the constrained graph of a company.

Additionally, nodes and edges have timestamps at a granularity of one day, corresponding to the granularity of our stock-market time series. Tweets are timestamped with the day they were posted. The rest of the nodes are timestamped with the day they were used for the first time in any tweet (i.e., for a user we set as a timestamp his first tweet). As every edge is incident on a tweet we use the timestamp of the tweet for the edge. For re-tweet edges we use the timestamp of the earliest tweet.

Figure 3 shows sample entries of events extracted for the company *Apple*. Each entry corresponds to a node in the constrained graph. For instance, the first line means the hash-tag #mkt was used on Jan 28 by some tweet related to Apple. The last line states that the Twitter account @CNNMoney was mentioned in some tweet related to Apple on June 15.

We are now ready to define the concept of *data graph*.

Definition [Data Graph] The *data graph* $G = (V,E)$ is a graph whose nodes and edges conform to the schemas in Tables 1.

Some statistics on our data graph are shown in Table 2.

We are interested in subgraphs constrained to a particular time interval and/or a particular company. A constrained subgraph, such as the one depicted in Figure 1, is a subgraph $G^c_{t1,t2}$ of G that only contains nodes with timestamps in time interval $[t1,t2]$, and is about company c. Our definition of constrained subgraph is the following.

Table 2: Data graph statistics for the normal and the expanded graph (which is described in Section 4.4)

	Normal	Expanded
Tweets	176 K	26.8 M
Nodes (Tweets+Users+URLs+Hashtags)	640 K	98.9 M
Edges	493 K	76.7 M
Compressed Size	48MB	1.4GB

Definition [Constrained Subgraph] Let G be a data graph. The *constrained subgraph* $G^c_{t1,t2} = (V,E)$ contains the nodes V of G that are either tweets with timestamps in interval $[t1,t2]$, or non-tweet nodes connected through an edge to the selected tweet nodes. All the edges E in G whose end-nodes are in V are added to $G^c_{t1,t2}$.

2.3 Graph post-processing

Most of the information that we include for each node and edge is straightforward to obtain from the Twitter stream. However, there are some data processing aspects that require special handling:

Mapping user names to IDs: The Twitter stream relates the tweets with internal user identifiers, while user mentions are expressed as user names. To match them, we use the Twitter API to resolve the user-id and user-name reference.

URL shortening: A tweet is constrained to 140 characters, so most URLs are shortened using a URL shortening service such as http://bit.ly/. The problem here is that a single URL can be referred to as several different short URLs. We solve this calling the interface of URL shortening services to get the original URLs.

Re-tweets: In the case of re-tweets, in most cases the original tweet of a re-tweet is referenced (by tweet-id). However, we found many cases where the reference to the original tweet is not present. To resolve those cases, instead of using just explicitly referenced re-tweets we augment the graph adding a new *similarity node* (see Figure 1) that links all similar tweets. We define two tweets to be similar if the Jaccard Distance between the bag of words for both tweets is greater than some value α. We set $\alpha = 0.8$ in our experiments, which is a conservative setting, meaning that tweets having this level of similarity are almost always re-tweets or minor variations of each other.

3. FEATURES

We extract two groups of features from the constrained subgraphs: activity features and graph features. Both are listed in Table 3. **Activity features** simply count the number of nodes of a particular type, such as number of tweets, number of users, number of hash-tags, etc. **Graph features** measure properties of the link structure of the graph. For scalability, feature computation is done using Map-Reduce (http://hadoop.apache.org/).

Feature normalization and seasonality: Most of the feature values are normalized to lie in the interval $[0,1]$. For example, if we consider all the constrained subgraphs within a k-days interval, we can normalize the number of tweets on such a subgraph by dividing by the maximum value across all such subgraphs. The same normalization strategy can be used for users and re-tweets. Other features like number of URLs, hash-tags, etc., are normalized using the number of tweets for the full day.

It is important to consider the effect of seasonality in this graph. The number of tweets is increasing (Twitter's user base grew during our observation period) and has a weekly seasonal effect. We normalize the feature values with a time-dependent normalization

Table 3: Features.

Activity features	Description
RTID	number of re-tweets in $G^c_{t1,t2}$
RTU	number of different users that have re-tweeted in $G^c_{t1,t2}$
TGEO	number of tweets with geo-location in $G^c_{t1,t2}$
TID	number of tweets in $G^c_{t1,t2}$
TUSM	number of tweets that mention any user in $G^c_{t1,t2}$
UFRN	average number of friends for user that posted in $G^c_{t1,t2}$
THTG	number of hash-tags used in all the tweets in $G^c_{t_1,t_2}$
TURL	number of tweets with URLs in $G^c_{t_1,t_2}$
UFLW	average number of followers for user that posted in $G^c_{t_1,t_2}$
UID	number different users that posted a tweet in $G^c_{t_1,t_2}$

Graph features	Description
NUM_NODES	number of nodes of $G^c_{t_1,t_2}$
NUM_EDGES	number of edges of $G^c_{t_1,t_2}$
NUM_CMP	number of connected components of $G^c_{t_1,t_2}$
MAX_DIST	maximum diameter for any component of $G^c_{t_1,t_2}$
PAGERANK	statistics on the page rank distribution for $G^c_{t_1,t_2}$ (AVG, STDV, QUARTILES, SKEWNESS, KURTOSIS)
COMPONENT	statistics on the connected component distribution for $G^c_{t_1,t_2}$ (same as above)
DEGREE	statistics on the node degree distribution for $G^c_{t_1,t_2}$ (same as above)

factor that considers seasonality. This factor is proportional to the total number of messages on each day.

4. TIME SERIES CORRELATION

In this section, we start by looking for correlations between the proposed features for a company, and the financial time series for its stock, in terms of volume traded or change in price. Next, we consider how this correlation changes under (*i*) an analysis isolating different types of companies, (*ii*) an analysis aggregating companies into an index, and (*iii*) changes to the filtering strategy.

4.1 Correlation with volume and price

We use the cross-correlation coefficient (CCF) to estimate how variables are related at different time lags. The CCF value at lag τ between two series X, Y, measures the correlation of the first series with respect to the second series shifted by an amount τ. This can be computed as

$$R_{xy}(t,\tau) = \frac{E[Y_{t+\tau}]E[X_t]}{\sigma[Y_{t+\tau}]\sigma[X_t]}.$$

If we find a correlation at a negative lag, this means that the input features could be used to predict the outcome series. Tables 4 and 5 report the average cross-correlation values for traded volume and price respectively, for the 50 companies with most tweets in the observation period, at different lags. We only report the top 5 features for each case, i.e., those having the higher correlation at lag 0. Interestingly, the top features are similar in both lists.

Table 4 shows that the number of components (NUM-CMP) of the constrained sub-graph is the feature that has the best correlation with traded volume. Other good features for this objective are the number of tweets, the number of different users and the total number of nodes on each graph. We also see that there is a positive correlation at lag -1, meaning that these features have some predictive power on the value on the next day. On the other hand, Table 5 shows that the price change is not strongly correlated with any of the proposed features.

Table 4: Average correlation of traded volume and features.

	Lag [days]						
Feature	-3	-2	-1	0	+1	+2	+3
NUM-CMP	0.09	0.11	0.21	0.52	0.33	0.16	0.10
TID	0.09	0.10	0.19	0.49	0.31	0.15	0.09
UID	0.09	0.11	0.21	0.49	0.31	0.15	0.10
NUM-NODES	0.09	0.10	0.20	0.49	0.31	0.15	0.09
NUM-EDGES	0.09	0.09	0.18	0.45	0.29	0.14	0.09

Table 5: Average correlation of price and features.

	Lag [days]						
Feature	-3	-2	-1	0	+1	+2	+3
NUM-CMP	0.08	0.09	0.10	0.13	0.07	0.07	0.07
NUM-NODES	0.07	0.09	0.10	0.11	0.08	0.07	0.07
TID	0.06	0.08	0.07	0.10	0.07	0.08	0.08
UID	0.07	0.08	0.08	0.10	0.07	0.08	0.07
NUM-EDGES	0.07	0.08	0.09	0.10	0.08	0.07	0.06

4.2 Separating companies by type

Figure 4 shows the cross-correlation coefficient (CCF) values for two selected companies (A.I.G. and Teradyne, Inc.) in our data-set. In Figure 4(a) we see a strong correlation of the stock volume with the four best features of Table 4. On the other hand, Figure 4(b) does not show this correlation.

The next question then is to find out factors that affect the correlation between micro-blogging activity and the companies' stock. We obtained a series of financial indicators for each company from Yahoo! Finance. For each such indicator, we separated the 50 companies in 3 quantiles.

The average correlation between NUM-CMP for each group is shown in Table 6, for the five financial indicators that exhibit the largest variance across their three groups. The "bounds" are the cut-off points of the quantiles. The table shows that the correlation is stronger for companies with low debt, regardless of whether their financial indicators are healthy or not. This could be related to stocks that are expected to surge or that may be candidates for short selling. The users' tweets also correlate better with the stocks for

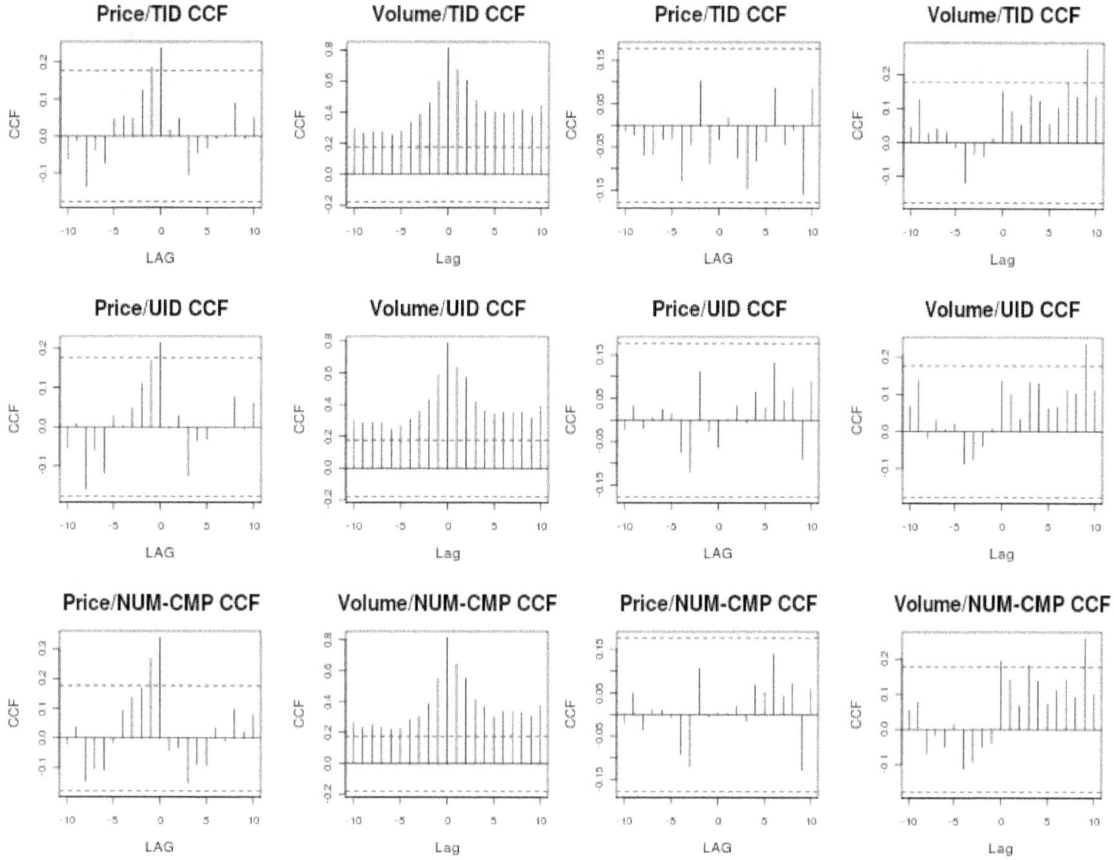

(a) A.I.G. (AIG) (b) Teradyne, Inc. (TER)

Figure 4: Correlations for two different companies.

Table 6: Average correlation of traded volumes for different companies according to several financial indicators. Financial indicators are discretized in 3 quantiles (low, medium, high) according to the bounds shown.

Indicator and bounds	Quantile Low	Medium	High
Current Ratio (mrq) bounds: 1.34,2.39,9.41	0.42	0.62	0.52
Gross Profit (ttm) bounds: \$2B,\$9B,\$103B	0.59	0.54	0.42
Enterprise Value/EBITDA (ttm) bounds: 6.22,11.78,20.21	0.54	0.43	0.59
PEG Ratio (5 yr expected) bounds: 1.04,1.51,35.34	0.51	0.44	0.61
Float bounds: \$272MM,\$914MM,\$10B	0.61	0.46	0.48
Beta bounds: 0.98,1.34,3.95	0.47	0.51	0.58

companies having high beta and low float, again suggesting that Twitter activity seems to be better correlated with traded volume for companies whose finances fluctuate a lot.

4.3 Aggregating companies in an index

In Sections 4.1 and 4.2 we built single-stock constrained sub-graphs, which are often too small to reliably compute graph features like PageRank. In this section, we consider a stocks index I consisting of the $n = 20$ biggest (in terms of market capitalization) companies $c_1, \cdots, c_n$ in our dataset, and build index-based constrained sub-graphs.

We can define the index change for each date d as follows:

$$\text{Idx}(I,d) = \sum_{c \in I} \text{priceChange}(c,d) \cdot \text{weight}(c)$$

where $\text{priceChange}(c,d)$ is the difference between the open and close price for c and d, and the weight is the importance (market capitalization) of each company. In particular, as usually done in financial indexes, we define the importance for each company as:

$$\text{weight}(c) = \frac{\text{MarketCap}(c)}{\max_{c' \in I} \text{MarketCap}(c')} .$$

We also define the index trade volume for a particular date as:

$$\text{VolumeIdx}(I,d) = \sum_{c \in I} \text{volumeTraded}(c,d) \cdot \text{weight}(c) .$$

The index data graph considers the tweets that are posted in the first half of 2010. The graph has 108,702 nodes and 209,714 edges. We repeat the correlation experiments of Section 4.1. The results are shown in Tables 7 and 8. The key difference from Tables 4 and 5 is that in the larger index constrained graphs, graph centrality measures like PAGERANK and DEGREE get more reliable estimations and

Table 7: Correlation of traded volume and features, for a synthetic index of top 20 companies.

Feature	Lag [days]						
	-3	-2	-1	0	+1	+2	+3
NUM-CMP	0.00	0.12	0.20	0.24	0.15	0.26	0.21
P.RANK-AVG	0.03	0.15	0.20	0.24	0.12	0.16	0.14
TID	-0.01	0.14	0.17	0.23	0.19	0.27	0.21
UID	-0.03	0.11	0.15	0.22	0.20	0.26	0.23
NUM-EDGES	0.02	0.12	0.14	0.22	0.19	0.24	0.20

Table 8: Correlation of price change and features, for a synthetic index of top 20 companies.

Feature	Lag [days]						
	-3	-2	-1	0	+1	+2	+3
DEG.-STD	0.08	0.05	0.10	0.12	0.10	0.07	-0.04
DEG.-SKW	0.04	0.02	0.07	0.11	0.06	0.03	0.02
P.RANK-SKW	0.02	0.03	0.08	0.10	0.06	0.02	0.03
DEG.-KURT	0.02	-0.01	0.05	0.10	0.08	0.05	-0.00
P.RANK-STD	0.08	-0.01	0.12	0.09	0.04	-0.03	0.05

are shown to be more strongly correlated to both price and traded volume.

Another interesting observation is that the trading volume is less correlated (Table 7) than in the case of individual stocks (Table 4). We have observed that increases in the activity of some companies is often compensated by the inactivity of others, leading to more stable constrained graphs. In particular, we measured that the variance of the number of connected components, which was the best feature, is lower compared to the average variance for individual companies.

4.4 Modifying the filtering strategy

In Section 2.1 we presented one strategy for filtering the stream. The rationale behind this strategy is that we only focus on tweets related to the financial domain. However, we may end up filtering out some messages that are related to a company but do not mention it explicitly. We study more loose filtering strategies, and obtain negative results: indeed, we degrade the quality of the correlations. We consider the following strategies:

1. **Restricted Graph**: Presented in Section 2.1.

2. **Expanded Graph**: We consider all tweets that: contain the ticker preceded by the $ or # character, or contain the full name of the company, or the short name version after removing common suffixes (e.g., *inc* or *corp*), or the short name as a hash-tag. For instance, for Yahoo! the new expression is: "#YHOO | $YHOO | #Yahoo | Yahoo | Yahoo Inc".

3. **RestExp**: This combines the previous two strategies. We add to the restricted graph the tweets of the expanded graph that are reachable from the nodes of the restricted graph through a path (e.g., through a common author or a re-tweet).

Again we do some visual inspections in a small sample to see if the rules were related with the company. If a rule was very generic (ambiguous) we remove it. For example for the company *APOL* we remove the rules that use *APOLO* as short name. The expanded graph size is shown in Table 2; it has about 150 times more nodes and edges than the normal graph for the same period of time.

The restricted graph is more precise than the expanded graph, but has lower recall. The expanded graph is more noisy, as it may contain many tweets that are related to spam, common conversation (e.g., "I want to eat an apple") or tweets related to non-financial discussions (e.g., complaints about customer service).

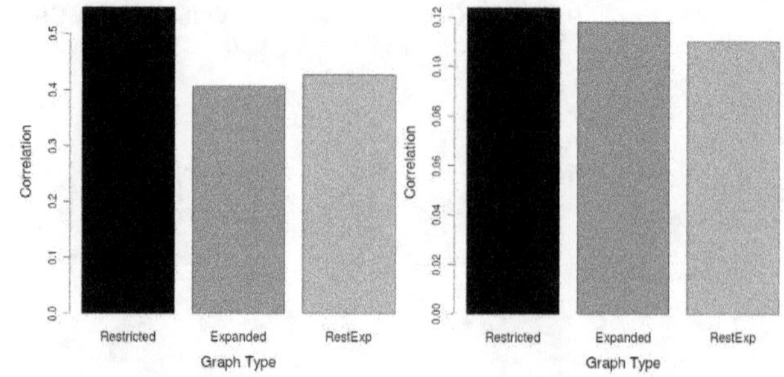

(a) Traded volume. (b) Price change.

Figure 5: Microblogging activity for different strategies, correlated with (a) traded volume (b) price change.

Figure 5 compares the volume and price correlation with the number of components (NUM-CMP), for the different filtering strategies. We observe that the restricted graph strategy has the best correlation, despite its smaller size. Using this expansion strategy of the graph, we add more noise than useful tweets.aaa

5. SIMULATION

In this section we study whether the correlation with price change can be used to develop a trading strategy in the stock market. We simulate daily trading [5, 22, 25] of stocks and try to predict the final price on each day of the simulation. We compare various trading strategies included simple regression models, augmented regression, random and fixed selection.

5.1 Strategies

We model an automated investor who buys and sells stock. The behavior model for this investor is the following:

1. The investor starts with an initial capital endowment C_0.

2. In the morning of every day t, she buys K different stocks using all of the available capital C_t. The investor uses various algorithms to select which stocks to buy and how many shares to buy from each of them. The companies in our simulated stock market are the same random selection from the S&P500 described in Section 2

3. The investor holds the stocks all day long.

4. She sells all the stocks at the closing time of day t. The amount she obtains will be her new capital C_{t+1} and will be used again in step 2. This process finishes on the last day of the simulation.

5. We compare the final capital against the initial investment. We plot the percent of money win or lossed each day against the original investment.

This simple simulation does not consider external effects like deficit of stocks, or the possibility of selling the stocks at the final price. Our aim is to determine if the proposed Twitter features have the potential of improving over other baseline strategies. The stock selection algorithms evaluated are the following:

Random: the investor selects K stocks at random each morning. To diversify the investment the amount of money invested in each stock is C_t/K (uniformly shared).

Fixed: the investor picks K stocks using a particular financial indicator (market capitalization, company size, total debt) and buys

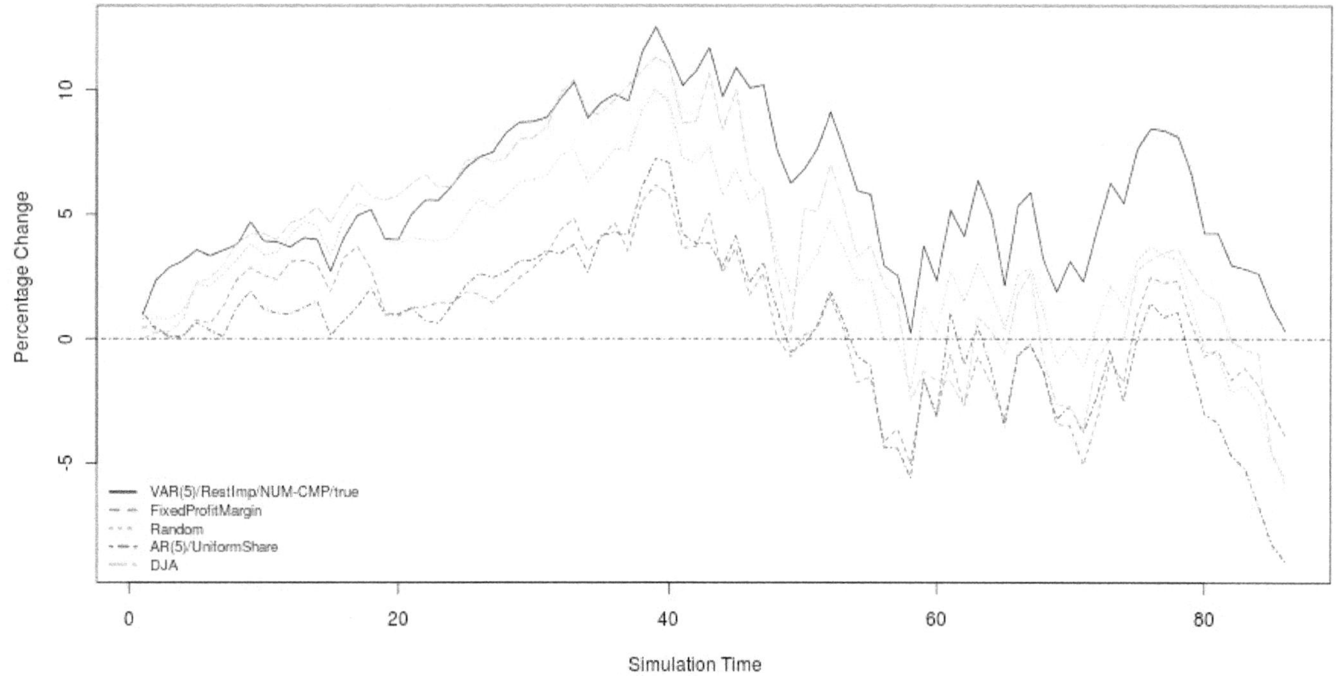

Figure 6: Simulation results for different trading strategies.

from the same companies every day. To diversify the investment the amount of money invested in each stock is C_t/K (uniformly shared).

Auto Regression: the investor buys the K stocks whose price changes will be larger, predicted using an auto-regression ($AR(s)$) model. This model predicts the price x_t of a company at time t using a linear combination of the price in the previous s days:

$$x_t = a_1 x_{t-1} + a_2 x_{t-1} \ldots a_m x_{t-m} + c,$$

where each a_i are the parameters of model and c is a constant. Parameters are learned with simple linear regression on a provided training data of L samples.

To diversify the market we have two options: the first one is the uniform split which we already discussed and the second one weighs each stock using the predicted price change. This last strategy is consistent with a very simple heuristic used for the bin packing problem where we prefer those items with high price-weight ratio. In our case:

$$weight = \frac{\text{price difference}}{\text{open price}}.$$

Twitter-Augmented Regression: the investor buys the best K stocks that are predicted using a vector auto-regressive (VAR(s)) model. This model considers, in addition to the price of the previous days, a Twitter feature (e.g., number of components) as observed in the previous days. The model predicts the price of a stock at time t using a linear combination of the price in the previous s days and the values of the augmenting series (Twitter feature) in the same dates:

$$x_t = a_1 x_{t-1} + a_1 x_{t-1} \ldots a_m x_{t-m} + \\ b_1 y_{t-1} + y_2 x_{t-1} \ldots y_m x_{t-m} + c.$$

Training details are similar to the one discussed for the $AR(s)$ model. The strategies to diversify are also the same (uniform and weighted).

5.2 Results

We simulate a series of investments between March 1, 2010 and June 30, 2010. We use the data from January 1, 2010 to February 28, 2010 as training data for the regression models. We keep a window of $L = 35$ training examples and use the previous $s = 5$ days to train. Each model is trained using the Ordinary Least Squares (OLS) method. The initial capital is $C_0 = 10000\$$. The investor buys stock from $K = 10$ different companies every day in every strategy.

For the Twitter-Augmented Regression we use the following features: TID, UID, NUM-CMP, NUM-NODES,NUM-EDGES. We use all the graphs that were described in Section 4.4. We also try the weighed and uniform share options for both the the AR and VAR model.

Figure 6 shows the simulation results for the discussed period. We show the behavior of a sample of all trading techniques discussed: specifically, we show the best approach for each category (e.g., for Twitter-Augmented Regression we only show the behavior of the NUM-CMP feature). Our two baselines for the rest of the discussion are the random strategy and the Auto-Regression strategy. The average loss for the random strategy is -5.52% and the one for the AR models are -8.9% (Uniform) and -13.08% (Weighted). Only one of the fixed models (Profit Margin) have a better behavior than the default random (-3.8%). All the rest of the models that improve the baseline are VAR models. The best one uses the number of tweets on the RestExp graph with a uniform share for a 0.32% gain. The models obtained with the restricted graph and number of components average a -2.4% loss that is still better that the random model.

Figure 6 also includes the Dow Jones Index Average (*DJA*) for the same period. As we can see the behavior of all the strategies is consistent with this index's behavior. Our proposed strategy is the only ones that manages to obtain a profit during this period in which the Dow Jones fell -5.8%. The best feature is again the number of components.

6. RELATED WORK

Microblogging data: In recent years several studies (e.g. [17, 19, 16]) have analyzed Twitter data to describe the different types of users, their behavior, the content of the tweets and the way that they are related to trends. In particular, [21] describe the relationship between tweets and trends in traditional news media, as well as query volume on major search engines. Our work is informed by this general knowledge about Twitter, but we focus our attention in a particular domain instead of attempting a general study.

The relations among users, entities and topics in Twitter have been described by a graph and exploited in previous work. For instance, [31] starts by identifying similar users based on their favorite topics and their social connections. Then, a modified version of PageRank is used to find the most influential authors on the Twitter graph. Yamaguchi et al. [32] extend the "Object Rank Algorithm" [1] to consider different types of vertices. These works only consider a fixed point in time and do not consider the changes on the graph structure over time.

News articles and the stock market: The literature relating news stories with financial events is vast. Here we outline some recent works on the subject. Hayo and Kutan [15] present a pure economic prediction model to study the effect of other markets on the Russian market. A variable in this model defines if the news were positive or negative in the past. Although the news classification is manual this study shows the importance of news on the market behavior.

Lavrenko et al. [23] present a model to predict the behavior of the stock of a company using news stories related to the company. The system builds a language model for positive and negative stories and predicts the future behavior checking the language model of the news that appear in the previous hours. Our work does not pretend to be a prediction model: we measure the correlation of the behavior of Twitter with the changes in the stock market. Schumaker and Chen [26] present a system that learns the importance of a news on the performance of a stock. Again, compared with this work we do not try to make a prediction but find a explanation of the change. Moreover, we use microblogging posts instead of news stories. DeChoudhury et al. [7] shows that discussions on blogpost are also correlated with the directions of the stock market.

Yi [33] presents a study to approximate the daily closing value of a stock using data from Twitter. This work also discusses several feature that can be used in the prediction and presents a model that can improve a simple moving average, reducing the error. Sprenger and Welpe [27] and Bollen et al. [3] also show the relations of the stock market or particular stocks with the sentiment of the tweets and how it can be used to improve the prediction. None of this work considers graph features.

Time series regression from Web data: The use of web data for predicting the behavior of a real time series is related with our work. Ginsberg et al. [12] present a method to approximate the cases of influenza of the US using the query log of a search engine. Corley et al. [6] makes a similar prediction using blog content. Other work [8] use search logs to predict the job market.

Hagedorn et al. [13] argue that while these prediction models are correct, they are not really competitive or add any information when compared with models that use domain knowledge. Their application on prediction of music, video games and movie hits shows that other, better-known and simple features are good enough.

Gayo et al. [11] have similar objections, and in addition show evidence of differences between the distribution of demographic characteristics of Twitter users from a country compared to the general population of that country. These differences are substantial and make it impossible to obtain a uniform random sampling of e.g. citizens voting in an ellection. Furthermore, Gayo [10] warns against jumping to conclusions too quickly when analyzing social media data, reminding that "just being large does not make such collections statistically representative of the population as a whole".

Data filtering and spam removal: The filtering of data can have an important effect in the performance of our method. This problem can be divided in two parts: finding related tweets and removing those that are spam.

In [14] the authors propose a supervised multi-classifier that can distinguish if an RSS feed is related with a particular company. We can use this kind of strategy to find better filters. Finin et al. [9] propose crowdsourcing strategies to annotate the entities that appear in the tweets. This knowledge could be used later to train Name Entity Recognizers that can be adapted to the particular twitter characteristics.

Our work could be extended by leveraging features used in the elimination of spam from tweets. Wang [30] and Benevenuto et al. [2] present features that can be used to detect spammers and how they differ from relevant users. Castillo et al. [4] go farther as they study the veracity of tweets for particular events. We think that our work can be improved if we utilize this knowledge to improve the filtering phase.

(Dynamic) graph features: The graph-based features we use are a subset of those present in previous work [18, 24]. We can extend our work by including more graph features. For instance, Kumar et al. [20] present a work on the evolution of social networks in the blogosphere. This work shows that there are changes on the structure that are related with changes in the real world. Other works [29, 28] propose algorithms to mine patterns on massive data graphs. In particular [28] shows how the structure of the graph changes over time.

7. CONCLUSIONS

We presented a framework to extract messages from Twitter about company stocks, and represent that information through graphs capturing different aspects of the conversation around those stocks.

We then used these time-constrained graphs to evaluate a wide range of features in terms of their degree of correlation to changes in stock price and traded volume. We show that the number of connected components of the constrained subgraph is generally the best feature in terms of correlation, especially in relation to traded volume. Graph centrality features like PageRank and average degree become effective for bigger graphs, which can be obtained for multi-company indexes.

Finally, we used simulation to show that these features are useful in order to improve a trading strategy in the stock market.

8. ACKNOWLEDGMENTS

Eduardo Ruiz and Vagelis Hristidis were supported in part by National Science Foundation grants OISE-0730065, IIS-0811922, IIS-0952347 and CNS-1126619. Carlos Castillo, Aristides Gionis and Alejandro Jaimes were partially supported by the Torres Quevedo Program of the Spanish Ministry of Science and Innovation, co-funded by the European Social Fund, and by the Spanish Centre for the Development of Industrial Technology under the CENIT program, project CEN-20101037, "Social Media" (http://www.cenitsocialmedia.es/).

9. REFERENCES

[1] A. Balmin, V. Hristidis, and Y. Papakonstantinou. Objectrank: authority-based keyword search in databases. In *Proceedings of the 13th international conference on Very Large Data Bases*, pages 564–575, 2004.

[2] F. Benevenuto, G. Magno, T. Rodrigues, and V. Almeida. Detecting Spammers on Twitter. *Collaboration, Electronic messaging, Anti-Abuse and Spam Conference (CEAS)*, 2010.

[3] J. Bollen, H. Mao, and X.-J. Zeng. Twitter mood predicts the stock market. *Journal of Computational Science*, abs/1010.3003, 2010.

[4] C. Castillo, M. Mendoza, and B. Poblete. Information Credibility on Twitter. In *Proceedings of World Wide Web Conference (WWW)*, 2011.

[5] A.-S. Chen, M. T. Leung, and H. Daouk. Application of neural networks to an emerging financial market: forecasting and trading the taiwan stock index. *Computers & Operations Research*, 30(6):901 – 923, 2003.

[6] C. Corley, A. R. Mikler, K. P. Singh, and D. J. Cook. Monitoring influenza trends through mining social media. In *BIOCOMP*, pages 340–346, 2009.

[7] M. DeChoudhury, H. Sundaram, A. John, and D. D. Seligmann. Can blog communication dynamics be correlated with stock market activity? In *Proceedings of the 20th ACM conference on Hypertext and Hypermedia*, 2008.

[8] M. Ettredge, J. Gerdes, and G. Karuga. Using web-based search data to predict macroeconomic statistics. *Communications of the ACM*, 48:87–92, 2005.

[9] T. Finin, W. Murnane, A. Karandikar, N. Keller, J. Martineau, and M. Dredze. Annotating named entities in twitter data with crowdsourcing. In *Proceedings of the NAACL HLT 2010 Workshop on Creating Speech and Language Data with Amazon's Mechanical Turk*, pages 80–88, 2010.

[10] D. Gayo-Avello. A warning against converting social media into the next literary digest. *Communications of the ACM*, 2011.

[11] D. Gayo-Avello, P. T. Metaxas, and E. Mustafaraj. Limits of electoral predictions using twitter. In *International AAAI Conference on Weblogs and Social Media (posters)*, 2011.

[12] J. Ginsberg, M. H. Mohebbi, R. S. Patel, L. Brammer, M. S. Smolinski, and L. Brilliant. Detecting influenza epidemics using search engine query data. *Nature*, 457(7232):1012–1014, 2009.

[13] S. Goel, J. M. Hofman, S. Lahaie, D. M. Pennock, and D. J. Watts. Whata can search predict? In *Proceedings of World Wide Web Conference (WWW)*, 2010.

[14] B. A. Hagedorn, M. Ciaramita, and J. Atserias. World knowledge in broad-coverage information filtering. In *Proceedings of the 30th annual International ACM SIGIR Conference on Research and Development in Information Retrieval*, pages 801–802, 2007.

[15] B. Hayo and A. M. Kutan. The impact of news, oil prices, and global market developments on russian financial markets. *The Economics of Transition*, 13(2):373–393, 2005.

[16] B. A. Huberman, D. M. Romero, and F. Wu. Social networks that matter: Twitter under the microscope. *First Monday*, 14(1), 2009.

[17] A. Java, X. Song, T. Finin, and B. Tseng. Why we twitter: understanding microblogging usage and communities. In *Proceedings of the 9th WebKDD and 1st SNA-KDD 2007 workshop on Web mining and social network analysis*, pages 56–65, 2007.

[18] J. M. Kleinberg, R. Kumar, P. Raghavan, S. Rajagopalan, and A. S. Tomkins. The web as a graph: measurements, models, and methods. In *Proceedings of the 5th annual international conference on Computing and combinatorics*, pages 1–17, 1999.

[19] B. Krishnamurthy, P. Gill, and M. Arlitt. A few chirps about twitter. In *Proceedings of the First Workshop on Online Social Networks*, pages 19–24, 2008.

[20] R. Kumar, J. Novak, P. Raghavan, and A. Tomkins. Structure and evolution of blogspace. *Communications of the ACM*, 47:35–39, December 2004.

[21] H. Kwak, C. Lee, H. Park, and S. Moon. What is twitter, a social network or a news media? In *Proceedings of the 19th international conference on World wide web*, pages 591–600, 2010.

[22] V. Lavrenko, M. Schmill, D. Lawrie, P. Ogilvie, D. Jensen, and J. Allan. Language models for financial news recommendation. In *Proceedings of the 9th international conference on Information and knowledge management*, pages 389–396, 2000.

[23] V. Lavrenko, M. Schmill, D. Lawrie, P. Ogilvie, D. Jensen, and J. Allan. Mining of concurrent text and time series. In *Proceedings of the 6th ACM SIGKDD International Conference on Knowledge Discovery and Data Mining Workshop on Text Mining*, pages 37–44, 2000.

[24] M. E. J. Newman. The structure and function of complex networks. *SIAM Review*, 45(2):167–256, 2003.

[25] T. Preis and H. E. Stanley. Trend switching processes in financial markets. In *Econophysics Approaches to Large-Scale Business Data and Financial Crisis*, pages 3–26. 2010.

[26] R. P. Schumaker and H. Chen. Textual analysis of stock market prediction using breaking financial news: The azfin text system. *ACM Transaction Information Systems*, 27:12:1–12:19, 2009.

[27] T. O. Sprenger and I. M. Welpe. Tweets and trades: The information content of stock micrologs. Work in progress in Social Science Research Network.

[28] J. Sun, C. Faloutsos, S. Papadimitriou, and P. S. Yu. Graphscope: parameter-free mining of large time-evolving graphs. In *Proceedings of the 13th ACM SIGKDD international conference on Knowledge discovery and data mining*, pages 687–696, 2007.

[29] H. Tong, S. Papadimitriou, J. Sun, P. S. Yu, and C. Faloutsos. Colibri: fast mining of large static and dynamic graphs. In *Proceeding of the 14th ACM SIGKDD International Conference on Knowledge Discovery and Data Mining*, pages 686–694, 2008.

[30] A. H. Wang. Don't follow me - spam detection in twitter. In *SECRYPT'10*, pages 142–151, 2010.

[31] J. Weng, E.-P. Lim, J. Jiang, and Q. He. Twitterrank: finding topic-sensitive influential twitterers. In *Proceedings of the 3rd ACM International Conference on Web Search and Data Mining*, pages 261–270, 2010.

[32] Y. Yamaguchi, T. Takahashi, T. Amagasa, and H. Kitagawa. Turank: Twitter user ranking based on user-tweet graph analysis. In *Web Information Systems Engineering-WISE 2010*, pages 240–253. 2010.

[33] A. Yi. Stock market prediction based on public attentions: a social web mining approach. Master's thesis, University of Edinburgh, 2009.

Harmony and Dissonance: Organizing the People's Voices on Political Controversies

Rawia Awadallah
Max-Planck Institute for Informatics
Saarbruecken, Germany
rawadall@mpi-inf.mpg.de

Maya Ramanath
Indian Institute of Technology, Delhi
New Delhi, India
ramanath@cse.iitd.ac.in

Gerhard Weikum
Max-Planck Institute for Informatics
Saarbruecken, Germany
weikum@mpi-inf.mpg.de

ABSTRACT

To understand the landscape of opinions on political controversies, it would be helpful to know which politician or other stakeholder takes which position - support or opposition - on specific aspects of these topics. We present a system, named OpinioNetIt, which aims to automatically derive a map of the opinions-people network from news and other Web documents. We build this network in four stages. First, we start with a few generic seeds to identify phrases denoting controversial topics from text. These phrases are then automatically organized and mapped into a DAG of topics. Second, opinion holders are identified for each topic, and their opinions (support or oppose) are extracted. Third, the acquired topics and opinion holders are used to construct a lexicon of phrases indicating support or opposition. Finally, we iterate this process, using the richer lexicon to identify more opinion holders, opinions and topics. We present a systematic evaluation which shows the high accuracy of OpinioNetIt. We also present use-case scenarios for identifying flip-flop politicians who change their opinions on the same topic, and for discovering people with divergent opinions on otherwise highly correlated topics.

Categories and Subject Descriptors

H.3.1 [**Information Storage and Retrieval**]: Content Analysis and Indexing—*Linguistic Processing*

General Terms

Algorithms, Experimentation

Keywords

Web Information Extraction, Political Opinion Mining

1. INTRODUCTION

1.1 Motivation

The crises in Libya and Syria, the debates about the economic crisis in Greece, and the downrating of the USA's creditworthiness are some of the controversial topics being played on the news everyday. Each of these topics has many different aspects, and there is no absolute, simple truth in answering questions such as: should the EU guarantee the financial stability of each member country, or should the countries themselves be solely responsible? To understand the landscape of opinions, it would be helpful to know which politician or other stakeholder takes which position - support or opposition - on these aspects of controversial topics. In order to navigate and analyze this complicated landscape of issues and opinions, it would be helpful if there were an *"opinion-base"* that organized controversial topics according to their various facets and stored information about who expressed an opinion on one or more topics and supported or opposed a certain direction.

This envisioned network goes beyond state-of-the-art sentiment mining in several ways. First, political controversies are much more complex and opinions are often expressed in subtle forms, which makes determining pro/con polarities much more difficult than with product reviews for cameras, movies, etc. - the typical objects in prior work on opinion mining [16, 13]. Second, most prior research focused on classifying individual sentences or reviews into pro/con categories or on aggregating (summarizing) opinions over a large number of observations (e.g., many different customers' reviews of some product). In contrast, our goal is to connect an opinion to an individual person (typically a politician) who expressed this position (multiple times, but often in very different wordings). Third, instead of merely finding a few or the most interesting pairs of opinion holders and topics, we aim at a systematic network of opinion holders and pro/con statements for a wide variety of fine-grained controversial topics. To the best of our knowledge, no prior work has addressed political opinion analysis in a similarly comprehensive manner.

Facet	Canonical Name
use of force against civilians in Libya	Muammer Gaddafi's response to the Libyan civil war
using military force against the regime of the Libyan leader	Military Action in Libya
No-Fly Zone over Libya	Military Action in Libya

Table 1: Example facets extracted for "Libyan Civil War"

⟨Nicolas Sarkozy⟩ ⟨support⟩ ⟨Military Action in Libya⟩
⟨Dmitry Medvedev⟩ ⟨oppose⟩ ⟨Muammer Gaddafi's Respponse to the Libyan Civil War⟩
⟨Angela Merkel⟩ ⟨support⟩ ⟨Military Action in Libya⟩

Table 2: Opinions about "Libyan Civil War"

In this paper, we present our system, called *OpinioNetIt* (pronounced similar to "opinionated"), which aims at building such an opinion-base for controversial topics by extracting and organizing information from online sources on the Web. For example, the first

Permission to make digital or hard copies of all or part of this work for personal or classroom use is granted without fee provided that copies are not made or distributed for profit or commercial advantage and that copies bear this notice and the full citation on the first page. To copy otherwise, to republish, to post on servers or to redistribute to lists, requires prior specific permission and/or a fee.
WSDM'12, February 8–12, 2012, Seattle, Washington, USA.
Copyright 2012 ACM 978-1-4503-0747-5/12/02 ...$10.00.

column of Table 1 shows some of the facets extracted by our system regarding the "Libyian Civil War". The outcome of analyzing these inputs should be a crisp set of structured records of the form: *person* (opinion holder), *polarity* (support/oppose), and *topic facet* (fine-grained controversial topic). Table 2 shows examples of people's opinions about various topic facets of the controversy. For example, ⟨Angela Merkel⟩ ⟨support⟩ ⟨Military Action in Libya⟩ could be a result in canonicalized form. This desired output involves aggregating statements, but only for the same pair of opinion holder and topic facet. The overall set of such records forms the OpinioNetIt network.

The challenge in building this network lies in the fact that the input is merely natural-language text, such as news articles, where it is difficult to spot phrases that denote individual politicians or controversial topics and map them into a canonical representation. For example, the opinions of Table 2, are extracted from text where the entity Vladimir Putin is mentioned several times with different wordings like "Mr. Putin", "the Russian President", "President Putin"etc. The same language diversity and ambiguity applies to the topic facets that we aim to detect and organize. Thus, the entire problem can be seen as an interleaved task of fact extraction, entity resolution, and opinion assessment.

1.2 Approach and Contribution

OpinioNetIt currently taps into 5 online news sources: Google News, Al-Jazeera, BBC, CNN, New York Times, and Wikipedia, and extracts 4-tuples of the following form:

⟨person⟩ ⟨support/oppose⟩ ⟨topic⟩*[⟨context⟩]*

where the triple: ⟨person⟩ ⟨support/oppose⟩ ⟨topic⟩ is extracted from the textual *context*.

We specifically choose the triple+context format since it is compatible with the RDF data model and recent efforts to extend RDF with contextual information [6]. The advantage of using RDF is that SPARQL, the query language for RDF, can be used to query the system. Queries of the form: "who opposes the military action in Libya", "who supports Muammer Gaddafi's respponse to the Libyan rebels", etc. can now be processed by the system.

Although our input is currently limited to 5 sources, our methods easily extend to additional Web sources. Our approach is to generate search-engine queries with site scope restricted to each of our sources, and extract opinions from the snippets returned by the search engine. The extraction is carried out in the following stages (see Figure 1 for an overview).

1. Acquisition and Organization of Topics: First, we manually construct a small list of seed patterns consisting of phrases denoting support and opposition. We query the Web with these seeds and acquire result snippets from the 5 sources listed previously. We then parse the snippets and extract phrases which correspond to facets of a controversial topic. Once we acquire a large number these phrases, we map them onto canonical topics and organize these in a topic hierarchy.

2. Acquiring Opinion Holders: Second, from the collected snippets, we identify opinion holders by deep natural-language parsing and judiciously designed heuristics. One of the assets harnessed here is the YAGO knowledge base [18] which provides us with many name variants and paraphrases of individual entities.

3. Building the Support/Oppose Lexicon: Third, given the facet and an opinion holder, we again query the Web and build a lexicon of support and oppose phrases. Some examples of such phrases are: "strongly against" (for oppose) and "acknowledged the validity of" (for support), etc.

4. Gathering More Opinions: Finally, by using the lexicon of support/oppose phrases as new seeds, we close the loop: we go back to the first step and iteratively acquire more topics and opinion holders, thus building the final OpinioNetIt network.

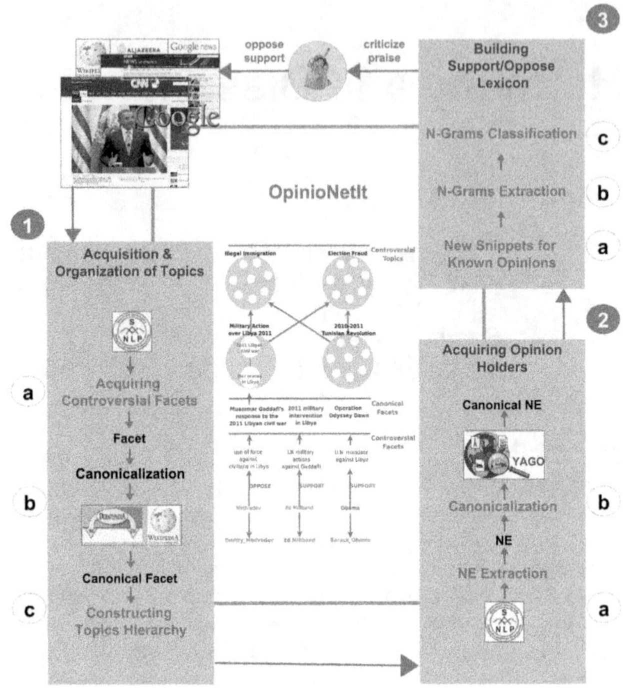

Figure 1: System architecture.

The contribution of this paper is the methodology for constructing this new style of opinion-base, like OpinioNetIt, which consists of controversial topics and their various facets and the people who hold opinions on it. We restrict our opinions to be of two types: support and oppose. Our methodology for achieving this makes use of a variety of building blocks and combines them in an innovative way. In particular, we integrate techniques for pattern-based information extraction with polarity classification, both customized to our setting of fine-grained political controversies. We present an experimental evaluation of our methods, and show that we achieve an overall precision of 72% on the extracted opinions. We also present experimental comparisons for alternative algorithms used in critical components (e.g. organizing facets and topics). Finally, we show use-case scenarios for identifying flip-flop politicians who change their opinions on the same topic, and for discovering people with divergent opinions on otherwise highly correlated topics.

The rest of the paper is organized as follows. Section 2 introduces our computational model. The different stages of our approach: acquiring and organizing controversial facets is in Section 3, identifying opinion holders is in Section 4, and building the support/oppose lexicon is in Section 5. The system implementation is described in Section 6. Section 7 presents our experimental evaluation, and Section 8 discusses use cases. Section 9 positions our contributions with regard to related work, and we conclude with Section 10.

2. COMPUTATIONAL MODEL

Our first major goal is to acquire politically controversial topics and to organize them into a hierarchy. For example, both "sanctions against Iran" as well as "military strikes on Iran" are different *facets* of the debate on "Iran's nuclear program" which in turn can be regarded as being a part of a larger debate on "nuclear power". Similarly, "Japan's nuclear disaster" is also part of the debate on "nuclear power". Constructing such a hierarchy, however, presents challenges. First, we have to acquire facets which are politically controversial. Second, since each facet can be expressed in different ways, we have to *canonicalize* these facets. That is, "military strikes against Iran" and "military action on Iran" are different ways of expressing the same topic and need to have a canonical form. Third, once we have canonical forms we need to identify the topics to which they belong. Before we describe each of these components in detail in Section 3, we first explain more precisely what we mean by terms such as "topic", "facet", etc. and formally define our goal.

A *topic* is informally defined as the subject matter of a particular piece of text. A *controversial topic* is a topic on which drastically varying opinions exist among people. A topic can be divided into a number of *subtopics* each of which can themselves be divided further. At the most basic level, we deal with *facets* (also referred to as *raw facets*) of a topic (or subtopic) and consider facets to be indivisible. Intuitively, the set of topics, subtopics and facets form a hierarchy.

With this understanding of the terms *topic*, *subtopic* and *facet*, we now introduce some formal terminology.

DEFINITION 2.1. *A* **facet** *f_i is denoted by a string $str(f_i)$. Examples of facets on the controversial topic "Iran's Nuclear Program, 2010" include "military strikes on Iran" and "sanctions on Iran". We use the term* facet name *to refer to $str(f_i)$.*

DEFINITION 2.2. *A* **canonicalized facet** *F_i, denoted by a string $str(F_i)$ corresponds to a set of facets $S(F_i) = \{f_1, f_2, \ldots, f_k\}$ where each f_j has the same semantic meaning. For example, "military strikes on Iran" and "military action against Iran" are both semantically the same and we may choose the former as the canonical form. Unless mentioned otherwise, we simply use the term "facet" to mean "canonicalized facet". We also use the term* canonicalized facet name *to refer to $str(F_i)$.*

DEFINITION 2.3. *A* **topic** *$T = \{Q_1, Q_2, \ldots, Q_n\}$ where Q_i denotes a facet or a subtopic. As an example, "Nuclear Proliferation" may have subtopics such as "Iran's Nuclear Program, 2010", "Nuclear Non-Proliferation Treaty", etc. And "Iran's Nuclear Program, 2010" in turn has facets such as "military strikes on Iran" and "sanctions on Iran". We denote the set of* all *topics, subtopics and facets by $\mathcal{T}$.*

DEFINITION 2.4. *An* **opinion holder** *P for a topic T or a facet f is an entity such as a person, organization or government that holds an opinion on T or f. We denote the set of all opinion holders as $\mathcal{P} = \{P_1, P_2, \ldots, P_n\}$.*

DEFINITION 2.5. *A* **topic hierarchy** *is a DAG consisting of topics, subtopics and facets. Formally, let $TH = \{V, E\}$, where $V = \{v_i | v_i \in \mathcal{T}\}$ and $E = \{(v_i, v_j) | v_j$ is a subtopic or facet of $v_i\}$.*

DEFINITION 2.6. *An* **opinion fact** *is denoted by:*
⟨P⟩ ⟨support/oppose⟩ ⟨Q⟩{⟨context⟩}
where the triple: ⟨P⟩ ⟨support/oppose⟩ ⟨Q⟩ is extracted from the textual context *and $P \in \mathcal{P}$ denotes the entity holding an opinion on $Q \in \mathcal{T}$.*

DEFINITION 2.7. *An* **opinion network** *is a node- and edge-labeled, directed graph $ON = (V, E, C)$ where $V = \{v_i | v_i \in \mathcal{T} \cup \mathcal{P}\}$ and $E = \{(v_i, v_j, l) | v_i \in \mathcal{P} \cup \mathcal{T}, v_j \in \mathcal{T}, l \in \{support, oppose, \epsilon\}\}$ and $C : E \rightarrow \{str_1, str_2, ..., str_n\}$ maps each edge to a context.*

The topic hierarchy TH is part of the opinion network (therefore, we have edges with both endpoints in $\mathcal{T}$ and with empty labels). Note that the triples *in* opinion facts *each correspond to a labeled edge in the graph and the mapping C associates each triple to its context.*

3. FACETS AND TOPICS

In this section, we describe our solutions to the problem of acquiring politically controversial topics and organizing them into a hierarchy.

3.1 Acquiring Controversial Facets

Our aim is to collect a large number of opinions (high recall). While using Wikipedia was an option we considered, we felt that comprehensive coverage of topics would be possible only on the Web. Therefore, we decided to use the Web to gather a large number of topics and opinions, while Wikipedia was used as a resource to help organize the topics.

Our initial approach to acquiring a candidate set of controversial facet used only two seed patterns: "support" and "oppose". These two patterns were fired as queries to a search engine and the resulting snippets were gathered. We parsed the individual sentences in each snippet using the Stanford parser [12] in order to identify phrases corresponding to facets. However, this initial approach proved insufficient for two reasons. First, simple "support" and "oppose" are not specific enough to i) return only political topics, and ii) return topics on which a *person* (or organization) could have an opinion. Second, simply firing these queries on the Web often returns snippets which are very difficult or even impossible to correctly parse (e.g., user comments in forums).

In order to solve the first problem, we refined our seed patterns. To ensure that the facets returned were those for which people could have opinions, we used the patterns "he supports" and "he opposes" (and their female counterparts). In order to keep the focus on political topics, we added the patterns "he voted for", "he voted against" on the intuition that most "voting" typically takes place in political forums. For the second problem of bad snippets, our pragmatic approach is to still query the Web, but limit the sites from which results are obtained. Our current sources are: Google News, Al-Jazeera, BBC, CNN, New York Times, and Wikipedia.

3.2 Canonicalization of Facets

Once the raw facets are collected, we organize them in two ways. First, in order to ensure uniformity in referring to semantically equivalent facets (e.g., "financial aid for Greece" and "EU loan to Greece" are equivalent), we automatically derive canonical names. Second, for convenient exploration and knowledge discovery at different granularities, we impose a topic hierarchy on the canonicalized facets. This subsection discusses our approach to the first issue, the second issue is addressed in Subsection 3.3. Figure 2 shows an example of what the final hierarchy looks like in the context of the recent Libyan crisis. Some of the raw facets we acquired are shown in blue (bottom level of the hierarchy) and include a variety of facets: "U.N. Mandate against Libya", "use of force against civilians in Libya", etc. These raw facets are then canonicalized to "2011 military intervention in Libya" and "Gaddafi's response to the 2011 Libyan Civil War" respectively which in turn are part of the larger topic "2011 Libyan Civil War".

For canonicalizing facets, we devised a *two-phase mapping technique*, based on Wikipedia and Debatepedia (`debatepedia.org`). Debatepedia consists of ca. 1700 debates organized into ca. 1300 topics such as Iranian nuclear crisis, Abortion, Homosexuality, etc. Each topic consists of a number of debates – for example, "Abortion" has debates on "Women's rights", "Fetus' rights" "Birth control", etc. The rationale for using both Debatepedia and Wikipedia is as follows. Debatepedia is focused on political controversies but not that large, whereas Wikipedia is much richer but controversial topics are only a small part of it. We use Debatepedia as a bootstrapping asset to focus on controversies, but eventually map facets to Wikipedia categories for a richer organization of topics.

Mapping Phase 1: To ensure that our facets are indeed of a controversial nature, we first build a classifier that maps facets onto Debatepedia debates (rather than trying to map directly to Wikipedia). To this end, we have built a nearest-neighbor classifier that uses statistical language models (LM) (an IR technique) as the basis for its distance measure. We also considered alternative classifiers like Bayesian or SVM models, but the emphasis here is on the feature space and the kNN method works very well.

DEFINITION 3.1. *Let $T = \{T_1, T_2, \ldots, T_m\}$ be the set of topics in Debatepedia and let D_T denote the set of all documents debating the topics in T. Recall that each topic has many different facets that may be debated. Let D_i be the set of documents which debate the various facets of the topic T_i. The* language model for a debate *D_i, smoothed with all debates D_T, is the following probability distribution over words (or phrases):*

$$P_{D_i}(w) = (1 - \lambda)P(w|D_i) + \lambda P(w|D_T)$$

where w is a word, $P_{D_i}(w)$ is the estimated probability of the word in the LM of D_i, $P(w|D_i)$ is the probability of the word in D_i and $P(w|D_T)$ is the probability of w in the "background corpus" D_T, consisting of all debates in T, and λ is a Jelinek-Mercer-style smoothing coefficient (or derived from a Dirichlet smoothing model).

We now map a raw facet f onto its nearest debate D (treating f as a query in LM-based IR terminology [8, 22]): that is, the D with maximum likelihood of generating f.

DEFINITION 3.2. *The* **ranking of debates** *D_i for a given facet f is in descending order of*

$$P(f|D_i) = \prod_{w_j \in f} P_{D_i}(w_j)$$

We compute the mean of the LM scores of the top-5 debates, and the mean of the LM scores of the bottom-5 debates. If the two means are statistically different using the T-test at $\alpha = 0.05$, the top-ranked debate is chosen as a candidate name for a canonical facet. Otherwise facets are discarded. We use the same heuristic for the Wikipedia articles ranking and for the Wikipedia categories ranking which we will describe later in this section.

Mapping Phase 2: Since, Debatepedia is smaller than Wikipedia, we extend the set of debates by mapping each debate to the 3 most similar articles in Wikipedia, again using an LM-based kNN method. The titles of these articles serve as candidates for canonical names of raw facets. For example, the recent Libyan civil war is covered in "No-fly zone over Libya", "Human rights violation in the 2011 Libyan civil war", and "National transitional council". These titles are different facets of the same topic.

For finding the 3 best Wikipedia articles, we would like to avoid LM comparisons with a large number of articles. Therefore, we first derive a Google query from the debate D and restrict the search results to Wikipedia. Since the entire text of D would be unsuitable as input to a search engine, we generate the query from the words in the title and 10 most frequent noun phrases in D. The top-10 search results $A_1, A_2, \ldots, A_{10}$ (corresponding to Wikipedia articles) are our candidates for the D-to-A mapping.

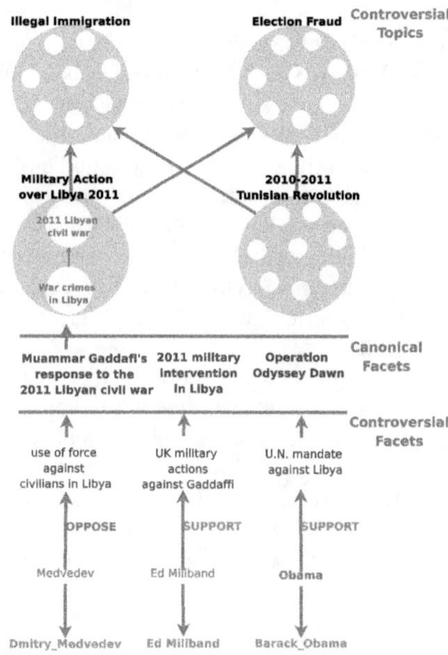

Figure 2: Organizing facets in different levels of granularities.

DEFINITION 3.3. *The* **language model for Wikipedia article** *A, smoothed with the entire Wikipedia as a background corpus W, is the probability distribution over words (or phrases):*

$$P_A(w) = (1 - \lambda)P(w|A) + \lambda P(w|W)$$

The **ranking of articles** *A_i for a given debate D is in descending order of*

$$P(D|A_i) = \prod_{w_j \in D} P_{A_i}(w_j)$$

3.3 Constructing the Topic Hierarchy

Once all raw facets have been mapped to canonical facet names and are associated with 3 Wikipedia articles, the next task is to organize them into a hierarchy of topics. A seemingly natural approach would be to use the Wikipedia category system. However, a major problem with such an approach is that not all categories to which an article belongs are really of controversial nature (e.g., "History of Greece", "European Union", etc.).

To make this important distinction, we devise the following approach. First we collect all Wikipedia categories associated with the 3 articles to which a facet F and its corresponding debate D were mapped, into candidates pool $C_w = \{c_{w_1}, c_{w_2}, \ldots\}$. Second, we use the Debatepedia categories $C_d = \{c_{d_1}, c_{d_2}, \ldots\}$ of the debate D to generate Google queries, restricted to Wikipedia categories (analogous to to the technique in Subsection 3.2). For each c_{d_i}, we obtain top-10 Wikipedia category pages but add only the 3 highest ranked ones to the candidates pool C_w . This step serves to reduce the candidate space. Subsequently, we employ LM-based kNN mapping to obtain the best 3 Wikipedia categories from C_w for the debate D.

DEFINITION 3.4. *The* **language model for Wikipedia category** *c_{w_i}, smoothed with the entire Wikipedia as a background corpus W, is the probability distribution over words (or phrases) in the collection of all Wikipedia articles $A_{c_{w_i}}$ under the category c_{w_i} and its subcategories:*

$$P_{c_{w_i}}(w) = (1 - \lambda)P(w|A_{c_{w_i}}) + \lambda P(w|W)$$

The **ranking of Wikipedia category** c_{w_i} *for a given debate* D *is in descending order of*

$$P(D|c_{w_i}) = \prod_{w_j \in D} P_{c_{w_i}}(w_j)$$

Note that these categories not only have the canonical facet name as a child, but may themselves be in a parent-child (or ancestor-descendant) relationship with each other. We retain these relationships as well, and later use them for the DAG structure of our **final topic graph**.

At this point we could directly use the hierarchy of the selected Wikipedia categories (perhaps, with heuristics to remove occasionally occurring cycles). However, this would yield a fairly noisy topic structure, as Wikipedia often exhibits unsystematic diversity (by its grassroots contributors) and does not enforce terminological standards (not to speak of ontological structures). For example, topics like "radioactive waste", and "nuclear safety" are part of a larger debate on "renewable energies", but Wikipedia does not organize them in this manner. Therefore, and inorder to build our **final topic graph**, we devises a clustering method on the Wikipedia categories, with preservation of whatever parent-child relationships are already present among categories.

Graph Coarsening Algorithm: To this end, we adopted and extended a *graph coarsening* algorithm, originally developed for the different task of multi-level graph partitioning [11]. We construct a weighted category graph as follows. For topology, we use the parent-child structure between Wikipedia categories.

DEFINITION 3.5. *We construct a node- and edge-weighted directed* **initial topic graph** $G_I = (V, E)$ *as follows. Each* $v_i \in V$ *corresponds to a wikipedia category produced by the previously described method. Let the category corresponding to* v_i *be denoted by* $c(v_i)$. $E = \{(v_i, v_j)|c(v_i)$ *is a parent of* $c(v_j)\}$.
The node weight *of* v_i*, denoted by* $w(v_i)$ *is the number of distinct facets that were mapped to* $c(v_i)$ *or one of its descendants.*
The edge weight for an edge $e_{ij} = (v_i, v_j)$*, denoted* $w(e_{ij})$ *is proportional to the number of common Wikipedia articles under* $c(v_i)$ *and* $c(v_j)$ *(and their subcategories). Let* $A_{c(i)}$ *and* $A_{c(j)}$ *denote the Wikipedia articles under* $c(v_i)$ *(and its subcategories) and* $c(v_j)$ *(and its subcategories), then* $w(e_{ij}) = \frac{|A_{c(i)} \cap A_{c(j)}|}{|A_{c(i)} \cup A_{c(j)}|}$, *the Jaccard co-efficient.*

So a category is considered more important if it transitively contains a large number of facets. We prune out very generic categories of portal nature and also very sparse categories of exotic specificity, by using upper and lower bounds α and β as thresholds for the category node weights.

From the initial topic graph constructed as described previously, we induce the final topic graph defined as follows.

DEFINITION 3.6. *A node- and edge-weighted DAG* **final topic graph** $G_F = (V, E)$ *is a hypergraph constructed such that each* $v_i \in V$ *corresponds to a topic denoted by* $t(v_i)$. $E = \{(v_i, v_j)|t(v_i)$ *is a parent of* $t(v_j)\}$. *Each topic* $t(v_i)$ *represents a graph* $G_S = (V', E')$ *such that* G_S *is a subgraph of the initial topic graph* G_I *(*$G_S \subset G_I$*) and* G_S *is induced by* V' *(*$G_S = G_I[V']$*).* V' *corresponds to a set of highly correlated Wikipedia categories.*

To construct the final topic graph, we run the graph coarsening algorithm of [11] on the initial topic graph, by gradually collapsing vertices and incident edges. In our experiments, we ran the algorithm until it arrived at around 500 clusters, and we generated a label (topic) for each cluster based on the most frequent n-gram in its underlying set of facet strings.

The graph coarsening algorithm works only with undirected graphs, it ignores edge orientation. So now we need to impose a DAG structure among the final clusters. This is done in two steps.

DAG Construction Phase 1: First, we aggregate the parent-child relations for two clusters A and B from their included categories $a \in A$, $b \in B$. For a being a parent of b in the original Wikipedia hierarchy, we compute the **average** of their edge weights into an aggregated weight $w(A \sqsupset B)$. For a being a child of b we analogously compute the aggregated $w(A \sqsubset B)$. Now the idea is to construct a parent-child edge from A to B if $w(A \sqsupset B) > 0$ and $w(A \sqsubset B) = 0$, and analogously for child-parent edges. Unfortunately, we cannot guarantee such conditions; we may have clusters with contradictory edges among their included categories.

DAG Construction Phase 2: As a second step, we, therefore, construct a priority order among all cluster pairs and then proceed in a greedy manner. We sort cluster pairs (A, B) in descending order of $priority(A, B) = w(A \sqsupset B) - w(A \sqsubset B)$. Now we construct parent-child edges between clusters in this order as long as $priority(A, B) > 0$. While doing this, we check for possible formation of cycles, and drop edges accordingly. Subsequently, we repeat this procedure for the dual priority order $w(A \sqsubset B) - w(A \sqsupset B)$ if it leads to additional edges without creating cycles. The greedy heuristic in this approach helps to ensure that the most prominent relationships between clusters are captured.

The outlined algorithm is our new way of constructing a topic DAG from Wikipedia categories, and completely mapping all collected facets onto these topics.

4. OPINION HOLDERS

We need to identify opinion holders who have expressed an opinion on these facets. For example, if we have extracted the facet "military action in Libya", then we need to find all people who support or oppose this particular facet. The problem here lies in reliably identifying, in the facet's surrounding text, the named entity who has expressed the opinion.

In order to identify these opinion holders, we again make use of the result snippets collected for extracting facets. Even though our seeds were of the form "he supports" (and variations thereof), it is often the case that the same sentence also names the opinion holder. For example, "Sarkozy said he supports military action in Libya" contains both the seed "he supports" as well as the opinion holder "Sarkozy". Our algorithm proceeds as follows:

1. Candidate identification: We run the Stanford dependency parser on the snippet's sentence that contains the support/oppose pattern, in order to identify the subject of the sentence.

2. Names-to-Entities mapping: In order to ensure that the subject is indeed a named entity, we made use of the YAGO ontology [18] which comprises all individual entities in Wikipedia and additionally provides a "means" relation which maps variations of names to the correct entities. For example, "B. Obama" and "President Obama" would both map to the entity Barack_Obama through the means relation. The means relation itself is constructed from Wikipedia cues like redirects and href anchor texts [9].

3. Disambiguation: As many names are ambiguous, YAGO actually connects the surface names to *all possible* meanings. For example, for "Obama"it provides both Barack_Obama as well as Michelle_Obama as entity candidates. Fortunately, YAGO comes with a simple but powerful heuristics for the *preferred meaning* of a name: the entity which most frequently occurs in Wikipedia as a link target for an href anchor text with the given name.

Using YAGO to identify names has the added advantage of canonicalizing the names of the opinion holders. In the case that YAGO does not know a name at all, then we discard the snippet. The disambiguation heuristics mentioned above may look crude, but it works amazingly well for important stakeholders like politicans or organizations. More advanced methods for named entity disambiguation can be easily plugged into our architecture.

We need also to consider the case when the parsing itself fails to identify a subject (e.g., because the subject is a pronoun or the snippet is not a grammatically correct sentence). In this case, we use the heuristics that the noun phrase identified by YAGO, which is closest to the seed is the opinion holder. This noun phrase may occur in the same sentence as the seed or in a previous sentence.

Finally, a candidate opinion is formed by adding the positively identified opinion holder, support or oppose (which is determined by the seed present in the sentence) and the facet. In addition, the snippet used to extract this opinion is added as its context.

5. SUPPORT/OPPOSE LEXICON

Using our initial seed set, we were able to extract ca. 7,000 opinion triples. However, the number of triples are limited by the initial seed set, since only those seeds are queried. For example, we find "she supports", but we would miss "she strongly supports" or "she is in favor of". Therefore, our next challenge is to *automatically* identify a large number of support and oppose patterns and create a lexicon of phrases. These phrases can then be used to collect more snippets from the Web and extract opinions from them. In this section we present several methods that we developed to automatically create a larger lexicon.

5.1 Unsupervised Method

Our first approach is an unsupervised method, bootstrapped from the initial seed set. We identify 10 support triples and 10 oppose triples from our initial list. From each triple, we isolate the person and the facet. Here we use the raw facets and entity names (not the canonicalized ones) because these are close to the variety of expressions used in news sources. Each ⟨person,facet⟩ pair is now viewed as a query submitted to a search engine. Examples of the resulting snippets are shown in Table 3. The bold text indicates phrases which could be used to populate the lexicon of support phrases. Our algorithm then processes these snippets in three steps:

1. We isolate the text in between the person and the facet phrase (e.g., "strongly defends US", "defended his decision to launch", etc). These substrings are now candidates for the lexicon, but still contain too much noise.

2. Therefore, we generate all n-grams (for $n = 1$ to 5) for the collected substrings, and each n-gram becomes a candidate.

3. Finally, the n-grams are ranked by their occurrence frequency in the collected snippets, and we retain the top-k.

Examples of collected phrases are shown in Table 4. We present an evaluation of their accuracy in Section 7.2.

Obama **strongly defends** US Military Action in Libya
Barack Obama has aligned himself with Nicolas Sarkozy by **committing to support** military action in Libya
US President Barack Obama **defended his decision to** launch military action in Libya
President Obama said Saturday that he **had authorized** limited military action in Libya
President Obama tells Americans that he **ordered** military action in Libya

Table 3: Examples of extracted snippets for (person,facet) pairs

support	approve, acknowledged, sponsored, campaigned for, strongly defends, had authorized, agree on
oppose	disapprove, campaigned against, criticize, overhaul, stand/speak against, to amend, attacks

Table 4: Examples of new seeds in the lexicon

5.2 Supervised Methods

We found that the unsupervised approach, despite its simplicity, is amazingly effective (see Section 7.2). Nonetheless, its recall and precision are limited. Moreover, we made the assumption that, if a query was formed by a "support" triple, then all snippets returned were candidates for the support set. However, the same ⟨person,facet⟩ query formulated from a support triple could also return an "oppose" snippet. To overcome these limitations, we developed methods based on supervised learning with different feature sets. These methods can be used to automaticly classify newly seen opinions.

Features. We explored the following features as inputs to the different supervised approaches.

1. NGRAMS: The NGRAMS feature for a snippet consists of all the n-grams extracted from its corresponding substring.

2. HMI: Hits Mutual Information: Consider an n-gram N (a candidate for a support or oppose phrase) and a *known support pair* s and a *known oppose pair* o. The number of times N co-occurs with s, and the number of times it co-occurs with o are indicators of whether the n-gram is a support or an oppose phrase. We formalize this approach into a measure HMI (derived from search-engine hits) as follows.
Let $S = \{s_i\}$ be the set of known support pairs and let $O = \{o_i\}$ be the set of known oppose pairs. Then,

$$HMI(N) = \frac{MI(S,N) - MI(O,N)}{MI(S,N) + MI(O,N)}$$

where $MI(S,N)$ is the mutual information of S and N, and computed as follows.

$$MI(S,N) = \sum_i P(s_i,N) \log \frac{P(s_i,N)}{P(s_i]P(N)}$$

where $P(s_i, N)$ is the probability that s_i and N co-occur and estimated as follows.

$$P(s_i,N) = \frac{hits(s_i,N)}{hits(s_i)hits(N)}$$

where $hits(s_i, N)$ is the number of hits returned by the search engine for a query formulated as "s_i AND N". If $HMI(N)$ is positive, it is more likely that N is a support phrase, otherwise, it is an oppose phrase.

3. SYN/ANT: Synonyms and Antonyms:

We add synonyms (SYN) to each verbal n-gram in the feature set (that is, any n-gram denoting a verbal phrase). Similarly, by substituting antonyms (ANT) in the verbal n-grams, we enhance the classifier in its ability to learn the opposite opinion. For example, for the n-gram "takes steps to change", we identify verbs "takes" and "to change". Adding synonyms to "to change", we arrive at a feature set that includes "takes steps to alter", "takes steps to modify", etc. Adding antonyms of "to change", gives us "takes steps to continue".

Classifiers. We trained two classifiers using different combinations of the features described above: a linear **SVM** and a J48 Decision Tree (**DT**). In addition, we developed a nearest-neighbor-style classifier based on a statistical language model (**LM**) (similar to

[2]). In this approach, we construct LMs for both the support and the oppose n-grams as follows.

DEFINITION 5.1. *Let $n^+ \in S$ be a* **support n-gram**. *The* **LM for** n^+, *using n^+ itself and the set S for smoothing, is defined as the following probability distribution over n-grams:*

$$P_{n^+}(p) = (1 - \lambda)P(p|n^+) + \lambda P(p|S)$$

where p is an n-gram, $P_{n^+}(p)$ is the estimated probability of the n-gram in the LM of n^+, $P(p|n^+)$ is the probability of p in n^+ and $P(p|S)$ is the probability of p in S.

Analogously, let $n^- \in O$ be an **oppose n-gram**. *The* **LM for** n^-, *using n^- itself and the set O for smoothing, is defined as:*

$$P_{n^-}(p) = (1 - \lambda)P(p|n^-) + \lambda P(p|O)$$

Both $P(p|n^+)$, and $P(p|n^-)$ are estimated based on the Jaccard similarity between p and n^+ or n^-, respectively. While $P(p|S)$, and $P(p|O)$ are estimated based on the max of the Jaccard similarities between p and each n-gram in S or O, respectively.

Let Q be a newly seen n-gram. We now construct two queries as follows. A *synonym query* $Q_s = \{Q\} \cup \{Q_{SYN}\}$ and an *antonym query* $Q_a = \{Q_{ANT}\}$, where Q_{SYN} and Q_{ANT} are constructed using the SYN/ANT technique described previously. For the synonym query Q_s, the probabilities of generating it given either the support LM or the oppose LM are,

$$P(Q_s|n_i^+) = \prod_{p_j \in Q_s} P_{n_i^+}(p_j)$$

$$P(Q_s|n_i^-) = \prod_{p_j \in Q_s} P_{n_i^-}(p_j)$$

Similarly, we compute the probabilities of the antonym query Q_a. The newly seen n-gram is then classified based on the highest of these computed probabilities. (e.g. Q is classified as a support n-gram if $P(Q_s|n_i^+)$ is the highest).

Our prototype system for OpinioNetIt supports all the above described supervised and unsupervised approaches.

6. SYSTEM IMPLEMENTATION

We have implemented OpinioNetIt in Java. Our system consists of three main components as numbered in Figure 1.

1. Acquisition & Organization of Topics: (a) uses the dependency parser of the Stanford NLP package (SNLP) to extract opinions facets from the collected snippets, (b) makes use of available online resources (e.g. Wikipedia, Debatepedia) and maps each facet to canonical name, (c) constructs the controversial topics hierarchy, making use of online resources (e.g. Wikipedia, Debatepedia), and using different algorithms (e.g. coarsening algorithm of Metis [11]).

2. Acquiring Opinion Holders: (a) uses (SNLP) and its NER to extract candidate opinions holders from the snippets, (b) uses YAGO to map each candidate opinion holder to a canonical name.

3. Building the Support/Oppose Lexicon: (a) takes as input, a query formulated from an opinion holder and a topic. Using Google, it collects a set of relevant snippets, (b) uses (SNLP) to extract candidate seeds, (c) uses different classification packages (e.g. SVM-light, Weka) to classify the candidate seeds into support or oppose. All outputs are saved in a relational database. Opinions are saved in the RDF+text format, where the text consists of the context from which an opinion triple was extracted.

7. EVALUATION

For evaluating the accuracy of our automated methods, we performed a series of experiments. We first present end-to-end studies of the output quality of OpinioNetIt (Subsection 7.1). Then we present results on the most important components, namely, the construction of the topic DAG and the classification into support vs. oppose, with comparison to alternative methods (Subsection 7.2).

7.1 End-to-End Experiments

Data. A lexicon of 17 support/oppose phrases, shown in Table 4, served as seeds to extract ca. 30,000 opinion statements. Our sources Al-Jazeera (**ALJ**), BBC, CNN, New York Times (**NY**), Wikipedia (**WP**), and Google News (**GN**). Table 5 shows the breakdown of the opinions.

We restricted the number of snippets collected to the first 2,000 search engine results for each seed. These snippets yielded ca. 14,000 named entities, 23,000 facets, 4,000 canonicalized facets mapped to 5,000 Wikipedia categories, and finally 500 controversial topics organized in a DAG with ca. 3,000 topic-subtopic edges.

Methodology. We performed the following experiments for which we present precision results:

1. A *random sample* of 2,000 opinion statements (topic-politician pairs). A total of 18 judges assessed these opinions as "correct" or "wrong". For opinions that the judges deemed wrong, they could indicate whether: i) named entity is wrong, ii) facet is wrong, iii) relation (support/oppose) is wrong.
2. A small *focused sample* of 50 opinion statements by prominent politicians on important contemporary topics.
3. We compared our opinion network to a *limited ground-truth set* on prominent US politicians and their opinions about major topics, available on `procon.org` and `ontheissues.org`.

Metrics. The main measure of interest is the precision of the opinion statements, the fraction of truly correct outputs that our methods yield. We estimate precision by samples, with Wilson confidence intervals for statistical significance [20]. It is not obvious how to define and estimate a notion of recall (and F1 score) here, without manually reading the entire corpus. Thus we restrict this aspect of our studies to giving absolute numbers of different outputs obtained by our methods.

1. Results for Random Sample. Table 5 shows precision values for each source, and the overall precision. For the entire set of 2,000 samples, the micro-averaged precision was 72.4%. Given the difficulty of this extraction task, these results are quite satisfying.

Of all the opinions that were judged wrong, only 9% were due to the support/oppose relation. We conclude that our process of constructing the support and oppose lexicon is reasonably robust. The extraction of named entities and facets both contributed ca. 45% of the cases of incorrect opinions.

For named entity extraction, we used a heuristics in cases where the subject cannot be identified by the parser, which considers as an opinion holder the closest person name identified by YAGO. We found that this heuristic is not very robust. For example, it failed for the sentence "Prime Minister David Cameron met *Mr Gates* in Downing Street on Monday and restated *his support* for *American strategy in Afghanistan*".

Some of the incorrectly judged facets were very generic (e.g. "*George Clooney* on why *he supports the protests*", while the others were in long sentences which are difficult to parse (e.g. "*Ivan*

Source	Overall	Support	Oppose	ALJ	BBC	CNN	GN	NY	WP
#Opinions	29648	16011	13637	970	3349	2650	6861	9877	5941
Precision	0.724	0.7	0.75	0.72	0.66	0.78	0.788	0.74	0.69

Table 5: Opinions & precision results grouped by source

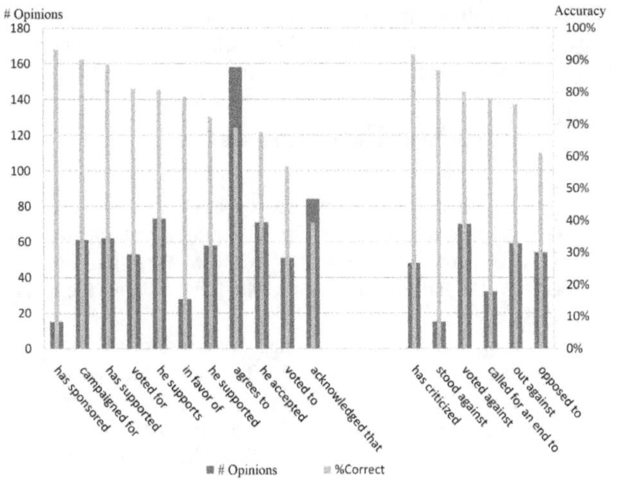

Figure 3: Accuracy of seeds.

Rojas said in Colombia that *he supports* Chavez's plan to secure *the release of his sister*").

The result that support opinions had lower accuracy than oppose opinions, is mostly due to difficult sentences with the pattern "acknowledged that" (e.g. "Kerry *acknowledged that* the bill would raise energy prices")

We notice significantly varying precision for different sources, with lower values for BBC and Wikipedia. For BBC, we encountered many snippets from user blogs with a different writing style compared to news. Wikipedia articles are long and detailed, and contain references to many different people. This writing style resulted in a lower accuracy in the extraction of the named entities.

2. Results for Focused Sample. We created a focused sample by manually identifying hot topics in each of the geo-political regions Africa, Asia, Europe, Middle East, and USA, and combining them with prominent politicians from these areas. An example subset of these pairs is shown in Table 6. For each cell of the table, we list the numbers of support (+) and oppose (−) opinions found in our corpus, and give the precision ($p = 0.93$) based on manual assessment by one of our judges.

	Africa: election in Cote d'Ivoire	Asia: nuclear power plants
Barack Obama	$2+, p = 1.0$	$2+, 2-, p = 1.0$
Laurent Gbagbo	$2-, p = 1.0$	
Binyamin Netanyahu		$1-, p = 0.0$
Nicolas Sarkozy	$2+, p = 1.0$	$1+, p = 1.0$
Manmohan Singh		$1+, p = 1.0$

Table 6: An example subset of the focused sample

3. Results for Ground-Truth Set. As the previous sample-based evaluation does not allow us to make any recall estimates, we also compared a subset of our automatically compiled opinions to a ground-truth dataset with largely aggregated and thus quasi-objective opinion polarities. To this end, we obtained the data on 8 US politicians (from both democratic and republican parties, e.g., Obama, McCain, etc.) on 19 controversial topics, from the two web sites `procon.org` and `ontheissues.org`. The topics were major themes such as abortion, same-sex marriage, death penalty, etc.

We aligned opinions triples in our database with ground-truth triples by first matching the named entities and then matching the ground-truth topics against i) the facets alone, ii) the Wikipedia topics of the facets, and iii) the Debatepedia topics of the facets. In the cases ii) and iii), we select the two topics with the highest Jaccard similarity to the ground-truth topic, based on the terms in the topics' facet strings.

Table 7 shows the results for precision and recall of this evaluation study. Note that the recall for facets is lower than for the Wikipedia or Debatepedia topics. This is caused by the inherent difficulty of matching fine-grained facets against coarse-grained main topics. For this situation, a recall of 30 percent is a satisfactory result.

	Facets	Debatepedia	Wikipedia
Precision	0.98	0.81	0.80
Recall	0.30	0.42	0.41

Table 7: Results for experiment with objective ground truth

We further investigated the reason behind the very high precision of both the focused set and the ground-truth set compared to the precision of the random set. Attributed to the nature of the topics in these sets, 96% of the matched triples were retrieved using the patterns: "support", "against', "voted for", "voted against". Sentences including these patterns are parsed with high accuracy. On the otherhand, different patterns with different parsing accuracies caused the low overall precision of the random set.

7.2 Components Experiments

1. Construction of Topic Hierarchy. We were interested in comparing our elaborate method for mapping facets to topics and for constructing the topic DAG against other alternatives like standard clustering. We presented judges with a randomly selected set of 500 facets along with: the top-3 canonical facets of each facet computed by the method of Subsection 3.2 (**LM-DebRank**), the corresponding top-3 Wikipedia categories of each canonical facet computed by the method of Subsection 3.3 (**LM-CatRank**), and the corresponding controversial topic of each category computed by the coarsening algorithm (**CO**) of Subsection 3.3).

Judges were asked to choose relevant: i) canonical facets for raw facets, ii) Wikipedia categories for canonical facets, iii) topics for Wikipedia categories. The 500 facets have 413 canonicalized facets, 387 Wikipedia categories, and 166 topics in the final topic DAG. In addition, the judges were asked to assess the correctness of 276 topic parent-child pairs from the topics in the final topic DAG. These topic pairs were collected using our DAG construction algorithm (**DAG**) described in Subsection 3.3. The main measure of interest is the precision of the assessed mappings.

Table 8 shows the results. **69%** of the raw facets f were assigned correctly to at least one of the top-3 canonicalized facets F, and **78%** of the presented F were correctly assigned to at least one of the top-3 Wikipedia categories C. Wrong (f, F) pairs were found mainly for very general facets (e.g., "the bill"). In such cases, informative LMs for facets require longer contexts.

For the (C,T) pairs obtained by the (**CO**) method, **73%** were correct, and **66%** of the facets have at least one correct complete path ($f \rightarrow F \rightarrow C \rightarrow T$). For the (T, T) pairs in the final topic DAG, **69%** were found to be correct, using the (**DAG**) approach.

As an alternative approach to both the (**CO**) and (**DAG**), we ran a hierarchical agglomerative clustering (**HAC**) algorithm on the collected Wikipedia categories. About **68%** of the 387 random (C, T) pairs were correct (**HAC-CT** vs. **CO**), while the 276 random (T, T) pairs have **71%** accuracy (**HAC-TT** vs. **DAG**). Since the construction of topics hierarchy depends on the construction of each topic cluster, the precision of these two components togother is computed. The precision of **CO** and **DAG** is higher than the precision of **HAC-CT** and **HAC-TT**. Also when comparing the judiciously constructed DAG vs. standard HAC, one also needs to consider the overall size and structure of the resulting graphs. DAG produces a compact and nicely explorable hierarchy with a total of 533 nodes and 299 edges (so that most nodes are leaves in the DAG). In contrast, HAC creates a much larger binary tree with 1056 nodes and 1055 edges in total. This graph is much more tedious to explore, and does not convey the same level of informativeness as our constructed DAG.

Items(#)-Pairs (#)	Approach	Precision
f **(500)-**(f,F) **(1500)**	LM-DebRank	0.69
F **(413)-**(F,C) **(1239)**	LM-CatRank	0.78
C **(387)-**(C,T) **(387)**	CO	0.73
nodes (137)-(T,T) **(276)**	DAG	0.69
-	CO&DAG	0.50
C **(387)-**(C,T) **(387)**	HAC-CT	0.68
nodes (532)-(T,T) **(276)**	HAC-TT	0.71
-	HAC-CT&HAC-TT	0.48

Table 8: Results for controversial topics graph

2. Support/Oppose Classifiers. For the unsupervised approach described in Section 5.1, our judges evaluated 460 n-grams out of 2,000 support or oppose n-grams. For the supervised approaches, 540 n-grams were manually labeled as support or oppose. Out of these, 400 n-grams for training, and 140 n-grams for testing different approaches (**SVM, DT, LM**) using different combinations of features (**NGRAMS, HMI, SYN, ANT**).

The main measures for the unsupervised approach are relative precision and relative recall (based on the 460 samples), while precision and recall are used for the supervised approaches (based on the withheld 140 test cases).

Table 9 shows the best results for the different methods using different combinations of features. The unsupervised approach outperforms the other methods, despite its simplicity. The LM method performs better than DT and SVM. Using n-grams only as features gives bad results because of data sparseness. For this reason, we used aggregated features (e.g., sum, max) over synonyms and antonyms features. Using synonyms only in the similarity measures gives better results than using antonyms as well while results with sum outperform the results of max function.

Approach	Precision	Recall
Unsupervised	**0.79**	**0.60**
SVM+Ngrams+HMI	0.47	0.21
SVM+SYN+SUM	0.61	0.60
DT+SYN+SUM	**0.63**	**0.62**
LM+SYN+SUM	**0.69**	**0.70**

Table 9: Results for support/oppose classifiers

8. USE CASES

As use cases for knowledge discovery and political analyses, we briefly discuss scenarios on the phenomena of so-called flip-flops and dissenters.

Flip-Flops Detection. A flip-flop according to Wikipedia is a sudden real or apparent change of policy or opinion by a public official. To detect flip-flops, we group opinions collected by our system by pairs of politicians and topics, both in canonicalized form. If a group contains both support and oppose opinions, we consider the politician to have flip-flopped. Table 10 shows some examples that we found in our collection (O denotes the opinion polarity: "+" for support, "-" for oppose).

Dissenters Detection. Our goal here is to detect interesting deviations from correlated opinions on different topics. Often, once you know that a person supports topic A, it is clear that she or he also supports topic B, given the semantic connection between A and B. To identify such topic pairs, we compute correlation coefficients and select the most positively correlated pairs. Then we aim to find notable dissenters: people who deviate from this pattern and support only one of A or B and oppose the other one. Table 11 shows some interesting examples that we found in our collection (dominant opinions: "++", "+-", "-+", or "–" with "+" denoting support and "-" denoting oppose).

9. RELATED WORK

Opinion mining (aka. sentiment mining) is a richly researched topic that gained a lot of attention in recent years for business intelligence, smart advertisements, marketing campaigns, etc. The standard model for these mining tasks is to identify objects (e.g., cameras or movies), facets (aspects, features) of these objects on which a sentiment is expressed (e.g., the camera's ease of use, or the movie's special effects), and a polarity of the opinionated statement (positive or negative), and sometimes also an opinion strength for quantifying the polarity. Typically, these cues are aggregated to form opinion profiles, based on many opinions like customer reviews or postings in discussion forums. [16, 13] are excellent surveys on the methodologies for doing this kind of opinion analysis. Our work uses specific techniques from this state of the art, but adapts them to our setting and combines them with new methods. Moreover, the opinion holder is crucial to our task, discriminating our goal from that of traditional sentiment mining: we are interested in the individual entities that express opinions rather than merely aggregating over many individuals.

Analyzing political opinions on controversial topics is inherently more difficult than standard sentiment mining (for products, movies, etc.), given the complexity of the topics and the subtleties in expressing opinions on them. For example, the SentiWordNet lexicon [7], although very useful for understanding product reviews, turned out to be of little help on political texts as these have much richer phrases, as opposed to polarity-bearing single words like adjectives and adverbs. Thus, the theme of political opinion mining is still in its infancy. The little prior work that we are aware of is scattered across specific sub-issues. There is some work on classifying political texts with regard to political parties [19, 15, 21], most notably, democrats vs. republicans in the US, but this stays at the crude level of general attitude and does not address positions on specific controversies. This theme of coarse-grained classification is taken further by the work of [10], which aims to annotate political speeches and parliament debates, but does not deal with fine-grained topics. Work on question answering has also tapped into opinion-related questions (e.g., [3]), but only for providing aggregated answers, not for constructing systematic opinion networks. [14] uses semantic taxonomies to identify aspects of topics, and analyzes opinions on these aspects rather than objects as whole. This applies to sentiment mining on politicians (with aspects such as Vietnam war, Watergate affair, etc.), but it does not address the more far-reaching

Politician	Topic	O	Example Snippet
Barack Obama	nuclear power	+	... Obama says he supports nuclear power ...
		−	... Obama criticized his rival McCain's proposal to encourage the building of 45 new nuclear reactors ...
Angela Merkel	nuclear power	+	... Dr. Merkel's government support for the nuclear energy sector ...
		−	... Chancellor Angela Merkel said she aimed to accelerate Germany's move away from nuclear energy ...

Table 10: Examples of flip-flops detected by our system

Topic Pair	Dominant (+−), (−+)	Dissenter (−−), (++)
Emissions Trading & Offshore Drilling	⟨Cynthia McKinney⟩ ⟨+⟩ ⟨Carbon Neutrality⟩ ⟨Cynthia McKinney⟩ ⟨-⟩ ⟨Offshore drilling⟩	⟨John McCain⟩ ⟨+⟩ ⟨Emissions trading⟩ ⟨John McCain⟩ ⟨+⟩ ⟨Offshore drilling⟩
George W. Bush Politics & Abortion	⟨Sarah Palin⟩ ⟨+⟩ ⟨George W. Bush⟩ ⟨Sarah Palin⟩ ⟨-⟩ ⟨Abortion⟩	⟨Joe Biden⟩ ⟨+⟩ ⟨George W. Bush⟩ ⟨Joe Biden⟩ ⟨+⟩ ⟨Abortion rights⟩

Table 11: Examples of topics correlations and dissenters

goal of connecting opinion holders with fine-grained controversial topics. Finally, the work described in [2] language models to classify pro/con statements, but disregarded the opinion holders.

For gathering statements that connect individual people (mostly politicians) with opinionated expressions, we make use of techniques for information extraction from text and Web sources. [5, 17] give overviews of state-of-the-art methods. Our approach builds specifically on the pattern-fact duality principle that goes back to [4, 1] and allows us to bootstrap the acquisition process with very few seeds. We customize this general framework to collect opinionated cues rather than general relational patterns. For matching names in text sources against canonical entities, we leverage existing knowledge bases like DBpedia, Freebase, or Yago. We specifically make use of the *means* relation that Yago [18] provides for individual entities and their lexical name variations. This information is in turn derived from anchor texts and redirects of Wikipedia. All these are building blocks of our methodology for constructing OpinioNetIt, but each ingredient has an auxiliary role only.

10. CONCLUSIONS AND FUTURE WORK

In this paper, we described OpinioNetIt, an opinion-base of facets, opinion holders and their opinions. First our system acquired opinions and extracted facets from Web result snippets using an initial set of seed patterns. These facets were then canonicalized and hierarchically organized. Second, for each facet, an opinion holder was identified from the same snippets. Third, using a small set of facts, a lexicon of support/oppose phrases was constructed. Finally, new patterns from the lexicon were used to collect further facts. Our evaluation showed an overall precision of 72%.

As future work, generic facets (such as "the bill", etc.) extracted for some opinions require a closer look at the snippet, and possibly the article itself. Also and in order to improve the accuracy of our system, we either need to predict an inaccurate extraction or use additional heuristics in addition to the deep parsing techniques which are sometimes limited when it comes to long sentences. Finally, we plan to expand our techniques to other kinds of sources such as blogs and online forums.

11. REFERENCES

[1] E. Agichtein and L. Gravano. Snowball: Extracting relations from large plain-text collections. In *ICDL*, 2000.

[2] R. Awadallah, M. Ramanath, and G. Weikum. Language-model-based pro/con classification of political text. In *SIGIR*, 2010.

[3] A. Balahur, E. Boldrini A. Montoyo, and P. Martínez-Barco. A unified proposal for factoid and opinionated question answering. In *COLING*, 2010.

[4] S. Brin. Extracting patterns and relations from the world wide web. In *Selected papers from the Intl. Workshop on The World Wide Web and Databases*, 1999.

[5] A. Doan, L. Gravano, R. Ramakrishnan, and S. Vaithyanathan. Special issue on managing information extraction. In *ACM SIGMOD Record*, 2008.

[6] S. Elbassuoni, M. Ramanath, R. Schenkel, and G. Weikum. Searching RDF graphs with SPARQL and keywords. In *IEEE Data Engg. Bulletin*, 2010.

[7] A. Esuli, S. Baccianella, and F. Sebastiani. Sentiwordnet 3.0: An enhanced lexical resource for sentiment analysis and opinion mining. In *LREC 2010*, 2010.

[8] D. Hiemstra. *Using Language Models for Information Retrieval*. PhD thesis, University of Twente, Enschede, 2001.

[9] J. Hoffart, M. Amir, I. Bordino, H. Fürstenau, M. Pinkal, M. Spaniol B. Taneva, S. Thater, and G. Weikum. Robust disambiguation of named entities in text. In *EMNLP 2011*, 2011.

[10] R. Kaptein, M. Marx, and J. Kamps. Who said what to whom?: capturing the structure of debates. In *SIGIR*, 2009.

[11] G. Karypis and V. Kumar. A Fast and High Quality Multilevel Scheme for Partitioning Irregular Graphs. *SIAM J. Sci. Comput.*, 20(1), 1998.

[12] D. Klein and C. Manning. Accurate unlexicalized parsing. In *ACL*, 2003.

[13] B. Liu. Sentiment analysis and subjectivity. In *Handbook of Natural Language Processing, Second Edition*. 2010.

[14] Y. Lu, H. Duan, H. Wang, and C. Zhai. Exploiting structured ontology to organize scattered online opinions. In *COLING*, 2010.

[15] T. Mullen and R. Malouf. Taking sides: User classification for informal online political discourse. *Internet Research*, 18(2), 2008.

[16] B. Pang and L. Lee. Opinion mining and sentiment analysis. *FnT in IR*, 2(1-2), 2008.

[17] S. Sarawagi. Information extraction. *FnT in Databases*, 1(3), 2008.

[18] F. Suchanek, G. Kasneci, and G. Weikum. Yago: A Core of Semantic Knowledge. In *WWW*, 2007.

[19] M. Thomas, B. Pang, and L. Lee. Get out the vote: Determining support or opposition from congressional floor-debate transcripts. In *EMNLP*, 2006.

[20] E. Wilson. Probable inference, the law of succession, and statistical inference. *Journal of the American Statistical Association*, 22(158), 1927.

[21] B. Yu, S. Kaufmann, and D. Diermeier. Classifying party affiliation from political speech. *Information Technology & Politics*, 5(1), 2008.

[22] C. Zhai. Statistical language models for information retrieval. *FnT in IR*, 2(3), 2008.

Identifying Content for Planned Events Across Social Media Sites

Hila Becker*†, Dan Iter†, Mor Naaman‡, Luis Gravano†

† Columbia University, 1214 Amsterdam Avenue, New York, NY 10027, USA
‡ Rutgers University, 4 Huntington St., New Brunswick, NJ 08901, USA

ABSTRACT

User-contributed Web data contains rich and diverse information about a variety of events in the physical world, such as shows, festivals, conferences and more. This information ranges from known event features (e.g., title, time, location) posted on event aggregation platforms (e.g., Last.fm events, EventBrite, Facebook events) to discussions and reactions related to events shared on different social media sites (e.g., Twitter, YouTube, Flickr). In this paper, we focus on the challenge of automatically identifying user-contributed content for events that are planned and, therefore, known in advance, across different social media sites. We mine event aggregation platforms to extract event features, which are often noisy or missing. We use these features to develop query formulation strategies for retrieving content associated with an event on different social media sites. Further, we explore ways in which event content identified on one social media site can be used to retrieve additional relevant event content on other social media sites. We apply our strategies to a large set of user-contributed events, and analyze their effectiveness in retrieving relevant event content from Twitter, YouTube, and Flickr.

Categories and Subject Descriptors

H.3.3 [**Information Storage and Retrieval**]: Information Search and Retrieval

General Terms

Experimentation, Measurement

Keywords

Event Identification, Social Media, Cross-site Document Retrieval

*Contact author: Hila Becker, hila@cs.columbia.edu. This author is currently at Google Inc.

Permission to make digital or hard copies of all or part of this work for personal or classroom use is granted without fee provided that copies are not made or distributed for profit or commercial advantage and that copies bear this notice and the full citation on the first page. To copy otherwise, to republish, to post on servers or to redistribute to lists, requires prior specific permission and/or a fee.
WSDM'12, February 8–12, 2012, Seattle, Washington, USA.
Copyright 2012 ACM 978-1-4503-0747-5/12/02 ...$10.00.

1. INTRODUCTION

Event-based information sharing and seeking are common user interaction scenarios on the Web today. The bulk of information from events is contributed by individuals through social media channels: on photo and video-sharing sites (e.g., Flickr, YouTube), as well as on social networking sites (e.g., Facebook, Twitter). This event-related information can appear in many forms, including status updates in anticipation of an event, photos and videos captured before, during, and after the event, and messages containing post-event reflections. Importantly, for known and upcoming events (e.g., concerts, parades, conferences) revealing, structured information (e.g., title, description, time, location) is often explicitly available on user-contributed event aggregation platforms (e.g., Last.fm events, EventBrite, Facebook events). In this paper, we explore approaches for identifying diverse social media content for planned events.

Suppose a user is interested in the "Celebrate Brooklyn!" festival, an arts festival that happens in Brooklyn, New York every summer. This user could obtain information about the various music performances during this year's "Celebrate Brooklyn!" using Last.fm, a popular site that contains information about music events. Fortunately, Last.fm offers useful details about concerts at "Celebrate Brooklyn!," including the time/date, location, title, and description of these concerts. However, since Last.fm only provides basic event information, the user may consider exploring a variety of complementary social media sites (e.g., Twitter, YouTube) to augment this information at different points in time. For instance, before the event the user might be interested in reading Twitter messages, or *tweets*, describing ticket prices and promotions, while after the event the user might want to relive the experience by exploring YouTube videos recorded by attendees. By automatically associating social media content with planned events we can greatly enhance a user's event-based information seeking experience.

Automatically identifying social media content associated with known events is a challenging problem due to the heterogenous and noisy nature of the data. These properties of the data present a double challenge in our setting, where both the known event information and its associated social media content tend to exhibit missing or ambiguous information, and often include short, ungrammatical textual features. In our "Celebrate Brooklyn!" example, event features (e.g., title, description, location) are supplied by a Last.fm user; therefore, these features may consist of generic titles (e.g., "Opening Night Concert"), missing descriptions, or insufficient venue information (e.g., "Prospect Park," with no exact address). Similarly, social media content associated with this event may be ambiguous (e.g., a YouTube video titled "Bird singing at the opening night gala") or not have a clear connection to the event (e.g., a tweet stating "#CB! starts next week, very excited!").

Existing approaches to find and organize social media content associated with known events are limited in the amount and types of event content that they can handle. Most related research relies on known event content in the form of manually selected terms (e.g., "earthquake," "shaking" for an earthquake) to describe the event [21, 24]. These terms are used to identify social media documents, with the assumption that documents containing these select terms will also contain information about the event. Unfortunately, manually selecting terms for any possible planned event is not a scalable approach. Improving on this point, a recent effort [7] used graphical models to label artist and venue terms in Twitter messages, identifying a set of related Twitter messages for concert events. While this work goes a step further in automating the process of associating events with social media documents, it is still tailored to a particular type of event (i.e., concerts) and restricted to a subset of the associated social media documents (i.e., documents containing venue and artist terms). Importantly, these related efforts focus on identifying site-specific event content, often tailoring their approaches to a particular site and its properties.

To address these limitations of the existing approaches, we leverage explicitly provided event features such as title (e.g., "Celebrate Brooklyn! Opening Gala"), description (e.g., "Singer/songwriter Andrew Bird will open the 2011 Celebrate Brooklyn! season"), time/date (e.g., June 10, 2011), location (e.g., Brooklyn, NY), and venue (e.g., "Prospect Park") to *automatically* formulate queries used to retrieve related social media content from *multiple* social media sites. Importantly, we propose a two-step query generation approach: the first step combines known event features into several queries aimed at retrieving *high-precision* results; the second step uses these high-precision results along with text processing techniques such as term extraction and frequency analysis to build additional queries, aimed at improving recall. We experiment with formulating queries for each social media site individually, and also explore ways to use retrieved content from one site to improve the retrieval process on another site. Our contributions are as follows:

- We pose the problem of identifying social media content for known event features as a query generation and retrieval task (Section 3).
- We develop precision-oriented query generation strategies using known event features (Section 4).
- We develop recall-oriented query generation strategies to improve the often low recall of the precision-oriented strategies (Section 5).
- We demonstrate how query generation strategies developed for one social media site can be used to inform the event content retrieval process on other social media sites (Section 6).

We evaluate our proposed query generation techniques on a set of known events from several sources and corresponding social media content from Twitter, Flickr, and YouTube (Section 7). Finally, we conclude with a discussion of our findings and directions for future work (Section 8).

2. RELATED WORK

We describe related work in three areas: quality content extraction in social media, event identification in textual news, and event identification in social media.

Research on extracting high-quality information from social media [1, 16] and on summarizing or otherwise presenting Twitter event content [11, 19, 23] has gathered recent attention. Agichtein et al. [1] examine properties of text and authors to find quality content in Yahoo! Answers, a related effort to ours but over fundamentally different data. In event content presentation, Diakopoulos et al. [11] and Shamma et al. [23] analyzed Twitter messages corresponding to large-scale media events to improve event reasoning, visualization, and analytics. Recently, we presented centrality-based approaches to extract high-quality, relevant, and useful Twitter messages from a given set of messages related to an event [6]. In this paper, we focus on identifying social media documents for known events, so the above approaches complement the work we present here, and can be used as a future extension to select among the social media documents that we collect for each event.

With an abundance of well-formed text, previous work on event identification in textual news (e.g., newswire, radio broadcast) [2, 13, 26] relied on natural language processing techniques to extract linguistically motivated features for identification of news events. Such techniques do not perform well over social media data, where textual content is often very short, and lacks reliable grammatical style and quality. More significantly, this line of research generally assumes that all documents contain event information. To identify events in social media, we have to consider and subsequently eliminate non-event documents when associating content with events.

While event detection in textual news documents has been studied in depth, the identification of events in social media sites is still in its infancy. Several related papers explored the idea of identifying *unknown* events in social media. We proposed an online clustering framework for identifying *unknown* events in Flickr [4]. As part of this framework, we explored the notion of multi-feature similarity for Flickr images and showed that combining a set of feature-driven similarity metrics yields better results for clustering social media documents according to events than using traditional text-based similarity metrics. Sankaranarayanan et al. [22] identified late breaking news events on Twitter using clustering, along with a text-based classifier and a set of news "seeders," which are handpicked users known for publishing news (e.g., news agency feeds). Petrović et al. [20] used locality-sensitive hashing to detect the first tweet associated with an event in a stream of Twitter messages. Finally, we used novel features to separate topically-similar message clusters into event and non-event clusters [5], thus identifying events and their associated social media documents on Twitter. In contrast with these efforts, we focus on identifying *known* events in social media, given a set of descriptive yet often noisy context features for an event.

Several recent efforts proposed techniques for identifying social media content for *known* events. Many of these techniques rely on a set of *manually* selected terms to retrieve event-related documents from a single social media site [21, 24]. Sakaki et al. [21] developed techniques for identifying earthquake events on Twitter by monitoring keyword triggers (e.g., "earthquake" or "shaking"). In their setting, the type of event must be known a priori, and should be easily represented using simple keyword queries. Most related to our work, Benson et al. [7] identified Twitter messages for concert events using statistical models to automatically tag artist and venue terms in Twitter messages. Their approach is novel and fully automatic, but it limits the set of identified messages for concert events to those with explicit artist and venue mentions. Our goal is to automatically retrieve social media documents for any known event, without any assumption about the textual content of the event or its associated documents. Importantly, all of these approaches are tailored to one specific social media site. In this paper we aim to retrieve social media documents across *multiple* sites with varying types of documents (e.g., photos, videos, textual messages).

3. MOTIVATION AND APPROACH

The problem that we address in this paper is how to identify social media documents across sites for a given planned event with known features (e.g., title, description, time/date, location). Records of planned events—including the event features on which we rely—abound on the Web, on platforms such as Last.fm events, EventBrite, and Facebook events. Figure 1 shows a snapshot of such a planned-event record on Last.fm.

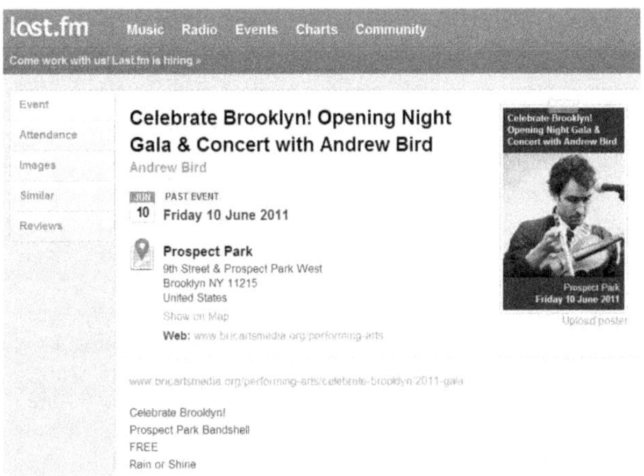

Figure 1: A Last.fm event record for the "Celebrate Brooklyn!" opening night gala and concert.

We regard a social media document (e.g., a photo, a video, a tweet) as relevant to an event if it provides a reflection on the event before, during, or after the event occurs. Consider the "Celebrate Brooklyn!" opening gala concert example (see Figure 1). This event's related documents can reflect anticipation of the event (e.g., a tweet stating "I'm so excited for this year's Celebrate Brooklyn! and the FREE opening concert!"), participation in the event (e.g., a video of Andrew Bird singing at the opening gala), and post-event reflections (e.g., a photo of Prospect Park after the concert titled "Andrew Bird really knows how to put on a show"). All of these documents may be relevant to a user seeking information about this event at different times.

The definition of "event" has received attention across fields, from philosophy [12] to cognitive psychology [25]. In information retrieval, the concept of event has prominently been studied for event detection in news [2]. We borrow from this research to define an event in the context of our work. Specifically, we define an *event* as a real-world occurrence e with (1) an associated time period T_e and (2) a time-ordered stream of social media documents D_e discussing the occurrence and published during time T_e.

Operationally, an event is any record posted to one of the public event planning and aggregation platforms available on the Web (e.g., Last.fm events, EventBrite). Unfortunately, not all user-contributed records on these sites are complete and coherent, and while we expect our approaches to handle some missing data, a small subset of these records lack critical features that would make them difficult to interpret by our system and humans alike. Therefore, we do not include in our analysis records that are potentially noisy and incomplete. Specifically, we ignore:

- Records that are missing both start time/date and end time/date
- Records that do not have any location information
- Records with non-English title or description
- Records for "endogenous" events [8, 18] (i.e., events that do not correspond to any real-world occurrence, such as "profile picture change," a Facebook-specific phenomenon with no real-world counterpart)

Regardless of the platform on which they are posted, user-contributed event records generally share a core set of *context features* that describe the event along different dimensions. These features include (see Figure 1): title, with the name of the event (e.g., "Celebrate Brooklyn! Opening Night Gala & Concert with Andrew Bird"); description, with a short paragraph outlining specific event details (e.g., "... Celebrate Brooklyn! Prospect Park Bandshell FREE Rain or Shine"); time/date, with the time and date of the event (e.g., Friday 10 June 2011); venue, with the site at which the event is held (e.g., Prospect Park); location, with the address of the event (e.g., Brooklyn, NY). These context features, collectively, can be helpful for constructing queries that can retrieve different types of social media documents associated with the event.

Problem Definition. *Consider any planned-event record posted on an event aggregation platform. Our goal is to retrieve relevant social media documents for this event on multiple social media sites, and identify the top-k such documents from each site, according to given site-specific scoring functions.*

We define the problem of associating social media documents with planned events as a query generation and retrieval task. Specifically, we design query generation strategies using the context features of events on the Web as defined above. For each event we generate a variety of queries, which we use *collectively* to retrieve matching social media documents from multiple sites. Since each event could potentially have many associated social media documents, we further filter the set of documents we present to a user to the top-k most similar documents, using given site-specific scoring functions (e.g., the multi-feature function in [4]). The similarity metrics that we use, and which are not the focus of this paper, might differ slightly across social media sites, since sites vary in their context features (e.g., documents from Flickr and YouTube have titles and descriptions whereas documents from Twitter do not).

Our approach for associating social media documents with planned events consists of two steps. First, we define precision-oriented queries for an event using its known context features (Section 4). These precision-oriented queries aim to collectively retrieve a set of social media documents with high-precision results. Then, to improve the (generally low) recall achieved in the first step, we use term extraction and frequency analysis techniques on the high-precision results to generate recall-oriented queries and retrieve additional documents for the event (Section 5). Figure 2 presents an overview of our query generation approach.

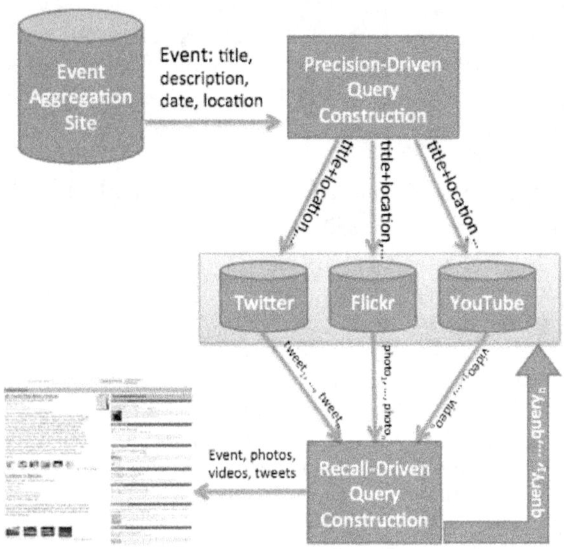

Figure 2: Our query-generation approach.

4. PRECISION-ORIENTED QUERY BUILDING STRATEGIES

Our first step towards retrieving social media documents for planned events consists of simple query generation strategies that are aimed at achieving high-precision results. These strategies form queries that touch on various aspects of an event (e.g., time/date and venue), following the intuition that these highly restrictive queries should only result in messages that relate to the intended event. We consider a variety of query generation strategies for this step, involving different combinations of the context features, namely, title, time/date, and location, of each event.

The precision-oriented queries for an event consist of combinations of one or more event features. One intuitive feature that we include in all strategies is a restriction on the time at which the retrieved social media documents are posted. In a study of trends on Twitter, Kwak et al. [15] discovered that most trends last for one week once they become "active" (i.e., once their associated Twitter messages are generated). Since our (planned) events can be anticipated, unlike the trends in [15], we follow a similar intuition and set the time period T_e that is associated with the event (see Section 3) to start a week prior to the event's start time/date and to end a week after the event's end time/date. For documents that contain digital media items (e.g., photos, videos), we only consider them if their associated media item was created during or after the event's start time. This step, while potentially eliminating a small number of relevant documents, is aimed at improving precision since we do not expect many digital media items associated with the event to be captured prior to the start of the event. We experimented with more restrictive time windows (e.g., one day after the event's end) but observed that relevant documents that contain digital media are generally posted within a week of the event, possibly due to a high barrier to post (e.g., having to upload photos from a camera that does not connect directly to the Internet).

In addition to restricting by time, we always include the title of the event in our precision-oriented strategies, as it often provides a precise notion of the subject of the event. As discussed in Section 3, title values exhibit substantial variations in specificity across event records. Some event titles might be too specific (e.g., "Celebrate Brooklyn! Opening Night Gala & Concert with Andrew Bird"); for any such specific title, any social media documents matching it exactly will likely be relevant to the corresponding event. If the titles are too specific, however, no matching documents might be available, which motivates the recall-oriented techniques described in the next section. In contrast, other event titles might be too general (e.g., "Opening Night Concert"). To automatically accommodate these variations in title values, we consider different query generation options for the title feature. Specifically, we generate queries with the original title as a phrase, to capture content for events with detailed titles. We also generate queries with the original title as a phrase augmented with (portions of[1]) the event location, to capture content for events with broad titles, for which the location helps narrow down the matching documents. Finally, we consider alternative query generation techniques that include the title keywords as a list of terms—rather than as a phrase—for flexibility, as well as variations of the non-phrase version that eliminate stop words from the queries.

The intuition for the precision-oriented strategies we define is motivated by the informal results of these strategies over planned events from a pilot system. Our system [3] has a customizable interface that allows a user to select among different retrieval strategies. We selected precision-oriented strategies that include three variations of the title (i.e., phrase, list of terms, and list of terms with removed stop words), optionally augmented with either the city or venue portion of the location. We use these precision-oriented strategies to retrieve social media documents for a set of planned events, and verify that they indeed return high-precision results (Section 7). The final set of selected precision-oriented strategies is listed in Table 1.

5. RECALL-ORIENTED QUERY BUILDING STRATEGIES

While the strategies outlined in Section 4 often return high-precision social media documents for an event, the number of these high-precision documents is generally low. To improve recall, we develop several strategies for constructing queries using term-frequency analysis. Specifically, we treat an event's title, description, and any retrieved results from

[1]We observed that social media documents usually mention a single, broad aspect of the event's location, such as city or venue, rather than a full address.

Strategy	Example
["title"+"city"]	["Celebrate Brooklyn! Opening Night Gala & Concert with Andrew Bird" "Brooklyn"]
[title+"city"]	[Celebrate Brooklyn! Opening Night Gala & Concert with Andrew Bird "Brooklyn"]
[title-stopwords+"city"]	[Celebrate Brooklyn! Opening Night Gala Concert Andrew Bird "Brooklyn"]
["title"+"venue"]	["Celebrate Brooklyn! Opening Night Gala & Concert with Andrew Bird" "Prospect Park"]
[title+"venue"]	[Celebrate Brooklyn! Opening Night Gala & Concert with Andrew Bird "Prospect Park"]
["title"]	["Celebrate Brooklyn! Opening Night Gala & Concert with Andrew Bird"]
[title]	[Celebrate Brooklyn! Opening Night Gala & Concert with Andrew Bird]
[title-stopwords]	[Celebrate Brooklyn! Opening Night Gala Concert Andrew Bird]

Table 1: Our selected precision-oriented strategies.

the precision-oriented techniques as "ground-truth" data for the event. We consider using the precision-oriented results from each social media site individually, and also from all social media sites collectively (Section 6).

Using the ground-truth data for each event, we design query formulation techniques to capture terms that uniquely identify each event. These terms should ideally appear in any social media document associated with the event but also be broad enough to match a larger set of documents than possible with the precision-oriented queries. We select these recall-oriented queries in two steps. First, we generate a large set of candidate queries for each event using two different *term analysis and extraction techniques*. Then, to select the most promising queries out of a potentially large set of candidates, we explore a variety of *query ranking strategies* and identify the top queries according to each strategy.

Frequency Analysis: The first query candidate generation technique aims to extract the most frequently used terms, while weighing down terms that are naturally common in the English language. The idea is based on the traditional term-frequency, inverse-document-frequency approach [17] commonly used in information retrieval. To select these terms, we compute term frequencies over the ground-truth data for word unigrams, bigrams, and trigrams. We then eliminate stop words and remove infrequent n-grams (determined automatically based on the size of the ground-truth corpus). We also eliminate any term that appears in the top 100,000 most frequent words indexed by Microsoft's Bing search engine as of April 2010[2], with the assumption that any of these queries would be too general to describe any event.

To normalize the n-gram term frequency scores, we use a language model built from a large corpus of Web documents (see Section 7). With this language model, we compute log probability values for any candidate n-gram term. The probability of a term in the language model provides an indication of its frequency on the Web and is used to normalize the term's computed frequency. We sort the n-grams extracted for each event according to their normalized term frequency values, and select the top 100 n-grams as candidate queries for the event.

Term Extraction: The second query candidate generation technique aims to identify meaningful event-related concepts in the ground-truth data using an external reference corpus. For this, we use a Web-based term extractor over our available textual event data [14]. This term extractor leverages a large collection of Web documents and query logs to construct an entity dictionary, and uses it along with statistical and linguistic analysis methodologies to find a list of significant terms. The extracted terms for each event serve as additional recall-oriented query candidates, along with the term-frequency query candidates described above.

Each of the techniques we describe could potentially generate a large set of candidate queries. However, many of these queries could be noisy (e.g., [@birdfan], with the name of a user that posts many updates about the event), too general (e.g., [concert tonight]), or describing a specific or non-central aspect of the event (e.g., [Fitz and the Dizzyspells], the name of an Andrew Bird song from the concert). Issuing hundreds of queries for each event is not scalable and could potentially introduce substantial noise, so we need to further reduce the set of queries to the most promising candidates. We explore a variety of strategies for selecting the top candidate queries out of all possible queries that we construct for each event. We consider two important criteria for ordering the event queries: specificity and temporal profile.

Specificity: Specificity assures that we rank long, detailed queries higher than broad, general ones. Since we use conjunctive query semantics, longer queries consisting of multiple terms (e.g., [a,b]), are more restrictive than shorter queries consisting of fewer terms (e.g., [a]). Particularly, since we use term n-gram shingles with n=1, 2, and 3 to construct the recall-oriented queries, our set of candidate queries often includes bigram queries that are subsets of trigram queries (e.g., [bird concert] and [andrew bird concert]). If both such candidates are present in the set, we favor the longer, more detailed version, as we observed that this level of specificity generally helps improve precision and yet is not restrictive enough to hurt recall.

Temporal Profile: The historical temporal profile of a query is another criterion we use to select among the candidate queries for an event. A local spike in document frequency around the time of the event might serve as an indication that the query is indeed associated with the event. We keep a record of the number of documents retrieved by each query during the week before and the week after the event, and compare this number to the query's document volume during shorter time periods (one or two days) around the event's time span. We used a similar signal successfully in our prior work [5] as an indicative feature for identifying events in textual streams of Twitter messages.

For example, Figure 3 shows a document volume histogram over Twitter documents for two recall-oriented queries retrieved around the week of Andrew Bird's concert at "Celebrate Brooklyn!" We can see that the volume of a general query such as [state farm insurance] is consistent over time, whereas the volume of [andrew bird concert], while lower, increases around the time of the event. While this temporal analysis is promising for some social media sites

[2]http://web-ngram.research.microsoft.com/info/

(e.g., Twitter) where the time of the messages generally coincides with the time of the event, it may be problematic for other sites (e.g., YouTube, Flickr) that tend to exhibit a delay between an event's time and upload time of the associated digital media documents for the event, because of the nature of these sites. Therefore, for sites containing digital media, we use the content creation time rather than the upload time, if possible. (This feature is, unfortunately, often noisy or missing, especially for YouTube videos.)

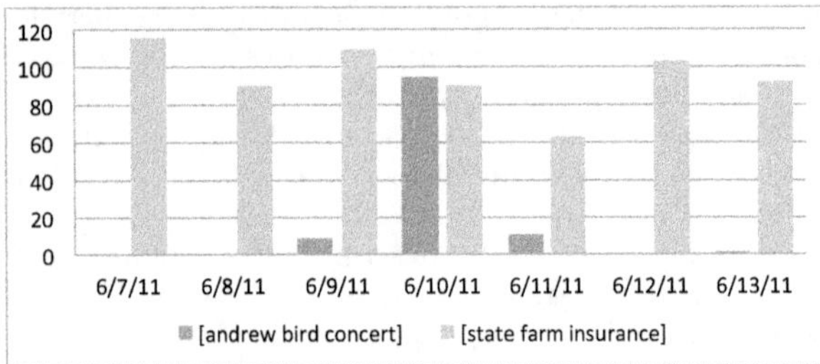

Figure 3: Histogram of Twitter document volume over time for two queries.

We consider using each of these query selection strategies individually, and also explore ways of combining them, to identify the top candidate queries for any given event. With these queries, we can retrieve associated social media documents from a variety of social media sites. Interestingly, content retrieved from the various sites can generate complementary signals for the recall-oriented query generation and retrieval process, as we will see next.

6. LEVERAGING CROSS-SITE CONTENT

Querying for event content from multiple social media sites can provide a holistic perspective on the event, complete with digital media and a variety of user perspectives. For the "Celebrate Brooklyn!" opening concert, for instance, we can use these different social media sites to learn about the event (e.g., via a Twitter message "Celebrate Brooklyn kicks off TONIGHT with Andrew Bird concert in Prospect Park!"), watch a video of a song performed at the event (e.g., "Andrew Bird - Effigy (Live) - Prospect Park - Brooklyn, NY" on YouTube), and see up-close photos of Andrew Bird on stage during the event (e.g., "Andrew Bird: Prospect Park Bandshell" photo set on Flickr).

Moreover, we can leverage event content from one social media site to help retrieve event documents from another social media site in different ways, following the query generation strategies proposed in the previous sections. One simple way is, of course, to generate recall-oriented queries for each site individually and use these queries across sites. Specifically, we can use the high-precision results obtained from an individual site to formulate recall-oriented queries as described in Section 5. We can then use these site-specific recall-oriented queries to obtain additional results from other social media sites. This is especially useful when the precision-oriented strategies do not retrieve results from all sites. This is the case for our "Celebrate Brooklyn!" example: since the event title is too specific, the precision-oriented queries fail to retrieve any documents from YouTube, and hence we cannot generate recall-oriented queries for the site. Fortunately, as is often the case, Twitter has a wealth of results for the precision-oriented queries for the event, and the resulting recall-oriented queries (e.g., [andrew bird concert], [brooklyn celebrate]) retrieve relevant videos from YouTube. In short, we manage to extract useful YouTube content through queries derived based on Twitter content.

An alternative way to leverage multi-site social media content is to generate recall-oriented queries using the high-precision results returned from all social media sites collectively. Whenever we obtain precision-oriented results from multiple sites, this approach yields a larger "ground-truth" corpus for the recall-oriented query generation than the ones obtained from each site individually, which may be helpful for identifying salient event terms that appear frequently across sites. At the same time, the results may be dominated by content from one site, possibly obscuring useful content from another site. This approach may also introduce noise or irrelevant content that is often present in some sites and not others (e.g., content-free titles of Flickr photos, Twitter username mentions).

Although content from different social media sites provides promising opportunities, it also presents challenges for our techniques. First, site-specific notations and conventions often introduce noise or inhibit recall. For example, Flickr users often tag photos with their camera settings (e.g., "canoneos5dmarkii"), which may be mistakenly identified as an important event term by the term frequency analysis, especially if the ground-truth corpus for the event is small. In addition, each Flickr tag must consist of a single term, so users often resort to very long multi-word tags (e.g., "greatcanadiancheesefestival"). In contrast, YouTube tags may each consist of several terms, so querying for such long multi-word tags on YouTube rarely yields results. We experimentally evaluate the merits of these alternative multi-site approaches in the next section.

7. EXPERIMENTS

We evaluated our query selection and retrieval techniques using a large dataset of real-world events from several event aggregation sites. For each event, we used our query generation strategies to collect related documents from popular social media sites. We performed three different sets of experiments:

- Comparison of the automatically generated queries against human-produced queries for the events
- Evaluation by human judges of the automatically generated queries
- Evaluation of the quality of the documents retrieved by the automatically generated queries

We report on the dataset and experimental settings, then turn to the results of our experiments.

7.1 Experimental Settings

Planned Event Dataset: We assembled a dataset of event records posted between May 13, 2011 and June 11, 2011 on four different event aggregation platforms: Last.fm events, EventBrite, LinkedIn events, and Facebook events. We used the Last.fm API with a location parameter set to "United States"[3] to collect musical performance events. To

[3]This was the only way to retrieve a set of events from Last.fm without issuing specific queries.

collect events from EventBrite, we used its API with the date parameters set to our specified date range. For LinkedIn events, where an API was not available, we retrieved and parsed event search pages in HTML format, using HTTP GET parameters to specify the date range.

Facebook events deserve special attention due to the difficulty of collecting such data via the site's API. Facebook events can only be retrieved in response to a specific search query or event id. To search for events, we used the most common event terms found in event titles collected by our event tracking system [3]. This list includes terms that describe specific types of events (e.g., [concert]) and also general terms commonly found in event titles (e.g., [national], [international]). We removed any returned event records that had no location or time information, and events that listed a virtual location (e.g., "everywhere") in their location or venue fields. Unfortunately, after filtering for these required fields we were left with very few events that matched our criteria. Still, we included these events in our experiments as they add diversity to our dataset.

To ensure that we collected events that would potentially have associated social media documents, we filtered out obscure events by requiring a minimum number of event attendees. We tuned this minimum threshold for each site given the observed distribution of attendees over all collected events. At the end of the process, we collected a total of 393 events, with 90 events from Last.fm, 94 events from EventBrite, 130 events from LinkedIn, and 25 events from Facebook. The above events constitute the test set over which we report our results. For training and tuning, we used a separate set of 329 event records, collected (in a similar fashion) between April 26 and May 11, 2011.

Social Media Documents: We collected social media documents for the events in our dataset from three social media sites: Twitter, YouTube, and Flickr. Specifically, we used each site's respective search API to issue precision-oriented (Section 4) and recall-oriented (Section 5) queries. From the retrieved results, we further eliminated any document that did not exactly match the search query since some site search engines (e.g., for Twitter) search for the query in any content that is linked from the document, and return matching documents as relevant results.

Note that part of our evaluation considers the quality of the top-k documents retrieved by the automatically generated queries (see problem definition in Section 3). The ranking of *documents* for an event is not the focus of this paper. For our evaluation, we rank the documents retrieved for an event by computing their similarity to the event record using (an adaptation of) the multiple-feature similarity function in [4]. As one additional component of the similarity, not present in [4], we consider the percentage of queries that retrieve a given document when we compute the score for the document and an event. Intuitively, we have observed that documents that are retrieved by several of our queries for an event should be preferred over documents that are retrieved by one such query.

Precision-Oriented Query Generation: For each event, we generated precision-oriented queries as defined in Section 4 using the event's context features, namely, title, time/date, city and venue. As an exception, we did not generate queries using the three title-only strategies for Last.fm events since we observed that many of the event titles on Last.fm consist of the name of a performer without any other context. Even though we restrict the social media documents that we retrieve to a specific time period around the event, it is often difficult in the Last.fm case to distinguish between two events held by the same performer in close time proximity. By forcing the location (i.e., city or venue) as part of the query for such events, we ensure that our precision-oriented queries produce results from the intended performance. For event records from the rest of the sites we use all precision-oriented queries from Section 4.

Recall-Oriented Query Generation: For each event, we generate recall-oriented queries as described in Section 5. To perform the frequency analysis, we index the documents using Lucene[4], with term n-grams, for n=1, 2, and 3. To normalize n-gram term frequency scores, we use the Microsoft Web n-gram Service[5], which provides n-gram log probability values. This service returns the joint probability of n-gram terms using a language model created from documents indexed by Microsoft's Bing search engine.

We extract meaningful queries from the high-precision results using the Yahoo! Term Extraction Web Service[6], which returns a list of significant terms or phrases given a segment of text. This term extractor leverages a large collection of documents and query logs to construct an entity dictionary and uses it along with a statistical and linguistic analysis [14] to process the given textual event data. This term extraction service has shown promising results on preliminary experiments with training data, to complement the first term frequency analysis technique above. It has also been successfully used in prior work for similar tasks [10, 14].

Query Generation and Ranking Techniques: Our experiments consider a subset of the (potentially many) queries generated using the precision- and recall-oriented strategies above. Different techniques will vary on how these subsets are selected. We consider two basic options to rank the queries for selection, namely, using (1) the "specificity" of the queries, as determined by the n-gram score on the Microsoft Web document corpus, or (2) variations of a "temporal" profile of the queries, determined by analyzing the volume of matching documents for the queries over time. Each alternative technique selects the top-10 queries according to the associated ranking criterion, as follows:

- MS n-gram Score (MS): n-gram score of the query from the Microsoft Web n-gram Service
- Time Ratio (TR): ratio of the number of documents created in the 48 hours before and after the event to the number of documents created in the week before and after the event
- Restricted Time Ratio (RTR): ratio of the number of documents created in the 24 hours before and after the event to the number of documents created in the week before and after the event
- MS n-gram Score and Time Ratio (MS-TR): MS score multiplied by TR score
- MS n-gram Score and Restricted Time Ratio (MS-RTR): MS score multiplied by RTR score

We apply the above techniques to documents from Twitter, YouTube, and Flickr individually, and also to documents

[4]http://lucene.apache.org/

[5]http://research.microsoft.com/web-ngram

[6]http://developer.yahoo.com/search/content/V1/termExtraction.html

from all three sites collectively. We use the site's name or "All," along with the strategy name (e.g., Twitter-MS, All-TR), to distinguish among these alternatives. We also compare the above techniques, which include both precision- and recall-oriented queries, against a technique that selects all precision-oriented queries. We refer to this technique as Precision.

Evaluation and Metrics: To evaluate our strategies, we collected annotations for a random sample of 60 events in our dataset. For each event, we used two annotators for three different tasks: comparison against human-produced queries, human evaluation of generated queries, and evaluation of document retrieval results. To compare our automatically generated queries against human-produced queries, we asked each annotator to provide 5 different queries that would be useful for collecting social media documents for each event. We use the Jaccard coefficient to measure the similarity of the set of automatically generated queries G to the set of human-produced queries H for each event. Specifically, for each query $q_g \in G$ and each query $q_h \in H$ we compute $J(q_g, q_h) = |q_g \cap q_h|/|q_g \cup q_h|$, with set operations performed over query terms. The Jaccard value that we report for G is then $\sum_{q_g \in G} max_{q_h \in H}(J(q_g, q_h))/|G|$. In other words, for each event, we computed the sum of maximum similarities between each automated query and the best-matching human-produced query.

For the human evaluation of the automatically generated queries, we asked two annotators to label 2,037 queries selected by our strategies for each event on a scale of 1-5, based on their relevance to the event. Here, we aim to gauge the potential of each query to retrieve results related to the event. For our "Celebrate Brooklyn!" example, the queries [celebrate], [celebrate brooklyn], and [andrew bird celebrate brooklyn] would receive scores of 1, 3, and 5, respectively. In cases of disagreement between annotators, we use the average rating. For two events in this set, our annotators were unable to provide queries due to ambiguous content (e.g., "ready film" as the title, without description), and content in a foreign language (e.g., queries in Italian for "FashionCamp," despite setting our API parameters for English-only content). These events were removed from the analysis.

Finally, for the evaluation of the quality of the documents retrieved by the automatically generated queries, we used Amazon's Mechanical Turk[7] to collect relevance judgments for the top-20 documents retrieved from Twitter, YouTube, and Flickr for each of our query selection techniques above. We collected two binary relevance judgments for each document. Agreement between our annotators was substantial, with Cohen's kappa coefficient values $\kappa = 0.85, 0.69$, and 0.93, for Twitter, YouTube, and Flickr documents, respectively. In cases of annotator disagreement, we collected a third judgment. To evaluate the retrieved documents, we use a standard metric, namely, normalized discounted cumulative gain, or *NDCG* [9], which captures the quality of ranked lists with focus on the top results. We use the binary version of NDCG [9], to measure how well our approach ranks the top documents relative to their ideal ranking.

7.2 Experimental Results

We begin by comparing the similarity of the automatically generated queries and human-produced queries for

[7]https://www.mturk.com

Strategy	Twitter	Flickr	YouTube	All
MS	0.571	0.216	0.181	0.272
TR	0.524	0.254	0.097	0.277
RTR	0.517	0.253	0.094	0.317
MS-TR	0.531	0.209	0.141	0.244
MS-RTR	0.523	0.209	0.141	0.263

Table 2: Jaccard coefficient for automatically generated queries and human-produced queries.

our events. Table 2 shows the results of our query generation methods using documents from Twitter, Flickr, and YouTube separately, and documents from all sites collectively. Across all strategies, queries generated using Flickr or YouTube documents were less similar to the human-produced queries compared to queries generated using Twitter documents. For Flickr, this result can be explained by the common use of long multi-word tags, which were often selected as the top queries by our strategies (e.g., [20110603musichallofwilliamsburgbrooklynny]). While these queries may not reflect human behavior, they could still be useful for retrieving event content, as we will see. In contrast, Precision had the highest Jaccard value at 0.705, indicating that the human-produced queries were most similar to the precision-oriented queries we defined in Section 4. Interestingly, using documents from all sites collectively did not improve the similarity, possibly due to the presence of Flickr tags among the selected queries for this strategy.

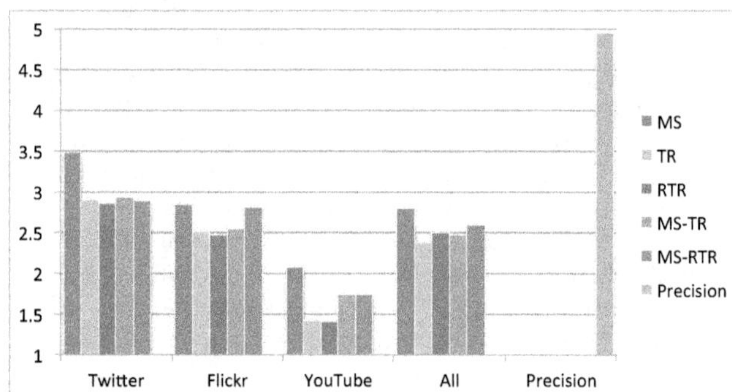

Figure 4: Average annotator rating of our automatically generated queries.

For the next step in our analysis, Figure 4 shows the average annotator rating for our alternative query generation approaches. Not surprisingly, Precision achieved the best average rating since, by design, it produced very detailed queries that are expected to return relevant results for their associated events. The query generation techniques that used Twitter documents, especially Twitter-MS, were again the most successful set of techniques. Based on our annotation guidelines, the score of Twitter-MS indicates that, on average, queries generated by this strategy are expected to retrieve some results for their associated event. The query generation techniques that used YouTube documents received the lowest scores in this evaluation. One possible explanation is that the query-generation strategies may not be effective when formulated using YouTube data alone, which may be related to the lack of reliable temporal information for YouTube documents, as we discussed in Section 5.

For our third set of experiments, we examined the rele-

Strategy	5 Docs	10 Docs	15 Docs	20 Docs
Twitter-MS	0.759	0.724	0.690	0.690
Twitter-RTR	0.828	0.793	0.759	0.759
Precision	0.414	0.293	0.241	0.224

Table 3: Percentage of events with Twitter results at different recall levels for alternative query strategies.

vance of documents retrieved by our query generation strategies to their associated events. Figure 5 shows the NDCG scores for the top 5, 10, 15, and 20 Twitter documents retrieved by Precision, Twitter-MS, and Twitter-RTR (Twitter-TR, Twitter-MS-TR, and Twitter-MS-RTR produced similar results to Twitter-MS and Twitter-RTR, and were therefore omitted). Validating our earlier observation (Section 4), Precision retrieved highly relevant results. Both Twitter-MS and Twitter-RTR also produced good results, demonstrating their effectiveness at retrieving Twitter documents for known events.

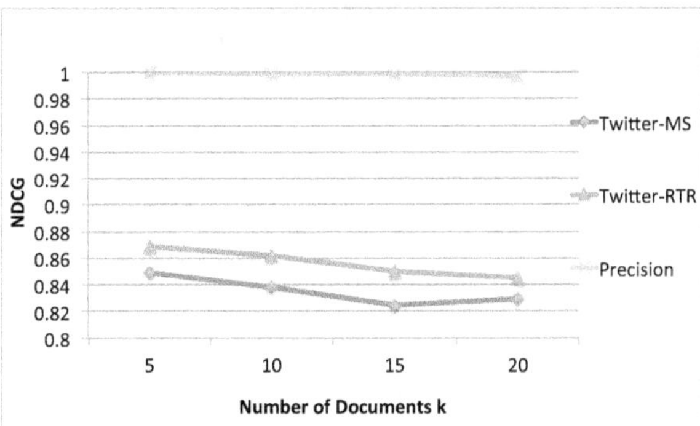

Figure 5: NDCG scores for top-k Twitter documents retrieved by our query strategies.

Note that the NDCG scores at each level of recall were averaged over the set of events that had some returned results for each strategy. Table 3 reports the percentage of events in our dataset for which each strategy returned results at various levels of recall. As expected, Precision returned results for a small fraction of the events. Interestingly, Twitter-RTR returned results for a larger proportion of the events than Twitter-MS. This can be explained by the way these alternative strategies select their top queries. Specifically, all queries selected for Twitter-RTR must have some matching documents, since we consider each query's document volume over time as the selection criterion. In contrast, Twitter-MS is biased towards rare terms (i.e., terms with lower probability scores), making it the second most precise among the strategies, following Precision.

Our next set of results examines the effectiveness of our approaches for retrieving event documents across social media sites. Given our observations from the query-based evaluations, we evaluated the relevance of documents retrieved by the best performing query generation approach, namely, Twitter-MS, from both YouTube and Flickr. Figure 6 shows the NDCG scores of Precision, Twitter-MS, and YouTube-MS for the top-k YouTube documents, averaged over all events. In addition, the size of each point reflects the number of events that had at least k documents retrieved by the strategy. As we can see, Twitter-MS performed better and retrieved results for more events than YouTube-MS, indicating that Twitter documents can be potentially used to improve both precision and recall of YouTube documents for planned events.

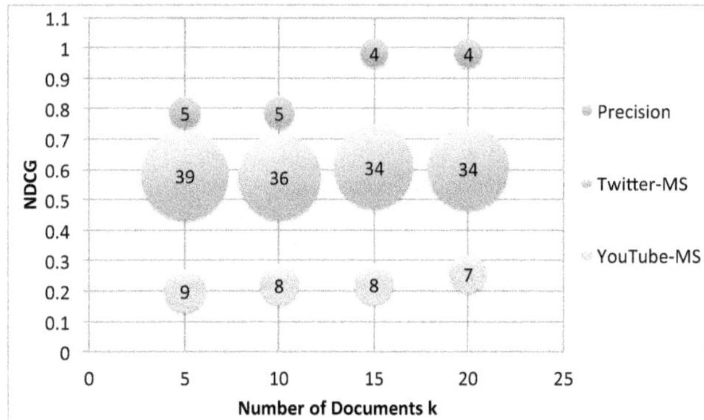

Figure 6: NDCG scores for top-k YouTube documents retrieved by our query strategies.

We performed a similar evaluation over documents from Flickr, using Precision, Twitter-MS, and Flickr-MS. Precision, expectedly, retrieved relevant results for a small number of events. Interestingly, unlike YouTube-MS, Flickr-MS achieved higher NDCG scores than Twitter-MS. However, the number of events covered by Flickr-MS is smaller than the number of events covered by Twitter-MS, showing that Twitter-MS can still retrieve relevant Flickr documents and can be particularly useful in cases where Flickr-MS returns no results.

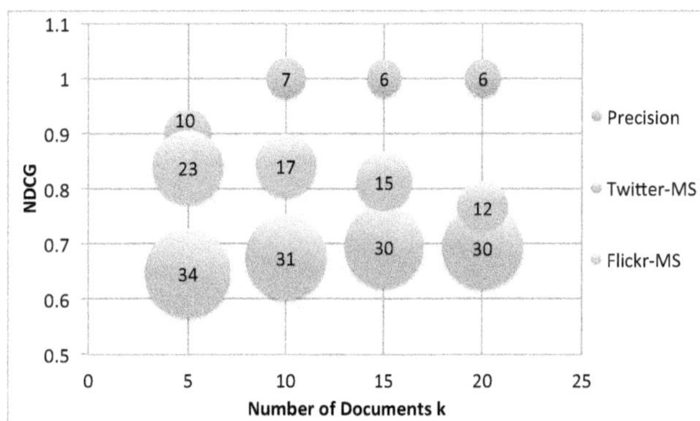

Figure 7: NDCG scores for top-k Flickr documents retrieved by our query strategies.

Overall, our evaluation showed that our query generation approaches can effectively retrieve relevant social media documents for planned events on multiple social media sites. In addition, we demonstrated that we can leverage social media documents on Twitter to generate a query strategy (i.e., Twitter-MS) that can retrieve relevant event documents on YouTube and Flickr.

8. CONCLUSIONS

In this paper, we presented a query-oriented solution for retrieving social media documents for planned events across different social media sites. This work provides an essential step in the process of organizing social media documents for events, towards improved browsing and search for event media. Using a combination of precision-oriented and recall-oriented query generation techniques, we showed how to automatically and effectively associate social media documents with planned events from various sources. Importantly, we demonstrated how social media documents from one social media site can be used to enhance document retrieval on another social media site, thus contributing to the diversity of information that we can collect for planned events. Many opportunities for future work remain to improve our general approach, such as learning how to exploit the content of pages linked from event-related documents and how to leverage direct links between such documents across social media sites, in an iterative cross-site retrieval process. Other future directions include sub-event content and topic analysis, so that multiple views or temporal variations represented in the data can be exposed. Overall, our techniques help unveil important information from, and about, planned events as they are reflected through the eyes of hundreds of millions of users of social media sites.

9. ACKNOWLEDGMENTS

This material is based on work supported by NSF Grants IIS-0811038, IIS-1017845, and IIS-1017389, and by two Google Research Awards. In accordance with Columbia University reporting requirements, Professor Gravano acknowledges ownership of Google stock as of the writing of this paper. We thank Feiyang Chen for his invaluable help with the precision-oriented strategies of Section 4, and our annotators Brandy Hartley and Emma Moore.

10. REFERENCES

[1] E. Agichtein, C. Castillo, D. Donato, A. Gionis, and G. Mishne. Finding high-quality content in social media. In *Proceedings of the First ACM International Conference on Web Search and Data Mining (WSDM '08)*, 2008.

[2] J. Allan, editor. *Topic Detection and Tracking: Event-based Information Organization.* Kluwer Academic Publisher, 2002.

[3] H. Becker, F. Chen, D. Iter, M. Naaman, and L. Gravano. Automatic identification and presentation of Twitter content for planned events. In *Proceedings of the Fifth International AAAI Conference on Weblogs and Social Media (ICWSM '11)*, 2011.

[4] H. Becker, M. Naaman, and L. Gravano. Learning similarity metrics for event identification in social media. In *Proceedings of the Third ACM International Conference on Web Search and Data Mining (WSDM '10)*, 2010.

[5] H. Becker, M. Naaman, and L. Gravano. Beyond trending topics: Real-world event identification on Twitter. In *Proceedings of the Fifth International AAAI Conference on Weblogs and Social Media (ICWSM '11)*, 2011.

[6] H. Becker, M. Naaman, and L. Gravano. Selecting quality Twitter content for events. In *Proceedings of the Fifth International AAAI Conference on Weblogs and Social Media (ICWSM '11)*, 2011.

[7] E. Benson, A. Haghighi, and R. Barzilay. Event discovery in social media feeds. In *Proceedings of the 49th Annual Meeting of the Association for Computational Linguistics: Human Language Technologies (ACL-HLT '11)*, 2011.

[8] R. Crane and D. Sornette. Robust dynamic classes revealed by measuring the response function of a social system. *Proceedings of the National Academy of Sciences*, 105(41):15649–15653, 2008.

[9] W. B. Croft, D. Metzler, and T. Strohman. *Search Engines: Information Retrieval in Practice.* Addison-Wesley Publishing Company, 2009.

[10] W. Dakka and P. G. Ipeirotis. Automatic extraction of useful facet hierarchies from text databases. In *Proceedings of the IEEE 24th International Conference on Data Engineering (ICDE '08)*, 2008.

[11] N. Diakopoulos, M. Naaman, and F. Kivran-Swaine. Diamonds in the rough: Social media visual analytics for journalistic inquiry. In *Proceedings of the IEEE Symposium on Visual Analytics Science and Technology (VAST '10)*, 2010.

[12] Events, 2002. In Stanford Encyclopedia of Philosophy. Retrieved June 2nd, 2010 from http://plato.stanford.edu/entries/events/.

[13] V. Hatzivassiloglou, L. Gravano, and A. Maganti. An investigation of linguistic features and clustering algorithms for topical document clustering. In *Proceedings of the 23rd ACM International Conference on Research and Development in Information Retrieval (SIGIR '00)*, 2000.

[14] R. Kraft, F. Maghoul, and C. C. Chang. Y!Q: Contextual search at the point of inspiration. In *Proceedings of the 14th ACM International Conference on Information and Knowledge Management (CIKM '05)*, 2005.

[15] H. Kwak, C. Lee, H. Park, and S. Moon. What is Twitter, a social network or a news media? In *Proceedings of the 19th International World Wide Web Conference (WWW '10)*, 2010.

[16] L. Liu, L. Sun, Y. Rui, Y. Shi, and S. Yang. Web video topic discovery and tracking via bipartite graph reinforcement model. In *Proceedings of the 17th International World Wide Web Conference (WWW '08)*, 2008.

[17] C. D. Manning, P. Raghavan, and H. Schütze. *Introduction to Information Retrieval.* Cambridge Univ. Press, 2008.

[18] M. Naaman, H. Becker, and L. Gravano. Hip and trendy: Characterizing emerging trends on Twitter. *Journal of the American Society for Information Science and Technology*, 62(5):902–918, 2011.

[19] M. Nagarajan, K. Gomadam, A. P. Sheth, A. Ranabahu, R. Mutharaju, and A. Jadhav. Spatio-temporal-thematic analysis of citizen sensor data: Challenges and experiences. In *Proceedings of the 10th International Conference on Web Information Systems Engineering (WISE '09)*, 2009.

[20] S. Petrović, M. Osborne, and V. Lavrenko. Streaming first story detection with application to Twitter. In *Proceedings of the 2010 Annual Conference of the North American Chapter of the Association for Computational Linguistics (NAACL '10)*, 2010.

[21] T. Sakaki, M. Okazaki, and Y. Matsuo. Earthquake shakes Twitter users: Real-time event detection by social sensors. In *Proceedings of the 19th International World Wide Web Conference (WWW '10)*, 2010.

[22] J. Sankaranarayanan, H. Samet, B. E. Teitler, M. D. Lieberman, and J. Sperling. Twitterstand: News in tweets. In *Proceedings of the 17th ACM International Conference on Advances in Geographic Information Systems (GIS '09)*, 2009.

[23] D. A. Shamma, L. Kennedy, and E. Churchill. Statler: Summarizing media through short-message services. In *Proceedings of the 2010 ACM Conference on Computer Supported Cooperative Work (CSCW '10)*, 2010.

[24] S. Yardi and d. boyd. Tweeting from the town square: Measuring geographic local networks. In *Proceedings of the Fourth International AAAI Conference on Weblogs and Social Media (ICWSM '10)*, 2010.

[25] J. M. Zacks and B. Tversky. Event structure in perception and conception. *Psychological Bulletin*, 127, 2001.

[26] K. Zhang, J. Zi, and L. G. Wu. New event detection based on indexing-tree and named entity. In *Proceedings of the 30th ACM International Conference on Research and Development in Information Retrieval (SIGIR '07)*, 2007.

Daily Deals: Prediction, Social Diffusion, and Reputational Ramifications

John W. Byers*
Computer Science Dept.
Boston University

Michael Mitzenmacher†
School of Eng. Appl. Sci.
Harvard University

Georgios Zervas*
Computer Science Dept.
Boston University

ABSTRACT

Daily deal sites have become the latest Internet sensation, providing discounted offers to customers for restaurants, ticketed events, services, and other items. We begin by undertaking a study of the economics of daily deals on the web, based on a dataset we compiled by monitoring Groupon and LivingSocial sales in 20 large cities over several months. We use this dataset to characterize deal purchases; glean insights about operational strategies of these firms; and evaluate customers' sensitivity to factors such as price, deal scheduling, and limited inventory. We then marry our daily deals dataset with additional datasets we compiled from Facebook and Yelp users to study the interplay between social networks and daily deal sites. First, by studying user activity on Facebook while a deal is running, we provide evidence that daily deal sites benefit from significant word-of-mouth effects during sales events, consistent with results predicted by cascade models. Second, we consider the effects of daily deals on the longer-term reputation of merchants, based on their Yelp reviews before and after they run a daily deal. Our analysis shows that while the number of reviews increases significantly due to daily deals, average rating scores from reviewers who mention daily deals are 10% lower than scores of their peers on average.

Categories and Subject Descriptors

K.4.4 [**Computers and Society**]: Electronic Commerce

General Terms

Economics, Measurement

1. INTRODUCTION

Groupon and LivingSocial are websites offering various deals-of-the-day, with localized deals for major geographic markets. Groupon in particular has been one of the fastest growing Internet sales businesses in history, with tens of millions of registered users and 2011 sales expected to exceed 1 billion dollars.

We briefly describe how daily deal sites work; additional details relevant to our measurement methodology will be given subsequently. In each geographic market, or city, there are one or more deals of the day. Generally, one deal in each market is the featured deal of the day, and receives the prominent position on the primary webpage targeting that market. The deal provides a coupon for some product or service at a substantial discount (generally 40-60%) to the list price. Deals may be available for one or more days. We use the term *size* of a deal to represent the number of coupons sold, and the term *revenue* of a deal to represent the number of coupons multiplied by the price per coupon. Groupon retains approximately half the revenue from the discounted coupons [11], and provides the rest to the seller, as does LivingSocial. Deals each have a minimum threshold size that must be reached for the deal to take hold, and sellers may also set a maximum threshold size to limit the number of coupons sold.

Daily deal sites represent a change from recent Internet advertising trends. While large-scale e-mail distributions for sale offers are commonplace (generally in the form of spam) and coupon sites have long existed on the Internet, Groupon and LivingSocial have achieved notable success with their emphasis on higher quality localized deals, as well as their marketing savvy both with respect to buyers and sellers (merchants). This paper represents an attempt to gain insight into the success of this business model, using a combination of data analysis and modeling.

The contributions of the paper are as follows:

- We compile and analyze datasets we gathered monitoring Groupon over a period of six months and LivingSocial over a period of three months in 20 large US markets. Our datasets will be made publicly available [4].
- We consider how the price elasticity of demand, as well as what we call "soft incentives", affect the size and revenue of Groupon and LivingSocial deals empirically. Soft incentives include deal aspects other than price, such as whether a deal is featured and what days of the week it is available.
- We study the predictability of the size of Groupon deals, based on deal parameters and on temporal progress. We show that deal sizes can be predicted with moderate accuracy based on a small number of parameters, and with substantially better accuracy shortly after a deal goes live.
- We examine dependencies between the spread of Groupon deals and social networks by cross-referencing our Groupon dataset with Facebook data tracking the frequency

*E-mail: {byers, zg}@cs.bu.edu. Supported in part by Adverplex, Inc. and by NSF grant CNS-1040800.

†E-mail: michaelm@eecs.harvard.edu. Supported in part by NSF grants CCF-0915922 and CNS-0721491, and in part by a research grant from Yahoo!

Permission to make digital or hard copies of all or part of this work for personal or classroom use is granted without fee provided that copies are not made or distributed for profit or commercial advantage and that copies bear this notice and the full citation on the first page. To copy otherwise, to republish, to post on servers or to redistribute to lists, requires prior specific permission and/or a fee.
WSDM'12, February 8–12, 2012, Seattle, Washington, USA.
Copyright 2012 ACM 978-1-4503-0747-5/12/02 ...$10.00.

with which users "like" Groupon deals. We offer evidence that propagation of Groupon deals is consistent with predictions of social spreading made by cascade models.

- We examine the change in reputation of merchants based on their Yelp reviews before and after they run a Groupon deal. We find that reviewers mentioning daily deals are significantly more negative than their peers on average, and the volume of their reviews materially lowers Yelp scores in the months after a daily deal offering.

We note that we presented preliminary findings based on a single month of Groupon data that focused predominantly on the issue of soft incentives in a technical report [3]. The current paper enriches that study in several ways, both in its consideration of LivingSocial as a comparison point, and especially in our use of social network data sources, such as Facebook and Yelp, to study deal sites. Indeed, we believe this use of multiple disparate data sources, while not novel as a research methodology, appears original in this context of gaining insight into deal sites.

Before continuing, we acknowledge that a reasonable question is why we gathered data ourselves, instead of asking Groupon for data; such data (if provided) would likely be more accurate and possibly more comprehensive. We offer several justifications. First, by gathering our own data, we can make it public, for others to use and to verify our results. Second, by relying on a deals site as a source for data, we would be limited to data they were willing to provide, as opposed to data we thought we needed (and was publicly available). Gathering our own data also motivated us to gather and compare data from multiple sources. Finally, due to fortuitous timing, Groupon's recent S-1 filing [11] allowed us to validate several aggregate measures of the datasets we collected.

We note that, due to space restrictions, we were able to include only a subset of our results in this paper. A full version is available at arXiv [5].

Related Work on Daily Deals: To date, there has been little previous work examining Groupon and LivingSocial specifically. Edelman et al. consider the benefits and drawbacks of using Groupon from the side of the merchant, modeling whether the advertising and price discrimination effects can make such discounts profitable [10]. Dholakia polls businesses to determine their experience of providing a deal with Groupon [9], and Arabshahi examines their business model [2]. Several works have studied other online group buying schemes that arose before Groupon, and that utilize substantially different dynamic pricing schemes [1, 12]. Ye et al. recently provide a stochastic "tipping point" model for sales from daily deal sites that incorporates social network effects [21]. They provide supporting evidence for their model using a Groupon data set they collected that is similar to, but less comprehensive, than ours, but they do not measure social network activity.

2. THE DAILY DEALS LANDSCAPE

In this section, we describe the current landscape of daily deal sites exemplified by Groupon and LivingSocial. We start by describing the measurement methodology we employed to collect longitudinal data from these sites, and provide additional background on how these sites operate. We then describe basic insights that can be gleaned directly from our datasets, including revenue and sales broken out by week, by deal, by geographic location, and by deal type. Moving on, we observe that given an offering, daily deal sites can optimize the performance of the offering around various parameters, most obviously price, but also day-of-week, duration, etc. We explore these through the lens of our datasets.

2.1 Measurement Methodology

We collected longitudinal data from the top two group deal sites, Groupon and LivingSocial, as well as from Facebook and Yelp. Our datasets are complex and we describe them in detail below.

Deal data: We collected data from Groupon between January 3rd and July 3rd, 2011. We monitored – to the best of our knowledge – all deals offered in 20 different cities during this period. Our criteria for city selection were population and geographic distribution. Specifically, our list of cities includes: Atlanta, Boston, Chicago, Dallas, Detroit, Houston, Las Vegas, Los Angeles, Miami, New Orleans, New York, Orlando, Philadelphia, San Diego, San Francisco, San Jose, Seattle, Tallahassee, Vancouver, and Washington DC. In total, our data set contains statistics for 16,692 deals.

Each Groupon deal is associated with a set of features: the deal description, the retail and discounted prices, the start and end dates, the threshold number of sales required for the deal to be activated, the number of coupons sold, whether the deal was available in limited quantities, and if it sold out. Each deal is also associated with a category such as "Restaurants", "Nightlife", or "Automotive". From these basic features we compute further quantities of interest such as the revenue derived by each deal, the deal duration, and the percentage discount.

With each Groupon deal, we collected intraday time-series data which monitors two time-varying parameters: cumulative sales, and whether or not a given deal is currently *featured*. To compile these time-series, we monitored each deal in roughly ten-minute intervals and downloaded the value of the sales counter. Occasionally some of our requests failed and therefore some gaps are present in our time-series data, but this does not materially affect our conclusions. The second parameter we monitored was whether a deal was featured or not, with featured deals being those deals that are presented in the subject line of daily subscriber e-mails while being given prominent presentation in the associated city's webpage. For example, visiting `groupon.com/boston`, one notices that a single deal occupies a significant proportion of the screen real-estate, while the rest of the deals which are concurrently active are summarized in a smaller sidebar.

Although Groupon has a public API[1] through which one can obtain some basic deal information, we decided also to monitor the Groupon website directly. Our primary rationale was that certain deal features, such as whether a link to reviews for the merchant offering the deal was present, were not available through the Groupon API. We used the API to obtain a category for each deal and to validate the sales data we collected. Observed discrepancies were infrequent and small: we used the API-collected data as the ground truth in these cases. We did not use the API to collect time-series data.

[1] `http://www.groupon.com/pages/api`

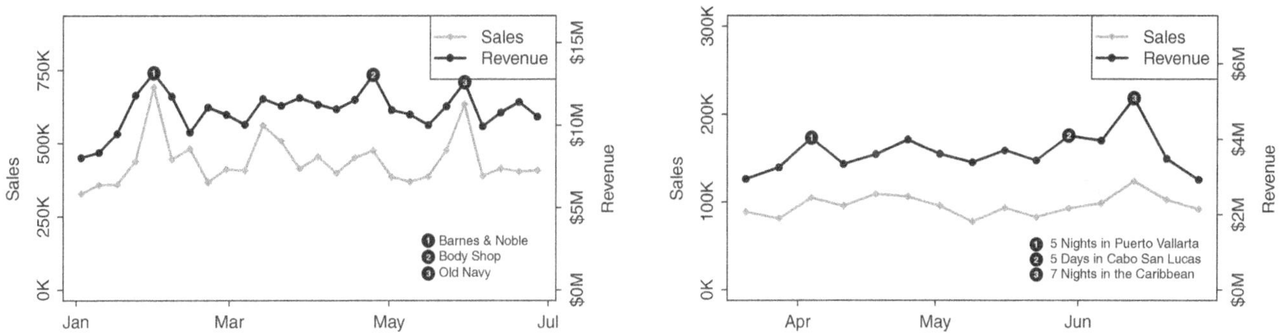

(a) Groupon (b) LivingSocial

Figure 1: Weekly revenue and sales in 20 selected cities (2011).

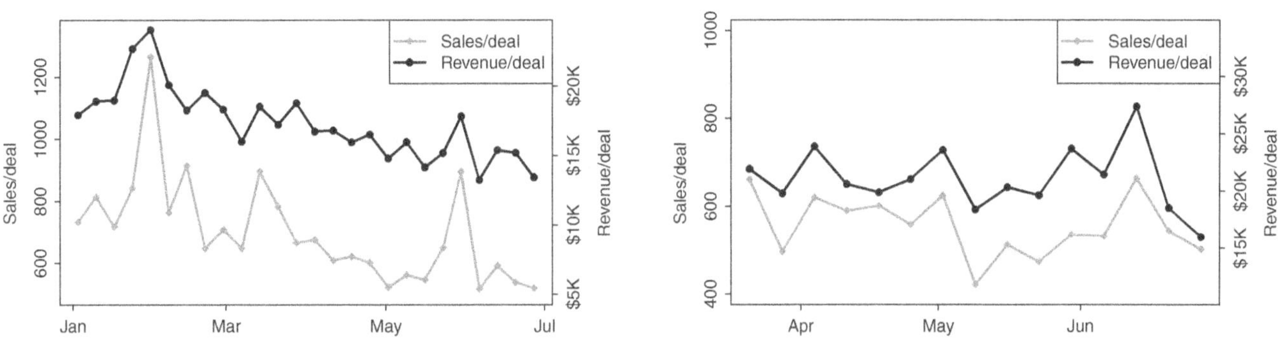

(a) Groupon (b) LivingSocial

Figure 2: Revenue and coupons sold per deal week-over-week.

We collected data from LivingSocial between March 21st and July 3rd, 2011 for the same set of 20 cities. In total, our LivingSocial dataset contains 2,609 deals. LivingSocial deals differ from their Groupon counterparts in that they have no tipping point, and in that they do not explicitly indicate whether they are available in limited quantities (although they do sell out occasionally). LivingSocial runs two types of deals: one featured deal per day, and a secondary "Family Edition" deal, which offers family-friendly activities, and receives less prominent placement on the LivingSocial website. For LivingSocial deals we only collected data on their outcomes; we did not collect time-series data.

Facebook data: Both Groupon and LivingSocial display a Facebook Like button for each deal, where the Like button is associated with a counter representing the number of Facebook users who have clicked the button to express their positive feedback. We refer to the value of the counter as the number of *likes* a deal has received, and we collected this value for each Groupon and LivingSocial deal in our dataset.

As a technical aside, we mention that Groupon and LivingSocial have different implementations of the Facebook Like button that necessitated our collecting data from them in different ways. Within each deal page, Groupon embeds code that dynamically renders the Facebook Like button. It does so by sending Facebook a request that contains a unique identifier associated with the corresponding deal page. We extracted the unique identifier from Groupon deal pages and directly contacted Facebook to obtain the number of likes for every deal. LivingSocial instead hard-codes the Like button and its associated counter within each page. As we could not obtain the identifier associated with each LivingSocial deal, we could not query Facebook to independently obtain the number of likes, and thus we collected the hard-coded number from LivingSocial deal pages.

Yelp data: Groupon occasionally displays reviews for the merchant offering the deal in the form of a star-rating, as well as selected reviewer comments. The reviews are sourced from major review sites such as Yelp, Citysearch, and TripAdvisor. For Groupon deals that were linked to Yelp reviews, we collected the individual reviewer ratings and comments left by customers on Yelp. We collected this dataset during the first week of October 2011. In total, our dataset contains 58,900 reviews, for 2,332 merchants who ran 2,486 deals on Groupon during our monitoring period. Yelp has a system in place to filter "spurious reviews", including for example those left by shills [18]. To see these filtered reviews, one has to solve a CAPTCHA which we did not attempt to circumvent. However, Yelp does report the number of filtered reviews for each merchant and using that we were able to estimate that approximately 23% of all reviews in our dataset were hidden from our collection.

2.2 Operational Insights

Figure 1 serves as an overview of insights we are able to gain using our dataset. It displays the weekly revenue as well as the weekly sales of coupons across all 20 cities we monitored for Groupon and LivingSocial, respectively. Notably, while both Groupon and LivingSocial are widely regarded as companies enjoying extremely rapid growth, our first take-

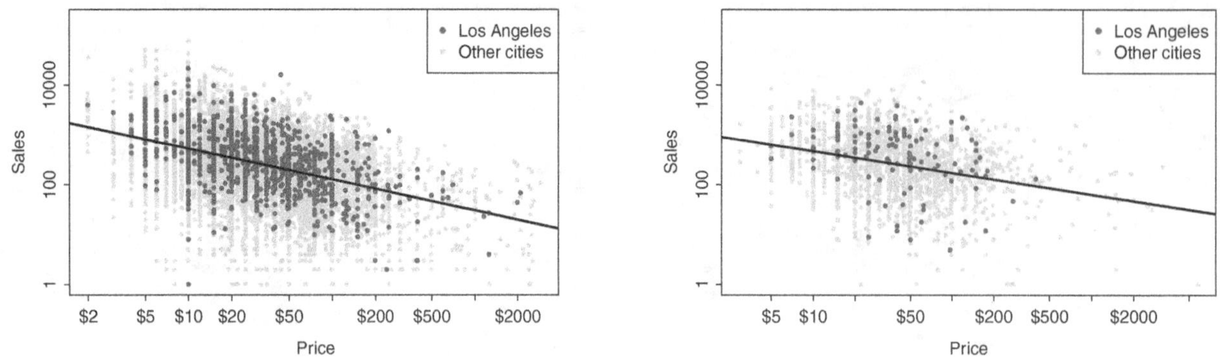

(a) Groupon, slope = −0.62

(b) LivingSocial, slope = −0.43

Figure 3: Deal size by price (in logarithmic scale.) Black dots highlight deals in LA; grey dots are used for other cities. A trend line fitted using OLS regression for all data is also shown.

away from these plots is that sales and revenue in these 20 established markets are relatively flat across the time period. We conjecture that much of the reported growth is in newer markets.

By happenstance, Groupon's recent S-1 filing [11] provided financial information that allowed us to validate some of the aggregate revenue data that we collected independently. For example, the filing states that in the three months ending March 31, 2011, Groupon had sold 950,689 deals in Chicago earning \$21.5M in revenues. Our dataset accounts for 967,244 deals sold and \$21.3M in revenues. For the same period in Boston, the filing reports 388,178 deals sold for total revenues of \$9.3M compared to 362,823 deals and \$8.7M in our dataset. In both cases, our observations closely match what the company reported. The small differences may have arisen for several reasons: we did not monitor all revenue generating activities (such as direct backchannels provided to merchants); some deals were offered at multiple prices but we only monitored the main one; our accounting methods might differ from Groupon's; our inability to account for refunds; and our monitoring infrastructure may have overlooked some deals.

Outliers in our plots are not due to especially strong performance in local markets, but instead seem to be generated by large national deals. The three most significant outliers for both Groupon and LivingSocial each correspond to a large national offer. Representative deals noted in Figure 1 include \$10 for \$20 in Barnes & Noble merchandise during the week of 1/31 for Groupon and 7 nights in the Caribbean during the week of 6/13 for LivingSocial.

A different phenomenon is captured in Figure 2, where we plot week-over-week sales and revenue on a *per-deal* basis. For Groupon, sales and revenue per deal in the 20 cities we monitored peaked in February 2011 and have trended steadily downward since. For LivingSocial, we observe much greater variability, obscuring any underlying trend, but per-deal sales and revenue appear flat or declining. While these trends could potentially point to underlying fragility in the daily deals business model (possibly the best revenue-producing merchants in a geographical area are becoming exhausted), more benign explanations exist. The trend could reflect a change in operational strategy to broaden the base of featured deals available to subscribers at any given time, for example, to provide better personalization of deals to subscribers. However, revenue growth in established markets appears to be a potential challenge facing daily deal sites.

2.3 Pricing and Other Incentives

We now consider a range of factors that influence the number of coupons sold and that daily deal sites can control. Our primary focus is on Groupon; we provide a complete analysis of LivingSocial in the full version of the paper. As daily deal sites have built their business around deeply discounted offers, one might expect that the discounted price associated with a deal would be the primary purchase incentive. Indeed, in the log-log scatterplots of deal sizes vs. deal prices depicted in Figure 3, the trend lines fitted using ordinary least-squares (OLS) regression indicate that the logarithm of price and the logarithm of sales are roughly linearly related. While there is a large amount of variance within individual price points, by controlling for other features, such as restricting attention to deals in Los Angeles (black points), the trend becomes clearer.

A closely related deal feature is the magnitude of the discount, which Groupon displays prominently in advertising a deal. While we conjecture that customers are sensitive to this quantity, most discounts presented fall in a relatively narrow range (three-quarters of all Groupon deals are discounted by 40 to 60%). This has the effect of making the list price highly correlated (0.90 correlation coefficient) with the discount price and therefore the discount is a weak distinguishing feature once price has been taken into account.

Deal sites can also control the length of time a deal runs. As shown in Table 1, while deal size varies minimally with duration, revenue increases, suggesting perhaps that Groupon is attempting to hit *sales*, instead of *revenue*, targets. Expensive deals may generally sell less quickly, and must be allowed more time to achieve the same sales goal.

At any point in time, and for each geographic market, one deal among the set of all available deals is featured by Groupon. Featured deals receive prominent placement both on the Groupon website and in the daily email that customers receive. In our dataset, 22% of deals were featured. The impact of featured placement is significant: the mean sales and revenue for featured deals are well in excess of twice the corresponding quantities for other deals. The effects of featuring a deal are summarized in the Table 2. However, we cannot assume that these outcomes are entirely causal effects from featuring a deal, as Groupon naturally has an incen-

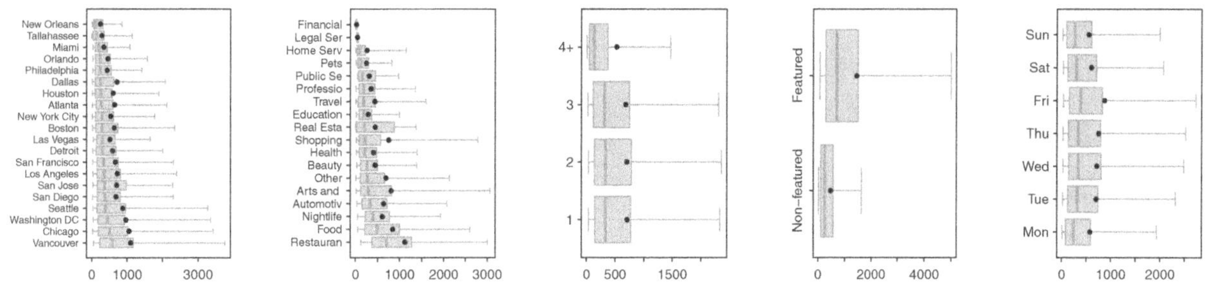

(a) By city (b) By category (c) By duration (days) (d) By placement (e) By start weekday

Figure 4: Groupon deal sizes are shown on the $x-$axis. On the $y-$axis deals are broken down by various deal features. The outer whiskers mark the 5% and 95% quantiles of the deal size, the sides of each grey rectangle the 1st and 3rd quartiles, the solid bar the median, and the solid dot the mean.

Duration (days)	1	2	3	4+
Mean price	$28	$42	$56	$139
Mean sales	712	707	685	529
Mean revenue	$12,576	$18,375	$20,010	$20,189
Number of deals	5,464	5,745	3,877	1,606

Table 1: Groupon deals by duration.

	Featured	Non-featured
Mean sales	1,443	475
Mean revenue	$34,181	$12,241
Number of deals	3,644	13,048

Table 2: Groupon deals by placement.

tive to feature those deals that will drive the most sales. We investigated whether certain *categories* of deals as a whole were featured more frequently. While there is some variation – 35% of all Travel deals are featured, while only 13% of Home Services deals are – most categories have deals featured between 15% and 25% of the time.

Another distinguishing characteristic is inventory size: some deals are available only in limited quantities. Groupon lets its customers know which deals are limited, but does not display the number of available units (while some competitors of Groupon display this prominently). Approximately 31% of all deals in our dataset are available in limited numbers, with wide variation across categories. Approximately 50% of all "Travel" deals and 39% of all "Arts and Entertainment" deals were available in limited quantities, as one might expect for these types of deals. Surprisingly, only about 18% of the limited deals in our dataset sold out. It is not that these deals are intrinsically less attractive: limited deals outperformed unlimited deals on average by 11% more coupon sales and 27% more revenue. It is possible that merchants (or Groupon) artificially limit deals as a strategy to exert pressure to customers, making them more likely to purchase on the spur of the moment.

Groupon also has a choice as to the days of the week that it schedules each offer. Figure 4e breaks down deals by the day of the week on which they began. Even though the differences are not striking, it appears that deals starting in the beginning of the week produce less revenue, and deals starting on Friday produce the most. One possible explanation is that on Fridays, Groupon starts more multi-day deals that span the weekend. For example, 45% of three-day deals start on a Friday. However, alternative explanations, such as that the best deals are run on Friday or that people are more likely to buy on Friday, may also apply.

Deals are said to be "on" when they surpass a sales threshold defined by Groupon, possibly in conjunction with the merchant. That is, for customers to get a discount, a minimum number of them must commit to the deal. In theory, this could drive a group dynamic whereby customers encourage their friends to buy a coupon to reach the threshold. However, current deal thresholds are very low. For example, in our dataset, the mean threshold to total sales ratio is approximately 19%. Deals that surpassed their threshold did so on average just after 8am, and only 2% of deals with thresholds failed to reach them. Like the relationship between price to deal size, the relationship between threshold and deal size also appears to be linear when plotted in logarithmic scale.

Deals can also be classified by two features that Groupon does not have direct control over: their geographic market, and their category. Figure 4a shows that while deal sizes vary considerably across cities, and not always in proportion to city population. This is in part due to localization: Long Island has a separate Groupon deal stream from New York; similarly Los Angeles is split into multiple subareas. As for deal categories, deals that are the most lucrative in terms of revenue for Groupon are not the most popular with their customers. For example, while "Travel" deals produce fewer sales than most other categories on average, they produce the most revenue; conversely "Restaurants" deals are the most popular, but produce much less revenue.

Finally, it is not especially surprising, but still notable that we observe heavy-tailed behavior throughout Figure 4, with the mean deal producing many more sales than the median in essentially all cases.

3. MODELING DEAL OUTCOMES

Having considered various deal features and their individual correlation with deal size and revenue individually, we now consider these characteristics collectively using regression. Our goal is both to better quantify the dependence of deal outcomes on the various features, and to determine if such models are sufficiently accurate to predict the outcomes of future deals. The model we use for Groupon deals, noting that all logarithms are base e, is:

$$\log q = \beta_0 + \beta_1 \log p + \beta_2 \log t + \beta_3 d + \beta_4 f + \beta_5 l + \bar{\beta}_6 \mathbf{w} + \bar{\beta}_7 \mathbf{c} + \bar{\beta}_8 \mathbf{g} \quad (1)$$

where q stands for the deal size, p for the coupon price, t for the threshold, d for whether the deal is run for multiple days or not, f for whether the deal is featured or not, and l for whether the deal inventory is limited or not. The values of p and t are centered to their corresponding medians (25 in both cases). This allows for a more intuitive interpretation of the regression's intercept but does not otherwise affect our results. The parameters $\mathbf{w}$, $\mathbf{c}$ and $\mathbf{g}$ are dummy-coded vectors representing the starting day of the week, category, and city relative to notional reference levels; their corresponding coefficients are also vectors. Dummy-coding refers to using binary vectors to encode categorical variables, where a variable that can take on k distinct values is encoded using a binary vector of length $k-1$ where at most one entry is set to one. We also fitted a similar log-log model to LivingSocial deals with similar results to those we report below.

The exact form the model takes upon is motivated by the observations of Section 2.3: $\log p$ and $\log t$ are well modeled as having a linear relationship to $\log q$, while the rest of the variables are either boolean or categorical in nature. Given the high correlation of the list price to the discounted price, we have chosen to exclude it from the model to avoid introducing multicollinearity. Also, since most multi-day deals last for two days, and there is little variance in the number of sales among multi-day deals, we have chosen (after experimentation) to encode duration as a boolean feature.

We fitted the model using ordinary least squares (OLS) regression. The parameter estimates, their standard errors, and their significance levels are not given for lack of space, but appear in detail in the full version.

The intercept of the model is the unconditional expected mean of the logarithm of the size of a deal. For example, the expected mean of the log-size of a deal in the "Other" category, priced at \$25, with a threshold of 25, not featured, with unlimited inventory, starting on Monday, and running for a single day in Atlanta, is 5.19. Equivalently, the expected *geometric* mean of the size of the same deal is $e^{5.19} \approx 179$.

The coefficient of $\log p$ is particularly interesting because its value is the *point-price elasticity of demand* for coupons. To see this, recall that the point-elasticity η_p is defined as:

$$\eta_p = (\partial q/q)/(\partial p/p) = \partial \log q / \partial \log p = \beta_1. \quad (2)$$

For deal size, the point-price elasticity given by our regression model is -0.48. Intuitively, this means that for a 1% increase in price, we expect a 0.48% decrease in demand. Since $\eta_p > -1$ the demand is said to be *inelastic*. This matches our intuition: coupons already represent heavy discounts and as such, changes in price should have a relatively less significant impact upon demand.

The coefficients of non-log-transformed variables represent differences in the expected means of log-sales, and their exponentiated values represent multiplicative increases (or decreases) in the expected geometric mean of sales. For example, the expected ratio of the geometric means of sales for multi-day deals to single-day deals is $e^{0.22} \approx 1.25$. A simple interpretation is that by running a deal for more than a day, we expect a 25% increase in sales. The effect of featuring a deal is, as anticipated, far greater: featured deals are expected to perform 141% better than their non-featured counterparts. Limiting a deal, in the presence of all the other parameters in our model, does not have a statistically significant effect.

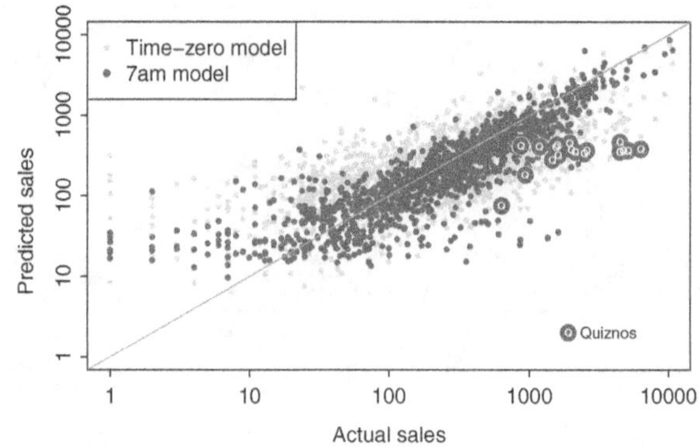

Figure 5: Actual vs. predicted sales for a test set of Groupon deals, in log-log scale for our plain regression model, as well as the the model incorporating early morning sales.

Overall, the F-statistic (345) and the p-value ($< 2 \cdot 10^{-16}$) of the model indicate that we can reject the null hypothesis (that there is no relation between sales and any of the explanatory variables in our model) with high confidence. However, the R^2 (0.49) value of the model suggests moderate predictive power. We tested this against a test set of 1,522 deals that ran in the same 20 cities between July 18th and 31st. Figure 5 shows the number of sales our model predicts against their actual sales. As anticipated by the R^2 value of our model, our predictions are generally well correlated with actual sales, with noticeably large errors for certain individual deals.

Not surprisingly, our model consistently overestimates weak deals with a very small number of actual sales, and tends to underestimate the strongest deals, indicating that there are additional factors at work not captured by our model. One such factor we study in Section 4.1 is how social networks can influence deal sales. Another possible influence on purchasing decisions could be merchant reputations, which we consider below, and in the other direction (how Groupon offers affect reputation) in Section 4.2. One clear major influence is that some deals are national in scope, and our largest underestimates appear to be for these deals. For example, as shown in in Figure 5, some of the larger errors in underestimating deal size correspond to a national deal for Quiznos sandwiches. Incorporating these additional refinements to improve the predictive power of our models is future work.

We consider two variations on our basic model:

Early-morning sales: We have incorporated first-day sales at 7am from our time-series dataset into our basic model. Our reasoning is that a deal site may want to obtain an improved prediction of deal performance early in the day (and perhaps adjust accordingly). We present data for 7am for 2 reasons. First, Groupon generally sends email between 4am and 6am, and we want to see effects after the e-mail is sent. Second, as shown in Figure 6, on average Groupon deals have sold less than 7% of their eventual *first* day sales by 7am, so the time is suitable for an early prediction. Unsurprisingly, the predictive power of our model is greatly improved with this feature, as indicated by an increased R^2 of 0.81, and as shown in Figure 5.

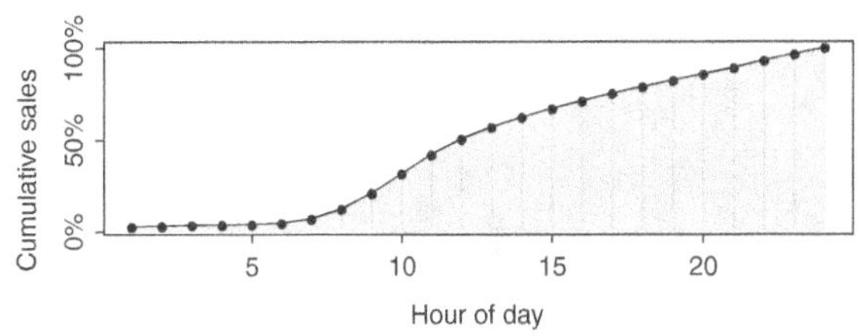

Figure 6: Average cumulative first day sales across all Groupon deals in our dataset.

Yelp merchant reviews: We also attempted to add the Yelp rating of merchants prior to their Groupon deal as a parameter to our model for the deals for which we had a rating available (2,522 of them). This failed to significantly improve our model. One explanation is that the average Yelp ratings may not be especially significant to Groupon buyers. Another is that there is only moderate variance in the merchants Groupon selects to give Yelp ratings for; 68% of the reviewed merchants had an average rating ranging between 3.5 and 4.5 stars, and 95% between 3 and 5 stars.

3.1 Deal Scheduling

One further optimization available to daily deal sites is managing how deals are *scheduled*. Our data shows that Groupon is already managing deal schedules in non-trivial ways. For example, there are far fewer deals offered on weekends, but more multi-day deals run over weekends.

We also find evidence that deals are scheduled according to their category; specifically, that Groupon avoids placing featured deals of the same category back-to-back over consecutive days in the same city. This is a natural strategy to maintain user interest, related to issues of ad fatigue (or advertising wear out) studied in other contexts [6, 8].

More details, including data analysis, are given in the full version of the paper. The problem of how deal sites should best schedule deals to optimize revenue or sales remains an interesting direction for future work.

4. THE IMPACT OF SOCIAL INFLUENCE

We now move from studying solely the deal data to considering the interplay between social networks and daily deal sites, specifically quantifying the impact of Facebook users while a deal is running, and of Yelp reviewers as they provide feedback about merchants.

4.1 Do Deals Propagate via Facebook Likes?

Groupon deals can be shared with friends by text, e-mail, Facebook, Twitter, and other means. Facebook offers a readily observable measure, which we use as a proxy for more general social sharing here: Groupon has added a Facebook Like button on each deal's web page. Should a Facebook user decide that he likes a Groupon deal (no purchase necessary) and clicks the Like button, a like counter shown next to the button is incremented, and a short message to that effect is distributed to the user's Facebook friends by means of their news feeds. These messages may then propagate recursively through Facebook, potentially creating a sales-enhancing word-of-mouth effect.

Here we examine whether Facebook likes correlate with the final deal size, and then ask whether the data appears consistent with current models for the effects of social networks on buying decisions. We note recent work also suggests social spreading as a significant determinant of final deal size, giving a model where once the tipping point of a deal is reached, it grows due to a stochastic process that models social spreading [21]. Their model appears orthogonal to our analysis.

We emphasize that we must be careful not to conflate correlation and causation; it is not clear that likes inspire purchases, even if the number of likes and deal sizes are correlated. As a strawman, consider a model where each purchaser ignores prior likes, and pushes the Like button with probability p after deciding to purchase. In this setting, likes and purchases would be closely (linearly) correlated, even though likes would not promote purchases. Indeed, this provides an interesting null hypothesis: are likes simply proportional to sales? Our data suggests that this is not the case: Figures 7a and 7b suggest a non-linear relationship, where the deal size is roughly proportional to the number of likes raised to a power much less than 1. Also, deals with approximately the same number of likes can vary significantly in terms of final deal size. (A more detailed breakdown appears in Figure 8.)

We can gain some further insight by adding likes to our regression model. (The complete fitted model again appears in the full paper.) Adding the logarithm of the number of likes as an additional variable on the right hand side of the model Equation 1 improves our R^2 statistic from 0.49 to 0.63 for Groupon and from 0.38 to 0.67 for LivingSocial. While this improvement is not directly useful for, for example, predicting deal size *a priori*, it demonstrates a strong correlation between the logarithms of likes and deal size.

Social Spreading: We do not currently have (and have not sought) *direct* evidence of social spreading of deals via likes; this would require either detailed knowledge of the Facebook social network, or a detailed user study. Both are beyond the scope of this paper, but are interesting questions for future work. Here, however, we examine whether our data is consistent with theoretical models of social spreading from the literature (e.g., [13, 16]). In such models, there is generally a *seed set* of users that initially recommend a product; then additional users *activate* and buy the product based on these recommendations. Here, we treat Facebook likes as recommendations for a specific deal.

Two key features of cascade models are how the seed set is selected, and how inactive users are activated by neighbors. In our setting, we consider the seed set to be Groupon subscribers who are informed of the daily deal through Groupon's daily email and proceed to like the deal on Facebook. (Likely, those in the seed set also purchase the deal, but this is irrelevant to the cascade dynamics we consider here.) Our data provides insight into the size of the seed set, but not into the how the seed set should be selected. Previous work [7, 19, 20] has established the correlation between degree and activity in social networks. In [20] the authors demonstrate that the top 50% of Facebook users by degree are responsible for most social interactions. Kwak et al. [14] make a similar case for Twitter, where they demonstrate that users with more followers are more like to tweet. The potential implication, translated to our setting, is that Groupon customers who have more friends on Facebook are more likely to belong to the seed set. We test this by simulating cascade models with the seed set selected uniformly at random, and as the top-k nodes by degree.

With regard to activation, we consider two standard vari-

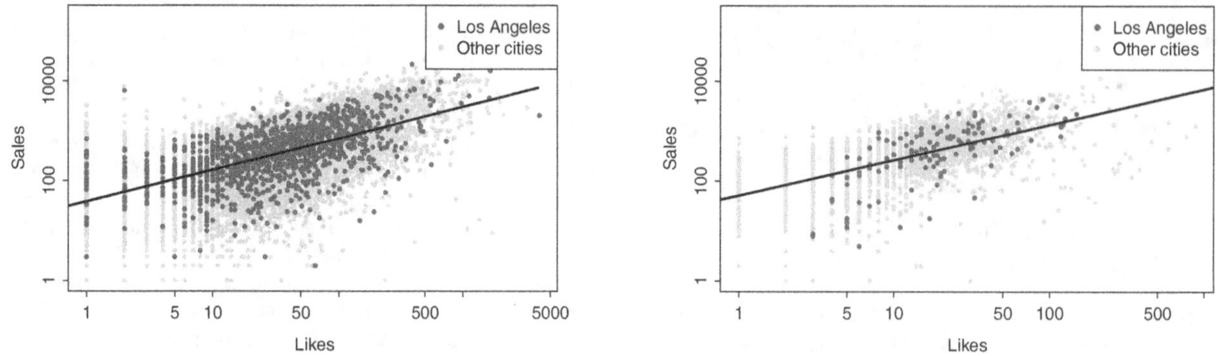

(a) Groupon, slope = 0.63

(b) LivingSocial, slope = 0.71

Figure 7: Deal size vs. number of Facebook likes (in logarithmic scale.) Black dots highlight deals in LA; grey dots are used for other cities. A trend line fitted using OLS regression is also shown.

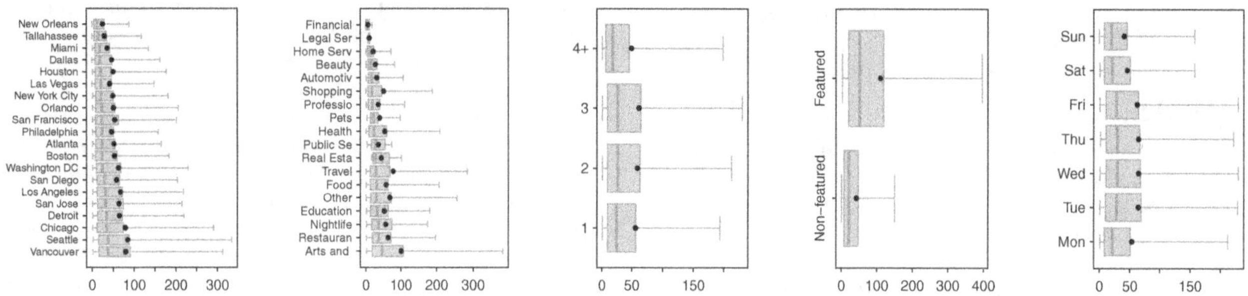

(a) By city (b) By category (c) By duration (days) (d) By placement (e) By start weekday

Figure 8: Number of Facebook likes are depicted on the $x-$axis. On the $y-$axis deals are broken down by various deal features. The outer whiskers mark the 5% and 95% quantiles of the deal size and revenue, the sides of each grey rectangle the 1st and 3rd quartiles, the solid bar the median, and the solid dot the mean.

ations: a user is activated with fixed probability p by each of his active neighbors, and each active user u activates user v with probability $1/d_v$, where d_v is the degree of user v. The first model activates high-degree nodes more frequently. These cases correspond to the Independent Cascade (IC) and Weighted Cascade (WC) models of Kempe et al. [13].

Finally, we model that each activated user purchases the deal with fixed probability q, which can be thought of as the conversion rate. Note that we separate the issues of activation and purchase; in our setting, activation corresponds to noticing the deal, rather than purchasing it.

We ran experiments based on these models on a network that has common characteristics with social network graphs, the arXiv High Energy Physics collaboration network from [15]. This network consists of 9,877 nodes and 51,971 edges. The results are shown in Figure 9. We plot the number of sales resulting by the cascade against the seed set size averaged over 100 trials per starting seed set size. We ran our experiments both by selecting a random seed set, and by selecting the top-k nodes by degree. The high-degree heuristic resembles our empirical findings more closely. For the IC model we set $p = 2\%$, and for both models $q = 5\%$. We observe that in both cases, when using top-k nodes as the seed set, we observe sublinear gains in the size of the cascade as the size of the seed set increases. These results match previous work such as [13], and give some insight into our empirical findings.

While these results suggest that social spreading is a fea-

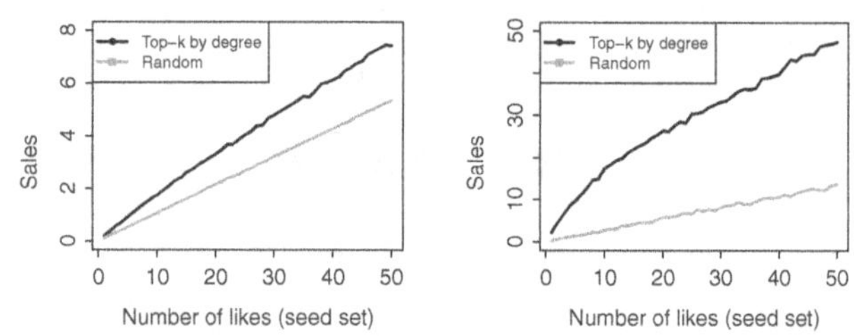

(a) Independent cascade (b) Weighted cascade

Figure 9: Sales as predicted by two diffusion models.

ture of daily deals, current theoretical models are too simplistic to capture the array of features we have found to be important in determining deal size, with price being the most obviously relevant. It may also be useful to specifically consider models for daily deals in the context of cascading recommendations (e.g., [16]); this could also be helpful in explaining the large observed variance in deal sizes across deals with the same number of likes.

4.2 Yelp Feedback on Groupon Merchants

A key selling point of a daily deals site is the promise of beneficial long-term effects for merchants participating in a deal offering. Since discounted deals typically result in a net short-term loss to the merchant as customers redeem the coupons, a merchant is pitched on the expectation that some

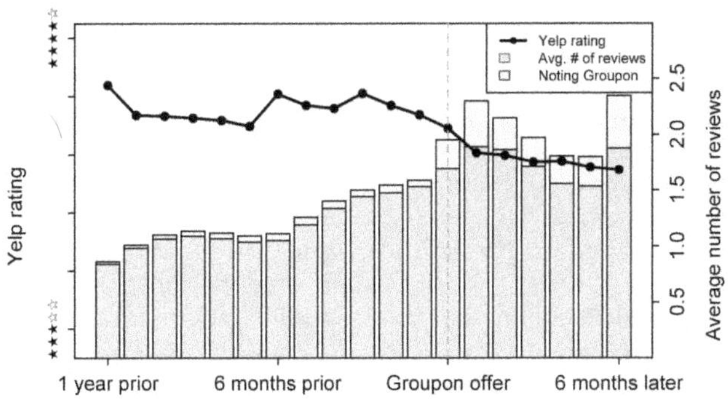

Figure 10: The average Yelp star-rating for merchants before and after their Groupon offers (line-chart), and the average number of reviews per merchant per month (bar-chart).

new customers, initially attracted by the deal, will become repeat customers, providing a long-term gain [10]. Participating merchants should determine that these gains outweigh the costs, which include providing discounts to their existing customer base.

While we do not have data to directly evaluate the long-term financial impact for Groupon merchants, we consider a novel, alternative approach to concretely quantify the impact of Groupon deals on a merchant's *reputation*. Specifically, we examine the extent to which a Groupon deal affects review scores at Yelp, a popular online review site. We view review scores as a useful proxy for both direct repeat business as well as for new business from word-of-mouth effects.

Groupon often displays a Yelp rating for the merchant offering a specific deal. For each Groupon deal associated with a Yelp rating, we collected all the individual reviews posted on Yelp up through September 2011. Yelp reviews are comprised of a star-rating ranging from one to five stars, the review text, and the date the review was written. We associated each review with an offset, measured in months, from the earliest Groupon deal in our dataset for the corresponding merchant, i.e., if a Groupon offer occurred in June 2011, a review for that merchant dated March 2011 would have an offset of -3. For each merchant, and for each integer offset (up through July 2011), we computed the merchant's average star-rating, thereby constructing a time-series of the star-rating value oriented around the first Groupon offer that we observed for a merchant. Figure 10 presents our findings. The line-chart displays the average star-rating across all Yelp-rated merchants in our dataset for each offset, with the x-axis depicting the offset from the time of the offer. The bar-chart depicts the average review volume over the same period, using the scale on the right-hand side of the y-axis, and measured in reviews per merchant per month. Lighter shading indicates total review volume, while darker shading indicates the volume of reviews that contain the keyword "Groupon". (Mentions of Groupon in reviews with negative offsets are mostly due to user reviews for merchants who ran an additional offer before we began collecting data. Excluding these merchants (results in full version) does not materially change our findings.)

In looking at Figure 10, we first consider the behavior *prior* to Groupon offers. While month to month scores vary, they appear essentially flat. The average number of reviews slowly increases (likely as Yelp itself is growing). There are

	Avg. Rating	Reviews
Before period (12 months)	3.72	34,212
After period (6 months)	3.58	20,159

Table 3: Yelp reviews around a merchant's Groupon offer.

few Groupon mentions. We think of these qualitative behaviors as our baseline.

Subsequent to the Groupon deal, we see marked changes in behavior. First, on average, the number of user-contributed reviews increases significantly after a Groupon offer, and based on the proportion of Groupon mentions, the Groupon deal appears to be the proximate cause. We quantify this change using the monthly number of Yelp reviews as a proxy. Our methodology is as follows: let Y_i be the average number of reviews merchant i received per month in the three months before the Groupon offer. Let Z_i be the number of reviews the month of the Groupon offer. We compute the percentage change in number of reviews for each merchant the month of the Groupon offer as $(Z_i - Y_i)/Y_i$. (This requires $Y_i > 0$.) Similarly, we can compute the percentage change for the month after the Groupon offer. We find that the average percentage increase in reviews across all merchants who had received at least one review in the 3 months prior to the Groupon offer is 44%. Meanwhile, the average month-over-month growth in number of reviews for deals prior to their Groupon offers is about 5%. Similarly, the average percentage increase in reviews the month after the Groupon offer is 71%. Roughly 20% of merchants in our dataset (470 out of 2,332) had received zero reviews in the 3 months prior to the Groupon offer. Of these, 271 received at least one review within two months after the Groupon offer.

Our second conclusion is that Yelp star ratings decline after a Groupon deal. To quantify the magnitude of the decline, we employed the following methodology: as our baseline, we computed the average of all reviews with a negative offset (before the Groupon offer). Similarly, we computed the average of all reviews with a positive offset (after the Groupon offer). We deemed reviews with offset zero as ambiguous, due to data collection granularity, and they were not considered. The results of the before and after comparison are depicted in Table 3. The average drop in ratings is 0.13. This could affect any sorted order produced according to Yelp rankings significantly. Also, Yelp scores are reported and displayed according to discretized half-star increments. Thus, an average drop of 0.13 suggests a significant number of merchants may lose a half-star due to rounding. This could have a potentially important effect on a business; a recent study reports that for independent restaurants a one-star increase in Yelp rating leads to a 9% increase in revenue [17]. However, the transitory nature of Groupon-driven reviews, in addition to complexities of modeling hidden factors like weighted moving averages, cloud our ability to pinpoint the reputational ramifications precisely.

To provide further attribution for the decline, we conducted additional text analysis on the content of individual reviews. The results are summarized in Table 4, which categorizes the user-contributed reviews according to occurrence of the keywords "Groupon" and "coupon". Reviews mentioning either keyword are associated with star ratings that are 10% lower on average than reviews that do not, while the

		Coupon mentioned	
		Yes	No
Groupon	Yes	2.91 (378)	3.34 (4,646)
mentioned	No	3.33 (1,261)	3.71 (52,615)

Table 4: Yelp reviews broken down by mentions of the keywords "Groupon" and "Coupon". The average rating as well as the number of reviews (in parentheses) are shown.

very small fraction of reviews mentioning both keywords are more than 21% lower on average.

Ultimately, the economic ramifications of reputational effects due to running a daily deal remain uncertain. The positive impact of quickly reaching a broad, new audience is precisely in line with the daily deals sales pitch, and is borne out by the surge in reviews that we witness in our dataset. However, the lower-on-average rating scores in those reviews mentioning Groupon provides a cautionary note: this could indicate that a more critical audience is being reached, or that the fit between the merchant and these new customers is more tenuous than with existing customers.

5. CONCLUSION AND FUTURE WORK

Our examination of daily deal sites, and particularly Groupon, has used data-driven analysis to investigate relationships between deal attributes and deal size beyond simple measures such as the offer price. Indeed, the scope of our investigation goes well outside of deal sites, to consider Groupon's relationship with the larger electronic commerce ecosystem, including Facebook and Yelp. We believe we expose significant complexity in understanding behavior in these systems. In particular, predicting deal sizes in settings where price, a multiplicity of other deal parameters, as well as the potential for social cascades to affect the outcome, provides a clear, albeit difficult, challenge. We also suggest the mining of publicly accessible Internet data, such as content on review sites, to benchmark the success of deal sites for merchants, in terms of the effect on their reputation. Expanding this approach to other data sources (such as Twitter or blogs) could yield further insights.

While our focus here has been on data analysis, we believe our work opens the door to several significant questions in both modeling and optimizing deal sites and similar electronic commerce systems.

Acknowledgements: The authors acknowledge Michalis Potamias for his work on data collection and for his contributions to Sections 2, 3, and 4.1.

6. REFERENCES

[1] K. S. Anand and R. Aron. Group buying on the web: A comparison of price-discovery mechanisms. *Manage. Sci.*, 49(11):1546–1562, November 2003.

[2] A. Arabshahi. Undressing Groupon: An Analysis of the Groupon Business Model. Available at `http://www.ahmadalia.com`, Dec. 2010.

[3] J. W. Byers, M. Mitzenmacher, M. Potamias, and G. Zervas. A Month in the Life of Groupon. Technical report arXiv:1105.0903, arXiv.org, May 4, 2011.

[4] J. W. Byers, M. Mitzenmacher, and G. Zervas. Daily Deals Dataset. `http://www.cs.yale.edu/homes/zg/daily-deals-dataset.html`.

[5] J. W. Byers, M. Mitzenmacher, and G. Zervas. Daily Deals: Prediction, Social Diffusion, and Reputational Ramifications. Technical report arXiv.org:1109.1530, arXiv.org, September 7, 2011.

[6] B. J. Calder and B. Sternthal. Television commercial wearout: An information processing view. *Journal of Marketing Research*, 17(2):pp. 173–186, 1980.

[7] H. Chun, H. Kwak, Y.-H. Eom, Y.-Y. Ahn, S. Moon, and H. Jeong. Comparison of online social relations in volume vs interaction: a case study of cyworld. In *Proc. of the 8th ACM SIGCOMM Conference on Internet Measurement*, pages 57–70, 2008.

[8] C. S. Craig, B. Sternthal, and C. Leavitt. Advertising wearout: An experimental analysis. *Journal of Marketing Research*, 13(4):pp. 365–372, 1976.

[9] U. M. Dholakia. How effective are groupon promotions for businesses? Available at `http://www.ruf.rice.edu/~dholakia`, Sept. 2010.

[10] B. Edelman, S. Jaffe, and S. D. Kominers. To Groupon or Not to Groupon: The Profitability of Deep Discounts. HBS Working Paper 11-063: `http://hbswk.hbs.edu/item/6597.html`, Aug. 2010.

[11] Groupon, Inc. S-1 Filing. Filed with the U.S. Securities and Exchange Commission, June 2, 2011.

[12] R. J. Kauffman and B. Wang. New buyers' arrival under dynamic pricing market microstructure: The case of group-buying discounts on the internet. *J. Manage. Inf. Syst.*, 18(2):157–188, October 2001.

[13] D. Kempe, J. M. Kleinberg, and É. Tardos. Maximizing the spread of influence through a social network. In *KDD*, pages 137–146, 2003.

[14] H. Kwak, C. Lee, H. Park, and S. Moon. What is Twitter, a social network or a news media? In *Proceedings of the 19th International Conference on the World Wide Web*, WWW '10, pages 591–600, New York, NY, USA, 2010. ACM.

[15] J. Leskovec, J. Kleinberg, and C. Faloutsos. Graph evolution: Densification and shrinking diameters. *ACM Trans. Knowl. Discov. Data*, 1(1), March 2007.

[16] J. Leskovec, A. Singh, and J. Kleinberg. Patterns of influence in a recommendation network. In *Advances in Knowledge Discovery and Data Mining*, volume 3918 of *LNCS*, pages 380–389. Springer-Verlag, 2006.

[17] M. Luca. Reviews, Reputation, and Revenues: The Case of Yelp.com. HBS Working Paper 12-016: `http://hbswk.hbs.edu/item/6833.html`, Sept. 2011.

[18] J. Stoppelman. Why Yelp has a Review Filter. `http://officialblog.yelp.com/2009/10/why-yelp-has-a-review-filter.html`.

[19] B. Viswanath, A. Mislove, M. Cha, and K. P. Gummadi. On the evolution of user interaction in Facebook. In *Proceedings of the 2nd ACM Workshop on Online Social Networks*, pages 37–42, 2009.

[20] C. Wilson, B. Boe, A. Sala, K. P. Puttaswamy, and B. Y. Zhao. User interactions in social networks and their implications. In *Proceedings of the 4th ACM European Conference on Computer Systems*, EuroSys '09, pages 205–218, New York, NY, USA, 2009. ACM.

[21] M. Ye, C. Wang, C. Aperjis, B. A. Huberman, and T. Sandholm. Collective Attention and the Dynamics of Group Deals. Technical report available at `http://papers.ssrn.com/sol3/papers.cfm?abstract_id=1949452`, October 25, 2011.

On Clustering Heterogeneous Social Media Objects with Outlier Links

Guo-Jun Qi
Department of Electrical and Computer Engineering
University of Illinois at Urbana-Champaign
Urbana, IL
qi4@illinois.edu

Charu C. Aggarwal
IBM T.J. Watson Research Lab
Hawthorne, NY
charu@us.ibm.com

Thomas S. Huang
Department of Electrical and Computer Engineering
University of Illinois at Urbana-Champaign
Urbana, IL
huang@ifp.uiuc.edu

ABSTRACT

The clustering of social media objects provides intrinsic understanding of the similarity relationships between documents, images, and their contextual sources. Both content and link structure provide important cues for an effective clustering algorithm of the underlying objects. While link information provides useful hints for improving the clustering process, it also contains a significant amount of noisy information. Therefore, a robust clustering algorithm is required to reduce the impact of noisy links. In order to address the aforementioned problems, we propose heterogeneous random fields to model the structure and content of social media networks. We design a probability measure on the social media networks which output a configuration of clusters that are consistent with both content and link structure. Furthermore, noisy links can also be detected, and their impact on the clustering algorithm can be significantly reduced. We conduct experiments on a real social media network and show the advantage of the method over other state-of-the-art algorithms.

Categories and Subject Descriptors

H.3.3 [**Information Search and Retrieval**]: Clustering

General Terms

Algorithms

Keywords

Social media networks, robust clustering, noisy links

1. INTRODUCTION

Social media networks represent social repositories for the sharing of multimedia objects between users, and a platform for interactions which are based on this content. The media objects may correspond to images, videos, or even text content. An example of such a network would be *Flickr* which provides a platform for the sharing of images between users. While the problem of clustering has been widely studied with the use of pure content, the social interactions in such networks provide vitally important information which can be used in order to improve the clustering process. The social links can be used as vital clues which can be used in order to cluster the media objects with consistent themes together. One interesting characteristic of such social media networks is that they provide a way to consistently cluster not just the social media objects, but also the users who contribute these objects. The content of the social media objects, and the user links to these objects provide mutually re-enforcing information which can be leveraged for a robust clustering process. In addition, user tagging information (or comments) are available to enhance the clustering process. A major challenge in this problem is that it requires us to simultaneously cluster data of many different kinds, such as images, user tags, user nodes and the links which represent the relationships between them. Clearly, an integrated and holistic approach to social media object clustering is required, which can help us understand the content themes in the different clusters with the help of user-centered social hints.

As illustrated in Figure 1, there are two types of links in generic social media networks - the links between the users and the social media objects, as well as the context links between media objects and their context objects such as user tags or comments. These links, along with the associated content of the media objects, play an important role in determining the clustering of the social media objects with a holistic approach. In this paper we will use a heterogeneous random field to model the natural clusters in the social media content and their underlying linkages in a seamless framework.

The social links between objects and users are often noisy, in which the links between users and objects could be spam, erroneous, or incidental links. Thus, the presence of such links may actually reduce the quality of the clustering, if such misleading social cues are used blindly. The detection and removal of such outlier links are useful in improving the underlying clustering quality. The traditional problem of clustering focusses on determining the outliers in the underlying *objects* rather than the links. However, since links form one of the key social cues in the clustering process, it implies

Permission to make digital or hard copies of all or part of this work for personal or classroom use is granted without fee provided that copies are not made or distributed for profit or commercial advantage and that copies bear this notice and the full citation on the first page. To copy otherwise, to republish, to post on servers or to redistribute to lists, requires prior specific permission and/or a fee.
WSDM'12, February 8–12, 2012, Seattle, Washington, USA.
Copyright 2012 ACM 978-1-4503-0747-5/12/02 ...$10.00.

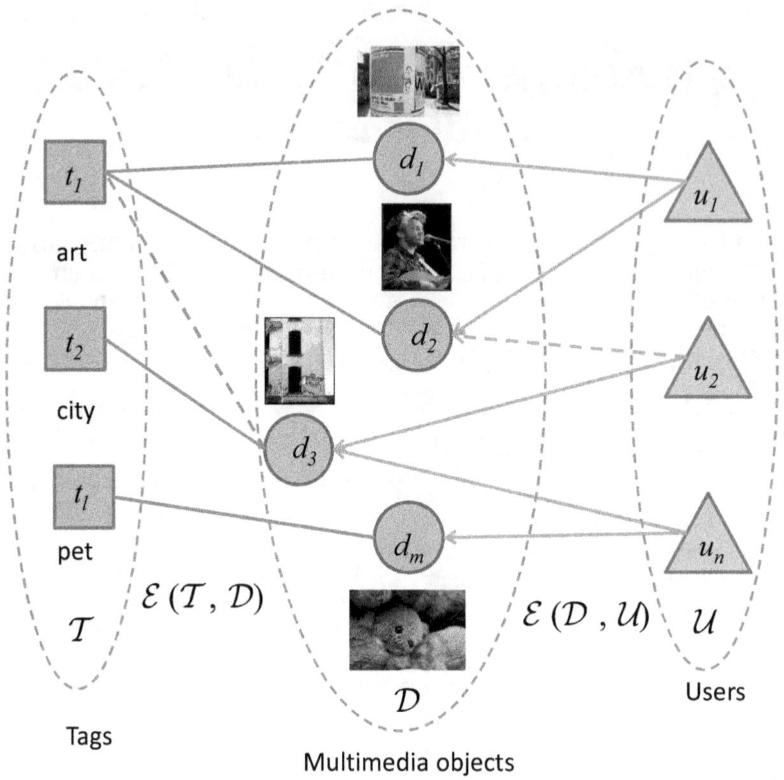

Figure 1: Illustration of social media network. Such network consists of three component graphs - the graphs of users, multimedia objects, and the annotated tags. Users indicate their preferences on media objects, while each object can be linked with multiple tags.

that the abnormalities in the linkages should be removed in order to enhance clustering quality. Our model will jointly detect the outlier links as well as model the underlying clustering structure. We will see that accurately identifying the abnormal links can improve the consistency of clustering the social media objects. On the other hand, a better understanding of the clustering structure can improve the accuracy of detecting of outlier links in the social networks. These two tasks enhance the effectiveness of each other, are therefore presented in a unified framework.

The remainder of this paper is organized as follows. In section 2, we introduce related work on clustering with social media networks. We formally define the problem in Section 3 and propose the heterogeneous random fields for clustering in Section 4. In Section 5 we present efficient inference algorithms for determining the cluster configuration with the highest probability. We present experiments on real data sets in Section 6. Finally, we present the conclusions in Section 7.

2. RELATED WORK

The problem of clustering has been studied extensively in the database, machine learning, multi-media and text literature. An extensive overview of clustering algorithms from a very generic context may be found in [14]. In the context of different kinds of multi-media data, especially text and images, a variety of content based algorithms have also been proposed [1, 5, 8, 13, 16, 20, ?]. However, such methods do not use the rich information which are available in a social network, such as the linkage information and user activity in the form of tags and comments.

On the other hand, from a linkage viewpoint, clusters may be considered as a group of nodes which are densely connected by edges in the networks. For example, a variety of node clustering algorithms for graphs have been proposed in [7, 12, 4, 6, 15, 18]. Some recent work [17, 21, 22, 23] uses a combination of content and link structure for clustering purpose, however, they do not consider the noisy links, and other kinds of social cues which are helpful for clustering social media objects. In particular, some recent work has been focussed on clustering web images [3, 10] with the use of surrounding text from the web page. However, this approach requires a copious amount of text unlike the tags and comments in social media, and also does not use social linkage structure for the clustering process. In this paper, we develop a robust clustering algorithm that is sensitive to the noisy links in the networks for determining the underlying clusters. Our approach is much more general than the methods discussed in earlier work in terms of combining data of many different kinds such as multi-media objects, tags, and social-linkage structure of actors to objects.

3. PROBLEM DEFINITION

In this paper, we consider jointly clustering the media objects, textual context objects, and users in social media networks. As a mathematical abstraction, we use a tri-partite graph $\mathcal{G} = (\mathcal{U}, \mathcal{D}, \mathcal{T})$ to denote the social media networks, where $\mathcal{U} = \{u_1, u_2, \cdots, u_n\}$ is the set of users, $\mathcal{D} = \{d_1, d_2, \cdots, d_m\}$ is the set of social media objects, and $\mathcal{T} = \{t_1, t_2, \cdots, t_l\}$ is a set of tags or comment keywords made by users on the social media objects $\mathcal{D}$. The users and objects in $\mathcal{U}$ and $\mathcal{D}$ are connected between each other by a set of links $\mathcal{E}(\mathcal{U}, \mathcal{D}) = \{(u_i, d_j)\}$ which correspond to user u_i interest in object d_j. In addition, collections of links $E(\mathcal{D}, \mathcal{T})$ exist between $\mathcal{D}$ and $\mathcal{T}$, which means one object d_j in $\mathcal{D}$ is annotated with user tag keyword t_l if the link $(d_j, t_l) \in \mathcal{E}(\mathcal{D}, \mathcal{T})$. In the event that the comment or tag contains multiple keywords, then a link exists from multiple nodes to the corresponding objects. The content of each object d_j in $\mathcal{D}$ is also summarized by a feature vector $\mathbf{x}_j \in \mathbb{R}^d$ of dimensionality d. For example, this feature vector could be the image features such as the visual words, or the tf-idf scores of a text document. The goal is to cluster the social media objects, users, and tags in this tri-partite graph simultaneously by investigating the associated link structure between component graphs as well as the object content. Associated with each user u_i, object d_j and tag t_l, there will be variables $c(u_i)$, $c(d_j)$ and $c(t_l)$ taking the same set of values from $\{1, 2, \cdots, k\}$ to indicate their cluster membership. Intuitively, the links between graphs should connect the objects in the same cluster.

While the social media objects may be clustered purely with the use of content, this ignores the fact that similar social cues for different objects can provide very useful hints. For example, images which are preferred by similar users, or have similar tags are much more likely to belong to the same cluster. One complicating factor with such an approach is that the social links between social media objects, users, and tags are quite noisy and often inconsistent. In order to mitigate this negative effect, we propose a robust clustering algorithm that can detect and remove the noisy links during the clustering process. Associated with each link in $\mathcal{E}(\mathcal{U}, \mathcal{D})$ we introduce the binary variable $n(u_i, d_j)$ to indicate that the link $e(u_i, d_j)$ is noisy if it makes on the value of 1. Similarly, we introduce the variable $n(d_j, t_l)$ to indicate that the link $e(d_j, t_l)$ is noisy.

4. HETEROGENEOUS RANDOM FIELD MODEL

In this section, we present our heterogeneous random field model (HRF), to determine the clusters of social media objects. In order to facilitate the random field model, we introduce an energy function on the edges. We show that minimizing the energy function will yield the most probable cluster configuration on $\mathcal{G}$, which is consistent with the social media content and link structure. The noise on the links are detected and utilized in order to determine their relevance to the clustering process.

We define the following energy functions for model construction. The first type of energy function is defined on the social links connecting users and media objects.

$$\begin{aligned} &E_{ij}\left(c\left(u_i\right), c\left(d_j\right), n\left(u_i, d_j\right)\right) \\ &= n\left(u_i, d_j\right)\varepsilon + \left(1 - n\left(u_i, d_j\right)\right)\delta\left[\!\left[c\left(u_i\right) \neq c\left(d_j\right)\right]\!\right] \\ &= \begin{cases} \delta\left[\!\left[c\left(u_i\right) \neq c\left(d_j\right)\right]\!\right], n\left(u_i, d_j\right) = 0 \\ \varepsilon, n\left(u_i, d_j\right) = 1 \end{cases} \end{aligned} \quad (1)$$

Here, $\delta[\![\cdot]\!]$ is the indicator function which outputs 1 when the condition in $[\![\cdot]\!]$ holds true and 0 otherwise. The variable $\varepsilon \geq 0$ denotes the confidence level of the links. A lower value of ε indicates a high level of noise on the links. In the extreme case, when $\varepsilon = 0$, all the links will be judged by the HRF as noisy links since the energy function will be minimized by $n(u_i, d_j) = 1$. On the other hand, when $\varepsilon = 1$, the links are treated as very relevant and the cluster membership of u_i and d_j will be regulated by this. We note that the clustering process outputs not just the membership of social media objects to clusters, but also the users to the analogous clusters. Thus, such an approach can also be used to facilitate recommendations in social media networks.

The second type of energy function is defined on the links between objects and tags.

$$\begin{aligned} &E_{jl}\left(c\left(d_j\right), c\left(t_l\right), n\left(d_j, t_l\right)\right) \\ &= n\left(d_j, t_l\right)\varepsilon + \left(1 - n\left(d_j, t_l\right)\right)\delta\left[\!\left[c\left(d_j\right) \neq c\left(t_l\right)\right]\!\right] \\ &= \begin{cases} \delta\left[\!\left[c\left(d_j\right) \neq c\left(t_l\right)\right]\!\right], n\left(d_j, t_l\right) = 0 \\ \epsilon, n\left(d_j, t_l\right) = 1 \end{cases} \end{aligned} \quad (2)$$

Here $\epsilon \geq 0$ denotes the confidence level on the quality of the context links between objects and tags. A larger value of ϵ indicates higher quality of the underlying social cues based on the context information for the clustering process.

In addition, we model the feature vector $\{\mathbf{x}_1, \mathbf{x}_2, \cdots, \mathbf{x}_m\}$ associated with the social media objects, given their cluster membership. For simplicity, we assume the objects are composed by a set of discrete features $\{w_1, w_2, \cdots, w_q\}$. For generality, we assume that such features may be of different kinds depending upon the kind of object at hand. For example, for an image object, the feature could correspond to visual words, whereas for a text object, it could correspond to the actual word. For each object d_j, each element of its content vector $\mathbf{x}_j = [x_{j1}, x_{j2}, \cdots, x_{jq}]^T$ counts the number of occurrences of this feature in the object. Now we use parameters $\gamma_k = \{\gamma_{k1}, \gamma_{k2}, \cdots, \gamma_{kq}\}$ to denote the probability of the features appearing in the k-th cluster, i.e., $\gamma_{cv} = P(w_v|c(d_j) = c), 1 \leq v \leq q$. Then the feature counts $\mathbf{x}_j$ of the object d_j are generated following the multi-nomial distribution as follows:

$$P\left(\mathbf{x}_j|c\left(d_j\right) = c\right) = \prod_{v=1}^{q} P\left(x_{jv}|c\left(d_j\right) = c\right) = \prod_{v=1}^{q} \gamma_{cv}^{x_{jv}} \quad (3)$$

Based on the above two types of energy functions and generative model of the feature vectors, we can define a random field on the heterogeneous tri-partite graph $\mathcal{G}$ as follows:

$$\begin{aligned} &P(\mathcal{C}, \mathcal{N}, \mathcal{X}) \propto \\ &\exp\left\{-\lambda \sum_{e(u_i, d_j) \in \mathcal{E}(\mathcal{U}, \mathcal{D})} E_{ij}\left(c\left(u_i\right), c\left(d_j\right), n\left(u_i, d_j\right)\right)\right\} \\ &\cdot \exp\left\{-\lambda \sum_{e(d_j, t_l) \in \mathcal{E}(\mathcal{D}, \mathcal{T})} E_{jl}\left(c\left(d_j\right), c\left(t_l\right), n\left(d_j, t_l\right)\right)\right\} \\ &\cdot \prod_{d_j \in \mathcal{D}} P\left(\mathbf{x}_j|c\left(d_j\right) = c\right) \end{aligned} \quad (4)$$

Here, $\mathcal{C} = \{c(u_i), c(d_j), c(t_l)|u_i \in \mathcal{U}, d_j \in \mathcal{D}, t_l \in \mathcal{T}\}$ is the configuration of the cluster membership over the whole graph $\mathcal{G}$, $\mathcal{N} = \{n(u_i, d_j), n(d_j, t_l)|e(u_i, d_j) \in \mathcal{E}(\mathcal{U}, \mathcal{D}), e(d_j, t_l) \in \mathcal{E}(\mathcal{D}, \mathcal{T})\}$ denotes the noisy links, and $\mathcal{X} = \{x_1, x_2, \cdots, x_m\}$ is the set of all feature vectors associated with the social media objects in the network. The optimal configuration of cluster memberships of the objects in $\mathcal{G}$, which is consistent with the link structure and object content, can be solved by

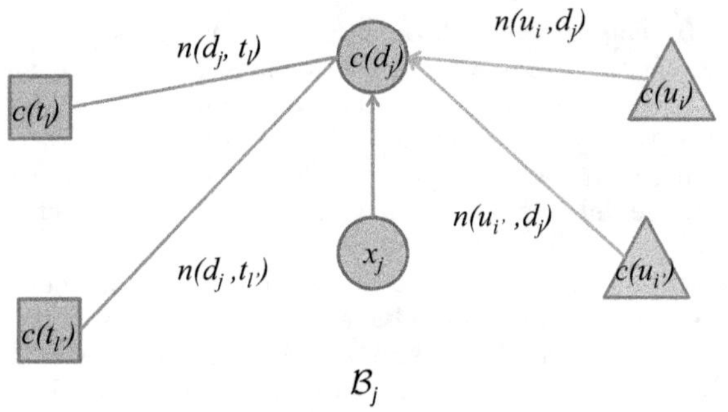

Figure 2: Illustration of the Markov blanket upon which $c(d_j)$ is dependent.

maximizing this probability measure given by $P(\mathcal{C},\mathcal{N},\mathcal{X})$. At the same time, the noise on the links can be detected by the edge-based variables, since these are included in the model.

4.1 Analysis

The probability measure given by Eq. (4) defines an interdependency structure between the cluster assignment $\mathcal{C}$, the noisy link detection $\mathcal{N}$ and the social media object content $\mathcal{D}$. Before giving the inference and learning algorithm of this probabilistic model, we discuss some of its properties which are beneficial to understanding the dependency between the cluster assignment task and the link relevance in the social media network.

From the probability measure in Eq. (4), we can obtain the conditional probability of the object d_j belonging to cluster k when the cluster membership of the other objects, and the corresponding link relevance variables:

$$\begin{aligned} & P(c(d_j)=c|\mathcal{C}\backslash c(d_j),\mathcal{N},\mathcal{X}) \propto P(c(d_j)=c|\mathcal{B}_j) \\ & \propto \prod_{e(u_i,d_j)\in\mathcal{E}(\mathcal{U},\mathcal{D})} P(c(d_j)=c|n(u_i,d_j),c(u_i)) \\ & \cdot \prod_{e(d_j,t_l)\in\mathcal{E}(\mathcal{D},\mathcal{T})} P(c(d_j)=c|n(u_i,d_j),c(u_i)) \\ & \cdot P(\mathbf{x}_j|c(d_j)=c) \end{aligned} \tag{5}$$

Here, $\mathcal{C}\backslash c(d_j)$ denotes the variables of cluster membership of the objects excluding the object d_j, and $\mathcal{B}_j$ is the Markov Blanket upon which $c(d_j)$ is dependent. As illustrated in Figure 2, $c(d_j)$ only depends on the objects which are linked to d_j as well as the noisy link variables that connect d_j. Formally, we have

$$\begin{aligned} \mathcal{B}_j = \{&x_j, c(u_i), c(t_l), n(u_i,d_j), n(d_j,t_l)\,|e(u_i,d_j) \\ &\in E(U,D), e(d_j,t_l)\in E(D,T)\} \end{aligned} \tag{6}$$

For each link $e(u_i,d_j)$ in $\mathcal{E}(\mathcal{U},\mathcal{D})$, there are the following two cases depending on the value of the associated link variable:

- when $n(u_i,d_j)=1$, it indicates $e(u_i,d_j)$ is a noisy link. Then, we have:

  $$P(c(d_j)=c|n(u_i,d_j),c(u_i)) \propto \exp\{-\lambda\varepsilon\} \tag{7}$$

  In this case, the membership of d_j is uniformly distributed over all the clusters since the cluster membership of its adjacent user u_i should not affect its membership since the link between the two is noisy.

- when $n(u_i,d_j)=0$, it is a normal link, and we have:

  $$P(c(d_j)=c|n(u_i,d_j),c(u_i)) \propto \exp\{-\lambda\delta\,[\![c(u_i)\neq c]\!]\} \tag{8}$$

  In this case, when the linked user u_i also belongs to the cluster k, the belief of the object d_i being in cluster k is enhanced; otherwise, such belief will be reduced.

On the other hand, the conditional probability of noisy link variables $n(u_i,d_j)$ and $n(d_j,t_l)$ is defined as follows:

$$P(n(u_i,d_j)|\mathcal{C},\mathcal{N}\backslash n(u_i,d_j),\mathcal{X}) \propto P(n(u_i,d_j)|c(u_i),c(d_j)) \tag{9}$$

with $c(u_i)$ and $c(d_j)$ in its Markov blanket. We differentiate two different cases for this conditional probability

- When $c(u_i)=c(d_j)$, user u_i and social media object d_j belong to the same cluster, and we have

  $$P(n(u_i,d_j)=0|c(u_i),c(d_j)) = \frac{1}{1+\exp(-\lambda\varepsilon)}$$

  The posterior that $e(u_i,d_j)$ is not a noisy link is greater than 0.5 in this case. This implies that the belief that the link is not noisy is greater than the opposite belief that the link is noisy.

- When $c(u_i)\neq c(d_j)$, user u_i and object d_j are in different clusters, we have:

  $$P(n(u_i,d_j)=0|c(u_i),c(d_j)) = \frac{1}{\exp(\lambda(1-\varepsilon))+1}$$

  This enhances the belief that $e(u_i,d_j)$ is a noisy link. Actually, when $0\leq\varepsilon\leq 1$, the posterior probability of $e(u_i,d_j)$ being a normal link is less than 0.5. While $\varepsilon>1$, the probability that $e(u_i,d_j)$ is a normal link is greater than 0.5. It is reasonable since a larger ε means a stronger belief on normal links. When $\varepsilon\rightarrow+\infty$, $P(n(u_i,d_j)=0|c(u_i),c(d_j))\rightarrow 1$.

A similar discussion can be applied to links between social media objects and tags. The above property of the probability measure is consistent with our intuition that the objects connected by normal links should have similar cluster membership and the belief of a normal link can be enhanced by the linked objects belong to the same cluster.

5. INFERENCE AND PARAMETRIC ESTIMATION WITH HRF

In this section, we present an efficient algorithm to infer the most probable configuration of clusters on social media networks based on the probability measure in Equation (4), as well as the model parameters.

5.1 Inference

The most probable configuration of clusters and the detection of noisy links in social media networks can be jointly inferred as follows:

$$\mathcal{C}^\star,\mathcal{N}^\star = \arg\max_{\mathcal{C},\mathcal{N}} P(\mathcal{C},\mathcal{N},\mathcal{X})$$

It is an NP-hard problem to find the exact solution to the above optimization problem. Fortunately, efficient algorithms exist to find the approximate solutions to the HRF model. In general, we use the Gibbs Sampling [11] algorithm to sample a sequence of values for the variables in

Algorithm 1 Gibbs Sampling of Heterogeneous Random Fields

input the number of sampling iterations T.

Initialize $s(u_i, c), s(d_j, c), s(t_l, c) \leftarrow 0$ for all $c \in \{1, 2, \cdots, K\}$, $u_i \in \mathcal{U}, d_j \in \mathcal{D}, t_l \in \mathcal{T}$; and $s(e(u_i, d_j), 0), s(e(u_i, d_j), 1), s(e(d_j, t_l), 0), s(e(d_j, t_l), 1) \leftarrow 0$ for each $e(u_i, d_j) \in \mathcal{E}(\mathcal{U}, \mathcal{D})$ and $e(d_j, t_l) in \mathcal{E}(\mathcal{D}, \mathcal{T})$.

Initialize the variables in $\mathcal{C}$ and $\mathcal{N}$.

for $t = 1, \cdots, T$ **do**

 for each u_i in $\mathcal{U}$ **do**

  Sample $c(u_i)$ from $\{1, 2, \cdots, k\}$ according to the posterior probability $P(c(u_i)|\mathcal{C}\backslash c(u_i), \mathcal{N}, \mathcal{X})$.

  $s(u_i, c(u_i)) \leftarrow s(u_i, c(u_i)) + 1$

 end for

 for each d_j in $\mathcal{D}$ **do**

  Sample $c(d_j)$ from $\{1, 2, \cdots, k\}$ according to the posterior probability $P(c(d_j)|\mathcal{C}\backslash c(d_j), \mathcal{N}, \mathcal{X})$.

  $s(d_j, c(d_j)) \leftarrow s(d_j, c(d_j)) + 1$.

 end for

 for each t_l in $\mathcal{D}$ **do**

  Sample $c(t_l)$ from $\{1, 2, \cdots, k\}$ according to the posterior probability $P(c(t_l)|\mathcal{C}\backslash c(t_l), \mathcal{N}, \mathcal{X})$.

  $s(t_l, c(t_l)) \leftarrow s(t_l, c(t_l)) + 1$.

 end for

 for each $e(u_i, d_j)$ in $\mathcal{E}(\mathcal{U}, \mathcal{D})$ **do**

  Sample $n(u_i, d_j)$ from $\{0, 1\}$ according to the posterior probability $P(n(u_i, d_j)|\mathcal{C}, \mathcal{N}\backslash n(u_i, d_j), \mathcal{X})$.

  $s(e(u_i, d_j), n(u_i, d_j)) \leftarrow s(e(u_i, d_j), n(u_i, d_j)) + 1$.

 end for

 for each $e(d_j, t_l)$ in $\mathcal{E}(\mathcal{U}, \mathcal{D})$ **do**

  Sample $n(d_j, t_l)$ from $\{0, 1\}$ according to the posterior probability $P(n(d_j, t_l)|\mathcal{C}, \mathcal{N}\backslash n(d_j, t_l), \mathcal{X})$.

  $s(e(d_j, t_l), n(d_j, t_l)) \leftarrow s(e(d_j, t_l), n(d_j, t_l)) + 1$.

 end for

end for

output $s(u_i, \cdot), s(d_j, \cdot), s(t_l, \cdot), s(e(u_i, d_j), \cdot), s(e(d_j, t_l), \cdot)$

HRF. Then the most probable cluster configuration can be obtained by the most frequent samples for each cluster variables in $\mathcal{C}$. Moreover, these sampled variables will also be used to estimate the model parameters as in the following subsection.

First, all the variables in $\mathcal{C}$ and $\mathcal{N}$ are randomly initialized. Then, in each sampling step, one variable is sampled based on the conditional probability of the current variable, given that others are fixed. In Eqn (5), we computes the conditional probability of cluster variables for each object given the other variables (including the other cluster variables in $\mathcal{C}$ and the link variables in $\mathcal{N}$) are fixed. A new variable is sampled according to this conditional probability. Algorithm 1 summarizes this sampling process and stores the number of sampled values in $s(u_i, c), s(d_j, c), s(t_l, c)$ and $s(e(u_i, d_j), 0), s(e(u_i, d_j), 1), s(e(d_j, t_l), 0), s(e(d_j, t_l), 0)$ for each variables in $\mathcal{C}$ and $\mathcal{N}$. Accordingly, the most probable cluster configuration can be inferred by the most frequently sampled cluster of each object as follows:

$$\begin{aligned} c^{\star}(u_i) &= \arg\max_c s(u_i, c) \\ c^{\star}(d_j) &= \arg\max_c s(d_j, c) \\ c^{\star}(t_l) &= \arg\max_c s(t_l, c) \end{aligned} \tag{10}$$

5.2 Parametric Estimation

The model parameters of the proposed HRF include $\Gamma = \{\gamma_c\}, 1 \leq q \leq k$, for the multinomial distribution of each cluster. The parameters can be obtained by maximizing the likelihood of the model from the observed social media objects $\mathcal{X}$ as follows:

$$\Gamma^{\star} = \arg\max_{\Gamma} \log P(\mathcal{X}|\Gamma) = \arg\max_{\Gamma} \sum_{\mathcal{C},\mathcal{N}} \log P(\mathcal{C}, \mathcal{N}, \mathcal{X}|\Gamma) \tag{11}$$

It is intractable to directly optimize the above likelihood to obtain $\Gamma^{\star}$ since the marginalization of the hidden variables $\mathcal{C}$ and $\mathcal{N}$ involve an exponentially large number of terms. In this subsection, we use Expectation-Maximization (EM) [9] algorithm based on Gibbs Sampling results in the above subsection to obtain an efficient solution to the model parameters. The parameter Γ is first initialized by $\Gamma^{(0)}$. At each step τ, an expectation of the complete joint distribution with respect to the posterior $P(\mathcal{C}, \mathcal{N}|\mathcal{X}, \Gamma^{(\tau)})$ is computed as follows:

$$Q\left(\Gamma|\Gamma^{(\tau)}\right) = \sum_{\mathcal{C},\mathcal{N}} P(\mathcal{C}, \mathcal{N}|\mathcal{X}, \Gamma^{(\tau)}) \log P(\mathcal{C}, \mathcal{N}, \mathcal{X}|\Gamma)$$

The new parameters are then updated by maximizing this expectation as follows:

$$\Gamma^{(\tau+1)} = \arg\max_{C,N} Q\left(\Gamma|\Gamma^{(\tau)}\right)$$

It is not trivial to compute $Q\left(\Gamma|\Gamma^{(\tau)}\right)$. Fortunately, we can approximate this expectation by the sampled values in Algorithm 1. It is not difficult to see that the model parameters Γ only depend on the variables $c(d_j)$ regarding the social media object clusters. Then, we have:

$$\begin{aligned} & Q\left(\Gamma|\Gamma^{(\tau)}\right) \\ = & \sum_{d_j \in D} \sum_{c=1}^{k} \frac{s(d_j, c) \log P(x_j|c(d_j) = c, \gamma_c)}{\sum_{c=1}^{k} s(d_j, c)} + \text{Const} \\ = & \sum_{d_j \in D} \sum_{c=1}^{k} \frac{s(d_j, c) \sum_{v=1}^{q} x_{jv} \log \gamma_{cv}}{\sum_{c=1}^{k} s(d_j, c)} + \text{Const} \end{aligned}$$

All the constant terms in the parameter set are merged into Const term above. Then we have:

$$\gamma_{cv}^{(\tau+1)} \leftarrow \frac{\sum_{d_j \in D} s(d_j, c) x_{jv}}{\sum_{d_j \in D} \sum_{c=1}^{k} s(d_j, c) x_{jv}}$$

for $1 \leq c \leq k, 1 \leq v \leq q$. It is equivalent to soft-counting the mean of the number of feature occurrences for each cluster in $\mathcal{D}$ based on the sampling results. The above update rule can iterate until convergence.

6. EXPERIMENTS

In this section, we will compare the effectiveness of the *HRF* model with the other state-of-the-art multimedia clustering algorithms on the social media networks. In the following, we will describe the data sets, performance metrics and the experimental setup in detail.

Group Name	Favored Images in the Group	Top 10 tags in the group
Family		family portrait children fun girl love hmmlargeart baby tucson child
Street Art		streetart art street tag graf pochoir peinture urban bombe arosol
Folk Music		music folk folkmusic concert festival guitar lastfm live performance singer
Magic City	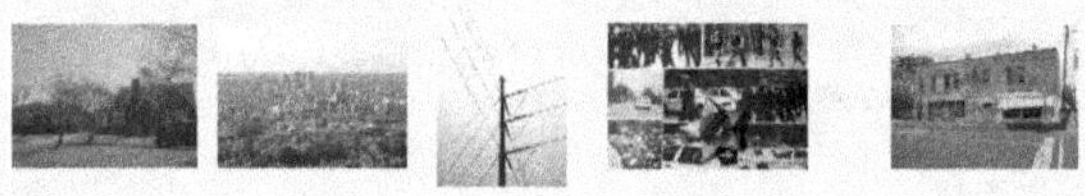	birmingham alabama al iphone iphoneography snow hdr stanroth urban downtown
Pet Portrait		dog pet cat portrait cute nikon animal puppy chien feline

Figure 3: Illustration of favored images and top 10 user tags in five user groups of *Flickr* social media network data set.

6.1 Data Set

We collected the following *Flickr* Social Network Data Set for evaluation purpose.

- *Flickr Social Network Data Set:* This data set contained 121 popular *Flickr* user groups, including "family", "auto" , "concerts", "pet portraits", "kids and nature", "street art," "wide party," "folk music," "magic city," "party favors", "British politics", "youth basketball", "fast food", "fancy dress party", and "great sky." These groups are collected using the keyword-based group search functionality provided by *Flickr*. The most popular tags were used as queries. This social media network has 13,826 users in these 121 groups, and each user can join more than one group. We note that users have the ability to mark their favored images in these groups. We use these favored images in order to create a graph of users in which the edges reflect an interest in the same image. In order to enable this, a total of 36,300 favored images were collected from *Flickr*. Since these images belong to user groups, we were able to use their group membership as the ground truth of the clustering. In order to construct the social media network, two users are linked by edges if they favor the same images. For each image, users also tag some keywords to describe its content. The user tags are stemmed and the stop words and meaningless keywords are removed. This results in 5,000 user tags in this *Flickr* data set. Figure 3 illustrates some favored images and top 10 user tags in five user groups of *Flickr* social media network data set. In general, the user tags provided a richly descriptive characterization of the underlying images as well as user sharing intention. These favored images and their associated user tags are collected to represent the edge content in social media graph. We also extract visual features in order to construct a multi-dimensional representation for image content. These include 8000 dimensional bag of words based on SIFT descriptions.

6.2 Performance Metrics

As mentioned in the previous section, each image is associated with cluster labels in addition to the content. These labels were used as the ground truth for measuring the effectiveness of the clustering process. Two metrics are used in the experiments. These were the *pairwise F-measure (P-*

Algorithm 2 Parametric Estimation for HRF model

input the sampled squences $s(u_i,\cdot), s(d_j,\cdot), s(t_l,\cdot), s(e(u_i,d_j),\cdot), s(e(d_j,t_l),\cdot)$ in Algorithm 1.

Uniformly initialize $\gamma_{cv}^{(0)} \leftarrow \frac{1}{q}$.

set $\tau \leftarrow 0$.

repeat

Sample a sequence of values from the current model, and count the occurrence of clusters for each object in $s(d_j,c)$.

Update the model parameters as

$$\gamma_{cv}^{(\tau+1)} \leftarrow \frac{\sum_{d_j \in D} s(d_j,c)x_{jv}}{\sum_{d_j \in D}\sum_{c=1}^{k} s(d_j,c)x_{jv}}$$

$\tau \leftarrow \tau + 1$.

until Convergence

output Model parameters Γ.

WF) and *average cluster purity (ACP)* respectively. These metrics are both supervised metrics, which are constructed with the use of the cluster ground truth (or class labels) collected in the data sets. Since clustering is an unsupervised problem, the ground truth information was not used during the clustering process. The class information about the communities is only used for evaluation purposes. This provides a robust evidentiary measure about the quality of the clustering.

Pairwise Precision, Recall and F-measure. We adopt the commonly used pairwise precision and recall measures for clustering algorithms [21], in order to create a meaningful measure. Let G denote the set of images that share one cluster class. Similarly, let H denote the set of images that are assigned to the same cluster by the algorithm. Then, we can compute the pairwise precision and recall as follows:

$$\text{pr} = \frac{|H \cap G|}{|H|}, \text{rc} = \frac{|H \cap G|}{|G|}$$

The afore-mentioned measures of precision and recall can be used in order to define the *pairwise F-measure* as follows:

$$\text{PWF} = \frac{2 \times \text{pr} \times \text{rc}}{\text{pr} + \text{rc}}$$

A higher value of the *pairwise F-measure (PWF)* suggests that the underlying clustering is of good quality.

Average Cluster Purity: The average cluster purity is computed as the average percentage of the *dominant community* in the different clusters. Formally, let $\mathcal{C} = \{C_1, \cdots, C_K\}$ be the k clusters determined by the algorithms. Let us assume that the number of points in C_i, are denoted by n_i. The corresponding set of n_i vertices is denoted by $\{v_{1,i}, \cdots, v_{n_i,i}\}$. Let $M_{l,i}$ denote the set of communities that $v_{l,i}$ truly belongs to in the ground truth of labels. Then, the *average cluster purity (ACP)* is defined as follows:

$$ACP = \frac{1}{k}\sum_{i=1}^{k}\sum_{l=1}^{n_i}\frac{\delta(dom_i \in M_{l,i})}{n_i}$$

Here, $\delta(\cdot)$ is an indicator function, which indicates whether the dominant class dom_i of cluster C_i matches with at least one of the labels for a vertex.

6.3 Compared Algorithms

In order to validate the effectiveness of our algorithms, we used the following baselines:

- We used a *pure content-based approach* where we are simply clustering the documents on the edges, with the use of a clustering approach. We used the *LDA-WORD* [2] algorithms in order to cluster the content of the data sets.
- We used some *link-based techniques* in which we cluster the nodes using known structural methods. In particular, we tested with the use of the normalized cut (*NCUT*) [19] which is a spectral clustering algorithm. In this algorithm, we consider two types of links - the user favor link and tag links. Specifically, for user favor links, two images are considered to be linked if they are favored by the same user. For tag links, two images are linked together if they are annotated by the same tag. The link weights are defined by the number of times that two images are either co-favored or annotated by the same tag keywords. We apply *NCUT* on a graph that combines these two kinds of links. The link structure is used to partition the images without any content information.
- We also compare with the clustering algorithm with both social links and the image content. In particular, we tested with a graph theoretical clustering algorithm, which simultaneously integrates visual and textual features in a trigraph for efficient Web image clustering [17]. This algorithm is referred to as *Consistent Isoperimetric High-order Co-clustering (*CIHC*)*, and it uses the user tags as well as image content to partition the object in social media networks.

We describe some implementation details about the initialization of the *HRF* clustering model. The Gibbs sampling approach needs to be be initialized with an initial cluster configuration. For this purpose, we apply the k-means clustering algorithm on the content of *Flickr* images without any link structure. Such content-based initialization may affect the first few iterations of Gibbs sampling process. However, the link structure will be gradually incorporated into the modeling process after several iterations.

6.4 Results

The results for the different algorithms on the *Flickr* image network are illustrated in Table 1. The value of the parameter λ was fixed at 0.5. We present the results in terms of pairwise precision, recall and F-measure. The proposed *HRF* clustering algorithm outperforms the other algorithms, including the pure content and pure link-based algorithms, and also the algorithms which combine both link and content. This demonstrates that the combination of the different kinds of content and linkage information in a social media network provides more effective results. For example, *CIHC*, which combines both image content and the links to user tags in a trigraph, outperforms the *LDA-WORD* and *NCUT*. However, the *CIHC* algorithm is not quite as effective at incorporating different kinds of heterogeneous

Table 1: Comparison of different clustering algorithms on *Flickr* social media data set.

Algorithms		*Flickr* Social Media Data Set			
		precision	recall	PWF	ACP
Content	*LDA-WORD*	0.4350	0.5569	0.4885	0.4989
Link only	*NCUT*	0.4960	0.7189	0.5870	0.5237
content + tags	*CIHC*	0.5504	0.7484	0.6343	0.6403
Our approach	*HRF*	**0.6350**	**0.8526**	**0.7279**	**0.8296**

content such as the tags, the social structure and the object content. As the result, the *HRF* algorithm outperforms *CIHC* as well. An interesting observation is that the pure link-based clustering algorithm *NCUT* obtain better performances than pure content-based information. This suggests that the linkage information in the networks often contain more useful semantic information for the clustering process than the content.

Our algorithm, which combines not only content but also the context and social links, achieves the best performances. This is because in social media networks, in addition to the content, both tag and social links provide important network structural information for the discovering the image clusters. In addition to modeling content and links, the proposed *HRF* algorithm detects and removes the noisy links from the clustering process. This improves the robustness of clustering algorithm, which avoids the negative effect of noisy links. Therefore, the *HRF* algorithm is able to determine the useful clustering by separating out the noise from the useful clustering hints. This is particularly important in social media networks which are known to be noisy for mining purposes.

One interesting aspect of the clustering algorithm is that it outputs user clusters, tag clusters, and object cluster simultaneously. This can be very useful for a wide variety of applications, because the tag clusters can be used in order to determine the semantic interpretability of the images, and the user clusters can be leveraged in order to do group recommendations. This is particularly useful in cases where the multi-media objects are available on social sharing platforms. For example, Figure 4 also illustrates five image clusters and the associated tag clusters obtained by the *HRF* clustering algorithm. We can find that the images and associated tags are well clustered based on their content and descriptive tag words. It is evident that the tag keywords provide the descriptive theme in each cluster very well. For example, the images in the first cluster correspond to restaurants, and the corresponding tag keywords reflect this semantic theme well. Such objects can be recommended to the corresponding users in this cluster. Furthermore, new images which are tagged with the corresponding keywords can also be immediately recommended to the users in the cluster. Alternatively, the new users containing the appropriate frequent keywords in their comments or profile can be recommended the appropriate images. Thus, this clustering process not only improves the quality of the clustering, but also provides useful social and semantic interpretability which can be leveraged for a wide variety of applications.

6.5 Parameter Sensitivity

We also tested the sensitivity of the *HRF* model to different choices of the parameter λ. This is a particularly important parameter, because it regulates the importance of linkage information in the clustering process. For the purposes of our previously presented results in Table 1, we set the value of λ to 0.5, so that an approximately equal amount of importance is placed on linkage and content. Nevertheless, it is interesting to test how the quality of clustering is influenced by varying the value of this parameter. We illustrate the variation of the algorithm with λ in Figure 5. The value of λ is illustrated on the X-axis, and it varies from 0.1 to 0.8 with 0.1 as the step size. The *F-measure* and *cluster purity* measures of clustering quality are illustrated on the Y-axis in the different charts. It is evident from the results that when little link information is incorporated ($\lambda = 0.1$), the *HRF* model does not perform well on the data sets. However, as λ increases, more link information is combined together with content and it performs better. However, the effectiveness starts reducing after a certain point, because the use of a value of λ which is too large discounts the importance of the content information. This verifies that both content and link information do help in modeling the clustering structure. One observation is that the two different measures provide slightly different peaks in terms of clustering quality, though they both suggest robustness within a wide range of parameter values. We find that in the interval $[0.1, 0.8]$, the proposed *HRF* model consistently outperforms the other algorithms in terms of both the ACP and PWF measures.

Table 2: Comparison of computing time spent by different clustering algorithms on *Flickr* social media data set.

Algorithm	Computing Time
LDA-WORD	457 min
NCUT	375 min
CIHC	421 min
HRF	189 min

6.6 Computational Efficiency

Finally, we also compare the computing time spent by different algorithms for performing the clustering. The comparison is performed on a Server platform with Intel Xeon CPU 2.4 GHz and 33 GM physical memory. For the sake of fair comparison, we apply all the algorithm to compute 50 clusters. Table 2 reports the computational time of the different algorithms. We find that the algorithm *HRF* is much faster than the other algorithms. In fact the the *HRF* algorithm was *twice* as fast as the next fastest algorithm, corresponding to the *NCUT* method. This is in spite of the fact that the *NCUT* method works with only the link struc-

Figure 4: Illustration of five image and tag clusters obtained by the *HRF* clustering algorithm.

ture, whereas our approach uses both the content and links for clustering. The *LDA-WORD* algorithm was the slowest, and was about 2.5 times slower than the *HRF* method. The efficiency of our approach is because of our use of the Gibbs sampling strategy, which is able to provide robust results for samples of reasonable size. Thus, the approach presented in this paper provides an effective tradeoff between the quality and efficiency of the results.

7. CONCLUSIONS AND SUMMARY

In this paper, we present a robust clustering algorithm on social media networks based on heterogeneous random fields. We use a combination of linkage information and social cues in order to perform the clustering. These are used to infer the highest probability cluster configuration in an efficient way. The algorithm is able to explicitly detect the noisy links, which is particularly important in the noisy social media scenario. We present experimental results, which network demonstrate the effectiveness of our algorithm compared to other state-of-the-art methods.

Acknowledgments

Research was sponsored by the Army Research Laboratory and was accomplished under Cooperative Agreement Number W911NF-09-2-0053. The views and conclusions contained in this document are those of the authors and should not be interpreted as representing the official policies, either expressed or implied, of the Army Research Laboratory or the U.S. Government. The U.S. Government is authorized to reproduce and distribute reprints for Government purposes notwithstanding any copyright notation here on. This work was also supported in part by National Science Foundation (NSF) Grant IIS-1144111. Guo-Jun Qi was supported in part by an IBM fellowship.

8. REFERENCES

[1] K. Barnard, P. Duygulu, and D. A. Forsyth. Clustering art. In *CVPR Conference*, 2001.

[2] D. M. Blei, A. Y. Ng, and M. I. Jordan. Latent dirichlet allocation. *Journal of Machine Learning Research*, (3):993–1022, January 2003.

[3] D. Cai, X. He, Z. Li, W.-Y. Ma, and J.-R. Wen. Hierarchical clustering of www image search results using visual, textual, and link information. In *ACM Multimedia Conference*, 2004.

[4] D. Chakrabarti, R. Kumar, and A. Tomkins. Evolutionary clustering. In *KDD*, 2006.

[5] Y. Chen, J. Z. Wang, and R. Krovetz. Clue: Cluster-based retrieval of images by unsupervised

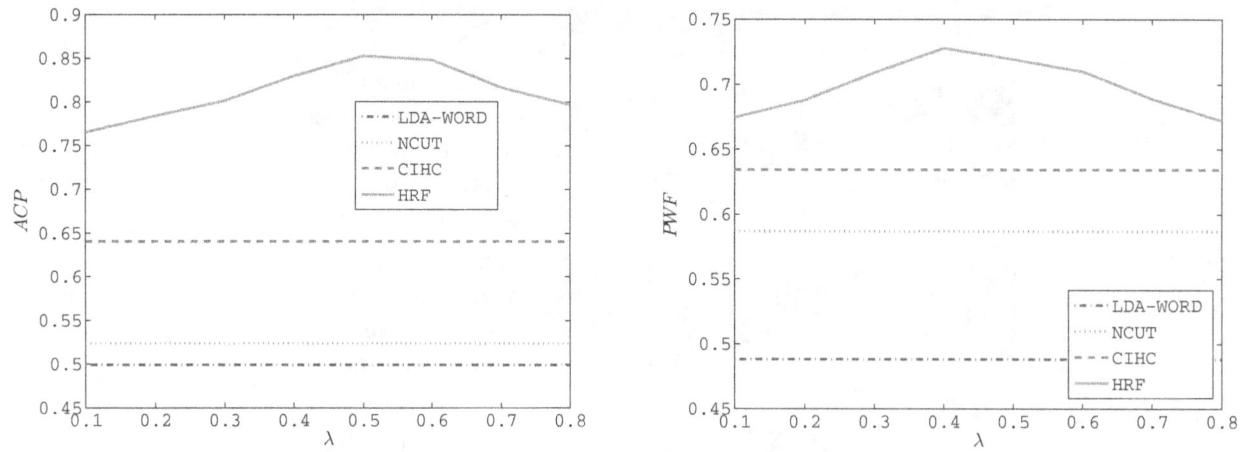

(a) (b)

Figure 5: Illustration of performance sensitivity with respect to the parameter λ for the *HRF* model in terms of pairwise F-measure (PWF) in subfigure (a) and cluster purity (ACP) in subfigure (b).

learning. In *IEEE Transactions on Image Processing, 14(8)*, 2005.

[6] Y. Chi, X. Song, D. Zhou, K. Hino, and B. Tseng. Evolutionary spectral clustering by incorporating temporal smoothness. In *KDD*, 2007.

[7] A. Clauset, M. E. J. Newman, and C. Moore. Finding community structure in very large networks. In *Phys.Rev. E 70, 066111*, 2004.

[8] D. Cutting, D. Karger, J. Pedersen, and J. Tukey. Scatter/gather: A cluster-based approach to browsing large document collections. In *Proceedings of the SIGIR*, 1992.

[9] A. P. Dempster, N. M. Laird, and D. B. Rubin. Maximum-likelihood from incomplete data via the em algorithm. *J. Royal Statist. Soc.*, B(39):1–38, 1977.

[10] B. Gao, T.-Y. Liu, T. Qin, X. Zheng, Q.-S. Cheng, and W.-Y. Ma. Web image clustering by consistent utilization of visual features and surrounding texts. In *ACM Multimedia Conference*, 2005.

[11] A. E. Gelfand and A. F. M. Smith. Sampling-based approaches to calculating marginal densities. *Journal of the American Statistical Association*, (85(410)):398ÍC409, 1990.

[12] D. Gibson, R. Kumar, and A. Tomkins. Discovering large dense subgraphs in massive graphs. In *VLDB*, 2005.

[13] J. Goldberger, S. Gordon, and H. Greenspan. Unsupervised image-set clustering using an information theoretic framework. In *IEEE Transactions on Image Processing, 15*, 2006.

[14] A. Jain and R. C. Dubes. Algorithms for clustering data. In *Prentice Hall*, 1988.

[15] Y.-R. Lin, J. Sun, P. Castro, R. B. Konuru, H. Sundaram, and A. Kelliher. Extracting community structure through relational hypergraphs. In *WWW Conference*, 2009.

[16] G. Qiu. Image ad feature co-clustering. In *ICPR Conference*, 2004.

[17] M. Rege, M. Dong, and J. Hua. Graph theoretical framework for simultaneously integrating visual and textual features for efficient web image clustering. In *Proc. of International Conference on World Wide Web*, 2008.

[18] V. Satuluri and S. Parthasarathy. Scalable graph clustering using stochastic flows: applications to community discovery. In *KDD Conference*, 2009.

[19] J. Shi and J. Malik. Normalized cuts and image segmentation, August 2000.

[20] C. Silverstein and J. Pedersen. Almost-constant time clustering of arbitrary corpus sets. In *Proceedings of the SIGIR*, 1997.

[21] T. Yang, R. Jin, Y. Chi, and S. Zhu. Combining link and content for community detection: a discriminative approach. In *ACM KDD Conference*, 2009.

[22] Y. Zhou, H. Cheng, and J. X. Yu. Graph clustering based on structural/attribute similarities. In *VLDB Conference*, 2009.

[23] S. Zhu, K. Yu, Y. Chi, and Y. Gong. Combining content and link for classification using matrix factorization. In *Proceedings of the 30th ACM SIGIR Conference on Research and Development in Information Retrieval*, 2007.

Adding Semantics to Microblog Posts

Edgar Meij
edgar.meij@uva.nl

Wouter Weerkamp
w.weerkamp@uva.nl

Maarten de Rijke
derijke@uva.nl

ISLA, University of Amsterdam
Amsterdam

ABSTRACT

Microblogs have become an important source of information for the purpose of marketing, intelligence, and reputation management. Streams of microblogs are of great value because of their direct and real-time nature. Determining what an individual microblog post is about, however, can be non-trivial because of creative language usage, the highly contextualized and informal nature of microblog posts, and the limited length of this form of communication.

We propose a solution to the problem of determining what a microblog post is about through semantic linking: we add semantics to posts by automatically identifying concepts that are semantically related to it and generating links to the corresponding Wikipedia articles. The identified concepts can subsequently be used for, e.g., social media mining, thereby reducing the need for manual inspection and selection. Using a purpose-built test collection of tweets, we show that recently proposed approaches for semantic linking do not perform well, mainly due to the idiosyncratic nature of microblog posts. We propose a novel method based on machine learning with a set of innovative features and show that it is able to achieve significant improvements over all other methods, especially in terms of precision.

Categories and Subject Descriptors

H.3 [**Information Storage and Retrieval**]: H.3.1 Content Analysis and Indexing; H.3.3 Information Search and Retrieval; H.3.4 Systems and Software

General Terms

Algorithms, Measurement, Performance, Experimentation

1. INTRODUCTION

In recent years Twitter has become one of the largest online microblogging platforms with over 65M unique visitors and around 200M tweets per day.[1] Microblogging streams have become invaluable sources for many kinds of analyses, including online reputation management, news and trend detection, and targeted marketing and customer services [4, 18, 32, 35]. Searching and mining microblog streams offers interesting technical challenges, because of the sheer volume of the data, its dynamic nature, the creative language usage, and the length of individual posts [17, 22].

In many microblog search scenarios the goal is to find out what people are saying about concepts such as products, brands, persons, et cetera [31]. Here, it is important to be able to accurately retrieve tweets that are on topic, including all possible naming and other lexical variants. So, it is common to manually construct lengthy keyword queries that (hopefully) capture all possible variants [2]. We propose an alternative approach, namely to determine what a microblog post is about by automatically identifying *concepts* in them. We take a concept to be any item that has a unique and unambiguous entry in a well-known large-scale knowledge source, Wikipedia.

Little research exists on understanding and modeling the semantics of individual microblog posts. Linking free text to knowledge resources, on the other hand, has received an increasing amount of attention in recent years. Starting from the domain of named entity recognition (NER), current approaches establish links not just to entity types, but to the actual entities themselves [15, 20, 30]. Instead of merely identifying types, we also aim to disambiguate the found concepts and link them to Wikipedia articles. With over 3.5 million articles, Wikipedia has become a rich source of knowledge and a common target for linking; automatic linking approaches using Wikipedia have met with considerable success [14, 25, 27, 28].

Most, if not all, of the linking methods assume that the input text is relatively clean and grammatically correct and that it provides sufficient context for the purposes of identifying concepts. Microblog posts are short, noisy, and full of shorthand and other ungrammatical text and provide very limited context for the words they contain [17, 22]. Hence, it is not obvious that automatic concept detection methods that have been shown to work well on news articles or web pages, perform equally well on microblog posts.

We present a robust method for automatically mapping tweets to Wikipedia articles to facilitate social media mining on a semantic level. The first research question we address is: What is the performance of state-of-the-art approaches for linking text to Wikipedia in the context of microblog posts? Our proposed approach involves a two-step method for semantic linking. The first step is recall-oriented where the aim is to obtain a ranked list of candidate concepts. In the next step, we enhance precision and determine which of the candidate concepts to keep. Our second research question concerns a comparison of methods for the initial concept ranking step; we consider lexical matching, language modeling, and other state-of-the-art baselines and compare their effectiveness. Our third

[1]http://blog.twitter.com/2011/06/200-million-tweets-per-day.html

Permission to make digital or hard copies of all or part of this work for personal or classroom use is granted without fee provided that copies are not made or distributed for profit or commercial advantage and that copies bear this notice and the full citation on the first page. To copy otherwise, to republish, to post on servers or to redistribute to lists, requires prior specific permission and/or a fee.
WSDM'12, February 8–12, 2012, Seattle, Washington, USA.
Copyright 2012 ACM 978-1-4503-0747-5/12/02 ...$10.00.

Tweet	Concepts
Is it me or does Google Instant encourage you to pay more attention to their Ads and Shopping links?	ADS, AND, ATTENTION, DOES, GOOGLE, GOOGLE INSTANT, IS, IT, LINKS, ME, MORE, *etc.*
Keep your eyes out for an actress called Judi Dench. She's a promising talent and I predict we'll be hearing more about her.	A, ABOUT, ACTRESS, AN, AND, AND I, BE, CALLED, DENCH, FOR, HEARING, HER, I, I PREDICT, JUDI DENCH, *etc.*

Table 1: Example tweets with concepts recognized using lexical matching on Wikipedia article titles.

research question concerns the second, precision-enhancing step. We approach this as a machine learning problem and consider a broad set of features, some of which have been proposed previously in the literature on semantic linking, some newly introduced. In addition to multiple features, we also consider multiple machine learning algorithms and examine which of these are most effective for our problem. Finally, we examine the relative effectiveness of the precision-enhancing step on top of different initial concept ranking methods. The paper focuses on the *effectiveness* of concept detection methods in the setting of microblog posts. In the conclusion to the paper we also discuss efficiency considerations.

Our main contributions are: (i) a robust, successful method for linking tweets to Wikipedia articles, based on a combination of high-recall concept ranking and high-precision machine learning, including state-of-the-art machine learning algorithms, (ii) insights into the influence of various features and machine learning algorithms on the task, and (iii) a reusable dataset, with which we aim to facilitate follow-up research. The remainder of this paper is organized as follows. In Section 2 we discuss related work, followed by a description of our method. In Section 4 we discuss the experimental setup and, in Section 5, the experiments with which we answer our research questions. We end with a concluding section.

2. RELATED WORK

In this section we review related work, pertaining to semantic linking and to Twitter in particular.

2.1 Linking Text

Links to a knowledge structure are often seen as a way of providing semantics to digital items. The idea has been used for different media types (such as text [27, 28] and multimedia [34]) and for different text genres (such as news pages [9], queries [23], archives [6], and radiology reports [14]). A simple and frequently taken approach for linking text to concepts is to perform lexical matching between (parts of the text) and the concept titles [10, 26], an approach related to keyword-based interfaces to databases [38]. However, merely matching an input text with concept titles suffers from many drawbacks, including ambiguity (where different concepts with the same label can be confused) and a possible lack of specificity (in which case less "meaningful" concepts are identified). Table 1 shows two example tweets with concepts identified using lexical matching between word n-grams in the tweets and Wikipedia titles. From these examples it is obvious that, while relevant concepts such as GOOGLE INSTANT and JUDI DENCH are identified, this approach also retrieves many false positives.

In general, such issues can be addressed on either the Wikipedia or on the textual side. That is, we can reduce the amount of "noisy" concepts, e.g., by applying some kind of filtering or weighing, or we can clean up the text, e.g., by identifying segments, key phrases, or by weighing terms based on various heuristics, including stopwords, document frequency, et cetera. Our approach incorporates both; it first determines a high-recall ranking of concepts for each part of the tweet and, next, applies machine learning on the concepts to improve precision. Since we adopt a machine learning framework, we can also include Twitter-specific features. The method proposed by Milne and Witten [28] yields accurate results on relatively clean input texts, such as those from Wikipedia entries and news articles. For comparative purposes, we include their method as one of the baselines and show that it does not perform well on tweets. Ferragina and Scaiella [11] propose an approach similar to [28], but with an explicit focus on short texts. They incorporate a voting scheme as well as pruning of n-grams unrelated to the input text. Since this method is geared towards short texts, we include it as a baseline below.

2.2 Twitter

Twitter provides its users facilities to share short text messages, comprising a maximum of 140 characters. Tweets are published publicly by default, making Twitter an enormous resource of casual information exchanges. As Twitter has grown, novel language use and standards such as mentions (to reference another user), hashtags (to refer to a topic), and retweets (similar to an e-mail forward) have emerged [37].

Various authors have attempted to "give meaning" to text in general [24] or to text contained in tweets. Liu et al. [20] focus on NER on tweets and use a semi-supervised learning framework to identify four types of entities. Benson et al. [3] try to match tweets to "records." These records are, for example, artist-venue pairs and can be obtained from sources like music guides. They train a model that extracts artists and venues from tweets and automatically match these to the extracted records. Our approach is more general and aims at enriching tweets rather than extracting information from them. Our approach could therefore simplify the task proposed in [3].

Abel et al. [1] aim at contextualizing tweets, a task very similar to ours. After adding context, the authors use the tweets to profile Twitter users. Their approach depends on matching tweets to news articles, followed by semantic enrichment based on the news article's content. Finally, the semantically enriched tweets are used for user modeling. For the second step, semantic enrichment, the authors use OpenCalais. Our approach differs from their approach in that we do not assume tweets to be related to news articles, making our approach more general.

Mendes et al. [26] propose Linked Open Social Signals, a framework that includes annotating tweets with information from Linked Data. Their approach is rather straightforward and involves either looking up hashtag definitions or lexically matching strings to recognize (DBpedia) entities in tweets. We include the former as a feature in our framework and evaluate the latter as a baseline.

Kwak et al. [18] show that hashtags are good indicators to detect events and trending topics and Laniado and Mika [19] explore the use of hashtags in Twitter and the relation to (Freebase) concepts. Using manual annotations, they find that about half of the hashtags can be mapped to Freebase concepts, most of them being named entities. In a few cases, more general hashtags are mapped to concepts. Assessors showed high agreement on the task of mapping tags to concepts. The authors make the assumption that hashtags are mainly used to "ground" tweets, an assumption we lift in our work, enabling us to add semantics to tweets without hashtags. Previous work has shown that hashtag usage is quite low and differs a lot per country and language [36]. Huang et al. [16] analyze the semantics of hashtags in more detail and reveal that hashtagging in Twitter is more commonly used to join public discussions than to organize content for future retrieval. In order to verify the relative contribution of hashtags, we include a feature that leverages the highest-voted hashtag definition.

3. LINKING POSTS TO CONCEPTS

As we have seen in the previous section, linking text to concepts is most commonly approached by lexically matching the input text with the concept labels, i.e., the titles of the Wikipedia articles. Due to the noisy nature of microblog posts, this approach does not work well on our task, as we will see below. Furthermore, a large number of concept titles will match with any part of the tweet, as illustrated by the example in Table 1.

We therefore need a mechanism to improve precision, not only by removing spurious target concepts but also by limiting the number of n-grams used to generate a mapping. We approach this in two steps. The goal of the first step is obtain high recall, so we generate a ranked list of candidate concepts for each n-gram in a tweet. Moreover, using n-grams in this step also means we can keep track of which n-gram links to which concept. In the second step we aim to improve precision by applying supervised machine learning. Here, each candidate concept c is classified as being relevant or not (in the context of the tweet and the user). In a way, this setup is a form of learning to rerank. Alternatively, we could forego the first step (in which we obtain a set of candidate concepts) and apply a form of learning to rank on *all* concepts for each n-gram. However, since semantic linking is akin to known-item finding and thus geared towards high precision—with only a relatively small number of relevant concepts per tweet—we reduce the set of candidate concepts prior to applying machine learning. Moreover, limiting the set of concepts to be used as input for the machine learning algorithm also reduces the number of feature vectors that need to be created, decreasing the runtime.

3.1 Concept Ranking

In order to be able to identify the part of the tweet that is the source for a semantic link, we first identify word n-grams in the tweet. That is, we extract all possible n-grams from a tweet Q (where $1 \leq n \leq |Q|$). For each n-gram q in this set of n-grams, $\{q_i\}_{i=1}^{|Q|!}$, we generate a ranked list of candidate concepts. Various methods exist for creating a ranked list of concepts for an n-gram and in our experiments below we compare three families of approaches that are further detailed in Section 4. They include lexical matching, language modeling, and other state-of-the-art methods.

3.2 Machine Learning

Once we have obtained a ranked list of candidate concepts for each n-gram, we turn to concept selection. In this stage we need to decide which of the concepts are most viable. We use supervised machine learning, that takes as input a set of labeled examples (tweet to concept mappings) and several features of these examples (detailed below).

For training, each n-gram q in each tweet Q is associated with a set of concepts C_q and a set of associated relevance assessments for the concepts. The latter is created by considering all concepts that an annotator identified for the tweet. If a concept was not selected by any annotator, we consider it to be non-relevant for Q. Section 4.3 further details the specifics of the manual annotations. As we are performing semantic linking at the tweet level (instead of doing named entity resolution) it is sufficient to have a mapping from tweets to concepts for our task. So, we consider each combination of n-gram and concept an instance, represented by a high-dimensional feature vector. Its label indicates the concept's binary relevance to the tweet and, hence, the n-gram. The goal of the machine learning algorithm is to learn a function that outputs a relevance status for any new n-gram and concept pair given a feature vector of this new instance. In the remainder of this section we detail the used features; in Section 4.6 we introduce the machine learning algorithms.

Since we consider each Wikipedia article to be a concept, we have an obvious textual representation to use for extracting our textual features. Below we discern different parts of this representation (which we call "fields") for feature extraction and concept ranking. The fields we include are: `title` (the title of the article associated with concept c), `sentence` (the first sentence of the article), `paragraph` (the first paragraph of the article), `content` (the full contents of the article), and `anchor` (the aggregated anchor texts of all incoming links in Wikipedia). We employ several types of features, each associated with either an n-gram, concept, or their combination. We also include a separate set of Twitter-specific features.

3.2.1 N-gram Features

This set of features is solely based on information from an n-gram and are listed in Table 2 (first group). Here, $IDF(q)$ indicates the relative number of concepts in which q occurs, which is defined as $IDF(q) = \log(|\mathcal{C}|/df(q))$, where $|\mathcal{C}|$ indicates the total number of concepts and $df(q)$ the number of concepts in which q occurs [21]. The subscript f denotes the field of the Wikipedia articles used, see above.

$WIG(q)$ indicates the weighted information gain [39], which can be considered a predictor of the retrieval performance of a query. It uses the set of all candidate concepts retrieved for this n-gram, C_q, and determines the relative probability of q occurring in these documents as compared to the collection. Formally:

$$WIG(q) = \frac{\frac{1}{|C_q|}\sum_{c \in C_q} \log(P(q|c)) - \log(P(q))}{\log P(q)}.$$

$SNIL(q)$ and $SNCL(q)$ are an indicator of the polysemy of an n-gram and determine the number of Wikipedia articles whose title matches (part of) q. Similarly, we leverage the Wikipedia anchors to determine the probability that q is used as an anchor in Wikipedia. Let $C_a(q)$ be the set of Wikipedia articles that contain the n-gram q as an anchor and $df(q)$ the total number of Wikipedia articles in which q appears. $KEYPHRASENESS(q)$, then, determines the probability $|C_a(q)|/df(q)$ [27]. Similarly, we determine this probability based on all occurrences, also including multiple occurrences in an article:

$$LINKPROB(q) = \frac{\sum_{c \in C_a(q)} n(q,c)}{\sum_{c' \in \mathcal{C}} n(q,c')},$$

where $n(q,c)$ is the count of q in the content of the textual representation of c.

3.2.2 Concept Features

Table 2 (second group) lists the concept-related features. This set relates to the knowledge we have of each candidate concept, such as the number of other Wikipedia articles linking to or from it, the number of associated categories, the number of redirect pages pointing to it, and the number of terms or characters in its title. The last two features in this set capture the relative popularity of an Wikipedia article and are based on Wikipedia access logs.[2] That is,

[2]See `http://dammit.lt/wikistats/`.

N-gram features	
$LEN(q) = \|q\|$	Number of terms in the n-gram q
$IDF_f(q)$	Inverse document frequency of q in representation f, where $f \in$ {title, anchor, content}
$WIG(q)$	Weighted information gain using top-5 retrieved concepts
$KEYPHRASENESS(q)$	Probability that q is used as an anchor text in Wikipedia
$LINKPROB(q)$	Probability that q is used as an anchor text in Wikipedia (all occurrences)
$SNIL(q)$	Number of articles whose title equals a sub-n-gram of q
$SNCL(q)$	Number of articles whose title match a sub-n-gram of q
Concept features	
$INLINKS(c)$	Number of Wikipedia articles linking to c
$OUTLINKS(c)$	Number of Wikipedia articles linking from c
$GEN(c)$	Function of depth of c in the Wikipedia category hierarchy
$CAT(c)$	Number of categories associated with c
$REDIRECT(c)$	Number of redirect pages linking to c
$WLEN(c)$	Number of terms in the title of c
$CLEN(c)$	Number of characters in the title of c
$WIKSTATS(c)$	Number of times c was visited in 2010
$WIKISTATSWK(c)$	Number of times c was visited in the seven days before the tweet was posted
N-gram + concept features	
$TF_f(c,q) = \frac{n_f(q,c)}{\|f\|}$	Relative phrase frequency of q in representation f of c, normalized by length of f, where $f \in$ {title, anchor, first sentence, first paragraph, content}
$POS_n(c,q) = pos_n(q)/\|c\|$	Position of nth occurrence of q in c, normalized by length of c
$SPR(c,q)$	Distance between the first and last occurrence of q in c
$TF \cdot IDF(c,q)$	Importance of q for c
$RIDF(c,q)$	Residual IDF (difference between expected and observed IDF)
$\chi^2(c,q)$	χ^2 test of independence between q in c and all concepts
$NCT(c,q)$	Does q contain the title of c?
$TCN(c,q)$	Does the title of c contain q?
$TEN(c,q)$	Does the title of c equal q?
$SCORE(c,q)$	Language modeling score of c with respect to q
$RANK(c,q)$	Retrieval rank of c with respect to q
$COMMONNESS(c,q)$	Probability of c being the target of a link with anchor text q
Tweet features	
$TWCT(c,Q)$	Does Q contain the title of c?
$TCTW(c,Q)$	Does the title of c contain Q?
$TETW(c,Q)$	Does the title of c equal Q?
$TAGDEF(q,Q)$	Number of times q appears in the hashtag definition of any hashtag in tweet Q
$URL(q,Q)$	Number of times q appears in a webpage linked to by Q

Table 2: Features used, grouped by type. More detailed descriptions in Section 3.2.

we determine for each Wikipedia article the normalized frequency with which it was visited in 2010 ($WIKSTATS(c)$) and the frequency with which it was visited in the seven days before the tweet was posted ($WIKSTATSWK(c)$).

3.2.3 N-gram + Concept Features

This set of features considers the combination of an n-gram and a concept (Table 2, third group). Here, we first consider the relative frequency of occurrence of q in separate concept fields, the position of the first occurrence of the n-gram, the distance between the first and last occurrence, and various IR-based measures [21]. Of these, $RIDF$ [8] is the difference between expected and observed IDF for a concept, which is defined as

$$RIDF(c,q) = \log\left(\frac{|\mathcal{C}|}{df(q)}\right) + \log\left(1 - \exp\left(\frac{-n(q,\mathcal{C})}{|\mathcal{C}|}\right)\right).$$

We also consider whether the title of the Wikipedia article matches q in any way.

For the features $SCORE(c,q)$ and $RANK(c,q)$ we adopt a language modeling framework, in which a query is viewed as having been generated from a multinomial language model and each document is scored according to the likelihood that the words in the query were generated by randomly sampling the document language model [21]. The word probabilities are estimated from the document itself (using maximum likelihood estimation) and combined with background collection statistics to overcome zero probability and data sparsity issues; a process known as smoothing. We calculate the score for a concept $c \in \mathcal{C}$ according to the probability that it was generated by the n-gram, $P(c|q)$, which can be rewritten using Bayes' rule as: $P(c|q) = P(q|c)P(c)P(q)^{-1}$. Here, for a fixed n-gram q, the term $P(q)$ is the same for all concepts and can be ignored for ranking purposes. The term $P(c)$ indicates the prior probability of selecting a concept, which we assume to be uniform. We consider each n-gram to be a phrase and determine the probability $P(q|c)$ using the following estimate:

$$P(q|c) = \frac{n(q,c) + \mu P(q)}{\mu + |c|}. \quad (1)$$

This is an estimate using Bayes smoothing with a Dirichlet prior, where $P(q)$ indicates the probability of observing q in a large background collection. Here, μ is a hyperparameter that controls the influence of the background corpus and $|c|$ is the length of the textual representation of the concept.

Finally, we consider the prior probability that c is the target of a link with anchor text q in Wikipedia:

$$COMMONNESS(c,q) = \frac{|L_{q,c}|}{\sum_{c'} |L_{q,c'}|}, \quad (2)$$

where $L_{q,c}$ denotes the set of all links with anchor text q and target c.

3.2.4 Tweet Features

Finally, we consider features related to the entire tweet (Table 2, last group), including three kinds of lexical matches. We also fetch the webpage(s) linked to by the tweet (if any) and determine the frequency of occurrence of q in them ($URL(q,Q)$). Finally, we use the TagDef API[3] to lookup the highest-voted hashtag definition of all hashtags in the tweet (if any) and determine the frequency of occurrence of q in them ($TAGDEF(q,Q)$).

4. EXPERIMENTAL SETUP

In order to answer the research questions introduced in Section 1, we have designed several experiments. In this section we detail our experimental setup, including how we sample tweets, the manual annotations, the Wikipedia version, and how we evaluate linking tweets to concepts.

4.1 Tweets

Out of a sample of 2000 tweets, Pear Analytics [32] classified 40% as containing "pointless babble," with another 37.55% as merely conversational. So, a significant portion of all tweets are non-informative and only a small fraction contains topics of general interest. In order to account for this possible bias, we randomly sample users from the "verified accounts" Twitter list and, for each of these users, we retrieve the last 20 tweets.[4] The Twitter users in this list can be considered influential and their tweets are more likely to be picked up by other Twitter users than from a random sample of Twitter users. As to preprocessing, we record all URLs, mentions, and hashtags in each tweet. URLs are removed from each tweet, whereas mentions and hashtags are kept without the leading '@' and '#' respectively.

4.2 Wikipedia

As our target for linking tweets, we use a dump of Wikipedia that is dated 11 Oct. 2010. In this particular snapshot, we have 3,483,213 articles proper, 4,526,685 redirects, 120,547 disambiguation pages, and 71,204,142 hyperlinks between articles. For the `anchor` field we include not only the anchor texts found in intra-Wikipedia hyperlinks, but also the titles of any redirect pages pointing to an article. As to retrieval, we use the entire Wikipedia document collection as background corpus and set μ (cf. Eq. 1) to the average length of a Wikipedia article.

[3]See `http://tagdef.com/`.

[4]See `http://twitter.com/help/verified/`.

4.3 Manual Annotations

In order to obtain manual annotations (both for training and evaluation), we have asked two volunteers to manually annotate 562 tweets, each containing 36.5 terms on average. They were presented with an annotation interface with which they could search through Wikipedia articles using any of the fields defined above. The annotation guidelines specified that the annotator should identify concepts contained in, meant by, or relevant to the tweet. They could also indicate that an entire tweet was either ambiguous (where multiple target concepts exist) or erroneous (when no relevant concept could be assigned). Out of the 562 tweets, 419 were labeled as not being in either of these two categories and kept for further analysis. For these, the annotators identified 2.17 concepts per tweet on average. In order to facilitate follow-up research, we make all annotations and derived data available.[5]

4.4 Evaluation

We approach the task of linking tweets to concepts as a ranking problem; given a tweet, the goal of a system implementing a solution to this problem is to return a ranked list of concepts meant by or contained in it, where a higher rank indicates a higher degree of relevance of the concept to the tweet. The best performing method puts the most relevant concepts towards the top of the ranking. Our method identifies relevant concepts for each tweet's constituent n-grams and, since the semantic linking task is defined at the tweet instead of the n-gram level, we need a way to aggregate potential duplicate concepts. In our experiments, we aggregate each duplicate concept (if any) by naively summing the confidence scores for each source n-gram. Future work should indicate whether more elaborate methods perform better. The manual annotations described above are then used to determine the relevance status of each of the concepts with respect to a tweet; a concept is considered relevant if it was linked by an annotator. If it was not selected by any annotator, we consider it to be non-relevant.

The evaluation measures we employ include precision at rank 1 (P1), r-precision (R-prec), recall, mean reciprocal rank (MRR), and mean average precision (MAP) [21]. Together, these measures provide a succinct summary of the quality of the retrieved concepts. We use the top-50 returned concepts for evaluation. To test for statistical significance, we use a paired two-sided t-test (with pairing at the run level). We indicate the best performing run using boldface and a significant improvement with $^\vartriangle$ and $^\blacktriangle$ (for $p < 0.05$ and $p < 0.01$ respectively) and, similarly, a significant decrease in performance with $^\triangledown$ and $^\blacktriangledown$ (again for $p < 0.05$ and $p < 0.01$ respectively). Unless indicated otherwise, we test for significance against the top-most row in a table.

4.5 Baselines

We employ three sets of baselines to which we compare our approach and to which we apply supervised machine learning. They include: (i) lexical matching of the n-grams with the concepts, (ii) a language modeling baseline, and (iii) a set of other methods, augmented with using solely the $COMMONNESS(c,q)$ feature.

4.5.1 Lexical Match

As our first baseline we consider a simple heuristic which is commonly used [10, 26] and select concepts whose title lexically matches any n-gram in the tweet, similar to the $NCT(c,q)$ and $TEN(c,q)$ features described in Section 3.2. We subsequently rank the concepts based on the language modeling score of their

[5]See `http://ilps.science.uva.nl/resources/wsdm2012-adding-semantics-to-microblog-posts/`.

associated Wikipedia article given the tweet. This method is the most naive, yet most commonly used approach; in sum, it returns concepts for which consecutive terms in the title of the Wikipedia article are contained in the n-gram.

An example is given in Table 1. As a variant, we apply the same approach to the `anchor` field. We also apply an heuristic to handle n-grams; this method starts with the largest n-grams in the tweet and checks to see if it lexically matches with a concept. If it does, it discards any smaller constituent n-grams. If the n-gram doesn't match it recurses with its constituent n-grams.

4.5.2 Retrieval

This baseline builds on the approach described by Eq. 1 and is similar to using a search engine and performing a search within Wikipedia. That is, we use language modeling to determine the similarity of a tweet with the concepts. In particular, we explore two different tweet representations and three different concept fields, resulting in six retrieval baseline runs. For the tweet representation we try either the full tweet or the constituent n-grams. In the case of ranking concepts for the entire tweets, we assume independence between the individual terms $t \in Q$:

$$P(c|Q) \propto P(c) \prod_{t \in Q} P(t|c)^{n(t,Q)}. \quad (3)$$

The probability $P(t|c)$ is again smoothed using Bayes smoothing with a Dirichlet prior, in this case formulated as:

$$P(t|c) = \frac{n(t,c) + \mu P(t)}{\mu + \sum_{t'} n(t',c)}. \quad (4)$$

As to the concept fields we use either the full Wikipedia article, its title, or its incoming anchor texts.

To combine the rankings produced by each constituent n-gram of a tweet, we use combMNZ [33]. CombMNZ is a result list merging method and a variant of CombSUM—which sums a document's scores from all lists where it was retrieved. CombMNZ multiplies the CombSUM score by the number of lists that contained the particular document. Formally, let $q_1, \ldots, q_K$ be the term n-grams in the tweet and $C_1, \ldots, C_K$ the concept rankings corresponding to each n-gram. Then,

$$\text{CombSUM}(c) = \sum_{k: c \in C_k} P(c|q_k), \quad (5)$$

$$\text{CombMNZ}(c) = \text{CombSUM}(c) \cdot |\{k : c \in C_k\}|. \quad (6)$$

4.5.3 Other Methods

The final set of baselines that we consider comprises three established methods, including the one proposed by Milne and Witten [28], denoted M&W, which represents the state-of-the-art in automatic linking approaches. We use the algorithm and best-performing settings as described in [28], trained on our version of Wikipedia. We also include a novel service provided by DBpedia, called DBpedia Spotlight.[6] The third baseline in this set (Tagme) is provided by Ferragina and Scaiella [11]. These first three baselines in this set do not perform optimally when linking individual n-grams. Therefore, we use the entire, cleaned tweet as input. Our last concept ranking method in this set (CMNS) corresponds to the $COMMONNESS(c, q)$ feature, detailed by Eq. 2. This method scores each concept based on the relative frequency with which the n-gram is used as an anchor text for that particular concept. We exclude OpenCalais from this set, since this webservice only recognizes entity types without performing any kind of disambiguation, similar to returning Wikipedia disambiguation pages. Moreover, the precise algorithmic details are not made public.

[6]See `http://dbpedia.org/spotlight`.

4.6 Machine Learning Methods

For all machine learning algorithms, we perform 5-fold cross-validation at the tweet level, in order to reduce the possibility of errors being caused by artifacts in the data and to verify the generalizability to unseen data. The reported scores are averaged over all testing folds. We experiment with multiple machine learning algorithms in order to confirm that our results are generally valid, i.e., not dependent on any specific algorithm. Following Milne and Witten [28], we include a Naive Bayes (NB), Support Vector Machines (SVM), and a C4.5 decision tree classifier.

Random forests (RFs) are a very efficient alternative to C4.5, since they are (i) relatively insensitive to parameter settings, (ii) resistant to overfitting, and (iii) easily parallelizable [5]. It is an ensemble-based decision tree classifier based on bagging, in which a learning algorithm is applied multiple times to a subset of the instances and the results averaged. In this case, for each iteration a bootstrap sample is taken and a full tree is constructed. For each node of the tree, m features are randomly selected to obtain the best split. This process reduces overfitting by averaging classifiers that are trained on different subsets of the data with the same underlying distribution. We set m to roughly 10% of the size of the feature set, i.e., $m = 4$. Besides m, RF has one additional parameter: the number of iterations, k. We set $k = 1000$, but also report on the effect of varying this setting on the linking effectiveness.

In recent years, gradient boosted regression trees (GBRTs) have been established as the de facto state-of-the-art learning paradigm for web search ranking [7, 12, 29]. It is a point-wise learning to rank algorithm that predicts the relevance score of a result to a query by minimizing a loss function (e.g., the squared loss) using stochastic gradient descent. It is similar to RF in that it is also based on tree averaging. In this case, however, many low-depth trees (instead of full ones) are sequentially created, each with a bias towards instances that are responsible for the current regression error. Let $\mathbf{q}_i$ be the feature vector associated with q_i, y_i the associated label, i.e., relevance status, and $\mathcal{T}(\mathbf{q}_i)$ the current prediction for q_i. Then assume we have a continuous, convex, and differentiable loss function $\mathcal{L}(\mathcal{T}(\mathbf{q}_1), \ldots, \mathcal{T}(\mathbf{q}_n))$ that reaches its minimum if $\mathcal{T}(\mathbf{q}_i) = y_i$ for all $\mathbf{q}_i$. GBRT performs gradient descent in the instance space, where the current prediction is updated with a gradient step,

$$\mathcal{T}(\mathbf{q}_i) \leftarrow \mathcal{T}(\mathbf{q}_i) - \alpha \frac{\mathcal{L}}{\mathcal{T}(\mathbf{q}_i)} \quad (7)$$

during each iteration. Here, $\alpha > 0$ denotes the learning rate. For our experiments we use the the square loss, which is defined as: $\mathcal{L} = \frac{1}{2} \sum_{i=1}^{n} (\mathcal{T}(\mathbf{q}_i) - y_i)^2$. So, GBRT depends on three parameters: the learning rate α, the depth of the tree, d, and the number of iterations, k. We set $\alpha = 0.02$ and $k = 1000$, and, following Hastie et al. [13], we set $d = 4$.

Finally, Mohan et al. [29] show that, since RF is resistant to overfitting and also often outperforms GBRT, the RF predictions can be used as starting point for GBRT. By doing so, GBRT starts at a point relatively close to the global minimum and is able to further improve the already good predictions. We also include this approach, labeled iGBRT.

5. RESULTS AND DISCUSSION

In this section we answer the research questions that we identified in Section 1 by presenting, comparing, and discussing the results of the baselines and our method.

	P1	R-prec	Recall	MRR	MAP
Lexical match					
`anchor`	0.0366	0.0422	0.1592	0.0796	0.0485
`title`	0.0262	0.0160	0.0616	0.0338	0.0205
Lexical match, longest n-gram					
`anchor`	**0.1990**	**0.1344**	0.2408	**0.2440**	**0.1405**
`title`	0.1885	0.1335	**0.2530**	0.2345	0.1372

Table 3: First set of baseline results, obtained using lexical matching on titles or anchor texts (first group) and applying the longest n-gram heuristic (second group).

	P1	R-prec	Recall	MRR	MAP
Tweet					
`content`	0.1492	0.1173	0.2464	0.2255	0.1396
`title`	0.1597	0.1185	0.1901▼	0.2106	0.1261
`anchor`	**0.2932**▲	**0.2147**▲	0.3719▲	0.3793▲	0.2415▲
N-grams					
`content`	0.2539	0.1939	**0.6864**▲	0.3910	0.2664
`title`	0.2120▼	0.1552▲	0.3985	0.2795▼	0.1818▼
`anchor`	0.2644	0.1994	0.6686▲	**0.4003**▲	**0.2810**▲

Table 4: Retrieval results using two tweet representations and three fields. Significance is tested against line 1 (first group) and line 3 (second group).

5.1 Establishing a Baseline

Since the machine learning step takes as input a ranked list of concepts for each n-gram in a tweet, the ideal baseline method should have a high recall with sufficient precision. Table 3 shows the results of using lexical matching to obtain a ranked list of concepts. Merely matching parts of the tweet with titles or anchors does not perform well. Note that this is a commonly taken approach, but these results indicate that it fails on tweets. When we apply the longest n-grams heuristic we observe a notable increase in concept ranking performance, in terms of recall and precision.

We now turn to the results for the retrieval baseline, using different fields and ways of handling the tweet as introduced earlier. Table 4 (first group) shows the results for ranking concepts based on the entire tweet, assuming independence between the terms in the tweet. This is a rather naive approach, but performs remarkably well. Especially when we only use the anchor texts of each Wikipedia article, we obtain a P1 value of 0.2932, i.e., the first returned concept is relevant for almost 30% of the tweets. Moreover, the average rank of of the first relevant concept lies around 3. Table 4 (second group) shows the results when we generate a ranking for each constituent n-gram and apply CombMNZ to merge these. We observe the following: First, recall improves significantly using n-grams and the `anchor` or `content` field. Second, both MAP and MRR increase significantly using the `anchor` field.

Table 5 shows the results of the last set of baselines. DBpedia Spotlight and the learning to link approach by Milne and Witten [28] achieve comparable results that slightly improve over the best language modeling baseline. The performance results for M&W are much lower than the results reported in [28], which can be attributed to the different nature of tweets as compared to Wikipedia and/or news articles. The Tagme system—designed especially for short texts—fares much better, achieving marked improvements.

	P1	R-prec	Recall	MRR	MAP
Spotlight	0.3717	0.2688	0.3068	0.4215	0.2658
M&W	0.3770	0.3033	0.3741	0.4255	0.3127
Tagme	0.5628	0.4643	0.5814	0.6339	0.4894
CMNS	**0.6021**	**0.5271**	**0.7775**	**0.7080**	**0.5853**

Table 5: Results for the third set of baselines.

	P1	R-prec	Recall	MRR	MAP
lex. match	0.1990	0.1344	0.2408	0.2440	0.1405
NB	0.3010▲	0.1996▲	0.2302	0.3440▲	0.2021▲
C4.5	0.4372▲	0.2553▲	0.2658	0.4503▲	0.2575▲
SVM	0.3194▲	0.2337▲	0.2943△	0.3878▲	0.2328▲
RF	**0.5681**▲	**0.4091**▲	**0.4872**▲	**0.6078**▲	**0.4222**▲
GBRT	0.5550▲	0.4034▲	0.4825▲	0.5964▲	0.4133▲
iGBRT	0.5654▲	0.4082▲	0.4819▲	0.6053▲	0.4209▲

Table 6: Results for the best lexical matching run with subsequent machine learning.

Simply applying the $COMMONNESS(c, q)$, i.e., CMNS, concept ranking method, however, achieves the highest scores so far, on all metrics. This relatively simple approach is able to retrieve over 75% of the relevant concepts and place the first relevant concept around rank 1.4 on average.

In conclusion, the results on the three baseline sets show that the task of linking tweets to concepts can be addressed relatively successfully; using a retrieval-based approach outperforms an approach based on mere lexical matching. Using the CMNS method obtains the highest performance, in terms of both precision and recall.

5.2 Applying Machine Learning

In this section we present the results of our approach, i.e., applying machine learning to further improve the results of the concept ranking step. That is, we take the best performing run per baseline set and apply the machine learning approaches introduced in Section 3.2. In particular, we select the "Lexical match, longest n-gram" for the first set and the "n-grams" retrieval for the second set, both using the `anchor` field. Finally, we select the CMNS run from the last set.

In Table 6 we show the results when we apply machine learning to the lexical matching baseline. All machine learning algorithms are able to significantly improve precision, MRR, and MAP. Only NB and C4.5 do not significantly improve in terms of recall. Here, RF obtains the highest scores overall, although the differences with GBRT and iGBRT are minimal and not significant.

Table 7 shows the results of the retrieval baseline, augmented by the machine learning step. Almost all machine learning algorithms are able to improve over the retrieval baseline, except for recall. Furthermore, iGBRT achieves the highest scores on most metrics, closely followed by RF.

Finally, in Table 8 we show the results of applying machine learning to the CMNS baseline. Of all the baselines, CMNS obtains the highest recall and precision levels; it does so by returning relatively few concepts per n-gram. We note that NB and C4.5 do not perform well in this case; their performance drops significantly for all metrics. Indeed, recall is significantly worse for NB, C4.5, and SVM, mainly due to the fact that a lot of concepts are identified as non-relevant by these algorithms. Interestingly, P1 improves significantly for SVM, while R-prec is significantly worse

	P1	R-prec	Recall	MRR	MAP
retrieval	0.2644	0.1994	**0.6686**	0.4003	0.2810
NB	0.4058▲	0.3212▲	0.4510▼	0.4911▲	0.3450▲
C4.5	0.3822▲	0.2294	0.2530▼	0.4106	0.2341▼
SVM	0.2958	0.2419△	0.4947▼	0.4138	0.2799
RF	0.5419▲	0.4197▲	0.6362▼	0.6195▲	**0.4662▲**
GBRT	0.5079▲	0.3978▲	0.6362▼	0.6012▲	0.4517▲
iGBRT	**0.5445▲**	**0.4209▲**	0.6349▼	**0.6229▲**	0.4660▲

Table 7: Results of applying machine learning, applied to the best performing retrieval baseline.

	P1	R-prec	Recall	MRR	MAP
CMNS	0.6021	0.5271	0.7775	0.7080	0.5853
NB	0.4921▼	0.4091▼	0.5292▼	0.5853▼	0.4294▼
C4.5	0.5209▼	0.3542▼	0.3774▼	0.5585▼	0.3528▼
SVM	0.6708▲	0.4670▼	0.4784▼	0.6846	0.4711▼
RF	**0.6780▲**	**0.5739△**	**0.8417▲**	**0.7676▲**	**0.6561▲**
GBRT	0.6649△	0.5624△	0.8361▲	0.7568▲	0.6421▲
iGBRT	0.6754△	0.5715△	0.8400▲	0.7644▲	0.6511▲

Table 8: Results of applying machine learning, with as input the best performing "other" baseline run, i.e. *COMMONNESS* (CMNS).

than CMNS. In many cases, SVM is able to push a single relevant concept to the top of the ranking, but fails to do so for all relevant concepts. RF, GBRT, and iGBRT obtain significant improvements over CMNS for all metrics; RF outperforms all other methods.

In sum, we find that the iterative machine learning methods obtain the best improvements overall and that they are able to significantly improve precision in all cases. In the remainder of this section we perform a more detailed analysis of the obtained results. We base these analyses mainly on the best performing method, i.e., machine learning using RF on the CMNS concept ranking, which we denote CMNS-RF.

5.3 Error Analysis

Figure 1 shows a per-tweet plot of the difference in terms of average precision (AP) between CMNS and CMNS-RF. As this figure indicates, most tweets are helped by applying machine learning, except for about a fifth of them. The tweets that are hurt most are mainly tweets with only a single relevant concept, that is retrieved by CMNS but classified as not relevant by CMNS-RF.

When we look at the errors being made in general, we observe that there are three typical cases of errors. First, there are concepts that are clearly relevant, but that were missed by the annotators. In some other cases, the concepts identified by the annotators do not always seem relevant. In a future study we intend to investigate this further, mainly by performing a post-hoc relevance analysis of annotated tweets. Second, we find that in some cases the machine learning algorithms seem to focus on a particular sense of an n-gram. E.g., in the case of "St. Patrick," most algorithms return various churches instead of the arguably more common concept SAINT PATRICK'S DAY. Finally, it also occurs that a non-content-bearing term in the tweet is being linked, such as the n-gram "wow" that gets linked to the concept WORLD OF WARCRAFT. In future work, we plan on tackling these two classes of errors, e.g., by including a post-ranking filter that first tries to match longer n-grams before moving on to shorter ones or by including more features that

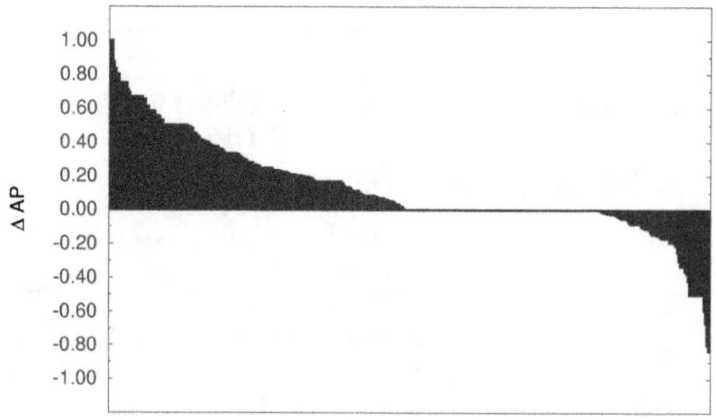

Figure 1: Per-tweet difference in AP between CMNS and CMNS-RF, where a positive value indicates an improvement over CMNS.

are related to the entire tweet; this way the remainder of the tweet might assist in disambiguating a particular n-gram.

5.4 Parameter Settings

In this section we consider the various parameters that are associated with the machine learning algorithms. For all of these, we have selected the top-ranked concepts returned by the concept ranking step, up to a maximum of 50 per n-gram. Varying this number does not significantly alter the obtained results.

Recall that RF, GBRT, and iGBRT have several parameters associated with them, including the number of iterations and the learning rate. In the case of gradient boosting there exists an inherent trade-off between the learning rate and the number of iterations. Ideally, the learning rate needs to be infinitesimally small and the number of iterations extremely large to obtain the true global minimum. In our case, varying the learning rate parameter α only influences the obtained end results very little.

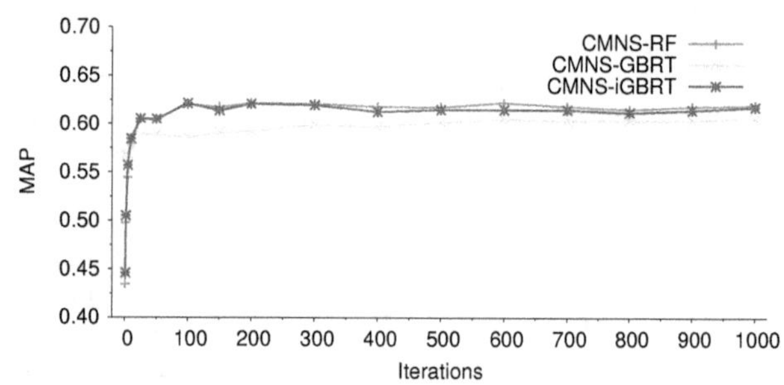

Figure 2: Effect of varying k on MAP.

Figure 2 shows the effect of varying the number of iterations using the RF, GBRT, and iGBRT machine learning algorithms on MAP. Both RF and iGBRT start at roughly the same level, since iGBRT uses the RF predictions as initialization weights. Both algorithms also reach their optimum after approximately 100 iterations, indicating that the iterative learning process can be stopped quite early. GBRT is not able to reach the same level of performance as iGBRT; it takes over 600 iterations to approach the others' scores.

5.5 Feature Analysis

Finally, we zoom in on the relative effectiveness of each of the features. The top-5 features with the highest discriminative power, measured using information gain, are, in decreasing order:

- $TEN(c, q)$,
- $TWCT(c, Q)$,
- $REDIRECT(c)$,
- $LINKPROB(q)$, and
- $IDF_{anchor}(q)$.

Interestingly, this is a mix between features that are based solely on the n-gram, the concept, and their combination. The binary feature that indicates whether the tweet contains the concept title is also a strong indicator for the relevance of a concept regarding a tweet.

In a follow-up experiment, we rank all features by their information gain and add each of them incrementally to the set of used features, starting with the features with the highest values. We keep the number of features RF selects at each iteration at $m = 4$ and thus start with selecting the 4 highest ranked features; Table 9 shows the results. CMNS-RF achieves MAP comparable to CMNS (on which this ranking is based) after adding the 12th feature, $TCN(c, q)$. When CMNS is subsequently added as a feature, we observe an improvement of 6% in retrieval performance. After $IDF_{content}(q)$ we truncate the table; MAP remains relatively constant around 0.65 after adding this feature. Almost all of the features shown here can be computed quite easily, either from an inverted index or from a cache that contains the link structure and anchor information of Wikipedia. The $URL(q, Q)$ and $WIG(q)$ features are the most costly features in this list. For the first an HTTP connection needs to be made and the web page content fetched, parsed, and matched with the n-gram. The second is a function over the n-gram and the top-ranked concepts for that n-gram. In a situation where the running time is of importance, we recommend removing these particular features.

Added feature	MAP	Δ
$TEN(c,q)$ / $TWCT(c,Q)$ / $REDIRECT(c)$ / $LINKPROB(q)$	0.4964	
+ $IDF_{anchor}(q)$	0.5452	9.83%
+ $KEYPHRASENESS(q)$	0.5523	1.30%
+ $SNIL(q)$	0.5502	-0.38%
+ $IDF_{title}(q)$	0.5547	0.82%
+ $SNCL(q)$	0.5593	0.83%
+ $TF_{paragraph}(c,q)$	0.5674	1.45%
+ $TF_{sentence}(c,q)$	0.5834	2.82%
+ $TCN(c,q)$	0.5866	0.55%
+ $COMMONNESS(c,q)$	0.6216	5.97%
+ $TF_{title}(c,q)$	0.6340	1.99%
+ $URL(q,Q)$	0.6405	1.03%
+ $POS_1(c,q)$	0.6435	0.47%
+ $GEN(c)$	0.6475	0.62%
+ $WIG(q)$	0.6491	0.25%
+ $IDF_{content}(q)$	0.6511	0.31%

Table 9: MAP of CMNS-RF after incrementally adding features proportional to their information gain (truncated to show only the top features).

6. CONCLUSION AND FUTURE WORK

Microblogging streams have become an invaluable resource for marketing, search, information dissemination, and online reputation management. Searching and mining microblog streams offers interesting challenges and in this paper we have presented a successful semantic linking method for microblog posts. The identified concepts, i.e., Wikipedia articles, can subsequently be used for, e.g., social media mining or advanced search result presentation. Our novel method uses machine learning and is based on a high-recall concept ranking and a high-precision concept selection step. Using a purpose-built test collection, we have shown that it significantly outperforms other methods, including various recently proposed approaches. Moreover, the concept selection step can be applied to any method that returns concepts for an input text. Our results show that this step, in particular using random forests or gradient boosted regression trees, can significantly improve a weak baseline, especially in terms of precision. It is even able to improve when the concept ranking performance is already strong on its own.

We have focused mainly on the effectiveness of semantic linking in the setting of microblog posts as opposed to the efficiency. Since both best performing machine learning algorithms are easily parallelizable, the bulk of the processing happens during feature extraction. From the results obtained during feature analysis, we note that not all features are equally important and that a minimal, easily computable set can already obtain good performance. Moreover, our analysis has shown that only a relatively small number of iterations is needed to achieve optimal performance. We finally note that, in the cases where a real-time analysis of a stream of microblog posts is required, merely using the low-cost CMNS feature already obtains very good performance.

Future work includes the following. First, although our method is not language-dependent in any way, the manual annotations are indeed language-specific. Wikipedia, on the other hand, already contains numerous, manually-curated inter-language links that we could use for this purpose. Second, we already mentioned a post-hoc evaluation of our semantic linking method for future work in Section 5.3. We also acknowledge that our sample of tweets, based on "authoritative users," is comparatively small and might be biased. Therefore, we intend to apply the best-performing methods to a much larger, random sample of microblog posts to see how it performs there. Further, in this paper we have focused on a domain-independent way of obtaining high-recall concept candidate rankings. We believe, however, that including additional information such as from NER could further improve semantic linking performance. For future work we also intend to consider bootstrapping or co-training, in which the concepts with the highest confidence are fed back as new training material. Finally we note that Wikipedia contains a few thousand links to Twitter in the articles' "External Links" sections and we intend to investigate to what extent we can use this information for semantic linking.

ACKNOWLEDGEMENTS

This research was supported by the European Union's ICT Policy Support Programme as part of the Competitiveness and Innovation Framework Programme, CIP ICT-PSP under grant agreement nr 250430, the European Community's Seventh Framework Programme (FP7/ 2007-2013) under grant agreements nr 258191 (PROMISE Network of Excellence) and 288024 (LiMoSINe project), the Netherlands Organisation for Scientific Research (NWO) under project nrs 612.061.814, 612.061.815, 640.004.802, 380-70-011, 727.011.005, the Center for Creation, Content and Technology (CCCT), the Hyperlocal Service Platform project funded by the Service Innovation & ICT program, the WAHSP project funded by the CLARIN-nl program, under COMMIT project Infiniti and by the ESF Research Network Program ELIAS.

REFERENCES

[1] F. Abel, Q. Gao, G.-J. Houben, and K. Tao. Semantic Enrichment of Twitter Posts for User Profile Construction on the Social Web. In *ESWC '11*, 2011.

[2] E. Amigó, J. Artiles, J. Gonzalo, D. Spina, B. Liu, and A. Corujo. WePS3 Evaluation Campaign: Overview of the On-line Reputation Management Task. In *2nd Web People Search Evaluation Workshop (WePS 2010), CLEF 2010 Conference*, 2010.

[3] E. Benson, A. Haghighi, and R. Barzilay. Event discovery in social media feeds. In *ACL '11*, 2011.

[4] D. Boyd, S. Golder, and G. Lotan. Tweet, tweet, retweet: Conversational aspects of retweeting on twitter. In *Hawaii Intern. Conf. on System Sciences*, 2010.

[5] L. Breiman. Random forests. *Mach. Learn.*, 45(1):5–32, 2001.

[6] M. Bron, B. Huurnink, and M. de Rijke. Linking archives using document enrichment and term selection. In *Research and Advanced Technology for Digital Libraries*. Springer Berlin / Heidelberg, 2011.

[7] C. J. C. Burges, K. M. Svore, P. N. Bennett, A. Pastusiak, and Q. Wu. Learning to rank using an ensemble of lambda-gradient models. *Journal of Machine Learning Research - Proceedings Track*, 14:25–35, 2011.

[8] K. W. Church and W. A. Gale. Inverse document frequency (IDF): A measure of deviations from poisson. In *Proc. Third Workshop on Very Large Corpora*, 1995.

[9] S. Cucerzan. Large-scale named entity disambiguation based on Wikipedia data. In *EMNLP '07*, 2007.

[10] S. Dill, N. Eiron, D. Gibson, D. Gruhl, R. Guha, A. Jhingran, T. Kanungo, S. Rajagopalan, A. Tomkins, J. Tomlin, and J. Zien. Semtag and seeker: Bootstrapping the semantic web via automated semantic annotation. In *WWW '03*, 2003.

[11] P. Ferragina and U. Scaiella. Tagme: on-the-fly annotation of short text fragments (by wikipedia entities). In *CIKM '10*, 2010.

[12] J. H. Friedman. Greedy function approximation: A gradient boosting machine. *Annals of Statistics*, 29:1189–1232, 2001.

[13] T. Hastie, R. Tibshirani, and J. H. Friedman. *The Elements of Statistical Learning*. Springer, 2003.

[14] J. He, M. de Rijke, M. Sevenster, R. van Ommering, and Y. Qian. Generating links to background knowledge: A case study using narrative radiology reports. In *CIKM '11*, 2011.

[15] D. W. C. Huang, Y. Xu, A. Trotman, and S. Geva. Overview of INEX 2007 Link the Wiki Track. In *INEX '07*, 2007.

[16] J. Huang, K. M. Thornton, and E. N. Efthimiadis. Conversational tagging in twitter. In *HT '10*, 2010.

[17] G. Inches, M. J. Carman, and F. Crestani. Statistics of online user-generated short documents. In *ECIR '10*, 2010.

[18] H. Kwak, C. Lee, H. Park, and S. Moon. What is Twitter, a social network or a news media? In *WWW '10*, 2010.

[19] D. Laniado and P. Mika. Making sense of twitter. In *ISWC '10*, 2010.

[20] X. Liu, S. Zhang, F. Wei, and M. Zhou. Recognizing named entities in tweets. In *ACL: HLT '11*, 2011.

[21] C. D. Manning, P. Raghavan, and H. Schütze. *Introduction to Information Retrieval*. Cambridge University Press, 2008.

[22] K. Massoudi, E. Tsagkias, M. de Rijke, and W. Weerkamp. Incorporating query expansion and quality indicators in searching microblog posts. In *ECIR '11*, 2011.

[23] E. Meij, M. Bron, B. Huurnink, L. Hollink, and M. de Rijke. Learning semantic query suggestions. In *ISWC '09*, 2009.

[24] E. Meij, D. Trieschnigg, M. de Rijke, and W. Kraaij. Conceptual language models for domain-specific retrieval. *Inf. Process. Manage.*, 46(4):448–469, 2010.

[25] E. Meij, M. Bron, L. Hollink, B. Huurnink, and M. de Rijke. Mapping queries to the Linking Open Data cloud: A case study using DBpedia. *Web Semantics: Science, Services and Agents on the World Wide Web*, 9(4):418 – 433, 2011.

[26] P. N. Mendes, A. Passant, P. Kapanipathi, and A. P. Sheth. Linked open social signals. In *WI-IAT '10*, 2010.

[27] R. Mihalcea and A. Csomai. Wikify!: Linking documents to encyclopedic knowledge. In *CIKM '07*, 2007.

[28] D. Milne and I. H. Witten. Learning to link with Wikipedia. In *CIKM '08*, 2008.

[29] A. Mohan, Z. Chen, and K. Q. Weinberger. Web-search ranking with initialized gradient boosted regression trees. *Journal of Machine Learning Research - Proceedings Track*, 14:77–89, 2011.

[30] D. Nadeau and S. Sekine. A survey of named entity recognition and classification. *Lingvisticae Investigationes*, 30(1):3–26, 2007.

[31] B. O'Connor, R. Balasubramanyan, B. R. Routledge, and N. A. Smith. From tweets to polls: Linking text sentiment to public opinion time series. In *ICWSM '10*, 2010.

[32] Pear Analytics. Twitter study – August 2009, 2009. `http://bit.ly/nYUJz7` [Online; accessed June 2011].

[33] J. A. Shaw and E. A. Fox. Combination of multiple searches. In *Text REtrieval Conference*, 1993.

[34] C. G. M. Snoek, B. Huurnink, L. Hollink, M. de Rijke, G. Schreiber, and M. Worring. Adding semantics to detectors for video retrieval. *IEEE Transactions on Multimedia*, 9(5):975–986, 2007.

[35] E. Tsagkias, M. de Rijke, and W. Weerkamp. Linking online news and social media. In *Fourth ACM Web Search and Data Mining (WSDM)*, Hong Kong, 2011.

[36] W. Weerkamp, S. Carter, and M. Tsagkias. How people use twitter in different languages. In *WebSci '11*, 2011.

[37] M. J. Welch, U. Schonfeld, D. He, and J. Cho. Topical semantics of twitter links. In *WSDM '11*, 2011.

[38] J. X. Yu, L. Qin, and L. Chang. Keyword search in relational databases: A survey. *IEEE Data Eng. Bull. Special Issue on Keyword Search*, 33(1):67–78, 2010.

[39] Y. Zhou and B. W. Croft. Query performance prediction in web search environments. In *SIGIR '07*, 2007.

Exploring Social Influence via Posterior Effect of Word-of-Mouth Recommendations

Junming Huang
Institute of Computing Technology, Chinese Academy of Sciences
Beijing, China
mail@huangjunming.com

Xue-Qi Cheng
Institute of Computing Technology, Chinese Academy of Sciences
Beijing, China
cxq@ict.ac.cn

Hua-Wei Shen
Institute of Computing Technology, Chinese Academy of Sciences
Beijing, China
shenhuawei@ict.ac.cn

Tao Zhou
Web Sciences Center, University of Electronic Science and Technology of China
Chengdu, China
zhutou@ustc.edu

Xiaolong Jin
Institute of Computing Technology, Chinese Academy of Sciences
Beijing, China
jinxiaolong@ict.ac.cn

ABSTRACT

Word-of-mouth has proven an effective strategy for promoting products through social relations. Particularly, existing studies have convincingly demonstrated that word-of-mouth recommendations can boost users' prior expectation and hence encourage them to adopt a certain innovation, such as buying a book or watching a movie. However, less attention has been paid to studying the posterior effect of word-of-mouth recommendations, i.e., whether or not word-of-mouth recommendations can influence users' posterior evaluation on the products or services recommended to them, the answer to which is critical to estimating user satisfaction when proposing a word-of-mouth marketing strategy. In order to fill this gap, in this paper we empirically study the above issue and verify that word-of-mouth recommendations are strongly associated with users' posterior evaluation. Through elaborately designed statistical hypothesis tests we prove the causality that word-of-mouth recommendations directly prompt the posterior evaluation of receivers. Finally, we propose a method for investigating users' social influence, namely, their ability to affect followers' posterior evaluation via word-of-mouth recommendations, by examining the number of their followers and their sensitivity of discovering good items. The experimental results on real datasets show that our method can successfully identify 78% influential friends with strong social influence.

Permission to make digital or hard copies of all or part of this work for personal or classroom use is granted without fee provided that copies are not made or distributed for profit or commercial advantage and that copies bear this notice and the full citation on the first page. To copy otherwise, to republish, to post on servers or to redistribute to lists, requires prior specific permission and/or a fee.
WSDM'12, February 8–12, 2012, Seattle, Washington, USA.
Copyright 2012 ACM 978-1-4503-0747-5/12/02 ...$10.00.

Categories and Subject Descriptors

J.4 [**SOCIAL AND BEHAVIORAL SCIENCES**]: Sociology; H.1.2 [**MODELS AND PRINCIPLES**]: User/Machine Systems—*Human factors*

General Terms

Design, Human Factors, Verification

Keywords

social influence, word-of-mouth recommendation, posterior evaluation

1. INTRODUCTION

Word-of-mouth recommendation, the process that an individual passes personal attitude to another (e.g., encouraging a potential customer to buy a product), has proven in decades to be an effective way to influence the latter's decision making. It was found that, for example, in the shopping site Amazon[1] an increase in book reviews, which is a kind of online word-of-mouth recommendations, results in an increase in relative sales [7]. Consequently, word-of-mouth marketing has been quickly developing via a variety of media including messages, blogs, microblogs and emails. In recent years, the integration of social network services and online sharing communities has gained a great success on a large number of web sites, such as Douban[2] and Goodreads[3], where millions of users cannot only rate books, music and movies, but also share their ratings and reviews with friends or followers. On those social network sites, the phenomenon that users recommend favorites to friends and followers plays an important role in shaping users' behaviors and their collections. Therefore, a deep understanding of word-of-mouth recommendations could be a key to designing a successful marketing strategy in online sharing communities.

[1]www.Amazon.com
[2]www.Douban.com
[3]www.Goodreads.com

The pervasive usage of word-of-mouth leads to a highly interesting research topic to understand its intrinsics. In decades various models, such as linear threshold, cascade model and spreading model, have been developed to explain why and how a word-of-mouth message encourages a receiver to adopt a certain innovation (e.g., a new product). It is widely believed that the reason encouraging a receiver to adopt an innovation is that a word-of-mouth message can raise his/her *prior expectation* on the concerned innovation, i.e., how valuable, useful and usable he/she expects the product to be. For example, when facing the question "to buy a BluRay player or an HD-DVD player", a person would more likely choose the former if many of his/her friends have already possessed BluRay players, which often provides a strong evidence in the quality of BluRay players.

However, less attention has been paid to investigating the *posterior effect* of word-of-mouth recommendations on a user's *posterior evaluation*, i.e., whether or not a word-of-mouth recommendation influences the evaluation (e.g., a rating) of the user on a product after he/she actually buys and experiences it. Without such knowledge, it is almost impossible to estimate user satisfaction, which is strongly related to user loyalty, before a word-of-mouth marketing strategy is proposed.

Intuitively, posterior evaluation depends only on how a product matches users' need, and is unlikely related to whether or not a friend has recommended it before. Nonetheless, in this paper we find a counter-intuitive phenomenon that a word-of-mouth recommendation surprisingly causes a change in the posterior evaluation of users. Upon this finding, we propose a framework to quantitatively measure *social influence*, i.e., the ability of an individual to affect a certain follower's posterior evaluation, and further develop a method for identifying individuals with great social influence. By properly estimating individuals' social influence, it is possible to leverage word-of-mouth recommendations in social networks to improve user satisfaction. In general, the main contributions of this paper can be summarized as follows:

1. This paper studies the relationship between word-of-mouth recommendations and users' posterior evaluation and find a counter-intuitive phenomenon that word-of-mouth recommendations are correlated to a raise in users' posterior evaluation.

2. Through elaborately designed hypothesis tests, we prove, for the first time, that word-of-mouth recommendations can significantly prompt users' posterior evaluation.

3. We propose a framework to quantitatively measure individuals' social influence by examining the number of their followers and their sensitivity of discovering good items.

4. We develop a method for identifying influential friends with strong social influence. Upon experiments on real datasets, we demonstrate that our method can identify up to 78% influential friends.

The rest sections are organized as follows: Section 2 summarizes existing studies on word-of-mouth recommendations. Section 3 describes how we find the phenomenon that word-of-mouth recommendations are correlated to a raise in users' posterior evaluation. Section 4 proposes two hypotheses to the reason that causes the phenomenon. The hypotheses are further tested in Section 5. In Section 6 we demonstrate that an influential individual can be identified with his/her sensitivity on good items and the number of followers.

2. RELATED WORKS

There is a long history of research focusing on the phenomenon, mechanics and usage of word-of-mouth recommendations. Earlier research observed the phenomenon that a word-of-mouth can effectively affect the receiver's decision making [16]. Consequently, word-of-mouth marketing, the strategy for promoting products with word-of-mouth recommendations, has been rapidly developing to encourage purchase by increasing a potential customer's prior expectation on the concerned product. The media of word-of-mouth recommendation is not limited to traditional oral conversation, but extended to online book reviews [7], emails [20], blogs [1], tweets [4], etc.

The wide usage of word-of-mouth has attracted great research attention to explain its intrinsic mechanics, which becomes practically possible with the availability of tremendous data from modern online communities [11]. Richardson and Domingos modeled the network value of individuals in social network when a word-of-mouth marketing is proposed [12, 24]. Lescovec empirically analyzed email promotions in a person-to-person network and figured out how purchase probability increases with incoming recommendations from friends [20]. Various models have been developed to explain the mechanism how a word-of-mouth message encourages a receiver to adopt a certain innovation, such as linear threshold [15], cascade model [13] and spreading model [23, 31, 8].

So far, lots of existing studies have been focusing on quantitatively estimating social influence of single nodes in social networks with topological and behavioral methods [26]. In many papers, it is believed that influence is related with the topological roles of the nodes in social networks, and can thus be calculated by link analysis, such as PageRank, HITS and LeaderRank [22]. More other studies attempted to estimate social influence by mining user behavior history to examine the effect of an individual on another's prior expectation and further decision making in a variety of scenarios, such as blogs [1], tweets [4], tags [14], books [17] and product reviews [3]. In addition, researchers have found that social influence could vary across different topics and items. Romero et al. found that tags of different types and topics spread in different mechanics on Twitter [25], Song and Tang found social influence can be of different strengths and directions given different topics [28, 29], and Cui et al. calculated social influence on item-level granularity with a modified matrix factorization algorithm [10].

Other research results focus on influence maximization, the task to find a small set of seed nodes to trigger a viral marketing that can reach a maximal range of nodes on an underlying social network, given the way information flows (e.g., defining the successful rate to propagate an innovation through every edge). Such a set of influential individuals are preferred when a merchant proposes a viral marketing. Many solutions have been developed to iteratively select seeds with a greedy algorithm, which guarantees a near-optimal selection, such as Kempe et al. [19] and Leskovec et al. [21].

Researchers also paid attention to discover influence hidden behind the correlation between a user's actions and his friends' behaviors. However, it is difficult to tell whether the correlation comes from influence or homophily, since the discovery of causality relation between variables is always a hard job and requires careful experimental design [18]. Crandall pointed out that influence and similarity can interplay [9]. Anagnostopoulos excluded influence with a high probability through an empirical analysis on the photo tagging website Flickr [2].

Sociologist analyzed the motive that why an individual sends a word-of-mouth recommendation in social networks. Many hints revealed that whether or not a word-of-mouth recommendation is presented mostly depends on the degree a recommender himself perceives the valuable, usefulness and usability of the referred product [6]. Wasko found reasons to share opinions also include reputation building or enjoyable feeling [30]. Those findings help us simplify our model in Section 5.1.

Although extensive studies have focused on addressing the prior expectation of word-of-mouth recommendations, less attention has been paid to investigating how word-of-mouth recommendations affect users' posterior evaluation. Bone found that a word-of-mouth comment from authority could bias users' post-usage performance judgments [5], i.e., users' posterior evaluation. However, a more common question, i.e., whether or not an ordinary user's word-of-mouth recommendation can affect his/her friends' posterior evaluation, is still unclear. We intend to answer it in this study.

3. PRELIMINARY STUDY

In this section, we demonstrate the counter-intuitive phenomenon that word-of-mouth recommendations can cause significant posterior effect on users. More specifically, word-of-mouth recommendations can obviously prompt users' posterior evaluation.

3.1 Data collection

We collect data from the aforementioned two online communities, Douban and Goodreads, where users can rate books and movies, and follow or make friends with other users. Friends are treated as mutual followers. The collected data contain user activities before Aug 2010 when we crawled the two web sites. We started crawling from the member lists of several hottest discussion groups on those web sites, and iteratively expanded to users who follow, or are followed by, the crawled ones. Among the 1,014,890 Douban users and 912,973 Goodreads users crawled, we remove inactive users who have rated less than 5 items and followed less than 5 other users, since their inactivity may lead to unreliable statistics. The detailed information about the datasets are presented in Table 1. In both datasets, the distribution of item popularity (how many times an item is collected) is observed in a power law as shown in Fig. 1.

On Douban, a user clicks the "recommend" button on an item's page to recommend it. Afterwards, all followers will get a notification of the recommendation. A total of 165,905(15.2%) Douban items are recommended by at least one user, as shown in Fig. 2. On Goodreads, when a user rates a book, all followers will get a recommendation message like "Adam loves *Harry Potter 7*". If a user rates an

Table 1: The two datasets crawled from Douban and Goodreads.

Property	Douban	Goodreads
Number of users	552,827	308,789
Number of directed edges	22,541,688	4,999,871
Number of items	1,089,914	1,648,546
Number of collections	111,001,250	26,900,929

item that has been *recommended* by anyone he/she follows, i.e. a Douban friend clicks the "recommend" button or a Goodreads friend rates it, we consider it as a *rating with word-of-mouth recommendation*. Otherwise, it is a *rating without word-of-mouth recommendation*.

In order to make ratings from different users comparable, we transform all ratings into Z-scores as follows, which will be used in the remained sections if no further specification is given.

$$r_{u,i} = \frac{R_{u,i} - \bar{R}_u}{\sigma_u}, \qquad (1)$$

where $r_{u,i}$ is the Z-score, corresponding to $R_{u,i}$ that is the observed rating user u posted on item i; $\bar{R}_u$ and σ_u are the mean and deviation among all ratings posted by user u, respectively.

3.2 Higher ratings on items with recommendations

Firstly, we take a glance at the ratings of two sample movies *The Pursuit of Happyness* and *Lost in Translation* on Douban. The former movie has been rated by over 200,000 users with a mean rating of 4.2 out of 5 stars, ranked top 30%, whilst the latter gets a relatively low mean rating of 3.9, ranked top 50%. Fig. 3 shows the rating distributions of these two movies and Table 2 reports ratings from 7 users who have rated both movies, where ratings with word-of-mouth recommendation are underlined. An obvious trend can be revealed that with word-of-mouth recommendations Douban users are more likely to present a higher rating to the recommended movies, indicating that they enjoy recommended movies more than unrecommended ones. This trend is even clearer on the lower-rated movie *Lost in Translation*. Specifically, the probability to rate it with 5 stars increases to 4 times if a recommendation is present.

To examine whether or not the above observed trend reflects a general tendency, we report the probability distributions of all (normalized) ratings with and without word-of-mouth recommendations on the two collected datasets. As

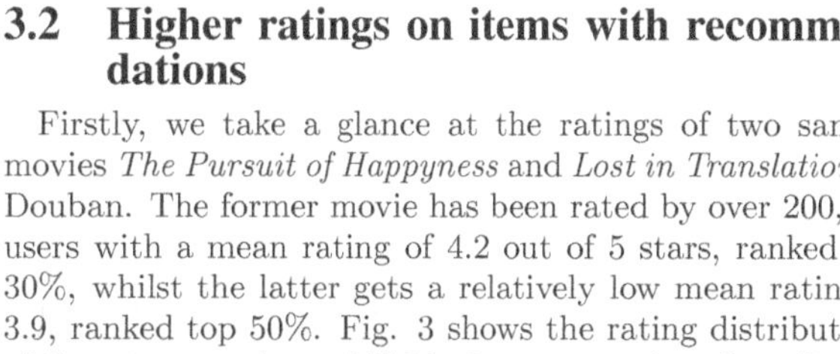

(a) Douban (b) Goodreads

Figure 1: The distributions of popularity (the times an item is collected).

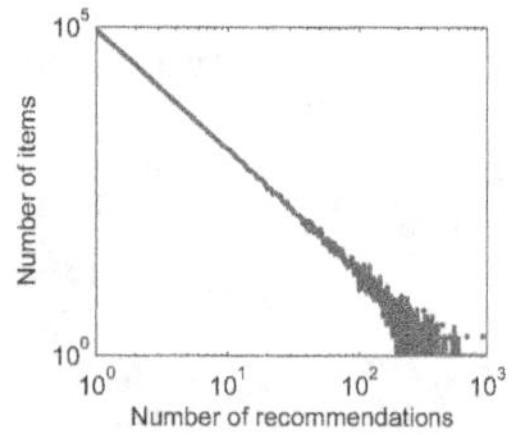

Figure 2: The distribution of recommendation count of Douban items.

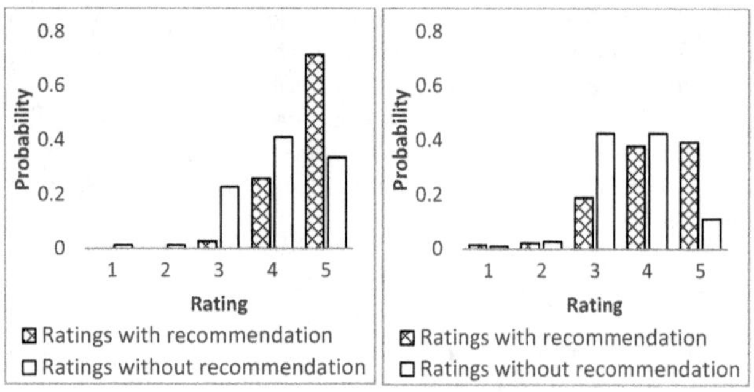

Figure 3: The probability distributions of Douban user ratings of a high-rated movie *The Pursuit of Happyness* (left) and a low-rated movie *Lost in Translation* (right).

shown in Fig. 4, an individual is more likely to present a high rating (less likely a low rating) to an item with a word-of-mouth recommendation, compared with an item without. Besides, the mean ratings without recommendations are almost zero in both Fig. 4(a) and 4(b), which is straightforward given the way we normalize ratings. In contrast, the mean ratings with recommendations are raised by 0.176 and 0.081 in two datasets respectively. Upon such observations, we can assert that as compared with an item without a word-of-mouth recommendation, an item recommended by a friend is tended to be given a higher rating, implying that ***a word-of-mouth recommendation is correlated to a raise in user posterior evaluation***.

An obvious explanation is that a recommendation implies the high quality of an item, which straightforwardly leads to a higher rating. Fig. 5(a) reveals that an item recommended at least once has a much larger collection count (solid curve) than than an item without any recommendation (dash curve), and the collection count of an item is strongly related to its recommendation count. Furthermore, the mean rating of items with at least one recommendation (solid curve and dash curve) is higher than that of items without recommendations (dash dot curve), as is shown in Fig. 5(b), although the ratings seem not correlated to the recommendation counts.

However, the above explanation only considers whether or not an item is recommended and ignores a possibly key factor that who recommends it. Therefore, in the following we examine the difference between the rating of an item recommended by the rater's friends, and that of an item recommended by a stranger that the rater never knows. Fig. 5(b) shows that a rating of an item with a word-of-mouth recommendation (solid curve) is even higher than that of an

Table 2: The ratings of two sample movies. The ratings with recommendation are underlined.

	Mean rating	u1	u2	u3	u4	u5	u6	u7
The Pursuit of Happyness	4.2	5	5	3	5	4	5	5
Lost in Translation	3.9	4	5	4	4	4	4	2

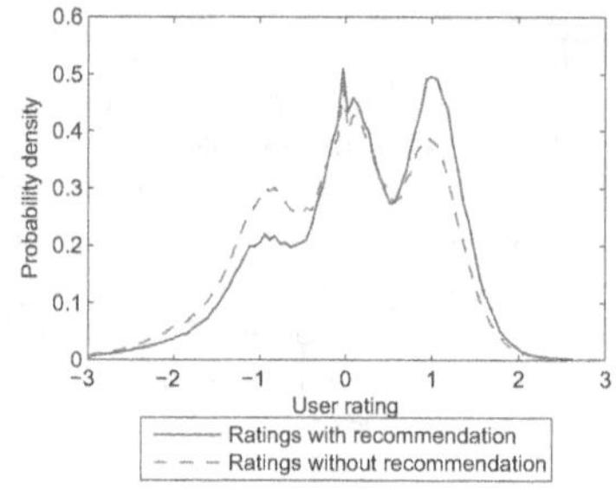

(a) Douban

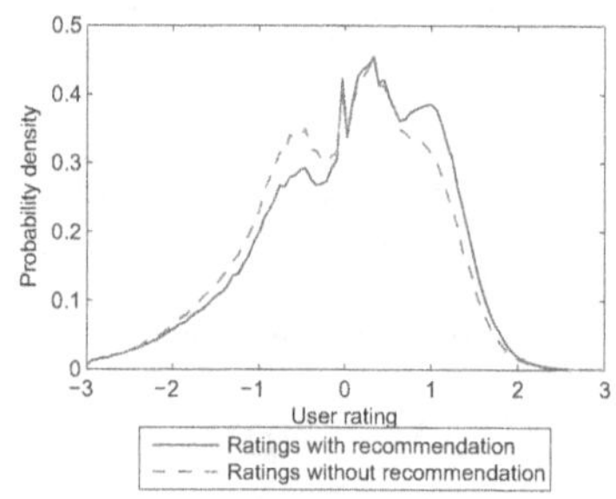

(b) Goodreads

Figure 4: The probability distributions of ratings, posted with (solid curves) or without (dash curves) a word-of-mouth recommendation.

item not directly recommended to the rater (dash curve). In a word, the tendency should not be simply explained with "a recommended item is preferred", since word-of-mouth recommendations play an indispensable role in influencing user ratings.

4. POSTERIOR EVALUATION MODELS

In this section we propose two possible models in order to formally explain the phenomenon observed in the previous section, whose validity and effectiveness will be further tested in the next section.

In the first model, a word-of-mouth recommendation and a higher rating of an item both attribute to certain common but unknown factors. In the other model, a word-of-mouth recommendation directly influences the rater to present a higher rating. The key difference between these two models lie in whether or not there is a *causality* relation between a word-of-mouth recommendation and an increase of the average user rating of an item.

The first model, which can be easily thought of, indicates that an individual's higher rating and his/her friend's rec-

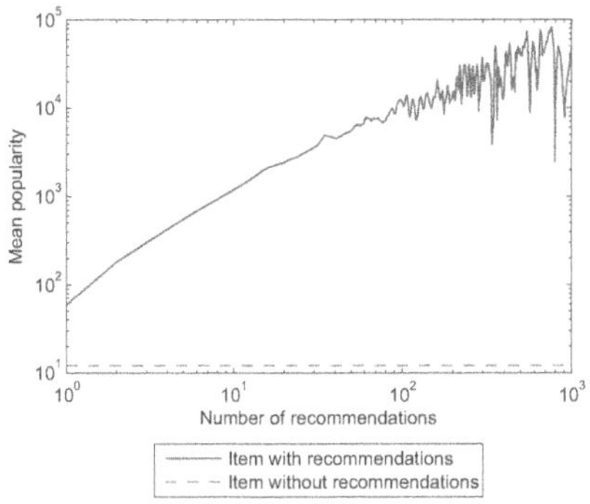

(a) Collection count w.r.t. recommendation count.

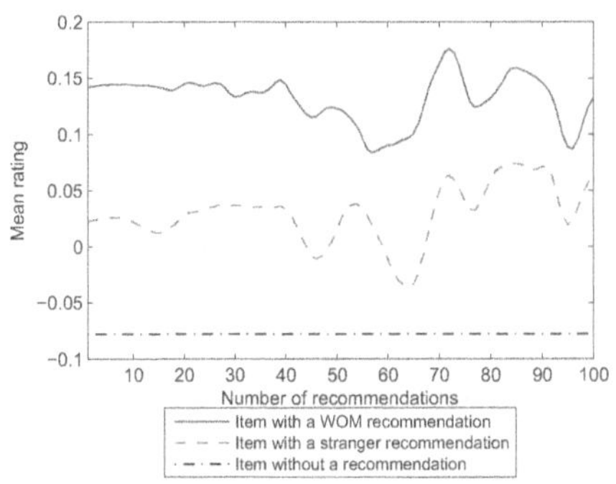

(b) Mean rating w.r.t. recommendation count.

Figure 5: The popularity and ratings w.r.t. recommendation count of items on Douban.

ommendation are both results of a group of unknown factors, including item quality, shared interests and any other reason. Take item quality for example. A recommendation can be viewed as a strong hint regarding the quality of the recommended item. If an item is recommended, it is more probable that the item is good enough to worth a higher rating. Another example is shared interests. It is observed in social networks that friends often share common interests more or less. If a friend of a user loves a movie and thus recommends it, it is quite probable that the movie also matches the user's taste, and thus a higher rating can be expected. Without loss of generality, we abstract such a model in Fig. 6(a), where a single variable c denotes a combination of all common factors. In this model, an individual's higher rating, denoted as r, and whether his/her friend recommends, denoted as m', are *independent* results from common unknown factors. Later on, we refer to this model as the ***independent model***.

The second explanation which sounds more consequential is that a friend's word-of-mouth recommendation is a direct cause of an individual's higher rating: m' directly influences r, as shown in Fig. 6(b).[4] For instance, the existence of a word-of-mouth recommendation may bring extra benefit to the receiver (e.g., reading a book that a friend recommends

[4]We ignore the inverse case that a user rating r leads to m' since we only consider a word-of-mouth recommendation when it is presented before the concerning user rates.

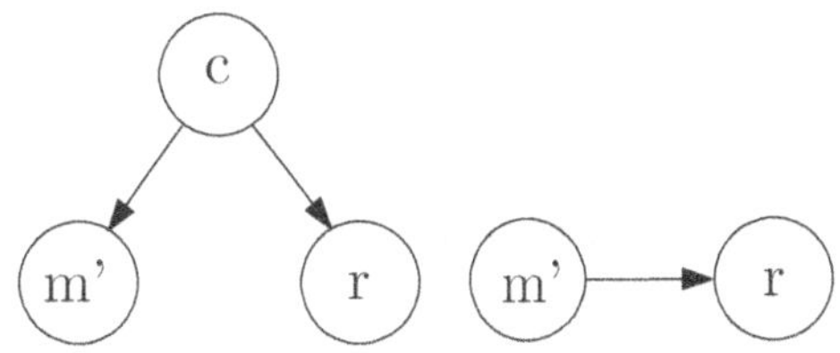

(a) Independent model (b) Influential model

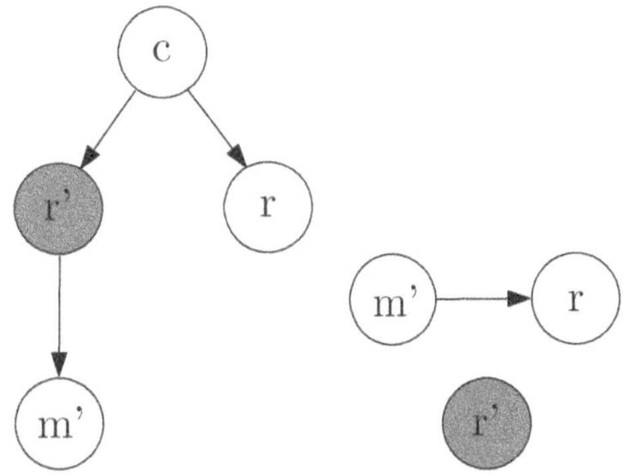

(c) Independent model with r' observed (d) Influential model with r' observed

Figure 6: Two possible models and corresponding conditional dependence relation between r and m', given r' observed.

might strengthen their friendship). Throughout the paper, this model is referred to as the ***influential model***. Note that we do not assume that a word-of-mouth recommendation is the only factor of user posterior evaluation.

5. MODEL VERIFICATION

In this section, we examine which of the two aforementioned models is supported by the real data using statistical hypothesis tests.

5.1 Designing statistical hypothesis tests

According to Fig. 6(a) and Fig. 6(b), in order to judge which model is more appropriate to explain the real data, we need to examine the conditional independence between m' and r given c. Unfortunately, such a conditional independence cannot be directly examined since the hidden variable c is unobservable. To circumvent this problem, we introduce the recommender's rating, denoted as r', to modify the models. In some cases an individual u rates an item previously recommended by his friend (i.e., $m' = 1$), r' denotes the rating that the friend posted to the item. In other cases an individual u rates an item with no friend recommendation (i.e., $m' = 0$), r' denotes the rating posted to the item by a randomly chosen friend of u who might have recommended the item to u. The modified independent model is shown in Fig. 6(c). Such a modification is reasonable from two aspects: 1) r' depends on c symmetrically as r in the original independent model; 2) m' fully depends on r' due to a common practice that whether or not a user recommends an item is determined by his/her rating on this item [6, 30]. In the modified independent model, whether m' and r are independent conditioned on r' is equivalent with whether they are independent conditioned on c, according to Bayesian network property. In addition, for the influential model where m' is a direct factor node of r, the dependence of r on m' always hold no matter any other variables are observed, as shown in Fig. 6(d). Therefore, we can judge which of the independent model and the influential model is more appropriate by examining the conditional independence between m' and r given r'.

Now we design a statistical hypothesis test to examine the conditional independence between m' and r given r'. In our test, each data point is a triple $\langle m', r, r' \rangle$. We first divide the observed data points into distinct partitions such that the data points in each partition share a unique or similar r' value and therefore follow, and can well approximate, the conditional probability distribution $p(m', r|r')$ if the partition size is large enough for convergence. For this purpose, we discretize the real-valued r' into distinct values in two ways, namely, equal-interval partitioning or equal-frequency partitioning. For the equal-interval partitioning, the values of r' in each partition are confined within a fixed small interval. We discard partitions containing less than 100 data points due to their low statistical reliability. For the equal-frequencies partitioning, each partition has a fixed number of data points. We ignore partitions where the interval of r' is too large (greater than 0.05) to guarantee the values of r' in the same partition are close enough.[5]

For each partition, we test the independence between $p(m'|r')$ and $p(r|r')$. Since m' can take only two values, namely, 0 and 1, $p(m'|r')$ is independent from $p(r|r')$ if and only if $p(r|m' = 0, r')$ is identical to $p(r|m' = 1, r')$ for any given r'. Whether or not $p(r|m' = 0, r')$ is identical to $p(r|m' = 1, r')$ can be examined by testing the empirical measure of two samples, $\{r|m' = 0, r'\}$ and $\{r|m' = 1, r'\}$, which serve as good estimators when the sample size is large enough. Specifically, we employ two different statistical hypothesis test methods to examine: the location t-test to examine whether there exists a significant difference between the means of the two samples, and the Kolmogorov-Smirnov test to examine whether there exists a significant difference between the empirical distribution functions of the two samples.

The null hypothesis in our test is that there exists no statistically significant difference between $p(r|m' = 1, r')$ and $p(r|m' = 0, r')$ for any given r'. If the null hypothesis holds, it implies that given a certain value of r', r identically distributes, regardless of the values of m' and therefore the independent model is supported. On contrary, the alternative hypothesis that the two samples are significantly different disproves the conditional independence and supports the influential model. We test the null hypothesis at the 0.05 significance level against the alternative hypothesis in all partitions for a consistent conclusion. We will declare the influential model holds if tests in almost all partitions reject the null hypothesis, and vice versa. In practice we report the reject ratio as a final result, i.e. the percentage of partitions where statistical hypothesis tests reject the null hypothesis.

In summary, the statistical hypothesis test is conducted as follows:

[5]The discretization of recommender rating r' is valid. Our normalization preprocess from integer ratings to real number Z-scores guarantees that the Z-score space of the whole dataset is still countable. Therefore, discretizing Z-scores does not greatly violate value dependence.

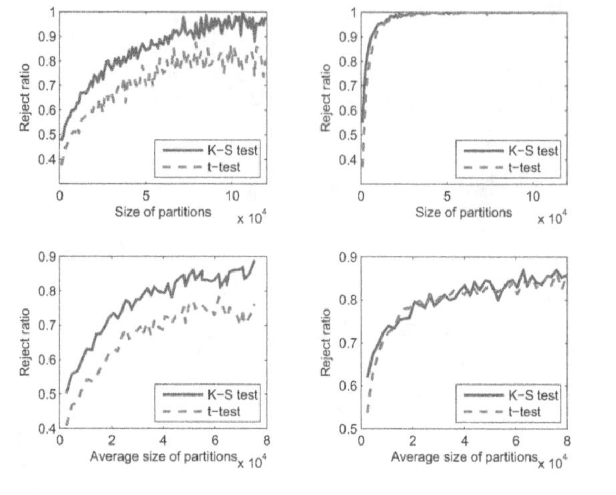

Figure 7: The reject ratio, the percentage of partitions where a two-sample test rejects the null hypothesis. Tests are conducted on two datasets (Left: Douban; Right: Goodreads) and with two partitioning ways (Top: equal-frequency; Bottom: equal-interval) respectively.

1. Slice data into partitions. All data points in each partition share a unique r' value.

2. Divide each partition into two samples, one with $m' = 1$ and the other with $m' = 0$.

3. In each partition, employ the two-sample t-test and a two-sample Kolmogorov-Smirnov test to examine the null hypothesis, i.e. the two samples are identically distributed.

4. Report the percentage of partitions where statistical hypothesis tests reject the null hypothesis.

5.2 Results of statistical hypothesis tests

In our test, we only consider the ratings falling into the range $[-3, 3]$ that accounts for most of the ratings from the Douban and Goodreads datasets. As a consequence, we obtain $186,054$ data points with $m' = 1$ and $2,278,023$ with $m' = 0$ for the Douban dataset. For Goodreads, the numbers of the data points are $6,759,850$ and $2,899,793$, respectively.

Fig. 7 illustrates the test result. When we divide Goodreads dataset into partitions with a fixed size of $20,000$ data points, the Kolmogorov-Smirnov test rejects the null hypothesis in 461(98.5%) partitions among 468 ones, and the t-test rejects in 97.2% of all partitions. Similarly, when the Goodreads dataset is divided into partitions with an equal interval of 0.03, which results in an average size of around $48,000$ data points in each partition as shown on the axis label, the Kolmogorov-Smirnov test rejects the null hypothesis in 155 partitions among 185 ones, covering 83.8% partitions and 97.5% data points, while the t-test rejects in 152(82.2%) partitions and 97.5% data points.

Test results are obvious positive, reading that on both datasets and with both partitioning ways, the two adopted statistical hypothesis tests consistently reject the null hypothesis in favor of the alternative hypothesis in a majority of partitions. The percentage of partitions where the null hypothesis is rejected increases with the number of data points contained in each partition, because larger samples can better establish a reliable result. When the partition size is large enough, the tests on almost all partitions consistently reject the null hypothesis, strongly supporting the influential model.

The fact that tests on Douban dataset fail to reject the null hypothesis in all partitions might attribute to the imbalance and size of Douban dataset. The Douban dataset is much more imbalanced than the Goodreads dataset, given less than 14% data points are observed with $m' = 1$. Besides, the number of Douban data points tested is less than one fourth of that of Goodreads dataset, therefore it is reluctant to afford a large amount of large partitions to establish reliable statistics results. With the obvious trend that a higher reject ratio comes with a larger size of partition, tests on Douban is expected to reach a almost-hundred-percent reject ratio with a larger dataset.

In summary, the two-sample tests in most partitions reject the null hypothesis in favor of the alternative hypothesis that r behaves differently with different m' values even when r' is observed, which suggests that the influential model correctly captures the causality relation hidden in the real data. That is to say, the posterior evaluation of a user directly depends on whether or not a friend has previously recommended the concerning item to him/her.

6. IDENTIFYING INFLUENTIAL FRIENDS

In the previous section, we have shown that word-of-mouth recommendations can influence users' posterior evaluation on the items they have experienced, which are specifically reflected by the increase of ratings presented by the receivers of the recommendations. Now it is of high interest to know what kind of persons are influential via their word-of-mouth recommendations and to identify the influential friends for each user.

6.1 Social influence measurement

Before proceeding, we need to quantify the raise in posterior evaluation brought by each word-of-mouth recommendation. We use $U^-_{u,i}$ to denote the rating on the item i from the user u without recommendations from his friends and $U^+_{u,i}$ to denote the rating with recommendations. Then the raise caused by word-of-mouth recommendation can be calculated by

$$x_{u,i} = U^+_{u,i} - U^-_{u,i}. \tag{2}$$

Unfortunately, we cannot observe $U^+_{u,i}$ and $U^-_{u,i}$ simultaneously. To address this problem, we consider only the cases where $U^+_{u,i}$ can be observed, i.e., the user u rated the item i after the item has been recommended by his/her friends at least once[6]. For the unobserved $U^-_{u,i}$, we estimate its value with $\hat{r}_{u,i}$, the expected rating a user would have posted without recommendations from his friends. In practice, $\hat{r}_{u,i}$ can be calculated with well-studied collaborative filtering recommendation algorithms. Actually, any recommendation algorithm can be used with the only constraint that the used algorithm should not leverage the knowledge about the friendships. In this paper, we employ the probabilistic matrix factorization algorithm [27], which has proven an effective and accurate algorithm especially for the sparse cases. For the sake of convenience, we also replace the $U^+_{u,i}$ with $r_{u,i}$ and the raise in posterior evaluation caused by word-of-mouth recommendation can be written as

$$\hat{x}_{u,i} = r_{u,i} - \hat{r}_{u,i}. \tag{3}$$

For the probabilistic matrix factorization algorithm, we train it with the training set consisting of only the ratings posted without recommendations. In this way, the trained model estimate the unobserved ratings $\hat{r}_{u,i}$ without the knowledge about friendships. Under such consideration, the two training datasets obtained for Douban and Goodreads contain 23,417,433 and 16,698,014 ratings, respectively. With the trained model, we estimate $\hat{r}_{u,i}$ for each observed $r_{u,i}$ and calculate the raise in posterior evaluation caused by word-of-mouth recommendations using Eq. (3).

Then, for any edge (u, v) which represents the friendship between two users u and v in the friendship network, we can measure the influence of u on v as the average raise in posterior evaluation over all items I_{uv} recommended to v by u and rated by v after the recommendation. Specifically, the *social influence* of u on v is calculated as

$$f_{u,v} = \frac{\sum_{i \in I_{uv}} \hat{x}_{v,i}}{|I_{uv}|}, \tag{4}$$

where $|I_{uv}|$ denotes the number of items in I_{uv}.

Given social influence calculated on all edges, salient asymmetry is observed that there usually exists an individual, between a pair of mutually connected friends, having a much greater social influence upon the other than what the other has on him. We quantify this phenomenon with the ratio of social influence on each pair of bidirectional edges, i.e., $\frac{max(f_{u,v}, f_{v,u})}{min(f_{u,v}, f_{v,u})}$. In 83% Douban pairs and 77% Goodreads pairs[7], there exists an individual whose social influence on the other is at least as twice as that in the reverse direction. As indicated by this phenomenon, the influence among two friends often acts in an one-way manner, although two friends can recommend favorite products to each other and thus have the potential to influence each other.

Furthermore, we label (u, v) an *influence edge*, if $f_{u,v}$ is larger than 0.1 and $|I_{uv}|$ is no less than 5. In this case, u serves as the *influential side* and v *influenced side*. Please note that those roles are assigned in a particular edge rather than a global setting. For the two used datasets, 0.095% and 2.19% edges are labeled as influence edges which involve 0.078% and 7.23% users, respectively.

6.2 Identification of influential friends

Now we check what correlates with the direction of influence among friends. Intuitively, there are possibly two kinds of factors, namely, the social positions of users in the friendship network and their personal characteristics independent on other individuals. Specifically, for the first kind of factors, we consider the out-degree[8], PageRank and Lead-

[6]For ease of identifying the influential source, in practice we ignore ratings posted with two or more friend recommendations, which are only a small portion of our observations.

[7]We ignore edges with $|I_{uv}| < 5$ whose f could be unreliable.

[8]We also analyze in-degree. Since Douban and Goodreads user-user networks are both observed with high reciprocity, the feature in-degree has almost the same result as out-degree.

erRank. For the second kind of factors, we consider the collection size, collection frequency (number of items collected per day) and sensitivity. Note that sensitivity, proposed in this paper, represents an individual's ability to quickly discover new valuable contents. Specifically, the sensitivity S_u of a user u is defined as

$$S_u = \frac{\sum_{i \in I(u)} |\{v : i \in I(v), T(v,i) > T(u,i)\}|}{\sum_{i \in I(u)} |\{v : i \in I(v)\}|}, \quad (5)$$

where $I(u)$ denotes the set of items collected by user u and $T(u,i)$ is the date when u collects item i. The sensitivity of a user can be explained as the percentage of other users who rates an item later than him/her. For example, if an individual u is the tenth one among all the 100 users who collect *The King's Speech* and the 20th among the 50 users collecting *Black Swan*, the sensitivity of u can then be calculated as $(90+30)/(100+50) = 0.8$.

With respect to each feature t, we examine the influential-side-to-influenced-side ratio $R^t_{u,v}$ on each influence edge pointing to v from u. Take the out-degree as example, $R^{out-degree}_{u,v} = k^{out}_u / k^{out}_v$. Fig. 8 shows the probability distribution of logarithm of $R^{out-degree}_{u,v}$ and $R^{sensitivity}_{u,v}$. It can be observed that the influential side of an influence edge is more probable to have a higher out-degree and sensitivity than the influenced side, reflected by the majority population of positive values of logarithm ratio (deep grey area in figure). The ratios with respect to other features also provide evidence on the effectiveness of these features when identifying the influential friends.

A more direct method for discriminating the effectiveness of these features is the accuracy in predicting which individual is the influential side in such a pair of friends, that are (a) mutually connected so that either might serve as the influential side, and (b) one edge between them is labeled as an influence edge. The results are shown in Table 3. We can see that almost all the considered features can correctly predict most of the pairs. This implies that a more active individual, from either the social perspective or the personal perspective, is more probable to be the influential side among two friends. We can also see that out-degree and sensitivity play the most important role in detecting influential sides. This tells us that an influential friend is more eager to explore new items and followed by many other users.

Table 3: The prediction accuracy of influence edges with user features.

Feature	Douban	Goodreads
Out-degree	**69.17%**	**71.16%**
Collection size	51.59%	59.18%
Collection frequency	46.18%	47.43%
Sensitivity	**69.41%**	**77.67%**
PageRank	68.98%	70.35%
LeaderRank	68.76%	70.28%
Random guess	50 %	50 %

Focusing on out-degree and sensitivity, we detail the experimental results. For each pair of mutually connected individuals u and v, with one and only one labeled influence edge (u, v), we define the gap between u and v as $G^f_{u,v} = f_u - f_v$ with respect to each feature f, where f_u is the value of feature f of user u. Given a threshold δ for the gap, we predict

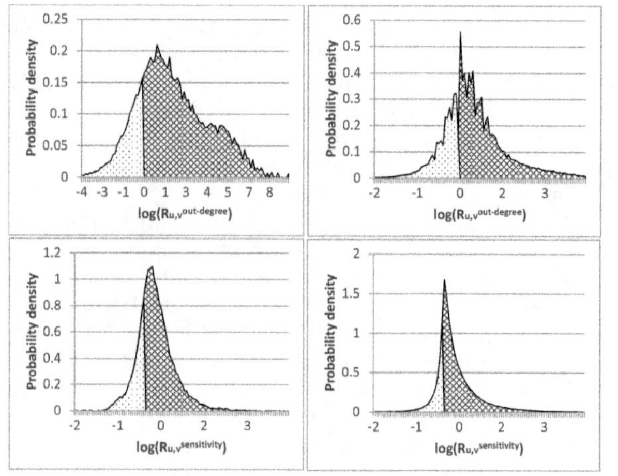

Figure 8: The out-degree and sensitivity of the influential and influenced sides in bidirectionally connected user pairs. Douban (left) and Goodreads (right).

edge (u, v) as an influence edge if $G^f_{u,v} > \delta$, or edge (v, u) as an influence edge if $G^f_{v,u} = -G^f_{u,v} > \delta$. Otherwise, we leave the pair unpredicted. Different gap thresholds lead to different prediction *accuracy*, i.e., the percentage of correctly predicted pairs among all predicted pairs, and *cover rate*, namely, the percentage of predicted pairs among all pairs. Generally speaking, a larger gap leads to a lower cover rate and a higher accuracy of prediction. This reflects that a tighter judge condition results in more confidence. That is to say, the more imbalanced that two friends are in their out-degrees or sensitivity, the more probable that the influence comes from the more social and sensitive side to the other. Fig. 9(a) depicts the accuracy and the cover rate for the two tested datasets. When the cover rate is 100%, the out-degree succeeds at predicting 69.17% or 71.16% of all predicted pairs for the two datasets. The accuracy of the feature sensitivity is slightly higher than the out-degree, being 69.41% or 77.67%. Note that the accuracy of both features are significantly higher than a random predictor with an expected accuracy of 50%.

Note that the out-degree characterizes the social position of an individual, while the sensitivity describes his/her personal characteristics. An interesting question is that whether these two kinds of features can complement each other when identifying the influential friends. In order to answer this question, we combine these two features to predict the influential side of each influence edge. Intuitively, an influential friend may have both higher out-degree and higher sensitivity. Therefore, we integrate these two features into one by combining their influential-to-influenced ratios as follows

$$R^{combined}_{u,v} = (R^{sensitive}_{u,v})^{\lambda} (R^{out-degree}_{u,v})^{(1-\lambda)}, \quad (6)$$

where the coefficient λ takes a real value in the range $[0, 1]$. Then, we predict the influential side as the one with a larger $R^{combined}_{u,v}$. Fig. 9(b) presents the prediction results with varied λ and the gap threshold $\delta = 0$. We can see that the prediction accuracy has a single maximum with respect to the value of λ for the two tested datasets. This indicates that a proper combination of out-degree and sensitivity can better distinguish an influential side than using only one of these two features. Therefore, it is necessary to combine the social position of individuals and their personal characteristics when identifying the influential friends for social recommendations.

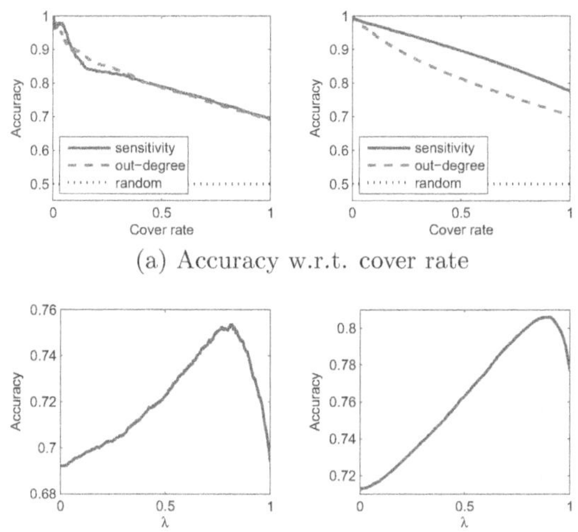

(a) Accuracy w.r.t. cover rate

(b) Accuracy w.r.t. combination coefficient λ

Figure 9: The prediction accuracy of influential sides with larger out-degree and sensitivity on Douban (left) and Goodreads (right), respectively.

7. CONCLUSIONS AND DISCUSSIONS

In this paper, we empirically analyzed the effects of word-of-mouth recommendations on real-world online social networks and content sharing communities. Specifically, our analysis indicates that word-of-mouth recommendations cannot only improve the prior expectation of users, who receive the recommendations, on the recommended items, but also raise their posterior evaluation. We further verified that the raise of the posterior evaluation is directly caused by word-of-mouth recommendations, through elaborately designed statistical hypothesis tests. Furthermore, we quantified the raise of posterior evaluation by comparing the real ratings presented by receivers of the word-of-mouth recommendations and the estimated ratings obtained by a classical collaborative filtering recommendation method. The latter are actually employed to approximate the ratings in the case without word-of-mouth recommendations. Based on the quantification, we proposed a method for investigating a user's social influence, i.e., the ability of the user to affect a follower's posterior evaluation, by examining his/her sensitivity of discovering good items and the number of his/her followers. Through experiments on the Douban and Goodreads datasets, we demonstrated that our method can successfully identify up to 78% influential friends.

This paper provides a new research perspective, i.e., the posterior evaluation, instead of the prior expectation which has been widely researched into. This new perspective is important for devising online word-of-mouth recommendation methods, aiming to enhance users' satisfaction and loyalty. However, it is still an open problem to identify the potential individuals whose opinions can influence their social contacts. In addition, it is of high interest to investigate how social influence propagates in social networks and how multiple word-of-mouth recommendations accumulate, which are critical to trigger a viral marketing cascade. Whether or not social influence changes across different topics is another interesting problem. Our future work will focus on these important research issues.

In addition, our findings are helpful to developing new applications. For example, shopping sites can promote a product to potential customers by asking their influential friends to make online word-of-mouth recommendations, instead of using an automatic recommendation system. More importantly, such a marketing strategy might have the potential to improve product sales and overcome the sparsity problem in personalized recommendation, as long as it is carefully designed to avoid fraudulent recommendations.

8. ACKNOWLEDGMENTS

We thank Professor Benjamin W. Wah for valuable comments. This work was funded by the National Natural Science Foundation of China under Grants No. 60873245, No. 60933005, No. 61003166, and No. 61173008. This work was also partly funded by the National High-Tech R&D Program of China (863 Program) with Grant No. 2010*AA*012502.

9. REFERENCES

[1] N. Agarwal, H. Liu, L. Tang, and P. S. Yu. Identifying the influential bloggers in a community. In *Proceedings of the international conference on Web search and web data mining*, WSDM '08, pages 207–218, New York, NY, USA, 2008. ACM.

[2] A. Anagnostopoulos, R. Kumar, and M. Mahdian. Influence and correlation in social networks. In *Proceeding of the 14th ACM SIGKDD international conference on Knowledge discovery and data mining*, KDD '08, pages 7–15, New York, NY, USA, 2008. ACM.

[3] C.-m. Au Yeung and T. Iwata. Strength of social influence in trust networks in product review sites. In *Proceedings of the fourth ACM international conference on Web search and data mining*, WSDM '11, pages 495–504, New York, NY, USA, 2011. ACM.

[4] E. Bakshy, J. M. Hofman, W. A. Mason, and D. J. Watts. Everyone's an influencer: quantifying influence on twitter. In *Proceedings of the fourth ACM international conference on Web search and data mining*, WSDM '11, pages 65–74, New York, NY, USA, 2011. ACM.

[5] P. F. Bone. Word-of-mouth effects on short-term and long-term product judgments. *Journal of Business Research*, 32(3):213 – 223, 1995.

[6] T. Brown, T. Barry, P. Dacin, and R. Gunst. Spreading the word: Investigating antecedents of consumers' positive word-of-mouth intentions and behaviors in a retailing context. *Journal of the Academy of Marketing Science*, 33(2):123–138, 2005.

[7] J. A. Chevalier and D. Mayzlin. The effect of word of mouth on sales: Online book reviews. *Journal of Marketing Research*, 43(3):345–354, 2006.

[8] G. Cimini, M. Medo, T. Zhou, D. Wei, and Y.-C. Zhang. Heterogeneity, quality, and reputation in an adaptive recommendation model. *The European*

Physical Journal B - Condensed Matter and Complex Systems, 80:201–208, 2011.

[9] D. Crandall, D. Cosley, D. Huttenlocher, J. Kleinberg, and S. Suri. Feedback effects between similarity and social influence in online communities. In *Proceeding of the 14th ACM SIGKDD international conference on Knowledge discovery and data mining*, KDD '08, pages 160–168, New York, NY, USA, 2008. ACM.

[10] P. Cui, F. Wang, S. Liu, M. Ou, S. Yang, and L. Sun. Who should share what?: item-level social influence prediction for users and posts ranking. In *Proceedings of the 34th international ACM SIGIR conference on Research and development in Information*, SIGIR '11, pages 185–194, New York, NY, USA, 2011. ACM.

[11] C. Dellarocas. The digitization of word of mouth: Promise and challenges of online feedback mechanisms. *Management Science*, 49(10):1407–1424, 2003.

[12] P. Domingos and M. Richardson. Mining the network value of customers. In *Proceedings of the seventh ACM SIGKDD international conference on Knowledge discovery and data mining*, KDD '01, pages 57–66, New York, NY, USA, 2001. ACM.

[13] J. Goldenberg, B. Libai, and E. Muller. Talk of the network: A complex systems look at the underlying process of word-of-mouth. *Marketing Letters*, 12(3):211–223, 2001.

[14] A. Goyal, F. Bonchi, and L. V. Lakshmanan. Learning influence probabilities in social networks. In *Proceedings of the third ACM international conference on Web search and data mining*, WSDM '10, pages 241–250, New York, NY, USA, 2010. ACM.

[15] M. Granovetter. Threshold models of collective behavior. *The American Journal of Sociology*, 83(6):1420–1443, 1978.

[16] P. M. Herr, F. R. Kardes, and J. Kim. Effects of word-of-mouth and product-attribute information on persuasion: An accessibility-diagnosticity perspective. *Journal of Consumer Research: An Interdisciplinary Quarterly*, 17(4):454–62, 1991.

[17] J. Huang, X.-Q. Cheng, J. Guo, H.-W. Shen, and K. Yang. Social recommendation with interpersonal influence. In *Proceedings of the 19th European Conference on Artificial Intelligence (ECAI 2010)*, pages 601–606, Amsterdam, The Netherlands, 2010. IOS Press.

[18] D. D. Jensen, A. S. Fast, B. J. Taylor, and M. E. Maier. Automatic identification of quasi-experimental designs for discovering causal knowledge. In *Proceedings of the 14th ACM SIGKDD international conference on Knowledge discovery and data mining*, KDD '08, pages 372–380, New York, NY, USA, 2008. ACM.

[19] D. Kempe, J. Kleinberg, and E. Tardos. Maximizing the spread of influence through a social network. In *Proceedings of the ninth ACM SIGKDD international conference on Knowledge discovery and data mining*, KDD '03, pages 137–146, New York, NY, USA, 2003. ACM.

[20] J. Leskovec, L. A. Adamic, and B. A. Huberman. The dynamics of viral marketing. *ACM Trans. Web*, 1, May 2007.

[21] J. Leskovec, A. Krause, C. Guestrin, C. Faloutsos, J. VanBriesen, and N. Glance. Cost-effective outbreak detection in networks. In *Proceedings of the 13th ACM SIGKDD international conference on Knowledge discovery and data mining*, KDD '07, pages 420–429, New York, NY, USA, 2007. ACM.

[22] L. Lu, Y.-C. Zhang, C. H. Yeung, and T. Zhou. Leaders in social networks, the delicious case. *PLoS ONE*, 6(6):e21202, 06 2011.

[23] M. Medo, Y.-C. Zhang, and T. Zhou. Adaptive model for recommendation of news. *EPL (Europhysics Letters)*, 88(3):38005, 2009.

[24] M. Richardson and P. Domingos. Mining knowledge-sharing sites for viral marketing. In *Proceedings of the eighth ACM SIGKDD international conference on Knowledge discovery and data mining*, KDD '02, pages 61–70, New York, NY, USA, 2002. ACM.

[25] D. M. Romero, B. Meeder, and J. Kleinberg. Differences in the mechanics of information diffusion across topics: idioms, political hashtags, and complex contagion on twitter. In *Proceedings of the 20th international conference on World wide web*, WWW '11, pages 695–704, New York, NY, USA, 2011. ACM.

[26] J. Sabater and C. Sierra. Review on computational trust and reputation models. *Artificial Intelligence Review*, 24:33–60, 2005. 10.1007/s10462-004-0041-5.

[27] R. Salakhutdinov and A. Mnih. Probabilistic matrix factorization. In *Advances in Neural Information Processing Systems*, volume 20, 2008.

[28] X. Song, B. L. Tseng, C.-Y. Lin, and M.-T. Sun. Personalized recommendation driven by information flow. In *Proceedings of the 29th annual international ACM SIGIR conference on Research and development in information retrieval*, SIGIR '06, pages 509–516, New York, NY, USA, 2006. ACM.

[29] J. Tang, J. Sun, C. Wang, and Z. Yang. Social influence analysis in large-scale networks. In *Proceedings of the 15th ACM SIGKDD international conference on Knowledge discovery and data mining*, KDD '09, pages 807–816, New York, NY, USA, 2009. ACM.

[30] M. M. Wasko and S. Faraj. Why should i share? examining social capital and knowledge contribution in electronic networks of practice. *MIS Quarterly*, 29(1):35–57, 2005.

[31] D. Wei, T. Zhou, G. Cimini, P. Wu, W. Liu, and Y.-C. Zhang. Effective mechanism for social recommendation of news. *Physica A: Statistical Mechanics and its Applications*, 390(11):2117 – 2126, 2011.

Find Me Opinion Sources in Blogosphere: A Unified Framework for Opinionated Blog Feed Retrieval

Xueke Xu[1,2], Songbo Tan[1], Yue Liu[1], Xueqi Cheng[1], Zheng Lin[1,2], Jiafeng Guo[1]
1. Institute of Computing Technology, Chinese Academy of Sciences, Beijing, China
2. Graduate School of Chinese Academy of Sciences, Beijing, China
{xuxueke, tansongbo}@software.ict.ac.cn, {cxq, liuyue, guojiafeng, linzheng }@ict.ac.cn

ABSTRACT
This paper aims to find blog feeds having a principal inclination towards making opinionated comments on the given topic, so that we can subscribe to them to track influential and interesting opinions in the blogosphere. One major challenge is assigning topic-related opinion scores to blog feeds, which is embodied in two aspects. Firstly, we should identify whether the blog feed has a principal opinionated inclination. This inclination should be collectively revealed by all posts of the feed. We should fully consider evidences from all the posts of the feed to identify salient information among many posts of the feed. Secondly, we should capture topic-related opinions in the blog feed while ignoring irrelevant opinions.

In this paper, we propose a unified framework for opinionated blog feed retrieval, which combines topic relevance and opinion scores with a generative model. Furthermore, we propose a language modeling approach to estimating opinion scores that is seamlessly integrated into the framework, where two language models, Topic-specific Opinion Model (TOM) and Topic-biased Feed Model (TFM), work collectively to reflect whether the blog feed shows a principal on-topic opinionated inclination. To estimate TFM, we propose a topic-biased random walk to exploit both content and structural information to capture topic-biased salient information in the feed. As for TOM estimation, we propose to use a generative mixture model with prior guidance to effectively capture topic-specific opinion expressing language usage. The conducted experiments in the context of the TREC 2009-2010 Blog Track show the effectiveness of our proposed approaches.

Categories and Subject Descriptors
H .3.3 [Information Search and Retrieval]: Retrieval Model

General Terms
Algorithms, Performance, Experimentation.

Keywords
opinionated blog feed retrieval, topic-related opinionatedness, mixture model, topic-biased random walk

1. INTRODUCTION
Nowadays, millions of bloggers are expressing their opinions about various topics, making blogosphere a major information source of public opinions. There has been a considerable amount of research on opinion retrieval from blogosphere, most of which takes blog posts as retrieval units [18, 11, 31, 19, 5, 32, 6, 4]. Individual blog posts, however, could only provide users with limited opinion pieces. Largely different from blog post, a blog feed can provide users with continuously updated information. Actually, each blog feed is associated with a blog site (or blog in short), and could refer to a stream of posts issued by the author of the blog site with time [21]. Considering such a scenario where a user wishes to track influential opinions in blogosphere about a specific topic such as the economic policy of Obama government, she/he may subscribe to blog feeds which are dedicated to issuing opinions about this topic. Aiming at this need, in this paper we take blog feeds as the retrieval units, and study the task of *Opinionated Blog Feed Retrieval* [27]. Our task aims to find blog feeds showing a principal inclination towards making opinionated comments on the given query topic. By subscribing to these top retrieved feeds with their RSS readers, users may easily track public opinions of interest in time.

According to the aim of the task, a relevant blog feed should satisfy following two criteria: 1) *Topic Relevance*: The blog feed should have a principal, recurring interest in the given topic [13]. This criterion is necessary since topic relevance is a good indicator of whether the opinions are indeed about the given topic [24]. 2) *Topic-related Opinionatedness*: The blog feed should show a principal inclination towards expressing opinions about the topic. Actually, our task can be considered as a particular type of the faceted blog distillation introduced by TREC 2009 Blog Track [13]. We focus on the "opinionated vs. factual" facet and only consider the first value (i.e., "opinionated"). Most approaches in TREC 2009-2010 Blog Track follow a two-stage framework [13, 20]. Firstly, they estimate topic relevance to produce a topic relevance baseline ranking regardless of the opinion features. Secondly, they estimate opinion scores and re-rank blog feeds by combining topic relevance and opinion scores using a heuristic manner.

This task turned out to be very challenging in TREC 2009-2010 Blog Track since many participating approaches failed to improve the underlying baseline rankings [13, 20]. We argue that there are two major challenges. The first challenge is assigning opinion scores to blog feeds to reflect whether the feeds show principal inclination to expressing opinions towards the topic. This challenge is mainly embodied in following two aspects.

- Firstly, we should determine whether the feeds show prevalence to opinionatedness, and a burst of opinions in few posts is not adequate. In other words, the opinionated inclination should be collectively revealed by all the posts published by the corresponding blogger, not few posts. Thus, we should fully consider evidences from the feed to capture

Permission to make digital or hard copies of all or part of this work for personal or classroom use is granted without fee provided that copies are not made or distributed for profit or commercial advantage and that copies bear this notice and the full citation on the first page. To copy otherwise, or republish, to post on servers or to redistribute to lists, requires prior specific permission and/or a fee.
WSDM'12, February 8-12, 2012, Seattle, Washington, USA.
Copyright 2012 ACM 978-1-4503-0747-5/12/02...$10.00.

salient content information which is shared among many posts of the feed, so that we can better identify whether the feed has a principal inclination to opinionatedness. To this end, we could exploit extra structural information in the blog feed beyond the content, such as relationships among the posts and words. Existing approaches usually ignore this valuable structural information and only take blog feed as a large document of the concatenation of all its constituent posts or a bag of independent posts.

- Secondly, we should take into account the query topic to capture opinions really related to topic at the granularity of blog feed, while ignoring irrelevant opinions. Many existing approaches in TREC consider opinions independently of the topic. Some other approaches consider topic-relatedness of opinions but not in an extensible and theoretical manner. They usually use heuristic techniques adapted from those for blog posts, such as "Near" information based [7], which may not be necessarily appropriate for the blog feeds.

In general, existing approaches to opinion scores estimation in TREC usually adopt lexicon-based [9, 10] or classification-based techniques [15, 7, 33] mostly adapted from those for individual blog posts. These approaches cannot well exploit special features of blog feeds, such as structural information. And most of these approaches have not been shown to be effective in the TREC results [13, 20], largely duo to the significant differences in the retrieval units and the aims between our task and blog post opinion retrieval.

The second challenge is finding a principled way to combine opinion scores and topic relevance to produce a final ranking. Existing approaches mostly estimate topic relevance and opinion scores in two separate stages and use a heuristic way to combine them, typically a linear summation [7, 9]. These two-stage approaches usually cannot well explore interaction between two factors of query topic and opinion to better balance between two criteria of topic relevance and topic-related opinionatedness for the final ranking. Indeed, heuristically considering opinion scores to re-rank the initial topic relevance ranking often largely harm topic relevance of the final ranking, to the point that it even deteriorates the overall performance compared with considering only topic relevance [13, 20].

This paper seeks to address these challenges in a unified framework. To this end, we specially introduce a hidden variable O_Q to denote the language usage of opinion expressions towards the given query topic Q, and rank blog feeds according to their generation probability given the query Q and O_Q, $P(F\,|\,Q,O_Q)$. Based on this generative model, we develop a unified probabilistic framework to estimate and combine topic relevance and opinion scores for blog feeds. In this unified framework, opinion scores are estimated using a language modeling approach. This approach determines whether the feed shows a clear on-topic opinionated inclination by how well the salient content information in the feed (with biased to the topic) fits the language usage of topic-related opinion expressions. The language usage of topic-related opinion expressions is captured by a language model, called Topic-specific Opinion Model (TOM). And the topic-biased salient content information is captured by another language model, Topic-biased Feed Model (TFM).

Language modeling approach provides an extensible, theoretical manner to fully and flexibly exploit various evidences from the blog feed, including both content information and structural information, to determine whether the blog feed show prevalence to opinionatedness towards the topic. We could take flexible ways to estimate the involved models. Specifically, in this paper, we propose a topic-biased random walk on Topic-specific Feed Graph to estimate TFM, which exploits topic-biased mutual reinforcement chain among posts and words to capture topic-biased salient content in the feed. As for TOM estimation, we propose to use a generative mixture model with prior guidance to effectively capture topic-specific opinion expression language usage.

We conduct empirical experiments in the context of the TREC 2009-2010 Blog Track. The results verify the unified framework and the proposed approaches to estimating the TFM and TOM. The results also largely outperform the best results in TREC 2009 and TREC 2010, respectively.

To sum up, the major contributions of this paper are:

- We propose a unified framework to estimate and combine topic relevance and opinion scores for opinionated blog feed retrieval.
- We propose a language modeling approach to estimating opinion scores, which is seamlessly integrated into the framework.
- We propose to use a generative probabilistic mixture model with prior guidance to estimate TOM.
- We propose a topic-biased random walk to exploits both content and structural information in the feed to estimate TFM.
- We conduct experiments in the context of the TREC 2009-2010 Blog Track to verify our models.

2. RELATED WORK

Blog post opinion retrieval. There has been a considerable amount of research on opinion retrieval from blogosphere, and most work takes blog posts as retrieval units [18, 11, 31, 5, 19, 32, 6, 22, 17, 23, 4, 25]. Blog post opinion retrieval aims at finding blog posts that have opinions about a given query topic [18]. At the first glance, our task is similar to blog post opinion retrieval in that they both consider topic and opinion for ranking respective retrieval objects. However, our task is largely different from that task in both retrieval units and the aims. We should fully exploit evidences from all posts of the feed, not a single post, to make a judge. These differences make our task especially challenging and the techniques adapted from those for individual blog posts are not necessarily effective as the results in TREC demonstrated [13, 20, 7, 9].

Opinionated blog feed retrieval. Most approaches in TREC 2009-2010 Blog Track follow a two-stage framework similar to that for blog post opinion retrieval [13, 20, 7, 9]. In the first stage, they estimate topic relevance and produce a topic relevance baseline ranking regardless of the opinionatedness criterion. In the next stage, they estimate opinion scores and re-rank blog feeds by combining topic relevance and opinion scores with a heuristic manner.

As for first stage, there is extensive research on topical blog feed retrieval (also referred to as blog distillation in TREC). Basically, the approaches may fall into two kinds according to their underlying blog representation models [2]: Small Document (SD) Model and Large Document (LD) Model. In SD Model, blog feeds are considered as collections of their constituent posts. The key issue is how to aggregate the topic relevance evidences of individual posts to infer the feed's topic relevance. To this end, various models have been explored such as blogger model [1], voting model [12] and resource selection model [2], etc. On the other hand, LD model treats a blog as a large document which is the concatenation of all its constituent posts. Generally, a language model (LM) is used to represent this large document, and ranking can be based on any LM based IR approaches [2].

As for second stage, most approaches in TREC adopt lexicon-based [9, 10] or classification-based [15, 7, 33] techniques that are similar to those devised for blog posts. Among those approaches, many consider opinions independently of the query topic, while some consider topic-relatedness of opinions using heuristic techniques adapted from those for blog post, such as "Near" information based [7]. Finally, topic relevance and opinion scores are combined using a heuristic manner, typically a linear summation [7, 9]

Here we present two typical approaches for the second stage in TREC, both failing to provide consistent and significant performance improvements over the underlying topic relevance baselines as our approaches. Keikha *et al.* [9] compute opinion score for each retrieved feed by averaging the opinionated weight for each word in the blog feed. Finally, the final ranking scores are computed as a linear combination of topic relevance scores estimated in the first stage and opinion scores. Jia *et al.* [7] use a topic-dependent SVM classifier to classify sentences into either opinionated or factual, and next use "NEAR" operator to determine whether the opinionated sentences are related to the topic. Opinion score is aggregated over all opinionated and topically relevant sentences in the blog feed. This opinion scores estimation approach is essentially adapted from that of [31] proposed for blog post opinion retrieval by treating each blog feed as a large document of the concatenation of all its constituent posts. Finally, topically retrieved blog feeds are re-ranked by linearly combining topic relevance and opinion scores.

To the best of our knowledge, Jiang *et al.*' work [8] is the only published work except for that in TREC. It uses a topic-opinion mixture model, constructed by linearly interpolating topic relevance model with opinion relevance model, to rank blog feeds according to KL divergence. Compared to our approach, it is essentially a linear combination of two factors of topic and opinion without solid theoretical justification. Besides, it simply treats each blog feed as a big document without fully consider structural information in the feed. In fact, that approach only managed to improve a very weak baseline.

3. THE UNIFIED FRAMEWORK

In this section, we will present the proposed unified framework that aims to effectively rank blog feeds by their likelihood of fulfilling both two criteria of topic relevance and topic-related opinionatedness discussed in Section 1. In particular, we will discuss in details the opinion scores estimation component in the framework.

According to the generative model in traditional information retrieval area, topic relevance can be estimated by probability of generating the blog feed F given the query Q, $P(F|Q)$. To consider the topic-related opinionatedness criterion in our task, we introduce a topic-specific variable O_Q to denote language usage of opinion expressions towards the query topic Q. Following the traditional generative model framework, we rank blog feeds according to their generation probability given the original query Q and O_Q, $P(F|Q,O_Q)$.

Formally, we have:

$$P(F|Q,O_Q) \propto P(F,Q,O_Q) = P(F)P(Q|F)P(O_Q|Q,F) \quad (1)$$

There are two major components in Equation (1): $P(F)P(Q|F)$ deals with topical relevance, while $P(O_Q|Q,F)$ deals with opinion scores. This equation provides a justifiable framework for combining topical relevance and opinion scores, which is naturally induced from a generative model with a solid probabilistic theoretical foundation. The framework fully considers the highly dependence of opinions on the topic to better balance between the two criteria of topic relevance and topic-related opinionatedness for the final ranking.

The topic relevance of the feed F is considered as query generation probability given the feed combined with the feed prior, $P(F)P(Q|F)$. This component is not focus of this paper, since it can be estimated by existing approaches to topical blog feed search (also referred to as blog distillation in TREC) which has been extensively studied [2].

We here focus on the opinion scores estimation component, where the opinion score of the feed F can be considered as the probability of O_Q given the query Q and F, $P(O_Q|Q,F)$.

We marginalize $P(O_Q|Q,F)$ across all words in the vocabulary:

$$P(O_Q|Q,F) = \sum_{w\in V} P(w|Q,F)P(O_Q|w,F,Q) \quad (2)$$

where V is the vocabulary, w is the word in V. By assuming conditional independence between O_Q and (Q,F) given the word w, Equation (2) reduces to:

$$P(O_Q|Q,F) = \sum_{w\in V} P(w|Q,F)P(O_Q|w) \quad (3)$$

By assuming the probability of each word w (i.e. $P(w)$) to be uniform, and eliminating $P(O_Q)$ that doesn't affect the ranking, we get the following equation:

$$P(O_Q|w) = \frac{P(w|O_Q)P(O_Q)}{P(w)} \propto P(w|O_Q) \quad (4)$$

Plugging Equation (4) into Equation (3), we come to:

$$P(O_Q|Q,F) \propto \sum_{w\in V} P(w|Q,F)P(w|O_Q) \quad (5)$$

According to Equation (5), opinion score of feed F is estimated by accumulating the relatedness of all words from the feed with expressing topic-relevant opinions (i.e. $\{P(w|O_Q)\}_{w\in V}$), weighted by the topic-sensitive prominence of each word w in the feed (i.e. $P(w|Q,F)$).

Equation (5) provides a language modeling approach to estimating opinion scores. Specifically, we use a language model (LM, i.e. a probability distribution over the vocabulary) to estimate the probability $P(w|O_Q)$. We call this LM as Topic-specific Opinion Model (TOM). Besides, for each blog feed F, we also use a LM to estimate $P(w|Q,F)$, called as Topic-biased Feed Model (TFM). TOM should be estimated to reflect language usage of topic-related opinion expressions which helps identify topic relevant opinions. And TFM should be estimated to capture salient content information in the blog feed with bias towards the topic, and consequently help reflect whether the feed shows principal inclination to expressing opinions about the topic. Our approach, intuitively speaking, determines whether the feed shows a clear on-topic opinionated inclination by how well the salient content information in the feed (with biased to the topic) fits the language usage of topic-related opinion expressions.

Language modeling approaches have been attracting much attention in IR area due to its solid statistical foundation and extensibility by leveraging various estimation approaches [9]. Our approach, therefore, provides an extensible, theoretical manner to fully and flexibly exploit various evidences from the blog feed, including both content information and structural information, to determine whether the blog feed show prevalence to opinionatedness towards the topic.

Note that, Zhang et al. [32] and Gerani *et al.* [4] have, respectively, proposed unified generation models for *blog post opinion retrieval*. The essential difference between their models and ours lies in how to deal with the challenge of opinion scores estimation. Their models use a general opinion word lexicon, and exploit the proximity based information (e.g. positional closeness of query terms to the general opinion words in the post documents) to capture the topic relevant opinions in the posts. However, it's non-trivial to adapt the proximity based approach for individual documents to blog feeds duo to their significant differences in granularity [7]. On the other hand, due to the specially introduced topic-specific opinion variable O_Q , our approach could fully exploit language usage information of opinion expressions about the topic to effectively capture relevant opinions in feeds [1]. More importantly, we could fully and flexibly exploit the special features of feeds for estimating their opinion scores under a language modeling framework.

Now, the key issue is to find a best way to estimate TOM and TFM, so that they can work together to reflect whether the blog feed shows prevalence to opinionatedness towards the topic. In following two sections, we will, respectively, discuss in details the requirements for better estimating TOM and TFM, and describe the estimation details.

4. TOM ESTIMATION

4.1 Requirements for Better Estimating TOM

TOM (i.e. $\{P(w|O_Q)\}_{w\in V}$) is required to reflect the language usage of topic-relevant opinion expressions. In other word, TOM should capture opinion words frequently used to express opinions towards the given topic. Indeed, people tend to use different opinion words to express opinions for different topics. And topic-specific opinion words are naturally more indicative of an opinion that is really towards the topic than other opinion words [4]. For instance, the word "rhythmic" may be used more for expressing opinion about music related topic than other topics, and it is in turn more indicative of an opinion about music than general opinion words like "great". Thus, we should assign a high probability value to a topic-specific opinion word, which is more likely to indicate a relevant opinion, and assign a relatively low value to a topic-unrelated general opinion word, which usually indicates an irrelevant opinion, and factual words, which doesn't indicate an opinion. In this way, TOM could help identify topic-related opinions, and ignore irrelevant opinions.

4.2 Mixture Model

In the context of opinion retrieval task, existing approaches usually learn a TOM by separately weighting words based on pseudo opinion relevance feedback [6, 17, 8], where the learned TOM could be easily "contaminated" by highly frequent, non-discriminative words or factual topic-related words. We here instead use a generative probabilistic mixture model, which could model topic-specific opinion expressions in a more effective and principled way. In particular, a background model that reflects general information in the background collection is used to prevent the learned model from being contaminated by general and usually topic-unrelated words and make the learned model more discriminative. Besides, we introduce a prior for TOM to discriminate opinionated content from factual content and prevent the learned model from being contaminated by factual topic-related words. Various variants of mixture models have been widely applied to different text analysis tasks [30, 16], we here extend the application of mixture models to modeling topic specific opinions in the context of opinion retrieval task.

Our model could be roughly considered as a simplification version of Topic Sentiment Mixture model [16], where only one topic and one sentiment are involved. Specifically, in our mixture model, the words in a topically relevant post are assumed to be generated by sampling from a mixture model involving TOM, Topic Relevance Model (TRM) and the background model. Formally, let θ_O be the TOM, θ_F be the TRM and θ_B be the background model. The generation likelihood of word *w* in post *d* is given as:

$$P_d(w)=\lambda_B P(w|\theta_B)+(1-\lambda_B)(\pi_{d,O}P(w|\theta_O)+\pi_{d,F}P(w|\theta_F)))$$

where λ_B is a fixed weight controlling the influence of the background model, $\pi_{d,O}$ ($\pi_{d,F}$) is the mixing weight of θ_O (θ_F) for post *d*, and $\pi_{d,F}+\pi_{d,O}=1$.

Let $C=\{d_1,d_2,....,d_m\}$ be a set of topically relevant posts, then the generation log-likelihood of C is given as:

$$\log P(C|\Lambda)=\sum_{d\in C}\sum_{w\in V}[c(w,d)\times \log(\lambda_B P(w|\theta_B)+(1-\lambda_B)(\pi_{d,O}P(w|\theta_O)+\pi_{d,F}P(w|\theta_F)))]$$

where $\Lambda=\{\theta_O,\theta_P,\pi_{d,O},\pi_{d,F}\}$ is the parameter set to estimate, V is the vocabulary, $c(w,d)$ is the frequency of word w in document *d*.

We set λ_B to 0.95 as Zhai *et al.* suggested [30] to alleviate the influence of general-purpose words and make the learned TOM more discriminative. Note that, θ_B is estimated beforehand using Maximum Likelihood Estimation (MLE) based on the whole Blogs08 collection [14] and will be fixed during the learning process. To obtain C , we use the original query terms to retrieve the top 500 topically relevant posts using the BM25 model from the Blogs08 collection.

We use Expectation-Maximization (EM) algorithm to compute a Maximum Likelihood Estimation of Λ as following updating formulas:

E-steps:

$$P(z(d,w,O))=\frac{\pi_{d,O}^{(n)}P^{(n)}(w|\theta_O)}{\sum_{\upsilon\in\{O,F\}}\pi_{d,\upsilon}^{(n)}P^{(n)}(w|\theta_\upsilon)},\ P(z(d,w,F))=1-P(z(d,w,O))$$

$$P(z(d,w,B))=\frac{\lambda_B P(w|\theta_B)}{\lambda_B P(w|\theta_B)+(1-\lambda_B)\sum_{\upsilon\in\{O,F\}}\pi_{d,\upsilon}^{(n)}P^{(n)}(w|\theta_\upsilon)}$$

M-steps:

$$\pi_{d,O}^{(n+1)}=\frac{\sum_{w\in V}c(w,d)P(z(d,w,O))}{\sum_{\upsilon\in\{O,F\}}\sum_{w\in V}c(w,d)P(z(d,w,\upsilon))},\ \pi_{d,F}^{(n+1)}=1-\pi_{d,O}^{(n+1)}$$

$$P^{(n+1)}(w|\theta_O)=\frac{\sum_{d\in \pounds}c(w,d)(1-P(z(d,w,B)))P(z(d,w,O))}{\sum_{w\in V}\sum_{d\in \pounds}c(w,d)(1-P(z(d,w,B)))P(z(d,w,O))}$$

$$P^{(n+1)}(w|\theta_F)=\frac{\sum_{d\in \pounds}c(w,d)(1-P(z(d,w,B)))P(z(d,w,F))}{\sum_{w\in V}\sum_{d\in \pounds}c(w,d)(1-P(z(d,w,B)))P(z(d,w,F))}$$

---

[1] Note that, we could also additionally use proximity based evidences in estimating TFM to help further capture topic-related opinions. And it will be very interesting in future to develop an appropriate way to exploiting such evidences for blog feeds. In this paper, we use "topic bias" in random walk in estimating TFM to help further capture topic-related opinions

where $z(d,w,O)$ ($z(d,w,F)$) is a hidden variable which denotes that word w in document d is generated from θ_O (θ_F).

Without any prior knowledge as guidance, the learned θ_O and θ_F can not differentiate with each other because opinionated content and factual content generally co-occur with each other even in a highly opinionated post. Thus the estimated θ_O would be biased towards factual topic-related words, and thus can't effectively reflect the characteristics of topic-related opinion expressions. To address this problem, we introduce a general opinion model $\bar{\theta}_O$ as prior knowledge for TOM to discriminate opinions from factual content. $\bar{\theta}_O$ is derived based on a general opinion lexicon (denoted as GO) with each opinion word in the lexicon uniformly distributed as:

$$P(w\mid\bar{\theta}_O)=\begin{cases}\frac{1}{|GO|}, & if\ w\in GO\\ 0\end{cases}$$

The general opinion lexicon is built based on two publicly available opinion knowledge bases. We first select from SentiWordNet [3] a list of words with a positive or negative score above a given threshold (i.e. 0.6). Then we extract from MPQA subjectivity lexicon[2] another list of words with corresponding type being "strongsubj". Finally we construct the opinion lexicon as union of these two word lists. To incorporate the prior knowledge, we define a conjugate Dirichlet prior for θ_O : $Dir(\{1+\mu P(w\mid\bar{\theta}_O)\}_{w\in V})$, and use uniform prior for other parameters, then the prior of all parameters is as:

$$P(\Lambda)\propto P(\theta_O)=\prod\nolimits_{w\in V}P(w|\theta_O)^{\mu P(w|\bar{\theta}_O)}$$

The parameter μ indicates the confidence of the prior. With this prior, we can use Maximum A Posteriori estimation: $\hat{\Lambda}=\arg\max_{\Lambda}(P(\Lambda)P(\mathbf{C}\mid\Lambda))$, and the corresponding updating formula for θ_O in M-steps of the above EM algorithm is modified as follows:

$$P^{(n+1)}(w\mid\theta_O)=\frac{\mu P(w|\bar{\theta}_O)+\sum_{d\in\pounds}c(w,d)(1-P(z(d,w,B)))P(z(d,w,O))}{\mu+\sum_{w\in V}\sum_{d\in\pounds}c(w,d)(1-P(z(d,w,B)))P(z(d,w,O))} \quad (6)$$

Intuitively, the impact of incorporating this prior is equivalent to adding $\mu p(w\mid\bar{\theta}_O)$ pseudo counts for word w in estimating θ_O . In this way, the opinion words frequently used within the □ will stand out in the learned TOM. For instance, for the TREC topic "jazz music", such words as "rhythmic", "melodic", "dreamy", and "superb" are among top words of the trained TOM.

5. TFM ESTIMATION

5.1 Requirements for Better Estimating TFM

TFM (i.e. $\{P(w\mid Q,F)\}_{w\in V}$) is estimated aiming to capture salient content information of the blog feed with bias towards the topic, and consequently, help better determine whether the blog feed is clearly inclined towards expressing opinions about the topic. We argue that, to this end, the specific requirements are embodied in following two aspects.

- *Salience.* We should capture salient content information shared among many posts of the feed, ignoring trivial content in only few posts, aiming to reflect whether the feed has a principal opinionated inclination. To this end, we should fully exploit all evidence from the feed, including content and structural information. Straightforwardly taking each feed as a large document of concatenation of its constituent posts is not appropriate. Because it would be easily biased to few long posts or influenced by trivial or noisy content in the feed, and cannot effectively reflect the principal inclination of the feed.
- *Topic Bias.* We should emphasize more topically relevant content in the feed, aiming to further capture relevant opinions and discard those irrelevant. Our assumption is that an opinion co-occurring with topically relevant content is more likely towards the target topic, and thus should be highlighted. On the other hand, an opinion within topically irrelevant content is less likely towards the target topic, and thus should be assigned with low weight.

5.2 Our Solution

Our proposed solution is to some degree inspired by [26], which exploits relationships among documents, sentences and words to identify topic-biased salient information within documents for topic-focused text summarization. Specifically, we use a Topic-specific Feed Graph to represent each feed under the specific query topic. We then propose a topic-biased random walk on the graph, which exploits topic-biased mutual reinforcement chain among posts and words. In this way, we consider the above two aspects of requirements simultaneously to balance between them for a better estimation of TFM.

5.2.1 Topic-specific Feed Graph

The graph includes two types of nodes representing posts and words respectively, and multiple types of edges corresponding to relationships among them. Specifically, give a feed F and the query Q, a weighted undirected graph is defined as: $\mathbf{G}^Q=(P,W,E^{PP},E^{PW},E^{WW},\mathbf{M}^{Q,PP},\mathbf{M}^{PW},\mathbf{M}^{WW})$, where P is the node set of all posts of feed F, and W is the node set of all words in the feed. E^{PP} is the edge set between posts and posts, E^{PW} between posts and words, and E^{WW} between words and words. All edges are associated with weights to measure the relationships between the corresponding objects, and the weighting matrices for E^{PP} , E^{PW} and E^{WW} are $\mathbf{M}^{Q,PP}$, $\mathbf{M}^{PW}$ and $\mathbf{M}^{WW}$, respectively.

We use the matrix $\mathbf{M}^{Q,PP}$ to reflect weights on $\mathbf{E}^{PP}$ under query Q, where $M_{i,j}^{Q,PP}$ measures topic-sensitive similarity relationship between post p_i and p_j . Specifically, $M_{i,j}^{Q,PP}(i\neq j)$ is computed as:

$$M_{i,j}^{Q,PP}=\sum\nolimits_{w\in V}\text{TF-IDF}(p_i,w)\cdot\text{Weight}(w,Q)\cdot\text{TF-IDF}(p_j,w) \quad (7)$$

here $\text{TF-IDF}(p,w)$ is L_2-normalized *TF-IDF* weight of word w in post p ,and $\text{Weight}(w,Q)$ indicates the relatedness of word w to the query topic. We use Bol model [5] to compute $\text{Weight}(w,Q)$, measuring how informative the word w is in a collection of pseudo relevance feedback posts[3] against the background collection (i.e. Blogs08 collection [14]). This equation highlights the contribution of topic-related words, and thus makes the similarity calculation topic sensitive. Note that, $M_{i,j}^{Q,PP}(i=j)$ is set to 0 to avoid self-reinforcement. Then $\mathbf{M}^{Q,PP}$ is normalized to $\tilde{\mathbf{M}}^{Q,PP}$ by making sum of each row equal to 1.

We use the matrix $\mathbf{M}^{WW}$ to reflect weights on E^{WW} , where $M_{i,j}^{WW}$ measures relationship between word w_i and word w_j in the feed. $M_{i,j}^{WW}(i\neq j)$ is computed as Pointwise Mutual Information between word w_i and w_j based on co-occurrence

---

[2] http://www.cs.pitt.edu/mpqa/

[3] In our experiments, we use original query terms to retrieve top 30 posts from Blogs08 collection using BM25 model.

statistics at sentence level in the feed as follow:

$$M^{WW}_{i,j} = \log(\frac{P(wi, wj)}{P(wi)\times P(wj)}) = \log(\frac{\text{count}(wi, wj)\times S}{\text{count}(wi)\times \text{count}(wj)})$$

where S is total number of sentences in the feed, count(w) is the count of sentences containing word w, and count(wi, wj) is the count of sentences containing both wi and wj .Note that, a very small number (i.e., $1/|W|$) is added to each count for smoothing. $M^{WW}_{i,j}(i=j)$ is set to 0 to avoid self-reinforcement. Then $\boldsymbol{M}^{WW}$ is normalized to $\tilde{\boldsymbol{M}}^{WW}$ by making the sum of each row equal to 1.

At last, we use the matrix $\boldsymbol{M}^{PW}$ to reflect weights on $\boldsymbol{E}^{PW}$, and $M^{PW}_{i,j}$ measures relationship between post p_i and word w_j. $M^{PW}_{i,j}$ is computed as TF-IDF(p_i, w_j). We use another matrix $\boldsymbol{M}^{WP}$ to denote the transpose of $\boldsymbol{M}^{PW}$.Then $\boldsymbol{M}^{PW}$ and $\boldsymbol{M}^{WP}$ are, respectively, normalized to $\tilde{\boldsymbol{M}}^{PW}$ and $\tilde{\boldsymbol{M}}^{WP}$ by making the sum of each row equal to 1.

5.2.2 *Topic-biased Random Walk*

We here propose a topic-biased random walk on the graph, which exploit topic-biased mutual reinforcement chain among posts and words to capture topic-biased salient content in the feed. The basic idea of mutual reinforcement principle is embodied in following assumptions.

1. A post is salient, if (1) it is similar to many other salient posts; (2) it contains many salient words.

2. A word is salient if (1) it is strongly associated with many other salient words; (2) it appears in many salient posts.

Besides the above assumptions, we will further consider "topic bias" to highlight more topically relevant content in the feed.

Specifically, let $\boldsymbol{R}_P = [R_P(p_i)]_{|P|\times 1}$ and $\boldsymbol{R}_W = [R_W(w_j)]_{|W|\times 1}$ denote salience score vectors for P and W, respectively. Then topic-biased mutual reinforcement principle can be encoded in following iterative equations.

According to assumption 1, the salience score computation for P is formulated in an iterative form as:

$$\begin{aligned} R_P(p_i) = &\lambda_{11}[\alpha\sum\nolimits_{j=1}^{|P|}\tilde{M}^{Q,PP}_{j,i}R_P(p_j) + (1-\alpha)A^Q_P(p_i)R_P(p_j)] \\ &+\lambda_{21}[\alpha\sum\nolimits_{j=1}^{|W|}\tilde{M}^{WP}_{j,i}R_W(w_j) + (1-\alpha)A^Q_P(p_i)R_W(w_j)] \end{aligned} \quad (8)$$

Likewise, according to assumption 2, the salience score computation for W is formulated in an iterative form as:

$$\begin{aligned} R_W(w_i) = &\lambda_{12}[\alpha\sum\nolimits_{j=1}^{|P|}\tilde{M}^{PW}_{j,i}R_P(p_j) + (1-\alpha)A_W(w_i)R_P(p_j)] \\ &+\lambda_{22}[\alpha\sum\nolimits_{j=1}^{|W|}\tilde{M}^{WW}_{j,i}R_W(w_j) + (1-\alpha)A_W(w_i)R_W(w_j)] \end{aligned} \quad (9)$$

where $\boldsymbol{A}^Q_P = [A^Q_P(p_i)]_{1\times|P|}$ and $\boldsymbol{A}_W = [A_W(w_i)]_{1\times|W|}$ is the preference probability vector for P and W, respectively. We use a uniform preference probability vector for W, but use a topic-biased preference probability vector for P, i.e. $A^Q_P(p_i) \propto \text{BM25}(p_i, Q)$ [4], to favor topically relevant posts.

The parameters $\lambda_{lm}(l=1,2; m=1,2)$ control the relative importance of different types of relationships, and we have: $\lambda_{11}+\lambda_{12}=\lambda_{21}+\lambda_{22}=1$. In our experiments, we simply set all λ_{lm} to 0.5 so as to fully exploit all types of relationship information. The parameter α is empirically set to 0.85 as the PageRank.

The initial $R_P(p_i)$ is set to $1/|P|$ for each post, and the initial $R_W(w_i)$ is set to $1/|W|$ for each word, so that $\|\boldsymbol{R}_P\|_1 = \|\boldsymbol{R}_W\|_1 = 1$.

Then, the salience scores computation could be conducted by iteratively running the Equations (8-9). Note that, it could be easily checked that $\|\boldsymbol{R}_P\|_1$ and $\|\boldsymbol{R}_W\|_1$ will keep being 1 during iteration process under our parameter setting (i.e. λ_{lm}=0.5).

This iterative process could be considered as a topic-biased random walk on the feed graph, where the states are nodes of the graph and the transition matrix is given as:

$$\tilde{\tilde{\boldsymbol{M}}}^Q = \begin{bmatrix} \lambda_{11}\tilde{\tilde{\boldsymbol{M}}}^{Q,PP} & \lambda_{12}\tilde{\tilde{\boldsymbol{M}}}^{PW} \\ \lambda_{21}\tilde{\tilde{\boldsymbol{M}}}^{WP} & \lambda_{22}\tilde{\tilde{\boldsymbol{M}}}^{WW} \end{bmatrix}.$$

The block matrix $\tilde{\tilde{\boldsymbol{M}}}^{Q,PP}$ in $\tilde{\tilde{\boldsymbol{M}}}^Q$ corresponds to the local transition probability from posts to posts, and we have $\tilde{\tilde{\boldsymbol{M}}}^{Q,PP} = \alpha\tilde{\boldsymbol{M}}^{Q,PP} + (1-\alpha)[1]_{|P|\times 1}\cdot \boldsymbol{A}^Q_P$. Similarly, $\tilde{\tilde{\boldsymbol{M}}}^{PW}$ corresponds to the local transition probability from posts to words, and we have $\tilde{\tilde{\boldsymbol{M}}}^{PW} = \alpha\tilde{\boldsymbol{M}}^{PW} + (1-\alpha)[1]_{|P|\times 1}\cdot \boldsymbol{A}_W$. The other block matrices in $\tilde{\tilde{\boldsymbol{M}}}^Q$ are constructed likewise. Then, the iterative Equation (8-9) could be rewritten in a matrix form as:

$$\begin{bmatrix} \boldsymbol{R}_P \\ \boldsymbol{R}_W \end{bmatrix} = (\tilde{\tilde{\boldsymbol{M}}}^Q)^T \cdot \begin{bmatrix} \boldsymbol{R}_P \\ \boldsymbol{R}_W \end{bmatrix}$$

It can be easily checked that the transition matrix is irreducible and aperiodic, thus a stationary score vector $\begin{bmatrix} \hat{\boldsymbol{R}}_P \\ \hat{\boldsymbol{R}}_W \end{bmatrix}$ can be obtained after adequate iterations[5]. Finally, we compute TFM as: $P(w_i | Q, F) \propto \hat{R}_W(w_i)$.

Note that, "topic biased" in this random walk is embodied in two aspects: 1) topic-sensitive similarity measure between posts as Equation (7), which makes the salience score transition sensitive to the topic to prevent topic-drift, and 2) topic-biased preference probability vector for P , which rewards those more topically relevant posts.

6. EXPERIMENTAL RESULTS

6.1 Experimental Setting

Test Collection. We conduct experiments in the context of faceted blog distillation task in TREC 2009-2010 Blog Track. In that task, each topic is associated with an additional "facet" field besides the traditional TREC topic fields. Each facet has two values, and each value corresponds to a separate ranking of blogs. An example topic is shown in Figure 1. Note that, we here focus on the "opinionated vs. factual" facet and only consider the first value (i.e. "opinionated").

There are totally 13 TREC 2009 topics and 7 TREC 2010 topics associated with "opinionated vs. factual" facet and officially used for evaluation. We use all these topics along with the corresponding official relevance judgments for test. The relevance judgments are in five scales [13], and we consider as being relevant the feeds that are topically relevant and clearly inclined towards first facet value (i.e. "opinionated") in the context of our task. Besides, we only use the "query" field of the topics as query terms discarding other fields such as "desc".

We use the TREC Blogs08 collection adopted in the TREC 2009-2010 Blog Track [14], which is a large scale of sample of blogosphere between 14/01/2008 and 10/02/2009. As for data preprocessing, we adopt a link tables removing algorithm [24] to detect valuable content blocks from post pages and discard noisy

[4] We add a small value to each BM25 score so that the preference value for each post is larger than 0.

[5] In our experiment, the iteration count is empirically set to 10.

blocks. We remove stop words from the extracted post content based on a stop word list[6], but not perform word stemming.

Topic Relevance Baselines. In order to facilitate fair comparisons among different opinion-based re-ranking techniques, TREC 2010 organizers selected three TREC standard baselines[7] from participating runs for baseline blog distillation task that considers only topic relevance as criterion [20]. Among these baselines, stabaseline1 is one of best performing runs for baseline blog distillation task in TREC 2010; stdbaseline3 could be treated as a weak run; while stdbaseline2 could represent a median run [20]. With TREC standard baselines in hand, we could evaluate the effectiveness and robustness of our proposed approaches by how much performance improvement over these baselines could be achieved. We adopt these standard baselines to implement topic relevance component in the unified framework (see Section 3). Specifically, we use the topic relevance scores provided by the corresponding baseline as topic relevance probability (i.e. $P(F)p(Q|F)$ in Equation (1)). Note that, more appropriate approaches to transforming topic relevance scores to topic relevance probability may further improve the performance [4], and this is a part of our future work.

<top>
<num> Number: 1162 </num>
<query> uzbekistan </query>
<desc> Description:
I am interested in news from Uzbekistan.
</desc>
<facet> opinionated </facet>
<narr> Narrative:
I am interested in information about what is happening in Uzbekistan (current events, not history). A blog that lists Uzbekistan in a list of countries is judged not relevant.
</narr>
</top>

Figure 1: Blog Track 2010, faceted blog distillation task, topic "1162".

Evaluation Metrics. The evaluation metrics we use are standard IR measures, such as mean average precision (MAP), R-Precision (R-prec), and precision at the top 10 results (p@10).

Approaches to Estimating TOM. Besides the approach presented in Section 4, referred to as **Mix,** we here introduce alternative approaches for comparisons. We will verify the reasonability of the requirements discussed in Section 4.1 for TOM estimation by comparing Mix with these additional approaches.

- **GEN.** This approach takes the general opinion model $\overline{\theta}_O$ (also used as prior in the mixture model, see Section 4) as TOM. This estimation is general across all topics, but cannot capture topic-specific characteristics of opinion expressions.
- **PRF.** The outline of this approach can be summarized in the following steps. Firstly, we use the original query terms to retrieve the top 5000 topically relevant posts from the Blogs08 collection with the BM25 model. Secondly we use all together the words in the opinion lexicon (also used in Section 4) as a query to re-retrieve top 30 posts from the 5000 posts as opinion relevance feedback posts. At last, we use divergence minimization algorithm [28] to estimate TOM, which weights each word by how discriminative the word is in opinion relevance feedback posts against the background collection (i.e. Blogs08 collection). This approach is quite similar to that used in [8], which also uses divergence minimization algorithm to estimate opinion relevance model based on opinion relevance feedback documents. The major limitation of this approach is that it can't effectively separate opinion words from factual topic-related word since they often co-occur with each other even in highly opinionated relevant posts. Thus the learned model may be biased towards factual topic-related words.

Approaches to Estimating TFM. Besides the approach presented in Section 5, which is referred to as **TRW,** we here further introduce alternative approaches. We will verify reasonability of the two aspects of requirements discussed in Section 5.1 for TFM estimation by comparing TRW with these additional approaches.

- **MLE.** It takes each feed as a large document of concatenation of all its constituent posts and uses Maximum Likelihood Estimation (MLE) with Jelinek-Mercer (JM) smoothing to estimate TFM. JM smoothing is more effective than other smoothing approaches for long and verbose queries according to Zhai & Lafferty's empirical study [29]. The smoothing parameter lambda is set empirically to 0.95. The limitation of this approach is that it would be easily influenced by trivial or noisy content in the feed, and cannot effectively reflect the salient information in the feed (i.e. not considering the first aspect of the requirements very well). Besides, it also ignores the second aspect of the requirements.
- **RW**. This approach is similar to TRW, but considering no "topic bias" by taking a uniform prior for *P,* and a non-topic-sensitive cosine similarity measure to compute $M_{i,j}^{Q,PP}$ (see Section 5). This approach can well capture the salient content information in the feed (i.e. considering the first aspect of the requirements), but ignore the second aspect.

Approaches to Estimating Opinion Score. An opinion score estimation approach could be a flexible combination of any TOM estimation approach and TFM estimation approach. Our proposed approach, referred to as Mix-TRW, uses Mix and TRW to estimate TOM and TFM, respectively. As comparisons, we introduce additional variants for our approach, which use different techniques to estimate the TOM and TFM. For instance, GEN-MLE refers to the approach using GEN and MLE to estimating TOM and TFM, respectively.

6.2 Results and Analysis

These are three groups of results in Table1, Table3 and Table4, respectively, each group corresponding to one of TREC standard baselines. For each group, we use the corresponding baseline to implement the topic relevance component in our unified framework (i.e. $P(F)P(Q|F)$ in Equation (1)). We will give comparisons among different TOM estimation approaches, as well as comparisons among different TFM estimation approaches. Through comparisons, we will verify the proposed requirements for an appropriate estimation of TOM and TFM, respectively (See Section 4.1, 5.1). And we will also show the effectiveness of approaches to estimating TOM and TFM presented in Section 4 and 5, respectively. Note that, the default value of parameter μ in Mix for estimating TOM (See Equation (6) in Section 4) is experimentally set to 100, 000.

Comparisons among TOM Estimation Approaches. Focusing on fairly comparing TOM estimation approaches, we fix

---

[6] http://ir.dcs.gla.ac.uk/resources/linguistic_utils/stop_words/

[7] The provided baselines cover both TREC 2009 and 2010 topics

the TFM estimation approach with MLE. We will observe that only Mix, which follows the requirements for TOM estimation discussed in Section 4.1, obtains consistent improvements over all standard baselines. Specifically, seen from Table 1, we observe that:

1. Gen-MLE improves very slightly or even deteriorates performance over these baselines. The major reason is that general opinion words are not effectively indicative of opinions relevant to the topic. Furthermore, the involvement of topic-unrelated opinion words may cause severe topic–drift when re-ranking the baselines, which largely decreases the topic relevance performance, and consequently, decreases the overall performance.
2. We also note that PRF-MLE shows very remarkable improvements over the two relatively weaker baselines (i.e., stdbaseline2 and stdbaseline3). We argue that this could be mainly attributed to the topic relevance improvements which usually increase the overall performance as well due to the opinionated nature of blogosphere [23]. Indeed, the TOM learned using PRF would highly overlap with factual topic-related words, which help improve topic relevance performance. However, it is infeasible to improve the overall performance over strong topic relevance baselines through only improving topic relevance, since there is very small room for improving topic relevance over these baselines. Thus, we observe slight performance decrease over the strongest baseline (i.e. stdbaseline1) for PRF-MLE. Furthermore, it's naturally more meaningful to improve over strong baselines. Thus, PRF, which could not improve strong baselines, is not a good choice for TOM estimation.
3. In comparison with Mix-MLE and PRF-MLE, Mix-MLE obtains consistent and remarkable improvements over all baselines. The major reason is that Mix can effectively capture language usage of topic-related opinion expressions, which help identify topic-related opinions. This observation verifies the reasonability of requirements for TOM estimation (see Section 4.1) and demonstrates the effectiveness of the proposed approach in Section 4.

Table 1: Performance comparisons among different TOM estimation approaches.

	MAP	p@10	R-prec	Δ MAP(%)
stdbaseline1	0.2427	0.2900	0.2579	–
Mix-MLE	**0.2684**	**0.2950**	**0.2974**	10.58
Gen-MLE	0.2551	**0.2950**	0.2851	5.12
PRF-MLE	0.2409	0.2650	0.2549	-0.75
stdbaseline2	0.1318	0.1700	0.1512	–
Mix-MLE	**0.1531**	**0.2400**	0.1734	16.18
Gen-MLE	0.1305	0.1900	0.1570	-0.98
RPF-MLE	0.1458	0.2050	**0.1837**	10.64
stdbaseline3	0.1001	0.1700	0.1281	–
Mix-MLE	0.1115	0.1800	0.1511	11.40
Gen-MLE	0.1042	0.1750	0.1470	4.14
PRF-MLE	**0.1442**	**0.1950**	**0.1650**	25.35

Table 2 present example results of TOM estimated using Mix and PRF for two TREC topics. Top 20 words with highest probabilities are showed in the table. We can clearly see that Mix can better capture language usage of topic-specific opinion expressions compared with PRF. For instance, for TREC topic 1111 "jazz music", most top words of the trained TOM using Mix are highly topic-specific opinion-bearing words, such as "rhythmic", "melodic", "dreamy", and "superb", while top words of TOM obtained by PRF are highly mixed with factual topic-related words.

Table2: Example results of TOM estimated using Mix and PRF for two TREC topics.

Topic 1111(Jazz music)		Topic 1162(Uzbekistan)	
Mix	PRF	Mix	PRF
musical	jazz	inconclusive	uzbekistan
groove	musicians	unsuitable	uzbek
rhythmic	musical	acne	karimov
mastering	music	foreigner	tashkent
melodic	classical	wealthy	regime
replica	bebop	hubris	fco
unbeatable	improvisation	infest	islamic
swing	chord	intelligible	murray
kindness	compositions	scabies	islam
dreamy	orchestra	unlimited	torture
vocal	composer	dictator	extremism
eclectic	composition	peacefully	asia
indie	genres	guardian	allies
nonesuch	sound	ambiguous	terror
learning	listened	tyranny	central
laughter	saxophone	oppose	western
strenuous	coltrane	unrest	democracy
superb	pop	whispering	samarkand
fiction	listening	servitude	muslims
comedy	soul	terror	foreign

Comparisons among TFM Estimation Approaches. To focus on fairly comparisons for TFM estimation approaches, we fix the TOM estimation approach with GEN. We will observe that TRW, which follows the requirements for TFM estimation discussed in Section 5.1, obtains consistent improvements over all baselines, and in general outperforms other approaches not fully following the requirements. Specifically, seen from Table 3, we observe that:

1. Gen-MLE improves very slightly or even deteriorates performance over three baselines, and Gen-RW outperforms Gen-MLE in terms of most merits over all baselines. This indicates that by capturing salient content in the feed using random walk, which fully exploits both content and structural information in the feed, we could better determine whether the feed has a principal opinionated inclination. This observation verifies reasonability of the first aspect of the requirements.
2. We also note that Gen-TRW further outperforms Gen-RW, and shows consistent improvements in almost all merits over all baselines. This indicates that further considering "topic bias" helps capture topic-related opinions in the feed to better determine whether the feed has a clear on-topic opinionated inclination. This observation verifies reasonability of the second aspect of requirements.

Overall Comparisons. From Table 4, we can observe that Mix-TRW can achieve consistent and remarkable improvements over all standard baselines. We also observe that Mix-TRW consistently outperforms Gen-TRW over all standard baselines in terms of all metrics. Likewise, Mix-TRW outperforms Mix-MLE except for p@10 over stdbaseline3. These observations show the effectiveness and flexibility of our proposed languages modeling approach to integrate both the language usage information of topic-specific opinion expressions and various evidences from the feed to determine whether the feed shows a principal on-topic opinionated inclination.

Tablel 3: Performance comparisons among different TFM estimation approaches.

	MAP	p@10	R-prec	Δ MAP(%)
stdbaseline1	0.2427	0.2900	0.2579	_
Gen-TRW	**0.2720**	**0.3050**	**0.2978**	12.09
Gen-MLE	0.2551	0.2950	0.2851	5.12
Gen-RW	0.2630	0.3000	0.2877	8.36
stdbaseline2	0.1318	0.1700	0.1512	_
Gen-TRW	**0.1399**	**0.2150**	**0.1614**	6.16
Gen-MLE	0.1305	0.1900	0.1570	-0.98
Gen-RW	0.1345	0.1950	0.1597	2.00
stdbaseline3	0.1001	0.1700	0.1281	_
Gen-TRW	**0.1151**	0.1700	**0.1470**	15.01
Gen-MLE	0.1042	**0.1750**	**0.1470**	4.14
Gen-RW	0.1148	0.1700	0.1458	14.75

Table4: Performance comparisons among different approaches. Paired t-tests are performed, significant improvements over the corresponding baseline (p-value < 0.05) are marked with *.

	MAP	p@10	R-prec	Δ MAP(%)
stdbaseline1	0.2427	0.2900	0.2579	_
Mix-TRW	**0.2855***	**0.3100***	**0.3036***	**17.61**
Mix-MLE	0.2684	0.2950	0.2974*	10.58
Gen-TRW	0.2720*	0.3050*	0.2978*	12.09
stdbaseline2	0.1318	0.1700	0.1512	_
Mix-TRW	**0.1710***	**0.2500***	**0.1917***	**29.74**
Mix-MLE	0.1531	0.2400*	0.1734*	16.18
Gen-TRW	0.1399	0.2150*	0.1614	6.16
stdbaseline3	0.1001	0.1700	0.1281	_
Mix-TRW	**0.1197***	0.1750	**0.1745***	**19.64**
Mix-MLE	0.1115*	**0.1800**	0.1511*	11.40
Gen-TRW	0.1151	0.1700	0.1470	15.01

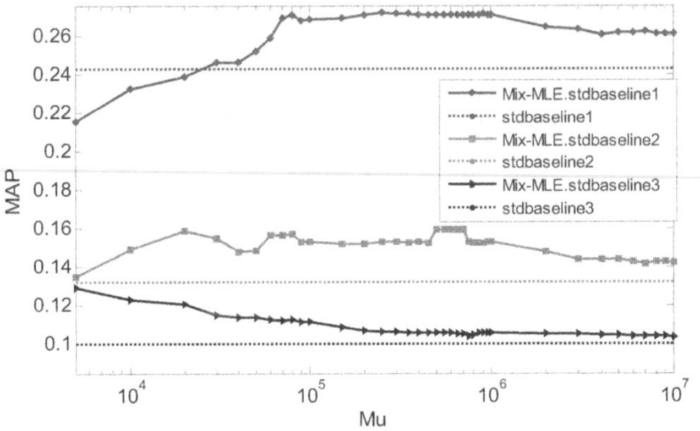

Figure 2: MAP curves with different μ based on standard baselines

Impact of Parameter μ for Estimating TOM with Mix. We here investigate the impact of parameter μ, which controls the influence of the prior for estimating TOM in the mixture model (see Section 4, Equation (6)). We fix the TFM estimation approach with MLE to focusing on purely investigating the impact of μ. We plot the MAP curves with different μ values based on three standard baselines in Figure 2, and from it we can observe that:

1. When μ values are around 100,000, Mix-MLE can obtain remarkable and consistent performance improvements over all standard baselines. And Mix-MLE still have consistent improvements over all baselines within a very large range of μ values (given μ >=60,000). It seems that it is not very sensitive to μ values within this range, especially for strong baselines. This shows the stability and robustness of our proposed mixture model to estimating TOM.
2. When μ values are extremely large (e.g. μ >=1,000,000), the performance go downwards but very smoothly. The major reason is that the learned TOM will be overwhelmed by general opinion words, and thus can not effectively capture topic-specific opinion words.
3. It seems that weaker baselines benefit more from low μ values. Indeed, when μ is very low (e.g., 5,000 and 10,000), Mix-MLE obtains very remarkable performance improvements over the weakest baseline (i.e., stdbaseline3). On the other hand, we observe a remarkable performance decrease over the strongest baseline (i.e., stdbaseline1). The major reason is that, with low μ values, the prior guidance is not adequate to effectively discriminate opinions from factual content. Thus, the learned TOM would highly overlap with factual topic-related words, which helps improve topic relevance performance and, consequently, overall performance for weak baselines, but not for strong baselines.

6.3 Comparisons with TREC approaches

TREC 2009. In TREC 2009, almost all submitted runs deteriorated the performance compared with underlying topic relevance baseline rankings. In fact, Mix-TRW based on stdbaseline1 outperforms the best run (i.e. *ICTNETBDRUN2*) by a large marine (0.2681 vs. 0.1259 in MAP).

TREC 2010. In TREC 2010, three standard baselines were provided by the organizers for fair comparisons of purely opinion-based re-ranking techniques. Mix-TRW based on stdbaseline1 largely outperforms the best run, i.e. *PKUTM111onB1*, among all runs (including those based on standard baselines and not) on 7 TREC 2010 topics (0.3177 vs. 0.2807 in MAP). Besides, most runs based on the standard baselines still provided deteriorated performance over the underlying standard baselines, although some systems managed to improve remarkably over their own baselines. And there was no participant managing to provide consistent and remarkable performance improvements over all standard baselines as our approaches. Table 5 gives the comparisons of Mix-TRW with the best runs based on three standard baselines, respectively. Note that, information in Table5 is based on appendix of the TREC 2010 Proceedings page[8]. Note that, only results on 5 TREC 2010 topics are available in the appendix, the results are based on these 5 topics. Seen from the table, Mix-TRW largely outperforms best runs based on two relatively strong baselines (i.e. stdbaseline1 and stdbaseline2), respectively. And Mix-TRW is defeated by the best run based on the weakest baseline (i.e. stdbaseline3). However, it's naturally more meaningful to improve over stronger baselines.

[8] http://trec.nist.gov/pubs/trec19/t19.proceedings.html

Table5: Performance comparisons with best runs based on standard baselines on TREC 2010 Topics

	MAP
stdbaseline1	0.2128
BIT10std1fd2	0.2240
Mix-TRW	**0.2915**
stdbaseline2	0.1179
ICTNETFBDs2	0.1372
Mix-TRW	**0.2301**
stdbaseline3	0.0927
uogTrfC919s3	**0.1233**
Mix-TRW	0.1086

7. CONCLUSIONS

In this paper, we study opinionated blog feed retrieval, and discuss the challenges of this task. To address these challenges, we propose a unified framework. In this the framework, we propose a language modeling approach to estimating opinion scores, where two language models, Topic-specific Opinion Model (TOM) and Topic-biased Feed Model (TFM), work collectively to reflect whether the blog feed shows a principal on-topic opinionated inclination. We discuss the requirements for an appropriate estimation of TOM and TFM, respectively. Following these requirements, we propose to use a mixture model with prior guidance to estimate TOM and a topic-biased random walk to estimate TFM. In our experiments, we show the reasonability of proposed approaches to estimating TOM and TFM. The experiments also show the effectiveness and flexibility of our proposed languages modeling approach to integrate both the language usage information of topic-specific opinion expressions and various evidences from the feed to improve the performance. As a preliminary work, there may be other ways to estimate the involved two language models better, which will be the focus of our future work.

Acknowledgments

This work was supported by following funds: National Natural Science Foundation of China under Grants, No. 60933005, No. 60873245, No. 60903139, No. 60803085, No.61100083, and No. 60873243; National High-Tech R&D Program of China (863 Program) with Grant No. 2010AA012502, and No. 2010AA012503; National Key Technology R&D program with Grant No. 2011BAH11B02.

8. REFERENCES

[1] Balog, K., Rijke, M., and Weerkamp, W. 2008.Bloggers as Experts Feed Distillation using Expert Retrieval Models. In *Proceedings of SIGIR 2008*.

[2] Elsas, J.L. , Arguello, J., Callan, J., and Carbonell, G.J. 2008. Retrieval and feedback models for blog feed search. In *Proceedings of SIGIR '08*.

[3] Esuli, A., and Sebastiani, F.2005.Determining the semantic orientation of terms through gloss classification. In *Proceedings of CIKM 2005*.

[4] Gerani, S., Carman, M.j., and Crestani, F. 2010. Proximity-based opinion retrieval. In *Proceeding of SIGIR '10*..

[5] He, B., Macdonald, C., He, J., and Ounis, I. 2008. An effective statistical approach to blog post opinion retrieval. In *Proceeding of CIKM '08*.

[6] Huang, X., and Croft, W. B. 2009. A unified relevance model for opinion retrieval. In *Proceedings of CIKM 2009*, pages 947–956.

[7] Jia, L., Yu, C.2010. UIC at TREC 2010 Faceted Blog Distillation.In *Proceedings of TREC 2010*.

[8] Jiang, P., Zhang, C., Yang, Q., and Niu, Z. 2010. Blog Opinion Retrieval Based on Topic-Opinion Mixture Model. In *Proceedings of PAKDD 2010*.

[9] Keikha, M., Mahdabi, P., Gerani, S., Inches, G., Carman, M., Crestani, F., and Parapar, J. 2010. University of Lugano at TREC 2010. In *Proceedings of TREC 2010*.

[10] Li, S., Gao, H., Sun, H., Chen, F., Feng, O., Gao, S., Zhang, H., Li, X., Tan, C., Xu, W., Chen, G., and Guo, J. 2009. A Study of Faceted Blog Distillation-- PRIS at TREC 2009 Blog Track. In *Proceedings of TREC 2009*.

[11] Macdonald, C., Ounis, I., and Soboroff, I. 2007. Overview of the TREC 2007 Blog track. In *Proceedings of TREC 2007*.

[12] Macdonald, C., and Ounis, I. 2008. Key blog distillation: ranking aggregates. In *Proceedings CIKM 2008*.

[13] Macdonald, C., Ounis, I., and Soboroff, I. 2009. Overview of the TREC-2009 Blog Track. In *Proceedings of TREC 2009*.

[14] Macdonald, C., Santos, R.L.T., Ounis, I., and Soboroff, I. 2010. Blog track research at TREC. SIGIR Forum 44, 58-75.

[15] McCreadie, R., Macdonald, C., Ounis, I., Peng, J., and Santos, R. 2009. University of Glasgow at TREC 2009: Experiments with Terrier. In *Proceedings of TREC 2009*.

[16] Mei, Q., Ling, X., Wondra, M., Su, H., and Zhai, C. 2007.Topic sentiment mixture: modeling facets and opinions in weblogs. In *Proceedings of WWW '07*, 171-180.

[17] Na, S.-H., Lee, Y. , Nam, S.-H., and Lee, J.-H. 2009. Improving opinion retrieval based on query-specific sentiment lexicon. In *Proceedings of ECIR 2009*, pages 734–738.

[18] Ounis, I., Macdonald, C., Rijke, M.de., Mishne, G., and Soboroff, I. 2006.Overview of the TREC 2006 Blog track. In *Proceedings of the 15th Text REtrieval Conference*.

[19] Ounis, I., Macdonald, C., and Soboroff, I.2008.Overview of the TREC-2008 Blog Track. In *Proceedings of TREC'08*.

[20] Ounis, I., Macdonald, C., and Soboroff, I. 2010. Overview of the TREC-2010 Blog Track (Preliminary). In *Proceedings of TREC 2010*.

[21] Sanderson, J.2008. The Blog is Serving Its Purpose: Self-Presentation Strategies on 38pitches.com. *Journal of Computer-Mediated Communication*. Jul 2008, Vol. 13, No. 4: 912-936.

[22] Santos, R. L. T. , He, B., Macdonald, C., and Ounis, I. 2009.Integrating proximity to subjective sentences for blog opinion retrieval. In *Proceedings of ECIR 2009*, pages 325–336.

[23] Seki, K., and Uehara, K. 2009. Adaptive subjective triggers for opinionated document retrieval. In *Proceedings WSDM '09*, 25-33.

[24] Song, L., Cheng, X., Guo, Y., Liu, L., and Ding, G. 2009. ContentEx: A Framework for Automatic Content Extraction Programs. In *Proceedings of ISI'2009*.

[25] Vechtomova, O. 2010.Facet-based opinion retrieval from blogs. *Information Processing and Management*, 46(1):71–88.

[26] Wei, F., Li, W., Lu, Q., and He, Y. 2008. Query-sensitive mutual reinforcement chain and its application in query-oriented multi-document summarization. In *Proceedings of SIGIR '08*.

[27] Xu, X., Meng, T., Cheng, X., and Liu, Y. 2011. A probabilistic model for opinionated blog feed retrieval. In *Proceedings of the 20th international conference companion on World wide web* (WWW '11).

[28] Zhai C., and Lafferty, J. 2001.Model-based feedback in the language modeling approach to information retrieval. In *Proceedings of CIKM 2001*.

[29] Zhai, C., and Lafferty, J. 2004.A study of smoothing methods for language models applied to information retrieval. *ACM Transactions on Information Systems*, Vol. 22, No. 2, 179-214.

[30] Zhai, C., Velivelli, A., and Yu, B.2004. A Cross-Collection Mixture Model for Comparative Text Mining. In *Proceedings of KDD 2004*.

[31] Zhang, W., Yu, C., and Meng, W. 2007. Opinion retrieval from blogs. In *Proceedings of CIKM 2007*, pages 831–840.

[32] Zhang, M., and Ye, X. 2008. A generation model to unify topic relevance and lexicon-based sentiment for opinion retrieval. In *Proceedings of SIGIR 2008*, pages 411–418.

[33] Zhou, Z., Zhang, X.,Vines, P.2010. RMIT at TREC 2010 Blog Track: Faceted Blog Distillation Task. *Online Proceedings of TREC 2010*.

Understanding Cyclic Trends in Social Choices

Anish Das Sarma
Google Research
anish.dassarma@gmail.com

Sreenivas Gollapudi
Microsoft Research
sreenig@microsoft.com

Rina Panigrahy
Microsoft Research
rina@microsoft.com

Li Zhang
Microsoft Research
lzha@microsoft.com

ABSTRACT

Motivated by trends in popularity of products, we present a formal model for studying trends in our choice of products in terms of three parameters: (1) their innate utility; (2) individual boredom associated with repeated usage of an item; and (3) social influences associated with the preferences from other people. Different from previous work, in this paper we introduce boredom to explain the cyclic pattern in individual and social choices. We formally model boredom and show that a rational individual would make cyclic choices when considering the boredom factor. Furthermore, we extend the model to social choices by showing that a society that votes for a particular style or product can be viewed as a single individual cycling through different choices.

We adopt a natural model of utility an individual derives from using an item, i.e., the utility of an item gets discounted by its repeated use and increases when the item is not used. We address the problem of optimally choosing items for usage, so as to maximize overall user satisfaction over a period of time. First we show that the simple greedy heuristic of always choosing the item with the maximum current composite utility can be arbitrarily worse than the optimal. Second, we prove that even with just a single individual, determining the optimal strategy for choosing items is NP-hard. Third, we show that a simple modification to the greedy algorithm is a provably close approximation to the optimal strategy. Finally, we present an experimental study over real-world data collected from query logs to compare our algorithms.

Categories and Subject Descriptors

F.0 [**Theory of Computation**]: General

General Terms

Algorithms, Theory, Human Factors, Economics

Keywords

fashion trends, cyclic trends, social choice

Permission to make digital or hard copies of all or part of this work for personal or classroom use is granted without fee provided that copies are not made or distributed for profit or commercial advantage and that copies bear this notice and the full citation on the first page. To copy otherwise, to republish, to post on servers or to redistribute to lists, requires prior specific permission and/or a fee.

WSDM'12, February 8–12, 2012, Seattle, Washington, USA.

Copyright 2012 ACM 978-1-4503-0747-5/12/02 ...$10.00.

1. INTRODUCTION

When an individual or a society is repeatedly presented with multiple substitutable choices, we often observe a recurring shift of user preferences over time. Many studies have observed that the choices of a society tend to be cyclic [11, 12, 5, 4]. While some trends are relatively easy to explain (e.g., sweater sales increasing in the winter), some other trends may result from a variety of factors, including social influence, novelty of an item, and its innate value to a user.

In this paper, we describe a utility model that combines different factors that may result in cyclic choices. We study the computational issues under the model and provide simple mechanisms by which consumers may make *close to optimal* decisions on which products to consume and when, in order to maximize their *overall utility*. In contrast, we give examples in which the (natural) greedy algorithm that maximizes short term utility can be much worse in long run. Further, we show that under a linear social influence model, the society can be viewed as an individual, and we can apply the algorithm designed for an individual to achieve nearly optimal social welfare. Therefore, our algorithm can be useful for a company or website in deciding which items to show to the users in order to maximize the total user satisfaction in long term. We also conduct experiments to show how various parameters in our model can be estimated as well as validate our algorithms.

In our model, a user lives in discrete time periods and at each time period chooses to consume one from a set of *items*, representing any product, good, or concept the user consumes repeatedly. We consider three broad categories of factors that may impact the user's utility of choosing an item. The first, and perhaps the most basic, cause of a product becoming trendy is its innate utility, intuitively capturing the value it gives an individual. Second, psychologically, a person's utility of consuming a product may be discounted by repeated consumption of the same item. This results in the user choosing new and different products as she gets tired of existing products.Third, while at an individual level, we have certain inclinations based on our tastes, these are influenced by social phenomena, such as friends' or celebrities' preferences. Our utility model is based on the aforementioned factors.

Innate utility: The utility of an item captures the innate value the item provides to an individual. We assume it is fixed, independent of other influences.

Individual boredom: If we use any item for too long, we

get bored of it, and our appreciation for it goes down. This is modeled as a negative component added to the utility. This factor grows if one repeatedly uses the same item and fades away when one stops consuming the item.

To model boredom on any item at any given time t, we associate with each past usage of the item, say at time t', a factor in the form of $(1-r)^{t-t'}$ for some $r < 1$. Then the total boredom on the item takes the sum of the this factor from all the past usage of the item. This definition captures the intuition that the boredom grows if an item is repeatedly used.

Utility maximization with boredom turns out to be hard — as we show in the paper, it is NP-hard to determine the optimal consumptions under the boredom model. One natural heuristic is the greedy algorithm in which the user, at each time t, always chooses the item with the maximum $u_i(t)$, based on the consumption history of the user. We construct an example to show that the natural greedy algorithm may result in overall utility far less than the optimum. On the other hand, we show a slightly adapted "greedy" algorithm can lead to close to the optimal utility. In the proposed algorithm, in addition to the past history, the user also factors in the boredom effect the item might have on the future consumption and calculates a "shadow" utility of each item by double the boredom. We show that by picking the item that maximize the "shadow" utility every time, the user can achieve close to optimal utility in long run when the boredom decay rate is small.

Social influence: Our valuation of an item can change significantly by the valuation of our friends or influencing people. For example, when we see that many people around us like something we may start liking it; or we may consciously want to differ from some other people around us. We model such influences as a weighted linear combination from other people.[1]

The effect of social influence can be formalized using a linear model. For example, to model social influence, consider one item and a society consisting of m people. Let G denote the influence graph on these people that is directed where each edge is labeled with a weight that indicates the strength of this influence. A high value on an edge, such as outgoing edges from celebrities indicates a strong outgoing influence; on the other hand a negative value indicates a desire to distance oneself or be different from the source node. Let A denote the corresponding influence matrix. let $u_i(t)$ denote the utility of the item to the ith person; let $\mathbf{u}(t)$ denote the vector of utilities. If we assume that for each time step the influence from all friends of a person add linearly then we may write $\mathbf{u}(t+1) = A\mathbf{u}(t)$, which is similar to [11]. Note that for stability of this iterative powers, we should assume that its top eigenvector has magnitude 1. We will show that under this influence model, we may treat the society as an individual making choices under the effect of boredom.

From a broader standpoint, one of the main points our model makes is that trends in social choices can be viewed as not just the effect of the influence of a privileged few but more as a democratic process that churns the social boredom

[1]Additional influence may come from the association of a product to things/concepts we like or dislike. For instance, someone may be very fond of green technologies or dislike things that are scary. We may simply model such concepts as individuals.

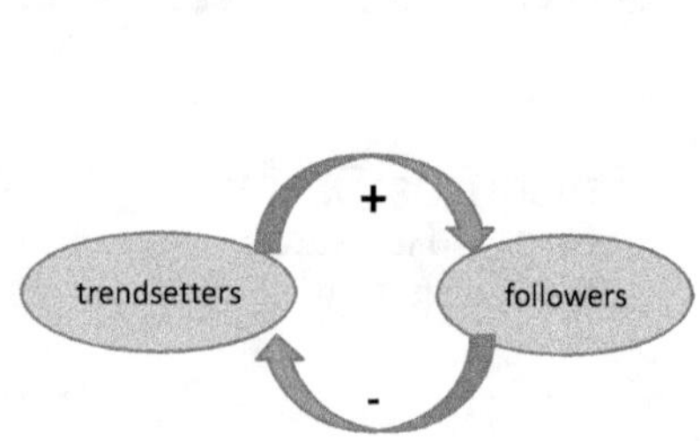

Figure 1: Cycles resulting from negative influences: Consider a system with two types of people: (1) followers, who always imitate the trendsetters, and (2) trendsetters who always attempt to distinguish themselves from the followers. Such a system will result in a cyclic preferences.

and channels the innate instinct for change. Boredom is the innate psychological force that dulls the effect of a constant stimulus over a period of time and make us look for newer stimuli. Thus the *coolness* of an item drops over time and things that we haven't seen or used in a long time begin to appear more *cool*. Another point the paper makes is that several scenarios involving individual and social choices are essentially driven by the same underlying principles. Boredom is thus the single most and simplest explanation for oscillations in individual and social choices. This is not at all surprising; indeed boredom is perhaps a strong influence when we make choices on items such as food, clothes, and songs. Social influence no doubt plays a large part in individual choices. But when we look at the social system as a whole the influences across individuals are forces within the system and in the net effect it simply gives a larger voice to the more influential individuals. We also note that influence by itself is not sufficient to create cyclic behavior. In fact, if all influences are positive then without any boredom the system $u(t+1) = Au(t)$ converges to a fixed value resulting in a fixed social choice.

Finally, we recognize that the factors we consider are by no means comprehensive; several other factors may change the values of nodes. Our decay model for boredom and linear model for influence may be too simplistic. Nonetheless, we believe boredom and social influence capture several important aspects of the underlying psychological processes that people use to value items.

Related work. Understanding social choices particularly in the context of fashion trends are of significant academic interest as well as commercial importance in various fields, including brand advertising and market economics. There's a large body of work in multiple disciplines – sociology (e.g. [5, 4]), economics (e.g. [7]), and marketing (e.g. [11, 12]), on theories for evolution of fashion. Our work is inspired by [11] in which the authors propose a mathematical model for unifying many existing explanations for fashion cycles. We will describe [11] in more details and contrast the difference of our work.

Reference [11] proposed a formal model of fashion based on association rules. Intuitively, an individual's utility for an item is impacted by how similar it is to items he likes, and how dissimilar it is to items he dislikes. Further, he is influenced by the society through other individuals' preferences for various items. Consider a single item, whose consumption vector is given by $c(t)$ at time t. Considering the recurrence $c(t+1) = Wc(t)$, where W is the weight influence matrix, [11] observed that if the matrix W has a complex top eigenvalue (corresponding to negative influences), then the item's consumption pattern may be periodic, producing cycles in preferences (as shown in Figure 1). Our model of utility is similar to the consumption model in [11]. However, we consider an additional parameter of boredom that is essential to explain fashion cycles in a society with non-negative influences as such a matrix W always has a real top eigenvalue. The following argument shows that a matrix with non-negative influences cannot result in cycles.

OBSERVATION 1.1. *The process $c(t+1) = Wc(t)$ converges to a fixed point if W has no non-negative entries and is eigen-decomposable where the magnitude of any eigenvalue is at most 1. That is, it cannot result in cyclic behavior where c takes different values repeatedly as $t \to \infty$*

PROOF. The basic idea is that if W is eigen decomposable, it can be written as $W = QDQ^{-1}$ where D is the diagonal matrix of eigenvalues and the columns of Q are the eigenvectors. Now $W^t = QD^tQ^{-1}$ which is dominated by the largest (in magnitude) eigenvalue. We already assumed the magnitudes are at most 1 for stability. If the top eigenvalue in magnitude is -1 (or complex) then we will see a behavior like $(-1)^t$ which cycles through the values $1, -1, 1, -1, ...$ If the top eigen values are the kth roots of 1 then we will get cyclic behavior with periodicity k.

But, if W is non-negative, the Perron-Frobenius theorem [2] states that there is a unique dominant positive eigenvalue. Then $W^t = QD^tQ^{-1}$ converges to 0 if eigenvalue of top magnitude is less than 1 and to $q_1'q_1$ if the unique top eigenvalue is 1, where q_1 is the eigenvector corresponding to the top eigenvalue. □

Some other recent work (e.g., [6]) study behavioral influences in social networks, such as in terms of information propagation. For instance, [8] studies how two competing products spread in society, [9] provides techniques for tracking and representing "memes", which may be used to analyze news cycles, and [10] studies how recommendations propagate in a network through social influence.

The focus of our paper is on formalizing a theory for social choices in the presence of boredom, combined with social influence. Therefore, for a large part of the paper we consider only a single individual and study cyclic trends based on boredom. In our extension to multiple individuals, we assume a linear weighting of influences from friends' preferences for particular items.

2. CONTRIBUTIONS OF OUR STUDY

2.1 Modeling individual boredom

We consider a user living in discrete time periods $0, 1, \ldots$ and consuming one item among n substitutable items at each time; for example, a person needs to decide which restaurant to go to every night or which political party to vote for every four years. We assume that each item i brings a base utility v_i to the user. Now if we assume that the utilities are fixed then the user would always choose the item with the maximum v_i. This would be inconsistent with the observed common behavior of cycling among multiple items. In order to explain cyclic choices, it is necessary to model the utility dependence of the consumptions across different time periods.

We propose a simple model in which the utility of an item at any time t is the base utility discounted by a boredom factor proportional to the "memory" the person has developed by using this item in the past. The more often or more recent the user has used the item, the more memory and boredom is developed for the item, and consequently the less utility the item has to the user.

We naturally assume that the memory drops geometrically over time, and the total memory of a person is bounded. This leads to the following definition of memory. Let $0 < r < 1$ be a memory decay rate, i.e., the rate at which a person "forgets" about things. Let $x_i(t) \in \{0, 1\}$ indicate if the user uses the item i at time t. Then the memory of i at time t is $M_i(t) = r \sum_{\tau=0}^{t-1} x_i(\tau)(1-r)^{t-\tau}$. We add the factor r so that $M_i(t) \leq 1$. This is equivalent to the recurrence $M_i(t+1) = (1-r)M_i(t) + rx_i(t)$. Note that r can be viewed as the decay rate because if an item is used once in the beginning and then never used then its memory after time t is $(1-r)^t \approx e^{-rt}$ (for small r).

Another important point to note is that a small decay rate is very different from a decay rate of 0. Look at the equation $M_i(t+1) = (1-r)M_i(t) + rx_i(t)$. If $r = 0$ then $M_i(t)$ is always 0 – there is no memory. If $r \to 0$, $M_i(t) = (1-r)M_i(t) + rx_i(t) = r \sum_{\tau=0}^{t-1} x_i(\tau)(1-r)^{t-\tau} = \frac{\sum_{\tau=0}^{t-1} x_i(\tau)(1-r)^{t-\tau}}{\sum_{\tau=0}^{t-1}(1-r)^{t-\tau}}$ which is like the weighted-average fraction of time the item was used where most of the weight is in the last $O(1/r)$ time steps. Thus if $r = 0$ memory is always 0, but if r is tiny then on continuous use of an item its memory will reach close to 1 in $O(1/r)$ time steps.

The boredom $b_i(t) = \alpha_i M_i(t)$ is proportional to the memory and depends on the item. The utility of item i is defined as $u_i(t) = v_i - b_i(t) = v_i - \alpha_i M_i(t)$. Henceforth, we will refer to v as the base utility and α as the boredom coefficient.

2.2 Utility optimization with boredom

With the above model, one natural question is to compute the choices of the items to maximize the user's overall utility. If we allow the user to choose at continuous time, the maximization problem becomes relatively easy as the best way to consume an item is to do it cyclically at regular time intervals. However, such regular placement may not be realizable in the discrete case or is hard to find. As we will show below, it is NP-hard to compute the best consumption sequence.

We also consider the natural greedy strategy and show that the under the greedy strategy, the utility of each item is always bounded in a narrow band and so each item is consumed approximately cyclically. The greedy strategy, however, may have produce a sequence giving poor overall utility. We provide a simple heuristics, called double-greedy strategy, and show that it emulates the cyclic pattern of the optimal solution on the real line and yields utility close to the optimal when r is small.

2.2.1 Greedy algorithm

In the greedy strategy, at each time t, the user consumes the item with the maximum utility $u_i(t)$. This strategy is intuitive and probably consistent with how we make our daily decisions. We show that the utility gap between any two items is small all the time. We provide an example to show it has poor performance in terms of utility maximization, even when $r \to 0$. Denote by $\alpha = \max_i \alpha_i$.

THEOREM 2.1. *There exists a time T such that for any $t \geq T$, $\mu \leq \max_i u_i(t) \leq \mu + O(r\alpha \log n)$ where μ is the unique solution to the following system:*

There is an $f_i \geq 0$ for each item such that (1) $\sum f_i = 1$; (2) if $f_i > 0$, $v_i - f_i\alpha_i = \mu$, and $v_i < \mu$ otherwise.

Intuitively, f_i is the long run frequency of the item i gets consumed. While the greedy algorithm has the nice property of keeping the utility gap between any items small, it may produce a sequence with poor overall utility.

OBSERVATION 2.1. *The Greedy strategy of always picking the highest utility item each day is not optimal.*

To see the non-optimality of greedy, simply consider two items for beverage, say "water" and "soda". Assume water has low innate utility say 1 and zero boredom coefficient. Soda on the other hand has high utility say 10 but also a high boredom coefficient say 10. So if one drank soda every day its utility would drop to below that of water. Observe that the greedy strategy will choose soda till its utility drops to that of water and then switch back to soda whenever its utility rises even slightly over 1. So the average utility of the greedy strategy is close to 1, as soda's utility fluctuates around 1. A smarter strategy is to hold off on the soda even if it is a better choice today so as to enjoy it even more on a later day. Thus it is possible to derive an average utility that is much higher than 1. For example, we can get average utility of at least 3 by alternating between water and soda in the above example. Since the memory on an item is at most 1, the memory on an item is at most $1/2$ if it is consumed every other day. Hence the utility on soda is $10-10/2 = 5$ in the above strategy. It can be easily seen that the parameters in the above example can be picked to create arbitrarily large gap between the greedy algorithm and the optimal solution. We emphasize that this gap exists for any value of r.

This naturally raises the question: what is the optimal strategy? More importantly is there an optimal strategy that is a simple 'rule of thumb' that is easy to remember and employ as we make the daily choices. Unfortunately it turns out that computing the optimal strategy is NP-hard.

THEOREM 2.2. *Given a period T, target utility U^*, and n items, it is NP-hard to determine whether there exists a selection of items with period T such that the total utility of the selection is at least U^*.*

The proof is detailed in the appendix.

2.2.2 Double-greedy algorithm

On the positive side we show that there is indeed a simple "rule of thumb" that gives an almost optimal solution when r is small. The strategy "double-greedy" waits longer for items that we get bored of too quickly. It is a simple twist on the greedy strategy: instead of picking the item that maximizes the utility $u_i(t) = u_i - b_i(t)$, it picks the one which maximizes $w_i(t) = u_i - 2b_i(t)$. Thus it doubles the boredom of all items and then runs the greedy strategy. We arrive at the double-greedy strategy by considering a continuous version of the problem. Intuitively, the double-greedy strategy tries to equalize the "marginal utility", rather than the utility as in the greedy algorithm, each item brings. Indeed, we will bound the gap between marginal utilities and show that it leads to close to optimal utility when r is small.

THEOREM 2.3. *Let $\overline{U}$ denote the average utility obtained by the double greedy algorithm and U^* the optimal utility. Then $\overline{U} \geq U^* - O(r\alpha \log n)$ where $\alpha = \max_i \alpha_i$.*

2.3 Fashion as a Social Choice

A choice is a fashion, if it is the choice of a large fraction of the society. Thus a society only supports a small number of fashions. Industries often target one type of fashion for each market segment. Consider a situation where the entire society consists of one fashion market segment. We will see how in this case such a society can be compared to an individual making choices to maximize utility under the effect of boredom. Each individuals utiltities depend not only on his base utility and boredom but also on the influence from other individuals.

Consider a society of n people and m possible item choices. The society needs to choose one item out of these at every time step. We will study the problem of the makiing the optimal choice so as to maximize welfare. This is applicable in the following scenarios: A business is launching the next fashion style for its market segment, or a radio channel is broadcasting songs in a sequence to maximize the welfare to its audience. Let $u_{ij}(t+1)$ denote the utility of item i to person j at time t; let $b_{ij}(t)$ denote the boredom value; let $\mathbf{u}_i(t)$ denote the vector of utitilities to the n people for item i, $\mathbf{v}_i(t)$ denote the vector of base utilities, and $\mathbf{b}_i(t)$ denote the vector of boredom values. In the absence of boredom we will say $\mathbf{u}_i(t+1) = A\mathbf{u}_i(t)$ where A is the influence matrix. Accounting for boredom we will say, $\mathbf{u}_i(t+1) = A\, u_i(t) - [\mathbf{b}_i(t+1) - \mathbf{b}_i(t)]$. Note that this is consistent with the case when there is only one individual where $u_i(t+1) = u_i(t) - [b(t+1) - b(t)]$. Observe that ignoring the effect of boredom we simply get the recurrence $\mathbf{u}_i(t+1) = A\mathbf{u}_i(t)$ or $\mathbf{u}_i(t) = A^t\mathbf{v}_i$. This recurrence reflects the diffusion of influence through the social network. Note that if the largest eigenvalue of A has magnitude more than 1 then the process will diverge and if all eigenvalues are < 1 it will eventually converge to 0. So we will assume the maximum eigenvalue of A is has magnitude 1. If the gap between the magnitude of the largest and the second largest eigenvalue is at least ϵ then this diffusion process converges quickly in about $\tilde{\Theta}(1/\epsilon)$ steps. We will focus on the case when rate of boredom r is much slower than the diffusion rate (this corresponds to the case where influences spread fast and the boredom grows slowly). We then study the problem of making social choices of items over time so as to maximize welfare.

We will assume that A is diagonlizable and has a real top eigenvalue of 1 and all the other eigenvalues are smaller in magnitude. In that case it is well known that for any vector x $A^t x$ converges to to a fixed point and the speed of convergence depends on the gap between the largest and second largest eigenvalue. We show that under certain conditions if r/ϵ is small then. the choices made by the society is comparable to the choices made by an individual with appropriate base utilities and boredom coefficients. Let $W_i(t)$ denote the welfare of the society at time t by choosing item i; then $W_i(t)/n$

THEOREM 2.4. *Consider a society with influence matrix A that has largest eigenvalue 1 and second largest eigenvalue of magnitude at most $1-\epsilon$. For computing the welfare over a a sequence of social choices approximately, such a society can be modelled as a single individual with base uitilities $\tilde{v}_i$ and boredom coefficients $\tilde{\alpha}_i$, where $\tilde{v}_i = \mathbf{c}'\mathbf{v}_i$ and $\tilde{\alpha}_i = \mathbf{c}'\alpha_i$ for some vector $\mathbf{c}$. Let $\tilde{u}_i(t)$ denote the utility of item i to such an individual at time t.*

More precisely, differences in the average utility of the society for the same sequence of choices until any time $|W_i(t)/n - \tilde{u}_i(t)| \le \frac{r}{\epsilon}O(|\alpha_i|_\infty)$ for any $t > T$ for some fixed T. The O notation hides factors that depends on A. For a real, symmetric matrix the constant is 1

3. TECHNICAL DETAILS

In this section, we include the proofs for Theorem 2.1, 2.3, and 2.4 and refer to Appendix B for the proof of Theorem 2.2.

3.1 Utility optimization with boredom

We will first show that the total memory $\sum_i M_i(t)$ approaches a constant over time. The following is straightforward from the definition.

LEMMA 3.1. *$\sum_i M_i(t) \le 1$, and $\sum_i M_i(t) \to 1$ for large t. When $t = \Omega(1/r)$, $\sum_i M_i(t) = 1 - O(\exp(-tr))$.*

Recall that $u_i(t) = u_i - \alpha_i M_i(t)$. The above lemma implies that $\sum_i (u_i - u_i(t))/\alpha_i = \sum_i M_i(t)$ is about constant for sufficiently large t. Together with the fact that the change to $u_i(t)$ is bounded by $r\alpha_i$, we are able to show that under the greedy strategy, the gap between $u_i(t)$'s cannot grow too large.

Before we prove Theorem 2.1, we prove the following Lemma that gives us an upper-bound on $\max_i u_i(t)$.

LEMMA 3.2. *For $t \ge T$ and any $i \in S_g$, $\max_j u_j(t) - u_i(t) = O(\alpha r \log n)$, where $\alpha = \max_i \alpha_i$.*

PROOF. The proof is by looking back at the times when each item is last picked and bound the gap iteratively. The details can be found in the appendix. □

We are now ready to prove Theorem 2.1.

PROOF. (**Theorem 2.1**) To see that the solution to the given system is unique, note that $f_i = (\frac{v_i-\mu}{\alpha_i})^+$ (where x^+ denotes $\max(x,0)$, and so $\sum_i(\frac{v_i-\mu}{\alpha_i})^+ = 1$. This must have a unique solution as $\sum_i(\frac{v_i-\mu}{\alpha_i})^+$ is decreasing function of μ and strictly decreasing as long as the sum is positive. Let μ denote the solution to the above system.

We now show $\max_i u_i(t) \ge \mu$ for any t. This is done by contradiction. Suppose that for all i $u_i(t) < \mu$. We have that $\sum_i(\frac{v_i-\mu}{\alpha_i})^+ < \sum_i \frac{v_i-u_i(t)}{\alpha_i}$. But $\sum_i \frac{v_i-u_i(t)}{\alpha_i} = \sum_i M_i(t) \le 1$. We have that $\sum_i(\frac{v_i-\mu}{\alpha_i})^+ < 1$, a contradiction.

Let S_g denote the set of all the items ever picked by the greedy algorithm. Let T be the time by which each item in S_g has been used at least once. By Lemma 3.1, after some steps $\sum_i M_i(t)$ converges to arbitrarily close to 1. Lets assume for simplicity of argument that it is exactly 1 with sufficiently large T. The upper-bound on $\max_i u_i(t)$ follows from Lemma 3.2.

Furthermore there exists $i \in S_g$ such that $u_i(t) \le \mu$ because otherwise it would be the case that $\sum_i(\frac{v_i-u}{\alpha_i})^+ > \sum_i \frac{v_i-u_i(t)}{\alpha_i} = \sum_i M_i(t) \approx 1$, a contradiction. Hence $\max_j u_j(t) = \mu + O(\alpha r \log n)$. □

Using the exactly same argument in the proofs of Theorem 2.1, we can prove that

LEMMA 3.3. *There exists a time T such that for any $t \ge T$, $\mu \le \max_i w_i(t) \le \mu + O(\alpha \log nr)$ where μ is the unique solution to the following system:*

There is an $f_i \ge 0$ for each item such that (1) $\sum f_i = 1$; (2) if $f_i > 0$, $v_i - 2f_i\alpha_i = \mu$, and $v_i < \mu$ otherwise.

To prove the approximation, we formulate a continuous version of the problem whose solution serves as an upper-bound to the utility in the discrete case. By using Lemma 3.3, we show that the double greedy strategy maintains each item's"marginal utility" close to that of the optimal solution from which we obtain the approximation bound.

PROOF. (**Theorem 2.3**) For $0 < f \le 1$, write $\Delta(f) = r \cdot \frac{(1-r)^{1/f}}{1-(1-r)^{1/f}}$.

Let U^* be the optimal value of the following program.

$$\max U = \sum_i f_i(v_i - \alpha_i f_i) \quad \text{s.t.} \quad \sum_i f_i \le 1 \quad \text{and } f_i \ge 0. \tag{1}$$

Let OPT denote the optimal average utility. We have that $OPT \le U^* + \alpha r$. This is by observing that for any $0 < f < 1$, placing an item $1/f$ apart gives an upper bound on the utility of consuming the item with frequency f. The bound is $v - \alpha\Delta(f) \le v - \alpha(r - f)$ by observing that $\Delta(f) > r - f$.

The objective of (1) is maximized when there exists λ such that $\frac{\partial U}{\partial f_i} = \lambda$ for $f_i > 0$ and $\frac{\partial U}{\partial f_i} < \lambda$ for $f_i = 0$, and $\sum_i f_i = 1$. Since $\frac{\partial U}{\partial f_i} = v_i - 2\alpha_i f_i$, λ is exactly the same as μ in the statement of Lemma 3.3. This explains the intuition of the double greedy heuristics — it tries to equalize the marginal utility gain of each item. Denote the optimal solution by f_i^*. Then for $f_i^* > 0$, $v_i - 2\alpha_i f_i^* = \mu$. Hence,

$$U^* = \sum_i f_i^*(v_i - \alpha_i f_i^*) = \sum_i f_i^*(\mu + \alpha_i f_i^*) = \mu + \sum_i \alpha_i {f_i^*}^2.$$

Let k_i denote the number of times item i is used in $[0,T]$ by the double-greedy algorithm, and $f_i = k_i/T$. Let $\overline{M}_i$ denote the average memory on i at the times when i is picked. Then we have that

$$\begin{aligned} \overline{U} &= \sum_{t=0}^{T} u_{x(t)}(t)/T = \sum_i \sum_{x(t)=i} u_i(t)/T \quad (2) \\ &= \sum_i \sum_{x(t)=i} (w_i(t) + \alpha_i M_i(t))/T \\ &\quad \text{(by Lemma 3.3, } w_i(t) \ge \mu) \\ &\ge \sum_i \sum_{x(t)=i} (\mu + \alpha_i M_i(t))/T \ge \mu + \sum_i \alpha_i f_i \overline{M}_i \,. \quad (3) \end{aligned}$$

Write $\delta = \alpha r \log n$. By Lemma 3.3, $w_i(t) = \mu + O(\delta)$ for each i, t. We will show that

Claim 1. $\alpha_i f_i = \alpha_i f_i^* - O(\delta)$. Observe that for any item i which is picked k_i times in $[0,T]$, $\min_{0 \le t \le T} M_i(t) \le$

$\Delta(k_i/T) \leq k_i/T = f_i$. Hence, $\max_t w_i(t) \geq v_i - 2\alpha_i M_i(t) \geq v_i - 2\alpha_i f_i$. On the other hand, $w_i(t) = \mu + O(\delta)$. We have $v_i - 2\alpha_i f_i = \mu + O(\delta)$. But $\mu = v_i - 2\alpha_i f_i^*$. Therefore $\alpha_i f_i \geq \alpha_i f_i^* - O(\delta)$.

Claim 2. $\alpha_i \overline{M}_i = \alpha_i f_i^* - O(\delta)$. Since $v_i - 2\overline{M}_i \leq \mu + \delta$, we obtain the bound by following the same argument as in the proof of Claim 1. Now, plugging both claims into (3), we have that

$$\begin{aligned}\overline{U} &\geq \mu + \sum_i \alpha_i (f_i^* - \frac{O(\delta)}{\alpha_i})^2 \geq \mu + \sum_i \alpha_i f_i^{*2} - O(\delta) \\ &= U^* - O(\delta) = OPT - O(\delta).\end{aligned}$$

This last equality follows from $U^* = OPT - \alpha r$. This completes the proof. □

3.2 Social Choice is equivalent to individual choice

Let **1** denote the vector with all coordinates set to 1 and α_i denote the vector of boredom coefficients α_{ij}.

OBSERVATION 3.1. *For any diagonalizable matrix A with largest eigenvalue 1 and the second largest eigenvalue is at most $1-\epsilon$, there is a vector c so that. $\mathbf{1}'A^t x - c'x \leq (1-\epsilon)^t \sqrt{n} O(|x|_2)$. The O notation hides factors that depends on A. For a real, symmetric matrix the constant is 1.*

PROOF. We will sketch the proof for real symmetric matrices. The same idea holds for non-symmetric matrices. If $p_1, \ldots, p_n$ denote the eigenvectors of A and $1 = \lambda_1, \ldots, \lambda_n$ denote the eigenvalues then $A^t x = \sum_j \lambda_j^t p_i v_i' x = p_1 v_1' x + \sum_{j>1} \lambda^t{}_j p_i' p_i x$. Now,$|\sum_{j>1} \lambda_j^t p_i' p_i x|_2 \leq (1-\epsilon)^t |x|_2$. So $|\mathbf{1}'(A^t x - p_1 p_1' x)| \leq |\mathbf{1}|_2 (1-\epsilon)^t |x|_2 = \sqrt{n}(1-\epsilon)^t |x|_2$ Setting $c = \mathbf{1}' v_1 v_1'$ completes the proof. □

We will now prove theorem 2.4

PROOF. (**Theorem 2.4**) Let $\Delta\mathbf{b}(t)$ denote $\mathbf{b}(t) - \mathbf{b}(t-1)$. Now $\mathbf{u}_i(t) = A\mathbf{u}_i(t-1) + \Delta\mathbf{b}(t)$. This gives, $\mathbf{u}_i(t) = A^t \mathbf{v}_i + \sum_{j=0}^{t-1} A^j \Delta\mathbf{b}(t)$. Note that $W_i(t) = \mathbf{1}'\mathbf{u}_i(t) = \mathbf{1}'A^t\mathbf{v} + \sum_{j=0}^{t-1} \mathbf{1}' A^j \Delta\ b(t-j)$

Note $\Delta b_{ij}(t) = \alpha_{ij}((1-r)M_{ij}(t) + rI_i(t) - M_{ij}(t)) = \alpha_{ij} r(x_i(t) - M_{ij}(t))$. So $|\Delta b_{ij}(t)|_2 \leq r|\alpha_i|_2$.

Now $|\mathbf{1}'A^t\mathbf{v}_i - c'\mathbf{v}_i| \leq (1-\epsilon)^t \sqrt{n} O(|\mathbf{v}_i|_2)$. For $t > (1/\epsilon)\Omega(\log(nr|\mathbf{v}_i|_2)$, this is at most r. Also $|\mathbf{1}A^j\Delta\mathbf{b}_i(t-j) - c'\Delta\mathbf{b}_i(t-j)| \leq (1-\epsilon)^j \sqrt{n} O(|\Delta\mathbf{b}_i(t-j)|_2) \leq (1-\epsilon)^j \sqrt{n} r O(|\alpha_i|_2)$. So, $|\sum_j \mathbf{1}A^j\Delta\mathbf{b}_i(t-j) - \sum_j c'\Delta\mathbf{b}_i(t-j)| \leq (r/\epsilon)\sqrt{n} O(|\alpha_i|_2)$. So, $|\sum_j \mathbf{1}A^j\Delta\mathbf{b}_i(t-j) - c'\ b_i(t)| \leq (r/\epsilon)\sqrt{n} O(|\alpha_i|_2)$. Therefore $|W_i(t) - (c'\mathbf{v}_i - c'\mathbf{b}_i(t))| \leq (r/\epsilon) O(\sqrt{n}|\alpha_i|_2)$. Dividing by n completes the proof. □

4. EXPERIMENTS

We now provide experimental results to study the techniques presented in the paper. Our primary objectives is to evaluate the quality of greedy and double-greedy algorithms for choosing items based on utility and boredom parameters estimated from the real data. In our experiments, we consider three faimilies of fashionable items, namely songs, movies, and popular events. Based on the data from Google Trends [1], we obtain parameters that describe the utility of various items. We then show that double-greedy algorithm outperforms the greedy algorithm consistently.

4.1 Setup

We obtain data on the popularity of songs, movies, and popular events from Google Trends [1]. We collected weekly aggregate counts from query logs for popular songs from the last 5 years. Similar data was collected for popular movies and events too. The event data was gathered by collecting trends on keywords related to major "events" in the last 5 years. While the popularity of each entity depends on additional factors such as awards won by an album or a movie, our goal was to perform a controlled experiment only based on overall utility and boredom. Therefore, for each item we collected weekly aggregate counts starting from the highest peak in logs till there was an "artificial peak" due to an external event such as an award. Further, we compare the utility obtained by our model with a baseline in which the user selects an item simply based on its utility without any discounting from boredom. We describe how we compute the values of α, v, and r in the next section.

Table 1 shows the v, α, and r values for a set of 10 songs used in our experiments while the corresponding data for the movie and event data set is shown in Tables 2 and 3; here we allow different values of r, but we notice that all r-values within the domain of songs and movies are similar. In the case of events, the lambda values are roughly similar (although there is a little more disparity compared to songs and movies).

Song	v	α	r
The Climb	12.3	9.9	0.097
Lucky	2.6	1.58	0.114
Snow Patrol - Chasing Cars	10.7	6.8	0.127
I know you want me	7.95	6.5	0.077
Viva la vida	12.4	9.1	0.16
Stop and stare	10.5	9.4	0.092
Disturbia	8	7.2	0.092
Pocket full of sunshine	7.6	6.3	0.14
Supernatural superserious	24.2	22	0.15
One step at a time	9.35	8.5	0.075

Table 1: v, α, r for the set of songs

4.2 Computing the model parameters

Figure 2 shows the trend observed for a specific song from our dataset, `I Know You Want Me`, over a 45-week period starting August 2, 2009. The first natural observation we make is that the total number of queries do indeed display a steady decline, which we attribute to boredom. From the data, we use the maximum count as the peak utility, v_{peak}, and let the final count be denoted v_{final}. We set $\alpha = v_{peak} - v_{final}$. Let $X(t)$ denote the aggregate count for the week t, we obtain the boredom parameter r using the following equation: $e^{-rt} = 1 - \frac{v_{peak} - X(t)}{v_{peak} - v_{min}}$.

We plot $rt = -\ln(1 - \frac{v_{peak} - X(t)}{v_{peak} - v_{min}})$, and fit a linear line on the resulting curve and obtain r from the slope. Figure 3 shows the curve for `I Know You Want Me`, from which we obtain the r value.

4.3 Results

We ran a set of experiments to verify the effectiveness of the greedy and double-greedy heuristics. We ran the experiments over 100000 steps for both the data sets. The

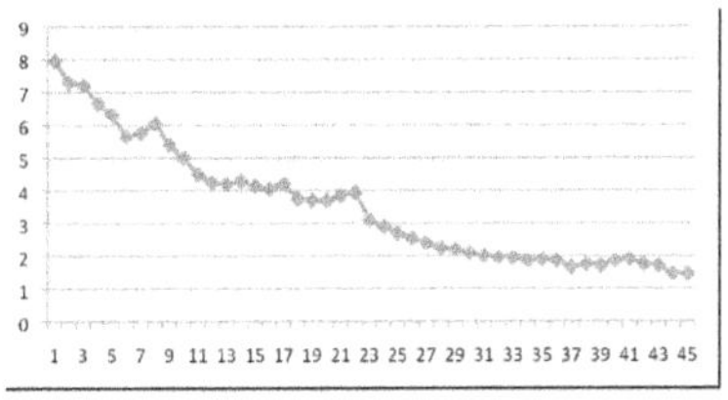

Figure 2: Weekly aggregate query counts for I Know You Want Me for a 45-week period from Google trends

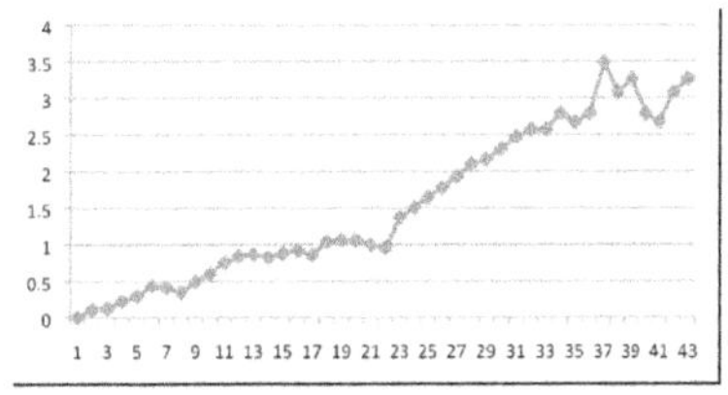

Figure 3: Approximate linear trend for I Know You Want Me, with slope giving r

Movie	v	α	r
Godfather	6.15	5.15	0.123
Hancock	9.6	8.8	0.128
The Bucket List	13.1	11.8	0.102
Quantum of Solace	29.8	29	0.111
Tropic Thunder	25.6	24.8	0.082

Table 2: v, α, r for the set of movies

Event	v	α	r
NASA phoeniz	4.02	3.96	0.32
Copenhagen Summit	27.8	27.4	0.14
H1N1	34.4	34	0.23
Lehman Brothers	33.8	33.6	0.09
Hudson River	18.9	18.1	0.3
Hurricane Katrina	6.3	6.2	0.3
Mumbai Terrorist	3.68	3.66	0.21
Michael Jackson	39.8	38.8	0.1
Haiti	80.5	79.5	0.25
Tsunami	186	184	0.19

Table 3: v, α, r for the set of popular events

average utility obtained by the user for both the data sets was computed and is shown in Table 4. We also show results for the baseline approach that always picks the same item with the highest base utility. Tables 5, 6, and 7 illustrate the average utility obtained by the user over the selected songs and movies respectively. The corresponding normalized frequencies are shown in parenthesis. As expected, in the baseline case where the user selects an item according to its base utility, the movie `Quantum of Solace` (with a base utility of 29.8) is always selected while in the case of songs, the song `supernatual superserious` (with a utility of 24.2) is selected. In the case of events, people always followed `Tsunami` (with a base utility of 186). Unsurprisingly, the average utility discounting boredom in all the cases is very low (see Table 4).

In another experiment, we measured the change in the average utility with time. Figure 4 illustrates the change in average utility as the user selects different items at each time step for movies. Naturally, the utility is highest at the very beginning as the user picks an item with the highest base utility and decreases subsequently as she picks items with highest discounted utility at each time step.

Dataset	Greedy	Double-Greedy	Baseline
Songs	11.94	13.53	5.62
Movies	16.12	17.30	4.25
Events	76.6	88.06	37.74

Table 4: Average utility over 100000 time steps

Song	Greedy	Double-Greedy
The Climb	11.17(0.17)	11.11(0.17)
Snow Patrol - Chasing Cars	- (0)	10.24(0.12)
Viva la vida	11.61(0.17)	11.24(0.21)
Stop and stare	- (0)	10.08(0.08)
Supernatural superserious	12.22(0.67)	17.52(0.40)

Table 5: Avg. utilities (frequencies) for selected songs

Movie	Greedy	Double-Greedy
Hancock	- (0)	9.56(0.04)
The Bucket List	- (0)	11.40(0.20)
Quantum of Solace	16.41(0.55)	20.37(0.40)
Tropic Thunder	15.77(0.45)	18.01(0.36)

Table 6: Avg. utilities (frequencies) for selected movies

Event	Greedy	Double-Greedy
H1N1	- (0)	34.4 (0.03)
Michael Jackson	- (0)	37.81 (0.094)
Haiti	71.35 (0.25)	62.80 (0.38)
Tsunami	78.34 (0.75)	119.60 (0.50)

Table 7: Avg. utilities (frequencies) for selected events

5. FUTURE WORK

As we mentioned, our model is by no means comprehensive. For example, boredom may come from consuming similar items, or there may be a cost when switching from item to item. Taking into account these factors raises some interesting algorithmic issues. Fully incorporating these extensions is left as future work.

Acknowledgments. We thank Atish Das Sarma for useful discussions.

6. REFERENCES

[1] Google Trends. *http://www.google.com/trends.*

[2] Perron Frobenius Theorem. `http://en.wikipedia.org/wiki/Perron-Frobenius_theorem`.

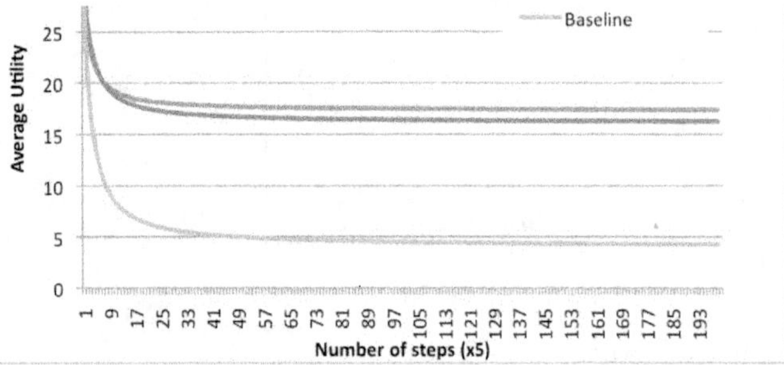

Figure 4: Change in average utility over time.

[3] A. Bar-Noy, R. Bhatia, J. Naor, and B. Schieber. Minimizing service and operation costs of periodic scheduling. *Math. Oper. Res.*, 27(3):518–544, 2002.

[4] B. Barber and L. S. Lobel. Fashion in womens clothing and the american social system. *Social Forces*, 1952.

[5] H. Blumer. Fashion: From class differentiation to collective selection. *Sociological Quarterly*, 1969.

[6] D. Easley and J. Kleinberg. *Networks, Crowds, and Markets: Reasoning About a Highly Connected World.* Cambridge University Press, 2010.

[7] M. P. Grindereng. Fashion diffusion. *Journal of Home Economics*, 1967.

[8] N. Immorlica, J. Kleinberg, M. Mahdian, and T. Wexler. The role of compatibility in the diffusion of technologies through social networks. In *Electronic Commerce*, 2007.

[9] J. K. J. Leskovec, L. Backstrom. Meme-tracking and the dynamics of the news cycle. In *Proc. 15th ACM SIGKDD Intl. Conf. on Knowledge Discovery and Data Mining*, 2009.

[10] J. Leskovec, A. Singh, and J. Kleinberg. Patterns of influence in a recommendation network. In *PAKDD*, 2006.

[11] C. M. Miller, S. H. Mcintyre, and M. K. Mantrala. Toward formalizing fashion theory. *Journal of Market Research*, 1993.

[12] W. H. Reynolds. Cars and clothing: Understanding fashion trends. *Journal of Marketing*, 1968.

APPENDIX

A. PROOF OF LEMMA 3.2

PROOF. Denote by $x(t)$ the item that has the maximum utility at time t. It suffices to show that $u_{x(t)} \leq u_i(t) + O(\alpha r \log n)$ for $i \in S_g$.

We recursively compute a decreasing sequence of t_j as follows. Let $t_1 = t$. For $j > 1$, suppose we have computed t_{j-1}. Let $S_{j-1} = \{x(t_1), x(t_2), \cdots, x(t_{j-1})\}$. Now let $t_j = \max_{t' < t_{j-1}, x(t') \notin S_{j-1}} t'$. We stop when there is k such that $x(t_k) = i$. Since $t > T$, the process is guaranteed to stop. By the above construction, we know only items in S_{j-1} are picked by the greedy algorithm in the interval $[t_j + 1, t_1]$. For any $S \subseteq \{1, \cdots, n\}$, let $A(S,t) = \sum_{\ell \in S} \frac{u_\ell(t)}{\alpha_\ell}$, and $B(S) = \sum_{\ell \in S} \frac{1}{\alpha_\ell}$. We will show that for $1 < j \leq k$,

$$A(S_{j-1}, t_{j-1}) \leq \frac{B(S_{j-1})}{B(S_j)} A(S_j, t_j) + r\,. \tag{4}$$

First observe that

$$A(S,t) = \sum_{\ell \in S} \frac{u_\ell(t)}{\alpha_\ell} = \sum_{\ell \in S} \frac{V_\ell - \alpha_\ell M_\ell(t)}{\alpha_\ell} = \sum_{\ell \in S} \frac{V_\ell}{\alpha_\ell} - \sum_{\ell \in S} M_\ell(t)\,. \tag{5}$$

(4) follows from the following claims.

Claim 1. $A(S_{j-1}, t_{j-1}) \leq A(S_{j-1}, t_j + 1)$.

Since any item picked by the greedy algorithm in $[t_j + 1, t_{j-1}]$ is in S_{j-1}, we have that for $t' \in [t_j + 1, t_{j-1})$,

$$\begin{aligned} \sum_{\ell \in S_{j-1}} M_\ell(t'+1) &= (1-r) \sum_{\ell \in S_{j-1}} M_\ell(t') + r \\ &\geq \sum_{\ell \in S_{j-1}} M_\ell(t')\,. \end{aligned}$$

The last inequality is by $\sum_\ell M_\ell(t') \leq 1$. Therefore

$$\sum_{\ell \in S_{j-1}} M_\ell(t_{j-1}) \geq \sum_{\ell \in S_{j-1}} M_\ell(t_j + 1)\,.$$

By (5), we have $A(S_{j-1}, t_{j-1}) \leq A(S_{j-1}, t_j + 1)$.

Claim 2. $A(S_{j-1}, t_j + 1) \leq A(S_j, t_j) + r$.

Since $t_j \notin S_{j-1}$ is the item picked by the greedy algorithm at t_j, $\sum_{\ell \in S_{j-1}} M_\ell(t_j + 1) = (1-r) \sum_{\ell \in S_{j-1}} M_\ell(t_j)$. Thus $\sum_{\ell \in S_{j-1}} M_\ell(t_j + 1) - \sum_{\ell \in S_{j-1}} M_\ell(t_j) = r \sum_{\ell \in S_{j-1}} M_\ell(t_j) \leq r$. Again by (5), we have $A(S_{j-1}, t_j + 1) \leq A(S_j, t_j) + r$.

Claim 3. $A(S_{j-1}, t_j) \leq \frac{B(S_{j-1})}{B(S_j)} A(S_j, t_j)$.

Immediately follows from $u_{t_j}(t_j) \geq u_\ell(t_j)$ for $\ell \in S_{j-1}$. Repeating (4), we have that

$$\begin{aligned} &A(S_{j-1}, t_{j-1}) \\ \leq\; & \frac{B(S_{j-1})}{B(S_j)} A(S_j, t_j) + r \\ \leq\; & \frac{B(S_{j-1})}{B(S_j)} \left(\frac{B(S_j)}{B(S_{j+1})} A(S_{j+1}, t_{j+1}) + r \right) + r \\ =\; & \frac{B(S_{j-1})}{B(S_{j+1})} A(S_{j+1}, t_{j+1}) + r \cdot \frac{B(S_{j-1})}{B(S_j)} + r \cdots \\ \leq\; & \frac{B(S_{j-1})}{B(S_k)} A(S_k, t_k) + r \cdot \sum_{\ell = j-1}^{k-1} \frac{B(S_{j-1})}{B(S_\ell)}\,. \end{aligned}$$

Hence, we have that

$$\begin{aligned} &u_{x(t_1)}(t_1) \\ =\; & \alpha_1 A(S_1, t_1) \leq \alpha_1 \left(\frac{B(S_1)}{B(S_k)} A(S_k, t_k) + r \cdot \sum_{\ell=1}^{k-1} \frac{B(S_1)}{B(S_\ell)} \right) \\ =\; & \frac{1}{B(S_k)} A(S_k, t_k) + r \cdot \sum_{\ell=1}^{k-1} \frac{1}{B(S_\ell)}\,. \end{aligned}$$

Since $i = x(t_k)$, for any i', $u_{i'}(t_k) \leq u_i(t_k)$. Therefore $A(S_k, t_k) = \sum_{j \in S_k} \frac{u_j(t_k)}{\alpha_j} \leq u_i(t_k) \sum_{j \in S_k} \frac{1}{\alpha_j} = u_i(t_k) B(S_k)$.

By that $\alpha = \max_i \alpha_i$, we have $B(S_\ell) \le \ell/\alpha$. Hence

$$\begin{aligned} u_{x(t_1)}(t_1) &\le \frac{1}{B(S_k)} A(S_k, t_k) + r \cdot \sum_{\ell=1}^{k-1} \frac{1}{B(S_\ell)} \\ &\le u_i(t_k) + \alpha r \sum_{\ell=1}^{k-1} 1/\ell \\ &= u_i(t_k) + O(\alpha r \log n)\,. \end{aligned}$$

Since item i is not used during the interval of $[t_k + 1, t_1]$, we have $u_i(t_k+1) \le u_i(t_1)$, and hence $u_i(t_k) \le u_i(t_k+1) + \alpha_i r \le u_i(t_1) + \alpha_i r$. Therefore we have that, $\max_j u_j(t_1) = u_{x(1)}(t_1) \le u_i(t_1) + O(\alpha r \log n)$.

□

B. PROOF OF THEOREM 2.2

Restatement of Theorem 2.2: It is NP-hard to decide, given T, and U^*, and n items, whether there exist a assignment Y with period T such that $U(Y) \ge U^*$.

PROOF. The reduction is from the following problem.

Regular assignment problem (RAP). Given positive integers $p_1, p_2, \cdots, p_n$, determine if there exists a sequence $y_0, y_1, \cdots$ where $y_t \in \{0, 1, \cdots, n\}$ such that for any $i \ne 0$, two consecutive appearances of i in the sequence are exactly p_i apart.

It is shown in [3] that the regular assignment problem is NP-complete. Note that for RAP, a regular assignment exists if and only if it does so on a cycle with length $T = \prod_i p_i$. We will now reduce it to the optimal fashion selection problem.

Given $p_1, \cdots, p_n$, we create $n+1$ items such that a regular assignment, if exists, maximizes the utility of any periodic selection with period T. Hence we can reduce RAP to the optimal selection problem. Item 0 is a special item with $v_0 = 1$ and $\alpha_i = 0$. For $1 \le i \le n$, we assign $v_i = \frac{2T}{p_i}$ and $\alpha_i = 1$. Further let $r_i = 1/T$ for $1 \le i \le n$. We claim that there exists U^* and $\epsilon \ge 1/T^2$ such that for a regular assignment Y, $U(Y) \ge U^*$, and $U(Y) < U^* - \epsilon$ otherwise.

Consider the case when there is only item and when the selections are made on the real line. Given T and an item with parameters v, α, r, let $\mathcal{Y}_k(v, \alpha, r)$ be the set of all the selections which have period T and choose the item exactly k times on the real interval $[0, T)$. Denote by $U_k(v, \alpha, r) = \max_{Y \in \mathcal{Y}_k(v,\alpha,r)} U(Y)$ and $\delta U_k(v, \alpha, r) = U_k(v, \alpha, r) - U_{k-1}(v, \alpha, r)$. The correctness of the reduction follows from the following claims.

Claim 1. $U_k(v, \alpha, r) = kv - k\alpha \frac{(1-r)^{T/k}}{1-(1-r)^{T/k}}$, and the maximum is achieved with the regular assignment.

Claim 2. For $1 \le v \le n$, $U_k(v_i, 1, 1/T) = kv_i - (k^2 - \frac{1}{2}k + \frac{1}{12} + o(1/k))$, and $\delta U_k(v_i, 1, 1/T) = v_i - (2k - \frac{3}{2} + o(1/k))$.

Claim 3. For any non-regular **integral** selection $Y \in \mathcal{Y}_k(v_i, 1, 1/T)$, $U(Y) < U_k(v_i, 1, 1/T) - 1/T^2$.

Claim 1 holds because the total memory is minimized when the k assignments are regularly spaced. Claim 2 is a direct consequence of Claim 1 by Taylor expansion on those particular parameters. Claim 3 follows by comparing the memory caused by adjacent items between regular and non-regular assignments.

From Claim 2, we can see that $\delta U_k(v_i, 1, 1/T) \ge 3/2$ for $k \le T/p_i$ and < 0 for $k \ge T/p_i + 1$ for $1 \le i \le n$, and $\delta U_k(v_0, 0, 1/T) = 1$. Combining it with Claim 3, we have that the utility gap between a regular and non-regular assignment is at least $1/T^2$. Therefore the reduction is correct and can be done in polynomial time.

□

Maximizing Product Adoption in Social Networks

Smriti Bhagat Amit Goyal Laks V. S. Lakshmanan

University of British Columbia
Vancouver, BC, Canada
{smritib,goyal,laks}@cs.ubc.ca

ABSTRACT

One of the key objectives of viral marketing is to identify a small set of users in a social network, who when convinced to adopt a product will influence others in the network leading to a large number of adoptions in an expected sense. The seminal work of Kempe et al. [13] approaches this as the problem of influence maximization. This and other previous papers tacitly assume that a user who is influenced (or, informed) about a product necessarily adopts the product and encourages her friends to adopt it. However, an influenced user may not adopt the product herself, and yet form an opinion based on the experiences of her friends, and share this opinion with others. Furthermore, a user who adopts the product may not like it and hence not encourage her friends to adopt it to the same extent as another user who adopted and liked the product. This is independent of the extent to which those friends are influenced by her. Previous works do not account for these phenomena.

We argue that it is important to distinguish product adoption from influence. We propose a model that factors in a user's experience (or projected experience) with a product. We adapt the classical Linear Threshold (LT) propagation model by defining an objective function that explicitly captures product adoption, as opposed to influence. We show that under our model, adoption maximization is NP-hard and the objective function is monotone and submodular, thus admitting an approximation algorithm. We perform experiments on three real popular social networks and show that our model is able to distinguish between influence and adoption, and predict product adoption much more accurately than the classical LT model.

Categories and Subject Descriptors H.2.8 [Database Management]: Database Applications - *Data Mining*
General Terms: Algorithms, Theory, Experimentation.
Keywords: Product adoption, Influence, Viral marketing.

1. INTRODUCTION

One of the fundamental problems in viral marketing is to identify a small set of individuals in a social network, who when convinced to adopt a product will influence others in the network through a word-of-mouth effect, leading to a large number of adoptions in an expected sense. Previous works such as [13] approached this as the problem of *influence maximization* where, given a social network represented by a directed graph with users as nodes, edges corresponding to social ties, and edge weights capturing influence probabilities, the goal is to find a *seed set* of k users such that by targeting these, the *expected influence spread* (defined as the expected number of influenced users) is maximized. Here, the expected influence spread of a seed set depends on the influence diffusion process which is captured by a model for influence propagation. While several propagation models exist, two classical models, namely Linear Threshold (LT) and Independent Cascade (IC), have been widely studied in the literature. In this work, we focus on the LT model. In the LT model, a user is either in an inactive or an active state. An active user influences each of its inactive neighbors. The activation of an inactive user depends on the influence probabilities associated with its active neighbors. Each user v picks an activation threshold θ_v uniformly at random from $[0, 1]$. At any time step, if the sum of incoming weights from its active neighbors exceeds the threshold, v becomes active. The process continues until no more activations are possible.

In the bulk of the influence maximization literature in data mining, it is assumed that once a user is active (i.e., is influenced), she will automatically and unconditionally adopt the product. In this sense, influence spread is viewed as equivalent to adoption spread (expected number of users who adopt the product). Clearly, product (or technology/innovation) adoption is the main goal in viral marketing, and influence spread is essentially used as a "proxy" for adoption. We argue that it is important to distinguish between influence and adoption, an idea well established in other domains like Sociology and Marketing. Bohlen et al. [2] in 1957 proposed five stages of product adoption in which the adoption stage is considered different than the awareness stage. Kalish [12] characterized the adoption of a new product as consisting of two steps – awareness and adoption – and argued that the awareness information spreads in an epidemic-like manner while the actual adoption depends on other factors such as price and individual's valuation of the product. Given these studies in other traditional domains, the current influence maximization work in the data mining community lags behind in modeling such phenomena. Our work is a step towards building a more realistic model of product adoption.

More concretely, previous literature (in data mining) on influence maximization makes three assumptions. First, once a user is influenced, she will immediately adopt the

Permission to make digital or hard copies of all or part of this work for personal or classroom use is granted without fee provided that copies are not made or distributed for profit or commercial advantage and that copies bear this notice and the full citation on the first page. To copy otherwise, to republish, to post on servers or to redistribute to lists, requires prior specific permission and/or a fee.
WSDM'12, February 8–12, 2012, Seattle, Washington, USA.
Copyright 2012 ACM 978-1-4503-0747-5/12/02 ...$10.00.

product. Second, it is assumed that once a user adopts a product, she encourages her friends to adopt it as well, irrespective of whether or how much she likes the product. In other words, adoption of a product implies that the user likes it regardless of her experience with it. Third, only after a user adopts a product, she shares her opinion on the product and attempts to influence her neighbors. That is, non-adopters either don't have any opinions on the product or such opinions are not visible to others. These assumptions may not hold in general as illustrated by the following examples.

Example 1. Bob buys an Amazon Kindle and dislikes the product. He posts his experience on his blog and describes the missing features. Kali, a friend of Bob, takes Bob's opinions on technology products seriously. She learns about the Kindle from the post and decides *not* to buy it. Furthermore, she blogs about the product not meeting her expectations and in turn influences the decisions of her friends. □

Example 2. Bob watches the movie "The Ring" and likes it. He tells his friend Kali that the movie is great. Kali doesn't get a chance to watch the movie, but tells her friend Charles about the movie. Charles gets influenced and watches it. □

In Example 1, Bob doesn't like the product and shares his opinion with his friends. Thus, opinions can emerge from a user experience with a product and can propagate from an adopter. Specifically, if a user does not like the product, their endorsement of the product is unlikely to be strong, a fact that may be noticed by their neighbors. Even when a user is strongly influenced by her neighbor, if the endorsement is weak, the user is less likely to adopt the product. The propagation of information to a user does not always lead to product adoption. There may be many factors that affect a user's adoption decision, including the user's interests, budget and time. Indeed, opinions can propagate from a non-adopter who is active (e.g., Kali in Example 2) and can promote adoption by others. In this example Kali acts as an "information bridge" or a *tattler*, who talks about the product without actually adopting it. How does the presence of such non-adopters who act as information bridges affect the overall adoption? Does the product adoption depend on the opinions, in addition to social influence? These are some of the questions this paper addresses.

In particular, we argue that the classical propagation models that make the three assumptions above may predict a product adoption quite different from reality, a point we will establish empirically using three real data sets. This motivates re-examining these assumptions and allowing for the following facts: (i) adopters' opinions may strongly affect the degree to which they influence their neighbors' adoption and (ii) non-adopters acting as an information bridge can contribute their own opinions, which too can affect influence propagation as well as adoption. We use user ratings of products as an abstraction of their opinions. Ratings are either provided by the user or can be predicted using collaborative filtering [14]. Therefore, the extent to which a user is influenced by her neighbors (to become active) is a function, not only of the influence probabilities but of the ratings of the neighbors as well. In this paper, we study an interesting variation of the classical influence maximization problem with an aim to *maximize the number of product adoptions* and make the following contributions.

- We study the novel problem of maximizing product adoption, a more natural goal of applications like viral marketing. We present an intuitive model called LT-C, for *LT with Colors*, that captures these intuitions. We show that the problem of product adoption maximization is NP-hard but the objective function, i.e., the expected number of product adoptions, is monotone and submodular; thus the greedy algorithm provides a $(1-1/e-\epsilon)$-approximation to the optimal solution. We also propose methods to learn parameters of our model (Section 3).
- We study two types of networks – movies networks (Section 4.1) and music networks (Section 4.2) using three real world datasets. We found that in almost all instances, the classical LT model significantly over-predicts the spread. Moreover, it predicts the same spread for all the products. We demonstrate that our LT-C model, by incorporating ratings, significantly improves the accuracy of these predictions.
- In all the three datasets, we found that there is a positive correlation between the number of initiators (users who first express opinions among their friend circles) and the final spread, suggesting that the network structure plays a significant role in the spread. We demonstrate that the choice of seed nodes is critical and can make a significant difference to the spread achieved. We also found that largely, the seed sets are different for different products, though some influential users are picked up consistently as seeds irrespective of the product being marketed (Section 4).

We review related work in Section 2 and present conclusions in Section 5.

2. BACKGROUND AND RELATED WORK

Background. In 2001, Domingos et al. [6] introduced the the problem of identifying influential users to the data mining community. Kempe et al. [13] formalized it as the problem of influence maximization as described above. In particular, their work focuses on two propagation models – Linear Threshold (LT) Model and Independent Cascade (IC) Model. The influence maximization problem is NP-hard under both the LT and IC models [13], and the expected influence spread function is monotone and submodular. Formally, a set function f is submodular iff $f(S+\{x\})-f(S) \geq f(T+\{x\})-f(T)$ whenever $S \subseteq T \subset V$ and $x \in V \setminus T$, where V is the set of all users. Exploiting these properties, Kempe et al. [13] showed that a simple greedy algorithm, which iteratively adds a user with the maximum marginal gain to the current seed set, guarantees a $(1-1/e-\epsilon)$-approximation to the optimal solution, for any $\epsilon > 0$. Our work adapts the framework of the LT model for product adoption in the presence of non-adopters who may promote or inhibit the adoption by sharing their opinions.

Related Work. One related problem is that of revenue maximization, studied by Hartline et al. [10]. They offer a family of strategies based on an *influence and exploit* paradigm that work as follows. In the first step, called the *influence* step, the seller gives the item to a chosen set of customers for free. Then in the *exploit* step, the seller visits the remaining buyers in a random sequence and offers each buyer a price that is expected to maximize her revenue. Their model allows the seller to bypass the network structure and visit arbitrary buyers at any time. While revenue maximization, in principle, is closely related to adoption maximization, and arguably should subsume the latter, there are the following key differences with our work. We explicitly model the following phenomena observed in real data sets: first, users may be activated but not necessarily adopt/buy a product and instead may tattle about it; second, opinions shared by tattlers may promote adoption by other users; third, sometimes, tattlers may choose to inhibit adoption by other users by sharing the poor ratings they gave for the product.

Another closely related problem is that influence maximization in the presence of negative opinions (see Chen et al. [3]). Their model, called IC-N, builds on the classical IC model by subdividing the active state into two sub-states, positive and negative, while preserving the properties of monotonicity and submodularity. They incorporate the spread of negative opinions with a parameter q that models the quality of the product. The model assumes that the parameter q is the same across all users, an assumption that is not always realistic. Unfortunately, this assumption is essential to their framework, since if the parameter q is allowed to be different for different users (indicating users like the product to differing degrees), their objective function is no longer monotone and submodular, thus, the greedy algorithm fails to provide any approximation guarantee. In our work, we argue that influence propagation depends on the extent to which a user likes the product, in addition to the influence weights among users. Furthermore, we claim that in a network, there exist information bridges, or *tattlers* who propagate the influence without adopting the product themselves. We show that these tattlers are indeed present in real data sets and their presence makes a significant difference to product adoption. A key feature of our model is that not only do we allow the probability of liking a product to be different for different users, we do so while retaining the monotonicity and submodularity of the objective function.

Tang et al. [18] recognize that influence varies with the domain/topic of an item. They present a scalable approach based on MapReduce for learning topic-specific social influence weights from a given social graph and topic distribution. By contrast, in our work, we recognize the reality that user tastes and opinions can be not just topic specific but even item specific and take that into account in our model.

In addition to social influence, *homophily* (or *selection*) has been shown to be a possible cause of users' actions. While some (e.g., [1]) focus on distinguishing the effects of influence and homophily, others (e.g., [5], [15]) showed the feedback effects that both factors have on each other. In particular, Crandall et al. [5] argued that both influence and homophily can be useful in predicting users' future behavior. In our work, we are interested in building a model that predicts the users' actions, in particular, users' adoption of products, without necessarily distinguishing the causes, and use it to develop algorithms that maximize the number of adoptions. Following [12], we argue that while information (or influence) spreads in an epidemic-like manner, actual adoption depends on various other factors. We separate the state of adoption from the state of being influenced (or active) in the LT model. Clearly, for the model to work, it is important that the underlying network structure represent the flow of information, irrespective of whether it corresponds to an explicit social graph (where the links are formed explicitly by users, e.g., friendship links in Facebook), an implicit social graph (where the information flows among users indirectly, e.g., as in recommendation engines like Movielens, Amazon etc.), or a combination of the two.

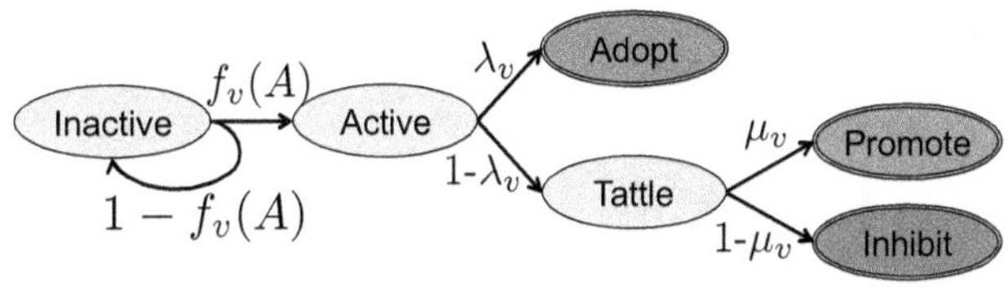

Figure 1: LT-C model with colored end states: adopt–green, promote–blue, inhibit–red

A recent work by Goyal et al. [8] also focuses on predicting the users' actions, while offering an alternative "data-based" approach that bypasses the propagation models to estimate the spread. The same authors [7] study the problem of learning influence probabilities based on the past propagation traces, paying special attention to the temporal nature of influence probabilities. In other work, Chen et al. [4] have proposed an efficient heuristic for influence maximization under the LT model, which is recently improved by [9].

3. PROPOSED FRAMEWORK

Let $G = (V, E, W)$ be a weighted, directed graph with nodes (users) V and edges (social ties) E, where the influence weights are captured by the function $W : E \to [0,1]$. The weight $w_{u,v}$ associated with an edge $(u,v) \in E$ represents the probability of user u influencing user v, such that the sum of incoming edge weights at any node is no greater than 1. That is, $\sum_{u \in N^{in}(v)} w_{u,v} \leq 1$, where $N^{in}(v)$ is the set of in-neighbors of user v. In addition, we assume that a matrix R of Users × Products is given where each entry $r_{u,i}$ denotes the rating given by user u to the product i. We assume whenever ratings are missing, they are predicted using collaborative filtering. The higher the rating, the more positive the opinion.

Intuitively, a user's decision to adopt a product should not only depend on the influence of neighbors, but also on what they think about the product, as captured by the ratings. Next, we describe our model that we call LT-C model, for *Linear Threshold with Colors.*

3.1 LT-C Model

Figure 1 gives an overview of our model in the form of a state diagram. An INACTIVE node v has not yet formed an opinion of the new product and is open to being influenced by neighbors. A node is ACTIVE if it is influenced by its neighbors. Let A be the set of ACTIVE in-neighbors of node v and $f_v(A)$ denote the activation function of v, that is, the total influence on v from nodes in A s.t. $0 \leq f_v(A) \leq 1$. Values of $f_v(A)$ close to 1 can be thought of as a collective "recommendation" of ACTIVE neighbors of u strongly favoring the product. On the hand, values of $f_v(A)$ that are close to 0 represent that neighbors of u collectively disapprove the product. As with the LT model, an INACTIVE node v picks an *activation threshold* θ_v uniformly at random from $[0,1]$ and if $f_v(A) \geq \theta_v$ then v becomes ACTIVE, else v remains INACTIVE. We instantiate the activation function as follows,

$$f_v(A) = \frac{\sum_{u \in A} w_{u,v}(r_{u,i} - r_{\min})}{r_{\max} - r_{\min}} \quad (1)$$

where $r_{\max}$ and $r_{\min}$ represent the maximum and minimum ratings in the system, respectively. Intuitively, this definition corresponds to treating, for each edge (u, v) in the graph, the effective influence weight of u on v as $w_{u,v}(r_{u,i} - r_{\min})/(r_{\max} - r_{\min})$, where i is the product being marketed.

Once a node is in the ACTIVE state, it has enough information about the product and has formed an opinion. At this stage, the node can choose to *adopt* the product and rate it, or decide to share its opinion without adopting the product i.e., *tattle*. With some probability λ_v, an activated node v enters the ADOPT state (or adopts) and is colored *green*, and with probability $1 - \lambda_v$, node v enters the TATTLE state (or tattles). Intuitively, the parameter λ_v models the likelihood of a node adopting the product after it has been activated by its neighbors. There are several real world factors that can be modeled into λ_v, such as a user's budget, interests and purchase history. Note that the parameter λ_v is specific to each node v. If the node decides to ADOPT, it provides a rating $r_{v,i}$ for the product i being marketed. In Section 3.4, we propose methods to learn these parameters.

The TATTLE state is an interesting one. It represents a typical gossipmonger who has not experienced the product but is expressing an *acquired* opinion. Such a node is likely to be biased one way or the other. We say a tattler (node in the TATTLE state) can either enter the PROMOTE state (color *blue*) or the INHIBIT state (color *red*) depending on its disposition parameterized by μ_v, specific to v. In other words, v enters the PROMOTE state with probability μ_v and INHIBIT stat with probability $1 - \mu_v$. For instance, consider a user who loves (or hates) the iPhone and owns one already. When the latest model is launched, even though the user is not ready to buy it, the user has some strongly biased opinion of the product which the user shares with his friends. We model this bias in opinion by representing it with a constant rating of $r_{\max}$ for a user in the PROMOTE state and $r_{\min}$ for a user in the INHIBIT state. A node in the PROMOTE or INHIBIT state propagates information but does not directly contribute to the revenue. The node's actions however may stimulate or inhibit adoption by its neighbors, thus proving to be an important information bridge in the network. Finally, we should mention that of the states in Figure 1, only the INACTIVE, ADOPT, PROMOTE and INHIBIT states may be observable in a real data set. The intermediate states are used for modeling purposes only.

The dynamics followed by the process of opinion propagation at discrete time steps are as follows. At time $t = 0$, a set S of k nodes is chosen as the *seed set* and are said to be active, and each seed node can choose any of the three states ADOPT, PROMOTE or INHIBIT. At $t > 0$, each node u that activated (ADOPT, PROMOTE or INHIBIT state) at time t, contributes to the activation of its neighbors v where $(u, v) \in E$. Let A_t denote the neighbors of v that are ACTIVE at time t, then the total influence on node v at time t is $f_v(A_t)$. If the ACTIVE neighbors push $f_v(A_t)$ over the threshold θ_v, then v becomes ACTIVE, else it remains INACTIVE. Once in ACTIVE state, the node follows the path to enter one of ADOPT, PROMOTE or INHIBIT states and stays in that state with corresponding probabilities. Also, each ACTIVE node provides a rating of the product that is factored into the activation function. Thus, once a node becomes active, it enters one of these states. A_{t+1} is the set of all nodes that become active as a result of the influence from their neighbors in A_t. The process of node activation stops if at some time step no new nodes can be activated.

3.2 Maximizing Product Adoption

We define the *expected spread* (or *spread* for short) of the seed set S as the expected number of ADOPT nodes in the network at the end of the propagation and denote it $\sigma(S)$. We sometimes refer to $\sigma(S)$ as the *coverage* of set S.

Problem 1 (Maximizing Product Adoption). *Given a social graph $G = (V, E, B)$, a parameter k, and a ratings matrix R and parameters $\lambda_v, \mu_v, \forall v \in V$, the problem of maximizing product adoption is to find a seed set S of k nodes such that by activating these nodes, the expected spread under LT-C model is maximized.*

Not surprisingly, the problem is NP-hard. However, as we will show, the spread function is monotone and submodular, so a simple greedy algorithm leads to a $(1 - 1/e - \epsilon)$-approximation to the optimum, for any $\epsilon > 0$.

Theorem 1. *Problem 1 is NP-hard.*

PROOF. Consider the restricted class of instances of the problem where $\forall v \in V, \lambda_v = 1$ and $r_{v,i} = r_{max}$. The problem of maximizing product adoption over this class of instances is equivalent to the classical problem of influence maximization under the LT model, which is known to be NP-hard [13]. The theorem follows. □

Theorem 2. *The spread function $\sigma(\cdot)$ under LT-C model is monotone and submodular.*

PROOF. It is straightforward to show that $\sigma(\cdot)$ is monotone. To establish submodularity, our proof outline follows that in [13]. The challenge in our case is two-fold: (1) There are four possible observable states of nodes – INACTIVE (gray), ADOPT (green), PROMOTE (blue), and INHIBIT (red) in place of just two; (2) The activation of a node depends on the state of its in-neighbors. The reason is that the influence of a node u on its neighbor v is a combination of the weight $w_{u,v}$ and the rating of u. This rating depends on u's state: it's r_{min} in the red state, r_{max} in the blue state, and a value $r_{u,i}$ obtained from R in the green state. Thus, u's state affects the extent of u's influence on its neighbors.

Borrowing the idea of a live edge model from [13], we define a timed version of the live edge selection process for the purpose of this proof. Start by activating the seed nodes S in G and color them as follows: for any $u \in S$, color u green w.p. λ_u, blue w.p. $(1-\lambda_u)\mu_u$, and red w.p. $(1-\lambda_u)(1-\mu_u)$. At any time $t > 0$, allow each uncolored out-neighbor v of a colored node to choose at most one of its in-neighbors z w.p. $p_{z,v}$ and no in-neighbor w.p. $\sum_{y \in N^{in}(v)} w_{y,v} = 1$. If the chosen in-neighbor is colored, then color v green w.p. λ_v, blue w.p. $(1 - \lambda_v)\mu_v$, and red w.p. $(1 - \lambda_v)(1 - \mu_v)$. Otherwise, don't record the choice. That is, if the chosen in-neighbor is not colored, we don't record the choice of the in-neighbor, but constrain future choices of in-neighbors by v, if any, to be outside the set of nodes colored by time $t - 1$. Term each chosen edge i.e., edge to the chosen colored neighbor as a *live edge*. Other edges are blocked/dead. A *live path* is a path made of only live edges. Stop the process when there is no change. This process produces a distribution over possible worlds. Let X be one such possible world. We will show that $\sigma(S) = \sum_X Pr[X]\sigma_X(S)$, where $\sigma_X(S)$ is the number of green nodes reachable from the seed nodes S via live paths in the possible world X. It is easy to see that $\sigma_X(.)$ is monotone and submodular, from which the theorem follows, since a non-negative linear combination of submodular functions is submodular. To show that $\sigma(S) = \sum_X Pr[X]\sigma_X(S)$, we will show that the probability distributions of sets of green/blue/red nodes obtained by running the LT-C model are identical to those obtained from the above process.

We step through the diffusion process according to the LT-C model and determine the probability with which any node v turns green, blue or red. Let each node v pick its threshold θ_v uniformly at random from $[0,1]$. Let S_t be the set of ACTIVE (colored) nodes at time $t = 0, 1, 2, \ldots$, with $S_0 = S$. The probability with which an uncolored node v will be colored at time $t+1$ is the likelihood that a neighbor u that got colored at time t pushes the total influence on v over the threshold θ_v. We denote this probability of v getting colored at time $t+1$ as ψ_v^{t+1}. Therefore,

$$Pr[v \text{ got colored at time } t+1] = \psi_v^{t+1} = \frac{\sum_{u \in S_t \setminus S_{t-1}} p_{u,v}}{1 - \sum_{u \in S_{t-1}} p_{u,v}}$$

Once a node v is ACTIVE, its color depends solely on the parameters λ_v and μ_v and so we have:

$$Pr[v \text{ turns green at } t+1] = \lambda_v \cdot \psi_v^{t+1}$$
$$Pr[v \text{ turns blue at } t+1] = (1-\lambda_v) \cdot \mu_v \cdot \psi_v^{t+1}$$
$$Pr[v \text{ turns red at } t+1] = (1-\lambda_v) \cdot (1-\mu_v) \cdot \psi_v^{t+1}$$

Next, we consider the timed version of the live edge selection process defined above and iterate through the corresponding process. Let $S'_0 = S$ be the seed set. Let S'_t, $t \geq 0$, denote the set of nodes that is colored at time t according to this process. Let $v \notin S$ be any node. The probability that it got colored at time $t+1$, denoted by ϕ_v^{t+1}, is the probability with which its chosen in-neighbor u got colored at time t, given that v was not colored before time $t+1$. More precisely,

$$Pr[v \text{ got colored at time } t+1] = \phi_v^{t+1} = \frac{\sum_{u \in S'_t \setminus S'_{t-1}} p_{u,v}}{1 - \sum_{u \in S'_{t-1}} p_{u,v}}$$

Applying induction on time, it is easy to see that the distributions of ACTIVE (i.e., colored) sets of nodes obtained from running the LT-C model, $S_t, t \geq 0$, and the sets of nodes reachable from the seed nodes S by live paths, $S'_t, t \geq 0$, are identical. Given the equivalence between the distributions over S_t and S'_t, it follows that $\phi_v^{t+1} = \psi_v^{t+1}$. Since the color acquired by an ACTIVE node solely depends on the parameters λ_v, μ_v, the distributions of nodes colored green, blue, and red under the LT-C model and under the timed live edge selection process are identical. This was to be shown. □

3.3 Choosing Optimal Seed Set

While product adption maximization is NP-hard, as shown by Theorem 2, the spread function $\sigma(S)$ under the LT-C model is monotone and submodular. Thus, we can employ a simple greedy algorithm which repeatedly picks a node with the maximum marginal gain and adds it to the seed set, until the budget k is reached. Furthermore, since the LT model is a special case of the LT-C model (corresponding to $\lambda_v = 1, \forall v$ and $r_{v,i} = r_{\max}, \forall v$), the #P-hardness [4] of computing the spread of a given seed set carries over to our setting. To mitigate this, we employ Monte Carlo simulation for estimating the spread. Finally, we adapt the CELF algorithm of Leskovec et al. [16]. The idea behind CELF is that the marginal gain of a node cannot increase in subsequent iterations (due to submodularity) and thus the spread of seed sets is computed in a lazy forward manner, speeding up the greedy algorithm considerably. Our implementation is based on these ideas. The adaptation of CELF to LT-C model is trivial and we omit the details. It is well known that this approach yields a $(1 - 1/e - \epsilon)$-approximation to the optimum, for any $\epsilon > 0$.

3.4 Learning Model Parameters

Edge Weights. As in [7], we learn influence weights from the past behavior of users. For example, consider a log of ratings in which each tuple is of the form $\langle u, i, t, r \rangle$, saying user u rated an item i at time t with rating r. There are several cases where such information is readily available in the real world. For example, consider a movie recommender system (see Section 4 for the complete case study), then an action can be considered as "user rating a movie". Seeing friends' ratings, one may be influenced to watch the movie and in turn, rate the movie at a later timestamp. Hence, the influence weight on an edge (u, v) is learnt as the fraction of times user v rated an item after u had done so, and normalized over all neighbors x of v such that $\sum_{x \in N^{in}(v)} w_{x,v} = 1$.

Ratings Matrix. We compute the ratings matrix R using collaborative filtering. Several sophisticated collaborative filtering methods have been proposed by the recommender systems community for predicting the rating of a user for a given item or product. Matrix factorization [14] is one such popular method. The input to matrix factorization is a very large sparse matrix of user ratings with a large number of missing values corresponding to users who have not rated a product. The main task is to predict these missing ratings. An assumption made is that some small number of ratings are available for each product. In the context of our problem, we maintain the assumption that the new product which we want to push in the market has been adopted by some small number of early adopters, who have assigned ratings to the product. This is commonly seen when new products are launched, for instance, technology bloggers get a sneak-peak of new products at tech-media events and they blog about those products. Often, linux operating system and even Google services are first released as beta versions to selected users for product analysis and to get initial feedback before launching to the public. In this paper, we make use of product ratings by users (either provided by users or predicted by recommender algorithms) as a way of modeling the user opinion of a product.

Node Parameters λ and μ. Recall that an active user v enters the ADOPT state with probability λ_v and it enters the TATTLE state with probability $1 - \lambda_v$. Typically, companies such as Netflix and Amazon have user logs which can be used to determine if a user reviewed the product without adopting it. Next to each review on Amazon, where the user bought the product being reviewed, there is a label that states "Amazon Verified Purchase" representing an adoption. The reviews without this label can be attributed to tattle nodes (states promote or inhibit). Given the user rating log, we learn λ_v as maximum likelihood estimate (MLE) which is the fraction of times a user provided an explicit rating for a product over the times the user provided any opinion including a comment, review and numeric rating.

The parameter μ_v models the inherent bias of user v. As with λ_v, we can rely on the rating log to compute this parameter. As an example, in the movie rating social network Flixster, there are special non-numeric ratings "want to see it" and "not interested" that map closely to the PROMOTE and INHIBIT states in our model respectively. Again, we use maximum likelihood estimate (MLE) to compute μ_v, that is, the fraction of times a user gave the rating "want to see it" over the number of times any such special rating was given by that user. We show the effectiveness of this choice by the means of extensive experiments in Section 4.

4. MODEL EVALUATION

We perform empirical analysis to study the adoption of two types of "products" – movies and artists. We analyze influence spread and actual adoption (viewing) of movies on two datasets, one from a social network for movies, Flixster[1], and the other from a movie recommender system, Movielens[2], presented in Section 4.1. Further, we analyze a music social network, Last.fm[3], and study the adoption (listening) of songs and artists, presented in Section 4.2. The table in Figure 2(a) presents the basic statistics of all these datasets. We compare the following models in our evaluation.

Classical LT. Linear Threshold model proposed in [13].

LT-C. Our proposed model.

LT Ratings. Our proposed model without TATTLE nodes. That is, all the nodes who are influenced adopt the product, and $\lambda_v = 1, \forall v \in V$. This is equivalent to modifying the activation function of the classical LT model to include ratings as defined in Eq. (1).

LT Tattle. Our proposed model without any ratings. That is, all the nodes in ADOPT state are assumed to rate the item as $r_{\max}$, as do those in PROMOTE state, while users in INHIBIT state rate $r_{\min}$.

We tested these variations of LT-C in order to understand the relative contribution of the different components to the overall accuracy of predicting the expected adoption spread. In all the experiments, we run 10K Monte Carlo simulations to estimate the coverage for $k = 50$ seeds. The data was divided into test and training sets randomly such that all the ratings of a movie fall in exactly one of training or test sets. All validation experiments are run on the test set.

4.1 Adoption of Movies

Datasets. Flixster is a social network for movies which enables users to share their opinion on movies with friends by rating and reviewing movies. This dataset, collected by Jamali et al. [11], in its raw form has 1M users, 14M (undirected) friendship relations among users, and 8.2M ratings that range from half a star (rating 0.5) to five stars (rating 5). Since running Monte Carlo (MC) simulations is very expensive (may take several hours even for 10K nodes), a graph of that size is difficult to handle, given the extensive set of experiments we perform in our study. We use the Graclus[4] software to extract a subgraph which contains 13K users and 192.4K (directed) edges among them. There are 4.14M ratings by these users of which 1.84M are numeric ratings and 2.3M are special ratings.

Our second dataset on movies is from the Movielens recommender system released by Grouplens[5] research group. The dataset consists of 6K users and 1M ratings (on scale of 1-5) on 3.7K movies. The dataset does not have an explicit social graph, so we construct an implicit one representing the flow of influence. In Movielens, influence flows indirectly via the recommendation engine that is based on collaborative filtering [14]. For instance, if a movie is recommended to Bob, it is likely that the "nearest neighbors" of Bob (as seen by the recommendation engine) must have given high ratings to the movie. We deduce these implicit relationships among users by computing similarity among users. Precisely, an edge is created between users u and v if the Jaccard index[6] w.r.t. the movies they rated is greater than a threshold (0.25 in experiments). The process resulted in a graph with 6K nodes and 209K edges.

The size of the training set is 19.9K for Flixster, and 2.9K for Movielens; and test set is 5.1K for Flixster, and 741 for Movielens. Our experiments were run on 650 movies randomly picked from the test set for Flixster, and the entire test set of 741 movies for Movielens.

Model Parameters from Data. For both the datasets, edge weights are learned as described in Section 3.4. Figures 2(b) and 2(c) show the distribution of edge weights for Flixster and Movielens respectively. Flixster allows ratings from 0.5 to 5 in steps of 0.5, while Movielens allows integer ratings from 1 to 5. Figures 2(d) and 2(e) show the distribution of ratings for Flixster and Movielens respectively. The complete ratings matrix R is computed using the matrix factorization method described in [14] for both the datasets.

Flixster allows two types of *special* ratings – "want to see it" and "not interested" – in addition to the numeric ratings. There are 2.3M special ratings in our dataset, of which 730K ratings are "want to see it" and 1.6M are "not interested". We map the "want to see it" and "not interested" ratings to the PROMOTE and INHIBIT states in our model and fix their numeric values to 0.5 and 5 respectively. For any user $v \in V$, the adoption probability λ_v is computed as the fraction of times v gave a numeric rating over the number of all (numeric and special) ratings given by v. Similarly, μ_v is computed as a fraction of times v gives a "want to see it" rating over the number of special ratings given by v. Figures 2(f) and 2(g) show the distribution of the λ and μ parameters learned using the special ratings. In both the distributions, a large majority of the users have λ and μ values close to the ends of the spectrum i.e., 0 and 1. A value of one (zero) for λ for a user indicates that she adopts (tattles about) each product which she learns about. Similarly, a value of one (zero) for μ indicates if the user decides to tattle, she promotes (inhibits) the product. The distributions in Figures 2(f) and 2(g) show these strong preferences of users. Over 1200 users gave only numeric ratings and have $\lambda = 1$. Considering the special ratings, 1400 users gave "want to watch" ratings only ($\mu = 1$) and 1500 users gave "not interested" ratings only ($\mu = 0$). The fact that over half of all ratings are special and represent opinions shared by users who have not watched the given movie emphasizes the need to study the effect of TATTLE nodes on adoption.

Movielens also features special ratings, such as, "want to see it" that corresponds to movies in a user's wishlist, and "hide this" that corresponds to "not interested". However, the actual dataset obtained from the Grouplens website did not include these ratings. In order to mitigate this, we use the distribution of λ and μ learned from Flixster for com-

[1]www.flixster.com

[2]www.movielens.org

[3]www.last.fm

[4]www.cs.utexas.edu/users/dml/Software/graclus.html

[5]www.grouplens.org/node/73

[6]Jaccard index for sets X, Y is $J(X, Y) = |X \cap Y|/|X \cup Y|$.

	Flixster	Movielens	Last.fm
#Nodes	13K	6040	1892
#Edges	192.4K	209K	25.4K
Avg. degree	14.8	34.6	13.4
#Movies or #Artists	25K	3706	17.6K
#Ratings	1.84M	1M	259K
#Edges with non-zero weight	75.7K	154K	157K

(a) Dataset statistics

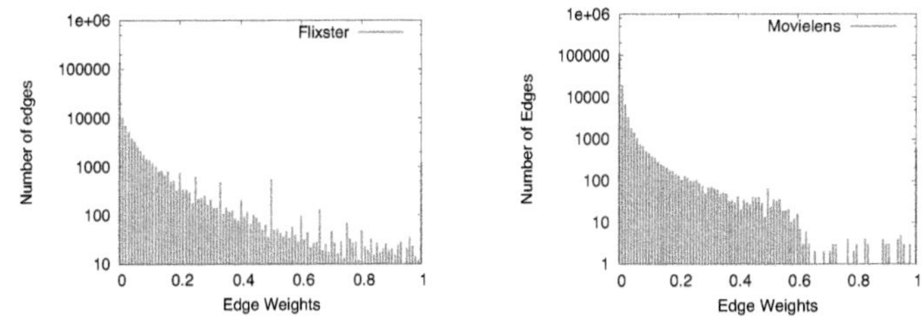

(b) Distribution of edge weights in Flixster

(c) Distribution of edge weights in Movielens

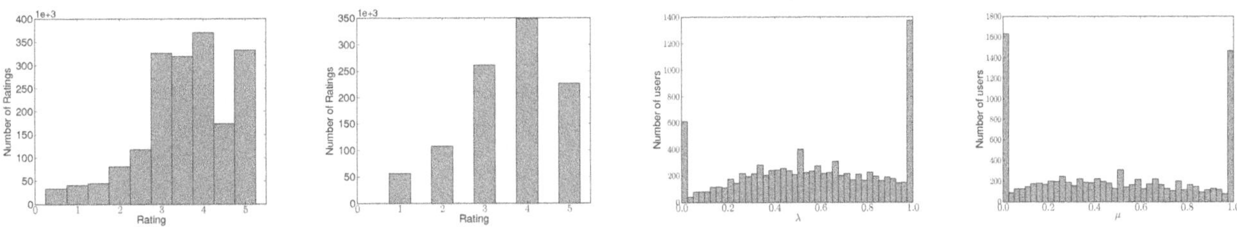

(d) Distribution of ratings in Flixster

(e) Distribution of ratings in Movielens

(f) Distribution of λ in Flixster

(g) Distribution of μ in Flixster

Figure 2: Summary of datasets and distributions of model parameters

puting the values and for users in the Movielens dataset. Though not ideal, we believe this is a reasonable approximation since both data sets represent users' opinions on movies. The shape of the distributions in Figures 2(f) and 2(g) suggests a Beta probability distribution as a natural choice for modeling both λ and μ. We learn the parameters for the Beta distribution by fitting a curve to the data from Flixster, and obtain the distributions $\lambda_u \sim \text{Beta}(0.3, 0.1)$ $\mu_u \sim \text{Beta}(0.001, 0.001)$, for any user $u \in V$.

Coverage with different models. We first analyze the effect of ratings on product adoption. Figures 3(a) and 3(b) show the coverage obtained for a seed set size $k = 50$ using the classical LT model, LT Ratings, LT Tattle and the LT-C model for maximizing product adoption. The figures show this comparison for a particular movie, and the results were similar for a set of 30 and 20 movies picked randomly from Flixster and Movielens, respectively. As can be seen, there is a huge gap between the prediction of classical LT and of LT-C model. For instance, on Flixster, LT model predicts a coverage of 4200 with a budget of 50, and LT-C predicts a coverage of only 701 for that budget. Which model is correct? Is LT-C too pessimistic or is the classical LT model too optimistic? Coverage is an important statistic used in estimating the revenue (and thus profit) and hence, it is important to have an accurate estimate of it. As shown next, gauging models based on the absolute coverage they predict can often lead to models that perform poorly.

Accuracy of estimated coverage. We evaluate the coverage obtained by different models against the actual adoption of a product. We define the *actual adoption coverage* (actual coverage, for short) as the number of users who adopted the product, in this case, gave a numeric rating for a given movie. Since the coverage estimated by a model depends on the size of the seed set, we fix the seed set for each movie and compute the coverage by each model given the seed set. The seed set for each movie is the set of *initiators* which includes all users who watched a given movie before any of their friends did. Figures 3(c) and 3(e) validate that the LT-C model estimates actual adoption coverage accurately on both datasets. Each point in the figures represents a movie and its coordinates correspond to the actual coverage vs. that estimated by a model, for the set of initiators as the seeds. The set of initiators and hence the size of the seed set may be different for each movie. Figure 3(d) shows that the actual coverage is positively correlated with the number of initiators in both the datasets (shown are all movies in the datasets). Moreover, the final coverage is much larger than the number of initiators, suggesting that the network structure plays a significant role in the final spread of adoption.

Table 1: Average RMSE for different models

Model	Flixster	Movielens
LT	1594.8	826.8
LT Ratings	269.3	301.8
LT Tattle	183	420.7
LT-C	144.6	301.7

Figure 3(c) shows 650 movies and 3(e) shows 741 movies of the test set for Flixster and Movielens, respectively. The $x = y$ line is the ideal scenario where the model estimate is identical to the actual coverage. As seen from the figures, the classical LT model over-estimates the coverage by large amounts. Both including tattle nodes and including ratings are useful in providing better estimates, while estimates of adoption using LT-C model are closest to reality. To quantify this error in estimating the coverage, we compute the average root mean square value (RMSE[7]) over the test set, for the coverage predicted by the different models w.r.t. actual coverage. We observe that the RMSE obtained using the classical LT model is over 10 times that by our model (on Flixster), as shown in Table 1. On Movielens, the LT-C and LT Ratings models have similar RMSE. This might be because we do not have data to learn values of λ and μ for various users, instead we draw their values from the Beta distribution whose parameters are taken from Flixster dataset (see above).

Another interesting trend observed in Figure 3(d) is that the choice of seeds is critical. For instance, we picked the 109 movies from Flixster where the number of the initiators

[7]For vectors x, y of size n, $\text{RMSE}(x, y) = \sqrt{\sum_1^n (x_i - y_i)^2 / n}$.

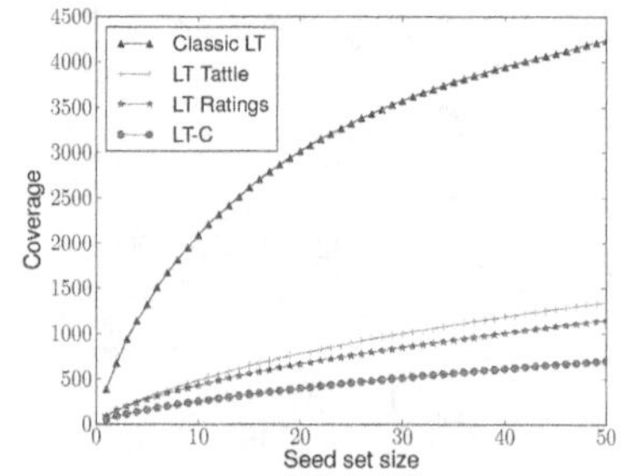

(a) Coverage obtained with different models on Flixster

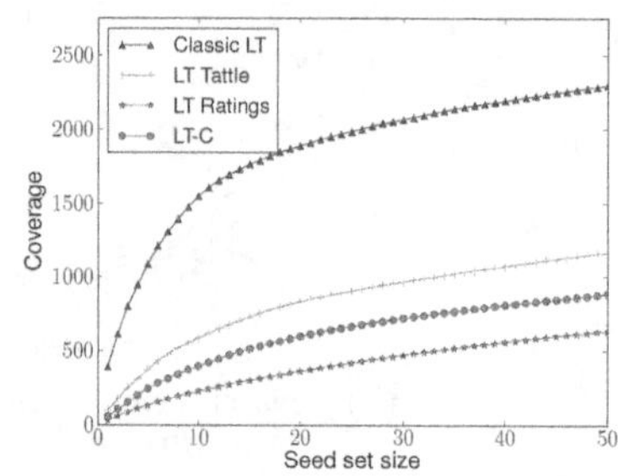

(b) Coverage obtained with different models on Movielens

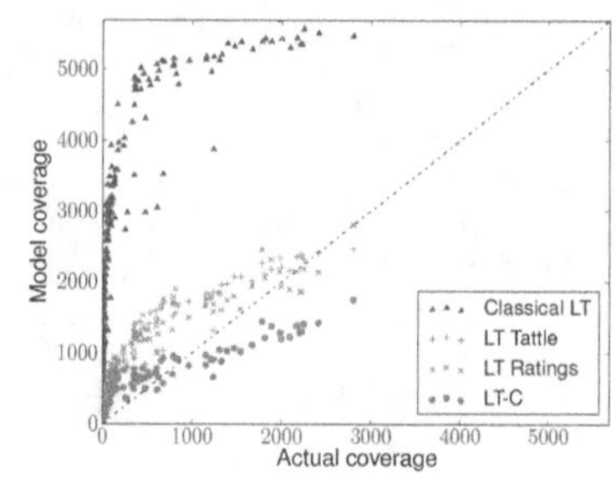

(c) Actual vs predicted coverage on Flixster

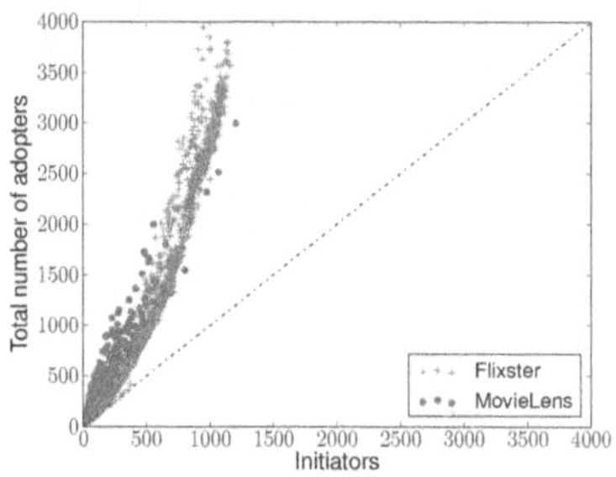

(d) Adoption Spread

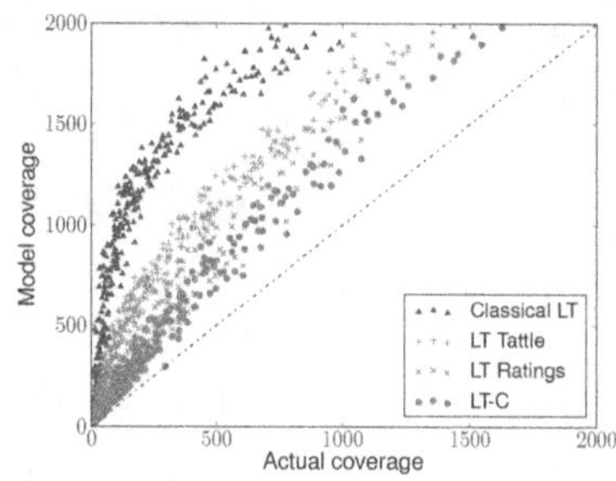

(e) Actual vs predicted coverage on Movielens

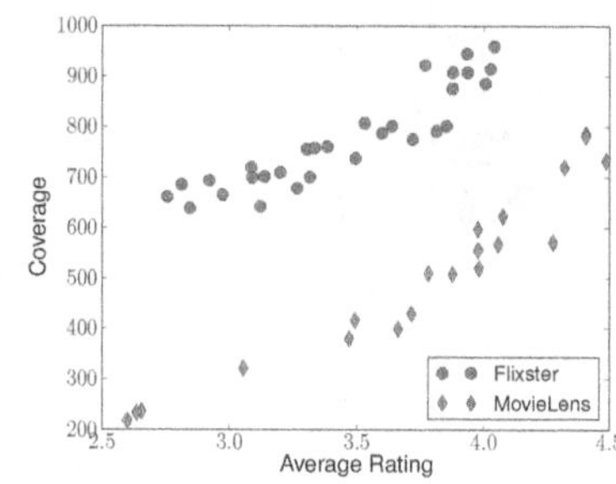

(f) Average rating of movie vs coverage for $k = 50$ on Flixster and Movielens

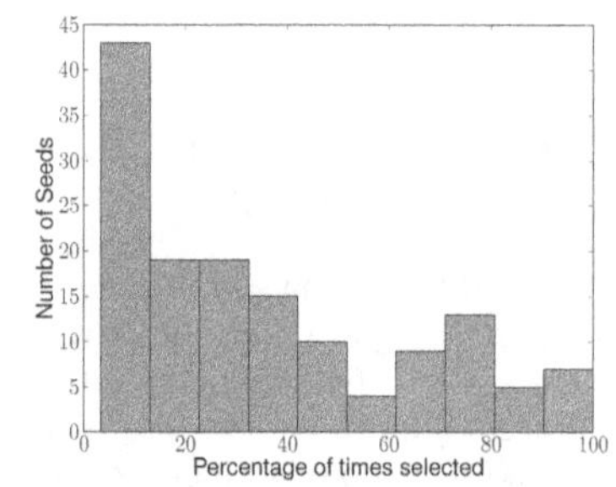

(g) Consistency of chosen seeds across actions on Flixster

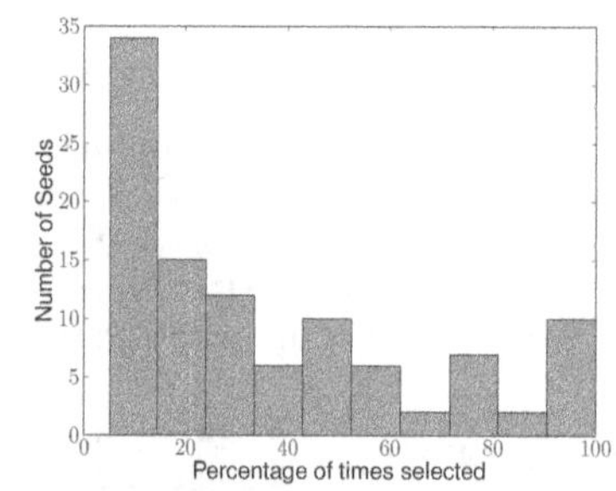

(h) Consistency of chosen seeds across actions on Movielens

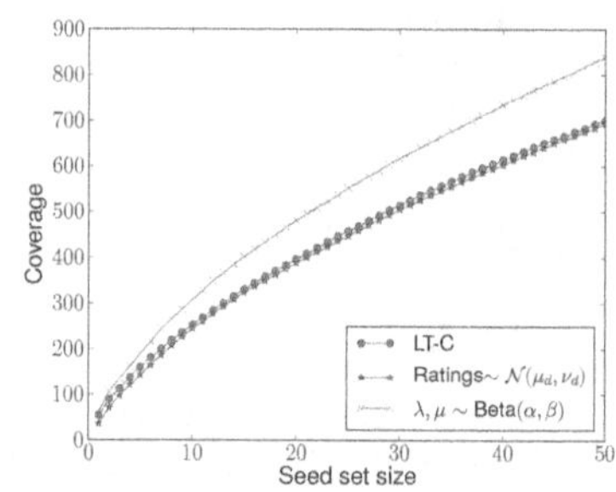

(i) Coverage with λ, μ and ratings from data and distributions on Flixster

Figure 3: Coverage and seed set analysis on Flixster and Movielens datasets

is 50. The average final coverage on these movies is 58.2, which is quite close to the number of initiators. On the other hand, if the initial seed set is picked carefully using the LT-C model, it is possible to achieve the coverage of even more than 500, as seen in Figure 3(a).

Product and seed set analysis. In Figure 3(f) we study the effect of ratings on the overall coverage given a budget of 50 seeds. Figure 3(f) shows the coverage for a set of 30 and 20 movies picked at random for the Flixster and Movielens datasets respectively. By taking ratings into account, the LT-C model predicts that good movies (rated high) are likely to have larger viewership compared with bad movies (rated low). By contrast, the coverage estimated using the LT model is the same across all movies, and is approximately 4200 nodes for movies in Flixster and 2300 for the Movielens dataset, significantly higher than the actual coverage in both cases.

A natural question to ask is whether there are some nodes that are influential across actions (movies) and are *consistently* selected as seeds. Figures 3(g) and 3(h) show a histogram of the percentage of times a node was selected as a seed for the same set of movies in Figure 3(f). For the Flixster dataset, there are 7 seeds among the 144 unique seeds that are consistently selected for 90% of the movies analyzed. The consistency decays exponentially where only a few seeds have high consistency and most seeds have low consistency. A similar trend was observed for the Movielens dataset, where 10 out of 104 unique seeds were consistently selected 90% of the times. Interestingly, these nodes are not the top high degree nodes in the graph. This observation is consistent with a recent study [17] on influence in Twitter.

Evaluating model parameters. During our study, we realized that sometimes we may not have access to the data required for computing λ and μ for each user in the network, instead, we may be able to infer the distribution of both these parameters. We evaluate the coverage obtained by drawing each model parameter from appropriate distributions and comparing it with that obtained when all parameters are computed from the data. The results are shown in Figure 3(i). We analyze the coverage when the ratings are drawn from a normal distribution $\mathcal{N}(\mu_d, \nu_d)$ where the distribution mean $\mu_d = 3.59$ and variance $\nu_d = 1.01$, as computed from the given numeric ratings. The obtained coverage is almost the same as that obtained when ratings are computed using matrix factorization from the available ratings. Next, we analyze the coverage when λ and μ are drawn from Beta distributions as $\lambda_u \sim \text{Beta}(0.3, 0.1)$ $\mu_u \sim \text{Beta}(0.001, 0.001)$, for each user $u \in V$. These distributions are learned by fitting a Beta probability distribution to the λ, μ values computed from the Flixster data. The obtained coverage comes close to that obtained from data. In conclusion, it is encouraging to observe that drawing the model parameters from a distribution that approximates the data may well give a good estimate of the coverage if access to user logs is limited.

4.2 Adoption of Music

Datasets. We study the adoption of music on a dataset from the popular music service Last.fm. The dataset we used was released for the Workshop on Information Heterogeneity and Fusion in Recommender Systems (HetRec 2011)[8]. The details of the dataset are presented in the table in Figure 2(a). It has 1892 users with 25.4K friendship relationships among them. The dataset includes the users' listening history in the form of number of times a user listened to songs by an artist, and users' tagging history for tagging artists.

Model Parameters from Data. We use both tagging and listening history as actions for computing edge weights. Since the listening history is only available as playcounts, it does not come with timestamps. We assume these are most recent actions and assign the current timestamp to all listening actions. Now, edge weights can be learned as before. The distribution of edge weights is shown in Figure 4(a). The data was divided into test and training sets, with the test set consisting of 3067 randomly picked artists.

A user's opinion of an artist is implicitly present in the form of playcounts, i.e., the number of times the user has listened to songs by that artist. To infer ratings on a scale of 0 to 5 for each user, we partition the artists into 5 buckets, where the top bucket represents artists in the top 20-percentile playcounts, the second bucket in the next 20-percentile and so on. Each artist in the top bucket is assigned a rating of 5, next bucket corresponds to rating 4 and so on. It is well known that listening history follows a power-law distribution where a few artists (or songs) are heard many times and many artists (songs) are heard very few times. This pattern is observed in the obtained ratings as shown in Figure 4(b).

Last.fm allows users to indicate their preference on songs by marking them as "loved" or "banned". For a given song, we regard the users who loved that song as being in the ADOPT state and those who banned that song as being in the INHIBIT state. Given this mapping, we can use the "loved" and "banned" songs for inferring a distribution of λ. However, the dataset for the HetRec workshop did not contain the information on loved and banned songs. We used the API from Last.fm to crawl this information for an arbitrary set of 10K users, and computed λ_u for a crawled user u as the fraction of loved songs over the number of loved and banned songs. Figure 4(c) shows the distribution of λ for the crawled users. A trend similar to that in Flixster is observed for values of λ in Last.fm, although with a larger skew towards adopting the product (in this case, an artist).

[8] `http://ir.ii.uam.es/hetrec2011`

We fit a Beta probability distribution to the values of λ and the best fit was obtained with Beta(0.5, 0.001). Since the consumption of songs from an online music service does not cost much, it is not natural for users to want to listen to a song but not actually listen to it. Therefore, for this domain, $\mu_u = 0$, for every user u.

Accuracy of estimated coverage. Figure 5(a) compares the coverage obtained using classical LT, LT Tattle, LT Ratings and LT-C models with the actual coverage obtained by the initiators. Since the distribution of λ as obtained from the data is highly skewed towards 1, including the TATTLE state does not make the coverage estimate much better than the classical LT model. On the other hand, most ratings are low and hence their inclusion into the LT model has a greater impact for this dataset. The estimated coverage of LT Ratings and LT-C are similar, and provide a far better estimate compared with the classical LT model. The RMSE values averaged over 3067 artists for the four models were as follows, classical LT:97.5, LT Tattle:93.6, LT Ratings:31.7 and LT-C:31.7. These errors in coverage estimation show that for the music domain as well (where adoption may not cost money), incorporating users' ratings in the propagation model provides better estimates of adoption, compared with accounting for tattling but not ratings. In Figure 4(d), we present the actual coverage against the number of initiators, for all the artists. Again, it can be seen that the two are positively correlated.

Product and seed set analysis. Figure 5(b) shows that the coverage varies for artists that have different popularity (or rating). The coverage estimated by the classical LT model is the 1230, regardless of the artist, again way off from reality. The trend in consistency of seeds observed for music domain is similar to that seen for movies. Figure 5(c) shows that few (i.e., 12) seeds are picked over 90% of the times and 62 out of 149 unique seeds are picked in less than 10% of the 20 artists analyzed. These two experiments show that using LT-C, it is not only the coverage that is different for different products, even the target seeds are different. In contrast, the classical model disregards these nuances. This suggests taking such nuances into account may lead to a more accurate and effective model for viral marketing.

5. CONCLUSIONS AND FUTURE WORK

Classical diffusion models such as IC and LT do not distinguish between influence and product adoption. Thus, they implicitly assume that once influenced, a node necessarily adopts a product and that adopters always influence other users to adopt the product. Our observations on real data show that sometimes influenced users, once they become active, may choose to not adopt but instead tattle about the product; by doing so, they may either promote or inhibit adoption by other users. Furthermore, adopters may endorse a product to varying degrees based on their experience with the product, as often reflected by the ratings they provide in several real data sets.

In this paper, we proposed a propagation model called LT-C model that accounts for these observations. We formalized the problem of adoption maximization as distinguished from influence maximization and showed that it is NP-hard. We also showed the expected adoption spread function under the LT-C model is monotone and submodular and thus, the classic greedy algorithm can be used to get an approximate

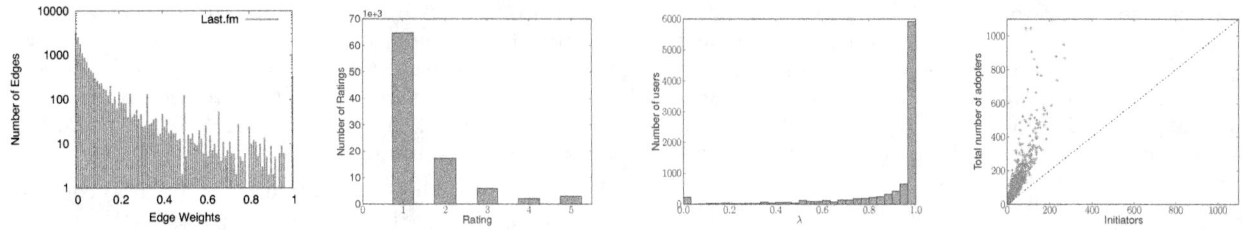

(a) Edge weight distribution (b) Distribution of ratings (c) Distribution of λ (d) Adoption Spread

Figure 4: Summary of dataset and distributions of model parameters for Last.fm

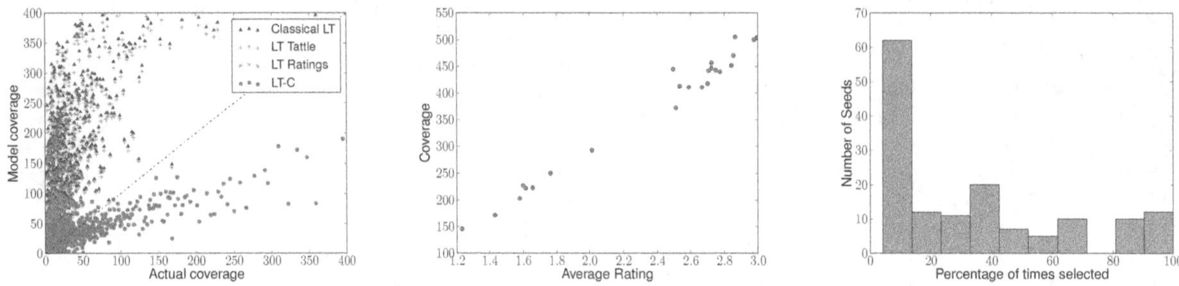

(a) Actual vs predicted coverage (b) Average rating of movie vs coverage for $k = 50$ (c) Consistency of chosen seeds across actions

Figure 5: Coverage and seed set analysis on Last.fm dataset

solution. We conducted extensive experiments on two domains – two data sets from movies and one from the music domain. Our results show that w.r.t. the accuracy of spread prediction, the LT-C model is consistently the best and the classical LT model is consistently the worst.

There is still a long way to go to develop a truly realistic product adoption model. It may be possible that the users are passive and may not express any opinion even after adopting a product [17]. One way to incorporate this is to split the ADOPT state into two sub-states, viz., "adopt and rate" and "adopt and not rate". However, it is not clear how we can identify the latter state (for learning the model parameters) in the datasets we can access. Similarly, users may not find tattlers' ratings as trustworthy as adopters' ratings. Marginalizing tattlers' ratings may improve the predictions. Extending the model by incorporating the five stages of product adoption [2] can be useful. Inclusion of negative opinions in the spirit of [3] within the framework of our model is interesting and may lead to an even more expressive model for product adoption. Next, it is important to validate the LT-C model against many more real data sets from diverse domains. Last but not the least, scalable heuristic algorithms need to be developed for the LT-C model in order to handle very large networks and seed sets. Our ongoing work addresses some of these questions.

Acknowledgments. This research was partially supported by a strategic network grant from NSERC Canada on Business Intelligence Network. We thank Mohsen Jamali and Martin Ester for sharing the Flixster dataset, and Mohammad Khabbaz for sharing the matrix factorization code.

6. REFERENCES

[1] S. Aral, L. Muchnik, and A. Sundararajan. Distinguishing influence-based contagion from homophily-driven diffusion in dynamic networks. In *PNAS*, 2009.

[2] J. M. Bohlen and G. M. Beal. The diffusion process. *Spl. Report No. 18, Agri. Extn. Serv., Iowa State College*, 1957.

[3] W. Chen, A. Collins, R. Cummings, T. Ke, Z. Liu, D. Rincon, X. Sun, Y. Wang, W. Wei, and Y. Yuan. Influence maximization in social networks when negative opinions may emerge and propagate. In *SDM*, 2011.

[4] W. Chen, Y. Yuan, and L. Zhang. Scalable influence maximization in social networks under the linear threshold model. In *ICDM*, 2010.

[5] D. Crandall, D. Cosley, D. Huttenlocher, J. Kleinberg, and S. Suri. Feedback effects between similarity and social influence in online communities. In *KDD*, 2008.

[6] P. Domingos and M. Richardson. Mining the network value of customers. In *KDD*, 2001.

[7] A. Goyal, F. Bonchi, and L. V. S. Lakshmanan. Learning influence probabilities in social networks. In *WSDM*, 2010.

[8] A. Goyal, F. Bonchi, and L. V. S. Lakshmanan. A data-based approach to social influence maximization. *PVLDB*, 5(1), 2011.

[9] A. Goyal, W. Lu, and L. V. S. Lakshmanan. Simpath: An efficient algorithm for influence maximization under the linear threshold model. In *ICDM*, 2011.

[10] J. Hartline, V. Mirrokni, and M. Sundararajan. Optimal marketing strategies over social networks. In *WWW*, 2008.

[11] M. Jamali and M. Ester. A matrix factorization technique with trust propagation for recommendation in social networks. In *RecSys*, 2010.

[12] S. Kalish. A new product adoption model with price, advertising, and uncertainty. *Management Science*, 31(12), 1985.

[13] D. Kempe, J. M. Kleinberg, and É. Tardos. Maximizing the spread of influence through a social network. In *KDD*, 2003.

[14] Y. Koren and R. Bell. Advances in collaborative filtering. In *Recommender Systems Handbook*. 2011.

[15] T. La Fond and J. Neville. Randomization tests for distinguishing social influence and homophily effects. In *WWW*, 2010.

[16] J. Leskovec, A. Krause, C. Guestrin, C. Faloutsos, J. VanBriesen, and N. Glance. Cost-effective outbreak detection in networks. In *KDD*, 2007.

[17] D. M. Romero, W. Galuba, S. Asur, and B. A. Huberman. Influence and passivity in social media. In *WWW*, 2011.

[18] J. Tang, J. Sun, C. Wang, and Z. Yang. Social influence analysis in large-scale networks. In *KDD*, 2009.

Answers, not Links

Extracting Tips from Yahoo! Answers to Address How-To Web Queries

Ingmar Weber
Yahoo! Research Barcelona
Avda. Diagonal 177
E-08018 Barcelona, Spain
ingmar@yahoo-inc.com

Antti Ukkonen
Yahoo! Research Barcelona
Avda. Diagonal 177
E-08018 Barcelona, Spain
aukkonen@yahoo-inc.com

Aris Gionis
Yahoo! Research Barcelona
Avda. Diagonal 177
E-08018 Barcelona, Spain
gionis@yahoo-inc.com

ABSTRACT

We investigate the problem of mining "tips" from Yahoo! Answers and displaying those tips in response to related web queries. Here, a "tip" is a short, concrete and self-contained bit of non-obvious advice such as "To zest a lime if you don't have a zester : use a cheese grater."

First, we estimate the volume of web queries with "how-to" intent, which could be potentially addressed by a tip. Second, we analyze how to detect such queries automatically without solely relying on literal "how to *" patterns. Third, we describe how to derive potential tips automatically from Yahoo! Answers, and we develop machine-learning techniques to remove low-quality tips. Finally, we discuss how to match web queries with "how-to" intent to tips. We evaluate both the quality of these direct displays as well as the size of the query volume that can be addressed by serving tips.

Categories and Subject Descriptors

H.3.1 [**Information Storage and Retrieval**]: Content Analysis and Indexing; H.3.3 [**Information Storage and Retrieval**]: Information Search and Retrieval

General Terms

Algorithms, Experimentation

1. INTRODUCTION

For millions of users, search engines constitute the main entry-point to the web, as well as a powerful tool to delve into a wealth of available information. The evolution of web-search engines has been very rapid. Over the years, not only the quality of search results has kept improving, but a large number of novel features has allowed users to find information directly, without the need to click on links away from the search-engine result page. Examples of such features include query recommendations, smart snippets, integration of rich content (images, videos, news, celebrities), direct displays (weather, stock quotes, calculators), and so on.

In this work, we take this approach further by attempting to answer common "how-to" queries *directly*, rather than serving links to sites that contain answers. For example, when a user searches for "how to round decimal in C" we would like to display "To round a decimal in C: add 0.5 and then floor the value – what you call dropping the decimal. Looks like this: int x = (my_float + 0.5);"[1]

We obtain potential answers by mining Yahoo! Answers,[2] the biggest online site for collaborative question-answering. However, rather than looking at all potential answers, including those that are long or those that are opinions rather than concrete solutions, we focus on extracting *tips*. In our context, a tip is a piece of advice that is (*i*) short (160 characters maximum[3]), (*ii*) concrete (it has to be actionable), (*iii*) self-contained (understandable without additional external sources), and (*iv*) non-obvious (otherwise it would be useless). Our focus on tips is mostly motivated by the limited screen real estate, in particular on mobile devices. Furthermore, short and to-the-point tips are often interesting even when they do not perfectly address the underlying problem. Hence, we expect users to be more forgiving than with, say, irrelevant web search results.

To materialize our idea into a functional system we need to address three sub-problems: (*i*) identify when a user query is a how-to query for which it is valuable to display a tip as an answer; (*ii*) extract tips from online resources and populate a large database of high-quality tips; and (*iii*) given a how-to query retrieve relevant tips for that query. Each of the three sub-problems has its own challenges which we we address in this paper. We address them independently creating a modular system, which is easier to build, evaluate, and improve. Figure 1 shows how the different modules connect to each other. The flow of the paper follows the decomposition of our problem into the three sub-problems. In particular, we make the following contributions:

- Using query logs we estimate a *clear how-to intent* in 2.0% of the total search volume of a commercial search engine (Section 3). This is done to demonstrate that directly answering such queries could have a significant

Permission to make digital or hard copies of all or part of this work for personal or classroom use is granted without fee provided that copies are not made or distributed for profit or commercial advantage and that copies bear this notice and the full citation on the first page. To copy otherwise, to republish, to post on servers or to redistribute to lists, requires prior specific permission and/or a fee.
WSDM'12, February 8–12, 2012, Seattle, Washington, USA.
Copyright 2012 ACM 978-1-4503-0747-5/12/02 ...$10.00.

[1] `http://yhoo.it/ly2f1S`

[2] `http://answers.yahoo.com`

[3] 160 characters is the maximum length for an SMS. See `http://latimesblogs.latimes.com/technology/2009/05/invented-text-messaging.html` for an explanation of this limitation.

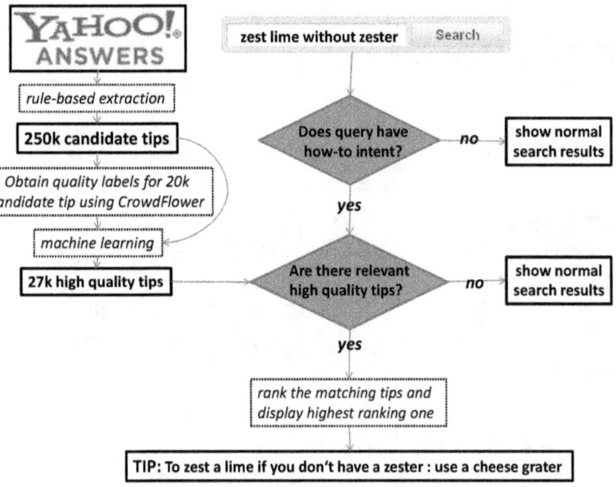

Figure 1: A schematic overview of the system.

impact, as most of the interesting open problems in web IR concern non-navigational queries [28].

- We develop methods to *automatically detect queries with how-to intent*, even when they do not match the literal "how to X" pattern (Section 4). Our best method annotates 1.13% of the total search volume as having a how-to intent. 83.5% of this volume has a clear how-to intent, according to human evaluators.
- We propose a *mechanism to automatically extract tips from Yahoo! Answers* (Section 5). We used a crowd-sourcing platform to evaluate 20 000 candidate tips found by our method. 25% of the candidate tips were judged as "very good," 48% as "ok," and 27% as "bad."
- Given the labeled set of tips, we use *machine learning techniques to filter tips of low quality* (Section 5). We obtain a precision of 0.94 (over 10-fold cross-validation) for the best method when separating potentially useful tips from candidates labeled as "bad."
- We *match the set of found how-to queries to the tips labeled by the classifier* (Section 6). The matching algorithm with the highest precision (0.92) returns a tip for 4.5% of the how-to queries. The coverage can be doubled to 10.0%, at the cost of precision dropping to 0.75.

To place our work in the context of question-answering and other related work we survey previous research in Section 7. Finally, we conclude by discussing drawbacks, strengths and future work in Section 8.

2. QUERY DATASET

We used a large sample of a query log of a commercial search engine. The sample contained queries submitted from May 1, 2010 to January 31, 2011. We used only queries by users who had an identifiable cookie related to their account with the search engine, which is also a major email provider. This selection was done to remove a large amount of search spam, typically issued by users who seek to avoid being identified. We also restricted our dataset to queries that led to at least one result click, which is the vast majority of queries. This selection was done since one of our techniques in Section 4 makes explicit use of click information.

The queries were anonymized by replacing potentially sensitive information by special symbols. An inspection of these cases lets us believe that this anonymization does not alter the results in our study as queries which underwent this process are practically never related to how-to intents. Finally, the queries were normalized for case, punctuation, stop-words, and word order.

In Section 4.4 we also made use of click information on a per-host basis and so, for completeness we explain how to obtain hostnames here. To map clicked URLs to hostnames we removed any prefix of the type (`http`|`https`|`ftp`)`://`. If the rest started with `www.`, this token was also removed.[4]

3. PREVALENCE OF HOW-TO QUERIES

Before embarking to solve the problem of finding tips for answering how-to queries, we need to convince ourselves that this is a meaningful problem. So our first question is whether how-to queries make up a large fraction of the search volume.

To answer this question, we sampled a few thousand distinct queries, which were then evaluated by human judges.[5] To obtain better insight whether how-to queries are more prominent among frequent head queries or rare tail queries, we sampled in different ways from the query distribution. The details are presented in the next section.

As far as what actually constitutes a query with a how-to intent, we used the following definition.

> A query is said to have how-to intent if the user is looking for information on solving a particular problem or performing a particular task.

How-to queries are *almost never navigational* and *rarely transactional*. A query such as "online calculator" already implies that the user knows of the existence of relevant online services and is just trying to find any of them. How-to queries are *mostly informational*. A query such as "compute logs in java" would fall into this category.

Judges were asked to evaluate if a query has a how-to intent using a 4-point scale:

2 – clear how-to intent;
1 – possible how-to intent;
0 – no how-to intent;
-1 – foreign language/character set or unintelligible.

The same scale is used in Section 4 where we discuss algorithms to automatically identify how-to queries. Table 1 lists a few queries for these classes.

3.1 Evaluation results

The three judges evaluated three distinct query sets. First, a set obtained by sampling 1 000 queries uniformly from the query volume. This set contains a noticeable fraction of (repeated) head queries. Second, a set obtained by sampling 1 000 queries uniformly from the set of distinct queries. This set has a stronger bias towards the tail of the query distribution than the previous one. Finally, the third set consists of the top 1 000 distinct queries, which are mostly navigational.

[4]These are not necessarily hostnames in a strict technical sense as "bbc.co.uk" and "www.bbc.co.uk" could be served by different hosts.

[5]The authors of this paper.

2: clear how-to	how to install a remington trigger, start a wiki, clean iphone screen, how to hook up tv vcr and dvd
1: possible how-to	copper cleaner homemade, paper match rocket, pizza dough, hair spiking
0: not how-to	my yahoo, mtv, cannon ef, women in war world 2, parkers uniforms houston

Table 1: Examples of queries that are clear how-to ("2"), possible how-to ("1"), and not how-to ("0"). Queries judged as unknown ("-1") largely contained non-Latin characters and are not displayed.

Metric	unif. volume	unif. distinct	top volume
cov. vol.	2.0/1.4/96.3	2.9/3.6/91.6	0.0/0.9/99.0
cov. dist.	2.3/1.7/95.7	3.6/5.2/90.1	0.0/1.2/98.7
agreement	93.9	88.4	96.6

Table 2: Percentage of queries falling into the classes "clear how-to query"/"possible how-to query"/"not a how-to query" when queries are (*i*) sampled uniformly at random over all occurrences, (*ii*) sampled uniformly at random over all distinct queries, or (*iii*) the most frequent 1 000 queries. "Agreement" is measured among the three judges as macro-average over all three pairs.

Each set of 1 000 queries was then randomly divided into one set of 100 and three sets of 300. Each of the three judges evaluated 400 queries: the set of 100 and one of the sets of 300. The common set was used to evaluate agreement among the judges. In computing the agreement, a negligible number of cases where at least one judge selected -1 (foreign language/character set or unintelligible) was skipped and not counted as disagreement. The results are shown in Table 2. We note that the fraction of strong disagreements, 2 vs. 0, was only a tiny fraction of all disagreements.

Overall, 2.0% of query volume and 2.3% of distinct queries were identified as having a clear how-to intent. These fractions are 0% for the most frequent queries though, but higher when sampling from the tail As previous work shows that the frequent queries, which are typically navigational, are "solved" by all major web search engines [28], we believe that a total of 2.0% is actually significant when it comes to giving search engines an opportunity to differentiate themselves from their competitors.

4. DETECTING HOW-TO WEB QUERIES

In the previous section, we showed that how-to queries make up a considerable part of the non-trivial search volume. In this section, we discuss different approaches to detect how-to queries automatically.

4.1 The obvious approach

The most basic approach to extract queries with a how-to intent is to look at queries starting with one of the literal strings "how to," "how do i," or "how can i." Though the precision for such an approach is very high, the recall will be as low as only 1.0% of query instances.

Examples: "how to safely extinguish a campfire," "how do you fix keys on a laptop," "how to do hair like audrey hepburn," "how to train your dragon," "how do you make your basement smell better," "how do i convert video formats."

4.2 Action queries

More experienced users are less likely to enter their information need in natural language with a "how to" prefix. Still, how-to queries could potentially be detected as they refer to an *action* and are likely to contain, or even start with, a verb. Hence, as another approach, we looked at all queries starting with an English verb in its infinitive. Queries were split on non-word characters and the first token was looked up in a verb dictionary.[6] Note that certain words such as "dream" or "sound" are both verbs and nouns.

Examples: "play my music on tool bar raido," "make your own oversized bag," "type of people who put christmas wreaths on cars," "dream symbols," "sound," "buy drawer handles."

4.3 Generalizing literal "how to" queries

As the simple baseline using literal "how to" queries has near-perfect precision, we try to come up with ways to improve its recall, possibly by trading a bit of precision. Concretely, from a query such as "how to fix a flat tire" we want to derive that the query "fix a flat tire" also has a how-to intent. Thus, for all the (literal) "how to" queries we extract, we drop the "how to" prefix, and consider the resulting normalized queries possibly having a how-to intent as well.[7]

However, this normalization alone is overly aggressive. For example, the query "google" is recognized as having a how-to intent, as our query log also contains the query "how to google." To avoid such incorrect generalizations, we look at the fraction of times the normalized query appears with and without the literal "how to" prefix. For example, the normalized query "lose weight" appears as part of a literal "how to" query in 80% of all occurrences. On the other hand, for the normalized query "google," the same fraction is roughly 0.0001%. We experimented with a minimum threshold of 1% (General-.01) and 10% (General-.10).

Examples: "how to dry corn," "fit baseball glove," "stop computer script," "craft ideas for boys," "how to make chocolate bars," "tune your guitar online."

4.4 Using typical how-to answer sites

One drawback of the previous approach is that it only recognizes queries that have been issued at least once as a literal "how to" query. To overcome this limitation we also tried to identify typical how-to *web sites*, such as `http://www.ehow.com/` or `http://www.wikihow.com/`. In analogy to the previous approach, for each clicked host name we looked at the fraction of literal "how to" queries leading to a click on this particular host name. Again we look at the *fraction* and not the *volume* of queries. For example, `http://www.youtube.com/` attracts a large volume of the literal "how to"

[6]Verbs used: `http://www.englishclub.com/vocabulary/regular-verbs-list.htm` and `http://www.englishclub.com/vocabulary/irregular-verbs-list.htm`.

[7]Whenever we refer to the literal "how to" string, we actual mean any of "how to," "how do i," and "how can i."

how-to hosts with largest search volume
wikihow.com
getridofthings.com
howtogetridofstuff.com
dragoart.com
howcast.com
hosts attracing almost exclusively how-to questions
deletepermanently.howto4pc.org
how-to-flirt.org
howtolosefatfast.org
howtogettallersecrets.com
askmethat.com

Table 3: Top how-to host names.

Method	Cover.	Top 500	Rand 500
Baseline	1.01%	99.0/0.0/1.0 (100)	95.8/3.5/0.7 (92)
Verb-first	3.22%	2.3/6.2/91.5 (82)	7.3/7.0/85.7 (83)
General-.10	1.13%	83.5/9.8/6.8 (90)	87.3/6.3/6.3 (89)
General-.01	1.48%	33.8/14.2/52.0 (82)	81.5/9.2/9.2 (86)
Host-.50-20	0.08%	3.3/2.0/94.2 (97)	61.3/14.8/22.8 (61)
Host-.25-10	0.88%	0.0/0.7/99.3 (93)	29.4/16.1/54.2 (64)

Table 4: Experimental results for the detection of how-to queries. The three numbers in the last two columns refer to the percentage of (distinct) queries voted "2", "1" and "0" respectively. Top 500 refers to the most frequent queries labeled as "how-to" by the particular method. The macro-averaged inter-judge agreement is given in parentheses.

queries but it is not a how-to site, as only 1% of queries leading to a click on it are literal "how to" queries.

To identify how-to hosts, we experimented with two different parameters: (*i*) a minimum threshold on the fraction of traffic-generating queries that are literal "how-to" queries, and (*ii*) a minimum threshold on the total number of clicks leading to a particular site.

Once how-to hosts were identified, we looked at their all incoming queries. From these, navigational queries such as "wikihow.com" were removed using a simple heuristic. This heuristic judged a query as navigational (for a given click) if all the tokens in the (normalized) query were also present in the host name. Here we allowed an edit distance of 1 to accommodate minor spelling mistakes. All remaining, non-navigational queries were labeled as "how-to." Host-.50-20 refers to a minimum how-to fraction of .50, where the actual fraction had to *surpass* this threshold, and a minimum traffic count of 20 for the host. Host-.25-10 is defined similarly.

Examples: "xbox 360 delete cache," "fixing a wet cell phone," "fried rice," "aspergers," "how to french braid," "what date is it right to make out."

4.5 Experimental evaluation

We evaluated the task of detecting how-to queries as a classification task. We used the sample of the query log described in Section 2. Our design principle is to put more emphasis on precision rather than on recall. Evaluating the exact recall would require annotating *all* distinct queries with ground truth labels, which is prohibitively expensive. Instead we report the fraction of total search volume that is labeled by a particular approach in the "Coverage" column in Table 4. To put the Coverage figures in perspective, we remind the reader that in Section 3 it was showed that about 2.0% of total web search traffic has a clear how-to intent. We evaluated the precision both for the 500 highest search volume queries labeled by each method, as well as for a set of 500 queries sampled uniformly among the distinct queries detected by this method. Each set of 500 was split into one set of 50 and three sets of 150. Each judge evaluated the set of 50 and one set of 150. The set of 50 was used to estimate inter-judge agreement. The same set of labels $(2, 1, 0, -1)$ as described in Section 3 was used.

As can be seen from Table 4, the simple baseline using the literal "how to" string performs at a reasonable level. Using the General-.10 approach, the coverage can be improved by 13% while still maintaining an acceptable level of precision. It is also worth noting that the precision of the verb-first approach could potentially be improved by removing navigational queries such as "chase online" or "face." Of course, there is also a large number of other applicable techniques for identifying "related queries," e.g., in the context of query suggestions [4, 15]. However, due to the fact that (*i*) the how-to detection is completely modular and (*ii*) the performance of General-.10 is sufficient, we decided to postpone evaluation of more involved schemes to a later stage.

We also considered alternative approaches for detecting how-to intent, such as using online sources, and in particular web-search results. We looked at result snippets and the page content to see if the query matches a "how to" string. Preliminary work showed that this approach works well for popular how-to queries, but as such queries are also detected by other techniques we decided to postpone this approach.

5. MINING TIPS FROM YAHOO! ANSWERS

The next step is to identify a set of potential answers, or tips. A tip is a piece of advice that is (*i*) short (160 characters maximum), (*ii*) concrete (it has to be actionable), (*iii*) self-contained, and (*iv*) non-obvious. The editorial guidelines used for evaluating tips are described in Section 5.3.

We chose to consider tips that have a specific structure "X : Y." Both parts X and Y are short pieces of text. X defines the *goal* of the tip, i.e., a specific situation for which ones requires an actionable solution. Y defines the *suggestion* of the tip, i.e., a proposed solution. The reason that we require tips to have the above structure, is because we find it expressive, easy for the user to parse and understand, and easier for our algorithms to extract and match to queries. As we mentioned before, tips are extracted from Yahoo! answers. Given a ⟨question, answer⟩ pair from Yahoo! answers, the 'question' is used to construct the goal X and the 'answer' to construct the suggestion Y.

Section 5.1 describes the data set from which we extracted our tips. Section 5.2 discusses the steps that were taken to construct candidate tips. In Section 5.3 we give details of the Crowdsource evaluation used to obtain ground-truth quality labels for a subset of candidate tips, which were then used as training data for machine-learning techniques to filter out low-quality tips. Details are given in Section 5.4. The performance results for this classification task are then discussed in Section 5.5.

5.1 Yahoo! answers dataset

We used data from Yahoo! Answers to extract candidate tips. Concretely, we used all ⟨question, best answer⟩ pairs, where the question was posted in the period between May 2006 and August 2010. Best answers are decided either (*i*) by the asker, or (*ii*) by popular vote among Yahoo! Answers users if the asker allows this, or (*iii*) automatically by the system after a certain amount of time. We only used *best* answers as we were interested in extracting high-quality tips, while potentially sacrificing coverage. We further filtered the data by requiring that the user who submitted the question used the English-language front-end.

For questions, only the title was used; the additional and optional information provided in the question description was ignored. Similarly, for answers, we did not use the optional reference field, which, when not empty, contains a justification for the given answer. We did, however, keep track of its binary presence/absence and this was later used as a feature in the machine-learning algorithms. Yahoo! Answers also comes with a topical hierarchy and we recorded the first two levels of this hierarchy for every ⟨question, answer⟩ pair.

We did *not* use any information about user points, which are awarded for contributing answers, nor did we attempt to detect key contributors. This was a deliberate choice in order to make our approach applicable to other sites where the contributor of a potential tip might not even be known.

5.2 Filtering and constructing tip candidates

From the initial set of ⟨question, answer⟩ pairs we constructed a set of candidate tips as follows.

First, we *check that both the question and answer are in English.* Even though we only considered ⟨question, answer⟩ pairs where the question was submitted through an English front-end to Yahoo! Answers, there was still a noticeable fraction of questions and answers in languages such as Spanish, or languages spoken in India. To filter out non-English content, we applied a stop-word-based language-detection technique [13]. Concretely, we used the following list of English stop words: *a, an, and, are, as, has, have, i, in, is, it, me, my, not, of, or, that, the, they, to, was, we, were, will, with, you, your.* Any ⟨question, answer⟩ pair that contained less than three instances of these tokens was removed from further consideration.

Second, we *only accept literal "how to" questions.* We only considered ⟨question, answer⟩ pairs where the question started with "how to," "how do i," or "how can i." This was done for three reasons: First, such questions are typically related to an actual problem or task, as opposed to opinion questions such as "Why have our country's politicians moved so far to the extreme right?"[8] or general knowledge questions such as "How do wildfires affect the ozone layer?"[9] Second, the tips generated from such questions can later more easily be matched against similarly structured web queries. Third, limiting the scope to questions of the given structure made it possible to convert passive "how to X?" questions into active "To X : ..." pieces of advice. We also removed *multi-part questions.* Some questions, such as "Does the truth set you free, or does it simply hurt your feelings? And how do you (usually) handle it?"[10] are made of several sentences, which make the construction of tips very hard. We used simple punctuation rules to keep only single-sentence questions.

Third, we *required that the answer starts with a verb.* We observed that concrete pieces of advice typically start with a verb in the imperative such as "Try this," "Go there," or "Do that." Remember again that our goal is to maximize precision, with a possible sacrifice in the coverage. We compiled a dictionary of English verbs and we used only the infinitive of the verbs. Conveniently, in English the imperative form of a verb agrees with its infinitive without the "to." Answers starting with "do you" or "have you" were ignored, even though both of these verbs were in our dictionary.

We also experimented with a part-of-speech (POS) tagger,[11] to identify answers where the first token of an answer was used as a verb. The performance of this POS-based approach was very similar to the simple method described above. In fact, due to malformed sentences, the POS-based approach incurred a slightly lower recall. Hence, we decided to stick with the simpler approach. We hypothesize that for textual corpora that contain more "proper" English and less online lingo and typos, POS-based methods and other more "semantic" approaches are likely to outperform the dictionary-based approach. Note that the use of an English verb dictionary provides additional filtering for non-English questions or answers.

After these filtering steps, we are left with a set of ⟨question, answer⟩ pairs to which we apply some syntactic transformations to the question, and construct a tip "X : Y" by concatenating the transformed question with the answer. The *tip goal* X is the transformed question, and the *tip suggestion* Y is the answer of the given ⟨question, answer⟩ pair.

To transform the question, we first *convert the questions to active advice* by replacing the initial "how (to | do i | can i)" in the question by a simple "to." Moreover, we *transform the question from ego-centered to user-centered.* Questions asked on Yahoo! Answers are often personal in nature and users bring themselves into the question by making use of first person pronouns such as *I, my, me* and so on. To turn an ego-centered question ("How can I improve my X?") into a user-centered tip ("To improve your X: ...") we replaced all occurrences of *I, my, me, am, 'm, myself, our, ours and we* with *you, your, you, are, 're, yourself, your, yours and you.* This replacement changed the tone of the tip from a dialogue to a more objective piece of advice.

Finally, any candidate tip longer than 160 characters was removed. There is a lot of motivation for doing this. First, it makes it easier to display our tips on mobile devices. Second, even on larger screens the "real estate" of a search result page, is very limited. And third, we believe that users will prefer to-the-point bits of advice, when they exist, over long and intricate solutions.

Note that we did not consider information about the age or recency of a tip. In some domains this might be a relevant signal though as, say, the answer to "how to change the default font in Microsoft Word" depends on the version of the corresponding software which, in turn, depends on the time when the query was issued and when a corresponding tip was created.

Example: The question-answer pair "Q: How can I get the mildew smell out of my towels? – A: Try soaking it

[8] `http://yhoo.it/kR31Z4`

[9] `http://yhoo.it/mf5NXO`

[10] `http://yhoo.it/ifn0jv`

[11] `http://search.cpan.org/~acoburn/Lingua-EN-Tagger/Tagger.pm`

	Very good	Ok	Bad
Very good	12.4%	22.9%	4.8%
Ok	–	25.7%	17.5%
Bad	–	–	16.6%

Table 5: Judge disagreement as computed by macro-averaging over all (judgment, judgment) pairs on a per-tip basis.

in a salt water solution, then washing with soap and cold water, that tends to get rid of smells."[12] was converted to the potential tip "To get the mildew smell out of your towels : try soaking it in a salt water solution, then washing with soap and cold water, that tends to get rid of smells."

5.3 Judging the quality of the tip candidates

The process described above generated a total of 249 675 candidate tips. However, these candidate tips were of a very mixed quality. In order to filter out tips of bad quality, we set to build a classifier for tip quality. To obtain training data for the classifier, we used the CrowdFlower[13] interface to Mechanical Turk.[14]

The workers were asked to label the quality of 20 000 candidate tips as "very good," "ok," or "bad." Those 20 000 tips were sampled uniformly at random from the set of 249 675 tips we constructed. The workers were given the following instructions.

"Very good" : The tip should be concrete and non-obvious. It may offer a likely solution for an issue.

"Ok" : The tip could be an opinion, it could be borderline obvious or its correctness is doubtful.

"Bad" : The tip can be unintelligible, joke advice, insulting, obviously wrong or crucial details are missing.

In addition to these short instructions, which were shown above each tip to evaluate, there was also a similar set of more explicit instructions which included four example for each of the three classes.

One of the advantages of CrowdFlower are so called "gold units," which in our case are tips for which the correct quality judgment is known in advance. These "gold units" are shown the workers at random intervals. If the workers' answers do not match the known correct response their trust score deteriorates. If the trust score becomes too low, the workers are excluded from further judgments and their previous judgments are ignored. To remove potential spammers or low quality workers we used a total of 78 "gold units" (22 very good, 21 ok, 35 bad).

We obtained at least 3 trusted judgments for each of the sampled 20 000 candidate tips. Applying a majority voting scheme, 25% of candidate tips were judged "very good," 48% "ok," and 27% "bad." Table 5 gives details about the inter-judge agreement. Note that there was very little disagreement of the type "very good" vs. "bad" but a substantial amount of disagreement between "very good" vs. "ok."

[12]http://yhoo.it/ClKuN

[13]http://crowdflower.com/

[14]https://www.mturk.com/mturk/welcome

5.4 Detecting high-quality tips using machine learning

Our next step is to use the ground-truth labels we obtained as training data in order to automatically detect high-quality tips. As we were mostly interested in having a high-precision classifier, we phrased the problem as a binary classification problem: can we separate the "very good" tips from the "ok" and "bad" tips? We chose this approach as we were less concerned about dropping a large fraction of "ok" tips than showing "bad" tips.

In the experiments we used standard machine learning algorithms: a support-vector machine with the RBF kernel,[15] a support-vector machine with a linear kernel, a decision tree,[16] and a simple k-nearest-neighbor classifier with Euclidean distance [3]. We made an effort to tune the parameters of each method to deliver best possible performance. Both the SVM and decision tree were configured to penalize more for misclassified instances of the negative (i.e., not "very good") class during training to increase precision.

We consider three types of features. The first feature set ("terms") is the tip-term matrix. This is a sparse matrix containing the number of times a term appears in a tip. Only terms occurring in at least 10 and at most 100K tips were included. Due to the high-dimensionality this set of features could not be used for all machine learning algorithms.

The second feature set ("topics") is derived from the first one. Here, we use the first singular vectors [25] of this matrix as the set of features. These can be interpreted as "topics" of a latent semantic space. More formally, if T is the $n \times m$ tip-term matrix, we have $T \approx U_h \Lambda_h V_h$, where h denotes the number of singular values to use, U_h is an $n \times h$ matrix, Λ_h is $h \times h$, and V_h is $h \times m$. The topic-features are given by the columns of the matrix U_h. In the experiments we set $h = 100$.

The last set ("textual") consists of various properties of the question and answer, such as reading level and sentiment. A few of these are specific to the question answering service, but the majority are easy to compute from any text snippet. To assess the quality of writing, we use the Flesch-Kincaid reading level[17] as computed by the "style" unix command.[18] The sentiment of the tip, both positive and negative, is computed using the SentiStrength[19] tool [24]. See Table 10 for further details.

5.5 Experimental evaluation

We evaluated all 9 combinations of the three classification algorithms and three sets of features. Performance is measured with precision and recall in two variants, hard and soft. The hard variant measures how well the classifier separates the class "very good" from the others. With the soft variant the class "ok" is also considered as relevant. All reported performance numbers are averages over stratified 10-fold cross-validation.

As can be seen in Table 7, differences among the classifiers and feature sets are rather small. All methods achieve a precision of at least 0.62 with at least one of the feature sets.

[15]LIBSVM: www.csie.ntu.edu.tw/~cjlin/libsvm/

[16]The classregtree function of Matlab's Statistics Toolbox.

[17]http://en.wikipedia.org/wiki/Flesch-Kincaid_readability_test

[18]http://www.gnu.org/software/diction/diction.html

[19]http://sentistrength.wlv.ac.uk/

Very good
To zest a lime if you don't have a zester : use a cheese grater
To round a decimal in c : add 0.5 and then floor the value - what you call dropping the decimal. looks like this: int x = (my_float + 0.5);
To access temporary internet files in windows vista : try clicking on start, run and then type in: %temp% and then press enter. cheers
Ok
To eliminate chapped lips : water water water, drink water alot, 8 and more glasses a day i use vaseline gel. it's the best for me!
To forget about a horror movie : sing a song over and over again to stop your mind from thinking about it
To prevent getting gastro : wash hands frequently and don't put them in nose/mouth/eyes.....
Bad
To make money at the age of 15 : hook up with your friends moms.
To make your computer super fast : tie it to the hood of your car and take it on the interstate
To you type a backwards e : use a 3. 3 look's like it

Table 6: Examples of candidate tips for the three quality classes. Poor quality tips are later filtered out by machine learning techniques (see Section 5.4).

	Method	terms	topics	textual
Hard	SVM		0.62/0.36	0.56/0.24
	linear SVM	0.61/0.39	0.67/0.30	0.59/0.16
	tree		0.63/0.13	0.60/0.08
	k-NN	0.65/0.14	0.64/0.20	0.57/0.18
Soft	SVM		0.95/0.18	0.93/0.13
	linear SVM	0.94/0.20	0.96/0.14	0.93/0.08
	tree		0.96/0.07	0.93/0.04
	k-NN	0.95/0.07	0.95/0.10	0.94/0.10

Table 7: Precision/recall for binary "very good" vs. "not very good" classification of potential tips. In the "soft" setting the evaluation was for "very good or ok" vs. "bad" for the *same* binary "very good" vs. "not very good" classifiers.

This is a good result, given that the fraction of the class "very good" is roughly 0.24, and that recognizing good tips can be a difficult problem even for humans. In the case of soft evaluation all methods reach at least 0.94 precision, albeit recall is now even lower. However, it must be emphasized that when tips are shown together with web search results, it is better to not show a tip than showing a tip of low quality. For this study we chose linear SVM with terms features as the combination to be used later when filtering good tips (a total of 26.7k) from our set of candidate tips.

Table 8 shows the hard evaluation across different categories in Yahoo! answers. (Note that these are computed from the training set!) First, the number of tips found in a category varies a lot. Categories rich in possible tips are e.g., "Computers & Internet" and "Family & Relationships," while tips about "Business & Finance" or "Society & Culture" are more rare. Also the fraction of "very good" tips varies considerably across the categories. Finally, the classifier performs a lot better in some categories than others. For example, despite the total fraction of tip candidates, as well as the fraction of "very good" tips being rather low in the "Entertainment & Music" category, the classifier achieves 0.63 precision. In summary, the difficulty of the classification task clearly depends on the topic of the tip in question.

6. MATCHING TIPS TO WEB QUERIES

As a final step, we discuss how to put together the components we described in the previous sections in order to complete the design of our system. In particular, in this step we show (*i*) how to decide which how-to queries to consider, (*ii*) how to find tips for those queries, and (*iii*) how to rank those tips. At heart, this is an information-retrieval task, however, care should be taken in order to account for the special structure of tips, their short length, and the fact that displaying a tip is optional and subject to quality.

Category	P,R	VG	size
Beauty & Style	0.52,0.06	0.16	0.08
Business & Finance	0.48,0.17	0.20	0.03
Cars & Transportation	0.81,0.11	0.23	0.03
Computers & Internet	0.69,0.44	0.45	0.15
Consumer Electronics	0.65,0.29	0.38	0.06
Entertainment & Music	0.63,0.32	0.15	0.05
Family & Relationships	0.64,0.05	0.06	0.14
Games & Recreation	0.65,0.34	0.24	0.04
Health	0.52,0.05	0.15	0.09
Home & Garden	0.39,0.05	0.27	0.04
Society & Culture	0.62,0.19	0.09	0.03
Sports	0.81,0.15	0.19	0.03
Yahoo! Products	0.73,0.53	0.45	0.07

Table 8: Category specific P(recision)/R(ecall) (hard) in training data for the 13 categories with the most tips, using a linear SVM with 100 topic features. VG refers to the fraction of labeled "very good" tips in the training data. Size refers to the total fraction of all identified high quality tips falling into the corresponding class.

6.1 Deciding which web queries to consider

Which queries should we consider as candidates for showing a tip? We decided to be fairly conservative and to even consider showing a tip only if the query was judged as a how-to query according to the "General-.10" approach (Section 4.3). Our motivation was that for such queries the tip could answer directly the underlying information need.

Note, however, that in many cases it might be interesting to show "related tips," even when no how-to intent is present. For example, for the query "sour cream" one could display the tip "To make fresh homemade sour cream : add a few drops of lemon juice to double cream."[20] This type of display would have more of a "Did you know ...?" flavor. It would

[20] http://yhoo.it/meI2YV

be interesting to evaluate through user studies how open users are for such kinds of serendipitous bits of advice.

6.2 Deciding which tips to consider for a query

Assume that we have decided to consider a query as candidate for showing a tip. The next question is to find a set of tips that could potentially be displayed in response to the query. Note that this binary decision of "Should I show anything at all?" does not arise in traditional web search where the search engine is *obliged* to return matching results, if any, even if they are of low quality.

For choosing a minimum "relatedness" threshold, there are many choices. In a strict scheme, for a query "how to do X" only tips of the form "To do X : . . . " would be considered. In this setting the query equals the goal of the tip.

Though this conservative approach has good precision (.72-.92 depending on the evaluation setting, see Table 9), it suffers on recall as it is overly conservative. To allow fuzzy matches and improve recall, we experimented with two parameters. First, we experimented with both AND and OR modes. In the AND mode *all* terms in the (normalized) query have to appear in the *goal* part of the tip. In the OR mode, partial matches are also counted. The first column in Table 9 refers to the matching mode. Second, we experimented with a parameter of *matching span*, which is defined as the fraction of distinct tokens in the tip goal that appear in the query. So, a minimum span of 0.5 requires at least half of the tokens in the tip goal to be in the query. The second column in Table 9 refers to this parameter.

We also experimented with matching using the *whole* text of the tip, not just the goal. However, this led to displaying tips that were only weakly related to the queries. We did not experiment further with this approach as we were interested in displaying answers to information needs, rather than "Did you know . . . ?" bits of advice.

6.3 Ranking tips for a given query

Once a set of candidate tips has been identified for a given query, a myriad of different ranking functions could be tried. Note that we are only interested in displaying a *single* tip and so precision at one (P@1) is a natural measure for the quality of a ranking function.

We used a simple ranking function. We rank according to the number of tokens in the query that are found in the tip goal, normalized by the goal's token length. Repeated tokens in the query are counted repeatedly. Note that stop words were previously removed. Ties were broken using `tf-idf` with simple logarithmic `idf`. Remaining ties were broken by giving preference to longer tips.

We deliberately decided against using more advanced features, such as the confidence of the classifier which labeled the tip as "very good" or signals such as the Yahoo! Answers point count of the person giving the underlying answer. This was done to keep our approach as modular as possible and work with arbitrary textual tips following the "To do X : try Y" structure. We also decided against using `tf-idf` as the primary ranking criteria as preliminary experiments showed that this often led to the preference of a single, rare term being present in both the query and the tip while giving too little importance to tokens such as "ipod" which were very common in our data set. Additionally, there were typically only very few tips to rank due to the minimum span threshold of .5 (see Section 6.2 and Table 9), in particular with an AND mode of query execution.

mode	span	vol.	dist.	P@1	med.	agr.
AND	.50	10.0%	3.2%	.497/.747	2	56%
AND	.66	7.3%	2.2%	.573/.840	2	49%
AND	1.0	4.5%	1.0%	.717/.922	1	63%
OR	.50	78.6%	85.6%	.057/.137	2	87%
OR	.66	33.5%	35.7%	.132/.247	2	83%
OR	1.0	12.2%	10.2%	.187/.394	2	56%

Table 9: The first two columns refer to different settings for the (binary) decision of whether to include a tip as a display candidate for a given query. Volume (vol.) and distinct (dist.) refer to the fraction of General-.10 "how-to" queries for which a tip was found. P@1 is the quality, averaged over 500 distinct (query, highest ranked tip) pairs. For the first number only 2's are counted as relevant, whereas for the second number 1's are also included. Median (med.) is the median number of display candidate tips to rank, when this set is non-empty. The ranking function was the same in all cases and is described in Section 6.3.

6.4 Experimental evaluation

We experimented with a total of six different parameter configurations for determining whether a tip should be shown for a query or not. For each of the six settings, 500 distinct (query, tip) pairs, sampled uniformly at random, were evaluated by three different judges with 50 pairs being evaluated by all three to estimate inter-judge agreement.

Judges were asked to evaluate the quality of the (query, tip) match on a 3-point scale by judging if the tip is ...

2 – ... both closely related to the query and very useful in addressing the user's information need;

1 – ... at least somewhat related to the query and potentially useful in addressing the user's information need;

0 – ... either not related to the query or is not useful in addressing the user's information need.

Results are shown in Table 9. Note that this evaluation does not only include the quality of the (query, tip) matching, but also the quality of the tip itself. Similarly, if the query lacks a how-to intent (e.g., "how to train your dragon") this will also hurt the performance.

7. RELATED WORK

This paper describes a system that (*i*) process a question-answering corpus to create a large database of *tips*, (*ii*) identifies how-to queries from a web query log, and (*iii*) serves those queries with tips. To our knowledge, this is a novel task. In this section we discuss work that is related to various components of our system.

Work on Yahoo! answers. We create a database of tips by processing automatically questions and answers from Yahoo! answers. Then we employ a machine-learning approach to assess the quality of those tips and filter our tips of bad quality. In the spirit of this task, Agichtein et al. [2] build a machine-learning approach to assess quality of questions and answers in Yahoo! answers. Similarly, Bouguessa et al. [6] apply link-analysis techniques to identify authoritative users in Yahoo! Answers. Both of these works employ user-centered and community-based features. In our work, we made the conscious decision not to consider such features to have our methods more generally applicable. Harper et al. [11] investigate the problem of classiying questions into informational vs. conversational and they observe that informational questions have a higher archival value and are more useful for future reference. They found that personal pronouns are useful features in this distinction and we included these in our feature set (see Table 10). In another line of work, Adamic et al. [1], Surdeanu et al. [22], and Kim and Oh [16] address the problem of finding automatically the best answer to a question in Yahoo! answers. The techniques and features used in all the above-mentioned papers could be potentially applied in our system in order to select more questions and answers of good quality, and thus, to enlarge our database of tips.

Question answering and databases of factoids. Contrasted with traditional information retrieval, where the goal is to retrieve full documents, the problem of *question answering* [18, 26] asks to locate possibly very fine-grained, targeted answers to questions given by the user. At a high level our work also falls in this framework, but there are important differences to existing approaches to question answering. In particular, we are not concerned with constructing an intermediary database of facts for assembling answers to questions, as done e.g., by Hildebrand et al. [12] or Denicia-Carral et al. [10]. Nor is our work about passage retrieval [9, 23], as we are not direcly using passages of text as the tips. A sophisticated passage retrieval system might also be useful to find tips for how-to questions, but so far research on passage retrieval has concentrated on factoid questions, not procedural knowledge, and are thus not directly applicable in our setting. Moreover, our system is inherently designed to work with a keyword search engine, as we can assign a how-to intent also to queries that are not explicitly formulated as a question by the user. Finally, many Q&A systems rely on proper punctuation but our approach also works with imperfect user-generated content.

Also related is the recent paper by Bian et al. [5], where the authors define the problem of *question-answering retrieval*, as the problem of retrieving high-quality question-answer pairs, from a question-answering portal, in response to a web query. This problem is again different than the one we address in this paper in many ways. Most importantly, we focus in how-to queries, and we provide a methodology to identify such queries. Also we combine questions and answers in a concise piece of advice that we call tip.

The idea of automatically extracting information from online sources to build datasets of factoids is another active area of research. A typical task in this line of work is ontolgy construction. Suchanek et al. [21] combine data from Wikipedia and WordNet to automatically build a large scale ontology of real world entities. Another popular application domain is biology, with the objective of assisting curators to mine different types facts from medical publications, in particular entities, and relationships between these entities [8, 27]. An important property that distinguishes our problem is that an ontology or any other database of factoids is unlikely to be sufficient to construct answers how-to queries. Our tips often describe a process that is not easily extracted from relationships between entities.

Query-indent classification. A component of our system is to automatically identify how-to queries. This component is related to a line of work on query-intent classification. Broder [7] defined a classification of web queries into three categories: informational, transactional, and navigational. Rose and Levinson [20] further extended the Broder's taxonomy and introduced goal hierarchy. Following Broder's taxonomy, several authors have focused on the automatic classification and characterization of user intent [14, 17]. In a somewhat related work, Radlinski et al. [19] find popular meanings of queries using web-search logs and user-click behavior. In our work, we do not aim to classify all queries in a hierarchy of intents, instead we are focusing on only identifying how-to queries. Again, we view the line of work on query-intent classification as complementary to our work, as techniques from these papers can be potentially employed to improve the accuracy of our query-identification task.

Existing services. The idea of serving tips for mobile devices with a focus on local/geographical events has been used in systems such as Foursquare[21] and View.[22] Differences between those services and our work are that (*i*) they do not extract tips automatically, and (*ii*) they exclusively focus on tips with a local/geographical context. So, for instance, they would not provide any tips such as "To change the default font in Microsoft Word do ...." The service most closely related to our system is probably *ClueDB*.[23] ClueDB allows users to submit tips (called "clues"), vote, and comment on each other's tips. However, ClueDB does not make use of any automatic extraction of tips but relies solely on a community effort. Even though we believe that a community of tip curators could add significant value, we also claim that automatic extraction of tips is a valuable tool to overcome the cold-start problem. In our work we also address the problem of matching queries to tips and ranking a set of candidate tips.

8. CONCLUSIONS

In this paper, we described a modular system that extracts high-quality tips from Yahoo! Answers and shows them as a direct display for matching web queries. We believe that such a system helps web search engines to differentiate themselves from competitors by providing "Answers, not Links"—an often heard phrase concerning the future of web search.

In the future we hope to improve our system along a number of dimensions. First, each of the individual parts (how-to identification, tip extraction, removal of low-quality tips, selecting candidate tips for web queries, ranking those candidate tips) could be improved by (*i*) incorporating additional features and (*ii*) combining our techniques with existing ones. Second, it seems feasible to extract tips from other data sources such as Twitter or travel sites. For Twitter, tip-related hash tags could be a useful signal. For Travel related and, in fact, arbitrary sites rules such as "Tips have to start with a verb." could be combined with part-of-speech tagging to ensure that the supposed tip is self-contained and does not refer to previous parts of text. Third, we would like to identify other query types which could be addressed by

[21] `http://foursquare.com`

[22] `http://view.io/`

[23] `http://www.cluedb.com/`

(Y! Answers specific) HAS-REFERENCE: Indicates whether the "reference" field in the answer was used. (Contents of this field *were not* used when constructing tips!)
(Y! Answers specific) AWARD-TYPE: Indicates whether the answer was selected "best answer" by the asker, by the community or automatically after a certain time.
WORD-IN-TIP: Occurrence counts for words in the tip that appear in at least 10 and in at most 100,000 tips.
FREQUENT-FRACTION: The fraction of words found in a frequent word dictionary. We used a list of 2 126 distinct words downloaded from `http://www.paulnoll.com/Books/Clear-English/English-3000-common-words.html` to compute the fraction of tokens that could be found in a dictionary of common English words;
READING-LEVEL: Flesch-Kincaid reading level.
POSITIVE-SENTIMENT-[Q|A]: The positive sentiment of the question according to SentiStrength.
NEGATIVE-SENTIMENT-[Q|A]: The negative sentiment of the question according to SentiStrength.
1ST-PERSON-SINGULAR-[Q|A]: The case insensitive count of "i", "my" etc. appearing in the question.
1ST-PERSON-PLURAL-[Q|A]: The case insensitive count of "we", "our" etc. appearing in the question.
2ND-PERSON-[Q|A]: The case insensitive count of "you", "yours" etc. appearing in the question.
3RD-PERSON-SINGULAR-[Q|A]: The case insensitive count of "he", "she", "his" etc. appearing in the question.
3RD-PERSON-PLURAL-[Q|A]: The case insensitive count of "they", "theirs" etc. appearing in the question;
FRACTION-UPPER-CASE-[Q|A]: Fraction of all uppercase characters (A-Z) in the question.
REPEATED-?!-COUNT-[Q|A]: The count of sequences matching /[!?]2,/
POSITIVE-EMOTICONS-[Q|A]: Number of emoticons from the set ":-)",":)", ";-)" and ";)".
NEGATIVE-EMOTICONS-[Q|A]: Number of emoticons from the set ":-(" and ":(".
URL-COUNT-[Q|A]: Count for the regular expression /[a-z]3, .(com|net|org|ca|uk)/ in the question.
TOKEN-COUNT-[Q|A]: Total number of tokens in the question when splitting on all white spaces and sentence punctuation.

Table 10: Textual features. The notation [Q|A] indicates that the feature appears separately for the question and answer parts of the tip.

similar techniques. To identify relevant query classes we envision applying a Jeopardy-like approach to answer the question "What type of web query should this short piece of text be returned to?"

Acknowledgements. This research was partially supported by the Torres Quevedo Program of the Spanish Ministry of Science and Innovation, co-funded by the European Social Fund, and by the Spanish Centre for the Development of Industrial Technology under the CENIT program, project CEN-20101037, "Social Media" `http://www.cenitsocialmedia.es/`.

9. REFERENCES

[1] L. A. Adamic, J. Zhang, E. Bakshy, and M. S. Ackerman. Knowledge sharing and yahoo answers: everyone knows something. In *WWW*, 2008.

[2] E. Agichtein, C. Castillo, D. Donato, A. Gionis, and G. Mishne. Finding high-quality content in social media. In *WSDM*, 2008.

[3] E. Alpaydin. *Introduction to Machine Learning.* 2004.

[4] I. Antonellis, H. G. Molina, and C. C. Chang. Simrank++: query rewriting through link analysis of the click graph. *VLDB*, 1, 2008.

[5] J. Bian, Y. Liu, E. Agichtein, and H. Zha. Finding the right facts in the crowd: factoid question answering over social media. In *WWW*, 2008.

[6] M. Bouguessa, B. Dumoulin, and S. Wang. Identifying authoritative actors in question-answering forums: the case of yahoo! answers. In *KDD*, 2008.

[7] A. Broder. A taxonomy of web search. *SIGIR Forum*, 2002.

[8] A. M. Cohen and W. R. Hersh. A survey of current work in biomedical text mining. *Briefings in Bioinformatics*, 6(1), 2005.

[9] H. Cui, R. Sun, K. Li, M.-Y. Kan, and T.-S. Chua. Question answering passage retrieval using dependency relations. In *SIGIR*, 2005.

[10] C. Denicia-Carral, M. Montes-Gómez, L. Villasenor-Pineda, and R. Hernández. A text mining approach for definition question answering. In *ANLP*, 2006.

[11] F. Harper, D. Moy, and J. Konstan. Facts or friends?: distinguishing informational and conversational questions in social Q&A sites. In *CHI*, 2009.

[12] W. Hildebrandt, B. Katz, and J. Lin. Answering definition questions with multiple knowledge sources. In *HLT/NAACL*, 2004.

[13] N. C. Ingle. A language identification table. *Incorporated Linguist*, 15(4), 1976.

[14] B. J. Jansen, D. L. Booth, and A. Spink. Determining the informational, navigational, and transactional intent of web queries. *Information Processing Management*, 44, 2008.

[15] R. Jones, B. Rey, O. Madani, and W. Greiner. Generating query substitutions. In *WWW*, 2006.

[16] S. Kim and S. Oh. Users' relevance criteria for evaluating answers in a social q&a site. *JASIST*, 60(4), 2009.

[17] U. Lee, Z. Liu, and J. Cho. Automatic identification of user goals in web search. In *WWW*, 2005.

[18] V. Moriceau, E. SanJuan, X. Tannier, and P. Bellot. Overview of the 2009 QA Track. *Focused Retrieval and Evaluation*, 2010.

[19] F. Radlinski, M. Szummer, and N. Craswell. Inferring query intent from reformulations and clicks. In *WWW*, 2010.

[20] D. E. Rose and D. Levinson. Understanding user goals in web search. In *WWW*, 2004.

[21] F. M. Suchanek, G. Kasneci, and G. Weikum. Yago: A large ontology from wikipedia and wordnet. *Journal of Web Semantics*, 6(3), 2008.

[22] M. Surdeanu, M. Ciaramita, and H. Zaragoza. Learning to rank answers on large online QA Cclections. In *ACL*, 2008.

[23] S. Tellex, B. Katz, J. Lin, A. Fernandes, and G. Marton. Quantitative evaluation of passage retrieval algorithms for question answering. In *SIGIR*, 2003.

[24] M. Thelwall, K. Buckley, G. Paltoglou, D. Cai, and A. Kappas. Sentiment in short strength detection informal text. *JASIST*, 61, 2010.

[25] L. Trefethen and D. Bau. *Numerical linear algebra.* Society for Industrial Mathematics, 1997.

[26] E. Voorhees. Question answering in TREC. In *CIKM*, 2001.

[27] R. Winnenburg, T. Wächter, C. Plake, A. Doms, and M. Schroeder. Facts from text: can text mining help to scale-up high-quality manual curation of gene products with ontologies? *Briefings in Bioinformatics*, 9(6), 2008.

[28] H. Zaragoza, B. B. Cambazoglu, and R. Baeza-Yates. Web search solved?: all result rankings the same? In *CIKM*, 2010.

A Straw Shows Which Way the Wind Blows: Ranking Potentially Popular Items from Early Votes

Peifeng Yin[†] [*] Ping Luo[§] Min Wang[♯] Wang-Chien Lee[‡]

[†,‡] Department of Computer Science & Engineering, Pennsylvania State University

[§,♯] Hewlett Packard Labs China, Beijing, China

{[†] pzy102, [‡] wlee} @cse.psu.edu, {[§] ping.luo, [♯] min.wang6}@hp.com

ABSTRACT

Prediction of popular items in online content sharing systems has recently attracted a lot of attention due to the tremendous need of users and its commercial values. Different from previous works that make prediction by fitting a popularity growth model, we tackle this problem by exploiting the latent *conforming* and *maverick* personalities of those who vote to assess the quality of on-line items. We argue that the former personality prompts a user to cast her vote conforming to the majority of the service community while on the contrary the later personality makes her vote different from the community. We thus propose a *Conformer-Maverick (CM)* model to simulate the voting process and use it to rank top-k potentially popular items based on the early votes they received. Through an extensive experimental evaluation, we validate our ideas and find that our proposed CM model achieves better performance than baseline solutions, especially for smaller k.

Categories and Subject Descriptors

H.4 [**Information Systems**]: Applications; J.4 [**Computer Applications**]: Social and Behavior Sciences

General Terms

Experimentation, Human Factors.

1. INTRODUCTION

The vision of Web 2.0 aims to encourage people to publish and share digital contents in the Internet. Many web and mobile services, e.g., YouTube[1], JokeBox[2], etc, have provided convenient tools to facilitate content sharing. Moreover, they support a voting function to allow users to express their positive/negative opinions, usually in simple binary format such as "like"/"dislike" in YouTube and "Thump up"/"Thump down" in JokeBox, on published items.

Due to the overwhelming quantity and diversity of published items, many of these services tend to put on their service front page the *popular items* that have received the most (positive) votes. By assuming that high-quality items receive more positive than negative votes, this simple strategy addresses the difficulty of assessing the quality of published items. Nevertheless, while putting those items on the front page may facilitate new or inactive users to find popular items easily, it does not help the loyal users who frequently return to the service since they probably have already accessed or even voted those so-called popular items. Moreover, it may lead to the situation of "rich-get-richer" [13], making these popular items difficult to be replaced. Furthermore, "popularity" may imply "obsolete" in some cases. Consider sales on Groupon[3] or Dealsea[4], where super deals usually come with a cap on limited number of participants. There is no doubt that many people will grab these deals, making them more popular and at the same time faster to reach the cap than other items. Business strategies that rely on the "known" popularity of items will unavoidably highlight near-expire deals, which is not desirable. We argue that user experience will be greatly improved if a system can predict the "potential" popularity of an item early without waiting until the popularity of the item becomes known through accumulating many votes. Additionally, being able to predict the popularity of items have tremendous value to not only service providers but also marketers who would bid for ad-space on items with high potential popularity in order to maximize the exposure. In this work, we aim to develop a popularity prediction technique that effectively predicts how likely a newly published item will become popular.

To predict popular items, a content-based technique has been proposed in [18]. In this work, a textual item is split into meaningful words which in turn forms a feature vector of the item. Next, a classification machine is learned to predict whether a new item, given its feature vector, will be popular or not. This method has several deficiencies. Firstly, this technique is not applicable to non-text contents, e.g., audio and video. Secondly, even for textual contents, it may not handle short messages such as tweets and short jokes where discriminative feature vectors are difficult to form due to the limited number of words or the subtle implications. Finally, the content-based method is unable to process items with new words that have not appeared in existing items.

Another idea for popularity prediction is to exploit the early votes. In [13], the trend of the vote growth is explored

[*]The work was done when Peifeng Yin was visiting HP Labs China.

[1]http://www.youtube.com

[2]http://itunes.apple.com/us/app/all-in-1-joke-box-no-ads-unlimited/id363494433?mt=8

[3]http://www.groupon.com

[4]http://dealsea.com

Permission to make digital or hard copies of all or part of this work for personal or classroom use is granted without fee provided that copies are not made or distributed for profit or commercial advantage and that copies bear this notice and the full citation on the first page. To copy otherwise, to republish, to post on servers or to redistribute to lists, requires prior specific permission and/or a fee.

WSDM'12, February 8–12, 2012, Seattle, Washington, USA.

Copyright 2012 ACM 978-1-4503-0747-5/12/02 ...$10.00.

and a logarithm linear model is learned to fit the correlation between early votes and the popularity. Thus, popularity prediction can be made by this model. However, designed for predicting the growth of item groups, this method is prune to possibly high inaccuracy when targeting on the individual item. Our approach, also exploiting the early votes, aims to rank the potential of individual item to become popular, instead of focusing on the popularity growth trend.

Through an empirical study we observe that, while there does exist correlation between early and final vote status, the people who contribute the early votes can be exploited to improve the prediction accuracy. Specifically, we observe that among early voters, some people's votes tend to be conforming to the opinions of the majority in the user community while some others exhibit contrary voting behavior. Thus, in this paper, we refer to the users exhibiting high degree of conforming behavior as *Conformer* and name those who tend to cast votes differently from the opinions of the society or social group (the user community of a service in our study) as *Maverick*. As shown in Figure 1, for Conformers, since their behaviors tend to be conforming to the group behavior, their votes usually can be amplified to represent the group opinions. On the other hand, the Mavericks give votes opposite to the majority, i.e., they favor items which do not attract the majority of users while giving negative ratings to items which are actually popular among the majority. For example, in the case of JokeBox where users share and rate funny jokes, Conformers are amused by funny jokes while the Mavericks may laugh at some clueless ones or shaggy-dog stories.

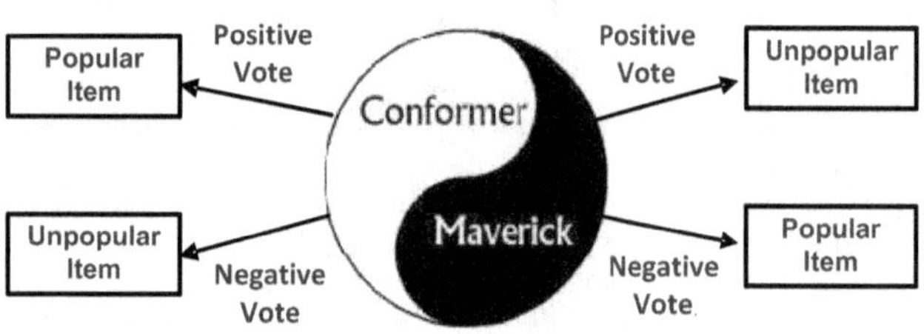

Figure 1: Illustration of Conformer and Maverick

We argue that each person has both conforming and maverick personalities in different degrees and thus propose a *Conformer-Maverick (CM)* model to capture the two personalities of a person. In this model, we assume that each person is equipped with these two personalities and one of them prevails when casting a vote. As mentioned, different people have these two personalities in varied degrees, which are learned by maximizing the probability of the observed vote data with EM algorithm. To predict whether an item will be popular or not, the conformer-maverick preference of its early voters are checked. Ideally, if positive votes come from more conformers and/or negative votes from more mavericks, the item is more likely to be welcomed by the majority, and vice versa.

Another challenge for popular-item prediction is how the popularity is measured based on the aggregated votes. In previous works [13, 18, 9, 14] only positive votes are available for an item and thus this number is naturally treated as its popularity. In this study, however, an item can receive both positive and negative votes and it remains a problem how such two-dimensional values are converted to a single dimensional popularity value. We designed a popularity measurement (detailed in Section 2) that considers both positive and negative votes and represent an item's popularity with a real number ranging from -1 to 1.

To sum up, our contribution is listed below:

- We designed a new popularity measure of items by combining both of their positive and negative votes.
- We proposed a Conformer-Maverick model to capture two personalities of a user in the voting process.
- With the CM model, we developed two ranking mechanisms, i.e., Aggregation-based ranking and Q-based ranking. The first one predicts the vote for each user and aggregates them while the second one directly predicts the item's popularity degree defined in Section 2.
- We conducted extensive experiments to evaluate the performance of the proposed solutions.

The rest of the paper is organized as follows. Section 2 defines the popularity measurement equation and formulates the problem, i.e., top-k popular item ranking. Section 4 and 5 respectively discuss the details of the proposed CM model and how it is adopted to accomplish the popularity prediction. Section 3 gives details of Naive CM model. Evaluation is put in Section 6. Section 7 gives related work and finally Section 8 concludes the paper and introduces our future work.

2. PRELIMINARIES

In this section we formally define a measure of item popularity and then formulate the research problem of *top-k popular item prediction*. Finally we analyze the problem and motivate our ideas behind the proposed solutions.

2.1 Popularity Measurement

In a content sharing and rating system, the popularity of a published item may be reflected by the votes it receives. Intuitively, the more positive votes it receives, the more popular it is and vice versa. While one may argue that an item receiving a large number of votes (whether they are positive or not) is popular, in this paper, we define popular items as those that are "liked" by the majority of the service users, i.e., those that receive many more positive than negative votes. To judge whether an item is liked by the majority, one precondition is that the item has received sufficient number of votes. For example, it is not reasonable to refer to an item receiving only 2 positive but 0 negative votes as popular. In other words, our measure of popularity aim to ensure that the number of votes exceeds certain threshold.

Formally, in a content sharing system, given pv positive votes and nv negative votes of an item where $pv + nv \geq \sigma$, a vote threshold, its *popularity* q is computed as in Equation (1).

$$q = \begin{cases} \frac{pv-nv}{pv+nv+1}; & pv - nv \neq 0 \\ \frac{\epsilon}{pv+nv+1}; & pv - nv = 0 \end{cases} \tag{1}$$

where ϵ is a small constant, e.g., 0.01. Note that this measure employs a threshold σ to govern the minimum total number of votes, which are system/service-dependent. We discuss how to determine the setting of σ in Section 6.

As shown Equation (1), the popularity ranges from -1 to 1. A measured popularity close to 1 indicates significant number of positive votes over the negative ones, and vice versa. On the other hand, a popularity value close to 0 suggests that the item is rather controversial, i.e., the number of positive and negative votes are quite even, and thus difficult to classify whether it is popular or not. Notice that, in Equation (1), we introduce a constant ϵ when an item receives equal number of positive and negative votes, aiming to incorporate the *controversial degree*, which is inversely proportional to the number of total votes, into the measure of item popularity.

We use an example in Table 1 to illustrate the popularity measures for different items. Suppose that there are six items and the votes they received are listed in the table. We can see that the popularity of items (i_1, i_2, i_3) are positive while that of items (i_4, i_5, i_6) are negative, which follows the common wisdom that more positive (negative) votes indicates higher (lower) popularity. Moreover, the items with popularity very close to 0 is more controversial than those with popularity less close to 0, e.g., item i_4 is more controversial than i_3.

Table 1: Illustration of Item Popularity

Item	Positive Vote	Negative Vote	Popularity
i_1	14	1	0.8125
i_2	97	2	0.95
i_3	4	3	0.125
i_4	99	100	-0.005
i_5	5	10	-0.3125
i_6	2	97	-0.95

2.2 Problem Formulation

Here we formulate the research problem of predicting the most popular items among newly created ones as a ranking problem. Our goal is to design a ranking function that quantifies the potential of a newly published item to become popular based on its early votes. Particularly, given N newly published items associated with their early n votes, the algorithm returns k items that are most likely to be popular.

Top-k Popular Item Ranking. Let the item i's first n votes be denoted by $\vec{V_i} = \langle(u_{i_1}, v_{i_1}), \cdots, (u_{i_n}, v_{i_n})\rangle$, where $u_{i_j}, 1 \le j \le n$ is a voter and $v_{i_j} \in \{-1, 1\}$ is the vote casted by u_{i_j}. Given a set of items $S = \{\vec{V_1}, \cdots, \vec{V_N}\}$, the *Top-k Popular Item Ranking* determines a sorted list of k items $S' \subseteq S, |S'| = k$ such that i) any item in S' is more likely to be popular than all the items in $S - S'$ ii) items in S' are non-increasingly sorted by their potential to be popular.

2.3 Problem Analysis

To predict a candidate item's potential to become popular based on its early votes, a natural question is whether there is a correlation between the early and final votes. To answer this question, we collect voting data from a popular iPhone application JokeBox[5] to conduct an analysis on the items which have received no less than 8 votes. We plot their early and final votes on a graph where x and y axis respectively represent the popularity computed according to early and final votes (as defined in Equation (1)). The results are shown in Figure 2, where Figure 2(a) displays the raw plot and Figure 2(b) shows the mean value and standard deviation. Generally speaking, items with good early votes may likely turn out to be popular. However, the scattered distribution of the data points in Figure 2(a) suggests potential inaccuracy if prediction is purely based on the votes. For example, given two newly published items, one with 3 positive and 2 negative early votes (i.e., $x \approx 0.1667$) while the other one's with 4 positive and 1 negative early votes (i.e., $x = 0.5$). It is however difficult to judge which one is more likely to be popular since statistically either one can turn out to be more popular than the other. Furthermore, if two items' early votes are exactly the same, it is unable to distinguish them.

[5]Details of the data are introduced in Section 6

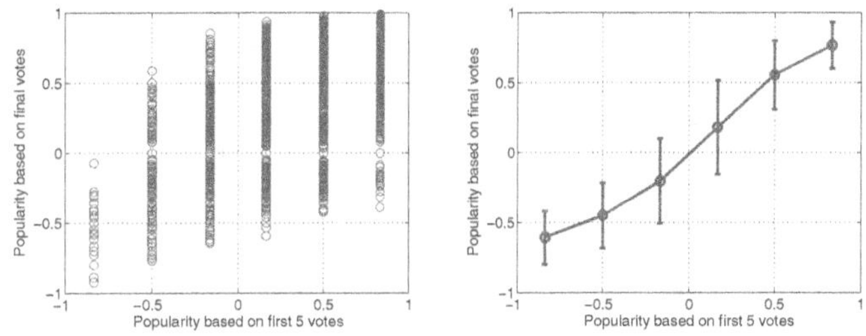

(a) Raw Data (b) Statistical Data

Figure 2: Statistical analysis on correlation where x and y axis respectively represent the popularity computed according to early and final votes.

In this study we resort to the voters to refine the prediction, aiming to find users who always give "conforming" (or "maverick") votes to items. Here the conforming votes mean that the casted positive/negative early votes later turn out to receive more positive/negative votes eventually. On the contrary, maverick votes mean that the casted positive/negative early votes leads to more negative/positive votes eventually. Thus, we aim to identify users whose votes are either positively or negatively correlated to the popularity of items. To this end, we calculate the *Pearson correlation coefficient*[6] of users' votes and items' popularity. Formally, given the votes of a user on multiple items (denoted by $\mathbf{X}$) and the corresponding items' popularity (denoted by $\mathbf{Q}$), we use Pearson correlation coefficient to measure the strength of linear dependence between $\mathbf{X}$ and $\mathbf{Q}$. The absolute value of Pearson correlation coefficients is no bigger than 1. Values equal to 1 or -1 correspond to purely linear positive and negative correlations respectively.

Using the voting data collected from JokeBox, we calculate the Pearson correlation coefficient for users randomly sampled from the whole user set. The distribution of this correlation values is plotted in Figure 3. We can see that most users have positive correlation values around 0.5. This indicates that people are not purely a conformer or a maverick but a combination of the two biased towards the conformer personality. Based on this observation, we propose a *Conformer-Maverick (CM)* model to capture these two personalities and adopt the model in popularity prediction.

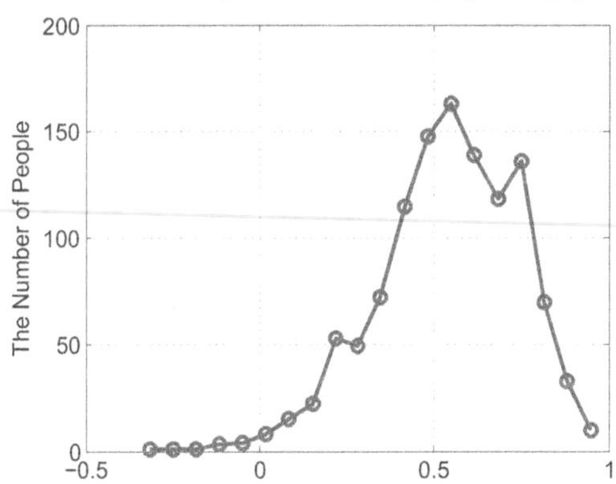

Figure 3: Pearson correlation of user's votes and items' quality

3. NAIVE CONFORMER-MAVERICK MODEL

In this section, we introduce a solution to the top-k popular item prediction problem. Based on our observations

[6]http://en.wikipedia.org/wiki/Pearson_product-moment_correlation_coefficient

discussed in Section 2.3, here we first propose a heuristic method to model the two user personalities of conformers and mavericks and develop a ranking function for popular item prediction. We refer to the method as *Naive Conformer-Maverick (NCM)* model to differentiate it from another solution discussed later in Section 4.

Recall that when a Conformer (Maverick) gives positive (negative) vote to an item, it turns out to be popular later, and vice versa. However, most people are not a pure Conformer or Maverick but their combinations (as shown in Figure 3). A question is how much we could rely on a person's view when she gives a positive (negative) vote to an item.

The NCM assumes that a person has a Conformer weight $w_c \in [0,1]$ and a Maverick weight $w_m \in [0,1]$. The difference of the two weights suggests how reliable the person's opinion is. A large value of $w_c - w_m$ indicates that the person's vote v reflects the popularity q of the item, i.e., $v = 1$ indicates a positive q while $v = -1$ a negative one. Formally, given a series of the votes $\mathbf{X} = \{x_1, \cdots, x_n\}$ casted by a user and the popularity of the voted items $\mathbf{Q} = \{q_1, \cdots, q_n\}$, the w_c and w_m of the user is defined in Equation (2).

$$w_c = \frac{C + \sum_{i=1}^{n} \mathbf{1}_{x_i \cdot q_i > 0} \cdot |q_i|}{2C + n}, w_m = \frac{C + \sum_{j=1}^{n} \mathbf{1}_{x_j \cdot q_j < 0} \cdot |q_i|}{2C + n} \tag{2}$$

where C is a constant larger than 1, serving as a prior weight and $\mathbf{1}_{\text{condition}} = \begin{cases} 1, & \text{condition is true} \\ 0, & \text{otherwise} \end{cases}$

Here we do not calculate w_c and w_m via the Pearson correlation of $\mathbf{X}$ and $\mathbf{Q}$ because the calculation of this correlation may fail when entries in $\mathbf{X}$ are all equal to a constant value (1 or -1) due to the issue of zero denominator.

For a new user who has not committed any single vote, her Conformer and Maverick weights are initialized as $w_c = w_m = \frac{C}{2C} = 0.5$, indicating an unclear personality. When she starts to vote on items, her weights will gradually change. Specifically, each time when her vote x is consistent with an item's final vote q, i.e., $x \cdot q > 0$, her Conformer weight w_c will increase. Otherwise, her Maverick weight w_m will increase as $x \cdot q < 0$.

As for the top-k popularity prediction, given an item's first n early votes $\vec{V_i} = \langle (u_{i_1}, v_{i_1}), \cdots, (u_{i_n}, v_{i_n}) \rangle$, where $v_{i_j} \in \{-1, 1\}$ is a vote and u_{i_j} is the voter with Conformer and Maverick weights as $w_c^{i_j}$ and $w_m^{i_j}$, respectively, the popularity ranking score is the weighted sum of those votes as defined in Equation (3).

$$\texttt{PopRank}(\vec{V_i}) = \sum_{j=1}^{n} (w_c^{i_j} - w_m^{i_j}) \cdot v_{i_j} \tag{3}$$

We use a simple example to illustrate the ranking function. Suppose there are two new items whose early votes are respectively $(u_1, 1)$ and $(u_2, 1)$, where the first voter's Conformer and Maverick weights are $w_c^1 = 0.9$ and $w_m^1 = 0.1$, while the second one's are $w_c^2 = 0.2$ and $w_m^2 = 0.8$. The ranking of the two items are shown below.

$$\begin{aligned} \texttt{PopRank}(\vec{V_1}) &= (0.9 - 0.1) \times 1 = 0.8 \\ \texttt{PopRank}(\vec{V_2}) &= (0.2 - 0.8) \times 1 = -0.6 \end{aligned} \tag{4}$$

Therefore the first item is more likely to be popular.

4. CONFORMER-MAVERICK MODEL

In this section we propose a probabilistic model, *Conformer-Maverick Model*, to simulate the voting process. Different from the NCM model that adopts a heuristic way to model the user profile and rank the item, this new model considers the voting behavior as a constrained random process. Based on the model, we aim to learn a better assignment of the conformer and maverick personalities for each user.

In an item voting process, a user firstly views an item, forms a judgement according to its quality, and casts a vote based on the judgement. For conformer-minded users, their votes usually are aligned with the general opinions of the user community while for maverick-dominated users, their votes are rather deviated. This explains why people with different personalities cast different votes on the same item, as shown in Figure 1. To model the voting behavior as a constrained random process, jointly determined by the voter's personality and the item's quality, we assume that one person's voting behavior is independent of others'. Figure 4 illustrates the process, where u stands for a user and z is her latent personality (i.e., conformer or maverick), which, together with the item's quality q, generates a parameter p. This p finally determines whether the vote v is positive or negative.

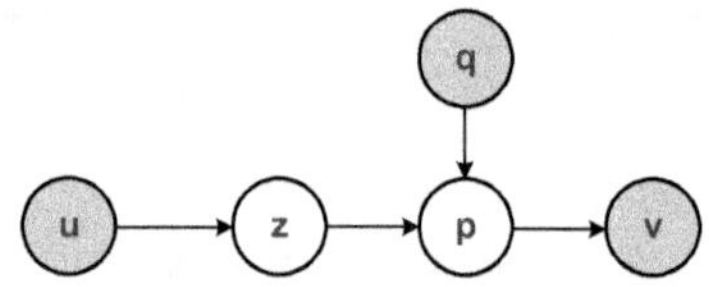

Figure 4: Generative Model for Voting

Specifically, the generating process is shown in Algorithm 1. To cast a vote in one trial, the voter first selects a latent personality from Conformer z_c and Maverick z_m in accordance with a multinomial distribution $\texttt{Multinomial}(\pi_c, \pi_m)$. Then, given the item quality q and the selected topic z, a parameter p, ranging from 0 to 1, is randomly generated from a generation function $\texttt{G}_p(z, q)$ (detailed later), where p indicates the probability that the person may give a positive vote. Finally, a vote is generated by a Bernoulli process.

Particularly, the key to the above generative process is the p-generation function $\texttt{G}_p(z, q)$, which should satisfy the following requirements. Firstly, the ranges of its output should be between 0 and 1 as the p represents the probability of casting a positive vote. Secondly, when the Conformer personality z_c is selected, the $p = \texttt{G}_p(z_c, q)$ should be positively proportional to q. Meanwhile, when the Maverick personality z_m is selected, p should be negatively correlated with q.

Algorithm 1 Process of vote generation

1. Choose a personality $z \sim \texttt{Multinomial}(\pi_c, \pi_m)$, $z \in \{z_c, z_m\}$
2. Choose a parameter $p \sim \texttt{G}_p(z, q)$, $p \in [0, 1]$
3. Choose a vote $v \sim \texttt{Bernoulli}(p)$, $v \in \{-1, 1\}$

In the rest of the section, we first introduce the modeling of latent topics, then describe the process of generating p with the parameters z and q, i.e., the function $\texttt{G}_p(z, q)$. Finally we discuss the methods of parameter learning.

4.1 Modeling the Latent Personalities

There are two latent personalities in the space for each person, corresponding to two inclinations of a person when she makes decisions. Specifically they are referred to as *Conformer* $z_1 = 1$ and *Maverick* $z_2 = -1$. The Conformer personality dictates that the person is more likely to conform with the majority when expressing her opinions, e.g., voting an item. On the other hand, the Maverick personality makes the person behave differently from most people. For instance, in a joke-sharing system where popular items are funny jokes, a person may give positive vote to jokes that are liked by many others and give negative vote to cold ones when Conformer is "active".On the contrary, a person may thumb up the cold jokes and thumb down funny jokes when her Maverick personality takes in charge.

We assume that all people have these two personalities and different people may have different probability distributions on Conformer and Maverick due their personalities. Two parameters $\pi_1, \pi_2 \in [0, 1]$ are used to respectively represent the probability that the person chooses z_1 or z_2 when she votes an item. It is easily seen that $\pi_1 + \pi_2 = 1$.

4.2 Modeling the p-Generation Process

As mentioned above, given a selected personality z and an item whose quality is q, a variable $p \in [0, 1]$ will be generated. We assume this generation process satisfies a Beta distribution shown in Equation (5).

$$\mathtt{Be}(p; a, b) = \frac{\Gamma(a+b)}{\Gamma(a)\Gamma(b)} p^{a-1}(1-p)^{b-1} = \frac{p^{a-1}(1-p)^{b-1}}{\mathtt{B}(a, b)} \quad (5)$$

where a and b are linearly associated with z and q.

In probability theory, Beta distribution is often used to describe a prior distribution of a parameter for some distribution, e.g., Bernoulli distribution. Specifically, the a and b jointly determine the probability distribution of p. When $a > b \geq 1$, the value of p is more likely to be large. In case of $1 \leq a < b$, the value of p is closer to 0.

Given z and q, the values of a and b are computed according to Equation (6).

$$a = f_a(z, q) = C \times H(z \cdot q), \; b = C - a \quad (6)$$

where C is a predefined constant bigger than 1 and function $H(x)$ is a normalized function defined in Equation (7).

$$H(z \cdot q) = \frac{z \cdot q - (-1)}{1 - (-1)} = \frac{z \cdot q + 1}{2} \quad (7)$$

It normalizes the original range $[-1, 1]$ of $z \cdot q$ into $[0, 1]$.

To sum up, the generation function is defined below.

$$\mathtt{G}_p(z, q) = \frac{\Gamma(C)}{\Gamma(\frac{q \cdot z+1}{2} \cdot C)\Gamma(\frac{-q \cdot z+1}{2} \cdot C)} p^{\frac{q \cdot z+1}{2} \cdot C-1}(1-p)^{\frac{-q \cdot z+1}{2}C-1} \quad (8)$$

As seen in Equations (6) and (7), a and b are respectively positively and negatively correlated with the value of $z \cdot q$. When the personality of Conformer z_c is selected, a large q indicates a large a and a small b, which thus leads to a high probability of positive vote. On the contrary, when Maverick z_m is selected, high quality results in small a and large b. Thus, a negative vote is more likely to happen. The probability density function for p with regarding to different q and z is shown in Figure 5 where C is set to 10. As you can see, the density functions coincide with our intuitive understandings on $\mathtt{G}_p(z, q)$. It is worth mentioning that, as to be shown next, all the derivations on this model is irrelevant to the parameter C.

4.3 Modeling the Voting Process

With a generated probability p, the voting is modeled as a Bernoulli process, i.e., $Pr(x = 1) = p$ and $Pr(x = -1) = 1 - p$. Aggregating all the processes, i.e., personality selection, p-generation and voting, we can obtain the complete

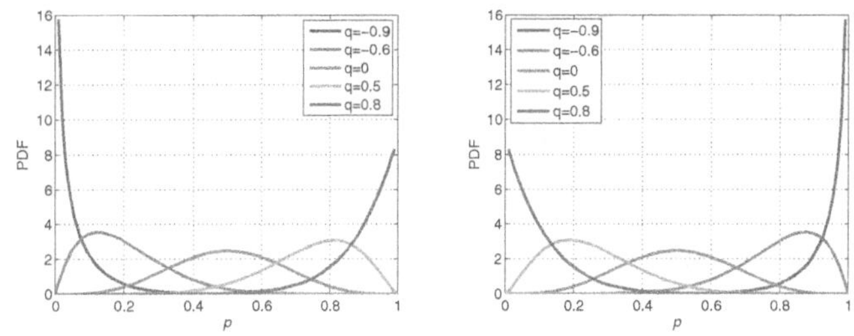

(a) $z = z_c$ (b) $z = z_m$

Figure 5: Illustration of $\mathtt{G}_p(z, q)$

probability that the person votes 1 in Equation (9).

$$\begin{aligned} Pr(x = 1, z|q) &= \sum_{j=1}^{2} I_{z=z_j} Pr(x = 1, z|q) \\ &= \sum_{j=1}^{2} I_{z=z_j} \left(\int_0^1 Pr(x = 1|p) Pr(p|z, q) dp \right) \pi_j \\ &= \sum_{j=1}^{2} I_{z=z_j} \left(\int_0^1 p \cdot \mathtt{Be}(p; f_a(z, q), f_b(z, q)) dp \right) \pi_j \end{aligned} \quad (9)$$

where $I_{z=z_j} = \begin{cases} 1 & z = z_j \\ 0 & \text{otherwise} \end{cases}$

Note that the expected value of Beta distribution $\mathtt{Be}(p; a, b)$ is $\frac{a}{a+b}$, i.e., $\int_0^1 p \cdot \mathtt{Be}(p; a, b) dp = \frac{a}{a+b}$. Equation (9) can thus be reduced to Equation (10).

$$\begin{aligned} Pr(x = 1, z|q) &= \prod_{j=1}^{2} \left(\frac{f_a(z, q)\pi_j}{f_a(z, q) + f_b(z, q)} \right)^{I_{z=z_j}} \\ &= \prod_{j=1}^{2} \left(\frac{\pi_j(z \cdot q + 1)/2}{(z \cdot q + 1 - z \cdot q + 1)/2} \right)^{I_{z=z_j}} = \prod_{j=1}^{2} (H(z \cdot q) \cdot \pi_j)^{I_{z=z_j}} \end{aligned} \quad (10)$$

Similarly, the probability that the person gives a negative vote is shown in Equation (11).

$$\begin{aligned} Pr(x = -1, z|q) &= \sum_{j=1}^{2} I_{z=z_j} \left(\int_0^1 Pr(x = -1|p) Pr(p|z, q) dp \right) \pi_j \\ &= \sum_{j=1}^{2} I_{z=z_j} \left(\int_0^1 (1 - p) \cdot \mathtt{Be}(p; f_a(z, q), f_b(z, q)) dp \right) \pi_j \\ &= \prod_{j=1}^{2} \left(\frac{f_b(z, q)\pi_j}{f_a(z, q) + f_b(z, q)} \right)^{I_{z=z_j}} = \prod_{j=1}^{2} ((1 - H(z \cdot q)) \cdot \pi_j)^{I_{z=z_j}} \end{aligned} \quad (11)$$

Note that $H(x) + H(-x) = 1$ and Equation (10) and (11) can thus be unified as in Equation (12).

$$Pr(x, z|q) = \prod_{j=1}^{2} (H(x \cdot z \cdot q) \cdot \pi_j)^{I_{z=z_j}} \quad (12)$$

Suppose that, in a rating system, a user rates a collection of items whose qualities are $\mathbf{Q} = \{q_1, \cdots, q_n\}$. Let $\mathbf{X} = \{x_1, \cdots, x_n\}$ denote the observed votes the user gives and $\mathbf{Z} = \{z_1, \cdots, z_n\}$ denote the particular topic that dominates the i_{th} voting. Note that $x_i, 1 \leq i \leq n$ are binary values, i.e., $x_i \in \{1, -1\}$.

Thus the probability of these votes can be computed as in Equation (13).

$$Pr(\mathbf{X},\mathbf{Z}|\mathbf{Q}) = \prod_{i=1}^{n} Pr(x_i, z_i|q_i) = \prod_{i=1}^{n}\prod_{j=1}^{2}(H(x_i \cdot z_i \cdot q_i)\cdot \pi_j)^{\tau_{ij}} \tag{13}$$

where the indicator $\tau_{ij}(1 \le i \le n, j \in \{1,2\})$ is defined as

$$\tau_{ij} = \begin{cases} 1 & \text{the } i^{th} \text{ vote is generated by } j^{th} \text{ topic} \\ 0 & \text{otherwise} \end{cases}$$

4.4 Learning the Model Parameters

We use maximum-likelihood to find the model parameters, i.e., finding proper parameter values to maximize the probability of observed data. The objective function is defined in Equation (14).

$$\mathfrak{L}(\pi_1, \pi_2; \mathbf{X}, \mathbf{Z}, \mathbf{Q}) = \log Pr(\mathbf{X},\mathbf{Z}|\mathbf{Q}; \pi_1, \pi_2) + \lambda(1-\pi_1-\pi_2)$$
$$= \sum_{i=1}^{n}\sum_{j=1}^{2}\tau_{ij}\{\log(H(x_i \cdot z_i \cdot q_i)) + \log \pi_j\} + \lambda(1-\pi_1-\pi_2) \tag{14}$$

where λ is a Lagrange multiplier.

We use Expectation-maximization (EM) algorithm [4] to solve the above equation. Let the parameters at t^{th} iteration be denoted by $\theta^{(t)}$. The two steps are shown below.

E-step

$$E(\tau_{ij}^{(t+1)}) = Pr(z_j|x_i, q_i) = \frac{Pr(x_i, z_j|q_i)}{Pr(x_i, z_1|q_i) + Pr(x_i, z_2|q_i)}$$
$$= \frac{H(x_i \cdot z_j \cdot q_i)\cdot \pi_j^{(t)}}{\sum_{k=1}^{2} H(x_i \cdot z_k \cdot q)\cdot \pi_k^{(t)}} \tag{15}$$

M-step

$$\pi_j^{(t+1)} = \frac{\sum_{i=1}^{n} E(\tau_{ij})}{\sum_{i=1}^{n} E(\tau_{i1}) + \sum_{i=1}^{n} E(\tau_{i2})} = \frac{\sum_{i=1}^{n} E(\tau_{ij})}{n} \tag{16}$$

In real situation, however, the quality of an item is usually impossible to measure. In this work we use the popularity degree defined in Equation (1) to represent the quality by assuming that a high-quality item often receives more positive and less negative votes.

Another issue worth attention is the difference between NCM and CM in modeling the user profiles. For NCM, each vote is either contributed to Conformer weight w_c or Maverick weight w_m, as shown in Equation (2). It is a coarse assignment method of weights. Compared to this "radical attitude" behind NCM, in CM each observed vote contributes probabilistically to both π_c and π_m as shown in Equations (15) and (16). Specifically, for a vote x_i on an item with the popularity q_i, the value of $Pr(z_c|x_i, q_i)$ contributes its conformer personality while that of $Pr(z_m|x_i, q_i)$ contributes its maverick personality. As such, CM provides a fine-grained assignment method of weights. It preserves the probability that a person can give "Conformer/Maverick-minded" vote even if the opposite personality is selected. This robustness leads to CM's better performance to NCM, as to be shown later in Section 6.4.

4.5 Discussion

In this section we provide a detailed discussion on the proposed model. We assume that the item quality satisfies a continuous uniform distribution over the interval $[-1, 1]$.

The CM model discussed above assumes that each person has two topics, i.e., Conformer and Maverick. In other words, the user profile is modeled as a suit of two topics together with the topic distribution. Formally, the ith user profile is denoted as $u_i = \langle \pi_1^i, \pi_2^i \rangle$, where $\pi_j^i, j \in \{1,2\}$ stands for $Pr(z_j|u_i)$, the probability of selecting topic z_j for the ith user.

With this model, we are particularly interested in the following two questions:

- Given an item j with *unknown* quality q_j, what is the probability for the person u_i to give a positive vote?
- Given an item j with *known* quality q_j, what is the probability for the person u_i to give a positive vote?

Let $v_{ij} \in \{-1, 1\}$ denote the vote user u_i gives to item j. For the first question, we can compute the probability of positive vote as in Equation (17).

$$Pr(v_{ij}=1|u_i) = \int_{-1}^{1}\sum_{k=1}^{2} Pr(v_{ij}=1|z_k, q)Pr(z_k|u_i)Pr(q)dq$$
$$= \frac{1}{2}\int_{-1}^{1}\sum_{k=1}^{2} H(z_k \cdot q)\pi_k^i dq = \frac{1}{2}\sum_{k=1}^{2}\pi_k^i\int_{-1}^{1}\frac{z_k \cdot q + 1}{2}dq$$
$$= \frac{1}{2}\sum_{k=1}^{2}\pi_k^i(\frac{(z_k+1)^2 - (-z_k+1)^2}{4z_k}) = \frac{1}{2} \tag{17}$$

Similarly, we can obtain that

$$Pr(v_{ij}=-1|u_i) = 1 - Pr(v_{ij}=1|u_i) = \frac{1}{2} \tag{18}$$

This result is reasonable because for a sensible person, her probability of liking or disliking an item should be equal as the quality of the item is unknown.

For a given item with known quality q_j, the probability of positive vote is computed in Equation (19).

$$Pr(v_{ij}=1|u_i, q_j) = \sum_{k=1}^{2} Pr(v_{ij}=1|z_k, q_j)Pr(z_k|u_i)$$
$$= \sum_{k=1}^{2}\int_{0}^{1} Pr(v_{ij}=1, p|z_k, q_j)dp \cdot Pr(z_k|u_i) = \sum_{i=1}^{2} H(z_i \cdot q_j)\pi_k^i$$
$$= \sum_{k=1}^{2}\frac{z_k \cdot q_j + 1}{2}\pi_k^i = \frac{(\pi_1^i - \pi_2^i)\cdot q_j + 1}{2} \tag{19}$$

Similarly the probability of negative vote is shown below.

$$Pr(v_{ij}=-1|u_i, q_j) = \frac{(\pi_2^i - \pi_1^i)\cdot q_j + 1}{2} \tag{20}$$

Suppose $\pi_1^i > \pi_2^i$, i.e., the person u_i is more of a conformer, the probability of positive (negative) vote increases (decreases) with the growth of the given item's quality q_j. On the other hand, if $\pi_1^i < \pi_2^i$, the person's vote is usually conflicted with the item's quality, suggesting her maverick personality. Finally, if $\pi_1^i = \pi_2^i$, the voting is purely random. Therefore, to help predict the popularity of the item, the favorite voters are those whose π_1^i and π_2^i differ a lot.

5. RANKING POTENTIAL POPULARITY

The key point behind our popularity prediction idea is to design a ranking function that can rank each candidate item's potential popularity based on its early votes. In this section, we give two ranking functions based on the proposed CM model introduced in Section 4.

The first one, referred to as *Aggregation-based Ranking Function*, aggregates the vote values over all the users given the early votes on item i (denoted by $\vec{V_i}$) and voters (denoted by U), i.e., $\sum_{j=1}^{|U|} E(v_{i_j}|u_{i_j}, \vec{V_i})$, where $E(v_{i_j}|u_{i_j}, \vec{V_i})$ is the expected value of user u_{i_j}'s vote on item i given $\vec{V_i}$. The second one, referred to as *Q-based Ranking Function*, defines an item's ranking score as $Pr(q_i \geq q^*|\vec{V_i})$, i.e., the probability that this item's popularity is no smaller than a predefined threshold q^* given the early votes and voters.

As seen from the definitions of these two ranking functions, we consider the early voting values and the personalities of the voters in this prediction. External factors such as social influence [10] and voting time [13] are out of scope of this work. Also, our prediction is focused on the newly published items which are typically listed reverse-chronologically in the "latest stories" list and and thus viewed by users with the same probability.[7]

5.1 Aggregation-based Ranking

To predict one item's potential popularity, an intuitive way is to predict the individual vote and aggregate all of them. Specifically, given an item i's early votes $\vec{V_i}$, we would like to compute the expected vote value for a user u_{i0}.

$$\begin{aligned} E(v_{i_0}|u_{i_0}, \vec{V_i}) &= Pr(v_{i_0} = 1|u_{i_0}, \vec{V_i}) - Pr(v_{i_0} = -1|u_{i_0}, \vec{V_i}) \\ &= 2Pr(1|u_{i_0}, \vec{V_i}) - 1 = 2\frac{\int_{-1}^{1}\prod_{j=0}^{n} Pr(v_{i_j}|u_{i_j}, q_i)dq_i}{\int_{-1}^{1}\prod_{j'=1}^{n} Pr(v_{i_{j'}}|u_{i_{j'}, q_i})dq_i} - 1 \end{aligned} \quad (21)$$

Now the key is to compute $\prod_{j=1}^{n} Pr(v_{i_j}|q_i, u_{i_j})$, which is shown in Equation (22).

$$\begin{aligned} \prod_{j=1}^{n} Pr(v_{i_j}|q_i, u_{i_j}) &= \prod_{j=1}^{n}\sum_{k=1}^{2} Pr(v_{i_j}|z_k, q_i)Pr(z_k|u_{i_j}) \\ &= \prod_{j=1}^{n}\sum_{k=1}^{2} H(v_{i_j}\cdot z_k\cdot q_i)\pi_k^{i_j} = \sum_{k_1\cdots k_n=1}^{2}\prod_{j=1}^{n} H(v_{i_j}\cdot z_{k_j}\cdot q_i)\cdot \pi_{k_j}^{i_j} \\ &= \sum_{k_1\cdots k_n=1}^{2} (H(q_i))^{\sum_{j=1}^{n}\mathbf{1}_{v_{i_j}z_{k_j}=1}}(H(-q_i))^{\sum_{j=1}^{n}\mathbf{1}_{v_{i_j}z_{k_j}=-1}}\prod_{j=1}^{n}\pi_{k_j}^{i_j} \\ &= \sum_{k_1\cdots k_n=1}^{2} (H(q_i))^{a_{\mathbf{k}}-1}(1-H(q_i))^{b_{\mathbf{k}}-1}\prod_{j=1}^{n}\pi_{k_i}^{i_j} \end{aligned} \quad (22)$$

where the function $a_{\mathbf{k}} - 1 = \sum_{j=1}^{n}\mathbf{1}_{v_{i_j}z_{k_j}=1}$ counts the number of positive ones when multiplying v_{i_j} by z_{k_j} while $b_{\mathbf{k}} - 1$ counts the number of negative ones.

The integration is computed as Equation (23).

$$\begin{aligned} &\int_{-1}^{1}\prod_{j=1}^{n} Pr(v_{i_j}|q_i, u_{i_j})dq_i \\ &= \sum_{k_1\cdots k_n=1}^{2} 2\prod_{j=1}^{n}\pi_{k_j}^{i_j}\int_{H(-1)}^{H(1)} t^{a_{\mathbf{k}}-1}(1-t)^{b_{\mathbf{k}}-1}dt \\ &= 2\sum_{k_1\cdots k_n=1}^{2}\prod_{j=1}^{n}\pi_{k_j}^{i_j}(\mathtt{B}(a_{\mathbf{k}}, b_{\mathbf{k}}) - \mathtt{B}_{H(-1)}(a_{\mathbf{k}}, b_{\mathbf{k}})) \end{aligned} \quad (23)$$

where $\mathtt{B}(a, b)$ and $\mathtt{B}_x(a, b)$ are respectively the complete and incomplete beta function defined in Equation (24).

$$\begin{aligned} \mathtt{B}(a, b) &= \int_0^1 t^{a-1}(1-t)^{b-1}dt = \frac{\Gamma(a)\Gamma(b)}{\Gamma(a+b)} \\ \mathtt{B}_x(a, b) &= \int_0^x t^{a-1}(1-t)^{b-1}dt \end{aligned} \quad (24)$$

Particularly, when a and b are both integers, $\mathtt{B}_x(a, b)$ can be computed as below:

$$\begin{aligned} \mathtt{B}_x(a, b) &= \mathtt{B}(a, b)\cdot\frac{\mathtt{B}_x(a, b)}{\mathtt{B}(a, b)} = \mathtt{B}(a, b)\cdot \mathtt{I}_x(a, b) \\ &= \frac{\Gamma(a)\Gamma(b)}{\Gamma(a+b)}(\sum_{j=a}^{a+b-1}\frac{(a+b-1)!}{j!(a+b-1-j)!}x^j(1-x)^{a+b-1-j}) \end{aligned} \quad (25)$$

Therefore, the ranking function in Equation (21) can be written as below.

$$E(v_{i_0}|u_{i_0}, \vec{V_i}) = 2\frac{\sum_{k_0\cdots k_n=1}^{2}\prod_{j=0}^{n}\pi_{k_j}^{i_j}\mathtt{B}(a_{\mathbf{k}}, b_{\mathbf{k}})}{\sum_{k'_1\cdots k'_n=1}^{2}\prod_{j'=1}^{n}\pi_{k'_{j'}}^{i_{j'}}\mathtt{B}(a_{\mathbf{k'}}, b_{\mathbf{k'}})} - 1 \quad (26)$$

The ranking score of the item is the aggregation of all individuals' expected votes, as shown in Equation (27).

$$\mathtt{PopRank}(\vec{V_i}) = \sum_{j=1}^{|U|} E(v_{i_j}|u_{i_j}, \vec{V_i}) \quad (27)$$

where $|U|$ is the total number of users in the system.

5.2 Q-based Ranking

An alternative way of popularity prediction, referred to as *Q-based ranking*, is to estimate a particular item's popularity degree q defined in Equation (1). For a predefined popularity threshold q^*, we want to calculate the probability that the particular item's popularity is larger than q^*.

Let $\vec{V_i} = \langle(u_{i_1}, v_{i_1}), \cdots, (u_{i_n}, v_{i_n})\rangle$ denote the first n votes for item i where $v_{i_j} \in \{1, -1\}$ is given by user u_{i_j}, whose personality distribution parameters are represented as $\langle\pi_{i_j}^1, \pi_{i_j}^2\rangle$. We also assume that the popularity of the item satisfies a uniform distribution between -1 to 1. The probability can be written as Equation (28).

$$\begin{aligned} Pr(q_i \geq q^*|\vec{V_i}) &= \int_{q^*}^{1} Pr(q_i|\vec{V_i})dq_i = \int_{q^*}^{1}\frac{Pr(\vec{V_i}|q_i)}{Pr(\vec{V_i})}Pr(q_i)dq_i \\ &= \frac{\int_{q^*}^{1}\prod_{j=1}^{n} Pr(v_{i_j}|q_i, u_{i_j})dq_i}{\int_{-1}^{1}\prod_{j'=1}^{n} Pr(v_{i_{j'}}|q'_i, u_{i_{j'}})dq'_i} \end{aligned} \quad (28)$$

With the knowledge of Equation (23), the $Pr(q_i \geq q^*|\vec{V_i})$ is computed in Equation (29).

$$\begin{aligned} Pr(q_i \geq q^*|\vec{V_i}) &= \frac{\int_{q^*}^{1}\prod_{j=1}^{n} Pr(v_{i_j}|q_i, u_{i_j})dq_i}{\int_{-1}^{1}\prod_{k=1}^{n} Pr(v_{i_k}|q'_i, u_{i_k})dq'_i} \\ &= \frac{\sum_{k_1\cdots k_n=1}^{2}\prod_{j=1}^{n}\pi_{k_j}^{i_j}(\mathtt{B}(a_{\mathbf{k}}, b_{\mathbf{k}}) - \mathtt{B}_{H(q^*)}(a_{\mathbf{k}}, b_{\mathbf{k}}))}{\sum_{k'_1\cdots k'_n=1}^{2}\prod_{j'=1}^{n}\pi_{k'_{j'}}^{i_{j'}}\mathtt{B}(a_{\mathbf{k'}}, b_{\mathbf{k'}})} \end{aligned} \quad (29)$$

Formally, given a popularity threshold q^* and a new published item's first n vote $\vec{V_i}$, the ranking score for its popularity is defined as $Pr(q_i \geq q^*|\vec{V_i})$, the probability that this item's popularity q_i is no smaller than a predefined q^*.

[7]Notice that we do not consider the impact of the item's position in the system as in [9].

We again use the example in Section 3 to illustrate this ranking function. The difference lies in the two voters' profiles where $u_1 = \langle 0.9, 0.1\rangle$ is a Conformer-dominated user and $u_2 = \langle 0.2, 0.8\rangle$ is a Maverick-dominated person. For $q^* = 0.8$, their popularity ranking scores are derived below.

Given the first item's early vote $\vec{V_1} = \langle (u_1, 1)\rangle$, the ranking score is computed as in Equation (30).

$$\begin{aligned} &Pr(q_1 \geq 0.8 | (u_1, 1)) \\ &= \frac{0.9(B(2,1) - B_{0.9}(2,1)) + 0.1(B(1,2) - B_{0.9}(1,2))}{0.9 \times B(2,1) + 0.1 \times B(1,2)} \\ &= 0.172 \end{aligned} \tag{30}$$

Similarly, the ranking score of the second item, given the early vote $\vec{V_2} = \langle (u_2, 1)\rangle$, is computed as in Equation (31).

$$\begin{aligned} &Pr(q_2 \geq 0.8 | (u_2, 1)) \\ &= \frac{0.2(B(2,1) - B_{0.9}(2,1)) + 0.8(B(1,2) - B_{0.9}(1,2))}{0.2 \times B(2,1) + 0.8 \times B(1,2)} \\ &= 0.046 \end{aligned} \tag{31}$$

Therefore the first item is ranked higher than the second one for top-k popular item prediction. This result also agrees with our intuition because the item favored by Conformer will probably be favored by the majority while the one liked by Maverick will usually not receive high attention.

Note that these two ranking functions have different time complexity. Suppose the time cost for computing complete Beta function $\mathtt{B}(a, b)$ is $O(1)$, then the Quality-based one only needs $O(1)$ while the Aggregation-based ranking function requires $O(|U|)$. As for the effectiveness, these two ranking functions show similar performance (as to be shown later in Section 6), suggesting their possible equivalence in the ranking process.

6. EVALUATION

In this section we show the experiment results from the evaluation of our proposed Conformer-Maverick models on top-k popular item prediction. Three algorithms, i.e., user-based collaborative filtering (UCF) [7], singular value decomposition (SVD), and biased SVD (SVD++) [8], are also evaluated for comparison.

In the following, Section 6.1 introduces the experiment data set as well as the preparation works. Section 6.2 gives the details of our evaluation measures and methodology. Section 6.3 shows the experiment results.

6.1 Data Preparation

The dataset used in our evaluation comes from a popular iPhone application *JokeBox*, a joke sharing platform where people can publish jokes as well as voting others' jokes. Voting an item, a user can only choose "like" or "dislike", corresponding to the positive and negative votes. Different from YouTube and Digg, JokeBox contains detailed information of each user's votes, which can be used to build user profiles for our CM model. The dataset used in this work spans from December 23, 2010 to May 3, 2011.

When preparing the dataset, we only kept items which had received "sufficient votes" and users who had committed "sufficient votes". The sufficient votes, i.e., the threshold σ in Section 2.1, aims to guarantee that i) the item's quality can be well reflected by the votes; and ii) there are enough data instances to learn the user's personality.

Figure 6(a) shows the votes received by an item follow a power-law distribution. As Pareto principle [8] indicates that 20% of members occupy 80% resources in a typical power-law distribution. Therefore, we adopt the minimum number of top 20% items' votes as the threshold (i.e., the "sufficient votes"), which is 8. After removing items whose votes are less than 8, we kept the users who had voted at least one of the remaining jokes. The vote distribution for each user is then shown in Figure 6(b). Again it is a power-law distribution and we set the threshold of votes for an "active" user to be 12 according to the Pareto rule. After this preparation phase, we get 16,490 items, 4,159 user and 353,721 votes.

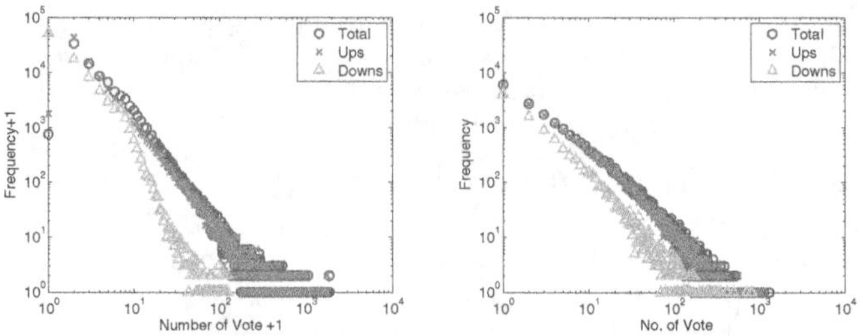

(a) Item-Vote (b) User-Vote

Figure 6: Vote Distribution

6.2 Evaluation Measures and Methodology

As formulated in Section 2.2, the top-k popular item prediction is a ranking problem. The evaluation is then to evaluate the returned list of k items. In the experiments, we use two widely used ranking measures, i.e., *Root Mean Squared Error (RMSE)* and *Normalized Discount Cumulative Gain (NDCG)*, as defined in Equation (32) and (33).

$$\mathtt{RMSE@}k = \sqrt{\frac{\sum_{i=1}^{k}(f_i - g_i)^2}{k}} \tag{32}$$

where the $f_i = i$ and g_i are respectively the predicted and actual rank of the i_{th} item.

$$\mathtt{NDCG@}k = \frac{\mathtt{DCG@}k}{\mathtt{iDCG@}k} \tag{33}$$

where DCG is defined as Equation (34) and iDCG is the maximum DCG.

$$\mathtt{DCG@}k = \begin{cases} G_k & k = 1 \\ \mathtt{DCG@}(k-1) + \frac{G_k}{log_b k} & k > 1 \end{cases} \tag{34}$$

where $G_k = 1 - \frac{k}{|T|}$ is "Gain" for k_{th} item and $|T|$ is the size of test data set.

Intuitively, for RMSE, a smaller value indicates a better performance while bigger NDCG suggests a better one.

In the experiments, we use collaborative filtering as the baseline solution, which works as follows. It uses the training data to learn either the user similarity (for UCF) or the feature vectors of users and items (for SVD and SVD++). To rank the items in the test data, this method first computes a score, or predicts a rating of each person to these items. The final ranking score is obtained by simply adding all users' predicted ratings.

N-Cross-validation is adopted as the evaluation methodology and the average performance is reported.

6.3 Experiment Results

This section discusses the experiment results. In the following, we first show the general performance of tested solutions. Then results on different n (the number of early votes) and different N (training-test data size) are shown.

[8]http://en.wikipedia.org/wiki/Pareto_principle

Figure 7 shows the general performance of the methods on top-k popular item prediction with regarding to different k. In this experiment set, the number of early vote n and the cross-validation group number N are both set to 5. By empirical study, the q^* is set to 0.8 where CM achieves best performance. The CM model with Aggregation-based ranking function is denoted as ACM while the one with Q-based denoted as QCM. As shown in Figure 7(a), the performance of ACM and QCM are nearly undistinguishable, suggesting the equivalence of the two ranking functions. However, the Q-based ranking function is preferred considering its higher efficiency. In the rest of the experiments, the Q-based ranking function is used for representing methods based on our CM model (and thus denoted as CM). Also from the figure we can see that when $k \leq 10$, our proposed CM model displays the best performance in terms of RMSE. After $k \geq 10$, the performance of CM model and SVD++ is hard to distinguish. However, for NDCG, the performance of the CM model is always better than the other solutions with regarding to all k, as shown in Figure 7(b). For the naive CM model, its performance is the second best when $k \leq 10$ but is worse than SVD++ for a bigger k. From this general performance comparison, we can see that our (naive) CM model does a good job in popularity prediction for smaller k. Although our models are no better than SVD++ for big k (i.e., $k \geq 10$), it is very valuable because users, especially mobile phone users, may only be able to consume items in a short top-ranking list instead of the whole long list of recommendation. We also argue that the failure of SVD++ may come from the cold start issue since the ranking is based on only the first 5 votes on a new item.

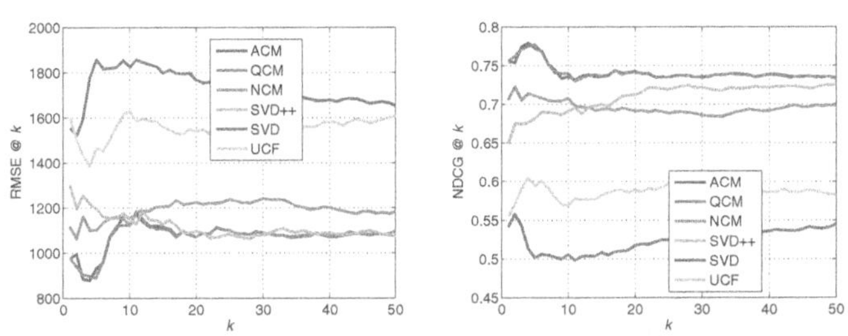

(a) RMSE (b) NDCG

Figure 7: General Comparison

The second experiment aims to show the impact of the number of early votes n on the performance. In this experiment set, we varies n from 1 to 5 and show the top-5 prediction performance in Figure 8. For both RMSE and NDCG, our proposed CM and NCM model outperforms the baseline solutions. More specifically, the performance of all solutions except for CM, degrade as n decreases. This shows the strength of our CM in making good prediction with few early votes. For NCM and collaborative filtering solutions, when more early votes are involved, more information can be relied on and thus the prediction will become more accurate, resulting in the performance improvement. Notice that it is not clear to us whether the performance of the CM model only prevail when the top-5 list is considered. To further demonstrate the superior performance of our CM model, we plot Figure 8(c) and 8(d) to display its performance under different n and k. We can see that its improvement is clear along the increase of n when k is bigger.

For the third set of experiments, we show the impact of training-test data size, i.e., N. A larger N means larger amount of training data and smaller quantity of test data and vice versa. The results are shown in Figure 9. Generally, the performance of all solutions shows some improvement

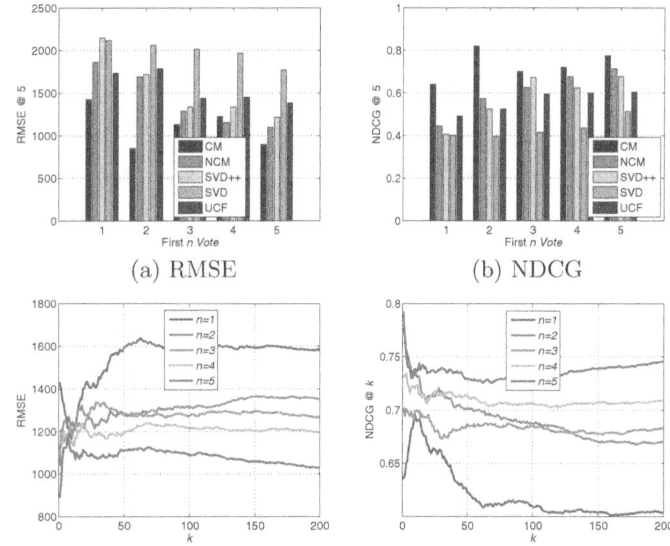

(a) RMSE (b) NDCG

(c) RMSE for CM (d) NDCG for CM

Figure 8: Evaluation on Different n

with larger N since there are more training data. The NCM outperforms the baseline solutions in all cases. On the other hand, the CM shows the best performance except for $N = 2$, where only 50% of data is available for training. In other words, the sparsity of the training data has an impact on the CM model, which suffers inaccuracy when modeling the user's CM personality with insufficient training data.

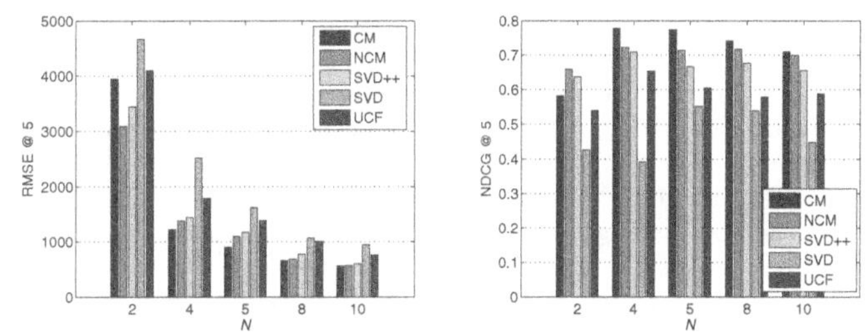

(a) RMSE (b) NDCG

Figure 9: Evaluation on Different N

6.4 Comparison of CM and NCM Models

As shown in previous results, the two proposed models, i.e., CM and NCM, display different performance. In this section, we made a detailed comparison of their differences.

Although their basic ideas are similar, CM adopts a more sophisticated process to model user's voting behavior while NCM is rather heuristic and straightforward. Specifically, the differences are attribute to two aspects: i) the modeling of user's personality, i.e., the learning of π_c, π_m for CM and the calculation of w_c, w_m for NCM; ii) the ranking function. Since the personality parameters have the same value range ($\pi_c, \pi_m, w_c, w_m \in [0, 1]$) and constraint ($\pi_c + \pi_m = 1, w_c + w_m = 1$), two new solutions can be "generated" by combing users' personality and ranking function from either model.

In the experiment we evaluate the performance of two new solutions: 1) *Combined CM Variance 1 (CCMV1)*, adopting the personality model of CM and the ranking function of NCM; and 2) *Combined CM Variance 2 (CCMV2)*, combing the personality model of NCM and the ranking function of CM. It can be seen from Figure 10 that i) the performances of CM and CCMV1 are significantly better than those of CCMV2 and NCM; ii) the performance of CM and CCMV1 are similar while the performance of CCMV2 is slightly better than that of NCM. Therefore we can safely conclude that the model of user personality is the major factor that affects the performance difference of CM and NCM.

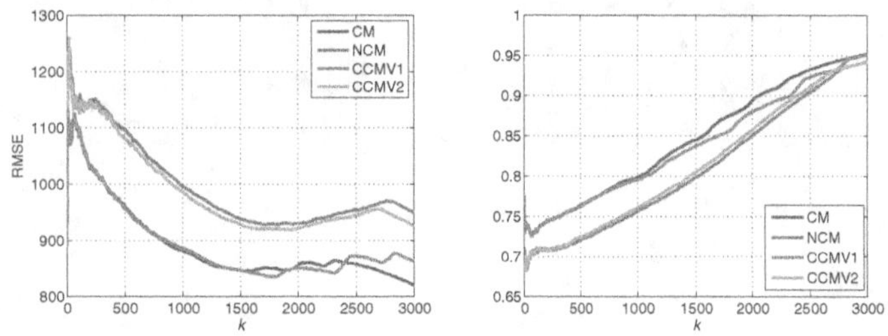

(a) RMSE (b) NDCG

Figure 10: Combined CM model

Recall in Section 4.4 we discuss the difference of NCM and CM in modeling user profiles. CM is more robust in handling the observed vote data while NCM is more "radical", attributing each vote to either Conformer weight w_c or Maverick weight w_m. The result here supports our claim that the CM model can better fit the data and outperforms NCM, although the two methods share the same basic ideas.

7. RELATED WORK

With the growing popularity of content-sharing services in web and mobile phones, research on the online contents' popularity evolution [3, 5, 17] and prediction are growing.

Szabo and Huberman [13] studied the change of votes for items in both Digg.com and YouTube. They analyzed the popularity evolution and found that the growth ratio is $(1 + rX)$, where r is a time-sensitive parameter and X is a variable that satisfies a normal distribution. This method aims to explore the popularity growing trend and can not rank the popularity of a single item. Also, prediction suffers inaccuracy if it is purely based on the number of early votes.

In [18], Yu et. al. exploited the content to judge whether a marketing message would be popular. Two classification methods, i.e., SVM and Naive Bayes are used and the feature is modeled as a vector of words. Their methods, however, are limited only to textual contents. Furthermore, the classification tools are unable to process the ranking problems addressed in this paper.

Lerman and Hogg [9] proposed a stochastic model that considers both social influence and the layout of the website. In this model, the increasing rate of the votes is related to the possibility that a user finds this item i) in font page, ii) in upcoming page and iii) through her friends. Prediction can then be made after learning the three parameters from the training data. This method, however, can not work in our scenario. Firstly, we are interested in the potential for newly published items to be popular instead of the position difference. Also, there is no social network in our data set and the voting is free of social influence. Finally, we focus on the voting process of a person, a key behavior that determines the popularity of an item.

Other existing works integrate user comments [12, 15, 16, 14]. This information, however, is not always available compared with votes. For example, a person is more likely to vote than leave a comment as the former one takes much less time and effort.

To improve the prediction precision, some works resort to information of other social media, e.g., web blog [6, 11], Twitter [1, 2]. While this is an interesting direction, this method works only when there are multiple sources containing the information of items, such as book sales [6], movie revenues [11, 1, 2] and stock markets [2]. Also, mining external web sites introduces high cost compared to methods that only rely on the information within the system.

8. CONCLUSION AND FUTURE WORK

In this work we propose a *Conformer-Maverick (CM)* model to rank potentially popular items. The CM assumes each person has two personalities, i.e., Conformer and Maverick, which guide the voting behavior. Conformers' votes are usually consistent with the majority's opinions while Mavericks' votes conflicting. Different people have different distributions of these two personalities, which can be learned from the voting history. By exploiting such behaviors, potentially popular items can be ranked by their early voters.

While people's topic distributions tend to be stable for items without many complex genres, e.g., jokes, they may vary when it comes to items with multiple genres, e.g., action, romance, horror and so on in movies. In our future work, we plan to adapt our CM model for such complex items and applications.

9. REFERENCES

[1] S. Asur and B. A. Huberman. Predicting the future with social media. *WIIAT*, 1:492–499, 2010.

[2] J. Bollen, H. Mao, and X. Zeng. Twitter mood predicts the stock market. *Journal of Computational Science*, 2(1):1–8, 2011.

[3] M. Cha, H. Kwak, P. Rodriguez, Y.-Y. Ahn, and S. Moon. Analyzing the video popularity characteristics of large-scale user generated content systems. *IEEE/ACM Trans. Netw.*, 17:1357–1370, 2009.

[4] A. Dempster, N. Laird, and D. Rubin. Maximum likelihood from incomplete data via the em algorithm. *Journal of the Royal Statistical Society*, 39(1):1–38, 1977.

[5] F. Figueiredo, F. Benevenuto, and J. M. Almeida. The tube over time: characterizing popularity growth of youtube videos. In *WSDM*, pages 745–754, 2011.

[6] D. Gruhl, R. Guha, R. Kumar, J. Novak, and A. Tomkins. The predictive power of online chatter. In *KDD*, pages 78–87, 2005.

[7] J. L. Herlocker, J. A. Konstan, A. Borchers, and J. Riedl. An algorithmic framework for performing collaborative filtering. In *SIGIR*, pages 230–237, 1999.

[8] Y. Koren. Factorization meets the neighborhood: a multifaceted collaborative filtering model. In *KDD*, pages 426–434, 2008.

[9] K. Lerman and T. Hogg. Using a model of social dynamics to predict popularity of news. In *WWW*, pages 621–630, 2010.

[10] J. Leskovec, L. A. Adamic, and B. A. Huberman. The dynamics of viral marketing. *ACM Trans. Web*, 2007.

[11] G. Mishne. Predicting movie sales from blogger sentiment. In *AAAI-CAAW*, 2006.

[12] G. Mishne and N. Glance. Leave a reply: An analysis of weblog comments. In *In Third annual workshop on the Weblogging ecosystem*, 2006.

[13] G. Szabo and B. o. A. Huberman. Predicting the popularity of online content. *Communications of the Acm*, 53(8):80–88, 2010.

[14] A. Tatar, J. Leguay, P. Antoniadis, A. Limbourg, M. D. de Amorim, and S. Fdida. Predicting the popularity of online articles based on user comments. In *WIMS*, pages 67:1–67:8, 2011.

[15] M. Tsagkias, M. Larson, and M. d. Rijke. Exploiting surface features for the prediction of podcast preference. *Advances in Information Retrieval*, 5478:473–484, 2009.

[16] M. Tsagkias, M. Larson, and M. d. Rijke. News comments:exploring, modeling, and online prediction. *Advances in Information Retrieval*, 5993:191–203, 2010.

[17] D. M. Wilkinson. Strong regularities in online peer production. In *EC*, pages 302–309, 2008.

[18] B. Yu, M. Chen, and L. Kwok. Toward predicting popularity of social marketing messages. *Computer Science*, 6589:317–324, 2011.

A Large-Scale Sentiment Analysis for Yahoo! Answers

Onur Kucuktunc
The Ohio State University
Columbus, OH, USA
kucuktunc.1@osu.edu

B. Barla Cambazoglu
Yahoo! Research
Barcelona, Spain
barla@yahoo-inc.com

Ingmar Weber
Yahoo! Research
Barcelona, Spain
ingmar@yahoo-inc.com

Hakan Ferhatosmanoglu
Bilkent University
Ankara, Turkey
hakan@cs.bilkent.edu.tr

ABSTRACT

Sentiment extraction from online web documents has recently been an active research topic due to its potential use in commercial applications. By sentiment analysis, we refer to the problem of assigning a quantitative positive/negative mood to a short bit of text. Most studies in this area are limited to the identification of sentiments and do not investigate the interplay between sentiments and other factors. In this work, we use a sentiment extraction tool to investigate the influence of factors such as gender, age, education level, the topic at hand, or even the time of the day on sentiments in the context of a large online question answering site. We start our analysis by looking at direct correlations, e.g., we observe more positive sentiments on weekends, very neutral ones in the Science & Mathematics topic, a trend for younger people to express stronger sentiments, or people in military bases to ask the most neutral questions. We then extend this basic analysis by investigating how properties of the (asker, answerer) pair affect the sentiment present in the answer. Among other things, we observe a dependence on the pairing of some inferred attributes estimated by a user's ZIP code. We also show that the best answers differ in their sentiments from other answers, e.g., in the Business & Finance topic, best answers tend to have a more neutral sentiment than other answers. Finally, we report results for the task of predicting the attitude that a question will provoke in answers. We believe that understanding factors influencing the mood of users is not only interesting from a sociological point of view, but also has applications in advertising, recommendation, and search.

Categories and Subject Descriptors

H.m [**Information Systems**]: Miscellaneous; J.4 [**Social and Behavioral Sciences**]: Psychology, Sociology

General Terms

Design, Experimentation, Human Factors, Measurement

Permission to make digital or hard copies of all or part of this work for personal or classroom use is granted without fee provided that copies are not made or distributed for profit or commercial advantage and that copies bear this notice and the full citation on the first page. To copy otherwise, to republish, to post on servers or to redistribute to lists, requires prior specific permission and/or a fee.
WSDM'12, February 8–12, 2012, Seattle, Washington, USA.
Copyright 2012 ACM 978-1-4503-0747-5/12/02 ...$10.00.

Keywords

Sentiment analysis, attitude, sentimentality, collaborative question answering, prediction

1. INTRODUCTION

The advance of Web 2.0 boosted the creation of personal web content involving sentiments, e.g., blogs, tweets, and other types of social media. Extraction and analysis of sentiments in this type of content do not only give an emotional snapshot of the online world but also have potential applications in electronic commerce, where the marketing strategy of a product might depend on the mood of the customer. Given both the sociological and financial motivations to understand sentiments, a large body of research has recently investigated the issues involved in sentiment analysis [18].

Despite the intense interest in sentiment analysis, however, relatively little has been done to understand the interplay between sentiments and other factors. In this work, we take the first step in this direction. In particular, we use a state-of-the-art sentiment extraction tool [22] to extract sentiments from a very large sample of questions and answers found in Yahoo! Answers.[1] Our sample provides a rich source for sentiments and also has rich meta-data, including demographic details of users and their degree of experience in the system. To facilitate our analysis, we introduce the metrics of attitude and sentimentality, which enable us to quantify the direction (i.e., positive or negative) and strength of sentiments, respectively.

Our analysis starts with a large-scale study on the correlation of various features with the observed attitude and sentimentality. We investigate textual, topical, demographical, spatial, and temporal features. We then take the analysis one step beyond and answer questions of the following kind:

- Topical context: Do sentiments depend on the context? For example, is there a difference in the attitude of answers related to Tiger Woods in the context of news and events versus the context of sports?
- Class interaction: Who answers how to whom? How do age groups differ in their answers to each other?
- Experience level: How does one's experience in Yahoo! Answers affect the expressed sentiments? Does high experience imply more positive attitude?
- Emotional congruence: How do one's own sentiments correlate with prior sentiments of others? Does a ques-

[1]`http://answers.yahoo.com`

tion with a strong sentimentality attract answers with a similar degree of sentimentality?

- Answer preference: How do sentiments within an answer influence an asker's preference? Do people tend to select positive or neutral answers as best answers?

In addition to seeking answers to such questions, we briefly elaborate on the predictability of sentiments. In particular, we build a machine learning model to predict the attitude that will be generated in response to a given question.

Some selected findings of our work are the following:

- There is a strong dependency on the topic. Topics such as Beauty & Style attract strong and generally positive sentiments, whereas Science & Mathematics attracts answers of low sentimentality.
- Demographic factors suggest a strong influence in our data, with women generally expressing stronger, more positive sentiments than men, young people being more positive than older people, and people from predominantly black neighborhoods expressing relatively more neutral sentiments. We also observe a trend for more educated people to give less sentimental answers.
- Sentiments show temporal variation. At a monthly level, the most positive sentiments are observed both during the summer and December. At a daily level, the most positive sentiments are expressed on Saturday and Sunday. At an hourly level, the attitude is at its lowest at around five in the morning.
- People have stronger tendency to give neutral answers as they gain more experience in the online world.
- Best answers differ significantly from other answers in terms of expressed sentiments with more neutral answers being preferred in Business & Finance and more positive ones in News & Events.

The rest of the paper is organized as follows. In Section 2, we provide some information about the Yahoo! Answers data used in our study. Section 3 summarizes the framework adopted for sentiment analysis. Potential caveats of our study are discussed in Section 4. We investigate the correlation between the sentiments and features extracted from the data in Section 5. In Section 6, we conduct various analyses involving sentiments. Section 7, as a representative prediction task, explores the predictability of the attitude a question will provoke in its answers. We survey the related work in Section 8. Finally, the paper is concluded in Section 9 with a brief discussion of potential future work.

2. YAHOO! ANSWERS

2.1 Background

Yahoo! Answers is the largest collaborative question answering site in the Web. People ask questions on different topics and share their knowledge, opinions, and personal experiences as answers to these questions. Questions are manually classified by askers into topics so that answerers can easily find them. Answerers can find questions by searching or browsing through a fixed hierarchy of categories.

Every question goes through a best answer selection process. A question remains open during four days for others to answer. The duration of the process can be shortened or extended by the asker of the question. The asker has the option to select a best answer, starting from one hour after the first answer is received, or he can leave the decision to the community vote. If he does neither and when there is only a single answer, then the system automatically selects the best answer after a certain time. Answerers whose answers are selected as the best answer gain experience points, which provide a motivation for answering others' questions.

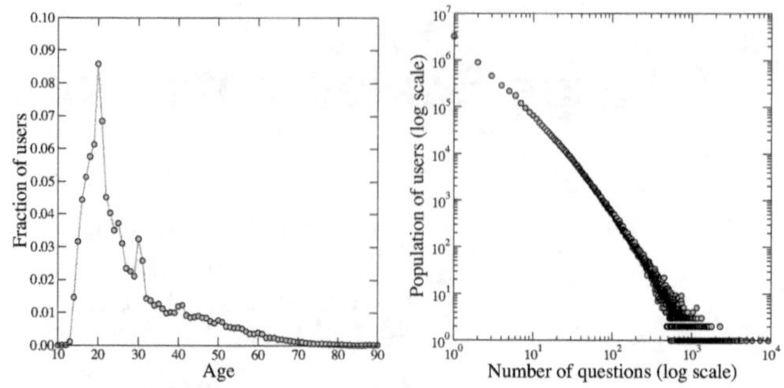

Figure 1: Fraction of user population with a certain age (left), population of users who posted a certain number of questions (right).

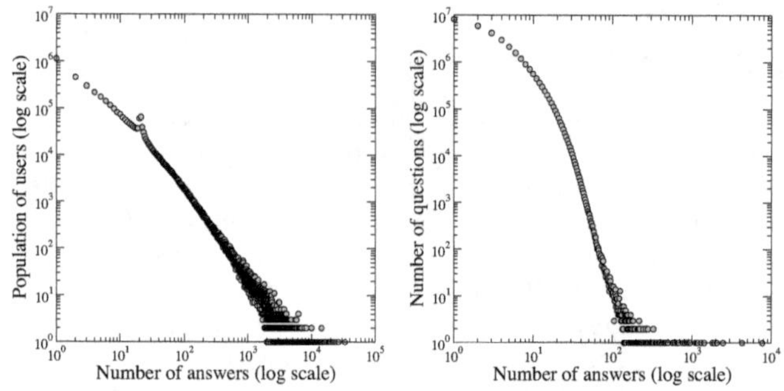

Figure 2: Population of users who posted a certain number of answers (left), number of questions receiving a certain number of answers (right).

2.2 Dataset Characteristics

We use a sample set of questions and answers posted in Yahoo! Answers during a 12-month period, from October 2009 to September 2010. The sample is restricted to posts originating from the US and contains 34M questions, 132M answers, and 412M sentences. In this sample, about 2.4M users have participated as either an asker or an answerer. We were able to obtain self-provided demographic information for about 1.5M users, of which 54.5% are females and 45.5% are males. The users in our sample are mainly young people, whose ages vary between 15 and 30 (Fig. 1 (left)).

In our data, a user posts 5.5 questions and 32.7 answers, on average.[2] Populations of users who posted a specific number of questions or answers both follow a power law distribution, as shown in Figs. 1 (right) and 2 (left), respectively. In Fig. 2 (left), it is interesting to note the sudden jump at 20 answers, due to many users aiming to post at least 20 answers since a new level is gained at this point. As seen in Fig. 2 (right), the distribution of the number of answers a question receives is also highly skewed (on average, 13.3 answers, excluding questions without any answer).

In Yahoo! Answers, there are 1676 editorially defined categories, 26 of which are top-level categories (e.g., Computers & Internet, Politics & Government). The rest are either second-level or third-level subcategories. A question is labeled with the lowest-level category selected by its asker.

[2]A user can provide only one answer to the same question.

3. ANALYSIS FRAMEWORK

Our analysis framework involves the following steps. We first process our sample data to extract questions posted in Yahoo! Answers and their corresponding answers. We then obtain the demographics information of users who posted these questions and answers. Within these two steps, we also extract a number of features that facilitate our analysis. Next, we compute the sentiment scores for individual sentences in the posts, using a state-of-the-art sentiment analysis software as a black box [22]. Based on the sentiment scores obtained at the sentence level, we compute two metrics, referred to as attitude and sentimentality, for different granularities of text. The details of these steps are provided in the rest of this section.

3.1 Question and Answer Extraction

In our framework, a question is represented by the sentences in the title section of the question,[3] i.e., the sentences in the abstract section, which provides more details about the question, are ignored. Together with the question text, we also extract some features related to the question (e.g., question length, category, time/date, asker's current experience, and ZIP code). Since the adopted tools cannot handle non-English text, we omit questions which are submitted to a frontend whose language is not English.

We represent an answer by the set of sentences it contains. To split answers into sentences, we use the Stanford parser.[4] Very short (less than 5 characters) or long sentences (more than 400 characters) are ignored. Since the language of the frontend is not always present in our data, we require that either the language is present and set to English or that the location is present and set to the US. Only answers given in response to questions submitted to an English frontend are considered. During the answer extraction process, we also extract some features related to answers (e.g., time/date, answerer's current experience, and ZIP code).

3.2 Demographics Extraction

To post either a question or an answer on Yahoo! Answers, a user must have an account and be logged in. Although initially Yahoo!-Answers-only accounts existed, for several years, a general Yahoo! account has been required. For these accounts, we obtain self-provided registration information, which includes birth year, gender, ZIP code, and country.

For users with an existing US ZIP code, we obtain demographic estimates of their income (as quantified by the annual per-capita income), their education level (as quantified by the fraction of the population holding a bachelor's degree or higher), and even their race via the 2000 Governmental Census Data,[5] using the same approach as in [26]. We classify ZIP codes and their corresponding users under the White, Black, and Asian classes[6] if the fraction of the corresponding race in that ZIP code surpasses 50%. In all plots and tables, we always report the results for the largest suitable user population. For example, if a user does not have a valid ZIP code, we do not involve the user in experiments about income, but the user contributes to statistics about the age distribution.

[3]Typically, the title contains a single question sentence.

[4]`http://nlp.stanford.edu/software/lex-parser.shtml`

[5]`http://factfinder.census.gov/`

[6]We use the terminology used in the US census.

Table 1: An example question and the first two sentences of the answer

Label	Text	Scores
Q1.1	Is Scotland a good place to live and start a small business?	+2/−1
A1.1	Yes, Edinburgh is always in the top 5 places to live in the UK and usually at the top.	+1/−1
A1.2	One problem regarding setting up a business is the competition is fierce and Edinburgh people are unusually highly qualified.	+1/−2

3.3 Sentiment Score Computation

To assign numerical scores to sentiments of an individual sentence, we use the SentiStrength[7] tool developed by Thelwall et al. [22]. This tool simultaneously assigns both a positive and a negative score to bits of English text, the idea being that users can express both types of sentiments at the same time, such as in "I love you, but I also hate you". Positive sentiment strength scores range from +1 (not positive) to +5 (extremely positive). Similarly, negative sentiment strength scores range from −1 to −5. The tool works by assigning scores to tokens in a dictionary which includes common emoticons. For example, "love" is mapped to +3/−1 and "stink" is mapped to +1/−3. Modifier words or symbols can boost the score such that "really love" is mapped to +4/−1 (the same for "love!!" or "looove"). The final positive sentiment strength for a bit of text is then computed by taking the maximum score among all individual positive scores. The negative sentiment strength is similarly calculated. Table 1 gives an example of a question, its answer, and the corresponding sentiment scores.

Fig. 3 (left) shows the distribution of sentiment scores given to sentences in answers. The vast majority of sentences are assigned a neutral +1/−1 sentiment score (58.26%). Slightly negative (+1/−2) and slightly positive (+2/−1) scores are also common (6.04% and 15.87%, respectively). Sentences with very strong sentiments, having either a positive score of +4 or higher or a negative score of −4 or lower, make up merely 4.18% of the total sentence volume.

3.4 Metrics: Attitude and Sentimentality

Before introducing the metrics of attitude and sentimentality, we introduce some notation. We use q_j, s_ℓ, A_k, $\mathcal{A}^j$, K_i, and R_i to represent the basic types in our data: a question, a particular sentence within an answer, an answer given to a question, the set of answers given to question q_j, an asker, and an answerer, respectively. We also use notation $\mathcal{S}^k$, $\mathcal{Q}^i$, and $\mathcal{P}^i$ to denote the set of sentences in A_k, the set of questions posted by asker K_i, and the set of answers posted by answerer R_i, respectively. Positive and negative sentiment scores generated by the sentiment analysis software for a given question q_j are denoted by $\varphi^+(q_j)$ and $\varphi^-(q_j)$. Similarly, $\varphi^+(s_\ell)$ and $\varphi^-(s_\ell)$ denote the positive and negative sentiment scores for a given sentence s_ℓ.

Based on this notation, we now define the attitude and sentimentality metrics. The attitude metric computes the inclination towards positive or negative sentiments. The sentimentality metric computes the amount of sentiments. In a sense, the former metric indicates the sign of sentiments while the latter indicates their magnitude. These metrics are computed by the formulas shown in Table 2, for differ-

[7]`http://sentistrength.wlv.ac.uk/`

Table 2: **The formulas used for computing the attitude and sentimentality metrics**

Input type	Symbol	Metrics: Attitude	Metrics: Sentimentality
Question	q_j	$\phi^q(q_j) = \varphi^+(q_j) + \varphi^-(q_j)$	$\psi^q(q_j) = \varphi^+(q_j) - \varphi^-(q_j) - 2$
Asker	K_i	$\Phi^K(K_i) = \frac{1}{\lvert\mathcal{Q}^i\rvert}\sum_{q_j \in \mathcal{Q}^i} \phi^q(q_j)$	$\Psi^K(K_i) = \frac{1}{\lvert\mathcal{Q}^i\rvert}\sum_{q_j \in \mathcal{Q}^i} \psi^q(q_j)$
Sentence in an answer	s_ℓ	$\phi^s(s_\ell) = \varphi^+(s_\ell) + \varphi^-(s_\ell)$	$\psi^s(s_\ell) = \varphi^+(s_\ell) - \varphi^-(s_\ell) - 2$
Answer to a question	A_k	$\Phi^A(A_k) = \frac{1}{\lvert\mathcal{S}^k\rvert}\sum_{s_\ell \in \mathcal{S}^k} \phi^s(s_\ell)$	$\Psi^A(A_k) = \frac{1}{\lvert\mathcal{S}^k\rvert}\sum_{s_\ell \in \mathcal{S}^k} \psi^s(s_\ell)$
Answerer	R_i	$\Phi^R(R_i) = \frac{1}{\lvert\mathcal{P}^i\rvert}\sum_{A_k \in \mathcal{P}^i} \Phi^A(A_k)$	$\Psi^R(R_i) = \frac{1}{\lvert\mathcal{P}^i\rvert}\sum_{A_k \in \mathcal{P}^i} \Psi^A(A_k)$
Answer set of a question	$\mathcal{A}^j$	$\Phi^A(\mathcal{A}^j) = \frac{1}{\lvert\mathcal{A}^j\rvert}\sum_{A_k \in \mathcal{A}^j} \Phi^A(A_k)$	$\Psi^A(\mathcal{A}^j) = \frac{1}{\lvert\mathcal{A}^j\rvert}\sum_{A_k \in \mathcal{A}^j} \Psi^A(A_k)$

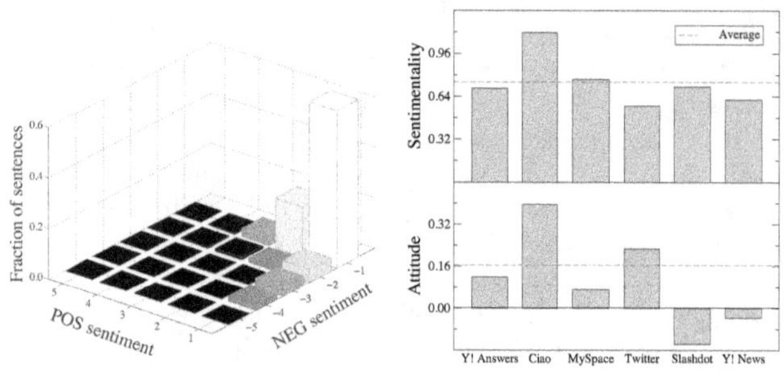

Figure 3: Distribution of sentiment scores for sentences in answers (left), average attitude and sentimentality for different web datasets (right).

ent fields of the data: question, asker, sentence in an answer, answer, answerer, and set of answers to a question. All results in the rest of the paper are reported by averaging the metrics shown in Table 2. At the beginning of each section, we indicate the specific formula we used in the experiments related to that section.

4. CAVEATS

4.1 Inferring Demographics

Certain online user attributes (e.g., race) can be inferred by aggregating real-life data, obtained from online Web resources. In our work, we aggregate the online data of people living in a region with a specific ZIP code to infer certain attributes of Yahoo! Answers users who provided the same ZIP code. Obviously, this kind of an inference can be quite noisy, especially if the demographical classes within a ZIP code are uniformly distributed (e.g., almost equal number of males and females in every ZIP code) or if the distribution of classes across the ZIP codes is highly skewed (e.g., very few regions where the Asians are the dominant race). We believe that the education level and income attributes, which we infer based on ZIP codes, are relatively less error-prone in this respect as the distribution of these attributes are typically neither uniform within a ZIP code nor very skewed across different ZIP codes.

4.2 Sentiment Analysis

We use sentiment analysis as the main technique to quantify the attitude and sentimentality. Obviously, there is no perfect sentiment analysis tool to date. The tool we use indeed performs a simple syntactical analysis over sentences rather than a sophisticated semantic analysis. However, we still hope the erroneous cases to be minimal as the accuracy of the tool has been shown to be good enough in another domain [22]. Moreover, the vast amount of data we use helps supporting the significance of the reported results.

4.3 User Bias

We emphasize that our results cannot be generalized to the entire population of the world as the user sample we have in our data may have a biased distribution. In particular, certain demographic classes may be under represented in the Internet. Even if they are represented in the Internet with similar likelihood, their distribution in Yahoo! Answers may be skewed. Finally, although they might be equally well presented in Yahoo! Answers, the rate at which they contribute to the posts may differ. Consequently, our findings are limited to the Yahoo! Answers users who actively participate in the questions and answers.

4.4 Site Bias

The generalizability of our results to other web sites may be questioned. To reveal any potential bias, we compute the attitude and sentimentality metrics over six web datasets,[8] each with different characteristics. The selected datasets include questions and answers from Yahoo! Answers, movie reviews from Ciao, forum discussions from MySpace, short messages from Twitter, comments on news-related posts from Slashdot, and news in English from Yahoo! News. For this experiment, we randomly sample 40K sentences from each dataset and compute the attitude and sentimentality metrics by averaging the respective scores over all sentences.

According to Fig. 3 (right), the Ciao dataset has the most positive attitude and a relatively higher sentimentality. The most negative attitude is observed in the Slashdot dataset. The Yahoo! Answers dataset stands very close to the average over all datasets, in terms of both the attitude and sentimentality metrics. This observation further justifies our use of Yahoo! Answers as a representative data source.

5. FEATURE ANALYSIS

We group the features used in our analysis under five headings: textual, topical, demographical, spatial, and temporal features (Table 3). All features are extracted from both questions and answers, except for the textual features, which are only extracted from questions. The rest of the section investigates the correlation of the extracted features with the previously defined attitude and sentimentality metrics. Due to space constraints, a detailed analysis of certain features is omitted. We note that, in all results presented in the paper, we report only the findings that are statistically significant according to a two-tailed t-test for equality of means at

[8] `http://caw2.barcelonamedia.org/node/7`

Table 3: Summary of extracted features

Type	Feature	Range	Applicable to Question	Applicable to Answer
Textual	Question length	ℕ	Yes	No
	# of ? symbols	ℕ		
	# of ! symbols	ℕ		
	First word	String		
Topical	Top category	1–26	Yes	Yes
	Leaf category	1–1676		
Demog.	Gender	{M, F}	Yes	Yes
	Age	ℕ		
	Race	{A, B, W}		
	Income	$\mathbb{R}^+$		
	Educ. degree	0-100%		
	Experience	ℕ		
Spatial	ZIP code	00000–99999	Yes	Yes
Temporal	Month	1–12	Yes	Yes
	Day of month	1–31		
	Day of week	1–7		
	Hour of day	1–24		

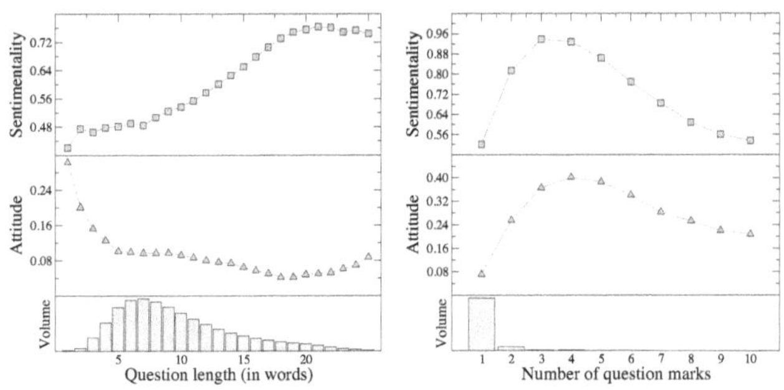

Figure 4: Attitude and sentimentality as the question's length (left) and the number of question marks it contains (right) increases.

the 95% confidence level. Similarly, we only display results where all of the three pairs (maximum, median), (maximum, minimum), and (median, minimum) differ at the 95% confidence level or above. This ensures that the reported results are "meaningful" and not merely noise.

5.1 Textual Features

The results reported in this section are obtained by averaging the ϕ^q and ψ^q values over all questions.

Question length. The sentimentality correlates positively with the question length in words (Fig. 4 (left)). This is somewhat expected as the probability of having sentimental words increases as new words are added to the question.[9] Interestingly, however, the attitude demonstrates a decreasing trend. This might suggest that shorter questions are more likely to contain positive sentiments and negative sentiments are more common in longer questions.

Number of question marks. We observe relatively higher sentimentality and attitude in questions that contain multiple question marks (Fig. 4 (right)). Both metrics reach a maximum value when there are three or four question marks in the question. This increase is simply because of question titles that contain multiple question sentences (remember that we do not split questions into sentences).

[9]Recall that the sentiment scores of a sentence are cumulated by taking the maximum over the words in the sentence. Hence, scores are not normalized by the sentence length.

Table 4: Attitude and sentimentality for the most popular question starting words

Word	Volume (%)	Questions ϕ^q	Questions ψ^q	Answers Φ^A	Answers Ψ^A
What	13.2	0.16	0.45	0.21	0.68
How	10.8	0.04	0.36	0.16	0.60
I	5.6	0.07	0.69	0.17	0.70
Is	4.9	0.05	0.62	0.14	0.69
Why	4.4	-0.17	0.66	-0.01	0.75
Can	3.4	0.10	0.38	0.14	0.59
Do	3.1	0.15	0.67	0.18	0.74
Does	2.2	0.11	0.55	0.18	0.69
Where	2.1	0.13	0.28	0.31	0.55
My	2.0	-0.09	0.70	0.07	0.70

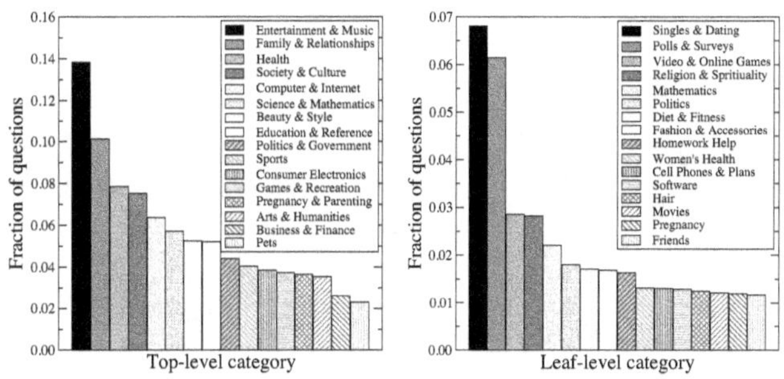

Figure 5: Most popular top-level (left) and leaf-level (right) categories.

Interestingly, however, the further increase in the number of question marks results in a decrease in the metrics.

Starting words. Table 4 shows the attitude and sentimentality of questions with the most popular starting words, listed in decreasing order of popularity. According to the table, the only words with negative attitude are "Why" and "My" while the rest imply mostly positive attitude. In terms of sentimentality, questions starting with words "What", "How", "Can", and "Where" have the lowest sentimentality. In general, we observe that questions seeking information have lower sentimentality than those asking for opinions.

5.2 Topical Features

The results reported in this section are obtained by averaging the ϕ^q and ψ^q values of questions and also by averaging the ϕ^A and ψ^A values of answers under specific categories.

Category. Fig. 5 shows the distribution of questions posted in the 16 most popular top-level and leaf-level categories. Table 5 shows the categories with the highest and lowest attitude, both for questions and answers. Similarly, Table 6 shows the categories with the highest and lowest sentimentality, again both for questions and answers. These results indicate that both the attitude and sentimentality of questions and answers are highly influenced by the category in which they are posted.

Since the dependence of the attitude and sentimentality on the topic is so pronounced, we test whether the topical differences induce all other differences. That is, we test if the differences between classes can be fully explained by the fact that class members have different topical interests. To test this hypothesis, we look at demographic differences for the attitude, averaged over all sentences in the set of an-

Table 5: Highest and lowest attitude values for top-level and leaf-level categories

	Top-level category				Leaf-level category			
	Questions		Answers		Questions		Answers	
	Category	ϕ^q	Category	$\Phi^{\mathcal{A}}$	Category	ϕ^q	Category	$\Phi^{\mathcal{A}}$
Highest	Beauty & Style	0.28	Beauty & Style	0.43	Baby Names	0.46	Baby Names	0.61
	Dining Out	0.24	Business & Finance	0.30	Beauty & Style	0.44	Valentine's Day	0.54
	Food & Drink	0.21	Dining Out	0.24	Valentine's Day	0.42	Makeup	0.51
	Arts & Humanities	0.20	Pregnancy & Parenting	0.24	Rock and Pop	0.36	Christmas	0.48
	Travel	0.18	Food & Drink	0.22	R&B & Soul	0.36	Fashion & Accessories	0.47
Lowest	Society & Culture	0.02	Health	0.05	Psychology	-0.38	Law Enforcement	-0.10
	Politics & Government	-0.13	Environment	0.04	Injuries	-0.40	Spam & Bulk Mail	-0.11
	News & Events	-0.14	Social Science	-0.03	Heart Diseases	-0.52	Pain Management	-0.11
	Social Science	-0.21	Politics & Government	-0.07	Mental Health	-0.71	Current Events	-0.14
	Health	-0.22	News & Events	-0.08	Pain Management	-1.35	Boxing	-0.19

Table 6: Highest and lowest sentimentality values for top-level and leaf-level categories

	Top-level category				Leaf-level category			
	Questions		Answers		Questions		Answers	
	Category	ψ^q	Category	$\Psi^{\mathcal{A}}$	Category	ψ^q	Category	$\Psi^{\mathcal{A}}$
Highest	Family & Relationships	0.91	Family & Relationships	0.91	Pain Management	1.74	Poetry	1.02
	Social Science	0.81	Social Science	0.83	Mental Health	1.25	Mental Health	0.97
	Health	0.68	Beauty & Style	0.78	Psychology	1.01	Singles & Dating	0.94
	Society & Culture	0.62	Pregnancy & Parenting	0.78	Friends	0.95	Friends	0.92
	News & Events	0.62	Business & Finance	0.76	Family & Relationships	0.95	Family & Relationships	0.91
Lowest	Home & Garden	0.32	Cars & Transportation	0.48	Yahoo! Mail	0.19	Astronomy & Space	0.36
	Business & Finance	0.32	Home & Garden	0.47	Embassies & Consulates	0.18	Biology	0.35
	Consumer Electronics	0.32	Science & Mathematics	0.46	Packing & Preparation	0.17	Accounts & Passwords	0.35
	Cars & Transportation	0.30	Local Businesses	0.46	Addr. Book & Calendar	0.17	Geography	0.32
	Local Businesses	0.27	Comp. & Internet	0.45	External Mail	0.17	Yahoo! Mail	0.32

Table 7: Differences in demographical features on a per-topic basis

Topic	Gender	Age	Race	Ed. level
Beauty & Style	**0.111**	**0.164**	**−0.049**	**0.028**
Business & Fin.	**−0.025**	**0.119**	0.010	**−0.047**
Arts & Human.	**0.180**	**0.233**	**0.015**	**0.103**
Pregn. & Parent.	**0.154**	**0.172**	**−0.020**	**−0.081**
News & Events	**0.015**	−0.018	**0.036**	−0.024
Games & Recr.	**0.090**	0.015	−0.008	−0.003
Science & Math.	−0.001	**0.103**	**0.018**	**0.034**

swers, on a per-topic basis. Table 7 shows the difference of the average attitudes for a selection of topics. In the table, differences that are significant at the 1% level for a two-sided t-test for equality of means are indicated in bold font. The attitude differences correspond to the numerical difference for the attitude of each of the following demographic group pairs: female versus male genders, [10, 20] versus [70, 80] age intervals, Black versus White races, and [0%, 5%) versus [50%, 55%) of population having a bachelor's degree or higher. The main finding of this experiment is that topical differences are not sufficient to explain the differences between demographic groups and that, even for the same topic, different groups express different sentiments.

5.3 Demographical Features

The results of this section are obtained by averaging the Φ^K and Ψ^K values of askers and also by averaging the Φ^R and Ψ^R values of answerers in a certain demographic group.

Gender. Our analysis suggest that women are more sentimental when answering a question than men (on average, $\Psi^R = 0.76$ and $\Psi^R = 0.66$ for women and men, respectively). We also observe that, in terms of attitude, men are more

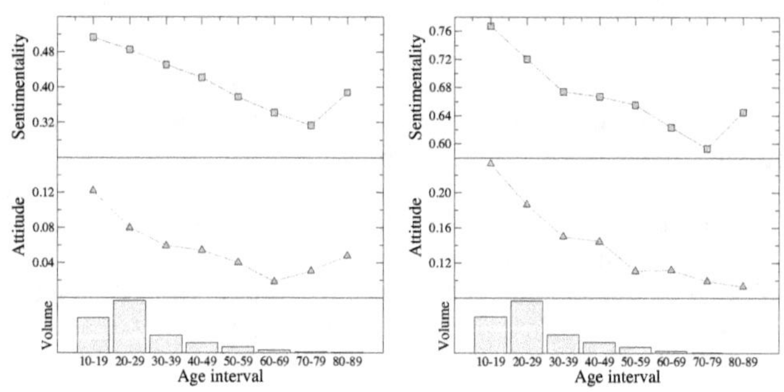

Figure 6: Attitude and sentimentality based on askers' (left) and answerers' (right) age.

neutral, whereas women have more positive attitude in their answers (on average, $\Phi^R = 0.23$ and $\Phi^R = 0.13$ for women and men, respectively). We observe a similar behavior in the questions they post.

Age. Fig. 6 shows the attitude and sentimentality values for askers and answerers of varying age. We observe that, in general, the sentimentality decreases with increasing age. We also observe a trend towards negative attitude as the reported age of the user increases.

Race. We observe that users from predominantly Black ZIP codes have more neutral attitude values (on average, $\Phi^R = 0.19$, $\Phi^R = 0.17$, and $\Phi^R = 0.19$, for Asian, Black, and White, respectively). Users from predominantly Asian ZIP code are less sentimental in both asking and answering among these race groups (on average, $\Phi^R = 0.67$, $\Phi^R = 0.71$, and $\Phi^R = 0.72$, for Asian, Black, and White, respectively).

Education level. As the education level increases, the data suggest that the sentimentality of askers tend to in-

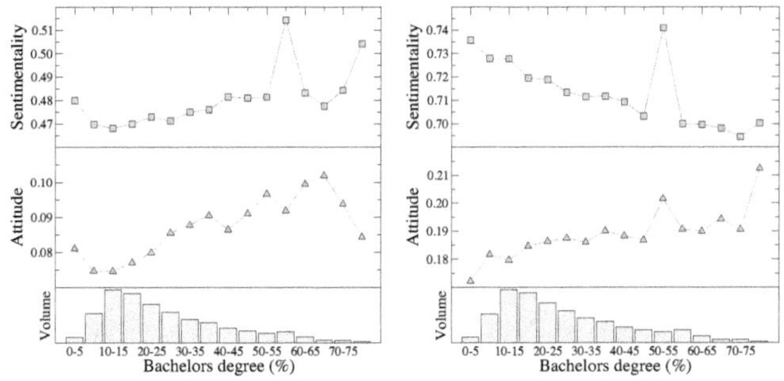

Figure 7: Attitude and sentimentality based on askers' (left) and answerers' (right) education level.

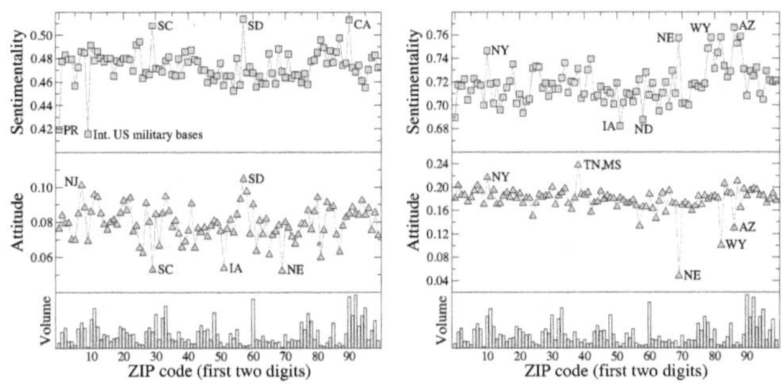

Figure 8: Attitude and sentimentality based on askers' (left) and answerers' (right) location.

crease (Fig. 7). However, answerers become more neutral as education level increases. On the other hand, the attitude shows a similar increasing trend for both askers and answerers with increasing education level. Irregularities in the 55%–60% interval are due to the relatively high volume of users with the self-provided ZIP code 90210 (Beverly Hills).

5.4 Spatial Features

The results of this section are obtained by averaging the Φ^K and Ψ^K values of askers and by averaging the Φ^R and Ψ^R values of answerers who reported a specific ZIP code.

ZIP code. We do not observe a clear effect of the location on sentimentality. Hence, we only display the two-digit ZIP code prefixes and corresponding states where the highest and lowest sentimentality values are observed (Fig. 8).[10] The attitude distribution is not very conclusive either, but it gives some hints about the user profiles of certain states.

5.5 Temporal Features

The results in this section are obtained by averaging the Φ^A and Ψ^A values of all answers posted in a specific time interval. In all cases, the Eastern Time Zone[11] is used as the timestamps in our data are in this timezone.

Month. The attitude and sentimentality show significant variation across the months. Answers posted during the summer and in the holiday season (i.e., December) have higher sentimentality and more positive attitude. Both the lowest sentimentality and attitude are observed in March.

Day of month. The variance over days of the month is very minor. Hence, we omit a discussion on this feature.

[10]Note that ZIP code prefixes typically correspond to geographically adjacent regions. See http://en.wikipedia.org/wiki/List_of_ZIP_code_prefixes.

[11]http://en.wikipedia.org/wiki/Eastern_Time_Zone

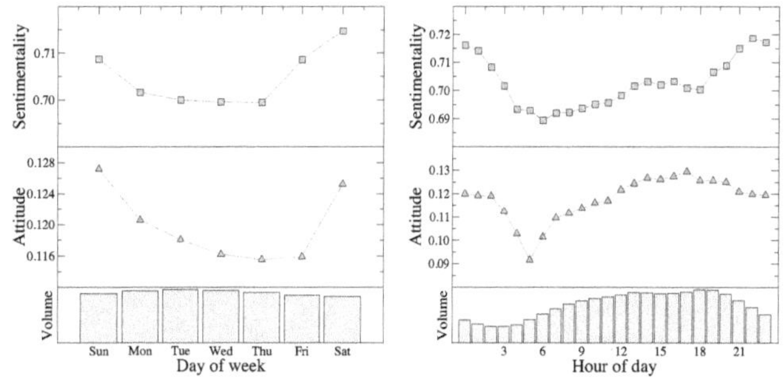

Figure 9: Answers' sentimentality and attitude versus day of week (left) and hour of day (right).

Day of week. Interesting behaviors are observed for day of the week. Answers posted during the weekends and on Friday are more sentimental than those posted during the weekdays (Fig. 9 (left)). The attitude moves from positive to neutral as the days go from Sunday to Thursday. Then, it changes its trend on Friday and Saturday.

Hour of day. Sentimentality shows a slightly increasing trend during the day (Fig. 9 (right)). Especially, a sharper increase is observed between the 18:00 and 23:00 hours, followed by a decreasing trend throughout the night. The attitude reaches its lowest value around 5:00 in the morning, which might correspond to an average of 3:00–4:00 on a national level when correcting for the fact that we use the Eastern Time for all users.

6. FURTHER ANALYSES

We determine five different concepts, for which we deepen our analysis on the attitude and sentimentality: topical context, class interaction, experience level, emotional congruence, and answer preference.

6.1 Topical Context

As mentioned in Section 5.2, the topical context plays an important role on the attitude and sentimentality of answers (Tables 5 and 6), i.e., the interpretation of a concept may differ according to the context. The same concept may be mentioned in a very positive sense in one category while the attitude can be quite negative in another. As a representative example, in our sample, the opinions about "Tiger Woods" show high variation based on the context of the discussion.[12] Questions about him receive answers with negative attitude in the News & Events ($\phi^s = -0.10$) category, whereas the answers are quite positive in the Sports ($\phi^s = 0.18$) and Games & Recreation ($\phi^s = 0.35$) categories. We observe a neutral attitude in Social Science ($\phi^s = -0.02$) and Family & Relationships ($\phi^s = 0.04$) categories. We further quantify the influence of the topical context in Section 7.

6.2 Class Interaction

Gender. We observe that the askers are more likely to receive answers from users with the same gender. Especially, female askers receive most answers from other females (%63.5). Female answerers have more positive attitude when the asker is a female ($\Phi^R = 0.17$). According to

[12]In our case, opinions refer to sentences that include a named entity extracted with the Stanford CoreNLP tool (http://nlp.stanford.edu/software/corenlp.shtml).

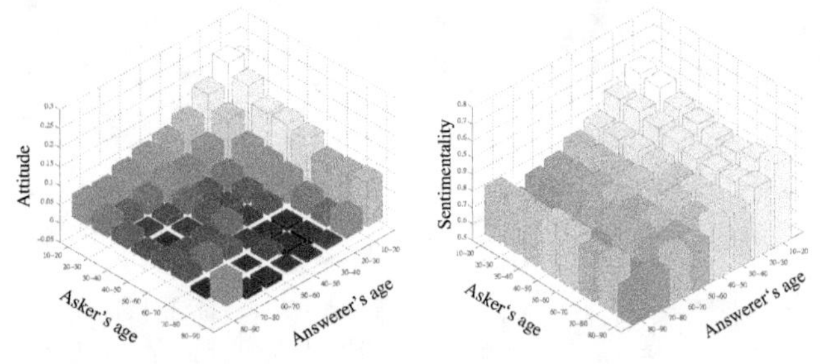

Figure 10: Class interaction: Attitude (left) and sentimentality (right) of answers versus ages of askers and answerers.

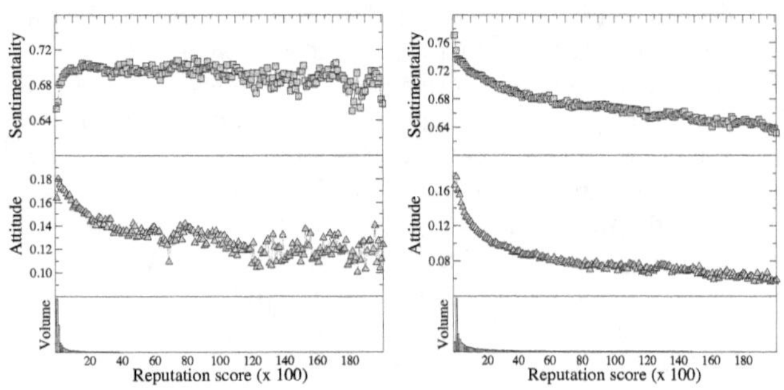

Figure 11: Experience level: Attitude and sentimentality for questions (left) and answers (right) based on users' experience.

our analysis, the lowest attitude is observed when both the asker and answerer are males ($\Phi^R = 0.03$).

Age. Younger people post and receive answers with a more positive attitude (Fig. 10). The attitude reaches the maximum when both the asker and answerer are less than 20 years old. In particular, people are likely to respond to people of the same age in a more positive manner. On the other hand, we do not observe a sentimentality change in answers given to different age groups.

Income. When both the asker and answerer are within the 30K–50K income range, the attitude of answers is slightly more positive. Otherwise, we do not observe any strong trend with the income level.

6.3 Experience Level

As discussed in Section 2.2, Yahoo! Answers awards points to its users for answering questions, with additional points being awarded for best answers. The total number of accumulated points can hence be seen as an indicator of the experience of the user in the system. Herein, we try to understand whether more experienced users differ in the sentiments they express in their questions and their answers.

As far as the questions are concerned, we observe that users with very little or no experience tend to issue the most positive questions, with the attitude of the question decreasing with an increase in experience (Fig. 11 (left)). On the other hand, as the experience increases, answerers become less sentimental in their answers (Fig. 11 (right)). This may indicate a correlation between the experience and the objectivity of answerers. This is also supported by the observation that the attitude becomes less positive as the experience increases.

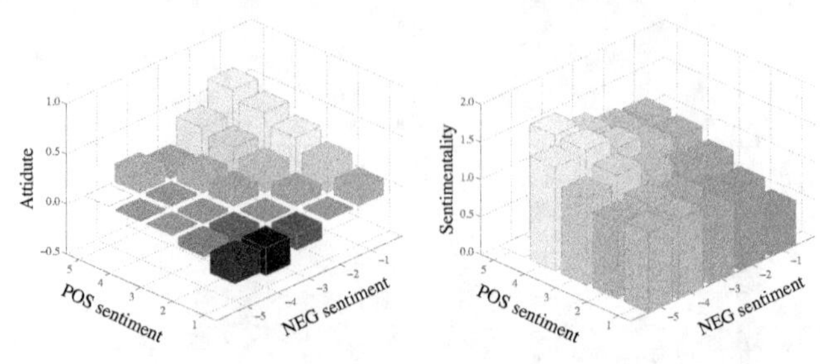

Figure 12: Emotional congruence: Questions' positive and negative sentiments versus the attitude (left) and sentimentality (right) of received answers.

Table 8: Answer preference: Answers selected as the best answer differ from other answers in terms of both attitude and sentimentality

		Answers		
	Category	Best	Other	Diff.
Attitude	Business & Finance	0.16	0.32	-0.16
	News & Events	-0.07	-0.14	0.08
	Environment	0.05	-0.01	0.07
	Entertainment & Music	0.21	0.15	0.06
	Health	-0.01	0.05	-0.06
Sentiment.	Business & Finance	0.47	0.77	-0.30
	News & Events	0.68	0.76	-0.08
	Travel	0.53	0.61	-0.08
	Local Business	0.44	0.51	-0.07
	Entertainment & Music	0.74	0.67	0.06

6.4 Emotional Congruence

Fig. 12 shows the attitude and sentimentality of answers that are posted in response to questions with different positive and negative sentiment scores.[13] In general, there is a strong positive correlation between the sentimentality of initial questions and received answers. That is, highly sentimental questions are more likely to receive very sentimental answers and vice versa. The way answers are created is also determined by the attitude of questions. More negative questions receive answers with negative attitude and vice versa, indicating a trend towards "emotional congruence" between the asker and the answerer.

6.5 Answer Preference

In general, the best answers, which are preferred over the other answers, have lower sentimentality ($\Psi^A = 0.67$ versus $\Psi^A = 0.71$, on average). At the same time, the best answers are more likely to be selected from answers with a more positive attitude ($\Phi^A = 0.16$ versus $\Phi^A = 0.14$, on average). For certain categories, the preference is even stronger (Table 8). As a striking example, in the Business & Finance category, the best answers are more inclined towards those with low sentimentality and neutral attitude. On the other hand, in the Entertainment & Music category, answers with higher sentimentality and more positive attitude seem to be preferred by the users.

[13]The data point $(-5, 5)$ is omitted from the two plots due to the very low volume of sentences.

Table 9: Feature importance

Feature	Importance
Leaf-level category	100.0
Negative sentiment score	63.0
Positive sentiment score	39.7
Starting word	19.7
Number of ! symbols	12.0
Month	9.1
Question length	7.2
Gender of asker	6.7
Age of asker	3.7
Experience of asker	2.2

Table 10: Prediction performance

Classifier	RMSE	Improv.
Baseline	0.5261	–
Topical	0.5096	3.14
Topical + Textual	0.4964	5.65
Topical + Demographical	0.5091	3.23
Topical + Spatial + Temporal	0.5091	3.23
Topical + Textual + Demographical	0.4962	5.68
Topical + Textual + Spatial + Temporal	0.4960	5.72
Topical + Demographical + Spatial + Temporal	0.5086	3.35
Topical + Textual + Demographical + Spatial + Temporal	0.4939	6.12

7. ATTITUDE PREDICTION

Is it possible to predict the attitude or sentimentality of the answers a particular question will attract before the answers are posted? Accurate prediction of attitude and sentimentality can have different practical use cases. For example, questions that are predicted to generate high sentimentality can be boosted in visible areas (in the main page or as hot topics) to increase page views. As another example, questions that have the potential to lead to very negative attitude in answers may be sent to moderators, beforehand.

Herein, we only focus on the problem of predicting the attitude in future answer posts. We formulate this particular task as a machine learning problem. In general, this is a very challenging task as the only information comes from the question and the asker. Features about the answerer, which the previous sections found to be correlated with the attitude in the answer, are not used as they are not available until the answers are posted. In addition to the features in Table 3, we also extract and use positive and negative sentiment scores of questions as features, which play a relatively important role in the prediction.[14] In our task, the value we try to predict for each question instance is the average attitude of the answers given to a question, i.e., average $\Phi^{\mathcal{A}}$.

We test the performance of the model over a dataset containing eight million question instances, obtained after filtering out questions whose askers' demographics information is missing. We train our machine learning model using gradient boosted decision trees [10, 27] and test on our data via 10-fold cross-validation.[15] The 10 most important features, as provided by the learning tool, are shown in Table 9.

We adopt the root mean square error (RMSE) to evaluate the performance. As the baseline technique, we use a simple yet effective predictor which always predicts the average attitude value observed in the training data. We build our classifier using different combinations of feature types to observe their individual contributions to the performance.

Table 10 shows the improvement, relative to the baseline, achieved by different classifiers trained with different combinations of feature types. When only the topical features are used, the prediction performance can be improved by 3.14%. Textual features also significantly improve the performance. The contributions of the asker's demographics and spatio-temporal features are relatively low. When all features are used the classifier can improve the baseline by 6.12%.

[14] We place these two features under the textual features category as they are obtained through text processing.

[15] In training, we set the number of trees to 40, the number of leaf nodes per tree to 40, and the learning rate to 0.5.

8. RELATED WORK

A large body of work so far have dealt with different aspects of sentiment analysis, mainly sentiment extraction [1, 2, 7, 28], classification [8, 19, 25], retrieval [11, 12, 29], summarization [3, 17], and presentation [14]. The core application areas are finance [5, 7, 9], reviews [8, 19, 25], politics [16, 24], and news [13]. Herein, we omit a discussion of these works and focus only on works that are directly relevant to our work. Interested reader may refer to [18], for a detailed survey on sentiment analysis.

A large number of studies apply sentiment analysis to Twitter [4, 21]. These works differ from ours as they omit demographic factors and Twitter messages are explicitly written in a non-anonymous manner for mass consumption. The "We feel fine" project[16] [15] is probably the most closely related work. In that project, the authors use a large number of blog posts and, wherever possible, annotate the posts with demographic information provided in public user profiles as well as weather data for profiles from which also the location could be extracted. The focus of their work is on interface design and on offering experimental data visualization. However, they also observe temporal patterns over the course of a day (lowest fraction of "joy" sentiments at night) and over the course of a week (high fraction of "relaxed" during the weekend). Similar to our finding, they observe a trend for older people to be less negative. As data mining is not their main focus, however, their quantitative findings are less comprehensive than ours and do not include features such as educational level or race in their analysis.

Apart from demographically annotated blogs, Facebook data is often used as it offers rich per-user profile information. Typically, sentiment analysis is applied to status messages of users. It has been observed, for example, that users with a relationship status "in a relationship" or "married" are more likely to have a positive status message [6].

We note that neither Facebook status messages nor blog posts have the question-response interaction available in our data, which allows investigation of the effect of the original sentiment on the induced sentiments in answers. A tendency towards "emotion homophily" for comments left by friends on blogs is observed in [20]. The gender differences that we observed are independently observed in a small-scale study using MySpace blog posts [23]. Given that both blog posts and status messages on Facebook are not anonymous and written for explicit consumption by an ideally large group of people, it is surprising to see the general trends of sentiments to be re-confirmed in a question answering site.

[16] `http://www.wefeelfine.org/`

9. FUTURE WORK AND EXTENSIONS

Given that we observed significant differences concerning sentiments between different demographic groups, this could be used to "normalize" individual sentiments to obtain a better idea about deviations from the expected behavior. For example, a "pretty good" by an older person might be equivalent to an "absolutely amazing" by a teenager. The availability of a topical classification makes it possible to differentiate sentiments attached to a particular entity according to the context. We plan to investigate this to obtain a more faceted representation of the opinions about an entity.

One interesting problem is to apply sentiment prediction techniques in other domains. For example, it would be interesting to predict the sentiments of comments left in response to a news article. Potentially, such techniques could even be used by blog writers to improve user engagement by providing them with indications about how to make their posts more controversial. Similarly, we deem it interesting to generalize our findings concerning the sentiments present in best answers to the more general problem of evaluating content quality. The presence/absence of sentiments in the text of, say, a news article might be an indication of its quality.

Finally, it seems promising to apply sentiment analysis to the content of pages from demographically annotated toolbar histories. Such a combination may help to back up claims about general trends, such as women preferring more positive sentiments or a general drop of positive attitude in the early morning hours. It may also make it possible to combine the sentiment analysis with analysis about click-through rates and even properties of the clicked/ignored ads.

10. ACKNOWLEDGMENTS

The authors thank Mike Thelwall for his kind support in making custom changes to the SentiStrength software. This work was partially supported by NSF grant, IIS-0546713 and by the Spanish Centre for the Development of Industrial Technology under the CENIT program, project CEN-20101037, "Social Media" (http://www.cenitsocialmedia.es)

11. REFERENCES

[1] A. Abbasi, H. Chen, and A. Salem. Sentiment analysis in multiple languages: feature selection for opinion classification in Web forums. *ACM Trans. Inf. Syst.*, 26:12:1–12:34, 2008.

[2] X. Bai. Predicting consumer sentiments from online text. *Decis. Support Syst.*, 50:732–742, 2011.

[3] P. Beineke, T. Hastie, C. Manning, and S. Vaithyanathan. Exploring sentiment summarization. In *Proc. AAAI Spring Symp. Exploring Attitude and Affect in Text: Theories and Applications*, pages 1–4, 2004.

[4] J. Bollen, H. Mao, and A. Pepe. Determining the public mood state by analysis of microblogging posts. In *Proc. Alife XII Conf.*, pages 667–668, 2010.

[5] J. Bollen, H. Mao, and X. Zeng. Twitter mood predicts the stock market. *J. Comput. Sci*, 2:1–8, 2011.

[6] S. I. Calderon. Facebook shares new data on relationship status and sentiment, 2010. `http://www.insidefacebook.com/2010/02/15/dr-facebook-is-in-people-in-relationships-are-happiest/`.

[7] S. R. Das and M. Y. Chen. Yahoo! for Amazon: sentiment extraction from small talk on the Web. *Manage. Sci.*, 53:1375–1388, 2007.

[8] K. Dave, S. Lawrence, and D. M. Pennock. Mining the peanut gallery: opinion extraction and semantic classification of product reviews. In *Proc. 12th Int'l Conf. World Wide Web*, pages 519–528, 2003.

[9] A. Devitt and K. Ahmad. Sentiment analysis in financial news: a cohesion-based approach. In *Proc. 45th Annual Meeting of the Assoc. for Computational Linguistics*, pages 984–991, 2007.

[10] J. H. Friedman. Greedy function approximation: a gradient boosting machine. *Ann. Stat.*, 29(5):1189–1232, 2001.

[11] S. Gerani, M. J. Carman, and F. Crestani. Investigating learning approaches for blog post opinion retrieval. In *Proc. 31th Eur. Conf. Information Retrieval*, pages 313–324,2009.

[12] S. Gerani, M. J. Carman, and F. Crestani. Proximity-based opinion retrieval. In *Proc. 33rd Int'l ACM SIGIR Conf. Research and Development in Information Retrieval*, pages 403–410, 2010.

[13] N. Godbole, M. Srinivasaiah, and S. Skiena. Large-scale sentiment analysis for news and blogs. In *Proc. Int'l Conf. Weblogs and Social Media*, 2007.

[14] M. L. Gregory, N. Chinchor, P. Whitney, R. Carter, E. Hetzler, and A. Turner. User-directed sentiment analysis: visualizing the affective content of documents. In *Proc. Workshop on Sentiment and Subjectivity in Text*, pages 23–30, 2006.

[15] S. D. Kamvar and J. Harris. We feel fine and searching the emotional web. In *Proc. 4th ACM Int'l Conf. Web Search and Data Mining*, pages 117–126, 2011.

[16] S.-M. Kim and E. H. Hovy. Crystal: analyzing predictive opinions on the Web. In *Proc. 2007 Joint Conf. Empirical Methods in Natural Language and Computational Natural Language Learning*, pages 1056–1064, 2006.

[17] K. Lerman, S. Blair-Goldensohn, and R. McDonald. Sentiment summarization: evaluating and learning user preferences. In *Proc. 12th Conf. European Chapter of the Assoc. for Computational Linguistics*, pages 514–522, 2009.

[18] B. Pang and L. Lee. Opinion mining and sentiment analysis. *Found. Trends Inf. Retr.*, 2:1–135, 2008.

[19] B. Pang, L. Lee, and S. Vaithyanathan. Thumbs up?: sentiment classification using machine learning techniques. In *Proc. 2002 Conf. Empirical Methods in Natural Language Processing*, pages 79–86, 2002.

[20] M. Thelwall. Emotion homophily in social network site messages. *First Monday*, 15(4-5), 2010.

[21] M. Thelwall, K. Buckley, and G. Paltoglou. Sentiment in Twitter events. *J.Am.Soc.Inf.Sci.Techn.*, 62:406–418, 2011.

[22] M. Thelwall, K. Buckley, G. Paltoglou, D. Cai, and A. Kappas. Sentiment in short strength detection informal text. *J. Am. Soc. Inf. Sci. Technol.*, 61:2544–2558, 2010.

[23] M. Thelwall, D. Wilkinson, and S. Uppal. Data mining emotion in social network communication: gender differences in MySpace. *J. Am. Soc. Inf. Sci. Technol.*, 61(1):190–199, 2010.

[24] M. Thomas, B. Pang, and L. Lee. Get out the vote: determining support or opposition from congressional floor-debate transcripts. In *Proc. Conf. Empirical Methods in Natural Language Processing*, pages 327–335, 2006.

[25] P. D. Turney. Thumbs up or thumbs down?: semantic orientation applied to unsupervised classification of reviews. In *Proc. 40th Annual Meeting on Assoc. for Computational Linguistics*, pages 417–424, 2002.

[26] I. Weber and C. Castillo. The demographics of web search. In *Proc. 33rd Int'l ACM SIGIR Conf. Research and Development in Information Retrieval*, pages 523–530,2010.

[27] J. Ye, J.-H. Chow, J. Chen, and Z. Zheng. Stochastic gradient boosted distributed decision trees. In *Proc. 18th ACM Conf. Information and Knowledge Management*, pages 2061–2064, 2009.

[28] J. Yi, T. Nasukawa, R. Bunescu, and W. Niblack. Sentiment analyzer: extracting sentiments about a given topic using natural language processing techniques. In *Proc. 3rd IEEE Int'l Conf. Data Mining*, pages 427–434, 2003.

[29] W. Zhang, C. Yu, and W. Meng. Opinion retrieval from blogs. In *Proc. 16th ACM Conf. Information and Knowledge Management*, pages 831–840, 2007.

What's in a Hashtag? Content based Prediction of the Spread of Ideas in Microblogging Communities

Oren Tsur
Department of Computer Science
The Hebrew University
Jerusalem 91904, Israel
oren@cs.huji.ac.il

Ari Rappoport
Department of Computer Science
The Hebrew University
Jerusalem 91904, Israel
arir@cs.huji.ac.il

ABSTRACT

Current social media research mainly focuses on temporal trends of the information flow and on the topology of the social graph that facilitates the propagation of information. In this paper we study the effect of the content of the idea on the information propagation. We present an efficient hybrid approach based on a linear regression for predicting the spread of an idea in a given time frame. We show that a combination of content features with temporal and topological features minimizes prediction error.

Our algorithm is evaluated on Twitter hashtags extracted from a dataset of more than 400 million tweets. We analyze the contribution and the limitations of the various feature types to the spread of information, demonstrating that content aspects can be used as strong predictors thus should not be disregarded. We also study the dependencies between global features such as graph topology and content features.

Categories and Subject Descriptors

H.4 [**Information Systems Applications**]: Miscellaneous

General Terms

Theory, Measurements

Keywords

Social media, information diffusion, microblogging, Twitter, hashtags

1. INTRODUCTION

Social media is a natural platform for the spread of thoughts and ideas, sometimes called *memes*. The spread and propagation of a meme through a social network attract a lot of research in recent years. Successful prediction of the spread of memes can improve "marketing" efforts, whether the target is a commercial product or an idea being promoted. It could also help in real time identification of new trends, both commercial and ideological.

From a graph topology perspective the social network is viewed as a graph of nodes (users/posts) connected by edges (readers in blogs, fans in Facebook, followers on Twitter etc.). Recent studies focused on the *topology* of the social graph, investigating what topologies and what activation patterns facilitate efficient propagation of memes. While graph topology plays an important role in the spread patterns of ideas, the *content* of the meme is also of great importance to the acceptance and promotion of a meme within the community. To the best of our knowledge, no prior work studies the way the inherent content features affect propagation.

In this work we propose a complementary framework: given an idea/meme m, and a time frame t, can we predict the acceptance of m in the community (a social network) within this horizon? We are interested in the following questions: can we accurately predict the acceptance of a meme based solely on the meme's content? Does the meme's context improve the prediction? What are the relations between the graph topology and the content and how do they integrate to facilitate efficient propagation?

Popularity is captured by the normalized count of the meme's occurrences in the given time frame. It is important to clarify that we are not interested in the temporal spreading patterns, although the temporal pattern serves as a feature type in our hybrid model.

The rationale behind focusing on content is threefold. First and foremost, there is a genuine interest in the way the content and structure of an idea drives its acceptance. Moreover, relying only on graph topology disregards content altogether, implicitly assuming all memes are born equal (if seeded equally). Second, the topology of the social graph is not always given, while the content is usually available online. Third, graph based algorithms are NP–hard and even approximation algorithms are ineffective for large graphs in real time.

A common definition of a meme is a short unit of text that passes relatively unchanged through many online sources [24]. We look at data from Twitter, considering hashtags as potential memes. A Twitter *hashtag* is a string of characters preceded by the hash (#) character. In many cases hashtags can be viewed as topical markers, an indication to the context of the tweet or as the core idea expressed

Permission to make digital or hard copies of all or part of this work for personal or classroom use is granted without fee provided that copies are not made or distributed for profit or commercial advantage and that copies bear this notice and the full citation on the first page. To copy otherwise, to republish, to post on servers or to redistribute to lists, requires prior specific permission and/or a fee.
WSDM'12, February 8–12, 2012, Seattle, Washington, USA.
Copyright 2012 ACM 978-1-4503-0747-5/12/02 ...$10.00.

in the tweet, therefore hashtags are adopted by other users that contribute similar content or express a related idea. A few examples of the use of hashtags are: "*ask GAGA anything using the tag #GoogleGoesGaga for her interview! RT so every monster learns about it!!*" referring to an exclusive interview for Google by Lady Gaga (singer), "*Whoever said 'youth is wasted on the young' must be eating his words right now. #March15 #Jan25 #Feb14*", referring to the protest movements in the Arab world[1], or "*Speaker refers to #Lanseys 'abysmal ignorance' as demonstrated on alcohol strategy; this SoS #notfitforpurpose #nhs #savethenhs #healthbill*", referring to the "national health services" and the "health bill".

The acceptance of a hashtag is captured by the (normalized) count of its appearance in a time interval. Given a hashtag, we aim at predicting its frequency after some time. We cast the problem of predicting the hashtag frequency as a regression task. We test our model on a large dataset which consists of more than 4 million tweets and thousands of hashtags. Our experiments show that there are three main factors to the acceptance of a meme: the meme's content, the meme's context and the social graph. A hybrid model combining all three factors performs best. In this paper we report several combinations of feature types, including models that incorporate early temporal patterns.

This work has two main contributions: (a) to the best of our knowledge, it is the first study that shifts the emphasis towards content features, and (b) we present a simple yet robust framework that efficiently models the exposure and acceptance of an idea/meme, using only global features, avoiding costly graph based algorithms.

This paper is arranged as follows. The next section surveys related work. Section 3 portrays the corpus we used and some preprocessing steps. Section 4 formally presents the prediction model and the feature types we employed, while Section 5 presents the experimental setup. Results are given in Section 6 and an elaborated discussion is offered in Section 7. In Section 8 we conclude and offer directions for future research.

2. RELATED WORK

Diffusion of information has become an active research area. Most works focus on the topology of the social graph, trying to model the propagation process, maximize the spread of information in a minimal effort by finding the most influential nodes, and maximize purchases induced by viral marketing and social recommendation networks [18, 19, 23, 4, 5, 13], or model temporal dynamics of information spread [12, 15, 34]. Collaborative filtering is used to predict the probability of a tweet to get retweeted [36].

Tweet's content is used in tasks such as profiling users according to substance, style, status, and social tendency [27] and for modeling the inter-influence of the linguistic style between participants in the discourse [7]. The effect of hashtag length (in characters) on its frequency is studied in [6][2].

Some works do refer to the topic of the information passed [14, 24, 34], though topic is addressed in coarse granularity (e.g. 'sports', 'news', 'professional blogs', 'Apple', 'Microsoft') and not very specific events or sentiment (e.g. 'save the national health service', 'Gaga Video Music Awards', 'free Iran'). Leskovec et al. [24] look at at the content in their meme–tracker, but textual content is only used in order to trace the evolution of a meme as it propagates.

Another line of works study the spread patterns of Twitter hashtags. Yang and Leskovec [34] propose a linear model that uses the implicit network rather than the explicit network. Cataldi et al. [3] detect emerging topics in Twitter although they refer to term frequency of tokens in Twitter. Although not using the explicit graph topology, both works use the level of influence of single nodes in order to model spread of information.

Romero, Meeder and Kleinberg [29] observe that different topical categories of hashtags have different propagation pattern. They introduce the distinction between 'stickiness' and 'persistence' arguing that some classes are more persistent than other. This work is the first to address attributes that are inherent to the meme and that goes beyond the most coarse topical propagation.

Our work shares these observations. However, it differs in a number of fundamental aspects. First, our task definition is different as we are interested in predicting the exposure of a meme in a given time frame while they are interested in the temporal spreading patterns. Second, we do not use annotators to classify hashtags, and third, while they model the spread patterns of only the most popular hashtags, we aim at predicting the spread of all hashtags but the least frequent ones.

Unlike other works, we are interested in the acceptance of a meme in a long time frame, as it is better to differentiate between sticky ideas (and successful campaigns) and short term trends that flare, infect many users but quickly disappear.

As we are interested in content based analysis, the sentiment of a tweet is of great importance. Sentiment analysis of Twitter data is studied in many works, [8, 9] among others. In this work we use the LIWC categories [32] and assign sentiment labels to tweets and hashtags based on the LIWC lexicons.

To the best of our knowledge, beyond the hashtag's coarse topic or its number of characters, there is no prior work addressing the features inherent to the information (meme, hashtag), such as location, orthography, number of words, lexicality, ease of cognitive process and emotional effect on various cognitive dimensions. These attributes are described in detail in Section 4.3.

3. DATA

Twitter & hashtags.

Twitter is a popular microblogging platform. A Twitter posting is called a *tweet.* A tweet is restricted to 140 characters in length. This length constraint makes characters "expensive", hence tweets present an informal, sometimes ungrammatical, language, as well as introducing many abbreviations. Twitter allows the usage of two meta characters: @ marking a user name (e.g. @BarackObama), and # marking a hashtag: a sequence of non whitespace characters preceded by the hash character (e.g. #healthCareReform). An extensive survey of Twitter, its uses and its social as-

[1]The protest movements are named after the date of the first demonstration, i.e. Jan25 is the Egyptian movement.

[2]This study refer to hashtags relevant to three events: Micheal Jackson death, the swine flu outbreak of 2009a nd to the Twitter idiom 'music–monday'.

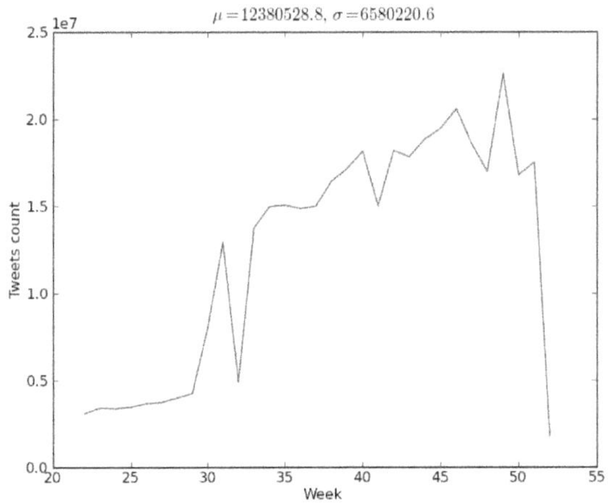

Figure 1: Plot of the number of tweets collected in weeks 22–52 (June–December) of 2009.

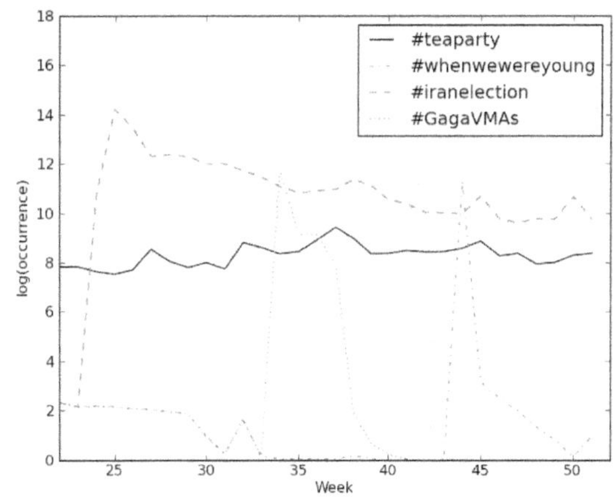

Figure 2: Four typical temporal trends (unnormalized counts).

pects in the first years can be found in [20][3]. The use of hashtags is a popular way to give the context of a tweet, an important function due to the length constraint. For example, the hashtag *#savethenhs*, reads as 'save the national health service', gives the context relevant to the tweet "*Speaker refers to #Lanseys 'abysmal ignorance' as demonstrated on alcohol strategy; this SoS #notfitforpurpose #nhs #savethenhs #healthbill*". The hashtags *#iranelections* and *#freeiran* give the context and ideology behind the tweet "*AP: Report: #Iran 's paramilitary launches cyber attack http://is.gd/HiCYJU #iranelections #freeiran*". Also note the use of *#Iran* both as a hashtag and as a crucial part of the sentence.

Analysis of the content of hashtags poses some interesting technical problems. The structure of the hashtag has no restrictions. A hashtag can be a lexical word (*#iran*), a compound of lexical words (*#freeiran*), or (compound with) abbreviations (*#savethenhs*). Moreover, while the Twitter engine is case insensitive, users do use variations such as *#freeiran* (2203), *#FreeIran* (729), *#freeIran* (319), *#Freeiran* (46), *#FREEIRAN* (44) or *#freeIRAN* (30). Although semantically identical, the usage frequencies of these hashtags differ greatly, as indicated in parenthesis.

The Corpus.

Our data consists of more than four hundred million tweets tweeted between June–December 2009[4]. The data was collected using Twitter API (the Spritzer and Gardenhose services) and was submitted to Twitter's streaming policy controlling the sample size collected every day (5%-15% sample of the non–private tweets, uniformly distributed). As Twitter gained popularity and as the sampling rate changed from time to time, the total number of tweets collected every week varies greatly. Figure 1 presents the weekly change in the sample size with standard deviation of 6.5 million.

We filtered out tweets that contain non–Latin characters,

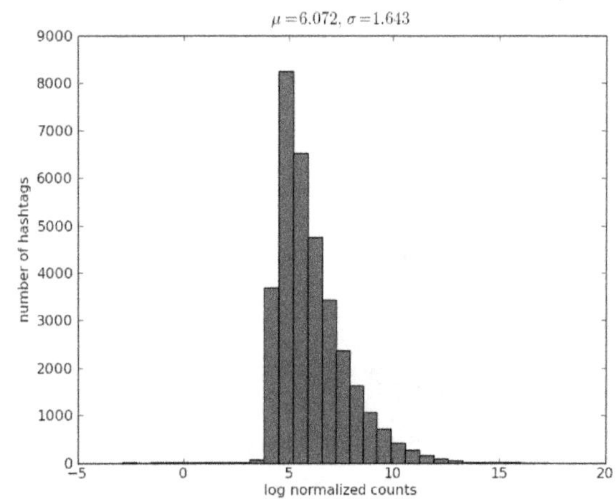

Figure 3: Histogram of the log count of all the hashtags in our dataset (7 monthes).

trying to maintain a corpus of only English tweets. Although we managed to remove all East Asian tweets, our corpus still contained some non–English tweets mainly in Spanish and Dutch. Non–English tweets can bias the results in case of hashtags that are composed of non–English words or English hashtags that appear in non–English content. A less noisy corpus can lead to improved results.

Another possible bias may be introduced due to spam tweets and spam hashtags. Identifying spam in Twitter is beyond the scope of this work, thus we cannot estimate the biased introduced by spammers.

Normalization of counts.

The great variance in the weekly sample size introduces some bias to the hashtag counts, unless one assumes that all hashtags have the same parametric distribution (over time). This assumption does not hold as different hashtags present different temporal patterns. The same hashtag could have gained different number of counts in our dataset in case it

[3]Their survey is based on about one million tweets in the span of three years. The current stream of Twitter messages is orders of magnitude larger.

[4]The data was collected and used for [26] and is generously shared at: http://www.ark.cs.cmu.edu/tweets/.

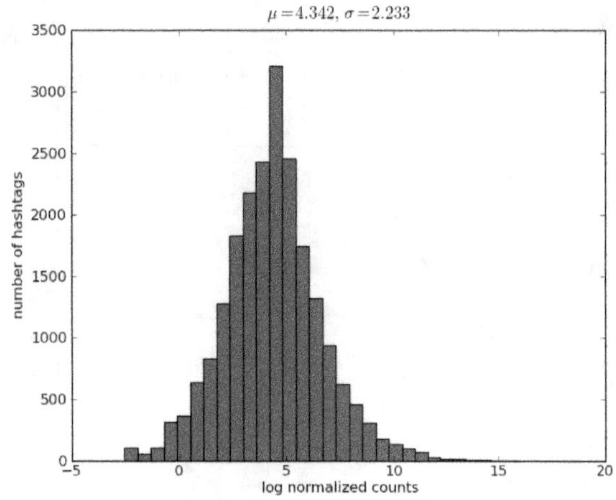

Figure 4: Histogram of the log count of 'fresh' hashtags in 10 weeks time frame.

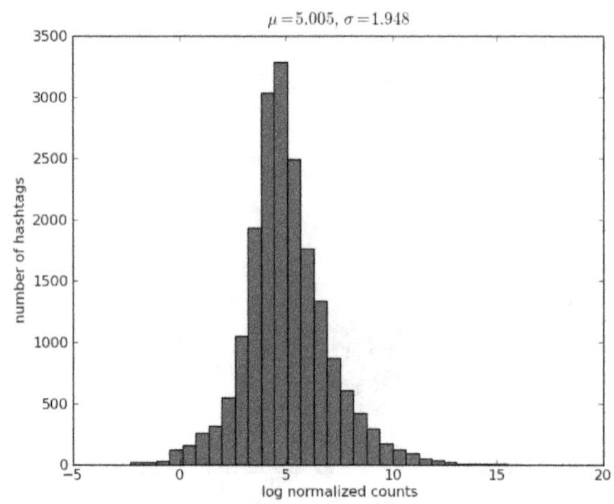

Figure 5: Histogram of the log count of 'fresh' hashtags in 15 weeks time frame.

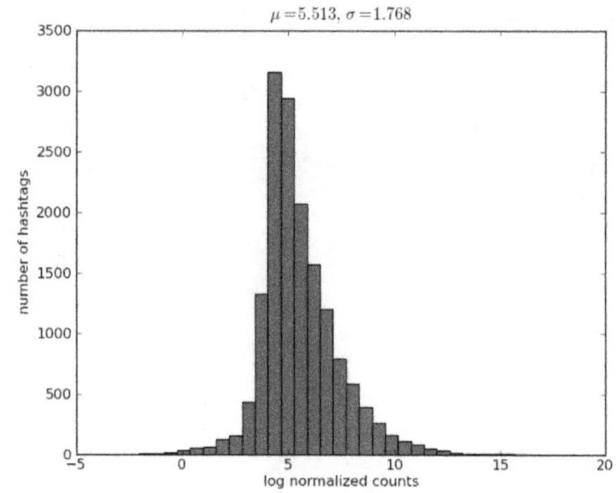

Figure 6: Histogram of the log count of 'fresh' hashtags in 20 weeks time frame.

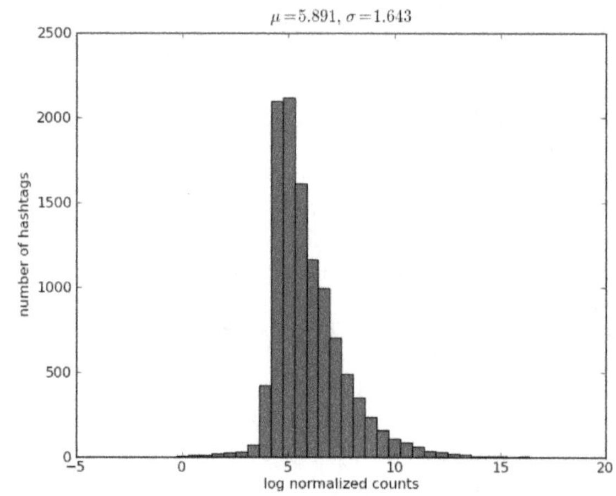

Figure 7: Histogram of the log count of 'fresh' hashtags in 25 weeks time frame.

was introduced in different weeks simply due to the variance in the sample size. See the weekly unnormalized counts of a few hashtags in Figure 2 (and compare to the weekly sample size in Figure 1). In order to address this bias we normalize the hashtag counts in the following way:

$$N(ht^i) = \sum_{j \in weeks} count(ht^i_j) \cdot \frac{w'}{w_j}$$

Where ht^i is the i–th hashtag, $weeks = \{22, ..., 52\}$, the sampled weeks, $count(ht^i_j)$ is the number of times hashtag i occurs in the sample of week j, w_j is the sample size in week j and w' is a constant, we use $w' = w_1$ so the sample size of the first week is the base for the normalization.

In our experiments we looked only at hashtags which occur over 100 times; assuming that less frequent hashtags are either typos (typically a missing trailing white space hence creating a concatenation of tokens that are not part of the tag), used only in a weakly connected component of the social graph or were introduced at the end of our date range therefore did not have the chance to be widely adopted (or ignored).

We look only on 'fresh' hashtags – hashtags that did not get popular before our corpus was collected (e.g. unlike *#teaParty* in Figure 2). We define a hashtag as fresh if it did not appear in the first week (week 22) or if its normalized count in the first week is less than 10% of its normalized count in its peak. Figures 3, 4, 5, 6 and 7 show the differences between the long tailed distributions of all the hashtags vs. the normal distribution of the fresh ones (we elaborate on the differences between different horizons in the General Discussion section).

As mentioned above, all hashtags that appear less than 100 times ($< 250e^{-9}\%$) were removed from the dataset.

Preprocessing.

Identifying the distinct words composing a hashtag is a mandatory step in order to process it and convert it to its vectorial representation. Matching hashtags against a lexicon of English words and using dynamic programming to perform segmentation of compound hashtags seems straightforward. However, many compound hashtags consists of non standard words and abbreviations that do not appear in standard dictionaries, e.g. 'luv' instead 'of love' in *#weluvjb* (reads as 'we love Justin Beiber'), and *#savethenhs* (reads as 'save the national health service'). In order to perform the segmentation of compound hashtags, besides matching hashtags against lexicons, we employed a simple heuristic algorithm that exploits redundancy of hashtags that differ only orthographically. The algorithm matches tuples like *#freeiran*, *#FreeIran* and *#FreeIran* and performs segmentation according to the capital letters, assuming they are used for visual segmentation (just like naming conventions of variables in programming). This heuristic algorithm achieves high precision and decent recall. However, we spend a few hours validating the results and manually fixing some untokenized hashtags.

4. PREDICTION MODEL

In order to predict the acceptance of a hashtag we learn a regression model. In this section we describe our regression model and the features we utilize in our model.

4.1 The Target Function

In a regression task, we want to learn a target function $f(ht) = n$, where ht is a vector space representation of a given hashtag, and $n \in \mathbb{N}_0$ is the normalized count of its occurrences in a time frame. Function f is typically learned from a training set of example hashtags and their counts, $\{ht_i, n_i\}$. In this work we learn the transformed target function $f'(ht) = \log(n)$.

Using f' instead of f serves two purposes: (a) We are interested in predicting the magnitude of the acceptance in a time frame, thus while a hashtag occurring 500 times is very different from a hashtag occurring 1000 times, occurrence of 30000 is similar to 30500. f' captures this observation. (b) f' allows us better smoothing of temporal variations induced due to different times of first appearance in the dataset.

4.2 Regression Model

We denote the training set by $(X, Y) = \{x_i, y_i\}$, where x_i is a feature vector representation of hashtag ht_i and $y_i = \log(n_i)$, is the log of the normalized number of its occurrences. A linear function $b + w^T X = b + \sum_j w_j^T X^j$ is a simple yet robust way to model the dependency of Y on X [11].

In its standard setting, the linear function is found analytically, however, this requires inversion of large matrices, thus impractical. Instead we use stochastic gradient descent. We use an $L1$ regularization to learn the optimal model parameters b and w:

$$L_r(b, w) = \frac{1}{2}\sum_i \left(y_i - (b + \sum_j w_j^T x_i^j)\right)^2 + \frac{1}{2}\lambda\|w\|$$

Where i denotes the i-th training example and j denotes the j-th attribute in x_i. Regularization is introduced in order to overcome sparsity and to lower the risk of overfitting.

To learn the parameter values we use Stochastic Gradient Descent (SGD) [2], for which the parameter update is as follows:

$$\begin{aligned} \Delta b &= \eta_t(y_i - (b + w^T x_i)) \\ \Delta w_i &= \eta_t(y_i - (b + w^T x_i)x_i - \lambda w_i) \end{aligned}$$

We cycle through random permutations of the observations to achieve convergence. For each learning rate we use a schedule of the form $\eta_t = \frac{\eta_0}{t+\tau}$ where $\tau > 0$, and t is the number of epochs. The schedule satisfies the Robbins-Monro conditions [28], $\sum \eta_t = \infty$ and $\sum \eta_t^2 < \infty$, hence convergence is guaranteed.

The final model strongly depends on a proper choice of hyper-parameters, η and λ. We use the Nelder-Mead [25] method in order to find the optimal values of the hyper parameters. Though not guaranteed to converge to the function's minimum [21], it is a widely used algorithm with excellent results on real world scenarios [33].

4.3 Model Features

In order to learn our regression models we represent each hashtag as a binary vector. We define four types of features:

1. Hashtag content – features that can be extracted from the hashtag itself.

2. Global tweet features – features related to the content of the tweets containing the hashtag.

3. Graph topology features – features related to graph topology and retweet statistics.

4. Global temporal features – features related to temporal pattern of the use of the hashtag.

All features are binary therefore each attribute in each feature type is represented by a short feature vector. The concatenation of these vectors spans our vectorial space. In the remaining of this section we give a detailed description of the extracted features along with the intuition behind using these features.

4.3.1 *Hashtag content*

For each hashtag we extract attributes belonging to a number of main categories: length (characters and words), hashtag orthography, emotional and cognitive dimension, hashtag location, and match with lexical lists such as general dictionary, proper names, holidays and celebrity names. These attributes are extracted based on the hashtag alone, e.g. *#freeIran* is 9 characters long, 2 words long, both words are listed lexical items, Iran is a state, the word free is a positive sentiment word etc.

Character length.

As a tweet's length is limited to 140 characters, each character becomes expensive. Using a hashtag as part of the tweet consumes space that could be used for the free text. On the other hand, if a hashtag is too short it might not be understood and will not serve its purpose. We used 7 bins for this attribute, bins capture hashtag of 2,3,4,5,6–9,10–14 and >14 characters long.

Number of words.

55% of the hashtags in our data are compounds of more than one word (e.g. *#freeIran, #GoogleGoesGaga*). A word compound can make a hashtag/meme clearer or too complex, thus more/less appealing to be adopted by users. Four bins were used for this feature: 1 word, 2,3 and 4 words or more. Acronyms (e.g. *#NYC*, *#nhs* and *#ff*) were considered one word.

Orthography.

Hashtags can be written in capital letters, contain some capital letters and/or digits, e.g. *#myheart4JB*, reads as 'my heart for Justin Beiber'. Using the 'right' writing style can make the hashtag readable (*savethenhs* vs. *saveTheNhs*), while on the other hand it requires more typing effort (requires using the shift key). We use four attributes for this group: no caps, some caps, all caps and contains digits.

Lexical items.

Working on a development set, we noticed that internet memes sometimes evolve around celebrities, holidays or locations. We match the hashtag or its words against five predefined lists: (1) a general lexicon containing all words from a large portion (612MB) of English Wikipedia (approximating that the hashtag is a proper English word), (2) a list of proper names taken from the name list compiled at the US census of 1995 and published online, (3) a list of celebrity names compiled from Forbes' 'The Celebrity 100' lists of 2008–2010[5]. (4) A short list of holidays and days of the week and (5) a list of all the world's countries. Each of these five lexicons is an attribute in our vector.

Location.

Hashtags can appear anywhere in a tweet. The location of a hashtag can give an indication to the way it is used[6]. For example, if located in the middle of the tweet, the hashtag also serves as part of the sentence and not only as a meta tag. We acknowledge three locations: prefix, infix and suffix. We treat sequences of hashtags as a single location, thus, for example, the two last hashtags in "*AP: Report: #Iran 's paramilitary launches cyber attack http://is.gd/HiCYJU #iranelections #freeiran*" are both considered to be suffixes, while *#Iran* is infix. Generally, if a hashtag has more that 25% of its occurrences in one position it is considered to fit this position role. We note that a hashtag can, therefore, have up to three locations.

Collocation.

Some hashtags tend to collocate with other hashtags. This was captured with one binary attribute, where the value 1 is assigned if more than 40% of the hashtag occurrences are collocated with other hashtags.

Cognitive dimension.

Words can be classified according to a number of psychological and cognitive dimensions. Some words trigger specific emotions and encourage specific behavior, such as increased empathy, involvement and cooperation [22]. The psychological dimensions in which a hashtag is located, are assumed to influence its spread. The LIWC project [32] assigns words to a number of emotional and cognitive dimensions in various granularities. Among the dimensions are positive sentiment, negative sentiment, physical, social, optimistic, self, anger etc., 69 attributes in total.

4.3.2 Global Tweet Features

Although an ideal meme is self contained, in the Twitter domain, the context in which the hashtag appears might contribute to its acceptance as discourse communities on Twitter (and offline) tend to converge linguistically and stylistically [7]. In order to capture the context in which hashtags appear, we looked on the cognitive dimension of the 1000 most frequent words each tag cooccurred with.

Cognitive dimension.

Similarly to the cognitive dimension for the hashtags, the most frequent words appearing with the hashtag are mapped to the 69 LIWC categories. Thus if a hashtag ht tends to appear with the word 'great' – the contextual positive sentiment attribute will be 1.

4.3.3 Graph Topology Features

It is clear that graph topology plays an important role in the spread patterns [18, 19, 23, 4, 5, 13, 29]. Since we are mainly interested in how the content of an idea affects its acceptance, we only use basic topological features with the strongest predictive power.

Average number of followers.

We divide the average number of followers of users who used the hashtag to 19 bins on a sub logarithmic scale.

Max number of followers.

Although a user with many followers does not necessarily has influence proportional to the number of his/her followers [4], the number of followers could be a crude estimator to the influential power of the user. We divide the max number of followers observed for users who used the hashtag to 19 bins on a logarithmic scale.

Retweets ratio.

This attribute captures the tendency of a hashtag to appear in retweeted messages. We are interested in this feature in order to create dependency with the orthographic feature set as retweeting is a simple operation that does not require extensive use of the shift key in case the hashtag has many capital letters. We used 25 bins for different retweet rates from less than 1% of retweets (first bin) to 60%-100% of retweets (last bin).

4.3.4 Global Temporal Features

Different hashtags are characterized by different temporal trends observed in close proximity to peak hours of usage of a hashtag [35]. We are modeling the acceptance of a hashtag in a longer time frame of weeks and month, therefore we model the temporal trend in the first few weeks to the appearance of a hashtag, using it to project about the future trend.

[5]Based on a development set we added 3 names of recently emerged celebrities to the celebrity lexicon.

[6]Ideally, we would like to know what POS tag is most suitable for a given hashtag, however, the informal nature of tweets along with the fact that hashtags can be composed of a number of words, sometime a complete clause, along with the lack of POS annotated Twitter data, makes current POS tagging techniques inapplicable.

Temporal features.

We sampled the normalized weekly counts of each hashtag in four time stamps: w_i, $i \in \{t, t+1, t+2, t+6\}$, where t is the first week the hashtag occurred in our data, and $t+j$ is the j–th week after the first occurrence. The four samples give three lag values, denoted as $d_{k\in 1,2,3}$. d_k is the ratio of change from the previous time stamp. These 3–lag values capture the change in the meme usage in the first two weeks and then again after another four weeks, approximating 'stickiness' and 'persistence'.

For each lag value we use 17 bins on a logarithmic scale from a change larger than -200% (decreased usage) to more than 200% change (increased usage). If the d ratio falls between -5% and 5% we consider the hashtag to be stable in that week.

We call this feature type 'global' since it is based on the global count of hashtags occurrences in a given week and not on occurrences induced locally by cascading from specific nodes.

5. EXPERIMENTAL SETUP

In our experiments we were trying to learn three aspects in the prediction: (i) what is the attribute combination that yields the best prediction? (ii) what are the strongest attributes and how do they complement each other? (iii) how does the prediction accuracy change given different time frames.

All our experiments were executed in a 10-fold cross validation manner. Performance is measured by the mean square error (MSE), a standard measure for regression tasks [1].

We note that when computationally possible, besides the stochastic gradient descent (SGD) described in Section 4.2, we also applied analytic regression algorithm and Support Vector Machine for regression (SVR) [31] with various kernels and optimization of hyper parameters (both implemented as part of the Weka toolkit [16]). Both SVR and analytic regression outperformed the SGD insignificantly. We backed to the SGD as it is orders of magnitude more efficient on high dimensional vectors and since the regression model produced by the SGD is more interpretable than some kernel models.

Baseline model.

Our basic model is a regression that optimizes only the intercept β, which always converges to the average, predicting the log–average normalized number of occurrences as a fixed function, keeping the error close to σ^2, the variance of the observed counts.

Other basic models.

Each of the four feature types in Section 4.3 was used in a different regression model.

Hybrid models.

Finally, we experimented with different combinations of the four feature types, studying the mutual effect of various feature types.

6. RESULTS

Table 1 shows our results for the baseline, the four basic models and the hybrid model. Results are presented for four different horizons. Each of the basic models out-

Model	MSE_{10}	MSE_{15}	MSE_{20}	MSE_{25}
baseline	4.988	3.796	3.125	2.698
HT_{all}	4.380	3.410	2.902	2.565
$TW_{content}$	4.776	3.509	2.743	2.221
Graph	4.295	3.144	2.404	1.923
Temporal	3.294	2.893	2.507	2.112
$Hybrid_{all}$	2.584	2.098	1.685	1.315

Table 1: MSE of basic models and the hybrid model in horizons. MSE_n indicates results for acceptance prediction in an n weeks time frame.

Time frame	$weeks_{10}$	$weeks_{15}$	$weeks_{20}$	$weeks_{25}$
Sample size	21683	19020	15635	10864
Mean avg.	4.342	5.005	5.513	5.891
STD	4.986	3.794	3.125	2.699

Table 2: Sample size, average log of normalized counts and standard deviation of 'fresh' hashtags in different time frames.

performs the baseline, while the global models (graph and temporal) outperforms the content based models. The hybrid model, combining all feature types is significantly better than all partial models. All models achieve better prediction as prediction horizon grows. This can be attributed to the decreased standard deviation of the counts as shown in Table 2 and in Figures 4,5,6 and 7.

Table 3 presents the contribution of different combinations of feature types, demonstrating that all feature types contribute to the prediction and no feature type is masked under a strong signal produced by other feature types. Table 3 also presents the correlation coefficient between the predicted values and the real values. The baseline, always optimized so the MSE is close to σ^2, presents no correlation with the target values as it is a fixed function. A correlation of 0.669, achieved in the all–inclusive hybrid model, shows that our linear model serves as a good approximation to the actual model. We also note that even the 0.268 correlation achieved by the HT_{all} is reasonable in real–world noisy data.

It is interesting to note that even though the content attributes of the hashtag and the tweet context show only a small improvement over the baseline with MSE of 3.41 and 3.509, combining both content types presents a much smaller error with MSE of 2.967.

7. GENERAL DISCUSSION

Model	MSE	Corr–coeff
baseline	3.796	-0.021
Ht_{all}	3.410	0.319
TW_{cont}	3.509	0.275
Graph	3.144	0.414
Temporal	2.893	0.487
$HT_{cont} + TW_{cont}$	2.967	0.467
$HT_{cont} + TW_{cont}$ + Graph	2.546	0.573
$HT_{cont} + TW_{cont}$ + Temp	2.321	0.6234
Graph+Temporal	2.450	0.594
$Hybrid_{all}$	2.098	0.669

Table 3: MSE and correlation coefficient for various combinations of feature types for a 15 weeks time frame.

Features	MSE	corr–coeff
baseline	3.796	-0.021
number of words	3.695	0.162
length chars	3.693	0.163
orthography	3.781	0.061
lexicons	3.667	0.183
lc+nw	3.662	0.187
collocation	3.651	0.195
cognitive	3.637	0.204
location	3.613	0.218
lc+nw+ortho	3.654	0.192
lc+nw+cog	3.637	0.204
lc+nw+lex	3.631	0.207
Ht_{all}	3.410	0.319
TW_{cont}	3.509	0.275
$HT_{all} + TW_{cont}$	2.967	0.467

Table 4: MSE and correlation coefficient of each single content feature set and combinations of content features for a 15 weeks time frame.

Model	MSE	Corr–coeff
d_1	3.236	0.383
d_2	3.39	0.326
d_3	3.44	0.303
$d_1 + d_2$	3.088	0.431
$d_1 + d_3$	2.97	0.464
$d_2 + d_3$	3.19	0.398
$d_1 + d_2 + d_3$	2.893	0.487

Table 5: MSE and correlation coefficient for different number of lags and different distances between sampling points in 15 weeks horizon. d_i indicates the the i-th lag described in Section 4.3.4.

In this section we discuss some of the results in greater detail.

Temporal based prediction.

Our temporal feature set (Section 4.3.4) is based on lags computed from samples in four time stamps, assuming that the lags portrait the tendency of a hashtag to stick around and propagate. Table 3 shows that hybrid models that include temporal features always outperform other models for a 15 weeks horizon. Table 1 shows that the temporal models performs better than other feature types in 10 and 15 weeks horizon while the graph–based model performs better in 20 and 25 weeks horizon.

Looking at our data, 4766 hashtags have a single spike. While our temporal features correctly model single–spiked hashtags, they fail to model hashtags with multiple spikes (see Figure 8), thus do not perform as well on longer horizons and hashtags with reoccurring spikes. An algorithm for clustering and predicting patterns of short temporal variations was proposed by [34, 35]. Table 5 illustrates the MSE for different numbers and distances of lags.

A close examination of spiked hashtags show that these are usually related to Twitter games and idioms that flare for an instant then quickly vanish, sometimes reoccurring for another playful round. Twitter games can be sometimes captured by our content features. An analysis of the information diffusion of (the most popular) Twitter idioms was done in [29].

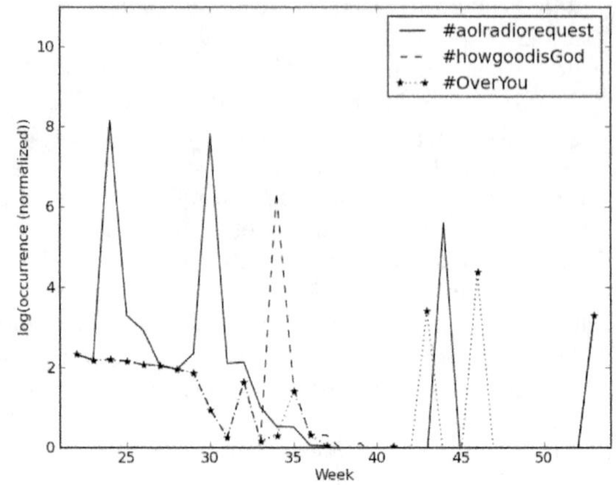

Figure 8: Hashtags with one, two and three spikes.

The effect of cognitive attributes.

Table 4 presents various combinations of attributes from the content type. While the baseline's MSE is 3.796, using all hashtag attributes (listed in Section 4.3) achieves MSE of 3.41, each attribute having a small contribution to the model. One of our hypotheses was that the hashtag's cognitive attributes have a great effect on the hashtag's popularity. While this hypothesis does not hold, the LIWC cognitive categories had a positive impact when applied to the context of the tweet (TW_{cont}), still supporting the intuition that the use of certain words drives users to adopt a hashtag or get involved in a certain discourse (defined by specific hashtags). We attribute the marginal contribution of the cognitive attributes of the hashtag to its 'sparseness', as these attributes were useful in the richer context.

These findings also validate sociolinguistic theories about the correlation between the use of certain words and personality traits such as the image of self and on team work [10, 30, 22, 17, 32].

Dependencies and collinearity.

In order to better understand the dependencies between attributes and feature types, we trained models with dummy attributes. Dummy attributes are second order attributes created by a Cartesian product over the feature space. Since all features are binary, a new feature type x_{ij} was added: $x_{ij} = 1$ iff $x_i = 1 \wedge x_j = 1$, where x_i and x_j are attributes in the standard model. For example, while in the standard (hybrid) model we have two different attributes *containsCaps* (some, but not all, letters in the hashtag are capitalized) and $rtRate_{0.4-0.6}$ (the hashtag has retweet rate of 40%–60% of its appearances); a dummy attribute in our new model is $containsCaps + rtRate_{0.4-0.6}$ which equals 1 iff both attributes had 1 in the hashtag's vector (e.g. the hashtag *#BoyFriends*). The dimension of our Cartesian models is very large (thousands) compared to the size of the sample (see Table 2), thus overfitted. While overfitted, analysis of model coefficients captures the relations between different variables.

Attribute	Coefficient
$chars_{long} + rtRate_{0.4-0.6}$	0.7677
$chars_5 + rtRate_{0.4-0.6}$	0.5718
$chars_3 + rtRate_{0.4-0.6}$	0.3543
$chars_2 + rtRate_{0.4-0.6}$	0.3469
$chars_{6-9} + rtRate_{0.4-0.6}$	0.3417
$chars_{10-14} + rtRate_{0.4-0.6}$	0.3060
$chars_4 + rtRate_{0.4-0.6}$	0.1266
$words_1 + rtRate_{0.4-0.6}$	0.6086
$words_2 + rtRate_{0.4-0.6}$	0.4224
$words_3 + rtRate_{0.4-0.6}$	0.2581
$words_{long} + rtRate_{0.4-0.6}$	0.0260
$containscaps + rtRate_{0.4-0.6}$	0.3131
$nocaps + rtRate_{0.4-0.6}$	0.002
$allcaps + rtRate_{0.4-0.6}$	-0.3437

Table 6: model coefficients dummy attributes of hashtag length and orthography combined with high retweet rates (40%-60% of the message containing these hashtags are retweeted), $char_{long}$ indicated hashtags longer than 14 characters, $words_{long}$ indicates hashtags that contain more than 3 distinct words.

Cognitive load and physical constraints.

Choosing attributes for our model we had several hypotheses about the the acceptance of hashtags. One such hypothesis is inspired by the optimality theory framework. A successful hashtag should be clear, informative and yet not too complex. The complexity of a hashtag can be measured by its length (in chars), the number of words it consists of and its orthographic features. Longer hashtags are harder to type, they are not economical unless very informative (due to the Twitter 140 characters policy) and they can be harder to interpret (a sequence of words with no white spaces). All these aspects can be broken down if one takes retweeting into account, as a retweeted message doesn't require retyping a complex hashtag. Table 6 illustrates the differences in the coefficients when the typing constraint is accounted for by looking only on hashtags with high retweet rate.

Examining the coefficients of the dummy attributes representing the hashtag length (chars and number of words) with the retweet rates, we observe an interesting phenomena. The coefficients show contradictory effects of the hashtag number of words and its character length. It seems that while users do not care so much about longer hashtags, they still prefer hashtags that are less complex. It might be because these are harder to remember or interpret (compare *#savethenhs* vs. *#technology*, both 10 characters long). While a larger number of words seems to be a burden, we observe that once capital letters are introduced to mark word boundaries, the coefficient of the dummy attribute that captures the dependency between number of words and retweets grows (compare *#savethenhs* vs. *#saveTheNHS*).

8. CONCLUSIONS

Predicting the spread of ideas in online communities is an interesting task from both commercial and psychological perspectives. Traditional approaches model the propagation of ideas in social media by analyzing the topology of the social graph. In this work we took a hybrid approach to predicting the spread of ideas according to their content as well as the topology of the social graph. We viewed Twitter hashtags as ideas and as potential memes and learned a regression model that predicts the spread of each hashtag/meme in a time frame. Our experiments demonstrated that the content of the idea plays an important role in its acceptance by the community. We demonstrated that an elegant hybrid approach, combining the meme's content, the meme's context, global temporal features and graph topology shows the best results, while maintaining computational efficiency. However, some of the feature types we used require more data that is not always available. In contrast, using the meme's content alone is free of the need of any global information but the meme itself. Our experiments also demonstrate some psychological and cognitive–linguistic principles on a large scale data.

There are many directions for future research. One of the main directions is to gain a better understanding of the mutual roles the different feature types play. Another direction is to better characterize psychological aspects and cognitive constraints and the ways they interact.

9. ACKNOWLEDGMENTS

We thank Gideon Dror and Idan Szpektor for valuable discussions and advice about this research.

10. REFERENCES

[1] J. Bibby and H. Toutenburg. *Prediction and Improved Estimation in Linear Models.* John Wiley & Sons, Inc., New York, NY, USA, 1 edition, 1978.

[2] L. Bottou. Stochastic learning. In O. Bousquet and U. von Luxburg, editors, *Advanced Lectures on Machine Learning,* Lecture Notes in Artificial Intelligence, LNAI 3176, pages 146–168. Springer Verlag, Berlin, 2004.

[3] M. Cataldi, L. Di Caro, and C. Schifanella. Emerging topic detection on Twitter based on temporal and social terms evaluation. In *Proceedings of the Tenth International Workshop on Multimedia Data Mining,* pages 1–10. ACM, 2010.

[4] M. Cha, H. Haddadi, F. Benevenuto, and K. P. Gummadi. Measuring User Influence in Twitter: The Million Follower Fallacy. In *In Proceedings of the 4th International AAAI Conference on Weblogs and Social Media (ICWSM),* Washington DC, USA, 2010.

[5] W. Chen, C. Wang, and Y. Wang. Scalable influence maximization for prevalent viral marketing in large-scale social networks. In *Proceedings of the 16th ACM SIGKDD international conference on Knowledge discovery and data mining,* pages 1029–1038. ACM, 2010.

[6] E. Cunha, G. Magno, G. Comarela, V. Almeida, M. Gonçalves, and F. Benevenuto. Analyzing the dynamic evolution of hashtags on twitter: a language-based approach. *ACL HLT 2011,* page 58, 2011.

[7] C. Danescu-Niculescu-Mizil, M. Gamon, and S. Dumais. Mark my words!: linguistic style accommodation in social media. In *Proceedings of the 20th international conference on World wide web,* pages 745–754. ACM, 2011.

[8] D. Davidov, O. Tsur, and A. Rappoport. Enhanced sentiment learning using twitter hashtags and smileys. In *Proceedings of the 23rd International Conference on*

Computational Linguistics: Posters, pages 241–249. Association for Computational Linguistics, 2010.

[9] D. Davidov, O. Tsur, and A. Rappoport. Semi-supervised recognition of sarcastic sentences in twitter and amazon. In *Proceedings of the Fourteenth Conference on Computational Natural Language Learning*, pages 107–116. Association for Computational Linguistics, 2010.

[10] D. Davis and T. Brock. Use of first person pronouns as a function of increased objective self-awareness and performance feedback. *Journal of Experimental Social Psychology*, 11(4):381–388, 1975.

[11] N. R. Draper and H. Smith. *Applied Regression Analysis (Wiley Series in Probability and Statistics)*. Wiley-Interscience, third edition, April 1998.

[12] M. Götz, J. Leskovec, M. McGlohon, and C. Faloutsos. Modeling blog dynamics. In *International Conference on Weblogs and Social Media*, 2009.

[13] A. Goyal, F. Bonchi, and L. Lakshmanan. Learning influence probabilities in social networks. In *Proceedings of the third ACM international conference on Web search and data mining*, pages 241–250. ACM, 2010.

[14] D. Gruhl, R. Guha, D. Liben-Nowell, and A. Tomkins. Information diffusion through blogspace. In *Proceedings of the 13th international conference on World Wide Web*, WWW '04, pages 491–501, New York, NY, USA, 2004. ACM.

[15] L. Guo, E. Tan, S. Chen, X. Zhang, and Y. Zhao. Analyzing patterns of user content generation in online social networks. In *Proceedings of the 15th ACM SIGKDD international conference on Knowledge discovery and data mining*, pages 369–378. ACM, 2009.

[16] M. Hall, E. Frank, G. Holmes, B. Pfahringer, P. Reutemann, and I. Witten. The WEKA data mining software: an update. *ACM SIGKDD Explorations Newsletter*, 11(1):10–18, 2009.

[17] J. Kahn, R. Tobin, A. Massey, and J. Anderson. Measuring emotional expression with the Linguistic Inquiry and Word Count. *The American journal of psychology*, pages 263–286, 2007.

[18] D. Kempe, J. Kleinberg, and É. Tardos. Maximizing the spread of influence through a social network. In *Proceedings of the ninth ACM SIGKDD international conference on Knowledge discovery and data mining*, pages 137–146. ACM, 2003.

[19] D. Kempe, J. Kleinberg, and É. Tardos. Influential nodes in a diffusion model for social networks. *Automata, Languages and Programming*, pages 1127–1138, 2005.

[20] H. Kwak, C. Lee, H. Park, and S. Moon. What is twitter, a social network or a news media? In *Proceedings of the 19th international conference on World wide web*, pages 591–600. ACM, 2010.

[21] J. C. Lagarias, J. A. Reeds, M. H. Wright, and P. E. Wright. Convergence properties of the nelder-mead simplex algorithm in low dimensions. *SIAM Journal of Optimization*, 9:112–147, 1996.

[22] G. Leshed, J. Hancock, D. Cosley, P. McLeod, and G. Gay. Feedback for guiding reflection on teamwork practices. In *Proceedings of the 2007 international ACM conference on Supporting group work*, pages 217–220. ACM, 2007.

[23] J. Leskovec, L. A. Adamic, and B. A. Huberman. The dynamics of viral marketing. *ACM Trans. Web*, 1, May 2007.

[24] J. Leskovec, L. Backstrom, and J. Kleinberg. Meme-tracking and the dynamics of the news cycle. In *Proceedings of the 15th ACM SIGKDD international conference on Knowledge discovery and data mining*, pages 497–506. Citeseer, 2009.

[25] J. A. Nelder and R. Mead. A Simplex Method for Function Minimization. *The Computer Journal*, 7(4):308–313, January 1965.

[26] B. O Connor, R. Balasubramanyan, B. Routledge, and N. Smith. From tweets to polls: Linking text sentiment to public opinion time series. In *Proceedings of the International AAAI Conference on Weblogs and Social Media*, pages 122–129, 2010.

[27] D. Ramage, S. Dumais, and D. Liebling. Characterizing microblogs with topic models. In *International AAAI Conference on Weblogs and Social Media*. The AAAI Press, 2010.

[28] H. Robbins and S. Monro. A stochastic approximation method. *Annals of Mathematical Statistics*, 22:400–407, 1951.

[29] D. M. Romero, B. Meeder, and J. Kleinberg. Differences in the mechanics of information diffusion across topics: Idioms, political hashtags, and complex contagion on twitter. In *Proceedings of the 13th international conference on World Wide Web*, WWW '11, 2011.

[30] S. Rude, E. Gortner, and J. Pennebaker. Language use of depressed and depression-vulnerable college students. *Cognition and Emotion*, 18(8):1121–1133, 2004.

[31] A. Smola and B. Scholkopf. A tutorial on support vector regression. *Statistics and computing*, 14(3):199–222, 2004.

[32] Y. R. Tausczik and J. W. Pennebaker. The Psychological Meaning of Words: LIWC and Computerized Text Analysis Methods. *Journal of Language and Social Psychology*, 29(1):24–54, Mar. 2010.

[33] M. Wright. Direct search methods: Once scorned, now respectable. In D. Griffiths and G. Watson, editors, *Numerical Analysis*, pages 191–208. Addison Wesley, Redwood City, 1995.

[34] J. Yang and J. Leskovec. Modeling Information Diffusion in Implicit Networks. In *2010 IEEE International Conference on Data Mining*, pages 599–608. IEEE, 2010.

[35] J. Yang and J. Leskovec. Patterns of temporal variation in online media. In *Proceedings of the fourth ACM international conference on Web search and data mining*, pages 177–186. ACM, 2011.

[36] T. Zaman, R. Herbrich, J. Van Gael, and D. Stern. Predicting information spreading in twitter. In *Workshop on Computational Social Science and the Wisdom of Crowds, NIPS*, 2010.

Tips, Dones and ToDos: Uncovering User Profiles in FourSquare

Marisa Vasconcelos
Universidade Federal de Minas Gerais
Belo Horizonte, Brazil
marisav@dcc.ufmg.br

Saulo Ricci
Universidade Federal de Minas Gerais
Belo Horizonte, Brazil
saulomrr@dcc.ufmg.br

Jussara Almeida
Universidade Federal de Minas Gerais
Belo Horizonte, Brazil
jussara@dcc.ufmg.br

Fabrício Benevenuto
Universidade Federal de Ouro Preto
Ouro Preto, Brazil
benevenuto@gmail.com

Virgílio Almeida
Universidade Federal de Minas Gerais
Belo Horizonte, Brazil
virgilio@dcc.ufmg.br

ABSTRACT

Online Location Based Social Networks (LBSNs), which combine social network features with geographic information sharing, are becoming increasingly popular. One such application is Foursquare, which doubled its user population in less than six months. Among other features, Foursquare allows users to leave tips (i.e., reviews or recommendations) at specific venues as well as to give feedback on previously posted tips by adding them to their to-do lists or marking them as done. In this paper, we analyze how Foursquare users exploit these three features – tips, dones and to-dos — uncovering different behavior profiles. Our study reveals the existence of very active and influential users, some of which are famous businesses and brands, that seem engaged in posting tips at a large variety of venues while also receiving a great amount of user feedback on them. We also provide evidence of spamming, showing the existence of users that post tips whose contents are unrelated to the nature or domain of the venue where the tips were left.

Categories and Subject Descriptors

H.3.5 [**Online Information Services**]: Web-based services; J.4 [**Computer Applications**]: Social and behavioral sciences

General Terms

Measurement, Human factors

Keywords

user behavior characterization, location based social networks, spamming

Permission to make digital or hard copies of all or part of this work for personal or classroom use is granted without fee provided that copies are not made or distributed for profit or commercial advantage and that copies bear this notice and the full citation on the first page. To copy otherwise, to republish, to post on servers or to redistribute to lists, requires prior specific permission and/or a fee.
WSDM'12, February 8–12, 2012, Seattle, Washington, USA.
Copyright 2012 ACM 978-1-4503-0747-5/12/02 ...$10.00.

1. INTRODUCTION

Online Location-Based Social Networks (LBSNs) is a new paradigm of online social networks that has been experiencing increasing popularity, attracting millions of users. In LBSNs, users can *check in*, broadcasting their location to their friends, through the social graph. Check ins are performed in special locations, named venues, which represent physical places, such as universities, monuments, or even business enterprises and commercial brands. Check ins may be converted into points that allow users to earn badges, venue mayorships as well as receive special offers. Examples of currently popular LBSNs are Foursquare, Gowalla and Brightkite[1], out of which Foursquare is perhaps the one with the largest user population. Indeed, it has doubled the number of users in only six months, having reportedly reached the mark of 10 million registered users [25].

In Foursquare, in particular, users may also post tips to specific venues, aiming at sharing information on any aspect related to the venue with others. For instance, a tip left at a restaurant may suggest a special dish or even complain about the service. Tips can thus be seen as reviews or *recommendations*, either positive or negative, about the tipped venues. A user who sees a tip may add it to her to-do list or mark it as done, as a sign of agreement as well as a feedback regarding the tip.

As such, tips, dones and to-do lists are valuable features for fostering interactions among users, who can share their experiences and learn from others. Similarly, business owners can also benefit from tips about their stores or products, as these tips are a means for them to reach and get feedback from potential customers. Some businesses, which are Foursquare users themselves, can also use tips for promoting their brands and products [5]. Indeed, according to [26], around two thirds of the users post tips to Foursquare venues, showing the wide usage of the feature. Unlike user check ins, which propagate through the social links, and thus are visible only to the user's friends, tips are visible to everybody. Thus, tips have the potential to significantly impact online information sharing and business marketing.

A few recent studies have analyzed the properties and user

[1]http://www.foursquare.com, http://gowalla.com, and http://brightkite.com/, respectively.

characteristics of LBSNs, particularly Foursquare. However, most of these studies focus on the user check in dynamics, on the properties of the social graph and related geographical information [17, 22, 18]. We are not aware of any previous analysis of how users exploit the tip, done and to-do features. An investigation of relevant user behavior patterns, when it comes to posting tips at venues and marking them as done or to-do, is key for future designs and developments. Given that LBSNs, and Foursquare in particular, are being increasingly used as forums for recommending places, services and products as well as for Internet marketing, understanding how these features are used can produce useful insights into the potential effectiveness and vulnerabilities of these actions.

To shed some light into the current use of tips, dones and to-dos, we here present a characterization of user behavior in Foursquare. Our analyses are performed over a dataset containing over 1.6 million venues and associated information crawled from Foursquare during 8 weeks of operation (May to July 2011). For each collected venue, we gathered its tips, the users who posted each tip, the number of dones and to-dos associated with each tip as well as the Foursquare category to which the venue was assigned and its geographical location.

Our study has two main phases. First, we characterized venues and users with respect to number of tips, number of dones and to-dos as well as percentage of tips containing links (i.e., URLs or email addresses). Next, we applied a clustering algorithm to group users into profiles based on three attributes, namely, number of venues tipped by the user, total number of dones and to-dos associated with the user's tips, and the percentage of the user's tips containing links. We further analyzed the clustering results by manually inspecting the contents of the tips posted by samples of users randomly selected from each cluster.

Our study revealed four different user profiles. Two profiles correspond to users with different levels of activity in the system: whereas one corresponds to occasional users that post tips to only a few venues and receive only a few dones and to-dos, the other, containing the vast majority of the clustered users, consists of more active users who also tend to get much more feedback regarding their tips. A third profile consists of users who are characterized by tipping a large number of different venues and receiving a very large number of dones and to-dos in return. Based on the feedback received on their tips, these users, many of which are famous businesses and brands, can be considered very influential in the system.

The last profile is characterized by a very large percentage of tips with links posted at many venues, a behavior that is consistent with spamming, according to the Foursquare's terms of service [8]. Indeed, our manual inspection revealed that the majority of the tips posted by *all* sampled users with this profile had contents that were unrelated to the nature or domain of the tipped venues. Moreover, we also found users who posted unrelated tips within the other three groups, in spite of the fact that most of their tips did not contain links. This is further evidence of spamming activity. Interestingly, some of these users received a large number of dones and to-dos in their tips, in spite of them being often posted at unrelated venues. In other words, such potential spammers did get a great amount of feedback from other users, indicating that dealing with tip spamming and spammers in Foursquare is a hard task that is subject to a high degree of controversy.

The rest of this paper is organized as follows. Section 2 discusses related work, whereas Section 3 introduces the main elements and features of Foursquare, our crawling methodology and a summary of the collected dataset. Section 4 analyzes how users exploit tips, dones and to-dos, characterizing attributes of venues and of individual users, whereas the identified user profiles are presented and discussed in Section 5. Section 6 summarizes the paper and discusses possible directions for future work.

2. RELATED WORK

Social interactions among individuals located within a short physical proximity has been used to explain a number of phenomena in society, such as the proliferation of specific industries in a certain region [24] and individuals employment status [29]. In the context of online social networks, Liben-Nowell *et al.* [16] showed a strong correlation between friendship links and geographic location of those friends for LiveJournal[2] users. More recently, some articles demonstrated that geographically identified social content, like chatter from Twitter[3], can be used to monitor real-world events and create interesting applications. Particularly, Gomide *et al.* [10] proposed a spatio-temporal approach to identify potential dengue epidemics, whereas Sakaki *et al.* [19] proposed to treat Twitter users as sensors and use them to create a mechanism for earthquake detection of earthquakes.

However, there is still a limited set of studies about location-based social networks, possibly because they are still at an infant stage. Next, we briefly survey some of these studies.

Scellato *et al* [21] analyzed the social, geographic and geo-social properties of four social networks that provide location information about their users, namely BrightKite, Foursquare, LiveJournal and Twitter. They showed that LBSNs are characterized by short-distance spatial-clustered friendships, while in the other types of networks, such as Twitter and LiveJournal, users have heterogeneous connection lengths. An analysis of Gowalla users showed that the number of friends follows a double Pareto-like distribution, whereas the numbers of check ins and places are better described by log-normal distributions [20]. The authors also analyzed the temporal variations of such distributions, observing that users tend to add new friends at a faster rate than they give check ins and go to new places. In [17], the authors analyzed the user check in dynamics and the presence of spatio-temporal patterns in Foursquare.

The link prediction problem in LBSNs, representing the task of recommending friends or places, has also been tackled. Using collaborative filtering techniques, Berjani and Strufe [4] proposed a personalized recommender for places in Gowalla based on the number of check ins at spots. In [15], the authors proposed a three-layered friend recommender model using attributes of user profiles (preferences), social graphs (friendship) and mobility patterns (distance of visited places) to recommend friends in Brightkite. Another supervised learning framework to recommend places and friends was proposed in [23] and evaluated in a longitudinal dataset collected from Gowalla. Using check in information regarding users who visited the same place and friends of

[2]http://www.livejournal.com
[3]http://www.twitter.com

friends, the authors were able to reduce the link prediction space. Both previous studies [23, 15] concluded that the inclusion of information about location-based activity leads to a better prediction than if only social data is used.

Human mobility patterns were investigated on Gowalla, Brightkite and cell phones trace datasets [6]. The authors observed, in the three datasets, that short-range spatially and temporally periodic movement is not influenced by the social network structure while the long-distance travel is more influenced by the social links. Thus, they proposed a mobility model that combines periodic daily movement patterns and the social movement effects caused by the friendship network.

We are aware of only two previous studies that aim at uncovering user profiles in LBSNs. In [14], the authors applied two different clustering approaches to identify user behavior patterns on BrightKite. One approach exploited the users update (i.e., check ins, photos and notes) geographic position to classify them into four groups according to their mobility, namely, home, home-vacation, home-work and other. The second approach clustered users based on multiple attributes such as total number of updates, social features and mobility characteristics, and led to the identification of five groups, namely, inactive, normal, active, mobile and trial (or non loyal) users. The second study was performed on Foursquare [18]. The authors used a spectral clustering algorithm to group users based on the categories of venues they had checked in, aiming at identifying communities and characterizing the type of activity in each region of a city.

Although the aforementioned studies offer important insights into properties of user interactions in LBSNs, none of them addressed how users exploit tips, dones and to-dos as means to review or recommend a place or a service as well as to give feedback regarding previously posted tips. Our work aims at contributing to fill this gap.

3. FOURSQUARE DATASET

In this section, we first describe Foursquare, its main elements and features. In particular, we introduce the tip, done and to-do features, which are target of our study (Section 3.1). Next, in Section 3.2, we describe the strategy adopted to crawl Foursquare and summarize the collected dataset used in the following sections.

3.1 Foursquare

Foursquare is a prime example of online Location-Based Social Network (LBSN) on which users share their location with friends. As videos and images are the main objects on YouTube and Flickr, respectively, the main objects on Foursquare are venues. A **venue** represents any physical location like a store, a restaurant, an university, an airport or a monument, where users can check in. Users may check in venues when they are physically close to those venues, using GPS-equipped mobile devices or SMS messages. Once users check in, they may choose to share their location with friends. Every time a user checks in a venue, she collects points, namely **badges**, on Foursquare. If a user has more "check ins" in a certain venue than any other user, she becomes the venues' mayor. Venues are created by Foursquare users who become owners of that place. However, venues can be claimed by real business owners. In this case, venues are verified by Foursquare and, if approved, the real owners of the venue can start offering promotions and special deals to users that frequently check in that venue. Foursquare also maintains a set of eight pre-defined venue categories, namely, "Arts & Entertainment", "Colleges & Universities", "Food", "Great Outdoors", "Nightlife Spots", "Travel Spots", "Shops", "Home, Work and Others".

In addition to checking in venues, users are also allowed to post tips at specific venues for other users that visit them in the future. **Tips** are pieces of information containing *recommendations* (or reviews), either positive or negative, about the venue. Examples of tips include the best option of a menu in a restaurant, the best place to have lunch in an airport, or even a complaint about a service in a venue. Tips have become extensively used in Foursquare as they allow one to share her opinion about nearby physical locations with others. When a user posts a tip, her immediate friends receive it as a message. Users may also see previously posted tips by searching nearby locations or accessing the venues.

After reading a tip, a user may add it to her **to-do** list or even mark it as **done**. Thus, tips, dones and to-dos foster interactions among users who accessed the same venue in the system. An illustrative example of such interactions is presented in Figure 1. User Ann posts a tip at a certain venue. After a while, user John searches for nearby locations, finds the venue tipped by Ann, reads it, and decides to add it to his to-do list. John may also mark the tip as done to indicate that he followed and agreed with Ann's recommendation. Thus, the total number of times a tip was marked as done or added to a user's to-do list (here referred to as, simply, the number of dones and to-dos the tip received) can be seen as an estimate of the amount of *feedback* from other users regarding that tip. Indeed, Foursquare maintains statistics about these numbers as an attempt to allow users to identify potentially good tips to follow.

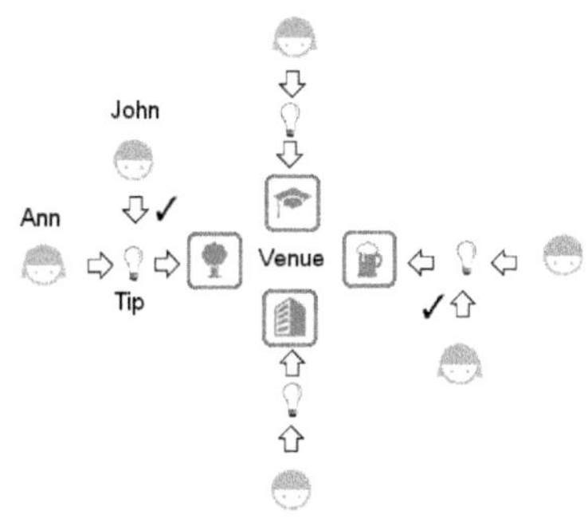

Figure 1: User Interactions Through Tips, Dones, and To-Dos: An Illustrative Example

Finally, it is important to mention that, in addition to ordinary user accounts, Foursquare also allows the creation of a special type of account, named brand user. **Brand users** are known business owners (e.g., "the History Channel", "Starbucks" and "The Wall Street Journal", among others) that are in the system to create content in the form of tips, comments, and photos [1], usually aiming at promoting themselves and their products. Towards that goal, they usually create special offers to attract users to their locations. Unlike ordinary users, who have friends, brand users have followers. The followers of a brand user receive all the tips posted by it.

3.2 Dataset

Ideally, we would like to have at our disposal data for each existing venue, including their tips, the user who posted each tip, the users who added each tip to their to-do lists, as well as the users who marked it as done. Since this data is not publicly available, we chose, instead, to crawl Foursquare to obtain a sample of it.

We used the Foursquare API to gather data about a sample of the existing venues and the users who interacted with them[4]. Our crawling strategy was based on the fact that each venue in Foursquare is assigned a unique and sequential numeric identifier (ID). Given (an estimate of) the largest ID assigned to a venue in the system, M, our crawler first randomly selects an ID between 0 and M, according to a uniform distribution. The random selection was performed to minimize the chance of bias in the sampled venues. Next, it sends a request to the Foursquare API to gather information about the corresponding venue. In particular, for each collected venue, the crawler collects all its tips, the identifications of the users who posted each of them, the number of dones and to-dos each tip received, the number of users who checked in the venue, the venue category as well as its geographic coordinates.

In order to estimate M, we ran a series of initial experiments consisting of sending HTTP GET requests to the pages of specific venues identified by their IDs. We tried increasing values of IDs, starting with 0. The largest ID for which we did get a response corresponding to a valid webpage was 20 million. We experiment with many IDs greater than that. In all those cases, the response was "Not Found". Thus, we speculate that, by the time of these experiments, this was the largest venue ID in the system, and was used as input to our crawler.

Our crawler ran from May 23rd to July 19th, gathering data corresponding to more than 1.6 million venues. Table 1 summarizes the collected dataset. Associated with the crawled venues, we were able to identify almost 1 million tips and more than half million unique users, out of whom 1,248 are brand users. Moreover, 3.8% of the venues are verified whereas 18.5% of them had received, by the time of the crawling, at least one tip. Since our focus is on understanding how users exploit tips, dones and to-dos, our analyses in the following sections are performed over the venues with at least one tip.

Table 1: Summary of our Foursquare Dataset

Number of venues	1,601,412
Number of venues with at least one tip	296,217
Number of verified venues	61,378
Number of users	526,651
Number of brand users	1,248
Number of tips	984,251
Total number of dones for all tips	1,407,835
Total number of to-dos for all tips	393,574

[4]We note that, alternatively, one might choose to crawl Foursquare by requesting user data. We opted to collect venues and their associated data instead, because user data is not publicly available.

4. USER INTERACTIONS THROUGH TIPS, DONES AND TO-DOS

In this section, we analyze how users exploit the tip, done and to-do features in Foursquare. We start by focusing on the venues, and analyze how users interact with them by posting tips and by marking them as done or to-do (Section 4.1). Next, we discuss how users interact through tips and how their tips are evaluated (Section 4.2).

4.1 Venue Analyses

We here characterize each venue in our dataset in terms of the number of tips and the total number of dones and to-dos associated with all the tips posted at the venue. The former represents the amount of reviews (i.e., recommendations) from the users regarding the venue, whereas the latter is here taken as an estimate of the amount of user feedback regarding those reviews. Figures 2(a) and 2(b) show the Complementary Cumulative Distribution Functions (CCDFs) of these measures. Note the log scale in both axes.

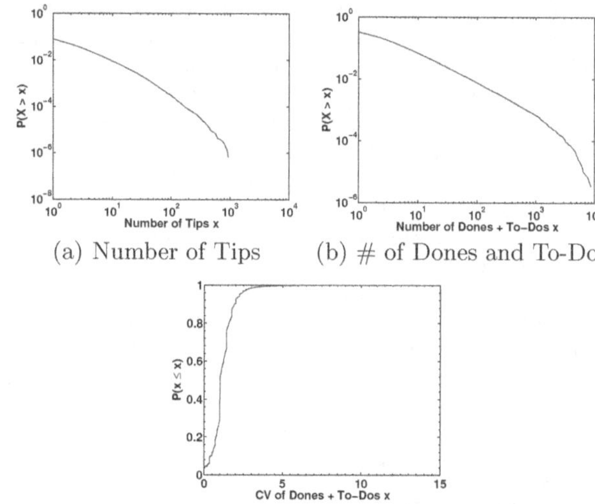

(a) Number of Tips (b) # of Dones and To-Dos

(c) CV of Number of Dones and To-Dos per Tip

Figure 2: Distributions of Venue Attributes

Figure 2(a) shows that around 57% of the venues have only one tip, whereas, some venues (around 500) are very popular among the users, receiving more than 100 tips each. Similarly, Figure 2(b) shows that there are a few venues (around 200) with tips that received a lot of feedback, with a total number of dones and to-dos exceeding 1,000. The Spearman's rank correlation coefficient, which is a non-parametric measure of statistical dependence between two variables [13], computed over the number of tips and the total number of dones and to-dos of each venue is 0.6. This reasonably strong positive correlation implies that tipping tends to be an effective mechanism to attract visibility to a venue: the larger the number of tips, the higher the amount of user feedback the venue tends to receive. Moreover, we also found a reasonably strong correlation (Spearman coefficient of 0.56) between the number of dones and to-dos and the number of distinct users who checked in each venue, indicating that user feedback is somewhat related to venue visitation in the system (i.e., check ins).

Recall that dones and to-dos are associated with tips.

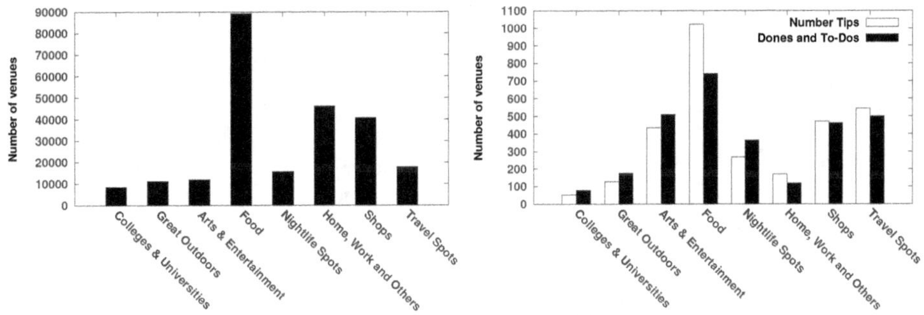

(a) All Venues

(b) Top 1% Venues According to Number of Tips and Number of Dones and To-Dos

Figure 3: Distribution of Venues Across Categories

Thus, different tips posted at the same venue may attract different feedback. To investigate this issue, we analyze the variability in the number of dones and to-dos across different tips of the same venue. Figure 2(c) shows the Cumulative Distribution Function (CDF) of the coefficient of variation - CV (ratio of standard deviation to the mean) of this number. We considered only venues with at least 2 tips and at least one done/to-do. Note that most (70%) of the venues have CVs larger than 1, and around 9% of our venues have CVs larger than 2, indicating reasonably high variability. These numbers imply that user feedback regarding a given venue does depend on the specific tip, and some tips do tend to attract more feedback than others.

As discussed in Section 3.1, Foursquare venues are grouped into 8 pre-defined categories. Figure 3(a) shows a histogram of the number of venues in each category, in our dataset. To understand which venue category attracts the largest number of tips, dones and to-dos, we ranked the venues according to the number of tips and according to the total number of dones and to-dos. We then selected the venues in the top 1% of each rank. Figure 3(b) shows the number of venues of each category in each selection. Note that "Food" contains the largest number of venues both in the top 1% more tipped venues (1024) and in the top 1% venues with more dones and to-dos (742). The second category with more venues is "Travel Spots" in the first rank and "Arts & Entertainment" in the second one. Indeed, the two venues with largest number of tips are "Super Bowl Event" ("Arts & Entertainment") and "Jakarta Airport" ("Travel Spots"), whereas "Grand Central Terminal" ("Travel Spots") and "Madison Square Garden" ("Arts & Entertainment") received the largest numbers of dones and to-dos.

4.2 User Analyses

We now turn our focus to the users, analyzing how they exploit tips, dones and to-dos. In particular, we characterize the number of tips posted by each user, the total number of dones and to-dos received by her tips, the number of venues tipped by her and the percentage of her tips containing links (i.e., URLs and e-mail addresses). The distributions of these measures are shown in Figure 4. Note that Figures 4(a,b,c) show CCDFs with both axes in logarithm scale.

Figures 4(a-b) shows that, like for the number of tips and the number of dones and to-dos per venue (Figures 2(a-b)), the the distributions of number of tips and number of tipped venues per user are heavy tailed. Most users posted a few tips at a few venues, whereas a few, very active users posted many tips at many different venues. Indeed, 66% of the users posted only one tip and 70% of the users posted tips at only one venue[5], whereas 67 users posted more than 100 tips and 39 posted tips at more than 100 venues. The distribution of the total number of dones and to-dos per user (Figure 4-c) is also heavy-tailed: around 103,348 users received only one to-do/done in their posted tips, whereas 90 users received at least 1,000 dones and to-dos.

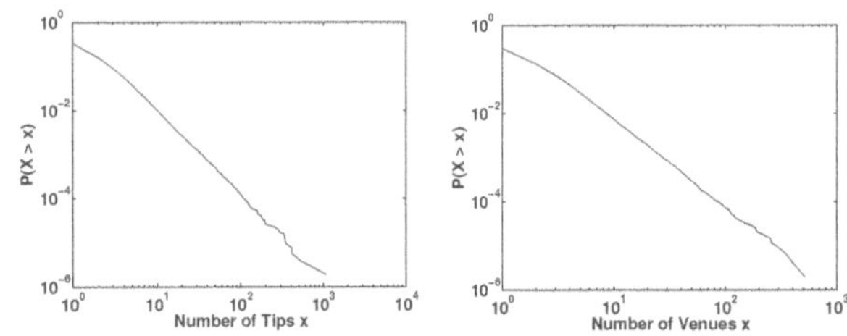

(a) Number of Tips (b) Number of Venues

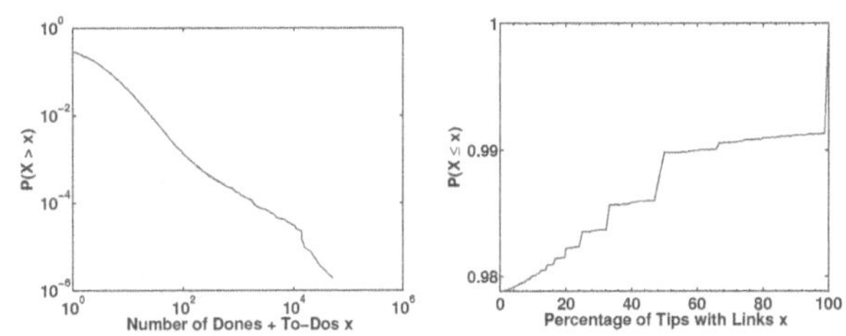

(c) # of Dones and To-Dos (d) % of Tips with Links

Figure 4: Distributions of User Attributes

The distribution of the percentage of tips containing links, shown in Figure 4(d), has a different pattern: the vast majority (98.7%) of all users who posted at least one tip did not add any link in their tips' contents. However, we do notice the presence of some users (around 200) with more than 60% of their tips containing links. These users are further discussed in Section 4.2.2.

We also analyzed how the four user attributes correlate. We found no significant correlation between the percentage of tips with links and any other attribute. In contrast, we did find a strong positive correlation (Spearman coeffi-

[5]Note that, since we collected users through venue tips, all analyzed users have posted at least one tip.

cient of 0.93) between the number of tips and the number of venues tipped by a user, suggesting that users who more often add tips do tend to spread them across more venues. The correlation remains very high (above 0.78) even when computed over selected groups of very active users, i.e., over the top 1% users with the largest number of (1) tips, (2) tipped venues, and (3) dones and to-dos in their tips.

We also found that the correlation between the number of tips and the total number of dones and to-dos received by a user's tips is only moderate (0.40), being even lower (0.23-0.30) if computed over the three aforementioned subsets of very active users. Thus, in general and in contrast to our finding regarding venues, users who tip more do not necessarily receive more feedback. If we take the total number of dones and to-dos received by a user's tips as an estimate of her influence in the system, such influence is only moderately correlated with her degree of tipping activity, seeming much more related to the tipped venue. We further analyze user influence next.

4.2.1 User Influence

Figure 5(a) shows the number of tipped venues versus the total number of dones and to-dos received by each user. Note the logarithm scale in both axes. In this plot, users are grouped into two sets based on the maximum geographical distance between any pair of venues tipped by them. We refer to such distance as the *diameter* of the venues tipped by the user, and use it to assess the scale (local or global) of the user's influence. We group users into those with diameter shorter than or larger than 40 kilometers. Figure 5(b) shows a similar graph, plotting the number of tips versus the total number of dones and to-dos of each user. To improve graph readability, both figures only show users with at least 10 tips. Note that, given the strong correlation between number of tips and number of tipped venues per user, the two graphs are similar.

Both graphs show the existence of different classes of users. On one hand, we find users who, despite posting a large number of tips and/or posting tips to a large number of venues, receive only a comparatively small number of dones and to-dos. One such user, marked as "User 1" in both graphs, posted approximately 104 tips at 100 different venues, but received only 4 to-dos and dones. By manually inspecting a sample of those users, located in the right bottom corner of the graphs, we found that they tend to be ordinary users who, in spite of being very active in the system and contributing with a lot of tips regarding many different venues, do not get a lot of feedback from others.

In contrast, the right top corner of the plots show users who not only post a large number of tips at a large number of different venues but also receive a lot of feedback on them. Those users, many of which are famous brands such as "Bravo", "History Channel", "The Wall Street Journal" and "National Post", seem engaged in providing many recommendations (tips) on a large variety of venues, and clearly succeed in reaching and attracting the attention of many users. Clearly, those users are very influential in the system. Note that, interestingly, the graphs show users with large number of tips (and tipped venues) and large number of dones and to-dos in both user sets, suggesting the presence of local and global influence.

Both graphs also show some users who, despite posting only a few tips at a few venues, received a comparatively very large amount of feedback, and thus can also be considered very influential. Examples are "User 2" and "User 3" in Figure 5(a), who received 2708 and 1337 dones and to-dos, respectively, despite targeting only a couple of venues with a few tips. Some of these highly focused influential users are brands, such as "Six Flags", while others are ordinary users (e.g., "User 4"). Once again, we found focused users with strong influence both locally and globally.

As a side note, we point out that, as expected, both graphs show a slight trend for users with larger numbers of tips and tipped venues also having larger diameter. Perhaps more interesting is the presence of some very active users, with tens to hundreds of tips and tipped venues, who are focused on venues in a local region (diameter under 40 kilometers).

4.2.2 Suspicious Behavior

According to the Foursquare's Terms of Service, the introduction of links to unrelated sites across various venues is considered *spamming*, and users who are caught doing it will have their accounts deactivated[8]. As previously discussed, we did find some users who had the majority of their tips containing links, i.e., URLs and email addresses. This finding raised a concern about suspicious behavior, particularly because only links included in the tip's text were accounted for. In other words, links placed in the "More info" field, expected to be directly related to the target venue (e.g., the venue's website), as well as related pictures, placed in a separate field, were disregarded.

To delve deeper into this issue, we selected users with at least 10 tips and at least 60% of their tips containing links for further analysis. This selection corresponded to 3% of all users that posted at least 10 tips. Figure 6(a) plots the percentage of tips with links versus the number of tipped venues for these users, whereas Figure 6(b) shows the percentage of tips with links versus the total number of dones and to-dos. As in the previous section, we group users based on the diameter of their tipped venues.

The graphs show no clear correlation between the percentage of tips with links and the total number of dones and to-dos or the number of tipped venues. Indeed, the Spearman coefficients are -0.17 and 0.13, respectively. In other words, there are many users with a large percentage of tips with links that posted tips at only a few venues, which cannot necessarily be configured as spamming according to Foursquare's rules. Moreover, there are also users that, despite the large percentage of tips with links, did receive a large number of dones and to-dos (see discussion below).

However, Figure 6(a) also shows that several of the selected users posted tips with links at a large number of venues. Take for instance "User 5", "User 6" and "User 7" in that figure. They posted tips at more than 100 different venues, and all tips contained links. These numbers reveal a behavior pattern that is consistent with spamming, and violates Foursquare's Terms of Service. Moreover, the total numbers of dones and to-dos for "User 5" and "User 7" are only 12 and 32, respectively, whereas "User 6" received no feedback. Interestingly, we found no clear correlation between suspicious behavior and diameter of the tipped venues. In other words, our results reveal potential spamming activity both locally and globally.

We note that not all users who posted tips with links at many venues are necessarily engaged in spamming activity, as the webpage linked to might be somewhat related to the

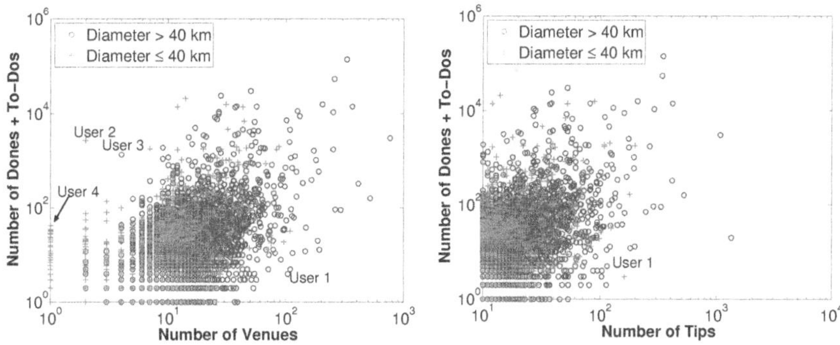

(a) Number of Venues vs. Number of Dones and To-Dos (b) Number of Tips vs. Number of Dones and To-Dos

Figure 5: Correlation between User Attributes (only users with at least 10 tips)

tipped venue. Take, for instance, "User 8" in Figure 6(a), that posted 286 tips, 90% of which containing links, at 261 different venues. Despite the large number of tips with links, those tips received a total 92 dones and to-dos. We manually investigated this user, finding that it corresponds to a large business chain that placed the same tip to all of its stores advertising a promotion. The tip contained a link to an external webpage that should be visited by those interested in participating to learn more about it. A reasonably large number of users (92) liked it enough to mark the tip as done or add it to their to-do lists. In this case, the link pointed to a content that was related to the tipped venue.

Moreover, as we further discuss in Section 5.2, some users that post many tips containing links at many venues aiming at spamming might still receive many dones and to-dos from others. In other words, they might succeed in triggering the interest of many users.

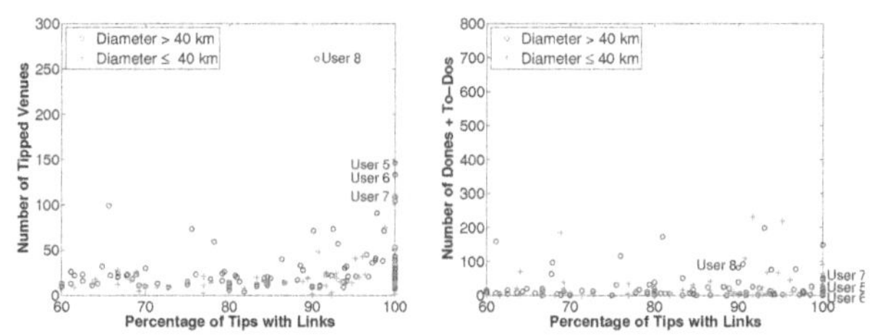

(a) # Tipped Venues vs. % of Tips with Links (b) # Dones and To-Dos vs. % of Tips with Links

Figure 6: Correlation between User Attributes (top 3% users with largest percentages of tips with links)

5. USER PROFILES

In the previous section, we discussed various user behavior patterns observed in our Foursquare dataset, with respect to the use of tips, dones and to-dos. We here go one step further and identify user profiles. We do so by applying a clustering algorithm to group users based on three attributes, namely the number of tipped venues, the total number of dones and to-dos and the percentage of tips with links[6].

[6]We did not include the number of tips as an attribute because of the strong correlation between number of tips and number of tipped venues (see section 4.2).

We selected the Expectation-Maximization (EM) clustering algorithm, which is a well-known algorithm used for clustering in the context of mixture models [7].We ran the EM implementation in Weka [30], which has a built-in iterative mechanism to determine the number of clusters. The mechanism is based on ten-fold cross-validation: for each candidate number of clusters, it breaks the data into 10 folds, 9 are used as training sets and 1 as testing set. It builds the clusters on the training sets and, given those clusters, computes the log-likelihood for each instance in the testing set. The log-likelihood values are summed and then averaged over all 10 folds. The number of clusters selected is the one with maximum (average) log-likelihood.

Because of the large variability observed in the values of the user attributes, particularly number of tipped venues and total number of dones and to-dos, which make the clustering task harder, we converted all values to a log scale, and normalized the results afterwards.

Next, we first present the clustering results (Section 5.1) and then discuss some findings of a manual inspection of selected users (Section 5.2).

5.1 Clustering Results

We applied the EM clustering algorithm over *all users with at least 10 tips*. The algorithm identified 4 clusters, referred to as, throughout this section, clusters 0, 1, 2 and 3. Table 2 shows, for each cluster, averages and CVs for each user attribute. It also shows the number of users in each cluster. Complementarily, Figure 7 shows, for each cluster, the CDF of each attribute.

Cluster 0, which includes around 3% of all clustered users, is characterized by a much larger percentage of tips with links (83% on average). This is consistent across most users of the cluster, as shown in Figure 7(c) and summarized by the low CV. Indeed, this attribute clearly distinguishes these users from the others. The number of tipped venues also tends to be large, though smaller than for users in cluster 3. These patterns are consistent with the suspicious, potential spamming, behavior discussed in Section 4.2.2. Moreover, in general, users in cluster 0 do not tend to receive a large number of dones and to-dos.

Cluster 1 consists of focused users who are neither very active nor influential: they tend to post tips at only a few venues and do not receive many dones and to-dos from oth-

Table 2: Summary of User Attributes Across Clusters

Attribute	Cluster 0		Cluster 1		Cluster 2		Cluster 3	
	avg	cv	avg	cv	avg	cv	avg	cv
Number of Venues	21.99	0.94	1.97	0.52	13.23	0.52	43.81	1.41
Percentage of Tips with Links	83.11	0.20	3.88	2.35	0.62	5.21	7.02	1.71
Number of Dones and To-Dos	20.41	1.82	7.35	1.52	29.53	2.09	1350.58	5.48
Number of Users	222		190		5660		477	

ers. These are mostly occasional users[7]. Users of cluster 2, on the contrary, are much more active: they tend to tip a larger number of venues, mostly with no links, getting many more dones and to-dos in return. Around 86% of all clustered users are in this group.

Finally, cluster 3, containing around 7% of the considered users, is characterized by the largest total number of dones and to-dos. These users also tend to post tips a large number of venues. Therefore, we expect that most very influential users that target a large number of venues fall into this cluster. Moreover, as shown in Figure 7(a), this cluster also contains users that post tips at only a few venues, indicating that this cluster also contains some very influential but focused users.

We also analyzed the distribution of venues tipped by users in each cluster across the several categories maintained by Foursquare. Figure 8 shows the distributions. The fractions of venues tipped by users from both clusters 0 and 3 vary only slightly across categories, except for "Colleges & Universities", which clearly attracts much fewer tips than the other categories. Indeed, it is the least popular category among users of all four clusters. In other words, neither users who seem engaged in suspicious activity (cluster 0) nor those who tend to be very influential in the system (cluster 3) are focused, collectively, on specific categories. In contrast, the venues tipped by the occasional users (cluster 1) are more concentrated in the "Food" category. The same can be said, to a lesser extent, for users of cluster 2.

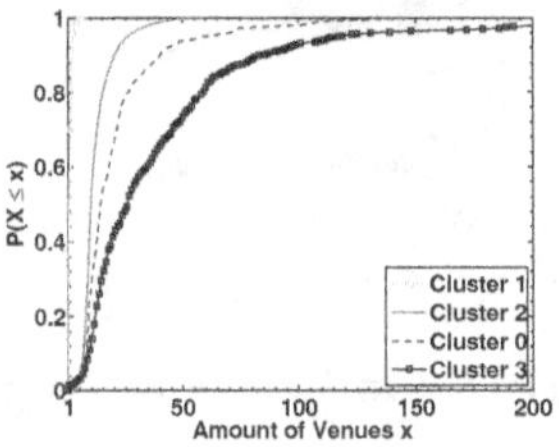

(a) Number of Tipped Venues

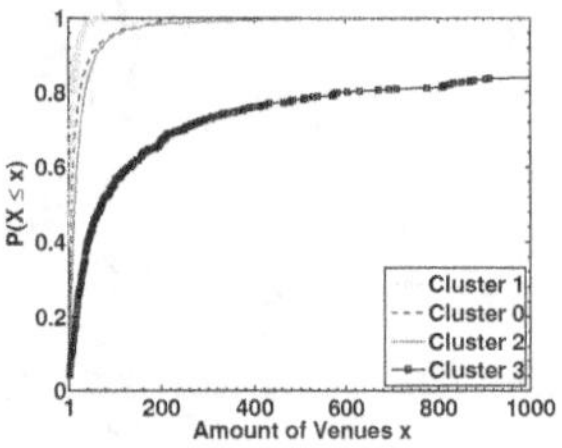

(b) Number of Dones and To-Dos

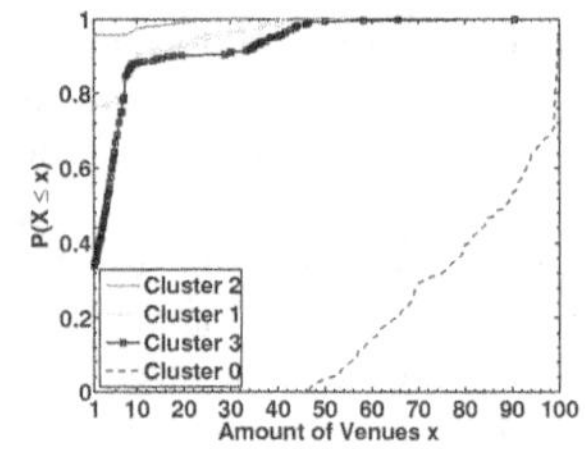

(c) Percentage of Tips with Links

Figure 7: User Attribute Distributions

5.2 Manual Inspection

As discussed in Section 4.2.2, we did find evidence of suspicious behavior, consistent with spamming activity. Note that this evidence was based only on the percentage of a user's tips containing links to external sites and email addresses and, to a lesser degree, on the feedback those tips received from other users. However, an interested spammer may find other ways of reaching users. For instance, a spammer interested in selling a product may write a text advertising it, and post it as a tip. One such case was a tip posted to various venues, including a japanese restaurant and an university, whose contents advertised a fitness center. The tip's text is completely unrelated to the nature and business domain of the venue.

We here consider as spam a tip whose content is unrelated to the tipped venue, typically an advertisement for a product that is, in nature, unrelated to that kind of venue. Given this definition, we note that, some spam tips might indeed be successful in getting a large number of dones and to-dos, since many users may find the advertised product interesting, despite it being unrelated to the venue where the tip was posted.

To further investigate the existence of tip spamming in Foursquare, we manually inspected a sample of users from each cluster. For each sampled user, we inspected the contents of her tips and the venues at which those tips were posted. In case the tip contained a link, the contents of the page pointed to by the link were also inspected.

Each sampled user was inspected independently by three volunteers, who labeled the user as either spammer or not. A user was labeled spammer if the contents of at least 50% of her tips were not related with the nature or domain of the tipped venues[8]. The volunteers were instructed to be conservative: in doubt, they should label the user as *not spammer*. Majority voting was used for final classification, although the volunteers agreed in the vast majority (93%) of the cases. The volunteers also counted down the number of inspected users who are brand users.

Table 3 presents our results, showing, for each cluster, the number of inspected users, the number and percentage of them labeled as spammers by the volunteers, and the number and percentage of them identified as brands. The sample size for each cluster was defined so as to have a maximum error in our estimates of 5% with 95% confidence [12].

Most of the users labeled as spammers are, as expected, in the cluster 0 sample. Indeed, all users sampled from

[7]We did observe, among users of cluster 1, many tips posted at the same venue within a very short time. For instance, around 10% of users of cluster 1 had an average inter-tip time below 2 seconds, suggesting that the user might have posted the same tip multiple times without knowing. This might reflect lack of experience with the application.

[8]Recall that, given our data collection methodology, our analysis is based only on a subset of all tips posted by each user.

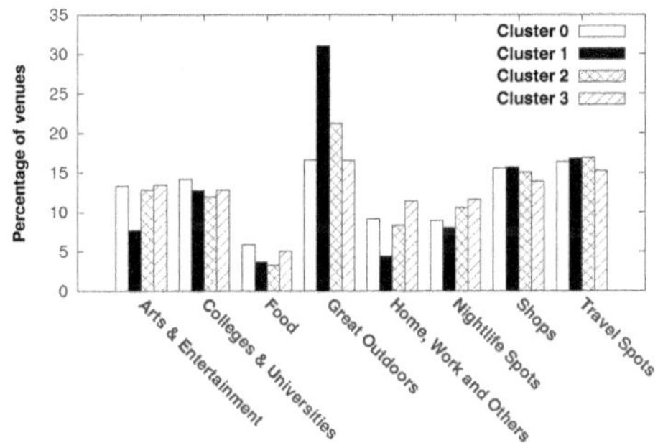

Figure 8: Venue Category Distributions

that cluster were labeled as spammers, mostly because they posted tips with links pointed to unrelated content. However, our results also show the presence of spammers in clusters 1, 2 and 3. Most of them were classified as such because the text of their tips advertised a product unrelated to the nature of the venue. Moreover, some users of cluster 3 labeled as spammers did receive a large number of dones and to-dos, indicating that, despite posting unrelated content, they did trigger the interest of many users[9].

Table 3 also shows that there are brand users in all four clusters, although the vast majority of them are in cluster 3. As discussed in Section 3, brand users are special Foursquare users that are expected to use the system to reach their followers and potential customers. The brand users of cluster 3 indeed succeeded in promoting themselves in Foursquare: they are very influential in the system, receiving a large number of dones and to-dos. Interestingly, we also found 4 brand users among the 127 users sampled from cluster 0 that were labeled as spammers.

We also analyzed the words commonly used by users labeled as spammers in their tips, contrasting them with the vocabulary of the remaining users. Figure 9 shows the word clouds of both user groups. Note that words related to service or product advertisement, such as *business*, *apartment*, *cellular*, *franchise*, *gadget* e *iphone* are more frequently used by users labeled as spammers.

Finally, we note that the concept of spamming in Foursquare is a very subjective and thus controversial matter, possibly even more than in other systems. What one classifies as spam, another person might interpret as creative marketing strategy. Take for instance the case, reported in [5], of a tip advertising a product sold by a certain venue v_i, posted at another venue v_j, which is indeed a business competitor of v_i. When customers check the tips left at v_j, they will see the advertisement and might indeed be drawn towards its competitor. In other words, the tip might contribute to steal business away from the venue at which it was left[10]. Moreover, obliviously of any marketing game, users might find the tip interesting and mark it as a to-do or done. This might happen even for tips advertising products completely unrelated to the tipped venues, as discussed above. Thus,

[9]We note that most of these users received only a couple of dones and to-dos in each tip. However, because they posted a large number of tips at various venues, collectively, those tips end up attracting a large number of users.

[10]During our manual inspection, we took a conservative approach and *did not* consider such cases spamming.

(a) Users Labeled as Spammers

(b) Users Labeled as Not Spammers

Figure 9: Words Commonly Used in Users' Tips

identifying and dealing with tip spamming and spammers is a hard task. The design of automatic detection mechanisms is a challenge we intend to pursue in the future.

6. CONCLUSIONS

This paper analyzes how users exploit tips, dones and to-dos in Foursquare. Based on a crawled dataset containing over 1.6 million venues and more than half million users, we have identified four groups of users with very different behaviors. Two profiles correspond to regular users that differ in terms of their levels of tipping activity in the system. A third profile consists of users that seem engaged in posting tips at a large variety of venues. These users, some of which are famous businesses and brands, are typically very influential in the system, receiving a large amount of feedback from others regarding their tips. Finally, we have identified a group of users characterized by posting tips containing links at many different venues. A manual inspection of a sample of these users confirmed them as potential spammers as they post tips that are unrelated to the venue. However, we also show that some spammers do succeed in attracting the attention of many users.

Our findings unveil various interesting findings with important implications. Two such findings are: (1) we provide the first pieces of evidence of spamming activity in Foursquare. Spam has been observed in many other online social systems, including Facebook [9],YouTube [3], and Twitter [11]. As a result, a number of efforts towards designing effective strategies to detect and remove spam from these systems are available [2, 28]. Although it is debatable whether the kind of spamming activity we uncovered here corresponds to malicious/opportunistic acts that deserves punishment, we hope that our analyses serve as motivation for future discussions on the matter and guide future developments to proper address such actions on Foursquare.

Finally, it is known that the democratization of technologies like Foursquare is fundamentally changing the way people interact with each other as well as with local opinion

Table 3: Results from Manually Inspecting a Sample of Users from Each Cluster

Cluster	Number of Sampled Users	Number of Spammers	Number of Brands
0	127	127 (100%)	4 (3.2%)
1	181	13 (7.2%)	2 (1.1%)
2	237	37 (15.6%)	7 (2.9%)
3	203	41 (20.2%)	58 (28.6%)

leaders, small businesses, and online customers. Unlike other social networks, Foursquare virtual interactions may reverberate in the real world. When a user posts a tip, he is interacting with a real business and exposing weaknesses or qualities about this business to everyone, including competitors. Thus, tips, dones and todos are valuable tools for registered businesses as they are sources of candid feedback from their customers, provide opportunity for improvements and may greatly impact future visitations and ultimately revenues. For the users, tips may act as filters to help them choose places to visit. While there are many skeptics who doubt that social networks will generate profits that match expectations [27], our study provides early pieces of evidence of the true "social" opportunity that lies on Foursquare in the role of brands, venues, local influential users and even opportunistic users that act like spammers. Furthermore, by analyzing the roles that different types of users play in Foursquare, we hope our findings may guide the design of future recommendation approaches.

7. ACKNOWLEDGMENTS

This research is partially funded by the Brazilian National Institute of Science and Technology for the Web (MCT/CNPq/ INCT grant number 573871/2008-6), and by the authors' individual grants from CNPq, CAPES and FAPEMIG.

8. REFERENCES

[1] 360i. Foursquare Brand Pages. http://blog.360i.com/social-media/foursquare-brand-pages.

[2] F. Benevenuto, T. Rodrigues, V. Almeida, J. Almeida, and M. Goncalves. Detecting Spammers and Content Promoters in Online Video Social Networks. In *Proc. ACM SIGIR'09*, 2009.

[3] F. Benevenuto, T. Rodrigues, V. Almeida, J. Almeida, and K. Ross. Video Interactions in Online Video Social Networks. *ACM TOMCCAP'09*, 5(4):1–25, 2009.

[4] B. Berjani and T. Strufe. A Recommendation System for Spots in Location-Based Online Social Networks. In *Proc. of SNS'11*, 2011.

[5] Catalyst Marketers Blog. Catalyst Marketers Blog. http://www.catalystmarketers.com/.

[6] E. Cho, S. Myers, and J. Leskovec. Friendship and Mobility: User Movement In Location-Based Social Networks. In *Proc. of KDD'11*, 2011.

[7] A. Dempster, N. Laird, and D. Rubin. Maximum Likelihood from Incomplete Data via the EM Algorithm. *Journal of the Royal Statistical Society. Series B (Methodological)*, 39(1):1–38, 1977.

[8] Foursquare. Foursquare house rules. http://support.foursquare.com/entries/386768-foursquare-house-rules.

[9] H. Gao, J. Hu, C. Wilson, Z. Li, Y. Chen, and B. Y. Zhao. Detecting and Characterizing Social Spam Campaigns. In *Proc. ACM IMC'10*, 2010.

[10] J. Gomide, A. Veloso, W. M. Jr., V. Almeida, F. Benevenuto, F. Ferraz, and M. Teixeira. Dengue Surveillance Based on a Computational Model of Spatio-Temporal Locality of Twitter. In *Proc. of the ACM WebSci'11*, 2011.

[11] C. Grier, K. Thomas, V. Paxson, and M. Zhang. @Spam: the Underground on 140 Characters or Less. In *ACM CCS'10*, 2010.

[12] R. Jain. *The Art of Computer Systems Performance Analysis: techniques for experimental design, measurement, simulation, and modeling.* Wiley, 1991.

[13] M. Kendall and J. D. Gibbons. *Rank Correlation Methods.* A Charles Griffin Title, fifth edition, 1990.

[14] N. Li and G. Chen. Analysis of a Location-based Network. In *Proc. of IEEE CSE'09*, 2009.

[15] N. Li and G. Chen. Multi-layer Friendship Modeling of Location-based Mobile Social Networks. In *Proc. of MobiQuitous'09*, 2009.

[16] D. Liben-Nowell, J. Novak, R. Kumar, P. Raghavan, and A. Tomkins. Geographic Routing in Social Networks. In *Proc. of PNAS*, volume 102, pages 11623–11628, 2005.

[17] A. Noulas, S. Scellato, C. Mascolo, and M. Pontil. An Empirical Study of Geographic User Activity Patterns in Foursquare. In *Proc. of ICWSM'11*, 2011.

[18] A. Noulas, S. Scellato, C. Mascolo, and M. Pontil. Exploiting Semantic Annotations for Clustering Geographic Areas and Users in Location-based Social Networks. In *Proc. of SMW'11*, 2011.

[19] T. Sakaki, M. Okazaki, and Y. Matsuo. Earthquake Shakes Twitter Users: Real-Time Event Detection by Social Sensors. In *Proc. of WWW'2010*, 2010.

[20] S. Scellato and C. Mascolo. Measuring User Activity on an Online Location-based Social Network. In *Proc. of NetSciCom'11*, 2011.

[21] S. Scellato, C. Mascolo, M. Musolesi, and V. Latora. Distance Matters: Geo-social Metrics for Online Social Networks. In *Proc. of WOSN'10*, 2010.

[22] S. Scellato, A. Noulas, R. Lambiotte, and C. Mascolo. Socio-spatial Properties of Online Location-based Social Networks. In *Proc. of ICWSM'11*, 2011.

[23] S. Scellato, A. Noulas, and C. Mascolo. Exploiting Place Features in Link Prediction on Location-based Social Networks. In *Proc. of KDD'11*, 2011.

[24] O. Sorenson. Social Networks and Industrial Geography. *Journal of Evolutionary Economics*, 13(5):513–527, 2003.

[25] Techcrunch. Foursquare now officially at 10-million-users. http://techcrunch.com/2011/06/20/foursquare-now-officially-at-10-million-users/.

[26] Techcrunch. Klout Adds Foursquare, But How Much Will It Boost My Score? http://techcrunch.com/2011/08/04/klout-adds-foursquare-but-how-much-will-it-boost-my-score/.

[27] The Economist. Where Networking Works. http://www.economist.com/node/21523437.

[28] K. Thomas, C. Grier, J. Ma, V. Paxson, and D. Song. Design and Evaluation of a Real-Time URL Spam Filtering Service. In *IEEE S&P'11*, 2011.

[29] G. Topa. Social Interactions, Local Spillovers and Unemployment. *Review of Economic Studies*, 68(2):261–95, 2001.

[30] Weka Machine Learning Project. Weka. http://www.cs.waikato.ac.nz/~ml/weka.

When Will It Happen? — Relationship Prediction in Heterogeneous Information Networks*

Yizhou Sun[†] [†] Jiawei Han[†] Charu C. Aggarwal[‡] Nitesh V. Chawla[§]
[†] University of Illinois at Urbana-Champaign, Urbana, IL, USA
[‡] IBM T. J. Watson Research Center, Yorktown Heights, NY, USA
[§] University of Notre Dame, Notre Dame, IN, USA
[†]{sun22, hanj}@illinois.edu [‡]charu@us.ibm.com [§]nchawla@nd.edu

ABSTRACT

Link prediction, i.e., predicting links or interactions between objects in a network, is an important task in network analysis. Although the problem has attracted much attention recently, there are several challenges that have not been addressed so far. First, most existing studies focus only on link prediction in homogeneous networks, where all objects and links belong to the same type. However, in the real world, *heterogeneous networks* that consist of multi-typed objects and relationships are ubiquitous. Second, most current studies only concern the problem of *whether* a link will appear in the future but seldom pay attention to the problem of *when* it will happen. In this paper, we address both issues and study the problem of *predicting when a certain relationship will happen in the scenario of heterogeneous networks*. First, we extend the link prediction problem to the relationship prediction problem, by systematically defining both the target relation and the topological features, using a meta path-based approach. Then, we directly model the distribution of relationship building time with the use of the extracted topological features. The experiments on citation relationship prediction between authors on the DBLP network demonstrate the effectiveness of our methodology.

Categories and Subject Descriptors

H.4 [**Information Systems Applications**]: Miscellaneous

General Terms

Algorithms

*The work was supported in part by the U.S. Army Research Laboratory under Cooperative Agreement No. W911NF-09-2-0053 (NS-CTA), MIAS, a DHS-IDS Center for Multimodal Information Access and Synthesis at UIUC, U.S. National Science Foundation grants IIS-0905215, and U.S. Air Force Office of Scientific Research MURI award FA9550-08-1-0265.
[†]The work was partially performed during Yizhou Sun's employment at IBM T. J. Watson Research Center.

Permission to make digital or hard copies of all or part of this work for personal or classroom use is granted without fee provided that copies are not made or distributed for profit or commercial advantage and that copies bear this notice and the full citation on the first page. To copy otherwise, to republish, to post on servers or to redistribute to lists, requires prior specific permission and/or a fee.
WSDM'12, February 8–12, 2012, Seattle, Washington, USA.
Copyright 2012 ACM 978-1-4503-0747-5/12/02 ...$10.00.

1. INTRODUCTION

Owing to the popularity of Web and social networks, link prediction, *i.e.*, predicting the emergence of links in a network in the future based on certain historical network information, has been a hot topic in recent years. Its applications range from social networks to biological networks, as it addresses the fundamental question of *whether* a link will form between two nodes in the future. Most of the existing link prediction methods [12, 7, 21, 13, 10] are designed for homogeneous networks, in which only one type of objects exists in the network. For example, friendship networks and co-author networks belong to homogeneous networks. However, most of the networks in the real world are heterogeneous, where multiple types of objects and links exist. For example, a movie network contains information about types of movies, actors, users, and comments, with links from types of view/viewed, post/posted, comment-on/commented-on, and so on. Other examples of heterogeneous networks include those extracted from social websites, such as YouTube, Flickr, and Delicious. A few studies [19] have worked on the problem of link prediction in heterogeneous networks, based on the observations of the attributes of the objects. However, the attribute values of objects are usually difficult to fully obtain in reality. For example, user profiles in the movie network is usually incomplete or unreliable.

The heterogeneity of objects and links makes it difficult to use well-known topological concepts in homogeneous networks for algorithmic design. For example, the number of the common neighbors is frequently used as a feature for link prediction in homogeneous networks. However, in heterogeneous networks, the neighbors of an object could come from different types, and the number of shared neighbors is not able to fully represent this heterogeneity. On the other hand, the focus of traditional link prediction tasks is on the fact about **whether** a link will happen in the future, *e.g.*, whether two people will become friends. However, in many applications, it may be more interesting to predict **when** the link will be built. Examples include: "what is the probability that two authors will co-write a paper within 5 years?", and "by when will a user in Netflix rent the movie *Avatar* with 80% probability?".

In this paper, we propose the problem of predicting the *relationship building time* between two objects, based on the topological structure in a heterogeneous network. Different from link prediction which predicts whether a link should exist between two homogeneous typed objects, *relationship prediction* predicts whether or when a relationship between two objects will be built, based on the relationships among *heterogeneous typed objects*. We first introduce our framework of relationship prediction in heterogeneous information networks, including the concepts of the target relation and topological features encoded in a meta-path [17]. Then, a generalized linear model (GLM) [5] based supervised framework is proposed to model the relationship building time. In this framework, the building time for relationships are treated as independent random variables with different observations and their expectation is modeled as a function of a linear predictor of the extracted topological features. We propose and compare models with different distribution assumptions for relationship building time, where the parameters for each model are learned separately.

We apply our methodology to predict citation relationship between authors in DBLP, a heterogeneous bibliographic network. The results show that our methodology can indeed handle the task of relationship prediction in heterogeneous networks, and detect the critical topological features in determining the timing of relationship building. By taking the relationship building time into consideration, one can obtain not only the relationship building probabilities within time constrains, but also richer information about the relationship building time, such as median, mean, and quantile intervals. The contributions of this paper are as follows:

- We extend the link prediction problem in homogeneous networks to relationship prediction in heterogeneous networks, by systematically defining the target relation and topological features in heterogeneous networks;
- We extend the traditional prediction problem from "whether it will happen" to "when it will happen", and directly model the relationship building time as a function of topological features; and
- Experiments on citation relationship prediction in the DBLP bibliographic network have validated our methodology.

The remaining of the paper is organized as follows. We introduce the concepts on heterogeneous information networks and define the task of relationship building time prediction in Section 2. Methods for design and calculation of topological features for relationship prediction are developed in Section 3. Relationship building time modeling is worked out in Section 4. We report our experiments in Section 5, discuss related work and other issues in Sections 6, and conclude the study in Section 7.

2. PROBLEM DEFINITION

In this section, we introduce the concepts related to heterogeneous information networks and define the relationship building time prediction task.

2.1 Heterogeneous Information Network

A **heterogeneous information network** is a network containing multiple types of objects and links, which is defined as a directed graph $G = (V, E)$ with a type mapping function $\phi : V \to \mathcal{A}$ and a link mapping function $\psi : E \to \mathcal{R}$. Each object $v \in V$ belongs to one particular type $\phi(v) \in \mathcal{A}$, and each link $e \in E$ belongs to a particular link type or relation $\psi(e) \in \mathcal{R}$. Notice that, if a relation exists between two types A and B, denoted as $A\ R\ B$, the reverse relation R^{-1} holds naturally for $BR^{-1}A$. In most cases, R and its reverse relation R^{-1} are not equal, unless the two types are the same and R is symmetric.

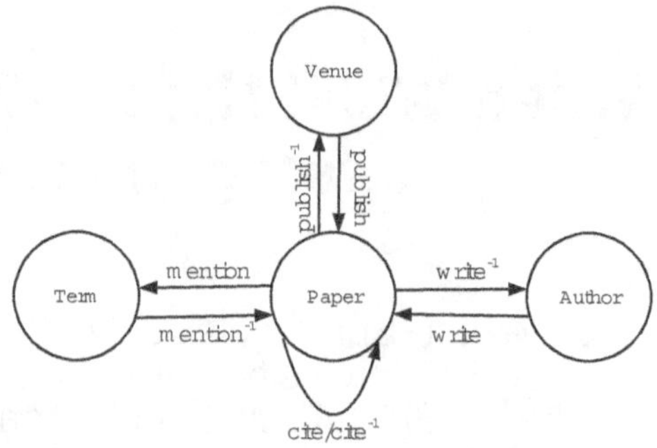

Figure 1: Schema for DBLP Bibliographic Network

Further, in order to describe a heterogeneous network at the meta-level, we use the concept of **network schema** following [17]. Let $G = (V, E)$ be a heterogeneous network with type mapping $\phi : V \to \mathcal{A}$ and relation mapping $\psi : E \to \mathcal{R}$, the network schema of G is a directed graph with nodes from object types $\mathcal{A}$ and edges from relation types $\mathcal{R}$, denoted as $T_G = (\mathcal{A}, \mathcal{R})$.

Here we give one example of heterogeneous networks, namely the DBLP bibliographic network, in its network schema form.

Example 3.1 (DBLP bibliographic network.) The DBLP bibliographic network integrated with citation relationships between papers, which is provided by [18], consists of rich information about publications. The network contains 4 types of objects, namely papers, authors, terms, and venues (conferences or journals). Links exist between authors and papers by the relation of "write" and "written by" (denoted as *write*$^{-1}$), between papers and terms by "mention" and "mentioned by" (denoted as *mention*$^{-1}$), between venues and papers by "publish" and "published by" (denoted as *publish*$^{-1}$), and between papers by "cite" and "cited by" (denoted as *cite*$^{-1}$). Its network schema is summarized in Fig. 1. ∎

For abbreviation, we use the first capital letters to denote these object types, namely P for papers, A for authors, T for terms, and V for venues.

2.2 Target Relation

Given a heterogeneous network, we generalize the link prediction task to **relationship** prediction, which is to predict whether two objects will build a relationship following a certain **target relation** in the future. Notice that target relationships between objects are instances of the target relation. For example, we say that Jim and Mike have built a co-author relationship, if they follow a co-author relation. The target relation can be either a relation in $\mathcal{R}$ or a composite relation concatenated from existing relations. For example, the co-author relation on author set is not defined in our original DBLP network schema, but can be defined through concatenation of two relations "*write*" and "*write*$^{-1}$", namely two authors a_i and a_j are co-authors, if and only if a_i has authored a paper p that is also authored by a_j.

Formally, we use the concept of **meta-path** [17, 16] defined over the network schema to describe the general relations that can be derived from the network. A meta-path is a path defined on the graph of network schema $T_G = (\mathcal{A}, \mathcal{R})$, and is denoted in the form of $A_1 \xrightarrow{R_1} A_2 \xrightarrow{R_2} \ldots \xrightarrow{R_l} A_{l+1}$, which defines a composite relation $R = R_1 \circ R_2 \circ \ldots \circ R_l$ over type A_1 and A_{l+1}, where $\circ$ denotes the composition operator. For example, in the DBLP network, the co-author relation can be described using the meta-path $A \xrightarrow{write} P \xrightarrow{write^{-1}} A$, and is short for $A - P - A$ if there is no ambiguity for either the meaning or order of the relations. Another example is $A - P \rightarrow P - A$, which is short for $A \xrightarrow{write} P \xrightarrow{cite} P \xrightarrow{write^{-1}} A$, and describes the citation relation between authors.

From the topological view, a target relationship is a path instance following the meta-path that defines the target relation. In real cases, the relationship building between two objects can be affected by many factors. In this paper, we are particularly interested in how topological structures in heterogeneous networks affect the relationship building. For example, for the co-authorship prediction, we want to know what kind of connections between two authors in the historical network can help build new co-author relationship in the future. We show that topological features in heterogeneous networks can be defined systematically using meta-paths, which is covered in Section 3.

2.3 Relationship Building Time Prediction

In addition, in this paper we aim at predicting the relationship building time between objects, which differs from the traditional link prediction problem in another aspect. Examples of relationship building time prediction tasks include predicting when two users will be friends in Delicious network; predicting when an author will publish papers in a conference in DBLP network; and predicting when a user will review a movie in IMDB network.

Generally, given a target relation $\langle A, B\rangle$ between two types $A \in \mathcal{A}$ and $B \in \mathcal{A}$, a history interval $T_0 = [t_0, t_1)$, we want to use the topological features extracted from the aggregated network in time period T_0, to predict the relationship building time t ($t \geq t_1$) in the future.

Following the seminal work of link prediction in homogeneous networks [12], we are interested in predicting the generation of new relationships rather than existing ones. Taking the co-authorship prediction as an example, we are interested in predicting the first time of relationship building between two authors who have never co-authored before rather than predicting how many times the existing co-authors will co-author again in the future.

3. TOPOLOGICAL FEATURES IN HETEROGENEOUS NETWORKS

In this section, we study how to systematically define the topological features in heterogeneous networks. Topological features are also called structural features, which are extracted connectivity properties for pairs of objects in the networks. Topological feature-based link prediction aims at inferring the future connectivity by the current connectivity of the network, namely, using the topology of the network itself to infer the evolution of the network.

There are some frequently used topological features defined in homogeneous networks, such as *common neighbors*, *preferential attachment* [2, 14], $katz_\beta$ [9], *Adamic/Adar* [1], and *PropFlow* [13]. Most of these features are either neighbor-based or path-based. Recently, frequent graph patterns are proposed as another topological feature in detecting the link formation rules [4, 11], which can be used for link prediction. However, most of these features are based on homogeneous networks. As there are multi-typed objects and multi-typed relations in heterogeneous networks, the neighbors of an object could belong to multiple types of objects, and the paths between two objects could follow different meta-paths and indicate different relations. For example, for the paths between two authors, it may follow the meta-paths $A - P \rightarrow P - A$, $A - P - V - P - A$, $A - P - T - P - A$ and so on. Thus, we need to design a more sophisticated strategy to generate topological features in heterogeneous networks.

To design the topological features in the heterogeneous networks, we first define the topology using the concept of meta-path, and then define measures to quantify the specific topology.

3.1 Meta Path-Based Topology

As introduced in Section 2, a meta-path is a path defined over a network schema, and denotes a composite relation over a heterogeneous network. Each meta-path defines a unique topology between objects, and can be used to define the topological features with different semantic meanings. In [16], a case study of meta-path preparation for co-authorship prediction is given. In this section, we give a general framework in preparing reasonable meta path-based topological features for the target relation.

In general, for a target relation $R_T = \langle A, B\rangle$, any meta-paths starting with type A and ending with type B other than the target relation itself can be used as the topological features. These meta-paths can be obtained by traversing on the network schema, for example, using BFS (breadth-first search). In particular, we are considering three forms of relations as topological features:

1. $AR_{sim}AR_TB$, where R_{sim} is a similarity relation defined between type A and R_T is the target relation. The intuition is that if a_i in type A is similar to many a_k's in type A that have relationships with b_j in type B, then a_i is likely to build a relationship with b_j in the future.

2. $AR_TBR_{sim}B$, where R_T is the target relation, and R_{sim} is a similarity relation between type B. The intuition is that if a_i in type A has relationships with many b_k's in type B that are similar to b_j in type B, then a_i is likely to build a relationship with b_j in the future.

3. AR_1CR_2B, where R_1 is some relation between A and C and R_2 is some relation between C and B. The intuition is that if a_i in type A has relationships with many c_k's in type C that have relationships with b_j in type B, then a_i is likely to build a relationship with b_j in the future. Notice that the previous two forms are special cases of this one, which can be viewed as triangle connectivity property. Also, $AR_{sim}A$ is another special case of this type.

For topological features, we confine similarity relations R_{sim} and other partial relations R_1 and R_2 to those that can be derived from the network using meta-paths. Moreover, we only consider similarity relations that are symmetric.

Taking the author citation relation, which is defined as $A - P \rightarrow P - A$, as the target relation, we consider 6 author-

Table 1: Meta-Paths Denoting Similarity Relations between Authors

Meta-path	Semantic meaning of the relation
$A-P-A$	a_i and a_j are co-authors
$A-P-A-P-A$	a_i and a_j have the same co-authors
$A-P-V-P-A$	a_i and a_j have publications in the same venues
$A-P-T-P-A$	a_i and a_j write the same terms
$A-P \rightarrow P \leftarrow P-A$	a_i and a_j cite the same papers
$A-P \leftarrow P \rightarrow P-A$	a_i and a_j are cited by the same papers

author similarity relations defined in Table 1. For each similarity relation, we can concatenate the target relation in its left side or in its right side. We then have 12 topology features with the form $AR_{sim}AR_TB$ and $AR_TBR_{sim}B$ in total. Besides, we can consider the concatenation of "author-cites-paper" relation ($A-P \rightarrow P$) and "paper-cites-author" relation ($P \rightarrow P-A$), as well as all the 6 similarity relations listed in Table 1, in the form of AR_1CR_2B. Now we have 19 topological features in total.

For each type of the meta-paths, we illustrate a concrete example to show the possible relationship building in Figure 2. In Figure 2(a), authors a_1 and a_2 are similar, as they publish papers containing similar terms, and a_2 cites papers published by a_3. In the future, a_1 is likely to cite papers published by a_3 as well, since she may follow the behavior of her fellows. In Figure 2(b), author a_1 cites a_2, and a_2 and a_3 are cited by common papers together (p_5, p_6, p_7). Then a_1 is likely to cite a_3 in the future, as she may cite authors similar to a_2. In Figure 2(c), a_1 and a_2 publish in the same venue, then a_1 is likely to cite a_2 in the future as they may share similar interests if publishing in the same conference.

By varying the similarity relations and partial relations, we are able to generate other topological features in arbitrary heterogeneous networks.

3.2 Quantify the Topology Features

Once the topologies defined by meta-paths are determined, the next stage is to propose measures on these meta-paths. We can use the count of the path instances, random walk-based measures, and others to define the measures between any two objects given the meta-path. For similarity relations, say $A-P-T-P-A$, we can treat each term as a 2-hop neighbor of authors and use weighted count or cosine similarity to measure the similarity between two authors. More discussion of measures defined on meta-paths can be found in [17] and [16].

In this paper, without loss of generality, we use the count of path instances as the default measure. Thus, each meta-path corresponds to a measure matrix. For a single relation in $R \in \mathcal{R}$, the measure matrix is just the adjacency matrix of the sub-network extracted by R. Given a composite relation, the measure matrix can be calculated by the matrix multiplication of the partial relations.

In Figure 2(a), the count of path instances between a_1 and a_3 following the given meta-path is 2, which are:

1. $a_1 - p_1 - t_1 - p_2 - a_2 - p_3 \rightarrow p_4 - a_3$;
2. $a_1 - p_1 - t_2 - p_2 - a_2 - p_3 \rightarrow p_4 - a_3$.

In Figure 2(b), the count of path instances between a_1 and a_4 following the given meta-path is 3, which are:

1. $a_1 - p_1 \rightarrow p_2 - a_2 - p_3 \leftarrow p_5 \rightarrow p_4 - a_4$;
2. $a_1 - p_1 \rightarrow p_2 - a_2 - p_3 \leftarrow p_6 \rightarrow p_4 - a_4$;
3. $a_1 - p_1 \rightarrow p_2 - a_2 - p_2 \leftarrow p_7 \rightarrow p_4 - a_4$.

In Figure 2(c), the count of path instances between a_1 and a_3 following the given meta-path is 1, which is:

1. $a_1 - p_1 - v_1 - p_2 - a_3$.

Measures for different meta-paths have different scales. For example, longer meta-paths usually have more path instances due to the adjacency matrix multiplication. We will normalize the measure using Z-score for each meta-path.

3.3 Discussions on Meta Path-based Feature Preparation

How to prepare the meta path-based features is an import issue from a feature engineering point of view. This can be done systematically as well. Note that each meta-path is a path defined on the graph of network schema. For $A\ R\ B$ type of meta-paths, we need to find a path starting from type A and ending with type B. We can use graph traverse algorithms such as BFS (breadth-first search) to enumerate all the possible meta-paths starting from A and ending with B with a length constraint. In particular, if we require $AR_{sim}A$ be a symmetric meta-path between type A to denote a similarity relation, we can confine the meta-path as a round trip path on the network schema. For example, $A-P \leftarrow P \rightarrow P-A$ is a round trip meta-path, which comes back from one type in a reverse manner, while $A-P \rightarrow P-A$ is not a round trip path.

4. MODELING RELATIONSHIP BUILDING TIME

So far, we have provided a systematic way to define the topological features in heterogeneous networks, which is a large space defined over $topology \times measure$.

In this section, we propose the generalized linear model-based prediction model, which directly model the relationship building time as a function of topological features, and provide methods to learn the coefficients of each topological feature, under different assumptions for relationship building time distributions. After that, we introduce how to use the learned model to make inferences.

4.1 Overview

We model the relationship building time prediction problem in a supervised learning framework. In the **training stage**, we first collect the topological features $\mathbf{x}_i$ in the history interval $T_0 = [t_0, t_1)$ for each sampled object pair $\langle a_i, b_i \rangle$, where $\phi(a_i) = A$ and $\phi(b_i) = B$. Then, we record their relative first relationship building time $y_i = t_i - t_1$, if t_i is in the future training interval $T_1 = [t_1, t_2)$; record the building time $y_i \geq t_2 - t_1$, if no new relationship has been observed in T_1. Note that in the training stage, we are only given limited time to observe whether and when two objects will build their relationship, it is very possible that two objects build their relationship after t_2, which needs careful handling in the training model. A generalized linear model (GLM) based relationship building time model is introduced in Section 4, and the goal is to learn the best coefficients associated with each topological feature that maximize the

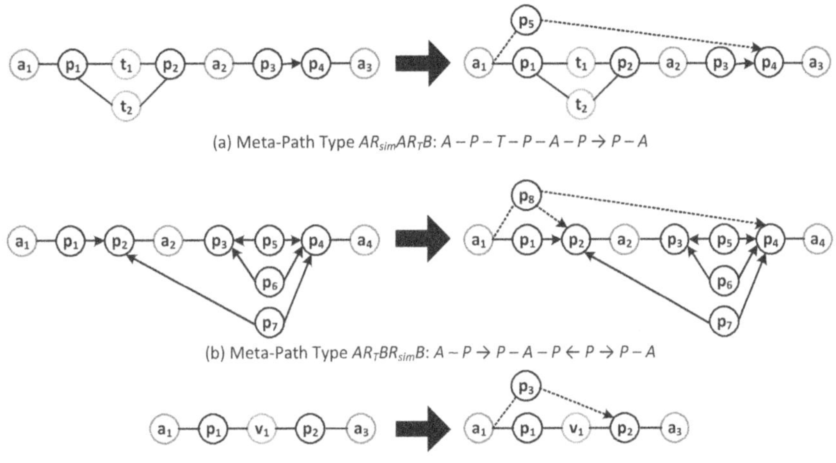

(a) Meta-Path Type $AR_{sim}AR_TB$: $A-P-T-P-A-P\rightarrow P-A$

(b) Meta-Path Type $AR_TBR_{sim}B$: $A-P\rightarrow P-A-P\leftarrow P\rightarrow P-A$

(c) Meta-Path Type AR_1CR_2B: $A-P-C-P-A$

Figure 2: Feature Meta-Path Illustration for Author Citation Relationship Prediction

current observations of the relationship building time. In the **test stage**, we apply the learned coefficients of the topological features to the test pairs, and compare the predicted relationship building time with the ground truth.

Different from the existing link prediction task, in the training stage, we are collecting relationship building time y_i for each training pair, which is a variable ranging from 0 to ∞, rather than a binary value denoting whether a link exists future interval or not. Similarly, in the test stage, we are predicting the relationship building time y_i for test pairs that range from 0 to ∞, rather than predicting whether the link exists or not in the given future interval.

4.2 The Relationship Building Time Prediction Model

We first introduce the generalized linear model [5] as a general framework to solve the relationship building time prediction problem. Then we propose several reasonable distributions for the relationship building time, and use generalized linear model to build the connection between the observed building time and the observed topological features, under different distribution assumptions. We provide the methods to learn the model as well as the model inference in Section 4.3 and 4.4.

4.2.1 The Generalized Linear Model Framework

The main idea of generalized linear model (GLM) [5] is to model the expectation of a dependent random variable Y, $E(Y)$, as some function ("link function") of the linear combination of features, *i.e.*, $\mathbf{X}\beta$, where $\mathbf{X}$ is the observed feature vector, and β is the coefficient vector. Then the goal is to learn β according to the training data set using maximum likelihood estimation. Under different distribution assumptions for Y, usually from the exponential family, $E(Y)$ has different forms of parameter set, and the link functions are with different forms too. Note that the most frequently used Least-Square regression and logistic regression are special cases of GLM, where Y follows Gaussian distribution and Bernoulli distribution respectively.

Suppose we have n training pairs for the target relation $\langle A, B\rangle$. We denote each labeled pair as $r_i = \langle a_i, b_i\rangle$, and y_i as the observed relative relationship building time in the future interval. We denote $\mathbf{X}_i$ as the d dimensional topological feature vector extracted for a_i and b_i in the historical interval plus a constant dimension.

4.2.2 Distributions for Relationship Building Time

The first issue of the prediction model is to select a suitable distribution for the relationship building time. Intuitively, a relationship building between two objects can be treated as an event, and we are interested in when this event will happen.

Let Y be the relationship building time relative to the beginning of the future interval ($y_i = t_i - t_1$), and let T be the length of future training interval. For training pairs, Y has the observations in $[0, T) \cup \{T^+\}$ in a continuous case, and $\{0, 1, 2, \ldots, T-1, T^+\}$ in a discrete case, where $y = T^+$ means no event happens within the future training interval; for testing pairs, Y has the observations in $[0, \infty]$ in a continuous case, and nonnegative integers in a discrete case. In this paper, we consider three types of distributions for relationship building time, namely exponential, Weibull and geometric distribution. For each of the distribution assumptions over y_i, we set up the models separately.

The first distribution is **exponential distribution**, which is the most frequently used distribution in modeling waiting time for an event. The probability density function of an exponential distribution is:

$$f_Y(y) = \frac{1}{\theta}\exp\{-\frac{y}{\theta}\} \tag{1}$$

where $y \geq 0$, and $\theta > 0$ is the parameter denoting the *mean waiting time* for the event. The cumulative distribution function is:

$$F_Y(y) = Pr(Y \leq y) = 1 - \exp\{-\frac{y}{\theta}\} \tag{2}$$

The second distribution is **Weibull distribution**, which is a generalized version of exponential distribution and is another standard way to model the waiting time of an event. The probability density function of a Weibull distribution is:

$$f_Y(y) = \frac{\lambda y^{\lambda-1}}{\theta^\lambda}\exp\{-(\frac{y}{\theta})^\lambda\} \tag{3}$$

where $y \geq 0$, and $\theta > 0$ and $\lambda > 0$ are two parameters related to *mean waiting time* for the event and *hazard of happening* of the event along with the time. λ is also called the shape parameter, as it affects the shape of probability function. When $\lambda > 1$, it indicates an increasing happening rate along the time (if an event does not happen at an early time, it is getting higher probability to happen at later time); and when $\lambda < 1$, it indicates a decreasing happening rate along the time (if an event does not happen at an early time, it is getting less possible in happening in later time). Notice that when $\lambda = 1$, Weibull distribution becomes exponential distribution with mean waiting time as θ, and the happening rate does not change along the time. The cumulative distribution function is:

$$F_Y(y) = Pr(Y \leq y) = 1 - \exp\{-(\frac{y}{\theta})^\lambda\} \quad (4)$$

The third distribution is the **geometric distribution**, which is a distribution that models how many times of failures it needs to take before the first-time success. As in our case, the time of failure is the discrete time that we need to wait before a relationship is built. The probability mass function of a geometric distribution is:

$$Pr(Y = k) = (1-p)^k p \quad (5)$$

where $k = 0, 1, 2, \ldots$, and p is the probability of the occurrence of the event at each discrete time. The cumulative distribution function is:

$$Pr(Y \leq k) = 1 - (1-p)^{k+1} \quad (6)$$

In our case, each relationship building is an independent event, and each relationship building time Y_i is an independent random variable, following the same distribution family, but with different parameters. With the distribution assumptions, we build relationship building time prediction models in the following.

4.2.3 Model under Exponential and Weibull Distribution

Notice that, as exponential distribution is a special case of Weibull distribution (with $\lambda = 1$), we only discuss prediction model with Weibull distribution.

In this case, we assume relationship building time Y_i for each training pair is independent of each other, following the same Weibull distribution family with the same shape parameter λ, but with different mean waiting time parameters θ_i. Namely, we assume that different relationships for the target relation share the same trend of hazard happening along with the time, but with different expectation in building time. Under this assumption, the expectation for each random variable Y_i, $E(Y_i) = \theta_i \Gamma(1 + \frac{1}{\lambda})$. We then use the link function $E(Y_i) = \exp\{-\mathbf{X}_i\boldsymbol{\beta}\}\Gamma(1 + \frac{1}{\lambda})$, that is $\log \theta_i = -\beta_0 - \sum_{j=1}^{d} X_{i,j}\beta_j = -\mathbf{X}_i\boldsymbol{\beta}$, where β_0 is the constant term.

Then we can write the log-likelihood function:

$$\log L = \sum_{i=1}^{n} (f_Y(y_i|\theta_i, \lambda) I_{\{y_i<T\}} + P(y_i \geq T|\theta_i, \lambda) I_{\{y_i \geq T\}})$$

where $I_{\{y_i<T\}}$ and $I_{\{y_i \geq T\}}$ are indicator functions, which equals to 1 if the predicate holds, otherwise 0. It is easy to see that the log-likelihood function includes two parts: if y_i is observed in the future interval, we use its real density in the function; otherwise, we are only able to use the probability of $y_i \geq T$ in the function. By plugging in $\log \theta_i = -\mathbf{X}_i\boldsymbol{\beta}$, we can get the log-likelihood with parameters $\boldsymbol{\beta}$ and λ:

$$LL_W(\boldsymbol{\beta}, \lambda) = \sum_{i=1}^{n} I_{\{y_i<T\}} \log \frac{\lambda y_i^{\lambda-1}}{e^{-\lambda \mathbf{X}_i\boldsymbol{\beta}}} - \sum_{i=1}^{n} (\frac{y_i}{e^{-\mathbf{X}_i\boldsymbol{\beta}}})^\lambda \quad (7)$$

We refer this model as Weibull model.

4.2.4 Model under Geometric Distribution

In this case, we assume relationship building time Y_i for each training pair is independent of each other, following the same geometric distribution family, but with different success probability p_i. Under this assumption, the expectation for each random variable Y_i, $E(Y_i) = \frac{1-p_i}{p_i}$. We then let $E(Y_i) = \exp\{-\mathbf{X}_i\boldsymbol{\beta}\}$, namely, $\log \frac{1-p_i}{p_i} = -\mathbf{X}_i\boldsymbol{\beta}$. The log-likelihood function is then:

$$\begin{aligned} & LL_G(\boldsymbol{\beta}) \\ &= \sum_{i=1}^{n} (Pr(Y_i = y_i) I_{\{y_i<T\}} + P(y_i \geq T) I_{\{y_i \geq T\}}) \\ &= \sum_{i=1}^{n} (-I_{\{y_i<T\}}(-\mathbf{X}_i\boldsymbol{\beta}) + (y_i+1)(-\mathbf{X}_i\boldsymbol{\beta} - \log(e^{-\mathbf{X}_i\boldsymbol{\beta}} + 1))) \end{aligned} \quad (8)$$

We refer this model as geometric model.

4.3 Model Learning

The learning of the models is becoming an optimization problem, which aims at finding $\hat{\boldsymbol{\beta}}$ and other parameters (*e.g.*, $\hat{\lambda}$ in the Weibull model) that maximize the log-likelihood. As there are no closed form solutions for Eq. 7 and Eq. 8, we use standard Newton-Raphson method to derive the update formulas, which are based on the first derivative and second derivative (Hessian matrix) of the log-likelihood function. The learning algorithms for Weibull model and geometric model are introduced as below.

4.3.1 The Learning Algorithm for Weibull Model

For Weibull model, there are two sets of parameters, namely, the coefficients for each topological feature $\boldsymbol{\beta}$ and the shape parameter λ. An iterative algorithm is proposed to solve this model, where $\boldsymbol{\beta}$ and λ are updated alternatively. Initially, we set $\lambda^{(0)} = 1$, and at the t-th iteration, $\boldsymbol{\beta}$ and λ are updated using the Newton-Raphson method:

- Updating $\boldsymbol{\beta}$ with $\lambda = \lambda^{(t)}$ by setting $\boldsymbol{\beta}^{(t+1)} = \max_{\boldsymbol{\beta}} LL_W(\boldsymbol{\beta}, \lambda^{(t)})$, where $\boldsymbol{\beta}^{(t+1)}$ is derived using an inner iteration of Newton-Raphson method:

  $$\boldsymbol{\beta}^{(t'+1)} = \boldsymbol{\beta}^{(t')} - [H\ LL_W(\boldsymbol{\beta}^{(t')}, \lambda^{(t)})]^{-1} \nabla LL_W(\boldsymbol{\beta}^{(t')}, \lambda^{(t)})$$

  where t' is the inner iteration number, H denotes the Hessian matrix and ∇ denotes the first derivative of function LL_W for $\boldsymbol{\beta}$.

- Updating λ with $\boldsymbol{\beta} = \boldsymbol{\beta}^{(t+1)}$ by setting $\lambda^{(t+1)} = \max_\lambda LL_W(\boldsymbol{\beta}^{(t+1)}, \lambda)$, where λ^{t+1} is derived using another inner iteration of Newton-Raphson method:

  $$\lambda^{(t'+1)} = \lambda^{(t')} - [H\ LL_W(\boldsymbol{\beta}^{(t+1)}, \lambda^{(t')})]^{-1} \nabla LL_W(\boldsymbol{\beta}^{(t+1)}, \lambda^{(t')})$$

  where t' is the inner iteration number, H denotes the Hessian matrix and ∇ denotes the first derivative of function LL_W for λ.

Please refer to Appendix A for the concrete formulas for Hessian matrices and first derivatives for β and λ. Note that, as for discrete time we may observe 0 for y_i's, which will cause ill-condition of the log-likelihood. Therefore, we will add a small time gap δy to all y_i's in the training period and extract the gap in the test period.

4.3.2 The Learning Algorithm for Geometric Model

For geometric model, there is only one set of parameters β, and we directly use Newton-Raphson method to optimize the objective function LL_G:

$$\beta^{(t+1)} = \beta^{(t)} - [H\ LL_G(\beta^{(t)})]^{-1} \nabla LL_G(\beta^{(t)})$$

where t is the iteration number, H denotes the Hessian matrix and ∇ denotes the first derivative of function LL_G for β.

Please refer to Appendix B for the concrete formulas for Hessian matrix and first derivative for β.

4.4 Model Inference

Once the parameters such as β and λ are learned from the training data set through MLE, we can apply the model to the test pairs of objects, as long as their topological features in the historical network are given. Let the learned parameter values be $\hat{\beta}$ and $\hat{\lambda}$ for β and λ, and let the topological feature vector for the test pairs be $\mathbf{X}_{test}$ (with constant 1 as the first dimension), we now consider three types of questions people may be interested in for the new relationship building time, and provide the solutions in the following.

1. Whether a new relationship between two test objects will be built within t years?

   This question is equal to the query for the probability $Pr(y_{test} \leq t)$, which can be evaluated by plugging in the MLE estimators to derive the distribution parameters. Notice that for traditional link prediction tasks, t should be the same as the length of training interval. For our task, t can be any nonnegative values. For Weibull model, we have:

$$\hat{\theta}_{test} = \exp\{-\mathbf{X}_{test}\hat{\beta}\}$$
$$Pr(y_{test} \leq t) = 1 - \exp\{-(\frac{t}{\hat{\theta}_{test}})^{\hat{\lambda}}\} \tag{9}$$

   For geometric model, we have:

$$\hat{p}_{test} = \frac{1}{\exp\{-\mathbf{X}_{test}\hat{\beta}\} + 1}$$
$$Pr(y_{test} \leq t) = 1 - (1 - \hat{p}_{test})^{t+1} \tag{10}$$

2. What is the average relationship building time for two test objects?

   This is simply the query for $E(Y_{test})$. Using the same estimators for $\hat{\theta}_{test}$ and $\hat{p}_{test}$ as above, we can have the estimator for $E(Y_{test})$ as $E(Y_{test}) = \hat{\theta}_{test}\Gamma(1 + \frac{1}{\hat{\lambda}})$ for Weibull model, where $\Gamma(\cdot)$ is the Gamma function, and $E(Y_{test}) = \frac{1-\hat{p}_{test}}{\hat{p}_{test}}$ for geometric model.

3. The quantile: by when a relationship will be built with a probability α?

   This is equal to query for the solution of $F_Y(y_{test}) = \alpha$, and we can get answers as $y_{test} = \hat{\theta}_{test}(-\log(1-\alpha))^{\frac{1}{\hat{\lambda}}}$ for Weibull model, and $y_{test} = \max\{\frac{\log(1-\alpha)}{\log(1-\hat{p}_{test})} - 1, 0\}$ for geometric model. When $\alpha = 0.5$, the quantile is just the median.

5. EXPERIMENTS

In this section, we apply our methodology on DBLP bibliographic network, and select the target relation as the author citation relationship ($A - P \rightarrow P - A$). The goal is to study the effectiveness of our time-involved relationship prediction model in the heterogeneous network scenario.

5.1 The Dataset

We select a subset of authors in the DBLP bibliographic network, who published more than 5 papers in top conferences in four areas[1] that are related to data mining between year 1996 and 2000 ($T_0 = [1996, 2000]$). The total number of the author set is 2721. Then we sampled 7000 pairs of authors in the form of $\langle a_i, a_j \rangle$ that a_i did not cite a_j in T_0, but have citation relationship between year 2001 and 2009 ($T_1 = [2001, 2009]$ and $T = 9$) as positive samples; and we sampled another 7000 pairs of authors that have no citation relationship during either T_0 or T_1. The citation relationship is defined if a_i cites papers written by a_j published before year 2000. Notice that, we have this time constraint for papers as we want to infer citation relationship via the historical network. 19 topological features introduced in Sec. 3 are calculated for each year in T_0 and then aggregated together. The first (relative) time of the citation relationship is recorded for each pair of authors; and if there is no citation relationship between them in T_1, the time is recorded as a value bigger than 9.

5.2 Experimental Setting

In order to show the power of using time-involved model in relationship prediction, we use logistic regression [15] (denoted as *logistic*) that is frequently used in binary link prediction tasks as the baseline. Notice that, the output of the logistic regression is a probability denoting whether a relationship will be built in T_1 for each test pair. In our models, the output is the parameter set for the distribution of the relationship building time, from which we can infer much more information rather than a simple probability. We denote our models with different distribution assumptions as *GLM_geo*, *GLM_exp*, and *GLM_weib* respectively.

To compare the four models, we use two sets of measures to evaluate the effectiveness of each model. First, we measure the effectiveness according to the predicted probability for each relationship. We define the *accuracy* of the relationship prediction as the ratio between the number of correctly predicted relationship (under the *cut-off* 0.5) and the total number of the test pairs. Also, another frequently used measure AUC (the area under ROC curve) [3] is used to compare the accuracy.

Second, we directly compare the predicted time with the ground truth, among our proposed models. Mean absolute error (MAE) that is the mean of the absolute error between predicted relationship building time and the ground truth is used. Also, we use the ratio of the relationships that occur in some confidence interval derived from the models as another measure to test the accuracy of the predicted time. Notice that, relationships yet to happen are not considered in these two measures.

[1]Data Mining: KDD, PKDD, ICDM, SDM, PAKDD; Database: SIGMOD Conference, VLDB, ICDE, PODS, EDBT; Information Retrieval: SIGIR, ECIR, ACL, WWW, CIKM; and Machine Learning: NIPS, ICML, ECML, AAAI, IJCAI.

Table 2: Relationship Prediction Accuracy Comparison

	$T = 1$		$T = 5$		$T = 9$	
	Acc.	AUC	Acc.	AUC	Acc.	AUC
logistic	**0.9312**	**0.7356**	**0.7097**	0.7751	0.6995	**0.8083**
GLM-geo	0.9310	0.7037	0.6909	**0.7758**	0.6659	0.8021
GLM-exp	0.9304	0.7262	0.6922	0.7680	**0.7096**	0.7917
GLM-weib	0.9304	0.7273	0.6915	0.7680	0.7031	0.7917

All the results in this section are the average results using 10-fold cross-validation.

5.3 Prediction Power Study

We now compare our time-involved models with the baseline logistic regression, using the first set of measures.

First, we vary the future interval used in the training stage T_1^{train} (with the length T^{train}) and test stage T_1^{test} (with the length T^{test}) but force them the same ($T = T^{train} = T^{test}$), and compare the predicted probability of the relationship building within time T ($Pr(y_{test}) < T$) for test pairs. The results are summarized in Table 2. From the results, we can see that logistic regression has the best overall performance in predicting the *probability* of relationship building, when the training future interval equals to the test future interval.

Next, we test the generality power for different models, namely, when the training future interval is not equal to the test future interval ($T^{train} \neq T^{test}$). On one hand, we may want to know the probability of relationship building within each year in the training interval ($T^{test} < T^{train}$); on the other hand, we may want to infer longer term probability given a short term training interval ($T^{test} > T^{train}$). We show the two cases in Table 3 and Table 4. Notice that, since logistic regression can only output the probability when $T^{test} = T^{train}$, we use the same predicted probability for different test intervals. In Table 3, we fix the training interval with length $T^{train} = 9$, namely, $T_1^{train} = [2001, 2009]$, and vary the test intervals with length from 1 to 4. We can see that when T^{test} is small, time-involved models can give much better prediction accuracy, especially in terms of the measure *accuracy*. In other words, time-involved models carry more information in telling the probability of relationship building in finer time periods. In Table 4, we fix the test interval with length $T^{test} = 9$ and vary the training intervals with length from 2 to 5. We can see that, time-involved models can better utilize the short term training than logistic regression, and output better prediction results for longer term relationship building behavior. It is interesting to notice that by using the measure AUC, which does not require users to specify a *cut-off* value in the predicted probabilities, the performance of logistic regression is still comparable with other models. This is due to AUC only uses the ranking order of the predicted values, while *accuracy* requires that the *absolute values* of the predicted probabilities are also correct.

In all, for time-involved model, it contains more information and can answer different questions and with strong generalization power. Logistic regression can only answer the question of whether a link will happen or not, given a fixed time interval, and the experiments show that it has the strength in answering this certain type of question. However, if we are asking more, it fails in most of the scenarios.

5.4 Time Prediction Accuracy Study

We now evaluate the predicted time using different time-involved models. Here, we use the predicted median time as the predicted time. Table 5 shows the MAE between the predicted median time and the ground truth under different training and test intervals. It turns out that *GLM-exp* has the lowest error. Also, both *GLM-exp* and *GLM-weib* perform even better using shorter interval as training, whereas *GLM-geo* has the opposite behavior, that is, longer term of training leads to better performance. Notice that, we only calculate the error for the positive relationships happened in the test interval.

Table 5: *MAE* of Predicted Time with the Ground Truth

	$T^{train} = 5, T^{test} = 9$	$T^{train} = 9, T^{test} = 9$
GLM-geo	4.9883	4.7219
GLM-exp	**2.7774**	**3.0685**
GLM-weib	3.1025	3.1692

In Table 6, we infer different confidence intervals from the predicted relationship building time distribution, and test the ratio of the true relationship in different confidence intervals. A confidence interval (range) rather than a simple value, say the median time, can give users a better view of the relationship building time. It is shown that *GLM-exp* and *GLM-weib* has a higher ratio of giving correct confidence intervals for the true relationship building time, especially when using a small confidence interval. This is very useful in practice as they can give tight bound estimations.

5.5 Case Studies

To better understand the output of our model, we now show a case study of citation relationship between "Philip S. Yu" and other candidates. The model is trained by *GLM-weib* using a training interval of 9 years ($T_1^{train} = [2001, 2009]$), with the learned parameter $\lambda = 0.9331$, slightly less than 1, which means the citation relationship has a higher hazard happening at an earlier time. The ground truth of the citation building time, and the predicted median, mean, 25% quantile and 75% quantile for several test pairs are shown in Table 7. It can be seen that the predicted median and confidence interval are very suggestive for predicting the true citation relationship building time. For those authors whose predicted being cited time is significantly different from the ground truth, in-depth studies may be needed. For example David Maier is a prolific researcher in database area, and by intuition as well as suggested by the model, Philip should cite him. However, the ground truth says otherwise. Furthermore, this function can be used to recommend authors to any author in DBLP for citation purpose.

For the above model, the learned *top-4* most important topological features with the highest coefficients are:

1. $A - P - T - P - A$, namely, if two authors are very similar in terms of writing similar topics, they tend to cite each other;
2. $A - P \leftarrow P \rightarrow P - A$, namely, if two authors are very similar in terms of being frequently co-cited by the common papers, they tend to cite each other;
3. $A - P - A - P \rightarrow P - A$, namely, an author tends to cite the authors that are frequently cited by her co-authors;
4. $A - P - T - P - A - P \rightarrow P - A$, namely, if two authors are similar in terms writing similar topics, they tend to cite the same authors.

These topological features provide insightful knowledge for people in understanding the citation relationship building.

Table 3: Prediction Generalization Power Comparison: $T^{test} < T^{train}$ and $T^{train} = 9$

	$T^{test} = 1$		$T^{test} = 2$		$T^{test} = 3$		$T^{test} = 4$	
	Accuracy	AUC	Accuracy	AUC	Accuracy	AUC	Accuracy	AUC
logistic	0.7106	0.7619	0.7246	**0.7535**	0.7669	0.7347	**0.7349**	**0.7731**
GLM-geo	0.9284	**0.7626**	0.8436	0.7532	**0.7829**	**0.7657**	0.7347	0.7696
GLM-exp	**0.9290**	0.7553	**0.8442**	0.7464	0.7821	0.7569	0.7328	0.7603
GLM-weib	0.9287	0.7273	0.8441	0.7452	0.7826	0.7559	0.7334	0.7597

Table 4: Prediction Generalization Power Comparison: $T^{test} > T^{train}$ and $T^{test} = 9$

	$T^{train} = 2$		$T^{train} = 3$		$T^{train} = 4$		$T^{train} = 5$	
	Accuracy	AUC	Accuracy	AUC	Accuracy	AUC	Accuracy	AUC
logistic	0.5157	0.7810	0.5379	0.7805	0.5599	0.7841	0.5952	0.7896
GLM-geo	0.5942	**0.7910**	0.6209	**0.7926**	0.6366	**0.7902**	0.6522	**0.7982**
GLM-exp	0.5015	0.7802	0.5214	0.7833	0.6709	0.7841	**0.7143**	0.7870
GLM-weib	**0.7081**	0.7816	**0.7021**	0.7832	**0.7002**	0.7833	0.7103	0.7862

6. RELATED WORK

The link prediction problem has been first studied on homogeneous networks. Early works mainly study unsupervised methods [1, 12], namely they propose different similarity measures according to either topological structures of the networks or proximity of object attributes that are consistent with the link appearance in the future. Later, supervised methods that are able to combine different features with different coefficients via training data sets are proposed by different studies [7, 21, 13]. A recent study [10] has discussed the link prediction problem when the network is not fully observed and thus is modeled in a probabilistic way. A survey in link prediction can be found in [6]. In this paper, we extend the link prediction problem to the more general heterogeneous networks, by extending link prediction to relationship prediction and exploring the topological features in such scenarios.

Recently, some studies [4, 11] propose frequent graph pattern mining-based methodology to detect graph evolution rules, which provides some clues for proposing new topological features in the network for link prediction. However, the focus on the two papers are still on homogeneous networks, and they have not considered how different frequent evolution patterns affect the link formation speed yet. That is, this methodology cannot answer the "when" problem of link formation.

Another line of study similar to our problem is the link prediction task in relational data [15, 19], as relational data also involves different types of objects and complex relationships between objects. However, these studies have a focus different from our paper. As in [15], they study feature selection in a relational environment using relational languages, and feed these features into supervised link prediction models; for [19], their goal is to model the relational data via a probabilistic model. In our paper, we aim at designing a model for relationship building time by systematically exploring the topological features in heterogeneous networks.

A novel meta path-based similarity measure called PathSim is proposed in [17], which also defines the framework of similarity measure in a heterogeneous network scenario. In [16], the authors study the relationship prediction problem using co-authorship prediction as a case study in the heterogeneous network. However, they have not systematically study the relationship prediction in a general case and they are only focus on the "whether" problem rather than the "when" problem. In this paper, we build a framework for general relationship prediction in heterogeneous networks by systematically extracting meta path-based topological features, and study when the relationship will happen in the future.

The general setting of link prediction task is set by Liben-Nowell and Kleinberg [12], which is to predict *whether* a link between two existing objects will be added to the network during the time interval $[t, t + \Delta t]$ given the snapshot of the network at time t. In other words, the task has not considered the issue *when* a link will appear in this time interval. Recently, several studies have considered the extension on usage of time. In [20], a methodology that assigns weights to events and edges according to their appearing time is proposed, which produces better link prediction accuracy by using more time information in the feature side. In [8], a time series model is proposed to predict the frequency of repeated links in networks. In comparison to these studies, our paper focuses on the new relationship prediction and aims at modeling the relationship building time in the future.

In all, in this paper, we extend the traditional link prediction in homogeneous networks into relationship prediction in the more complex heterogeneous networks, and aims at modeling the relationship building time in the future.

7. CONCLUSIONS AND FUTURE WORK

In this paper, we propose a new problem of study relationship building time prediction in heterogeneous networks. This problem on one hand extends the traditional link prediction problem in homogeneous networks into relationship prediction in heterogonous networks; and on the other hand it extends the traditional "whether a link will happen in a fixed future interval" to "when it will happen." We systematically study how to define relationship and how to select topological features in heterogeneous networks, using a meta path-based concept. Time-involved relationship prediction models are proposed. Experiments have shown the effectiveness of our proposed models.

Predicting relationship building time is still an open problem. It is worth of considering a broader range of target relations in different heterogeneous networks, and propose a systematic methodology of model selection and model comparison. More future work can be done along this line.

8. REFERENCES

[1] L. A. Adamic and E. Adar. Friends and neighbors on the web. *SOCIAL NETWORKS*, 25:211–230, 2001.

Table 6: Ratio of the True Relationship Occurring in Different Confidence Intervals: $T^{test} = 9$

	25%-75%		10%-90%		0%-80%	
	$T^{train} = 9$	$T^{train} = 5$	$T^{train} = 9$	$T^{train} = 5$	$T^{train} = 9$	$T^{train} = 5$
GLM-geo	0.5489	0.5336	**0.8936**	**0.8947**	0.9650	0.9743
GLM-exp	0.7167	0.7246	0.8619	0.8634	0.9880	0.9889
GLM-weib	**0.7278**	**0.7314**	0.8680	0.8686	**0.9884**	**0.9896**

Table 7: Case Studies of Relationship Building Time Prediction

a_i	a_j	Ground Truth	Median	Mean	25% quantile	75% quantile
Philip S. Yu	Ling Liu	1	2.2386	3.4511	0.8549	4.7370
Philip S. Yu	Christian S. Jensen	3	2.7840	4.2919	1.0757	5.8911
Philip S. Yu	C. Lee Giles	0	8.3985	12.9474	3.2450	17.7717
Philip S. Yu	Stefano Ceri	0	0.5729	0.8833	0.2214	1.2124
Philip S. Yu	David Maier	9+	2.5675	3.9581	0.9920	5.4329
Philip S. Yu	Tong Zhang	9+	9.5371	14.7028	3.6849	20.1811
Philip S. Yu	Rudi Studer	9+	9.7752	15.0698	3.7769	20.6849

[2] A. L. Barabasi, H. Jeong, Z. Neda, E. Ravasz, A. Schubert, and T. Vicsek. Evolution of the social network of scientific collaborations. *arXiv:cond-mat/0104162v1*, Apr 2001.

[3] A. P. Bradley. The use of the area under the ROC curve in the evaluation of machine learning algorithms. *Pattern Recognition*, 30(7):1145–1159, July 1997.

[4] B. Bringmann, M. Berlingerio, F. Bonchi, and A. Gionis. Learning and predicting the evolution of social networks. *IEEE Intelligent Systems*, 25:26–35, 2010.

[5] A. J. Dobson. *An Introduction to Generalized Linear Models, Second Edition.* Chapman & Hall/CRC, November 2001.

[6] L. Getoor and C. P. Diehl. Link mining: a survey. *SIGKDD Explor. Newsl.*, 7:3–12, December 2005.

[7] M. A. Hasan, V. Chaoji, S. Salem, and M. Zaki. Link prediction using supervised learning. In *Proc. of SDM '06 workshop on Link Analysis, Counterterrorism and Security*, 2006.

[8] Z. Huang and D. K. J. Lin. The time-series link prediction problem with applications in communication surveillance. *INFORMS J. on Computing*, 21:286–303, April 2009.

[9] L. Katz. A new status index derived from sociometric analysis. *Psychometrika*, 18(1):39 – 43, 1953.

[10] V. Leroy, B. B. Cambazoglu, and F. Bonchi. Cold start link prediction. In *KDD '10*, 2010.

[11] C. W.-k. Leung, E.-P. Lim, D. Lo, and J. Weng. Mining interesting link formation rules in social networks. In *CIKM '10*, 2010.

[12] D. Liben-Nowell and J. Kleinberg. The link prediction problem for social networks. In *CIKM '03*, pages 556–559, 2003.

[13] R. N. Lichtenwalter, J. T. Lussier, and N. V. Chawla. New perspectives and methods in link prediction. In *KDD '10*, 2010.

[14] M. E. J. Newman. Clustering and preferential attachment in growing networks. *Physical Review Letters E*, 64, 2001.

[15] A. Popescul, R. Popescul, and L. H. Ungar. Statistical relational learning for link prediction. In *Proc. of the Workshop on Learning Statistical Models from Relational Data at IJCAI-2003.*, 2003.

[16] Y. Sun, R. Barber, M. Gupta, C. C. Aggarwal, and J. Han. Co-author relationship prediction in heterogeneous bibliographic networks. In *ASONAM' 11*, 2011.

[17] Y. Sun, J. Han, X. Yan, P. S. Yu, and T. Wu. Pathsim: Meta path-based top-k similarity search in heterogeneous information networks. In *VLDB' 11*, 2011.

[18] J. Tang, J. Zhang, L. Yao, J. Li, L. Zhang, and Z. Su. Arnetminer: extraction and mining of academic social networks. In *KDD '08*, 2008.

[19] B. Taskar, M. fai Wong, P. Abbeel, and D. Koller. Link prediction in relational data. In *NIP '03*, 2003.

[20] T. Tylenda, R. Angelova, and S. Bedathur. Towards time-aware link prediction in evolving social networks. In *Proceedings of the 3rd Workshop on Social Network Mining and Analysis*, SNA-KDD '09, pages 9:1–9:10, 2009.

[21] C. Wang, V. Satuluri, and S. Parthasarathy. Local probabilistic models for link prediction. In *ICDM '07*, pages 322–331, 2007.

APPENDIX

A. FORMULAS FOR WEIBULL MODEL

- First derivative and Hessian matrix for $\boldsymbol{\beta}$:

$$\nabla LL_W(\boldsymbol{\beta}) = -(-\lambda \mathbf{X}'(I_{\{Y<T\}}) + \lambda \mathbf{X}' \exp\{\lambda(\log(Y)\mathbf{X}\boldsymbol{\beta})\})$$

$$H\ LL_W(\boldsymbol{\beta}) = -\lambda^2((\mathbf{X}. * (\exp\{\lambda(\log(Y) + \mathbf{X}\boldsymbol{\beta})\}\mathbf{1}_{1\times p}))'\mathbf{X})$$

- First derivative and second derivative for λ:

$$\nabla LL_W(\lambda) = \sum_i (\frac{I_{\{y_i<T\}}}{\lambda} + \lambda(\log(y_i) + \mathbf{X}_i\boldsymbol{\beta}) - (\log(y_i) + \mathbf{X}\boldsymbol{\beta}) \exp\{\lambda(\log(y_i) + \mathbf{X}_i\boldsymbol{\beta})\})$$

$$H\ LL_W(\lambda) = \sum_i (-\frac{I_{\{y_i<T\}}}{\lambda^2} - (\log(y_i) + \mathbf{X}_i\boldsymbol{\beta})^2 \exp\{\lambda(\log(y_i) + \mathbf{X}_i\boldsymbol{\beta})\})$$

B. FORMULAS FOR GEOMETRIC MODEL

- First derivative and Hessian matrix for $\boldsymbol{\beta}$:

$$\eta = \exp\{-\mathbf{X}\boldsymbol{\beta}\}$$

$$\nabla LL_G(\boldsymbol{\beta}) = -\mathbf{X}'(-(I_{\{Y<T\}}) + Y + \mathbf{1}_{n\times 1})./(\eta + \mathbf{1}_{n\times 1})$$

$$H\ LL_G(\boldsymbol{\beta}) = -((Y + \mathbf{1}_{n\times 1}). * \eta./(\eta + \mathbf{1}_{n\times 1}).^2))\mathbf{X}\mathbf{1}_{1\times p})'\mathbf{X}$$

The Life and Death of Online Groups: Predicting Group Growth and Longevity

Sanjay Kairam
Stanford University
Computer Science
sanjay.kairam@gmail.com

Dan J. Wang
Stanford University
Sociology
djwang@stanford.edu

Jure Leskovec
Stanford University
Computer Science
jure@cs.stanford.edu

ABSTRACT

We pose a fundamental question in understanding how to identify and design successful communities: What factors predict whether a community will grow and survive in the long term? Social scientists have addressed this question extensively by analyzing offline groups which endeavor to attract new members, such as social movements, finding that new individuals are influenced strongly by their ties to members of the group. As a result, prior work on the growth of communities has treated growth primarily as a diffusion processes, leading to findings about group evolution which can be difficult to explain. The proliferation of online social networks and communities, however, has created new opportunities to study, at a large scale and with very fine resolution, the mechanisms which lead to the formation, growth, and demise of online groups.

In this paper, we analyze data from several thousand online social networks built on the Ning platform with the goal of understanding the factors contributing to the growth and longevity of groups within these networks. Specifically, we investigate the role that two types of growth (growth through diffusion and growth by other means) play during a group's formative stages from the perspectives of both the individual member and the group. Applying these insights to a population of groups of different ages and sizes, we build a model to classify groups which will grow rapidly over the short-term and long-term. Our model achieves over 79% accuracy in predicting group growth over the following two months and over 78% accuracy in predictions over the following two years. We utilize a similar approach to predict which groups will die within a year. The results of our combined analysis provide insight into how both early non-diffusion growth and a complex set of network constraints appear to contribute to the initial and continued growth and success of groups within social networks. Finally we discuss implications of this work for the design, maintenance, and analysis of online communities.

Categories and Subject Descriptors: H.2.8 [**Database Management**]: Database applications – *Data mining*

General Terms: Measurement; Theory.

Keywords: Social Networks, Group Formation, Online Communities, Information Diffusion

Permission to make digital or hard copies of all or part of this work for personal or classroom use is granted without fee provided that copies are not made or distributed for profit or commercial advantage and that copies bear this notice and the full citation on the first page. To copy otherwise, to republish, to post on servers or to redistribute to lists, requires prior specific permission and/or a fee.
WSDM'12, February 8–12, 2012, Seattle, Washington, USA.
Copyright 2012 ACM 978-1-4503-0747-5/12/02 ...$10.00.

1. INTRODUCTION

The formation and evolution of groups has long been a focus in social science research. While the proliferation of online communities has made it possible to study the dynamics of group membership in richer detail than ever before [2, 15, 19, 31], several important questions about the factors that influence group growth remain unresolved. Why do some groups grow faster than others? Why do some groups continue to attract new members over time while others do not? What causes groups to *stop* growing? These fundamental questions in the study of group dynamics have important implications for research on communities, both online and offline.

Motivation. Researchers have only recently begun to take advantage of large-scale data from online social networks and communities to study the dynamics of group formation and evolution. A key motivation in this paper is not only to contribute to the understanding of the relationship between structural features of a group and its future growth, but also to understand how this relationship might change over time. While past work has measured growth rates over a fixed period of time, there is no reason to expect that what makes groups grow fast in the short-term is the same as what makes them grow fast or continue growing over longer periods. In addition, past research has not examined future growth rates as a function of past growth or a group's current size or age. These gaps represent important issues in the study of online communities.

We also seek to address unresolved questions from the more recent work on social networks and group evolution. Prior research on online community growth has resulted in sometimes puzzling findings indicating that ties spanning group boundaries may induce individuals to join a group while also slowing down overall growth. In this work, we are motivated in part by the desire to explain these seemingly inconsistent results.

An Empirical Puzzle. Past research in the social sciences has advanced important, but sometimes, conflicting hypotheses about the relationship between group growth and group network structure. Citing the example of a Boston community which failed to cultivate enough support to preserve itself aganst a threat, Granovetter hypothesizes that this community failed to grow because it was too clustered, though this hypothesis is not tested empirically [12]. The intuition is that if the members of a group have a disproportionate amount of friendship or communication ties with people within the group (as opposed to with individuals outside the group) then the group is too inwardly focused to ever grow. For Granovetter, weak ties outside of the group could have facilitated the mobilization of resources from members outside the community to defend against being taken over by adjacent neighborhoods.

The strength of Granovetter's 'weak ties' traditionally lies in their ability to facilitate the spread of information. Centola and Macy, however, identify that the act of joining a group may be

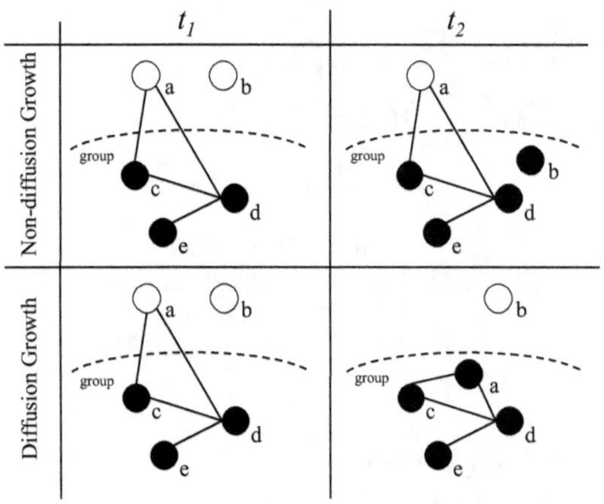

Figure 1: Illustration of diffusion vs. non-diffusion growth

categorically different from simply being informed of it [6]; using simulated networks, they provide examples of how such 'complex' contagions may not spread via weak ties in the same way [5, 6]. In contrast to Granovetter, Centola and Macy's results suggest that diffusion and growth processes in groups are facilitated by the presence of strong ties and clustering within the group.

Backstrom, et al. provide one of the first empirical investigations of group evolution using data from online social networks [2]. Examining the LiveJournal friendship network and DBLP coauthorship network, the authors identify how certain network structural features of a group influence its growth patterns over time. Their work casts group growth mainly as a diffusion process similar to Centola [6] and Granovetter [12] — that is, they assume that a group grows through the ties its members have to individuals outside the group. In other words, researchers envision membership status spreading through the network structure of a given community. Among other insights, they uncover the seemingly paradoxical finding that clustering in a group both attracts new members and decreases overall group growth, bearing out the predictions made by both Centola [6] and Granovetter [12].

Specifically, for an individual with social ties to members of a group, Backstrom, et al. find that the probability of joining the group increases with the number of ties among the individual's in-group friends. This suggests that as the clustering of a group increases, individuals with ties to the group will be more likely to join, boosting group growth. At the same time, however, the authors also find that as the ratio of open to closed triads in a group (a measure of clustering) increases, the average four-month growth rate of a group decreases. Thus, they leave a key question about their findings unresolved: If individuals with prior connections to a group are more likely to join a highly clustered group, then why do highly clustered groups experience lower growth rates overall?

1.1 Overview of Results

In this paper, we contribute to research on group evolution in social networks by making a conceptual difference between diffusion and non-diffusion growth in groups. Diffusion growth describes the process in which groups attract new members through ties to existing members; in these cases, the ties form the 'skeleton' over which membership spreads. In non-diffusion growht, individuals with no prior ties to any group members become members themselves. Here, group membership apepars to 'jump' across the community network. This is an important distinction not explicitly made in prior work, but vital to understanding why some groups grow larger, faster, and for longer preiods than others.

Figure 1 illustrates the difference between diffusion and non-diffusion growth in a group. In both scenarios at time t_1, nodes c, d, e are members of a group, and nodes a and b are not members. a, however, is connected to two of the group's members, whereas b has no ties to the group (borrowing the language of [2], we explain in section 3 that a is part of the group's *fringe*). The group experiences diffusion growth if at time t_2, a joins the group. The group experiences non-diffusion growth if b joins the group at time t_2.

Analysis of Diffusion and Non-Diffusion Growth. Our analysis focuses on the differences in the processes which govern diffusion and non-diffusion growth. In our two main analytical exercises, we explore the tension between these two types of growth as both outcomes and inputs in models of group formation and future growth. We conduct our analysis using data on online groups drawn from communities built on a common platform, Ning. Through empirical study of these networks, we explain the puzzling finding that clustering within a group can both increase the probability of a non-member joining and decrease the overall growth rate of a group.

We gain this insight by examining the mediating role that diffusion growth plays in explaining the relationship between clustering and group growth. Our main finding is that group clustering does increase the diffusion growth of a group, but that groups which grow primarily through diffusion reach smaller sizes eventually. In this way, the apparent inverse relationship between clustering and overall group growth is actually moderated by the different effects of group clustering on diffusion and non-diffusion growth. If a group is highly clustered, it is more likely to experience diffusion growth, but if more of a group's growth comes from diffusion, then it is also less likely to grow larger overall. In addition, we find that small groups within smaller communities tend to experience more diffusion growth than similarly sized groups in larger communities. This suggests that understanding group growth requires attention not only to aspects of individuals and the group, but also to the wider network setting in which these groups are situated.

Predicting Group Growth and Longevity. The second part of our analysis uses these insights about diffusion and non-diffusion growth to generate models which predict the growth and longevity of groups mined from a diverse set of thousands of independent networks. We analyze the predictive accuracy of various group structural features for two outcomes: (1) the *rate* of group growth over a fixed period of time, and (2) the *longevity* of a group's growth (i.e. the amount of time that passes before a group stops growing). Our models incorporate features capturing the rate of growth and the proportion of that growth occurring due to diffusion processes, as well as network features such as the group's transitivity and the size of cliques within groups. We demonstrate the effects of these features on group growth and longevity. In addition, we extend past work on group growth by predicting growth for groups at different stages of evolution (i.e. groups of different ages and sizes).

Specifically, we find that the predictive accuracy of certain group features is contingent on the current size and age of a group. For predicting short-term growth, models that incorporate past growth rates have the greatest accuracy. Models that include network structural features predict long-term growth more accurately. Regarding longevity, we find that the size of the largest clique within a group predicts positive growth more accurately than all other features. Our models using all features generally achieve AUC values greater than 0.78, meaning that we consistently perform better than chance, and our most accurate models achieves AUC close to 0.87. We utilize our findings to first show how features relevant to growth may vary depending on specific prediction goals and discuss how the results of our analysis can help inform insights about the struc-

Feature	All Groups	Small Grps	Large Grps
Number of Nodes	32.9	14.9	51.6
Number of Edges	108.2	25.4	194.3
Giant Component	.89	.86	.91
Transitivity	.30	.33	.28
Fringe Size	488.2	344.2	638.1
Longevity	336.4	283.9	390.9

Table 1: Network descriptive statistics for Ning group sample (mean values).

tural properties which predispose certain groups to continue growing and others to stop.

Finally, we conclude our paper with a discussion of the implications of our findings for future work on online communities and group evolution. We generalize our results to other settings and describe how past work can be reinterpreted in light of our findings. By paying closer attention to different types of growth processes, researchers can better focus their analysis on linking individual online behavior to macro dynamics of group formation and evolution. In addition, we contextualize our findings in practical applications by explaining how understanding group growth can help architects of online communities design platforms that better promotes membership and participation. We also discuss limitations of our work, open questions, and future directions for research.

2. RELATED WORK

The growth of groups in social networks has often been viewed as a diffusion process. Consequently, many researchers treated growth as a process similar to the diffusion of innovations [26] and other behaviors. Early studies, such as Milgram's small-world experiment [18], demonstrated that information could spread along social networks quickly, and Granovetter's theory of the "strength of weak ties" [12] provided a conceptual framework for how this might occur. Granovetter's theory explained these global patterns of information transmission using local features built into the structure of the network. It was natural, then, that social scientists interested in group evolution used the language of diffusion to describe how group growth.

Research on social movements is one area which has emphasized the importance of diffusion growth in groups. A *social movement* refers to the phenomenon in which a group of individuals join to take collective action in order to press for some social change or express some grievance against an authority figure. Consider, for example, the protest activity in the Middle East in February 2011 and the role played by social networks in mobilizing protestors [27]. Past work has shown that such movements grow by attracting individuals with prior ties to group members [9, 17]. Most social movement studies share the view that participants are recruited through pre-existing ties with group members [28], with estimates that 74-100% of members of such movements joining due to such ties [16].

Diffusion processes in group growth has also been the focus social science research in other settings. For example, sociologists and economists have investigated how pressure from co-workers can make individuals more likely to join labor unions [30]. In addition, in political parties and civic associations, membership growth is linked to the influence of existing members who recruit friends and families as new members [25]. Even studies of religious conversion take into account the effect of being associated with existing members of a given religion [29].

The shift to online tools for social organization has provided a host of new opportunities to study the dynamics of communities.

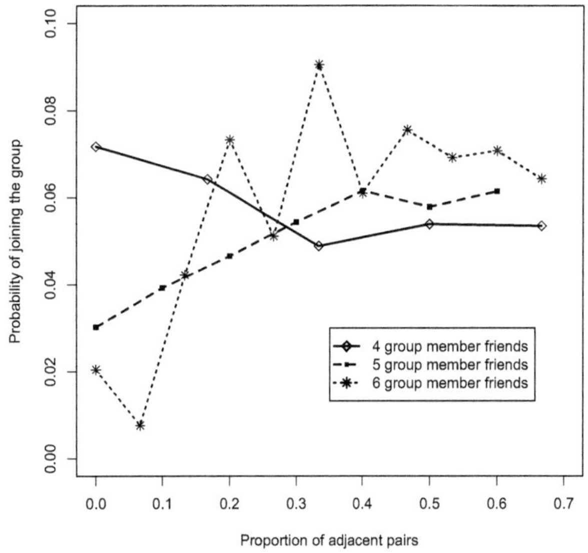

Figure 2: Proportion adjacent pairs vs. probability of fringe member joining.

While extensive research has focused on identifying implicit communities within networks [10, 15, 21], this is not our present goal. Other work has focused on capturing properties of explicitly defined groups within networks. Mislove, et al. analyze groups occuring in a variety of networks (Flickr, YouTube, Orkut, and LiveJournal) finding that they tend to overlap with highly clustered subgraphs of the network and that smaller groups exhibit higher clustering than larger ones [19]. Zheleva, et al. develop a theoretical model of how users in an evolving social network might affiliate which closely matches the observed properties of groups in Flickr [31].

Ducheneaut, et al. examine the impact of network features on the longevity of groups, finding that guilds in World of Warcraft with smaller subgroups and higher density survive longer; given the intensely goal-directed nature of these groups, they hypothesize that such structures reduce coordination problems [7]. As mentioned, our work is informed by Backstrom, et al.'s investigation of the formation and growth of groups in large social networks [2]. Our analysis starts by answering the open questions left by this prior work and goes on to develop a more comprehensive view of what predisposes some groups to rapid and continued growth. We also analyze groups within thousands of independently-formed social networks, which we believe improves the robustness and generalizability of our findings.

3. NING COMMUNITY DATA

The data for our analysis comes from the membership lists of communities built using Ning (`http://www.ning.com`), a web platform that allow users to create their own online social networks similar to Facebook. These online communities, which we call *Ning communities* serve a variety of interests ranging from small private networks for friends and families to public networks for larger organizations. Some of the largest networks belong to entertainment properties such as the Dallas Mavericks NBA Team (`http://friends.mavs.com`) and the rapper 50 Cent (`http://thisis50.com`).

Ning communities include a variety of social features including user profiles, forums, blogs, and groups. For each user in a Ning community, we observe their group affiliations and when they joined these groups. Only some communities in our data al-

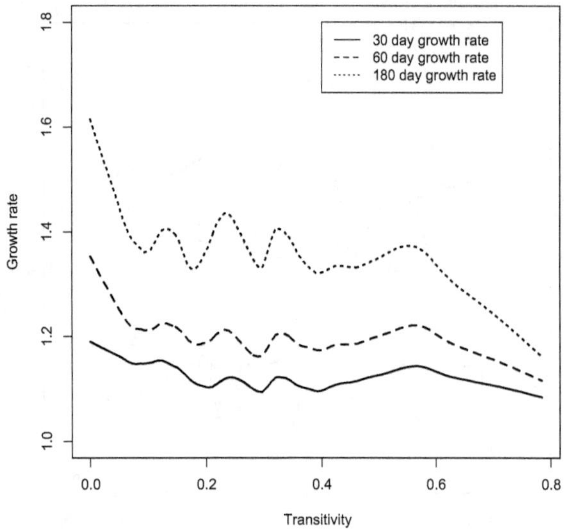

Figure 3: Future growth rates vs. transitivity for Ning groups with 50 members.

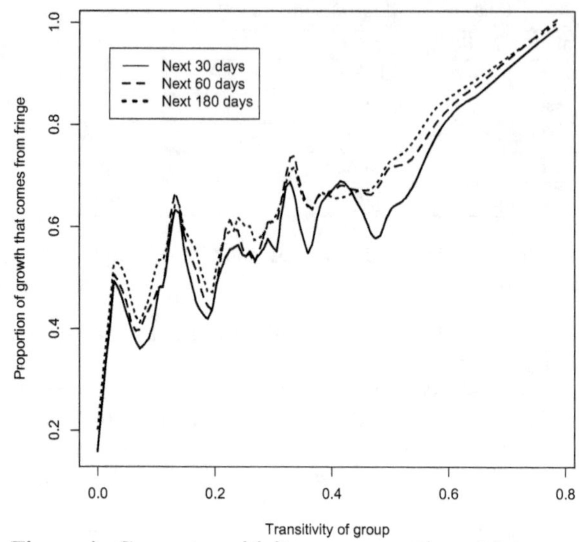

Figure 4: Group transitivity vs. proportion of future growth from the fringe.

low users to explicitly 'friend' other users. For all communities, however, social interactions on a page, such as replying to a user in a forum, are stored as user-to-user comments. In our analysis, we consider an edge to have been created between two users when they have exchanged at least one comment in each direction (reciprocal communication). We found that this formulation reduced issues due to spam messages which are often unreciprocated. While these implicit edges are different from the explicit edges based on 'friend' relationships, we find that they serve as suitable network structures for our analysis. Using the group affiliation data and the comment networks, it is possible to reconstruct the day-by-day evolution of groups within a Ning community.

4. GROUP GROWTH AND DIFFUSION

In the following subsections, we provide definitions for diffusion and non-diffusion growth. We then discuss how data was collected from Ning communities and groups to analyze how these interact with network clustering and overall growth.

4.1 Diffusion and Non-Diffusion Growth

We define diffusion growth as the addition to a group of new members with existing social ties to one or more group members (see Figure 1). Non-diffusion growth comes from new members with no prior ties to group members. This conceptual distinction leads to two hypotheses about why users join a group. Under diffusion growth, users may be influenced to join due to the behavior of their friends. In non-diffusion growth, users may join because there is a feature of the group itself (i.e. a common interest) which appeals to them. In these cases, a Ning community user might be exposed to the group through some means other than an invitation from a friend, such as banner ads on the Ning community website or a search for similar groups. It is, of course, possible that some users join groups based both on shared interests and influence from a friendship tie — which can be difficult to separate — but for our purposes, we designate users who join groups as part of either diffusion or non-diffusion growth to simplify our analysis [1].

To measure diffusion growth in a Ning group, we first consider a snapshot of the friendship network containing the members of a Ning group, G, at a given moment in its evolution, t_1. Second, we identify all users in the Ning community who are not members of the Ning group but who have *at least one tie* to the members of the Ning group. This set of users is what [2] call the group's fringe, f_G. Finally, we then obtain a snapshot of the Ning group network at t_2, where t_2 represents some fixed time after t_1 — call this new snapshot of the Ning group, G'. We then identify the members of G' that were not part of G as m, representing the overall growth of G from t_1 to t_2. The proportion of Ning users in m that were also in f_G signals the amount of growth in G attributable to diffusion growth whereas $(|m|/|m \cap f_G|)$ gives the total amount of non-diffusion growth in G from t_1 to t_2.

4.2 Sampling Ning Communities and Groups

For the analysis in this section, we sampled Ning groups and communities using the following rules. First, based on an examination of several groups, we set a lower threshold of 10 members for the final group size. Groups which did not grow larger than 10 members may represent 'failed attempts' or 'tire-kicking' by creators and thus would not be sensible to include in our sample. We also excluded all groups which grew to be larger than 50% of the surrounding community, as these may represent groups which are not distinct from the overall community (and thus would grow artificially large). In order to eliminate 'right-censoring' issues in assessing group growth over time, we considered only groups which had stopped adding new members 2 months prior to the end of the data collection period; while this may form an artificial constraint, it allows us to analyze groups according to their final size. Table 1 reports descriptive statistics for the sample of 4,051 Ning groups from 418 Ning communities used in the analysis below. In Table 1, 'small' groups are those smaller than the median group size in our sample (22 eventual members) 'small', and 'large' are those larger than the median.

4.3 Resolving the Clustering-Growth Paradox

Using our sample of Ning groups, we replicated experiments by Backstrom, et al. [2] concerning the effects of group clustering on future group growth and the probability of an individual in a group's fringe joining the group [2]. First, for each group, G, with 50 or more members, we obtain a snapshot of the group on the date, time t, on which it gained its 50th member. We then calculate the proportion of members in G's fringe, f_G, who joined the group after 180 days — we treat this as the probability of a fringe member joining the group. Then, for each group, we calculate the average

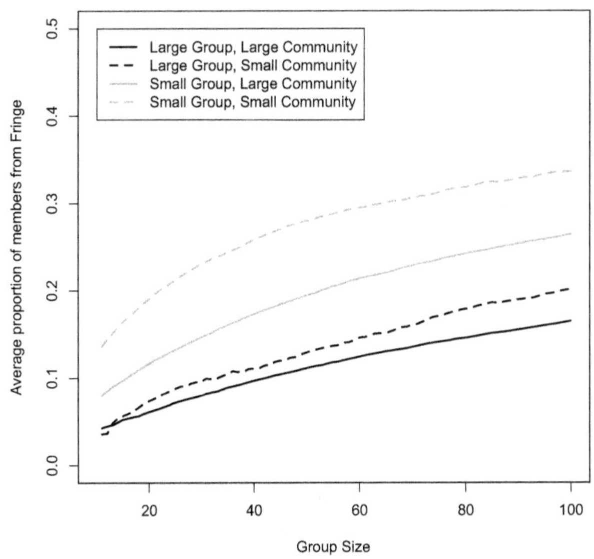

Figure 5: Proportion of group membership from fringe vs. current group size (by eventual group size).

proportion of adjacent pairs among a fringe member's group member friends. The proportion of adjacent pairs refers to the number of ties between a fringe member's group member friends divided the by the possible number of ties between them.

Figure 2 plots the average probability of a fringe member joining a group against the average proportion of adjacent pairs among this individual's in-group friends for all of the groups in our sample (with separate lines for fringe members with 4, 5, and 6 friends in the group). We observe a generally positive relationship between the proportion of adjacent pairs and the probability of a fringe member joining a group which strengthens with the number of friends that the fringe member has in the group. The explanation for this is intuitive. If non-member has six friends in the group who are highly clustered, the social pressure to join the group is stronger than that for a non-member who has only three friends in the group who are highly clustered.

In Figure 3, we also plotted the 30-, 60-, and 180-day future growth rates of Ning groups at size 50 against their clustering as measured by transitivity. The transitivity of a graph, G, is equal to the number of closed triads in G divided by the possible number of closed triads in G. According to Figure 3, the average future growth rate of a Ning group (of size 50) decreases as the current transitivity of a group increases. For example, for Ning groups that have transitivity = 0, 180-day growth rates exceed 1.6, whereas a highly clustered group, with transitivity = .8, experiences a 180-day growth rate of only 1.2.

The findings shown in Figures 2 and 3 show that group clustering appears to both increase and decrease future group growth across the wide range of groups and diverse communities available in the Ning data. Thus, the relationships that Backstrom, et al discover in their work are not particular to the LiveJournal or DBLP communities [2]. Having shown the general nature of this pattern, we now move on to explaining how it arises.

4.4 Network Clustering and Growth

Comparing diffusion and non-diffusion growth for Ning groups sheds light on these contradictory findings. In Figure 4, we plot the transitivity of a group at t, where t is equal to the time where a group reaches 50 members, against the proportion of its growth in the next 30, 60, and 180 days that comes from the fringe (i.e. diffu-

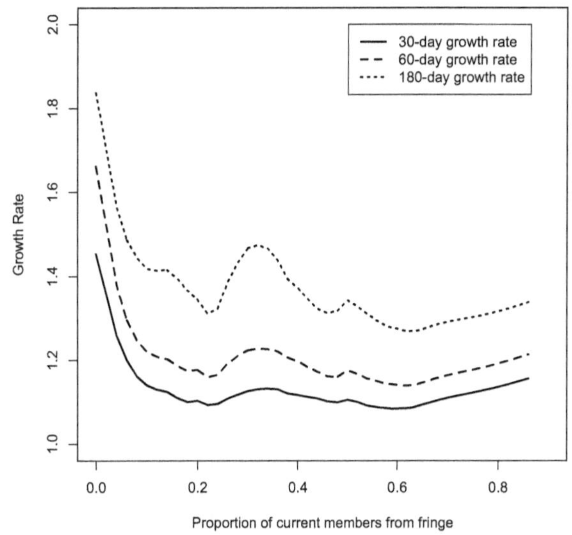

Figure 6: Proportion of current membership from fringe vs. future overall growth.

sion growth). We calculate the proportion of growth attributable to diffusion growth as described above. Figure 4 contains smoothed versions of line plots to facilitate interpretation.

The results from Figure 4 are clear. As the clustering of a group increases, the proportion of its future growth from its fringe also increases. However, even though group clustering promotes diffusion growth, this is not enough evidence to claim that higher clustering leads to greater overall growth. In fact, most of the confusion associated with the clustering-growth paradox comes from assuming that group growth is primarily achieved through diffusion growth.

Higher group clustering therefore leads to a greater proportion of its members joining diffusion growth. This, in turn, influences future rates of overall growth. Figure 5 illustrates the differences between small and large groups (embedded within small and large communities) in terms of their fringe and non-fringe membership composition over their first 100 members. To generate this graph, we divided groups into four categories based on 'final' group sizes and 'final' community sizes. We classify any group which never gains more than 113 members as 'small', and those which surpass 630 as 'large'. Communities with more than 2000 users are large, while those with less are small.

Figure 5 shows that in groups which eventually grow large, a smaller proportion of membership comes from the fringe than in groups which eventually grow small; moreover, this is true at any point in a group's growth from 10 to 100 members. In small Ning communities, groups which eventually grow larger than 630 members will gain only 10% of their first 40 members from the fringe, on average (black dotted line in Figure 5). In these same communities, groups which never grow larger than 113 members will gain 25% of their first 40 members from the fringe (gray dotted line in Figure 5).

The resolution to the growth-clustering paradox is evident from the patterns shown in Figures 4 and 6. Figure 4 shows that higher group clustering increases the proportion of growth which happens as a result of diffusion processes. Figure 6 shows that the group's overall growth rate decreases as the proportion of group membership coming from the fringe increases. Thus, we infer that higher clustering increases the amount of diffusion growth happening in a group, but decreases a group's growth rate overall.

We attribute this pattern to the notion that some groups grow by appealing to common interests and identities (non-diffusion growth) while other groups grow by virtue of its extra-group connections

Category	Feature	Description
Growth	Monthly Growth Rate	Fraction of users who joined in the prior month
	Fringe Growth Rate	Fraction of users who joined in the prior month who joined from the fringe
Connectivity	Group Transitivity	Transitivity of network formed by group members
	Transitivity Ratio	Ratio of group transitivity to transitivity of entire community
	Group Density	Density of network formed by group members
	Density Ratio	Ratio of group density to density of entire community
Structural	Clique Ratio	Largest fraction of group members whose edges form a clique
	Disconnected Ratio	Fraction of group members who are not a part of the group's largest connected component

Table 2: Features used in all growth and longevity models.

(diffusion growth). If a group relies on diffusion growth, it can only grow as much as the number of ties its members have to non-members. At some point, a group relying on diffusion growth, might run out of such ties, constraining its eventual growth. Thus, while clustering in a group can increase joining activity from the group's fringe, it can also diminish the group's overall growth.

Group growth and Ning community size. While Figure 5 offers insight into the relationship between the amount of growth a group experienced through diffusion and its future growth, it also shows how this dynamic operates for groups in different settings. While groups that reach eventually smaller sizes tend to experience more diffusion growth, we can also compare growth rates for eventually small groups in large communities and small communities.

According to Figure 5, among eventually small groups, those that were established in Ning communities that are eventually small tend to experience a greater proportion of diffusion growth than those in Ning communities that are eventually large. For example, in an eventually small group with 40 current members, an average of 28% of its current members will have come from the fringe if the group is in an eventually small community. By contrast, if the same group were in an eventually large community, only 16% of its current members will have come from the fringe on average.

These observations lead to the hypothesis that smaller communities may foster greater familiarity among individuals, and thus, stronger social pressures to adopt behaviors such as group membership. This is consistent with social science research finding that participation rates in civic groups or clubs, such as voter registration organizations, in small towns and rural areas is far higher than in big cities [22]. Part of the explanation is that individuals experience more peer pressure in smaller, more intimate communities than in big cities where they may be more isolated.

Figure 5 also shows the same contrast between small and large communities for eventually large groups, but the difference is much smaller. This is likely because eventually large groups generally attract many members through wider appeal. That is, individuals join not because they were invited by a 'friend' in the group; instead, they join because they have some broad interest shared by the members of the group. For example, consider the differences between a Ning group that serves as an online fan club for a professional sports team and a group used by close friends to exchange private group messages. Regardless of where the online fan club group is established–i.e. a small or large Ning community–its growth primarily comes from its appeal to other fans rather than through the influence of its members' external friendship ties.

Diffusion Growth and Future Overall Growth. Figure 6 further clarifies the relationship between the proportion of a group's current members who came from the fringe and the group's future growth rate. Specifically, in Figure 6, if no members of a 50 member group joined from the fringe, then on average, we expect the group to grow by a factor of 1.6 over the next 180 days. However, if 90% of the group joined from the fringe, then we expect the group to only grow by a factor of 1.2 in the same amount of time. We observe the same pattern when examining growth rates over periods of 30 or 60 days. Again, this suggests that fringe growth early in a group's existence can diminish the eventual size of the group. One hypothesis about why groups which grow primarily through diffusion would be eventually smaller concerns the purposes of these groups. Prior work has shown that group dynamics can differ greatly for groups based on a *common bond* versusthose based on a *common identity* [23, 24]. We discuss the connection between these attachment types in Section 6.

5. PREDICTING GROWTH & LONGEVITY

Building on these empirical observations, we engage in two machine learning tasks aimed at predicting which groups will be successful in attracting new members. The goal of our first task is to understand what group and network characteristics predict whether a group will grow faster or slower than others. Specifically, we explore how the predictive value of these features vary along three dimensions: *group age*, *group size*, and *prediction interval*.

We test the effects of age by taking snapshots of groups at 60 and 180 days after their creation. For each age group, we separate these snapshots into two categories according to size, resulting in a total of 4 age-size 'buckets' of data; for each of these buckets, we generate two models, one aimed at predicting short-term growth and the other at predicting long-term growth. Building these 8 models in this manner provides results which are cleaner and more interpretable as they allow us to clearly observe how coefficients change across groups of different ages and sizes and for the two prediction intervals without having to explain complex interaction effects. Comparing these models provides a rich picture of how diffusion processes, group transitivity, and other features predict short-term and long-term growth of groups. In our second modeling task, we utilize these same features to predict whether groups will 'die' or cease to grow within a given period of time, shedding additional light on how these group and network characteristics affect group dynamics.

5.1 Features for Learning

We begin by defining a set of features to be used in our predictive models, described in Table 2. We divide these features into three rough categories which describe the data at different levels. The first category, labeled *growth* features, capture how quickly and by what means the group was growing when the snapshot was taken. These features serve as a baseline, capturing both the current 'velocity' of growth, as well as insights from the prior section about the role of diffusion processes in subsequent growth.

In addition, we consider a set of *connectivity* features, capturing the probability of edges among members of the group absolutely and relative to the community as a whole, and *structural* features, chosen because they succinctly summarize aspects of higher-level structure within the group. As most features approximated a log-

Size	Statistics	60 Days	180 Days
Small	Number of Groups	5871	5312
	2-Month Growth	1.333	1.165
	2-Year Growth	2.613	1.934
Large	Number of Groups	1602	2884
	2-Month Growth	1.147	1.076
	2-Year Growth	1.494	1.267

Table 3: Number of groups, short-term (2-month) and long-term (2-year) median growth rates for each age*size bucket.

normal distribution, values were log-transformed as part of our anlaysis. *Monthly growth rate* and *group transitivity* more closely approximated normality after being power-transformed.

5.2 Predicting Group Growth

We now describe in more detail the procedure used in our first task of generating predictions about short-term and long-term group growth. We started with a sample of 11,944 groups mined from 1,713 distinct Ning communities. These groups were selected using the same criteria for group size, community size, and expiration date as in our prior analysis. To aid in generalizability, we limited data collection to no more than 50 groups within any single community in order to avoid over-representing a single, large community in our analysis.

As mentioned above, we generated snapshots for groups at two ages (60 and 180 days) and then separated groups of the same age into 'small" (10-100 members) and 'large' (150-1000) members. Rather than including group size as a dependent variable, we bin groups in this manner for two reasons: (1) results from prior work indicate a natural threshold for group size around 150 members [8, 15], (2) our dependent variable, growth rate, does not exhibit equal variance for small and large groups (a small group can feasibly grow 100x in size, while a large group can not).

For each group, we define the 'growth rate' to be the ratio of the group size at prediction time to the group size at the time of the first snapshot. For each group at a given age, we calculate the short-term (2 month) and long-term (2 year) growth rates. Table 3 shows median growth rates over these two prediction intervals. For each combination of age, size, and prediction interval, we structure our problem as a binary classification task, with class 1 representing groups growing more quickly than the median rate, a formulation which provides a balanced sample without excluding groups from our analysis. We generate predictions using a classifier based on logistic regression.

5.2.1 Growth: Results

Below, we summarize and compare results from the 8 models (for each combination of group age, size, and prediction interval) described above. In evaluating our models, we consider two different evaluation measures: the classification accuracy and the area under the ROC curve (AUC). In each task, we generate models for each category of features and a fourth combining all features.

Short-term growth. In Figure 7, we show the accuracy of model predictions for short-term growth. Rows show results for groups of the same age, and columns show groups of the same size. In each cell, the four bars correspond to the four models: (G)rowth, (C)onnectivity, (S)tructural, and (ALL) features. For short-term growth, we can clearly see that the growth features contribute the most to the accuracy of the models and that predictions are more accurate for larger, younger groups, perhaps where the growth rate from the prior month provides more signal. For large groups at 60 days, for instance, the combined model achieves 79.2% accuracy (AUC = 0.868), with predictions driven almost entirely by the growth metrics. As shown in Figure 7, models based on growth metrics alone consistently achieved prediction accuracy over 68.6% (consistently over 77.3% for large groups).

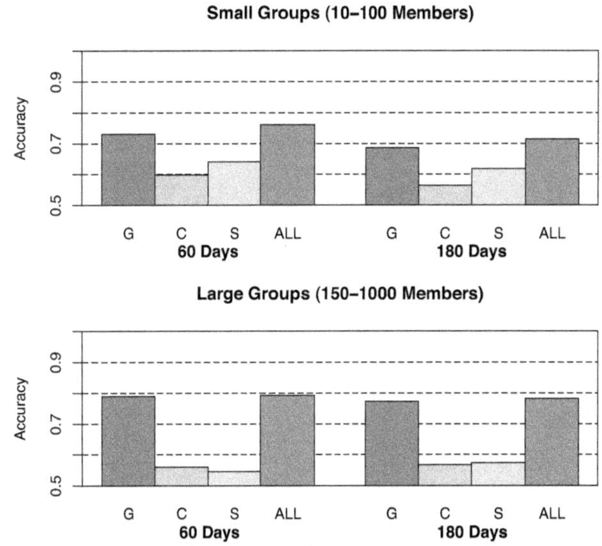

Figure 7: Short-term (2-month) prediction accuracy of models. Rows show groups of the same size, columns show groups of the same age. Note that the y-axis starts at 0.5, the expected accuracy of a random model.

Table 4 shows regression coefficents for the models combining all features. Within each age-size bucket, distributions for each feature were standardized to have a mean of 0 and standard deviation of 1, allowing us to directly compare regression coefficients. Here, we see clearly that short-term predictions are heavily dependent on monthly growth rate, especially for large groups. For small groups, we find that increased group transitivity and growth from the fringe signal a decreased likelihood that a group will grow rapdily, matching earlier observations about diffusion processes, transitivity and growth. An intriguing finding seemingly at odds with this observation about transitivity is that a larger clique seems to predict an increased likelihood that a group will grow rapidly, with this effect stronger for small groups. Furthermore, groups with more individuals outside the largest connected component seem to grow more quickly as well. Together, these findings hint at a more nuanced picture of how network properties predispose groups to growth, which we will discuss later on in our analysis.

Long-term growth. Figure 8 shows prediction accuracy achieved by our models for long-term growth. Again, rows correspond to group size, columns to group age, and the bars in each cell represent the four models. In general, our models still achieve relatively high accuracy, up to 78.6% (AUC = 0.868) for small groups at 60 days and consistently over 71.9% (AUC = 0.782), in predicting whether groups will grow rapidly over the subsequent two years. We see an interesting pattern where model fit for small groups is better at 60 days and for large groups at 180 days; looking more closely, we see that this is because different features appear to be contributing to predictions for small and large groups. For small groups, we see that the models based on structural features are more accurate than those based on growth metrics.

In Table 5, we show coefficients for the combined models (as with the short-term models, distributions for feature values are standardized). Again, we see a pattern where increased growth from the fringe predicts decreased growth rates for small groups and increased transitivity predicts decreased growth for all groups. In

	Small		Large	
Feature	60 Days	180 Days	60 Days	180 Days
Monthly Growth	1.19***	0.88***	1.94***	2.00***
Fringe Growth	-0.20***	-0.10*	—	—
Group Trans.	-0.68***	-0.67***	—	—
Trans. Ratio	0.22***	0.12*	—	—
Group Dens.	0.24*	—	—	—
Dens. Ratio	-0.14**	-0.11	—	—
Clique Ratio	0.95***	1.10***	—	0.32**
Disconnected	0.34***	0.38***	—	0.33***

Table 4: Regression coefficients for combined models predicting short-term growth (For this and following tables: * $p < 0.01$, ** $p < 0.005$, *** $p < 0.001$). Coefficients with $p > 0.05$ are not reported.

addition, the presence of larger cliques and more members outside the giant component is predictive of increased growth for groups of all sizes and ages. Interestingly, at least for small groups, these structural features now appear to play a very large role regarding the outcome of our predictions.

Predictive Value of Features. As expected, groups which were growing quickly at the time of the first snapshot were likely to continue to do so over the short-term, though the extent to which this feature predicted long-term growth for large groups may have been surprising. Of greater interest to us, however, were the findings pertaining to fringe growth, which confirm the results of our prior empirical investigation concerning the role that diffusion processes play in the growth of groups. We find that the negative effect of diffusion processes on subsequent growth is significant only for small groups, suggesting some support for our initial hypothesis about differences between groups smaller and larger than 150 members.

Similarly, for small groups, our models confirmed prior observations concerning group transitivity and growth, with increased transitivity predicting decreased growth over the short-term for small groups and over the long-term for all groups. An interesting result seemingly at odds with these findings about transitivity was that, over both prediction intervals, the presence of a large clique appeared to predict a greater likelihood of subsequent growth. The estimated effect of clique size on subsequent growth was especially high for small groups, hinting that these structural features may be important at the early stages of group formation. In the discussion, we provide hypotheses about types of network structures which could lead to these combinations of features. Our finding that having more members outside of the largest connected component appears to be a good predictor of growth coincides with our notion of non-diffusion growth (membership 'jumps' across the network rather than following existing connections).

We chose this classification approach to match the real-world analysis task of identifying groups which will be 'successful' in the future; an alternative approach would be to utilize linear regression to predict final group size. Though space does not permit a full exposition of these linear models, our experiments showed that group size could be predicted with some accuracy (for long-term growth predictions, we achieved adjusted R^2 values around 0.5 for models combining all features). While these final size predictions were driven heavily by growth features, an analysis of deviance revealed that adding features pertaining to network connectivity and structure provided a better model fit despite the added complexity.

5.3 Predicting Group Longevity

In this section, we focus on the closely related problem of predicting when groups will 'die', or cease to attract new members.

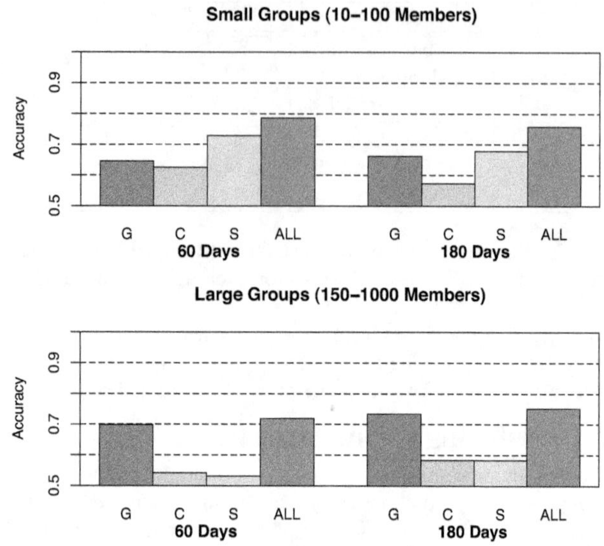

Figure 8: Long-term (2-year) prediction accuracy of models.

Instead of predicting when groups will cease to grow, we again avoid right-censoring problems by focusing on the binary classification task of predicting whether they will continue to grow after 1 year (360 days). In order to simplify our analysis in this section, we focus on groups at a single age (90 days), selecting the 1818 groups which stopped growing within a year (Class 0) and the 1818 groups which grew the fastest after 1 year (Class 1) to obtain a balanced sample. We utilize the same features and logistic regression approach used before. As our goal is now to predict which groups will 'die', we expect that the feature coefficeints learned by the model will have signs opposite those in the growth analysis (i.e. features which positively predict growth should negatively predict death).

Results. Coefficients estimated by our five models, as well as the accuracy and AUC for each, are summarized succinctly in Table 6. For the task of predicting whether groups would stop growing within a year, the group size at the time of the snapshot again provided the most information, followed by the structural metrics. The model using only structural metrics achieved a favorable 70.4% accuracy (AUC = 0.759) compared to random chance (50.0%) and the models utilizing only growth (62.0% accuracy) or connectivity (61.9% accuracy) features. Our combined model achieves 77.4% accuracy (AUC = 0.834) in predicting whether groups will 'die' within a year. Observing the magnitude and sign of learned coefficients for the longevity model, we see that they match closely the findings from the growth analysis. We summarize these observations in the list below and then in more detail in our discussion.

- A higher proportion of growth from diffusion corresponds to a higher likelihood that a group will die.
- Clique Ratio is the strongest feature: a large clique makes a group significantly less likely to die.
- We see similar patterns as with growth with respect to the Group Transitivity and Disconnected Ratio features – low transitivity and fewer members in the large connected component make a group significantly less likely to die.
- One finding which differs from the growth analysis is that groups which are more dense than their surrounding community are more likely to die.
- Groups with a high monthly growth rate are more likely to continue growing a year later.

	Small		Large	
Feature	60 Days	180 Days	60 Days	180 Days
Monthly Growth	0.49***	0.62***	1.24***	1.55***
Fringe Growth	-0.27***	-0.31***	—	—
Group Trans.	-1.34***	-1.37***	-0.31**	-0.25*
Trans. Ratio	0.37***	0.33***	—	0.21**
Group Dens.	—	—	-0.41	—
Dens. Ratio	-0.32***	-0.49***	—	-0.17
Clique Ratio	2.64***	2.33***	0.67***	0.48***
Disconnected	0.75***	0.78***	0.20	0.47***

Table 5: Regression coefficients for combined models predicting long-term growth.

Feature	Model G	Model C	Model S	Model ALL
Prior Month	-0.46***			-0.39***
Fringe Growth	0.26***			0.27***
Group Transitivity		0.23***		0.30***
Transitivity Ratio		-0.18***		-0.12
Group Density		-0.67***		0.27
Density Ratio		0.41***		0.65***
Clique Ratio			-1.05***	-1.59***
Disconnected Ratio			-0.62***	-0.47***
Accuracy	0.622	0.619	0.701	0.744
AUC	0.656	0.647	0.758	0.809

Table 6: Coefficients and prediction outcomes for modles predicting at 90 days whether groups would cease to grow within a year. Note that coefficient signs differ from the prior analysis.

6. DISCUSSION

Core-Periphery Structures. Building off of these findings, we could hypothesize that groups with one or more cores of tightly connected members and a periphery of members loosely connected or entirely disconnected from this core should experience increased and prolonged growth (low transitivity, small connected components, and large cliques). Such core-periphery structures have been observed empirically in many large, real-world networks such as communication and transportation systems [13], online media sites [11], and social networks [15]. The densely connected core allows for the swift transmission of resources [13] and the loose periphery allows for the presence of structural holes [3], or ties which bridge clusters, allowing members on the periphery to bring new information or members to the core. When all members are too tightly bound to the core, as they are in groups with high fringe growth and high transitivity, groups might become too inwardly focused, precluding the possibility of gaining new information and members outside the group.

Common-Bond vs. Common-Identity Groups. Qualitative research on online and offline groups has detailed differences between groups based on *common bond*, where group members form attachments to one another, and those based on *common identity*, in which group members form attachments to the group itself. Our results imply that groups with high transitivity and high diffusion growth represent common-bond groups due to the strong relationship between group members. Prior research on offline communities [23] has argued that common-identity groups may adapt better to changes in membership, as attachment is not so dependent on who is or is not in the group. This resilience may play a greater role in online communities, where membership can change much more dramatically. Research on online communities has shown that groups which accrue more traffic witness greater membership turnover [4, 14]. Ren, et al. [24] hypothesize that change of this type may be unsettling for members of bond-based communities, leading these communities to falter.

7. CONCLUSION

Summary. We investigated the relationship between a group's network features and its future growth using online community data from Ning.com social networks. We considered two types of growth: 1) diffusion growth, wherein a group attracts new members through the friendship ties of its current members to outsiders, and 2) non-diffusion growth, wherein individuals without pre-existing ties to any group members join a group. First, we showed that while group clustering increases diffusion growth, groups that grow more from diffusion tend to reach smaller eventual sizes. This explains the empirical puzzle that group clustering can increase the probability of an individual joining a group (given that the individual has ties to the group) while decreasing a group's overall growth rate.

Second, we generated a set models which use a group's structural features and past growth experience to predict its eventual size and longevity. We found that past growth features predict short-term growth more accurately while, for small groups at least, network structural features better predict long-term growth. In terms of growth rates, we find that while a group's higher transitivity leads to slower long-term growth, the larger a group's largest clique, the more likely the group will experience fast growth over a 2-year period. In addition, structural features predict a group's longevity better than a group's past growth and connectivity features. We note, finally, that we were able to achieve robust results using networks based on implicit (comment) reciprocal edges rather than explicitly defined (friend) edges.

Areas for Future Research. Our findings have useful practical implications and serve as a springboard for future research. For architects and administrators of online communities, understanding the dynamics of group growth is important for sustaining and promoting interaction [20]. Knowing how groups form within networks helps community managers assess the future growth prospects of the community. In addition, it helps administrators decide whether to implement certain features, like membership invitation requests, in online groups to regulate group growth. Because our results were based on data from a wide array of online social network settings, our insights are also generalizable to many online environments.

Our findings raise several important open research questions. While we explored one measure of group longevity, studies of group growth would benefit from research that better specifies the key moments of a group's life-cycle. In addition, we welcome further investigation into the relationship between group growth and the group content. Finally, we encourage analysis on how groups within the same community network setting interact with one another — what role do members that have multiple group affiliations play in promoting diffusion growth? Under what conditions do groups 'compete' for members? We invite future research on these questions to enhance our knowledge about the relationship between networks, group growth, and online community evolution.

8. ACKNOWLEDGMENTS

Research was supported in-part by NSF CNS 1010921, NSF-IIS-1016909, Albert Yu & Mary Bechmann Foundation, IBM, Lightspeed, Yahoo! and the Microsoft Faculty Fellowship.

9. REFERENCES

[1] S. Aral, L. Muchnik, and A. Sundararajan. Distinguishing influence-based contagion from homophily-driven diffusion in dynamic networks. *Proceedings of the National Academy of Sciences*, 106(51):21544–21549, Dec. 2009.

[2] L. Backstrom, D. Huttenlocher, J. Kleinberg, and X. Lan. Group formation in large social networks: membership, growth, and evolution. In *Proceedings of the 12th ACM SIGKDD international conference on Knowledge discovery and data mining*, KDD '06, pages 44–54, New York, NY, USA, 2006. ACM.

[3] R. Burt. Structural holes versus network closure as social capital. *Social capital: Theory and research*, pages 31–56, 2001.

[4] B. Butler. Membership size, communication activity, and sustainability: The internal dynamics of networked social structures. *Information Systems Research*, 12(4):346–362, 2001.

[5] D. Centola. The spread of behavior in an online social network experiment. *Science (New York, N.Y.)*, 329(5996):1194–1197, Sept. 2010.

[6] D. Centola and M. Macy. Complex Contagions and the Weakness of Long Ties. *American Journal of Sociology*, 113(3):702–734, Nov. 2007.

[7] N. Ducheneaut, N. Yee, E. Nickell, and R. J. Moore. The life and death of online gaming communities: a look at guilds in world of warcraft. In *Proceedings of the SIGCHI conference on Human factors in computing systems*, CHI '07, pages 839–848, New York, NY, USA, 2007. ACM.

[8] R. Dunbar. Coevolution of neocortex size, group size, and language in human. *Behavioral and Brain Sciences*, 16(4):681–735, 1993.

[9] R. M. Fernandez and D. McAdam. Social networks and social movements: Multiorganizational fields and recruitment to mississippi freedom summer. *Sociological Forum*, 3:357–382, 1988. 10.1007/BF01116431.

[10] M. Givan and M. E. J. Newman. Community structure in social and biological networks. *PNAS*, 99(12):7821–7826, June 2002.

[11] M. Gomez Rodriguez, J. Leskovec, and A. Krause. Inferring networks of diffusion and influence. In *Proceedings of the 16th ACM SIGKDD international conference on Knowledge discovery and data mining*, KDD '10, pages 1019–1028, New York, NY, USA, 2010. ACM.

[12] M. Granovetter. The Strength of Weak Ties. *The American Journal of Sociology*, 78(6):1360–1380, 1973.

[13] P. Holme. Core-periphery organization of complex networks. *Physical Review E*, 72(046111), 2005.

[14] Q. Jones, G. Ravid, and S. Rafaeli. Information overload and the message dynamics of online interaction spaces. *Information Systems Research*, 15(2):194–210, 2004.

[15] J. Leskovec, K. J. Lang, A. Dasgupta, and M. W. Mahoney. Statistical properties of community structure in large social and information networks. In *Proceeding of the 17th international conference on World Wide Web*, WWW '08, pages 695–704, New York, NY, USA, 2008. ACM.

[16] G. Marwell and P. Oliver. *The Critical Mass in Collective Action: A Micro-Social Theory*. Cambridge University Press, 1993.

[17] D. McAdam and R. Paulsen. Specifying the relationship between social ties and activism. In D. McAdam and D. A. Snow, editors, *Social Movements: Readings on Their Emergence, Mobilization, and Dynamics*, pages 145–157. Roxbury Publishing Co., 2007.

[18] S. Milgram. The small-world problem. *Psychology Today*, pages 60–67, 1967.

[19] A. Mislove, M. Marcon, K. P. Gummadi, P. Druschel, and B. Bhattacharjee. Measurement and analysis of online social networks. In *Proceedings of the 7th ACM SIGCOMM conference on Internet measurement*, IMC '07, pages 29–42, New York, NY, USA, 2007. ACM.

[20] E. D. Mynatt, A. Adler, M. Ito, and V. L. O'Day. Design for network communities. In *Proceedings of the SIGCHI conference on Human factors in computing systems*, CHI '97, pages 210–217, New York, NY, USA, 1997. ACM.

[21] M. E. J. Newman. Detecting community structure in networks. *Eur. Phys. J. B*, 38:321–330, 2004.

[22] J. E. Oliver. The Strength of Weak Ties. *The American Political Science Review*, 94(2):361–373, 2000.

[23] D. Prentice, D. Miller, and J. Lightdale. Asymmetries in attachments to groups and to their members: Distinguishing between common-identity and common-bond groups. *Personality and Social Psychology Bulletin*, 20(5):484–493, 1994.

[24] Y. Ren, R. Kraut, and S. Kiesler. Applying Common Identity and Bond Theory to Design of Online Communities. *Organization Studies*, 28(3):377–408, Mar. 2007.

[25] C. T. Reviews. *Making Democracy Work: Civic Traditions in Modern Italy*. Cram 101. Academic Internet Publishers Incorporated, 2007.

[26] E. M. Rogers. *Diffusion of Innovations, 5th Edition*. Free Press, 5th edition, 2003.

[27] F. Salem and R. Mourtada. Civil movements: The impact of facebook and twitter. *The Arab Social Media Report*, 1(2), 2011.

[28] D. A. Snow, L. A. Zurcher, and S. Ekland-Olson. Social networks and social movements: A microstructural approach to differential recruitment. In D. McAdam and D. A. Snow, editors, *Social Movements: Readings on Their Emergence, Mobilization, and Dynamics*, pages 122–131. Roxbury Publishing Co., 2007.

[29] R. Stark and W. S. Bainbridge. Networks of faith: Interpersonal bonds and recruitment to cults and sects. *American Journal of Sociology*, 85:1376–1395, 1980.

[30] J. Waddington and C. Whitston. Why do people join unions in a period of membership decline? *British Journal of Industrial Relations*, 35(4):515–546, 1997.

[31] E. Zheleva, H. Sharara, and L. Getoor. Co-evolution of social and affiliation networks. In *Proceedings of the 15th ACM SIGKDD international conference on Knowledge discovery and data mining*, KDD '09, pages 1007–1016, New York, NY, USA, 2009. ACM.

Evaluating Search in Personal Social Media Collections

Chia-Jung Lee, W. Bruce Croft and Jin Young Kim
Center for Intelligent Information Retrieval
Department of Computer Science
University of Massachusetts, Amherst
{cjlee, croft, jykim}@cs.umass.edu

ABSTRACT

The prevalence of social media applications is generating potentially large personal archives of posts, tweets, and other communications. The existence of these archives creates a need for search tools, which can be seen as an extension of current desktop search services. Little is currently known about the best search techniques for personal archives of social data, because of the difficulty of creating test collections. In this paper, we describe how test collections for personal social data can be created by using games to collect queries. We then compare a range of retrieval models that exploit the semi-structured nature of social data. Our results show that a mixture of language models with field distribution estimation can be effective for this type of data, with certain fields, such as the name of the poster, being particularly important. We also analyze the properties of the queries that were generated by users with two versions of the games.

Categories and Subject Descriptors

H.3.3 [**Information Storage and Retrieval**]: Information Search and Retrieval

General Terms

Design, Performance, Experimentation

Keywords

Personal social media collections, Facebook, Twitter, search evaluation, semi-structured document, desktop search

1. INTRODUCTION

The growing popularity of social media applications such as Facebook, Twitter and Google+ has generated huge archives of potentially useful information. From an individual's point of view, these social media services provide frequent updates, and considerable personal archives of posts, tweets, and other communications can accumulate. The existence of these personal archives creates a potential search problem that is not addressed by global search mechanisms such as Twitter search[1] and Facebook search[2]. In this paper, we focus on studying the personal search tools that can be viewed as an extension of current desktop search services.

Research on desktop search has focused on the problems of developing test collections[6], retrieval models, and evaluation methods. Despite this research, results are currently only known for more "conventional" document types such as email or office documents; information about search techniques for personal social archives is quite limited. To understand this new type of personal search, we explore and evaluate a range of search techniques on test collections created using personal archives from social applications. In particular, we focus on the task of known-item search on personal social archives, as known-item queries are the most frequent type of request in a desktop environment[5]. Moreover, according to Teevan et al [15], people have reported that attempting to re-find previously encountered information with global Twitter archives usually ended in failure, showing that this is both a real and difficult problem.

Another property of social media data is the rich set of fields associated with the content, which is usually presented in the form of semi-structured documents. Exploiting this structure can be helpful for improving retrieval performance as well as understanding field characteristics. Several field-based retrieval techniques [12][13][6] have been proposed to deal with semi-structured text for typical desktop data. The common principle among these approaches is to estimate the weights representing the query intent over structural components for query terms. Specifically, the probabilistic retrieval model for semi-structured data (PRMS) [6] has reported effectiveness improvements based on per-term weight estimation. However, little is known about suitable retrieval models for social media data, which has some significant differences such as document length compared to typical desktop data.

In this paper, we propose a method for building test collections from personal social media data. We collect personal archives from Facebook or Twitter as the document collections. Two types of human computation games, DocTrack[7] and MemRecap, are proposed for collecting known-item queries from real users. Based on the test collections, we are able to compare a range of retrieval models that exploit the semi-structured nature of social data. Our results

Permission to make digital or hard copies of all or part of this work for personal or classroom use is granted without fee provided that copies are not made or distributed for profit or commercial advantage and that copies bear this notice and the full citation on the first page. To copy otherwise, to republish, to post on servers or to redistribute to lists, requires prior specific permission and/or a fee.
WSDM'12, February 8–12, 2012, Seattle, Washingtion, USA.
Copyright 2012 ACM 978-1-4503-0747-5/12/02 ...$10.00.

[1]http://twitter.com/
[2]https://www.facebook.com/srch.php

show that a mixture of language models with field distribution estimation can be effective for this type of data.

To better understand our data, we analyze the properties of the queries as well as the associated field distribution information. In sum, we find that (1.) the queries collected using the MemRecap game could potentially be more realistic. (2.) Further analysis of field importance indicates that certain fields, such as the name of the poster, can be particularly important for retrieval. (3.) There is a high correlation between manual-specified query fields and fields estimated using field distribution models, which can be the key to better retrieval performance.

In the rest of the paper, we first introduce related work in Section 2 and detail the approach to building test collections in Section 3. The retrieval models studied are described in Section 4. Sections 5 and 6 respectively analyze the query set and the field information. In section 7, we show retrieval performance using different approaches, and conclude the paper in Section 8.

2. RELATED WORK

The task of searching personal social media collections is related to a number of research areas including building test collections, semi-structured document retrieval, known-item search, desktop search, and microblog search.

The difficulty of evaluating search on personal social data results from the lack of available test collections. Human computation games [8, 7] suggest a way of collecting queries based on an interaction that involves asking users to search in response to displayed documents. We extend the DocTrack game [7] by enabling users to manually specify field information. We further propose another type of game, MemRecap, as an attempt to obtain realistic queries in the absence of real query logs.

Social media data is usually described with a rich set of fields in the form of semi-structured documents. Previous work [6, 9, 12, 13] has explored modeling field importance for retrieval, as associating words with fields can be viewed as a hidden process in query formulation. Kim et al.[6] proposed a probabilistic retrieval model based on collection statistics. We explore several new ways to estimate field weights, as well as the feasibility of interpolating various language models based on a series of field distribution estimations.

Searching personal archives including email and documents on desktop machines has been studied to some extent [9, 18, 3, 4], and is usually modeled as a task of known-item search[5]. The accumulation of personal social data can be viewed as a new type of collection on the desktop; however, little is currently known about the best search techniques for this type of data. The emergence of new tools such as Greplin[3] has provided web services for personal search engines.

Our work is related to microblog search such as the official Twitter Search which globally retrieves documents (tweets) from the entire collection. However, the focus of Twitter Search is not on individuals or personal archives and documents may often be ranked based solely on time[2]. Other aspects of searching Twitter have been explored, including event detection [14][17], locating topics of interest[10][19], and mining opinions[16]. Facebook search emphasizes social relationships, and provides search based mainly on people or organizations. Our research, while using data collected from Twitter and Facebook, differs from the previous work in that we focus on searching personal archives.

[3]https://www.greplin.com/

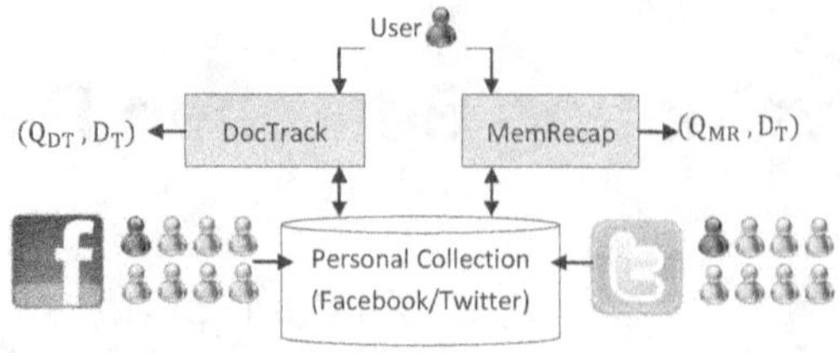

Figure 1: Overview of a personal social media collection.

Table 1: Statistics of Facebook and Twitter data.

Facebook			Twitter		
User	#Q	#Doc	User	#Q	#Doc
user0	35	19741	user5	41	127512
user1	67	165068	user6	58	24835
user2	36	47067	user7	50	92891
user3	62	28128	user8	62	14805
user4	60	42224	user9	60	32714

3. BUILDING PERSONAL SOCIAL MEDIA COLLECTIONS

In this section, we detail the steps taken to build personal social media collections, which include documents, queries, and relevance judgments. A personal document collection contains a set of documents that an individual could have seen previously by using social media applications. In practice, we assume the possible set of viewed documents for a user is composed of his own postings as well as all other postings of his friends from either Facebook or Twitter. For each personal document collection, we also collect two types of known-item queries, Q_{DT} and Q_{MR}, based on the human computation games DocTrack and MemRecap. Figure 1 provides a high level overview of a personal social media collection.

3.1 Document Collection – Facebook

To collect the set of documents that a user may have viewed, we obtained authorization to gather the postings related to a set of users and their friends within a period of time[4] using the Graph API [5] supported by Facebook. We store each posting as a XML file, which is regarded as a document in the collection. Table 1 shows the total number of documents collected for each of the 5 individuals involved in our experiments.

Facebook data is rich both in terms of the various types of postings as well as XML fields. The most common types are "status", "link", "photo" and "video". The XML fields contain nested information over a collection of sources. Given that our focus is on conducting known-item search on the social media collections, we flatten the field structure and keep only the more informative and interesting content. Specifically, we merge some of the fields and in total use 14 single-layered fields including uname (usernames of the posters

[4]07/01/2010-02/01/2011

[5]https://developers.facebook.com/docs/reference/api/

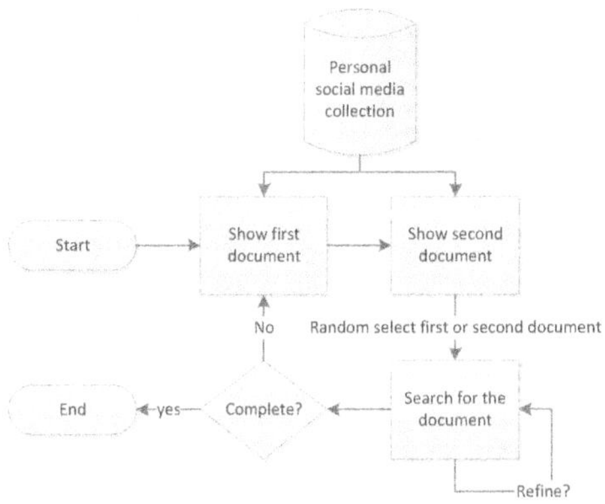

Figure 2: Flowchart of collecting Q_{DT} based on the DocTrack game.

and/or receivers), msg (main body of text in the post), pct (post created time), put (post updated time), cmtname (usernames involved in the comments), cmtmsg (all comment texts), ct (comments created time), likename (usernames who "like" the post), link (content of the post is typed as "link"), description (texts describing link content), caption (title of links), olink (other links that may appear any place in the post), pname (usernames involved in photos), and aname (usernames involved in albums).

3.2 Document Collection – Twitter

Similar to Facebook, we construct a personal document collection for Twitter by gathering postings of a set of individuals together with postings from the people they follow. We have collected 5 personal collections from Twitter. The statistics are shown in Table 1.

Again, we discard XML field information such as "the background color of a user profile" that is unlikely to be used in a query by users. In total, we keep 11 flattened single-layered fields consisting of text (main body of tweet text), uname (usernames of poster), replyname (usernames of people being replied), src (source of media used for tweeting such as smart phones or web), time (post created time), link (links that may appear any place in the post), re-text (main body of retweeted text), re-uname (usernames of poster being retweeted), re-replyname, re-src, and re-time.

3.3 Query Set – DocTrack

To complete the test collections for known-item search, test queries along with the corresponding relevance judgments are required. The task can be done with human computation games that reduce the cost of collecting data as well as providing higher motivation for users' participation. The DocTrack game proposed by Kim et al [7] functions by first showing two documents to users within a limited period of time, and asking them to randomly search one of the documents by typing in a query. Following [7], the search system was implemented using Apache Lucene[6] which differs from the retrieval models in Section 4 and avoids biased results towards certain models. Users can refine their queries for about 3 times if they cannot find the target documents. DocTrack simulates the situation that a user has seen a document before, and tries to recall it later. The randomness

[6]http://lucene.apache.org/

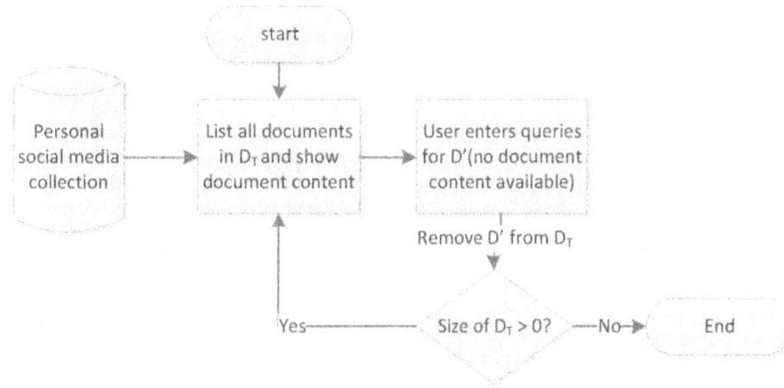

Figure 3: Flowchart of collecting Q_{MR} based on the MemRecap game.

of choosing one of the two documents is designed to make it more difficult for users to formulate queries. Following this procedure, pairs of DocTrack query and target documents $\{(Q_{DT}, D_T)\}$ can be collected. For a known-item query, the relevance judgments are also provided by the association between each pair of (Q_{DT}, D_T). Figure 2 illustrates the flow chart of the DocTrack game.

Occasionally, users remember information such as "the person who wrote a message" or "the time when a posting was posted". We assume that this type of structural information could potentially help retrieve target documents. We therefore extended the DocTrack interface by allowing users to specify fields from which a query term comes during the process of typing queries. For example, given a query "Jessica basketball game", we provide an optional method for users to specify a structured query as "Jessica.user basketball.message game.message".

3.4 Query Set – MemRecap

Despite the effectiveness of DocTrack as demonstrated in previous research [7], the queries Q_{DT} can still be different from real queries that can only be gathered via a real search log system on personal collections. Moreover, we found some potential improvements that can be made for the DocTrack game. The time restriction on reading documents is different from a typical scenario of reading social media postings on the web. In addition, as DocTrack requires users to search the target document after reading, the search algorithm could potentially affect how users formulate queries. Also, we follow the original design of DocTrack game in [7] that all the query terms should be exactly matched with the terms in documents. That is, in order to retrieve the target documents, users need to formulate queries using words that are 100% from the target documents.

In an attempt to produce more realistic queries, we designed the second game, MemRecap, as illustrated in Figure 3. MemRecap takes the same set of target documents $\{D_T\}$ previously collected by DocTrack as input. During each round of MemRecap, users are asked to read as many $d \in \{D_T\}$ as they want without time limitation, under the constraint that users are confident of memorizing all of them. The set of documents read is denoted as D'. After users finish reading, they are directed to another page where the contents of the documents are no longer available and where they can type queries for D'. As users may have read quite a few documents in each round, we provide users with hints which help them correctly remember the documents. In particular, we show the profile pictures of people involved in each document to the users, which could strike a balance of providing hints as well as keeping the words in the document hidden. Users can start another round of reading documents after they finish formulating queries, and the process repeats until there is no more $d \in \{D_T\}$ unspecified.

MemRecap gathers a new set of queries $\{Q_{MR}\}$ based on the target documents D_T previously collected by DocTrack. This makes us possible to compare the queries $\{Q_{DT}\}$ and $\{Q_{MR}\}$ that share the same source document. Moreover, MemRecap makes modifications based on DocTrack by removing the time constraint and the search requirement. Also, MemRecap provides a free-text interface for users to type their queries. In such case, users are not required to formulate queries using only the words from target documents, which can be realistic in some cases where users have vague memories.

For MemRecap, we do not collect field information as in the DocTrack game. As users can choose as many documents to read as they want, it could be difficult for them to accurately remember which field a query word should belong to, as opposed to the two documents in DocTrack. The average number of documents that users read in each around is four.

4. RETRIEVAL MODELS

Social media documents contain richer field information and fewer words than typical documents. In this section, we propose several retrieval methods that could potentially be suited to the search task. We denote $Q = \{q_1, q_2, \ldots, q_n\}$ as a query sample from either Q_{DT} or Q_{MR}, and use $f = \{f_1, f_2, \ldots, f_m\}$ to represent the fields of a document. Further, $F = \{F_1, F_2, \ldots, F_m\}$ denotes the fields from the perspective of collections; that is, each F_j is composed of f_j across all the documents in the collections.

4.1 Query likelihood model (QLM)

We use the well-known query likelihood model as a baseline for retrieval, which ranks documents according to the probability of generating a term q_i from a document d.

$$P(Q|d) = \prod_{i=1}^{n} P_{QL}(q_i|d)$$

4.2 Proximity model (Prox)

A proximity model helps identify phrases by emphasizing words appearing within a pre-defined window[7]. The Prox model helps to test the assumption that query terms are likely to appear in close proximity to one another in relevant documents, and is formulated as:

$$P_{Prox}(Q|d) = P_{unordered}(q_1 \ldots q_k|d)$$

4.3 Field specific model (FSM)

The correct association of a query term with its source field could potentially help retrieval performance. Given information about the association (q_i, f_j), we can retrieve documents by taking into account only the appearance of query term q_i in a certain field f_j as:

$$P_{FSM}(Q|d) = \prod_{i=1}^{n} P_{QL}(q_i|f_j, d)$$

[7]The window size is 8 in our experiments.

Specifically, the probability $P_{QL}(q_i|f_j, d)$ is calculated by dividing the number of times q_i appearing in f_j by the length of entire document. In our experiments, FSM is only used for the Q_{DT} queries as we collect field information using the DocTrack game.

4.4 Field distribution model (FDM)

Since the correct association of words and fields is not always available, an alternative that estimates field weights for semi-structured documents has been shown to be effective in previous research [6, 9, 12, 13]. In this approach, a set of weights $w = \{w_1, w_2, \ldots, w_m\}$ over a set of fields $f = \{f_1, f_2, \ldots, f_m\}$ is estimated for each of query term q_i; that is, a probability distribution over the fields is estimated for each q_i. Mathematically, the family of FMD models can be formulated as:

$$P_{FDM}(Q|d) = \prod_{i=1}^{n} \sum_{j=1}^{m} w_{ij} P_{QL}(q_i|f_j, d)$$

In the following sections, we describe an existing weight estimation technique as well as several proposed estimators. Alternatives exist for the calculation of $P_{QL}(q_i|f_j, d)$: to divide the number of times q_i in f_j by the length of field f_j or by the length of entire document d. Finally, we combine together all of the FDM models.

4.4.1 *Probabilistic Retrieval Model for Semi-structured Data* (PRMS)

The PRMS model proposed by Kim et al [6] estimates field importance based on statistical information from document collections. Kim et al [6] reported improvements in effectiveness for PRMS compared to several other field-based retrieval methods[12, 13]. The PRMS model computes a weight as follows:

$$w_{ij} = P(F_j|q_i) = \frac{P_M(q_i|F_j)P_M(F_j)}{\sum_{F_j \in F} P_M(q_i|F_j)P_M(F_j)}$$

Specifically, the weight w_{ij} corresponds to a posterior probability $P(F_j|q_i)$ that calculates the probability of mapping a query term q_i to a field F_j. The PRMS model focuses on the term distribution in each field by considering the probability $P_M(q_i|F_j)$ that measures how many times a q_i is included in a F_j. $P_M(F_j)$ is a prior representing how much belief one has in the field F_j, and is uniformly set according to Kim et al.

PRMS calculates the $P_{QL}(q_i|f_j, d)$ by division by the length of field f_j. For comparison, we add a variation of PRMS using the division by the entire document length, and denote this variation as FDM_{prms}. Except for PRMS, we adopt the definition of division by the entire document length thorough the paper.

4.4.2 *Probabilistic Model using All Fields* (FDM_{AllF})

In contrast to PRMS, we can also use the term distribution over all fields, with the advantage of estimating field importance according to the entire collection. In particular, we calculate the probability, $P(q_i \in F_j|q_i \in F)$, that measures how likely a term q_i belongs to a field F_j compared to all other fields F in the collection. $P(q_i \in F_j|q_i \in F)$ can be efficiently calculated based on the number of times q_i appears in each F_j. w_{ij} can be computed accordingly by normalizing over all possible fields for a q_i.

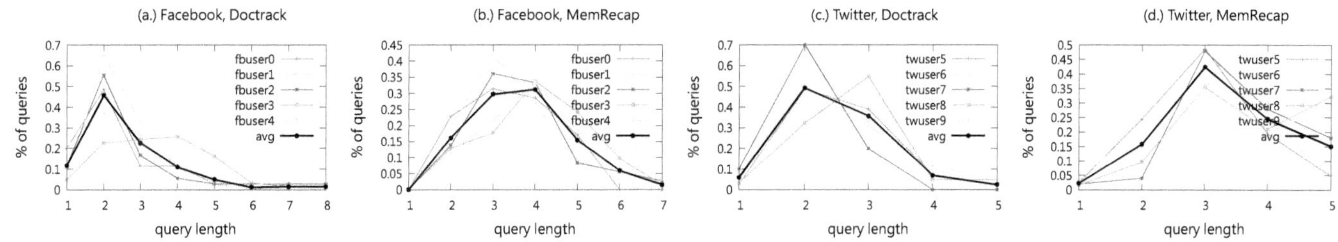

Figure 4: Query length distribution for DocTrack and MemRecap queries on Facebook and Twitter.

$$w_{ij} = \frac{P(q_i \in F_j | q_i \in F)}{\sum_{F_j \in F} P(q_i \in F_j | q_i \in F)}$$

4.4.3 *Probabilistic Model using Field Size* ($\text{FDM}_{\text{Fsize}}$)

We further study the feasibility of using the size of fields as an indicator for weight estimation. We assume that the more words a field contains, the more likely it is that a query term belongs to that field. We also normalize the weight by Z:

$$w_{ij} = \frac{1}{Z} \frac{|F_j|}{\sum_{F_j \in F} |F_j|}, \quad Z = \sum_{F_j \in F} \frac{|F_j|}{\sum_{F_j \in F} |F_j|}$$

4.4.4 *Probabilistic Model on Field Prior* ($\text{FDM}_{\text{Fprior}}$)

Different characteristics of the fields make them not equally important for search. We can incorporate prior knowledge concerning the effectiveness of different fields in the retrieval process. The $Prior(F_j)$ can be viewed a function for estimating how much belief one has for a certain field, and can be estimated in various ways. In Section 6.2, we show the estimation of $Prior(F_j)$ based directly on retrieval effectiveness.

$$w_{ij} = \frac{Prior(F_j)}{\sum_{F_j \in F} Prior(F_j)}$$

4.4.5 *Mixture of Field distribution model* (FDM_{mix})

Correct field importance estimation can be challenging. To this end, we incorporate together all of the FDM with each as a basic indicator, where the aim is to potentially combine the advantages and reduce the disadvantages of each of the models. We linearly combine the confidence over the fields by specifying a set of parameters $\Gamma = \{\gamma_k\}$ to each FDM. Mathematically, w_{ij} is estimated as,

$$w_{ij} = \frac{1}{Z} \sum_{k} \gamma_k w_{ij}^k, \quad Z = \sum_{F_j \in F} \sum_{k} \gamma_k w_{ij}^k$$

where w_{ij}^k corresponds to the estimation of the kth FDM. In total, we use the models FDM_{prms}, FDM_{AllF}, $\text{FDM}_{\text{Fsize}}$, and $\text{FDM}_{\text{Fprior}}$, and $\Gamma = \{\gamma_k\}$ are uniformly distributed without prior knowledge.

4.5 Mixture of language models

A linear interpolation of individual retrieval models helps estimate the overall joint conditional probability based on several conditional probabilities. Accordingly, we combine QLM, field-related models(FSM/FDM) and Prox models using either two (Mix_{LM2}) or three (Mix_{LM3}) of them.

Mix_{LM2} linearly combines QLM with FSM, Prox, or FDM_{mix} models, which rank documents in proportion to the interpolated probabilities. $\lambda \in [0, 1]$ is a free parameter specifying the importance for each model, and is cross-validated and set to 0.8 in this paper, which is consistent with [1].

QLM+FSM: $rank(d) \propto \lambda P(Q|d) + (1 - \lambda) P_{fsm}(Q|d)$

QLM+Prox: $rank(d) \propto \lambda P(Q|d) + (1 - \lambda) P_{prox}(Q|d)$

QLM+FDM_{mix}: $rank(d) \propto \lambda P(Q|d) + (1 - \lambda) P_{Fmix}(Q|d)$

Mix_{LM3} further combines 3 types of language models together. λ_Q, λ_F and λ_P are parameters controlling the weights of different models, with the sum of them equal to 1. λ_Q, λ_F and λ_P are empirically set to 0.8, 0.1 and 0.1, which is consistent with [11] in a sense that QLM is most highly weighted.

QLM+FSM+Prox:
$rank(d) \propto \lambda_Q P(Q|d) + \lambda_F P_{fsm}(Q|d) + \lambda_P P_{prox}(Q|d)$

QLM+FDM_{mix}+Prox:
$rank(d) \propto \lambda_Q P(Q|d) + \lambda_F P_{Fmix}(Q|d) + \lambda_P P_{prox}(Q|d)$

5. ANALYSIS ON DOCTRACK AND MEMRECAP QUERY SETS

In this section, we compare the two types of test queries, Q_{DT} and Q_{MR}, from statistical and retrieval effectiveness perspectives. Our finding suggests that the Q_{MR} queries can potentially be regarded as more similar to real queries than Q_{DT} queries in our environment.

5.1 Query length distribution

We first examine the distributions of query lengths for the DocTrack and MemRecap queries. Figure 4(a)(b) show the percentage of queries of different lengths for Q_{DT} and Q_{MR} in Facebook collections. It can be observed that there is around 10% of Q_{DT} queries with length 1, compared to 0% in Q_{MR}. When users are formulating Q_{DT} queries, it is more likely for them to randomly pick a word to remember as a result of time limitations on reading documents. In this case, the intention of users, according to the design of the DocTrack game, is to find the target document rather than to recall something that they have seen in the past. Another reason for the one-word queries in DocTrack is because users tend to refine the query by downsizing and dropping query words if they could not retrieve the target documents; this may imply the querying behavior is influenced by the search system in DocTrack.

For Q_{MR}, users formulate their queries using at least two words. The time restriction of DocTrack also makes the

Table 2: Average t-test p-values between MRR samples of DocTrack and MemRecap queries. Results are reported for Facebook and Twitter collections using various retrieval models.

p-value	QLM	Prox	PRMS	F_{prms}	F_{AllF}	F_{Fsize}	F_{Fprior}	F_{mix}	Q+P	Q+F_m	Q+F_m+P
Facebook avg	0.9989	0.0018	0.7658	0.7836	0.9989	0.9989	0.9989	0.9807	0.9989	0.9989	0.9989
Twitter avg	0.9766	0.0001	0.7612	0.7712	0.9677	0.9677	0.9677	0.9612	0.9767	0.9877	0.9877

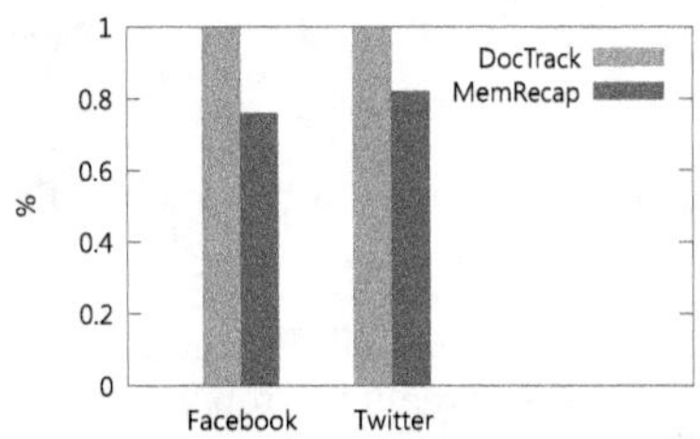

Figure 5: Average term overlap rate for DocTrack and MemRecap queries on Facebook and Twitter.

query length of Q_{DT} (average 2.68) shorter than Q_{MR} (average 3.69). Similarly, we find that 45% of DocTrack queries have query length 2, while query lengths of 3 (29%) and 4 (31%) are more common in MemRecap queries. For example, "pic" and "pic being tan" are the DocTrack and MemRecap queries for the same target document.

Moreover, a small portion of DocTrack queries (3% averagely) were very long because users could randomly memorize a sentence under the pressure of limited time, which can be unrealistic. For example, "not getting enough sleep is bad" and "lecture sleeping" are the DocTrack and MemRecap queries for the same target document. For the case of MemRecap queries, long queries of length 6 or 7 are mainly composed of "uname" together with several other words describing the content of "msg". One example of long queries in Q_{MR} is "bon jovi suffer olympic stadium finland".

Similarly, Figures 4(c)(d) show the distribution of query lengths for Q_{DT} and Q_{MR} in the Twitter collections. The length of the majority of Q_{MR} queries is one word longer than Q_{DT} queries. It can also be observed that, comparing queries across Facebook and Twitter, queries for Facebook are usually longer as a result of postings having more information in Facebook archives.

5.2 Term overlap rate

We examined the rate of exact matches between query and document words in Figure 5. According to the design of DocTrack game, there is 100% term overlap rate in all cases, while there is about 20% of query words in Q_{MR} that are not included in D_T. We believe both types of queries can be useful for testing the effectiveness of our retrieval algorithms. Q_{DT} can represent the case that users have sharp memories about the known documents, whereas Q_{MR} provides some degree of uncertainty to represent the case where users could have vague memories. Also, we examine the non-matched words of Q_{MR} and find that reasons such as misspelling, different verb tenses, synonyms, or simply errors can account for much of the 20% mismatch.

From Figure 5, we can see that the term overlap rate of Q_{MR} is higher for Twitter collections. This is because the length of Twitter documents are usually shorter which makes it easier for users to recap the document content.

Table 3: Statistics of field information for Q_{DT}.

Facebook			Twitter		
user	#words	Perc%	user	#words	Perc%
0	78	0.9487	5	106	0.9528
1	160	0.9937	6	141	1.0000
2	78	0.5512	7	105	0.9904
3	217	0.9493	8	171	1.0000
4	139	0.9064	9	124	0.9012
avg	134.4	0.8699	avg	129.4	0.9686

5.3 Retrieval performance deviation

Comparison of the retrieved results is useful for understanding the degree of compatibility between queries from the perspective of search systems. Accordingly, we compare the distribution of retrieval scores between DocTrack and MemRecap queries. Specifically, the two-tailed student's t-test, which has the advantage of being suitable for small datasets and being sensitive if the data meets the requirements of the test, determines if two datasets differ significantly based on the null hypothesis. Based on this test, we conclude that two distributions are not significantly different from each other if the resulting p-value of the two empirical samples is greater than a certain threshold.

Table 2[8] reports the average p-values over 5 users between Q_{DT} and Q_{MR} respectively for both Facebook and Twitter collections. From Table 2, the two types of queries consistently agree with each other, except for the Prox model. The significant difference (p-value < 0.05) for the Prox model suggests that users tend to memorize consecutive words from target documents in order to generate queries in DocTrack games. However, in the MemRecap game, users do not exhibit the same tendency as they were given sufficient time to go through the content of the documents in detail. For the other retrieval models, Q_{DT} and Q_{MR} are similar to each other.

6. ANALYSIS ON FIELD INFORMATION

Another focus of this paper is to analyze the field distribution of query words and how this distribution can potentially affect retrieval performance. In this section, we describe the distributions for the manual-specified fields as well as the estimated fields based on the retrieval model FDM_{mix}. Note that we collect manual-specified field information only based on the DocTrack game, and therefore we focus on the Q_{DT} queries here.

6.1 Statistics of Field Information

Though not required, users are recommended to specify fields for query words in DocTrack game. In Table 3, we show the total number of words and the percentage of words that are specified with fields. We can see that users are generally willing to specify fields when formulating queries

[8]Abbreviations: Q(QLM), P(Prox), F_m(FDM_{mix}).

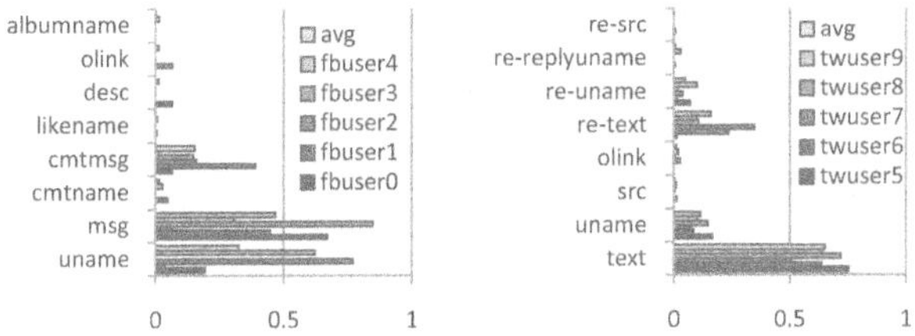

Figure 6: Field distribution for manual-specified queries for Facebook (left) nd Twitter (right).

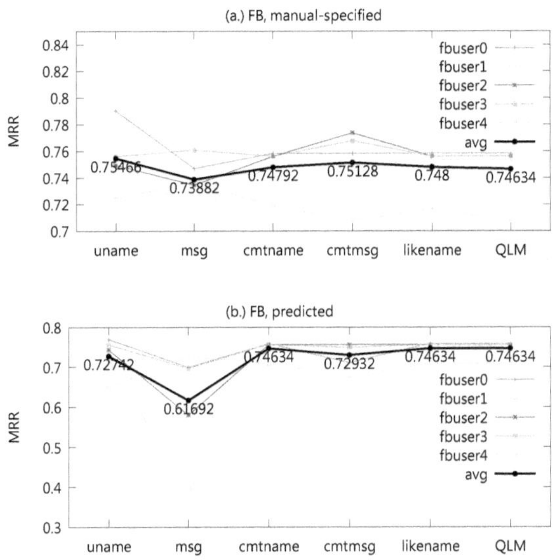

Figure 7: MRR of QLM and FSM using human-specified/predicted field information on Facebook

(more than 85%), which makes the following analysis more reliable.

Moreover, for the set of query words manually specified with fields, we are interested in how the field information is distributed. From Figure 6 [9], it can be observed that most query words are associated with the "msg"/"text" (46% in Facebook and 65% in Twitter) or "uname" (32% in Facebook and 11% Twitter) fields. Words specified with "cmtmsg" (15%) or "re-text" (15%) also share a fair portion of all the fields, while the rest of fields are seldom addressed. The fields involving time information are never specified.

6.2 Field importance for retrieval

A straightforward approach to understanding the importance of fields for retrieval is to search using each of the fields individually. As a baseline for comparison, we first retrieve documents using Q_{DT} based on QLM where fields do not get involved. Then for each field F_j, we search with a FSM model where words specified with F_j are restricted to that field while others remain the same as in QLM. For example, "Jessica basketball.message game.message" would be the query we issue if we were to inspect the performance impact of field "message". Figure 7(a) and Figure 8(a) show

[9]Fields that are never specified are omitted in the figures

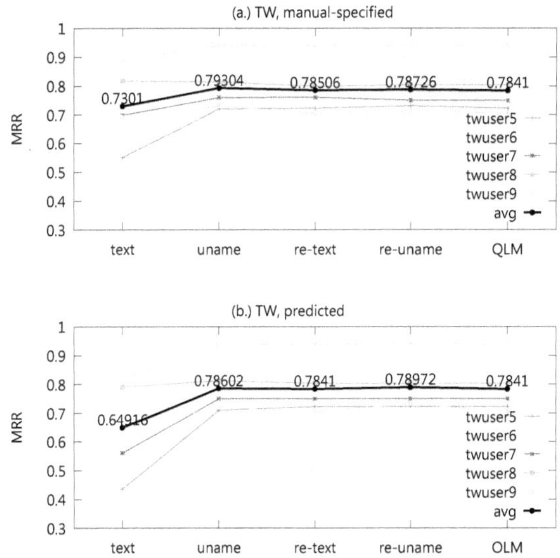

Figure 8: MRR of QLM and FSM using human-specified/predicted field information on Twitter.

the MRR results of search using the F_j-field-specific FSM model as well as the QLM model[10].

We also explore the impact of fields when the manual-specified field information is no longer available. In this case, for each query term q_i, as an approximation, we adopt the top-weighted field $F_{top1} = \arg\max_{w_j} F_j$ as the field which q_i belongs to. Specifically, we use the FDM$_{\text{mix}}$ model to estimate field weights and select F_{top1} for each q_i. Similarly, we conduct search based on field-specific FSM model for each F_j, and the retrieval performance can be found in Figure 7(b) and Figure 8(b). From these figures, we summarize several findings:

- Comparing manual-specified and predicted fields, the retrieval performance using predicted information is worse. This indicates that using only a single field suffers from incorrect prediction and inevitably decreases performance.
- The agreement rates between manual-specified and predicted fields are 64% and 70% for Facebook and Twitter collections.
- For facebook data, "uname" is more helpful than other fields both with (Fig. 7(a)) or without (Fig. 7(b)) manual specifications. This supports the intuition that named entities such as person names show strong correlation with better performance, and that an interface design that emphasizes specifying person names in the query could potentially help retrieve relevant documents. The specification of "msg" field, contrary to our expectation, is no better than simple QLM. This may be because that the words in message fields are more common and can be found in several fields, and therefore restricting to the message field does not provide further information.

[10]The default Dirichlet smoothing with mu=2500 is used.

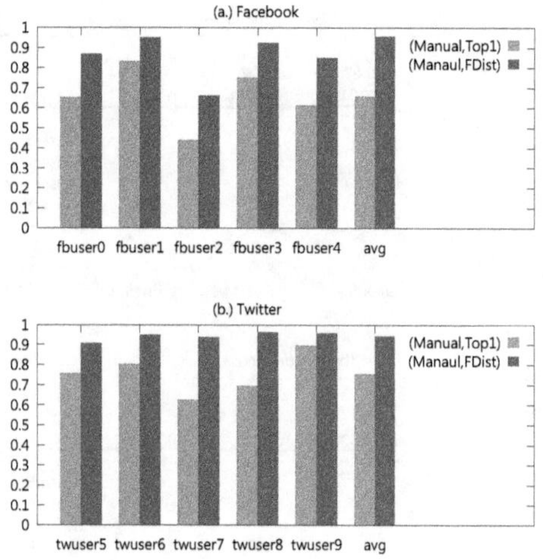

Figure 9: Correlation of (V_{avg}^{man}, V_{avg}^{top1}) and (V_{avg}^{man}, V_{avg}^{FDM}) on Facebook and Twitter.

- For Twitter data, similar trends, such as better effectiveness from "uname" can be found. In particular, the restriction to "text" results in a large drop of performance compared to QLM. This could be the result of frequent retweets in the Twitter corpus. For the case of retweets, QLM considers a query term q_i twice in "text" and "re-text"while FSM counts just once for either of the 2 fields.

Finally, let us recall the FDM_{Fprior} model in Section 4. In this paper, we normalize the retrieval performance across the fields to estimate the function $Prior(F_j)$. Specifically, we take 20% of queries from each user for $Prior(F_j)$ estimation.

6.3 Field distribution of query terms

In addition to associating q_i with only a single field as in Section 6.2, we now focus on understanding the field distribution for each query term. First we introduce the notations: vector $V_i^{man} = (v_1, v_2, \ldots, v_m)$ describes the manual-specified field distribution for a query term q_i. For example, $(1, 0, \ldots, 0)$ can be used to describe q_i is manually specified "uname" in Facebook. If q_i is not manually specified with a field, V_i^{man} is then uniformly distributed. Vector V_i^{top1} on the other hand represents the estimated field distribution for q_i, and is always composed of a series of "0" or "1" as only the top-weighted field is considered. Finally, the vector V_i^{FDM} records the real-valued field distribution for each q_i based on the estimation of FDM_{mix} model.

For each query term q_i, we may describe it using the three vectors V_i^{man}, V_i^{top1}, and V_i^{FDM}. We are then able to summarize the characteristic of each personal collection with 3 average vectors V_{avg}^{man}, V_{avg}^{top1}, and V_{avg}^{FDM} by taking the average over the set of query terms. Moreover, we compute the Pearson product-moment correlation coefficient of (V_{avg}^{man}, V_{avg}^{top1}) and (V_{avg}^{man}, V_{avg}^{FDM}) for each personal collection, as shown in Figure 9. The two figures show a consistently higher correlation of (V_{avg}^{man}, V_{avg}^{FDM}) than (V_{avg}^{man}, V_{avg}^{top1}). This finding shows that modeling q_i using a field distribution is reasonable. Also, in the following section, we show the retrieval performance based on field distributions can be very effective and even better than manual specifications.

7. RETRIEVAL EXPERIMENTS

In this section, we compare the retrieval effectiveness of the various models described previously. Firstly, we describe the experimental setup. Then, we detail the retrieval performance of the models for the Facebook and Twitter collections.

7.1 Experimental Setup

The test collections used for evaluation include 10 personal social media collections, with 5 gathered from Facebook and the other 5 from Twitter. For each personal collection, the query set is composed of two types of queries, Q_{DT} and Q_{MR}, which are collected based on DocTrack and MemRecap respectively. To ensure the quality of queries, we keep queries that have their target documents ranked in the top 50 by the DocTrack game as suggested in Kim et al, which may cause different numbers of queries for each user. Table 1 details the statistics of the collections. Moreover, we use the mean reciprocal rank (MRR) for effectiveness measurement as we focus on the task of known-item search. There is only one relevant document for each query, and the relevance judgments are the same for the Q_{DT} and Q_{MR} queries.

We index the personal collections using the Indri toolkit[11], where documents are stemmed with the Krovetz stemmer and no stopwords are eliminated. We show the effectiveness across various retrieval models discussed in Section 4, including QLM, FSM, FDM with different estimators, and finally the mixture of the language models. Specifically, we cross-validated and fixed the smoothing parameters for each retrieval model.

7.2 Performance on Facebook Collections

In the following, we summarize several observations from Table 4 and Table 5. Table 4[12] shows the retrieval performance for Q_{DT} on the Facebook collections. (1.) We see that the simple QLM model (the baseline model) can be very effective with an average MRR of 0.7519. FSM, though with extra field information, is merely comparable to QLM as field specification can sometimes be too restrictive. The Proximity model alone is not as effective, indicating that query words can sometimes be scattered in the documents. (2.) For the FDM models, including PRMS, FDM_{PRMS}, FDM_{AllF}, FDM_{Fsize}, and FDM_{Fprior}, have similar results and are close to the performance of QLM. We further take a uniform mixture of FDM models to form FDM_{mix}, whose performance is the second best of all FDM models. Though FDM_{mix} is not the top-performing FDM model, the effect of combining different FDM estimations can be complementary, and reduces the risk of being biased to current collections.

From Table 4, (3.) we see that combining different language models including Mix_{LM2} and Mix_{LM3} can significantly improve retrieval effectiveness, with Mix_{LM3} outperforming Mix_{LM2}. This shows that combining evidence from the document, the fields, and the words location is beneficial to retrieval. (4.) The use of manual-specified fields can be more precise than field distribution estimated by FDM_{mix} for the combined models, and thus QLM+FSM and QLM+FSM+Prox are consistently better than QLM+FDM_{mix} and QLM+FDM_{mix}+Prox.

[11]http://www.lemurproject.org/indri/

[12]Abbreviations:Q(QLM), F(FSM), P(Prox), F_m(FDM_{mix}).

Table 4: **MRR of Q_{DT} on Facebook collections. * is marked for p-value < 0.05 compared to QLM.**

user	QLM	FSM	Prox	PRMS	F_{prms}	F_{AllF}	F_{Fsize}	F_{Fprior}	F_{mix}	Q+F	Q+P	Q+F_m	Q+F+P	Q+F_m+P
0	0.7581	0.7833	0.7254	0.7643	0.7842	0.7603	0.7825*	0.7851*	0.7892*	0.7963*	0.7967*	0.7798	0.8102*	0.8110*
1	0.7643	0.7012*	0.5360*	0.6474*	0.7225*	0.6791*	0.7218	0.7333	0.7057*	0.7846	0.7723	0.7617	0.7891	0.7663
2	0.7608	0.7743	0.4844*	0.7397	0.7504	0.7638	0.7589	0.7706	0.7799	0.7654	0.7513	0.7951	0.7875	0.7851
3	0.7712	0.8142*	0.7585	0.8351*	0.7377*	0.7582	0.7636	0.7716	0.7634	0.8046*	0.8328*	0.7623	0.8430*	0.8337*
4	0.7051	0.7114	0.5201*	0.7037	0.7026	0.7190	0.7190	0.7383*	0.7422	0.7829*	0.7398	0.7134	0.7735*	0.7439*
Avg	0.7519	0.7568	0.6048*	0.7380	0.7394	0.7360	0.7491	0.7597	0.7560	0.7867	0.7785	0.7624	0.8006*	0.7880*

Table 5: **MRR of Q_{MR} on Facebook collections. * is marked for p-value < 0.05 compared to QLM.**

user	QLM	Prox	PRMS	F_{prms}	F_{AllF}	F_{Fsize}	F_{Fprior}	F_{mix}	Q+P	Q+F_m	Q+F_m+P
0	0.7781	0.5101*	0.7631	0.7558	0.7822	0.7930	0.8009	0.7916	0.8000	0.8167*	0.8236*
1	0.7824	0.4225*	0.6928*	0.7472	0.7425*	0.7756	0.7756	0.7493	0.7725	0.7929	0.7834
2	0.7447	0.2092*	0.7460	0.7399	0.7216	0.7137	0.7430	0.7268	0.7446	0.7447	0.7582
3	0.7995	0.5364*	0.7978	0.8129	0.8303*	0.8212	0.8214*	0.8231*	0.8573*	0.8044	0.8745*
4	0.7239	0.3164*	0.6859	0.7122	0.6753*	0.7092	0.7071	0.7132	0.7417	0.7415	0.7533
Avg	0.7657	0.3989*	0.7371	0.7536	0.7503	0.7625	0.7696	0.7608	0.7832	0.7800	0.7986*

For the other test query set Q_{MR}, we report the MRR in Table 5 for each retrieval model except for the ones associated with manual-specified fields (e.g., FSM, QLM+FSM and QLM+FSM+Prox). From Table 5, (5.) similar trends such as that the basic QLM sets a high baseline and Mix_{LM3} outperforms all other approaches can be observed. There are, however, differences compared to Q_{DT}. (6.) The Prox model works significantly worse for Q_{MR}, which we believe is because users have more time on reading in MemRecap and formulate queries based on the entire document. In this case, the query words of Q_{MR} can be more scattered than Q_{DT}, causing poor effectiveness for the Prox model alone.

Finally, (7.) comparing performance across Q_{DT} and Q_{MR}, we can see that queries collected based on MemRecap tend to be more effective despite the fact that words in Q_{DT} are exactly matched with the target documents. Several reasons have been discovered for this. Users have more time to understand document contents in MemRecap. Also, with a search-based mechanism, users tend to downsize the query length in the DocTrack game if they have incorrectly memorized document content and couldn't locate the target document. It seems more natural for users to formulate queries using stemmed (root) vocabularies, as can be observed in MemRecap queries. Considering the exact match approach in DocTrack, non-stemmed vocabularies such as past tense verbs could cause word mismatch between queries and documents.

7.3 Performance on Twitter Collections

We also show the retrieval performance of Q_{DT} and Q_{MR} for Twitter personal collections, respectively in Table 6 and Table 7. The overall trend of performance is consistent with the results of Facebook collections. The QLM model sets a high baseline for finding the target documents. The individual FDM models do not outperform the QLM model; however, together Mix_{LM2} and Mix_{LM3} can significantly improve the baseline performance. The Prox model alone works poorly for MemRecap queries as previously.

Comparing performance across the Facebook and Twitter collections, we can see that the effectiveness of retrieving Twitter documents is on average higher than that of Facebook collections. In this case, the shorter length of Twitter documents makes it easier for retrieval models to identify the target documents as there is less information contained in the tweets. For the same reason, we find it is challenging to improve baseline performance using the mixture of language models. The limitation comes from the fact that exploiting field structures as well as proximity information can still be similar to just using the plain text of document, as the document can be too short to contain extra text information.

8. CONCLUSION

In this paper, we propose the viewpoint that social media archives can serve as a new type of personal documents in the desktop environment. It is clear that providing search tools can be important; however, the lack of publicly available test collections makes evaluation difficult. To address this, we describe how text collections for personal social data can be created. In particular, we use human computation games, Doctrack and MemRecap, to collect known-item queries from real users. We also explore a range of retrieval models that exploit the semi-structured nature of social data.

Our results have several interesting aspects. The retrieval experiments show that a mixture of language models Mix_{LM3} with field distribution estimation can be effective for this type of data. Also, we see that certain fields, such as poster name, can be particularly important for retrieval. This provides a hint for future search applications that letting users specify names can potentially enhance retrieval performance.

This work has focused on evaluating search using a single collection from either Facebook or Twitter. In future work, it would be important to deal with multiple types of social media documents simultaneously, which can involve the task of type prediction as in the desktop environment. In addition, the nested XML structures could potentially contain information that could improve retrieval, but is currently not being considered in this paper. Finally, we are implementing a personal search application on desktop and mobile platforms. With this search tool, not only can we satisfy the user needs of retrieving known items, but real queries can be acquired for further research.

Table 6: MRR of Q_{DT} on Twitter collections. * is marked for p-value < 0.05 compared to QLM.

user	QLM	FSM	Prox	PRMS	F_{prms}	F_{AllF}	F_{Fsize}	F_{Fprior}	F_{mix}	Q+F	Q+P	Q+F_m	Q+F+P	Q+F_m+P
5	0.7305	0.5841*	0.5728*	0.6831	0.7154	0.7215	0.6078*	0.7125	0.7051	0.7431	0.7516	0.7488	0.7541	0.7338
6	0.9402	0.9103	0.8678*	0.9389	0.9329	0.9326	0.9114	0.9431	0.9431	0.9454	0.9402	0.9431	0.9454	0.9402
7	0.7753	0.7148*	0.7319	0.7761	0.7624	0.7124*	0.6965*	0.7550	0.7320	0.7751	0.7702	0.7719	0.7584	0.7660
8	0.8353	0.8245	0.6855*	0.8002	0.8568	0.8264	0.7848	0.8156	0.8197	0.8393	0.8237	0.8286	0.8393	0.8259
9	0.7133	0.7012	0.6027*	0.7059	0.6984	0.7399	0.7053	0.7098	0.7286	0.7401	0.7339	0.7356	0.7531*	0.7459
Avg	0.7989	0.7469	0.6921*	0.7808	0.7931	0.7865	0.7411	0.7872	0.7857	0.8086	0.8039	0.8056	0.8100*	0.8023

Table 7: MRR of Q_{MR} on Twitter collections. * is marked for p-value < 0.05 compared to QLM.

user	QLM	Prox	PRMS	F_{prms}	F_{AllF}	F_{Fsize}	F_{Fprior}	F_{mix}	Q+P	Q+F_m	Q+F_m+P
5	0.7802	0.5102*	0.7396	0.7496	0.7419	0.7353	0.7310*	0.7401	0.7966	0.8056	0.8086
6	0.9064	0.6810*	0.8873	0.8943	0.8928	0.8814	0.9063	0.9031	0.9043	0.9064	0.9043
7	0.8443	0.5975*	0.8498	0.8203	0.7979*	0.8464	0.8484	0.8245	0.8475	0.8420	0.8475
8	0.9395	0.5376*	0.9307	0.9276	0.9260	0.9327	0.9327	0.9327	0.9395	0.9395	0.9395
9	0.7361	0.5668*	0.7204	0.7313	0.7200	0.7361	0.7457	0.7413	0.7638*	0.7519	0.7710*
Avg	0.8413	0.5786*	0.8255	0.8246	0.8157	0.8263	0.8328	0.8283	0.8503	0.8490	0.8541

9. ACKNOWLEDGMENTS

This work was supported in part by the Center for Intelligent Information Retrieval and in part by ARRA NSF IIS-9014442. Any opinions, findings and conclusions or recommendations expressed in this material are those of the authors and do not necessarily reflect those of the sponsor.

10. REFERENCES

[1] M. Bendersky and W. B. Croft. Discovering key concepts in verbose queries. In *SIGIR '08*, pages 491–498, 2008.

[2] C. Chen, F. Li, B. C. Ooi, and S. Wu. Ti: an efficient indexing mechanism for real-time search on tweets. In *SIGMOD '11*, pages 649–660, New York, NY, USA, 2011. ACM.

[3] E. Cutrell, D. Robbins, S. Dumais, and R. Sarin. Fast, flexible filtering with phlat. In *SIGCHI'06*, pages 261–270, New York, NY, USA, 2006. ACM.

[4] S. Dumais, E. Cutrell, J. Cadiz, G. Jancke, R. Sarin, and D. C. Robbins. Stuff i've seen: a system for personal information retrieval and re-use. In *SIGIR'03*, pages 72–79, New York, NY, USA, 2003. ACM.

[5] D. Elsweiler and I. Ruthven. Towards task-based personal information management evaluations. In *SIGIR '07*, pages 23–30, New York, NY, USA, 2007. ACM.

[6] J. Kim and W. B. Croft. Retrieval experiments using pseudo-desktop collections. In *CIKM '09*, pages 1297–1306, 2009.

[7] J. Kim and W. B. Croft. Ranking using multiple document types in desktop search. In *SIGIR '10*, pages 50–57, New York, NY, USA, 2010. ACM.

[8] H. Ma, R. Chandrasekar, C. Quirk, and A. Gupta. Improving search engines using human computation games. In *CIKM '09*, pages 275–284, New York, NY, USA, 2009. ACM.

[9] C. Macdonald and I. Ounis. Combining fields in known-item email search. In *SIGIR '06*, pages 675–676, New York, NY, USA, 2006. ACM.

[10] K. Massoudi, M. Tsagkias, M. de Rijke, and W. Weerkamp. Incorporating query expansion and quality indicators in searching microblog posts. In *ECIR'11*, pages 362–367, Berlin, Heidelberg, 2011. Springer-Verlag.

[11] D. Metzler and W. B. Croft. A Markov random field model for term dependencies. In *SIGIR '05*, pages 472–479, New York, NY, USA, 2005. ACM.

[12] P. Ogilvie and J. Callan. Combining document representations for known-item search. In *SIGIR '03*, pages 143–150, New York, NY, USA, 2003. ACM.

[13] S. Robertson, H. Zaragoza, and M. Taylor. Simple bm25 extension to multiple weighted fields. In *Information and knowledge management*, CIKM '04, pages 42–49, New York, NY, USA, 2004. ACM.

[14] T. Sakaki, M. Okazaki, and Y. Matsuo. Earthquake shakes twitter users: real-time event detection by social sensors. In *WWW '10*, pages 851–860, New York, NY, USA, 2010. ACM.

[15] J. Teevan, D. Ramage, and M. R. Morris. #twittersearch: a comparison of microblog search and web search. In *WSDM '11*, pages 35–44, New York, NY, USA, 2011. ACM.

[16] A. Tumasjan, T. O. Sprenger, P. G. Sandner, and I. M. Welpe. *Predicting elections with Twitter: What 140 characters reveal about political sentiment*, pages 178–185. 2010.

[17] S. Vieweg, A. L. Hughes, K. Starbird, and L. Palen. Microblogging during two natural hazards events: what twitter may contribute to situational awareness. In *Human factors in computing systems*, CHI '10, pages 1079–1088, New York, NY, USA, 2010. ACM.

[18] S. Yahyaei and C. Monz. Applying maximum entropy to known-item email retrieval. In *ECIR'08*, pages 406–413, Berlin, Heidelberg, 2008. Springer-Verlag.

[19] X. Zhou, H. Chen, Q. Jin, and J. Yong. Generating associative ripples of relevant information from a variety of data streams by throwing a heuristic stone. In *ICUIMC'11*, pages 59:1–59:7, New York, NY, USA, 2011. ACM.

Learning Evolving and Emerging Topics in Social Media: A Dynamic NMF approach with Temporal Regularization

Ankan Saha*
Department of Computer Science
University of Chicago, Chicago, IL 60637
ankans@cs.uchicago.edu

Vikas Sindhwani
IBM T.J. Watson Research Center
Yorktown Heights, NY 10598
vsindhw@us.ibm.com

ABSTRACT

As massive repositories of real-time human commentary, social media platforms have arguably evolved far beyond passive facilitation of online social interactions. Rapid analysis of information content in online social media streams (news articles, blogs,tweets etc.) is the need of the hour as it allows business and government bodies to understand public opinion about products and policies. In most of these settings, data points appear as a stream of high dimensional feature vectors. Guided by real-world industrial deployment scenarios, we revisit the problem of online learning of topics from streaming social media content. On one hand, the topics need to be dynamically adapted to the statistics of incoming datapoints, and on the other hand, early detection of rising new trends is important in many applications. We propose an online nonnegative matrix factorization framework to capture the evolution and emergence of themes in unstructured text under a novel temporal regularization framework. We develop scalable optimization algorithms for our framework, propose a new set of evaluation metrics, and report promising empirical results on traditional TDT tasks as well as streaming Twitter data. Our system is able to rapidly capture emerging themes, track existing topics over time while maintaining temporal consistency and continuity in user views, and can be explicitly configured to bound the amount of information being presented to the user.

Categories and Subject Descriptors

H.3.3 [**Information Storage and Retrieval**]: Information Search and RetrievalRetrieval Models

General Terms

Algorithms, Experimentation

Keywords

Dictionary Learning, NMF, Topic Models, Time Series Analysis

*Work done as a summer intern at IBM Research

Permission to make digital or hard copies of all or part of this work for personal or classroom use is granted without fee provided that copies are not made or distributed for profit or commercial advantage and that copies bear this notice and the full citation on the first page. To copy otherwise, to republish, to post on servers or to redistribute to lists, requires prior specific permission and/or a fee.
WSDM'12, February 8–12, 2012, Seattle, Washington, USA.
Copyright 2012 ACM 978-1-4503-0747-5/12/02 ...$10.00.

1. INTRODUCTION

Over the last few years, the growth and ease of internet access accompanied by the advent of various facets of online social media *viz.* blogs, social networks and lately, twitter, has provided a vast continuous supply of dynamic diverse information content. When analyzed with appropriate statistical and computational tools, social media content can be turned into invaluable scientific and business insights. A recent large-scale study [9] of 500 million tweets generated in 2009, for example, concluded that the appearance of flu-related topics in Twitter was highly predictive of future influenza rates in the general population.

While the early years of social media platforms were focussed on developing software infrastructure for connecting people, the emphasis has only very recently begun to shift towards understanding collective public opinion by using deep, data-driven *social media analytics* [21]. One of the most basic and necessary tasks that arises in this setting is to organize streaming social media into coherent threads of discussion that can be easily analyzed and utilized to improve various services that are affected by social media. In this paper, we argue that traditional topic detection and tracking methodologies historically rooted in Information Retrieval literature need to be revisited in the context of the demands of these emerging applications.

Over regular intervals of time (which might be per day or even every few hours), any user who is continuously mining social media content, has the following natural expectations from the system: (1) to be alerted to any new emerging themes of discussion that is fast gathering steam in social media, (2) to be able to follow the evolution of existing topics that have already been identified as being of particular interest and (3) not to be overloaded with excessive bits of information that is time consuming to sift through. Several tradeoffs become naturally evident in the design of a satisfactory system. By definition, an emerging theme is one that has not been observed before and is somewhat of an anomaly in the data stream, not necessarily distinguishable from noise when first encountered. Yet, not every anomaly can be presented to the user as an "early warning" as this would lead to excessive information overload in a large-scale setting. At the same time, information presented in the past sets up expectations for what the user expects in the future, e.g., the ability to clearly see how a topic has evolved possibly in response to marketing or PR interventions. What is needed, is an ability to distinguish valid emerging topics (with steep information content) from "noise" and some method to continuously summarize essential data characteristics in terms of a small number of human interpretable components.

Several social media monitoring tools rely on communicating individual keywords whose usage has rapidly increased in recent time, as proxies for emerging topics. Such a methodology has obvious limitations in characterizing the separate strands of conversations that may have simulatenously Jo-emerged in the data stream. In this paper, we describe a system for online analysis of streaming text using more rigorous machine learning and optimization methodologies in the form of powerful topic modeling and non negative matrix factorization techniques. Unlike previously proposed IR techniques, our approach incorporates special algorithmic constructs to attempt to detect emerging topics early, maintains temporal continuity while evolving existing topics in response to the statistics of incoming data, and allows the amount of information being presented to the user to be explictly configured. While we demonstrate these ideas in the context of online topic modeling, our methods apply much more broadly to early detection problems in more general signal separation and decomposition settings. A preliminary version of this work appeared in the NIPS 2010 workshop on Social Computing.

2. RELATED WORK AND OVERVIEW

Over the last decade, different methods have been used for topic modeling and detection from a corpus of documents available as a batch or an online stream. Early impetus in this research was provided by DARPA sponsorship of Topic Detection and Tracking evaluations which led to the design of several TDT engines [26, 1]. One of the best performing engines, GAC-INCR [26], uses a clustering algorithm (GAC) to cluster incoming new data in the first phase, and then, based on a similarity/novelty threshold, either merges each of these clusters with those discovered in the past or treat them as a new cluster/topic to be tracked going forward.

Probabilistic latent semantic indexing (pLSI) [16] and Latent Dirichlet Allocation (LDA) [5] are probabilistic methods that have found remarkable success in building topic models of text. Both of them characterize topics as a multinomial distribution over a vocabulary of words rather than clusters of documents. The topics are treated as latent variables and the joint probability of the terms and documents is represented as the mixture of conditional probabilities over the latent topics which are typically inferred by maximum likelihood or Bayesian procedures that involve either variational inference or Gibbs sampling techniques. The notion of a "topic" is then communicated to a user via keywords that have highest mass in these learnt distributions.The two models are essentially equivalent [12], the key difference being that while the PLSI approach may be viewed as maximum likelihood estimation of model parameters, LDA applies a Dirichlet prior on them. Variants of pLSI and LDA have been proposed for online and dynamic topic modeling (see [6, 13, 15, 4, 2] and references therein).

Another line of seemingly unrelated work which finds use in topic modeling is that of dictionary learning and non-probabilistic matrix factorizations[20]. Dictionary Learning is the problem of estimating a collection of basis vectors over which a given data collection can be accurately reconstructed, often with sparse encodings. It may be formulated in terms of uncovering low-rank structure in the data using matrix factorizations possibly with sparsity-inducing priors [20]. These are closely related to probabilistic topic models (pLSI, LDA) for textual datasets.

In this paper, we propose a framework for online topic detection to handle streaming non-negative data matrices with possibly growing number of components. Our methods are rooted in non-negative matrix factorizations (NMF) [18, 25] whose unregularized variants for (generalized) KL-divergence minimization can be shown to be equivalent to pLSI [10]. For squared loss, NMF finds a low-rank approximation to a data matrix $\mathbf{X}$ by minimizing the Frobenius norm of $\|\mathbf{X} - \mathbf{WH}\|_{fro}^2$ under non-negativity and scaling constraints on the factors $\mathbf{W}$ and $\mathbf{H}$. Finding the minimum rank NMF of $\mathbf{X}$ is a non-convex problem and the general algorithm used is due to the multiplicative weight methods of [18]. It is common to add some form of l_1/l_2 regularization, generally to encourage sparse factors and prevent overfitting. If $\mathbf{X}$ is an $N \times D$ document-term matrix, then $\mathbf{W}$ is a $N \times K$ matrix of topic encodings of documents where each column corresponds to a topic and represents the contribution of the documents to the particular topic. $\mathbf{H}$ is a $K \times D$ matrix of topic-word associations, whose rows are the dictionary elements learnt by the NMF approach.

Figure 1: A snapshot of the online NMF system for tracking and capturing topics

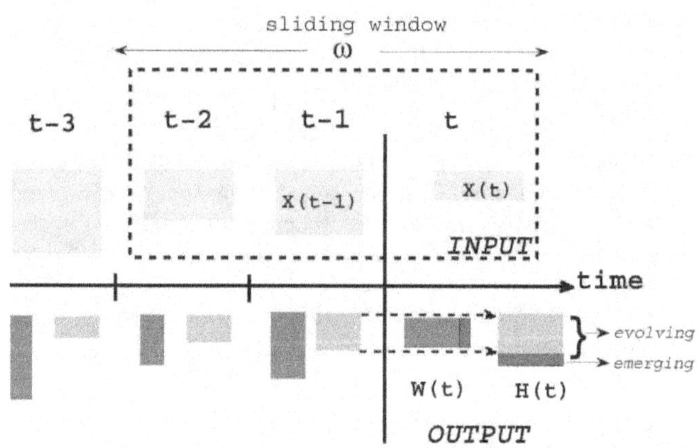

We give a preview of our online learning framework in Figure 1. At any given timepoint, our system consumes the incoming data together with recently seen documents over a short time window. The output is an NMF that yields a new set of topics together with encodings for the most recently seen documents. These topics can be divided into two sets, which we call *evolving* and *emerging* sets. The evolving set is a smooth evolution of previously discovered topics. This evolution is constrained to prevent excessive drift or change that can negatively affect user interpretability. The emerging set comprises of a small number of topics injected into the model for the purpose of detecting emerging themes. This is done by finding the *optimal* word distributions that show rising temporal trends after correcting for spurious discontinuities. We show that constrained topic evolution and trend estimation can be posed naturally as extended matrix factorization problems that infact also have a link to margin-based learning methods such as SVMs. We then develop scalable alternating optimization algorithms using efficient schemes to solve rank-one subproblems. Once the online model is learnt, the emerging set (whose size can be configured) is presented to the user who may choose to explicitly discard a subset from current consideration. Going forward in time, the emerging set becomes part of the evolving set, and new emerging bandwidth is introduced for the next timepoint. The use of explicit temporal regularizers for emerging topic detection in a matrix factorization framework in this manner is novel to the best of our knowledge. Prior work on online matrix factorization has not dealt with low-rank approximations with gradually increasing rank. In the next section, we describe the details of our online models.

Notation: In the sequel we abuse notation to denote $\mathbf{h}_i$ as the ith row of $\mathbf{H}$ and $\mathbf{h}_{ij} = \mathbf{H}_{ij}$. Δ_D denotes the D dimensional simplex. $[K]$ refers to the set $\{1, 2 \ldots K\}$ and $\mathbf{0}_d, \mathbf{1}_d$ refers to the vector of all 0's and 1's of dimension d.

3. DYNAMIC NMF FRAMEWORK

Let $\{\mathbf{X}(t) \in \mathbb{R}^{N(t) \times D(t)}, t = 1, 2 \ldots t, ..\}$ denote a sequence of streaming matrices where each row of $\mathbf{X}(t)$ represents an observation whose time stamp is t. For simplicity in notation and exposition, we will assume that $D(t) = D$ for all t. In topic modeling applications over streaming documents, $\mathbf{X}(t)$ will represent the highly sparse document-term matrix observed at time t [1]. We will use the conventional vector space model [23] used in the information retrieval literature. Terms in a document are statistically weighted using standard measures Term Frequency(TF) and Inverse-Document Frequency(IDF). The (d, r)-th entry of $\mathbf{X}(t)$ corresponding to document d and term r is given by

$$\mathbf{X}(t)(d, r) = \frac{(1 + \log_2 TF(d, r)) \times \log_2 IDF(r)}{C}$$

where C normalizes the representation to unit norm l_2 norm vectors. We use $\mathbf{X}(t_1, t_2)$ to denote the document-term matrix formed by vertically concatenating $\{\mathbf{X}(t), t_1 \leq t \leq t_2\}$. Since we operate in an online framework, we introduce a short sliding time window ω over which trends are estimated at every time point.

At the current time point t, our model consumes the incoming data $\mathbf{X}(t)$ and appends to documents seen in a recent ω-window, $\mathbf{X}(t - \omega + 1, t)$. It generates a factorization $(\mathbf{W}^\star, \mathbf{H}(t))$ comprising of $K(t)$ topics (see equation (1)). Each column of $\mathbf{W}^\star$ and each row of $\mathbf{H}(t)$ corresponds to a topic. Note that $\mathbf{W}^\star$ has the same number of rows as all the documents accumulated over the ω-window ending at time point t. The last $N(t)$ rows of $\mathbf{W}^\star$(corresponding to $\mathbf{X}(t)$) represent the weight matrix $\mathbf{W}(t)$ at time t. Furthermore, since $\mathbf{H}(t)$ is the matrix of topic-term dependence at time t, we normalize each row of $\mathbf{H}(t)$ so that it resembles a probability distribution of words over the corresponding topic. This online factorization mechanism is designed to satisfy two considerations:

- The first $K(t-1)$ topics in $\mathbf{H}(t)$ must be smooth evolutions of the $K(t-1)$ topics found upto the previous time point in $\mathbf{H}(t-1)$. These topics are assumed to be gradually changing over time (with steady temporal profile). We call this the *evolving set* and introduce an evolution parameter, δ, which constrains the evolving set so that each entry of these $K(t-1)$ topics in $\mathbf{H}(t)$ resides within a box of size δ on the probability simplex around their previous values in $\mathbf{H}(t-1)$ (see equation (4)). With minor modifications, δ can also be made topic or word-specific e.g., to take topic volatility or word dominance into account.
- The second consideration is the fast detection of emerging topics. At each time point, we inject additional topic bandwidth for this purpose which constitute the $K(t) - K(t-1)$ remaining rows of $\mathbf{H}(t)$. This represents the *emerging set*.

[1]As new documents come in and new terms are identified, we expand the vocabulary and zero-pad the previous matrices so that at the current time t, all previous and the current documents have a representation over the same vocabulary space.

Thus the topic variable $\mathbf{H}(t)$ can be partitioned into an evolving set of $K(t-1)$ topics, $\mathbf{H}^{ev}$, and an emerging set of K^{em} topics $\mathbf{H}^{em}$ where $K(t) = K(t-1) + K^{em}$. It should be noted that the set $\mathbf{H}^{ev}$ is an increasing set over time. Older topics that are no longer active may be removed for efficiency, but for simplicity, we do not discuss such a removal process in this paper. As new discussions take place over social forums, new topics emerge and are added to the system. Furthermore, we assume that emerging topics can be distinguished from noise based on their temporal profile. In other words, the number of documents that a true emerging topic associates with rapidly increases. This may occur due to a sudden large increase in discussions about the topic in documents over time.

The discussion above motivates the following objective function that is optimized at every time point t.

$$(\mathbf{W}^\star, \mathbf{H}(t)) = \underset{\mathbf{W}, \mathbf{H}}{\operatorname{argmin}} \|\mathbf{X}(t - \omega + 1, t) - \mathbf{W}\mathbf{H}\|_{fro}^2 + \mu\Omega(\mathbf{W}) \tag{1}$$

where Ω plays the role of a temporal emergence regularizer (described in section 4) which penalizes static temporal profiles and encourages the discovery of topics whose temporal profiles exhibit steep increase. These intuitively correspond to the emerging topics. This objective function is minimized under the following non-negativity, normalization and evolution constraints as discussed above.

$$\mathbf{W}, \mathbf{H} \geq 0 \tag{2}$$

$$\sum_{j=1}^{D} \mathbf{H}_{ij} = 1 \qquad \forall i \in [K(t-1) + K^{em}] \tag{3}$$

$$\min(\mathbf{H}_{ij}(t-1) - \delta, 0) \leq \mathbf{H}_{ij} \leq \max(\mathbf{H}_{ij}(t-1) + \delta, 1), \tag{4}$$
$$\forall i \in [K(t-1)], \forall j \in [D]$$

The last equation (4) enforces the smoothness condition for the evolving topics $\mathbf{H}^{ev}$ by forcing the individual topic components at time t to stay within δ of their value at the previous time step.

We then extract $\mathbf{W}(t)$ from the bottom rows of $\mathbf{W}^\star$ that correspond to $\mathbf{X}(t)$ which came in at time t. Since $\mathbf{W}(t)$ stores the weights assigned to each topic by the documents, the ith document (row) in $\mathbf{X}(t)$ is tagged in the following way:

$$\pi_{system}(i) = \underset{j}{\operatorname{argmax}}\, \mathbf{W}(t)(i, j) \tag{5}$$

Figure 2:

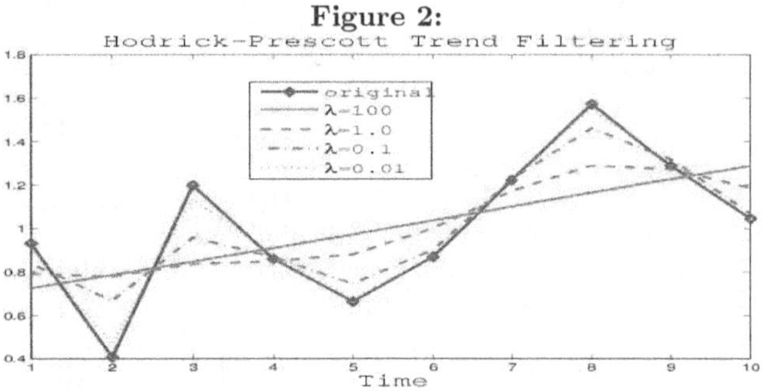

. Thus each document at time t is assigned to the corresponding most dominating topic by the system. Note that this gives a clustering of the documents per topic. In the next section, we define the emergence regularization operator $\Omega(\mathbf{W})$ that forms an essential component of our optimization algorithm.

4. EMERGENCE REGULARIZATION

In this section, we formulate the temporal regularization operator $\Omega(\mathbf{W})$ by chaining together trend extraction with a margin-based loss function to penalize static or decaying topics. We begin with a brief introduction to trend filtering.

4.1 Hodrick-Prescott (HP) Trend Filtering

Let $\{y_t\}_{t=1}^T$ be a univariate time-series which is composed of an unknown, slowly varying trend component $\{x_t\}_{t=1}^T$ perturbed by random noise $\{\alpha_t\}_{t=1}^T$. Trend Filtering is the task of recovering the trend component $\{x_t\}$ given the observations $\{y_t\}$. The Hodrick-Prescott filter is an approach to estimate the trend assuming that it is smooth and that the random residual is small. It is based on solving the following optimization problem:

$$\operatorname*{argmin}_{\{x_t\}} \frac{1}{2}\sum_{i=1}^{T}(y_i - x_i)^2 + \lambda \sum_{t=2}^{T-1}((x_{t+1} - x_t) - (x_t - x_{t-1}))^2 \tag{6}$$

The first term tries to minimize the reconstruction error while the second term penalizes the change in the underlying time series over successive time points thus enforcing the concept that the underlying trend component is smooth.

Let us introduce the second order difference matrix $\mathbf{D} \in \mathbb{R}^{(T-2)\times T}$ such that $\mathbf{D}_{ii} = 1, \mathbf{D}_{i,i+1} = -2$ and $\mathbf{D}_{i,i+2} = 1$ for all $i \in [T-2]$. It is easy to see that the solution to the optimization problem of Equation 6 is given by:

$$\mathbf{x} = [I + 2\lambda \mathbf{D}^\top \mathbf{D}]^{-1}\mathbf{y}$$

where we use the notation $\mathbf{y} = (y_1 \dots y_T)^\top, \mathbf{x} = (x_1 \dots x_T)^\top$. In the sequel, we use F to denote $[I + 2\lambda \mathbf{D}^\top \mathbf{D}]^{-1}$, the linear smoothing operator associated with the Hodrick-Prescott Filter. Given the time series $\mathbf{y}$, the Hodrick-Prescott (HP) trend estimate simply is $\mathbf{x} = F\mathbf{y}$. Figure 2 captures the notion of Hodrick-Prescott trend filtering where a smooth reconstruction of the observed signal is demonstrated for different values of the parameter λ. In our experiments, we use $\lambda = 10$.

4.2 Loss Function for Emerging Trends

Let $\mathbf{x} = F\mathbf{y}$ be the HP trend of the time series $\mathbf{y}$. Let $\mathcal{D}$ be the forward difference operator, i.e., the only non-zero entries of $\mathcal{D}$ are: $\mathcal{D}_{i,i} = -1$ and $\mathcal{D}_{i,i+1} = 1$. If $\mathbf{z} = \mathcal{D}\mathbf{x}$, then $z_i = x_{i+1} - x_i$ reflects the discrete numerical gradient in the trend x. Given z_i, we define a margin based loss function (the ℓ_2 hinge loss), $L(z_i) = c_i \max(0, \nu - z_i)^2$. If the growth in the trend at time i is *sufficient*, i.e., greater than ν, the loss evaluates to 0. If the growth is insufficient, the loss evaluates to $c_i(\nu - z_i)^2$ where c_i is the weight of timepoint i. We observed experimentally that the best results are given by weights c_i's which typically increase with i. For a vector $\mathbf{z}$, the loss is added over the time components. In terms of the original time series $\mathbf{y}$, this loss function is,

$$L(\mathbf{y}) = \sum_{i=1}^{T-1} c_i \max(0, \nu - (\mathcal{D}F\mathbf{y})_i)^2 \tag{7}$$

Optimization Problem: As documents arrive over $t \in \{1, 2, \dots T\}$, we use $\mathbf{S}$ to denote a $T \times N$ time-document matrix, where $\mathbf{S}(i,j) = 1$ if the document j has time stamp i. Noting that each column $\mathbf{w}$ of $\mathbf{W}$, denotes the document associations for a given topic, $\mathbf{Sw}$ captures the time series of total contribution of the topic corresponding to $\mathbf{w}$, which is analogous to the temporal profile of the topic and is expected to rapidly grow for emerging topics. Finally, we concretize (1) as the following optimization problem

$$\operatorname*{argmin}_{\mathbf{W},\mathbf{H}\geq \mathbf{0}} \|\mathbf{X} - \mathbf{WH}\|_{fro}^2 + \mu \sum_{\mathbf{w}_i \in \mathbf{W}^{em}} L(\mathbf{Sw}_i) \tag{8}$$

subject to constraints in equations 3 and 4. Note that the sum in the penalization term only runs over the emerging topic variables.

5. OPTIMIZATION ALGORITHMS

We approximate $\mathbf{X}$ as the sum of rank-one matrices $\mathbf{w}_i\mathbf{h}_i^\top$ and optimize cyclically over individual $\mathbf{w}_i$ and $\mathbf{h}_i$ variables while keeping all other variables fixed. This results in three specific sub-problems, each of which requires an efficient projection of a vector onto an appropriate space. Optimization of rank-one subproblems has been previously shown to be very effective for standard NMFs [14, 7] and is also reminiscent of the K-SVD approach for dictionary learning [11].

Optimization over $\mathbf{h}_i$: Firstly note that since the regularization term is independent of $\mathbf{h}_i$, it does not contribute to this optimization problem. Holding all variables except $\mathbf{h}_i$ fixed and omitting additive constants independent of $\mathbf{h}_i$, (8) can be reduced to $\operatorname{argmin}_{\mathbf{h}_i \in \mathfrak{C}} \|R - \mathbf{w}_i\mathbf{h}_i^\top\|_{fro}^2$ where

$$R = \mathbf{X} - \sum_{j\neq i} \mathbf{w}_j \mathbf{h}_j^\top \tag{9}$$

is the residual matrix independent of $\mathbf{h}_i$. Note that R is the difference of a sparse matrix and rank one matrices. While it can possibly be a dense matrix, we never need to evaluate it explicitly. In particular, our algorithm only needs to compute matrix vector products against R, namely

$$R\mathbf{h}_i = \mathbf{X}\mathbf{h}_i - \sum_{j\neq i} \mathbf{w}_j(\mathbf{h}_j^\top \mathbf{h}_i) \quad \text{and}$$

$$R^\top \mathbf{w}_i = \mathbf{X}^\top \mathbf{w}_i - \sum_{j\neq i} \mathbf{h}_j(\mathbf{w}_j^\top \mathbf{w}_i)$$

We use sparse matrix computations to evaluate $\mathbf{X}\mathbf{h}_i$ and $\mathbf{X}^\top\mathbf{w}_i$ thus allowing us to efficiently compute the updates without evaluating R explicitly.

Algorithm 1: Online Learning Algorithm for Topic Evolution and Emergence.

Input: New data $\mathbf{X}(t) \in \mathbb{R}^{N(t)\times D}$, Old data $\mathbf{X}(t-\omega+1, t-1)$, Previous topic matrix $\mathbf{H}(t-1)$ of size $K(t-1)\times D$, Emerging Topic Bandwidth B, Hyperparameters: Evolution δ, Emergence μ, Hinge ν.
Output: $\mathbf{W}(t) \in \mathbb{R}^{N(t)\times K(t)}$, $\mathbf{H}(t) \in \mathbb{R}^{K(t)\times D}$
$\epsilon = 10^{-6}$
Set $K(t) = K(t-1) + B$
Define $\mathbf{X} = \mathbf{X}(t-\omega+1, t) \in \mathbb{R}^{N\times D}$
Initialize $\mathbf{W} = \mathbf{W}_{\text{init}}, \mathbf{H} = \mathbf{H}_{\text{init}}$ where $\mathbf{W}_{\text{init}} \in \mathbb{R}^{N\times K(t)}, \mathbf{H}_{\text{init}} \in \mathbb{R}^{K(t)\times D}$ (details in Section 5).
while not(converge) **do**
  for $i = 1, \ldots K(t)$ **do**
    if $i \leq K(t-1)$ **then**
      $R\mathbf{h}_i = \mathbf{X}\mathbf{h}_i - \sum_{j\neq i} \mathbf{w}_j(\mathbf{h}_j^\top \mathbf{h}_i)$
      Evolving $\mathbf{w}_i$: $\mathbf{w}_{ij} = \max\left(0, \frac{1}{\|\mathbf{h}_i\|^2}(R\mathbf{h}_i)_j\right)$.
    else
      Emerging $\mathbf{w}_i$ (use Projected Gradient):
      $\mathbf{w}_i = \text{argmin}_{\mathbf{w}\geq \mathbf{0}} \left\|\mathbf{w} - R\mathbf{h}_i / \|\mathbf{h}_i\|^2\right\|^2 + \frac{\mu}{\|\mathbf{h}_i\|^2}\sum_{j=1}^{T-1} c_j \max(0, \nu_j - \mathbf{q}_j^\top \mathbf{w}_i)^2$ (see Section 5).
    end if
  end for
  for $i = 1, \ldots K(t)$ **do**
    $R^\top \mathbf{w}_i = \mathbf{X}^\top \mathbf{w}_i - \sum_{j\neq i} \mathbf{h}_j(\mathbf{w}_j^\top \mathbf{w}_i)$
    if $i \leq K(t-1)$ **then**
      $l_{ij} = \max(0, \mathbf{h}_{ij}(t-1) - \delta)$,
      $u_{ij} = \min(\mathbf{h}_{ij}(t-1) + \delta, 1)$.
      Evolving $\mathbf{h}_i$ (Simplex projection with box constraints):
      $\mathbf{h}_i = \text{argmin}_{\mathbf{h}\in\mathfrak{C}_1} \left\|\mathbf{h} - R^\top \mathbf{w}_i / \|\mathbf{w}_i\|^2\right\|^2$
      where $\mathfrak{C}_1 = \{\mathbf{h} : \mathbf{h} \in \Delta_D, \quad l_{ij} \leq \mathbf{h}_j \leq u_{ij}\}$.
    else
      Emerging $\mathbf{h}_i$ (use Simplex Projection):
      $\mathbf{h}_i = \text{argmin}_{\mathbf{h}\in\Delta_D} \left\|\mathbf{h} - R^\top \mathbf{w}_i / \|\mathbf{w}_i\|^2\right\|^2$
    end if
  end for
  Convergence Check: Relative change in Objective value $< \epsilon$
end while
$\mathbf{H}(t) = \mathbf{H}$ and $\mathbf{W}(t)$ is last $N(t)$ rows of $\mathbf{W}$.

Simple linear algebraic operations yield that the above is equivalent to

$$\underset{\mathbf{h}_i\in\mathfrak{C}}{\text{argmin}} \left\|\mathbf{h}_i - R^\top \mathbf{w}_i / \|\mathbf{w}_i\|^2\right\|^2 \tag{10}$$

Note that the domain of dependence $\mathfrak{C}$ changes according to different constraints on $\mathbf{h}_i$ depending on whether it is an emerging or evolving topic.

Evolving $\mathbf{h}_i$: For an evolving topic, the optimization needs to be performed under the smoothness and the normalization constraints ((4) and (3) respectively). Thus the optimum $\mathbf{h}_i^\star$ is obtained by optimizing the above objective over the set $\mathfrak{C} = \{\mathbf{h}_i : \mathbf{h}_i \in \Delta_D, l_j \leq \mathbf{h}_{ij} \leq u_j\}$ for appropriate lower and upper bounds l_j and u_j determined by (4). This is equivalent to a projection onto a simplex with box constraints. Adapting a method due to [22], we can find the minimizer in $O(D)$ time *i.e.* linear in the number of coordinates.

Emerging $\mathbf{h}_i$: For an emerging topic, we do not have the smoothness constraints and the domain $\mathfrak{C} = \{\mathbf{h}_i : \mathbf{h}_i \in \Delta_D\}$ is just the D dimensional simplex. The optimization (10) becomes equivalent to a projection onto the simplex Δ_D. The same algorithm [22] again gives us the minimizer in linear time $O(D)$.

Evolving $\mathbf{w}_i$: When $\mathbf{w}_i \in \mathbf{W}^{ev}$, the regularization term in (8) does not contribute and the corresponding optimization problem boils down to $\mathbf{w}_i^\star = \text{argmin}_{\mathbf{w}_i\geq\mathbf{0}} \left\|R - \mathbf{w}_i\mathbf{h}_i^\top\right\|^2$. Similar to (10), simple algebraic operations yield that the above minimization is equal to the following simple projection problem,

$$\underset{\mathbf{w}_i\geq\mathbf{0}}{\text{argmin}} \left\|\mathbf{w}_i - R\mathbf{h}_i / \|\mathbf{h}_i\|^2\right\|^2 .$$

The projection set now is just the non-negative orthant, for which there is a closed form minimizer: $\mathbf{w}_{ij} = \max\left(0, \frac{1}{\|\mathbf{h}_i\|^2}(R\mathbf{h}_i)_j\right)$.

Emerging $\mathbf{w}_i$: When $\mathbf{w}_i \in \mathbf{W}^{em}$, the second term in (8) is active and the corresponding optimization problem looks like

$$\underset{\mathbf{w}_i\geq\mathbf{0}}{\text{argmin}} \left\|R - \mathbf{w}_i\mathbf{h}_i^\top\right\|^2 + \mu L(S\mathbf{w}_i)$$

Omitting the terms independent of $\mathbf{w}_i$, simple algebra yields that the above is equivalent to

$$\underset{\mathbf{w}_i\geq\mathbf{0}}{\text{argmin}} \left\|\mathbf{w}_i - R\mathbf{h}_i / \|\mathbf{h}_i\|^2\right\|^2 + \mu L(S\mathbf{w}_i) / \|\mathbf{h}_i\|^2 \tag{11}$$

Noting that we choose L to be the ℓ_2 hinge loss, (11) can be rewritten as

$$\underset{\mathbf{w}_i\geq\mathbf{0}}{\text{argmin}} \left\|\mathbf{w}_i - R\mathbf{h}_i / \|\mathbf{h}_i\|^2\right\|^2 + \frac{\mu}{\|\mathbf{h}_i\|^2}\sum_{j=1}^{T-1} c_j \max(0, \nu_j - \mathbf{q}_j^\top \mathbf{w}_i)^2$$

where $\mathbf{q}_j^\top = (\mathcal{D}F\mathbf{S})_{j,:}$, the jth row of $\mathcal{D}F\mathbf{S}$ where the operators are defined in (7) and (8) respectively. Assimilating the $\mu / \|\mathbf{h}_i\|^2$ into the constant c_i, the above optimization problem can be written in the following generic form

$$\min_{\mathbf{w}\geq\mathbf{0}} \quad J(\mathbf{w}) \qquad \text{where}$$

$$J(\mathbf{w}) = \sum_i \max(0, c_i(\nu_i - \langle \mathbf{w}, \mathbf{x}_i\rangle))^2 + \frac{\lambda}{2}\|\mathbf{w} - \mathbf{w}_0\|^2 \tag{12}$$

where $\mathbf{w}_0$ refers to the term $R\mathbf{h}_i / \|\mathbf{h}_i\|^2$. Note that this is the same as the L2-SVM optimization problem with additional non-negativity constraints on $\mathbf{w}_i$ and the regularizer measuring distance from the vector $\mathbf{w}_0$ instead of the origin.

This objective is minimized using a projected gradient algorithm (due to the non-negativity constraint) [19] on the primal objective directly, as it is smooth and therefore the gradient is well defined. The update is given by

$$\mathbf{w}^{(k+1)} = \prod(\mathbf{w}^{(k)} - \eta_k \nabla J(\mathbf{w}^{(k)}))$$

where $\prod$ is the projection operator $\prod(s) = \max(s, 0)$ and

$$\nabla J(\mathbf{w}^{(k)}) = -2\sum_i \max\left[c_i\left(\nu_i - \left\langle \mathbf{w}^{(k)}, \mathbf{x}_i\right\rangle\right), 0\right]\mathbf{x}_i + \lambda(\mathbf{w}^{(k)} - \mathbf{w}_0)$$

The main trick lies in choosing the best rate η_k at the kth step. Following [19], we start with $\eta_0 = 1$ and at every step hot start $\eta_k = \eta_{k-1}$. If η_k satisfies

$$J(\mathbf{w}^{(k+1)}) - J(\mathbf{w}^{(k)}) \leq \sigma \left\langle \nabla J(\mathbf{w}^{(k)}), \mathbf{w}^{(k+1)} - \mathbf{w}^{(k)} \right\rangle \quad (13)$$

we continuously increase $\eta_k \leftarrow \eta_k/\beta$ as long it satisfies (13). If η_k initially does not satisfy (13), we continuously decrease $\eta_k \leftarrow \eta_k\beta$ until the condition is satisfied. For our experiments, we choose $\beta = 0.05$ and $\sigma = 0.01$.

Our online learning algorithm can now be composed as in the table labeled Algorithm 1.

Initializations: Note that in the algorithm above, $\mathbf{H}_{\text{init}} = \begin{pmatrix} \mathbf{H}^{ev} \\ \mathbf{H}^{em} \end{pmatrix}$ where $\mathbf{H}^{ev}$, the evolving set is initialized from $\mathbf{H}(t-1)$ and $\mathbf{H}^{em}$ is initialized to random distributions.

The corresponding parts of $\mathbf{W}_{\text{init}} = \begin{pmatrix} \mathbf{W}_{11} & \mathbf{W}_{12} \\ \mathbf{W}_{21} & \mathbf{W}_{22} \end{pmatrix}$ are initialized in the following way: $\mathbf{W}_{11}$ is extracted from previous runs (previous association of old documents with existing topics), $\mathbf{W}_{12} = 0$ (old documents have weak association with emerging topics), $\mathbf{W}_{21}$ optimizes

$$\underset{\hat{\mathbf{W}} \geq 0}{\text{argmin}} \|\mathbf{X}(t) - \hat{\mathbf{W}}\mathbf{H}^{ev}\|_{fro}^2$$

In other words, existing topics are allowed to first reconstruct new documents. Finally, $\mathbf{W}_{22}$ is chosen to be the columns of $\mathbf{W}$ corresponding to emerging topics where $\mathbf{W}$ is chosen randomly and scaled appropriately with

$$\alpha = \underset{\beta > 0}{\text{argmin}} \|\mathbf{X}(t) - \beta\mathbf{W}\mathbf{H}_{init}\|_{fro}^2$$

(see [14] for simple expressions for α).

Convergence: Using a general result on convergence of Block Coordinate Descent, from [3], we can show that the limit point $(\mathbf{W}^*, \mathbf{H}(t))$ generated by algorithm 1 is a stationary point of the objective function (1). This follows from the uniqueness of the projection onto a closed convex set (simplex, or simplex with box constraints) and the strict convexity of Eq. 12.

6. PERFORMANCE EVALUATION

We conducted a comprehensive empirical evaluation of our system on both traditional topic detection and tracking datasets comprising of streaming news stories, as well as a twitter stream filtered for tweets relevant to IBM that was collected over a span of 6 weeks.

It should be noted that the goal of our experiments is to empirically understand the effectiveness of the temporal regularizers. As a result, most of our experiments try to demonstrate the role of these temporal regularizers on traditional news datasets as well as twitter streams as opposed to exhaustive comparison with existing TDT algorithms. However we still perform comparisons with a simple baseline TDT model to put our models into perspective. We begin with a discussion on appropriate evaluation metrics, some of which are new to the best of our knowledge.

6.1 Metrics and Methodology

For performance evaluation, we assume that documents in the corpus have been manually identified with a set of E events. For simplicity, we assume that each document i is tagged with a single, most dominant event that it associates with $\pi_{true}(i) \in \{1 \dots E\}$. In the description below, we call these human labeled topics as events or "true topics" and assume them to be the ground truth.

Microaveraged F1: This measure has been commonly reported in topic detection and tracking (TDT) literature (see, e.g., [6]). Let us assume that the system generates S topics where in general $S \neq E$ i.e., the system is allowed to generate any number of topics. We first construct the $E \times S$ confusion matrix CM between events and system topics, i.e., $CM_{e,s}$ is the number of documents that were tagged e by the human and tagged s by the system. From this matrix, for each event e, we identify $top_k(e)$ – the set of top-k most frequently co-occuring system topics. We can then compute the *microaveraged* F1 measure as follows:

$$Precision_k = \frac{\sum_{e=1}^{E} |D_{true}(e) \cap D_{system}(e)|}{\sum_{e=1}^{E} |D_{system}(e)|} \quad (14)$$

$$Recall_k = \frac{\sum_{e=1}^{E} |D_{true}(e) \cap D_{system}(e)|}{\sum_{e=1}^{E} |D_{true}(e)|} \quad (15)$$

$$F1_k = \frac{Precision * Recall}{Precision + Recall} \quad (16)$$

where $D_{true}(e)$ is the set of documents human-tagged e and $D_{system}(e)$ is the set of documents system-tagged with a topic in $top_k(e)$, $|\cdot|$ denotes the cardinality and $\cap$ denotes intersection operators on sets. Note that while k in top_k is typically chosen to be 1, higher values may also be meaningful to study particularly when multiple system topics attempt to capture the same semantic event. Also note that the F1 score also implicitly measures topic continuity which is important in providing a stable, consistent association across time between events and system topics.

Miss Rate @ First Detection: This measure attempts to intuitively capture the following notion: *how much of an event has been "missed" before the system is able to communicate its existence to the user via the word-distribution of a topic.* It is a direct measure of the quality of an online topic detection model to serve as an early warning system for emerging themes. To compute this measure, we find the *first detection timepoint*: the earliest timepoint when the word-distribution of a system generated topic gets *sufficiently near* the word distribution of the event e (which is itself evolving temporally). We then compute the percentage of documents tagged with e that have streamed away prior to first detection. This fraction is called the *miss rate @ first detection.* To operationalize this measure, we define the following:

(a) *Word distribution of an event* e at time t: the normalized centroid of all documents on event e upto time t. Note that this distribution is also obtained from the solution to the optimization problem

$$\mathbf{H}_{true}(t) = \underset{\mathbf{H} \geq 0, \mathbf{H}\mathbf{1}_D = \mathbf{1}_E}{\text{argmin}} \|\mathbf{X}(1:t) - \mathbf{W}_{true}\mathbf{H}\|_{fro}^2$$

where $\mathbf{W}_{true}$ is simply the matrix encoding for π_{true}, i.e., $\mathbf{W}_{true}(i, e) = 1$ *if* $\pi_{true}(i) = e$ and 0 otherwise. $\mathbf{H}_{true}(t)$ serves as a proxy for the word distributions of the true topics.

(b) *Similarity measure for Topic nearness*: Given two discrete distributions $\mathbf{p}$ and $\mathbf{q}$, we use the Jensen-Shannon Divergence (JSD) as a measure of topic proximity,

$$JSD(\mathbf{p}, \mathbf{q}) = \frac{1}{2}(KL(\mathbf{p}||\mathbf{m}) + KL(\mathbf{q}||\mathbf{m}))$$

Figure 3: Metrics for TDT2 (note that F1 score for independent models (not plotted) is 0.21).

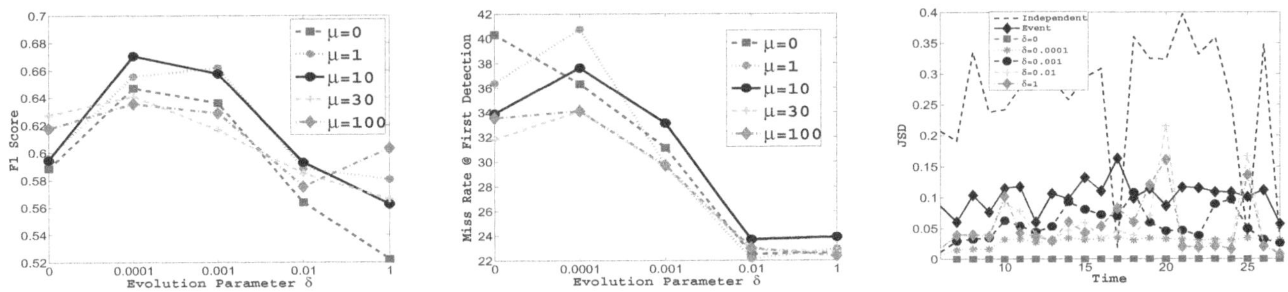

where $\mathbf{m} = \frac{1}{2}(\mathbf{p}+\mathbf{q})$. Other measures (KL-divergence, Symmetric KL-divergence, Overlap in top words etc) are also possible. However, we chose JSD because it is always numerically well defined and bounded between 0 and 1.
(c) *First detection Time* for an event e is defined as:

$$t_{detect}(e) = \operatorname*{argmin}_t \left[t : \min_s JSD\left(h_{true}(e;t), h_{sys}(s;t)\right) < \theta \right]$$

where θ is a detection threshold and $h_{true}(e;t)$ is the word distribution for event e at time t *i.e.* the row corresponding to event e in $\mathbf{H}_{true}(t)$, and $h_{sys}(s;t)$ is a row of $\mathbf{H}(t)$, i.e., a system topic s at time t. Hence, t_{detect} simply measures the first timepoint at which a system topic comes θ-close to an event as measured by JSD. In our experiments, we either set θ to a small value (0.2) or study variation with respect to its choice. The miss rate for event e can now be defined as:

$$\frac{|d : d \in D_{true}(e), timestamp(d) < t_{detect}(e)| * 100}{|D_{true}(e)|} \quad (17)$$

We study miss rates for individual events or report an average across all events.

Topic Continuity: We adapt a direct measure of topic continuity suggested in [6]. This measure essentially reports the JSD between word-distributions in consecutive timepoints both for events (true topics) as well as for system-topics. It therefore measures temporal smoothness in topic distributions.

Emerging Bandwidth: The topics in the emerging set can a) either all become part of the evolving set going forward in time, b) can be manually selected with some of them being discarded as noise by the user or c) can be selected using criteria such as net current strength (sum of the document weights of a topic from the corresponding column of $\mathbf{W}$). In our experiments, we choose (a) and retain all topics in the emerging set.

6.2 Threshold Based TDT model

We adopt a simple baseline model (Threshold Based TDT) based on a body of work in topic detection [1, 8] which corresponds to one of the classic topic detection frameworks. We adapt these body of algorithms for comparison to our experimental setup by using analogous concepts like adhoc period and emerging topics. In particular, we learn an initial set of topics by k-means clustering of the documents over an adhoc period. New documents then stream in one time unit at a time and if their similarity to the existing topics exceed a certain threshold (**Yes/No threshold**), they are allocated to those topics. We also incorporate adaptation [8] so that if the similarity of an incoming document to a topic exceeds a certain **adaptation threshold** τ, we modify the corresponding cluster (topic) center to incorporate the effect of the new document. The threshold values are treated as tunable parameters. The remaining documents which are not similar to the existing topics are then considered as belonging to emerging topics. We perform another k-means clustering to cluster these documents into a set of emerging topics. The documents which are very far from these cluster centers are assigned to singleton topics. Similar to our temporal model, the emerging topics are absorbed into the evolving set going forward in time.

6.3 TDT2 Dataset

Our first dataset is drawn from the NIST Topic Detection and Tracking (**TDT2**) corpus[2] which consists of news stories in the first half of 1998. In our evaluation, we used a set of 9394 documents represented over 19528 terms and distributed into the top 30 TDT2 human-labeled topics over a period of 27 weeks. We choose the hinge parameter to be $\nu = 20$ and emerging bandwidth of 2 per week for this dataset. In our experiments, we use a sliding window of $\omega = 4$ weeks. The left panel of Figure 3 shows tracking performance ($F1$) as a function of the evolution parameter δ for various values of μ. When $\delta = 0$, the system freezes a topic as soon as it is detected not allowing the word distributions to change as the underlying topic drifts over time. When $\delta = 1$, the system has complete freedom in retraining topic distributions causing no single channel to remain consistently associated with an underlying topic. It can be seen that both these extremes are suboptimal. Tracking is much more effective when topic distributions are allowed to evolve under sufficient constraints in response to the statistics of incoming data. Moreover, the presence of emergence regularizer $\mu > 0$ tends to lead to higher F1-score also. In the middle panel of Figure 3 we turn to the miss rate at first detection. Higher values of μ typically reduces miss rates helping emerging topics to be detected early. As δ is increased, topics become less constrained and therefore provide additional bandwidth to drift towards emerging topics, therefore lowering the miss rate curves. However, this comes at the price of reduced tracking performance. Thus, for a fixed amount of available topic bandwidth (which also corresponds to user information overload), there is a tradeoff between tracking and early detection that can be navigated

[2]http://www.nist.gov/speech/tests/tdt/tdt98/index.htm

with the choice of μ and δ. The rightmost panel of Figure 3 shows topic continuity. Choosing $\delta = 0$ leads to no evolution of word distributions while $\delta = 1$ can lead to abrupt changes than can cause user confusion. For other values of δ we see that the system allows drift that is of the same scale as the drift in the true word distributions. Figure 3 also plots the metrics for a simple online methodology where a fresh NMF is learnt at every timepoint over all the data seen so far, independent of previous runs. This model is labeled *independent* in the Figure. As can be seen, independent runs lead to high miss rate (see middle panel) since small emerging topics can be swamped by the goal of reconstructing the ever expanding set of historical documents. Due to complete temporal independence, no system topic can maintain a stable association with an event leading to low F1 score (0.20, not plotted in the left panel) and high temporal discontinuity (see right panel). In Figure 4, we see that, as expected, training online models across short sliding windows takes much lesser time overall than training fresh batch models at every timepoint.

Figure 4: Training time on TDT2

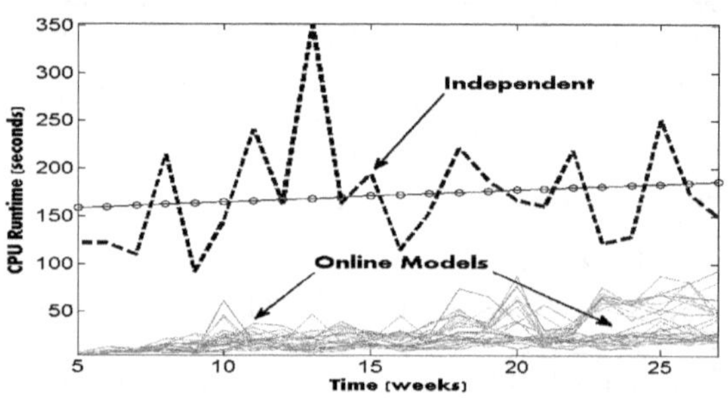

We perform baseline experiments with the Threshold Based TDT model over the TDT2 dataset. Due to space constraints, we just report the tracking performance using F1 score (left panel on Figure 5) as a function of the Yes/No threshold for various values of the Adaptation threshold, τ. The F1 scores obtained by our temporal model are clearly much better than the simple baseline.

Figure 5: Metrics for Threshold Based TDT: F1 score on TDT2 and Twitter

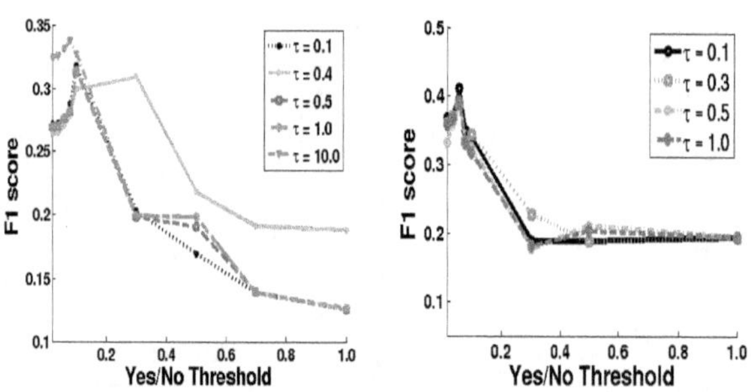

6.4 IBM Twitter Archive

We used the Twitter Search API to collect all tweets mentioning "IBM" in the time period Dec 21, 2010 to Feb 2, 2011. Our dataset comprises of 198029 tweets spread over 43 days. The first 7 days are used to build an initial adhoc model after which the data is streamed into our models for online analysis. In order to facilitate quantitative benchmarking, we labeled approximately 23% of this data in a semi-automatic fashion. First, we learnt a batch NMF model over the entire dataset with 100 topics. From this model, we identified 10 salient events in this time period concerning IBM, listed in the table below together with an estimate of date of peak strength from the model.

Table 1: 10 events comprising roughly 23% of 198029 tweets between Dec 21, 2010 and Feb 2, 2011.

ID	Event	Size	Peak Date
1	Lotusphere 2011 Conference	5020	Jan 31, 2011
2	Watson Jeopardy Contest	16388	Jan 14, 2011
3	Graphene Transistors	874	Jan 24, 2011
4	IBM Patents	2459	Jan 10, 2011
5	IBM Virtual Desktop Offering	1889	Jan 24, 2011
6	IBM Cloud Computing Data Center	2823	Jan 26, 2011
7	IBM Centennial	2558	Jan 22, 2011
8	IBM Quarterly Earnings	6944	Jan 18, 2011
9	IBM Analytics Study	3413	Jan 14, 2011
10	IBM ARM Partnership	3168	Jan 20, 2011

Several topics in the batch model were found to cover these events and induced a partial clustering of tweets which was treated as ground truth. Note, the online model needs to make a real-time judgement of emerging topics and online tracking of evolving ones, and does not have the benefit of retrospective hindsight that the batch model does. It is important to note that our online models are trained on the entire dataset, and only the evaluation is restricted to these labeled events. In other words, these events need to each be teased apart from the entire data collection as they emerge. These 10 events are quite diverse and cover the victory of the IBM Watson supercomputer in a practice Jeopardy! round in January, IBM's quarterly earnings statement, announcements such as creation of the largest cloud computing data center in Asia and a new virtual desktop offering, new partnerships, market studies, patent leadership, centennial celebrations and super fast Graphene transistors. In our empirical study, we fixed the hinge parameter $\nu = 20$, evolution parameter $\delta = 0.001$, sliding window of one week ($\omega = 7$) and emerging topic bandwidth to be 4. regularization. Figure 6 shows that the miss rate at first detection

Figure 6: Miss Rate at First Detection as a function of Detection Threshold on IBM Twitter data

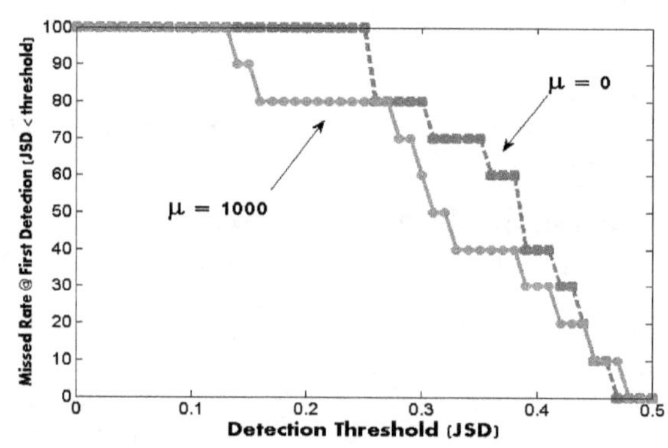

curve as a function of detection threshold (θ in Equation 17) is significantly lower when the emergence regularizer is used.

Table 2: Tracking Performance on Twitter

	top_1		top_5	
Measure	$\mu = 0$	$\mu = 1000$	$\mu = 0$	$\mu = 1000$
Precision	92.10	91.50	71.03	82.09
Recall	36.72	30.73	65.05	62.01
F1	52.51	46.00	67.91	70.65

In Figures 7, 8 we see the effect of emergence regularization: on several events, the online model with $\mu = 1000$ shows a much sharper dip (see bottom panel for each event) as compared to $\mu = 0$ in terms of JSD with respect to the true word distribution, around the time the event emerges (see top panel for each event). These results clearly show the effectiveness and potential value of emergence regularization. The training time is 3.8 minutes per day for $\mu = 0$ and 4.5 minutes per day for $\mu = 1000$ on a commodity desktop running MATLAB. In the Table 2, we report $F1$ scores at $k = 1$ and $k = 5$ respectively. We see that the models tend to have high precision and in particular, the presence of the emergence regularizer also significantly improves precision when upto 5 best matched system topics are associated with each event. Finally, in Figure 9, we show a visualization of topic temporal rivers [24] populated by keyword clouds (the words with highest mass) associated with system topics generated by our model. We show two different time points each spanning 1 week that has some coverage for most of the events. We see that the system is able to communicate the semantic essence (in terms of words) as well as the temporal profile of each event very effectively.

We perform baseline experiments with Threshold Based TDT as described in section 6.2 for both $k = 1$ and $k = 5$ just like our model. For $k = 1$, the maximum F1 score for the thresholds considered is 41.12 obtained for precision and recall values of 71.65 and 28.83 respectively. The corresponding numbers for $k = 5$ is F1 of 48.16 with precision 39.30 and recall 62.19 respectively. We plot the F1 score in the same way as for the TDT2 dataset for the $k = 1$ case(Figure 5 right panel).

7. CONCLUSION AND FUTURE WORK

We have developed a new framework for modeling the evolution of topics and aiding the fast discovery of emerging themes in streaming social media content. We have shown the effectiveness and value of novel temporal regularizers in analyzing twitter streams. There are several avenues for future work including a detailed large-scale empirical study of the interplay between the model parameters as well as the tradeoff between evolution and emergence, coming up with convex formulations to avoid local minima problems possibly using nuclear norm regularization[17], and effective means to do model selection in the online setting. Other fascinating directions include incorporating topic volatility into the evolution constraints, and building sparser models using l_0/l_1-regularizers.

Figure 7: Emerging Topics in IBM Tweets

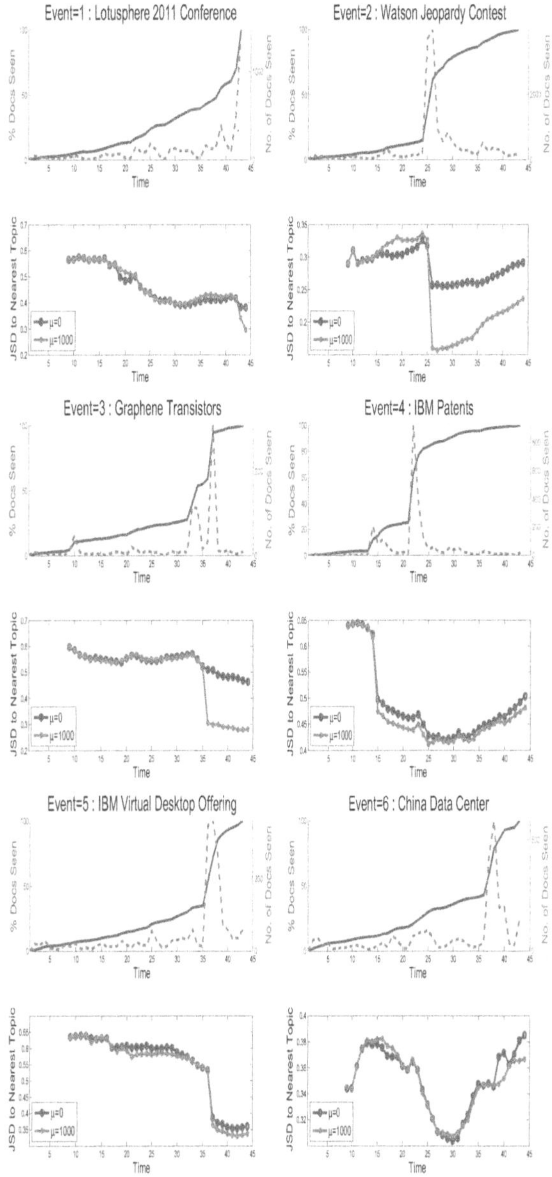

8. REFERENCES

[1] J. Allan, editor. *Topic Detection and Tracking: Event-based Information Organization.* Kluwer Academic Publ, 2002.

[2] L. AlSumait, D. Barbara, and C. Domeniconi. On-line lda: Adaptive topic models for mining text streams. In *ICDM*, 2008.

[3] D. Bertsekas. *Non-linear Programming.* Athena Scientific, 1999.

[4] D. Blei and J. Lafferty. Dynamic topic models. In *ICML*, 2006.

[5] D. Blei and M.Jordan. Latent dirichlet allocation. *JMLR*, 3:993–1022, 2003.

[6] Tzu-Chuan Chou and Meng Chang Chen. Using Incremental PLSI for Treshhold-Resilient Online Event Analysis. *IEEE transactions on Knowledge and Data Engineering*, 2008.

[7] A. Cichocki, R. Zdunek, A. H. Phan, and S. Amari. *Non-negative and Tensor Factorizations: Applications to Exploratory Multiway Data Analysis and Blind Source Separation.* Wiley, 2009.

Figure 8: Emerging Topics in IBM Tweets

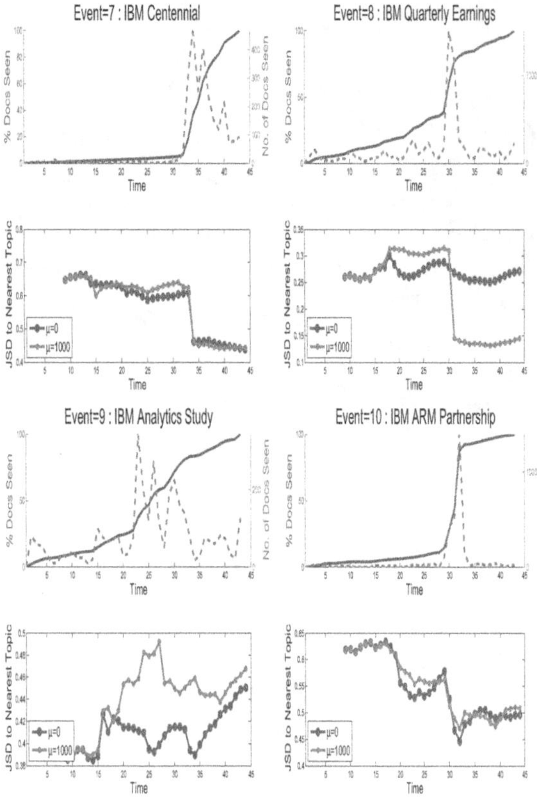

Figure 9: TIARA visualizations [24]: Topics are organized as stacked rivers with width proportional to strength. Top keywords for each topic are also show.

[8] Margaret Connell, Ao Feng, Giridhar Kumaran, Hema Raghavan, Chirag Shah, and James Allan. UMass at TDT 2004. 2004.

[9] Aron Culotta. Towards detecting influenza epidemics by analyzing twitter messages, 2010.

[10] C. Ding, T. Li, and W. Peng. On the equivalence between non-negative matrix factorizations and probabilistic latent semantic analysis. *Computational Statistics and Data Analysis*, 2008.

[11] M. Elad. *Sparse and Redundant Representations: From Theory to Applications in Signal and Image Processing*. Springer, 2010.

[12] Mark Girolami and A. Kaban. On an equivalence between plsi and lda. *SIGIR*.

[13] A. Gohr, A. Hinneburg, R. Schult, and M. Spiliopoulou. Topic evolution in a stream of documents. In *SDM*, 2009.

[14] Ngoc-Diep Ho, Paul Van Dooren, and Vincent D. Blondel. Descent methods for nonnegative matrix factorization. *Numerical Linear Algebra in Signals*, abs/0801.3199, 2007.

[15] Matthew D. Hoffman, David M. Blei, and Frances Bach. Online learning for latent dirichlet allocation. In *NIPS*, 2010.

[16] T. Hoffman. Probabilistic latent semantic analysis. In *UAI*, 1999.

[17] M. Jaggi and M. Sulovský. A simple algorithm for nuclear norm regularized problems. In *ICML*, 2010.

[18] D. Lee and H.S. Seung. Learning the parts of objects using non-negative matrix factorizations. *Nature*, 1999.

[19] C.J. Lin. Projected gradient methods for non-negative matrix factorization. In *Neural Computation*, 2007.

[20] J. Mairal, F. Bach, J. Ponce, and G. Sapiro. Online learning for matrix factorization and sparse coding. *JMLR*, 2010.

[21] P. Melville, V. Sindhwani, and R. Lawrence. Social media analytics: Channeling the power of the blogosphere for marketing insight. *Workshop on Information in Networks*, 2009.

[22] P. M. Pardalos and N. Kovoor. An algorithm for singly constrained class of quadratic programs subject to upper and lower bounds. *Mathematical Programming*, 46:321–328, 1990.

[23] G. Salton. *Automatic Text Processing: The Transformation, Analysis, and Retrieval of Information by Computer*. Addison-Wesley, 1989.

[24] Furu Wei Shimie Pan Michelle X. Zhou Weihong Qian Lei Shi Li Tan Qiang Zhang Shixia Liu, Yangqiu Song. Tiara: Visually analyzing topic evolution in large text collections. In *KDD*, 2010.

[25] Wei Xu, Xin Liu, and Yihong Gong. Document clustering based on non-negative matrix factorization. In *SIGIR*, 2003.

[26] Yiming Yang, Tom Pierce, and James Carbonell. A Study on Retrospective and Online Event Detection. In *SIGIR*, 1998.

Effects of User Similarity in Social Media

Ashton Anderson
Stanford University
ashton@cs.stanford.edu

Daniel Huttenlocher
Cornell University

Jon Kleinberg
Cornell University

{dph, kleinber}@cs.cornell.edu

Jure Leskovec
Stanford University
jure@cs.stanford.edu

ABSTRACT

There are many settings in which users of a social media application provide evaluations of one another. In a variety of domains, mechanisms for evaluation allow one user to say whether he or she trusts another user, or likes the content they produced, or wants to confer special levels of authority or responsibility on them. Earlier work has studied how the *relative status* between two users — that is, their comparative levels of status in the group — affects the types of evaluations that one user gives to another.

Here we study how *similarity* in the characteristics of two users can affect the evaluation one user provides of another. We analyze this issue under a range of natural similarity measures, showing how the interaction of similarity and status can produce strong effects. Among other consequences, we find that evaluations are less status-driven when users are more similar to each other; and we use effects based on similarity to provide a plausible mechanism for a complex phenomenon observed in studies of user evaluation, that evaluations are particularly low among users of roughly equal status.

Our work has natural applications to the prediction of evaluation outcomes based on user characteristics, and the use of similarity information makes possible a novel application that we introduce here — to estimate the chance of a favorable overall evaluation from a group knowing only the attributes of the group's members, but not their expressed opinions.

Categories and Subject Descriptors: H.2.8 [**Database Management**]: Database applications—*Data mining*

General Terms: Algorithms; Experimentation.

Keywords: User-to-User Evaluations, User Similarity, Status, Ballot-Blind Prediction.

1. INTRODUCTION

Many on-line social applications include mechanisms for users to express evaluations of one another, or of the content they create. These evaluations of users are defined in different ways, depending on the application; for example, one user can say that they trust another user's reviews on a product rating site such as Epinions [7, 9]; or that they like the answer another user provides to a question on a community discussion site such as Stack Overflow or Yahoo! Answers [1]; or that they are in favor of granting special levels of privilege to another user on a site built around large-scale collaboration such as Wikipedia or a massive open-source project [3, 14]. Such evaluations serve a crucial purpose in the functioning of these sites, directing users toward content that is highly favored, and — as in Wikipedia and other collaborative domains — enabling the formation of cohorts of highly trusted users who guide the operation of the site.

The synthesis of these types of evaluations is an important problem: when multiple people all provide evaluations of the same "target" person, how do we create a composite description of these evaluations that accurately reflects some type of cumulative opinion of the community? Several recent studies have approached this question through the observation that at an aggregate level, user-to-user evaluations seem to reflect overall levels of *status* in the community [7, 16] — that is, the extent of users' past contributions or achievement. Moreover, the process is further affected by the *relative status* between the user providing the evaluation and the user being evaluated [14]. At the same time, this framework has thus far provided only a first approximation to the factors affecting evaluations, and as we discuss below, there are a number of basic phenomena related to evaluation that it seems unable to explain.

In this paper, we show that the analysis of user-to-user evaluations can be significantly strengthened by taking into account the *similarity* in characteristics of users — such as the extent to which their contributions to the site have involved similar content, or have involved interactions with a common set of other users. We identify some fundamental principles that guide the ways in which similarity affects evaluations, and the way in which it acts in combination with relative status. Then we develop new methods demonstrating how community judgments can be more accurately extrapolated from a small set of evaluations when we have information about the similarity levels among users.

For our analysis, we focus on three primary domains that exemplify distinct forms of user evaluation: Wikipedia, Stack Overflow, and Epinions. On Wikipedia, we study the admin promotion process. When a user wants to acquire special adminship privileges on Wikipedia, she submits her credentials to a review and promotion process, involving public discussion followed by a public vote on the promotion [3]. On Stack Overflow, a question and answering site, a central mechanism allows users to vote for or against different user-contributed answers to a question, thereby collectively "up-voting" better answers and "down-voting" worse ones. On Epinions, users write reviews of various products and a similar mechanism to Stack Overflow's allows others to rate these reviews on a scale of 1 to 5.

Permission to make digital or hard copies of all or part of this work for personal or classroom use is granted without fee provided that copies are not made or distributed for profit or commercial advantage and that copies bear this notice and the full citation on the first page. To copy otherwise, to republish, to post on servers or to redistribute to lists, requires prior specific permission and/or a fee.
WSDM'12, February 8–12, 2012, Seattle, Washington, USA.
Copyright 2012 ACM 978-1-4503-0747-5/12/02 ...$10.00.

We find a range of common phenomena occurring across these domains, despite some differences in the way evaluations work across them. On Wikipedia, the target of the evaluation is the user herself, whereas on Stack Overflow and Epinions the target is a piece of content produced by the user, but in a setting where it is still clearly associated with the user's identity. We will thus speak of a user A evaluating a user B as shorthand either for a direct evaluation of B herself, or for an indirect evaluation via content that B has authored. Moreover, on Wikipedia, the evaluations we study are synthesized into a cumulative *outcome* — whether the user is promoted to adminship or not — whereas on Epinions the result of the evaluations is an unsynthesized composite of individual ratings.

We now provide a brief overview of some of our main findings about the effect of similarity, as well as our results on the use of similarity information to infer outcomes.

Overview of Results: The Effect of Similarity. As noted above, we measure similarity between users A and B using two different types of characteristics: similarity of interests using a distance metric capturing overlap in the types of content they produce; and similarity of social ties using a measure of the overlap in the sets of people they have evaluated. We measure status by the number of actions taken on the site, where "action" is defined in a way that fits the use of each site.

Across all the domains, we find an aggregate pattern in which users with more similar interests or social ties are more positive toward one another, and — more subtly — in which status differences matter less for evaluations among users who are more similar to each other. In other words, when people have more in common with each other, status seems to play a less important role in evaluation. This overall pattern varies in strength according to the specific site that we study and also the particular characteristics that are measured. For instance on Stack Overflow we observe only marginally more positive evaluations from more similar users when we measure similarity based on content, whereas evaluations are much more positive for highly similar users when using our social measure of similarity. Such distinctions can provide useful insights into the ways that different types of judgments — evaluating a user versus evaluating their content — affect the overall behavior we see on these sites.

Moreover, on Wikipedia, we see a further important effect: among the users who choose to provide evaluations of B, the high-status evaluators have overall more similarity to B than the low-status evaluators do. This suggests a selection effect where "elite" or high status individuals are more likely to participate in evaluations in their areas of interest or expertise.

The combination of these effects offers a novel explanation for the following intriguing observation from earlier work by three of us on admin promotion in Wikipedia [14] that we now also find in Stack Overflow and Epinions. A key finding in this earlier study was that the probability of A providing a positive evaluation of B has a pronounced local minimum when the status difference Δ between A and B is near zero — a striking effect where the aggregate evaluations are particularly negative among users of comparable status levels. It was an open question to explain the mechanism behind this effect. In Section 5 we illustrate how this effect is well explained by the combination of two underlying aggregate factors. The first is based on the role played by low-status users, who tend to be judged differently than those with moderate or high status. However, on Wikipedia the local minimum near $\Delta = 0$ persists (in a milder form) even when low-status users are not considered, and we argue that this can arise from the fact that users more similar to the target B tend to be more positive about B, and such high-similarity users are overrepresented among the high status evaluators. These findings suggest that much of the observed effect may be due to aggregate factors such as the set of people who show up to evaluate a given user, as well as the fact that status-consciousness decreases with greater similarity, rather than any individual effects of how users evaluate those of comparable status.

Overview of Results: Ballot-Blind Prediction. In the settings we study, users provide explicit evaluations (positive or negative). But there are many domains where users interact with a piece of content (or another user), and we know attributes of these users but not their evaluation of the content. Do our results have relevance for these types of domains?

In fact, we find that they do: using the principles developed earlier in the paper, we show in Section 6 that knowing only the first few users $A_1, A_2, \ldots, A_k$ who evaluate another user B and their attributes (similarity to B and relative status) – but *not* the actual evaluations – we can make accurate predictions about the outcome of the election. The crucial point is that in this prediction task, we do not have access to the evaluations provided by $A_1, A_2, \ldots, A_k$, but only to their attributes as individuals relative to user B. As a result, we refer to this as the problem of *ballot-blind prediction*.

The results we obtain for ballot-blind prediction suggest that there is considerable power in the use of similarity information, and that the potential applicability of our framework for reasoning about the interplay of similarity and status extends beyond settings in which users provide explicit, observable evaluations.

2. RELATED WORK

The issue of evaluations in social media is a very general one, and it splits into several themes depending on the nature of what is being evaluated. A large amount of work has studied the evaluation of items such as products, movies, or Web sites; for example, the area of collaborative filtering and recommendation systems focuses on this issue (e.g., [8, 10, 17, 20]). In these settings, there is an inherent asymmetry between the people doing the evaluating and the items being evaluated, and hence the evaluation is best modeled in different ways — as a function of intrinsic properties of the item, or of some notion of the match of person to item. In our setting, on the other hand, the evaluators and the targets of evaluation are both people, and everyone can both evaluate and be evaluated. Thus in addition to user A judging user B purely based on B's characteristics, A can also take into account her own characteristics relative to B's ("Is B similar to me? Is B better than I am?"). This latter form is unique to our setting: when evaluating products such as a microwave oven, it doesn't make sense to compare the microwave to oneself – but in user-to-user evaluation, it is not only valid but natural to compare the subject of evaluation to oneself.

Other areas have also considered the evaluation of people in contexts different from ours. This includes the inference of opinion from natural-language text [19], as well as "higher-order" modeling of opinions about opinions [6]; it also includes the use of norms to control deviant behavior in on-line communities [5]. If we view evaluation as providing positive and negative signs on the edges of an underlying graph (denoting positive and negative evaluations between people), then we obtain a signed social network; recent work has considered the characteristic properties of such networks [2, 12, 16, 15, 21]. In contrast, our work here focuses on how attributes of the individuals comprising the nodes, and in particular their levels of similarity, affect the signs expressed on the links.

Finally, notions of similarity and status appear in a number of contexts throughout the sociology literature. The principle of *homophily* provides a principled basis for reasoning about the ways

Wikipedia language	N	$P_0(+)$	U
English	119,489	74.5%	10,558
German	78,647	67.7%	3,560
French	22,534	78.0%	1,552
Spanish	8,641	83.4%	917

Table 1: Wikipedia statistics. N = number of votes, $P_0(+)$ = baseline fraction of positive votes, U = number of users.

in which people tend to favor those who are similar to themselves [13]. Burt considers the ways in which differential status comparisons take place among people who view themselves as belonging to a set of peers — and how the fear of "falling behind" in comparison to this set can motivate people to succeed [4]. Work in network exchange theory has also produced experiments showing how perceived status differences between parties to an interaction can affect the balance of power in the interaction [22, 23].

3. DATASET DESCRIPTION

We use data from online social media applications where users explicitly evaluate other users, either directly (evaluating the users themselves) or indirectly (evaluating the content they produce).

Wikipedia is a collaboratively authored free encyclopedia. Active users can be nominated for promotion to admin status (admins have access to privileges that aid the maintenance of the site). Once nominated, a public deliberation process begins and other Wikipedia users cast either positive, negative, or neutral votes on the candidate. Votes are public, signed by the voter, and timestamped. After enough time has passed, a Wikipedia official reviews the votes and discussion and decides whether the election was successful or not. A public record of the election is archived online. We collected data from English Wikipedia on 3,422 elections that took place between September 17, 2004 and January 30, 2010. We extracted a total of 153K votes, but use a subset of 120K votes for which we could obtain similarity and status information. We collected similar data from French, German, and Spanish Wikipedias as well. Basic stats are shown in Table 1.

Stack Overflow is a popular question-answering site for programmers. Users post questions and answers, and can upvote or downvote other users' questions and answers. Heavily upvoted answers are prominently displayed on the question page, and heavily upvoted questions are publicized on the site. There is a visible reputation system that assigns a score to each user on the site. Users gain/lose reputation by receiving upvotes/downvotes on the content they produce. Users cannot downvote freely; it costs them a small amount of reputation to do so.

There are 1.1M questions, 3.2M answers, and 7.5M votes (1.8M on questions, 5.7M on answers) from the site's inception on July 31, 2008 to January 3, 2011. 93.4% of the votes are positive, and for each vote we know the identity of the voter and the time it occurred. Who voted on what is not publicly displayed on the site. Questions are annotated with tags describing relevant topics. There are 31K unique tags and 3.6M tag events.

Epinions is an online reviewing site where users can review products and rate each others' reviews. Our dataset has 132K users, 1.5M reviews, and 13.6M ratings of those reviews (on a scale of 1-5 stars) [18]. The ratings are overwhelming positive (78% are 5-star ratings), so we call a 5-star rating a "positive" evaluation and all others "negative".

In the results that follow, we have performed the analyses on all these datasets (four languages of Wikipedia, plus Stack Overflow and Epinions), except for analyses, where noted, that were specific to certain features of one of the sites. Due to the space limits, we will often report the results only for subsets of the datasets, designed to cover the space of different outcomes; the datasets where results are not reported have outcomes very similar to what is shown here. In particular, the results on Stack Overflow and Epinions are very similar; we only report Stack Overflow and comment on differences where there are any.

4. THE INTERPLAY BETWEEN SIMILARITY AND STATUS

Definitions of Similarity. To explore how user similarity affects evaluations, we first formalize a notion of similarity that measures how much two users' interests overlap.

In each dataset, we can think of users as being represented by the actions they take. By *action*, we will be referring to editing an article on Wikipedia, asking or answering a question on Stack Overflow, and rating a review on Epinions. Let user u's *binary action vector* be a vector of length M (where M is the number of all possible actions a user can take) with a 1 in the ith position if u took action i at least once, and 0 otherwise. The similarity between users u and v is then the cosine between their respective binary action vectors: $s(u,v) = \frac{u_a \cdot v_a}{||u_a|| \cdot ||v_a||}$ (where u_a is u's binary action vector). If either $||u_a|| = 0$ or $||v_a|| = 0$ (either u or v hasn't taken any actions), then we say $s(u,v)$ is undefined and exclude it from our calculations. Notice that a user's action vector changes over time as they make more actions. Whenever we compute the similarity $s(E,T)$ between an evaluator E and target T, we use the action vectors corresponding to the time at which E evaluated T.

On Wikipedia, we make one modification. The similarity metric defined above works well for most users, but breaks down for "typo-fixer" editors who make large numbers of minor edits, for example by writing automated bots that find and fix typos (since they edit a lot of articles, they are artificially similar to virtually everyone). To account for this, when computing user similarity for Wikipedia we restrict a user's binary action vector to only include the top k articles he edits the most. This eliminates the long tail of edits that typo-fixers make and limits our similarity measure to only take a user's main area of interest into account. After some experimentation we use $k = 100$.

On Stack Overflow, questions are annotated with tags that represent relevant topics. These can be used to provide a summary description of a user's interests by considering tags that annotate the questions a user evaluates as well as those annotating the parent questions of answers the user evaluates. We represent user u as a binary tag vector with a 1 in the ith position if tag i annotated a question u evaluated or a parent question to an answer u evaluated. "Tag similarity" refers to the cosine between binary tag vectors. Similarly, on Epinions, we measure similarity between users' binary action vectors (recall that on Epinions an action corresponds to rating a review).

Additionally, on all of our datasets, we also define another type of user-to-user similarity. We can characterize a user by a vector of other users that a user has evaluated and define similarity between two users as the cosine between their corresponding binary evaluation vectors. We call this *social similarity*.

We experimented with a number of standard similarity measures, including weighted cosine (where position i is assigned the number of times user u took action i), Jaccard, and others. For all of them, either the results are not qualitatively different, or if they are, it is due to an idiosyncrasy of the particular measure.

Similarity and Evaluations. Now that we have formally defined similarity, we can investigate how similarity affects the probability of a positive evaluation. Although it is natural to expect a relationship between status and similarity, it is not a priori obvious the

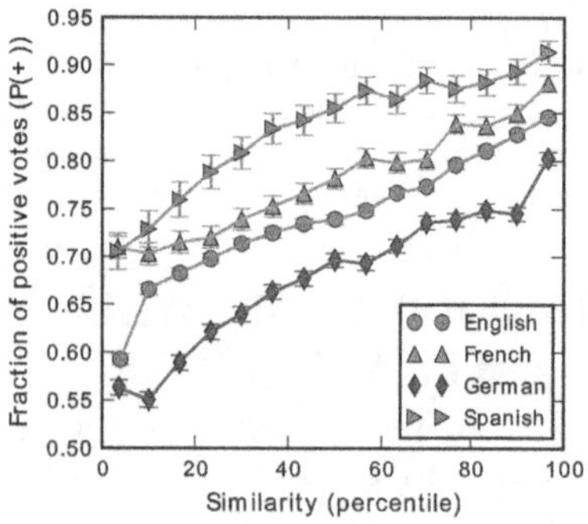

Figure 1: (Wikipedia) Probability of a positive evaluation ($P(+)$) as a function of the similarity (binary cosine) between the evaluator and target edit vectors ($s(e,t)$).

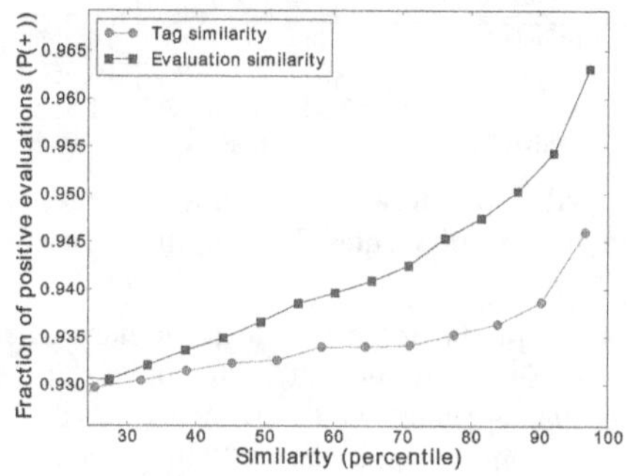

Figure 2: (Stack Overflow) Probability of E positively evaluating T as a function of similarity (note that errorbars are still plotted, but they are too small to be visible).

relationship is positive or negative. It could be that evaluators are more supportive of targets in their area of expertise. For instance, it's possible that evaluators on Wikipedia "cheerlead" their area's most promising editors into administrative positions. An alternative theory is that the more familiar the evaluator is with the target's work, the more likely the evaluator is to know about mistakes and weaknesses, or other negative things not uncovered by the type of superficial appraisal that evaluators from other domains can give, and are consequently harsher in their evaluations. Another reason evaluators could be harsher on similar targets is simple competition; an evaluator's power in their area can only diminish as the number of other admins around increases.

On Wikipedia we find strong evidence for the former theory – that the probability of a positive evaluation grows with the (content as well as social) similarity between the evaluator and the target. On average, overlapping interests with the target make it more likely that an evaluator will cast a positive vote. In Figure 1, we show the probability of a positive vote as a function of the cosine between the evaluator and target binary edit vectors (averaging over all values of Δ). (Note that throughout this paper, $P(+)$ is simply the fraction of positive evaluations in a given set of evaluations.) The monotonically-increasing, diminishing-returns relationship between them is clearly present. We plot results not only for English Wikipedia but also for French, German and Spanish as examples of how the results are similar for several datasets. The qualitative trend is the same across all of them. For ease of presentation, we will restrict Wikipedia plots to English Wikipedia for the remainder of the paper. The results are similar across all Wikipedia datasets, except where noted otherwise.

On Stack Overflow, the effect of similarity on evaluations is more nuanced. We still find that the more similar an evaluator-target pair is, the more likely the evaluation is positive. But in contrast to Wikipedia, the strength of this relationship depends on which notion of similarity we use. As discussed above, we can consider similarity on tags, which is a measure of content similarity, or we can consider similarity on evaluations, which is a measure of social similarity. These measure two fundamentally different things: similarity in the content two people are interested in and similarity in the users they have evaluated. In Figure 2, we plot the fraction of positive evaluations as a function of these two measures of similarity. Since the scale of the cosine values are different for the two measures, we normalize by their respective cumulative distribution functions so that we compare percentiles instead of raw values on the x-axis. We find that $P(+)$ increases with tag-similarity very gradually for most of the data (from the 25th to the 80th percentile, $P(+)$ only increases by 0.5%, a relative gain of 7%). But for evaluation-similarity, $P(+)$ is both everywhere higher than it is for tag-similarity (except for $s = 0$) and rises much more significantly (for the same range, $P(+)$ increases 1.5%, a relative gain of 21% – 3 times as much). This suggests that the social orbits users travel in influence evaluations much more than the topics they're interested in. Since social similarity is more informative on Stack Overflow, we will use it for the rest of the paper. As alluded to above, there is no strong difference on Wikipedia (and thus, we henceforth only consider action similarity on the Wikipedia datasets). We find similar effects for content similarity on Epinions. However, social similarity turns out to be too sparse to be meaningful in Epinions.

So far we have demonstrated that evaluator-target similarity is directly correlated with the probability of a positive evaluation. Next we examine how similarity and status jointly interact with user evaluations.

Similarity and status. We now consider some of the interactions between similarity and status; to do this, we first provide some definitions underpinning the measures of status. A user's status, or standing in the community, is an intricate function of the community's perception of his contributions. In this work, we follow previous research on notions of status in networks [3, 14] and use volumetric measures of contribution, or *activity level*, as simple yet reasonable approximations of status.[1] In particular, we consider user u's status at time t as the number of actions u has taken before time t (i.e. the number of non-zero entries in her corresponding binary action vector u_a at time t). Thus on Wikipedia, we use the total number of edits made by a user u before time t as u's status at time t; on Stack Overflow, we use the total number of questions asked and answers given[2]; and on Epinions, we use the number of ratings given. For the rest of the paper, "status" refers to the number of actions, and we use σ_A to refer to user A's status.

Previous research showed that evaluation behavior does not just vary with target status alone, but rather it varies with the evaluator

[1]This is consistent with sociological work showing how overt surface-level *markers* of status tend to serve as proxies in everyday interactions for more subtle forms of status [22]. Extending the simple formulations of status we use here to encompass the community's opinion and perception of one's status is an interesting direction for future work.

[2]A tempting definition of status on Stack Overflow would be the reputation score that is assigned to each user based on their activity on the site. However, since our main interest is in investigating the relationship between status and user evaluations, reputation is not an ideal measure. This is due to the fact that users directly gain reputation from positive evaluations and lose reputation from negative evaluations – and hence for this definition, status and user evaluations would be correlated in an uninteresting way.

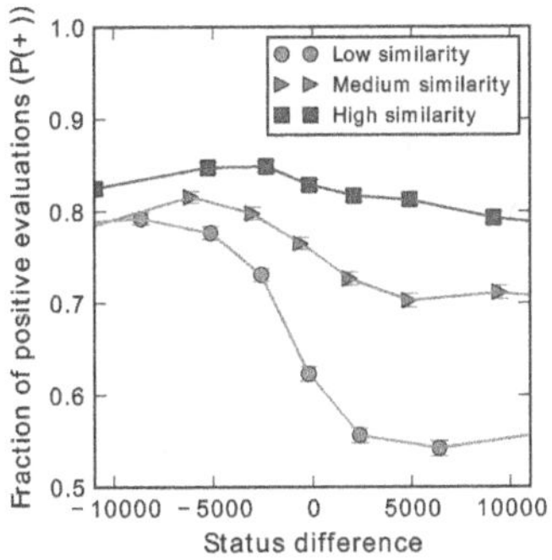

Figure 3: (English Wikipedia) Probability of E voting positively on T as a function of Δ for different levels of similarity

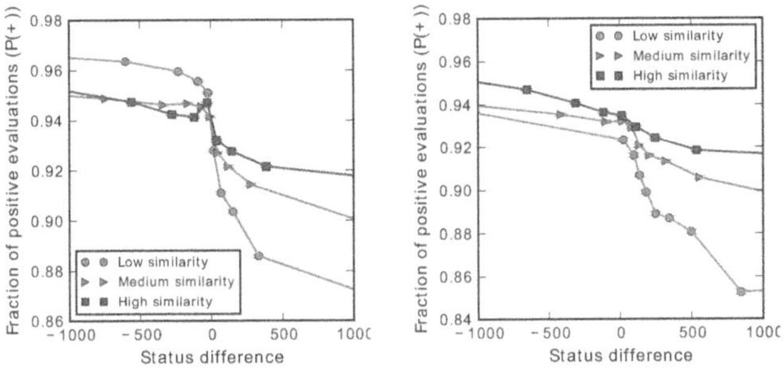

(a) All evaluators (b) No low-status evaluators

Figure 4: (Stack Overflow) Probability of E voting positively on T as a function of Δ for different levels of similarity (errorbars are plotted but are too small to be visible).

status and target status together [14]. We therefore need a way to compare the evaluator's status with the target's status. We use the *differential status* $\Delta = \sigma_E - \sigma_T$ to do this. Note that it is not a priori clear whether this is the right measure or not; for example, the ratio of their respective statuses could plausibly be a better measure. We show that the differential status is the appropriate way to compare statuses at the end of the section.

We now turn to a subtle effect that arises from the interplay of the similarity and differential status between two users. Previous work has found $P(+)$ depends on Δ, and that the relationship is natural: evaluators with higher status than the target tend to be harsher than the evaluators with lower status than the target. However, we find that this effect is significantly moderated by the similarity between the evaluator and the target. The more similar E and T are, the less their difference in status affects the vote. That is, if an evaluator and target have similar action profiles, the vote varies less with their status difference than if the evaluator and target operate in different domains. This suggests evaluators use status as a proxy for quality in the absence of more direct knowledge of the target, and depend less on status when they are more well-informed, i.e., more similar to the target. Evidence for this is shown in Figure 3, where $P(+)$ is plotted as a function of Δ for different levels of similarity in English Wikipedia. Notice that for low-similarity pairs status plays a major role, as can be seen by comparing the curves on left half of $\Delta = 0$ to the right half: for $\Delta < 0$, votes are about 80% positive, but for $\Delta > 0$, the fraction of positive votes plummets to below 60%. As similarity is increased however, the votes get more positive across all values of Δ and the curve becomes increasingly flat. This shows that status difference is less critical when the evaluator and target tend to edit the same articles.

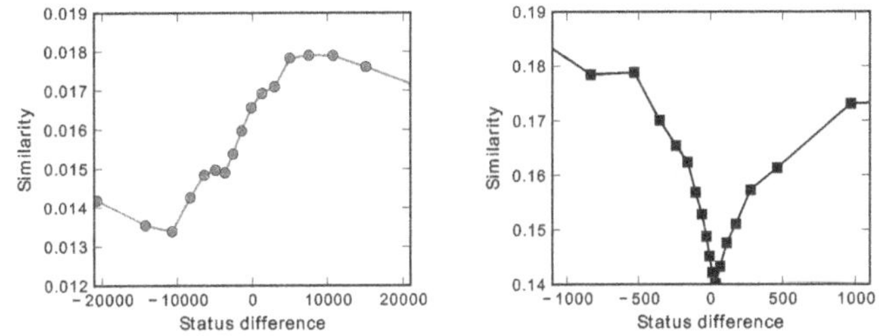

(a) English Wikipedia (b) Stack Overflow

Figure 5: Similarity between E and T pairs as a function of Δ. On English Wikipedia we screen out low-status targets (those below 3000 edits) to show the trend doesn't depend on them, but the curve doesn't qualitatively change for any threshold on target status. On Stack Overflow, similarity on tags is shown, but the curve is robust to changes in the similarity and status metrics used.

The story on Stack Overflow is similar, but has an additional subtlety. The $P(+)$ vs. Δ curves for different levels of social similarity are shown in Figure 4a. When $\Delta > 0$, the picture is qualitatively the same as in Wikipedia: the higher the similarity, the higher $P(+)$ is. But for $\Delta < 0$, the situation is very different: the similarity curves are in the opposite order from before: evaluators with low similarity to the higher-status targets (since $\Delta < 0$) are more positive than evaluators with high similarity.

This is due to a particular property of Stack Overflow's reputation system, in which it costs a user a small amount of reputation to downvote a question or answer (issue a negative evaluation). This creates a disincentive to downvote which is most strongly felt by users with lower reputation scores (which correlates with our measure of status on Stack Overflow). When we remove low-status evaluators ($\sigma_E < 100$), this effect disappears and the overall picture looks the same as it does on Wikipedia (see Figure 4b).

We have just shown that similarity significantly controls the extent to which differential status influences evaluations. Now we highlight another key observation relating similarity and status.

In Wikipedia elections, we find that the evaluator's similarity to the target depends strongly on Δ (Figure 5a). In particular, the evaluators who have higher status than the target are significantly more similar to the target than are the evaluators who have lower status. This is an important *selection effect*: in aggregate, users with higher status than the target only tend to show up and vote on targets who are active in the same areas as they are. This means that voters who show up to evaluate a particular target are not necessarily representative of the voting population on Wikipedia. This effect is independent of the target's status – it holds and is quantitatively similar for both relatively high- and low-status targets.

This selection effect does not happen on Stack Overflow or Epinions (see Figure 5b). The shape of how s varies with Δ for evaluator-target pairs is almost identical to how it looks for pairs of random users, implying that there is no similar selection effect. The one difference between the two curves is that for random users the curve is symmetric across $\Delta = 0$, whereas for evaluator-targets pairs the similarity is a bit higher the left of $\Delta = 0$. Thus, there is a slight selection effect in the opposite direction on Stack Overflow: evaluators with lower status than the target tend to be more similar than when they have higher status. But we emphasize that this selection effect is slight in comparison to the one on Wikipedia, which completely overwhelms the baseline shape with a global minimum at $\Delta = 0$.

We hypothesize that the lack of a significant selection effect on

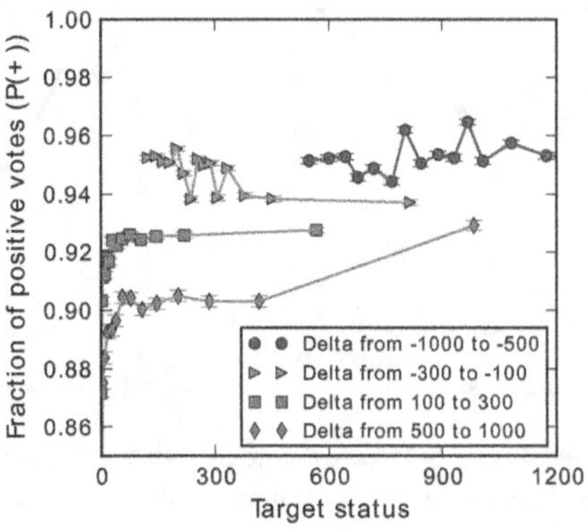

Stack Overflow

Figure 6: (Stack Overflow) Probability of E positively evaluating T versus σ_T for various fixed levels of Δ.

Stack Overflow similar to one we see on Wikipedia is due to the very different contexts that the evaluations occur in on Stack Overflow compared to Wikipedia. On Wikipedia, the vote is the central focus of the evaluator-target interaction we observe. An evaluator needs to care enough about the target's potential adminship in order to show up and vote – he must intend to vote. On Stack Overflow, evaluating questions and answers is a by-product of organic browsing behavior. Users mainly visit a question/answer page to learn something specific, and only then decide whether to offer an evaluation or not.

Absolute and Differential Status. Earlier we discussed the methodological question of how to compare an evaluator's status with a target's status, and we return to this issue now. For all of our datasets we find that status difference is the main factor determining evaluation outcome, as opposed to the absolute status or, for example, the ratio of the statuses. That is, the probability of evaluator E giving a positive assessment of target T conditioned on a status difference between them of $\Delta = \sigma_E - \sigma_T$ depends primarily on Δ, and not on their absolute status levels σ_E or σ_T.

This is illustrated in Figure 6, where we plot the fraction of positive evaluations $P(+)$ against the target's status σ_T within several narrow Δ ranges on Stack Overflow. If the status difference is really how users compare their status against others, then we would expect to see two things. First, that these curves are approximately flat (i.e. $P(+)$ doesn't depend on σ_T for a fixed Δ), because this would imply that for pairs separated by Δ, evaluation positivity does not depend on what their individual statuses are. Second, that the level of these constant curves depends on Δ, so that different Δ values result in different evaluation behavior. In Figure 6, this is exactly what we see. The fraction of positive votes does not significantly vary with absolute status level, meaning that even users of vastly different absolute status levels treat differences of Δ the same; and this constant level depends monotonically on Δ (the higher the Δ range, the lower $P(+)$ is). Neither of these observations hold if we consider narrow status ratio σ_E/σ_T ranges instead of status difference ranges. The last point on the $\Delta \in [500, 1000]$ curve is an outlier far from the rest of the curve and can be ignored.

Note that Δ does not control the result well for extremely low target status values, where evaluators are much more negative than just the difference in status would otherwise suggest. This is because the poor quality of targets with low status overwhelms the difference in status between evaluator and target. Thus absolute status, and not differential status, is the main criterion evaluators use to evaluate very low-status targets.

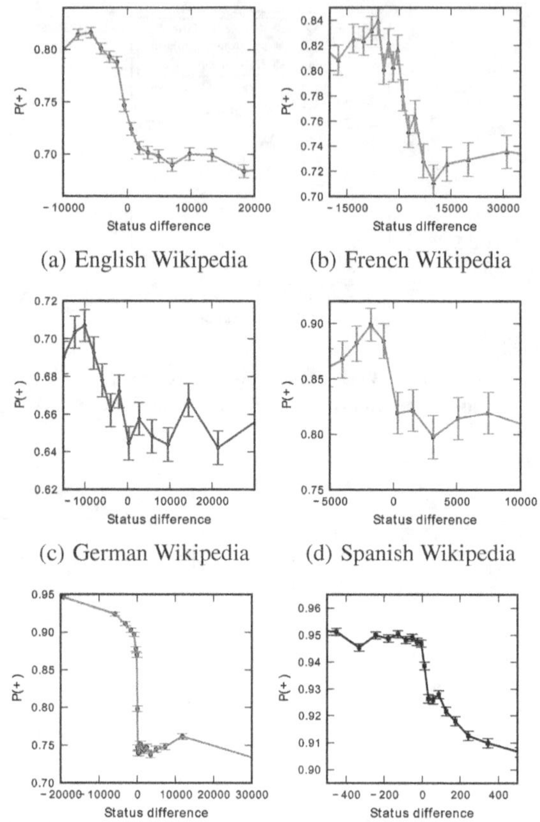

(a) English Wikipedia (b) French Wikipedia

(c) German Wikipedia (d) Spanish Wikipedia

(e) Epinions (f) Stack Overflow

Figure 7: Examples of the "dip" in various datasets.

To summarize, in this section we have analyzed how similarity affects user evaluation in various social media domains. The main insights we've discovered are: (1) positive evaluation is strongly positively correlated with similarity, (2) the more similar the evaluator is to the target, the less status-conscious he is, (3) there is a strong selection effect of high-similarity, higher-status evaluators showing up to vote on targets on Wikipedia (but not on Stack Overflow or Epinions), (4) methodologically, Δ is the correct measure for relative status, and (5) for low enough levels of target status, the target's low status overwhelms other factors.

5. MODELS OF AGGREGATE USER EVALUATION

We now turn our attention to designing a model that explains an interesting phenomenon first observed in our previous research [14]. As noted in Section 1, this work found that the probability of positive evaluation $P(+)$ is consistently non-monotonic in status difference Δ to the right of 0. We also observe this effect in our datasets as shown in Figure 7, with the "dip" emerging at small positive Δ. This phenomenon is intriguing because it applies across every user evaluation dataset we consider here, and it suggests that in aggregate, users are particularly harsh on each other when they have approximately the same status. Understanding why this happens, however, is challenging. In particular, the fact that users of comparable status are harsh on each other is intuitively at odds with our findings in the previous section that users who are similar in other dimensions tend to be more positive toward each other. Can we use our insights into how similarity affects evaluations to explain this dip and subsequent rebound in $P(+)$?

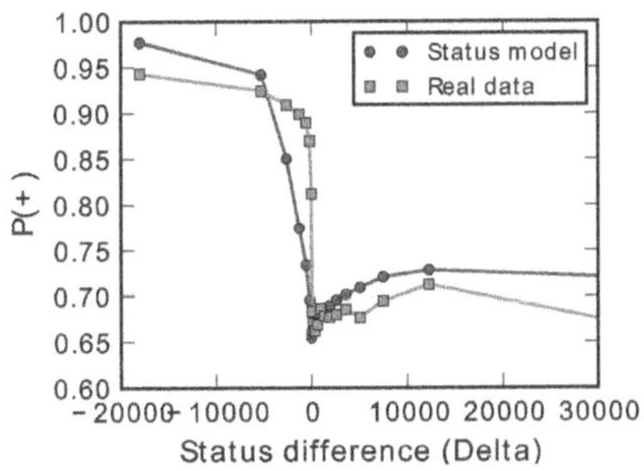

Figure 8: (Epinions) Fraction of positive votes versus status difference Δ.

In this section, we propose such an explanation. The explanation is two-pronged, designed to capture what appear to be two distinct aspects of this dip in $P(+)$. Recall first that there are two main regimes of user evaluations: (A) low-status targets tend to garner evaluations that depend mainly on the target's absolute status, whereas (B) evaluations of higher-status targets are functions of the differential status between the pair.

The distinction between (A) and (B) is reflected in two different behaviors for the dip in $P(+)$ across the datasets. For Stack Overflow and Epinions, we find that the dip disappears when low-status targets are filtered out, but for Wikipedia the dip persists even on the population consisting only of higher-status users. This provides an indication that different mechanisms may be contributing to the dip across different datasets. We now propose a pair of models that capture these different aspects.

Status model. First we present a model that is consistent with behavior on Stack Overflow and Epinions. When we examine $P(+)$ as a function of Δ, we are aggregating over the two different regimes of user evaluations. In Section 4, we showed that evaluation behavior is qualitatively different for low-status targets. Since most evaluators in the data have relatively low status, this implies that most evaluations in the absolute status evaluation regime will have small positive Δ values. And since these evaluations are much more negative than those made in the relative status regime, this can cause a dip slightly to the right of 0.

More concretely, we propose the following simple absolute-status-based mechanism that can generate the dip. We assume that evaluators do not discriminate among high-status targets, but for low-status targets they are increasingly negative as the target's status decreases. We capture this with a simple function: in the high-status target range ($\sigma_T > \sigma_{min}$) evaluators evaluate positively with a constant probability $P_E(+|T) = p^*$. In the low-status target range ($\sigma_T < \sigma_{min}$), evaluators evaluate a target positively with probability proportional to their status, $P_E(+|T) \propto \sigma_T$. We semi-simulate this process where we use real status values and $P_E(+|T) = (p^* - p_0)\sigma_T/\sigma_{min} + p_0$ where we set $p^* = 95\%$, $p_0 = 65\%$, $\sigma_{min} = 8000$. For each evaluation in our dataset, we use the real status values σ_E and σ_T (and hence real Δ) values, but replace the evaluation with a synthetic one sampled from the above $P_E(+|T)$. The resulting synthetic curve is overlayed with the real curve in Figure 8. Note that the model does not have a simple parametric form because the real σ_E and σ_T values were used.

Similarity model. The previous status-based model aligns well with the behavior of the dip in $P(+)$ on Stack Overflow and Epinions. On Wikipedia, however, the dip persists even when we eliminate targets of low status. Here we propose a mechanism that takes similarity into account in order to fully explain the phenomenon.

In Section 4 we observed that high similarity between evaluator and target yields more positive votes, and that Wikipedia elections have a persistent selection effect: higher-status evaluators are more similar to the target than lower-status evaluators are. In the following we show that these two effects alone are sufficient to cause the non-monotonicity we observe. Note that the function we are seeking to model is $\Pr[+ \mid \Delta]$, and that this aggregates over all levels of similarity. We also know that for small positive Δ values, the mix of similarities shifts more towards high-similarity pairs than it does elsewhere. Finally, we know that higher similarity correlates well with positive evaluations. The combination of these two observations leads us to the following model where we aim to recreate a dip at $\Pr[+ \mid \Delta = 0]$: We write:

$$\Pr[+ \mid \Delta] = \sum_s \Pr[+ \mid \Delta, s] \cdot \Pr[s \mid \Delta]$$

where the summation ranges over the domain of similarity s. By Bayes' Rule the right-hand side can be written as

$$\Pr[+ \mid \Delta] = \sum_s \frac{\Pr[+, \Delta, s]}{\Pr[\Delta, s]} \cdot \frac{\Pr[\Delta, s]}{\Pr[\Delta]}$$

Next we show how to model $\Pr[+ \mid \Delta, s]$. Figure 3 showed that the change in $P(+)$ as a function of status difference is more drastic for low values of similarity. This suggests that we can model $\Pr[+ \mid \Delta, s]$ with a function of the form

$$\Pr[+ \mid \Delta, s] = (a - bh(s)\Delta),$$

for constants $a, b > 0$ and a function $h(\cdot)$ that is monotone decreasing in s. In other words, for each fixed s, the probability $\Pr[+ \mid \Delta, s]$ is approximately linearly decreasing in Δ, with a slope controlled by s in such a way that larger values of s produce shallower downward slopes. Since the definition of similarity is arbitrary, we can re-parametrize the definition of similarity so that this monotone function $h(\cdot)$ becomes $h(s) = 1 - s$. We use this functional form and now we have:

$$\begin{aligned} \Pr[+ \mid \Delta] &= \sum_s \Pr[+ \mid \Delta, s] \cdot \Pr[s \mid \Delta] \\ &= \sum_s (a - b(1-s)\Delta) \cdot \Pr[s \mid \Delta] \\ &= \sum_s (a - b\Delta + b\Delta s) \cdot \Pr[s \mid \Delta] \\ &= (a - b\Delta) \sum_s \Pr[s \mid \Delta] + b\Delta \sum_s s \cdot \Pr[s \mid \Delta] \\ &= (a - b\Delta) + b\Delta E[s \mid \Delta]. \end{aligned}$$

The advantage of working with this last expression is that one does not need to work with the full set of conditional probabilities $\Pr[s \mid \Delta]$, but instead only with the conditional expectations $E[s \mid \Delta]$ as a function of Δ. The conditional expectation $E[s \mid \Delta]$ is simply the mean similarity among evaluator-target pairs (A, B) for which the status difference is Δ. We write $f(\Delta) = E[s \mid \Delta]$.

Function $f(\cdot)$ can be approximated from the data. Based on our findings in Figure 5 we know that $f(\cdot)$ has a roughly inverted unimodal shape with a unique local minimum near 0, and that it rises higher to the right of 0 than to the left. It is also natural to assume that the similarity eventually saturates as Δ moves away from 0 in either direction — in other words, that

$$\lim_{x \to -\infty} f'(x) = \lim_{x \to \infty} f'(x) = 0.$$

A natural function that has a unique local minimum at $x = 0$ and

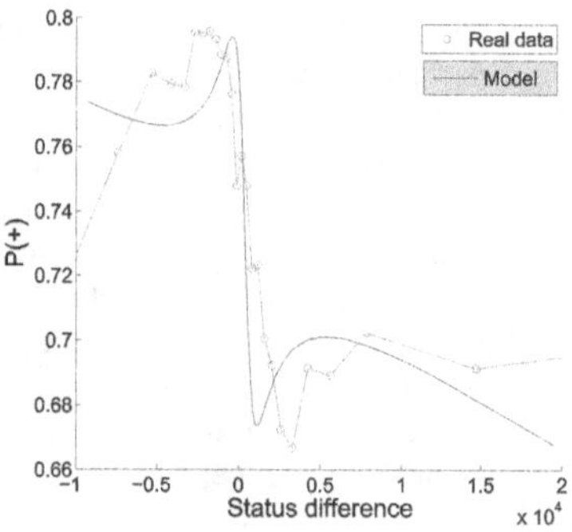

Figure 9: (English Wikipedia) The dip in real data versus the differential status model.

the saturation phenomenon is

$$f(x) = \frac{c(\alpha x)^2}{1 + (\alpha x)^2}$$

for positive constants c and α.

We show results for this model in Figure 9 and compare it to the real Wikipedia "dip". For $f(x)$ we set parameters $c = 0.98$ and $\alpha = 40$. Notice that the behavior qualitatively well matches the real data. Moreover, we also note that in our model for any fixed level of similarity, the probability of positive evaluation decreases monotonically with Δ. The more similar the evaluation-pair, the less steeply $P(+)$ drops off. This is consistent with our previous observations in Figure 3.

Thus although any individual $P(+)$-vs.-Δ curve for a particular similarity level is monotonically decreasing (as in Figure 3), the persistent dip on Wikipedia can be obtained by a weighted average over all these curves with the selection effect observed in Section 4. This highlights the importance of the selection effect and explains why the dip persists after thresholding out low-status targets on Wikipedia but not on Stack Overflow or Epinions (because the selection effect only occurs on Wikipedia).

In this section, we applied the insights we explained in Section 4 to theoretically model the mechanism behind the interesting "dip" phenomenon first observed in [14]. Now we turn our attention to showing that Section 4's discoveries are also useful in a practical learning setting.

6. BALLOT-BLIND PREDICTION

Here we aim to show that evaluator-target similarity has predictive power. The task we focus on is predicting administrator promotion on Wikipedia from the early voters, without looking at the sign of their votes. Just by looking at properties of the first few voters who show up (and importantly, their similarity with the candidate up for election), we are able to predict whether the election succeeds or not with accuracy that significantly improves on a number of natural baselines. Since we're not allowed to look at the actual votes to make our prediction, we call this task *ballot-blind prediction*.

Inferring information from a small prefix of users can be useful for any application with implicit user feedback. Our results raise the possibility of being able to infer an audience's approval or disapproval of a piece of content purely from the makeup of the audience (e.g., readers of a news article, viewers of a video, etc.).

We are interested in predicting a final outcome about a particular user from the first few evaluations we see. For this task we focus on Wikipedia because it has the most natural outcome variable that is a direct result of the evaluations we observe (election success).

Experimental setup. The Wikipedia data consists of public elections where users vote whether candidates should be granted administrative status or not. Formally, an election (T, Ω, R) is specified by a target (or *candidate*) T, a set of ordered votes Ω, and a result $R \in \{+1, -1\}$ denoting whether T was promoted or not. Each vote $v_i \in \Omega$ is a tuple (E_i, s_i, t_i) where E_i is the evaluator, $s_i \in \{+1, -1\}$ denotes whether the vote is positive or negative (we disregard neutral votes), and t_i is the time when E_i cast the vote. The votes are sorted by time, so $t_1 < t_2 < \ldots < t_m$, where m is the number of votes cast in the election. The task then is to predict R from the first k votes $v_1, \ldots, v_k$ (without looking at the sign s_i of each vote) using the similarity and status of the evaluators relative to the target. Our key finding is that knowledge of the similarity and status of the early voters alone (and not what they actually voted) provides enough useful information to successfully predict the final result.

We evaluate performance using accuracy on leave-one-out cross-validation, where we train on the entire dataset minus one example and test on the example for every example in the dataset.

In English Wikipedia, we have approximately 120,000 votes made by approximately 7,600 unique voters across 3,422 elections on 2,953 distinct candidates. (The number of elections exceeds the number of distinct candidates since some candidates go up for election more than once). We use $k = 5$ in our experiments, so that we're only looking at the first 5 voters. This ballot-blind prediction is difficult for two reasons: first, we are only using information from the first 5 voters (the average election length on English Wikipedia is 44 votes, so we only see the first 11% of the votes), and second, we aren't allowed to look at the actual sign of the vote.

Features for learning. We work with the following information. For each vote v_i, we know the identity of the evaluator E_i, her similarity $s(E_i, T)$ with the target, her status σ_{E_i}, and the status difference $\Delta_i = \sigma_{E_i} - \sigma_T$ between her and the target.

Note that in the previous sections our analysis and models have focused on aggregate behavior. Since we're now predicting on a per-instance basis, it makes sense to use per-instance features. We use each voter's historical fraction of positive votes P_i (excluding the current vote, since we aren't allowed to look at it), which we call their *positivity*. If they have no other votes in the dataset, we define their positivity to be the global positivity across the entire dataset (the overall fraction of positive votes across all voters).

We use two classes of features:

- Simple Summary Statistics (**S**) of the status and similarity of the target and the evaluators: $\log(\sigma_T)$, mean similarity $\bar{s} = \sum_{i=1}^{k} s(v_i, T)/k$, and $\bar{\Delta} = \sum_{i=1}^{k} (\sigma_{E_i} - \sigma_T)/k$.
- Δ-s quadrants: We partition the Δ-s space into into four quadrants (shown in Figure 10), divided by $\Delta = 0$ and a similarity value that roughly splits the evaluations into two equally-sized buckets (for example, $s = 0.025$ in English Wikipedia). This gives us four features where each simply counts the number of voters coming from a particular Δ-s quadrant.

Baselines. Before developing our final approach in detail, we describe three baselines we compare against.

The first baseline is a logistic regression classifier that uses all of the features we described above: 4 features of Δ-s quadrants and the **S** statistics. We consider this a very strong baseline as it uses a wide range of basic features that describe the voter population in a given election. We refer to this model as **B1**.

The second baseline models the probability of voter E_i voting positively (without considering his relation to the candidate). We estimate the probability of user E_i voting positively $P(E_i = 1)$ as

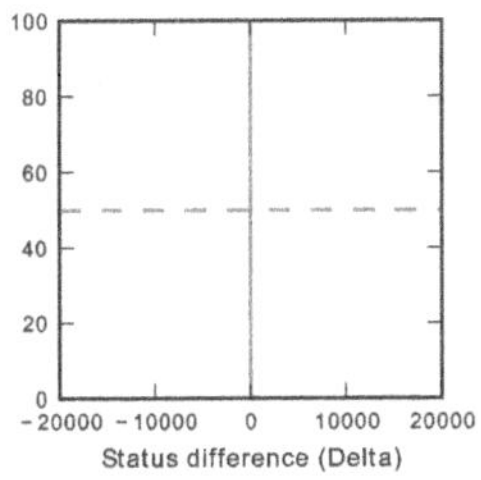

Figure 10: The Delta-similarity half-plane. Votes in each quadrant are treated as a group.

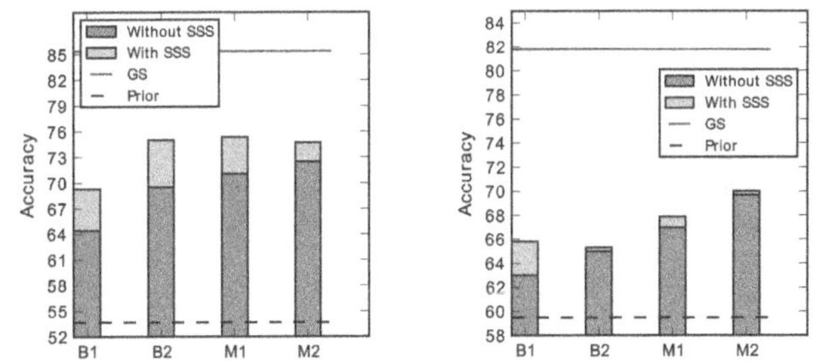

(a) English Wikipedia (b) German Wikipedia

Figure 11: Ballot-blind prediction results.

the empirical fraction E_i's votes that are positive. The estimated fraction of positive votes in a election is then simply the average $\frac{1}{k}\sum_{i=1}^{k} P_i$ of first k voters. We then learn the optimal threshold to predict election outcome. We call this baseline **B2**.

We also define a "gold-standard" (**GS**) that represents the best possible performance we can hope to achieve. It "cheats" by examining the values of actual votes themselves (s_i, for $i \leq k$), computes the empirical fraction of positive votes and learns the optimal threshold to predict the election outcome.

Proposed methods. Now we develop our main methods. The main idea is to directly incorporate how similarity and relative status drive deviations from default voting behavior. Thus, our models have two components: (1) P_i, which captures the overall positivity of user i, and (2) a deviation component that quantifies the deviation in the positivity of user i as a function of her similarity s_i and status difference Δ_i with the target.

In the first method (**M1**), we model the probability that E_i votes positively as $P(E_i = 1) = P_i + d(\Delta_i, s_i)$, where P_i is E_i's positivity, and $d(\Delta_i, s_i)$ is the average deviation of the fraction of positive votes in the Δ_i, s_i bucket compared to the overall fraction of positive votes across the entire dataset. This way we are using the evaluator's positivity as an "absolute" level and then adjusting it, based on how s and Δ affect the probability of positive votes across the *entire* population. We compute the average $P(E_i = 1)$ for $i = 1 \dots k$ and then threshold it to make a prediction. **M1** thus uses 4 deviation parameters (one for each Δ-s quadrant), the threshold, and P_i for each user i.

In the second method (**M2**), we extend the model to factor in how s and Δ affect a voter's behavior at the *individual* level. We model $P(E_i = 1)$ as $P(E_i = 1) = \alpha \cdot P_i(\Delta_i, s_i) + (1 - \alpha) \cdot d(\Delta_i, s_i)$, where d is the same as above, and $P_i(\Delta_i, s_i)$ is E_i's positivity in the Δ, s_i bucket. This can be thought of as establishing an absolute level of the evaluator's positivity (as above), but then making relative adjustments based on personal as well as global deviations based on s and Δ. Now we are directly modeling how s and Δ affect E_i's likelihood of voting positively. We use $\alpha = 0.6$ in the results below, but the results are essentially the same with α anywhere between 0.6 and 0.9. **M2**'s parameters are: 4 deviation parameters for each user, P_i of each user, α, and the threshold.

Discussion of results. We find that the performance of the different approaches varies across our datasets, reflecting the different attitudes towards voting displayed by the various Wikipedia populations we're studying. Here we examine both the results on English Wikipedia as well as German Wikipedia to illustrate the differences (French and Spanish Wikipedia results were very similar to the German results).

Figure 11 plots the classification accuracy of our models. In English Wikipedia, where the prior on elections (i.e., the accuracy of random guessing) is around 54%, **B1** trained on Δ-s features alone give us 64% accuracy (and using the simple summary statistics **S** boosts its performance close to 70%). This shows how surprisingly informative similarity and status are, since we're not utilizing voter identities here.

Baseline **B2**, which looks at the identities of the individual evaluators and uses their positivity, gives an additional significant boost. On English Wikipedia, using just the positivities alone (**B2** without the **S** features) does as well as **B1** with **S** (70%). Adding the **S** features to **B2** gives an unusually large boost to 75%, which we only observed on English Wikipedia. On German Wikipedia, **B2** performs about as well as **B1** and hardly benefits from **S**.

Our best results come from the personal approaches that explicitly model deviations from voters' positivities (models **M1**, **M2**). In German Wikipedia, both models improve significantly on the baselines, with the **M2** approach improving on both **B1** and **B2** almost as much as the baselines improve on the prior (70% versus 64% and 66%, where the prior is just below 60%). In English Wikipedia, both models **M1** and **M2** significantly outperform **B1**, and marginally out-perform **B2** (the gain is smaller because of **B2**'s significant, idiosyncratic gain from the summary statistics).

Furthermore, notice that on German Wikipedia **M2** without the informative **S** features beats both baselines with access to **S**. Adding **S** to our second model gives us performance that is halfway to even the gold standard. This means that by only using s, Δ, and P_i values of the early voters – and ignoring the votes they casted – we can still recover half of the information contained in their votes.

We also ran experiments to measure how much predictive power similarity and status each contribute. We created two versions of our best model (**M2**): one which only uses similarity and one which only uses status. Thus instead of splitting the Δ-s space into quadrants, the first just splits along the similarity dimension (creating two buckets) and the second splits along the Δ dimension. In English Wikipedia, the original **M2** without **S** achieves 72.7% accuracy. Using only status, it achieves 70.7%; using only similarity, it scores 68.1%. Similarity's 2% contribution is the majority of **M2**'s gain over **B1**. On German Wikipedia, the full **M2** model scores 70%, whereas it scores 65.3% using only status and 68.5% using only similarity. In both cases, similarity contributes a significant amount of predictive power, and in German Wikipedia it is even more predictive than status. This experiment shows that similarity is a major component in the success of our models.

All of our approaches give us a quantitative picture of how evaluations depend on where they fall in the Δ-s space. For example, in our first model **M1**, where we model $P(E_i = 1) = P_i + d(\Delta_i, s_i)$, the $d(\Delta_i, s_i)$ function imposes an ordering over quadrants indicating which quadrants have the highest fraction of positive evaluations. Baseline **B1**, which learns weights corresponding to each Δ-s quadrant, also learns coefficients that impose a similar ordering. In all the experiments we ran on all of the models we introduced in this section, the relative importance of the quadrants remained

	$\Delta < 0$	$\Delta > 0$
High s	4	3
Low s	2	1

Table 2: Relative importance of quadrants in Δ-s space (1 = highest weight, 4 = lowest weight). This ranking is robust to changes in the election prefix length, similarity metric, etc.

unchanged. This ranking, shown in Table 2, agrees with all of the observations we made in Section 4: votes from evaluators with low similarity to the target are more predictive of election success than those with high similarity, and this split between high and low similarity is more important than the differential status between evaluator and target — a further indication of the important role that similarity is playing in this analysis. Also, votes from higher-status evaluators are more predictive of election success than those from lower-status evaluators.

These results demonstrate that without even looking at the actual votes, it is possible to derive a lot of information about the outcome of the election from a small prefix of the evaluators. As we mentioned at the start of this section, our results suggest that very informative implicit feedback could be gleaned from a small sampling of the audience consuming the content in question, especially if previous evaluation behavior by the audience members is known.

7. CONCLUSION

We have investigated a number of fundamental ways in which similarity affects how users evaluate each other on-line. This has enabled us both to explain open theoretical questions — such as the low aggregate evaluations given by users to others of comparable status [14] — and also to provide new methods for predicting the outcome of group evaluations from observing only the attributes of the evaluators and not their individual evaluations, which we term ballot-blind prediction.

Our work suggests several promising directions for further research. One direction is based on the fact that we can predict outcomes simply from the statuses and similarities of the users who show up to provide evaluations, without ever seeing the positive/negative values of the evaluations themselves. This suggests intriguing potential applications in which the composition of an audience can tell us something about the audience's reaction; it also may have potential synergies with recent techniques for modeling users in collaborative filtering contexts [11]. Another direction is to explore the spectrum of evaluation ranging from judgments about the content produced by individuals to overt judgments about the individuals themselves. We have seen that many of the underlying phenomena are remarkably similar across domains (Wikipedia and Stack Overflow) that occupy different points along this spectrum. Nonetheless different kinds of evaluation bring contrasts into play as well, and developing an understanding of these contrasts can help shed further insight into the ways in which users form collective judgments in social applications.

Acknowledgements. We thank Stack Overflow for providing us with their data. This research has been supported in part by a Google Research Grant, a Yahoo Research Alliance Grant, NSF grants IIS-0910664, CCF-0910940, IIS-1016099, IIS-1016909 and CNS-1010921, the Albert Yu & Mary Bechmann Foundation, IBM, Lightspeed, Microsoft and Yahoo.

8. REFERENCES

[1] L. A. Adamic, J. Zhang, E. Bakshy, and M. S. Ackerman. Knowledge sharing and yahoo answers: everyone knows something. In *Proc. WWW*, pages 665–674, 2008.

[2] M. J. Brzozowski, T. Hogg, and G. Szabó. Friends and foes: ideological social networking. In *Proc. CHI*, pages 817–820, 2008.

[3] M. Burke and R. Kraut. Mopping up: Modeling wikipedia promotion decisions. In *Proc. CSCW*, pages 27–36, 2008.

[4] R. S. Burt. *Neighbor Networks: Competitive Advantage Local and Personal*. Oxford University Press, 2009.

[5] D. Cosley, D. Frankowski, S. B. Kiesler, L. G. Terveen, and J. Riedl. How oversight improves member-maintained communities. In *Proc. CHI*, pages 11–20, 2005.

[6] C. Danescu-Niculescu-Mizil, G. Kossinets, J. M. Kleinberg, and L. Lee. How opinions are received by online communities: a case study on amazon.com helpfulness votes. In *Proc. WWW*, pages 141–150, 2009.

[7] R. V. Guha, R. Kumar, P. Raghavan, and A. Tomkins. Propagation of trust and distrust. In *Proc. WWW*, 2004.

[8] W. Hill, L. Stead, M. Rosenstein, and G. Furnas. Recommending and evaluating choices in a virtual community of use. In *Proc. CHI*, pages 194–201, 1995.

[9] S. Kamvar, M. Schlosser, and H. Garcia-Molina. The eigentrust algorithm for reputation management in p2p networks. In *Proc. WWW*, pages 640–651. ACM, 2003.

[10] J. A. Konstan, B. N. Miller, D. Maltz, J. L. Herlocker, L. R. Gordon, and J. Riedl. Grouplens: Applying collaborative filtering to usenet news. *Commun. ACM*, 40(3):77–87, 1997.

[11] Y. Koren. Factor in the neighbors: Scalable and accurate collaborative filtering. *TKDD*, 4(1), 2010.

[12] J. Kunegis, A. Lommatzsch, and C. Bauckhage. The Slashdot Zoo: Mining a social network with negative edges. In *Proc. WWW*, pages 741–750, 2009.

[13] P. Lazarsfeld and R. K. Merton. Friendship as a social process: A substantive and methodological analysis. In M. Berger, T. Abel, and C. H. Page, editors, *Freedom and Control in Modern Society*, pages 18–66. Nostrand, 1954.

[14] J. Leskovec, D. Huttenlocher, and J. Kleinberg. Governance in social media: A case study of the Wikipedia promotion process. In *Proc. ICWSM*, 2010.

[15] J. Leskovec, D. Huttenlocher, and J. Kleinberg. Predicting positive and negative links in on-line social networks. In *Proc. WWW*, pages 641–650, 2010.

[16] J. Leskovec, D. Huttenlocher, and J. Kleinberg. Signed networks in social media. In *Proc. CHI*, pages 1361–1370, 2010.

[17] G. Linden, B. Smith, and J. York. Amazon.com recommendations: Item-to-item collaborative filtering. *IEEE Internet Computing*, 7(1):76–80, 2003.

[18] P. Massa and P. Avesani. Trust metrics in recommender systems. *Computing with social trust*, pages 259–285, 2009.

[19] B. Pang and L. Lee. *Opinion Mining and Sentinment Analysis*. Number 2(1-2) in Foundations and Trends in Information Retrieval. Now Publishers, 2008.

[20] U. Shardanand and P. Maes. Social information filtering: Algorithms for automating "word of mouth". In *Proc. CHI*, volume 1, pages 210–217, 1995.

[21] M. Szell, R. Lambiotte, and S. Thurner. Multirelational organization of large-scale social networks in an online world. *Proc. Natl. Acad. Sci.*, 107(31):13636–13641, 2010.

[22] S. Thye, D. Willer, and B. Markovsky. From status to power: New models at the intersection of two theories. *Social Forces*, 84:1471–1495, 2006.

[23] D. Willer (editor). *Network Exchange Theory*. Praeger, 1999.

How User Behavior is Related to Social Affinity

Rina Panigrahy
Microsoft Research
1065 La Avenida
Mountain View, CA 94043, USA
rina@microsoft.com

Marc Najork
Microsoft Research
1065 La Avenida
Mountain View, CA 94043, USA
najork@microsoft.com

Yinglian Xie
Microsoft Research
1065 La Avenida
Mountain View, CA 94043, USA
yxie@microsoft.com

ABSTRACT

Previous research has suggested that people who are in the same social circle exhibit similar behaviors and tastes. The rise of social networks gives us insights into the social circles of web users, and recommendation services (including search engines, advertisement engines, and collaborative filtering engines) provide a motivation to adapt recommendations to the interests of the audience. An important primitive for supporting these applications is the ability to quantify how connected two users are in a social network. The shortest-path distance between a pair of users is an obvious candidate measure. This paper introduces a new measure of "affinity" in social networks that takes into account not only the distance between two users, but also the number of edge-disjoint paths between them, i.e. the "robustness" of their connection. Our measure is based on a sketch-based approach, and affinity queries can be answered extremely efficiently (at the expense of a one-time offline sketch computation). We compare this affinity measure against the "approximate shortest-path distance", a sketch-based distance measure with similar efficiency characteristics. Our empirical study is based on a Hotmail email exchange graph combined with demographic information and Bing query history, and a Twitter mention-graph together with the text of the underlying tweets. We found that users who are close to each other – either in terms of distance or affinity – have a higher similarity in terms of demographics, queries, and tweets.

Categories and Subject Descriptors

G.2.2 [**Graph Theory**]: Graph algorithms, path and circuit problems

General Terms

Algorithm, Experimentation, Performance

Permission to make digital or hard copies of all or part of this work for personal or classroom use is granted without fee provided that copies are not made or distributed for profit or commercial advantage and that copies bear this notice and the full citation on the first page. To copy otherwise, to republish, to post on servers or to redistribute to lists, requires prior specific permission and/or a fee.
WSDM'12, February 8–12, 2012, Seattle, Washington, USA.
Copyright 2012 ACM 978-1-4503-0747-5/12/02 ...$10.00.

Keywords

Social networks, distance, affinity, influence, sketching

1. INTRODUCTION

Are the activities and preferences of people correlated to or influenced by their position in a social network? Do two users that are "nearby" in the network tend to have similar preferences, browse the same web sites, or speak the same language? If so, exactly what is the right measure of "social affinity"? While a natural choice may the shortest-path distance, this doesn't capture the number of paths between the pair of users. An alternate choice is the min-cut or the connectivity, which is also the number of edge-disjoint paths between two users. Furthermore, an affinity measure should preferably be robust – it should not change much with a small change in the edges of the network.

This paper introduces a social affinity measure that can be viewed as an intermediate measure between the shortest-path distance and the number of paths connecting a pair of nodes. Such a notion of affinity is not only useful for studying user behavior, but it has commercial applications in web search, targeted advertising, and collaborative filtering. For example, on a web search query, it may be desirable to bias the results towards documents that are authored by or preferred by nearby users (such as the Facebook "liked" documents). For this reason it is important that the distance measure should be easy to compute in an online fashion at run-time. Our affinity measure not only takes into account the lengths and the number of paths between two users, but is also efficient in the sense that it can be easily computed online (with some one-time offline precomputation).

The second contribution of this paper consists of two empirical studies of the relationship between social affinity and user characteristics and behavior, and a comparison of social affinity to approximate shortest path (ASP) distance, another efficiently computable measure. The first study is based on the email exchange graph between Hotmail users, their self-declared demographic information, and queries they issued to the Bing search engine. We found that users who are nearby in the email exchange graph tend to have similar demographic characteristics, and more interestingly, that their queries were more similar to each other than those of far-apart users. Moreover, we found that both ASP distance and social affinity between two users are correlated to their profile and query similarity. While ASP had a higher correlation for most user properties, affinity was better in one that changes over short distances. This suggests that the affinity measure may be better-suited for capturing short-distance effects in a social graph, whereas ASP may be preferable for capturing long-distance effects. The second study is based on the graph induced by two Twitter users mutually mentioning each other in their tweets, using the textual similarities between their collected tweets as ground truth. We found that the affinity between two users is strongly correlated with the similarity between their tweets, while ASP distance in the mention-graph is less strongly correlated. We speculate that textual similarity between tweets is high in a short range of distances, and that affinity captures this better than ASP does.

There is a growing body of work on the impact of social influence on consumer preferences. Domingos and Richardson [10] proposed to model markets as social networks of consumers, and derived how to optimize profit by focusing on the most influential consumers, validating their model against a movie recommendation database; others (for example, Kempe et al. [14] and Leskovec et al. [17]) expanded on this work. Crandall et al. [8] studied the interplay between social influence and selection (individuals forming associations with like-minded people) based on a edit history of Wikipedia articles. Kossinets et al. [15] proposed a temporal notion of distance in social graphs, by quantifying how long it takes for information to propagate along a given edge. Cosley et al. [9] subsequently proposed a model of how influence propagates through a social network. The topic has also attracted much interest from disciplines other than Computer Science. For example, the medical community has investigated the correlation between social connections and public-health issues such as obesity [6], smoking [7], and alcohol consumption [20], as well as positive factors such as happiness [12].

Similarly, there is a large body of work on using sketching for estimating distances in graphs. Bourgain [3] showed how any graph can be embedded into a Euclidean space while preserving distances to a factor of $O(\log n)$; Matousek [19] obtained a tighter analysis of Bourgain's result. Thorup and Zwick [24] gave an alternate algorithm for estimating distances to within a factor of $2k-1$ by using sketches of size $\tilde{O}(n^{1/k})$. Sketching is also commonly used in comparing documents, see for example work by Broder et al. [5, 4]. Spielman and Teng [23] showed how a method known as graph sparsification can be used to estimate resistance across edges; improved in follow-on work [22, 1, 16]. Von Luxburg et al. [18] argued that resistance may not be a good measure of distance in large graphs.

2. MEASURES OF SOCIAL AFFINITY

As stated earlier, a good social affinity measure should take into account not only the length of the shortest path between two nodes (users) but also the number of paths and their lengths. Some candidate measures are:

1. Max flow (or min cut) between the pair of nodes
2. Commute time (or effective resistance) between the pair in a random walk
3. Using probabilities of reaching one node from another in a random walk

Unfortunately, all the above measures are very difficult to compute efficiently online. An alternative approach is to employ sketching. It involves a one-time precomputation that produces a compact "sketch" for each node in the graph (user in the social network). During the online phase, given a pair of users, it suffices to read the sketches stored for these users and perform some simple computation on these sketches. In the context of this paper, this computation produces the social distance between two users, or an approximation of it. Not all distance measures are sketchable. For example, the shortest-path distance cannot be sketched unless one is willing to make use of a gross approximation. On a graph with n nodes, if one is willing to obtain a $2k-1$-approximation to the shortest-path distance, then this can be achieved with a sketching algorithm that stores a sketch of size $O(n^{1/k})$ per node. In recent years, theoretical algorithms research has produced sketching algorithms for computing the commute-time between a pair of nodes [23, 16] – however, despite a low asymptotic time complexity, these algorithms are very complicated and perhaps have large constants hidden in the asymptotics. The social affinity measure introduced in this paper employs sketching to approximate the probability that the pair of nodes remain connected when a certain fraction of the edges are removed randomly. We compare this measure to the approximate shortest-path (ASP) measure [11], another sketch-based technique for estimating the shortest-path distance in a graph; ASP has been observed to have small additive error for certain real-world graphs.

2.1 Affinity based distance measure

The affinity measure introduced in this paper is essentially a quantification of the probability that a given pair of nodes remain connected when a certain fraction of the edges are removed randomly. For example, if 50% of the edges are removed randomly, then it is reasonable to conclude that pairs of nodes remaining in the same connected component have a higher affinity than the ones that got separated. If there is only one path of a certain length between a pair it is less likely to survive sampling as compared to a case when there are many paths of that length. Also, longer paths are less likely to survive than shorter paths. Thus, our measure accounts for both length and breadth of the set of paths. We formalize this intuition below.

Given a graph G, let G_p denote the graph obtained by sampling the edges of the graph with probability p (so $G_1 = G$). The affinity, parameterized by p, between a pair of nodes is defined as follows

DEFINITION 1. $A_p(u, v)$ = *probability that* u *and* v *are connected in* G_p.

One method to get a parameter-free version of affinity is to look at the mean (or expected) value when p is chosen from a distribution D such as the uniform distribution on the range $[0, 1]$.

DEFINITION 2. $A(u, v) = E_{p \in D}[A_p(u, v)]$

The above definition captures the mean of A_p over a distribution. Alternatively, we could capture the median, or more generally a percentile quantified by a threshold θ. Formally,

DEFINITION 3. $A^{\theta}(u, v) = 1 - \min\{p : A_p(u, v) > \theta\}$

Thus $A^{\theta}(u, v)$ measures the fraction of edges from the graph that must be removed so that the probability of the two points being connected is no more than θ.

2.2 Relation to other measures

The following theorems show the connection between the affinity measure and other connectivity and distance measures. It has some relations to the shortest-path distance, to the minimum cut and to strong-connectivity, which is a variant of minimum cut. Assume that $A(u,v)$ is computed by drawing p uniformly from $[0,1]$.

We will use $d(u,v)$ to denote the shortest-path distance measure between u and v.

DEFINITION 4. *(Connectivity) A pair of nodes u,v is k-connected if there are k edge-disjoint paths between u and v. The connectivity $C(u,v)$ between a pair u,v is the maximum value of k for which the pair is k-connected. It is also equal to the minimum cut between the pair (by the max-flow min-cut theorem).*

DEFINITION 5. *(Strong Connectivity [2]) A pair u,v is k-strongly connected if it lies in a subset U of nodes, so that every pair of nodes in the subgraph induced by U is k-connected. The strong-connectivity $S(u,v)$ between a pair u,v is the maximum value of k for which the pair of k-strongly-connected.*

Use $\bar{A}_p(u,v)$ to denote $1 - A_p(u,v)$. Similarly for $A(u,v)$ and $A^\theta(u,v)$.

THEOREM 6.

$$\Omega\left(\frac{S(u,v)}{\log n}\right) \le \frac{1}{1 - A(u,v)} \le 1 + C(u,v)$$

$$lim_{p\to 0}\frac{\log A_p(u,v)}{\log p} = d(u,v).$$

$$lim_{p\to 1}\frac{\log(1 - A_p(u,v))}{\log(1-p)} = C(u,v).$$

$$\theta\bar{A}^\theta(u,v) \le \bar{A}(u,v) \le \frac{1}{\theta}\bar{A}^\theta(u,v)$$

PROOF. Look at the minimum cut of size $C(u,v)$ between u and v. At sampling probability p, the probability that none of the edges of the cut are chosen resulting in a disconnection is $(1-p)^{C(u,v)}$, implying that $1 - A_p(u,v) \ge (1-p)^{C(u,v)}$. Therefore if p is chosen uniformly from $[0,1]$ then $1 - A(u,v) = E_p[1 - A_p(u,v)] \ge E[(1-p)^{C(u,v)}] \ge \int_0^1 (1-p)^{C(u,v)}dp = \frac{1}{1+C(u,v)}$.

It is known that if you sample edges with probability $p = \Omega(\log n/S(u,v))$ then the pair (u,v) remains connected with high probability, which means that $A_p(u,v)$ is close to 1 for such p [2, 13]. This implies $1 - A(u,v) \le O(\log n/S(u,v))$.

Note that in the $lim_{p\to 0}$, the probability that all the edges on the shortest path between u and v are sampled is $p^{d(u,v)}$, and this is the least set of edges that need to be sampled and hence is a dominating factor in the probability of staying connected.

$A_p(u,v) = \sum_{i=1}^m N(i).p^i(1-p)^{m-1}$ where $N(i)$ is the number of edge subsets of size i in which u and v are connected. As $p \to 0$, $\frac{\log A_p(u,v)}{\log p}$ is equal to the minimum i for which $N(i)$ is non-zero which is $d(u,v)$.

A similar argument holds when $p \to 1$. In this case the smallest set of edges that disconnects u and v has size $C(u,v)$. So $(1-p)^{C(u,v)}$ is a dominating factor in the probability of disconnection.

At sampling probability $h = \bar{A}^\theta(u,v)$, $A_h(u,v) = \theta$. So at any probability $p \le h$, $\bar{A}_p(u,v) \ge \theta$ implying that $\bar{A}(u,v) = E_p[\bar{A}_p(u,v)] \ge h\theta = \theta\bar{A}^\theta(u,v)$.

Recall that G_p denotes a subgraph of G where each edge is sampled with probability p. Note that for any integer x, G_{px} stochastically dominates the union of x independently sampled graphs G_p, because the union will contain each edge with probability at most px implying that $\bar{A}_{px}(u,v)$ is at most the probability that u and v are disconnected in all the copies, which happens with probability $(\bar{A}_p(u,v))^x$. Since $\bar{A}_p(u,v)$ is decreasing in p, we have $\bar{A}(u,v) = E_p[\bar{A}_p(u,v)] \le \int_{x=0}^{\frac{1}{h}-1} h(\bar{A}_{hx}(u,v))dx \le \int_{x=0}^{\frac{1}{h}-1} h(1-\theta)^x dx \le \frac{h}{\theta} = \frac{\bar{A}^\theta(u,v)}{\theta}$ □

2.3 Affinity Sketching Algorithm

We now show that the affinity measure is easily sketchable. The algorithm computes a short sketch (a summary) per node as a precomputation offline. At runtime the sketch of two nodes is used to estimate their affinity $A(u,v)$.

The rough idea of the off-line sketch generation phase is to sample the edges of the graph at different probabilities and record the connected component a node belongs to. The probabilities could be values chosen geometrically such as $1, \frac{1}{2}, \frac{1}{4}, \frac{1}{8}, \cdots$ or from some other discrete set of values between 0 and 1. For each value of probability we can sample the edges of the graph and record the connected component of each node (e.g. the ID of a canonical "representative" node in the connected component). We repeat this for all probabilities, a few times for each value. The sketch $C(u)$ is simply the vector (or matrix) of component IDs for this node u over all these sampling experiments.

At runtime, to estimate $A^\theta(u,v)$ we retrieve $C(u)$ and $C(v)$. For each sampling probability find the fraction of times they were in the same component. We find the two consecutive sampling probabilities p and p' that cross over the threshold θ (one can ensure that these fractions are monotonically decreasing in the sampling probability by making the sampled sets as a telescoping sequence of sets one contained in the next one). $A^\theta(u,v)$ is concentrated between p and p'.

Now, let us give a formal definition of an affinity sketch. Let (V,E) be a social graph with vertex (user) set V and edge (relationship) set E, such that $E \subseteq V \times V$. For simplicity, we assume that the graph is undirected and that the edge set reflects this, i.e. $(u,v) \in E \equiv (v,u) \in E$.

We write $\text{Conn}(v,v',V,E)$ to denote that v and v' are connected in graph (V,E). We define a partitioning of a (sub)graph (V,E) into connected components as follows:

$\text{Part}(V,E) = \{V_1,\cdots,V_t\}$ such that

1. $V_1 \cup \cdots \cup V_t = V$
2. $\forall V_i, V_j s.t. V_i \ne V_j : V_i \cap V_j = \emptyset$
3. $\forall V_i \forall v, v' \in V_i : \text{Conn}(v,v',V,E)$
4. $\forall V_i, V_j s.t. V_i \ne V_j : \forall v \in V_i, v' \in V_j : \neg\text{Conn}(v,v',V,E)$

We define the component of a vertex v given a partitioning of a (sub)graph (V,E) as follows:

$$\text{Comp}(v,V,E) = V_i \text{ where } V_i \in \text{Part}(V,E) \wedge v \in V_i$$

The sketch construction phase of our algorithm takes three parameters: integers q and r and a sampling probability vector $p_1, \cdots, p_r$. Given these parameters, we generate a matrix of edge subsets

$$\begin{pmatrix} E_{1,1} & \cdots & E_{1,r} \\ \vdots & \ddots & \vdots \\ E_{q,1} & \cdots & E_{q,r} \end{pmatrix}$$

such that $E \subseteq E_{i,1} \subseteq \cdots \subseteq E_{i,r}$ (i.e. each row of the matrix is a telescoping sequence of subsets) and $|E_{i,j}| = p_j|E|$ (the cardinality of $E_{i,j}$ is p_j that of the cardinality of the full edge set E). Using this definition, we define the sketch C of a vertex v to be the matrix

$$\begin{pmatrix} c_{1,1} & \cdots & c_{1,r} \\ \vdots & \ddots & \vdots \\ c_{q,1} & \cdots & c_{q,r} \end{pmatrix}$$

where $c_{i,j} = \text{Comp}(v, V, E_{i,j})$, i.e. based on the graph partitioning induced by the edge subset matrix defined above.

In order to describe how sketches are used to estimate the affinity between two vertices, we employ Iverson bracket notation: $[a = b]$ is 1 if $a = b$ and 0 otherwise, and $[a < b]$ is 1 if $a < b$ and 0 otherwise. Using this notation, we define the affinity estimates $\tilde{A}$ and $\tilde{A}^\theta$ of two vertices v and v' with sketch matrices C and C' to be as follows:

$$\tilde{A}(v, v') = \frac{1}{qr} \sum_{j=1}^{r} \sum_{i=1}^{q} [c_{i,j} = c'_{i,j}]$$

$$\tilde{A}^\theta(v, v') = \frac{1}{r} \sum_{j=1}^{r} \left[\theta < \frac{1}{q} \sum_{i=1}^{q} [c_{i,j} = c'_{i,j}] \right]$$

By setting the sampling probabilities $p_1, \cdots, p_r$ to the values $1, (1-\epsilon), (1-\epsilon)^2, ...(1-\epsilon)^r$ where $r = O(\log m/\epsilon)$ one can obtain a $1 \pm \epsilon$ approximation to the affinity between a pair of nodes.

THEOREM 7. *There is an algorithm that estimates $\tilde{A}^\theta(u, v)$ between any pair of nodes (u, v), for any constant θ within a $1 \pm \epsilon$ factor with high probability. using sketches of size $O(\log m \log n/\epsilon^2)$ per node. The sketches can be computed in time $\tilde{O}(m/\epsilon^2)$.*

PROOF. Let $h = \tilde{A}^\theta(u, v)$ be the sampling probability at which the probability that u and v are connected is θ. If a sampling probability p is more than $h(1+\epsilon)$ then we will argue that $A_p(u, v) \geq \theta(1 + \Omega(\epsilon))$: Note that the graph G_p stochastically dominates the union of the graph G_h and $G_{\epsilon h}$ as the sampling probability in the former is no lower than the sampling probability in the union. So $A_p(u, v)$ is at least the probability that u and v are connected in either of G_h or $G_{\epsilon h}$ which is $1 - (\bar{A}_h(u, v))(\bar{A}_{\epsilon h}(u, v))$. But again the union of $(1+\epsilon)/\epsilon$ independent copies of $G_{\epsilon h}$ stochastically dominates G_h as the sampling probability in the union is no lower. So $\bar{A}_h(u, v) \geq (\bar{A}_{\epsilon h}(u, v))^{(1+\epsilon)/\epsilon}$. This gives, $A_p(u, v) \geq 1 - (\bar{A}_h(u, v))^{1+\epsilon/(1+\epsilon)} \geq A_h(u, v)(1 + \Omega(\epsilon)) \geq \theta(1 + \Omega(\epsilon))$. Since each sampling probability is repeated $q = \Theta(\log n/\epsilon^2)$ times, by Chernoff bounds, the observed fraction of times the pair stays connected will be more than θ with high probability. Similarly we can argue that if $p \leq h(1-\epsilon)$ then the observed fraction will be less than θ. Therefore our sampling probability vector will contain two probability values that sandwich h within a $1 \pm O(\epsilon)$ factor. By appropriately adjusting the constants in the $O(.)$ notation, we get the theorem statement. □

2.4 Affinity Implementation

We built single-machine implementations of both the off-line and the on-line phase of the affinity sketch algorithm. The off-line phase consists of several steps: First, we map user IDs into a dense integer space suitable as array indices. Second, we load the edge set of the graph into an in-memory array and permute this array, either uniformly at random or biased by the weight of each edge. Third, we perform q iterations, each computing one row of the sketch matrix $C(v)$ for each vertex v. Each iteration starts with an empty edge set, and consumes the content of the permuted edge array in order, adding each new edge to a union-find forest. Whenever a sampling threshold as specified by the vector $p_1, \cdots, p_r$ is crossed, we write the connected-component ID of each node v (which corresponds to a cell $c_{i,j}$ in $C(v)$) to disk, eventually producing $q \times r$ streams of connected component IDs. Fourth, we merge these $q \times r$ streams into a single stream of sketches, each sketch being a matrix of $q \times r$ component IDs. The online phase, given a pair of user IDs, simply converts them into two integers using the same mapping as the off-line phase, and uses each integer to seek to the right position of the sketch file and to read the sketch from disk.

2.5 Approximate Shortest Path

In Section 3, we will compare the effectiveness of the affinity measure to that of the approximate shortest path measure, another sketch-based measure of distances in graphs [11]. The ASP measure is a variant of the algorithm introduced by Thorup and Zwick [24].

The idea behind the approximate shortest path (ASP) algorithm is to sample, in the off-line phase, a small number of sets of "seed" nodes in the graph. Then, for each node in the graph, find the closest seed node in each of these seed sets. The sketch for a node simply consists of the closest seeds (one per seed set), and the distance to each closest seed. Then, in the online computation, one can use the distance to these closest seeds to estimate the distance between a given pair of nodes by checking for a common seed between the two sketches. Given a pair of nodes u and v one can estimate the distance between them by looking for a common seed in their sketches. If w is a common seed in the sketch of u and v then the distance can be estimated by adding up the distances to the common seed w.

3. EXPERIMENTS

We performed two studies to evaluate the effectiveness of the Affinity measure and to compare it to ASP distance. The first study was conducted on the Hotmail email exchange graph, and used user-supplied demographic information as well as Bing query history as its ground truth; the second study was conducted on the Twitter mention-graph, and used the text of tweets as its ground truth.

3.1 The Hotmail experiment

Our first experiment is based on three data sets:

1. An anonymized data set containing a pair of user ID hashes for any two email users (at least one of which is a Hotmail user) that had a mutual email exchange (that is, both users sent email to one another). This data set induces a graph with 312,548,443 nodes and 574,434,516 undirected edges, implying an average de-

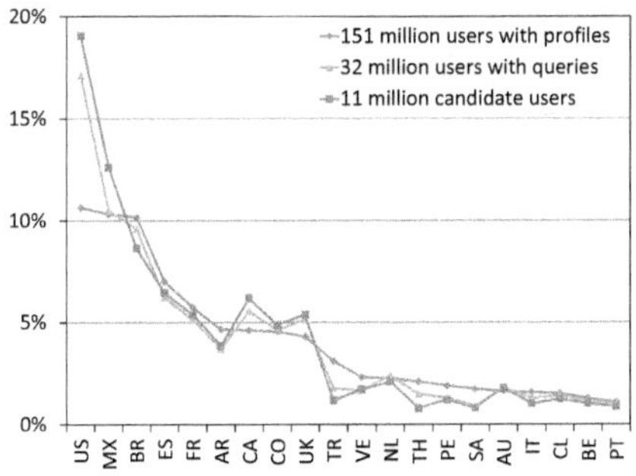

Figure 1: Country distribution of Hotmail users

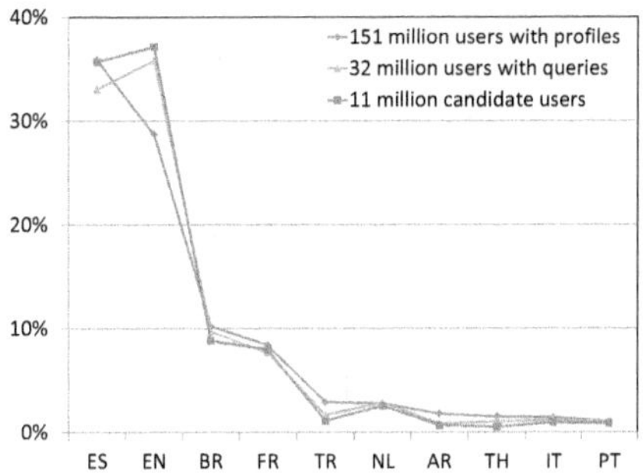

Figure 2: Language distribution of Hotmail users

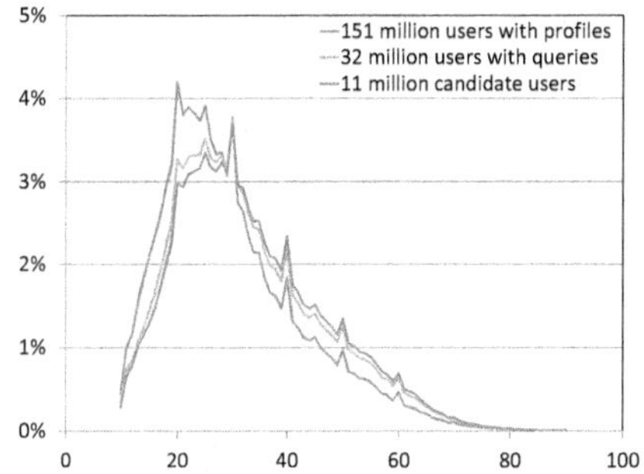

Figure 3: Age distribution of Hotmail users

gree of about 3.676. The graph is highly-connected, with 309,065,428 of the nodes (close to 99%) being part of a giant connected component. The data was collected between October 2007 and April 2010, and represents a sample of the email traffic (condensed to a hash of the sender's and receiver's email address) going through Hotmail during that timeframe. Assuming that user u sent a messages to user v and v sent b messages to u, the edge (u, v) in the graph has a weight of $\min\{u, v\}$ associated with it.

2. A data set containing basic, self-reported demographic information (including country of residence, primary language, and age) for a subset of 151,265,301 Hotmail users in the first dataset.

3. A data set containing the Bing query history for a subset of 32,212,592 users in the second data set.

We furthermore restricted this set of 32,212,592 users covered by all three data sets (that is, for whom we have email exchange history, demographic information, and Bing query history) to contain only users who had issued at least five queries so as to be able to make meaningful comparisons between two users' query histories, and we restrict who had a minimum of two email partners in order to compensate for the vagaries of email traffic sampling. This left us with a set of 10,974,103 "candidate" users.

Figure 1 shows the distribution of the top twenty countries of residence of Hotmail users (the top twenty countries being those with at least 1% of users in the overall data set). The horizontal axis shows the country, ordered by decreasing frequency in the overall data set; the vertical axis shows the percentage of users from a given country. The blue curve plots the distribution of the 151 million users for whom we have demographic information; the green curve shows the distribution of the 32 million users for which we also have queries; and the red curve shows the distribution of the 11 million "candidate" users from which we sampled pairs. While the largest portion of Hotmail users resides in the United States, a surprisingly large portion resides in Latin America (Mexico, Brazil, Argentina, Columbia, Venezuela, Peru, and Chile). It is also worth noting that users from the US are overrepresented in the users-with-queries set relative to their representation in the overall data set. This is due the fact that Bing is particularly popular in the US. Users from the US and Mexico yet more overrepresented in the candidate set, suggesting that they either issue more queries or maintain a larger set of email partners.

Figure 2 shows the distribution of the top ten primary languages of Hotmail users (the top ten languages being those with at least 1% of users in the overall data set), using the same encoding as the previous figure. The largest portion of users in the overall set are Spanish-speakers (consistent with the popularity of Hotmail in Latin America and Spain), while the users-with-queries and candidate sets are dominated by English-speakers. We attribute this to the overrepresentation of US users in the candidate set.

Figure 3 shows the distribution of (self-declared) ages of Hotmail users, using the same encoding as the previous two figures. The graph shows only ages from 10 to 90 years, which accounts for 98.4% of the overall user base. The overall user base is dominated by people in their early twenties, users in the users-with-queries and candidate sets are slightly older. Notice the peaks at ages that are a multiple of ten, and minor peaks at multiples of five, which suggests that users round their ages before reporting.

We used the implementation described in section 2.4 to compute sketches for each node in the email exchange graph, using a machine with a dual-core AMD Opteron 285 processor clocked at 2.6 GHz, 16 GB of RAM, and a RAID-5 array composed of eight 1 TB, 7200 RPM Seagate Barracuda SATA drives. We set q to 10 and r to 100, yielding sketches of 4000 bytes per node. We computed three sets of sketches: one where edges were permuted uniformly at random, one where edges were permuted biased by their weight (the count of email exchanges), and one where edges were permuted biased by the log of their weight. The computation took 14 days. Most of the time was spent on disk I/O; indeed, the final merge phase (which merged a thousand files into a single 1.13 TB file) took 11 days. We also ran a variant of this program that performs the same computation, but records statistics instead of writing out sketches. Running this variant over the same input data took slightly less than 22 hours.

Instead of choosing a geometric progression for the sampling probability vector $p_1, \cdots, p_r$ as suggested in in Theorem 7, we calibrated it such that the affinity value between a random pair of nodes is uniformly distributed in the range $[0, 1]$.

We randomly sampled 5 million pairs of users from the set of 10,974,103 candidate users, and computed the ASP distances and affinities between each pair. Using the hardware described above and the 1.13 TB sketch file produced by the off-line phase, computing the affinity value for each pair of Hotmail user IDs takes about 17 milliseconds; this time is dominated by the cost of performing two disk seeks.

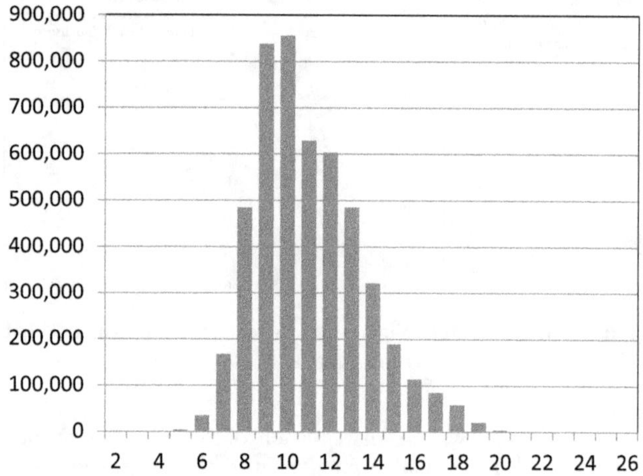

Figure 4: Distribution of ASP distances for the sampled 5 million pairs of users

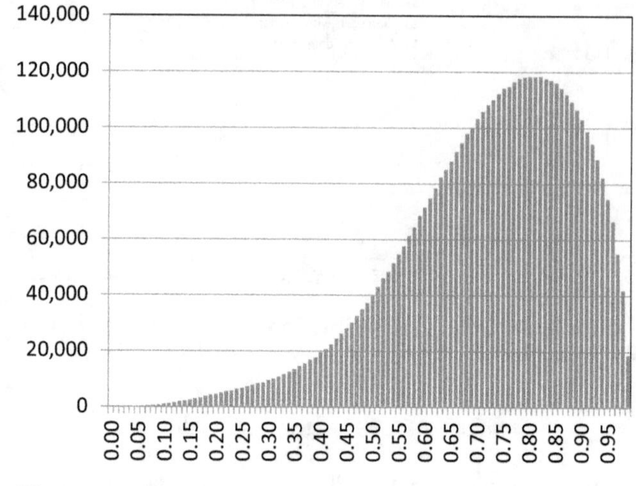

Figure 5: Distribution of affinities for the sampled 5 million pairs of users

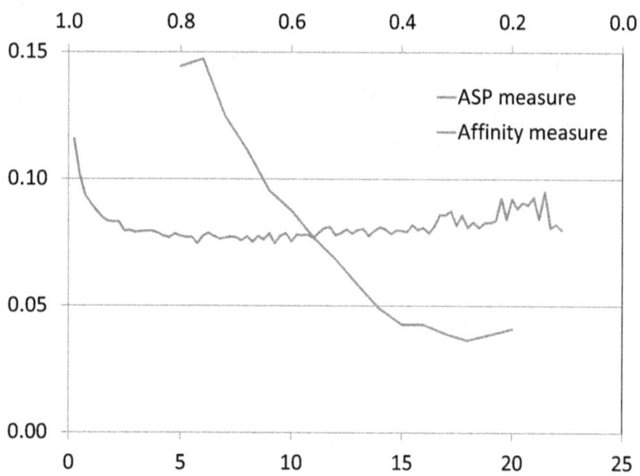

Figure 6: Fraction of pairs of users in same country as a function of ASP or affinity measure

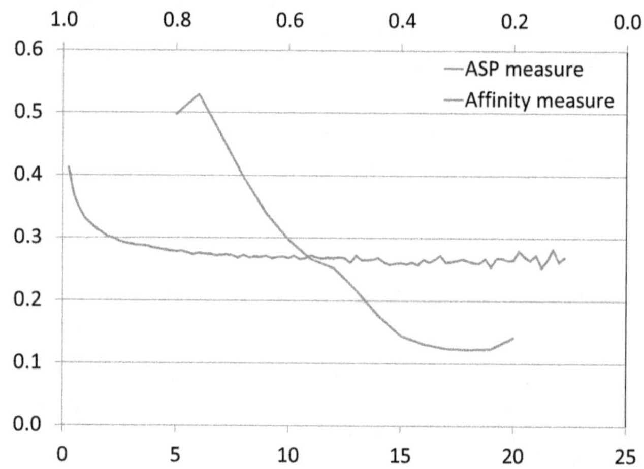

Figure 7: Fraction of pairs of users speaking same language as a function of ASP or affinity measure

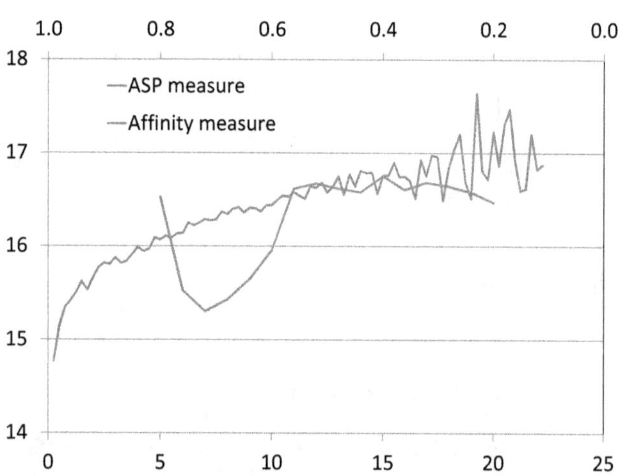

Figure 8: Average age difference between pairs of users as a function of ASP or affinity measure

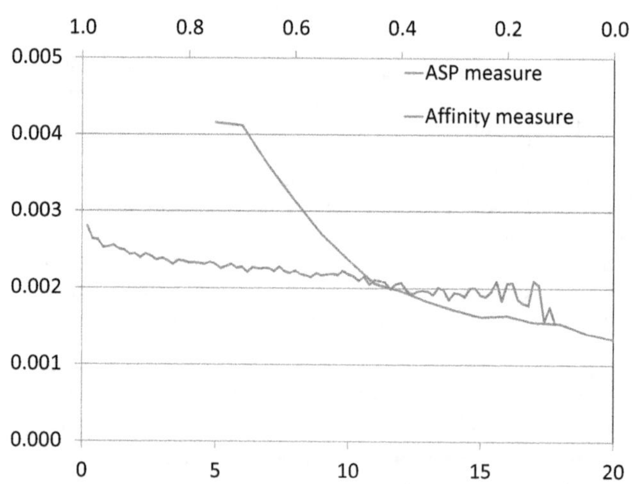

Figure 9: Average cosine similarity of queries of users as a function of ASP or affinity measure

	negative ASP distance	A^θ unweighted	A unweighted	A^θ weighted	A weighted	A^θ log-weighted	A log-weighted
Country similarity	0.0828	0.0020	0.0020	0.0255	0.0258	0.0179	0.0181
Language similarity	0.1794	0.0324	0.0329	0.0430	0.0439	0.0424	0.0432
Age similarity	-0.0290	0.0241	0.0242	-0.0110	-0.0110	-0.0015	-0.0011
Query similarity	0.0616	0.0200	0.0205	0.0155	0.0161	0.0186	0.0191

Table 1: Correlation coefficient between similarity of pairs of users and their proximity in the email exchange graph.

Figure 4 shows the distribution of ASP distances. The mode of the distribution is at distance 10, and the bulk is between 5 and 15. It should be pointed out that in earlier work we found ASP to overestimate distance by a constant additive amount (about 2 to 3 in the case of undirected web graphs), so we assume the distribution of true distances to be shifted accordingly. Figure 5 shows the distribution of A^θ affinity values (for $\theta = 0.5$) of the sketches for the graph with unweighted edges. The mode of the distribution is at 0.82. Given that the sampling probability vector $p_1, \cdots, p_r$ was calibrated to produce a uniform distribution of affinity values across the entire set of 312 million users in the email exchange graph, the non-uniformity of the distribution in Figure 5 indicates that our set of candidate users is biased towards users with affinity towards each other.

Figure 6 shows the fraction of pairs of users (drawn from the candidate set) residing in the same country, as a function of the distance and affinity between the pair of users. The vertical axis shows the fraction of pairs coming from the same country; the bottom scale of the horizontal axis shows ASP distance values (in increasing order) whose distribution is plotted by the blue curve; the top scale shows the estimated A^θ affinity values (in decreasing order, for $\theta = 0.5$ and based on the sketches formed using unweighted edges) whose distribution is plotted by the red curve. Each (x, y) point of a curve shows the fraction y of all pairs at distance/affinity x who reside in the same country. In order to reduce noise, we restricted the curves to only those distance and affinity values with at least 1000 (out of 5 million) pairs of users. Both distance and affinity measures are discrete, but since the set of possible distance values is smaller than the set of possible affinity values, the affinity curve appears smoother. The ASP curve is far more slanted than the affinity curve, suggesting that the correlation between ASP and country of residence is far stronger than between affinity and country. Indeed, this is borne out by the correlation coefficients shown in Table 1.

Figure 7 shows the fraction of pairs of users speaking the same language, using the same encoding as the previous figure. Again, we restricted the curve to points with at least 1000 pairs of users. As in the previous figure, the ASP curve is far more slanted than the affinity curve, suggesting stronger correlation between distance and language than between affinity and language. This is also borne out by the correlation coefficients in the second row of Table 1.

Figure 8 shows the age difference between pairs of users as a function of the distance and affinity between the pair of users. The vertical axis plots the age difference, the horizontal axis plots distance and affinity as it did in Figures 6 and 7. Each (x, y) point of a curve shows the average age difference y of all pairs at distance/affinity x. Again, the curve only shows points with at least 1000 pairs of users so as to reduce noise. The graph has several features worth pointing out: First, note that the vertical axis does not start at 0, but rather at 14 years – the average age difference between pairs of users is ranges between about 15 and 18 years regardless of distance or affinity. Putting it differently, email is a social medium that connects generations. Second, age difference and affinity are negatively correlated – users with high affinity are on average closer in age. Third, the distance curve is non-monotonic – there is no clear relationship between the ASP distance of two users in the email graph and their age difference. Referring to the third row of Table 1, the correlation coefficients of ASP distance and age vs. affinity and age are quite low and fairly close to each other, with ASP having a slight edge.

The previous three figures examined the connection between two users' demographic background (namely country, language and age) and their distance and affinity in the email exchange graph. Next, we examine whether the distance or affinity between two users is predictive of shared *interests*. To that end, we aggregate all the queries issued by a given user into a bag of terms, and we weigh each term in the bag by its tf-idf value [21]. We compute the cosine similarity between the tf-idf weighted queries for each of the 5 million pairs of users, and we treat this similarity as a proxy of the similarity of their interests. Figure 9 depicts the results of this experiment. The vertical axis plots the similarity between a pair's queries, the horizontal axis plots distance and affinity as it did in the previous three figures. Each (x, y) point of a curve shows the average similarity y of all pairs at distance/affinity x. As in Figures 6 and 7, the ASP curve is more slanted than the affinity curve, suggesting stronger correlation between distance and query similarity than between affinity and query similarity. This is also borne out by the correlation coefficients in the fourth row of Table 1.

Table 1 shows the correlation coefficient between user demographic and interest profiles and the different types of social proximity measures we are considering in this study. In addition to the approximate shortest path distance, we are considering six different variants of the affinity measure: A^θ (for $\theta = 0.5$) and A, computed on the email exchange graph with unweighted edges, edges weighted (and sampled) by the number of reciprocal email exchanges, and edges weighted by the logarithm of that number. Consistent with Figures 6–9, we find that the correlation coefficients of the ASP measure are higher than those of A^θ and A for all user characteristics. The weighted versions of affinity also have a higher correlation than the unweighted ones for all characteristics except age. This might indicate that age changes differently over the network than language or country. Language and country probably change over long distances, whereas age per-

	negative ASP distance	A^{θ} unweighted	A unweighted	A^{θ} weighted	A weighted	A^{θ} log-weighted	A log-weighted
Country similarity	75.27	6.67	10.00	15.00	15.18	16.27	15.08
Language similarity	81.55	13.50	13.71	12.29	12.19	11.46	11.68
Age similarity	13.81	7.09	7.33	7.86	8.46	15.00	11.00
Query similarity	23.69	6.90	7.32	10.33	9.47	7.15	7.64

Table 2: Statistical significance of the correlations: Ratio of correlation for the same pair to correlation for random pairs.

haps changes more quickly; that is, the ball around a point with similar age is probably smaller than the ball around a point with the same language or country. This could be an indication that the unweighted variants of affinity are better measures to capture "small" social distances whereas ASP is better for "large" social distances. This is consistent with our earlier observation that ASP has a higher percentage error on shorter distances [11]. It is an open question of how well *precise* shortest-path distance would perform; unfortunately we do not know how to perform five million precise shortest-path computations within a reasonable time frame.

While it may seem that the correlation coefficients in Table 1 are small, we show that they are much higher than the values we would expect if the properties were completely uncorrelated. In Table 2, we compare the correlation coefficients computed in Table 1 to the correlation coefficients between the same properties for two independently chosen sequences of 5 million pairs. For example, to compute the correlation coefficient between affinity and cosine similarity ($C_{A,cs}$), we computed it between the vector of cosine similarities and affinities on the same set of 5 million pairs. Now we compute it between the vector of cosine similarities for one random set of pairs and vector of affinities for another random set of pairs ($C^{r}_{A,cs}$). We compute the ratio $|C_{A,cs}|/|C^{r}_{A,cs}|$. If this ratio is high it means that the values of affinity and cosine similarities for the same pair are much more correlated than for two random pairs. Table 2 shows this ratio for the different pairs of properties. As can be seen, the ratio is about 7 to 16 for the affinity variants and about 13 to 80 for the ASP measure, which means that the statistical significance of the correlations is not negligible.

3.2 The Twitter experiment

Our second experiment is based on one month worth of Twitter postings (*tweets*), 1,475,522,405 in total. Twitter is a popular micro-blogging service that allows users to post messages up to 140 characters in length. The Twitter community follows a number of stylistic conventions when composing tweets, one of them the convention of mentioning other Twitter users by prefixing their Twitter user IDs with the @ character. A single *mention* in itself does not indicate a social connection between the mentioner and the mentioned, but we assert that if two users mutually mention each other, a social bond does indeed exist.

We first ran an initial data extraction process on our collection of tweets that identified all pairs of (distinct) users mutually mentioning each other at least once during August 2011, and extracted all tweets (whether containing mentions or not) authored by these users. This extracted 1,265,660,845 tweets authored by 10,410,144 users.

Next, we constructed the mention-graph using the following process: First, we constructed an intermediate weighted directed graph containing a vertex for each user whose tweets we extracted during the data extraction phase, and an edge (u, v) with weight w if user u mentioning user v a total of w times. Next, we constructed the actual mention graph, an undirected weighted graph, by taking the vertex set of the directed graph, and introducing an edge between u and v with weight $mean(w_1, w_2)$ if the directed graph contained an edge (u, v) with positive weight w_1 and an edge (v, u) with positive weight w_2. We constructed one variant of the mention graph using the arithmetic mean of weights, and another variant using the geometric mean. The mention-graph contained 10,410,144 vertices and 176,551,621 edges.

As in the previous experiment, we drew a random sample of 5 million pairs of users, and computed affinity values and ASP distances between each pair of users in the mention graph. We also computed the cosine similarity between the tf-idf vectors of the collected tweets of each pair of users, and we computed correlation coefficients between the graph-based measures and the text-based ground truth. 880,564 of the 5,000,000 pairs (or 17.6% of all sampled pairs) were in separate connected components of the mention-graph, with no path between them. These pairs have an affinity value of 0 and an ASP distance of ∞.

In computing affinity values and ASP distances, we experimented with different transform functions for edge weights. In the case of affinity, where heavier edges are more likely to be included in G_p and thus denote closeness, we tried the constant transform $T(w) = 1$ (effectively ignoring weights), the identity transform $T(w) = w$ (directly using the mean of the mention frequency), and the logarithmic transform $T(w) = \log w$ (discounting excessive "mutual admiration"). In the case of ASP distance, where edge weight denote social distance, we tried the constant transform $T(w) = 1$ (effectively ignoring weights), the reciprocal transform $T(w) = \frac{1}{w}$, and the reciprocal logarithmic transform $T(w) = \frac{1}{\log w}$.

Figure 10 shows the distribution of ASP distances computed using the constant edge weight transform (i.e. an unweighted graph); Figure 11 shows the distribution of A^{θ} affinity values (for $\theta = 0.5$) of the sketches for the graph with unweighted edges. In both figures, we do not show the 880,564 disconnected pairs of users in the sample. The mode of the ASP distance distribution is at distance 9, and the bulk is between 6 and 12.

Figure 12 is the analogous version of Figure 9 for the Twitter mention graph. We compute the cosine similarity between the tf-idf weighted tweets of each of the 5 million pairs of users, and we treat this similarity as a proxy of the similarity of their interests. The vertical axis plots the similarity between a pair's queries, the horizontal axis plots distance

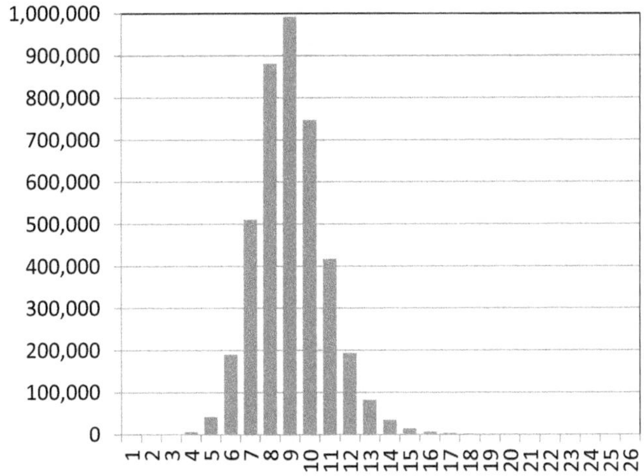

Figure 10: Distribution of ASP distances for the sampled 5 million pairs of users in the Twitter graph

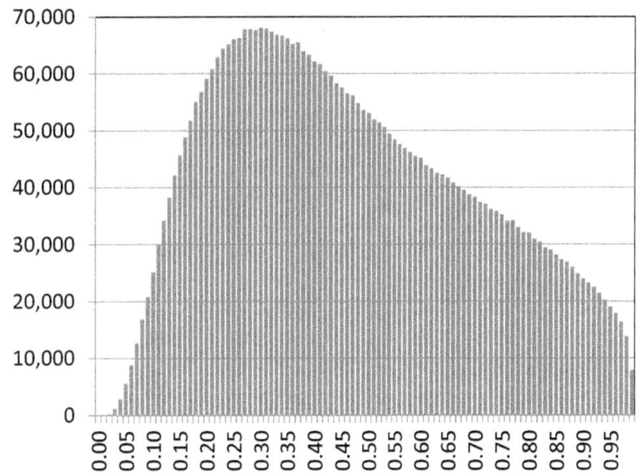

Figure 11: Distribution of affinities for the sampled 5 million pairs of users in the Twitter graph

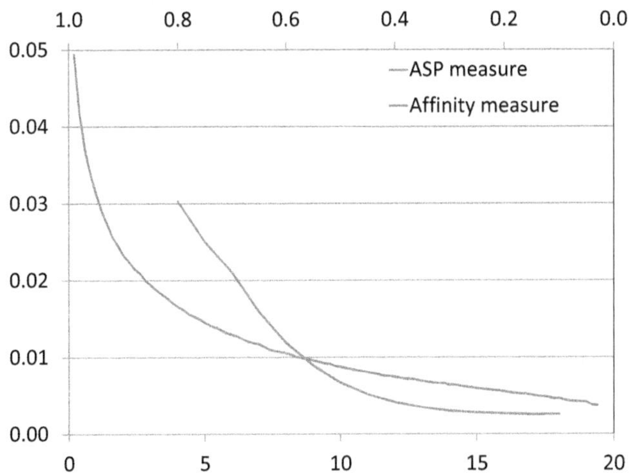

Figure 12: Average cosine similarity of queries of users as a function of ASP or affinity measure

	arithmetic mean	geometric mean
ASP, $T(w) = 1$	0.216	0.216
ASP, $T(w) = \frac{1}{w}$	0.206	0.207
ASP, $T(w) = \frac{1}{\log w}$	0.209	0.210
A^θ, $T(w) = 1$	0.472	0.468
A^θ, $T(w) = w$	0.489	0.487
A^θ, $T(w) = \log w$	0.488	0.484
A, $T(w) = 1$	0.472	0.469
A, $T(w) = w$	0.492	0.490
A, $T(w) = \log w$	0.489	0.486

Table 3: Correlation coefficient between similarity of pairs of users and their proximity in the Twitter mention graph.

and affinity. Each (x, y) point of a curve shows the average similarity y of all pairs at distance/affinity x. Unlike what we observed for the Hotmail graph, the affinity curve is more slanted than the ASP curve, suggesting stronger correlation between affinity and tweet similarity than between distance and tweet similarity. This is also borne out by the correlation coefficients in Table 3. The table shows correlation coefficients between textual cosine similarity (our ground truth) and different variants of our graph-distance measures. Specifically, it explores the impact of using an arithmetic vs. a geometric mean when combining edge weights during the mapping from a directed to an undirected graph; the impact of multiple edge weight transforms; and of course the distance measure itself – negated ASP distance, A^θ affinity, and A affinity. We can draw several conclusions from the data presented in this table:

- Similarity is much more highly correlated to affinity than to ASP distance.
- For affinity measures, the identity transform performs slightly better than the other transforms.
- In the context of the affinity measures, combining edge weights using their arithmetic mean is slightly better than using their geometric mean.
- The A affinity measure performs slightly better than the A^θ affinity measure.

4. CONCLUSION

In this paper, we introduced "social affinity" as a new measure of how robustly two users are connected within a social network. Intuitively, affinity captures how robust the connection between a pair of users is to random deletion of edges in the graph. The affinity value can be efficiently estimated through a sketch-based algorithm, which requires only two table lookups to retrieve the sketch for each user, plus a simple computation on the pair of sketches. We compare this new affinity measure against "approximate shortest path" distance, another sketch-based measure estimating the shortest-path distance between two nodes in a graph. We evaluated our measure on two social graphs. First, we used a sampling of the Hotmail email exchange graph as our social network, and user profiles and query history as independent measures of user similarity. We found that both ASP distance and social affinity between two users are correlated to their profile and query similarity. While ASP had a higher correlation for most user properties, affinity was better in one that changes over short distances. This suggests that the affinity measure may be better-suited for capturing short-distance effects in a social graph, whereas ASP may be preferable for capturing long-distance effects. Second, we constructed a Twitter mention graph from one month worth of tweets, and the collection of tweets written by a given user as the ground truth. We found that the textual similarity between two users' tweets was strongly correlated to their affinity, and somewhat more weakly correlated to their approximate distance in the mention-graph.

We hypothesize that some of the weaknesses we observed for ASP are due to the fact that ASP is an approximation of the true distance. We are still investigating whether it is reasonably feasible to compute *precise* shortest path distances for the five million pairs we used to compare our measures.

5. REFERENCES

[1] Joshua D. Batson, Daniel A. Spielman, and Nikhil Srivastava. Twice-Ramanujan sparsifiers. In *41st Annual ACM Symposium on Theory of Computing*, 2009.

[2] András A. Benczúr and David R. Karger Approximating $s-t$ minimum cuts in $\tilde{O}(n^2)$ time. In *28th Annual ACM Symposium on the Theory of Computing*, 1996.

[3] Jean Bourgain. On Lipschitz embeddings of finite metric spaces in Hilbert space. *Israel Journal of Mathematics*, 52(1-2):46–52 (1985).

[4] Andrei Z. Broder. Identifying and filtering near-duplicate documents. In *11th Annual Symposium on Combinatorial Pattern Matching*, 2000.

[5] Andrei Z. Broder, Steven C. Glassman, Mark S. Manasse, and Geoffrey Zweig. Syntactic clustering of the web. *Computer Networks*, 29(8):1157–1166 (1997).

[6] Nicholas A. Christakis and James H. Fowler. The spread of obesity in a large social network over 32 years. *New England Journal of Medicine* 357(4): 370-379 (July 2007).

[7] Nicholas A. Christakis and James H. Fowler. The collective dynamics of smoking in a large social network. *New England Journal of Medicine*, 358(21): 2249-2258 (May 2008).

[8] David J. Crandall, Dan Cosley, Daniel P. Huttenlocher, Jon M. Kleinberg, and Siddharth Suri. Feedback effects between similarity and social influence in online communities. In *14th ACM SIGKDD International Conference on Knowledge Discovery and Data Mining*, 2008.

[9] Dan Cosley, Daniel P. Huttenlocher, Jon M. Kleinberg, Xiangyang Lan, and Siddharth Suri. Sequential influence models in social networks. In *4th International Conference on Weblogs and Social Media*, 2010.

[10] Pedro Domingos and Matthew Richardson. Mining the network value of customers. In *7th ACM SIGKDD International Conference on Knowledge Discovery and Data Mining*, 2001.

[11] Atish Das Sarma, Sreenivas Gollapudi, Marc Najork, and Rina Panigrahy. A sketch-based distance oracle for Web-scale graphs. In *3rd International Conference on Web Search and Web Data Mining*, 2010.

[12] James H. Fowler and Nicholas A. Christakis. The dynamic spread of happiness in a large social network: Longitudinal analysis over 20 years in the Framingham Heart Study. *British Medical Journal* 2008; 337: a2338.

[13] Wai Shing Fung, Ramesh Hariharan, Nicholas J. A. Harvey, and Debmalya Panigrahi. A general framework for graph sparsification. In *43rd ACM Symposium on Theory of Computing*, 2011.

[14] David Kempe, Jon M. Kleinberg, and Éva Tardos. Maximizing the spread of influence through a social network. In *9th ACM SIGKDD International Conference on Knowledge Discovery and Data Mining*, 2003.

[15] Gueorgi Kossinets, Jon M. Kleinberg, and Duncan J. Watts. The structure of information pathways in a social communication network. In *14th ACM SIGKDD International Conference on Knowledge Discovery and Data Mining*, 2001.

[16] Ioannis Koutis, Gary L. Miller, and Richard Peng. Approaching optimality for solving SDD linear systems. In *51st Annual IEEE Symposium on Foundations of Computer Science*, 2010.

[17] Jure Leskovec, Ajit Singh, and Jon M. Kleinberg. Patterns of influence in a recommendation network. In *10th Pacific-Asia Conference on Knowledge Discovery and Data Mining*, 2006.

[18] Ulrike von Luxburg, Agnes Radl, Matthias Hein. Getting lost in space: Large sample analysis of the commute distance. In *24th Annual Conference on Neural Information Processing Systems*, 2010.

[19] Jiri Matousek. On the distortion required for embedding finite metric spaces into normed spaces. *Israel Journal of Mathematics*, 93(1):333–344 (1996).

[20] J. Niels Rosenquist, Joanne Murabito, James H. Fowler, and Nicholas A. Christakis. The spread of alcohol consumption behavior in a large social network. *Annals of Internal Medicine* 152(7): 426-433 (April 2010).

[21] Gerard Salton and Christopher Buckley. Term-weighting approaches in automatic text retrieval. *Information Processing & Management* 24 (5): 513–523 (1988).

[22] Daniel A. Spielman and Nikhil Srivastava. Graph sparsification by effective resistances. In *40th Annual ACM Symposium on Theory of Computing*, 2008.

[23] Daniel A. Spielman and Shang-Hua Teng. Nearly-linear time algorithms for graph partitioning, graph sparsification, and solving linear systems. In *36th Annual ACM Symposium on Theory of Computing*, 2004.

[24] Mikkel Thorup and Uri Zwick. Approximate distance oracles. *Journal of the ACM*, 52(1):1–24 (January 2005).

Finding Your Friends and Following Them to Where You Are

Adam Sadilek
Dept. of Computer Science
University of Rochester
Rochester, NY, USA
sadilek@cs.rochester.edu

Henry Kautz
Dept. of Computer Science
University of Rochester
Rochester, NY, USA
kautz@cs.rochester.edu

Jeffrey P. Bigham
Dept. of Computer Science
University of Rochester
Rochester, NY, USA
jbigham@cs.rochester.edu

ABSTRACT

Location plays an essential role in our lives, bridging our online and offline worlds. This paper explores the interplay between people's location, interactions, and their social ties within a large real-world dataset. We present and evaluate Flap, a system that solves two intimately related tasks: link and location prediction in online social networks. For link prediction, Flap infers social ties by considering patterns in friendship formation, the content of people's messages, and user location. We show that while each component is a weak predictor of friendship alone, combining them results in a strong model, accurately identifying the majority of friendships. For location prediction, Flap implements a scalable probabilistic model of human mobility, where we treat users with known GPS positions as noisy sensors of the location of their friends. We explore supervised and unsupervised learning scenarios, and focus on the efficiency of both learning and inference. We evaluate Flap on a large sample of highly active users from two distinct geographical areas and show that it (1) reconstructs the entire friendship graph with high accuracy even when no edges are given; and (2) infers people's fine-grained location, even when they keep their data private and we can only access the location of their friends. Our models significantly outperform current comparable approaches to either task.

Categories and Subject Descriptors

H.1.m [**Information Systems**]: Miscellaneous

General Terms

Algorithms, Experimentation, Human Factors

Keywords

Location modeling, link prediction, social networks, machine learning, graphical models, visualization, Twitter

Permission to make digital or hard copies of all or part of this work for personal or classroom use is granted without fee provided that copies are not made or distributed for profit or commercial advantage and that copies bear this notice and the full citation on the first page. To copy otherwise, to republish, to post on servers or to redistribute to lists, requires prior specific permission and/or a fee.
WSDM'12, February 8–12, 2012, Seattle, Washington, USA.
Copyright 2012 ACM 978-1-4503-0747-5/12/02 ...$10.00.

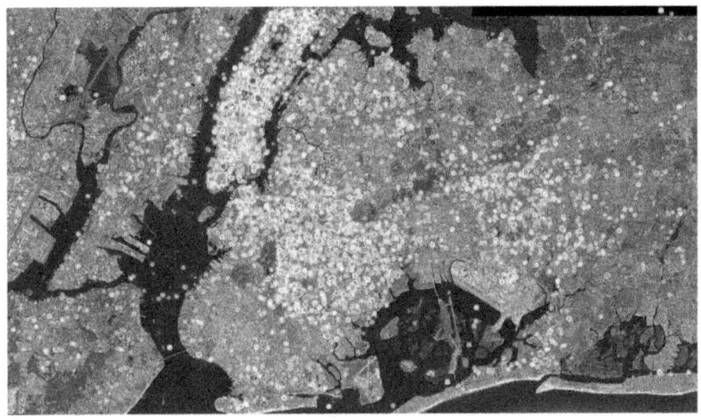

Figure 1: A snapshot of a heatmap animation of Twitter users' movement within New York City that captures a typical distribution of geo-tagged messaging on a weekday afternoon. The hotter (more red) an area is, the more people have recently tweeted from that location. Full animation is at http://cs.rochester.edu/u/sadilek/research/.

1. INTRODUCTION

Our society is founded on the interplay of human relationships and interactions. Since every person is tightly embedded in our social structure, the vast majority of human behavior can be fully understood only in the context of the actions of others. Thus, not surprisingly, more and more evidence shows that when we want to model the behavior of a person, the best predictors are often not based on the person herself, but rather on her friends, relatives, and other *connected* people. For instance, behavioral patterns of people taking taxis, rating movies, choosing cell phone providers, or sharing music are often best predicted by the habits of related people, rather than by the attributes of the individual such as age, ethnicity, or education [3, 24].

Until recently, it was nearly impossible to gather large amounts of data about the connections that play such important roles in our lives. However, this is changing with the explosive increase in the use, popularity, and significance of *online* social media and *mobile* devices.[1] The online aspect makes it practical to collect vast amounts of data, and the mobile element bridges the gap between our online and offline activities. Unlike other computers, phones are aware of the location of their users, and this information is often included in users' posts. In fact, major online social networks

[1]http://www.comscore.com/

are fostering location sharing. Twitter added an explicit GPS tag that can be specified for each tweet (AKA Twitter message update) in early 2010 and is continually improving the location-awareness of its service. Google+, Facebook, FourSquare, and Gowalla allow people to share their location, and to "check-in" at venues. With Google Latitude and Bliin, users can *continually* broadcast their location.

Thus, we now have access to colossal amounts of real-world data containing not just the text and images people post, but also their location. Of course, these three data modalities are not necessarily mutually independent. For instance, photos are often GPS-tagged and locations can also be mentioned, or alluded to, in text.

While the information about users' *location* and *relationships* is important to accurately model their behavior and improve their experience, it is not always available. This paper explores novel techniques of inferring this latent information from a stream of message updates. We present a unified view on the interplay between people's location, message updates, and their social ties on a large real-world dataset. Our approaches are robust and achieve significantly higher accuracy than the best currently known methods, even in difficult experimental settings spanning diverse geographical areas.

1.1 Significance of Results

Consider the task of determining the exact geographic location of an arbitrary user of an online social network. If she routinely geo-tags her posts and makes them public, the problem is relatively easy. However, suppose the location information is hidden, and you only have access to public posts by her friends. By leveraging social ties, our probabilistic location model—the first component of this work—infers where any given user is with high accuracy and fine granularity in both space and time *even when the user keeps his or her posts private.* Since this work shows that once we have location information for some proportion of people, we can infer the location of their friends, one can imagine doing this recursively until the entire target population is covered. To our knowledge, no other work attempts to predict locations in a comparably difficult setting.

The main power of our link prediction approach—the second major component of this work—is that it accurately reconstructs the entire friendship graph even when no "seed" ties are provided. Previous work either obtained very good predictions at the expense of large computational costs (*e.g.*, [28]), thereby limiting those approaches to very small domains, or sacrificed orders of magnitude in accuracy for tractability (*e.g.*, [19, 7]). By contrast, we show that our model's performance is comparable to the most powerful relational methods applied in previous work [28], while at the same time being applicable to large real-world domains with tens of millions (as opposed to hundreds) of possible friendships. Since our model leverages users' locations, it not only encompasses virtual friendships, but also begins to tie them together with their real-life groundings.

Prediction of people's location and social ties—especially when considered together—has a number of important applications. They range from improved local content with better social context, through increased security (both personal and electronic) via detection of abnormal behavior tied with one's location, to better organization of one's relationships and connecting virtual friendships with the real-world. We note that even when friends participate in the same social networking platform, their relationship may not be exposed—either because the connections are hidden or because they have not yet connected online. Flap can also help contain disease outbreaks [12]. Our model allows identification of highly mobile individuals as well as their most likely meeting points, both in the past and in the future. These people can be subsequently selected for targeted treatment or preemptive vaccination. Given people's inferred locations, and limited resource budget, a decision-theoretic approach can be used to select optimal emergency policy. Clearly, strong privacy concerns are tied to such applications, as we discuss in the conclusions.

2. RELATED WORK

Recent research in **location-based reasoning** explored harnessing data collected on regular smart phones for modeling human behavior [10]. Specifically, they model individuals' general location from nearby cell towers and Bluetooth devices at various times of day. Eagle *et al.* show that predicting if a person is at home, at work, or someplace else can be achieved with more than 90% accuracy. Besides scalability and practicality—social network data is much more readily available than cell phone logs—our work differs in that we include dynamic relational features (location of friends), focus on a finer time granularity, and consider a substantially larger set of locations (hundreds per user, rather than three). Additionally, the observations in our framework (people's self-published locations) are significantly noisier and less regular than cell tower and Bluetooth readings. Finally, our location estimation applies even in situations, where the target people decide to keep their data private.

Backstrom *et al.* predict the home address of Facebook users based on provided addresses of one's friends [2]. An empirically extracted relationship between geographical distance and the probability of friendship between pairs of users is leveraged in order to find a maximum likelihood assignment of addresses to hidden users. The authors show that their method of localizing users is in general more accurate than an IP address-based alternative. However, even their strongest approach captures only a single static home location for each user and the spatial resolution is low. For example, less than 50% of the users are localized within 10 miles of their actual home. By contrast, we consider much finer temporal resolution (20 minute intervals) and achieve significantly greater spatial precision, where up to 84% of people's exact dynamic location is correctly inferred.

Very recently, Cho *et al.* focus on modeling user location in social networks as a dynamic Gaussian mixture, a generative approach postulating that each check-in is induced from the vicinity of either a person's home, work, or is a result of social influence of one's friends [6]. By contrast, our location model is inherently discrete, which allows us to predict the *exact* location rather than a sample from a generally high-variance continuous distribution; operates at a finer time granularity; and learns the candidate locations from noisy data. Furthermore, our approach leverages the complex temporal and social dependencies between people's locations in a more general, discrete fashion. We show that our model outperforms that of Cho *et al.* in the experiments presented below.

A number of geolocating applications demonstrate emerging privacy issues in this area. The most impactful ones are arguably Creepy[2], ICanStalkU.com, and PleaseRobMe.com (currently disabled). The purpose of these efforts is to raise awareness about the lack of location privacy in online social networks. Given a username from an online social network, Creepy aggregates location information about the target individual from her GPS-tagged posts and photos, and displays it on a map. ICanStalkU.com scans public Twitter timeline, and extracts GPS metadata from uploaded photos, which often reveal people's current location without them realizing it. PleaseRobMe.com used to extract people's geographic check-ins that imply they are not at home and therefore vulnerable to burglaries.

However, all these applications work only with *publicly available* data. By contrast, this paper shows that we can *infer* people's precise location even when they keep their data private, as long as some of their friends post their location publicly. Therefore, simply turning off the geolocation features of your phone—which may seem to be a reliable way to keep your whereabouts secret—does not really protect your privacy unless your friends turn theirs off as well.

While our work concentrates on Twitter users, recent research shows that the predictability of human mobility remains virtually unchanged across a number of demographical attributes such as age and gender [27]. This strongly suggests that our approach achieves similar accuracy for other geographical areas and different samples of users. Finally, we note that although it has been shown that possibly as many as 34% of accounts provide either wrong or misleading symbolic (*e.g.*, city, state) location information in their profiles, our work is largely shielded from this phenomenon since we focus only on raw GPS data that can be more readily verified and is not fed into a geocoder [15].

The problem of **link prediction** has been studied in a large number of domains and contexts; here we mention the ones that are most relevant to our work. Liben-Nowell *et al.* models the *evolution* of a graph solely from its topological properties [19]. The authors evaluate a number of methods of quantifying the probability of a link in large graphs, and conclude that while no single technique is substantially better than the rest, their models outperform a random predictor by a significant margin. This shows that there is important information to be mined from the graph structure alone.

An alternative approach is to leverage the topology as well as attributes of the individual entities [28]. They model friendships of students in an online university community using relational Markov networks. Similarly to our approach, their probabilistic model encompasses a number of features, some of which are based on the attributes of individual users while others model the structure of the friendship graph. Their inference method is standard belief propagation (BP), whereas we develop an efficient and specialized version of BP, which in practice quickly converges. Their domain contains only several hundred candidate social ties. This size restriction is apparently due to the computational challenges posed by their relational model. We, in contrast, consider thousands of individuals who can be connected in arbitrary fashion, which results in tens of millions potential friendships. Furthermore, Taskar *et al.* assume that some friendships are given to the model at testing time. In this work, we show that it is possible to achieve good performance even with no observed links.

Crandall *et al.* explore the relationship between co-location of Flickr users and their social ties [7]. They model the relationship as an exponential probability distribution and show it fits well to the observed, empirical distribution. They show that the number of distinct places where two users are co-located within various periods of time has the potential to predict a small fraction of the ties quite well. However, the recall is dramatically low. In their Flickr data, only 0.1% of the friendships meet the condition for being predicted with at least 60% confidence. By contrast, with our approach we can predict over 90% of the friendships with confidence beyond 80% (see Figure 4). This is consistent with our experiments, where we show that location alone is generally a poor predictor of friendship (consider the "commuter train" example described below on one end of the spectrum, and a pair of friends that never share their location on the other end). We therefore leverage textual similarity and network structure as well, and evaluate the predictive power of our model in terms of AUC while inferring the friendship graph. Additionally, our model does not require setting subtle parameters, such as cell size and time granularity. When we apply the method of Crandall *et al.* to our Twitter data, the results are (as one would expect) poor; see Figure 5 and its analysis in text.

The relationship between social ties and distance has recently received considerable attention [20, 2, 25]. Even though online interactions are in principle not hampered by physical distance, all works agree that in any social network studied, the probability of friendship generally decreases as the distance between people increases. However, a significant portion of social ties often cannot be explained by location alone. We observe the same pattern in our Twitter data and show that location can be augmented with text and structural features to infer social ties with high accuracy.

Backstrom *et al.* present a method for predicting links cast as a random walk problem [1]. A key difference between our approaches is that we can construct the entire social network with high accuracy even when *none* of the edges are observed, whereas Backstrom *et al.*'s approach depends upon already knowing most of the links in the network along with a set of source and candidate nodes, and only needs to predict relatively few new links. Furthermore, unlike our work, Backstrom *et al.*'s approach requires many parameters to be selected. In contrast with random walks, approaches related to our belief propagation method for enforcing and chaining soft transitive constraints have been validated in many areas in the machine learning literature, and are implicitly used in many works on link prediction as a way to solve the underlying probabilistic models [26, 28].

We note that no work to date focused on capturing both directions of the relationship between location and social ties. This paper concentrates on predicting, in turn, both location and social structure from the remaining data modality.

3. BACKGROUND

Our experiments are based on data obtained from Twitter, a popular micro-blogging service where people post at most 140 characters long message updates. The forced brevity encourages frequent mobile updates, as we show below. Relationships between users on Twitter are not necessarily sym-

[2]https://github.com/ilektrojohn/creepy

metric. One can follow (subscribe to receive messages from) a user without being followed back. When users do reciprocate following, we say they are *friends* on Twitter. There is anecdotal evidence that Twitter friendships have a substantial overlap with offline friendships [14]. Twitter launched in 2006 and has been experiencing an explosive growth since then. As of March 2011, approximately 200 million accounts are registered on Twitter.[3] For an excellent general overview of computational analysis of social networks at large see [11].

Decision trees are models of data encoded as rules induced from examples [4]. Intuitively, in the Twitter domain, a decision tree represents a series of questions that need to be asked and answered in order to estimate the probability of friendship between any two people, based on their attributes. During decision tree learning, features are evaluated in terms of information gain with respect to the labels and the best candidates are subsequently selected for each inner node of the tree. Our implementation uses *regression* decision trees, where each leaf contains the probability of a friendship. As described below, we also employ decision trees for feature selection, since they intrinsically rank features by their information content.

Belief propagation (BP) is a family of message passing algorithms that perform inference in graphical models. BP is proven to be exact and to converge for certain classes of graphs, such as trees, but its behavior on general cyclic graphs is poorly understood [23]. However, in many practical applications, BP performs surprisingly well [22].

Dynamic Bayesian networks (DBNs) are generative probabilistic graphical models of sequential data [21]. Nodes in the graph represent random variables and edges represent conditional dependencies. In a typical setting, a subset of the random variables is *observed*, while the others are *hidden* and their values have to be inferred. A DBN is composed of *slices*—in our case each slice represents a time interval. In order to specify a DBN, we either write down or learn intra- and inter-slice conditional probability distributions (CPDs). The intra-slice CPDs typically constitute the observation model while the inter-slice CPDs model transitions between hidden states.

There are a number of parameter learning and inference techniques for DBNs. In a supervised learning scenario, where the hidden labels are known at training time, maximum likelihood estimates can be calculated directly. On the other hand, when the state of the hidden nodes is not known, the CPDs have to be learned without supervision. We achieve this via expectation-maximization described below. Exact inference is usually intractable in general DBNs and one has to resort to sampling techniques such as Markov chain Monte Carlo. However, our model is sufficiently efficient to afford exact inference using dynamic programming.

In this work, we apply DBNs because they naturally model time series data (time flows in one direction), we can highly optimize both learning and inference. Since the hidden nodes in our models are discrete, we perform both parameter learning and exact inference efficiently by customized versions of the Baum-Welch algorithm and Viterbi decoding, respectively. For a detailed treatment of these methods see [17]. We exaplain how we apply DBNs to our Twitter domain in Section 5.2.

[3]http://www.bbc.co.uk/news/business-12889048

4. THE DATA

Using the Twitter Search API[4], we collected a sample of public tweets that originated from two distinct geographic areas: Los Angeles (LA) and New York City (NYC). The collection period was one month long and started on May 19 2010. Using a Python script, we periodically queried Twitter with requests of all recent tweets within 150 kilometers of LA's city center, and 100 kilometers within the NYC city center. In order to avoid exceeding Twitter's query rate limits and subsequently missing some tweets, we distributed the work over a number of machines with different IP addresses that asynchronously queried the server and merged their results. Twitter does not provide any guarantees as to what sample of existing tweets can be retrieved through their API, but a comparison to official Twitter statistics shows that our method recorded nearly all of the publicly available tweets in those two regions. Altogether, we have logged over 26 million tweets authored by more than 1.2 million unique users (see Table 1). To put these statistics in context, the entire NYC and LA metropolitan areas have an estimated population of 19 and 13 million people, respectively.[5]

In this work, we concentrate on accounts that posted more than 100 GPS-tagged tweets during the one-month data collection period. We refer to them as *geo-active users*.

New York City & Los Angeles Dataset

Unique users	1,229,611
Unique geo-active users	11,380
Tweets total	26,118,084
GPS-tagged tweets	7,566,569
GPS-tagged tweets by geo-active users	4,016,286
Unique locations	89,077
Significant locations	25,830
"Follows" relationships between geo-active users	123,182
"Friends" relationships between geo-active users	52,307

Table 1: Summary statistics of the data collected from NYC and LA. Geo-active users are ones who geo-tag their tweets relatively frequently (more than 100 times per month). Note that following reciprocity is about 42%, which is consistent with previous findings [18, 16]. Unique locations are the result of iterative clustering that merges (on a per-user basis) all locations within 100 meters of each other. Significant location is defined as one that was visited at least five times by at least one person.

5. THE SYSTEM: FLAP

Flap (Friendship + Location Analysis and Prediction), has three main components responsible for downloading Twitter data, visualization, and learning and inference. The data collection component was described in the previous section. Figure 2 shows Flap's visualization a sample of geo-active users in NYC. People are represented by pins on the map and the red links denote friendships (either ground truth or inferred). Beyond standard Google Maps user interface elements, the visualization is controlled via the black toolbar

[4]http://search.twitter.com/api/
[5]http://www.census.gov/popest/metro/

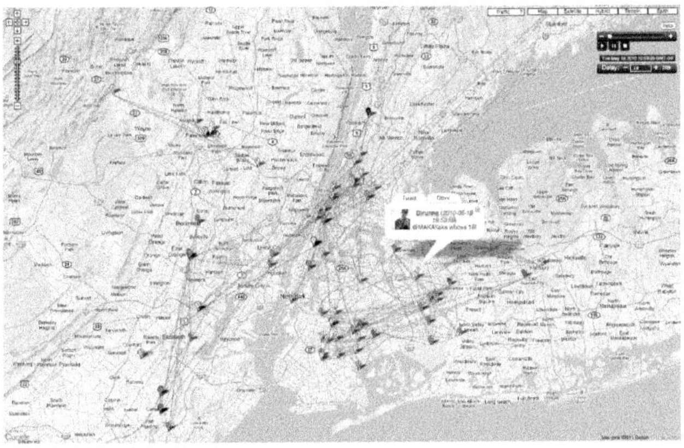

Figure 2: Flaps's visualization of a sample of geo-active friends in NYC. Red links between users represent friendships.

in the upper-right corner. Flap can animate arbitrary segments of the data at various speeds. Selecting a user displays additional information such as his profile, time and text of his recent tweets, and a more detailed map of his current surroundings.

Now we turn to the third—machine learning—module of Flap that has two main tasks. First, it is responsible for learning a model of people's friendships and subsequently revealing hidden friendships. And second, it learns models of users' mobility and predicts their location at any given time. We will now discuss these two tasks and our solutions in turn.

5.1 Friendship Prediction

The goal of friendship prediction is to reconstruct the entire social graph, where vertices represent users and edges model friendships. We achieve this via an iterative method that operates over the current graph structure and features of pairs of vertices. We first describe the features used by our model of social ties, and then focus on its structure, learning, and inference. In agreement with prior work, we found that no single property of a pair of individuals is a good indicator of the existence or absence of friendship [20, 6]. Therefore, we combine multiple disparate features—based on text, location, and the topology of the underlying friendship graph.

5.1.1 *Features*

The text similarity coefficient quantifies the amount of overlap in the vocabularies of users u and v, and is given by

$$\mathcal{T}(u,v) = \sum_{w \in W(u) \cap W(v) \setminus S} f_u(w) f_v(w), \tag{1}$$

where $W(u)$ is the set of words that appear in user u's tweets, S is the set of stop-words (it includes the standard stop words augmented with words commonly used on Twitter, such as RT, im, and lol), and $f_u(w)$ is the frequency of word w in u's vocabulary.

Interestingly, in the Twitter domain, the mentions tags (@) give a clue to user's friendships. However, in the experiments presented here, we *eliminate* all user names that appear in the tweets in order to report results that generalize to other social networks.

Our co-location feature ($\mathcal{C}$) is based on the observation that at least some people who are online friends also meet in the physical world [14]. We make an assumption that once a user tweets from a location, he or she remains at that location until they tweet again. Even though people generally do not tweet from every single place they visit, this approximate co-location measure still captures how much time pairs of users tend to spend close to each other. The co-location score is given by

$$\mathcal{C}(u,v) = \sum_{\ell_u, \ell_v \in L} \frac{t(\ell_u, \ell_v)}{d(\ell_u, \ell_v)}, \tag{2}$$

where L is the union of all locations from which users u and v send messages, $t(\ell_u, \ell_v)$ is the amount of time u spends at location ℓ_u while v is at location ℓ_v. In short, we add up the time overlaps two users spend at their respective locations and we scale each overlap by the distance between the locations. Thus, two individuals spending a lot of common time at nearby places receive a large co-location score, while people who always tweet from two opposite ends of a city have a small co-location score. We have implemented an efficient algorithm that calculates $\mathcal{C}(u,v)$ for a pair of users in time $O(n)$ where n is the minimum number of GPS-tagged messages created by either user u or v. Note that unlike previous work (*e.g.*, [7, 1]), our co-location feature is continuous and does not require discretization, thresholding, or parameter selection.

As a graph structure feature, we use the meet/min coefficient ($\mathcal{M}$) and its generalized version ($\mathcal{M}_{\mathbb{E}}$) defined in equations 3 and 4 respectively.

$$\mathcal{M}(u,v) = \frac{|N(u) \cap N(v)|}{\min\Big(|N(u)|, |N(v)|\Big)} \tag{3}$$

$$\mathcal{M}_{\mathbb{E}}(u,v) = \frac{\sum_{n \in N(u) \cap N(v)} p_{nu} p_{nv}}{\min\Big(\sum_{n \in N(u)} p_{nu}, \sum_{n \in N(v)} p_{nv}\Big)} \tag{4}$$

$N(u)$ is the set of neighbors of node u and p_{nu} is the probability of edge (n,u). The standard meet/min coefficient counts the number of common neighbors of u and v (this quantity is equal to the number of triads that the edge (u,v) would complete, an important measure in structural balance theory [11]), and scales by the size of the neighborhood of either u or v, whichever is smaller. Intuitively, $\mathcal{M}(u,v)$ expresses how extensive is the overlap between friendlists of users u and v with respect to the size of the shorter friendlist. The expectation of the meet/min coefficient $\mathcal{M}_{\mathbb{E}}$ calculates the same quantities but in terms of their expected values on a graph where each edge is weighted by its probability. Neither measure depends on the existence or probability of edge (u,v) itself.

Since the $\mathcal{T}$ and $\mathcal{C}$ scores are always observed, we use a regression decision tree to unify them, in a pre-processing step, into one feature $\mathcal{DT}(u,v)$, which is the decision tree's prediction given $\mathcal{T}(u,v)$ and $\mathcal{C}(u,v)$. Thus, we end up with one feature function for the observed variables ($\mathcal{DT}$) and one for the hidden variables ($\mathcal{M}_{\mathbb{E}}$).

We have experimented with other features, including the Jaccard coefficient, preferential attachment, hypergeometric coefficient, and others. However, our work is motivated by having an efficient and scalable model. A decision tree-based feature selection showed that our three measures ($\mathcal{T}$, $\mathcal{C}$, and

$\mathcal{M}_{\mathbb{E}}$) jointly represent the largest information value. Finally, while calculating the features for all pairs of n users is an $O(n^2)$ operation, it can be significantly sped up via locality-sensitive hashing [8].

5.1.2 Learning and Inference

Our probabilistic model of the friendship network is a Markov random field that has a hidden node for each possible friendship. Since the friendship relationship is symmetric and irreflexive, our model contains $n(n-1)/2$ hidden nodes, where n is the number of users. Each hidden node is connected to an observed node ($\mathcal{DT}$) and to all other hidden nodes.

Ultimately, we are interested in the probability of existence of an edge (friendship) given the current graph structure and the pairwise features of the vertices (users) the edge is incident on. Applying Bayes' theorem while assuming mutual independence of features $\mathcal{DT}$ and $\mathcal{M}_{\mathbb{E}}$, we can write

$$\begin{aligned} &P(E=1|DT=d, M_{\mathbb{E}}=m) = \\ &= P(DT=d|E=1)P(M_{\mathbb{E}}=m|E=1)P(E=1)/Z \\ &= P(DT=d|E=1)P(E=1|M_{\mathbb{E}}=m)/Z \end{aligned} \tag{5}$$

where

$$Z = \sum_{i\in\{0,1\}} P(DT=d|E=i)P(E=i|M_{\mathbb{E}}=m).$$

E, DT, and $M_{\mathbb{E}}$ are random variables that represent edge existence, $\mathcal{DT}$ score, and $\mathcal{M}_{\mathbb{E}}$ score, respectively. In equation 5, we applied the equality

$$P(M_{\mathbb{E}}|E) = P(E|M_{\mathbb{E}})P(E)/P(M_{\mathbb{E}})$$

and subsequent simplifications so that we do not need to explicitly model $P(E)$.

At learning time, we first train a regression decision tree $\mathcal{DT}$ and prune it using ten-fold cross-validation to prevent overfitting. We also perform maximum likelihood learning of the parameters $P(DT|E)$ and $P(E|M_{\mathbb{E}})$. We chose the decision tree pre-processing step for several reasons. First, the text and location-based features considered individually or independently have very poor predictive power. Therefore, models such as logistic regression tend to have low accuracy. Furthermore, the relationships between the observed attributes of a pair of users and the their friendship is often quite complex. For example, it is not simply the case that a friendship is more and more likely to exist as people spend larger and larger amounts of time near each other. Consider two strangers that happen to take the same train to work, and tweet every time it goes through a station. Our dataset contains a number of instances of this sort. During the train ride, their co-location could not be higher and yet they are not friends on Twitter. This largely precludes success of classifiers that are looking for a simple decision surface.

At inference time, we use $\mathcal{DT}$ to make preliminary predictions on the test data. Next, we execute a customized loopy belief propagation algorithm that is initialized with the probabilities estimated by $\mathcal{DT}$ (see Algorithm 1). Step 6 is where an edge receives belief updates from the other edges as well as the $\mathcal{DT}$ prior. Even though the graphical model is dense, our algorithm converges within several hundred iterations, due in part to the sufficiently accurate initialization and regularization provided by the decision tree. Note that the algorithm can also function in an online fashion: as new active users appear in the Twitter public timeline, they are processed by the decision tree and added to Q. This is an attractive mode, where the model is always up to date and takes advantage of all available data.

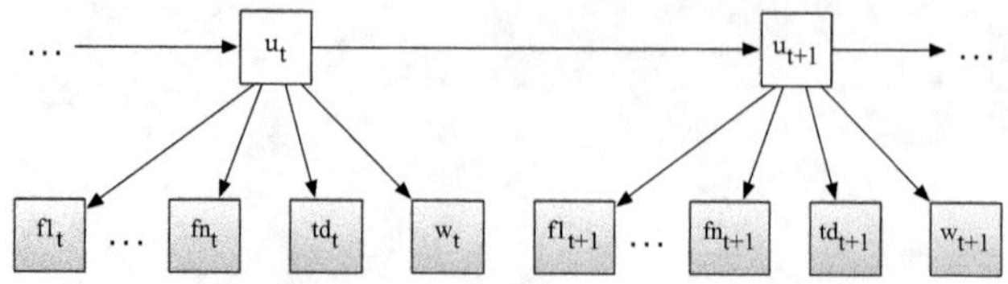

Figure 3: Two consecutive time slices of our dynamic Bayesian network for modeling motion patterns of Twitter users from n friends. All nodes are discrete, shaded nodes represent observed random variables, unfilled denote hidden variables.

Algorithm 1 : refineEdgeProbabilities(Q)

Input: Q: list containing all potential edges between pairs of vertices along with their preliminary probabilities
Output: Q: input list Q with refined probabilities

1: **while** Q has not converged **do**
2: sort Q high to low by estimated edge probability
3: **for each** $\langle e, P(e)\rangle$ **in** Q **do**
4: $dt \Leftarrow \mathcal{DT}(e)$
5: $m \Leftarrow \mathcal{M}_{\mathbb{E}}(e)$
6: $P(e) \Leftarrow \frac{P(DT=dt|E=1)P(E=1|\mathcal{M}_{\mathbb{E}}=m)}{\sum_{i\in\{0,1\}} P(DT=dt|E=i)P(E=i|\mathcal{M}_{\mathbb{E}}=m)}$
7: **end for**
8: **end while**
9: **return** Q

5.2 Location Prediction

The goal of Flap's location prediction component is to infer the most likely location of person u at any time. The input consists of a sequence of locations visited by u's friends (and for supervised learning, locations of u himself over the training period), along with corresponding time information. The model outputs the most likely sequence of locations u visited over a given time period.

We model user location in a dynamic Bayesian network shown in Figure 3. In each time slice, we have one hidden node and a number of observed nodes, all of which are discrete. The hidden node represents the location of the target user (u). The node td represents the time of day and w determines if a given day is a work day or a free day (weekend or a national holiday). Each of the remaining observed nodes ($f1$ through fn) represents the location of one of the target user's friends. Since the average node degree of geo-active users is 9.2, we concentrate on $n \in \{0, 1, 2, \ldots, 9\}$, although our approach works for arbitrary nonnegative values of n. Each node is indexed by time slice.

The domains of the random variables are generated from the Twitter dataset in the following way. First, for each user, we extract a set of distinct locations they tweet from. Then, we iteratively merge (cluster) all locations that are within 100 meters of each other in order to account for GPS sensor noise, which is especially severe in areas with tall buildings, such as Manhattan. The location merging is done separately for each user and we call the resulting locations *unique*. We subsequently remove all merged locations that the user visited fewer than five times and assign a unique label to each remaining place. These labels are the domains of u and fi's. We call such places *significant*.

The above place indexing yields a total of 89,077 unique locations, out of which 25,830 were visited at least five times by at least one user. There were 2,467,149 tweets total posted from the significant locations in the 4 week model evaluation period. Table 1 lists summary statistics.

We model each person's location in 20 minute increments, since more than 90% of the users tweet with lower frequency. Therefore, the domain of the time of day random variable t_d is $\{0, \ldots, 71\}$ (total of 24/0.3 time intervals in any given day).

5.2.1 Learning

We explore both supervised and unsupervised learning of user mobility. In the earlier case, for each user, we train a DBN on the first three weeks of data with known hidden location values. In the latter case, the hidden labels are unknown to the system.

During *supervised* learning, we find a set of parameters (discrete probability distributions) θ that maximize the log-likelihood of the training data. This is achieved by optimizing the following objective function.

$$\theta^\star = \underset{\theta}{\text{argmax}} \ \log\left(\Pr(x_{1:t}, y_{1:t}|\theta)\right), \quad (6)$$

where $x_{1:t}$ and $y_{1:t}$ represent the sequence of observed and hidden values, respectively, between times 1 and t, and $\theta^\star$ is the set of optimal model parameters. In our implementation, we represent probabilities and likelihoods with their log-counterparts to avoid arithmetic underflow.

For *unsupervised* learning, we perform expectation-maximization (EM) [9]. In the E step, the values of the hidden nodes are inferred using the current DBN parameter values (initialized randomly). In the subsequent M step, the inferred values of the hidden nodes are in turn used to update the parameters. This process is repeated until convergence, at which point the EM algorithm outputs a maximum likelihood point estimate of the DBN parameters. The corresponding optimization problem can be written as

$$\theta^\star = \underset{\theta}{\text{argmax}} \ \log \sum_{y_{1:t}} \Pr(x_{1:t}, y_{1:t}|\theta)), \quad (7)$$

where we sum over all possible values of hidden nodes $y_{1:t}$. Since equation 7 is computationally intractable for sizable domains, we simplify by optimizing its lower bound instead, similar to [13].

The random initialization of the EM procedure has a profound influence on the final set of learned parameter values. As a result, EM is prone to getting "stuck" in a local optimum. To mitigate this problem, we perform deterministic simulated annealing [29]. The basic idea is to reduce the undesirable influence of the initial random set of parameters by "smoothing" the objective function so that it hopefully has fewer local optima. Mathematically, this is written as

$$\theta^\star(\tau_1, \ldots, \tau_m) = \underset{\theta}{\text{argmax}} \ \tau_i \log \sum_{y_{1:t}} \Pr(x_{1:t}, y_{1:t}|\theta)^{\frac{1}{\tau_i}}. \quad (8)$$

Here, $\tau_1, \ldots, \tau_m$ is a sequence of parameters, each of which corresponds to a different amount of smoothing of the original objective function (shown in equation 7). The sequence is often called a *temperature schedule* in the simulated annealing literature, because equation 8 has analogs to free energy in physics. Therefore, we start with a relatively high temperature τ_1 and gradually lower it until $\tau_m = 1$, which recovers the original objective function.

5.2.2 Inference

At inference time, we are interested in the most likely explanation of the observed data. That is, given a sequence of locations visited by one's friends, along with the corresponding time and day type, our model outputs the most likely sequence of locations one visited over the given time period.

Flap runs a variant of Viterbi decoding to efficiently calculate the most likely state of the hidden nodes. In our model, Viterbi decoding is given by

$$y^\star_{1:t} = \underset{y_{1:t}}{\text{argmax}} \ \log\left(\Pr(y_{1:t}|x_{1:t})\right), \quad (9)$$

where $\Pr(y_{1:t}|x_{1:t})$ is conditional probability of a sequence of hidden states $y_{1:t}$ given a concrete sequence of observations $x_{1:t}$ between times 1 and t.

In each time slice, we coalesce all observed nodes with their hidden parent node, and since we have one hidden node in each time slice, we apply dynamic programming and achieve polynomial runtimes in a way similar to [17]. Specifically, the time complexity of our inference is $O(T|Y|^2)$, where T is the number of time slices and Y is the set of possible hidden state values (potential locations).

Therefore, the overall time complexity of learning and inference for any given target user is $O(kT|Y|^2)$, where k is the number of EM iterations ($k = 1$ for supervised learning). This renders our model tractable even for very large domains that evolve over long periods of time with fine granularity. Next, we turn to our experiments, and analysis of results.

6. EVALUATION

For clarity, we discuss experimental results for each of the two Flap's tasks separately.

6.1 Friendship Prediction

We evaluate Flap on friendship prediction using two-fold cross-validation in which we train on LA and test on NY data, and vice versa. We average the results over the two runs. We varied the amount of randomly selected edges provided to the model at testing time from 0 to 50%.

Flap reconstructs the friendship graph well over a wide range of conditions—even when given no edges (Figure 4 and Table 2). It far outperforms the baseline model (decision tree) and the precision/recall breakeven points are comparable to those of [28], even though our domain is orders of magnitude larger and our model is more tractable.

We also compare our model to that of Crandall *et al.* [7], summarized in Section 2. Figure 5 shows the results of their contemporaneous events counting procedure on our Twitter data for various spatial and temporal resolutions. We see that in our dataset, the relationship between co-location and friendship is much more complex and non-monotonic as compared to their Flickr dataset. As a result, the predictive performance of Crandall *et al.*'s model on our data is poor. When probabilistically predicting social ties based on the number of contemporaneous events, the accuracy is 0.001%, precision 0.008, and recall 0.007 (in the best case,

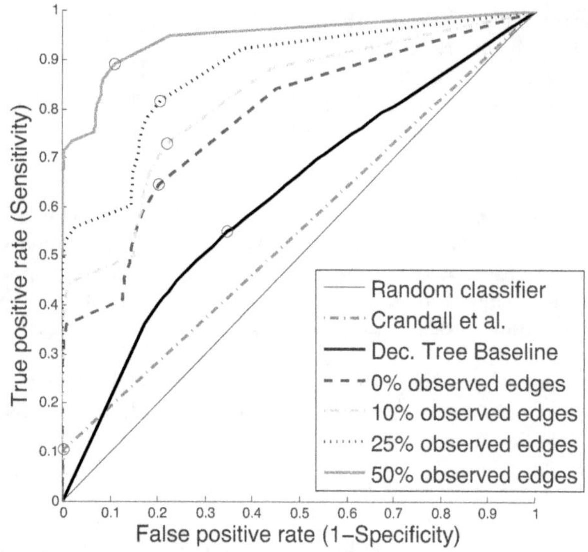

Figure 4: Averaged ROC curves for decision tree baseline, Crandall *et al.*'s model with the most favorable setting of parameters ($s = 0.001$ and $t = 4$ hours), and Flap.

	#E	0%	10%	25%	50%
AUC Flap	6.5×10^7	0.78	0.82	0.88	0.95
AUC Crandall *et al.*	6.5×10^7	0.55	-	-	-
P=R Flap	6.5×10^7	0.28	0.36	0.47	0.64
P=R Crandall *et al.*	6.5×10^7	0.05	-	-	-
P=R Taskar *et al.*	$\sim 4 \times 10^2$	N/A	0.47	0.58	0.73

Table 2: Summary of model evaluation. The #E column represents the number of candidate edges that exist in the social graph. The remaining columns denote the proportions of friendships given to the models at testing time. AUC is the area under the ROC curve; P=R denotes precision/recall breakeven points. All results are based on our Twitter dataset, except for the P=R results for Taskar *et al.*, which are based on their—much smaller—university dataset as their model does not scale to larger networks; see text for details.

where $s = 0.001$ and $t = 4$ hours). There are two conclusions based on this result. First, similarly to Liben-Nowell *et al.* [20], we observe that geographic distance alone is not sufficient to accurately model social ties. And second, looking at the performance of [7]'s approach on the Flick data comprising the entire world, versus its performance on our LA and NYC data, we see that inferring relationships from co-location data in dense and relatively small geographical areas can be a more challenging task. This is important, as the majority of population lives and interacts in such metropolitan areas. However, our work shows that when we leverage additional information channels beyond co-location, and embed them in a probabilistic model, we can infer social ties quite well.

In order to explore how our model performs in the context of *strong* ties, in both LA and NYC, we selected a subgraph that contains only active users who are members of a clique of size at least eight. We again evaluated via cross-validation as above. Flap reconstructs the friendship network of the

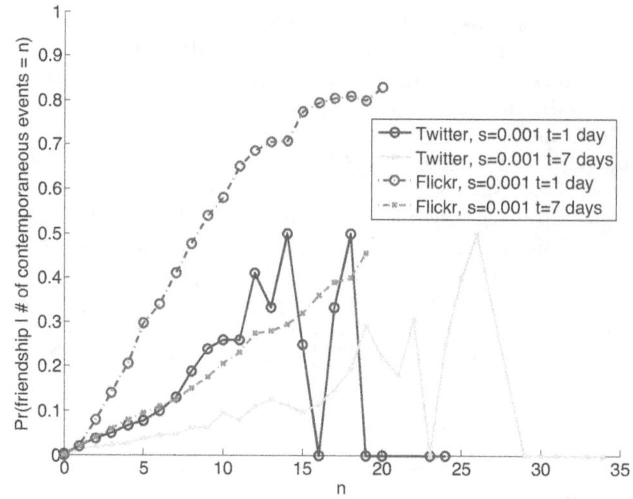

Figure 5: Comparison of the intensity of co-location of pairs of users versus the probability of their friendship in our Twitter and Crandall *et al.*'s Flickr datasets. We see that the relationship is more complex on Twitter, causing a simple model of social ties to achieve very low predictive accuracy. (s is the size of cells in degrees in which we count the co-located events and t is the time slack; compare with Figure 2 in [7].)

83 people with 0.92 precision and 0.85 recall, whereas the baseline decision tree achieves precision of 0.83 and recall of 0.51. Interestingly, the co-location feature plays a major role here because the cliques of friends spend most of their time in relatively small areas.

6.2 Location Prediction

Our evaluation is done in terms of *accuracy*—the percentage of timeslices for which the model infers the correct user location. We have a separate dynamic Bayesian network model for each user.

In order to evaluate the models learned in a *supervised* fashion, we train each model on three weeks worth of data (5/19/2010 00:00:00 – 6/8/2010 23:59:59) and test on the following fourth week (6/9/2010 00:00:00 – 6/15/2010 23:59:59). We always use the respective local time: PDT for LA, and EDT for NYC. We vary the number of friends (n) that we harness as sensors for each individual from 0 to 9. We always use the n most geo-active friends, and introduce a special missing value for users who have fewer than n friends. We evaluate the overall performance via cross-validation. In each fold of cross-validation, we designate a target user and run learning and inference for him. This process is repeated for all users, and we report the average results over all runs for a given value of n (Figure 6).

For models learned in an *unsupervised* manner, we also apply cross-validation as above. The hidden locations are learned via unsupervised clustering as described above. The temperature schedule for the EM procedure is given by $\tau_{i+1} = \tau_i \times 0.8$, with initial temperature $\tau_1 = 10$ (see equation 8). This results in calculating the likelihood at 11 different temperatures for each EM run. The EM procedure always converged within one thousand iterations, resulting in runtimes under a minute per user even in the largest domain.

We compare the results obtained by our DBN models to

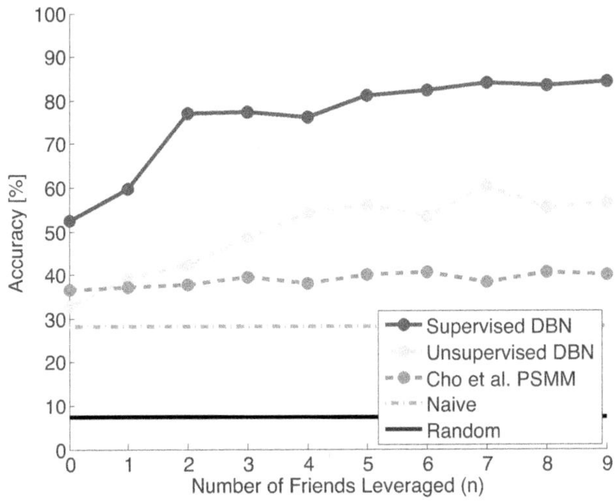

Figure 6: Predictive accuracy of location models. The performance of the two baseline models is by design independent of number of friends considered.

random and naïve baselines, and to the currently *strongest* mobility model of Cho *et al.* [6]. The random model is given the number of hidden locations for each user and guesses target user's location uniformly at random for each time slice. The naïve model always outputs the location at which the target user spends most of his time in the training data. We consider a prediction made by Cho *et al.*'s model accurate if it lies within 100 meters (roughly a city block) of the true user location.

Figure 6 summarizes the results. As expected, the supervised models perform better than their unsupervised counterparts. However, given the complexity of the domain and the computational efficiency of our models during training as well as testing, even the unsupervised models achieve respectable accuracy. The DBN approaches are significantly better than both random and naïve baselines, and they also dominate [6]'s social mobility model (PSMM) by a large margin. We believe this is mainly because people's mobility in condensed metropolitan areas often does not nicely decompose into "home" and "work" states, and the social influence on user location is not simply an attractive force (*i.e.*, one does not necessarily tend to appear closer to one's friends). For instance, consider two co-workers, one having a morning shift and the other a night shift in the same store. Their mobility is certainly intertwined, but the force between their location is a repulsive one, as when the first one is working, the other is sleeping at home. Unlike other approaches, our DBN model correctly learns such nonlinear patterns (both temporal and social).

The results are very encouraging. For example, even when the model is given information only about one's two friends, and no information about the target user (Unsupervised, $n = 2$ in Figure 6), it infers the correct location 47% of the time. As we increase the number of available friends to nine (Unsupervised, $n = 9$), we achieve 57% accuracy. When historical data about the mobility of the target user and his friends is available, we can estimate the correct location 77% of the time when two friends are available (Supervised, $n = 2$) and 84.3% with nine friends (Supervised, $n = 9$). As n increases, the accuracy generally improves. Specifically, we see that there is a significant boost from $n = 0$ to $n = 2$, after which the curves plateau. This suggests that a few active friends explain one's mobility well. We also see that simply outputting the most commonly visited location (Naïve) yields poor results since people tend to lead fairly dynamic lives.

7. CONCLUSIONS AND FUTURE WORK

Location information linked with the content of users' messages in online social networks is a rich information source that is now accessible to machines in massive volumes and at ever-increasing real-time streaming rates. This data became readily available only very recently. In this work, we show that there are significant patterns that characterize locations of individuals and their friends. These patterns can be leveraged in probabilistic models that infer people's locations as well as social ties with high accuracy. Moreover, the prediction accuracy degrades gracefully as we limit the amount of observed data available to the models, suggesting successful future deployment of Flap at a scale of an entire social network.

Our approach is quite powerful, as it allows us to reason even about the location of people who keep their messages and GPS data private, or have disabled the geo-features on their computers and phones altogether. Furthermore, unlike all existing approaches, our model of social ties reconstructs the entire friendship network with high accuracy even when the model is not "seeded" with a sample of known friendships. At the same time, we show that the predictions improve as we provide more observed edges at testing time.

By training the model on one geographical area and testing on the other using cross-validation (total of 4 million geo-tagged public tweets we collected from Los Angeles and New York City metropolitan areas), we show that Flap discovers robust patterns in the formation of friendships that transcend diverse and distant areas of the USA. We conclude that no single property of a pair of individuals is a good indicator of the existence or absence of friendship. And no single friend is a good predictor of one's location. Rather, we need to combine multiple disparate features—based on text, location, and the topology of the underlying friendship graph—in order to achieve good performance.

In our current work, we are extending the model to leverage the textual content of the tweets, as it contains hints about locations that are not captured by our existing features. We are currently exploring language understanding and toponym resolution techniques vital for tapping this information. We also focus on casting the two problems explored in this paper in a unified formalism and solving them *jointly*, perhaps in a recursive fashion.

We recognize that there are substantial ethical questions ahead, specifically concerning tradeoffs between the values our automated systems create versus user privacy. For example, our unsupervised experiments show that location can be inferred even for people who keep their tweets and location private, and thus may believe that they are "untrackable." These issues will need to be addressed in parallel with the development of our models. Other researchers have started exploring solutions to privacy concerns through data obfuscation [5].

However, we believe that the benefits of Flap—in helping to connect and localize users, and in building smarter systems—outweigh the possible dangers. There are many exciting practical applications that have the potential to change people's lives that rely on location and link estimation. These include context-aware crowdsourcing, timely and accurate recommendations, better local content, disease prevention and containment, security, traffic modeling, emergency response, and others.

8. ACKNOWLEDGMENTS

This research was partly funded by ARO grant W911NF-08-1- 0242, ONR grant N00014-11-10417, OSD grant W81X WH-08-C0740, and a gift from the Kodak Company. The views and conclusions contained in this document are those of the authors and should not be interpreted as necessarily representing the official policies, either expressed or implied, of any of these organizations.

9. REFERENCES

[1] L. Backstrom and J. Leskovec. Supervised random walks: predicting and recommending links in social networks. In *Proceedings of the fourth ACM international conference on Web search and data mining*, pages 635–644. ACM, 2011.

[2] L. Backstrom, E. Sun, and C. Marlow. Find me if you can: improving geographical prediction with social and spatial proximity. In *Proceedings of the 19th international conference on World wide web*, pages 61–70. ACM, 2010.

[3] R. Bell, Y. Koren, and C. Volinsky. Modeling relationships at multiple scales to improve accuracy of large recommender systems. In *KDD*, pages 95–104, New York, NY, USA, 2007. ACM.

[4] L. Breiman et al. *Classification and Regression Trees*. Chapman & Hall, New York, 1984.

[5] A. B. Brush, J. Krumm, and J. Scott. Exploring end user preferences for location obfuscation, location-based services, and the value of location. In *Ubicomp*, Ubicomp '10, pages 95–104, New York, NY, USA, 2010. ACM.

[6] E. Cho, S. A. Myers, and J. Leskovec. Friendship and mobility: User movement in location-based social networks. *ACM SIGKDD International Conference on Knowledge Discovery and Data Mining (KDD)*, 2011.

[7] D. Crandall, L. Backstrom, D. Cosley, S. Suri, D. Huttenlocher, and J. Kleinberg. Inferring social ties from geographic coincidences. *Proceedings of the National Academy of Sciences*, 107(52):22436, 2010.

[8] M. Datar, N. Immorlica, P. Indyk, and V. Mirrokni. Locality-sensitive hashing scheme based on p-stable distributions. In *Proceedings of the twentieth annual symposium on Computational geometry*, pages 253–262. ACM, 2004.

[9] A. P. Dempster, N. M. Laird, and D. B. Rubin. Maximum likelihood from incomplete data via the em algorithm. *Journal of the Royal Statistical Society*, 39(1):1–38, 1977.

[10] N. Eagle and A. Pentland. Reality mining: sensing complex social systems. *Personal and Ubiquitous Computing*, 10(4):255–268, 2006.

[11] D. Easley and J. Kleinberg. *Networks, Crowds, and Markets: Reasoning About a Highly Connected World*. Cambridge University Press, 2010.

[12] S. Eubank, H. Guclu, V. Anil Kumar, M. Marathe, A. Srinivasan, Z. Toroczkai, and N. Wang. Modelling disease outbreaks in realistic urban social networks. *Nature*, 429(6988):180–184, 2004.

[13] Z. Ghahramani. Learning dynamic Bayesian networks. In *Adaptive Processing of Sequences and Data Structures*, page 168. Springer, 1998.

[14] A. Gruzd, B. Wellman, and Y. Takhteyev. Imagining twitter as an imagined community. In *American Behavioral Scientist, Special issue on Imagined Communities*, 2011.

[15] L. Hong, B. Suh, and E. H. Chi. Tweets from justin bieber's heart: the dynamics of the "location" field in user profiles. In *ACM CHI*, 2011.

[16] A. Java, X. Song, T. Finin, and B. Tseng. Why we twitter: understanding microblogging usage and communities. In *WebKDD/SNA-KDD*, pages 56–65, New York, NY, USA, 2007. ACM.

[17] M. Jordan. *Learning in graphical models*. Kluwer Academic Publishers, 1998.

[18] H. Kwak, C. Lee, H. Park, and S. Moon. What is Twitter, a Social Network or a News Media? In *WWW*, April 2010.

[19] D. Liben-Nowell and J. Kleinberg. The link-prediction problem for social networks. *J. Am. Soc. Inf. Sci. Technol.*, 58:1019–1031, May 2007.

[20] D. Liben-Nowell, J. Novak, R. Kumar, P. Raghavan, and A. Tomkins. Geographic routing in social networks. *Proceedings of the National Academy of Sciences of the United States of America*, 102(33):11623, 2005.

[21] K. Murphy. *Dynamic bayesian networks: representation, inference and learning*. PhD thesis, University of California, Berkeley, 2002.

[22] K. P. Murphy, Y. Weiss, and M. I. Jordan. Loopy belief propagation for approximate inference: An empirical study. In *In Proceedings of Uncertainty in AI*, pages 467–475, 1999.

[23] J. Pearl. *Probabilistic Reasoning in Intelligent Systems: Networks of Plausible Inference*. Morgan Kaufmann Publishers Inc., San Francisco, CA, USA, 1988.

[24] A. S. Pentland. *Honest Signals: How They Shape Our World*. The MIT Press, 2008.

[25] S. Scellato, A. Noulas, R. Lambiotte, and C. Mascolo. Socio-spatial properties of online location-based social networks. *Proceedings of ICWSM*, 11, 2011.

[26] D. Smith and J. Eisner. Dependency parsing by belief propagation. In *Proceedings of the Conference on Empirical Methods in Natural Language Processing*, pages 145–156. Association for Computational Linguistics, 2008.

[27] C. Song, Z. Qu, N. Blumm, and A. Barabási. Limits of predictability in human mobility. *Science*, 327(5968):1018, 2010.

[28] B. Taskar, M.-F. Wong, P. Abbeel, and D. Koller. Link prediction in relational data. In *in Neural Information Processing Systems*, 2003.

[29] N. Ueda and R. Nakano. Deterministic annealing em algorithm. *Neural Networks*, 11(2):271 – 282, 1998.

How to Win Friends and Influence People, Truthfully: Influence Maximization Mechanisms for Social Networks

Yaron Singer
Computer Science Division
University of California at Berkeley, CA, 94720 USA
yaron@cs.berkeley.edu

ABSTRACT

Throughout the past decade there has been extensive research on algorithmic and data mining techniques for solving the problem of influence maximization in social networks: if one can incentivize a subset of individuals to become early adopters of a new technology, which subset should be selected so that the word-of-mouth effect in the social network is maximized? Despite the progress in modeling and techniques, the incomplete information aspect of the problem has been largely overlooked. While data can often provide the network structure and influence patterns may be observable, the inherent cost individuals have to become early adopters is difficult to extract.

In this paper we introduce mechanisms that elicit individuals' costs while providing desirable approximation guarantees in some of the most well-studied models of social network influence. We follow the mechanism design framework which advocates for allocation and payment schemes that incentivize individuals to report their true information. We also performed experiments using the Mechanical Turk platform and social network data to provide evidence of the framework's effectiveness in practice.

Categories and Subject Descriptors

H.2.8 [**Database Management**]: Database applications – Data mining

General Terms

Algorithms, Economics, Experimentation, Theory

1. INTRODUCTION

The emergence of online social networks in the past decade has given birth to the study of information propagation in social networks. Motivated by marketing applications, a central problem that received considerable attention in this domain is the *influence maximization problem*, where the goal is to identify a small subset of individuals in a social network that can serve as early adopters of a new technology and trigger a large word-of-mouth cascade in the network.

The main focus in the study of the influence maximization problem has been on descriptive influence models and efficient optimization machinery. Since the problem is known to be NP-hard, there has been substantial focus on characterization of influence models and their approximation guarantees (e.g. [19, 18, 26, 5]). To enable better predictions, a different line of work studies techniques for inferring influence models from observable data and analyzing large scale information cascades (e.g. [8, 30, 11, 23, 14, 13, 25, 4]).

These developments in algorithmic and data mining techniques focus on identifying influencers and predicting their potential influence in the social network. To execute viral marketing campaigns, however, an important question remains: *How do we influence the influencers?*

For concreteness, consider *Ticketbuster*, a (fictitious) online retailer that sells concert tickets and wishes to promote a concert through word-of-mouth in a social network (e.g. Google+). To do this, Ticketbuster is willing to provide discounts to individuals who purchase tickets and are willing to announce their purchase to their friends in the social network. Given that it is limited by the total amount of discounts it can offer and that individuals respond differently to incentives, Ticketbuster needs to decide who should be offered a discount for announcing their purchase to their friends, and importantly, how much they should be offered.

The above example is an illustration of the kind of problems we wish to address in this work: how to design algorithms for viral marketing campaigns that provide appropriate incentives for individuals to become early adopters[1]. The challenge lies in the fact that individuals attribute different costs for becoming early adopters, and our algorithms must somehow be designed to account for this.

The Influence Maximization Model

In the influence maximization model, as formalized by Kempe, Kleinberg and Tardos in [19] we are given a social network graph and an *influence function* that takes a subset of nodes of initial adopters and returns the expected number of nodes influenced in the graph. Given some parameter k the goal is to find k initial adopters that will maximize the expected number of nodes influenced. This elegant model captures the decisions often made in viral marketing campaigns where a set of consumers is chosen to receive incentives for being

[1]The term *early adopters* here is used to generally describe the subset of individuals we are seeking to incentivize in order to create the word-of-mouth effect.

Permission to make digital or hard copies of all or part of this work for personal or classroom use is granted without fee provided that copies are not made or distributed for profit or commercial advantage and that copies bear this notice and the full citation on the first page. To copy otherwise, to republish, to post on servers or to redistribute to lists, requires prior specific permission and/or a fee.
WSDM'12, February 8–12, 2012, Seattle, Washington, U SA.
Copyright 2012 ACM 978-1-4503-0747-5/12/02 ...$10.00.

early adopters of a technology (e.g. receive a product at a discounted price), so that their experiences would be advertised by word-of-mouth through the social network.

The underlying assumption in the influence maximization model is that each node in the graph has some inherent *cost* for being an initial adopter[2] and that the word-of-mouth process described by the influence function does not depend on additional incentives. In simple cases one may assume that costs are uniform (e.g. the cost for being an initial adopter may simply be the cost of buying the technology at an advertised market price), or that the incentives can be rewarding enough to cover any reasonable cost that may be associated with being an initial adopter. In general however, as in the case of our example, costs may be subjective and must be considered in the input to the problem.

Challenges of Inferring Incentives

Despite the growing availability of personalized data and the emergence of sophisticated machine learning techniques, inferring personal costs is a difficult task: individuals often have subjective costs that heavily depend on various aspects that are difficult to observe like personal history or opinions.

A reasonable approach may be to estimate an optimal reward value and use this estimate as an offer to individuals. The problem however is that this approach leads to poor results both in theory and in practice. In Appendix A we show that even when given access to individuals' costs, no mechanism that offers uniform rewards can approximate the optimal solution within a factor better than $\Omega(\frac{\log n}{\log \log n})$. In Section 4 we show that such mechanisms perform poorly in practice as well. This implies that even under the strong assumption that costs are known, the influence maximization techniques that use the optimal reward perform poorly.

Finally, we can consider algorithms that pay individuals their declared costs. This naïve approach, however, is susceptible to manipulation: individuals may declare higher costs to increase their reward.

A Mechanism Design Approach

To address the above challenges, we introduce machinery from mechanism design theory. The theory is based on the idea of designing mechanisms[3] that are *incentive compatible* (aka *truthful*): mechanisms for which it is provably in each agent's best interest to report her true private information, regardless of the other agents' reports. Thus, by assuming that agents are rational[4], an incentive compatible mechanism extracts the agents' true information and uses it to identify and reward the subset of initial adopters. Our goal is therefore to design *incentive compatible* mechanisms that compare favorably against the optimal influence maximization solution.

1.1 Our Results

In this paper we introduce incentive compatible mechanisms for the influence maximization problem in some of the most well-studied models of influence in social networks. In particular we show constant-factor approximation mechanisms [5] for the Coverage, Linear Threshold, Independent Cascades, the Voter and general submodular influence models. To evaluate their practical performance, we provide experimental evidence of the mechanisms' effectiveness on real data sets. In our experiments we used network data that has almost a million nodes and over 72 million edges, together with a representative cost distribution that was obtained by running a simulated campaign on Amazon's Mechanical Turk platform [1].

1.2 Related Work

The problem of maximizing influence was first posed by Domingos and Richardson in [8, 30] and has been extensively studied since. In their seminal work [19], Kempe, Kleinberg and Tardos characterize some of the main models of influence in terms of their computational approximability. While they show that the optimization problem in many of the models is NP-hard, their work identifies important classes of influence models in which the objective function is submodular – a condition that allows providing desirable approximation guarantees. The approximation frontiers of the influence problem in more general models have been further explored in [5, 26].

Incentives have been considered in mechanisms for finding information within a social network in [21] using payments at Nash-equilibrium. In [17] a game theoretic influence model is suggested, where incentives for adoption in the influence process are considered. Network externalities were considered for pricing mechanisms in [16] and revenue maximizing auctions in [15]. There has been recent work on incentives in social network motivated by marketing applications [3, 9], though not in the influence maximization framework, nor are the mechanisms incentive compatible.

The theoretical work in this paper follows recent work in [31], which establishes a theory for designing incentive compatible mechanisms under a budget constraint on payments. The main result shows that for any submodular optimization function, there exists a randomized incentive compatible mechanism with a constant factor approximation guarantee. In this paper we rely on the characterization of payments from this line of work to develop improved mechanisms for the standard models in social networks.

2. THE MODEL

In our model there is a social network that is represented by a graph $G = (\mathcal{N}, \mathcal{E})$ and an influence function $f : 2^{\mathcal{N}} \rightarrow \mathcal{R}_{\geq 0}$. Given a subset $S \subseteq \mathcal{N}$ the value $f(S)$ represents the expected number of nodes influenced in the social graph. Each node in the graph represents an agent a_i that has a *private* cost $c_i \in \mathcal{R}_{\geq 0}$ of being an initial adopter, and this cost is not known to the mechanism designer. We assume that agents are rational and strategic in a game theoretic sense. That is, given a choice of payments an agent will choose to maximize her profit[6] and may misreport her cost to do so. In particular, an agent can become an initial adopter only if the payment it receives is greater or equal to her cost.

[2]Otherwise no incentives would be necessary to become an initial adopter and there would be no restriction on the number of nodes that can be selected.

[3]A mechanism is simply an algorithm that decides who is allocated and how much they are paid.

[4]In our case, rationality simply means that an agent wishes to maximize her profit.

[5]Our comparisons follow the strictest benchmarks one can consider: We compare our mechanisms against the computationally unbounded optimal solution that has full information about the agents' true costs.

[6]The profit of an agent with cost c that receives payment p is simply $p - c$.

Given a budget $B \geq 0$ our goal is to maximize the influence by paying a subset of agents to be the initial adopters of the technology. A solution to the problem is a subset of agents and a payment vector that describes the payments to each agent in the subset. A mechanism is simply a pair $M = (A, p)$ where A is an algorithm and p is a payment rule. We sometimes refer to the algorithm of the mechanism as the *allocation rule*. The mechanism takes the social network, the influence function, the budget and the agents' reported costs as input [7].

Approximation

Since the problem is known to be NP-hard, as in the case of standard algorithms, we restrict our mechanisms to run in polynomial time, and seek solutions that are provably close as possible to optimal. For $\alpha \geq 1$ we say that a mechanism $M = (A, p)$ is α-approximate if A is an α approximation algorithm: A returns a solution S such that $f(S^*) \leq \alpha f(S)$, where S^* is the optimal solution in the full-information case (i.e. the same benchmark that is used for an algorithm when the costs are known and the payment equals the costs).

Incentive Compatible Mechanisms

An incentive compatible mechanism is a mechanism in which the algorithm and payment rule are designed in such a way so that each agent maximizes her profit by revealing her true cost. Rather than proving that a mechanism is incentive compatible directly we will rely on a well known characterization from the literature that will reduce incentive compatibility to a simple condition on the algorithm.

In our setting, where each agent's private information is her cost we can use a characterization for incentive compatible mechanisms by Myerson [28]. According to this characterization, a mechanism is incentive compatible in our setting if and only if it is *monotone* and uses threshold payments. Informally, this means that as long as other agents do not change their bids, an agent that is selected should remain selected when declaring a lower cost and that her payment is the maximal cost she can declare and remain selected. Formally, given an algorithm A and an agent a_i let $A(c_i, c_{-i})$ be the subset selected by the algorithm when a_i declares cost c_i and the rest of the agents' costs are denoted by the vector c_{-i}. The monotonicity rule requires that if $a_i \in A(c_i, c_{-i})$ then $a_i \in A(c_i', c_{-i})$, for any $c_i' < c_i$. The threshold payment that ensures incentive compatibility is $p_i = \inf\{b_i : a_i \notin A(b_i, c_{-i})\}$.

To prove that a mechanism is incentive compatible we will therefore show that the algorithm is monotone. An important requirement is that the mechanism's payments do not exceed the budget. Fortunately, the main component of our mechanisms will be the proportional share allocation rule, for which a result in [31] gives a characterization of its incentive compatible payments that can be immediately translated to a condition on the algorithm. We will therefore use the characterization as a black box and discuss the restrictions the payments impose in the appropriate sections.

[7]This is known as a *direct revelation mechanism:* agents report their cost to the mechanisms. On Ticketbuster, for example, once completing her purchase, an individual would report how much she would like to be rewarded for sharing her purchase on Google+. Note that we assume that the social network and budget are known to the mechanism.

3. MECHANISMS FOR MAX INFLUENCE

In this section we present several mechanisms for some of the well-studied models of influence in social networks. To simplify the exposition, we begin with the Coverage influence model and later show how the mechanism can be adapted to accommodate other influence models.

The Coverage Model

In the Coverage model, each agent a_i in the network is associated with a subset of nodes R_i and the influence in this model is $f(S) = |\cup_{i \in S} R_i|$. The optimization problem is the well known NP-hard Max-k-Cover problem, and it can be easily verified that this influence model is submodular. It is a fundamental model that serves as a basis for many of the well-studied submodular influence models.

Intuitively, a good mechanism will select agents that yield high coverage while the incentive compatible payments will not exceed the given budget. The main component of our mechanism achieves this by greedily selecting agents based on their marginal contributions and enforcing an appropriate stopping condition. The greedy selection uses the weighted marginal contribution sorting: an ordering in which at each stage the agent selected is the one that has the maximal weighted contribution given the previously selected agents. That is, under this ordering, the jth agent is:

$$a \in \text{argmax}_{a_i \in \mathcal{N}} \frac{f(S_{j-1} \cup \{a_i\}) - f(S_{j-1})}{c_i} \tag{1}$$

where S_{j-1} denotes the set of $j-1$ agents that have been previously selected by this rule. This is the generalized version of the sorting rule used in the celebrated greedy algorithm for submodular function maximization [29], and it has beed used to obtain constant factor approximation guarantees in [20, 22, 24].

To enforce a stopping condition with desirable payment guarantees, after sorting the agents we will include them into the solution as long as the ratio between their cost and the budget is smaller than half of the ratio between their marginal contribution and the value of the subset already selected. That is, we consider agent a_i that meets the condition:

$$c_i \leq \frac{B}{2} \cdot \Big(\frac{f(S_i) - f(S_{i-1})}{f(S_i)}\Big). \tag{2}$$

This allocation rule is a variation of *proportional share* rule which is the basis for mechanisms under a budget [31, 6, 7, 32]. Observe that if k agents are selected according to this rule and each selected agent is paid according to their proportional contribution, the total payments do not exceed the budget:

$$\sum_{i=1}^{k} B \cdot \Big(\frac{f(S_i) - f(S_{i-1})}{f(S_i)}\Big) \tag{3}$$

$$\leq \frac{B}{f(S_k)} \cdot \sum_{i=1}^{k} \Big(f(S_i) - f(S_{i-1})\Big) \tag{4}$$

$$= \frac{B}{f(S_k)} \cdot f(S_k) = B. \tag{5}$$

The desirable property of this allocation rule is that for

any submodular function, it can be proved that the incentive compatible payments do not exceed the agents' proportional contributions. We will further discuss payments after describing the entire mechanism below. Importantly, this allocation rule provides desirable guarantees in terms of approximation as well. We use OPT to denote the optimal solution and denote the agent with maximal value by a^*. The main idea behind the proof is similar to that in [31] and compares the proportional allocation rule against the standard greedy algorithm which is known to have a good approximation guarantee.

LEMMA 3.1. *Let S_k be the set that is selected by the algorithm that sorts agents according to their weighted marginal contribution as in (1) and selects the maximal number of agents that respect the proportional allocation rule as in (2). Then, $OPT \leq (\frac{5e}{e-1}) \max\{f(S_k), f(a^*)\}$.*

PROOF. Let the agents be sorted as describes above, and let ℓ be the maximal index s.t. $\sum_{i=1}^{\ell} c_i \leq B$. For sake of the analysis, consider adding a new agent, a' which does not share any friends with the agents in $\mathcal{N}$, declares cost $B - \sum_{i=1}^{\ell} c_i$ and $f(a') = \left(\frac{B-\sum_{i=1}^{\ell} c_i}{c_{\ell+1}}\right) \cdot \left(f(S_{\ell+1}) - f(S_\ell)\right)$. Observe that the weighted marginal contribution of this agent is identical to that of agent $a_{\ell+1}$ and that the solution $f(S_\ell \cup \{a'\})$ is feasible. Obviously, the optimal solution over all agents in $\mathcal{N}' = \mathcal{N} \cup \{a\}$ is an upper bound on the optimal solution over all agents in $\mathcal{N}$. Due to the decreasing marginal utilities property, we are guaranteed that the first ℓ agents selected in both $\mathcal{N}$ and $\mathcal{N}'$ are identical. We can therefore analyze our solution over the set of agents $\mathcal{N}'$. For notational convenience in the following analysis we will denote agent a' as $a_{\ell+1}$.

In [20] and its generalization [22], it is shown that for any submodular function we have that $f(S_{\ell+1}) \geq (1 - \frac{1}{e})OPT$. We will use $S_{\ell+1}$ as a benchmark. Since $S_{\ell+1}$ is feasible:

$$\begin{aligned}
&\sum_{i=k+1}^{\ell+1} \left(\frac{c_i}{f(S_i) - f(S_{i-1})}\right)\left(f(S_i) - f(S_{i-1})\right) \\
&\leq \sum_{i=1}^{\ell+1} \left(\frac{c_i}{f(S_i) - f(S_{i-1})}\right)\left(f(S_i) - f(S_{i-1})\right) \\
&= \sum_{i=1}^{\ell+1} c_i = B.
\end{aligned}$$

Since agents are sorted according to their weighted marginal contributions, for every $i \in \{k+1, \ldots, \ell+1\}$ we have that:

$$\frac{f(S_i) - f(S_{i-1})}{c_i} \leq \frac{f(S_{k+1}) - f(S_k)}{c_{k+1}}. \tag{6}$$

Putting the above inequalities together we get:

$$\begin{aligned}
&\tfrac{c_{k+1}}{f(S_{k+1})-f(S_k)}\left(\textstyle\sum_{i=k+1}^{\ell+1} f(S_i) - f(S_{i-1})\right) \\
&= \left(\tfrac{c_{k+1}}{f(S_{k+1})-f(S_k)}\right) \cdot \left(f(S_{\ell+1}) - f(S_{k+1})\right) \leq B.
\end{aligned}$$

Note that this implies that $2f(S_{k+1}) > f(S_{\ell+1}) - f(S_k)$ as otherwise $c_{k+1} \leq \frac{B}{2}\left(\frac{\cdot(f(S_{k+1})-f(S_k)}{f(S_{k+1})}\right)$ which contradicts the maximality of k. Thus, together with submodularity this implies that:

$$\begin{aligned}
f(S_{\ell+1}) &= f(S_{\ell+1}) - f(S_k) + f(S_k) \\
&< 2f(S_{k+1}) + f(S_k) \\
&\leq 2f(a_{k+1}) + 3f(S_k).
\end{aligned}$$

In conclusion, we get:

$$OPT \leq (\tfrac{e}{e-1})f(S_{\ell+1}) \leq \left(\tfrac{5e}{e-1}\right)\max\{f(S_k), f(a^*)\}. \quad \square$$

The above lemma suggests that the approximation guarantee of the proportional share allocation rule depends on the selected subset S_k being larger than a^*. If it were not for incentive constraints, one could simply compare $f(S_k)$ and $f(a^*)$ and by selecting the solution that yields the higher value, guarantee a constant-factor approximation. In our case however, one can show that this process would violate incentive compatibility. This happens since there are cases where by declaring a lower cost, an agent changes the allocation of the mechanism which may reduce the value of the proportional share solution. That is, letting A denote the proportional share allocation, there may be cases where $f(A(c_i, c_{i-1})) > f(a^*)$ but $f(A(c_i', c_{i-1})) < f(a^*)$ when $c_i' < c_i$. To address this, we develop the following methodology. We will compare between a^* and a solution to a nonlinear relaxation program that doesn't suffer from this property while the value of its solution is provably "close" to that of the proportional share mechanism. Observe that the Coverage optimization problem can be reformulated as the following integer program:

$$\begin{aligned}
\max \quad & \textstyle\sum_{j=1}^{m} z_j & j \in U \quad & (7)\\
& \textstyle\sum_{i \in C_j} x_i \geq z_j, & j \in U, \quad & (8)\\
& \textstyle\sum_{i=1}^{n} c_i x_i \leq B, & & (9)\\
& 0 \leq x_i, z_j \leq 1 & i \in \mathcal{N}, j \in \mathcal{U}, \quad & (10)\\
& x_i \in \{0,1\} & i \in \mathcal{N} \quad & (11)
\end{aligned}$$

where z_j are variables representing the agents we wish to cover, x_i are the variables representing the agents we can select, and C_j denotes the subset of agents that cover an agent $a_j \in \mathcal{N}$. In our case $z_i = x_i$ and C_j is the set of friends of agent a_j. For a relaxation we will use:

$$\begin{aligned}
\max \quad & \textstyle\sum_{j=1}^{m} \min\left\{1, \sum_{i \in C_j} x_i\right\} & j \in U \quad & (12)\\
& \textstyle\sum_{i \in C_j} x_i \geq z_j, & j \in U, \quad & (13)\\
& \textstyle\sum_{i=1}^{n} c_i x_i \leq \frac{B}{2}, & & (14)\\
& 0 \leq x_i, z_j \leq 1 & i \in \mathcal{N}, j \in \mathcal{U}, \quad & (15)\\
& x_i \in [0,1] & i \in \mathcal{N} \quad & (16)
\end{aligned}$$

The optimal solution to this relaxation, denoted x^* is computable in polynomial time and is a relaxation of the integer program in the sense that for all $x \in \{0,1\}$ it is equivalent to the integer program. In our mechanism we will compare a^* and this relaxation to circumvent the problem with incentive compatibility. We denote this relaxation as L, and use $L(x)$ to denote a solution that respects the constraints above where $x \in [0,1]^n$. We will show that the solution of $L(x)$ is "close" to $f(S_k)$, which guarantees that comparing a^* to $L(x)$ rather than $f(S_k)$ does not hurt the solution by more than a constant factor. We will use $L(x^*)$ to denote the value of the optimal solution to the relaxation over the subset $\mathcal{N}_- = \mathcal{N} \setminus \{a^*\}$. After describing the mechanism we show how this is used to maintain incentive compatibility and the approximation guarantee.

3.1 Influence Maximization in Coverage

We can now formally describe the mechanism:

An Approximation Mechanism for Coverage

Require: $< G = (\mathcal{N}, \mathcal{E}), c, B >$

$a^* \longleftarrow \text{argmax}_{j\in[n]} f(a_j)$;

$a_i \longleftarrow \text{argmax}_{j\in[n]} \frac{f(a_j)}{c_j}$;

while $c_i \leq \frac{B}{2} \cdot \left(\frac{f(S_i)-f(S_{i-1})}{f(S_i)}\right)$ **do:**

$a_i \longleftarrow \text{argmax}_{j\in[n]} \frac{f(S_i\cup\{a_j\})-f(S_i)}{c_j}$;

$S_i \longleftarrow S_i \cup \{a_i\}$;

if $L(x^*) > \left(\frac{6e^2}{(e-1)^2}\right) f(a^*)$

$S \longleftarrow S_i$

else do: $S \longleftarrow \{a^*\}$

Output: S

The mechanism above uses the proportional share algorithm with budget $\frac{B}{2}$, and returns the set selected by this algorithm if the value of the relaxation is greater than a factor of $f(a^*)$. The payment characterization in [31] shows that the incentive compatible payments are bounded by a constant factor of the proportional contributions, which implies that when using this constant fraction of the budget in the stopping condition the payments do not violate the budget constraint. The subsequent improved analysis in [6] shows that this constant factor is no more than 2, and thus by using $\frac{B}{2}$ in the stopping condition we are guaranteed that the payments do not exceed the budget. We defer the proof of the to the full version of the paper.

LEMMA 3.2. *The mechanism is monotone.*

PROOF. To see that the mechanism is indeed monotone assume for purpose of contradiction that for a given cost profile c there is an agent $a_i \in S$ with declared cost c_i, that is not allocated when declaring $c_i' \leq c_i$ while the rest of the agents declare the same cost as in c. Let $\alpha = \frac{6e^2}{(e-1)^2}$. If $a_i \neq a^*$ then it has been selected by the proportional share allocation rule and $L(x^*) > \alpha f(a^*)$. By decreasing her cost the agent will move ahead in the sorting to place $j \leq i$, and due to the decreasing marginal contribution property her marginal contribution will only increase. Thus, $f(S_{j-1} \cup \{a_i\}) - f(S_{j-1}) \geq f(S_{i-1} \cup \{a_i\}) - f(S_{-1})$ and since f is an increasing function $f(S_{j-1} \cup \{a_i\}) \leq f(S_i)$. This implies:

$$c_i' < c_i \leq \frac{B}{2}\Big(\frac{f(S_i) - f(S_{i-1})}{f(S_i)}\Big)$$
$$\leq \frac{B}{2}\Big(\frac{f(S_{j-1} \cup \{a_i\}) - f(S_{j-1})}{f(S_{j-1}) \cup \{a_i\}}\Big)$$

and thus a_i will meet the proportional share allocation rule. Since $L(x^*)$ is the value of the *optimal* fractional solution, it can only increase when the costs are reduced, and therefore its value will be larger than that of a^* in this case as well. In case $a_i = a^*$, it is allocated only if $L(x^*) < \alpha f(a^*)$. Note that her cost does not change the value of $f(a^*)$, nor that of $L(x^*)$ which computes its solution over $\mathcal{N} \setminus \{a^*\}$. Thus, $\alpha f(a^*)$ remains larger and a^* is allocated. In summary, in all cases we get a contradiction. □

The argument for showing that the mechanism has a constant factor guarantee depends on showing that $L(x^*)$ and the value of the proportional share solution $f(S_k)$ are close. Consider the nonlinear program relaxation:

$$\begin{aligned}
\max \quad & \textstyle\sum_{j=1}^m (1 - \Pi_{i\in C_j}(1 - x_i)) && j \in U && (17)\\
& \textstyle\sum_{i\in C_j} x_i \geq z_j, && j \in U, && (18)\\
& \textstyle\sum_{i=1}^n c_i x_i \leq \frac{B}{2}, && && (19)\\
& 0 \leq x_i, z_j \leq 1 && i \in \mathcal{N}, j \in \mathcal{U}, && (20)\\
& x_i \in [0, 1] && i \in \mathcal{N} && (21)
\end{aligned}$$

Let F denote the above relaxation. Note that both $F(x)$ and $L(x)$ identify with our integer program over integral solutions. The following lemma can be shown directly using the pipage rounding technique in [2], and we reserve the proof to the full version of the paper.

LEMMA 3.3. *Let x^* be the optimal solution for L. Then, there exists an integral solution $\bar{x}$ s.t. $L(x^*) \leq (\frac{2e}{e-1})F(\bar{x})$.*

Using the above lemmas, we can now conclude with our main theorem.

THEOREM 3.4. *The mechanism is incentive compatible and guarantees an approximation ratio of $\frac{12e^2}{(e-1)^2} + 1$.*

PROOF. Incentive compatibility is a direct result of the monotonicity and the threshold payments discussed. Recall that the optimal *fractional* solution $L(x^*)$ is computed over $\mathcal{N}_- = \mathcal{N} \setminus \{a^*\}$ with budget $\frac{B}{2}$. Let OPT' be the optimal solution over the set of agents $\mathcal{N}_-$ with budget $\frac{B}{2}$.

First, in a similar way to the proof of Lemma 3.1 we can prove that $OPT' < \frac{3e}{e-1} \max\{f(S_k), f(a^*)\}$. Since F is equivalent to our integer program over integral solutions, then OPT' is an upper bound on any of its integral solutions. Together with Lemma 3.3 these two bounds imply:

$$L(x^*) \leq \Big(\frac{2e}{e-1}\Big)OPT' < \Big(\frac{6e^2}{(e-1)^2}\Big) \max\{f(S_k), f(a^*)\}.$$

If $L(x^*) \geq \left(\frac{6e^2}{(e-1)^2}\right) f(a^*)$, the above inequality implies that $f(a^*) < f(S_k)$, and by Lemma 3.1 we have that $OPT \leq (\frac{5e}{e-1}) f(S_k)$, and we're done.

Otherwise, if $L(x^*) \leq \left(\frac{6e^2}{(e-1)^2}\right) f(a^*)$, let $L(x^*, \mathcal{N}', B')$ denote the optimal solution of the relaxation L over the set of agents $\mathcal{N}'$ and budget B'. In this case we have:

$$\begin{aligned}
OPT \leq L(x^*, \mathcal{N}, B) &\leq L(x^*, \mathcal{N}_-, B) + f(a^*)\\
&= 2L(x^*, \mathcal{N}_-, \frac{B}{2}) + f(a^*)\\
&\leq \Big(\frac{12e^2}{(e-1)^2} + 1\Big) f(a^*)
\end{aligned}$$

and we obtain the desired bound. □

3.2 Submodular Influence Models

In the main models studied in the past, influence is described as a step-by-step procedure that is governed by some probabilistic interaction rule. The seminal work of [19] shows that many of the probabilistic influence models considered in the literature are characterized by their submodularity. The two basic diffusion models studied there are the Linear Threshold and Independent Cascades models.

The Linear Threshold Model

In this model, for each neighbor w a node v associates a weight $b_{v,w} \geq 0$ where $\sum_{w \in N(v)} b_{v,w} \leq 1$, and chooses some threshold $\theta_v \in [0,1]$ uniformly at random. The node v is activated at time step t if $\sum_{w \in N_t(v)} b_{v,w} \geq \theta_v$, where $N_t(v)$ denotes the neighbors of v that are active at time step t.

The Independent Cascades Model

Here we assume that each node v is independently influenced by each neighbor w with some probability $p_{v,w}$. When a node w is activated at some time step t it has a single chance to activate each neighbor v with probability $p_{v,w}$.

In each realization of the above models, the influence maximization problem becomes equivalent to the problem in the Coverage model. In the Independent Cascades Model, a realization of the probabilities of each interaction creates a graph that deterministically describes the spread of influence. We can therefore construct a reachability graph that describes for each node v the subset of nodes it influences, and the nodes influenced by a subset S is its coverage in the reachability graph. In the Linear Threshold case [19] show that the model is equivalent to a process in which each node v picks one incoming edge with probability $b_{v,w}$ and does not pick any edges with probability $1 - \sum_w b_{v,w}$ which also reduces to the Coverage model. Therefore, for both models, in any realization we can apply the mechanism described for the Coverage model.

While the Linear Threshold and the Independent Cascades models can be used to describe many influence functions considered in the literature, there are more general submodular influence functions that are not captured by these models. For such models we can obtain a constant factor approximation mechanism by allowing for randomization:[8] Since Lemma 3.1 applies to any submodular function, randomly choosing between the most influential agent and the proportional share allocation, guarantees, in expectation, a constant factor approximation mechanism.

COROLLARY 3.5. *For any submodular influence function there is a randomized incentive compatible constant-factor approximation mechanism. Furthermore, for any realization of the Linear Threshold and Independent Cascades models there is a deterministic constant factor approximation mechanisms that is incentive compatible.*

The Voter Model

In the Voter model, at each time step, each agent is influenced with probability that is proportional to the number of friends that were influenced in the previous time step. This influence model has been extensively covered in the past and recently also in the computer science community [27, 10]. More formally, assuming a set of nodes has been activated at step $t = 0$, the probability of v to be influenced at time step $t > 1$ is $p_{v,t} = \frac{|\{u : u \in N_{t-1}(v)\}|}{|N(v)|}$, where $N_{t-1}(v)$ denotes the subset of neighbors of v that are influenced at time step $t-1$ and $N(v)$ denotes the set of neighbors of v.

An equivalent formulation of the Voter model can be stated in terms of a random walk on the graph that represents the social network: if u is activated at time step 0, the probability of some node v in the graph to be activated by u after t time steps is equivalent to the probability of a random walk on the graph that starts at v and terminates at u after t steps. To see this, observe that if w is activated at step 0 for $t = 1$ the probability of v to be influenced by its neighbor w is $\frac{1}{|N(v)|}$, and that the probability of v to be influenced at a general time step t can be recursively computed.

The random walk process can be computed by associating a transition matrix M_G with the graph. In this matrix $M_G(u,v) = \frac{1}{|N(u)|}$ if v is a neighbor of u and 0 otherwise, and the probability of a random walk that starts at node v and terminates at node u after t steps is $M_G^t(v,u)$. Using this representation we can easily compute the expected number of nodes that terminate at u after t time steps, or equivalently the number of nodes influenced by u: $f_t(u) = \sum_v M_G^t(v,u)$. Importantly, the matrix formulation implies that we can compute the expected influence of a given subset S additively:

$$f_t(S) = \sum_{u \in S} \sum_v M^t(v,u).$$

The linearity allows using variation of the mechanism from Section 3 with a better approximation guarantee.

THEOREM 3.6. *For the Voter Model there is an incentive compatible 4-approximation mechanism.*

PROOF SKETCH. The mechanism is similar to the mechanism for Coverage, except that it uses the entire budget in the stopping condition of the proportional allocation rule, and an integer programming relaxation suitable for this linear problem rather than the relaxation used in the previous mechanism. The proportional contribution of an agent a_i in this case is:

$$\frac{B \cdot f_t(a_i)}{\sum_{j \leq i} f_t(a_j)} \tag{22}$$

and can be efficiently computed by $\sum_v M_G^t(v,u)$, and the total marginal contribution of a subset S is $\sum_{u \in S} \sum_v M^t(v,u)$. Due to linearity, by case analysis we can prove that an agent that declares a cost that is larger than her proportional contribution will not be allocated. This implies that the incentive compatible payments can be bounded by agents' proportional contributions, thus allowing us to use the proportional share allocation rule with the entire budget. The approximation guarantee then follows with an analysis similar to the one in Lemma 3.1 that can be used to show that the optimal solution is bounded by $2\sum_{i=1}^{k} f(a_i) + f(a_{k+1}) + f(a^*)$ when k agents selected and a^* is the agent with maximal influence. Similar arguments to those used above can be used to show the mechanism is monotone and incentive compatible. □

[8]In general submodular functions may require a description that is exponential in the size of the problem. In such cases we can apply our mechanisms efficiently in the *value query* model where it is assumed that any subset can be evaluated by an oracle in polynomial time.

4. EXPERIMENTAL EVALUATION

Given the theoretical guarantees discussed above, we would like to show that our mechanisms also work well in practice. While it may be the case that our mechanisms provide theoretical guarantees in the worst case, it is not obvious a priori that they outperform simpler heuristics on representative instances. Furthermore, as we discussed above, one may argue that mechanisms with differential prices like the ones suggested here, are too complex or alternatively that eliciting costs from individuals is an unnecessary procedure.

To examine these issues we performed an experimental evaluation of our mechanisms in different influence models over a large sample of a social network, and compared their performance against other mechanisms. While network data that is representative of real social networks is relatively accessible, the greatest crux in performing this experiment was the lack of knowledge about individuals' costs for making a recommendation in their social network. To address this, we performed an experiment on Amazon's Mechanical Turk platform to obtain a descriptive cost distribution.

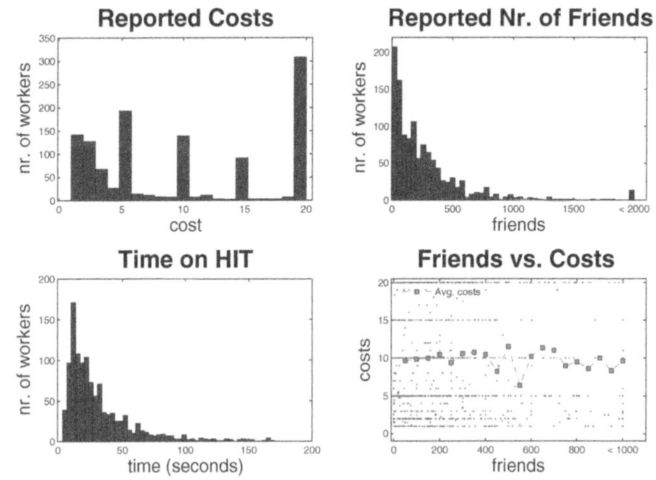

Figure 1: Results from the MTurk experiment.

4.1 The MTurk Experiment

To obtain a distribution that is reflective of individuals' costs to make recommendations in their social network we ran an experiment for a period of three months on Amazon's Mechanical Turk platform (henceforth MTurk)[1]. The experiment was presented as a competition for receiving bonus money. The workers were explained that a small number of individuals will be selected to advertise a travel agency by posting a message with commercial content in their Facebook page, and that they need to specify how much they want be rewarded and how many friends they have on Facebook. Since a posted message is automatically displayed to an individual's friends in Facebook, the reports on rewards in this experiment represent the reported costs we address in this work. We ran the competition with a small budget to enable cost-effective data collection. Each worker who participated in the competition was paid, and the workers who won the competition received a bonus reward at least as high as their bid. [9]

The experiment ran for a period of three months. The payments for participating in the experiment varied from \$0.05 to \$0.50, and the mean payment was approximately \$0.26. We limited the experiment to workers based in the US with high approval rate (above 97%). The main reason was to increase the likelihood that the worker is an active Facebook user and understands the experiment. Due to individuals' privacy concerns we did not use verification methods provided by Facebook (e.g. Facebook applications) to establish the workers' Facebook identities.

In the Human Intelligence Task (HIT) the competition details were clearly described in two sentences. An image of an example post that advertises a travel agency was provided and workers were asked to give a value of how much they would like to be rewarded for posting the message on Facebook, as well as to provide the number of friends. The example message displayed had clear commercial content, similar to content generated when users share a message of an online retailer on the Facebook platform. We chose advertising for a travel agency as it is rather generic, and is not likely to introduce significant gender or age biases. The main reason for requesting the number of friends was to see whether there is a corellation between cost and reported number of friends. We collected over 1,178 bids from over 1,000 different MTurk workers. In Figure 1 we plot distributions of reported costs, reported friends, time required to complete the task, as well as a plot of costs vs. reported number of friends.

To avoid biases, we used a single bid from each worker by choosing between bids at random if a user bid more than once. The mean cost that users bid was \$9.77 and the median was \$8. There were 307 workers who bid the maximal allowed bid (\$20), and 364 who bid below \$5. The mean time to complete the HIT was 32.25 seconds.

In our experiment, in order to use the cost distribution generated by MTurk on the sampled Facebook graph, we wanted to verify that there is no correlation between the number of friends and the reported cost. First, we observed that the reported number of friends generated a distribution that is similar to the distribution of friends from crawling Facebook with a BFS search [12]. This leads us to believe that, in general, workers reported an accurate estimate of their number of friends on Facebook. We assume this is due to the fact that workers were told that if they give a false report on the number of friends they will not be eligible for the reward. The mean number of reported friends was 271.3, the median was 185. We then tested to see whether there is any correlation between the number of friends and the reported cost, and found no evidence for such correlation ($corr = 0.04$). We see this as support to the methodology in our data simulation, where we take a cost at random from the data gathered in the MTurk experiment and assign it to a node from the Facebook sampled graph. We plot the costs as a function of friends in Figure 1.

4.2 Computational Experiments

Network Data

To represent the social network we used a graph of 957,459 nodes and over 72 million edges which was sampled from the

[9] Winners were selected by running the mechanism with the influence function $f(S) = \sum_{i \in S} f_i$, where f_i is the reported number of friends of agent a_i. The goal in this experiment was not to test the mechanism, but rather collect bids.

Facebook social graph via a random walk [12]. The average degree of this graph is 95.2 and the median degree is 40.

Influence Models

To compare the mechanisms over different influence models we implemented the Coverage, Independent Cascades, and the Linear Threshold influence models. The Coverage model was implemented by using each agent's friends as its reachable set. In this implementation a node that's selected activates all of its friends, and the influence process does not propagate further. In the Independent Cascades model we ran two separate trials with uniform probabilities of an edge being activated. In one trial the probability of an edge being activated was 1% and in the other trial the probability was 10%. These choices correspond to the distributions used in [19]. In the Linear Threshold model we chose weights based on the degree distribution of nodes in the social graph. For each node v the value d_v was drawn independently at random from an estimated degree distribution of the social graph. For each of its neighbors w we applied the weight $b_{v,w} = d_v^{-1}$. Since we used a subgraph of the larger Facebook social graph, we did not have the degrees of all of the nodes in the graph and therefore used the degree distribution of the subgraph as an estimate.

To have comparable reachability sets, we limited the time steps of the influence process to 5, 10 and 25 steps in the Independent Cascades with probability 10%, 1% and the Linear Threshold model, respectively. Limiting the time steps seems to be reasonable in light of experimental evidence (see e.g. [33], who report that less than 5% of diffusion processes they studied in Twitter are longer than 5 steps).

After applying the influence model on the graph, to simulate the bidding procedure, we randomly selected 5,000 nodes and randomly assigned them costs from the distribution generated using the MTurk data. We ran several iterations with different budgets ranging from \$100 to \$5000.

Mechanisms

OPS: optimized proportional share mechanism. For the incentive compatible mechanism, we used an optimized version of the mechanisms presented above which allows us to use almost the entire budget in the allocation. Recall that the mechanism presented above uses half the budget, since this way it can ensure the total payments are within budget. Informally, the potential overpayment that imposes the budget reduction is proportional to the effect a selected agent has on the quality of the solution (see the characterization in [31] for more details). Since the network structure, budget and range of bids are known to the mechanism designer, the budget used in the proportional contribution allocation can be optimized accordingly. This optimization step enabled using almost the entire budget in the allocation rule.

Benchmarks

Our main goal in this experimental evaluation is to understand the implication of our lack of knowledge of the agents' costs (we compare the mechanism against the greedy algorithm that has full knowledge of the costs) and whether knowing agents' costs is indeed necessary (we compare against a near-optimal uniform price mechanism that is given access to the costs to establish the optimal reward). In both cases we conducted theoretical comparisons (see Corollary 3.5 and Appendix A) and our goal here is to conduct an empirical

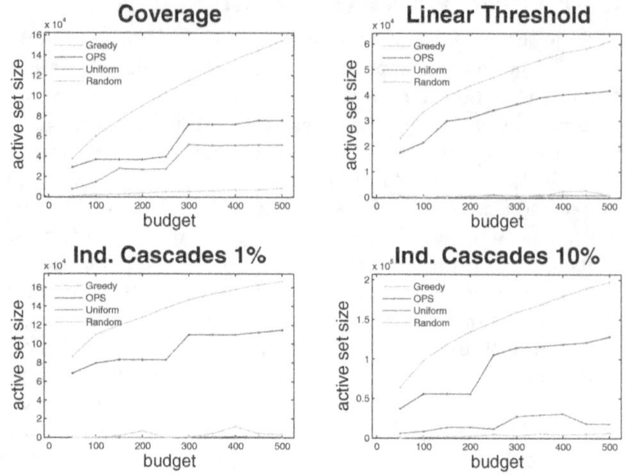

Figure 2: Figures of the different mechanisms with budgets ranging from 50 to 500.

comparison. We further discuss alternative mechanisms in Section 5.

Greedy: algorithmic upper bound. To draw an algorithmic upper bound, we ran the greedy algorithm for maximizing a submodular function under a budget constraint, which is known to work very well both in theory and in practice [20, 24]. Of course, the algorithm is not incentive compatible and assumes full knowledge of the agents' costs.
Uniform-price: cost-oblivious upper-bound. In order to gain insight to whether differential pricing is necessary in practice, we compared against a near-optimal uniform-price mechanism. We describe the mechanism in Appendix A. The mechanism provides an $O(\log n)$ approximation guarantee, which is nearly optimal in the class of uniform price mechanisms (see lower bound in Appendix A). It is important to emphasize that this mechanism represents an upper bound on how well influence maximization algorithms can do assuming uniform rewards are sufficient.

Random: lower bound on algorithmic performance. Finally, we also compared against a random assignment mechanism. The mechanism chooses agents at random and pays them their declared cost. We use this mechanisms to describe how well one can do without any algorithmic machinery. Despite its poor theoretical guarantees, our evaluation shows that in practice this lower bound outperforms the uniform price mechanism in some cases. Note that this mechanism is not incentive compatible since it pays agents their bids. To make the existing mechanism incentive compatible one would need to pay each agent \$20, which gives a uniform price mechanism or alternatively offer random rewards. The random assignment mechanism is an upper bound on both of these mechanisms.

4.3 Results

In Figure 2 we plot the results from the experiments with budgets in the range 50–500. In the Coverage model, for a small budget the proportional share mechanism is comparable with the greedy algorithm. As the budget increases one can witness the growing gap. Similar behavior is apparent when running with larger budgets, as further discussed be-

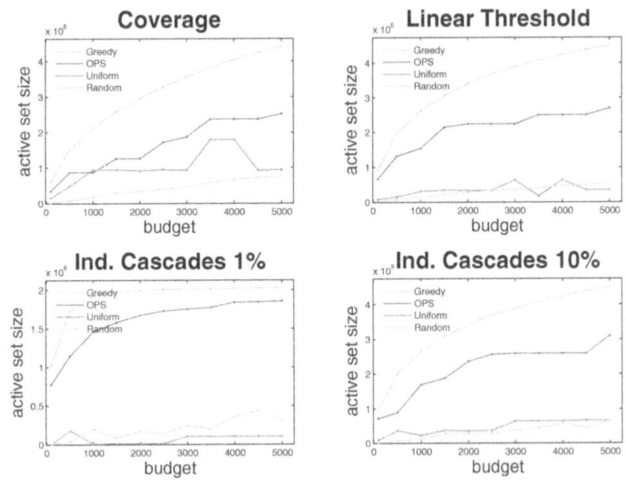

Figure 3: Figures of the different mechanisms with budgets ranging from 100 to 5000.

low. In this model the uniform price mechanism is comparable with the proportional share. Thus, for Coverage it seems that despite its theoretically poor guarantees, the uniform price mechanism seems to be at least a constant fraction from the proportional share and greedy mechanisms. This is mainly due to the fact that the budgets are rather small in comparison to the variance in cost distribution and the marginal value of individuals. Note that in this mechanism in some cases the value in performance decreases while the budget increases. This is due to the fact that at each budget iteration the mechanism uses the given cost distribution to estimate a threshold price, and while the budget may increase, using the value-maximizing bin is not optimal.

In the Independent Cascades model, Figure 2 shows experimental evidence of the poor performance of the uniform price mechanism, in sharp contrast to the Coverage model. This shows that in cases where nodes have larger reachability sets, the uniform price mechanism provides poor guarantees that correspond to its theoretical performance. Furthermore, it seems that this mechanism is not a strict improvement over the random assignment one.

The poor performance of the uniform price mechanism can be further observed in the Independent Cascades models with probabilities set to 10% and the Linear Threshold model in Figure 2 as well as in the experiments with the larger budgets. These results imply that even when one has perfect knowledge about the cost distribution and can extract a near-optimal uniform threshold value, the resulting solution will have poor quality not only in theory but also in practice. We consider this to be a strong argument for the use of differential price mechanisms in these settings.

Observe that the proportional share mechanism exhibits a "step function" behavior: at certain points it levels off, and continues in a steep ascent. This implies that there are budgets which are exhausted well by the mechanism, and exploring these optimal budget points can be crucial when designing viral marketing campaigns.

In Figure 3 we plot the performance of the different mechanisms when the budgets are in the 100–5000 ranges. In the seed graph of 5000 nodes we used, the average degree was 170.3. Recall that in this model the number of nodes influenced is the number of friends that is covered by the selected subset. In this experiment, for almost all of the different budgets, the performance of the mechanisms had the same ordering: greedy, proportional share, uniform price and the random assignment. As one may expect the random assignment mechanism follows an almost perfect linear increase in performance as the budget increases. While the proportional share mechanism dominates the uniform price method, the gap is less dramatic in this model.

When comparing against the greedy benchmark, it seems that in this model, as the budget increases, the gap between the two mechanisms grows. The analysis in Lemma 3.1 guarantees that if the contribution of the agent with highest influence is not greater than the rest, the gap between the two mechanisms will converge to a factor of two. Interestingly, this gap is almost achieved when the budget is 5000. Since the proportional share solution is a subset of the greedy solution, this effect implies that the "least valuable" half of the greedy solution is as valuable as the "most valuable" half. In the Coverage model on this graph there is little overlap between the nodes' reachability sets, which can explain this phenomenon. This effect implies that the budget is well exhausted. To test this we applied the same experiment in this model with larger budgets and discovered that the ratios begin to shrink at a budget of about 10000. In the other influence models, the gap between the greedy and the proportional share mechanisms is relatively small.

5. DISCUSSION

In this paper we presented mechanisms that incentivize individuals to become early adopters in some of the well-studied models of influence maximization. The negative results presented here for uniform-price mechanisms suggest that differential price mechanisms are necessary.

An alternative to the bidding approach used here would be *posted price* mechanisms, where agents receive take-it-or-leave-it offers, and the mechanism can adjust its offers based on their responses. Such mechanisms are by default incentive compatible. The positive results we presented here can serve as foundations for natural next steps in this direction.

In our experimental evaluation, to compensate for the lack of data on agents' costs, we simulated a competition on Mechanical Turk. Ideally, we would have used data in which the network also includes agent's costs, though we are not aware of any publicly available data sets. As discussed above however, the lack of correlation between costs and number of friends leads us to believe this approach produces a representative data set, at a relatively low cost. We believe similar methodologies can be used in the future.

Lastly, it seems that beyond the scope of influence maximization, mechanism design can be useful in data mining. The emergence of crowdsourcing and user-generated content on the web present challenges that are similar to the ones addressed in this work, and it seems that incentive-based mechanisms can become an important addition to the arsenal of powerful techniques in the data mining realm.

6. ACKNOWLEDGMENTS

The author was supported by the Microsoft Research graduate student fellowship and the Facebook fellowship.

7. REFERENCES

[1] Mechanical turk. In *https://www.mturk.com/*.

[2] A. A. Ageev and M. Sviridenko. Pipage rounding: A new method of constructing algorithms with proven performance guarantee. *J. Comb. Optim.*, 8(3):307–328, 2004.

[3] D. Arthur, R. Motwani, A. Sharma, and Y. X. 0002. Pricing strategies for viral marketing on social networks. In *WINE*, pages 101–112, 2009.

[4] E. Bakshy, J. M. Hofman, W. A. Mason, and D. J. Watts. Everyone's an influencer: quantifying influence on twitter. In *WSDM*, 2011.

[5] N. Chen. On the approximability of influence in social networks. In *SODA*, pages 1029–1037, 2008.

[6] N. Chen, N. Gravin, and P. Lu. On the approximability of budget feasible mechanisms. 2011.

[7] S. Dobzinski, C. Papadimitriou, and Y. Singer. Mechanisms for complement-free procurement. In *EC*, 2011.

[8] P. Domingos and M. Richardson. Mining the network value of customers. In *KDD*, pages 57–66, 2001.

[9] P. Dütting, M. Henzinger, and I. Weber. How much is your personal recommendation worth? In *WWW*, pages 1085–1086, 2010.

[10] E. Even-Dar and A. Shapira. A note on maximizing the spread of influence in social networks. *Inf. Process. Lett.*, 111(4):184–187, 2011.

[11] C. Faloutsos, K. S. McCurley, and A. Tomkins. Fast discovery of connection subgraphs. In *KDD*, pages 118–127, 2004.

[12] M. Gjoka, M. Kurant, C. T. Butts, and A. Markopoulou. Walking in Facebook: A Case Study of Unbiased Sampling of OSNs. In *Proceedings of IEEE INFOCOM '10*, San Diego, CA, March 2010.

[13] M. Gomez-Rodriguez, J. Leskovec, and A. Krause. Inferring networks of diffusion and influence. In *KDD*, pages 1019–1028, 2010.

[14] A. Goyal, F. Bonchi, and L. V. S. Lakshmanan. Learning influence probabilities in social networks. In *WSDM*, pages 241–250, 2010.

[15] N. Haghpanah, N. Immorlica, V. S. Mirrokni, and K. Munagala. Optimal auctions with positive network externalities. In *ACM Conference on Electronic Commerce*, pages 11–20, 2011.

[16] J. D. Hartline, V. S. Mirrokni, and M. Sundararajan. Optimal marketing strategies over social networks. In *WWW*, pages 189–198, 2008.

[17] M. O. Jackson and L. Yariv. Diffusion of behavior and equilibrium properties in network games. *American Economic Review*, 2007.

[18] A. R. Karlin, D. Kempe, and T. Tamir. Beyond VCG: Frugality of truthful mechanisms. In *FOCS*, pages 615–626, 2005.

[19] D. Kempe, J. M. Kleinberg, and É. Tardos. Maximizing the spread of influence through a social network. In *KDD*, pages 137–146, 2003.

[20] S. Khuller, A. Moss, and J. S. Naor. The budgeted maximum coverage problem. *Inf. Process. Lett.*, 70(1):39–45, 1999.

[21] J. Kleinberg and P. Raghavan. Query incentive networks. In *Proc. 46th IEEE Symposium on Foundations of Computer Science*, pages 132–141, 2005.

[22] A. Krause and C. Guestrin. A note on the budgeted maximization of submodular functions. In *Technical Report*, pages CMU- CALD- 0 5 - 1 0 3, 2005.

[23] J. Leskovec, L. A. Adamic, and B. A. Huberman. The dynamics of viral marketing. In *ACM Conference on Electronic Commerce*, pages 228–237, 2006.

[24] J. Leskovec, A. Krause, C. Guestrin, C. Faloutsos, J. M. VanBriesen, and N. S. Glance. Cost-effective outbreak detection in networks. In *KDD*, pages 420–429, 2007.

[25] M. Mathioudakis, F. Bonchi, C. Castillo, A. Gionis, and A. Ukkonen. Sparsification of influence networks. In *KDD*, 2011.

[26] E. Mossel and S. Roch. On the submodularity of influence in social networks. In *STOC*, pages 128–134, 2007.

[27] E. Mossel and G. Schoenebeck. Reaching consensus on social networks. In *ICS*, pages 214–229, 2010.

[28] R. Myerson. Optimal auction design. *Mathematics of Operations Research*, 6(1), 1981.

[29] G. L. Nemhauser, L. A. Wolsey, and M. L. Fisher. An analysis of approximations for maximizing submodular set functions ii. *Math. Programming Study 8*, pages 73–87, 1978.

[30] M. Richardson and P. Domingos. Mining knowledge-sharing sites for viral marketing. In *KDD*, pages 61–70, 2002.

[31] Y. Singer. Budget feasible mechanisms. In *FOCS*, pages 765–774, 2010.

[32] Y. Singer and M. Mittal. Mechanisms for online labor markets. In *Workshop on Human Computation*, 2011.

[33] J. Yang and S. Counts. Predicting the speed, scale, and range of information diffusion in twitter. In *ICWSM*, 2010.

APPENDIX

A. BOUNDS ON UNIFORM PRICES

THEOREM A.1. *Even for $f(S) = \sum_{i \in S} f(a_i)$ no uniform-price mechanism can approximate better than $\Omega(\frac{\log n}{\log(\log n)})$.*

PROOF. Consider the instance in which $c_i = f(a_i) = 1/i$ for all $i \in [n]$ and we have a budget of $B = \log n$. For any uniform price mechanism that uses the price p, the solution will include $\lfloor \log n/p \rfloor$ items. The value from this will be:

$$\sum_{i=1/p}^{\log n/p} 1/i = \sum_{i=1}^{\log n/p} 1/i - \sum_{i=1}^{1/p} 1/i = O(\log(\log n))$$

Note that the optimal solution which pays each agent her declared cost has value $O(\log n)$. □

A Near-optimal Uniform Price Mechanism. The algorithm divides the agents into bins based on their cost, where an agent i is binned in bin j if her cost is between $B/2^j$ and $B/2^{j+1}$, and uses the greedy algorithm to find the optimal solution in each bin. The bin that returns the highest value is used as the optimal uniform price. It is easy to show that this algorithm is a $O(\log n)$ approximation.

Inferring Social Ties across Heterogeneous Networks

Jie Tang
Department of Computer Science
Tsinghua University
Beijing 100084, China
jietang@tsinghua.edu.cn

Tiancheng Lou
Institute for Interdisciplinary Information Sciences
Tsinghua University
Beijing 100084, China
ltc08@tsinghua.edu.cn

Jon Kleinberg
Department of Computer Science
Cornell University
Ithaca NY 14853
kleinber@cs.cornell.edu

ABSTRACT

It is well known that different types of social ties have essentially different influence on people. However, users in online social networks rarely categorize their contacts into "family", "colleagues", or "classmates". While a bulk of research has focused on inferring particular types of relationships in a specific social network, few publications systematically study the generalization of the problem of inferring social ties over multiple heterogeneous networks. In this work, we develop a framework for classifying the type of social relationships by learning across heterogeneous networks. The framework incorporates social theories into a factor graph model, which effectively improves the accuracy of inferring the type of social relationships in a target network by borrowing knowledge from a different source network. Our empirical study on five different genres of networks validates the effectiveness of the proposed framework. For example, by leveraging information from a coauthor network with labeled advisor-advisee relationships, the proposed framework is able to obtain an F1-score of 90% (8-28% improvements over alternative methods) for inferring manager-subordinate relationships in an enterprise email network.

Categories and Subject Descriptors

J.4 [**Social and Behavioral Sciences**]: Miscellaneous; H.2.8 [**Database Management**]: Data Mining; H.3.3 [**Information Search and Retrieval**]: Text Mining

General Terms

Algorithms, Experimentation

Keywords

Inferring social ties, Social network, Predictive model, Social influence analysis

1. INTRODUCTION

Our social networks are complex and consist of many overlapping parts. Nobody exists merely in one social network. People are connected via different types of social ties in different networks. For example, in an enterprise email network, where people are connected by sending/receiving emails to/from others, relationships between people can be categorized into manager-subordinate, colleague, etc.; in a mobile communication network, the relationship types could include family, colleagues, and friends. It is well known that the different types of social ties have essentially different influence on people. A graduate's research topic may be mainly influenced by his or her advisor, while other parts of his everyday life will be more influenced by his close friends. Awareness of these different types of social relationships can benefit many applications. For example, if we could have extracted friendships between users from a mobile communication network, we can leverage the friendships for a "word-of-mouth" promotion of a new product.

However, in most online networks (e.g., Facebook, Twitter, LinkedIn, YouTube, and Slashdot), such information (relationship type) is usually unavailable. Users may easily add links to others by clicking "friend request", "follow" or "agree", but do not often take the time to create labels and maintain their friend list. Indeed, one survey of mobile phone users in Europe shows that only 16% of users have created contact groups on their mobile phones [10, 26]; our preliminary statistics on the LinkedIn data also shows that more than 70% of the connections have not been well labeled. In addition, the availabilities of labeled relationships in different networks are very unbalanced. In some networks, such as Slashdot, it might be easy to collect the labeled relationships (e.g., trust/distrust relationships between users). However, in most other networks, it may be infeasible to obtain the labeled information. A challenging question is: can we leverage the labeled relationships from one network to infer the type of relationships in another totally different network?

Motivating Examples To clearly illustrate the problem, Figure 1 gives an example of inferring social ties across a product-reviewer network and a mobile communication network. In Figure 1, the left sub-figure is the input to our problem: a reviewer network, which consists of reviewers and relationships between reviewers; and a mobile network, which consists of mobile users and their communication relationships (via calling or texting message). The right sub-figure shows the output of our problem: the inferred social ties in the two networks. In the reviewer network, we infer the trust/distrust relationships and in the communication network, we identify friendships, colleagues, and families. The middle of Figure 1 is the component of knowledge transfer for inferring social ties in different networks. This is the key objective of this work. The fundamental challenge is how to bridge the available knowledge from different networks to help infer the different types of social relationships.

The problem is non-trivial and poses a set of unique challenges. First, what are the fundamental factors that form the structure of different networks? Second, how to design a generalized frame-

Permission to make digital or hard copies of all or part of this work for personal or classroom use is granted without fee provided that copies are not made or distributed for profit or commercial advantage and that copies bear this notice and the full citation on the first page. To copy otherwise, to republish, to post on servers or to redistribute to lists, requires prior specific permission and/or a fee.
WSDM'12, February 8–12, 2012, Seattle, Washington, USA.
Copyright 2012 ACM 978-1-4503-0747-5/12/02 ...$10.00.

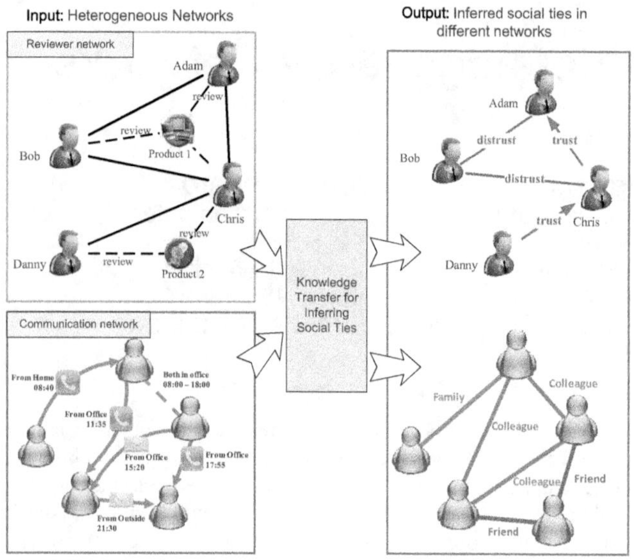

Figure 1: Example of inferring social ties across two heterogeneous networks: a product-reviewer network and a mobile communication network.

work to formalize the problem in a unified way? Third, as real social networks are getting larger with hundreds of millions of nodes, how to scale up the model learning algorithm to adapt to the growth of large real networks?

Results In this work, we aim to conduct a systematic investigation of the problem of inferring social ties across heterogeneous networks. We precisely define the problem and propose a transfer-based factor graph (TranFG) model. The model incorporates social theories into a semi-supervised learning framework, which can be used to transfer supervised information from a source network to help infer social ties in a target network.

We evaluate the proposed model on five different genres of networks: Epinions, Slashdot, Mobile, Coauthor, and Enron. We show that the proposed model can significantly improve the performance (averagely +15% in terms of F1-Measure) for inferring social ties across different networks comparing with several alternative methods. Our study also reveals several interesting phenomena for social science:

- Social balance is satisfied well on friendship (or trust) networks; but not ($< 20\%$ with a large variance) on user communication networks (e.g., mobile communication network).
- Users are more likely (up to +152% higher than chance) to have the same type of relationship with a user who spans a structural hole. Disconnected users have an even higher likelihood.
- It was validated that social status is satisfied in many networks. We further discover that several frequent forms of triads have a similar distribution in different networks (Coauthor and Enron).
- Opinion leaders are more likely (+71%-+84%) to have a higher social status than ordinary users.

Organization Section 2 formulates the problem; Section 3 introduces the data set and our observations over different networks. Section 4 explains the proposed model and describes the algorithm for learning the model; Section 5 gives the experimental setup and Section 6 presents the results; finally, Section 7 discusses related work and Section 8 concludes.

2. PROBLEM DEFINITION

In this section, we first give several necessary definitions and then present the problem formulation. To simplify the explanation, we frame the problem with two social networks: a source network and a target network, although the generalization of this framework to multiple-network setting is straightforward.

Let $G = (V, E^L, E^U, \mathbf{X})$ denote a partially labeled social network, where E^L is a set of labeled relationships and E^U is a set of unlabeled relationships with $E^L \cup E^U = E$; $\mathbf{X}$ is an $|E| \times d$ attribute matrix associated with edges in E with each row corresponding to an edge, each column an attribute, and an element x_{ij} denoting the value of the jth attribute of edge e_i. The label of edge e_i is denoted as $y_i \in \mathcal{Y}$, where $\mathcal{Y}$ is the possible space of the labels (e.g., family, colleague, classmate).

Input: The input to our problem consists of two partially labeled networks G_S (source network) and G_T (target network) with $|E_S^L| \gg |E_T^L|$ (with an extreme case of $|E_T^L| = 0$). Please note that the two networks might be totally different (with different sets of vertexes, i.e., $V_S \cap V_T = \varnothing$, and different attributes defined on edges).

In real social networks, the relationship could be undirected (e.g., friendships in a mobile network) or directed (e.g., manager-subordinate relationships in an enterprise email network). To keep things consistent, we will concentrate on the undirected network. In addition, the label of a relationship may be static (e.g., the family-member relationship) or change over time (e.g., the manager-subordinate relationship). In this work, we focus on static relationships.

Learning Task: Given a source network G_S with abundantly labeled relationships and a target network G_T with a limited number of labeled relationships, the goal is to learn a predictive function $f : (G_T|G_S) \rightarrow Y_T$ for inferring the type of relationships in the target network by leveraging the supervised information (labeled relationships) from the source network.

Without loss of generality, we assume that for each possible type y_i of relationship e_i, the predictive function will output a probability $p(y_i|e_i)$; thus our task can be viewed as obtaining a triple $(e_i, y_i, p(y_i|e_i))$ to characterize each link e_i in the social network. There are several key issues that make our problem formulation different from existing works on social relationship mining [4, 6, 27, 29, 30]. First, the source network and the target network may be very different, e.g., a coauthor network and an email network. What are the fundamental factors that form the structure of the networks? Second, the label of relationships in the target network and that of the source network could be different. How reliably can we infer the labels of relationships in the target network by using the information provided by the source network? Third, as both the source and the target networks are partially labeled, the learning framework should consider not only the labeled information but also the unlabeled information.

3. DATA AND OBSERVATIONS

3.1 Data Collection

We try to find a number of different types of networks to investigate the problem of inferring social ties across heterogenous networks. In this study, we consider five different types of networks: Epinions, Slashdot, Mobile, Coauthor, and Enron. Table 1 lists statistics of the five networks. All data sets and codes used in this work are publicly available.[1]

Epinions is a network of product reviewers. Each user on the site can post a review on any product and other users would rate the review with trust or distrust. In this data, we created a network of reviewers connected with trust and distrust relationships. The data set consists of 131,828 nodes (users) and 841,372 edges, of which about 85.0% are trust links. 80,668 users received at least one trust or distrust edge. Our goal on this data set is to infer the trust relationships between users.

Slashdot is a network of friends. Slashdot is a site for sharing technology related news. In 2002, Slashdot introduced the Slashdot Zoo which allows users to tag each other as "friends" (like) or "foes" (dislike). The data set is comprised of 77,357 users and 516,575 edges of which 76.7% are "friend" relationships. Our goal on this data set is to infer the "friend" relationships between users.

Mobile is a network of mobile users. The data set is from [7]. It consists of the logs of calls, blue-tooth scanning data and cell tower IDs of 107 users during about ten months. If two users communicated (by making a call and sending a text message) with each other or co-occurred in the same place, we create an edge between them. In total, the data contains 5,436 edges. Our goal is to infer whether two users have a friend relationship. For evaluation, all users are required to complete an online survey, in which 157 pairs of users are labeled as friends.

Coauthor is a network of authors. The data set, crawled from Arnetminer.org [28], is comprised of 815,946 authors and 2,792,833 coauthor relationships. In this data set, we attempt to infer advisor-advisee relationships between coauthors. For evaluation, we created a smaller ground truth data in the following ways: (1) collecting the advisor-advisee information from the Mathematics Genealogy project[2] and the AI Genealogy project[3]; (2) manually crawling the advisor-advisee information from researchers' homepages. Finally, we have created a data set with 1,534 coauthor relationships, of which 514 are advisor-advisee relationships. The data set was used in [30].

Enron is an email communication network. It consists of 136,329 emails between 151 Enron employees. Two types of relationships, i.e., manager-subordinate and colleague, were annotated between these employees. The data set was provided by [6]. Our goal on this data set is to infer manager-subordinate relationships between users. There are in total 3,572 edges, of which 133 are manager-subordinate relationships.

Please note that for the first three data sets (i.e., Epinions, Slashdot, and Mobile), our goal is to infer undirected relationships (friendships or trustful relationships); while for the other two data sets (i.e., Coauthor and Enron), our goal is to infer directed relationships (the source end has a higher social status than the target end, e.g., advisor-advisee relationships and manager-subordinate relationships).

3.2 Observations

As a first step, we engage in some high-level investigation of how different factors influence the formation of different social ties in different networks. Generally, if we consider inferring particular social ties in a specific network (e.g., mining advisor-advisee relationships from the Coauthor network), we can define domain-specific features and learn a predictive model based on labeled training data. The problem becomes very different, when handling

Table 1: Statistics of five data sets.

Relationship	Dataset	#Nodes	#Edges
Trust	Epinions	131,828	841,372
Friendship	Slashdot	77,357	516,575
Friendship	Mobile	107	5,436
Advisor-advisee	Coauthor	815,946	2,792,833
Manager-subordinate	Enron	151	3,572

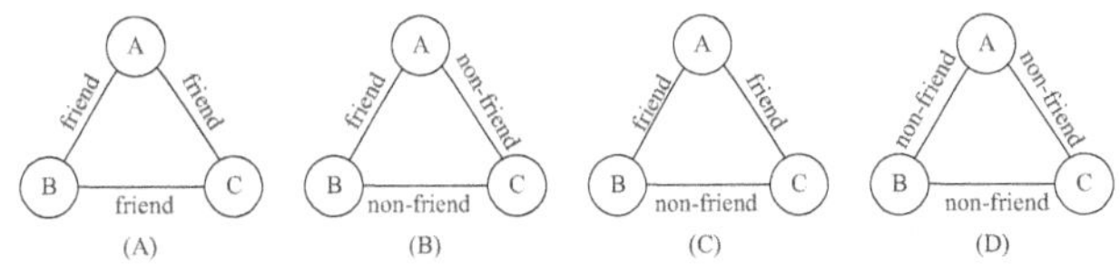

Figure 2: Illustration of structural balance theory. **(A) and (B) are balanced, while (C) and (D) are not balanced.**

multiple heterogeneous networks, as the defined features in different networks may be significantly different. To solve this problem, we connect our problem to several basic social psychological theories and focus our analysis on the network based correlations via the following statistics:

1. *Social balance [8].* How is the social balance property satisfied and correlated in different networks?
2. *Structural hole [3].* Would structural holes have a similar behavior pattern in different networks?
3. *Social status [5, 11, 20].* How do different networks satisfy the properties of social status?
4. *"Two-step flow" [18].* How do different networks follow the "two-step flow" of information propagation?

Social Balance Social balance theory suggests that people in a social network tend to form into a balanced network structure. Figure 2 shows such an example to illustrate the structural balance theory over triads, which is the simplest group structure to which balance theory applies. For a triad, the balance theory implies that either all three of these users are friends or only one pair of them are friends. Figure 3 shows the probabilities of balanced triads of the three undirected networks (Epinions, Slashdot, and Mobile). In each network, we compare the probability of balanced triads based on communication links and that based on friendships (or trust relationships). For example, in the Mobile network, the communication links include making a call or sending a message between users. We find it interesting that different networks have very different balance probabilities based on the communication links, e.g., the balance probability in the mobile network is nearly 7 times higher than that of the slashdot network, while based on friendships (or trustful relationships) the three networks have relatively similar balance probabilities (with a maximum of +28% difference).

Structural Hole Roughly speaking, a person is said to span a *structural hole* in a social network if he or she is linked to people in parts of the network that are otherwise not well connected to one another [3]. Arguments based on structural holes suggest that there is an informational advantage to have friends in a network who do not know each other. A sales manager with a diverse range of connections can be considered as spanning a structural hole, with a number of potentially *weak ties* [9] to individuals in different communities. More generally, we can think about Web sites such as eBay as spanning structural holes, in that they facilitate economic

[1]http://arnetminer.org/socialtieacross/

[2]http://www.genealogy.math.ndsu.nodak.edu

[3]http://aigp.eecs.umich.edu

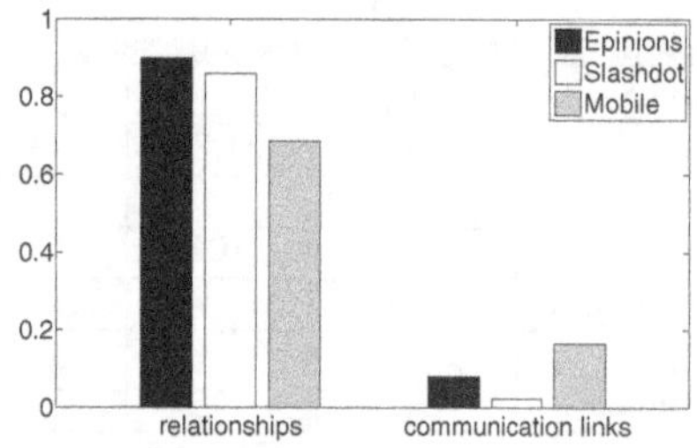

Figure 3: Social balance. **Probabilities of balanced triads in different networks based on communication links and friendships (or trustful relationships). Based on communication links, different networks have very different balance probabilities (e.g., the balance probability in the mobile network is nearly 7 times higher than that of the slashdot network). While based on friendships the three networks have a relatively similar probabilities.**

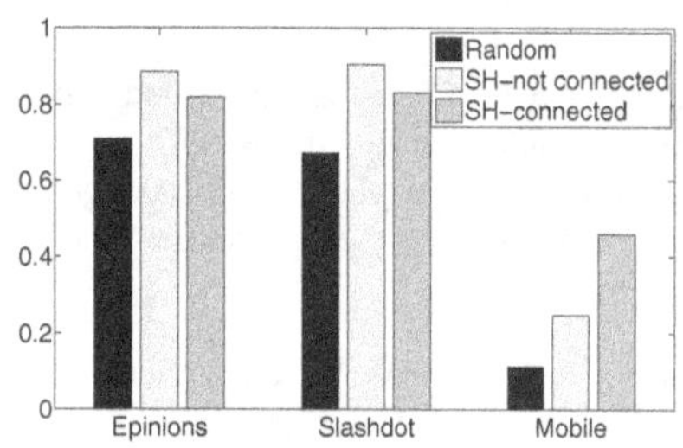

Figure 4: Structural hole. **Probabilities that two connected (or disconnected) users (A and B) have the same type of relationship with user C, conditioned on whether user C spans a structural hole or not. It is clear that (1) users are more likely (averagely +70% higher than chance) to have the same type of relationship with C if C spans a structural hole; and (2) disconnected users are more likely than connected users to have the same type of relationship with a user who spans a structural hole (except the mobile network).**

interactions between people who would otherwise not be able to find each other.

Our idea here is to test if a structural hole tends to have the same type of relationship with the other users. We first employ a simple algorithm to identify structural hole users in a network. Following the informal description of structural holes [3], for each node, we count the number of pairs of neighbors who are not directly connected. All users are ranked based on the number of pairs and the top 1% users[4] with the highest numbers are viewed as structural holes in the network. Figure 4 shows the probabilities that two users (A and B) have the same type of relationship with another user (say C), conditioned on whether user C spans a structural hole or not. We have two interesting observations: (1) users are more likely (on average +70% higher than chance) to have the same type of relationship with C if C spans a structural hole; (2) disconnected users are more likely than connected users to have the same type of relationship with a user classified as spanning a structural hole. One exception is the mobile network, where most mobile users in the data set are university students and thus friends frequently communicate with each other.

Social Status Another social psychological theory is the theory of status [5, 11, 20]. This theory is based on the directed relationship network. Suppose each directed relationship labeled by a pos-

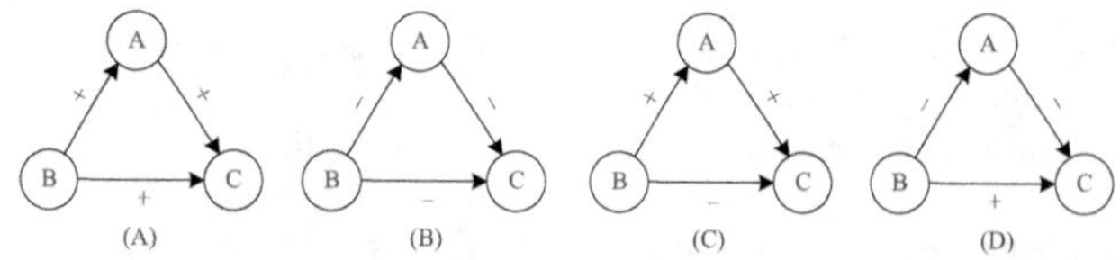

Figure 5: Illustration of status theory. (A) and (B) satisfy the status theory, while (C) and (D) do not satisfy the status theory. Here positive "+" denotes the target node has a higher status than the source node; and negative "-" denotes the target node has a lower status than the source node. In total there are 16 different cases.

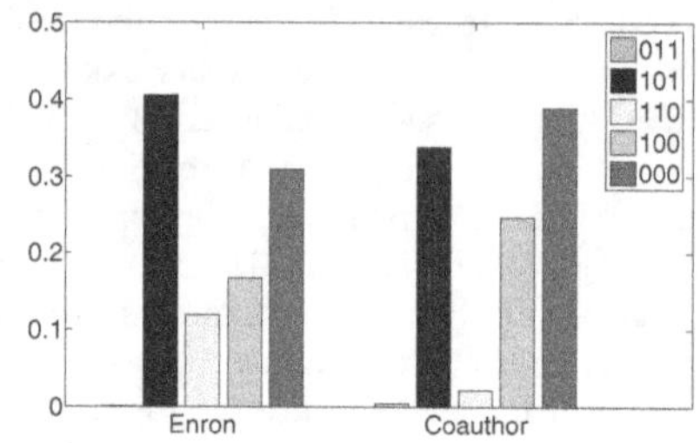

Figure 6: Social status. **Distribution of five most frequent formations of triads with social status. Given a triad (A, B, C), let us use 1 to denote the advisor-advisee relationship and 0 colleague relationship. Thus the number 011 to denote A and B are colleagues, B is C's advisor and A is C's advisor.**

itive sign "+" or a negative sign "-" (where sign "+"/"-" denotes the target node has a higher/lower status than the source node). Then status theory posits that if, in a triangle on three nodes (also called triad), we take each negative edge, reverse its direction, and flip its sign to positive, then the resulting triangle (with all positive edge signs) should be acyclic. Figure 5 illustrates four examples. The first two triangles satisfy the status ordering and the latter two do not satisfy it. We conducted an analysis on the Coauthor and the Enron networks, where we aim to find directed relationships (advisor-advisee and manager-subordinate). We found nearly 99% of triads in the two networks satisfy the social status theory, which was also validated in [20]. We investigate more by looking at the distribution of different forms of triads in the two networks. Specifically, there are in total 16 different forms of triads [20]. We select five most frequent forms of triads in the two networks. For easy understanding, given a triad (A, B, C), we use 1 to denote the advisor-advisee relationship and 0 colleague relationship, and three consecutive numbers 011 to denote A and B are colleagues, B is C's advisor and A is C's advisor. It is striking that although the two networks (Coauthor and Enron) are totally different, they share a similar distribution on the five frequent forms of triads (as plotted in Figure 6).

Opinion Leader The two-step flow theory is first introduced in [18] and further elaborated in literature [14, 15]. The theory suggests that ideas (innovations) usually flow first to *opinion leaders*, and then from them to a wider population. In the enterprise email network, for example, managers may act as opinion leaders to help spread information to subordinates.

Our basic idea here is to examine whether "opinion leaders" are more likely to have a higher social status (manager or advisor) than ordinary users. To do this, we first categorize users into two groups (opinion leaders and ordinary users) by PageRank[5]. With PageRank, according to the network structure, we select as opin-

[4]This is based on the observation that less than 1% of the Twitter users produce 50% of its content [31].

[5]PageRank is an algorithm to estimate the importance of each node in a network [25].

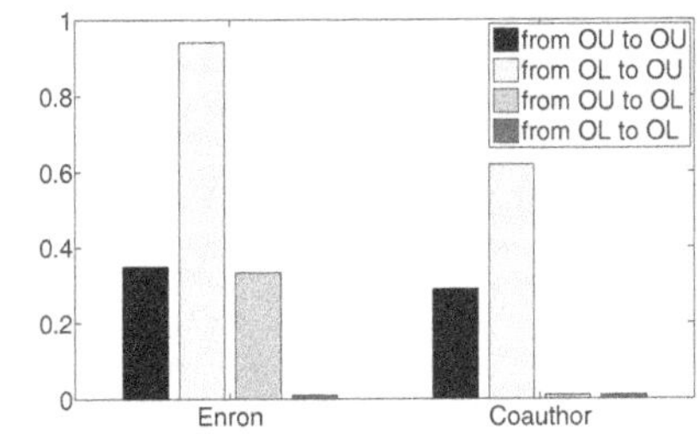

Figure 7: Opinion leader. OL - Opinion leader; OU - Ordinary user. Probability that two types of users have a directed relationship (from higher social status to lower status, i.e., manager-subordinate relationship in Enron and advisor-advisee relationship in Coauthor). It is clear that opinion leaders (detected by PageRank) are more likely to have a higher social-status than ordinary users.

ion leaders the top 1% users who have the highest PageRank scores and the rest as ordinary users. Then, we examine the probabilities that two users (A and B) have a directed social relationship (from higher social-status user to lower social-status user) such as advisor-advisee relationship or manager-subordinate relationship. Figure 7 shows some interesting discoveries. First, in both of the Enron and Coauthor networks, opinion leaders (detected by PageRank) are more likely (+71%-+84%) to have a higher social status than ordinary users. Second and also more interestingly, in Enron, it is likely that ordinary users have a higher social status than opinion leaders. Its average likelihood is much larger (30 times) than that in the Coauthor network. The reason might be in the enterprise email network (Enron), some managers may be inactive, and most management-related communications were done by their assistants.

Summary According to the statistics above, we have the following intuitions:

1. Probabilities of balanced triads based on communication links are very different in different networks, while the balance probabilities based on friendships (or trustful relationships) are similar with each other.
2. Users are more likely (+25%-+152% higher than chance) to have the same type of relationship with a user who spans a structural hole.
3. Most triads (99%) satisfy properties of the social status theory. For the 5 most frequent formations of triads, the Coauthor and the Enron networks share a similar distribution.
4. Opinion leaders are more likely (+71%-+84% higher than chance) to have a higher social status than ordinary users.

4. MODEL FRAMEWORK

We propose a transfer-based factor graph (TranFG) model for learning and predicting the type of social relationships across networks. We first describe the model in the context of a single network, and then explain how to transfer the supervised information provided by one network to another network.

4.1 The Predictive Model

Given a network $G = (V, E^L, E^U, \mathbf{X})$, each relationship (edge) e_i is associated with an attribute vector $\mathbf{x}_i$ and a label y_i indicates the type of the relationship. Let $\mathbf{X} = \{\mathbf{x}_i\}$ and $Y = \{y_i\}$. Then we have the following formulation:

$$P(Y|\mathbf{X}, G) = \frac{P(\mathbf{X}, G|Y)P(Y)}{P(\mathbf{X}, G)} \quad (1)$$

Here, G denotes all forms of network information. This probabilistic formulation indicates that labels of edges depend on not only local attributes associated with each edge, but also the structure of the network. According to Bayes' rule, we have

$$P(Y|\mathbf{X}, G) = \frac{P(\mathbf{X}, G|Y)P(Y)}{P(\mathbf{X}, G)} \propto P(\mathbf{X}|Y) \cdot P(Y|G) \quad (2)$$

where $P(Y|G)$ represents the probability of labels given the structure of the network and $P(\mathbf{X}|Y)$ denotes the probability of generating attributes $\mathbf{X}$ associated to all edges given their labels Y. We assume that the generative probability of attributes given the label of each edge is conditionally independent, thus we have

$$P(Y|\mathbf{X}, G) \propto P(Y|G) \prod_i P(\mathbf{x}_i|y_i) \quad (3)$$

where $P(\mathbf{x}_i|y_i)$ is the probability of generating attributes $\mathbf{x}_i$ given the label y_i. Now, the problem is how to instantiate the probability $P(Y|G)$ and $P(\mathbf{x}_i|y_i)$. In principle, they can be instantiated in different ways, for example by the Bayesian theory or Markov random fields. In this work, we choose the latter. Based on Markov random fields, for any node v_i, the conditional property holds: $P(y_i|G\backslash v_i) = P(y_i|NB(i))$, where $NB(i)$ are neighborhood of y_i in the graph G. The Hammersley-Clifford theorem [12] tells us that the probability of a Markov random field is equivalent to a Gibbs distribution which is factorized into positive function defined on cliques $\{Y_c\}$ that cover all the nodes and edges of G. Thus the two probabilities in Eq. 3 can be rewritten as:

$$P(\mathbf{x}_i|y_i) = \frac{1}{Z_1} \exp\{\sum_{j=1}^{d} \alpha_j g_j(x_{ij}, y_i)\} \quad (4)$$

$$P(Y|G) = \frac{1}{Z_2} \exp\{\sum_c \sum_k \mu_k h_k(Y_c)\} \quad (5)$$

where Z_1 and Z_2 are normalization factors. Eq. 4 indicates that we define a feature function $g_j(x_{ij}, y_i)$ for each attribute x_{ij} associated with edge e_i and α_j is the weight of the jth attribute. It can be defined as either a binary function or a real-valued function. For example, for inferring advisor-advisee relationships from the publication network, we can define a real-valued feature function as the difference of years when authors v_i and v_j respectively published his first paper. In Eq. 5, we define a set of correlation feature functions $\{h_k(Y_c)\}_k$ over each clique Y_c in the network. Here μ_k is the weight of the kth correlation feature function. The simplest clique is an edge, thus a feature function $h_k(y_i, y_j)$ can be defined as the correlation between two edges (e_i, e_j), if the two edges share a common end node. We also consider triads as cliques in the TranFG model, in that several social theories we discussed in §3 are based on triads.

If we are given a single network G with labeled information Y, learning the predictive model is to estimate a parameter configuration $\theta = (\{\alpha\}, \{\mu\})$ to maximize the log-likelihood objective function $\mathcal{O}(\theta) = \log P_\theta(Y|\mathbf{X}, G)$, i.e.,

$$\theta^\star = \arg\max \mathcal{O}(\theta) \quad (6)$$

4.2 Learning across Heterogeneous Networks

We now turn to discuss how to learn the predictive model with two heterogeneous networks (a source network G_S and a target network G_T). Straightforwardly, we can define two separate objective functions for the two networks. The challenge is then how to bridge the two networks, so that we can transfer the labeled information from the source network to the target network. As the source and target networks may be from arbitrary domains, it is difficult to define correlations between them based on prior knowledge.

To this end, we propose a transfer-based factor graph (TranFG) model. Our idea is based on the fact that the social theories we discussed in §3 are general over all networks. Intuitively, we can leverage the correlation in the extent to which different networks satisfy each of the social theories to transfer the knowledge across networks. In particular, for social balance, we define triad based features to denote the proportion of different balanced triangles in a network; for structural hole, we define edge correlation based features, i.e., correlation between two relationships e_i and e_j; for social status, we define features over triads to respectively represent the probabilities of the seven most frequent formations of triads; for opinion leaders, we define features over each edge.

Finally, by incorporating the social theories into our predictive model, we define the following log-likelihood objective function over the source and the target networks:

$$\begin{aligned}\mathcal{O}(\alpha, \beta, \mu) &= \mathcal{O}_S(\alpha, \mu) + \mathcal{O}_T(\beta, \mu) \\ &= \sum_{i=1}^{|V_S|}\sum_{j=1}^{d} \alpha_j g_j(x_{ij}^S, y_i^S) + \sum_{i=1}^{|V_T|}\sum_{j=1}^{d'} \beta_j g'_j(x_{ij}^T, y_i^T) \\ &\quad + \sum_k \mu_k(\sum_{c\in G_S} h_k(Y_c^S) + \sum_{c \in G_T} h_k(Y_c^T)) \\ &\quad - \log Z\end{aligned} \tag{7}$$

where d and d' are numbers of attributes in the source network and the target network respectively. In this objective function, the first term and the second term respectively define the likelihood over the source network and the target network; while the third term defines the likelihood over common features defined in the two networks. The common feature functions are defined according to the social theories. Such a definition implies that attributes of the two networks can be entirely different as they are optimized with different parameters $\{\alpha\}$ and $\{\beta\}$, while the information transferred from the source network to the target network is the importance of common features that are defined according to the social theories. Finally, we define four (real-valued) balance based features, seven (real-valued) status based features, four (binary) features for opinion leader and six (real-valued) correlation features for structural hole. More details about feature function are given in Appendix.

Model Learning and Inferring The last issue is to learn the TranFG model and to infer the type of unknown relationships in the target network. Learning the TranFG model is to estimate a parameter configuration $\theta = (\{\alpha\}, \{\beta\}, \{\mu\})$ to maximize the log-likelihood objective function $\mathcal{O}(\alpha, \beta, \mu)$. We use a gradient decent method (or a Newton-Raphson method) to solve the objective function. We use μ as the example to explain how we learn the parameters. Specifically, we first write the gradient of each μ_k with regard to the objective function:

$$\begin{aligned}\frac{\mathcal{O}(\theta)}{\mu_k} &= \mathbb{E}[h_k(Y_c^S) + h_k(Y_c^T)] \\ &\quad - \mathbb{E}_{P_{\mu_k}(Y_c|\mathbf{X}_S, \mathbf{X}_T, G_S, G_T)}[h_k(Y_c^S) + h_k(Y_c^T)]\end{aligned} \tag{8}$$

Input: a source network G_S, a target network G_T, and the learning rate η
Output: estimated parameters $\theta = (\{\alpha\}, \{\beta\}, \{\mu\})$
Initialize $\theta \leftarrow 0$;
Perform statistics according to social theories;
Construct social theories based features $h_k(Y_c)$;
repeat
- **Step 1:** Perform LBP to calculate marginal distribution of unknown variables in the source network $P(y_i|x_i, G_S)$;
- **Step 2:** Perform LBP to calculate marginal distribution of unknown variables in the target network $P(y_i|x_i, G_T)$;
- **Step 3:** Perform LBP to calculate the marginal distribution of clique c, i.e., $P(y_c|\mathbf{X}_c^S, \mathbf{X}_c^T, G_S, G_T)$;
- **Step 4:** Calculate the gradient of μ_k according to Eq. 8 (for α_j and β_j with a similar formula);
- **Step 5:** Update parameter θ with the learning rate η:

$$\theta_{\text{new}} = \theta_{\text{old}} + \eta \cdot \frac{\mathcal{O}(\theta)}{\theta}$$

until *Convergence*;

Algorithm 1: Learning algorithm for TranFG.

where $\mathbb{E}[h_k(Y_c^S) + h_k(Y_c^T)]$ is the expectation of factor function $h_k(Y_c^S) + h_k(Y_c^T)$ given the data distribution (i.e., the average value of the factor function $h_k(Y_c)$ over all triads in the source and the target networks); and the second term $\mathbb{E}_{P_{\mu_k}(Y_c|\mathbf{X}_S, \mathbf{X}_T, G_S, G_T)}[\cdot]$ is the expectation under the distribution $P_{\mu_k}(Y_c|\mathbf{X}_S, \mathbf{X}_T, G_S, G_T)$ given by the estimated model. Similar gradients can be derived for parameter α_j and β_j.

As the graphical structure can be arbitrary and may contain cycles, we use loopy belief propagation (LBP) [23] to approximate the gradients. It is worth noting that in order to leverage the unlabeled relationships, we need to perform the LBP process twice in each iteration, one time for estimating the marginal distribution of unknown variables $y_i =?$ and the other time for marginal distribution over all cliques. Finally with the gradient, we update each parameter with a learning rate η. The learning algorithm is summarized in Algorithm 1. We see that in the learning process, the algorithm uses an additional loopy belief propagation to infer the label of unknown relationships. After learning, all unknown relationships are assigned with labels that maximize the marginal probabilities.

5. EXPERIMENTAL SETUP

The proposed framework is very general and can be applied to many different networks. For experiments, we consider five different types of networks: Epinions, Slashdot, Mobile, Coauthor, and Enron. On the first three networks (Epinions, Slashdot, and Mobile), our goal is to infer undirected relationships (e.g., friendships), while on the other two networks (Coauthor and Enron), the goal is to infer directed relationships (e.g., advisor-advisee relationships).

Comparison Methods We compare the following methods for inferring the type of social relationships.

SVM: similar to the logistic regression model used in [19], SVM uses attributes associated with each edge as features to train a classification model and then employs the classification model to predict edges' labels in the test data set. For SVM, we employ SVM-light.

CRF: it trains a conditional random field [17] with attributes associated with each edge and correlations between edges.

PFG: the method is also based on CRF, but it employs the unla-

Table 2: Performance comparison of different methods for inferring friendships (or trustful relationships). (S) indicates the source network and (T) the target network. For the target network, we use 40% of the labeled data in training and the rest for test.

Data Set	Method	Prec.	Rec.	F1-score
Epinions (S) to Slashdot (T) (40%)	SVM	0.7157	**0.9733**	0.8249
	CRF	0.8919	0.6710	0.7658
	PFG	0.9300	0.6436	0.7607
	TranFG	**0.9414**	0.9446	**0.9430**
Slashdot (S) to Epinions (T) (40%)	SVM	0.9132	**0.9925**	0.9512
	CRF	0.8923	0.9911	0.9393
	PFG	**0.9954**	0.9787	**0.9870**
	TranFG	**0.9954**	0.9787	**0.9870**
Epinions (S) to Mobile (T) (40%)	SVM	0.8983	0.5955	0.7162
	CRF	0.9455	0.5417	0.6887
	PFG	**1.0000**	0.5924	0.7440
	TranFG	0.8239	**0.8344**	**0.8291**
Slashdot (S) to Mobile (T) (40%)	SVM	0.8983	0.5955	0.7162
	CRF	0.9455	0.5417	0.6887
	PFG	**1.0000**	0.5924	0.7440
	TranFG	0.7258	**0.8599**	**0.7872**

beled data to help learn the predictive model. The method is proposed in [29].

TranFG: the proposed approach, which leverages the label information from the source network to help infer the type of relationship in the target network.

We also compare with the method TPFG proposed in [30] for mining advisor-advisee relationships in the publication network. This method is domain-specific and thus we only compare with it on the Coauthor network.

In all experiments, we use the same feature definitions for all methods. On the Coauthor network, we do not consider some domain-specific correlation features[6].

Evaluation Measures To quantitatively evaluate the performance of inferring the type of social relationships, we conducted experiments with different pairs of (source and target) networks, and evaluated the approaches in terms of Precision, Recall and F1-Measure.

All codes were implemented in C++, and all experiments were performed on a PC running Windows 7 with Intel (R) Core (TM) 2 CPU 6600 (2.4GHz) and 4GB memory. It took about 1-30 minutes to train the TranFG model over different data sets (e.g., 30 minutes for learning over the Epinions and the Slashdot networks). For incorporating social balance and social status into the TranFG model, we need count all triads in the source and the target networks. We design an efficient linear algorithm[1], which takes 1-5 minutes to enumerate all triads for the five networks.

6. RESULTS AND ANALYSIS

We first evaluate the inferring accuracy of the proposed approach and then analyze how social theories help improve the inferring performance. Finally, we give a qualitative case study to further demonstrate the effectiveness of the proposed approach.

6.1 Inferring Accuracy Analysis

We compare the performance of the four methods for inferring friendships (or trustful relationships) on four pairs of networks:

[6]We conducted experiments, but found that those features will lead to overfitting.

Table 3: Performance comparison of different methods for inferring directed relationships (the source end has a higher social status than the target end). (S) indicates the source network and (T) the target network. For the target network, we use 40% of labeled data in training and the rest for test.

Data Set	Method	Prec.	Rec.	F1-score
Coauthor (S) to Enron (T) (40%)	SVM	0.9524	0.5556	0.7018
	CRF	0.9565	0.5366	0.6875
	PFG	**0.9730**	0.6545	0.7826
	TranFG	0.9556	**0.7818**	**0.8600**
Enron (S) to Coauthor (T) (40%)	SVM	0.6910	0.3727	0.4842
	CRF	**1.0000**	0.3043	0.4666
	PFG	0.9916	0.4591	0.6277
	TPFG	0.5936	**0.7611**	0.6669
	TranFG	0.9793	0.5525	**0.7065**

Epinions (S) to Slashdot (T), Slashdot (S) to Epinions (T), Epinions (S) to Mobile (T), and Slashdot (S) to Mobile (T).[7] In all experiments, we use 40% of the labeled data in the target network for training and the rest for test. For transfer, we consider the labeled information in the source network. Table 2 lists the performance of the different methods on the four test cases. Our approach shows better performance than the three alternative methods. We conducted sign tests for each result, which shows that all the improvements of our approach TranFG over the three methods are statistically significant ($p \ll 0.01$).

Table 3 shows the performance of the four methods for inferring directed relationships (the source end has a higher social status than the target end) on two pairs of networks: Coauthor (S) to Enron (T) and Enron (S) to Coauthor (T). We use the same experimental setting as that for inferring friendships on the four pairs of networks, i.e., taking 40% of the labeled data in the target network for training and the rest for test, while for transfer, analogously, we consider the labeled information from the source network. We see that by leveraging the supervised information from the source network, our method clearly improves the performance (about 15% by F1-score on Enron and 10% on Coauthor).

The method PFG can be viewed as a non-transferable counterpart of our method, which does not consider the labeled information from the source network. From both Table 2 and Table 3, we can see that with the transferred information, our method can clearly improve the relationship categorization performance. Another phenomenon is that PFG has a better performance than the other two methods (SVM and CRF) in most cases. PFG could leverage the unlabeled information in the target network, thus enhances the inferring performance. The only exception is the case of Epinions (S) to Slashdot (T), where it seems that users in Slashdot have a relatively consistent pattern, thus a classification based method (SVM) with only general features (e.g., in-degree, out-degree, and number of common neighbors) can achieve very high performance.

Factor contribution analysis We now analyze how different social theories (social balance, social status, structural hole, and two-step flow (opinion leader)) can help infer social ties. For inferring friendships, we consider social balance (SB) and structural hole (SH) based transfer and for inferring directed friendships, we consider social status (SS) and opinion leader (OL) based transfer.

[7]We did try to use Mobile as the source network and Slashdot/Epinions as the target network. However as the size of Mobile is much smaller than the other two networks, the performance was considerably worse.

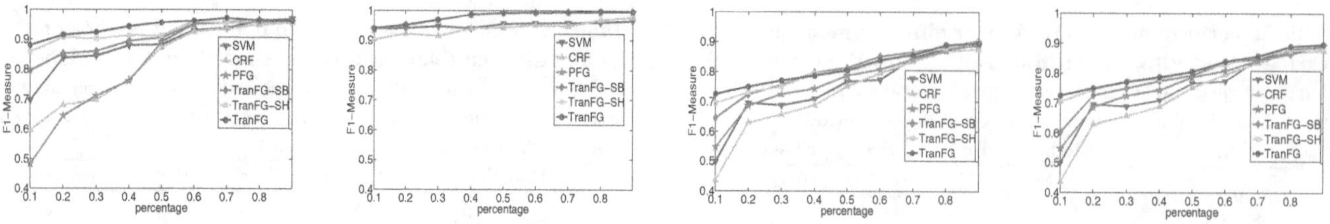

(a) Epinions-to-Slashdot (b) Slashdot-to-Epinions (c) Epinions-to-Mobile (d) Slashdot-to-Mobile

Figure 9: Performance of inferring friendships with and w/o the balance based transfer by varying the percent of labeled data in the target network.

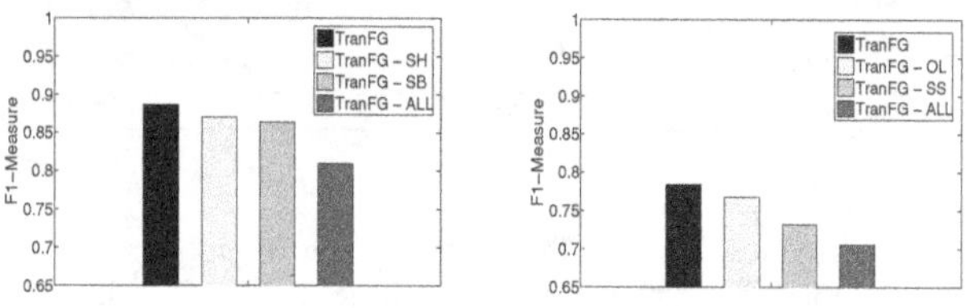

(a) Friendship (b) Directed

Figure 8: Factor contribution analysis. TranFG-SH denotes our TranFG model by ignoring the structural hole based transfer. TranFG-SB stands for ignoring the structural balance based transfer. TranFG-OL stands for ignoring the opinion leader based transfer and TranFG-SS stands for ignoring social status based transfer.

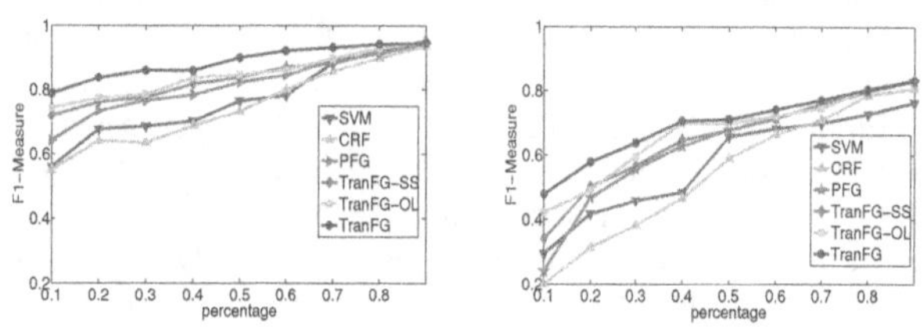

(a) Coauthor-to-Enron (b) Enron-to-Coauthor

Figure 10: Performance of inferring directed relationship with and w/o the status based transfer by varying the percent of labeled data in the target network.

Here we examine the contribution of the different factors defined in our TranFG model. Figure 8 shows the average F1-Measure score over the different networks, obtained by the TranFG model for inferring friendships and directed relationships. In particular, TranFG-SB represents TranFG without social balance based features and TranFG-All denotes that we remove all the transfer features. It can be clearly observed that the performance drops when ignoring each of the factors. We can also see that for inferring friendships the social balance is a bit more useful than structural hole, and for inferring directed relationships the social status factor is more important than the factor of opinion leader. The analysis also confirms that our method works well (further improvement is obtained) when combining different social theories.

Social balance and structural hole based transfer. We present an in-depth analysis on how the social balance and structural hole based transfer can help by varying the percent of labeled training data in the target network. We see that in all cases except Slashdot-to-Epinions, clear improvements can be obtained by using the social balance and structural hole based transfer, when the labeled data in the target network is limited ($\leq 50\%$). Indeed, in some case such as Epinions-to-Slashdot, with merely 10% of the labeled relationships in Slashdot, our method can obtain a good performance (88% by F1-score). Without transfer, the best performance is only 70% (obtained by SVM). We also find that structural balance based transfer is more helpful than structural hole based transfer for inferring friendships in most cases with various percents of labeled relationships. This result is consistent with what we obtained in the factor contribution analysis.

A different phenomenon is found in the case of Slashdot-to-Epinions, where all methods can obtain a F1-score of 94% with only 10% of the labeled data. The knowledge transfer seems not helpful. By a careful investigation, we found simply with those features (Cf. Appendix for details) defined on the edges, we could achieve a high performance (about 90%). The structure information indeed helps, but the gained improvement is limited.

Social status and opinion leader based transfer. Figure 10 shows an analysis for inferring directed relationships on the two cases (Enron-to-Coauthor and Coauthor-to-Enron). Here, we focus on testing how social status and opinion leader based transfer can help infer the type of relationships by varying the percent of labeled relationships in the target network. In both cases (Coauthor-to-Enron and Enron-to-Coauthor), the TranFG model achieves consistent improvements. For example, when there is only 10% of labeled advisor-advisee relationships in the Coauthor network, without considering the status and opinion leader based transfer, the F1-score is only 24%. By leveraging the status and opinion leader based transfer from the email network (Enron), the score is doubled (47%). Moreover, we find that the social status based transfer is more helpful than the opinion leader based transfer with various percents of the labeled data.

6.2 Case Study

Now we present a case study to demonstrate the effectiveness of the proposed model. Figure 11 shows an example generated from our experiments. It represents a portion of the Coauthor network. Black edges and arrows respectively denote labeled colleague relationships and advisor-advisee relationships in the training data. Colored arrows and edges indicate advisor-advisee and colleagues relationships detected by three methods: SVM, PFG and TranFG, with red color indicating mistake ones. The numbers associated with each author respectively denote the number of papers and the score of h-index.

We investigate more by looking at a specific example. SVM mistakenly classifies three advisor-advisee relationships and two colleague relationships. SVM trains a local classification model without considering the network information. PFG considers the network information as well as the unlabeled data, thus obtains a better result. Our proposed TranFG model further corrects two mistakes ("Fait-Leonardi" and "Ausiello-Laura") by leveraging properties of

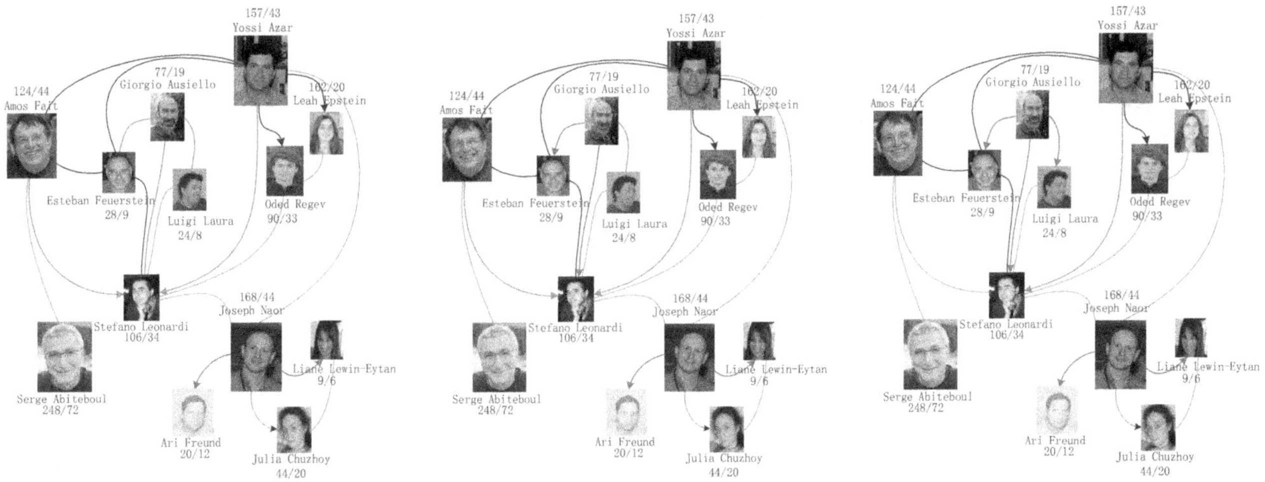

(a) SVM (b) PFG (c) Our approach (TranFG)

Figure 11: Case study. Illustration of inferring advisor-advisee relationships on the Coauthor network. Directed edges indicate advisor relationships, and undirected ones indicate coauthor relationships. Black edges indicate labeled data. Red colored edges indicates wrong predictions.

social status and opinion leader. For example, the results obtained by PFG among "Azar", "Amos" and "Leonardi" form a triad of ("011"). Although it satisfies the property of social status, the probability of such triad is much lower (0.4% vs. 24.6%) than the form ("100"). However, the limitation of the training data leads PFG to result in a bias mistake (5.8% vs. 12.6%). TranFG smoothes the results by transferring knowledge from the source (Enron) network.

7. RELATED WORK

Inferring social ties is an important topic in social network analysis. Liben-Nowell et al. [21] present an unsupervised method for link prediction. Tang et al. [27] propose a topical affinity propagation to quantify the social influence between users. Backstrom et al. [2] propose a supervised random walk algorithm to estimate the strength of social links. Leskovec et al. [19] employ a logistic regression model to predict positive and negative links in online social networks. Hopcroft et al. [13] study the extent to which the formation of a reciprocal relationship can be predicted in a dynamic network. However, most existing works focus on predicting and recommending unknown links in social networks, but ignore the type of relationships.

Recently, there are several works on inferring the meanings of social relationships. Diehl et al. [6] try to identify the manager-subordinate relationships by learning a ranking function. Wang et al. [30] propose an unsupervised probabilistic model for mining the advisor-advisee relationships from the publication network. Crandall et al. [4] investigate the problem of inferring friendship between people from co-occurrence in time and space. Eagle et al. [7] present several patterns discovered in mobile phone data, and try to use these patterns to infer the friendship network. However, these algorithms mainly focus on specific domains, while our model is general and can be applied to different domains. More importantly, our work takes the first step to incorporate social theories for inferring social ties across heterogeneous networks.

Our work is related to link prediction, which is one of the core tasks in social networks. Existing work on link prediction can be broadly grouped into two categories based on the learning methods employed: unsupervised link prediction and supervised link prediction. Unsupervised link predictions usually assign scores to potential links based on the intuition - the more similar the pair of users are, the more likely they are linked. Various similarity measures of users are considered, such as the Adamic and Adar measure [1], the preferential attachment [24], and the Katz measure [16]. A survey of unsupervised link prediction can be found in [21]. Recently, [22] designs a flow based method for link prediction. There are also a few works which employ supervised approaches to predict links in social networks, such as [2, 19]. The main difference between existing work on link prediction and our effort lies in that existing work mainly focuses on one single network, while our proposed model combines social theories (such as structural balance, structural hole, and social status) into a transfer learning framework and can be applied to different domains.

8. CONCLUSION

In this paper, we study the novel problem of inferring social ties across heterogeneous networks. We precisely define the problem and propose a transfer-based factor graph (TranFG) model. The model incorporates social theories into a semi-supervised learning framework, which is used to transfer supervised information from the source network to help infer social ties in the target network. We evaluate the proposed model on five different genres of networks. We show that the proposed model can significantly improve the performance for inferring social ties across different networks comparing with several alternative methods. Our study also reveals several interesting phenomena.

The general problem of inferring social ties represents a new and interesting research direction in social network analysis. There are many potential future directions of this work. First, some other social theories can be further explored and validated for analyzing the formation of different types of social relationships. Next, it is interesting to study how to further correct the inferring mistakes by involving users into the learning process (e.g., via active learning). Another potential issue is to validate the proposed model on some other social networks.

Acknowledgements Jie Tang is supported by the Natural Science Foundation of China (No. 61073073), Chinese National Key Foundation Research (No. 60933013, No.61035004). Tiancheng Lou is supported in part by the National Basic Research Program of China Grant 2011CBA00300, 2011CBA00301, the National Natural Science Foundation of China Grant 61033001, 61061130540, 61073174. Jon Kleinberg has been supported in part by a Google Research Grant, a Yahoo Research Alliance Grant, and NSF grants IIS-0910664, CCF-0910940, and IIS-1016099.

9. REFERENCES

[1] L. A. Adamic and E. Adar. Friends and neighbors on the web. *SOCIAL NETWORKS*, 25:211–230, 2001.

[2] L. Backstrom and J. Leskovec. Supervised random walks: predicting and recommending links in social networks. In *WSDM'11*, pages 635–644, 2011.

[3] R. S. Burt. *Structural Holes : The Social Structure of Competition*. Cambridge, Mass.: Harvard University Press, 1995.

[4] D. J. Crandall, L. Backstrom, D. Cosley, S. Suri, D. Huttenlocher, and J. Kleinberg. Inferring social ties from geographic coincidences. *PNAS*, 107:22436–22441, Dec. 2010.

[5] J. A. Davis and S. Leinhardt. The structure of positive interpersonal relations in small groups. In J. Berger, editor, *Sociological Theories in Progress*, volume 2, pages 218–251. Houghton Mifflin, 1972.

[6] C. P. Diehl, G. Namata, and L. Getoor. Relationship identification for social network discovery. In *AAAI*, pages 546–552, 2007.

[7] N. Eagle, A. S. Pentland, and D. Lazer. Inferring social network structure using mobile phone data. *PNAS*, 106(36), 2009.

[8] D. Easley and J. Kleinberg. *Networks, Crowds, and Markets: Reasoning about a Highly Connected World*. Cambridge University Press, 2010.

[9] M. Granovetter. The strength of weak ties. *American Journal of Sociology*, 78(6):1360–1380, 1973.

[10] R. Grob, M. Kuhn, R. Wattenhofer, and M. Wirz. Cluestr: Mobile social networking for enhanced group communication. In *GROUP'09*, 2009.

[11] R. Guha, R. Kumar, P. Raghavan, and A. Tomkins. Propagation of trust and distrust. In *WWW'04*, pages 403–412, 2004.

[12] J. M. Hammersley and P. Clifford. Markov field on finite graphs and lattices. *Unpublished manuscript*, 1971.

[13] J. E. Hopcroft, T. Lou, and J. Tang. Who will follow you back? reciprocal relationship prediction. In *CIKM'11*, 2011.

[14] E. Katz. The two-step flow of communication: an up-to-date report of an hypothesis. *In Enis and Cox(eds.), Marketing Classics*, pages 175–193, 1973.

[15] E. Katz and P. F. Lazarsfeld. *Personal Influence*. The Free Press, New York, USA, 1955.

[16] L. Katz. A new status index derived from sociometric analysis. *Psychometrika*, 18(1):39–43, 1953.

[17] J. D. Lafferty, A. McCallum, and F. C. N. Pereira. Conditional random fields: Probabilistic models for segmenting and labeling sequence data. In *ICML'01*, pages 282–289, 2001.

[18] P. F. Lazarsfeld, B. Berelson, and H. Gaudet. *The people's choice: How the voter makes up his mind in a presidential campaign*. Columbia University Press, New York, USA, 1944.

[19] J. Leskovec, D. Huttenlocher, and J. Kleinberg. Predicting positive and negative links in online social networks. In *WWW'10*, pages 641–650, 2010.

[20] J. Leskovec, D. Huttenlocher, and J. Kleinberg. Signed networks in social media. In *CHI'10*, pages 1361–1370, 2010.

[21] D. Liben-Nowell and J. M. Kleinberg. The link-prediction problem for social networks. *JASIST*, 58(7):1019–1031, 2007.

[22] R. Lichtenwalter, J. T. Lussier, and N. V. Chawla. New perspectives and methods in link prediction. In *KDD'10*, pages 243–252, 2010.

[23] K. P. Murphy, Y. Weiss, and M. I. Jordan. Loopy belief propagation for approximate inference: An empirical study. In *UAI'99*, pages 467–475, 1999.

[24] M. E. J. Newman. Clustering and preferential attachment in growing networks. *Phys. Rev. E*, 64(2):025102, 2001.

[25] L. Page, S. Brin, R. Motwani, and T. Winograd. The pagerank citation ranking: Bringing order to the web. Technical Report SIDL-WP-1999-0120, Stanford University, 1999.

[26] M. Roth, A. Ben-David, D. Deutscher, G. Flysher, I. Horn, A. Leichtberg, N. Leiser, Y. Matias, and R. Merom. Suggesting friends using the implicit social graph. In *KDD'10*, pages 233–242, 2010.

[27] J. Tang, J. Sun, C. Wang, and Z. Yang. Social influence analysis in large-scale networks. In *KDD'09*, pages 807–816, 2009.

[28] J. Tang, J. Zhang, L. Yao, J. Li, L. Zhang, and Z. Su. Arnetminer: Extraction and mining of academic social networks. In *KDD'08*, pages 990–998, 2008.

[29] W. Tang, H. Zhuang, and J. Tang. Learning to infer social ties in large networks. In *ECML/PKDD'11*, 2011.

[30] C. Wang, J. Han, Y. Jia, J. Tang, D. Zhang, Y. Yu, and J. Guo. Mining advisor-advisee relationships from research publication networks. In *KDD'10*, pages 203–212, 2010.

[31] S. Wu, J. M. Hofman, W. A. Mason, and D. J. Watts. Who says what to whom on twitter. In *WWW'11*, pages 705–714, 2011.

Appendix

There are two categories of features. The first category includes local features defined for each specific network, and the second includes transfer features defined based on the social theories. Tables 4-7 give a summary of local feature definitions for the five networks. For a more detailed description of the feature definitions, please refer to literature [6, 7, 19, 29].

For the transfer features, in Epinions, Slashdot and Mobile, we define four (real-valued) balance triad based features and six (real-valued) structural hole based features. In the Coauthor and Enron, we define seven (real-valued) social status based features and four (binary) opinion leader based features.

Table 4: Features defined for edge (v_i, v_j) in Epinions/Slashdot.

Feature	Description
in-degree	$d_{in}(v_i), d_{in}(v_j)$
out-degree	$d_{out}(v_i), d_{out}(v_j)$
total-degree	$d_{in}(v_i) + d_{out}(v_i), d_{in}(v_j) + d_{out}(v_j)$
common neighbors	the total number of common neighbors of v_i and v_j in an undirected sense.

Table 5: Features defined for edge (v_i, v_j) in Mobile.

Feature	Description
Total Proximity	Number of proximity events between a and b
In-Role	Number of proximity events at working place in day time from Monday to Friday
Extra-Role	Number of proximity events at home or elsewhere at night of weekends
Total Communication	Number of communication logs between a and b
Night Call Ratio	The ratio of communication logs at night

Table 6: Features defined for edge (v_i, v_j) in Coauthor. P_i denotes a set of papers published by author v_i.

Feature	Description
paper count	$\|P_i\|, \|P_j\|$
paper ratio	$\|P_i\|/\|P_j\|$
coauthor ratio	$\|P_i \cap P_j\|/\|P_i\|, \|P_i \cap P_j\|/\|P_j\|$
conference coverage	The proportion of the conferences which both v_i and v_j attended among conferences v_j attended.
first-pub-year diff	The difference in year of the first earliest publication of v_i and v_j.

Table 7: Features defined for edge (v_i, v_j) in Enron.

From	Sent-To + CC	From	Sent-To + CC
v_i	v_j	v_j	v_i
v_i	v_k and not v_j	v_j	v_k and not v_i
v_k	v_i and not v_j	v_k	v_j and not v_i
v_k	v_i and v_j		

The Secret Life of Social Links

Hilary Mason
bitly
416 W 13th St. Suite 203
New York, NY
hmason@gmail.com

ABSTRACT

The social web is a messy place! At bitly, we see hundreds of millions of shares and clicks per day—clicks that contain all sorts of wonderful content from lolcats to spacecraft launches. I'll discuss our philosophy, tools, and techniques for looking at the data, and new research opportunities that weren't possible before.

Categories and Subject Descriptors
H.3.5 [On-line Information Services]: *Web-based services*

General Terms:
Experimentation, Human Factors, Measurement

Keywords:
social web, social content

BIOGRAPHY

Hilary Mason is the Chief Scientist at bitly, where she finds sense in vast data sets. Her work involves both pure research and development of product-focused features.

She's also a co-founder of HackNY (hackny.org), a non-profit organization that connects talented student hackers from around the world with startups in NYC.

Hilary recently started the data science blog Dataists (dataists.com) and is a member of hacker collective NYC Resistor.

She has discovered two new species, loves to bake cookies, and asks way too many questions.

Copyright is held by the author/owner(s).
WSDM'12, February 8–12, 2012, Seattle, Washington, USA.
ACM 978-1-4503-0747-5/12/02.

Exploration and Discovery of User-generated Content in Large Information Spaces

Luca Chiarandini*
Web Research Group
Universitat Pompeu Fabra
Tànger, 122-140
Barcelona, Spain
chiarluc@yahoo-inc.com

ABSTRACT

The accumulation of large collections of social media data poses new challenges for the design of exploratory experiences, such as when a user browses through a collection to discover content (*e.g.* exploring photo collections, network of friends, etc). Cardinality and characteristics of the set, together with volatility of the information, resulting from fast and continuous creation, deletion and updating of entries, trigger novel research questions. In this context, we plan to investigate and contribute to the data analysis, and user interface design of exploratory experiences. The proposed approach is an iterative process where analysis and design phases are performed in cycles. The long-term vision is to understand the underlying reasoning in order to be able to automatically replicate it.

Categories and Subject Descriptors

I.2 [**Computing Methodologies**]: Artificial Intelligence; H.5.2 [**Information Systems**]: Information Interfaces and Presentation—*User Interfaces*

General Terms

Design, Human Factors

Keywords

Human Computer Interaction, Data mining, Social media

1. INTRODUCTION

Exploration and discovery of content is a research topic that deals with the traveling through possibly unfamiliar data in order to making sense of it. Nowadays the amount of content is very large and increasing, rendering the problem more challenging, especially in the field of *social media*. Traditional ways of representing information (such as tables, lists, etc.), which have been suitable for a small amount of data, fail to scale. Information representation needs to account for the users' need, inherent capabilities and particular skills.

*Also Yahoo! Research Barcelona

Copyright is held by the author/owner(s).
WSDM'12, February 8–12, 2012, Seattle, Washington, USA.
ACM 978-1-4503-0747-5/12/02.

Good methods for exploring and presenting the content of a collection may help in many ways. Firstly, they help the user understanding how the collection is composed or how it evolves over time. Secondly, in search, it is sometimes hard when not even impossible for the user to formulate the query in the required form (*e.g.* text, keywords); therefore, the user needs to browse through content. In addition, it helps the user not only in finding what she needs but also retrieving content she did not expect but is interested in (*serendipity*). Finally, browsing through a collection can give the *sense of space*, *i.e.* make the user aware of how this is structured and being able to orientate herself in it [3].

During the Ph.D. we plan to investigate how the characteristics of large collections of *user-generated content* could be used in order to design the exploratory experience. The methodology uses techniques from *data mining* and *machine learning* to analyze the data and *human-computer interaction* to design the interaction. We will exploit an iterative approach in which the result of the analysis phase drives the design process. At the same time, collecting data about how users interact with the machine, allows us to trigger again the analytical step.

2. CONTEXT AND RELATED WORK

Morse [7] defined browsing as *search, hopefully serendipitous*). Bawden [1] identifies three kinds of browsing: *a) purposive*, *i.e.* the deliberate seeking for new information in a defined (albeit broad) subject area; *b) capricious*, *i.e.* random examination of material without a definite goal; and *c) exploratory* or *semi-purposive*, *i.e.* in search, quite literally, of inspiration. We will mainly consider the third kind.

Kaplan and Haenlein [6] define social media as *a group of Internet-based applications that build on the ideological and technological foundations of Web 2.0, which allows the creation and exchange of user-generated content.* They use two dimensions for the categorization (Table 1). On the one hand, the categorization considers *media richness* [2], *i.e.* the amount of information they allow to be transmitted in a given time interval. On the other hand, we consider *self-disclosure*, *i.e.* the conscious or unconscious revelation of personal information (*e.g.*, thoughts, feelings, likes, dislikes).

In the context of User Interfaces (UI), many authors devised methods in order to automatically build interfaces and adapt them to different devices. Nichols et al. [8] present a run-time, fully-autonomous UI generator based on a declarative language. More recently, Gajos and Weld [4] describe

		Media-richness		
Self-disclosure		*Low*	*Medium*	*High*
	High	Blogs	Facebook	Virtual social networks (*e.g.* Second life)
	Low	Wikipedia	Youtube	Virtual game worlds

Table 1: Social media categorization with examples for each category.

SUPPLE, which interprets the process of generating the UI as an optimization problem. Several design criteria may be expressed as cost functions. Our work differs from existing solutions under multiple aspects: *a)* the design of the interface is not static but *dynamically adapts* to users' behavior *b)* the goal of the interface is not just accessing or editing the data but should allow the user to browse through the dataset; therefore, the correspondence between the data point and interface is not trivial *c)* in our work, the context is the Web and in particular Social Media applications; this changes many aspects of the interaction (*e.g.* the user may want to read more than write).

3. RESEARCH QUESTIONS

The research task requires the understanding of the two sides of the interaction: *a) Large information spaces*: Which are the characteristics of large content-rich collections? How do they change over time? Understanding this may also suggest new ways of indexing, summarizing or querying the collection as well as give hints about possible UIs and exploration mechanisms. *b) User*: What does the user look for when browsing? Could we model or predict serendipity? What changes in the behavior of the user between browsing and accessing to information (*e.g.* web search, catalog querying, etc.)? User modeling has been extensively analyzed in the context of websites.

In parallel, many questions are related to the *interface* between these two entities: How could we increase the frequency of serendipitous encounters? Could we take into account intuitive knowledge of the user in the design of interfaces? How could dataset and user behavior models enhance the design process? Can UIs adapt to user's behavior to improve usability? Can browsing be a *social* experience?

4. METHODOLOGY

We address two aspects in this thesis: *a) Analysis* (Machine learning and data mining), in order to understand the characteristics of the dataset and model user's behavior *b) Design* (Human-computer interaction), to improve the user experience on the the basis of the results of the previous phase. The results of the analysis are used to extract design guidelines and improve both user experience and interaction mechanism. The integration of an automated data collection mechanisms not only allows us to evaluate the goodness of the method but also to extract information to iterate the process. Whereas in a first moment the iterations are done manually through studies and data mining, we aim at the automation of the process.

This methodology will be applied in different fields to test its generality. We have access to data about heterogeneous websites in the form of click- and pageview-logs (*i.e.* the information about where the user clicks and which pages she views). We plan to apply the analysis/design methodology to: *a) News sites*: portals where users are able to find the latest news, be informed about the happenings in the world or simply browse interesting content *b) Media and document browsing sites*: systems in which users are able to browse or optionally search for informative or multimedia content.

5. CONCLUSION

The Ph.D. research will contribute in settings in which the user browses through and explores a content-rich dataset. Social media is a particularly suitable context for this research since it involves very heterogeneous content and datasets (multimedia data, social network graphs, etc.).

Acknowledgement

This Ph.D. is under the supervision of Dr. Ricardo Baeza-Yates and Dr. Alejandro Jaimes.

References

[1] D. Bawden. Information systems and the stimulation of creativity. *Journal of Information Science*, 12(5):203, 1986.

[2] R. Daft and R. Lengel. Organizational information requirements, media richness and structural design. *Management science*, 32(5):554–571, 1986.

[3] M. Dörk, S. Carpendale, and C. Williamson. The information flaneur: A fresh look at information seeking. In *Proceedings of the 2011 annual conference on Human factors in computing systems*, pages 1215–1224. ACM, 2011.

[4] K. Gajos and D. S. Weld. Supple: automatically generating user interfaces. In *Proceedings of the 9th international conference on Intelligent user interfaces*, IUI '04, pages 93–100, New York, NY, USA, 2004. ACM.

[5] E. Goffman. The presentation of self in everyday life. 1959. *Garden City, NY*, 2002.

[6] A. Kaplan and M. Haenlein. Users of the world, unite! the challenges and opportunities of social media. *Business Horizons*, 53(1):59–68, 2010.

[7] P. Morse. On browsing: the use of search theory in the search for information. *Bulletin of the Operations Research Society of America, Vol. 19 supplement, p.1*, 1971.

[8] J. Nichols, Myers, B. A., M. Higgins, J. Hughes, Harris, T. K., R. Rosenfeld, and M. Pignol. Generating remote control interfaces for complex appliances. In *Proceedings of the ACM Symposium on User Interface Software and Technology*, Papers: infrastructure for ubicomp, pages 161–170, 2002.

[9] J. Short, E. Williams, and B. Christie. *The social psychology of telecommunications.* John Wiley and Sons Ltd, 1976.

[10] R. Spence. A framework for navigation. *International Journal of Human-Computer Studies*, 51(5):919–945, 1999.

Computational Advertising: Leveraging User Interaction & Contextual Factors for Improved Ad Relevance & Targeting

Kushal Dave
Language Technologies Research Centre
International Institute of Information Technology
Hyderabad, India
kushal.dave@research.iiit.ac.in

ABSTRACT

Computational advertising refers to finding the most relevant ads matching a particular context on the web. The core problem attacked in computational advertising (*CA*) is of the match making between the ads and the context.

My research work aims at leveraging various user interaction, ad and advertiser related information and contextual information for improving the relevance, ranking and targeting of ads. The research work focuses on the identification of various factors that contribute in retrieving and ranking the most relevant set of ads that match best with the context. Specifically, information associated with the user, publisher and advertiser is leveraged for this purpose.

Categories and Subject Descriptors

I.2.6 [**Artificial Intelligence**]: Learning—*Induction*; H.1.1 [**Information Systems**]: Models and Principles

General Terms

Algorithm, Experimentation, Performance, Economics

Keywords

Sponsored Search, Viral Marketing, Contextual Advertising

1. INTRODUCTION

The central problem addressed in *CA* is: Retrieving a set of ads that best matches the context (of the page) and then ranking these retrieved ads. Based on the context, *CA* can be divided into following three areas: 1) Sponsored search 2) Contextual advertising 3) Social advertising. *Sponsored search (SS)* refers to the placement of ads on a search results page. 2) *Contextual advertising (ConAd)* deals with the placement of ads on third-party web pages. 3) *Social advertising (SA)* is the newest of all the siblings and it refers to placement of ads on the personalized home pages of the users of the social network.

My research work focuses on exploring various user-level, ad-level and context level factors that can help improve the process of retrieving the most relevant and best matched ads for a context. The first step is identifying such factors for all three areas - *SS*, *ConAd* and *SA*. Next step is to empirically analyze the contribution of all these factors towards better ad retrieval, ranking and targeting.

Copyright is held by the author/owner(s).
WSDM'12, February 8–12, 2012, Seattle, Washington, USA.
ACM 978-1-4503-0747-5/12/02.

2. SPONSORED SEARCH

Sponsored search refers to the placement of a ranked list of ads on the search page contextually matching the user query. Usually, this is done in a two-step fashion. First, an initial set of k ads contextually matching the query are fetched from the database. Next, these k-ads are ranked according to some relevance measure.

Retrieving Relevant Ads: Queries and ads (bid terms) are short fragments of text, hence traditional information retrieval techniques are not sufficient to retrieve a larger pool of relevant ads. In this work, we propose a topic modeling approach to overcome this vocabulary mis-match. Topic models can be a good way to bridge the vocabulary mismatch between the query and the ad. Latent Dirichlet Allocation (LDA) can be used for modeling the latent topics in query and ads. The idea is to first train a model on a set of documents comprising past queries and ads retrieved for those queries. Using this trained model, each query and ad is reduced into low dimensional topic vectors representing their topic distribution. For the LDA model to perform well, it needs comprehensive training data which needs to be carefully crafted to account for the vocabulary gap between the query and ads. This learned model can then be used to transform the test ads and test queries to topical vectors in lower dimension. The ads are augmented using queries similar to the original query to overcome the sparseness of the ad text. Once the expanded query and ads are transformed into topical vectors, retrieving similar ads can be done in various ways: 1. Retrieving relevant ads based on the cosine similarity of the expanded query and the ad text topic vectors. 2. Using a machine learning algorithm to predict the relevance of the ads for a query by considering the topic probabilities as features. 3. Combining LDA with other retrieval techniques like language modeling.

Ranking the Ads: Once the top-k relevant ads are retrieved, the next task deals with ranking these ads. The ranking needs to be done in such a way that it maintains high relevance at the top positions and also maximizes the expected revenue. Keeping this in mind, the ranking is usually done on the product of the bid amount and the relevance of the ad. Relevance of ad usually is derived from several measures like the similarity (both syntactic and semantic) between the ad and the query the popularity of the ad/advertiser and the query. One widely used and largely contributing measure for assessing relevance of an ad for ranking is its click-through rate (CTR). CTR can be calculated from historical click-logs. For new ads, we do not have any historical information. In order to rank these ads in conjunction with the established ads it is very important to accurately predict the CTR for new ads. Most of the earlier work predicted CTR as a function of the ad text only. An ad's CTR can vary across different queries. To account for these differences, it is also important to consider the query associated with the ad in predicting the CTR value. Thus, CTR of an ad is a function of both ad and the query. We performed our experiments on a dataset of about 1.5M unique query-ad pairs from the click log. The prediction model uses following set of features:

Features from Query-ad click graph: These features are based on finding similar ads and queries to the given ad and query. Similar ads and queries are found by representing them as transitional probabilities to ad/query.

Features from Ad Hierarchy: Advertisements on an ad engine are typically maintained in some kind of a hierarchy. For example, a typical hierarchy would contain ads from same advertiser but different business unit organized in different *Accounts*. Within each account, ads from different *Campaigns* can be organized in different campaign sets. Ad groups, Terms and Creative gives more granular hierarchical classification of ads from an advertiser. CTR of other ads in the same group are used as features.

Features from Ad Hierarchy: This set comprises of query-ad syntactic matching features, like textual overlap, query length etc. The model with these features gave a good 28.61% improvement over the baseline (average CTR). Further details on this work can be found at [2].

3. CONTEXTUAL ADVERTISING

Keyword Extraction: The web page content usually contains noise, hence typically advertisement keywords are extracted from the web page text and then the ads are matched against the extracted keywords. We propose a new chunking approach that employs part-of-speech knowledge for selecting candidates from the text. Only these potential advertising keywords can be considered for classification. Using this approach, the average reduction in the number of candidates is found to be 86% in comparison with N-Gram approach. For a detailed explanation please refer [3].

Topic modeling and External resources: We propose to leverage topic modeling by using ODP (Open Directory Project) documents as a training set for training the LDA model. ODP documents are a good sample of web pages that represent various categories from the web. The LDA model gives a topic distribution for a test page and an ad. This topic distribution can be leveraged to retrieve relevant ads for a web page. In addition, we also propose to learn a language model on these ODP documents and use them with the topic modeling approach. We also plan to compare the topical approach with a semantic approach. The idea is to use the ODP or the Wikipedia category tree to classify each ad and the page into a taxonomy and use the classification into a category as a feature.

Advertising on micro blogs: Micro blogs such as Twitter, Facebook, Google+ have rapidly become a prominent medium for users to share information. These micro blogs can be used to do contextual advertising. Micro blogs have the added advantage of being personal to the user as the source is usually the friend network. If the advertising is properly channeled towards the right micro blogs, it can be very effective. However, as the micro blogs are very small in length the challenge with advertising on these micro blogs is that very little content is available to decide whether to advertise or not. Hence, it is important to learn when the content is desirable for advertising. In this work, we plan to learn a model to decide if the micro blog content is appropriate for advertising. We Propose features pertaining to the tweet like count of hash tags, count of nouns, features using external knowledge like query logs, features gathered from user tweet statistics etc.

4. SOCIAL ADVERTISING

Social advertising (*SA*) goes one step further beyond *SS* and *ConAd*. In SA, the rich neighborhood information can be leveraged to achieve better *reach* for the ads. The idea is to target certain special individuals in the network who can influence others to perform a similar action (say, click the advertisement). This is commonly known as *viral marketing*. Targeting these influentials usually leads to a vast spread of the information across the network.

We hypothesize that a user's influencing capability depends on the information/action that disseminates across the network, the user and their social neighborhood's influencing capabilities. Hence the problem of identification of influencers should also take the particular action into account while identifying the influencers. To confirm this hypothesis, we first empirically analyze how factors like user's and their neighborhood's influencing ability and action popularity affect a cascade by a user for an action.

We first quantify the average number of cascade a user u triggers for an action a as its reach. Let $reach^a(u)$ be the reach of a user u for an action a, which quantifies the past influence of a user for that action. First, we analyze the co-relation of $reach^a(u)$ with various user-level, action-level and user's neighborhood-level factors. In the user level features, we study, how $reach^a(u)$ of u changes with the number of friends of u and with the influencing capability of a user u (*influence probability*) p_u^{inf}. In the neighborhood level factors, we consider the average of the influencing capabilities of all the neighbors at hop k from the user u ($P_{u:hopk}^{inf}$), which is the average of influencing probabilities of all the users at hop k from user u. In addition, we also consider, how prone is a user's neighborhood at hop k to getting influenced for any action (P_u^{prone}, $P_{u:hopk}^{prone}$). In the action level factors, we define action's influencing ability (p_a^{inf}) as the ratio of number of users doing action a under a friend's influence by the total number of users doing action a.

The analysis of various factors yields several interesting insights - There is a direct association between the reach and various user, action and neighborhood factors. The analysis confirms that more contagious the factors, bigger is the reach for that user and the action. Also, we empirically showed that the action, user and the neighborhood features combined together give a good prediction of the average reach of a user in the graph. A detailed description of the paper can be found out in [1].

5. REFERENCES

[1] K. S. Dave, R. Bhatt, and V. Varma. Modeling action cascades in social networks. ICWSM '11. AAAI, 2011.

[2] K. S. Dave and V. Varma. Learning the click-through rate for rare/new ads from similar ads. SIGIR '10, 2010.

[3] K. S. Dave and V. Varma. Pattern based keyword extraction for contextual advertising. In *CIKM*, pages 1885–1888, 2010.

The Early Bird Gets the Buzz: Detecting Anomalies and Emerging Trends in Information Networks *

Brian Thompson
Rutgers University
110 Frelinghuysen Road
Piscataway, NJ 08854
bthom@cs.rutgers.edu

ABSTRACT

In this work we propose a novel approach to anomaly detection in streaming communication data. We first build a stochastic model for the system based on temporal communication patterns across each edge, which we call the REWARDS (REneWal theory Approach for Real-time Data Streams) model. We then define a measure of anomaly for an arbitrary subgraph based on the likelihood of its recent activity given past behavior. Finally, we develop an algorithm to efficiently identify subgraphs with the most anomalous activity. Although our work has until now focused on the cybersecurity domain, the model we present is more broadly applicable to information retrieval in data streams and information networks.

Categories and Subject Descriptors

E.1 [**Data Structures**]: Graphs and networks; G.2.2 [**Graph Theory**]: Graph algorithms; G.3 [**Probability and Statistics**]: Time series analysis; G.3 [**Probability and Statistics**]: Renewal theory

General Terms

Algorithms, Design, Experimentation, Performance

1. RELATED WORK

Anomaly detection has been studied extensively in a variety of domains, from detecting credit card fraud to monitoring activity in computer networks. For an overview of anomaly detection methods, we refer the reader to a recent survey by Chandola et. al. [1]. In their classification, our approach can be described as using statistical methods for identifying collective, contextual anomalies. That means that we define an anomaly to be a set of objects whose collective behavior is rare or improbable within the context of their environment. In this work, we focus on applications to the domain of time-evolving networks. Please see the full version of this paper for a survey of recent approaches and comparison to our work.

2. MODEL AND APPROACH

2.1 The REWARDS Model

We consider data in the form of a stream of time-stamped events (TSEs). We use $\langle(v,u);t\rangle$ to denote communication between entities v and u at time t, and refer to the pair as a *network edge*.

*This is an abridged version of joint work with James Abello. The full version can be found at `www.cs.rutgers.edu/~bthom`.

Copyright is held by the author/owner(s).
WSDM'12, February 8–12, 2012, Seattle, Washington, USA.
ACM 978-1-4503-0747-5/12/02.

For each network edge $e=(v,u)$, let $T_{e,t}$ denote the sequence of timestamps $t_i \leq t$ during which v and u communicated.

We model communication across a network edge $e=(v,u)$ as a *renewal process*, a continuous-time Markov process where new events occur with inter-arrival times (IATs) sampled independently from a fixed distribution μ_e. In the absence of prior knowledge of the true distribution, we approximate μ_e based on $T_{e,t}$, the sequence of IATs previously seen. For details, see the full paper.

We say network edge $e=(v,u)$ is *alive* at time t if the elapsed time since their last communication is less than $iat_{e,t}^{max}$, the maximum inter-arrival time previously seen for that pair, and *dead* otherwise. We define the graph $G_t=(V_t,E_t)$, where $V_t=\{\text{entities}\}$ and $E_t \subseteq V_t \times V_t$ consists of all network edges alive at time t.

The IAT distribution summarizes the long-term behavior of a network edge. The second part of our REWARDS model assigns greater relevance to communication that happened more recently.

2.2 Recency

The *age* of a renewal process is the time elapsed since the last event. Adapting this terminology, we define $Age(e,t)=t-t_e^{last}$, the time elapsed since the last communication across edge e. Consider the cumulative distribution function for values of $Age(e,t)$, sampled uniformly over all times at which e is alive:

$$CDF_e^{Age}(\tau)=\mathbf{P}(Age(e,t)\leq\tau).$$

We now define the recency of an edge e at time t:

$$Rec(e,t)=1-CDF_e^{Age}(Age(e,t)).$$

We observe that Rec is a decreasing function on the age of a network edge, having value 1 at the time of a new event, 0 when iat_e^{max} time has elapsed, and taking values uniformly in $[0,1]$ when sampled over times at which e is alive. (In fact, it is the unique such function.) Formally, the uniformity property states that for any edge e and time t, $Pr(Rec(e,t)\leq z)=z$ for all $z\in[0,1]$. Next, we consider the collective behavior of a subset of edges.

2.3 Divergence

Given a graph $G=(V,E)$ with weight function $w:E\rightarrow[0,1]$, $E'\subseteq E$, and threshold $\theta\in[0,1]$, let $X_{E',\theta}=|\{e\in E':w(e)\geq\theta\}|$. We define the θ-divergence of E' as follows:

$$\begin{aligned} Div_\theta(E') &= \frac{1}{\mathbf{P}(X\geq X_{E',\theta})} \\ &= \left(\sum_{i=X_{E',\theta}}^{|E'|}\binom{|E'|}{i}(1-\theta)^i\theta^{|E'|-i}\right)^{-1} \end{aligned}$$

where $X\sim Bin(|E'|,1-\theta)$ is a Binomial random variable representing the sum of Bernoulli trials, one for each edge in E'.

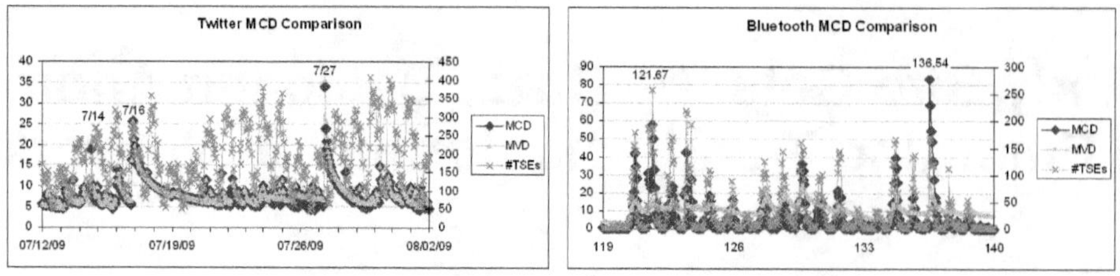

Figure 1: Plots of $\log_{10}$(MCD), $\log_{10}$(MVD), and # of TSEs over time for TWITTER and BLUETOOTH networks.

However, a challenge still remains in choosing the threshold value. In fact, we claim that a high-divergence edge set at any threshold is meaningful. We address this by introducing the concept of *max-divergence*, which is defined as follows:

$$Div_{max}(E') = \max_{\theta \in [0,1]} Div_{\theta}(E').$$

Now that we have defined divergence for an arbitrary set of edges, we consider specifically the edges incident to a vertex or to the set of vertices in a *maximal θ-component* of G (connected component formed by edges with $w(e) \geq \theta$). We define the *maximum vertex divergence* and *maximum component divergence* of a graph:

$$\begin{aligned} MVD(G) &= \max_{v \in V(G)} Div_{max}(v) \\ MCD(G) &= \max_{C \subseteq \mathcal{C}(G)} Div(C) \end{aligned}$$

where $\mathcal{C}(G)$ is the set of all maximal θ-components of G for any θ.

This leads us to our last step, the MCD Algorithm, which takes as input a weighted graph $G = (V, E)$ with weight function $w : E \rightarrow [0, 1]$, and outputs a list of disjoint θ-components that partition $V(G)$, in order of decreasing divergence. This is accomplished by running a variant of the Union-Find Algorithm [2], incrementally adding edges in order of decreasing weight. Details of the MCD Algorithm can be found in the full version of the paper.

3. EXPERIMENTS

To evaluate our approach, we perform experiments on 4 datasets: ENRON (email records over 2 years), BLUETOOTH (proximity of 100 mobile devices over 9 months), LBNL (IP traffic over 1 hour), and TWITTER (directed messages over 1 year). The number of edges ranged from 2k to 300k, and the number of timestamps ranged from 5k to 9 million. More extensive experiments and validation of our approach can be found in the full version of the paper.

3.1 Understanding the Results

In Figure 1 we examine plots of MCD and MVD over time for the TWITTER and BLUETOOTH networks, and compare them with the total network activity (number of time-stamped events). In both datasets, the number of TSEs follows a clear weekly and daily pattern. For TWITTER, the MCD and MVD values are almost always identical, indicating that the dataset is composed of disjoint stars, so that the divergence of each component is equal to the divergence of the vertex at the center of the star. Manual inspection of the data confirms that this is indeed the case (the top MCD values correspond to spammers), and similarly for the ENRON and LBNL datasets (corresponding to multiple-recipient emails and scanning activity, respectively). On the other hand, MCD values do not seem to be heavily dependent on the number of TSEs for TWITTER or LBNL. This is likely due to the large number of TSEs in the dataset, and highlights the ability of our approach to find local regions of heightened recent activity in large networks.

Due to the nature of the BLUETOOTH dataset (measuring physical proximity), denser subgraphs are more common, so heightened activity within a component can not necessarily be attributed to a single individual. This is most noticable on Day 136, where the MCD reaches its peak, yet the MVD and number of TSEs at that time are not significantly greater than on other days or weeks.

3.2 Network Visualization

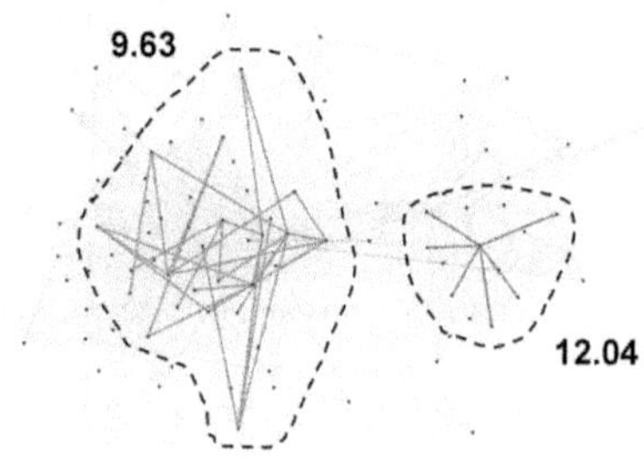

A visual representation of the network can be especially helpful to a human analyst, highlighting the individuals and groups with the most anomalous behavior for further inspection. Figure 3.2 shows the graph of all live edges in the BLUETOOTH network in the early afternoon on Day 99, along with the output from the MCD Algorithm: a disjoint set of connected components, each with a corresponding divergence value. This demonstrates the ability of our method to identify anomalous activity in different parts of the network simultaneously.

4. COMPLEXITY ANALYSIS

Our REWARDS model requires only $O(m)$ space, with constant-time updates (per communication event). The MCD Algorithm runs in $O(n + m \log m)$ time, and $O(n + m)$ time in practice. Detailed analysis can be found in the full version of the paper.

5. QUESTIONS & FUTURE DIRECTIONS

Until recently our work has centered on anomaly detection in the communication domain, where traffic or message contents may be encrypted or unavailable. Our current interest is to apply our techniques in the context of web search in information networks, where semantic information is readily available. Namely, how do we identify emerging trends and patterns of information diffusion in a streaming fashion? How do we find information that is both time-relevant and of likely interest to an individual? We suggest that our REWARDS model can be a good first step in this direction.

6. REFERENCES

[1] V. Chandola, A. Banerjee, and V. Kumar. Anomaly detection: A survey. *ACM Comput. Surv.*, 41(3), 2009.

[2] R. E. Tarjan. Efficiency of a good but not linear set union algorithm. *J. ACM*, 22:215–225, April 1975.

Characterizing and Harnessing Peer-Production of Information in Social Tagging Systems

Elizeu Santos-Neto
University of British Columbia
2332 Main Mall, Room 4075
Vancouver, BC, Canada
elizeus@ece.ubc.ca

ABSTRACT

Assessing the value of individual users' contributions in peer-production systems is paramount to the design of mechanisms that support collaboration and improve users' experience. For instance, to incentivize contributions, file sharing systems based on the BitTorrent protocol equate value with volume of contributed content and use a prioritization mechanism to reward users who contribute more. This approach and similar techniques used in resource sharing systems rely on the fact that the physical resources shared among users are easily quantifiable.

In contrast, information-sharing systems, like social tagging systems, lack the notion of a physical resource unit (e.g., content size, bandwidth) that facilitates the task of evaluating user contributions. For this reason, the issue of estimating the value of user contributions in information sharing systems remains largely unexplored. This paper outlines a research project to tackle the problem of assessing the value of contributions in social tagging systems.

Categories and Subject Descriptors

H.1.1 [**Models and Principles**]: Systems and Information Theory—*value of information*

General Terms

Algorithms, Experimentation, Measurement

Keywords

social, tagging, systems, information value, peer-production

1. INTRODUCTION

The wide adoption of social media services has transformed online information production from a centralized, proprietary, and hierarchical editorial model to a decentralized, non-proprietary, and collaborative model. Benkler [3] defines systems with the above characteristics as commons-based peer production systems (or, simply, peer production systems) – e.g., car pooling, Wikipedia, del.icio.us, Flickr.

Quantifying the value of individual user contributions in peer production systems is instrumental for a number of mechanisms that enable their efficient functioning and even their long-term survival. One direct application of methods to quantify the value of individual user contributions is to support incentive mechanisms to boost participation and collaboration. For instance, in offline peer production systems like car pooling, drivers have an incentive to share their cars (i.e., give rides to other people), as cars with a higher occupancy are allowed to use a dedicated faster lane [3]. Similarly, in online peer production systems, like BitTorrent [1], for instance, users who contribute more (i.e., they upload more) have higher download priority. Similarly, the value of contributions can also be used to deter malicious and opportunistic users by marginalizing those users who do not contribute at all.

In peer production systems designed for the shared use of a single type of resource, which embeds an easily measurable physical quantity, quantifying users' contributions is generally straightforward. In Folding@Home, for instance, users donate CPU cycles, thus user contributions can simply be calculated by estimating the number of (normalized) CPU/hours donated by a user (http://folding.stanford.edu). Analogously, in BitTorrent-based systems contributions can be evaluated by estimating the volume of uploaded traffic. Thus, to a great extent, quantifying contributions in these systems reduces to counting the units of donated resources. Even in peer production systems that deal with multiple types of resources, accounting for the amounts of physical resources produced by one user and consumed by others is at the core of techniques that quantify the value of contributions [7].

However, some systems lack a clear mapping between the amount of physical resources donated and the value of a contribution. This is the case of peer production systems designed to support the production of information goods, such as social tagging systems (e.g., del.icio.us) and wikis (e.g., Wikipedia.org). In particular, the lack of a quantifiable resource unit creates a new challenge: *the value of each user's contributions cannot anymore be directly linked to some amount of resource they donate.* For example, whereas a user may produce a large number of tags, only a few of them may indeed help their peers (i.e., other users of the system) in particular tasks such as navigation. Moreover, the value of information is contextual to the consumer. Some users may find the tag 'agneta' valuable when exploring a set of items (e.g., books or articles related to someone named Agneta such as Pedro Juan Gutierrez's novel Tropical Animal [5]), while others may find the tag 'cuba' more useful to discover a similar subset of items.

Assessing the value of peer-produced information in tag-

Copyright is held by the author/owner(s).
WSDM'12, February 8–12, 2012, Seattle, Washington, USA.
ACM 978-1-4503-0747-5/12/02.

ging systems is an instance of the problem of assessing the value of information goods. In this topic, Hirshleifer [6] describes five aspects that affect the value of information: *certainty, diffusion, applicability, content, and decision-relevance.* Stigler [10] and Bates [2] complement the list presented by Hirshleifer [6] by stating that the value of information is only fully determined by its use. Thus, to estimate value of tags and items, this work must consider the context in which they are used.

Therefore, to take the first steps towards designining methods to assess the value of user contributions in social tagging systems, this work focuses on the use of tags for exploratory search (e.g., *del.icio.us*, MrTaggy [4], StackOverflow.com).

2. METHODOLOGY

To guide the efforts towards realizing the benefits of methods to assess the value of user contributions, this work uses the methodology described below, where each phase is guided by a particular research question. It is worth mentioning that most of the methodology is based on the analysis of real-world social tagging systems like *del.icio.us.*

Q1. *How to assess the value of user contributions in social tagging systems?* – To address this question, I will design a novel method as well as adapt tag ranking functions used in recent studies to select tags to construct tag clouds [11, 9]. Besides evaluating the methods' computational complexity (i.e., feasibility), measuring whether the methods produce accurate estimates of value requires a user study, where users will be given navigation tasks and tags, and are asked to rank the tags according to how helpful they are for the completion of the task.

Q2. *How the methods to assess the value of contributions compare according to different application-level metrics (e.g., precision, recall, selectivity)?* – To address this question we look for correlations between the value of a tag measured according to a particular method (e.g., usage frequency) and application-level metrics such as navigation cost. Answering this question helps understanding whether the methods that assess the value of user contributions capture important aspects of the application.

Q3. *What are the existing types of contributors in social tagging systems?* – The goal is to characterize the user population of a social tagging system to observe whether users contribute equally to different aspects of the application or they concentrate more on few aspects. For instance, some information producers may create tags that are efficient in reducing the cost of a navigation task to information seekers, while other producers generate tags that maximize the diversity of items retrieved by information seekers. To answer this question, I will characterize the tag vocabularies of each user according to the application-level metrics in the context of navigation.

Q4. *Can the user population of social tagging systems divided into contributors vs. consumers of value?* – The goal is to understand whether the value of contributions are spread across the user population or concentrated on few users. To this end, I will measure the distribution of contributions over the participants of social tagging systems to understand its concentration.

Q5. *Are the devised methods to assess the value of user contributions robust against tag spam or malicious attempts to boost the perceived contribution value?* – To address this question, I will use labeled traces such as those provided by Bibsonomy (http://www.bibsonomy.org) to evaluate whether ranking users according to the value of their contributions is sufficient to marginalize spammers on the bottom of the ranking.

By addressing the above questions, this work foresees the following contributions:

- The design of new methods that assess the value of user contributions in social tagging systems.
- Definition of new models of navigation strategies that can be used to evaluate both the methods proposed in this work and future methods in the context of navigation.
- Characterization of user contributions in social tagging systems.
- Analysis of robustness of methods that quantify the value of user contribution against spam and strategic malicious users together with strategies to mitigate their impact.

3. SUMMARY

This work introduces the problem of assessing the value of user contribution in online peer production systems designed for information-sharing such as social tagging systems. In particular, the focus is on describing the methodology and potential contributions of this research project.

The main challenge is that quantifying user contributions in information-sharing systems lacks the straightforward quantifiable unit of value that is present in resource-sharing peer production systems. For more details on initial steps towards addressing the research questions presented above, we refer the reader to an extended version of this report [8].

4. REFERENCES

[1] N. Andrade, E. Santos-Neto, F. Brasileiro, and M. Ripeanu. Resource demand and supply in BitTorrent content-sharing communities. *Comput. Netw.*, 53(4):515–527, Nov. 2009.

[2] B. J. Bates. *Mediation, information, and communication.* Information and behavior series, 3. Transaction Publ., New Brunswick, NJ [u.a.], 1990.

[3] Y. Benkler. *The Wealth of Networks: How Social Production Transforms Markets and Freedom.* Yale University Press, May 2006.

[4] E. Chi, P. Pirolli, and S. Lam. *Aspects of Augmented Social Cognition: Social Information Foraging and Social Search,* pages 60–69. 2007.

[5] P. J. Gutierrez. *Tropical Animal.* Avalon, January 2005.

[6] J. Hirshleifer. Where Are We in the Theory of Information? *The American Economic Review,* 63(2):31–39, 1973.

[7] M. Mowbray, F. Brasileiro, N. Andrade, J. Santana, and W. Cirne. A reciprocation-based economy for multiple services in peer-to-peer grids. In *Proceedings of the Sixth IEEE International Conference on Peer-to-Peer Computing,* pages 193–202, Washington, DC, USA, 2006. IEEE Computer Society.

[8] E. Santos-Neto, F. Figueiredo, J. Almeida, M. Mowbray, M. Gonçalves, and M. Ripeanu. Assessing the Value of Contributions in Tagging Systems. *2010 IEEE International Conference on Social Computing,* 0:431–438, Aug. 2010.

[9] D. Skoutas and M. Alrifai. Tag clouds revisited. In *Proceedings of the 20th ACM international conference on Information and knowledge management,* CIKM '11, pages 221–230, New York, NY, USA, 2011. ACM.

[10] G. J. Stigler. *The Organization of Industry.* University Of Chicago Press, Mar. 1983.

[11] P. Venetis, G. Koutrika, and H. G. Molina. On the selection of tags for tag clouds. WSDM '11, pages 835–844, Hong Kong, China, 2011. ACM.

Mining, Searching and Exploiting Collaboratively Generated Content on the Web

Tutorial Abstract

Eugene Agichtein
Math & CS Department
Emory University, Atlanta, GA, USA
eugene@mathcs.emory.edu

Evgeniy Gabrilovich
Yahoo! Research
Santa Clara, CA, USA
gabr@yahoo-inc.com

Categories and Subject Descriptors

H.3.3 [**Information Storage and Retrieval**]: Information Search and Retrieval; H.3.1 [**Information Storage and Retrieval**]: Content Analysis and Indexing

General Terms

Algorithms, Experimentation, Human Factors

Keywords

Collaboratively-generated content

ABSTRACT

Proliferation of ubiquitous access to the Internet enables millions of Web users to collaborate online on a variety of activities. Many of these activities result in the construction of large repositories of knowledge, either as their primary aim (e.g., Wikipedia) or as a by-product (e.g., Yahoo! Answers). In this tutorial, we will discuss organizing and exploiting Collaboratively Generated Content (CGC) for information organization and retrieval. Specifically, we intend to cover two complementary areas of the problem: (1) using such content as a powerful enabling resource for knowledge-enriched, intelligent representations and new information retrieval algorithms, and (2) development of supporting technologies for extracting, filtering, and organizing collaboratively created content.

The unprecedented amounts of information in CGC enable new, knowledge-rich approaches to information access, which are significantly more powerful than the conventional word-based methods. Considerable progress has been made in this direction over the last few years. Examples include explicit manipulation of human-defined concepts and their use to augment the bag of words (cf. Explicit Semantic Analysis), using large-scale taxonomies of topics from Wikipedia or the Open Directory Project to construct additional class-based features, or using Wikipedia for better word sense disambiguation.

However, the quality and comprehensiveness of collaboratively created content vary significantly, and in order for this resource to be useful, a significant amount of preprocessing, filtering, and organization is necessary. Consequently, new methods for analyzing CGC and corresponding user interactions are required to effectively harness the resulting knowledge. Thus, not only the content repositories can be used to improve IR methods, but the reverse pollination is also possible, as better information extraction methods can be used for automatically collecting more knowledge, or verifying the contributed content. This natural connection between modeling the generation process of CGC and effectively using the accumulated knowledge suggests covering both areas together in a single tutorial.

The intended audience of the tutorial includes IR researchers and graduate students, who would like to learn about the recent advances and research opportunities in working with collaboratively generated content. The emphasis of the tutorial is on comparing the existing approaches and presenting practical techniques that IR practitioners can use in their research. We also cover open research challenges, as well as survey available resources (software tools and data) for getting started in this research field.

Copyright is held by the author/owner(s).
WSDM'12, February 8–12, 2012, Seattle, Washingtion, USA.
ACM 978-1-4503-0747-5/12/02.

Presenters' bios

Dr. Eugene Agichtein is an Assistant Professor in the Math & Computer Science Department at Emory University, where he founded and directs the Emory Intelligent Information Access Laboratory (IR Lab). His research interests are in web search and information retrieval, text and data mining, social media, and medical informatics. Eugene's is a recipient of several awards, including the "Best Paper" award at SIGIR 2011. He is a Program Co-Chair of the WSDM 2012 conference, and served as a Senior PC member or Area Chair of SIGIR, ICWSM, ICDM, AAAI, and ACL/HLT conferences. Eugene earned a Ph.D. in Computer Science from Columbia University.
URL: `http://www.mathcs.emory.edu/~eugene/`

Dr. Evgeniy Gabrilovich is a Principal Research Scientist and Head of the NLP & IR Group at Yahoo! Research. His research interests include information retrieval, machine learning, and computational linguistics. Evgeniy is a recipient of the 2010 Karen Spärck Jones Award for his contributions to natural language processing and information retrieval. He served as a Senior PC member or Area Chair at SIGIR, AAAI, IJCAI, ACL, WWW, WSDM, EMNLP, ICDM, and ICWSM. Evgeniy earned his PhD degree in Computer Science from the Technion—Israel Institute of Technology. **URL:** `http://research.yahoo.com/~gabr`

Collaborative Information Seeking: Understanding Users, Systems, and Content

Chirag Shah
School of Communication & Information (SC&I)
Rutgers, The State University of New Jersey
chirags@rutgers.edu

Abstract

The course will introduce the student to theories, methodologies, and tools that focus on information retrieval/seeking in collaboration. The student will have an opportunity to learn about the social aspect of IR with a focus on collaborative information seeking (CIS) situations, systems, and evaluation techniques.

Traditionally, IR is considered an individual pursuit, and not surprisingly, the majority of tools, techniques, and models developed for addressing information need, retrieval, and usage have focused on single users. The assumption of information seekers being independent and IR problem being individual has been challenged often in the recent past. This course will introduce such works to the students, with an emphasis on understanding models and systems that support collaborative search or browsing. In addition, the course will provide samples of data collected through several experiments to demonstrate various mining and analysis techniques.

Specifically, the course will (1) outline the research and latest developments in the field of collaborative IR, (2) list the challenges for designing and evaluating collaborative IR systems, and (3) show how traditional single user IR models and systems could be mapped to those for CIS. This will be achieved through introduction to appropriate literature, algorithms and interfaces that facilitate CIS, and methodologies for studying and evaluating them. Thus, the course will offer a balance between theoretical and practical elements of CIS.

Categories and Subject Descriptors:
H.3.3 [**Information Storage and Retrieval**]: Information Search and Retrieval: *Search process* H.5.3 [**Information Interfaces and Presentation**]: Group and Organization Interfaces: *Computer-supported cooperative work; Theory and models; Evaluation/methodology; Web-based interaction; Synchronous interaction; Asynchronous interaction*

General Terms: Design, Experimentation, Measurement

Keywords: Collaborative information seeking

Bio:

Chirag Shah is an assistant professor at the Dept. of Library & Information Science (LIS) within the School of Communication & Information (SC&I) at Rutgers University. He received his PhD from the School of Information & Library Science (SILS) at UNC Chapel Hill (advisor: Gary Marchionini). He holds an MTech, Computer Science & Engineering from IIT Madras, India and an MS, Computer Science from UMass Amherst (advisor: W. Bruce Croft).

His research interests include various aspects of interactive information retrieval/seeking, especially in the context of online social networks and collaborations, contextual information mining, and applications of social media services for exploring critical socio-political issues. At Rutgers, he runs a research group on Information Seeking and Behavior, as well as special interest groups on Collaborative Information Seeking and Social Information Seeking. He has published numerous papers in journals and conferences relating to these topics, and specific to collaborative information seeking (CIS). His co-authored paper for SIGIR 2008 titled "Algorithmic Mediation for Collaborative Exploratory Search" won the best paper award. He co-organized workshops on CIS at ACM Group 2010 and ASIST 2011 conferences. He has developed Coagmento, which allows a group of users to search and share information in collaboration. He recently received the Yahoo! Campus Innovation Award for his project titled "Reimagining and Reinvigorating Information Seeking with a Novel Approach to Collaborative Information Seeking". He also taught a short course on collaborative IR at the Russian Summer School of Information Retrieval (RuSSIR) in St. Petersburg, Russia this summer.

References

Baeza-Yates, R., & Pino, J. A. (1997). A First Step to Formally Evaluate Collaborative Work. *Proceedings of GROUP* (pp. 56-60).

Fidel, R., Bruce, H., Pejtersen, A. M., Dumais, S. T., Grudin, J., & Poltrock, S. (2000). Collaborative Information Retrieval (CIR). *The New Review of Information Behaviour Research*, 235-247.

Golovchinsky, G., Pickens, J., & Back, M. (2008). A taxonomy of collaboration in online information seeking. *Proceedings of JCDL 2008 Workshop on Collaborative Exploratory Search*. Pittsburgh, PA.

Grudin, J. (1994). Groupware and social dynamics: eight challenges for developers. *Communications of the ACM, 37*(1), 92-105.

Morris, M. R., & Horvitz, E. (2007). SearchTogether: An Interface for Collaborative Web Search. *ACM Symposium on User Interface Software and Technology (UIST)* (pp. 3-12). Newport, RI.

Shah, C. (2010). Collaborative Information Seeking: A Literature Review. *Advances in Librarianship, 32*, 3-33. doi:10.1108/S0065-2830(2010)0000032004

Twidale, M. B. T., Nichols, D. M. N., & Paice, C. D. (1997). Browsing is a Collaborative Process. *Information Processing and Management, 33*(6), 761-783.

Copyright is held by the author/owner(s).
WSDM'12, February 8–12, 2012, Seattle, Washington, USA.
ACM 978-1-4503-0747-5/12/02.

Machine Learning for Query-Document Matching in Search

Hang Li
Microsoft Research Asia
No. 5 Danling street, Haidian District
Beijing, China 100080
hangli@microsoft.com

Jun Xu
Microsoft Research Asia
No. 5 Danling street, Haidian District
Beijing, China 100080
junxu@microsoft.com

Categories and Subject Descriptors

H.3.3 [**Information Storage and Retrieval**]: Information Search and Retrieval—*Retrieval models, Query formulation*

General Terms

Algorithms, Theory

Keywords

web search, machine learning, query-document matching

1. INTRODUCTION

In web search, relevance is one of the most important factors to meet users' satisfaction, and the success of a web search engine heavily depends on its performance on relevance. It has been observed that many hard cases in search relevance are due to term mismatch between query and document (e.g., query 'ny times' does not match well with document only containing 'new york times'), and thus it is not exaggerated to say that dealing with mismatch between query and document is one of the most critical research problems in web search. Recently researchers have spent significant effort to address the grand challenge. The major approach is to conduct more query and document understanding, and perform better matching between enriched query and document representations. With the availability of large amount of log data and advanced machine learning techniques, this becomes more feasible and significant progress has been made recently.

In this tutorial, we will give a systematic and detailed presentation on newly developed machine learning technologies for query document matching in search. We will focus on the fundamental problems, as well as the novel solutions for query document matching at word form level, word sense level, topic level, and structure level. We will talk about novel technologies about query spelling error correction [3, 13], query rewriting [1, 4, 6, 7], query classification [2], topic modeling of documents [5, 9], query document matching [8, 10, 11, 12], and query document-title translation. The ideas and solutions introduced in this tutorial may motivate industrial practitioners to turn the research fruits into product reality. The summary of the state-of-the-art methods and the discussions on the technical issues in this tutorial may stimulate academic researchers to find new research directions and solutions.

Matching between query and document is not limited to search, and similar problems can be observed at online advertisement, recommendation system, and other applications, as matching between objects from two spaces. The technologies we introduce can be generalized into more general machine learning techniques, which we call learning to match.

Copyright is held by the author/owner(s).
WSDM'12, February 8–12, 2012, Seattle, Washington, USA.
ACM 978-1-4503-0747-5/12/02.

2. REFERENCES

[1] M. Bendersky, D. Metzler, and W. B. Croft. Parameterized concept weighting in verbose queries. In *SIGIR*, pp. 605–614, 2011.

[2] P. N. Bennett, K. Svore, and S. T. Dumais. Classification-enhanced ranking. In *WWW*, pp. 111–120, 2010.

[3] E. Brill and R. C. Moore. An improved error model for noisy channel spelling correction. In *ACL*, 2000.

[4] A. Broder, P. Ciccolo, E. Gabrilovich, V. Josifovski, D. Metzler, L. Riedel, and J. Yuan. Online expansion of rare queries for sponsored search. In *WWW*, pp. 511–520, 2009.

[5] J. Gao, K. Toutanova, and W.-t. Yih. Clickthrough-based latent semantic models for web search. In *SIGIR*, pp. 675–684, 2011.

[6] J. Guo, G. Xu, X. Cheng, and H. Li. Named entity recognition in query. In SIGIR, pp. 267–274, 2009.

[7] D. Sheldon, M. Shokouhi, M. Szummer, and N. Craswell. Lambdamerge: merging the results of query reformulations. In WSDM, pp. 795–804, 2011.

[8] C. Wang, R. Raina, D. Fong, D. Zhou, J. Han, and G. Badros. Learning relevance from heterogeneous social network and its application in online targeting. In SIGIR, pp. 655–664, 2011.

[9] Q. Wang, J. Xu, H. Li, and N. Craswell. Regularized latent semantic indexing. In *SIGIR'11*, pp. 685–694.

[10] Z. Wang, G. Xu, H. Li, and M. Zhang. A fast and accurate method for approximate string search. In ACL-HLT, pp. 52–61, 2011.

[11] W. Wu, H. Li, J. Xu, and S. Oyama. Learning a robust relevance model for search using kernel methods. *JMLR*, pp. 1429–1458, 2011.

[12] J. Xu, W. Wu, H. Li, and G. Xu. A kernel approach to addressing term mismatch. In *WWW*, pp. 153–154, 2011.

[13] J. Xu and G. Xu. Learning similarity function for rare queries. In *WSDM*, pp. 615–624, 2011.

2nd International Workshop on Diversity in Document Retrieval (DDR 2012)

Craig Macdonald
Univ. of Glasgow, UK
craigm@dcs.gla.ac.uk

Jun Wang
Univ. College London, UK
j.wang@cs.ucl.ac.uk

Charles Clarke
Univ. of Waterloo, Canada
claclark@plg.uwaterloo.ca

ABSTRACT

When an ambiguous query is received, a sensible approach is for the information retrieval (IR) system to diversify the results retrieved for this query, in the hope that at least one of the interpretations of the query intent will satisfy the user. Diversity is an increasingly important topic, of interest to both academic researchers (such as participants in the TREC Web and Blog track diversity tasks, or the NTCIR INTENT task), as well as to search engines professionals. In the 2nd edition of the Diversity in Document Retrieval workshop (DDR 2012), we solicited submissions both on approaches and models for diversity, the evaluation of diverse search results, and on applications of diverse search results. This workshop builds upon a successful 1st edition of DDR which was held at ECIR 2011 in Dublin, Ireland [6].

Categories and Subject Descriptors: H.3.3 [Information Storage & Retrieval]: Information Search & Retrieval

General Terms: Performance, Experimentation

Keywords: Diversity, Search, Information Retrieval

1. BACKGROUND AND MOTIVATION

The query is often the only evidence of the user's underlying information need available to an IR system. However, if the query is ambiguous, a sensible approach is to diversify the results retrieved for this query, in the hope that at least one of the interpretations of the query intent will satisfy the user. Diversification is now becoming an important topic in IR (driven by the TREC & NTCIR tracks, and through deployment by search engines), and hence research is appearing in areas such as modelling, applications and evaluation.

Modelling Diversity: Diversifying search results usually involves a departure from the independent document relevance assumption underlying the well-known probability ranking principle. An IR system should consider not only the relevance of each individual document, but also how relevant the document is in light of the other retrieved documents. Various models exist, but often form around two schools [9], namely implicit [2, 11] and explicit [1, 8], depending on how the query aspects are accounted for in the retrieved documents.

Modelling Risk: Search for information is a risky business. The risk lies in the fact we may not know exactly the users' specific information needs, the languages used in the documents, and/or the relevance matching between documents and queries. Therefore, any retrieval decision we make is always a balance between risk and reward. Various models have theoretically demonstrated that diversifying the documents in the ranked list is also an effective way of reducing the retrieval risk [11].

Applications: Diverse rankings have applications in various areas. One primary application is of course in Web search (as investigated by the TREC Web track [3] or NTCIR INTENT task [10]). However, applications are also possible in social search (e.g. find me diverse opinions of a topic on the blogosphere - c.f. TREC Blog track [5]), in product search (e.g. I'm not sure what kind of digital camera I want to buy, show me a selection of different types), and in summarisation [2].

Evaluation: A diverse ranking of results should have documents matching as many of the possible aspects underlying a query (known as diversity or coverage), while still promoting novelty, whereby one aspect does not become over-represented. Various evaluation measures for diversity have been proposed, such as α-NDCG [4], Intent Aware-Precision [1], as well as the more recent D# measures [7] that have recently been deployed in the NTCIR INTENT task. The advent of the diversity tasks in both TREC and NTCIR have created means for the evaluation of diversification approaches [3, 5, 10]. Other problems include how the importance of different query aspects should be taken into account during evaluation.

2. GOALS & OBJECTIVES

As diversity is, in general, an emerging topic, there is no consensus on various aspects of the topic. For instance, there are several evaluation measures in common use (α-NDCG, D#-nDCG, Intent Aware-Precision, etc.), with no clear consensus on the most suitable. In terms of modelling, there are various competing schools, based on implicit or explicit modelling of the query aspects in the retrieved documents.

This workshop differs from an IR conference in that while diversity papers may be accepted to such venues, usually covering the modelling or evaluation aspects of diversity, papers on applications aspects of diversity are less well-represented. Moreover, in a conference venue, there is not the volume to tackle each and all of these aspects in depth, in an interactive environment.

After the 2nd DDR workshop, there will be a special issue of the Information Retrieval journal on "Search Intents and Diversification", which has a submission deadline of 2nd

Copyright is held by the author/owner(s).

WSDM'12, February 8–12, 2012, Seattle, Washington, USA.
ACM 978-1-4503-0747-5/12/02.

April 2012. Given there is two months between the workshop and the submission, we hope that workshop authors will take the opportunity to use the feedback at the workshop on their submissions to extend for the special issue.

3. TOPICS OF INTEREST

In terms of author audience, we solicited technical and position paper submissions with the following (but not limited to) research topics:

- Modelling Diversity: Implicit diversification approaches
- Modelling Diversity: Explicit diversification approaches
- Modelling Diversity: Query log mining for diversity
- Modelling Diversity: Learning-to-rank for diversification
- Modelling Diversity: Clustering of results for diversification
- Modelling Diversity: Query intent understanding
- Modelling Diversity: Query type classification
- Modelling Risk: Probability ranking principle
- Modelling Risk: Risk minimization frameworks and role diversity
- Evaluation: Test collections for diversity
- Evaluation: Evaluating of diverse search results
- Evaluation: Measuring the ambiguity of queries
- Evaluation: Measuring query aspects importance
- Applications: Product & review diversification
- Applications: Opinion and sentiment diversification
- Applications: Summarisation
- Applications: Legal precedents & patents
- Applications: Diverse recommender systems
- Applications: Diversifying in real-time & news search

4. PROGRAMME COMMITTEE

We are thankful to our programme committee, listed below.

- Ben Carterette, University of Delaware, USA
- Hui Fang, University of Delaware, USA
- Ben He, Chinese Academy of Science, China
- Jaap Kamps, University of Amsterdam, the Netherlands
- Jian-Yun Nie, Université de Montréal, Canada
- Iadh Ounis, University of Glasgow, UK
- Filip Radlinski, Microsoft, Canada
- Tetsuya Sakai, Microsoft Research Asia, China
- Rodrygo Santos, University of Glasgow, UK
- Ryen White, Microsoft Research, USA

5. REFERENCES

[1] R. Agrawal, S. Gollapudi, A. Halverson, and S. Ieong. Diversifying search results. In *Proceedings of the 2nd ACM International Conference on Web Search and Data Mining*, pages 5–14, Barcelona, Spain, 2009. ACM.

[2] J. Carbonell and J. Goldstein. The use of MMR, diversity-based reranking for reordering documents and producing summaries. In *SIGIR '98: Proceedings of the 21st annual international ACM SIGIR conference on Research and development in information retrieval*, pages 335–336, Melbourne, Australia, 1998. ACM.

[3] C. L. A. Clarke, N. Craswell, and I. Soboroff. Overview of the TREC 2009 Web track. In *Proceedings of the 18th Text REtrieval Conference (TREC 2009)*, Gaithersburg MD, USA, 2010. NIST.

[4] C. L. A. Clarke, M. Kolla, G. V. Cormack, O. Vechtomova, A. Ashkan, S. Büttcher, and I. MacKinnon. Novelty and diversity in information retrieval evaluation. In *Proceedings of the 31st Annual International ACM SIGIR Conference on Research and Development in Information Retrieval*, pages 659–666, Singapore, Singapore, 2008. ACM.

[5] C. Macdonald, I. Ounis, and I. Soboroff. Overview of the trec-2009 blog track. In *Proceedings of the 18th Text REtrieval Conference (TREC 2009)*, Gaithersburg MD, USA, 2010. NIST.

[6] C. Macdonald, J. Wang, and C. Clarke, editors. *Proceedings of the 1st international workshop on Diversity in Document Retrieval (DDR 2011)*, Dublin, Ireland, 2011.

[7] T. Sakai and R. Song. Evaluating diversified search results using per-intent graded relevance. In *Proceedings of the 34th international ACM SIGIR conference on Research and development in Information*, SIGIR '11, pages 1043–1052, Beijing, China, 2011. ACM.

[8] R. L. T. Santos, C. Macdonald, and I. Ounis. Exploiting query reformulations for Web search result diversification. In *Proceedings of the 19th International Conference on World Wide Web*, pages 881–890, Raleigh NC, USA, 2010. ACM.

[9] R. L. T. Santos, J. Peng, C. Macdonald, and I. Ounis. Explicit search result diversification through sub-queries. In *Proceedings of the 31st European Conference on Information Retrieval*, pages 87–99, Milton Keynes, UK, 2010. Springer.

[10] R. Song, M. Zhang, T. Sakai, M. Kato, L. Y., M. Sugimoto, Q. Wang, and N. Orii. Overview of the NTCIR-9 INTENT task. In *NTCIR-9 Proceedings*, Tokyo, Japan, 2011. NII.

[11] J. Wang and J. Zhu. Portfolio theory of information retrieval. In *Proceedings of the 32nd International ACM SIGIR Conference on Research and Development in Information Retrieval*, pages 115–122, Boston MA, USA, 2009. ACM.

WSCD2012: Workshop on Web Search Click Data 2012

Pavel Serdyukov
Yandex
16 Leo Tolstoy Street
Moscow, Russia 119021
pserdukov@yandex.ru

Nick Craswell
Microsoft Corporation
One Microsoft Way
Redmond, WA USA 98052
nickcr@microsoft.com

Georges Dupret
Yahoo! Labs
701 First Avenue
Sunnyvale, CA USA 94089
gdupret@yahoo-inc.com

ABSTRACT
WSCD2012 is the second workshop on Web Search Click Data, following WSCD2009. It is a forum for new research relating to Web search usage logs and for discussing desirable properties of publicly released search log datasets. Research relating to search logs has been hampered by the limited availability of click datasets. This workshop comes with a new click dataset based on click logs and an accompanying challenge to predict the relevance of documents based on clicks.

Categories and Subject Descriptors
H.3.3 [**Information Storage and Retrieval**]: Information Search and Retrieval – *relevance feedback, search process.*

General Terms
Measurement, Experimentation.

Keywords
Web search, click data.

1. OVERVIEW
Web search click data has caught the interest of a growing community of professional during the last five years. It provides a snapshot of the typical information access patterns of the user population, unlike a group of relevance judges or the tags provided on collaborative sites. Issued queries and clicked document records have the potential to give an accurate view of millions of people's daily interests, how these interests evolve, and how these interest are related, etc. Yet this information is not easily extracted because in spite of its abundance it is sparse, most queries are repeated only a few time if at all, and clicks cannot be interpreted as document relevance directly. Moreover, user clicks are strongly biased by the search engine ranking, which mean that many documents are never seen in spite of being relevant.

Copyright is held by the author/owner(s).
WSDM'12, February 8–12, 2012, Seattle, Washington, USA.
ACM 978-1-4503-0747-5/12/02.

Of particular interest is the relation between click data and editorial relevance judgments. A large body of Literature exists on how to use editorial judgments to evaluate and train Machine Learned Ranking functions. This describes what has been and continues to be a largely successful technology that serves millions of users every day, yet relying on editorial judgments as the Gold Standard against which to learn has its limits: 1) The metrics used to evaluate rankings are heuristics and hard to relate to user behavior, 2) As search technologies are extended to new areas, it is ever harder for editors to provide accurate judgments. This applies to most verticals like "local search" and to newer research areas like "diversity" where the question is how to introduce diversity in document ranking or "personalization" where the goal is to adapt the search results to take into account what is known from the user who issued the query.

In this workshop, we will attempt to address these issues but we will also explore novel applications and use of these data for enhancing the user search experience.

Research on the incorporation of click data into information retrieval systems, and for understanding user search, has been hampered by a lack of shared datasets. This workshop provides a common click dataset and a forum for presenting new results and analysis in the area. The dataset includes user sessions extracted from Yandex logs, with queries, URL rankings and clicks. Unlike previous click datasets, it also includes relevance judgments for the ranked URLs, for the purposes of training relevance prediction models. To allay privacy concerns the user data is fully anonymized. So, only meaningless numeric IDs of queries, sessions, and URLs are released. The queries are grouped only by sessions and no user IDs are provided. More details are available at http://imat-relpred.yandex.ru/en.

Author Index

www.ingramcontent.com/pod-product-compliance
Lightning Source LLC
LaVergne TN
LVHW080105011026
849160LV00013B/1034
* 9 7 8 1 4 5 0 3 1 3 6 7 4 *